OCP: Oracle Database 1
Professional Study Gui

OBJECTIVE	...APTER
Database Architecture and ASM	
Describe Automatic Storage Management (ASM)	1
Set up initialization parameter files for ASM and database instances	1
Start up and shut down ASM instances	1
Administer ASM disk groups	1
Configuring for Recovery	
Configure multiple archive log file destinations to increase availability	2
Define, apply and use a retention policy	4
Configure the Flash Recovery Area	4
Use Flash Recovery Area	4
Using the RMAN Recovery Catalog	
Identify situations that require RMAN recovery catalog	5
Create and configure a recovery catalog	5
Synchronize the recovery catalog	5
Create and use RMAN stored scripts	5
Back up the recovery catalog	5
Create and use a virtual private catalog	5
Configuring Backup Specifications	
Configure backup settings	2
Allocate channels to use in backing up	4
Configure backup optimization	4
Using RMAN to Create Backups	
Create image file backups	4
Create a whole database backup	4
Enable fast incremental backup	4
Create duplex backup and back up backup sets	4
Create an archival backup for long-term retention	4

Sybex®
An Imprint of
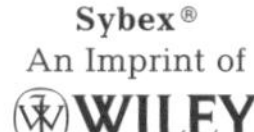
WILEY

OBJECTIVE	CHAPTER
Create a multi-section compressed and encrypted backup	4
Report on and maintain backups	7
Performing User-Managed Backup and Recovery	
Recover from a lost TEMP file	3
Recover from a lost redo log group	3
Recover from the loss of password file	3
Perform user-managed complete database recovery	3
Perform user-managed incomplete database recovery	3
Perform user-managed backups and server-managed backups	2
Identify the need of backup mode	2
Back up and recover a control file	2, 3
Using RMAN to Perform Recovery	
Perform complete recovery from a critical or non-critical data file loss using RMAN	6
Perform incomplete recovery using RMAN	6
Recover using incrementally updated backups	6
Switch to image copies for fast recovery	6
Restore a database onto a new host	8
Recover using a backup control file	6
Perform disaster recovery	8
Using RMAN to Duplicate a Database	
Creating a duplicate database	8
Using a duplicate database	8
Performing Tablespace Point-in-Time Recovery	
Identify the situations that require TSPITR	8
Perform automated TSPITR	8
Monitoring and Tuning RMAN	
Monitoring RMAN sessions and jobs	7
Tuning RMAN	7
Configure RMAN for Asynchronous I/O	7

Exam objectives are subject to change at any time without prior notice and at Oracle's sole discretion. Please visit Oracle's Training and Certification website (`http://www.oracle.com/education/certification/`) for the most current exam objectives listing.

Sybex®
An Imprint of
WILEY

OCP

Oracle® Database 11*g* Administrator Certified Professional

Study Guide

OCP

Oracle® Database 11*g* Administrator Certified Professional

Study Guide

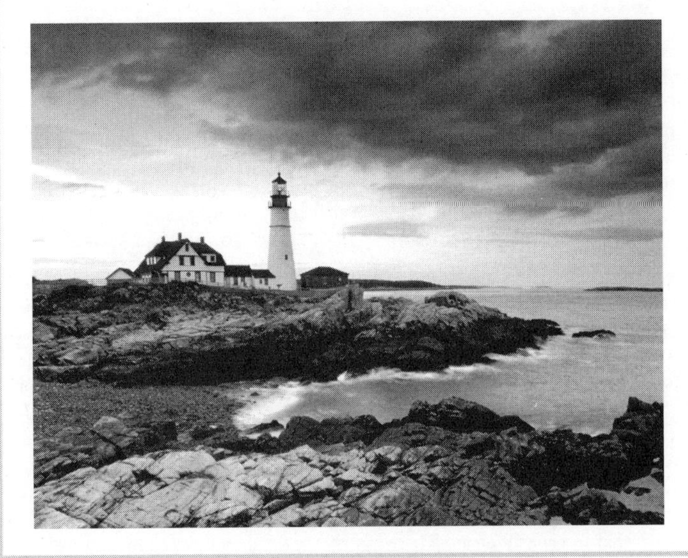

Robert G. Freeman

Charles A. Pack

Doug Stuns

Tim Buterbaugh

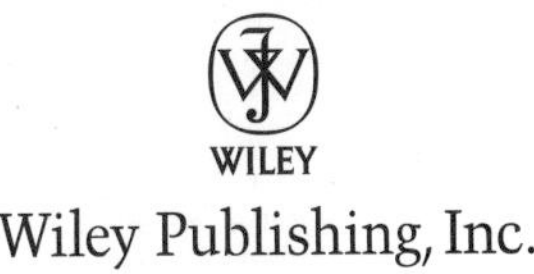

Wiley Publishing, Inc.

Acquisitions Editor: Jeff Kellum
Development Editor: Kim Wimpsett
Technical Editors: Arup Nanda and Bob Bryla
Production Editor: Christine O'Connor
Copy Editor: Judy Flynn
Production Manager: Tim Tate
Vice President and Executive Group Publisher: Richard Swadley
Vice President and Publisher: Neil Edde
Assistant Project Manager: Jenny Swisher
Associate Producer: Angie Denny
Quality Assurance: Josh Frank
Book Designer: Judy Fung, Bill Gibson
Compositor: Craig Woods, Happenstance Type-O-Rama
Proofreader: Candace English
Indexer: Nancy Guenther
Project Coordinator, Cover: Lynsey Stanford
Cover Designer: Ryan Sneed

Published simultaneously in Canada

ISBN: 978-0-470-39513-4

For general information on our other products and services or to obtain technical support, please contact our Customer Care Department within the U.S. at (877) 762-2974, outside the U.S. at (317) 572-3993 or fax (317) 572-4002.

Wiley also publishes its books in a variety of electronic formats. Some content that appears in print may not be available in electronic books.

Library of Congress Cataloging-in-Publication Data is available from the publisher.

10 9 8 7 6 5 4 3 2 1

Dear Reader,

Thank you for choosing *OCP: Oracle Database 11g Administrator Certified Professional Study Guide*. This book is part of a family of premium-quality Sybex books, all of which are written by outstanding authors who combine practical experience with a gift for teaching.

Sybex was founded in 1976. More than thirty years later, we're still committed to producing consistently exceptional books. With each of our titles we're working hard to set a new standard for the industry. From the paper we print on, to the authors we work with, our goal is to bring you the best books available.

I hope you see all that reflected in these pages. I'd be very interested to hear your comments and get your feedback on how we're doing. Feel free to let me know what you think about this or any other Sybex book by sending me an email at `nedde@wiley.com`, or if you think you've found a technical error in this book, please visit `http://sybex.custhelp.com`. Customer feedback is critical to our efforts at Sybex.

Best regards,

Neil Edde
Vice President and Publisher
Sybex, an Imprint of Wiley

This book is dedicated to my wife, Lisa; my children; and my father.
—Robert G. Freeman

For my wife, Donna, and our daughter, Jenny.
—Charles A. Pack

Acknowledgments

Writing a book is such a vast undertaking that it's hard to know where to start with the acknowledgments. I also hate writing this part because, frankly, someone always gets forgotten. That being said, here we go.

Thanks to my patient wife, Lisa, who sits across from me in our office and typically gets as little sleep as I do. Thanks to my kids who are still managing to grow up into wonderful adults in spite of this crazy world. Thanks to all my great friends at work who support me, who uplift me (imagine working at a job where you can start a meeting with a prayer!), and who are some very smart people. In particular, thanks to David Wright, Bill Johnson, Heber Allen, Jed Brunson, Dan Dredge, and Mandy Cosper. Additional thanks to Dave Prestwich, Mike Bowers, Stephen Shaffer, Brent Moody, and John Harper. Thanks also to my Core team guys Scott Black, Dennis Carlson, Ryan Allen, and Randy Knight. Also thanks to my way cool DBE team members Curt Workman, Bill Francis, Mike Noble, Ben Beishline, and Matthew Newman. You are all awesome. Thanks also to the rest of the EIM team at the church; you are awesome but too numerous to mention in the space I have here. I've worked with more awesome people that I can list in these pages. If I could list all your names here, I would. As it is, just know that I appreciate you and loved working with you over the years.

Writing books is a long, complex, and often frustrating task. Thanks to all the folks at Sybex that participated in the making of this book. Thanks to Jeff Kellum, who was my acquisitions editor, for getting me involved in this project. I'd worked with Jeff before on my very first book, and apparently he didn't remember the pain I caused him well enough, since he asked me to write this book anyway. Thanks to Kim Wimpsett for awesome editing and being the best development editor ever! Thanks to Christine O'Connor for doing a bang-up job with the book and to Judy Flynn, copy editor extraordinaire, the proofreader Candace English, and to Nancy Guenther, indexer.

Finally, a very important thanks goes out to YOU. Thanks for buying this book. Thanks for wanting to become an Oracle Certified Professional. Thanks for any nice comments you might leave on websites here and there. Thanks for trusting us to help you succeed at the test!

—Robert G. Freeman

Thanks to Robert Freeman and Jeff Kellum for the opportunity to write this book. Thanks to David May, Gary Baird, and Greg Sinclair for providing a rock-solid infrastructure, not only in which to practice my art but also to the great benefit of my employer, CSX. Thanks to my capacity management team Chris Roessler, Harry Price, Brian Horan, Jan Shane, Joe Zuleger, and Derryck Zimmerman; my storage team Andy Brackett, Scott Gunter, Joe Fredrickson, Mike Able, John Anderson, Chris Griffith, Rick Ferry, Gene Pate, and Jim Gouvernante. To my coworkers Benny Kronz, Maritza Gonzalez, Chris Wilson, John Kall, Sandra Merwin, Duard Williams, Rich McClain, and Frank Lamon, for building a world-class Oracle database environment at CSX and for making it possible for me to continuously learn, develop, and teach.

This book would not have been written without my wife's permission, of course. Thank you, Donna, for being by my side through these projects, especially during the summer months in Florida. Thank you to my daughter, Jenny, who is 7 and sitting next to me on the sofa writing stories on her MacBook about Chihuahuas and leopard geckos while I write about "the Oracle."

—Charles A. Pack

About the Authors

Robert G. Freeman lives in Salt Lake City, Utah, and is a principle database engineer with the Church of Jesus Christ of Latter-day Saints. Robert has been working with Oracle for some 20 years now. After the latest economic explosion, Robert expects that he will continue to be working for at least another 20 years. He has shelved his pending midlife career-change plans to become a maniacal recluse living in a cabin out in the middle of nowhere due to the economic crisis and current state of his 401(k).

Besides working with Oracle databases (that's his story and he's sticking to it), Robert writes an occasional book (at last count 12 or so), flies airplanes, enjoys karate, and has a family that is awesome. He met Charles Pack, who is a fellow Okie (even if he sometimes roots for the wrong school) years ago and to this day wonders if Charles will ever walk around without wearing sunglasses to hide his eyes and the deep meaning contained in them. Robert is the husband of the patient Lisa and father of five wonderful, if not occasionally misguided, children.

If you liked this book and want to email Robert, you can do so at `dbaoracle@aol.com`. If you didn't like this book, then make sure you remember that Charles A. Pack wrote it and email him instead.

Charles A. Pack is an Oracle Certified Professional DBA with over 20 years of IT experience. His career has included the roles of PC repairman, network administrator, systems operator, COBOL programmer, backup and storage engineer, DBA, architect, project manager, and people manager. He earned the Bachelor of Science degree from Oklahoma State University, the MBA from the University of Oklahoma, and the Master of Science in Computer Science from Texas A&M University – Corpus Christi. He has taught Oracle DBA classes at Florida Community College Jacksonville and has presented on the subject at universities and to professional organizations. He authored the Oracle Press *Oracle9i Database: OCP 9i Performance Tuning Exam Guide* and collaborated with coauthor Robert Freeman on the *Oracle 8 to 8i Upgrade Exam Cram*. In his current role as technical director of hardware provisioning at CSX Technology in Jacksonville, Florida, he and his teams are responsible for enterprise storage, backups, capacity planning, and performance. He is a true Cowboy at heart, and he loves to barbecue.

Contents at a Glance

Contents

Table of Exercises

Introduction

There is high demand for professionals in the information technology (IT) industry, and Oracle certifications are the hottest credentials in the database world. You have made the right decision to pursue your Oracle certification because it will give you a distinct advantage in this highly competitive market.

Most readers should already be familiar with Oracle and do not need an introduction to the Oracle database world. For those who aren't familiar with the company, here are the basics: Oracle, founded in 1977, sold the first commercial relational database and is now the world's leading database company and largest enterprise software company, with 2008 fiscal year revenues of more than $22 billion.

Oracle databases are the de facto standard for large Internet sites, and Oracle advertisers are boastful but honest when they proclaim, "The Internet Runs on Oracle." Almost all big Internet sites run Oracle databases. Oracle's penetration of the database market runs deep and is not limited to dot-com implementations. Enterprise resource planning (ERP) application suites, data warehouses, and custom applications at many companies rely on Oracle. The demand for DBA resources remains higher than the demand for others during weak economic times.

This book is intended to help you pass the Oracle Database 11*g*: Administration II exam, which will establish your credentials as an Oracle Certified Professional (OCP). The OCP certification is a prerequisite for obtaining an Oracle Certified Master (OCM) certification. Using this book and a practice database, you can learn the necessary skills to pass the 1Z0-053 Oracle Database 11*g*: Administration II exam.

Why Become Oracle Certified?

The number-one reason to become an OCP is to gain more visibility and greater access to the industry's most challenging opportunities. Oracle certification is the best way to demonstrate your knowledge and skills in Oracle database systems.

Certification is proof of your knowledge and shows that you have the skills required to support Oracle core products. The Oracle certification program can help a company to identify proven performers who have demonstrated their skills and who can support the company's investment in Oracle technology. It demonstrates that you have a solid understanding of your job role and the Oracle products used in that role.

OCPs are among the best paid in the IT industry. Salary surveys consistently show the OCP certification to yield higher salaries than other certifications, including Microsoft, Novell, and Cisco.

So whether you are beginning your career, changing your career, or looking to secure your position as a DBA, this book is for you!

Oracle Certifications

Oracle certifications follow a track that is oriented toward a job role. These are database administration, application developer, and web application server administrator tracks. Within each track, Oracle has a multitiered certification program.

Within the administration track there are three tiers:

- The first tier is the Oracle 11*g* Certified Associate (OCA). To obtain OCA certification, you must pass the 1Z0-052 Oracle Database 11*g*: Administration I exam.
- The second tier is the Oracle 11*g* Certified Professional (OCP), which builds on and requires OCA certification. To obtain OCP certification, you must attend an approved Oracle University hands-on class and pass the 1Z0-053 Oracle Database 11*g*: Administration II exam.
- The third and highest tier is the Oracle 11*g* Certified Master (OCM), which builds on and requires OCP certification. To obtain OCM certification, you must attend advanced-level classes and take a two-day, hands-on practical exam.

The material in this book addresses only the Administration II exam. Other Wiley books—which can be found at `http://www.wiley.com`—can help students new to the DBA world prepare for the OCA exam 1Z0-052 Oracle Database 11*g*: Administration I. You can also get information on the Oracle upgrade exam for the Oracle 10*g* OCP, Oracle Database 11*g*: New Features for Administrators (exam 1Z0-050).

See the Oracle website at `http://www.oracle.com/education/certification` for the latest information on all of Oracle's certification paths, along with Oracle's training resources.

Oracle DBA Certification

The role of the DBA has become a key to success in today's highly complex database systems. The best DBAs work behind the scenes but are in the spotlight when critical issues arise. They plan, create, maintain, and ensure that the database is available for the business. They are always watching the database for performance issues and to prevent unscheduled downtime. The DBA's job requires broad understanding of the architecture of Oracle database, and expertise in solving problems.

Because this book focuses on the DBA track, we will take a closer look at the different tiers of the DBA track.

Oracle Database 11*g* Administrator Certified Associate

The Oracle 11g Administrator Certified Associate (OCA) certification is a streamlined, entry-level certification for the database-administration track and is required to advance toward the more senior certification tiers. This certification requires you to pass one of the following exams:

- 1Z0-001 Introduction to Oracle: SQL & PL/SQL
- 1Z0-007 Introduction to Oracle9*i* SQL
- 1Z0-047 Oracle Database SQL Expert
- 1Z0-051 Oracle Database 11*g*: SQL Fundamentals I

And then you must pass the following exam:

- 1Z0-052 Oracle Database 11*g*: Administration I

Oracle Database 11*g* Administrator Certified Professional

The OCP tier of the database-administration track challenges you to demonstrate your enhanced experience and knowledge of Oracle technologies. The Oracle 11*g* Administrator Certified Professional (OCP) certification requires achievement of the OCA certification, completion of one or more approved Oracle University classes, and successful completion of the following exam:

- 1Z0-053 Oracle Database 11*g*: Administration II

The approved courses for OCP candidates include the following:

- Oracle Database 11*g*: Advanced PL/SQL
- Oracle Database 11*g*: Data Guard Administration
- Oracle Database 11*g*: Performance Tuning
- Oracle Database 11*g*: Administration Workshop I
- Oracle Database 11*g*: Administration Workshop II
- Oracle Database 11*g*: Introduction to SQL
- Oracle Database 11*g*: New Features for Administrators
- Oracle Database 11*g*: Program with PL/SQL
- Oracle Database 11*g*: Develop PL/SQL Program Units
- Oracle Database 11*g*: Implement Streams
- Oracle Database 11*g*: SQL Tuning Workshop
- Oracle Spatial 11*g*: Essentials
- Oracle Database 11*g*: RAC Administration
- Oracle Database 11*g*: SQL Fundamentals 1

If you already have your OCP in 10*g* or earlier and have elected to take the upgrade path, you are not required to take the Oracle University class to obtain your OCP for Oracle 11*g*.

You should verify the list of approved courses for OCP candidates against the Oracle education website (`www.oracle.com/education`) because it can change without any notice.

Oracle Database 11*g* Certified Master

The Oracle Database 11*g* Administration Certified Master (OCM) is the highest level of certification that Oracle offers. To become a certified master, you must first obtain OCP certification; then complete two advanced-level classes at an Oracle Education facility; pass a hands-on, two-day exam at an Oracle Education facility; and then submit the Hands On Course Requirement form. The classes and practicum exam are offered only at an Oracle Education facility and may require travel.

Details on the required coursework for the OCM exam were not available when this book was written.

Oracle 11*g* Upgrade Paths

Existing Oracle Professionals can upgrade their certification in several ways:

- An Oracle10*g* OCP can upgrade to 11*g* certification by passing the 1Z0-050 Oracle Database 11g: New Features for Administrators exam.
- An Oracle9*i* OCP can upgrade to 11*g* certification by passing the 1Z0-055 Oracle Database 11*g*: New Features for 9*i* OCPs exam.
- An Oracle8*i* OCP can upgrade to 10*g* by passing the 1Z0-045 Oracle Database 10*g* DBA New Features for Oracle8*i* OCPs exam, then separately passing the 10*g* to 11*g* upgrade exam.
- Oracle 7.3 and Oracle 8 DBAs must first upgrade to an Oracle9*i* certification with the 1Z0-035 Oracle9*i* DBA New Features for Oracle 7.3 and Oracle 8 OCPs exam and then upgrade the 9*i* certification to 11*g* with the 1Z0-055 Oracle Database 11*g*: New Features for 9*i* OCPs exam.

Oracle Exam Requirements

The Oracle Database 11*g*: Administration II exam covers several core subject areas. As with many typical multiple-choice exams, there are several tips that you can follow to maximize your score on the exam.

Skills Required for the Oracle Database 11*g*: Administration II Exam

To pass the Oracle 11*g* Administration II exam, you need to master the following subject areas in Oracle 11*g*:

Database Architecture and ASM

Describe Automatic Storage Management (ASM)

Set up initialization parameter files for ASM and database instances

Start up and shut down ASM instances

Administer ASM disk groups

Configuring for Recoverability

Configure multiple archive log file destinations to increase availability

Define, apply, and use a retention policy

Configure the Flash Recovery Area

Use Flash Recovery Area

Using the RMAN Recovery Catalog

Identify situations that require RMAN recovery catalog

Create and configure a recovery catalog

Synchronize the recovery catalog

Create and use RMAN stored scripts

Back up the recovery catalog

Create and use a virtual private catalog

Configuring Backup Specifications

Configure backup settings

Allocate channels to use in backing up

Configure backup optimization

Using RMAN to Create Backups

Create image file backups

Create a whole database backup

Enable fast incremental backup

Create duplex backup and back up backup sets

Create an archival backup for long-term retention

Create a multisection, compressed and encrypted backup

Report on and maintain backups

Performing User-Managed Backup and Recovery

Recover from a lost TEMP file

Recover from a lost redo log group

Recover from the loss of password file

Perform user-managed complete database recovery

Perform user-managed incomplete database recovery

Perform user-managed and server-managed backups

Identify the need of backup mode

Back up and recover a control file

Using RMAN to Perform Recovery

Perform complete recovery from a critical or noncritical datafile loss using RMAN

Perform incomplete recovery using RMAN

Recover using incrementally updated backups

Switch to image copies for fast recovery

Restore a database onto a new host

Recover using a backup control file

Perform disaster recovery

Using RMAN to Duplicate a Database

Creating a duplicate database

Using a duplicate database

Performing Tablespace Point-in-Time Recovery

Identify the situations that require TSPITR

Perform automated TSPITR

Monitoring and Tuning RMAN

Monitoring RMAN sessions and jobs

Tuning RMAN

Configure RMAN for Asynchronous I/O

Using Flashback Technology

Restore dropped tables from the Recycle Bin

Perform Flashback Query

Use Flashback Transaction

Additional Flashback Operations

Perform Flashback Table Operations

Configure, monitor Flashback Database and perform Flashback Database operations

Set up and use a Flashback Data Archive

Diagnosing the Database

Set up Automatic Diagnostic Repository

Using Support Workbench

Perform block media recovery

Managing Memory

Implement Automatic Memory Management

Manually configure SGA parameters

Configure automatic PGA memory management

Managing Database Performance

Use the SQL Tuning Advisor

Use the SQL Access Advisor to tune a workload

Understand Database Replay

Space Management

Manage resumable space allocation

Describe the concepts of transportable tablespaces and databases

Reclaim wasted space from tables and indexes by using the segment shrink functionality

Managing Resources

Understand the database resource manager

Create and use Database Resource Manager Components

Automating Tasks with the Scheduler

Create a job, program, and schedule

Use a time-based or event-based schedule for executing Scheduler jobs

Create lightweight jobs

Use job chains to perform a series of related tasks

Administering the Scheduler

Create Windows and Job Classes

Use advanced Scheduler concepts to prioritize jobs

Globalization

Customize language-dependent behavior for the database and individual sessions

Working with database and NLS character sets

Tips for Taking the Administration II Exam

Use the following tips to help you prepare for and pass the exam:

- The exam contains about 55 to 80 questions to be completed in 90 minutes. Answer the questions you know the answers to first so that you do not run out of time.
- Many questions on the exam have answer choices that at first glance look identical. Read the questions carefully. Do not just jump to conclusions. Make sure you clearly understand exactly what each question asks.
- Some of the questions are scenario-based. Some of the scenarios contain nonessential information and exhibits. You need to be able to identify what's important and what's not important.
- Do not leave any questions unanswered. There is no negative scoring. After selecting an answer, you can mark a difficult question or one that you're unsure of and come back to it later.
- When answering questions that you're not sure about, use a process of elimination to get rid of the obviously incorrect answers first. Doing this greatly improves your odds if you need to make an educated guess.
- If you're not sure of your answer, mark it for review and then look for other questions that may help you eliminate any incorrect answers. At the end of the test, you can go back and review the questions that you marked for review.

You should be familiar with the exam objectives, which are included in the front of this book as a perforated tear-out card. You can also find them at `http://education.oracle.com/pls/web_prod-plq-dad/db_pages.getpage?page_id=41&p_exam_id=1Z0_053`.

Where Do You Take the Certification Exam?

The Oracle Database 11*g* certification exams are available at any of the more than 900 Thomson Prometric Authorized Testing Centers around the world. For the location of a testing center near you, call 1-800-891-3926. Outside the United States and Canada, contact your local Thomson Prometric Registration Center.

To register for a proctored Oracle Certified Professional exam:

- Determine the number of the exam you want to take. For the OCP exam, it is 1Z0-053.
- Register with Thomson Prometric online at `www.prometric.com` or, in North America, by calling 1-800-891-EXAM (1-800-891-3926). At this point, you will be asked to pay in advance for the exam. At the time of this writing, the exams are $125 each and must be taken within one year of payment.
- When you schedule the exam, you'll get instructions regarding all appointment and cancellation procedures, the ID requirements, and information about the testing-center location.

You can schedule exams up to six weeks in advance or as soon as one working day before the day you wish to take it. If something comes up and you need to cancel or reschedule your exam appointment, contact Thomson Prometric at least 24 hours or one business day in advance.

What Does This Book Cover?

This book covers everything you need to pass the Oracle Database11*g*: Administration II exam. Each chapter begins with a list of exam objectives.

Chapter 1 In this chapter, you'll learn about Automatic Storage Management (ASM). It introduces the ASM architecture and how to create a special type of Oracle instance: an ASM instance. In addition, this chapter describes in detail how to create and manage disk volumes in an ASM environment.

Chapter 2 This chapter introduces oracle user managed backup and recovery. A review of Oracle's architecture with respect to backup and recovery is presented. Management of the Oracle database with respect to backup and recovery is included in the chapter. The chapter covers putting the database in ARCHIVELOG mode. Finally the chapter covers Oracle offline and online backups.

Chapter 3 This chapter introduces the reader to Oracle user managed recoveries. Both complete and incomplete recoveries are covered in this chapter. Backup and recovery of the database control file is included along with the re-creation of the temporary tablespace datafiles. Finally, recovery from the loss of online redo logs and the password files are covered.

Chapter 4 This chapter introduces the reader to RMAN. The chapter discusses configuration of RMAN for backup and recovery operations. Both offline and online backups are discussed in the chapter. The chapter then proceeds to cover backups of an Oracle database by RMAN.

Chapter 5 This chapter provides an introduction to the RMAN recovery catalog. The chapter provides information on when you might want to use a recovery catalog, how to setup a recovery catalog, and register a database with the recovery catalog. We also discuss the use of RMAN's new virtual private catalog.

Chapter 6 This chapter dives into RMAN recoveries. RMAN recoveries in both NOARCHIVELOG and ARCHIVELOG mode are covered. Recoveries using both full backups and incremental backups are discussed. Faster recoveries using image copies are discussed and recoveries using a backup control file are also covered.

Chapter 7 This chapter covers RMAN reporting, monitoring, and tuning. Use of various views to monitor and report on RMAN operations is discussed in this chapter. The RMAN report and list commands are also covered in this chapter. Various RMAN administration commands are covered in the chapter.

Chapter 8 This chapter covers advanced RMAN recovery topics. This includes incomplete recoveries using RMAN. The chapter also discusses using RMAN for database duplication and tablespace point-in-time recoveries. The chapter also includes a discussion on using RMAN in disaster recovery situations.

Chapter 9 In this chapter, you'll learn about flashback technologies, including restoring dropped tables, performing flashback queries, flashback transactions, flashback table operations, flashback database operations, and setting up and using the Flashback Data Archive.

Chapter 10 This chapter discusses database diagnosis and performance management. You will learn about the Automatic Diagnostic Repository, the Support Workbench, performing block media recovery, and using the SQL Tuning Advisor, the SQL Access Advisor, and the Database Replay feature.

Chapter 11 This chapter discusses the management of Oracle resources. You will learn about automatic memory management features, including Automatic Memory Management (AMM), Automatic Shared Memory Management (ASMM), and Automatic PGA Memory Management (APMM) features. You will learn about resumable space allocation, transportable tablespaces, transportable databases, and shrinking segments to recover unused space.

You will learn about the Database Resource Manager (DRM) and how it can be used to manage resources. You will learn to create resource plans, resource consumer groups, and resource plan directives.

Chapter 12 In this chapter, we discuss the Oracle Scheduler. You will learn how the Scheduler can be used to automate repetitive DBA tasks. You will also learn to create the objects necessary to schedule jobs, including job, schedule, program, window, job group, and window group objects.

Chapter 13 This chapter describes Oracle's globalization support features. You will learn about linguistic sorting and searching, datetime datatypes, and how to configure the database to support different language and territorial conventions.

Throughout each chapter, we include Real World Scenario sidebars, which are designed to give a real-life perspective on how certain topics affect our everyday duties as DBAs. Each chapter ends with a list of exam essentials, which give you a highlight of the chapter, with an emphasis on the topics that you need to be extra familiar with for the exam. The chapter concludes with 20 review questions, specifically designed to help you retain the knowledge presented. To really nail down your skills, read and answer each question carefully.

How to Use This Book

This book can provide a solid foundation for the serious effort of preparing for the Oracle 11g: Administration II exam. To best benefit from this book, use the following study method:

1. Take the assessment test immediately following this introduction. (The answers are at the end of the test.) Carefully read over the explanations for any questions you get wrong, and note which chapters the material comes from. This information should help you plan your study strategy.
2. Study each chapter carefully, making sure you fully understand the information and the test objectives listed at the beginning of each chapter. Pay extra close attention to any chapter related to questions you missed in the assessment test.

3. Complete all hands-on exercises in the chapter, referring back to the chapter text so that you understand the reason for each step you take. If you do not have an Oracle database available, be sure to study the examples carefully.
4. Answer the review questions related to each chapter. (The answers appear at the end of each chapter, after the review questions.) Note the questions that confuse or trick you, and study those sections of the book again.
5. Take the two bonus exams that are included on the accompanying CD. This will give you a complete overview of what you can expect to see on the real test.
6. Remember to use the products on the CD included with this book. The electronic flashcards and the Sybex Test Engine exam-preparation software have been specifically designed to help you study for and pass your exam.

To learn all the material covered in this book, you'll need to apply yourself regularly and with discipline. Try to set aside the same time period every day to study, and select a comfortable and quiet place to do so. If you work hard, you will be surprised at how quickly you learn this material. All the best!

What's on the CD?

We have worked hard to provide some really great tools to help you with your certification process. All of the following tools should be loaded on your workstation when you're studying for the test.

The Wiley Test Engine Preparation Software

This test-preparation software prepares you to pass the 1Z0-053 Oracle Database 11*g*: Administration II exam. In this test, you will find all of the questions from the book, plus two additional bonus exams that appear exclusively on the CD. You can take the assessment test, test yourself by chapter, or take the practice exams. The test engine will run on either a Microsoft Windows or Linux platform.

Here is a sample screen from the Wiley Test Engine:

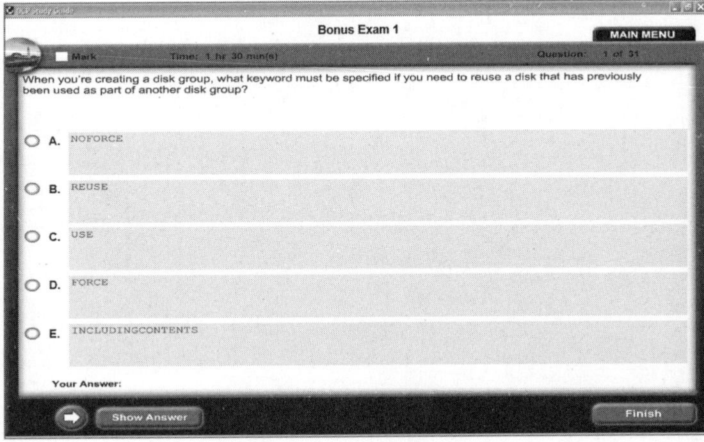

Electronic Flashcards for PC and Palm Devices

After you read the *OCP: Oracle Database 11*g *Administrator Certified Professional Study Guide*, read the review questions at the end of each chapter and study the practice exams included in the book and on the CD. You can also test yourself with the flashcards included on the CD.

The flashcards are designed to test your understanding of the fundamental concepts covered in the exam. Here is what the Sybex flashcards interface looks like:

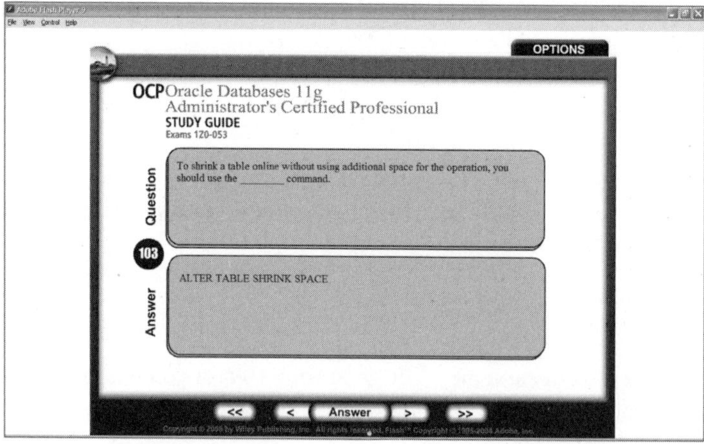

*OCP: Oracle 11*g *Administrator Certified Professional Study Guide* in PDF

Many people like the convenience of being able to carry their Study Guide on a CD, which is why we included the book in PDF format. This will be extremely helpful to readers who fly or commute on a bus or train and prefer an e-book, as well as to readers who find it more comfortable reading from their computer. We've also included a copy of Adobe Acrobat Reader on the CD.

Assessment Test

1. ASM supports all but which of the following file types? (Choose all that apply.)
   - A. Database files
   - B. Spfiles
   - C. Redo-log files
   - D. Archived log files
   - E. RMAN backup sets
   - F. Password files
   - G. `init.ora` files

2. After executing the command

   ```
   alter diskgroup disk group2 drop disk dg2a;
   ```

   you issue the following command from the ASM instance:

   ```
   Select group_number, count(*) from v$asm_operation;
   ```

   What is the implication if the query against `V$ASM_OPERATION` returns zero rows?
   - A. The `drop disk` operation is still proceeding and you cannot yet run the `undrop disks` operation.
   - B. The `drop disk` operation is complete and you can run the `undrop disks` command if needed.
   - C. The `drop disk` operation is complete and you cannot run the `undrop disk` command.
   - D. The query will fail since there is not a `V$ASM_OPERATION` view available in an ASM instance.
   - E. None of the above is true.

3. What is the net effect of the following command?

   ```
   alter diskgroup dgroup1 drop disk abc;
   ```

   - A. The disk ABC will be dropped from the disk group. Since you did not issue a rebalance command, the data on that disk will be lost.
   - B. The command will raise an error indicating that you need to rebalance the disk group to remove the data from that disk prior to dropping the disk.
   - C. The disk group will be automatically rebalanced during the drop operation. Once the rebalancing is complete, the disk will be dropped.
   - D. This command will fail because you cannot drop a specific disk in an ASM disk group.
   - E. The `disk drop` command will be suspended for a predetermined amount of time, waiting for you to also issue an `alter diskgroup rebalance` command. Once you have issued the rebalance command, ASM will proceed to rebalance the disk group and then drop the disk.

4. Which of the following is not a configurable attribute for an individual disk group?
   A. AU_SIZE
   B. COMPATIBLE.RDBMS
   C. COMPATIBLE.ASM
   D. DISK_REPAIR_TIME
   E. DG_DROP_TIME
5. What Oracle process runs when the database is in ARCHIVELOG mode but not when it is in NOARCHIVELOG mode?
   A. MMON
   B. LGWR
   C. ARCH
   D. ARWR
   E. COPY
6. You are peer reviewing a fellow DBA's backup plan for his NOARCHIVELOG mode database, as shown here:
   1. Put the tablespaces in backup mode.
   2. Back up the datafiles for all tablespaces.
   3. Take the tablespaces out of backup mode.
   4. Back up all archived redo logs.

   Your colleague asks for you to comment on his plan. Which response would be correct?
   A. The plan will work as is.
   B. The plan needs to be modified to allow for an archive-log switch after step 3.
   C. The plan needs to be modified so that a backup of the archived redo logs occurs before step 1.
   D. The plan needs to be adjusted to shut down the database after step 1 and to restart the database after step 2.
   E. The plan cannot work as presented.
7. Which of the following statements is true when the database is in ARCHIVELOG mode and tablespaces are in hot backup mode?
   A. Archive log generation is suspended until the tablespaces are taken out of hot backup mode.
   B. Datafiles are not written to during hot backups.
   C. Changes to the database are cached during the backup and not written to the datafiles to ensure that the datafiles are consistent when recovered.
   D. The datafile headers are not updated during the backup.
   E. The way data is written to the online redo logs is unchanged during the backup.

8. When you create a backup control file, where is the resulting file written to?
   - A. The database user dump destination directory
   - B. The database diagnostic destination directory
   - C. To `$ORACLE_HOME/rdbms`
   - D. To `$ORACLE_HOME/admin`
   - E. To the directory and filename you specify in the command

9. If a log file becomes corrupted, it may cause the database to stall. How would you correct such a situation?
   - A. Recover the online redo log from backup.
   - B. Delete and re-create the log file.
   - C. Use the `alter database clear logfile` command to clear the log file.
   - D. Shut down the database and restart it.
   - E. Shut down the database and then mount it. Clear the log file with the `alter database clear logfile` command and then restart the database with `alter database open resetlogs`.

10. You have lost datafiles 1 and 3 from your database, and the database has crashed. In what order should you perform the following steps to recover your database?
    1. Take the datafiles that were lost offline.
    2. `startup mount` the database
    3. Issue the `alter database open` command.
    4. Restore the datafiles that were lost
    5. Recover the datafiles with the `recover datafile` command.
    6. Bring the datafiles back online.
    7. Recover the database with the `recover database` command.

    - A. 2, 1, 3, 4, 5, 6
    - B. 2, 4, 5, 3
    - C. 4, 7, 3
    - D. 2, 4, 7, 3
    - E. 2, 7, 3

11. Which command is used to open the database after an incomplete recovery?
    - A. `alter database open`
    - B. `alter database open repairlog`
    - C. `alter database open resetlogs`
    - D. `alter database open resetlog`
    - E. `alter database resetlogs open`

12. Your database has a backup that was taken yesterday (Tuesday) between 13:00 and 15:00 hours. This is the only backup you have. You have lost all the archived redo logs generated since the previous Monday, but you have archived redo logs available from the previous Sunday and earlier. You now need to restore your backup due to database loss. To which point can you restore your database?

    A. 13:00 on Tuesday.
    B. 15:00 on Tuesday.
    C. Up until the last available archived redo log on Sunday.
    D. To any point; all the redo should still be available in the online redo logs.
    E. The database is not recoverable.

13. Which of the following files cannot be backed up by RMAN? (Choose all that apply.)

    A. Database datafiles
    B. Control files
    C. Online redo logs
    D. Database pfiles
    E. Archived redo logs

14. Which of the following RMAN structures can data from a datafile span?

    A. RMAN backup-set pieces spanning backup sets
    B. RMAN backup-set pieces within a given backup set
    C. RMAN backups
    D. RMAN channels
    E. None of the above

15. Which RMAN backup command is used to create the block-change tracking file?

    A. `alter database create block change tracking file`
    B. `alter database enable block change file`
    C. `alter database enable block change tracking using file '/ora01/opt/block_change_tracking.fil'`
    D. `alter system enable block change tracking using file '/ora01/opt/block_change_tracking.fil'`
    E. `alter system block change tracking on`

16. A shoot-out has erupted between your MS development teams using .NET and your Linux development teams using Java. Knowing that your database is in danger, which command would you use to back up your NOARCHIVELOG mode database using RMAN with compression?

    A. `backup database all`
    B. `backup compressed database`
    C. `backup as compressed backupset database;`
    D. `backup as compressed backup database plus archivelog all;`
    E. `backup as compressed backupset database plus compress archivelog all;`

17. What is the purpose of the RMAN recovery catalog? (Choose all that apply.)
    - **A.** Make backups faster
    - **B.** Store RMAN metadata
    - **C.** Store RMAN scripts
    - **D.** Provide the ability to do centralized backup reporting.
    - **E.** Make recovery faster

18. RMAN provides more granular catalog security through which feature?
    - **A.** Virtual private database
    - **B.** Virtual private catalog
    - **C.** RMAN virtual database
    - **D.** RMAN secure catalog
    - **E.** Oracle Database Vault

19. True of false? You can back up the RMAN recovery catalog with RMAN.
    - **A.** True
    - **B.** False

20. What RMAN command must you use before you can back up a database using the recovery catalog?
    - **A.** `create catalog`
    - **B.** `install database`
    - **C.** `catalog database`
    - **D.** `merge Catalog with database`
    - **E.** `register database`

21. You have control-file autobackups enabled. When starting your database from SQL*Plus, you receive the following error message:

```
SQL> startup
ORA-01078: failure in processing system parameters
LRM-00109: could not open parameter file
'C:\ORACLE\PRODUCT\11.1.0\DB_1\DATABASE\INITORCL.ORA'
```

    Using RMAN, how would you respond to this error?
    - **A.** Issue the `startup nomount` command and then issue the `restore parameter file` command from the RMAN prompt.
    - **B.** Issue the `startup nomount` command and then issue the `restore spfile` command from the RMAN prompt.
    - **C.** Issue the `startup nomount` command and then issue the `restore spfile from autobackup` command from the RMAN prompt.
    - **D.** Issue the `startup nomount` command and then issue the `restore spfile from backup` command from the RMAN prompt.
    - **E.** Issue the `restore spfile from autobackup` command from the RMAN prompt.

22. While working on a data problem, Curt, Bill, Ben, Mike, and Matt introduced a vast amount of corrupted data into the database. Pablo has discovered this problem and he needs you to recover the database to the point in time prior to the introduction of the corruption. The logical corruption was introduced at 6:30 p.m. on September 6, 2008. Which of the following would be the correct commands to use to restore the database to a point in time before the corruption?

   A.
   ```
   restore database until time
   '06-SEP-2008 06:30:00');
   recover database until time
   '06-SEP-2008 06:30:00');

   alter database open;
   ```

   B.
   ```
   restore database until time
   '06-SEP-2008 06:30:00');
   recover database until time
   '06-SEP-2008 06:30:00');

   alter database open resetlogs;
   ```

   C.
   ```
   restore database until time
   '06-SEP-2008 18:29:55');
   recover database until time
   '06-SEP-2008 18:29:55');
   alter database open resetlogs;
   ```

   D.
   ```
   restore database until time '06-SEP-2008 18:29:55');
       alter database open resetlogs;
   ```

   E.
   ```
   restore database until time '06-SEP-2008 18:29:55');
   recover database;
   alter database open resetlogs;
   ```

23. What is the purpose of the `until change` option of the restore command?

   A. It allows you to select the SCN that you want to restore to.

   B. It allows you to select the log sequence number you want to restore to.

   C. It allows you to select the timestamp you want to restore to.

   D. It allows you to manually stop the restore at any time as online redo logs are applied.

   E. None of the above.

24. What is the purpose of the `recover` command? (Choose all that apply.)

   A. Recover database datafiles from physical disk backup sets.

   B. Recover required incremental backups from physical disk backup sets.

   C. Recover required archived redo logs from physical disk backup sets.

   D. Apply incremental backups to recover the database.

   E. Apply archived redo logs to recover the database.

25. What is an obsolete backup set?

- **A.** A backup set that is missing one or more backup set pieces
- **B.** A backup that has exceeded the retention criteria and is no longer needed
- **C.** A backup set that does not include archived redo logs
- **D.** A backup set that can not be recovered due to corruption
- **E.** A backup set superceded by a datafile copy

26. What is the purpose of the `list expired backup` command?

- **A.** Lists all backups impacted by a `resetlogs` command
- **B.** Lists all backups that are subject to retention criteria
- **C.** Lists all backups that are missing associated physical backup set pieces
- **D.** Lists the status of datafile backup failures due to the use of the `duration` command
- **E.** Lists backups that cannot be used by the restore command because they have been marked as disabled

27. What is the purpose of the `catalog` command?

- **A.** To review RMAN control file and recovery catalog metadata and ensure that it's correct
- **B.** To delete RMAN backup-related metadata from the recovery catalog
- **C.** To create metadata in the control file and the recovery catalog related to backup set pieces
- **D.** To create a report that lists database backups
- **E.** To rebuild the recovery catalog

28. Which of the following commands will fail?

- **A.** `report schema;`
- **B.** `report need backup;`
- **C.** `report need backup days 3;`
- **D.** `report user;`
- **E.** `report obsolete;`

29. What are the two different types of database duplication? (Choose two.)

- **A.** Active
- **B.** Passive
- **C.** Online
- **D.** Backup-based
- **E.** Failure driven

30. When you're performing a tablespace point-in-time recovery, which tablespaces will always be restored to the auxiliary instance? (Choose all that apply.)

   A. The SYSTEM tablespace.

   B. The UNDO tablespace.

   C. All tablespaces with tables.

   D. All tablespaces with indexes.

   E. No tablespaces are automatically restored.

31. Which operation requires that you create an auxiliary instance manually before executing the operation? (Choose all that apply.)

   A. Backup-based database duplication.

   B. Active database duplication.

   C. Tablespace point-in-time recovery.

   D. No operation requires the creation of an auxiliary instance.

32. What RMAN command is used to execute a tablespace point-in-time recovery?

   A. `recover`

   B. `duplicate`

   C. `restore`

   D. `copy`

   E. None of the above

33. A user performs an update on a table. Shortly after committing the transaction, they realize that they had an error in their WHERE clause causing the wrong rows to be updated. Which Flashback option would allow you to undo this transaction and restore the table to its previous state?

   A. Flashback Drop

   B. Flashback Query

   C. Flashback Versions Query

   D. Flashback Transaction Query

   E. Flashback Table

34. A developer calls and reports that he accidentally dropped an important lookup table from a production database. He needs the table to be recovered. What action would you take?

   A. Initiate an incomplete recovery operation using RMAN.

   B. Copy the table from a development database.

   C. Advise the user to rekey the data.

   D. Perform a Flashback Drop operation.

   E. Perform a Flashback Recovery operation.

35. In a Database Replay workload capture, what client request information is gathered? (Choose all that apply.)

A. SQL text

B. Shared server requests (Oracle MTS)

C. Bind variable values

D. Information about transactions

E. Remote `DESCRIBE` and `COMMIT` operations

36. Which of the following are true concerning block media recovery? (Choose all that apply.)

A. Any gap in archive logs ends the recovery.

B. If a gap in archive logs is encountered, RMAN will search forward for newer versions of the blocks that are not corrupt.

C. Uncorrupted blocks from the flashback logs may be used to speed recovery.

D. The database can be in NOARCHIVELOG mode.

E. None of the above.

37. The DBA has chosen to manage SGA and PGA memory separately in an OLTP database because of his unique knowledge of the application. Which of these are good starting points to use when configuring the maximum values for SGA and PGA, based on the amount of memory available on the system?

A. 20% SGA, 80% PGA

B. 25% SGA, 75% PGA

C. 50% SGA, 50% PGA

D. 75% SGA, 25% PGA

E. 80% SGA, 20% PGA

38. You notice that a long-running transaction is suspended due to a space constraint, and there is no `AFTER SUSPEND` triggered event addressing the issue. You also note that the critical transaction is just about to reach the `RESUMABLE_TIMEOUT` value. Which of these actions is appropriate?

A. Abort the session, fix the space problem, then resubmit the transaction.

B. Use the `DBMS_RESUMABLE.SET_SESSION_TIMEOUT` procedure to extend the time-out for the session while you fix the problem.

C. Do nothing, let the transaction fail, then fix the problem.

D. Use Segment Shrink to clean up the table.

E. Use the `DBMS_RESUMABLE.SET_TIMEOUT` procedure to extend the time-out for the session while you fix the problem.

39. Which of the following are not disabled by default?
    - A. Jobs
    - B. Chains
    - C. Windows
    - D. Window groups
    - E. Schedule

40. You notice that a job in a chain has not completed on a nonconstrained RAC database. Which of these are valid reasons why that might occur?
    - A. The job priority is 1 and the resource consumer group CPU emphasis allocation is a low percentage.
    - B. The job affinity is to a service and one node in that service is unavailable.
    - C. The job affinity is to an instance and that instance is unavailable.
    - D. There is no service affinity.
    - E. None of the above.

41. The NLS_LANGUAGE parameter specifies the default conventions to be used for which of the following globalization elements?
    - A. Languages for server messages
    - B. Day and month names and abbreviations
    - C. Symbols to represent a.m., p.m., AD, and BC
    - D. Affirmative and negative response strings (YES, NO)
    - E. None of the above
    - F. All of the above

42. The NLS_TERRITORY parameter specifies the default conventions to be used for which of the following globalization elements? (Choose all that apply.)
    - A. Date format
    - B. Decimal character
    - C. Group separator
    - D. First day of the month
    - E. None of the above
    - F. All of the above

Answers to Assessment Test

1. F, G. ASM supports datafiles, log files, control files, archive logs, RMAN backup sets, spfiles, and other Oracle database file types, but not password files or `init.ora` files. For more information, see Chapter 1, "Using Oracle ASM."

2. C. The V$ASM_OPERATION view will indicate if the `drop disk` operation is still in progress. If no rows are returned by the view, then the `drop disk` operation is complete. If the drop disk operation is complete you cannot run the `undrop disks` command. For more information, see Chapter 1, "Using Oracle ASM."

3. C. The disk group will be automatically rebalanced during a drop (or add) disk operation. Once the rebalancing is complete then the disk is dropped. For more information, see Chapter 1, "Using Oracle ASM."

4. E. DG_DROP_TIME is not a valid configuration attribute for a disk group. For more information, see Chapter 1, "Using Oracle ASM."

5. C. The ARCH process starts up when the database is in ARCHIVELOG mode. It is responsible for moving the online redo logs to the various archived redo log destination directories. For more information, see Chapter 2, "Performing Oracle User-Managed Backups."

6. E. Since the database is in NOARCHIVELOG mode, the entire plan will not work since you can not perform hot backups in NOARCHIVELOG mode. If the database was in ARCHIVELOG mode, then you would choose option B. For more information, see Chapter 2, "Performing Oracle User-Managed Backups."

7. D. When a tablespace is in hot backup mode, the related datafile headers are not updated. The headers will be updated after the tablespaces are taken out of hot backup mode. For more information, see Chapter 2, "Performing Oracle User-Managed Backups."

8. E. When you issue the `alter database backup controlfile to 'directory/filename'`, Oracle will write the backup control file to the directory and filename that you choose. For more information, see Chapter 2, "Performing Oracle User-Managed Backups."

9. C. Use the `alter database clear logfile` command to clear the log file and free up the database. If the log file has not been archived, you may have to use the `alter database clear unarchived logfile` command instead. For more information, please see Chapter 3, "Performing Oracle User-Managed Database Recoveries."

10. B. You will have to startup mount the database and then restore the database datafiles that were lost (you could, of course, restore the files first). You then need to recover the datafiles with the `recover datafile` command. Once the datafiles are recovered, you can then open the database. You may wonder why online recovery is not possible in this case. Datafile 1 is always the SYSTEM tablespace. The database cannot be opened if the SYSTEM tablespace is not available. Also the use of the `recover database` command is not the best choice in this case. Oracle always wants you to answer the question that is the best choice. In this case, datafile recovery is the better choice. For more information, please see Chapter 3, "Performing Oracle User-Managed Database Recoveries."

11. C. The `alter database open resetlogs` command is used to open an Oracle database after an incomplete recovery. For more information, please see Chapter 3, "Performing Oracle User-Managed Database Recoveries."

12. E. The database is not recoverable. You would need all the archived redo logs generated during the backup on Tuesday, at least, to restore the database after that backup. The online redo logs are very unlikely to have all the redo that would be required. For more information, please see Chapter 3, "Performing Oracle User-Managed Database Recoveries."

13. C, D. RMAN will not back up online redo logs or database parameter files. RMAN will back up database server parameter files (spfiles) however. For more information, see Chapter 4, "Configuring and Backing Up Using RMAN."

14. B. RMAN backup set pieces within the same backup set can contain data from a given datafile. For more information see Chapter 4, "Configuring and Backing Up Using RMAN."

15. C. Use the `alter database enable block change tracking using file` command, followed by the path and filename in single quotes, to create the block change tracking file. For more information, see Chapter 4, "Configuring and Backing Up Using RMAN."

16. C. You would use the `backup as compressed backupset database plus archivelog all` command to back up your database. Of course, the command is so long-winded that the war would be over by the time you finished typing it all in. For more information, see Chapter 4, "Configuring and Backing Up Using RMAN."

17. B, C, D. The RMAN recovery catalog provides a centralized location for all RMAN-related metadata. Thus it makes centralized reporting much easier. Additionally, you can store scripts in the recovery catalog for use across all databases that use RMAN. For more information, see Chapter 5, "Using the RMAN Recovery Catalog."

18. B. The RMAN virtual private catalog provides the ability to allow users granular access to RMAN recovery catalog records based on database name. Thus, specific users can see only records they are allowed to see. For more information, see Chapter 5, "Using the RMAN Recovery Catalog."

19. A. You can back up any database without connecting to the recovery catalog, including the recovery catalog database. In fact, you can back up the recovery catalog database while connected to the recovery catalog. For more information, see Chapter 5, "Using the RMAN Recovery Catalog."

20. E. The `register database` command is used to indicate that the target database should be registered in the recovery catalog. For more information, see Chapter 5, "Using the RMAN Recovery Catalog."

21. C. You would first need to start the database with the `startup nomount` command from the RMAN prompt. Then you restore the spfile using the `restore spfile from autobackup` command. For more information, see Chapter 6, "Recovering Databases with RMAN."

22. C. You would first need to restore the database to the correct point in time with the `restore database` command. You would include the `until time` parameter to indicate what point in time you want to restore to. You then recover the database with the `recover database` command, which will apply the appropriate incremental backups and archived redo logs. Again, you use the `until time` command to indicate the time to recover to. Finally, you would open the database with the `alter database open resetlogs` command. For more information, see Chapter 6, "Recovering Databases with RMAN."

23. A. The `until change` option of the restore command provides the ability to restore the database to a specific SCN. For more information, see Chapter 6, "Recovering Databases with RMAN."

24. B, C, D, E. The recover command will recover the needed incremental backup and archived redo logs from backup sets for recovery purposes. The recover command will then apply the incremental backups and archived redo logs as needed to recover the database. For more information, see Chapter 6, "Recovering Databases with RMAN."

25. B. An obsolete backup set is one that has exceeded the retention criteria. As a result, it is subject to automatic removal in the flash recovery area. For more information, see Chapter 7, "Reporting, Monitoring, and Tuning with RMAN."

26. C. An expired backup is one that is missing one or more physical backup set pieces. The `list expired backup` command lists these types of backups. For more information, see Chapter 7, "Reporting, Monitoring, and Tuning with RMAN."

27. C. The `catalog` command is used to catalog backup set pieces or image copies in both the control file and the recovery catalog so RMAN can use those backup set pieces or image copies. For more information, see Chapter 7, "Reporting, Monitoring, and Tuning with RMAN."

28. D. There is no `report user` command. For more information, see Chapter 7, "Reporting, Monitoring, and Tuning with RMAN."

29. A, D. Active database duplication takes place using network connections between the target database and the auxiliary database instance. Backup-based duplication requires that the RMAN backup set pieces be available on the server where the duplicate database will be created. For more information, see Chapter 8, "Performing Oracle Advanced Recovery."

30. A, B. The `SYSTEM` and `UNDO` tablespaces will always be restored during a tablespace point-in-time recovery operation. For more information, see Chapter 8, "Performing Oracle Advanced Recovery."

31. A, B. Database duplication (either backup-based or active) requires that you create the parameter files for the auxiliary database instance and have the auxiliary database instance started in NOMOUNT mode. For more information, see Chapter 8, "Performing Oracle Advanced Recovery."

32. A. You use the recover tablespace command to perform a tablespace point-in-time recovery. For more information, see Chapter 8, "Performing Oracle Advanced Recovery."

33. E. Only the Flashback Table option recovers a table to a previous point in time. The other options allow viewing of past states of the data (B, C, D) or restoration from the Recycle Bin (A), but they do not recover a table to a previous point in time. For more information, see Chapter 9, "Understanding Flashback Technology."

34. D. A Flashback Drop option would allow you to restore the table from the Recycle Bin. Although A, B, and C may all be valid recovery options, they are much less desirable than Flashback Drop. E is an invalid option altogether. For more information, see Chapter 9, "Understanding Flashback Technology."

35. A, C, D. Shared server requests and remote `DESCRIBE` and `COMMIT` operations are not captured in a workload. For more information, see Chapter 10, "Diagnosing the Database and Managing Performance."

36. B, C. Option A is incorrect because a gap in archive logs does not automatically end the recovery. RMAN will search forward for uncorrupted newer blocks; if RMAN finds one, it will continue with the restore and recovery operation. RMAN will check the flashback logs for uncorrupted copies of the block before it checks the backups. Option D is incorrect because the database must be in ARCHIVELOG mode. For more information, see Chapter 10, "Diagnosing the Database and Managing Performance."

37. E. A good starting point is to use approximately 20 percent of the available memory for the PGA and approximately 80 percent for the SGA. For more information, see Chapter 11, "Managing Database Resources."

38. B. Since you're running short on time, extend the time-out for the session that's in jeopardy and fix the space problem. Don't put the transaction at risk while you try to find free space and run the commands, and don't kill the transaction—unless you know that the space condition and extended suspend has caused other issues. For more information, see Chapter 11, "Managing Database Resources."

39. E. A schedule is enabled by default. The others are disabled by default. For more information, see Chapter 12, "Using the Scheduler to Automate Tasks."

40. C. Since we've established that the RAC is not performance constrained, option A is not valid—if the resource group were not able to obtain adequate CPU, this might be a valid answer. Option B is not correct because service affinity guarantees that if one instance in the service is available, the Scheduler will attempt to use it to run the job. If there is no service or instance affinity, the Scheduler will attempt to balance the load across surviving nodes. For more information, see Chapter 12, "Using the Scheduler to Automate Tasks."

41. F. The `NLS_LANGUAGE` parameter specifies the default sorting sequence for character data. For more information, see Chapter 13, "Implementing Globalization Support."

42. A, B, C. The `NLS_TERRITORY` parameter specifies conventions for local currency symbol, ISO currency symbol, dual currency symbol, credit/debit symbols, ISO week flag, and the list separator. Option D is incorrect because the default first day of the week is specified; the first day of the month is the 1st, not a specific day of the week. For more information, see Chapter 13, "Implementing Globalization Support."

Using Oracle ASM

ORACLE DATABASE 11*g*: ADMINISTRATION II EXAM OBJECTIVES COVERED IN THIS CHAPTER:

✓ **Database Architecture and ASM**

- Describe Automatic Storage Management (ASM)
- Set up initialization parameter files for ASM and database instances
- Start up and shut down ASM instances
- Administer ASM diskgroups

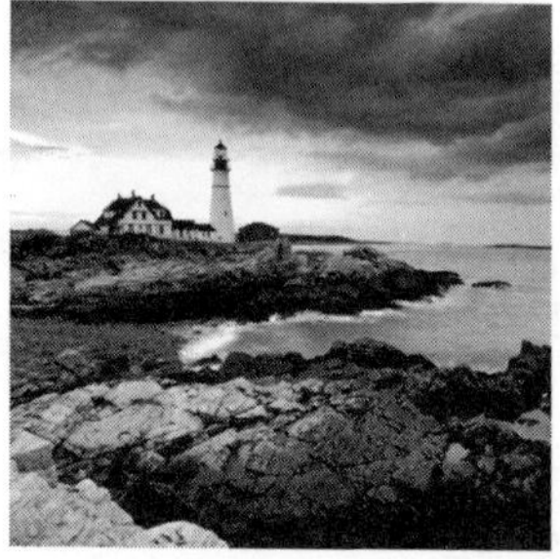

Automatic Storage Management (ASM) provides a centralized way to manage Oracle Database disk storage. The Oracle Database 11*g* OCP exam will test your knowledge of ASM, and thus ASM is the first topic we will tackle in this book.

In this chapter, we will discuss what ASM is, how to configure an ASM instance, how to manage an ASM instance, and finally, how to use ASM from within an Oracle database. As is true in the rest of this book, we will conclude with a review of the chapter, and we will tell you, in the section "Exam Essentials," what you need to know about ASM for the exam. Finally, we will present chapter review questions and answers so you can determine whether you have gained sufficient knowledge of ASM to pass the Oracle Database 11*g* OCP exam.

On with the show!

Exam objectives are subject to change at any time without prior notice and at Oracle's sole discretion. Please visit Oracle's Training and Certification website (`http://www.oracle.com/education/certification/`) for the most current exam-objectives listing.

What Is ASM?

ASM is designed to simplify Oracle database storage administration. Database environments have become more and more complex, with large numbers of (and larger) datafiles, storage area networks (SANs), and high-availability requirements. ASM is somewhat like a logical volume manager, allowing you to reduce the management of Oracle files into ASM disk groups. It also provides redundancy configurations, rebalancing operations, and, when installed on top of clusterware, the ability to share database-related files.

ASM stores files in *disk groups*, which are logical entities made up of one or more physical disk drives. ASM is good for more than just storing database datafiles. In an ASM instance, you can store database datafiles, online redo logs, archived redo logs, backup files, and data-pump dumpfiles as well as change-tracking files and control files of one or several Oracle databases, though these databases and the ASM instance must have affinity to a given machine or cluster. ASM also provides the ability to locate the flash recovery area on an ASM disk group, so your backups to disk can be made to ASM.

Here are some features of ASM:

- Automatic software data striping (RAID-0)
- Load balancing across physical disks
- Software RAID-1 data redundancy with double or triple mirrors
- Elimination of fragmentation
- Simplification of file management via support for Oracle Managed Files (OMF)
- Ease of maintenance

ASM fits perfectly into a Real Application Clusters (RAC) environment, but you can use ASM in a non-RAC environment too. In the following sections we will cover these ASM-related topics:

- The ASM instance
- Configuring ASM disks
- Accessing ASM from the database
- Managing ASM
- ASM data dictionary views

You should be aware of a few ASM limitations:

- ASM limits you to 63 disk groups in a given storage system. A disk group is a logical storage entity that is made up of one or more physical disks (we discuss adding ASM disk groups later in this chapter).
- You can have a maximum of 10,000 ASM disks in a given storage system.
- Each ASM disk can be a maximum of 4 petabytes (PB) in size.
- Each ASM instance can manage up to 40 exabytes of storage.
- Each disk group can contain up to one million files.
- Maximum file sizes vary by the type of disk group:
  - External-redundancy disk group: 140PB maximum file size
  - Normal-redundancy disk group: 42PB maximum file size
  - High-redundancy disk group: 15PB maximum file size

Working with the ASM Instance

Driving ASM is the *ASM instance*, which is a separate instance from any database instance. The ASM instance is mounted but never open like an Oracle database. It is, essentially, just a bunch of programs (daemons) running. You will create only one ASM instance per node. You can use the *Oracle Database Configuration Assistant (DBCA)* to create the ASM instance for you, or you can choose to create the ASM instance yourself.

Real World Scenario

Using ASM in the Real World

If you are an Oracle database administrator, ASM will very much be on your mind if you have to deal with Oracle database clustering (RAC). Early on in the architecting process, you will have to decide how to store shared files because RAC depends on sharing of database datafiles among the different nodes of the cluster.

You have several options, including shared raw devices and vendor-supplied products. Another option is ASM sitting on top of Oracle Clusterware. This combination can often provide a less-expensive solution over the vendor-supplied options and is easier to manage than raw disk storage. ASM and Clusterware are very popular options, and it is likely you will encounter them in your Oracle career.

One very positive thing, from a business point of view, is that ASM is included as part of your Oracle database license. This makes Oracle Clusterware/ASM an attractive alternative to products from other vendors that charge extra for their clustering solutions.

At one location we are familiar with, the move to ASM was cautious but direct. Oracle Clusterware was installed and ASM was sitting on top. All new Oracle RAC installs started using ASM instead of shared raw disk partitions. The flash recovery area (FRA) was also moved to ASM. Older RAC databases were moved to ASM over time, and now all clustered databases are using ASM.

We also note that Oracle's future direction calls for the elimination of raw devices for storage of database datafiles. This will make movement to an ASM solution even more attractive.

Creating the ASM Instance

In the following sections, we will review how to create an ASM instance. First we will cover creating the ASM instance with the Oracle Database Configuration Assistant. Then we will cover how to manually create an ASM instance.

Creating the ASM Instance with the DBCA

The DBCA is a Java-based tool that you can use to create or remove Oracle databases. Fortunately for us, it can also be used to create or remove ASM instances. You can create the ASM instance at any time, regardless of whether a database already exists. In Exercise 1.1, you will see how to create an ASM instance.

EXERCISE 1.1

Creating an ASM Instance with the DBCA.

To create the ASM instance with the DBCA, do the following:

1. Start the Oracle DBCA.
2. The DBCA presents a list of options for you to choose from. Select Configure Automatic Storage Management and click Next.
3. The DBCA then prompts you for the SYS password for the new ASM instance to be created. Enter the password for the SYS account.
4. Oracle then creates the ASM instance. A new window appears giving you the option to create new disk groups. You can choose to create disk groups (we will cover that shortly) or you can click Finish to complete the ASM instillation.
5. The name of the resulting instance will be +ASM. You can log into the ASM instance from SQL*Plus, as shown in this example:

```
C:\Documents and Settings\Robert>Set ORACLE_SID=+ASM
C:\Documents and Settings\Robert>Sqlplus sys/Robert as sysasm
SQL*Plus: Release 11.1.0.6.0 - Production on Mon Jul 14 19:55:33 2008
Copyright (c) 1982, 2007, Oracle.  All rights reserved.
Connected to:
Oracle Database 11g Enterprise Edition Release 11.1.0.6.0 - Production
With the Partitioning, OLAP and Data Mining options
SQL> select instance_name from v$instance;
INSTANCE_NAME
----------------
+asm
```

When we logged into the ASM instance, we did so using the SYSASM role. This role is much like the SYSDBA role when logging into a database and should be used when logging into an ASM instance for administrative purposes.

Creating the ASM Instance Manually

Manual creation of an ASM instance is fairly straightforward. If you have ever manually created a database, then manually creating an ASM instance should be easy for you. To manually create an ASM instance, you would follow these steps:

1. Create directories for the ASM instance.
2. Create the instance parameter file.

3. Perform any Microsoft Windows–specific configuration.
4. Start the ASM instance.
5. Create the ASM server parameter file (spfile).

Let's look at each of these steps in a bit more detail.

Step 1: Creating Directories for the ASM Instance

An ASM instance is almost always called +ASM. An exception exists in RAC environments where the ASM instance will be called +ASM1, +ASM2, and so on. Create the admin directories for the instance using Oracle's OFA standards. In the following examples, we assume that you have defined the ORACLE_BASE parameter.

The following are examples of the commands you might issue:

For Unix

```
mkdir -p $ORACLE_BASE/admin/+ASM/bdump
mkdir -p $ORACLE_BASE/admin/+ASM/cdump
mkdir -p $ORACLE_BASE/admin/+ASM/hdump
mkdir -p $ORACLE_BASE/admin/+ASM/pfile
mkdir -p $ORACLE_BASE/admin/+ASM/udump
```

For Microsoft Windows

```
mkdir %ORACLE_BASE%\admin\+ASM\bdump
mkdir %ORACLE_BASE%\admin\+ASM\cdump
mkdir %ORACLE_BASE%\admin\+ASM\hdump
mkdir %ORACLE_BASE%\admin\+ASM\pfile
mkdir %ORACLE_BASE%\admin\+ASM\udump
```

Of course, you could use a tool such as Windows Explorer to create the directories.

Step 2: Creating the Instance Parameter File

The ASM instance will require a *parameter file*, just as any other Oracle instances does. The number of parameters that you will need to set for an ASM instance is relativity small, so the parameter file typically is smaller than that of a normal Oracle database. You will also find that some parameters that you will set are unique to ASM. Let's look at a sample parameter file, and then we will discuss ASM-specific parameters and what they are for.

First, here is an example ASM parameter file:

```
###############################################
# ASM Parameter File - Unix
# Note, the ASM_DISKGROUPS parameter is commented out for now.
# ASM_DISKGROUPs='DISK GROUP_ROB1'
###############################################
```

```
# Diagnostics and Statistics
###########################################
background_dump_dest=/u01/app/oracle/admin/+ASM/bdump
core_dump_dest=/u01/app/oracle/admin/+ASM/cdump
user_dump_dest=/u01/app/oracle/admin/+ASM/udump
###########################################
# Miscellaneous
# Of course - set compatible to your version of Oracle
###########################################
instance_type=asm
compatible=11.1.0.6.0
remote_login_passwordfile=exclusive
```

Note the following Oracle parameters that are specific to ASM instances:

- INSTANCE_TYPE: Used only with an ASM instance, this parameter indicated to Oracle that this is an ASM instance. The default value is RDBMS, which indicates the instance is an Oracle database instance. This parameter is not dynamic and is the only mandatory parameter in an ASM instance.
- ASM_DISKSTRING: This parameter indicates where Oracle should search for disk devices to be used by ASM. We will discuss this parameter in more detail later in this section. This parameter can be dynamically changed.
- ASM_DISKGROUPS: This parameter lists ASM disk groups that ASM should mount when it is started. You can also use the `alter diskgroup all mount` command to cause these disk groups to be mounted. This parameter can be dynamically changed.
- ASM_POWER_LIMIT: This parameter controls the rate at which ASM can rebalance disks by increasing or decreasing the degree of parallelism used. Lower values will slow rebalancing but will also result in less of an IO impact by those operations. Higher values may speed up rebalancing by parallelizing the rebalance operation. The default is 1, and this is typically sufficient. This parameter can be set dynamically.

Did you notice that we did not include any of the memory settings (for example, SHARED_POOL_SIZE or DB_CACHE_SIZE) in this parameter file? While ASM does allocate memory, the default settings for the memory parameters are often quite enough.

Step 3: Performing Any Microsoft Windows–Specific Configuration

If you are running in a Windows environment, you will need to create the ASM service with the oradim utility. Here is an example of this operation:

```
C:Oracle\> oradim -new -asmsid +ASM -syspwd my_password
    -pfile C:\oracle\product\11.1.0.6\admin\+ASM\pfile\init.ora -spfile
    -startmode manual -shutmode immediate
```

Note in this example that we made the start mode manual so the service will not start automatically when the system is started. You will want to configure the service startup as required by your system.

Step 4: Starting the ASM Instance

You are now ready to start the Oracle ASM instance. Note that until you have added a disk group, you will get an error when the ASM instance is started. This is expected. In Exercise 1.2, you will see how to start an ASM instance.

EXERCISE 1.2

Starting an ASM Instance

Starting an ASM instance is quite easy, as shown in this exercise.

1. The name of the resulting instance will be +ASM. You can log into the ASM instance from SQL*Plus, as shown in this example:

```
C:\Documents and Settings\Robert>Set ORACLE_SID=+ASM
C:\Documents and Settings\Robert>Sqlplus sys/Robert as sysasm
SQL*Plus: Release 11.1.0.6.0 - Production on Mon Jul 14 19:55:33 2008
Copyright (c) 1982, 2007, Oracle.  All rights reserved.
Connected to:
Oracle Database 11g Enterprise Edition Release 11.1.0.6.0 - Production
With the Partitioning, OLAP and Data Mining options
```

2. Now, start the ASM instance with the `startup` command:

```
SQL> startup
ASM instance started
Total System Global Area   83886080 bytes
Fixed Size                  1247420 bytes
Variable Size              57472836 bytes
ASM Cache                  25165824 bytes
ORA-15110: no disk groups mounted
```

You will get an ORA-15110 error, but this is no concern at this time. This error is expected because you have not yet created any ASM disk groups. We will cover the creation and management of ASM disk groups later in this chapter.

Step 5: Creating the ASM Spfile

Having started the ASM instance, create the instance spfile from the pfile created in step 2. Here is an example:

```
create spfile from pfile='/u01/opt/oracle/admin/+ASM/pfile/init.ora';
```

Managing the ASM Instance

Management of the ASM instance is typically done from the command-line prompt. In the following sections, we will discuss these topics:

- Starting and stopping the ASM instance
- ASM processes
- ASM disk discovery
- Redundancy, striping, and templates
- Adding an ASM disk group
- Dropping an ASM disk group
- Altering an ASM disk group
- Using the ASMCMD command-line utility

Starting and Stopping the ASM Instance

Starting and stopping the ASM instance is pretty straightforward and much like starting and stopping an Oracle database. Oracle knows that you are starting an ASM instance, so it knows that when you issue the `startup` command, it needs to do something a bit different from what it would with a normal database. Exercise 1.2, shown earlier in this chapter, walks you through starting an ASM instance.

Shutting down the ASM instance is just as easy. A `shutdown immediate`, `shutdown abort`, or just a plain `shutdown` will do fine. If you execute a normal or immediate `shutdown` command on an ASM instance, that shutdown will fail if there is any database using that ASM instance. An error will be returned and the ASM instance will stay up. As a result, before you shut down the ASM instance, you will need to shut down all databases using that ASM instance.

You can perform a `shutdown abort` on the ASM instance. This will cause the ASM instance to shut down immediately and all of the associated databases will be shut down in an inconsistent state. This will require instance recovery when the databases are restarted, which can increase the time it takes to reopen the database. Oracle recommends that you not use the `shutdown abort` command when stopping an ASM instance.

ASM Processes

After you start your ASM instance, you will find that several of the Oracle processes you are acquainted with will be running, such as PMON and DBWR. Additional ASM processes will be started too. These processes include the following:

- The ARB*n* process, used to perform disk group rebalance operations. There may be one or more of these processes running.
- The ASMB process manages ASM storage and provides statistics.
- The GMON process maintains disk membership in ASM disk groups.
- The KATE process performs proxy I/O to ASM metadata files when a disk is offlined.

- The MARK process is responsible for marking ASM allocation units as stale following a missed write to an offline disk.
- The RBAL process runs in both database and ASM instances. RBAL is responsible for performing a global open of ASM disks in normal databases. RBAL coordinates rebalance activity for disk groups in ASM instances.

ASM Disk Discovery

ASM disk discovery is the first step to setting up an ASM disk group. In this section, we will cover configuring the ASM_DISKSTRING parameter, which helps with ASM disk discovery, and then we will discuss the topic of ASM disk discovery in general.

Setting the *ASM_DISKSTRING* Parameter

When you configured the parameter file for your ASM instance, you configured a parameter called ASM_DISKSTRING. This parameter contains the paths that Oracle will use to try to find the various candidate disks available for ASM's use. The process of ASM finding disks in the ASM_DISKSTRING path is known as *discovery*.

You may not need to set ASM_DISKSTRING. ASM_DISKSTRING has a number of different default values depending on the platform you are using. Table 1.1 lists the platform-specific default values (these will be set if ASM_DISKSTRING is set to a NULL value only).

TABLE 1.1 Default ASM Disk String

Platform Name	Default ASM_DISKSTRING Value
AIX	/dev/rhdisk*
HP-UX	/dev/rdsk/*
Linux	/dev/raw/*
Mac OS X	/dev/rdisk*s*s1
Solaris	/dev/rdsk/*
Tru64UNIX	/dev/rdisk/*

You can have multiple locations in the ASM_DISKSTRING parameter (we will provide an example of this in just a moment). If you insert a ? placeholder at the beginning of the string, Oracle will expand that out to represent the location of ORACLE_HOME in the parameter values. The ASM_DISKSTRING can be dynamically altered, which is nice if your friendly system administrator adds some storage to your system that you want Oracle to be able to use. If you happen to change ASM_DISKSTRING dynamically and the new disk path is not present, it will revert to the old disk path. Removing an existing disk path, when that disk path is in use, will result in a failure of the command.

Another thing to consider when determining how to configure the ASM_DISKSTRING parameter is performance. Leaving this parameter set to NULL, and thus taking the Oracle default, will often be sufficient. However, if you set ASM_DISKSTRING using a more restrictive set of parameters, you may find that discovery of disks will be faster. For example, using the default Linux setting of /dev/raw/* will result in ASM scanning the entire /dev/raw file system structure (it does not search subfolders). If you have a large number of devices in this structure, this may take some time. If, however, your disk devices in this structure are all prefixed with the word *raw* (raw1, raw2, raw3, and so on), then setting the ASM_DISKSTRING to /dev/raw/raw* could reduce the time it take ASM to perform discovery and improve performance of the startup of the ASM instance.

Something you will see common to all ASM_DISKSTRING parameters is the use of the asterisk. The asterisk is required when defining the ASM_DISKSTRING parameter. Here are some examples of setting the ASM_DISKSTRING parameter. In this first example, ASM will look for disks in devices when we create disk groups:

```
Alter system set ASM_DISKSTRING='/devices/*';
```

In the next example, we are pointing ASM_DISKSTRING to ORACLE_HOME/disks:

```
Alter system set ASM_DISKSTRING='?/disks/*';
```

In this example, we are pointing ASM_DISKSTRING to two different locations:

```
Alter system set ASM_DISKSTRING='?/disks/d1/*,?/disks/d21/*';
```

We could also use some adjunctive regular expressionish–type extensions and perform the allocation this way:

```
Alter system set ASM_DISKSTRING='?/disks/d[12]/*';
```

ASM Disk Discovery on Instance Start

When the ASM instance is started, it will use the paths listed in the ASM_DISKSTRING parameter and discover the disks that are available. These disks can then be added to ASM disk groups that we will discuss in the next section. Once discovery is complete and the ASM instance is open, you can review the disks discovered by looking at the V$ASM_DISK view, as shown in this example:

```
column path format a20
set lines 132
set pages 50
select path, group_number group_#, disk_number disk_#, mount_status,
header_status, state, total_mb, free_mb
from v$asm_disk
order by group_number;
```

```
PATH            GROUP_# DISK_# MOUNT_S HEADER_STATU STATE  TOTAL_MB   FREE_MB
--------------- ------- ------ ------- ------------ ----- -------- ----------
/dev/raw/raw4         0      1 CLOSED  FOREIGN      NORMAL      39          0
/dev/raw/raw5         0      0 CLOSED  FOREIGN      NORMAL      39          0
/dev/raw/raw3         0      2 CLOSED  FOREIGN      NORMAL      39          0
/dev/raw/raw6         0      2 CLOSED  CANIDATE     NORMAL    2048       2048
ORCL:ASM01_004        1      3 CACHED  MEMBER       NORMAL   34212      30436
ORCL:ASM01_005        1      4 CACHED  MEMBER       NORMAL   34212      30408
ORCL:ASM01_006        1      5 CACHED  MEMBER       NORMAL   34212      30420
ORCL:ASM01_007        1      6 CACHED  MEMBER       NORMAL   34212      30297
ORCL:ASM01_008        1      7 CACHED  MEMBER       NORMAL   34212      30507
ORCL:ASM01_009        1      8 CACHED  MEMBER       NORMAL   34212      30404
ORCL:ASM01_010        1      9 CACHED  MEMBER       NORMAL   34212      30509
ORCL:ASM01_011        1     10 CACHED  MEMBER       NORMAL   34212      30449
ORCL:ASM01_012        1     11 CACHED  MEMBER       NORMAL   34212      30340
ORCL:ASM01_013        1     12 CACHED  MEMBER       NORMAL   34212      30357
```

In this view, you see that there are three disks that are not assigned to any group (those with `GROUP_#` set to 0). These are unassigned disks that ASM has discovered but that have not been assigned to a disk group. Note the mount status of `CLOSED` on those three disks, which also indicates that the disk is not being accessed by ASM. The `HEADER_STATUS` of `FOREIGN` indicates that these disks contain data already and are owned by some process other than ASM (in this case, these are voting disks for a RAC). If the `HEADER_STATUS` says `CANIDATE`, as with `/dev/raw/raw6`, then we could add this disk to an ASM disk group.

Notice that most of the disks have a `MOUNT_STATUS` of `CACHED` and a `HEADER_STATUS` of `MEMBER`. This means that the disk is currently part of an ASM disk group (which we will discuss more in the next section).

There are some cases where the `V$ASM_DISK` view will not report any disks. For example, on our Windows XP system there are no raw disks to discover, so the `V$ASM_DISK` view will simply be blank. This is not a problem because we can use an existing file system as a location for an ASM disk. We will discuss that in the next section as we show you how to add disk groups to ASM.

Here are some things to be aware of with regard to ASM disk discovery:

- ASM can discover no more than 10,000 disks. If you have more than that, ASM will discover only the first 10,000 disks. This can occur when your ASM disk string is not sufficiently restrictive and the directory that you are searching in has a number of raw devices but many of them are not going to be assigned to ASM.
- ASM will not discover any disk that contains an operating-system partition table.
- ASM may discover disks that already contain Oracle data (as in our previous example with the voting disks).

Redundancy, Striping, and Other ASM Topics

When configuring ASM disk groups, you need to consider recoverability, performance, and other attributes. We will first cover recoverability by discussing the concept of redundancy. We will then discuss striping of ASM disk groups and ASM disk templates. Then we'll discuss ASM disk group attributes, ASM fast disk resync features, and ASM preferred mirror read features. We will end this section with a discussion of ASM Allocation Unit (AU) size and extents in ASM.

Redundancy

When configuring an ASM disk group, you can use one of three different *ASM redundancy* setting options to protect the data in your disk group:

- *Normal*: Typically employs two-way mirroring by default and thus requires allocation of two failure groups.
- *High*: Typically employs three-way mirroring by default and thus requires allocation of three failure groups.
- *External*: Does not employ any mirroring. This setting is typically used when the disk group is being assigned to an external disk that is attached to some device that already employs some disk redundancy.

The Costs of Redundancy

Keep in mind that there is a cost to everything, and this includes redundancy. If you have two 100GB ASM disks that you will be assigning to an ASM disk group, you will be able to effectively use only 100GB of overall space if you use normal redundancy, because each disk will have to go into an individual failure group. If you were to use external redundancy, you would be able to use all 200GB (at a cost, of course, of loss of protection).

Redundancy is supported by one or more *failgroups* (or failure groups) assigned to the ASM disk group when it is created. If you are using external redundancy, you typically would just have one failure group. If you are using the Normal redundancy setting, then the ASM disk group typically will need two failure groups. Each failure group represents a logical allocation of one or more disks to the ASM disk group and provides for mirroring within that disk group. Thus, when you create an ASM disk group, you might have one disk assigned to failure group 1 and one disk assigned to failure group 2. This way your data is protected from failure.

When you're using ASM mirroring, ASM will allocate an extent on a disk that becomes the primary copy (one of the failure groups) and then allocate copies of that extent to the mirrored copies (the other failure groups). When you create a disk group, you can indicate which disk goes in which failure group or you can let Oracle decide for you.

When you define the redundancy setting for a disk group, you are defining things such as what kind of striping occurs and whether the data will be mirrored. These attributes are defined based on which template you have assigned to the ASM disk group. By default, when you create a disk group, Oracle will assign it the default template setting. You can optionally assign another ASM template to a given disk group (We discuss templates later in this chapter).

Table 1.2 gives you some guidance about the redundancy-related settings defined within the default template.

TABLE 1.2 Default-Template Redundancy Settings

Template Name	Striping	Mirroring with Normal Redundancy	Mirroring with High Redundancy	Mirroring with Extended Redundancy
Control file	Fine	Three-way mirroring	Three-way mirroring	No mirroring
Datafile	Coarse	Two-way mirroring	Three-way mirroring	No mirroring
Onlinelog	Fine	Two-way mirroring	Three-way mirroring	No mirroring
Archivelog	Coarse	Two-way mirroring	Three-way mirroring	No mirroring
Tempfile	Coarse	Two-way mirroring	Three-way mirroring	No mirroring
Backupset	Coarse	Two-way mirroring	Three-way mirroring	No mirroring
Parameterfile	Coarse	Two-way mirroring	Three-way mirroring	No mirroring
Dataguardconfig	Coarse	Two-way mirroring	Three-way mirroring	No mirroring
Flashback	Fine	Two-way mirroring	Three-way mirroring	No mirroring
Changetracking	Coarse	Two-way mirroring	Three-way mirroring	No mirroring
Dumpset	Coarse	Two-way mirroring	Three-way mirroring	No mirroring
Xtransport	Coarse	Two-way mirroring	Three-way mirroring	No mirroring
Autobackup	Coarse	Two-way mirroring	Three-way mirroring	No mirroring

Default ASM Template Redundancy Settings

So, if you create a disk group with normal redundancy using the default template and you put datafiles on it, the datafile template would be used by default. In this case, a datafile would use two-way mirroring and coarse striping (see the section "Striping"). This means you would have to allocate at least two disks to an ASM disk group when it was created, one assigned to a different failure group. We will discuss failure groups later in this chapter.

Dealing with ASM Disk Loss

If you lose an ASM disk, then one of two situations will occur. First, ASM will take the lost/damaged disk offline and then automatically drop it. ASM will attempt a rebalance operation to maintain redundancy, using the mirror copies as required. The disk group and its associated data will remain available during this time.

If the disk group cannot be rebalanced, then ASM will take the whole disk group offline and the data in that disk group will not be available until the damaged disk is restored and the disks can be rebalanced.

Striping

Table 1.2 includes a *striping* column. There are two values there, fine and coarse. This refers to the stripe size that ASM applies to the disks that the disk groups are assigned to. If fine striping is selected, the ASM will use a 128KB stripe size. If coarse is selected, then Oracle uses the AU size of the disk group for the stripe size.

Templates

When you create an ASM disk group, Oracle will assign a default *template* to that disk group (see Table 1.2). A template is simply a named collection of attributes. For example, if you create a disk group using the default template and then create datafiles in that disk group, the datafile template will define the redundancy and striping for that data.

There may be cases where you want to define your own template for a disk group. You will need to first create the disk group and then alter it using the `add template` parameter of the `alter diskgroup` commands, as shown in this example:

```
CREATE DISKGROUP sp_dgroup2 NORMAL REDUNDANCY
failgroup diskcontrol1 DISK 'c:\oracle\asm_disk\_file_disk3' NAME file_diska1
failgroup diskcontrol2 DISK 'c:\oracle\asm_disk\_file_disk4' NAME file_diskb1;
ALTER DISKGROUP sp_dgroup2 ADD TEMPLATE new_template ATTRIBUTES (mirror);
```

After the mirror template has been added, you can create files in that disk group using the new template. When you add a template to a disk group, the template cannot be retroactively applied to files already in that disk group. As a result, you will need to use RMAN to back up and then restore files that already exist in the disk group in order for them to take on the attributes of the new template.

You can see the templates associated with a given disk group by querying the V$ASM_TEMPLATE view, as shown in this example:

```
SQL> select * from v$asm_template
  2  where group_number=2;
GROUP_NUMBER ENTRY_NUMBER REDUND STRIPE S NAME
------------ ------------ ------ ------ - --------------------
           2            0 MIRROR COARSE Y PARAMETERFILE
           2            1 MIRROR COARSE Y DUMPSET
           2            2 HIGH   FINE   Y CONTROLFILE
           2            3 MIRROR COARSE Y ARCHIVELOG
           2            4 MIRROR FINE   Y ONLINELOG
           2            5 MIRROR COARSE Y DATA FILE
           2            6 MIRROR COARSE Y TEMPFILE
           2            7 MIRROR COARSE Y BACKUPSET
           2            8 MIRROR COARSE Y AUTOBACKUP
           2            9 MIRROR COARSE Y XTRANSPORT
           2           10 MIRROR COARSE Y CHANGETRACKING
           2           11 MIRROR FINE   Y FLASHBACK
           2           12 MIRROR COARSE Y DATAGUARDCONFIG
           2           13 MIRROR COARSE N NEW_TEMPLATE
```

In this output, you can see that our new template (new_template) has been created and is ready for use. You can drop a template with the alter diskgroup command using the drop template parameter, as shown in this example:

```
ALTER DISKGROUP sp_dgroup2
DROP TEMPLATE new_template;
```

And you can alter a user-defined template with the alter template parameter of the alter diskgroup command. Notice in this example that we are actually changing one of the attributes of the default templates. You cannot drop the default templates, but you can modify them, as shown here:

```
ALTER DISKGROUP sp_dgroup2
ALTER TEMPLATE datafile
ATTRIBUTES (coarse);
```

ASM Disk Group Attributes

We have discussed ASM templates that define a set of attributes to the disk group assigned to them. Oracle Database 11*g* also allows you to define specific *disk group attributes*. Disk group attributes are set using the `attribute` clause of the `create diskgroup` and `alter diskgroup` commands. The following attributes can be set on a specific ASM disk group:

`Au_size` This is the disk group allocation unit (AU) size. The value defaults to 1MB and can be set only when the disk group is created. You must modify the AU size of the disk group if you want the disk group to be able to hold larger amounts of data. A disk group with the default AU size will be able to grow to 35TB (normal redundancy). Increasing the AU size will significantly increase the maximum size of the disk group. The maximum AU size is 64MB.

`Compatible.rdbms` Indicates the database version that the disk group is compatible with at a minimum (default is 10.1). This value should be equal to or greater than the compatibility parameter of the database(s) accessing the ASM disk group. This value cannot be rolled back once set.

`Compatible.asm` Indicates the ASM instance version that the disk group is compatible with at a minimum (default is 10.1). `Compatible.asm` must always be set to a value equal to or greater than `compatible.rdbms`. Once `compatible.asm` is set for a disk group, it can not be rolled back to an earlier value.

`Disk_repair_time` Indicates the length of time that the disk resync process should maintain change tracking before dropping an offline disk. The default for this parameter is 3.6 hours.

Disk group attributes can be viewed using the `V$ASM_ATTRIBUTE` view. You can see some examples of setting compatibility here:

```
Create diskgroup robert01 external redundancy
Disk '/oracle/asm/ASM_DISKGROUP_robert01.asm'
Attribute 'ccompatible.asm'='11.1.0';
Alter diskgroup robert01 set attribute 'DISK_REPAIR_TIME'='1200M';
Alter diskgroup robert01 set attribute 'compatible.asm'='11.1.0';
```

ASM Fast Disk Resync

The redundancy features of ASM make it possible for an ASM disk group to survive the loss of a disk associated with that disk group. Disk loss can result from a number of reasons, such as loss of controller cards, cable failures, or power-supply errors. In many cases, the disk itself is still intact. To allow for sufficient time to recover from disk failures that do not involve the actual failure of a disk, ASM provides the *ASM fast disk resync* feature.

By default, when a disk in an ASM disk group fails (including any associated infrastructure pieces), the disk will be taken offline automatically. The disk will be dropped some 3.6 hours later. As a result, you have only 3.6 hours by default to respond to a disk outage. If you correct the problem and the physical disk media is not corrupted, then ASM fast disk resync will quickly resynchronize the disk when it comes back online, correcting the problem very quickly. This type of resynchronization is much faster than rebuilding a newly added disk should the disk media be corrupted.

You can change the amount of time that Oracle will wait to automatically drop the disk by setting the `disk_repair_time` attribute (see the discussion on attributes earlier, in the section "ASM Disk group Attributes") for the individual disk groups using the `alter diskgroup` command, as shown in this example, where we set the `disk_repair_time` attribute to 18 hours:

```
Alter diskgroup dgroup1 set attribute 'disk_repair_time'='18h';
```

ASM Preferred Mirror Read

The *ASM preferred mirror read* feature allows you to define a primary set of disks that are the preferred disks to read from for a given instance. This is most prevalent when using RAC databases. In a RAC configuration, you could have two or more sets of disk arrays. Each disk array might be local to a given RAC instance. ASM preferred mirror read allows you to indicate which disk array is local to a specific RAC instance. As a result, it become the preferred disk set for the instance and thus is likely to be more performant.

The ASM preferred local disk is defined using the optional parameter `asm_preferred_read_failure_groups`.

ASM AU Size and Extents

ASM files are stored in disk groups. In each disk group, space is allocated in *extents*, and an extent consists of one or more units of space called *allocation units (AUs)*. Allocation units default to a size of 10MB and can be configured from 1 to 64MB at the time the disk group is created. Once the AU size has been determined for a given disk group, it cannot be changed.

To enable support for larger ASM datafiles, to reduce the memory overhead of large databases, and to improve file open and close operations, ASM uses a variable-extent sizing policy. Extents will be initially sized at the size of the AU (for the first 20,000 extents) of the ASM disk group in which the extent is created. The extent size will be increased to 8 times the AU size for the next 20,000 extents and then will increment to 64 times the AU size for subsequent extent allocations.

Adding an ASM Disk Group

We have now talked about discovering disks, and we have talked about templates, redundancy, and striping. Now we need to talk about actually creating a disk group. You use the `create diskgroup` command to create an ASM disk group. When you issue the command, you will assign the disk group its name, and you will add one or more discovered (unallocated) disks to that disk group. Here is an example of the use of the `create diskgroup` command:

```
CREATE DISKGROUP dgroup1 NORMAL REDUNDANCY
failgroup diskcontrol1 DISK
'/devices/diska1'
failgroup diskcontrol2 DISK
'/devices/diskb1';
```

In this case, we have created a disk group called dgroup1. It is using normal redundancy and the default template. Two named failure groups are assigned, diskcontrol1 and diskcontrol2. Each failure group represents one physical or logical disk unit, which has been discovered by ASM. Two separate disks and failure groups are required because of the normal redundancy. If we used high redundancy, we would need to add a third disk to the command, as shown here:

```
CREATE DISKGROUP dgroup1 HIGH REDUNDANCY
failgroup diskcontrol1 DISK
'/devices/diska1' NAME diska1
failgroup diskcontrol2 DISK
'/devices/diskb1' NAME diskb1
failgroup diskcontrol3 DISK
'/devices/diskc1' NAME diskc1;
```

You might have noticed the `name` clause in the `create diskgroup` command example earlier. You can also name the disks being assigned to the ASM disk group using the `name` clause of the `create diskgroup` command. Failure to use the `name` clause will result in each disk receiving its own system-default assigned name.

When you create an ASM disk group, Oracle will add that disk group to the `ASM_DISKGROUPS` parameter on the ASM instance only if you are using an spfile. If you are not using an spfile, you will need to manually add the disk group to the `ASM_DISKGROUPS` parameter. The `ASM_DISKGROUPS` parameter tells Oracle which disk groups it should mount when the ASM instance is started. You can see the `ASM_DISKGROUPS` parameter setting by using the `show parameter` command from SQL*Plus, as shown here:

```
SQL> show parameter ASM_DISKGROUPS
NAME                                 TYPE        VALUE
------------------------------------ ----------- -------------------------
ASM_DISKGROUPS                       string      COOKED_DGROUP1, SP_DGROUP2
```

If you do not add the disk group to the `ASM_DISKGROUPS` parameter, you will need to manually mount the disk group.

You might have noticed that each time we create a new disk group (and when we add new disks to a disk group), we give the disk a name. For example, here we create a new disk group called `DGROUP1`:

```
CREATE DISKGROUP dgroup1 EXTERNAL REDUNDANCY
failgroup diskcontrol1 DISK
'/oracle01/oradata/asm/disk group1.dsk' NAME dgroup1_0000;
```

You can reference the disk group and the disk name by joining the V$ASM_DISK and V$ASM_DISKGROUP views, as shown in this query:

```
select adg.name dg_name, ad.name fg_name, path
from v$asm_disk ad
right outer join v$ASM_DISKGROUP adg
on ad.group_number=adg.group_number
where adg.name='DGROUP1';
DG_NAME  FG_NAME          PATH
-------- ---------------  ----------------------------------------
DGROUP1  DGROUP1_0000     /oracle01/oradata/asm/disk group1.dsk
```

 **Real World Scenario**

Why Tiered Storage?

Tiered database storage attempts to reduce the overall costs of disk storage in databases. When you configure ASM, you might want to consider configuring different disk groups for different kinds of tiered storage.

For example, suppose you work at Amalgamated General Consolidated. You have a new database that you are designing. You can choose from fast and expensive solid-state disks that costs $50 a gigabyte. Then there are the Fibre Channel disks that are a bit slower but only $30 a gigabyte. Finally, there are the slow SATA drives at $20 a gigabyte.

You can, of course, architect your 1 terabyte database with all solid-state disks at a cost of $50 million. It will be fast, no doubt, but is this the best choice for Amalgamated?

Amalgamated decides to analyze the needs of the database and determine if it can benefit from a tiered storage approach. If you determined that you need only 100GB of solid-state disk and that you could store the remaining 900GB on your $20 SATA drives, that would be cost savings of $27 million. That's quite a big savings.

This type of architecture requires that you architect physical database objects to sit across these layers using partitioning, creating the more heavily used partitions on better-performing disk; the infrequently used partitions can be moved over time to the cheaper/slower disks. This might take more time and effort, but in the end the dollar savings can be significant! Tiered storage is an idea that is very much taking off!

Dropping an ASM Disk Group

To remove an ASM disk group, you use the drop diskgroup command. By default, if any files exist in the disk group, ASM will not allow you to drop it unless you use the including contents clause. The drop diskgroup statement is synchronous in nature, so once the prompt returns, the deed is done ... no Recycle Bin here. When the drop diskgroup command is executed, ASM will unmount the disk from the ASM instance and write over all the ASM-related information on that disk. The ASM_DISKGROUPS parameter will also be changed if you are using an spfile. Here is an example of removing an ASM disk group with the drop diskgroup command:

```
Drop diskgroup sp_dgroup2;
```

If the ASM disk group has files in it, use this version:

```
Drop diskgroup sp_dgroup2 including contents;
```

Altering an ASM Disk Group

The alter diskgroup command is used to modify ASM disk groups. With the alter diskgroup command, you can do the following:

- Add disks to an ASM disk group
- Remove disks from an ASM disk group
- Add and drop disks from an ASM disk group
- Undrop disks from an ASM disk group
- Resize disks in a disk group
- Manually rebalance a disk group
- Mount and unmount disk groups
- Check the consistency of a disk group
- Create ASM disk group directories
- Manage ASM disk group directories

Adding Disks to an ASM Disk Group

As databases grow, you need to add disk space. The alter diskgroup command allows you to add disks to a given disk group to increase the amount of space available. Adding a disk to an existing disk group is easy with the alter diskgroup command, as shown in this example:

```
alter diskgroup cooked_dgroup1
add disk 'c:\oracle\asm_disk\_file_disk3'
name new_disk;
```

When you add a disk to a disk group, Oracle will start to rebalance the load on that disk group. Also, notice that in the preceding example we did not assign the disk to a specific failure group. As a result, each disk will be assigned to its own failure group when it's created. For example, when we added the disk to the cooked_dgroup1 disk group, a new failure group called cooked_dgroup1_0002 was created, as shown in this output:

```
SQL> select disk_number, group_number, failgroup from v$asm_disk;
DISK_NUMBER GROUP_NUMBER failgroup
----------- ------------ ------------------------------
          1            0
          0            1 DISKCONTROL1
          1            1 DISKCONTROL2
          2            1 COOKED_DGROUP1_0002
```

We can add a disk to an existing failure group by using the failgroup parameter, as shown in this example:

```
alter diskgroup cooked_dgroup1
add failgroup DISKCONTROL1
disk 'c:\oracle\asm_disk\_file_disk4'
name new_disk;
```

Removing Disks from an ASM Disk Group

The alter diskgroup command allows you to remove disks from an ASM disk group using the drop disk parameter. ASM will first rebalance the data on the disks to be dropped, assuming enough space is available. If insufficient space is available to move the data from the disk to be dropped to another disk, then an error will be raised. You can use the force parameter to force ASM to drop the disk, but this can result in data loss. Here is an example of dropping a disk from a disk group:

```
alter diskgroup cooked_dgroup1
drop disk 'c:\oracle\asm_disk\_file_disk4';
```

The alter diskgroup command also gives you the option to drop from a failure group all disks that are assigned to the disk group. Use the in failgroup keyword and then indicate the name of the failure group, as shown in this example:

```
alter diskgroup cooked_dgroup1
drop disks in failgroup diskcontrol1;
```

When you drop a disk from a disk group, the operation is asynchronous. Therefore, when the SQL prompt returns, this does not indicate that the operation has completed. To determine if the operation has completed, you will need to review the V$ASM_DISK view. When the disk drop is complete the column HEADER_STATUS will take on the value of FORMER, as shown in this example:

```
SQL> select disk_number, header_status from v$asm_disk;
DISK_NUMBER HEADER_STATU
----------- ------------
          0 FORMER
          1 FORMER
          1 MEMBER
          2 MEMBER
```

If the drop is not complete (the V$ASM_DISK column STATE will read dropping), you can check the V$ASM_OPERATION view and it will give you an idea of how long the operation is expected to take before it is complete. Here is an example query that will provide you with this information:

```
select group_number, operation, state, power, est_minutes
from v$asm_operation;
```

Adding and Dropping Disks from an ASM Disk Group

The alter diskgroup command will allow you to add and drop a disk from a disk group at the same time. Assuming you want to add a disk /dev/raw/raw6 and drop a disk called d2c, you could issue this command:

```
alter diskgroup mydisk group
add failgroup fg4 disk '/dev/raw/raw6/ name d2d
drop disk d2c;
```

Undropping Disks from an ASM Disk Group

You know you are having a bad day when you accidentally drop a disk from a disk group and you realize your mistake only after the drop operation has completed. Fortunately, this is not one of those mistakes that you cannot recover from. If you have accidentally dropped a disk, simply use the alter diskgroup command with the undrop disks parameter, as shown here:

```
alter diskgroup sp_dgroup2 undrop disks;
```

This will cancel the pending drop of disks from that disk group. You can not use this command to restore disks dropped if you dropped the entire disk group with the drop diskgroup command.

Resizing Disks in an ASM Disk Group

Sometimes when more space is needed, all a disk administrator needs to do is add that additional space to the disk devices that are being presented for ASM to use. If this is the case, you will want to indicate to ASM that it needs to update its metadata to represent the correct size of the disks it's using so you get the benefit of the additional space. This is accomplished using the `alter diskgroup` command with the `resize all` parameter, as shown in this example:

```
alter diskgroup cooked_dgroup1 resize all;
```

This command will query the operating system for the current size of all of the disk devices attached to the disk group and will automatically resize all disks in that disk group accordingly. You can indicate that a specific disk needs to be resized by including the disk name (from the `NAME` column in `V$ASM_DISK`), as shown in this example:

```
alter diskgroup cooked_dgroup1 resize disk FILE_DISKB1;
```

You can also resize an entire failure group at one time:

```
alter diskgroup cooked_dgroup1 resize disks in failgroup DISKCONTROL2;
```

Manually Rebalancing Disks Assigned to an ASM Disk Group

Manually rebalancing disks within ASM is typically not required since ASM will perform this operation automatically. However, in cases where you might want to have some more granular control over the disk-rebalance process, you can use the `alter diskgroup` command along with the `rebalance` parameter to manually rebalance ASM disks.

When we discuss rebalancing disks in ASM, we often discuss the power level that is assigned to that rebalance operation. Setting power with regard to a rebalance operation really defines the urgency of that operation with respect to other operations occurring on the system (for example, other databases or applications). When a rebalance operation occurs with a low power (for example, 1, the typical default), then that operation is not given a high priority on the system As a result, the rebalance operation can take some time. When a higher power setting is used (for example, 11, the maximum), the ASM is given higher priority. This can have an impact on other operations on the system. If you use a power of 0, this will have the effect of suspending the rebalance operation. You can set the default power limit for the ASM instance by changing the `asm_power_limit` parameter.

Here is an example of starting a manual rebalance of a disk group:

```
alter diskgroup cooked_dgroup1 rebalance power 5 wait;
```

In this example, you will notice that we used the `wait` parameter. This makes this rebalance operation synchronous for our session. Thus, when the SQL prompt returns, we know that the rebalance operation has completed. The default is `nowait`, which will cause the operation to be synchronous in nature. You can check the status of the rebalance operation using the `V$ASM_OPERATION` view during asynchronous rebalance operations. If you use the `wait` parameter and you want to convert the operation to an asynchronous operation, you can simply press Ctrl+C on most platforms and an error will be returned along with the SQL prompt. The rebalance operation will continue, however.

If you do not use the `power` parameter during a manual rebalance operation, or if an implicit rebalance operation is occurring (because you are dropping a disk, for example), you can affect the power of that rebalance operation by dynamically changing the `ASM_POWER_LIMIT` parameter to a higher value with the `alter system` command.

Finally, you can also use the `rebalance` parameter along with the `power` parameter when adding, dropping, or resizing disks within a disk group, as shown in this example:

```
alter diskgroup cooked_dgroup1 resize all rebalance power 5;
```

Manually Mounting and Unmounting an ASM Disk Group

If an ASM disk group is not assigned to the `ASM_DISKGROUPS` parameter, or if the disk group is unmounted for some other reason, you will need to mount the ASM disk group. You can use the `alter diskgroup` command with the `mount` clause to mount the disk group.

Additionally, if you need to dismount an ASM disk group, you can use the `alter diskgroup` command. Here are some examples:

```
alter diskgroup sp_dgroup2 dismount;
alter diskgroup sp_dgroup2 mount;
```

Note that when you dismount a disk group, that disk group will be automatically removed from the `ASM_DISKGROUPS` parameter if you are using an spfile. This means that when ASM is restarted, that disk group will not be remounted. If you are using a regular text parameter file, you will need to remove the disk group manually (assuming it's in the parameter file to begin with) or ASM will try to remount the disk group when the system is restarted.

Checking the Consistency of a Disk Group

On occasion you might wonder if there is some problem with an ASM disk group, and you will want to check the consistency of the ASM disk group metadata. This need might arise because of an error that occurs when the ASM instance is started or as the result of an Oracle database error that might be caused by some ASM corruption. To perform this check, simply use the `alter diskgroup` command with the `check all` parameter, as shown in this example:

```
alter diskgroup sp_dgroup2 check all;
```

When you execute the `alter diskgroup check all` command the results are written to the alert log of the instance. ASM will attempt to correct any errors that are detected.

Creating ASM Disk Group Directories

When you create an ASM disk group, it includes a system-generated directory structure for the ASM files that will be stored in that disk group. The system-generated directory structure takes on the following format, where disk_group is the root of the directory hierarchy:

```
+disk_group/database_name/object_type/ASM_file_name
```

The database name will be the name of the database that the data is associated with. The object_type is the type of object being stored (for example, datafile) and the ASM_file_name is the system-generated filename assigned to that ASM file.

ASM allows you to create your own directories within these predefined structures. This allows you to give alias names to the ASM files that you will create. This can make working with ASM files easier.

To create a directory structure, you use the alter diskgroup command with the add directory parameter, as shown in this example:

```
ALTER DISKGROUP cooked_dgroup1
ADD DIRECTORY '+cooked_dgroup1/stuff';
```

Managing ASM Disk Group Directories

The alter diskgroup command is also used to manage ASM disk group directories. If you want to drop an ASM disk group directory, simply use the drop directory clause of the alter diskgroup command, as shown in this example:

```
alter diskgroup cooked_dgroup1
drop directory '+cooked_dgroup1/stuff';
```

You can also rename directories with the alter diskgroup command using the rename directory clause, as shown in this example:

```
alter diskgroup cooked_dgroup1
rename directory '+cooked_dgroup1/stuff' to '+cooked_dgroup1/badstuff';
```

You can see the ASM disk group directories in the V$ASM_ALIAS view, as shown in this example:

```
select a.name "Alias Name", b.name "Disk group"
from v$asm_alias a, v$ASM_DISKGROUPS b
where a.group_number=b.group_number;
Alias Name                                        Disk group
------------------------------------------------ ---------------
badstuff                                          COOKED_DGROUP1
```

Using the ASMCMD Command-Line Utility

The ASMCMD tool is a command-line utility that allows you to manage ASM instances and the disk structures and files within those instances. With ASMCMD, you can do the following:

- List contents of ASM disk groups
- Perform searches (like directory listings)
- Add or remove directories
- Display space availability and utilization

ASMCMD allows you to traverse the ASM disks as you would a directory structure. From the root of the ASM instance, you can move down the various disk structures to find the disks you are interested in. Many of the commands in ASMCMD are Unix-like (in other words, `ls`, `cd`) and therefore the ASMCMD is fairly easy to learn how to use.

Starting ASMCMD

To start ASMCMD, simply set your `ORACLE_SID` to +ASM and then type **`asmcmd`** from the command line, as shown here:

```
C:\>set ORACLE_SID=+ASM
C:\>asmcmd
```

Or from Unix:

```
/opt/oracle>export ORACLE_SID=+ASM
/opt/oracle>asmcmd
```

You will need to make sure that `perl.exe` is in the path before you run ASMCMD. If you have installed more than one `ORACLE_HOME`, it may take some setup to get the pathing set correctly. Make sure the following is set to the correct `ORACLE_HOME`:

- `ORACLE_HOME`
- `PATH`
- `PERL5LIB`
- `PERLBIN`

When ASMCMD starts, you will see the ASMCMD prompt, as shown here:

```
ASMCMD>
```

You can start ASMCMD with the -p option and it will display the current directory level, as shown in this example:

```
C:\oracle\product\11.1.0.6\DB01\BIN>asmcmd -p
ASMCMD [+] >
```

ASMCMD Commands

ASMCMD has a basic set of commands, many of which mimic Unix commands. You can see these commands from the ASMCMD prompt if you type in **help**. The commands are pretty straightforward and easy to use. In the next section, we will introduce each command and provide an example of its use. Table 1.3 lists the different ASMCMD commands and their purposes.

TABLE 1.3 ASMCMD Commands

Command	Purpose	Example
cd	Changes ASM directory.	cd +group1
du	Gets disk use.	du
find	Finds directory or file.	find + rob11g
help	Displays the help screen.	help
ls	Lists files in directory.	ls -l
lsct	Lists all clients using the ASM instance.	lsct
lsdg	Lists information on disk groups in the ASM instance.	lsdg
lsdsk	Lists ASM visible disks. Supported only in Unix.	lsdsk -k -d DATA *
mkalias	Creates an ASM alias for a given ASM filename.	mkalias +cooked_dgroup1/11gDB/controlfile/Current.258.613087119 +cooked_dgroup1/control01.ctl
mkdir	Creates an ASM directory.	mkdir old
md_backup	Backs up ASM metadata.	md_backup -b /tmp/dgbackup070222 -g dgroup1 -g dgroup2

TABLE 1.3 ASMCMD Commands *(continued)*

Command	Purpose	Example
`md_restore`	Restores ASM metadata.	`md_restore -t full -g dgroup1 -i /tmp/dgbackup070222`
`pwd`	Locates where you are on the ASM directory tree.	`pwd`
`remap`	Remaps a range of physical blocks on disk.	`remap data data_0003 6000-8000`

`rm`	Removes an ASM directory or file.	`rm Current.258.613087119`
		`rm current*`
		`rm -r current*`

`rmalias`	Removes an ASM alias.	`rmalias +cooked_dgroup1/11gDB/datafile/alias_tbs_01.dbf`

Overview of ASM Data Dictionary Views

You were introduced to Oracle's data dictionary as a part of your OCA studies. Recall that the data dictionary provides views on the operation and performance of the database. The data dictionary also provides a great deal of metadata about database structures. Several data-dictionary views are available for use with ASM. Table 1.4 lists those views and gives descriptions of their use.

You can learn more about the Oracle data dictionary in Chapter 2, "Performing Oracle User-Managed Backups."

TABLE 1.4 ASMCMD Commands

View Name	In ASM Instance	In Database
V$ASM_DISKGROUP	This view will describe a given disk group.	This view contains a single row for each ASM disk group that is mounted by the local ASM instance. Note that discovery will occur each time you query this view. This can have performance impacts.

TABLE 1.4 ASMCMD Commands *(continued)*

View Name	In ASM Instance	In Database
V$ASM_DISK	This view describes each disk that was discovered by the ASM instance. All disks are reported, even those not assigned to disk groups.	This view describes each disk that is assigned to a database. Note that discovery will occur each time you query this view. This can have performance impacts.
V$ASM_DISKGROUP_STAT	This view is equivalent to the V$ASM_DISKGROUP view.	This view contains a single row for each ASM disk group that is mounted by the local ASM instance. No discovery will occur when this view is queried.
V$ASM_FILE	Displays each ASM file contained in the ASM instance.	Not used in a database instance.
V$ASM_DISK_STAT	This view is equivalent to the V$ASM_DISK view.	This view describes each disk that is assigned to a database. No discovery will occur when this view is queried.
V$ASM_TEMPLATE	Displays each ASM template contained in the ASM instance by disk group.	Not used in a database instance.
V$ASM_ALIAS	Displays each alias contained in the ASM instance by disk group.	Not used in a database instance.
V$ASM_OPERATION	Displays each long-running operation occurring on the ASM instance.	Not used in a database instance.
V$ASM_CLIENT	Displays each database that is using at least one disk group managed by the ASM instance.	Not used in a database instance.

Using ASM Storage

We have discussed management of an ASM instance. This section covers how to actually use ASM from an Oracle instance. You can put all sorts of Oracle-related files into an ASM instance, including these:

- Oracle datafiles
- Database tempfiles
- Online redo logs
- Archived redo logs
- Control files
- Spfiles
- RMAN backup sets
- The flash recovery area (FRA)
- Data-pump dump sets

When you create one of these objects, you can decide to create it in an ASM disk group. You can also define default file-creation locations that point to ASM disk groups. Finally, you can mix and match the use of ASM and cooked file systems if you prefer. In the following sections, we will review these topics:

- Defining what ASM files are
- Defining ASM as the default destination for database files
- Creating a tablespace using an ASM disk group as the destination
- Creating a control file in an ASM disk group location
- Creating spfiles or parameter files on an ASM disk group
- Creating online redo logs in an ASM disk group location
- Defining an ASM disk group location as an archived redo-log storage area
- Creating RMAN backup sets on an ASM disk
- Defining an ASM disk group as the location for the FRA

What Are ASM Files?

We have already created ASM disk groups. To actually use the ASM disk groups, we have to populate them with ASM files. In this section, we will discuss what ASM files are and then we will discuss the different kinds of ASM filenames that you might deal with.

ASM Files

ASM files are created in a number of different ways; for example, when you execute the `create tablespace` command and you indicate that the resulting datafile(s) should be stored in an ASM disk group, the result will be the creation of ASM files in that ASM disk group.

A goodly number of Oracle file types can be stored in ASM, including datafiles, control files, redo logs, and archived redo logs. There are some Oracle files that cannot be stored in an ASM group. These are mostly the administrative files like trace files, the alert log, and so on.

ASM Filename Types

When a file is created on an ASM disk, the filename is generated by ASM. There is a number of different kinds of ASM filename types:

- Fully qualified ASM filenames
- Numeric ASM filenames
- Alias ASM filenames
- Alias filenames with templates
- Incomplete filenames
- Incomplete filenames with templates

Let's look at each of these types in a bit more detail.

Fully Qualified ASM Filenames

The full filename is known as the *fully qualified ASM filename*. Here is an example of a fully qualified ASM filename:

```
+sp_dgroup2/mydb/controlfile/Current.56.544956473
```

The naming format for a fully qualified ASM filename is as follows:

- The `+group` is listed (in our case, `+sp_dgroup2`). Note that the + indicates the root of the ASM filename.
- The database name (in our case `mydb`).
- The file type (in our case, this is a control file).
- Next we have the start of the actual ASM file. First we have the file type flag (in our case, `Current`). This provides additional information on the file type in question. In this case, this is a current control file, as opposed to a control-file backup, which would be listed as `backup`.
- Finally we have two numbers delineated by a period (56.544956473), which represent the file number and an incarnation number. These two numbers combined guarantee that the ASM filename will be unique from any other ASM filename on the system.

ASM Numeric Filenames

The *ASM numeric filename* is a subset of the fully qualified filename, as you might have noticed. The numeric filename for the fully qualified filename in the preceding section would be

```
+sp_dgroup2.56.544956473
```

Alias ASM Filenames

An *ASM alias filename* takes on the following format:

```
+group_name/your_assigned_alias
```

In this case, if you assign the alias to the file when it's created filenames might look like this:

```
+sp_dgroup2/ctrl_files/control_file_01
+sp_dgroup2/datafile/mydbf_user_data_01
```

Alias ASM Filenames with Templates

You can also reference an alias ASM filename with a template name. Simply include the ASM template name in parentheses next to the alias-name definition, as shown here:

```
+sp_dgroup2/ctrl_files/control_file_01(special)
```

Incomplete ASM Filenames

There are times you will use an *incomplete ASM filename*. An ASM filename is incomplete when the name of the ASM disk group is all that is referenced, as in this case:

```
+Sp_dgroup1
```

So, the incomplete ASM filename really is just a + followed by the disk group name. This is the most commonly used ASM filename type because this type is used when defining default destinations for database files (see more on that in the next section) in parameters, creating tablespaces, or performing RMAN database backups.

Incomplete ASM Filenames with Templates

As with alias filenames, you can also reference a template in an incomplete filename definition, as shown here:

```
+sp_dgroup1(special_template)
```

Adding ASM Filename Aliases to Existing Files

You can add filename aliases to ASM files that have already been created. To add the alias, use the `alter diskgroup` command with the `add alias` parameter. For example, if you wanted to create an alias for `ALIAS_TBS.260.613168611`, you would issue the following command:

```
Alter diskgroup cooked_dgroup1
add alias '+cooked_dgroup1/alias_dir/alias_tbs_01.dbf'
FOR '+cooked_dgroup1/11GDB/datafile/alias_tbs. 260.613168611';
```

Managing ASM File Alias Names

You can change ASM file alias names with the `rename alias` parameter of the `alter diskgroup` command, as shown in this example:

```
Alter diskgroup cooked_dgroup1
Rename alias '+cooked_dgroup1/alias_dir/alias_tbs_01.dbf'
To '+cooked_dgroup1/datafiles/alias_tbs_01.dbf';
```

You can use the `drop alias` command to drop ASM aliases, as in this example:

```
Drop alias '+cooked_dgroup1/datafiles/alias_tbs_01.dbf';
```

Drop Files from an ASM Disk Group

There may be cases where you will need to drop files from an ASM disk group (for example, the database is removed in an unorderly fashion). To remove ASM files, use the `alter diskgroup` command with the `drop file` clause. Here is an example of removing a file from an ASM disk group (in this case, using an alias name):

```
alter diskgroup cooked_dgroup1
drop file '+cooked_dgroup1/alias_dir/alias_tbs_01.dbf';
```

Defining ASM as the Default Destination for Database Files

If you decide you want to allow Oracle to create all file types as ASM file types, you can set the values of various parameters such that ASM will automatically be employed. One of the big benefits of this feature is the standardization of your database, ensuring that all files get placed where they belong and in the ASM structure to which they belong. You can define default ASM destinations be defining incomplete ASM filenames. The following database parameters take incomplete ASM filenames:

- DB_CREATE_FILE_DEST
- DB_CREATE_ONLINE_LOG_DEST_n
- DB_RECOVERY_FILE_DEST
- CONTROL_FILES
- LOG_ARCHIVE_DEST_n (log_archive_dest_format will be ignored)
- LOG_ARCHIVE_DEST (log_archive_dest_format will be ignored)
- STANDBY_ARCHIVE_DEST

Here is an example of using an incomplete name when setting the DB_CREATE_FILE_DEST parameter so that it will use the ASM disk group +sp_dgroup1:

```
alter system set db_create_file_dest='+cooked_dgroup1' scope=both;
```

Creating a Tablespace Using an ASM Disk Group as the Destination

There are different ways to create tablespaces using ASM disks. In this section, we will first look at creating an ASM tablespace, allowing the default ASM disk location to be used (as a result of having set the DB_CREATE_FILE_DEST parameter as we did earlier). We will then look at how to create a tablespace datafile by explicitly referencing the ASM disk group that it is supposed to be assigned to.

Creating Tablespaces Using Default ASM Assignments

Now that you have seen how to define a default ASM location, you can use the create tablespace command to create a tablespace that will have a file in the ASM disk group by default, as shown in this example:

```
create tablespace test_rgf datafile size 100k;
```

Let's see where Oracle put the datafile now by querying the DBA_DATA_FILES view:

```
Select tablespace_name, file_name
from dba_data_files Where tablespace_name='TEST_RGF';

TABLESPACE FILE_NAME
---------- ---------------------------------------------------------
TEST_RGF   +COOKED_DGROUP1/11gDB/datafile/test_rgf.256.613064385
```

Note in this example that Oracle went ahead and filled out the rest of the path, giving us a complete filename in the DBA_DATA_FILES view to work with. We can also see this new file in the ASM instance using the V$ASM_FILES view, as shown here:

```
SQL> select group_number, file_number, type, blocks, bytes from v$asm_file;

GROUP_NUMBER FILE_NUMBER TYPE                     BLOCKS      BYTES
------------ ----------- -------------------- ---------- ----------
           1         256 DATAFILE                     14     114688
```

If you want to drop a tablespace that contains ASM files, you need only issue the drop tablespace command. Oracle will clean up all of the ASM datafiles associated with that tablespace. You can have a mix of ASM datafiles and normal datafiles assigned to a tablespace, as shown in this create table statement:

```
Create tablespace part_asm_tbs
Datafile 'c:\oracle\oradata\11gDB\part_asm_tbs_01.dbf' size 10m,
'+COOKED_DGROUP1' size 100k;
```

Let's look and see where the datafiles were created:

```
Select tablespace_name, file_name
from dba_data_files Where tablespace_name='PART_ASM_TBS';

TABLESPACE_NAME FILE_NAME
--------------- ------------------------------------------------------------
PART_ASM_TBS    C:\ORACLE\ORADATA\11GDB\PART_ASM_TBS_01.DBF
PART_ASM_TBS    +COOKED_DGROUP1/11GDB/datafile/part_asm_tbs.256.613066047
```

Note that in this case, if you drop the PART_ASM_TBS tablespace, only the ASM files related to that tablespace would be removed from the disk when you issue the drop tablespace command. In cases such as these, you need to make sure you include the including contents and datafiles parameter with the drop tablespace command.

Creating Tablespaces Referencing Specific ASM Disk Groups

There are going to be many times when you will not want to define a default ASM disk group to write all tablespaces to. In this case, you will want to reference the specific ASM disk group that you want a datafile created in when you issue the create tablespace command. Here is an example:

```
create tablespace another_test
datafile '+COOKED_DGROUP1' size 100k;
```

Let's see where Oracle put the datafile now by querying the DBA_DATA_FILES view:

```
select tablespace_name, file_name
from dba_data_files Where tablespace_name='ANOTHER_TEST';

TABLESPACE_NAME FILE_NAME
--------------- ------------------------------------------------------------
ANOTHER_TEST    +COOKED_DGROUP1/11GDB/datafile/another_test.256.613065911
```

The create tablespace command comes with a number of different options when you are using cooked file systems, and there is no reason you cannot use those options when you are using ASM file systems. For example, you can create a tablespace with autoextend enabled, as shown here:

```
create tablespace another_test
datafile '+COOKED_DGROUP1' size 100k
autoextend on next 10m maxsize 300m;
```

If you want to create a tablespace using a template other than the default template, this is easy too, as shown in this example:

```
create tablespace different_template
datafile '+COOKED_DGROUP1(alternate_template)';
```

Tablespace Maintenance When Using Tablespaces Referencing Specific ASM Disk Groups

Tablespace maintenance is basically unchanged when using ASM disks. For example, you can add a datafile with the alter tablespace command as you normally would:

```
alter tablespace part_asm_tbs Add datafile '+COOKED_DGROUP1' size 100k;
```

Creating a Database Using ASM Disk Group Locations

You can create a database that completely uses ASM disk group locations. You can do this when creating the database through the DBCA interface or if you are going to manually create the database. In the following sections, we will look at both options.

Creating a Database Using ASM Disks with DBCA

If you are creating the database with the DBCA, you will have the opportunity to indicate that you want to use ASM disks for the database as a part of the DBCA workflow.

After you indicate that you want to use ASM, you will be prompted to create the SYS password to the ASM instance. DBCA will then present to you a list of available disk groups that you can use to create the database.

DBCA will confirm your selection in the next screen. You will then be presented with a screen that asks you where you want the flash recovery area to be assigned. It will prepopulate this screen with one of the disk groups that you selected to use in the previous screen (typically it will be the second disk group in the list).

The DBCA will set all of the different file location parameters to those in the ASM disk groups that you selected (for example, CONTROL_FILES, DB_CREATE_FILE_DEST, DB_RECOVERY_FILE_DEST, and LOG_ARCHIVE_DEST_1). You can edit these choices if you want to use a mix of ASM and cooked file systems for some reason.

You complete the DBCA screens as normal and DBCA will then create a database that is totally (or partially, if you prefer) using ASM.

Creating a Database Manually Using ASM Disks

It can actually be easier to create a database using ASM than to create a database with DBCA, if only because less typing is required! To create an Oracle database with ASM, follow the standard procedures, but when you are creating the parameter file, make sure you assign the following parameters to an ASM disk group:

- DB_CREATE_FILE_DEST
- DB_RECOVERY_FILE_DEST

Once you have done this, issuing the `create database` command requires no parameters at all! Simply issue the command and that's it! Oracle will create the various database files on ASM disk.

Creating a Control File in an ASM Disk Group Location

When you create a database from the DBCA or manually, you can opt to create the database control files in an ASM location by setting the CONTROL_FILES parameter to an ASM disk group. A note about moving control files, or any other database-related files: be very careful. It's dangerous to re-create the control file because it is a rather central part of your database!

If you have an existing database and you want to move the control files to ASM, it gets a bit stickier. You will pretty much have to use the `create controlfile` command to move the database control files to ASM disks. You will need to change the database CONTROL_FILES parameter before you run the create `controlfile` command. Here is an example of this operation:

```
SQL> alter system set control_files='' scope=SPFILE;
SQL> alter system set
DB_CREATE_FILE_DEST='+COOKED_DGROUP1','+COOKED_DGROUP2' scope=spfile;
SQL> shutdown immediate
SQL> startup nomount
SQL>CREATE CONTROLFILE REUSE DATABASE "11GDB"
```

```
NORESETLOGS  NOARCHIVELOG
    MAXLOGFILES 16
    MAXLOGMEMBERS 3
    MAXDATAFILES 100
    MAXINSTANCES 8
    MAXLOGHISTORY 292
LOGFILE
  GROUP 1 'C:\ORACLE\ORADATA\11GDB\REDO01.LOG'  SIZE 50M,
  GROUP 2 'C:\ORACLE\ORADATA\11GDB\REDO02.LOG'  SIZE 50M,
  GROUP 3 'C:\ORACLE\ORADATA\11GDB\REDO03.LOG'  SIZE 50M
-- STANDBY LOGFILE
DATAFILE
  'C:\ORACLE\ORADATA\11GDB\SYSTEM01.DBF',
  'C:\ORACLE\ORADATA\11GDB\UNDOTBS01.DBF',
  'C:\ORACLE\ORADATA\11GDB\SYSAUX01.DBF',
  'C:\ORACLE\ORADATA\11GDB\USERS01.DBF',
  'C:\ORACLE\ORADATA\11GDB\EXAMPLE01.DBF',
  'C:\ORACLE\ORADATA\11GDB\PART_ASM_TBS_01.DBF',
  '+COOKED_DGROUP1/11GDB/datafile/part_asm_tbs.256.613066047',
  '+COOKED_DGROUP1/11GDB/datafile/part_asm_tbs.257.613083267'
CHARACTER SET WE8MSWIN1252;
SQL>RECOVER DATABASE;
SQL>ALTER DATABASE OPEN NORESETLOGS;
```

You can also use RMAN to restore the control file to an ASM disk location, as shown in this example (this assumes you are connected to a recovery catalog):

```
SQL> alter system set control_files='' scope=SPFILE;
SQL> alter system set
DB_CREATE_FILE_DEST='+COOKED_DGROUP1' scope=spfile;
RMAN>shutdown
RMAN>startup nomount
RMAN>restore controlfile;
RMAN>recover database;
RMAN>alter database open resetlogs;
```

If you are using autobackups, then the process is slightly different:

```
SQL> alter system set control_files='' scope=SPFILE;
SQL> alter system set
DB_CREATE_FILE_DEST='+COOKED_DGROUP1' scope=spfile;
```

```
RMAN>shutdown
RMAN>startup nomount
RMAN>restore controlfile from autobackup;
RMAN>recover database;
RMAN>alter database open resetlogs;
```

Note that instead of setting the DB_CREATE_FILE_DEST parameter, you could set the CONTROL_FILES parameter, as shown here:

```
alter system set control_files=
'+COOKED_DGROUP1/11GDB/controlfile/current.259.613088323',
'+COOKED_DGROUP2/11GDB/controlfile/current.257.613088325';
```

If you have restored the control files to a disk group, you may not know what the filenames are in order to set the CONTROL_FILES parameter (the RMAN output does not give you the ASM filenames that are created). In this case, you can query the V$ASM_FILE view from the ASM instance and derive the filename for the newly created control file.

Recall that the format for an ASM filename is file_type_flag.file#.incarnation#. Knowing this, you can derive the control-file names. For example, here is a query against the V$ASM_FILE view in our database after we restored the control files to our ASM instance:

```
SQL> select a.group_number, b.name, a.incarnation, a.file_number, a.type
  2  from v$ASM_DISKGROUPS b, v$asm_file a
  3  where a.group_number= b.group_number
  4  and a.type='CONTROLFILE';

GROUP_NUMBER NAME                          INCARNATION FILE_NUMBER TYPE
------------ ----------------------------- ----------- ----------- -----------
           1 COOKED_DGROUP1                  613087119         258 CONTROLFILE
           2 COOKED_DGROUP2                  613087131         256 CONTROLFILE
```

From this, we can surmise that our CONTROL_FILES parameter should be set to the following:

```
alter system set control_files=
'+COOKED_DGROUP1/11GDB/controlfile/current.258.613087119',
'+COOKED_DGROUP1/11GDB/controlfile/current.258.613087131'
Scope=spfile;
```

Of course, you can reverse this process and move control files out of ASM and put them into cooked file systems at any time. As should always be standard practice, make sure you back up your database before you begin moving any database-related files around.

Creating Spfiles or Parameter Files on an ASM Disk Group

You can create pfiles or spfiles on an ASM disk group using the `create pfile` or `create spfile` command with the ASM disk group as the location for the parameter file. For example, you could issue this command:

```
create spfile '+COOKED_DGROUP1' from pfile;
```

Creating Online Redo Logs in an ASM Disk Group Location

Creation of redo logs on ASM disks is straightforward. If the database was configured to use ASM from the beginning, then the existing online redo logs will already be on ASM disk groups. Assuming that the parameter `DB_ONLINE_CREATE_LOG_DEST_n` or `DB_CREATE_FILE_DEST` is set, you can simply issue the `alter database add logfile` command and Oracle will add a new redo log group to your database for you, as shown in this example:

```
alter database add logfile size 100m;
```

You can also manually add a redo log file group to a disk group if you prefer using SQL, such as in the following, which will create a new log file group, and multiplex it, between two ASM disk groups:

```
alter database add logfile ('+COOKED_DGROUP1','+COOKED_DGROUP2') size 100m;
```

Defining an ASM Disk Group Location as an Archived Redo Log Storage Area

Once you have created an ASM disk, it's easy to use it as the storage for archived redo logs. Simply set one of the `LOG_ARCHIVE_DEST_n` parameters to point to that ASM disk group, as shown in this example:

```
alter system
set log_archive_dest_1='location=+COOKED_DGROUP2';
```

You can check the ASM instance and see the new archived logs being created, as shown in this example code:

```
SQL> select a.group_number, b.name, a.incarnation, a.file_number, a.type
  2  from v$ASM_DISKGROUPS b, v$asm_file a
  3  where a.group_number=b.group_number
  4  and a.type='ARCHIVELOG';
```

```
GROUP_NUMBER NAME                           INCARNATION FILE_NUMBER TYPE
------------ ------------------------------ ----------- ----------- -----------
           2 COOKED_DGROUP2                   613091705         258 ARCHIVELOG
```

Creating Database Objects Using ASM Filename Aliases

An alias includes the disk group name and then appends a user-defined name to the filename. This makes it possible to reference an ASM file with a name that makes some sense. ASM aliases start with the disk group name, followed by a slash and then the alias name as in this example:

```
+COOKED_DGROUP1/datafiles/myfile.dbf
```

Aliases can be created at the time the file is created (such as when you issue the `create tablespace` command), or you can add the alias later. Here is an example of creating a tablespace with an alias filename:

```
create tablespace alias_tbs
Datafile'+COOKED_DGROUP1/myalias.dbf' size 10m;
```

The resulting ASM file would be as follows:

```
+COOKED_DGROUP1/11GDB/datafile/alias_tbs.256.613066047
```

You can see this through the following query executed in the ASM instance:

```
SQL> select b.name gname, a.name aname, a.system_created, a.alias_directory,
  2              c.type file_type
  3         from v$asm_alias a, v$ASM_DISKGROUPS b, v$asm_file c
  4         where a.group_number = b.group_number
  5               and a.group_number = c.group_number(+)
  6               and a.file_number = c.file_number(+)
  7               and a.file_incarnation = c.incarnation(+)
  8               and b.name='COOKED_DGROUP1'
  9               and c.type='DATAFILE';

GNAME                          ANAME                          S A FILE_TYPE
------------------------------ ------------------------------ - - -----------
COOKED_DGROUP1                 ALIAS_TBS.260.613168611        Y N DATAFILE
```

Using RMAN with ASM

You can use RMAN in conjunction with ASM. In the following sections, we will cover the following RMAN-related operations:

- Copying database datafiles to an ASM disk with RMAN
- Creating RMAN backups on ASM

Copying Database Datafiles to an ASM Disk with RMAN

If you want to move your entire database to ASM, you can easily do this with RMAN. First you make an image copy of the database, copying it to an ASM disk group. Then use the RMAN `switch database to copy` command to switch the database from using the old datafiles to using the new datafiles that were copied onto the ASM drives. Here is an example of moving the database datafiles using the following commands:

```
RMAN>shutdown
RMAN>startup mount
RMAN>backup as copy database format '+COOKED_DGROUP1';
RMAN>switch database to copy;
RMAN>alter database open;
```

Creating RMAN Backups on ASM

RMAN backup sets can be made to ASM disks. This means that the database, archived redo logs, control-file backups, and spfiles can all be backed up to ASM disks. There are two different ways of using ASM for backups. You can send individual backups directly to an ASM disk group, or you can define the flash recovery area to be a disk group and cause backups to be sent to the flash recovery area. Let's look at these two options in a bit more detail.

Backing Up from RMAN to ASM Directly

Backing up to an ASM disk group with RMAN is quite easy. Use the RMAN `backup` command and add the `format` parameter indicating the disk group to which you want to back up the database. Here is an example:

```
RMAN>backup as compressed backupset database format '+COOKED_DGROUP1';
```

You can also back up archived redo logs and database control files using RMAN via the same method.

Configuring and Backing Up to an ASM Flash Recovery Area

The flash recovery area is a directory structure that centralizes Oracle backups in one Oracle-defined backup structure (see Chapter 2 for more on the flash recovery area). You define the flash recovery area by setting the `DB_ RECOVERY_FILE_DEST` and `DB_RECOVERY_FILE_DEST_SIZE` parameters as required. Here is an example of using the `alter system` command to point the flash recovery area to an ASM disk group.

```
alter system set db_recovery_file_dest='+COOKED_DGROUP1';
alter system set db_recovery_file_dest_size=4G;
```

Once these parameters have been set, RMAN backups will start using the flash recovery area and ASM since the flash recovery area has been configured to use an ASM disk group.

Summary

In this chapter, we showed you how Automatic Storage Management (ASM) can reduce or eliminate the headaches involved in managing the disk space for all Oracle file types, including online and archived logs, RMAN backup sets, flashback logs, and even initialization parameter files (spfiles).

We reviewed the concepts related to a special type of instance called an ASM instance along with the initialization parameters specific to an ASM instance. In addition, we described the dynamic performance views that allow you to view the components of an ASM disk group as well as to monitor the online rebalancing operations that occur when disks are added to or removed from a disk group. Starting and stopping an ASM instance is similar to starting and stopping a traditional database instance. Of course, other databases that use disk groups within the ASM instance will not be available to users if the ASM instance is not available to service disk group requests.

ASM filenames have a number of different formats and are used differently depending on whether existing ASM files or new ASM files are being referenced. ASM templates are used in conjunction with ASM filenames to ease the administration of ASM files.

Additionally, we reviewed ASM disk group architecture, showing how failure groups can provide redundancy and performance benefits while eliminating the need for a third-party logical volume manager. Dynamic disk group rebalancing automatically tunes I/O performance when a disk is added or deleted from a disk group or a disk in a disk group fails.

Exam Essentials

Enumerate the benefits and characteristics of Automatic Storage Management (ASM). Understand how ASM can relieve you of manually optimizing I/O across all files in the tablespace by using ASM disk groups. Show how ASM operations can be performed online with minimal impact to ongoing database transactions.

Be able to create an ASM instance and configure its initialization parameters. Understand the initialization parameters `INSTANCE_TYPE`, `ASM_POWER_LIMIT`, `ASM_DISKSTRING`, and `ASM_DISKGROUPS`. Configure `DB_UNIQUE_NAME` for an ASM instance. Start up and shut down an ASM instance, noting the dependencies with database instances that are using the ASM instance's disk groups.

Understand the architecture of an ASM instance. Enumerate the different states for an ASM instance. Describe what happens when an ASM instance is shut down normally or is aborted. Understand and describe the differences between an RDBMS instance and an ASM instance.

Understand redundancy and resync. Describe what redundancy is and how it's implemented in ASM. Understand what a failure group is and how it is created. Know what ASM fast disk resync and preferred mirror read are.

Understand how ASM filenames are constructed and used when creating Oracle objects. Differentiate how different ASM filename formats are used and how files are created depending on whether the file is an existing ASM file, whether a new ASM file is being created, or whether multiple ASM files are being created. Understand the different system templates for creating ASM files with the associated filename and how the characteristics are applied to the ASM files. Show how ASM files are used in SQL commands.

Be able to create, drop, and alter ASM disk groups. Define multiple failure groups for new disk groups and make sure you understand how the number of failure groups is different for two-way and three-way mirroring. Show how disk rebalancing can be controlled or rolled back. Understand the ASM disk group attributes and how they are used.

Identify the steps involved in converting non-ASM files to ASM files using RMAN. Migrate a database to ASM disk groups by shutting down the database, running an RMAN script for each file to be converted, and opening the database with `RESETLOGS`.

Review Questions

1. What are three benefits of using ASM? (Choose three.)
   - A. Ease of disk administration and maintenance
   - B. Load balancing across physical disks
   - C. Software RAID-1 data redundancy with double or triple mirrors
   - D. Automatic recovery of failed disks
2. What components are present in an ASM instance? (Choose three.)
   - A. SGA
   - B. Database processes
   - C. Database datafiles
   - D. Control files
   - E. Database parameter file or spfile
3. Which of the following is a benefit of ASM fast disk resync?
   - A. Failed disks are taken offline immediately but are not dropped.
   - B. Disk data is never lost.
   - C. By default, the failed disk is not dropped from the disk group ever, protecting you from loss of that disk.
   - D. The failed disk is automatically reformatted and then resynchronized to speed up the recovery process.
   - E. Hot spare disks are automatically configured and added to the disk group.
4. What is the result of increasing the value of the parameter `ASM_POWER_LIMIT` during a rebalance operation?
   - A. The ASM rebalance operation will likely consume fewer resources and complete in a shorter amount of time.
   - B. The ASM rebalance operation will consume fewer resources and complete in a longer amount of time.
   - C. The ASM rebalance operation will be parallelized and should complete in a shorter amount of time.
   - D. There is no `ASM_POWER_LIMIT` setting used in ASM.
   - E. None of the above.

5. What is the default AU size of an ASM disk group? What is the maximum AU size in an ASM disk group?

   A. 100KB default, 10TB maximum

   B. 256KB default, 1024MB maximum

   C. 10MB default, 126PB maximum

   D. 64KB default, 1EB maximum

   E. 1MB default, 64MB maximum

6. Which initialization parameter in an ASM instance specifies the disk groups to be automatically mounted at instance startup?

   A. `ASM_DISKMOUNT`

   B. `ASM_DISKGROUP`

   C. `ASM_DISKSTRING`

   D. `ASM_MOUNTGROUP`

7. When an ASM instance receives a `SHUTDOWN NORMAL` command, what command does it pass on to all database instances that rely on the ASM instance's disk groups?

   A. `TRANSACTIONAL`

   B. `IMMEDIATE`

   C. `ABORT`

   D. `NORMAL`

   E. None of the above

8. When starting up your ASM instance, you receive the following error:

```
SQL> startup pfile=?/dbs/init+ASM.ora
ASM instance started
Total System Global Area  104611840 bytes
Fixed Size                  1298220 bytes
Variable Size              78147796 bytes
ASM Cache                  25165824 bytes
ORA-15032: not all alterations performed
ORA-15063: ASM discovered an insufficient number of disks for disk group
"DGROUP3"
ORA-15063: ASM discovered an insufficient number of disks for disk group
"DGROUP2"
ORA-15063: ASM discovered an insufficient number of disks for disk group
"DGROUP1"
```

In trying to determine the cause of the problem, you issue this query:

```
SQL> show parameter asm
NAME                                 TYPE        VALUE
------------------------------------ ----------- ------------------------_
asm_allow_only_raw_disks             boolean     FALSE
asm_diskgroups                       string      DGROUP1, DGROUP2, DGROUP3
asm_diskstring                       string
asm_power_limit                      integer     1
asm_preferred_read_failure_groups    string
```

What is the cause of the error?

A. The ASM_DISKGROUPS parameter is configured for three disk groups: DGROUP1, DGROUP2, and DGROUP3. The underlying disks for these disk groups have apparently been lost.

B The format of the ASM_DISKGROUPS parameter is incorrect. It should reference the disk group numbers, not the names of the disk groups.

C. The ASM_POWER_LIMIT parameter is incorrectly set to 1. It should be set to the number of disk groups being attached to the ASM instance.

D. The ASM_DISKSTRING parameter is not set; therefore disk discovery is not possible.

E. There is insufficient information to solve this problem.

9. As DBA for the Rebel Alliance you have decided that you need to facilitate some redundancy in your database. Using ASM, you want to create a disk group that will provide for the greatest amount of redundancy for your ASM data (you do not have advanced SAN mirroring technology available to you, unfortunately). Which of the following commands would create a disk group that would offer the maximum in data redundancy?

A.
```
CREATE DISKGROUP dg_alliance1 NORMAL REDUNDANCY
failgroup diskcontrol1 DISK 'c:\oracle\asm_disk\_file_disk3' NAME file_
diska1
failgroup diskcontrol2 DISK 'c:\oracle\asm_disk\_file_disk4' NAME file_
diskb1;
```

B.
```
CREATE DISKGROUP dg_alliance1 EXTERNAL REDUNDANCY
failgroup diskcontrol1 DISK 'c:\oracle\asm_disk\_file_disk3' NAME file_
diska1;
```

C.
```
CREATE DISKGROUP dg_alliance1
HIGH REDUNDANCY
failgroup diskcontrol1 DISK 'c:\oracle\asm_disk\_file_disk1' NAME file_
disk1
failgroup diskcontrol2 DISK 'c:\oracle\asm_disk\_file_disk2' NAME file_
disk2
failgroup diskcontrol2 DISK 'c:\oracle\asm_disk\_file_disk3' NAME file_
disk3;
```

D. ```
CREATE DISKGROUP dg_alliance1
MAXIMUM REDUNDANCY
failgroup diskcontrol1 DISK 'c:\oracle\asm_disk_file_disk1' NAME file_
disk1
failgroup diskcontrol2 DISK 'c:\oracle\asm_disk_file_disk2' NAME file_
disk2
failgroup diskcontrol2 DISK 'c:\oracle\asm_disk_file_disk3' NAME file_
disk3
failgroup diskcontrol2 DISK 'c:\oracle\asm_disk_file_disk4' NAME file_
disk4;
```

**E.** None of the above

**10.** You want to migrate your database to ASM, so you've done a clean shutdown, made a closed backup of the entire database, noted the location of your control files and online redo log files, and changed your spfile to use OMF. The last step is to run an RMAN script to do the conversion. Using the following steps, what is the correct order in which the following RMAN commands should be executed?

1. `STARTUP NOMOUNT`
2. `ALTER DATABASE OPEN RESETLOGS`
3. `SQL "ALTER DATABASE RENAME 'logfile1 path' TO '+dgrp4 '"   # plus all other logfiles`
4. `SWITCH DATABASE TO COPY`
5. `BACKUP AS COPY DATABASE FORMAT '+dgrp4'`
6. `ALTER DATABASE MOUNT`
7. `RESTORE CONTROLFILE FROM 'controlfile_location'`

**A.** 2, 5, 3, 1, 7, 6, 4

**B.** 1, 7, 6, 5, 4, 3, 2

**C.** 5, 1, 2, 7, 4, 6, 3

**D.** 7, 3, 1, 5, 6, 2, 4

**11.** How can you reverse the effects of an `ALTER DISKGROUP ... DROP DISK` command if it has not yet completed?

**A.** Issue the `ALTER DISKGROUP ... ADD DISK` command.

**B.** Issue the `ALTER DISKGROUP ... UNDROP DISKS` command.

**C.** Issue the `ALTER DISKGROUP ... DROP DISK CANCEL` command.

**D.** Retrieve the disk from the Recycle Bin after the operation completes.
```

12. To reference existing ASM files, you need to use a fully qualified ASM filename. Your development database has a disk group named DG2A, the database name is DEV19, and the ASM file that you want to reference is a datafile for the USERS02 tablespace. Which of the following is a valid ASM filename for this ASM file?

    A. dev19/+DG2A/datafile/users02.701.2

    B. +DG2A/dev19/datafile/users02.701.2

    C. +DG2A/dev19/users02/datafile.701.2

    D. +DG2A.701.2

    E. +DG2A/datafile/dev19.users.02.701.2

13. Which background process coordinates the rebalance activity for disk groups?

    A. ORB*n*

    B. OSMB

    C. RBAL

    D. ASM*n*

14. On the development database rac0, there are six raw devices: /dev/raw/raw1 through /dev/raw/raw6. /dev/raw/raw1 and /dev/raw/raw2 are 8GB each, and the rest are 6GB each. An existing disk group +DATA1, of NORMAL REDUNDANCY, uses /dev/raw/raw1 and /dev/raw/raw2. Which series of the following commands will drop one of the failure groups for +DATA1, create a new disk group +DATA2 using two of the remaining four raw devices, and then cancel the drop operation from +DATA1?

    A. ALTER DISKGROUP DATA1 DROP DISK DATA1_0001;CREATE DISKGROUP DATA2 NORMAL REDUNDANCY FAILGROUP DATA1A DISK '/dev/raw/raw3' FAILGROUP DATA1B DISK '/dev/raw/raw4';ALTER DISKGROUP DATA1 UNDROP DISKS;

    B. ALTER DISKGROUP DATA1 DROP DISK DATA1_0001;CREATE DISKGROUP DATA2 HIGH REDUNDANCY FAILGROUP DATA1A DISK '/dev/raw/raw3' FAILGROUP DATA1B DISK '/dev/raw/raw4;'ALTER DISKGROUP DATA1 UNDROP DISKS;

    C. ALTER DISKGROUP DATA1 DROP DISK DATA1_0001;CREATE DISKGROUP DATA2 NORMAL REDUNDANCY FAILGROUP DATA1A DISK '/dev/raw/raw3' FAILGROUP DATA1B DISK '/dev/raw/raw4';ALTER DISKGROUP DATA1 UNDROP DATA1_0001;

    D. ALTER DISKGROUP DATA1 DROP DISK DATA1_0001 ADD DISK GROUP DATA2 NORMAL REDUNDANCY FAILGROUP DATA1A DISK '/dev/raw/raw3' FAILGROUP DATA1B DISK '/dev/raw/raw4';ALTER DISKGROUP DATA1 UNDROP DISKS;

15. Which type of database file is spread across all disks in a disk group?

    A. All types of files are spread across all disks in the disk group.

    B. Datafiles

    C. Redo log files

    D. Archived redo log files

    E. Control files

16. How can you reverse the effects of an ALTER DISKGROUP … DROP DISK command if it has already completed?

A. Issue the ALTER DISKGROUP … ADD DISK command.

B. Issue the ALTER DISKGROUP … UNDROP DISKS command.

C. Issue the ALTER DISKGROUP … DROP DISK CANCEL command.

D. Retrieve the disk from the Recycle Bin after the operation completes.

17. Which of the following ALTER DISKGROUP commands does *not* use V$ASM_OPERATION to record the status of the operation?

A. ADD DIRECTORY

B. DROP DISK

C. RESIZE DISK

D. REBALANCE

E. ADD FAILGROUP

18. If you use ALTER DISKGROUP … ADD DISK and specify a wildcard for the discovery string, what happens to disks that are already a part of the same or another disk group?

A. The command fails unless you specify the FORCE option.

B. The command fails unless you specify the REUSE option.

C. The command must be reissued with a more specific discovery string.

D. The other disks, already part of the disk group, are ignored.

19. You are an Oracle DBA responsible for an ASM instance. The disk controller on your system fails. You suspect that the disk itself is okay. You know it will take 24 hours to replace the controller and you don't want to have to rebuild the disks from scratch. What do you do?

A. Take the whole disk group offline and wait for the controller card to be installed. Once it's installed, bring the disk group online again.

B. Change the ASM parameter ASM_PREFERRED_READ_FAILURE_GROUPS to indicate that you want to read from the non-failed disk. Once the disk controller is replaced, reset the parameter to its original value.

C. You have no choice but to rebuild the disk. Drop the disk from the disk group and wait for the controller to be replaced. Once the controller is replaced, add the disk back into the disk group and allow ASM to rebuild it.

D. If you are using any setting other than REDUNDANCY EXTERNAL for your disk group, you will have to recover any data on that disk from a backup. The database will be unavailable until you can correct the problem and perform recovery.

E. Change the attribute DISK_REPAIR_TIME on the disk group to a time greater than 24 hours.

20. As the DBA, you run the following query on your ASM instance. What is the implication of the results of the query? (Choose two.)

```
SQL> select group_number, name, state from v$ASM_DISKGROUP;

GROUP_NUMBER NAME                           STATE
------------ ------------------------------ -----------
           0 DGROUP1                        DISMOUNTED
           2 DGROUP2                        MOUNTED
           3 DGROUP3                        MOUNTED
```

A. The DGROUP1 disk group was unmounted by another DBA.

B. A datafile has been lost, causing the ASM disk group DGROUP1 to go into the DISMOUNTED state.

C. One of the redundant disks (DGROUP1) has been lost in a disk group.

D. This query has no meaning in an ASM instance.

E. A disk associated with a disk group was discovered after the ASM instance initially opened.

Answers to Review Questions

1. A, B, C. Option A is correct because ASM makes administration and maintenance of disks much easier. Option B is correct because ASM provides for load balancing across the physical disks for better performance. Answer C is correct because ASM provides RAID-1 redundancy via double or triple mirrors.

2. A, B, E. Option A is correct because the SGA is allocated when the ASM instance is started. Option B is correct because the Oracle processes are also started when the ASM instance is started. Option E is correct because the ASM instance requires either a parameter file or an spfile.

3. A. When a disk fails, it is taken offline immediately but it is not dropped at that time. By default, you will have 3.6 hours to correct the problem before ASM will automatically drop the disk. You can configure this time by modifying the disk attributes.

4. C. Increasing the value of `ASM_POWER_LIMIT` will increase the degree of parallelism of the rebalance operation, which may help to increase the performance of that operation.

5. E. The default AU size is 1MB, and 64MB is the maximum AU size for a disk group.

6. B. The initialization parameter `ASM_DISKGROUP`, valid only in an ASM instance, specifies the disk groups to be automatically mounted when the ASM instance starts. `ASM_DISKSTRING` is operating system–dependent and restricts the file-system devices that can be used to create disk groups. `ASM_DISKMOUNT` and `ASM_MOUNTGROUP` are not valid initialization parameters.

7. E. If you do a normal shutdown of the ASM instance, an error will be returned if any Oracle database is using that ASM instance. Use the `shutdown abort` command to force the ASM instance to shut down. This will cause all other Oracle databases attached to the ASM instance to be shut down with the equivalent of a `shutdown abort` command.

8. D. The `ASM_DISKSTRING` parameter is not set correctly. When the ASM instance is started, it will use the `ASM_DISKSTRING` to do ASM disk discovery. Correct the `ASM_DISKSTRING` parameter, and restart the instance to correct the problem.

9. C. High redundancy is the highest redundancy setting available in ASM, or to the Alliance in this case. This will result in a double-mirrored ASM disk group.

10. B. After the RMAN script is run and the database is up and running successfully, you may delete the old database files.

11. B. If the `DROP DISK` operation has not yet completed, you can cancel and roll back the entire `DROP DISK` operation by using `ALTER DISKGROUP ... UNDROP DISKS`, with the disk group still being continuously available to all users.

12. B. A fully qualified existing ASM filename has the format *`+group/dbname/filetype/tag.file.incarnation`*. In this case, *`filetype`* is `datafile`, and *`tag`* is the tablespace name to which it belongs, or `users02`.

13. C. RBAL coordinates rebalance activity for a disk group in an ASM instance.

14. A. Note that the UNDROP operation will cancel a drop operation in progress but cannot reverse a drop operation that has already completed. For HIGH REDUNDANCY, at least three failure groups must be specified. While you can combine a drop and add operation into one command, the command can reference only one disk group.

15. A. All types of database files are spread across all disks in the disk group to ensure redundancy unless the redundancy is set to EXTERNAL.

16. A. If the DROP DISK operation has already completed, you must use ALTER DISKGROUP ... ADD DISK to add the disk back to the disk group. In any case, the disk group is continuously available to all users and no data is lost.

17. A. The ADD DIRECTORY command is not likely to use V$ASM_OPERATION to track its progress, because this operation adds only a small amount of metadata—a directory object—to the disk group and takes a minimal amount of time to complete. The V$ASM_OPERATION view provides the status of long-running ASM operations.

18. D. The ALTER DISKGROUP ... ADD DISK command adds all disks that match the discovery string but are not already part of the same or another disk group.

19. E. The DISK_REPAIR_TIME attribute will prevent Oracle from automatically dropping the disk in the disk group for a specific period of time. This gives you time to replace the controller indicated in the question.

20. A, E. Apparently, for some reason DGROUP1 was not mounted when the ASM instance was started, or the disk was missing and then reappeared (hardware failure perhaps) after the ASM instance was started. ASM will discover new disks, even after the ASM instance is opened.

Performing Oracle User-Managed Backups

ORACLE DATABASE 11*g*: ADMINISTRATION II EXAM OBJECTIVES COVERED IN THIS CHAPTER:

✓ **Configuring Backup Specifications**

- Configure backup settings

✓ **Configuring for Recovery**

- Configure multiple archive log file destinations to increase availability

✓ **Performing User-Managed Backup and Recovery**

- Identify the need of backup mode
- Perform user-managed backups and server-managed backups
- Back up and recover a control file

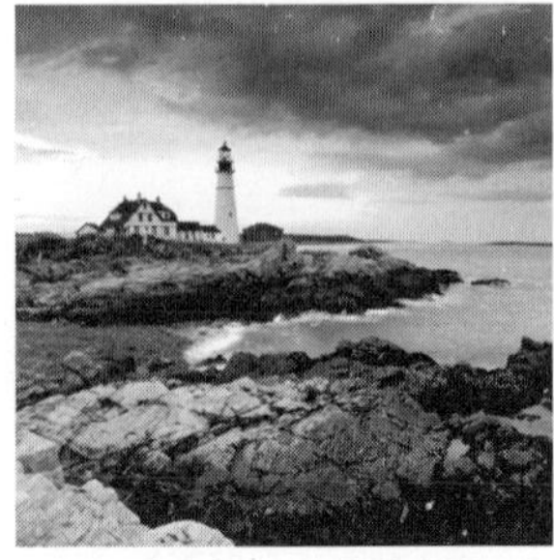

With this chapter, you will begin to dive into Oracle backup and recovery. The ability to restore an Oracle database is perhaps one of the DBA's more important jobs. In this chapter, we will do the following:

- Discuss the architecture of the Oracle database with respect to backup and recovery
- Discuss Oracle user-managed backup and recovery
- Show how to configure the database for backup and recovery
- Show how to perform user-managed backups both online and offline

Regarding the objectives listed in this chapter, server-managed backups are covered in Chapter 4, and manually recovering a control file is covered in Chapter 3.

Exam objectives are subject to change at any time without prior notice and at Oracle's sole discretion. Please visit Oracle's Training and Certification website (`http://www.oracle.com/education/certification/`) for the most current exam-objectives listing.

Understanding the Oracle Database as It Relates to Backup and Recovery

As a DBA, recovering your database should be important to you. Correspondingly, recovery is also important to Oracle, so the database product has been built to be robust with respect to backup and recovery. We'll start this chapter with a quick primer on how Oracle supports backup and recovery. In this section, we'll give you the background you need to understand backup and recovery and to be successful with your OCP exam. In the following sections, we will discuss these topics:

- Oracle processes related to backup and recovery
- Oracle memory structures related to backup and recovery
- The data dictionary

- Oracle datafiles and tablespaces
- Online redo logs
- Control files
- Parameter files
- NOARCHIVELOG and ARCHIVELOG modes
- The Oracle instance and the Oracle database
- Backup and recovery, the big picture

Note this is not the "kitchen sink" when it comes to an Oracle architecture discussion. We assume you are already somewhat familiar with the Oracle database architecture (since to take the OCP exam you must first have passed the OCA exam), so this is just a review of the pieces of it that are involved in backup and recovery in some way.

There are two different kinds of Oracle recoveries: instance/crash recovery and media recovery. *Instance recovery* is automatically managed by Oracle when you restart the database. Since the OCP exam objectives do not include instance recovery as a topic, we will not be discussing it in any detail. *Media recovery* is a manual process done by the DBA and involves the use of Oracle database backups. In this text and the OCP exam, media recovery will be the principal topic to be discussed.

Oracle Processes Related to Backup and Recovery

The front-line support for Oracle backup and recovery is the Oracle architecture. One part of this architecture is the processes related to the Oracle database. Although the Oracle database has a number of processes, only a few really matter with respect to backup and recovery and will be mentioned in this text. These processes are as follows:

- LGWR
- DBWR
- ARCH
- User processes

Let's discuss each of these processes next so you can better understand how they impact database recovery.

LGWR Process

The *log writer process (LGWR)* is responsible for keeping the online redo logs up-to-date. The job of the LGWR process is to move redo from the volatile (nonpersistent) redo log buffer in the System (sometimes called Shared) Global Area (SGA) to the persistence of the online redo logs. A number of different things cause LGWR to wake up and write the redo data, among them commits and when the redo log buffer fills to a certain point.

DBWR Process

The *database writer process DBWn* is responsible for writing to the database datafiles. This writing occurs during events called *checkpoints*. A database checkpoint may, in reality, happen at just about any time while the database is running. DBWR has very little to do with recovery of the database (other than to support it by writing to the datafiles) because database datafile writes are often delayed and the blocks within the datafiles themselves are not consistent with the current state of the data inside of the SGA.

ARCH Process

The *archiver process ARCn* is responsible for the creation of archived redo logs. In a later section in this chapter on redo logs, we will discuss how redo logs are filled with redo. Once the redo log file fills, a log switch occurs and Oracle will begin to write to the next online redo log. If the database is in ARCHIVELOG mode (see the section "NOARCHIVELOG and ARCHIVELOG Modes"), the ARCH process will be responsible for taking that filled archived redo log and copying it to one or more backup locations.

In Oracle Database 11*g*, the ARCH process starts automatically. Oracle can also start more than one ARCH process if multiple redo logs need to be archived. For ARCH to work properly, you will need to configure the appropriate archiving locations (see "Configuring the Database for Backup and Recovery" later in this chapter for more). The ARCH process is so vital to backup and recovery of the database that if it cannot copy the archived redo logs to the mandatory archived log destinations, the database will eventually stall until the problem is corrected.

User Processes

At first glance, it might seem that the user processes are not all that important to backup and recovery. As you will see, user processes are actually an integral part of backup and recovery since you have to be able to connect to the database instance to actually do a database backup or recovery.

Oracle Memory Structures Related to Backup and Recovery

The principle SGA memory structure to be aware of when it comes to backup and recovery is the *redo log buffer*. This is typically a small area of memory that is configured for Oracle to store redo in. This is a very transient area of memory and its size can impact the performance of your database. Although the redo log buffer will not have a direct impact on backup and recovery, it's still important to be aware of it in the light of any discussion on backup and recovery.

The Oracle Data Dictionary

The *Oracle data dictionary* is a critical piece of the backup and recovery landscape. In the following sections, we will first introduce you to the data dictionary. We will then give you some information on the basic format of the data dictionary so it will be more familiar to you when you actually use it. Finally, we will provide a list of views that you will find useful during your backup and recovery efforts.

Overview of the Data Dictionary

The data dictionary is a set of views and tables that expose metadata about your Oracle database. For example, if you want to know the name of your database, you can look at the NAME column in a view called V$DATABASE.

The data dictionary is critical because it will give you information on the following critical components of the database:

- Tablespaces
- Datafiles
- Redo logs
- RMAN backup–related information
- Database configuration

This information will be critical when configuring for backups and also when it comes time to recover your database from failure. Throughout this book you will be using the data dictionary, and it behooves you to become comfortable with it.

Forms of the Data Dictionary

The data dictionary views are named using a common naming convention. This convention can be used to identify the source of the data and when a view can be queried. The main types of data dictionary views are as follows:

Static data dictionary views The *static data dictionary views* are sourced from tables and views created when the database was first created. These tables and views are owned by the SYS schema and are located in the SYSTEM tablespace. The views typically contain structural metadata about the database, including such things as tables, indexes, and other database objects. The names of these views are all prefixed to indicate the scope of the data contained within that view. There are three main prefixes:

DBA_* **The** DBA_* views allow those with DBA privileges to see all data contained in the view. For example, if you were a DBA and you wanted to see all tables in the database named MY_DATA, you could query the DBA_TABLES view, as shown here:

```
Select owner, table_name from dba_tables
Where owner='MY_DATA';
```

ALL_* **The scope of the** ALL_* views is more reduced than that of the DBA_* views. When you query the ALL_* views, you see only those objects that you have been granted some form of access to. For example, if you wanted to see all instances of a table called MY_DATA that you had access to, you could query the ALL_TABLES view, as shown here:

```
Select owner, table_name from all_tables;
```

USER_* The USER_* views are the most restrictive of the data dictionary views. When you query the USER_* views, you see only those objects that are in the schema you are currently logged into. For example, if you wanted to see if there was a table called MY_DATA in your schema, you could query the USER_TABLES view, as shown here:

```
Select table_name from user_tables;
```

Notice in the example query against USER_TABLES that you removed the owner column. It is quite common that the DBA_* and ALL_* views will have an owner column but that the USER_* views will not. This is because the user in the USER_* views is assumed to be the user you are logged in as.

Dynamic performance data dictionary views The *dynamic performance data dictionary views* typically start with a V$ prefix, such as V$DATABASE or V$SESSION. The views are often used for database monitoring and tuning, but there are times when they will be the only database views available to you for recovery purposes.

The data in these views source from either the database control file or C structures that are part of the Oracle database kernel. Typically these views are available when the database instance is mounted (see "Oracle Database Startup and Shutdown" later in this chapter), but some views are available only after the instance has started.

Real World Scenario

Using Data Dictionary Views

In the real world, DBAs use the data dictionary a great deal. Although Oracle offers a nice graphical database administration tool called OEM that helps reduce the DBAs' need to use the data dictionary, the typical DBA will often find a need to access the data dictionary.

For example, the other day we needed to know which users were on the system and what their OS process IDs were so we could kill a process. We were already in SQL*Plus and it was going to be easier to just query the data dictionary than to open a browser, log into OEM, and surf to the page that would give us the information we wanted.

Our boss thought we were crazy for not using OEM, so we had a race to see who could get the information faster. Want to guess who won? Often DBAs will create their own set of scripts to access the data dictionary views. This makes it even faster to get the information you want without having to switch back and forth to OEM. OEM is a great tool, but sometimes it just pays to know the data dictionary.

Common Data Dictionary and Dynamic Performance Views You Will Use

During your backup and recovery experiences as an Oracle DBA, you will have occasion to use the data dictionary. Table 2.1 provides a list of some data dictionary views that you will want to be aware of and that will be helpful to you on your OCP exam.

TABLE 2.1 Examples of Data Dictionary/Dynamic Performance Views Useful for Recovery

View Name	Description
V$DATABASE	Provides basic database-related information, including the logging mode
V$INSTANCE	Provides basic instance information
V$DATAFILE	Provides database datafile information stored in the control file
V$LOGFILE	Provides information on the individual redo log file members from the control file
V$LOG	Provides information on the redo log groups from the control file
V$ARCHIVED_LOG	Provides archive log information from the control file
V$LOG_HISTORY	Provides information on redo log switches in the database
DBA_DATA_FILES	Provides datafile information from the data dictionary
DBA_TABLESPACES	Provides information on tablespaces in the database

You can find all the data dictionary views available in Oracle by looking at the Oracle reference guide in the Oracle documentation available at `http://tahiti.oracle.com`.

Oracle Datafiles and Tablespaces

Oracle data is stored in tablespaces, which comprise one or more datafiles. It is very important to understand datafiles and tablespaces and their relationships when it comes to backup and recovery. In the following sections, we will briefly reintroduce you to the important components of the Oracle database.

Oracle Datafiles

The Oracle database *datafiles* are critical database physical files that are used to store all your Oracle data (well, almost all!). The physical datafiles are the structures most likely to be lost and subsequently recovered during a database-recovery operation. You are probably aware that database datafiles are preallocated in size and that they can be configured to grow automatically.

When you perform a physical backup of your database, the database datafiles will be the principle structures you back up. When you restore your database due to a media failure, you will be restoring one or more datafiles. You may also have to restore other database files such as the control file, the online redo logs, and the archived redo logs, which we will discuss later in this section.

Oracle Tablespaces

A *tablespace* is a logical, named, entity in the database that is used to store database objects. For example, your database might have a table called STORES that contains data about stores in your organization. The table STORES will be assigned to a tablespace, perhaps called STORE_DATA.

A tablespace is assigned to one or more database datafiles, and the size of the tablespace is related to the size of the underlying database datafiles. Several recovery options exist with respect to tablespaces, including tablespace point-in-time recovery, which we will discuss in Chapter 8 of this book.

Redo Logs

The redo logs of the database are the principle vehicle for backup and recovery. In the following sections, we will cover two different types of redo logs. First we will discuss the online redo log, and then we will discuss the archived redo log.

Online Redo Logs

Online redo logs are used by Oracle to store all the changes that occur in the database. Think of them as something akin to a videotape recording everything that is going on. Later on, you can rewind that videotape and replay it to see what happened. During recovery, Oracle does just that using the online redo logs.

In this section we will discuss online redo log file basics, redo log file groups, redo log file members, and redo log file sequence numbers.

Redo Log File Basics

Online redo logs are created when the database is created. You must have a minimum of two redo logs in any Oracle database. When the database starts running, it will write to the first redo log. Once that log fills up, it will switch over and begin to write to the next log. Once the second log fills up, the database will clear the first log and begin to write redo into that log. Thus, redo log files are used in a round-robin style.

Redo Log File Groups

Each online redo log file is a member of a specific *redo log file group*. In the case where there are just two online redo logs (the minimum allowed), there will be two groups, likely named group 1 and group 2. You can create new online redo log groups and drop existing groups (until you are down to just two groups) anytime online.

Redo Log File Members

As you might gather, the online redo log files are an important component of the database. If you loose the online log files, you could actually permanently loose data. To protect against this, Oracle provides for multiplexing of online redo logs within each group. Each copy of the online redo log is considered a *redo log file member*, often called just a member.

Multiplexing allows you to indicate to Oracle that it should create and maintain duplicate copies of the online redo log files. When multiplexing online redo logs, it's a good idea to put each member on a different disk for many reasons, even on a SAN.

Redo Log Sequence Numbers

Each time an online redo log group is used, that group is assigned a unique *redo log sequence number* (typically 1 for a new database). As you can see in Figure 2.1, you have two online redo log groups. You start writing to the first online redo log group, which is log sequence 1. Once that log group fills up, you start writing to online group 2, which was assigned sequence number 2. Once that group fills up, you switch back to redo log group one, reusing that redo log group. The sequence number is incremented, though, and the redo associated with that online redo log group will be part of sequence 3. Once that group fills up, Oracle will switch to online log group 3. Once that group fills up, Oracle switches back to redo log group 1, reusing that redo log group.

FIGURE 2.1 Redo log file round-robin writing

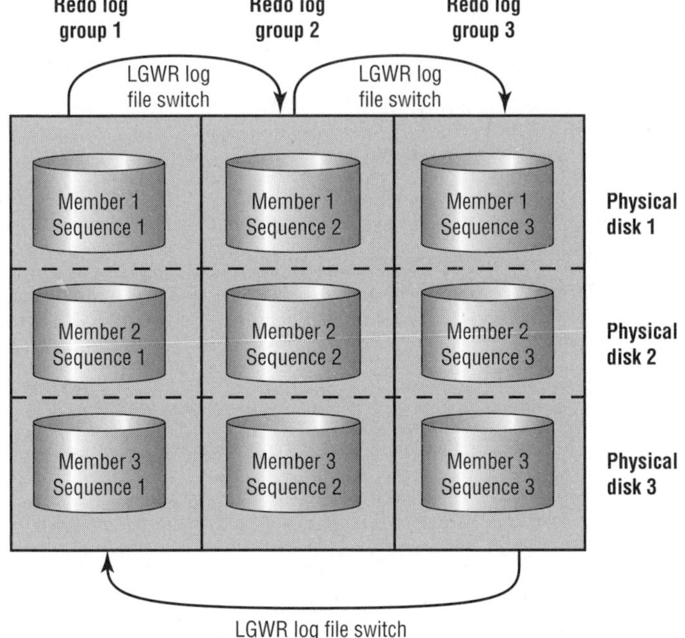

Sequence numbers can be very important when it comes to recovering your database, as you will see in Chapters 3, 6, and 8.

Archived Redo Logs

You may have noticed from the previous discussion on online redo logs that the redo log files get reused over and over. As a result, the records in those log files will be lost forever when the log file is reused. This overwriting of the online redo logs limits the recovery options available for you to use with Oracle.

When the database is put in ARCHIVELOG mode (see the section "NOARCHIVELOG and ARCHIVELOG Modes"), Oracle will make copies of the online redo logs after they have been filled and after Oracle starts to write to the next online redo log group. The copies of the online redo logs are called *archived redo logs*. Archived redo logs are critical to advanced recoveries such as point-in-time recoveries and point-of-failure recoveries.

Control Files

The *control file* of the database is kind of the master control file, if you will. It's a binary file that contains information about physical database structures, redo logs, and archived redo logs, and RMAN information is stored here too. The control file is critical to a good backup and recovery strategy, as you will see in this chapter and other chapters of this book.

Parameter Files

In this section we will address what parameter files and parameters are. We will then discuss the two types of parameter files available in Oracle, the parameter file (pfile) and server parameter file (spfile).

Parameter Files and Parameters

Every Oracle database has a *parameter file*. Inside the parameter file you'll find a variety of parameters that define global settings for that database. Parameter files are stored, by default, in `ORACLE_HOME/dbs` or `ORACLE_HOME/database`, depending on the operating system in use.

Each parameter file will contain many different parameters. Parameters are used to configure memory settings, auditing settings, destination directories for log files, and archived redo log files. When configuring a database for backup and recovery, you will configure several parameters, as you will see in the section titled "Configuring the Database for Backup and Recovery."

Parameters come in two flavors, static and dynamic. You must change static parameters and restart the database in order for the parameters to take effect. Dynamic parameters can be changed on the fly, without the need to restart the database.

You can find all the database parameters available in Oracle by looking at the Oracle reference guide in the Oracle documentation available at `http://tahiti.oracle.com`.

Parameter Files (pfiles)

The pfile parameter file is a text-based parameter file. To modify settings in this file, you simply open the file with your editor and change it. Once your changes are complete, save the file. You will then need to bounce the database to have those settings take effect.

pfiles are kept, by default, in the `$ORACLE_HOME/dbs` (UNIX) or `%ORACLE_HOME%\database` (Windows) directory. The default name for a pfile is `init<oracle_sid>.ora`. So if your Unix database is called ORCL, your pfile will be called `initORCL.ora` by default. Note that case sensitivity applies here based on the operating system.

Server Parameter Files (spfiles)

The spfile is a parameter file managed by the Oracle server. We will first look closer at the spfile itself, and then we will discuss how to set parameters when using an spfile.

What Is an spfile?

An Oracle spfile differs from a text-based parameter file in that the Oracle server manages it, and you as the DBA should never edit the file directly. The spfile is partly nontext (it has a header and a footer), but the actual parameter settings are in plain text (so you can view the file if you like and see what parameters are set to in the spfile).

spfiles are kept, by default, in the `$ORACLE_HOME/dbs` (Unix) or `%ORACLE_HOME%\database` (Windows) directory. The spfile naming convention is `sp<oracle_sid>.ora` by default. When the DBA starts the Oracle database/instance, Oracle will first look for an spfile using the default filename. If one is not found, it will look for a file called `spfile<oracle_sid>.ora` in the same default directory. Finally, if no spfile is found, Oracle will look for a regular pfile as described previously. If no parameter file is found, then the database will signal an error and the startup will abort.

Note that if you try to start the database from RMAN without an spfile or pfile available, Oracle will use default parameter settings and actually start the database. This does not happen if you try to start the database from SQL*Plus or OEM. We will discuss RMAN more in Chapter 4.

How Do You Set Parameter Values When Using an spfile?

To modify a parameter when using an spfile, you use the `alter system` command. For example, if you want to change the parameter `DB_RECOVERY_FILE_DEST_SIZE`, which is dynamic (so it can be changed on the fly), you would issue the following `alter system` command:

```
Alter system set db_recovery_file_dest_size=100m;
```

As we said earlier, some parameters are not dynamic. In this case, you have to indicate that you want to change only the parameter file. To do this, use the `alter system` command and include the `scope=spfile` keyword, as shown here:

```
Alter system set memory_max_target=200m scope=spfile;
```

In some cases, you may want to change the parameter in just the current instance of the database, but you will not want that change to persist after the next shutdown. In this case, use the `scope=memory` keyword when issuing the `alter system` command, as shown here:

```
Alter system set db_recovery_file_dest_size=100m scope=memory;
```

NOARCHIVELOG and ARCHIVELOG Modes

The Oracle database runs in two principal modes, NOARCHIVELOG (the default) and ARCHIVELOG. The logging bit has to do with archived redo logs and if they are saved or not, which makes a difference in the kinds of recoveries that you can do. Let's look at each mode in a bit more detail.

NOARCHIVELOG MODE *NOARCHIVELOG* mode is the default logging mode. In NOARCHIVELOG mode, the online redo logs are overwritten over time and no backups are created. Because of this, you are limited in the way you can back up your database and how you can recover it.

Backups are limited to cold or offline backups. This means that you must shut down your database before you can back it up. As you will see in later sections of this chapter, you will back up all the datafiles of the database plus the online redo logs and the control file(s).

Recovery in NOARCHIVELOG is equally limited. In NOARCHIVELOG mode, you can restore the database only to the point in time that the backup was taken. Thus you will lose any changes to the database that took place after the backup was complete and the database was opened for business. This is typically not an acceptable solution for production databases.

We will discuss how to back up your database in NOARCHIVELOG mode later in this chapter. In Chapter 3 we will discuss recovering your database with backups taken in NOARCHIVELOG mode. In Chapter 4 we will discuss using RMAN to perform offline backups, and in Chapter 6 we will discuss using RMAN to restore these backups.

ARCHIVELOG MODE *ARCHIVELOG* mode is a much more flexible method of operating your database. In this mode, you can back up your database while it's up and running, allowing users to work at the same time that the backups are running.

When the database is in ARCHIVELOG mode, changes are recorded in the online redo logs as usual. What is different is that the archived redo logs are copied to a backup directory once they have filled up. These copies of the redo log files are called *archived redo logs* and the Oracle database process that copies them is called the *ARCH process*. In Oracle Database 11*g*, the ARC*n* process starts automatically when the database is in ARCHIVELOG mode.

The archived redo logs may be copied to one or a number of different destinations. We will discuss configuring where Oracle should copy these archived redo logs to in the section "Configuring the Database for Backup and Recovery."

We will discuss how to back up your database in ARCHIVELOG mode later in this chapter. In Chapter 3 we will discuss recovering your database with backups taken in ARCHIVELOG mode. In Chapter 4 we will discuss using RMAN to perform online backups, and in Chapter 6 we will discuss using RMAN to restore these backups. Finally, in Chapter 8 we will discuss more-advanced recoveries with backups taken in ARCHIVELOG mode.

The Oracle Instance and the Oracle Database

In the following sections, we will first review knowledge you should already have on the basics of the Oracle instances and the Oracle database. Then we will discuss the startup and shutdown of the Oracle instance and the Oracle database.

Oracle Instances and Oracle Databases: A Review

With respect to backup and recovery of Oracle databases, it is important to understand that there is a difference between an Oracle instance and an Oracle database. This is because certain backup and recovery operations must occur while the Oracle instance is running and the database is not. Other operations will require that the database be open (which presumes the instance is already running).

No doubt you are already somewhat familiar with the notion of the instance from your OCA experience as well as your actual database experience. To review, an Oracle *instance* is the collection of shared memory (SGA) and processes (LGWR, DBWR, and so on). When these are all up and running, the instance is said to be started (see the next section for more details on starting and stopping a database).

The Oracle *database* is essentially the collection of database datafiles. When the instance is running, Oracle will attach to the database and open it for business. Once the database is open, users can begin to do their work, assuming there are no problems during the database open process that prevents it from opening.

Sybex's *OCA: Oracle Database 11*g *Administrator Certified Associate Study Guide* provides complete coverage on the Oracle database memory and processes. In this text, we assume you have already taken and passed the OCA exam and that you understand the body of knowledge consanguineous to that exam.

Oracle Database Startup and Shutdown

It is important to understand the startup and shutdown process of an Oracle database. In this section we will first discuss the different stages of the Oracle database startup and shutdown processes. We will then discuss the mechanics of actually starting and stopping the database in its different phases. We will quickly discuss restricted-mode database operations, and finally we will discuss the different stages the database must be in for specific types of backup and recovery operations to occur.

Exploring the Stages of Database Startup and Shutdown

When an Oracle database is started, it goes through four different and distinct stages:

Shutdown When the database and instance are shut down, they are at rest. There are no processes present, no memory allocated, nothing is going on. It is important to note that even though the database/instance may be shut down and closed, other Oracle processes (like the listener or OEM agents) maybe still running.

Nomount When the database is in nomount mode, the instance has been started. Thus, processes have been started and memory allocated.

Mount When the database is in mount mode (or mounted), the instance is started and the database has opened the control file. The control file is read, but is contents are not validated.

Open When the database is opened, the control-file contents have been validated against the physical database. The datafiles are all confirmed to be present, and they are opened. Oracle will then analyze the datafiles to determine if the database is in a consistent state. If the database is not in a consistent state, some form of recovery will be required.

Typically, the form of recovery required, *crash or instance recovery*, does not require any DBA involvement. If instance recovery is not possible, then *media recovery* is required. Media recovery requires the application of backups and recovery operations to bring the database current to the point of failure (if this is possible). The principal determining factors for media recovery is the presence of the needed datafiles and the availability in the online redo logs of the redo needed to bring those files current. If either of these conditions does not exist, then media recovery is required.

Database shutdowns occur in much the same way as startups, except in reverse. There are two different kinds of shutdowns, however: consistent and inconsistent.

Consistent shutdowns If your database shutdown is a *consistent shutdown*, then the database datafiles and the database control file will be synchronized upon shutdown. The dirty buffers in the database buffer cache will be flushed out to the database datafiles, making them consistent. A consistent shutdown is a nice, tidy shutdown.

Inconsistent shutdowns An *inconsistent shutdown* is another term for a mess. When your database is shut down in an inconsistent manner, it is in a indeterminate state and will require some form of recovery (typically instance recovery, which requires no DBA intervention) when it is restarted. Inconsistent shutdowns, however bad they might sound, often are the only way to shut down a database in a timely manner.

Sybex's OCA preparation guide for Oracle Database 11*g* *(OCA: Oracle Database 11g Administrator Certified Associate Study Guide*, 2009) provides complete coverage on starting the Oracle database and the different stages of opening the Oracle database, so this is just a quick review.

Starting and Stopping the Database

During backup and recovery operations, you will need to know how to start up and shut down your database correctly. To start up the database in any of the modes described in the previous section, you will use the `startup` command or the `alter database` command, as required. To stop the database, you will use the `shutdown` command. Typically, database startup operations are performed from SQL*Plus or Oracle Enterprise Manager.

The `startup` command This command is used to start the instance and/or database when the database is in a shutdown state only. The `startup` command can be used to completely open the database, as shown in this code snippet:

```
SQL> startup
```

The `startup` command also has options that you can use to indicate that you want Oracle to start the startup operation at a certain point. For example, you can indicate that you want the instance to be started only by using the `startup nomount` command:

```
SQL> startup nomount
```

Or perhaps you want to start the instance and mount the database. In this case, the command would be as follows:

```
SQL> startup mount
```

Sometimes you want to shut down the database and start it up in one command. You can use the `startup force` command to perform this action. Note that the `startup force` command will shut down your database in an inconsistent manner (which we discussed earlier in this chapter), and some operations (such as putting the database in ARCHIVELOG mode) will not complete successfully if the database was shut down in an inconsistent manner. Here is an example of the `startup force` command:

```
SQL> startup force
```

The `shutdown` command The `shutdown` command does what it says; it shuts down the database. As with the `startup` command, it comes with a few options. First there is the plain-Jane `shutdown` command, which will shut down the database if absolutely nothing is going on and if absolutely no one is logged in. You can guess how often those conditions happen in reality! Until its conditions are met, the `shutdown` command will just sit there, waiting for its opportunity to shut down the database.

Here is an example of the `shutdown` command:

```
SQL> shutdown
```

If waiting is not your forte, then you may want to try the `shutdown immediate` command. The `shutdown immediate` command will prevent new logons, roll back any uncommitted transactions, and then bring the database down. It's a consistent-shutdown, no-waiting approach to stopping the database and lots of DBAs like it. Here is an example:

```
SQL> shutdown immediate
```

The cousin of `shutdown immediate` is `shutdown transactional` (we are not sure if it's a first cousin or second cousin; Oracle has not defined this within the body of the Oracle documentation yet). The main difference here is that the `shutdown transactional` command will wait for active transactions to complete (commit) before shutting down those sessions. As a result, the `shutdown transactional` command can take a while longer to complete its task, but on the positive side, users might be a little bit happier (if they are actually able to be happy anytime the database comes down). Here is an example of the `shutdown transactional` command:

```
SQL> shutdown transactional
```

The bad boy of database shutdowns is the `shutdown abort` command. If you want your database to come down without debate, this is the way to do it. This is like pulling the power cord on your database; it is a crash of the database, shutting it down in an inconsistent manner. Here is an example of the `shutdown abort` command:

```
SQL>shutdown abort
```

The *shutdown abort* Command: The Truth Is Out There

As long as the `shutdown abort` command has been around it has been surrounded in controversy. It is believed by some that the Seven-Day War was actually started as the result of a disagreement between DBAs over the `shutdown abort` command (they conveniently ignore the fact that Oracle didn't even exist then). The truth is that the `shutdown abort` command is the fastest way to shut down your database. Because the database will be shut down in an inconsistent manner, it may result in a delayed database startup because of the recovery process that Oracle must go through internally. Often, though, `shutdown abort` may well be the way to get your database shut down and started back up in the shortest amount of time possible.

The `alter database` command The `alter database` command is used to move the instance/database from one state to another. For example, if the instance was started with the `startup nomount` command, you may want to mount the database. To do so, you would use the `alter database mount` command, as shown here:

```
SQL>alter database mount;
```

If the database is already mounted and you want to open it, then the `alter database mount` command would be appropriate, as shown in this example:

```
SQL>alter database open;
```

Performing Database Restricted-Mode Operations

Sometimes it's nice to have the house to yourself, isn't it? Oracle allows you the equivalent of having the house to yourself when you put the database in restricted mode. When the database is in restricted mode, only those with the restricted session privilege can access it. Since DBA accounts have restricted session privileges, this means you can log into the database and do your work, feeling secure that other users won't get in and cause problems. You may find that during certain recovery operations restricted session will help when you need to get into the database to perform some DBA-related activities but you don't want other users to log in yet.

To open the database in restricted mode you will issue the `startup restrict` command. If your database is already open, you can put it in restricted mode with the `alter database enable restricted session` command. To disable restricted session and allow users to connect to the database, use the `alter database disable restricted session` command.

Performing Backup and Recovery Operations and Getting Database Status

So, what kind of operations would you do given the different open or closed combinations of the database and instance? Here are some examples:

Operations while the instance is down and the database is not open:

- Copy the spfile to a pfile.
- Copy the pfile to a spfile.
- Perform manual cold backups.

Operations while the instance is open and the database is not open:

- Create a database.
- Create a database control file.
- Restore the database control file or spfile from RMAN.

Operations while the instance is mounted and the database is not open:

- Cold backup with RMAN
- Recovery of critical datafiles (SYSTEM, UNDO tablespaces).
- Offline recovery of entire database.

Operations while the instance is mounted and the database is open:

- Online datafile or tablespace recovery of noncritical tablespaces.
- Online backups of the database.

Configuring the Database for Backup and Recovery

The ARCHIVELOG and NOARCHIVELOG modes of the database really boil down to what your backup and recovery needs and requirements are. If your recovery needs are simple, you just want to restore to the point of your last backup; then you can leave your database in NOARCHIVELOG mode and do offline backups. If your database uptime requirements provide time to shut down the database for your backup, then NOARCHIVELOG mode will work fine for you.

If you are going to do offline backups of your database in NOARCHIVELOG mode, then you can pretty much ignore this section. All you will need to do there (as we will cover in the next section) is determine the location of the files you need to back up and the location to which you want to back them up, shut down the database, and back it up.

When you want to perform online backups, or if you want to be able to recover offline backups beyond the time of the backup, then the database needs to be in ARCHIVELOG mode. Putting the database in ARCHIVELOG mode requires some configuration, which we will discuss first. Once you have configured the database, you will then actually put it in ARCHIVELOG mode, which we will cover next.

In the following sections we will discuss configuring the database for ARCHIVELOG mode operations (no additional configuration for NOARCHIVELOG mode operations is required unless you want to configure the flash recovery area for RMAN, which is covered in Chapter 4), and then we will discuss actually putting the database in ARCHIVELOG mode. Finally we will discuss some database views that will be useful when managing a database in ARCHIVELOG mode.

Real World Scenario

Mixing NOARCHIVELOG and ARCHIVELOG Modes

In the real world, you might find that some of your databases are running in NOARCHIVELOG mode and some of your databases are running in ARCHIVELOG mode. For example, your development and test databases may be able to be shut down at night for backups. Additionally, they might not have a need for point-in-time or point-of-failure recovery. Thus, NOARCHIVELOG mode is just fine for them.

You may find that your production databases have different requirements. First, it may be that shutting down your production systems for backups at any time is not acceptable to your customer. Further, you probably will also find that people prefer not to lose data in production and that they would prefer to be able to restore the database and then recover all work that occurred after the last backup. You will have to put your database in ARCHIVELOG mode to satisfy those requirements.

Configuring for ARCHIVELOG Mode

The first step to putting the database in ARCHIVELOG mode is to set the database parameters. You need to set the database parameters so that the ARCH process will work correctly when it needs to archive the online redo logs, creating archived redo logs.

You will want to consider setting several parameters when you are going to put the database in ARCHIVELOG mode. A number of parameters are directly associated with user-managed backup and recovery in ARCHIVELOG mode. Table 2.2 describes these parameters.

Perhaps you are asking yourself, "What about this flash recovery area thing I've been hearing about?" We will discuss the flash recovery area (FRA) in more detail in Chapter 4. As a result, the parameters related to the RMAN and the FRA are not included in Table 2.2.

TABLE 2.2 Oracle Parameters Associated with User-Managed Backup and Recovery

Parameter Name	Description
LOG_ARCHIVE_DEST	Indicates the destination to copy archived redo logs to. Typically this parameter is not set and the LOG_ARCHIVE_DEST_N parameter is set instead.
LOG_ARCHIVE_DEST_*n*	Indicates one of up to 10 destinations to copy archived redo logs to. The first destination starts with 1 (LOG_ARCHIVE_DEST_01).
LOG_ARCHIVE_DEST_STATE_n	Indicates the state of LOG_ARCHIVE_DEST_N (ENABLED, DEFERRED, or ALTERNATE).]
LOG_ARCHIVE_FORMAT	Indicates the format of the archived redo log filenames.

Assume that you have a database called `orcl` and you have decided that you want Oracle to back up your archived redo logs to a directory called `c:\oracle\archivelog\orcl` (in Unix, perhaps it's called `/oracle/archivelog/orcl`). You would first have to create the file-system directory structures and then you would need to set the appropriate parameters. In this case, you would use the `alter system` command to set the LOG_ARCHIVE_DEST_1 parameter to point to `c:\oracle\archivelog\mydb`, as shown in this code example:

```
Alter system set log_archive_dest_1='location=c:\oracle\archivelog\orcl';
```

You can also clear this parameter setting by just using blank quotes, as shown in this example:

```
Alter system set log_archive_dest_1='';
```

With the LOG_ARCHIVE_DEST_*n* parameter, you can configure up to 10 different archive-log destination directories. This feature can be used to provide redundant backup locations for your archive logs to protect them in the event of a failure of one or more of those locations. For example, you could archive to a local disk, and you could archive to an NFS-mounted disk. In that case, you would have two LOG_ARCHIVE_DEST parameters set like this:

```
-- Local mount on C: drive
Alter system set log_archive_dest_1='location=c:\oracle\archivelog\orcl';
-- NFS Mount on Z: drive
Alter system set log_archive_dest_2='location=Z:\oracle\archivelog\orcl';
```

Oracle will archive to both destinations, in parallel. This type of configuration is also used in more advanced database setups such as standby databases.

Archive-log destination directories can take on different states, such as ENABLED, DEFERRED, or ALTERNATE (I tried to get the folks at Oracle to add a state of EXAUSTION or FRUSTRATION; they said no, but they did seem to like the suggestion of a state of CONFUSION). They can also be defined as MANDATORY or OPTIONAL. You will not need to be aware of these advanced settings for your OCP exam, but you might need to use these options as a part of your normal duties. You can find more information on these different attributes in the Oracle documentation.

You may also want to control how Oracle names the archived redo logs. This is done with the LOG_ARCHIVE_FORMAT parameter. For example, you may want to put the database name in the name of the archive logs being created, but you also want them to be numbered in such a way that the name will always be unique. You can set the LOG_ARCHIVE_FORMAT string to a value of `orcl_%s_%t_%r.arc`, as shown in this example:

```
Alter system set log_archive_format='orcl_%s_%t_%r_%d.arc';
```

You may wonder what the %s, %t, %r, and %d represent. These are variables that represent values for particular components of the archived redo log. The %s represents the sequence number, which is always unique for a given database (until a `resetlogs` command occurs, which we will discuss in Chapter 3). The %t is the thread number that represents an individual node on a cluster when your database is running on Oracle's Real Application Clusters (RAC). The %r represents the resetlogs number (see Chapter 3). Finally, the %d represents the DBID that should be unique for each database. Together, this string of variables will make the archive log filenames unique for every database on your system.

Every database in Oracle has a DBID, which is a unique identifier for the database (see the DBID column in V$DATABASE to see your DBID). Be careful, though! It is possible to have databases on two different boxes with the same name and even with the same DBID. If you will be sharing an ARCHIVELOG mount point between boxes (say, via NFS), you will need to make sure you do not accidentally overwrite archived redo logs originating from databases with the same name and/or DBID! You won't need to know about the DBID for your OCP exam, but we thought we'd tell you anyway!

Putting the Database in ARCHIVELOG Mode

Putting the database in ARCHIVELOG mode is as easy as following these steps:

1. Configure archiving-related parameters as shown in the previous section.
2. Shut down the database in a consistent state using the `shutdown`, `shutdown immediate`, or `shutdown transactional` command.
3. Mount the database with the `startup mount` command.
4. Put the database in ARCHIVELOG mode with the `alter database archivelog` command.
5. Open the database with the `alter database open` command.

One thing to be aware of when the database is in ARCHIVELOG mode is that if you have not configured archiving correctly, you could find yourself with a database that just stops running. If Oracle cannot archive the online redo logs, it will suspend all database operations once it cycles through all the online redo log groups. So, for example, if your database does log switches every 10 minutes and has three redo log groups, your database will mysteriously freeze after 30 minutes. Lack of configuration is not as big of a problem in Oracle Database 11*g* as it was in earlier versions since Oracle defaults to using the flash recovery area (discussed in Chapter 4).

Similar problems can occur if the archive-log destination directory runs out of space or if the permissions are not set correctly. If Oracle starts to have problems of this sort, it will log an error in the alert log of the database. Here is an example of an error you might see in the alert log:

```
All online logs needed archiving
ARCH: Archival stopped, error occurred. Will continue retrying
ORA-16014: log 2 sequence# 29 not archived, no available destinations
ORA-00312: online log 2 thread 1: 'C:\ORACLE\ORADATA\ORCL\REDO02.LOG'
```

Also, users logging into the database will find their logins just hanging until the archive-log problems are solved.

We've covered the parameters needed to put the database in ARCHIVELOG mode and the basic steps involved in the process. Let's look at an example of actually putting the database in ARCHIVELOG mode. Exercise 2.1 provides an example of doing just that.

Real World Scenario

Online Redo Logs Stop Being Archived

We can't tell you how many times this has happened to us as DBAs. You are busy designing some cool model and the operations guys call. "Hey," they say, "we are getting calls. The database isn't working anymore."

"What?" you respond, "What do you mean it's not working?"

"The user sessions are just stalled, sitting there not doing anything. It's like the database has gone out to lunch or something," the operations guy says.

Immediately you are pretty sure you know what's wrong. So you ask the operations guy, "So, the mount point for the archived redo logs. Are you possibly getting an alert that it's full?"

The operations guy fumbles around to look at the alerts. Sure enough, the archived redo log destination is filled up. "Oh, yeah...I was going to call you about that but I forgot."

So, you proceed to back up the archived redo logs and then remove them from the system to free up space. You also follow up to make sure some additional disk space is added to the file system.

This kind of situation happens a lot if you do not have enough space available for your archived redo logs or if your backups stop working. I've seen this happen a lot in shops where the database was originally designed for a certain amount of use and that usage has increased significantly.

EXERCISE 2.1

Putting a Database in ARCHIVELOG Mode

In this exercise you will take a database that is in NOARCHIVELOG mode and put it in ARCHIVELOG mode.

1. First, validate that the database is in NOARCHIVELOG mode using the V$DATABASE column LOG_MODE:

```
SQL> Select log_mode from v$database;
LOG_MODE
```

EXERCISE 2.1 *(continued)*

```
------------
NOARCHIVELOG
```

2. Next, look at the settings for the parameters LOG_ARCHIVE_DEST_1 and LOG_ARCHIVE_FORMAT:

```
SQL> show parameter log_archive_dest_1
NAME                                 TYPE        VALUE
------------------------------------ ----------- -----------
log_archive_dest_1                   string
log_archive_dest_10                  string
SQL> show parameter log_archive_format
NAME                                 TYPE        VALUE
------------------------------------ ----------- -----------
log_archive_format                   string      ARC%S_%R.%T
```

3. Create the archive log directory `c:\oracle\arch\orcl`:

```
SQL> host mkdir c:\oracle\arch\orcl
```

4. You want to modify LOG_ARCHIVE_DEST_1 and LOG_ARCHIVE_FORMAT so that they are set correctly. LOG_ARCHIVE_DEST_1 should be set to `c:\oracle\arch\orcl` and LOG_ARCHIVE_FORMAT should be `orcl_%r_%t_%s.arc`. You will use the `alter system` command to set these parameters. You will then check to make sure they are set correctly.

```
Alter system set log_archive_dest_1='location=c:\oracle\arch\orcl';
-- Note that we have to use the scope=spfile on this next parameter.
-- This is because it's not dynamic!
Alter system set log_archive_format='orcl_%r_%t_%s.arc' scope=spfile;
```

5. Next, shut down the database in a consistent manner with the `shutdown immediate` command:

```
SQL> shutdown immediate
Database closed.
Database dismounted.
ORACLE instance shut down.
```

6. Now nomount the database with the `startup nomount` command:

```
SQL> startup nomount;
ORACLE instance started.
Total System Global Area  418484224 bytes
Fixed Size                  1333592 bytes
Variable Size             348128936 bytes
```

EXERCISE 2.1 *(continued)*

```
Database Buffers            62914560 bytes
Redo Buffers                 6107136 bytes
Database Mounted.
```

7. Put the database in ARCHIVELOG mode with the `alter database archivelog` command:

```
SQL> alter database archivelog;
Database altered.
```

8. Open the database for operations:

```
SQL> alter database open;
Database altered.
```

9. Make sure the database is in ARCHIVELOG mode:

```
SQL> Select log_mode from v$database;
LOG_MODE
------------
ARCHIVELOG
```

10. It is a good idea to make sure that everything is configured correctly and that the archived redo logs are getting generated in the place you expect them to be getting generated in. So, first you will force an archive-log switch with the `alter system switch logfile` command. This will cause a log switch to the next redo log group and ARCH will need to copy the redo log to an archived redo log.

```
SQL> alter system switch logfile;
System altered.
```

11. Look in the `c:\oracle\arch\orcl` directory. You should see a file in that directory.

```
SQL> host dir c:\oracle\arch\orcl
 Volume in drive C has no label.
 Volume Serial Number is 08DE-E1AB
 Directory of c:\oracle\arch\orcl
08/02/2008  12:44 PM    <DIR>          .
08/02/2008  12:44 PM    <DIR>          ..
08/02/2008  12:44 PM        41,032,192 ORCL_658485967_1_2.ARC
               1 File(s)     41,032,192 bytes
               2 Dir(s)  17,065,476,096 bytes free
```

The `ORCL_659495967_1_2.ARC` file is your archive-log file, so ARCH is copying the log file to the correct location. Excellent job!

What If the Archived Redo Logs Are Not Getting Created?

So, what if you don't see an archived redo log in the directory where you think it's supposed to be? Double-check the `log_archive_dest_1` parameter and make sure it's set correctly. This is usually the problem. You can issue the command `show parameter log_archive_dest_1` from SQL*Plus to do this. Make sure the directory exists, check the security permissions on the directory, and make sure you have enough space available on the file system.

If the archive logs are not getting created correctly, you will need to quickly figure out why. If Oracle switches through all of the available online redo logs and tries to switch into one that has previously been used and is waiting to be archived, all database activity will be suspended until the archived redo log can be completely written out.

Using ARCHIVELOG Mode Data Dictionary Views

Oracle provides several data dictionary views that can be used to monitor and manage the online and archived redo logs. Table 2.3 describes those views.

TABLE 2.3 Oracle dynamic Performance Views Associated with User-Managed Backup and Recovery

View Name	Description
V$ARCHIVE	The V$ARCHIVE view provides information on redo logs that are in need of being archived.
V$ARCHIVE_DEST	The V$ARCHIVE_DEST view provides information on each individual archive-log destination. Typically this view is used for Oracle Data Guard.
V$ARCHIVE_DEST_STATE	The V$ARCHIVE_DEST_STATE view provides status information on each of the individual archive-log destination directories.
V$ARCHIVE_PROCESSES	The V$ARCHIVE_PROCESSES view provides information on the different ARCH processes running on your system.
V$ARCHIVED_LOG	The V$ARCHIVED_LOG view provides information on individual archived redo logs.
V$LOG	The V$LOG view provides information on the online redo log groups.
V$LOGFILE	The V$LOGFILE view provides information on specific online redo logs.
V$LOG_HISTORY	The V$LOG_HISTORY view provides historical information on all online/archived redo logs.

Using the V$ views is easy to do, and they can tell you a lot about the status of both online and archived redo logs, as shown in Exercise 2.2.

EXERCISE 2.2

Putting the V$ Views to Work

The V$ views are very useful when want to find out something about your database related to backup or recovery. In this exercise we will look at some V$ views related to the database online redo logs.

1. Let's look at the current redo logs that have been archived:

```
SQL> select name, thread#, sequence# from v$archived_log;
NAME                                          THREAD#  SEQUENCE#
-------------------------------------------- ---------- ----------
C:\ORACLE\ARCH\ORCL\ORCL_658485967_1_2.ARC            1          2
C:\ORACLE\ARCH\ORCL\ORCL_658485967_1_3.ARC            1          3
C:\ORACLE\ARCH\ORCL\ORCL_658485967_1_4.ARC            1          4
C:\ORACLE\ARCH\ORCL\ORCL_658485967_1_5.ARC            1          5
```

   In the output you will find the name of the archived redo log. You also display the thread number (in case you are running RAC) and the log sequence number. Note that since you have put the database in ARCHIVELOG mode, you have generated four archived redo logs.

2. You can see where your online redo logs are by using the V$LOGFILE view, as shown in this example:

```
SQL> select group#, status, member from v$logfile;
    GROUP# STATUS  MEMBER
---------- ------- ----------------------------------
         3         C:\ORACLE\ORADATA\ORCL\REDO03A.LOG
         2         C:\ORACLE\ORADATA\ORCL\REDO02.LOG
         1         C:\ORACLE\ORADATA\ORCL\REDO01.LOG
         3         C:\ORACLE\ORADATA\ORCL\REDO03B.LOG
```

   In this output, you can see you have three online redo log groups. It is interesting to note that group 3 actually has two members, whereas groups 1 and 2 have one member each.

3. You can see which is the current online redo log group by querying the V$LOG view, as shown here:

```
SQL> select group#, sequence#,  status from v$log;
    GROUP#  SEQUENCE# STATUS
```

EXERCISE 2.2 *(continued)*

```
---------- ---------- ----------------
         1         13 CURRENT
         2         11 ACTIVE
         3         12 ACTIVE
```

In this example, log group 1 is (marked with a CURRENT status) is the group that Oracle is currently writing to. Note that sequences 11 and 12 are marked active. This implies that they have not been archived yet or that they are being archived. They will be marked inactive once ARCH has finished archiving them.

Performing Oracle Offline Backups

We have been talking a lot about ARCHIVELOG mode and preparing for online backups, but we first need to talk about how to do offline backups in Oracle. Offline backups are actually quite easy to do, as you will see in the Exercise 2.3, where you will be backing up a database with an offline backup.

EXERCISE 2.3

Executing an Offline Backup

In this exercise you will be executing an offline backup of your database. Follow these steps to back up a database with an offline backup:

1. First you need to determine which files to back up. You will need to know the location of the datafiles, the control file, and the online redo logs. You use the FILE_NAME column of the DBA_DATA_FILES view to find the datafiles first.

```
SQL> Select file_name from dba_data_files;
FILE_NAME
--------------------------------------------
C:\ORACLE\ORADATA\ORCL\USERS01.DBF
C:\ORACLE\ORADATA\ORCL\UNDOTBS01.DBF
C:\ORACLE\ORADATA\ORCL\SYSAUX01.DBF
C:\ORACLE\ORADATA\ORCL\SYSTEM01.DBF
C:\ORACLE\ORADATA\ORCL\REVEAL_DATA_01.DBF
C:\ORACLE\ORADATA\ORCL\REVEAL_INDEX_01.DBF
C:\ORACLE\ORADATA\ORCL\USERS02.DBF
7 rows selected.
```

EXERCISE 2.3 *(continued)*

2. You use the MEMBER column in the V$LOGFILE view to find the location of all the online redo logs:

```
SQL> select member from v$logfile;
MEMBER
-----------------------------------
C:\ORACLE\ORADATA\ORCL\REDO03A.LOG
C:\ORACLE\ORADATA\ORCL\REDO02.LOG
C:\ORACLE\ORADATA\ORCL\REDO01.LOG
C:\ORACLE\ORADATA\ORCL\REDO03B.LOG
```

3. You use the NAME column in V$CONTROLFILE to find the control files:

```
SQL> select name from v$controlfile;
NAME
-------------------------------------
C:\ORACLE\ORADATA\ORCL\CONTROL01.CTL
C:\ORACLE\ORADATA\ORCL\CONTROL02.CTL
C:\ORACLE\ORADATA\ORCL\CONTROL03.CTL
C:\ORACLE\ORADATA\ORCL\CONTROL04.CTL
```

4. Having found all the files you will need for your backup, create a directory to back up all your files to. Of course, you might back your files up to tape or a thumb drive or some such thing. In this case, you will just copy the files to a directory that you will create called c:\backup\orcl\backup1.

```
SQL> host mkdir c:\backup\orcl\backup1
```

5. Having created your backup directory, you need to shut down the database with the shutdown immediate command before you start your backup.

```
SQL> shutdown immediate
Database closed.
Database dismounted.
ORACLE instance shut down.
```

6. Now copy the files that you found in steps 1, 2, and 3 to the backup directory created in step 4. Notice that all the files in this example reside in one directory, c:\oracle\oradata\orcl, so the copy command is quite easy. Backups can take a while, so be patient. It's probably a good time to go grab a cool refreshment from the vending machine!

```
C:\>copy c:\oracle\oradata\orcl\*.* c:\backup\orcl\backup1
c:\oracle\oradata\orcl\CONTROL01.CTL
```

EXERCISE 2.3 *(continued)*

```
c:\oracle\oradata\orcl\CONTROL02.CTL
c:\oracle\oradata\orcl\CONTROL03.CTL
c:\oracle\oradata\orcl\CONTROL04.CTL
c:\oracle\oradata\orcl\REDO01.LOG
c:\oracle\oradata\orcl\REDO02.LOG
c:\oracle\oradata\orcl\REDO03A.LOG
c:\oracle\oradata\orcl\REDO03B.LOG
c:\oracle\oradata\orcl\REVEAL_DATA_01.DBF
c:\oracle\oradata\orcl\REVEAL_INDEX_01.DBF
c:\oracle\oradata\orcl\SYSAUX01.DBF
c:\oracle\oradata\orcl\SYSTEM01.DBF
c:\oracle\oradata\orcl\TEMP01.DBF
c:\oracle\oradata\orcl\UNDOTBS01.DBF
c:\oracle\oradata\orcl\USERS01.DBF
c:\oracle\oradata\orcl\USERS02.DBF
       16 file(s) copied.
```

7. Once the copy is complete, verify that the backup is where you expect it to be:

```
C:\>dir c:\backup\orcl\backup1
 Volume in drive C has no label.
 Volume Serial Number is 08DE-E1AB
 Directory of c:\backup\orcl\backup1
08/02/2008  02:16 PM    <DIR>          .
08/02/2008  02:16 PM    <DIR>          ..
08/02/2008  02:02 PM        10,174,464 CONTROL01.CTL
08/02/2008  02:02 PM        10,174,464 CONTROL02.CTL
08/02/2008  02:02 PM        10,174,464 CONTROL03.CTL
08/02/2008  02:02 PM        10,174,464 CONTROL04.CTL
08/02/2008  02:02 PM        52,429,312 REDO01.LOG
08/02/2008  02:02 PM        52,429,312 REDO02.LOG
08/02/2008  02:02 PM       104,858,112 REDO03A.LOG
08/02/2008  02:02 PM       104,858,112 REDO03B.LOG
08/02/2008  02:02 PM        15,736,832 REVEAL_DATA_01.DBF
08/02/2008  02:02 PM        15,736,832 REVEAL_INDEX_01.DBF
08/02/2008  02:02 PM       851,386,368 SYSAUX01.DBF
08/02/2008  02:02 PM       754,982,912 SYSTEM01.DBF
08/02/2008  02:02 PM        50,339,840 TEMP01.DBF
08/02/2008  02:02 PM       519,053,312 UNDOTBS01.DBF
```

EXERCISE 2.3 *(continued)*

```
08/02/2008  02:02 PM        581,246,976 USERS01.DBF
08/02/2008  02:02 PM         10,493,952 USERS02.DBF
              16 File(s)  3,154,249,728 bytes
               2 Dir(s)  13,330,685,952 bytes free
```

8. Start the database. Your backup is complete!

```
SQL> startup
ORACLE instance started.
Total System Global Area  418484224 bytes
Fixed Size                  1333592 bytes
Variable Size             348128936 bytes
Database Buffers           62914560 bytes
Redo Buffers                6107136 bytes
Database mounted.
Database opened.
```

You could always decide to compress the backup files with a utility like PKZIP to save space if you wanted. By the way, RMAN can do this for you!

That's all there is to an offline database backup. In the next chapter, you will see that recovering the database using this backup is just as easy!

Temporary Tablespaces and Backups

Temporary tablespaces created with the `create temporary tablespace` command do not need to be backed up. The tempfiles associated with temporary tablespaces can be re-created on the fly as needed. This is true with both online backups and offline backups. If you are using the old-style temporary tablespaces that are not using tempfiles, you will still need to back up those datafiles.

To re-create tempfiles, simply use the `alter tablespace` command with the add `tempfile` keyword, as shown here:

```
Alter tablespace my_temp
Add tempfile '/u01/db01/mytempfile01.dbf' size 100m;
```

Performing Oracle Online Backups

Oracle online backups are not difficult to do; they just require a few additional steps. In this section, we will introduce you to Oracle online backups. First we will discuss online backups and generally how to do them. We will then present an example of actually performing an online backup.

The Mechanics of Online Backups

To do Oracle online backups, your database must be in ARCHIVELOG mode. You can back up the entire database or you can choose to back up a specific tablespace or set of tablespaces. If you choose to back up only specific tablespaces, you will not be able to recover your database until you have at least a base backup of all of its tablespaces. That said, you can back up the tablespaces at different times if you prefer (though this is not common practice). For example, you could back up the SYSTEM tablespace on Monday, the USERS tablespace on Tuesday, and so on. As long as you have a complete cumulative backup of the database (taken at different times), you can recover it.

To start an online backup, you will need to put each tablespace in hot backup mode. This can be done by using the `alter database begin backup` command, or you can individually put tablespaces in hot backup mode with the `alter tablespace begin backup` command. After you have put the tablespaces in hot backup mode, you back up the underlying datafiles of that tablespace. If you need to know where the datafiles related to that tablespace reside, you can use the DBA_DATA_FILES view.

When a Tablespace Is in Hot Backup Mode

When you put a tablespace in hot backup mode, Oracle will start writing block-sized records to the redo logs. These records are much bigger than the normal-sized records, so this can cause performance problems.

One odd misconception we hear from time to time is that Oracle will stop writing to the database datafiles during a hot backup. In fact Oracle will continue to write changes to the datafiles; however, it will not update the datafile headers until the backup is complete.

When you put a tablespace in hot backup mode, you are really putting the underlying datafiles of the that tablespace in hot backup mode. You can determine if a datafile is in hot backup mode by querying the V$BACKUP view. The STATUS column will indicate ACTIVE if the given datafile is in hot backup mode. Here is an example of such a query where our users tablespace is in hot backup mode, as indicated by the ACTIVE status.

```
SQL> select a.tablespace_name, b.status
  2  from dba_data_files a, v$backup b
```

```
  3   where a.file_id=b.file#
  4  order by tablespace_name;
TABLESPACE_NAME               STATUS
----------------------------- -----------
REVEAL_DATA                   NOT ACTIVE
REVEAL_INDEX                  NOT ACTIVE
SYSAUX                        NOT ACTIVE
SYSTEM                        NOT ACTIVE
UNDOTBS1                      NOT ACTIVE
USERS                         ACTIVE
USERS                         ACTIVE
```

Another thing to be aware of is what happens if the database is shut down while datafiles are in hot backup mode. First, Oracle will not allow you to shut down a database with most shutdown commands (`shutdown`, `shutdown immediate`, `shutdown transactional`, or `startup force`) while a tablespace is in hot backup mode. Instead it will generate an error, as shown here:

```
ORA-01149: cannot shutdown - file 4 has online backup set
ORA-01110: data file 4: 'C:\ORACLE\ORADATA\ORCL\USERS01.DBF'
```

This error identifies the datafile that is in hot backup mode. You would need to determine which tablespace the datafile is assigned to by looking at the DBA_DATA_FILES view. You would then issue the `alter tablespace end backup` command to take it out of hot backup mode.

If you issue a `shutdown abort` or if the database crashes for some reason or the server shuts down without shutting down the database in a natural fashion, Oracle will not restart with a datafile in hot backup mode. You will see the following error when you try to restart the database:

```
ORA-10873: file 4 needs end backup before opening a database
ORA-01110: data file 4: 'C:\ORACLE\ORADATA\ORCL\USERS01.DBF'
```

You simply issue the command `alter database end backup` to take the datafiles out of hot backup mode and then `alter database open` to open the database.

Once the backup is complete, you will take the tablespaces out of hot backup mode with the `alter database end backup` command, or you can individually take each tablespace out of hot backup mode by issuing the `alter tablespace end backup` command.

Once you complete the online backup, one more very important step is to back up the archived redo logs that were generated during the backup. You will need each log that was generated from the time you issued the `alter database begin backup` command until you issued the `alter database end backup` command. After the backup, use the `alter system switch logfile` command to force a log switch to cause the current online redo log (which contains redo generated during the backup) to be archived after you have completed the backup. You will need the redo in this log file, and any other archived redo logs that might have been generated during the backup, in order to recover the database from the backup you just completed.

In addition to regular online backups, you will want to schedule regular backups of your archived redo logs to protect them as much as possible. For example, if the online backup in the exercise ended at 4 p.m., you would be able to restore the database up to 4 p.m. with the archived redo logs you backed up. Archived redo logs will continue to be generated, though, and if you want to be able to recover your database to a point beyond 5 p.m., you will need to have those later-generated archived redo logs available (more on recovery in the next chapter). Thus it is a good idea to have regular backups of your archived redo logs!

In Exercise 2.4, we walk you through the process of doing an online backup.

EXERCISE 2.4

Executing an Online Backup

In this exercise we will be performing an online database backup. As mentioned in the text, your database will need to be in ARCHIVELOG mode to successfully execute this backup.

1. We assume your database is already running in ARCHIVELOG mode. If it's not, return to Exercise 2.1 and put your database in ARCHIVELOG mode.
2. As with the previous offline/cold backup, you need to know what datafiles need to be backed up.

```
SQL> Select file_name from dba_data_files;
FILE_NAME
--------------------------------------------
C:\ORACLE\ORADATA\ORCL\USERS01.DBF
C:\ORACLE\ORADATA\ORCL\UNDOTBS01.DBF
C:\ORACLE\ORADATA\ORCL\SYSAUX01.DBF
C:\ORACLE\ORADATA\ORCL\SYSTEM01.DBF
C:\ORACLE\ORADATA\ORCL\REVEAL_DATA_01.DBF
C:\ORACLE\ORADATA\ORCL\REVEAL_INDEX_01.DBF
C:\ORACLE\ORADATA\ORCL\USERS02.DBF
7 rows selected.
```

3. Having determined which datafiles need to be backed up, you need to know where the archived redo logs are being copied to.

```
SQL> show parameter log_archive_dest_1
NAME                        TYPE        VALUE
--------------------------- ----------- ------------------------------
log_archive_dest_1          string      location=c:\oracle\arch\orcl
```

EXERCISE 2.4 *(continued)*

4. You should note the current online redo log sequence number at this point. You will need this, plus all log sequences generated during the backup, in order to be able to perform your recovery. You can get this number from the v$log view:

```
SQL> select group#, sequence#, status from v$log;
    GROUP#  SEQUENCE# STATUS
---------- ---------- ----------------
         1         13 INACTIVE
         2         14 CURRENT
         3         12 INACTIVE
```

In this case, you see that you will need all log files from sequence number 14 on in order to restore the backup you are preparing to use.

5. You now need to put the database in hot backup mode. Oracle Database 11*g* provides the command `alter database begin backup` for this purpose. You can also back up specific tablespaces with the `alter tablespace begin backup` command.

```
SQL> alter database begin backup;
Database altered.
-- ALTERNATE - Run this for each tablespace to be backed up.
-- alter tablespace users begin backup;
```

6. The database datafiles are now ready to be backed up. You will copy the files to a directory that you will create called `c:\backup\orcl\backup2`.

```
SQL> host mkdir c:\backup\orcl\backup2
```

7. Now copy all the database datafiles to this directory. In this case, all the files are in the directory `c:\oracle\oradata\orcl`, and the filenames all end with an extension of `.DBF`, so the command to copy them is pretty easy. Once you have started the datafile copy, go get something to eat. It might take a while.

```
SQL> host copy c:\oracle\oradata\orcl\*.dbf c:\backup\orcl\backup2
c:\oracle\oradata\orcl\REVEAL_DATA_01.DBF
c:\oracle\oradata\orcl\REVEAL_INDEX_01.DBF
c:\oracle\oradata\orcl\SYSAUX01.DBF
c:\oracle\oradata\orcl\SYSTEM01.DBF
c:\oracle\oradata\orcl\TEMP01.DBF
c:\oracle\oradata\orcl\UNDOTBS01.DBF
c:\oracle\oradata\orcl\USERS01.DBF
c:\oracle\oradata\orcl\USERS02.DBF
        8 file(s) copied.
```

EXERCISE 2.4 *(continued)*

8. Having patiently waited for the backup to complete, you now need to take the database out of hot backup mode. Oracle Database 11*g* provides the command `alter database end backup` for this purpose. You can also back up specific tablespaces with the `alter tablespace end backup` command.

```
SQL> alter database end backup;
Database altered.
-- ALTERNATE - Run this for each tablespace to be backed up.
-- alter tablespace users end backup;
```

9. Next you need to determine the current log file sequence number. You will need the earlier log file that you identified and all log files generated during the backup up to the current log file in order to be able to restore this backup. The query is the same against V$LOG that you saw earlier:

```
SQL> select group#, sequence#, status from v$log;
    GROUP#  SEQUENCE# STATUS
---------- ---------- ----------------
         1         13 INACTIVE
         2         14 ACTIVE
         3         15 CURRENT
```

In this example, you can see that during the backup you had a log file switch, from sequence number 14 to sequence number 15. You see that log sequence 15 is the current sequence number. You know now that you will need to back up the logs with sequence numbers 14 and 15 in order to be able to restore this backup.

10. You now need to force a log switch so the log with sequence number 15 (the current online redo log sequence number) will be archived. To do this, you issue the `alter system switch logfile` command. This will cause Oracle to switch to the next log file (sequence 16), and the current archive log (Sequence 15) will be copied to the archive-log directory by the ARCn processes.

```
SQL> Alter system switch logfile;
System altered.
```

11. Having switched log files, you need to wait for ARCH to complete copying the last log file to the archive-log directory. You can check for this completion by looking at the V$ARCHIVED_LOG view.

```
SQL> Select sequence#, archived, status from v$archived_log
  2  Where sequence# between 14 and 15;
 SEQUENCE# ARC S
---------- --- -
```

EXERCISE 2.4 *(continued)*

```
14 YES A
15 YES A
```

Here you see that the logs with sequence numbers 14 and 15 (already identified as critical to restoring this backup) have been archived successfully. The ARCHIVED column indicates this with the use of the YES value.

12. Now back up all archived redo logs, ensuring that all logs with numbers between sequence *x and sequence y* are backed up. You will simply copy all archived redo logs from the directory identified in step 3 (c:\oracle\arch\orcl) to your backup directory.

```
SQL> Host copy c:\oracle\arch\orcl\*.* c:\backup\orcl\backup2
c:\oracle\arch\orcl\ORCL_658485967_1_10.ARC
c:\oracle\arch\orcl\ORCL_658485967_1_11.ARC
c:\oracle\arch\orcl\ORCL_658485967_1_12.ARC
c:\oracle\arch\orcl\ORCL_658485967_1_13.ARC
c:\oracle\arch\orcl\ORCL_658485967_1_14.ARC ← Log sequence 14
c:\oracle\arch\orcl\ORCL_658485967_1_15.ARC ← Log sequence 15
c:\oracle\arch\orcl\ORCL_658485967_1_2.ARC
c:\oracle\arch\orcl\ORCL_658485967_1_3.ARC
c:\oracle\arch\orcl\ORCL_658485967_1_4.ARC
c:\oracle\arch\orcl\ORCL_658485967_1_5.ARC
c:\oracle\arch\orcl\ORCL_658485967_1_6.ARC
c:\oracle\arch\orcl\ORCL_658485967_1_7.ARC
c:\oracle\arch\orcl\ORCL_658485967_1_8.ARC
c:\oracle\arch\orcl\ORCL_658485967_1_9.ARC
        14 file(s) copied.
```

You can tell that the logs with sequence numbers 14 and 15 were backed up since you know that the log sequence number is part of the filename (it's the number right before the extension). We also marked them for you in the output just because we are nice guys. After copying the archived redo logs to the backup location, you can delete the source location if you want to save space. Once the backup of the archived redo logs is complete, your database backup is done.

We hope you also realize that you will need to back up files like the database parameter file, any other Oracle-related configuration files (like for networking), and the Oracle database software itself. Backing up these structures (except for the spfile, which is a special RMAN case we cover in Chapter 4) is beyond the scope of the OCP exam.

Backing Up the Control File

Finally, we need to talk about control-file backups. We introduced you to the control file in Chapter 1. In Oracle there are three ways to manually back up a control file (again, RMAN methods will be covered in Chapter 4):

- Backing up the original control file during a cold backup
- Creating a backup control file
- Creating a trace file with the `create control file` command in it

We have really already covered the first method in this chapter. Let's look at the remaining two methods in some more detail. We will address recovering from a lost control file in Chapter 3.

Creating a Backup Control File

The backup control file is almost the same as a regular control file. It has some areas in it that are marked such that Oracle recognizes that it's a backup control file. When a backup control file is used, some form of recovery will be required (typically just involving the use of the archived and online redo logs if the database is otherwise intact).

To create the backup control file simply issue the `alter database backup controlfile to` command, indicating at the end of the command where you want the control file to be created.

For example, if you wanted to create a backup control file after the online backup you performed in Exercise 2.4, you would simply need to issue the following command:

```
SQL> alter database backup controlfile to
'c:\backup\orcl\backup2\backup_control.ctl';
Database altered.
```

The result is the creation of a backup control file called `backup_control.ctl` found in the `c:\backup\orcl\backup2` directory, as you can see here:

```
SQL> host dir c:\backup\orcl\backup2\backup_control.ctl
 Volume in drive C has no label.
 Volume Serial Number is 08DE-E1AB
 Directory of c:\backup\orcl\backup2
08/02/2008  03:24 PM        10,174,464 BACKUP_CONTROL.CTL
               1 File(s)     10,174,464 bytes
               0 Dir(s)   9,930,571,776 bytes free
```

We will cover recovering from control-file loss using a backup control file in Chapter 3.

Creating a Trace File with the *Create Control File* Command in It

If all else fails and you do not have a backup control file, don't worry; you have another option, the `create controlfile` command. Normally, manually executing the command can be challenging because you need to know a lot of information about your database (like the names and locations of all the database datafiles). However, you can prepare for the possibility of having to use the `create controlfile` command by creating one in advance. The `alter database backup controlfile to trace` command will create a trace file with the `create controlfile` command in it for you. The trace file is stored in the new diagnostic directory structure in Oracle Database 11*g*.

The diagnostic directory structure is a new standard introduced in Oracle Database 11*g* that defines where Oracle stores files related to database troubleshooting and diagnostics. The base directory of this structure is defined by the parameter `DIAGNOSTIC_DEST`. Here is an example of the setting of `DIAGNOSTIC_DEST` on an Oracle database:

```
SQL> show parameter diag
NAME                                 TYPE        VALUE
------------------------------------ ----------- ---------
diagnostic_dest                      string      C:\ORACLE
```

A whole book could be written on the new 11*g* diagnostic capabilities, but what we are interested in is where user-generated trace files get created, because when we issue the `alter database backup controlfile to trace` command, the resulting file will be a user-generated trace file.

In this case, the trace file will be created in `$DIAGNOSTIC_BASE\diag\rdbms\orcl\orcl\trace` as shown in this code example:

```
SQL> alter database backup controlfile to trace;
Database altered.
C:\oracle\diag\rdbms\orcl\orcl\trace>dir
 Volume in drive C has no label.
 Volume Serial Number is 08DE-E1AB
 Directory of C:\oracle\diag\rdbms\orcl\orcl\trace
08/02/2008  03:38 PM    <DIR>          .
08/02/2008  03:38 PM    <DIR>          ..
08/02/2008  03:38 PM         1,027,520 alert_orcl.log
08/02/2008  03:38 PM             9,572 orcl_ora_12120.trc
08/02/2008  03:38 PM                91 orcl_ora_12120.trm
               4 File(s)      1,037,183 bytes
               4 Dir(s)   9,964,507,136 bytes free
```

The trace file is called `orcl_ora_12120.trc` (it's easy to tell since there are no other trace files in the directory). Another option with the `alter database backup controlfile to trace` command is to define an alternate location for the trace file. The syntax for this command is as follows:

```
alter database backup controlfile to trace as '/tmp/my_control_trace.trc';
```

If you look in the file, you will find a trace-file header in it first. Later down the trace file you will find two different versions of the `create controlfile` command. Here is an example of the `create control file` command that you might find in this file:

```
CREATE CONTROLFILE REUSE DATABASE "ORCL" NORESETLOGS  ARCHIVELOG
    MAXLOGFILES 16
    MAXLOGMEMBERS 3
    MAXDATAFILES 100
    MAXINSTANCES 8
    MAXLOGHISTORY 292
LOGFILE
  GROUP 1 'C:\ORACLE\ORADATA\ORCL\REDO01.LOG'  SIZE 50M,
  GROUP 2 'C:\ORACLE\ORADATA\ORCL\REDO02.LOG'  SIZE 50M,
  GROUP 3 (
    'C:\ORACLE\ORADATA\ORCL\REDO03A.LOG',
    'C:\ORACLE\ORADATA\ORCL\REDO03B.LOG'
  ) SIZE 100M
-- STANDBY LOGFILE
DATAFILE
  'C:\ORACLE\ORADATA\ORCL\SYSTEM01.DBF',
  'C:\ORACLE\ORADATA\ORCL\SYSAUX01.DBF',
  'C:\ORACLE\ORADATA\ORCL\UNDOTBS01.DBF',
  'C:\ORACLE\ORADATA\ORCL\USERS01.DBF',
  'C:\ORACLE\ORADATA\ORCL\REVEAL_DATA_01.DBF',
  'C:\ORACLE\ORADATA\ORCL\REVEAL_INDEX_01.DBF',
  'C:\ORACLE\ORADATA\ORCL\USERS02.DBF'
CHARACTER SET WE8MSWIN1252;
```

You will notice that this output includes the datafile names, the location and names of the online redo logs, and other information needed by the `create controlfile` command. The trace file contains other output that will be required to complete the recovery process, so you should back up the trace file as it is. In Chapter 3 we will address the process of recovering from a control-file loss using the output contained in the trace files.

Summary

In this chapter, we covered all aspects of user-managed Oracle database backups. We started with a quick review of the Oracle architecture related to backup and recovery so you could have a good foundation on which to build your knowledge. In that review, we discussed processes and memory in Oracle. We discussed ARCHIVELOG and NOARCHIVELOG mode. We also discussed startup and shutdown of the database, the different modes the database is in while starting up or shutting down, and why those modes are important during a recovery exercise.

We then reviewed configuring your database for backup and recovery, which mostly pertained to backups in ARCHIVELOG mode. We talked about archive logs, and the archive-log destination parameters. We talked about how an archive log is named when its created. We provided you with a list of parameters that are commonly used when configuring Oracle online backups, and we also provided you with a list of data dictionary views you might need to use to manage archived redo logs.

We then moved on to the topic of offline (cold) backups. We demonstrated how you could do an offline backup of your database. We proceeded to the topic of online backups, demonstrating that they are almost as simple as offline backups. Finally, we discussed backup control files and how they could be created.

Exam Essentials

Be able to configure a database of user-initiated online backups. Understand the different parameters that need to be configured when you are going to back up a database with user-based online backups. You will need to understand parameters such as `LOG_ARCHIVE_DEST_1` and how to configure them. You will need to understand what happens if you have two archive-log destination directories defined.

Be able to back up your database with an offline backup. Understand the steps that need to be performed to do an offline backup. Understand the difference between an offline backup and an online backup and how these differences can be used to decide the optimal backup strategy.

Be able to back up your database with an online backup. Know how to configure your database for an online backup. Understand how to put the database in ARCHIVELOG mode so you can do online backups. Understand how to determine which archived redo logs you will need to back up when doing an online backup.

Be able to back up your database control file. Understand why it is important to back up your control file. Understand the different methods of backing up your control file. Understand what a backup control file is.

Review Questions

1. Your database is in NOARCHIVELOG mode. You start to do a backup, but your users complain that they don't want you to shut down the database to perform the backup. What options are available to you?

   A. Put the database in hot backup mode and perform an online backup, including backing up the archived redo logs.

   B. Just back up the database datafiles without shutting down the database.

   C. You will have to wait until you can shut down the database to perform the backup.

   D. Mark each datafile as backup in progress, back them up individually, and then mark them as backup not in progress. No archived redo logs will need to be backed up.

   E. Only back up the datafiles that the user will not be touching. Once the user has finished what they were doing, you can shut down the database and back up the datafiles the user changed during the course of the remaining backup.

2. When performing an online backup, what is the proper order of the following steps?

   a. Issue the `alter database end backup` command.

   b. Back up the archived redo logs.

   c. Issue the `alter database begin backup` command.

   d. Back up the database files.

   e. Determine the beginning log sequence number.

   f. Determine the ending log sequence number.

   g. Force a log switch with the `alter system switch logfile` command.

   A. a, b, c, d, e, f, g

   B. c, d, a, b, e, g, f

   C. f, d, b, g, a, c, e

   D. e, c, d, a, g, f, b

   E. a, f, b, g, e, c, d

3. You want to put a specific tablespace called MY_DATA in hot backup mode so you can back it up. What command would you use?

   A. `alter tablespace MY_DATA begin backup;`

   B. `alter tablespace MY_DATA start backup;`

   C. `alter tablespace MY_DATA backup begin;`

   D. `alter MY_DATA begin backup;`

   E. You cannot back up individual tablespaces.

4. You backed up the database at 8 a.m. today using an online backup. Accounting made a large change to the underlying data between 10 a.m. and noon. Which of the following actions would ensure that the changes could be recovered using the 8 a.m. backup?

   A. Create a manual incremental online database backup.

   B. Back up all the archived redo logs generated since the 8 a.m. backup.

   C. Create a brand-new backup after all the changes have been applied.

   D. There is no way to make the changes recoverable based on the 8 a.m. backup.

   E. Perform an online backup of the tablespace(s) that contained changed data.

5. What are the different logging modes available in Oracle Database 11*g*? (Choose two.)

   A. NOLOG mode

   B. NOARCHIVELOG mode

   C. LOGGING mode

   D. HOTDATABASE mode

   E. ARCHIVELOG mode

6. Which is the correct command to put the database in ARCHIVELOG mode?

   A. `alter database archivelog`

   B. `alter system enable archivelog mode`

   C. `alter database enable archive`

   D. `alter database archivelog enable`

   E. None of the above

7. What is the correct order of steps to perform an online database backup?

   a. `alter database begin backup;`

   b. `alter database end backup;`

   c. Back up the database datafiles.

   d. Back up the archive log files.

   e. `alter system switch logfile;`

   A. a, b, c, d, e

   B. e, d, a, b, c

   C. a, c, b, d, e

   D. d, b, c, a, e

   E. a, c, b, e, d

8. Which command will result in a trace file being created with the `create controlfile` command contained in it?

   A. `alter database backup controlfile;`

   B. `alter database backup controlfile to trace;`

   C. `alter database controlfile backup;`

   D. `alter database controlfile backup to '/ora01/oracle/ctrl_backup.ctl';`

   E. `alter database begin controlfile backup;`

9. Which of the following is a valid way of putting a tablespace named DAVE_TBS into hot backup mode?

   A. `alter tablespace DAVE_TBS backup mode;`

   B. `alter tablespace DAVE_TBS start backup;`

   C. `alter tablespace DAVE_TBS begin backup;`

   D. `alter tablespace DAVE_TBS backup begin;`

   E. `alter tablespace DAVE_TBS backup;`

10. Every Sunday the Unix system administrator has a job that executes a full backup of the entire Unix system your database is on. Is this backup usable for backup and recovery of your database?

    A. Yes, if the database is in ARCHIVELOG mode.

    B. Yes, if the database is in NOARCHIVELOG mode.

    C. No, the backup is not usable in any way.

    D. Only if the ENABLE_ONLINE_BACKUP parameter is set to TRUE.

11. Which is not a valid way of backing up a control file?

    A. Backing up the control file to trace

    B. Copying the existing control file of the database to the backup location during a hot backup

    C. Copying the existing control file of the database to the backup location during a cold backup

    D. Creating a backup control file

    E. Using the `create controlfile` command

12. Which of the following parameters defines the location where Oracle should create archived redo logs?

    A. LOG_ARCHIVE_1

    B. LOG_DESTINATION_1

    C. LOG_ARCHIVED_DESTINATION_1

    D. LOG_ARCHIVE_DEST_1

    E. LOG_ARCHIVE_SOURCE_1

13. True or false? Archived redo logs can be copied to more than one destination by Oracle.
    A. True
    B. False

14. What will be the result of the following configuration?

```
Log_archive_dest_1='location=c:\oracle\arch\mydb'
Log_archive_dest_2='location=z:\oracle\arch\mydb'
```

    A. An error will occur during database startup because the second parameter is not valid.
    B. An error will occur during database startup since you are trying to create archived redo logs in two different locations.
    C. Archived redo logs will be created in two different locations by the ARCH process.
    D. Archived redo logs will be created in two different locations by the LGWR process.
    E. Neither parameter setting is valid, so the database will not start up.

15. Which view provides information on the backup status of the datafiles in the database?
    A. `V$BACKUP`
    B. `V$BACKUP_STATUS`
    C. `V$BACKUP_DATAFILE`
    D. `V$DATAFILE_BACKUP`
    E. `V$TABLESPCE_BACKUP`

16. Another DBA issues a `shutdown abort` command on a database on which you were running an online backup. What will happen when you try to restart the database?
    A. Oracle will automatically take the datafile out of hot backup mode, generate a warning message, and then open the database.
    B. Oracle will automatically take the datafile out of hot backup mode and then open the database.
    C. Oracle will generate an error when trying to open the database, indicating that a datafile is in hot backup mode. You will need to correct this error before you can open the database.
    D. The database will open with the file in hot backup mode. You can restart the backup at any time.
    E. The datafile in hot backup mode will be corrupted and you will have to recover it.

17. What is the proper command to shut down the database in a consistent manner?
    A. `Shutdown abort`
    B. `Shutdown kill`
    C. `Shutdown nowait`
    D. `shutdown immediate`
    E. `shutdown halt`

18. If you issue the command `shutdown abort` prior to trying to put the database in ARCHIVELOG mode, what will be the result when you issue the command `alter database archivelog`?

A. The `alter database archivelog` command will fail.

B. The `alter database archivelog inconsistent` command must be used to put the database in ARCHIVELOG mode.

C. The `alter database archivelog` command will succeed.

D. The `alter database archivelog` command will ask if you want to make the database consistent first.

E. There is no `alter database archivelog command`. The correct command is `alter database alterlogging`.

19. Your archive-log destination directory runs out of space. What is the impact of this on the database?

A. None. The database will switch over to the stand-by archive-log destination directory.

B. A warning message will be written to the alert log of the database, but no adverse impacts to the database will be experienced.

C. The database will shut down, and will not restart until you correct the out-of-space situation.

D. The database will continue to try to write to the archive-log destination directory for one hour. After one hour, the database will shut down normally.

E. Once Oracle has cycled through all online redo logs, it will stop processing any DML or DDL until the out-of-space condition is corrected.

20. How many individual archive-log destination directories are supported by Oracle Database 11g?

A. 7

B. 1

C. 10

D. 11

E. 21

Answers to Review Questions

1. C. You will have to wait until you can shut down the database since it's in NOARCHIVELOG mode. No other option will give you a backup that is recoverable.

2. D. The correct answer is D. First you determine the beginning log sequence number, then you issue the `alter database begin backup` command, then you back up the database files, and then you issue the `alter database end backup` command. Next you force a log switch with the `alter system switch logfile` command, and then you determine the ending log sequence number. Finally, you back up the archived redo logs.

3. A. The correct answer is A. The `alter tablespace` command is followed by the name of the tablespace and then the `begin backup` keyword.

4. B. The most correct answer is B. This is because the question asked you what would be done using the 8 a.m. backup.

5. B, E. B and E are the correct answers because ARCHIVELOG and NOARCHIVELOG are the two logging modes available in Oracle Database 11*g*.

6. A. The `alter database archivelog` will put the database in ARCHIVELOG mode.

7. E. The correct answer is E. You first put the database in ARCHIVELOG mode with the `alter database begin backup` command. You then back up the database datafiles. Then take the database out of backup mode with the `alter database end backup` command. Issue the `alter system switch logfile` command and then back up the archived redo logs.

8. B. The `alter database backup controlfile to trace` command will create a trace file in the `DIAGNOSTIC_DEST` directory structure that contains your control file.

9. C. The correct command would be `alter tablespace DAVE_TBS begin backup;`.

10. C. The correct answer is C. Regardless of the logging mode, the backup would not be usable since the tablespaces were not put in hot backup mode.

11. B. The correct answer is B. You would never back up the actual control file during an online database backup.

12. D. The correct answer is D. The `LOG_ARCHIVE_DEST_1` parameter is a parameter that would be used to define the location where Oracle would create your archived redo logs.

13. A. Oracle can be configured to copy archived redo logs to up to 10 different locations.

14. C. The archived redo logs will be created in two different locations. The ARCH process is responsible for the creation of the archived redo logs.

15. A. The `V$BACKUP` view provides information on the online backup status for datafiles in the database.

16. C. Oracle will generate an error indicating that a datafile is in hot backup mode. You will need to issue the `alter database end backup` command to make sure all datafiles in hot backup mode are no longer in hot backup mode. You can then use the `alter database open` command to open the database.

17. D. The `shutdown immediate` command is used to shut down the database in a consistent manner.

18. A. The `alter database archivelog` command will fail. You will need to open the database and then shut it down in a consistent manner.

19. E. Oracle will cycle through all of the online redo logs, trying to archive them after they have been filled. After cycling through the last online redo log, Oracle will suspend all database operations until the out-of-space condition is corrected.

20. C. Oracle provides support for up to 10 different archive-log destination directories.

Performing Oracle User-Managed Database Recoveries

ORACLE DATABASE 11*g*: ADMINISTRATION II EXAM OBJECTIVES COVERED IN THIS CHAPTER:

✓ **Performing User-Managed Backup and Recovery**

- Perform user-managed complete database recovery
- Perform user-managed incomplete database recovery
- Backup and recover a control file
- Recover from a lost TEMP file
- Recover from a lost redo log group
- Recover from the loss of a password file

In Chapter 2 we showed you how to perform user-based database backups. Of course, those backups are of little good if you don't know how to use them to restore your database. In this chapter, we will show you how to restore your database with user-based backups. First we will show you how to use the offline backup you took in NOARCHIVELOG mode and use it to restore your database. We will then address online backups taken in ARCHIVELOG mode and show you how to restore them. We will then talk about different kinds of user-based incomplete recoveries, also called *point-in-time* recoveries.

Finally, we will cover other recovery processes, such as recovering from a lost control file and a lost temporary tablespace tempfile, recovering from the loss of an online redo log group, and how to recover from loss of a password file. So, buckle in, keep your hands and arms inside the vehicle at all times, and enjoy the ride!

Exam objectives are subject to change at any time without prior notice and at Oracle's sole discretion. Please visit Oracle's Training and Certification website (`http://www.oracle.com/education/certification/`) for the most current exam-objectives listing.

Performing a Recovery in NOARCHIVELOG Mode

Recovering a database that was backed up in NOARCHIVELOG mode is perhaps the easiest recovery task to do. The thing to keep in mind is that there are no archived redo logs to apply. You simply will be restoring your database to the point in time of the backup you took. It does not matter if you lost one datafile or the entire enchilada; you have to restore all the files you backed up to recover the database.

The process is simple. You copy all the files you backed up during your offline backup (datafiles, control files, redo logs) and then start the database. You simply must copy all of these files; you can't pick and choose what to recover. Exercise 3.1 provides an example of such a recovery operation.

EXERCISE 3.1

Restoring a Database Using a Cold Backup

In this exercise you will be restoring the database with a cold backup. It is assumed the database is in NOARCHIVELOG mode.

1. Make sure the database is shut down.

2. Copy the files on the backup media to the original location. You would copy the following files:

   - Database datafiles
   - Database control files
   - Database online redo logs

   If the original location of the database files is not available, copy them to an alternate location. Having copied the files to an alternate location, you will likely need to execute an optional step 3 for the control files and optional step 4 for all database files and/or online redo logs. Here is an example of the copy command:

   ```
   C:\Documents and Settings\Robert>copy c:\oracle\oradata\orcl\cold\*.*
   c:\backup\orcl\backup1
   ```

3. (Optional) If you copied the database control files to a location other than their original location, you will need to modify the database parameter CONTROL_FILES to point to the control files in their new location.

   If you are using a text-based parameter file (pfile), simply edit the file and change the CONTROL_FILES parameter value contained within that file.

   If you are using a server-based parameter file (spfile), then you will need to start the database in NOMOUNT mode and change the SPFILE entry for the CONTROL_FILES parameter using the `alter system` command. We will have to use the `scope=spfile` keyword when issuing the `alter system` command since changing the CONTROL_FILE parameter is not supported as a dynamic change.

   After you have changed the parameter file (manually or using the `alter system` command), use the shutdown command to shut down the database (the parameter file will be reread when you open it again in the next steps). Here is an example:

   ```
   SQL> startup nomount
   ORACLE instance started.
   Total System Global Area  397557760 bytes
   Fixed Size                  1333452 bytes
   Variable Size             289408820 bytes
   Database Buffers          100663296 bytes
   ```

EXERCISE 3.1 *(continued)*

```
Redo Buffers                6152192 bytes
SQL> alter system set control_files='C:\ORACLE\ORADATA\ORCL\CONTROL01.CTL',
'C:\ORACLE\ORADATA\ORCL\CONTROL02.CTL',
'C:\ORACLE\ORADATA\ORCL\CONTROL03.CTL' scope=spfile;
System altered.
SQL> shutdown immediate
ORA-01507: database not mounted
ORACLE instance shut down.
```

4. (Optional) If you copied the database online redo logs or the database datafiles to a different location, you will need to indicate to Oracle that you have done so. This is so Oracle will know where the files are now so it can open them. This is known as a rename operation. (Don't be fooled, though. It renames only the files inside of Oracle; it does not rename them on the operating system).

   To rename the database files (redo log and datafiles) you must have the database mounted first. Once the database is mounted, you will issue the `alter database rename file` command for each database file that needs to be changed.

   Here is an example where we have moved the online redo logs and database datafiles from `c:\oracle\oradata\orcl` to `c:\oracle\oradata\orclnew`. You need to indicate to Oracle that you have made this change by using the `alter database rename file` command. This will change the pointers to the database files inside the control file so Oracle will be looking for the files in the correct location.

   Note that for the rest of this exercise we will assume that the files were moved to their original locations. In this example, you rename the online redo logs and then you rename the database datafiles:

```
SQL> startup mount
ORACLE instance started.
Total System Global Area  397557760 bytes
Fixed Size                  1333452 bytes
Variable Size             272631604 bytes
Database Buffers          117440512 bytes
Redo Buffers                6152192 bytes
Database mounted.
SQL>alter database rename file 'c:\oracle\oradata\orcl\RED001.LOG' to
 'c:\oracle\oradata\orclnew\RED001.LOG';
SQL>alter database rename file 'c:\oracle\oradata\orcl\RED002.LOG' to
 'c:\oracle\oradata\orclnew\RED002.LOG';
```

EXERCISE 3.1 *(continued)*

```
SQL>alter database rename file 'c:\oracle\oradata\orcl\REDO03.LOG' to
 'c:\oracle\oradata\orclnew\REDO03.LOG';
SQL>alter database rename file 'c:\oracle\oradata\orcl\SYSAUX01.DBF' to
 'c:\oracle\oradata\orclnew\SYSAUX01.DBF';
SQL>alter database rename file 'c:\oracle\oradata\orcl\SYSTEM01.DBF' to
 'c:\oracle\oradata\orclnew\SYSTEM01.DBF';
SQL>alter database rename file 'c:\oracle\oradata\orcl\TEMP01.DBF' to
 'c:\oracle\oradata\orclnew\TEMP01.DBF';
SQL>alter database rename file 'c:\oracle\oradata\orcl\UNDOTBS01.DBF' to
 'c:\oracle\oradata\orclnew\UNDOTBS01.DBF';
SQL>alter database rename file 'c:\oracle\oradata\orcl\USERS01.DBF' to
 'c:\oracle\oradata\orclnew\USERS01.DBF';
```

5. Now that the files are copied into place, you can start up the database:

```
SQL> startup
ORACLE instance started.
Total System Global Area  418484224 bytes
Fixed Size                  1333592 bytes
Variable Size             348128936 bytes
Database Buffers           62914560 bytes
Redo Buffers                6107136 bytes
Database mounted.
Database opened.
```

That's it. You have recovered your database! Query to your heart's delight!

Real World Scenario

Recovering in NOARCHIVELOG Mode

Because of its limitations, you might ask yourself whether anyone really uses a database in NOARCHIVELOG mode. The answer is yes.

The main benefit to running in NOARCHIVELOG mode is that you are not generating archived redo logs. Archived redo logs require more space (sometimes a lot more space). Often development or test databases do not require online backups or point-in-time recovery, so running them in NOARCHIVELOG mode might make sense. Most bigger shops will run all databases in ARCHIVELOG mode because of the added flexibility it gives you.

Performing a Full Database Recovery in ARCHIVELOG Mode

You might think there's something slightly mystical about database recoveries in ARCHIVELOG mode the first few times you do them. You take a backup that may be days or even weeks old, apply some magic in the form of application of the archived redo logs, and *voila* (Robert's wife, the French expert, will appreciate that word), your database is up-to-date and ready to roll.

It's true that some DBAs (and managers) actually don't believe that you can back up a database while it's up and running and be able to restore it fully without losing any data. Well, we're here to tell you that you can, that it works, and it's not magic but just some good programming. It's reliable too. We've been working with Oracle for a very long time. We've yet to see an online backup that's not recoverable unless someone did something wrong, and it's pretty hard to do something wrong unless you are just not paying attention.

In the following sections, we will talk about user-based recovery of your database when it's in ARCHIVELOG mode. We will talk about preparing for the recovery and then we will talk about the actual recovery process. Note that we are discussing a full database recovery to the point of failure of the database and not a point-in-time recovery. We assume that the online redo logs are intact since full point-of-failure recovery requires this.

The OCP exam may ask you about conditions where the online redo logs have been lost, you have to use a backup control file, or all the files associated with the database are lost. See the sections "Performing Incomplete Recoveries" and "Performing Other Types of Recoveries" for more details on these special types of database recoveries.

Loss of Online Redo Logs or Control Files

Remember, if you have lost your online redo logs, then recovery becomes more complex (and the OCP exam is likely to ask you questions about these kinds of losses). We will discuss these kinds of losses later in this chapter.

Preparing for the Recovery

When preparing for recovery, you have to consider what kind of datafile loss you have experienced. There are three types you might experience:

- Loss of all datafiles
- Loss of one or more non-SYSTEM or -UNDO tablespace datafiles.
- Loss of the SYSTEM or UNDO tablespace datafile

The recovery for each of these types of datafile losses is similar. Some recoveries can be done online (with the database up and running) and other recoveries will require that the database be shut down (though in these cases it's likely going to have crashed anyway). We will cover each of these types of loss in the following sections.

Restoring Datafiles After the Loss of All Datafiles

If you have lost all of your database datafiles, then you will need to perform a database recovery with the database down. It is most likely in these cases that the database will have already crashed anyway (or refused to restart); Oracle does not do well if all of the database datafiles go missing.

The procedure in this case is simple. Restore the datafile backups from your backup media. You can restore these datafiles to their original locations or to new locations depending on your needs. Once you have restored the datafiles, you are ready to recover the entire database. We discuss full database recovery in the section "Recovering the Database" (an original title, we know).

Restoring Datafiles After the Loss of the *SYSTEM or UNDO* Tablespace Datafile

If you have lost only datafiles related to the SYSTEM or UNDO tablespace, then you should restore only those datafiles. You will still need to do an offline recovery, but the recovery will be much quicker since all you will need to do is recover those database datafiles. Once you have recovered the datafiles from your backup media, perform a tablespace- or datafile-level recovery, which is covered in the section "Recovering the Database."

Specific Recovery Actions

The OCP exam expects you to answer a question with the best answer. For example, in the case of the loss of a single, non-SYSTEM or -UNDO tablespace datafile, the best answer is to restore just that datafile and not all database datafiles. Sure you can restore all the datafiles, but that would not be the best course of action.

Restoring Datafiles After the Loss of One or More Non-*SYSTEM or -UNDO* Tablespace Datafiles

If you lose a datafile related to a tablespace other than the SYSTEM or UNDO tablespace, then you can actually perform online recovery of the database. In these cases, it is unlikely that the database will crash, and if the database is started up, it will seem to start up normally. To perform this kind of recovery, you will need to first indicate to the database that the file is in an offline state. You do this by using the `alter database` command, as shown here:

```
alter database datafile 4 offline;
alter database datafile 'C:\ORACLE\ORADATA\ORCL\USERS01.DBF' offline;
```

Now you will find that the STATUS column for this datafile in V$DATAFILE will show that the file has a RECOVER status as seen here:

```
SQL> select file#, status from v$datafile;
     FILE# STATUS
---------- -------
         1 SYSTEM
         2 ONLINE
         3 ONLINE
         4 RECOVER
```

You should also note that the status of the datafile in the DBA_DATA_FILES view does not change when you offline a file. It will still show as AVAILABLE. A row will also appear for the datafile you have taken offline in the V$RECOVER_FILE view.

Datafile IDs

Did you notice in the alter system command where we used a number instead of the location of the datafile? This is the datafile ID, and you can use the datafile ID in lieu of the entire path many times. You can find the datafile ID in the V$DATAFILE and DBA_DATA_FILES views as shown here:

```
SQL> select file_id, file_name from dba_data_files;
   FILE_ID FILE_NAME
---------- ----------------------------------------
         4 C:\ORACLE\ORADATA\ORCL\USERS01.DBF
         3 C:\ORACLE\ORADATA\ORCL\UNDOTBS01.DBF
         2 C:\ORACLE\ORADATA\ORCL\SYSAUX01.DBF
         1 C:\ORACLE\ORADATA\ORCL\SYSTEM01.DBF
```

Recovering the Database

If you restore the database files to different locations, you will need to modify the database parameter file and/or the database control file with the new file locations using the alter system command as demonstrated in optional steps 3 and 4 of Exercise 3.1.

Recovering the database depends, again, on the type of datafile outage you have experienced. In the next sections, we will cover the recover database command first. Then we'll cover restoring the database after loss of all datafiles, loss of SYSTEM or UNDO tablespace datafiles, and loss of non-SYSTEM or -UNDO tablespace datafiles.

Renaming Database files

Sometimes during a recovery you will need to restore database files to different locations. If this is the case, you will need to indicate to Oracle where the new location is. The types of files you are likely to move are control files, online redo logs, and database datafiles.

If you are restoring control files to a different location, then simply change the `CONTROL_FILES` parameter.

If the relocation involves the online redo logs or the database datafiles, then you will need to use the `alter database rename file` command. This command works only when the database is mounted, and in some cases when it's open (like when datafiles to be renamed are offline).

To rename a file, restore the files to the new location and issue the `alter database rename file` command, as shown here:

```
alter database rename file '/ora01/oracle/oradata/orcl/system01.dbf'
To '/ora02/oracle/oradata/orcl/system01.dbf';
```

This will rename the file in the control file. Note that it has no impact on the actual physical file.

Using the *recover database* Command

The `recover database` command is used in Oracle to recover the database from the SQL prompt. When you issue the `recover database` command without any parameters, Oracle will assume a *point-of-failure recovery* or *complete recovery*. That is, it will try to recover the database up to the last redo-log entry. This results in a complete recovery of your database down to the last transaction. During recovery operations, Oracle will inspect the datafile headers and the control file and determine where datafile recovery needs to begin for each datafile. To do this, Oracle will inspect the SCN contained in each database datafile. It will use the SCN to determine where it needs to start recovering the datafile.

What is the SCN? The System Change Number (SCN) is a counter, and its job is to keep track of everything going on inside the database and assign it a temporal identity. This serves to keep transactions that occurred in a particular order in the same order later down the road (such as during recovery). We need to preserve the order of transactions because of dependencies that occur between transactions. For example, if you have a parent and child table, you want to make sure that during recovery all `inserts` into the parent table occur before `inserts` into the child table. This is because of the foreign key constraint that exists between the two tables to ensure the integrity of that parent/child relationship. The SCN helps Oracle to track the temporal flow of those changes, and thus the parent table `insert` will have a lower SCN than the child table `insert`. As a result, in the end, all is right with the world.

SCNs are loosely coupled with time. Thus, 12:30pm local time would be associated with a specific SCN in a given individual database. The thing to remember is that 12:30pm local time will most likely be associated with a different SCN in each database, so the coupling is very loose. The concept of the SCN is very important because there may be times when you will want to restore your database back to a specific SCN. This is supported during recovery operations. Also, Oracle's Flashback features support the use of the SCN when flashing back the database. See Chapter 9 for more information on the vast number of features available with Oracle Flashback Database.

When you issue the `recover database` command from the SQL prompt, you have a number of options. You can recover the entire database with `recover database`, you can recover a specific tablespace with `recover tablespace`, and you can recover a datafile with `recover datafile`. As you progress through this chapter, you will see several examples of the use of the `recover database` command, including the use of the database SCN to recover your database.

After you have issued the `recover database` command, you will be prompted for the archived redo log it thinks it needs to apply. You can simply press the Enter key and Oracle will apply the redo in that archived redo log. Once the redo has been applied, the `recover database` command will prompt you for the next redo log in the sequence, and you press Enter again.

As you can imagine, this can get a little long-winded if you have to apply a number of archived redo logs. Another thing you can do at the prompt is type in `auto`. This will cause the `recover database` command to automatically start applying archived redo-log files without prompting you for the name or location of those files. This is much easier!

Recovering the Database After the Loss of All Datafiles

You can use the `recover database` command to recover the entire database all at once. Having restored all the database datafiles from the backup media, you would follow these steps:

1. Log into the database as SYS.
2. Mount the database with the `startup mount` command.
3. Issue the `recover database` command from the SQL prompt.
4. The `recover database` command will recommend to you the correct archived redo log to apply. At the prompt, type **AUTO**; the `recover database` command automatically starts applying all redo until the database is recovered.
5. Once database recovery is complete, the `recover database` command will return you to the SQL prompt. You can then issue the `alter database open` command to open the database for business.

Note that in this case you have performed a full recovery. Your database should have been completely restored without any data loss. There is no need to perform a special backup after this recovery (other than your regularly scheduled backups). In Exercise 3.2, you'll be doing a full recovery of your database after it has lost all datafiles.

EXERCISE 3.2

Recovering the Database from the Loss of All Datafiles

In this exercise, you will perform a full (complete) database recovery, restoring all datafiles. It is important to note that this recovery presupposes that the online redo logs and control files of the database are intact.

1. Back up the database. Details on how to do a full online database backup are found in Chapter 2.
2. In summary, follow these steps:
   - First put the database in hot backup mode.
   - Copy all database datafiles to a backup location.
   - Take the database out of hot backup mode.
   - Force a log switch. Back up the archived redo logs.

   Here is an example of a backup:

```
[oracle@localhost orcl]$ sqlplus "/ as sysdba"
SQL*Plus: Release 11.1.0.6.0 - Production on Sun Aug 17 15:35:48 2008
Copyright (c) 1982, 2007, Oracle.  All rights reserved.
Connected to:
Oracle Database 11g Enterprise Edition Release 11.1.0.6.0 - Production
With the Partitioning, OLAP, Data Mining and Real Application Testing options
SQL> alter database begin backup;
Database altered.
SQL> host cp /oracle01/oradata/orcl/*.dbf /oracle01/backup/orcl
SQL> alter database end backup;
Database altered.
SQL> alter system switch logfile;
System altered.
SQL> host cp /oracle01/backup/arch/* /oracle01/backup/orcl/*
SQL> alter database backup controlfile to trace;
Database altered.
SQL> alter database backup controlfile to '/oracle01/oradata/orcl/control1.bak';
Database altered.
```

3. Now remove all datafiles from the database. On some operating-system platforms (Linux, for example), you can do this with the database up and running, and on others (Windows) you will have to shut down the database.

```
SQL> quit
Disconnected from Oracle Database 11g Enterprise Edition Release
```

EXERCISE 3.2 *(continued)*

```
11.1.0.6.0 - Production
With the Partitioning, OLAP, Data Mining and Real Application Testing options
[oracle@localhost orcl]$ pwd
/oracle01/oradata/orcl
[oracle@localhost orcl]$ ls -al *.dbf
-rw-r----- 1 oracle oinstall  104865792 Aug 17 15:49 example01.dbf
-rw-r----- 1 oracle oinstall  104865792 Aug 17 15:49
my_second_secure_tbs_01.dbf
-rw-r----- 1 oracle oinstall  104865792 Aug 17 15:49 my_secure_tbs_01.dbf
-rw-r----- 1 oracle oinstall  104865792 Aug 17 15:49 retention_archives_01.
dbf
-rw-r----- 1 oracle oinstall  778051584 Aug 17 15:49 sysaux01.dbf
-rw-r----- 1 oracle oinstall  744497152 Aug 17 15:49 system01.dbf
-rw-r----- 1 oracle oinstall  182525952 Aug 17 14:03 temp01.dbf
-rw-r----- 1 oracle oinstall 1121984512 Aug 17 15:49 undotbs01.dbf
-rw-r----- 1 oracle oinstall  159326208 Aug 17 15:49 users01.dbf
[oracle@localhost orcl]$ rm *.dbf
```

4. Connect to the database and shut down the database. It may be possible that you will not be able to connect to the database, and yet the database will still be running. In this case you will have to manually kill the Oracle processes if you are running in Unix or shut down the database service in Windows. In our case, we are not able to log into the database, so we kill the LGWR process.

```
[oracle@localhost trace]$ sqlplus "/ as sysdba"
SQL*Plus: Release 11.1.0.6.0 - Production on Sun Aug 17 15:58:16 2008
Copyright (c) 1982, 2007, Oracle.  All rights reserved.
ERROR:
ORA-01075: you are currently logged on
Enter user-name:
ERROR:
ORA-01017: invalid username/password; logon denied
Enter user-name:
ERROR:
ORA-01017: invalid username/password; logon denied
SP2-0157: unable to CONNECT to ORACLE after 3 attempts, exiting SQL*Plus
[oracle@localhost trace]$ ps -ef|grep orcl|grep lgwr
oracle   23118     1  0 15:48 ?        00:00:01 ora_lgwr_orcl
[oracle@localhost trace]$ kill -9 23118
```

EXERCISE 3.2 *(continued)*

5. Once you are sure the database is down, restore the database datafiles from their backup location to the location where the database files belong.

```
[oracle@localhost orcl]$ pwd
/oracle01/backup/orcl
[oracle@localhost orcl]$ cp *.dbf /oracle01/oradata/orcl/*
```

6. Now connect to the database and issue the `startup mount` command.

```
[oracle@localhost orcl]$ sqlplus / as sysdba
SQL*Plus: Release 11.1.0.6.0 - Production on Sun Aug 17 16:26:56 2008
Copyright (c) 1982, 2007, Oracle.  All rights reserved.
Connected to an idle instance.
SQL> startup mount
ORACLE instance started.
Total System Global Area  167395328 bytes
Fixed Size                  1298612 bytes
Variable Size             142610252 bytes
Database Buffers           20971520 bytes
Redo Buffers                2514944 bytes
Database mounted.
SQL>
```

7. To recover the database, issue the `recover database` command. The command may return a response that says "media recovery complete," as shown here:

```
SQL> recover database
Media recovery complete.
```

You may also be prompted to apply archived redo logs. Simply enter **AUTO** at the prompt.

```
SQL> recover database
ORA-00279: change 5071334 generated at 08/17/2008 15:35:51 needed for thread 1
ORA-00289: suggestion :
/oracle01/flash_recovery_area/ORCL/archivelog
/2008_08_17/o1_mf_1_5_4bk6onh8_.arcORA-00280:
change 5071334 for thread 1 is in sequence #5
Specify log: {<RET>=suggested | filename | AUTO | CANCEL}
auto
ORA-00279: change 5071583 generated at 08/17/2008
15:40:04 needed for thread 1
```

EXERCISE 3.2 *(continued)*

```
ORA-00289: suggestion :
/oracle01/flash_recovery_area/ORCL/archivelog
/2008_08_17/o1_mf_1_6_4bk76kwk_.arcORA-00280:
change 5071583 for thread 1 is in sequence #6
ORA-00279: change 5091960 generated at 08/17/2008
15:49:05 needed for thread 1
ORA-00289: suggestion :
/oracle01/flash_recovery_area/ORCL/archivelog
/2008_08_17/o1_mf_1_7_4bk9ksb4_.arcORA-00280:
change 5091960 for thread 1 is in sequence #7
ORA-00279: change 5112317 generated at 08/17/2008
16:29:13 needed for thread 1
ORA-00289: suggestion :
/oracle01/flash_recovery_area/ORCL/archivelog
/2008_08_17/o1_mf_1_8_4bk9p236_.arcORA-00280:
change 5112317 for thread 1 is in sequence #8
ORA-00279: change 5112647 generated at 08/17/2008
16:31:29 needed for thread 1
ORA-00289: suggestion :
/oracle01/flash_recovery_area/ORCL/archivelog
/2008_08_17/o1_mf_1_9_4bk9p2mz_.arcORA-00280:
change 5112647 for thread 1 is in sequence #9
Log applied.
Media recovery complete.
```

8. Oracle will apply the needed redo and then return you to the SQL prompt. Assuming no errors occur, you can now open the database with the `alter database open` command as shown here:

```
SQL> alter database open;
Database altered.
```

Recovering the Database After the Loss of the *SYSTEM or UNDO* Tablespace Datafile

In this case, we will just restore the tablespaces or datafiles that were lost. Of course, because these are critical tablespace objects, the database itself is down. After restoring the datafiles that were lost (do not restore any datafiles that are intact), recover the database following these steps:

1. Log into the database as SYS.
2. Mount the database with the `startup mount` command.
3. For recovery, you have two options. You can use the `recover tablespace` or the `recover datafile` command to recover the datafiles that were lost. It's kind of up to you which one you want to use (we like the `recover tablespace` command in this situation more).
4. The `recover database` command will recommend to you the correct archived redo log to apply. At the prompt, type **AUTO**; the `recover database` command automatically starts applying all redo until the database is recovered.
5. Once database recovery is complete, the `recover database` command will return you to the SQL prompt. You can then issue the `alter database open` command to open the database for business.

Recovery of the *UNDO* Tablespace

There are cases where the UNDO tablespace can be recovered online. If the database was shut down in a consistent manner before the UNDO tablespace was lost, it may be that all you will need to do is take the UNDO tablespace datafiles offline (you won't be able to take the tablespace itself offline) and then open the database.

Oracle has a default SYSTEM tablespace that would be used in this case, when the database initially comes up. You could then just create a new UNDO tablespace and drop the old one. This might be a quicker recovery method in some cases.

Recovering the Database After the Loss of One or More Non-*SYSTEM or -UNDO* Tablespace Datafiles

If the tablespace/datafile you lost is not associated with the SYSTEM or UNDO tablespaces, then you are in luck. You don't even need to shut down the database to recover! All you need to do is take the datafiles offline, restore the impacted datafiles, recover the datafiles (or the tablespace), and bring them back online.

The nice thing about this is if your users are not using the tablespace, they will never know there was a problem. If the users are using the tablespace, they will be impacted only if they try to use the datafiles that are offline (which is one good reason in some cases to take just datafiles offline rather than the whole tablespace).

The first question is, How do you know which datafiles are missing? There are a couple of things that will give you a clue. First of all, your users will start getting these messages:

```
SQL> select * from scott.emp;
select * from scott.emp
                    *
```

```
ERROR at line 1:
ORA-00376: file 4 cannot be read at this time
ORA-01110: data file 4: 'C:\ORACLE\ORADATA\ORCL\USERS01.DBF'
```

You can also look at the V$RECOVER_FILE view for more information on datafiles that need recovery. Here is an example of such a query:

```
SQL> select * from v$recover_file;
     FILE# ONLINE  ONLINE_ ERROR                   CHANGE# TIME
---------- ------- ------- -------------------- ---------- ---------
         4 ONLINE   ONLINE FILE NOT FOUND                0
```

Missing Datafiles

Don't expect that these errors indicating datafiles are missing will always show up in the alert log. Sometimes they will (for example, on database startup), but often they won't (for example, when a query fails because a datafile is offline). If you want to monitor for this problem reliably, then the V$RECOVER_FILE view is the way to go.

So, here is the general recovery process from such an error. In this case we assume the database is up and running:

1. Take the datafile offline using the `alter database datafile offline` command as shown here:

   ```
   alter database datafile 'C:\ORACLE\ORADATA\ORCL\USERS01.DBF' offline;
   ```

   As an alternative, you can use FILE_ID as shown in this example:

   ```
   alter database datafile 4 offline;
   ```

   FILE_ID will appear in the error message, or you can use the FILE_ID column of DBA_DATA_FILES or the FILE# column in the V$DATAFILE view.
2. Restore the missing datafiles.
3. Restore all archived redo logs that will be needed for recovery. This would be all archived redo logs generated from the beginning of the backup image you restored in step 2.

When you are restoring backup files, never restore backed-up online redo logs over the existing online redo logs. This is so important, in fact, that when we talked about hot backups in Chapter 2, we did not even back up the online redo logs. Restoring old online redo logs over your existing ones will lead to data loss. Fair warning!

4. Recover the missing datafiles with the `recover datafile` or `recover tablespace` command.
5. Bring the datafiles or the tablespace online with the `alter database` or `alter tablespace` command.

So, what do you do if your database was down and you discover the files are lost when you start it up? That's simple too.

1. Log in as SYS and start up the database. If a datafile is missing, you will get an error message that looks something like this:

```
SQL> startup
ORACLE instance started.
Total System Global Area  397557760 bytes
Fixed Size                  1333452 bytes
Variable Size             289408820 bytes
Database Buffers          100663296 bytes
Redo Buffers                6152192 bytes
Database mounted.
ORA-01157: cannot identify/lock data file 4 - see DBWR trace file
ORA-01110: data file 4: 'C:\ORACLE\ORADATA\ORCL\USERS01.DBF'
```

2. It may be that you are missing more than datafile 4, since Oracle will alert you to only the first datafile that it finds missing. Use the V$RECOVER_FILE, V$DATAFILE, and V$TABLESPACE views to determine exactly which datafiles are missing and which tablespaces they are associated with, as shown in this example:

```
SQL> l
  1  select b.name ts_name, a.error, c.name datafile
  2  from v$recover_file a, v$tablespace b, v$datafile c
  3  where a.file#=c.file#
  4* and b.ts#=c.ts#
SQL> /
```

```
TS_NAME   ERROR                DATAFILE
--------- -------------------- ------------------------------------
USERS     FILE NOT FOUND       C:\ORACLE\ORADATA\ORCL\USERS01.DBF

select
```

3. Review the results of the query. As long as the missing datafiles are not part of the SYSTEM or UNDO tablespace, you can simply take those datafiles offline and open the database. The intent will be to recover those tablespaces/datafiles with the database open. First use the `alter database datafile offline` command to take the tablespaces offline:

```
SQL> alter database
datafile 'C:\ORACLE\ORADATA\ORCL\USERS01.DBF' offline;
Database altered.
```

4. Next, open the database with the `alter database open` command:

```
alter database open
```

5. Now restore the database backup datafiles from your hot backup media.
6. Restore all archived redo logs that will be needed for recovery. You will need to restore all archived redo logs generated from the beginning of the backup image you restored in step 2.

Figuring Out Which Archived Redo Logs You Need

If you need to figure out exactly which archived redo logs you need to restore your backup (so, perhaps, you can restore those files off of backup media), you can use the V$RECOVER_FILE and the V$LOG_HISTORY views. The V$RECOVER_FILE view provides the last change number (in the CHANGE# column) present in the file(s) needing recovery. The V$LOG_HISTORY view will tell you which archived redo logs the changes are in. Here is an example:

```
ORA-01157: cannot identify/lock data file 4 - see DBWR trace file
ORA-01110: data file 4: 'C:\ORACLE\ORADATA\ORCL\USERS01.DBF'
SQL> host copy users01.dbf.backup users01.dbf
        1 file(s) copied.
SQL> Select a.file#, a.change#, b.first_change#, b.next_change#, b.sequence#
  2  From v$recover_file a, v$log_history b
```

```
  3  Where a.change#<=b.next_change#;
     FILE#    CHANGE# FIRST_CHANGE# NEXT_CHANGE#  SEQUENCE#
---------- ---------- ------------- ------------ ----------
         4    1418889       1417349      1438925         20
```

You could also find the name of the actual archived redo logs needed for recovery by querying the V$ARCHIVED_LOG view. In some cases, the log sequence number will not show up here if the associated online redo log file has not yet been archived.

```
SQL> Select a.file#, a.change#, b.first_change#, b.next_change#,
  2  b.sequence#, b.name
  3  From v$recover_file a, v$archived_log b
  4  Where a.change#<=b.next_change#;
     FILE#    CHANGE# FIRST_CHANGE# NEXT_CHANGE#  SEQUENCE#
---------- ---------- ------------- ------------ ----------
NAME
-----------------------------------------------
         4    1418889       1417349      1438925         20
C:\ORACLE\ARCH\ORCL\ARC00020_0662757171.001
```

7. Recover the datafiles or tablespaces using the `recover datafile` or `recover tablespace` command.

   ```
   SQL> recover datafile 4;
   ```

8. Bring the datafiles or tablespaces online using the `alter database datafile online` or `alter tablespace online` command. Once you have done this, you have recovered the missing tablespace datafiles and your database is back to normal.

   ```
   SQL>Alter database datafile 4 online;
   ```

Backing Up After the Recovery

There really is no requirement to do a special backup after a datafile or tablespace recovery. All your backup files are still usable, and Oracle will keep generating archived redo logs just like before.

 **Real World Scenario**

Performing Database Recoveries in the Real World

In this book, we are providing you with some of the most common recovery situations that you might face and that appear on the OCP exam. The reality is that in the real world, recovery can quickly become very complex and overwhelming. You have people looking over your shoulder, 200 opinions on how to fix the problem (all of them different, of course), and you face an issue that does not quite neatly fit into the backup and recovery case studies that you have experienced in your training.

The key to figuring out what to do is to sit back and think about what the problem is and why it is happening. Another key is if you feel that you might be getting in over your head, get Oracle support on the line. Sometimes it takes a while to get them geared up to really help you, and the sooner you get them engaged, the better you will be in the end.

Finally, when you are troubleshooting, don't shotgun solutions. If you are not sure about your solution, think it out very carefully. Talk to other DBAs around you and get their opinions. Nothing makes a bad day worse like having a database failure and then realizing that you just made it a bigger problem by screwing up the recovery process.

Performing Incomplete Recoveries

Incomplete recovery (also called *point-in-time recovery*) is the process of recovering the database to a different point in time than the most current point in time. Why would one do such a thing, you ask? There may be a number of reasons:

- Loss of one of the online redo log groups making full recovery impossible
- User error requiring a recovery of the database to a different point in time
- Creation of a duplicate database to a point in time other than that of the source database.

In the following sections, we will cover the basics of incomplete recovery. First we will discuss the requirements for and mechanics of incomplete recovery, and then we will cover preparation for incomplete recovery. Finally, we will walk through the process of an actual incomplete recovery.

Requirements for and Mechanics of an Incomplete Recovery

The requirements for incomplete recovery are much like those of a complete recovery from an online backup. First, the database must be in ARCHIVELOG mode. Second, you have to have a backup of the database (online or offline) and all of the archived redo logs required to get your database to the point in time that you are interested in.

Preparing for an Incomplete Recovery

The first step in performing an incomplete recovery is to restore the database from a backup that was taken before the point in time to which you want to restore the database.

Notice that you have to restore the entire database. This can sometimes confuse less-experienced DBAs. With incomplete recovery, you must restore the entire database, and it must be restored to a point in time before the point in time that you wish to recover to.

For example, suppose it's 2 p.m. and you wish to recover just the USERS tablespace objects to 1 p.m. because someone messed something up. To do so, it's not just as simple as restoring the USERS tablespace datafiles to 1 p.m. You have to restore the entire database to 1 p.m.

Tablespace Point-in-Time Recovery

There is a concept of tablespace point-in-time recovery that allows you to restore just a tablespace to a point in time different from that of the database. We will discuss tablespace point-in-time recovery using RMAN in Chapter 8. The OCP exam does not require that you know how to do tablespace point-in-time recovery manually, so we are not covering that topic in this book.

Oracle is persnickety about datafile consistency. Recall the concept of the SCN, which is Oracle's internal counter for all operations. When you do an insert, it is assigned an SCN. When you then commit that insert, it is assigned a different, higher SCN. This way, Oracle knows the insert came first and the commit came second.

When you start the Oracle database, it's a demanding bit of software. It requires that the SCN in each datafile be the same before it will open the database (there is an exception to this with read-only tablespaces). Also, there are SCNs stored in the control file that have to jibe with the SCNs in the datafiles. If the SCNs don't jibe, then some form of recovery is required.

So, if the entire database is at SCN 12345 (see Figure 3.1) and you restore the USERS tablespace to SCN 1234, that will be a problem. Oracle will detect the different SCNs and require a complete recovery. Not quite what we hoped for.

So, when you want to perform an incomplete database recovery, you have to restore all the datafiles to a point in time at or before the point in time that you actually want to recover to. In Figure 3.2, you can see that all the datafiles are recovered to SCN 1230 or less, so you can now begin an incomplete recovery to SCN 1234 as you wish.

Note that you do not need to restore the control file to a previous version for incomplete recovery to work. Once you have finished the incomplete-recovery process, Oracle will reset the control file so that it will correctly reflect the current state of the database.

FIGURE 3.1 Database with datafiles restored incorrectly for incomplete recovery

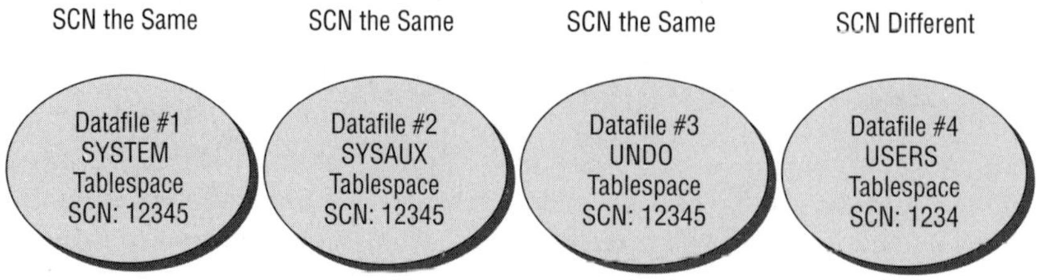

SCN the Same | SCN the Same | SCN the Same | SCN Different

Datafile #1 SYSTEM Tablespace SCN: 12345

Datafile #2 SYSAUX Tablespace SCN: 12345

Datafile #3 UNDO Tablespace SCN: 12345

Datafile #4 USERS Tablespace SCN: 1234

You want to recover to SCN 1234. Datafiles 1, 2, and 3 are at SCN 12345, which is after SCN 1234. Incomplete recovery to SCN 1234 is not possible because recovery rolls forward SCNs, not backward.

FIGURE 3.2 Database with datafiles restored correctly for incomplete recovery

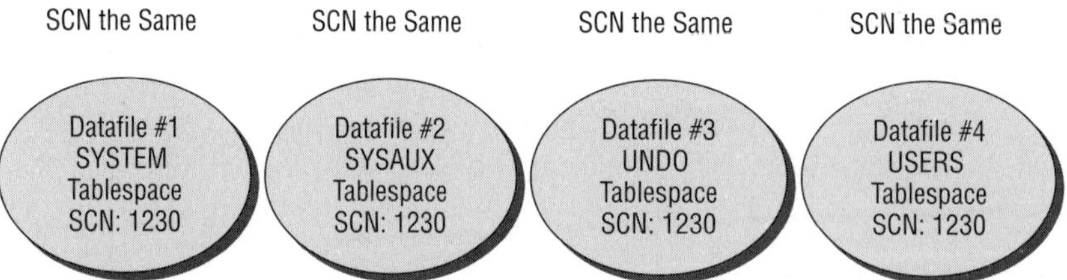

You want to recover to SCN 1234. All datafiles are at SCN 1230. It's now easy to recover them all to SCN 1234.

You will also need to restore all archived redo logs that were generated from the time of the backup image until the point that you want to restore to. You can determine which archived redo log sequence numbers you want to restore by looking at the `V$ARCHIVED_LOG` view (we provided a query using the `V$ARCHIVED_LOG` view in a note earlier in this chapter). Keep in mind that you may also need redo contained in an online redo log that has not been archived yet. Since you will not be restoring any online redo logs, this won't be a problem.

Now that you have restored all the database datafiles and the needed archived redo logs, you are ready to execute your incomplete database recovery.

Performing an Incomplete Recovery

Having restored the database datafiles, recovery is pretty easy. First you determine the type of recovery that you want to do, and then you perform the recovery using the `recover database` command. Finally, you open the database. Let's look at these steps in some more detail next.

Determining the Type of Point-in-Time Recovery

There are three types of point-in-time recovery that you can perform:

Time-based recovery *Time-based recovery* is based on the time that you want to recover your database to. Time-based recovery is granular to the nearest second.

Log sequence–based recovery *Log sequence–based recovery* is based on defining the log sequence number you wish the database to be recovered to. You will need to determine the correct log sequence number. The `V$ARCHIVED_LOG` and `V$LOG` views may be helpful in making this determination.

Change-based recovery *Change-based recovery* is based on the SCN that you wish to restore your database to. You can determine what the current SCN of the database is by querying the `CURRENT_SCN` column of the `V$DATABASE` view. You can also associate a given time to an approximate SCN by using the `TIMESTAMP_TO_SCN`, `SCN_TO_TIMESTAMP`, or `SMON_SCN_TIME` view.

Perform Your Point-in-Time Recovery

Regardless of which of the three point-in-time recoveries you choose to perform, the overall process is very similar. You will use the `recover database` command for your recovery. Each recovery type will take a different keyword, as shown here:

Time-based recovery To perform time-based recovery use the `recover database until time` command. The format of the time in the command is `'yyyy-mm-dd:hh24:mi:ss'`, which is consistent in each Oracle database (so it is not dependent on parameters such as `NLS_DATE_FORMAT`). Here is an example of the use of the `recover database until time` command:

```
Recover database until time '2008-10-23:13:00:00'
```

In this example, the database will be recovered up to October 23, 2008 at 1 p.m. Any transaction that are committed after that point will be rolled back.

Log sequence–based recovery To perform log sequence–based recovery, use the `recover database until sequence` command. This example recovers to log sequence 34:

```
Recover database until sequence 34;
```

Change-based recovery To perform change-based recovery, use the `recover database until change` command followed by the SCN you wish to recover to. In this example, we recover to SCN 226250:

```
Recover database until change 226250;
```

Once the recovery begins, you will be prompted for the appropriate archived redo logs to apply just as with a complete database recovery. The main difference is that the application of archived redo logs (and possibly online redo logs) will automatically cease once the point in time, change, or SCN has been reached. Once the redo has been applied, the database is ready to be opened.

Opening the Database

Having recovered the database, you will want to open it. A point-in-time recovery will result in a new incarnation of the database. A new incarnation is a new logical version of the database. The data remains the same, of course, but the redo stream essentially starts over. The log sequence number is reset to 1 (the SCN is not reset) and a new life begins for the database.

To indicate to Oracle that you are doing an incomplete recovery, you will open the database in a slightly different way. You will still use the `alter database open` command, but you will also include the keyword `resetlogs`. The `resetlogs` command indicates to Oracle that it should reset the control file and the redo log sequence number and open the database as a brand-new incarnation. The entire command looks like this:

```
alter database open resetlogs;
```

Through Oracle Database 10g, Oracle recommended that you back up the database anytime you issue a `resetlogs` operation. This was because Oracle did not support recovering a database through a `resetlogs` operation. In Oracle Database 11g, Oracle has been modified to allow for a recovery through `resetlogs`. This is supported through the new `%r` format string available in the `LOG_ARCHIVE_FORMAT` parameter (see Chapter 2 for more on this parameter). This format string will include a resetlogs number in the naming of each archived redo log. This will help Oracle keep the redo-log stream straight.

If you should need to do a recovery after a resetlogs operation, simply restore the same backup that you used to do the point-in-time recovery and recover using that backup. You can do full recovery or point-in-time recovery using the redo associated with the new incarnation. In Exercise 3.3, you'll perform a point-in-time recovery.

EXERCISE 3.3

Performing a Point-in-Time Recovery

In this exercise, you will do a point-in-time recovery by restoring the database to a previous SCN.

1. Back up the database. Details on how to do a full online database backup are found in Chapter 2. In summary, follow these steps:
   - First put the database in hot backup mode.
   - Copy all database datafiles to a backup location.
   - Take the database out of hot backup mode.
   - Force a log switch. Back up the archived redo logs.

EXERCISE 3.3 *(continued)*

Here is an example of a backup:

```
[oracle@localhost orcl]$ sqlplus "/ as sysdba"
SQL*Plus: Release 11.1.0.6.0 - Production on Sun Aug 17 15:35:48 2008
Copyright (c) 1982, 2007, Oracle.  All rights reserved.
Connected to:
Oracle Database 11g Enterprise Edition Release 11.1.0.6.0 - Production
With the Partitioning, OLAP, Data Mining and Real Application Testing options
SQL> alter database begin backup;
Database altered.
SQL> host cp /oracle01/oradata/orcl/*.dbf /oracle01/backup/orcl
SQL> alter database end backup;
Database altered.
SQL> alter system switch logfile;
System altered.
SQL> host cp /oracle01/backup/arch/* /oracle01/backup/orcl/*
SQL> alter database backup controlfile to trace;
Database altered.
SQL> alter database backup controlfile to '/oracle01/oradata/orcl/control1.bak';
Database altered.
```

2. Next, log into the database as `scott/tiger` and create a new table. Insert two records into the new table and commit the insert.

```
SQL> connect scott/tiger
Connected.
SQL> create table test_table (id number);
Table created.
SQL> insert into test_table values (1);
1 row created.
SQL> insert into test_table values (2);
1 row created.
SQL> commit;
Commit complete.
```

3. Now log in as SYS and determine the current SCN by using the CURRENT_SCN column of the V$DATABASE table. Your SCN will be different from that in the example.

```
SQL> connect sys as sysdba
Enter password:
```

EXERCISE 3.3 *(continued)*

```
Connected.
SQL> select current_scn from v$database;
CURRENT_SCN
-----------
    5135413
```

4. Log back in as `scott/tiger` and add two more records. Commit the inserts.

```
SQL> connect scott/tiger
Connected.
SQL> insert into test_table values (3);
1 row created.
SQL> insert into test_table values (4);
1 row created.
SQL> commit;
Commit complete.
```

5. Log in as SYS again and query the current SCN by using the CURRENT_SCN column of the V$DATABASE table. Notice that the SCN has changed.

```
SQL> connect sys as sysdba
Enter password:
Connected.
SQL> select current_scn from v$database;
CURRENT_SCN
-----------
    5135522
```

6. Shut down the database.

```
SQL> shutdown immediate
Database closed.
Database dismounted.
ORACLE instance shut down.
```

7. Once you are sure the database is down, restore the database datafiles from their backup location to the location where the database files belong.

```
[oracle@localhost orcl]$ pwd
/oracle01/backup/orcl
[oracle@localhost orcl]$ cp *.dbf /oracle01/oradata/orcl/*
```

EXERCISE 3.3 *(continued)*

8. Mount the database.

```
[oracle@localhost orcl]$ sqlplus "/ as sysdba"
SQL*Plus: Release 11.1.0.6.0 - Production on Sun Aug 17 17:53:14 2008
Copyright (c) 1982, 2007, Oracle.  All rights reserved.
Connected to an idle instance.
SQL> startup mount
ORACLE instance started.
Total System Global Area  167395328 bytes
Fixed Size                  1298612 bytes
Variable Size             142610252 bytes
Database Buffers           20971520 bytes
Redo Buffers                2514944 bytes
Database mounted.
```

9. Recover the database using the `recover database until change` command. You will use the SCN you queried in step 3 as the SCN to recover to. Enter **AUTO** when prompted for an archived redo log to apply.

```
SQL> Recover database until change 5135413;
ORA-00279: change 5071334 generated at 08/17/2008 15:35:51 needed for thread 1
ORA-00289: suggestion :
/oracle01/flash_recovery_area/ORCL/archivelog/2008_08_17
/o1_mf_1_5_4bk6onh8_.arc
ORA-00280: change 5071334 for thread 1 is in sequence #5
Specify log: {<RET>=suggested | filename | AUTO | CANCEL}
auto
ORA-00279: change 5071583 generated at 08/17/2008 15:40:04 needed for thread 1
ORA-00289: suggestion :
/oracle01/flash_recovery_area/ORCL/archivelog/2008_08_17
/o1_mf_1_6_4bk76kwk_.arc
ORA-00280: change 5071583 for thread 1 is in sequence #6
ORA-00279: change 5091960 generated at 08/17/2008 15:49:05 needed for thread 1
ORA-00289: suggestion :
/oracle01/flash_recovery_area/ORCL/archivelog/2008_08_17
/o1_mf_1_7_4bk9ksb4_.arc
ORA-00280: change 5091960 for thread 1 is in sequence #7
ORA-00279: change 5112317 generated at 08/17/2008 16:29:13 needed for thread 1
ORA-00289: suggestion :
/oracle01/flash_recovery_area/ORCL/archivelog/2008_08_17
/o1_mf_1_8_4bk9p236_.arc
```

EXERCISE 3.3 *(continued)*

```
ORA-00280: change 5112317 for thread 1 is in sequence #8
ORA-00279: change 5112647 generated at 08/17/2008 16:31:29 needed for thread 1
ORA-00289: suggestion :
/oracle01/flash_recovery_area/ORCL/archivelog/2008_08_17
/o1_mf_1_9_4bk9p2mz_.arc
ORA-00280: change 5112647 for thread 1 is in sequence #9
ORA-00279: change 5112649 generated at 08/17/2008 16:31:30 needed for thread 1
ORA-00289: suggestion :
/oracle01/flash_recovery_area/ORCL/archivelog/2008_08_17
/o1_mf_1_10_4bk9p3gz_.arc
ORA-00280: change 5112649 for thread 1 is in sequence #10
Log applied.
Media recovery complete.
```

10. Open the database with the `alter database open resetlogs` command. Note that once you have done this you will not be able to recover any data that was entered after the point of the recovery.

```
SQL> alter database open resetlogs;
Database altered.
```

11. Log into the `scott` schema. Do a `select * from test_table`. You should have only two records in the table.

```
SQL> Connect scott/tiger
Connected.
SQL> Select * from test_table;
        ID
----------
         1
         2
```

Performing Other Types of Recoveries

You will need to be prepared for other types of user-managed recoveries when taking your OCP exam or just in the course of managing your Oracle database. In the following sections, we will talk about the following types of user-managed recoveries:

- Loss of a tempfile
- Loss of an online redo log group

- Loss of the control file
- Loss of the password file
- Loss of everything

Recovering from the Loss of a Tempfile

Tempfiles are used with temporary tablespaces. As discussed in Chapter 2, you do not need to back up a tempfile. Because of its temporary nature, the contents of a tempfile are not needed during a recovery. You will need to re-create the tempfile after any recovery that includes the temporary tablespace. This is done by using the `alter tablespace add tempfile` command as shown in this example, where we add a tempfile to the TEMP tablespace:

```
ALTER TABLESPACE TEMP ADD TEMPFILE '/oracle01/oradata/orcl/temp01.dbf'
SIZE 200m  REUSE AUTOEXTEND ON;
```

Recovering from the Loss of an Online Redo Log Group

Loss of the online redo logs comes in four different flavors.

- Loss of a redo log file group member
- Loss of an inactive online redo log group
- Loss of an active but not current online redo log group
- Loss of the current online redo log group

Any loss of an entire online redo log group makes for a very bad day. Loss of the last two categories (loss of an active or current online redo log) is often a disaster.

Recall that the redo logs are written to as soon as there is a commit (and other events can cause writes too). Remember also that the database datafiles are written to later, sometimes much later. Thus, the database datafiles are often way out of synchronization with the actual current state of the database. If the database crashes, then often the database datafiles are not up-to-date and this forces Oracle to apply redo to get them current when you start up the database. Normally, Oracle will do this automatically in a process called *instance recovery*.

As a result of the fact that the database datafiles are often out of synch with the actual state of the database, loss of an active or the current online redo log group can be disastrous. Loss of an *active online redo log* can result in loss of data. Loss of the current online redo log will likely result in data loss, but this is not always the case. As a result, redo logs are quite important. You may wonder what the difference between the current, active, and inactive redo logs is:

- Current: Current online redo log group.

- Active: Not currently in use but the dirty blocks associated with the redo in the log file still need to be written to the datafiles by DBWR. Also, the group may still need to be archived.
- Inactive: Not currently in use and dirty blocks associated with the redo in the log file have been written to datafiles by DBWR.

You can see the status of an online redo log group by querying the `STATUS` column of the `V$LOG` view. Let's look at what to do when it comes to recovering from loss of redo log groups.

Dealing with the Loss of an Inactive Online Redo Log Group Member

If you have lost one or more members of an online redo log group (but not the entire group) then the response is pretty easy. You can simply re-create the member using the `alter database add logfile member` command. For example, you might see this error in the alert log:

```
ORA-00313: open failed for members of log group 2 of thread 1
ORA-00312: online log 2 thread 1: 'C:\ORACLE\ORADATA\ORCL\REDO02.LOG'
```

If the database has not shut down, you should immediately attempt to checkpoint the database using the `alter system checkpoint` command. The `alter system checkpoint` command forces the database to write any dirty blocks from the database buffer cache to the database datafiles in an urgent manner. This will be helpful in the event the database crashes because of this missing online redo log.

Once the checkpoint has completed, you would issue the `alter database add logfile` command to re-create the redo log group member redo02.log:

```
SQL>alter database add logfile 'C:\ORACLE\ORADATA\ORCL\REDO02.LOG' reuse to
group 2;
```

If the database happened to crash before you could add the log file, you would mount the database and then issue the `alter database add logfile` command. You should then be able to open the database.

Another option is to shut down the database in a consistent manner (`shutdown`, `shutdown transactional`, `shutdown normal`) and then copy another member of the redo log group to the location of the missing member. You can then restart the database normally.

Dealing with the Loss of an Inactive Online Redo Log Group

Loss of an inactive online redo log group is not a terribly big deal in and of itself and is quite easy to recover from. There are two different situations you will need to be prepared for. First is loss of an inactive online redo log group during database startup. Second is loss of an inactive online redo log group during database operations. Let's look at these two situations in more detail.

Dealing with the Loss of an Inactive Online Redo Log Group on Startup

First, if you start up the database and the inactive online redo log group can not be opened, you will get the following error message:

```
ORA-00313: open failed for members of log group 2 of thread 1
ORA-00312: online log 2 thread 1: 'C:\ORACLE\ORADATA\ORCL\REDO02.LOG'
```

The response to this condition is to drop the log-file group using the `alter database` command as shown here:

```
SQL> alter database drop logfile group 2;
```

You can then re-create the online redo log group using the `alter database add logfile` command:

```
SQL> alter database add logfile
2  group 2 'c:\oracle\oradata\orcl\redo02.log' size 50m;
SQL> alter database add logfile
2  group 2 'c:\oracle\oradata\orcl\redo02.log' size 50m;
```

Dealing with the Loss of an Inactive Online Redo Log Group When the Database Is Running

If you lose an inactive online redo log group (or it becomes corrupted) while the database is running, the database will sometimes keep operating. It will sometimes skip the online redo log group that went missing and continue to operate normally. In this case, you can issue an `alter system checkpoint` command and then clear the log-file group with the `alter database clear logfile group` command as shown here:

```
SQL>alter system checkpoint;
SQL>alter database clear logfile group 1;
```

It may be that when you try to clear the log file you will receive an error that indicates that the log file needs to be archived:

```
SQL> alter database clear logfile group 1;
alter database clear logfile group 1
*
ERROR at line 1:
ORA-00350: log 1 of instance orcl (thread 1) needs to be archived
ORA-00312: online log 1 thread 1: '/oracle01/oradata/orcl/redo01.log'
```

Since the log file is not there, it cannot be archived. You can use the `alter database clear unarchived logfile` command to clear the unarchived log file, and rebuild the log file in its current location as shown here:

```
SQL> alter database clear
2 unarchived logfile '/oracle01/oradata/orcl/redo01.log';
```

You will need to back up your database in this case, since an archived redo log will have been lost.

Sometimes the database will not crash but will freeze. In this case, you will open another SQL*Plus session and issue the `alter database checkpoint` command followed by either the `alter database clear logfile` or the `alter database clear unarchived logfile` command, depending on the type of recovery required. After issuing these commands, the database should operate as usual.

Back Up the Database After Clearing Unarchived Log Files

Sometimes the database will crash as a result of the loss of the online redo log group. In this case, you will need to follow this procedure:

- From the SQL*Plus, log in as SYS using SYSDBA privileges.
- Mount the database using the `startup mount` command.
- Issue the `alter database clear logfile group` SQL command.
- Open the database with the `alter database open` command.

Dealing with the Loss of an Active but Not Current Online Redo Log Group

Loss of an ACTIVE (as shown in V$LOG column status) online redo log group requires the use of the `alter database clear unarchived logfile` command as shown in the previous section. This is because the active online redo log will not have been archived and you need to indicate to Oracle that this is okay. This command will rebuild the online redo log and allow Oracle to proceed with normal operations. You should always back up the database after this operation.

Dealing with the Loss of the Current Online Redo Log Group

Losing the current online redo log group is, perhaps, the worst disaster your Oracle database could encounter. This is because there is a significant risk of loss of data in such cases. When you lose the current online redo log group, you can expect that the database will shut down.

If the database has not yet shut down, you should immediately attempt to checkpoint the database using the `alter system checkpoint` command and then shut down the database afterward as soon as practical. The `alter system checkpoint` command forces the database to write any dirty blocks from the database buffer cache to the database datafiles in an urgent manner.

It may be that you can open the database without any recovery being required. This is the best-case situation. To try to restart the database do the following:

- Issue the `startup mount` command
- Issue the `alter database clear unarchived logfile` for the redo log group that was lost. Examples of this command can be seen in earlier sections of this chapter.
- Issue the `alter database open` command.

If the database opens successfully, you are in luck. If the database fails to open, you are in a bad way. You will need to perform incomplete recovery of the database as discussed in the section "Performing an Incomplete Recovery." You can see an example of recovering the database as a result of the loss of the current online redo log group in Exercise 3.1.

Recovering from the Loss of a Control File

Recovery from loss of a control file depends on the nature of the loss. There are two different situations you might encounter. You might lose one or more but not all control files. You might also lose all control files. Let's look at what to do in these cases.

Dealing with the Loss of One or More Control Files but Not All

If you have but one control file left, recovery is quite simple. Follow these steps:

- Shut down the database normally.
- Copy one of the remaining control files to the location of the lost control files and give it the same name as the lost control file.
- Restart the database.

Recovering from Loss of All Control Files

If you lose your control files, Oracle is not shy about telling you. If you are trying to start up your database and your control files are missing, you will see an error like this:

```
SQL> startup
ORACLE instance started.
Total System Global Area  171581440 bytes
Fixed Size                  1298640 bytes
Variable Size             146804528 bytes
Database Buffers           20971520 bytes
Redo Buffers                2506752 bytes
ORA-00205: error in identifying control file, check alert log for more info
```

This error will occur on startup if any of your control files are missing. If your database is running, loss of some of your control files will not cause it to stop operating. As a result, you can plan to shut down your database and then simply copy a surviving copy of the control file to the location of the lost control file. If the location is no longer available, you can modify the `CONTROL_FILES` parameter so that it points to the location of the new control file.

If you lose your control files while the database is running, it is quite likely that the database will crash in short order. There are some cases where it might stay up for a little while, but it will eventually come down on you.

Loss of all control files will require that you use a backup control file or issue the `create control file` command from the SQL prompt. We discussed the creation of a backup control file in Chapter 2. We also discussed how to create a trace file with the `create control file` command in it in Chapter 2. Let's look at each of these recoveries in a bit more detail.

Recovering Lost Control Files with a Backup Control File

If you have a backup control file, follow these steps to recover from the loss of all your control files:

1. Copy the backup control file to the location of each control file defined by the parameter `CONTROL_FILES`. Modify the `CONTROL_FILES` parameter if required.
2. Mount the database with the `startup mount` command.
3. Recover the database using the `recover database using backup controlfile` command. At the prompt, type in **AUTO** to apply all archived redo logs.
4. Recovery will end, likely with an error. This is because the final redo log sequence number you need to apply is not in an archived redo log but is in one of the online redo logs. Issue the `recover database using backup controlfile` command again. This time, when prompted for the archived redo log to apply, enter one of your online redo log names (for example, `redo01.log`). Continue to attempt to apply each online redo log group until you find the correct log sequence number.
5. Once the final online redo log is applied, recovery will complete automatically and without error.
6. You can now open the database using the `alter database open resetlogs` command.

Recovering Lost Control Files Using the *create control file* Command

In Chapter 2, we introduced the `alter database backup controlfile to trace` command. This created a trace file that you can use to re-create your control file. If you lose your control files, a backup control file is the easiest way to manually recover. However, if you do not have a backup control file, you have two options:

- Use the contents of the script created as a result of the `alter database backup controlfile to trace` command.
- Manually issue the `create control file` command.

As already discussed in Chapter 2, the `alter database backup controlfile to trace` command creates a script that you can use to recover your control file. The script will need to be modified before it can be used.

The script contains the following sections:

- Trace-file header
- List of parameters related to archiving
- NORESETLOGS case for re-creating the control file
- RESETLOGS case for re-creating the control file

As you can see, the script has two different versions of the `create controlfile` command. One is for recoveries where the online redo logs are intact. You will want to edit the script so that the correct type of recovery is done. Each version of the script also contains code to register archived redo logs, recover the database, and then open the database automatically.

Let's look at the following code, which is an example of using the NORESETLOGS case. The script is designed to do it all without any DBA interference. First it starts the database instance. It then proceeds to issue the `create control file` command. The script records some archived redo log records in the control file that will be needed for recovery. The database is then recovered and opened. Finally, the temporary tablespace tempfile is re-created.

```
STARTUP NOMOUNT
CREATE CONTROLFILE REUSE DATABASE "ORCL" NORESETLOGS  ARCHIVELOG
    MAXLOGFILES 16
    MAXLOGMEMBERS 3
    MAXDATAFILES 100
    MAXINSTANCES 8
    MAXLOGHISTORY 292
LOGFILE
  GROUP 1 (
    '/oracle01/oradata/orcl/redo01.log',
    '/oracle01/oradata/orcl/redo01a.log'
  ) SIZE 100M,
  GROUP 2 (
    '/oracle01/oradata/orcl/redo02.log',
    '/oracle01/oradata/orcl/redo02a.log'
  ) SIZE 50M,
  GROUP 3 (
    '/oracle01/oradata/orcl/redo03.log',
    '/oracle01/oradata/orcl/redo03a.log'
  ) SIZE 50M
-- STANDBY LOGFILE
DATAFILE
  '/oracle01/oradata/orcl/system01.dbf',
```

```
  '/oracle01/oradata/orcl/sysaux01.dbf',
  '/oracle01/oradata/orcl/undotbs01.dbf',
  '/oracle01/oradata/orcl/users01.dbf',
  '/oracle01/oradata/orcl/example01.dbf',
  '/oracle01/oradata/orcl/retention_archives_01.dbf',
  '/oracle01/oradata/orcl/my_secure_tbs_01.dbf',
  '/oracle01/oradata/orcl/my_second_secure_tbs_01.dbf'
CHARACTER SET WE8MSWIN1252
;
-- Configure RMAN configuration record 1
VARIABLE RECNO NUMBER;
EXECUTE :RECNO :=
SYS.DBMS_BACKUP_RESTORE.SETCONFIG('COMPRESSION ALGORITHM','''BZIP2''');
-- Configure RMAN configuration record 2
VARIABLE RECNO NUMBER;
EXECUTE :RECNO := SYS.DBMS_BACKUP_RESTORE.SETCONFIG('CONTROLFILE
AUTOBACKUP','ON');
-- Commands to re-create incarnation table
-- Below log names MUST be changed to existing filenames on
-- disk. Any one log file from each branch can be used to
-- re-create incarnation records.
-- ALTER DATABASE REGISTER LOGFILE
'/oracle01/flash_recovery_area/ORCL/archivelog/2008_08_16/o1_mf_1_1_%u_.arc';
-- ALTER DATABASE REGISTER LOGFILE
 '/oracle01/flash_recovery_area/ORCL/archivelog/2008_08_16/o1_mf_1_1_%u_.arc';
-- ALTER DATABASE REGISTER LOGFILE
 '/oracle01/flash_recovery_area/ORCL/archivelog/2008_08_16/o1_mf_1_1_%u_.arc';
-- Recovery is required if any of the datafiles are restored backups,
-- or if the last shutdown was not normal or immediate.
RECOVER DATABASE
-- Set Database Guard and/or Supplemental Logging
ALTER DATABASE ADD SUPPLEMENTAL LOG DATA (PRIMARY KEY) COLUMNS;
-- All logs need archiving and a log switch is needed.
ALTER SYSTEM ARCHIVE LOG ALL;
-- Database can now be opened normally.
ALTER DATABASE OPEN;
-- Commands to add tempfiles to temporary tablespaces.
-- Online tempfiles have complete space information.
-- Other tempfiles may require adjustment.
ALTER TABLESPACE TEMP ADD TEMPFILE '/oracle01/oradata/orcl/temp01.dbf'
     SIZE 182517760  REUSE AUTOEXTEND ON NEXT 655360  MAXSIZE 32767M;
```

Recovering from the Loss of the Password File

If you lose the database password file, it is simple to recover. First, if you have backed up the password file and it has not changed since the backup, you can simply restore it. If you did not have a backup of the password file, all you need to do is rerun the orapwd command to re-create the password file. The orapwd command is used to create password files. It's executed from the command line as shown in this example:

```
[oracle@localhost dbs]$ cd $ORACLE_HOME/dbs
[oracle@localhost dbs]$ orapwd file=orapwtest entries=20 password=Robert
```

In this example, we first changed to the $ORACLE_HOME/dbs directory where password files are stored. Next we ran the orapwd command to create the password file. We passed the name of the password file using the file= parameter. Password files always start with orapw followed by the name of the database (test in this case). The entries parameter indicates the number of SYSADM entries that are allowed for, and password indicated the password associated with the SYS account.

Recovering from the Loss of Everything

Loss of everything might rightly be called the "full-meal deal." It's the worst possible case of data loss. If you have lost everything, you will need the following to recover your database when running in ARCHIVELOG mode:

- Oracle software
- Oracle networking–related parameter files
- Oracle database parameter file
- Oracle database datafiles
- Backup control file or create controlfile command ready to run

The procedure to fully restore your database is as follows:

1. Create any new directories required.
2. Restore the Oracle software.
3. Restore or re-create the Oracle networking parameter files.
4. Restore the Oracle paramcter file.
5. Rebuild the Oracle password file if required.
6. Restore the Oracle database datafiles.
7. Start up the database.
8. Recover the database using the procedure outlined in the section titled "Recovering from Loss of All Control Files."

Summary

As you can see, backup and recovery in Oracle can be a big deal. There are a number of different situations you will find yourself in. Sometimes these situations take some deep thinking to get out of. Often, understanding how Oracle actually works will help guide you through the problem and find a solution.

The Oracle 11*g* OCP exam contains a number of recovery-related questions, so you will want to know this stuff well. You should also work through the different exercises so that you understand what to do in different situations. In this chapter, we discussed a number of recovery cases:

- NOARCHIVELOG recovery
- ARCHIVELOG recovery
- Point-in-time recoveries
- Special recovery cases

It is probably clear to you that recovery in Oracle can be quite complex. It becomes even harder when you are actually doing it under the gun, when people are breathing down your neck to get that database up.

Exam Essentials

Restore and recover your database in NOARCHIVELOG mode. Understand how to restore and recover your database in NOARCHIVELOG mode. Understand that you have to shut down the database and that you have to restore all the datafiles, the control files, and the online redo logs from your backup.

Restore and recover your database to the point of failure in ARCHIVELOG mode. Understand how to restore and recover your database in ARCHIVELOG mode. Understand that you can recover the entire database or just a given tablespace or datafile. Understand what recoveries can be done with the database up and which require that the database be shut down.

Restore and recover your database to a different point in time. Understand how to perform point-in-time recovery with your database. Understand how to restore the datafiles. Understand the types of recovery that are available (time-based, change-based, and SCN-based). Understand how to use the `recover database` command to perform point-in-time recovery and how to open the database after recovery has been completed.

Recover your database in the event of a lost online redo log. Understand how to recover your database if you lose an inactive or current online redo log file. Understand the benefit of using the `alter database checkpoint` command if you have lost an online redo log group and the database is still running. Understand how to use the `alter database clear` command to clear unarchived redo log files and to re-create lost online redo log files. Understand the impacts of losing the current or an active online redo log file.

Recover your database in the event of a lost control file. Understand how to recover your database if you lose one or more control files. Learn how to recover a lost control file by using a backup control file. Learn how to recover a lost control file by using the `create controlfile` command contained in the trace file resulting from the `alter database backup controlfile to trace` command.

Review Questions

1. Your database has experienced a loss of datafile `users_01.dbf`, which is associated with a tablespace called USERS. The database is still running. Which answer properly describes the order of the steps that you would use to recover from this error?
   a. Shut down the database.
   b. Take the `users_01.dbf` datafile offline with the `alter database` command.
   c. Restore the `users_01.dbf` datafile from backup media with the required archived redo logs.
   d. Restore all users tablespace-related datafiles from backup media.
   e. Issue the `recover tablespace users` command.
   f. Issue the `recover datafile users_01.dbf` command.
   g. Start up the database.
   h. Bring the `users_01.dbf` datafile online with the `alter database` command.
   A. a, c, f, g
   B. b, c, f, h
   C. a, b, c, f, g
   D. a, b, c, f, g, h
   E. b, c, f, e, g
2. As soon as you discover that you have lost an online redo log, if the database is still functioning, what should be your first action?
   A. Shut down the database.
   B. Clear the online redo log.
   C. Back up the database.
   D. Checkpoint the database.
   E. Call Oracle support.
3. You have lost all your SYSTEM tablespace datafiles (`system_01.dbf` and `system_02.dbf`) and the database has crashed. What would be the appropriate order of operations to correct the situation?
   a. Mount the database with the `startup mount` command.
   b. Take the SYSTEM datafile offline with the `alter database` command.
   c. Restore the SYSTEM_01.dbf datafile from backup media with the required archived redo logs.
   d. Restore all SYSTEM tablespace–related datafiles from backup media.
   e. Issue the `recover tablespace SYSTEM` command.
   f. Issue the `recover datafile SYSTEM_01.dbf` command.

g. Open the database with the `alter database open` command.

h. Open the database with the `alter database open resetlogs` command.

A. a, c, f, g

B. b, d, e, h

C. a, b, c, f, g

D. d, a, e, g

E. b, c, f, e, g

4. You have discovered that one of three control files has been lost. What steps would you follow to recover that control file?

a. Shut down the database.

b. Restore a control-file copy from backup media.

c. Use the `create control file` command to create a new control file.

d. Copy the backup control file into place.

e. Create a new copy of the control file from one of the surviving control files.

f. Recover the database using the `recover database using backup controlfile` command.

g. Start up the database.

A. a, b, f, g

B. c, f, g

C. a, d, f, g

D. a, f, g

E. a, e, g

5. Which files will you need to perform a full recovery of a database backed up in NOARCHIVELOG mode? (Choose all that apply.)

A. Database datafiles

B. Control files

C. Archived redo logs

D. Online redo logs

E. Flashback logs

6. Which are the correct steps, in order, to deal with the loss of an online redo log if the database has not yet crashed?

a. Issue a checkpoint.

b. Shut down the database.

c. Issue an `alter database open` command to open the database.

d. `Startup mount` the database.

e. Issue an `alter database clear logfile` command.

f. Recover all database datafiles.

A. a, b, c, d
B. b, d, e, c
C. a, b, d, e, c
D. b, f, d, f, c
E. b, d, a, c

7. What methods of point-in-time recovery are available? (Choose all that apply.)
   A. Change-based
   B. Cancel-based
   C. Time-based
   D. Sequence number-based
   E. Transaction number-based

8. Which files are required for a full recovery of the database in ARCHIVELOG mode? (Choose three.)
   A. Database datafiles
   B. Online redo logs
   C. Archived redo logs
   D. Backup control file
   E. Control file from a backup

9. What is the proper procedure to recover a lost tempfile?
   A. Restore the backup copy of the tempfile from the backup media.
   B. Re-create the tempfile with the `create tempfile` command.
   C. Copy an existing tempfile from another database.
   D. Re-create the tempfile with the `create tablespace` command.
   E. Re-create the tempfile with the `alter tablespace` command.

10. Upon starting your database, you receive the following error:

```
SQL> startup
ORACLE instance started.
Total System Global Area  171581440 bytes
Fixed Size                  1298640 bytes
Variable Size             146804528 bytes
Database Buffers           20971520 bytes
Redo Buffers                2506752 bytes
Database mounted.
ORA-00313: open failed for members of log group 1 of thread 1
ORA-00312: online log 1 thread 1: '/oracle01/oradata/orcl/redo01.log'
ORA-00312: online log 1 thread 1: '/oracle01/oradata/orcl/redo01a.log'
```

You can choose from the following steps:

a. Restore the database datafiles.

b. Issue the `alter database clear unarchived logfile group 1` command.

c. Issue the `alter database open` command.

d. Issue the `alter database open resetlogs` command.

e. Recover the database using point-in-time recovery.

f. Issue the `Startup Mount` command to mount the database.

g. Back up the database.

Which is the correct order of these steps in this case?

A. a, f, e, d, g

B. f, e, d

C. f, b, c, g

D. a, f, c

E. The database cannot be recovered.

11. A user sends you an email with the following error message:

```
create table idtable(id number)
*
ERROR at line 1:
ORA-01116: error in opening database file 4
ORA-01110: data file 4: '/oracle01/oradata/orcl/users01.dbf'
ORA-27041: unable to open file
Linux Error: 2: No such file or directory
Additional information: 3
```

You can choose from the following steps:

a. Restore the missing database datafiles.

b. Take the missing datafile offline.

c. Shut down the database.

d. Issue the `recover tablespace USERS` command.

e. Issue the `Startup Mount` command to mount the database.

f. Bring the `USERS` tablespace online.

g. Issue the `alter database open` command.

Which is the correct order of these steps in this case?

A. b, a, d, f

B. c, a, e, b, d, f, g

C. c, e, d, g

D. b, d, f

E. e, d, g

12. You have lost all your database control files. To recover them, you are going to use the results of the `alter database backup controlfile to trace` command. Your datafiles and your online redo logs are all intact. Which of the following is true regarding your recovery?

    A. You will need to open the database with the `resetlogs` command.

    B. All you need to do is execute the trace file from SQL*Plus and it will perform the recovery for you.

    C. You will use the `resetlogs` version of the `create controlfile` command.

    D. You will use the `noresetlogs` version of the `create controlfile` command.

    E. You will use the trace file to create a backup control file, and then you will recover the database with the `recover database using backup controlfile` command.

13. Your developers have asked you to restore the development database, which is in NOARCHIVELOG mode, back to last Tuesday the 20th. Your last backup is from Monday the 19th. What do you do?

    A. Restore the 19th's backup, restore all archived redo logs, recover the database to the 20th, and open the database.

    B. Tell them that their request cannot be met with the current backup strategy.

    C. Restore the 19th's backup, apply the online redo logs, and open the database.

    D. Switch the database into ARCHIVELOG mode, restore the 19th's backup, restore all archived redo logs, and recover the database to the 20th.

    E. Use the `recover database` command to roll back the database from today to the 19th of the month.

14. What methods are available to recover lost control files? (Choose all that apply.)

    A. Backup control file.

    B. Emergency control file.

    C. The `create controlfile` command.

    D. The `restore controlfile` SQL*Plus command.

    E. No backup is required. The database will re-create the control file when it is discovered to be lost.

15. Your ARCHIVELOG-mode database has lost three datafiles and shut down. One is assigned to the SYSTEM tablespace and two are assigned to the USERS tablespace. You can choose from the following steps to recover your database:

    a. Restore the three database datafiles that were lost.

    b. Issue the `Startup Mount` command to mount the database.

    c. Issue the `alter database open` command.

    d. Issue the `alter database open resetlogs` command.

    e. Recover the database using the `recover database` command.

    f. Recover the datafiles with the `recover datafile` command.

    g. Take the datafiles offline.

Which is the correct order of these steps in this case?

A. a, b, e, c

B. b, e, d

C. a, b, d, c

D. b, g, c, f

E. a, b, d, f

16. You have lost all your online redo logs. As a result, your database has crashed. You have tried to restart the database and clear the online redo log files, but when you try to open the database you get the following error.

```
SQL> startup
ORACLE instance started.
Total System Global Area  167395328 bytes
Fixed Size                  1298612 bytes
Variable Size             142610252 bytes
Database Buffers           20971520 bytes
Redo Buffers                2514944 bytes
Database mounted.
ORA-00313: open failed for members of log group 2 of thread 1
ORA-00312: online log 2 thread 1: '/oracle01/oradata/orcl/redo02a.log'
ORA-27037: unable to obtain file status
Linux Error: 2: No such file or directory
Additional information: 3
ORA-00312: online log 2 thread 1: '/oracle01/oradata/orcl/redo02.log'
ORA-27037: unable to obtain file status
Linux Error: 2: No such file or directory
Additional information: 3
SQL> alter database clear logfile group 2;
alter database clear logfile group 2
*
ERROR at line 1:
ORA-01624: log 2 needed for crash recovery of instance orcl (thread 1)
ORA-00312: online log 2 thread 1: '/oracle01/oradata/orcl/redo02.log'
ORA-00312: online log 2 thread 1: '/oracle01/oradata/orcl/redo02a.log'
```

What steps must you take to resolve the error?

a. Issue the `recover database redo logs` command.

b. Issue the `Startup Mount` command to mount the database.

c. Restore the last full database backup.

d. Perform a point-in-time recovery, applying all archived redo logs that are available.

e. Restore all archived redo logs generated during and after the last full database backup.

f. Open the database using the `alter database open resetlogs` command.

g. Issue the `alter database open` command.

A. b, a, f

B. e, b, a, f

C. e, b, a, g

D. b, a, g

E. c, e, b, d, f

17. What does the SCN represent?

A. The system change number, which is a point in time relative to transactions within a given database.

B. A number that represents time. Thus, at 1300 hours, the SCN is the same on all databases.

C. The security change number, which represents the security code that is needed to access any database structure.

D. A conversion factor that converts internal database time to external clock time.

E. UTC time in the database, providing a standardized way of tracking time in Oracle.

18. You have lost datafile 4 from your database. Which is typically the fastest way to restore your database?

A. Restore and recover the datafile.

B. Restore and recover the tablespace.

C. Restore and recover the database.

D. Restore and recover the control file.

E. Restore and recover the parameter file.

19. You are trying to recover your database. During the recovery process, you receive the following error:

```
ORA-00279: change 5033391 generated at 08/17/2008 06:37:40
needed for thread 1
ORA-00289: suggestion :
/oracle01/flash_recovery_area/ORCL/archivelog/2008_08_17
/o1_mf_1_11_%u_.arc
ORA-00280: change 5033391 for thread 1 is in sequence #11
ORA-00278: log file
'/oracle01/flash_recovery_area/ORCL/archivelog/2008_08_17
/o1_mf_1_10_4bj6wnqm_.arc' no longer needed for this recovery
Specify log: {<RET>=suggested | filename | AUTO | CANCEL}
ORA-00308: cannot open archived log
```

```
'/oracle01/flash_recovery_area/ORCL/archivelog/2008_08_17
/o1_mf_1_11_%u_.arc'
ORA-27037: unable to obtain file status
Linux Error: 2: No such file or directory
Additional information: 3
```

How do you respond to this error? (Choose two.)

A. Restore the archived redo log that is missing and attempt recovery again.

B. Recovery is complete and you can open the database.

C. Recovery needs redo that is not available in any archived redo log. Attempt to apply an online redo log if available.

D. Recover the entire database and apply all archived redo logs again.

E. Recovery is not possible because an archived redo log has been lost.

20. During recovery, you need to know if log sequence 11 is in the online redo logs, and if so, you need to know the names of the online redo logs so you can apply them during recovery. Which view or views would you use to determine this information? (Choose all that apply.)

A. V$LOGFILE

B. V$RECOVER_LOG

C. V$RECOVER_DATABASE

D. V$LOG_RECOVER

E. V$LOG

Answers to Review Questions

1. B. First you would take the `users_01.dbf` datafile offline. You would then restore the `users_01.dbf` datafile from the most current backup. Once you have restored the datafile, recover the datafile with the `recover datafile` command. Finally, bring the datafile online with the `alter database` command.

2. D. When you discover that you have lost an online redo log, and if the database is still up, the first action should be to checkpoint the database. This can serve to reduce the overall risk of data loss. After you checkpoint the database, you can then attempt to clear the online redo log. A backup afterward is highly recommended.

3. D. First you would restore the missing datafiles. Notice in the question that there are two datafiles that were lost. Next you would mount the database and then you would recover the SYSTEM tablespace. Since it is the SYSTEM tablespace, you would not be able to open the database first. Then you open the database with the `alter database open` command.

4. E. If you lose one or more control files but at least one remains, you should shut down the database. Then use any remaining control file as the source to create new control-file copies for the control files that were lost. Then restart the database. No recovery is required in this situation.

5. A, B, D. You will need the database datafiles, the control files, and the online redo logs all in place to be able to restore the database when it's in NOARCHIVELOG mode.

6. C. If the database has not shut down yet, you have an opportunity to preserve your data changes. Issue a checkpoint, which will flush dirty buffers to disk. Then shut down the database normally, if possible (`shutdown`, `shutdown immediate`). You then should mount the database with the `startup mount` command followed by clearing and rebuilding the log file with the `alter database clear logfile` command. Finally, attempt to open the database with the `alter database open` command.

7. A, B, C, D. Change-based application allows you to recover the database to a specific SCN. Cancel-based recovery provides the ability for you to cancel recovery after each archived redo log application. Time-based recovery provides the ability to recover the database up to a specific point in time. Sequence number–based recovery allows you to recover the database up to a specific log sequence number.

8. A, C, D. To perform a full recovery of the database that is in ARCHIVELOG, you would need the database datafiles, the archived redo logs, and a backup control file.

9. E. You use the `alter tablespace add tempfile` command to re-create a missing tempfile or add a new tempfile to a temporary tablespace.

10. C. You should first start the database in mount mode using the `startup mount` command. You then issue the `alter database clear unarchived logfile` command. This will clear the log file if it needs to be archived and re-create the online redo log group. If that command is successful, then you issue the `alter database open` command. The last step, backing up the database, is very important since your previous backup will not be able to recover the database beyond the point of the cleared redo log sequence number. This is because you have skipped a redo log in the redo log stream.

11. A. You would first take the missing datafile offline with the `alter database datafile 4 offline` command. You should then restore the datafiles that have been lost. Then issue the `recover tablespace USERS` command to recover the USERS tablespace. Use the `alter database datafile 4 online` command to bring the USERS tablespace online.

12. D. Since the online redo logs are intact, you will be able to use the `noresetlogs` version of the `create controlfile` command.

13. B. Since the database is in NOARCHIVELOG mode, their request cannot be met because point-in-time recovery is supported only in ARCHIVELOG mode.

14. A, C. You can create a backup control file with the `alter database backup controlfile` command. You can create a trace file that contains the `create controlfile` command.

15. A. First you would want to restore the three datafiles that were lost. Then you would want to issue the `startup mount` command to mount the database to prepare for recovery. You would then recover the database (you could opt to recover just the datafiles if you wished). Finally, open the database with the `alter database open` command.

16. E. In this situation, you have gotten yourself in real trouble and you will have data loss. First you will need to restore the last full database backup and also all archived redo logs that were generated during the backup and since the backup was completed. You will then issue the `startup mount` command to mount the database, and then issue the `recover database until cancel` command. Apply all the archived redo logs you can. Then cancel the recovery and open the database using the `alter database open resetlogs` command.

17. A. The SCN is a number that represents a point in time in the database relative to transactions within a given database.

18. A. If you have only lost a datafile, you should just restore and then recover the datafile.

19. A, C. This error will appear if an archived redo log is not available. In this case you need sequence 11. First you would try to restore archived redo log sequence 11. If log sequence 11 is not available as an archived redo log, you might find that it is available in one of the online redo logs.

20. A, E. The V$LOGFILE view will give you the name of the online redo logs associated with each group. The V$LOG view will provide the current sequence number assigned to each group.

Chapter 4

Configuring and Backing Up Using RMAN

ORACLE DATABASE 11*g*: ADMINISTRATION II EXAM OBJECTIVES COVERED IN THIS CHAPTER:

✓ **Configuring Backup Specifications**

- Allocate channels to use in backing up
- Configure backup optimization

✓ **Configuring for Recovery**

- Define, apply and use a retention policy
- Configure the Flash Recovery Area
- Use Flash Recovery Area

✓ **Using RMAN to Create Backups**

- Create image file backups
- Create a whole database backup
- Enable fast incremental backup
- Create duplex backup and back up backup sets
- Create an archival backup for long-term retention
- Create a multi-section compressed and encrypted backup

Backup and recovery is one of the central themes in the Oracle Database 11*g* OCP exam. In Chapters 2 and 3 we talked about user-managed backup and recovery in Oracle, and now we will move on to what is termed *server-managed* backups, which are managed by RMAN. RMAN is like SQL*Plus in some ways. RMAN is a client. It connects to the Oracle database and issues a few commands to the server, and the server actually does the work (hence the term *server-based backups*). The server reports the results to RMAN and RMAN reports those results to you.

In this chapter we will introduce you to RMAN. We will discuss the features and configuration of RMAN, including configuration of the flash recovery area (FRA). We will also discuss using RMAN to back up your Oracle database. In Chapter 5 we will continue with a discussion of using RMAN to restore and recover your Oracle database.

Exam objectives are subject to change at any time without prior notice and at Oracle's sole discretion. Please visit Oracle's Training and Certification website (`http://www.oracle.com/education/certification/`) for the most current exam-objectives listing.

Why Use RMAN?

RMAN has many capabilities to facilitate the backup and recovery process. It comes in both web-based GUI and command-line versions. In general, RMAN performs and standardizes the backup and recovery process, which can reduce mistakes made during this process. The following are just a few of the exciting RMAN features:

- It's free with the Oracle license.
- You can perform full and incremental backups of the entire database, specific tablespaces, and datafiles. You can also back up control files and archive logs.
- RMAN offers persistent parameter configuration for easy backup and recovery.
- RMAN offers automated backups of control files and spfiles.
- You can validate your database backups without actually recovering your database.
- RMAN offers actual compression of backup images through various means.
- RMAN offers actual encryption of database backups.
- RMAN provides various backup reporting capabilities.

- RMAN provides scripting capabilities when you are using a recovery catalog.
- With the Media Management Library (MML) you can integrate easily with third-party tape media software.
- RMAN provides for parallel processing of backups and restores.
- With RMAN, you can create duplicate databases.
- RMAN helps you migrate datafiles across operating-system platforms.
- With RMAN, you can perform tablespace point-in-time recovery (TSPITR).
- RMAN allows you to recover datafiles that aren't backed up.
- RMAN will automatically recover tempfiles during a database recovery.

Exploring the RMAN Architecture

As you can see, RMAN has a rich feature set, and with each version of Oracle, the feature set becomes even richer. Oracle Database 11*g* offers a very full-featured backup and recovery tool in the form of RMAN.

RMAN is based on a robust architecture consisting of the following main components:

- The RMAN client interface
- The database server
- The database control file
- The optional recovery catalog
- Database pfile or spfile
- Backup media and the Media Management Library (MML)
- Backup sets and backup set pieces
- RMAN channels
- Snapshot control file

Let's look at each component in a bit more detail:

RMAN client interface The *RMAN command-line interface (RCLI)* provides access to Recovery Manager. This process spawns off-server sessions that connect to the *target database*, which is the database that will be backed up. From the RMAN client interface you will issue RMAN commands to execute RMAN backup, recovery, and restore operations.

Previous versions of this text (and OCP exams) contained significant coverage of Oracle Enterprise Manager (OEM). The Oracle Database 11*g* OCP exam contains no coverage specific to OEM, and much more coverage on user-based backup and recovery. As a result, there is little coverage of OEM within this text.

Database server The database server is the principal mechanism used to back up the database. Built into the core of the Oracle kernel code are stored packages used by RMAN to back up, restore, and recover the database. RMAN cannot execute back up, restore, or recover operations without having first attached to the database server. Depending on the operation, the database will need to be opened in NOMOUNT, MOUNT, or OPEN mode.

Control file The *database control file* is used to store RMAN-related information for each database. The control file is the principal storage mechanism for all RMAN-related records. All records with respect to database backups, archive-log backups, and control-file backups are stored in the control file. Control files have limitations with respect to how many RMAN records they can hold, and as a result, certain retention requirements may call for the use of a recovery catalog to augment a control file. RMAN provides an automated means of backing up the control file and restoring it when a control file is not readily available. This method is called a control-file autobackup.

Recovery catalog The *recovery catalog* is an optional component that stores RMAN-related information inside an Oracle database. This is similar to the RMAN repository stored in the control file, but the recovery catalog provides some additional features and longer-term storage of RMAN records. The recovery catalog is a special schema that contains backup-related information in a set of tables. During normal database operations, RMAN will synchronize the database control file with the recovery catalog, ensuring that the recovery-catalog schema is in synchronization with the database control file.

Database pfile or spfile You should already be familiar with the *database parameter file (pfile)* and the *server parameter file (spfile)*. These files are critical to RMAN operations because they contain parameters that impact RMAN operations. RMAN can be used to back up and recover an spfile using an option called autobackups. Pfiles can not be backed up with RMAN.

Backup media and the Media Management Library Obviously, if RMAN is going to back up your database, it needs to back it up somewhere. RMAN, out of the box, allows you to back up your database to disk. This can be the local disk, or a network-attached disk (in other words, NFS) can be used. RMAN also offers the *Media Management Library (MML)*. The MML is an API set that media vendors (for example, tape-drive vendors) can write to and that allows RMAN to communicate directly with their products.

Backup sets and backup set pieces Backup sets are logical entities that consist of one or more backup set pieces. Backup set pieces are physical files that actually store the RMAN backup data.

RMAN channels *Channels* are used in RMAN to indicate the device to back up to. They are also used to partition a backup operation, essentially parallelizing the operation. For example, if you had two tape units, you could create two different RMAN channels and stream your backup to the two different tape devices in parallel. This can reduce backup and recovery times significantly.

RMAN offers *automated channel failover* for both backup and recovery operations. With automated channel failover, if a channel in a multichannel backup fails, the other channels will continue to back up the remainder of the database. This can be helpful when, for example, a tape device fails. In addition, Oracle will retry to back up the data that was on the failed channel across the remaining channels.

Snapshot control file When RMAN does its business, it bases its knowledge of the database on information in the database control file. That's fine and well, but if the control file changes during an RMAN operation, what is RMAN to do, use the old information or the new information? The answer to this dilemma is the snapshot control file.

When RMAN performs any operation that requires a consistent view of the control file (such as a backup), it will first create a copy of the control file. This copy is called the *snapshot control file*. The snapshot control file will be used for the duration of that operation and will be overwritten by any subsequent operation. Even related operations (say, during a backup database plus archive-log operation that does an archive log backup, a database backup, and then another archive log backup) will use newly created snapshot control files, one for each operation.

Connecting to RMAN

Connecting to the RMAN client is quite simple. RMAN is a command-line tool, so you would want to open a command-line window for your operating system. Once you have done that you will set your ORACLE_HOME environment to the database that you want to connect to. Now you can start RMAN and connect to the target database (or the database that you want to backup and recover). Here is an example of connecting to a database with the RMAN client:

```
C:\oracle\admin\ORCL\wallet>set oracle_sid=orcl
C:\oracle\admin\ORCL\wallet>rman target=/
Recovery Manager: Release 11.1.0.6.0 - Production on Thu Sep 11 18:28:24 2008
Copyright (c) 1982, 2007, Oracle.  All rights reserved.
connected to target database: ORCL (DBID=1190537904)
```

Sometimes you may need to connect to your target database using Oracle Net connection strings. If you are using a recovery catalog or an auxiliary database you will normally connect to those using Oracle Net connection strings, as seen in these examples:

```
C:\oracle\admin\ORCL\wallet>rman target=sys/robert@orcl
C:\oracle\admin\ORCL\wallet>rman target=sys/robert@orcl
catalog=rcat_user/robert@rcat
```

The RMAN command line contains a number of different command-line parameters. You will see many of these in use throughout these next few chapters. Table 4.1 provides an overview of the most commonly used command-line parameters you might use:

Putting Files in *ORACLE_HOME* Is Not a Best Practice

You might have noticed that RMAN puts the snapshot control file in an ORACLE_HOME location by default. This is not unusual; Oracle does this for other types of files (for example, the FRA defaults to ORACLE_HOME) by default.

In the real world, defaults like this are never acceptable, and we never allow ORACLE_HOME to be the destination for any type of file other than those associated with the Oracle install and certain configuration files (thus its size is fairly static). This is because you do not want the disk space in ORACLE_HOME to unexpectedly become exhausted because Oracle databases are writing files into it. This becomes even more important as you add more databases to your server and those databases are using the same ORACLE_HOME concurrently. Allowing those databases to write to ORACLE_HOME can cause problems for all databases on the server.

RMAN snapshot control files, files and directories associated with the Automatic Diagnostic Repository (ADR), database datafiles, and most other database-related files should be created in directories specific to each database other than ORACLE_HOME. (See Chapter 10 for more on ADR.)

The real-world solution generally involves the creation of different mount points for database-specific data. These mount points might be shared among different databases, or there might be a unique mount point for each database (or perhaps several mount points for one or more databases). For example, if your database is ORCL, you might have the following mount points/directories created:

- `/oracle01/oracle/product/11.1.0/db_1`: ORACLE_HOME
- `/oracle02/oracle/oradata/orcl` (for Oracle Database datafiles)
- `/oracle03/oracle/oradata/orcl` (for Oracle Database datafiles)
- `/oracle04/oracle/diag` (for the ADR)

For more information, you may want to review Oracle's OFA recommendations. OFA is outside the scope of the OCP exam and this book, but it provides some guidance from Oracle on directory naming and placement for Oracle-related files.

TABLE 4.1 RMAN Command-Line Parameters

Parameter Name	Description
`Target`	Connection string for the target database
`Catalog`	Connection string for the recovery catalog database
`Nocatalog`	Indicates no recovery catalog is to be used. Default.
`Cmdfile`	Name of command file to run.
`Log`	Name of log file to log RMAN output.
`Trace`	Name of file for debugging messages.
`Append`	Append to log file rather than overwrite.
`Auxiliary`	The connection string for the auxiliary database.

Configuring RMAN for Use

RMAN will work out of the box without any configuration. Unfortunately, this is generally not a good idea. RMAN tends to throw things into `ORACLE_HOME` if you have not configured the database and RMAN correctly. In this section, we will address configuring RMAN correctly.

In the following sections, we will introduce you to the flash recovery area (FRA) in RMAN. We will then address RMAN persistent configuration settings to allow for streamlined backups followed by using nonpersistent settings when required. Finally, we will cover configuring RMAN for its first use.

The Flash Recovery Area

The Oracle *flash recovery area (FRA)* was introduced in Oracle Database 10*g* as the central repository for all files related to Oracle backup and recovery. In this section, we will discuss the flash recovery area. First we will have a quick overview of what the FRA is generally used for. Then you'll learn about configuring the FRA for your Oracle database.

Introducing the FRA

The FRA is the principal store for all Oracle database backup–related files. The FRA can be stored on disk or within an ASM instance. It cannot be stored on tape, but files backed up in the FRA can be backed up to tape via the RMAN `backup recovery area` command.

The FRA stores the following types of Oracle database files:

- Backup set pieces
- Archive log backups
- Database archive logs
- Control-file autobackups
- Image copies
- Database online redo logs
- Database control files
- Flashback logs

The FRA supports RMAN's backup and retention policies by automatically removing files when they are no longer needed and when FRA space is required (obsolete RMAN backups to non-FRA locations will not be removed by RMAN automatically).

Configuring the FRA

Configuring the FRA is easy. First you create the base directory of the FRA from the OS, and then you set the following parameters in any database that will use the FRA:

- DB_RECOVERY_FILE_DEST
- DB_RECOVERY_FILE_DEST_SIZE

The DB_RECOVERY_FILE_DEST parameter defines the FRA base directory location. This is the only directory you will need to create when configuring the FRA. You will need to make sure that this directory is owned by the owner of the Oracle executable so that Oracle can create other subdirectories beneath it.

The DB_RECOVERY_FILE_DEST_SIZE parameter defines the total amount of space for this database instance is allowed to consume in the FRA. This is a logical limit, which can be greater than or less than the actual physical limit of space on that device. For example, you may have a file system with 500GB of space available on it. However, you may want to indicate that your database can consume only up to 100GB of space within the FRA while assigning the FRA to the 500GB file system.

You use the `alter system` command to configure the FRA. Note that DB_RECOVERY_FILE_DEST is not dynamic, while DB_RECOVERY_FILE_DEST_SIZE is dynamic. To configure the FRA, do the following:

1. Create the base FRA directory:

```
/u01>mkdir /oracle01/fra
```

2. Log into SQL*Plus:

```
C:\oracle\orabackup\orcl>sqlplus sys as sysdba
SQL*Plus: Release 11.1.0.6.0 - Production on Thu Aug 14 18:57:13 2008
Copyright (c) 1982, 2007, Oracle.  All rights reserved.
Enter password:
Connected to:
Oracle Database 11g Enterprise Edition Release 11.1.0.6.0 - Production
With the Partitioning, OLAP, Data Mining and Real Application
Testing options
SQL>
```

3. Now use the `alter system` command to set the parameter `DB_RECOVERY_FILE_DEST` to `/oracle01/fra` and `DB_RECOVERY_FILE_DEST_SIZE` to 2GB.

```
sql>alter system set db_recovery_file_dest_size=2GB;
sql>alter system set db_recovery_file_dest='/oracle01/fra' scope=spfile;
```

4. Now shut down and restart the database. Once the database has been restarted, the FRA will become operational.

```
SQL> shutdown immediate
Database closed.
Database dismounted.
ORACLE instance shut down.
SQL> startup
ORACLE instance started.
Total System Global Area  397557760 bytes
Fixed Size                  1333452 bytes
Variable Size             268437300 bytes
Database Buffers          121634816 bytes
Redo Buffers                6152192 bytes
Database mounted.
Database opened.
```

Managing the FRA

Management of the FRA is done principally by Oracle based on backup retention settings for RMAN (see the section "Retention Policies" later in this chapter). Thus, as backups become obsolete and as FRA space is exhausted by an instance, Oracle will remove those obsolete backups automatically. As a result, over time FRA space tends to reach an equilibrium, assuming that the database datafiles do not grow at a great rate.

Real World Scenario

Really Using the FRA

In the real world, it's hard to get things right the first time. Using the FRA is no exception. One of us had a client that had a few problems when they first switched to using the FRA. The databases were not set up correctly, so the FRA would fill up.

Over time, the FRA became more stable as we understood the load profile and its relationship to the creation of archived redo logs and backups. We eventually found the sweet spot with respect to how much disk space we needed to allocate to the FRA. This is actually a good thing because it forced them to realize that understanding the disk-usage profile of their databases was important.

Monitoring of the FRA is another real-world issue to be aware of. Many companies that are using the FRA are investing some time in scripts to monitor FRA disk-space usage. OEM can be used for this too.

The FRA does require some care and feeding by the DBA, however, particularly at first. Sometimes it's hard to properly estimate the correct setting for the `DB_RECOVERY_FILE_DEST_SIZE` and you will find the FRA filling up. Archived redo logs are stored in the FRA, so if the FRA fills up, archived redo logs will no longer be able to be written.

If this occurs, Oracle will first try to free space in the FRA by removing obsolete backups. If Oracle cannot free up enough space, then eventually the inability to archive will cause the database to freeze until the out-of-space condition can be rectified. In this case, you can free up space by changing `DB_RECOVERY_FILE_DEST_SIZE` to a higher value. This parameter is dynamic, so the change can be made immediately.

You can use the `V$DB_RECOVERY_FILE_DEST` view to determine the state of the FRA. In the following example, we find that the FRA is sized to 2GB and that we have used 251MB in total. We also see that 41MB of that space is reclaimable. In short, this FRA looks pretty good at this point.

```
SQL> select name, space_limit, space_used, space_reclaimable
2 from v$recovery_file_dest;
NAME                              SPACE_LIMIT   SPACE_USED SPACE_RECLAIMABLE
------------------------------ -------------- ------------ -----------------
c:\oracle\flash_recovery_area   2,147,483,648  251,173,376        41,127,424
```

If you manually remove files from the FRA, you will have to let Oracle know that you have done so. By default Oracle will not detect that the files have been removed. Oracle can detect the file removals by using the RMAN `crosscheck` and `delete expired` commands. See Chapter 7 for more information on using these commands.

RMAN Persistent Configuration Settings

When RMAN first came out in Oracle version 8.0, you had to manually indicate in each backup where the backup destination was to be, any limits related to the backup (such as the maximum size of backup set pieces), and so on. This required a lot of work and made RMAN a bit more archaic-looking and difficult to use.

Oracle Database version 9*i* introduced the concept of persistent configuration in RMAN. *RMAN persistent configuration settings* are settings that are configured through the RMAN interface, stored in the control file, and automatically used during each backup unless they are overridden.

Oracle Database 11*g* provides for a number of persistent settings, including the following:

- Backup (database and archive log) retention criteria
- Backup optimization
- Default channel/device configuration
- Control-file autobackup configuration
- Datafile and archive log backup-copy configuration
- Default encryption settings
- Default compression settings
- Default location for the snapshot control file

You can see the current settings for all persistent parameters in RMAN by using the RMAN `show all` command, as shown here:

```
RMAN> show all;
using target database control file instead of recovery catalog
RMAN configuration parameters for database with db_unique_name ORCL are:
CONFIGURE RETENTION POLICY TO REDUNDANCY 1; # default
CONFIGURE BACKUP OPTIMIZATION OFF; # default
CONFIGURE DEFAULT DEVICE TYPE TO DISK; # default
CONFIGURE CONTROLFILE AUTOBACKUP OFF; # default
CONFIGURE CONTROLFILE AUTOBACKUP FORMAT FOR DEVICE TYPE DISK TO '%F'; #default
CONFIGURE DEVICE TYPE DISK PARALLELISM 1 BACKUP TYPE TO BACKUPSET; # default
CONFIGURE DATAFILE BACKUP COPIES FOR DEVICE TYPE DISK TO 1; # default
CONFIGURE ARCHIVELOG BACKUP COPIES FOR DEVICE TYPE DISK TO 1; # default
CONFIGURE CHANNEL DEVICE TYPE DISK MAXPIECESIZE 100 M;
CONFIGURE MAXSETSIZE TO UNLIMITED; # default
CONFIGURE ENCRYPTION FOR DATABASE OFF; # default
CONFIGURE ENCRYPTION ALGORITHM 'AES128'; # default
CONFIGURE COMPRESSION ALGORITHM 'BZIP2'; # default
```

```
CONFIGURE ARCHIVELOG DELETION POLICY TO NONE; # default
CONFIGURE SNAPSHOT CONTROLFILE NAME TO
 'C:\ORACLE\PRODUCT\11.1.0\DB_1\DATABASE\SNCFORCL.ORA'; # default
```

You can also look at an individual setting by using the `show` command followed by the setting you are interested in. In this example, we are interested in the retention policy:

```
RMAN> show retention policy;
RMAN configuration parameters for database with db_unique_name ORCL are:
CONFIGURE RETENTION POLICY TO REDUNDANCY 1; # default
```

You can clear configuration settings using the `configure clear` command, as shown in this example:

```
RMAN>configure device type disk clear;
```

Unique RMAN Configuration Settings

Sometimes you need to do something different. Perhaps you have configured your default channels to go to tape but you want a particular backup to go to disk one time. You can configure unique one-time-only settings in RMAN through the use of a combination of the `set` command, a *run block*, and individual keywords available in specific commands. Here is an example of using a run block to override channel defaults. We also use the `allocate channel` command to manually allocate channels:

```
run {
allocate channel c1 device type disk format 'c:\oracle\oraback1\orcl\%U';
allocate channel c2 device type disk format 'c:\oracle\oraback2\orcl\%U';
backup database plus archivelog;
};
```

You can also use options within the backup command to override default settings. For example, by default RMAN will write backups to the FRA, so the backup command (which we will discuss later in this chapter) is as simple as `backup database plus archivelog`. If you want to write to a directory other than the FRA for a single backup, you would include the `format` keyword to override the default setting, as in this example:

```
backup database format 'c:\oracle\backup\backup\%U.bak' plus archivelog
format 'c:\oracle\backup\arch\%U.bak';
```

The RMAN Backup and Recovery Manuals

Oracle provides some great sources of information within the Oracle documentation set. We strongly recommend you acquaint yourself with the Oracle documentation and especially the Oracle RMAN documentation. The place to go for the online Oracle documentation is `http://tahiti.oracle.com`. For RMAN backup and recovery, look at the following books while you are preparing for your OCP exam:

- Backup and Recovery Reference - Part Number B28273-02
- Backup and Recovery Users Guide - Part Number B27270-02

And finally, if we may pat our own backs a little bit, a great book on getting to know RMAN is *Oracle Database 10g* RMAN Backup & Recovery by Robert G. Freeman and Matthew Hart (Oracle Press/McGraw-Hill, 2007). It's a comprehensive guide to all things RMAN. The Oracle Database 11*g* version should be available sometime in 2009.

Preparing RMAN for Use

Before you use RMAN, you will want to customize it to use your preferences. This makes the backup process easy and repeatable with a minimum of effort. In this section, we will discuss a number of configurable features of RMAN:

- Setting the `control_file_record_keep_time` parameter
- Backup retention policies
- Backup compression
- Backup encryption
- Specific channel configurations
- Control-file autobackups
- Backup optimization
- Setting the location of the snapshot control file

Let's look at each of these in some more detail.

Setting the *control_file_record_keep_time* Parameter

When using RMAN without a recovery catalog (which we discuss in Chapter 5), you will need to make sure that you have set the `CONTROL_FILE_RECORD_KEEP_TIME` parameter correctly. This parameter is used to determine how long RMAN-related control-file records are maintained in the control file. Make sure this parameter is set high enough so that it will not interfere with your retention-policy requirements (see the next section for more on retention policies).

You can set the CONTROL_FILE_RECORD_KEEP_TIME (defined in days) parameter using the alter system command, as shown here:

```
-- Set control_file_record_keep_time to 14 days.
SQL> alter system set control_file_record_keep_time=14;
```

The parameter is a dynamic parameter; therefore, you can change it without having to shut down the database.

Retention Policies

RMAN *retention policies* are used to manage how long Oracle will maintain backups. When you're using the FRA, retention policies are used for automated cleanup of unneeded backup sets, which eliminates the need to manually manage space usage. When you're not using the FRA, retention policies can be used to manually manage space usage. In the following sections, you'll learn about the two different kinds of retention policies and how to configure them.

Types of Retention Policies

These are the different types of retention policies that you can set in RMAN:

- None
- Redundancy (the default)
- Recovery window

Let's look at the redundancy and recovery window retention criteria in a bit more detail. Then we will cover how to override the retention criteria with the keep operand.

REDUNDANCY RETENTION POLICY

The redundancy retention policy ensures that there will be a certain number of backups available for recovery. Once a backup is no longer needed, Oracle will mark it as obsolete, making it eligible for removal. For example, if the retention criterion is set to redundancy 2, then the following happens as you back up your database:

- Backup 1 occurs; when successful, it is considered current.
- Backup 2 occurs. Backups 1 and 2 are considered current.
- Backup 3 occurs. Backup 1 is marked as obsolete and backups 2 and 3 are considered current.

The default retention setting in RMAN is a redundancy retention policy of 1 copy.

If an FRA is configured, the backup will be removed when space is needed. If an FRA is not used, you will need to use the RMAN command delete obsolete (discussed in Chapter 8) to remove the backup metadata and physical files.

RECOVERY WINDOW RETENTION POLICY

The recovery retention policy provides the ability to define a recovery window to be applied to your backups in a period of days. For example, if you want to be sure you can restore your database to 14 days ago, you would establish a recovery retention policy of 14 days and earlier. Note that this setting does not impact the lifetime of a specific backup based on when the backup occurred but rather ensures that all backups that are retained can be restored based on the retention policy. This means that backups taken 15, 16, or 30 days ago may remain valid backups as demonstrated here and in Figure 4.1:

- Your database retention policy is 14 days.
- You perform database backup #1 on day 1; it is of course valid.
- Archive log backups are taken on days 1 through 14. Backup #1 is now 15 days old. It remains valid because it is needed to restore the database to days 0 through 14.
- Database backup #2 is taken on day 16. Database backup #1 is still valid. Why? Because we need database backup #1 to restore the database to day 10, or day 9, since database backup #2 is valid for only day 16 and beyond.
- Archive log backups are taken on days 17 through 29, which is the 14th day since backup #2.
- On day 29, backup #1 and all the associated archived redo logs are finally eligible for removal.

FIGURE 4.1 Recovery-window retention-policy example: 14 days

Day	1	2	3	4	5	6	7
	Full Backup Taken	Arch Backup	Arch Backup	Arch Backup	Arch Backup	Arch Backup	Arch Backup

Day	8	9	10	11	12	13	14
	Arch Backup	Arch Backup	Arch Backup	Arch Backup	Arch Backup	Arch Backup	Arch Backup

Day	15	16	17	18	19	20	21
	No Backup	Full Backup Taken	Arch Backup	Arch Backup	Arch Backup	Arch Backup	Arch Backup

(Still need day 1 backup to restore to day 15; day 1 backup is still valid.)

Day	22	23	24	25	26	27	28	29	30
	No Backup	Full Backup Taken	Arch Backup	Arch Backup	Arch Backup	Arch Backup	Arch Backup	Arch Backup	Backup on Day 1 No Longer Needed

When the backup is marked obsolete, it is eligible for removal. If it exists in the FRA, then Oracle will remove it automatically. If it is not in the FRA, you can use the `list obsolete` command to list those backups subject to removal based on the retention policy and then use the `delete obsolete` command to remove those backups. Here is an example:

```
RMAN> report obsolete;
RMAN retention policy will be applied to the command
RMAN retention policy is set to redundancy 2
Report of obsolete backups and copies
Type                 Key   Completion Time Filename/Handle
-------------------- ----- --------------- --------------------
Backup Set           19    05-SEP-08
  Backup Piece       36    05-SEP-08        C:\ORACLE\BACKUP\0MJPS3LL_3_1.ORCL
Backup Set           19    05-SEP-08
  Backup Piece       35    05-SEP-08        C:\ORACLE\BACKUP\0MJPS3LL_2_1.ORCL
Backup Set           19    05-SEP-08
  Backup Piece       34    05-SEP-08        C:\ORACLE\BACKUP\0MJPS3LL_1_1.ORCL
Backup Set           20    05-SEP-08
  Backup Piece       37    05-SEP-08        C:\ORACLE\BACKUP\0NJPS3VG_1_1.ORCL
Backup Set           21    05-SEP-08
  Backup Piece       38    05-SEP-08        C:\ORACLE\BACKUP\0OJPS402_1_1.ORCL
Backup Set           22    07-SEP-08
  Backup Piece       39    07-SEP-08       C:\ORACLE\FLASH_RECOVERY_AREA\ORCL
\BACKUPSET\2008_09_07\O1_MF_ANNNN_TAG20080907T170612_4D8QMNYR_.BKP
RMAN> delete noprompt obsolete;
RMAN retention policy will be applied to the command
RMAN retention policy is set to redundancy 2
using channel ORA_DISK_1
Deleting the following obsolete backups and copies:
Type                 Key   Completion Time Filename/Handle
-------------------- ----- --------------- --------------------
Backup Set           19    05-SEP-08
  Backup Piece       36    05-SEP-08        C:\ORACLE\BACKUP\0MJPS3LL_3_1.ORCL
Backup Set           19    05-SEP-08
  Backup Piece       35    05-SEP-08        C:\ORACLE\BACKUP\0MJPS3LL_2_1.ORCL
Backup Set           19    05-SEP-08
  Backup Piece       34    05-SEP-08        C:\ORACLE\BACKUP\0MJPS3LL_1_1.ORCL
Backup Set           20    05-SEP-08
  Backup Piece       37    05-SEP-08        C:\ORACLE\BACKUP\0NJPS3VG_1_1.ORCL
Backup Set           21    05-SEP-08
  Backup Piece       38    05-SEP-08        C:\ORACLE\BACKUP\0OJPS402_1_1.ORCL
Backup Set           22    07-SEP-08
```

```
  Backup Piece       39     07-SEP-08        C:\ORACLE\FLASH_RECOVERY_AREA\ORCL
\BACKUPSET\2008_09_07\01_MF_ANNNN_TAG20080907T170612_4D8QMNYR_.BKP
deleted backup piece
backup piece handle=C:\ORACLE\BACKUP\0MJPS3LL_3_1.ORCL RECID=36
STAMP=664670185
deleted backup piece
backup piece handle=C:\ORACLE\BACKUP\0MJPS3LL_2_1.ORCL RECID=35
STAMP=664670069
deleted backup piece
backup piece handle=C:\ORACLE\BACKUP\0MJPS3LL_1_1.ORCL RECID=34
STAMP=664669886
deleted backup piece
backup piece handle=C:\ORACLE\BACKUP\0NJPS3VG_1_1.ORCL RECID=37
STAMP=664670208
deleted backup piece
backup piece handle=C:\ORACLE\BACKUP\0OJPS402_1_1.ORCL RECID=38
STAMP=664670216
deleted backup piece
backup piece handle=C:\ORACLE\FLASH_RECOVERY_AREA\ORCL
\BACKUPSET\2008_09_07\01_MF_ANNNN_TAG20080907T170612_4D8QMNYR_.BKP RECID=39
STAMP=664823188
Deleted 6 objects
```

USING THE *KEEP* OPTION

If you have a defined retention policy, you may well want to override it for specific backups. Perhaps you have a policy that says at the end of the year you will make a backup of the database and keep it forever, or perhaps you have a "gold" copy backup that you want to keep for a longer period of time than the default retention policy allows. The `keep` option provides the ability to override the default retention policy. You can define a different retention policy for the specific backup (for example, remove it in 180 days) or you can choose to keep the backup until you decide to obsolete it manually with the `unkeep` command.

For example, if you wanted to create a backup with a retention criterion of 365 days, you would issue the following command:

```
RMAN> backup database plus archivelog delete input
keep until time 'sysdate + 365';
```

Using the `keep forever` option, you could keep the backup indefinitely, as shown here:

```
RMAN> backup database plus archivelog tag=gold_copy
delete input keep forever;
```

Note that the use of the keep option does not require that you back up archived redo logs at the same time. Issuing the keep command will cause RMAN to back up the archived redo logs needed to restore the backup you are indicating you want to keep. So you could avoid the plus archivelog option if you wanted, as shown here:

```
RMAN> backup database format 'c:\oracle\backup\%U'
keep until time "sysdate+300" tag='DavidW_HeberA_BillJ_JedB_DanD_MandyC';
```

The keep forever option requires that you use a recovery catalog. The keep until time option does not require the use of a recovery catalog.

You can use the change command to subsequently decide to keep a backup or to change the setting on a backup so that the status of the backup is no longer set to keep. For example, you can take a backup with a tag of gold_backup that was backed up with the keep command and start to enforce the retention criteria on that backup by using the change nokeep command, as shown here:

```
RMAN>backup database plus archivelog tag=gold_copy delete input format
'c:\oracle\backup\%U' keep until time "sysdate+300";
RMAN>change backupset tag gold_backup nokeep;
```

You cannot create backups on which you've used the keep option in the FRA. If you want to create backups that have nonstandard retention criteria, you will have to use a non-FRA location to create them. This often requires the use of the format parameter, as shown in this example:

```
backup database format 'c:\oracle\backup\%U' keep until time
"sysdate+300" ;
```

Configuring Retention Policies

Retention policies are configured in RMAN using the configure command. When configuring a redundancy configuration policy, you will use the configure command with the retention policy to redundancy keywords, as shown here:

```
RMAN> configure retention policy to redundancy 1 ;
```

To configure a recovery-window retention policy, you use the configure command with the retention policy to recovery window of days keywords, as shown here:

```
RMAN> configure retention policy to recovery window of 2 days;
```

To disable the retention policy, use the configure command with the retention policy to none keywords, as shown here:

```
RMAN> configure retention policy to none;
```

Compression

RMAN has long offered *white-space compression*. Essentially, this means that blocks in a datafile that are not used do not get backed up. White-space compression is quite helpful for a database that is sized quite large but contains little data. It is less helpful for well-packed databases.

In these cases, you will want to take advantage of actual *backup set compression*. This is compression not unlike that available with operating system programs like pkzip, gzip, and compress. Oracle Database 11*g* offers two flavors of compression, zlib and bzip2 (the default). Zlib is designed to compress with a minimum of CPU impact. The result is often a slightly bigger backup image than you get with the bzip2 compression format.

You can configure compression as a default value with the `configure compression algorithm` command followed by the compression format name, as shown in this example:

```
RMAN> configure compression algorithm 'zlib';
```

To actually perform a backup with compression, you will need to configure the default device type to use compression, or you will have to use the `as compressed` keyword when issuing the backup command. Here is an example of configuring the default device type to use compression:

```
RMAN> configure device type disk backup type to compressed backupset;
```

And here is an example of using the `as compressed` keyword when creating a backup:

```
backup as compressed backupset database plus archivelog;
```

Real World Scenario

The Hidden Talents of Compression

Sometimes there's a product feature that has hidden benefits. Compression is one of these. While compression can help reduce the size of your backup sets, there is another potential feature that we look at in the real world, and that is an overall reduction in I/O. With compression enabled, we often see a reduction in backup and recovery times since there is less disk I/O associated with the backup. This can result in reduced backup times, and the backups may have less impact on the overall system.

Everything comes with a price, though, and in this case it's CPU. Compression comes with a high CPU cost. On systems where there was plenty of CPU to go around, we have seen compression significantly reduce backup times and I/O impacts.

Encryption

You can choose to encrypt your backups in Oracle Database 11*g*. Several encryption options are available to you, and they can be found by querying the V$RMAN_ENCRYPTION_ALGORITHMS view. You can use the configure command to define the default level of encryption that you want to use. You then use the configure command to enable encryption for the entire database or for specific tablespaces.

For example, if you wanted to configure encryption for the entire database, you would use the following commands:

```
RMAN> configure encryption algorithm "AES128";
RMAN> configure encryption for database on;
```

Encryption options for a given tablespace will take precedence over the database global settings. Thus, you can enable global encryption for the database and disable it for a specific tablespace.

There are three different modes of encryption (as opposed to the algorithm used). These are transparent mode, password-based encryption, and dual-mode encryption, which encompasses both modes of encryption. For transparent encryption, you will need to create a wallet, and it must be open. Transparent encryption will then occur automatically after you have issued the configure encryption for database on or configure encryption for tablespace on command.

For password authentication, you will need to use the set encryption identified by command first to enable password-based authentication. If you are restoring you will have to use the set decryption identified by command to set the password to decrypt a backup. You can also use the set command to change the type of encryption for a specific backup or to turn off encryption. Here is an example of the use of the set encryption command:

```
RMAN> set encryption identified by my_pass only on for all tablespaces;
```

Channel Configuration

When you initiate an RMAN backup, RMAN will create one or more channels that connect the database to a backup device. By default, RMAN will create a single channel to back up or recover to or from the FRA. You can override the defaults using the configure command. Along with backup locations, the configure command allows you to define other settings for your backup channels, including parallelism and backup-set and piece-set sizing. In the following sections, you'll learn about using the configure command to define default backup locations, about configuring parallelism, and then about using the configure command to set other channel-related parameters.

Configuring Backup Locations

The `configure default device` command is used to configure a backup location other than the default location. If, for example, you wanted to back up to a directory called `/oracle01/backup/orcl`, you would issue the following command:

```
RMAN> configure channel device type disk format '/oracle01/backup/orcl/%U';
```

RMAN will use this path for future backups. You can configure multiple channels with the `configure` command by specifying each individual channel, as shown here where we have indicated different default backup locations for each channel:

```
RMAN> configure channel 1 device type disk format '/oracle01/backup/orcl/%U';
RMAN> configure channel 2 device type disk FORMAT '/oracle02/backup/orcl/%U';
```

You might have wondered about the `%U` in the backup location format. The `%U` is an *RMAN backup format specification*. There are a number of different format specifications. `%U` is the most common because it ensures a unique filename for each backup set piece created by RMAN. Table 4.2 provides a list of the most common format specifications.

TABLE 4.2 Format Options

Option	Description
%a	Specifies the activation ID of the database
%c	Specifies the copy number of the backup piece within a set of duplexed backup pieces
%d	Specifies the name of the database
%D	Specifies the current day of the month from the Gregorian calendar
%e	Specifies the archived log sequence number
%f	Specifies the absolute file number
%F	Combines the database ID (DBID), day, month, year, and sequence into a unique and repeatable generated name
%h	Specifies the archived redo log thread number
%I	Specifies the DBID
%M	Specifies the month in the Gregorian calendar in *MM* format

TABLE 4.2 Format Options *(continued)*

Option	Description
%N	Specifies the tablespace name.
%n	Specifies the name of the database, padded on the right with *n* characters to a total length of eight characters.
%p	Specifies the piece number within the backup set.
%s	Specifies the backup-set number.
%t	Specifies the backup-set timestamp.
%T	Specifies the year, month, and day in the Gregorian calendar.
%u	Specifies an eight-character name constituted by compressed representations of the backup-set or image-copy number.
%U	Specifies a system-generated unique filename (this is the default setting).

Configuring Parallelism

Now that you can configure multiple channels, you might want to use them! To do so, you use the `configure` command along with the `parallelism` keyword, as shown here:

```
RMAN> configure device type disk parallelism 2;
```

This will cause any `backup database` command to use two channels, performing the backup in parallel.

Other Channel Configuration Options

You have already seen how to configure channels for alternate backup locations and parallelism, but there are other things you might want to configure for a given channel. In this section we will discuss the following channel-configuration options, which you will want to be aware of:

- SBT channel configuration
- `Maxsetsize` and `Maxpiecesize` configuration

SBT CHANNEL CONFIGURATION

First, most of our examples in this chapter have identified disk-based locations for backups. You may well want to have your backup go to tape instead. To do so, you will need to install the vendor's interface into RMAN's MML API, following the vendor's instructions. Once you have done so, you would then allocate a channel (or more if you want parallel backups) to a device called SBT to send it to the tape device. Here is an example where we use the `configure` command to make the SBT device the default device:

```
configure device type sbt parallelism 2;
```

Or you could configure individual channels like this:

```
RMAN> configure channel 1 device type sbt;
RMAN> configure channel 2 device type sbt;
```

During the backup, you could manually allocate channels to SBT also within a run block:

```
run {
allocate channel c1 device type sbt;
allocate channel c2 device type sbt;
backup database plus archivelog;
};
```

MAXSETSIZE AND *MAXPIECESIZE* CONFIGURATION

You may find that you need to limit the size of your backups. For example, you may find that the OS that you are working on has a maximum file-size limit of 2GB. Thus, you need to make sure your backup set pieces are no larger than 2GB. This is facilitated through the use of the `maxsetsize` and `maxpiecesize` operators.

The `maxsetsize` operator will limit the size of any backup set. The `maxpiecesize` operator will limit the size of any individual backup set piece. Here is an example of configuring a default channel with a `maxpiecesize` setting:

```
RMAN> configure channel 1 device type disk maxpiecesize 2g;
```

The main use of the `maxpiecesize` parameter is to ensure that your backup set pieces do not grow bigger than some OS, file system, or storage device limit. For example, if each of your tapes can hold only 200GB of data, then you would want to limit the size of each backup set piece to 200GB.

`Maxsetsize` has essentially the same purpose, to limit the overall size of one backup set. The downside to using `maxsetsize` is that if you end up with a datafile that is larger than `maxsetsize`, it will never get backed up since each datafile must be backed up within the scope of one backup set.

Control-File Autobackups

When enabled, RMAN will perform automatic control-file autobackups after each backup. Additionally, RMAN/Oracle will automatically create a backup of the control file to disk anytime a database change occurs that impacts the control file and the database physical structure, such as adding a tablespace or datafile.

To enable control-file autobackups through RMAN, use the `configure` command with the `controlfile autobackup on` keyword, as shown here:

```
RMAN> configure controlfile autobackup on;
```

Control-file autobackups are stored in the FRA if one is configured. You can also use the `configure` command to configure RMAN to create the control-file autobackup in a different location, as shown in this example:

```
configure controlfile autobackup format for device type disk to
'/oracle01/oracle/controfilebackup/%F';
```

In this example, notice the use of the `%F` format specifier. `%F` is required when defining the location of the backup control file. This will ensure that the backup control file name is unique each time the backup is created.

Backup Optimization

Sometimes things don't change, like some of our T-shirts (they are older than we are!) and read-only datafiles. When this happens, you don't need to back them up if they have already been backed up. *Backup optimization* provides the ability to tell RMAN that you don't want to back up a database datafile if that backup is not needed. This saves time and effort on the part of RMAN. RMAN still follows all the rules of retention, backup files are expired when they are set to expire, and if the retention policy calls for two copies of a datafile, then the datafile will be backed up two times. However, on the third backup of the database, the read-only datafile will not be backed up, because the two identical copies are sufficient for recovery.

To configure backup optimization, use the `configure` command with the `backup optimization on` keyword, as shown here:

```
RMAN> configure backup optimization on;
```

Snapshot Control-File Location

As we mentioned earlier, Oracle places the snapshot control file in the `ORACLE_HOME/dbs` directory. As a part of the setup of RMAN, you should change the location of the snapshot control file by using the `configure` command, as shown here:

```
configure snapshot controlfile name to '/oracle01/backup/sncf/sncforcl.ora';
```

Backup Tags

When you create backups, you can optionally tag them. If you do not tag a backup, RMAN will tag it for you. A *tag* is a name that you assign to the backup, such as, for example, Gold Copy (perhaps you re-create your database every day with the backup tagged Gold Copy). You can easily restore and recover the database using the tag as the key for the recovery. We will discuss using tags to recover your database in Chapter 6. Here is an example of performing a backup with a tag included:

```
RMAN> backup database tag 'DPrestwich' plus archivelog
tag='ARCH_GOLD' delete input;
```

Duplexing Backups

You may want to create duplicate copies of backup sets when they are created. This is called *duplexing*. Duplexing of backup sets can be configured as a default setting by using the `configure` command, as shown here:

```
RMAN>configure datafile backup copies for device type disk to 2;
```

You can also configure duplexing for archive log backups, as shown here:

```
RMAN>configure archivelog backup copies for device type disk to 2;
```

Note that you can duplex across similar devices only. So you can duplex across tape devices or across disk devices but not both.

If you want to duplex an individual backup rather than set a persistent configuration setting, you would use the `set backup copies` command within a RUN block, as in this example:

```
RMAN> run
2> {
3> allocate channel d1 device type disk format 'c:\oracle\backup\%U';
4> set backup copies 2;
5> backup incremental level 0 database plus archivelog delete input;
6> }
```

In Exercise 4.1, you'll configure some RMAN settings.

EXERCISE 4.1

Configuring RMAN

1. Start RMAN from the command line:

```
C:\oracle\admin\ORCL\wallet>rman target=/
Recovery Manager: Release 11.1.0.6.0 - Production
```

EXERCISE 4.1 *(continued)*

```
on Thu Sep 11 18:28:24 2008
Copyright (c) 1982, 2007, Oracle.  All rights reserved.
connected to target database: ORCL (DBID=1190537904)
```

2. Display your RMAN configuration (yours may look different than our output—that's okay):

```
RMAN> show all;
RMAN configuration parameters for database with db_unique_name ORCL are:
CONFIGURE RETENTION POLICY TO REDUNDANCY 1;
CONFIGURE BACKUP OPTIMIZATION ON;
CONFIGURE DEFAULT DEVICE TYPE TO DISK; # default
CONFIGURE CONTROLFILE AUTOBACKUP OFF;
CONFIGURE CONTROLFILE AUTOBACKUP FORMAT FOR DEVICE
TYPE DISK TO '%F'; # default
CONFIGURE DEVICE TYPE DISK PARALLELISM 1 BACKUP
TYPE TO BACKUPSET; # default
CONFIGURE DATAFILE BACKUP COPIES FOR DEVICE TYPE DISK TO 1; # default
CONFIGURE ARCHIVELOG BACKUP COPIES FOR DEVICE TYPE DISK TO 1; # default
CONFIGURE MAXSETSIZE TO UNLIMITED; # default
CONFIGURE ENCRYPTION FOR DATABASE OFF;
CONFIGURE ENCRYPTION ALGORITHM 'AES128';
CONFIGURE COMPRESSION ALGORITHM 'zlib';
CONFIGURE ARCHIVELOG DELETION POLICY TO NONE; # default
CONFIGURE SNAPSHOT CONTROLFILE NAME TO 'C:\ORACLE\PRODUCT\11.1.0\DB_1\
DATABASE\SNCFORCL.ORA'; # default
```

3. Configure the retention policy to redundancy of 2:

```
RMAN> CONFIGURE RETENTION POLICY TO REDUNDANCY 2;
old RMAN configuration parameters:
CONFIGURE RETENTION POLICY TO REDUNDANCY 1;
new RMAN configuration parameters:
CONFIGURE RETENTION POLICY TO REDUNDANCY 2;
new RMAN configuration parameters are successfully stored
```

4. Configure control-file autobackups on:

```
RMAN> CONFIGURE CONTROLFILE AUTOBACKUP on;
old RMAN configuration parameters:
CONFIGURE CONTROLFILE AUTOBACKUP OFF;
new RMAN configuration parameters:
```

EXERCISE 4.1 *(continued)*

```
CONFIGURE CONTROLFILE AUTOBACKUP ON;
new RMAN configuration parameters are successfully stored
```

5. Configure for compressed backup sets:

```
RMAN> CONFIGURE DEVICE TYPE DISK PARALLELISM 1 BACKUP
TYPE TO COMPRESSED BACKUPSET;
new RMAN configuration parameters:
CONFIGURE DEVICE TYPE DISK PARALLELISM 1 BACKUP TYPE
TO COMPRESSED BACKUPSET;
new RMAN configuration parameters are successfully stored
```

6. Create a directory to hold the snapshot control file (you will want to use your own directory paths, of course):

```
RMAN> host "mkdir \oracle01";
host command complete
RMAN> host "mkdir \oracle01\snapshot";
host command complete
```

7. Configure RMAN so the snapshot control file will be created in the new directory:

```
RMAN> CONFIGURE SNAPSHOT CONTROLFILE NAME TO 'c:\oracle01\snapshot';
new RMAN configuration parameters:
CONFIGURE SNAPSHOT CONTROLFILE NAME TO 'c:\oracle01\snapshot';
new RMAN configuration parameters are successfully stored
```

8. Exit RMAN:

```
RMAN> exit
Recovery Manager complete.
```

Backing Up Your Database with RMAN

We will discuss backups of your database using RMAN in the following sections. We will first talk about the different types of backups that you can make with RMAN. Then we will discuss what you can back up using RMAN, such as the database, archived redo logs, and so forth.

Using the RMAN Command Line

Like SQL and SQL*Plus, RMAN has its own unique command set. You use these commands to do a number of things:

- Configure RMAN
- Back up database structures (tablespaces, datafiles, control files, and so on)
- Restore and recover your database
- Produce various reports and lists that contain backup-related information.
- Create duplicate databases
- Restore specific tablespaces

This is just a partial list of all the things RMAN can do for you. Table 4.3 describes the RMAN commands you will need to be aware of for the OCP exam.

TABLE 4.3 RMAN Commands

RMAN Command	Description
@	Run a command file.
@@	Run a command file in the same directory as another command file that is currently running. The @@ command differs from the @ command only when run from within a command file.
ALLOCATE CHANNEL	Establish a channel, which is a connection between RMAN and a database instance.
ALLOCATE CHANNEL FOR MAINTENANCE	Allocate a channel in preparation for issuing maintenance commands such as DELETE.
allocOperandList	A subclause that specifies channel control options such as PARMS and FORMAT.
ALTER DATABASE	Mount or open a database.
archivelogRecordSpecifier	Specify a range of archived redo-log files.
BACKUP	Back up database files, copies of database files, archived logs, or backup sets.
BLOCKRECOVER	Recover an individual data block or set of data blocks within one or more datafiles.
CATALOG	Add information about a datafile copy, archived redo log, or control file copy to the repository.

TABLE 4.3 RMAN Commands *(continued)*

RMAN Command	Description
CHANGE	Mark a backup piece, image copy, or archived redo log as having the status UNAVAILABLE or AVAILABLE; remove the repository record for a backup or copy; override the retention policy for a backup or copy.
completedTimeSpec	Specify a time range during which the backup or copy completed.
CONFIGURE	Configure persistent RMAN settings. These settings apply to all RMAN sessions until explicitly changed or disabled.
CONNECT	Establish a connection between RMAN and a target, auxiliary, or recovery catalog database.
connectStringSpec	Specify the username, password, and net service name for connecting to a target, recovery catalog, or auxiliary database. The connection is necessary to authenticate the user and identify the database.
CONVERT	Convert datafile formats for transporting tablespaces across platforms.
CREATE CATALOG	Create the schema for the recovery catalog.
CREATE SCRIPT	Create a stored script and store it in the recovery catalog.
CROSSCHECK	Determine whether files managed by RMAN, such as archived logs, datafile copies, and backup pieces, still exist on disk or tape.
datafileSpec	Specify a datafile by filename or absolute file number.
DELETE	Delete backups and copies, remove references to them from the recovery catalog, and update their control-file records to status DELETED.
DELETE SCRIPT	Delete a stored script from the recovery catalog.
deviceSpecifier	Specify the type of storage device for a backup or copy.
DROP CATALOG	Remove the schema from the recovery catalog.
DROP DATABASE	Delete the target database from disk and unregister it.

TABLE 4.3 RMAN Commands *(continued)*

RMAN Command	Description
DUPLICATE	Use backups of the target database to create a duplicate database that you can use for testing purposes or to create a standby database.
EXECUTE SCRIPT	Run an RMAN stored script.
EXIT	Quit the RMAN executable.
fileNameConversionSpec	Specify patterns to transform source to target filenames during BACKUP AS COPY, CONVERT, and DUPLICATE.
FLASHBACK	Return the database to a previous state as defined by a previous time or system change number (SCN).
formatSpec	Specify a filename format for a backup or copy.
HOST	Invoke an operating-system command-line subshell from within RMAN or run a specific operating-system command.
keepOption	Specify that a backup or copy should or should not be exempt from the current retention policy.
LIST	Produce a detailed listing of backup sets or copies.
listObjList	A subclause used to specify which items will be displayed by the LIST command.
maintQualifier	A subclause used to specify additional options for maintenance commands such as DELETE and CHANGE.
maintSpec	A subclause used to specify the files operated on by maintenance commands such as CHANGE, CROSSCHECK, and DELETE.
obsOperandList	A subclause used to determine which backups and copies are obsolete.
PRINT SCRIPT	Display a stored script.
QUIT	Exit the RMAN executable.
recordSpec	A subclause used to specify the objects on which the maintenance commands should operate.

TABLE 4.2 RMAN Commands Description *(continued)*

RMAN Command	Description
RECOVER	Apply redo logs and incremental backups to datafiles restored from backup or datafile copies in order to update them to a specified time.
REGISTER	Register the target database in the recovery catalog.
RELEASE CHANNEL	Release a channel that was allocated with an ALLOCATE CHANNEL command.
releaseForMaint	Release a channel that was allocated with an ALLOCATE CHANNEL FOR MAINTENANCE command.
REPLACE SCRIPT	Replace an existing script stored in the recovery catalog. If the script does not exist, then REPLACE SCRIPT creates it.
REPORT	Perform detailed analyses of the content of the recovery catalog.
RESET DATABASE	Inform RMAN that the SQL statement ALTER DATABASE OPEN RESETLOGS has been executed and that a new incarnation of the target database has been created, or reset the target database to a prior incarnation.
RESTORE	Restore files from backup sets or from disk copies to the default or to a new location.
RESYNC	Perform a full resynchronization, which creates a snapshot control file and then copies any new or changed information from that snapshot control file to the recovery catalog.
RUN	Execute a sequence of one or more RMAN commands, which are one or more statements executed within the braces of a RUN block.
SEND	Send a vendor-specific quoted string to one or more specific channels.
SET	Set the value of various attributes that affect RMAN behavior for the duration of a RUN block or a session.
SHOW	Display the current CONFIGURE settings.
SHUTDOWN	Shut down the target database. This command is equivalent to the SQL*Plus SHUTDOWN command.

TABLE 4.2 RMAN Commands Description *(continued)*

RMAN Command	Description
SPOOL	Write RMAN output to a log file.
SQL	Execute a SQL statement from within RMAN.
STARTUP	Start up the target database. This command is equivalent to the SQL*Plus STARTUP command.
SWITCH	Specify that a datafile copy is now the current datafile; that is, the datafile pointed to by the control file. This command is equivalent to the SQL statement ALTER DATABASE RENAME FILE as it applies to datafiles.
UNREGISTER DATABASE	Unregister a database from the recovery catalog.
untilClause	A subclause specifying an upper limit by time, SCN, or log sequence number. This clause is usually used to specify the desired point in time for an incomplete recovery.
UPGRADE CATALOG	Upgrade the recovery-catalog schema from an older version to the version required by the RMAN executable.
VALIDATE	Examine a backup set and report whether its data is intact. RMAN scans all of the backup pieces in the specified backup sets and looks at the checksums to verify that the contents can be successfully restored.

Types of RMAN Backups

There are two principle types of RMAN backups. The first type is called backup sets. *Backup sets* are a very flexible way of backing up your Oracle database. The downside is that backup sets are not direct copies of Oracle database datafiles. As a result, you need RMAN to put the backup sets back together to restore your database.

Oracle also supports *image copies*. Image copies are direct copies of database datafiles. Image copies offer faster recovery options but typically take up a great deal more space. In the following sections, we will address these two types of RMAN backups in more detail.

RMAN Backup Sets

By default, when you create a backup in RMAN, it writes the backups to physical files. These physical files are called *backup set pieces* (RMAN can also create backups called image copies, which we will discuss later in this section). A given backup may create more than one backup set piece. A collection of related backup set pieces is called a *backup set*. A backup set is a logical entity that is used to maintain the association of independent backup set pieces.

In addition to multiple backup set pieces, you may have more than one backup set. This occurs when you parallelize a backup. Each channel will represent one backup set, each with its own backup set pieces. New backup sets will also be created on a channel if a backup set exceeds the backup set size limitations.

Note that a given datafile can span backup set pieces but cannot span backup sets. The ability of a given datafile to span backup set pieces is known as *multiplexing*. Multiplexing is another form of parallelization, as it allows RMAN to read from multiple datafiles in parallel and write them to a single backup set piece. Thus a given backup set piece may have data from many datafiles in it.

In the default RMAN configuration, a given tablespace/datafile backup may find itself in more than one backup set piece. However, each individual tablespace/datafile backup can be associated with only a single RMAN backup set and thus will be backed up by only one channel.

Oracle Database 11*g* has a new feature called multisection backups. *Multisection backups* allow you to parallelize the backup of large datafiles (bigfile tablespaces or normal tablespaces). You may well find questions on multisection backups on your OCP exam.

Figure 4.2 demonstrates the relationship between backups, backup sets, and backup set pieces.

FIGURE 4.2 Relationship between RMAN backups, backup sets, and backup set pieces

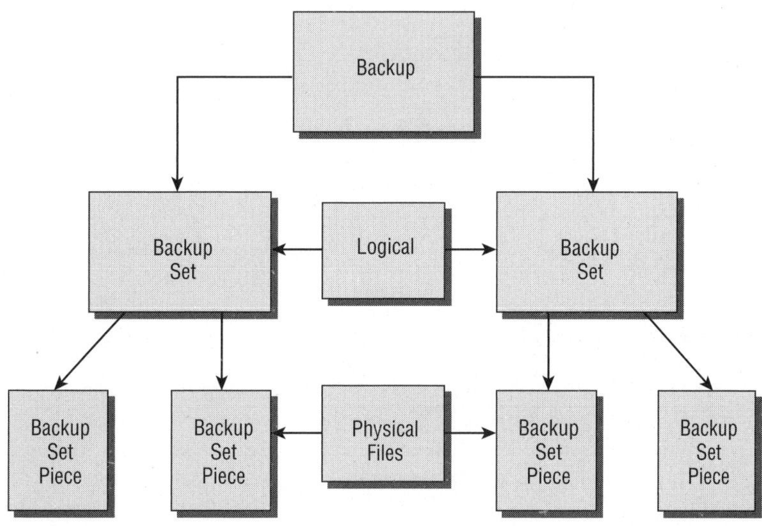

RMAN Image Copies

RMAN image copies are one-to-one copies of database datafiles. When you do an image-copy backup of your database, you will receive no benefits of compression, so the disk-space requirement is a one-to-one requirement. Image copies must be made to disk. Figure 4.3 shows the difference between image and regular backups.

FIGURE 4.3 Image vs. regular backups

The upside to an image copy is that it can be much faster to restore. RMAN will always choose to restore image copies over backup sets if an image copy is available. In fact, using the `switch to copy` command makes it even faster, as RMAN will simply switch to the image copy on disk and start using that copy (applying redo as required). To make an image copy, use the `backup as copy` command, as shown in this example:

```
RMAN> Backup as copy database;
```

You can also make image copies of datafiles or tablespaces, as shown in these examples:

```
RMAN>backup as copy datafile 4;
RMAN>Backup as copy tablespace users;
```

If you prefer to always use image copies rather than backup sets, you can configure RMAN to do so by default with the `configure` command, as seen here:

```
configure device type disk backup type to copy;
```

RMAN can use a mixture of image copies, incremental backups, and archived redo logs when performing recovery (which we will discuss in more detail in Chapter 5). This can make total recovery of your database, a tablespace, or a datafile much quicker.

RMAN Offline Backups

We discussed manual offline backups in Chapter 2. Offline backups in RMAN are not much different except that you use the RMAN interface to actually do the backup rather than an OS file-copy utility. You will still need to close the database, but your backup will be done with the database in mount mode rather than completely shut down.

No parameter-file adjustments are required for an RMAN offline backup. We recommend that you configure and use the FRA (discussed earlier in this chapter) even if you are doing offline backups. This makes for a standardized backup location and also allows the Oracle database to manage the overall backup space utilization more efficiently.

To perform an offline backup of your database with RMAN, follow these steps:

1. Start the RMAN client.
2. Shut down the database from the RMAN client, SQL*Plus, or OEM. The shutdown should be a consistent shutdown, so use the `shutdown`, `shutdown immediate`, or `shutdown transactional` command.
3. Start up the database in mount mode using the `startup mount` command.
4. Back up the database with the RMAN `backup` command:

   ```
   RMAN>backup database;
   ```

5. When the backup is complete, open the database with the `alter database open` command.

RMAN Online Backups

For online backups in RMAN, the database must be configured in ARCHIVELOG mode (see Chapter 2 for more on configuring the database for ARCHIVELOG-mode operations). Once the database is configured properly, and RMAN is configured properly (as discussed earlier in this chapter), you can do online backups.

Online backups with RMAN are easy. You need to make sure the database and the archived redo logs are backed up; thus you issue the command `backup database plus archivelog`. That's it. That command will create a recoverable backup of the database. This is known as a *whole database backup*.

If you want to delete the archived redo logs after the backup, you would append the `delete input` clause to the command. Other options are available depending on your needs.

In the following example we perform an online backup of our database using the `backup as compressed backupset database plus archivelog delete input` command. This will create a compressed backup of the database, backing up the archived redo logs and then deleting those backed-up archived redo logs after the backup is complete. Also note that we have configured control-file autobackups.

```
RMAN> backup as compressed backupset database plus archivelog delete input;
Starting backup at 05-SEP-08
current log archived
allocated channel: ORA_DISK_1
channel ORA_DISK_1: SID=131 device type=DISK
channel ORA_DISK_1: starting compressed archived log backup set
channel ORA_DISK_1: specifying archived log(s) in backup set
input archived log thread=1 sequence=41 RECID=40 STAMP=664583178
input archived log thread=1 sequence=42 RECID=41 STAMP=664621168
```

```
input archived log thread=1 sequence=43 RECID=42 STAMP=664650496
input archived log thread=1 sequence=44 RECID=43 STAMP=664655636
channel ORA_DISK_1: starting piece 1 at 05-SEP-08
channel ORA_DISK_1: finished piece 1 at 05-SEP-08
piece handle=C:\ORACLE\FLASH_RECOVERY_AREA\ORCL\BACKUPSET\2008_09_05\
O1_MF_ANNNN_TAG20080905T183357_4D3N085C_.BKP tag=TAG20080905T183357
comment=NONE
channel ORA_DISK_1: backup set complete, elapsed time: 00:00:15
channel ORA_DISK_1: deleting archived log(s)
archived log file name=C:\ORACLE\ARCH\ORCL\ARC00041_0662757171.001
RECID=40 STAMP=664583178
archived log file name=C:\ORACLE\ARCH\ORCL\ARC00042_0662757171.001
RECID=41 STAMP=664621168
archived log file name=C:\ORACLE\ARCH\ORCL\ARC00043_0662757171.001
RECID=42 STAMP=664650496
archived log file name=C:\ORACLE\ARCH\ORCL\ARC00044_0662757171.001
RECID=43 STAMP=664655636
Finished backup at 05-SEP-08
Starting backup at 05-SEP-08
using channel ORA_DISK_1
channel ORA_DISK_1: starting compressed full datafile backup set
channel ORA_DISK_1: specifying datafile(s) in backup set
input datafile file number=00002 name=C:\ORACLE\ORADATA\ORCL\SYSAUX01.DBF
input datafile file number=00001 name=C:\ORACLE\ORADATA\ORCL\SYSTEM01.DBF
input datafile file number=00005 name=C:\ORACLE\ORADATA\ORCL\UNDOTBS02.DBF
input datafile file number=00004 name=C:\ORACLE\ORADATA\ORCL\USERS01.DBF
channel ORA_DISK_1: starting piece 1 at 05-SEP-08
channel ORA_DISK_1: finished piece 1 at 05-SEP-08
piece handle=C:\ORACLE\FLASH_RECOVERY_AREA\ORCL\BACKUPSET\2008_09_05\
O1_MF_NNNDF_TAG20080905T183432_4D3N0Z0Z_.BKP tag=TAG20080905T183432
comment=NONE
channel ORA_DISK_1: starting piece 2 at 05-SEP-08
channel ORA_DISK_1: finished piece 2 at 05-SEP-08
piece handle=C:\ORACLE\FLASH_RECOVERY_AREA\ORCL\BACKUPSET\2008_09_05
\O1_MF_NNNDF_TAG20080905T183432_4D3N63Y8_.BKP tag=TAG20080905T183432
comment=NONE
channel ORA_DISK_1: starting piece 3 at 05-SEP-08
channel ORA_DISK_1: finished piece 3 at 05-SEP-08
```

```
piece handle=C:\ORACLE\FLASH_RECOVERY_AREA\ORCL\BACKUPSET\2008_09_05\
O1_MF_NNNDF_TAG20080905T183432_4D3N9PY8_.BKP tag=TAG20080905T183432
comment=NONE
channel ORA_DISK_1: backup set complete, elapsed time: 00:04:48
channel ORA_DISK_1: starting compressed full datafile backup set
channel ORA_DISK_1: specifying datafile(s) in backup set
including current control file in backup set
including current SPFILE in backup set
channel ORA_DISK_1: starting piece 1 at 05-SEP-08
channel ORA_DISK_1: finished piece 1 at 05-SEP-08
piece handle=C:\ORACLE\FLASH_RECOVERY_AREA\ORCL\BACKUPSET\2008_09_05\
O1_MF_NCSNF_TAG20080905T183432_4D3NBHXS_.BKP tag=TAG20080905T183432
comment=NONE
channel ORA_DISK_1: backup set complete, elapsed time: 00:00:02
Finished backup at 05-SEP-08
Starting backup at 05-SEP-08
current log archived
using channel ORA_DISK_1
channel ORA_DISK_1: starting compressed archived log backup set
channel ORA_DISK_1: specifying archived log(s) in backup set
input archived log thread=1 sequence=45 RECID=44 STAMP=664655986
channel ORA_DISK_1: starting piece 1 at 05-SEP-08
channel ORA_DISK_1: finished piece 1 at 05-SEP-08
piece handle=C:\ORACLE\FLASH_RECOVERY_AREA\ORCL\BACKUPSET\2008_09_05\
O1_MF_ANNNN_TAG20080905T183946_4D3NBS89_.BKP tag=TAG20080905T183946
comment=NONE
channel ORA_DISK_1: backup set complete, elapsed time: 00:00:01
channel ORA_DISK_1: deleting archived log(s)
archived log file name=C:\ORACLE\ARCH\ORCL\ARC00045_0662757171.001
RECID=44 STAMP=664655986
Finished backup at 05-SEP-08
```

You can also do backups of tablespaces and datafiles using the backup command, as shown in these examples:

```
RMAN>Backup tablespace users;
RMAN>Backup datafile 3;
```

In Exercise 4.2, you'll execute an online backup using RMAN.

EXERCISE 4.2

Executing an Online Backup

In this exercise you will perform an online backup of your ARCHIVELOG mode database. Your database should already be in ARCHIVELOG mode (see Exercise 2.1). Once the database is in ARCHIVELOG mode you can do this exercise.

1. Log into the database using SQL*Plus:

```
C:\oracle\admin\ORCL\wallet>set oracle_sid=orcl
C:\oracle\admin\ORCL\wallet>sqlplus "/ as sysdba"
SQL*Plus: Release 11.1.0.6.0 - Production on Thu Sep 11 18:56:27 2008
Copyright (c) 1982, 2007, Oracle.  All rights reserved.
Connected to:
Oracle Database 11g Enterprise Edition Release 11.1.0.6.0 - Production
With the Partitioning, OLAP, Data Mining and Real Application
Testing options
SQL>
```

2. Query the LOG_MODE column of the V$DATABASE view to confirm that the database is in ARCHIVELOG mode. If the database is not in ARCHIVELOG mode, refer to Chapter 2 for information on how to put the database in ARCHIVELOG mode.

```
SQL> Select log_mode from v$database;
LOG_MODE
------------
ARCHIVELOG
```

3. Exit SQL*Plus and start RMAN:

```
SQL> exit
Disconnected from Oracle Database 11g Enterprise Edition
Release 11.1.0.6.0 - Production
With the Partitioning, OLAP, Data Mining and Real Application
Testing options
C:\oracle\admin\ORCL\wallet>rman target=/
Recovery Manager: Release 11.1.0.6.0 - Production on
Thu Sep 11 18:58:55 2008
Copyright (c) 1982, 2007, Oracle.  All rights reserved.
connected to target database: ORCL (DBID=1190537904)
```

4. Execute the RMAN backup using the `backup database` command. Back up the archived redo logs at the same time with the `plus archivelog` option. Remove the archived redo logs after they are backed up using the `delete input` option.

```
RMAN> Backup database plus archivelog delete input;
```

EXERCISE 4.2 *(continued)*

5. Review the output, and make sure the backup was successful. Here is an example of our output. We bolded the messages that indicate a successful backup.

```
RMAN> Backup database plus archivelog delete input;
Starting backup at 11-SEP-08
current log archived
using target database control file instead of recovery catalog
allocated channel: ORA_DISK_1
channel ORA_DISK_1: SID=128 device type=DISK
channel ORA_DISK_1: starting compressed archived log backup set
channel ORA_DISK_1: specifying archived log(s) in backup set
input archived log thread=1 sequence=87 RECID=86 STAMP=665092065
input archived log thread=1 sequence=88 RECID=87 STAMP=665138962
input archived log thread=1 sequence=89 RECID=88 STAMP=665172239
input archived log thread=1 sequence=90 RECID=89 STAMP=665172313
input archived log thread=1 sequence=91 RECID=90 STAMP=665172466
input archived log thread=1 sequence=92 RECID=91 STAMP=665175694
channel ORA_DISK_1: starting piece 1 at 11-SEP-08
channel ORA_DISK_1: finished piece 1 at 11-SEP-08
piece handle=C:\ORACLE\FLASH_RECOVERY_AREA\ORCL
\BACKUPSET\2008_09_11\O1_MF_ANNNN_TAG20080911T190135_4DMHVZFK_.BKP
tag=TAG20080911T190135 comment=NONE
channel ORA_DISK_1: backup set complete, elapsed time: 00:00:07
channel ORA_DISK_1: deleting archived log(s)
archived log file name=C:\ORACLE\ARCH\ORCL\
ARC00087_0662757171.001 RECID=86 STAMP=665092065
archived log file name=C:\ORACLE\ARCH\ORCL\
ARC00088_0662757171.001 RECID=87 STAMP=665138962
archived log file name=C:\ORACLE\ARCH\ORCL\
ARC00089_0662757171.001 RECID=88 STAMP=665172239
archived log file name=C:\ORACLE\ARCH\ORCL\
ARC00090_0662757171.001 RECID=89 STAMP=665172313
archived log file name=C:\ORACLE\ARCH\ORCL\
ARC00091_0662757171.001 RECID=90 STAMP=665172466
archived log file name=C:\ORACLE\ARCH\ORCL\
ARC00092_0662757171.001 RECID=91 STAMP=665175694
Finished backup at 11-SEP-08
Starting backup at 11-SEP-08
using channel ORA_DISK_1
```

EXERCISE 4.2 *(continued)*

```
channel ORA_DISK_1: starting compressed full datafile backup set
channel ORA_DISK_1: specifying datafile(s) in backup set
input datafile file number=00002
name=C:\ORACLE\ORADATA\ORCL\SYSAUX01.DBF
input datafile file number=00001
name=C:\ORACLE\ORADATA\ORCL\SYSTEM01.DBF
input datafile file number=00005
name=C:\ORACLE\ORADATA\ORCL\UNDOTBS02.DBF
input datafile file number=00004
name=C:\ORACLE\ORADATA\ORCL\USERS01.DBF
channel ORA_DISK_1: starting piece 1 at 11-SEP-08
channel ORA_DISK_1: finished piece 1 at 11-SEP-08
piece handle=C:\ORACLE\FLASH_RECOVERY_AREA\ORCL
\BACKUPSET\2008_09_11\O1_MF_NNNDF_TAG20080911T190200_4DMHWM1T_.BKP
tag=TAG20080911T190200 comment=NONE
channel ORA_DISK_1: backup set complete, elapsed time: 00:05:36
Finished backup at 11-SEP-08
Starting backup at 11-SEP-08
current log archived
using channel ORA_DISK_1
channel ORA_DISK_1: starting compressed archived log backup set
channel ORA_DISK_1: specifying archived log(s) in backup set
input archived log thread=1 sequence=93 RECID=92 STAMP=665176062
channel ORA_DISK_1: starting piece 1 at 11-SEP-08
channel ORA_DISK_1: finished piece 1 at 11-SEP-08
piece handle=C:\ORACLE\FLASH_RECOVERY_AREA\ORCL
\BACKUPSET\2008_09_11\O1_MF_ANNNN_TAG20080911T190742_4DMJ7H29_.BKP
tag=TAG20080911T190742 comment=NONE
channel ORA_DISK_1: backup set complete, elapsed time: 00:00:01
channel ORA_DISK_1: deleting archived log(s)
archived log file name=C:\ORACLE\ARCH\ORCL
\ARC00093_0662757171.001 RECID=92 STAMP=665176062
Finished backup at 11-SEP-08
Starting Control File and SPFILE Autobackup at 11-SEP-08
piece handle=C:\ORACLE\FLASH_RECOVERY_AREA\ORCL
\AUTOBACKUP\2008_09_11\O1_MF_S_665176080_4DMJ7SOT_.BKP comment=NONE
Finished Control File and SPFILE Autobackup at 11-SEP-08
```

RMAN Incremental Backups

Incremental database backups are a way to quickly back up your database. In the following sections, we will discuss incremental backups. First you'll learn about configuring for incremental backups, next we will look at the two different kinds of incremental backups that are available, and then you'll learn how to actually do incremental backups.

Configuring for Incremental Backups

Technically, you don't have to configure anything to do an incremental backup. RMAN will perform an incremental backup when you issue the appropriate backup command. However, without any configuration, RMAN must inspect each block and determine whether it has indeed changed since the last backup and if it must go into the backup image.

Optionally you can create a *block-change tracking file* that will keep track of blocks that have changed since the last full or incremental backup. This can significantly reduce the time it takes to perform an incremental backup of your database, because it removes the need for Oracle to inspect each data block to determine if it's been changed since the last backup. Figure 4.4 demonstrates the block-change tracking file.

FIGURE 4.4 The block-change tracking file

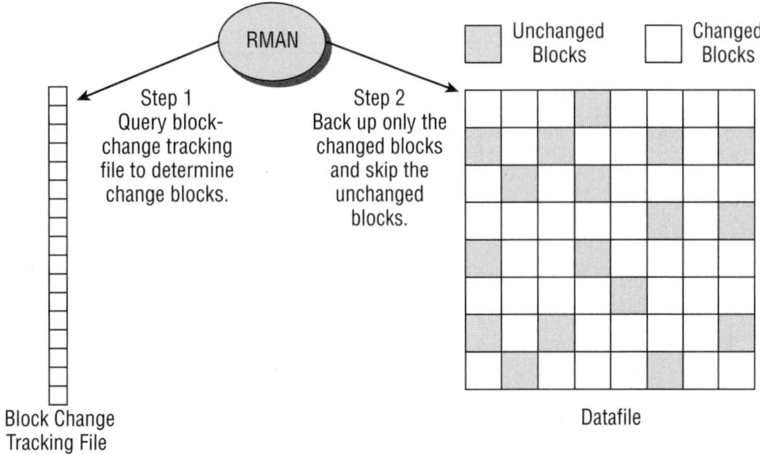

The block-change tracking file can track only a maximum of seven different incremental level-1 backups. After the seventh backup, the initial level-0 backup records will be overwritten in the block-change tracking file. This will result in RMAN having to scan all database blocks on subsequent incremental backups. As a result, limit incremental backups without an intervening level 0 to a maximum of seven.

To create the block-tracking file, use the `alter database enable block change tracking` command. By default, Oracle will create the block-change tracking file in the location defined by the `DB_CREATE_FILE_DEST` parameter. If that parameter is not set, Oracle will require that you provide a destination and filename for the block-change tracking file. Here is an example of the creation of a block-change tracking file:

```
SQL> alter database enable block change tracking using file
'c:\oracle\block_change_tracking\orcl_block_change.fil';
```

You can find the location of the current block-change tracking file by looking at the `FILENAME` column of the `V$BLOCK_CHANGE_TRACKING` view. You can use the `STATUS` column of the `V$BLOCK_CHANGE_TRACKING` view to determine if block-change tracking is enabled.

You should perform a level 0 incremental backup after creating the block-change tracking file. This is because the parent level-0 backup bitmap must be in the block-change tracking file.

Types of Incremental Backups

Two types of incremental backups are available for you to choose from:

- Level-0 incremental backup
- Level-1 incremental backup

The level-0 backup is like a full backup (sometimes it's called a base backup), except that incremental backups can be based on it (they can not be based on a regular full backup).

The level-1 backup is the incremental backup that backs up changed blocks. There are two different kinds of level-1 backups:

- Differential incremental backup
- Cumulative incremental backup

The *differential incremental backup* will back up all changed blocks since the last level-1 backup. These images are typically smaller. The *cumulative incremental backup* is one where the data backed up is the data that changed since the last level-0 full backup. Thus it is a cumulative backup of all changed blocks since the last level-0 backup. This makes for faster recoveries since you don't have to apply several incremental backups during the database restore. Figure 4.5 provides a visual example of the differences between these types of backups.

Performing Incremental Backups

Performing incremental backups is almost exactly like performing regular backups except that you include the `incremental level` option in the backup command. For example, to create a base, level-0 backup, you would issue this command:

```
RMAN> Backup as compressed backupset incremental level 0 database plus archivelog
delete input;
```

When you are ready to run your first incremental backup you would use the backup command with the incremental level-1 option, as shown here:

```
RMAN> Backup as compressed backupset incremental level 1 database plus
archivelog delete input;
```

FIGURE 4.5 Differential vs. cumulative incremental backups

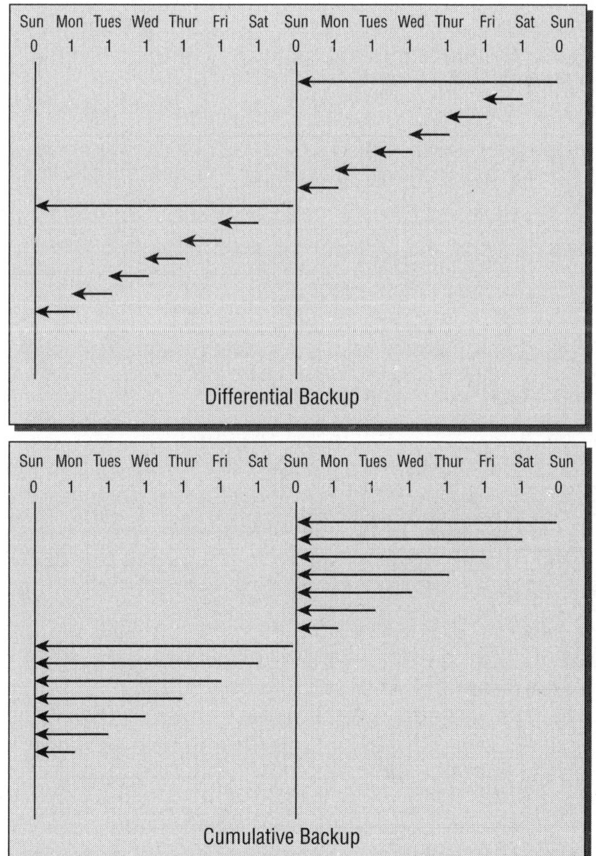

Differential backups are the default type of incremental backup in Oracle. If you want to perform a cumulative backup, you will need to include the `cumulative` keyword, as shown here:

```
RMAN> Backup as compressed backupset incremental level 1 cumulative database
plus archivelog delete input;
```

Note that if you try to do a level-1 backup and a level-0 does not exist, RMAN will not generate an error. It will simply perform a level-0 backup for you instead.

RMAN Incrementally Updated Backups

Incrementally updated backups involve a combination of a full image backup of the database and then subsequent level-1 incremental backups of the database, which are applied to the image-copy backup. An incrementally updated backup makes for a quicker restore but for a bigger backup image.

To create an incrementally updated backup, all you need do is run the following script:

```
RUN { # the recover copy command does not really recover anything.
      # it simply tells RMAN that the incremental to be executed should
      # be applied to the database copy we made above.
      Recover copy of database with tag 'Jacob_Jared_Lizzie';
      Backup incremental level 1
      for recover of copy with tag 'Jacob_Jared_Lizzie' Database; }
```

On the first execution of this script, RMAN will detect that no backup copy exists. Warnings will be generated, but no errors. RMAN will proceed to create the initial copy of the database. No incremental copy will be created.

On subsequent executions, RMAN will detect that an image copy does exist, and it will then apply the previous level-1 incremental-and then execute another level-1 incremental backup. Note that on the second run, RMAN will detect that no incremental backup exists to apply to the datafile copy and a warning will be raised because of this. That is normal.

This method limits the recovery window for your database to one day. For example, if you executed this script on day 1, day 2, and day 3, after day 3's execution you would not be able to restore your database to any point before day 3's backup.

You could provide for longer recovery windows by including the `until time` clause. In this example, we allow for a recovery window of five days:

```
run {
  recover copy of database with tag 'lisa' until time 'sysdate - 5';
  backup  incremental level 1 for recover of copy with tag 'lisa' database;
}
```

RMAN Multisection Backups

Prior to Oracle Database 11g, you could not parallelize the backup of a given database datafile. Since datafiles had to be contained wholly within a single backup set, this meant that the backup of that datafile was serialized. This can be a bit of a problem if your database consists of one or two huge datafiles and several smaller datafiles. Also, if you are using bigfile tablespaces, the lack of inner-file backup parallelization could be a big issue.

Oracle Database 11*g* provides a new feature called *multisection backups* that provides the ability to parallelize the backup of a single datafile. This feature is supported by the section size clause in the backup command followed by the desired section size. Here is an example:

```
RMAN> backup section size 40m database;
```

In this example, RMAN will chunk up each datafile into 40MB chunks, and each allocated channel can process those individual 40MB chunks. Note that if you allocate only one channel, only one chunk at a time will get backed up! Also note that the size parameter does not indicate the size of the resulting backup set piece. Rather, it is the equivalent amount of data within the datafile that each RMAN channel will process. The resulting pieces can vary wildly in size.

RMAN Backup of Archived Redo Logs

Backing up archived redo logs is an important task since it serves to protect the database's principal recovery mechanism, which is redo. Backing up archived redo logs is done via the `backup archivelog` command. This command requires that you include keywords from the `archivelog specifier` clause, which is used to indicate the archived redo logs that you want to back up. Common keywords that you might use include the following:

- `All`: Backs up all archived redo logs currently on disk
- `Sequence between n and o`: Backs up all archived redo logs available on disk between sequence number n and sequence number o
- `Time between t1 and t2`: Backs up all archived redo logs available on disk between time t1 (the earlier time) and time t2 (the later time)

Here is an example of backing up all archived redo logs, still on disk, that were generated in the last 24 hours:

```
RMAN> backup archivelog time between "sysdate-1" and "sysdate";
Starting backup at 05-SEP-08
using channel ORA_DISK_1
channel ORA_DISK_1: starting archived log backup set
channel ORA_DISK_1: specifying archived log(s) in backup set
input archived log thread=1 sequence=46 RECID=45 STAMP=664657241
channel ORA_DISK_1: starting piece 1 at 05-SEP-08
channel ORA_DISK_1: finished piece 1 at 05-SEP-08
piece handle=C:\ORACLE\FLASH_RECOVERY_AREA\ORCL\BACKUPSET\2008_09_05\
O1_MF_ANNNN_TAG20080905T190103_4D3OLO2G_.BKP tag=TAG20080905T190103
comment=NONE
channel ORA_DISK_1: backup set complete, elapsed time: 00:00:01
Finished backup at 05-SEP-08.
```

Be Careful What You Ask For...You Might Just Get It (Or Not)

Look at the example where we backed up the archived redo logs for the last 24 hours. The command was as follows:

```
backup archivelog time between "sysdate-1" and "sysdate";
```

But guess what happens if you change this command just slightly:

```
RMAN> backup archivelog time between "sysdate" and "sysdate-1";
Starting backup at 05-SEP-08
using channel ORA_DISK_1
RMAN-00571: ===========================================================
RMAN-00569: =============== ERROR MESSAGE STACK FOLLOWS ===============
RMAN-00571: ===========================================================
RMAN-03002: failure of backup command at 09/05/2008 19:02:56
RMAN-20242: specification does not match any archived log in the
recovery catalog
```

If you didn't know any better, you might just think that there are no archived redo logs to back up and assume the backup `archivelog` command worked fine and dandy. In fact, the command failed because you had the from/to dates in the wrong order. This highlights how important it is to make sure you carefully review the syntax of the command you are getting ready to execute and then review the output of RMAN commands and make sure RMAN did what you thought you told it to do.

RMAN Backup of the Spfile and Control Files

We have already discussed control-file autobackups in this chapter. You may find that on occasion you want to do an individual backup of the control file or the spfile.

You have two options in RMAN for control-file backups, using the `backup current controlfile` command or the `backup controlfilecopy` command.

The `backup as copy` command will cause the current control file to be backed up. This is a copy of the control file, so it's like a backup control file. Thus, you could just copy the file into place and treat it as a backup control file. By default the backup will be created in the FRA as would happen in this example:

```
RMAN> backup as copy current controlfile;
```

Or you can choose to define the location of the output control file, as shown in this example:

```
RMAN>backup as copy current controlfile format
'c:\oracle\controlfilebackup\contrf_backup.ctl';
```

The `backup controlfilecopy` command will back up a control-file copy (created with the `alter database backup controlfile to` command or the `backup as copy current controlfile` command). Here is an example of the use of the `backup controlfilecopy` command:

```
SQL>Alter database backup controlfile to
'c:\oracle\controlfilebackup\contrf_backup.ctl';
RMAN>backup controlfilecopy 'c:\oracle\controlfilebackup\contrf_backup.ctl';
```

You can also back up spfiles with RMAN using the `backup spfile` command, as shown in this example:

```
RMAN>Backup spfile;
```

Backing Up RMAN Backup Sets

Often database backups will be initially made to disk, and then later those backups will be backed up to tape. The reason for this is that backing up to disk is generally much faster than backing up to tape. Yet you want to back up to tape so you can offsite the media and because tape tends to be less expensive for longer-term storage (though this is quickly becoming less true).

To back up a backup set, you use the `backup backupset` command, as shown here:

```
RMAN> backup device type sbt backupset all;
```

Summary

In this chapter, we introduced you to RMAN, Oracle's backup and recovery tool of choice. We discussed the many features that make RMAN truly a power backup and recovery tool. We discussed the architecture of RMAN, including backup set pieces, which are the critical component of any RMAN backup.

We then talked about how to configure RMAN so that it is easy to use. Persistent configuration parameters are the key to RMAN's ease of use, and understanding what they are and what they do is key to understanding how RMAN works. There is a number of different configuration options to consider, including parallelism, compression, and encryption, and the OCP exam is poised to ask you about all of them.

Finally, we talked about actually backing up your database with RMAN. We talked about the various kinds of backups available to you, from complete database backups to incremental backups. We covered backing up tablespaces and datafiles and backing up archived redo logs. We even talked about backing up the backups themselves if we were not already talking you into circles enough.

In the following chapters, we will be covering the RMAN recovery catalog, recovering your database with RMAN, reporting from RMAN, and finally, advanced RMAN recovery topics. So there is plenty of fun yet to go. Hang tight—it's going to be a fun ride!

Exam Essentials

Be able to describe the basic RMAN architecture. Understand what backup sets and backup set pieces are. Understand that backup set pieces are physical files that contain the data that has actually been backed up. Understand what the flash recovery area is, what its benefits are, and what parameters are required to configure it.

Be able to configure RMAN. Understand what the RMAN `configure` command does and how to use it. Understand how to use the `show` command to display persistent configuration settings. Understand the use of the different persistent configuration settings, such as compression, encryption, and devices. Know the difference between a disk device and the SBT device (tape). Explain how RMAN retention policies work and how to configure them. Explain what backup optimization is and how it works. Understand how to configure for duplexed backups.

Know how to back up your database with RMAN. Understand the different kinds of backups available in RMAN. Know what a whole database backup is and how to perform it both with configured settings and using a run block. Know how to use the `keep` command to override retention policies. Know what an incremental database backup is and how to perform it. Understand the different kinds of incremental database backups and how to create a block-change tracking file. Know what multiselection backups are and how to create them. Know what image copies are and how to create them. Know how to back up archived redo logs, control files, and spfiles. Know how to back up backup sets.

Review Questions

1. How is block-change tracking enabled?
   A. With `alter database enable block change tracking`
   B. With `alter system enable block change tracking`
   C. With an `init.ora` parameter change
   D. With an spfile parameter change

2. What type of backup is stored in a proprietary RMAN format?
   A. Backup set
   B. Image copy
   C. Backup section
   D. Backup group

3. Consider the following command:

   ```
   Backup database plus archivelog delete input;
   ```

   How many backup sets would be created by this command if the following were true:
   - Control-file auto backups were enabled.
   - The size of backup sets was not restricted.
   - One channel was allocated.

   A. 1
   B. 2
   C. 3
   D. 4
   E. 5

4. Which command creates an image copy?
   A. `backup as copy`
   B. `backup copy`
   C. `copy as backup`
   D. `copy back`

5. Compressed backups work with which of the following commands?
   - **A.** `copy as backup`
   - **B.** `backup as copy`
   - **C.** `backup`
   - **D.** `copy`

6. Which is the correct command to back up the database, back up the archived redo logs, and then remove the backed-up archived redo logs?
   - **A.** `backup database`
   - **B.** `backup database and archivelogs`
   - **C.** `backup database plus archivelogs`
   - **D** `backup database plus archivelog delete input`
   - **E.** `backup database and archivelog delete input`

7. Which of the following best describes a full backup?
   - **A.** All datafiles of a database
   - **B.** All datafiles, archive logs, and control files
   - **C.** All datafiles and control files
   - **D.** All the used blocks in a datafile

8. Which type of backup backs up only data blocks modified since the most recent backup at the same level or lower?
   - **A.** Differential incremental backup
   - **B.** Different incremental backup
   - **C.** Cumulative backup
   - **D.** Cumulative incremental backup

9. Which type of backup must be performed first with an incremental backup?
   - **A.** Level 1
   - **B.** Level 0
   - **C.** Level 2
   - **D.** Level 3

10. Which backup option defines a user-defined name for a backup?
    - **A.** `FORMAT`
    - **B.** `NAME`
    - **C.** `TAG`
    - **D.** `FORMAT U%`

11. Given the following steps, which would be the correct order to create a backup of an Oracle database in NOARCHIVELOG mode?
   a. `shutdown immediate` from RMAN
   b. Log into RMAN
   c. `startup mount` from RMAN
   d. `backup database`
   e. `alter database open`
   f. `backup database plus archivelog delete input`
   A. b, c ,a, d, e
   B. b, a, c, f, e
   C. a, c, e, d
   D. b, a, c, e, f
   E. b, a, c, d, e
12. Which of the following most closely represents an image copy?
   A. Unix `cp` command of a file
   B. Bit-by-bit copy of a file
   C. Windows `COPY` command of a file
   D. All of the above
13. Which dynamic view displays the status of block-change tracking?
   A. `V$BLOCK_CHANGE`
   B. `V$BLOCK_CHANGE_TRACKING`
   C. `V$BLOCKCHANGE`
   D. `V$BLOCK_TRACKING`
14. What feature comes into play to help ensure the completion of the backup should one of three backup devices fail during a backup that is using three different channels?
   A. Channel failover
   B. Restartable backups
   C. Rescheduable backups
   D. Automatic backup recovery
   E. Channel recovery
15. What command would you use to set a persistent setting in RMAN so that backups are all written to a tape device?
   A. `CONFIGURE DEFAULT DEVICE TYPE TO TAPE MEDIA`
   B. `CONFIGURE DEFAULT DEVICE TYPE TO TAPE`
   C. `CONFIGURE DEFAULT DEVICE TYPE TO SBT`
   D. `CONFIGURE DEFAULT DEVICE TYPE TO SBT_TAPE`

16. The CONTROL_FILE_RECORD_KEEP_TIME initialization parameter should be set to what value? (Choose all that apply.)
   - A. The initialization parameter should be set to 0 when the RMAN repository is being used.
   - B. The initialization parameter should be set to greater than 0 with the RMAN repository utilizing the recovery catalog only.
   - C. The initialization parameter should be set to greater than 0 with the RMAN repository utilizing the control file or the recovery catalog.
   - D. The initialization parameter should be set to 0 with the RMAN repository utilizing the control file or the recovery catalog.
   - E. The initialization parameter should never be set to 0 if you are using RMAN.

17. Given the following steps, which would be the correct order to create a backup of an Oracle database in ARCHIVELOG mode with control-file autobackups enabled?
   - a. `backup archivelog all;`
   - b. `backup database all;`
   - c. `backup controlfile;`
   - d. `backup archivelog, database, controlfile delete input;`
   - e. `backup database plus archivelog delete input`
   - A. e
   - B. a, b, a, c
   - C. d
   - D. b, a, c
   - E. b, a, c, d, e

18. Which of the following statements are true about the BACKUP command? (Choose all that apply.)
   - A. The BACKUP command can not be used to make image copies of a datafile.
   - B. The BACKUP command can improve performance by multiplexing backup files.
   - C. The BACKUP can take advantage of the block-change tracking capability.
   - D. The BACKUP command cannot store data in incremental backups.
   - E. The BACKUP command can store data in cumulative incremental backups only.

19. Which command is used to configure RMAN to perform a compressed backup for every backup executed?
   - A. BACKUP AS COMPRESSED BACKUPSET DATABASE
   - B. BACKUP AS COMPRESSED COPY OF DATABASE
   - C. CONFIGURE DEVICE TYPE DISK BACKUP TYPE TO COMPRESSED BACKUPSET
   - D. CONFIGURE DEVICE TYPE DISK BACKUP TYPE COMPRESS
   - E. BACKUP DATABASE COMPRESS

20. You issue the following command:

```
RMAN>CONFIGURE BACKUP OPTIMIZATION ON;
```

What is the result of this command on your backups?

A. An incremental backup strategy will be used automatically.

B. Read-only datafiles will not be backed up as long as backups of those files already exist and those backups meet established retention criteria.

C. RMAN will configure itself for maximum performance at the cost of CPU.

D. RMAN will configure itself for minimal OS/CPU impact at the cost of time to back up the database.

E. RMAN will automatically compress backups.

Answers to Review Questions

1. A. Block-change tracking must be enabled with `alter database enable block change tracking`. The physical location and name of the block-change tracking file must be supplied.
2. A. The backup set is stored in a proprietary RMAN format, where only used blocks are backed up.
3. D. The following backup sets would be created:
   - One for an archive log backup before the main backup.
   - One for the main backup. Since we are using a single channel with no backup-set size restriction, RMAN would create a single backup set.
   - One for an archive log backup after the main backup.
   - One for the control-file autobackup.
4. A. The `backup as copy` command is used to create an image-copy backup.
5. C. Compressed backups work only with backup sets, not image copies. Thus, compressed backups will work only with the `backup` command.
6. D. The correct answer is to use the `backup database plus archivelog delete input` command.
7. D. A full backup is best described by backing up all the used blocks in a datafile or any database file. A full backup can be taken on one database file.
8. A. A differential incremental backup backs up only blocks that have been modified since a backup at the same level or lower.
9. B. A level-0 backup is the first backup that is performed when implementing an incremental backup strategy. A level-0 backup copies all the used blocks as a baseline.
10. C. The `TAG` option is used to name a backup with a user-defined character string.
11. E. The correct order of operations is to log into RMAN and then shut down the database with the `shutdown immediate` command. You then mount the database with the `startup mount` command. Once the database is mounted, you back up the database with the `backup database` command. Finally, after the backup is complete, you open the database.
12. D. Image copies are similar to operating-system copy commands. These equate to bit-by-bit copies of a file.
13. B. The `V$BLOCK_CHANGE_TRACKING` dynamic view shows the filename, status, and size of the block-change tracking file.
14. A. Channel failover is the RMAN feature that provides the ability for other channels to take over the work of a failed channel during backup and recovery operations. Obviously, channel failover requires the allocation of more than one channel.

15. C. The command that sets the persistent setting that directs RMAN to back up to tape is `CONFIGURE DEFAULT DEVICE TYPE TO SBT`.

16. C, E. The `CONTROL_FILE_RECORD_KEEP_TIME` initialization parameter should never be set to 0 if you are using RMAN. If this value is set to 0, there is a potential to lose backup records.

17. A. Backing up in ARCHIVELOG mode is as easy as issuing the `backup database plus archivelog delete input` command.

18. B, C. The `BACKUP` command can take advantage of multiplexing datafiles to the same backup set. The `BACKUP` command can also use the block-change tracking capability.

19. C. Use the `CONFIGURE DEVICE TYPE DISK BACKUP TYPE TO COMPRESSED BACKUPSET` command to configure RMAN to always create a compressed backup by default.

20. B. Backup optimization is a feature whereby Oracle will not back up a read-only tablespace as long as that tablespace has been backed up such that it meets the backup retention criteria.

Using the RMAN Recovery Catalog

ORACLE DATABASE 11*g*: ADMINISTRATION II EXAM OBJECTIVES COVERED IN THIS CHAPTER:

✓ **Using the RMAN Recovery Catalog**

- Identify situations that require RMAN recovery catalog
- Create and configure a recovery catalog
- Synchronize the recovery catalog
- Create and use RMAN stored scripts
- Back up the recovery catalog
- Create and use a virtual private catalog

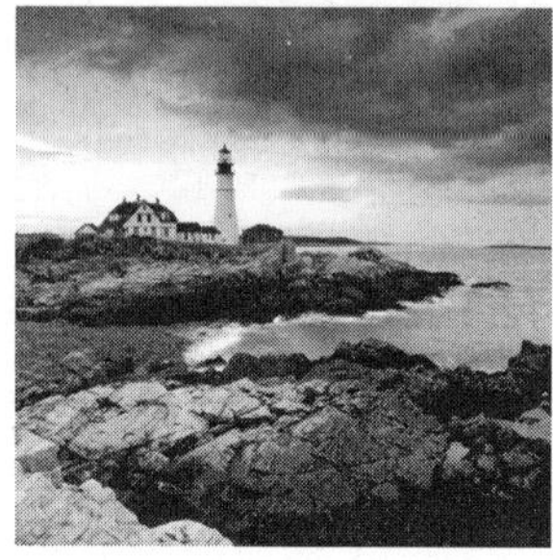

The RMAN recovery catalog is an optional component that you can use with RMAN. In this chapter, we will review the recovery catalog so you will be prepared to answer recovery-catalog OCP exam questions. This chapter will contain the following information on the recovery catalog:

- Introducing the recovery catalog
- Creating the recovery catalog
- Using the recovery catalog
- Recovery-catalog RMAN scripting
- Recovery-catalog maintenance
- Virtual private catalog

So, let's get on with learning about the recovery catalog!

Exam objectives are subject to change at any time without prior notice and at Oracle's sole discretion. Please visit Oracle's Training and Certification website (`http://www.oracle.com/education/certification/`) for the most current exam-objectives listing.

Introducing the Recovery Catalog

The *RMAN recovery catalog* is a schema that sits in an Oracle database. This schema is designed to store RMAN-related information. The information stored in the recovery catalog is in large part just like that stored in the control file. Since most RMAN information is stored in the control file of a database, the recovery catalog serves as a backup repository for RMAN information.

Using the recovery catalog has some clear benefits that need to be carefully considered. The first is that it acts as a single location to store all your RMAN backup-related information. The views of the recovery catalog are well documented, and as a result you can build reports off of those views that will help you to understand the current status of your database backups.

The second benefit is that the recovery catalog also makes global scripting of RMAN operations much easier. You simply store the scripts in the recovery catalog and call them as needed.

Another benefit is that the recovery catalog enables a few RMAN operations not available without a recovery catalog, like using the `keep forever` option (discussed in Chapter 4) or keeping RMAN-related records for a period of time greater than a year.

As you can see, the recovery catalog adds to the overall RMAN architecture nicely. It provides redundancy and additional features that make it very useful. Not all environments will need a recovery catalog. If you have just one or two databases, then a recovery catalog may be more trouble than it's worth. If you have a large environment though, the recovery catalog can make managing that environment much easier.

Database duplication can cause the recovery catalog all sorts of problems if you are not careful. This is because each database in the recovery catalog is uniquely identified by its database ID, or DBID. If you duplicate a database manually, you must change the DBID of the newly created duplicate database with the Oracle NID utility. If you do not do this and you register the new database in the recovery catalog, RMAN will get confused as to who the individual catalog records belong to. This can put your ability to recover your database with RMAN at risk. Note that when you do an RMAN database duplication, it will change the DBID for you automatically when the duplication is complete.

The recovery catalog provides a number of views (called *recovery catalog views*) into the metadata contained therein. The OCP exam will likely not expect you to memorize these views, but it's still best to be aware of them. All the recovery catalog views start with an RC_ prefix and then end with a descriptive name of the data contained in the view. The following are some more popular recovery catalog views:

- RC_DATABASE
- RC_BACKUP_PIECE
- RC_PIECE_DETAILS
- RC_ARCHIVED_LOG
- RC_BACKUP_ARCHIVELOG_SUMMARY
- RC_BACKUP_SET
- RC_BACKUP_SET_DETAILS
- RC_BACKUP_SPFILE

Creating the Recovery Catalog User and Schema Objects

As we mentioned, the recovery catalog is a schema in an existing Oracle database. This schema typically will have its own tablespace, where the RMAN recovery-catalog schema data will be stored. Creating the recovery catalog user and schema is fairly easy. You use the `create user` command to create the database user first. You will then need to create the tablespace that will store the recovery catalog data.

Real World Scenario

To Use the Recovery Catalog or Not to Use the Recovery Catalog; That Is the Question

Adding components to any system has the potential to inject problems into that system. The same is true with the recovery catalog. One database shop implemented the Oracle recovery catalog at the same time they started using RMAN (this was using Oracle Database 10*g*).

Initially things worked great, but over time backup performance became slower and slower. These performance problems were not seen when the recovery catalog was not in use. In the end, after lots of troubleshooting, it was discovered that a couple of queries being issued against the recovery-catalog schema were not tuned well and that these queries would slow down a great deal as the catalog schema got larger. They opened a service request with Oracle and after some time Oracle found the problem and made a patch available.

The moral of this story, in our minds, is to use the KISS (keep it simple, stupid) principle when deciding if you need a recovery catalog or not. If you can justify the additional component because it will provide significant benefit, then by all means use it. Just understand that it's something else that may well break, and things always break at the most inopportune times.

In Exercise 5.1, you'll create a recovery-catalog schema.

How much space you will need for the recovery-catalog schema is a function of how often you back up the database and how long you retain the RMAN backup database in the recovery catalog. Oracle indicates that for one database with one backup per day and one archive-log backup per day, you can estimate metadata storage requirements of between 15MB and 120MB per year, per database, depending on how many backups (database, archive log, and so on) you do per day. The Oracle documentation provides more guidelines. You will not need to be familiar with these sizing guidelines when taking your OCP exam.

EXERCISE 5.1

Creating a Recovery-Catalog Schema

Here are the steps to follow when creating the recovery-catalog schema:

1. Open a command-line window. For this example, you will use a database called RCAT. You need to set the ORACLE_SID to RCAT as shown here:

```
C:\Documents and Settings\dstuns>set ORACLE_SID=RCAT
```

2. Sign into the database using SQL*Plus:

```
C:\Documents and Settings\Robert>sqlplus sys/robert as sysdba
SQL*Plus: Release 11.1.0.6.0 - Production on Mon Sep 15 21:48:06 2008
Copyright (c) 1982, 2007, Oracle.  All rights reserved.
Connected to:
Oracle Database 11g Enterprise Edition Release 11.1.0.6.0 - Production
With the Partitioning, OLAP, Data Mining and Real Application Testing
options
SQL>
```

3. Create a tablespace called RCAT_DATA. This tablespace will be used to store the recovery-catalog schema data:

```
SQL> create tablespace rcat_data
  2  datafile 'c:\oracle\oradata\rcat\rcat_data_01.dbf' size 60m
  3  autoextend on next 10m maxsize 200m;
Tablespace created.
```

4. Create the user that will store the catalog. Use the name RMAN with the password RMAN. Make RCAT_DATA the default tablespace (we assume you have a default temporary tablespace already defined). Also, you will grant an unlimited quota on RCAT_DATA to RCAT_USER:

```
SQL> create user rcat_user identified by rcat_user
  2  default tablespace rcat_data
  3  quota unlimited on rcat_data;
User created.
```

5. The recovery catalog–owning user requires only a grant to the RECOVERY_CATALOG_OWNER role using the grant command:

```
SQL> grant recovery_catalog_owner to rcat_user;
Grant succeeded.
```

EXERCISE 5.1 *(continued)*

6. Test to see whether you can connect to the recovery-catalog schema that you have just created:

```
SQL> connect rcat_user/rcat_user
Connected.
```

7. Now you need to create the recovery-catalog schema. To do this, use the `create catalog` command as shown in this example:

```
C:\Documents and Settings\Robert>Rman catalog=rcat_user/rcat_user@rcat
Recovery Manager: Release 11.1.0.6.0 - Production on
Mon Sep 15 23:10:13 2008
Copyright (c) 1982, 2007, Oracle.  All rights reserved.
connected to recovery catalog database
RMAN> create catalog
recovery catalog created
```

Some texts may show you granting connect or resource roles to the recovery catalog–schema owner. This is not required in Oracle Database 11*g* and may represent a security risk.

Using a Recovery Catalog

Using a recovery catalog is pretty straightforward with RMAN. You simply indicate that you want to connect to the recovery catalog when you start RMAN. You will also have to register the database before your first RMAN operation when connected to the recovery catalog. Most RMAN operations when connected to the recovery catalog are pretty much the same; it's just that RMAN metadata will now be stored in both the control file and the recovery catalog. In the following sections, we will discuss these topics:

- Connecting to the recovery catalog from RMAN
- Registering the database with the recovery catalog
- Unregistering a database from the recovery catalog

Connecting to the Recovery Catalog from RMAN

When you start RMAN, you will need to indicate that you want to connect to a recovery catalog if you want the session to use the recovery catalog. There are a couple of ways of connecting to the recovery catalog. The first is to use the `catalog` RMAN command-line parameter, as shown in this example:

```
C:\Documents and Settings\Robert>Set oracle_sid=orcl
C:\Documents and Settings\Robert>Rman target=sys/Robert
catalog=rcat_user/rcat_user@rcat
Recovery Manager: Release 11.1.0.6.0 - Production on Mon Sep 15 22:17:11 2008
Copyright (c) 1982, 2007, Oracle.  All rights reserved.
connected to target database (not started)
connected to recovery catalog database
RMAN>
```

Note the use of the terms `target` and `catalog`. As we first mentioned in Chapter 4, the database you are intending to back up is called the *target database*. In the previous example, you connected directly to the target database with RMAN. At the same time, you connected to the catalog database through Oracle Net. If you desired, you could connect directly to the catalog database and connect to the target database via Oracle Net, or you could connect to both databases via Oracle Net. Since the server itself does the backup work via locally allocated channels, connecting to the server or the recovery catalog through Oracle Net should not impose any undue performance constraints on the performance of your backups.

Another way of connecting to the recovery catalog is to do so from the RMAN command-line prompt using the `connect` command, as shown in this example:

```
C:\Documents and Settings\Robert>Rman target=sys/Robert
Recovery Manager: Release 11.1.0.6.0 - Production on Mon Sep 15 22:18:05 2008
Copyright (c) 1982, 2007, Oracle.  All rights reserved.
connected to target database (not started)
RMAN> Connect catalog rcat_user/rcat_user@rcat
connected to recovery catalog database
```

Registering the Target Database with the Recovery Catalog

Once you have connected to the recovery catalog, you will have to register the database with the `register database` command. To be registered, the database must be mounted or open. In this example, you connect to the target database and the recovery catalog and then register the database with the recovery catalog:

```
C:\Documents and Settings\Robert>Rman target=sys/Robert
catalog=rcat_user/rcat_user@rcat
```

```
Recovery Manager: Release 11.1.0.6.0 - Production on Mon Sep 15 23:12:51 2008
Copyright (c) 1982, 2007, Oracle.  All rights reserved.
connected to target database: ORCL (DBID=1190537904, not open)
connected to recovery catalog database
RMAN> register database;
database registered in recovery catalog
starting full resync of recovery catalog
full resync complete
```

Unregistering a Database

If you are preparing to remove a database, you will want to remove its metadata from the recovery catalog. This is done with the `unregister` command, as shown in this example:

```
C:\Documents and Settings\Robert>Rman target=sys/Robert
catalog=rcat_user/rcat_user@rcat
Recovery Manager: Release 11.1.0.6.0 - Production on Mon Sep 15 23:13:45 2008
Copyright (c) 1982, 2007, Oracle.  All rights reserved.
connected to target database: ORCL (DBID=1190537904, not open)
connected to recovery catalog database
RMAN> unregister database;
database name is "ORCL" and DBID is 1190537904
Do you really want to unregister the database (enter YES or NO)? yes
database unregistered from the recovery catalog
```

Unregistering a database from the recovery catalog will cause all recovery catalog–related records to be removed from the recovery catalog. Control-file records for that database will be retained, of course. You might have had older backup records stored in the recovery catalog, though. When you unregister a database, those old records will be lost if the age of the backups exceeds the setting of the `CONTROL_FILE_RECORD_KEEP_TIME` parameter. Also, any scripts related to the database in the recovery catalog will be lost (we will talk more about scripting later in this chapter).

Using Scripts in the RMAN Recovery Catalog

One benefit of the recovery catalog is the ability to store RMAN scripts. In the following sections, these topics will be addressed:

- Executing external scripts
- Creating stored scripts

- Replacing stored scripts
- Removing stored scripts
- Executing stored scripts
- Printing stored scripts
- Using script-substitution variables

Executing External Scripts

RMAN provides the ability to execute external scripts. You can do so from the RMAN command line using the `cmdfile` option, as shown here:

```
Rman target=/ cmdfile=run_me.rman
```

You can also run an external script from within RMAN using the `@` command, as shown here:

```
RMAN> @run_me.rman
```

Creating Stored Scripts

Recovery catalog stored scripts provide the ability to centrally manage your backup and recovery scripts. Using global stored scripts allows you to use common scripts across the entire enterprise.

Use the `create script` RMAN command to store scripts in the recovery catalog. You will assign a name to the stored script when you create it. Stored scripts can be created to do many RMAN operations, including backups, recoveries, and database-maintenance operations. As mentioned earlier, you must be connected to the recovery catalog to be able to create a script.

Here is an example of using the `create script` command to create a script. This script does a backup of the database and the archived redo logs:

```
create script db_backup_script
{ backup database plus archivelog delete input;}
```

Note that if you are using virtual private catalogs (see more on these later in this chapter), you will need to create the script as a global script as shown here:

```
create global script db_delete_obsolete
{ delete obsolete;}
```

Replacing Stored Scripts

The `replace script` command is used to replace stored RMAN scripts. The following example demonstrates the use of the `replace script` command:

```
Replace script db_delete_obsolete
{ delete noprompt obsolete;}
```

Removing Stored Scripts

If you need to remove a stored script permanently, you can use the `delete script` command as shown here:

```
Delete script db_delete_obsolete;
```

Executing Stored Scripts

Once you have created the script, it might be nice to actually run it! To run the script, you will use the `execute script` command. This command must be run within the confines of an RMAN run block, as shown in this example:

```
Run {execute script db_delete_obsolete;}
```

Printing Stored Scripts

The `print script` command will print your script to the standard output device, allowing you to cut and paste its contents. Here is an example of the `print script` command:

```
RMAN> Print script db_delete_obsolete;
printing stored script: db_delete_obsolete
{ delete obsolete;}
```

Using Script Substitution Variables

Oracle Database 11*g* provides for the use of *substitution variables* in RMAN scripts or command files. You define the substitution variables using the ampersand (&) character followed by a number, as shown in this example:

```
Restore database from tag &1;
```

The RMAN executable includes the `using` command-line parameter that allows you to define the value of the substitution variable. For example, if the previous `restore` command were in a file called `restore.cmd` and you wanted to restore a backup with the tag `MINE`, you would call RMAN in this manner:

```
Rman target=/ @restore.cmd using MINE
```

You can also use substitution variables with stored scripts. For example, you can create a script to back up your database and use a tag as shown here:

```
RMAN> create script db_backup_script
2> { backup database tag  '&1' plus archivelog delete input;}
Enter value for 1: test
created script db_backup_script
```

You can then execute the script, setting the variable with the `using` command, as shown here:

```
RMAN> Run {execute script db_backup_script using 'TEST';}
```

Maintaining the Recovery Catalog

If you are running the recovery catalog, you will need to know how to synchronize it with the control file of the database. Additionally, you will need to back up the recovery catalog. We briefly cover these two topics next.

Synchronizing the Recovery Catalog

Typically during an RMAN operation, the recovery catalog will be synchronized with the control file. New records will be updated or added during this synchronization process. There may be times you will want to synchronize the recovery catalog yourself manually. You can use the `resync catalog` command to perform manual catalog synchronization. Here is an example of using the `resync` command:

```
RMAN> resync catalog;
starting full resync of recovery catalog
full resync complete
```

Backing Up the Recovery Catalog

You can actually back up the recovery catalog using RMAN. You would simply use the control file of the recovery catalog to store the backup-related information. You can do online or offline backups and complete or point-in-time restores as your needs dictate.

You can also use Oracle's flashback features (see Chapter 9 for more on Oracle Flashback Database) on the recovery catalog.

Real World Scenario

Why Resync the Catalog?

You might be asking yourself, "If RMAN resynchronizes the catalog automatically after a backup, why would I ever need to use the `resync catalog` command?" That's a fair question.

One place where one of us was employed had a large number of databases and used RMAN and the recovery catalog. As more and more records were added to the recovery catalog, we found our backups were taking longer. This ended up being because of a bug in RMAN. To work around the problem until Oracle could give us a fix, we did our backups without connecting to the recovery catalog. These made the backups perform much faster. We would then connect to the recovery catalog in a different operation and resync the control file to the recovery catalog.

This corrected the performance problem while still allowing us to use the recovery catalog to store our database backup metadata.

Using the RMAN Virtual Private Catalog

You might have noticed that the catalog-schema owner has access to all data in the recovery catalog. You may want to allow other users access to the recovery catalog, but you may want them to see information on only specific databases. Oracle provides the RMAN virtual private catalog for just such cases. In the following sections, we will discuss how to create a virtual catalog and how to grant users access to databases contained within it. We will discuss how to create the RMAN virtual private catalog first, and then we will discuss administration of the virtual private catalog.

Creating the RMAN Virtual Private Catalog

If you want to use the *RMAN virtual private catalog (RVPC)*, you start with a regular recovery catalog. The recovery-catalog schema should have been created and the databases registered (you can, of course, register databases later), and it can be brand-new or already have been in use.

Now that you have a recovery catalog, let's assume you have registered two databases in the recovery catalog; one is called orcl and one is called secret. Let's assume you have a DBA named Ed who you don't quite trust (he's a seedy-looking guy with tattoos of the Smurfs all over his arms). Because you don't trust him, you want him to be able to access only the orcl database RMAN records. The secret database records will remain a mystery to him (you assume, of course, that he does not have SYS access to your recovery catalog, or all is lost!).

To create the RVPC account for Ed, you would execute the following steps:

Step 1: Create the RVPC database account. First you create the RVPC database account log in the recovery-catalog database as a privileged user (for example, SYS) and issue the create user command. You will also need to grant the recovery_catalog_owner privilege to the new user.

Step 2: Create the RVPC. Once the RVPC user has been created, you need to create the virtual catalog. To do this, you log into RMAN and use the create virtual catalog command, as shown here:

```
Create virtual catalog;
```

Step 3: Grant the RVPC access to the appropriate catalog databases. Now that you have created the RVPC account, you need to indicate to the recovery-catalog database which databases this account will have access to. You will use the RMAN command to perform this operation as shown here, where we grant access to the ORCL database catalog metadata:

```
grant catalog for database orcl to rcat_001;
```

Administering the RMAN Virtual Private Catalog

Once you have set up RVPC, there are other administrative activities you can perform. For example, you can grant the register database privilege to RVPC owners using the RMAN grant command as shown here:

```
RMAN> grant register database to rcat_002;
Grant succeeded.
```

The revoke RMAN command is used to revoke privileges to databases in the RVPC or other privileges, such as the register database privilege, as shown here:

```
RMAN>Revoke catalog for database abcs;
RMAN>Revoke register database from rcat_002;
```

Finally, you can drop the RVPC with the `drop catalog` command as shown in this example:

```
RMAN>connect catalog rcat_002/rcat002@rcat;
RMAN> drop catalog;
```

After using the `drop catalog` command, it's safe to drop the RVPC catalog user with the `drop user` SQL command:

```
SQL> drop user rcat_001;
```

Summary

The recovery catalog is an optional but very powerful tool in your RMAN arsenal. It can make your life as a DBA easier by providing a centralized repository for all your RMAN-related data. The recovery catalog is easy to create and maintain. Oracle's new virtual private catalog features make the recovery catalog even more powerful, increasing the security within the catalog.

Exam Essentials

Identify situations that will require the RMAN recovery catalog. Understand that the recovery catalog is largely optional. A recovery catalog will be needed for storing scripts, and it will be required if you want to store backup records longer than one year or beyond the setting of `CONTROL_FILE_RECORD_KEEP_TIME`.

Create and configure an RMAN recovery catalog. Understand the process required to create the RMAN recovery catalog. Know how to create the recovery-catalog user and what privileges are required. Understand how to register and unregister databases with the recovery catalog and how to create a virtual private catalog and configure users to use it.

Maintain the RMAN recovery catalog. Understand how to back up the recovery catalog. Know how to synchronize the target database with the recovery catalog.

Review Questions

1. What is the purpose of the RMAN recovery catalog? (Choose all that apply.)
   - **A.** It must be used because all RMAN-related backup and recovery metadata information is contained in it.
   - **B.** It provides a convenient, optional, repository of backup- and recovery-related metadata.
   - **C.** It provides the ability to store RMAN scripts for global use by any database that has access to the repository.
   - **D.** It provides a means of storing all RMAN backup sets physically in an Oracle database server.
   - **E.** It provides the ability to store backup records for more than a year.
2. What privileges must be granted to allow an account to create the recovery catalog? (Choose all that apply.)
   - **A.** `RECOVERY_CATALOG_OWNER`
   - **B.** `DBA`
   - **C.** `RESOURCE`
   - **D.** `SELECT ANY DICTIONARY`
   - **E.** `CONNECT`
3. Which command do you use to create a recovery-catalog schema?
   - **A.** `create recovery catalog`
   - **B.** `create catalog`
   - **C.** `build catalog`
   - **D.** `catalog create`
   - **E.** `mount catalog`
4. If you back up a database without connecting to the recovery catalog, which operations will cause the recovery catalog to be updated? (Choose all that apply.)
   - **A.** The next time you back up the database when you are also connected to the recovery catalog and the target database
   - **B.** The next time you are connected to the target database and the recovery catalog database and issue the `resync` command
   - **C.** The next time you connect RMAN to just the recovery catalog
   - **D.** The next time you connect to the recovery catalog and the target database with RMAN
   - **E.** Connecting to the recovery catalog and issuing the `resync all databases` command

5. You have created a script in the recovery catalog called backup_database. Which of the following commands would successfully execute that script?

   A.

```
run {
      open script backup_database;
      run script backup_database
    }
```

   B.

```
run {
      engage script backup_database;
    }
```

   C.

```
run {
      run script backup_database;
    }
```

   D.

```
Run {
      execute script backup_database;
    }
```

   E. The name backup_database is an invalid name for an RMAN script. Trying to run it from RMAN would result in an error.

6. In what order would you execute the following steps to create a recovery catalog?

   a. Issue the create catalog command.

   b. Create the recovery-catalog database.

   c. Create the recovery-catalog user.

   d. Grant the recovery_catalog_owner privilege to the recovery-catalog user.

   e. Issue the register database command from the target database.

   A. a, b, c, d, e

   B. b, a, d, c, e

   C. b, c, d, a, e

   D. b, c, d, e, a

   E. b, d, c, a, e

7. How would you grant the RVPC user access to specific RMAN database records in the RMAN virtual private catalog?

   A. Issue the `grant` command from the SYS user (or equivalent) of the target database.

   B. Issue the `grant` command from the SYS user (or equivalent) of the recovery-catalog database.

   C. Issue the `grant` command from the recovery catalog–owning schema user account in the recovery catalog.

   D. Issue the `grant` command from RMAN when connected to the recovery catalog–owning schema.

   E. Issue the `grant` command from RMAN when connected to the target database.

8. The RVPC user can do which of the following? (Choose all that apply.)

   A. Register databases if granted the `register database` privilege

   B. See all databases in the recovery-catalog schema

   C. See all database-related metadata in the recovery catalog if they are granted access to that database

   D. Unregister databases from the RVPC catalog that were not granted to the RVPC catalog owner with the `grant` command

   E. Not be connected to with the RMAN command-line catalog parameter for backup or recovery purposes

9. Given the script

   ```
   create script db_backup_datafile_script
   {backup datafile &1, &2 plus archivelog delete input;}
   ```

   what is the result of running this command?

   ```
   Run {execute script db_backup_datafile_script using 2;}
   ```

   A. The script will fail since you instructed RMAN to back up only one datafile rather than two.

   B. The script will successfully back up datafile 3 without error.

   C. The script will fail since it uses a substitution variable which is not supported.

   D. The `execute script` command will prompt for the value of &2 since it's not included in the command.

   E. The script will fail because you cannot use the `plus archivelog` command when backing up database datafiles.

10. Which is the correct way to connect to both the target database and the recovery catalog from the RMAN command line? Assume that the target database is called ORCL and that the recovery catalog database is called RCAT. Also assume that the recovery-catalog owner is called RCAT_OWN. Assume the environment is configured for the ORCL database. (Choose all that apply.)

A. `rman target=/ catalog=/@rcat`

B. `rman target=/ catalog=rcat_own/rcat_own`

C. `rman target=/ catalog=rcat_own/rcat_own@RCAT`

D. `rman target=sys/robert@orcl catalog=rcat_own/rcat_own@RCAT`

E. You cannot connect to the target database and the recovery catalog at the same time.

Answers to Review Questions

1. B, C, E. The recovery catalog provides a means of storing metadata related to a database's RMAN backup and recovery operations. Additionally, it provides the ability to store scripts that can be used by any database connecting to the repository via RMAN. Finally, the recovery catalog provides the means to store backup records for longer than a year.

2. A, C. The `RECOVERY_CATALOG_OWNER` and `RESOURCE` privileges are required to create the recovery catalog. The `DBA` privilege includes `RESOURCE` and `CONNECT` and will work, but this role has many additional privileges that are unneeded. `SELECT ANY DICTIONARY` is not required.

3. B. Use the `create catalog` command to create the recovery-catalog schema.

4. A, B. Anytime you execute an RMAN backup operation when connected to the recovery catalog, RMAN will automatically resynchronize the recovery-catalog metadata with the database control file. The `resync` command is used to manually resynchronize the recovery catalog with the database.

5. D. You would use the `execute script` RMAN command, contained within a `run` block, to execute the `backup_database` script.

6. C. You would first create the recovery catalog database. Then you create the recovery catalog user, granting that user the `RECOVERY_CATALOG_OWNER` role. You then issue the `create catalog` command from RMAN, which will create the recovery-catalog schema. Finally, you connect to the target database and register the database with the `register database` command.

7. D. To give the RVPC user rights to specific databases, you must connect to the recovery catalog with RMAN. You then grant those rights to that user from the RMAN prompt using the `grant` command.

8. A, C. The RVPC user can **`register database`** if they are granted the `register database` privilege. They can also see all recovery-catalog database metadata to which they are granted access.

9. D. The script will prompt for the missing substitution variable. The script will return an error if you do not put in a value for the second substitution variable.

10. C, D. Options C and D show the correct format for the RMAN command line. Option C connects to the database locally, while option D connects through Oracle Net. Both methods are completely legal.

Recovering Databases with RMAN

ORACLE DATABASE 11*g*: ADMINISTRATION II EXAM OBJECTIVES COVERED IN THIS CHAPTER:

✓ **Using RMAN to Perform Recovery**

- Perform complete recovery from a critical or non-critical data file loss using RMAN
- Perform incomplete recovery using RMAN
- Recover using incrementally updated backups
- Switch to image copies for fast recovery
- Recover using a backup control file

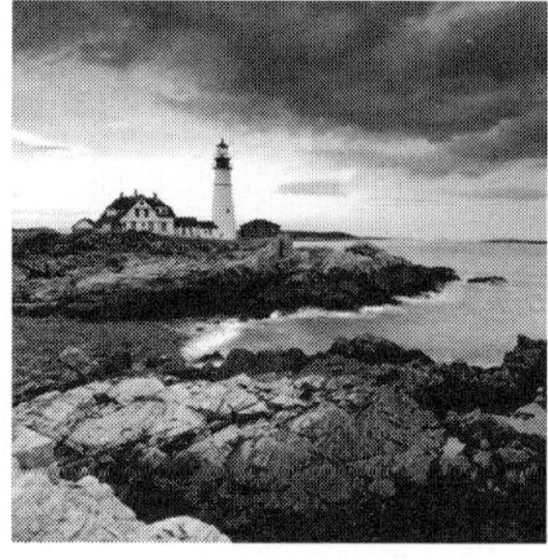

Database recovery ought to be easy in our minds. You have enough problems when your database has unexpectedly left the building, and those problems should not be made worse by a bad piece of database-backup-and recovery software. RMAN makes recovery of your database easy as long as you have crafted a solid backup and recovery strategy (discussed in previous chapters). Additionally, the old adage that practice makes perfect very much applies to database recoveries. So take some time and practice a recovery or two before you have to deal with the real thing. All too often, people wait for disaster to strike rather than learning what to do beforehand.

This chapter is about what to do when disaster strikes and you are under the gun to get your backup restored. In this chapter, we will discuss the following topics:

- RMAN database-recovery basics
- Recovering a database in NOARCHIVELOG mode
- Recovering a database in ARCHIVELOG mode
- Recovering datafiles or tablespaces in ARCHIVELOG mode
- Recovering a database using incomplete recovery
- Using image copies to recover your database
- Other recovery topics

The best way to really learn about backup and recovery is to do it. A lot. The exercises in this chapter along with the examples of the various forms of recovery will certainly get you on your way.

Exam objectives are subject to change at any time without prior notice and at Oracle's sole discretion. Please visit Oracle's Training and Certification website (`http://www.oracle.com/education/certification/`) for the most current exam-objectives listing.

In this chapter and in Chapter 8 we have opted not to use a recovery catalog in our examples. The functionality demonstrated is the same with or without a recovery catalog. Where there are exceptions to this rule, we will note them or provide additional examples.

RMAN Database-Recovery Basics

There is a common theme or pattern when recovering databases in RMAN that you will want to be familiar with. This pattern for recovery is as follows:

Step 1: Put the database in the proper mode. Putting the database in the proper mode is the first step to recovering it. The proper mode is dependent on the type of recovery you want to be able to make. For example, in NOARCHIVELOG mode your database must always be in MOUNT mode to perform a recovery. We will cover the modes the database should be in for individual recovery in the later sections of this chapter.

RMAN provides commands that you can use to put the database in the mode you want it to be in (you'll find a summary of the RMAN commands in Chapter 4). If you want the database mounted, then you can use the RMAN `startup mount` command, for example. RMAN recoveries will occur in almost any mode, NOMOUNT for control-file or spfile recoveries, MOUNT for offline database recoveries or OPEN for ARCHIVELOG noncritical datafile or tablespace recoveries. For the OCP exam, it will be a very good idea if you learn which modes are required for which recovery types.

The RMAN client is full-featured. There should be few times when any recovery operation will require you to use anything other than RMAN. If you do have to use something else, it probably means you have made a mistake, you are having a really bad day, or you have run into a bug (which in and of itself means you are having a really bad day).

Putting the database in the proper mode may also require restoring files required to put it in that mode. For example, if the spfile is missing, you may need to restore it. Perhaps the control file will need to be restored. You will find more information on these kinds of recoveries later in this chapter.

Step 2: Restore the database datafiles. After the database has been put in the correct mode for the recovery chosen, you will use the RMAN `restore` command to begin the database recovery. The `restore` command will determine which backup set pieces or image copies need to be used to recover the database to the point in time that you direct. By default, RMAN will restore the database to the point of failure if you are running in ARCHIVELOG mode. If you are in NOARCHIVELOG mode, the restore will be to the point of the last backup. Once the datafiles have been restored, you will be returned to the RMAN prompt so you can issue the `recover database` command.

The `restore` command comes in different flavors, allowing you to restore the entire database, datafiles, or tablespaces. We understand that a future version will also allow you to restore your broken heart, but that's still in beta.

Step 3: Recover the database. One the database datafiles are restored, the RMAN `recover` command is used to start the actual recovery process. During the execution of the `recover` command, RMAN will extract the needed archived redo logs (if running in ARCHIVELOG mode) and apply them as needed. Obviously during a NOARCHIVELOG-mode recovery no redo will be applied (and in fact, you will indicate this when you do the recovery, as you will see later in this chapter). Once the `recover` command has completed its job, you will be returned to the RMAN prompt so you can complete the recovery process by opening the database or bringing the tablespace or datafile online.

As with the `restore` command, the `recover` command has a number of different variations, such as `recover database`, `recover tablespace`, and `recover datafile`. You will see these demonstrated throughout the rest of this chapter.

Step 4: Complete the recovery. If your restore and recovery required the database to be in MOUNT mode, then all you need to do is open the database for business and you are the hero of the day. To do so, issue the `alter database open` command from the RMAN prompt. If you did everything correctly, your database should open and your users will erect a statue in your honor. At one time we had upward of 15 statues erected in our honor, only to be toppled by DBAs who succeeded us. Statues are, in the end, highly overrated.

Of course, if you didn't get your backup strategy right, your users may well throw another party in your honor—the going-away party, if your boss even allows that. So, you'll want to make sure you get it right the first time and even test it a few times before the real deal comes to town.

If your restore and recovery permitted the database to be open, then you probably had a tablespace or a datafile offline. In this case, you will use the RMAN `sql` command, embedding the `alter tablespace online` or `alter datafile online` command within the confines of that command. With the successful completion of those commands, your recovery will be complete and you can celebrate!

Now that we have showed you the basic pattern for recovering from a downed database, let's talk in some more specifics about the different kinds of database recoveries you will encounter.

Recovering a Database in NOARCHIVELOG Mode

Recovering your NOARCHIVELOG-mode database is perhaps the easiest thing you could do. There is no application of redo to worry about; only restoring the database datafiles and getting the database up and running. One important thing to understand is that your best recovery situation is from a database backup that is consistent. Fortunately RMAN will force you to do consistent database backups when the database is in NOARCHIVELOG mode, so this isn't a problem. We discussed this situation in detail in Chapter 3, so please make sure you reference that chapter and understand this important concept in backup and recovery. Oftentimes knowing how something works and why will help you answer an OCP exam question that you otherwise don't really know the answer to.

So, how easy is recovery of your database in NOARCHIVELOG mode? Here are the steps in summary form. We will give you more detail as this chapter progresses:

1. If you have lost your control file or spfile (or database parameter file), you will need to reference the section on recovering your control file or spfile with RMAN, which appears later in this chapter. To start any RMAN recovery, you must have a control file and an spfile (or database parameter file).
2. If you are not already logged into RMAN (for example, if you had to restore your control file), then log into RMAN now. You will see lots of examples of this later in this chapter.
3. Mount your database with the `startup mount` command.
4. Issue the RMAN `restore database` command.
5. Issue the RMAN `recover database` command. Because this is a NOARCHIVELOG-mode database recovery, you will need to include the `noredo` keyword to indicate that there is no redo to be applied.
6. Open the database with the `alter database open` command.

Here is an example of an RMAN restore of a database in NOARCHIVELOG mode:

```
RMAN> connect target /
RMAN> shutdown abort
using target database control file instead of recovery catalog
Oracle instance shut down
RMAN> startup mount
connected to target database (not started)
Oracle instance started
database mounted
Total System Global Area     397557760 bytes
Fixed Size                     1333452 bytes
Variable Size                339740468 bytes
Database Buffers              50331648 bytes
Redo Buffers                   6152192 bytes
RMAN> restore database;
Starting restore at 28-SEP-08
allocated channel: ORA_DISK_1
channel ORA_DISK_1: SID=154 device type=DISK
channel ORA_DISK_1: starting datafile backup set restore
channel ORA_DISK_1: specifying datafile(s) to restore from backup set
channel ORA_DISK_1: restoring datafile 00002 to
C:\ORACLE\ORADATA\ORCL\SYSAUX01.DBF
```

```
channel ORA_DISK_1: reading from backup piece
 C:\ORACLE\FLASH_RECOVERY_AREA\ORCL\BACKUPSET\2008_09_22
\O1_MF_NNNDF_TAG20080922T182631_4FJFXXVT_.BKP
channel ORA_DISK_1: piece
handle=C:\ORACLE\FLASH_RECOVERY_AREA\ORCL\BACKUPSET\2008_09_22
\O1_MF_NNNDF_TAG20080922T182631_4FJFXXVT_.BKP tag=TAG20080922T182631
channel ORA_DISK_1: restored backup piece 1
channel ORA_DISK_1: restore complete, elapsed time: 00:02:25
channel ORA_DISK_1: starting datafile backup set restore
channel ORA_DISK_1: specifying datafile(s) to restore from backup set
channel ORA_DISK_1: restoring datafile 00001 to
C:\ORACLE\ORADATA\ORCL\SYSTEM01.DBF
channel ORA_DISK_1: restoring datafile 00004 to
C:\ORACLE\ORADATA\ORCL\USERS01.DBF
channel ORA_DISK_1: restoring datafile 00005 to
C:\ORACLE\ORADATA\ORCL\UNDOTBS02.DBF
channel ORA_DISK_1: reading from backup piece
C:\ORACLE\FLASH_RECOVERY_AREA\ORCL\BACKUPSET\2008_09_28\
O1_MF_NNNDF_TAG20080928T165801_4GO2ZZC7_.BKP
channel ORA_DISK_1: piece
 handle=C:\ORACLE\FLASH_RECOVERY_AREA\ORCL\BACKUPSET\2008_09_28
\O1_MF_NNNDF_TAG20080928T165801_4GO2ZZC7_.BKP tag=TAG20080928T165801
channel ORA_DISK_1: restored backup piece 1
channel ORA_DISK_1: restore complete, elapsed time: 00:02:55
Finished restore at 28-SEP-08
RMAN> recover database noredo;
Starting recover at 28-SEP-08
using channel ORA_DISK_1
Finished recover at 28-SEP-08
RMAN> alter database open;
database opened
```

Recovering a Database in ARCHIVELOG Mode

If your database is in ARCHIVELOG mode, then your recovery options might include a complete database recovery or an online datafile or tablespace recovery. Another option is point-in-time recovery, which we discuss later in this chapter. Other more advanced options, including tablespace point-in-time recovery, are also available. These are covered in Chapter 8 of this book.

Complete recovery is called for when all or most of the datafiles of the database have been lost. Tablespace or datafile recovery is a better solution if you have lost only a few datafiles or perhaps all datafiles of one or two tablespaces. Let's look at each of these recovery methods in more detail next.

Complete Database Recovery in ARCHIVELOG Mode

A *complete* database recovery in ARCHIVELOG mode is required when most or all of the database datafiles have been lost. In this mode, the database is shut down (if it has not already done so itself because of the loss of datafiles). It is then mounted and recovered. Here are the steps to follow for a complete database recovery in ARCHIVELOG mode:

1. Shut down the database if it is not already down.
2. If you have lost your control file or spfile, you will need to reference the section, "Other Basic Recovery Topics" which appears later in this chapter. To start any RMAN recovery, you must have a control file and an spfile or parameter file.
3. If you are not already logged into RMAN (for example, if you had to restore your control file), then log into RMAN now.
4. Mount your database with the `startup mount` command.
5. Issue the RMAN `restore database` command.
6. Issue the RMAN `recover database` command. The command will restore the needed incremental backups and archived redo logs, recovering the database to the point of failure.
7. Open the database with the `alter database open` command. If you restored your control file, you will need to use the `alter database open resetlogs` command.

Here is an example of a recovery in ARCHIVELOG mode:

```
RMAN> shutdown abort
using target database control file instead of recovery catalog
Oracle instance shut down
RMAN> startup mount
connected to target database (not started)
Oracle instance started
database mounted
Total System Global Area     397557760 bytes
Fixed Size                     1333452 bytes
Variable Size                339740468 bytes
Database Buffers              50331648 bytes
Redo Buffers                   6152192 bytes
RMAN> restore database;
```

```
Starting restore at 28-SEP-08
allocated channel: ORA_DISK_1
channel ORA_DISK_1: SID=154 device type=DISK
channel ORA_DISK_1: starting datafile backup set restore
channel ORA_DISK_1: specifying datafile(s) to restore from backup set
channel ORA_DISK_1: restoring datafile 00002 to
C:\ORACLE\ORADATA\ORCL\SYSAUX01.DBF
channel ORA_DISK_1: reading from backup piece
 C:\ORACLE\FLASH_RECOVERY_AREA\ORCL\BACKUPSET\2008_09_22
\O1_MF_NNNDF_TAG20080922T182631_4FJFXXVT_.BKP
channel ORA_DISK_1: piece
handle=C:\ORACLE\FLASH_RECOVERY_AREA\ORCL\BACKUPSET\2008_09_22
\O1_MF_NNNDF_TAG20080922T182631_4FJFXXVT_.BKP tag=TAG20080922T182631
channel ORA_DISK_1: restored backup piece 1
channel ORA_DISK_1: restore complete, elapsed time: 00:02:35
channel ORA_DISK_1: starting datafile backup set restore
channel ORA_DISK_1: specifying datafile(s) to restore from backup set
channel ORA_DISK_1: restoring datafile 00001 to
 C:\ORACLE\ORADATA\ORCL\SYSTEM01.DBF
channel ORA_DISK_1: restoring datafile 00004 to
 C:\ORACLE\ORADATA\ORCL\USERS01.DBF
channel ORA_DISK_1: restoring datafile 00005 to
 C:\ORACLE\ORADATA\ORCL\UNDOTBS02.DBF
channel ORA_DISK_1: reading from backup piece
C:\ORACLE\FLASH_RECOVERY_AREA\ORCL\BACKUPSET\2008_09_28
\O1_MF_NNNDF_TAG20080928T172015_4G049OQX_.BKP
channel ORA_DISK_1: piece
handle=C:\ORACLE\FLASH_RECOVERY_AREA\ORCL\BACKUPSET\2008_09_28
\O1_MF_NNNDF_TAG20080928T172015_4G049OQX_.BKP tag=TAG20080928T172015
channel ORA_DISK_1: restored backup piece 1
channel ORA_DISK_1: restore complete, elapsed time: 00:02:45
Finished restore at 28-SEP-08
RMAN> recover database;
Starting recover at 28-SEP-08
using channel ORA_DISK_1
starting media recovery
media recovery complete, elapsed time: 00:00:03
Finished recover at 28-SEP-08
RMAN> Alter database open;
database opened
```

If you added a datafile or a tablespace to the database after your last RMAN backup, RMAN will add that tablespace or datafile for you automatically during a restore. Additionally, RMAN will re-create any tempfiles needed during a restore process automatically.

In Exercise 6.1, you'll restore your ARCHIVELOG-mode database with RMAN.

EXERCISE 6.1

Restoring Your ARCHIVELOG-Mode Database with RMAN

This activity builds on the backup done in Exercise 4.2 from Chapter 4. You should have completed Exercise 4.2 prior to executing this activity. Please note that the output you experience from this exercise will probably differ from the output shown in this exercise.

1. Complete Exercise 4.2.
2. Log into the database as SYS using SQL*Plus:

```
C:\oracle>set oracle_sid=orcl
C:\oracle>sqlplus sys as sysdba
SQL*Plus: Release 11.1.0.6.0 - Production on Fri Oct 3 00:31:07 2008
Copyright (c) 1982, 2007, Oracle.  All rights reserved.
Enter password:
Connected to:
Oracle Database 11g Enterprise Edition Release 11.1.0.6.0 - Production
With the Partitioning, OLAP, Data Mining and
Real Application Testing options
SQL>
```

3. Determine the location of the database datafiles by issuing the `select file_name from dba_data_files;` query:

```
SQL> select file_name from dba_data_files;
FILE_NAME
--------------------------------------------------------------------
C:\ORACLE\FLASH_RECOVERY_AREA\ORCL\DATAFILE\O1_MF_USERS_4G2Q1YTC_.DBF
C:\ORACLE\ORADATA\ORCL\UNDOTBS01.DBF
C:\ORACLE\ORADATA\ORCL\SYSAUX01.DBF
C:\ORACLE\ORADATA\ORCL\SYSTEM01.DBF
```

4. Shut down the database:

```
SQL> shutdown abort
ORACLE instance shut down.
```

EXERCISE 6.1 (continued)

5. Exit SQL*Plus:

```
SQL> quit
Disconnected from Oracle Database 11g Enterprise Edition
Release 11.1.0.6.0 - Production
With the Partitioning, OLAP, Data Mining and
Real Application Testing options
C:\oracle>
```

6. From the operating system prompt, delete all the database datafiles listed in step 3. Be careful not to do a wildcard delete because you might delete files in that directory that you do not want to remove, such as the online redo logs or the database control files.

```
C:\oracle>Del C:\ORACLE\FLASH_RECOVERY_AREA\ORCL\DATAFILE\O1_MF_
USERS_4G2Q1YTC_.DBF
C:\oracle>Del C:\ORACLE\ORADATA\ORCL\UNDOTBS01.DBF
C:\oracle>Del C:\ORACLE\ORADATA\ORCL\SYSAUX01.DBF
C:\oracle>Del C:\ORACLE\ORADATA\ORCL\SYSTEM01.DBF
```

7. Log into the database as SYS using SQL*Plus:

```
C:\oracle>sqlplus sys as sysdba
SQL*Plus: Release 11.1.0.6.0 - Production on Fri Oct 3 00:35:25 2008
Copyright (c) 1982, 2007, Oracle.  All rights reserved.
Enter password:
Connected to an idle instance.
```

8. Start the database. Notice the error that you receive:

```
SQL> startup
ORACLE instance started.
Total System Global Area  364081152 bytes
Fixed Size                  1333228 bytes
Variable Size             264243220 bytes
Database Buffers           92274688 bytes
Redo Buffers                6230016 bytes
Database mounted.
ORA-01157: cannot identify/lock data file 1 - see DBWR trace file
ORA-01110: data file 1: 'C:\ORACLE\ORADATA\ORCL\SYSTEM01.DBF'
```

9. Shut down the database:

```
SQL> shutdown abort
ORACLE instance shut down.
```

EXERCISE 6.1 *(continued)*

10. Exit SQL*Plus:

```
SQL> quit
Disconnected from Oracle Database 11g Enterprise Edition
Release 11.1.0.6.0 - Production
With the Partitioning, OLAP, Data Mining and
Real Application Testing options
C:\oracle>
```

11. Start RMAN. We will assume you are not using a recovery catalog during this exercise.

```
C:\oracle>rman target=/
Recovery Manager: Release 11.1.0.6.0 -
Production on Fri Oct 3 00:37:44 2008
Copyright (c) 1982, 2007, Oracle.  All rights reserved.
connected to target database (not started)
```

12. Start up the database with the Startup mount command from RMAN:

```
RMAN> startup mount
Oracle instance started
database mounted
Total System Global Area     364081152 bytes
Fixed Size                     1333228 bytes
Variable Size                264243220 bytes
Database Buffers              92274688 bytes
Redo Buffers                   6230016 bytes
```

13. Restore the database files with the restore database command:

```
RMAN> restore database;
Starting restore at 10/03/2008 00:38:55
using target database control file instead of recovery catalog
allocated channel: ORA_DISK_1
channel ORA_DISK_1: SID=155 device type=DISK
channel ORA_DISK_1: starting datafile backup set restore
channel ORA_DISK_1: specifying datafile(s) to restore from backup set
channel ORA_DISK_1: restoring datafile 00001 to
C:\ORACLE\ORADATA\ORCL\SYSTEM01.DBF
channel ORA_DISK_1: restoring datafile 00002 to
C:\ORACLE\ORADATA\ORCL\SYSAUX01.DBF
channel ORA_DISK_1: restoring datafile 00003 to
```

EXERCISE 6.1 *(continued)*

```
C:\ORACLE\ORADATA\ORCL\UNDOTBS01.DBF
channel ORA_DISK_1: restoring datafile 00004 to
C:\ORACLE\FLASH_RECOVERY_AREA\ORCL\DATAFILE\O1_MF_USERS_4G2Q1YTC_.DBF
channel ORA_DISK_1: reading from backup piece
C:\ORACLE\FLASH_RECOVERY_AREA\ORCL\BACKUPSET\2008_10_03
\O1_MF_NNNDF_TAG20081003T001928_4GCGCQQ4_.BKP
channel ORA_DISK_1: piece
handle=C:\ORACLE\FLASH_RECOVERY_AREA\ORCL\BACKUPSET\2008_10_03
\O1_MF_NNNDF_TAG20081003T001928_4GCGCQQ4_.BKP tag=TAG20081003T001928
channel ORA_DISK_1: restored backup piece 1
channel ORA_DISK_1: restore complete, elapsed time: 00:04:05
Finished restore at 10/03/2008 00:43:02
RMAN>
```

14. Recover the database with the `recover database` command:

```
RMAN> recover database;
Starting recover at 10/03/2008 01:43:59
using channel ORA_DISK_1
starting media recovery
media recovery complete, elapsed time: 00:00:04
Finished recover at 10/03/2008 01:44:05
RMAN>
```

15. Open the database with the `alter database open` command:

```
RMAN> alter database open;
database opened
```

The database is open.

Datafile or Tablespace Recovery in ARCHIVELOG Mode

If you have lost one or a few database datafiles, or perhaps all the datafiles lost are part of a tablespace, you can perform recovery actions specific to those few lost datafiles rather than to the database as a whole. *Datafile recoveries* and *tablespace recoveries* can be far faster than recovering the entire database with a complete recovery.

Some datafile and tablespace recoveries require that the database be in MOUNT mode. If you have lost the SYSTEM tablespace or the active UNDO tablespace (or an inactive tablespace that contained transactions when the database was shut down), then your recovery will have to be done with the database mounted.

The best recoveries (if there is really any kind of recovery that is even considered good) are those that your users know nothing about. If the datafile or tablespace that was lost was not the SYSTEM or active UNDO tablespace, then you can recover that datafile or tablespace while the rest of the database is still online. Thus, unless the users need access to the tablespace that is being restored, they will never know that you were in the throes of some form of recovery.

In the following sections, we will address these two kinds of datafile and tablespace recoveries. First we will address recovery of a datafile or tablespace when the SYSTEM or active UNDO tablespace is down and the database is not open. We will then address datafile and tablespace recoveries when the database is open and running.

Recovering Critical Database Datafiles and/or Tablespaces with the Database Down

If the SYSTEM or the active UNDO tablespace, or datafiles associated with those tablespaces, are lost, then you will have to recover with the database shut down. In fact, if datafiles associated with these tablespaces are lost, it's likely that the database will have crashed anyway. You can use the `restore datafile` or `restore tablespace` RMAN command to restore the lost datafiles or tablespaces quickly, in turn getting the database recovered as quickly as possible.

To restore a database datafile or tablespace with the database shut down, follow these steps.

1. If the database is not already shut down, try to force a checkpoint and then shut down the database as normally as possible. It is possible that when you force the checkpoint, the database will crash.
2. If you have lost your control file or spfile, you will need to reference the section, "Other Basic Recovery Topics" which appears later in this chapter. To start any RMAN recovery, you must have a control file and an spfile or parameter file.
3. Mount your database with the `startup mount` command.
4. You will use the RMAN `restore` command to restore the datafiles or tablespaces. If you have lost all or most of the datafiles related to a given tablespace, then issue the RMAN `restore tablespace` command. If you have lost one or just a few datafiles, use the `restore datafile` command. Once the restore is complete, you will be returned to the RMAN prompt.
5. You now need to recover the database with the RMAN `recover` command. This will apply any incremental backups and any archived redo logs to the datafiles being restored. If you used the `restore tablespace` command, recover the tablespace with the `recover tablespace` command. If you used the `restore datafile` command, use the `recover datafile` command to start recovery. Once recovery is complete, you will be returned to the RMAN prompt.
6. Open the database with the `alter database open` command. If you restored your control file, you will need to use the `alter database open resetlogs` command.

In this example, we will try to start up our database from the RMAN prompt only to find that the SYSTEM tablespace datafile is missing for some odd reason:

```
RMAN> startup
Oracle instance started
database mounted
RMAN-00571: ===========================================================
RMAN-00569: =============== ERROR MESSAGE STACK FOLLOWS ===============
RMAN-00571: ===========================================================
RMAN-03002: failure of startup command at 09/28/2008 17:37:53
ORA-01157: cannot identify/lock data file 1 - see DBWR trace file
ORA-01110: data file 1: 'C:\ORACLE\ORADATA\ORCL\SYSTEM01.DBF'
```

We could, of course, restore the entire database, but the size of the SYSTEM tablespace/datafile is a very small part of the overall size of the database. So we will just restore and recover the SYSTEM tablespace. Note that the SYSTEM tablespace is a critical tablespace; thus, this recovery cannot be done online:

```
RMAN> startup
Oracle instance started
database mounted
RMAN-00571: ===========================================================
RMAN-00569: =============== ERROR MESSAGE STACK FOLLOWS ===============
RMAN-00571: ===========================================================
RMAN-03002: failure of startup command at 09/28/2008 17:37:53
ORA-01157: cannot identify/lock data file 1 - see DBWR trace file
ORA-01110: data file 1: 'C:\ORACLE\ORADATA\ORCL\SYSTEM01.DBF'
RMAN> restore tablespace system;
Starting restore at 28-SEP-08
using target database control file instead of recovery catalog
allocated channel: ORA_DISK_1
channel ORA_DISK_1: SID=153 device type=DISK
channel ORA_DISK_1: starting datafile backup set restore
channel ORA_DISK_1: specifying datafile(s) to restore from backup set
channel ORA_DISK_1: restoring datafile 00001 to
C:\ORACLE\ORADATA\ORCL\SYSTEM01.DBF
channel ORA_DISK_1: reading from backup piece
C:\ORACLE\FLASH_RECOVERY_AREA\ORCL\BACKUPSET\2008_09_28
\O1_MF_NNNDF_TAG20080928T172015_4G049OQX_.BKP
channel ORA_DISK_1: piece
handle=C:\ORACLE\FLASH_RECOVERY_AREA\ORCL\BACKUPSET\2008_09_28
```

```
\01_MF_NNNDF_TAG20080928T172015_4G049OQX_.BKP tag=TAG20080928T172015
channel ORA_DISK_1: restored backup piece 1
channel ORA_DISK_1: restore complete, elapsed time: 00:03:35
Finished restore at 28-SEP-08
RMAN> recover tablespace system;
Starting recover at 28-SEP-08
using channel ORA_DISK_1
starting media recovery
media recovery complete, elapsed time: 00:00:03
Finished recover at 28-SEP-08
RMAN> alter database open;
database opened
```

Restoring Datafiles to Different Locations

If during a recovery you need to restore datafiles to a different location, you will need to use the RMAN `set newname` command to reset the location of each datafile that is to be relocated. For example, if you wanted to relocate the `USERS01.DBF` datafile from `c:\oracle\oradata\orcl` to `d:\oracle\oradata\orcl` during an RMAN recovery, you would issue this command:

```
set newname for 'c:\oracle\oradata\orcl\users01.dbf' to
'd:\oracle\oradata\orcl\users01.dbf';
```

Note that if you use the `set newname` command, you will have to include it and all restore-and-recovery-related commands within a run block, as shown here:

```
run { set newname for datafile 'c:\oracle\oradata\orcl\users01.dbf' to
'c:\oracle\oradata\orcltwo\users01.dbf';
restore database;
recover database; }
```

Recovering Noncritical Database Datafile and/or Tablespaces with the Database Open

When you have lost a datafile or a few datafiles or all the datafiles of one or several tablespaces, RMAN provides the ability to restore those datafiles online without having to shut down the database. This is known as an *online datafile recovery* or *online tablespace recovery*. Online recoveries allow users to access unaffected tablespaces/datafiles of the database without knowing that other parts of the database are unavailable. To be sure, anyone who tries to use the parts of the database that are being recovered will know that something is not right, but something is better than nothing, right?

The SYSTEM and active UNDO tablespaces are considered critical tablespaces and thus are the only tablespaces that will require recovery of the database with the database down (see the previous section for a discussion on recovery of these critical tablespaces). Any other tablespace can be restored with the database running. Let's look at online database recoveries with datafiles and then tablespaces in the next sections.

You never need to restore temporary files that are associated with temporary tablespaces. First, RMAN will never back up the temporary tablespace, because it does not need to. All RMAN needs to know is that the temporary tablespace exists, and it knows this by virtue of reading the control file of the database. Knowing what temporary tablespace and what tempfiles are needed, RMAN will simply add the tempfiles to the temporary tablespace after a complete or point-in-time database restore. No datafile restore needed!

Preparing to Restore Datafiles or Tablespaces Online

It may be that your database is already shut down and will not start because of the missing datafiles. It may or may not make sense to open the database before starting the restore so users can access unaffected data. To open the database when noncritical datafiles are missing, follow these steps:

1. From the RMAN prompt, issue the `startup` command. An error will appear indicating the datafile that is missing. This will report on just a single missing datafile. You can use the `report schema` command to report on any other missing datafiles. Any datafile with a size of 0 will be a missing datafile and will likely need to be restored. Here is an example of the output from the `list schema` command that indicates the USERS01.DBF datafile is missing. Note the 0 value in the `Size(MB)` column:

```
RMAN> report schema;
Report of database schema for database with db_unique_name ORCL
List of Permanent Datafiles
===========================
File Size(MB) Tablespace           RB segs Datafile Name
---- -------- -------------------- ------- ------------------------
1    700      SYSTEM               ***
C:\ORACLE\ORADATA\ORCL\SYSTEM01.DBF
2    716      SYSAUX               ***
C:\ORACLE\ORADATA\ORCL\SYSAUX01.DBF
4    0        USERS                ***
C:\ORACLE\ORADATA\ORCL\USERS01.DBF
5    30       UNDOTBS2             ***
C:\ORACLE\ORADATA\ORCL\UNDOTBS02.DBF
```

2. From the RMAN prompt, take all the datafiles or tablespaces to be recovered offline. You do this by using the RMAN `sql` command followed by the appropriate `alter database datafile offline` command or the `alter tablespace offline` command.
3. From the RMAN prompt, issue the `alter database open` command. The database should open without complaining about any missing datafiles.

Here is a case where we have tried to start our database and the `USERS01.DBF` datafile is not available. We will make sure that this is the only datafile that needs to be restored. We then take the datafile offline and open the database:

```
RMAN> startup
Oracle instance started
database mounted
RMAN-00571: ===========================================================
RMAN-00569: =============== ERROR MESSAGE STACK FOLLOWS ===============
RMAN-00571: ===========================================================
RMAN-03002: failure of startup command at 09/28/2008 17:50:49
ORA-01157: cannot identify/lock data file 3 - see DBWR trace file
ORA-01110: data file 3: 'C:\ORACLE\ORADATA\ORCL\USERS01.DBF'
RMAN> report schema;
Report of database schema for database with db_unique_name ORCL
List of Permanent Datafiles
===========================
File Size(MB) Tablespace         RB segs Datafile Name
---- -------- ------------------ ------- ------------------------
1    700      SYSTEM             ***     C:\ORACLE\ORADATA\ORCL\SYSTEM01.DBF
2    716      SYSAUX             ***     C:\ORACLE\ORADATA\ORCL\SYSAUX01.DBF
3    0        USERS              ***     C:\ORACLE\ORADATA\ORCL\USERS01.DBF
5    30       UNDOTBS2           ***     C:\ORACLE\ORADATA\ORCL\UNDOTBS02.DBF

List of Temporary Files
=======================
File Size(MB) Tablespace        Maxsize(MB) Tempfile Name
---- -------- ----------------- ----------- --------------------
1    20       TEMP              32767       C:\ORACLE\ORADATA\ORCL\TEMP01.DBF
RMAN> sql 'alter database datafile 3 offline';
sql statement: alter database datafile 3 offline
RMAN> alter database open;
database opened
```

Restoring Database Datafiles Online

Once the database is up and running or if the database was already running, follow these steps to restore one or more missing datafiles:

1. From the RMAN prompt, take the datafile or datafiles offline using the RMAN `sql` command calling the `alter database datafile offline` command. Do this for each datafile that you need to take offline.
2. From the RMAN prompt, restore the datafiles using the `restore datafile` command. You can restore one or multiple datafiles in one shot. You will be returned to the RMAN prompt once the restore is complete.
3. Having restored the datafiles, use the `recover datafile` command to recover each specific datafile. This will apply any incremental backups and archived redo logs to the restored datafile. You will be returned to the RMAN prompt once the recovery is complete.
4. Bring the datafile(s) back online using the RMAN `sql` command to issue the `alter database datafile online` SQL command. This will bring each datafile online, completing the recovery process.

In this example, the `USERS01.DBF` datafile is already offline (we offlined the datafile in the earlier example). We will restore that datafile (referring to it by its datafile number) and then recover it. Finally, we will bring the datafile online so that the database may access it:

```
RMAN> restore datafile 3;
Starting restore at 28-SEP-08
allocated channel: ORA_DISK_1
channel ORA_DISK_1: SID=136 device type=DISK
channel ORA_DISK_1: starting datafile backup set restore
channel ORA_DISK_1: specifying datafile(s) to restore from backup set
channel ORA_DISK_1: restoring datafile 00003 to
C:\ORACLE\ORADATA\ORCL\USERS01.DBF
channel ORA_DISK_1: reading from backup piece
C:\ORACLE\FLASH_RECOVERY_AREA\ORCL\BACKUPSET\2008_09_28
\O1_MF_NNNDF_TAG20080928T185206_4G09OW7B_.BKP
channel ORA_DISK_1: piece
handle=C:\ORACLE\FLASH_RECOVERY_AREA\ORCL\BACKUPSET\2008_09_28
\O1_MF_NNNDF_TAG20080928T185206_4G09OW7B_.BKP tag=TAG20080928T185206
channel ORA_DISK_1: restored backup piece 1
channel ORA_DISK_1: restore complete, elapsed time: 00:00:15
Finished restore at 28-SEP-08
RMAN> recover datafile 3;
Starting recover at 28-SEP-08
using channel ORA_DISK_1
```

```
starting media recovery
media recovery complete, elapsed time: 00:00:02
Finished recover at 28-SEP-08
RMAN> sql 'alter database datafile 3 online';
sql statement: alter database datafile 3 online
```

Restoring Database Tablespaces Online

If you have lost most or all datafiles related to one or more tablespaces, it might be easier to recover the entire tablespace rather than individual datafiles. Of course, a tablespace recovery really is a datafile recovery; it just makes RMAN do the extra legwork to figure out which datafiles need to be restored. Once the database is up and running or if the database was already running, follow these steps to restore one or more tablespaces:

1. From the RMAN prompt, take the tablespace(s) offline using the RMAN `sql` command calling the `alter tablespace offline` command. Do this for each tablespace that you need to take offline.
2. From the RMAN prompt, restore the tablespace using the `restore tablespace` command. You can restore one or multiple tablespaces in one shot. You will be returned to the RMAN prompt once the restore is complete.
3. Having restored the tablespace datafiles, use the `recover tablespace` command to recover the tablespace and its associated datafiles. This will apply any incremental backups and archived redo logs to the restored tablespace. You will be returned to the RMAN prompt once the recovery is complete.
4. Bring the datafile(s) back online using the RMAN `sql` command to issue the `alter database datafile online` SQL command. This will bring each datafile online, completing the recovery process.

Here is an example of a recovery of the USERS tablespace from RMAN (note that if the database was running, we could use the `alter tablespace offline` command to take the tablespace offline):

```
RMAN> startup
Oracle instance started
database mounted
RMAN-00571: ===========================================================
RMAN-00569: =============== ERROR MESSAGE STACK FOLLOWS ===============
RMAN-00571: ===========================================================
RMAN-03002: failure of startup command at 09/28/2008 20:01:30
ORA-01157: cannot identify/lock data file 3 - see DBWR trace file
ORA-01110: data file 3: 'C:\ORACLE\ORADATA\ORCL\USERS01.DBF'
RMAN> sql 'alter tablespace users datafile offline';
sql statement: alter tablespace users datafile offline
```

```
RMAN> alter database open;
database opened
RMAN> restore tablespace users;
Starting restore at 28-SEP-08
using target database control file instead of recovery catalog
allocated channel: ORA_DISK_1
channel ORA_DISK_1: SID=153 device type=DISK
channel ORA_DISK_1: starting datafile backup set restore
channel ORA_DISK_1: specifying datafile(s) to restore from backup set
channel ORA_DISK_1: restoring datafile 00003 to
C:\ORACLE\ORADATA\ORCL\USERS01.DBF
channel ORA_DISK_1: reading from backup piece
C:\ORACLE\FLASH_RECOVERY_AREA\ORCL\BACKUPSET\2008_09_28
\O1_MF_NNNDF_TAG20080928T185206_4G09OW7B_.BKP
channel ORA_DISK_1: piece
handle=C:\ORACLE\FLASH_RECOVERY_AREA\ORCL\BACKUPSET\2008_09_28
\O1_MF_NNNDF_TAG20080928T185206_4G09OW7B_.BKP tag=TAG20080928T185206
channel ORA_DISK_1: restored backup piece 1
channel ORA_DISK_1: restore complete, elapsed time: 00:00:15
Finished restore at 28-SEP-08
RMAN> recover tablespace users;
Starting recover at 28-SEP-08
using channel ORA_DISK_1
starting media recovery
media recovery complete, elapsed time: 00:00:02
Finished recover at 28-SEP-08
RMAN> sql 'alter tablespace users online';
sql statement: alter tablespace users online
```

Recovering a Database Using Incomplete Recovery

We discussed *incomplete recovery* or *point-in-time recovery* back in Chapter 3. It is, essentially, restoring the database to some point in time that is not the current point in time. If you are not familiar with what incomplete recovery is, please review Chapter 3 for more details. In the following sections we will discuss point-in-time recoveries. First we will discuss the types of recoveries that are available and then we will discuss the mechanics of such recoveries.

Real World Scenario

What Happens If the Control File Has Lost the Backup Records

Most RMAN restores are easy and require only the use of the RMAN client. However, we've seen cases where the RMAN client was not enough. In one case, the database site had lost its recovery catalog, and the `CONTROL_FILE_RECORD_KEEP_TIME` parameter was set to 7 days. Guess what happened to all the RMAN metadata after 7 days when the recovery catalog was lost.

At the same time, we had a need to restore a database to a point in time of perhaps 30 days before to check on the state of some data. Of course, the metadata for the restore was not available. This was clearly a bad day.

There are several ways to address this problem. The Oracle Database 11*g* *RMAN catalog* command provides the ability to catalog backup set pieces in the database (this was not available prior to Oracle Database 10*g*). In the case of the loss listed earlier, we opted to write some PL/SQL and use the PL/SQL packages that RMAN uses itself to restore the backups from tape. RMAN uses a PL/SQL package called *dbms_backup_restore* to perform most backup and restore operations. Using this package (documented pretty well on Oracle's support site at `metalink.oracle.com`), we were able to restore a database from an older backup.

The bottom line is that as long as you have the backup set pieces, any RMAN backup can be restored. It just might take some time and effort and perhaps a bit of help from Oracle support.

Remember that point-in-time backups must be consistent. That means you have to restore the whole database to the specific point in time you are aiming for. Oracle offers the ability to do tablespace point-in-time recoveries, which we will discuss in Chapter 8.

Types of Point-in-Time Recovery

RMAN supports point-in-time recovery using the `until` clause of the `restore` and `recover` commands as seen in this example, where we will be restoring to 9/30/2008 at 18:00 hours:

```
Restore database until time '09/30/2008:18:00:00';
Recover database until time '09/30/2008:18:00:00';
```

When using a run block, you will use the set command to set the recovery window for RMAN, as shown in this example:

```
Run {
Set until time until time '09/30/2008:18:00:00';
Restore database;
Recover database;
}
```

You can do point-in-time recovery using the following:

Time The *Time-based point-in-time recovery* method is based on the timestamps in the online redo logs. RMAN will restore the database to the closest possible timestamp listed in the command. You can find the timestamp ranges contained in specific online redo logs by querying the FIRST_TIME column of the V$LOG_HISTORY view for each redo log. In this example, RMAN will restore the database to 9/29/2008 at 15:00:00:

```
restore database until time '09/29/2008:15:00:00';
recover database until time '09/29/2008:15:00:00';
alter database open resetlogs;
```

SCN The *SCN-based point-in-time recovery* method is based on recovery to a specific SCN in the database. You can determine the current SCN of the database from the CURRENT_SCN column of the V$DATABASE view. You can determine the SCN range contained within a given redo log by querying the FIRST_CHANGE# and NEXT_CHANGE# columns of the V$LOG_HISTORY view. Here is an example of an SCN-based point-in-time recovery:

```
restore database until SCN 12345;
recover database until SCN 12345;
alter database open resetlogs;
```

Log sequence number The *log sequence number point-in-time recovery* method is based on recovery up to, and including, a specific log sequence number. Log sequence numbers for individual redo logs can be found in the V$LOG_HISTORY and V$LOG views. Here is an example of a point-in-time recovery based on a log sequence number:

```
restore database until sequence 12345;
recover database until sequence 12345;
alter database open resetlogs;
```

In Exercise 6.2, you'll perform a point-in-time recovery with RMAN.

EXERCISE 6.2

Perform a Point-in-Time Recovery with RMAN

This activity builds on the backup done in Exercise 4.2 in Chapter 4. You should have completed Exercise 4.2 prior to executing this activity. Please note that the output you experience from this exercise will probably differ from the output shown in this exercise.

1. Complete Exercise 4.2.
2. Set the NLS_DATE_FORMAT environment variable from the operating system.

   In Unix (may vary based on the shell you are using):

   ```
   export NLS_DATE_FORMAT='mm/dd/yyyy hh24:mi:ss'
   ```

   In DOS:

   ```
   set NLS_DATE_FORMAT=mm/dd/yyyy hh24:mi:ss
   ```

3. Start RMAN. We will assume you are not using a recovery catalog during this exercise.

   ```
   C:\oracle>rman target=/
   Recovery Manager: Release 11.1.0.6.0 -
   Production on Fri Oct 3 00:37:44 2008
   Copyright (c) 1982, 2007, Oracle.  All rights reserved.
   connected to target database (not started)
   ```

4. Start up the database with the `startup force mount` command from RMAN.

   ```
   RMAN> startup force mount
   Oracle instance started
   database mounted
   Total System Global Area     364081152 bytes
   Fixed Size                     1333228 bytes
   Variable Size                264243220 bytes
   Database Buffers              92274688 bytes
   Redo Buffers                   6230016 bytes
   ```

5. Determine the current backups that are available for restore with the `list backup of database summary` command (to be discussed in Chapter 7):

   ```
   RMAN> list backup of database summary;
   List of Backups
   ===============
   Key     TY LV S Device Type Completion Time     #Pieces #Copies Compressed Tag
   ------- -- -- - ----------- ------------------- ------- ------- ---------- ---
   6       B  F  A DISK        09/29/2008 14:07:23 1       1       NO
   SILVER_COPY
   11      B  F  A DISK        10/02/2008 00:46:25 1       1       YES
   ```

EXERCISE 6.2 *(continued)*

```
GOLD_COPY
17      B  F  A DISK        10/03/2008 00:25:19 1       1       YES
TAG20081003T001928
```

6. From the output generated in step 5, choose the date and time of the most current backup (in our case, it's 10/03/2008 at 00:25:19). We will restore the database to 10 minutes after this date and time (in our case, 10/03/2008 at 00:35:19).

7. Issue the `restore database until time` command to restore the database to the date and time selected. In our case, the command will be `restore database until time '10/03/2008:00:35:19'`; your command will have a different date and time (unless you have reset the clock so precisely that you got the same date!).

```
RMAN> restore database until time '10/03/2008:00:35:19';
Starting restore at 10/03/2008 01:57:31
allocated channel: ORA_DISK_1
channel ORA_DISK_1: SID=155 device type=DISK
channel ORA_DISK_1: starting datafile backup set restore
channel ORA_DISK_1: specifying datafile(s) to restore from backup set
channel ORA_DISK_1: restoring datafile 00001 to
C:\ORACLE\ORADATA\ORCL\SYSTEM01.DBF
channel ORA_DISK_1: restoring datafile 00002 to
C:\ORACLE\ORADATA\ORCL\SYSAUX01.DBF
channel ORA_DISK_1: restoring datafile 00003 to
C:\ORACLE\ORADATA\ORCL\UNDOTBS01.DBF
channel ORA_DISK_1: restoring datafile 00004 to
C:\ORACLE\FLASH_RECOVERY_AREA\ORCL\DATAFILE\O1_MF_USERS_4G2Q1YTC_.DBF
channel ORA_DISK_1: reading from backup piece
C:\ORACLE\FLASH_RECOVERY_AREA\ORCL\BACKUPSET\2008_10_03
\O1_MF_NNNDF_TAG20081003T001928_4GCGCQQ4_.BKP
channel ORA_DISK_1: piece
handle=C:\ORACLE\FLASH_RECOVERY_AREA\ORCL\BACKUPSET\2008_10_03
\O1_MF_NNNDF_TAG20081003T001928_4GCGCQQ4_.BKP tag=TAG20081003T001928
channel ORA_DISK_1: restored backup piece 1
channel ORA_DISK_1: restore complete, elapsed time: 00:07:15
Finished restore at 10/03/2008 02:04:47
```

8. Recover the database with the `recover database until time` command. Our command would be `recover database until time '10/03/2008:00:35:19'`; your command will have a different date and time.

```
RMAN> recover database until time '10/03/2008:00:35:19';
Starting recover at 10/03/2008 02:06:01
```

EXERCISE 6.2 *(continued)*

```
using channel ORA_DISK_1
starting media recovery
media recovery complete, elapsed time: 00:00:03
Finished recover at 10/03/2008 02:06:05
```

9. Open the database with the `alter database open resetlogs` command:

```
RMAN> alter database open resetlogs;
database opened
```

The database is open.

What Can I Recover To?

You may want to make sure you can actually recover to the point in time that you are interested in before you haul off and try the recovery. Nothing makes for a worse day than trying to do a point-in-time restore, after having removed the existing datafiles, than finding out that you can't do the restore.

The `restore validate` command can come in handy here. You can use this command to make sure that all of the backup set pieces you will need to restore your database are available. This includes backup sets for datafile backups and archived redo logs as well as any datafile image copies. Here is an example of the `restore validate` command for a point-in-time database recovery:

```
RMAN> restore database until time 'sysdate -1/24' validate;
Starting restore at 28-SEP-08
using channel ORA_DISK_1
channel ORA_DISK_1: starting validation of datafile backup set
channel ORA_DISK_1: reading from backup piece
C:\ORACLE\FLASH_RECOVERY_AREA\ORCL\BACKUPSET\2008_09_28
\O1_MF_NNNDF_TAG20080928T185206_4G09OW7B_.BKP
channel ORA_DISK_1: piece
handle=C:\ORACLE\FLASH_RECOVERY_AREA\ORCL\BACKUPSET\2008_09_28
\O1_MF_NNNDF_TAG20080928T185206_4G09OW7B_.BKP tag=TAG20080928T185206
channel ORA_DISK_1: restored backup piece 1
channel ORA_DISK_1: validation complete, elapsed time: 00:00:25
Finished restore at 28-SEP-08
```

Point-in-Time Recovery Mechanics

Regardless of the type of point-in-time recovery you are going to do, the mechanics are the same. During a point-in-time recovery, the database must be in MOUNT mode. There is no online point-in-time recovery for an entire Oracle database (though RMAN does offer tablespace point-in-time recovery, which can be done online).

Once the point-in-time recovery is complete, you will open the database with the `alter database open resetlogs` command. This will reset (or re-create if need be) the online redo logs of the database and open it for business. The end result is a new incarnation of the database (see Chapter 3 for more on database incarnations), which can impact future backups. Oracle Database 11*g* and RMAN will be able to use the same backup to restore the database (as well as any old and new archived redo logs). Still, it's probably a good idea to perform another backup of your database, as it just makes things cleaner and easier.

Here is a list of the RMAN commands needed to perform a time-based point-in-time recovery to September 29, 2008, at 15:00 hours:

```
shutdown abort
startup mount
restore database until time '09/29/2008:15:00:00';
recover database until time '09/29/2008:15:00:00';
alter database open resetlogs;
```

And here is the result of the execution of those commands:

```
C:\Documents and Settings\Robert>rman target=/
Recovery Manager: Release 11.1.0.6.0 - Production on Wed Oct 1 22:30:48 2008
Copyright (c) 1982, 2007, Oracle.  All rights reserved.
connected to target database: ORCL (DBID=1194488809)
RMAN> shutdown abort
Oracle instance shut down
RMAN> startup mount
connected to target database (not started)
Oracle instance started
database mounted
Total System Global Area     364081152 bytes
Fixed Size                     1333228 bytes
Variable Size                239077396 bytes
Database Buffers             117440512 bytes
Redo Buffers                   6230016 bytes
RMAN> restore database until time '09/29/2008:15:00:00';
Starting restore at 10/01/2008 22:32:44
allocated channel: ORA_DISK_1
channel ORA_DISK_1: SID=151 device type=DISK
```

```
channel ORA_DISK_1: starting datafile backup set restore
channel ORA_DISK_1: specifying datafile(s) to restore from backup set
channel ORA_DISK_1: restoring datafile 00001 to
C:\ORACLE\ORADATA\ORCL\SYSTEM01.DBF
channel ORA_DISK_1: restoring datafile 00002 to
C:\ORACLE\ORADATA\ORCL\SYSAUX01.DBF
channel ORA_DISK_1: restoring datafile 00003 to
C:\ORACLE\ORADATA\ORCL\UNDOTBS01.DBF
channel ORA_DISK_1: restoring datafile 00004 to
C:\ORACLE\FLASH_RECOVERY_AREA\ORCL
\DATAFILE\O1_MF_USERS_4G2Q1YTC_.DBF
channel ORA_DISK_1: reading from backup piece
C:\ORACLE\FLASH_RECOVERY_AREA\ORCL
\BACKUPSET\2008_09_29\O1_MF_NNNDF_SILVER_COPY_4G2DQT1Y_.BKP
RMAN> recover database until time '09/29/2008:15:00:00';
Starting recover at 10/02/2008 00:09:47
using channel ORA_DISK_1
starting media recovery
archived log for thread 1 with sequence 5 is already on disk as file
C:\ORACLE\PRODUCT\11.1.0\DB_1\RDBMS\ARC00005_0666708076.001
archived log for thread 1 with sequence 6 is already on disk as file
C:\ORACLE\FLASH_RECOVERY_AREA\ORCL\ARCHIVELOG\2008_09_30
\O1_MF_1_6_4G4QPYYR_.ARC
archived log file name=
C:\ORACLE\PRODUCT\11.1.0\DB_1\RDBMS\ARC00005_0666708076.001
thread=1 sequence=5
media recovery complete, elapsed time: 00:00:14
Finished recover at 10/02/2008 00:10:03
RMAN> alter database open resetlogs;
database opened
```

You could also have executed this restore using the following commands:

```
shutown abort
startup mount
run {
set until time '09/30/2008:18:00:00';
restore database;
recover database;
}
sql 'alter database open resetlogs';
```

One time that you might need to perform point-in-time recovery is during a database recovery after a complete loss of the online redo logs of the database. This might include cases where just the online redo logs were lost or cases when the entire database was lost, including the online redo logs. While it is possible to save your database data in the event of such a loss (see Chapter 3 for more information on such a case), it is likely that you will have to perform a point-in-time recovery to get your database operational again. This will, of course, result in some data loss.

You can also restore databases using tags. A tag allows you to choose a specific backup image that you want to use for the restore. You can also use a tag during a recovery to indicate specific incremental backups that you want to use for a restore. When you use tags, Oracle will still do a complete recovery unless you use the `until time` parameter to indicate that you want to recover to a specific point in time.

Here is an example where we are restoring the database using the tag `gold_copy`:

```
shutdown immediate
startup mount
restore database from tag 'gold_copy';
recover database from tag 'gold_copy';
alter database open;
```

We discussed database incarnations in Chapter 3. Sometimes for specific types of RMAN recoveries you will need to reset the database incarnation. We will cover this in more detail in Chapter 8.

Using Image Copies to Recover Your Database

Recall that an *image copy* is an exact copy of a given database datafile. You can use image copies to restore your database. This can provide for quick database recovery, though the image copies will require much more storage than a compressed backup set piece.

Oracle provides the `switch` command to use in place of the `restore` command. This will essentially change the control file so it will point to the datafile copy(ies). You then would call the `recover` command to apply any incremental backups and archived redo logs to restore the datafile(s) or tablespace(s). You can switch the entire database, tablespaces, or specific datafiles depending on your needs. Here is an example where we are restoring datafile 4:

```
Sql 'alter database datafile 4 offline';
Switch datafile 4 to copy '/oracle/backup/users_01.dbf';
Recover datafile 4;
Sql 'alter database datafile 4 online';
```

Note that if you are making image copies and backup-set copies, RMAN will determine which to use during a normal restore operation. This includes image copies that are updated with incremental backups (discussed in Chapter 4). So, with image copies you have two options for restore and recovery really:

- Use the `restore` command to have RMAN copy the image copies to the original location of the database datafiles. This will not result in any changes to datafile locations in the database control file.
- Use the `switch` command to cause RMAN to instantly start using the image copy of the datafile in its current location. This will cause the database control file to be changed with locations of the new database datafiles.

Other Basic Recovery Topics

There are other recovery-related topics you will need to be aware of. In the following sections, we will cover some of those, and in Chapter 8 we will cover other, more advanced recovery topics. In this section we will discuss block media recovery and recovering from lost control files and lost spfiles with RMAN.

Block Media Recovery

Sometimes one or a few blocks will become corrupt. It's rare, but it happens. RMAN provides the ability to do online block media recovery. With *block media recovery*, RMAN will recover the corrupted blocks online. The only user impact will be to those users who want to access the corrupt blocks, and they will have been impacted anyway.

In Oracle Database 11g you use the `recover` command with the `datafile...block` option to perform block media recovery. To use the `recover block` command the following requirements must be met:

- The database must be in ARCHIVELOG mode.
- The database must be mounted or open.
- There must be a current database control file in place.
- All redo logs must be accessible.
- Only blocks marked as `MEDIA_CORRUPT` can be recovered.

For example, sometimes you will issue a DML or DDL statement and get an error such as the one found here:

```
ORA-01578: ORACLE data block corrupted (file # 6, block # 55)
ORA-01110: data file 6: '/oracle/oradata/trgt/users01.dbf'
```

In this case, you could issue the `recover datafile` command using the block parameter as seen in this example:

```
Recover datafile 6 block 55;
```

In some cases, you may want to repair a range of blocks, as shown here:

```
Recover datafile 6 block 55 to 105;
```

You can also recover a range of blocks and several datafiles at one time:

```
Recover datafile 6 block 55 to 105 datafile 7 block 27 to 44;
```

You can also run the `backup database validate` command to determine if any blocks are media corrupt. Any blocks that are corrupt will be listed in the `V$DATABASE_BLOCK_CORRUPTION` view. The column `CORRUPTION_TYPE` will indicate if they are media corrupt.

You can attempt to recover all corrupted blocks listed in the `V$DATABASE_BLOCK_CORRUPTION` view by using the `recover` command with the `corruption list` parameter from RMAN, as seen in this example:

```
RMAN> recover corruption list;
Starting recover at 28-OCT-08
using target database control file instead of recovery catalog
allocated channel: ORA_DISK_1
channel ORA_DISK_1: SID=153 device type=DISK
starting media recovery
media recovery complete, elapsed time: 00:00:01
Finished recover at 28-OCT-08
```

Recovering the Control File

One recovery that you need to be prepared for is the recovery of a lost control file. There are two different situations that come into play here. The first is recovering the control file from a control-file autobackup; the second is recovering a control file if you are not using control-file autobackups. Let's look at each of these methods in more detail.

Recovering Control Files with Control-File Autobackups

We talked about RMAN *control-file autobackups* in Chapter 4. They are a way of automating the backup of database control files. Recovering the control file is quite easy if you are using control-file autobackups. There are two different situations that you will deal with when using control-file autobackups: one when you are using the flash recovery area (FRA) and the other when you are not using the FRA. Let's look at these in a bit more detail.

Control-File Backups Using the FRA

If you are using the FRA and have enabled control-file autobackups, then restoring the current control file is easy. Simply do the following:

- Start the database instance with the `startup nomount` command.
- Issue the `restore controlfile from autobackup` command. RMAN will proceed to restore the control file from the latest automated control-file backup on disk.
- Mount the database after the restore is complete.
- Recover the database with the RMAN `recover` command.
- Open it using the `alter database open resetlogs` command.

Here is an example of the RMAN code:

```
RMAN> Startup nomount;
connected to target database (not started)
Oracle instance started
Total System Global Area     535662592 bytes
Fixed Size                     1334380 bytes
Variable Size                369099668 bytes
Database Buffers             159383552 bytes
Redo Buffers                   5844992 bytes
RMAN> Restore controlfile from autobackup;
Starting restore at 28-SEP-08
allocated channel: ORA_DISK_1
channel ORA_DISK_1: SID=153 device type=DISK
channel ORA_DISK_1: looking for AUTOBACKUP on day: 20080928
channel ORA_DISK_1: AUTOBACKUP found:
c:\oracle\controlfilebackup\c-437680418-20080928-00
channel ORA_DISK_1: restoring control file from AUTOBACKUP
 c:\oracle\controlfilebackup\c-437680418-20080928-00
channel ORA_DISK_1: control file restore from AUTOBACKUP complete
output file name=C:\ORACLE\ORADATA\RCAT\CONTROL01.CTL
output file name=C:\ORACLE\ORADATA\RCAT\CONTROL02.CTL
output file name=C:\ORACLE\ORADATA\RCAT\CONTROL03.CTL
Finished restore at 28-SEP-08
RMAN> alter database mount;
database mounted
released channel: ORA_DISK_1
RMAN> recover database;
Starting recover at 28-SEP-08
allocated channel: ORA_DISK_1
```

```
channel ORA_DISK_1: SID=153 device type=DISK
starting media recovery
archived log for thread 1 with sequence 13 is already on disk as file
C:\ORACLE\ORADATA\RCAT\REDO01.LOG
archived log for thread 1 with sequence 14 is already on disk as file
C:\ORACLE\ORADATA\RCAT\REDO02.LOG
archived log file name=C:\ORACLE\ORADATA\RCAT\REDO01.LOG thread=1 sequence=13
archived log file name=C:\ORACLE\ORADATA\RCAT\REDO02.LOG thread=1 sequence=14
media recovery complete, elapsed time: 00:00:01
Finished recover at 28-SEP-08
RMAN> alter database open resetlogs;
Database opened
```

When you use the `restore controlfile from autobackup` command, Oracle will start searching for the most current control-file autobackup by default. If you have used the `set until` command to perform a point-in-time recovery, RMAN will start searching for the most current control file starting with that day/time and moving backwards.

The `restore controlfile` command also comes with the `maxseq` and `maxdays` parameters to further control how much effort is used to search for a backup control file.

The `maxseq` parameter Each control-file backup on a given day is assigned a sequence number. That number increments by one for each additional control-file autobackup, until the next day when the sequence resets itself. The maximum sequence number is 256 and the minimum number is 0. RMAN will always search for the highest sequence number (or the most current file) first. The `maxseq` parameter indicates to RMAN which sequence number it should start with when looking for the correct control-file autobackup. This allows you to skip certain sequence numbers if you know you do not want to use them. Here is an example of using `maxseq`:

```
Restore controlfile from autobackup maxseq 200;
```

The `maxdays` parameter By default RMAN will look back 7 days (from the current date or the `set until` date) to find the correct control-file autobackup. If you want to change this default setting, use the `maxdays` parameter when calling the `restore controlfile from autobackup` command. You can search from 0 until 366 days for the current control-file autobackup. Here is an example of using `maxdays` where we will go back 30 days to find the correct control-file autobackup.

```
Restore controlfile from autobackup maxdays 30;
```

The maxdays and maxseq parameters also apply to spfile autobackup restore operations.

Control-File Backups Not Using the FRA

If you are not using the FRA but have enabled control-file autobackups, you will need to determine the database ID (DBID) of the database. Each database has a DBID, which uniquely identifies it. You should maintain a list of DBIDs for each of your databases if you are not using the FRA but want to use control-file autobackups. You can find the DBID in the DBID column of the V$DATABASE view as seen in this query:

```
SQL> select dbid from v$database;
      DBID
----------
437680418
```

The database DBID is included in the filename of the control-file autobackup backup set pieces (if you're not using the FRA). Thus, in a worst-case situation, you can determine the DBID for your database by looking at these files and determining the DBID from the filenames. If you are not using the FRA, this is one very good reason to have control-file autobackups be put in different directories for different databases!

Now that you have the DBID, you are ready to restore the database control file. To do so, follow these steps:

1. Start up the database in NOMOUNT mode. This will start the database and load the database parameter file. The FRA parameters will be set at this point.
2. Issue the `set dbid` command to set the database DBID that RMAN will look for.
3. Set the control-file autobackup location with the `set controlfile autobackup format` command.
4. Restore the control file with the `restore` command.
5. Mount the database for recovery.
6. Issue the `recover database` command.
7. Open the database using the `alter database open resetlogs` command.

Here is an example of recovering a control file when the FRA is not in use:

```
RMAN> startup force nomount;
Oracle instance started
Total System Global Area     535662592 bytes
Fixed Size                     1334380 bytes
Variable Size                369099668 bytes
Database Buffers             159383552 bytes
Redo Buffers                   5844992 bytes
RMAN> Set dbid 437680418;
```

```
executing command: SET DBID
RMAN> set controlfile autobackup format for device type
disk to 'c:\oracle\controlfilebackup\%F';
executing command: SET CONTROLFILE AUTOBACKUP FORMAT
RMAN> Restore controlfile from autobackup;
Starting restore at 28-SEP-08
using channel ORA_DISK_1
channel ORA_DISK_1: looking for AUTOBACKUP on day: 20080928
channel ORA_DISK_1: AUTOBACKUP found:
c:\oracle\controlfilebackup\c-437680418-20080928-04
channel ORA_DISK_1: restoring control file from AUTOBACKUP
c:\oracle\controlfilebackup\c-437680418-20080928-04
channel ORA_DISK_1: control file restore from AUTOBACKUP complete
output file name=C:\ORACLE\ORADATA\RCAT\CONTROL01.CTL
output file name=C:\ORACLE\ORADATA\RCAT\CONTROL02.CTL
output file name=C:\ORACLE\ORADATA\RCAT\CONTROL03.CTL
Finished restore at 28-SEP-08
RMAN> Alter database mount;
database mounted
released channel: ORA_DISK_1
RMAN> Recover database;
Starting recover at 28-SEP-08
allocated channel: ORA_DISK_1
channel ORA_DISK_1: SID=153 device type=DISK
starting media recovery
archived log for thread 1 with sequence 1 is already on disk as file
C:\ORACLE\ORADATA\RCAT\REDO01.LOG
archived log for thread 1 with sequence 2 is already on disk as file
C:\ORACLE\ORADATA\RCAT\REDO02.LOG
archived log file name=C:\ORACLE\ORADATA\RCAT\REDO01.LOG thread=1 sequence=1
archived log file name=C:\ORACLE\ORADATA\RCAT\REDO02.LOG thread=1 sequence=2
media recovery complete, elapsed time: 00:00:02
Finished recover at 28-SEP-08
RMAN> alter database open resetlogs;
database opened
```

You can also use the `restore controlfile` command to restore a control file to a different location and filename using the to keyword as seen in this example:

```
Restore controlfile to '/tmp/orcl.ctl' from autobackup;
```

Recovering Control Files When Not Using Control-File Autobackups

If you have not enabled control-file autobackups you need to use the recovery catalog to restore a control file (there are other ways—see the sidebar "Emergency Control-File Recoveries"). Simply follow these steps:

1. Start RMAN and connect to the recovery catalog.
2. Use the `startup force nomount` command to start the database instance.
3. Issue the `restore controlfile` command and RMAN will restore the control file.
4. Mount the database with the `alter database mount` command.
5. Issue a `recover database` command
6. Open the database with the `alter database open resetlogs` command.

Here is an example of the commands you would use to perform a control-file restore using the recovery catalog:

```
Startup force nomount
restore controlfile;
alter database mount;
recover database;
Alter database open resetlogs;
```

You can also use the `restore controlfile` command to restore a control file to a different location and filename using the `to` keyword, as seen in this example:

```
Restore controlfile to '/tmp/orcl.ctl';
```

Emergency Control-File Recoveries

If you are not using control-file autobackups and you are not using a recovery catalog, what are you to do when you lose your control file? You can always re-create the control file with the `create controlfile` command (see Chapter 2 for more on this command). You can then use the `catalog` command to catalog the backup set pieces. One complication may be if you are backing up to tape. In this case, you may have to restore your backups from tape to local disk before you can run the `catalog` command.

It is not a fun exercise to have to create your own `create controlfile` command from scratch and we strongly recommend that you configure control-file autobackups instead.

Recovering the Spfile

If you have enabled control-file autobackups, then RMAN will back up the current spfile each time a control-file autobackup occurs. To restore your spfile, you will first need to start the database from RMAN without a parameter file of any sort. Just simply type in **startup nomount** and the database will start using default parameter settings. This positions the database to be able to restore the spfile from the autobackup. RMAN will display a message when it's using default parameter settings as seen in this output:

```
RMAN> startup nomount
connected to target database (not started)
startup failed: ORA-01078: failure in processing system parameters
LRM-00109: could not open parameter file
'C:\ORACLE\PRODUCT\11.1.0\DB_1\DATABASE\INITORCL.ORA'
starting Oracle instance without parameter file for retrieval of spfile
Oracle instance started
Total System Global Area     159019008 bytes
Fixed Size                     1331852 bytes
Variable Size                 67112308 bytes
Database Buffers              83886080 bytes
Redo Buffers                   6688768 bytes
```

The restore process for an spfile differs a bit depending on if you have been using the FRA or not using the FRA. We will look into these two different options in the next sections.

Restoring the spfile When Using the FRA

Restoring the spfile when using the FRA is a bit more complex than restoring the control file. First you will need to start the database instance, as demonstrated previously. Then you will need to configure the FRA location. Because the FRA parameter DB_RECOVERY_FILE_DEST is not dynamic, you need to create a temporary pfile based on the current memory settings and then update it with the correct FRA location.

First, you create the temporary pfile from the in-memory settings using the SQL command `create pfile from memory`. This command will create a database parameter file that you will edit. The parameter settings in this file will be based on the default, in-memory settings used when RMAN started the database. Here is an example of the creation of the pfile from memory:

```
RMAN> sql 'create pfile from memory';
using target database control file instead of recovery catalog
sql statement: create pfile from memory
```

Note that you must create a pfile and not an spfile. This is because you cannot restore over an existing spfile that is in use. Using your editor of choice, edit the pfile you just created. The pfile will typically be created in `ORACLE_HOME/database` in Win and `$ORACLE_HOME/dbs` in linux.

You will want to set the `DB_RECOVERY_FILE_DEST` parameter to the location of the FRA and `DB_RECOVERY_FILE_DEST_SIZE` to the size of the FRA. When setting the `DB_RECOVERY_FILE_DEST_SIZE` parameter, don't worry about how big you need to size it because this is just a temporary parameter setting for the spfile restore. The real value of the parameter will be set after the spfile has been restored. Here is an example of what those parameters would look like in a pfile:

```
db_recovery_file_dest='c:\oracle\flash_recovery_area'
db_recovery_file_dest_size=10g
```

Once the parameter has been set correctly, save the file and restart the database using the temporary pfile, as shown here:

```
C:\Documents and Settings\Robert>rman target=/
Recovery Manager: Release 11.1.0.6.0 - Production on Sun Sep 28 14:56:38 2008
Copyright (c) 1982, 2007, Oracle.  All rights reserved.
connected to target database (not started)
RMAN> startup force nomount pfile=?/database/initorcl.ora
Oracle instance started
Total System Global Area     163213312 bytes
Fixed Size                     1331852 bytes
Variable Size                 71306612 bytes
Database Buffers              79691776 bytes
Redo Buffers                  10883072 bytes
```

You can now restore the spfile backed up in the last control-file autobackup using the `restore spfile from autobackup` command, as shown here:

```
RMAN> restore spfile from autobackup;
Starting restore at 28-SEP-08
using target database control file instead of recovery catalog
allocated channel: ORA_DISK_1
channel ORA_DISK_1: SID=98 device type=DISK
recovery area destination: c:\oracle\flash_recovery_area
database name (or database unique name) used for search: ORCL
channel ORA_DISK_1: AUTOBACKUP
C:\ORACLE\FLASH_RECOVERY_AREA\ORCL\AUTOBACKUP\2008_09_28
\O1_MF_S_666628278_4FZTDYVC_.BKP found in the recovery area
AUTOBACKUP search with format "%F" not attempted because DBID was not set
```

```
channel ORA_DISK_1: restoring spfile from AUTOBACKUP
C:\ORACLE\FLASH_RECOVERY_AREA\ORCL\AUTOBACKUP\2008_09_28
\01_MF_S_666628278_4FZTDYVC_.BKP
channel ORA_DISK_1: SPFILE restore from AUTOBACKUP complete
Finished restore at 28-SEP-08
```

Now all you need to do is shut down and start up the database (assuming further restore and/or recovery operations are not required) or use the `startup force` command, as shown here:

```
RMAN> startup force
Oracle instance started
database mounted
database opened
Total System Global Area      397557760 bytes
Fixed Size                      1333452 bytes
Variable Size                 335546164 bytes
Database Buffers               54525952 bytes
Redo Buffers                    6152192 bytes
```

Just to summarize the steps needed to perform this recovery, here they are:

1. `startup nomount` the database from RMAN.
2. Issue the `create pfile from memory` command from SQL*Plus or using the `SQL` RMAN command.
3. Edit the pfile so that it contains the correct setting for the parameter `DB_RECOVERY_FILE_DEST` and the parameter `DB_RECOVERY_FILE_DEST_SIZE`.
4. Shut down and restart the database instance using the newly created pfile.
5. Use the `restore spfile from autobackup` command to restore the spfile.
6. Restart the database using the `startup force` command.

Restoring the Spfile When Not Using the FRA

If you are not using the FRA, the procedure to restore the spfile from an autobackup is actually slightly easier. First, you have already started the database instance. You will have to set two RMAN parameters. The first parameter identifies the DBID of the database (discussed earlier in this chapter). You use the `set dbid` command to do this, as shown here:

```
RMAN> Set dbid= 437680418
executing command: SET DBID
```

Now you need to use the `set controlfile autobackup format` parameter to indicate where the control-file autobackups can be found, as shown here:

```
RMAN> SET CONTROLFILE AUTOBACKUP FORMAT FOR DEVICE TYPE DISK TO
2> 'c:\oracle\controlfilebackup\%F';
executing command: SET CONTROLFILE AUTOBACKUP FORMAT
using target database control file instead of recovery catalog
```

All that remains is the restore of the spfile:

```
RMAN> Restore spfile from autobackup;
Starting restore at 28-SEP-08
allocated channel: ORA_DISK_1
channel ORA_DISK_1: SID=98 device type=DISK
channel ORA_DISK_1: looking for AUTOBACKUP on day: 20080928
channel ORA_DISK_1: AUTOBACKUP found:
c:\oracle\controlfilebackup\c-437680418-20080928-00
channel ORA_DISK_1: restoring spfile from AUTOBACKUP
c:\oracle\controlfilebackup\c-437680418-20080928-00
channel ORA_DISK_1: SPFILE restore from AUTOBACKUP complete
Finished restore at 28-SEP-08
```

You can also include the `set` commands within the confines of a run block, as shown here:

```
RUN
{
  SET CONTROLFILE AUTOBACKUP FORMAT FOR DEVICE TYPE DISK TO
   'c:\oracle\controlfilebackup\%F';
  RESTORE CONTROLFILE FROM AUTOBACKUP MAXSEQ 100;
}
```

You can now open the database with the `startup force` command, as shown here:

```
RMAN> startup force
Oracle instance started
database mounted
database opened
Total System Global Area      535662592 bytes
Fixed Size                      1334380 bytes
Variable Size                 369099668 bytes
Database Buffers              159383552 bytes
Redo Buffers                    5844992 bytes
```

To summarize the steps for this recovery, here they are:

1. Start up the database in NOMOUNT mode.
2. Set the database DBID.
3. Use the `set` command to set the RMAN parameter `controlfile autobackup format` to point to the correct control-file autobackup location.
4. Restore the spfile with the `restore spfile from autobackup` command.
5. Recycle the database to reread the newly recovered spfile parameter file.

Summary

As you can see, there are several ways to recover a database with RMAN. From database recoveries to tablespace recoveries to datafile recoveries and beyond, there is a lot that can go wrong—and a number of different ways to fix what may go wrong.

For your OCP exam, you will want to be familiar with the different kinds of database restores and recoveries that are possible. In this chapter we have provided you with the information you need to successfully answer the RMAN-recovery-oriented questions.

We strongly recommend that you practice these recovery techniques before you take the test. This is particularly important if you have not have any experience with RMAN restore and recovery operations. You might attempt to follow the exercises in this chapter to give you more experience with recovery of your database and to better prepare you for the exam.

Backup and recovery is the lifeblood of being a DBA. Truly there is nothing more important than knowing not only how to recover your database but also how to craft an overall backup and recovery strategy for your database.

Exam Essentials

Describe the basic process used when performing an RMAN database restore and recovery. Understand the essentials behind RMAN backup and recovery. Know what might be required to prepare for an RMAN recovery. Understand the basic steps of a typical RMAN recovery and what they are for.

Know how to use the `restore` command. Understand the use of the `restore` command. Know the different options of the `restore` command, such as `restore database`, `restore tablespace`, and `restore datafile`. Understand what happens when you call the `restore` command.

Know how to use the `recover` command. Understand and be able to successfully use the `recover` command. Know the different options of the `recover` command, such as `recover database`, `recover tablespace`, and `recover datafile`. Understand what happens when you call the `recover` command.

Understand point-in-time recovery. Understand and be able to perform point-in-time recovery with RMAN. Know how to use the `until time` parameter of the `recover` and `restore` commands to perform a point-in-time recovery. Know how to use the `set until time` command to perform a point-in-time recovery.

Understand how to perform other recoveries. Understand how to recover from loss of a control file. Understand how to recover from loss of an spfile.

Review Questions

1. What command would you issue to enable automated backups of control files?
   A. `alter database controlfile autobackup on`
   B. `alter system controlfile autobackup on`
   C. `configure controlfile autobackup on`
   D. `enable controlfile autobackup`

2. Given the following RMAN commands, choose the option that reflects the order required to restore your currently operational ARCHIVELOG-mode database.
   a. `restore database;`
   b. `recover database;`
   c. `shutdown immediate`
   d. `startup`
   e. `restore archivelog all;`
   f. `alter database open`
   A. a, b, c, d, e, f
   B. c, b, a, d, e, f
   C. c, b, a, d, f
   D. c, a, b, d
   E. c, a, e, b, d, f

3. Which commands are used for RMAN database recovery? (Choose all that apply.)
   A. `restore`
   B. `repair`
   C. `copy`
   D. `recover`
   E. `replace`

4. Given a complete loss of your database, in what order would you need to perform the following RMAN operations to restore it?
   a. `restore controlfile`
   b. `restore database`
   c. `restore spfile`
   d. `recover database`
   e. `alter database open`
   f. `alter database open resetlogs`

A. b, a, c, d, e
B. a, c, b, d, f
C. c, a, b, d, e
D. c, a, b, d, f
E. e, a, b, d, c

5. If you lost your entire database, including the database spfile, control files, online redo logs, and database datafiles, what kind of recovery would be required with RMAN?
   A. Complete database recovery.
   B. Incomplete database recovery.
   C. Approximate database recovery.
   D. Archived database recovery.
   E. The database could not be recovered with RMAN.

6. Which command will restore all datafiles to the date 9/30/2008 at 18:00 hours?
   A. `restore datafiles until time '09/28/2008:21:03:11';`
   B. `restore database files until time '09/28/2008:18:00:00';`
   C. `restore database until time '09/28/2008:18:00:00';`
   D. `recover database until time '09/28/2008:18:00:00';`
   E. `recover database until timestamp '09/28/2008:18:00:00';`

7. What is the end result of these commands if they are successful?

```
RMAN> show retention policy;
RMAN configuration parameters for database with db_unique_name ORCL are:
CONFIGURE RETENTION POLICY TO REDUNDANCY 1; # default
Backup database tag='gold_copy' plus archivelog
tag='gold_copy' delete input;
Backup database tag='silver_copy' plus archivelog
tag='silver_copy' delete input;
```

   A. Attempting to restore `silver_copy` will fail.
   B. Attempting to restore `gold_copy` will fail.
   C. Both backups will be available for restore without question.
   D. Attempting to restore `gold_copy` may or may not succeed.
   E. You will not be able to restore either `gold_copy` or `silver_copy`.

8. You are using RMAN to backup your ARCHIVELOG mode database. You have enabled control-file autobackups. Which files are not backed up during the RMAN backup?

   A. Database Datafiles

   B. Database Control Files

   C. Online redo logs

   D. Archived redo logs

   E. The database SPFILE

   F. None of the above, all these files are backed up.

9. True or false: RMAN offers the equivalent of the SQL command `alter database backup controlfile to trace`.

   A. True

   B. False

10. You need to restore your database back to 9/30/2008 at 18:00. In what order would you run the following commands to compete this task?

    a. `restore controlfile until time '09/30/2008:18:00:00';`

    b. `restore database until time '09/30/2008:18:00:00';`

    c. `restore spfile until time '09/30/2008:18:00:00';;`

    d. `recover database until time '09/30/2008:18:00:00';`

    e. `alter database open resetlogs;`

    f. `alter database open;`

    A. b, d, e

    B. b, d, f

    C. c, a, b, d, e

    D. c, a, b, d, f

    E. a, b, d, e

11. What is the correct order of the following commands if you wanted to restore datafile 4, which was accidentally removed from the file system?

    a. `sql 'alter database datafile 4 online';`

    b. `restore datafile 4;`

    c. `recover datafile 4;`

    d. `sql 'alter database datafile 4 offline';`

    e. `startup`

    f. `shutdown`

A. a, c, b, d

B. d, b, c, a

C. f, d, b, c, a, e

D. c, a, b, d, f

E. a, b, d, e

12. Your database is up and running and one of your three control files is accidentally erased. You start RMAN and run the following command:

```
RESTORE CONTROLFILE FROM AUTOBACKUP;
```

Which of the following statements is true? (Choose all that apply.)

A. The command restores only the missing control file.

B. The command restores all the control files.

C. The command fails because the database is running.

D. This is the correct way to address this problem.

E. This is not the correct way to address this problem.

13. Which of the following are valid `until` command options when attempting point-in-time recovery in RMAN? (Choose all that apply.)

A. `until time`

B. `until change`

C. `until sequence`

D. `until SCN`

E. `until commit`

14. Which of the following does the `recover` command not do?

A. Restore archived redo logs.

B. Apply archived redo logs.

C. Restore incremental backups.

D. Apply incremental backups.

E. Restore datafile images.

15. You have a database with the following tablespaces: SYSTEM, SYSAUX, UNDO, USERS, TEMP. You want to "roll back" the data in the USERS tablespace to the way it looked yesterday. Which tablespaces do you need to perform a point-in-time restore operation on in order to complete this task? (Choose all that apply.)

A. SYSTEM

B. SYSAUX

C. UNDO

D. USERS

E. TEMP

F. This restore is not possible.

16. You have backed up your database using image copies. You have lost the SYSTEM tablespace and need to restart your database as quickly as possible. What is the correct solution?

    A. Restore the SYSTEM tablespace from the last backup set and then recover the database.

    B. Restore the SYSTEM tablespace image copy using the `restore` command and then restore the database.

    C. Use the `switch datafile` command to instantly switch to the datafile copy, recover the tablespace, and open the database.

    D. The database is not recoverable in this situation with image copies.

    E. Manually copy the datafile image copy to the correct location and then manually restore the database from SQL*Plus.

17. If you find errors in the view V$DATABASE_BLOCK_CORRUPTION with a status of MEDIA_CORRUPT, what RMAN command would you run to correct the problem?

    A. `recover lost blocks;`

    B. `recover corrupt blocks;`

    C. `recover media corrupt blocks from list;`

    D. `recover corrupt blocks from list;`

    E. `recover corruption list;`

18. What will be the end result of this set of RMAN commands?

```
shutdown abort
startup mount
restore datafile 4 until time '09/30/2008:15:00:00';
recover datafile 4 until time '09/29/2008:15:00:00';
alter database open resetlogs;
```

    A. Datafile 4 will be recovered until 9/30/2008 at 15:00 and the database will open.

    B. The `restore` command will fail.

    C. The `recover` command will fail.

    D. The `alter database open resetlogs` command will fail.

    E. All these commands will fail because they must be in the confines of a run block.

19. Which of the following represents the correct way to perform an online recovery of datafile 4, which is assigned to a tablespace called USERS?

A.
```
shutdown
restore datafile 4;
recover datafile 4;
alter database open;
```

B.
```
Sql 'alter database datafile 4 offline';
restore datafile 4;
recover datafile 4;
alter database open;
```

C.
```
Sql 'alter database datafile 4 offline';
restore datafile 4;
Sql 'alter database datafile 4 online';
```

D.
```
Sql 'alter database datafile 4 offline';
restore database datafile 4;
recover database datafile 4;
Sql 'alter database datafile 4 online';
```

E.
```
Sql 'alter database datafile 4 offline';
restore datafile 4;
recover datafile 4;
Sql 'alter database datafile 4 online';
```

20. David managed to accidentally delete the datafiles for database called DSL. He called Heber and Heber tried to help but he managed to delete the control files of the database. Heber called Bill and Bill saved the day. They are using a recovery catalog for this database. What steps did Bill perform to recover the database and in what order?

a. Restored the control file with the RMAN `restore controlfile` command.

b. Mounted the DSL instance with the `alter database mount` command.

c. Restored the datafiles for the DSL database with the RMAN `restore` command.

d. Opened the DSL database with the `alter database open resetlogs` command.

e. Recovered the datafiles for the DSL database with the RMAN `recover` command.

f. Started the DSL instance.

g. Connected to the recovery catalog with RMAN.

A. a, b, c, d, e, f, g

B. b, c, d, g, f, e, a

C. g, f, a, b, c, e, d

D. c, a, d, b, f, e, g

E. g, f, a, b, e, c, d

Answers to Review Questions

1. C. Enable control-file autobackups by executing the command `configure controlfile autobackup on`.

2. D. You would shut down the database with the `shutdown immediate` command before the recovery. You would then issue the `restore database` command followed by the `recover database` command. After you have recovered the database, you will want to open it with the `startup` command.

3. A, D. The `restore` command is used to restore datafiles during a database recovery. The `recover` command is used to apply incremental backups and archived redo logs to recover the database to the needed point in time.

4. D. In the event of complete loss of your database, you will need to first restore the database spfile. Once you have restored the database spfile, you will need to restore the database control file. Having restored the database control file, you would restore the database and then recover the database. Finally, since this would be an incomplete recovery (because you lost the entire database, the online redo logs are gone too), you would need to open the database using the `alter database open resetlogs` command.

5. B. A loss of the entire database will result in a requirement for an incomplete database recovery. This is because the online redo logs would not be available to perform a complete recovery.

6. C. The `restore database` command is used to restore database datafiles. The `until time` parameter is used to indicate the point in time to which you want to restore the database datafiles.

7. D. Since the retention policy is set to redundancy of 1, the `gold_copy` backup is not required to meet the retention criteria. Since the backup was not made in a way that will exclude or alter the retention criteria, then the `gold_copy` backup is no longer needed and may be removed at any time. It is possible that it will still be available for restore purposes, however.

8. C. The online redo logs are never backed up by Oracle no mater what kind of backup you are performing.

9. B. There is no equivalent RMAN command that creates a trace file with the `create controlfile` statement in it.

10. A. In this case you would first issue the `restore database` command using the `until time` option. You would then use the `recover database` command using the same `until time` option. Finally, since this is an incomplete recovery, you would need to open your database with the `alter database open` resetlogs command.

11. B. To perform the restore of datafile 4, you would first need to take the datafile offline with the `alter database` command. Once the datafile is offline, use the `restore datafile` and `recover datafile` commands to restore and recover the datafile in question. After the restore and recover, you will need to bring the datafile back online.

12. C, E. This is not the correct way to address this problem. The command will fail because the database is running. Additionally, this is not the correct way to approach the loss of one of several control files. The better way to approach this loss is to shut down the database and simply copy one of the surviving control files over to where the missing control file existed.

13. A, C, D. The `until time` clause provides the ability to restore to a specific point in time. The `until sequence` clause provides the ability to restore to a specific redo log sequence number, and `until SCN` provides the ability to restore to a specific database SCN number.

14. E. The recover command does not restore datafile images. It does restore and apply archived redo logs and incremental backup images during the recovery process.

15. A, B, C, D, E. You will need to restore the datafiles associated with each tablespace in the database in order to successfully complete the point-in-time database restore operation.

16. C. You would use the `switch datafile` command (for example, `switch datafile 1 to copy`) to instantly switch to the image copy. Issue the `restore` command and then start up the database.

17. E. You would run the RMAN command `recover corruption list` to recover the corrupted blocks using block media recovery.

18. D. The commands will run without error until you attempt to open the database. At that time, the `alter database open resetlogs` command will fail. This will be because datafile 4 and the rest of the database will be inconsistent with each other and Oracle does not allow this. If you are going to restore and recover an Oracle database using point-in-time recovery, you must do so with the entire database.

19. E. For this recovery, you would use the RMAN `sql` command to issue an `alter database datafile offline` command. You would then use the RMAN `restore` and `recover` commands to recover the lost datafile. Finally, you would use the RMAN `sql` command to issue the `alter database datafile online` command.

20. C. To restore the database, in this case they needed to connect to the recovery catalog with RMAN. They then started the DSL instance with the `startup nomount` command and restored the control file with the `restore controlfile` command. After restoring the control file, they mounted the database with the `alter database mount` command and then restored the database with the `restore database` command. After restoring the database, they recovered it with the `recover database` command and then opened it with the `alter database open` resetlogs command.

Reporting, Monitoring, and Tuning with RMAN

ORACLE DATABASE 11*g*: ADMINISTRATION II EXAM OBJECTIVES COVERED IN THIS CHAPTER:

✓ **Monitoring and Tuning RMAN**

- Monitoring RMAN sessions and jobs
- Tuning RMAN
- Configure RMAN for Asynchronous I/O

✓ **Using RMAN to Create Backups**

- Report on and maintain backups

Overview of the RMAN Report and List Commands

RMAN provides a wealth of reporting with respect to backups, the database, and other various RMAN-related information. In the following sections, we will discuss the RMAN `report` command and the RMAN `list` command. You will need to be familiar with both commands.

Exam objectives are subject to change at any time without prior notice and at Oracle's sole discretion. Please visit Oracle's Training and Certification website (`http://www.oracle.com/education/certification/`) for the most current exam-objectives listing.

Using the RMAN *report* Command

First we will cover the RMAN `report` command. We will describe the purpose of the `report` command in RMAN, and then we will provide several examples of its use.

Introducing the RMAN *report* Command

The RMAN `report` command provides information on records within the database control file or the RMAN recovery catalog. The `report` command provides the following information:

- Database, tablespace, or datafiles that need to be backed up.
- Obsolete backups. These are backups that meet the retention criteria and can be removed with the `delete obsolete` commands.
- Objects in the database that need to be backed up because of unrecoverable SQL operations.
- Information on the database schema.

Let's look at some examples of how to use the `report` command.

Seeing the RMAN *report* Command in Action

Now we will show a number of examples of the use of the RMAN `report` command. First we will show the `report backup` command, and we will then show the `report schema` command.

Example of the *report need backup* Command

For example, if you wanted to know which datafiles need to be backed up in your database based on the retention criteria, you could use the `report need backup` command:

```
RMAN> report need backup;
RMAN retention policy will be applied to the command
RMAN retention policy is set to redundancy 1
Report of files with less than 1 redundant backups
File #bkps Name
---- ----- -----------------------------------------
5    0     C:\ORACLE\ORADATA\ORCL\MY_DATA_01.DBF
```

In this example you see that datafile 5 is in need of backup with respect to the retention policy. You also see that it has 0 backups (in the `#bkps` column). In this case, this is a new datafile that has never been backed up.

You can use various options with the `report need backup` command to customize the report. For example, you could say that you want to see a report of all files that have not been backed up in the last three days. The report would look like this:

```
RMAN> report need backup days 3;
Report of files whose recovery needs more than 3 days of archived logs
File Days  Name
---- ----- -----------------------------------------------------
1    6     C:\ORACLE\ORADATA\ORCL\SYSTEM01.DBF
2    6     C:\ORACLE\ORADATA\ORCL\SYSAUX01.DBF
3    6     C:\ORACLE\ORADATA\ORCL\UNDOTBS01.DBF
4    6     C:\ORACLE\ORADATA\ORCL\USERS01.DBF
```

There are other reporting options besides `days`:

`Incremental` Maximum number of incrementals to apply.

`Recovery window of` Indicates the recovery-window criteria to apply. This can be handy when trying to determine the impacts of changing the recovery-window retention policy.

`Redundancy` Indicates the level of backup redundancy for datafiles. This can be handy when trying to determine the impacts of changing the redundancy retention policy.

Example of the *report obsolete* Command

The `report obsolete` command is used to list backup sets that are marked as obsolete in the control file or the recovery catalog. Depending on your configuration, you might look at the report obsolete command output and ensure that the backups listed in that command are supposed to be deleted. If so, you could remove them with the delete obsolete command (discussed later in this chapter).

In this example, you can see that several backup set pieces are obsolete and no longer needed. If these were present in a flash recovery area (FRA), then Oracle would automatically delete the backup set pieces when space was needed or when you ran the delete obsolete command. If you were not using the FRA, you would need to run the delete obsolete command to remove those pieces.

```
RMAN> report obsolete;
RMAN retention policy will be applied to the command
RMAN retention policy is set to redundancy 1
Report of obsolete backups and copies
Type                 Key    Completion Time    Filename/Handle
-------------------- ------ ------------------ --------------------
Backup Set           424    11-OCT-08
  Backup Piece       432    11-OCT-08
C:\ORACLE\FLASH_RECOVERY_AREA\ORCL\BACKUPSET\
2008_10_11\O1_MF_ANNNN_TAG20081011T142547_4H22YYOO_.BKP
Backup Set           426    11-OCT-08
  Backup Piece       434    11-OCT-08
C:\ORACLE\FLASH_RECOVERY_AREA\ORCL\BACKUPSET\
2008_10_11\O1_MF_NCSNF_TAG20081011T142622_4H23CVNJ_.BKP
Backup Set           429    11-OCT-08
  Backup Piece       437    11-OCT-08
C:\ORACLE\FLASH_RECOVERY_AREA\ORCL\AUTOBACKUP\
2008_10_11\O1_MF_S_667838162_4H23KXWB_.BKP
Backup Set           430    12-OCT-08
  Backup Piece       438    12-OCT-08
C:\ORACLE\FLASH_RECOVERY_AREA\ORCL\AUTOBACKUP\
2008_10_12\O1_MF_S_667915771_4H4HCM7L_.BKP
```

Example of the *report schema* Command

The report schema command provides information on the tablespaces and related datafiles (and tempfiles) in the database. Displayed by the report schema command is the datafile ID, the size of the datafile, and the tablespace that the datafile is associated with. An example of the use of the report schema command is shown next:

```
RMAN> report schema;
using target database control file instead of recovery catalog
Report of database schema for database with db_unique_name ORCL
```

```
List of Permanent Datafiles
===========================
File Size(MB) Tablespace       RB segs Datafile Name
---- -------- ---------------- ------- ------------------------
1    680      SYSTEM           ***     C:\ORACLE\ORADATA\ORCL\SYSTEM01.DBF
2    612      SYSAUX           ***     C:\ORACLE\ORADATA\ORCL\SYSAUX01.DBF
3    25       UNDOTBS1         ***     C:\ORACLE\ORADATA\ORCL\UNDOTBS01.DBF
4    5        USERS            ***     C:\ORACLE\ORADATA\ORCL\USERS01.DBF
5    50       MY_DATA          ***     C:\ORACLE\ORADATA\ORCL\MY_DATA_01.DBF
List of Temporary Files
=======================
File Size(MB) Tablespace           Maxsize(MB) Tempfile Name
---- -------- -------------------- ----------- --------------------
1    20       TEMP                 32767       C:\ORACLE\ORADATA\ORCL\TEMP01.DBF
```

Note the report in its header indicates that the control file is being used instead of the recovery catalog.

Example of the *report unrecoverable* Command

Certain types of SQL operations can make an object unrecoverable. This is because these operations do not produce redo, in an effort to make the process more performant. Since there is no redo, there is no recovering the object, and what you end up with after a recovery is a shell of an object with no data in it. Here is an example.

First, you log into RMAN and issue the command `report unrecoverable database`:

```
RMAN> report unrecoverable database;
starting full resync of recovery catalog
full resync complete
Report of files that need backup due to unrecoverable operations
File Type of Backup Required Name
---- ----------------------- -----------------------------------
```

Next, you create an object in the SCOTT schema and load it with data:

```
SQL> create table unrecover_table (id number);
SQL> begin
 2  for dd in 1..50
 3  loop
 4  insert into unrecover_table values (dd);
 5  end loop;
 6* end;
SQL>commit;
```

Now you will crate a table based on the UNRECOVER_TABLE. You will make the operation an unrecoverable operation:

```
SQL> Create table test_norecover nologging as select * from unrecover_table;
```

Now you see that the RMAN report unrecoverable command indicates that your USERS tablespace needs a backup:

```
C:\>rman target=/ catalog=rcat_user/rcat_user@rcat
Recovery Manager: Release 11.1.0.6.0 - Production on Sat Oct 18 01:15:17 2008
Copyright (c) 1982, 2007, Oracle.  All rights reserved.
connected to target database: ORCL (DBID=1195614221)
connected to recovery catalog database
RMAN> report unrecoverable database;
Report of files that need backup due to unrecoverable operations
File Type of Backup Required Name
---- ---------------------- ----------------------------------
4    full or incremental     C:\ORACLE\ORADATA\ORCL\USERS01.DBF
```

To fix this problem, you back up the USERS tablespace, as shown here:

```
RMAN> backup tablespace users;
Starting backup at 18-OCT-08
allocated channel: ORA_DISK_1
channel ORA_DISK_1: SID=134 device type=DISK
channel ORA_DISK_1: starting datafile copy
input datafile file number=00004 name=C:\ORACLE\ORADATA\ORCL\USERS01.DBF
output file name=C:\ORACLE\FLASH_RECOVERY_AREA\ORCL\DATAFILE\
O1_MF_USERS_4HM3CGQX_.DBF tag=TAG20081018T011646 RECID=1
STAMP=668395023
channel ORA_DISK_1: datafile copy complete, elapsed time: 00:00:03
Finished backup at 18-OCT-08
Starting Control File and SPFILE Autobackup at 18-OCT-08
piece handle=C:\ORACLE\FLASH_RECOVERY_AREA\ORCL\AUTOBACKUP\2008_10_18\
O1_MF_S_668395027_4HM3CWNZ_.BKP comment=NONE
Finished Control File and SPFILE Autobackup at 18-OCT-08
RMAN> report unrecoverable database;
Report of files that need backup due to unrecoverable operations
File Type of Backup Required Name
---- ---------------------- ----------------------------------
```

In Exercise 7.1, you will get to experiment with the report command.

EXERCISE 7.1

Using the *report* Command

1. Log into RMAN, connecting to your recovery catalog.

```
C:\>rman target=/ catalog=rcat_user/rcat_user@rcat
Recovery Manager: Release 11.1.0.6.0 -
Production on Sun Oct 19 14:51:06 2008
Copyright (c) 1982, 2007, Oracle.  All rights reserved.
connected to target database: ORCL (DBID=1195614221)
connected to recovery catalog database
```

2. Just type in the command **report;**. Review the output. Notice how RMAN prompts you for the syntax it is expecting. For example, in this case it's expecting something akin to `report device`, `report need`, `report obsolete`, and so on.

```
RMAN> report;
RMAN-00571: ===========================================================
RMAN-00569: =============== ERROR MESSAGE STACK FOLLOWS ===============
RMAN-00571: ===========================================================
RMAN-00558: error encountered while parsing input commands
RMAN-01009: syntax error: found ";": expecting one of:
"device, need, obsolete, schema, unrecoverable"
RMAN-01007: at line 1 column 7 file: standard input
```

3. See what datafiles and tempfiles are in the database by using the `report schema` command:

```
RMAN> report schema;
Report of database schema for database with db_unique_name ORCL
List of Permanent Datafiles
===========================
File Size(MB) Tablespace        RB segs Datafile Name
---- -------- ----------------- ------- ------------------------
1    680      SYSTEM            YES     C:\ORACLE\ORADATA\ORCL\SYSTEM01.DBF
2    631      SYSAUX            NO      C:\ORACLE\ORADATA\ORCL\SYSAUX01.DBF
3    25       UNDOTBS1          YES     C:\ORACLE\ORADATA\ORCL\UNDOTBS01.DBF
4    5        USERS             NO      C:\ORACLE\ORADATA\ORCL\USERS01.DBF
5    50       MY_DATA           NO      C:\ORACLE\ORADATA\ORCL\MY_DATA_01.DBF
List of Temporary Files
=======================
File Size(MB) Tablespace        Maxsize(MB) Tempfile Name
---- -------- ----------------- ----------- --------------------
1    20       TEMP              32767       C:\ORACLE\ORADATA\ORCL\TEMP01.DBF
```

EXERCISE 7.1 *(continued)*

4. See what backups in the database have become obsolete because they do not meet the retention criteria. To do so, you will use the `report obsolete` command:

```
RMAN> report obsolete;
RMAN retention policy will be applied to the command
RMAN retention policy is set to redundancy 1
Report of obsolete backups and copies
Type                 Key    Completion Time    Filename/Handle
-------------------- ------ ------------------ --------------------
Archive Log          926    18-OCT-08
C:\ORACLE\PRODUCT\11.1.0\DB_1\RDBMS\ARC00022_0667833490.001
Backup Set           978    18-OCT-08
  Backup Piece       980    18-OCT-08
C:\ORACLE\FLASH_RECOVERY_AREA\ORCL\AUTOBACKUP\2008_10_18
\O1_MF_S_668446569_4HNOPMRF_.BKP
Backup Set           1252   18-OCT-08
  Backup Piece       1260   18-OCT-08          C:\ORACLE\FLASH_RECOVERY_AREA\
ORCL\BACKUPSET\2008_10_18
\O1_MF_ANNNN_TAG20081018T153543_4HNOP6OH_.BKP.OLD
Backup Set           1253   18-OCT-08
  Backup Piece       1261   18-OCT-08          C:\ORACLE\FLASH_RECOVERY_AREA\
ORCL\BACKUPSET\2008_10_18\
O1_MF_NNNDF_TAG20081018T152908_4HNO9DX9_.BKP.OLD
```

5. Log out of RMAN and log into the database with SQL*Plus:

```
RMAN> quit
Recovery Manager complete.
C:\Documents and Settings\Robert>sqlplus "/ as sysdba"
SQL*Plus: Release 11.1.0.6.0 - Production on Sun Oct 19 15:37:03 2008
Copyright (c) 1982, 2007, Oracle.  All rights reserved.
Connected to:
Oracle Database 11g Enterprise Edition Release 11.1.0.6.0 - Production
With the Partitioning, OLAP, Data Mining
and Real Application Testing options
SQL>
```

6. Add a tablespace to the database, and then log out of SQL*Plus. You may want to put your tablespace in a different location; this is fine.

```
SQL> create tablespace testtbs
  2  datafile 'c:\oracle\oradata\orcl\testtbs.dbf' size 20m;
```

EXERCISE 7.1 *(continued)*

```
Tablespace created.
SQL> exit
Disconnected from Oracle Database 11g Enterprise Edition
Release 11.1.0.6.0 - Production
With the Partitioning, OLAP, Data Mining and
Real Application Testing options
```

7. Log into RMAN, connecting to your recovery catalog:

```
C:\>rman target=/ catalog=rcat_user/rcat_user@rcat
Recovery Manager: Release 11.1.0.6.0 -
Production on Sun Oct 19 14:51:06 2008
Copyright (c) 1982, 2007, Oracle.  All rights reserved.
connected to target database: ORCL (DBID=1195614221)
connected to recovery catalog database
```

8. Now generate a report of datafiles that need to be backed up with the `report need backup` command. You will see that the new datafile shows up as needing a backup. Note that as long as you have the archived redo logs that were generated since the datafile was created, you can still recover this datafile and any data in it.

```
RMAN> report need backup;
RMAN retention policy will be applied to the command
RMAN retention policy is set to redundancy 1
Report of files with less than 1 redundant backups
File #bkps Name
---- ----- -----------------------------------------
6    0     C:\ORACLE\ORADATA\ORCL\TESTTBS.DBF
```

Using the RMAN *list* Command

The RMAN `list` command provides information on backups in your Oracle database. The `list` command has the following functionality:

- Listing expired backups
- Listing the database incarnation
- Listing database restore points
- Listing scripts
- Listing information on database backups and image copies

Additionally, information can often be listed in two formats, detail and summary, as you will see in the following sections.

Seeing the *list expired backup* Command in Action

When you run the crosscheck command (discussed later in this chapter), any missing backup files will be marked as EXPIRED, meaning that they are no longer on the media where they are expected to be. The list expired command will show you the backups that are expired. You can review this list and then use the delete command to mark the backup files as deleted in the control file and the recovery catalog. Here is an example of the list expired backup command in use:

```
RMAN> list expired backup of database;
List of Backup Sets
===================
BS Key  Type LV Size       Device Type Elapsed Time Completion Time
------- ---- -- ---------- ----------- ------------ ---------------
425     Full    176.72M    DISK        00:06:02     11-OCT-08
BP Key: 433   Status: EXPIRED  Compressed: YES  Tag: TAG20081011T142622
Piece Name: C:\ORACLE\FLASH_RECOVERY_AREA\ORCL\BACKUPSET\2008_10_11\
O1_MF_NNNDF_TAG20081011T142622_4H22ZOMK_.BKP
  List of Datafiles in backup set 425
  File LV Type Ckp SCN    Ckp Time  Name
  ---- -- ---- ---------- --------- ----
  1       Full 903859     11-OCT-08 C:\ORACLE\ORADATA\ORCL\SYSTEM01.DBF
  2       Full 903859     11-OCT-08 C:\ORACLE\ORADATA\ORCL\SYSAUX01.DBF
  3       Full 903859     11-OCT-08 C:\ORACLE\ORADATA\ORCL\UNDOTBS01.DBF
  4       Full 903859     11-OCT-08 C:\ORACLE\ORADATA\ORCL\USERS01.DBF
```

In this case, you have one backup set that is expired. Each backup set has its own unique backup-set key that you will find in many reports. In this report, the backup-set key 425 is missing. This backup includes backups of four datafiles. Since it's expired, this essentially means it's missing from the database. Expired backups will not show up on this report until the crosscheck command detects they are missing. You can find more information on the crosscheck command later in this chapter. If you want to mark these as deleted in the recovery catalog, you can use the delete expired command. You can find more information on the delete expired command later in this chapter.

Seeing the *list incarnation* Command in Action

In previous chapters, we gave you a little bit of a preview of the list incarnation command. The list incarnation command provides information related to database incarnation from the control file or the recovery catalog. You can use this command to guide you in situations in which you need to reset the database incarnation for certain types of database recoveries (see Chapter 6 for more on this topic).

The `list incarnation` command output is slightly different depending on whether you are connected to a recovery catalog or the database control file. For example, here is some sample output from the `list incarnation` command when we were connected to the control file of the database:

```
RMAN> list incarnation;
List of Database Incarnations
DB Key  Inc Key DB Name  DB ID            STATUS  Reset SCN  Reset Time
------- ------- -------- ---------------- --- ---------- ----------
1       1       ORCL     1195614221       PARENT  1          15-OCT-07
2       2       ORCL     1195614221       CURRENT 886308     11-OCT-08
```

Note that there are two records here, and the DBID for each record is the same. When you execute the same command from the recovery catalog, you may get different results, as shown here:

```
RMAN> list incarnation;
List of Database Incarnations
DB Key  Inc Key DB Name  DB ID            STATUS  Reset SCN  Reset Time
------- ------- -------- ---------------- --- ---------- ----------
1       15      ORCL     1194488809       PARENT  1          15-OCT-07
1       16      ORCL     1194488809       PARENT  886308     29-SEP-08
1       17      ORCL     1194488809       ORPHAN  907851     02-OCT-08
1       2       ORCL     1194488809       PARENT  953055     02-OCT-08
1       270     ORCL     1194488809       CURRENT 988211     02-OCT-08
321     335     ORCL     1195614221       PARENT  1          15-OCT-07
321     322     ORCL     1195614221       CURRENT 886308     11-OCT-08
```

This is a case where we have two databases called ORCL in our recovery catalog. Notice that each of those databases has a different DBID. Oracle will be able to separate the databases based on this unique ID, but both databases show up in the report because the report is generated based on the database name, not the DBID.

Seeing the *list restore point* Command in Action

Database restore points are a function of Oracle Flashback Database technologies (see Chapter 9 for more information on Oracle Flashback Database). You can set restore points from the SQL prompt with the `create restore point` command. In this example, we use the `list restore point all` command to list all restore points:

```
RMAN> list restore point all;
SCN              RSP Time  Type       Time      Name
---------------- --------- ---------- --------- ----
1219891                               18-OCT-08 ROBERT
```

You could also list a specific restore point as in this example:

```
RMAN> list restore point robert;
SCN              RSP Time  Type       Time      Name
---------------- --------- ---------- --------- ----
1219891                               18-OCT-08 ROBERT

RMAN> list restore point davep;
SCN              RSP Time  Type       Time      Name
---------------- --------- ---------- --------- ----
```

Seeing the *list all script names* Command in Action

The `list all script names` command generates a report with the names of all scripts in the recovery catalog. This command is available for use only when you are connected to the recovery catalog. Here is an example of the `list all script names` command where you find you have one script in the recovery catalog called `db_backup_script`:

```
RMAN> list all script names;
List of Stored Scripts in Recovery Catalog
    Scripts of Target Database ORCL
       Script Name
       Description
       -----------------------------------
       db_backup_script
```

Examples of Listing Backup-Related Information

DBAs will, from time to time, want to know what backups have been made on their database. The `list` command provides all sorts of information on database backups. For example, if you want to see what full backups of your database are available, then you can run the `list backup of database` command:

```
RMAN> list backup of database;
List of Backup Sets
```

```
===================
BS Key  Type LV Size       Device Type Elapsed Time Completion Time
------- ---- -- ---------- ----------- ------------ ---------------
2       Full    176.72M    DISK        00:06:02     11-OCT-08
        BP Key: 2   Status: EXPIRED  Compressed: YES  Tag: TAG20081011T142622
        Piece Name: C:\ORACLE\FLASH_RECOVERY_AREA\ORCL\BACKUPSET\2008_10_11\
O1_MF_NNNDF_TAG20081011T142622_4H22ZOMK_.BKP
  List of Datafiles in backup set 2
  File LV Type Ckp SCN    Ckp Time  Name
  ---- -- ---- ---------- --------- ----
  1       Full 903859     11-OCT-08 C:\ORACLE\ORADATA\ORCL\SYSTEM01.DBF
  2       Full 903859     11-OCT-08 C:\ORACLE\ORADATA\ORCL\SYSAUX01.DBF
  3       Full 903859     11-OCT-08 C:\ORACLE\ORADATA\ORCL\UNDOTBS01.DBF
  4       Full 903859     11-OCT-08 C:\ORACLE\ORADATA\ORCL\USERS01.DBF

BS Key  Type LV Size       Device Type Elapsed Time Completion Time
------- ---- -- ---------- ----------- ------------ ---------------
11      Full    186.89M    DISK        00:04:43     18-OCT-08
      BP Key: 11   Status: AVAILABLE  Compressed: YES  Tag: TAG20081018T032019
        Piece Name: C:\ORACLE\FLASH_RECOVERY_AREA\ORCL\BACKUPSET\2008_10_18\
O1_MF_NNNDF_TAG20081018T032019_4HMBLT5V_.BKP
  List of Datafiles in backup set 11
  File LV Type Ckp SCN    Ckp Time  Name
  ---- -- ---- ---------- --------- ----
  1       Full 1195239    18-OCT-08 C:\ORACLE\ORADATA\ORCL\SYSTEM01.DBF
  2       Full 1195239    18-OCT-08 C:\ORACLE\ORADATA\ORCL\SYSAUX01.DBF
  3       Full 1195239    18-OCT-08 C:\ORACLE\ORADATA\ORCL\UNDOTBS01.DBF
  4       Full 1195239    18-OCT-08 C:\ORACLE\ORADATA\ORCL\USERS01.DBF
  5       Full 1195239    18-OCT-08 C:\ORACLE\ORADATA\ORCL\MY_DATA_01.DBF

BS Key  Type LV Size       Device Type Elapsed Time Completion Time
------- ---- -- ---------- ----------- ------------ ---------------
15      Full    187.63M    DISK        00:05:37     18-OCT-08
      BP Key: 15   Status: AVAILABLE  Compressed: YES  Tag: TAG20081018T134250
        Piece Name: C:\ORACLE\FLASH_RECOVERY_AREA\ORCL\BACKUPSET\2008_10_18\
O1_MF_NNNDF_TAG20081018T134250_4HNH25TC_.BKP
  List of Datafiles in backup set 15
  File LV Type Ckp SCN    Ckp Time  Name
  ---- -- ---- ---------- --------- ----
  1       Full 1218699    18-OCT-08 C:\ORACLE\ORADATA\ORCL\SYSTEM01.DBF
  2       Full 1218699    18-OCT-08 C:\ORACLE\ORADATA\ORCL\SYSAUX01.DBF
  3       Full 1218699    18-OCT-08 C:\ORACLE\ORADATA\ORCL\UNDOTBS01.DBF
```

```
  4        Full 1218699    18-OCT-08 C:\ORACLE\ORADATA\ORCL\USERS01.DBF
  5        Full 1218699    18-OCT-08 C:\ORACLE\ORADATA\ORCL\MY_DATA_01.DBF
```

Of course, when you read the output of the previous example, you probably said to yourself, "Wow! That's a lot more output than I needed!" You can use the summary keyword to produce summary output that is often all you need, as shown in this example:

```
RMAN> list backup of database summary;
List of Backups
===============
Key     TY LV S Device Type Completion Time #Pieces #Copies Compressed Tag
------- -- -- - ----------- --------------- ------- ------- ---------- ---
2       B  F  X DISK        11-OCT-08       1       1       YES
TAG20081011T142622
11      B  F  A DISK        18-OCT-08       1       1       YES
TAG20081018T032019
15      B  F  A DISK        18-OCT-08       1       1       YES
TAG20081018T134250
```

Now that's a lot easier to read! Here you see that there are three backups of the database, when they were taken, the type, and other interesting information on the backups.

You can get the following details on the various types of backups that you might be taking with RMAN:

- Lists of all backups
- Lists of backup-set backups
- Lists of archive-log backups
- Lists of image copies
- Lists of control-file backups
- Backups of specific tablespaces or datafiles

For example, here is a list of the backup of all archive logs. Note that the `list backup of archivelog` command provides the ability to list specific archive logs based on numerous criteria, such as a log-sequence number range, time range, and SCN range, or you can just list them all as we do in this example:

```
RMAN> list backup of archivelog all summary;
List of Backups
===============
Key     TY LV S Device Type Completion Time #Pieces #Copies Compressed Tag
------- -- -- - ----------- --------------- ------- ------- ---------- ---
1       B  A  A DISK        11-OCT-08       1       1       YES
TAG20081011T142547
```

```
4        B  A  A DISK        11-OCT-08       1        1         YES
TAG20081011T143308
5        B  A  A DISK        11-OCT-08       1        1         NO
TAG20081011T143528
10       B  A  A DISK        18-OCT-08       1        1         YES
TAG20081018T031922
12       B  A  A DISK        18-OCT-08       1        1         YES
TAG20081018T032513
14       B  A  A DISK        18-OCT-08       1        1         YES
TAG20081018T134136
16       B  A  A DISK        18-OCT-08       1        1         YES
TAG20081018T134839
```

In Exercise 7.2, you will get to experiment with the `list` command.

EXERCISE 7.2

Using the *list* Command

1. Log into RMAN, connecting to your recovery catalog:

```
C:\>rman target=/ catalog=rcat_user/rcat_user@rcat
Recovery Manager: Release 11.1.0.6.0 -
Production on Sun Oct 19 14:51:06 2008
Copyright (c) 1982, 2007, Oracle.  All rights reserved.
connected to target database: ORCL (DBID=1195614221)
connected to recovery catalog database
```

2. You can see what backups are available by calling the `list backup of database summary` command:

```
RMAN> list backup of database summary;
List of Backups
===============
Key  TY LV S Device Type Completion Time #Pieces #Copies Compressed Tag
---- -- -- - ----------- --------------- ------- ------- ---------- ---
1253 B  F  A DISK        18-OCT-08       1       1       YES
TAG20081018T152908
1342 B  F  A DISK        18-OCT-08       1       1       YES
TAG20081018T163034
```

3. To look at one of these backups in more detail, call the `list` backup command:

```
RMAN> list backup of database;
List of Backup Sets
```

EXERCISE 7.2 *(continued)*

```
===================
BS Key  Type LV Size       Device Type Elapsed Time Completion Time
------- ---- -- ---------- ----------- ------------ ---------------
1253    Full    187.77M    DISK        00:00:00     18-OCT-08
        BP Key: 1261   Status: AVAILABLE  Compressed: YES
Tag: TAG20081018T152908
    Piece Name: C:\ORACLE\FLASH_RECOVERY_AREA\ORCL\BACKUPSET\2008_10_18
\O1_MF_NNNDF_TAG20081018T152908_4HNO9DX9_.BKP.OLD
List of Datafiles in backup set 1253
File LV Type Ckp SCN    Ckp Time  Name
---- -- ---- ---------- --------- ----
1       Full 1222465    18-OCT-08 C:\ORACLE\ORADATA\ORCL\SYSTEM01.DBF
2       Full 1222465    18-OCT-08 C:\ORACLE\ORADATA\ORCL\SYSAUX01.DBF
3       Full 1222465    18-OCT-08 C:\ORACLE\ORADATA\ORCL\UNDOTBS01.DBF
4       Full 1222465    18-OCT-08 C:\ORACLE\ORADATA\ORCL\USERS01.DBF
5       Full 1222465    18-OCT-08 C:\ORACLE\ORADATA\ORCL\MY_DATA_01.DBF

BS Key  Type LV Size       Device Type Elapsed Time Completion Time
------- ---- -- ---------- ----------- ------------ ---------------
1342    Full    187.87M    DISK        00:56:47     18-OCT-08
        BP Key: 1348   Status: AVAILABLE  Compressed: YES
Tag: TAG20081018T163034
     Piece Name: C:\ORACLE\FLASH_RECOVERY_AREA\ORCL\BACKUPSET\2008_10_18
\O1_MF_NNNDF_TAG20081018T163034_4HNRWKVC_.BKP
List of Datafiles in backup set 1342
File LV Type Ckp SCN    Ckp Time  Name
---- -- ---- ---------- --------- ----
1       Full 1224452    18-OCT-08 C:\ORACLE\ORADATA\ORCL\SYSTEM01.DBF
2       Full 1224452    18-OCT-08 C:\ORACLE\ORADATA\ORCL\SYSAUX01.DBF
3       Full 1224452    18-OCT-08 C:\ORACLE\ORADATA\ORCL\UNDOTBS01.DBF
4       Full 1224452    18-OCT-08 C:\ORACLE\ORADATA\ORCL\USERS01.DBF
5       Full 1224452    18-OCT-08 C:\ORACLE\ORADATA\ORCL\MY_DATA_01.DBF
```

4. Next, simulate the loss of a backup set piece by using the host command and deleting the backup set piece. In this case, you will remove the backup set piece called O1_MF_NNNDF_TAG20081018T163034_4HNRWKVC_.BKP, which showed up in the report in step 3. Your backup set piece will probably be named differently.

```
RMAN> Host 'del C:\ORACLE\FLASH_RECOVERY_AREA\ORCL\BACKUPSET\2008_10_18
\O1_MF_NNNDF_TAG20081018T163034_4HNRWKVC_.BKP';
```

EXERCISE 7.2 *(continued)*

5. Now you need to use the crosscheck command so RMAN will detect that you have deleted the backup set piece. Note that the backup set piece you removed is now marked as expired.

```
RMAN> crosscheck backup;
allocated channel: ORA_DISK_1
channel ORA_DISK_1: SID=122 device type=DISK
crosschecked backup piece: found to be 'AVAILABLE'
backup piece handle=C:\ORACLE\FLASH_RECOVERY_AREA\ORCL\AUTOBACKUP\
2008_10_18\01_MF_S_668446569_4HNOPMRF_.BKP RECID=29 STAMP=668446579
crosschecked backup piece: found to be 'AVAILABLE'
backup piece handle=C:\ORACLE\FLASH_RECOVERY_AREA\ORCL\BACKUPSET\
2008_10_18\01_MF_ANNNN_TAG20081018T153543_4HNOP6OH_.BKP.OLD RECID=31
STAMP=668449007
crosschecked backup piece: found to be 'AVAILABLE'
backup piece handle=C:\ORACLE\FLASH_RECOVERY_AREA\ORCL\BACKUPSET\
2008_10_18\01_MF_NNNDF_TAG20081018T152908_4HNO9DX9_.BKP.OLD RECID=32
STAMP=668449009
crosschecked backup piece: found to be 'EXPIRED'
backup piece handle=C:\ORACLE\FLASH_RECOVERY_AREA\ORCL\BACKUPSET\
2008_10_18\01_MF_NNNDF_TAG20081018T163034_4HNRWKVC_.BKP RECID=33
STAMP=668449841
crosschecked backup piece: found to be 'AVAILABLE'
backup piece handle=C:\ORACLE\FLASH_RECOVERY_AREA\ORCL\AUTOBACKUP\
2008_10_18\01_MF_S_668453268_4HNW82VT_.BKP RECID=34
STAMP=668453282
crosschecked backup piece: found to be 'AVAILABLE'
backup piece handle=C:\ORACLE\FLASH_RECOVERY_AREA\ORCL\AUTOBACKUP\
2008_10_19\01_MF_S_668533219_4HQBBXCQ_.BKP RECID=35 STAMP=668533245
Crosschecked 6 objects
```

6. Now issue the `list expired` backup command to get a report of expired RMAN backup set pieces:

```
RMAN> list expired backup;
List of Backup Sets
===================
BS Key  Type LV Size       Device Type Elapsed Time Completion Time
------- ---- -- ---------- ----------- ------------ ---------------
1342    Full    187.87M    DISK        00:56:47     18-OCT-08
```

EXERCISE 7.2 *(continued)*

```
BP Key: 1348   Status: EXPIRED  Compressed: YES Tag: TAG20081018T163034
        Piece Name: C:\ORACLE\FLASH_RECOVERY_AREA\ORCL\BACKUPSET\2008_10_18
\01_MF_NNNDF_TAG20081018T163034_4HNRWKVC_.BKP
  List of Datafiles in backup set 1342
  File LV Type Ckp SCN  Ckp Time  Name
  ---- -- ---- -------- --------- ----
  1       Full 1224452  18-OCT-08 C:\ORACLE\ORADATA\ORCL\SYSTEM01.DBF
  2       Full 1224452  18-OCT-08 C:\ORACLE\ORADATA\ORCL\SYSAUX01.DBF
  3       Full 1224452  18-OCT-08 C:\ORACLE\ORADATA\ORCL\UNDOTBS01.DBF
  4       Full 1224452  18-OCT-08 C:\ORACLE\ORADATA\ORCL\USERS01.DBF
  5       Full 1224452  18-OCT-08 C:\ORACLE\ORADATA\ORCL\MY_DATA_01.DBF
```

7. Now, mark the backup set piece as deleted by using the `delete expired backup` command. You will need to respond when prompted to verify that you want to delete the backup set piece:

```
RMAN> delete expired backup;
using channel ORA_DISK_1
List of Backup Pieces
BP Key  BS Key  Pc# Cp# Status      Device Type Piece Name
------- ------- --- --- ----------- ----------- ----------
1348    1342    1   1   EXPIRED     DISK        C:\ORACLE\FLASH_RECOVERY_AREA\
ORCL\BACKUPSET\2008_10_18
\01_MF_NNNDF_TAG20081018T163034_4HNRWKVC_.BKP
Do you really want to delete the above objects (enter YES or NO)? yes
deleted backup piece
backup piece handle=C:\ORACLE\FLASH_RECOVERY_AREA\ORCL\BACKUPSET\
2008_10_18\01_MF_NNNDF_TAG20081018T163034_4HNRWKVC_.BKP RECID=33
STAMP=668449841
Deleted 1 EXPIRED objects
```

Monitoring, Administering, and Tuning RMAN

For the OCP exam, you will be expected to know a little bit about how to monitor RMAN operations. The exam will also test your knowledge of RMAN administration and tuning options. In the following sections, we will address all of these items.

Monitoring RMAN Operations

More often than not, RMAN works just fine. However, there are times when you will want to be able to monitor RMAN operations. In the next sections, we will discuss RMAN tuning, including enabling asynchronous I/O and monitoring RMAN operations with data dictionary views.

Configuring for Asynchronous I/O

In most cases, your operating system (OS) will already support asynchronous I/O operations natively. In these cases, no special configuration is required.

If your OS does not support native asynchronous I/O operations, then you may want to consider configuring your database, and RMAN, to simulate asynchronous I/O. Oracle provides Oracle slave I/O processes, which are individual processes that Oracle starts that are used to simulate asynchronous I/O.

You can enable these asynchronous I/O processes by configuring the parameter `dbwr_io_slaves`. This parameter indicates to Oracle how many I/O slaves should be started when the database is started. When this parameter is zero, simulated asynchronous I/O is disabled. When the parameter is greater than zero, Oracle will automatically start four backup I/O slaves.

When using IO slaves to simulate asynchronous I/O, you will also want to configure the large pool using the `large_pool_size` parameter. RMAN will use the large pool, if configured, instead of the shared pool. If the large pool is allocated when you're using I/O slaves but insufficient memory exists, then RMAN will generate an error and will not use asynchronous I/O. If the large pool is not allocated and IO slaves are enabled, RMAN will use the shared pool and try to simulate asynchronous I/O operations. If the large pool is not allocated and there is not enough shared-pool memory, then Oracle will use the PGA. In this case, simulated asynchronous I/O operations will not occur.

Using the *V$SESSION_LONGOPS* View to Monitor RMAN

Oracle provides the `V$SESSION_LONGOPS` view as a means to monitor long-running processes within the Oracle database. Since RMAN uses internal database calls, records for long-running RMAN operations will appear in `V$SESSION_LONGOPS`. This view can be useful when you're trying to determine just how long a database backup or restore is likely to take. In this example, you first start an RMAN backup in one session. And as the backup is running, you will query the `V$SESSION_LONGOPS` view with this query:

```
SQL> Select sid, serial#, opname, time_remaining
  2  From v$session_longops
  3  Where sid in (select sid from v$session
  4                              Where program like '%rman%')
  5  And time_remaining > 0;
     SID     SERIAL# OPNAME                                TIME_REMAINING
```

```
---------- ---------- ------------------------------ --------------
       129        415 RMAN: aggregate input                     188
       121        269 RMAN: full datafile backup                161
```

In the output from this example, it appears that the overall time for the RMAN backup in question is about 188 seconds (the `aggregate input` figure is the one to use here). Keep in mind that these figures are just for the individual backup operation that is currently running. The output is not cumulative for the entire backup command.

For example, if you executed a backup using a command like `backup as compressed backup database plus archivelog delete input`, the output displayed would be only for the database backup or the archived redo-log backup. Keep in mind that the `backup database plus archivelog` command can show a series of backups. These would include two individual archive-log backups, the database backup, and then the control-file autobackup. Each of these operations will appear in the `V$SESSION_LONGOPS` view differently. Notice in the previous example that `OPNAME` is displayed as full datafile backup. The value for `OPNAME` would be different for different stages in the RMAN backup operation.

Real World Scenario

Tuning RMAN: It's the Little Things That Count

In the real world, tuning RMAN can make a huge difference. RMAN works fine as it is out of the box, but very often there is a lot you can do to make things run faster. Sometimes even the smallest things can make a huge difference. One place where one of us worked had limited tape drives for performing backups.

The problem was that individual DBAs were scheduling their backups for each of their individual databases and there wasn't a lot of coordination of schedules going on. We started getting complaints because backups were taking a long time.

It turned out that everyone was hitting the tape drives all at the same time. The tape drives would be working a specific backup, and all the other backups would sit and wait for a tape device to become available. Once we worked out a reasonable schedule, the backups started working better and everyone was much happier!

Using the *V$SESSION* and *V$SESSION_WAIT_HISTORY* Views to Troubleshoot RMAN Problems

Trouble. We hate trouble. Sometimes you get into problems with RMAN and are not sure what the trouble is. The `V$SESSION` and `V$SESSION_WAIT` views can be a big help in your troubleshooting efforts. These views can help identify the cause of RMAN processes that are not running as fast as you would like. In this example, we have an RMAN backup running, rather slowly at that. We query the `V$SESSION` view to determine the total number of waits that the session has experienced and the wait event that the session is currently experiencing:

```
SQL> Select sid, serial#, event, seconds_in_wait
  2  From v$session
  3  Where sid in (select sid from v$session
  4                  Where program like '%rman%');
       SID    SERIAL# EVENT                          SECONDS_IN_WAIT
---------- ---------- ------------------------------ ---------------
       121        269 RMAN backup & recovery I/O                   2
       129        415 SQL*Net message from client                 63
       130        270 SQL*Net message from client                  8
```

Here you see that the backup-and-recovery I/O on SID 121 appears to be a problem. It's been waiting 2 seconds, which is a long time for an I/O request. Note that the two other wait events are considered idle waits and are likely not a problem. Later we might run the query again and see something like this:

```
       SID    SERIAL# EVENT                          SECONDS_IN_WAIT
---------- ---------- ------------------------------ ---------------
       121        269 control file sequential read                 3
       129        415 SQL*Net message from client                  3
       130        270 SQL*Net message from client                  3
```

The control-file sequential read is now the main wait.

The V$SESSION view lists waits that are occurring at that moment. We could query V$SESSION_WAIT_HISTORY and find out all waits for the session since it started, as shown here:

```
SQL> Select sid, event, wait_time
  2  From v$session_wait_history
  3  Where sid in (select sid from v$session
  4                  Where program like '%rman%')
  5 And wait_time>0;
       SID EVENT                           WAIT_TIME
---------- ------------------------------ ----------
       121 RMAN backup & recovery I/O             11
       129 SQL*Net message from client             1
       129 SQL*Net message from client             2
       129 SQL*Net message from client             2
       130 SQL*Net message from client           400
       130 SQL*Net message from client           200
       130 SQL*Net message from client           100
       130 SQL*Net message from client           766
```

This gives us the cumulative wait times for a given session. You might wait for a few moments and run the query again. Perhaps you would get these results:

```
       SID EVENT                          WAIT_TIME
---------- ------------------------------ ----------
       121 RMAN backup & recovery I/O             85
       121 RMAN backup & recovery I/O             47
       129 SQL*Net message from client             1
       129 SQL*Net message from client             2
       129 SQL*Net message from client             2
       130 SQL*Net message from client          1000
       130 SQL*Net message from client          1000
       130 SQL*Net message from client          1000
       130 SQL*Net message from client          1000
       130 SQL*Net message from client          1000
```

The difference in session 121's wait titled RMAN backup & recovery I/O might indicate a problem with the disk subsystem that we are backing up to (which is quite correct in this situation, as we ran this on a slow computer).

Administering RMAN Operations

For the OCP exam, you will be expected to know how to administer RMAN. The principal commands used to administer RMAN are the `delete` command, the `crosscheck` command, the `catalog` command, and finally, the `resync` command.

Using the *delete* Command

The `delete` command is used to mark backup set pieces, image copies, or archived redo logs as deleted if they have been previously marked as expired (missing) or obsolete (retention criteria–related). Previously in this chapter you saw the `list expired` command used to indicate which backup set pieces were expired. After running the `list expired` command, we would use the `delete expired backup` command to mark those as permanently deleted from the control file and the recovery catalog.

When the delete expired command is executed, all records for those backup set pieces in the control file and/or the recovery catalog are marked as deleted. When the delete obsolete command is executed, that command will mark the records for the backupset pieces as deleted in the control file and recovery catalog. The delete obsolete command will also remove any physical-backup set pieces present on the backup media.

Here is an example where we list the expired (missing) backup set pieces and then delete them:

```
RMAN> list expired backup;
List of Backup Sets
```

```
===================
BS Key  Type LV Size       Device Type Elapsed Time Completion Time
------- ---- -- ---------- ----------- ------------ ---------------
425      Full    176.72M    DISK        00:06:02     11-OCT-08
      BP Key: 433   Status: EXPIRED  Compressed: YES  Tag: TAG20081011T142622
      Piece Name: C:\ORACLE\FLASH_RECOVERY_AREA\ORCL\BACKUPSET\2008_10_11
\O1_MF_NNNDF_TAG20081011T142622_4H22ZOMK_.BKP
  List of Datafiles in backup set 425
  File LV Type Ckp SCN    Ckp Time  Name
  ---- -- ---- ---------- --------- ----
  1       Full 903859     11-OCT-08 C:\ORACLE\ORADATA\ORCL\SYSTEM01.DBF
  2       Full 903859     11-OCT-08 C:\ORACLE\ORADATA\ORCL\SYSAUX01.DBF
  3       Full 903859     11-OCT-08 C:\ORACLE\ORADATA\ORCL\UNDOTBS01.DBF
  4       Full 903859     11-OCT-08 C:\ORACLE\ORADATA\ORCL\USERS01.DBF
RMAN> delete expired backup;
using channel ORA_DISK_1
List of Backup Pieces
BP Key  BS Key  Pc# Cp# Status      Device Type Piece Name
------- ------- --- --- ----------- ----------- ----------
433     425      1   1   EXPIRED     DISK
C:\ORACLE\FLASH_RECOVERY_AREA\ORCL\BACKUPSET\2008_10_11
\O1_MF_NNNDF_TAG20081011T142622_4H22ZOMK_.BKP
Do you really want to delete the above objects (enter YES or NO)? yes
deleted backup piece
backup piece handle=C:\ORACLE\FLASH_RECOVERY_AREA\ORCL\BACKUPSET\2008_10_11\
O1_MF_NNNDF_TAG20081011T142622_4H22ZOMK_.BKP RECID=2 STAMP=667837589
Deleted 1 EXPIRED objects
```

One important thing to note is that once you have marked a backup set with a DELETED status, that status cannot be changed. Thus, if you ever needed to restore that backup set piece, you would have to use the catalog command to reimport it into the database control file and recovery catalog (assuming it was still available).

Using the *crosscheck* Command

The crosscheck command is used to validate RMAN records in the database control file and the recovery catalog against what is physically on the backup media. The crosscheck command can be used on both disk backups and tape backups. In this example, we are using it to validate that all the backups set pieces recorded in the control file of our database are actually on the media where they are supposed to be:

```
RMAN> crosscheck backup of database;
using channel ORA_DISK_1
crosschecked backup piece: found to be 'EXPIRED'
```

```
backup piece handle=C:\ORACLE\FLASH_RECOVERY_AREA\ORCL\BACKUPSET\2008_10_18
\01_MF_NNNDF_TAG20081018T152908_4HNO9DX9_.BKP RECID=27 STAMP=668446156
Crosschecked 1 objects
```

In this case, we had some bad news because one of our backup set pieces is marked EXPIRED, or missing. If we know that it's permanently gone, we can use the `delete expired` command (discussed earlier in this chapter) to mark it as deleted. Sometimes the backup set piece is expired just because the backup media is offline (for example, a bad disk cable). Once the backup media is back online, you would rerun the `crosscheck` command and the backup set piece would be marked as AVAILABLE once it is again accessible by RMAN.

As with other administration commands, you can cross-check the gambit of backups. From database backups and archive-log backups to image copies, the `crosscheck` command covers them all.

Using the *catalog* Command

The `catalog` command is used to import one or more backup set pieces, image copies, control-file copies, or archived redo logs into the recovery catalog. For example, say we had executed a `crosscheck` of our database backups and then deleted the expired backup set pieces with the `delete expired` command. That would mark the expired backup set piece as deleted in our control file and recovery catalog. This is okay until the missing backup set piece reappears (say we restore it from a tape backup). In this case, you will have to use the `catalog` command to reregister the backup set piece in the control file and recovery catalog. Here is an example of the use of the `catalog` command:

```
RMAN> crosscheck backup of database;
using channel ORA_DISK_1
crosschecked backup piece: found to be 'EXPIRED'
backup piece handle=C:\ORACLE\FLASH_RECOVERY_AREA\ORCL\BACKUPSET\2008_10_18
\01_MF_NNNDF_TAG20081018T152908_4HNO9DX9_.BKP RECID=27 STAMP=668446156
Crosschecked 1 objects
RMAN> catalog backuppiece
'C:\ORACLE\FLASH_RECOVERY_AREA\ORCL\BACKUPSET\2008_10_18
\01_MF_NNNDF_TAG20081018T152908_4HNO9DX9_.BKP';
cataloged backup piece
backup piece handle=C:\ORACLE\FLASH_RECOVERY_AREA\ORCL\BACKUPSET\2008_10_18
\01_MF_NNNDF_TAG20081018T152908_4HNO9DX9_.BKP RECID=30 STAMP=668447953
```

The `crosscheck` command can also import complete directories, as shown in this example:

```
RMAN> catalog start with
'C:\ORACLE\FLASH_RECOVERY_AREA\ORCL\BACKUPSET\2008_10_18\';
```

```
searching for all files that match the pattern
C:\ORACLE\FLASH_RECOVERY_AREA\ORCL\BACKUPSET\2008_10_18\
List of Files Unknown to the Database
=====================================
File Name: C:\ORACLE\FLASH_RECOVERY_AREA\ORCL\BACKUPSET\2008_10_18\
01_MF_ANNNN_TAG20081018T153543_4HNOP6OH_.BKP.old
File Name: C:\ORACLE\FLASH_RECOVERY_AREA\ORCL\BACKUPSET\2008_10_18\
01_MF_NNNDF_TAG20081018T152908_4HNO9DX9_.BKP.old
Do you really want to catalog the above files (enter YES or NO)? yes
cataloging files...
cataloging done
List of Cataloged Files
=======================
File Name: C:\ORACLE\FLASH_RECOVERY_AREA\ORCL\BACKUPSET\2008_10_18\
01_MF_ANNNN_TAG20081018T153543_4HNOP6OH_.BKP.old
File Name: C:\ORACLE\FLASH_RECOVERY_AREA\ORCL\BACKUPSET\2008_10_18\
01_MF_NNNDF_TAG20081018T152908_4HNO9DX9_.BKP.old
RMAN> list backup of database summary;
List of Backups
===============
Key     TY LV S Device Type Completion Time #Pieces #Copies Compressed Tag
------- -- -- - ----------- --------------- ------- ------- ---------- ---
1253    B  F  A DISK        18-OCT-08       1       1       YES
TAG20081018T152908
```

The `catalog` command can come in quite handy during disaster-recovery exercises when all you have are backup set pieces and an Oracle database instance. You can create the instance, catalog the backup set pieces (including control-file autobackups), and then restore your database. The `catalog` command works only with disk devices, so in disaster-recovery cases you might first have to restore datafiles from tape before you can catalog them.

Using the *resync* Command

The `resync` command is used to synchronize the recovery catalog with the control file. RMAN will often perform automatic resync operations, but there may be times when you will want to perform a manual resync operation. Simply issue the `resync catalog` command and the catalog will be synchronized with the recovery catalog, as shown in this example:

```
RMAN> resync catalog;
starting full resync of recovery catalog
full resync complete
```

Tuning RMAN Operations

The final topic in this chapter is how to tune RMAN operations. Of course, standard Oracle tuning methodologies apply here; use enough backup devices to get good I/O performance. Allocate enough memory to the database, and make sure your CPUs can handle the load.

Another method of tuning your RMAN operations is through parallel channel operations. Recall that using channels is the method that RMAN uses to write backup-related information from the database to the backup device. If you can create multiple channels to different backup devices (say two channels to two different disk drives or tape devices), then you can speed up the performance of your backups in many cases.

Oracle also provides the `duration` parameter associated with the `backup` command, which allows you to indicate to Oracle how much overall impact it should allow the backup to have on the database as a whole. When using the `duration` parameter, you indicate the overall duration that you want the backup to run. If it runs over that (say 5 hours), then RMAN will terminate the backup. The datafiles already backed up will still be valid, but there may be datafiles that are not backed up. RMAN will prioritize any missed datafile backups on the subsequent backup operation.

Note that if a backup does not complete after the amount of time identified in the `duration` parameter, then the whole backup will be considered to have failed. Other backup operations within a run block will not be executed as a result. You can use the `partial` keyword to indicate to RMAN that it should consider the backup to have been successful and not return an error. This will allow subsequent commands (like archive-log backups) to execute. Here is an example of the use of the `partial` keyword:

```
RMAN> Backup as compressed backupset duration 1:00
partial minimize load database ;
```

If you use the `duration minimize load` parameter when performing a backup, then you will be indicating to Oracle that you want it to reduce the load that the backup has on the database as a whole. When `minimize load` is used, Oracle will try to spread the backup over the entire time identified in the `duration` parameter. This will result in slower backup times but improved overall database performance. Here is an example of the use of the `duration` parameter in the backup command:

```
RMAN> Backup as compressed backupset duration 1:00 minimize load database;
```

Summary

In some ways, this is the most important chapter when it comes to RMAN overall. In previous chapters we have shown you that typical backup and recovery is not a very complex task most of the time in RMAN. When things go wrong, however, RMAN can become a bit trickier. Of course, things tend to go wrong just when the stress is the highest and the need to get your database up and running is the highest.

To help you with these difficult moments and prepare you for the OCP exam, we covered RMAN reporting, tuning, and monitoring. Reporting is quite important because you need to be able to see what backups are available (for example, to determine what types of incomplete recovery are actually available).

Tuning is important because we want our backups and our recoveries to go as fast as possible. Everyone wants the backups to go fast, and the longer they take the more impact they have on the system. Of course, everyone wants restores to go fast. That's where strategies like parallelism come in handy.

Monitoring is important too because we need to be able to look at backup or restore operations as they are happening and answer the question, Does this look normal? Monitoring gives us that ability. It's important to know what is normal for your backups and your recoveries so that when the time comes, you will be able to understand just what is not normal and how deviant a statistic actually is from the norm. Then you can address the problem.

This is the last chapter on RMAN in this book. Questions on RMAN will be a significant portion of your OCP exam. Study it hard, and practice backup and recovery a lot before you take your test (both RMAN and user-managed). If you do so, we suspect you will do well on your exam.

Exam Essentials

Be able to use the `list` and `report` commands. Understanding the `list` and `report` commands is very important to RMAN operations and to being successful on your OCP exam. They allow you to review metadata contained within the database control file and recovery catalog, understand backups that have been taken, and take corrective action when certain conditions arise.

Be able to administer the RMAN environment. Understanding how to administer RMAN is quite important. Knowing how to use commands like `catalog`, `delete`, and `crosscheck` is critical to properly administering the RMAN environment. These commands will come in especially handy after disaster recovery when you need to get your database up and running quickly.

Be able to performance-tune your RMAN operations. Understanding how parallelism can make your database backups and restores perform faster is critical to making RMAN performant. Understand how to control the duration of a backup and how to reduce the overall I/O load with the `duration` command.

Review Questions

1. Which command would you use to determine what database backups are currently available for restore?

   A. `list database backup;`

   B. `report database backup;`

   C. `list backup of database;`

   D. `list summary backup;`

   E. `report backup of database;`

2. What command would you use to ensure that backup records in the control file are pointing to actual physical files on the backup media?

   A. `crosscheck`

   B. `list backup`

   C. `confirm`

   D. `resync`

   E. `backup validate`

3. You have backed up your database twice without connecting to the recovery catalog. What command do you issue to transfer the control-file metadata to the recovery catalog?

   A. `synch catalog`

   B. `resync catalog`

   C. `replicate catalog`

   D. `update catalog`

   E. `restore catalog`

4. You want to make sure that your database backup does not exceed 10 hours in length. What command would you issue that would meet this condition?

   A. `backup database plus archivelog;`

   B. `backup database plus archivlog until time '10:00';`

   C. `backup database plus archivelog timeout '10:00';`

   D. `backup database plus archivelog duration 10:00;`

   E. `backup database plus archivelog timeout 10:00;`

5. You have lost all your RMAN backup set pieces due to a disk failure. Unfortunately, you have an automated cross-check script that also does a `delete expired backupset` command. You have restored all the backup set pieces from tape. What command would you use to get those backup set pieces registered in the recovery catalog and the control file of the database again?

   A. `register database`

   B. `recover catalog`

   C. `load backupset`

   D. `synch metadata`

   E. `catalog start with`

6. You run the following commands:

   ```
   RMAN> list expired backup;
   RMAN> delete expired backup;
   ```

   What will happen to the backup set pieces associated with the backups that appear in the `list expired backup` command?

   A. They will be renamed.

   B. Nothing will happen to them. The backup set pieces do not exist.

   C. They will be deleted immediately since they are not in the flash recovery area.

   D. You will need to manually remove the physical files listed in the output of the commands.

   E. They will become hidden files and removed 10 days later.

7. Why would you run the `delete obsolete` command? (Choose all that apply.)

   A. To remove missing backup set pieces physically from disk

   B. To remove metadata related to backup set pieces in the control file and the recovery catalog

   C. To mark as deleted records in the control file and the recovery catalog associated with obsolete backup sets

   D. To delete backup set pieces associated with backups that are no longer needed due to retention criteria

   E. To remove old versions of RMAN backups

8. What does it mean if a backup is expired?

   A. The backup set has exceeded the retention criteria set in RMAN and is eligible for removal.

   B. The backup set has one or more invalid blocks in it and is not usable for recovery.

   C. The backup set contains one or more tablespaces no longer in the database.

   D. The backup set contains one or more missing backup set pieces.

   E. The backup set is from a previous version of RMAN and was not upgraded.

9. If a backup set is expired, what can you do to correct the problem?
   A. Change the retention criteria.
   B. Make the lost backup set pieces available to RMAN again.
   C. Run the `crosscheck` command to correct the location for the backup set piece contained in the metadata.
   D. Nothing. The backup set piece is lost forever.
   E. Call Oracle support. Their assistance is required.

10. How long will this backup be allowed to run?

```
Backup as compressed backupset duration 2:00 minimize load database ;
```

   A. 2 minutes
   B. 2 hours
   C. 2 days
   D. The command will generate an error.
   E. This backup is not constrained by any time limitation.

11. What is the impact of the following backup if it exceeds the duration allowance? (Choose all that apply.)

```
Backup as compressed backupset duration 2:00 partial minimize load database ;
```

   A. The entire backup will fail. It will not be usable for recovery.
   B. The entire backup will fail, but any datafile successfully backed up will be usable for recovery.
   C. If this backup fails, subsequent backups will prioritize datafiles not backed up.
   D. If this backup fails, an error will be raised and any other commands will not be executed.
   E. If this backup fails, no error will be raised and any other commands will be executed.

12. In what view are you likely to see the following output?

```
       SID    SERIAL# EVENT                          SECONDS_IN_WAIT
---------- ---------- ------------------------------ ---------------
       121        269 RMAN backup & recovery I/O                   2
       129        415 SQL*Net message from client                 63
       130        270 SQL*Net message from client                  8
```

   A. V$SESSION_EVENT
   B. V$SESSION
   C. V$WAITS
   D. V$WAITSTAT
   E. V$SYSSTAT

13. What view might you use to try to determine how long a particular backup will take?

    A. V$SESSION_EVENT

    B. V$SESSION

    C. V$WAITS

    D. V$WAITSTAT

    E. V$SESSION_LONGOPS

14. What is the impact of the results of the output of the following command?

```
RMAN> report unrecoverable database;
Report of files that need backup due to unrecoverable operations
File Type of Backup Required Name
---- ----------------------- -----------------------------------
4    full or incremental     C:\ORACLE\ORADATA\ORCL\USERS01.DBF
```

    A. There are no backup sets with any backups of the users01.dbf datafile.

    B. The users01.dbf datafile has had unrecoverable operations occur in it. It will need to be backed up or some data loss is possible during a recovery.

    C. The users01.dbf datafile is corrupted.

    D. The users01.dbf datafile backup exceeds the retention criteria.

    E. The last backup of the users01.dbf datafile failed and must be rerun.

15. What does the output on this report indicate?

```
RMAN> report need backup;
RMAN retention policy will be applied to the command
RMAN retention policy is set to redundancy 1
Report of files with less than 1 redundant backups
File #bkps Name
---- ----- -----------------------------------------
5    0     C:\ORACLE\ORADATA\ORCL\MY_DATA_01.DBF
```

    A. The my_data_01.dbf datafile is corrupted and needs to be restored.

    B. The my_data_01.dbf datafile has not yet been backed up. This report does not imply that the data in the datafile can not be recovered.

    C. The my_data_01.dbf datafile has not yet been backed up. This report implies that the data in the datafile can not be recovered.

    D. The my_data_01.dbf datafile no longer meets the retention criteria for backups.

    E. Datafile 5 is missing.

16. What does the `minimize load database` parameter mean when backing up a database?

   A. RMAN will attempt to make the backup run as fast as possible without any IO limitations.

   B. RMAN will automatically restrict the number of channels in use to one.

   C. RMAN will spread the backup IO over the total duration stated in the `backup` command.

   D. RMAN will skip any datafile that currently is involved in an IO operation. RMAN will retry backing up the datafile later and an error will be raised at the end of the backup if the datafile cannot be backed up.

   E. Datafiles will be backed up; those having the lowest current number of IO operations will be backed up first.

17. What is the result of this command?

   `RMAN> Report need backup days 3;`

   A. Lists all datafiles created in the last three days that are not backed up.

   B. Lists all datafiles not recoverable based on the current retention criteria.

   C. Lists all datafiles not backed up in the last three days. The datafile is not recoverable.

   D. Lists all datafiles that need to be backed up due to unrecoverable operations.

   E. Lists all datafiles not backed up in the last three days. It does not imply that the datafile is not recoverable.

18. Why would you execute the `report obsolete` command?

   A. To list all backups that were no longer available for restore operations

   B. To list all backups that had aged beyond the RMAN retention criteria

   C. To list all backup set pieces listed in control-file or recovery-catalog metadata that are not on the backup media

   D. To list all datafiles that are no longer part of the database and thus do not need to be backed up

   E. To list all archived redo logs that are no longer needed for any database recovery

19. What information does the `report schema` command not provide? (Choose all that apply.)

   A. Size of the datafiles

   B. Size of the tempfiles

   C. Date of last backup for datafiles and tempfiles

   D. Filenames for each datafile

   E. Checkpoint SCN associated with the last RMAN backup

20. If a backup is expired, which of the following is true?

   A. It can never be used for a restore/recover operation.

   B. Oracle will remove the backup set pieces from the flash recovery area.

   C. The backup has been used at least once to restore and recover the database.

   D. The backup is no longer valid because of a `resetlogs` operation.

   E. The physical backup set pieces are missing from the media.

Answers to Review Questions

1. C. The `list backup of database` command provides information on all database backups that are available for restore via RMAN.

2. A. The `crosscheck` command is used to validate all RMAN-related metadata with associated physical backups on backup media.

3. B. The `resync catalog` command is used to synchronize the recovery catalog with the database control file.

4. D. The `duration` command is used to limit the overall time of a database backup.

5. E. The `catalog` command is used to load backup set pieces that do not already exist into the recovery catalog or the control file.

6. B. Expired backup set pieces are those backup set pieces that do not exist. They are discovered via the `crosscheck` command and marked as expired. The `list expired` command reports backup set records that are marked as expired. The `delete expired backup` command marks the backup metadata in the control file and recovery catalog with a status of `DELETED`.

7. C, D. The `delete obsolete` command will mark the related metadata records for the backups as `DELETED` in the control file and the recovery catalog.

8. D. If a backup is expired, it means that a `crosscheck` command has detected that one or more backup set pieces associated with that backup are missing.

9. B. You would make the lost backup set available again by running the `crosscheck` command once the backup set piece becomes available on the backup media.

10. B. The backup will be allowed to run for 2 hours.

11. B, C, E. The backup will fail after the duration period expires, but the datafiles that were backed up successfully will be able to be used in any restore operation. RMAN will prioritize any datafiles not backed up in subsequent backups. Also, the backup will not return an error when the duration expires and other commands will be executed.

12. B. This output would be from the `V$SESSION` view. It contains the current wait event for each session as well as how long the wait has been occurring.

13. E. The `V$SESSION_LONGOPS` view is used to estimate how long a given running operation has until it is complete.

14. B. The `users01.dbf` database datafile has had an unrecoverable operation occur. Because an unrecoverable operation does not generate redo records, the data involved in that operation will be lost in the event of a recovery. The datafile should be backed up.

15. B. The #bkps columns shows zero, which indicates that the datafile has not been backed up. The datafile may yet still be recoverable as long as the archived redo logs are available.

16. C. RMAN will attempt to spread the overall IO over the total stated duration of the backup listed in the `duration` parameter. This will have the effect of limiting the overall load on the database and reducing the performance impacts of the backup.

17. E. This command lists all database datafiles that would require that more than three days of archived redo logs be applied in order to be restored.

18. B. The `report obsolete` command will list all RMAN backups that have aged beyond the RMAN retention criteria and are eligible for removal.

19. C, E. The `report schema` command does not contain the date of the last backup of the datafiles and tempfiles. Also, the `report schema` command does not report the checkpoint SCNs associated with each RMAN backup.

20. E. If a backup is expired, then the physical backup set pieces are missing from the backup media. This backup cannot be restored unless the physical backup set pieces are found, and either re-cataloged or re-crosschecked.

Performing Oracle Advanced Recovery

ORACLE DATABASE 11*g*: ADMINISTRATION II EXAM OBJECTIVES COVERED IN THIS CHAPTER:

- ✓ **Using RMAN to Perform Recovery**
  - Restore a database onto a new host
  - Perform disaster recovery
- ✓ **Using RMAN to Duplicate a Database**
  - Creating a duplicate database
  - Using a duplicate database
- ✓ **Performing Tablespace Point-in-Time Recovery**
  - Identify the situations that require TSPITR
  - Perform automated TSPITR

We have already discussed the basics of recovering your Oracle database. You now know how to use the `restore` and `recover` commands to recover your database to the point of failure. In this chapter, we will cover more advanced recovery topics. First we will cover RMAN incarnations, and then we will introduce you to RMAN database duplication. After that we will discuss tablespace point-in-time recovery, and we will close the chapter with some discussion of disaster recovery of your Oracle database.

Exam objectives are subject to change at any time without prior notice and at Oracle's sole discretion. Please visit Oracle's Training and Certification website (`http://www.oracle.com/education/certification/`) for the most current exam-objectives listing.

Switching Between RMAN Incarnations

We introduced you to the idea of RMAN incarnations in Chapter 2 and have talked about incarnations in several other chapters. A *database incarnation* is the measure of the logical lifetime of an Oracle database. A database's first incarnation begins when it is created and ends whenever the `resetlogs` option is used to open the database. The next incarnation starts at the point of the `resetlogs` operation and ends at the point of the next `resetlogs` operations and so on. When a new incarnation is started, the log sequence numbers are reset, the online redo logs are flushed, and the database literally has a new future.

Sometimes when performing RMAN operations it is necessary to reset to a previous database incarnation. This is pretty rare and is typically done in cases where you have restored your database using point-in-time recovery. After such cases, if you need to perform another restore and that restore needs to be to an SCN that is before the current resetlog SCN, then you will have to reset the database incarnation.

For example, look at this output of this `list incarnation` command:

```
RMAN> list incarnation;
using target database control file instead of recovery catalog
List of Database Incarnations
DB Key  Inc Key DB Name  DB ID       STATUS  Reset SCN  Reset Time
------- ------- -------- ----------- ------  ---------- ----------
1       1       ORCL     1194923408  PARENT  1          10/15/2007 10:08:59
2       2       ORCL     1194923408  PARENT  886308     10/03/2008 13:24:36
3       3       ORCL     1194923408  CURRENT 904361     10/03/2008 14:05:15
```

If you wanted to restore the database to a point in time before 10/03/2008 at 14:05:15 (or SCN 904361), you would need to reset the database to one of the previous incarnations. If, however, you wanted to restore the database to the resetlog time/SCN or after that time, then you would not need to reset the database incarnation.

To reset the database incarnation, you would need to mount the database first. Then use the `reset database to incarnation` command. You include the incarnation number that you want to switch to in the command. This number comes from the `Inc Key` column displayed in the `list incarnation` command output. Here is an example of switching the database to incarnation number 2:

```
RMAN> shutdown immediate
database closed
database dismounted
Oracle instance shut down
RMAN> startup mount
connected to target database (not started)
Oracle instance started
database mounted
Total System Global Area     364081152 bytes
Fixed Size                     1333228 bytes
Variable Size                239077396 bytes
Database Buffers             117440512 bytes
Redo Buffers                   6230016 bytes
RMAN> Reset database to incarnation 2;
database reset to incarnation 2
```

Figure 8.1 provides a graphic example of database incarnations. In this graphic, the database crashes at SCN 40000 (shown in point A in the figure). We restore the database from a backup taken at SCN 10000 (shown in point B in the figure) and recover it to SCN 25000 (shown in point C). Perhaps we have lost the redo logs needed to restore the database beyond SCN 25000, and so we open the database at SCN 25000 with the `alter database open resetlogs` command. This creates a new incarnation of the database. Note that the SCNs are greater than 40000 (because the SCN does not change), but notice that there is a new timeline with which the changes are being recorded (the tangent line heading to the northeast in the figure). This is the new incarnation of the database (demonstrated in point D). It's a completely new life for the database, and everything that happened in the database in the previous life after the previous SCN 25000 is as if it had never happened. There will now actually be two SCN 25000s in the redo stream.

FIGURE 8.1 Example of an Oracle incarnation

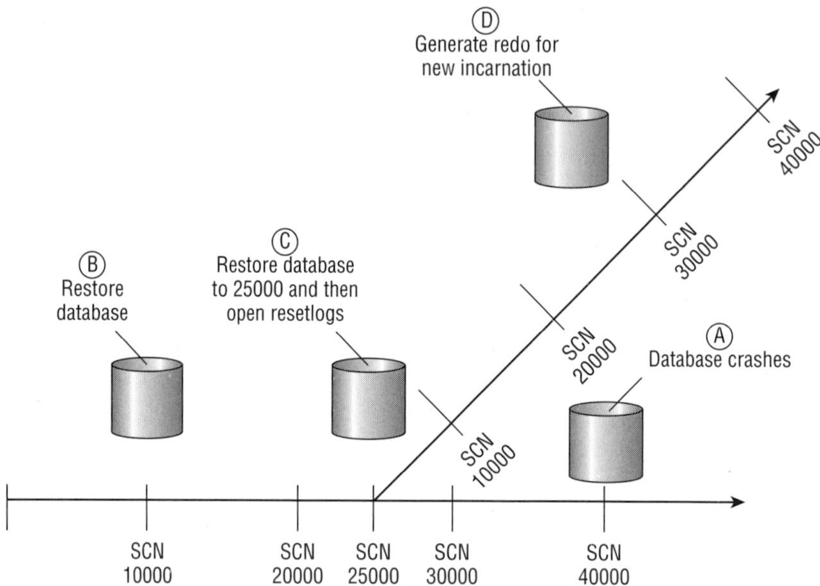

Overview of RMAN Database Duplication

One frequent use of RMAN is to duplicate an existing database. *Database duplication* can be used for a number of different purposes, such as creating development and test databases from production databases or creating a database to test upgrades. In the following sections, we will discuss RMAN duplication basics. Then we will cover how to use the RMAN `duplicate database` command to duplicate a database. We will fist look at how to prepare to duplicate the database. We will then walk you through actually duplicating the database, and finally we will discuss things to do after.

RMAN Database Duplication Basics

The host from which the database is being duplicated is the *source host*. The host to which the database is being duplicated is called the *destination host*. The source host and destination host can be the same computer or a different computer, depending on your needs. One requirement is that the source and destination host must be on the same platform. The target or source database is the database that you will be duplicating from. You will be duplicating to a database instance that will be associated with the new database. This instance is called the *auxiliary instance*.

Two types of database duplication exist:

Active database duplication Active database duplication duplicates the live target database to the auxiliary instance over the network. As a result, no backup of the target database is required and the destination host need not have access to the RMAN backup set pieces.

Backup-based database duplication Backup-based database duplication requires that a backup of the database being duplicated be available. This backup can be an RMAN backup set or image copy. The target host must have access to these backup sets in order to complete the database duplication.

Database duplication takes place over what is called the auxiliary channel. This channel is created during the duplication process and is a server process associated with the auxiliary instance.

When you connect to RMAN to start a database duplication, you will connect to both the target database and the auxiliary instance. This implies that network connectivity to the auxiliary instance is available, and as you will see, getting the auxiliary instance up and running is one prerequisite to starting a database-duplication operation.

Performing an RMAN Database Duplication

Duplicating a database is an operation that many DBAs find themselves doing. RMAN provides the `duplicate database` command to help ease the database-duplication process.

Preparing to Duplicate Your Database

Preparing to duplicate your database requires a few steps:

1. Backing up the target database (backup-based database duplication only)
2. Making backup images available to the destination host (backup-based database duplication only)
3. Deciding where to put the duplicate-database-related files
4. Preparing the auxiliary instance for the duplication

Let's look at each of these steps in more detail next.

Backing up the target database is not required if you are using active database duplication. If you are doing backup-based duplication, you will need a complete backup of the target database. Follow the steps outlined in Chapter 3 to perform an RMAN backup of your database. The database can be in NOARCHIVELOG or ARCHIVELOG mode.

Making backup images available to the destination host is not required if you are using active database duplication. If you are doing backup-based duplication, you will need to make the backup set pieces associated with the backup of the target database, and all associated archived redo logs, available to the destination host. This is so they can be read by RMAN during the duplication process. You can make everything available to the destination host by putting the backup set pieces on shared devices (such as Network File System, or NFS) or some other shared disk environment. You could also manually copy the needed files to the destination host via Secure File Transfer Protocol (SFTP) or some equivalent file-copy protocol.

You will need to decide where you want to put the database files that will be associated with the newly duplicated database. Files like the control files, the online redo logs, and the database datafiles need a home, and you have to know where that will be before you start the duplication process. In the next step, you will use this information to configure the auxiliary instance for duplication.

Before you can begin the duplication process, you must configure the auxiliary instance so that it will start. To do so, follow these steps:

Step 1: Configure any OS-specific requirements. Different operating systems require that certain prerequisites be completed before you can start a database instance. For example, in Windows you must create the Windows service, and in most Unix flavors you will need to configure shared memory. You will need to make sure that these preconfiguration steps are complete before you can start the auxiliary instance and begin the duplication process.

Step 2: Configure the database password file for the auxiliary instance. The auxiliary instance will require a password file. Use the `orapwd` command (see Chapter 3 for more on `orapwd`) to create the password file. If you prefer, you can instruct Oracle to copy the password file from the target database to the duplicated database when you issue the duplication command.

Step 3: Configure Oracle networking for the auxiliary instance. If you will be executing the `duplicate` command from a host other than the destination host, or if you are going to use active database duplication, you will have to configure Oracle networking so that you can connect to the auxiliary instance via Oracle Net. You can use the Oracle Net Configuration Assistant to configure both the database listener and the `tnsnames.ora` file for naming resolution.

Step 4: Configure the database parameter file for the auxiliary instance. Configuring the database parameter file correctly can make for successful database duplication. Incorrectly configuring the parameter file can make for a frustrating exercise in futility. The parameter file must be configured to be able to start the auxiliary instance. The parameters listed in Table 8.1 are available for use during the database-duplication process. You may not need to use all of the parameters listed in Table 8.1 when duplicating databases. In some cases these parameters can also be defined on the RMAN command line as parameters of the duplication command.

Step 5: Start the auxiliary instance. The auxiliary instance should be ready to start at this time. To start it, simply connect to the auxiliary instance from SQL*Plus and issue the `startup nomount` command. Once you have been able to get the auxiliary instance started, you are ready to duplicate to it.

TABLE 8.1 Auxiliary Database Parameters Related to Database Duplication

Parameter Name	Purpose
DB_NAME	The name of the duplicated database. This same name will be used in the RMAN duplicate command. This name should be unique for databases on a given host. This parameter is a required parameter for any database duplication.
CONTROL_FILES	Identifies the location of the control files for the auxiliary instance. This parameter is required unless you are using OMF.
DB_BLOCK_SIZE	Block size of the database to be created. This parameter is required if the same parameter has been defined on the source database.
DB_FILE_NAME_CONVERT	Contains pairs of strings that indicate the conversion path for database files from the source database to the target database. For example, if the parameter were set to '/ora01/oracle/oradata','/ora02/oracle/oradata', all files contained in /ora01/oracle/oradata would be re-created on the duplicate database in /ora02/oracle/oradata. This parameter can also be defined as part of the call to the RMAN duplicate command.
LOG_FILE_NAME_CONVERT	Contains pairs of strings that indicate the conversion path for database redo-log files from the source database to the target database. For example, if the parameter were set to '/ora01/oracle/oradata','/ora02/oracle/oradata', all online redo-log files contained in /ora01/oracle/oradata would be re-created on the duplicate database in /ora02/oracle/oradata.

This parameter can also be defined as part of the call to the RMAN duplicate command.

Duplicating Your Database

As mentioned previously, there are two different modes of database duplication. They are active database duplication and backup-based database duplication. Both duplication methods are achieved via the use of the `duplicate database` command. Let's look at the `duplicate database` command in more detail. Following that we will look at both database-duplication modes in more detail.

Connecting to RMAN for a Database Duplication

Before starting database duplication, you will need to start RMAN and connect to the correct databases. When starting RMAN, you will need to connect to the following:

- The target database
- The auxiliary database

Typically you will connect to the target database locally and connect to the auxiliary database via Oracle Net, but this is not a requirement. Here is an example of connecting to RMAN to perform a database duplication. In this example, we are connecting to a local target database called `orcl`. We use the auxiliary command-line parameter to indicate that we are connecting to an auxiliary database. In this case, it is the database pointed to by the net service name of `mydb`.

```
set oracle_sid=orcl
rman target=/ auxiliary=sys/password@mydb
```

You could also use these variations to connect with RMAN for a database duplication:

```
rman target=sys/robert auxiliary=sys/password@mydb
rman target=sys/robert@orcl auxiliary=sys/password@mydb
```

You might have noticed that we don't use SYSDBA when connecting to RMAN. That is because all connections from RMAN to any database are always with SYSDBA privileges.

The RMAN *duplicate database* Command

The RMAN `duplicate database` command is used when performing either mode of database duplication. The command comes with a number of different options that give you ability to complete the following operations:

- Copy the source spfile to the auxiliary instance.
- Change specific parameters when copying a source spfile to the auxiliary instance.
- Indicate the location that the duplicated files should be copied to using the database filename conversion options `DB_FILE_NAME_CONVERT` and `LOG_FILE_NAME_CONVERT`.
- Create a stand-by database environment on the auxiliary instance.
- Open the duplicated database in a restricted session.
- Use the password file from the target database to create the password file on the auxiliary instance (active database duplication only).
- Skip read-only tablespaces.
- Include or exclude specific tablespaces.
- Restore to a specific restore point or use the `until` clause to restore to a specific time, SCN, or log sequence number (backup-based database duplication only).

During the duplication process, RMAN will automatically create the needed tempfiles for any temporary tablespaces. Here is an example of the RMAN duplication command:

```
Duplicate target database to neworcl nofilenamecheck spfile;
```

The duplicate command comes with a number of options, including the ability to exclude tablespaces, as shown here:

```
Duplicate target database to neworcl nofilenamecheck spfile skip tablespace users;
```

You can also define a restore point, as seen in this example:

```
Duplicate target database to neworcl nofilenamecheck spfile skip
tablespace users to restore point 'Test';
```

You can have Oracle open the duplicated database in restricted mode by adding the open restricted parameter, as shown here:

```
Duplicate target database to neworcl nofilenamecheck spfile open restricted;
```

As with pretty much everything else Oracle, the duplicate command is well documented. We strongly recommend that you review the Oracle Database Backup and Recovery Reference (Oracle part number B28273-02) for more information on all RMAN-related commands.

Active Database Duplication

Active database duplication is started by issuing the RMAN duplicate database command and including the from active database parameter. Active database duplication is not the default.

When you perform active database duplication, Oracle will create the auxiliary channel to the auxiliary database. An additional target-database RMAN channel will also be required. If you have configured automated channels, this should be sufficient. If not, you will need to allocate a channel manually with the allocate channel command.

Finally, the until and to restore point clauses are not valid when doing an active database duplication. Here is an example of the RMAN duplicate command performing an active database duplication:

```
duplicate target database to neworcl from active database nofilenamecheck
spfile set control_files 'c:\oracle\oradata\neworcl\control01.ctl',
'c:\oracle\oradata\neworcl\control02.ctl'
set db_file_name_convert 'c:\oracle\oradata\orcl','c:\oracle\oradata\neworcl'
set log_file_name_convert
'c:\oracle\oradata\orcl','c:\oracle\oradata\neworcl';
```

Backup-Based Database Duplication

Using the duplicate database command without the from active database parameter starts backup-based database duplication. The auxiliary channel will be allocated automatically. No additional channel is required with backup-based database duplication.

When executing a backup-based database duplication, RMAN will determine the last archived redo log available. RMAN will then restore the duplicate database to the point of that last available archived redo log by default. You can use the `until` or `to restore point` parameter to change this behavior. Here is an example of the RMAN `duplicate` command performing a backup-based database duplication:

```
duplicate target database to neworcl
spfile
set control_files 'c:\oracle\oradata\neworcl\control01.ctl',
'c:\oracle\oradata\neworcl\control02.ctl'
set db_file_name_convert 'c:\oracle\oradata\orcl','c:\oracle\oradata\neworcl'
set log_file_name_convert 'c:\oracle\oradata\orcl',
'c:\oracle\oradata\neworcl';
```

After the Duplication

Once the database duplication is complete, the duplicated database will be opened and operational. You can use the `restricted session` parameter of the `duplicate` command to indicate that RMAN should open the database in a restricted session only. You should, of course, consider backing up the newly created database on a regular basis.

In Exercise 8.1, you'll be duplicating a database using backup-based database duplication.

EXERCISE 8.1

Duplicating a Database Using Backup-Based Duplication

In this exercise, you will use backup-based duplication to create a database on the same system that the target database resides on. For this exercise, your database should be running in ARCHIVELOG mode and all networking to the target database should be already configured.

1. Back up your database as shown in Exercise 4.2.
2. Start RMAN and confirm that you have a valid backup with the `list backup of database summary` command and with the `restore database validate` command. Note that your output will likely look very different from ours.

```
C:\Documents and Settings\Robert>rman target=/
Recovery Manager: Release 11.1.0.6.0 -
Production on Sat Oct 4 22:56:10 2008
Copyright (c) 1982, 2007, Oracle.  All rights reserved.
connected to target database: ORCL (DBID=1194923408)
RMAN> list backup of database summary;
```

EXERCISE 8.1 *(continued)*

```
using target database control file instead of recovery catalog
List of Backups
===============
Key     TY LV S Device Type Completion Time #Pieces #Copies Compressed
------- -- -- - ----------- --------------- ------- ------- ----------
Tag
---
2       B  F  A DISK        03-OCT-08       1       1       YES
TAG20081003T135426
RMAN> restore database validate;
Starting restore at 04-OCT-08
allocated channel: ORA_DISK_1
channel ORA_DISK_1: SID=127 device type=DISK
channel ORA_DISK_1: starting validation of datafile backup set
channel ORA_DISK_1: reading from backup piece C:\ORACLE\FLASH_RECOVERY_AREA\
ORCL\BACKUPSET\2008_10_03
\O1_MF_NNNDF_TAG20081003T135426_4GDY3S9H_.BKP
channel ORA_DISK_1: piece handle=C:\ORACLE\FLASH_RECOVERY_AREA\ORCL\
BACKUPSET\2008_10_03
\O1_MF_NNNDF_TAG20081003T135426_4GDY3S9H_.BKP tag=TAG20081003T135426
channel ORA_DISK_1: restored backup piece 1
channel ORA_DISK_1: validation complete, elapsed time: 00:01:36
Finished restore at 04-OCT-08
C:\Documents and Settings\Robert>set oracle_sid=orcl
```

3. If you are running in Windows, create the service for the new database with `oradim`. In this example, you are creating a new database instance called `neworcl`:

```
C:\>oradim -new -sid neworcl
Instance created.
```

If there are any other OS-specific operations required to create a database instance, complete them now.

4. Create the password file for the `neworcl` instance:

```
C:\>orapwd file=c:\oracle\product\11.1.0\db_1\database\pwdneworcl.ora
Enter password for SYS:
```

EXERCISE 8.1 *(continued)*

5. Create a temporary pfile for the neworcl auxiliary instance using your editor of choice. The pfile should be contained in the ORACLE_HOME\database directory of the auxiliary instance and should be named initneworcl.ora. The pfile should have these parameters in it:

```
db_name=neworcl
memory_target=300m
control_files='c:\oracle\oradata\neworcl\control01.ctl',
'c:\oracle\oradata\neworcl\control02.ctl'
```

   We will do the actual file-location conversions during the duplication.

6. Create the directory c:\oracle\oradata\neworcl:

```
mkdir c:\oracle\oradata\neworcl
```

7. Start up the auxiliary instance:

```
C:\oracle\product\11.1.0\db_1\database>set oracle_sid=neworcl
C:\oracle\product\11.1.0\db_1\database>sqlplus "/ as sysdba"
SQL*Plus: Release 11.1.0.6.0 - Production on Sat Oct 4 23:09:52 2008
Copyright (c) 1982, 2007, Oracle.  All rights reserved.
Connected to an idle instance.
SQL> startup nomount
ORACLE instance started.
Total System Global Area  313860096 bytes
Fixed Size                  1332892 bytes
Variable Size             192940388 bytes
Database Buffers          113246208 bytes
Redo Buffers                6340608 bytes
```

8. Configure service name resolution for your new auxiliary database. The method of this configuration will vary based on your site. In our case, we created an entry in the tnsnames.ora file on our server that looked like this:

```
NEWORCL =
  (DESCRIPTION =
    (ADDRESS = (PROTOCOL = TCP)(HOST = 192.168.2.2)(PORT = 1521))
    (CONNECT_DATA =
      (SERVER = DEDICATED)
      (SERVICE_NAME = neworcl)
    ) )
```

EXERCISE 8.1 *(continued)*

9. Now you will need to hard-code the instance name into the listener.ora file until the duplication of the database has been completed. You will get network errors if you do not hard-code the auxiliary instance in the listener.ora file. An example of the entry in our listener.ora is as follows:

```
SID_LIST_LISTENER =
   (SID_LIST =
     (SID_DESC =
        (ORACLE_HOME=C:\oracle\product\11.1.0\db_1\NETWORK\ADMIN)
        (SID_NAME=neworcl)
     ) )
LISTENER =
  (DESCRIPTION_LIST =
    (DESCRIPTION =
      (ADDRESS = (PROTOCOL = TCP)(HOST = 192.168.2.2)(PORT = 1521))
      (ADDRESS = (PROTOCOL = IPC)(KEY = EXTPROC1521))
    ) )
```

10. Test the network connectivity to the auxiliary instance:

```
C:\>sqlplus sys/robert@neworcl as sysdba
SQL*Plus: Release 11.1.0.6.0 - Production on Sat Oct 4 23:17:50 2008
Copyright (c) 1982, 2007, Oracle.  All rights reserved.
Connected to:
Oracle Database 11g Enterprise Edition Release 11.1.0.6.0 - Production
With the Partitioning, OLAP, Data Mining and
Real Application Testing options
SQL> select instance_name from v$instance;
INSTANCE_NAME
----------------
neworcl
```

If the connection fails, review the network configuration and ensure that the new auxiliary instance is running.

11. Start RMAN, connecting to the target and the auxiliary databases:

```
C:\oracle\product\11.1.0\db_1\database>Set oracle_sid=orcl
C:\oracle\product\11.1.0\db_1\database>Rman target=/ auxiliary=sys/Robert@
neworcl
```

EXERCISE 8.1 *(continued)*

```
Recovery Manager: Release 11.1.0.6.0 -
Production on Sat Oct 4 23:19:55 2008
Copyright (c) 1982, 2007, Oracle.  All rights reserved.
connected to target database: ORCL (DBID=1194923408)
connected to auxiliary database: NEWORCL (not mounted)
```

12. You are now ready to start the database duplication. Issue the `duplicate database` command, as shown here:

```
duplicate target database to neworcl nofilenamecheck
spfile set control_files=
'c:\oracle\oradata\neworcl\control01.ctl',
'c:\oracle\oradata\neworcl\control02.ctl'
set db_file_name_convert 'c:\oracle\oradata\orcl',
'c:\oracle\oradata\neworcl'
set log_file_name_convert 'c:\oracle\oradata\orcl',
'c:\oracle\oradata\neworcl';
```

This command does the following:

- It starts the duplication process.
- The `spfile` parameter will result in the target database spfile being copied over to the duplicate database. The duplicate database will use this spfile.
- The set commands (`set control_files`, `set db_file_name_convert`, and `set log_file_name_convert`) modify or add parameters to the spfile being copied to the duplicate database.

This `duplicate` command will result in a great deal of output, which we have decided not to include here as it seems a great waste of a perfectly good tree. Here is the output that you hopefully will see at the end of the database duplication:

```
database opened
Finished Duplicate Db at 04-OCT-08
```

13. Connect to the duplicated database to verify it is open:

```
C:\oracle\product\11.1.0\db_1\database>set oracle_sid=neworcl
C:\oracle\product\11.1.0\db_1\database>sqlplus sys/Robert as sysdba
SQL*Plus: Release 11.1.0.6.0 - Production on Sun Oct 5 00:04:02 2008
```

EXERCISE 8.1 *(continued)*

```
Copyright (c) 1982, 2007, Oracle.  All rights reserved.
Connected to:
Oracle Database 11g Enterprise Edition Release 11.1.0.6.0 - Production
With the Partitioning, OLAP, Data Mining and
Real Application Testing options
SQL> select name, open_mode from v$database;
NAME      OPEN_MODE
--------- ----------
AUXDB     READ WRITE
```

If you want to run this exercise again after the first successful run, you will need to perform these steps:

1. Shut down the auxiliary instance (now it's a new database!).
2. Remove the spfile assigned to the auxiliary instance.
3. `Startup nomount` the auxiliary instance.
4. Run this exercise again starting at step 11.

Performing an RMAN Tablespace Point-in-Time Recovery

As you may recall, when you do a point-in-time recovery of an Oracle database, you have to restore the entire database to the point in time selected. There are times when you may want to restore a specific tablespace to a specific point in time. DBAs have been doing this type of recovery manually for a long time. Simply, they restore a backup to another database on the same or a different server to the point in time they want to restore the tablespace to. They then export the objects they want to restore (or use transportable tablespaces) to the original database.

Of course, this is a lot of manual work. RMAN automates *tablespace point-in-time recovery (TSPITR)* for you, making recovery much easier to perform. In this section we will address TSPITR. We will first look at the TSPITR-related prerequisites and considerations and then look at the aftereffects of a TSPITR. We will then look into setting up for and executing a TSPITR.

For the `until time` commands shown in this chapter, we set NLS_DATE_FORMAT at the Windows OS level to a value of mm/dd/yyyy hh24:mi:ss as seen in this example:

```
Set nls_date_format=mm/dd/yyyy hh24:mi:ss
```

How you set the NLS_DATE_FORMAT OS `level` parameter will vary by platform.

If you are using a date format other than ours, you will need to reformat the date/time in the commands to meet that format. You can also use the to_date function to format the date as seen in this example:

```
recover tablespace users
until time "to_date('10/06/2008:22:42:00','mm/dd/yyyy:hh24:mi:ss')"
auxiliary destination 'c:\oracle\auxiliary';
```

TSPITR Overview

RMAN provides the ability to do a full TSPITR on a given tablespace or set of tablespaces with minimal user interaction. This is known as fully automated TSPITR. You may want to exercise more granular control over TSPITR, in which case you might want to choose to perform customized RMAN TSPITR where you have more control over the creation of the auxillary instance and other aspects of the operation. For the purposes of this book, we will be concerned with only fully automated TSPITR.

Before starting TSPITR Since TSPITR creates an auxiliary-instance database, it needs to know where you want to put the files associated with that database. For automated TSPITR, you are going to use the `auxiliary destination` parameter of the `recover tablespace` command (discussed shortly); then you will need to create the directory associated with the auxiliary destination before executing the TSPITR.

Starting TSPITR You will start TSPITR using the RMAN command `recover tablespace`. Special syntax (which we will cover shortly) that you will include in the body of the command will indicate to RMAN that this is a tablespace TSPITR rather than a normal tablespace recovery. Here is an example of the use of the `recover tablespace` command to start a TSPITR recovery:

```
recover tablespace users
until time '10/06/2008:22:42:00'
auxiliary destination 'c:\oracle\auxiliary';
```

In this case, we are executing a TSPITR of the USERS tablespace. We want to recover the entire USERS tablespace to 10/6/2008 at 22:42:00 hours. The `auxiliary destination` clause, discussed earlier, indicates where we want RMAN to create the auxiliary instance database files—in this case, the directory `c:\oracle\auxiliary`.

Now that we have executed the `recover tablespace` command, what happens next?

The TSPITR auxiliary instance TSPITR requires the use of an auxiliary instance just as database duplication does. The *auxiliary instance* (in RMAN output, it's called an *automatic* *instance*) is the database that will be used to perform the TSPITR. It is a transient database, used just long enough to restore the tablespaces, export the database, and finish the TSPITR. The main difference here is that once RMAN is done with the TSPITR, the auxiliary instance will no longer be needed.

TSPITR transport-set check When you start the TSPITR with the `recover tablespace` command, RMAN will check that the tablespace you want to recover can actually be recovered. It does this by checking the transport set to ensure that it's wholly self-contained. See the next section, "Checking the Transport Set," for more information on this process and why it's needed.

Create the auxiliary instance Once RMAN confirms that the tablespace set can be transported, it will create the auxiliary instance, start it, and connect to it. This is nice since you will not have to create the auxiliary instance. You can opt to create the auxiliary instance yourself if there are specific reasons to do so. RMAN will create a control file for the auxiliary instance.

Target database tablespaces are taken offline Once the auxiliary instance has been created, the tablespaces on the target database to be moved will be taken offline. This implies that the data in these databases will not be available to users until the tablespaces are brought back online. Since you are restoring these tablespaces to a different point in time, the data the users will see the next time the tablespaces are brought back online will possibly be very different. Keep this in mind when doing a TSPITR: You are impacting the entire tablespace or set of tablespaces. If someone is not aware of what you are doing, you might get a very nasty phone call.

Transport the source tablespaces Now that the tablespace(s) has been taken offline, RMAN will restore the recovery set and the auxiliary set from the target database to the auxiliary instance. The *recovery set* is the set of tablespaces that you are going to recover with TSPITR. The *auxiliary set* is the set of datafiles that are required to get the auxiliary instance running. This includes files for the `SYSTEM` tablespace, the `UNDO` tablespace, and the `SYSAUX` tablespace and temporary tablespace tempfiles.

Recover the auxiliary-instance database Once the auxiliary set and the recovery set are restored, RMAN will proceed to recover the auxiliary-instance database to the point in time identified when the RMAN `recover` command was issued. Once the restore is complete, the auxiliary-instance database will be opened.

Transport the tablespace set TSPITR uses transportable tablespaces to facilitate the movement of the tablespace datafiles from the auxiliary database instance to the target database instance. To perform this action, RMAN will first export needed metadata from the auxiliary database instance. It will then shut down the auxiliary database instance. On the target system, RMAN `switch` commands are executed to cause the datafile locations in the target database control file to be switched to the newly recovered datafiles. Finally, the backed-up metadata will be restored to the target database so the data in the restored tablespaces will be accessible to the target database.

Complete the operation The auxiliary database files will be removed after the operation is completed. The target database tablespaces will be offline. You should back up those tablespaces, and then you will need to bring those tablespaces online manually. Once you do, you will find that the tablespaces contain the data in the version it existed in at the restore time indicated in the `recover` command.

TSPITR does not restore the point-in-time statistics for the objects contained in the restored tablespaces. Thus, you should analyze the objects in the tablespaces after completing the TSPITR.

Checking the Transport Set

When you perform a TSPITR, you want a transport set that is self-contained. This means that the tablespaces in the transport set do not have external object references; that is, they don't refer to objects that are not in the transport set. For example, suppose you are transporting the USERS tablespace, and a table in that tablespace has an index in the INDEX tablespace. In this case, you will not be able to transport the USERS tablespace unless you also transport the INDEX tablespace. When you transport both the USERS and the INDEX tablespace, you are transporting a wholly self-contained transport set.

RMAN will determine if the transport set is fully self-contained, but you may want to check beforehand to save some time. You can query the TS_PITR_CHECK view. In our example, USERS and INDEX_TBS are self-contained. If USERS is not transported with INDEX_TBS, then the TSPITR will error out. To determine if USERS and INDEX_TBS are self-contained, we would issue this query:

```
SQL> SELECT ts1_name, ts2_name, reason
  2  FROM SYS.TS_PITR_CHECK
  3  WHERE (
  4          TS1_NAME IN ('USERS','INDEX_TBS')
  5          AND TS2_NAME NOT IN ('USERS','INDEX_TBS')
  6       )
  7  OR   (
  8          TS1_NAME NOT IN ('USERS','INDEX_TBS')
  9          AND TS2_NAME IN ('USERS','INDEX_TBS')
 10*      )
SQL> /
no rows selected
```

If you were to plan to transport only the USERS tablespace, then you would see the following error:

```
SQL> SELECT ts1_name, ts2_name, reason
  2  FROM SYS.TS_PITR_CHECK
```

```
  3  WHERE (
  4          TS1_NAME IN ('USERS')
  5          AND TS2_NAME NOT IN ('USERS')
  6        )
  7  OR    (
  8          TS1_NAME NOT IN ('USERS')
  9          AND TS2_NAME IN ('USERS')
 10*       )
SQL> /

TS1_NAME   TS2_NAME
---------- ----------
REASON
---------------------------------------------------------------------
USERS      INDEX_TBS
Tables and associated indexes not fully contained in the recovery set
```

Lost Objects

When you perform a TSPITR recovery, it is possible that you will lose objects in the tablespace that were created after the point in time to which you restore the tablespace. You can export these objects before the TSPITR with Oracle Data Pump and then import them after the TSPITR has completed.

By querying the view TS_PITR_OBJECTS_TO_BE_DROPPED, you can determine which objects will be lost, as shown in this example:

```
SQL> SELECT OWNER, NAME, TABLESPACE_NAME,
  2         TO_CHAR(CREATION_TIME, 'YYYY-MM-DD:HH24:MI:SS')
  3         FROM TS_PITR_OBJECTS_TO_BE_DROPPED
  4  WHERE TABLESPACE_NAME IN ('USERS')
  5  AND CREATION_TIME >
  6  TO_DATE('07-OCT-08:22:35:30','YY-MON-DD:HH24:MI:SS')
  7  ORDER BY TABLESPACE_NAME, CREATION_TIME;
OWNER                          NAME
------------------------------ -----------------------------
TABLESPACE_NAME                TO_CHAR(CREATION_TI
------------------------------ -------------------
SCOTT                          TESTTABLE
USERS                          2008-10-07:19:34:39
```

Rules, Rules, and More Rules

Finally, TSPITR involves a few rules you need to be aware of:

- The target database must be in ARCHIVELOG mode.
- You must have a backup that was taken before the point in time that you want to perform the TSPITR.
- You must have all archived redo logs generated since the last backup (complete or incremental) up to the point to which you want to restore the transport set.
- If you rename a tablespace, you cannot perform a TSPITR to any point in time before that rename operation occurred.
- If you have tables in `tablespace_1` that have associated constraints in `tablespace_2`, then you must transport both tablespaces.
- If a tablespace contains the following objects, then that tablespace can not be used during a TSPITR.
  - Replicated master tables.
  - Incomplete tables; you must transport complete tables, including all partitions of a partitioned table.
  - Any tables that contain `VARRAY` columns, nested tables, or external tables.
  - Snapshot-related objects (snapshot logs and snapshots).
  - Tablespaces with `UNDO` or rollback segments.
  - Any tablespace with objects owned by the `SYS` schema.

TSPITR Aftereffects

Some interesting things happen after a TSPITR:

- If a datafile was added to the tablespace on the target database after the point in time for the recovery, then the resulting tablespace after the TSPITR process will have an empty datafile restored.
- Once the TSPITR is complete, all backups associated with tablespaces in the transport set taken before the point in time that you restored the tablespaces to are no longer valid. You should run a backup after the TSPITR.
- Once a TSPITR is complete, you will not be able to run another TSPITR on that tablespace to any time before the point to which you restored the tablespace.
- Once a TSPITR is complete, you will not be able to use the control file to restore any part of the database to any point in time before the time that you restored the tablespaces to during the TSPITR.

In Exercise 8.2, you'll perform a tablespace point-in-time recovery with RMAN.

EXERCISE 8.2

Performing a Tablespace Point-in-Time Recovery

In this exercise, you will perform a tablespace point-in-time recovery of the USERS tablespace.

1. Log into the scott account in the database with SQL*Plus:

```
C:\Documents and Settings\Robert>set oracle_sid=orcl
C:\Documents and Settings\Robert>sqlplus scott/tiger
SQL*Plus: Release 11.1.0.6.0 - Production on Thu Oct 9 21:06:00 2008
Copyright (c) 1982, 2007, Oracle.  All rights reserved.
Connected to:
Oracle Database 11g Enterprise Edition Release 11.1.0.6.0 - Production
With the Partitioning, OLAP, Data Mining and
Real Application Testing options
SQL>
```

2. Create a table called TSPITR for this exercise. It will be created in the USERS tablespace (create the USERS tablespace if required):

```
SQL> create table tspitr (id number, the_date date)  tablespace users;
Table created.
```

3. Exit SQL*Plus and start RMAN. Back up the database with RMAN:

```
RMAN> backup as compressed backupset database plus archivelog delete input;
```

4. Exit RMAN and connect to the scott schema again with SQL*Plus:

```
RMAN> exit
Recovery Manager complete.
C:\Documents and Settings\Robert>sqlplus scott/tiger
SQL*Plus: Release 11.1.0.6.0 - Production on Thu Oct 9 21:15:39 2008
Copyright (c) 1982, 2007, Oracle.  All rights reserved.
Connected to:
Oracle Database 11g Enterprise Edition Release 11.1.0.6.0 - Production
With the Partitioning, OLAP, Data Mining and
Real Application Testing options
SQL>
```

5. Insert a record into the TSPITR table and commit:

```
SQL> insert into tspitr values (1,sysdate);
1 row created.
SQL> commit;
```

EXERCISE 8.2 *(continued)*

```
Commit complete.
SQL>
```

6. Wait a minute and insert another record into TSPITR. Commit the record:

```
SQL> insert into tspitr values (2,sysdate);
1 row created.
SQL> commit;
Commit complete.
SQL>
```

7. Select from the TSPITR table. Record the time/date of both records for a later step:

```
SQL> select * from tspitr;

        ID THE_DATE
---------- -------------------
         1 10/09/2008 22:09:02
         1 10/09/2008 22:10:04
```

8. Exit SQL*Plus.

9. From the operating system, create a directory for the auxiliary database files. In our case we are using `c:\oracle\oradata\auxiliary`.

```
c:>mkdir c:\oracle\oradata\auxiliary
```

10. Start RMAN. Connect to the target database:

```
C:\Documents and Settings\Robert>rman target=/
Recovery Manager: Release 11.1.0.6.0 -
Production on Thu Oct 9 21:30:01 2008
Copyright (c) 1982, 2007, Oracle.  All rights reserved.
connected to target database: ORCL (DBID=1194923408)
RMAN>
```

11. Perform a tablespace point-in-time recovery of the USERS tablespace to a point in time between insert #1 and insert #2.

```
RMAN> recover tablespace users
2> until time '10/09/2008:22:09:20' auxiliary destination 'c:\oracle\
auxiliary';
< we have decided to remove the output here to save a few trees.>
```

12. Back up the USERS tablespace:

```
RMAN> backup tablespace users;
```

EXERCISE 8.2 *(continued)*

```
Starting backup at 10/09/2008 22:28:51
using channel ORA_DISK_1
channel ORA_DISK_1: starting full datafile backup set
channel ORA_DISK_1: specifying datafile(s) in backup set
input datafile file number=00004
name=C:\ORACLE\ORADATA\ORCL\USERS01.DBF
channel ORA_DISK_1: starting piece 1 at 10/09/2008 22:28:58
channel ORA_DISK_1: finished piece 1 at 10/09/2008 22:28:59
piece handle=C:\ORACLE\FLASH_RECOVERY_AREA\ORCL\BACKUPSET\2008_10_09
\O1_MF_NNNDF_TAG20081009T222851_4GXPJB5V_.BKP
tag=TAG20081009T222851 comment=NONE
channel ORA_DISK_1: backup set complete, elapsed time: 00:00:01
Finished backup at 10/09/2008 22:28:59
Starting Control File and SPFILE Autobackup at 10/09/2008 22:28:59
piece handle=C:\ORACLE\FLASH_RECOVERY_AREA\ORCL\AUTOBACKUP\2008_10_09
\O1_MF_S_667693739_4GXPJMNZ_.BKP comment=NONE
Finished Control File and SPFILE Autobackup at 10/09/2008 22:29:14.
```

13. Connect to SYS with SQL*Plus:

```
C:\Documents and Settings\Robert>sqlplus sys/robert as sysdba
SQL*Plus: Release 11.1.0.6.0 - Production on Thu Oct 9 22:31:40 2008
Copyright (c) 1982, 2007, Oracle.  All rights reserved.
Connected to:
Oracle Database 11g Enterprise Edition Release 11.1.0.6.0 - Production
With the Partitioning, OLAP, Data Mining and
Real Application Testing options
```

14. Bring the USERS tablespace online:

```
SQL> alter tablespace users online;
Tablespace altered.
```

15. Select from the TSPITR table. Notice that only the first record is now in the table. This concludes this exercise.

```
SQL> select * from tspitr;

        ID THE_DATE
---------- -------------------
         1 10/09/2008 22:09:02
```

Performing a Database Disaster Recovery

In the previous several chapters, we discussed user-based backup and recovery and RMAN-based (or server-based) backup and recovery. So what happens if there is a complete disaster and you lose everything? First, you need to plan for such an event. Taking backups and moving them offsite is the first step. You will need to make sure that you not only have backups of your database offsite, but that you have copies of the Oracle software available offsite too. Any parameter files that are not backed up by RMAN (say, your `tnsnames.ora` or your `listener.ora` files) should be backed up offsite.

We thought we would close this chapter with a review of what you would need to do if you had to recover from offsite backups following a disaster. If you are using RMAN and you find you need to do a complete database recovery, you would follow the steps listed below. Chapter 6 provides more detail on the individual RMAN recovery steps and how to execute them:

1. Restore the OS.
2. Restore the Oracle software.
3. Configure Oracle networking.
4. Ensure that you have access to the RMAN backup set pieces that you need.
5. Restore the database spfile from the control-file autobackup. We assume that if you are doing control-file autobackups to disk, you will move those backups to tape and offsite them.
6. Once the database spfile is restored, you can mount the database and restore the control files of the database from the autobackups.
7. Once the database control file is restored, you would begin the restore and recovery of the database proper. This would complete your disaster-recovery operation. If you need to restore database files to a different location, you would use the `set newname` RMAN command as discussed in Chapter 6.
8. After you have completed the restore and recovery of the database datafiles, you would open the database with the `alter database open resetlogs` command.

If you are doing user-managed backup and recovery, the process is not all that different, as you can see here:

1. Restore the OS.
2. Restore the Oracle software.
3. Configure Oracle networking.
4. Ensure that you have access to the database backups that you will be restoring.
5. Restore the database parameter file or spfile from your backup media.

6. Once the database parameter file or spfile is restored, you can mount the database with the `alter database mount` command. You would then use a backup control file or the `create controlfile` command to re-create the control file of the database.
7. Once the database control file is restored, you would move the backups of the database datafiles from the backup media.
8. If you are restoring the database datafiles to a different location, you would need to rename them in the database control file. Use the `alter database rename file` command for this operation.
9. You will need to restore the needed archived redo logs from the backup media.
10. Use the `recover database` command to complete the database recovery. You will need to perform an incomplete recovery, since the online redo logs are not available. See Chapter 3 for more on incomplete user-managed recoveries.
11. Once the `recover database` command has completed its work, open the database with the `alter database open resetlogs` command.

Summary

In this chapter, we talked about some advanced RMAN recovery concepts. First we talked about changing database incarnations. You will want to know how to change incarnations of your database, as this provides the ability to restore your database from previous incarnations in certain cases.

The ability of RMAN to duplicate databases is very powerful. The Oracle OCP exam will include questions about this functionality, and we strongly suggest you go through the exercise of actually performing database duplication. The first few times, it can be a frustrating exercise, but it's well worth the experience.

Tablespace point-in-time recovery is an RMAN feature that makes recovering tablespaces to specific points in time easy to do. We covered the basics of TSPITR, which you will need to know for your OCP exam, but we encourage you to do further research into more customized methods of doing TSPITR that might meet your unique needs.

Finally, we concluded this chapter with a discussion of disaster recovery. This is the end game of backup and recovery (or as one person once told us, it should be called recovery and backup since *recovery* is the really important part). We gave you an outline of the process to follow to get your database back up to speed should you lose the whole database server.

Exam Essentials

Describe database incarnations. Understand how to use the `set database incarnation` command. Know what a database incarnation is and when a given incarnation changes.

Describe database duplication. There are two kinds of database duplication, active and backup-based. Understand that when you use backup-based duplication, the backup set pieces must be available on the host to which you are duplicating. Understand that active database duplication occurs over the network. Know how to set up for database duplication.

Describe tablespace point-in-time recovery. Be able to list the benefits of tablespace point-in-time recovery. Understand how to perform a tablespace point-in-time recovery and what the restrictions are.

Describe disaster-recovery basics. Understand how to restore a system from a complete disaster using both RMAN-based backup sets and user-managed recovery.

Review Questions

1. True or false: tablespace point-in-time recovery is possible only with RMAN.
   A. True
   B. False

2. Which command is used to begin a tablespace point-in-time recovery?
   A. `Restore tablespace`
   B. `Recover tablespace`
   C. `Tablespace recover`
   D. `Recover to time`
   E. `recover datafile`

3. When you're performing active database duplication, a backup of what kind is required?
   A. A current RMAN backup-set backup is required.
   B. No backup is required.
   C. An RMAN image backup is required.
   D. A manual backup is required.
   E. A "duplicate" preparatory backup is required.

4. Which of the following commands will perform an active database duplication of the ORCL database to the ORCL2 database?

   A.

```
Set oracle_sid=orcl
rman target=sys/robert auxname=sys/Robert@orcl2
create duplicate target database to neworcl from
active database nofilenamecheck
spfile set control_files 'c:\oracle\oradata\neworcl\control01.ctl',
'c:\oracle\oradata\neworcl\control02.ctl'
set db_file_name_convert
'c:\oracle\oradata\orcl','c:\oracle\oradata\neworcl'
set log_file_name_convert
'c:\oracle\oradata\orcl','c:\oracle\oradata\neworcl';
```

   B.

```
Set oracle_sid=orcl
rman target=sys/robert auxname=sys/Robert@orcl2
duplicate target database nofilenamecheck
spfile set control_files 'c:\oracle\oradata\neworcl\control01.ctl',
'c:\oracle\oradata\neworcl\control02.ctl'
```

```
set db_file_name_convert
'c:\oracle\oradata\orcl','c:\oracle\oradata\neworcl'
set log_file_name_convert
'c:\oracle\oradata\orcl','c:\oracle\oradata\neworcl';
```

C.

```
Set oracle_sid=orcl
rman target=sys/robert auxname=sys/Robert@orcl2
duplicate target database to neworcl nofilenamecheck
spfile set control_files 'c:\oracle\oradata\neworcl\control01.ctl',
'c:\oracle\oradata\neworcl\control02.ctl'
set db_file_name_convert
'c:\oracle\oradata\orcl','c:\oracle\oradata\neworcl'
set log_file_name_convert
'c:\oracle\oradata\orcl','c:\oracle\oradata\neworcl';
```

D.

```
Set oracle_sid=orcl
rman target=sys/robert auxname=sys/Robert
duplicate target database to neworcl from active database nofilenamecheck
spfile set control_files 'c:\oracle\oradata\neworcl\control01.ctl',
'c:\oracle\oradata\neworcl\control02.ctl'
set db_file_name_convert
'c:\oracle\oradata\orcl','c:\oracle\oradata\neworcl'
set log_file_name_convert
'c:\oracle\oradata\orcl','c:\oracle\oradata\neworcl';
```

E.

```
Set oracle_sid=orcl
rman target=sys/robert auxname=sys/Robert@orcl2
duplicate target database to neworcl from active database nofilenamecheck
spfile set control_files 'c:\oracle\oradata\neworcl\control01.ctl',
'c:\oracle\oradata\neworcl\control02.ctl'
set db_file_name_convert
'c:\oracle\oradata\orcl','c:\oracle\oradata\neworcl'
set log_file_name_convert
'c:\oracle\oradata\orcl','c:\oracle\oradata\neworcl';
```

5. How many database instances are used during a database-duplication process?

A. One

B. Two

C. Three

D. Four

E. Five

6. What command is used to reset a database to a previous incarnation?

   A. `reset incarnation`

   B. `incarnation reset`

   C. `reset database to incarnation`

   D. `reset database incarnation`

   E. `reset databse incarnation number`

7. What view would you use to determine if a given tablespace is fully self-contained for the execution of a tablespace point-in-time recovery?

   A. TS_CHECK

   B. TPITR_CHECK

   C. TS_PITR_CHECK

   D. CHECK_TSPITR

   E. PITR_TS_CHECK

8. When performing a full database disaster recovery with RMAN, in what order would you execute these steps?

   a. Restore the control file from autobackups.

   b. Run the RMAN restore and recover command.

   c. Restore the database spfile from autobackups.

   d. Make the RMAN backup set pieces available.

   e. Open the database with the `alter database open resetlogs` command.

   f. Open the database with the `alter database open` command.

   A. a, b, c, d, e, f

   B. c, d, a, b, f

   C. d, c, a, b, f

   D. d, b, d, c, e

   E. d, c, a, b, e

9. When performing a database duplication, which `duplicate database` parameter would you set to ensure that the online redo logs are created in the correct location?

   A. `log_file_name_convert`

   B. `convert_log_file_name`

   C. `file_name_convert_log`

   D. `redo_log_file_name_convert`

   E. `logfile_convert_directory`

10. Which command would correctly start a TSPITR of the USERS tablespace?

    A.
    ```
    recover tablespace users
    until time '10/06/2008:22:42:00' auxiliary 'c:\oracle\auxiliary';
    ```
    B.
    ```
    recover tablespace users
    time '10/06/2008:22:42:00' auxiliary destination 'c:\oracle\auxiliary';
    ```
    C.
    ```
    recover tablespace users
    to point-in-time '10/06/2008:22:42:00'
    auxiliary destination 'c:\oracle\auxiliary';
    ```
    D.
    ```
    recover tablespace users
    except time '10/06/2008:22:42:00'
     auxiliary destination 'c:\oracle\auxiliary';
    ```
    E.
    ```
    recover tablespace users
    until time '10/06/2008:22:42:00'
    auxiliary destination 'c:\oracle\auxiliary';
    ```

11. True or false: you can perform an active database duplication when the database is in NOARCHIVELOG mode.

    A. True

    B. False

12. When running the tablespace point-in-time command
    ```
    recover tablespace users
    until time '10/06/2008:22:42:00'
    auxiliary destination 'c:\oracle\auxiliary';
    ```
    you receive the following error:
    ```
    RMAN-00571: ===========================================================
    RMAN-00569: =============== ERROR MESSAGE STACK FOLLOWS ===============
    RMAN-00571: ===========================================================
    RMAN-03002: failure of recover command at 10/08/2008 16:00:30
    RMAN-20202: Tablespace not found in the recovery catalog
    RMAN-06019: could not translate tablespace name "USERS"
    ```

What is the likely cause of the error?

A. The database is in ARCHIVELOG mode.

B. There is not a current backup of the database available.

C. The `USERS` tablespace has dependent objects in other tablespaces and can not be a part of a TSPITR alone.

D. The `USERS` tablespace is not eligible for TSPITR because it has invalid objects.

E. The `recover tablespace` command is incorrect and generates the error.

13. Which of the following restrictions are not true with respect to tablespace point-in-time recovery? (Choose all that apply.)

A. The target database must be in NOARCHIVELOG mode.

B. No backup is required of the database before you perform a TSPITR.

C. You must have all archived redo logs generated since the last backup up to the point to which you want to restore the transport set.

D. If you rename a tablespace, you can not perform a TSPITR to any point in time before that rename operation occurred.

E. If you have tables in `tablespace_1` that have associated constraints in `tablespace_2`, then you must transport both tablespaces.

14. If you are going to run a TSPITR recovery, which view will help you to determine which objects will be lost during the TSPITR?

A. `TS_OBJECTS_TO_BE_DROPPED`

B. `TS_PTTR_OBJECT_DROPPED`

C. `TS_PITR_OBJECTS_TO_BE_DROPPED`

D. `TS_OBJECTS_DROPPED`

E. `TS_DROPPED_OBJECTS`

15. You're performing tablespace point-in-time recovery on a tablespace called `USERS`. If an object in that tablespace has a foreign key constraint owned by another object in the `INDEX_TBS`, which statement is true?

A. You cannot perform the TSPITR with the constraints enabled.

B. You must perform the TSPITR recovery of both tablespaces for it to be successful.

C. You can perform TSPITR only on the `USERS` tablespace.

D. RMAN will determine if the `INDEX_TBS` tablespace must also be duplicated and will duplicate it automatically.

E. The TSPITR will only be successful if the constraint is enabled.

16. When issuing the `duplicate database` command, you use the parameter DB_FILE_NAME_CONVERT. For what purpose do you use this parameter?

    A. To indicate the location of the auxiliary-instance online redo logs.

    B. To indicate the location of the target database datafiles.

    C. To indicate the location of the auxiliary-instance control file and online redo logs.

    D. To indicate the location of the auxiliary-instance database datafiles.

    E. This is not a valid parameter when duplicating a database.

17. What is the end result of the following commands?

```
recover tablespace users
until time '10/06/2008:22:42:00'
auxiliary destination 'c:\oracle\auxiliary';
sql 'alter tablespace users online';
recover tablespace users
until time '10/06/2008:20:40:00'
auxiliary destination 'c:\oracle\auxiliary';
sql 'alter tablespace users online';
```

    A. The commands will be successful. The USERS tablespace will be recovered until 10/06/2008 at 20:40.

    B. The first `recover tablespace` command will fail because the syntax is incorrect.

    C. The first `alter tablespace users online` command will fail because the tablespace will already be online after the `recover` command.

    D. The second `recover tablespace` command will fail because it will be unable to complete the recovery.

    E. The second `alter tablespace users online` command will fail because you cannot perform two TSPITRs in a row without backing up the database between the first and the last recovery.

18. Why should you back up a duplicated tablespace after a TSPITR is complete?

    A. The tablespace cannot be duplicated or restored to any point in time after the duplication.

    B. The tablespace cannot be duplicated or restored to the point in time before the duplication.

    C. The entire database cannot be restored after a TSPITR, so a backup is required.

    D. You cannot bring the tablespace online until it's been backed up.

    E. There is no requirement to do so, as RMAN will back up the tablespace after the TSPITR.

19. In what state are the datafiles of a tablespace after a TSPITR has been successfully completed?

 A. The datafiles have an ONLINE status.

 B. The datafiles have an OFFLINE status.

 C. The datafiles have an ONLINE status and are in hot backup mode prepared for an online backup.

 D. The datafiles have an OFFLINE status and are in hot backup mode for an online backup.

 E. The datafiles are in STANDBY mode.

20. Which command do you use to generate a report of database incarnations?

 A. `list incarnation of database`

 B. `report incarnation of database`

 C. `list database incarnation`

 D. `database incarnation list`

 E. `report database incarnation`

Answers to Review Questions

1. B. Tablespace point-in-time recovery has been done in Oracle for some time, using various means and methods. RMAN simply automates and simplifies the process for you.

2. B. The `recover tablespace` command is used to start a TSPITR recovery.

3. B. Active database duplication does not require any backup before the duplication is run.

4. E. The commands in option E are the correct commands to perform an active database duplication given the conditions listed.

5. B. You will use two databases. The first is be the target database, and the second is the auxiliary database instance.

6. C. The `reset database to incarnation` command is used to reset the database incarnation.

7. C. The TS_PITR_CHECK view is used to determine if a given tablespace (or tablespaces) can be independently transported or if there are other dependencies that will require the transport of additional tablespaces.

8. E. You would first need to restore the RMAN backup set pieces. Then you would restore the database spfile followed by the database control file. You would then run the RMAN `restore` and `recover` command. Finally, you would open the database with the `alter database open resetlogs` command.

9. A. The correct answer is `log_file_name_convert`. This setting will direct RMAN to the directory in which it should create the online redo logs.

10. E. The correct command is shown in option E. You would issue the `recover tablespace` command and list the tablespaces to be recovered. You would then use the `until time` parameter to define the point in time to restore the tablespace to. Finally, you would define the location for the auxiliary database instance with the `auxiliary destination` parameter.

11. B. Any database to be duplicated in active mode must be in ARCHIVELOG mode.

12. B. This error message alludes to the fact that there is not a backup of the database available to perform TSPITR. A backup before the point in time of the recovery is required to perform TSPITR.

13. A, B. The database must be in ARCHIVELOG mode to perform a TSPITR. Additionally, you must have a backup of the database that occurred at a point in time before the point in time to which you want to perform the TSPITR.

14. C. Use the TS_PITR_OBJECTS_TO_BE_DROPPED view to determine which objects will be lost as a result of the pending tablespace point-in-time recovery operation. To preserve the objects, you will want to export them before the TSPITR and import them after the recovery is complete with the Oracle Data Pump or Imp/Exp utility.

15. B. If there is a constraint between two objects in two different tablespaces, you must perform a TSPITR between the two tablespaces. As an alternative, you could disable or drop the constraint. You may not be able to reenable the constraint with validation after the TSPITR, however.

16. D. The `DB_FILE_NAME_CONVERT` parameter is used to define the location in which the datafiles for the auxiliary-database datafiles should be created.

17. D. The second `recover tablespace` command will fail because it is trying to perform a recovery to a point in time before the time to which the tablespace was recovered during the first recovery.

18. B. After you perform a TSPITR, you should back up the tablespace/datafile. If you do not, you will not be able to do a TSPITR to any point in time before the original TSPITR.

19. B. After a TSPITR each datafile associated with the TSPITR will be offline. Oracle recommends you back up the datafile before bringing it online.

20. A. The `list incarnation of database` command is used to produce a report of database incarnations.

Understanding Flashback Technology

ORACLE DATABASE 11*g*: ADMINISTRATION II EXAM OBJECTIVES COVERED IN THIS CHAPTER:

✓ **Using Flashback Technology**

- Restore dropped tables from the Recycle Bin
- Perform Flashback Query
- Use Flashback Transaction Query

✓ **Additional Flashback Operations**

- Perform Flashback Table Operations
- Configure, Monitor Flashback Database and perform Flashback Database operations
- Set up and use a Flashback Data Archive

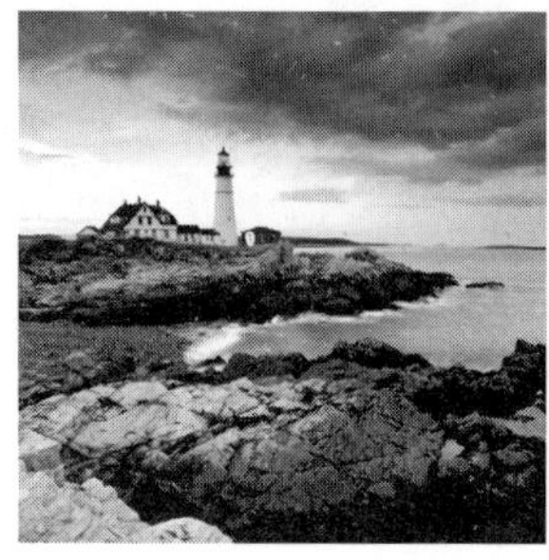

If you have been working through this book chapter by chapter, you should have a pretty firm grasp of Oracle backup and recovery methods available through RMAN. For the most part, RMAN works in the physical realm. It provides recovery from physical problems such as physical block corruption, failed hardware, missing files, and so on. It is vital for a database administrator to be able to recover from these types of problems, and RMAN is definitely the tool for the job.

But database administrators must also have tools to deal with *logical corruption* in the database. Logical corruption, for the most part, is synonymous with the term *user error.* Rather than having a physical problem with your database, you have a problem with the data in your database. Here are some examples:

- A developer accidentally drops a table.
- A programming bug causes data updates to populate the wrong records.
- The DBA is purging data and accidentally deletes the wrong rows.
- An inadvertent table `TRUNCATE` takes place.

Logical corruption is far more common than physical corruption. And although RMAN could certainly be used to recover from logical corruption, a full-blown recovery effort is time-consuming and generally involves database downtime.

In these situations, Flashback technology provides the solution. It allows dropped objects to be recovered. It allows queries to view data as it existed at a point in time in the past, and it allows queries to view a history of changes made to data. It even allows returning the entire database to a point in time or SCN. Having a thorough understanding of the many Flashback options will not only help you pass your OCP exam; it will help you to be a better DBA.

This chapter offers a detailed explanation of the functionality provided by Flashback technology as it exists in Oracle Database 11*g* (Oracle 11*g*).

Initially, we will provide a brief overview of Flashback functionality and where it fits in the database administrator's arsenal. We will also examine Automatic Undo Management, the cornerstone upon which key Flashback technologies rely. Next, we will examine the various Flashback options:

- Flashback Drop (and the Recycle Bin)
- Flashback Query
- Flashback Versions Query
- Flashback Transaction
- Flashback Table

- Flashback Database
- Flashback Data Archive

For each of these options, we will discuss the requirements, capabilities, and limitations in detail.

Exam objectives are subject to change at any time without prior notice and at Oracle's sole discretion. Please visit Oracle's Training and Certification website (`http://www.oracle.com/education/certification/`) for the most current exam-objectives listing.

Overview of Flashback Technology

Flashback technology was first introduced in Oracle Database 9*i*. Since then, it has been steadily improved with each successive Oracle release. In Oracle Database 11*g*, it represents a mature and time-tested technology.

Flashback technology consists of a set of tools that allow users to recover from logical data errors without resorting to a database recovery. However, Flashback can do much more.

The Recycle Bin allows dropped objects to persist in the database, and the Flashback Drop option allows the objects to be restored.

The Flashback Query option allows the user to query tables as they looked at a specific point in the past.

The Flashback Versions Query option allows the user to retrieve a historical view of data as it changed over time. In other words, if a column had been updated multiple times, Flashback Versions Query could provide a list of each of the values and the date and time that they were changed.

Flashback Transaction Query is a useful diagnostic tool that allows the user to retrieve detailed transaction information for previously executed transactions. It can run for a single transaction or for all transactions that occurred during a specified time frame.

Flashback Table allows point-in-time recovery (recovering one or more tables to a specified point in the past) without the need to take any part of the database offline. This offers a very desirable alternative to performing a full-blown point-in-time recovery.

Flashback Database is best used as a replacement for incomplete recovery of the entire database. The main benefit of Oracle Flashback Database over incomplete database recovery is that Flashback Database is much quicker and more efficient. Flashback Database is not based on undo data but on flashback logs. It is best suited to recover from errors such as truncating a large table, an incomplete batch job, or a dropped user.

As you can see, Flashback offers a wide variety of tools for the DBA. However, these options are not exclusive to the DBA. In fact, one of the key advantages to the various Flashback technologies is that they do not require DBA-level privileges. Users and developers can utilize them to recover from their own errors without DBA intervention (except for Flashback Database).

Using Automatic Undo Management

Before we can delve too deeply into Flashback technologies, it is important to understand that all of the Flashback options covered in this chapter, except for Flashback Database and Flashback Drop, work in conjunction with Oracle's undo functionality. Without undo, there would be no Flashback. In fact, without undo, transaction processing as we know it would not exist.

The topics of undo and undo management should not be new to you and will not be covered in depth here. However, we believe that a brief overview of the subject will be helpful in better understanding Flashback technologies and how they work.

In the following sections, you will take a look at undo and *Automatic Undo Management (AUM)*. First we will define undo and its purpose. You will discover how Oracle can automatically manage undo on your behalf. Then you will learn how undo sizing and undo record retention play a key role in Flashback technologies.

Uncovering Undo

So what exactly is "undo" and why does it need to be managed? Undo is a key component of the Oracle database that stores a record of every change made to data in the database. This record contains the data necessary to "undo" the change (in other words, roll back the transaction) and restore the data to its previous condition. For example, when a row in a table is updated, Oracle will create an undo record that stores the data that was changed. If a new row is inserted into a table, an undo record will be created that would effectively delete the row.

Maintaining undo records serves multiple purposes in the database:

- Transaction processing
- Failed-transaction recovery
- Read consistency
- Flashback functionality

Let's look at each of these individually.

Transaction Processing

Transaction processing allows SQL statements to be grouped into discrete units of work that can be committed or rolled back as one. The classic example is that of woman walking into a bank and asking to transfer $500 from her checking account to her savings account. Behind the scenes, two SQL statements are executed: one that subtracts $500 from her checking-account balance and one that adds $500 to her savings-account balance.

Now, suppose the bank's computer system crashed after completing the first statement but not the second. The money would be gone from her checking account but never added to her savings account. She would be out $500 on the deal. Instead, the two statements must be treated as a single, logical unit of work (in other words, a transaction). Only when both statements have completed successfully should the changes be committed. If either fails, they must both be rolled back.

When a user changes data in a table (via insert, update, or delete), the change does not occur immediately. The user must either commit the change (finalize it) or roll it back (undo it). Until they do, the database must keep track of both versions of the data (before the change and after the change).

In order to meet this requirement, the database will modify the data in the table to reflect the change. It will then create an *undo record* in the undo tablespace that contains any data needed to undo the change.

Although the transaction remains in limbo (neither committed nor rolled back), other users who query the table will see the data as it looked prior to the change. If the user decides to roll back the transaction, the undo information is used to modify the table data to revert it to its previous value. If the user decides to commit the transaction, the change becomes permanent.

From strictly a transaction-processing standpoint (allowing a transaction the option of committing or rolling back), the undo records for a transaction are useless after the transaction finishes. They have served their purpose and could be deleted. However, by retaining undo information for a period of time after a commit, many new options become available to us.

As you will see, as you continue through this chapter, the whole host of Flashback options becomes available by the simple act of retaining undo records for a period of time after they have been committed.

Failed-Transaction Recovery

A failed transaction is a transaction that never completes; that is, it never commits or rolls back. This can happen for a variety of reasons, but they all boil down to a session closing with a transaction still in progress.

Since most (if not all) Oracle clients are designed to either commit or roll back automatically when a session is closed, simply forgetting to finish a transaction before exiting will rarely result in a failed transaction. In general, a failed transaction occurs because of an abnormal server shutdown (because of hardware failure, loss of power, or even a `shutdown abort`).

When a failed transaction is discovered (generally at startup time following an abnormal shutdown), Oracle will undo the transaction automatically using the data stored in the undo tablespace.

Read Consistency

When a user issues a query, the database is required to process the query and return the data as it looked at the moment the query started. In other words, if you kicked off a long-running query at 10 a.m. and it finished at 10:15 a.m., the data should not reflect changes (committed or uncommitted) made by other users in the interim.

To fulfill this requirement, Oracle must retain undo records after their associated transaction has been committed. The length of time that it chooses to retain this data is governed by the undo retention period, which will be covered later in this chapter.

Flashback Functionality

Flashback functions allow users to view elements of the database as they appeared at a certain point in time. These functions will be described in much more detail later in this chapter.

Much like the read-consistency requirements, Flashback requires that undo records be retained for a period of time after the associated transaction has completed.

In short, the undo feature creates and maintains records of all transactions that occur in the database and stores the data necessary to undo them. By maintaining these records throughout the life of a transaction, undo provides transaction management and read-consistency capabilities. By maintaining these records after the transaction has been committed, undo provides read-consistency and Flashback options.

Working with Automatic Undo Management

Undo data is temporary. In that respect, the undo tablespace is similar to a temporary tablespace. Information is written there to fulfill a temporary need. As soon as the information is no longer needed, it can be removed to make room for new undo data. To keep things running smoothly requires a considerable amount of management. Luckily, Oracle offers the Automatic Undo Management feature.

Automatic Undo Management (AUM) is a feature whereby Oracle will handle all undo management tasks without interaction from the DBA. Although this is not a new feature in Oracle Database 11g, one important aspect has changed. In previous Oracle versions, manual undo management was the default setting. In order to enable AUM, configuration changes were required by the DBA. Beginning with Oracle Database 11g, AUM will be enabled by default.

When creating a new database with the Database Configuration Assistant (DBCA), Oracle will perform the following actions:

- Create an undo tablespace named UNDOTBS1
- Configure the undo tablespace to auto-extend.
- Add an UNDO_MANAGEMENT=AUTO initialization parameter

These three steps ensure that Oracle will automatically manage the undo needs for the database

Automatic Undo Management must ensure that Oracle can store undo information for all new transactions as they occur. This means that adequate space must be available in the undo tablespace.

By creating an auto-extending undo tablespace, Oracle can extend the size as needed to maintain adequate undo information.

So how long should Oracle retain committed undo information? The simple answer is, long enough to satisfy the undo retention period. The undo retention period represents the minimum amount of time that Oracle will attempt to retain committed undo information before allowing it to be overwritten.

Please note that it is still possible to run the database in manual undo management mode. This can be done by changing the initialization parameter to UNDO_MANAGEMENT=MANUAL. However, Oracle strongly advises against it.

In Oracle Database 11*g*, if the UNDO_MANAGEMENT initialization parameter is set to NULL, the database will default to AUTO. However, it was just the opposite in earlier Oracle versions. Therefore, if you are upgrading to version 11*g*, be aware that a NULL setting will have the opposite effect that it had in the prior version.

Understanding Undo Retention

The undo functionality of Oracle Database 11*g* is governed by a setting known as the undo retention period. The undo retention period represents the minimum time (expressed in seconds) that committed undo information should be retained in the undo tablespace.

To ensure read consistency, the undo retention period should be set to a value larger than the runtime of your longest-running query. If your longest running query takes 60 minutes to run and you retain undo information for 65 minutes, your system should not encounter any `ORA-01555 Snapshot too old` errors.

To ensure that undo data is available for Flashback operations, the undo retention period should be set long enough to retain adequate data to support your Flashback needs. For example, if you want to always maintain a 4-hour window in which to undo data changes, then the setting should be at least 14400 (4 hours expressed in seconds).

It is important to understand that the undo retention setting is actually a target for AUM to achieve; it does not guarantee that data will actually be retained for the entire time. There are circumstances under which AUM may choose to violate the undo retention period.

Undo data is considered to be in one of three possible states at any given time: uncommitted, unexpired, or expired.

Uncommitted data is undo data corresponding to a transaction that has been neither committed nor rolled back. Undo data in this state will remain in the undo tablespace indefinitely. It will never be removed based on the retention period.

Once data has been committed, it enters the unexpired state. This effectively starts the timer running on the retention-period clock. It will remain in this state until the retention period has elapsed.

When the retention period has elapsed, the data will enter the expired state, meaning the data has been retained for the requested amount of time. The expired state tells Oracle that the data is now eligible to be purged from the Undo tablespace to make room for new data.

By keeping track of the state of all undo data, AUM can manage the space and ensure adequate space for new transactions. But suppose a new transaction begins when the undo tablespace is full and none of the undo data is expired? Oracle will attempt to extend the tablespace (if it is enabled) to make more space. If auto-extend is not possible (because it is not enabled or it has reached the MAXSIZE), Oracle must make a choice. It can either forego the retention period by removing unexpired data or honor the retention period, thereby causing the new transaction to fail. By default, Oracle will choose to sacrifice the unexpired data to make room for the new transaction.

In the following sections, you will learn how an undo retention period can be established and what effect it will have. You will also learn about the power and the pitfalls of guaranteeing undo retention.

Establishing an Undo Retention Period

As part of its management duties, AUM monitors system activity and available undo space to derive an optimum undo retention time. This setting may change over time as activity and available space change. Since AUM takes care of this, there is no action required by the DBA to establish an undo retention period.

However, AUM will also allow you to specify the retention period yourself. It can be done by setting the UNDO_RETENTION initialization parameter, as shown here:

```
SQL> ALTER SYSTEM SET UNDO_RETENTION=14400
     SCOPE=BOTH;

System altered
```

When AUM encounters a manual undo retention setting, it will honor the setting *only if it is using an auto-extending tablespace.* If AUM is configured with a fixed-size tablespace, it will ignore the setting and will instead follow its default behavior of dynamically setting the retention time based on system activity and available disk space.

Because of this behavior, it is highly recommended that you allow AUM to use an auto-extending undo tablespace. If you are concerned that an errant long-running query could cause it to extend too much, use the MAXSIZE option to limit its growth.

Guaranteeing Retention

As mentioned previously, Oracle will violate the undo retention period if it is required to prevent transactions from failing. For most users, it is a fair trade-off. However, there may be situations where it is more important to guarantee the retention period, even at the expense of failed transactions. This can be accomplished by specifying the RETENTION GUARANTEE clause on the undo tablespace. This can either be done when initially creating the tablespace or by altering the tablespace, as shown here:

```
SQL> ALTER TABLESPACE UNDOTBS1 RETENTION
     GUARANTEE;

System altered
```

When the RETENTION GUARANTEE clause is invoked on the undo tablespace, Oracle will never remove unexpired data from the undo tablespace, even if it means allowing new transactions to fail.

Using the `RETENTION GUARANTEE` option is a mixed blessing, and one that must be carefully considered. On the one hand, you ensure that undo records necessary for all of your Flashback and read-consistency needs will be retained. On the other hand, if space runs out and the undo tablespace cannot be extended, Oracle will stubbornly enforce the guarantee and allow new transactions to fail.

To summarize, these sections offered you a brief overview of undo and AUM. First you learned about undo and its purpose. You saw how Oracle automatically manages undo on your behalf. And you learned how undo sizing and undo record retention play a key role in Flashback technologies. But what exactly are Flashback technologies? You are about to find out.

Using Flashback Technologies

In the following sections, we will explore each of the various Flashback options and provide examples of how they can be used in the real world. First, we will discuss the Flashback Drop option and the Recycle Bin and how the two work together to recover dropped objects in the database. Next, we will use the Flashback Query option to view data as it existed at a point in the past.

We will continue on to discuss Flashback Versions Query, and you'll learn how to retrieve a historical view of changes made to the database. We will show how to use the Flashback Transaction Query option to retrieve information about past transactions and then show how to use the Flashback Transaction functionality to reverse those transactions.

Using Flashback Drop and the Recycle Bin

In Oracle Database 10*g*, the *Recycle Bin* feature was added to the Oracle Database. This feature enabled tables (and their associated objects) to persist in the database after they were dropped. Oracle 10*g* also introduced the Flashback Drop feature, which allows objects to be recovered from the Recycle Bin. These features remain largely unchanged in Oracle Database 11*g*.

In the following sections, we will provide an overview of the Recycle Bin feature. We will also demonstrate how to use the *Flashback Drop* feature to recover objects from the Recycle Bin.

Using the Recycle Bin

The Recycle Bin is a logical container for dropped tables and their associated objects (indexes, constraints, triggers, nested tables, large-object [LOB] segments, and LOB index segments).

When a table is dropped in Oracle Database 11*g*, it is not actually removed from the database. Instead, it is moved into the Recycle Bin. These objects remain in the Recycle Bin until they are purged explicitly or due to space pressure (permanently removed) or restored via the Flashback Drop feature.

In this section, we will cover the usage of the Recycle Bin, including how to use it, how to purge objects from it, how to enable and disable it, and how to recover objects from it using Flashback Drop.

The Recycle Bin is a logical container, as opposed to a physical container. There is no Recycle Bin tablespace or datafile into which the dropped objects are moved. Instead, the objects remain in their original tablespace and are simply renamed using a special naming convention. This naming convention ensures that database objects with the same name will not be assigned duplicate identifiers when they are moved into the Recycle Bin.

To demonstrate how objects interact with the Recycle Bin, this section will provide a series of examples showing how a dropped table is represented in the Recycle Bin. To begin, we first must drop a table, as shown here:

```
SQL> drop table job_history;

Table dropped.
```

Once the table has been dropped, our next step is to view the contents of the Recycle Bin to verify that the table is truly there. One simple way to do this is to use the `SHOW RECYCLEBIN` command, as shown here:

```
SQL> show recyclebin
ORIGINAL NAME    RECYCLEBIN NAME
OBJECT TYPE  DROP TIME
---------------- ------------------------------
------------ -------------------

JOB_HISTORY      BIN$F2JFfMq8Q5unbC0ceE9eJg==$0
TABLE        2008-04-07:11:52:36
```

The `SHOW RECYCLEBIN` command confirms that our table now resides in the Recycle Bin, as expected. It also provides several other pieces of useful information. These are described in Table 9.1.

TABLE 9.1 SHOW RECYCLEBIN Columns

Column Name	Description
ORIGINAL NAME	This column stores the original name of the object (at the time when it was dropped).
RECYCLEBIN NAME	This column shows the system-assigned name of the object. This is the object's unique identifier within the Recycle Bin.
OBJECT TYPE	This column shows the type of the object (TABLE, INDEX, and so on).
DROP_TIME	This column shows the timestamp corresponding to the dropping of the object.

Next, we will create a new table named JOB_HISTORY, insert some data, and then drop it. We will then look in the Recycle Bin to verify that both tables are there, even though both tables had the same name.

```
SQL> create table job_history (job_id number);

Table created.

SQL> insert into job_history values(1);

1 row created.

SQL> commit;

Commit complete.

SQL> drop table job_history;

Table dropped.

SQL> show recyclebin
ORIGINAL NAME    RECYCLEBIN NAME
OBJECT TYPE  DROP TIME
---------------- ------------------------------
------------ -------------------

JOB_HISTORY      BIN$XwEOKAONSRGwYREWXnjkKw==$0
TABLE        2008-04-07:12:16:55

JOB_HISTORY      BIN$F2JFfMq8Q5unbC0ceE9eJg==$0
TABLE        2008-04-07:11:52:36
```

As promised, Oracle assigned the second version of the JOB_HISTORY table a unique identifier (RECYCLEBIN NAME). This ensures that either version of the table could be restored if required.

Besides the SHOW RECYCLEBIN command, Oracle also offers views named USER_RECYCLEBIN and DBA_RECYCLEBIN, which can be used to query objects in the Recycle Bin. These views offer much more information than the simple SHOW RECYCLEBIN command. For example, look at the following query:

```
SQL> select original_name, object_name, type, droptime from user_recyclebin;
```

```
ORIGINAL_NAME      OBJECT_NAME
------------------ ------------------------------
TYPE        DROPTIME
---------- -------------------
JHIST_JOB_IX       BIN$1h6Ja8caSluy+7vvQjANHA==$0
INDEX      2008-04-07:11:52:35

JHIST_EMPLOYEE_IX  BIN$Ju6RtfJiTYagKJqj50PgUQ==$0
INDEX      2008-04-07:11:52:35

JHIST_DEPT_IX      BIN$ZX4rQYBwTgyHPpTlC8JH+Q==$0
INDEX      2008-04-07:11:52:35

JHIST_EMP_ID_PK    BIN$ngQEsBNrRqSUad0WnyBQUg==$0
INDEX      2008-04-07:11:52:35

JOB_HISTORY        BIN$F2JFfMq8Q5unbC0ceE9eJg==$0
TABLE      2008-04-07:11:52:36

JOB_HISTORY        BIN$XwE0KAONSRGwYREWXnjkKw==$0
TABLE      2008-04-07:12:16:55

6 rows selected.
```

Upon first glance, you might have assumed that this query would have returned the exact same results as the SHOW RECYCLEBIN command. Instead we see four additional rows showing the indexes that were moved to the Recycle Bin when we dropped the first JOB_HISTORY table.

The SHOW RECYCLEBIN command shows only tables that reside in the Recycle Bin. It filters out the dependent objects such as indexes and constraints. Furthermore, the USER_RECYCLEBIN view also offers many other columns, as listed in Table 9.2.

TABLE 9.2 USER_RECYCLEBIN Columns

Column Name	Description
OBJECT_NAME	The system-assigned name of the object. This is the object's unique identifier within the Recycle Bin.
ORIGINAL_NAME	The original name of the object (at the time when it was dropped).
OPERATION	The type of operation that occurred to move the object into the Recycle Bin (in other words, DROP, TRUNCATE). Currently, only dropped objects can be restored.

TABLE 9.2 USER_RECYCLEBIN Columns *(continued)*

Column Name	Description
OBJECT_NAME	The system-assigned name of the object. This is the object's unique identifier within the Recycle Bin.
ORIGINAL_NAME	The original name of the object (at the time when it was dropped).
OPERATION	The type of operation that occurred to move the object into the Recycle Bin (in other words, DROP, TRUNCATE). Currently, only dropped objects can be restored.
TYPE	The type of object (TABLE, INDEX, and so on).
TS_NAME	The name of the tablespace where the object resides.
CREATETIME	Timestamp reflecting when the object was created.
DROPTIME	Timestamp reflecting when the object was dropped.
DROPSCN	The system change number (SCN) corresponding to the dropping of the object.
PARTITION_NAME	If the dropped object was partitioned, the name of the partition.
CAN_UNDROP	This object can be undropped (restored) using the Flashback Drop option. This is true only for table objects. Dependent objects can be restored, but not by themselves. They will be restored only if their related table is restored.
CAN_PURGE	This object can be purged from the Recycle Bin.
RELATED	Object number of the parent object.
BASE_OBJECT	Object number of the base object (in other words, the original table that was dropped).
PURGE_OBJECT	Object number of the current Recycle Bin object. This is the object number that will be purged.
SPACE	Number of blocks used by the object.

Tables residing in the Recycle Bin can be queried directly, just like any other table. The only caveat is that they cannot have any Data Definition Language (DDL) or Data Manipulation Language (DML) statements performed on them. Any attempt to do so will result in an error.

To query a table currently residing in the Recycle Bin, simply use the system-assigned name (OBJECT_NAME), not the original name. Also, since this name consists of mixed-case characters, you must enclose the name in double quotes in your select statement. Here's an example:

```
SQL> select * from "BIN$XwEOKAONSRGwYREWXnjkKw==$0";

    JOB_ID
----------
         1
```

Purging the Recycle Bin

As was mentioned previously, objects are never physically moved into the Recycle Bin. Therefore, there is no tablespace associated with it. Instead, the objects remain in their respective tablespaces but are no longer listed in the data dictionary. So, they appear to have been dropped, yet they are still available for recovery.

However, this poses a problem for a user who is dropping tables to reclaim tablespace. Or perhaps you have a temporary table that you have no further need for and will never need to restore. For situations like these, the purge option should be used. Purging objects from the Recycle Bin will remove them permanently and release the storage space that they were occupying. However, it also means that they cannot be restored.

Purging can be accomplished in several ways. The first is by adding the PURGE option to the DROP command, as shown here:

```
SQL> drop table employees purge;
Table dropped
```

By adding PURGE to the end of the DROP command, you make the table will bypass the Recycle Bin altogether. It will not be recoverable, so proceed with caution.

To purge objects that already reside in the Recycle Bin, you have several options. First, you can purge a specific table, as shown:

```
SQL> purge table employees;

Table purged
```

When purging a single table, you can reference the table by using either the original table name or the system-assigned name. If you use the system-assigned name, be sure to use double quotes around the name.

You can also purge all objects from a specific tablespace by using the TABLESPACE option, as shown:

```
SQL> purge tablespace users;

Tablespace purged
```

You can also purge the entire Recycle Bin (all objects you have dropped, regardless of tablespace) as shown here:

```
SQL> purge recyclebin;

Recyclebin purged
```

This command will purge all of the objects from the Recycle Bin. By the same token, a DBA can purge all of the objects from all users' Recycle Bins at once using the following:

```
SQL> purge dba_recyclebin;

DBA Recyclebin purged
```

There may also be times when Oracle itself will purge objects from the Recycle Bin. This will occur when Oracle can no longer allocate new extents in a tablespace where the dropped objects reside without extending the tablespace. This is referred to as *space pressure*. Before extending the tablespace, Oracle will choose to purge Recycle Bin objects.

When space pressure occurs, Oracle will purge the oldest objects first, and it will purge dependent objects (in other words, indexes and triggers) before purging the table itself.

Because of the threat of space pressure, objects in the Recycle Bin are not guaranteed to be recoverable.

In Exercise 9.1, you'll purge a table from the Recycle Bin.

EXERCISE 9.1

Purging a Table from the Recycle Bin

To purge a table from the recycle bin, do the following:

1. Create a table and add rows of data.
2. Drop the table.
3. Purge the table from the Recycle Bin.
4. Verify that the table is no longer in the Recycle Bin:

```
SQL> create table foo (x number, y varchar2(10));
Table created.

SQL> insert into foo values (1,'test1');
1 row created.
SQL> insert into foo values (2,'test2');
1 row created.
SQL> insert into foo values (3,'test3');
1 row created.
```

EXERCISE 9.1 *(continued)*

```
SQL> commit;
Commit complete.
SQL> drop table foo;
Table dropped.
SQL> select * from recyclebin;

OBJECT_NAME                    ORIGINAL_NAME
OPERATION
------------------------------ --------------------------------
---------
TYPE                      TS_NAME
CREATETIME
------------------------- ------------------------------
-------------------
DROPTIME                DROPSCN PARTITION_NAME                   CAN CAN
------------------- ---------- -------------------------------- --- ---
   RELATED BASE_OBJECT PURGE_OBJECT      SPACE
---------- ----------- ------------ ----------
BIN$dKC+/rixR5GZmNzTPnUNnw==$0 FOO                               DROP
TABLE                     USERS
2008-11-04:20:50:28
2008-11-04:20:50:37    6048081                                   YES YES
     72654       72654        72654          8


SQL> purge table foo;
Table purged.
SQL> select * from recyclebin;
no rows selected
SQL>
```

Disabling and Enabling the Recycle Bin

It is important to understand that even though the Recycle Bin is extremely useful, its use is entirely optional. Though it is enabled by default, it can be turned off at either the system or session level to suit the users' needs. For instance, if you work in an environment that is very tight on space, the Recycle Bin might be more of a hindrance than a help.

The Recycle Bin feature is governed by an initialization parameter named RECYCLEBIN. As with other initialization parameters, it can be set in the INIT.ORA file as shown:

```
RECYCLEBIN=OFF
```

For a database using spfiles, the same thing can be accomplished as shown here:

```
SQL>  alter system set recyclebin = off scope=spfile;

System altered.
```

It can also be set at the session level, as shown in the following example:

```
SQL>  alter session set recyclebin = off;

Session altered.
```

And, as you can probably guess, the Recycle Bin feature can be reenabled by all the same methods; just substitute ON for OFF.

Using Flashback Drop

Now that you've seen how the Recycle Bin works, it's time to use the Flashback Drop feature to restore objects from it. The syntax for the Flashback Drop command is as follows:

```
FLASHBACK TABLE table_name
TO BEFORE DROP
[RENAME TO new_table_name];
```

By default, a Flashback Table operation will restore the table using the same name it had originally. The optional rename clause allows you to restore the table under a different name. This may be required if an object with the original name already exists in your schema.

Let's take a look at how it all works. In this example, we will restore the JOB_HISTORY table and rename it JOB_HIST:

```
SQL> flashback table job_history to before drop rename to job_hist;

Flashback complete.
```

Now we'll query the restored table, as shown here:

```
SQL> select * from job_hist;

    JOB_ID
----------
         1
```

As you can see, the Flashback Drop feature was successful in restoring the table. However, we had two different versions of the JOB_HISTORY table in the Recycle Bin. Why did Oracle choose to restore this one instead of the other one? The answer is that Oracle will always choose to restore the most recently dropped version of the table (if it has two identically named tables).

To recover the previous version of the JOB_HISTORY table, we have two options. Since we already recovered the first one, we can simply execute the Flashback Drop command again to restore the second version (however, we must rename one of them). However, a better alternative is to use the system-assigned object name whenever you want to recover a specific version of a table. Here's an example:

```
SQL> flashback table "BIN$F2JFfMq8Q5unbC0ceE9eJg==$0" to before drop;

Flashback complete.
```

By specifying the system-assigned object name in your Flashback Drop, you avoid duplicate-name issues and ensure that only the specific table that you've selected (and the specific version of that table) will be restored.

Flashback Drop functionality offers a simple way to recover from logical corruption caused when a table has been dropped in error. It is simple, fast, and works well. But there are other types of logical corruption that you must also be able to deal with, and those will require different tools. In the next section, we will introduce you to the next one: Flashback Query.

Regarding the Behavior of Dependent Objects after Undropping

When you recover a table from the Recycle Bin, the triggers, constraints, and indexes are also brought back; however, the names of the dependent objects remain as they were in the Recycle Bin. For example, if table T has an index IN_T, a primary key constraint PK_T, and a trigger named TR_T and the table is dropped and later flashed back, all these dependent objects will revert back to table T but with different names:

```
SQL> select trigger_name from user_triggers where table_name = 'T';
 TRIGGER_NAME
------------------------------
BIN$VJSEh1G2cMngQA4KH2h7+A==$0
 SQL> select index_name from user_indexes where table_name = 'T';
 INDEX_NAME
------------------------------
BIN$VJSEh1G0cMngQA4KH2h7+A==$0
BIN$VJSEh1G1cMngQA4KH2h7+A==$0
 SQL> select constraint_name from user_constraints where table_name = 'T';
 CONSTRAINT_NAME
------------------------------
BIN$VJSEh1GzcMngQA4KH2h7+A==$0
```

You will need to explicitly rename these objects to their former names, if you so choose. Additionally, the following statements are true:

- Some constraints, such as FK, can't be flashed back; they are lost.
- Bitmap join indexes are not flashed back.
- Materialized view logs are not placed in the Recycle Bin, so they are lost.
- It's possible that some indexes may have been erased from the Recycle Bin, even when the table remained (typically under space pressure). So, it's not guaranteed that all the indexes will be reverted back when the table is flashed back before drop.

Using Flashback Query

In the previous section you learned how to restore tables that had been dropped by accident. But oftentimes, logical corruption issues are not as blatant as a dropped table. It is much more common that a user will make a mistake on a data-entry form, delete a row by accident, or make any of a number of other mistakes. When a problem like this occurs, wouldn't it be nice to be able to go back in time to fix it? Flashback Query allows you to do just that—in a manner of speaking.

Flashback Query provides a method of viewing data as it existed at a prior point in time. So when a user makes a mistake, you can just go back in time and fix it.

Flashback Query is implemented through the AS OF clause of the SELECT statement. The AS OF clause is used to specify a particular point in time (either a timestamp or an SCN number) for one or more tables in the query. When the query is executed, Flashback Query will return the data exactly as it existed at a specified point in time. It is important to note that Flashback Query will return only committed data. It will never return uncommitted data. So if the query happened to specify a point in time that fell in the middle of a transaction, Flashback Query will ignore the transaction and simply return the committed data.

As you can imagine, Flashback Query can be used in many situations encountered by a DBA in the course of their duties:

- Recovering from data changes that were committed by mistake
- Comparing current data values to past values
- Simplifying certain programming tasks by alleviating the need to store certain types of temporary data
- Allowing users to correct their own mistakes

In the past, these types of problems could be addressed only through a costly and time-consuming recovery process. With Flashback Query, they can be handled with ease. Also, Flashback Query functionality is not limited to the DBA. Any user who has been granted SELECT and FLASHBACK privileges can take advantage of it.

Let's take a look at Flashback Query in action. To begin with, we will look at the JOB_HISTORY table:

```
SQL> select * from job_history;

EMPLOYEE_ID START_DAT END_DATE  JOB_ID     DEPARTMENT_ID
----------- --------- --------- ---------- -------------
        102 13-JAN-93 24-JUL-98 IT_PROG               60
        101 21-SEP-89 27-OCT-93 AC_ACCOUNT           110
        101 28-OCT-93 15-MAR-97 AC_MGR               110
        201 17-FEB-96 19-DEC-99 MK_REP                20
        114 24-MAR-98 31-DEC-99 ST_CLERK              50
        122 01-JAN-99 31-DEC-99 ST_CLERK              50
        200 17-SEP-87 17-JUN-93 AD_ASST               90
        176 24-MAR-98 31-DEC-98 SA_REP                80
        176 01-JAN-99 31-DEC-99 SA_MAN                80
        200 01-JUL-94 31-DEC-98 AC_ACCOUNT            90

10 rows selected.
```

Now, let's simulate a user accidentally dropping a row:

```
SQL> delete from job_history where employee_id = 102;

1 row deleted.

SQL> commit;

Commit complete.
```

You can see that the row has indeed been deleted:

```
SQL> select * from job_history;

EMPLOYEE_ID START_DAT END_DATE  JOB_ID     DEPARTMENT_ID
----------- --------- --------- ---------- -------------
        101 21-SEP-89 27-OCT-93 AC_ACCOUNT           110
        101 28-OCT-93 15-MAR-97 AC_MGR               110
        201 17-FEB-96 19-DEC-99 MK_REP                20
        114 24-MAR-98 31-DEC-99 ST_CLERK              50
        122 01-JAN-99 31-DEC-99 ST_CLERK              50
        200 17-SEP-87 17-JUN-93 AD_ASST               90
        176 24-MAR-98 31-DEC-98 SA_REP                80
```

```
        176 01-JAN-99 31-DEC-99 SA_MAN                80
        200 01-JUL-94 31-DEC-98 AC_ACCOUNT            90

9 rows selected.
```

Now, we can use Flashback Query to view the data that existed prior to the delete, as shown here:

```
SQL> select *
from job_history as of timestamp(
to_timestamp('08-MAY-2008 11:50:00','DD-MON-YYYY HH24:MI:SS'))
where employee_id = 102;

EMPLOYEE_ID START_DAT END_DATE  JOB_ID     DEPARTMENT_ID
----------- --------- --------- ---------- -------------
        102 13-JAN-93 24-JUL-98 IT_PROG               60
```

The Flashback Query successfully returned the missing row, but we have only displayed it. We haven't actually recovered it. To do so, we can simply run the same query but wrap it inside an INSERT statement as shown here:

```
SQL> insert into job_history
(select * from job_history
as of timestamp(
to_timestamp('08-MAY-2008 11:50:00','DD-MON'))
where employee_id = 102);

1 row created.

SQL> commit;

Commit complete.

SQL> select * from job_history;

EMPLOYEE_ID START_DAT END_DATE  JOB_ID     DEPARTMENT_ID
----------- --------- --------- ---------- -------------
        102 13-JAN-93 24-JUL-98 IT_PROG               60
        101 21-SEP-89 27-OCT-93 AC_ACCOUNT           110
        101 28-OCT-93 15-MAR-97 AC_MGR               110
        201 17-FEB-96 19-DEC-99 MK_REP                20
        114 24-MAR-98 31-DEC-99 ST_CLERK              50
        122 01-JAN-99 31-DEC-99 ST_CLERK              50
```

```
    200 17-SEP-87 17-JUN-93 AD_ASST                   90
    176 24-MAR-98 31-DEC-98 SA_REP                    80
    176 01-JAN-99 31-DEC-99 SA_MAN                    80
    200 01-JUL-94 31-DEC-98 AC_ACCOUNT                90

10 rows selected.
```

We have now successfully recovered from the accidental deletion and, as you can see, the effort was minimal.

In the example, our Flashback query pulled data only from a single table, and at a single point in time. Flashback Query is not limited to such simple queries. It can be used in multi-table join queries as well. It can also be mixed and matched with tables that are not flashed back as well as tables that are flashed back to a different point in time. Look at the following example:

```
SQL> select e.last_name, d.department_name, j.job_title
from employees as of timestamp(to_timestamp(
'08-MAY-2008 11:50:00','DD-MON-YYYY HH24:MI:SS')) e,
departments as of timestamp(
to_timestamp('08-MAY-2008 11:53:00','DD-MON-YYYY
HH24:MI:SS')) d,
jobs j
where e.department_id = d.department_id
and e.job_id = j.job_id
and e.employee_id = 200;

LAST_NAME  DEPARTMENT_NAME      JOB_TITLE
---------- -------------------- ----------------------
Whalen     Administration       Administration Assistant
```

This query joined a total of three tables. Two of these tables were flashed back to different points in time. The third table was not flashed back at all. This demonstrates the flexibility of Flashback Query. In fact, a single table could even be joined multiple times, each join flashed back to a different point in time. As has been discussed before, the only limitation is how far back in time you can flash back, and that is determined by the undo retention period.

It is important to understand that the data present in the undo segment governs the ability to flash back to a point in time. Undo retention is only a guideline.

In this section, you've seen a sample of what Flashback Query can do and what a powerful tool it can be in a DBA's arsenal. It allows you to look into the past to view data as it existed at a specific point in time. But what if you're not sure exactly when a change was made? Or suppose you wanted to see all the changes that were made to a column over a period of time. Those are different types of problems and require a different type of tool—Flashback Versions Query.

In Exercise 9.2, you'll practice using the Flashback Query feature.

EXERCISE 9.2

Using Flashback Query

To practice using the Flashback Query feature, perform the following:

1. Create a table, insert rows of data, and commit.
2. Select all rows from the table.
3. Select the system time.
4. Insert more rows of data into the table, and commit.
5. Select all rows from the table prior to the system time returned in step 3:

```
SQL> create table foo (x number, y varchar2(10));

Table created.

SQL> insert into foo values (1,'test1');

1 row created.

SQL> insert into foo values (2,'test2');

1 row created.

SQL> insert into foo values (3,'test3');

1 row created.

SQL> commit;

Commit complete.

SQL> alter session set nls_date_format = 'DD-MON-YY HH24:MI:SS';

Session altered.

SQL> select sysdate from dual;

SYSDATE
------------------
04-NOV-08 20:31:19
```

EXERCISE 9.2 *(continued)*

```
SQL> insert into foo values (4,'test4');

1 row created.

SQL> insert into foo values (5,'test5');

1 row created.

SQL> commit;

Commit complete.

SQL> select * from foo;

         X Y
---------- ----------
         1 test1
         2 test2
         3 test3
         4 test4
         5 test5
SQL> select * from foo as of timestamp(to_timestamp(
'04-NOV-08 20:31:19','DD-MON-YY HH24:MI:SS'));
         X Y
---------- ----------
         1 test1
         2 test2
         3 test3
SQL>
```

Using Flashback Versions Query

Flashback Versions Query allows you to query a table and retrieve all of the versions of the data that have existed between two specific points in time (specified by a timestamp or an SCN). What's more, Flashback Versions Query offers a host of metadata columns that can also be included in your query, allowing you to view details regarding each change, such as the date/time that the change took place and the SCN that governed the change.

Like Flashback Query, Flashback Versions Query returns only the committed occurrences of the data. Uncommitted data will be ignored. Also just like Flashback Query, Flashback Versions Query works by retrieving data from the UNDO tablespace and is therefore limited by the undo retention period. It also requires the same privileges as Flashback Query: SELECT and FLASHBACK.

Flashback Versions Query is implemented by adding a VERSIONS BETWEEN clause to a SELECT statement. Just like the AS OF clause in Flashback Query, the VERSIONS BETWEEN clause allows the starting point in time to be expressed as either a timestamp or as an SCN.

Let's look at Flashback Versions Query in action. First, we will update a single row in our table several times to simulate changes that may have occurred over time:

```
SQL> update employees
    set salary=salary*1.03
    where employee_id = 193;

1 row updated.

SQL> commit;

Commit complete.

SQL> update employees
    set salary=salary*1.05
    where employee_id = 193;

1 row updated.

SQL> commit;

Commit complete.

SQL> update employees
    set salary=salary/2
    where employee_id=193;

1 row updated.

SQL> commit;

Commit complete.
```

As you can see, our sample employee received a 3 percent raise, a 5 percent raise, and then had his salary cut in half. Next, we will query the table using the `versions between` clause to view the history of changes:

```
SQL> select salary
  from employees
  versions between scn minvalue and maxvalue
  where employee_id = 193;

    SALARY
----------
   2108.93
   4217.85
      4017
      3900
```

The results show us, from most to least recent, the history of our employee's salary changes. He started off at a salary of $3,900, his 3 percent raise boosted him to $4,017, and his 5 percent raise boosted him to $4,217.85. Finally, our hapless employee's salary was cut in half, to $2,018.93 (presumably after he was unable to quickly restore the rows his boss deleted since he didn't know about Flashback technologies).

You will also notice that the sample query used the clause between `scn minvalue` and `maxvalue` to identify the range of versions to select. This construct allows the user to quickly select all versions that are available in the undo tablespace. This is a much cleaner solution than using artificially low and high date ranges such as `BETWEEN TIMESTAMP TO_TIMESTAMP('01-JAN-1700','DD-MON-YYYY')`

`AND`

`TO_TIMESTAMP('31-DEC-2999', 'DD-MON-YYYY').`

As mentioned earlier, there are several pseudocolumns available in conjunction with Flashback Versions Query that can be used to identify when and how the changes were originally made. These columns are identified in Table 9.3.

TABLE 9.3 Flashback Versions Query Pseudocolumns

Column Name	Description
VERSIONS_STARTTIME	The timestamp of the first version of the rows returned from the query.
VERSIONS_ENDTIME	The timestamp of the last version of the rows returned from the query.

TABLE 9.3 Flashback Versions Query Pseudocolumns *(continued)*

Column Name	Description
VERSIONS_STARTSCN	The SCN of the first version of the rows returned from the query.
VERSIONS_ENDSCN	The SCN of the last version of the rows returned from the query.
VERSIONS_XID	The unique transaction ID under which the data was originally changed. In Oracle 11*g* this is a raw value, whereas in 10*g* it was a character value.
VERSIONS_OPERATION	The type of operation that caused the change. Valid values are as follows: I - Insert U - Update D - Delete

In our next example, we will use some of these pseudocolumns to create a simple history report covering the salary changes of our sample employee. The query is shown here:

```
SQL> select to_char(versions_starttime,'DD-MON HH:MI') "START DATE",
   to_char (versions_endtime, 'DD-MON HH:MI') "END DATE",
   versions_operation,
   employee_id,
   salary
   from employees
   versions between scn minvalue and maxvalue
   where employee_id = 123;

START DATE   END DATE     V EMPLOYEE_ID SALARY
------------ ------------ - ----------- ----------
08-MAY 09:13              U         123    2108.93
08-MAY 09:12 08-MAY 09:13 U         123    4217.85
08-MAY 09:08 08-MAY 09:12 U         123       4017
08-MAY 08:15 08-MAY 09:08 I         123       3900
```

This simple query has produced a comprehensive report showing a wealth of information regarding this employee's salary history. By reading from the bottom up, you can see the date and time that the employee was first inserted into the EMPLOYEES table (presumably the day he was hired), as well as his starting salary.

The next lines show the dates, times, amounts, and durations of each salary change for the employee. You will notice that the last line (the top one) has no value for END DATE. This shows that this value still represents the current salary for the employee.

The Flashback Versions Query can also be used in DDL and DML subqueries.

So, in conclusion, Flashback Versions Query allows you to see into the past to view the history of data changes in the database. It takes the power of Flashback Query a step further and provides you with additional metadata to identify changes in further detail. It even allows you to identify the specific transaction that made the change.

But wouldn't it be nice if you could drill down even further, to see specific details about that transaction? Unfortunately, Flashback Versions Query does not allow you to do that. Instead, you need to move ahead to the next section and learn about the tool that *will* allow you to do that: Flashback Transaction Query.

Using Flashback Transaction Query

Flashback Transaction Query is a diagnostic tool used to identify changes made to the database at the transaction level. Much like Flashback Versions Query, Flashback Transaction Query allows you to identify all changes made between two specific points in time. But Flashback Transaction Query goes a step further, allowing you to perform transactional recovery of tables. In other words, it provides you with the SQL that could be used to undo the transaction.

Before you can begin using Flashback Transaction Query functionality, there are two configuration steps that must be completed.

1. Ensure that the database is running with version 10.0 compatibility.
2. Supplemental logging must be enabled (in other words, ALTER DATABASE ADD SUPPLEMENTAL LOG DATA;).

In addition to these systemwide settings, users who want to take advantage of this feature must be granted the SELECT ANY TRANSACTION privilege. They must also be granted the FLASHBACK privilege on the specific tables they want to flash back, or they must have the broader FLASHBACK ANY TABLE privilege.

Flashback Transaction Query is implemented through the use of the FLASHBACK_TRANSACTION_QUERY view. The data in this view allows analysis of a specific transaction to identify what changes were made to the data. This view can be large, so it is helpful to use a filter when querying the view. This will generally be the transaction identifier (XID column).

Be sure to note that the transaction identifier is stored as a raw value in Oracle 11*g*. This is a change from Oracle 10*g*, which stored it as a character value. Because of this, you can't simply pass in a string representation of a transaction identifier; you must provide a raw value. You can use Flashback Versions Query to provide it for you. For example, let's use the FLASHBACK_TRANSACTION_QUERY view to analyze the transactions that created the changes we viewed in the previous section. To do this, we will join a Flashback Versions Query with the FLASHBACK_TRANSACTION_QUERY view as shown here:

```
SQL> select table_name, operation, undo_sql
from flashback_transaction_query t,
(select versions_xid as xid
 from employees versions between scn minvalue and maxvalue
 where employee_id = 123) e
where t.xid = e.xid
and operation = 'UPDATE';

TABLE_NAME OPERATION UNDO_SQL
---------- --------- --------------------------------------
EMPLOYEES  UPDATE    update "HR"."EMPLOYEES" set "SALARY" =
                     '2108.93' where ROWID =
                     'AAARAgAAFAAAABYABd';
EMPLOYEES  UPDATE    update "HR"."EMPLOYEES" set "SALARY" =
                     '4217.85' where ROWID =
                     'AAARAgAAFAAAABYABd';
EMPLOYEES  UPDATE    update "HR"."EMPLOYEES" set "SALARY" =
                     '4017' where ROWID =
                     'AAARAgAAFAAAABYABd';

3 rows selected.
```

This query shows you the three update transactions you ran earlier to modify our employee's salary. It also provides you with a SQL statement that could be run to effectively offset the transaction.

The example query selected only a few of the columns available in the view. Table 9.4 shows the complete list.

TABLE 9.4 FLASHBACK_TRANSACTION_QUERY View Columns

Column Name	Description
XID	Transaction identifier.
START_SCN	Current SCN at start of transaction.
START_TIMESTAMP	Timestamp at start of transaction.
COMMIT_SCN	SCN at commit of transaction. This is the SCN associated with the transaction.

TABLE 9.4 FLASHBACK_TRANSACTION_QUERY View Columns *(continued)*

Column Name	Description
COMMIT_TIMESTAMP	Timestamp at commit of transaction.
LOGON_USER	User who executed the transaction.
UNDO_CHANGE#	Link to the related undo information.
OPERATION	DML operation performed by the transaction.
TABLE_NAME	Name of the table to which the DML is being applied.
TABLE_OWNER	Owner of the table to which the DML is being applied.
ROW_ID	Row ID of the row modified by the DML.
UNDO_SQL	SQL to undo the transaction.

If you've ever used Oracle Log Miner, the columns listed in Table 9.4 may look familiar to you. In fact, Flashback technology offers functionality that is very similar to Log Miner, but is much simpler to use. It allows you to drill down to the transactional level to analyze data changes. It also provides the SQL necessary to undo any transaction, provided the necessary undo records still exist in the undo tablespace.

Using Additional Flashback Operations

In the following sections, you will first learn how to perform Flashback Table operations and then learn how to perform point-in-time recovery on tables in a live database. Then you will learn how to configure, monitor, and perform Flashback Database operations. Lastly, you will learn to set up and use a Flashback Data Archive.

Using Flashback Table

All of the previous Flashback options we've covered in this chapter have allowed you to view and correct specific data elements within a table. They have not affected the table as a whole. Flashback Table is a little different in that regard.

Flashback Table is a Flashback technology that allows you to recover an entire table (or set of tables) to a specific point in time without the hassle of performing an incomplete recovery. This means that rather than rolling back a single transaction, the entire table will be rolled back. If the table has dependent objects associated with it, they are also rolled back automatically.

So why would you choose to use Flashback Table instead of performing an incomplete recovery? There are several reasons:

Speed It is much faster than incomplete recovery.

Simplicity It is much easier than incomplete recovery.

Availability Flashback Table does not impact the availability of the database. Unlike with other recovery methods, the database remains available, and the tablespace remains online the entire time.

Accessibility Users can flash back their own tables, so DBA involvement is not required.

Like other Flashback technologies, Flashback Table is limited only by the availability of undo data. Flashback Table also uses `RETENTION GUARANTEE` in the same manner as the previously discussed Flashback options.

There are two main clauses that are used with the Flashback Table:

- The `TO SCN` clause can recover the Flashback Table to a certain SCN.
- The `TO TIMESTAMP` clause can recover the Flashback Table to a certain point in time.

To flash back a table, the table must have `ROW MOVEMENT` enabled. This can be accomplished with the following command: `ALTER TABLE` *`tablename`* `ENABLE ROW MOVEMENT`.

It is important to get the current SCN from the database. The current SCN can be identified by querying the `CURRENT_SCN` column in the `V$DATABASE` view. To show that Flashback Table is recovered, you can create a change to the data. In the following example, you will update the `SALARY` value for an employee and commit the transaction. Then you will perform a Flashback Table operation to recover the table to its state prior to the update. This change will be missing if the table is recovered to an SCN before the change is introduced.

Let's walk through performing a Flashback Table operation with SCN:

1. Enable `row movement` on the `employees` table:

```
SQL> alter table employees enable row movement;

Table altered.
```

2. Retrieve the current SCN from the database. This is for reference, so make a note of it:

```
SQL> select current_scn from v$database;

CURRENT_SCN
-----------
     623411
```

3. Query the employees table to verify the current salary for the employee with an employee_id = 110:

```
SQL> select employee_id, salary
from employees
where employee_id = 110;

EMPLOYEE_ID SALARY
----------- ----------
110                3000
```

4. Update the employees table as shown. Be sure to commit the change too:

```
SQL> update employees set salary=4000 where
   employee_id = 110;

1 row updated.

SQL> commit;

Commit complete.
```

5. Query the employees table to verify the new salary for our sample employee:

```
SQL> select employee_id, salary
from employees
where employee_id = 110;

EMPLOYEE_ID SALARY
----------- ----------
110                4000
```

6. Perform a Flashback Table operation to recover the table to the SCN retrieved in step 2:

```
SQL> flashback table employees
       to scn 623411;
```

7. Query the employees table again to verify that the change was eliminated because of the Flashback Table operation:

```
SQL> select employee_id, salary
from employees
where employee_id = 110;
```

```
EMPLOYEE_ID SALARY
----------- ----------
110               3000
```

As the example shows, the table has been recovered to its previous state, as it existed back at SCN 623411. Also, if any dependent objects such as indexes existed on the table, they would have also been recovered to maintain consistency.

If a table contains triggers, however, there are some special rules that apply when a Flashback Table operation is performed. All triggers are disabled during a Flashback Table operation. By default, they will remain disabled after the operation is complete, regardless of whether the trigger was previously enabled or not.

If a table has one or more enabled triggers and you want them to remain enabled after the Flashback Table operation is complete, you can add the ENABLE TRIGGERS clause to the statement, as shown here:

```
SQL> flashback table employees
  to scn 623411
     enable triggers;
```

When you specify the ENABLE TRIGGERS option, all triggers that were previously enabled will be reenabled after the operation is complete. Note that the trigger did not remain enabled during the Flashback Table operation. As stated before, all triggers are disabled during the operation (they will not fire in conjunction with the recovery operation). They are then reenabled only after the operation is complete.

As you can see, the Flashback Table operation is a valuable recovery method. Now when a user updates a table using an incorrect WHERE clause, you can simply undo the change using Flashback Table. They could even do it themselves. And, best of all, the availability of the database is not impacted by the operation. Please keep in mind that more complex flashback operations may be required, depending on the number of objects and relations impacted.

In Exercise 9.3, you'll practice using the Flashback Table feature; continue using the table created in Exercise 9.2.

EXERCISE 9.3

Using Flashback Table

To practice using the Flashback Table feature, continue using the table created in Exercise 9.2, and perform the following:

1. Select all rows from the table.
2. Verify the system time at which the last two rows were inserted.
3. Flash back the table to the system time returned in step 2:

```
SQL> alter table foo enable row movement;
Table altered.
```

EXERCISE 9.3 *(continued)*

```
SQL> select * from foo;

         X Y
---------- ----------
         1 test1
         2 test2
         3 test3
         4 test4
         5 test5

SQL> flashback table foo to timestamp to_timestamp(
'04-NOV-08 20:31:19','DD-MON-YY HH24:MI:SS');

Flashback complete.

SQL> select * from foo;

         X Y
---------- ----------
         1 test1
         2 test2
         3 test3

SQL>
```

Configuring and Monitoring Flashback Database and Performing Flashback Database Operations

Flashback Database was introduced in Oracle 10*g*. There is one main difference between the other Flashback technologies and Flashback Database: Flashback Database relies on "before" images in the flashback logs, whereas the other Flashback features rely on the undo data.

Flashback Database allows you to flash the entire database back to a specific point in time. This is extremely useful to recover from errors such as truncating a large table, not completing a batch job, or dropping a user. Flashback Database recovery is also the best choice for most logical corruptions such as a bad complex transaction that gets propagated throughout the database.

Before you can use Flashback Database, you must set up the *flash recovery area*. Please refer to Chapter 2 for an introduction to the flash recovery area, and refer to Chapter 3 to learn how to configure it.

One major technological benefit of Flashback Database is that it allows you to reverse user errors or logical corruption much quicker than performing a traditional incomplete recovery or using the Oracle Log Miner utility. The reason Flashback Database recovery is much quicker than traditional recovery operations is that recovery is no longer impacted by the size of the database. The mean time to recovery (MTTR) for traditional recovery is dependent on the size of the datafiles and archive logs that need to be restored and applied. Using Flashback Database recovery, recovery time is proportional to the number of changes that need to be backed out of the recovery process, not the size of datafiles and archive logs. This makes the Flashback Database recovery process the most efficient recovery process in most user-error or logical-corruption situations.

The Flashback Database architecture consists of the recovery writer *RVWR* background process and Flashback Database logs. When the Flashback Database is enabled, the RVWR process is started. *Flashback Database logs* are a new type of log file that contain a "before" image of physical database blocks. The RVWR writes the Flashback Database logs in the flash recovery area. Enabling the flash recovery area is a prerequisite to using Flashback Database because the Flashback Database logs are written to the flash recovery area.

Configuring the Flashback Database

The database must have multiple features configured prior to configuring Flashback Database. The database must have `ARCHIVE LOG` enabled. As mentioned earlier, the flash recovery area must be configured to store the Flashback Database logs.

First, make sure the database is shut down. Next, the database must be started in MOUNT mode. Then, the database parameter `DB_FLASHBACK_RETENTION_TARGET` can be set to the desired value, which is based on minutes. This value determines how far back in time you can flash back the database. This is like a baseline for Flashback Database. Next, Flashback Database can be enabled with the `ALTER DATABASE FLASHBACK ON` command. Finally, the database can be opened for normal use.

Let's walk through these steps in more detail:

1. Start the database in MOUNT mode:

```
SQL> connect / as sysdba
SQL> startup mount
ORACLE instance started.
Total System Global Area  535662592 bytes
Fixed Size                  1334380 bytes
Variable Size             171967380 bytes
Database Buffers          356515840 bytes
Redo Buffers                5844992 bytes
```

```
Database mounted.
```

2. Set the DB_FLASHBACK_RETENTION_TARGET parameter to the desired value. This value is in minutes, which equates to three days:

   ```
   SQL> alter system set db_flashback_retention_target=4320;
   ```

3. Enable the flashback capability:

   ```
   SQL> alter database flashback on;
   ```

4. Now the database can be opened for normal use:

   ```
   SQL> alter database open;
   ```

As you can see, enabling Flashback Database is fairly simple. A key point for you to know is how far back in time you need to be able to flash back from, or know the DB_FLASHBACK_RETENTION_TARGET parameter value. The DB_FLASHBACK_RETENTION_TARGET value will determine how far you can flash back the database in minutes. In the preceding example, you specified the value of 4,320, which is for three days; the default value is 1,440, or one day.

Monitoring Flashback Database

The Flashback Database can be monitored by using a few dynamic views: V$DATABASE, V$FLASHBACK_DATABASE_LOG, and V$FLASHBACK_DATABASE_STAT. These views provide some valuable information regarding the status of the Flashback Database and the supporting operations.

The V$DATABASE view displays if the Flashback Database is on or off. This tells you whether the Flashback Database is enabled or not.

Let's query the V$DATABASE view and see the results:

```
SQL> select flashback_on from v$database;

FLASHBACK_ON
------------
YES
SQL>
```

Query the V$FLASHBACK_DATABASE_LOG to determine the amount of space required in the recovery area to support the flashback activity generated by changes in the database. The values in the OLDEST_FLASHBACK_SCN and OLDEST_FLASHBACK_TIME columns give you information regarding how far back you can use Flashback Database. This view also shows the size of the flashback data in the FLASHBACK_SIZE column. The column ESTIMATED_FLASHBACK_SIZE can be used to identify the estimated size of flashback data that you need for your current target retention. Shown next is an example of querying the V$FLASHBACK_DATABASE_LOG:

```
SQL> select
  2.  oldest_flashback_scn,
  3.  oldest_flashback_time,
  4.  retention_target,
  5.  estimated_flashback_size
  6.  from v$flashback_database_log;

OLDEST_FLASH_SCN OLDEST_FLASH_TIME RET_TARGET EST_FLASHBACK_SIZE
---------------- ----------------- ---------- ------------------
979720           20-JUL-08         4320       298967040

SQL>
```

The V$FLASHBACK_DATABASE_STAT view is used to monitor the overhead of maintaining the data in the Flashback Database logs. This view allows you to make estimates regarding future Flashback Database operations. This is done by coming up with an estimate about potential required space.

Let's look at the V$FLASHBACK_DATABASE_STAT:

```
SQL> select * from v$flashback_database_stat;

BEGIN_TIM END_TIME  FLASHBACK_DATA    DB_DATA  REDO_DATA
--------- --------- -------------- ---------- ----------
ESTIMATED_FLASHBACK_SIZE
------------------------
20-JUL-08 20-JUL-08       61784064   35880960   99203072
                       0
SQL>
```

As you can see, the V$FLASHBACK_DATABASE_STAT dynamic view shows the utilization of the Flashback Database log. This is determined by the begin and end times.

Using Flashback Database

The Flashback Database can be used with SQL*Plus to perform recoveries. Once the database is configured for the Flashback Database, you just need to start the database in MOUNT mode, and you are ready to perform a Flashback Database recovery. You also need to get either OLDEST_FLASHBACK_SCN or OLDEST_FLASHBACK_TIME from the V$FLASHBACK_DATABASE_LOG view. This will allow you to utilize the TO SCN or TO TIME clause in the FLASHBACK DATABASE clause. If you have established a *restore point*, you can recover to it if it is newer than the oldest_flashback_scn.

Let's walk through performing a Flashback Database recovery to an SCN:

1. First, query the V$FLASHBACK_DATABASE_LOG view to retrieve the OLDEST_FLASHBACK_SCN:

```
SQL> select oldest_flashback_scn, oldest_flashback_time
  2  from v$flashback_database_log;

OLDEST_FLASHBACK_SCN OLDEST_FLASHBACK_TIME
-------------------- --------------------
              979720 20-JUL-08

SQL>
```

2. Next, shut down and start the database in MOUNT mode:

```
SQL> shutdown
Database closed.
Database dismounted.
ORACLE instance shut down.
SQL>
SQL> startup mount
ORACLE instance started.
Total System Global Area  535662592 bytes
Fixed Size                  1334380 bytes
Variable Size             171967380 bytes
Database Buffers          356515840 bytes
Redo Buffers                5844992 bytes
Database mounted.
SQL>
```

3. Next, issue the Flashback Database recovery command:

```
SQL> flashback database to scn 979721;
Flashback complete.
SQL>
```

4. Finally, open the database with the RESETLOGS option, because you recovered to a time prior to the current database:

```
SQL> alter database open resetlogs;
Database altered.
SQL>
```

As you can see, the Flashback Database recovery is a fairly simple process. The V$FLASHBACK_DATABASE_LOG dynamic view is useful for both TO SCN and TO TIME recoveries. The Flashback Database recovery is a quick and efficient method for recovering from user errors or logical corruptions in the database. This is a great alternative to performing a traditional incomplete recovery.

Flashback Database recovery can also be performed in SQL*Plus with the FLASHBACK DATABASE command as well as with RMAN.

Limitations with the Flashback Database

Flashback Database recovery cannot recover through some common occurrences such as resizing a datafile to a smaller size or a deleted datafile. In these cases, the datafile would need to be restored with traditional methods to a point in time prior to its deletion or resizing. Then you could use Flashback Database recovery to recover the rest of the database.

Flashback Database is a nice substitute for incomplete recovery for logical corruption and user errors. However, there are some limitations to Flashback Database that you should be aware of:

- Media failure cannot be resolved with Flashback Database. You will still need to restore datafiles and recover archived redo logs to recover from media failure.
- Resizing datafiles to a smaller size, also called shrinking datafiles, cannot be undone with the Flashback Database.
- You cannot use Flashback Database if the control file has been restored or re-created.
- Dropping a tablespace and recovery through resetlogs cannot be performed.
- You cannot flash back the database to an SCN prior to the earliest available SCN in the flashback logs.

Setting Up and Using a Flashback Data Archive

The *Flashback Data Archive*, also known as *Oracle Total Recall*, allows you to retain and track all transactional changes to a record over its lifetime. This eliminates the need to write custom programs to archive all transactional changes to data. The uses of the Flashback Data Archive are many, but auditing and compliance are two key areas where this technology can be useful.

To utilize the Flashback Data Archive capabilities, create one or more tablespaces as an archive. Each archive has a retention time that determines how long data is retained within it. The DBA can designate a default Flashback Data Archive for the database.

Once you have a created a Flashback Data Archive, you can enable flashback data archiving on a per-table basis. By default, flashback archiving is turned off.

Configuring the Flashback Data Archive

Setting up the Flashback Data Archive is straightforward. Simply name the archive and assign a tablespace, an optional space quota, and the retention time:

```
SQL> create flashback archive audit_flash_archive
tablespace audit_archive quota 20g retention 7 year;


SQL> create flashback archive audit_flash_archive_2
Tablespace audit_archive quota 10m retention 90 day;
SQL>
```

To establish a default Flashback Data Archive, simply add the `default` keyword in the `create` clause:

```
SQL> create flashback archive default default_flash_archive
Tablespace audit_archive quota 10m retention 90 day;
SQL>
```

After you've created a Flashback Data Archive, of course you will need to alter it. As DBA, you may alter the storage quota and retention time and add, drop, or modify tablespaces in a data archive using the `alter flashback archive` command. Here are a few examples:

```
SQL> alter flashback archive default_flash_archive
Modify tablespace audit_archive quota 100m;
SQL>
SQL> alter flashback archive default_flash_archive
retention 180 day;
SQL>
SQL> alter flashback archive default_flash_archive
Remove Tablespace audit_archive;
SQL>
```

To clean up or purge data to an SCN or timestamp from a Flashback Data Archive, use the `alter` command with the `purge` clause:

```
SQL> alter flashback archive default_flash_archive
Purge before SCN 979271;
SQL>
```

```
SQL> alter flashback archive default_flash_archive
Purge before timestamp (SYSDATE - 180);
SQL>
```

And if you have established a deletion policy for archives, you can drop an archive quite easily:

```
SQL> drop flashback archive default_flash_archive;
SQL>
```

Using the Flashback Data Archive

Once the Flashback Data Archive is created, you can begin archiving data from specific tables. To enable archiving for an existing table, use the ALTER TABLE command with the FLASHBACK ARCHIVE clause:

```
SQL> alter table employee_history flashback archive audit_flash_archive;
SQL>
```

If you have created a default flashback archive and want to use it, then you don't need to specify the name of the archive.

Equally straightforward, create a new table with the archive feature to utilize the default Flashback Data Archive:

```
SQL> create table shipments (ship_id number(9),
shipper number(9), ship_date date),
flashback archive;
SQL>
```

To disable archiving for a table, simply alter the table using the NO FLASHBACK ARCHIVE clause:

```
SQL> alter table shipments no flashback archive;
SQL>
```

Now that you have established all the structures, query the base table to retrieve archive data using the AS OF TIMESTAMP clause:

```
SQL> select * from shipments AS OF TIMESTAMP
('2008-05-01 12:00:00', 'YYYY-MM-DD HH24:MI:SS');
SQL>
```

Certain DDL is not allowed on archived tables: TRUNCATE, DROP, and RENAME as well as ALTER commands that drop, rename, or modify a column, change a long raw to a LOB, perform a partition or subpartition operation, or use the UPGRADE TABLE clause.

Monitoring the Flashback Data Archive

The Flashback Data Archiver process, FBDA, archives the historical rows of tables enabled for archiving to the Flashback Data Archive. FBDA writes a pre-image of a row and metadata on current rows into the flashback archive when a transaction that changes data commits. FBDA manages the Flashback Data Archive retention and space.

Several views are available for monitoring the Flashback Data Archive. See Table 9.5 for an description of the views.

TABLE 9.5 Flashback Data Archive Views

View Name	Description
DBA_FLASHBACK_ARCHIVE	Information about Flashback Data Archive
DBA_FLASHBACK_ARCHIVE_TS	Tablespaces used for Flashback Data Archive
DBA_FLASHBACK_ARCHIVE_TABLES	Tables that are enabled for archive

Summary

In this chapter, you learned about Flashback technologies and their dependence on Oracle's undo functionality. You learned about Automatic Undo Management (AUM) and how it aids the DBA in managing undo information.

We discussed the Recycle Bin in detail, and you learned how dropped objects are moved to the Recycle Bin. We showed you how to query the contents of the Recycle Bin and how to recover objects using the Flashback Drop feature.

Next, you learned about Flashback Query and its ability to show you data as it appeared at a specific time in the past.

The next section discussed the Flashback Versions Query, which retrieves all versions of the rows that existed between two specific points in time.

You then used the Flashback Transaction Query to view transactional changes in data. You saw examples of how you can use this tool to perform transactional analysis, including producing SQL statements that will undo the transaction.

You used Flashback Table to recover a table to a specific point in time without performing an incomplete recovery. You also learned how all dependent objects are recovered when using Flashback Table.

The Flashback Database is best used to recover from logical corruption and user error. This is an alternative to incomplete recovery or the Log Miner utility. The Flashback Database can be enabled and configured fairly easily. You must have the flash recovery area enabled to implement the Flashback Database.

The last Flashback technology discussed in this chapter was the Flashback Data Archive, which Flashback Data Archive can be used to track all DML changes to a table and keep the changes for a specific retention period.

Exam Essentials

Know how to restore dropped tables from the Recycle Bin. Make sure that you understand how the Recycle Bin handles dropped objects. You should be able to locate objects in the Recycle Bin. You should be able to perform a Flashback Drop recovery of a dropped object.

Know how to perform a Flashback query. You must understand how Flashback Query works. Know which options are available in the `AS OF` clause (timestamp and SCN). Be able to execute a Flashback query and understand what the results represent.

Know how to use Flashback Transaction Query. Know how to use Flashback Transaction Query to expose transactional information relating to changes in the database. Be sure that you are familiar with the contents of the `FLASHBACK_TRANSACTION_QUERY` view. Be able to access the undo SQL required to roll back a transaction.

Understand how to perform Flashback Table operations. Understand the basics of how Flashback Table works. Know how to perform a Flashback Table operation with a timestamp or an SCN. Be aware of how undo data is used in Flashback Table and how to protect this data.

Understand the Flashback Database architecture. Make sure you are aware of the components that make up the Flashback Database architecture. Understand the Flashback Database logs and RVWR background-process functionality.

Understand how to enable and disable the Flashback Database. Know how to configure the Flashback Database. Understand the flash recovery area and how it is configured.

Know how to monitor the Flashback Database. Know the dynamic views that monitor the Flashback Database. Understand what each view contains.

Know how to create and use a Flashback Data Archive. Know the syntax to create a Flashback Data Archive in a tablespace, alter the storage and retention parameters, purge and drop, archive a table, and query the results.

Review Questions

1. Which of the following Oracle features utilize the undo tablespace? (Choose all that apply)
   - **A.** Flashback Query
   - **B.** Flashback Drop
   - **C.** Flashback Table
   - **D.** Flashback Database
   - **E.** Transaction Processing
   - **F.** Recycle Bin
2. Which of the following statements are true regarding the Recycle Bin? (Choose all that apply.)
   - **A.** The Recycle Bin is a physical storage area for dropped objects.
   - **B.** The Recycle Bin is a logical container for dropped objects.
   - **C.** The Recycle Bin stores the results of a Flashback Drop operation.
   - **D.** The objects in the Recycle Bin are stored in the tablespace in which they were created.
3. Over the course of a day, a department performed multiple DML statements (inserts, updates, deletes) on multiple rows of data in multiple tables. The manager would like a report showing the time, table name, and DML type for all changes that were made. Which Flashback technology would be the best choice to produce the list?
   - **A.** Flashback Drop
   - **B.** Flashback Query
   - **C.** Flashback Transaction Query
   - **D.** Flashback Versions Query
   - **E.** Flashback Table
4. A user named Arren is executing this query:

```
select table_name, operation, undo_sql
    from
    flashback_transaction_query t,
     (select versions_xid as xid
 from employees versions between scn minvalue
 and maxvalue
     where employee_id = 123) e
    where t.xid = e.xid;
```

When the query runs, he receives an `ORA-01031: insufficient privileges` error. Since the user owns the `employees` table, you know that it is not the problem. Which of the following SQL statements will correct this problem?

A. `GRANT SELECT ANY TRANSACTION TO ARREN;`

B. `GRANT SELECT ON FLASHBACK_TRANSACTION_QUERY TO ARREN;`

C. `GRANT SELECT_ANY_TRANSACTION TO ARREN;`

D. `GRANT FLASHBACK TO ARREN;`

E. `GRANT SELECT ANY VIEW TO ARREN;`

5. AUM has been retaining about 15 minutes' worth of undo. You want to double the retention period, but not at the expense of new transactions failing. You decide to alter the system to set the parameter `UNDO_RETENTION=18000`. However, AUM still retains only about 15 minutes' worth of undo. What is the problem? (Choose the best answer.)

   A. You need to alter the undo tablespace to add the `RETENTION GUARANTEE` setting.

   B. You need to increase the size of the undo tablespace.

   C. The undo tablespace is not set to auto-extend.

   D. You need to alter the Recycle Bin to add the `RETENTION GUARANTEE` setting.

6. In order to perform Flashback Transaction Query operations, which of these steps are required? (Choose all that apply.)

   A. Ensure that database is running with version 10.1 compatibility.

   B. Enable Flashback Logging.

   C. Enable Supplemental Logging.

   D. Ensure that the database is running with version 10.0 compatibility.

   E. Ensure that the database is in ARCHIVELOG mode

7. Users notify you that their application is failing every time they try to add new records. Because of poor application design, the actual ORA error message is unavailable. What might be the problem? (Choose the best answers.)

   A. The application user has exceeded their undo quota.

   B. The `FLASHBACK GUARANTEE` option is set on the undo tablespace.

   C. The table is currently being queried by a Flashback Transaction Query operation.

   D. The table is currently being queried by a Flashback Versions Query operation.

   E. The `RETENTION GUARANTEE` option is set on the undo tablespace.

8. Which of the following statements best describes Flashback Versions Query?

   A. Flashback Versions Query is used to make changes to multiple versions of data that existed between two points in time.

   B. Flashback Versions Query is used to view all version changes on rows that existed between the time the query was executed and a point in time in the past.

   C. Flashback Versions Query is used to view version changes and the SQL to undo those changes on rows that existed between two points in time.

   D. Flashback Versions Query is used to view all version changes on rows that existed between two points in time.

9. Which pseudocolumn could you use to identify a unique row in a Flashback Versions Query?
   A. XID
   B. VERSIONS_PK
   C. VERSIONS_XID
   D. VERSIONS_UNIQUE

10. Which of the following can be used in conjunction with a Flashback Versions Query to filter the results? (Choose all that apply.)
    A. A range of SCN values
    B. A list of SCN values
    C. A starting and ending timestamp
    D. Minimum and maximum sequence values
    E. A list of sequence values

11. At the request of a user, you issue the following command to restore a dropped table:

    ```
    flashback table "BIN$F2JFfMq8Q5unbCOceE9eJg==$0" to
    ```

    `before drop;` Later, the user notifies you that the data in the table seems to be very old and out of date. What might be the problem?
    A. Because a proper range of SCNs was not specified, the wrong data was restored.
    B. A proper range of timestamps was not specified, so the wrong data was restored.
    C. A previous Flashback Drop operation had been performed, resulting in multiple versions of the table being stored in the Recycle Bin.
    D. Either option A or B could be correct. Not enough information was provided to determine which.
    E. None of the above.

12. Which of the following statements is true regarding the VERSIONS BETWEEN clause?
    A. The VERSIONS BETWEEN clause may be used in DML statements.
    B. The VERSIONS BETWEEN clause may be used in DDL statements.
    C. The VERSIONS BETWEEN clause may not be used to query past DDL changes to tables.
    D. The VERSIONS BETWEEN clause may not be used to query past DML statements to tables.

13. Which of the following statements is true regarding implementing a Flashback Table recovery?
    A. An SCN is never used to perform a Flashback Table recovery.
    B. If a significant number of changes have been made to the table, row movement must be enabled.
    C. The tablespace must be offline before performing a Flashback Table recovery.
    D. Flashback Table recovery is completely dependent on the availability of undo data in the undo tablespace.

14. You have just performed a FLASHBACK TABLE operation using the following command:

```
flashback table employees
to scn 123456;
```

The employees table has triggers associated with it. Which of the following statements is true regarding the state of the triggers during the Flashback Table operation?

   A. All the triggers are disabled.
   B. All the triggers are enabled by default.
   C. Enabled triggers remain enabled and disabled triggers remain disabled.
   D. Triggers are deleted when a Flashback Table operation is performed.

15. Which method could be utilized to identify both DML operations and the SQL statements needed to undo those operations for a specific schema owner? (Choose all that apply.)

   A. Query DBA_TRANSACTION_QUERY for TABLE_NAME, OPERATION, and UNDO_SQL. Limit rows by START_SCN and TABLE_OWNER.
   B. Query FLASHBACK_TRANSACTION_QUERY for TABLE_NAME, OPERATION, and UNDO_SQL. Limit rows by START_SCN and TABLE_OWNER.
   C. Query FLASHBACK_TRANSACTION_QUERY for TABLE_NAME, OPERATION, and UNDO_SQL. Limit rows by START_TIMESTAMP and TABLE_OWNER.
   D. Query DBA_TRANSACTION_QUERY for TABLE_NAME, OPERATION, and UNDO_SQL. Limit rows by START_SCN and TABLE_OWNER.

16. Flashback Database relies on which technologies to recover to a point in time?

   A. Flashback Data Archive
   B. Flashback logs in the flash recovery area
   C. Undo tablespace
   D. RMAN command line
   E. None of the above

17. The _______ writes the Flashback Database logs in the flash recovery area.

   A. FLSH
   B. FLDB
   C. RVWR
   D. RVRW
   E. FBDA

18. Which of these are valid Flashback Database recovery point parameters? (Choose all that apply.)

    A. SCN
    B. Timestamp
    C. Named recovery point
    D. Transaction ID
    E. Session ID

19. When setting up the Flashback Data Archive, which of these key parameters are required? (Choose all that apply.)

    A. Tablespace name
    B. Storage quota
    C. Retention
    D. Table name
    E. Create a default archive

20. To clean up old records that are in a Flashback Data Archive and are past the retention period, what must the DBA do?

    A. `TRUNCATE` the archive table.
    B. `DROP` the Flashback Data Archive.
    C. Nothing; expired rows are automatically removed.
    D. Nothing; expired rows are moved to an archive table.
    E. Delete entries from the archive where the metadata date retained is greater than the retention period.

Answers to Review Questions

1. A, C, E. Flashback Drop utilizes the Recycle Bin, which does not use the undo tablespace; therefore options B and F are incorrect. Flashback Database is a physical recovery method and does not use undo; therefore option D is incorrect.

2. B, D. The Recycle Bin is a logical container of Flashback dropped objects. The objects in the Recycle Bin are stored in the tablespace they were created in.

3. C. Flashback Transaction Query could provide the data requested in a single query. Option A is an invalid choice because the table wasn't dropped. Option B is incorrect because Flashback Query returns data at only a specific point in time, not for a range of times. Option D is incorrect because, although it could produce the data needed for the report, Flashback Versions Query would have to be run for each table individually. Option E is incorrect because the user does not want to recover the table at all.

4. A. The user needs to have the `SELECT ANY TRANSACTION` privilege granted to him. All of the other choices are incorrect.

5. C. AUM will ignore the `UNDO_RETENTION` parameter if the undo tablespace is not set to auto extend. Option A is incorrect because guaranteeing retention could result in failed transactions, which you are specifically wanting to avoid. Option B is not the best answer because the size of the undo tablespace is not the cause of the issue, but increasing the size of the undo tablespace could increase the amount of undo retained. Option D is wrong because this question is not dealing with the Recycle Bin and because it has no guaranteed retention setting.

6. C, D. Version 10.0 compatibility must be set, so option A is incorrect. Option B is incorrect because there is no such thing as Flashback Logging. Option E is incorrect because ARCHIVELOG mode has no effect on Flashback Transaction Query functionality.

7. A, E. The likely causes are that the `RETENTION GUARANTEE` option has been set on the undo tablespace and there are no expired transactions to remove to make room for new transactions, or that the user has exceeded the undo quota that has been set by the database resource manager. `FLASHBACK GUARANTEE` is not a valid option, so option B is incorrect. Flashback queries would not interfere with transactions entering the system, so options C and D are incorrect.

8. D. Flashback Versions Query does not change data at all, so option A is incorrect. B could be correct, but only if one of the specified points in time was the current timestamp. Therefore, B is not the best description. Option C is incorrect because Flashback Versions Query does not provide the SQL to undo the changes.

9. C. The `VERSIONS_XID` column contains the unique transaction identifier for the row. None of the other choices are valid column names.

10. A, C. Lists of values are not valid, so both B and E are incorrect. Also, sequence values are not valid, so D is also incorrect.

11. E. A Flashback Drop operation restores dropped objects from the Recycle Bin. It does not use SCN or timestamp ranges, so options A, B, and D are incorrect. Also, Flashback Drop operations don't create objects in the Recycle Bin (they move them out of the Recycle Bin), so C is incorrect. The likely cause is that multiple versions of the table existed in the Recycle Bin and the wrong one was restored.

12. C. The `VERSIONS BETWEEN` clause of the Flashback Versions Query cannot query past table modifications or DDL changes to a table.

13. D. Like the other Flashback options, Flashback Table must be able to find the necessary undo records in order to recover. The use of SCNs is valid in Flashback Table; therefore option A is incorrect. Row Movement must be enabled in all cases, not just when a significant number of changes have been made. Therefore option B is incorrect. One of the main features of Flashback Table is that the tablespace can remain online, so option C is incorrect.

14. A. The default action for the `FLASHBACK TABLE` command is to disable all triggers regardless of their previous state. If the `ENABLE TRIGGER` clause is added to the `FLASHBACK TABLE` command, then triggers that were previously enabled will be reenabled after the operation completes.

15. B, C. `FLASHBACK_TRANSACTION_QUERY` is the correct view to query, and it can be done using either timestamps or SCN ranges. `DBA_TRANSACTION_QUERY` is not a valid view; therefore options A and D are incorrect.

16. B. Flashback Database relies on flashback logs in the flash recovery area. The Flashback Data Archive and Undo tablespace are not required. The RMAN command line is not required to recover to a flashback point; the DBA can execute the Flashback Database command from within SQL Plus.

17. C. The Flashback Database architecture consists of the recovery writer RVWR background process and Flashback Database logs. When the Flashback Database is enabled, the RVWR process is started. The RVWR writes the Flashback Database logs in the flash recovery area. FBDA is the Flashback Data Archive background process; the remaining options are fictitious.

18. A, B, C. The DBA can use Flashback Database to recover to an SCN, a point in time, or a named recovery point that is within the recovery window. Transaction ID and Session ID will not help you recover using the Flashback Database feature.

19. A, C. When creating a Flashback Data Archive, you need to specify the tablespace name and a retention period. The storage quota is optional. You add tables to an archive after the archive is created, not as a prerequisite. You don't need to name a default Flashback Data Archive.

20. C. Do nothing. Once the retention period has passed, rows will be automatically removed from the Flashback Data Archive. `TRUNCATE` on a table that is archived is not allowed. Dropping the archive will definitely clear the old records, but it will also eliminate the ones you wanted to keep.

Diagnosing the Database and Managing Performance

ORACLE DATABASE 11*g*: ADMINISTRATION II EXAM OBJECTIVES COVERED IN THIS CHAPTER:

✓ **Diagnosing the Database**

- Set up Automatic Diagnostic Repository
- Using Support Workbench
- Perform block media recovery

✓ **Managing Database Performance**

- Use the SQL Tuning Advisor
- Use the SQL Access Advisor to tune a workload
- Understand Database Replay

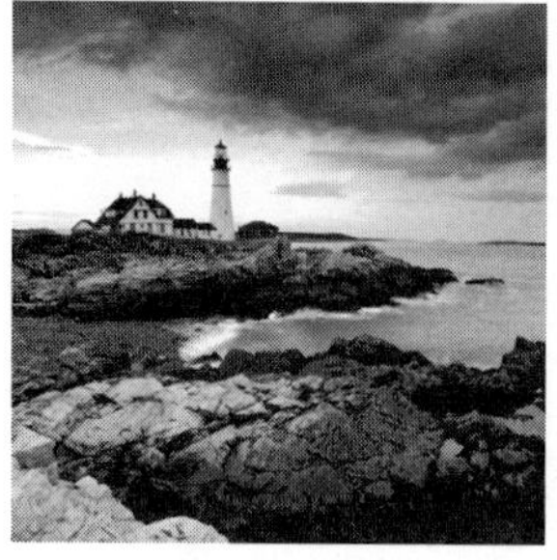

This chapter is divided into two sections; the first section is dedicated to tools that help the DBA diagnose problems in the database, and the second part is dedicated to tools that assist with detecting and resolving performance issues.

In the first part, we introduce the Automatic Diagnostic Repository, the new central repository for all database diagnostic information, and the Support Workbench, which the DBA uses for problem recognition, reporting, and resolution. We also discuss and demonstrate block media recovery.

In the second part, we introduce the SQL Tuning Advisor and the SQL Access Advisor and also teach you the fundamentals of Database Replay. The SQL Tuning Advisor may recommend SQL profiles and indexes, rewriting your SQL statements, or using statistics to improve query performance. The SQL Access Advisor may recommend indexes, partitioning, and materialized views to improve the performance of a workload. Database Replay allows the DBA to capture a workload on a production system and replay it on a different system, simulating the behavior of the production application in a different environment.

Exam objectives are subject to change at any time without prior notice and at Oracle's sole discretion. Please visit Oracle's Training and Certification website (`http://www.oracle.com/education/certification/`) for the most current exam-objectives listing.

Diagnosing the Database

One of the most important day-to-day tasks of the DBA is to monitor system activity and diagnose, report, and repair problems. In Oracle 11*g*, the toolset has improved dramatically. The Automatic Diagnostic Repository provides a central location for storing problem-incident-related information. The Support Workbench improves DBA productivity when it is time to report, analyze, and seek help from Oracle Support to resolve a problem. Block media recovery improvements in 11*g* make it easier for the DBA to recognize and recover from a data-corruption incident.

Setting Up the Automatic Diagnostic Repository

The Automatic Diagnostic Repository (ADR) is a hierarchical file-based systemwide and system-managed repository for storing and organizing dump files, trace files, alert logs, health monitor reports, network tracing, and all other error diagnostic data. In Oracle 11*g*, ADR is the diagnostic data repository for Automatic Storage Management (ASM), the database, and all other Oracle products.

The ADR stores information in files outside the database so the information is available whether or not the database is up. The files are stored in a directory structure that includes a home directory for each instance of each product.

ADR Initialization Parameters

Since the Oracle 11*g* ADR provides a single repository location for the alert log and all dump files and trace files, there is no longer a need for the BACKGROUND_DUMP_DEST, CORE_DUMP_DEST, and USER_DUMP_DEST initialization parameters. They are deprecated and ignored. Now you use the initialization parameter DIAGNOSTIC_DEST to designate the location of the ADR.

```
SQL> show parameter diag
NAME                                 TYPE        VALUE
------------------------------------ ----------- ---------
diagnostic_dest                      string      C:\ORACLE
```

The default value for DIAGNOSTIC_DEST is $ORACLE_BASE. If the ORACLE_BASE environment variable is not set, then $ORACLE_HOME is used for DIAGNOSTIC_DEST.

Directory Structure of the Automatic Diagnostic Repository

Within the DIAGNOSTIC_DEST directory, Oracle builds the hierarchy of directories to support the ADR. The ADR home directory is located in this directory structure:

```
<diagnostic_dest>/diag/rdbms/<dbname>/<instname>
```

For the examples used in this chapter, the following represents the correct ADR home:

```
C:\oracle\diag\rdbms\orcl\orcl
```

These are some important directories that you need to know about:

- Incident: Each incident gets its own subdirectory within the incident directory.
- Alert: The alert log is written to the alert directory.
- Cdump: Core dumps are written to this directory.
- Trace: Trace files are written to the trace directory.

See Figure 10.1 for an example directory structure.

The DBA can set the value of DIAGNOSTIC_DEST on each instance in Real Application Clusters. The recommendation from Oracle is for each instance in a cluster to have the same value for DIAGNOSTIC_DEST.

FIGURE 10.1 Folders within the ADR home directory

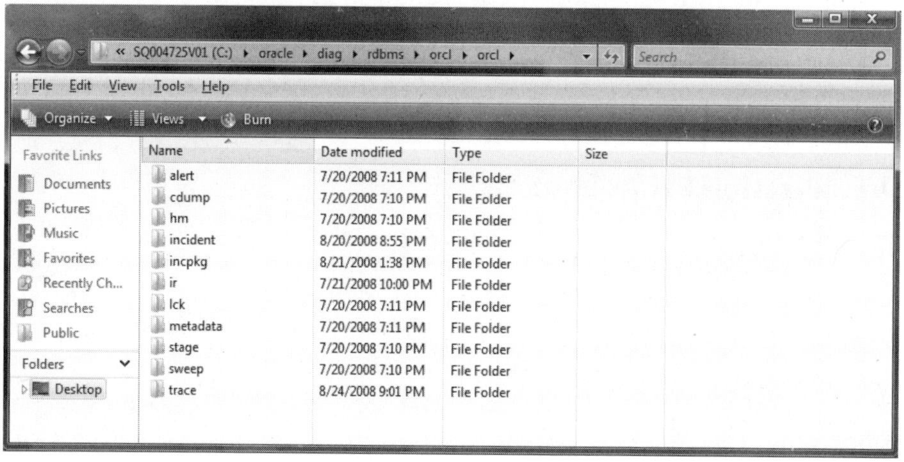

In Exercise 10.1, you'll set the diagnostic destination.

EXERCISE 10.1

Setting the Diagnostic Destination

To set the value for the diagnostic destination, do the following:

1. Verify the current setting for DIAGNOSTIC_DEST.
2. Determine the new destination.
3. Set the value for DIAGNOSTIC_DEST.
4. Verify that the directory structure has been created.
5. Verify the current setting for DIAGNOSTIC_DEST.

```
SQL> show parameter diag

NAME                                 TYPE        VALUE
------------------------------------ ----------- ---------
diagnostic_dest                      string      C:\ORACLE
```

6. Determine the new destination. Check the new destination for security, access, and sufficient space. In this example, we're moving the diagnostic destination from c:\oracle to c:\temp.
7. Set the value for DIAGNOSTIC_DEST.
8. Use the ALTER SYSTEM command to change the value of DIAGNOSTIC_DEST:

```
SQL> alter system set diagnostic_dest="c:\temp";
```

EXERCISE 10.1 *(continued)*

9. Verify that the directory structure has been created.

10. Oracle creates the `diag` directory under the `diagnostic_dest` directory and creates the directory tree under the `diag` directory:

```
SQL> host

c:\temp>cd diag

c:\temp\diag>tree
Folder PATH listing for volume SQ004725V01
Volume serial number is 000DF7CC 8E02:02B8
C:.
rdbms
    orcl
        orcl
            alert
            cdump
            hm
            incident
            incpkg
            ir
            lck
            metadata
            stage
            sweep
            trace

c:\temp\diag>
```

Using the Support Workbench

New to Oracle 11g, the Enterprise Manager Support Workbench (Support Workbench) is a central location for the DBA to see reported problems, investigate the problems, report the problem to Oracle support, and follow up through problem resolution. This is a vast improvement over previous versions, where there was no central location and no defined process for reporting, tracking, and resolving problem incidents.

To access the Support Workbench, start from the Enterprise Manager Database home page, click the Software and Support tab, and then in the Support section, click Support Workbench.

Fundamental Tasks of the Support Workbench

The Support Workbench provides a framework for problem resolution: investigate, report, and resolve a problem. The following are the basic tasks within the Support Workbench:

- View critical error alerts.
- View problem details.
- Gather additional diagnostic information.
- Create a service request.
- Package and upload diagnostic data to Oracle Support.
- Track the service request and implement any repairs.
- Close the incident.

Task 1: View Critical Error Alerts

In most cases, you'll discover a critical alert on the Enterprise Manager home page and then work your way to the Support Workbench page. On the EM Database Instance home page, critical-error alerts and warnings will be displayed in the Alerts section. A red *X* in the Severity column and an incident in the Category column indicate a critical-error alert. See Figure 10.2 for an example.

FIGURE 10.2 Alerts on the Enterprise Manager home page

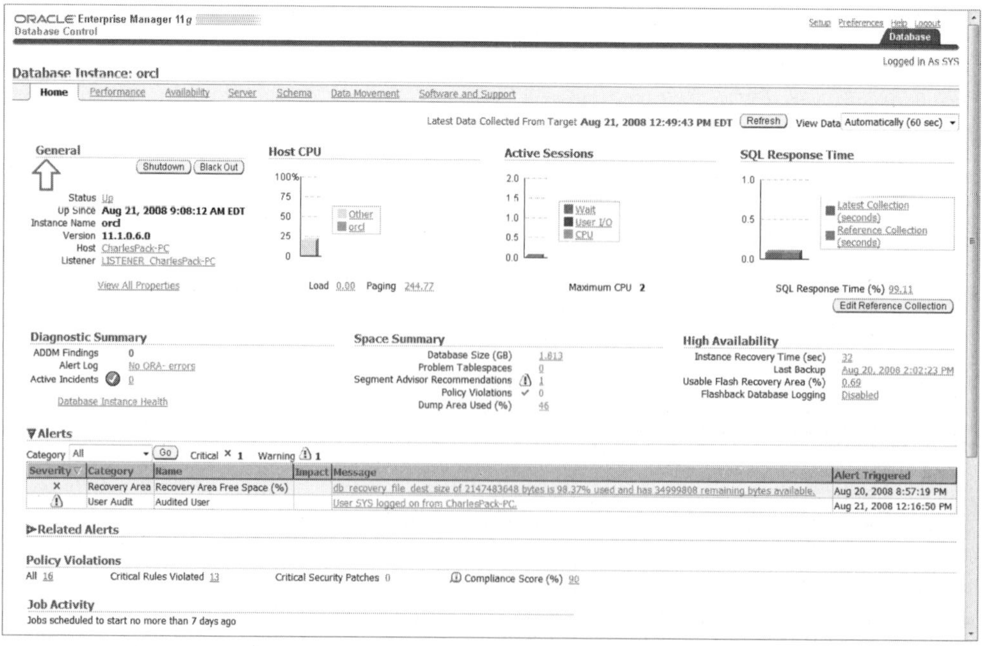

When you select the Message link, EM will direct you to the details for the critical alert, indicating by default any incidents in the last 24 hours. As you can see in Figure 10.3, changing the View Data option to Last 7 Days shows a lingering problem that needs to be addressed. You can add a comment to the most recent alert, or you can click one of the alert messages and add a comment to that specific alert.

FIGURE 10.3 Critical alert

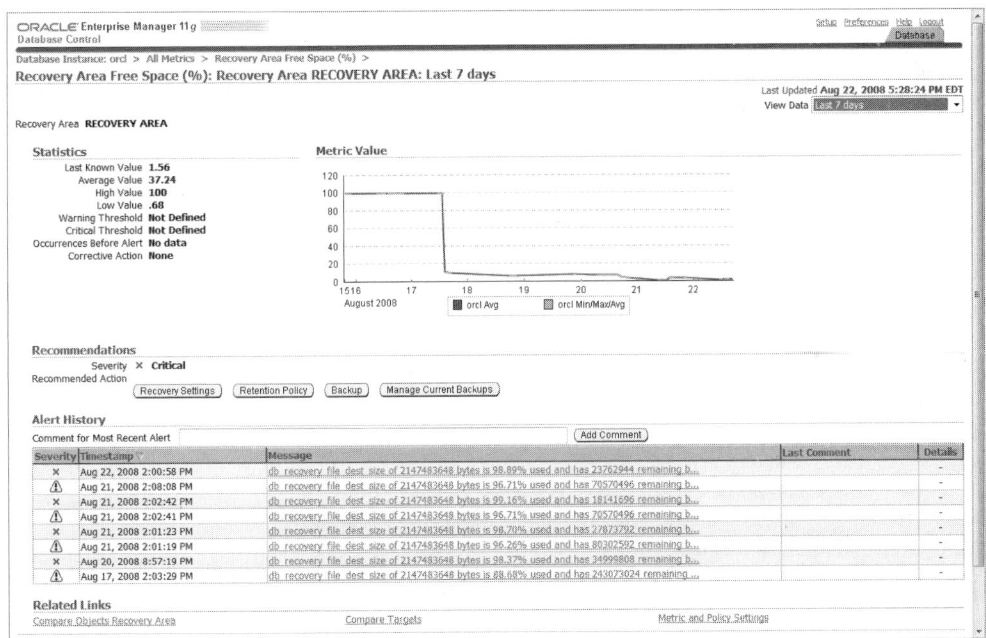

Return to the Database home page and go to the Support Workbench home page as described previously. Figure 10.4 shows one problem and two incidents. In Oracle 11*g*, a *problem* is a critical error in the database. An *incident* is a single occurrence of a *problem*. By default, incidents of a problem that have occurred within the last 24 hours are displayed on the page. To change the date range displayed, click the View drop-down menu and select your preference. To view all of the incidents for a problem, click the Details column's Show icon or the Show All Details link.

Task 2: View Problem Details

Click the Select check box for the problem, and click the View button to see the problem details and, by default, all open incidents of the problem. To view all open, all closed, or all incidents associated with the problem, select the appropriate values from the Status drop-down menu options. There is also a Data Dumped drop-down menu; the options are yes and no. For the example shown in Figure 10.5, we want to see open incidents with data dumped.

FIGURE 10.4 Support Workbench

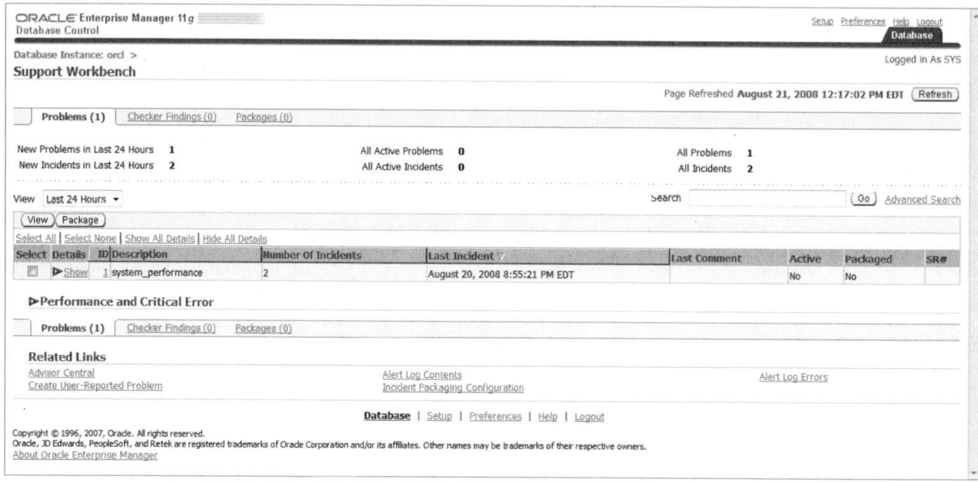

FIGURE 10.5 Problem details

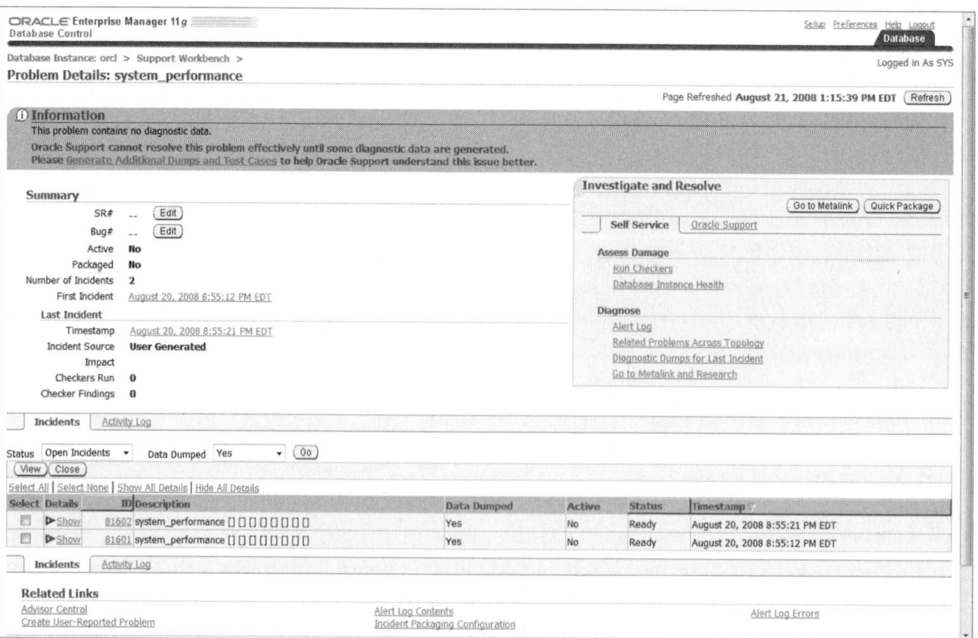

You can view the details for an incident of this problem by clicking the Show icon in the Details column of the Incidents section.

Task 3: Gather Additional Diagnostic Information

With this problem, the DBA needs to generate additional dumps and test cases before engaging Oracle Support, as noted at the top of the Problem Details subpage. Now would be a good time to perform self-service. In the Investigate and Resolve Section on the Self Service tab, select Run Checkers. For the example shown in Figure 10.6, there are no recommended checkers to run.

FIGURE 10.6 Run Checkers

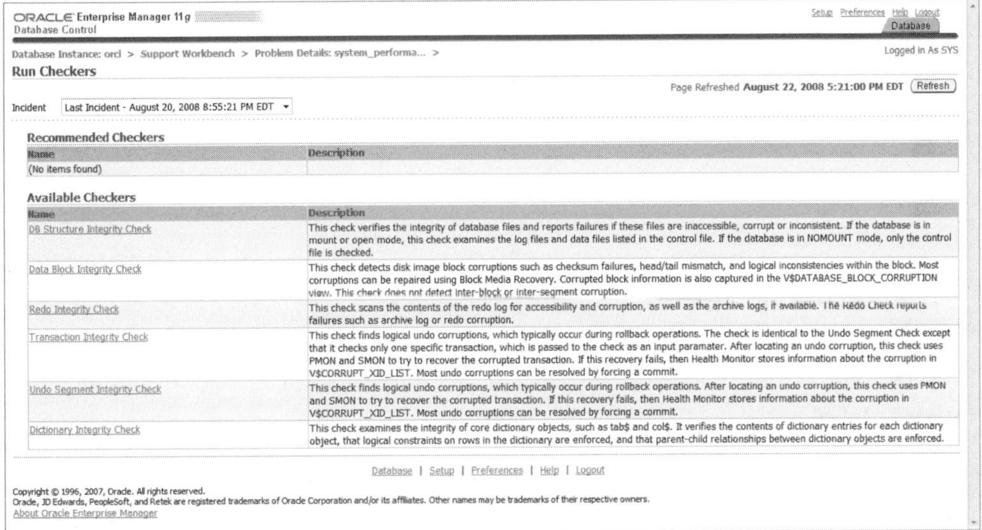

Task 4: Create a Service Request

If you would like to open a service request with Oracle Support, click the Go to Metalink button in the Investigate and Resolve section; your browser will take you to Oracle's Metalink home page. From there, you can open a service request and then return to EM.

Task 5: Package and Upload Diagnostic Data to Oracle Support

The Support Workbench has solved one very annoying problem for the active DBA: packaging all of the related data for an incident and getting it to Oracle. In the past, we searched for relevant files, compressed them, batched them, and either FTPed them to Oracle Support or attached the files to the Technical Assistance Request (TAR). Oracle 11*g* Incident Packaging Service (IPS) makes it easy. It identifies all files associated with a critical error and adds them to a zip file so you can easily send it to Oracle Support.

IPS is built into the Support Workbench, meant to make the DBA more productive and help Oracle Support to receive a complete set of data before advising on action steps.

From the Investigate and Report section on the Problem Details page, click Quick Package. This will allow you to zip files related to the problem and send them to Oracle Support. We start the process in Figure 10.7.

Enter your package description, Metalink credentials, and customer-support identifier. Click Next to view the package contents, shown in Figure 10.8.

FIGURE 10.7 Quick Packaging: Create New Package

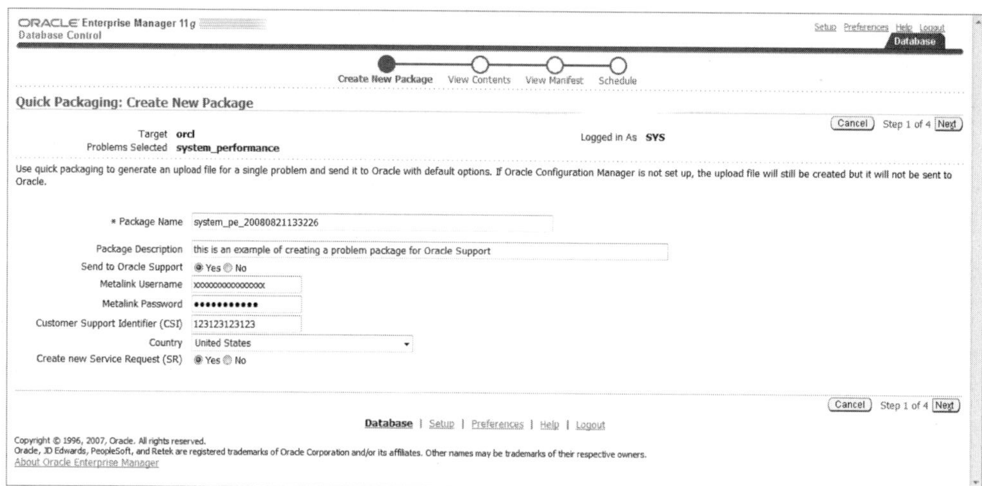

FIGURE 10.8 Viewing the package contents

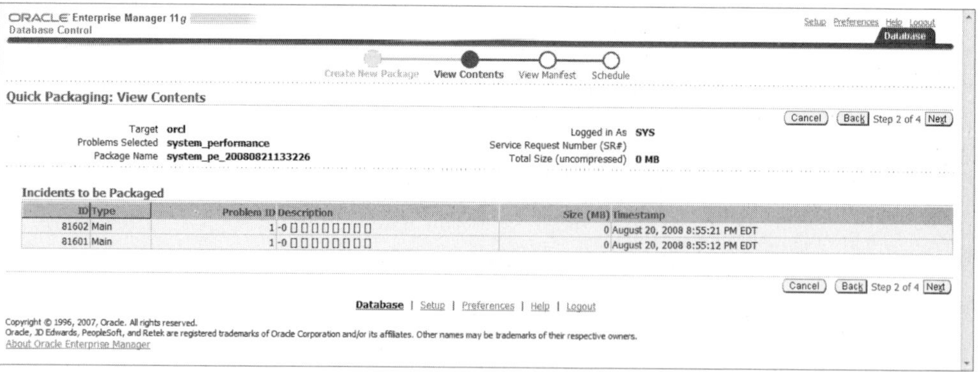

The View Manifest screen, shown in Figure 10.9, displays the package information that will be sent to Oracle Support.

After you verify that the information is correct, click Next to schedule the job that will submit the information to Oracle Support. Once you verify the job send time, click the final Submit button. Then click the OK button to return to the Problem Details page.

To view the details of a package in the Support Workbench, choose packages from the Support Workbench home page, and then choose a package by clicking on the package name. You can view the list of files included in the package, as shown in Figure 10.10, by clicking the Files tab from the Incident Package Details screen.

FIGURE 10.9 The View Manifest screen

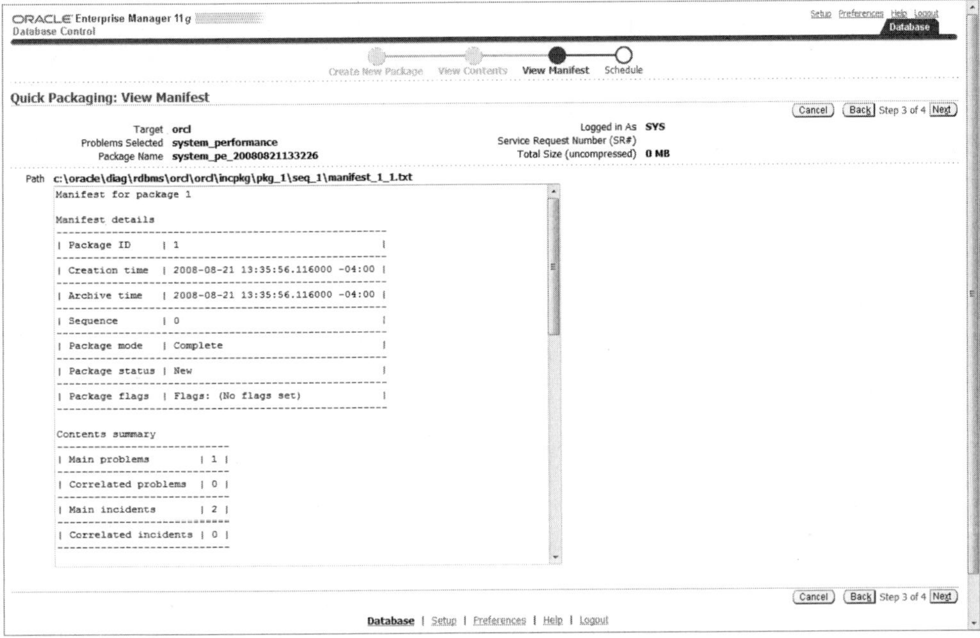

FIGURE 10.10 The Customize Package screen

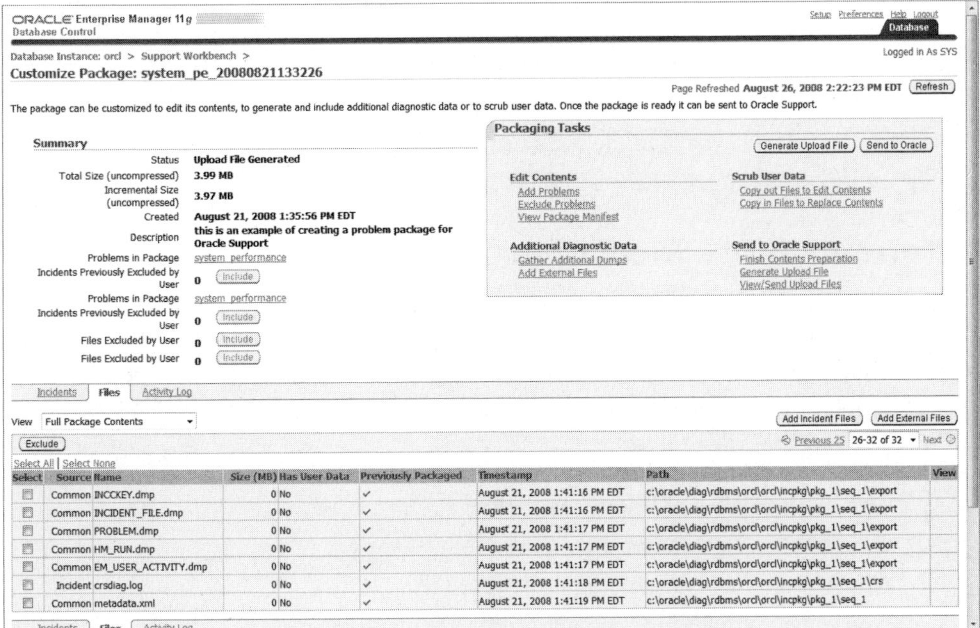

Task 6: Track the Service Request and Implement Any Repairs

From the Problem Details page, click the Activity Log link to view the list of activities performed in response to this problem, as shown in Figure 10.11. On the Problem Details page, you can add the Oracle SR number as well as the Oracle bug number related to the problem by clicking on the Edit button next to the item.

FIGURE 10.11 Viewing the activity log

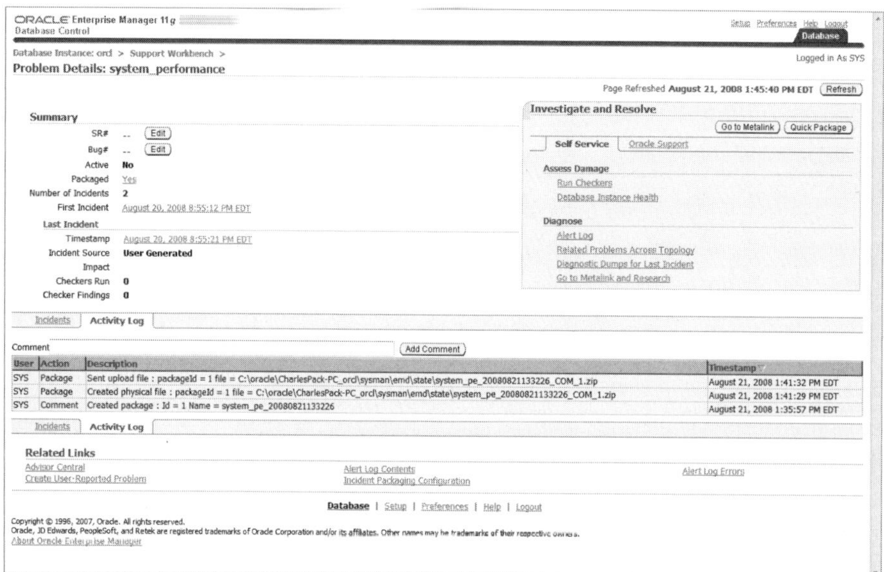

Task 7: Close the Incident

From the Problem Details page in the Incidents section, select the incident close, then click the Close button. You will be asked to confirm.

Performing Block Media Recovery

Block media recovery (BMR) is used to repair corrupt blocks within a datafile. It allows you to recover corrupt blocks while keeping the datafile online, as opposed to datafile media recovery, which requires taking the file offline during the restore and recovery operation. You can perform BMR only on blocks that are identified as corrupt. Block media recovery requires Enterprise Edition.

Advantages of Block Media Recovery

The advantages of block media recovery are straightforward:

- The mean time to recovery (MTTR) is reduced.
- Datafiles remain online while corrupt blocks are repaired.

These advantages are related to recovery performance and returning the customer to normal operating mode.

Detecting Block-level Corruption

Data-block corruption can occur because of memory corruption that is written to disk or because of I/O errors. Corruption is detected by dbv, SQL that accesses corrupt blocks, RMAN, ANALYZE operations, and any other operation that attempts to read data from a corrupt block, including DBMS_REPAIR.CHECK_OBJECT. Once a corrupt block is detected, the database will not allow access to that block until it is repaired.

The aid the DBA in diagnosis of datafile corruption, Oracle provides the dbv "DB Verify" OS utility program. The dbv program takes, for example, a database file name as a command-line parameter, and performs an analysis of the structure and contents of the file and determines if there is any block corruption. At the command line, execute dbv to see the following help screen:

```
C:\>dbv

DBVERIFY: Release 11.1.0.6.0 - Production on Sun Nov 23
18:30:28 2008

Copyright (c) 1982, 2007, Oracle.  All rights reserved.

Keyword     Description                    (Default)
----------------------------------------------------
FILE        File to Verify                 (NONE)
START       Start Block                    (First Block of
File)
END         End Block                      (Last Block of File)
BLOCKSIZE   Logical Block Size             (8192)
LOGFILE     Output Log                     (NONE)
FEEDBACK    Display Progress               (0)
PARFILE     Parameter File                 (NONE)
USERID      Username/Password              (NONE)
SEGMENT_ID  Segment ID (tsn.relfile.block) (NONE)
HIGH_SCN    Highest Block SCN To Verify    (NONE)
            (scn_wrap.scn_base OR scn)
```

Physical and logical block corruption are recorded in V$DATABASE_BLOCK_CORRUPTION. Physical block corruption is when the database does not recognize the block because the block header is damaged, the checksum is invalid, or the block contains all zeros. This is often due to disk hardware or OS failures and often is not acknowledged as corruption by the OS or underlying storage devices. Logical block corruption is when the contents of the block are logically inconsistent, sometimes the result of an Oracle internal error. Logical block corruption checking is enabled by using the RMAN BACKUP, RESTORE, RECOVER, or VALIDATE command with the CHECK LOGICAL clause. Logical block corruption is not repairable by BMR.

Performing Block Media Recovery

Oracle 11*g* can restore prior uncorrupted versions of the corrupt block from the flashback logs, improving recovery performance over restore from tape or disk backups. In previous versions of the database, block media recovery required restoring the uncorrupted blocks from a backup and then applying any necessary archive logs. A gap in archive logs meant the end of the recovery process. In Oracle 11*g*, if BMR encounters a gap in archive logs, it will continue forward to search for newer versions of the corrupted blocks. If a newer version is available, the restore and recovery can continue. If there are no uncorrupted newer versions of the block, the operation will fail.

To perform BMR, the database must be open or mounted and in ARCHIVELOG mode, and must have a current, usable control file. The database must not be a standby database. You must use level 0 or full backups for the restore. All of the required archived redo logs must be available for the recovery process.

If you have enabled Flashback Database and logging, then RMAN will search the flashback logs for uncorrupted versions of the required blocks.

The steps to recover blocks using BMR are fairly simply. From SQL*Plus, determine which blocks need recovery by viewing the alert log or querying the V$DATABASE_BLOCK_CORRUPTION view:

```
SQL> SELECT NAME, VALUE FROM V$DIAG_INFO;


SQL> SELECT FILE#, BLOCK#, BLOCKS, CORRUPTION_TYPE "TYPE"
FROM V$DATABASE_BLOCK_CORRUPTION;

     FILE#     BLOCK#     BLOCKS CORRUPTION_CHANGE# TYPE
---------- ---------- ---------- ------------------ ---------
      1201       1968          2                    PHYSICAL
```

Now that you have the blocks required for recovery, connect to the target database with RMAN and begin the recovery:

```
RMAN> RECOVER DATAFILE 1201 BLOCK 1968;
```

RMAN also allows you to recover all corrupt blocks in a database using BMR. Query the V$DATABASE_BLOCK_CORRUPTION view to measure the extent of the damage, then launch RMAN to perform the recovery:

```
RMAN> RECOVER CORRUPTION LIST;
```

When a block is repaired, it is removed from the V$DATABASE_BLOCK_CORRUPTION view.

Block media recovery will fail if there is physical corruption in the redo logs that results in a checksum failure.

Managing Database Performance

In the following sections, you will learn how to use the SQL Tuning Advisor, the SQL Access Advisor, and Database Replay. Each of these tools can be used by the DBA to analyze and improve database performance. The Advisors operate directly on the database you wish to tune, while the Database Replay feature allows you to test a production workload on a test system to determine ways to improve performance without directly impacting the production system.

Using the SQL Tuning Advisor

The SQL Tuning Advisor is a tool that you can use to analyze the performance of one or more SQL statements. To improve SQL performance, the Advisor may suggest new or modified indexes, SQL profiles, restructuring your SQL statements, or gathering statistics. The SQL Tuning Advisor runs in one of two modes, Automatic or Manual. The Automatic Tuning Advisor is scheduled to run during the maintenance window, finds ways to improve high-load SQL statements, and automatically takes action. Use the SQL Tuning Advisor in Manual mode to analyze collections of SQL statements or individual SQL statements. In Manual mode, the SQL Tuning Advisor is used to analyze a collection of SQL statements called a SQL Tuning Set.

From the database home page in EM, in the Related Links section, choose the Advisor Central link, then SQL Advisors, and you'll see the page in Figure 10.12.

Automatic SQL Tuning Advisor

From the SQL Advisors page, click the Automatic SQL Tuning Results Summary link. The page that appears, shown in Figure 10.13, will display the results from the most recent Automatic SQL Tuning Advisor job.

From the results page, you can click the Configure button to configure the Automatic SQL Tuning tasks that will run during each daily maintenance window, as shown in Figure 10.14.

FIGURE 10.12 SQL Advisors home page

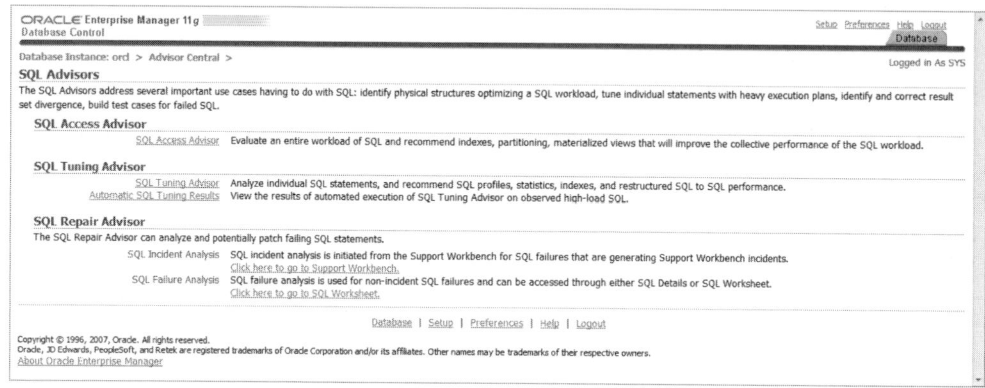

FIGURE 10.13 Automatic SQL Tuning results

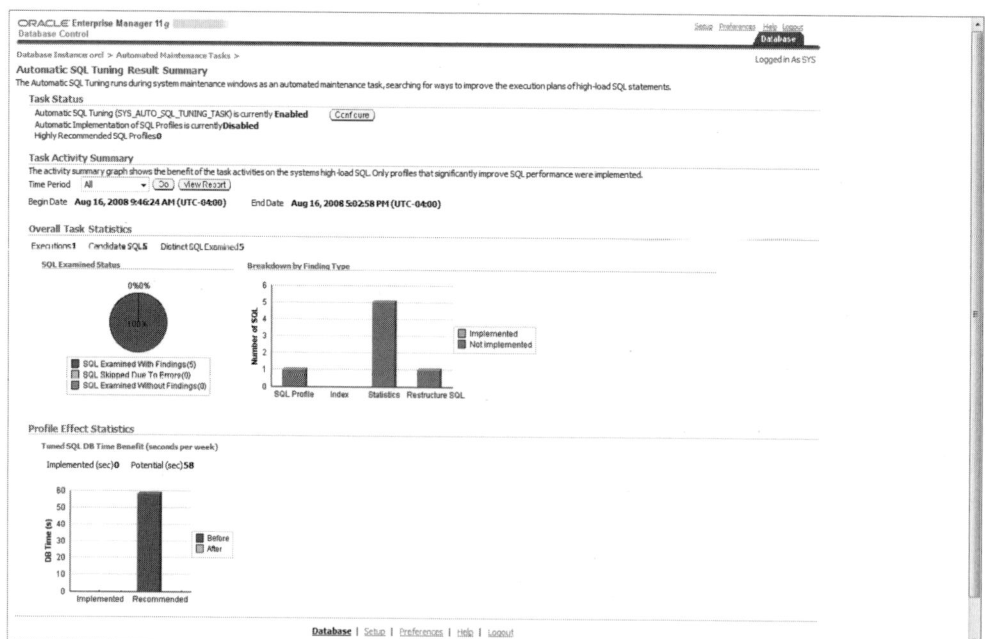

You can view the Automatic SQL Tuning result details, shown in Figure 10.15, by clicking the View Report button in the Task Activity Summary section of the Automatic SQL Tuning Result Summary page.

And you can view the recommendations made by the Tuning Advisor, as shown in Figure 10.16.

FIGURE 10.14 Automatic Maintenance Task Configuration page

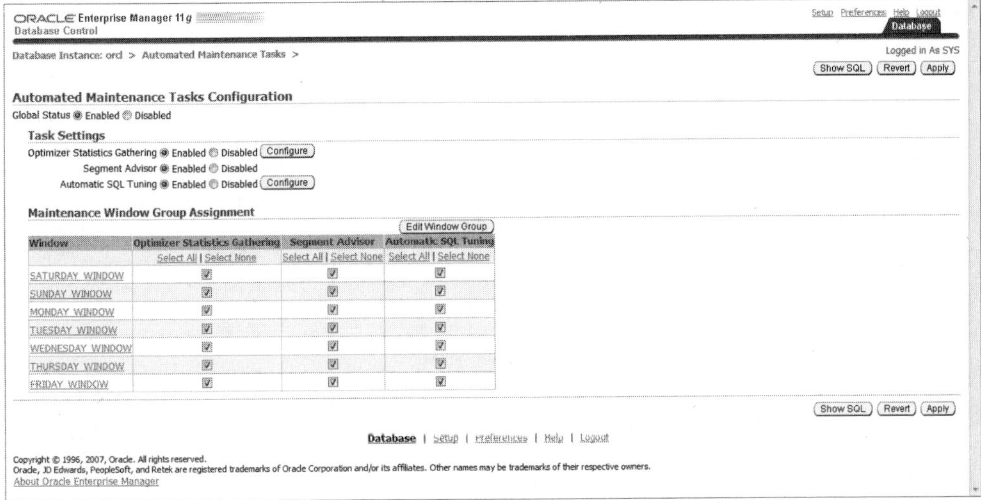

FIGURE 10.15 Automatic SQL Tuning Result Details page

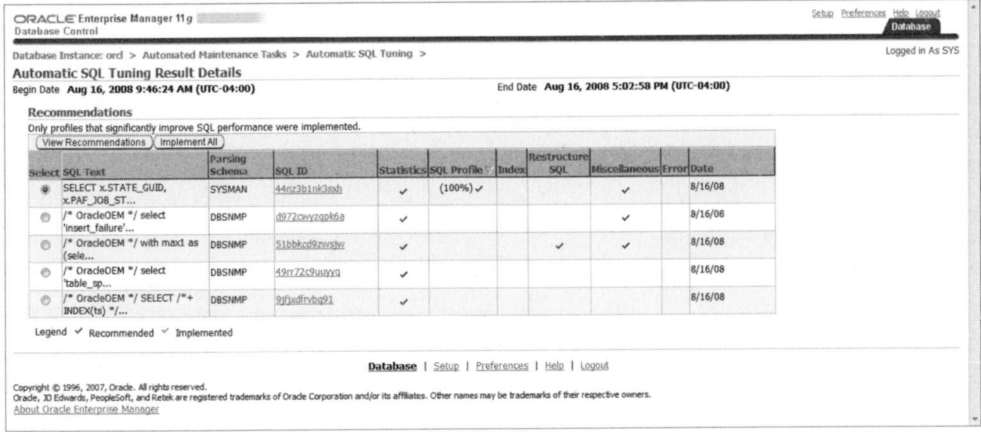

FIGURE 10.16 Automatic SQL Tuning recommendations

Manual SQL Tuning Advisor

From the SQL Advisors page, select the SQL Tuning Advisor to configure manual tuning. On the SQL Tuning Advisor page you will input the parameters for collecting SQL statement information, including scheduling information for task-data collection.

If there are no defined SQL tuning sets, then you have the opportunity to create a new one. On the SQL Tuning Sets page, click the Create button; this will begin a five-step process to create a new SQL tuning set, as shown in Figure 10.17.

FIGURE 10.17 Creating a new SQL tuning set

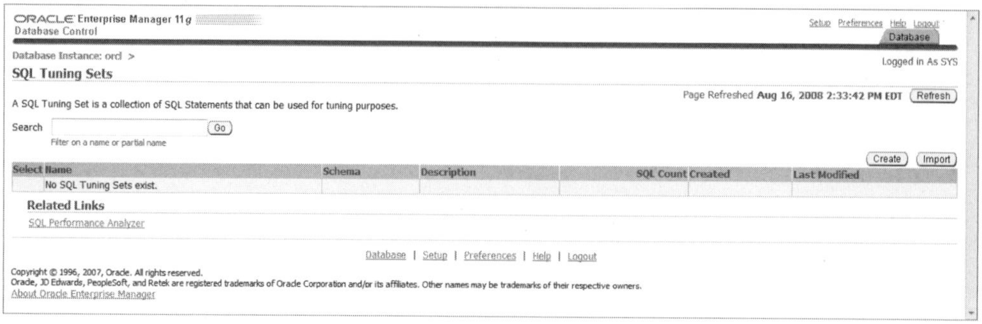

Step 1 is to type a name for your tuning set, the schema owner, and a description, as shown in Figure 10.18.

Step 2 is to choose the load methods; in the case, as shown in Figure 10.19, a duration of 24 hours with samples taken at 5-minute intervals.

FIGURE 10.18 SQL tuning set options

ORACLE Enterprise Manager 11*g*
Database Control

Setup Preferences Help Logout
Database

Options Load Methods Filter Options Schedule Review

Logged in As SYS

Create SQL Tuning Set: Options

Database **orcl**

Cancel Step 1 of 5 Next

* SQL Tuning Set Name SampleExercise

Owner SCOTT

Description this is a test

Create an empty SQL tuning set

Cancel Step 1 of 5 Next

Database | Setup | Preferences | Help | Logout

Copyright © 1996, 2007, Oracle. All rights reserved.
Oracle, JD Edwards, PeopleSoft, and Retek are registered trademarks of Oracle Corporation and/or its affiliates. Other names may be trademarks of their respective owners.
About Oracle Enterprise Manager

FIGURE 10.19 SQL tuning set load methods

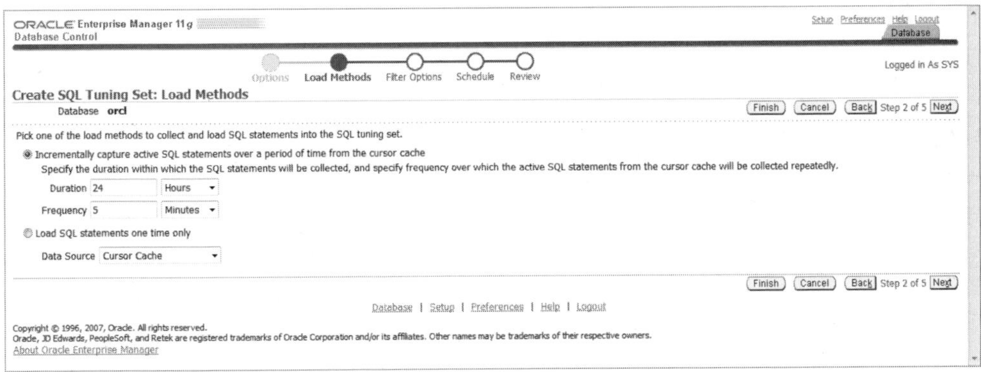

In step 3 you set criteria for SQL statements to include in the tuning set, as shown in Figure 10.20. The drop-down menu allows you to select from a predefined list to add additional filter attributes.

In step 4 (Figure 10.21), you create and schedule a job to collect the SQL statement information and load it into a SQL tuning set. We want to start collecting immediately for this example. Click Next for the final review.

In step 5 we review, confirm, and submit to begin collection to the tuning set, shown in Figure 10.22.

FIGURE 10.20 SQL tuning set filter options

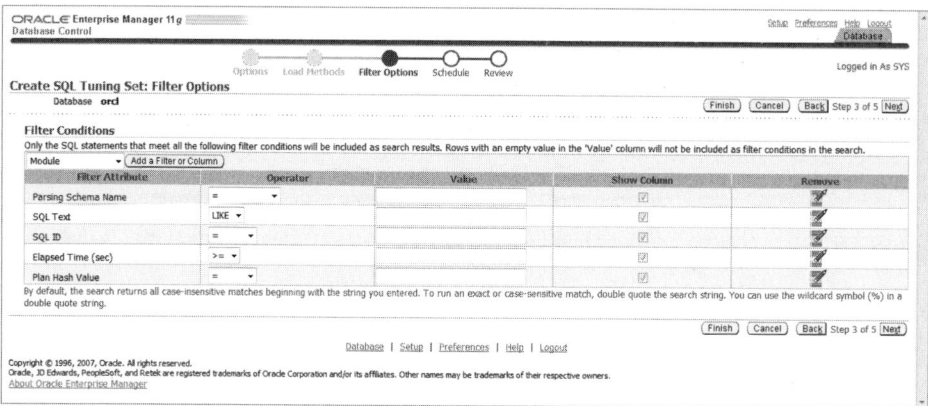

FIGURE 10.21 SQL tuning set schedule

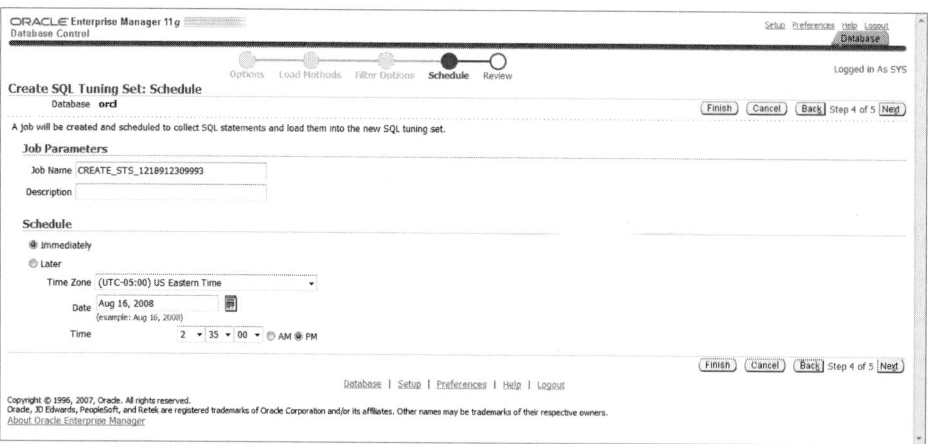

FIGURE 10.22 SQL tuning set review

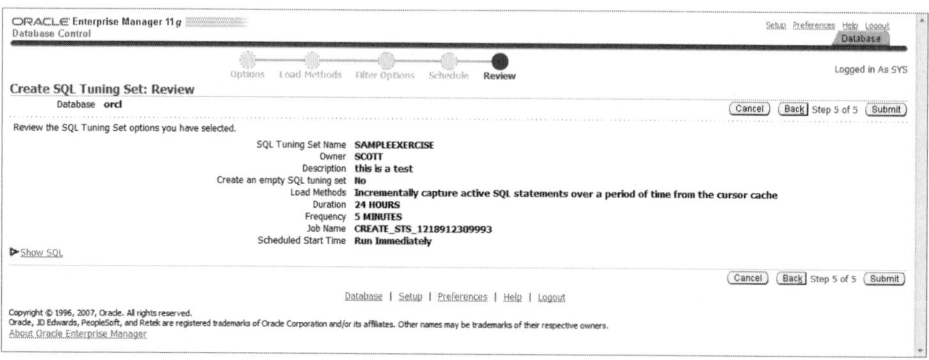

The confirmation page, shown in Figure 10.23, indicates that the SQL tuning set and collection job have been successfully created.

Return to the SQL Advisor page and select the name of this SQL tuning set; you should receive quick confirmation that SQL collection is in progress—the SQL statements count will increase. After you have collected SQL statements in a set, you can run the SQL Tuning Advisor using the tuning set. In Figure 10.24, we identify which SQL tuning set to process, the scope of analysis, and when to schedule the Advisor process. For this example, we will use a comprehensive scope of analysis and schedule it to run immediately.

FIGURE 10.23 SQL tuning set confirmation

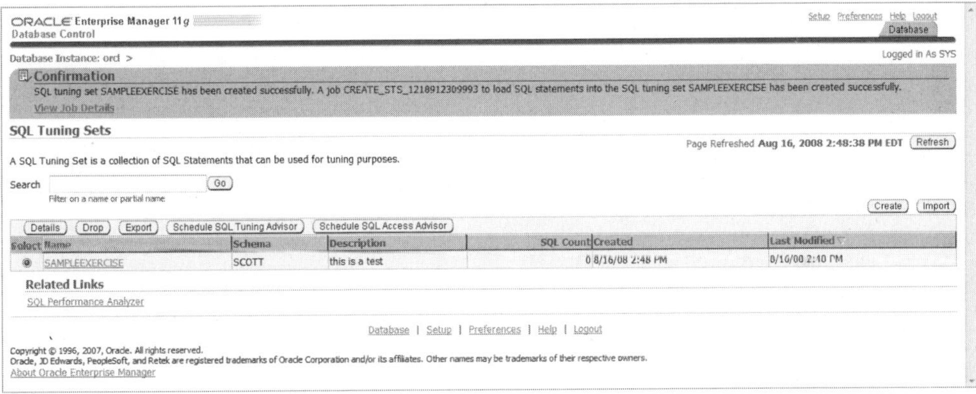

FIGURE 10.24 SQL tuning advisor schedule

ORACLE Enterprise Manager 11g
Database Control
Setup Preferences Help Logout
Database
Database Instance: orcl > Advisor Central > SQL Advisors >
Logged in As SYS
Schedule SQL Tuning Advisor
Cancel Submit
Specify the following parameters to schedule a job to run the SQL Tuning Advisor.
* Name SQL_TUNING_1218915743634
Description
* SQL Tuning Set SYS.ANOTHERTEST
SQL Tuning Set Description another test
SQL Statements Counts 10
Overview
The SQL Tuning Advisor analyzes individual SQL statements, and suggests indexes, SQL profiles, restructured SQL, and statistics that improve the performance of the SQL statements.
The SQL Tuning Advisor operates on a collection of SQL. You can choose a SQL Tuning Set to run the advisor. If you do not have a SQL Tuning Set with the desired SQL for running the advisor, you can create a new one.
You can click on one of the following sources, which will lead you to a data source where you can tune SQL statements using the SQL Tuning Advisor.
Top Activity Historical SQL (AWR) SQL Tuning Sets
SQL Statements
Scope
Total Time Limit (minutes) 30
Scope of Analysis Limited
The analysis is done without SQL Profile recommendation and takes about 1 second per statement.
Comprehensive
This analysis includes SQL Profile recommendation, but may take a long time.
Time Limit per Statement (minutes) 5
Schedule
Time Zone America/New_York
Immediately
Later
Date Aug 16, 2008
(example: Aug 16, 2008)
Time 3 30 00 AM PM
Cancel Submit
Database | Setup | Preferences | Help | Logout

When you submit the analysis, you will be directed to the SQL Tuning Advisor task status page, shown in Figure 10.25. The page will refresh automatically.

When the task completes, the status will change to completed and the SQL information will be displayed on the SQL Tuning Results page. See Figure 10.26 for the Tuning Advisor results for this example.

FIGURE 10.25 SQL Tuning Advisor task processing

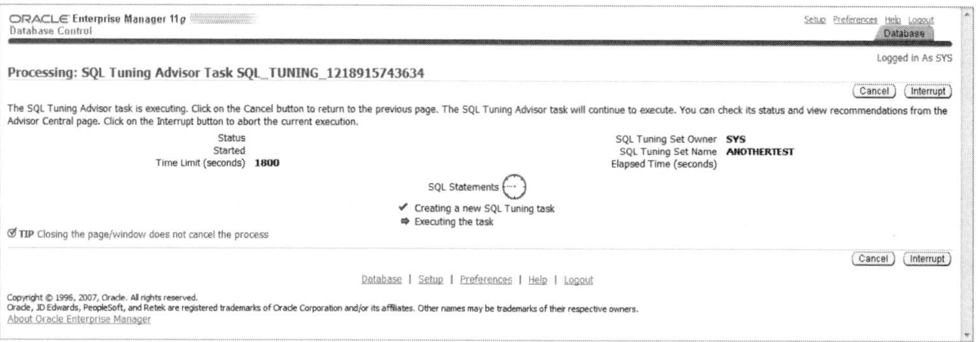

FIGURE 10.26 SQL Tuning Advisor results

ORACLE Enterprise Manager 11g
Database Control

Setup Preferences Help Logout
Database

Database Instance: orcl > Advisor Central >

Logged in As SYS

SQL Tuning Results:SQL_TUNING_1218915561760

Page Refreshed **Aug 16, 2008 3:41:05 PM EDT** (Refresh)

Status **COMPLETED**
Started **Aug 16, 2008 3:40:54 PM**
Completed **Aug 16, 2008 3:41:02 PM**

Tuning Set Owner **SYS**
Tuning Set Name **ANOTHERTEST**
Time Limit (seconds) **1800**
Running Time (seconds) **8**

Recommendations

(View)

Select	SQL Text	Parsing Schema	SQL ID	Statistics	SQL Profile	Index	Restructure SQL	Miscellaneous	Error
◉	select table_name from user_tables	SCOTT	cpm405mcw3bkj				✓		
○	select * from emp	SCOTT	a2dk8bdn0ujx7						
○	SELECT ATTRIBUTE,SCOPE,NUMERIC_VALUE,CHAR_VALUE,DATE_VALUE FROM SYSTEM.PRODUCT_PRIVS WHERE (UPPER('S...	SCOTT	1uzhrfn574t12						
○	BEGIN DBMS_OUTPUT.DISABLE; END;	SCOTT	5qgz1p0cut7mx					✓	
○	select * from dept	SCOTT	3154rqzb8xudy						
○	select empno, ename, job, mgr, hiredate, sal, comm, e.deptno, dname, loc from emp e, dept d where e....	SCOTT	5yswsc1puy0vh						
○	BEGIN DBMS_APPLICATION_INFO.SET_MODULE(:1,NULL); END;	SCOTT	g4y6nw3tts7cc					✓	
○	SELECT CHAR_VALUE FROM SYSTEM.PRODUCT_PRIVS WHERE (UPPER('SQL*Plus') LIKE UPPER (PRODUCT)) AND ((...	SCOTT	c4pc3jhzjcmc7						
○	SELECT USER FROM DUAL	SCOTT	d6vwqbw6r2ffk						
○	SELECT DECODE('A','A','1','2') FROM DUAL	SCOTT	dyk4dprp70d74						

(View)

Database | Setup | Preferences | Help | Logout

About Oracle Enterprise Manager

Select a SQL statement to view, and as shown on the details page in Figure 10.27, the Advisor will recommend a course of action. We selected the first query listed in Figure 10.26, and in Figure 10.27 the Advisor cautions that we have a Cartesian product.

If we then click the findings, we can see the detailed execution plan, as shown in Figure 10.28, and determine an action plan.

FIGURE 10.27 SQL Tuning Advisor recommendations for a SQL statement

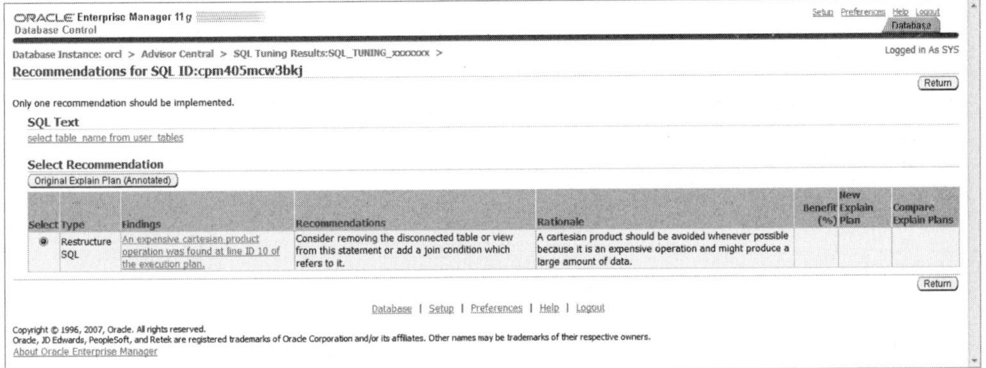

FIGURE 10.28 SQL Tuning Advisor recommendations: SQL statement original explain plan

ORACLE Enterprise Manager 11g
Database Control

Setup Preferences Help Logout
Database

Database Instance: orcl > Advisor Central > SQL Tuning Results:SQL_TUNING_xxxxxxx > Recommendations for SQL ID:cpm405mcw3bkj >

Logged in As SYS

Original Explain Plan (Annotated)

Expand All | Collapse All

Operation	Line ID	Object	Object Type	Order	Rows	Bytes	Cost	Time	CPU Cost	I/O Cost
▼ SELECT STATEMENT	0			20		401.060	510	7	151,334,400	503
▼ HASH JOIN RIGHT OUTER	1			19		401.060	510	7	151,334,400	503
INDEX FULL SCAN	2	SYS.I_USER2	INDEX (UNIQUE)	1		0.352	1	1	7,321	1
▼ HASH JOIN OUTER	3			18		391.337	508	7	139,989,232	502
▼ HASH JOIN OUTER	4			16		371.892	452	6	120,174,920	447
▼ HASH JOIN RIGHT OUTER	5			14		359.738	396	5	100,360,608	392
TABLE ACCESS FULL	6	SYS.SEG$	CLUSTER	2		79.138	61	1	2,945,082	61
▼ HASH JOIN	7			13		333.001	335	5	84,986,120	331
TABLE ACCESS FULL	8	SYS.TS$	CLUSTER	3		0.021	4	1	50,900	4
▼ NESTED LOOPS	9			12		325.709	330	4	73,609,816	327
▼ MERGE JOIN CARTESIAN	10			9		252.789	237	3	68,125,304	234
▼ HASH JOIN	11			6		0.066	1	1	11,790,607	0
FIXED TABLE FULL	12	SYS.X$KSPPI	TABLE (FIXED)	4		0.054	0	1	355,000	0
FIXED TABLE FULL	13	SYS.X$KSPPCV	TABLE (FIXED)	5		1.270	0	1	350,000	0
▼ BUFFER SORT	14			8		87.504	237	3	67,775,304	234
TABLE ACCESS FULL	15	SYS.OBJ$	TABLE	7		87.504	237	3	56,334,696	234
▼ TABLE ACCESS CLUSTER	16	SYS.TAB$	CLUSTER	11		0.029	1	1	10,051	1
INDEX UNIQUE SCAN	17	SYS.I_OBJ#	INDEX (CLUSTER)	10			0	1	1,900	0
INDEX FAST FULL SCAN	18	SYS.I_OBJ1	INDEX (UNIQUE)	15		340.317	55	1	1,395,802	55
INDEX FAST FULL SCAN	19	SYS.I_OBJ1	INDEX (UNIQUE)	17		544.508	55	1	1,395,802	55

Database | Setup | Preferences | Help | Logout

About Oracle Enterprise Manager

SQL Tuning Advisor Supplied Package and Views

Oracle 11*g* includes the DBMS_SQLTUNE package to manually execute the SQL Tuning Advisor. Instead of point and click from Oracle EM, you can manually configure the steps from SQL*Plus or another SQL front end.

Oracle also provides SQL tuning informational views, if you prefer to use them instead of EM:

- DBA_ADVISOR_TASKS
- DBA_ADVISOR_EXECUTIONS
- DBA_ADVISOR_FINDINGS
- DBA_ADVISOR_RECOMMENDATIONS
- DBA_ADVISOR_RATIONALE
- DBA_SQLTUNE_STATISTICS
- DBA_SQLTUNE_BINDS
- DBA_SQLTUNE_PLANS
- DBA_SQLSET
- DBA_SQLSET_BINDS
- DBA_SQLSET_STATEMENTS
- DBA_SQLSET_PREFERENCES
- DBA_SQLSET_PLANS
- USER_SQLSET_PLANS
- DBA_SQL_PROFILES

Using the SQL Access Advisor to Tune a Workload

The SQL Access Advisor is a tuning tool that assists the DBA by offering recommendations for indexes, partitioning, and materialized view logs for a workload.

Indexing recommendations may include B-tree, bitmap, and function-based indexes. The SQL Access Advisor may recommend partitioning tables, new partitioned indexes, and new partitioned materialized views. It also provides recommendations on how to improve the performance of materialized views by using Fast Refresh and Query Rewrite.

You can manually execute the SQL Access Advisor functions and procedures included in the DBMS_ADVISOR package. For this exercise, we will use Enterprise Manager. From the database home page in EM, in the Related Links section, chose the Advisor Central link, then SQL Advisors. From the SQL Advisors home page, shown in Figure 10.29, choose the SQL Access Advisor.

From the Initial Options page, shown in Figure 10.30, choose the Recommend New Access Structures option.

First, select the workload source. We'll use a tuning set that we've already created, shown in Figure 10.31.

Next, choose the depth and breadth of recommendation options, shown in Figure 10.32. For this exercise, we just want to view index recommendations. The Advanced Options link allows you to select space restrictions, tuning prioritization, workload scope and volatility, default storage schema and tablespace names for indexes and materialized views, and tablespace names for materialized view logs and partitions.

FIGURE 10.29 SQL Advisors home page

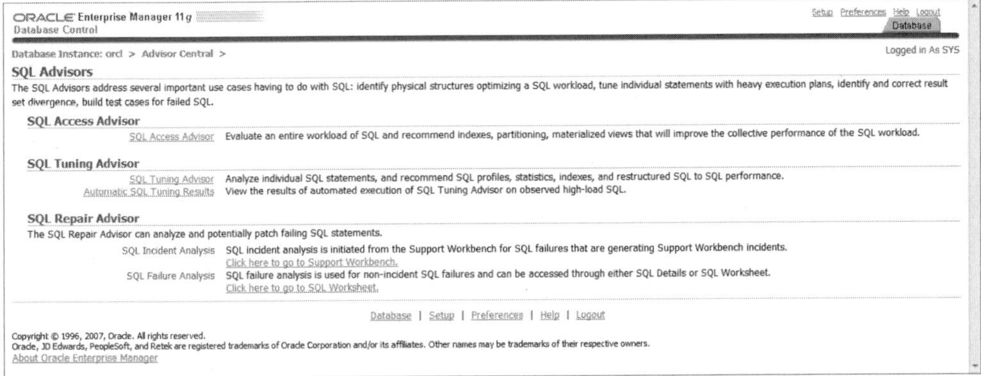

FIGURE 10.30 SQL Access Advisor initial options

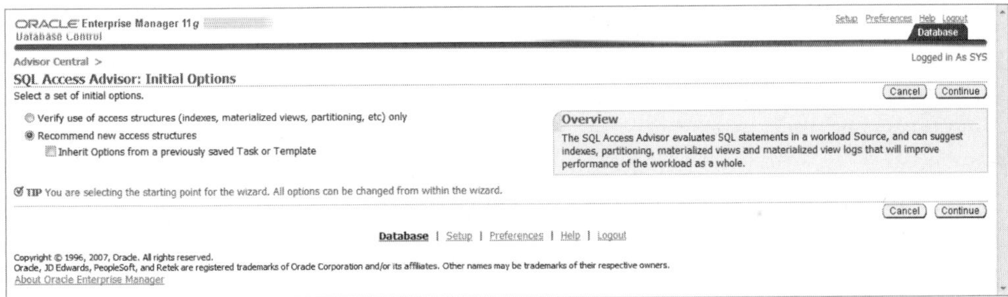

FIGURE 10.31 Choose Workload Source for SQL Access Advisor

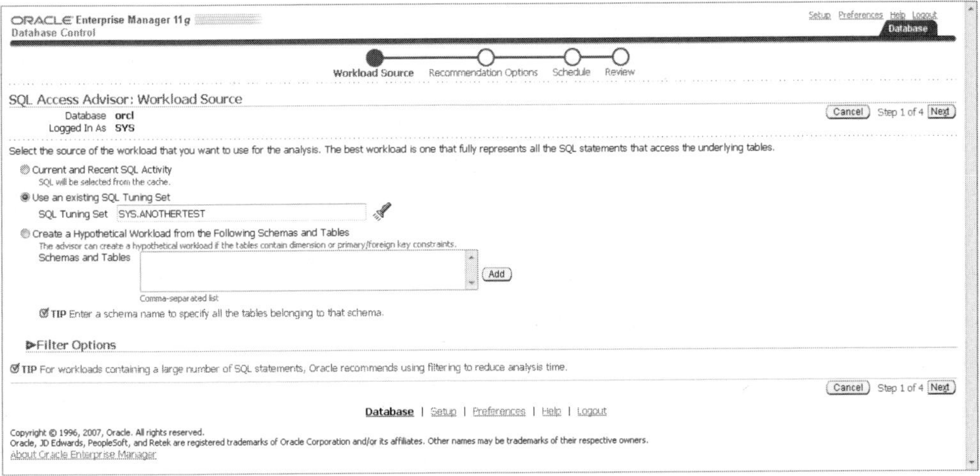

FIGURE 10.32 Recommendation options for SQL Access Advisor task

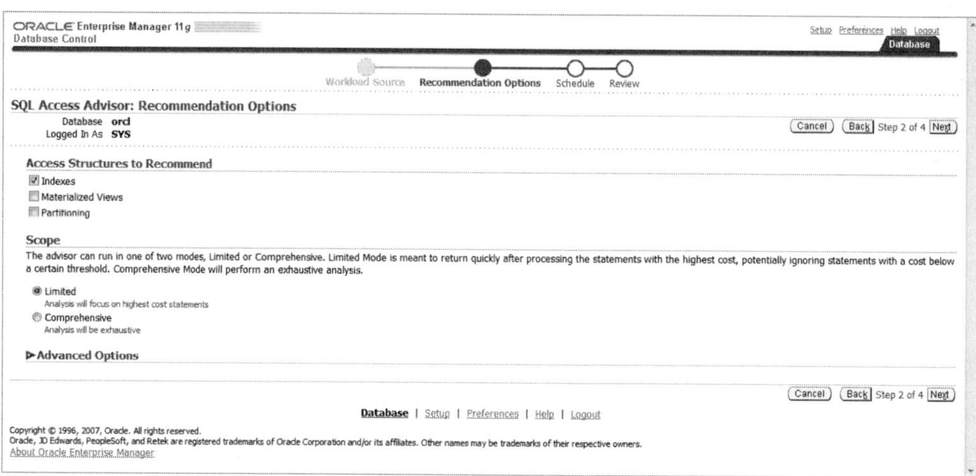

Step 3 is to schedule the SQL Access Advisor task, shown in Figure 10.33.

FIGURE 10.33 Scheduling the SQL Access Advisor task

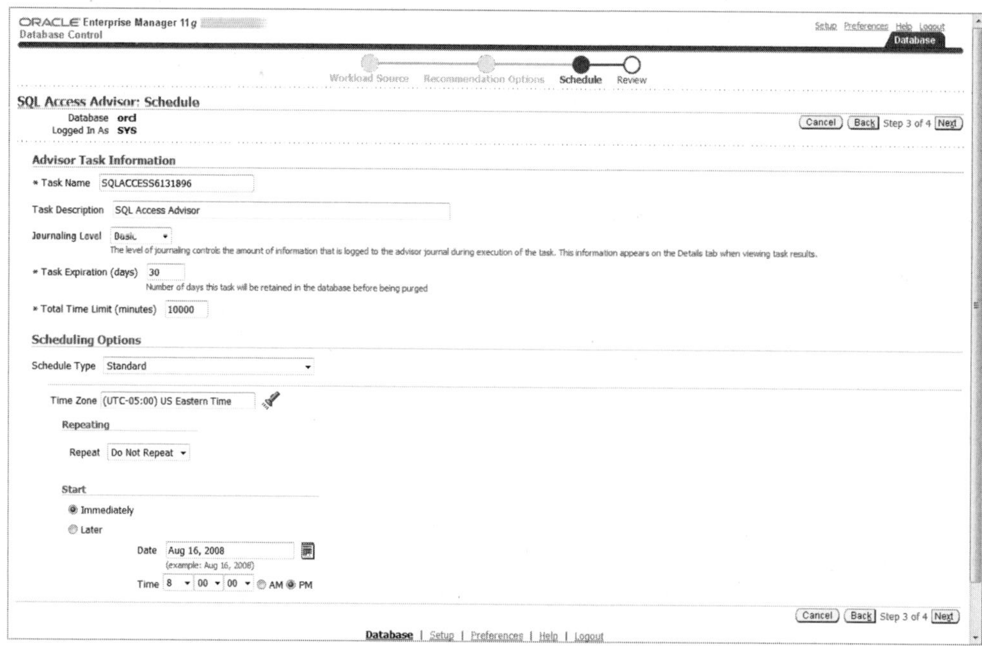

In step 4, we review, verify, and submit, as shown in Figure 10.34.

Once the task is submitted, you receive confirmation that the task was submitted successfully. You can monitor the task through completion from the Advisor Central home page, shown in Figure 10.35.

Once the task is complete, in the Advisor Tasks section, click the Results Name link to view the detailed recommendations for the task. The results of our task are shown in Figure 10.36.

FIGURE 10.34 Review and submit the SQL Access Advisor task

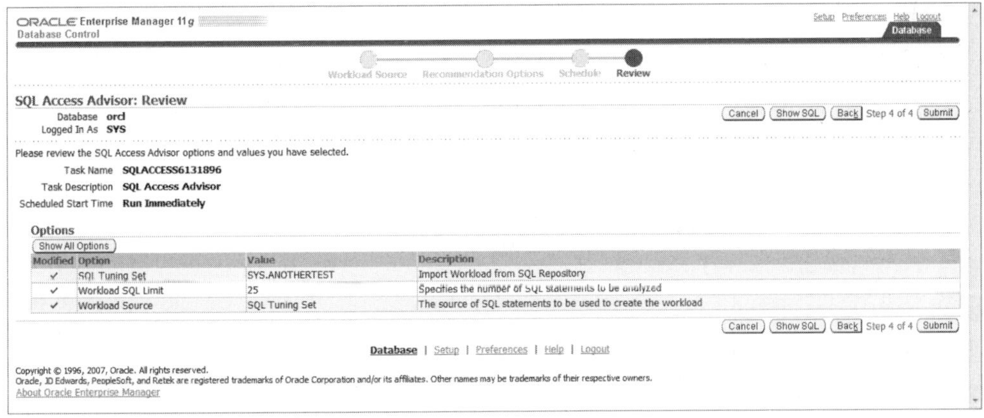

FIGURE 10.35 Monitor the SQL Access Advisor task

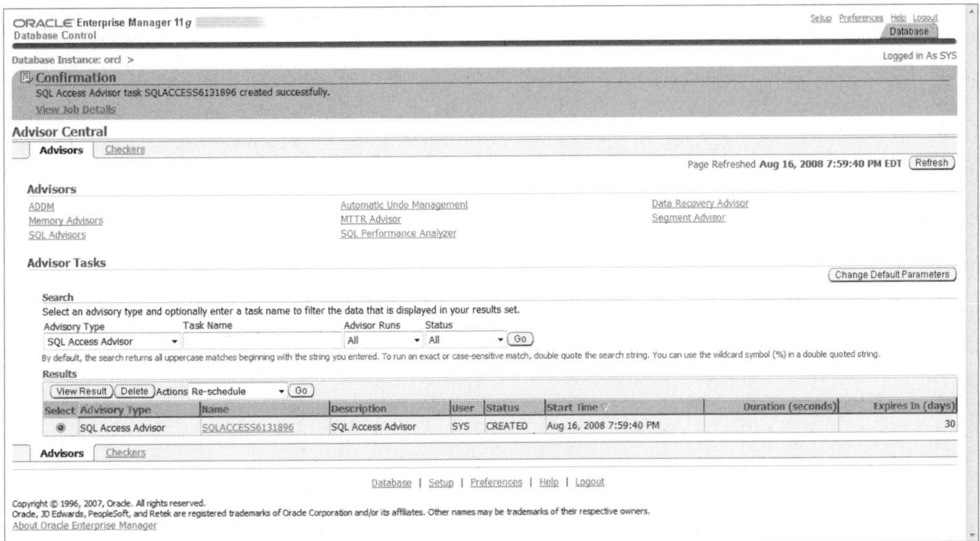

FIGURE 10.36 Results for SQL Access Advisor task

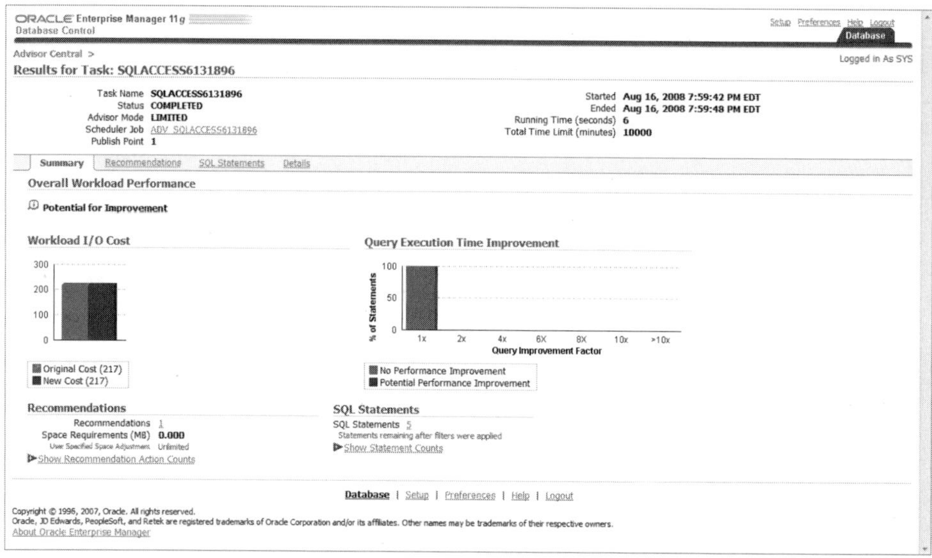

For this simplified example, there were no recommendations, as shown in Figure 10.37, because the sample tables are too small. With larger tables and more SQL statements to work with, we would see legitimate recommendations.

FIGURE 10.37 Recommendations for the SQL Access Advisor task

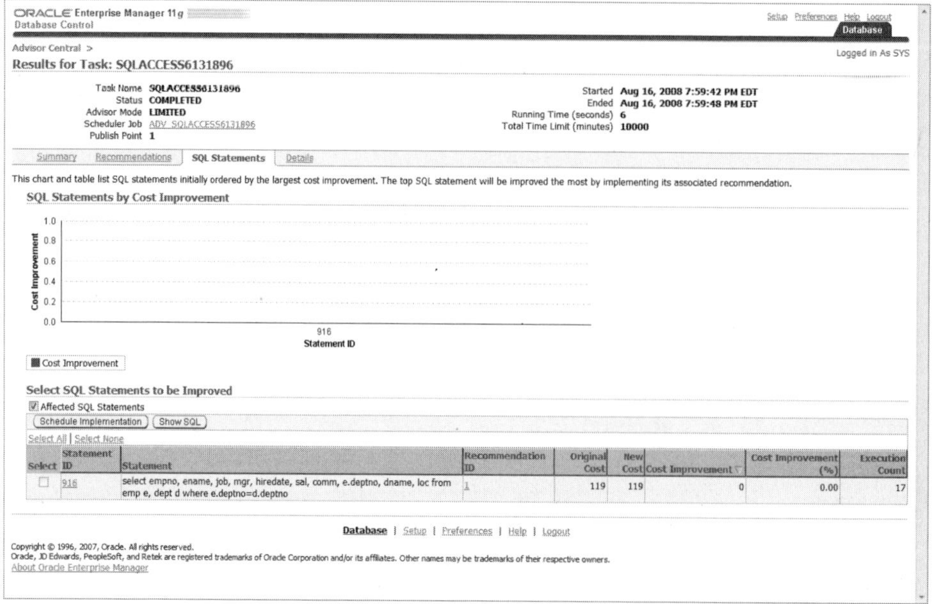

To implement the recommendations, select the recommended items and then click the Schedule Implementation button. Figure 10.38 shows the Schedule Implementation page.

Click the Submit button to implement the recommendations. The confirmation note will appear on the Results page, shown in Figure 10.39.

FIGURE 10.38 Implement recommendations for the SQL Access Advisor task

ORACLE Enterprise Manager 11g
Database Control
Setup Preferences Help Logout
Database
Advisor Central > Results for Task: SQLACCESS6131896 >
Logged in As SYS
Schedule Implementation
SQL Access Advisor will implement all recommendations from this task that are currently selected and have not yet been implemented. This implementation task will be submitted and run as a job. Go to Scheduler Jobs to check on the job status.
Cancel Show SQL Submit
* Job Name SQLACCESSIMPL1916955
Stop on Error
If checked, this implementation job will stop processing if an error occurs. If not checked, this job will ignore errors and will continue processing all actions of selected recommendations.
Scheduling Options
Schedule Type Standard
Time Zone (UTC-05:00) US Eastern Time
Repeating
Repeat Do Not Repeat
Start
Immediately
Later
Date Aug 16, 2008
(example: Aug 16, 2008)
Time 8 40 00 AM PM
Cancel Show SQL Submit
Database | Setup | Preferences | Help | Logout
Copyright © 1996, 2007, Oracle. All rights reserved.
Oracle, JD Edwards, PeopleSoft, and Retek are registered trademarks of Oracle Corporation and/or its affiliates. Other names may be trademarks of their respective owners.
About Oracle Enterprise Manager

FIGURE 10.39 Results confirmed for the SQL Access Advisor task

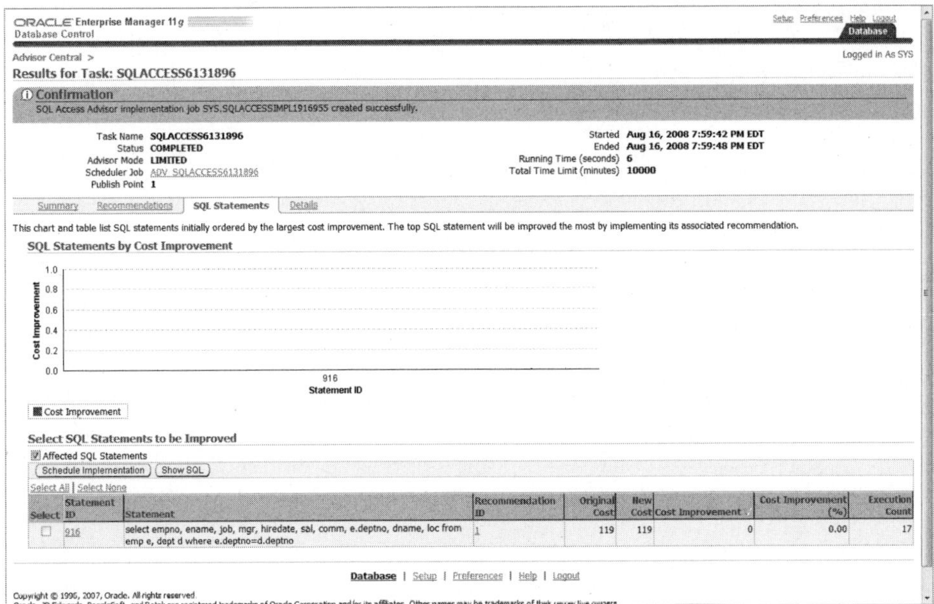

When implementing recommendations in SQL Access Advisor, be aware that certain operations will take time to complete. Partitioning an existing large table may take a long time, so keep that in mind before implementing it. The partitioning process creates a copy of the existing unpartitioned table, so make sure you have sufficient disk space for the operation.

In Exercise 10.2, you will run the SQL Access Advisor on your database instance and determine which tuning steps should be applied.

EXERCISE 10.2

Using the SQL Access Advisor

In this exercise, you will utilize the SQL Access Advisor to tune a workload. Since the workload is highly dependent on your database configuration, you will need to provide a workload, execute the advisor, and take the recommended actions.

1. Select a workload that you've already created, or create a new workload.
2. For the depth and breadth of recommendation options, you want to review only indexing recommendations.
3. Review the recommendations. If they make sense to you for your database, then implement them.

Understanding Database Replay

One of the most difficult tasks for the professional DBA is setting up and conducting valid workload performance tests. It's easy to test the performance of a single query but often very challenging to test how an entire workload will perform in a different environment. For many organizations, the cost to test a platform migration is prohibitive, and the perceived risk of not testing is too high. Organizations need to know how infrastructure changes will affect database application performance and if there's any impact to service-level agreements.

Database Replay allows the DBA to capture a workload on one database and replay it on another. Database Replay is platform-independent, so it is very useful when planning a hardware or operating-system change to understand how workload performance might also change. If you have multiple platforms or components available to test, you can conduct a valid and repeatable performance comparison. The DBA and team can utilize Database Replay to identify performance bottlenecks in the workload; determine if storage, CPU, memory, or OS changes can remove the bottlenecks; then run additional comparisons after the changes are made.

These are the basic steps of Database Replay:

- Capture the database workload.
- Preprocess the workload.
- Replay the workload.
- Analyze the workload.

Let's look at each of these individually.

Capture a Workload

We start by capturing all the external client requests performed against a database and writing the information to a platform-independent binary capture file. The workload capture contains the following client request info:

- SQL text
- Bind variable values
- Information about transactions

Workload capture can be initiated from Oracle Enterprise Manager or through the DBMS_WORKLOAD_CAPTURE package. For this text, we will focus on EM.

There a few basic steps that should be followed before capturing a workload:

- Make sure you have a replay database that is similar in data content to the capture system. You can accomplish this by using Oracle or third-party tools to keep the data synchronized close to the capture start time. Consider RMAN, a standby database, or export/import.
- Oracle recommends a clean shutdown and restart of the capture database before beginning workload capture. Start the database instance in RESTRICTED mode, start the capture, and the instance will automatically switch to UNRESTRICTED. If a database instance restart is not feasible, then quiesce the database or verify that there are no transactions running at the time the workload capture begins.
- Define either inclusion or exclusion workload filters to include or exclude specific user sessions. The default is to capture all user sessions; you can use include or exclude filters, but not both.
- Set up a capture directory, and make sure it's empty and has plenty of space. The workload capture will stop if it runs out of space.

Using Enterprise Manager, click the Software and Support tab. From the page shown in Figure 10.40, choose the Database Replay link under the Real Application Testing heading.

Note that EM provides an overview and lists the typical steps to perform a database replay, as shown in Figure 10.41.

Once all of the prerequisites are verified, you can start the workload capture by clicking on the Go to Task icon in the rightmost column of task 1, shown in Figure 10.41. In step 1, you acknowledge that the prerequisites have been met (see Figure 10.42).

Restrictions and Limitations of Workload Capture

- Only one workload capture can run at a time.
- Distributed transactions will be replayed as local transactions

The following are not captured:

- Background activities and database scheduler jobs
- Direct path load of data from external files using utilities such as SQL*Loader
- Shared server requests (Oracle MTS)
- Oracle streams
- Advanced replication streams
- Non-PL/SQL-based Advanced Queuing (AQ)
- Flashback queries
- Object navigations based on Oracle Call Interface (OCI)
- Non-SQL-based object access
- Remote DESCRIBE and COMMIT operations

In an Oracle Real Application Cluster (RAC) database, workload capture is for the database, not for a single instance. Following Oracle's recommendation to capture a clean workload, you will need to shut down and restart all instances in this manner:

1. Shut down all instances associated with the database.
2. Start one of the instances.
3. Begin the workload capture.
4. Start the remaining instances.

In step 2, you choose to restart the database and select workload filters, as shown in Figure 10.43.

In step 3, shown in Figure 10.44, you specify the name of the capture file, the directory object, and the database-instance shutdown and startup options. If the directory doesn't exist, you can create it using an OS program, and then click the Create Directory button to assign the directory to a directory object. Figure 10.44 shows confirmation that the directory object was created successfully.

FIGURE 10.40 Software and support home page

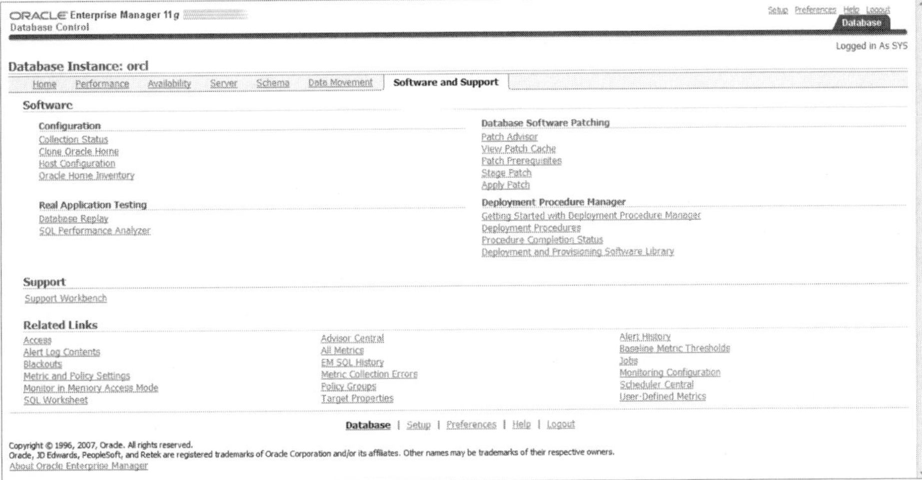

FIGURE 10.41 Database replay home page

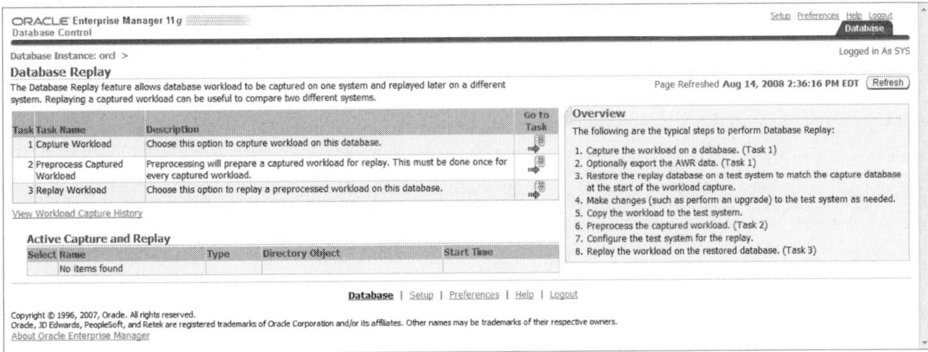

FIGURE 10.42 The Capture Workload: Plan Environment screen

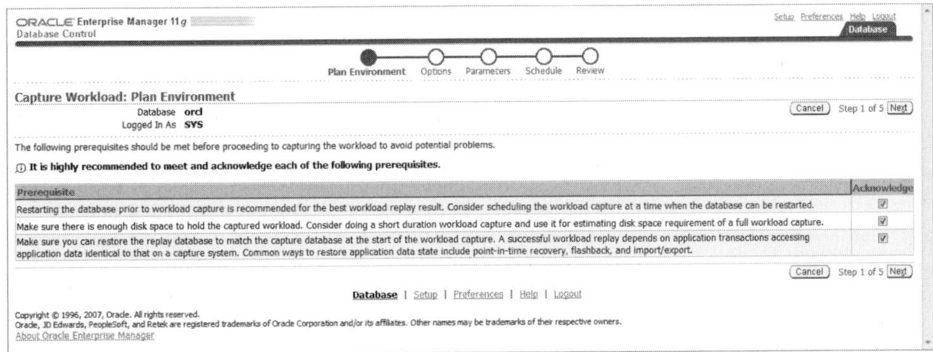

FIGURE 10.43 The Capture Workload: Options screen

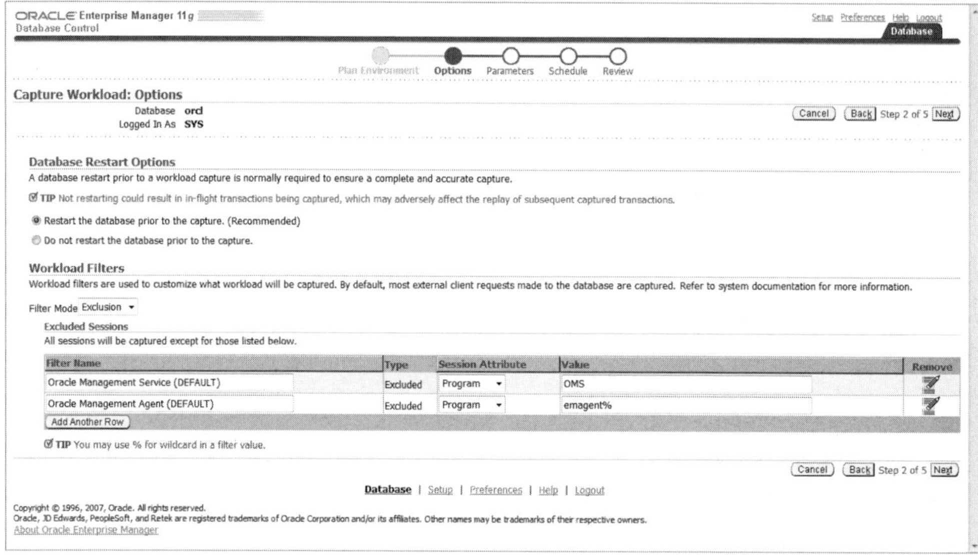

FIGURE 10.44 The Capture Workload: Parameters screen

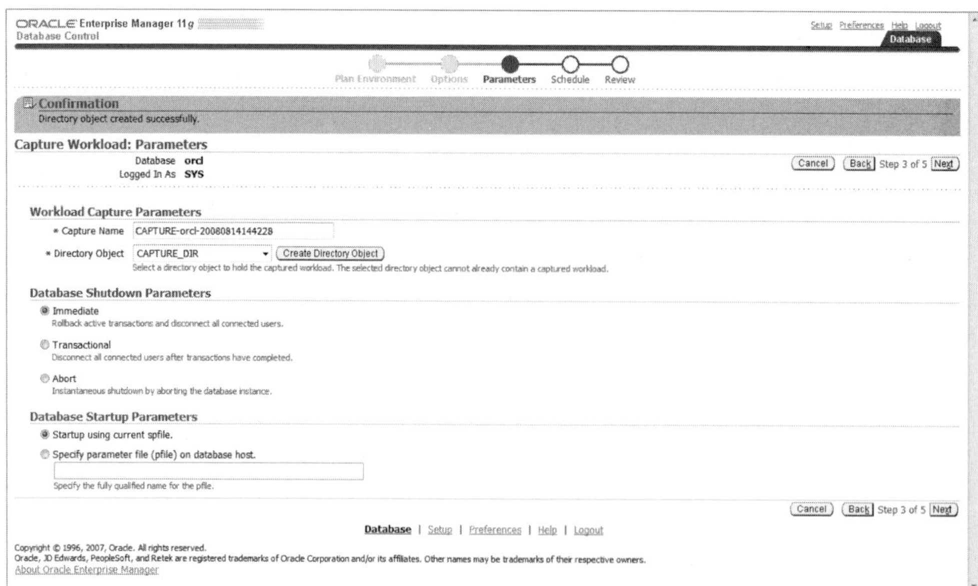

Specify the job schedule, parameters, and credentials in step 4, shown in Figure 10.45.

Step 5 is the final review and acknowledgement, shown in Figure 10.46. Click the Submit button to begin the workload capture. You will be asked to confirm that you wish to restart the database and begin the capture. If you wish to continue, click the Yes button.

FIGURE 10.45 The Capture Workload: Schedule screen

FIGURE 10.46 The Capture Workload: Review screen

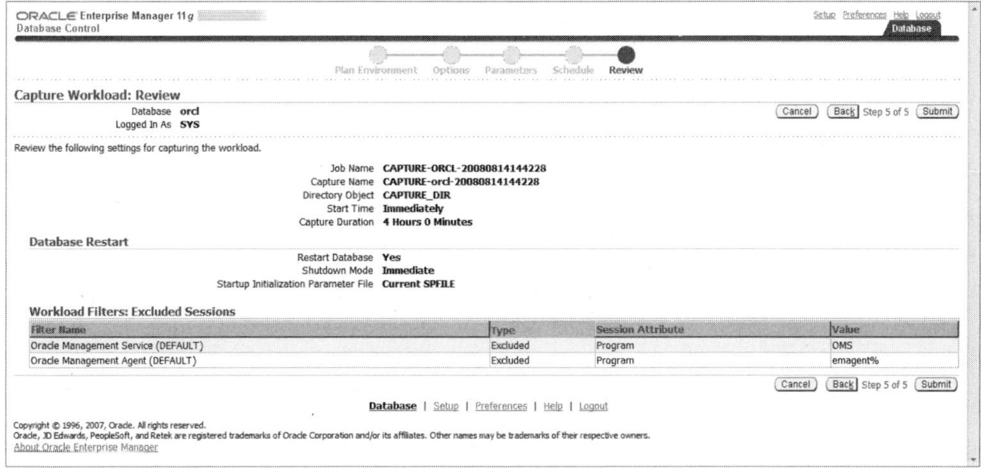

After you select yes, you will be directed to an information page (see Figure 10.47) while the database is restarted.

Click Refresh to log on to the database after it has restarted. When you log on, you will be directed to the View Workload Capture screen, shown in Figure 10.48, where you may observe the capture in progress. Click the summary icon to change the view. Click the Report button to see the detailed workload capture report. Click Stop Capture to end the workload capture. You will be asked to acknowledge before the capture is stopped. Once you stop the capture, you will be presented with the option to export the workload to the AWR workload directory. If you choose not to save the AWR data at this time, you may do so later. Click the OK button to return to the Database Replay page.

FIGURE 10.47 The Confirmation screen

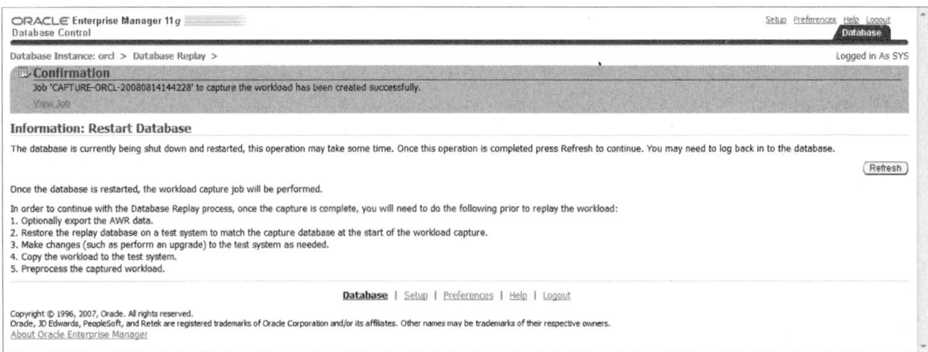

FIGURE 10.48 The View Workload Capture screen

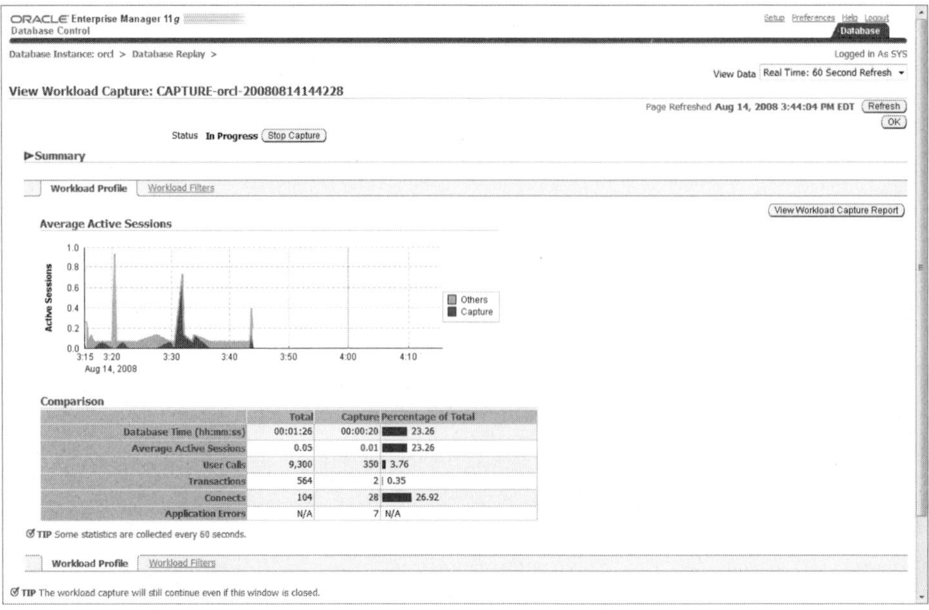

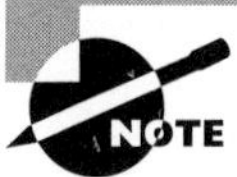

For this example, we used the general-purpose database supplied with Oracle 11*g*. We ran queries from three SQL*Plus sessions and from an MS-Access session.

Preprocess a Captured Workload

The next task is to preprocess the captured workload. Launch the task by clicking the Go to Task icon at the end of the row on task 2 (see Figure 10.49).

To preprocess a workload, select a workload directory and the relevant data will be populated to the EM screen, as shown in Figure 10.50. Once you have acknowledged the correct workload, click Preprocess Workload

FIGURE 10.49 Database Replay preprocess

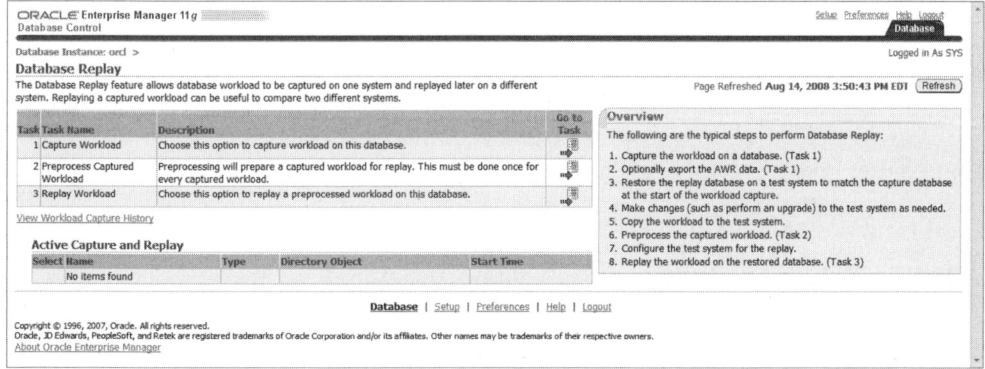

FIGURE 10.50 The Preprocess Captured Workload screen

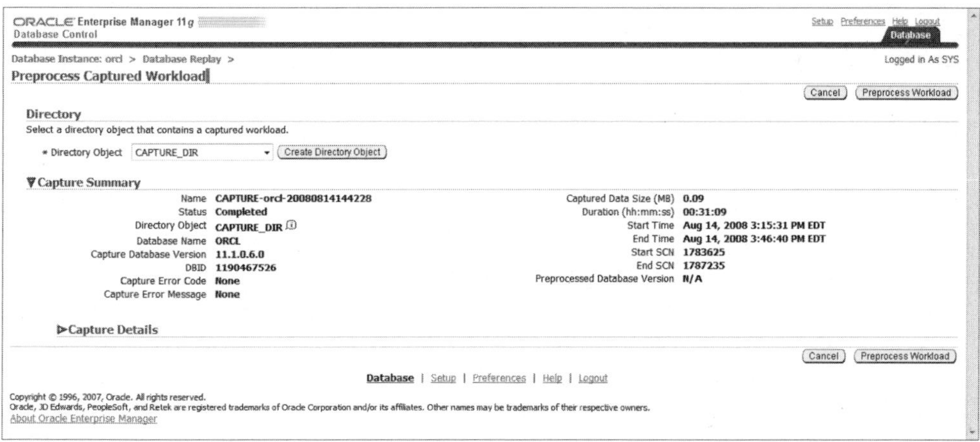

The next screen is shown in Figure 10.51; in step 1, you confirm the capture database version, username, and instance name.

In step 2, you schedule the preprocess job, as shown in Figure 10.52. For this exercise, we will start immediately upon completion of these steps. You will need to provide host OS credentials for the host machine where the database replay capture directory object resides.

In step 3, you review the preprocess job and submit it, as shown in Figure 10.53.

When the job is submitted, you will be returned to the Database Replay screen and receive confirmation that the preprocess job has been submitted, as seen in Figure 10.54. Click the refresh button to verify that the job has completed successfully.

FIGURE 10.51 The Preprocess Captured Workload: Database Version screen

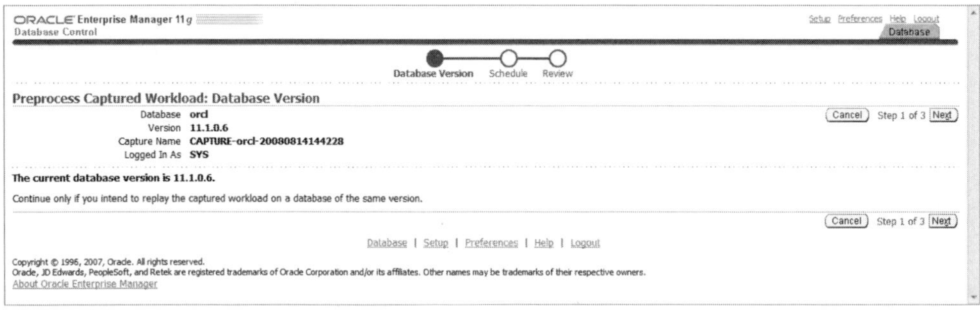

FIGURE 10.52 The Preprocess Captured Workload: Schedule screen

ORACLE Enterprise Manager 11g
Database Control
Setup Preferences Help Logout
Database
Database Version Schedule Review
Preprocess Captured Workload: Schedule
Database orcl
Version 11.1.0.6
Capture Name CAPTURE-orcl-20080814144228
Logged In As SYS
Cancel Back Step 2 of 3 Next
Specify the following to schedule the preprocessing job.
Job Parameters
* Job Name PREPROCESS-ORCL-20080814155752
Description
Start
Immediately
Later
Date Aug 14, 2008
(example: Aug 14, 2008)
Time 3 55 00 AM PM
Host Credentials
* Username Charles Pack
* Password ••••••
* Confirm Password ••••••
Save as Preferred Credential
Cancel Back Step 2 of 3 Next
Database | Setup | Preferences | Help | Logout
Copyright © 1996, 2007, Oracle. All rights reserved.
Oracle, JD Edwards, PeopleSoft, and Retek are registered trademarks of Oracle Corporation and/or its affiliates. Other names may be trademarks of their respective owners.
About Oracle Enterprise Manager

FIGURE 10.53 The Preprocess Captured Workload: Review screen

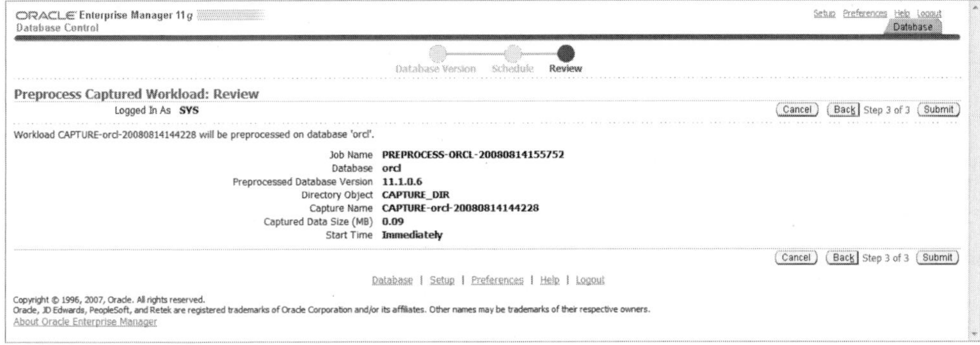

FIGURE 10.54 The job Confirmation screen

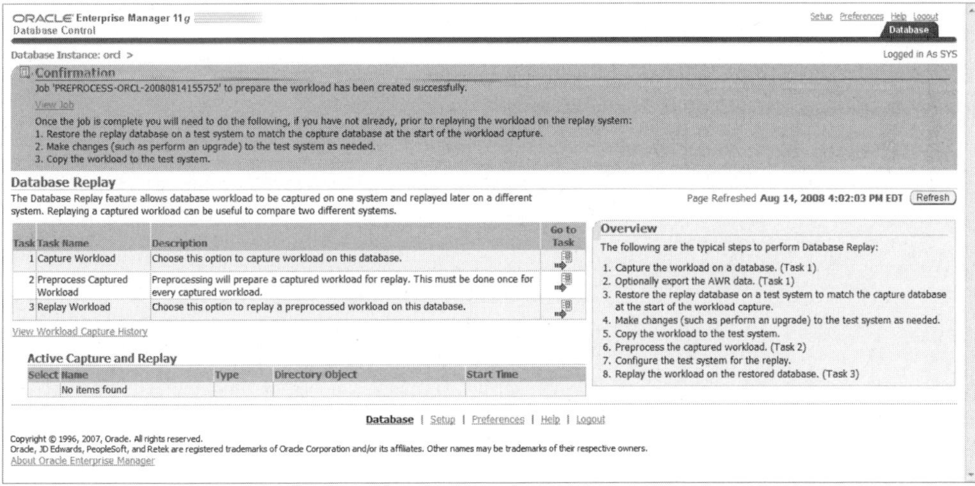

From the Database Replay home page, click the View Workload Capture History link to see the status of captured workloads, shown in Figure 10.55.

FIGURE 10.55 The View Workload Capture History screen

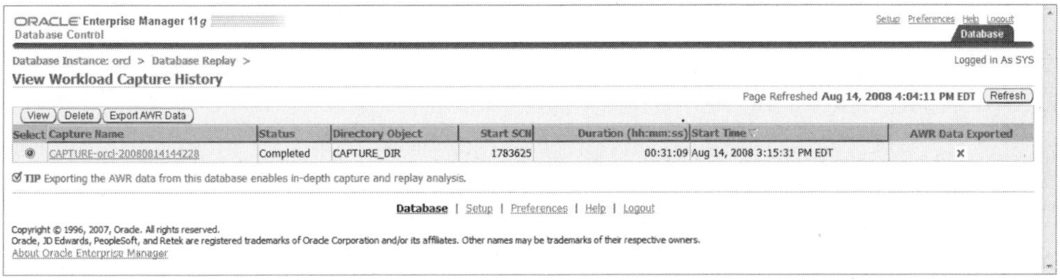

Replay a Captured Workload

To replay a workload, you need a test database that has data that's similar to the data in the capture database. We created a general-purpose database named STDB using the Database Configuration Assistant, and it is basically the same as the ORCL database we used to capture the workload.

You can perform Workload Replay using the DBMS_WORKLOAD_REPLAY supplied package, but for this example, we will use EM. From the test database EM home page, choose the Software and Support tab, and under Real Application Testing, click the Database Replay. The next page presented is the Database Replay page; in this example, we chose task 3, replay workload. Note that in Figure 10.56, there are no active captures or replays at this time.

As we did during workload capture, we need to specify a directory object, as shown in Figure 10.57, and provide OS credentials to create the directory. Once it's created, click the Test File System button to verify and then click OK.

The confirmation page in Figure 10.58 gives you the chance to verify the playback information before continuing. Click the Setup Replay button to continue.

FIGURE 10.56 Database Replay home page

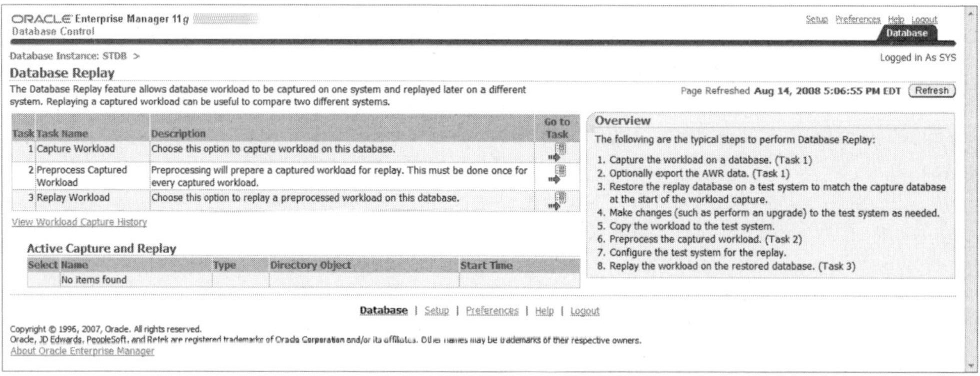

FIGURE 10.57 The Create Directory Object screen

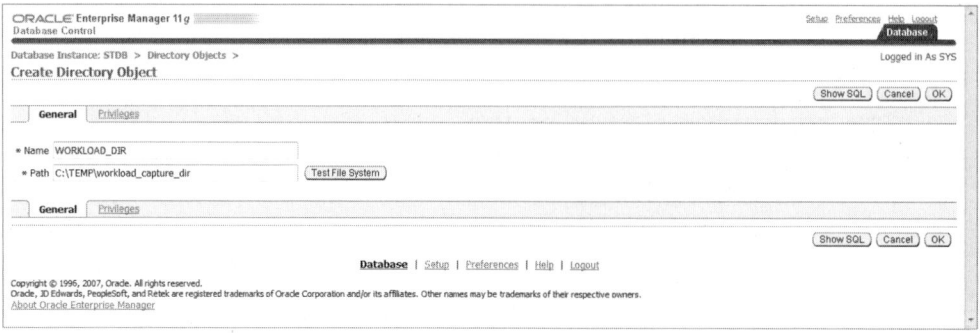

ORACLE Enterprise Manager 11g
Database Control
Setup Preferences Help Logout
Database
Database Instance: STDB > Directory Objects >
Logged in As SYS
Create Directory Object
Show SQL Cancel OK
General Privileges
* Name WORKLOAD_DIR
* Path C:\TEMP\workload_capture_dir Test File System
General Privileges
Show SQL Cancel OK
Database | Setup | Preferences | Help | Logout
Copyright © 1996, 2007, Oracle. All rights reserved.
Oracle, JD Edwards, PeopleSoft, and Retek are registered trademarks of Oracle Corporation and/or its affiliates. Other names may be trademarks of their respective owners.
About Oracle Enterprise Manager

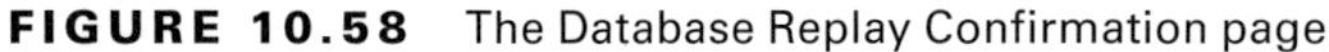

FIGURE 10.58 The Database Replay Confirmation page

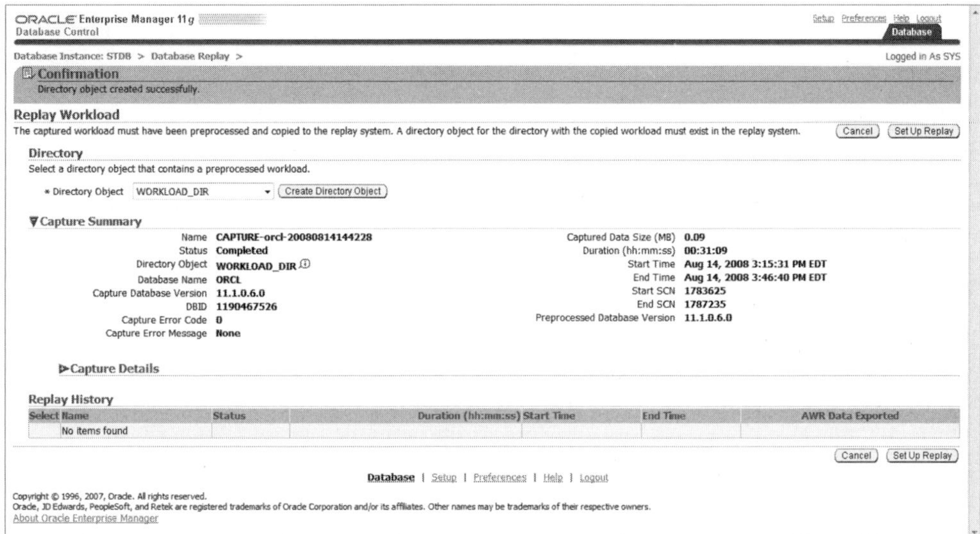

The next page, shown in Figure 10.59, reminds you to verify each of the prerequisites before continuing. If you have verified that each of the prerequisites has been met and you're ready to continue, click the Continue button.

The page shown in Figure 10.60 reminds you that Database Replay should be performed on an isolated test system and to make sure there are no external references on the target test database. Verify that there are no DB links, directory objects, or streams. When you're ready to proceed, click the Continue button.

FIGURE 10.59 Database Replay prerequisites

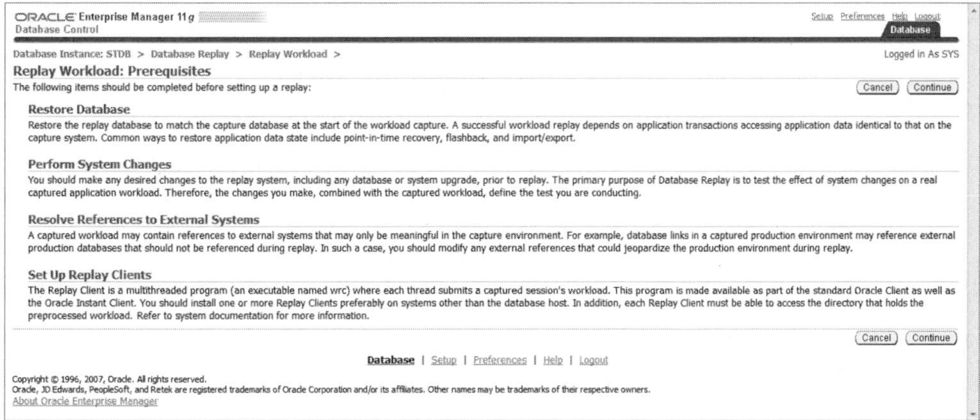

FIGURE 10.60 Database Replay external references

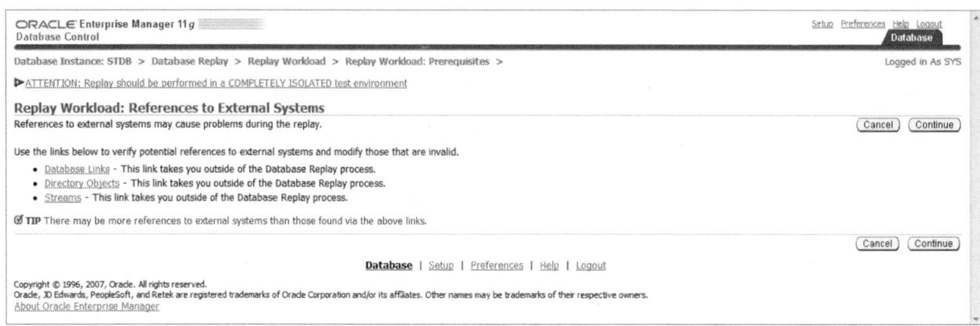

Step 1 of the replay options, Choose Initial Options, allows you to add a custom name for the replay. See Figure 10.61.

In step 2, Customize Options, you can modify the connection mappings on the first page, shown in Figure 10.62, and choose the replay parameters on the second page, shown in Figure 10.63. On the Connection Mappings page, you can designate a connect descriptor and test it; use a single TNS net service name for each client, or use separate connect descriptors for each client.

In step 3, shown in Figure 10.64, you are reminded to prepare the replay clients. You will run the replay clients from the OS, not within Enterprise Manager, so now is a good time to make sure you're ready to run the clients. Click Next to continue.

FIGURE 10.61 The Choose Initial Options screen

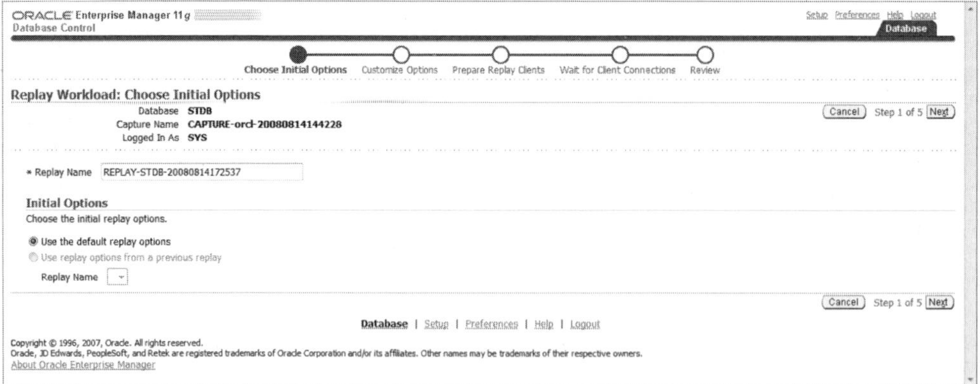

FIGURE 10.62 Database Replay connection mappings

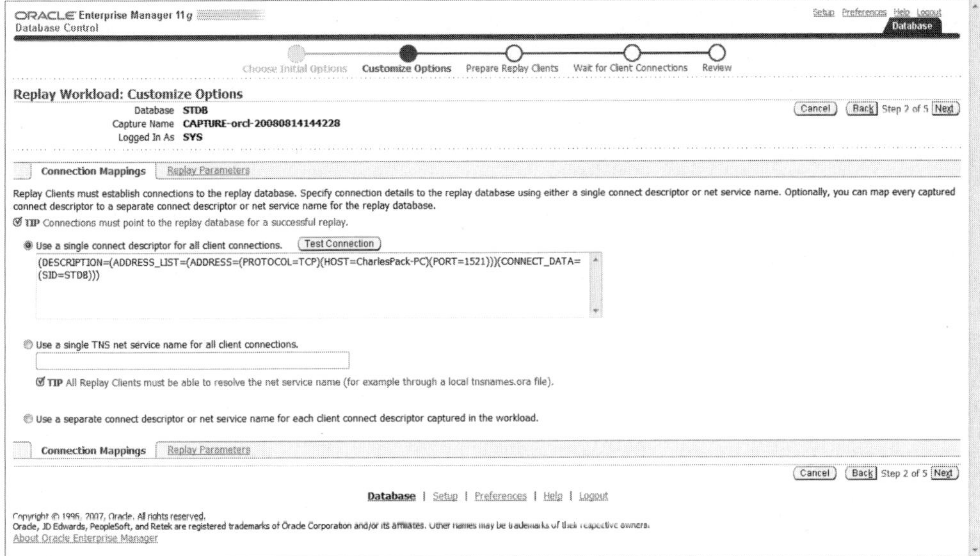

FIGURE 10.63 Database Replay replay parameters

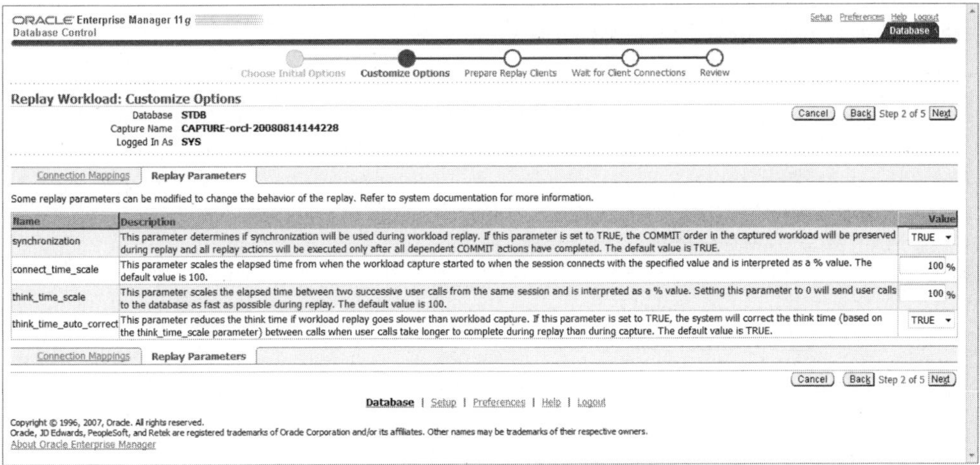

FIGURE 10.64 The Prepare Replay Clients screen

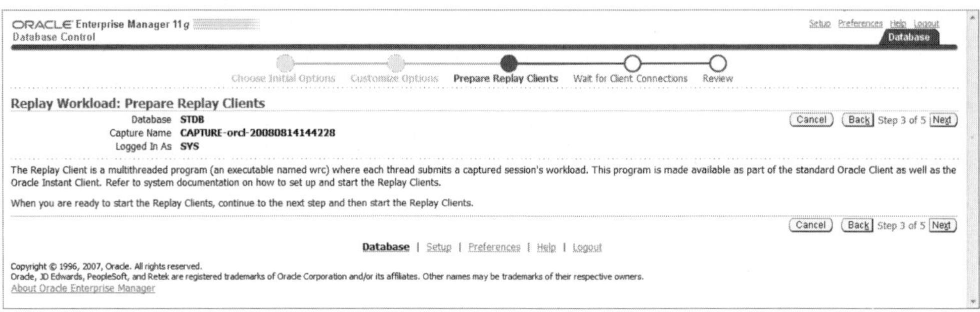

In step 4, shown in Figure 10.65, you start the replay clients externally, wait on them to connect, and confirm when they do. To start a replay client, you'll need to execute the `$ORACLE_HOME\bin\wrc` program with the appropriate parameters. For this basic exercise, we'll pass the username and password parameters as well as the replay directory:

```
c:\oracle\bin\WRC system/stdb@stdbreplaydir=c:\temp\workload_capture_dir
Workload Replay Client: Release 11.1.0.6.0 - Production
on Thu Aug 14 19:10:56 2008
Copyright (c) 1982, 2007, Oracle. All rights reserved.
Wait for the replay to start (19:10:56)
```

FIGURE 10.65 Database Replay client connections

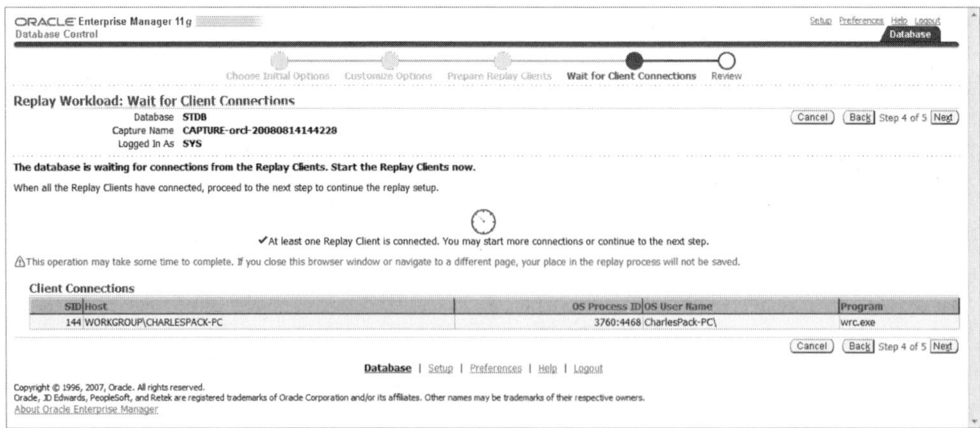

Once the clients have connected, click Next to continue.

On the Review page, shown in Figure 10.66, you are instructed to reset the system time on the test database server to match the start time of the workload capture. You then begin the replay by clicking the Submit button.

FIGURE 10.66 Database Replay review

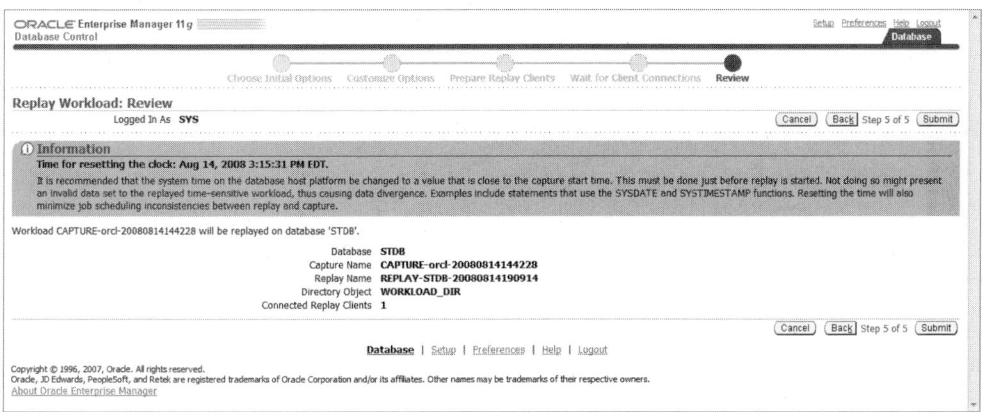

Once the replay has begun, you can monitor the progress, as shown in Figure 10.67. At the OS prompt where you ran the wc command, you'll notice an acknowledgement that the replay has started, and the replay start time matches the system time:

```
Replay started (15:16:51)
```

FIGURE 10.67 The View Workload Replay screen

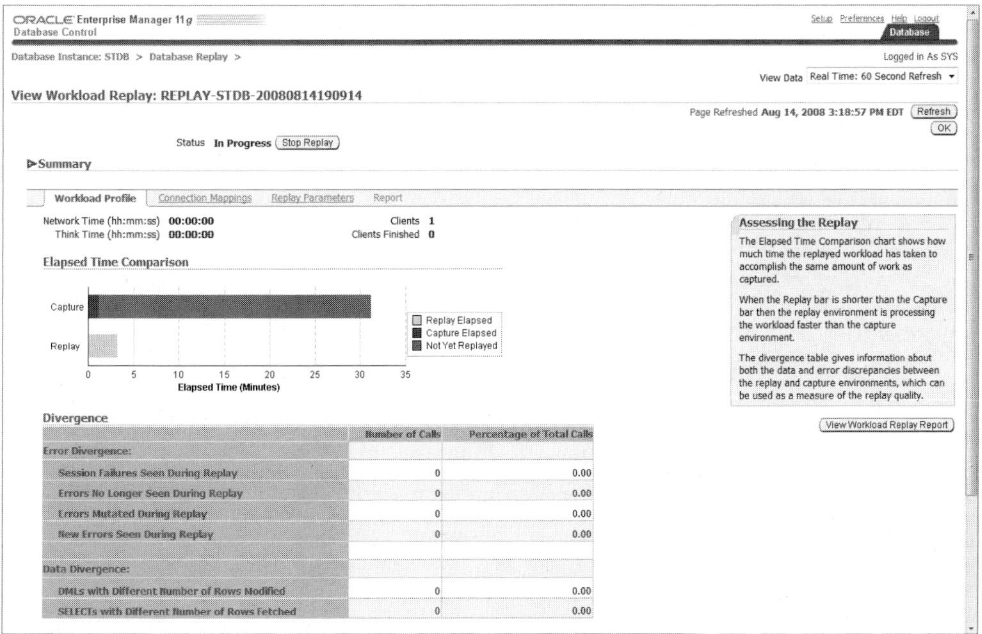

When the replay is complete, the command window will indicate replay completion time. You can then view the report and analyze the results:

```
Replay finished (15:51:19)
```

Analyze the Workload Replay Results

The basic steps to analyze the results are to view the capture report, view the replay report, and compare the results. To view the capture report from the database replay page in EM, click the View Workload Capture History link, select the capture report you wish to analyze, and then click the View button. On the subsequent capture summary page, click the View Workload Capture Report button.

We will not go into a detailed analysis of the report, but there are a few key sections of the report to review:

- Workload Captured
- Workload Not Captured
- SQL Text
- Workload Filters

To view the replay report, connect to the replay database using EM. From the database replay page, click the replay workload Go to Task icon. From the drop-down box, choose the directory object for the replay. When the Replay Workload page is populated with capture summary and replay history information, select the appropriate replay name and then click the Replay History View button. Once the workload replay summary is presented, click the View Workload Replay Report button, shown in Figure 10.68.

FIGURE 10.68 The View Workload Replay summary

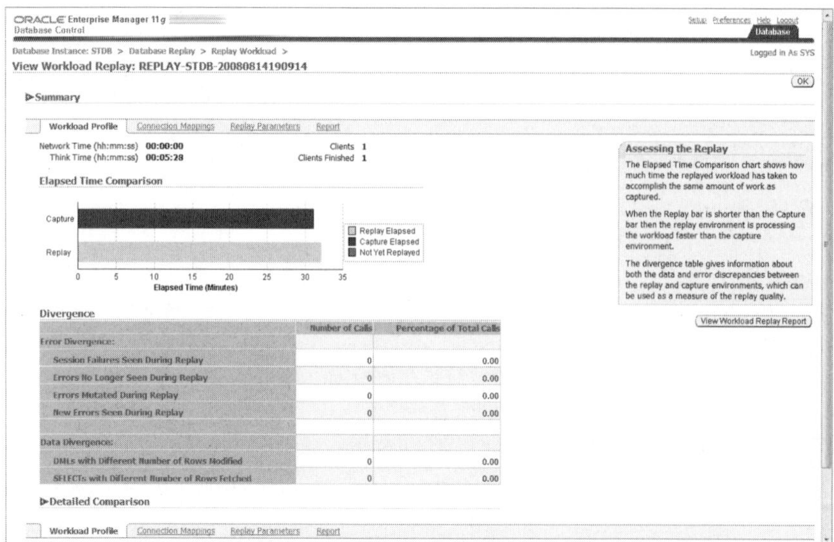

Key items to look for in the replay report are top SQL statements, performance divergence, data divergence, and error divergence. Performance divergence is usually due to infrastructure or configuration differences between the capture and replay environments. In this example, the replay took longer than the capture, so we need to further investigate to determine the bottlenecks in the test system. Data divergence occurs when the DML and SQL statement results in the replay system and capture system do not match. Error divergence is when the errors that occur do not match.

In Exercise 10.3, you will capture a Database Replay workload on a source database and replay it on a destination database.

EXERCISE 10.3

Performing Database Replay

In this exercise you will use the Database Replay feature to compare workload performance between a source database and a destination database.

1. Create a replay database as a copy of the capture database. One method is to use RMAN to make a clone. You could also use the DBCA to create a new capture database and a replay database.
2. Capture a workload on the source database.
3. Preprocess the workload capture.
4. Replay the workload on the destination database.
5. Analyze the results.

Summary

In this chapter, you learned about tools that help the DBA diagnose problems in the database and tools that assist with detecting and resolving performance issues.

In the first part, we introduced the Automatic Diagnostic Repository (ADR), the new central repository for storing all database diagnostic information, and the Support Workbench, which the DBA uses for problem recognition, reporting, and resolution. The Support Workbench improves DBA productivity by providing a process and web pages to report, analyze, and send diagnostic information to Oracle Support for problem resolution. Block media recovery improvements in 11*g* include faster automatic recognition of corrupt blocks and faster block recovery using the flashback logs.

In the second part, we introduced the SQL Tuning Advisor, the SQL Access Advisor, and Database Replay. To help improve the performance of SQL statements, the SQL Tuning Advisor recommends new or modified indexes, SQL profiles, rewriting your SQL statements, or using statistics. The SQL Access Advisor looks at workgroups and recommends indexes, partitioning, and materialized views to improve the performance of a workload. Database Replay is an extremely useful tool that allows the DBA to capture and replay a workload to compare the performance of one system to another.

Exam Essentials

Know how to set up the Automatic Diagnostic Repository. Make sure you understand the new initialization parameter for ADR, which parameters are deprecated, and the basic directory structure of the ADR.

Know how to use the Support Workbench to report an incident. Know the steps required to open a service request with Oracle Support. Know how to package and submit the files related to a problem incident.

Know how to perform block media recovery. Know how to discover corrupt data blocks, what causes data corruption, and how to repair corrupt data blocks. Know what can contribute to faster recoveries. Know what is required to perform block media recovery.

Understand automatic and manual SQL tuning. Understand the differences between automatic and manual SQL tuning using the Tuning Advisor. Understand the advantages and potential dangers of automatic SQL tuning. Understand how to use the SQL Tuning Advisor in manual mode.

Understand the SQL Access Advisor. Know what types of changes and types of indexes the SQL Access Advisor may recommend. Understand the impact of implementing recommendations.

Know when to use Database Replay. Know the purpose and uses for Database Replay. Know what is required to set up and perform Database Replay. Know how to compare results from the production workload and the replay workload.

Review Questions

1. Which of the following initialization parameters have been deprecated in Oracle 11*g* because of the introduction of the Automatic Workload Repository? (Choose all that apply.)

   A. BACKGROUND_DUMP_DEST

   B. FOREGROUND_DUMP_DEST

   C. CORE_DUMP_DEST

   D. USER_DUMP_DEST

   E. DIAGNOSTIC_DEST

   F. All of the above

2. Which of the following statements is true regarding the initialization parameter DIAGNOSTIC_DEST?

   A. The default value is the value of the environment variable $ORACLE_HOME; if $ORACLE_HOME isn't set, then the default is set to $ORACLE_BASE.

   B. The default value is the value of the environment variable $ORACLE_BASE; if $ORACLE_BASE isn't set, then it is set to $ORACLE_HOME.

   C. DIAGNOSTIC_DEST is always equal to $ORACLE_HOME.

   D. DIAGNOSTIC_DEST is always equal to $ORACLE_BASE.

3. Which of these formats represents the correct hierarchy for the ADR?

   A. <diagnostic_dest>/rdbms/diag/<dbname>/<instname>

   B. <diagnostic_dest>/diag/rdbms/<instname>/<dbname>

   C. <diagnostic_dest>/diag/rdbms/<dbname>/<instname>

   D. None of the above

4. Which of the following are not fundamental tasks of the Support Workbench? (Choose all that apply.)

   A. View long-running SQL workloads

   B. View problem details

   C. Gather additional diagnostic information

   D. Create a Service Request

   E. Clean up incident data after upload to Oracle Support

5. Which of the following tasks does the tool Incident Packaging Service (IPS) perform?
   A. Cleans up the ADR by deleting files not associated with an incident uploaded to Oracle Support.
   B. Identifies all files associated with a critical error and adds them to a zip file to be sent to Oracle Support.
   C. Automatically opens a Service Request with Oracle Support for each critical error and sends all relevant files.
   D. Displays a high-level view of critical errors on the database home page.

6. Choose the correct order to package and upload data for an incident to Oracle Support.
   A. Schedule, create new package, view manifest, view contents
   B. Create new package, view manifest, view contents, schedule
   C. Schedule, create new package, view contents, view manifest
   D. Create new package, view contents, view manifest, schedule
   E. None of the above.

7. Which of the following is *not* an advantage of block media recovery (BMR)?
   A. Reduced MTTR.
   B. Datafiles remain offline while corrupt blocks are repaired.
   C. Datafiles remain online while corrupt blocks are repaired.
   D. A and C

8. Which of the following methods can be used to detect block corruption?
   A. ANALYZE operations
   B. dbv
   C. SQL queries that access the potentially corrupt block
   D. RMAN
   E. All of the above

9. Which of the following are correct about block media recovery? (Choose all that apply.)
   A. Physical and logical block corruption is recorded automatically in `V$DATABASE_BLOCK_CORRUPTION`.
   B. Logical corruptions are repairable by BMR.
   C. Physical corruptions are repairable by BMR.
   D. RMAN can use any backup for a BMR restore.
   E. ARCHIVELOG mode is not required if you have both a full and incremental backup for restore.

10. While querying the EMPLOYEES table, you receive an ORA-01578 message indicating block corruption in File# 1201 and Block# 1968. You analyze the table and the corruption is verified. Which RMAN command do you use to perform BMR and repair the corrupt block?

    A. `RECOVER FILE=1201 BLOCK=1968;`

    B. `RECOVER CORRUPTION LIST;`

    C. `RECOVER DATAFILE 1201 BLOCK 1968;`

    D. `RECOVER BLOCK CORRUPTION LIST;`

    E. None of the above

11. To view the results of the most recent Automatic SQL Tuning Advisor task, which sequence should you follow?

    A. EM Database home page, Software and Support, SQL Advisors, Automatic SQL Tuning Advisor.

    B. EM Database home page, Software and Support, Advisor Central, SQL Advisors, Automatic SQL Tuning Advisor.

    C. EM Database home page, Software and Support, Support Workbench, Advisor Central, SQL Advisors, Automatic SQL Tuning Advisor.

    D. Either B or C.

    E. All of the above

12. When creating a SQL tuning set, which of the following steps allows the DBA to reduce the size of the SQL set by selecting specific operators and values?

    A. Filter versions

    B. Filter loads

    C. Filter tasks

    D. Filter options

13. To view the results of a manual SQL Tuning Advisor task, which steps should the DBA take?

    A. From the Advisor Central home page, select the tuning task from the Advisor Tasks section.

    B. From Advisor Central, choose SQL Advisors, SQL Tuning Advisors, Manual Tuning Task Results.

    C. From Advisor Central, choose SQL Advisors, Manual SQL Tuning Advisors, Tuning Task Results.

    D. Either B or C.

14. Which of these appropriately describes the results of a manual SQL Tuning Advisor task?

    A. A list of SQL statements and recommendations for tuning

    B. A list of SQL statements that have been tuned by the Advisor, with before and after metrics

    C. Graphs showing the actual performance improvement made by the Advisor after it implemented the recommended changes

    D. All of the above

15. Which of the following is a potential performance tuning recommendation from the SQL Access Advisor?
    A. Create new indexes.
    B. Modify existing indexes.
    C. Implement partitioning on a nonpartitioned table.
    D. Create materialized views.
    E. All of the above

16. Which statement most accurately describes the implementation of a SQL Access Advisor recommendation?
    A. SQL Access Advisor recommendations are automatically implemented.
    B. Individual SQL Access Advisor recommendations can be scheduled for implementation.
    C. All SQL Access Advisor recommendations for a specific task must be implemented at the same time.
    D. SQL Access Advisor recommendations are automatically scheduled for implementation during the maintenance window.
    E. None of the above.

17. Which of the following represents the correct sequence of events for Database Replay?
    A. Capture, analyze, preprocess, replay
    B. Capture, preprocess, analyze, replay
    C. Capture, preprocess, replay, analyze
    D. Analyze, capture, preprocess, replay
    E. None of the above

18. Which of these recommendations should be followed before capturing a workload? (Choose all that apply.)
    A. Make sure your replay database has the same structure as the capture database, except without data.
    B. Make sure the replay and capture databases are similar in data content.
    C. Perform a clean shutdown and restart of the capture database before beginning a workload capture.
    D. Start the capture database in UNRESTRICTED mode, then start the capture.
    E. Define inclusion and exclusion filters.

19. Which is true concerning Database Replay in an Oracle Real Application Cluster (RAC) database?

A. Workload capture is per instance.

B. You only need to restart one instance to begin workload capture.

C. Specifically in RAC, you shut down all instances, restart them individually, and begin workload capture with the last instance started.

D. RAC does not support workload capture, but it does support workload replay.

E. None of the above.

20. Performance divergence indicated in the Workload Replay report is most likely due to what?

A. DML and SQL statement results that do not match between the capture and replay systems

B. When errors that occur in the capture system don't occur in the replay system

C. Top SQL statements

D. Infrastructure or system-configuration differences

E. Time-of-day differences between capture and replay systems

Answers to Review Questions

1. A, C, D. FOREGROUND_DUMP_DEST is not a valid initialization parameter, so option B is incorrect. DIAGNOSTIC_DEST is the new parameter that replaces the parameters in options A, C, and D, so E is incorrect.

2. B. When $ORACLE_BASE is set, it is the default value for DIAGNOSTIC_DEST.

3. C. Option A is incorrect because the correct order is diag/rdbms. Option B is incorrect because the correct order is <dbname>/<instname>.

4. A, E. Options B, C, and D are each fundamental tasks of the Support Workbench problem-resolution process.

5. B. Option A is incorrect because IPS does not delete files not associated with a package that will be sent to Oracle Support. Option C is incorrect because IPS does not open an Oracle service request for each critical error. D is incorrect because IPS does not display critical errors on the database home page.

6. D. All other sequences are incorrect. D is the correct sequence. First create the new package, then view the package contents. Next view the manifest, then schedule the job to upload the data for the incident to Oracle Support.

7. B. Option A is incorrect because reduced MTTR is an advantage of BMR. Option C is incorrect because the datafiles remaining online is an advantage of BMR. Since A and C are advantages, D is also incorrect. Option B is the correct choice because it is not an advantage of BMR.

8. E. Option A is correct because if you attempt to analyze a table or index that has a corrupt block, the ANALYZE command will indicate it. Option B is correct because the dbv command (DBVERIFY utility) is used to verify the data-structure integrity of an offline datafile. DBVERIFY will let you know if the datafile fails the integrity check. Option C is correct unless you have used DBMS_REPAIR.SKIP_CORRUPT_BLOCKS to permit queries to skip corrupt blocks. D is correct because the RMAN BACKUP command will detect corruption by default.

9. A, C. Option B is incorrect because logical corruptions are not repairable by BMR. Option D is incorrect because you must use a level 0 or full backup for the restore. Option E is incorrect because ARCHIVELOG mode is a requirement for BMR.

10. B, C. Option A is incorrect because the syntax is wrong. Option D is incorrect because BLOCK doesn't belong. B is how we recover all corrupt blocks listed in V$DATABASE_BLOCK_CORRUPTION. C is the correct syntax to recover just the one block that we've identified as corrupt.

11. D. Option A is incorrect because there is no direct link on the Software and Support home page to the SQL Advisors. You use either sequence B or C to get to the SQL Advisors and to the Automatic SQL Tuning Advisor page; from there, you can see the results of the most recent Automatic SQL Tuning Advisor task.

12. D. Options A, B, and C are not valid choices when creating a SQL tuning set. During the filter options step, the DBA can choose the SQL attributes, the operator, and the values to use as filter conditions.

13. A. Option B is incorrect because there is no Manual Tuning Task Results option. C is incorrect because there is no Manual SQL Tuning Advisors option.

14. A. Option B is incorrect because the manual SQL Tuning Advisor task does not tune the SQL statements. C is incorrect for the same reason.

15. E. All of the options are correct. The SQL Access Advisor recommends indexing, partitioning, and materialized view changes to improve performance.

16. B. Option A is incorrect because SQL Access Advisor recommendations are not automatically implemented. Option C is incorrect because the DBA can choose which recommendations to schedule and implement from the task result set. D is incorrect because the recommendations are not automatically scheduled for implementation.

17. C. The correct sequence is capture, preprocess, replay, analyze.

18. B, C. Option A is incorrect because the data divergence between the capture and replay databases should be minimized. Option D is incorrect because the database should be started in RESTRICTED mode, and then the workload capture process will switch the database to UNRESTRICTED. Option E is incorrect because you can define either inclusion or exclusion filters for a workload capture, but not both.

19. E. Option A is incorrect because workload capture is for the database, not for individual instances. B is incorrect because the correct procedure is to shut down all instances before you begin workload capture. Option C is incorrect; after the shutdown of all instances, start one instance to begin workload capture, and then start the remaining instances after capture begins. Workload capture and replay are supported in RAC, so D is incorrect.

20. D. Option A is incorrect; DML and SQL results drive data divergence. Option B is incorrect because error divergence, not performance divergence, happens when errors that occur in the capture system don't occur in the replay system. Top SQL statements should behave the same in the capture and replay systems, unless there is a data-divergence issue, so C is incorrect. E is incorrect because the time of day should have no impact on differences between the capture and replay systems. It is possible that other workloads running on the capture and replay systems that have a time-of-day trend might impact performance, but that is an extraneous variable, not a cause.

Managing Database Resources

ORACLE DATABASE 11*g*: ADMINISTRATION II EXAM OBJECTIVES COVERED IN THIS CHAPTER:

✓ **Managing Memory**

- Implementing Automatic Memory Management
- Manually configure SGA parameters
- Configuring automatic PGA memory management

✓ **Space Management**

- Managing resumable space allocation
- Describe the concepts of transportable tablespaces and databases
- Reclaim wasted space from tables and indexes by using the segment shrink functionality

✓ **Managing Resources**

- Understand the Database Resource Manager
- Create and use Database Resource Manager Components

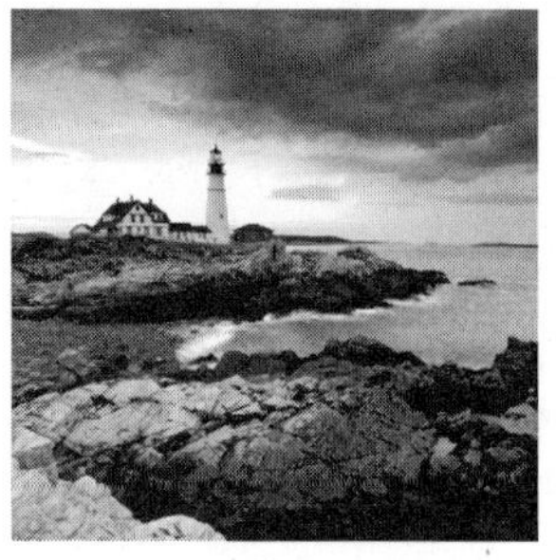

In this chapter, we will discuss how to most effectively manage memory, space, and resources. For memory management, we will discuss the Oracle 11*g* feature Automatic Memory Management, which enables the DBA to set one memory parameter for management of the instance memory. For space management, we will discuss resumable space allocation, transportable tablespaces and databases, and shrinking segments. For resource management, we will discuss the Database Resource Manager functionality and components.

Memory management is critical to database instance performance and has often been a source of frustration for Oracle DBAs. With Oracle 11g, much of the manual memory management has been replaced with automatic memory options—either to automatically manage all of the instance memory or to automatically manage the SGA and PGA as two separate pools.

We'll cover two features (resumable space allocation and shrinking segments) for managing the efficient utilization of space resources and two features (transportable tablespaces and transportable databases) for managing large-scale data movement. The resumable space allocation feature allows you to efficiently utilize space resources and prevent transaction aborts when space limitations are encountered. Shrinking segments allow you to eliminate white space in a segment in place while the segment remains online and available for application use. For large-scale movement of tablespaces from one database to another, the DBA can use the transportable tablespaces feature. To move an entire database, even to another platform, you can use the transportable database feature.

The Database Resource Manager is a robust and mature feature that allows the DBA to manage scarce session, I/O, and CPU resources within an Oracle instance. The Database Resource Manager allows you to create groups, policies, and plans to control the utilization of system resources.

Throughout this chapter, we will show command-line and Oracle Enterprise Manager methods for managing memory, space, and resources.

Exam objectives are subject to change at any time without prior notice and at Oracle's sole discretion. Please visit Oracle's Training and Certification website (`http://www.oracle.com/education/certification/`) for the most current exam-objectives listing.

Managing Memory

In the following sections, we will first cover Automatic Memory Management, new to Oracle 11*g*, which allows the DBA to set one initialization parameter and then leave the memory management up to the Oracle instance. Our next topic for memory management is manually configuring System Global Area (SGA) parameters. DBAs who need more granular control over the SGA pools will find this discussion useful. We will then discuss configuring automatic Program Global Area (PGA) memory management.

Implementing Automatic Memory Management

In Oracle 11g, the DBA has the opportunity to set one initialization parameter and allow Oracle to manage the size of the SGA and instance PGA automatically. When you set the value of MEMORY_TARGET, Oracle will automatically resize the SGA and PGA components dynamically based on processing demands for optimal database performance. The instance will automatically deallocate and allocate memory between the SGA and instance PGA as needed. Automatic Memory Management, when enabled, automatically adjusts the cache and pool sizes as needed to keep the database performing optimally.

Automatic Memory Management is supported on Linux, Solaris, Windows, HP-UX, and AIX.

When you create a new database in Oracle 11g, the default is to use Automatic Memory Management. You can adjust individual SGA component minimum values to ensure that minimum performance thresholds are not compromised. However, the instance monitors the performance of each memory component and adjusts as necessary as workloads change to provide optimal performance.

Automatic Memory Management Options

To enable Automatic Memory Management for the instance, set the value of MEMORY_TARGET in the spfile. Also, MEMORY_MAX_TARGET sets the upper bound for MEMORY_TARGET. You can adjust MEMORY_TARGET dynamically up to the value of MEMORY_MAX_TARGET; however, MEMORY_MAX_TARGET is not a dynamic initialization parameter and will require an instance restart for a modification to take effect.

```
NAME                                 TYPE        VALUE
------------------------------------ ----------- ------
...
memory_max_target                    big integer 1000M
memory_target                        big integer 816M
...
SQL>
```

If you don't set MEMORY_MAX_TARGET, it will default to the value of MEMORY_TARGET. By setting these values, you have set the maximum memory size that will be used by Oracle to manage all instance PGA and SGA objects.

If you would like more granular control over the SGA or instance PGA, Oracle will allow you to manage them manually with the Automatic Shared Memory Management, Manual Shared Memory Management, Automatic PGA Memory Management, or Manual PGA Memory Management option.

Oracle strongly recommends that you enable Automatic Memory Management and let the Oracle instance manage the memory components on your system. If you choose not to use Automatic Memory Management, use the Memory Advisor in Enterprise Manager to assist you with your instance memory configuration.

Automatic Shared Memory Management

To exercise control over the SGA, you'll need to disable Automatic Memory Management and enable Automatic Shared Memory Management for the SGA by setting MEMORY_TARGET to zero and setting the values for SGA_MAX_SIZE and SGA_TARGET. You will also need to verify that the value of STATISTICS_LEVEL is set to TYPICAL or ALL. These parameters are dynamic, with the exception of SGA_MAX_SIZE, which requires an instance restart to take effect.

```
NAME                                 TYPE        VALUE
------------------------------------ ----------- -----
lock_sga                             boolean     FALSE
...
sga_max_size                         big integer 600M
sga_target                           big integer 0
SQL>
```

Now that you have set the values for SGA_TARGET and SGA_MAX_SIZE, Oracle will manage the individual components of the SGA for optimal performance up to the SGA_TARGET value. You can dynamically increase the size of the SGA up to the value of SGA_MAX_SIZE, and Oracle will resize the pools as needed to take advantage of the additional memory.

When setting the value for SGA_TARGET, you'll need to consider the combined sizes of the different SGA memory pools:

- Default pool of database buffer cache DB_CACHE_SIZE
- Shared pool SHARED_POOL_SIZE
- Large pool LARGE_POOL_SIZE
- Java pool JAVA_POOL_SIZE
- Streams pool STREAMS_POOL_SIZE

You can set the value for each of the associated initialization parameters to a nonzero value, and that value will indicate the minimum size for each pool. If you dynamically set SGA_TARGET to zero, you will disable Automatic Shared Memory Management and the current sizes of the pools will not change dynamically. You can manually change the sizes of the pools as needed by using the ALTER SYSTEM command.

The following pools are not impacted by Automatic Shared Memory Management; they are manually sized:

- KEEP, RECYCLE, and non-default block-size buffer cache pools
- Fixed SGA and other internal memory structures
- Log buffer

The values of these manually configured pools are subtracted from the value of SGA_TARGET.

When you disable Automatic Memory Management and enable Automatic Shared Memory Management, you also enable Automatic PGA Memory Management. We'll discuss Automatic PGA Memory Management later in this chapter.

Automatic Memory Management and Enterprise Manager

To use Enterprise Manager to configure and manage the Automatic Memory Management features, access the Memory Advisors page from the Advisor Central home page. You'll see the following information, also displayed in Figure 11.1:

- Whether Automatic Memory Management is enabled and the ability to toggle between enabled and disabled
- The current total and maximum memory size and advice
- Memory allocation history
- Tabs for SGA and PGA memory configuration details

FIGURE 11.1 Memory Advisors page

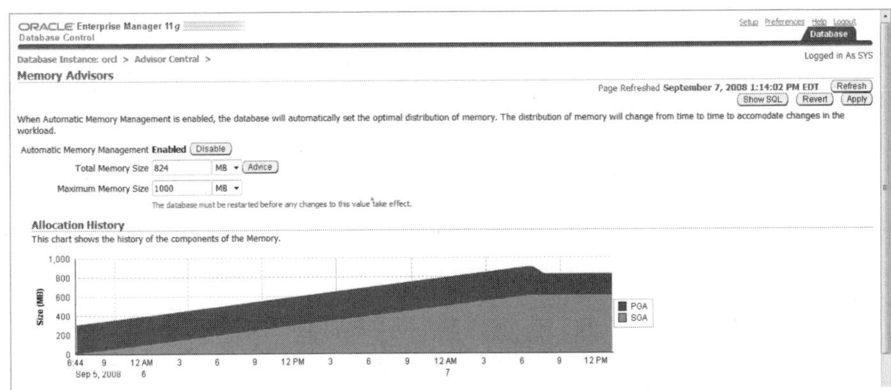

In Figure 11.2, we show the default lower half of the page displayed in Figure 11.1. This half of the page displays the detailed SGA configuration, which includes the SGA allocation history chart, the current SGA component MB allocated, and a pie chart showing the current SGA pool percentages:

- Shared pool
- Buffer cache
- Large pool
- Java pool
- Other

FIGURE 11.2 Memory Advisor SGA detail

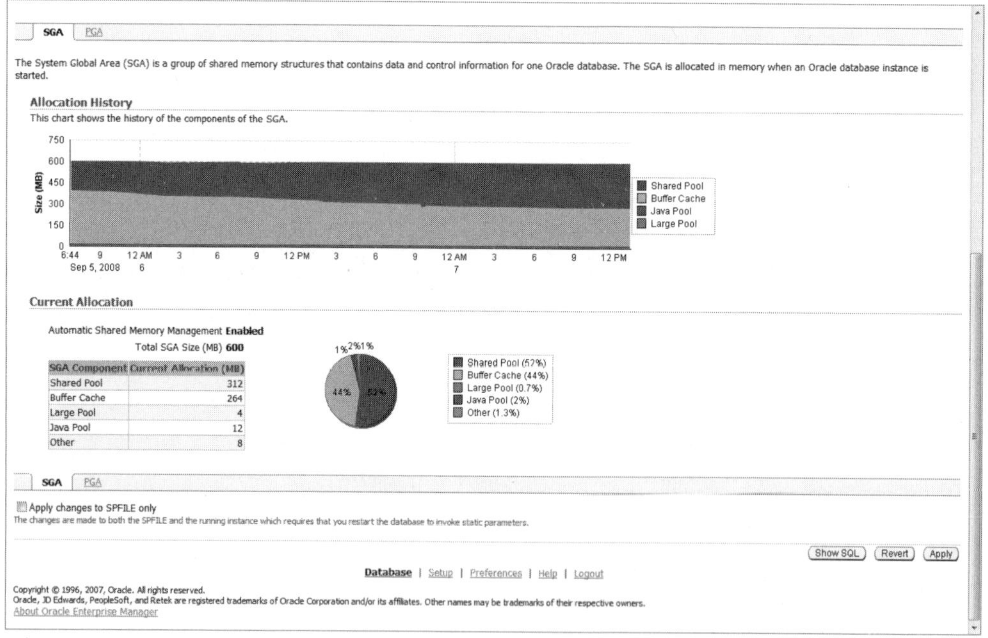

SGA Component	Current Allocation (MB)
Shared Pool	312
Buffer Cache	264
Large Pool	4
Java Pool	12
Other	8

In Figure 11.3, we show the PGA details, which are viewed by clicking the PGA tab of the Memory Advisors page. Shown are the aggregate PGA target, current PGA allocated, maximum PGA allocated, and the cache hit percentage.

You can click the PGA Memory Usage Details button to see the current work area size executions, as shown in Figure 11.4. The chart shows the following:

- Optimal executions
- One-pass executions
- Multipass executions

On this page you have the options to change the chart view to see execution percentages and number of executions and also show memory-usage details for the PGA target that you choose from the drop-down list.

FIGURE 11.3 Memory Advisor PGA detail

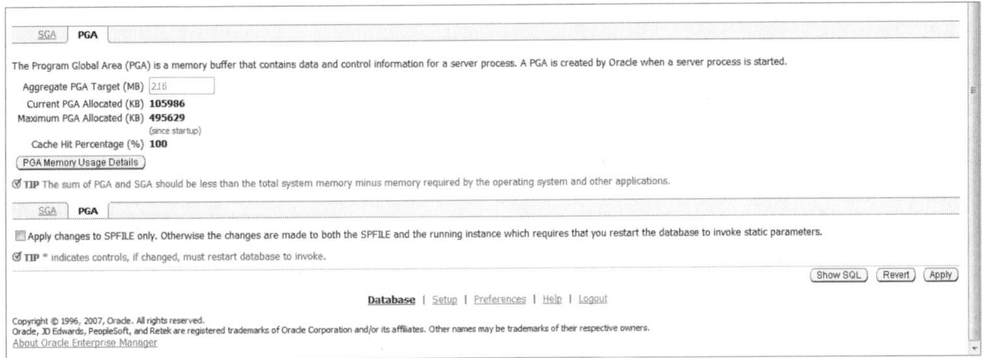

FIGURE 11.4 PGA work area size detail

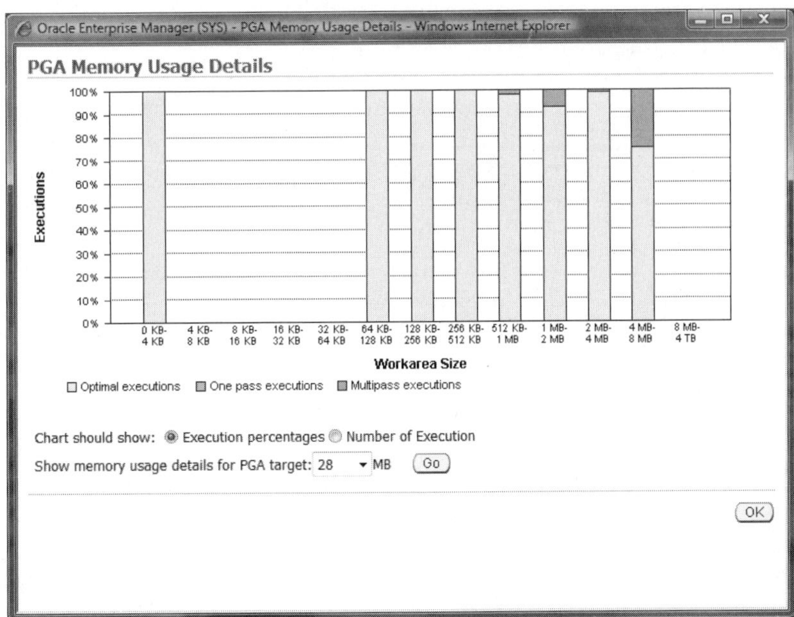

Disabling Automatic Memory Management Using Enterprise Manager

From the Memory Advisors page, you can disable Automatic Memory Management by clicking the Disable button. The change takes effect immediately. You can revert to

Automatic Memory Management by clicking the Enable button. We'll discuss enabling in a later section titled "Enabling Automatic Memory Management Using Enterprise Manager."

When you disable Automatic Memory Management, the Memory Advisors page changes to reflect that Automatic Memory Management is disabled, as shown in Figure 11.5. Now you have an SGA tab that gives you the ability to enable or disable Automatic Shared Memory Management as well as request advice (see Figure 11.6) and modify the total and maximum SGA sizes.

FIGURE 11.5 Automatic Memory Management SGA configuration

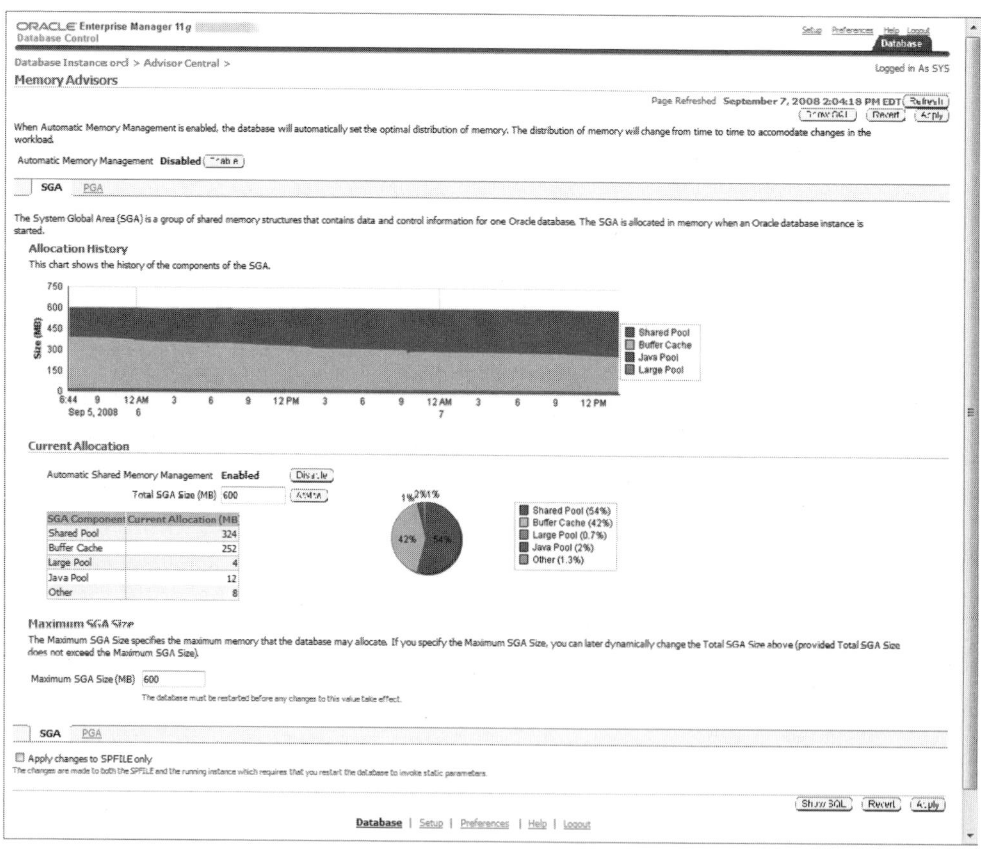

If you click the PGA tab, you'll see (Figure 11.7) that you can now request advice, as shown in Figure 11.8, and modify the aggregate PGA target based on the recommendations.

FIGURE 11.6 Automatic Memory Management SGA size advice

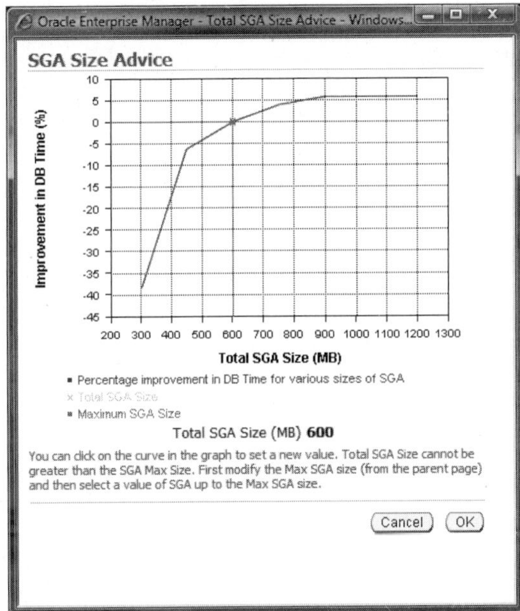

FIGURE 11.7 Automatic Memory Management PGA configuration

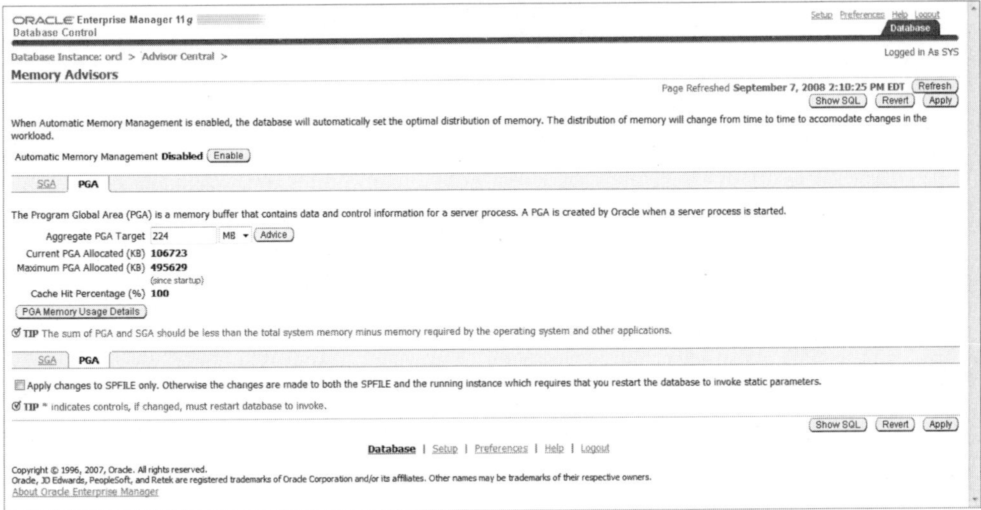

FIGURE 11.8 Automatic Memory Management PGA size advice

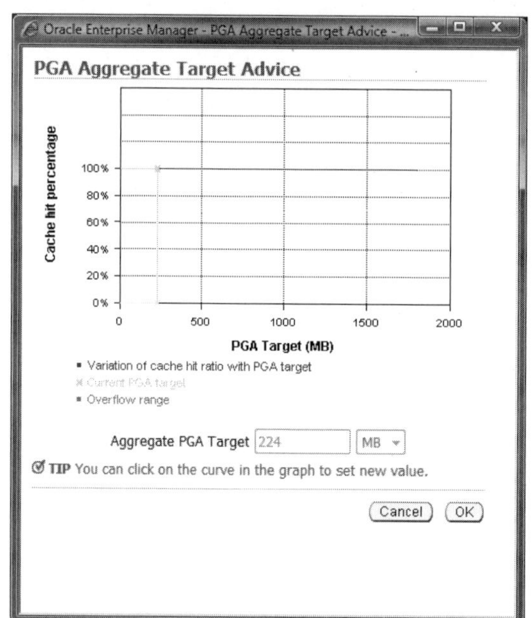

Disabling Automatic Shared Memory Management Using Enterprise Manager

If you now want to disable Automatic Shared Memory Management and manually set the values for the various SGA pools, you can do so by clicking the Disable button in the Current Allocation section on the SGA tab. This action opens the Disable Automatic Shared Memory Management page, shown in Figure 11.9, where you can manually set the values for each component. You may revert to Automatic Shared Memory Management by canceling from this page, or click OK to continue and begin manually managing the SGA.

FIGURE 11.9 Manually configuring the SGA

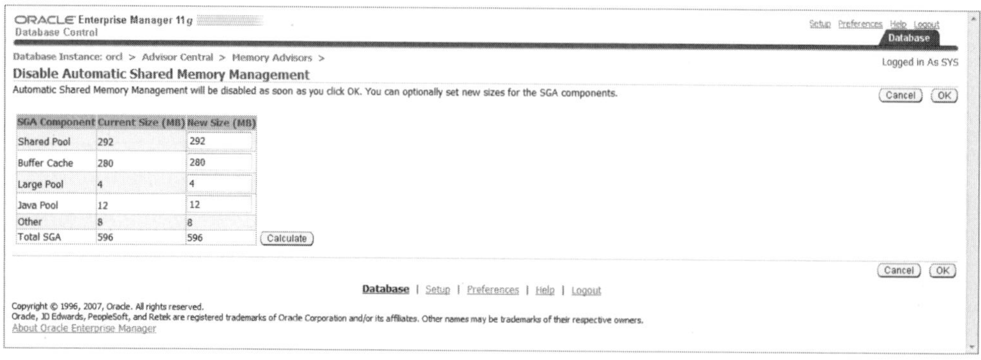

If you disable Automatic Shared Memory Management, you will manually configure and manage each of the SGA pools. We'll discuss manual SGA memory management later in this chapter, in the section titled "Manually Configuring SGA Parameters."

Enabling Automatic Shared Memory Management Using Enterprise Manager

Stepping back from full manual configuration of the SGA to Automatic Shared Memory Management is straightforward; simply click the Enable button presented next to the Automatic Shared Memory Management Disabled header in the SGA section of the Memory Advisors page, as shown in Figure 11.10.

FIGURE 11.10 Enabling Automatic Shared Memory Management

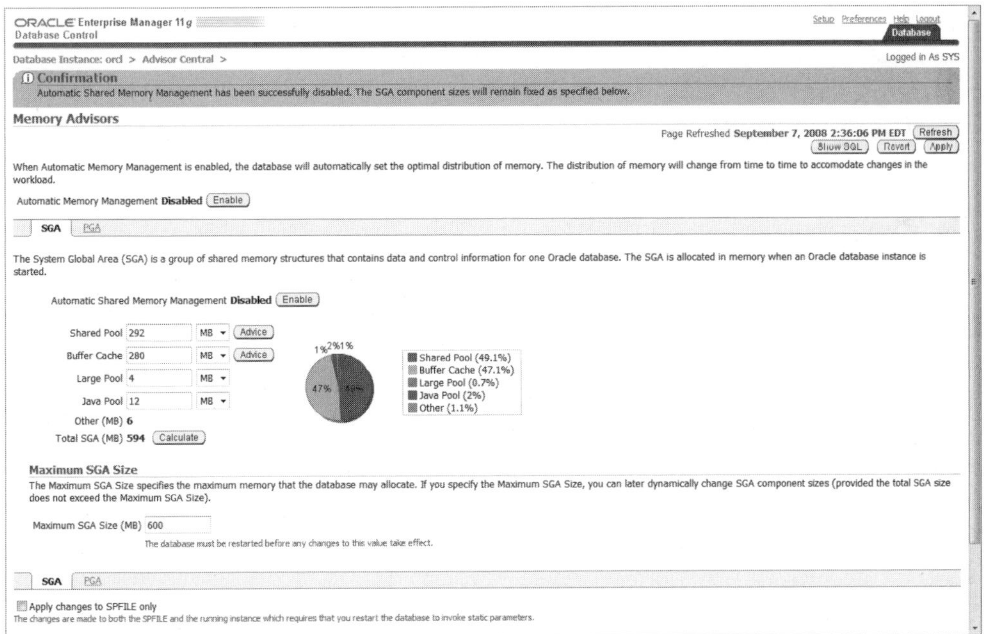

Enabling Automatic Memory Management Using Enterprise Manager

You can also go directly from manual SGA management to Automatic Memory Management by clicking the Enable button next to the Automatic Memory Management Disabled line directly under the Memory Advisors header on the Memory Advisors page (shown earlier, in Figure 11.10).

If you are currently running the instance in Automatic Shared Memory Management mode and want to enable Automatic Memory Management, click the Enable button, shown in Figure 11.11.

You'll have the opportunity to modify the maximum memory size and the total size of automatic shared memory, as shown in Figure 11.12.

Figure 11.13 shows confirmation that the instance is now running in Automatic Memory Management mode.

FIGURE 11.11 Enabling Shared Memory Management

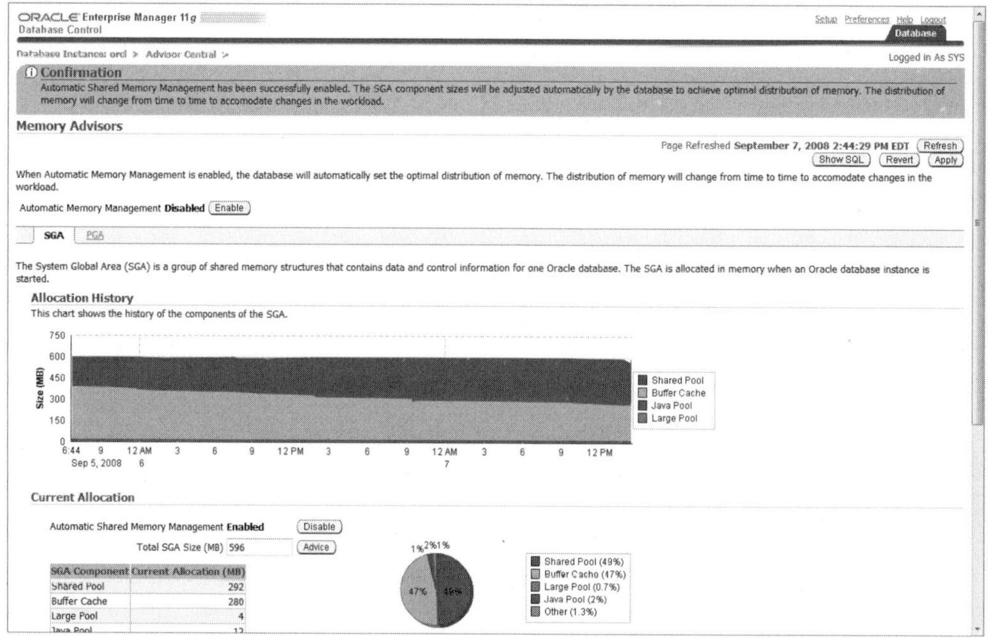

FIGURE 11.12 Configuring Automatic Memory Management

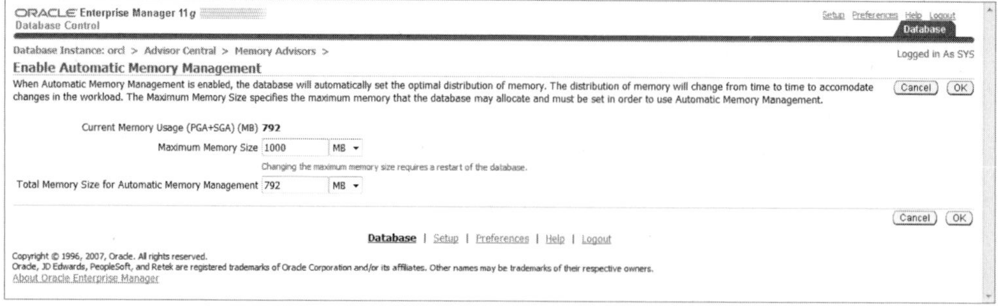

FIGURE 11.13 Automatic Memory Management enabled

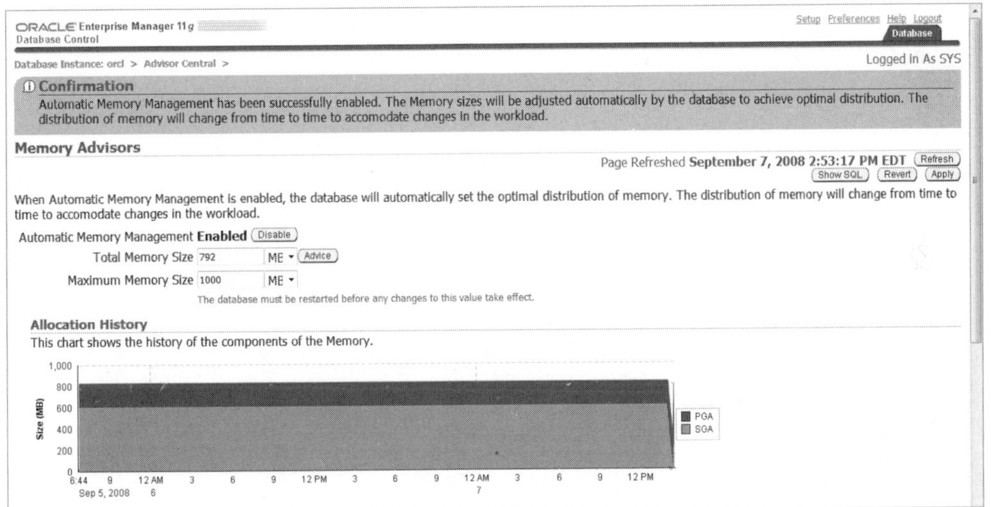

Manually Configuring SGA Parameters

If you don't want to let the Oracle instance manage the SGA memory allocations for you and you want greater control over the individual pools, Oracle provides the option for you to bypass both Automatic Memory Management and Automatic Shared Memory Management. By setting `MEMORY_TARGET` and `SGA_TARGET` initialization parameters to zero, you in effect force the manual configuration of each of the SGA memory pools and enable manual shared memory management.

While Oracle strongly recommends that you allow the instance to manage memory automatically, Oracle also understands that the DBA in some cases needs to manually configure specific pools based on specific knowledge of the application workload.

So when manually setting the SGA components, you'll need to plan and verify that each pool is given sufficient memory to meet performance requirements. As shown previously, in Figure 11.9, you can specify values for the following SGA components:

- Default pool of database buffer cache `DB_CACHE_SIZE`
- Shared pool `SHARED_POOL_SIZE`
- Large pool `LARGE_POOL_SIZE`
- Java pool `JAVA_POOL_SIZE`

Additionally, you'll need to set the value of `SGA_MAX_SIZE` to a value that represents the maximum amount of memory you would use for the SGA.

If you choose to manually configure the SGA components using Enterprise Manager after you have been running with Automatic Shared Memory Management, the SGA components are sized based on the current Memory Advisors advice. Additionally, you may seek advice after you have manually set the values, as shown earlier, in Figure 11.10. Figure 11.14 shows the advice for the shared pool, launched by clicking the Advice button next to the Shared Pool line on the Memory Advisors page.

Figure 11.15 shows the same exercise for the default database buffer pool, also known as the *buffer cache*.

FIGURE 11.14 Shared pool size advice

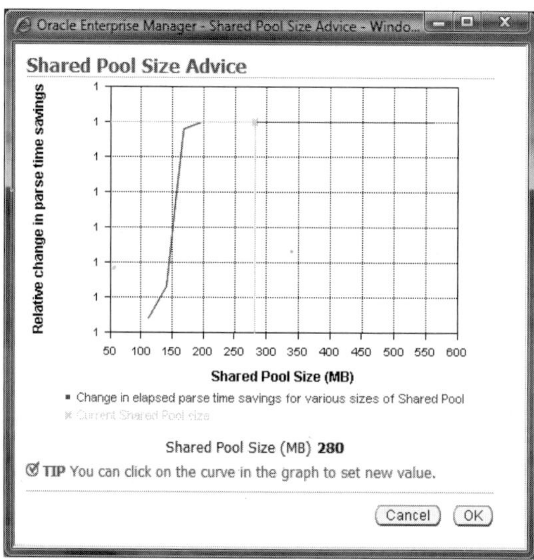

FIGURE 11.15 Buffer cache size advice

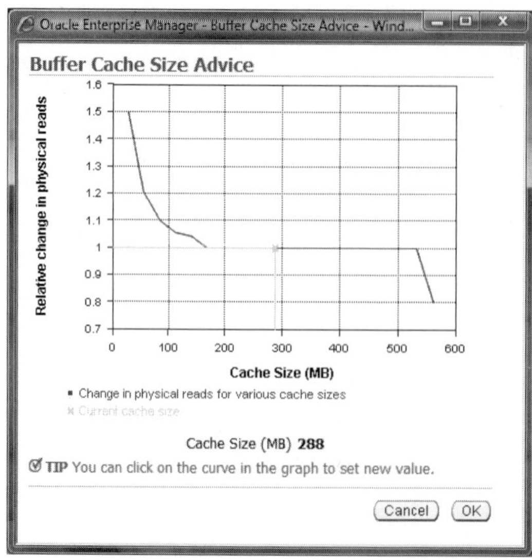

If you attempt to manually size the SGA pools to a total SGA size greater than or equal to the value for Maximum SGA Size (SGA_MAX _SIZE), you will receive the messages "ORA-02097: Parameter cannot be modified because specified value is invalid" and "ORA-04033: Insufficient memory to grow pool." If you attempt to grow the buffer cache too large, you will receive the ORA-02097 error and the message "ORA-00384: Insufficient memory to grow cache." In either case, you will not be able to make the total size of the SGA greater than or equal to the Maximum SGA Size value. See Figure 11.16.

FIGURE 11.16 Attempting to manually resize beyond the maximum SGA size

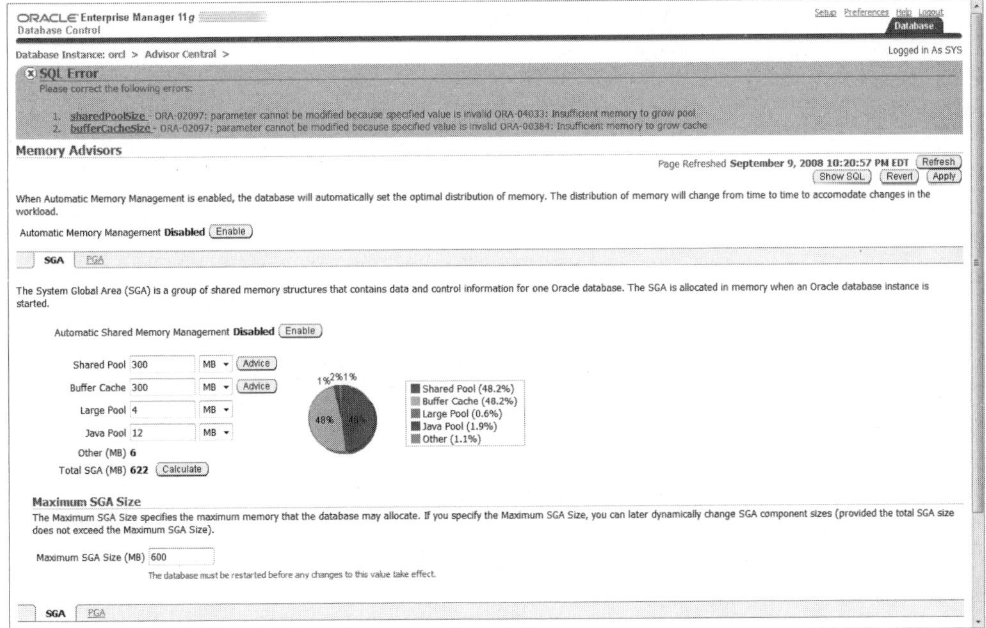

Also note in Figure 11.16 that you can change the Maximum SGA Size value, SGA_MAX_SIZE, but this will require a database-instance restart to take effect. Also on this screen you have the option to apply changes to the spfile only. If you do so, you will receive an update message indicating that changes were made to the spfile, as shown in Figure 11.17.

FIGURE 11.17 Save SGA size changes to the spfile

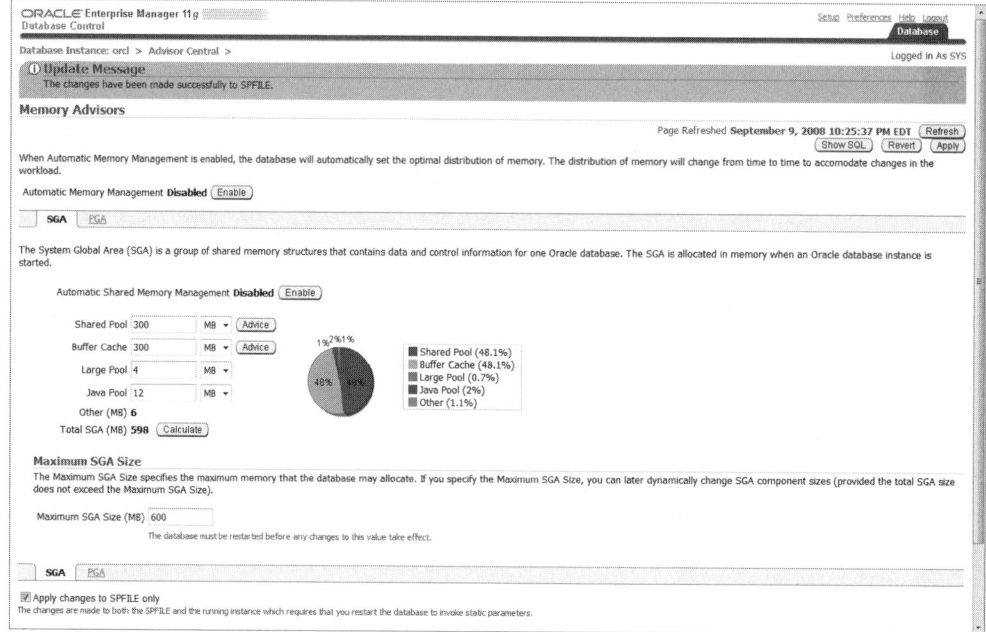

Configuring Automatic PGA Memory Management

Remember that when you configure the database instance for Automatic Memory Management, PGA memory is automatically allocated and deallocated from MEMORY_TARGET as needed. If you determine that you need greater control over the PGA, then you can go to Automatic Shared Memory Management or manual shared memory management, thereby being forced to choose between automatic or manual PGA memory management. In Automatic PGA Memory Management, you set the value of PGA_AGGREGATE_TARGET and the Oracle instance manages memory allocation to work areas as needed. If you choose manual PGA memory management, you will need to configure each of the work areas manually, which requires you to keep up with workload changes and modify the work areas accordingly.

If you choose to not utilize Automatic Memory Management for the instance, Oracle strongly recommends that you enable Automatic PGA Memory Management and let the Oracle instance manage the PGA components on your system. If you choose not to use Automatic PGA Memory Management, use the Memory Advisor in Enterprise Manager to assist you with your instance PGA memory configuration.

Automatic PGA Memory Management

In the following sections, we'll discuss how to enable Automatic PGA Memory Management in Enterprise Manager, how to monitor Automatic PGA Memory Management, and how you can tune Automatic PGA Memory Management. We will also discuss how you can disable Automatic PGA Memory Management and tune the individual work areas manually.

Enabling Automatic PGA Memory Management Using Enterprise Manager

If you're currently running your instance in Automatic or manual Shared Memory Management mode, then you are by default running Automatic PGA Memory Management. You can verify that the instance is in Automatic PGA Memory Management mode, and not manual mode, by viewing the PGA tab in the Memory Advisors page, as shown in Figure 11.18. On this page you can change the value of the PGA aggregate target based on the recommendations received when you click the Advice button.

FIGURE 11.18 Automatic PGA Memory Management

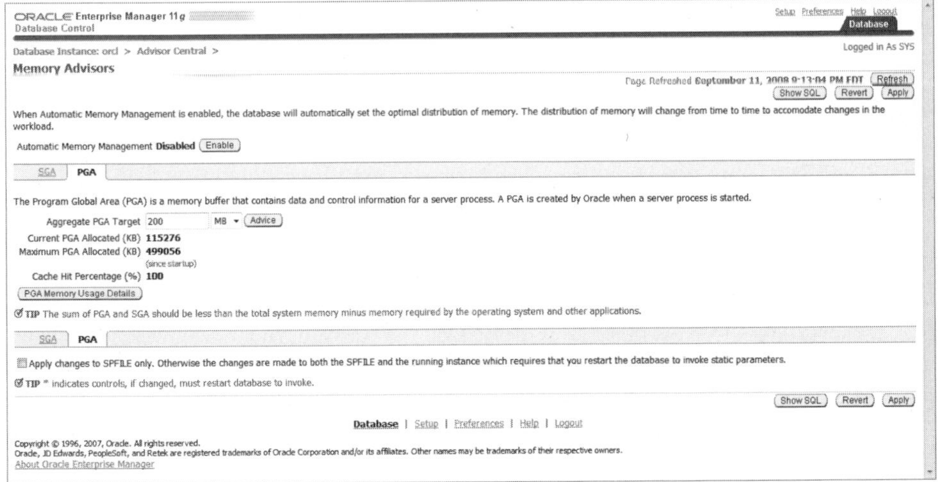

The minimum value for PGA_AGGREGATE_TARGET is 10MB, and the maximum value is 256GB.

If your database instance was running in Automatic Memory Management mode and you converted to Automatic Shared Memory Management mode, then the PGA_AGGREGATE_TARGET was set at the value determined by the instance when it was running in Automatic Memory Management mode.

For an online transaction processing (OLTP) system, a good starting point for the PGA size, the value of the PGA_AGGREGATE_TARGET, should be approximately 20 percent of the memory available on the system; conversely, the value of the SGA should be about 80 percent of the available memory. For a decision support system, data warehouse, or analytical database, a good starting point is 50 percent of available memory for PGA and 50 percent for SGA. Of course, you will need to tune the PGA_AGGREGATE_TARGET value based on advice from the Memory Advisors page or by querying dynamic views. Also note that if you run multiple instances on the same server, it is easy to overallocate the SGA and PGA so that the combined memory used by all the instances is larger than real memory on the server, which can lead to memory paging and significant performance degradation.

Monitoring Automatic PGA Memory Management

You can monitor the PGA performance using several dynamic performance views:

- V$PGASTAT
- V$PROCESS
- V$PROCESS_MEMORY
- V$SQL_WORKAREA_ACTIVE
- V$SQL_WORKAREA
- V$SQL_WORKAREA_HISTOGRAM

A key statistic to look for in the V$PGASTAT view is the overallocation count, which tells you the cumulative number of times you have overallocated the PGA since instance startup; a large number indicates that the PGA_AGGREGATE_TARGET may be too small.

The V$PROCESS view has one row for each Oracle process for this instance. You can monitor PGA usage by observing the columns that start with PGA_*.

The V$PROCESS_MEMORY view goes into greater detail for each process, showing PGA memory used for these six categories: PL/SQL, SQL, Java, OLAP, Freeable, and "other."

V$SQL_WORKAREA_ACTIVE shows currently active work areas in the instance, excluding sorts that are less than 64KB. When a SQL operation is complete, the work area is deallocated from V$SQL_WORKAREA_ACTIVE and the V$SQL_WORKAREA view is updated to include the cumulative execution statistics for each work area.

The V$SQL_WORKAREA_HISTOGRAM view shows the cumulative statistics for the number of work areas executed since instance startup for optimal, one-pass, and multipass memory sizes. The columns for low and high optimal size bytes represent the work-area size buckets that were used. Your expectation should be to run as many work areas as possible in the OPTIMAL_EXECUTIONS column.

Tuning Automatic PGA Memory Management

The PGA advice performance views are available to help you tune the value of PGA_AGGREGATE_TARGET. The dynamic views V$PGA_TARGET_ADVICE and V$PGA_TARGET_ADVICE_HISTOGRAM are supplied to help you tune Automatic PGA Memory Management.

Set the value of STATISTICS_LEVEL to TYPICAL or ALL and set the value of PGA_AGGREGATE_TARGET to between 10MB and 256GB to enable the automatic generation of PGA advice statistics and population of the advice views.

The V$PGA_TARGET_ADVICE view shows the predicted cache hit-ratio improvement as you increase the size of the PGA_AGGREGATE_TARGET. In this case, the small workload indicates you could reduce the size of the 200MB PGA_AGGREGATE_TARGET and still have a good PGA hit ratio.

```
SQL> SELECT PGA_TARGET_FOR_ESTIMATE/1024/1024 "target mb",
  2  ESTD_PGA_CACHE_HIT_PERCENTAGE "cache_hit%"
  3  FROM V$PGA_TARGET_ADVICE
  4  /

 target mb cache_hit%
---------- ----------
        25         99
        50         99
       100        100
       150        100
       200        100
       240        100
       280        100
       320        100
       360        100
       400        100
       600        100
       800        100
      1200        100
      1600        100
14 rows selected.
SQL>
```

Similarly, the V$PGA_TARGET_ADVICE_HISTOGRAM view forecasts how the V$SQL_WORKAREA_HISTOGRAM will change if you modify the value of PGA_AGGREGATE_TARGET. It shows the predicted number of executions in each of the optimal, one-pass, and multipass work areas for each setting of PGA_AGGREGATE_TARGET.

Disabling Automatic PGA Memory Management Using Enterprise Manager

If you want to manually control the sizes of the individual work areas, going against the strong recommendation from Oracle, you will need to set the value of PGA_AGGREGATE_TARGET to zero and set the following parameters to a positive value:

- SORT_AREA_SIZE
- HASH_AREA_SIZE
- BITMAP_MERGE_AREA_SIZE
- CREATE_BITMAP_AREA_SIZE

Then restart the instance and enjoy tuning the work areas manually.

If you're using OEM, set the PGA Aggregate Target value to zero and choose to make the changes to the spfile, as shown in Figure 11.19.

Once you've stopped and started the instance and returned to the PGA tab of the OEM Memory Advisor, you'll notice that the page has changed from the view in Figure 11.18 to what you see in Figure 11.20.

FIGURE 11.19 Disabling Automatic PGA Memory Management

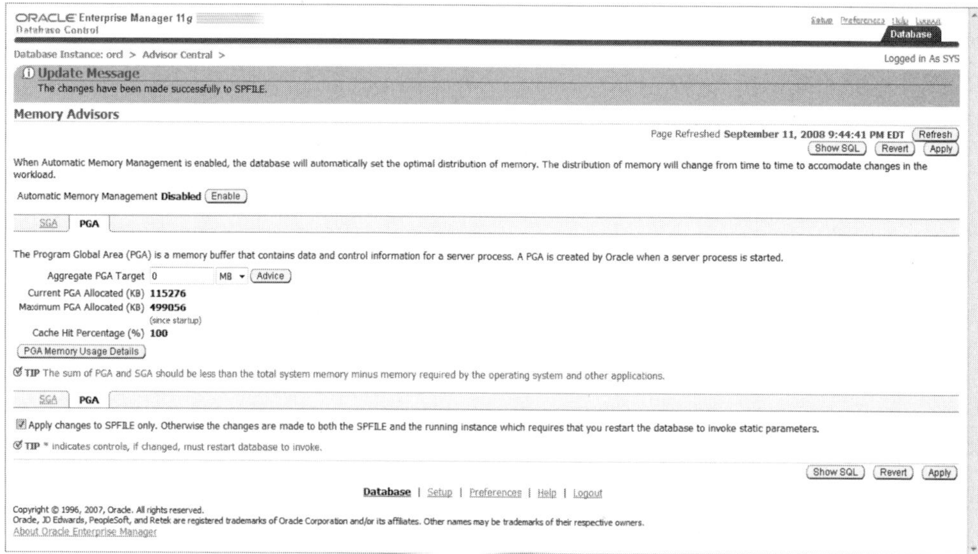

FIGURE 11.20 Manual PGA Memory Management

ORACLE Enterprise Manager 11g
Database Control

Setup Preferences Help Logout

Database

Database Instance: orcl > Advisor Central >

Logged in As SYS

Memory Advisors

Page Refreshed September 11, 2008 9:52:05 PM EDT (Refresh)

(Show SQL) (Revert) (Apply)

When Automatic Memory Management is enabled, the database will automatically set the optimal distribution of memory. The distribution of memory will change from time to time to accomodate changes in the workload.

Automatic Memory Management **Disabled** (Enable)

SGA | PGA

Manual Mode

Max Concurrent Users* 700

The maximum number of users who can be concurrently connected to the database at any given time. The PROCESSES initialization parameter is based on the value of the maximum number of users and the number of background processes.

Sort Area Size 64 KB

The maximum amount of memory to use for a sort. Larger value of SORT_AREA_SIZE improves efficiency of large sorts.
Under peak load when all concurrent users are utilizing their max sort size allocation, the overall pga memory consumption will be at least 44800 KB

Enable Automatic Mode

In this mode Oracle manages the size of SQL work areas automatically for the entire instance.

Aggregate PGA Target 0 B

SGA | PGA

Apply changes to SPFILE only. Otherwise the changes are made to both the SPFILE and the running instance which requires that you restart the database to invoke static parameters.

TIP * indicates controls, if changed, must restart database to invoke.

(Show SQL) (Revert) (Apply)

Database | Setup | Preferences | Help | Logout

About Oracle Enterprise Manager

You'll note that the only work area that you can modify with OEM is the SORT_AREA_SIZE, but you can also set the value for the maximum number of concurrent users; the product of the two determines the maximum total size of memory that will be used for the sort work area. Also, from the command-line interface you can show the *_AREA_SIZE parameters and modify them in the spfile as needed. Please note that HASH_AREA_SIZE and SORT_AREA_SIZE can be modified at the session level and that they are not dynamically modifiable for the instance.

```
SQL> show parameter area_size

NAME                                 TYPE        VALUE
------------------------------------ ----------- -------
bitmap_merge_area_size               integer     1048576
create_bitmap_area_size              integer     8388608
hash_area_size                       integer     131072
sort_area_size                       integer     65536
```

You can very easily return to Automatic PGA Memory Management mode by clicking the Enable Automatic Mode button and then Apply.

Managing Space

In the following sections, we will explore resumable space allocation, transportable tablespaces, transportable databases, and shrinking segments. Resumable space allocation allows you to temporarily suspend operations that run out of space while you correct the space issue without aborting the operation. With the transportable tablespace feature, you can copy a set of tablespaces from a source database to a destination database. With the transportable database feature, you can copy an entire database from one platform to another. And finally, you'll learn how to shrink segments dynamically.

Managing Resumable Space Allocation

If the Oracle database encounters a space problem during the execution of an operation, it can suspend the operation and then later resume the operation. This feature is called *resumable space allocation*, and it allows the DBA to fix a problem prior to the database returning an error message to the user process. Once you've fixed the problem, the database automatically resumes the suspended operation.

Enabling resumable space allocation is simple: you can set the initialization parameter RESUMABLE_TIMEOUT to a value greater than zero, or you can issue the ALTER SESSION ENABLE RESUMABLE statement.

Understanding Resumable Space Allocation

A resumable statement suspends when an object runs out of space, it reaches the maximum number of extents, or a space quota is exceeded. An object running out of space or reaching maximum extents applies to tables, indexes, temporary segments, undo segments, large objects (LOBs), clusters, and table or index partitions. When a resumable statement is suspended, an error is reported in the alert log and the system issues the resumable session suspended alert, and if an AFTER SUSPEND trigger is in place, it will be executed. When the statement is suspended, the transaction will be suspended and all transaction resources held until rolled back or the suspend operation is resumed to completion. When the suspend condition is resolved, it will automatically resume and the associated resumable session suspended alert is cleared; of course, the original error message logged in the alert log remains.

In a distributed transaction, the remote RESUMABLE_TIMEOUT initialization parameter applies to the remote part of the transaction, and the remote session resumable setting applies. Also, local resumable settings do not apply to the remote part of the distributed transactions.

Resumable Space Operations

Specific Data Definition Language (DDL), Import/Export, Data Manipulation Language (DML), and query statements are candidates for resumable executions:

- SELECT statements that run out of sort area temporary space
- INSERT, UPDATE, DELETE, and INSERT INTO...SELECT
- Export/import and SQL*Loader
- The following DDL statements:

```
CREATE TABLE AS SELECT
CREATE INDEX
ALTER TABLE MOVE PARTITION
ALTER TABLE SPLIT PARTITION
ALTER INDEX REBUILD
ALTER INDEX REBUILD PARTITION
ALTER INDEX SPLIT PARTITION
CREATE MATERIALIZED VIEW
CREATE MATERIALIZED VIEW LOG
```

For parallel operations, each process is handled independently. If one suspends, an error is logged and the associated AFTER SUSPEND trigger is executed. Meanwhile, the other parallel processes continue. However, if one aborts, the parallel operation aborts. As with all resumable processing, when a suspend condition is repaired, it will continue and join up with the others.

Enabling and Disabling Resumable Operations

You enable resumable operations and configure the suspend time-out for the instance and for a session. For the instance, configure the initialization parameter RESUMABLE_TIMEOUT. For the session, set the session parameter RESUMABLE_TIMEOUT to a numeric value greater than zero, or issue the ALTER SESSION command.

Enabling and Disabling Resumable Operations for an Instance

To enable resumable operations for the instance, alter the instance parameter RESUMABLE_TIMEOUT to a numeric value greater than zero. The default value is 0, which in effect initially disables resumable operations for all sessions. This represents the number of seconds that an operation may suspend while you take corrective action. After the time-out is reached, the operation will abort. In this example, we alter the system RESUMABLE_TIMEOUT from 1 minute to 10 minutes:

```
SQL> show parameter resumable

NAME                                 TYPE        VALUE
------------------------------------ ----------- -------
resumable_timeout                    integer     60
SQL> alter system set resumable_timeout=600 scope=both;

System altered.
```

Enabling and Disabling Resumable Operations for a Session

Before you can enable or disable resumable operations at the session level, the user must have been granted the RESUMABLE system privilege. Once that's granted, resumable operations are enabled within a session when the following command is issued:

```
SQL> alter session enable resumable;

Session altered.
```

The default resumable time-out for a session is 7,200 seconds. To disable resumable operations within a session, issue the following command:

```
SQL> alter session disable resumable;

Session altered.
```

Additionally, the user session can control the suspend time-out in one of three ways: by altering the RESUMABLE_TIMEOUT parameter for the session, by executing the DBMS_RESUMABLE.SET_TIMEOUT procedure (covered later, in the section "The DBMS_RESUMABLE Supplied Package") or by appending to the ALTER SESSION ENABLE RESUMABLE command as follows:

```
SQL> alter session set resumable_timeout=3600;
```

```
Session altered.

SQL> show parameter resumable;

NAME                                 TYPE        VALUE
------------------------------------ ----------- -----
resumable_timeout                    integer     3600
SQL>

SQL> alter session enable resumable timeout 7200;

Session altered.
SQL> show parameter resumable;

NAME                                 TYPE        VALUE
------------------------------------ ----------- -----
resumable_timeout                    integer     3600
SQL>
```

The `alter session enable resumable timeout nnnn` command does not alter the value of the session-initialization parameter `RESUMABLE_TIMEOUT`.

Procedurally, you can also enable resumable operations for a session with a logon trigger.

Identifying Resumable Sessions

By default, if a session is enabled for resumable space allocation, the session is identified in the `NAME` column of the `DBA_` and `USER_RESUMABLE` views by the username, session ID, and instance number, as follows:

```
SQL> select name from user_resumable;

NAME
------------------------------------
User SYS(0), Session 108, Instance 1

SQL>
```

You can alter the session identifier by issuing the `ALTER SESSION` command and adding the `NAME` clause, as follows:

```
SQL> alter session enable resumable name 'LEB test';
Session altered.
SQL> select name from user_resumable;
NAME
```

```
----------------------------------------------------
LEB test
SQL>
```

This changed name remains in effect until it's altered by the ENABLE RESUMABLE NAME command, until resumable is disabled by the session, or until the session ends.

Working with Resumable Operations

Once you've enabled resumable operations, you'll need to monitor and take action on suspended resumable operations. You'll monitor specific views to determine the status of resumable operations, and you'll write AFTER SUSPEND triggers and utilize the DBMS_RESUMABLE supplied package to take action within a session when a suspend occurs.

Additionally, Enterprise Manager reports resumable alerts and provides the mechanism for resolving resumable space issues.

Views for Monitoring Resumable Space Allocation

The DBA_RESUMABLE and USER_RESUMABLE views contain rows for suspended resumable statements as well as those that are executing as normal. The key information columns are described in Table 11.1. The USER_ID column is not included in the USER_RESUMABLE view, and as with all USER_ views, only the current session information is shown.

TABLE 11.1 DBA_RESUMABLE Columns

Column Name	Description
STATUS	Status of the RESUMABLE statement: RUNNING, SUSPENDED, TIMEOUT, ERROR, ABORTED.
TIMEOUT	Time-out value of the resumable statement.
START_TIME	Start time of the resumable statement.
SUSPEND_TIME	The last time the resumable statement was suspended.
RESUME_TIME	The last time the statement resumed.
SQL_TEXT	The resumable statement.
ERROR_NUMBER	The error number of the last error logged or this resumable statement. If no errors, the value will be NULL.
ERROR_PARAMETERn	Error parameter columns 1 through 5.
ERROR_MSG	The error message associated with the ERROR_NUMBER.

The DBA can also use the V$SESSION_WAIT view to catch suspended resumable operations. The EVENT column will contain a statement indicating that the operation is suspended and waiting for the error to be cleared.

Monitoring Resumable Space Alerts with Enterprise Manager

Oracle Enterprise Manager will display alerts on the database home page when there are resumable space suspends. In the example shown in Figure 11.21, we have created a suspend condition by attempting to insert into a table that is in a space-constrained tablespace.

FIGURE 11.21 Resumable space suspend alert on database home page

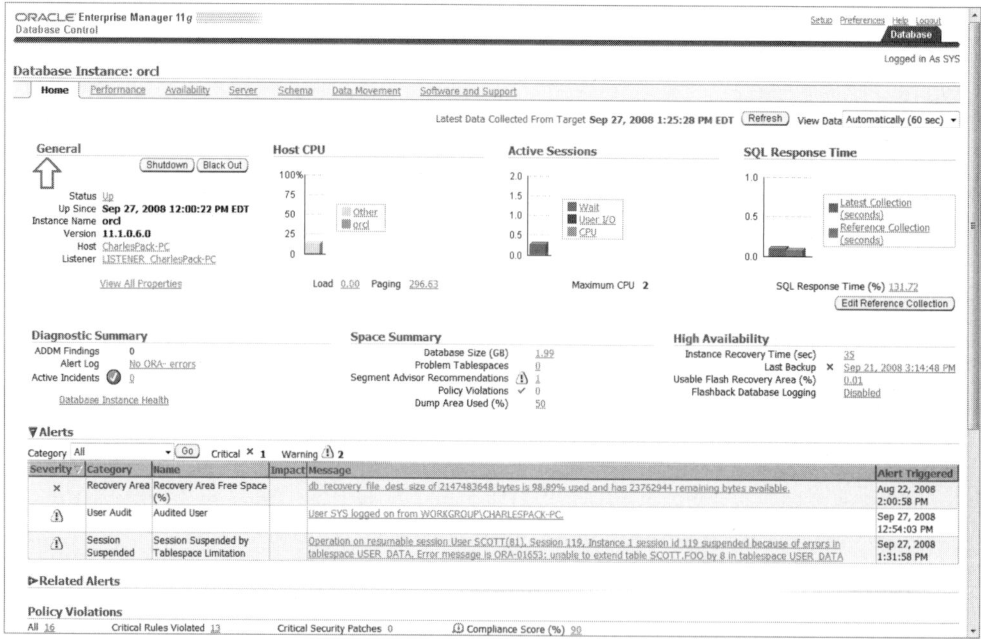

Click the Message link to see the details, shown in Figure 11.22.

Now from the database home page, under the Space Summary caption, click on the value to the right of Database Size" to display the database tablespaces, shown in Figure 11.23.

Choose the constrained tablespace, shown in Figure 11.24. From there, choose to add a new datafile to the tablespace or edit the datafile and increase the size.

For this example, we will click the link on the datafile name, and we can either increase the size of the datafile or change the datafile to AUTOEXTEND ON to resolve the suspend issue.

FIGURE 11.22 Resumable space suspended session details

ORACLE Enterprise Manager 11*g*
Database Control

Setup Preferences Help Logout
Database

Database Instance: orcl > All Metrics > Session Suspended by Tablespace Limitation >

Session Suspended by Tablespace Limitation: Object Causing USER_DATA: Last 24 hours

Last Updated **Sep 27, 2008 1:39:03 PM EDT**
View Data Last 24 hours

Current Alert

Object Causing **Tablespace USER_DATA**
Alert Triggered **Sep 27, 2008 1:31:58 PM**
Message **Operation on resumable session User SCOTT(81), Session 119, Instance 1 session id 119 suspended because of errors in tablespace USER_DATA. Error message is ORA-01653: unable to extend table SCOTT.FOO by 8 in tablespace USER_DATA**

Recommendations

Severity **Warning**
Recommended Action Please check view dba_resumable.

Top Sessions

Alert History

Comment for Most Recent Alert Add Comment

Severity	Timestamp	Message	Last Comment	Details
⚠	Sep 27, 2008 1:31:58 PM	Operation on resumable session User SCOTT(81), Session 119, Instance 1 session id 119 susp...		-

Related Links

Metric and Policy Settings

Database | Setup | Preferences | Help | Logout

About Oracle Enterprise Manager

FIGURE 11.23 Database tablespaces

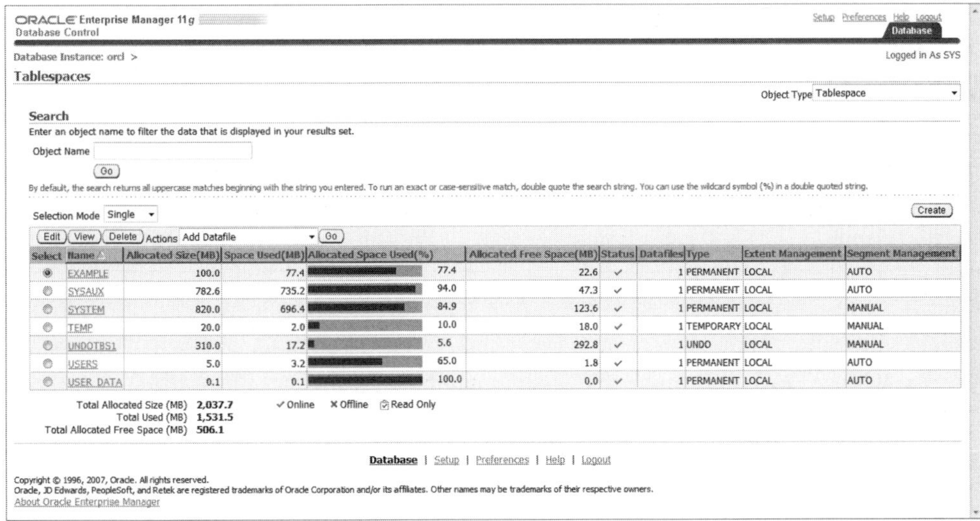

ORACLE Enterprise Manager 11*g*
Database Control

Setup Preferences Help Logout
Database

Database Instance: orcl >
Logged in As SYS

Tablespaces

Object Type Tablespace

Search

Enter an object name to filter the data that is displayed in your results set.

Object Name
Go

By default, the search returns all uppercase matches beginning with the string you entered. To run an exact or case-sensitive match, double quote the search string. You can use the wildcard symbol (%) in a double quoted string.

Selection Mode Single Create

Edit View Delete Actions Add Datafile Go

Select	Name	Allocated Size(MB)	Space Used(MB)	Allocated Space Used(%)	Allocated Free Space(MB)	Status	Datafiles	Type	Extent Management	Segment Management
◉	EXAMPLE	100.0	77.4	77.4	22.6	✓	1	PERMANENT	LOCAL	AUTO
○	SYSAUX	782.6	735.2	94.0	47.3	✓	1	PERMANENT	LOCAL	AUTO
○	SYSTEM	820.0	696.4	84.9	123.6	✓	1	PERMANENT	LOCAL	MANUAL
○	TEMP	20.0	2.0	10.0	18.0	✓	1	TEMPORARY	LOCAL	MANUAL
○	UNDOTBS1	310.0	17.2	5.6	292.8	✓	1	UNDO	LOCAL	MANUAL
○	USERS	5.0	3.2	65.0	1.8	✓	1	PERMANENT	LOCAL	AUTO
○	USER_DATA	0.1	0.1	100.0	0.0	✓	1	PERMANENT	LOCAL	AUTO

Total Allocated Size (MB) **2,037.7**
Total Used (MB) **1,531.5**
Total Allocated Free Space (MB) **506.1**

✓ Online ✗ Offline Read Only

Database | Setup | Preferences | Help | Logout

About Oracle Enterprise Manager

FIGURE 11.24 Tablespaces datafile details

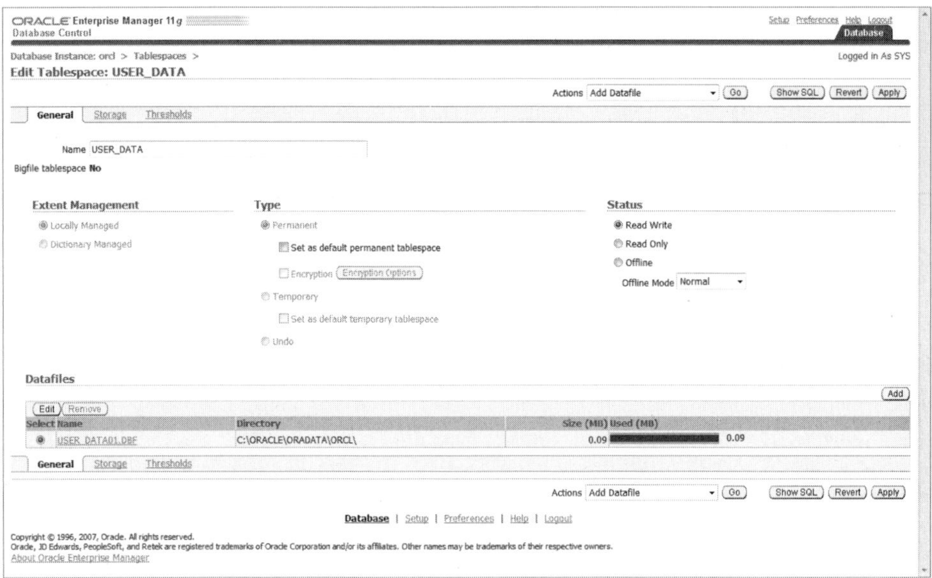

The *DBMS_RESUMABLE* Supplied Package

The DBMS_RESUMABLE package allows you to get and set time-out parameters for a session, abort a suspended resumable session, and query the error stack for specific resumable space errors. Table 11.2 describes the package functions and subprograms.

TABLE 11.2 DBMS_RESUMABLE Package Programs

Program Name	Description
ABORT	Procedure that allows you to abort a suspended resumable operation
GET_SESSION_TIMEOUT	Function that when passed the session ID returns the current resumable time-out
GET_TIMEOUT	Function that returns resumable time-out for the current session
SET_SESSION_TIMEOUT	Procedure that when passed the session ID and time-out value sets the time-out for a session
SET_TIMEOUT	Procedure that sets the time-out for the current session
SPACE_ERROR_INFO	Function that allows you to search the error stack on error_type, object_type, object_owner, object_name, sub_object_name, and table_space_name

In the following code, you see an example that enables resumable for the session, gets the session time-out value; changes the value; queries the value; disables resumable; and then queries, modifies, and enables it. You'll note that the resumable time-out value is retained by the session even though resumable was disabled. Also note that the default time-out is 7,200 seconds.

```
SQL> alter session enable resumable;

Session altered.

SQL> select dbms_resumable.get_timeout from dual;

GET_TIMEOUT
-----------
       7200

SQL> exec dbms_resumable.set_timeout (9600);

PL/SQL procedure successfully completed.

SQL> select dbms_resumable.get_timeout from dual;

GET_TIMEOUT
-----------
       9600

SQL> alter session disable resumable;

Session altered.

SQL> select dbms_resumable.get_timeout from dual;

GET_TIMEOUT
-----------
       9600

SQL> alter session enable resumable timeout 7200;

Session altered.

SQL> select dbms_resumable.get_timeout from dual;
```

```
GET_TIMEOUT
-----------
       7200

SQL>
```

Triggered Events to Respond to Suspends

Oracle has created the AFTER SUSPEND trigger to help you resolve suspend conditions programmatically. By registering an AFTER SUSPEND trigger on the database as user SYS using the ON DATABASE clause, you can take action regardless of who owns the resumable operation.

Managing Transportable Tablespaces

The transportable tablespace feature allows you to copy or move a tablespace from one database to another. Using transportable tablespaces is faster than copying rows or using export/import or unload/load. With Oracle 10*g* or higher, it is possible to transport tablespaces across some but not all platforms. Transportable tablespaces are useful for, but not limited to, the following:

- Database migrations
- Sharing tablespaces with other database users (for example, remote customers)
- Tablespace point-in-time recovery (TSPITR)
- Archiving data from one database to another
- Exporting and importing partitions

Transporting a tablespace is straightforward, but there are caveats and limitations. You can use Enterprise Manager, or you can use SQL*Plus and the OS command line. We will take you through the basic process and list the major considerations.

The first step is to determine what will be transported. If your intent is to transport objects that exist only in one tablespace and have no dependencies in other tablespaces, then the process is simplified. If, however, you intend to transport a set of objects that are spread across multiple tablespaces or have dependencies on objects in other tablespaces, then the task becomes slightly more complex.

Transportable Tablespace Sets

A transportable tablespace set is a self-contained group of tablespaces that encapsulate the objects that you wish to transport from one database to another. For example, if you wish to transport several tables that reside in different tablespaces, then you would include each of the tablespaces in the tablespace set. If you wish to transport a partitioned table and the different partitions are in different tablespaces, then you would need to include each of the tablespaces in the tablespace set.

We'll discuss tablespace sets in detail and show examples a bit later.

Requirements of Transportable Tablespaces

Transportable tablespaces must meet the following requirements:

- The tablespaces can be locally managed or dictionary managed.
- In Oracle9*i* or higher, the transported tablespace does not have to be the same block size as the target database's standard block size. However, the target database must have a *DB_nK_CACHE_SIZE* initialization parameter set, where *n* is the block size of the transportable tablespace.
- The tablespace must be placed in read-only mode during the transport process.
- Starting with Oracle 11*g*, data pump is used instead of export/import to move the metadata from the source to the target.
- You can't import a transported tablespace that has the same name as an existing tablespace in the target database. You can rename the transported tablespace as part of the import process.
- In order for an object to be transportable, all of the partitions that contain its dependent objects such as indexes, materialized views, and partitioned tables must be included in the tablespace set.
- Tablespaces that do not use block encryption but have tables that have encrypted columns are not transportable.
- You can't transport the SYSTEM tablespace or objects owned by the SYS user.
- Tablespaces with 8.0-compatible advanced queues with multiple recipients are not transportable.
- If you're transporting across platforms, RAW, BFILE, and AnyTypes are not converted from one endian type to another as part of the transport process.

Manually Transporting a Tablespace

In this section, we will demonstrate how to manually transport a tablespace using a combination of SQL*Plus, the OS command line, and data pump.

The basic steps are as follows:

1. Check compatibility and endian format.
2. Choose the transportable tablespace set.
3. Generate the transportable tablespace set.
4. Transport the tablespace set.
5. Import the tablespace set.

Database Requirements for Transportable Tablespaces

To utilize the transportable tablespace feature, you must make sure the database meets the following criteria:

- To create a transportable tablespace set, the source database must be Oracle 8*i* or later, and it must be Enterprise Edition.
- To import a tablespace set from the same platform, the target database can be any edition of Oracle8*i* or higher.
- To create a transportable tablespace set for import into a database on a different platform, the source database must have compatibility set to 10.0 or higher.
- To import a transportable tablespace set from a different platform, both the source and target databases must have compatibility set to 10.0 or higher.
- The source and target database must have the same character set and national character set.

Step 1: Check Compatibility and Endian Format

If the source and target are different versions of the database, you'll need to verify the minimum compatibility for transportable tablespaces. When you create a transportable tablespace set, Oracle determines the minimum compatibility level for the target. Oracle throws an error if the target database's compatibility level is lower than the minimum compatibility. If you're transporting a tablespace to the same platform, the minimum compatibility must be 8.0 for both the source and target. Both source and target must have a minimum compatibility of 9.0 if the transportable tablespace's block size is different than the target's standard block size. For different platforms, the minimum compatibility must be 10.0 for both source and target.

If your source and target are different platforms, it will be necessary to check for endian compatibility. If the source and target are not directly compatible—for example, the source is big endian and the target is little endian—then you will need to use RMAN to convert the copy of each tablespace datafile on either the source or target platform. To determine which platforms you can transport to, run this query:

```
SQL> select * from v$transportable_platform;
PLATFORM_ID PLATFORM_NAME                    ENDIAN_FORMAT
----------- -------------------------------- --------------
          1 Solaris[tm] OE (32-bit)          Big
          2 Solaris[tm] OE (64-bit)          Big
          7 Microsoft Windows IA (32-bit)    Little
         10 Linux IA (32-bit)                Little
```

```
          6 AIX-Based Systems (64-bit)        Big
          3 HP-UX (64-bit)                    Big
          5 HP Tru64 UNIX                     Little
          4 HP-UX IA (64-bit)                 Big
         11 Linux IA (64-bit)                 Little
         15 HP Open VMS                       Little
          8 Microsoft Windows IA (64-bit)     Little
          9 IBM zSeries Based Linux           Big
         13 Linux 64-bit for AMD              Little
         16 Apple Mac OS                      Big
         12 Microsoft Windows 64-bit for AMD Little
         17 Solaris Operating System (x86)    Little
         18 IBM Power Based Linux             Big
         19 HP IA Open VMS                    Little
         20 Solaris Operating System (AMD64) Little
19 rows selected.
SQL>
```

If you only want to see target platforms that are endian-compatible with the source platform, run this query at your source database:

```
SQL> COL "Source" FORM A32
SQL> COL "Compatible Targets" FORM A32
SQL> BREAK ON "Source"

SQL> select d.platform_name "Source", t.platform_name
 "Compatible Targets", endian_format
 from v$transportable_platform t, v$database d
 where t.endian_format = (select endian_format
                          from v$transportable_platform t,
                           v$database d
                          where d.platform_name =
                           t.platform_name)
SQL> /

Source                             Compatible Targets
             ENDIAN_FORMAT
-------------------------------- -------------------------
------ --------------

Microsoft Windows IA (32-bit)    Microsoft Windows IA (32-bit)    Little
```

```
                              Linux IA (32-bit)                  Little
                              HP Tru64 UNIX                      Little
                              Linux IA (64-bit)                  Little
                              HP Open VMS                        Little
                              Microsoft Windows IA (64-bit)      Little
                              Linux 64-bit for AMD               Little
                              Microsoft Windows 64-bit for AMD Little
                              Solaris Operating System (x86)     Little
                              HP IA Open VMS                     Little
                              Solaris Operating System (AMD64) Little

11 rows selected.

SQL>
```

If the source and target have the same endian format, no RMAN conversion is necessary. If they are different, you will need to use RMAN to convert the tablespace datafiles in the transportable set to the correct endian format.

Step 2: Choose the Transportable Tablespace Set

In order for a tablespace set to be transportable, it must be self-contained; that is, objects in the tablespace set must have no dependencies in tablespaces outside the tablespace set. Here are some basic rules:

- The tablespace set must contain all of the partitions of a partitioned table if any of the table's partitions are included in the tablespace set.
- If an index is included in a tablespace set, its corresponding table must also be included in the tablespace set.
- If you choose to include referential integrity constraints in the tablespace set, then all tablespaces required to support the constraints must be included in the set.
- If you have tables with LOB columns in the set, the tablespace that contains the LOBs must be included.

The easy way to determine if the set of tablespaces is self-contained is to execute the DBMS_TTS.TRANSPORT_SET_CHECK procedure, supplying the list of tablespaces in the tablespace set, as in this example:

```
SQL> create table scott.foo_1 (x number, y varchar2(20)) tablespace users;
Table created.
SQL> create index scott.foo_1_indx on scott.foo_1 (x) tablespace user_data;
Index created.
SQL> SET SERVEROUTPUT ON
SQL> exec dbms_tts.transport_set_check ('USER_DATA');
```

```
PL/SQL procedure successfully completed.
SQL> SELECT * FROM TRANSPORT_SET_VIOLATIONS;
VIOLATIONS
ORA-39907: Index SCOTT.FOO_1_INDX in tablespace USER_DATA points to table
SCOTT.FOO_1 in tablespace USERS.
SQL>
```

This simple verification showed that the index foo_1_indx was built in the USER_DATA tablespace but the corresponding foo_1 table is in the USERS tablespace, which is not included in the transportable tablespace set. You must remedy this situation before you can transport tablespace USER_DATA.

It is important at this time to discuss the concept of referential integrity constraints relative to transportable tablespace sets. By default, referential integrity constraints are not required to be included in the transportable set; however, you can test for constraint containment with the DBMS_TTS.TRANSPORT_SET_CHECK procedure. For the following example, we have created the table FOO in the USER_DATA tablespace and checked the transportability. We then add an index on FOO in the USERS tablespace and create a primary key constraint on the indexed column. We check the transportability of the USER_DATA tablespace as follows:

```
SQL> exec dbms_tts.transport_set_check ('USER_DATA',TRUE);
PL/SQL procedure successfully completed.

SQL> SELECT * FROM TRANSPORT_SET_VIOLATIONS;
no rows selected
SQL>
SQL> CREATE INDEX SCOTT.FOO_INDX
  2  ON SCOTT.FOO (X)
  3  TABLESPACE USERS;
Index created.
SQL> ALTER TABLE SCOTT.FOO ADD (PRIMARY KEY (x));
Table altered.
SQL> exec dbms_tts.transport_set_check ('USER_DATA',TRUE);
PL/SQL procedure successfully completed.
SQL> SELECT * FROM TRANSPORT_SET_VIOLATIONS;

VIOLATIONS
----------------------------------------------------------

ORA-39908: Index SCOTT.FOO_INDX in tablespace USERS
 enforces primary constraints
of table SCOTT.FOO in tablespace USER_DATA.
SQL>
```

Before we can transport the USER_DATA tablespace, we need to resolve this constraint issue by including the USERS tablespace, by rebuilding the index into the USER_DATA tablespace, by dropping the primary key constraint, or by deciding not to include constraints in the transportable set.

The SYSAUX tablespace is not transportable. Also, if the SYSTEM tablespace is locally managed, you can plug in a dictionary-managed tablespace, but it will be read-only and cannot be made writable.

Step 3: Generate the Transportable Tablespace Set

As introduced earlier, a transportable tablespace set is a self-contained group of tablespaces that encapsulate the objects that you wish to transport from one database to another. The transportable set must include all datafiles for each of the tablespaces to transport. The remaining component of the transportable set is a data pump export file that contains metadata about the transportable set. Here are the basic steps required to generate the transportable set:

1. Make all of the tablespaces in the transportable set read-only.
2. Use data pump on the source system to specify which tablespaces are included in the transportable set.
3. If converting to a different endian format, use the RMAN `convert` command to convert the files in a temporary location on the source system.

With these basic steps, we can show you a straightforward example. Remember, the tablespaces are placed in read-only mode and remain read-only until the files have been copied to the target or to their temporary location for endian conversion.

You must have the EXP_FULL_DATABASE role to export a transportable tablespace. You must use a valid DIRECTORY in your data pump export command.

First, place the tablespaces in the transportable set in read-only mode:

```
SQL>alter tablespace user_data read only;
Tablespace altered.
```

Now exit or "host" to the command line and execute the data pump export command:

```
SQL>host
C:\>expdp dumpfile=expdat.dmp DIRECTORY=exp_dir
 TRANSPORT_TABLESPACES= user_data

Export: Release 11.1.0.6.0 - Production on Sunday, 28 September, 2008 14:40:19
```

```
Copyright (c) 2003, 2007, Oracle.  All rights reserved.

Username: sys as sysdba
Password:

Connected to: Oracle Database 11g Enterprise Edition
 Release 11.1.0.6.0 - Production
With the Partitioning, OLAP, Data Mining and Real Application Testing options
Starting "SYS"."SYS_EXPORT_TRANSPORTABLE_01":
sys/******** AS SYSDBA dumpfile=e
xpdat.dmp DIRECTORY=EXP_DIR TRANSPORT_TABLESPACES= user_data
Processing object type TRANSPORTABLE_EXPORT/PLUGTS_BLK
Processing object type TRANSPORTABLE_EXPORT/TABLE
Processing object type TRANSPORTABLE_EXPORT/INDEX
Processing object type TRANSPORTABLE_EXPORT/CONSTRAINT/CONSTRAINT
Processing object type TRANSPORTABLE_EXPORT/INDEX_STATISTICS
Processing object type TRANSPORTABLE_EXPORT/TABLE_STATISTICS
Processing object type TRANSPORTABLE_EXPORT/POST_INSTANCE/PLUGTS_BLK
Master table "SYS"."SYS_EXPORT_TRANSPORTABLE_01" successfully loaded/unloaded
******************************************************************************
Dump file set for SYS.SYS_EXPORT_TRANSPORTABLE_01 is:
  C:\TEMP\EXPDAT.DMP
******************************************************************************
Datafiles required for transportable tablespace USER_DATA:
  C:\ORACLE\ORADATA\ORCL\USER_DATA01.DBF
Job "SYS"."SYS_EXPORT_TRANSPORTABLE_01" successfully completed at 14:41:47
```

Once the export is complete, if no endian conversion is required you can move on to the step of transporting the tablespace set. If endian conversion is required and you want to run the conversion on the target system, move on to that step. Otherwise, endian conversion is required locally and you'll need to invoke RMAN on the source system as follows:

```
C:\>RMAN TARGET /
RMAN> convert tablespace user_data
2> to platform 'Solaris[tm] OE (32-bit)'
3> format 'c:\temp\%U';

Starting conversion at source at 28-SEP-08
using channel ORA_DISK_1
channel ORA_DISK_1: starting datafile conversion
input datafile file number=00006 name=C:\ORACLE\ORADATA\ORCL\USER_DATA01.DBF
converted datafile=C:\TEMP\DATA_D-ORCL_I-1190467526_TS-
```

```
USER_DATA_FNO-6_3RJRNU8G
channel ORA_DISK_1: datafile conversion complete, elapsed time: 00:00:01
Finished conversion at source at 28-SEP-08

RMAN>
```

At this point you can exit from RMAN and return to SQL*Plus; you have a transportable set that consists of the export dump file and the converted tablespace datafile on the local source system. You can exit to SQL*Plus and return the tablespaces in the transportable set to read-write mode:

```
SQL>alter tablespace user_data read write;
Tablespace altered.
SQL>
```

Step 4: Transport the Tablespace Set

Now you will need to copy the export dump file and datafiles in the tablespace set to the target system. If the datafiles didn't need endian conversion or if you converted the datafiles using RMAN on the source system, copy the datafiles from the source to the target destination using an operating-system copy utility or FTP binary mode, RMAN, or the DBMS_FILE_TRANSFER package. If the files require target-side conversion, copy the files into the temporary staging directory on the target.

Once you have copied the datafiles from the source system, you can return to SQL*Plus on the source and return the tablespaces in the transportable set to read-write mode:

```
SQL>alter tablespace user_data read write;
Tablespace altered.
SQL>
```

If the files do not need conversion, move on to step 5 at this time. If the datafiles require target-side endian conversion, invoke RMAN to perform the conversion, as in this example:

```
RMAN> CONVERT DATAFILE
'/orastage/user_data01.dbf'
TO PLATFORM="Solaris[tm] OE (32-bit)"
FROM PLATFORM="Microsoft Windows IA (32-bit)"
DB_FILE_NAME_CONVERT="/oracle/oradata/LNEB/";
```

Now that the datafiles are converted locally and in the correct target destination, you can move on to step 5.

Step 5: Import the Tablespace Set

As mentioned in an earlier note, either the transportable tablespace's block size must match the standard block size of the target database or the target database must have a cache configured for the same block size as the transportable set.

In the previous target-side endian conversion example, we copied the tablespace datafile and converted it into the /oracle/oradata/LNEB directory. Make sure that you have a DIRECTORY created for the target database and that you have copied the export metadata file referenced by DUMPFILE into that location. Now we'll import the datafiles:

```
IMPDP DUMPFILE=expdat.dmp DIRECTORY=imp_dir
TRANSPORT_DATAFILES=/oracle/oradata/LNEB/user_data01.dbf
```

If the schema owner on the source does not exist on the target, you must either create the schema owner on the target or use the REMAP_SCHEMA import clause to specify a new schema owner. You must use a valid Directory object in your data pump import command.

Once you have verified that the import completed successfully, it would be a good time to verify that the source tablespaces are in read-write mode.

In Exercise 11.1, you will see how to export a transportable tablespace set.

EXERCISE 11.1

Exporting a Transportable Tablespace Set

To export a transportable tablespace set, do the following:

1. Check source and destination compatibility.
2. Select the tablespaces for the transportable tablespace set and verify that the set is self-contained.
3. Generate the transportable tablespace set.

Using Enterprise Manager to Transport a Tablespace

In this section we will show you how to transport a tablespace using Enterprise Manager. From the Enterprise Manager database home page, click the Data Movement tab, then click the Transport Tablespaces link under Move Database Files, shown in Figure 11.25.

From the Transport Tablespaces page, select the Generate a Transportable Tablespace Set option, provide the host credentials, then click the Continue button, all shown in Figure 11.26.

Now, in the screen shown in Figure 11.27, add the tablespaces required in the transportable tablespace set, and choose Self or Full under Containment Type. For self-contained, determine if you need to include constraints. You can also check containment at this time.

Once you have checked containment, you will be given the opportunity to select the destination database platform and character set, shown in Figure 11.28.

FIGURE 11.25 The Transport Tablespace link in Enterprise Manager

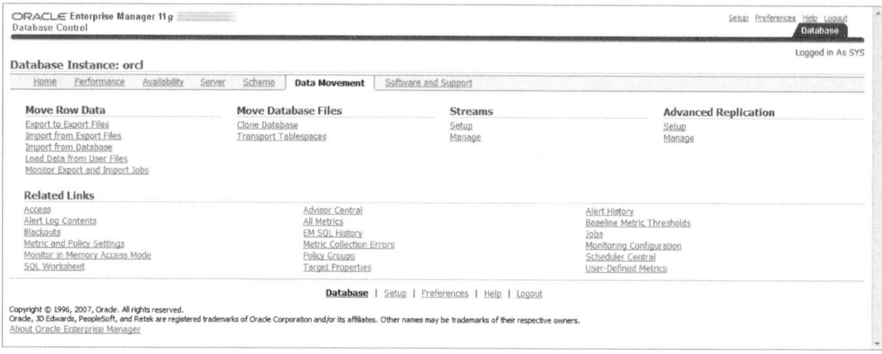

FIGURE 11.26 Transport tablespaces using Enterprise Manager.

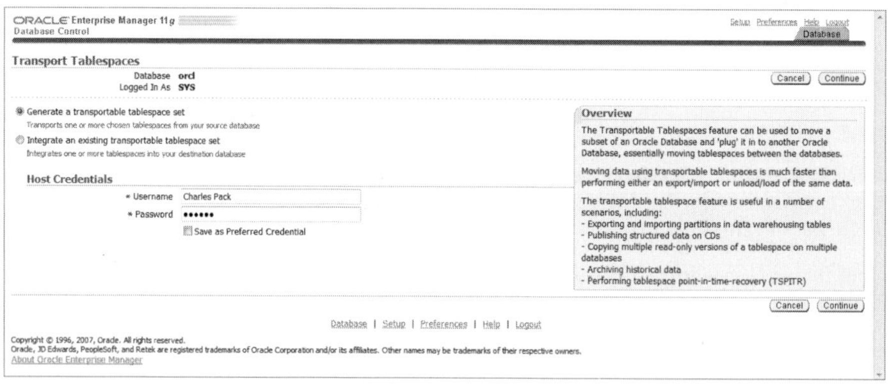

FIGURE 11.27 Generate Transportable Tablespaces: Select Tablespaces

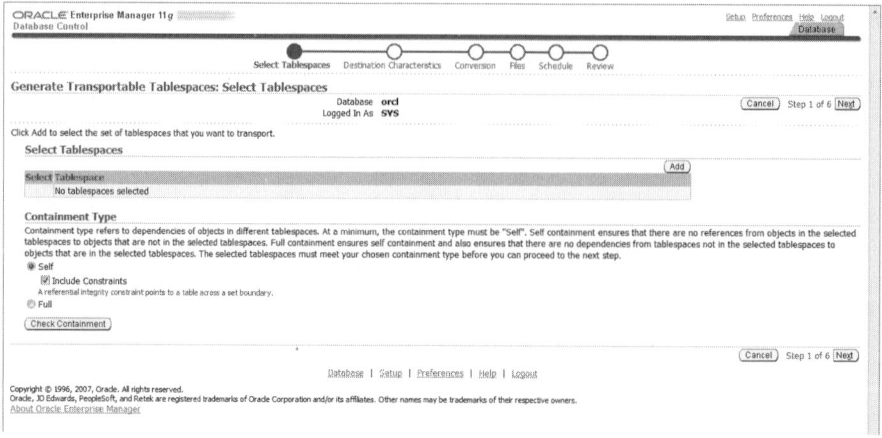

FIGURE 11.28 Generate Transportable Tablespaces: Destination Characteristics

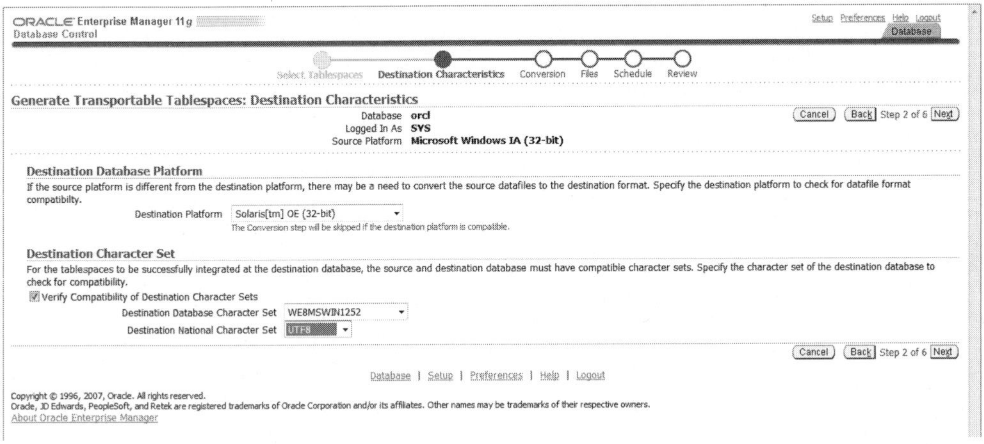

The next step is to choose the conversion process, either convert at destination or convert at source, as shown in Figure 11.29. For this exercise, we'll choose to convert at the source.

Now we choose the dump-file directory and dump-file name, as shown in Figure 11.30.

Now you can schedule the export and conversion, and then review as shown in Figure 11.31.

Submit the job. You will be returned to the Data Movement home page, and you can view the job details if you choose. At this point, you have a transportable tablespace set that you can import into a target database using Enterprise Manager or the command line.

FIGURE 11.29 Generate Transportable Tablespaces: Conversion

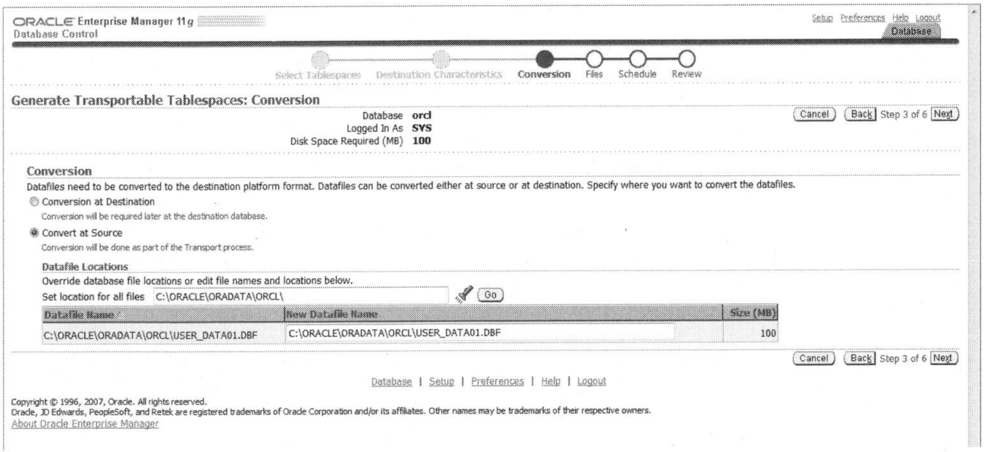

FIGURE 11.30 Generate Transportable Tablespaces: Files

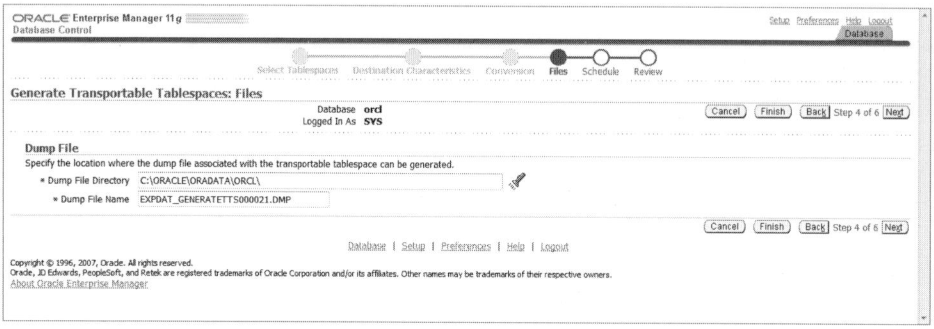

FIGURE 11.31 Generate Transportable Tablespaces: Review

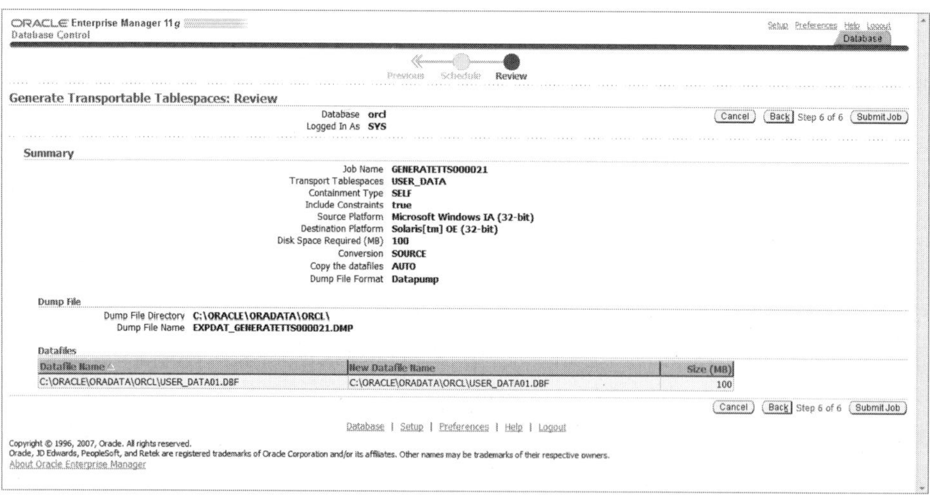

Managing Transportable Databases

Transportable Database (TDB) allows you to migrate an entire database from one platform to another as long as the source and destination platforms have the same endian format. You must use a tool other than TDB for database migration if the source and destination are not of the same endian format.

TDB utilizes RMAN to convert all datafiles from the source to the destination platform. You can use TDB to create a copy of the database on the source system in the format of the destination system and then copy to the files to the destination, or you can copy the source files to the destination system into a staging area and then use RMAN to convert the datafiles and copy them to their intended final destination.

The basic steps for TDB to migrate a database to a new platform are as follows:

1. Verify the prerequisites.

2. Identify all external files and directories.
3. Start the source database in read-only mode.
4. Verify that the source database is ready for migration.
5. Run RMAN CONVERT DATABASE.
6. Move files to the destination system.
7. Complete the migration.

A large amount of the time required to complete the migration will be spent writing files, with RMAN converting files and transferring files from the source to the destination. If you have a time constraint, consider manually copying files across a LAN instead; utilize your storage area network (SAN)–attached storage, network attached storage (NAS), or network file system (NFS)–mounted file systems to speed the process. Allowing source and destination to share the staging area will reduce your transfer time. Also consider running the RMAN CONVERT process on the system that has the better throughput.

Checking Prerequisites

Before you begin TDB, you'll need to verify that your source and destination database platforms are supported. From your source database, query the V$DB_TRANSPORTABLE_PLATFORM view. If you don't see the destination platform, you'll need to skip TDB and choose another migration method.

```
SQL> select platform_name from v$db_transportable_platform;

PLATFORM_NAME
-------------------------------
Microsoft Windows IA (32-bit)
Linux IA (32-bit)
HP Tru64 UNIX
Linux IA (64-bit)
HP Open VMS
Microsoft Windows IA (64-bit)
Linux 64-bit for AMD
Microsoft Windows 64-bit for AMD
Solaris Operating System (x86)
HP IA Open VMS
Solaris Operating System (AMD64)

11 rows selected.

SQL>
```

The query results show that you can transport the database on this server to any of those platforms listed.

The remaining prerequisite steps are as follows:

1. Verify that there are no restrictions or limitations that the source or destination database may encounter.
2. Verify that the destination and source systems have the same Oracle version, critical patch updates, patch-set version, and patch-set exceptions. Verify using the OPatch utility.
3. Determine if you will use the source or destination system to perform the conversion.

Identifying all External Files and Directories

Verify that you have created all necessary directories on the destination system as well as determined which external database files, such as BFILES and external tables, need to migrate to the destination. Query DBA_DIRECTORIES to report file system locations. Execute the supplied function DBMS_TDB.CHECK_EXTERNAL to identify external tables, directories, and BFILES that you'll need to move as part of the migration. Here's an example:

```
SQL> set serveroutput on
SQL> declare
         tdb_check boolean;
      begin
         tdb_check := dbms_tdb.check_external();
      end;
/
The following external tables exist in the database:
SYS.WRR$_REPLAY_CONN_DATA_EXT, SYS.WRR$_REPLAY_SEQ_DATA_EXT,
SYS.WRR$_REPLAY_SCN_ORDER_EXT, SH.SALES_TRANSACTIONS_EXT
The following directories exist in the database:
SYS.EM_TTS_DIR_OBJECT, SYS.EXP_DIR, SYS.IDR_DIR, SYS.CAPTURE_DIR, SYS.SUBDIR,
SYS.XMLDIR, SYS.MEDIA_DIR, SYS.LOG_FILE_DIR, SYS.DATA_FILE_DIR, SYS.AUDIT_DIR,
SYS.DATA_PUMP_DIR
The following BFILEs exist in the database:
PM.PRINT_MEDIA

PL/SQL procedure successfully completed.

SQL>
```

Once you start the migration, don't create any new external objects in the source database.

Starting the Source Database in Read-Only Mode

When you're ready to start the migration, you'll need to shut down the source database and open it in read only mode.

```
SQL> shutdown immediate;
SQL> startup mount;
SQL> alter database open read only;
```

At this point in time you have not started the migration to the destination system, and you haven't made any changes to the source system. If you run into problems and need to return to normal operations in the source system, this would be your "rollback" point.

Verifying that the Database Is Ready for Migration

Now you need to verify that the source database is in fact ready for migration to the destination. Execute the DBMS_TDB.CHECK_DB function, providing the destination system PLATFORM_NAME exactly as shown in the V$DB_TRANSPORTABLE_PLATFORM view. If the CHECK_DB function returns an error condition, you must fix it before you can continue the migration.

```
SQL> set serveroutput on
SQL> declare
        tdb_check boolean;
     begin
        tdb_check := dbms_tdb.check_db
        ('Linux IA (64-bit)',dbms_tdb.skip_none);
     end;
Database is not open in READ-ONLY mode. Open the database
 in READ-ONLY mode and retry.
PL/SQL procedure successfully completed.
```

The results show that you didn't start the database in read-only mode, so you must fix that and rerun the PL/SQL block before moving to the next step.

If you're using a physical standby database for the migration source, run the DBMS_TDB.CHECK_DB function on the standby, not the primary. Follow this general rule for the remainder of this section unless otherwise indicated. If you're migrating from a physical standby database, use the physical standby, not the primary database, wherever we refer to the source.

Running RMAN *CONVERT DATABASE*

With the RMAN conversion, you'll run either a source-system or destination-system conversion. We'll describe the process for both, starting with the source-system, then the destination-system approach.

Database Conversion on the Source System

To create the converted copy of the source database on the source system, connect to RMAN on the source system and execute the `CONVERT DATABASE` command. In this example, we converted the small `orcl` sample database on a Windows 32-bit system to Linux 64-bit. The database files are converted and placed into the `c:\temp\stage` directory on the source system, and the transport script and the `init.ora` file are placed in the `c:\temp` directory.

```
RMAN> convert database
2> transport script 'c:\temp\transport_db_orclnx.sql'
3> new database 'orclnx'
4> to platform 'Linux IA (64-bit)'
5> parallelism 4
6> format 'c:\temp\%d%f'
7> db_file_name_convert 'c:\oracle\oradata\orcl\','c:\temp\stage\';

Starting conversion at source at 31-AUG-08
using channel ORA_DISK_1
using channel ORA_DISK_2
using channel ORA_DISK_3
using channel ORA_DISK_4

External table SYS.WRR$_REPLAY_CONN_DATA_EXT found in the database
External table SYS.WRR$_REPLAY_SEQ_DATA_EXT found in the database
External table SYS.WRR$_REPLAY_SCN_ORDER_EXT found in the database
External table SH.SALES_TRANSACTIONS_EXT found in the database

Directory SYS.IDR_DIR found in the database
Directory SYS.CAPTURE_DIR found in the database
Directory SYS.SUBDIR found in the database
Directory SYS.XMLDIR found in the database
Directory SYS.MEDIA_DIR found in the database
Directory SYS.LOG_FILE_DIR found in the database
Directory SYS.DATA_FILE_DIR found in the database
Directory SYS.AUDIT_DIR found in the database
Directory SYS.DATA_PUMP_DIR found in the database
Directory SYS.ORACLE_OCM_CONFIG_DIR found in the database

BFILE PM.PRINT_MEDIA found in the database

User SYS with SYSDBA and SYSOPER privilege found in password file
channel ORA_DISK_1: starting datafile conversion
```

```
input datafile file number=00005 name=C:\ORACLE\ORADATA\ORCL\EXAMPLE01.DBF
channel ORA_DISK_2: starting datafile conversion
input datafile file number=00002 name=C:\ORACLE\ORADATA\ORCL\SYSAUX01.DBF
channel ORA_DISK_3: starting datafile conversion
input datafile file number=00001 name=C:\ORACLE\ORADATA\ORCL\SYSTEM01.DBF
channel ORA_DISK_4: starting datafile conversion
input datafile file number=00003 name=C:\ORACLE\ORADATA\ORCL\UNDOTBS01.DBF
converted datafile=C:\TEMP\STAGE\EXAMPLE01.DBF
channel ORA_DISK_1: datafile conversion complete, elapsed time: 00:00:41
channel ORA_DISK_1: starting datafile conversion
input datafile file number=00004 name=C:\ORACLE\ORADATA\ORCL\USERS01.DBF
converted datafile=C:\TEMP\STAGE\USERS01.DBF
channel ORA_DISK_1: datafile conversion complete, elapsed time: 00:00:26
converted datafile=C:\TEMP\STAGE\UNDOTBS01.DBF
channel ORA_DISK_4: datafile conversion complete, elapsed time: 00:02:18
converted datafile=C:\TEMP\STAGE\SYSAUX01.DBF
channel ORA_DISK_2: datafile conversion complete, elapsed time: 00:03:17
converted datafile=C:\TEMP\STAGE\SYSTEM01.DBF
channel ORA_DISK_3: datafile conversion complete, elapsed time: 00:03:15
Edit init.ora file C:\TEMP\INIT_ORCLNX4294967295.ORA.
This PFILE will be used to
 create the database on the target platform
Run SQL script C:\TEMP\TRANSPORT_DB_ORCLNX.SQL on the
 target platform to create
database
To recompile all PL/SQL modules, run utlirp.sql and
 utlrp.sql on the target plat
form
To change the internal database identifier, use DBNEWID Utility
Finished conversion at source at 31-AUG-08

RMAN>
```

Verify the accuracy of the filenames and directories in the script files before you run them and attempt to start up your new destination database.

Database Conversion on the Destination System

To create the converted copy of the source database on the destination system, run RMAN on the destination system and execute the `CONVERT DATABASE ON DESTINATION PLATFORM` command. The command produces the convert script necessary to convert the database files on the destination system, the pfile, and a transport script.

```
rman connect target /
RMAN> convert database on destination platform
2>convert script '/tmp/convert_orclnx.rman'
3>transport script '/tmp/transport_orclnx.sql'
4>new database 'orclnx'
5>format '/tmp/orclnx%U'
6>db_file_name_convert '/ora100/oradata/orclnx/datafile','/tmp/stage/';
```

Moving Files to the Destination System

If you converted the datafiles at the source, you should now copy them to the destination system. If you used your SAN, NAS, or NFS storage, now's the time for the destination system to take ownership of the database files. Copy the transport SQL script, pfile, external table files, and BFILES to the destination.

If you chose to convert the files at the destination, you will now need to copy the convert script to the destination and move the unconverted datafiles to the staging area. Again, SAN, NAS, and/or NFS storage should be made read/write for the destination at this time.

Completing the Migration

If you converted the datafiles at the destination, you'll need to run the RMAN convert script on the destination system.

Whether you converted at the source or at the destination, review and modify the pfile as required. Now review the transport script created by the `RMAN CONVERT DATABASE` command. Verify that the directory locations are correct for the pfile, datafiles, log files, and tempfile. After you make corrections and verify, execute the transport script and check for any error messages.

Using Shrinking Segments

As with the files on the hard drive in your personal computer, the data within Oracle database segments can become fragmented with use. Data Manipulation Language (DML) operations—namely delete, update, and insert—can cause fragmentation of data and free space. Fragmentation of free space leads to wasted free space as well as performance issues such as the following:

Cache utilization Sparsely populated (fragmented) data blocks in memory require more reads to get the same amount of data as densely populated (defragmented) data blocks.

Table and index scans A full segment scan of fragmented data blocks requires more physical reads than a scan of defragmented blocks, so full table scans must read more fragmented blocks than defragmented blocks to get the same results.

There are two methods to defragment a segment online; use either Table Redefinition, also referred to as *reorganization*, or Segment Shrink. Table Redefinition copies a table to a new location and consolidates the data. This operation requires space for the new copy of the table and its dependent objects. Also worth mentioning is the method to deallocate unused space above the high-water mark by issuing the `DEALLOCATE UNUSED` command. See Table 11.3 for a comparison of these methods.

TABLE 11.3 Comparing Space-Reclamation Methods

Method	Reclamation Method
Segment Shrink	Reclaims space above and below the high-water mark without using additional space
Reorganization	Moves rows to a new physical location, resetting the high-water mark but using additional space during the operation
Deallocate Unused	Deallocates space above the high-water mark that is currently not in use

For segments in dictionary-managed tablespaces or for locally managed tablespaces with manual segment space management, segment reorganization is the only permitted operation for reclaiming fragmented free space.

Online Segment Shrink compacts the segment in place and does not require additional space to perform the operation. Segment Shrink can be performed on the dependent objects like indexes and partitions. Segment Shrink works on the following objects:

- Heap tables
- Index-organized tables and their overflow segments
- LOBs and LOB segments
- Materialized views and materialized view logs
- Indexes
- Partitions and subpartitions

To be eligible for segment shrink, the segment must have row movement enabled and reside in a tablespace that is locally managed and utilizes Automatic Segment Space Management (ASSM). The following objects in an ASSM tablespace are not eligible for Segment Shrink:

- SecureFile LOBs
- Index-organized table mapping tables
- Tables that have ROWID-based materialized views
- Tables with function-based indexes

To enable row movement for a table, issue the ALTER TABLE ... ENABLE ROW MOVEMENT command.

Performing an Online Segment Shrink Operation

Because Segment Shrink moves rows and changes the ROWIDs, before you perform the online Segment Shrink operation, you will need to do the following:

- Enable row movement.
- Disable any ROWID-based triggers defined on the object.
- Determine if the application uses any ROWID-based DML or queries.

By default, online Segment Shrink performs the following:

- Compacts the segment
- Resets the high-water mark
- Releases the reclaimed free space

Since Segment Shrink is an online operation, DML and queries can continue as normal. There is a brief block of concurrent DML operations on the segment when the space is released at the end of the shrink operation. Indexes remain usable throughout the operation.

Here's an example of shrinking a table:

```
SQL> ALTER TABLE HR.EMPLOYEES SHRINK SPACE;
ALTER TABLE HR.EMPLOYEES SHRINK SPACE
*
ERROR at line 1:
ORA-10636: ROW MOVEMENT is not enabled
SQL> ALTER TABLE HR.EMPLOYEES ENABLE ROW MOVEMENT;
Table altered.
SQL> ALTER TABLE HR.EMPLOYEES SHRINK SPACE;
Table altered.
```

There are two optional clauses with the SHRINK SPACE command: COMPACT and CASCADE. The COMPACT clause defragments and compacts but does not reset the high-water mark or return the free space. Execute the SHRINK SPACE command without the COMPACT clause at a later time to complete the task.

The CASCADE clause performs the Shrink Space operation on all dependent objects, as reported by the DBMS_SPACE.OBJECT_DEPENDENT_SEGMENT procedure.

Partitions in a partitioned table are automatically shrunk with the SHRINK SPACE command, so you don't need to specify the CASCADE clause.

Here's an example of a small sample table called HR.EMPLOYEES_HIST, built as a copy of the Oracle-provided HR.EMPLOYEE table. We've inserted rows until we've allocated 40 blocks, then deleted about 70 percent of the rows. The shrink operation should reduce the number of blocks to 16. We'll perform the two-step COMPACT process and CASCADE so that you can see how they work:

```
SQL> SELECT COUNT(1) from hr.employees_hist;

  COUNT(1)
----------
      2943

SQL> SELECT SEGMENT_NAME, BLOCKS FROM DBA_SEGMENTS
WHERE OWNER = 'HR' and SEGMENT_NAME LIKE 'EMPL%';

SEGMENT_NAME                 BLOCKS
------------------------ ----------
EMPLOYEES                         8
EMPLOYEES_HIST                   40
EMPLOYEES_HIST_IX                16

SQL> ALTER TABLE HR.EMPLOYEES_HIST SHRINK SPACE COMPACT;
Table altered.
SQL> SELECT SEGMENT_NAME, BLOCKS FROM DBA_SEGMENTS
WHERE OWNER = 'HR' and SEGMENT_NAME LIKE 'EMPL%';

SEGMENT_NAME                 BLOCKS
------------------------ ----------
EMPLOYEES                         8
EMPLOYEES_HIST                   40
EMPLOYEES_HIST_IX                16

SQL> ALTER TABLE HR.EMPLOYEES_HIST SHRINK SPACE;
Table altered.
SQL> SELECT SEGMENT_NAME, BLOCKS FROM DBA_SEGMENTS
WHERE OWNER = 'HR' and SEGMENT_NAME LIKE 'EMPL%';

SEGMENT_NAME                 BLOCKS
------------------------ ----------
EMPLOYEES                         8
EMPLOYEES_HIST                   16
```

```
EMPLOYEES_HIST_IX                  16

SQL> ALTER TABLE HR.EMPLOYEES_HIST SHRINK SPACE CASCADE;
Table altered.
SQL> SELECT SEGMENT_NAME, BLOCKS FROM DBA_SEGMENTS
WHERE OWNER = 'HR' and SEGMENT_NAME LIKE 'EMPL%';

SEGMENT_NAME                   BLOCKS
------------------------ ----------
EMPLOYEES                           8
EMPLOYEES_HIST                     16
EMPLOYEES_HIST_IX                   8

SQL> SELECT COUNT(1) from hr.employees_hist;

  COUNT(1)
----------
       910

SQL>
```

Using Enterprise Manager Segment Space Advisor to Perform an Online Segment Shrink Operation

After repopulating and deleting from our test table HR.EMPLOYEES_HIST, we want to use EM to shrink the segment. From the Enterprise Manager database home page, in the Related Links section, find the Advisor Central. From the Advisor Central, choose the Segment Advisor. From the Segment Advisor Scope page, shown in Figure 11.32, choose Schema Objects and then click Next.

FIGURE 11.32 The Automatic Segment Advisor: Scope page

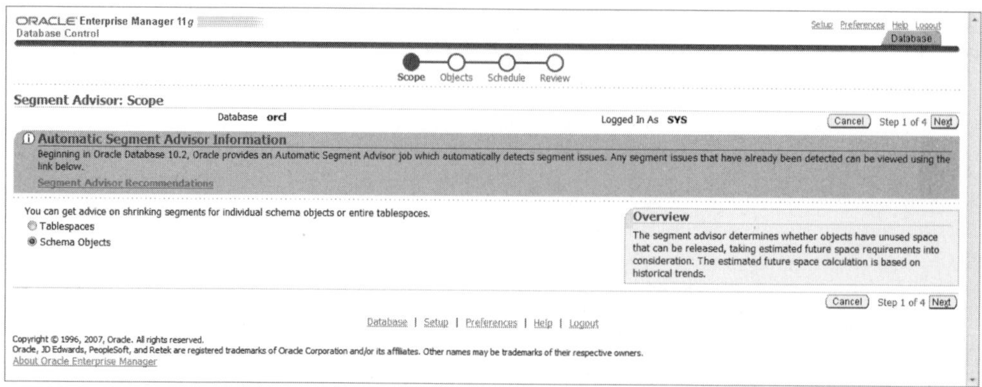

Next choose the objects to add to the advisor by clicking the check box in the Select column next to the object name on the Schema Objects page, shown in Figure 11.33. You can also set the time limit for analysis under the advanced options, shown in Figure 11.34.

FIGURE 11.33 The Automatic Segment Advisor: Schema Objects page

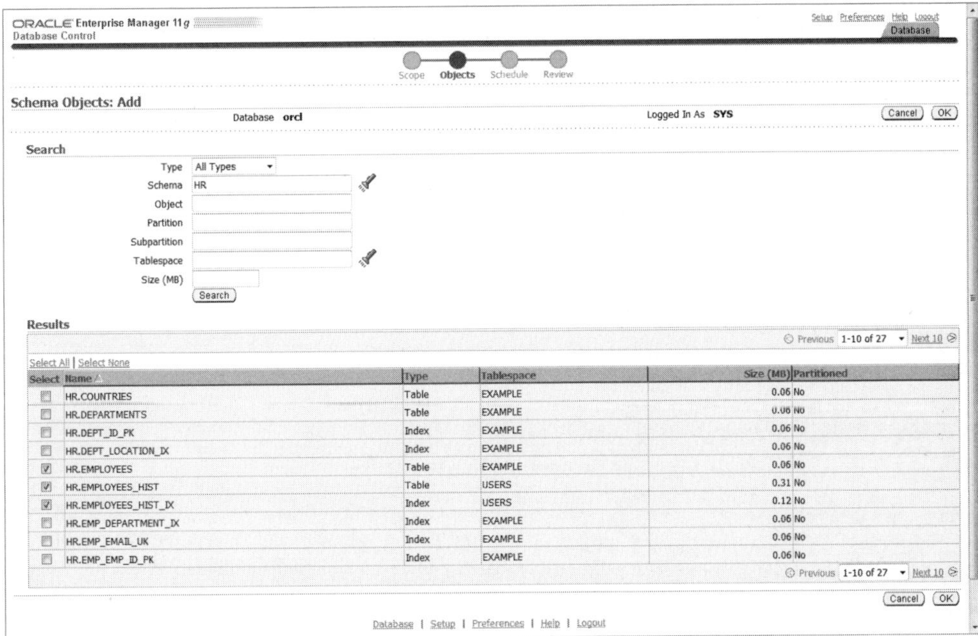

FIGURE 11.34 The Automatic Segment Advisor: Schema Objects page

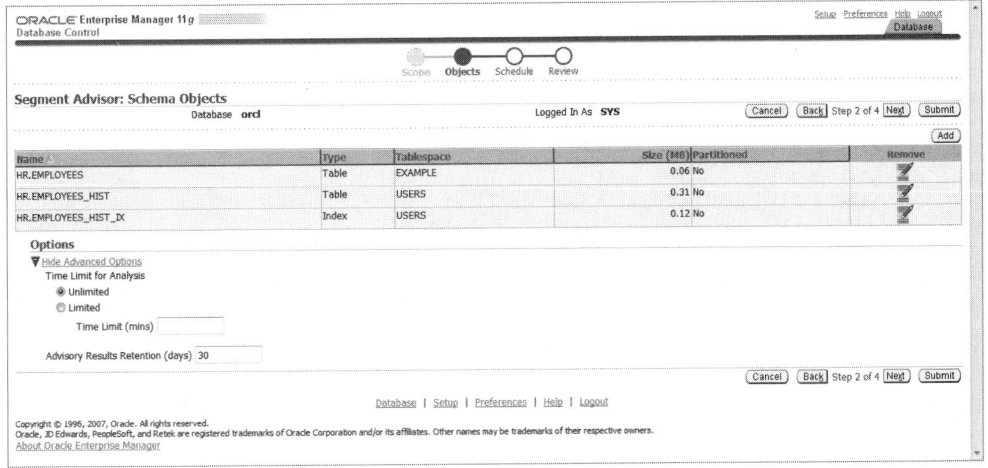

Once you set the schedule and review it, return to the Advisor Central page to monitor the Auto Space Advisor task results. For the example, the Segment Space Advisor chose not to shrink our `HR.EMPLOYEES_HIST` table. Since we're really persistent about shrinking this table, from the EM database home page we will go to the Schema page, click Tables, enter the schema and object information for `HR.EMPLOYEES_HIST`, and then click the Go button. The basic information for the object will be displayed as in Figure 11.35.

Figure 11.36 shows that we chose the Shrink Segment operation from the Actions drop-down menu.

FIGURE 11.35 Selecting a table

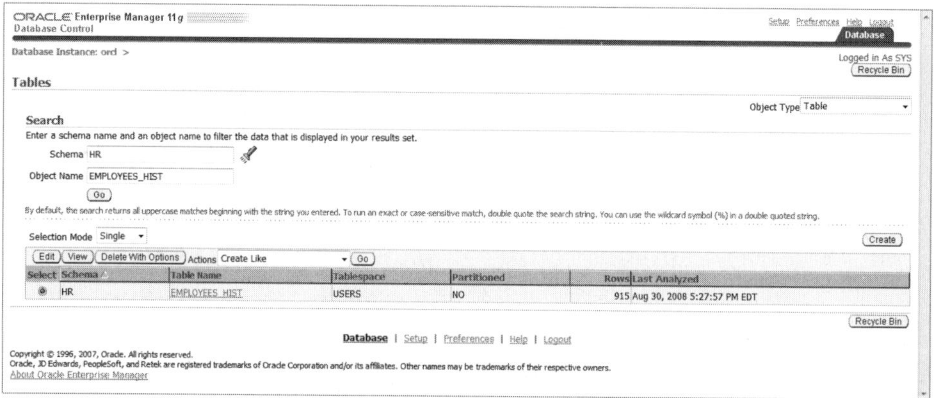

FIGURE 11.36 Selecting the shrink operation

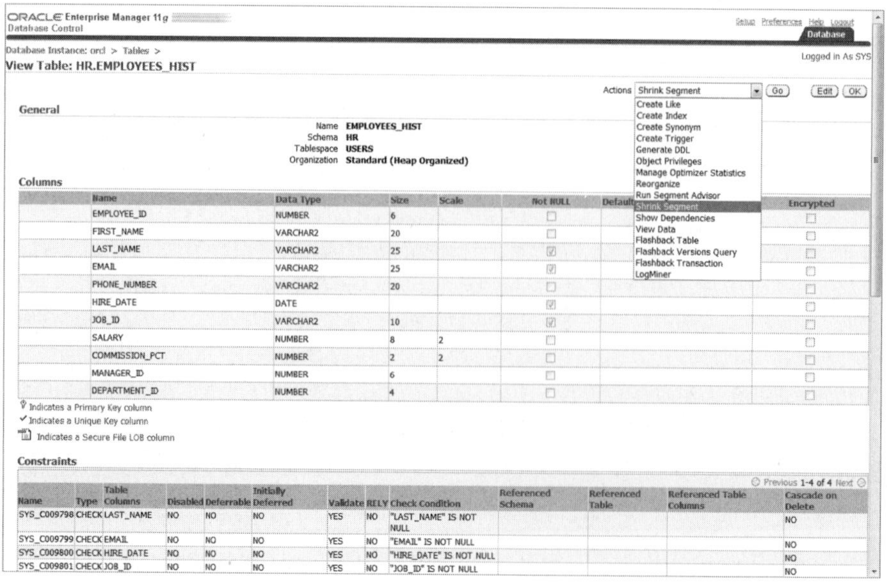

ORACLE Enterprise Manager 11g
Database Control

Setup Preferences Help Logout

Database

Database Instance: orcl > Tables >

Logged in As SYS

View Table: HR.EMPLOYEES_HIST

Actions: Shrink Segment (Go) (Edit) (OK)

Create Like
Create Index
Create Synonym
Create Trigger
Generate DDL
Object Privileges
Manage Optimizer Statistics
Reorganize
Run Segment Advisor
Shrink Segment
Show Dependencies
View Data
Flashback Table
Flashback Versions Query
Flashback Transaction
LogMiner

General

Name **EMPLOYEES_HIST**
Schema **HR**
Tablespace **USERS**
Organization **Standard (Heap Organized)**

Columns

Name	Data Type	Size	Scale	Not NULL	Default	Encrypted
EMPLOYEE_ID	NUMBER	6				
FIRST_NAME	VARCHAR2	20				
LAST_NAME	VARCHAR2	25		✓		
EMAIL	VARCHAR2	25		✓		
PHONE_NUMBER	VARCHAR2	20				
HIRE_DATE	DATE			✓		
JOB_ID	VARCHAR2	10		✓		
SALARY	NUMBER	8	2			
COMMISSION_PCT	NUMBER	2	2			
MANAGER_ID	NUMBER	6				
DEPARTMENT_ID	NUMBER	4				

Indicates a Primary Key column
Indicates a Unique Key column
Indicates a Secure File LOB column

Constraints

Previous 1-4 of 4 Next

Name	Type	Table Columns	Disabled	Deferrable	Initially Deferred	Validate	RELY	Check Condition	Referenced Schema	Referenced Table	Referenced Table Columns	Cascade on Delete
SYS_C009798	CHECK	LAST_NAME	NO	NO	NO	YES	NO	"LAST_NAME" IS NOT NULL				NO
SYS_C009799	CHECK	EMAIL	NO	NO	NO	YES	NO	"EMAIL" IS NOT NULL				NO
SYS_C009800	CHECK	HIRE_DATE	NO	NO	NO	YES	NO	"HIRE_DATE" IS NOT NULL				NO
SYS_C009801	CHECK	JOB_ID	NO	NO	NO	YES	NO	"JOB_ID" IS NOT NULL				NO

Under Shrink Options (shown in Figure 11.37), choose to compact only or to compact and release freed space, and also choose an option under Segment Selection, synonymous with the CASCADE clause we used at the command line. Schedule a job to shrink the table by clicking the Continue button; then submit the job. You can see in Figure 11.38 that the job completed successfully, and you can view the SQL statement executed to shrink the segment.

FIGURE 11.37 Selecting the shrink options

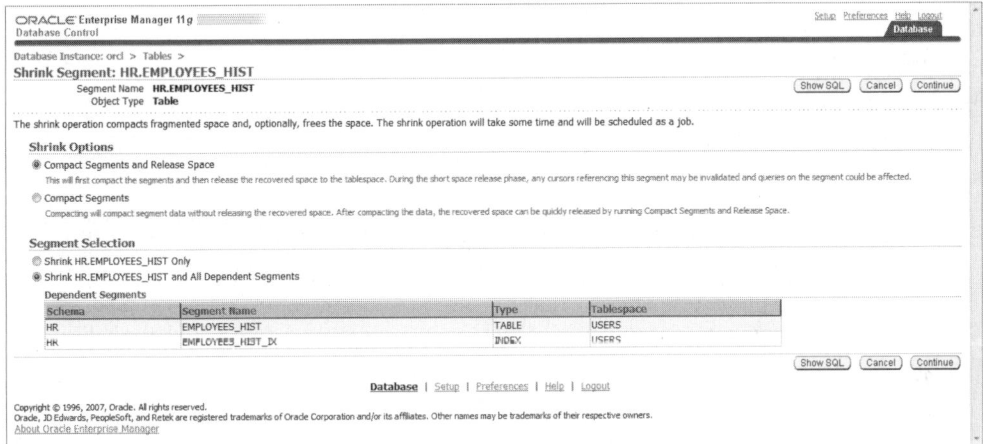

FIGURE 11.38 Viewing the shrink job

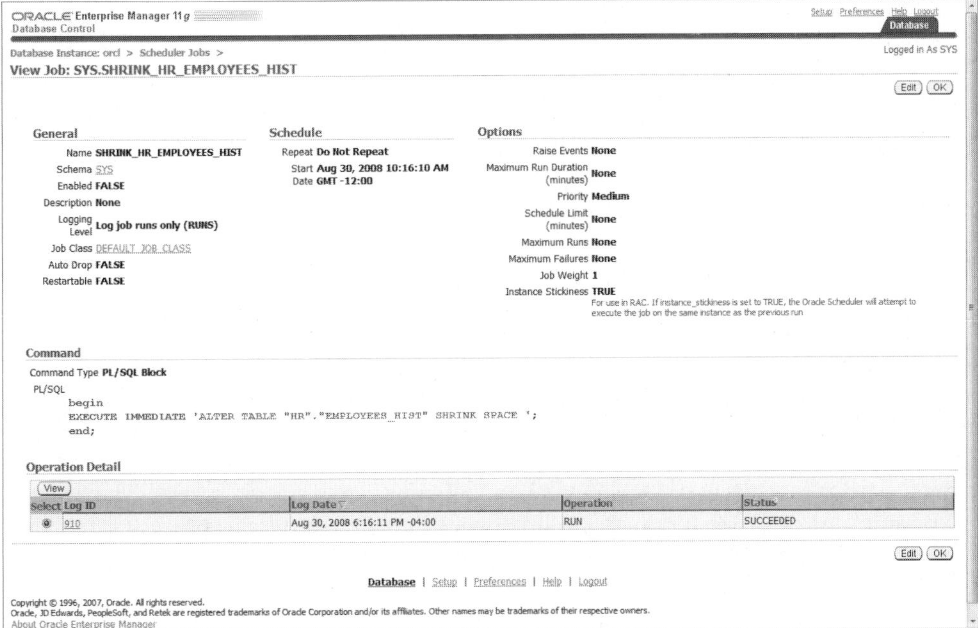

We want to verify the operation was successful, so in SQL*Plus, run the query we ran before to validate the results.

```
SQL> SELECT SEGMENT_NAME, BLOCKS FROM DBA_SEGMENTS
WHERE OWNER = 'HR' and SEGMENT_NAME LIKE 'EMPL%';

SEGMENT_NAME                  BLOCKS
------------------------- ----------
EMPLOYEES                          8
EMPLOYEES_HIST                    16
EMPLOYEES_HIST_IX                  8
```

In Exercise 11.2, you'll learn how to shrink a segment.

EXERCISE 11.2

Shrinking a Segment

For this exercise, you'll create a table, populate it, delete rows, and then shrink the table segment:

1. Create a table named `shrink_test` with two columns: a NUMBER column named X and a VARCHAR2 (10) column named Y. Enable row movement for the table.
2. Insert two rows with a unique value for X for each row.
3. Now, using the `insert into shrink_test select * from shrink_test` SQL statement repeatedly, grow the table to 1 million rows (or more), and commit. Verify that every other row has the same value.
4. Query DBA_SEGMENTS to determine the size of the segment.
5. Delete half the rows from the table, using one of the values of X as the delete criteria.
6. Now shrink the segment online, and verify that the number of blocks decreases.

Managing Resources

As a database administrator, it is your job to maintain a given level of performance from the database. Successfully accomplishing this mission requires close management of scarce hardware resources.

In the past, management of Oracle resources fell upon the operating system. The operating system had to juggle resources not only between the different Oracle processes, but also between Oracle and all other processes running on the system. As if that weren't enough, it also had no way of differentiating one Oracle process from another. Therefore, allocating resources between user groups or applications was impossible.

In addition, resource management performed by the operating system has a tendency to cause certain performance problems. Excessive context switching can occur when the number of server processes is high. Server processes holding latches can be descheduled, resulting in further inefficiency. And inappropriate resource allocation is common due to the inability to prioritize Oracle tasks.

Oracle's Database Resource Manager (DRM) circumvents the inefficient operating system management process by giving the Oracle database server more control over resource-management decisions. It also allows you to distribute available system resources among your users and applications based on business needs (or whatever criteria you wish to base it on).

The following sections describe the different elements of DRM and how to use them. In the overview section, you'll learn about the elements that DRM comprises and see, at a high level, how they interact. You will be introduced to the pending area, a work area that must be established prior to the creation or modification of DRM objects.

Next, you will learn about resource consumer groups, which allow you to classify users based on their resource requirements. You'll learn how to set up resource plans that direct the allocation of resources among the resource consumer groups. You'll learn about resource-allocation options offered by the database, and the methods you can define to apply them.

You will also learn about resource-plan directives that associate resource consumer groups, resource plans, and resource-allocation methods. Finally, you'll learn the PL/SQL interface to manage DRM as well as the views available to query DRM information.

Keep in mind that the elements of DRM constitute a "chicken or the egg" situation in terms of the ordering of the topics. For instance, the pending area must be established before anything else is done. However, discussion of the pending area assumes knowledge of the objects defined later. In the interest of organization and ease of use, each topic will be covered separately in its own section. Then, a final section will show how the elements integrate.

The DRM offers a component-based approach to resource allocation management. When you define distinct, independent components representing the DRM elements, the result is an extremely flexible and easy-to-use system.

There are three main elements that make up the DRM:

- Resource consumer groups
- Resource plans
- Resource-plan directives

DRM allocates resources among resource consumer groups based on a resource plan. A resource plan consists of resource-plan directives that specify how resources should be distributed among the groups. Resource consumer groups are categories to which user sessions can be assigned. These groups can then be allocated resources through plan directives.

Plan directives define resource-allocation rules by assigning resource-allocation methods to specific resource consumer groups. They connect resource plans to consumer groups and define the resource-allocation method to be used.

Resource-allocation methods are methods that can be used to allocate resources such as CPU usage, number of sessions, idle time, operation execution time, and so on. Resource-allocation methods are predefined by Oracle, but plan directives determine which ones to apply and the allocation amounts. For example, a plan named NIGHT_PLAN may contain a directive allocating a percentage of CPU to a consumer group named MANAGERS.

Working with the Pending Area

Before defining or updating any DRM objects, you must first establish a pending area. A *pending area* is a staging area where resource-management objects can be defined and validated before they are activated. If you forget to create the pending area, you will receive the following error message if you try to create or update a DRM object:

```
ERROR at line 1:
ORA-29371: pending area is not active
ORA-06512: at "SYS.DBMS_RMIN", line 115
ORA-06512: at "SYS.DBMS_RESOURCE_MANAGER", line 108
ORA-06512: at line 1
```

The next sections explain how to manage pending areas. You will learn to create, validate, submit, and clear them.

Creating a Pending Area

To create a pending area, simply execute the DBMS_RESOURCE_MANAGER.CREATE_PENDING_AREA procedure. This procedure accepts no parameters, so it can be called as follows:

```
SQL> exec dbms_resource_manager.create_pending_area();

PL/SQL procedure successfully completed.
```

Once a pending area has been created, all changes will automatically be stored there until they are validated and submitted.

Validating Changes to the Pending Area

After changes have been made in the pending area, they need to be checked for validity before being activated. This can be accomplished through the DBMS_RESOURCE_GROUP.VALIDATE_PENDING_AREA procedure.

The validation process verifies that any changes in the pending area will not result in a violation of any of the following rules:

- No plan schema can contain a loop.
- All DRM objects identified in a plan directive must exist.
- All plan directives refer to either plans or resource groups.
- Allocation percentages for a given level cannot exceed 100.

- Deletes are not allowed for top plans being used by an active instance.
- Only plan directives that refer to resource consumer group are allowed to set the following parameters:
  - ACTIVE_SESS_POOL_P1
  - MAX_EST_EXEC_TIME
  - MAX_IDLE_BLOCKER_TIME
  - MAX_IDLE_TIME
  - PARALLEL_DEGREE_LIMIT_P1
  - QUEUEING_P1
  - SWITCH_ESTIMATE
  - SWITCH_GROUP
  - SWITCH_TIME
  - SWITCH_FOR_CALL
  - SWITCH_IO_MEGABYTES
  - SWITCH_IO_REQS
  - UNDO_POOL
- An active plan schema can contain no more than 32 resource consumer groups.
- Plan names cannot conflict with resource consumer group names.
- There must be a plan directive for the OTHER_GROUPS group to allocate resources for sessions not identified in the active plan.

If any of the preceding rules are violated, the VALIDATE_PENDING_AREA procedure will return errors for each violation. Here's an example:

```
SQL> exec dbms_resource_manager.validate_pending_area;
BEGIN dbms_resource_manager.validate_pending_area; END;

*
ERROR at line 1:
ORA-29382: validation of pending area failed
ORA-29377: consumer group OTHER_GROUPS is not part of top-plan OLTP_PLAN
ORA-29383: all leaves of top-plan OLTP_PLAN must be consumer groups
ORA-29374: resource plan OLTP_PLAN in top-plan OLTP_PLAN
 has no plan directives
ORA-29377: consumer group OTHER_GROUPS is not part of top-plan OFF_HOURS_PLAN
ORA-29383: all leaves of top-plan OFF_HOURS_PLAN must be consumer groups
ORA-29374: resource plan OFF_HOURS_PLAN in top-plan OFF_HOURS_PLAN has no plan
  directives
```

```
ORA-29377: consumer group OTHER_GROUPS is not part of top-plan DAY_PLAN
ORA-29383: all leaves of top-plan DAY_PLAN must be consumer groups
ORA-29374: resource plan DAY_PLAN in top-plan DAY_PLAN has no plan directives
ORA-06512: at "SYS.DBMS_RMIN", line 402
ORA-06512: at "SYS.DBMS_RESOURCE_MANAGER", line 437
ORA-06512: at line 1
```

If validation is successful, no error messages will be returned.

Submitting the Pending Area

When you are ready to make your changes active, you can use the DBMS_RESOURCE_MANAGER .SUBMIT_PENDING_AREA procedure, as shown here:

```
SQL> exec dbms_resource_manager.submit_pending_area;

PL/SQL procedure successfully completed.
```

As you can see, no parameters are required when submitting the pending area.

Submitting the contents of the pending area will activate those objects (move them to the data dictionary). Active objects are stored in the data dictionary and can be enabled by DRM.

Just because a DRM object is active does not mean it is enabled. It simply means it can be enabled or be included in an enabled plan.

Submitting the pending area actually performs three distinct actions: it validates, submits, and clears the pending area. Therefore, it is not required to perform a separate validation before submitting. However, from a debugging standpoint, it is beneficial to validate changes on an incremental basis rather than waiting until submit time.

Clearing the Pending Area

To clear the pending area without submitting your changes, you can use the DBMS_RESOURCE_MANAGER.CLEAR_PENDING_AREA procedure, as shown here:

```
SQL> exec dbms_resource_manager.clear_pending_area;

PL/SQL procedure successfully completed.
```

Clearing the pending area drops everything in the pending area irretrievably, so use this procedure with caution. As mentioned earlier, submitting the pending area also clears the pending area, so it is not necessary to use this procedure after a successful submit is performed.

The name of this procedure is somewhat misleading. It seems to imply that the objects in the pending area will be cleared but that the pending area will remain intact. This is not true. Once the pending area is cleared, a new pending area must be created before you make any new changes.

Resource Consumer Groups

Resource consumer groups represent the next step in defining a DRM strategy. They allow you to classify users into logical groupings based on resource-consumption requirements or business needs.

There are two ways to define *resource consumer groups*:

- A resource consumer group is a method of classifying users based on their resource-consumption tendencies or requirements.
- A resource consumer group is a method of prioritizing database resource usage by classifying users based on business needs.

For instance, in most companies, payroll users tend to have high priority because no one wants their paychecks to be late. Therefore, a resource consumer group named `PAYROLL` can be created and all payroll users assigned to it.

This does not imply anything about the resource-consumption tendencies or the requirements of payroll users. Instead, it identifies them based on a business need.

On the other hand, a group of inexperienced users may have a habit of executing queries without first checking join conditions. Their resultant Cartesian products tend to run for hours, wasting system resources. For these users, a group named `NOVICE` could be created. This group could then have resource limitations placed upon it.

In this situation, group classification is directly related to the consumption tendencies of the users.

In either situation, users can be assigned to one or more resource consumer groups, although each active session can be assigned to only one resource consumer group at a time. A user may, for example, use the system in an online transaction processing (OLTP) capacity for part of the day, perhaps entering orders or doing account maintenance. The rest of the day, the same user may switch to an online analytical processing (OLAP) capacity, running reports and statistical queries. This user could be a member of both the `OLTP` and `OLAP` resource consumer groups but could be assigned to only one for any session.

The following sections explain how to manage resource consumer groups using PL/SQL packages.

Managing Resource Consumer Groups

Resource consumer groups can be managed by using the `DBMS_RESOURCE_MANAGER` PL/SQL package. This package offers procedures that allow the creation, deletion, and modification of resource consumer groups. It also provides functionality for assigning users to groups and switching the group for user sessions.

In the next few sections, you'll learn how to add, modify, and delete resource consumer groups using the `DBMS_RESOURCE_MANAGER` package. You will also learn to assign users to groups as well as how to switch user sessions between groups.

You must have the `ADMINISTER_RESOURCE_MANAGER` system privilege to administer Database Resource Manager. This privilege is granted by default to the DBA role.

Creating Resource Consumer Groups

To create a new resource consumer group, use the DBMS_RESOURCE_MANAGER.CREATE_CONSUMER_GROUP procedure. All that is required when defining a new group is a unique name and a description. It is not necessary (nor possible) to define how this group will be used at this point.

There are three parameters that you can specify when creating a resource consumer group. Table 11.4 describes these parameters.

TABLE 11.4: CREATE_CONSUMER_GROUP PARAMETERS

Parameter	Description
CONSUMER_GROUP	Consumer group name.
COMMENT	Any comment (usually a description of the group).
CPU_MTH	Deprecated. Use MGMT_MTH.
MGMT_MTH	Method used to schedule CPU resources between sessions in the group. Valid values are as follows: ROUND_ROBIN (the default) ensures fair distribution by using a round-robin schedule; RUN_TO_COMPLETION schedules the most active sessions ahead of other sessions.

The CPU_MTH parameter defines the resource scheduling method used between sessions within a resource group. This method governs only CPU resources between group members.

Be aware that a CPU-allocation method can also be defined at the plan level. Therefore, the total CPU available to the resource group may already have been limited by the active resource plan.

To create a new resource consumer group named DEVELOPERS that uses a round-robin CPU methodology, see the following example:

```
SQL> begin
  dbms_resource_manager.create_consumer_group('developers',
    'application developers');
 end;
SQL>/


PL/SQL procedure successfully completed.
```

To verify that the command succeeded, you can use the DBA_RSRC_CONSUMER_GROUPS view:

```
SQL>  select consumer_group, cpu_method, comments from
```

```
 dba_rsrc_consumer_groups
  where consumer_group = 'DEVELOPERS';

CONSUMER_GROUP  CPU_METHOD      COMMENTS
--------------- --------------- ------------------------
DEVELOPERS      ROUND-ROBIN     application developers
```

By default, there are 14 resource consumer groups predefined in the database. They are described in Table 11.5.

TABLE 11.5 Predefined Resource Consumer Groups

Group Name	Description
DEFAULT_CONSUMER_GROUP	Default group for all users/sessions not assigned to an initial consumer group.
OTHER_GROUPS	Catchall group for users assigned to groups that are not part of the currently active plan. This group cannot be explicitly assigned to users.
SYS_GROUP	Used by the Oracle-provided SYSTEM_PLAN plan.
LOW_GROUP	Used by the Oracle-provided SYSTEM_PLAN plan.
BATCH_GROUP	Consumer group for batch operations.
ORA$DIAGNOSTICS	Consumer group for diagnostics.
ORA$AUTOTASK_HEALTH_GROUP	Consumer group for health checks.
ORA$AUTOTASK_SQL_GROUP	Consumer group for SQL tuning.
ORA$AUTOTASK_SPACE_GROUP	Consumer group for space-management advisors.
ORA$AUTOTASK_STATS_GROUP	Consumer group for gathering optimizer statistics.
ORA$AUTOTASK_MEDIUM_GROUP	Consumer group for medium-priority maintenance tasks.
INTERACTIVE_GROUP	Consumer group for interactive OLTP operations.
AUTO_TASK_CONSUMER_GROUP	System-maintenance task consumer group.
ORA$AUTOTASK_URGENT_GROUP	Consumer group for urgent maintenance tasks.

As you can see in the description, all users who are not assigned to a group will become part of the DEFAULT_CONSUMER_GROUP group. And users who are not assigned to a group in the currently active plan will be assigned to the OTHER_GROUPS group.

The remaining groups were defined to support predefined resource plans provided by Oracle.

Updating Resource Consumer Groups

Resource consumer groups can be updated using the DBMS_RESOURCE_MANAGER.UPDATE_CONSUMER_GROUP procedure. This procedure allows you to change the comment and/or the CPU-allocation method for a particular group. Table 11.6 describes the parameters for the DBMS_RESOURCE_MANAGER.UPDATE_CONSUMER_GROUP procedure.

TABLE 11.6: UPDATE_CONSUMER_GROUP Procedure Parameters

Parameter	Description
CONSUMER_GROUP	Name of the consumer group.
NEW_COMMENT	Updated comment.
NEW_CPU_MTH	Deprecated. Use NEW_MGMT_MTH.
NEW_MGMT_MTH	Updated method for CPU resource allocation.

For instance, to change the CPU-allocation method for the DEVELOPERS group, the following SQL could be used:

```
SQL> begin
  dbms_resource_manager.update_consumer_group(
  CONSUMER_GROUP => 'DEVELOPERS',
  NEW_MGMT_MTH => 'RUN-TO-COMPLETION');
 end;
SQL> /

PL/SQL procedure successfully completed.
```

As you can see in this example, the NEW_COMMENT parameter was omitted because no change was being made to it. By the same token, the NEW_MGMT_MTH parameter could be omitted if only the comment was being updated.

Deleting a Resource Consumer Group

Resource consumer groups can be deleted using the DBMS_RESOURCE_MANAGER.DELETE_CONSUMER_GROUP procedure. Deleting a resource group has a couple of implications that are important to understand:

- Users assigned to the deleted group as their initial resource consumer group will be assigned to the DEFAULT_CONSUMER_GROUP group.
- Current sessions assigned to the deleted group will be switched to the DEFAULT_CONSUMER_GROUP group.

Don't worry if you don't understand the implications of these changes right now. They will be made clear as this chapter progresses.

The single parameter required by the DBMS_RESOURCE_MANAGER.DELETE_CONSUMER_GROUP procedure is CONSUMER_GROUP, the name of the consumer group to be deleted.

Only the name of the group to be deleted needs to be passed to the procedure, as you can see in this example:

```
SQL> begin
  dbms_resource_manager.delete_consumer_group('DEVELOPERS');
 end;
SQL>/

PL/SQL procedure successfully completed.
```

The DEVELOPERS group should now be deleted from the system.

Assigning User Sessions to Consumer Groups

Creating resource consumer groups is only half the battle. You still need a method of assigning consumer groups to user sessions. DRM can be configured to automatically assign consumer groups to sessions based on specific session attributes. This process is called *consumer group mapping*. In the following sections, you will learn how to create consumer group mappings. You will also learn how to set priorities so DRM knows which mapping has precedence in case of conflicts.

CREATING CONSUMER GROUP MAPPINGS

Consumer group mappings can be created by using the DBMS_RESOURCE_MANAGER.SET_CONSUMER_GROUP_MAPPING procedure to create the mapping and the DBMS_RESOURCE_MANAGER.SET_CONSUMER_GROUP_MAPPING_PRI procedure to create the attributes for the mapping. These procedures allow you to map sessions to consumer groups based on login or runtime *session attributes*. Table 11.7 shows the available attributes that can be mapped.

TABLE 11.7: SET_CONSUMER_GROUP_MAPPING_PRI Session Attributes

Attribute	Type	Description
ORACLE_USER	Login	Oracle Database username.
SERVICE_NAME	Login	Service name used by the client to establish a connection.
CLIENT_OS_USER	Login	Operating-system username of the client that is logging in.
CLIENT_PROGRAM	Login	Name of the client program used to log in to the server.
CLIENT_MACHINE	Login	Name of the computer from which the client is making the connection.
MODULE_NAME	Runtime	Module name that is currently executing, as defined by the DBMS_APPLICATION_INFO.SET_MODULE_NAME procedure.
MODULE_NAME_ACTION	Runtime	Module name and module action that are currently executing, as defined by the DBMS_APPLICATION_INFO.SET_MODULE_NAME/SET_ACTION procedures. Attribute is specified in the format *SERVICE_NAME .ACTION*.
SERVICE_MODULE	Runtime	Service name and module name in the format *SERVICE_NAME.MODULE_NAME*.
SERVICE_MODULE_ ACTION	Runtime	Service name, module name, and action name in the format *SERVICE_NAME.MODULE_NAME.ACTION_NAME*.

Mappings simply define a session attribute, a value for the attribute, and a consumer group. For example, if the session attribute CLIENT_OS_USER has a value of graciej, then assign the OLAP_GROUP to the session. The following code would create this mapping:

```
SQL> begin
  dbms_resource_manager.set_consumer_group_mapping(
ATTRIBUTE => CLIENT_OS_USER,
    VALUE => 'graciej', CONSUMER_GROUP => 'OLAP_GROUP');
 end;
SQL>/

PL/SQL procedure successfully completed.
```

Note that session attributes are defined as Oracle constants and are therefore specified without surrounding single quotes.

ESTABLISHING MAPPING PRIORITIES

It is possible that a session may map to more than one consumer group based on mapping rules. Therefore, Oracle allows the creation of *mapping priorities* through the use of the DBMS_RESOURCE_MANAGER.SET_CONSUMER_GROUP_MAPPING_PRI procedure, as follows:

```
SQL> begin
  dbms_resource_manager.set_consumer_group_mapping_pri(
    EXPLICIT => 1,
    CLIENT_OS_USER => 2,
    CLIENT_MACHINE => 3,
    CLIENT_PROGRAM => 4,
    ORACLE_USER => 5,
    MODULE_NAME => 6,
    MODULE_NAME_ACTION => 7,
    SERVICE_NAME => 8,
    SERVICE_MODULE => 9,
    SERVICE_MODULE_ACTION => 10);
 end;
SQL>/

PL/SQL procedure successfully completed.
```

The priorities defined in the SET_CONSUMER_GROUP_MAPPING_PRI procedure are used to resolve any conflicting mapping rules. The EXPLICIT attribute refers to an explicit consumer-group switch (using one of the switching methods described in the next section).

Changing Resource Consumer Groups

Two procedures are provided in the DBMS_RESOURCE_MANAGER package to allow you to explicitly change consumer groups for currently active user sessions: the SWITCH_CONSUMER_GROUP_FOR_SESS and SWITCH_CONSUMER_GROUP_FOR_USER procedures.

In addition, users can be granted the privilege to change their own consumer group. When a user is granted the *switch privilege*, they can use the DBMS_SESSION.SWITCH_CURRENT_CONSUMER_GROUP procedure to change the consumer group for their current session.

In the following sections, you will learn how to use each of these methods to explicitly change consumer groups. You will also learn how to grant and revoke the switch privilege.

SWITCHING GROUPS USING *DBMS_RESOURCE_MANAGER PROCEDURES*

The first procedure, SWITCH_CONSUMER_GROUP_FOR_SESS, explicitly assigns an active session to a new consumer group. The session is identified by the session identifier (SID) and serial number (SERIAL#), both of which can be derived from the V$SESSION table. This procedure is described in Table 11.8.

TABLE 11.8: SWITCH_CONSUMER_GROUP_FOR_SESS Procedure Parameters

Parameter	Description
SESSION_ID	Session identifier (SID column from the view V$SESSION)
SESSION_SERIAL	Serial number of the session (SERIAL# column from view V$SESSION)
CONSUMER_GROUP	Name of the target consumer group

For example, the following SQL switches a session to the LOW_GROUP group:

```
SQL> begin
  dbms_resource_manager.switch_consumer_group_for_sess (
     SESSION_ID => '56',
     SESSION_SERIAL=> '106',
     CONSUMER_GROUP => 'LOW_GROUP');
 end;
SQL>/

PL/SQL procedure successfully completed.
```

The second method of changing the consumer group for an active session is the SWITCH_CONSUMER_GROUP_FOR_USER procedure. This procedure changes all active sessions for a given Oracle username. Here's an example:

```
SQL> begin
  dbms_resource_manager.switch_consumer_group_for_user (
     USER => 'BRANDON',
     CONSUMER_GROUP => 'LOW_GROUP');
 end;
SQL>/

PL/SQL procedure successfully completed.
```

This procedure identifies all sessions running under the username of BRANDON and switches them to the LOW_GROUP.

Both of these procedures also switch all parallel sessions that may have been spawned by the session or user.

Explicit consumer-group changes are not persistent. They affect only current sessions.

SWITCHING GROUPS USING *DBMS_SESSION*

If a user has been granted the switch privilege, they can use the DBMS_SESSION.SWITCH_CURRENT_CONSUMER_GROUP procedure to explicitly change the group for their current session. Table 11.9 describes the parameters for this procedure.

TABLE 11.9: SWITCH_CURRENT_CONSUMER_GROUP Procedure Parameters

Parameter	Description
NEW_CONSUMER_GROUP	The name of the consumer group to which the session is switching.
OLD_CONSUMER_GROUP	An output parameter that returns the name of the original consumer group (before the switch).
INITIAL_GROUP_ON_ERROR	If the switch fails, this parameter controls the outcome. If TRUE, the session reverts to its original group. If FALSE, an error is raised.

When this procedure completes, it returns the name of the original consumer group back to the calling program. This is presumably so the program can retain the original group and use it to revert later in the program, if so desired. The following example shows how to call this procedure from a PL/SQL block:

```
DECLARE
   original_group varchar2(30);
   junk           varchar2(30);
BEGIN
  DBMS_SESSION.SWITCH_CURRENT_CONSUMER_GROUP(
  'MARKETING', original_group, FALSE);

< execute some SQL>

  DBMS_SESSION.SWITCH_CURRENT_CONSUMER_GROUP(
  original_group, junk, FALSE);

END;
```

This PL/SQL block switches from the current consumer group to the MARKETING group and saves the original group name in a variable named ORIGINAL_GROUP. After executing some SQL, it uses the ORIGINAL_GROUP variable to switch back to the original group.

MANAGING THE SWITCH PRIVILEGE

Before a user can switch their own consumer group, they must have been granted the switch privilege directly or have been granted a role that has been granted the switch privilege.

The switch privilege is granted to users and/or to roles through the DBMS_RESOURCE_MANAGER_PRIVS.GRANT_SWITCH_CONSUMER_GROUP procedure. The parameters for this procedure are described in Table 11.10.

TABLE 11.10: GRANT_SWITCH_CONSUMER_GROUP Procedure Parameters

Parameter	Description
GRANTEE_NAME	Username or role name receiving the grant.
CONSUMER_GROUP	Name of the consumer group to which the grantee will be allowed to switch.
GRANT_OPTION	Determines whether the grantee can, in turn, grant the switch privilege to another user. If TRUE, the grantee can grant the switch privilege to another user. If FALSE, the grantee cannot grant the switch privilege to another user.

By granting the switch privilege to roles, it is much easier to grant the privilege to entire groups of users, as shown here:

```
SQL> begin
  dbms_resource_manager_privs.grant_switch_consumer_group(
    'PROG_ROLE', 'DEVELOPERS', FALSE);
 end;
SQL>/

PL/SQL procedure successfully completed.
```

In this example, the switch privilege is granted to the PROG_ROLE role. Any user granted that role will be able to switch to the DEVELOPERS group, but they cannot grant the privilege to any other users. If the GRANT_OPTION parameter was set to TRUE, the user could, in turn, grant the same privilege to another user.

If the switch privilege is granted to PUBLIC for any consumer group, any user will be able to switch to the specified consumer group.

The switch privilege can also be revoked by using the DBMS_RESOURCE_MANAGER_PRIVS.REVOKE_SWITCH_CONSUMER_GROUP procedure. The parameters for this procedure are described in Table 11.11.

TABLE 11.11: REVOKE_SWITCH_CONSUMER_GROUP Procedure Parameters

Parameter	Description
REVOKEE_NAME	Name of user or role with privileges being revoked
CONSUMER_GROUP	Name of consumer group being revoked

This procedure revokes a user's or role's privilege to switch to the specified consumer group. Here's an example:

```
SQL> begin
  dbms_resource_manager_privs.revoke_switch_consumer_group(
    'PROG_ROLE', 'DEVELOPERS');
 end;
SQL>/

PL/SQL procedure successfully completed.
```

This example revokes the privileges granted in the preceding example.

Resource Plans

DRM allocates resources among resource consumer groups based on a resource plan. A *resource plan* consists of directives specifying how resources should be distributed among resource consumer groups or other resource plans.

Resource plans prioritize resource allocation through the use of levels, with level 1 being the highest priority and level 8 being the lowest.

Simple resource plans are limited to allocating only CPU resources to a small number of consumer groups. However, they are very simple to set up, and they represent a good starting place if you're new to DRM. Simple resource plans define the resource plan, resource plan directives, and resource consumer groups all with one procedure, whereas complex plans define each separately. Simple resource plans are also classified as *single-level resource plans* because there are no subplans involved.

Complex resource plans can use any of Oracle's predefined resource-allocation methods and can include up to 32 consumer groups. Complex resource plans can also contain *subplans*. If subplans are defined, the plan would be classified as a multilevel resource plan.

There is no difference between a plan and a subplan. They are defined in exactly the same manner. A subplan is simply a plan that is nested within the scope of a top-level plan, so it is allocated resources from the top-level plan.

Resource plans have two options regarding the CPU-allocation method—EMPHASIS and RATIO—as described in Table 11.12.

TABLE 11.12 Resource Plan CPU-Allocation Methods

CPU-Allocation Method	Description
EMPHASIS	The allocated amount is treated as a percentage (in other words, 80 = 80 percent) of available CPU. EMPHASIS is valid for both single- and multilevel plans and is the only option for simple resource plans (the default).
RATIO	The allocated amount is treated as a ratio of the total CPU resources. The RATIO method can be defined only on single-level plans.

The EMPHASIS method is used most often and can be used for either single- or multilevel plans. Under the EMPHASIS method, CPU resource allocations are expressed as percentages in the plan directives.

The RATIO method can be used only on single-level plans (plans that contain directives that allocate CPU resources at level 1 only). Under the RATIO method, the CPU resource allocations are expressed as a weight in the plan directives.

For example, assume a plan containing plan directives for the PAYROLL, MARKETING, and OTHER_GROUPS consumer groups. The plan is defined to use the RATIO method for CPU allocation. Assume that the directives contain the allocations listed in Table 11.13.

TABLE 11.13 Plan Directives Using the RATIO Method

Consumer Group	CPU_P1 Parameter Setting
PAYROLL	10
MARKETING	2
OTHER_GROUPS	1

The result of these directives will allocate CPU resources using a 10:2:1 ratio. The MARKETING group will get only two CPU cycles for every 10 that the PAYROLL group receives. The OTHER_GROUPS group will get one cycle for every for every two that the MARKETING group receives.

Examples of resource directives using both the EMPHASIS and RATIO methods are provided in the section "Resource Plan Directives" later in this chapter.

In the following sections, you will learn how to create both simple and complex resource plans. You'll also learn how to update and delete resource plans.

Creating Simple Resource Plans

Simple resource plans, though limited in their abilities and scope, offer an adequate solution for environments with only basic resource-management needs. They are distinct from complex plans in that they create a resource plan, resource-plan directives, and resource consumer groups in one simple procedure.

Simple resource plans are limited to using only the CPU resource-plan directive. This means that the only resource that can be allocated is the CPU. Simple plans also limit the total number of resource groups to eight.

Oracle provides the DBMS_RESOURCE_MANAGER.CREATE_SIMPLE_PLAN procedure for creating a simple resource plan; its parameters are described in Table 11.14 (deprecated parameters not listed).

TABLE 11.14: CREATE_SIMPLE_PLAN Procedure Parameters

Parameter	Description
SIMPLE_PLAN	The name assigned to the plan
CONSUMER_GROUP1	The name of the first consumer group
GROUP1_PERCENT	The CPU allocation for the first consumer group
CONSUMER_GROUP2	The name of the second consumer group
GROUP2_PERCENT	The CPU allocation for the second consumer group
CONSUMER_GROUP3	The name of the third consumer group
GROUP3_PERCENT	The CPU allocation for the third consumer group
CONSUMER_GROUP4	The name of the fourth consumer group
GROUP4_PERCENT	The CPU allocation for the fourth consumer group
CONSUMER_GROUP5	The name of the fifth consumer group
GROUP5_PERCENT	The CPU allocation for the fifth consumer group
CONSUMER_GROUP6	The name of the sixth consumer group
GROUP6_PERCENT	The CPU allocation for the sixth consumer group
CONSUMER_GROUP7	The name of the seventh consumer group
GROUP7_PERCENT	The CPU allocation for the seventh consumer group

TABLE 11.14: CREATE_SIMPLE_PLAN Procedure Parameters *(continued)*

Parameter	Description
CONSUMER_GROUP8	The name of the eighth consumer group
GROUP8_PERCENT	The CPU allocation for the eighth consumer group

This procedure allows for the creation of up to eight consumer groups, along with their CPU allocations.

Simple resource plans always use the EMPHASIS CPU resource-allocation policy. This means that the value entered for the CPU allocations will be interpreted as a percentage of total CPU. For example, if you want to implement the specifications shown in Table 11.15, a simple resource plan can be created as in the example that follows.

```
SQL>  begin
DBMS_RESOURCE_MANAGER.CREATE_SIMPLE_PLAN(
  SIMPLE_PLAN => 'DEPARTMENTS',
  CONSUMER_GROUP1 => 'PAYROLL',
  GROUP1_PERCENT => 50,
  CONSUMER_GROUP2 => 'SALES',
  GROUP2_PERCENT => 25,
  CONSUMER_GROUP3 => 'MARKETING',
  GROUP3_PERCENT => 25);
end;
SQL> /

PL/SQL procedure successfully completed.
```

TABLE 11.15: DEPARTMENTS Plan Specification

Group	CPU Allocation
PAYROLL	50%
SALES	25%
MARKETING	25%

When a simple plan is created, the results might be somewhat surprising. Table 11.16 shows the finished plan, and you can see that Oracle has added two additional consumer groups to it: SYS_GROUP and OTHER_GROUPS.

TABLE 11.16 Final DEPARTMENTS Plan

Level	SYS_GROUP	PAYROLL	SALES	MARKETING	OTHER_GROUPS
1	100%				
2		50%	25%	25%	
3					100%

SYS_GROUP represents the users SYS and SYSTEM.

OTHER_GROUPS is a required group that must be included in any resource plan. It ensures that users who are not assigned to any group in the active resource plan will still have resources allocated.

Notice also that the final plan is a multilevel plan and the elements that you defined are assigned to the second level. This ensures that members of the SYS_GROUP (at level 1) will have no CPU restrictions. Groups at level 2 will share CPU resources not used by level-1 groups. Likewise, users not assigned to any group in the plan (at level 3) will receive CPU time only after levels 1 and 2 have satisfied their requirements.

Creating Complex Resource Plans

Complex resource plans differ from simple resource plans in how they are defined. When you create a simple plan, you can create the plan, resource groups, and plan directives in one operation. For complex plans, each of these elements is defined and stored separately. This method offers more flexibility when building resource plans.

This method also allows for the nesting of plans, so one plan can act as a subplan of another. When plans are nested in this manner, it is referred to as a multilevel plan.

Creating a plan involves defining the name of the plan, a comment or description regarding the plan, and the methods that the plan will follow when allocating specific resources. Notice that the plan does not determine which resources it will manage. Those are predefined by Oracle. A plan defines only the method it will apply when allocating those resources.

To create a new plan, use the DBMS_RESOURCE_MANAGER.CREATE_PLAN procedure, whose parameters are described in Table 11.17.

TABLE 11.17: CREATE_PLAN Procedure Parameters

Parameter	Description
PLAN	The name of the resource plan.
COMMENT	A comment or a description of the plan.

TABLE 11.17: CREATE_PLAN Procedure Parameters *(continued)*

Parameter	Description
CPU_MTH	Deprecated. Use MGMT_MTH.
ACTIVE_SESS_POOL_MTH	The method of allocating session pool resources (limiting the number of active sessions). ACTIVE_SESS_POOL_ABSOLUTE is the only method available. Treats the number specified in a plan directive as the maximum number of active sessions allowed.
PARALLEL_DEGREE_LIMIT_MTH	The method of specifying degree of parallelism for any operation. PARALLEL_DEGREE_LIMIT_ABSOLUTE is the only method available. Treats the number specified in plan directives as the maximum degree of parallelism that will be allowed.
QUEUEING_MTH	The Method of allocating execution of queued sessions. FIFO_TIMEOUT is the only method available. Uses a first-in/first-out method for prioritizing sessions waiting in queue due to resource limitations.
MGMT_MTH	The method of allocating CPU resources. EMPHASIS (default): CPU will be distributed on a percentage basis for single and multilevel plans. RATIO: CPU will be distributed on a ratio basis for single-level plans.
SUB_PLAN	If TRUE, the plan can't be used as the top-level plan. Default is FALSE.

As you can see, only the PLAN, COMMENT, and MGMT_MTH parameters actually have any effect on the plan. The others (ACTIVE_SESS_POOL_MTH, PARALLEL_DEGREE_LIMIT_MTH, and QUEUEING_MTH) offer only one option, which is also the default. It is expected that future releases will expand the choices for these parameters. For the SUB_PLAN parameter, you can specify if this plan cannot be used as a top-level plan.

Therefore, a plan can be created as follows:

```
SQL> begin
  dbms_resource_manager.create_plan(
    PLAN => 'DAY',
    COMMENT => 'Use during daytime');
  end;
SQL>/

PL/SQL procedure successfully completed.
```

To verify that the resource plan was actually created, you can use the DBA_RSRC_PLANS view:

```
SQL> select plan, num_plan_directives, cpu_method
  2  from dba_rsrc_plans;

PLAN                 NUM_PLAN_DIRECTIVES CPU_METHOD
-------------------- ------------------- ----------
SYSTEM_PLAN                            3 EMPHASIS
INTERNAL_QUIESCE                       2 EMPHASIS
INTERNAL_PLAN                          1 EMPHASIS
DAY                                    1 EMPHASIS
```

As you can see, the plan was indeed created, and in fact it already has one plan directive assigned to it. Remember that Oracle requires all plans to have a directive for the OTHER_GROUPS resource group. Therefore, Oracle automatically creates this directive for you.

Creating Resource Subplans

A resource subplan is created in exactly the same manner as a resource plan. That's because there is no difference between them. A subplan is a plan. It becomes a subplan only if a higher-level plan allocates resources to it (through a resource plan directive) or if you explicitly define that it can be only a subplan when you create the plan.

For example, plan A can allocate resources to consumer groups X and Y and to plan B. Plan B is now classified as a subplan. The difference is that a top-level plan always has 100 percent of the resources available to allocate, whereas a subplan can allocate only the resources that have been allocated to it by the top-level plan.

Modifying Resource Plans

Resource plans can be modified by using the DBMS_RESOURCE_MANAGER.UPDATE_PLAN procedure. The parameters for this procedure are described in Table 11.18.

TABLE 11.18: UPDATE_PLAN Procedure Parameters

Parameter	Description
PLAN	Name of the resource plan
NEW_COMMENT	New comment
NEW_CPU_MTH	Deprecated. Use NEW_MGMT_MTH
NEW_ACTIVE_SESS_POOL_MTH	New method of allocating session pool resources
NEW_PARALLEL_DEGREE_LIMIT_MTH	New method of specifying the degree of parallelism for any operation

TABLE 11.18: UPDATE_PLAN Procedure Parameters *(continued)*

Parameter	Description
NEW_QUEUEING_MTH	New method of allocating the execution of queued sessions
NEW_MGMT_MTH	New method of allocating CPU resources

Again, keep in mind that only the first three parameters in the UPDATE_PLAN procedure will have any effect on resource plans because there are no other valid options for the others. To verify this, you can use any of the following views:

- V$ACTIVE_SESS_POOL_MTH
- V$PARALLEL_DEGREE_LIMIT_MTH
- V$QUEUEING_MTH
- V$RSRC_PLAN_CPU_MTH

These views display the valid values for each of the resource-plan allocation methods.

To change the comment on the DAY plan, see the following example:

```
SQL>  exec dbms_resource_manager.update_plan(
  PLAN => 'DAY',
  NEW_COMMENT => 'Plan for scheduled work hours');

PL/SQL procedure successfully completed.
```

Deleting Resource Plans

Resource plans can be deleted by using either the DBMS_RESOURCE_MANAGER.DELETE_PLAN procedure or the DBMS_RESOURCE_MANAGER.DELETE_PLAN_CASCADE procedure. The former removes the resource plan but leaves all subordinate objects (consumer groups, plan directives, and subplans) intact. The latter removes the resource plan, along with all subordinate objects.

If the DELETE_PLAN_CASCADE procedure attempts to delete a subordinate object that happens to also be part of the currently active plan, the delete will fail and the entire plan will be restored.

The only parameter accepted by these procedures is a valid resource plan name, as shown in this example:

```
SQL>  exec dbms_resource_manager.delete_plan('DAY');

PL/SQL procedure successfully completed.
```

Resource-Plan Directives

Resource-plan directives are the key element in creating complex resource plans. As you saw earlier in this chapter, a resource plan by itself does very little until it has resource-plan directives assigned to it. Resource-plan directives assign consumer groups to resource plans and define the resource allocations for each. In addition to consumer groups, plan directives can allocate resources to subplans.

Resource-plan directives work by specifying the owning resource plan, the target consumer group or subplan, and the resource allocations assigned to the target. Resources are allocated to the target by setting parameters for the various resource-allocation methods.

Resource-allocation methods are predefined by Oracle and, as such, are not modifiable. They represent the various methods available to DRM to allocate resources. The following methods are available:

CPU The CPU method specifies how CPU resources are to be allocated among consumer groups or subplans. Up to eight levels can be defined, allowing for the prioritization of CPU resources. For example, level 2 gets CPU only if level 1 is unable to utilize all of its allocated CPU. Therefore, level 1 has the highest priority, while level 8 has the lowest priority.

Active session pool with queuing This method limits the number of concurrent active sessions available to a consumer group. If the allocated number of sessions is reached, new session requests will be placed in a queue until an active session completes.

Degree of parallelism limit This method specifies the maximum parallel degree for any operation within a consumer group. If a higher degree is specified, it will automatically be altered down to the value specified for this parameter.

Automatic consumer-group switching This switching method allows sessions exceeding certain execution-time criteria to be dynamically switched to a different group. For example, if a session exceeds the defined execution-time threshold, it can be automatically switched to a lower priority group. This method can also be used to automatically cancel the operation or even kill the offending session.

Canceling SQL and terminating sessions This method specifies that long-running queries or long-running sessions will be automatically terminated if the execution-time threshold is exceeded.

Execution time limit The execution time-limit method specifies the maximum estimated execution time allowed for any operation. If Oracle estimates that an operation will exceed the specified execution time, it will terminate the operation and return an error. It does this before actual execution begins.

Undo pool The undo-pool method specifies the amount of undo that can be generated by a consumer group. If the group exceeds the allocated amount, the current DML statement is terminated and no other group members may perform data manipulation until undo space is freed.

Idle time limit This method specifies the maximum amount of time that a session can remain idle. If this limit is exceeded, the session will automatically be terminated. This method can also be limited to terminating only idle sessions that are blocking other sessions.

Resource-plan directives can set levels for one or more of these methods for each consumer group or subplan. However, only CPU methods may be defined for subplans. The other methods are invalid for assigning resources to subplans.

In the following sections, you will learn how to create the various types of resource-plan directives. You'll also learn how plan directives can be used to monitor and manage long-running operations. Finally, you'll learn to update and delete plan directives.

Creating Resource-Plan Directives

To create a resource-plan directive, the DBMS_RESOURCE_MANAGER.CREATE_PLAN_DIRECTIVE procedure is used. Table 11.19 describes the interface for this procedure.

TABLE 11.19: CREATE_PLAN_DIRECTIVE Procedure Parameters

Parameter	Description
PLAN	The name of the resource plan to which this directive belongs.
GROUP_OR_SUBPLAN	The name of the consumer group or subplan being allocated resources by this directive.
COMMENT	A comment or a description of the plan directive.
CPU_P1	Deprecated. Use MGMT_P1.
CPU_P2	Deprecated. Use MGMT_P2.
CPU_P3	Deprecated. Use MGMT_P3.
CPU_P4	Deprecated. Use MGMT_P4.
CPU_P5	Deprecated. Use MGMT_P5.
CPU_P6	Deprecated. Use MGMT_P6.
CPU_P7	Deprecated. Use MGMT_P7.
CPU_P8	Deprecated. Use MGMT_P8.
ACTIVE_SESS_POOL_P1	Specifies the maximum number of concurrently active sessions for a consumer group or subplan. The default is NULL, which means unlimited.

TABLE 11.19: CREATE_PLAN_DIRECTIVE Procedure Parameters *(continued)*

Parameter	Description
QUEUEING_P1	The number of seconds before a job in the inactive session queue times out. The default is NULL, meaning that queued jobs will never time out.
PARALLEL_DEGREE_LIMIT_P1	The maximum degree of parallelism that can be defined for any operation. The default is NULL, meaning that no limit is imposed.
SWITCH_GROUP	The consumer group to which this session will be switched if the switch criteria is met. The default is NULL. Other options are CANCEL_SQL, which will kill the query when switch criteria is met, and KILL_SESSION, which will kill the session when the switch criteria is met.
SWITCH_TIME	The number of seconds for which a session can execute an operation before a group switch will occur. The default is NULL, meaning that there is no limit on execution time. After the operation is complete, the session remains in the new consumer group rather than reverting to its original consumer group.
SWITCH_ESTIMATE	Directs Oracle to estimate the execution time for an operation before execution begins. If the estimated time exceeds the value set for SWITCH_TIME, Oracle will perform the switch before execution of the query begins. Valid settings are TRUE and FALSE. The default is FALSE.
MAX_EST_EXEC_TIME	Directs Oracle to estimate the execution time for an operation before execution begins. If the estimated time exceeds the number of seconds defined in this parameter, the operation is not started and an ORA-07455 error is issued. The default is NULL, meaning that no estimate limit is imposed.
UNDO_POOL	Maximum kilobytes (KB) of undo that can be generated by the consumer group/subplan. The default is NULL, meaning that no limit is imposed.
MAX_IDLE_TIME	The number of seconds that a session can remain idle before the session is killed. The default is NULL, meaning that no idle time limit is imposed.
MAX_IDLE_BLOCKER_TIME	The number of seconds that a blocking session can remain idle before the session is killed. (A blocking session is a session that is locking a resource that is needed by another session.) The default is NULL, meaning that no idle time limit is imposed.

TABLE 11.19: CREATE_PLAN_DIRECTIVE Procedure Parameters *(continued)*

Parameter	Description
SWITCH_TIME_IN_CALL	Deprecated. Use SWITCH_FOR_CALL.
MGMT_P1	If the resource plan uses the EMPHASIS allocation method, this parameter defines the percentage of CPU allocated at level 1 for the group/subplan. If the plan uses the RATIO allocation method for CPU resources, this parameter defines the weight of CPU usage for the group/subplan. The default is NULL for all MGMT_Pn parameters, which provides no allocation of CPU resources.
MGMT_P2	The percentage of CPU allocated at level 2 for the group/subplan (if the plan uses the EMPHASIS method). Not applicable for the RATIO method. The default is NULL.
MGMT_P3	The percentage of CPU allocated at level 3 for the group/subplan (if the plan uses the EMPHASIS method). Not applicable for the RATIO method. The default is NULL.
MGMT_P4	The percentage of CPU allocated at level 4 for the group/subplan (if the plan uses the EMPHASIS method). Not applicable for the RATIO method. The default is NULL.
MGMT_P5	The percentage of CPU allocated at level 5 for the group/subplan (if the plan uses the EMPHASIS method). Not applicable for the RATIO method. The default is NULL.
MGMT_P6	The percentage of CPU allocated at level 6 for the group/subplan (if the plan uses the EMPHASIS method). Not applicable for the RATIO method. The default is NULL.
MGMT_P7	The percentage of CPU allocated at level 7 for the group/subplan (if the plan uses the EMPHASIS method). Not applicable for the RATIO method. The default is NULL.
MGMT_P8	The percentage of CPU allocated at level 8 for the group/subplan (if the plan uses the EMPHASIS method). Not applicable for the RATIO method. The default is NULL.
SWITCH_IO_MEGABYTES	The number of megabytes of I/O that a session can transfer (read and write) before action is taken. The default is UNLIMITED. Action specified by SWITCH_GROUP.
SWITCH_IO_REQS	Specifies the number of I/O requests that a session is allowed to execute before action is taken. The default is UNLIMITED. Action specified by SWITCH_GROUP.

TABLE 11.19: CREATE_PLAN_DIRECTIVE Procedure Parameters *(continued)*

Parameter	Description
SWITCH_FOR_CALL	When set to TRUE, a user session that was automatically switched to another consumer group (based on SWITCH_IO_MEGABYTES, SWITCH_IO_REQS, or SWITCH_TIME) is returned to its original consumer group when the top-level call completes. Default is NULL.

Both SWITCH_TIME_IN_CALL and SWITCH_TIME cannot be specified in the same resource directive because they represent conflicting actions.

The following example creates a resource-plan directive for the DAY plan, which limits the parallel degree settings for the DEVELOPERS group:

```
SQL> begin
  dbms_resource_manager.create_plan_directive(
    PLAN => 'DAY',
    COMMENT => 'DEVELOPERS DAY PLAN',
    GROUP_OR_SUBPLAN => 'DEVELOPERS',
    PARALLEL_DEGREE_LIMIT_P1 => '4');
  end;
SQL> /

PL/SQL procedure successfully completed.
```

In the following sections, you will learn to create directives that define subplans. You'll also learn to create directives that create multilevel plans. Finally, you'll learn to create plans that use the consumer group switching method to manage long-running operations.

Creating Subplan Directives

To create a subplan directive, you first create a plan directive, which allocates CPU resources to another plan (which is then referred to as a subplan). The subplan still retains all of its original functionality. However, the total CPU resources it can allocate are limited to those it receives from the top-level plan.

For example, to define a subplan under the DAY plan, you would set the GROUP_OR_SUBPLAN parameter to the name of the target plan, as follows:

```
SQL> begin
  dbms_resource_manager.create_plan_directive(
    PLAN => 'DAY',
```

```
    COMMENT => 'DEPARTMENTS SUB-PLAN',
    GROUP_OR_SUBPLAN => 'DEPARTMENTS',
    MGMT_P2=> 50);
  end;
SQL> /

PL/SQL procedure successfully completed.
```

In this example, the plan DEPARTMENTS was defined as a subplan of the DAY plan and limited to 50 percent of the level-2 CPU resources.

Subplan directives can allocate only CPU resources to a subplan.

Creating Multilevel Plan Directives

Multilevel plan directives are used to prioritize CPU allocation for consumer groups and subplans. When a plan directive is created, the parameters CPU to MGMT determine the level at which the CPU resources will be allocated to the specified group or subplan. The total resources allocated at any one level cannot exceed 100 percent.

Up to eight levels can be specified, with level 1 being the highest priority and level 8 being the lowest. Level-1 recipients share the total available CPU based on their respective MGMT_P1 parameter value. Level-2 recipients share only the CPU resources that are not consumed at level 1, and so on.

Consider this example:

```
SQL> begin
  dbms_resource_manager.create_plan_directive(
    PLAN => 'DAY',
    COMMENT => 'SYSTEM USERS',
    GROUP_OR_SUBPLAN => 'SYS_GROUP',
    MGMT_P1=> 100);
  end;
SQL> /

PL/SQL procedure successfully completed.

SQL> begin
  dbms_resource_manager.create_plan_directive(
    PLAN => 'DAY',
    COMMENT => 'DEPARTMENTS SUB-PLAN',
    GROUP_OR_SUBPLAN => 'DEPARTMENTS',
```

```
    MGMT_P2=> 50);
  end;
SQL> /

PL/SQL procedure successfully completed.

SQL> begin
  dbms_resource_manager.create_plan_directive(
    PLAN => 'DAY',
    COMMENT => 'DEVELOPERS GROUP CPU ALLOCATION',
    GROUP_OR_SUBPLAN => 'DEVELOPERS',
    MGMT_P2=> 50);
  end;
SQL> /

PL/SQL procedure successfully completed.

SQL> begin
  dbms_resource_manager.create_plan_directive(
    PLAN => 'DAY',
    COMMENT => 'OTHER_GROUPS CPU ALLOCATION',
    GROUP_OR_SUBPLAN => 'OTHER_GROUPS',
    MGMT_P3=> 100);
  end;
SQL> /

PL/SQL procedure successfully completed.
```

In this example, four directives are created for the DAY plan. The first directive allocates 100 percent of level-1 CPU resources to the SYS_GROUP group. The second directive allocates 50 percent of level-2 CPU resources to the DEPARTMENTS subplan. The third directive allocates the other 50 percent of level-2 CPU resources to the DEVELOPERS consumer group. Finally, the fourth directive allocates 100 percent of level-3 CPU resources to the OTHER_GROUPS group.

Creating Automatic Consumer Group Switching Directives

Plan directives can include options for automatically switching resource consumer groups for sessions that exceed defined thresholds. For example, a directive can dictate that any session that has an operation executing for more than 10 minutes should automatically be switched into a lower-priority group. They can also dictate that Oracle will automatically kill the query or even the session when switching thresholds are exceeded.

The key parameters in defining automatic consumer group switching are as follows:

SWITCH_TIME The SWITCH_TIME parameter sets the maximum execution time (in seconds) allowed for any operation. A session violating this threshold is automatically switched to the group defined by the SWITCH_GROUP parameter.

The switch group is generally a group with lower priority so that the long-running operation will be allocated fewer resources. However, the switch group can also be set to the Oracle constant KILL_SESSION or CANCEL_SQL, which would result in the offending session being killed or the offending SQL operation being canceled.

Once a session has been switched to another group using this method, it will not switch back to its original consumer group, even after the offending operation has completed.

The SWITCH_TIME and SWITCH_TIME_IN_CALL methods are mutually exclusive. Only one method may be defined in a plan directive.

SWITCH_ESTIMATE The SWITCH_ESTIMATE parameter specifies that the Oracle optimizer should estimate the execution time of an operation before actually executing it. If the estimated time exceeds the value set in the SWITCH_TIME parameter, then the consumer group switch will occur prior to execution of the operation.

When a session is switched using this method, it will not revert to its original consumer group if the SWITCH_TIME parameter is set.

SWITCH_IO_MEGABYTES The SWITCH_IO_MEGABYTES parameter specifies that the session that exceeds the number of megabytes transferred will be switched.

SWITCH_FOR_CALL The SWITCH_FOR_CALL parameter, when TRUE, specifies that the session will be returned to the original consumer group after the PL/SQL block completes.

To create a plan directive that automatically cancels operations that execute for more than one hour, see the following example:

```
SQL> begin
  dbms_resource_manager.create_plan_directive(
    PLAN => 'DAY',
    COMMENT => 'LIMIT DEVELOPERS EXECUTION TIME',
    GROUP_OR_SUBPLAN => 'DEVELOPERS',
    SWITCH_GROUP => 'CANCEL_SQL',
    SWITCH_TIME => 3600);
  end;
SQL> /

PL/SQL procedure successfully completed.
```

To create a plan directive that temporarily moves DEVELOPERS sessions to a lower-priority group whenever the actual I/O transferred in exceeds 3,000 megabytes, then returns them to their original group following the completion of the PL/SQL block, see this example:

```
SQL> begin
  dbms_resource_manager.create_plan_directive(
    PLAN => 'DAY',
    COMMENT => 'SWITCH DEVELOPERS TEMPORARILY',
    GROUP_OR_SUBPLAN => 'DEVELOPERS',
    SWITCH_IO_MEGABYTES => 3000,
    SWITCH_GROUP => 'LOW_GROUP',
    SWITCH_FOR_CALL => TRUE);
  end;
SQL> /

PL/SQL procedure successfully completed.
```

This example switches the session to the LOW_GROUP consumer group prior to execution of any operation that Oracle estimates will exceed 15 minutes (900 seconds). When the operation has completed, the session will revert to the DEVELOPERS group.

Updating Resource Plan-Directives

Resource-plan directives can be updated using the DBMS_RESOURCE_MANAGER.UPDATE_PLAN_DIRECTIVE procedure. The parameters for this procedure are identical to the parameters for the CREATE_PLAN_DIRECTIVE procedure, except that the prefix NEW_ has been added to all of the modifiable parameters (for example, NEW_COMMENT, NEW_MGMT_P1, and so on).

The only parameters that cannot be modified are PLAN and GROUP_OR_SUBPLAN. All of the others can be updated.

Consider the following example:

```
SQL> begin
  dbms_resource_manager.update_plan_directive(
    PLAN => 'DAY',
    GROUP_OR_SUBPLAN => 'DEVELOPERS',
    NEW_SWITCH_ESTIMATE => FALSE);
 end;
SQL>/

PL/SQL procedure successfully completed.
```

In this example, the SWITCH_ESTIMATE setting is updated to a value of FALSE. Notice that the parameter used is NEW_SWITCH_ESTIMATE rather than SWITCH_ESTIMATE.

Runaway Processes

In our current job, our team administers (among other things) a data warehouse totaling approximately five billion rows. Due to the size of many of the tables, parallel queries drastically reduce runtime most of the time. However, we seem to encounter our share of Oracle bugs, resulting in runaway parallel processes.

For example, a query will spawn eight parallel processes and proceed normally until very near the end of the processing. Then, one process will slowly start spinning CPU cycles. If not caught early, it will eventually consume all CPU and bring the system grinding to a halt.

We've applied several patches that seem to fix the problem, but in reality we just encounter the bug (or a different one with similar effects) less often.

By using Database Resource Monitor, we were able to devise a relatively simple plan that killed sessions if they reached a very high CPU-percentage threshold. Now the runaway processes are automatically killed, and the beauty of it is that no DBA involvement is required.

Deleting Resource-Plan Directives

Resource-plan directives can be deleted using the DBMS_RESOURCE_MANAGER.DELETE_PLAN_DIRECTIVE procedure. The only parameters required are the PLAN and GROUP_OR_SUBPLAN parameters, as shown here:

```
SQL> begin
  dbms_resource_manager.delete_plan_directive(
    PLAN => 'DAY',
    GROUP_OR_SUBPLAN => 'DEVELOPERS');
 end;
SQL>/

PL/SQL procedure successfully completed.
```

Creating and Using Database Resource Manager Components

Now that you've learned about all of the various elements of DRM individually, it's time to put them all together.

For most companies, database requirements differ depending on the time of day. For example, during normal daytime business hours, online transaction processing (OLTP) may be mission-critical, along with a small amount of report processing. After hours, however, bulk data loads and online analytical processing (OLAP) reports may take priority.

In the following sections, you'll learn how to develop complex multilevel resource plans to accommodate these types of business requirements. You'll see how all of the elements are created and associated to the plan. You'll also learn how to enable the finalized plan.

You will be provided step-by-step instructions for the creation of the plans. First, the pending area will be created. Next, the resource consumer groups will be created. After that, the resource plans will be created. And, finally, the resource-plan directives will be created to tie them all together.

Once all of the elements are in place, they will be validated and activated. Finally, you'll learn to enable the resource plans, as well as how to switch the enabled resource plan.

Creating the Pending Area

Before any new DRM elements are created, a pending area must be established to hold your new plans. The pending area is a development area where you can work on DRM elements without affecting the active DRM plan. It can be created as shown here:

```
SQL> exec dbms_resource_manager.create_pending_area();


PL/SQL procedure successfully completed.
```

Once the pending area is in place, new elements will reside there until the plan is enabled.

Creating the Resource Consumer Groups

Next, the resource consumer groups can be created. In this step, all resource consumer groups required by both resource plans will be created.

These groups can be created as follows:

```
SQL> begin
  dbms_resource_manager.create_consumer_group(
  'OLTP_GROUP','Incoming orders');
 end;
SQL>/

PL/SQL procedure successfully completed.

SQL> begin
  dbms_resource_manager.create_consumer_group(
  'DAY_REPORTS_GROUP','DAYTIME REPORTS');
 end;
SQL>/

PL/SQL procedure successfully completed.

SQL> begin
  dbms_resource_manager.create_consumer_group(
```

```
  'NIGHTLY_PROCESSING_GROUP','BULK LOADS, ETL, ETC.');
 end;
SQL>/

PL/SQL procedure successfully completed.

SQL> begin
  dbms_resource_manager.create_consumer_group(
  'OLAP_REPORTS_GROUP','OFF HOURS REPORTS');
 end;
SQL>/

PL/SQL procedure successfully completed.
```

Because the SYS_GROUP and the OTHER_GROUPS consumer groups are created automatically at Oracle installation time, there is no need to create them.

Creating the Resource Plans

Now that all the necessary consumer groups are in place, the next step is to create the resource plans. Three distinct plans are required. Both the DAY_PLAN and the OLTP_PLAN plan use the default EMPHASIS CPU-allocation method, whereas the OFF_HOURS_PLAN plan utilizes the RATIO method. Remember that the CPU resource-allocation method (CPU_MTH) sets the type of allocation used only if there is a resource-plan directive that specifies CPU allocation.

These plans can be created as shown here:

```
SQL> begin
  dbms_resource_manager.create_plan(
    PLAN => 'DAY_PLAN',
    COMMENT => 'GOVERNS NORMAL WORKING HOURS ');
   end;
SQL> /

PL/SQL procedure successfully completed.

SQL> begin
  dbms_resource_manager.create_plan(
    PLAN => 'OLTP_PLAN',
    COMMENT => 'ORDER ENTRY SUB-PLAN');
   end;
```

```
SQL> /

PL/SQL procedure successfully completed.

SQL> begin
  dbms_resource_manager.create_plan(
    PLAN => 'OFF_HOURS_PLAN',
    COMMENT => 'GOVERNS NON-WORKING HOURS',
    MGMT_MTH => 'RATIO');
   end;
SQL> /

PL/SQL procedure successfully completed.
```

Because the default CPU-allocation method is EMPHASIS, the MGMT_MTH parameter was left out when creating the first two plans. For the OFF_HOURS_PLAN plan, the CPU_MTH parameter was explicitly set.

Creating the Resource-Plan Directives

Next, the resource-plan directives need to be created. This will be done in three steps. First, the directives for the OFF_HOURS_PLAN plan will be created. Next, the directives for the OLTP_PLAN plan will be created. Finally, the directives for the DAY_PLAN plan will be created.

CREATING THE *OFF_HOURS_PLAN* PLAN DIRECTIVES

The OFF_HOURS_PLAN plan is a single-level plan using the RATIO method for CPU allocation. The plan directives can be created as follows:

```
SQL> begin
  dbms_resource_manager.create_plan_directive(
    PLAN => 'OFF_HOURS_PLAN',
    GROUP_OR_SUBPLAN => 'SYS_GROUP',
    COMMENT => 'CPU ALLOCATION FOR SYS_GROUP',
    MGMT_P1 => 10);
 end;
SQL>/

PL/SQL procedure successfully completed.

SQL> begin
   dbms_resource_manager.create_plan_directive(
     PLAN => 'OFF_HOURS_PLAN',
     GROUP_OR_SUBPLAN => 'NIGHTLY_PROCESSING_GROUP',
```

```
      COMMENT => 'CPU ALLOCATION FOR NIGHTLY JOBS',
      MGMT_P1 => 5);
  end;
SQL>/

PL/SQL procedure successfully completed.

SQL> begin
    dbms_resource_manager.create_plan_directive(
      PLAN => 'OFF_HOURS_PLAN',
      GROUP_OR_SUBPLAN => 'OLAP_REPORTS_GROUP',
      COMMENT => 'CPU ALLOCATION FOR NIGHTLY REPORTS',
      MGMT_P1 => 2);
  end;
SQL>/

PL/SQL procedure successfully completed.

SQL> begin
    dbms_resource_manager.create_plan_directive(
      PLAN => 'OFF_HOURS_PLAN',
      GROUP_OR_SUBPLAN => 'OTHER_GROUPS',
      COMMENT => 'CPU ALLOCATION FOR OTHER_GROUPS',
      MGMT_P1 => 1);
  end;
SQL>/

PL/SQL procedure successfully completed.
```

The CPU-allocation ratio for the OFF_HOURS_PLAN plan will be 10:5:2:1.

CREATING THE *OLTP_PLAN* PLAN DIRECTIVES

Next, the plan directives for the OLTP_PLAN plan can be created:

```
SQL> begin
  dbms_resource_manager.create_plan_directive(
    PLAN => 'OLTP_PLAN',
    GROUP_OR_SUBPLAN => 'OLTP_GROUP',
    COMMENT => 'CPU ALLOCATION FOR OLTP USERS',
    MGMT_P1 => 90);
 end;
SQL>/
```

```
PL/SQL procedure successfully completed.

SQL> begin
  dbms_resource_manager.create_plan_directive(
    PLAN => 'OLTP_PLAN',
    GROUP_OR_SUBPLAN => 'DAY_REPORTS_GROUP',
    COMMENT => 'CPU ALLOCATION FOR DAYTIME REPORTING',
    MGMT_P1 => 10);
 end;
SQL>/

PL/SQL procedure successfully completed.

SQL> begin
  dbms_resource_manager.create_plan_directive(
    PLAN => 'OLTP_PLAN',
    GROUP_OR_SUBPLAN => 'OTHER_GROUPS',
    COMMENT => 'CPU ALLOCATION FOR OTHER_GROUPS',
    MGMT_P2 => 100);
 end;
SQL>/

PL/SQL procedure successfully completed.
```

As you can see, the directives for the OLTP_PLAN plan allocate 90 percent of level-1 CPU resources to the OLTP_GROUP group and the other 10 percent to the DAY_REPORTS_GROUP group. One hundred percent of level-2 CPU resources are allocated to the OTHER_GROUPS group.

CREATING THE *DAY_PLAN* PLAN DIRECTIVES

Now the directives for the DAY_PLAN plan can be created:

```
SQL> begin
  dbms_resource_manager.create_plan_directive(
    PLAN => 'DAY_PLAN',
    GROUP_OR_SUBPLAN => 'SYS_GROUP',
    COMMENT => 'CPU ALLOCATION FOR SYS_GROUP',
    MGMT_P1 => 100);
 end;
SQL>/

PL/SQL procedure successfully completed.
```

```
SQL> begin
  dbms_resource_manager.create_plan_directive(
    PLAN => 'DAY_PLAN',
    GROUP_OR_SUBPLAN => 'OLTP_PLAN',
    COMMENT => 'CPU ALLOCATION FOR OLTP_PLAN SUB-PLAN',
    MGMT_P2 => 100);
 end;
SQL>/

PL/SQL procedure successfully completed.

SQL> begin
  dbms_resource_manager.create_plan_directive(
    PLAN => 'DAY_PLAN',
    GROUP_OR_SUBPLAN => 'OTHER_GROUPS',
    COMMENT => 'CPU ALLOCATION FOR OTHER_GROUPS',
    MGMT_P3 => 100);
 end;
SQL>/

PL/SQL procedure successfully completed.
```

You may have noticed that both the DAY_PLAN and OLTP_PLAN plans allocate resources to the OTHER_GROUPS group. Remember that *every* resource plan must have an allocation to the OTHER_GROUPS group. In fact, any consumer group can be assigned to more than one plan, as long as no loops are created as a result.

Validating the Pending Area

Now that all of the necessary elements have been created and defined, the contents of the pending area must be validated. Validation checks for any rule violations that may exist when the elements are grouped under their respective plans.

Validation will be done for all elements in the pending area, as shown here:

```
SQL> exec dbms_resource_manager.validate_pending_area;

PL/SQL procedure successfully completed.
```

When you're validating the pending area, no news is good news. As long as the procedure completes and no error messages are returned, the pending area has passed inspection.

If you are using SQL*Plus, make sure the SERVEROUTPUT option is on before validating. Otherwise, no error messages will be displayed onscreen. Use the SET SERVEROUTPUT ON statement to turn it on.

Submitting the Pending Area

The final step is to activate the plans by submitting the pending area. This step moves the DRM elements to the data dictionary. Once the elements are in the data dictionary, they are considered active and eligible to be enabled (resource plans) or referenced by enabled plans (resource consumer groups and resource-plan directives). Remember that this step does not actually enable a plan; it only makes it eligible to be enabled.

Also, when you're submitting a pending area, Oracle automatically performs the same validation that was done in the previous step. Therefore, the validation step discussed earlier is technically unnecessary. However, it is still a good idea from a debugging standpoint, especially when designing very complex plans.

The pending area can be submitted as shown:

```
SQL> exec dbms_resource_manager.submit_pending_area;


PL/SQL procedure successfully completed.
```

Again, the absence of error messages signifies successful submission of the pending area to the data dictionary. The plans are now active (in other words, residing in the data dictionary) and can be enabled at any time.

Enabling the Resource Plans

When a resource plan is enabled, it governs all resource allocation for the Oracle instance. Only one resource plan may be enabled at any given time, and the enabled plan can be switched at any time.

There are two methods in which resource plans can be enabled:

- Initialization parameter (at instance startup time)
- `ALTER SYSTEM` statement

Initialization parameter method In the `init.ora` file, the `RESOURCE_MANAGER_PLAN` initialization variable can be set to the name of any active plan. For example, the following code can be added to the `init.ora` file:

```
RESOURCE_MANAGER_PLAN = DAY_PLAN;
```

When the instance is restarted, `DAY_PLAN` will be the enabled plan for the instance.

`ALTER SYSTEM` statement method Resource plans can also be enabled dynamically by using the `ALTER SYSTEM` statement, as shown here:

```
ALTER SYSTEM SET RESOURCE_MANAGER_PLAN = 'DAY_PLAN' [SCOPE = BOTH];
```

This dynamically enables the `DAY_PLAN` plan for the instance. There is no need to shut down the instance in this case. The optional `SCOPE` clause can be used in an spfile environment to change the setting both in memory and in the spfile (to make the change persist through a shutdown).

Switching the Enabled Resource Plan

The top-level plans that were created in this section are designed to govern specific times of the day. The DAY_PLAN plan is to be used during normal business hours, while the OFF_HOURS_PLAN plan is to be used on nights and weekends.

The enabled plan can be changed at any time by using the ALTER SYSTEM command, as you saw earlier, but it would be very inconvenient to have to always make this change manually. Instead, you can use Oracle's scheduler to schedule the switch so that it is executed automatically based on a specific schedule.

One caveat of scheduling resource-plan switches, however, is that you may encounter a situation in which you don't want the plans to change.

For instance, if your nightly data loads are larger than normal and might exceed the cutoff time, you may want to delay the switch until the loads have finished. This will ensure that the loads have all the resources necessary to complete.

Rather than having to alter the job in the scheduler, you can simply execute the following statement:

```
SQL> ALTER SYSTEM
  SET RESOURCE_MANAGER_PLAN = 'FORCE:OFF_HOURS_PLAN';

System altered.
```

When the prefix FORCE: is added to the name of the plan, Oracle will restrict the active plan from being changed by the scheduler. The scheduler will still attempt to make the change, but it will fail.

When the nightly loads are finished, the restriction can be lifted by reissuing the identical ALTER SYSTEM statement without the FORCE: prefix, as shown here:

```
SQL> ALTER SYSTEM
  SET RESOURCE_MANAGER_PLAN = 'OFF_HOURS_PLAN';

System altered.
```

With the restriction lifted, the resource plan can now be changed manually (or by the scheduler).

I/O Calibration with DRM

Also included in the DRM is a procedure that enables the DBA to test the I/O performance of the database's storage system. The supplied DBMS_RESOURCE_MANAGER.CALIBRATE_IO procedure executes an I/O intense read of the database files and determines the maximum sustainable IOPS (I/O requests per second) and MBPS (megabytes of I/O per second). The results are written to the DBA_RSRC_IO_CALIBRATE table. Because it is an intense workload, choose to run this procedure when it will have the least impact on your customers. This tool is a valid representative of storage performance capabilities using the Oracle database engine.

Resource Manager Statistics in AWR

The Automatic Workload Repository (AWR) introduces new views for DRM statistics. The DBA_HIST_RSRC_PLAN and DBA_HIST_RSRC_CONSUMER_GROUP views retain historical versions of the statistics in V$RESOURCE_PLAN and V$RESOURCE_CONSUMER_GROUP. The view V$RSRCMGRMETRIC shows resource utilization and waits due to DRM.

DBRM is the background process for the Database Resource Manager.

Summary

In this chapter, you learned about Automatic Memory Management, Automatic Shared Memory Management, manually configuring SGA parameters, Automatic PGA Memory Management, resumable space operations, transportable tablespaces, transportable databases, Segment Shrink operations, and the Database Resource Manager.

With memory management, you learned that Oracle highly recommends that you configure Automatic Memory Management and leave memory tuning and management to the Oracle instance. If you as the DBA for a database understand the application and know how to tune the SGA and PGA to achieve better results, then choose Automatic Shared Memory Management and Automatic PGA Memory Management. If you need more granular control, then manually configure your SGA and/or PGA.

You learned about resumable space allocations and how to configure, detect, and remedy suspended transactions.

You learned about transportable tablespaces and transportable databases. With transportable tablespaces, you can convert a tablespace set to run on a different platform with a different endianness using the RMAN convert clause. You cannot transport an entire database to a different endian format, but you can convert it to run on a different platform with the same endianness.

The Segment Shrink feature can be used to reclaim space both above and below the high-water mark while a segment remains online and in use.

You learned about the Oracle Database Resource Manager (DRM) and how to configure it to manage resources on your Oracle database. You can set up a pending area to hold all of the DRM objects as they are created or modified. Objects in the pending area need to be validated before moving them into the data dictionary. We discussed the requirements that each object must pass before being declared valid by the DRM. You learned that submitting the pending area activates all the objects therein and moves them into the data dictionary. To put all of the elements together, you can build a complex resource-plan schema using PL/SQL packages and then enable the plan on the database.

Exam Essentials

Know the difference between Automatic Memory Management and Automatic Shared Memory Management. Be able to distinguish the characteristics, pros, and cons of Automatic Memory Management. Understand how to configure Automatic Memory Management vs. Automatic Shared Memory Management. Understand the difference between the MEMORY_TARGET and MAX_MEMORY_TARGET and the difference between SGA_TARGET and SGA_MAX_SIZE. Understand how to dynamically increase or decrease the amount of memory usable by the instance.

Know how to manually configure the SGA. Understand how to disable Automatic Memory Management and Automatic Shared Memory Management and how to manually configure the individual SGA pools. Know the names of the pools you can configure manually.

Know how to configure Automatic PGA Memory Management. Understand how to explicitly and implicitly configure Automatic PGA Memory Management. Understand what instance PGA memory is used for. Understand the meaning of and how to configure Automatic PGA Memory using PGA_AGGREGATE_TARGET.

Know how to configure the Database Resource Manager. Be able to create, update, and delete DRM objects. Be aware of the pending area and the need to validate and submit objects to the data dictionary to make them active. Know that submitting the pending area enforces validation, so it isn't strictly necessary to validate as a separate step. Know the various methods of enabling DRM (through ALTER SYSTEM and through initialization parameters). Understand the various allocation methods.

Be able to assign users to Database Resource Manager groups. Know all the methods of assigning user sessions to DRM groups. Know the names of the DBMS_RESOURCE_MANAGER procedures for assigning groups. Be aware of the switch privilege and how it is granted. Be aware of the DBMS_SESSION procedure that users can use to change their own group.

Know how to create resource plans within groups. Understand all the steps involved in creating resource plans, both simple and complex. Know the difference between single- and multilevel resource plans. Understand the allocation methods used. Know what constitutes a top-level plan and a subplan.

Be able to specify directives for allocating resources to consumer groups. Know how to create and manage plan directives to allocate resources to consumer groups and subplans. Understand which allocation methods are available for directives to groups as opposed to directives to subplans.

Review Questions

1. Which of the following Oracle features is enabled by setting a nonzero value for the MEMORY_TARGET initialization parameter?
   A. Automatic PGA Memory Management
   B. Automatic SGA Memory Management
   C. Automatic Shared Memory Management
   D. Automatic Memory Management
   E. Manual SGA Memory Management
   F. None of the above

2. By setting the value of MEMORY_TARGET to zero and setting the value of SGA_TARGET to a nonzero value, you will enable which of the following memory-management options?
   A. Automatic PGA Memory Management
   B. Automatic SGA Memory Management
   C. Automatic Shared Memory Management
   D. Automatic Memory Management
   E. Manual SGA Memory Management
   F. None of the above

3. For Oracle 11*g*, Oracle strongly recommends that you configure your database to use which of the following memory-management features?
   A. Automatic PGA Memory Management
   B. Automatic SGA Memory Management
   C. Automatic Shared Memory Management
   D. Automatic Memory Management
   E. Manual SGA Memory Management
   F. None of the above

4. To manually configure the SGA components using Oracle Enterprise Manager Memory Advisor, you can set values for which of the following initialization parameters? (Choose all that apply.)
   A. DB_CACHE_SIZE
   B. SHARED_POOL_SIZE
   C. LARGE_POOL_SIZE
   D. JAVA_POOL_SIZE
   E. SGA_MAX_SIZE
   F. SORT_AREA_SIZE

5. When manually configuring the SGA, which of the following parameter changes requires an instance restart to take effect?

   A. DB_CACHE_SIZE

   B. SHARED_POOL_SIZE

   C. LARGE_POOL_SIZE

   D. JAVA_POOL_SIZE

   E. SGA_MAX_SIZE

   F. SORT_AREA_SIZE

6. Using Oracle Enterprise Manager to set SGA pool values manually, for which of the following pools does Oracle EM offer advice to set the value appropriately? (Choose all that apply.)

   A. DB_CACHE_SIZE

   B. SHARED_POOL_SIZE

   C. LARGE_POOL_SIZE

   D. JAVA_POOL_SIZE

   E. SGA_MAX_SIZE

   F. SORT_AREA_SIZE

7. In Oracle 11g, by default which one of the following conditions implicitly enables Automatic PGA Memory Management?

   A. Setting a nonzero value for SGA_TARGET

   B. Configuring Automatic Shared Memory Management

   C. Configuring Automatic Memory Management

   D. Setting a nonzero value for SGA_MAX_SIZE and PGA_AGGREGATE_TARGET

   E. None of the above

8. Automatic PGA Memory Management eliminates the need to manually configure which of the following initialization parameters? (Choose all that apply.)

   A. SORT_AREA_SIZE

   B. HASH_AREA_SIZE

   C. BITMAP_MERGE_AREA_SIZE

   D. CREATE_BITMAP_AREA_SIZE

   E. PGA_AGGREGATE_TARGET

9. When tuning Automatic PGA Memory Management, which of the following views will provide the information specified?

   A. The V$PGA_TARGET_ADVICE view shows the predicted cache hit-ratio improvement if you increase PGA_AGGREGATE_TARGET.

   B. The V$PGA_TARGET_ADVICE view shows how the V$SQL_WORKAREA histogram will change if you change the value of PGA_AGGREGATE_TARGET.

   C. The V$PGA_TARGET_ADVICE_HISTOGRAM view shows how the V$SQL_WORKAREA_HISTOGRAM will change if you switch between Manual and Automatic PGA Memory Management.

   D. The V$PGA_TARGET_ADVICE view shows how performance will improve for the different work areas if you switch from Manual to Automatic PGA Memory Management.

10. To enable resumable space allocation for the instance, which of the following initialization parameters should you set to a nonzero value?

    A. RESUMABLE_SPACE_TIME

    B. RESUMABLE_SPACE

    C. RESUMABLE_TIME

    D. RESUMABLE_TIMEOUT

    E. TIME_RESUMABLE

11. Which of the following describes how a distributed resumable transaction behaves?

    A. The resumable setting on the initiating session determines the resumable conditions for the entire distributed transaction.

    B. The resumable setting for the initiating instance determines the resumable conditions for the entire distributed transaction.

    C. The resumable setting on the initiating session controls only that part of the transaction that occurs within the local instance; remote resumable settings determine the behavior of the distributed parts of the transaction.

    D. None of the above.

12. Which of these components correctly identify the unique value of the NAME column in the DBA_RESUMABLE view?

    A. Username, instance number, session ID

    B. Instance number, username, session ID

    C. Instance number, session ID, username

    D. Username, session ID, instance number

    E. None of the above

13. Which of the following are included in a transportable tablespace set? (Choose all that apply.)
    A. The datafiles that make up a self-contained group of tablespaces required for copy
    B. The system tablespace
    C. An export of the tablespace metadata
    D. The spfile
    E. All of the above

14. The following query will provide what information about transportable tablespaces for the current database? (Choose all that apply.)

```
select d.platform_name "Source", t.platform_name
 "Compatible Targets", endian_format
 from v$transportable_platform t, v$database d
 where t.endian_format = (select endian_format
   from   v$transportable_platform t,
                          v$database d
                         where d.platform_name =
                          t.platform_name);
```

    A. The list of target platforms having the same endian format as the source database
    B. The list of target platforms requiring endian conversion
    C. The list of target platforms that will not require endian conversion
    D. The list of all target platforms that can receive transportable tablespaces from the source database
    E. None of the above

15. When exporting metadata for the transportable tablespaces, what is the correct next step after confirming endian format?
    A. Export the tablespaces using data pump.
    B. Determine if the transportable set is self-contained.
    C. Convert the datafiles using RMAN.
    D. Copy the datafiles from source to destination.

16. Which of the following are prerequisite steps to transport a database? (Choose all that apply.)
    A. Query the V$TRANSPORTABLE_PLATFORMS view in the source database to determine if the intended destination is listed.
    B. Verify that there are no restrictions or limitations that the source or destination database may encounter.
    C. Verify that the source and destination have the same Oracle version, critical updates, patch-set version, and patch-set exceptions.
    D. Determine if you will perform the conversion on the source or destination platform.
    E. None of the above.

17. Which of the following supplied functions is used to identify external tables, directories, and BFILES?

    A. DBMS_TDB.CHECK_DIRECTORIES

    B. DBMS_TDB.CHECK_EXTERNAL

    C. DBMS_TDB.CHECK_BFILE

    D. DBMS_TDB.CHECK_EXT

18. Which of the following is a prerequisite for running DBMS_TDB.CHECK_DB to a successful completion?

    A. The database must be in read-write mode.

    B. The database must have no external files.

    C. The database must open in read-only mode.

    D. The database must be mounted but not opened.

19. Which of the following options describes Segment Shrink?

    A. Reclaims space above and below the high-water mark without using additional space

    B. Moves rows to a new physical location, resetting the high-water mark, but uses additional space during the operation

    C. Deallocates space above the high-water mark that is currently not in use

    D. None of the above

20. For which of the following can you use Segment Shrink? (Choose all that apply.)

    A. Heap tables

    B. Tables with function-based indexes

    C. Indexes

    D. Partitions and subpartitions

    E. None of the above

21. When shrinking a table segment, you choose to shrink all the indexes for that table using the SHRINK SPACE command. Which clause should you use?

    A. INCLUDING DEPENDENCIES

    B. INCLUDING DEPENDENCIES CASCADE

    C. COMPACT

    D. CASCADE

    E. None of the above

22. Which of these represent the main components of Database Resource Manager? (Choose all that apply.)
    A. Resource consumer groups
    B. Resource plans
    C. Resource-plan groups
    D. Resource-plan directives
    E. All of the above

23. Every resource plan must contain an allocation to which consumer group?
    A. LOW_GROUP
    B. SYS_GROUP
    C. DEFAULT_GROUP
    D. BASE_GROUP
    E. OTHER_GROUPS

24. Which DBMS_RESOURCE_MANAGER procedure prioritizes consumer-group mappings?
    A. CREATE_MAPPING_PRIORITY
    B. SET_MAPPING_PRIORITY
    C. SET_MAPPING_ORDER
    D. PRIORITIZE_MAPPING_ORDER
    E. This functionality is not available through the DBMS_RESOURCE_MANAGER package.

25. Within a resource-plan definition, what differentiates a top-level plan from a subplan?
    A. A subplan has the PLAN_SUB parameter value set to SUB.
    B. A top-level plan has the GROUP_OR_PLAN parameter set to the name of the subplan in the resource-plan definition.
    C. There is no difference in the resource-plan definition.
    D. A subplan always has the CPU_MTH parameter value set to RATIO.
    E. The string TOP_LEVEL is appended to the name of top-level resource plans.

Answers to Review Questions

1. D. The MEMORY_TARGET initialization parameter is used to set the total memory shared between SGA and PGA for Automatic Memory Management.

2. C. The SGA_TARGET initialization parameter is used to set the total memory for the SGA for Automatic Shared Memory Management.

3. D. For Oracle 11*g*, Oracle highly recommends that you let the instance manage all the memory automatically, using the Automatic Memory Management feature.

4. A, B, C, D. Each of these are SGA components that are configured manually if you choose not to manage the SGA using Automatic Shared Memory Management or all memory using Automatic Memory Management. The SGA_MAX_SIZE is not an SGA component but represents the maximum value for the combined SGA pool sizes. The SORT_AREA_SIZE is a manual PGA initialization parameter.

5. E. The SGA_MAX_SIZE parameter can be changed in the spfile using OEM, but it cannot be changed dynamically for the instance. It requires an instance restart to take effect. You can change options A, B, C, and D without requiring a restart as long as the sum of the values remains less than the value for SGA_MAX_SIZE. SORT_AREA_SIZE is not an SGA parameter.

6. A, B. Advice can be obtained for the buffer cache DB_CACHE_SIZE parameter and the shared pool SHARED_POOL_SIZE parameter. Advice is not offered for the large pool, Java pool, or the maximum SGA size. SORT_AREA_SIZE is not an SGA parameter.

7. B. By default, Oracle 11*g* is configured for Automatic Memory Management. If you configure Automatic Shared Memory Management and make no other changes, you will implicitly enable Automatic PGA Memory Management. Setting SGA_TARGET to a nonzero value doesn't immediately enable Automatic Shared Memory Management because you may still have Automatic Memory Management enabled. Setting the parameter SGA_MAX_SIZE to nonzero puts a cap on manual SGA configuration, but again it does not implement Manual Shared Memory Management. The value of PGA_AGGREGATE_TARGET is relevant only if Automatic Memory Management is not configured, so you must also set MEMORY_TARGET to zero for it to take effect.

8. A, B, C, D. Each of these are work areas in the PGA is configured manually if Automatic PGA Memory Management is not enabled. You enable Automatic PGA Memory Management when you disable Automatic Memory Management and set a nonzero value for the PGA_AGGREGATE_TARGET parameter.

9. A. When operating in Automatic PGA Memory Management mode, you can seek advice on increasing or decreasing the value of PGA_AGGREGATE_TARGET to influence the hit ratio for the PGA work areas.

10. D. For the instance, set the initialization parameter RESUMABLE_TIMEOUT to a nonzero value, representing the number of seconds for which an operation will suspend until an action is taken to repair the condition or the operation aborts due to the condition.

11. C. In a distributed transaction, the remote RESUMABLE_TIMEOUT initialization parameter applies to the remote part of the transaction, and the remote-session resumable setting applies. Also, local resumable settings do not apply to the remote part of the distributed transactions.

12. D. For the DBA_RESUMABLE view, the NAME column is populated with the username, session ID, and instance number.

13. A, C. The transportable tablespace set is the self-contained group of tablespaces that encapsulate the objects that you wish to transport along with the exported metadata for the tablespaces.

14. A, C. The SQL query returns the list of target platforms that have the same endian format and do not require RMAN conversion between source and destination databases.

15. B. Execute the DBMS_TTS.TRANSPORT_SET_CHECK procedure using the proposed list of tablespaces for the transportable set. Optionally, the last parameter should be TRUE to verify referential integrity constraints.

16. B, C, D. Option A is incorrect because the correct view name is V$DB_TRANSPORTABLE_PLATFORM. You'll need to verify that there are no restrictions or limitations such as storage or memory, verify that the version levels are the same, and determine where you will perform the conversion.

17. B. The DBMS_TDB.CHECK_EXTERNAL function returns the list of external files that will need to be copied to the destination system. The other answers are not valid.

18. C. The DBMS_TDB.CHECK_DB function must execute with the database open and in read-only mode.

19. A. The Segment Shrink feature reclaims space above and below the high-water mark without using additional space to perform an operation.

20. A, C, D. The Segment Shrink feature can be used on tables, indexes, and partitions, but not on tables with function-based indexes.

21. D. The Segment Shrink SHRINK SPACE command specifying the table name, and then including the CASCADE clause, will reclaim space from the table segment and all dependent index segments, as reported by the DBMS_SPACE.OBJECT_DEPENDENT_SEGMENT function.

22. A, B, D. The main components are resource consumer groups, resource plans, and resource-plan directives. There is no such thing as a resource-plan group.

23. E. The OTHER_GROUPS consumer group is assigned to sessions whose assigned group is not contained in the enabled plan. Therefore, Oracle requires that an allocation be made so that no sessions will be completely deprived of resources.

24. B. The SET_MAPPING_PRIORITY procedure allows for prioritization based on the session attribute type.

25. C. There is no concept of a subplan in the resource-plan definition. Only in a resource-plan directive can a subplan be identified.

Using the Scheduler to Automate Tasks

ORACLE DATABASE 11*g*: ADMINISTRATION II EXAM OBJECTIVES COVERED IN THIS CHAPTER:

✓ **Automating Tasks with the Scheduler**

- Create a job, program, and schedule
- Use a time-based or event-based schedule for executing Scheduler jobs
- Create lightweight jobs
- Use job chains to perform a series of related tasks

✓ **Administering the Scheduler**

- Create Windows and Job Classes
- Use advanced Scheduler concepts to prioritize jobs

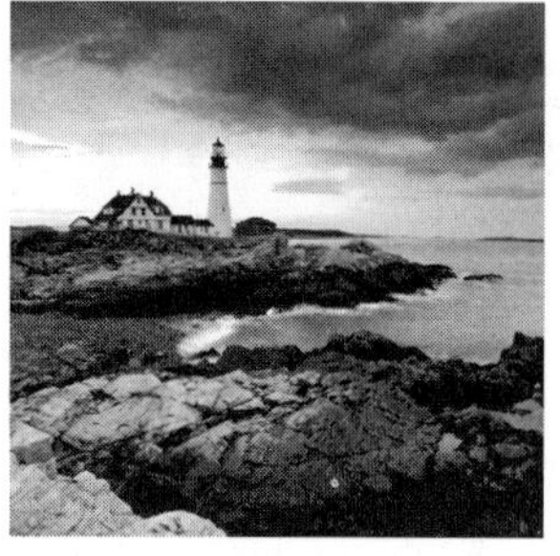

As an Oracle database administrator, you might find that an inordinate amount of your time is spent performing routine tasks. Unfortunately, routine tasks come with the territory, and that is unlikely to change in the foreseeable future. Handling these routine tasks manually is an invitation for problems. Mistakes can be made, or even worse, the tasks will be forgotten and not run at all.

The Oracle Scheduler feature makes the scheduling of routine tasks a simple matter. The Oracle Scheduler is a major advancement over the old `DBMS_JOB` scheduling system found in previous Oracle versions. It corrects many of the nagging idiosyncrasies while adding powerful new features such as the calendaring syntax, a flexible method of defining repeat intervals for Scheduler jobs. `DBMS_JOB` is now deprecated, so we will focus on using the Scheduler to manage jobs in the Oracle database.

In this chapter, you will learn how the Scheduler works and how to create and manage Scheduler elements. First, you will get an overview of the terminology and components that make up the Scheduler. You will learn the underlying architecture of the Scheduler and how all the pieces fit together.

Next, you will learn about Scheduler jobs and how to create and manage them. You will also learn about job groups and how they can be used to simplify the management of jobs as well as to prioritize job execution.

You will also learn about Scheduler programs, which define the work that will be performed. You'll learn to create and manage schedules, which define when jobs will be run and how often they will be repeated. You'll learn how to define complex repeat intervals using Oracle's calendaring syntax.

Next, you will learn about windows and window groups, which allow you to switch resource plans based on a schedule. You'll learn about job classes, which allow you to group jobs together based on business requirements. You'll learn about lightweight jobs, which are used for high-frequency, low-utilization programs. We'll introduce the concept of the job chain, which allows you to implement dependency-based scheduling. And, last, you will learn about the Scheduler views that are available to you.

Exam objectives are subject to change at any time without prior notice and at Oracle's sole discretion. Please visit Oracle's Training and Certification website (`http://www.oracle.com/education/certification/`) for the most current exam-objectives listing.

Automating Tasks with the Scheduler

The main functionality of any enterprise scheduling system is the ability to schedule tasks to execute at a specific date and time. These can be recurring tasks that run at preset intervals or one-time tasks set to execute immediately or at some point in the future.

To achieve this functionality, the Scheduler uses several distinct components to specify scheduled tasks:

Jobs A *job* instructs the Scheduler to run a specific program at a specific time on a specific date.

Programs A *program* contains the code (or a reference to the code) such as PL/SQL code or a binary executable that needs to be run to accomplish a task. It can also contain parameters that should be passed to the program at runtime. A program can be stored as an independent object that can be referenced by many jobs.

Schedules A *schedule* contains a start date, an optional end date, and a repeat interval. With these elements, an execution schedule can be calculated. A schedule can be stored as an independent object that can be referenced by many jobs.

Windows A *window* identifies a recurring block of time during which a specific resource plan should be enabled to govern resource allocation for the database. For instance, the weekend may be classified as a maintenance window, and you can enable a resource plan that allocates the bulk of the system resources to administrative users.

Job classes A *job class* is a logical method of classifying jobs with similar attributes. Job groups define specific attributes that will be inherited by all jobs assigned to the group. They also simplify management by allowing collections of jobs to be manipulated as one object.

Window groups A *window group* is a logical method of grouping windows. They simplify the management of windows by allowing the members of the group to be manipulated as one object. Unlike job groups, window groups don't set default characteristics for windows that belong to the group.

Chains A *chain* consists of two or more Scheduler programs that are linked together to meet an objective. A chain is an implementation of dependency scheduling, where the outcome of one job determines which job or jobs will execute next.

These basic components make up the bulk of Oracle's Scheduler facility. Their design encourages building flexible, reusable components shared by many scheduled jobs.

The Scheduler also offers a powerful and flexible *calendaring syntax* that is used to specify recurring task executions. This new syntax allows for the specification of complex date and time requirements. It also eliminates many of the shortcomings of `DBMS_JOB`, such as schedule creep (where the start time of a task was directly affected by the start time of the previous execution of that task).

Last, the Scheduler allows the execution of non-Oracle-related programs and scripts. This means that the Scheduler can be used not only to execute SQL and PL/SQL, but also operating-system executable programs. Therefore, most of your tasks can be scheduled in a common place.

Exploring the Scheduler Architecture

Understanding how to use the Scheduler begins with understanding the underlying architecture upon which the Scheduler functionality is built. This is not to say that you have to be able to name every locking mechanism and memory structure used in the Scheduler, any more than a person needs to know the ignition sequence of their car in order to drive it. Rather, it implies that a high-level knowledge of the underlying Scheduler processes will help you create more logical Scheduler objects and enable you to troubleshoot problems associated with the Scheduler.

In the following sections, you will learn about these topics:

- The job table, which houses all the active jobs within the database
- The job coordinator, a key Oracle process that ensures that jobs are being run on schedule
- Job slaves, processes that carry out the execution of jobs under the guidance of the job coordinator
- The architecture in Real Application Clusters (RAC) environments and how it differs only slightly from a stand-alone database environment
- Special considerations for Data Guard

The Job Table

The Scheduler *job table* is the master container for all enabled jobs in the database. This table stores information about all jobs, including the objects referenced by the job, the owner of the job, and the next run date. It also stores statistical information about jobs, such as the number of times the job has run and the number of times the job has failed. And it contains the STATE column, which contains the current state of the job (for example, RUNNING, SCHEDULED, BROKEN).

The information stored in the job table can be viewed through the *_SCHEDULER_JOBS view. For example, the following query will show the state of all jobs in the table as well as their next run date:

```
SQL> select owner, job_name, state
  2  from dba_scheduler_jobs;

OWNER      JOB_NAME             STATE
---------- -------------------- ------------
SYS        PURGE_LOG            SCHEDULED
SYS        GATHER_STATS_JOB     RUNNING
```

As you can see in this example, the GATHER_STATS_JOB is currently running, while the PURGE_LOG job is scheduled to run at some point in the future. If you really want to know when the PURGE_LOG job will run, you could include the NEXT_RUN_DATE column in your query and see exactly when it will run next.

The Job Coordinator

The *job coordinator* is an Oracle background process with the responsibility of ensuring that jobs are run on schedule. The job coordinator regularly queries the job table and copies job information to a memory cache for improved performance when the job is executed.

The Oracle database itself monitors job schedules and starts the job-coordinator process (if it is not already started) when a job needs to be executed. The job coordinator pulls the job information from the memory cache and passes it to a job-slave (described in the next section) process for execution.

The job coordinator controls all aspects of the job-slave pool of processes, so it can remove dormant slave processes and spawn new processes as needed to meet the needs of the Scheduler.

The background process for the job coordinator is cjqNNN. There is one job-coordinator process per instance.

The Job-Slave Processes

Job-slave processes are tasked with carrying out the execution of job programs assigned to them by the Scheduler. When a job slave receives the job information from the coordinator, it sets to work collecting all the metadata that it needs to carry out the request. This metadata includes things such as the program arguments and privilege information.

When it is ready to execute the program, the job slave creates a new session as the owner of the job, starts a transaction within the session, and then executes the job. When the job is complete, the transaction is committed and the session is closed by the job slave. Next, the slave performs the following actions:

- Reschedules the job if required.
- Updates the STATUS column to a value of COMPLETED in the job table for the current job.
- Updates the RUN_COUNT column to increment the current value by 1 in the job table for the current job. If necessary, updates the failure and retry count.
- Inserts an entry into the job log table.
- Cleans up.
- Looks for any new work that needs to be done.

If no new work is found, the job-slave process will sleep until it is called again by the coordinator or until it is removed from the system by the job coordinator.

RAC Considerations

The Scheduler architecture in an Oracle Real Application Clusters (RAC) environment is the same as in a stand-alone instance, with the following exceptions:

- Each instance in the cluster will have its own job coordinator.
- The job coordinators can communicate with one another to share information.
- Jobs can be defined with a service affinity (they should run on a specific service) as opposed to an instance affinity (they should run on a specific instance). If a job is assigned to a service consisting of two instances, even if one instance is down, the other can execute the job normally.
- If there is service affinity and more than one instance in the service is available, the Scheduler will attempt to balance job workload across instances in the service.
- If there is no service affinity, the Scheduler will attempt to balance the workload across all available instances.
- If there is instance affinity and the instance is down, none of the jobs with an affinity to that instance will run until the instance is back up.

Aside from these exceptions, the Scheduler architecture in a RAC environment is the same as described previously.

As mentioned earlier, there is one job-coordinator process per instance. There is only one job table per database.

Data Guard Considerations

With Oracle 11g, the Scheduler can run jobs taking into consideration whether the database is a physical or logical standby in an Oracle Data Guard configuration.

- Changes made to the Scheduler on the primary database are applied to the physical standby.
- If you want the job to run on the logical standby only after it becomes the primary, then set the `database_role` attribute to `PRIMARY` using the `DBMS_SCHEDULER.SET_ATTRIBUTE` procedure.
- If you want the job to run on the logical standby only if it is in the logical-standby role, then set the `database_role` attribute to `LOGICAL STANDBY` using the `DBMS_SCHEDULER.SET_ATTRIBUTE` procedure.

Aside from these exceptions, the Scheduler architecture in a RAC environment is the same as described previously.

Exploring Common Administration Tools

The Oracle Scheduler is implemented through a PL/SQL package named DBMS_SCHEDULER. This package offers a collection of procedures that are used to create and manage Scheduler objects (jobs, programs, schedules, windows, job classes, window groups, and chains). Each of these object types will be covered thoroughly in this chapter.

Most of the procedures in the DBMS_SCHEDULER package are specific to a certain object type. The object type can be derived from the name of the procedure. For example, the CREATE_PROGRAM procedure is obviously specific to program objects.

However, because all Scheduler objects share some common attributes, there are also procedures that work with any Scheduler object type. These procedures play an important role in the management of Scheduler objects, so they warrant thorough coverage. However, due to their "global" nature, they will be covered in the following sections, separate from any specific object type.

You will learn about the following DBMS_SCHEDULER procedures:

- ENABLE
- DISABLE
- SET_ATTRIBUTE
- SET_ATTRIBUTE_NULL

You will also learn about any special cases that may exist within the different Scheduler object types.

Using the *ENABLE* Procedure

With the exception of schedules, all Scheduler objects have a common attribute named ENABLED. The attribute is a Boolean (TRUE or FALSE) value that identifies whether the object is eligible for use by the Scheduler.

Because schedule objects do not have an ENABLED attribute, they cannot be enabled or disabled. They are always enabled by default.

Therefore, to be eligible for use in the Scheduler, the ENABLED attribute must be set to TRUE. By default, only schedule objects are enabled at creation time, because they cannot be disabled. All other objects will be disabled by default when they are created.

To enable an object, the DBMS_SCHEDULER.ENABLE procedure is used. The procedure accepts only one argument, NAME, which designates one of the following:

- The name of one specific object
- A comma-separated list of objects

For example, here's how to enable one specific object:

```
SQL> begin
  2  dbms_scheduler.enable('BACKUP_JOB');
  3  end;
  4  /

PL/SQL procedure successfully completed.
```

To enable multiple objects, a comma-separated list can be passed in. Note that the entire list is enclosed in single quotes. Therefore, the list is submitted as a single parameter, as shown here:

```
SQL> begin
  2  dbms_scheduler.enable(
  3    'BACKUP_PROGRAM, BACKUP_JOB, STATS_JOB');
  4  end;
  5  /

PL/SQL procedure successfully completed.
```

The list of objects can also contain both groups and individual objects:

```
SQL> begin
  2  dbms_scheduler.enable(
  3    'BACKUP_JOB_GROUP, STATS_JOB, SYS.WINDOW_GROUP_1');
  4  end;
  5  /

PL/SQL procedure successfully completed.
```

There are a couple of special cases that should be noted about enabling group objects:

- When a job group is enabled, all members of that job group will be enabled.
- When a window group is enabled, only the window group object is enabled. Windows that are members of the group are not enabled.
- When a window or window group is referenced in the ENABLE procedure, it must always be prefixed with the SYS schema name as shown in the preceding example (SYS.WINDOW_GROUP_1).

Using the *DISABLE* Procedure

When a Scheduler object is disabled, it is ineligible for use by the Scheduler. Disabling a Scheduler object is accomplished by setting the object's ENABLED attribute to FALSE.

To disable an object, the `DBMS_SCHEDULER.DISABLE` procedure is used. This procedure accepts two parameters: `NAME` and `FORCE`. The `NAME` parameter designates one of the following:

- The name of one specific object
- A comma-separated list of objects

The `FORCE` parameter is a Boolean (`TRUE` or `FALSE`) value that tells the procedure how to handle the request if dependencies exist. The default value is `FALSE`.

There are two situations that could be classified as dependencies:

- A job object that references a program object is considered to be dependent on that object.
- If an instance of an object is currently running (for example, a window is open or a job is running), there may be a dependency issue.

If any dependencies are found, the value of the `FORCE` parameter will determine the ultimate outcome of the `DISABLE` procedure.

The purpose of the FORCE parameter is not to cascade the changes to dependent objects. The purpose is to make you aware of dependencies. No changes will be made to dependent objects.

The effect of the `FORCE` option varies between object types. The differences are listed in Table 12.1.

TABLE 12.1 Effects of DISABLE with the FORCE Option

Object Type	Effect
Job	If the FORCE attribute is FALSE: If an instance of the job is currently running, the procedure will fail. If the FORCE attribute is TRUE: The job is disabled, but the currently running instance is allowed to finish.
Schedule	N/A
Program	If the FORCE attribute is FALSE: If the program is referenced by any job, the procedure will fail. If the FORCE attribute is TRUE: The program will be disabled. Jobs that reference the program will not be disabled but will fail at runtime if the program is still disabled.
Window	If the FORCE attribute is FALSE: If the window is open or referenced by any job, the procedure will fail. If the FORCE attribute is TRUE: The procedure will succeed in disabling the window. If that window is open at the time the DISABLE procedure is called, it will not be affected. Jobs that reference the window will not be disabled.
Window group	If the FORCE attribute is FALSE: If any member windows are open or if any member windows are referenced by a job object, the DISABLE procedure will fail. If the FORCE attribute is TRUE: The window group will be disabled. Any open window that is a member of the group will continue to its end. Jobs that reference the window group as their schedule will not be disabled.

If an object has no dependencies, using the DISABLE procedure will disable any valid Scheduler object regardless of the value of the FORCE parameter.

For example, use the following command to disable one specific object:

```
SQL> begin
dbms_scheduler.disable('BACKUP_JOB');
end;
/

PL/SQL procedure successfully completed.
```

To disable multiple objects, a comma-separated list can be passed in. Note that the entire list is enclosed in single quotes. Therefore, the list is submitted as a single parameter. In this example, the FORCE option is also set to TRUE:

```
SQL> begin
dbms_scheduler.disable(
  'BACKUP_PROGRAM, BACKUP_JOB, STATS_JOB',TRUE);
end;
/

PL/SQL procedure successfully completed.
```

The list of objects can also contain both groups and individual objects:

```
SQL> begin
dbms_scheduler.disable(
  'BACKUP_JOB_GROUP, STATS_JOB, SYS.WINDOW_GROUP_1');
end;
/

PL/SQL procedure successfully completed.
```

There are a couple of special cases that should be noted about disabling group objects:

- Disabling a window group does not disable jobs that reference the group. However, those jobs will fail when they try to execute.
- Disabling a window group does not affect members of the group. They will continue to function normally.

Setting Attributes

You might be surprised to find that the DBMS_SCHEDULER package does not have an ALTER procedure of any kind. This is because Scheduler objects are collections of attributes. To make a change to an object requires setting its *attributes*. Therefore, to alter a Scheduler object, the DBMS_SCHEDULER.SET_ATTRIBUTE and DBMS_SCHEDULER.SET_ATTRIBUTE_NULL procedures are used.

In the following sections, you will learn to use these procedures with all types of Scheduler objects.

The SET_ATTRIBUTE procedure sets an attribute for any type of Scheduler object. The SET_ATTRIBUTE_NULL procedure, on the other hand, sets any attribute to NULL for any type of Scheduler object. This is useful for "unsetting" an attribute.

The only attribute that cannot be altered (for any type of Scheduler object) is the name of the object.

When the attributes on an object are changed, Oracle will attempt to disable the object before making the changes. When the attribute has been successfully altered, Oracle will reenable the object automatically. If the SET_ATTRIBUTE procedure fails, the object will remain disabled (and an error message is returned).

Using the SET_ATTRIBUTE procedure does not affect instances of the object that are currently executing. Changes made will affect only future instantiations of the object.

The SET_ATTRIBUTE procedure accepts three parameters:

NAME The name of the Scheduler object.

ATTRIBUTE The name of the attribute to be changed.

VALUE The new value for the attribute. The procedure is overloaded to accept a value of any applicable datatype, so no conversion is necessary when setting values for different datatypes.

The SET_ATTRIBUTE_NULL procedure accepts only two parameters:

NAME The name of the Scheduler object.

ATTRIBUTE The name of the attribute, which should be set to NULL.

In the preceding section, you learned that an object was considered enabled when the ENABLED attribute was set to a value of TRUE. Therefore, you can enable or disable an object by using the SET_ATTRIBUTE procedure, as shown here:

```
SQL> begin
  2  dbms_scheduler.set_attribute (
  3  name => 'TEST_JOB',
  4  attribute => 'ENABLED',
  5  value => TRUE);
  6 end;
  7 /

PL/SQL procedure successfully completed.
```

To remove the end date from a schedule, the SET_ATTRIBUTE_NULL procedure can be used to set the attribute to NULL, as shown here:

```
SQL> begin
dbms_scheduler.set_attribute_null (
name => 'TEST_SCHEDULE',
attribute => 'END_DATE');
end;
/

PL/SQL procedure successfully completed.
```

Using Scheduler Jobs

A Scheduler job defines a specific program to be executed, the arguments (or parameters) to be passed to the program, and the schedule defining when the program should be executed. It also specifies other characteristics, such as logging options, job priority, and so on.

Many of these characteristics are explicitly set at job-creation time through the CREATE_JOB procedure. However, others are inherited from the job class to which the job is assigned. If a job is not explicitly assigned to a job class, these characteristics will be inherited from a job class named DEFAULT_JOB_CLASS.

In the following sections, you will learn how to administer the various aspects of Scheduler jobs. You will learn to create, copy, and alter jobs to achieve your scheduling needs. You will learn how to run jobs and how to stop jobs that are running. You will learn how to enable and disable jobs and, finally, how to drop jobs that are no longer needed.

Creating Jobs

Scheduler jobs can be created by using the DBMS_SCHEDULER.CREATE_JOB procedure. As you will recall, a job combines a program and a schedule for execution of that program. Therefore, these are the elements that you must define when creating a new job.

Depending on the program that the job uses, you may also need to set job arguments. These are parameters that will be passed to the program at execution time. Job arguments can be set by using the SET_JOB_ARGUMENT and/or SET_JOB_ANYDATA_VALUE procedures in the DBMS_SCHEDULER package.

Jobs also have *job attributes* that control certain behaviors of the job. Many of these can be set through the CREATE_JOB procedure, while others are inherited from the job class to which the job is assigned (or from the DEFAULT_JOB_CLASS class, as mentioned previously).

For example, job attributes such as JOB_TYPE, JOB_ACTION, and REPEAT_INTERVAL can all be defined at job-creation time. Other attributes, such as MAX_FAILURES, LOGGING_LEVEL, and JOB_PRIORITY, are inherited from the job class.

A job is stored like any other database object, so it is vital that a valid object name is used when creating jobs. The job name must also be unique within the schema in which it is created. Like other database objects, jobs can be created in a different schema by prefixing the job name with a schema name.

In the following sections, you will learn which attributes define a Scheduler job. You will also learn how to administer all aspects of Scheduler job objects.

Job Attributes

Scheduler jobs have a specific set of attributes that you can set to define the characteristics of the job. These attributes can be set at job-creation time through the following `CREATE_JOB` procedure parameters:

JOB_NAME The `JOB_NAME` parameter specifies the name assigned to the new job. Because jobs are stored like any other database object, standard Oracle naming requirements are enforced for jobs. This means that the job name must not only be a valid Oracle object name; it must also be unique within the schema.

JOB_TYPE The `JOB_TYPE` parameter specifies the type of job that will be created. This is a required parameter and cannot be excluded. It can be any one of the following:

- **PLSQL_BLOCK** The job will execute an anonymous PL/SQL block. Anonymous PL/SQL block jobs do not accept job or program arguments, so the number of arguments must be set to 0.
- **STORED_PROCEDURE** The job will execute a PL/SQL stored procedure. When you use PL/SQL's External Procedure feature, the PL/SQL procedure could be a wrapper to call a Java stored procedure or an external C routine.
- **EXECUTABLE** The job will execute a program that is external to the database. An external job is any program that can be executed from the operating system's command line. `ANYDATA` arguments are not supported with a job or program type of executable.

JOB_ACTION The `JOB_ACTION` attribute specifies the code to be executed for this job.

For a PL/SQL block, the Scheduler will automatically wrap the `JOB_ACTION` code in its own PL/SQL block prior to execution. Therefore, `JOB_ACTION` can be a complete PL/SQL block or one or more lines of valid PL/SQL code. Therefore, both of the following examples are valid:

```
'BEGIN update employee set salary = salary*2
where employee_name like 'EVANS'; commit; END;'
```

```
'update employee set salary = salary*2
where employee_name like 'EVANS'; commit;'
```

For a stored procedure, the value should be the name of the stored procedure, as in this example:

```
'DBMS_SESSION.SET_ROLE(''PAYROLL_USER'');'
```

For an executable, the value is the name of the executable, including the full path name and applicable command-line arguments. If environment variables are required, we suggest that the executable be wrapped in a shell script that defines the environment before executing the program.

For example, specifying '/prod/bin/big_load.sh full' would execute the big_load.sh script and pass in one argument with the value of full.

NUMBER_OF_ARGUMENTS The NUMBER_OF_ARGUMENTS parameter specifies the number of arguments that the job accepts. The range is 0 (default) to 255.

PROGRAM_NAME The PROGRAM_NAME parameter specifies the name of the program associated with this job. The program name must be the name of an existing program object.

START_DATE The START_DATE parameter specifies the first date that the job should be run. If both the START_DATE and REPEAT_INTERVAL parameters are NULL, the job will be run as soon as it is enabled.

The START_DATE parameter is used as a reference date when the REPEAT_INTERVAL parameter uses a calendaring expression. In this situation, the job will run on the first date that matches the calendaring expression *and* is on or after the date specified in the START_DATE parameter.

The Scheduler cannot guarantee that a job will execute at an exact time because the system may be overloaded and thus resources may be unavailable.

REPEAT_INTERVAL The REPEAT_INTERVAL parameter specifies how often the job should be repeated. This parameter can be specified using either a calendaring or a PL/SQL expression. If this parameter is NULL, the job will run only once (at the scheduled start time).

SCHEDULE_NAME The SCHEDULE_NAME parameter specifies the name of the schedule associated with this job. It can optionally specify a window or window group associated with the job.

END_DATE The END_DATE parameter specifies the date when the job will expire. After the date specified, the job will no longer be executed; the STATE of the job will be set to COMPLETED, and the ENABLED flag will be set to FALSE.

If this parameter is set to NULL, the job will repeat forever. However, if the MAX_RUNS or MAX_FAILURES parameters are set, the job will stop if either of these thresholds is met.

COMMENTS The COMMENTS parameter allows the entry of a comment to document the job.

ENABLED The ENABLED parameter specifies whether the job is created in an enabled state. A value of TRUE means the job will be enabled. By default, all jobs are created disabled, so the default value for this parameter is FALSE. A disabled job will exist as an object in the database, but it will never be processed by the job coordinator.

AUTO_DROP The AUTO_DROP parameter specifies whether the job will be automatically dropped once it has been executed (for nonrepeating jobs) or when its status is changed to COMPLETED (for repeating jobs).

The default value for this parameter is TRUE, meaning the job will be dropped from the database. If it is set to FALSE, the jobs are not dropped and their metadata is retained in the database until they are explicitly dropped using the DBMS_SCHEDULER.DROP_JOB procedure.

Identifying the *CREATE_JOB* Procedure Options

Jobs are created by using the DBMS_SCHEDULER.CREATE_JOB procedure. The CREATE_JOB procedure is an *overloaded procedure*. If you are not familiar with procedure overloading, it simply means that the procedure can accept a variety of different parameter combinations. Oracle will execute the version of the procedure that matches the parameter list that is passed in. For a more thorough explanation, see the sidebar "Overloading Procedures and Functions."

Overloading Procedures and Functions

Overloading allows you to create multiple versions of a procedure or function. Each version has the same name but a different parameter list. When an overloaded procedure or function is called, Oracle will execute the version with the parameter list matching the parameters that have been passed in.

The power of overloading lies in the ability to make a single function or procedure that will work with differing datatypes or data elements. For example, if you want to create a function that returns a date in *DD-MM-YYYY* format, you could overload the function to accept date, string, or numeric datatypes. The function could be defined as shown here:

```
FUNCTION conv_date (dt IN DATE)
   <CODE GOES HERE>
   RETURN VARCHAR2;

FUNCTION conv_date (dt IN VARCHAR2)
   <CODE GOES HERE>
   RETURN VARCHAR2;

FUNCTION conv_date (
   mon IN NUMBER,
   day IN NUMBER,
   year IN NUMBER
   )
   <CODE GOES HERE>
   RETURN VARCHAR2;
```

By overloading the function, you can use the same function name regardless of how the date is passed in.

Using the *CREATE_JOB* Procedure

Now that you have been introduced to the options available with the CREATE_JOB procedure, you should have a feel for how Scheduler jobs are created. The following example creates a job that will run once every year to enact cost-of-living adjustments for all employees:

```
SQL> begin
dbms_scheduler.create_job (
job_name => 'LNE_job',
job_type => 'PLSQL_BLOCK',
job_action => 'update employee set salary = salary*1.05;',
start_date => '10-OCT-2008 06:00:00 AM',
repeat_interval => 'FREQ=YEARLY',
comments => 'Cost of living adjustment');
end;
/

PL/SQL procedure successfully completed.
```

To verify that the job was created, you can query the DBA|ALL|USER_SCHEDULER_JOBS view, as shown here:

```
SQL> select job_name, enabled, run_count
  from user_scheduler_jobs;

JOB_NAME                 ENABLED   RUN_COUNT
------------------------ ----------
LNE_JOB                 FALSE              0
```

As you can see from the results, the job was indeed created, but it's not enabled because the ENABLE attribute was not explicitly set in the CREATE_JOB procedure.

By default, jobs are created disabled. You must explicitly enable a job before it will become active and scheduled.

Copying Jobs

Jobs can be copied by using the DBMS_SCHEDULER.COPY_JOB procedure. This procedure accepts only two parameters: OLD_JOB and NEW_JOB. These parameters represent the name of the source and destination job names, respectively.

A copied job will be identical to the original job, with the following exceptions:

- The new job will have a different name.
- The new job will be created in a disabled state.

The COPY_JOB procedure can be used as shown in the following example:

```
SQL> begin
  2  dbms_scheduler.copy_job('LNE_JOB','RAISE_JOB');
  3  end;
  4  /

PL/SQL procedure successfully completed.
```

In the example, a new job named RAISE_JOB was created as a copy of the LNE_JOB job. To verify, the USER_SCHEDULER_JOBS view can be queried, as shown here:

```
SQL> select job_name, enabled
  2  from user_scheduler_jobs;

JOB_NAME                       ENABL
------------------------------ -----
LNE_JOB                        TRUE
RAISE_JOB                      FALSE
```

As you can see, the job was indeed created, and even though the LNE_JOB job is enabled, the RAISE_JOB job is disabled.

Running Jobs

The Scheduler allows scheduled jobs to be run outside of their normal schedule through the DBMS_SCHEDULER.RUN_JOB procedure. This procedure is useful for testing a newly created job or for re-executing a job that failed previously. It doesn't affect the existing schedule of the job, nor does it require the creation of a separate, one-time-only job.

The RUN_JOB procedure accepts the JOB_NAME and USE_CURRENT_SESSION parameters. The USE_CURRENT_SESSION parameter is a Boolean (TRUE or FALSE) value that determines the method in which the job will be run. If this parameter is set to FALSE (the default value), the job will be submitted to the job Scheduler for normal asynchronous execution.

If the parameter is set to TRUE, the job will be executed synchronously using the current user session. This means that as soon as the procedure is executed, the job will run. Therefore, control will not be returned to your user session until the job execution is complete, as you can see here:

```
SQL> begin
  2  dbms_scheduler.run_job('DAILY_ETL',TRUE);
  3  end;
  4  /

<JOB RUNS HERE>
```

```
PL/SQL procedure successfully completed.
SQL>
```

Keep in mind that only an enabled job may be run using the RUN_JOB procedure.

Stopping Jobs

A running job can be stopped by using the DBMS_SCHEDULER.STOP_JOB procedure. When a job is stopped in this manner, the Scheduler attempts to stop the job in a graceful manner by means of an interrupt mechanism. When that's successful, control is returned to the slave process running the job, which will set the status of the job to STOPPED.

Optionally, a user with the MANAGE_SCHEDULER privilege can set the FORCE parameter to TRUE. This causes Oracle to terminate the process running the job and stops the job much faster, in most cases.

The STOP_JOB procedure can be called as follows:

```
SQL> begin
dbms_scheduler.stop_job(job_name => 'LNE_JOB',
force => TRUE);
end;
/

PL/SQL procedure successfully completed.
```

When a job is stopped using the STOP_JOB procedure, only the most recent transaction is rolled back. If the job has performed any commits prior to the time when it is stopped, data inconsistency may result.

Dropping Jobs

Jobs can be dropped by using the DBMS_SCHEDULER.DROP_JOB procedure. This procedure removes the job object completely from the database. If an instance of the job is running when you issue the DROP_JOB procedure, an error will result. If you set the FORCE option to TRUE, Oracle will issue an implicit STOP_JOB procedure to kill the current instance and then drop the job.

The DROP_JOB procedure can be called as follows:

```
SQL> begin
dbms_scheduler.drop_job(job_name => 'LNE_JOB',
force => TRUE);
end;
/

PL/SQL procedure successfully completed.
```

In Exercise 12.1, you'll create a job, copy it, run it, stop it, and then drop it.

EXERCISE 12.1

Getting Comfortable with Jobs

For this exercise, we'll create a job, copy it, run it, stop it, then drop it.

1. Create a table, and then create a job using dbms_scheduler.create_job.

```
create table LNE_TEST (x DATE);
begin
  dbms_scheduler.create_job (
  job_name => 'LNE_job',
  job_type => 'PLSQL_BLOCK',
  job_action => 'insert into LNE_TEST select sysdate from dual;',
  start_date => '30-NOV-2008 10:05:00 PM',
  repeat_interval => 'FREQ=YEARLY',
  comments => 'Cost of living adjustment');
end;
/
```

2. Copy the newly created job using dbms_scheduler.copy_job.

```
begin
   dbms_scheduler.copy_job('LNE_JOB','CSTAY_JOB');
end;
/
```

3. Now run the job using dbms_scheduler.run_job.

```
begin
  dbms_scheduler.run_job('LNE_JOB',TRUE);
end;
/
```

4. Try stopping the job using dbms_scheduler.stop_job. If the job already finished, modify the program so that the job will run longer so that you have the opportunity to stop it. (Hint, modify the program to loop, so that you have a chance to stop it).

```
begin
  dbms_scheduler.stop_job(job_name => 'LNE_JOB',
  force => TRUE);
end;
/
```

EXERCISE 12.1 *(continued)*

5. Now drop the job using dbms_scheduler.drop_job.

```
begin
  dbms_scheduler.drop_job(job_name => 'LNE_JOB',
  force => TRUE);
end;
/
```

Using Scheduler Programs

A program defines the action that will occur when a job runs. It can be a PL/SQL block, a stored procedure, or an operating-system executable. In the previous section, you learned to define a program within the confines of the CREATE_JOB procedure. However, programs can also be created as independent objects that can be reused by many different jobs. And because programs can also accept arguments, they offer flexibility and encourage reuse.

In the following sections, you will learn the different attributes that define a Scheduler program object. You will learn how to create new programs and how to drop them. You will also learn to define arguments for programs.

Program Attributes

Scheduler programs have a specific set of attributes that you can set to define their characteristics. These attributes can be set at creation time through the following CREATE_PROGRAM procedure parameters:

PROGRAM_NAME The PROGRAM_NAME parameter specifies the name assigned to the new program. Because programs are stored like any other database object, standard Oracle object-naming requirements are enforced for programs. This means that the program name must not only be a valid Oracle object name; it must also be unique within the schema.

PROGRAM_TYPE The PROGRAM_TYPE parameter specifies the type of program that will be created. This is a required parameter and cannot be excluded. It can be any one of the following:

> **PLSQL_BLOCK** The program is an anonymous PL/SQL block. Anonymous PL/SQL block jobs do not accept job or program arguments, so the NUMBER_OF_ARGUMENTS attribute must be set to 0.
>
> **STORED_PROCEDURE** The program is a PL/SQL stored procedure. When you use PL/SQL's External Procedure feature, the PL/SQL procedure could be a wrapper to call a Java stored procedure or an external C routine.

EXECUTABLE The program is external to the database. An external program is any program that can be executed from the operating system's command line.

PROGRAM_ACTION The PROGRAM_ACTION attribute specifies the code to be executed. For a PL/SQL block, the Scheduler automatically wraps the PROGRAM_ACTION code in its own PL/SQL block prior to execution. Therefore, this attribute can be a complete PL/SQL block or one or more lines of valid PL/SQL code.

NUMBER_OF_ARGUMENTS The NUMBER_OF_ARGUMENTS parameter specifies the number of arguments that the job accepts. The range is 0 (the default) to 255.

ENABLED The ENABLED parameter specifies whether the job is created in an enabled state. A value of TRUE means the program will be enabled. By default, all programs are created disabled, so the default value for this parameter is FALSE.

COMMENTS The COMMENTS parameter allows the entry of a comment to document the program.

Creating Programs

New programs can be created by using the DBMS_SCHEDULER.CREATE_PROGRAM procedure. This procedure creates a new program object that can in turn be called by job objects. The procedure's parameters match the list of attributes described in the previous section.

Programs, like jobs, are stored as independent schema objects. Therefore, they must have unique names within the schema, and they must conform to Oracle's standards for valid object naming.

To create a program that executes a stored procedure, see the following example:

```
SQL> begin
dbms_scheduler.create_program(
program_name => 'STATS_PROGRAM',
program_type => 'STORED_PROCEDURE',
program_action => 'DBMS_STATS.GATHER_SCHEMA_STATS',
number_of_arguments => 1,
comments => 'Gather stats for a schema');
end;
/

PL/SQL procedure successfully completed.
```

This example creates a reusable program that will gather statistics for a schema. As you can see, the program requires one argument, which is the name of the schema. The argument can be defined by using the DEFINE_PROGRAM_ARGUMENT procedure, as shown here:

```
SQL> begin
dbms_scheduler.define_program_argument(
```

```
  3  program_name => 'STATS_PROGRAM',
  4  argument_position => 1,
  5  argument_type => 'VARCHAR2');
  6  end;
SQL> /

PL/SQL procedure successfully completed.
```

You may have noticed that the example of the DEFINE_PROGRAM_ARGUMENT procedure doesn't specify a name for the argument. The ARGUMENT_NAME parameter is available, but it's completely optional.

This program can now be used by a job object, and the schema name can be passed in as an argument. Therefore, the same program can be used by many jobs, each gathering statistics for a different schema.

Arguments can be dropped from programs as well. The DBMS_SCHEDULER.DROP_PROGRAM_ARGUMENT procedure allows arguments to be dropped either by name or by the position of the argument. The following examples show how an argument may be dropped by specifying its position:

```
SQL> begin
  2  dbms_scheduler.drop_program_argument(
  3  program_name => 'STATS_PROGRAM',
  4  argument_position => 1);
  5  end;
SQL> /

PL/SQL procedure successfully completed.
```

This example shows how an argument may be dropped by specifying its name:

```
SQL> begin
  2  dbms_scheduler.drop_program_argument(
  3  program_name => 'STATS_PROGRAM',
  4  argument_name => 'SCHEMA_NAME');
  5  end;
SQL> /

PL/SQL procedure successfully completed.
```

Dropping Programs

Program objects can be dropped through the use of the DBMS_SCHEDULER.DROP_PROGRAM procedure. This procedure removes the program entirely from the database. If existing job definitions include the program that you are attempting to drop, the drop will fail. However, if you set the FORCE parameter to TRUE, the program will be dropped and the referencing jobs will become disabled.

The following example drops the STATS_PROGRAM program and disables any referencing jobs:

```
SQL> begin
dbms_scheduler.drop_program (
program_name => 'STATS_PROGRAM',
force => TRUE);
end;
SQL> /

PL/SQL procedure successfully completed.
```

Using Schedules

Schedules define when jobs run as well as when windows are opened. (Windows will be covered later in this chapter.) Like jobs and programs, schedules are stored objects and follow all the same naming requirements. When schedules are saved as independent objects, they can be used by multiple jobs.

Schedules define not only when a job will start, but also how often the job will be repeated. This is known as the repeat interval. Oracle's Scheduler offers two ways to define the interval: using PL/SQL expressions or using the powerful new calendaring syntax introduced in Oracle 10*g*.

The Scheduler can schedule job execution based on the following methods:

- Time-based
- Event-based
- Dependency

In time-based scheduling, you define the time and date that you would like a job to run and repeat. Event-based scheduling allows you to start a job based on some event that signals the Scheduler. In dependency scheduling, the Scheduler runs jobs based on the results of previous jobs in a defined chain.

In the following sections, you will learn which attributes define a schedule object. You will learn how to create and drop schedules. You will also learn how to define repeat intervals using the calendaring syntax.

Schedule Attributes

Schedule objects have a specific set of attributes that you can set to define the characteristics of the schedule. These attributes can be set at creation time through the following CREATE_SCHEDULE procedure parameters:

SCHEDULE_NAME The SCHEDULE_NAME parameter specifies the name of the schedule. Because schedules are stored like any other database object, standard Oracle object-naming requirements are enforced for schedules. This means that the schedule name must not only be a valid Oracle object name it must also be unique within the schema.

START_DATE The START_DATE parameter specifies the first date that the schedule is valid. The START_DATE parameter is used as a reference date when the REPEAT_INTERVAL parameter uses a calendaring expression. In this situation, the job runs on the first date that matches the calendaring expression *and* is on or after the date specified in the START_DATE parameter.

END_DATE The END_DATE parameter specifies the date when the schedule will expire. After the date specified, the job will no longer be executed; the STATE of the job will be set to COMPLETED, and the ENABLED flag will be set to FALSE.

If this parameter is set to NULL, the job will repeat forever. However, if the MAX_RUNS or MAX_FAILURES parameter is set, the job will stop if either of these thresholds is met.

REPEAT_INTERVAL The REPEAT_INTERVAL parameter specifies how often the schedule should be repeated. This parameter can be specified using either a calendaring or a PL/SQL expression. If this parameter is NULL, the job will run only once (at the scheduled start time).

COMMENTS The COMMENTS parameter allows the entry of a comment to document the schedule.

Creating Schedules

Schedules are created using the DBMS_SCHEDULER.CREATE_SCHEDULE procedure. By default, schedules are created with access to the PUBLIC role. Therefore, no privileges need to be granted to allow other users to use the schedule.

The following example creates a schedule that repeats every night at 8:00 p.m.:

```
SQL> begin
  dbms_scheduler.create_schedule(
  schedule_name => 'NIGHTLY_8_SCHEDULE',
  start_date => SYSTIMESTAMP,
  repeat_interval => 'FREQ=DAILY; BYHOUR=20',
  comments => 'Runs nightly at 8:00 PM');
  end;
SQL> /

PL/SQL procedure successfully completed.
```

Setting Repeat Intervals

Oracle's calendaring syntax offers tremendous flexibility when it comes to defining repeat intervals. The syntax includes a set of elements that offer different methods of specifying repeating dates. By mixing and matching these elements, you can generate fairly complex repeat intervals. Table 12.2 describes the clauses and their usage.

TABLE 12.2 Calendaring Syntax Element Descriptions

Name	Description
FREQ	The FREQ parameter defines the frequency type. This parameter is required. The following values are valid: YEARLY, MONTHLY, WEEKLY, DAILY, HOURLY, MINUTELY, and SECONDLY.
INTERVAL	The INTERVAL element specifies how often the recurrence repeats. For example, if FREQ is set to DAILY, then an INTERVAL value of 1 (the default value) means that the job will execute every day. A value of 2 means that the job would execute every other day, and so on. The maximum value is 999.
BYMONTH	The BYMONTH element specifies the month or months in which you want the job to execute. The months can be represented numerically (1–12) or using three-letter abbreviations (JAN–DEC). Multiple months should be separated by commas.
BYWEEKNO	The BYWEEKNO element specifies the week of the year as a number. It follows the ISO-8601 standard, which defines the week as starting with Monday and ending with Sunday. It also defines the first week of a year as the first week in which most days fall within the Gregorian year.
BYYEARDAY	The BYYEARDAY element specifies the day of the year as a number. Positive numbers that are greater than 59 will be affected by leap day. For example, 60 would evaluate to March 1 on non-leap years but would evaluate to February 29 on leap years. Instead, negative numbers can be used. For example, –7 will always evaluate to December 25.
BYMONTHDAY	The BYMONTHDAY element specifies the day of the month as a number. Negative numbers can be used to count backward. For example, –1 will always evaluate to the last day of the month.
BYDAY	The BYDAY element specifies the day of the week using a three-letter abbreviation (MON, TUE, and so on). Monday is always the first day of the week. You can also prepend the BYDAY element with a number representing the occurrence of the specified day. For example, if FREQ is set to MONTHLY, you can specify the last Friday of the month by using -1FRI.
BYHOUR	The BYHOUR element specifies the hour on which the job is to run. Valid values are 0–23.

TABLE 12.2 Calendaring Syntax Element Descriptions *(continued)*

Name	Description
BYMINUTE	The BYMINUTE element specifies the minute on which the job is to run. Valid values are 0–59.
BYSECOND	The BYSECOND element specifies the second on which the job is to run. Valid values are 0–59.

Keep in mind that certain rules apply when using the calendaring syntax. These rules will aid you in creating accurate schedules:

- The first element defined must always be the frequency. All other elements are optional and can appear in any order.
- Elements should be separated by a semicolon, and each element can be represented no more than once.
- Lists of values within an element should be separated by commas. They do not need to be ordered.
- Calendaring statements are not case sensitive, and white space is allowed between elements.
- The BYWEEKNO element can be used only when the FREQ element is set to YEARLY. By default, it returns all days in the week, so a BYDAY setting would be required to limit the days.
- Negative numbers are allowed with certain BY elements. For example, months have different numbers of days, so defining the last day of every month is not possible by using a single, positive number. Instead, you can specify BYMONTHDAY=-1, which will always return the last day of the month. Fixed-size elements such as BYMONTH, BYHOUR, and so on do not support negative numbers.
- The BYDAY element generally specifies the day of the week. However, when used in conjunction with a frequency of YEARLY or MONTHLY, you can add a positive or negative number in front of the day to achieve greater specificity. For example, a FREQ value set to MONTHLY and a BYDAY value set to -1SAT would specify the last Saturday of every month.
- The calendaring syntax always considers Monday the first day of the week.
- The calendaring syntax does not allow you to specify time zones or daylight savings time adjustments. Instead, the region defined in the schedule's START_DATE attribute is used to determine the time zone/daylight savings time adjustments.

To help you get more familiar with the calendaring syntax, Table 12.3 provides examples that demonstrate different repeat intervals and the syntax used to achieve them.

TABLE 12.3 Calendaring Syntax Examples

Goal	Expression
Every Monday	FREQ=WEEKLY; BYDAY=MON;
Every other Monday	FREQ=WEEKLY; BYDAY=MON; INTERVAL=2;
Last day of each month	FREQ=MONTHLY; BYMONTHDAY=-1;
Every January 7	FREQ=YEARLY; BYMONTH=JAN; BYMONTHDAY=7;
Second Wednesday of each month	FREQ=MONTHLY; BYDAY=2WED;
Every hour	FREQ=HOURLY;
Every 4 hours	FREQ=HOURLY; INTERVAL=4;
Hourly on the first day of each month	FREQ=HOURLY; BYMONTHDAY=1;
15th day of every other month	FREQ=MONTHLY; BYMONTHDAY=15; INTERVAL=2

Testing Repeat Intervals

One issue inherent in defining schedule repeat intervals is testing. How do you make sure you didn't make a mistake in your logic? To address that issue, Oracle offers the DBMS_SCHEDULER .EVALUATE_CALENDAR_STRING procedure. This procedure allows you to pass in a calendaring syntax expression and a start date, and it will return the time and date that the job will execute next. Optionally, you can also instruct the procedure to show the next execution time after a certain date, thereby allowing you to see execution dates in the future. Table 12.4 lists the parameters for the EVALUATE_CALENDAR_STRING procedure and describes their usage.

TABLE 12.4: EVALUATE_CALENDAR_STRING Procedure Parameters

Parameter	Description
CALENDAR_STRING	The calendar expression to be evaluated.
START_DATE	The date after which the repeat interval becomes valid.
RETURN_DATE_AFTER	Instructs the procedure to return only execution dates that will occur after the date specified in this parameter. This allows you to see dates and times far out into the future. By default, Oracle uses the current SYSTIMESTAMP.

TABLE 12.4: EVALUATE_CALENDAR_STRING Procedure Parameters *(continued)*

Parameter	Description
NEXT_RUN_DATE	This is an out parameter (the procedure will return this value to the calling program) of type TIMESTAMP that shows the date and time of the next execution.

To use the EVALUATE_CALENDAR_STRING procedure, you will need to use PL/SQL that accepts a return value of type TIMESTAMP, as shown here:

```
SQL> DECLARE
  2   start_date TIMESTAMP;
  3   return_date_after TIMESTAMP;
  4   next_run_date TIMESTAMP;
  5  BEGIN
  6   start_date := to_timestamp_tz(
  7  '10-OCT-2008 10:00:00','DD-MON-YYYY HH24:MI:SS');
  8   DBMS_SCHEDULER.EVALUATE_CALENDAR_STRING(
  9   'FREQ=MONTHLY; INTERVAL=2; BYMONTHDAY=15',
 10   start_date, null, next_run_date);
 11   DBMS_OUTPUT.PUT_LINE('next_run_date: ' ||
 12   next_run_date);
 13   END;
SQL> /
next_run_date: 15-OCT-08 10.00.00.000000 AM

PL/SQL procedure successfully completed.
```

As you can see, line 9 contains the actual calendar expression that is being evaluated. Also, because a value of NULL was submitted for the RETURN_DATE_AFTER parameter, Oracle uses the current date and time as the default.

The procedure returns only a single value for NEXT_RUN_DATE, but you may want to see more than one. If so, you can use the SQL shown here:

```
SQL> DECLARE
 start_date TIMESTAMP;
 return_date_after TIMESTAMP;
 next_run_date TIMESTAMP;
BEGIN
 start_date := to_timestamp_tz(
 '10-OCT-2008 10:00:00','DD-MON-YYYY HH24:MI:SS');
```

```
  return_date_after := start_date;
  FOR i IN 1..10 LOOP
  DBMS_SCHEDULER.EVALUATE_CALENDAR_STRING(
  'FREQ=MONTHLY; INTERVAL=2; BYMONTHDAY=15',
  start_date, return_date_after, next_run_date);
  DBMS_OUTPUT.PUT_LINE(
   'next_run_date: ' || next_run_date);
  return_date_after := next_run_date;
  END LOOP;
 END;
SQL> /
next_run_date: 15-OCT-08 10.00.00.000000 AM
next_run_date: 15-DEC-08 10.00.00.000000 AM
next_run_date: 15-FEB-09 10.00.00.000000 AM
next_run_date: 15-APR-09 10.00.00.000000 AM
next_run_date: 15-JUN-09 10.00.00.000000 AM
next_run_date: 15-AUG-09 10.00.00.000000 AM
next_run_date: 15-OCT-09 10.00.00.000000 AM
next_run_date: 15-DEC-09 10.00.00.000000 AM
next_run_date: 15-FEB-10 10.00.00.000000 AM
next_run_date: 15-APR-10 10.00.00.000000 AM

PL/SQL procedure successfully completed.
```

This example calls the procedure inside of a loop, and each time through, it uses the NEXT_RUN_DATE returned from the prior call as the value for the RETURN_DATE_AFTER parameter. This tells Oracle to only return a date that is farther in the future than the date specified. Therefore, you will get each successive execution date.

Creating Lightweight Jobs

New to Oracle 11g, a *lightweight job* is defined by indicating LIGHTWEIGHT as the value for job_style when creating the job. Lightweight jobs have the following characteristics:

- They are not schema objects
- Because they are not schema objects, they have lower overhead and better create and drop time when compared to regular jobs.
- They store less metadata and job runtime data than regular jobs.
- They must reference an enabled 'PLSQL_BLOCK' or 'STORED_PROCEDURE' program to specify a job action.

Lightweight jobs inherit their privileges from the program; you cannot grant privileges to lightweight jobs. Consider using a lightweight job when you have a high-frequency short-duration job.

Here's an example of a PL/SQL block that creates a lightweight job.

```
BEGIN
DBMS_SCHEDULER.CREATE_JOB (
   job_name => 'example_lightweight_job',
   program_name => 'lne_prog',
   repeat_interval => 'FREQ=SECONDLY;INTERVAL=30',
   job_style => 'LIGHTWEIGHT',
   comments => 'Heartbeat monitor job');
END;
/
```

In Exercise 12.2, you'll create a lightweight job and execute it.

EXERCISE 12.2

Creating and Executing a Lightweight Job

For this exercise, we'll create a lightweight job and execute it. Use the table LNE_TEST created in Exercise 12.1.

1. Create a stored procedure that inserts sysdate into a row in a table.

```
create or replace procedure LNE_TEST_PROC
as
begin
insert into LNE_TEST select sysdate from dual;
end;
/
```

2. Create and enable a program for the stored procedure using dbms_scheduler.create_program, and dbms_scheduler.enable.

```
begin
  dbms_scheduler.create_program(
  program_name => 'LNE_PROGRAM',
  program_type => 'STORED_PROCEDURE',
  program_action => 'LNE_TEST_PROC',
  number_of_arguments => 0,
  comments => 'Insert SYSDATE into LNE_TEST table');
end;
```

EXERCISE 12.2 *(continued)*

```
/

exec dbms_scheduler.enable('LNE_PROGRAM');
```

3. Create a lightweight job using dbms_scheduler.create_job to execute the stored procedure every 30 seconds.

```
begin
  dbms_scheduler.create_job (
  job_name => 'LNE_LIGHTWEIGHT_JOB',
  program_name => 'LNE_PROGRAM',
   repeat_interval => 'FREQ=SECONDLY;INTERVAL=30',
  job_style => 'LIGHTWEIGHT',
  comments => 'Lightweight job exercise');
end;
/
```

4. Now run the job using dbms_scheduler.run_job.

```
begin
  dbms_scheduler.run_job('LNE_LIGHTWEIGHT_JOB',TRUE);
end;
/
```

5. Finally, stop the job using dbms_scheduler.stop_job.

```
begin
  dbms_scheduler.stop_job(job_name => 'LNE_LIGHTWEIGHT_JOB',
  force => TRUE);
end;
/
```

Using Job Chains

Chains are used to implement dependency scheduling. A chain consists of two or more Scheduler programs that are linked together to meet an objective. These multiple steps, when combined with dependency rules or conditions, create a chain or decision tree. Here's an example:

- Run program A.
- If program A completes successfully, run program B.

- If both programs A and B complete successfully, run program C.
- If program A or B does not succeed, run program F.
- Run program ZZ.

Chains are useful for complex business transactions that require multiple dependent programs to complete successfully or take predefined steps when a step in the process fails. Financial reporting and a daily ETL load and report process are both examples of these kinds of business transactions.

A chain job is a type of scheduler job that references a job chain as the job action, can reference a chain instead of a program to start the process. Each step in the chain can be one of the following:

- A program
- Another chain
- An inline event or event schedule

When a chain job is running you can view its progress by querying the `*_SCHEDULER_RUNNING_JOBS`, `*_SCHEDULER_JOB_LOG`, `*_SCHEDULER_JOB_RUN_DETAILS`, and `*_SCHEDULER_RUNNING_CHAINS` views.

Creating a Chain

Create a chain by using the `CREATE_CHAIN` procedure, as follows:

```
BEGIN
DBMS_SCHEDULER.CREATE_CHAIN (
   chain_name => 'lne_chain',
   rule_set_name => NULL,
   evaluation_interval => NULL,
   comments => 'Never break the chain');
END;
/
```

Once you've created the chain, you'll define the steps and rules.

Defining Chain Steps

Now that you've created a chain, you need to add steps to it. Remember that each step can point to a program, another chain, an inline event, or an event schedule. Here's an example that adds three steps, each of which points to a specific program:

```
BEGIN
DBMS_SCHEDULER.DEFINE_CHAIN_STEP (
   chain_name => 'lne_chain',
```

```
    step_name => 'lne_step1',
    program_name => 'start_lne');
DBMS_SCHEDULER.DEFINE_CHAIN_STEP (
    chain_name => 'lne_chain',
    step_name => 'lne_step2',
    program_name => 'lne_run_stage1');
DBMS_SCHEDULER.DEFINE_CHAIN_STEP (
    chain_name => 'lne_chain',
    step_name => 'lne_step3',
    program_name => 'lne_run_stage2');
END;
/
```

It is not mandatory that the program exist when you define the chain step, but it must exist and be enabled before you execute the chain. If the program is an external executable, you must use the ALTER_CHAIN procedure to set the credentials for the step. If the program is a remote external executable, use ALTER_CHAIN to set the destination.

Defining a Chain That Waits for an Event

Use the DEFINE_CHAIN_EVENT_STEP procedure to define a step that waits for an event. In this example, we add a chain step to the previously defined lne_chain chain that will wait for a specific event to occur:

```
BEGIN
DBMS_SCHEDULER.DEFINE_CHAIN_EVENT_STEP (
    chain_name => 'lne_chain',
    step_name => 'lne_step4',
    event_schedule_name => 'lne_event_schedule');
END;
/
```

Adding Rules to a Chain

Chain rules define dependencies between steps and determine when steps run. A rule has a condition and an action. When a condition is evaluated true, the associated action is taken. The condition can contain a valid SQL WHERE clause or Scheduler chain condition syntax.

The Scheduler chain condition syntax takes one of the following two forms:

```
stepname [NOT] {SUCCEEDED|FAILED|STOPPED|COMPLETED}
stepname ERROR_CODE {comparision_operator|[NOT] IN} {integer|list_of_integers}
```

You can create complex conditions by using Boolean operators AND, OR, and NOT().

Step Attributes

When using the SQL WHERE clause to evaluate a condition, you can include the following step attributes: completed, state, start_date, end_date, error_code, and duration. When the state attribute is SUCCEEDED, FAILED, or STOPPED, the completed attribute is set to TRUE.

Conditions

Here are some examples of the chain condition syntax:

```
Credentials_confirm_step COMPLETED
Credentials_confirm_step SUCCEEDED
Credentials_confirm_step FAILED and
 credentials_confirm_step ERROR_CODE != 21000
```

In the first example, the step completed, with one of the following conditions: STOPPED, FAILED, or SUCCEEDED. In the second example, the step must have succeeded for the condition to be met. In the third example, the step must have failed and the returned error code must not be equal to 21000.

Defining Rules

In the following example, the rule starts the chain at step 1 and on completion starts step 2:

```
BEGIN
DBMS_SCHEDULER.DEFINE_CHAIN_RULE (
   chain_name => 'lne_chain',
   condition => 'TRUE',
   action => 'START lne step1',
   rule_name => 'lne_rule1',
   comments => 'start the chain');
DBMS_SCHEDULER.DEFINE_CHAIN_RULE (
   chain_name => 'lne_chain',
   condition => 'lne step1 completed',
   action => 'START lne step2',
   rule_name => 'lne_rule2');
END;
/
```

Starting and Ending the Chain

To start the chain, at least one rule must always evaluate to TRUE. The easiest way to do this is to simply set the condition to '1=1' if you're using SQL syntax or 'TRUE' if you using Scheduler chain condition syntax.

For the chain to end, at least one chain rule must have an action of 'END' when a condition evaluates to TRUE. If a chain has no more running steps and no END action has been determined to be TRUE, then the chain job will go into the CHAIN_STALLED state.

Enabling a Chain

Enabling a chain is straightforward:

```
BEGIN
DBMS_SCHEDULER.ENABLE ('lne_chain');
END;
/
```

The chain must be enabled before a job can run it.

Creating Jobs for Chains

There are two ways you can run a chain: either by using the RUN_CHAIN procedure or, as in this example, by creating and scheduling a job of type CHAIN:

```
BEGIN
DBMS_SCHEDULER.CREATE_JOB (
   job_name => 'lne_chain_job1',
   job_type => 'CHAIN',
   job_action => 'lne_chain',
   repeat_interval => 'freq=daily;byhour=7;byminute=30;bysecond=0',
   enabled => TRUE);
END;
/
```

The Scheduler creates a step job for each step of a chain job that is running. Each step job is uniquely identified by a job subname. To monitor the job steps, query the *_SCHEDULER_RUNNING_JOBS, *_SCHEDULER_JOB_LOG, and *_SCHEDULER_JOB_RUN_DETAILS views.

In Exercise 12.3, you'll create a job chain.

EXERCISE 12.3

Creating and Executing a Job Chain

For this exercise, you'll create a job chain. Reuse components from the previous exercises when possible.

1. Create a simple chain, and set up the starting chain step as described in the section "Starting and Ending the Chain."

```
BEGIN
DBMS_SCHEDULER.CREATE_CHAIN (
   chain_name => 'LNE_CHAIN',
   rule_set_name => NULL,
   evaluation_interval => NULL,
   comments => 'Never break the chain');
END;
/
```

2. Create chain steps for the stored procedures created earlier, and enable the job chain.

```
BEGIN
DBMS_SCHEDULER.DEFINE_CHAIN_STEP (
   chain_name => 'lne_chain',
   step_name => 'lne_step1',
   program_name => 'LNE_LIGHTWEIGHT_JOB');
DBMS_SCHEDULER.DEFINE_CHAIN_STEP (
   chain_name => 'lne_chain',
   step_name => 'lne_step2',
   program_name => 'LNE_JOB');
END;
/


BEGIN
DBMS_SCHEDULER.DEFINE_CHAIN_RULE (
   chain_name => 'LNE_CHAIN',
   condition => 'TRUE',
   action => 'START LNE_STEP1',
   rule_name => 'LNE_RULE1',
   comments => 'start the chain');
DBMS_SCHEDULER.DEFINE_CHAIN_RULE (
   chain_name => 'LNE_CHAIN',
   condition => 'LNE_STEP1 completed',
```

EXERCISE 12.3 *(continued)*

```
   action => 'START LNE_STEP2',
   rule_name => 'LNE_RULE2');
END;
/


BEGIN
   DBMS_SCHEDULER.ENABLE ('LNE_CHAIN');
END;
/
```

3. Execute the job chain, then drop the chain.

```
BEGIN
   DBMS_SCHEDULER.RUN_CHAIN (
   chain_name => 'LNE_CHAIN',
   job_name => 'impromptu_job_chain',
   start_steps => 'LNE_STEP1');
END;
/

BEGIN
   DBMS_SCHEDULER.DROP_CHAIN (
   chain_name => 'LNE_CHAIN',
   force => TRUE);
END;
/
```

Using Scheduler Windows

In Chapter 11, "Managing Database Resources," you learned to create and manage resource plans to allocate system resources. Scheduler windows allow you to change the active resource plan based on defined schedules. In general, resource plans tend to be created with specific time windows in mind. For instance, assume that your system performs heavy transaction processing between the hours of 8:00 a.m. and 5:00 p.m. but runs mostly batch processing and reports after hours. It would make sense to create a separate resource plan to govern resource allocation for each time period. Scheduler windows can then be used to switch automatically between the two.

Unlike most of the other Scheduler objects that you've seen so far, windows are created in the SYS schema. They are stored as database objects and therefore must have a valid name that is unique within the SYS schema.

In the following sections, you will learn to create, open, and close scheduler windows. You'll also learn about scheduler window logging and how to manage window logs. Last, you'll learn about purging scheduler logs.

Creating Windows

Windows can be created by using the DBMS_SCHEDULER.CREATE_WINDOW procedure. When creating a window, you have the choice of either using an existing schedule or defining an inline schedule. However, an existing schedule may not be used if the schedule has a repeat interval based on a PL/SQL expression.

The parameters for the CREATE_WINDOW procedure are described here:

WINDOW_NAME The WINDOW_NAME parameter uniquely identifies the window in the SYS schema. The name has to be unique in the SYS schema.

RESOURCE_PLAN The RESOURCE_PLAN parameter specifies the name of the resource plan that will govern the timeframe of the window. When the window opens, the system switches to the specified resource plan. When the window closes, the system either switches back to the prior resource plan or, if another window is opening, to the resource plan of the new window. If the current resource plan has been set through the use of the ALTER SYSTEM SET RESOURCE_MANAGER_PLAN FORCE statement, the Scheduler will not be allowed to change the resource plan. If no resource plan is defined for the window, the current resource plan will remain in effect when the window opens and will stay in effect for the duration of the window.

START_DATE The START_DATE parameter specifies the first date that the window is scheduled to open. If START_DATE is NULL or references a date in the past, the window will open as soon as it is created. The START_DATE parameter is used as a reference date when the REPEAT_INTERVAL parameter uses a calendaring expression. In this situation, the window will open on the first date that matches the calendaring expression *and* is on or after the date specified in the START_DATE parameter.

DURATION The DURATION attribute specifies how long the window will remain open. There is no default value, so a value must be provided. The value should be specified as an INTERVAL DAY TO SECOND datatype (for example, `interval '10' hour` or `interval '20' minute`).

SCHEDULE_NAME The SCHEDULE_NAME parameter specifies the name of the schedule associated with the window.

REPEAT_INTERVAL The REPEAT_INTERVAL parameter specifies how often the window should repeat. It is defined using the calendaring syntax only; PL/SQL expressions cannot be used in conjunction with a window. If the REPEAT_INTERVAL parameter is NULL, the window will open only once at the specified start date.

END_DATE The END_DATE parameter specifies the date when the window will be disabled. If the END_DATE parameter is NULL, a repeating window will repeat forever.

WINDOW_PRIORITY The WINDOW_PRIORITY parameter is relevant only when two windows overlap each other. Because only one window can be in effect at a time, the window priority determines which window will be opened. The valid values are LOW (the default) and HIGH. A high-priority window has precedence.

COMMENTS The COMMENTS parameter specifies an optional comment about the window.

The following example creates a window that activates the DAY_PLAN resource plan and uses a schedule named WORK_HOURS_SCHEDULE:

```
SQL>  begin
dbms_scheduler.create_window (
window_name => 'WORK_HOURS_WINDOW',
resource_plan => 'DAY_PLAN',
schedule_name => 'WORK_HOURS_SCHEDULE',
duration => INTERVAL '10' HOUR,
window_priority => 'HIGH');
end;
SQL> /

PL/SQL procedure successfully completed.
```

This newly created window will be started based on a schedule named WORK_HOURS_SCHEDULE and will remain in effect for 10 hours. During those 10 hours, the DAY_PLAN resource plan will be in effect. Also, because the priority for this window is set to HIGH, it will take precedence over any overlapping window that has a priority setting of LOW.

Opening and Closing Windows

There are two distinct ways that a window can be opened. The first is based on the window's schedule. The second is by opening it manually by using the DBMS_SCHEDULER.OPEN_WINDOW procedure.

The OPEN_WINDOW procedure opens a window independent of its schedule. The associated resource plan is enabled immediately, and currently executing jobs are subjected to the change in resource plan, just as if the window had opened based on its schedule.

When opening a window manually, you can specify a new duration for the window to remain open; otherwise it will remain open for the duration defined when the window was created.

If the FORCE parameter is set to TRUE in the OPEN_WINDOW procedure, the Scheduler will automatically close any currently open window, even if it has a higher priority. Also, it will not allow any other windows to be opened during the time the manually opened window is open.

The OPEN_WINDOW procedure accepts only three parameters: WINDOW_NAME, DURATION, and FORCE. Here is an example of its usage:

```
SQL>  begin
  2  dbms_scheduler.open_window (
  3  window_name => 'WORK_HOURS_WINDOW',
  4  duration => INTERVAL '20' MINUTE,
  5  force => TRUE);
  6  end;
  SQL> /

PL/SQL procedure successfully completed.
```

This example forces the WORK_HOURS_WINDOW to be opened and any current window to close. The new window will remain open for a duration of 20 minutes.

In a similar manner, windows can be manually closed by using the DBMS_SCHEDULER .CLOSE_WINDOW procedure. This procedure accepts the window name as a parameter, as shown here:

```
SQL>  begin
  2  dbms_scheduler.close_window (
  3  window_name => 'WORK_HOURS_WINDOW');
  4  end;
  SQL> /

PL/SQL procedure successfully completed.
```

Window Logging

The Oracle Scheduler maintains *window logs* of all window activities. The DBA_SCHEDULER_WINDOW_LOG view can be used to view log entries for all of the following window activities:

- Creating a new window
- Dropping a window
- Opening a window
- Closing a window
- Overlapping windows
- Disabling a window
- Enabling a window

For example, use the following query to view window log entries:

```
SQL> select log_id, trunc(log_date) log_date,
  window_name, operation
```

```
from dba_scheduler_window_log;

LOG_ID LOG_DATE   WINDOW_NAME          OPERATION
------ --------- -------------------- ---------
   527 25-SEP-04  WEEKEND_WINDOW       OPEN
   544 28-SEP-04  WEEKNIGHT_WINDOW     OPEN
   547 28-SEP-04  WEEKNIGHT_WINDOW     CLOSE
   548 29-SEP-04  WEEKNIGHT_WINDOW     OPEN
   551 29-SEP-04  WEEKNIGHT_WINDOW     CLOSE
   552 30-SEP-04  WEEKNIGHT_WINDOW     OPEN
   559 01-OCT-04  WEEKNIGHT_WINDOW     CLOSE
   560 02-OCT-04  WEEKNIGHT_WINDOW     OPEN
   563 02-OCT-04  WEEKNIGHT_WINDOW     CLOSE
   555 30-SEP-04  WEEKNIGHT_WINDOW     CLOSE
   564 02-OCT-04  WEEKEND_WINDOW       OPEN
```

For each CLOSE operation logged in the DBA_SCHEDULER_WINDOW_LOG view, there will be an associated record in the DBA_SCHEDULER_WINDOW_DETAILS view, as shown here:

```
SQL> select log_id, trunc(log_date) log_date,
  window_name, actual_duration
  from dba_scheduler_window_details;

 LOG_ID LOG_DATE   WINDOW_NAME          ACTUAL_DURATION
------- ---------- -------------------- ---------------
    547 28-SEP-04  WEEKNIGHT_WINDOW     +000 08:00:00
    551 29-SEP-04  WEEKNIGHT_WINDOW     +000 08:00:00
    559 01-OCT-04  WEEKNIGHT_WINDOW     +000 08:00:00
    563 02-OCT-04  WEEKNIGHT_WINDOW     +000 08:00:00
    555 30-SEP-04  WEEKNIGHT_WINDOW     +000 07:59:58
```

Purging Logs

As with any automatic logging system, window logs must be purged on a regular basis to prevent excessive table growth. Oracle provides an automatic method to purge the log files after a specified number of days.

Scheduler job logs and window logs will be automatically purged based on the setting of the LOG_HISTORY attribute of the Scheduler itself. The value of this parameter determines the number of days that log data should be retained, after which it will be purged. To set this value, use the SET_SCHEDULER_ATTRIBUTE procedure, as in the following example:

```
SQL> begin
  2    DBMS_SCHEDULER.SET_SCHEDULER_ATTRIBUTE(
```

```
  3   'LOG_HISTORY','60');
  4  end;
SQL> /

PL/SQL procedure successfully completed.
```

This example instructs Oracle to automatically purge all records that are over 60 days old.

By default, this procedure sets the history retention period for both Scheduler window logs and Scheduler job logs. To set only one, you may include the WHICH_LOG parameter to specify either WINDOW_LOG or JOB_LOG.

Creating and Using Job Classes

A job class is a container object for the logical grouping of jobs into a larger unit. Classifying jobs in this manner offers several advantages:

- From an administrative perspective, it is easier to manage a small number of job groups than to manage a large number of individual jobs. Certain job characteristics can be assigned at the group level and will be inherited by all jobs within the group. Certain administrative procedures will also operate at the group level, making administrative functions easier.
- Job classes can be assigned to a resource consumer group. This allows you to control resource allocation for all jobs within the group.
- Jobs can be prioritized within the job class. This gives you more control over which jobs should take precedence in case of a conflict. For example, if a conflict occurs, the JOB_PRIORITY attribute of each job will be evaluated. A job with a value of HIGH takes priority over a job with a value of LOW.

All jobs must belong to exactly one job class. Any job not explicitly assigned to a job class will belong to the DEFAULT_JOB_CLASS class and will inherit the characteristics of that job class. In the following sections, you will learn to create and administer job classes.

Job Class Parameters

Job classes have a specific set of attributes that you can set to define the characteristics of the class. These attributes will be inherited by all jobs assigned to the job class, thereby saving you the work of setting them individually on each job. The available attribute parameters are described here:

JOB_CLASS_NAME The JOB_CLASS_NAME parameter uniquely identifies the job class in the SYS schema. The name has to be unique in the SYS schema.

RESOURCE_CONSUMER_GROUP The RESOURCE_CONSUMER_GROUP parameter associates the job group with a specific consumer group. All jobs assigned to the job group will automatically be governed by this consumer group.

SERVICE The SERVICE parameter specifies the service to which the job class belongs. This means that, in a RAC environment, the jobs in this class will have affinity to the particular service specified. Therefore, they will run only on those database instances that are assigned to the specific service. If this attribute is not set, the default service will be used, meaning that the jobs have no service affinity and can be run by any instance within the cluster. If the SERVICE parameter is specified, the RESOURCE_CONSUMER_GROUP attribute cannot be set. They are mutually exclusive.

LOGGING_LEVEL The Oracle Scheduler can optionally maintain *job logs* of all job activities. Job logging is determined by the setting of the LOGGING_LEVEL attribute of the job class. The LOGGING_LEVEL parameter specifies how much job information is logged. There are four valid settings for this attribute:

DBMS_SCHEDULER.LOGGING_OFF No logging will be performed for any jobs in this class.

DBMS_SCHEDULER.LOGGING_RUNS Detailed information will be written for all runs of each job in the class.

DBMS_SCHEDULER.LOGGING_FULL Detailed information will be written for all runs of each job in the class, and every operation performed on any job in the class (create, enable, drop, and so on) will be logged.

DBMS_SCHEDULER.LOGGING_FAILED_RUNS Logs only jobs that failed and the reason for failure. If the job class has a higher logging level the higher level takes precedence.

Note that the valid values for this parameter are all constants defined within the DBMS_SCHEDULER package. Therefore, they must be referenced exactly as shown, with no quotes around them.

LOG_HISTORY The LOG_HISTORY parameter determines the number of days logged information should be retained. The default value is 30 days. Valid values are 1 to 999. When records have exceeded this limit, the Scheduler will automatically purge them.

COMMENTS The COMMENTS parameter specifies an optional comment about the job class.

Creating Job Classes

Job classes can be created through the DBMS_SCHEDULER.CREATE_JOB_CLASS procedure, as shown in the following example:

```
SQL> begin
  dbms_scheduler.create_job_class(
job_class_name => 'LOW_PRIORITY_CLASS',
resource_consumer_group => 'LOW_GROUP',
```

```
  logging_level => DBMS_SCHEDULER.LOGGING_FULL,
  log_history => 60,
  comments => 'LOW PRIORITY JOB CLASS');
end;
SQL> /

PL/SQL procedure successfully completed.
```

In this example, a job class named LOW_PRIORITY_CLASS was created that will assign all jobs in the group to the LOW_GROUP consumer group.

Dropping Job Classes

Job classes can be dropped by using the DBMS_SCHEDULER.DROP_JOB_CLASS procedure. Dropping a job class that has jobs assigned to it will result in an error. However, it is allowed if the FORCE parameter is set to TRUE. In this case, the job class will be dropped and the jobs assigned to the class will be disabled. Dropping the class has no effect on any currently running instances of member jobs.

Several job classes can also be dropped at the same time by separating the names of the job classes by a comma, as shown in the following example:

```
SQL> begin
  dbms_scheduler.drop_job_class(
    'LOW_PRIORITY_CLASS, HIGH_PRIORITY_CLASS');
  end;
SQL> /

PL/SQL procedure successfully completed.
```

Note that if a list of job classes is used, as in the example in the section "Dropping Job Classes," there is no rollback available. For instance, if the first job class dropped but the second job class failed to drop, the procedure will return an error, but the first job class will not be restored.

Using Advanced Scheduler Concepts to Prioritize Jobs

The Scheduler allows you to prioritize jobs based on your unique business requirements. It gives you control over resource allocation through job classes, as described earlier. It also allows you to change the prioritization based on a schedule.

When working with a job class, you can define a resource consumer group and take advantage of the Database Resource Manager capabilities, as described earlier in this chapter. You can also prioritize jobs within a job class.

Prioritizing Jobs within a Job Class

Within a job class, you can assign priority values from 1 to 5 to individual jobs so that if more than one job within the same class starts at the same time, the job with the highest priority will take precedence over the others. If two jobs have the same priority, the one that had the earlier start date gets the higher priority. Priority rules apply only when comparing jobs within the same class. The default priority for a job is 3; 1 is the highest, and 5 is the lowest.

To change a job priority, use the SET_ATTRIBUTE procedure. For example, here's how to raise the priority of the LNE_JOB1 job to priority 1:

```
BEGIN
DBMS_SCHEDULER.SET_ATTRIBUTE (
   name => 'lne_job1',
   attribute => 'job_priority',
   value => 1);
END;
/
```

The job_priority attribute is set by default to 3 when you create the job; use the SET_ATTRIBUTE procedure to change the job priority.

Using Scheduler Views

Oracle offers a wide variety of views to access information regarding the Scheduler and its associated objects. These views allow you to see information about currently running jobs and past runs of jobs. Table 12.5 describes the available Scheduler views.

TABLE 12.5 Scheduler Views Available

View	Description
*_SCHEDULER_SCHEDULES	Shows information on all defined schedules.
*_SCHEDULER_PROGRAMS	Shows information on all defined programs.

TABLE 12.5 Scheduler Views Available *(continued)*

View	Description
*_SCHEDULER_PROGRAM_ARGUMENTS	Shows all registered program arguments and the default values if they exist.
*_SCHEDULER_JOBS	Shows all defined jobs, both enabled and disabled.
*_SCHEDULER_GLOBAL_ATTRIBUTE	Shows the current values of all Scheduler attributes.
*_SCHEDULER_JOB_ARGUMENTS	Shows the arguments for all defined jobs.
*_SCHEDULER_JOB_CLASSES	Shows information on all defined job classes.
*_SCHEDULER_WINDOWS	Shows information about all defined windows.
*_SCHEDULER_JOB_RUN_DETAILS	Shows information about all completed (failed or successful) job runs.
*_SCHEDULER_WINDOW_GROUPS	Shows information about all window groups.
*_SCHEDULER_WINGROUP_MEMBERS	Shows the members of all window groups.
*_SCHEDULER_RUNNING_JOBS	Shows the state information on all jobs that are currently being run.

To see information on completed instances of a job, use the code shown here:

```
SQL> select job_name, status, error#
  2  from dba_scheduler_job_run_details
  3   where job_name = 'FAIL_JOB';

JOB_NAME        STATUS              ERROR#
--------        --------------      ------
FAIL_JOB        FAILURE              20000
```

To see the current state of all jobs, use the following code:

```
SQL> select job_name, state
  2  from dba_scheduler_jobs;

JOB_NAME          STATE
----------------- ---------------
PURGE_LOG         SCHEDULED
GATHER_STATS_JOB  SCHEDULED
```

```
LNE_JOB            SCHEDULED
RAISE_JOB           DISABLED
```

To view windows and their next start dates, the following SQL can be used:

```
SQL> select window_name, next_start_date
  2  from dba_scheduler_windows;

WINDOW_NAME          NEXT_START_DATE
-------------------- -----------------------------------
WEEKNIGHT_WINDOW     12-OCT-04 10.00.00.300000 PM -08:00
WEEKEND_WINDOW       16-OCT-04 12.00.00.500000 AM -08:00
```

The DBA_SCHEDULER_JOB_LOG view can be used to view log entries for previously executed jobs, as shown here:

```
SQL> select log_id, trunc(log_date) log_date, owner, job_name, operation from
dba_scheduler_job_log;

LOG_ID LOG_DATE   OWNER JOB_NAME            OPERATION
------- ---------- ----- -----------------  ---------
    522 25-SEP-04  SYS     PURGE_LOG         RUN
    524 25-SEP-04  SYS     ADV_SQL_TUNING    SUCCEEDED
    525 25-SEP-04  SYS     ADV_SQL_TUNING    DROP
    528 25-SEP-04  SYS     GATHER_STATS_JOB  RUN
    484 18-SEP-04  SYS     GATHER_STATS_JOB  RUN
    541 26-SEP-04  SYS     PURGE_LOG         RUN
    543 27-SEP-04  SYS     PURGE_LOG         RUN
    545 28-SEP-04  SYS     GATHER_STATS_JOB  RUN
    546 28-SEP-04  SYS     PURGE_LOG         RUN
    553 30-SEP-04  SYS     GATHER_STATS_JOB  RUN
    622 10-OCT-04  SYS     LNE_JOB           RUN
    549 29-SEP-04  SYS     GATHER_STATS_JOB  RUN
```

Summary

In this chapter, you learned about the new Oracle 11*g* Scheduler. You learned how it resolves issues such as schedule creep that existed in its predecessor, the DBMS_JOB package.

This chapter also explained the new architecture that underlies the Scheduler. You learned how the job table stores all enabled jobs within the database and how the job-coordinator process queries the job table on a regular basis and stores the job information in a memory cache for faster access. When a job is scheduled to run, the job-coordinator process is automatically started (if it is not already active). It will pass the job information to a job-slave process for execution.

You learned that the job-slave process will gather all the metadata for the job, start a session as the owner of the job, begin a transaction within the session, and then execute the job. When the job completes, the slave commits the transaction and closes the session. The slave then updates the job entry in the job table to show a COMPLETE status. It inserts a new entry into the job log, updates the run count for the job, and then looks for any new work that needs to be done. If none is found, the job-slave process returns to a sleep state.

You also learned that, in a RAC environment, each instance has its own job coordinator, and the job coordinators have the ability to communicate with each other to keep information current. You learned that a RAC environment will still have only one job table that is shared by all the instances. You also learned that jobs can be assigned to a service, as opposed to an instance, ensuring that the job can be run by a different node if an instance is down.

We showed you how, in a Data Guard environment, changes made to the primary are applied to the physical standby. For a logical standby, you have the option to run jobs based on the databases role—either primary or logical standby.

Next, you learned about job objects and how they are created and administered. You saw how the CREATE_JOB procedure is overloaded. You also learned to set job arguments using the SET_JOB_ARGUMENT_VALUE and the SET_JOB_ANYDATA_VALUE procedures as well as how to copy, run, disable, enable, and drop jobs.

We discussed program objects and how they define PL/SQL blocks, stored procedures, or external operating-system executables as well as their arguments and other metadata. You also learned to administer all aspects of program objects.

This chapter also covered schedule objects and how they are created. Schedules specify a start date, an optional end date, and a repeat interval. Together, these elements are used to calculate run dates. You can use the new calendaring syntax to define repeat intervals within the schedules.

You learned about lightweight jobs and the special conditions that may lead you to choose a lightweight job instead of a regular job.

Next you learned about job chains and how to create dependencies between job steps in a chain.

Finally, we discussed windows and how they can be used to switch resource plans at scheduled intervals to control resource allocation for the system. You learned that only one window can be open at any given time and that, when overlapping windows exist, a window with a priority of HIGH will take precedence over a window with a priority of LOW.

Exam Essentials

Know how to simplify management tasks by using the Scheduler. Understand how the Scheduler can be used to automate routine management tasks to run on a repeating basis. Know the types of programs that can be run through the Scheduler (PL/SQL blocks, stored procedures, and external operating-system executables).

Be able to create a job, program, schedule, and window. Know the various CREATE procedures in the DBMS_SCHEDULER package (CREATE_JOB, CREATE_PROGRAM, CREATE_SCHEDULE, and CREATE_WINDOW). Understand the different options that can be used when creating a job (inline definitions versus stored objects). Understand that only a subset of attributes can be defined at creation time. The other attributes can be set by altering the object through the SET_ATTRIBUTE and SET_ATTRIBUTE_NULL procedures.

Know how to create and use job chains. Understand the difference between dependency rules, conditions, and actions. Know how to define chain steps. Know how to create a chain. Know how to add rules to a chain. Know how to enable, start, and stop a chain.

Know how to prioritize jobs. Understand the difference between job class priorities and individual job priorities within a class. Know how to set a job attribute to change the job priority.

Know how to reuse Scheduler components for similar tasks. Understand the difference between inline schedule and program definitions and stored Scheduler object components. Know that a job can reference stored schedule and program objects. Know that a window can reference a stored schedule object. Understand that a job can be reused with different parameters.

Understand how to view information about job executions and job instances. Be aware of the different views available to view Scheduler information. Know that the views use the naming convention of DBA|ALL|USER_SCHEDULER_ as a prefix for all views (for example, DBA_SCHEDULER_JOBS, DBA_SCHEDULER_PROGRAMS, and so on). Know that the DBA_SCHEDULER_JOB_RUN_DETAILS view shows information about job executions and that the DBA_SCHEDULER_RUNNING_JOBS view shows information on jobs that are currently running.

Review Questions

1. When setting arguments for a job, which procedure do you use for types that cannot be implicitly converted to and from a VARCHAR2 datatype?
   - **A.** SET_JOB_ARGUMENT_VALUE
   - **B.** SET_JOB_VALUE_ANYDATA
   - **C.** SET_JOB_ANYDATA_VALUE
   - **D.** SET_SPECIAL_JOB_VALUE
   - **E.** SET_JOB_ANYTYPE_VALUE

2. Which DBMS_SCHEDULER procedures can be used to enable a program? (Choose all that apply.)
   - **A.** ENABLE
   - **B.** ENABLE_PROGRAM
   - **C.** VALIDATE_PROGRAM
   - **D.** SET_ATTRIBUTE
   - **E.** SET_ENABLED

3. Which of the following is not a valid calendaring syntax element?
   - **A.** FREQ
   - **B.** BYHOUR
   - **C.** RUNDATE
   - **D.** INTERVAL
   - **E.** BYMINUTE

4. Which Scheduler view(s) can be queried to see which jobs are currently executing? (Choose all that apply.)
   - **A.** DBA_SCHEDULER_JOB_RUN_DETAILS
   - **B.** DBA_SCHEDULER_RUNNING_JOBS
   - **C.** DBA_SCHEDULER_CURRENT_JOBS
   - **D.** DBA_SCHEDULER_JOBS
   - **E.** DBA_SCHEDULER_EXECUTING_JOBS

5. A schedule defined entirely within the confines of a Scheduler job object is known as a(n) ____________________.
   - **A.** Fixed schedule
   - **B.** Inline schedule
   - **C.** Stored schedule
   - **D.** Hard-coded schedule
   - **E.** None of the above

6. Which DBMS_SCHEDULER procedure(s) can be used to alter an existing job? (Choose all that apply.)
   A. SET_ATTRIBUTE_NULL
   B. ALTER_JOB
   C. ALTER_JOB_PARAMETERS
   D. ALTER
   E. SET_ATTRIBUTE

7. What is the default value for the ENABLED attribute of a job or program when it is created?
   A. TRUE
   B. FALSE
   C. There is no default. It must be defined at creation time.
   D. PENDING
   E. NULL

8. To set the history retention period for either window logging or job logging individually, which parameters of the SET_SCHEDULER_ATTRIBUTE procedure need to be used? (Choose all that apply.)
   A. LOG_HISTORY
   B. JOB_LOG_RETENTION
   C. WINDOW_LOG_RETENTION
   D. WHICH_LOG
   E. LOG_NAME

9. Consider the following code snippet:

```
BEGIN
DBMS_SCHEDULER.SET_ATTRIBUTE (
   name => 'lne_job1',
   attribute => 'job_priority',
   value => 1);
END;
/
```

   If this code were executed, which of the following statements would be true?
   A. The priority of the lne_job1 job would be set to 1.
   B. The lne_job1 job would be executed synchronously.
   C. The lne_job1 job would run immediately in the user's current session.
   D. The lne_job1 job would retain its current priority.
   E. The job will immediately take priority over all running jobs.

10. Which of the following calendaring syntax expressions would evaluate to the last day of every month?
    A. `FREQ = MONTHLY; BYMONTHDAY = 31`
    B. `FREQ = MONTHLY; BYMONTHDAY = -1`
    C. `FREQ = DAILY; BYDAY = -1`
    D. `FREQ = MONTHLY; BYDAY = 31`
    E. `FREQ = DAILY; BYMONTHDAY = LAST_DAY`

11. Which of the following tasks is *not* performed by the job coordinator?
    A. Update job log when a job completes
    B. Spawn and remove job slaves
    C. Write/read job info to/from memory cache
    D. Query job table
    E. Pass job information to job slaves

12. Which of the following objects can be directly referenced by a window object? (Choose all that apply.)
    A. Schedule object
    B. Program object
    C. Job object
    D. Resource plan
    E. Resource consumer group

13. Which of the following are valid program types for a lightweight job? (Choose all that apply.)
    A. `PLSQL_BLOCK`
    B. `EXECUTABLE`
    C. `JAVA_STORED_PROCEDURE`
    D. `STORED_PROCEDURE`
    E. `EXTERNAL`

14. Which of the following is not a valid setting for the `PROGRAM_TYPE` parameter in a program object or the `JOB_TYPE` parameter in a job object?
    A. `PLSQL_BLOCK`
    B. `JAVA_STORED_PROCEDURE`
    C. `STORED_PROCEDURE`
    D. `EXECUTABLE`
    E. None of the above are invalid settings.

15. Which of the following Scheduler elements encourage object reuse? (Choose all that apply.)
    - A. Schedule objects
    - B. Program arguments
    - C. Job classes
    - D. Job arguments
    - E. All of the above

16. What is the danger associated with stopping a running job by using the STOP_JOB procedure?
    - A. The job will need to be reenabled before it will execute again.
    - B. The job may hold locks on objects referenced within it.
    - C. All jobs within the job group will also be stopped.
    - D. The job may leave data in an inconsistent state.
    - E. There is no danger in using the STOP_JOB procedure.

17. If a job references a schedule that has been disabled, what will be the result?
    - A. The job will be automatically disabled.
    - B. The job will never execute.
    - C. The job will attempt to execute but will fail.
    - D. The job will inherit the DEFAULT_SCHEDULE schedule.
    - E. A schedule object cannot be disabled.

18. When a job exceeds the date specified in its END_DATE attribute, which of the following will happen? (Choose all that apply.)
    - A. The job will be dropped automatically if the value of the AUTO_DROP attribute is TRUE.
    - B. The job will only be disabled if the value of the AUTO_DROP attribute is FALSE.
    - C. The STATE attribute of the job will be set to COMPLETED if the value of the AUTO_DROP attribute is FALSE.
    - D. All objects referenced by the job will be dropped if the value of the AUTO_DROP attribute is TRUE and the value of the CASCADE attribute is TRUE.
    - E. The STATE column of the job table will be set to COMPLETED for the job.

19. Which of the following is true about job chains?
    - A. They consist of one or more Scheduler programs.
    - B. They are used to implement dependency scheduling.
    - C. They are used to implement time-based scheduling.
    - D. They are used to implement event-based scheduling.
    - E. None of the above.

20. If two windows overlap, which window attribute will determine whether one should be chosen over the other?

A. `WINDOW_PRIORITY`

B. `PRIORITY`

C. `PRIORITY_LEVEL`

D. `WINDOW_PRIORITY_LEVEL`

E. `OVERLAP_RULE`

Answers to Review Questions

1. C. The SET_JOB_ANYDATA_VALUE procedure allows you to set job arguments that don't easily convert to and from a string (VARCHAR2) datatype.

2. A, D. Programs (as well as jobs) can be enabled in two ways: by using the ENABLE procedure or by using the SET_ATTRIBUTE procedure to set the ENABLED attribute to TRUE.

3. C. The calendaring syntax does not support an element named RUNDATE. It does not support the concept of specifying a single run date at all. The purpose of the calendaring syntax is to define repeat intervals that will be used to calculate run dates.

4. B, D. The DBA_SCHEDULER_RUNNING_JOBS view shows detailed information about all jobs currently executing. The DBA_SCHEDULER_JOBS view contains the STATE column, which shows a value of RUNNING for an executing job.

5. B. A schedule defined within a job object is known as an inline schedule, whereas an independent schedule object is referred to as a stored schedule. Inline schedules cannot be referenced by other objects.

6. A, E. A job can be altered only by changing the value of one or more of its attributes. This is accomplished by using the SET_ATTRIBUTE and SET_ATTRIBUTE_NULL procedures.

7. B. Jobs and programs are created in a disabled state by default. They must be enabled by setting the ENABLE parameter to TRUE in their respective CREATE statements, or by altering the object after creation.

8. A, D. The LOG_HISTORY parameter defines the retention period for both job logging and window logging by default. However, the WHICH_LOG parameter can be used to specify either JOB_LOG or WINDOW_LOG.

9. A. Executing the SET_ATTRIBUTE procedure with the job_priority attribute changes the priority of a job, with 1 being the highest priority and 5 the lowest. This procedure does not give the job priority over running jobs with the same priority (1).

10. B. The BYMONTHDAY element accepts negative values that represent a specific count of days from the end of the month. Also, the FREQ parameter must be set to MONTHLY because it will execute every month.

11. A. The job coordinator does not update the job log when a job completes. That function is performed by the job slave that has been assigned to the job.

12. A, D. A window does not execute programs or jobs. It specifies a resource plan that will be enabled based on a schedule. Therefore, it can reference both a schedule object and a resource-plan object. And while the resource plan may reference one or more resource consumer groups, the window object does not directly reference them.

13. A, D. PLSQL_BLOCK and STORED_PROCEDURE are the only valid program types that can be used with a lightweight job.

14. B. Java stored procedures cannot be executed by the job Scheduler unless they are called from within a PL/SQL procedure wrapper. This can be done in a stored procedure using PL/SQL's External Procedure feature. Therefore, the job or program type setting would be `STORED_PROCEDURE`.

15. A, B, D. Schedule objects do not specify any action to be performed; they simply generate execution dates that any job can use. Program and job arguments allow the jobs and programs to be reused by simply changing the arguments that are passed in. Job classes simplify the management of jobs, but they do not specifically encourage job reuse.

16. D. The Scheduler will attempt to wrap the job within a transaction and will execute a rollback if a job is stopped. However, if the job has performed commits, the rollback will roll back only uncommitted changes. This could result in inconsistent data.

17. E. A schedule object does not possess the `ENABLED` attribute. It is therefore enabled upon creation and can never be disabled.

18. A, B, E. When a job exceeds its end date, it will be dropped only if the `AUTO_DROP` attribute is set to `TRUE`. Otherwise, it will be disabled. In either case, the `STATE` column will be set to `COMPLETED` in the job table. A job object does not possess a `CASCADE` attribute or a `STATE` attribute.

19. B. Job chains are used to implement dependency-based scheduling. A job chain consists of two or more Scheduler programs.

20. A. The `WINDOW_PRIORITY` attribute can be set to either `HIGH` or `LOW` for a window. If two windows overlap and only one of the windows has a priority of `HIGH`, it will be chosen.

Implementing Globalization Support

ORACLE DATABASE 11*g*: ADMINISTRATION II EXAM OBJECTIVES COVERED IN THIS CHAPTER:

✓ **Globalization**

- Customize language-dependent behavior for the database and individual sessions
- Working with database and NLS character sets

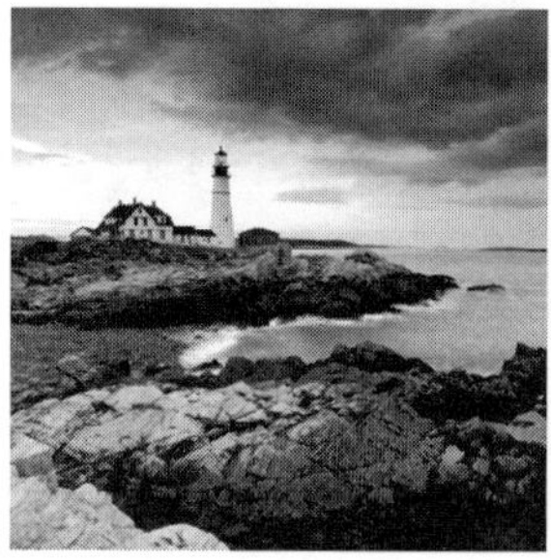

Doing business on a global scale presents a new set of challenges to any company, especially to the DBA. Beyond the obvious issues of language lie a host of less obvious but equally important issues that must be addressed—time-zone differences, mixed currency types, and differing calendars, just to name a few. But Oracle's globalization support features provide the tools needed to meet these challenges.

Globalization support enables you to manage data in multiple languages. It provides the functionality to ensure that native language and locale conventions are followed when dealing with date, time, currency, numeric, and calendar data.

Globalization support also offers datetime datatype options for handling transactions crossing time zones. And it provides a rich set of options for linguistic sorts and searching.

In this chapter, you'll learn what globalization support entails and how it all fits together. You'll see how National Language Support (NLS) parameter settings can change the functionality of many of Oracle's operations. You will learn about datetime datatypes and how they can be used to synchronize data around the globe. You'll also learn about new linguistic sorting and searching options that allow multilingual data to be searched, sorted, and managed simply and efficiently.

Exam objectives are subject to change at any time without prior notice and at Oracle's sole discretion. Please visit Oracle's Training and Certification website (`http://www.oracle.com/education/certification/`) for the most current exam-objectives listing.

An Overview of Globalization Support

Oracle's globalization support is a collection of features that allow you to manage data in multiple native languages within the same database instance. It also greatly simplifies application development by offering a rich set of globalization functionality to the developer.

Globalization support provides the character sets and datatypes needed to store multilingual data. It ensures that date, time, monetary, numeric, and calendar data will follow any supported *locale* conventions and display properly. It provides utilities and error messages translated to many different languages. It also provides the internal functionality to sort and to query multilingual data using proper linguistic rules.

In the following sections, you will learn about Oracle's globalization support features. You will get an overview of each feature and the functionality that it provides.

You will learn about the architecture upon which globalization support is built. You'll be introduced to the *National Language Support Runtime Library (NLSRTL)* and see how its modular design provides flexibility and saves resources.

You will also learn how applications interact with Oracle from a globalization perspective.

And finally, you will be introduced to *Unicode* and the advantages that it offers in a multilingual environment.

Globalization Support Features

Globalization support provides a rich set of functionality to the Oracle database. But it is important to make two distinctions perfectly clear regarding what globalization support does not do:

- Globalization support does not translate text into different languages.
- Globalization does not control how multilingual text is displayed on client machines.

Globalization support simply provides the infrastructure to allow text to be stored, manipulated, sorted, and searched in many languages using linguistically significant means. It also allows the data to be displayed using the standard conventions for a specific region.

Globalization support includes these features:

Language support Globalization support allows data to be stored, processed, and retrieved in virtually any scripted language. For many of these languages, Oracle provides additional support such as text-sorting conventions, date-formatting conventions (including translated month names), and even error-message and utility-interface translation.

Territory support Cultural conventions often differ between geographical locations. For example, local time format, date format, and numeric and monetary conventions can differ significantly between regions even though they may share a common language. To allow for these differences, the `NLS_TERRITORY` parameter can be used to define which conventions to follow.

However, these default settings can still be overridden through the use of NLS parameter settings. Overriding the default settings allows finer granularity in defining and customizing display formats to account for special circumstances. For example, it is possible to set the primary currency to the Japanese yen and the secondary currency to the dollar even with the territory defined as India.

Linguistic sorting and searching Globalization support offers culturally accurate case conversion, sorting, and searching for all supported languages. It offers the ability to search and sort based on the rules of language rather than simply on the order in which the characters are encoded in the character set. It also offers *case-insensitive sorts* and searches as well as *accent-insensitive sorts* and searches.

Linguistic sorts are defined separately from the language itself, allowing the ability to share sort definitions between languages. Linguistic sort defaults can also be overridden through the use of NLS parameter settings. This gives you the flexibility to customize your environment as needed.

Character sets and semantics Oracle supports a vast number of character sets based on national and international standards, including Unicode. Because of the wide variety of *character sets*, users can often find a single set that supports all of the languages they need to support.

Unicode is a universal character set that supports all known written languages. Oracle offers full support of the Unicode 5.0 standard and offers several Unicode encoding options.

Unicode can be defined as the database character set, making it the default datatype for all character columns. If Unicode is not defined as the database character set, it can still be used by defining specific columns as *Unicode datatypes* (in other words, NCHAR, NVARCHAR2, NCLOB).

Many multibyte character sets use variable widths when storing data. This means that, depending on the character being stored, Oracle may use anywhere from 1 to 4 bytes to store it. Therefore, defining column widths in terms of the number of characters, rather than the number of bytes, becomes crucial. *Character semantics* allow character data to be specified in terms of the number of characters regardless of the number of bytes actually required. *Byte semantics*, the default, assume a single-byte character set, where one character always requires 1 byte of storage.

While Unicode may seem like the logical choice for any database, the decision to use it needs to be weighed carefully. There are performance and space-usage penalties associated with using Unicode. If a smaller code set is available that encompasses all of the languages you are likely to ever need, then the overhead of Unicode makes it an illogical choice.

Calendars Different geographic areas often utilize different calendar systems, which can make international transactions hard to synchronize. Oracle supports seven distinct calendar systems: Gregorian, Japanese Imperial, ROC (Republic of China) Official, Thai Buddha, Persian, English Hijrah, and Arabic Hijrah. Globalization support offers functionality to resolve calendar-system differences.

Locale and calendar customization Oracle's Locale Builder utility allows customization of globalization definitions, including language, character set, territory, and linguistic sorting. Calendars can also be customized using the NLS Calendar utility. Coverage of Locale Builder and the NLS Calendar utilities fall outside the scope of this book.

Globalization Support Architecture

Globalization support in Oracle 11*g* is implemented through the Oracle National Language Support Runtime Library (NLSRTL). The NLSRTL offers a set of language-independent text and character-processing functions as well as functions for language-convention manipulation. The behavior of these algorithms is determined at runtime (database startup), as the name suggests.

At database startup time, NLSRTL looks for a file named `lx1boot.nlb`. This file defines the set of locale definitions available to the database. To determine where to look for this file, NLSRTL will first check the environment for the existence of an `ORA_NLS10` variable.

If `ORA_NLS10` is defined, it will contain the path to where the `lx1boot.nlb` file resides. If the variable is not set, the default location of `$ORACLE_HOME/nls/data` will be used instead.

By default, ORA_NLS10 is not set. It should be set only in a multihomed environment where the locale-specific files are shared.

The `lx1boot.nlb` file identifies the set of locales available to the NLSRTL. These locales are defined in a collection of *locale definition files* that reside in the same directory as the `lx1boot.nlb` file.

There are four types of locale definition files:

- Language
- Territory
- Character set
- Linguistic sort

Each file contains data relating to only one particular locale type. For each locale type, there can be many different definition files.

This modular design of the locale definition files offers several distinct benefits:

- By using only the set of locales that you need, memory won't be wasted on unnecessary locales.
- Locale definitions can be mixed and matched.
- Locale files can be modified without affecting any other files.
- New locale files can be created without affecting existing files.

All the locale definition files follow the common naming convention:

Code	Position	Meaning
`Lx`	1–2	The standard prefix for all locale definition files
T	3	Represents the locale type: 0 = language, 1 = territory, 2 = character set, 3 = linguistic sort
Nnnn	4–7	The object ID (in hex)
`.nlb`	8–11	The standard extension for all locale definition files

For example, the file `lx00001.nlb` is the language file for American, as shown in the Locale Builder in Figure 13.1.

FIGURE 13.1 Locale Builder file `lx00001.nlb`

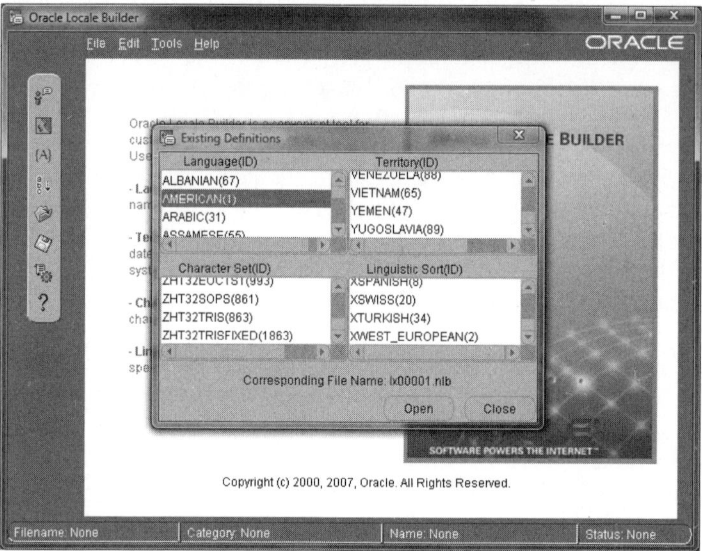

The complete set of locale definition files represents the globalization options available inside the database. Locale definitions can also be added or modified to support new functionality.

Supporting Multilingual Applications

Globalization allows the database to support multitier and client/server applications in any language for which it is configured. Locale-dependent operations are governed by NLS parameters and NLS environment variables set on both the client and server sides.

In the following sections, you will learn how client applications interact with the server from a globalization viewpoint. You will learn the purpose of the character sets defined at database-creation time. You'll learn how data-conversion issues can affect session performance. And finally, you'll learn how clients resolve globalization environment differences when they connect to a server.

Database Character Sets

When a database is created, two session-independent NLS parameters are specified: the database character set and the national character set.

The *database character set* defines the character set that will govern default text storage in the database. This includes all CHAR, VARCHAR2, LONG, and CLOB data as well as all SQL and PL/SQL text.

The *national character set* is an alternate Unicode character set that governs NCHAR, NVARCHAR2, and NCLOB data. You may want to store characters in the database from a character set that is not the database default; for example, the default character set may be US7ASCII, but you may also wish to store Chinese characters in the database. Use the national character set NCHAR, NVARCHAR2, and NCLOB data types to store this non-default character-set data.

Together, these two settings define the available character sets for the database.

Setting the Database Character Set

When you create the database, you specify the database character set thusly using the CHARACTER SET clause, and set the national character set using the NATIONAL CHARACTER SET clause:

```
SQL> CREATE DATABASE LNETEST
...
CHARACTER SET AL32UTF8
NATIONAL CHARACTER SET AL16UTF16
...
```

To identify SQL and PL/SQL source code, the database character set must have either EBCDIC or 7-bit ASCII, depending on the underlying platform, as a subset. Since it is not possible to use a fixed-width multibyte character set as the database character set, you cannot specify AL16UTF16 as the database character set. You can, however, specify AL16UTF16 as the national character set.

Changing the Database Character Set

Once you've created the database, you must re-create it to change the database character sets. The only exception is that if the new character set is a strict superset of all of the schema data, you can use the CSALTER script to change the database character set.

If it is not possible to utilize the CSALTER script, then you can perform a full export of the database, create the new database with the new character set, then import the full database.

Automatic Data Conversion

When a client makes a connection to a database server, the character sets used on both the client and server are compared. If they do not match, Oracle will need to perform automatic data conversion to resolve the difference. There is overhead involved in this conversion process as well as a risk of data loss. Performance will be affected relative to the level of conversion required.

The exception to this rule is when the database character set is a strict *superset* of the client character set. Two things must be true in order to classify a character set as a strict superset of another:

- The superset must contain all of the characters defined in the subset.
- The encoded values of all characters defined in the subset must match their encoded values in the superset.

If Oracle determines that both of these requirements are met, it will not perform automatic data conversion because it is not necessary.

Resolving Client/Server Settings

Any application that connects to the server is considered to be a client, in terms of globalization. Even if the application lives on the same physical machine as the server, it will still be classified as a client. This includes middle-tier application servers. Therefore, from a globalization perspective, all applications are governed by client-side NLS parameters.

When a client application is run, the client NLS environment is initialized from the environment variable settings. All local NLS operations are executed using these settings. *Local NLS operations* are client operations performed independently of any Oracle server session (for example, display formatting in Oracle Developer applications).

When the application completes a connection to the database server, the resulting session is initialized with the NLS environment settings of the server.

However, immediately after the session is established, the client implicitly issues an `ALTER SESSION` statement to synchronize the session NLS environment to match the client's NLS environment. In fact, the session environment can be modified at any time by using the `ALTER SESSION` statement, as shown here:

```
SQL*Plus: Release 11.1.0.6.0 - Production on Dim. Oct. 19 20:46:55 2008

Copyright (c) 1982, 2007, Oracle.  All rights reserved.


Connected to:
Oracle Database 11g Enterprise Edition Release 11.1.0.6.0 - Production
With the Partitioning, OLAP, Data Mining and Real Application Testing options

SQL>select sysdate from dual;

SYSDATE
---------
28-AUG-08

SQL> alter session set NLS_LANGUAGE=French;

Session altered.

SQL> select sysdate from dual;

SYSDATE
-----------
28-AOÛT -08
```

```
SQL> alter session set NLS_LANGUAGE=Italian;

Session altered.

SQL> select sysdate from dual;

SYSDATE
---------
28-AGO-08
```

Remember, however, that using `ALTER SESSION` changes only the session NLS environment. It does not change the client NLS environment.

Using Unicode in a Multilingual Database

Unicode is a universal character set that encompasses all known written languages in the world. Historically, dealing with multiple languages in a database or an application has been a difficult proposition. Existing character sets have always been too limited. Many don't even offer all the characters required for a single language, much less for all languages!

To support a wide variety of languages, it often meant that applications, databases, and programs using different character sets would have to be able to interact and exchange data, all with proper data conversion taking place every step of the way.

To address this problem, Unicode was created with this simple motto:

> Unicode provides a unique number for every character, no matter what the platform, no matter what the program, no matter what the language.
>
> Source: `www.unicode.org/standard/WhatIsUnicode.html`

Unicode assigns a guaranteed unique value (known as a *code point*) to every character to assure that no conflicts exist. Oracle supports version 5.0 of Unicode and offers the encoding methods listed in Table 13.1.

TABLE 13.1 Oracle-Supported Unicode Encoding Methods

Encoding Method	Description
UTF-8	An 8-bit encoding method that uses 1 to 4 bytes to store characters, as needed. UTF-8 is a strict superset of ASCII, meaning that every character in the ASCII character set is not only represented in the UTF-8 character set, but it also has the same code point value in both character sets. UTF-8 is supported on Unix platforms, HTML, and most Internet browsers.

TABLE 13.1 Oracle-Supported Unicode Encoding Methods *(continued)*

Encoding Method	Description
UCS-2	A fixed-width, 16-bit encoding method, meaning that each character is stored in 2 bytes. Both Microsoft Windows NT and Java support UCS-2 encoding. UCS-2 supports the older Unicode 3 standard; therefore, it does not support supplementary characters.
UTF-16	A strict superset of UCS-2. Offers support of supplementary characters by using two UCS-2 code points for each supplementary character. Newer versions of Windows (2000, XP, Vista) are based on this encoding method.

Unicode can be used in Oracle in several ways:

- It can be defined as the database character set, thereby becoming the default for all SQL CHAR datatypes (CHAR, VARCHAR2, CLOB, and LONG). In this setup, the UTF-8 encoding method will be used.
- It can be used as needed by creating columns using the NCHAR datatypes, also known as Unicode datatypes (NCHAR, NVARCHAR2, and NCLOB). Unicode data can be encoded as either UTF-8 or UTF-16 when used in this scenario.

Using NLS Parameters

Ultimately, Oracle globalization support options are defined by NLS parameter settings. By assigning values to specific NLS parameters, you can control when, where, and how Oracle will utilize globalization support functionality. These settings can be specified in a variety of ways, and their effects may vary accordingly.

On the server side, NLS parameters are read from initialization parameter settings at instance-startup time. The values are stored in the data dictionary, as are the database and national character-set settings.

On the client side, NLS parameters can be defined as environment variables (such as `NLS_LANG`), or they can be set at the session level by using the `ALTER SESSION` statement. NLS parameters can also be defined inside SQL function calls with a scope limited to only the current function. Therefore, it is vital to understand the order of precedence that Oracle follows concerning NLS parameter settings.

In the following sections, you'll learn about many of the different NLS parameters, how to set them, and what effect they will have on the system. You'll also learn how Oracle prioritizes NLS parameter settings. Last, you will learn how to use NLS data dictionary and dynamic performance views to access NLS information from the database.

Setting NLS Parameters

Oracle's globalization support is designed to be very simple to use. In many environments, globalization needs can be met by setting a single client-side parameter (NLS_LANG). This is because Oracle automatically derives lower-level specifics from the high-level settings. For instance, if the NLS_TERRITORY parameter is set to AMERICA, Oracle assumes that currency should be displayed as dollars, comma separators should be used, and so on.

However, the granularity provided by Oracle's globalization support allows almost unlimited variations for users with even the most demanding globalization needs.

NLS parameters can be classified into the following categories:

- Language and territory parameters
- Date and time parameters
- Calendar parameters
- Numeric, list, and monetary parameters
- Length semantics

Each category offers one or more individual parameters that can be set to meet your exact globalization needs.

In the following sections, you will learn how to set the NLS_LANG client-side environment variable to specify the NLS environment for your session. You'll also learn about each of the different categories of NLS parameter settings and the different options they offer.

Using the *NLS_LANG* Parameter

NLS_LANG is a client-side environment variable that defines the language, territory, and character set for the client. It is functionally equivalent to setting the NLS_LANGUAGE, NLS_TERRITORY, and NLS_CHARACTERSET parameters individually.

For most clients, the NLS_LANG parameter is all that needs to be set to define the entire globalization environment. This is true because the NLS_LANGUAGE and NLS_TERRITORY settings define the default settings for nearly all other NLS parameters.

The NLS_LANGUAGE parameter, for instance, specifies the default conventions to be used for all of the following globalization elements:

- Language for server messages
- Day and month names and abbreviations
- Symbols to represent a.m., p.m., , AD, and BC
- Sorting sequence for character data
- Affirmative and negative response strings (YES, NO)

The NLS_TERRITORY parameter specifies the default conventions used for these globalization elements:

- Date format
- Decimal character

- Group separator
- Local currency symbol
- ISO currency symbol
- Dual currency symbol
- First day of the week
- Credit/debit symbols
- ISO week flag
- List separator

Therefore, no other NLS parameters need to be set unless the default settings don't meet your needs.

The format for setting the NLS_LANG parameter is as follows:

```
NLS_LANG = language_territory.characterset
```

For example, the following are all valid:

```
NLS_LANG=AMERICAN_AMERICA.US7ASCII
NLS_LANG=JAPANESE_JAPAN.JA16EUC
NLS_LANG=FRENCH_CANADA.WE8ISO8859P1
```

The language element controls the conventions used for Oracle messages, sorting, and day and month names. If language is not set, Oracle will default to AMERICAN. Each language is identified by a unique name, such as FRENCH or GERMAN. Languages also impose a default territory and character set that will be used unless overridden.

The territory element determines the default date, monetary format, and numeric format conventions. If the territory is not defined, the default territory value from the language setting will be used. Territories carry distinct names such as AMERICA, CANADA, and GERMANY.

The character-set element determines the client character set. Normally this would be the Oracle character set that matches the character set of the operating system or terminal. Character sets have unique identifiers such as WE8ISO8859P1, US7ASCII, and JA16EUC.

All NLS_LANG definition components are optional. For example, the following is valid to set the language component independently of the other components:

```
NLS_LANG=FRENCH
```

It is also possible to set the territory and character-set components independently, but the following conventions must be followed:

- Territory must be preceded by an underscore character (_)
- Character set must be preceded by a period (.)

For example, to set the territory to AMERICA, you could use this syntax:

```
NLS_LANG=_AMERICA
```

Oracle Character-Set Naming Convention

The naming convention for Oracle character sets is as follows:

region number_of_bits standard_character_set_name [S][C]

The elements of the naming convention have the following meanings:

- *region* is generally a two-character abbreviation (US, WE, JA).
- *number_of_bits* represents the number of bits used to store one character.
- *standard_character_set_name* represents the common name for the character set. This name can vary in length (ASCII, ISO8859P1, SJIS).
- The optional S and C are used to specify character sets that are exclusive to the server (S) or the client (C) side.

For example, US7ASCII is a 7-bit United States code commonly referred to as ASCII (American Standard Code for Information Interchange).

The Unicode character sets UTF-8 and UTF-E defy Oracle's standard character-set naming convention.

To set the client character set to UTF-8, you could use this syntax:

```
NLS_LANG=.UTF8
```

Use caution when setting NLS_LANG. It is possible to make combinations that will not function correctly, such as specifying a character set that does not support the specified language.

In the following example, you'll set the NLS_LANG parameter to FRENCH_FRANCE .WE8ISO8859P1 and see how this affects your session. Remember that NLS_LANG is an environment variable setting, so it must be set in the operating system before connecting to Oracle:

```
$ export NLS_LANG=French_France.WE8ISO8859P1
$ sqlplus "/ as sysdba"

SQL*Plus: Release 11.1.0.6.0 - Production on Dim. Oct. 19 20:46:55 2008

Copyright (c) 1982, 2007, Oracle.  All rights reserved.
```

```
Connected to:
Oracle Database 11g Enterprise Edition Release 11.1.0.6.0 - Production
With the Partitioning, OLAP, Data Mining and Real Application Testing options

SQL> select prod_id, time_id,
round(sum(amount_sold),2) amount
from sh.sales
group by prod_id, time_id;

PROD_ID TIME_ID      AMOUNT
---------- -------- ----------
…
       127 19/10/01      87,88
        18 22/12/01    1478,83
        21 29/11/01    1047,02
        22 28/12/01      75,15
        23 22/10/01      21,15
        32 26/10/01      68,94
        45 02/12/01      47,74
       113 13/12/01      23,89
       114 08/12/01      19,05
       121 01/10/01      10,59
       121 20/12/01      32,43
       122 06/11/01      20,86
       128 03/11/01      30,16
       134 23/10/01      43,38

36292 rows selected.
SQL>
```

As you can see in this example, the date and number formats follow the conventions established in the NLS_LANG settings.

Using Language and Territory Parameters

NLS language and territory functionality can also be defined individually using the NLS_LANGUAGE and NLS_TERRITORY parameters.

On the server side, these parameters can be set as initialization parameters. They will then become the default settings for the Oracle instance. For example, the following lines could be inserted into the INIT.ORA file:

```
NLS_LANGUAGE=French
NLS_TERRITORY=France
```

When the database instance is next started, these settings will become the default settings for the instance.

On the client side, these parameters can be set within a session by using the ALTER SESSION statement, as shown here:

```
SQL> alter session set NLS_LANGUAGE=French;

Session altered.

SQL> alter session set NLS_TERRITORY=France;

Session altered.
```

NLS parameters modified using ALTER SESSION have a higher precedence than those set through environment variables such as NLS_LANG. Therefore, they will override the previously set parameter values. This topic will be covered later in this chapter. Of course, the value for NLS_LANGUAGE and NLS_TERRITORY must be legitimate; for example, attempting to set the NLS_TERRITORY to Fredonia will result in an error:

```
SQL> alter session set NLS_TERRITORY=Fredonia;
ERROR:
ORA-12705: Impossible d'acc_der aux fichiers de donn_es
NLS ou l'environnement indiqu_ n'est pas valide
```

And if you don't read French but you wish to know what the error message translates to in American English, simply set your NLS_LANGUAGE to American and then attempt to set the NLS_TERRITORY to Fredonia.

```
SQL> alter session set NLS_LANGUAGE=American;

Session altered.

SQL> alter session set NLS_TERRITORY=Fredonia;
ERROR:
ORA-12705: Cannot access NLS data files or invalid environment specified
```

Using Date and Time Parameters

NLS date and time functionality can also be defined individually using the following NLS parameters:

- NLS_DATE_FORMAT
- NLS_DATE_LANGUAGE
- NLS_TIMESTAMP_FORMAT
- NLS_TIMESTAMP_TZ_FORMAT

All of these parameters can be set within a session by using the ALTER SESSION statement. They can also be defined as initialization parameters and will then become default settings for the entire instance.

NLS_DATE_FORMAT

The NLS_DATE_FORMAT parameter specifies the default format for dates in the current session. It can be defined as any valid date-format mask, such as in this example:

```
SQL> ALTER SESSION SET NLS_DATE_FORMAT = MM/DD/YY;

Session altered.
```

You can even append text literals into the date format, if you wish, by enclosing the literal in double quotes. You must also enclose the entire format string in apostrophes (single quotes), as shown here:

```
SQL> alter session set NLS_DATE_FORMAT =' "Today' 's date is "MM/DD/YYYY';

Session altered.

SQL> select sysdate from dual;

SYSDATE
--------------------------
Today's date is 10/19/2008
```

Note that normal quoting rules apply inside the text literal. Therefore, two apostrophes were required to create the string "Today's".

NLS_DATE_LANGUAGE

The NLS_DATE_LANGUAGE parameter governs the language used in the following situations:

- Day and month names and abbreviations displayed by the functions TO_CHAR and TO_DATE
- Day and month names returned by the default date format (NLS_DATE_FORMAT)
- Abbreviations for a.m., p.m., AD, and BC

NLS_DATE_LANGUAGE accepts any valid language as a value and can be set as shown here:

```
SQL> alter session set nls_date_language=Italian;

Session altered.

SQL> select to_char(sysdate,'Day:Dd Month YYYY') from dual;
```

```
TO_CHAR(SYSDATE,'DAY:DDMONT
---------------------------
Domenica :19 Ottobre   2008
```

NLS_TIMESTAMP_FORMAT

The NLS_TIMESTAMP_FORMAT parameter is used to set the default date format for both TIMESTAMP and TIMESTAMP WITH TIME ZONE datatypes. An example is shown here:

```
SQL> alter session set nls_timestamp_format='MM/DD/YYYY HH24:MI:SS.FF';

Session altered.

SQL> select startup_time
from sys.dba_hist_snapshot
where rownum < 3;

STARTUP_TIME
-----------------------------------------------------------------------
10/11/2008 11:32:33.000
10/11/2008 11:32:33.000

SQL> select next_run_date
from sys.dba_scheduler_jobs;

NEXT_RUN_DATE
-----------------------------------------------------------------------
20/10/08 03:00:00,000000 US/CENTRAL
20/10/08 03:00:00,000000 US/CENTRAL
01/11/08 01:01:01,400000 -05:00
19/10/08 21:26:27,000000 -04:00
19/10/08 20:40:30,000000 -05:00

5 rows selected.
SQL>
```

The TIMESTAMP and TIMESTAMP WITH TIME ZONE datatypes will be covered later in this chapter.

NLS_TIMESTAMP_TZ_FORMAT

Like the NLS_TIMESTAMP_FORMAT parameter, the NLS_TIMESTAMP_TZ_FORMAT parameter is used to set the default date format for TIMESTAMP and TIMESTAMP WITH TIME ZONE datatypes. However, as the name suggests, it adds the option of time-zone formatting, as shown here:

```
SQL> alter session set nls_timestamp_tz_format = 'YYYY/MM/DD HH:MI TZH:TZM';

Session altered.

SQL> select startup_time
from sys.dba_hist_snapshot
where rownum < 3;

STARTUP_TIME
------------------------------------------------------------------------
10/11/2008 11:32:33.000
10/11/2008 11:32:33.000

SQL> select next_run_date
 from sys.dba_scheduler_jobs;

NEXT_RUN_DATE
------------------------------------------------------------------------
2008/10/20 03:00 -05:00
2008/10/20 03:00 -05:00
2008/11/01 01:01 -05:00
2008/10/19 09:26 -04:00
2008/10/19 08:40 -05:00

5 rows selected.
SQL>
```

As you can see in the example, the `TZH:TZM` element shows the time-zone offset in hours and minutes.

Using Calendar Parameters

Different geographical areas can use different calendaring systems. Oracle 11*g*'s globalization support defines seven distinct calendars, all of which are fully supported:

- Gregorian
- Japanese Imperial
- ROC Official
- Persian

- Thai Buddha
- Arabic Hijrah
- English Hijrah

For each of these calendars, the following information is maintained:

First day of the week While the United States and many other countries consider Sunday to represent the first day of the week, other countries, such as Germany, consider Monday to be the first day of the week.

First calendar week of the year Many countries use the week number for things like bookkeeping and scheduling. However, an International Standards Organization (ISO) week can differ from the calendar-week number. (ISO weeks run from Monday through Sunday.) Oracle supports both conventions. Here are the definitions provided by Oracle:

- If January 1 falls on a Friday, Saturday, or Sunday, then the ISO week that includes January 1 is the last week of the previous year because most of the days in the week belong to the previous year.
- If January 1 falls on a Monday, Tuesday, Wednesday, or Thursday, then the ISO week is the first week of the new year because most of the days in the week belong to the new year.

Number of days/months in a year The number of days and months in a year can differ between calendars, as shown in Table 13.2.

First year of the era Different regions may also choose a notable year in which to start, much like the Gregorian calendar starts with Anno Domini (Latin for "the year of the Lord"), also known as the Common Era. The Islamic calendar, for example, starts with the year of the Hegria (622 AD, when the prophet Mohammed and his followers migrated from Mecca to Medina). The Japanese Imperial calendar starts from the first year of an Emperor's reign.

The `NLS_CALENDAR` parameter is used to specify which calendar Oracle should use, as shown here:

```
SQL> alter session set NLS_CALENDAR = 'Persian';
Session altered.

SQL> select sysdate from dual;

SYSDATE
------------------
28 Mehr        1387
```

TABLE 13.2 International Calendar Days/Months in a Year

Calendar	Description
Gregorian	The standard calendar used by most of the world. The Gregorian calendar has 365 days in each year, with 366 days on leap years. The number of days in a month varies. Years are counted from the beginning of the Common Era, or Anno Domini.
Japanese Imperial	Same as Gregorian, but the year starts with the beginning of each Imperial era.
ROC Official	Same as Gregorian, but the year starts with the founding of the Republic of China: Gregorian year 1912 is ROC Official year 1. For example, Gregorian year 2008 is ROC Official year 97.
Persian	The first six months have 31 days each. The next five have 30 days each. The last month has 29 days (30 in a leap year).
Thai Buddha	Same as Gregorian, but the year begins with BE (Buddhist Era), which starts with the death of Gautama Buddha; for example, Gregorian year 2008 is Thai Buddha year 2551, or Gregorian plus 543 years.
Arabic Hijrah	Has 12 months, with 354 or 355 days.
English Hijrah	Has 12 months, with 354 or 355 days.

Using Numeric, List, and Monetary Parameters

Number-formatting conventions define how Oracle should display large numbers and numeric lists.

In the United States, for example, the following convention is followed:

1,234,567.89

Germany, on the other hand, uses a convention that is diametrically opposite:

1.234.567,89

In the following sections, you'll learn to use the various numeric, list, and monetary NLS parameters.

NLS_NUMERIC_CHARACTERS

The `NLS_NUMERIC_CHARACTERS` parameter defines the characters that represent the decimal and group separator (for example, thousands, millions, and so on) elements in the number-format mask. These elements are represented by the letters *D* and *G*, respectively, in the number-format mask. Any single-byte character can be assigned, with the following exceptions:

- The decimal character and the group separator cannot be the same character.
- They cannot be numeric.
- They cannot have mathematical significance (+, –, <, >).

When this parameter is set, the decimal character comes before the group separator, as shown here:

```
SQL> alter session set NLS_NUMERIC_CHARACTERS=",.";

Session altered.

SQL> select cust_id, to_char(sum(amount_sold), '9G999G999D99') big_sales
from sh.sales
group by cust_id
having sum(amount_sold) > 30000;
CUST_ID    BIG_SALES
---------- -------------
...
      6960     33.407,59
      7680     33.528,24
      3080     43.395,67
     12600     49.980,28
850 rows selected.
SQL>
```

As you can see, the decimal character is now represented by a comma. The group separator, on the other hand, is now represented by a period.

NLS_LIST_SEPARATOR

The NLS_LIST_SEPARATOR parameter specifies the character used to separate values in a list of values. The following restrictions apply to the NLS_LIST_SEPARATOR parameter:

- It cannot be numeric.
- It cannot be the same character as the numeric or monetary decimal character.
- It cannot have mathematical significance (+, –, <, >).

The NLS_LIST_SEPARATOR parameter is strictly a client-side setting. It has no meaning on the server. Therefore, it is set through a client-side environment variable but does not execute an implicit ALTER SESSION when a server connection is established.

NLS_CURRENCY

The NLS_CURRENCY parameter defines the currency symbol that will be displayed by the element *L* in the number-format mask, as shown here:

```
SQL> alter session set NLS_CURRENCY = "£";

Session altered.

SQL> select to_char(123.45,'L9G999G999D99') amount
from dual;

AMOUNT
-----------------------
                £123.45
```

The NLS_CURRENCY parameter is not limited to a single character. It can be set to a string as well:

```
SQL> alter session set NLS_CURRENCY = " USD";

Session altered.

SQL>  select to_char(123.45,'9G999G999D99L') amount
  2   from dual;

AMOUNT
-----------------------
             123.45 USD
```

Notice in the example that a space is embedded at the beginning of the string. Without the space, the output would appear as shown here:

```
AMOUNT
-----------------------
             123.45USD
```

NLS_ISO_CURRENCY

The NLS_ISO_CURRENCY parameter is used to prevent ambiguity in the currency symbol. For example, the dollar sign ($) can be used for both Australian and American dollars. NLS_ISO_CURRENCY uses a unique text string in place of the currency sign. Several common examples are shown here:

USD: United States

AUD: Australia

EEK: Estonia

EUR: Germany

GBP: United Kingdom

The NLS_ISO_CURRENCY parameter defines the currency symbol that will be displayed by the *C* element of the number-format mask. It can be modified using the ALTER SESSION statement, but instead of a text string, it requires a valid territory name, as follows:

```
SQL>  alter session set NLS_ISO_CURRENCY=France;

Session altered.

SQL> select to_char(123.45,'9G999G999D99C') amount
  2  from dual;

AMOUNT
--------------------
           123.45EUR
```

Using the *NLS_LENGTH_SEMANTICS* Parameter

Single-byte character sets always use one byte to store one character. This makes storage calculation a breeze. But when you're using a multibyte character set, such as Unicode, a single character may use several bytes of storage. Column sizing becomes much more difficult in this situation.

Length semantics, originally introduced in Oracle9*i*, make it possible to size columns using either bytes or characters. The method of calculating the length of character strings in bytes is known as byte semantics. Calculating the length in characters is referred to as character semantics.

The NLS_LENGTH_SEMANTICS parameter defines the default method of length semantics to either BYTE (the default) or CHAR. An example is shown here:

```
SQL> alter system set NLS_LENGTH_SEMANTICS = CHAR;

System altered.
```

Consider the following example:

```
SQL> create table test_table (
Last_name VARCHAR2(25));

Table created.
```

When length semantics are set to CHAR, the LAST_NAME column in this table will hold 25 characters, no matter how many actual bytes of storage are required.

When length semantics are set to BYTE, the LAST_NAME column will allocate 25 bytes of storage. If the character set requires 3 bytes to store a single character (or symbol), only 8 characters can be stored.

The default setting can be overridden by declaring the length semantics directly in the CREATE TABLE statement. For example, when you're defining a character column, character semantics can be forced using the following syntax:

```
SQL> create table test_table (
Last_name VARCHAR2(25 CHAR));

Table created.
```

This example forces the use of character semantics, regardless of the setting of the NLS_LENGTH_SEMANTICS parameter.

There are a few exceptions to consider when dealing with length semantics:

- NCHAR, NVARCHAR, CLOB, and NCLOB datatypes are not affected by the NLS_LENGTH_SEMANTICS parameter value. These are datatypes designed specifically for multi-byte character data; therefore they will always use character semantics.
- Tables in the SYS and SYSTEM tablespaces are not governed by the NLS_LENGTH_SEMANTICS parameter. All data dictionary tables always use byte semantics.

Prioritizing NLS Parameters

Oracle databases often represent only one tier in a multitier environment. For instance, let's assume that Arren is a user in France. He uses a custom, client-side application that connects to an application server in Italy. The application server connects to a transaction-processing gateway in Sweden. The transaction-processing gateway connects to the Oracle database in the United States.

Each of these machines may have NLS settings appropriate for their respective locale, but none match the settings of the database server. How does the database server determine the NLS settings to honor?

There are several different ways in which NLS parameters can be specified. Therefore, when conflicting settings are issued, Oracle needs to have a method of prioritizing to determine which setting will ultimately be used.

NLS parameters can be defined using any of the following methods:

- Setting server-initialization parameters
- Setting client-environment variables
- Using the ALTER SESSION statement
- By executing SQL functions
- As default values

In the following sections, you will learn about each of the methods of setting NLS parameter values as well as how Oracle chooses to prioritize them.

Setting Server-Initialization Parameters

NLS settings can be defined as initialization parameters on the server. Initialization parameters are loaded at instance-startup time, as in this example:

```
NLS_LANGUAGE=FRENCH
```

The effect of initialization-parameter settings will be seen only on the server. They have no effect on the client side. They will, however, govern sessions created by the client to the server, unless the client NLS environment overrides them.

Setting Client Environment Variables

Environment variables on the client side will govern local client-side NLS operations (operations that don't involve the database). They will also override server-side NLS settings for sessions created from the client.

In the following example, the environment variable `NLS_LANGUAGE` is set to French before a session is opened. Note that in a Windows environment, the environment variable could be set either using the `set` command or in the Environment tab in the System Properties window.

```
$ export NLS_LANGUAGE=French

$ sqlplus "/ as sysdba"

SQL*Plus: Release 11.1.0.6.0 - Production on Dim. Oct. 19 21:22:15 2008

Copyright (c) 1982, 2007, Oracle.  All rights reserved.


Connected to:
Oracle Database 11g Enterprise Edition Release 11.1.0.6.0 - Production
With the Partitioning, OLAP, Data Mining and Real Application Testing options
SQL> select to_char(sysdate, 'Mon') from dual;
TO_CH
-----
Oct.
```

When the client-side environment variable `NLS_LANG` was set, the server's NLS settings were overridden for the session. The client program accomplishes this by issuing an implicit `ALTER SESSION` statement when a new session is opened.

Using the *ALTER SESSION* Statement

Setting NLS parameters using the ALTER SESSION statement also overrides the server-side NLS settings for the current session, as in this example:

```
SQL> ALTER SESSION set NLS_SORT = FRENCH;

Session altered.
```

Using ALTER SESSION also overrides any previous ALTER SESSION settings. Therefore, an explicit ALTER SESSION statement overrides settings from the client environment variables (which perform an implicit ALTER SESSION call).

Setting NLS Parameters in SQL Functions

NLS parameters can also be set inside certain SQL functions. Inline NLS parameter settings have the highest priority and will override any other NLS settings. However, their scope is limited to the immediate SQL function, as shown here:

```
SQL> select to_char(sysdate, 'DD/MON/YYYY','nls_date_language=Italian')
from dual;
TO_CHAR(SYS
-----------
19/OTT/2008

SQL> select to_char(sysdate, 'DD/MON/YYYY') from dual;

TO_CHAR(SYSDA
-------------
19/OCT./2008
```

As you can see in this example, the inline NLS parameter setting affected only the function in which it was called. It had no effect on the subsequent statement.

Only specific SQL functions will accept inline NLS parameter settings.

Prioritization Summary

As you learned in the preceding sections, there are five distinct methods in which NLS parameters can be specified. Oracle prioritizes these methods to ensure that conflicting settings can be resolved. Table 13.3 summarizes these methods for NLS parameter prioritization as well as the scope for each method.

TABLE 13.3 NLS Parameter–Setting Precedence

Method	Priority	Scope
Set in SQL functions	1	Current SQL function
Explicit ALTER SESSION statement	2	Current session
Client environment variable (implicit ALTER SESSION statement)	3	Current session
Set by server-initialization parameter	4	Instance
Default	5	Instance

Using NLS Views

Information relating to Oracle NLS settings is stored in the data dictionary and inside fixed tables in memory. This information consists of NLS settings for the session, instance, and database. You can also view a list of the valid values that may be specified when setting NLS parameters.

The following views can be queried to find NLS information from the data dictionary and from dynamic performance tables:

- NLS_SESSION_PARAMETERS
- NLS_INSTANCE_PARAMETERS
- NLS_DATABASE_PARAMETERS
- V$NLS_VALID_VALUES

We will look at each of these views in the following sections.

NLS_SESSION_PARAMETERS

The NLS_SESSION_PARAMETERS view offers an insight into the current NLS settings for your session. Here is an example, continuing with the environment and session NLS parameters set earlier:

```
SQL> select * from nls_session_parameters;

PARAMETER                      VALUE
------------------------------ ---------------------------
NLS_LANGUAGE                   FRENCH
NLS_TERRITORY                  FRANCE
```

```
NLS_CURRENCY
NLS_ISO_CURRENCY                FRANCE
NLS_NUMERIC_CHARACTERS          ,
NLS_CALENDAR                    GREGORIAN
NLS_DATE_FORMAT                 DD/MM/RR
NLS_DATE_LANGUAGE               FRENCH
NLS_SORT                        FRENCH
NLS_TIME_FORMAT                 HH24:MI:SSXFF
NLS_TIMESTAMP_FORMAT            DD/MM/RR HH24:MI:SSXFF
NLS_TIME_TZ_FORMAT              HH24:MI:SSXFF TZR
NLS_TIMESTAMP_TZ_FORMAT         DD/MM/RR HH24:MI:SSXFF TZR
NLS_DUAL_CURRENCY
NLS_COMP                        BINARY
NLS_LENGTH_SEMANTICS            BYTE
NLS_NCHAR_CONV_EXCP             FALSE

17 rows selected.
```

You will notice that the NLS_SESSION_PARAMETERS view is restricted to show only the current session and nothing more. You may also see settings here that you don't remember specifying. If so, the values represent either the default setting or the value derived from a higher-level NLS parameter. For example, if NLS_TERRITORY is set to AMERICA, the NLS_CURRENCY parameter will automatically be set to use dollars.

NLS_INSTANCE_PARAMETERS

The NLS_INSTANCE_PARAMETERS view returns NLS settings for the entire instance rather than for a single session. These are settings that have been set explicitly through initialization parameters or ALTER SYSTEM statements. Here is an example:

```
SQL> select * from nls_instance_parameters;

PARAMETER                       VALUE
------------------------------ --------------
NLS_LANGUAGE                    AMERICAN
NLS_TERRITORY                   AMERICA
NLS_SORT
NLS_DATE_LANGUAGE
NLS_DATE_FORMAT
NLS_CURRENCY
NLS_NUMERIC_CHARACTERS
NLS_ISO_CURRENCY
NLS_CALENDAR
```

```
NLS_TIME_FORMAT
NLS_TIMESTAMP_FORMAT
NLS_TIME_TZ_FORMAT
NLS_TIMESTAMP_TZ_FORMAT
NLS_DUAL_CURRENCY
NLS_COMP                       BINARY
NLS_LENGTH_SEMANTICS           BYTE
NLS_NCHAR_CONV_EXCP            FALSE

17 rows selected.
```

The results from the NLS_INSTANCE_PARAMETERS view show that many parameters have not been explicitly set. Instead, they derive their value from higher-level parameters. For example, NLS_SORT derives its value from NLS_LANGUAGE, while the currency-, date-, and time-related parameters are derived from NLS_TERRITORY.

NLS_DATABASE_PARAMETERS

The NLS_DATABASE_PARAMETERS view shows NLS settings for the database itself. These represent the default values that will govern the instance, unless they are overridden by initialization parameter settings.

An example is shown here:

```
SQL> select * from nls_database_parameters;

PARAMETER                      VALUE
------------------------------ ----------------------------
NLS_LANGUAGE                   AMERICAN
NLS_TERRITORY                  AMERICA
NLS_CURRENCY                   $
NLS_ISO_CURRENCY               AMERICA
NLS_NUMERIC_CHARACTERS         .,
NLS_CHARACTERSET               WE8MSWIN1252
NLS_CALENDAR                   GREGORIAN
NLS_DATE_FORMAT                DD-MON-RR
NLS_DATE_LANGUAGE              AMERICAN
NLS_SORT                       BINARY
NLS_TIME_FORMAT                HH.MI.SSXFF AM
NLS_TIMESTAMP_FORMAT           DD-MON-RR HH.MI.SSXFF AM
NLS_TIME_TZ_FORMAT             HH.MI.SSXFF AM TZR
NLS_TIMESTAMP_TZ_FORMAT        DD-MON-RR HH.MI.SSXFF AM TZR
NLS_DUAL_CURRENCY              $
NLS_COMP                       BINARY
```

```
NLS_LENGTH_SEMANTICS            BYTE
NLS_NCHAR_CONV_EXCP             FALSE
NLS_NCHAR_CHARACTERSET          AL16UTF16
NLS_RDBMS_VERSION               11.1.0.6.0

20 rows selected.
```

The values shown in the NLS_DATABASE_PARMETERS view are set at database-creation time and based on the parameters used in the CREATE DATABASE statement.

V$NLS_VALID_VALUES

The V$NLS_VALID_VALUES dynamic performance view lists all valid values for each of the following NLS parameters: NLS_LANGUAGE, NLS_SORT, NLS_TERRITORY, and NLS_CHARACTERSET.

The following example shows a truncated listing:

```
SQL>  select *
  from v$nls_valid_values
  where value like '%GER%';

PARAMETER        VALUE           ISDEP
---------------- --------------- -----
LANGUAGE         GERMAN          FALSE
LANGUAGE         GERMAN DIN      FALSE
TERRITORY        GERMANY         FALSE
TERRITORY        ALGERIA         FALSE
SORT             GERMAN          FALSE
SORT             XGERMAN         FALSE
SORT             GERMAN_DIN      FALSE
SORT             XGERMAN_DIN     FALSE

8 rows selected.
SQL>
```

Using Datetime Datatypes

A challenge in managing data in a global environment is synchronizing transactions that occur across time zones. Oracle's globalization support offers special datatypes and functionality to manage dates and times across differing time zones.

In the following sections, you'll learn about the Oracle datatypes that store date and time information. The data stored using these datatypes are often called datetimes, and you'll learn about the following:

- DATE
- TIMESTAMP
- TIMESTAMP WITH TIME ZONE
- TIMESTAMP WITH LOCAL TIME ZONE

You'll also be introduced to several datetime SQL functions. Last, time-zone parameters and files will be covered.

Using the DATE Datatype

The DATE datatype is used to store date information as well as time information in the database. In fact, every date stored as a DATE datatype will have an accompanying time, even if no time was specified when the date was stored. See Exercise 13.1, "Time Elements in DATE Datatypes," for further information on time elements.

To define a column using the DATE datatype, use the DATE keyword as shown here:

```
SQL>  create table birthdates (
  client_id NUMBER,
  birthdate DATE);

Table created.
```

Oracle dates consist of seven parts: century, year, month, day, hours, minutes, and seconds (elapsed since midnight). In fact, they are stored internally in the database as seven separate one-byte elements.

To demonstrate, insert a row into the BIRTHDATES table that was created earlier:

```
SQL> insert into birthdates
  values(1, TO_DATE('01-DEC-68'));

1 row created.

SQL> commit;

Commit complete.
```

Next, select the date from the table using the following TO_CHAR formatting option:

```
SQL> select to_char(birthdate,'YYYY-MM-DD:HH24:MI:SS')
from birthdates;
```

```
TO_CHAR(BIRTHDATE,'
-------------------
1968-12-01:00:00:00
```

You can see the elements displayed clearly when using this formatting option. However, that doesn't tell you anything about how the data is stored internally. To see that, use the DUMP function, as shown here:

```
SQL> select dump(birthdate)
 from birthdates;

DUMP(BIRTHDATE)
--------------------------------------------------
Typ=12 Len=7: 119,168,12,1,1,1,1
```

The DUMP function shows the datatype, the length (number of bytes), and the actual byte values for a particular element. So, the example shows that the BIRTHDATE element is stored internally as a DATE datatype (typ=12). It occupies 7 bytes (Len=7) of storage, and the values stored in those bytes are 119, 168, 12, 1, 1, 1, and 1. The century is recorded in the first byte as 100 + the century. The year is recorded in the second byte as 100 + the year. The month and day of the month are stored in subsequent bytes. The hour, minute, and second are each incremented by 1.

Oracle stores the century and the year elements using excess-100 notation, which means that it adds 100 to the number before storing it. Also, the hours, minutes, and seconds elements are stored using excess-1 notation. As you probably guessed, that means that it adds 1 to each number before storing it.

Therefore, if the stored values were converted to standard decimal notation, this is what we would see:

```
DUMP(BIRTHDATE)
--------------------------------------------------
Typ=12 Len=7: 19,68,12,1,1,1,1
```

Now, you can see that the stored values do indeed match the original date, as shown here:

```
SQL> select to_char(birthdate,'YYYY-MM-DD:HH24:MI:SS')
 from birthdates;

TO_CHAR(BIRTHDATE,'
-------------------
1968-12-01:00:00:00
```

By better understanding how the data is stored internally, you can think of dates as collections of individual elements that can be accessed together or individually. In Exercise 13.1, we will practice storing date and time values in columns with different data types, then query and compare the results.

EXERCISE 13.1

Time Elements in DATE Datatypes

DATE datatypes always store both a date and a time. If no time is specified when storing a date, Oracle will use a default time of midnight. This can be problematic if you're not careful, as this exercise will demonstrate.

1. First, confirm the date by selecting SYSDATE from dual:

```
SQL> select sysdate from dual;

SYSDATE
---------
19-OCT-08
```

2. Create a table with a VARCHAR2 column to contain a date string and a DATE column:

```
SQL> create table conv_dates (datestring varchar2(15),
converted_date date);
Table created.
```

3. Insert the current date into a table column defined as a datatype of DATE:

```
SQL> insert into conv_dates
  values ('10-19-2008', to_date('10-19-2008','MM-DD-YYYY'));

1 row created.

SQL> commit;

Commit complete.
```

4. Execute the following SQL:

```
SQL> select * from conv_dates where converted_date = sysdate;

no rows selected
```

Even though the two dates appear identical, the query fails to return any matching rows. The following queries will show you the reason:

```
SQL> select
 to_char(converted_date, 'MM-DD-YYYY HH24:MI')
 from conv_dates;
```

EXERCISE 13.1 *(continued)*

```
TO_CHAR(CONVERTE
----------------
10-19-2008 00:00
12-01-1968 00:00

SQL> select
  to_char(sysdate,'MM-DD-YYYY HH24:MI')
  from dual;

TO_CHAR(SYSDATE,
----------------
10-19-2008 22:22
```

Because no time element was defined when you inserted the rows into the CONV_DATES table, Oracle defaulted the time to midnight. SYSDATE, on the other hand, returns the current date and the current time. Therefore, unless you happen to run the query at exactly midnight, the query returns no rows.

To resolve this problem, you can use the TRUNC function, as shown here:

```
SQL> select * from conv_dates
  where trunc(converted_date) = trunc(sysdate);

DATESTRING      CONVERTED_
--------------- ----------
10-19-2008      19/10/08
```

The TRUNC function removes the time element from the date element in a DATE value. With the time element gone, the query returns one row, as expected.

When entering date information into a DATE datatype, you can specify it in several ways:

Literal The date can be entered as a literal, which matches the NLS_DATE_FORMAT format. For example, if NLS_DATE_FORMAT is defined as 'MM-DD-YYYY', then a literal of '12-21-2000' would be acceptable, as shown in this example:

```
SQL> alter session set NLS_DATE_FORMAT = "MM-DD-YYYY";

Session altered.
```

```
SQL> insert into birthdates
values(2, '12-21-2000');

1 row created.
```

Note that in this example, because no time portion was specified, Oracle will set the time elements to represent midnight.

ANSI date literal An American National Standards Institute (ANSI) date literal contains no time element. It must be formatted exactly as shown here:

```
DATE 'YYYY-MM-DD'
```

Dates can be entered using the ANSI date-literal format at any time, regardless of the NLS_DATE_FORMAT setting. Here's an example:

```
SQL> insert into birthdates
  2  values(3, DATE '1969-08-23');

1 row created.
```

TO_DATE function Dates can also be entered by using the **TO_DATE** function. This function converts text strings to DATE types based on the format specified. An example is shown here:

```
SQL> insert into birthdates
  values(4, to_date('04-19-1977 13:45', 'MM-DD-YYYY HH24:MI');
```

This example specifies not only the date, but also the hours and minutes elements of the time.

The TO_DATE function can also be handy for converting dates that have been stored as character types. Consider the following examples using the CONV_DATES table created earlier in this section. This table will hold a string of 15 characters and a date. Now, a string representation of two dates will be inserted in the table. Note that they are being stored as VARCHAR2 character data, not as dates:

```
SQL> insert into conv_dates (datestring)
  values ('12-01-1968');

1 row created.

SQL> insert into conv_dates (datestring)
  values ('04-09-1965');

1 row created.
```

```
SQL> commit;

Commit complete.
```

Next, the strings will be converted and stored as dates by using the TO_DATE function:

```
SQL> update conv_dates
  set converted_date =
  to_date(datestring,'MM-DD-YYYY');

2 rows updated.

SQL> commit;

Commit complete.
```

Now both will be selected, as shown here:

```
SQL> select * from conv_dates;

DATESTRING      CONVERTED_D
--------------- -----------
12-01-1968      01-DEC-1968
04-09-1965      09-APR-1965
```

As you can see in this example, the TO_DATE function converted the dates stored as VARCHAR2 data in the DATESTRING column into the DATE datatype format, which was subsequently stored in the CONVERTED_DATE column.

Using the TIMESTAMP Datatype

The TIMESTAMP datatype offers all the date and time elements found in the DATE datatype in addition to the extended functionality of storing fractional seconds.

By default, the TIMESTAMP datatype stores fractional seconds to six digits of precision. This can be changed, however, by specifying a number from 0 and 9 in parentheses after the TIMESTAMP keyword. This number determines the digits of precision for the fractional seconds, as shown here:

```
SQL> create table test_stamp (stamp timestamp(2));

Table created.
```

```
SQL> insert into test_stamp
select to_timestamp('19-OCT-2008 17:54.38.92',
'DD-MON-YYYY HH24:MI:SS:FF')
from dual;

1 row created.

SQL> commit;

Commit complete.

SQL> select * from test_stamp;

STAMP
------------------------------------
19-OCT-08 05.54.38.92 PM
```

As you can see, the timestamp was entered using the `TO_TIMESTAMP` function (which is similar to the `TO_DATE` function). Notice that fractional seconds can be specified by using the `FF` element in the date mask.

The TIMESTAMP datatype should be used when locale information (time zone) is not required but fractional-second granularity is. For example, application event logging is a common use of the TIMESTAMP datatype.

Using the TIMESTAMP WITH TIME ZONE Datatype

The TIMESTAMP WITH TIME ZONE datatype extends the functionality of the TIMESTAMP datatype by including time-zone information. The time-zone data is stored as an offset (hours and minutes) between the local time and the UTC (Coordinated Universal Time, formerly known as Greenwich mean time). It can be displayed either in this form or in the form of a region name.

Like the TIMESTAMP datatype, the TIMESTAMP WITH TIME ZONE datatype stores fractional seconds to six digits of precision. This can be changed by specifying a number from 0 and 9 in parentheses between the `TIMESTAMP` keyword and the `WITH TIME ZONE` keywords. This number determines the digits of precision for the fractional seconds, as in this example:

```
SQL> create table stamp_tz (stamp_tz TIMESTAMP(4) WITH TIME ZONE);
Table created
```

The TIMESTAMP WITH TIME ZONE is recommended when local information and precise time transactions across time zones need to be synchronized. For example, a bank with branches in different time zones needs to post transactions in real time, regardless of location.

Using the TIMESTAMP WITH LOCAL TIME ZONE Datatype

The TIMESTAMP WITH TIME ZONE datatype doesn't actually store time-zone information at all. Instead, when a record is inserted into a column defined with a datatype of TIMESTAMP WITH LOCAL TIME ZONE, the following happens:

- If the incoming data has no time-zone element, it is assumed to be local time and is stored as is.
- If the incoming data has a time-zone element but the time zone matches the local time zone, the time-zone element is dropped and the data is stored.
- If the incoming data has a time-zone element and the time zone does not match the local time zone, the timestamp is adjusted to local time. The data is then stored without a time-zone element.

Using this method synchronizes all time elements to the local time, allowing a company that spans multiple time zones to see data in real time relative to the local time zone. One way to utilize this datatype is to use the supplied `CURRENT_TIMESTAMP` function, which returns the current date and time in the session time zone, in a value of datatype TIMESTAMP WITH TIME ZONE.

Real World Scenario

Using the TIMESTAMP WITH LOCAL TIME ZONE Datatype

Suppose your company is headquartered in London and you have a branch office in New York. Transactions from the branch office need to be stored in your London database and synchronized to London time.

The time-zone information for London is as follows:

Element	Value
Standard time zone	No UTC offset
Daylight Savings Time	+1 hour
Current time-zone offset	UTC +1 hour
Time-zone abbreviation	BST (British summer time)
Current time	Friday, September 3, 2008, at 1:15:14 p.m. BST

The time-zone information for New York is as follows:

Element	**Value**
Standard time zone	UTC –5 hours
Daylight Savings Time	+1 hour
Current time-zone offset	UTC –4 hours
Time-zone abbreviation	EDT (eastern daylight time)
Current time	Friday, September 3, 2008, at 8:15:14 a.m. EDT

As you can see, London is currently one hour ahead of UTC, whereas New York is four hours behind. Therefore, London's time is five hours ahead of New York's.

Now, suppose a transaction comes in from your New York branch to your London office. The timestamp data will be stored in a column defined with the TIMESTAMP WITH LOCAL TIME ZONE datatype. Before storing the data, Oracle synchronizes the time by adding five hours to the timestamp value and drops the time-zone element.

In Exercise 13.2, you'll see the functionality of the TIMESTAMP WITH LOCAL TIME ZONE datatype.

EXERCISE 13.2

Using TIMESTAMP WITH LOCAL TIME ZONE

To demonstrate the functionality of the TIMESTAMP WITH LOCAL TIME ZONE datatype, perform the following steps:

1. Create table `timezone_test` with two columns: x as TIMESTAMP and y as TIMESTAMP WITH LOCAL TIME ZONE. Set your server time zone to UTC –5:

```
SQL> create table timezone_test (x timestamp,
y timestamp with local time zone);
Table created.
```

2. Alter the session time zone to 5 hours behind UTC, and then insert sysdate into both columns in the `timezone_test` table.

```
SQL> ALTER SESSION SET TIME_ZONE = '-5:00';
SQL> insert into timezone_test values (sysdate, sysdate);
1 row created.
```

EXERCISE 13.2 *(continued)*

3. Insert the client time into both columns using the `current_timestamp` function, and query the results:

```
SQL> insert into timezone_test values (current_timestamp,
current_timestamp);
1 row created.
SQL> select * from timezone_test;
X                              Y
------------------------------ ------------------------------
11-NOV-08 07.25.31.000000 PM   11-NOV-08 07.25.31.000000 PM
11-NOV-08 07.25.36.897000 PM   11-NOV-08 07.25.36.897000 PM
SQL>
```

4. Modify your local time zone to UTC –7, and repeat step 3:

```
SQL> ALTER SESSION SET TIME_ZONE = '-7:00';
SQL> insert into timezone_test values (current_timestamp,
current_timestamp);
1 row created.
SQL> select * from timezone_test;
X                              Y
------------------------------ ------------------------------
11-NOV-08 07.25.31.000000 PM   11-NOV-08 05.25.31.000000 PM
11-NOV-08 07.25.36.897000 PM   11-NOV-08 05.25.36.897000 PM
11-NOV-08 05.31.35.104000 PM   11-NOV-08 05.31.35.104000 PM
```

5. Modify your local time zone to UTC –5, and query the `timezone_test` table:

```
SQL> ALTER SESSION SET TIME_ZONE = '-5:00';
SQL> select * from timezone_test;
X                              Y
------------------------------ ------------------------------
11-NOV-08 07.25.31.000000 PM   11-NOV-08 07.25.31.000000 PM
11-NOV-08 07.25.36.897000 PM   11-NOV-08 07.25.36.897000 PM
11-NOV-08 05.31.35.104000 PM   11-NOV-08 07.31.35.104000 PM
```

Note that column y, the TIMESTAMP WITH TIMEZONE column, shows the corrected time based on the local time zone because the time-zone data was retained. Note that column x does not retain the time-zone data and is not corrected if the time zone changes.

Using Linguistic Sorts and Searches

Different languages follow different rules when it comes to sorting text. Unfortunately, that means that there is no "one-size-fits-all" algorithm that can be used. Instead, Oracle's global support functionality allows not only binary sorting methods but also linguistic sorting and searching methodologies to provide the flexibility to support the needs of many languages.

In the following sections, you will learn the methods that Oracle uses when it performs text-sorting operations. You will also learn about the different NLS parameters that impact linguistic sorting and searching. Next, you will learn about the different types of linguistic sorts supported by Oracle. Last, you will learn about linguistic text searches.

An Overview of Text Sorting

There are many ways in which text sorting can be accomplished. Sort order can be case sensitive or case can be ignored. *Diacritics* (accent marks) can be considered or ignored. Sorting can be done phonetically or based on the appearance of the character.

Some languages even consider groupings of characters to have a specific sort order. For example, traditional Spanish treats *ch* as a character that sorts after the letter C. Therefore, when sorting the words *cat*, *dog*, *cow*, and *chinchilla*, the correct sort sequence would be *cat*, *cow*, *chinchilla*, and *dog*.

To support these different sorting methods, Oracle offers two basic categories of sorting: binary and linguistic.

Binary Sorts

Binary sorts are the fastest and most efficient sorting method offered by Oracle. However, they are also the most limited. Binary sorts perform a numeric sort based on the encoded value (in the character set) for each character. As long as the character set encodes all of the characters in the proper sort order, this method works very well. The performance is also exceptional.

For example, in the US7ASCII character set, alphabetical characters are encoded as shown in Table 13.4. Note that this is just a subset of the character set.

TABLE 13.4 US7ASCII Alphabetical Characters

Char	Value	Char	Value	Char	Value	Char	Value
A	65	N	78	a	97	n	110
B	66	O	79	b	98	o	111
C	67	P	80	c	99	p	112

TABLE 13.4 US7ASCII Alphabetical Characters *(continued)*

Char	Value	Char	Value	Char	Value	Char	Value
D	68	Q	81	d	100	q	113
E	69	R	82	e	101	r	114
F	70	S	83	f	102	s	115
G	71	T	84	g	103	t	116
H	72	U	85	h	104	u	117
I	73	V	86	i	105	v	118
J	74	W	87	j	106	w	119
K	75	X	88	k	107	x	120
L	76	Y	89	l	108	y	121
M	77	Z	90	m	109	z	122

Because the encoded values ascend in correlation with the characters, a binary sort will always perform a proper alphabetical sort. In addition, uppercase characters will always sort higher than lowercase characters.

However, different languages may share the same alphabet (and therefore, the same character set) yet utilize a sort order that deviates from the encoding order of the character set. In this situation, binary sorting will fail to produce an acceptable result.

Binary sorting is Oracle's default sorting method.

Linguistic Sorts

Linguistic sorts, unlike binary sorts, operate independently of the underlying encoded values. Instead, they allow character data to be sorted based on the rules of specific languages. Linguistic sorts offer the flexibility to deal with the caveats imposed by different languages.

Oracle provides a rich set of linguistic sort definitions that cover most of the languages of the world. However, it also provides the ability to define new definitions or to modify existing definitions. The Oracle Locale Builder, a graphical tool that ships with Oracle 11*g*, can be used to view, create, and modify sort definitions and other locale definitions. However, as mentioned earlier, Locale Builder is not covered in this book.

Linguistic sorts are defined using a variety of rules that govern the sorting process. The following elements are available and can be used to create a comprehensive linguistic sort:

Base letters Base letters are the individual letters upon which other characters are based. The derived characters would map back to the base letter to determine the sorting value. For example, the character *A* is a base letter, while *À*, *Á*, *Ã*, *Ä*, *a*, *à*, *á*, and *ä* would all map to *A* as a base letter.

Ignorable characters Ignorable characters, just as the name implies, can be defined as having no effect on sort order. Diacritics, such as the umlaut, can be classified as ignorable, as can certain punctuation characters, such as the hyphen. Therefore, a word such as *e-mail* would be sorted the same as *email*.

Contracting characters Contracting characters represent two or more characters that are treated linguistically as a single character. An example—the traditional Spanish *ch* string—was explained earlier in this section. Contracting characters require flexibility in the sorting algorithm to read ahead to the next character to determine if a contracting character has been found.

Expanding characters With some locales, repeating or commonly occurring strings of characters are compressed into a single character for brevity's sake. However, the character needs to sort as if all characters are present. These are referred to as expanding characters.

For example, the *ö* character should be treated as the string *oe* for sorting purposes.

Context-sensitive characters With certain languages, characters are sorted differently based upon their relationship to other characters. These are generally characters that modify the preceding character. For example, a Japanese length mark is sorted according to the vowel that precedes it.

Canonical equivalence When a Unicode character set is used, the character *ö* and the string *o¨* can be considered equal from a sorting perspective. This is because the code points of the two-character string match the code point of the individual character. The two are said to have canonical equivalence.

In situations of canonical equivalence, the value of the `CANONICAL_EQUIVALENCE` linguistic flag (with a value of `TRUE` or `FALSE`) determines whether the rules of canonical equivalence should be followed.

Reverse secondary sorting In some languages, strings containing diacritics will be sorted from left to right on the base characters and then from right to left on the diacritics. This is referred to as reverse secondary sorting. For example, resumé would sort before résume because of the position of the diacritic from left to right.

The `REVERSE_SECONDARY=TRUE` linguistic flag enables this functionality.

Character rearrangement In certain languages (notably Thai and Laotian dialects), sorting rules declare that certain characters should switch places with the following character before sorting. This generally happens when a consonant is preceded by a vowel sound. In this case, the consonant is given priority, forcing the characters to be switched before the sort begins.

The SWAP_WITH_NEXT linguistic flag can determine whether character rearrangement will occur within a sort definition.

Don't confuse linguistic flags with Oracle parameter settings. Linguistic flags are defined for specific sort-order definitions when they are created.

These different sorting methods represent the toolset available to sort and search text. Different languages may use one or more of the linguistic methods listed here. But as long as the rules of a language can be described using these methods, Oracle is able to perform linguistic sorts, either through an existing sort definition or through a custom sort definition.

Using Linguistic Sort Parameters

Linguistic sorts are generally applicable to a specific language or to a specific character set. And, as mentioned previously, there are many predefined linguistic sort definitions that may be utilized. Therefore, it is unlikely that you would ever need to define your own.

You can instruct Oracle to utilize specific linguistic sorts by setting the appropriate NLS sort parameters. In this section, you will learn about the NLS_SORT and NLS_COMP parameters and how they affect linguistic sorting operations.

NLS_SORT

The NLS_SORT parameter defines which type of sorting—binary or linguistic—should be performed for SQL sort operations. By default, the value for NLS_SORT is the default sort method defined for the language identified in the NLS_LANGUAGE parameter. For example, if the NLS_LANGUAGE parameter is set to AMERICAN, the default value for the NLS_SORT parameter will be BINARY.

To instruct Oracle to use linguistic sorting, this parameter can be set to the name of any valid linguistic sort definition, as shown here:

```
SQL> alter session set NLS_SORT = German;
Session altered.
```

A list of valid sort definition names is shown here. You could also query the V$NLS_VALID_VALUES view (as shown earlier in this chapter).

ARABIC	GERMAN	SWISS
ARABIC_ABJ_MATCH	GERMAN_DIN	TCHINESE_RADICAL_M
ARABIC_ABJ_SORT	GREEK	TCHINESE_STROKE_M
ARABIC_MATCH	HEBREW	THAI_DICTIONARY
ASCII7	HKSCS	THAI_M

AZERBAIJANI
BENGALI
BIG5
BINARY
BULGARIAN
CANADIAN FRENCH
CANADIAN_M
CATALAN
CROATIAN
CZECH
CZECH_PUNCTUATION
DANISH
DANISH_M
DUTCH
EBCDIC
EEC_EURO
EEC_EUROPA3
ESTONIAN
FINNISH
FRENCH
FRENCH_M
GBK
GENERIC_BASELETTER
GENERIC_M
HUNGARIAN
ICELANDIC
INDONESIAN
ITALIAN
JAPANESE
JAPANESE_M
KOREAN_M
LATIN
LATVIAN
LITHUANIAN
MALAY
NORWEGIAN
POLISH
PUNCTUATION
ROMANIAN
RUSSIAN
SCHINESE_PINYIN_M
SCHINESE_RADICAL_M
SCHINESE_STROKE_M
SLOVAK
SLOVENIAN
SPANISH
SPANISH_M
SWEDISH
THAI_TELEPHONE
TURKISH
UKRAINIAN
UNICODE_BINARY
VIETNAMESE
WEST_EUROPEAN
XAZERBAIJANI
XCATALAN
XCROATIAN
XCZECH
XCZECH_PUNCTUATION
XDANISH
XDUTCH
XFRENCH
XGERMAN
XGERMAN_DIN
XHUNGARIAN
XPUNCTUATION
XSLOVAK
XSLOVENIAN
XSPANISH
XSWISS
XTURKISH
XWEST_EUROPEAN

By using the NLS_SORT parameter, you can make the following changes to Oracle's default functionality:

- Set the default sort method for all ORDER BY operations.
- Set the default sort value for the NLSSORT function.

It is important to note that not all SQL functionality supports linguistic sorting. Certain functions support only binary sorts. However, most of the commonly used methods are supported. Also, all NLS-specific SQL functions (for example, NLSSORT) will support linguistic sorts.

The methods listed here support linguistic sorting:

- ORDER BY
- BETWEEN
- CASE WHEN
- HAVING
- IN/OUT
- START WITH
- WHERE

By default, all of these operations will perform binary sorts. When you set the NLS_SORT parameter, SQL statements using the WHERE operation will perform linguistic sorts by default.

The following example demonstrates the use of the NLS_SORT parameter. Initially, you can see that your session has no value set for NLS_SORT. Therefore, it will inherit the default setting from the NLS_LANGUAGE parameter (BINARY).

```
SQL> show parameters NLS_LANGUAGE

NAME                                 TYPE        VALUE
------------------------------------ ----------- ----------
nls_language                         string      AMERICAN

SQL> show parameters NLS_SORT

NAME                                 TYPE        VALUE
------------------------------------ ----------- ----------
nls_sort                             string
```

As you learned earlier, the default sort for the language AMERICAN is BINARY. The default setting for NLS_COMP is BINARY as well. Therefore, you can expect that, by default, Oracle will perform a binary sort unless otherwise specified, as shown here:

```
SQL> select * from sort_test
  order by name;

NAME
--------------------------------
Finsteraarhornhutte
Grünhornlücke
einschließlich
```

```
finsteraarhornhütte
grünhornlücke

5 rows selected.
```

As expected, Oracle sorted the rows based on the encoded value of the characters in the US7ASCII character set. Therefore, all uppercase characters sort before lowercase characters.

Because the words in this table are of German origin, it is logical that you might want to sort them using a German sorting method. To change the sorting method for a GROUP BY clause, the NLS_SORT parameter can be set as shown here:

```
SQL> alter session set NLS_SORT=German_din;

Session altered.

SQL> select * from sort_test
  order by name;

NAME
-------------------------------------------
einschließlich
Finsteraarhornhutte
finsteraarhornhütte
Grünhornlücke
grünhornlücke

5 rows selected.
```

As you can see, setting the NLS_SORT parameter changed the default sorting method to a linguistic sort instead of a binary sort.

In the next step, another query is executed, this time using a WHERE condition rather than an ORDER BY clause:

```
SQL> select * from sort_test
  2  where name > 'einschließlich';

NAME
---------------------------------------
finsteraarhornhütte
grünhornlücke

2 rows selected.
```

The result of this query might not be what you expect. Instead of the expected four rows (which a linguistic sort would have returned), only two rows are returned, indicating that a binary sort took place instead.

Remember, the NLS_SORT parameter overrides the default sorting method for ORDER BY operations and for the NLSSORT function, but it has no effect on other sort operations, such as WHERE conditions. Therefore, this query ignored the parameter entirely.

To perform a linguistic sort, you call the NLSSORT function. Normally, the function would be called like this:

```
SQL> select * from sort_test
  where nlssort(name, 'NLS_SORT=German_din') >
  nlssort('einschließlich','NLS_SORT=German_din');

NAME
--------------------------------------------------
Finsteraarhornhutte
finsteraarhornhütte
Grünhornlücke
grünhornlücke

4 rows selected.
```

However, because the NLS_SORT parameter defines the default sort for the NLSSORT function, specifying the sort inside the function is unnecessary. The following method works as well:

```
SQL> select * from sort_test
  where nlssort(name) > nlssort('einschließlich');

NAME
--------------------------------------------------
Finsteraarhornhutte
finsteraarhornhütte
Grünhornlücke
grünhornlücke

4 rows selected.
```

As you can see, in both queries the sort was performed linguistically and returned the expected rows.

The NLS_SORT parameter is very limited in relation to linguistic sorting. The NLS_COMP parameter, on the other hand, makes linguistic sorting much easier.

NLS_COMP

The NLS_COMP parameter works in conjunction with the NLS_SORT parameter to make linguistic sorts easier to use. When the NLS_COMP parameter is set to a value of ANSI, all of the following SQL operations will default to linguistic sorting (using the language specified in NLS_SORT parameter):

- ORDER BY
- BETWEEN
- CASE WHEN
- HAVING
- IN/OUT
- START WITH
- WHERE

Setting the NLS_COMP parameter makes it unnecessary to call the NLSSORT function when using these sort operations. As you can guess, this makes linguistic sorting much easier to perform.

The NLS_COMP parameter can be set to either BINARY (the default) or ANSI.

The following example shows the usage of the NLS_COMP parameter:

```
SQL> alter session set NLS_SORT=German_din;

Session altered.

SQL> alter session set NLS_COMP=ANSI;

Session altered.

SQL> select * from sort_test
  2  where name > 'einschließlich';

NAME
----------------------------------------
Finsteraarhornhutte
finsteraarhornhütte
Grünhornlücke
grünhornlücke

4 rows selected.
```

As you can see, the query performed the linguistic sort and returned the expected results, even without using the NLSSORT function.

If the NLS_COMP parameter is set back to BINARY, binary sorting occurs once again:

```
SQL> alter session set NLS_COMP=BINARY;

Session altered.

SQL> select * from sort_test
  2  where name > 'einschließlich';

NAME
----------------------------------------
finsteraarhornhütte
grünhornlücke

2 rows selected.
```

Linguistic Sort Types

When performing linguistic sorts, Oracle uses different methodologies, depending upon the number of languages involved in the sort. If character data in only one language is being sorted, this is classified as a monolingual linguistic sort. If more than one language is involved in the sort, it is classified as a multilingual linguistic sort.

In the following sections, you will learn the methodology that Oracle implements in performing both monolingual and multilingual linguistic sorts. You will also learn about accent-insensitive and case-insensitive linguistic sorts.

Monolingual Linguistic Sorts

When dealing with only a single language inside a sort, Oracle performs a two-step process to compare character strings. First, the major value of the strings is compared. Next, if necessary, the minor value of the strings is compared.

Major and minor values are sort values assigned to letters in the character set. A base letter and those derived from it will generally share a common major value, but they will have different minor values based on the desired sort order.

Here's an example:

Letter	Major Value	Minor Value
A	30	10
A	30	20
Ä	30	30
Ä	30	40
B	40	10

The example shows that all four variations of the letter *A* have identical major values, but differing minor values. When two letters share a major value, the minor value will determine the sort order.

The major-value numbers are assigned to a *Unicode code point* (a 16-bit binary value that defines a character in a Unicode character set).

Multilingual Linguistic Sorts

Multilingual sorts offer the ability to sort mixed languges within the same sort. For example, if you have a table that stores names in both English and Spanish, a multilingual sort should be used.

Multilingual sorts perform three levels of evaluation: primary, secondary, and tertiary.

Primary sorts assign a primary sort value based on the base letter of each character (diacritics and case are ignored). If a character is defined as ignorable, it is assigned a primary value of zero.

Secondary-level sorts consider diacritics to differentiate accented letters from base letters in assigning a secondary sort level. For example, *A* and *ä* share the same base letter, so they have the same primary sort level but they will have different secondary levels.

Tertiary-level sorts consider character case to differentiate uppercase and lowercase letters. Tertiary sorts also handle special characters such as *, +, and -.

Consider the following words:

Fahrvergnügen

Fahrvergnugen

farhrvergnugen

fahrvergnügen

Because all of these words share the same base letters in the same order, all of them would be considered equivalent at the primary sort level. After a secondary-level sort, they would be ordered similarly to the following list:

Fahrvergnugen

farhrvergnugen

Fahrvergnügen

fahrvergnügen

The secondary-level sort is concerned only with diacritics, so it will sort characters without diacritics above those with diacritics. After that, the words are displayed in their primary sort order. Because the words in this example have identical primary sort orders, there is no guarantee which word will appear before the other. The only guarantee is that those with diacritics will sort after those without.

After the tertiary-level sort is performed, the list should look exactly like this:

farhrvergnugen

Fahrvergnugen

fahrvergnügen

Fahrvergnügen

The tertiary-level sort applies the case rule to the data, forcing lowercase letters to sort before uppercase letters. This is the final result of the sort after applying all three multilingual sorting levels.

In keeping with the ISO 14651 standard for multilingual sorting, Oracle appends an _M to the sort name to identify it as multilingual. For example, FRENCH_M identifies a French multilingual sort, whereas FRENCH identifies a French monolingual sort. Table 13.5 shows the multilingual sorts predefined in Oracle 11g.

TABLE 13.5 Multilingual Sorts Available in Oracle 11g

Multilingual Sort Name	Description
CANADIAN_M	Canadian French
DANISH_M	Danish
FRENCH_M	French
GENERIC_M	Generic based on ISO 14651
JAPANESE_M	Japanese
KOREAN_M	Korean
SPANISH_M	Traditional Spanish
THAI_M	Thai
SCHINESE_RADICAL_M	Simplified Chinese
SCHINESE_STROKE_M	Simplified Chinese
SCHINESE_PINYIN_M	Simplified Chinese
TCHINESE_RADICAL_M	Traditional Chinese
TCHINESE_STROKE_M	Traditional Chinese

Case-Insensitive and Accent-Insensitive Linguistic Sorts

Oracle, by default, will always consider both the case of the characters and any diacritics when performing sort operations. As you've seen in previous examples, linguistic sorts have rules to govern precedence between uppercase and lowercase words, as well as those words containing diacritics.

However, you may wish to override this functionality from time to time and choose to ignore case and/or diacritics. Oracle 11*g* offers case-insensitive and accent-insensitive sorting options to allow for these cases.

To specify case-insensitive or accent-insensitive sorts, the NLS_SORT parameter is used, but with the following changes:

- For a case-insensitive linguistic sort, append the string _CI to the sort name.
- For an accent-insensitive linguistic sort, append the string _AI to the sort name.

Accent-insensitive sorts are also case insensitive by default.

For example, to specify a French, multilingual, accent-insensitive sort, use the following:

```
NLS_SORT = French_M_AI
```

Here is how to specify a German, monolingual, case-insensitive sort:

```
NLS_SORT = German_CI
```

Case-Insensitive and Accent-Insensitive Binary Sorts

Binary sorts can also be designated as case insensitive or accent insensitive. The NLS_SORT parameter can be set to BINARY_CI or BINARY_AI. Table 13.6 shows how the sort will be affected by these settings.

TABLE 13.6 Binary Case and Accent-Insensitive Sort Options

Sort Name	Sort Type	Case Insensitive?	Accent Insensitive?
BINARY_CI	Binary	Yes	No
BINARY_AI	Binary	Yes	Yes

As you can see, using the BINARY_AI sort will result in both an accent-insensitive and case-insensitive sort.

Searching Linguistic Strings

Linguistic searches are closely related to linguistic sorts and are directly affected by the NLS_SORT setting. To accomplish linguistically meaningful searches, Oracle must apply the same rules it applies for linguistic sorts.

Earlier in this section, you saw several examples of linguistic string searching, including the following:

```
SQL> select * from sort_test
  2  where name > 'einschließlich';

NAME
----------------------------------------
Finsteraarhornhutte
finsteraarhornhütte
Grünhornlücke
grünhornlücke

4 rows selected.
```

When you set the NLS_COMP parameter to ANSI and the NLS_SORT parameter to the desired sort language, the WHERE operator (as well as several others) will perform linguistic searching by default.

And, just as you did with sorts, if the NLS_SORT is set to ignore case or accents, linguistic searches will follow suit, as in this example:

```
SQL> alter session set NLS_COMP=ANSI;

Session altered.
SQL> alter session set NLS_SORT=German_din_ci;

Session altered.

SQL> select * from sort_test
  2  where name = 'Grünhornlücke';

NAME
----------------------------------------
Grünhornlücke
grünhornlücke
```

As you can see, the search ignored the case and returned both rows that matched. This is the expected functionality of the case-insensitive search.

In the next example, the NLS_SORT parameter will be set to define an accent-insensitive search:

```
SQL> alter session set NLS_SORT=German_din_ai;

Session altered.
```

```
SQL> select * from sort_test
  where name = 'Finsteraarhornhutte';

NAME
-----------------------------------------------
Finsteraarhornhutte
finsteraarhornhütte
```

When the NLS_SORT parameter defined an accent-insensitive search, both accents and case were ignored. This is the expected functionality for accent-insensitive searches.

Summary

In this chapter, you learned about Oracle's global support functionality and how it simplifies the issues related to multilingual databases. You learned about the internal architecture that makes globalization support possible. You saw how the NLS Runtime Library (NLSRTL) integrates with the Oracle locale definition files to provide functionality. You also learned that the modular nature of the locale definition files provides great flexibility while reducing memory usage.

You learned about the main components of globalization support: language, territory, character set, and linguistic sorts. You saw how these four components provide default settings for all the other NLS options. You then learned that those default settings can be overridden with a variety of methods.

We introduced you to the many character sets that Oracle supports, including the important Unicode character set. You saw how the Unicode character set can support all known written languages in the world.

You also learned about using NLS parameters to modify your globalization environment as needed. You learned about the different categories of NLS parameters, including language and territory parameters, date and time parameters, linguistic sort parameters, calendar parameters, and more.

This chapter introduced you to the datetime datatypes and explained how the TIMESTAMP WITH TIME ZONE and TIMESTAMP WITH LOCAL TIME ZONE datatypes can be used to synchronize transactions occurring across time zones.

Last, you learned about linguistic sorting and searching and how globalization support allows culturally appropriate sorting and searching. You also learned about monolingual and multilingual sorts and how each evaluates text strings when performing a sort operation. You learned that multilingual sorts can be identified by the _M appended to the sort definition name.

You learned how, in conjunction with linguistic sorting and searching, you can perform case-insensitive and accent-insensitive operations by appending _CI or _AI to the end of the NLS_SORT parameter value.

Exam Essentials

Be able to customize language-dependent behavior for the database and individual sessions. Be aware of the different NLS parameters and the different ways that they can be set (initialization parameters, environment variables, the `ALTER SESSION` statement). Know the order of precedence for NLS parameter settings. Know which parameters apply only to the client or the server.

Know how to specify different linguistic sorts for queries. Understand the mechanisms for producing linguistic sorts versus binary sorts. Know how to specify both case-insensitive and accent-insensitive linguistic sorts. Know how to differentiate between multilingual and monolingual sort definitions.

Understand how to use datetime datatypes. Understand the purpose of datetime datatypes. Know the different datetimes covered in this chapter: DATE, TIMESTAMP, TIMESTAMP WITH TIME ZONE, and TIMESTAMP WITH LOCAL TIME ZONE. Understand the differences between the various datetime datatypes and how they relate to globalization.

Know how to query data using case-insensitive and accent-insensitive searches. Know the syntax for specifying case-insensitive and accent-insensitive operations. Understand which SQL operations support linguistic operations. Know which NLS parameters control case-insensitive and accent-insensitive searching.

Understand how to obtain globalization support configuration information. Know the views available to see globalization information: `NLS_SESSION_PARAMETERS`, `NLS_INSTANCE_PARAMETERS`, `NLS_DATABASE_PARAMETERS`, and `V$NLS_VALID_VALUES`. Understand the information returned by each of these views.

Understand globalization support architecture. Know the purpose of the NLSRTL. Understand the location, purpose, and file-naming conventions of locale definition files. Know the four types of locale definition files: language, territory, character set, and linguistic sort.

Review Questions

1. Globalization support is implemented through the text- and character-processing functions provided by which Oracle feature?
   A. RSTLNE
   B. NLSRTL
   C. LISTENER
   D. NLSSORT
   E. Linguistic sorts
2. What elements of globalization can be explicitly defined using the NLS_LANG environment variable? (Choose all that apply.)
   A. NLS_LANGUAGE
   B. NLS_SORT
   C. NLS_CALENDAR
   D. NLS_CHARACTERSET
   E. NLS_TERRITORY
3. Given two different character sets (*A* and *B*), which of the following must be true for *A* to be considered a strict superset of *B*? (Choose all that apply.)
   A. *A* must contain all of the characters defined in *B*.
   B. *A* must be Unicode.
   C. The encoded values in *A* must match the encoded values in *B* for all characters defined in *B*.
   D. *A* must be a multibyte character set.
   E. The encoded values in *A* must match the encoded values in *B* for all numeric and alphabetic characters in *B*.
4. The NLS_SORT parameter sets the default sort method for which of the following operations? (Choose all that apply.)
   A. WHERE clause
   B. ORDER BY clause
   C. BETWEEN clause
   D. NLSSORT function
   E. NLS_SORT function
5. Which view shows all valid values for the NLS_LANGUAGE, NLS_SORT, NLS_TERRITORY, and NLS_CHARACTERSET parameters?
   A. V$VALID_NLS_VALUES
   B. NLS_VALID_VALUES
   C. NLS_VALUE_OPTIONS
   D. V$NLS_VALUE_OPTIONS
   E. V$NLS_VALID_VALUES

6. Which of the following datatypes store time-zone information in the database?
   A. TIMESTAMP
   B. DATE
   C. TIMESTAMP WITH TIME ZONE
   D. TIMESTAMP WITH LOCAL TIME ZONE
   E. DATETIME

7. Which of the following are valid settings for the `NLS_COMP` parameter? (Choose all that apply.)
   A. `ASCII`
   B. `ANSI`
   C. `BINARY`
   D. `MONOLINGUAL`
   E. `MULTILINGUAL`

8. NLS parameters can be set using the five methods listed. Put the methods in order from highest to lowest according to Oracle's order of precedence:
   a. Default setting
   b. Client environment variable
   c. Explicit `ALTER SESSION` statement
   d. Inside SQL function
   e. Server initialization parameter
   A. b, d, e, a, c
   B. e, a, b, c, d
   C. d, c, b, e, a
   D. a, b, d, c, e
   E. d, c, b, a, e

9. What can you determine about the following linguistic sorts based only on their names?
   1. `GERMAN`
   2. `FRENCH_M`
   A. 1 is a monolingual sort.
   B. 2 is a monolingual sort.
   C. 1 is case insensitive.
   D. Both 1 and 2 are case insensitive.
   E. Case sensitivity is unknown.

10. In a database with the database character set of US7ASCII and a national character set of UTF-8, which datatypes would be capable of storing Unicode data by default?
    A. VARCHAR2
    B. CHAR
    C. NVARCHAR2
    D. CLOB
    E. LONG

11. Automatic data conversion will occur if which of the following happens?
    A. The client and server have different NLS_LANGUAGE settings.
    B. The client and server character sets are not the same, and the database character set is not a strict superset of the client character set.
    C. The client and server are in different time zones.
    D. The client requests automatic data conversion.
    E. The AUTO_CONVERT initialization parameter is set to TRUE.

12. Which of the following NLS_SORT parameter values would result in case-insensitive and accent-insensitive binary sorts?
    A. NLS_SORT = BINARY
    B. NLS_SORT = BINARY_AI
    C. NLS_SORT = BINARY_CI
    D. NLS_SORT = BINARY_AI_CI
    E. Binary sorts are case insensitive and accent insensitive by default.

13. Which NLS parameter can be used to change the default Oracle sort method from binary to linguistic for the SQL SELECT statement?
    A. NLS_LANG
    B. NLS_SORT
    C. NLS_COMP
    D. NLS_SORT
    E. None of the above

14. Which of the following would be affected by setting NLS_LENGTH_SEMANTICS=CHAR?
    A. All objects in the database
    B. Tables owned by SYS and SYSTEM
    C. Data dictionary tables
    D. NCHAR columns
    E. CHAR columns

15. Which is not a valid locale definition file type?

A. Language

B. Linguistic sort

C. Calendar

D. Territory

E. Character set

16. How many different calendars does Oracle 11*g* support?

A. 22

B. 7

C. 6

D. 15

E. 2

17. Which NLS parameter directly governs linguistic searches?

A. `NLS_SEARCH_L`

B. `NLS_SORT`

C. `NLS_SEARCH`

D. `NLS_SORT_L`

E. None of the above

18. True or false? Case-insensitive sorts are always accent insensitive by default.

A. True

B. False

19. What is the name of the file that identifies the set of available locale definitions?

A. `locale.def`

B. `lxdef.ora`

C. `lx1boot.nlb`

D. `lx1boot.ora`

E. `lang.def`

20. Which of the following is not a valid linguistic sort element?

A. Accent expansion

B. Canonical equivalence

C. Reverse secondary sorting

D. Ignorable characters

E. Character rearrangement

Answers to Review Questions

1. B. The NLS Runtime Library (NLSRTL) provides the language-independent text- and character-processing functionality for Oracle.

2. A, D, E. The client-side NLS_LANG parameter can define language, territory, and character set all at once. Though the value for NLS_SORT is derived from the NLS_LANGUAGE parameter setting, it is not *explicitly* set by NLS_LANG. NLS_CALENDAR is not affected by the setting of NLS_LANG.

3. A, C. A strict superset must contain all characters found in the other character set and have matching encoded values for those characters.

4. A, D. The NLS_SORT parameter defines the default sort method (binary or linguistic) for both SQL WHERE clause operations and NLSSORT function operations. The default sort method for ORDER BY and BETWEEN (and all other SQL operations that support linguistic sorts) is defined by the NLS_COMP parameter. NLS_SORT is an invalid function name.

5. E. The V$NLS_VALID_VALUES view shows the names of all language, territory, sort, and character-set definitions that are available in the database.

6. C. Only the TIMESTAMP WITH TIME ZONE datatype actually stores time-zone information in the database. The TIMESTAMP WITH LOCAL TIME ZONE datatype converts the timestamp to local time and drops the time-zone information before storing it in the database. DATE and TIMESTAMP datatypes do not deal with time-zone information at all. DATETIME is not a valid datatype.

7. B, C. The NLS_COMP parameter can be set to BINARY or ANSI. This parameter determines the default sort type for certain SQL functions. (A setting of ANSI specifies that linguistic sorts should be used.)

8. C. NLS settings embedded in a SQL function have the highest precedence, followed by explicit ALTER SESSION statements, client environment variables (which execute an implicit ALTER SESSION statement), server-initialization parameters, and finally default settings.

9. A. A is the only true statement. An _M appended to the end of a sort name denotes a multilingual sort. Its absence denotes a monolingual sort. Case-sensitive and accent-insensitive sorts have _CI or _AI appended to the name. Its absence denotes case sensitivity and accent sensitivity.

10. C. NLS datatypes (NCHAR, NVARCHAR, and NCLOB) store data using the character set defined as the national character set by default. Because the national character set is UTF-8 (a Unicode character set), data stored in these datatypes will be Unicode data by default. All other datatypes use the character set defined as the database character set. Because US7ASCII is not a Unicode character set, it does not store Unicode data by default.

11. B. Automatic data conversion occurs when data is moved between character sets. However, if the server character set is a strict superset of the client character set, no conversion is necessary.

12. B. The _AI suffix implies that an accent-insensitive sort will be performed. Accent-insensitive sorts are also case insensitive by default. The _CI suffix implies that a case-insensitive sort will be performed, but it will not be accent insensitive. Specifying both suffixes (_AI_CI) is illegal.

13. E. The SQL SELECT statement does not invoke a sort.

14. E. Only option E is correct. Tables owned by the SYS and SYSTEM users are not affected by default-length semantics. Data dictionary tables always use byte semantics, and NCHAR columns always use character semantics. Therefore, neither is affected by the setting of the NLS_LENGTH_SEMANTICS parameter.

15. C. Calendar definitions are not stored as locale definition files. Only languages, linguistic sorts, territories, and character set definitions are stored as locale definition files.

16. B. Oracle supports seven distinct calendars: Gregorian, Japanese Imperial, ROC Official, Persian, Thai Buddha, Arabic Hijrah, and English Hijrah.

17. B. Linguistic searches are closely related to linguistic sorts and are governed by the NLS_SORT parameter.

18. B. Accent-insensitive sorts are always case insensitive, not the other way around.

19. C. The lx1boot.nlb file identifies the available locale definitions to the NLSRTL.

20. A. Linguistic sort elements define the rules for linguistic sorting. There is no linguistic sort element named "accent expansion." The other choices are all valid rules.

Appendix A

Lab Exercises

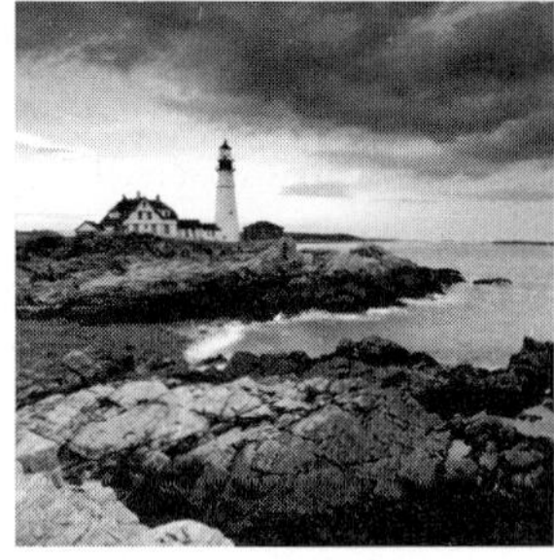

This appendix contains lab exercises for each chapter so that you can practice your skills before the exam.

Lab 1.1: Creating an ASM Instance

This lab was created using Windows XP. However, it should also work using Unix (and in fact was tested using Linux). We have taken certain liberties in this lab to make the use of Automatic Storage Management (ASM) as easy as possible. We will note them as the lab proceeds. Where there is a difference between the use of Windows and Unix, we will note that difference and provide some guidance. The RMAN labs will be using ASM as the flash recovery area (FRA), so this lab and Lab 1.2 will be prerequisites to future labs.

To create your ASM instance, do the following:

1. Start the Oracle Database Configuration Assistant (DBCA). You should be familiar with this tool as it was covered as a part of your OCA studies.
2. Click though the Welcome page and select Configure Automatic Storage Management from the DBCA Operations page.
3. A window appears indicating that you need to install Oracle Cluster Synchronization Service (CSS) and that it needs to be running. The window will instruct you on how to install this service (running `localconfig reset`). Open a command-line window and run the command to configure CSS. Here is an example of the output from this command after a successful execution:

```
C:\>c:\oracle\product\11.1.0\db_1\bin\localconfig reset
Step 1:  stopping local CSS stack
Step 2:  deleting OCR repository
Step 3:  creating new OCR repository
Successfully accumulated necessary OCR keys.
Creating OCR keys for user 'robert', privgrp ''..
Operation successful.
Step 4:  creating new CSS service
successfully created local CSS service
successfully reset location of CSS setup
```

After configuring CSS, click OK in the DBCA pop-up window and then Next on the DBCA Operations page to continue.

4. You will be prompted for the SYS password in the DBCA. Enter the password you want to use for SYS. Click Next.
5. A pop-up window appears indicating that DBCA will create the ASM instance. Click OK to create the instance.
6. The DBCA ASM Disk Groups page appears. We will add disk groups to our ASM instance in the next lab, so simply click Finish to complete the ASM instance creation. A pop-up window appears asking if you want to perform another operation. Click the No button to exit DBCA.
7. Check to see whether you can connect to your ASM instance. In Windows, from a command line set your ORACLE_SID=+ASM and connect to the ASM instance, as shown here:

```
C:\Documents and Settings\Robert>sqlplus sys as sysasm
SQL*Plus: Release 11.1.0.6.0 - Production on Sun Aug 10 13:21:17 2008
Copyright (c) 1982, 2007, Oracle.  All rights reserved.
Enter password:
Connected to:
Oracle Database 11g Enterprise Edition Release 11.1.0.6.0 - Production
With the Partitioning, OLAP, Data Mining
and Real Application Testing options
SQL>
```

8. Shut down and then start up your ASM service with the shutdown command:

```
C:\Documents and Settings\Robert>sqlplus sys as sysasm
SQL*Plus: Release 11.1.0.6.0 - Production on Sun Aug 10 18:37:11 2008
Copyright (c) 1982, 2007, Oracle.  All rights reserved.
Enter password:
Connected to:
Oracle Database 11g Enterprise Edition Release 11.1.0.6.0 - Production
With the Partitioning, OLAP, Data Mining
and Real Application Testing options
SQL> shutdown immediate
ORA-15100: invalid or missing diskgroup name
ASM instance shutdown
SQL> startup
ASM instance started
Total System Global Area  535662592 bytes
Fixed Size                  1334380 bytes
Variable Size             509162388 bytes
ASM Cache                  25165824 bytes
ORA-15110: no diskgroups mounted
```

Lab 1.2: Creating ASM Disk Groups

In this lab, you will create two ASM disk groups that you will be able to use. Because of the wide variety of ways that disks might be presented, we will use a rather simplified way of creating ASM disk groups. While Oracle/ASM does not directly support creation of ASM disk groups on existing file systems, we can use a hidden parameter and some simple OS magic to get it to do so.

The method we will use in this lab is not supported by Oracle, so you should not use it in any kind of production install. Rather, refer to the Oracle documentation for the appropriate way of creating disk groups based on the disk setup that you have and your operating system. Don't worry if this method is not directly supported by Oracle from the point of view of the OCP exam. You will not be tested on using tools such as asmtool or asmtoolg (which you might use in an actual install) in your OCP exam.

This lab is still important, though. It will give you your first experiences managing an ASM instance. You will use ASM commands and query ASM views. As a result, the material within the lab itself is fully relevant to the OCP exam.

1. Ensure that your ASM service is running (on Windows) by running net start and look for the Oracle service called `OracleASMService+ASM`. If you are running Unix, from the command line use the `ps` command (`ps -ef|grep +ASM`) to determine if ASM is running. If ASM is not running, start up the ASM instance as shown in Lab 1.1, step 7.

2. If ASM is running, set the following parameter so that you can create disk groups. Note that the parameter we are setting called `_ASM_ALLOW_ONLY_RAW_DISKS` is not supported by Oracle. We are only using is in this lab to provide a consistent way of creating a disk group that can be used on all operating systems. Never do this in an actual production database.

```
Alter system set "_asm_allow_only_raw_disks"=false scope=spfile;
```

3. Restart your Oracle ASM instance so the parameter change will take effect:

```
SQL> startup force
ASM instance started
Total System Global Area  535662592 bytes
Fixed Size                  1334380 bytes
Variable Size             509162388 bytes
ASM Cache                  25165824 bytes
ORA-15110: no diskgroups mounted
```

4. Create a directory to hold the files you will be creating for ASM.

```
Mkdir c:\oracle\oradata\asmfiles
```

5. You now need to create three files that can attach to your ASM instance. These three files will simulate three disk devices that might appear if you had added a disk to your system. To create these files, you will need to use the Perl interpreter that comes with Oracle.

6. CD to your `ORACLE_HOME` directory where your Oracle software is installed.

7. Continue to the directory where `perl.exe` is located. This is typically `ORACLE_HOME\perl\5.8.3\bin\MSWin32-x86-multi-thread` in a Windows environment. You can quickly find the correct home on your operating system by using the `dir` command or the `ls` command and recursively finding `perl.exe`, as shown in this example:

```
C:\oracle\product\11.1.0\db_1>dir perl.exe /s
 Volume in drive C has no label.
 Volume Serial Number is 08DE-E1AB
 Directory of C:\oracle\product\11.1.0\db_1\perl\5.8.3\
bin\MSWin32-x86-multi-thread
11/15/2004  12:35 PM            16,384 perl.exe
               1 File(s)         16,384 bytes
```

8. Having found the `perl.exe` executable, you will need to run the following code through the interpreter three times, one time for each of the ASM files you will be using. Each ASM file in this example will be 1GB in size. Here is the code that you will execute:

```
my $s='0' x 2**20;
open(DF1,">C:/oracle/oradata/asm_disk/_file_disk1") ||
die "Cannot create file - $!\n";
open(DF2,">C:/oracle/oradata/asm_disk/_file_disk2") ||
die "Cannot create file - $!\n";
open(DF3,">C:/oracle/oradata/asm_disk/_file_disk3") ||
die "Cannot create file - $!\n";
for (my $i=1; $i<1000; $i++) {
  print DF1 $s;
  print DF2 $s;
  print DF3 $s;
}
exit
```

9. Save this code to a file called `create_files.pl` and execute this file with Perl, as shown here:

```
Perl create_files.pl
```

Having executed this Perl program, you have in essence created three virtual disks. At least, that's what they will look like to ASM.

10. Having created your three "disks," you are ready to create disk groups and associate them with your files. ASM will need to know where to find the files. You set the parameter ASM_DISKSTRING to indicate to ASM where it will find files associated with ASM. Here you set ASM_DISKSTRING to the appropriate location:

```
SQL>Alter system set ASM_DISKSTRING='c:\oracle\oradata\asmfiles\_file*';
```

11. Having set the ASM_DISKSTRING parameter, you should now be able to see the "fake" disk devices you just created by querying the V$ASM_DISK view, as shown in this example:

```
SQL> SELECT group_number "GROUP", disk_number "DISK", mount_status,
  2  header_status, state, path
  3  FROM    v$asm_disk;
GROUP DISK MOUNT_S HEADER_STATU STATE     PATH
----- ---- ------- ------------ -------- ---------------------------------
0        0 CLOSED  CANDIDATE    NORMAL   C:\ORACLE\ORADATA\ASMFILES\_FILE_DISK1
0        2 CLOSED  CANDIDATE    NORMAL   C:\ORACLE\ORADATA\ASMFILES\_FILE_DISK3
0        1 CLOSED  CANDIDATE    NORMAL   C:\ORACLE\ORADATA\ASMFILES\_FILE_DISK2
```

12. You can now create ASM disk groups. Notice that each disk group is listed as a CANDIDATE disk. This does not mean it's running for office, but rather that it can be used in the creation of a disk group. Let's create our first disk group!

    You will use the `create diskgroup` command from SQL*Plus to create two disk groups. You will call them dgroup1 and dgroup2. Dgroup1 will use two of the "disks." They will be mirrored copies of each other, providing redundancy. Dgroup2 will use external redundancy and just use one of the "disks." Here are the `create diskgroup` commands:

```
CREATE DISKGROUP dgroup1 NORMAL REDUNDANCY
failgroup diskcontrol1 DISK
'C:\ORACLE\ORADATA\ASMFILES\_FILE_DISK1' NAME file_disk1
failgroup diskcontrol2 DISK
'C:\ORACLE\ORADATA\ASMFILES\_FILE_DISK2' NAME file_disk2;
CREATE DISKGROUP dgroup2 EXTERNAL REDUNDANCY
DISK 'C:\ORACLE\ORADATA\ASMFILES\_FILE_DISK3' NAME file_disk3;
```

13. You should now be able to see the disk groups that you just created by querying the V$ASM_DISKGROUP view, as shown here.

```
SQL> select group_number, name from v$ASM_DISKGROUP;
GROUP_NUMBER NAME
------------ ------------------------------
           1 DGROUP1
           2 DGROUP2
```

14. Use show parameter to display the ASM_DISKGROUPS parameter to see that it has been updated with the new disk groups.

```
SQL> show parameter asm_diskgroups
NAME                                 TYPE        VALUE
------------------------------------ ----------- -----------------
asm_diskgroups                       string      DGROUP1, DGROUP2
```

In the next lab, you will actually create tablespaces using these disk groups!

Lab 1.3: Using ASM Disk Groups from a Database

This lab will walk you through the creation of a tablespace using ASM. This lab assumes you have a database called ORCL created, and that your ASM instance is up and running.

1. Make sure your ASM instance is up and running. Log into the ASM instance and ensure that its status is STARTED.

```
C:\set ORACLE_SID=+ASM
C:\>sqlplus sys as sysasm
SQL*Plus: Release 11.1.0.6.0 - Production on Mon Aug 11 20:43:28 2008
Copyright (c) 1982, 2007, Oracle.  All rights reserved.
Enter password:
Connected to:
Oracle Database 11g Enterprise Edition Release 11.1.0.6.0 - Production
With the Partitioning, OLAP, Data Mining
and Real Application Testing options
SQL> select status from v$instance;
STATUS
------------
STARTED
```

2. Using the V$ASM_DISKGROUP view, make sure you have sufficient space in your disk groups and that they are mounted.

```
SQL> select name, state, free_mb, total_mb
  2  from v$asm_diskgroup;
NAME                           STATE          FREE_MB   TOTAL_MB
------------------------------ ----------- ---------- ----------
DGROUP1                        MOUNTED           1896       1998
DGROUP2                        MOUNTED            949        999
```

3. Log into the ORCL database.

```
C:\>set oracle_sid=orcl
C:\>sqlplus sys as sysdba
SQL*Plus: Release 11.1.0.6.0 - Production on Mon Aug 11 20:50:06 2008
Copyright (c) 1982, 2007, Oracle.  All rights reserved.
Enter password:
Connected to:
Oracle Database 11g Enterprise Edition Release 11.1.0.6.0 - Production
With the Partitioning, OLAP, Data Mining
and Real Application Testing options
```

4. Create the first tablespace called ASM_TBS_ONE. We will use the ASM disk group DGROUP1 to store the underlying database datafile.

```
SQL> Create tablespace ASM_TBS_ONE Datafile '+DGROUP1' size 200m;
Tablespace created.
```

5. Once the tablespace is created, look at the filename information in DBA_DATA_FILES.

```
SQL> select file_name from dba_data_files
where tablespace_name='ASM_TBS_ONE';
FILE_NAME
------------------------------------------------------------------------
+DGROUP1/orcl/datafile/asm_tbs_one.256.662503917
```

Note the file-naming convention. When you used just the DGROUP1 in the CREATE TABLESPACE command, Oracle created a default directory structure and also a default file-naming convention.

6. Create the second tablespace ASM_TBS_TWO in DGROUP2. This time we will use our own directory structure and file-naming convention.

```
SQL> Create tablespace ASM_TBS_TWO
  2  Datafile '+DGROUP2/oradata/orcl/dbf/asm_tbs_two.dbf' size 200m;
Create tablespace ASM_TBS_TWO
*
ERROR at line 1:
ORA-01119: error in creating database file
'+DGROUP2/oradata/orcl/dbf/asm_tbs_two.dbf'
ORA-17502: ksfdcre:4 Failed to create file
+DGROUP2/oradata/orcl/dbf/asm_tbs_two.dbf
ORA-15173: entry 'oradata' does not exist in directory '/'
```

The error occurred because we did not create the underlying directory structure. We will need to do this from the ASM instance.

7. Connect to the ASM instance.

```
C:\set ORACLE_SID=+ASM
C:\>sqlplus sys as sysasm
SQL*Plus: Release 11.1.0.6.0 - Production on Mon Aug 11 20:43:28 2008
Copyright (c) 1982, 2007, Oracle.  All rights reserved.
Enter password:
Connected to:
Oracle Database 11g Enterprise Edition Release 11.1.0.6.0 - Production
With the Partitioning, OLAP, Data Mining
and Real Application Testing options
```

8. Using the ALTER DISKGROUP command, create the directory structure in DGROUP2.

```
SQL> Alter diskgroup dgroup2
  2  Add directory '+DGROUP2/oradata';
Diskgroup altered.
SQL> Alter diskgroup dgroup2
  2  Add directory '+DGROUP2/oradata/orcl';
Diskgroup altered.
SQL> Alter diskgroup dgroup2
  2  Add directory '+DGROUP2/oradata/orcl/dbf';
Diskgroup altered.
```

9. Now log into the ORCL database and try again.

```
C:\>set oracle_sid=orcl
C:\>sqlplus sys as sysdba
SQL*Plus: Release 11.1.0.6.0 - Production on Mon Aug 11 20:50:06 2008
Copyright (c) 1982, 2007, Oracle.  All rights reserved.
Enter password:
Connected to:
Oracle Database 11g Enterprise Edition Release 11.1.0.6.0 - Production
With the Partitioning, OLAP, Data Mining
and Real Application Testing options
Create tablespace ASM_TBS_TWO
Datafile '+DGROUP2/oradata/orcl/dbf/asm_tbs_two.dbf' size 200m;
```

Lab 2.1: Executing a Manual Offline (Cold) Backup

In this lab, you will perform an offline backup. This lab will work if your database is in NOARCHIVELOG or ARCHIVELOG mode. In the Chapter 3 lab exercises, you will use the backup created in this lab to restore your database.

This exercise assumes that you do not have any tablespaces using space in an ASM instance. Though offline backups are possible with ASM, we strongly advise that you use RMAN to perform your backups. The OCP exam will not test your knowledge of manual backups of databases using ASM.

1. Create a directory to copy your backup-related files to. In this example, we will be using `c:\oracle\orabackup\orcl\cold`.

```
C:\>mkdir oracle
C:\>cd oracle
C:\oracle>mkdir orabackup
C:\oracle>cd orabackup
C:\oracle\orabackup>mkdir orcl
C:\oracle\orabackup>cd orcl
C:\oracle\orabackup\orcl>mkdir cold
```

2. Log into your database using SQL*Plus.

```
C:\oracle\orabackup\orcl>sqlplus sys as sysdba
SQL*Plus: Release 11.1.0.6.0 - Production on Thu Aug 14 18:57:13 2008
Copyright (c) 1982, 2007, Oracle.  All rights reserved.
Enter password:
Connected to:
Oracle Database 11g Enterprise Edition Release 11.1.0.6.0 - Production
With the Partitioning, OLAP, Data Mining
and Real Application Testing options
SQL>
```

3. Using the DBA_DATA_FILES view, determine the datafiles that you will need to back up.

```
SQL> select tablespace_name, file_name from dba_data_files;
TABLESPACE_NAME FILE_NAME
--------------- ----------------------------------------
USERS           C:\ORACLE\ORADATA\ORCL\USERS01.DBF
UNDOTBS1        C:\ORACLE\ORADATA\ORCL\UNDOTBS01.DBF
```

```
SYSAUX          C:\ORACLE\ORADATA\ORCL\SYSAUX01.DBF
SYSTEM          C:\ORACLE\ORADATA\ORCL\SYSTEM01.DBF
```

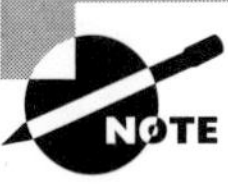

Note, for the purpose of this lab, that all of our datafiles, control files, and online redo logs are in the same directory. Also note that the number of files in your database may be different than those shown in this lab.

4. Using the V$LOGFILE view, determine the online redo logs that will require a backup.

```
SQL> select member from v$logfile;
MEMBER
----------------------------------
C:\ORACLE\ORADATA\ORCL\REDO03.LOG
C:\ORACLE\ORADATA\ORCL\REDO02.LOG
C:\ORACLE\ORADATA\ORCL\REDO01.LOG
```

Again, the number of online redo logs in your database may be different than the number in this lab.

5. Using the V$CONTROLFILE view, determine the location of the database control files that will be backed up.

```
SQL> select name from v$controlfile;
NAME
-------------------------------------
C:\ORACLE\ORADATA\ORCL\CONTROL01.CTL
C:\ORACLE\ORADATA\ORCL\CONTROL02.CTL
C:\ORACLE\ORADATA\ORCL\CONTROL03.CTL
```

6. From the SQL*Plus prompt, shut down the database with the `shutdown immediate` command.

```
SQL> shutdown immediate
Database closed.
Database dismounted.
ORACLE instance shut down.
```

7. Once the database is shut down, exit SQL*Plus.

```
SQL>exit
C:\oracle\orabackup\orcl>
```

8. Using the OS Copy command, copy the database datafiles, control files, and online redo logs to the backup directory created in step 1. In our example, they are all in the same directory, so this is easy to do.

```
        C:\oracle\orabackup\orcl>Copy c:\oracle\oradata\orcl\*.*
        c:\oracle\orabackup\orcl\cold
c:\oracle\oradata\orcl\CONTROL01.CTL
c:\oracle\oradata\orcl\CONTROL02.CTL
c:\oracle\oradata\orcl\CONTROL03.CTL
c:\oracle\oradata\orcl\REDO01.LOG
c:\oracle\oradata\orcl\REDO02.LOG
c:\oracle\oradata\orcl\REDO03.LOG
c:\oracle\oradata\orcl\SYSAUX01.DBF
c:\oracle\oradata\orcl\SYSTEM01.DBF
c:\oracle\oradata\orcl\TEMP01.DBF
c:\oracle\oradata\orcl\UNDOTBS01.DBF
c:\oracle\oradata\orcl\USERS01.DBF
        11 file(s) copied.
```

You will notice that we backed up a file called TEMP01.DBF that didn't show up in the list of files. This is the tempfile associated with the temporary tablespace. Technically, we didn't need to back this file up because when we do a restore, we just re-create it.

9. Start SQL*Plus connecting as sys as sysdba. Restart the database with the startup command. You have completed your backup.

```
C:\oracle\orabackup\orcl>sqlplus sys as sysdba
SQL*Plus: Release 11.1.0.6.0 - Production on Thu Aug 14 19:31:56 2008
Copyright (c) 1982, 2007, Oracle.  All rights reserved.
Enter password:
Connected to an idle instance.
SQL> startup
ORACLE instance started.
Total System Global Area  397557760 bytes
Fixed Size                  1333452 bytes
Variable Size             268437300 bytes
Database Buffers          121634816 bytes
Redo Buffers                6152192 bytes
Database mounted.
Database opened.
```

Lab 2.2: Putting the Database in ARCHIVELOG Mode

In this exercise, you will configure the database for ARCHIVELOG mode. You will then actually put the database in ARCHIVELOG mode.

1. Create a directory called `c:\oracle\arch\arch`.

```
C:\>mkdir oracle
C:\>cd oracle
C:\oracle>mkdir arch
C:\oracle>cd arch
C:\oracle\arch>mkdir orcl
C:\oracle\arch>cd orcl
C:\oracle\arch\orcl>
```

2. Log into your database using SQL*Plus. Check the log mode the database is in by querying the `LOG_MODE` column in `V$DATABASE`.

```
C:\oracle\orabackup\orcl>sqlplus sys as sysdba
SQL*Plus: Release 11.1.0.6.0 - Production on Thu Aug 14 19:37:19 2008
Copyright (c) 1982, 2007, Oracle.  All rights reserved.
Enter password:
Connected to:
Oracle Database 11g Enterprise Edition Release 11.1.0.6.0 - Production
With the Partitioning, OLAP, Data Mining
and Real Application Testing options
SQL> select log_mode from v$database;
LOG_MODE
------------
NOARCHIVELOG
```

3. Using the `alter system` command, set the `LOG_ARCHIVE_DEST_1` parameter to point to the new directory you created in step 1.

```
SQL> Alter system set log_archive_dest_1='location=c:\oracle\arch\orcl';
System altered.
```

4. Shut down the database using the `shutdown immediate` command.

```
SQL> shutdown immediate
Database closed.
```

```
Database dismounted.
ORACLE instance shut down.
```

5. Put the database in MOUNT mode with the `startup mount` command. Confirm that the database is in MOUNT mode by querying the `OPEN_MODE` column in `V$DATABASE`.

```
SQL> startup mount
ORACLE instance started.
Total System Global Area  397557760 bytes
Fixed Size                  1333452 bytes
Variable Size             272631604 bytes
Database Buffers          117440512 bytes
Redo Buffers                6152192 bytes
Database mounted.
SQL> select open_mode from v$database;
OPEN_MODE
----------
MOUNTED
```

6. Now put the database in ARCHIVELOG mode using the `alter database archivelog` command.

```
SQL> alter database archivelog;
Database altered.
```

7. Open the database with the `alter database open` command. Check the `LOG_MODE` parameter of the `V$DATABASE` view to ensure that the database is in ARCHIVELOG mode.

```
SQL> alter database open;
Database altered.
SQL> select log_mode from v$database;
LOG_MODE
------------
ARCHIVELOG
```

8. To ensure that the database is configured correctly, force a log switch.

```
SQL> Alter system switch logfile;
System altered.
```

9. Now check the directory `c:\oracle\arch\orcl` to ensure that the archived redo logs are being created correctly.

```
SQL> Host dir c:\oracle\arch\orcl
 Volume in drive C has no label.
```

```
 Volume Serial Number is 08DE-E1AB
 Directory of c:\oracle\arch\orcl
08/14/2008  07:48 PM    <DIR>          .
08/14/2008  07:48 PM    <DIR>          ..
08/14/2008  07:48 PM             1,024 ARC00003_0662757171.001
               1 File(s)          1,024 bytes
               2 Dir(s)  12,981,006,336 bytes free
```

Lab 2.3: Executing a Manual Online (Hot) Backup

In this lab, you will perform an online/hot backup of your database, with the database still running.

1. Create a directory for the backups. In this lab, we use `c:\oracle\orabackup\orcl\hot`. We assume that the directory structure `c:\oracle\orabackup\orcl` is already created from the work you did in Lab 2.1.

```
C:\>cd oracle\orabackup\orcl
C:\oracle\orabackup\orcl> mkdir hot
```

2. Log into your database using SQL*Plus. Check the log mode the database is in by querying the `LOG_MODE` column in `V$DATABASE`. It should be in ARCHIVELOG mode.

```
C:\oracle\orabackup\orcl>sqlplus sys as sysdba
SQL*Plus: Release 11.1.0.6.0 - Production on Thu Aug 14 19:37:19 2008
Copyright (c) 1982, 2007, Oracle.  All rights reserved.
Enter password:
Connected to:
Oracle Database 11g Enterprise Edition Release 11.1.0.6.0 - Production
With the Partitioning, OLAP, Data Mining
and Real Application Testing options
SQL> select log_mode from v$database;
LOG_MODE
------------
ARCHIVELOG
```

3. Using the `DBA_DATA_FILES` view, determine the datafiles that you will need to back up.

```
SQL> select tablespace_name, file_name from dba_data_files;
```

```
TABLESPACE_NAME FILE_NAME
--------------- ----------------------------------------
USERS           C:\ORACLE\ORADATA\ORCL\USERS01.DBF
UNDOTBS1        C:\ORACLE\ORADATA\ORCL\UNDOTBS01.DBF
SYSAUX          C:\ORACLE\ORADATA\ORCL\SYSAUX01.DBF
SYSTEM          C:\ORACLE\ORADATA\ORCL\SYSTEM01.DBF
```

4. Using the V$LOG view, determine which sequence is the current online redo log sequence. You must ensure that you have this log sequence and all logs generated during the backup in order to be able to restore the backup.

```
SQL> select group#, sequence#, status from v$log;
    GROUP#  SEQUENCE# STATUS
---------- ---------- ----------------
         1          4 CURRENT
         2          2 INACTIVE
         3          3 INACTIVE
```

5. Put the database in hot backup mode with the `alter database begin backup` command.

```
SQL> alter database begin backup;
Database altered.
```

6. Copy all database datafiles (in our case, they all have an extension of `.dbf`) to the backup directory created in step 1.

```
SQL>host C:\oracle\orabackup\orcl>>Copy c:\oracle\oradata\orcl\*.dbf
 c:\oracle\orabackup\orcl\hot\*.*

c:\oracle\oradata\orcl\SYSAUX01.DBF
c:\oracle\oradata\orcl\SYSTEM01.DBF
c:\oracle\oradata\orcl\TEMP01.DBF
c:\oracle\oradata\orcl\UNDOTBS01.DBF
c:\oracle\oradata\orcl\USERS01.DBF
        5 file(s) copied.
```

7. Using the V$LOG view, determine which sequence is the current online redo log sequence. You must ensure that you have this log sequence and all logs generated during the backup in order to be able to restore the backup. In our case, we need log sequences starting with 4 (the sequence when we started our backup) and continuing through log sequence 7.

```
SQL> select group#, sequence#, status from v$log;

    GROUP#  SEQUENCE# STATUS
```

```
---------- ---------- ----------------
         1          7 CURRENT
         2          5 INACTIVE
         3          6 INACTIVE
```

8. Take the database out of hot backup mode with the `alter database end backup` command.

```
SQL> alter database end backup;
Database altered.
```

9. Use the `alter system switch logfile` command to force a switch from log sequence 7.

```
SQL> alter system switch logfile;
```

There may be times when you will need to use the `alter system archive log all;` command to get the latest archived redo-log files archived in a timely manner.

10. Check the archive-log directory to make sure log-file sequences 4 through 7 have been created. Note that we also checked the `LOG_ARCHIVE_FORMAT` parameter value. This is so we can know in the filename of the archived redo logs where the sequence number is.

```
SQL> show parameter log_archive_format
NAME                                 TYPE        VALUE
------------------------------------ ----------- -----------
log_archive_format                   string      ARC%S_%R.%T
SQL> show parameter log_archive_dest_1
NAME                                 TYPE     VALUE
------------------------------------ -------- -------------------------
log_archive_dest_1                   string   location=c:\oracle\arch\orcl
log_archive_dest_10                  string

SQL> host dir c:\oracle\arch\orcl
 Volume in drive C has no label.
 Volume Serial Number is 08DE-E1AB
 Directory of c:\oracle\arch\orcl
08/16/2008  05:25 PM    <DIR>          .
08/16/2008  05:25 PM    <DIR>          ..
08/14/2008  07:48 PM             1,024 ARC00003_0662757171.001
08/15/2008  05:01 AM        49,038,848 ARC00004_0662757171.001
08/15/2008  10:12 PM        48,250,880 ARC00005_0662757171.001
08/16/2008  09:00 AM        48,244,736 ARC00006_0662757171.001
08/16/2008  05:25 PM        34,351,104 ARC00007_0662757171.001
```

```
               5 File(s)    179,886,592 bytes
               2 Dir(s)   9,701,888,000 bytes free
```

Note in this output that the filename convention has the sequence number of the archived redo log right after the ARC value. Thus we have ARC00003 for log sequence 3, ARC00004 for log sequence 4, and so on. In the preceding output, we appear to have all log sequences that are required to recover this backup.

11. Copy the archived redo logs to the backup location.

```
SQL> Host copy c:\oracle\arch\orcl\arc*.* c:\oracle\orabackup\orcl\hot\*.*
c:\oracle\arch\orcl\ARC00003_0662757171.001
c:\oracle\arch\orcl\ARC00004_0662757171.001
c:\oracle\arch\orcl\ARC00005_0662757171.001
c:\oracle\arch\orcl\ARC00006_0662757171.001
c:\oracle\arch\orcl\ARC00007_0662757171.001
        5 file(s) copied.
```

12. Check the backup directory to ensure that all the files needed are in place.

```
SQL> Host dir c:\oracle\orabackup\orcl\hot\*.*
 Volume in drive C has no label.
 Volume Serial Number is 08DE-E1AB
 Directory of c:\oracle\orabackup\orcl\hot
08/16/2008  05:36 PM    <DIR>          .
08/16/2008  05:36 PM    <DIR>          ..
08/14/2008  07:48 PM             1,024 ARC00003_0662757171.001
08/15/2008  05:01 AM        49,038,848 ARC00004_0662757171.001
08/15/2008  10:12 PM        48,250,880 ARC00005_0662757171.001
08/16/2008  09:00 AM        48,244,736 ARC00006_0662757171.001
08/16/2008  05:25 PM        34,351,104 ARC00007_0662757171.001
08/15/2008  05:40 PM       594,485,248 SYSAUX01.DBF
08/15/2008  05:40 PM       723,525,632 SYSTEM01.DBF
08/14/2008  10:03 PM        20,979,712 TEMP01.DBF
08/15/2008  05:40 PM        26,222,592 UNDOTBS01.DBF
08/15/2008  05:40 PM         5,251,072 USERS01.DBF
              10 File(s)  1,550,350,848 bytes
               2 Dir(s)   9,521,692,672 bytes free
```

Here is a checklist:

- Datafiles: Check
- Redo log sequences 4 through 7: Check

13. This is an optional step. Now that we know our archived redo logs were copied successfully, we can remove them from the archive-log directory if we want.

```
SQL> Host del c:\oracle\arch\orcl\ARC00003_0662757171.001
SQL> Host del c:\oracle\arch\orcl\ARC00004_0662757171.001
SQL> Host del c:\oracle\arch\orcl\ARC00005_0662757171.001
SQL> Host del c:\oracle\arch\orcl\ARC00006_0662757171.001
SQL> Host del c:\oracle\arch\orcl\ARC00007_0662757171.001
```

This completes your online backup. You will use this backup to recover your database in a Chapter 3 lab.

In the Chapter 3 labs, we will be doing full database recoveries. This will require all of the archived redo logs generated by the database, including those created after this backup. Make sure you do not delete any archived redo logs that are not backed up. If you want to back up later archived redo logs, simply repeat step 8 of Lab 2.3 as often as needed.

Lab 3.1: Executing a Time-Based Point-in-Time Recovery

In this exercise, you will do a point-in-time recovery by restoring the database to a given point in time.

1. Back up the database. Details on how to do a full online database backup are found in Chapter 2. In summary, follow these steps:
   a. Put the database in hot backup mode.
   b. Copy all database datafiles to a backup location.
   c. Take the database out of hot backup mode.
   d. Force a log switch. Back up the archived redo logs.

   Here is an example of a backup:

```
[oracle@localhost orcl]$ sqlplus "/ as sysdba"
SQL*Plus: Release 11.1.0.6.0 - Production on Sun Aug 17 15:35:48 2008
Copyright (c) 1982, 2007, Oracle.  All rights reserved.
Connected to:
Oracle Database 11g Enterprise Edition Release 11.1.0.6.0 - Production
With the Partitioning, OLAP, Data Mining
```

```
and Real Application Testing options
SQL> alter database begin backup;
Database altered.
SQL> host cp /oracle01/oradata/orcl/*.dbf /oracle01/backup/orcl
SQL> alter database end backup;
Database altered.
SQL> alter system switch logfile;
System altered.
SQL> host cp /oracle01/backup/arch/* /oracle01/backup/orcl/*
SQL> alter database backup controlfile to trace;
Database altered.
SQL> alter database backup controlfile to
 '/oracle01/oradata/orcl/control1.bak';
Database altered.
```

2. Next, log into the database as `scott/tiger` and create a new table. Insert two records into the new table and commit the insert.

```
SQL> connect scott/tiger
Connected.
SQL> create table time_table (col_one date);
Table created.
SQL> insert into time_table values (sysdate);
1 row created.
SQL> insert into time_table values (sysdate);
1 row created.
SQL> commit;
Commit complete.
SQL> alter session set nls_date_format='mm/dd/yyyy hh24:mi:ss';
Session altered.
SQL> select * from time_table;
COL_ONE
-------------------
08/17/2008 22:03:59
08/17/2008 22:03:59
```

3. Wait a minute or so (however long you like) and add two more records. Commit the inserts.

```
SQL> insert into time_table values (sysdate);
1 row created.
SQL> insert into time_table values (sysdate);
```

```
1 row created.
SQL> commit;
Commit complete.
SQL> select * from time_table;
COL_ONE
-------------------
08/17/2008 22:03:59
08/17/2008 22:03:59
08/17/2008 22:04:45
08/17/2008 22:04:45
```

4. Shut down the database.

```
SQL> connect sys as sysdba
Enter password:
Connected.
SQL> shutdown immediate
Database closed.
Database dismounted.
ORACLE instance shut down.
```

5. Once you are sure the database is down, restore the database datafiles from their backup location to the location where the database files belong.

```
[oracle@localhost orcl]$ pwd
/oracle01/backup/orcl
[oracle@localhost orcl]$ cp *.dbf /oracle01/oradata/orcl/*
```

6. Mount the database.

```
[oracle@localhost orcl]$ sqlplus "/ as sysdba"
SQL*Plus: Release 11.1.0.6.0 - Production on Sun Aug 17 17:53:14 2008
Copyright (c) 1982, 2007, Oracle.  All rights reserved.
Connected to an idle instance.
SQL> startup mount
ORACLE instance started.
Total System Global Area  167395328 bytes
Fixed Size                  1298612 bytes
Variable Size             142610252 bytes
Database Buffers           20971520 bytes
Redo Buffers                2514944 bytes
Database mounted.
```

7. Recover the database using the `recover database until time` command. Use a time that is after the time listed in the second insert in the TIME_TABLE (22:03:59 in our example). In this case, we will recover to 22:04:00. Enter **AUTO** if prompted for an archived redo log to apply.

```
SQL> recover database until time '2008-08-17:22:04:00';
Media recovery complete.
```

8. Open the database with the `alter database open resetlogs` command. Note that once you have done this, you will not be able to recover any data that was entered after the point of the recovery.

```
SQL> alter database open resetlogs;
Database altered.
```

9. Log into the scott schema. Do a `select * from test_table`. You should have only two records in the table.

```
SQL> Connect scott/tiger
Connected.
SQL> select * from time_table;
COL_ONE
-------------------
08/17/2008 22:03:59
08/17/2008 22:03:59
```

Lab 3.2: Recovering from Control-File Loss with a Backup Control File

In this lab we will be recovering a database that has experienced the complete loss of its control files. We will be using a backup control file to perform the recovery.

1. Back up the database. Details on how to do a full online database backup are found in Chapter 2. In summary, follow these steps:
   a. Put the database in hot backup mode.
   b. Copy all database datafiles to a backup location.
   c. Take the database out of hot backup mode.
   d. Force a log switch. Back up the archived redo logs.

Here is an example of a backup:

```
[oracle@localhost orcl]$ sqlplus "/ as sysdba"
SQL*Plus: Release 11.1.0.6.0 - Production on Sun Aug 17 15:35:48 2008
Copyright (c) 1982, 2007, Oracle.  All rights reserved.
Connected to:
Oracle Database 11g Enterprise Edition Release 11.1.0.6.0 - Production
With the Partitioning, OLAP, Data Mining
and Real Application Testing options
SQL> alter database begin backup;
Database altered.
SQL> host cp /oracle01/oradata/orcl/*.dbf /oracle01/backup/orcl
SQL> alter database end backup;
Database altered.
SQL> alter system switch logfile;
System altered.
SQL> host cp /oracle01/backup/arch/* /oracle01/backup/orcl/*
SQL> alter database backup controlfile to trace;
Database altered.
SQL> alter database backup controlfile to
 '/oracle01/oradata/orcl/control1.bak';
Database altered.
```

2. Find the location of the control files.

```
SQL> select name from v$controlfile;
NAME
--------------------------------------------------------------------------
/oracle01/oradata/orcl/control01.ctl
/oracle01/oradata/orcl/control02.ctl
/oracle01/oradata/orcl/control03.ctl
```

3. Shut down the database.

```
SQL> connect sys as sysdba
Enter password:
Connected.
SQL> shutdown immediate
Database closed.
Database dismounted.
ORACLE instance shut down.
```

4. Remove all control files.

```
SQL> host rm /oracle01/oradata/orcl/control01.ctl
SQL> host rm /oracle01/oradata/orcl/control02.ctl
SQL> host rm /oracle01/oradata/orcl/control03.ctl
```

5. Start up the database. Notice the error resulting from loss of all control files.

```
SQL> startup
ORACLE instance started.
Total System Global Area  159027200 bytes
Fixed Size                  1298556 bytes
Variable Size             134221700 bytes
Database Buffers           20971520 bytes
Redo Buffers                2535424 bytes
ORA-00205: error in identifying control file, check alert log for more info
```

6. Copy the backup control file into place.

```
SQL>Host cp /oracle01/backup/orcl/control.bak
/oracle01/oradata/orcl/control01.ctl
SQL>Host cp /oracle01/backup/orcl/control.bak
/oracle01/oradata/orcl/control02.ctl
SQL>Host cp /oracle01/backup/orcl/control.bak
/oracle01/oradata/orcl/control03.ctl
```

7. Mount the database with the `alter database mount` command.

```
SQL> alter database mount;
Database altered.
```

8. Recover the database by issuing the `recover database using backup controlfile` command. Since you have all the online redo logs, you can do a complete recovery. If prompted to recover using archived redo logs, enter **AUTO**.

```
SQL> recover database using backup controlfile;
ORA-00279: change 5026597 generated at 08/19/2008 16:23:33
needed for thread 1
ORA-00289: suggestion :
/oracle01/flash_recovery_area/ORCL/archivelog/2008_08_19/o1_mf_1_10_%u_.arc
ORA-00280: change 5026597 for thread 1 is in sequence #10
Specify log: {<RET>=suggested | filename | AUTO | CANCEL}
auto
ORA-00308: cannot open archived log
```

```
'/oracle01/flash_recovery_area/ORCL/archivelog/2008_08_19
/o1_mf_1_10_%u_.arc'
ORA-27037: unable to obtain file status
Linux Error: 2: No such file or directory
Additional information: 3
ORA-00308: cannot open archived log
'/oracle01/flash_recovery_area/ORCL/archivelog/2008_08_19
/o1_mf_1_10_%u_.arc'
ORA-27037: unable to obtain file status
Linux Error: 2: No such file or directory
Additional information: 3
```

9. (This step is not required if step 8 completed with a message that said media recovery successful.) If you get the error message we got above (you may not), determine which online redo log contains the sequence number needing to be restored by querying V$LOG and V$LOGFILE as shown here.

```
SQL> select a.group#, a.member, b.sequence#
  2  from v$logfile a, v$log b
  3* where a.group#=b.group#;
    GROUP# MEMBER                                    SEQUENCE#
---------- ---------------------------------------- ----------
         1 /oracle01/oradata/orcl/redo01.log                10
         1 /oracle01/oradata/orcl/redo01a.log               10
         2 /oracle01/oradata/orcl/redo02a.log                8
         2 /oracle01/oradata/orcl/redo02.log                 8
         3 /oracle01/oradata/orcl/redo03a.log                9
         3 /oracle01/oradata/orcl/redo03.log                 9
```

In this case, the online redo-log file /oracle01/oradata/orcl/redo01.log contains sequence 10, which we need to restore. Start recovery again, and apply the online redo-log file as shown here.

```
SQL> recover database using backup controlfile;
ORA-00279: change 5026597 generated at 08/19/2008 16:23:33
needed for thread 1
ORA-00289: suggestion :
/oracle01/flash_recovery_area/ORCL/archivelog/2008_08_19/o1_mf_1_10_%u_.arc
ORA-00280: change 5026597 for thread 1 is in sequence #10
Specify log: {<RET>=suggested | filename | AUTO | CANCEL}
/oracle01/oradata/orcl/redo01.log
Log applied.
Media recovery complete.
```

10. Open the database with the `alter database open resetlogs` command. Since you are using a backup control file, you must use the `resetlogs` command.

```
SQL> alter database open resetlogs;
Database altered.
```

Lab 3.3: Recovering from Loss of the Current Online Redo Log

In this lab we will be recovering from the loss of the current online redo log. This is perhaps one of the worst-case situations that you would face as an Oracle DBA!

1. Back up the database. Details on how to do a full online database backup are found in Chapter 2. In summary, follow these steps:
   a. Put the database in hot backup mode.
   b. Copy all database datafiles to a backup location.
   c. Take the database out of hot backup mode.
   d. Force a log switch. Back up the archived redo logs.

   Here is an example of a backup:

```
[oracle@localhost orcl]$ sqlplus "/ as sysdba"
SQL*Plus: Release 11.1.0.6.0 - Production on Sun Aug 17 15:35:48 2008
Copyright (c) 1982, 2007, Oracle.  All rights reserved.
Connected to:
Oracle Database 11g Enterprise Edition Release 11.1.0.6.0 - Production
With the Partitioning, OLAP, Data Mining
and Real Application Testing options
SQL> alter database begin backup;
Database altered.
SQL> host cp /oracle01/oradata/orcl/*.dbf /oracle01/backup/orcl
SQL> alter database end backup;
Database altered.
SQL> alter system switch logfile;
System altered.
SQL> host cp /oracle01/backup/arch/* /oracle01/backup/orcl/*
SQL> alter database backup controlfile to trace;
Database altered.
SQL> alter database backup controlfile to
 '/oracle01/oradata/orcl/control1.bak';
Database altered.
```

2. Determine the location of the online redo logs by querying the MEMBER column of the V$LOGFILE view.

```
SQL> select member from v$logfile;
MEMBER
--------------------------------------------------------------------------
/oracle01/oradata/orcl/redo03.log
/oracle01/oradata/orcl/redo02.log
/oracle01/oradata/orcl/redo01.log
/oracle01/oradata/orcl/redo01a.log
/oracle01/oradata/orcl/redo02a.log
/oracle01/oradata/orcl/redo03a.log
```

3. While the database is still running, remove all of the online redo logs.

```
SQL> host rm /oracle01/oradata/orcl/redo03.log
SQL> host rm /oracle01/oradata/orcl/redo02.log
SQL> host rm /oracle01/oradata/orcl/redo01.log
SQL> host rm /oracle01/oradata/orcl/redo01a.log
SQL> host rm /oracle01/oradata/orcl/redo02a.log
SQL> host rm /oracle01/oradata/orcl/redo03a.log
```

Note that this lab is set up to demonstrate recovering a database from an actual crash as a result of the loss of the online redo logs. If the database has not actually crashed, you would issue an `alter database checkpoint` command and then try an `alter database clear logfile` command to try to save the database from crashing.

4. If the database is still running, simulate a crash using the `shutdown abort` command.

```
SQL> shutdown abort
ORACLE instance shut down.
```

5. Start up the database to see the error you will receive.

```
SQL> startup
ORACLE instance started.
Total System Global Area  159027200 bytes
Fixed Size                  1298556 bytes
Variable Size             134221700 bytes
Database Buffers           20971520 bytes
Redo Buffers                2535424 bytes
Database mounted.
ORA-00313: open failed for members of log group 1 of thread 1
```

```
ORA-00312: online log 1 thread 1: '/oracle01/oradata/orcl/redo01a.log'
ORA-27037: unable to obtain file status
Linux Error: 2: No such file or directory
Additional information: 3
ORA-00312: online log 1 thread 1: '/oracle01/oradata/orcl/redo01.log'
ORA-27037: unable to obtain file status
Linux Error: 2: No such file or directory
Additional information: 3
```

6. Restore the database from the backup taken in step 1.

```
[oracle@localhost orcl]$ cp /oracle01/backup/orcl/*.gz . &
```

7. Mount the database using the `startup mount` command.

```
[oracle@localhost orcl]$ sqlplus / as sysdba
SQL*Plus: Release 11.1.0.6.0 - Production on Sun Aug 17 16:26:56 2008
Copyright (c) 1982, 2007, Oracle.  All rights reserved.
Connected to an idle instance.
SQL> startup mount
ORACLE instance started.
Total System Global Area  167395328 bytes
Fixed Size                  1298612 bytes
Variable Size             142610252 bytes
Database Buffers           20971520 bytes
Redo Buffers                2514944 bytes
Database mounted.
```

8. Using the `V$ARCHIVED_LOG`, determine the last log sequence number archived.

```
SQL> select max(sequence#) from v$archived_log
  2 where resetlogs_change#=
  3 (select max(resetlogs_change#) from v$archived_log);
MAX(SEQUENCE#)
--------------
             9
```

9. Recover the database using the `recover database until cancel` command. Use the last archived redo log sequence number found in step 8 as the sequence to recover to. Once you reach that sequence number, cancel the recovery.

```
SQL> recover database using backup controlfile until cancel;
SQL> recover database until cancel using backup controlfile;
ORA-00279: change 5026562 generated at 08/19/2008 16:23:14
```

```
needed for thread 1
ORA-00289: suggestion :
/oracle01/flash_recovery_area/ORCL/archivelog/2008_08_19/
o1_mf_1_9_4bpm2cgp_.arcORA-00280: change 5026562
for thread 1 is in sequence #9
Specify log: {<RET>=suggested | filename | AUTO | CANCEL}
ORA-00279: change 5026597 generated at 08/19/2008 16:23:33
needed for thread 1
ORA-00289: suggestion :
/oracle01/flash_recovery_area/ORCL/archivelog/2008_08_19/
o1_mf_1_10_4bpm2bt3_.arc
ORA-00280: change 5026597 for thread 1 is in sequence #10
ORA-00278: log file
'/oracle01/flash_recovery_area/ORCL/archivelog/2008_08_19/
o1_mf_1_9_4bpm2cgp_.arc' no longer needed for this recovery
Specify log: {<RET>=suggested | filename | AUTO | CANCEL}
cancel
Media recovery cancelled.
```

10. Open the database with the `alter database open resetlogs` command. Your recovery is complete.

```
SQL> alter database open resetlogs;
Database altered.
```

Lab 4.1: Creating an RMAN Offline Backup

In this lab, you will be creating an RMAN offline backup. You can back up databases in NOARCHIVELOG or ARCHIVELOG mode with offline backups.

1. Start RMAN.

```
C:\>rman target=/
Recovery Manager: Release 11.1.0.6.0 - Production on
Thu Sep 11 18:58:55 2008
Copyright (c) 1982, 2007, Oracle.  All rights reserved.
connected to target database: ORCL (DBID=1190537904)
```

2. Shut down the database from RMAN using the RMAN `shutdown immediate` command. Then start the database in MOUNT mode with the RMAN `startup mount` command.

```
RMAN> shutdown immediate
using target database control file instead of recovery catalog
database closed
database dismounted
Oracle instance shut down
RMAN> startup mount
connected to target database (not started)
Oracle instance started
database mounted
Total System Global Area     397557760 bytes
Fixed Size                     1333452 bytes
Variable Size                281020212 bytes
Database Buffers             109051904 bytes
Redo Buffers                   6152192 bytes
```

3. Back up the database using the backup command. In this case, we are not going to back up the database archived redo logs if the database is in ARCHIVELOG mode. Since it was shut down in a consistent manner, we don't need to back up any archived redo logs to restore this backup.

```
RMAN> Backup database;
Starting backup at 11-SEP-08
allocated channel: ORA_DISK_1
channel ORA_DISK_1: SID=155 device type=DISK
channel ORA_DISK_1: starting compressed full datafile backup set
channel ORA_DISK_1: specifying datafile(s) in backup set
input datafile file number=00002 name=C:\ORACLE\ORADATA\ORCL\SYSAUX01.DBF
input datafile file number=00001 name=C:\ORACLE\ORADATA\ORCL\SYSTEM01.DBF
input datafile file number=00005 name=C:\ORACLE\ORADATA\ORCL\UNDOTBS02.DBF
input datafile file number=00004 name=C:\ORACLE\ORADATA\ORCL\USERS01.DBF
channel ORA_DISK_1: starting piece 1 at 11-SEP-08
channel ORA_DISK_1: finished piece 1 at 11-SEP-08
piece handle=C:\ORACLE\FLASH_RECOVERY_AREA\ORCL
\BACKUPSET\2008_09_11\01_MF_NNNDF_TAG20080911T204331_4DMOTSN1_.BKP
tag=TAG20080911T204331 comment=NONE
channel ORA_DISK_1: backup set complete, elapsed time: 00:05:26
Finished backup at 11-SEP-08
Starting Control File and SPFILE Autobackup at 11-SEP-08
```

```
piece handle=C:\ORACLE\FLASH_RECOVERY_AREA\ORCL
\AUTOBACKUP\2008_09_11\O1_MF_S_665181628_4DMP5C9P_.BKP comment=NONE
Finished Control File and SPFILE Autobackup at 11-SEP-08
```

4. Restart the database with the RMAN command `alter database open`.

```
RMAN> Alter database open;
database opened
```

Lab 4.2: Creating an RMAN Incremental Backup

In this lab, we will be creating an incremental backup. We will also be looking at the size of the resulting backup sets to compare the backup set sizes and the impacts of the level-0 and level-1 incremental backups.

1. Log into the database using SQL*Plus.

```
C:\oracle\admin\ORCL\wallet>set oracle_sid=orcl
C:\oracle\admin\ORCL\wallet>sqlplus "/ as sysdba"
SQL*Plus: Release 11.1.0.6.0 - Production on Thu Sep 11 18:56:27 2008
Copyright (c) 1982, 2007, Oracle.  All rights reserved.
Connected to:
Oracle Database 11g Enterprise Edition Release 11.1.0.6.0 - Production
With the Partitioning, OLAP, Data Mining
and Real Application Testing options
SQL>
```

2. Query the `LOG_MODE` column of the `V$DATABASE` view to confirm that the database is in ARCHIVELOG mode. If the database is not in ARCHIVELOG mode, refer to Chapter 2 for information on how to put the database in ARCHIVELOG mode.

```
SQL> Select log_mode from v$database;
LOG_MODE
------------
ARCHIVELOG
```

3. Exit SQL*Plus and start RMAN.

```
SQL> exit
Disconnected from Oracle Database 11g Enterprise Edition
```

```
Release 11.1.0.6.0 - Production
With the Partitioning, OLAP, Data Mining
and Real Application Testing options
C:\oracle\admin\ORCL\wallet>rman target=/
Recovery Manager: Release 11.1.0.6.0 - Production
on Thu Sep 11 18:58:55 2008
Copyright (c) 1982, 2007, Oracle.  All rights reserved.
connected to target database: ORCL (DBID=1190537904)
```

4. Execute the RMAN backup using the `backup database` command. Include the `incremental level 0` option. You will back up the archived redo logs at the same time with the `plus archivelog` option. Remove the archived redo logs after they are backed up using the `delete input` option.

```
RMAN> Backup incremental level 0 database plus archivelog delete input;
```

5. Exit RMAN and log into SQL*Plus.
6. Query the `V$BACKUP_DATAFILE` and `V$BACKUP_SET` views to determine the size of the backup image (found in the `BLOCKS` column).

```
SQL> select a.set_count, a.start_time, a.completion_time, sum(b.blocks)
  2  from v$backup_set a, v$backup_datafile b
  3  where a.set_count=b.set_count
  4  and to_char(a.start_time, 'mm/dd/yyyy hh24:mi:ss')=
  5  (select to_char(max(start_time), 'mm/dd/yyyy hh24:mi:ss')
  6   from v$backup_set
  7   where incremental_level=0)
  8  group by a.set_count, a.start_time, a.completion_time ;
 SET_COUNT START_TIM COMPLETIO SUM(B.BLOCKS)
---------- --------- --------- -------------
       155 11-SEP-08 11-SEP-08        144318
```

7. Exit RMAN. Sign into the database using SQL*Plus. Add a table to the `scott` (or any other) schema. Insert and commit records into that table.

```
RMAN> Exit
Recovery Manager complete.
C:\Documents and Settings\Robert>Sqlplus scott/tiger
SQL*Plus: Release 11.1.0.6.0 - Production on
Thu Sep 11 20:37:39 2008
Copyright (c) 1982, 2007, Oracle.  All rights reserved.
Connected to:
Oracle Database 11g Enterprise Edition
Release 11.1.0.6.0 - Production
```

```
With the Partitioning, OLAP, Data Mining and Real Application
Testing options
SQL> Create table my_new_table (id number);
Table created.
SQL> Insert into my_new_table values (1);
1 row created.
SQL> Commit;
Commit complete.
SQL> Exit
```

8. Sign into RMAN. Perform a level-1 incremental backup.

```
RMAN> Backup incremental level 1 database plus archivelog delete input;
```

9. Query the V$BACKUP_DATAFILE and V$BACKUP_SET views again to determine the size of the backup image (found in the BLOCKS column). Since we are not doing an outer join here, the query will not return any rows until the backup in step 8 has completed. Note that the level-1 incremental backup is much smaller in the output than that in step 6.

```
SQL> select a.set_count, a.start_time, a.completion_time, sum(b.blocks)
  2  from v$backup_set a, v$backup_datafile b
  3  where a.set_count=b.set_count
  4  and to_char(a.start_time, 'mm/dd/yyyy hh24:mi:ss')=
  5  (select to_char(max(start_time), 'mm/dd/yyyy hh24:mi:ss')
  6   from v$backup_set
  7   where incremental_level=1)
  8   group by a.set_count, a.start_time, a.completion_time ;
 SET_COUNT START_TIM COMPLETIO SUM(B.BLOCKS)
---------- --------- --------- -------------
       159 11-SEP-08 11-SEP-08            45
```

Lab 4.3: Creating an Image-Copy Backup

In this lab, you will create an image-copy backup of your database. We assume your database is in ARCHIVELOG mode for this backup.

1. Log into the database using SQL*Plus.

```
C:\oracle\admin\ORCL\wallet>set oracle_sid=orcl
C:\oracle\admin\ORCL\wallet>sqlplus "/ as sysdba"
SQL*Plus: Release 11.1.0.6.0 - Production on Thu Sep 11 18:56:27 2008
Copyright (c) 1982, 2007, Oracle.  All rights reserved.
```

```
Connected to:
Oracle Database 11g Enterprise Edition Release 11.1.0.6.0 - Production
With the Partitioning, OLAP, Data Mining
and Real Application Testing options
SQL>
```

2. Using the backup as copy command, create an image copy of the database.

```
RMAN> Backup as copy database;
Starting backup at 11-SEP-08
using channel ORA_DISK_1
channel ORA_DISK_1: starting datafile copy
input datafile file number=00002 name=C:\ORACLE\ORADATA\ORCL\SYSAUX01.DBF
output file name=C:\ORACLE\FLASH_RECOVERY_AREA\ORCL
\DATAFILE\O1_MF_SYSAUX_4DMQJBMK_.DBF tag=TAG20080911T211158
RECID=23 STAMP=665183712
channel ORA_DISK_1: datafile copy complete, elapsed time: 00:03:16
channel ORA_DISK_1: starting datafile copy
input datafile file number=00001 name=C:\ORACLE\ORADATA\ORCL\SYSTEM01.DBF
output file name=C:\ORACLE\FLASH_RECOVERY_AREA\ORCL
\DATAFILE\O1_MF_SYSTEM_4DMQPMC7_.DBF tag=TAG20080911T211158
RECID=24 STAMP=665184016
channel ORA_DISK_1: datafile copy complete, elapsed time: 00:04:56
channel ORA_DISK_1: starting datafile copy
input datafile file number=00005 name=C:\ORACLE\ORADATA\ORCL\UNDOTBS02.DBF
output file name=C:\ORACLE\FLASH_RECOVERY_AREA\ORCL
\DATAFILE\O1_MF_UNDOTBS2_4DMRO3BY_.DBF tag=TAG20080911T211158
RECID=25 STAMP=665184046
channel ORA_DISK_1: datafile copy complete, elapsed time: 00:00:15
channel ORA_DISK_1: starting datafile copy
input datafile file number=00004 name=C:\ORACLE\ORADATA\ORCL\USERS01.DBF
output file name=C:\ORACLE\FLASH_RECOVERY_AREA\ORCL
\DATAFILE\O1_MF_USERS_4DMROS6S_.DBF tag=TAG20080911T211158
RECID=26 STAMP=665184058
channel ORA_DISK_1: datafile copy complete, elapsed time: 00:00:03
Finished backup at 11-SEP-08
Starting Control File and SPFILE Autobackup at 11-SEP-08
piece handle=C:\ORACLE\FLASH_RECOVERY_AREA\ORCL
\AUTOBACKUP\2008_09_11\O1_MF_S_665184060_4DMR163F_.BKP comment=NONE
Finished Control File and SPFILE Autobackup at 11-SEP-083.
```

Lab 5.1: Implementing RVPC

In this lab, you will implement RMAN virtual private catalog (RVPC) in the recovery catalog.

1. First you need to create the RVPC database account. Log into the recovery-catalog database as a privileged user (for example, SYS) and issue the `create user` command.

```
C:\Documents and Settings\Robert>sqlplus rcat_user/rcat_user@rcat
SQL*Plus: Release 11.1.0.6.0 - Production on Tue Sep 16 20:33:07 2008
Copyright (c) 1982, 2007, Oracle.  All rights reserved.
Connected to:
Oracle Database 11g Enterprise Edition Release 11.1.0.6.0 - Production
With the Partitioning, OLAP, Data Mining
and Real Application Testing options
SQL> create user rcat_001 identified by rcat_001
  2  default tablespace rcat_data
  3  quota unlimited on rcat_data;
User created.
```

2. Grant the `recovery_catalog_owner` privilege to the new user. Here is an example of this operation:

```
SQL> grant recovery_catalog_owner to rcat_001;
Grant succeeded.
```

3. Create the virtual catalog. To do this, you log into RMAN and use the `create virtual catalog` command, as shown in this example:

```
C:\Documents and Settings\Robert>rman catalog=rcat_001/rcat_001@rcat
Recovery Manager: Release 11.1.0.6.0 - Production
on Tue Sep 16 20:30:04 2008
Copyright (c) 1982, 2007, Oracle.  All rights reserved.
connected to recovery catalog database
RMAN> Create virtual catalog;
found eligible base catalog owned by RCAT_USER
created virtual catalog against base catalog owned by RCAT_USER
```

4. Now that you have created the RVPC account, you need to indicate to the recovery-catalog database which databases this account will have access too. Log into RMAN

and connect to the recovery catalog. Use the grant command and register the ORCL database to rcat_001.

```
C:\Documents and Settings\Robert>rman catalog=rcat_user/rcat_user@rcat
Recovery Manager: Release 11.1.0.6.0 - Production
on Tue Sep 16 20:25:32 2008
Copyright (c) 1982, 2007, Oracle.  All rights reserved.
connected to recovery catalog database
RMAN> grant catalog for database orcl to rcat_001;
Grant succeeded.
```

5. Query the RC_DATABASE view and see that only the ORCL database can be seen in the RVPC.

```
C:\Documents and Settings\Robert>sqlplus rcat_001/rcat_001@rcat
SQL*Plus: Release 11.1.0.6.0 - Production on Tue Sep 16 20:33:07 2008
Copyright (c) 1982, 2007, Oracle.  All rights reserved.
Connected to:
Oracle Database 11g Enterprise Edition Release 11.1.0.6.0 - Production
With the Partitioning, OLAP, Data Mining and Real Application
Testing options
SQL> Select name from rc_database;
NAME
--------
ORCL
```

Lab 6.1: Restoring a Datafile Online

In this activity, we will restore a datafile while the rest of the database is online. This activity builds on the backup done in Exercise 4.2 in Chapter 4. You should have completed Exercise 4.2 prior to executing this activity. Please note that the output you experience from this exercise will probably differ from the output shown here.

1. Log into the database as SYS using SQL*Plus.

```
C:\oracle>set oracle_sid=orcl
C:\oracle>sqlplus sys as sysdba
SQL*Plus: Release 11.1.0.6.0 - Production on Fri Oct 3 00:31:07 2008
Copyright (c) 1982, 2007, Oracle.  All rights reserved.
Enter password:
Connected to:
```

```
Oracle Database 11g Enterprise Edition Release 11.1.0.6.0 - Production
With the Partitioning, OLAP, Data Mining
and Real Application Testing options
SQL>
```

2. Determine the location of the database datafiles and their associated FILE_ID's.

```
SQL> select file_id, file_name from dba_data_files;
FILE_ID FILE_NAME
------- ------------------------------------------------------------
      4
C:\ORACLE\FLASH_RECOVERY_AREA\ORCL\DATAFILE\O1_MF_USERS_4G2Q1YTC_.DBF
          3 C:\ORACLE\ORADATA\ORCL\UNDOTBS01.DBF
          2 C:\ORACLE\ORADATA\ORCL\SYSAUX01.DBF
          1 C:\ORACLE\ORADATA\ORCL\SYSTEM01.DBF
```

3. Shut down the database.

```
SQL> shutdown abort
ORACLE instance shut down.
```

4. Exit SQL*Plus.

```
SQL> quit
Disconnected from Oracle Database 11g Enterprise Edition
Release 11.1.0.6.0 - Production
With the Partitioning, OLAP, Data Mining
and Real Application Testing options
C:\oracle>
```

5. From the operating prompt, delete one of the database datafiles listed in step 3. Make sure, before you delete the file, that you note its datafile number, the filename, and the location. In our example, we will delete datafile 4, which is the datafile associated with the USERS tablespace.

```
C:\oracle>Del
C:\ORACLE\FLASH_RECOVERY_AREA\ORCL\DATAFILE\O1_MF_USERS_4G2Q1YTC_.DBF
```

6. Log into the database as SYS using SQL*Plus.

```
C:\oracle>sqlplus sys as sysdba
SQL*Plus: Release 11.1.0.6.0 - Production on Fri Oct 3 00:35:25 2008
Copyright (c) 1982, 2007, Oracle.  All rights reserved.
Enter password:
Connected to an idle instance.
```

7. Start the database. Notice the error that you receive.

```
SQL> startup
ORACLE instance started.
Total System Global Area  364081152 bytes
Fixed Size                  1333228 bytes
Variable Size             264243220 bytes
Database Buffers           92274688 bytes
Redo Buffers                6230016 bytes
Database mounted.
ORA-01157: cannot identify/lock data file 4 - see DBWR trace file
ORA-01110: data file 4:
'C:\ORACLE\FLASH_RECOVERY_AREA\ORCL\DATAFILE\O1_MF_USERS_4G2Q1YTC_.DBF'
```

8. Use the `alter database datafile offline` command to take datafile 4 offline.

```
SQL> Alter database datafile 4 offline;
Database altered.
```

9. Open the database with the `alter database open` command. Exit SQL*Plus after the database has opened.

```
SQL> Alter database datafile 4 offline;
Database altered.
SQL> alter database open;
Database altered.
SQL> exit
Disconnected from Oracle Database 11g Enterprise Edition
Release 11.1.0.6.0 - Production
With the Partitioning, OLAP, Data Mining
and Real Application Testing options
```

10. Start RMAN. We will assume you are not using a recovery catalog during this exercise.

```
C:\oracle>rman target=/
Recovery Manager: Release 11.1.0.6.0 - Production
on Fri Oct 3 00:37:44 2008
Copyright (c) 1982, 2007, Oracle.  All rights reserved.
connected to target database (not started)
```

11. Restore database datafile 4 with the `restore datafile` command.

```
RMAN> restore datafile 4;
Starting restore at 10/03/2008 02:16:38
```

```
using target database control file instead of recovery catalog
allocated channel: ORA_DISK_1
channel ORA_DISK_1: SID=133 device type=DISK
channel ORA_DISK_1: starting datafile backup set restore
channel ORA_DISK_1: specifying datafile(s) to restore from backup set
channel ORA_DISK_1: restoring datafile 00004 to
C:\ORACLE\FLASH_RECOVERY_AREA\ORCL\DATAFILE\O1_MF_USERS_4G2Q1YTC_.DBF
channel ORA_DISK_1: reading from backup piece
 C:\ORACLE\FLASH_RECOVERY_AREA\ORCL\BACKUPSET\2008_10_03
\O1_MF_NNNDF_TAG20081003T001928_4GCGCQQ4_.BKP
channel ORA_DISK_1: piece
handle=C:\ORACLE\FLASH_RECOVERY_AREA\ORCL\BACKUPSET\2008_10_03
\O1_MF_NNNDF_TAG20081003T001928_4GCGCQQ4_.BKP tag=TAG20081003T001928
channel ORA_DISK_1: restored backup piece 1
channel ORA_DISK_1: restore complete, elapsed time: 00:00:03
Finished restore at 10/03/2008 02:16:42
```

12. Recover datafile 4 with the `recover datafile` command.

```
RMAN> recover datafile 4;
Starting recover at 10/03/2008 02:17:53
using channel ORA_DISK_1
starting media recovery
archived log for thread 1 with sequence 3 is already on disk as file
C:\ORACLE\PRODUCT\11.1.0\DB_1\RDBMS\ARC00003_0667012858.001
archived log for thread 1 with sequence 4 is already on disk as file
 C:\ORACLE\FLASH_RECOVERY_AREA\ORCL\ARCHIVELOG\2008_10_03
\O1_MF_1_4_4GCMC8GV_.ARC
archived log for thread 1 with sequence 1 is already on disk as file
C:\ORACLE\FLASH_RECOVERY_AREA\ORCL\ARCHIVELOG\2008_10_03
\O1_MF_1_1_4GC04G15_.ARC
archived log file
name=C:\ORACLE\PRODUCT\11.1.0\DB_1\RDBMS\ARC00003_0667012858.001
thread=1 sequence=3
archived log file
name=C:\ORACLE\FLASH_RECOVERY_AREA\ORCL\ARCHIVELOG\2008_10_03
\O1_MF_1_4_4GCMC8GV_.ARC thread=1 sequence=4
media recovery complete, elapsed time: 00:00:01
Finished recover at 10/03/2008 02:17:55
```

13. Bring the datafile online using the RMAN `sql` command calling the SQL statement `alter database datafile online`.

```
RMAN> sql 'alter database datafile 4 online';
sql statement: alter database datafile 4 online
```

The datafile has been restored online and the lab is complete.

Lab 6.2: Performing a Change-Based Recovery with RMAN

In this activity, you will restore the database to a specific SCN, or system change number. This activity builds on the backup done in Exercise 4.2 in Chapter 4. You should have completed Exercise 4.2 prior to executing this activity. Please note that the output you experience from this exercise will probably differ from the output shown here.

1. Start SQL*Plus.

```
C:\oracle>sqlplus sys as sysdba
SQL*Plus: Release 11.1.0.6.0 - Production on Fri Oct 3 00:35:25 2008
Copyright (c) 1982, 2007, Oracle.  All rights reserved.
Enter password:
```

2. The database should already be started. If not, start it with the `startup` command. To determine the current SCN, issue the following query:

```
SQL> select current_scn from v$database;
CURRENT_SCN
-----------
    1095172
```

This is the SCN that we will recover to. Your SCN is likely to be very different.

3. Start RMAN. We will assume you are not using a recovery catalog during this exercise.

```
C:\oracle>rman target=/
Recovery Manager: Release 11.1.0.6.0 - Production on Fri Oct 3 00:37:44 2008
Copyright (c) 1982, 2007, Oracle.  All rights reserved.
```

4. To prepare for the restore, put the database in MOUNT mode with the `startup force mount` RMAN command.

```
RMAN> startup force mount
Oracle instance started
```

```
database mounted
Total System Global Area     364081152 bytes
Fixed Size                     1333228 bytes
Variable Size                289409044 bytes
Database Buffers              67108864 bytes
Redo Buffers                   6230016 bytes
```

5. Issue the `restore database until scn` command to restore the database to the SCN identified in step 3. In our case, the command will be `restore database until scn 1095172`; your command will have a different change number.

```
RMAN> restore database until scn 1095172;
Starting restore at 10/03/2008 11:48:17
using target database control file instead of recovery catalog
allocated channel: ORA_DISK_1
channel ORA_DISK_1: SID=155 device type=DISK
channel ORA_DISK_1: starting datafile backup set restore
channel ORA_DISK_1: specifying datafile(s) to restore from backup set
channel ORA_DISK_1: restoring datafile 00001 to
C:\ORACLE\ORADATA\ORCL\SYSTEM01.DBF
channel ORA_DISK_1: restoring datafile 00002 to
C:\ORACLE\ORADATA\ORCL\SYSAUX01.DBF
channel ORA_DISK_1: restoring datafile 00003 to
C:\ORACLE\ORADATA\ORCL\UNDOTBS01.DBF
channel ORA_DISK_1: restoring datafile 00004 to
C:\ORACLE\FLASH_RECOVERY_AREA\ORCL\DATAFILE\O1_MF_USERS_4G2Q1YTC_.DBF
channel ORA_DISK_1: reading from backup piece
C:\ORACLE\FLASH_RECOVERY_AREA\ORCL\BACKUPSET\2008_10_03
\O1_MF_NNNDF_TAG20081003T001928_4GCGCQQ4_.BKP
channel ORA_DISK_1:
piece handle=C:\ORACLE\FLASH_RECOVERY_AREA\ORCL\BACKUPSET\2008_10_03
\O1_MF_NNNDF_TAG20081003T001928_4GCGCQQ4_.BKP tag=TAG20081003T001928
channel ORA_DISK_1: restored backup piece 1
channel ORA_DISK_1: restore complete, elapsed time: 00:07:25
Finished restore at 10/03/2008 11:55:44
```

6. Recover the database with the `recover database until scn` command. Our command would be `recover database until scn 1095172`; your command will have a different date and time.

```
RMAN> recover database until scn 1095172;
Starting recover at 10/03/2008 11:57:24
```

```
using channel ORA_DISK_1
starting media recovery
archived log for thread 1 with sequence 3 is already on disk as file
C:\ORACLE\PRODUCT\11.1.0\DB_1\RDBMS\ARC00003_0667012858.001
archived log for thread 1 with sequence 4 is already on disk as file
C:\ORACLE\FLASH_RECOVERY_AREA\ORCL\ARCHIVELOG\2008_10_03
\O1_MF_1_4_4GCMC8GV_.ARC
archived log for thread 1 with sequence 1 is already on disk as file
C:\ORACLE\FLASH_RECOVERY_AREA\ORCL\ARCHIVELOG\2008_10_03
\O1_MF_1_1_4GCO4G15_.ARC
archived log file
name=C:\ORACLE\PRODUCT\11.1.0\DB_1\RDBMS\ARC00003_0667012858.001
thread=1 sequence=3
archived log file
name=C:\ORACLE\FLASH_RECOVERY_AREA\ORCL\ARCHIVELOG\2008_10_03
\O1_MF_1_4_4GCMC8GV_.ARC thread=1 sequence=4
media recovery complete, elapsed time: 00:00:28
Finished recover at 10/03/2008 11:57:54
```

7. Open the database with the `alter database open resetlogs` command.

```
RMAN> alter database open resetlogs;
database opened
```

The database is open. This concludes the exercise.

Lab 6.3: Restoring a Control File from an Autobackup

In this activity, we will simulate loss of a control file and subsequent recovery. This activity builds on the backup done in Exercise 4.2. We assume that you have configured control-file autobackups as done in Exercise 4.1. You should have completed Exercises 4.1 and 4.2 prior to executing this activity. Please note that the output you experience from this exercise will probably differ from the output shown here.

1. Start SQL*Plus.

```
C:\oracle>sqlplus sys as sysdba
SQL*Plus: Release 11.1.0.6.0 - Production on Fri Oct 3 00:35:25 2008
Copyright (c) 1982, 2007, Oracle.  All rights reserved.
Enter password:
```

2. The database should be started. If not, start the database with the `startup force` command. From the SQL*Plus prompt, determine the current location of the database control files by issuing the query `select name from v$controlfile;`.

```
SQL> select name from v$controlfile;
NAME
------------------------------------
C:\ORACLE\ORADATA\ORCL\CONTROL01.CTL
C:\ORACLE\ORADATA\ORCL\CONTROL02.CTL
C:\ORACLE\ORADATA\ORCL\CONTROL03.CTL
```

3. Shut down the database and exit SQL*Plus.

```
SQL> shutdown immediate
Database closed.
Database dismounted.
ORACLE instance shut down.
SQL> exit
Disconnected from Oracle Database 11g Enterprise Edition Release
11.1.0.6.0 - Production
With the Partitioning, OLAP, Data Mining
and Real Application Testing options
```

4. From the OS, remove all of the database control files.

```
C:\oracle>del C:\ORACLE\ORADATA\ORCL\CONTROL01.CTL
C:\oracle>del C:\ORACLE\ORADATA\ORCL\CONTROL02.CTL
C:\oracle>del C:\ORACLE\ORADATA\ORCL\CONTROL03.CTL
```

5. Start RMAN.

```
C:\oracle>rman target=/
Recovery Manager: Release 11.1.0.6.0 - Production
on Fri Oct 3 00:37:44 2008
Copyright (c) 1982, 2007, Oracle.  All rights reserved.
connected to target database (not started)
```

6. Try to start up the database. What error do you get?

```
RMAN> startup
Oracle instance started
RMAN-00571: ===========================================================
RMAN-00569: =============== ERROR MESSAGE STACK FOLLOWS ===============
RMAN-00571: ===========================================================
```

```
RMAN-03002: failure of startup command at 10/03/2008 12:09:57
ORA-00205: error in identifying control file, check alert log for more info
```

7. Issue the `restore controlfile from autobackup` command from RMAN to restore the control files.

```
RMAN> restore controlfile from autobackup;
Starting restore at 10/03/2008 12:10:24
using target database control file instead of recovery catalog
allocated channel: ORA_DISK_1
channel ORA_DISK_1: SID=155 device type=DISK
recovery area destination: c:\oracle\flash_recovery_area
database name (or database unique name) used for search: ORCL
channel ORA_DISK_1: AUTOBACKUP
C:\ORACLE\FLASH_RECOVERY_AREA\ORCL\AUTOBACKUP\2008_09_28
\O1_MF_S_666651824_4G0KDSG5_.BKP found in the recovery area
AUTOBACKUP search with format "%F" not attempted because DBID was not set
channel ORA_DISK_1: restoring control file from AUTOBACKUP
C:\ORACLE\FLASH_RECOVERY_AREA\ORCL\AUTOBACKUP\2008_09_28
\O1_MF_S_666651824_4G0KDSG5_.BKP
channel ORA_DISK_1: control file restore from AUTOBACKUP complete
output file name=C:\ORACLE\ORADATA\ORCL\CONTROL01.CTL
output file name=C:\ORACLE\ORADATA\ORCL\CONTROL02.CTL
output file name=C:\ORACLE\ORADATA\ORCL\CONTROL03.CTL
Finished restore at 10/03/2008 12:10:33
```

8. Mount the database.

```
RMAN> alter database mount;
database mounted
released channel: ORA_DISK_1
```

9. Recover the database with the `recover database` command.

```
RMAN> recover database;
Starting recover at 10/03/2008 14:03:49
Starting implicit crosscheck backup at 10/03/2008 14:03:49
allocated channel: ORA_DISK_1
channel ORA_DISK_1: SID=150 device type=DISK
Crosschecked 3 objects
Finished implicit crosscheck backup at 10/03/2008 14:03:54
Starting implicit crosscheck copy at 10/03/2008 14:03:54
using channel ORA_DISK_1
Finished implicit crosscheck copy at 10/03/2008 14:03:54
```

```
searching for all files in the recovery area
cataloging files...
cataloging done
List of Cataloged Files
=======================
File Name: C:\ORACLE\FLASH_RECOVERY_AREA\ORCL\AUTOBACKUP\2008_10_03
\O1_MF_S_667144857_4GDYJ29H_.BKP
using channel ORA_DISK_1
starting media recovery
archived log for thread 1 with sequence 4 is already on disk as file
C:\ORACLE\ORADATA\ORCL\REDO01.LOG
archived log file
name=C:\ORACLE\ORADATA\ORCL\REDO01.LOG thread=1 sequence=4
media recovery complete, elapsed time: 00:00:00
Finished recover at 10/03/2008 14:03:59
```

10. Open the database with the `alter database open resetlogs` command.

```
RMAN> alter database open resetlogs;
database opened
```

The database is open. This concludes the exercise.

Lab 7.1: Monitoring RMAN Backups

In this exercise, we will monitor the progress of RMAN backups. We will also experiment with the `duration` command.

1. Log into RMAN, connecting to your recovery catalog.

```
C:\Documents and Settings\Robert>set oracle_sid=orcl
C:\Documents and Settings\Robert>rman target=/
catalog=rcat_user/rcat_user@rcat
Recovery Manager: Release 11.1.0.6.0 - Production
on Sun Oct 19 14:51:06 2008
Copyright (c) 1982, 2007, Oracle.  All rights reserved.
connected to target database: ORCL (DBID=1195614221)
connected to recovery catalog database
```

2. From another command-line window, log into SQL*Plus.

```
C:\Documents and Settings\Robert>set oracle_sid=orcl
C:\Documents and Settings\Robert>sqlplus / as sysdba
```

```
SQL*Plus: Release 11.1.0.6.0 - Production on Sun Oct 19 22:07:29 2008
Copyright (c) 1982, 2007, Oracle.  All rights reserved.
Connected to:
Oracle Database 11g Enterprise Edition Release 11.1.0.6.0 - Production
With the Partitioning, OLAP, Data Mining
and Real Application Testing options
SQL>
```

3. From the RMAN session, start an RMAN backup. We assume you have configured RMAN for backups as discussed in Chapter 2.

```
RMAN> Backup as compressed backupset database plus archivelog delete input;
```

4. While the RMAN backup is running, change to the SQL*Plus session and query the V$SESSION_LONGOPS view, as shown here.

```
SQL> Select sid, serial#, opname, time_remaining
  2  From v$session_longops
  3  Where sid in (select sid from v$session
  4                        Where program like '%rman%')
  5 And time_remaining > 0;
       SID    SERIAL# OPNAME                         TIME_REMAINING
---------- ---------- ------------------------------ --------------
       133         14 RMAN: aggregate input                      87
       126         33 RMAN: full datafile backup                179
```

5. Rerun the query listed in step 4, monitoring the TIME_REMAINING column. This will give you an idea of how long the backup will take.

6. When the backup completes, note how long it took to run. Ours took 4 minutes and 55 seconds, as shown here.

```
channel ORA_DISK_1: backup set complete, elapsed time: 00:04:55
Finished backup at 19-OCT-08
```

7. Once the RMAN backup is complete, run a second RMAN backup using the duration command with the minimize load database option as shown here.

```
RMAN> Backup as compressed backupset duration 1:00 minimize load database;
```

8. Monitor the backup with the V$SESSION_LONGOPS view again. How has the TIME_REMAINING column changed since you used the duration command? Here is what we saw when we queried the view. Note that TIME_REMAINING is now much higher.

```
SQL> Select sid, serial#, opname, time_remaining
  2  From v$session_longops
```

```
  3  Where sid in (select sid from v$session
  4                           Where program like '%rman%')
  5 And time_remaining > 0;
       SID     SERIAL# OPNAME                          TIME_REMAINING
---------- ---------- ------------------------------ --------------
       126          33 RMAN: full datafile backup              3130
```

9. When the backup ends, note how the runtime has changed.

Lab 7.2: One of My Backups Is Missing!

Sometimes it happens—the unexpected. This lab is about one of those cases.

1. Log into RMAN, connecting to your recovery catalog.

```
C:\Documents and Settings\Robert>set oracle_sid=orcl
C:\Documents and Settings\Robert>rman target=/
catalog=rcat_user/rcat_user@rcat
Recovery Manager: Release 11.1.0.6.0 - Production
on Sun Oct 19 14:51:06 2008
Copyright (c) 1982, 2007, Oracle.  All rights reserved.
connected to target database: ORCL (DBID=1195614221)
connected to recovery catalog database
```

2. List all of the archived redo logs currently in the control file. Note that these are not backups of the archived redo logs, but the actual archived redo logs themselves.

```
RMAN> list archivelog all;
List of Archived Log Copies for database with db_unique_name ORCL
=====================================================================
Key     Thrd Seq     S Low Time
------- ---- ------- - ---------
1773    1    23      A 18-OCT-08
        Name: C:\ORACLE\PRODUCT\11.1.0\DB_1\RDBMS\ARC00023_0667833490.001
1779    1    24      A 19-OCT-08
        Name: C:\ORACLE\PRODUCT\11.1.0\DB_1\RDBMS\ARC00024_0667833490.001
1787    1    25      A 19-OCT-08
        Name: C:\ORACLE\PRODUCT\11.1.0\DB_1\RDBMS\ARC00025_0667833490.001
```

3. Next, remove the last archived redo log listed.

```
RMAN> Host 'del C:\ORACLE\PRODUCT\11.1.0\DB_1\RDBMS\
ARC00025_0667833490.001';
host command complete
```

4. Now try to execute a backup.

```
RMAN> Backup as compressed backupset database plus archivelog delete input;
Starting backup at 20-OCT-08
current log archived
using channel ORA_DISK_1
RMAN-00571: ===========================================================
RMAN-00569: =============== ERROR MESSAGE STACK FOLLOWS ===============
RMAN-00571: ===========================================================
RMAN-03002: failure of backup plus archivelog command
at 10/20/2008 00:34:26
RMAN-06059: expected archived log not found, lost
of archived log compromises
recoverability
ORA-19625: error identifying file
C:\ORACLE\PRODUCT\11.1.0\DB_1\RDBMS\ARC00025_0667833490.001
ORA-27041: unable to open file
OSD-04002: unable to open file
O/S-Error: (OS 2) The system cannot find the file specified.
```

5. Notice that the backup failed because of the missing archived redo log. Run the command `crosscheck archivelog all` to mark the archived redo log as expired. This will allow you to rerun the backup.

```
RMAN> Crosscheck archivelog all;
released channel: ORA_DISK_1
allocated channel: ORA_DISK_1
channel ORA_DISK_1: SID=126 device type=DISK
validation succeeded for archived log
archived log file name=C:\ORACLE\PRODUCT\11.1.0\DB_1\RDBMS\
ARC00023_0667833490.001 RECID=43 STAMP=668556384
validation succeeded for archived log
archived log file name=C:\ORACLE\PRODUCT\11.1.0\DB_1\RDBMS\
ARC00024_0667833490.001 RECID=45 STAMP=668556995
validation failed for archived log
archived log file name=C:\ORACLE\PRODUCT\11.1.0\DB_1\RDBMS\
ARC00025_0667833490.001 RECID=47 STAMP=668557334
```

```
validation succeeded for archived log
archived log file
name=C:\ORACLE\FLASH_RECOVERY_AREA\ORCL\ARCHIVELOG\2008_10_20\
O1_MF_1_26_4HR9MCQX_.ARC RECID=50 STAMP=668565264
validation succeeded for archived log
archived log file name=C:\ORACLE\PRODUCT\11.1.0\DB_1\RDBMS\
ARC00026_0667833490.001 RECID=49 STAMP=668565264
Crosschecked 5 objects
```

6. Run the `list archivelog all` command. Notice that the status column (so clearly named S) is now X (expired) instead of A (available):

```
RMAN> list archivelog all;
List of Archived Log Copies for database with db_unique_name ORCL
=====================================================================
Key     Thrd Seq     S Low Time
------- ---- ------- - ---------
1773    1    23      A 18-OCT-08
        Name: C:\ORACLE\PRODUCT\11.1.0\DB_1\RDBMS\ARC00023_0667833490.001
1779    1    24      A 19-OCT-08
        Name: C:\ORACLE\PRODUCT\11.1.0\DB_1\RDBMS\ARC00024_0667833490.001
1787    1    25      X 19-OCT-08
        Name: C:\ORACLE\PRODUCT\11.1.0\DB_1\RDBMS\ARC00025_0667833490.001
1898    1    26      A 19-OCT-08
        Name: C:\ORACLE\FLASH_RECOVERY_AREA\ORCL\ARCHIVELOG\2008_10_20\
O1_MF_1_26_4HR9MCQX_.ARC
1897    1    26      A 19-OCT-08
        Name: C:\ORACLE\PRODUCT\11.1.0\DB_1\RDBMS\ARC00026_0667833490.001
```

Lab 8.1: Duplicating a Database Using Active Database Duplication

In this exercise, we will use backup-based duplication to create a database on the same system that the target database resides on. For this exercise, your database should be running in ARCHIVELOG mode and all networking to the target database should already be configured.

1. If you are running in Windows, create the service for the new database with `oradim`. In this example, we are creating a new database instance called `neworcl`.

```
C:\>oradim -new -sid neworcl
Instance created.
```

If there are any other OS-specific operations required to create a database instance, complete those now.

2. Create the password file for the neworcl instance.

```
C:\>orapwd file=c:\oracle\product\11.1.0\db_1\database\pwdneworcl.ora
Enter password for SYS:
```

3. Create a temporary pfile for the neworcl auxiliary instance using your editor of choice. The pfile should be contained in the ORACLE_HOME\database directory of the auxiliary instance and should be named initneworcl.ora. The pfile should have these parameters in it:

```
db_name=neworcl
memory_target=300m
control_files='c:\oracle\oradata\neworcl\control01.ctl',
'c:\oracle\oradata\neworcl\control02.ctl'
```

We will do the actual file-location conversions during the duplication.

4. Create the directory c:\oracle\oradata\neworcl

```
mkdir c:\oracle\oradata\neworcl
```

5. Startup nomount the auxiliary instance.

```
C:\oracle\product\11.1.0\db_1\database>set oracle_sid=neworcl
C:\oracle\product\11.1.0\db_1\database>sqlplus "/ as sysdba"
SQL*Plus: Release 11.1.0.6.0 - Production on Sat Oct 4 23:09:52 2008
Copyright (c) 1982, 2007, Oracle.  All rights reserved.
Connected to an idle instance.
SQL> startup nomount
ORACLE instance started.
Total System Global Area  313860096 bytes
Fixed Size                  1332892 bytes
Variable Size             192940388 bytes
Database Buffers          113246208 bytes
Redo Buffers                6340608 bytes
```

6. Configure service name resolution for your new auxiliary database. The method of this configuration will vary based on your site. In our case, we created an entry in the tnsnames.ora file on our server that looked like this:

```
NEWORCL =
  (DESCRIPTION =
    (ADDRESS = (PROTOCOL = TCP)(HOST = 192.168.2.2)(PORT = 1521))
    (CONNECT_DATA =
```

```
        (SERVER = DEDICATED)
        (SERVICE_NAME = neworcl)
    ) )
```

7. Now you will need to hard-code the instance name into the `listener.ora` file until the duplication of the database has been completed. You will get network errors if you do not hard-code the auxiliary instance in the `listener.ora` file. Here's an example of the entry in our `listener.ora`:

```
SID_LIST_LISTENER =
   (SID_LIST =
     (SID_DESC =
        (ORACLE_HOME=C:\oracle\product\11.1.0\db_1\NETWORK\ADMIN)
        (SID_NAME=neworcl)
     )  )
LISTENER =
  (DESCRIPTION_LIST =
    (DESCRIPTION =
      (ADDRESS = (PROTOCOL = TCP)(HOST = 192.168.2.2)(PORT = 1521))
      (ADDRESS = (PROTOCOL = IPC)(KEY = EXTPROC1521))
    ) )
```

8. Test the network connectivity to the auxiliary instance.

```
C:\oracle\product\11.1.0\db_1\database>sqlplus sys/robert@neworcl as sysdba
SQL*Plus: Release 11.1.0.6.0 - Production on Sat Oct 4 23:17:50 2008
Copyright (c) 1982, 2007, Oracle.  All rights reserved.
Connected to:
Oracle Database 11g Enterprise Edition Release 11.1.0.6.0 - Production
With the Partitioning, OLAP, Data Mining
and Real Application Testing options
SQL> select instance_name from v$instance;
INSTANCE_NAME
----------------
neworcl
```

If the connection fails, review the network configuration and ensure that the new auxiliary instance is running.

9. Start RMAN and connect to the target and the auxiliary databases.

```
C:\oracle\product\11.1.0\db_1\database>Set oracle_sid=orcl
C:\oracle\product\11.1.0\db_1\database>Rman target=sys/robert
```

```
auxiliary=sys/Robert@neworcl
Recovery Manager: Release 11.1.0.6.0 - Production
on Sat Oct 4 23:19:55 2008
Copyright (c) 1982, 2007, Oracle.  All rights reserved.
connected to target database: ORCL (DBID=1194923408)
connected to auxiliary database: NEWORCL (not mounted)
```

10. We are now ready to start the database duplication. Issue the `duplicate database` command, as shown here:

```
duplicate target database to neworcl from active database
nofilenamecheck
spfile set control_files 'c:\oracle\oradata\neworcl\control01.ctl',
'c:\oracle\oradata\neworcl\control02.ctl'
set db_file_name_convert
 'c:\oracle\oradata\orcl','c:\oracle\oradata\neworcl'
set log_file_name_convert 'c:\oracle\oradata\orcl','c:\oracle\oradata\
neworcl';
```

This command does the following:

- It starts the duplication process. We are using active database duplication, so no database backup is required.
- The SPFILE parameter will result in the target database spfile being copied over to the duplicate database. The duplicate database will use this spfile.
- The set commands (`set control_files`, `set db_file_name_convert`, and `set log_file_name_convert`) modify or add parameters to the spfile being copied to the duplicate database.

This `duplicate` command will result in a great deal of output, which we have decided not to include here as it seems a great waste of a perfectly good tree. Here is the output that you hopefully will see at the end of the database duplication:

```
database opened
Finished Duplicate Db at 04-OCT-08
```

There are several bugs in 11.1.0.6 that may cause a failure of active database duplications. We experienced one or two of these when writing this book. This exercise should work well on a new database that has just been created or a database with the latest patch sets installed.

11. Connect to the duplicated database to verify it is open.

```
C:\oracle\product\11.1.0\db_1\database>set oracle_sid=neworcl
C:\oracle\product\11.1.0\db_1\database>sqlplus sys/Robert as sysdba
```

```
SQL*Plus: Release 11.1.0.6.0 - Production on Sun Oct 5 00:04:02 2008
Copyright (c) 1982, 2007, Oracle.  All rights reserved.
Connected to:
Oracle Database 11g Enterprise Edition Release 11.1.0.6.0 - Production
With the Partitioning, OLAP, Data Mining
and Real Application Testing options
SQL> select name, open_mode from v$database;
NAME      OPEN_MODE
--------- ----------
AUXDB     READ WRITE
```

Lab 8.2: Duplicating a Database Using Backup-Based Duplication to a Different Point in Time

In this exercise, you will use backup-based duplication to create a database on the same system that the target database resides on. For this exercise, your database should be running in ARCHIVELOG mode and all networking to the target database should already be configured.

1. Back up your database as shown in Exercise 4.2.
2. Start RMAN and confirm that you have a valid backup with the `list backup of database summary` command and the `restore database validate` command. Note that your output will likely look very different from ours.

```
C:\Documents and Settings\Robert>rman target=/
Recovery Manager: Release 11.1.0.6.0 - Production
on Sat Oct 4 22:56:10 2008
Copyright (c) 1982, 2007, Oracle.  All rights reserved.
connected to target database: ORCL (DBID=1194923408)
RMAN> list backup of database summary;
using target database control file instead of recovery catalog
List of Backups
===============
Key     TY LV S Device Type Completion Time #Pieces #Copies Compressed Tag
------- -- -- - ----------- --------------- ------- ------- ---------- ---
2       B  F  A DISK        03-OCT-08       1       1       YES
TAG20081003T135426
RMAN> restore database validate;
```

```
Starting restore at 04-OCT-08
allocated channel: ORA_DISK_1
channel ORA_DISK_1: SID=127 device type=DISK
channel ORA_DISK_1: starting validation of datafile backup set
channel ORA_DISK_1: reading from backup piece
C:\ORACLE\FLASH_RECOVERY_AREA\ORCL\BACKUPSET\2008_10_03
\O1_MF_NNNDF_TAG20081003T135426_4GDY3S9H_.BKP
channel ORA_DISK_1: piece
handle=C:\ORACLE\FLASH_RECOVERY_AREA\ORCL\BACKUPSET\2008_10_03
\O1_MF_NNNDF_TAG20081003T135426_4GDY3S9H_.BKP tag=TAG20081003T135426
channel ORA_DISK_1: restored backup piece 1
channel ORA_DISK_1: validation complete, elapsed time: 00:01:36
Finished restore at 04-OCT-08
C:\Documents and Settings\Robert>set oracle_sid=orcl
```

3. If you are running in Windows, create the service for the new database with `oradim`. In this example, we are creating a new database instance called `neworcl`.

```
C:\>oradim -new -sid neworcl
Instance created.
```

If there are any other OS-specific operations required to create a database instance, complete those now.

4. Create the password file for the `neworcl` instance.

```
C:\>orapwd file=c:\oracle\product\11.1.0\db_1\database\pwdneworcl.ora
Enter password for SYS:
```

5. Create a temporary pfile for the `neworcl` auxiliary instance using your editor of choice. The pfile should be contained in the `ORACLE_HOME\database` directory of the auxiliary instance and should be named `initneworcl.ora`. The pfile should have these parameters in it:

```
db_name=neworcl
memory_target=300m
control_files='c:\oracle\oradata\neworcl\control01.ctl',
'c:\oracle\oradata\neworcl\control02.ctl'
```

We will do the actual file-location conversions during the duplication.

6. Create the directory `c:\oracle\oradata\neworcl`.

```
mkdir c:\oracle\oradata\neworcl
```

7. Start up the auxiliary instance.

```
C:\oracle\product\11.1.0\db_1\database>set oracle_sid=neworcl
C:\oracle\product\11.1.0\db_1\database>sqlplus "/ as sysdba"
SQL*Plus: Release 11.1.0.6.0 - Production on Sat Oct 4 23:09:52 2008
Copyright (c) 1982, 2007, Oracle.  All rights reserved.
Connected to an idle instance.
SQL> startup nomount
ORACLE instance started.
Total System Global Area  313860096 bytes
Fixed Size                  1332892 bytes
Variable Size             192940388 bytes
Database Buffers          113246208 bytes
Redo Buffers                6340608 bytes
```

8. Configure service name resolution for your new auxiliary database. The method of this configuration will vary based on your site. In our case, we created an entry in the `tnsnames.ora` file on our server that looked like this:

```
NEWORCL =
  (DESCRIPTION =
    (ADDRESS = (PROTOCOL = TCP)(HOST = 192.168.2.2)(PORT = 1521))
    (CONNECT_DATA =
      (SERVER = DEDICATED)
      (SERVICE_NAME = neworcl)
    ) )
```

9. Now you will need to hard-code the instance name into the `listener.ora` file until the duplication of the database has been completed. You will get network errors if you do not hard-code the auxiliary instance in the `listener.ora` file. Here's an example of the entry in our `listener.ora`:

```
SID_LIST_LISTENER =
   (SID_LIST =
     (SID_DESC =
        (ORACLE_HOME=C:\oracle\product\11.1.0\db_1\NETWORK\ADMIN)
        (SID_NAME=neworcl)
     )   )
LISTENER =
  (DESCRIPTION_LIST =
    (DESCRIPTION =
      (ADDRESS = (PROTOCOL = TCP)(HOST = 192.168.2.2)(PORT = 1521))
      (ADDRESS = (PROTOCOL = IPC)(KEY = EXTPROC1521))
    ) )
```

10. Test the network connectivity to the auxiliary instance.

```
C:\oracle\product\11.1.0\db_1\database>sqlplus sys/robert@neworcl as sysdba
SQL*Plus: Release 11.1.0.6.0 - Production on Sat Oct 4 23:17:50 2008
Copyright (c) 1982, 2007, Oracle.  All rights reserved.
Connected to:
Oracle Database 11g Enterprise Edition Release 11.1.0.6.0 - Production
With the Partitioning, OLAP, Data Mining
and Real Application Testing options
SQL> select instance_name from v$instance;
INSTANCE_NAME
----------------
neworcl
```

If the connection fails, review the network configuration and ensure that the new auxiliary instance is running.

11. Connect to the ORCL database using the scott account.

```
C:\Documents and Settings\Robert>sqlplus scott/tiger
SQL*Plus: Release 11.1.0.6.0 - Production on Sat Oct 11 14:43:14 2008
Copyright (c) 1982, 2007, Oracle.  All rights reserved.
Connected to:
Oracle Database 11g Enterprise Edition Release 11.1.0.6.0 - Production
With the Partitioning, OLAP, Data Mining
and Real Application Testing options
SQL>
```

If you are using a new database, you may need to unlock the scott account.

```
SQL> alter user scott account unlock;
User altered.
SQL> alter user scott identified by tiger;
User altered.
```

12. In the scott schema, create a table called DUPE_TABLE.

```
SQL> create table dupe_table(id number, the_date date);
Table created.
```

13. Insert a record in the DUPE_TABLE table and commit.

```
SQL> Insert into dupe_table values (1, sysdate);
1 row created.
SQL> commit;
Commit complete.
```

14. Wait for a minute or so. Insert a second record in the DUPE_TABLE table and commit.

```
SQL> Insert into dupe_table values (1, sysdate);
1 row created.
SQL> commit;
Commit complete.
```

15. Select from the DUPE_TABLE table.

```
SQL> select * from dupe_table;
        ID THE_DATE
---------- -------------------
         1 10/11/2008 14:46:14
         1 10/11/2008 14:48:25
```

16. Connect as sys and force a log switch. This is because database duplications from backup will use only archived redo logs to recover a database. Online redo logs are not used. This is not true with active database duplications.

```
SQL> connect sys/robert as sysdba
Connected.
SQL> alter system switch logfile;
System altered.
```

17. Start RMAN and connect to the target and the auxiliary databases.

```
C:\oracle\product\11.1.0\db_1\database>Set oracle_sid=orcl
C:\oracle\product\11.1.0\db_1\database>Rman target=/
auxiliary=sys/Robert@neworcl
Recovery Manager: Release 11.1.0.6.0 - Production
on Sat Oct 4 23:19:55 2008
Copyright (c) 1982, 2007, Oracle.  All rights reserved.
connected to target database: ORCL (DBID=1194923408)
connected to auxiliary database: NEWORCL (not mounted)
```

18. We are now ready to start the database duplication. Issue the `duplicate database` command, recovering the database to a time in between the two insert records. We recommend you recover to about 5 seconds before the second record, as shown here:

```
duplicate target database to neworcl
until time "to_date('10/11/2008 14:48:20','mm/dd/yyyy hh24:mi:ss')"
nofilenamecheck
spfile set control_files=
'c:\oracle\oradata\neworcl\control01.ctl',
```

```
'c:\oracle\oradata\neworcl\control02.ctl'
set db_file_name_convert
'c:\oracle\oradata\orcl','c:\oracle\oradata\neworcl'
set log_file_name_convert
'c:\oracle\oradata\orcl','c:\oracle\oradata\neworcl';
```

This command does the following:

- It starts the duplication process.
- It starts the duplication process restoring the database to the specific point in time using backups of the database and archived redo logs. The restore will be to the point in time listed in the `until time` clause.
- The SPFILE parameter will result in the target database spfile being copied over to the duplicate database. The duplicate database will use this spfile.
- The `set` commands (`set control_files`, `set db_file_name_convert`, and `set log_file_name_convert`) modify or add parameters to the spfile being copied to the duplicate database.

This `duplicate` command will result in a great deal of output, which we have decided not to include here as it seems a great waste of a perfectly good tree. Here is the output that you hopefully will see at the end of the database duplication:

```
database opened
Finished Duplicate Db at 04-OCT-08
```

19. Connect to the duplicated database to verify that it is open.

```
C:\oracle\product\11.1.0\db_1\database>set oracle_sid=neworcl
C:\oracle\product\11.1.0\db_1\database>sqlplus sys/Robert as sysdba
SQL*Plus: Release 11.1.0.6.0 - Production on Sun Oct 5 00:04:02 2008
Copyright (c) 1982, 2007, Oracle.  All rights reserved.
Connected to:
Oracle Database 11g Enterprise Edition Release 11.1.0.6.0 - Production
With the Partitioning, OLAP, Data Mining
and Real Application Testing options
SQL> select name, open_mode from v$database;
NAME      OPEN_MODE
--------- ----------
AUXDB     READ WRITE
```

20. Connect to the `scott` schema. Query the DUPE_TABLE and ensure that only one record now exists.

```
SQL> connect scott/tiger
Connected.
```

```
SQL> select * from dupe_table;
        ID THE_DATE
---------- ---------
         1 11-OCT-08
```

If you want to run this exercise again after the first successful run, you will need to perform these steps:

1. Shut down the auxiliary instance (now it's a new database!).
2. Remove the spfile assigned to the auxiliary instance.
3. Mount the auxiliary instance with the `Startup nomount` command.

Lab 9.1: Using the Recycle Bin

This lab was created using Windows XP. However, it should also work using Unix (and in fact was tested using Linux). This lab shows you how to set up the Recycle Bin and use it to restore a dropped table. The overall steps are as follows: create a table, insert data into the table, enable the Recycle Bin, drop the table, restore the table from the Recycle Bin, and query the table to verify the contents.

1. Create the table.

   ```
   SQL> create table recycle_test (x number, y varchar2(10));
   Table created.
   SQL>
   ```

2. Next, we'll add some rows and commit the transaction.

   ```
   SQL>
   insert into recycle_test values (1, 'row 1');
   insert into recycle_test values (2, 'row 2');
   insert into recycle_test values (3, 'row 3');
   insert into recycle_test values (4, 'row 4');
   insert into recycle_test values (5, 'row 5');
   Commit;
   SQL>
   ```

3. Then, enable the Recycle Bin for the session.

   ```
   SQL> ALTER SESSION SET recyclebin = ON;
   Session altered.
   ```

4. Now drop the table.

```
SQL> drop table recycle_test;
Table dropped.
```

5. Restore the table from the Recycle Bin.

```
SQL> flashback table recycle_test to before drop;
Flashback complete.
```

6. Finally, query the table and verify the contents.

```
SQL> select * from recycle_test;

         X Y
---------- ----------
         1 row 1
         2 row 2
         3 row 3
         4 row 4
         5 row 5
```

Lab 9.2: Performing a More Complex Flashback Query Analysis

This lab shows you how to perform a more complex analysis using the Flashback Query feature. We'll create and populate a table, then step through adding rows and querying the table at various points in time to demonstrate the feature.

1. Create the table.

```
SQL> create table flashback_query_test
         (x number,
          y varchar2(10),
          z date
         );
Table created.
```

2. Now insert five rows of data and commit.

```
SQL>
insert into flashback_query_test values (1, 'row 1', sysdate);
```

```
insert into flashback_query_test values (2, 'row 2', sysdate);
insert into flashback_query_test values (3, 'row 3', sysdate);
insert into flashback_query_test values (4, 'row 4', sysdate);
insert into flashback_query_test values (5, 'row 5', sysdate);
commit;
Commit complete.
```

3. Now query the table to view the results.

```
SQL> alter session set nls_date_format = 'dd-mon-yy hh24:mi:ss';

Session altered.

SQL> select * from flashback_query_test;
         X Y          Z
---------- ---------- --------------------
         1 row 1      21-nov-2008 13:48:51
         2 row 2      21 nov 2008 13:48:51
         3 row 3      21-nov-2008 13:48:51
         4 row 4      21-nov-2008 13:48:51
         5 row 5      21-nov-2008 13:48:51
SQL>
```

4. Query the table, specifying a timestamp after the table was created but prior to inserting the first five rows:

```
SQL> select * from flashback_query_test
     as of timestamp(to_timestamp(
     '21-nov-2008 13:48:50','DD-MON-YYYY HH24:MI:SS'));

no rows selected

SQL>
```

5. Now insert five more rows, wait five minutes, then insert five more rows, then commit. The results should look similar to this:

```
insert into flashback_query_test values (6, 'row 6', sysdate);
insert into flashback_query_test values (7, 'row 7', sysdate);
insert into flashback_query_test values (8, 'row 8', sysdate);
insert into flashback_query_test values (9, 'row 9', sysdate);
insert into flashback_query_test values (10, 'row 10', sysdate);
commit;
```

Wait here five minutes.

```
insert into flashback_query_test values (11, 'row 11', sysdate);
insert into flashback_query_test values (12, 'row 12', sysdate);
insert into flashback_query_test values (13, 'row 13', sysdate);
insert into flashback_query_test values (14, 'row 14', sysdate);
insert into flashback_query_test values (15, 'row 15', sysdate);
commit;

SQL> select * from flashback_query_test;
         X Y          Z
---------- ---------- --------------------
         1 row 1      21-nov-2008 13:48:51
         2 row 2      21-nov-2008 13:48:51
         3 row 3      21-nov-2008 13:48:51
         4 row 4      21-nov-2008 13:48:51
         5 row 5      21-nov-2008 13:48:51
         6 row 6      21-nov-2008 13:50:00
         7 row 7      21-nov-2008 13:50:00
         8 row 8      21-nov-2008 13:50:00
         9 row 9      21-nov-2008 13:50:00
        10 row 10     21-nov-2008 13:50:00
        11 row 11     21-nov-2008 13:55:00
        12 row 12     21-nov-2008 13:55:00
        13 row 13     21-nov-2008 13:55:00
        14 row 14     21-nov-2008 13:55:00
        15 row 15     21-nov-2008 13:55:00

15 rows selected.

SQL>
```

6. Now that you have different discrete insert times, you can run queries that show the state of the table at various points in time. Run an AS OF query that will show only rows 1 through 10, based on the timestamp that was inserted.

```
SQL> select * from flashback_query_test
     as of timestamp(to_timestamp(
     '21-nov-2008 13:51:00','DD-MON-YYYY HH24:MI:SS'));

         X Y          Z
---------- ---------- --------------------
         1 row 1      21-nov-2008 13:48:51
```

```
         2 row 2      21-nov-2008 13:48:51
         3 row 3      21-nov-2008 13:48:51
         4 row 4      21-nov-2008 13:48:51
         5 row 5      21-nov-2008 13:48:51
         6 row 6      21-nov-2008 13:50:00
         7 row 7      21-nov-2008 13:50:00
         8 row 8      21-nov-2008 13:50:00
         9 row 9      21-nov-2008 13:50:00
        10 row 10     21-nov-2008 13:50:00

10 rows selected.

SQL>
```

7. Now insert five more rows, but don't commit. Run a query showing the new rows in the table, and then an AS OF query with a timestamp following the insert that shows that the data is not committed and not available for Flashback Query.

```
SQL>
insert into flashback_query_test values (16, 'row 16', sysdate);
insert into flashback_query_test values (17, 'row 17', sysdate);
insert into flashback_query_test values (18, 'row 18', sysdate);
insert into flashback_query_test values (19, 'row 19', sysdate);
insert into flashback_query_test values (20, 'row 20', sysdate);

SQL> select * from flashback_query_test;

         X Y          Z
---------- ---------- --------------------
         1 row 1      21-nov-2008 13:48:51
         2 row 2      21-nov-2008 13:48:51
         3 row 3      21-nov-2008 13:48:51
         4 row 4      21-nov-2008 13:48:51
         5 row 5      21-nov-2008 13:48:51
         6 row 6      21-nov-2008 13:50:00
         7 row 7      21-nov-2008 13:50:00
         8 row 8      21-nov-2008 13:50:00
         9 row 9      21-nov-2008 13:50:00
        10 row 10     21-nov-2008 13:50:00
        11 row 11     21-nov-2008 13:55:00
        12 row 12     21-nov-2008 13:55:00
```

```
        13 row 13     21-nov-2008 13:55:00
        14 row 14     21-nov-2008 13:55:00
        15 row 15     21-nov-2008 13:55:00
        16 row 16     21-nov-2008 14:00:00
        17 row 17     21-nov-2008 14:00:00
        18 row 18     21-nov-2008 14:00:00
        19 row 19     21-nov-2008 14:00:00
        20 row 20     21-nov-2008 14:00:00

20 rows selected.

SQL>
SQL> select * from flashback_query_test
        as of timestamp(to_timestamp(
       '21-nov-2008 14:05:00','DD-MON-YYYY HH24:MI:SS'));

         X Y          Z
---------- ---------- --------------------
         1 row 1      21-nov-2008 13:48:51
         2 row 2      21-nov-2008 13:48:51
         3 row 3      21-nov-2008 13:48:51
         4 row 4      21-nov-2008 13:48:51
         5 row 5      21-nov-2008 13:48:51
         6 row 6      21-nov-2008 13:50:00
         7 row 7      21-nov-2008 13:50:00
         8 row 8      21-nov-2008 13:50:00
         9 row 9      21-nov-2008 13:50:00
        10 row 10     21-nov-2008 13:50:00
        11 row 11     21-nov-2008 13:55:00
        12 row 12     21-nov-2008 13:55:00
        13 row 13     21-nov-2008 13:55:00
        14 row 14     21-nov-2008 13:55:00
        15 row 15     21-nov-2008 13:55:00

15 rows selected.

SQL>
```

8. Commit and then requery, noting that the `AS OF` timestamp must be after the commit for you to see the committed data using Flashback Query.

```
SQL> commit;
SQL> select sysdate from dual;
SYSDATE
--------------------
21-nov-2008 14:21:41

SQL> select * from flashback_query_test
        as of timestamp(to_timestamp(
       '21-nov-2008 14:21:41','DD-MON-YYYY HH24:MI:SS'));

         X Y          Z
---------- ---------- --------------------
         1 row 1      21-nov-2008 13:48:51
         2 row 2      21-nov-2008 13:48:51
         3 row 3      21-nov-2008 13:48:51
         4 row 4      21-nov-2008 13:48:51
         5 row 5      21-nov-2008 13:48:51
         6 row 6      21-nov-2008 13:50:00
         7 row 7      21-nov-2008 13:50:00
         8 row 8      21-nov-2008 13:50:00
         9 row 9      21-nov-2008 13:50:00
        10 row 10     21-nov-2008 13:50:00
        11 row 11     21-nov-2008 13:55:00
        12 row 12     21-nov-2008 13:55:00
        13 row 13     21-nov-2008 13:55:00
        14 row 14     21-nov-2008 13:55:00
        15 row 15     21-nov-2008 13:55:00
        16 row 16     21-nov-2008 14:00:00
        17 row 17     21-nov-2008 14:00:00
        18 row 18     21-nov-2008 14:00:00
        19 row 19     21-nov-2008 14:00:00
        20 row 20     21-nov-2008 14:00:00

20 rows selected.
SQL>
```

Lab 9.3: Using Flashback Data Archive

In this lab you'll exercise the Flashback Data Archive feature. You'll create an archive table for a populated base table and observe the audit migrations to the archive table, then observe purging from the archive table.

1. Create the flashback data archive.

```
SQL>create flashback archive default default_flash_archive
tablespace user_data quota 10m retention 1 day;
```

2. Now we'll use the previously created `flashback_query_test` table as the base table for the archive.

```
SQL> alter table flashback_query_test flashback
 archive default_flash_archive;
Table altered.
```

3. Now we'll manipulate the data and observe the flashback data archive.

```
SQL> select sysdate from dual;

SYSDATE
--------------------
21-nov-2008 15:58:44

SQL> delete from flashback_query_test where x > 15;

5 rows deleted.

SQL> commit;

Commit complete.

SQL> select * from flashback_query_test;

         X Y          Z
---------- ---------- --------------------
         1 row 1      21-nov-2008 13:48:51
         2 row 2      21-nov-2008 13:48:51
         3 row 3      21-nov-2008 13:48:51
         4 row 4      21-nov-2008 13:48:51
         5 row 5      21-nov-2008 13:48:51
```

```
         6 row 6      21-nov-2008 13:50:00
         7 row 7      21-nov-2008 13:50:00
         8 row 8      21-nov-2008 13:50:00
         9 row 9      21-nov-2008 13:50:00
        10 row 10     21-nov-2008 13:50:00
        11 row 11     21-nov-2008 13:55:00
        12 row 12     21-nov-2008 13:55:00
        13 row 13     21-nov-2008 13:55:00
        14 row 14     21-nov-2008 13:55:00
        15 row 15     21-nov-2008 13:55:00

15 rows selected.
```

4. Query the base table using the AS OF clause, specifying a timestamp prior to the delete timestamp. You'll observe that all the rows are returned.

```
SQL> select * from flashback_query_test
as of timestamp(to_timestamp('21-nov-2008 15:58:00',
'DD-MON-YYYY HH24:MI:SS'));

         X Y          Z
---------- ---------- --------------------
        16 row 16     21-nov-2008 15:08:54
        17 row 17     21-nov-2008 15:08:54
        18 row 18     21-nov-2008 15:08:54
        19 row 19     21-nov-2008 15:08:54
        20 row 20     21-nov-2008 15:08:54
         2 row 2      21-nov-2008 13:48:51
         4 row 4      21-nov-2008 13:48:51
        14 row 14     21-nov-2008 13:55:00
         1 row 1      21-nov-2008 13:48:51
         7 row 7      21-nov-2008 13:50:00
        13 row 13     21-nov-2008 13:55:00
        15 row 15     21-nov-2008 13:55:00
         3 row 3      21-nov-2008 13:48:51
         8 row 8      21-nov-2008 13:50:00
         6 row 6      21-nov-2008 13:50:00
         9 row 9      21-nov-2008 13:50:00
        10 row 10     21-nov-2008 13:50:00
         5 row 5      21-nov-2008 13:48:51
        11 row 11     21-nov-2008 13:55:00
```

```
        12 row 12     21-nov-2008 13:55:00

20 rows selected.
```

5. Verify the timestamp for the delete.

```
SQL> select * from flashback_query_test
as of timestamp(to_timestamp('21-nov-2008 16:00:00',
'DD-MON-YYYY HH24:MI:SS'));

         X Y          Z
---------- ---------- --------------------
         2 row 2      21-nov-2008 13:48:51
         4 row 4      21-nov-2008 13:48:51
        14 row 14     21-nov-2008 13:55:00
         1 row 1      21-nov-2008 13:48:51
         7 row 7      21-nov-2008 13:50:00
        13 row 13     21-nov-2008 13:55:00
        15 row 15     21-nov-2008 13:55:00
         3 row 3      21-nov-2008 13:48:51
         8 row 8      21-nov-2008 13:50:00
         6 row 6      21-nov-2008 13:50:00
         9 row 9      21-nov-2008 13:50:00
        10 row 10     21-nov-2008 13:50:00
         5 row 5      21-nov-2008 13:48:51
        11 row 11     21-nov-2008 13:55:00
        12 row 12     21-nov-2008 13:55:00

15 rows selected.
```

6. Now run the query again as many times as you like prior to the end of the 10-day retention period, and you should see the following results:

```
SQL> select * from flashback_query_test
as of timestamp(to_timestamp('21-nov-2008 15:58:00',
'DD-MON-YYYY HH24:MI:SS'));

         X Y          Z
---------- ---------- --------------------
        16 row 16     21-nov-2008 15:08:54
        17 row 17     21-nov-2008 15:08:54
        18 row 18     21-nov-2008 15:08:54
```

```
        19 row 19      21-nov-2008 15:08:54
        20 row 20      21-nov-2008 15:08:54
         2 row 2       21-nov-2008 13:48:51
         4 row 4       21-nov-2008 13:48:51
        14 row 14      21-nov-2008 13:55:00
         1 row 1       21-nov-2008 13:48:51
         7 row 7       21-nov-2008 13:50:00
        13 row 13      21-nov-2008 13:55:00
        15 row 15      21-nov-2008 13:55:00
         3 row 3       21-nov-2008 13:48:51
         8 row 8       21-nov-2008 13:50:00
         6 row 6       21-nov-2008 13:50:00
         9 row 9       21-nov-2008 13:50:00
        10 row 10      21-nov-2008 13:50:00
         5 row 5       21-nov-2008 13:48:51
        11 row 11      21-nov-2008 13:55:00
        12 row 12      21-nov-2008 13:55:00

20 rows selected.
SQL>
```

Just to verify that you are using the flasback data archive and not undo, you can shut down and start up the database to clear the undo tablespace, and you will still see the query results demonstrated in this section.

Lab 10.1: Using Support Workbench to Report a Problem to Oracle Support

This lab was created using Oracle Enterprise Manager (OEM) running on Windows XP. However, it should also work using Unix.

This lab shows you the basic steps to follow to use the Oracle Support Workbench to open a support ticket with Oracle. Using the OEM user interface, the directions will be presented to you on each page, so you should have no problem opening the support ticket—that is, if you have an Oracle support agreement. If you have an Oracle support agreement, perform the following steps to completion. If you don't have an Oracle support agreement, follow until step 5.

1. Open Support Workbench.
2. View your alerts and select a critical error alert.
3. View the problem details.
4. Gather any additional diagnostic information.

5. Create a service request.
6. Package and upload the data to Oracle Support.
7. Track the service request and implement any recommended changes.
8. Close the incident.

Lab 10.2: Performing Block Media Recovery

In this lab, you will perform block media recovery of a corrupt data file. This lab was created on Windows XP and uses a tool specifically for Windows. However, it should also work using Unix, using Unix-specific commands.

These are the basic prerequisites and steps for this exercise:

1. Make sure you have a hex editor.
2. Ensure that the database is in ARCHIVELOG mode.
3. Create a new tablespace called USER_DATA.
4. Create a new table in the USER_DATA tablespace.
5. Take a hot full backup of the database.
6. Use the hex editor to corrupt the datafile for the USER_DATA tablespace.
7. Run the dbv command and the SQL queries to identify the corrupt blocks.
8. Perform the block media recovery.
9. Validate the results.

Here are the specific steps:

1. If using Windows, download and install a hex editor.
2. Make sure the database is in ARCHIVELOG mode.

```
SQL> show parameter log_archive_start
NAME                                 TYPE        VALUE
------------------------------------ ----------- -----------
log_archive_start                    boolean     FALSE

SQL> shutdown immediate;
Database closed.
Database dismounted.
ORACLE instance shut down.
SQL> exit

sqlplus sys/orcl as sysdba
```

```
SQL*Plus: Release 11.1.0.6.0 - Production on Sat Nov 22 17:55:34 2008

Copyright (c) 1982, 2007, Oracle.  All rights reserved.

Connected to an idle instance.

SQL> startup mount
ORACLE instance started.

Total System Global Area  732352512 bytes
Fixed Size                  1335696 bytes
Variable Size             444599920 bytes
Database Buffers          281018368 bytes
Redo Buffers                5398528 bytes
Database mounted.
SQL> alter database archivelog;

Database altered.

SQL> archive log start;
Statement processed.
SQL> alter database open;

Database altered.

SQL>
```

3. Create a new tablespace called USER_DATA.

```
SQL> create tablespace user_data datafile
'c:\oracle\oradata\orcl\user_data01.dbf' size 10 m;

Tablespace created.
SQL>
```

4. Create a new table in the USER_DATA tablespace.

```
SQL> create table block_corruption_test
tablespace user_data
as select * from flashback_query_test;

Table created.
SQL>
```

5. Take a hot full RMAN backup of the database.

```
rman target=sys/orcl

Recovery Manager: Release 11.1.0.6.0 - Production on
 Sat Nov 22 18:17:45 2008

Copyright (c) 1982, 2007, Oracle.  All rights reserved.

connected to target database: ORCL (DBID=1190467526)

RMAN> backup database plus archivelog;
Starting backup at 22-NOV-08
current log archived
allocated channel: ORA_DISK_1
channel ORA_DISK_1: SID=130 device type=DISK
channel ORA_DISK_1: starting archived log backup set
channel ORA_DISK_1: specifying archived log(s) in backup set
input archived log thread=1 sequence=210 RECID=184 STAMP=670763775
input archived log thread=1 sequence=211 RECID=185 STAMP=670765527
input archived log thread=1 sequence=212 RECID=186 STAMP=670847849
input archived log thread=1 sequence=213 RECID=187 STAMP=671056681
input archived log thread=1 sequence=214 RECID=188 STAMP=671313636
input archived log thread=1 sequence=215 RECID=189 STAMP=671387999
input archived log thread=1 sequence=216 RECID=190 STAMP=671459676
input archived log thread=1 sequence=217 RECID=191 STAMP=671461419
input archived log thread=1 sequence=218 RECID=192 STAMP=671481182
input archived log thread=1 sequence=219 RECID=194 STAMP=671481209
channel ORA_DISK_1: starting piece 1 at 22-NOV-08
channel ORA_DISK_1: finished piece 1 at 22-NOV-08
piece handle=C:\TEMP\ORABACKUP\41K0BVRH_1_1
tag=TAG20081122T183330 comment=NONE
channel ORA_DISK_1: backup set complete, elapsed time: 00:03:46
Finished backup at 22-NOV-08

Starting backup at 22-NOV-08
using channel ORA_DISK_1
channel ORA_DISK_1: starting full datafile backup set
channel ORA_DISK_1: specifying datafile(s) in backup set
```

```
input datafile file number=00001 name=C:\ORACLE\ORADATA\ORCL\SYSTEM01.DBF
input datafile file number=00002 name=C:\ORACLE\ORADATA\ORCL\SYSAUX01.DBF
input datafile file number=00003 name=C:\ORACLE\ORADATA\ORCL\UNDOTBS01.DBF
input datafile file number=00005 name=C:\ORACLE\ORADATA\ORCL\EXAMPLE01.DBF
input datafile file number=00006
name=C:\ORACLE\ORADATA\ORCL\USER_DATA01.DBF
input datafile file number=00004 name=C:\ORACLE\ORADATA\ORCL\USERS01.DBF
channel ORA_DISK_1: starting piece 1 at 22-NOV-08
channel ORA_DISK_1: finished piece 1 at 22-NOV-08
piece handle=C:\TEMP\ORABACKUP\42K0C03A_1_1
 tag=TAG20081122T184601 comment=NONE
channel ORA_DISK_1: backup set complete, elapsed time: 00:02:26
channel ORA_DISK_1: starting full datafile backup set
channel ORA_DISK_1: specifying datafile(s) in backup set
including current control file in backup set
including current SPFILE in backup set
channel ORA_DISK_1: starting piece 1 at 22-NOV-08
channel ORA_DISK_1: finished piece 1 at 22-NOV-08
piece handle=C:\TEMP\ORABACKUP\43K0C08F_1_1
 tag=TAG20081122T184601 comment=NONE
channel ORA_DISK_1: backup set complete, elapsed time: 00:00:02
Finished backup at 22-NOV-08

Starting backup at 22-NOV-08
current log archived
using channel ORA_DISK_1
channel ORA_DISK_1: starting archived log backup set
channel ORA_DISK_1: specifying archived log(s) in backup set
input archived log thread=1 sequence=220 RECID=195 STAMP=671482150
channel ORA_DISK_1: starting piece 1 at 22-NOV-08
channel ORA_DISK_1: finished piece 1 at 22-NOV-08
piece handle=C:\TEMP\ORABACKUP\44K0C097_1_1
 tag=TAG20081122T184910 comment=NONE
channel ORA_DISK_1: backup set complete, elapsed time: 00:00:01
Finished backup at 22-NOV-08

RMAN>
```

In Step 6 you will use a hex editor to corrupt a datafile. You will lose data, so complete Step 6 only in an isolated testing environment!

6. Use the hex editor to corrupt the datafile for the USER_DATA tablespace. First issue the SQL command to make the USER_DATA tablespace offline, then use the hex editor to search for a text string found in the target table (for example, `row 1`), and then replace the data with zeroes. Save the file, exit, then issue the command to make the tablespace online.

```
SQL> alter tablespace user_data offline;

Tablespace altered.

SQL>
```

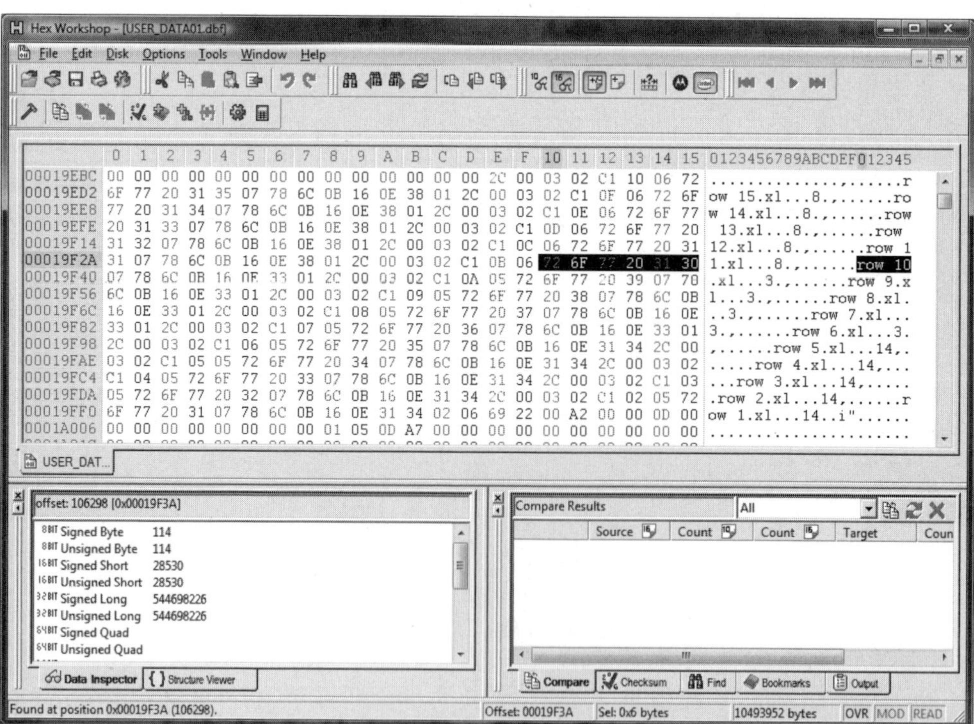

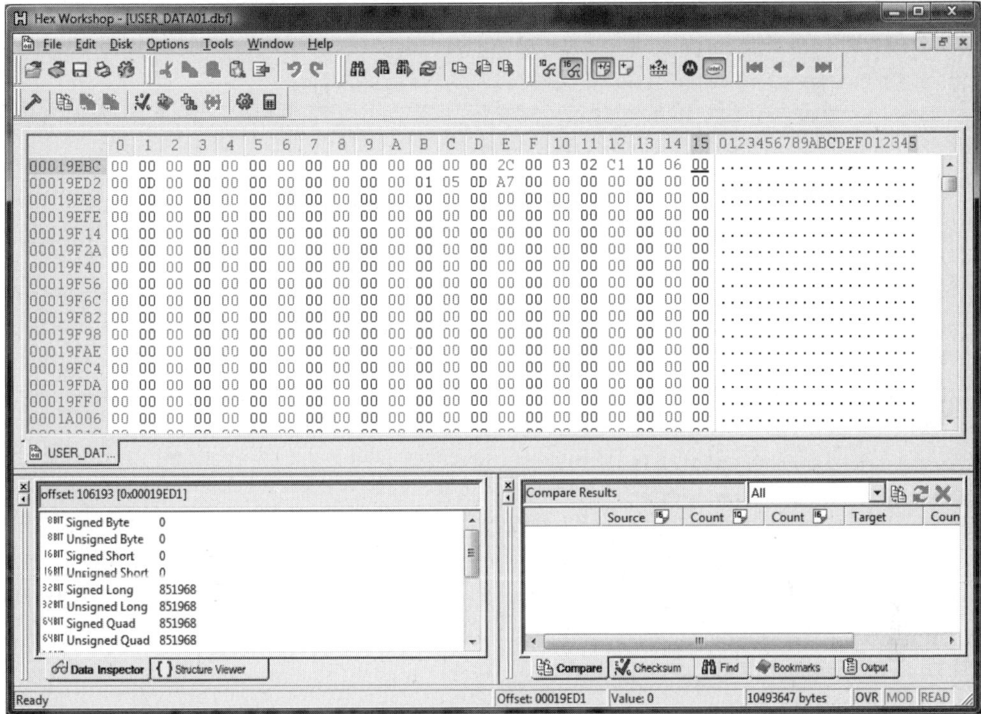

```
SQL> alter tablespace user_data online;

Tablespace altered.

SQL>
```

7. Run the dbv command and the SQL queries to identify the corrupt blocks.

```
c:\dbv file=c:\oracle\oradata\orcl\user_data01.dbf
DBVERIFY: Release 11.1.0.6.0 - Production on Sat Nov 22 19:27:57 2008

Copyright (c) 1982, 2007, Oracle.  All rights reserved.

DBVERIFY - Verification starting : FILE =
 c:\oracle\oradata\orcl\user_data01.dbf

Page 12 is influx - most likely media corrupt
Corrupt block relative dba: 0x0180000c (file 6, block 12)
Fractured block found during dbv:
```

```
Data in bad block:
 type: 6 format: 2 rdba: 0x0180000c
 last change scn: 0x0000.00622269 seq: 0x2 flg: 0x04
 spare1: 0x0 spare2: 0x0 spare3: 0x0
 consistency value in tail: 0x00000000
 check value in block header: 0xc476
 computed block checksum: 0xdd1e



DBVERIFY - Verification complete

Total Pages Examined         : 1280
Total Pages Processed (Data) : 0
Total Pages Failing   (Data) : 0
Total Pages Processed (Index): 0
Total Pages Failing   (Index): 0
Total Pages Processed (Other): 11
Total Pages Processed (Seg)  : 0
Total Pages Failing   (Seg)  : 0
Total Pages Empty            : 1268
Total Pages Marked Corrupt   : 1
Total Pages Influx           : 1
Total Pages Encrypted        : 0
Highest block SCN            : 6431341 (0.6431341)



SQL> select * from block_corruption_test;
select * from block_corruption_test
              *
ERROR at line 1:
ORA-01578: ORACLE data block corrupted (file # 6, block # 12)
ORA-01110: data file 6: 'C:\ORACLE\ORADATA\ORCL\USER_DATA01.DBF'


SQL>
SQL> select file#, block#, blocks, corruption_type "TYPE"
```

```
from v$database_block_corruption;

     FILE#     BLOCK#     BLOCKS TYPE
---------- ---------- ---------- ---------
         6         12          1 FRACTURED

SQL>
```

8. Perform the block media recovery using RMAN. Either recover the specific block or recover all the blocks in the corruption list.

```
RMAN> recover datafile 6 block 12;

RMAN> recover corruption list;
C:\rman target=sys/orcl

Recovery Manager: Release 11.1.0.6.0 - Production on
 Sat Nov 22 19:37:52 2008

Copyright (c) 1982, 2007, Oracle.  All rights reserved.

connected to target database: ORCL (DBID=1190467526)

RMAN> recover datafile 6 block 12;

Starting recover at 22-NOV-08
using target database control file instead of recovery catalog
allocated channel: ORA_DISK_1
channel ORA_DISK_1: SID=138 device type=DISK

channel ORA_DISK_1: restoring block(s)
channel ORA_DISK_1: specifying block(s) to restore from backup set
restoring blocks of datafile 00006
channel ORA_DISK_1: reading from backup piece
 C:\TEMP\ORABACKUP\42K0C03A_1_1
channel ORA_DISK_1: piece handle=C:\TEMP\ORABACKUP\42K0C03A_1_1
 tag=TAG20081122T
184601
channel ORA_DISK_1: restored block(s) from backup piece 1
channel ORA_DISK_1: block restore complete, elapsed time: 00:00:01
```

```
starting media recovery
media recovery complete, elapsed time: 00:00:03

Finished recover at 22-NOV-08

RMAN>
```

9. Validate the results.

```
SQL>select file#, block#, blocks, corruption_type "TYPE"
from v$database_block_corruption;

no rows selected

SQL> select * from block_corruption_test;

         X Y          Z
---------- ---------- ---------
         1 row 1      22-NOV-08
         2 row 2      22-NOV-08
         3 row 3      22-NOV-08
         4 row 4      22-NOV-08
         5 row 5      22-NOV-08
         6 row 6      22-NOV-08
         7 row 7      22-NOV-08
         8 row 8      22-NOV-08
         9 row 9      22-NOV-08
        10 row 10     22-NOV-08
        11 row 11     22-NOV-08
        12 row 12     22-NOV-08
        13 row 13     22-NOV-08
        14 row 14     22-NOV-08
        15 row 15     22-NOV-08

15 rows selected.

SQL>
```

Lab 11.1: Exporting a Transportable Tablespace

This lab was created using Windows XP. However, it should also work using Unix (and in fact was tested using Linux). In this lab, you'll export a transportable tablespace set.

1. Query the v$transportable_platform view to determine which destination platforms are compatible with the source database platform.

```
SQL> select * from v$transportable_platform;
PLATFORM_ID PLATFORM_NAME                    ENDIAN_FORMAT
----------- -------------------------------- --------------
          1 Solaris[tm] OE (32-bit)          Big
          2 Solaris[tm] OE (64-bit)          Big
          7 Microsoft Windows IA (32-bit)    Little
         10 Linux IA (32-bit)                Little
          6 AIX-Based Systems (64-bit)       Big
          3 HP-UX (64-bit)                   Big
          5 HP Tru64 UNIX                    Little
          4 HP-UX IA (64-bit)                Big
         11 Linux IA (64-bit)                Little
         15 HP Open VMS                      Little
          8 Microsoft Windows IA (64-bit)    Little
          9 IBM zSeries Based Linux          Big
         13 Linux 64-bit for AMD             Little
         16 Apple Mac OS                     Big
         12 Microsoft Windows 64-bit for AMD Little
         17 Solaris Operating System (x86)   Little
         18 IBM Power Based Linux            Big
         19 HP IA Open VMS                   Little
         20 Solaris Operating System (AMD64) Little
19 rows selected.
SQL>
```

2. After you have identified the names of the tablespaces you want to transport, execute the DBMS_TTS.TRANSPORT_SET_CHECK procedure. Next, query the TRANSPORT_SET_VIOLATIONS view.

```
SQL> SET SERVEROUTPUT ON
SQL> exec dbms_tts.transport_set_check ('USER_DATA');
PL/SQL procedure successfully completed.
```

```
SQL> SELECT * FROM TRANSPORT_SET_VIOLATIONS;
SQL>
```

3. To generate the transportable tablespace set, you'll need to place the tablespaces in read-only mode.

```
SQL>alter tablespace user_data read only;
Tablespace altered.
```

4. Exit to the host prompt and execute the data pump export utility to export the metadata.

```
SQL>host
C:\>expdp dumpfile=expdat.dmp DIRECTORY=exp_dir
 TRANSPORT_TABLESPACES= user_data

Export: Release 11.1.0.6.0 - Production on Sunday, 28
 September, 2008 14:40:19

Copyright (c) 2003, 2007, Oracle.  All rights reserved.

Username: sys as sysdba
Password:

Connected to: Oracle Database 11g Enterprise Edition
 Release 11.1.0.6.0 - Produc
tion
With the Partitioning, OLAP, Data Mining and Real
 Application Testing options
Starting "SYS"."SYS_EXPORT_TRANSPORTABLE_01":
  sys/******** AS SYSDBA dumpfile=e
xpdat.dmp DIRECTORY=EXP_DIR TRANSPORT_TABLESPACES= user_data
Processing object type TRANSPORTABLE_EXPORT/PLUGTS_BLK
Processing object type TRANSPORTABLE_EXPORT/TABLE
Processing object type TRANSPORTABLE_EXPORT/INDEX
Processing object type TRANSPORTABLE_EXPORT/CONSTRAINT/CONSTRAINT
Processing object type TRANSPORTABLE_EXPORT/INDEX_STATISTICS
Processing object type TRANSPORTABLE_EXPORT/TABLE_STATISTICS
Processing object type TRANSPORTABLE_EXPORT/POST_INSTANCE/PLUGTS_BLK
Master table "SYS"."SYS_EXPORT_TRANSPORTABLE_01"
 successfully loaded/unloaded
*************************
Dump file set for SYS.SYS_EXPORT_TRANSPORTABLE_01 is:
```

```
  C:\TEMP\EXPDAT.DMP
*************************
Datafiles required for transportable tablespace USER_DATA:
  C:\ORACLE\ORADATA\ORCL\USER_DATA01.DBF
Job "SYS"."SYS_EXPORT_TRANSPORTABLE_01" successfully completed at 14:41:47
```

5. Now copy the tablespace database files to the staging area, either local or remote. Once the copy is complete, return to SQL*Plus and place the tablespaces in read-write mode:

```
SQL>alter tablespace user_data read write;
Tablespace altered.
SQL>
```

Lab 11.2: Testing Resumable Space Allocation

In this lab, you will perform a more detailed resumable-space-allocation exercise. You will create a table, start an insert operation that will create a resumable condition, monitor the table's space utilization, and then remedy the condition.

1. Shrink the existing USER_DATA tablespace and create a table with minimal storage values.

```
SQL> alter database datafile
'c:\oracle\oradata\orcl\user_data01.dbf'
resize 10 m;

Database altered.

SQL> create table scott.resumable_test
(x number, y varchar2(10))
storage (initial 1k maxextents 1)
tablespace user_data;

Table created.
```

2. Start an insert operation.

```
SQL> insert into resumable_test values (1, 'testtest');
SQL> insert into resumable values (1, 'testtest');
1 row created.
SQL> insert into resumable select * from resumable;
1 row created.
```

```
SQL> /
2 rows created.
SQL> /
4 rows created.
SQL> /
8 rows created.
SQL> /
16 rows created.
SQL> /
32 rows created.
SQL> /
64 rows created.
SQL> /
128 rows created.
SQL> /
256 rows created.
SQL> /
512 rows created.
SQL> /
1024 rows created.
SQL> /
2048 rows created.
SQL> /
4096 rows created.
SQL> /
8192 rows created.
SQL> /
16384 rows created.
SQL> /
32768 rows created.
SQL> /
65536 rows created.
SQL> /
131072 rows created.
SQL> /
```

The session should hang at this point.

3. Monitor the operation from another SQL*Plus session:

```
SQL> select session_id, sql_text, error_msg from dba_resumable;
```

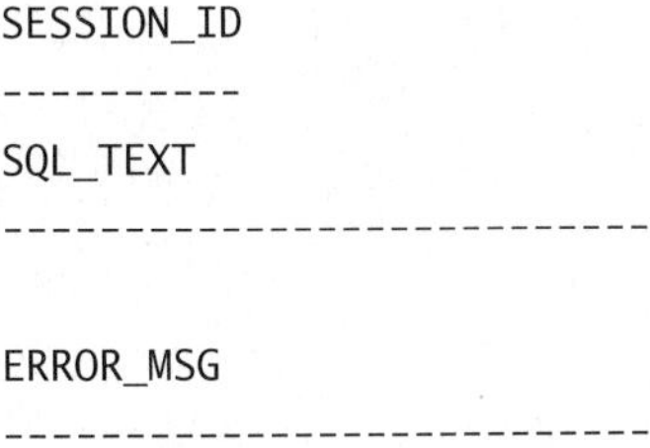

```
SESSION_ID
----------
SQL_TEXT
--------------------------

ERROR_MSG
--------------------------

       125
insert into resumable select * from resumable
ORA-01653: unable to extend table
 SCOTT.RESUMABLE_TEST by 128 in tablespace
USER_DATA

SQL>
```

4. Remedy the resumable condition.

```
SQL> alter database datafile
'c:\oracle\oradata\orcl\user_data01.dbf'
resize 100 m;
```

5. Verify the resumable condition.

```
SQL> select session_id, sql_text, error_msg from dba_resumable;
no rows selected
SQL>
```

Lab 11.3: Manually Configuring the SGA

In this lab, you will modify initialization parameters and configure the SGA. You will start with an instance that uses Automatic Memory Management, then you'll step through modifying the parameters to utilize Automatic Shared Memory Management, and finally you'll manually configure each of the SGA components. This is the basic procedure:

Here's an example:

1. Configure the instance for Automatic Memory Management.

```
SQL> show parameter memory
```

```
NAME                                 TYPE        VALUE
------------------------------------ ----------- -----
hi_shared_memory_address             integer     0
memory_max_target                    big integer 1000M
memory_target                        big integer 0
shared_memory_address                integer     0
SQL>
SQL>alter system set memory_target=1000m scope=both;

System altered.

SQL>show parameter memory

NAME                                 TYPE        VALUE
------------------------------------ ----------- -----
hi_shared_memory_address             integer     0
memory_max_target                    big integer 1000M
memory_target                        big integer 1000M
shared_memory_address                integer     0
SQL>
```

Since both memory_target and memory_max_target are set to a nonzero value, the instance is running in Automatic Memory Management mode.

2. Modify the configuration to use Automatic Shared Memory Management.

```
SQL> show parameter sga

NAME                                 TYPE        VALUE
------------------------------------ ----------- -----
lock_sga                             boolean     FALSE
pre_page_sga                         boolean     FALSE
sga_max_size                         big integer 700M
sga_target                           big integer 0
SQL>
SQL>alter system set sga_target=700m scope=both;

System altered.
SQL>alter system set memory_target=0 scope=both;
```

```
System altered.

SQL>
```

Since SGA_TARGET and SGA_MAX_SIZE are set to a nonzero value and MEMORY_TARGET is set to zero, you're now running the instance in Automatic Shared Memory Management mode.

3. Manually configure each of the SGA components.

```
SQL> show parameter pool

NAME                                 TYPE        VALUE
------------------------------------ ----------- --------
_shared_io_pool_size                 big integer 0
buffer_pool_keep                     string
buffer_pool_recycle                  string
global_context_pool_size             string
java_pool_size                       big integer 12M
large_pool_size                      big integer 0
olap_page_pool_size                  big integer 0
shared_pool_reserved_size            big integer 14050918
shared_pool_size                     big integer 0
streams_pool_size                    big integer 32M
SQL>
SQL>alter system set large_pool_size=4m scope=both;
SQL>alter system set shared_pool_size=268m scope=both;
SQL>alter system set sga_target=0 scope=both;
```

By setting the value of SGA_TARGET to zero, you effectively begin managing the SGA manually. You'll need to set the individual pool sizes to nonzero values, as shown earlier.

Lab 12.1: Creating a Local External Job

This lab was created using Windows XP. However, it should also work using Unix (and in fact was tested using Linux).

This lab shows you how to create a local external job that is also a detached job. A detached job starts another process and then exits. Use a detached job when it is impractical or impossible to wait for the job to complete. A detached job must point to a program that has its detached attribute set to TRUE. These are the overall steps: create the external shell script that invokes an RMAN script, create the RMAN script that performs an archive log backup, and create the job and use a detached local external program.

1. Create the shell script that executes the RMAN script.

```
$ORACLE_HOME/scripts/archivelogbackup.sh
#!/bin/sh
export ORACLE_HOME=/ora01/oracle/product/11.1.0
export ORACLE_SID=orcl
export LD_LIBRARY_PATH=$LD_LIBRARY_PATH:$ORACLE_HOME/lib
$ORACLE_HOME/bin/rman TARGET / @$ORACLE_HOME/scripts/archivelogbackup.rman
trace /ora01/oracle/orcl/backup/logs/archivelogbackup.out &
exit 0
```

2. Next, create the RMAN script that runs the archive log backup.

```
$ORACLE_HOME/scripts/archivelogbackup.rman
run {
BACKUP DEVICE TYPE sbt
ARCHIVELOG LIKE '/oraarc01/orcl%arc%'
DELETE ALL INPUT;
# Let the scheduler know that the detached job completed
sql " BEGIN DBMS_SCHEDULER.END_DETACHED_JOB_RUN(''sys.archivelog_backup'',
0,null); END; ";
}
```

3. Finally, return to SQL*Plus and execute the following PL/SQL block. Note that the ? embedded in the program_action field is a shortcut value for ORACLE_HOME:

```
BEGIN
DBMS_SCHEDULER.CREATE_PROGRAM(
   program_name => 'sys.archivelog_backup',
   program_type => 'executable',
   program_action => '?/scripts/archivelogbackup.sh',
   enabled => TRUE);
DBMS_SCHEDULER.SET_ATTRIBUTE('sys.archivelog_backup', 'detached', TRUE);
DBMS_SCHEDULER.CREATE_JOB(
   job_name => 'sys.archivelog_backup',
   program_name => 'sys.archivelog_backup',
```

```
    repeat_interval => 'FREQ=HOURLY;INTERVAL=4');
  DBMS_SCHEDULER.ENABLE('sys.archivelog_backup');
  END;
  /
```

Lab 12.2: Creating a Job Window

This lab shows you how to create and use a job window in the Scheduler. Here are the steps:

1. Create a simple resource plan.
2. Create a job schedule.
3. Create a job window to utilize the resource plan.
4. Open the job window explicitly.
5. Close the job window explicitly.

Here's a specific example:

1. Create a simple resource plan.

```
SQL>begin
   dbms_resource_manager.create_simple_plan(simple_plan => 'LNE_PLAN1',
   consumer_group1 => 'LNEGROUP1', group1_percent => 80,
   consumer_group2 => 'LNEROUP2', group2_percent => 20);
end;
/
PL/SQL procedure successfully completed.

SQL>
```

2. Create a job schedule.

```
SQL>begin
  dbms_scheduler.create_schedule(
  schedule_name => 'NIGHTLY_BATCH_SCHEDULE',
  start_date => SYSTIMESTAMP,
  repeat_interval => 'FREQ=DAILY; BYHOUR=20',
  comments => 'Runs nightly at 9:00 PM');
  end;
 /
```

```
PL/SQL procedure successfully completed.

SQL>
```

3. Create a job window to utilize the resource plan.

```
SQL>begin
   dbms_scheduler.create_window (
   window_name => 'NIGHTLY_BATCH_WINDOW',
   resource_plan => 'LNE_PLAN1',
   schedule_name => 'NIGHTLY_BATCH_SCHEDULE',
   duration => INTERVAL '10' HOUR,
   window_priority => 'HIGH');
   end;
/
PL/SQL procedure successfully completed.

SQL>
```

4. Open the job window explicitly for a 10-hour duration.

```
SQL>begin
  dbms_scheduler.open_window (
  window_name => 'NIGHTLY_BATCH_WINDOW',
  duration => INTERVAL '600' MINUTE,
  force => TRUE);
  end;
SQL> /

PL/SQL procedure successfully completed.
```

5. Close the job window explicitly.

```
SQL> begin
  dbms_scheduler.close_window (
  window_name => 'NIGHTLY_BATCH_WINDOW');
  end;
SQL> /

PL/SQL procedure successfully completed.
```

Lab 13.1: Using the Locale Builder to Create a New Linguistic Sort

This lab was created using Windows XP. However, it should also work using Unix (and in fact was tested using Linux).

This lab shows you how to use the Oracle Locale Builder to create a new linguistic sort.

1. Open Oracle Locale Builder.
2. Choose to create a new file, and then choose Linguistic Sort.

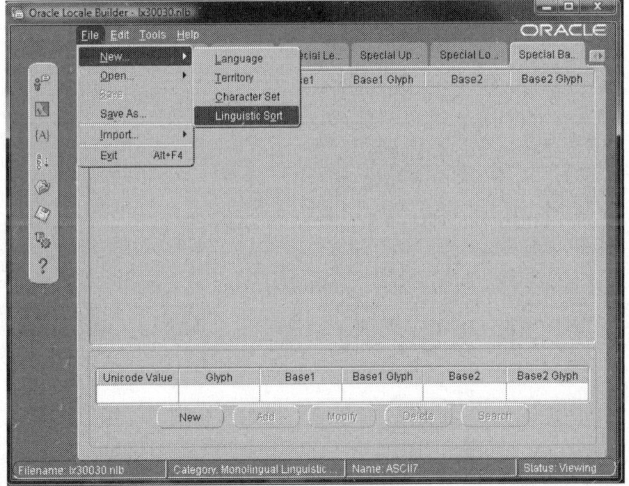

3. Select Monolingual Linguistic Sort.

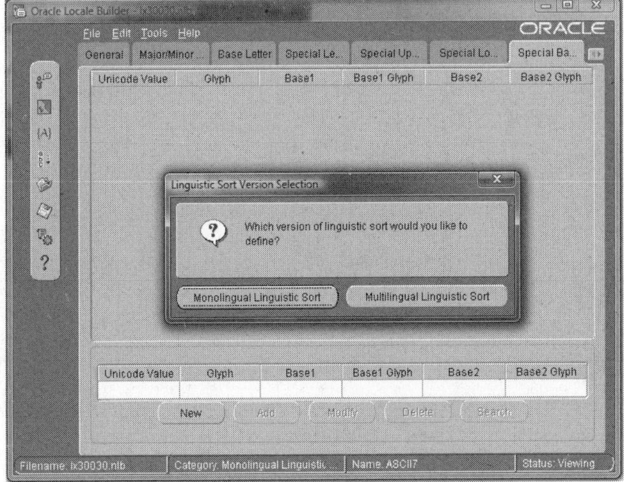

4. Click the Show Existing Definitions button.
5. Choose ASCII7 as the character set/collation name, and then click Open.
6. Change the collation name to your choice, and change the collation ID to a number between 1000 and 2000.

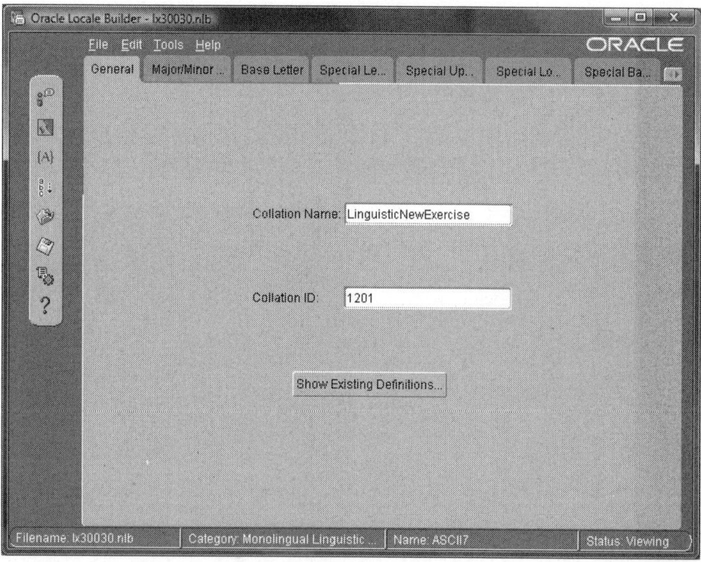

7. Modify a few of the special letters by choosing the Unicode value or copying the glyph.

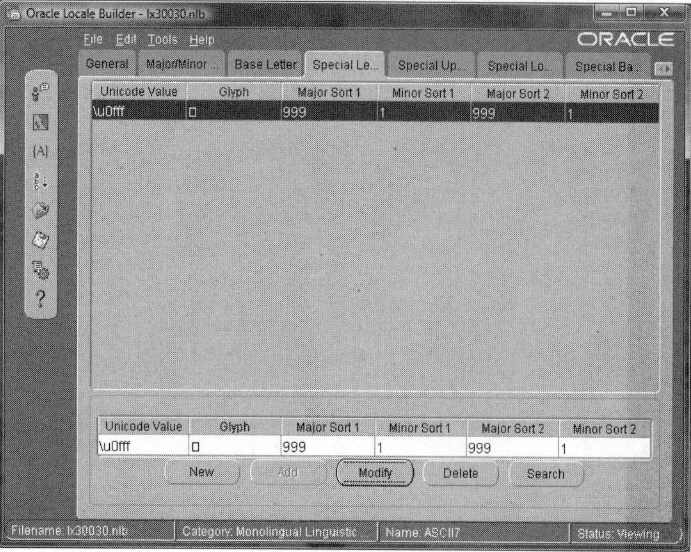

8. Save the file with a new unique name.

Lab 13.2: Setting NLS Parameters

In this lab, you will practice setting NLS parameters for the instance and for the session and observe how parameters are prioritized. Here are the general steps:

1. Show and modify instance NLS parameters.
2. Modify and observe the effects of setting session NLS variables.
3. Demonstrate NLS-parameter priorities.

Here's an example:

1. Show and modify instance NLS parameters.

```
SQL> show parameter nls

NAME                                 TYPE        VALUE
------------------------------------ ----------- --------
nls_calendar                         string
nls_comp                             string      BINARY
nls_currency                         string
nls_date_format                      string
nls_date_language                    string
nls_dual_currency                    string
nls_iso_currency                     string
nls_language                         string      AMERICAN
nls_length_semantics                 string      BYTE
nls_nchar_conv_excp                  string      FALSE
nls_numeric_characters               string
nls_sort                             string
nls_territory                        string      AMERICA
nls_time_format                      string
nls_time_tz_format                   string
nls_timestamp_format                 string
nls_timestamp_tz_format              string
SQL>
```

Only `nls_nchar_conv_excp` and `nls_lenght_semantics` are dynamically system modifiable or instance modifiable. You can, however, modify the parameter with `scope=spfile` and restart the instance to take effect.

```
SQL> alter system set nls_date_format='dd-mon-yyyy hh24:mi:ss'
  scope=spfile;
/
```

```
System altered.
SQL> shutdown immediate;
Database closed.
Database dismounted.
ORACLE instance shut down.

SQL> startup
ORACLE instance started.

Total System Global Area  732352512 bytes
Fixed Size                  1335696 bytes
Variable Size             444599920 bytes
Database Buffers          281018368 bytes
Redo Buffers                5398528 bytes
Database mounted.
Database opened.
SQL> show parameter nls

NAME                                 TYPE        VALUE
------------------------------------ ----------- ----
--------------------------
nls_calendar                         string
nls_comp                             string      BINARY
nls_currency                         string
nls_date_format                      string      dd-mon-yyyy hh24:mi:ss
nls_date_language                    string
nls_dual_currency                    string
nls_iso_currency                     string
nls_language                         string      AMERICAN
nls_length_semantics                 string      BYTE
nls_nchar_conv_excp                  string      FALSE
nls_numeric_characters               string
nls_sort                             string
nls_territory                        string      AMERICA
nls_time_format                      string
nls_time_tz_format                   string
nls_timestamp_format                 string
nls_timestamp_tz_format              string
SQL>
```

You can also observe the system NLS parameters by querying the NLS_INSTANCE_PARAMETERS view.

2. Modify and observe the effects of setting session NLS variables. Query the NLS_SESSION_PARAMETERS view to see your session parameter settings.

```
SQL> select * from nls_session_parameters
SQL> /

PARAMETER                      VALUE
------------------------------ ----------------------------
NLS_LANGUAGE                   AMERICAN
NLS_TERRITORY                  AMERICA
NLS_CURRENCY                   $
NLS_ISO_CURRENCY               AMERICA
NLS_NUMERIC_CHARACTERS         .,
NLS_CALENDAR                   GREGORIAN
NLS_DATE_FORMAT                DD-MON-RR
NLS_DATE_LANGUAGE              AMERICAN
NLS_SORT                       BINARY
NLS_TIME_FORMAT                HH.MI.SSXFF AM
NLS_TIMESTAMP_FORMAT           DD-MON-RR HH.MI.SSXFF AM
NLS_TIME_TZ_FORMAT             HH.MI.SSXFF AM TZR
NLS_TIMESTAMP_TZ_FORMAT        DD-MON-RR HH.MI.SSXFF AM TZR
NLS_DUAL_CURRENCY              $
NLS_COMP                       BINARY
NLS_LENGTH_SEMANTICS           BYTE
NLS_NCHAR_CONV_EXCP            FALSE

17 rows selected.

SQL> select sysdate from dual;

SYSDATE
---------
23-NOV-08

SQL>
```

Modify the session NLS_DATE_FORMAT, and query.

```
SQL> alter session set nls_date_format='dd-mon-yyyy hh24:mi:ss';
Session altered.
```

```
SQL> select * from nls_session_parameters;

PARAMETER                      VALUE
------------------------------ ----------------------------
NLS_LANGUAGE                   AMERICAN
NLS_TERRITORY                  AMERICA
NLS_CURRENCY                   $
NLS_ISO_CURRENCY               AMERICA
NLS_NUMERIC_CHARACTERS         .,
NLS_CALENDAR                   GREGORIAN
NLS_DATE_FORMAT                dd-mon-yyyy hh24:mi:ss
NLS_DATE_LANGUAGE              AMERICAN
NLS_SORT                       BINARY
NLS_TIME_FORMAT                HH.MI.SSXFF AM
NLS_TIMESTAMP_FORMAT           DD-MON-RR HH.MI.SSXFF AM
NLS_TIME_TZ_FORMAT             HH.MI.SSXFF AM TZR
NLS_TIMESTAMP_TZ_FORMAT        DD-MON-RR HH.MI.SSXFF AM TZR
NLS_DUAL_CURRENCY              $
NLS_COMP                       BINARY
NLS_LENGTH_SEMANTICS           BYTE
NLS_NCHAR_CONV_EXCP            FALSE

17 rows selected.

SQL> select sysdate from dual;

SYSDATE
--------------------
23-nov-2008 00:11:38

SQL>
```

3. Demonstrate NLS-parameter priorities. Modify the session NLS_LANGUAGE, and query.

```
SQL> alter session set nls_language='GERMAN';

Session altered.

SQL> select * from nls_session_parameters;
```

```
PARAMETER                      VALUE
------------------------------ ----------------------------
NLS_LANGUAGE                   GERMAN
NLS_TERRITORY                  AMERICA
NLS_CURRENCY                   $
NLS_ISO_CURRENCY               AMERICA
NLS_NUMERIC_CHARACTERS         .,
NLS_CALENDAR                   GREGORIAN
NLS_DATE_FORMAT                dd-mon-yyyy hh24:mi:ss
NLS_DATE_LANGUAGE              GERMAN
NLS_SORT                       GERMAN
NLS_TIME_FORMAT                HH.MI.SSXFF AM
NLS_TIMESTAMP_FORMAT           DD-MON-RR HH.MI.SSXFF AM
NLS_TIME_TZ_FORMAT             HH.MI.SSXFF AM TZR
NLS_TIMESTAMP_TZ_FORMAT        DD-MON-RR HH.MI.SSXFF AM TZR
NLS_DUAL_CURRENCY              $
NLS_COMP                       BINARY
NLS_LENGTH_SEMANTICS           BYTE
NLS_NCHAR_CONV_EXCP            FALSE

17 rows selected.

SQL>
```

Notice that when you set the NLS_LANGUAGE, the NLS_DATE_LANGUAGE and NLS_SORT also changed but the NLS_TERRITORY and NLS_ISO_CURRENCY did not. Now change the NLS_LANGUAGE back and observe.

```
SQL> alter session set nls_language='AMERICAN';

Session altered.

SQL> select * from nls_session_parameters;

PARAMETER                      VALUE
------------------------------ ----------------------------
NLS_LANGUAGE                   AMERICAN
NLS_TERRITORY                  AMERICA
NLS_CURRENCY                   $
NLS_ISO_CURRENCY               AMERICA
```

```
NLS_NUMERIC_CHARACTERS         .,
NLS_CALENDAR                   GREGORIAN
NLS_DATE_FORMAT                dd-mon-yyyy hh24:mi:ss
NLS_DATE_LANGUAGE              AMERICAN
NLS_SORT                       BINARY
NLS_TIME_FORMAT                HH.MI.SSXFF AM
NLS_TIMESTAMP_FORMAT           DD-MON-RR HH.MI.SSXFF AM
NLS_TIME_TZ_FORMAT             HH.MI.SSXFF AM TZR
NLS_TIMESTAMP_TZ_FORMAT        DD-MON-RR HH.MI.SSXFF AM TZR
NLS_DUAL_CURRENCY              $
NLS_COMP                       BINARY
NLS_LENGTH_SEMANTICS           BYTE
NLS_NCHAR_CONV_EXCP            FALSE

17 rows selected.

SQL>
```

Note the NLS_LANGUAGE sets a default for NLS_DATE_LANGUAGE and NLS_SORT; however, you can modify NLS_DATE_LANGUAGE and NLS_SORT independently.

```
SQL> alter session set nls_sort='GERMAN';

Session altered.

SQL> select * from nls_session_parameters;

PARAMETER                      VALUE
------------------------------ ----------------------------
NLS_LANGUAGE                   AMERICAN
NLS_TERRITORY                  AMERICA
NLS_CURRENCY                   $
NLS_ISO_CURRENCY               AMERICA
NLS_NUMERIC_CHARACTERS         .,
NLS_CALENDAR                   GREGORIAN
NLS_DATE_FORMAT                dd-mon-yyyy hh24:mi:ss
NLS_DATE_LANGUAGE              AMERICAN
NLS_SORT                       GERMAN
NLS_TIME_FORMAT                HH.MI.SSXFF AM
NLS_TIMESTAMP_FORMAT           DD-MON-RR HH.MI.SSXFF AM
NLS_TIME_TZ_FORMAT             HH.MI.SSXFF AM TZR
```

```
NLS_TIMESTAMP_TZ_FORMAT        DD-MON-RR HH.MI.SSXFF AM TZR
NLS_DUAL_CURRENCY              $
NLS_COMP                       BINARY
NLS_LENGTH_SEMANTICS           BYTE
NLS_NCHAR_CONV_EXCP            FALSE

17 rows selected.

SQL>
```

If I now set the NLS_LANGUAGE to American, it will overlay the NLS_SORT value with BINARY:

```
SQL> alter session set nls_language='AMERICAN';

Session altered.

SQL> select * from nls_session_parameters;

PARAMETER                      VALUE
------------------------------ ----------------------------
NLS_LANGUAGE                   AMERICAN
NLS_TERRITORY                  AMERICA
NLS_CURRENCY                   $
NLS_ISO_CURRENCY               AMERICA
NLS_NUMERIC_CHARACTERS         .,
NLS_CALENDAR                   GREGORIAN
NLS_DATE_FORMAT                dd-mon-yyyy hh24:mi:ss
NLS_DATE_LANGUAGE              AMERICAN
NLS_SORT                       BINARY
NLS_TIME_FORMAT                HH.MI.SSXFF AM
NLS_TIMESTAMP_FORMAT           DD-MON-RR HH.MI.SSXFF AM
NLS_TIME_TZ_FORMAT             HH.MI.SSXFF AM TZR
NLS_TIMESTAMP_TZ_FORMAT        DD-MON-RR HH.MI.SSXFF AM TZR
NLS_DUAL_CURRENCY              $
NLS_COMP                       BINARY
NLS_LENGTH_SEMANTICS           BYTE
NLS_NCHAR_CONV_EXCP            FALSE

17 rows selected.

SQL>
```

Lab 13.3: Performing Linguistic Sorts

In this exercise, you will create a table and populate it with values that are easily sorted. You will then modify the NLS parameters that affect linguistic sorts and query the table, observing how the NLS-parameter settings modify the sort results. Here are the steps:

1. Create a table for linguistic sorts, and populate it.
2. Verify your session NLS parameters.
3. Query the sort table.
4. Modify the sort parameter.
5. Query the table and observe the differences in the sort results.

Here's an example:

1. Create a table for linguistic sorts, and populate it.

```
SQL> create table linguistic_sort_test (x number, y varchar2(1));

Table created.

SQL>

insert into linguistic_sort_test values (1,'A');
insert into linguistic_sort_test values (2,'B');
insert into linguistic_sort_test values (3,'C');
insert into linguistic_sort_test values (4,'D');
insert into linguistic_sort_test values (5,'E');
insert into linguistic_sort_test values (6,'F');
insert into linguistic_sort_test values (7,'G');
insert into linguistic_sort_test values (8,'H');
insert into linguistic_sort_test values (9,'I');
insert into linguistic_sort_test values (10,'J');
insert into linguistic_sort_test values (11,'a');
insert into linguistic_sort_test values (12,'b');
insert into linguistic_sort_test values (13,'c');
insert into linguistic_sort_test values (14,'d');
insert into linguistic_sort_test values (15,'e');
insert into linguistic_sort_test values (16,'f');
insert into linguistic_sort_test values (17,'g');
insert into linguistic_sort_test values (18,'h');
insert into linguistic_sort_test values (19,'i');
insert into linguistic_sort_test values (20,'j');
commit;
```

2. Verify your session NLS parameters.

```
SQL> select * from nls_session_parameters;

PARAMETER                      VALUE
------------------------------ ----------------------------
NLS_LANGUAGE                   AMERICAN
NLS_TERRITORY                  AMERICA
NLS_CURRENCY                   $
NLS_ISO_CURRENCY               AMERICA
NLS_NUMERIC_CHARACTERS         .,
NLS_CALENDAR                   GREGORIAN
NLS_DATE_FORMAT                dd-mon-yyyy hh24:mi:ss
NLS_DATE_LANGUAGE              AMERICAN
NLS_SORT                       BINARY
NLS_TIME_FORMAT                HH.MI.SSXFF AM
NLS_TIMESTAMP_FORMAT           DD-MON-RR HH.MI.SSXFF AM
NLS_TIME_TZ_FORMAT             HH.MI.SSXFF AM TZR
NLS_TIMESTAMP_TZ_FORMAT        DD-MON-RR HH.MI.SSXFF AM TZR
NLS_DUAL_CURRENCY              $
NLS_COMP                       BINARY
NLS_LENGTH_SEMANTICS           BYTE
NLS_NCHAR_CONV_EXCP            FALSE

17 rows selected.

SQL>
```

3. Query the sort table. Order by the numeric value as a baseline or control query, and then order by the character column using the default BINARY sort.

```
SQL> select * from linguistic_sort_test order by x;

         X Y
---------- -
         1 A
         2 B
         3 C
         4 D
         5 E
         6 F
         7 G
```

```
         8 H
         9 I
        10 J
        11 a
        12 b
        13 c
        14 d
        15 e
        16 f
        17 g
        18 h
        19 i
        20 j

20 rows selected.

SQL>


SQL> select * from linguistic_sort_test order by y;

         X Y
---------- -
         1 A
         2 B
         3 C
         4 D
         5 E
         6 F
         7 G
         8 H
         9 I
        10 J
        11 a
        12 b
        13 c
        14 d
        15 e
        16 f
        17 g
```

```
        18 h
        19 i
        20 j

20 rows selected.
```

4. Modify the sort parameter. The default was BINARY; we'll modify it to EBCDIC to demonstrate the simple difference.

```
SQL>
SQL> alter session set nls_sort='EBCDIC';

Session altered.
```

5. Query the table and observe the differences in the sort results from the previous query.

```
SQL> select * from linguistic_sort_test order by y;

         X Y
---------- -
        11 a
        12 b
        13 c
        14 d
        15 e
        16 f
        17 g
        18 h
        19 i
        20 j
         1 A
         2 B
         3 C
         4 D
         5 E
         6 F
         7 G
         8 H
         9 I
        10 J

20 rows selected.
```

Notice that the EBCDIC sort placed the lowercase letters at the beginning of the sort because they have a lower EBCDIC value than their uppercase counterparts.

If we now set the NLS_SORT value to ASCII7, you'll see the same results as BINARY for this simple sort.

```
SQL> alter session set nls_sort='ASCII7';

Session altered.

SQL> select * from linguistic_sort_test order by y;

         X Y
---------- -
         1 A
         2 B
         3 C
         4 D
         5 E
         6 F
         7 G
         8 H
         9 I
        10 J
        11 a
        12 b
        13 c
        14 d
        15 e
        16 f
        17 g
        18 h
        19 i
        20 j

20 rows selected.
```

Now if you set the NLS_SORT to CROATIAN, you'll see something really interesting.

```
SQL> alter session set nls_sort='CROATIAN';
```

```
Session altered.

SQL> select * from linguistic_sort_test order by y;

         X Y
---------- -
         1 A
        11 a
         2 B
        12 b
         3 C
        13 c
         4 D
        14 d
         5 E
        15 e
         6 F
        16 f
         7 G
        17 g
         8 H
        18 h
         9 I
        19 i
        10 J
        20 j

20 rows selected.

SQL>
```

And when you set NLS_SORT to THAI_M, you'll see the opposite pattern from the one for CROATIAN.

```
SQL> alter session set nls_sort='THAI_M';

Session altered.

SQL> select * from linguistic_sort_test order by y;
```

```
         X Y
---------- -
        11 a
         1 A
        12 b
         2 B
        13 c
         3 C
        14 d
         4 D
        15 e
         5 E
        16 f
         6 F
        17 g
         7 G
        18 h
         8 H
        19 i
         9 I
        20 j
        10 J

20 rows selected.

SQL>
```

Remember that setting NLS_LANGUAGE will override the NLS_SORT setting, but NLS_SORT can be set to whatever valid setting you choose following a change to NLS_LANGUAGE.

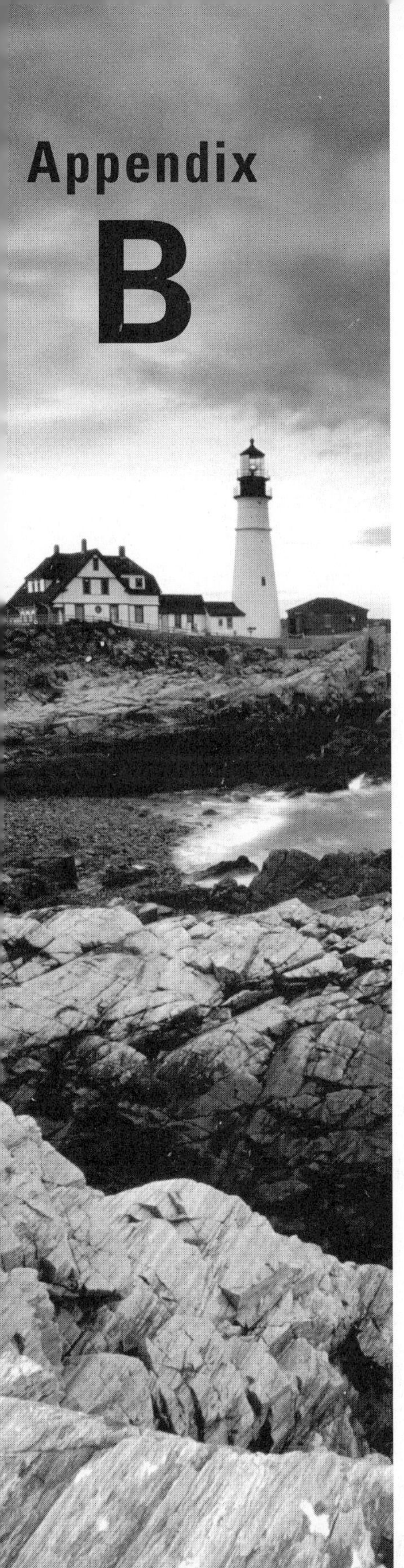

Appendix B

About the Companion CD

IN THIS APPENDIX:

- ✓ What you'll find on the CD
- ✓ System requirements
- ✓ Using the CD
- ✓ Troubleshooting

What You'll Find on the CD

The following sections are arranged by category and summarize the software and other goodies you'll find on the CD. If you need help with installing the items provided on the CD, refer to the installation instructions in the "Using the CD" section of this appendix.

Some programs on the CD might fall into one of these categories:

Shareware programs are fully functional, free, trial versions of copyrighted programs. If you like particular programs, register with their authors for a nominal fee and receive licenses, enhanced versions, and technical support.

Freeware programs are free, copyrighted games, applications, and utilities. You can copy them to as many computers as you like—for free—but they offer no technical support.

GNU software is governed by its own license, which is included inside the folder of the GNU software. There are no restrictions on distribution of GNU software. See the GNU license at the root of the CD for more details.

Trial, *demo*, or *evaluation* versions of software are usually limited either by time or by functionality (such as not letting you save a project after you create it).

Sybex Test Engine

For Windows

The CD contains the Sybex test engine, which includes all of the assessment test and chapter review questions in electronic format, as well as two bonus exams located only on the CD.

PDF of the Book

For Windows

We have included an electronic version of the text in `.pdf` format. You can view the electronic version of the book with Adobe Reader.

Adobe Reader

For Windows

We've also included a copy of Adobe Reader so you can view PDF files that accompany the book's content. For more information on Adobe Reader or to check for a newer version, visit Adobe's website at `www.adobe.com/products/reader/`.

Electronic Flashcards

For PC, Pocket PC, and Palm

These handy electronic flashcards are just what they sound like. One side contains a question or fill-in-the-blank question, and the other side shows the answer.

System Requirements

Make sure your computer meets the minimum system requirements shown in the following list. If your computer doesn't match up to most of these requirements, you may have problems using the software and files on the companion CD. For the latest and greatest information, please refer to the ReadMe file located at the root of the CD-ROM.

- A PC running Microsoft Windows 98, Windows 2000, Windows NT4 (with SP4 or later), Windows Me, Windows XP, or Windows Vista
- An Internet connection
- A CD-ROM drive

Using the CD

To install the items from the CD to your hard drive, follow these steps:

1. Insert the CD into your computer's CD-ROM drive. The license agreement appears.

Windows users: The interface won't launch if you have autorun disabled. In that case, click Start ➤ Run (for Windows Vista, Start ➤ All Programs ➤ Accessories ➤ Run). In the dialog box that appears, type **`D:\Start.exe`**. (Replace *D* with the proper letter if your CD drive uses a different letter. If you don't know the letter, see how your CD drive is listed under My Computer.) Click OK.

2. Read the license agreement, and then click the Accept button if you want to use the CD.

The CD interface appears. The interface allows you to access the content with just one or two clicks.

Troubleshooting

Wiley has attempted to provide programs that work on most computers with the minimum system requirements. Alas, your computer may differ, and some programs may not work properly for some reason.

The two likeliest problems are that you don't have enough memory (RAM) for the programs you want to use or you have other programs running that are affecting installation or running of a program. If you get an error message such as "Not enough memory" or "Setup cannot continue," try one or more of the following suggestions and then try using the software again:

Turn off any antivirus software running on your computer. Installation programs sometimes mimic virus activity and may make your computer incorrectly believe that it's being infected by a virus.

Close all running programs. The more programs you have running, the less memory is available to other programs. Installation programs typically update files and programs; so if you keep other programs running, installation may not work properly.

Have your local computer store add more RAM to your computer. This is, admittedly, a drastic and somewhat expensive step. However, adding more memory can really help the speed of your computer and allow more programs to run at the same time.

Customer Care

If you have trouble with the book's companion CD-ROM, please call the Wiley Product Technical Support phone number at (800) 762-2974. Outside the United States, call +1(317) 572-3994. You can also contact Wiley Product Technical Support at `http://sybex.custhelp.com`. John Wiley & Sons will provide technical support only for installation and other general quality-control items. For technical support on the applications themselves, consult the program's vendor or author.

To place additional orders or to request information about other Wiley products, please call (877) 762-2974.

Glossary

A

active database duplication Active database duplication is an RMAN duplication process that occurs over the network and does not use RMAN backups as the source of the duplication.

active online redo log group This is an online redo log that is not currently in use by the database but has not been archived.

archived redo logs Copies of the online redo logs. Critical to database recovery when the database is in ARCHIVELOG mode.

ARCHIVELOG mode When in ARCHIVELOG mode, the database will generate archived redo logs and, by applying those files and the online redo logs, can be recovered to any point other than the point of the last backup.

archiver process (ARCH) The process responsible for copying an online redo log to an archived redo log after a log switch has completed.

ASM See Automatic Storage Management.

ASM fast disk resync Method of quickly recovering from hardware failures that impact disk availability but do not corrupt the data on the disk itself.

ASM instance Running Oracle instance specific to ASM functionality.

ASM preferred mirror read When one set of disks is local and the other remote, this allows you to indicate to ASM that it should read from a specific failure group set of disks (typically the local set).

ASM redundancy Method of protecting data on ASM disks by mirroring the data on one or more ASM failure groups.

ASM_DISKSTRING Parameter that indicates to the Oracle ASM instance where to look for ASM disks upon instance startup.

ASMCMD Command-line tool used to manage ASM instances.

automated channel failover The ability of other channels to automatically restart failed RMAN activities from a channel that has failed.

Automatic Diagnostic Repository (ADR) File-based repository for database diagnostic data.

automatic instance Temporary instance created automatically when performing RMAN tablespace point-in-time recovery.

Automatic Memory Management Default memory-management model in Oracle 11*g*; when you set a nonzero value for MEMORY_TARGET and MEMORY_MAX_TARGET, Oracle will manage SGA and PGA memory pools, caches, and work-area sizes dynamically.

Automatic PGA Memory Management When you set the value of MEMORY_TARGET and MAX_MEMORY_TARGET to zero and set a nonzero value for PGA_AGGREGATE_TARGET, Oracle will manage PGA memory components automatically, resizing as needed within the value specified.

Automatic Shared Memory Management When you set the value of MEMORY_TARGET and MAX_MEMORY_TARGET to zero and set a nonzero value for SGA_MAX_SIZE and SGA_TARGET, Oracle will manage SGA memory components automatically, resizing as needed within the value specified.

Automatic Storage Management An Oracle native file system management system that provides a volume manager, fault tolerance, and load balancing of disks assigned to Oracle databases. Both stand-alone and clustered databases are supported.

Automatic Undo Management (AUM) Oracle functionality that simplifies management of undo tablespaces. AUM works to meet undo retention goals while ensuring that adequate space is available for new transactions.

auxiliary instance Instance manually created when database duplication is performed or automatically created during tablespace point-in-time recovery. This instance is used as the destination database and will become the duplicated database during a database duplication, or is temporarily used during a tablespace point-in-time recovery.

auxiliary set The set of database datafiles required to create the automatic instance during a tablespace point-in-time recovery.

B

backup-based database duplication Database duplication dependent on the presence of RMAN backups and archived redo logs.

backup optimization When enabled, will prevent unnecessary backups of read-only database datafiles.

backup set A logical entity representing a single backup of specific database tablespace datafiles. Individual database datafiles are always contained within a single RMAN backup set. A backup set comprises one or more physical files called backup-set pieces.

backup-set compression Zip-like compression of RMAN backup sets used to reduce the size of the RMAN backup-set pieces, and thus the entire backup.

backup-set piece Default physical file used by RMAN to back up a database. Backup-set pieces are physical files. Many backup-set pieces may belong to one logical structure called a backup set.

binary sorting Ordering character strings based on their binary coded values.

block-change tracking file Physical file used to track changed blocks. Level-1 incremental backups use these files to improve performance of incremental backups by avoiding unnecessary datafile IO.

block media recovery A technique for restoring and recovering individual data blocks that have been identified as corrupt while all database files remain online and available.

byte semantics Assumes a single-byte character set, where one character always requires one byte of storage; treatment of strings as a sequence of bytes.

C

chain Two or more Scheduler programs that are linked together to meet an objective, where the outcome of one job determines the next steps in the chain.

change-based recovery Recovery of the database based on a specific system change number (SCN).

channel A connection from the database server to the backup destination (disk or MML layer). Each RMAN backup or recovery has at least one channel allocated. Multiple channels provide for parallel backup and recovery in RMAN.

character semantics Allows character data to be specified in terms of the number of characters regardless of the number of bytes required.

character set A collection of elements that represent textual information for a specific language or group of languages.

complete database recovery Recovering the database to the point of failure by applying all archived redo logs and all redo in the online redo logs.

complete recovery A recovery of the database to the point of the last completed transaction. This kind of recovery involves no data loss. Complete recovery is synonymous with point-of-failure recovery.

consistent shutdown A shutdown of the database that leaves the datafiles in a consistent state.

control file A critical database file that contains metadata related to the database, such as the location of the database datafiles, redo logs, and archived redo logs.

control-file autobackups An RMAN feature providing automatic backup and restore of the database control files and spfiles. Also provides for easy recovery of these database-related files.

`convert` The RMAN command that allows the DBA to transport databases and tablespaces from one platform to another where the source and destination platforms have different endianness.

corrupt block An Oracle block that is not in a recognized Oracle format or whose contents are not internally consistent. Corruption is usually caused by hardware or operating-system problems. In Oracle, block corruption is classified as either logical, caused by an Oracle internal error, or physically corrupt media, meaning the block format is not correct.

crash or instance recovery A recovery from a database that has been shut down in an inconsistent manner. This kind of recovery does not require user intervention because the Oracle database uses the online redo logs to bring the database to a consistent state.

cumulative incremental backup An incremental backup that contains all database data blocks changed since the last level 0 backup.

current online redo log group The online redo log group that is currently in use by the database.

D

datafile recoveries The recovery of specific database datafiles instead of the entire database or a specific tablespace.

database A collection of datafiles that is used to store data.

database character set The character set that will govern default text storage in the database.

database control file The file that contains configuration information on the database associated with the control file, such as the location of datafiles, redo logs, and RMAN-related information.

database datafiles The physical media used to store database data. Tablespaces are assigned to one or more database datafiles.

database duplication The process of creating one database from another.

database incarnation Indicates the logical life of a given database. The first incarnation begins at the creation of a database and ends at the point the `resetlogs` command is used when creating a database.

database parameter file (pfile) A text-based file that contains database-related parameters and their settings.

Database Replay An Oracle feature that allows the capture of a workload and replay on a similar database in a test environment.

Database Resource Manager The Oracle feature that allows the DBA to manage resource allocation by creating directives, plans, and groups.

database writer process (DBWR) The process responsible for writing database changes to the database datafiles.

DBID Stands for database ID. This number uniquely identifies an Oracle database.

dependency scheduling Scheduling jobs based on the outcomes of previous jobs. In the Oracle Scheduler, job chains are used to implement dependency-based scheduling.

destination host The host that is the destination of a duplicate operation.

differential incremental backup An incremental backup that contains all database data blocks changed since the last level-1 differential incremental backup.

disk group Equivalent to a logical volume in ASM. Individual LUNs (disks) are assigned to disk groups. Fault tolerance is supported at the disk-group level through mirroring.

disk-group attributes Attributes assigned individually to specific disk groups, such as disk repair time.

duplexing A method of creating more than one copy of a database backup during the backup.

dynamic performance data dictionary views Views that provide near-real-time information on the database, including metadata about database structures. Much of the data in dynamic performance views comes from the database control file.

E

endianness Or endian format. The byte order used by a particular hardware platform. When the sequence of bytes with increasing significance is stored with increasing memory addresses, this is referred to as little endian. If the most significant byte is stored first, this is referred to as big endian. When bytes are exchanged between platforms with different endianness, a conversion process must occur before the bytes will make sense to the destination computer.

event-based scheduling The concept of executing a job based on an event that signals the Scheduler, regardless of time or dependencies.

F

failure groups (or FAILGROUPS) Failure groups provide for data redundancy in an ASM disk group. Each failure group is assigned one or more disks. Data in one failure group is redundantly copied to the other failure groups in the disk group.

flash recovery area (FRA) File system dedicated to back-up and recovery purposes. Can contain many recovery-related components, such as backup set pieces, archived redo logs, and copies of the database control files.

Flashback Data Archive An Oracle feature that allows one to archive all DML changes to a table and retain those changes for a specified retention period. The archive is queryable; the retention period is automatically enforced.

Flashback Database An Oracle feature that allows a point-in-time logical recovery of the entire database to a timestamp, SCN, or named recovery point. Flashback Database uses flashback logs stored in the flash recovery area. It can't be used for media recovery.

Flashback Drop An Oracle feature that allows dropped objects to be recovered from the Recycle Bin instead of requiring an expensive incomplete recovery process to be performed.

Flashback Table An Oracle feature that allows tables (and their dependent objects) to be recovered to an earlier point in time while the tablespace remains online and without the overhead of an incomplete recovery.

Flashback Transaction Query An Oracle feature that allows users to identify changes made to tables at a transactional level.

Flashback Versions Query A feature that allows users to view all versions of data that have existed over a period of time for a specific table.

I

image copies Exact byte-for-byte copies of database datafiles backed up by RMAN. Image copies are made with the `backup as copy` command. Can be used for quick database restores.

inactive online redo log group One of the online redo log groups of the database that is not in use and has been archived.

incident In Oracle 11g, a single occurrence of a problem.

Incident Packaging Service (IPS) Enables you to automatically gather the diagnostic data pertaining to a critical error into a zip file for transmission to Oracle Support.

incomplete recovery Also called point-in-time recovery. Recovery of the database to a earlier point in time, SCN, or log sequence number than the current ones.

inconsistent shutdown A shutdown of the database that leaves the datafiles in an inconsistent state. An inconsistent shutdown of the database will definitely result in an instance recovery. In some cases, an inconsistent shutdown (due to loss of a datafile, for example) could lead to media recovery.

incremental database backups Backups of an Oracle database by RMAN. Includes a level-0 backup, which is a full backup of the database, and a level-1 backup, which incrementally backs up only changed database blocks.

incrementally updated backups Combination of a backup image copy and incremental backups that allow for very fast recovery of the Oracle database.

instance Collection of database processes and memory.

J

job An instruction to the Scheduler to execute a specific program at a specific time on a specific date, for example.

job class A logical way of grouping jobs that have similar business or performance attributes.

job coordinator The Oracle background process that is responsible for ensuring that jobs are run on schedule.

job table The master table in the Oracle database that contains the information for all enabled jobs in the database.

L

length semantics Determines how you treat the length of a character string. The length can be treated as a sequence of characters or bytes.

level-0 incremental backup Essentially, a full backup of the Oracle database. A level-0 incremental backup is required to be able to perform subsequent level-1 incremental backups. Whole-database backups are not the same as incremental level-0 backups.

level-1 incremental backup Backups of changed blocks in Oracle databases. Can be based on either a differential backup strategy or a cumulative incremental strategy.

log sequenced–based recovery Recovery of the database based on a specific log sequence number.

log sequence number point-in-time recovery A method of incomplete recovery used to restore the database to a specific log sequence number.

log writer process (LGWR) The process responsible for writing redo data from the redo log buffer in the SGA to the online redo logs of the database.

logical corruption Data inconsistencies caused by user error (where a user can be a user, developer, DBA, or program that modifies data in the database).

M

Media Management Library (MML) An Oracle-created API that allows media-product vendors to write interfaces into RMAN. RMAN channels that are allocated to SBT instead of disk will be directed to the MML layer. This layer must first be configured according to vendor instructions.

media recovery Recovery of the database, typically by means of database backups, that requires DBA intervention.

MOUNT mode One of three modes that the database can be in. When the database is open in MOUNT mode, it has read the database control file but not yet opened the database datafiles.

multibyte character A character whose character code consists of two or more bytes under a certain encoding scheme.

multiplexing The ability to create more than one copy of a database backup to a different location (but on the same type of media). It is essentially making parallel copies of the backup.

multiselection backups Multiselection backups provide the ability to chunk up large database datafiles into individual backup channels. This allows for parallelization of backups of individual datafiles.

N

national character set An character set that is an alternative to the database character set that governs NCHAR, NVARCHAR2, and NCLOB data.

National Language Support (NLS) Allows users to interact with the database in their native language.

NOARCHIVELOG mode When in NOARCHIVELOG mode, the database will not generate archived redo logs and can not be recovered to any point other than the point of the last backup.

O

online datafile recovery Recovery of a database datafile while the database is open.

online redo logs Persistent mechanism that stores redo copied from the redo-log buffer by the LGWR process.

online tablespace recovery Recovery of all tablespace datafiles while the database is open.

Oracle data dictionary Views in the database that provide metadata information about the database, including database configuration, objects, users, and other information.

Oracle Database Configuration Assistant (DBCA) Oracle graphical interface used to create both ASM instances and Oracle databases.

orapwd The program that creates the Oracle database password file.

P

parameter file A file that defines global database settings such as memory allocations. Can be either a pfile, which is text-based, or an spfile, which is managed by the Oracle server.

point-in-time recovery Recovery of the database based on a specific point in time. Also called incomplete recovery. Recovery of the database to an earlier point in time, SCN, or log sequence number than the current ones.

point-of-failure recovery This is a recovery of the database to the point of the last completed transaction. This kind of recovery involves no data loss. Point-of-failure recovery is synonymous with complete recovery.

problem In Oracle 11g, a critical error in the database.

program Defines the action that will occur when a job runs.

R

recover command RMAN command used to recover a database, tablespace, or datafile. Causes the application of incremental backups and archived redo logs to complete the database recovery.

recovery catalog The recovery catalog is an optional database schema that maintains a record of all RMAN backup operations.

recovery catalog stored scripts These are scripts stored in the recovery catalog. These scripts can be called by RMAN for backup, recovery, or reporting purposes.

recovery catalog views Views that can be queried by the DBA to look at RMAN-related metadata in the recovery catalog.

recovery set Set of tablespaces to be recovered during tablespace point-in-time recovery.

Recycle Bin A logical container that stores objects dropped from the database. The Recycle Bin (in conjunction with the Flashback Drop feature) offers users a simple method of querying and recovering objects that may have been dropped by accident.

redo-log buffer The memory area in the SGA to which redo is initially written.

redo log sequence number A unique number assigned to each online redo log to define the order in which it was written to.

redo logfile group A set of one or more online redo logs. Each redo logfile group is written to one at a time and may have one or more copies of the redo log called members.

Redo logfile member One or more files in a redo logfile group. These files are written to in parallel and are used to protect each online redo log from failure.

resource consumer group A logical grouping of users based on resource-consumption requirements and business needs.

resource plan A group of resource-plan directives that specify how resources should be distributed among the consumer groups.

resource-plan directive Defines resource allocation rules and connects resource plans to consumer groups.

restore command RMAN command used to restore the database from a previous RMAN backup. This command will cause RMAN to restore datafiles from backup-set pieces or image copies.

resumable space allocation The Oracle feature that enables transactions to suspend and wait for a space condition to be resolved within a specified time without aborting the transaction. When the space condition is resolved, the transaction will resume.

`RETENTION GUARANTEE` An option that, when enabled, will guarantee that unexpired undo records will never be removed from the undo tablespace. They will be maintained until they expire (at the end of the retention period), even at the expense of new transactions failing because of lack of undo space.

retention policies Retention policies determine how long database backups will be considered valid in RMAN. After the retention period expires, backups will be marked as obsolete and be eligible for removal.

RMAN Oracle's provided backup and recovery tool.

RMAN backup-format specification The backup-format specification is used to indicate the file-naming convention to be used when creating an RMAN backup-set piece.

RMAN command-line interface (RCLI) Used to access RMAN and perform RMAN-related activities.

RMAN persistent configuration settings Provide the ability to configure backup- and recovery-related settings that become the default value for RMAN backup and recovery operations.

RMAN virtual private catalog An optional feature of the RMAN recovery catalog that provides the ability to limit access to records in the recovery catalog to specific sets of users.

run block A block of RMAN commands that starts with a run command. The commands are enclosed in braces.

S

schedule A schedule contains a start date, an optional end date, and a repeat interval.

SBT Device designation that indicates the backup, restore or maintenance operation will use the MML layer instead of a disk device.

SCN-based point-in-time recovery A method of recovery that restores the database to a specific point in time based on a database SCN.

Segment Shrink An online Segment Shrink operation reduces the size of a segment by moving rows and consolidating the space used, eliminating unused space above and below the high-water mark.

service request A request to Oracle Support to assist with a technical problem.

snapshot control file A consistent copy of the control file created at the beginning of an RMAN backup operation.

source host The database host machine where the target database is located.

space pressure A situation that occurs when Oracle cannot allocate any further extents in a tablespace without extending the tablespace. When this situation occurs, Oracle will purge objects from the Recycle Bin rather than extend the tablespace.

SQL Access Advisor The SQL advisor that analyzes the schema design for a workload and recommends indexes, partitions, and materialized views to improve performance.

SQL Tuning Advisor One of the SQL advisors; it takes one or more SQL statements as input and produces tuning advice.

SQL tuning set (STS) A database object that stores a set of SQL statements along with their execution context and statistics.

static data dictionary views Data dictionary views that provide metadata information on various database structures such as tables, indexes, and other database objects.

substitution variables Variables used in place of literal values. Each time you execute code with the substitution variable, you can indicate the value of that variable or RMAN will prompt you for the value of that variable when you run the code.

Support Workbench An environment within Oracle Enterprise Manager that provides a workflow for investigating, diagnosing, reporting, submitting service requests to Oracle Support, and resolving problems.

suspended transaction A transaction that has encountered a space condition and is waiting for the space condition to be resolved. The transaction will abort if the suspend condition is not resolved within the time-out.

system change number (SCN) An internal counter that is used to maintain the order and dependency of transactions within a given database.

T

tablespace A logical storage area that is assigned to one or more database datafiles. Oracle objects (such as tables) are assigned to a tablespace when they are created.

tablespace point-in-time recovery The process of recovering one or more tablespaces in a database to a previous point in time.

tablespace recoveries See online tablespace recovery.

tag A specific name given to an RMAN backup. It can be referenced during subsequent RMAN operations such as recoveries.

time-based point-in-time recovery A method of recovery that restores the database to a specific point in time based on a time defined in the `restore` and `recover` commands.

transportable database In Oracle 11g, the feature that allows the DBA to copy an entire database from one platform to another.

transportable tablespace set The datafiles associated with a group of tablespaces along with the exported metadata that encapsulates the self-contained set of objects that are to be transported.

U

undo record A row stored in the undo tablespace that contains the data necessary to undo a transaction (or a piece of a transaction).

`UNDO_RETENTION` An Oracle parameter that governs the length of time that undo records will be retained in the undo tablespace after their associated transaction has completed.

Unicode The universal character set that supports all known written languages.

W

white-space compression RMAN's default behavior, attempting to reduce the size of backup sets by not including blocks that are unused in the backup.

whole-database backup A complete backup of an Oracle database using the `backup` command.

window A recurring block of time during which a specific resource plan should be enabled to govern resource allocation for the database.

window group A logical method of grouping windows to simplify management by allowing them to be managed as one object.

Index

Note to the reader: Throughout this index **boldfaced** page numbers indicate primary discussions of a topic. *Italicized* page numbers indicate illustrations.

Symbols

A

B

C

D

E

F

G

H

I

J

K

L

M

N

O

P

Q

R

S

T

U

V

W

Z

Wiley Publishing, Inc.
End-User License Agreement

READ THIS. You should carefully read these terms and conditions before opening the software packet(s) included with this book "Book". This is a license agreement "Agreement" between you and Wiley Publishing, Inc. "WPI". By opening the accompanying software packet(s), you acknowledge that you have read and accept the following terms and conditions. If you do not agree and do not want to be bound by such terms and conditions, promptly return the Book and the unopened software packet(s) to the place you obtained them for a full refund.

1. License Grant. WPI grants to you (either an individual or entity) a nonexclusive license to use one copy of the enclosed software program(s) (collectively, the "Software," solely for your own personal or business purposes on a single computer (whether a standard computer or a workstation component of a multi-user network). The Software is in use on a computer when it is loaded into temporary memory (RAM) or installed into permanent memory (hard disk, CD-ROM, or other storage device). WPI reserves all rights not expressly granted herein.

2. Ownership. WPI is the owner of all right, title, and interest, including copyright, in and to the compilation of the Software recorded on the physical packet included with this Book "Software Media". Copyright to the individual programs recorded on the Software Media is owned by the author or other authorized copyright owner of each program. Ownership of the Software and all proprietary rights relating thereto remain with WPI and its licensers.

3. Restrictions On Use and Transfer.

(a) You may only (i) make one copy of the Software for backup or archival purposes, or (ii) transfer the Software to a single hard disk, provided that you keep the original for backup or archival purposes. You may not (i) rent or lease the Software, (ii) copy or reproduce the Software through a LAN or other network system or through any computer subscriber system or bulletin-board system, or (iii) modify, adapt, or create derivative works based on the Software.

(b) You may not reverse engineer, decompile, or disassemble the Software. You may transfer the Software and user documentation on a permanent basis, provided that the transferee agrees to accept the terms and conditions of this Agreement and you retain no copies. If the Software is an update or has been updated, any transfer must include the most recent update and all prior versions.

4. Restrictions on Use of Individual Programs. You must follow the individual requirements and restrictions detailed for each individual program in the About the CD-ROM appendix of this Book or on the Software Media. These limitations are also contained in the individual license agreements recorded on the Software Media. These limitations may include a requirement that after using the program for a specified period of time, the user must pay a registration fee or discontinue use. By opening the Software packet(s), you will be agreeing to abide by the licenses and restrictions for these individual programs that are detailed in the About the CD-ROM appendix and/or on the Software Media. None of the material on this Software Media or listed in this Book may ever be redistributed, in original or modified form, for commercial purposes.

5. Limited Warranty.

(a) WPI warrants that the Software and Software Media are free from defects in materials and workmanship under normal use for a period of sixty (60) days from the date of purchase of this Book. If WPI receives notification within the warranty period of defects in materials or workmanship, WPI will replace the defective Software Media.

(b) WPI AND THE AUTHOR(S) OF THE BOOK DISCLAIM ALL OTHER WARRANTIES, EXPRESS OR IMPLIED, INCLUDING WITHOUT LIMITATION IMPLIED WARRANTIES OF MERCHANTABILITY AND FITNESS FOR A PARTICULAR PURPOSE, WITH RESPECT TO THE SOFTWARE, THE PROGRAMS, THE SOURCE CODE CONTAINED THEREIN, AND/OR THE TECHNIQUES DESCRIBED IN THIS BOOK. WPI DOES NOT WARRANT THAT THE FUNCTIONS CONTAINED IN THE SOFTWARE WILL MEET YOUR REQUIREMENTS OR THAT THE OPERATION OF THE SOFTWARE WILL BE ERROR FREE.

(c) This limited warranty gives you specific legal rights, and you may have other rights that vary from jurisdiction to jurisdiction.

6. Remedies.

(a) WPI's entire liability and your exclusive remedy for defects in materials and workmanship shall be limited to replacement of the Software Media, which may be returned to WPI with a copy of your receipt at the following address: Software Media Fulfillment Department, Attn.: *OCP, Oracle Database 11*g *Administrator Certified Professional Study Guide*, Wiley Publishing, Inc., 10475 Crosspoint Blvd., Indianapolis, IN 46256, or call 1-800-762-2974. Please allow four to six weeks for delivery. This Limited Warranty is void if failure of the Software Media has resulted from accident, abuse, or misapplication. Any replacement Software Media will be warranted for the remainder of the original warranty period or thirty (30) days, whichever is longer.

(b) In no event shall WPI or the author be liable for any damages whatsoever (including without limitation damages for loss of business profits, business interruption, loss of business information, or any other pecuniary loss) arising from the use of or inability to use the Book or the Software, even if WPI has been advised of the possibility of such damages.

(c) Because some jurisdictions do not allow the exclusion or limitation of liability for consequential or incidental damages, the above limitation or exclusion may not apply to you.

7. U.S. Government Restricted Rights. Use, duplication, or disclosure of the Software for or on behalf of the United States of America, its agencies and/or instrumentalities "U.S. Government" is subject to restrictions as stated in paragraph (c)(1)(ii) of the Rights in Technical Data and Computer Software clause of DFARS 252.227-7013, or subparagraphs (c) (1) and (2) of the Commercial Computer Software - Restricted Rights clause at FAR 52.227-19, and in similar clauses in the NASA FAR supplement, as applicable.

8. General. This Agreement constitutes the entire understanding of the parties and revokes and supersedes all prior agreements, oral or written, between them and may not be modified or amended except in a writing signed by both parties hereto that specifically refers to this Agreement. This Agreement shall take precedence over any other documents that may be in conflict herewith. If any one or more provisions contained in this Agreement are held by any court or tribunal to be invalid, illegal, or otherwise unenforceable, each and every other provision shall remain in full force and effect.

The Best OCP: Oracle Database 11*g* Book/CD Package on the Market!

Get ready for your Oracle Certified Professional for Oracle Database 11g certification and the Oracle Database 11g: Administration II (1Z0-053) exam with the most comprehensive and challenging sample tests anywhere!

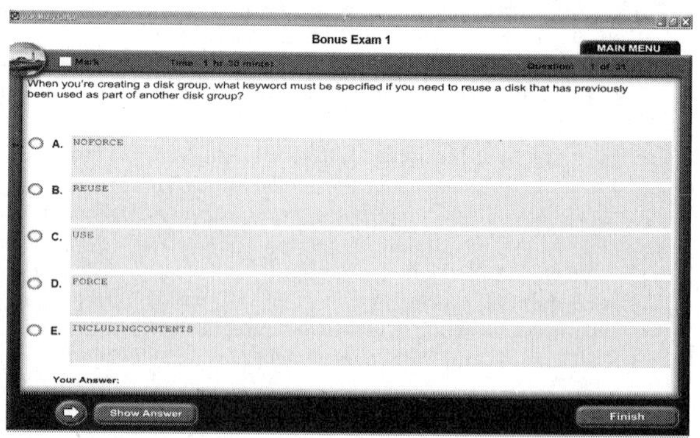

The Sybex Test Engine features:

- All the review questions, as covered in each chapter of the book.
- Challenging questions representative of those you'll find on the real exam.
- Two full-length bonus exams available only on the CD.
- An Assessment Test to narrow your focus to certain objective groups.

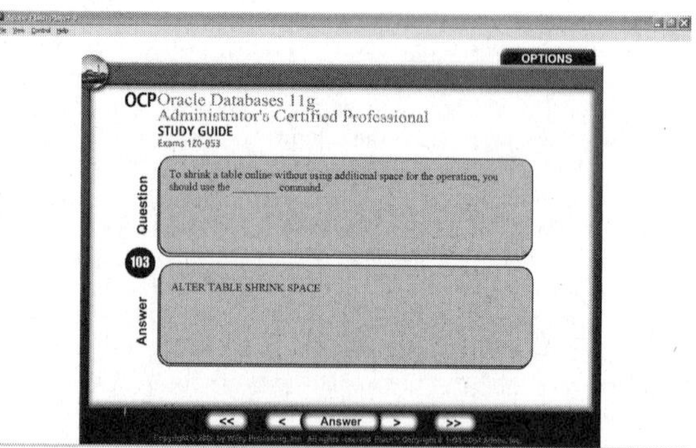

Use the Electronic Flashcards for PCs or Palm devices to jog your memory and prep last-minute for the exam!

- Reinforce your understanding of key concepts with these hardcore flashcard-style questions.
- Download the Flashcards to your Palm device and go on the road. Now you can study for the Oracle Database 11*g*: Administration II (1Z0-053) exams anytime, anywhere.

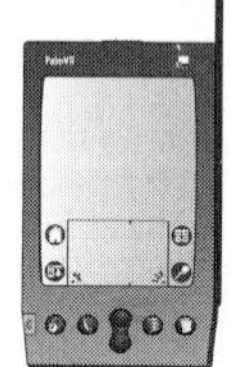

Search through the complete book in PDF!

- Access the entire *OCP: Oracle Database 11g Administrator Certified Professional Study Guide* complete with figures and tables, in electronic format.
- Search the *OCP: Oracle Database 11g Administrator Certified Professional Study Guide* chapters to find information on any topic in seconds.

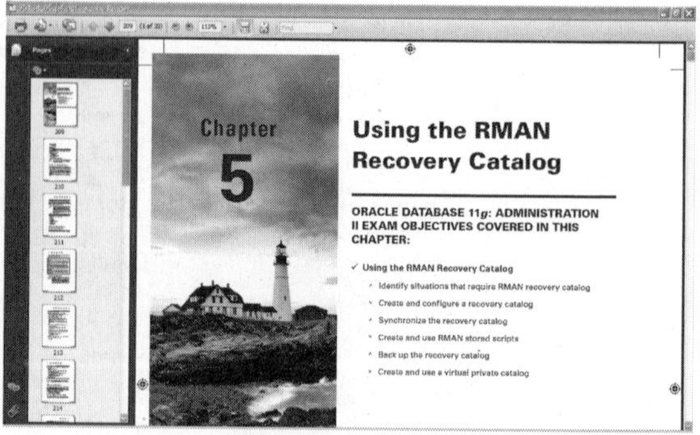

OCA

Oracle® Database 11*g* Administrator Certified Associate

Study Guide

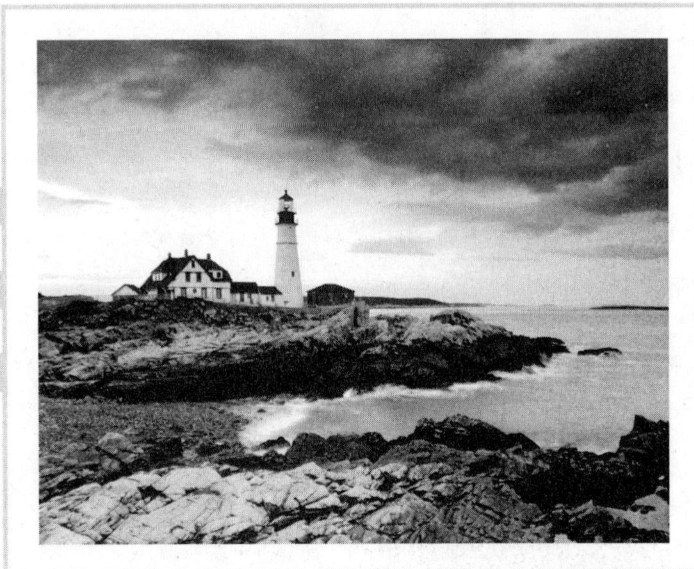

OCA

Oracle® Database 11*g* Administrator Certified Associate

Study Guide

Biju Thomas

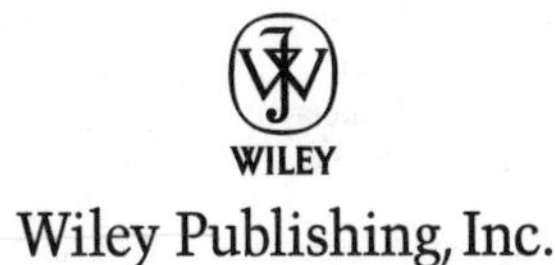

Wiley Publishing, Inc.

Acquisitions Editor: Jeff Kellum
Development Editor: Denise Santoro Lincoln
Technical Editors: Arup Nanda and Bob Bryla
Production Editor: Eric Charbonneau
Copy Editor: Kim Wimpsett
Production Manager: Tim Tate
Vice President and Executive Group Publisher: Richard Swadley
Vice President and Publisher: Neil Edde
Media Project Manager 1: Laura Moss-Hollister
Media Associate Producer: Josh Frank
Media Quality Assurance: Kit Malone
Book Designer: Judy Fung
Compositor: Craig Johnson, Happenstance Type-O-Rama
Proofreader: Candace English
Indexer: Ted Laux
Project Coordinator, Cover: Lynsey Stanford
Cover Designer: Ryan Sneed

Published simultaneously in Canada

ISBN: 978-0-470-39512-7

Library of Congress Cataloging-in-Publication Data

Thomas, Biju.
OCA : Oracle database 11g administrator certified associate study guide (1Z0-051 and 1Z0-052) / Biju Thomas. — 1st ed.
p. cm.
ISBN 978-0-470-39512-7 (paper/cd-rom)
1. Electronic data processing personnel—Certification. 2. Database management—Examinations—Study guides. 3. Oracle (Computer file) I. Title.
QA76.3.T5136 2009
005.75'75—dc22

2008052085

10 9 8 7 6 5 4 3 2 1

Dear Reader,

Thank you for choosing *OCA: Oracle Database 11g Administrator Certified Associate Study Guide* (1ZO-051 and 1ZO-052). This book is part of a family of premium-quality Sybex books, all of which are written by outstanding authors who combine practical experience with a gift for teaching.

Sybex was founded in 1976. More than thirty years later, we're still committed to producing consistently exceptional books. With each of our titles we're working hard to set a new standard for the industry. From the paper we print on, to the authors we work with, our goal is to bring you the best books available.

I hope you see all that reflected in these pages. I'd be very interested to hear your comments and get your feedback on how we're doing. Feel free to let me know what you think about this or any other Sybex book by sending me an email at `nedde@wiley.com`, or if you think you've found a technical error in this book, please visit `http://sybex.custhelp.com`. Customer feedback is critical to our efforts at Sybex.

Best regards,

Neil Edde
Vice President and Publisher
Sybex, an Imprint of Wiley

To the loving memory of my father

To Joshua and Jeanette

Acknowledgments

Thanks first to Jeff Kellum and to Sybex for their faith in me to write this book. I would also like to thank the following wonderful people at Sybex for their support, patience with my slipping schedules, and good work: Denise Santoro Lincoln (developmental editor) for her valuable comments, thoughtful edits, patience, and making sure the chapters have a smooth flow; Eric Charbonneau (production editor) for making sure the various pieces of the book tie together; Candace English for proofreading; and Pete Gaughan for managing the project.

I thank Kim Wimpsett (copy editor) for her edits and making sure the same standard is followed across the book. I'm sure her edits made a difference to the look and feel of the chapters. I also thank Sybex and authors of the *Introduction to Oracle9*i *SQL* and *Oracle Database 10*g *Administration I* study guides for letting me reuse content from their books.

I am very fortunate and honored to have Arup Nanda as the technical editor. Thank you very much for all your valuable suggestions and for pointing out the errors and inaccuracies in the book. Your comments are invaluable. Thank you, Bob Bryla, for tech-reviewing the book and making sure the chapters are technically accurate.

I could not have completed this book without the endless support and love of my wife, Shiji. Thank you for engaging and taking care of the kids while I spent nights and weekends in front of the computer.

Last but not least, I thank all my colleagues and management at OneNeck IT Services for their friendship and support. My special thanks to Joe Hanna for all the encouragement.

About the Author

Biju Thomas is an Oracle 7.3, Oracle8, Oracle8*i*, Oracle9*i*, Oracle 10*g*, and Oracle 11*g* OCP certified professional. He is also a certified Oracle Database SQL Expert. Biju has been developing and administering Oracle databases since 1993, starting with Oracle version 6. He is a senior database consultant at OneNeck IT Services Corporation (`www.oneneck.com`) and resides in Keller, Texas. He maintains a website for DBAs at `www.bijoos.com/oracle`.

Contents at a Glance

Contents

Introduction

There is high demand for professionals in the information technology (IT) industry, and Oracle certifications are the hottest credential in the database world. You have made the right decision to pursue certification, because being Oracle Database 11*g* certified will give you a distinct advantage in this highly competitive market.

Many readers may already be familiar with Oracle and do not need an introduction to Oracle databases. Oracle, founded in 1977, sold the first commercial relational database and is now the world's leading database company and second-largest independent software company with annual revenues of more than $22 billion, and is headquartered in Redwood City, California.

Oracle databases are the de facto standard for large Internet sites and mission-critical enterprise applications. Oracle advertisers are boastful but honest when they proclaim, "The Internet runs on Oracle." Almost all the big Internet sites run on Oracle databases. Oracle's penetration of the database market runs deep and is not limited to Internet implementations. Enterprise resource planning (ERP) application suites, data warehouses, and custom applications at many large and medium companies rely on Oracle. The demand for DBA resources remains higher than others during weak economic times.

This book is intended to help you on your exciting path toward becoming an Oracle Database 11*g* Administrator Certified Associate (OCA), which is the first step on the path toward the Oracle Certified Professional (OCP) and Oracle Certified Master (OCM) certifications. This book covers the two exams required for the OCA certification. Using this book and a practice database, you can start learning Oracle 11*g* and pass the Oracle Database 11*g*: SQL Fundamentals I (1Z0-051) and Oracle Database 11*g*: Administration I (1Z0-052) exams.

Why Become Oracle Certified?

The number-one reason to become OCA or OCP certified is to gain more visibility and greater access to the industry's most challenging opportunities. Oracle certification is the best way to demonstrate your knowledge and skills in Oracle database systems.

Certification is proof of your knowledge and shows that you have the skills required to support Oracle core products. The Oracle certification program can help a company identify proven performers who have demonstrated their skills and who can support the company's investment in Oracle technology. It demonstrates that you have a solid understanding of your job role and the Oracle products used in that role.

The certification tests are scenario-based, which is the most effective way to assess your hands-on expertise and critical problem-solving skills. OCPs are among the best paid in the IT industry. Salary surveys consistently show the OCP certification to yield higher salaries than the other certifications, including Microsoft, Novell, and Cisco.

So, whether you are beginning a career, changing careers, securing your current position, or seeking to refine and promote your position, this book is for you!

Oracle Certifications

Oracle certifications follow a track that is oriented toward a job role. The certification tracks are Database, Middleware, Applications, and Linux. Within each track, Oracle has a tiered certification program of OCA and OCP. Only the Database track has OCM.

The Database track is clearly for the database administrator job role. The Middleware track has certifications on many products, such as Oracle 10*g* Application Server, Oracle Essbase, Oracle Forms, Oracle PL/SQL, Oracle WebLogic, and Service-Oriented Architecture (SOA) and is intended for application developers, system administrators, consultants, and architects.

The Applications track is for ERP administrators and functional consultants. This track covers the Oracle E-Business Suite, Siebel, Hyperion, and PeopleSoft applications. The Linux track is for Linux administrators.

For the latest certification information on all of Oracle certification paths, please visit the Oracle website at `http://education.oracle.com/pls/web_prod-plq-dad/db_pages.getpage?page_id=39&p_org_id=1001&lang=US`.

The role of database administrator (DBA) has become a key to success in today's highly complex database systems. The best DBAs work behind the scenes but are in the spotlight when critical issues arise. They plan, create, maintain, and ensure that the database is available for the business. They have tools to proactively monitor the database for performance issues and to prevent unscheduled downtime. The DBA's job requires a broad understanding of the architecture of Oracle Database and an expertise in solving problems.

Sybex has Oracle certification study guides for the Database track. In the following sections, I'll introduce you to the different tiers in the Oracle Database 11*g* certification track.

Oracle Database 11*g* Administrator Certified Associate

The Oracle Certified Associate (OCA) credential is the first step toward achieving the Oracle Certified Professional (OCP) certification. OCA shows that you have the fundamental knowledge and skills to support an Oracle 11*g* database. This certification requires you to pass two exams that demonstrate your Oracle basics:

- 1Z0-051: Oracle Database 11g: SQL Fundamentals I
- 1Z0-052: Oracle Database 11g: Administration I

If you have already passed any one of the following tests, you need not take the 1Z0-051 test; you need to pass only 1Z0-052:

- 1Z0-001: Introduction to Oracle: SQL and PL/SQL
- 1Z0-007: Introduction to Oracle9*i* SQL
- 1Z0-047: Oracle Database SQL Expert

You can take the 1Z0-051 exam at a testing location or from your home using the Internet. The 1Z0-052 test is offered only at a Prometric facility.

To register for the test or find the location of a testing center, visit Prometric at www.prometric.com/oracle, or call 1-800-891-3926. At the time of writing this book, the exam fee was $95 USD for the online exam and $125 USD for the in-facility exam.

Oracle Database 11*g* Administrator Certified Professional

The Oracle Certified Professional credential shows that you have the skill and technical expertise to manage and implement enterprise databases. The OCP tier challenges you to demonstrate your continuing experience and knowledge of Oracle technologies. The Oracle Database 11g Administrator Certified Professional certification requires you to have the OCA certification as well as to pass the following exam at a Prometric facility.

- 1Z0-053: Oracle Database 11g Administration II

In addition, the OCP candidate must take one instructor-led Oracle University hands-on requirement class from the following list:

- Oracle Database 11*g*: Advanced PL/SQL
- Oracle Database 11*g*: Data Guard Administration
- Oracle Database 11*g*: Performance Tuning
- Oracle Database 11*g*: Administration Workshop I
- Oracle Database 11*g*: Administration Workshop II
- Oracle Database 11*g*: Introduction to SQL
- Oracle Database 11*g*: New Features for Administrators
- Oracle Database 11*g*: Program with PL/SQL
- Oracle Database 11*g*: Develop PL/SQL Program Units
- Oracle Database 11*g*: Implement Streams
- Oracle Database 11*g*: SQL Tuning Workshop
- Oracle Spatial 11*g*: Essentials
- Oracle Database 11*g*: RAC Administration
- Oracle Database 11*g*: SQL Fundamentals I

You should verify the list of approved hands-on course at the Oracle University website at http://education.oracle.com/pls/web_prod-plq-dad/db_pages.getpage?page_id=244#5. This list may change without notice.

Oracle Database 11*g* Administrator Certified Master

The highest level of certification available in any track is the Oracle Certified Master. The OCM certification credential shows that you have the highest level of expertise in an Oracle product. To become an Oracle Certified Master, you must first achieve OCP status and then complete two advanced instructor-led classes at an Oracle University facility. You must also pass a hands-on examination at an Oracle University facility. At the time of writing this book, the Oracle Database 11*g* Certified Master exam has not been released yet.

More Information and Resources

You can find most current information about Oracle certifications at www.oracle.com/global/us/education/certification. You may be asked to choose your country of residence before being directed to the site. Follow the links under Certifications to choose the track and learn more.

Choose the Database track to view the different certification versions available. Choose Oracle 11*g* Administrator Certified Associate, and then click the test to learn more about the test contents, the objectives covered on the test, and the passing score. You can also register for the test here.

Oracle also provides sample practice questions for the OCA and OCP exams. You can find Oracle Database 11*g* SQL Fundamentals I exam practice questions at www.oracle.com/global/us/education/certification/sample_questions/exam_1z0-051.html. You can find the sample questions for the Oracle Database 11*g* Administration I exam at www.oracle.com/global/us/education/certification/sample_questions/exam_1z0-052.html.

The Oracle documentation is available online at http://tahiti.oracle.com. The Oracle documentation contains a wealth of information, which can be used to supplement what you learn from this book.

Oracle provides training series with step-by-step instructions to perform a variety of Oracle Database 11*g* tasks. You can find the Oracle by example (OBE) tutorial at www.oracle.com/technology/obe/11gr1_db/otn_all_db11gr1.html.

The Oracle Technology Network (www.oracle.com/technology/index.html) is also a great resource for database administrators and developers. You can read articles, view sample code, access documentation, participate in forums, and, most important, download a trial version of Oracle Database 11*g* and other Oracle products.

OCA/OCP Study Guides

The Oracle Database 11*g* administration certification consists of three tests: two for OCA and one for OCP. Sybex offers study guides to help you achieve OCA and OCP certification:

- *OCA: Oracle Database 11*g* Administrator Certified Associate Study Guide* (ISBN 9780470395127) covers the exams Oracle Database 11*g*: SQL Fundamentals I (1Z0-051) and Oracle Database 11*g*: Administration I (1Z0-052).
- *OCP: Oracle Database 11*g* Administrator Certified Professional Study Guide* (ISBN 9780470395134) covers the exam Oracle Database 11*g*: Administration II (1Z0-053).

These two books are offered in a boxed set as *OCP: Oracle Database 11*g* Administrator Certified Professional Certification Kit* (ISBN 9780470395141).

Oracle Exam Requirements

The Oracle Database 11*g* Database Administrator Certified Associate certification tests your basic SQL skills for the SQL exam and your database architecture and administration skills for the DBA exam. The SQL exam tests your knowledge of writing SQL and using the functions available in Oracle 11*g*. The Administration I exam concentrates on the architecture and the basic administration of Oracle 11*g* database. The following sections detail the skills needed to pass the SQL Fundamentals I and Administration I exams.

OCA SQL (1Z0-051) Requirements

To pass the Oracle Database 11*g* SQL Fundamentals I exam, you must have the following skills:

- Write SQL SELECT statements that display data from one or more tables.
- Join tables using ANSI syntax and Oracle traditional syntax.
- Restrict, sort, and aggregate data using single-row, conversion, and group functions.
- Write subqueries and queries using SET operators.
- Manipulate data via insert, update, and delete.
- Create and manage tables, indexes, views, synonyms, and sequences.

OCA Admin I (1Z0-052) Requirements

To pass the Oracle Database 11*g* Administration I exam, you must have the following skills:

- Understand the Oracle server architecture (database and instance).
- Be able to install the Oracle 11*g* software and create a database.
- Use the Database Configuration Assistant and Enterprise Manager Database Control tools.
- Understand the physical and logical storage of the database and be able to manage space allocation and growth.
- Use the data dictionary views and set database parameters.
- Manage and manipulate data, including its storage, loading, and reorganization.
- Create and manage tables, constraints, and indexes.
- Manage redo logs, archive logs, and automatic undo.
- Configure Oracle Net on the server side and the client side.
- Understand the backup and recovery architecture.
- Secure the database and audit database usage.
- Use advisors to tune and manage the database.
- Be able to contact Oracle Support for problem resolution and patches.

Tips for Taking the OCA Exams

The following tips will help you prepare for and pass each exam:

- Each OCP test consists of about 70 questions to be completed in 90 (120 for the SQL exam) minutes. Answer the questions you are sure of first, before you run out of time. Mark the difficult questions or the ones you are not sure of and return to them later.
- Many questions on the exam have answer choices that at first glance look identical. Read the questions carefully. Do not jump to conclusions. Make sure you clearly understand what each question asks.
- Most questions are based on scenarios. Some of the scenarios contain nonessential information and exhibits. You need to be able to identify what's important and what's not.
- Do not leave any questions unanswered. There is no negative scoring.
- When answering questions you are not sure about, use a process of elimination to get rid of the obviously incorrect answers first. Doing this greatly improves your odds if you need to make an educated guess.
- If you are not sure of your answer, mark it for review, and then look for other questions that may help you eliminate any incorrect answers. At the end of the test, you can review the questions you marked earlier.

You should be familiar with the exam objectives, which are included at the beginning of each chapter. Please check the objectives listing on the Oracle University website (`http://education.oracle.com/pls/web_prod-plq-dad/db_pages.getpage?page_id=244#5`) for any changes or updates. The detail page for each exam shows the passing score, the number of questions, the minutes allocated, and any exam fees or other requirements.

What Is Covered in This Book

This book covers everything you need to pass the Oracle Database 11*g* Certified Associate exams. Part I includes the first eight chapters that cover the objectives for the Oracle Database 11*g* SQL Fundamentals I exam. Part II of the book includes the remaining 10 chapters that cover the objectives for the Oracle Database 11*g* Administration I exam.

Part I: Oracle Database 11*g* SQL Fundamentals I

Chapter 1: Introducing SQL introduces you to writing simple queries using the SELECT statement. It also introduces you to filtering and sorting data.

Chapter 2: Using Single-Row Functions discusses the single-row functions and conversion functions available in Oracle 11g, with details on how and where to use them.

Chapter 3: Using Group Functions explains data aggregations, Oracle's built-in group function, and how to nest functions.

Chapter 4: Using Joins and Subqueries explains how data from multiple tables can be related via joins, subqueries, and SET operators.

Chapter 5: Manipulating Data explores how to manipulate data—adding, removing, and updating data. The chapter also covers how transaction control works.

Chapter 6: Creating Tables and Constraints explains how to create and manage tables and constraints. It also discusses the various data types available in Oracle 11*g* to store data.

Chapter 7: Creating Schema Objects introduces you to creating and managing views, sequences, and synonyms.

Part II: Oracle Database 11*g* Administration I

Chapter 8: Introducing Oracle Database 11*g* Components and Architecture is the first chapter to read if you're studying for the Administration I exam. This chapter introduces you to the Oracle 11*g* database architecture and how to install the Oracle 11*g* software.

Chapter 9: Creating an Oracle 11*g* Database explains how you can create an Oracle 11*g* database. It discusses the initialization parameters, stages of database startup and shutdown, where to find log and trace files, and how to use the data dictionary.

Chapter 10: Allocating Database Storage and Creating Schema Objects explores the logical and physical storage of the database. You will learn space management and the various types of tablespaces. This chapter also talks about creating and managing tables and constraints, but does not repeat what was covered in Chapter 6.

Chapter 11: Understanding Network Architecture introduces you to the Oracle Net configuration and setup. You will learn to set up network architecture on the server and client.

Chapter 12: Implementing Security and Auditing shows how you can secure your database using privileges, profiles, and roles. You will also learn how to audit database usage.

Chapter 13: Managing Data and Undo shows you how you can add, update, and remove data from tables as well as how transactions work. It also introduces you to undo data and undo management. Be sure to read Chapter 5 before you read this chapter.

Chapter 14: Maintaining the Database and Managing Performance explores the tools available in Oracle 11*g* to manage the performance of the database. You will learn about optimizer statistics, Automatic Workload Repository, various advisors, and Automatic Memory Management.

Chapter 15: Implementing Database Backups introduces you to the backup architecture concepts. It discusses the various backup modes and how to use RMAN.

Chapter 16: Recovering the Database explores the various recovery scenarios and how best to get the data back. It introduces you to the Data Recovery Advisor, a new tool in Oracle 11*g* that helps in finding the recovery-related errors in the database, gives you advice, and helps you recover the database.

Chapter 17: Moving Data and Using EM Tools introduces you to two tools available in Oracle 11*g* to move and load data: Data Pump and SQL*Loader. This chapter also covers the intelligent infrastructure of Enterprise Manager that helps DBAs manage patches and contact Oracle Support.

Each chapter ends with review questions that are specifically designed to help you retain the knowledge presented. To really nail down your skills, read and answer each question carefully.

How to Use This Book

This book provides a solid foundation for the serious effort of preparing for the Oracle 11*g* Certified Associate exams. To best benefit from the book, use the following study method:

1. Take the assessment test immediately following this introduction (the answers are at the end of the test). Carefully read the explanations for any questions you get wrong, and note in which chapters the material is covered. This information should help you plan the study strategy.
2. Study each chapter carefully, making sure you fully understand the information and the test objectives listed at the beginning of each chapter. Pay close attention to any chapter related to questions you missed on the assessment test.
3. Complete all examples in the chapter, referring to the chapter so that you understand the reason for each step you take. It is best to have an Oracle 11*g* database available to try the examples and code provided in the book. Answer the review questions related to that chapter.
4. Note the review questions that confuse or trick you, and study those sections of the book again.
5. Two bonus exams for each exam are included on the accompanying CD. They will give you a complete overview of what you can expect to see on the real test.
6. Answer all the flashcard questions on the CD.

Remember to use the products on the CD included with this book. The electronic flashcards and Sybex test engine exam-preparation software have been specifically designed to help you study and pass your exams.

To learn all the material covered in this book, you will need to apply yourself regularly and with discipline. Try to set the same time period every day to study, and select a comfortable and quiet place to do so. If you work hard, you will be surprised at how quickly you learn this material. All the best!

The companion CD is home to all the demo files, samples, and bonus resources mentioned in the book. See the CD appendix for more details on the contents and how to access them.

How to Contact the Author

I welcome feedback from you about this book or about books you'd like to see from me in the future. You can reach me by writing to `biju.thomas.sybex@gmail.com`. For more information about database administration and Oracle 11g, please visit my website at `www.bijoos.com/oracle`.

Sybex strives to keep you supplied with the latest tools and information you need for your work. Please check the website at `www.sybex.com`, where we'll post additional content, errata, and updates that supplement this book if the need arises. Enter **OCA Oracle 11g** in the Search box (or type the book's ISBN—**9780470395127**), and click Go to get to the book's update page.

SQL Fundamentals I Assessment Test

1. Which operator will be evaluated first in the following SELECT statement?

   ```
   SELECT (2+3*4/2-5) FROM dual;
   ```

   A. +

   B. *

   C. /

   D. -

2. Which two of the following statements are true?

   A. A view can be created before creating the base table.

   B. A view cannot be created before creating the base table.

   C. A view will become invalid if the base table's column referred to in the view is altered.

   D. A view will become invalid if any column in the base table is altered.

3. Which function can return a non-NULL value if passed a NULL argument?

   A. NULLIF

   B. LENGTH

   C. CONCAT

   D. INSTR

   E. TAN

4. The following statement will raise an exception on which line?

   ```
   select dept_name, avg(all salary)
         ,count(*) "number of employees"
   from emp , dept
   where deptno = dept_no
     and count(*) > 5
   group by dept_name
   order by 2 desc;
   ```

   A. `select dept_name, avg(all salary), count(*) "number of employees"`

   B. `where deptno = dept_no`

   C. `and count(*) > 5`

   D. `group by dept_name`

   E. `order by 2 desc;`

5. Review the code segment. Which line has an error?

```
1 INSERT INTO salaries VALUES (101, 23400, SYSDATE);
2 UPDATE salaries
3 SET salary = salary * 1.1
4 AND effective_dt = SYSDATE
5 WHERE empno = 333;
```

   A. 2

   B. 4

   C. 5

   D. There is no error.

6. Review the following SQL, and choose the most appropriate option.

```
SELECT job_id, COUNT(*)
FROM employees
GROUP BY department_id;
```

   A. The statement will show the number of jobs in each department.

   B. The statement will show the number of employees in each department.

   C. The statement will generate an error.

   D. The statement will work if the GROUP BY clause is removed.

7. Which datatype stores data outside Oracle Database?

   A. UROWID

   B. BFILE

   C. BLOB

   D. NCLOB

   E. EXTERNAL

8. The DEPT table has the following data:

```
SQL> SELECT * FROM dept;

    DEPTNO DNAME          LOC
---------- -------------- ----------
        10 ACCOUNTING     NEW YORK
        20 RESEARCH       DALLAS
        30 SALES          CHICAGO
        40 OPERATIONS     BOSTON
```

Consider this INSERT statement, and choose the best answer:

```
INSERT INTO (SELECT * FROM dept WHERE deptno = 10)
VALUES (50, 'MARKETING', 'FORT WORTH');
```

A. The INSERT statement is invalid; a valid table name is missing.

B. 50 is not a valid DEPTNO value, since the subquery limits DEPTNO to 10.

C. The statement will work without error.

D. A subquery and a VALUES clause cannot appear together.

9. Which two of the following queries are valid syntax that would return all rows from the EMPLOYEES and DEPARTMENTS tables, even if there are no corresponding/related rows in the other table?

A.
```
SELECT last_name, first_name, department_name
FROM   employees e FULL JOIN departments d
ON     e.department_id = d.department_id;
```

B.
```
SELECT last_name, first_name, department_name
FROM   employees e OUTER JOIN departments d
ON     e.department_id = d.department_id;
```

C.
```
SELECT e.last_name, e.first_name, d.department_name
FROM   employees e
LEFT OUTER JOIN departments d
ON     e.department_id = d.department_id
RIGHT OUTER JOIN employees f
ON     f.department_id = d.department_id;
```

D.
```
SELECT e.last_name, e.first_name, d.department_name
FROM   employees e
CROSS JOIN departments d
ON     e.department_id = d.department_id;
```

E.
```
SELECT last_name, first_name, department_name
FROM   employees
FULL OUTER JOIN departments USING (department_id);
```

10. Which of the following statements could use an index on the columns PRODUCT_ID and WAREHOUSE_ID of the OE.INVENTORIES table? (Choose all that apply.)

   A.
   ```
   select count(distinct warehouse_id)
   from oe.inventories;
   ```

   B.
   ```
   select product_id, quantity_on_hand
   from oe.inventories
   where product_id = 100;
   ```

   C.
   ```
   insert into oe.inventories values (5,100,32);
   ```

   D. None of these statements could use the index.

11. The following statements are executed:

   ```
   create sequence my_seq;
   select my_seq.nextval from dual;
   select my_seq.nextval from dual;
   rollback;
   select my_seq.nextval from dual;
   ```

   What value will be returned when the last SQL SELECT statement is executed?

   A. 0

   B. 1

   C. 2

   D. 3

   E. NULL

12. Which of the following statements are true? (Choose two.)

   A. Primary key constraints allow NULL values in the columns.

   B. Unique key constraints allow NULL values in the columns.

   C. Primary key constraints do not allow NULL values in the columns.

   D. A nonunique index cannot be used to enforce primary key constraints.

13. The current time in Dubai is 04-APR-2008 08:50:00, and the time in Dallas is 03-APR-2008 23:50:00. A user from Dubai is connected to a session in the database located on a server in Dallas. What will be the result of his query?

   ```
   SELECT TO_CHAR(SYSDATE,'DD-MON-YYYY HH24:MI:SS') FROM dual;
   ```

   A. 04-APR-2008 08:50:00

   B. 03-APR-2008 23:50:00

   C. 03-APR-2008 2324:50:00

   D. None of the above

14. The FIRED_EMPLOYEE table has the following structure:

```
EMPLOYEE_ID  NUMBER (4)
FIRE_DATE DATE
```

How many rows will be counted from the last SQL statement in the code segment?

```
SELECT COUNT(*) FROM FIRED_EMPLOYEES;
COUNT(*)
--------
     105

INSERT INTO FIRED_EMPLOYEE VALUES (104, TRUNC(SYSDATE);
SAVEPOINT A;
INSERT INTO FIRED_EMPLOYEE VALUES (106, TRUNC(SYSDATE);
SAVEPOINT B;
INSERT INTO FIRED_EMPLOYEE VALUES (108, TRUNC(SYSDATE);
ROLLBACK TO A;
INSERT INTO FIRED_EMPLOYEE VALUES (104, TRUNC(SYSDATE);
COMMIT;
SELECT COUNT(*) FROM FIRED_EMPLOYEES;
```

A. 109

B. 106

C. 105

D. 107

15. At a minimum, how many join conditions should be there to avoid a Cartesian join if there are three tables in the FROM clause?

A. 1

B. 2

C. 3

D. There is no minimum.

16. Why does the following statement fail?

```
CREATE TABLE FRUITS-N-VEGETABLES
(NAME VARCHAR2 (40));
```

A. The table should have more than one column in its definition.

B. NAME is a reserved word, which cannot be used as a column name.

C. Oracle does not like the table name.

D. The column length cannot exceed 30 characters.

17. Which two statements are true about NULL values?
   - A. You cannot search for a NULL value in a column using the WHERE clause.
   - B. If a NULL value is returned in the subquery or if NULL is included in the list when using a NOT IN operator, no rows will be returned.
   - C. Only = and != operators can be used to search for NULL values in a column.
   - D. In an ascending-order sort, NULL values appear at the bottom of the result set.
   - E. Concatenating a NULL value to a non-NULL string results in a NULL.

18. Table CUSTOMERS has a column named CUST_ZIP that could be NULL. Which of the following functions include the NULL rows in its result?
   - A. COUNT (CUST_ZIP)
   - B. SUM (CUST_ZIP)
   - C. AVG (DISTINCT CUST_ZIP)
   - D. None of the above

19. Using the following EMP table, you need to increase everyone's salary by 5 percent of their combined salary and bonus. Which of the following statements will achieve the desired results?

Column Name	emp_id	name	salary	bonus
Key Type	pk	pk		
NULLs/Unique	NN	NN	NN	
FK Table				
Datatype	VARCHAR2	VARCHAR2	NUMBER	NUMBER
Length	9	50	11,2	11,2

   - A. UPDATE emp SET salary = (salary + bonus)*1.05;
   - B. UPDATE emp SET salary = salary*1.05 + bonus*1.05;
   - C. UPDATE emp SET salary = salary + (salary + bonus)*0.05;
   - D. A, B, and C will achieve the desired results.
   - E. None of these statements will achieve the desired results.

20. Which option is not available in Oracle when modifying tables?
   - A. Adding new columns
   - B. Renaming existing columns
   - C. Dropping existing columns
   - D. None of the above

21. The following data is from the EMPLOYEES table:

```
DEPARTMENT_ID      EMPNO FIRST_NAME
------------- ---------- -------------
           30        119 Karen
           50        124 Kevin
           50        135 Ki
           80        146 Karen
                     178 Kimberely
           50        188 Kelly
           50        197 Kevin
```

Which EMPNO will be returned last when the following query is executed?

```
select department_id, employee_id empno, first_name
from employees
order by 1, 2
```

A. 188

B. 178

C. 146

D. 119

22. INTERVAL datatypes store a period of time. Which components are included in the INTERVAL DAY TO SECOND datatype column? (Choose all that apply.)

A. Years

B. Quarters

C. Months

D. Days

E. Hours

F. Minutes

G. Seconds

H. Fractional seconds

23. The primary key of the STATE table is STATE_CD. The primary key of the CITY table is STATE_CD/CITY_CD. The STATE_CD column of the CITY table is the foreign key to the STATE table. There are no other constraints on these two tables. Consider the following view definition:

```
CREATE OR REPLACE VIEW state_city AS
SELECT a.state_cd, a.state_name, b.city_cd, b.city_name
FROM   state a, city b
WHERE  a.state_cd = b.state_cd;
```

Which of the following operations are permitted on the base tables of the view? (Choose all that apply.)

A. Insert a record into the CITY table.

B. Insert a record into the STATE table.

C. Update the STATE_CD column of the CITY table.

D. Update the CITY_CD column of the CITY table.

E. Update the CITY_NAME column of the CITY table.

F. Update the STATE_NAME column of the STATE table.

24. The table CUSTOMERS has the following data:

```
ID   NAME                   ZIP UPD_DATE
---- --------------- ---------- ---------
L921 LEEZA                75252 01-JAN-00
B023 WILLIAMS             15215
K783 KATHY                75252 15-FEB-00
B445 BENJAMIN             76021 15-FEB-00
D334 DENNIS               12443
```

You issue the following command to alter the table. Which line of code will cause an error?

```
1  ALTER TABLE CUSTOMERS
2  MODIFY
3  (UPD_DATE DEFAULT SYSDATE NOT NULL,
4  ZIP NOT NULL);
```

A. Line 2 will cause an error.

B. Line 3 will cause an error.

C. Line 4 will cause an error.

D. There will be no error.

25. In ANSI SQL, a self-join can be represented by using which of the following? (Choose the best answer.)

A. NATURAL JOIN clause

B. CROSS JOIN clause

C. JOIN...USING clause

D. JOIN...ON clause

E. All of the above

26. What will be result of `trunc(2916.16, -1)`?

A. 2916.2

B. 290

C. 2916.1

D. 2900

E. 2910

27. The table ADDRESSES is created using the following syntax. How many indexes will be created automatically when this table is created?

```
CREATE TABLE ADDRESSES (
NAME   VARCHAR2 (40) PRIMARY KEY,
STREET VARCHAR2 (40),
CITY   VARCHAR2 (40),
STATE  CHAR     (2) REFERENCES STATE (ST_CODE),
ZIP    NUMBER   (5) NOT NULL,
PHONE  VARCHAR2 (12) UNIQUE);
```

A. 0

B. 1

C. 2

D. 3

28. Which line of the following code has an error?

```
SELECT *
FROM emp
WHERE comm = NULL
ORDER BY ename;
```

A. SELECT *

B. FROM emp

C. WHERE comm = NULL

D. There is no error in this statement.

29. Which of the following statements will raise an exception?

A. `alter sequence emp_seq nextval 23050;`

B. `alter sequence emp_seq nocycle;`

C. `alter sequence emp_seq increment by -5;`

D. `alter sequence emp_seq maxvalue 10000;`

30. What order does Oracle use in resolving a table or view referenced in a SQL statement?

A. Table/view within user's schema, public synonym, private synonym

B. Table/view within user's schema, private synonym, public synonym

C. Public synonym, table/view within user's schema, private synonym

D. Private synonym, public synonym, table/view within user's schema

31. Which two options are not true when you execute a COMMIT statement?

A. All locks created by DML statements are released in the session.

B. All savepoints created are erased in the session.

C. Queries started before COMMIT in other sessions will show the current changes after COMMIT.

D. All undo information written from the DML statements is erased.

32. Which two operators are used to add more joining conditions in a multiple-table query?

A. NOT

B. OR

C. AND

D. Comma (,)

33. What is wrong with the following SQL?

```
SELECT  department_id, MAX(COUNT(*))
FROM employees
GROUP BY  department_id;
```

A. Aggregate functions cannot be nested.

B. The GROUP BY clause should not be included when using nested aggregate functions.

C. The department_id column in the SELECT clause should not be used when using nested aggregate functions.

D. The COUNT function cannot be nested.

34. Which types of constraints can be created on a view?

A. Check, NOT NULL

B. Primary key, foreign key, unique key

C. Check, NOT NULL, primary key, foreign key, unique key

D. No constraints can be created on a view.

35. Which two declarations define the maximum length of a CHAR datatype column in bytes?

A. CHAR (20)

B. CHAR (20) BYTE

C. CHAR (20 BYTE)

D. BYTE (20 CHAR)

E. CHAR BYTE (20)

36. A view is created using the following code. Which of the following operations are permitted on the view?

```
CREATE VIEW USA_STATES
AS SELECT * FROM STATE
WHERE  CNT_CODE = 1
WITH READ ONLY;
```

A. SELECT

B. SELECT, UPDATE

C. SELECT, DELETE

D. SELECT, INSERT

37. You query the database with the following:

```
SELECT PRODUCT_ID FROM PRODUCTS
WHERE PRODUCT_ID LIKE '%S\_J\_C' ESCAPE '\';
```

Choose the two PRODUCT_ID strings that will satisfy the query.

A. BTS_J_C

B. SJC

C. SKJKC

D. S_J_C

38. The EMPLOYEE table is defined as follows:

```
EMP_NAME    VARCHAR2(40)
HIRE_DATE   DATE
SALARY      NUMBER (14,2)
```

Which query is most appropriate to use if you need to find the employees who were hired before January 1, 1998 and have a salary greater than 5,000 or less than 1,000?

A.
```
SELECT emp_name FROM employee
WHERE hire_date > TO_DATE('01011998','MMDDYYYY')
AND SALARY < 1000 OR > 5000;
```

B.
```
SELECT emp_name FROM employee
WHERE hire_date < TO_DATE('01011998','MMDDYYYY')
AND SALARY < 1000 OR SALARY > 5000;
```

C.
```
SELECT emp_name FROM employee
WHERE hire_date < TO_DATE('01011998','MMDDYYYY')
AND (SALARY < 1000 OR SALARY > 5000);
```

D.
```
SELECT emp_name FROM employee
WHERE hire_date < TO_DATE('01011998','MMDDYYYY')
AND SALARY BETWEEN  1000 AND 5000;
```

39. What happens when you issue the following command? (Choose all that apply.)

```
TRUNCATE TABLE SCOTT.EMPLOYEE;
```

A. All the rows in the table EMPLOYEE owned by SCOTT are removed.

B. The storage space used by the table EMPLOYEE is released (except the initial extent).

C. If foreign key constraints are defined to this table using the ON DELETE CASCADE clause, the rows from the child tables are also removed.

D. The indexes on the table are dropped.

E. You cannot truncate a table if triggers are defined on the table.

40. Which two statements will drop the primary key defined on table EMP? The primary key name is PK_EMP.

A. ALTER TABLE EMP DROP PRIMARY KEY;

B. DROP CONSTRAINT PK_EMP;

C. ALTER TABLE EMP DROP CONSTRAINT PK_EMP;

D. ALTER CONSTRAINT PK_EMP DROP CASCADE;

E. DROP CONSTRAINT PK_EMP ON EMP;

Answers to SQL Fundamentals I Assessment Test

1. B. In the arithmetic operators, unary operators are evaluated first, then multiplication and division, and finally addition and subtraction. The expression is evaluated from left to right. For more information about order of evaluation, see Chapter 1.

2. A, C. The CREATE FORCE VIEW statement can be used to create a view before its base table is created. In versions prior to Oracle 11*g*, any modification to the table will invalidate the view. In Oracle 11*g*, the view will be invalidated only if the columns used in the view are modified in the base table. Use the ALTER VIEW <view name> COMPILE statement to recompile the view. See Chapter 7 to learn more about views.

3. C. CONCAT will return a non-NULL if only one parameter is NULL. Both CONCAT parameters would need to be NULL for CONCAT to return NULL. The NULLIF function returns NULL if the two parameters are equal. The LENGTH of a NULL is NULL. INSTR will return NULL if NULL is passed in and the tangent of a NULL is NULL. For more information about NULL values, see Chapter 2.

4. C. Group functions cannot appear in the WHERE clause. To learn more about group functions, see Chapter 3.

5. B. When updating multiple columns in a single UPDATE statement, the column assignments in the SET clause must be separated by commas, not AND operators. To read more about DML statements (INSERT, UPDATE, and DELETE), refer to Chapter 5.

6. C. Since job_id is used in the SELECT clause, it must be used in the GROUP BY clause also. To learn more about the rules of using the GROUP BY clause and aggregate functions, read Chapter 3.

7. B. The BFILE datatype stores only the locator to an external file in the database; the actual data is stored as an operating system file. BLOB, NCLOB, and CLOB are the other large object data types in Oracle 11*g*. UROWID is Universal ROWID datatype and EXTERNAL is a not a valid datatype. See Chapter 6 for information about datatypes.

8. C. The statement will work without error. Option B would be correct if you used the WITH CHECK OPTION clause in the subquery. See Chapter 4 for more information about subqueries.

9. A, E. An outer join on both tables can be achieved using the FULL OUTER JOIN syntax. You can specify the join condition using the ON clause to specify the columns explicitly or using the USING clause to specify the columns with common column names. Options B and D would result in errors. In option B, the join type is not specified; OUTER is an optional keyword. In option D, CROSS JOIN is used to get a Cartesian result, and Oracle does not expect a join condition. To learn more about joins, read Chapter 4.

10. A, B. The index contains all the information needed to satisfy the query in option A, and a full-index scan would be faster than a full-table scan. A subset of index columns is specified in the WHERE clause of option B; hence, Oracle 11*g* can use the index. For more information on indexes, see Chapter 7.

11. D. The CREATE SEQUENCE statement will create an increasing sequence that will start with 1, will increment by 1, and will be unaffected by the rollback. A rollback will never stuff vales back into a sequence. See Chapter 7 to learn more about sequences.

12. B, C. Primary and unique key constraints can be enforced using nonunique indexes. Unique constraints allow NULL values in the columns, but primary keys do not. Read Chapter 6 to learn more about constraints.

13. B. The SYSDATE function returns the date and time on the server where the database instance is started. CURRENT_DATE returns the local date and time. For information on the built-in date functions, read Chapter 2.

14. D. The first INSERT statement and last INSERT statement will be saved in the database. The ROLLBACK TO A statement will undo the second and third inserts. To know more about transaction control and ROLLBACK, read Chapter 5.

15. B. There should be at least *n*-1 join conditions when joining *n* tables to avoid a Cartesian join. To learn more about joins, see Chapter 4.

16. C. The table and column names can include only three special characters: #, $, and _. No other characters are allowed in the table name. You can have letters and numbers in the table name. To learn more about table and column names, read Chapter 6.

17. B, D. You can use the IS NULL or IS NOT NULL operator to search for NULLs or non-NULLs in a column. Since NULLs are sorted higher, they appear at the bottom of the result set in an ascending-order sort. See Chapter 1 for more information about sorting NULL values.

18. D. COUNT (<column_name>) does not include the NULL values, whereas COUNT (*) includes the NULL values. No other aggregate function takes NULL into consideration. To learn more about aggregate functions, read Chapter 3.

19. E. These statements don't account for possible NULL values in the BONUS column. For more information about NULL values, see Chapter 2.

20. D. Using the ALTER TABLE statement, you can add new columns, rename existing columns, and drop existing columns. To learn more about managing tables, read Chapter 6.

21. B. Since DEPARTMENT_ID is NULL for employee 178, NULL will be sorted after the non-NULL values when doing an ascending-order sort. Since I did not specify the sort order or the NULLS FIRST clause, the defaults are ASC and NULLS LAST. Read Chapter 1 for more information on SELECT and sort orders.

22. D, E, F, G. The INTERVAL DAY TO SECOND datatype is used to store an interval between two datetime components. See Chapter 6 for more information on the INTERVAL and TIMESTAMP datatypes.

23. D, E. In the join view, CITY is the key-preserved table. You can update the columns of the CITY table, except STATE_CD, because STATE_CD is not part of the view definition (the STATE_CD column in the view is from the STATE table). Since I did not include the STATE_CD column from the CITY table, no INSERT operations are permitted (STATE_CD is part of the primary key). If the view were defined as follows, all the columns of the CITY table would have been updatable, and new records could be inserted into the CITY table.

```
CREATE OR REPLACE VIEW state_city AS
SELECT b.state_cd, a.state_name, b.city_cd, b.city_name
FROM   states a, cities b
WHERE  a.state_cd = b.state_cd;
```

See Chapter 7 for more information about views.

24. B. When altering an existing column to add a NOT NULL constraint, no rows in the table should have NULL values. In the example, there are two rows with NULL values. Creating and modifying tables are discussed in Chapter 6.

25. D. NATURAL JOIN and JOIN…USING clauses will not allow alias names to be used. Since a self-join is getting data from the same table, you must include alias names and qualify column names. To learn more about ANSI join syntax, read Chapter 4.

26. E. The TRUNC function used with a negative second argument will truncate to the left of the decimal. To learn more about TRUNC and other numeric functions, read Chapter 2.

27. C. Oracle creates unique indexes for each unique key and primary key defined in the table. The table ADDRESSES has one unique key and a primary key. Indexes will not be created for NOT NULL or foreign key constraints. Constraints are discussed in Chapter 6.

28. D. Although there is no error in this statement, the statement will not return the desired result. When a NULL is compared, you cannot use the = or != operator; you must use the IS NULL or IS NOT NULL operator. See Chapter 1 for more information about the comparison operators.

29. A. You cannot explicitly change the next value of a sequence. You can set the MAXVALUE or INCREMENT BY value to a negative number, and NOCYCLE tells Oracle to not reuse a sequence number. See Chapter 7 for more information.

30. B. Private synonyms override public synonyms, and tables or views owned by the user always resolve first. To learn more about synonyms, see Chapter 7.

31. C, D. When COMMIT is executed, all locks are released, all savepoints are erased, and queries started before the COMMIT will constitute a read-consistent view using the undo information. To learn more about COMMIT, read Chapter 5.

32. B, C. The operators OR and AND are used to add more joining conditions to the query. NOT is a negation operator, and a comma is used to separate column names and table names. Read more about joins and join conditions in Chapter 4.

33. C. Since you are finding the aggregate of the aggregate, you should not use nonaggregate columns in the SELECT clause. To read more about nesting of aggregate functions, see Chapter 3.

34. B. You can create primary key, foreign key, and unique key constraints on a view. The constraints on views are not enforced by Oracle. To enforce a constraint, it must be defined on a table. Views can be created with the WITH CHECK OPTION and READ ONLY attributes during view creation. Read Chapter 7 to learn more.

35. A, C. The maximum lengths of CHAR and VARCHAR2 columns can be defined in characters or bytes. BYTE is the default. To learn more about CHAR and VARCHAR2 datatypes, read Chapter 6.

36. A. When the view is created with the READ ONLY option, only reads are allowed from the view. See Chapter 7 to learn more about creating views as read-only.

37. A, D. The substitution character % can be substituted for zero or many characters. The substitution character _ does not have any effect in this query because an escape character precedes it, so it is treated as a literal. Read Chapter 1 to learn more about substitution characters.

38. C. You have two main conditions in the question: one on the hire date and the other on the salary. So, you should use an AND operator. In the second part, you have two options: the salary can be either more than 5,000 or less than 1,000, so the second part should be enclosed in parentheses and should use an OR operator. Option B is similar to option C except for the parentheses, but the difference changes the meaning completely. Option B would select the employees who were hired before January 1, 1998 *or* have a salary greater than 5,000 or less than 1,000. Read Chapter 1 to learn more about writing queries using filtering conditions.

39. A, B. The TRUNCATE command is used to remove all the rows from a table or cluster. By default, this command releases all the storage space used by the table and resets the table's high-water mark to zero. No indexes, constraints, or triggers on the table are dropped or disabled. If there are valid foreign key constraints defined to this table, you must disable all of them before truncating the table. Chapter 5 includes a comparison between using TRUNCATE and the DELETE statement to remove rows.

40. A, C. Since there can be only one primary key per table, the syntax in option A works. Any constraint (except NOT NULL) can be dropped using the syntax in option C. Learn more about constraints in Chapter 6.

Administration I Assessment Test

1. Which of the following is not considered part of Oracle Database?

   A. Data files

   B. Redo logs

   C. Pfile and spfile

   D. Control files

2. The following are the steps required for relocating a data file belonging to the `USERS` tablespace. Order the steps in their proper sequence.

   A. Copy the `file /disk1/users01.dbf` to `/disk2/users01.dbf` using an OS command.

   B. `ALTER DATABASE RENAME FILE '/disk1/users01.dbf' TO '/disk2/users01.dbf'`

   C. `ALTER TABLESPACE USERS OFFLINE`

   D. `ALTER TABLESPACE USERS ONLINE`

3. You manage one non-Oracle Database and several Oracle Databases. An application needs to access the non-Oracle database as if it were part of the Oracle database. What tool allows you to do this? (Choose the best answer.)

   A. Oracle Advanced Security

   B. Oracle Connection Manager

   C. Heterogeneous Services

   D. Oracle Net

   E. None of the above

4. Choose two utilities that can be used to apply CPU patches on an Oracle 11*g* database.

   A. Oracle Universal Installer

   B. OPatch

   C. EM Database Control

   D. DBCA

5. The loss of a data file in which two tablespaces requires an instance shutdown to recover the tablespace?

   A. `TEMP`

   B. `SYSTEM`

   C. `UNDO`

   D. `SYSAUX`

6. Which of the following statements is not always true? (Choose two.)
   - A. Every database should have at least two tablespaces.
   - B. Every database should have at least two data files.
   - C. Every database should have at least three multiplexed redo logs.
   - D. Every database should have at least three control files.

7. Which statement about the initialization-parameter files is true?
   - A. The pfile and spfile can be modified using the `ALTER SYSTEM` statement.
   - B. You cannot have both an spfile and a pfile under the `$ORACLE_HOME/dbs` directory.
   - C. The pfile is used only to read by the Oracle instance, whereas the spfile is used to read and write to.
   - D. On Windows systems, pfile and spfiles are not used because parameters are modified using the system registry.

8. Which initialization parameter determines the location of the alert log file?
   - A. `DIAGNOSTIC_DEST`
   - B. `BACKGROUND_DUMP_DEST`
   - C. `ALERT_LOG_DEST`
   - D. `USER_DUMP_DEST`

9. Which parameter is used to set up the directory for Oracle to create data files if the `DATAFILE` clause does not specify a filename when creating or altering tablespaces?
   - A. `DB_FILE_CREATE_DEST`
   - B. `DB_CREATE_FILE_DEST`
   - C. `DB_8K_CACHE_SIZE`
   - D. `USER_DUMP_DEST`
   - E. `DB_CREATE_ONLINE_LOG_DEST_1`

10. Which component of the SGA has the dictionary cache?
    - A. Buffer cache
    - B. Library cache
    - C. Shared pool
    - D. Program global area
    - E. Large pool
    - F. Result cache

11. A constraint is created with the `DEFERRABLE INITIALLY IMMEDIATE` clause. What does this mean?

    A. Constraint checking is done only at commit time.

    B. Constraint checking is done after each SQL, but you can change this behavior by specifying `SET CONSTRAINTS ALL DEFERRED`.

    C. Existing rows in the table are immediately checked for constraint violation.

    D. The constraint is immediately checked in a DML operation, but subsequent constraint verification is done at commit time.

12. You have just made changes to the `listener.ora` file for the listener called `listener1` using Oracle Net Manager. Which of the following commands or combinations of commands would you use to put the changes into effect with the least amount of client disruption?

    A. `lsnrctl stop listener1` followed by `lsnrctl start listener1`

    B. `lsrnctl restart listener1`

    C. `lsnrctl reload listener1`

    D. `lsnrctl reload`

13. What is the prefix for dynamic performance views?

    A. X$

    B. V$

    C. ALL_

    D. DBA_

14. If you are updating one row in a table using the `ROWID` in the `WHERE` clause (assume that the row is not already in the buffer cache), what will be the minimum amount of information copied to the database buffer cache?

    A. The entire table is copied to the database buffer cache.

    B. The extent is copied to the database buffer cache.

    C. The block is copied to the database buffer cache.

    D. The row is copied to the database buffer cache.

15. When you are configuring Shared Server, which initialization parameter would you likely need to modify?

    A. DB_CACHE_SIZE

    B. DB_BLOCK_BUFFERS

    C. LARGE_POOL_SIZE

    D. BUFFER_SIZE

    E. None of the above

16. To grant the SELECT privilege on the table HR.CUSTOMERS to all users in the database, which statement would you use?

    A. `GRANT SELECT ON HR.CUSTOMERS TO ALL USERS;`

    B. `GRANT SELECT ON HR.CUSTOMERS TO ALL;`

    C. `GRANT SELECT ON HR.CUSTOMERS TO ANONYMOUS;`

    D. `GRANT SELECT ON HR.CUSTOMERS TO PUBLIC;`

17. Which of the following commands is most likely to generate an error message? (Choose two.)

    A. `ALTER SYSTEM SET UNDO_MANAGEMENT=AUTO SCOPE=MEMORY;`

    B. `ALTER SYSTEM SET UNDO_MANAGEMENT=AUTO SCOPE=SPFILE;`

    C. `ALTER SYSTEM SET UNDO_MANAGEMENT=MANUAL SCOPE=MEMORY;`

    D. `ALTER SYSTEM SET UNDO_MANAGEMENT=MANUAL SCOPE=SPFILE;`

    E. `ALTER SYSTEM SET UNDO_TABLESPACE=RBS1 SCOPE=BOTH;`

18. The Automatic Workload Repository (AWR) is primarily populated with performance statistics by which Oracle 11*g* background process?

    A. MMNL

    B. QMN1

    C. MMON

    D. MMAN

19. You performed a SHUTDOWN ABORT on the database. What happens when you issue the STARTUP command?

    A. Startup will fail because you have not completed the instance recovery.

    B. Oracle automatically performs recovery; all committed changes are written to data files.

    C. During instance recovery you have the option to selectively commit uncommitted transactions.

    D. After the database starts, you have to manually clean out uncommitted transactions from the transaction table.

20. Which storage parameter is used to make sure that each extent is a multiple of the value specified on dictionary-managed tablespaces?

    A. MINEXTENTS

    B. INITIAL

    C. MINIMUM EXTENT

    D. MAXEXTENTS

21. Which of the following is the utility that you can use to test the network connections across TCP/IP?
    A. `trcasst`
    B. `lsnrctl`
    C. `namesctl`
    D. `ping`
    E. None of the above

22. What is the difference between a unique key constraint and a primary key constraint?
    A. A unique key constraint requires a unique index to enforce the constraint, whereas a primary key constraint can enforce uniqueness using a unique or nonunique index.
    B. A primary key column can be `NULL`, but a unique key column cannot be `NULL`.
    C. A primary key constraint can use an existing index, but a unique constraint always creates an index.
    D. A unique constraint column can be `NULL`, but the primary key column(s) cannot be `NULL`.

23. Which of the following conditions prevents you from being able to insert into a view?
    A. A `TO_NUMBER` function on one of the base table columns
    B. A `CONNECT BY` clause in the view definition
    C. A column of type `RAW`
    D. All of the above

24. Which parameter is used to enable the Automatic Memory Management feature of the Oracle 11*g* database?
    A. `MEMORY_MANAGEMENT`
    B. `MEMORY_TARGET`
    C. `SGA_TARGET`
    D. `MEMORY_SIZE`

25. Undo data in an undo tablespace is *not* used for which of the following purposes?
    A. Providing users with read-consistent queries
    B. Rolling forward after an instance failure
    C. Flashback queries
    D. Recovering from a failed transaction
    E. Restoring original data when a `ROLLBACK` is issued

26. Which initialization parameter determines the window of flashback database operation?
   A. DB_RECOVERY_FILE_DEST_SIZE
   B. DB_FLASHBACK_RETENTION_TARGET
   C. FAST_START_MTTR_TARGET
   D. No initialization parameter; the window is determined by the RMAN backups.

27. When you started the Oracle 11*g* database, you got an "ORA-01157: cannot identify data file..." error. After invoking RMAN, which command would you use before performing REPAIR FAILURE?
   A. RECOVER FAILURE
   B. ADVISE FAILURE
   C. LIST FAILURE
   D. CHANGE FAILURE

28. Who is the owner of a directory object?
   A. SYSTEM
   B. SYSMAN
   C. SYS
   D. The user who creates the directory

29. Which of the following types of statements can use a temporary tablespace?
   A. An index creation
   B. SQL statements with a GROUP BY clause
   C. A hash join operation
   D. All of the above

30. Which of the following is false about shared servers?
   A. Shared servers can process requests from many users.
   B. Shared servers receive their requests directly from dispatchers.
   C. Shared servers place completed requests on a dispatcher response queue.
   D. The SHARED_SERVERS parameter configures the number of shared servers to start at instance startup.

31. What is accomplished when you issue the following statement?

   ```
   ALTER USER JOHN DEFAULT ROLE ALL;
   ```

   A. John is assigned all roles created in the database.
   B. Existing roles remain the same, but future roles created will be enabled.
   C. All of John's roles are enabled except the roles with passwords.
   D. All of John's roles are enabled, including the roles with passwords.

32. Which initialization parameter determines the location of the alert log file?

A. LOG_ARCHIVE_DEST

B USER_DUMP_DEST

C. BACKGROUND_DUMP_DEST

D. DIAGNOSTIC_DEST

33. The highest level at which a user can request a lock is the ________ level.

A. schema

B. table

C. row

D. block

34. How can you prevent someone from using an all-numeric password?

A. Set the initialization parameter PASSWORD_COMPLEXITY to ALPHANUM.

B. Alter that user's profile setting PASSWORD_COMPLEXITY to ALPHNANUM.

C. Alter the user's profile to use a password-verify function that performs comparisons to validate the password.

D. There is no mechanism that lets you prevent an all-numeric password.

35. Which of the following advisors is used to determine whether the database read-consistency mechanisms are properly configured?

A. Undo Management Advisor

B. SQL Access Advisor

C. SQL Tuning Advisor

D. Memory Advisor

36. Where does Oracle Database record all changes made to the database that can be used for recovery operations?

A. Control files

B. Redo log files

C. Alert log file

D. Parameter file

37. In the Disk Settings section of EM Database Control's Configure Backup Settings page, which of the following backup settings is not configurable?

A. Disk Backup Type

B. Control File Autobackup Format

C. Disk Backup Location

D. Parallelism

38. You need to copy the GL schema from production to qa_test, changing the tablespace for indexes from gl_index to fin_indx. What is the best way to satisfy these requirements?

    A. First, use Data Pump to copy the schema without indexes. Then, change the default tablespace for user GL in qa_test to fin_indx. Next, use Data Pump to copy the indexes. Finally, change the default tablespace for user GL back to gl_data.

    B. Use the dbms_metadata package to extract table and index DDL. Then, use Notepad (or sed) to edit this DDL, changing the tablespace for the indexes. Finally, run the DDL in the qa_test database.

    C. Use Data Pump import, specifying a remap_datafile parameter to change the data file location for indexes.

    D. Use Data Pump import, specifying a remap_tablespace parameter to change the tablespace location for indexes.

39. Identify the statement that is not true about checkpoints.

    A. Instance recovery is complete when the data from the last checkpoint up to the latest SCN in the control file has been written to the data files.

    B. A checkpoint keeps track of what has already been written to the data files.

    C. The redo log group writes must occur before a Commit complete is returned to the user.

    D. The distance between the checkpoint position in the redo log file and the end of the redo log group can never be more than 90 percent of the size of the largest redo log group.

    E. How much the checkpoint lags behind the SCN is controlled by both the size of the redo log groups and by setting the parameter FAST_START_MTTR_TARGET.

40. The STATUS column of the dynamic performance view V$LOG contains what value if the redo log file group has just been added?

    A. INVALID

    B. STALE

    C. UNUSED

    D. NULL

41. When performing Data Pump import using impdp, which of the following options is not a valid value to the TABLE_EXISTS_ACTION parameter?

    A. SKIP

    B. APPEND

    C. TRUNCATE

    D. RECREATE

42. What would you do to reduce the time required to start the instance after a database crash?

A. Multiplex the redo log files.

B. Increase the size of the redo log files.

C. Set the `FAST_START_MTTR_TARGET` parameter to 0.

D. All of the above.

E. None of the above.

Answers to Administration I Assessment Test

1. C. Although pfiles and spfiles are physical files used to configure the Oracle instance, they are not considered part of the database. To learn more about Oracle Database structure, read Chapter 8.

2. C, A, B, D. To rename a data file, you need to make the tablespace offline so that Oracle does not try to update the data file while you are renaming. Using OS commands, copy the data file to the new location, and using the `ALTER DATABASE RENAME FILE` command or the `ALTER TABLESPACE RENAME FILE` command, rename the file in the database's control file. To rename the file in the database, the new file should exist. Bring the tablespace online for normal database operation. See Chapter 10 for more information.

3. C. Heterogeneous Services is the correct answer because these services provide cross-platform connectivity to non-Oracle databases. Oracle Advanced Security would not solve this application problem because it addresses security and is not accessibility to non-Oracle databases. Oracle Net would be part of the solution, but another Oracle Network component is necessary. Connection Manager would also not be able to accommodate this requirement on its own. Read Chapter 11 to learn more.

4. B, C. CPU patches and interim patches can be applied using the OPatch utility or using EM Database Control. EM Database Control also includes patch search and download options. See Chapter 17 for more information.

5. B, C. Only the `SYSTEM` and `UNDO` tablespaces require the instance to be shut down when their data files need recovery. Read Chapter 16 to learn about database recovery.

6. C, D. Every database must have at least two redo log files, which may or may not be multiplexed. Every database must have one control file. It is a good idea to have more than one control file for redundancy. Since `SYSTEM` and `SYSAUX` are mandatory tablespaces in Oracle 11*g*, there will be at least two data files. See Chapter 8 for more information.

7. C. A pfile is a read-only file, and no database changes are written to the pfile. There is no harm in having both an spfile and a pfile in the `$ORACLE_HOME/dbs` directory; Oracle will only read the spfile when starting the database. On Windows systems also, you will need a parameter-initialization file; the registry is not used. Read more about parameter files in Chapter 9.

8. A. Oracle 11*g* uses the Automatic Diagnostic Repository to maintain the alert log and other diagnostic information. In pre–Oracle 11*g* databases, the `BACKGROUND_DUMP_DEST` parameter determined the alert log location; in Oracle 11*g*, this parameter value is ignored. To learn more about the alert log and its contents, read Chapter 9.

9. B. `DB_CREATE_FILE_DEST` specifies the directory to create data files and temp files. This directory is also used for control files and redo log files if the `DB_CREATE_ONLINE_LOG_DEST_1` parameter is not set. Learn more in Chapter 10.

10. C. The shared pool has three components: the library cache, the result cache, and the dictionary cache. Read Chapter 8 to learn more about SGA and Oracle instances.

11. B. DEFERRABLE specifies that the constraint can be deferred using the SET CONSTRAINTS command. INITIALLY IMMEDIATE specifies that the constraint's default behavior is to validate the constraint for each SQL. Constraints are discussed in Chapters 7 and 10.

12. C. Although you can use option A to stop and start the listener, doing so temporarily disrupts clients attempting to connect to the database. Option D is fine if you are starting and stopping the default listener called LISTENER, but you are using a nondefault listener here. Option B is not valid because RESTART is not a valid command-line argument for lsnrctl. Therefore, the best method is to use the lsnrctl reload listener1 command to load the new set of values in for the listener without disrupting connection service to the databases that the listener is servicing. For more information, read Chapter 11.

13. B. Dynamic performance views begin with V$. The actual views have a prefix of V_$, and the synonyms have a prefix of V$. The V$ views are based on the X$ tables, known as dynamic performance tables. To learn more about dynamic performance views and tables, read Chapter 9.

14. C. The block is the smallest unit that can be copied to the buffer cache. Information in the dictionary cache is copied as rows. To learn about buffer cache and dictionary cache, read Chapter 8.

15. C. Shared Server requires a shift of memory away from individual session processes to the SGA. More information has to be kept in the SGA (in the UGA) within the shared pool. A large pool is configured and is responsible for most of the SGA space allocation. Option C is the correct answer. The cache size and block buffers settings do not affect Shared Server. Read Chapter 11 for more information.

16. D. PUBLIC is the group or class of database users where all existing and future database users belong. See Chapter 12 for more information.

17. A, C. You cannot dynamically change the parameter UNDO_MANAGEMENT after the instance has started. You can, however, change the UNDO_TABLESPACE parameter to switch to another undo tablespace while the instance is up and running. Read Chapter 13 to learn more.

18. C. The Manageability Monitor (MMON) process gathers performance statistics from the system global area (SGA) and stores them in the AWR. Manageability Monitor Light (MMNL) also does some AWR-related statistics gathering, but not to the extent that MMON does. QMN1 is the process that monitors Oracle advanced queuing features. Memory Manager (MMAN) is the process that dynamically manages the sizes of each SGA component when directed to make changes by the Automatic Database Diagnostic Monitor (ADDM). For more information, see Chapter 14.

19. B. Oracle automatically performs instance recovery after a database crash or SHUTDOWN ABORT. All uncommitted changes are rolled back, and committed changes are written to data files during instance recovery. Read Chapter 9 for more information.

20. C. The MINIMUM EXTENT parameter is used to make sure each extent is a multiple of the value specified on dictionary-managed tablespaces. This parameter is useful to reduce fragmentation in the tablespace. Oracle discourages the use of dictionary-managed tablespaces. You should use locally managed tablespaces. Read Chapter 10 for more information.

21. D. Protocols come with tools that allow you to test network connectivity. One such utility for TCP/IP is ping. The user supplies either an IP address or a hostname to the ping utility. It then searches the network for this address. If it finds one, it displays information on data that is sent and received and how quickly it found this address. The other choices are Oracle-supplied utilities. Read Chapter 11 for more information.

22. D. Columns that are part of the primary key cannot accept NULL values. Read Chapters 7 and 10 to learn more.

23. B. You cannot insert into a view that contains a CONNECT BY, ORDER BY, or GROUP BY clause. Read Chapter 13 to learn more.

24. B. A nonzero value for the MEMORY_TARGET parameter enables Automatic Memory Management. SGA_TARGET enables Automatic Shared Memory Management. Automatic Memory Management tunes both SGA and PGA components of the memory. To learn more, read Chapter 14.

25. B. The online redo log files are used to roll forward after an instance failure; undo data is used to roll back any uncommitted transactions. Read Chapter 13 to learn more.

26. B. The DB_FLASHBACK_RETENTION_TARGET parameter determines the window for the flashback database operation. The value is specified in minutes. So, a value of 1440 specifies that the flashback database window is 1 day. To learn more, read Chapter 15.

27. B. REPAIR FAILURE works only after ADVISE FAILURE. Option A, RECOVER FAILURE, is invalid. CHANGE FAILURE can be used to lower or raise the priority of a failure. To learn more about automatically recovering from failures, read Chapter 16.

28. C. SYS is always the owner of directory object. You can grant read and write privileges on the directory to users. See Chapter 17 to learn more.

29. D. Any operation that requires a large sort or other creation of temporary segments will create, alter, and drop those temporary segments in the TEMPORARY tablespace. See Chapter 12 for more information.

30. B. Shared servers can process requests from many users. The completed requests are placed into the dispatchers' response queues. The servers are configured with the SERVERS parameter. However, shared servers do not receive requests directly from dispatchers. The requests are taken from the request queue. Read Chapter 11 to learn more.

31. D. Default roles are enabled when a user connects to the database, even if the roles are password-protected. See Chapter 12 for more information.

32. D. DIAGNOSTIC_DEST is new to Oracle 11*g*, and it determines the location of the alert log file and trace files. Read Chapter 14 to learn more about alert log and trace file locations.

33. B. The highest level at which a user can request a lock is the table level; the only other lock level available to a user is a row-level lock. Users cannot lock at the block or schema level. Read Chapter 13 to learn more.

34. C. There are no standard password-complexity settings in either the initialization parameters or the profiles. A password-verify function can validate new passwords against any rules that you can code in PL/SQL, including regular-expression comparisons. See Chapter 12 for more information.

35. A. You can use the Undo Management Advisor to monitor and manage the undo segments to ensure maximum levels of read consistency and minimize occurrences of "ORA-01555: Snapshot Too Old" error messages. For more information, see Chapter 14.

36. B. Redo log files record all the changes made to Oracle Database, whether the changes are committed or not. To learn more about redo log files and database recovery, read Chapters 15 and 16.

37. B. Settings such as the control file autobackup filename format and the snapshot-control file destination filename must be configured using the RMAN command-line interface. To learn more, read Chapter 15.

38. D. Options A and B are a lot of work. The `remap_datafile` parameter applies only to `CREATE TABLESPACE` and `CREATE DIRECTORY` statements, not indexes. The `remap_tablespace` parameter tells Data Pump import to change the tablespace that objects are stored in between the source and the target database. See Chapter 17 for more information.

39. D. The distance between the checkpoint position in the redo log file and the end of the redo log group can never be more than 90 percent of the size of the *smallest* redo log group. Read Chapter 16 to learn more about checkpoints and instance recovery.

40. C. If the redo log file group has never been used, the value of `STATUS` is `UNUSED` until the log file member is used to record redo information. Read Chapter 16 for more information.

41. D. `REPLACE` is the valid value; it drops the existing table and creates the table using the definition from the dump file. `SKIP` leaves the table untouched. `APPEND` inserts rows to the existing table. `TRUNCATE` leaves the structure but removes all existing rows before inserting rows. See Chapter 17 to learn more.

42. E. To tune the instance-recovery time, configure the `FAST_START_MTTR_TARGET` parameter to a nonzero value. The default is 300 seconds. A lower value will reduce the instance-recovery time but may cause frequent checkpoints. A value of 0 turns off MTTR tuning. To learn more, read Chapter 15.

Oracle Database 11*g*: SQL Fundamentals I

Introducing SQL

ORACLE DATABASE 11*g*: SQL FUNDAMENTALS I EXAM OBJECTIVES COVERED IN THIS CHAPTER:

✓ **Retrieving Data Using the SQL SELECT Statement**

- List the capabilities of SQL SELECT statements
- Execute a basic SELECT statement

✓ **Restricting and Sorting Data**

- Limit the rows that are retrieved by a query
- Sort the rows that are retrieved by a query
- Use ampersand substitution to restrict and sort output at runtime

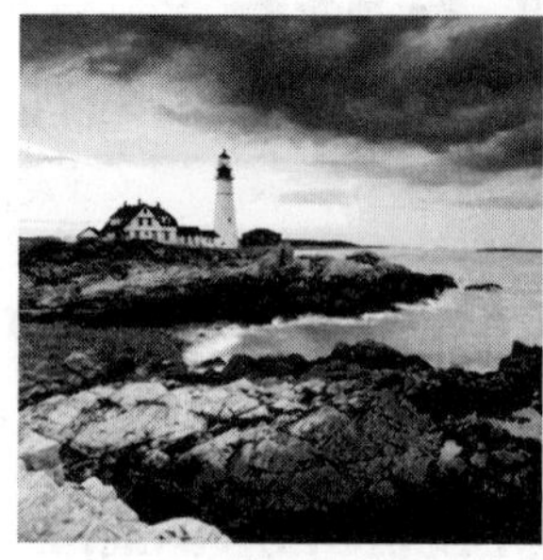

Oracle 11*g* is a very powerful and feature-rich relational database management system (RDBMS). SQL has been adopted by most RDBMSs for the retrieval and management of data, schema creation, and access control. The American National Standards Institute (ANSI) has been refining standards for the SQL language for more than 20 years. Oracle, like many other companies, has taken the ANSI standard of SQL and extended it to include much additional functionality.

SQL is the basic language used to manipulate and retrieve data from the Oracle Database 11*g*. SQL is a nonprocedural language, meaning it does not have programmatic constructs such as loop structures. PL/SQL is Oracle's procedural extension of SQL, and SQLJ allows embedded SQL operations in Java code. The scope of the Oracle Database 11*g* SQL Fundamentals I test includes only SQL.

In this chapter, I will discuss Oracle SQL fundamentals such as the various types of SQL statements, introduce SQL*Plus and a few SQL*Plus commands, and discuss `SELECT` statements.

You will learn how to write basic SQL statements to retrieve data from tables. This will include coverage of SQL `SELECT` statements, which are used to query data from the database-storage structures, such as tables and views. You will also learn how to limit the information retrieved and to display the results in a specific order.

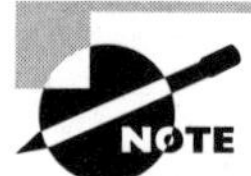

Exam objectives are subject to change at any time without prior notice and at Oracle's sole discretion. Please visit Oracle's Training and Certification website at `http://education.oracle.com/pls/web_prod-plq-dad/db_pages.getpage?p_exam_id=1Z0_051` for the most current exam objectives.

SQL Fundamentals

SQL is the standard language to query and modify data as well as manage databases. SQL is the common language used by programmers, database administrators, and users to access and manipulate data as well as to administer databases. To get started with SQL in this chapter, I will show how to use the sample `HR` schema supplied with the Oracle Database 11*g*.

When you install Oracle software, you can choose the Basic Installation option and select the Create Starter Database check box. This database will have the sample schemas used in this book. The password you specify will be applicable to the SYS and SYSTEM accounts. The account SYS is the Oracle dictionary owner, and SYSTEM is a database administrator (DBA) account. Initially, the sample schemas are locked. You need to log in to the database using SQL*Plus as the SYSTEM user and then unlock the account using the ALTER USER statement. To unlock the HR schema, use `ALTER USER hr IDENTIFIED BY hrpassword ACCOUNT UNLOCK;`. Now you can log in to the database using the hr user with the password hrpassword. Remember, the password is case sensitive.

For detailed information on installing Oracle 11*g* software and creating Oracle Database 11*g*, please refer to the Oracle Technology Network at `www.oracle.com/technology/obe/11gr1_db/install/dbinst/windbinst2.htm`.

To install the sample schemas in an existing Oracle Database 11*g*, please follow the instructions in the Oracle document "Oracle Database Sample Schemas 11*g* Release 1" at `http://download.oracle.com/docs/cd/B28359_01/server.111/b28328/toc.htm`.

Chapter 2 of the "Oracle Database Sample Schemas 11*g* Release 1" manual on the Oracle Technology Network will provide instructions on how to install the sample schemas using Database Configuration Assistant (DBCA) as well as running scripts. The same chapter also gives you steps to reinitialize the sample schema data.

SQL statements are like plain English but with specific syntax. SQL is a simple yet powerful language used to create, access, and manipulate data and structures in the database. SQL statements can be categorized as listed in Table 1.1.

TABLE 1.1 SQL Statement Categories

SQL Category	Description
Data Manipulation Language (DML)	Used to access, create, modify, or delete data in the existing structures of the database. DML statements include those to query information (SELECT), add new rows (INSERT), modify existing rows (UPDATE), delete existing rows (DELETE), perform a conditional update or insert operation (MERGE), see an execution plan of SQL (EXPLAIN PLAN), and lock a table to restrict access (LOCK TABLE). Including the SELECT statement in the DML group is debatable within the SQL community, since SELECT does not modify data.

TABLE 1.1 SQL Statement Categories *(continued)*

SQL Category	Description
Data Definition Language (DDL)	Used to define, alter, or drop database objects and their privileges. DDL statements include those to create, modify, drop, or rename objects (CREATE, ALTER, DROP, RENAME), remove all rows from a database object without dropping the structure (TRUNCATE), manage access privileges (GRANT, REVOKE), audit database use (AUDIT, NOAUDIT) and add a description about an object to the dictionary (COMMENT).
Transaction Control	Used to group a set of DML statements as a single transaction. Using these statements, you can save the changes (COMMIT) or discard the changes (ROLLBACK) made by DML statements. Also included in the transaction-control statements are statements to set a point or marker in the transaction for possible rollback (SAVEPOINT) and to define the properties for the transaction (SET TRANSACTION).
Session Control	Used to control the properties of a user session. (A session is the point from which you are connected to the database until you disconnect.) Session-control statements include those to control the session properties (ALTER SESSION) and to enable/disable roles (SET ROLE).
System Control	Used to manage the properties of the database. There is only one statement in this category (ALTER SYSTEM).

Table 1.1 provides an overview of all the statements that will be covered in this book. Do not worry if you do not understand certain terms, such as *role*, *session*, *privilege*, and so on. I will cover all the statements in the coming chapters with many examples. In this chapter, I will begin with writing simple statements to query the database (SELECT statements). But first I'll go over some fundamentals.

SQL Tools: SQL*Plus

The Oracle Database 11*g* software comes with two primary tools to manage data and administer databases using SQL. SQL*Plus is a character-based command-line utility. SQL Developer is a graphical tool that has the capability to browse, edit, and manage database objects as well as to execute the SQL statements. On Windows platforms, these tools are located under the Application Development subfolder in the Oracle 11*g* program group.

On Linux and Unix platforms, you can find these tools in the `bin` directory under the Oracle software installation (`$ORACLE_HOME/bin`).

Since the test is on SQL and the tool used throughout the book for executing SQL is SQL*Plus, I will discuss some fundamentals of SQL*Plus in this section.

SQL*Plus, widely used by DBAs and developers to interact with the database, is a powerful tool from Oracle. Using SQL*Plus, you can execute all SQL statements and PL/SQL programs, format results from queries, and administer the database.

SQL*Plus is packaged with the Oracle software and can be installed using the client software installation routine on any machine. This tool is automatically installed when you install the server software.

On Unix/Linux platforms, you can invoke SQL*Plus using the `sqlplus` executable found in the `$ORACLE_HOME/bin` directory. On Windows and Unix/Linux platforms, when you start SQL*Plus, you will be prompted for a username and password, as shown in Figure 1.1.

FIGURE 1.1 SQL*Plus screen

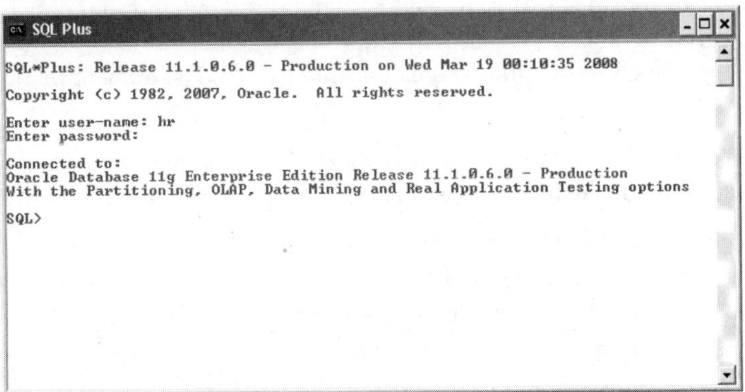

Once you are in SQL*Plus, you can connect to another database or change your connection by using the `CONNECT` command, with this syntax:

```
CONNECT <username>/<password>@<connectstring>
```

The slash separates the username and password. The connect string following `@` is the database alias name. If you omit the password, you will be prompted to enter it. If you omit the connect string, SQL*Plus tries to connect you to the local database defined in the `ORACLE_SID` variable.

You can invoke and connect to SQL*Plus using the `sqlplus` command, with this syntax:

```
sqlplus <username>/<password>@<connectstring>
```

If you invoke the tool with just `sqlplus`, you will be prompted for a username and password. If you invoke SQL*Plus with a username, you will be prompted for a password.

Once you are connected to SQL*Plus, you get the `SQL>` prompt. This is the default prompt, which can be changed using the `SET SQLPROMPT` command. Type the command you want to execute at this prompt. With SQL*Plus, you can enter, edit, and execute SQL statements; perform database administration; and execute statements interactively by accepting user input. You can also format query results and perform calculations.

`sqlplus -help` displays a help screen to show the various options available with starting SQL*Plus.

To exit from SQL*Plus, use the `EXIT` command. On platforms where a return code is used, you can provide a return code while exiting. You can also use the `QUIT` command to complete the session. `EXIT` and `QUIT` are synonymous.

Entering SQL Statements

A SQL statement can spread across multiple lines, and the commands are case insensitive. The previously executed SQL statement will always be available in the *SQL buffer.* The buffer can be edited or saved to a file. You can terminate a SQL statement in any of the following ways:

- End with a semicolon (;): The statement is completed and executed.
- Enter a slash (/) on a new line by itself: The statement in the buffer is executed.
- Enter a blank line: The statement is saved in the buffer.

You can use the `RUN` command instead of a slash to execute a statement in the buffer. The SQL prompt returns when the statement has completed execution. You can enter your next command at the prompt.

Only SQL statements and PL/SQL blocks are stored in the SQL buffer; SQL*Plus commands are not stored in the buffer.

Entering SQL*Plus Commands

SQL*Plus has its own commands to perform-specific tasks on the database, as well as to format the query results. Unlike SQL statements, which are terminated with a semicolon or a blank line, SQL*Plus commands are entered on a single line. Pressing Enter executes the SQL*Plus command.

If you want to continue a SQL*Plus command onto the next line, you must end the current line with a hyphen (-), which indicates command continuation. This is in contrast to SQL statements, which can be continued to the next line without a continuation operator. For example, the following SQL statement gives an error, because SQL*Plus treats the hyphen operator (-) as a continuation character:

```
SQL> SELECT 800 -
> 400 FROM dual;
```

```
SELECT 800  400 FROM dual
           *
ERROR at line 1:
ORA-00923: FROM keyword not found where expected
SQL>
```

You need to put the hyphen in the next line for the query to succeed:

```
SQL> SELECT 800
  2  - 400 FROM dual;

   800-400
----------
       400
SQL>
```

Getting Information with the DESCRIBE Command

You can use the DESCRIBE command to get information about the database objects. Using DESCRIBE on a table or view shows the columns, its datatypes, and whether each column can be NULL. Using DESCRIBE on a stored program such as procedure or function shows the parameters that need to be passed in/out, their datatype, and whether there is a default value. You can abbreviate this command to the first four characters or more—DESC, DESCR, and DESCRIB are all valid.

If you're connected to the HR schema and need to see the tables and views in this schema, use the following query:

```
SQL> SELECT * FROM tab;

TNAME                          TABTYPE  CLUSTERID
------------------------------ ------- ----------
COUNTRIES                      TABLE
DEPARTMENTS                    TABLE
EMPLOYEES                      TABLE
EMP_DETAILS_VIEW               VIEW
JOBS                           TABLE
JOB_HISTORY                    TABLE
LOCATIONS                      TABLE
REGIONS                        TABLE

8 rows selected.
SQL>
```

Editing the SQL Buffer

The most recent SQL statement executed or entered is stored in the SQL buffer of SQL*Plus. You can run the command in this buffer again by simply typing a slash or using the RUN command.

SQL*Plus provides a set of commands to edit the buffer. Suppose you want to add another column or add an ORDER BY condition to the statement in the buffer. You do not need to type the entire SQL statement again. Instead, just edit the existing statement in the buffer.

One way to edit the SQL*Plus buffer is to use the EDIT command to write the buffer to an operating-system file named afiedt.buf (this is the default filename, which can be changed) and then use a system editor to make changes.

You can use your favorite text editor by defining it in SQL*Plus. For example, to make Notepad your favorite editor, just issue the command DEFINE _EDITOR = NOTEPAD. You need to provide the entire path if the program is not available in the search path.

Another way to edit the buffer is to use the SQL*Plus editing commands. You can make changes, delete lines, add text, and list the buffer contents using the commands described in the following sections. Most editing commands operate on the current line. You can change the current line simply by typing the line number. All commands can be abbreviated except DEL (which is already abbreviated).

LIST

The LIST command lists the contents of the buffer. The asterisk indicates the current line. The abbreviated command for LIST is L.

```
SQL> L
  1  SELECT empno, ename
  2* FROM emp
SQL> LIST LAST
  2* FROM emp
SQL>
```

The command LIST *m n* displays lines from *m* through *n*. If you substitute * for *m* or *n*, it implies the current line. The command LIST LAST displays the last line.

APPEND

The APPEND *text* command adds text to the end of line. The abbreviated command is A.

```
SQL> A  WHERE empno <> 7926
  2* FROM emp WHERE empno <> 7926
SQL>
```

CHANGE

The CHANGE */old/new* command changes an old entry to a new entry. The abbreviated command is C. If you omit *new*, *old* will be deleted.

```
SQL> C /<>/=
  2* FROM emp WHERE empno = 7926
SQL> C /7926
  2* FROM emp WHERE empno =
SQL>
```

INPUT

The INPUT *text* command adds a line of text. Its abbreviation is I. If *text* is omitted, you can add as many lines you want.

```
SQL> I
  3  7777 AND
  4  empno = 4354
  5
SQL> I ORDER BY 1
SQL> L
  1  SELECT empno, ename
  2  FROM emp WHERE empno =
  3  7777 AND
  4  empno = 4354
  5* ORDER BY 1
SQL>
```

DEL

The DEL command used alone or with * deletes the current line. The DEL *m n* command deletes lines from *m* through *n*. If you substitute * for *m* or *n*, it implies the current line. The command DEL LAST deletes the last line.

```
SQL> 3
  3* 7777 AND
SQL> DEL
SQL> L
  1  SELECT empno, ename
  2  FROM emp WHERE empno =
  3  empno = 4354
  4* ORDER BY 1
SQL> DEL 3 *
```

```
SQL> L
  1  SELECT empno, ename
  2* FROM emp WHERE empno =
SQL>
```

CLEAR BUFFER

The CLEAR BUFFER command (abbreviated CL BUFF) clears the buffer. This deletes all lines from the buffer.

```
SQL> L
  1  SELECT empno, ename
  2* FROM emp WHERE empno =
SQL> CL BUFF
buffer cleared
SQL> L
No lines in SQL buffer.
SQL>
```

Using Script Files

SQL*Plus provides commands to save the SQL buffer to a file, as well as to run SQL statements from a file. SQL statements saved in a file are called a *script file*.

You can work with script files as follows:

- To save the SQL buffer to an operating-system file, use the command SAVE *filename*. If you do not provide an extension, the saved file will have an extension of .sql.
- By default, the SAVE command will not overwrite an existing file. If you want to overwrite an existing file, you need to use the keyword REPLACE.
- To add the buffer to the end of an existing file, use the SAVE *filename* APPEND command.
- You can edit the saved file using the EDIT *filename* command.
- You can bring the contents of a *script file* to the SQL buffer using the GET *filename* command.
- If you want to run a script file, use the command START *filename*. You can also run a script file using @*filename*.
- An @@*filename* used inside a script file looks for the filename in the directory where the parent *script file* is saved and executes it.

Exercise 1.1 will familiarize you with the script file commands, as well as the other topics I have covered so far.

EXERCISE 1.1

Practicing SQL*Plus File Commands

In this exercise, you will learn how to edit the SQL*Plus buffer using various buffer edit commands.

1. Enter the following SQL; the third line is a blank line so that the SQL is saved in the buffer:

```
SQL> SELECT employee_id, first_name, last_name
  2  FROM    employees
  3
SQL>
```

2. List the SQL buffer:

```
SQL> L
  1  SELECT employee_id, first_name, last_name
  2* FROM    employees
SQL>
```

3. Save the buffer to a file named `myfile`; the default extension will be `.sql`:

```
SQL> SAVE myfile
Created file MYFILE.sql
SQL>
```

4. Choose to edit the file:

```
SQL> EDIT myfile
SQL>
```

5. Add `WHERE EMPLOYEE_ID = 106` as the third line to the SQL statement.

6. List the buffer:

```
SQL> LIST
  1  SELECT employee_id, first_name, last_name
  2* FROM    employees
SQL>
```

   The buffer listed is still the old buffer. The edited changes are not reflected because you edited the file MYFILE, which is not yet loaded to the buffer.

7. Bring the file contents to the buffer:

```
SQL> GET myfile
  1  SELECT employee_id, first_name, last_name
```

EXERCISE 1.1 *(continued)*

```
  2  FROM    employees
  3* WHERE employee_id = 106
SQL>
```

8. List the buffer to verify its contents:

```
SQL> LI
  1  SELECT employee_id, first_name, last_name
  2  FROM    employees
  3* WHERE employee_id = 106
SQL>
```

9. Change the employee number from 106 to 110:

```
SQL> C/106/110
  3* WHERE employee_id = 110
SQL>
```

10. Save the buffer again to the same file:

```
SQL> SAVE myfile
SP2-0540: File "MYFILE.sql" already exists.
Use "SAVE filename[.ext] REPLACE".
SQL>
```

An error is returned, because SAVE will not overwrite the file by default.

11. Save the file using the REPLACE keyword:

```
SQL> SAVE myfile REPLACE
Wrote file MYFILE.sql
SQL>
```

12. Execute the file:

```
SQL> START myfile

EMPLOYEE_ID FIRST_NAME           LAST_NAME
----------- -------------------- ---------
        110 John                 Chen
SQL>
```

13. Change the employee number from 110 to 106, and append this SQL to the file; then execute it using @:

```
SQL> C/110/106
  3* WHERE employee_id = 106
```

EXERCISE 1.1 (continued)

```
SQL> SAVE myfile APPEND
Appended file to MYFILE.sql
SQL> @MYFILE
EMPLOYEE_ID FIRST_NAME           LAST_NAME
----------- -------------------- ---------
        110 John                 Chen

EMPLOYEE_ID FIRST_NAME           LAST_NAME
----------- -------------------- ---------
        106 Valli                Pataballa
SQL>
```

Saving Query Results to a File

You can use the SPOOL *filename* command to save the query results to a file. By default, the SPOOL command creates an .lst file extension. SPOOL overwrites an existing file by default. If you include the APPEND option as in SPOOL *filename* APPEND, the results are added to an existing file. A new file will be created if the file does not exist already.

SPOOL OFF stops writing the output to the file. SPOOL OUT stops the writing of output and sends the output file to the printer.

Adding Comments to a Script File

Having comments in the script file improves the readability and understandability of the code. You can enter comments in SQL*Plus using the REMARKS (abbreviated REM) command. Lines in the script file beginning with the keyword REM are comments and are not executed. You can also enter a comment between /* and */. Comments can also be entered following -- (double hyphen), all characters following -- in the line are treated as comment by Oracle.

While executing a script file with comments, the remarks entered using the REMARKS command are not displayed on the screen, but the comments within /* and */ are displayed on the screen with the prefix DOC> when there is more than one line between /* and */. You can turn this off by using SET DOCUMENT OFF.

This section provided an overview of SQL*Plus, the tool you will be using to enter and execute SQL statements in Oracle Database 11*g*. In the next sections, I will discuss some of the Oracle 11*g* SQL fundamentals before showing you how to write your first SQL query (a SELECT statement).

Oracle Datatypes

The basic structure of data storage in the Oracle Database 11*g* is a table. A table can be considered as a spreadsheet with columns and rows. Data is stored in the table as rows. Each column in the table has storage characteristics such as the type of data contained in the column. Oracle has several built-in datatypes to store different kinds of data. In this section, I will go over the built-in datatypes available in Oracle 11*g*. Detailed discussion on datatypes as well as creating and maintaining tables are discussed in Chapter 6, "Creating Tables and Constraints."

When you create a table to store data in the database, you need to specify a datatype for all the columns you define in the table. Oracle has many datatypes to suit application requirements. Oracle 11*g* also supports ANSI and DB2 datatypes. The Oracle built-in datatypes can be broadly classified as shown in Table 1.2.

TABLE 1.2 Oracle Built-in Datatypes

Category	**Datatypes**
Character	CHAR, NCHAR, VARCHAR2, NVARCHAR2
Number	NUMBER, FLOAT, BINARY_FLOAT, BINARY_DOUBLE
Long and raw	LONG, LONG RAW, RAW
Date and time	DATE, TIMESTAMP, TIMESTAMP WITH TIME ZONE, TIMESTAMP WITH LOCAL TIME ZONE, INTERVAL YEAR TO MONTH, INTERVAL DAY TO SECOND
Large object	CLOB, NCLOB, BCLOB, BFILE
Row ID	ROWID, UROWID

In the following sections, I will discuss only a few of the built-in datatypes to get you started with SQL. I discuss all the datatypes and their usage in detail in Chapter 6.

CHAR(<size>)

The *CHAR* datatype is a fixed-length alphanumeric string, which has a maximum length in bytes (to specify length in characters, use the CHAR keyword inside parentheses along with a size; see Chapter 6). Data stored in CHAR columns is space-padded to fill the maximum length. Its size can range from a minimum of 1 byte to a maximum of 2,000 bytes. The default size is 1.

When you create a column using the CHAR datatype, the database will ensure that all data placed in this column has the defined length. If the data is shorter than the defined length, it is space-padded on the right to the specified length. If the data is longer, an error is raised.

VARCHAR2(<size>)

The *VARCHAR2* datatype is a variable-length alphanumeric string, which has a maximum length in bytes (to specify the length in characters, use the CHAR keyword inside parentheses along with a size; see Chapter 6). VARCHAR2 columns require only the amount of space needed to store the data and can store up to 4,000 bytes. There is no default size for the VARCHAR2 datatype. An empty VARCHAR2(2000) column takes up as much room in the database as an empty VARCHAR2(1) column.

The default size of a CHAR datatype is 1. For a VARCHAR2 datatype, you must always specify the size.

The VARCHAR2 and CHAR datatypes have different comparison rules for trailing spaces. With the CHAR datatype, trailing spaces are ignored. With the VARCHAR2 datatype, trailing spaces are not ignored, and they sort higher than no trailing spaces. Here's an example:

CHAR datatype: `'Yo' = 'Yo   '`

VARCHAR2 datatype: `'Yo' < 'Yo   '`

NUMBER (<p>, <s>)

The *NUMBER* datatype stores numbers with a precision of *<p>* digits and a scale of *<s>* digits. The precision and scale values are optional. Numeric datatypes are used to store negative and positive integers, fixed-point numbers, and floating-point numbers. The precision can be between 1 and 38, and the scale has a range between –84 and 127. If the precision and scale are omitted, Oracle assumes the maximum of the range for both values.

You can have precision and scale digits in the integer part. The scale rounds the value after the decimal point to *<s>* digits. For example, if you define a column as NUMBER(5,2), the range of values you can store in this column is from –999.99 to 999.99; that is, 5 – 2 = 3 for the integer part, and the decimal part is rounded to two digits. Even if you do not include the decimal part for the value inserted, the maximum number you can store in a NUMBER(5,2) definition is 999.

Oracle will round numbers inserted into numeric columns with a scale smaller than the inserted number. For example, if a column were defined as NUMBER(4,2) and you specified a value of 12.125 to go into that column, the resulting number would be rounded to 12.13 before it was inserted into the column. If the value exceeds the precision, however, an Oracle error is returned. You cannot insert 123.1 into a column defined as NUMBER(4,2). Specifying the scale and precision does not force all inserted values to be a fixed length.

If the scale is negative, the number is rounded to the left of the decimal. Basically, a negative scale forces *<s>* number of zeros just to the left of the decimal.

If you specify a scale that is greater than the precision value, the precision defines the maximum number of digits to the right of the decimal point after the zeros. For example, if a column is defined as NUMBER(3,5), the range of values you can store is from –0.00999 to 0.00999; that is, it requires two zeros (*<s>*-*<p>*) after the decimal point and rounds the decimal part to three digits (*<p>*) after zeros. Table 1.3 shows several examples of how numeric data is stored with various definitions.

TABLE 1.3 Precision and Scale Examples

Value	Datatype	Stored Value	Explanation
123.2564	NUMBER	123.2564	The range and precision are set to the maximum, so the datatype can store any value.
1234.9876	NUMBER(6,2)	1234.99	Since the scale is only 2, the decimal part of the value is rounded to two digits.
12345.12345	NUMBER(6,2)	Error	The range of the integer part is only from –9999 to 9999.
123456	NUMBER(6,2)	Error	The precision is larger than specified; the range is only from –9999 to 9999.
1234.9876	NUMBER(6)	1235	The decimal part is rounded to the next integer.
123456.1	NUMBER(6)	123456	The decimal part is rounded.
12345.345	NUMBER(5,-2)	12300	The negative scale rounds the number <*s*> digits left to the decimal point. –2 rounds to hundreds.
1234567	NUMBER(5,-2)	1234600	Rounded to the nearest hundred.
12345678	NUMBER(5,-2)	Error	Outside the range; can have only five digits, excluding the two zeros representing hundreds, for a total of seven digits: $(s - (-p) = s + p = 5 + 2 = 7)$.
123456789	NUMBER(5,-4)	123460000	Rounded to the nearest 10,000.
1234567890	NUMBER(5,-4)	Error	Outside the range; can have only five digits, excluding the four trailing zeros.
12345.58	NUMBER(*, 1)	12345.6	The use of * in the precision specifies the default limit (38).
0.1	NUMBER(4,5)	Error	Requires a zero after the decimal point (5 – 4 = 1).
0.01234567	NUMBER(4,5)	0.01235	Rounded to four digits after the decimal point and zero.

TABLE 1.3 Precision and Scale Examples *(continued)*

Value	Datatype	Stored Value	Explanation
0.09999	NUMBER(4,5)	0.09999	Stored as it is; only four digits after the decimal point and zero.
0.099996	NUMBER(4,5)	Error	Rounding this value to four digits after the decimal and zero results in 0.1, which is outside the range.

DATE

The *DATE* datatype is used to store date and time information. This datatype can be converted to other forms for viewing, but it has a number of special functions and properties that make date manipulation and calculations simple. The time component of the DATE datatype has a resolution of one second—no less. The DATE datatype occupies a storage space of 7 bytes. The following information is contained within each DATE datatype:

- Century
- Year
- Month
- Day
- Hour
- Minute
- Second

Date values are inserted or updated in the database by converting either a numeric value or a character value into a DATE datatype using the function `TO_DATE`. Oracle defaults the format to display the date as `DD-MON-YY`. This format shows that the default date must begin with a two-digit day, followed by a three-character abbreviation for the month, followed by a two-digit year. If you specify the date without including a time component, the time is defaulted to midnight, or 00:00:00 in military time. The `SYSDATE` function returns the current system date and time from the database server to which you're currently connected.

TIMESTAMP [<precision>]

The TIMESTAMP datatype stores date and time information with fractional precision for seconds. The only difference between the DATE and TIMESTAMP datatypes is the ability to store fractional seconds up to a precision of nine digits. The default precision is 6 and can range from 0 to 9. Similar to the `SYSDATE` function, the `SYSTIMESTAMP` function returns the current system date and time, with fractional precision for seconds.

Operators and Literals

An *operator* is a manipulator that is applied to a data item in order to return a result. Special characters represent different operations in Oracle (+ represents addition, for example). Operators are commonly used in all programming environments, and you should already be familiar with the following operators, which may be classified into two types:

Unary operator A unary operator has only one operand. Examples are +2 and –5. They have the format <operator><operand>.

Binary operator A binary operator has two operands. Examples are 5+4 and 7*5. They have the format <operand1><operator><operand2>. You can insert spaces between the operand and operator to improve readability.

I'll now discuss the various types of operators available in Oracle.

Arithmetic Operators

Arithmetic operators operate on numeric values. Table 1.4 shows the various arithmetic operators in Oracle and how to use them.

TABLE 1.4 Arithmetic Operators

Operator	Purpose	Example
+ -	Unary operators: Use to represent positive or negative data item. For positive items, the + is optional.	`-234.44`
+	Addition: Use to add two data items or expressions.	`2+4`
-	Subtraction: Use to find the difference between two data items or expressions.	`20.4-2`
*	Multiplication: Use to multiply two data items or expressions.	`5*10`
/	Division: Use to divide a data item or expression with another.	`8.4/2`

Do not use two hyphens (--) to represent double negation; use a space or parentheses in between, as in `-(-20)`. Two hyphens represent the beginning of a comment in SQL.

Concatenation Operator

The *concatenation operator* is used to concatenate or join two character (text) strings. The result of concatenation is another character string. Concatenating a zero-length string ('')

or a NULL with another string results in a string, not a NULL (NULL in Oracle 11*g* represents unknown or missing data). Two vertical bars (||) are used as the concatenation operator.

Here are two examples:

'Oracle11g' || 'Database' results in 'Oracle11gDatabase'.

'Oracle11g ' || 'Database' results in 'Oracle11g Database'.

Operator Precedence

If multiple operators are used in the same expression, Oracle evaluates them in the *order of precedence* set in the database engine. Operators with higher precedence are evaluated before operators with lower precedence. Operators with the same precedence are evaluated from left to right. Table 1.5 lists the precedence.

TABLE 1.5 SQL Operator Precedence

Precedence	Operator	Purpose
1	- +	Unary operators, negation
2	* /	Multiplication, division
3	+ - ||	Addition, subtraction, concatenation

Using parentheses changes the order of precedence. The innermost parenthesis is evaluated first. In the expression 1+2*3, the result is 7, because 2*3 is evaluated first and the result is added to 1. In the expression (1+2)*3, 1+2 is evaluated first, and the result is multiplied by 3, giving 9.

Literals

Literals are values that represent a fixed value (constant). There are four types of literals:

- Text (or character)
- Numeric (integer and number)
- Datetime
- Interval

You can use literals within many of the SQL functions, expressions, and conditions.

Text Literals

A *text literal* must be enclosed in single quotation marks. Any character between the quotation marks is considered part of the text value. Oracle treats all text literals as though they were CHAR datatypes for comparison (blank padded). The maximum length of a text literal is 4,000 bytes. Single quotation marks can be included in the literal text value by preceding it with another single quotation mark. Here are some examples of text literals:

```
'The Quick Brown Fox'
'That man''s suit is black'
'And I quote: "This will never do." '
'12-SEP-2001'
```

Alternatively, you can use `Q` or `q` quoting, which provides a range of delimiters. The syntax for using the `Q/q` quoting with a quote-delimiter text literal is as follows:

```
[Q|q]' <quote_delimiter> <text literal> <quote_delimiter>'
```

`<quote_delimiter>` is any character except a space, tab, or carriage return. The quote delimiter can be a single quotation mark, but make sure inside the text literal a single quotation mark is not immediately followed by another single quotation mark. If the opening quote delimiter is `[` or `{` or `<` or `(`, then the closing quote must be the corresponding `]` or `}` or `>` or `)`. For all other quote delimiters, the opening quote delimiter must be the same as the closing quote delimiter. Here are some examples of text literals using the alternative quoting mechanism:

```
q'<The Quick Brown Fox>'
Q'#The Quick Brown Fox#'
q'{That man's suit is black}'
Q'(And I quote: "This will never do." )'
Q'"And I quote: "This will never do." "'
q'[12-SEP-2001]'
```

Numeric Literals

Integer literals can be any number of numerals, excluding a decimal separator and up to 38 digits long. Here are two examples:

- 24
- –456

Number and *floating-point literals* can include scientific notation, as well as digits and the decimal separator. `E` or `e` represents a number in scientific notation; the exponent can be in the range of –130 to 125. If the literal is followed by an `f` or `F`, it is treated as a `BINARY_FLOAT` datatype. If the literal is followed by a `d` or `D`, it is treated as a `BINARY_DOUBLE` datatype. Here are some examples:

- 24.0
- –345.65
- 23E-10

- 1.5f
- –34.567D
- –4d
- –4.0E+0

Datetime Literals

You can specify a date value as a string literal using the *datetime literals*. The most common methods to represent the datetime values are to use the conversion function TO_DATE or TO_TIMESTAMP with the appropriate format mask. For completeness of literals, I will discuss the datetime literals briefly.

The DATE literal uses the keyword DATE followed by the date value in single quotes, and the value must be specified in *YYYY-MM-DD* format with no time component. The time component will be defaulted to midnight (00:00:00). The following are examples of the DATE literal:

```
DATE '2008-03-24'
DATE '1999-12-31'
```

Similar to the TIMESTAMP datatype, the TIMESTAMP literal can be used to specify the year, month, date, hour, minute, second, and fractional second. You can also include timezone data along with the TIMESTAMP literal. The time zone information can be specified using the UTC offset or using the time zone region name. The literal must be in the format YYYY-MM-DD HH24:MI:SS TZ. Here are some examples of the TIMESTAMP literal:

```
TIMESTAMP '2008-03-24 03:25:34.123'
TIMESTAMP '2008-03-24 03:25:34.123 -7:00'
TIMESTAMP '2008-03-24 03:25:34.123 US/Central'
TIMESTAMP '2008-03-24 03:25:34.123 US/Central CDT'
```

Interval Literals

Interval literals specify a period of time in terms of years and months or in terms of days and seconds. These literals correspond to the Oracle datatypes INTERVAL YEAR TO MONTH and INTERVAL DAY TO SECOND. I'll discuss these datatypes in more detail in Chapter 6.

Writing Simple Queries

A *query* is a request for information from the database tables. Queries do not modify data; they read data from database tables and views. Simple queries are those that retrieve data from a single table or view. A table is used to store data and is stored in rows and columns. The basis of a query is the SELECT statement. The SELECT statement can be used to get data from a single table or from multiple tables. Queries using multiple tables are discussed in later chapters.

Using the SELECT Statement

The SELECT statement is the most commonly used statement in SQL. It allows you to retrieve information already stored in the database. The statement begins with the keyword SELECT, followed by the column names whose data you want to query. You can select information either from all the columns (denoted by *) or from name-specific columns in the SELECT clause to retrieve data. The FROM clause provides the name of the table, view, or materialized view to use in the query. These objects are discussed in detail in later chapters. For simplicity, I will use tables for the rest of this chapter.

Let's use the JOBS table defined in the HR schema of the Oracle 11*g* sample database. You can use SQL*Plus tool to connect to the database as discussed earlier in the chapter. The JOBS table definition is provided in Table 1.6.

TABLE 1.6 JOBS Table Definition

Column Name	Datatype	Length
JOB_ID	VARCHAR2	10
JOB_TITLE	VARCHAR2	35
MIN_SALARY	NUMBER	6,0
MAX_SALARY	NUMBER	6,0

The simple form of a SELECT statement to retrieve all the columns and rows from the JOBS table is as follows (only part of output result set is shown here):

```
SQL> SELECT * FROM jobs;

JOB_ID     JOB_TITLE                       MIN_SALARY MAX_SALARY
---------- ------------------------------- ---------- ----------
AD_PRES    President                            20000      40000
AD_VP      Administration Vice President         15000      30000
AD_ASST    Administration Assistant              3000       6000
FI_MGR     Finance Manager                       8200      16000
FI_ACCOUNT Accountant                            4200       9000
… … … … …
IT_PROG    Programmer                            4000      10000
```

```
MK_MAN     Marketing Manager                    9000     15000
MK_REP     Marketing Representative             4000      9000
HR_REP     Human Resources Representative       4000      9000
PR_REP     Public Relations Representative      4500     10500

19 rows selected.
```

The keywords, column names, and table names are case insensitive. Only literals enclosed in single quotation marks are case sensitive in Oracle.

How do you list only the job title and minimum salary from this table? If you know the column names and the table name, writing the query is simple. Here, the column names are JOB_TITLE and MIN_SALARY, and the table name is JOBS. Execute the query by ending the query with a semicolon. In SQL*Plus, you can execute the query by entering a slash on a line by itself or by using the RUN command.

```
SQL> SELECT job_title, min_salary FROM jobs;

JOB_TITLE                           MIN_SALARY
----------------------------------- ----------
President                                20000
Administration Vice President            15000
Administration Assistant                  3000
Finance Manager                           8200
Accountant                                4200
Accounting Manager                        8200
Public Accountant                         4200
… … … … …
Programmer                                4000
Marketing Manager                         9000
Marketing Representative                  4000
Human Resources Representative            4000
Public Relations Representative           4500

19 rows selected.
```

Notice that the numeric column (MIN_SALARY) is aligned to the right and the character column (JOB_TITLE) is aligned to the left. Does it seem that the column heading MIN_SALARY should be more meaningful? Well, you can provide a *column alias* to appear in the query results.

Column Alias Names

The column alias name is defined next to the column name with a space or by using the keyword AS. If you want a space in the column alias name, you must enclose it in double quotation marks. The case is preserved only when the alias name is enclosed in double quotation marks; otherwise, the display will be uppercase. The following example demonstrates using an alias name for the column heading in the previous query:

```
SELECT job_title AS Title, min_salary AS "Minimum Salary"
FROM jobs;

TITLE                               Minimum Salary
----------------------------------- --------------
President                                    20000
Administration Vice President                15000
Administration Assistant                      3000
Finance Manager                               8200
Accountant                                    4200
Accounting Manager                            8200
... ... ... ... ...
Programmer                                    4000
Marketing Manager                             9000
Marketing Representative                      4000
Human Resources Representative                4000
Public Relations Representative               4500

19 rows selected.
```

In this listing, the column alias name Title appears in all capital letters because I did not enclose it in double quotation marks.

The asterisk (*) is used to select all columns in the table. This is useful when you do not know the column names or when you are too lazy to type all the column names.

Ensuring Uniqueness

The DISTINCT keyword (or UNIQUE keyword) following SELECT ensures that the resulting rows are unique. Uniqueness is verified against the complete row, not the first column. If you need to find the unique departments in the EMPLOYEES table, issue this query:

```
SELECT DISTINCT department_id
FROM employees;
```

```
DEPARTMENT_ID
-------------
          100
           30

           20
           70
           90
          110
           50
           40
           80
           10
           60

12 rows selected.
```

To demonstrate that uniqueness is enforced across the row, let's do one more query using the SELECT DISTINCT clause. Notice DEPARTMENT_ID repeating for each JOB_ID value in the following example:

```
SELECT DISTINCT department_id, job_id
FROM employees;

DEPARTMENT_ID JOB_ID
------------- ----------
          110 AC_ACCOUNT
           90 AD_VP
           50 ST_CLERK
           80 SA_REP
          110 AC_MGR
… … …
           10 AD_ASST
           20 MK_REP
           40 HR_REP
           30 PU_MAN

20 rows selected.
```

SELECT * FROM TAB; shows all the tables and views in your schema. Don't be alarmed if you see a table name similar to BIN$PJV23QpwQfu0zPN9uaXw+w==$0. These are tables that belong to the Recycle Bin (or dropped tables). The tasks of creating tables and managing tables are discussed in Chapter 6.

The DUAL Table

The DUAL table is a dummy table available to all users in the database. It has one column and one row. The DUAL table is used to select system variables or to evaluate an expression. Here are few examples. The first query is to show the contents of the DUAL table.

```
SQL> SELECT * FROM dual;

DUMMY
-----
X

SQL> SELECT SYSDATE, USER FROM dual;

SYSDATE   USER
--------- ------------------------------
18-SEP-07 HR

SQL> SELECT 'I''m ' || user || ' Today is ' || SYSDATE
  2  FROM dual;

'I''M'||USER||'TODAYIS'||SYSDATE
-----------------------------------------------------
I'm HR Today is 18-SEP-07
```

SYSDATE and USER are built-in functions that provide information about the environment. These functions are discussed in Chapter 2, "Using Single-Row Functions."

Limiting Rows

You can use the WHERE clause in the SELECT statement to limit the number of rows processed. Any logical conditions of the WHERE clause use the comparison operators. Rows are returned or operated upon where the data satisfies the logical condition(s) of the WHERE clause. You can use column names or expressions in the WHERE clause, but not column alias names. The WHERE clause follows the FROM clause in the SELECT statement.

How do you list the employees who work for department 90? The following example shows how to limit the query to only the records belonging to department 90 by using a WHERE clause:

```
SELECT first_name || ' ' || last_name "Name", department_id
FROM   employees
WHERE  department_id = 90;

Name                                       DEPARTMENT_ID
------------------------------------------ -------------
Steven King                                           90
Neena Kochhar                                         90
Lex De Haan                                           90
```

You need not include the column names in the SELECT clause to use them in the WHERE clause.

You can use various operators in Oracle 11*g* in the WHERE clause to limit the number of rows.

Comparison Operators

Comparison operators compare two values or expressions and give a Boolean result of TRUE, FALSE, or NULL. The comparison operators include those that test for equality, inequality, less than, greater than, and value comparisons.

= (Equality)

The = operator tests for equality. The test evaluates to TRUE if the values or results of an expression on both sides of the operator are equal.

```
SELECT first_name || ' ' || last_name "Name", department_id
FROM   employees
WHERE  department_id = 90;

Name                                       DEPARTMENT_ID
------------------------------------------ -------------
Steven King                                           90
Neena Kochhar                                         90
Lex De Haan                                           90
```

!=, <>, or ^= (Inequality)

You can use any one of these three operators to test for inequality. The test evaluates to TRUE if the values on both sides of the operator do not match.

```
SELECT first_name || ' ' || last_name "Name", commission_pct
FROM   employees
WHERE  commission_pct != .35;

Name                                     COMMISSION_PCT
---------------------------------------- --------------
John Russell                                         .4
Karen Partners                                       .3
Alberto Errazuriz                                    .3
Gerald Cambrault                                     .3
… … … … …
Jack Livingston                                      .2
Kimberely Grant                                     .15
Charles Johnson                                      .1

32 rows selected.
```

< (Less Than)

The < operator evaluates to TRUE if the left side (expression or value) of the operator is less than the right side of the operator.

```
SELECT first_name || ' ' || last_name "Name", commission_pct
FROM   employees
WHERE  commission_pct < .15;

Name                                     COMMISSION_PCT
---------------------------------------- --------------
Mattea Marvins                                       .1
David Lee                                            .1
Sundar Ande                                          .1
Amit Banda                                           .1
Sundita Kumar                                        .1
Charles Johnson                                      .1

6 rows selected.
```

> (Greater Than)

The > operator evaluates to TRUE if the left side (expression or value) of the operator is greater than the right side of the operator.

```
SELECT first_name || ' ' || last_name "Name", commission_pct
FROM   employees
WHERE  commission_pct > .35;

Name                                     COMMISSION_PCT
---------------------------------------- --------------
John Russell                                         .4
```

<= (Less Than or Equal to)

The <= operator evaluates to TRUE if the left side (expression or value) of the operator is less than or equal to the right side of the operator.

```
SELECT first_name || ' ' || last_name "Name", commission_pct
FROM   employees
WHERE  commission_pct <= .15;

Name                                     COMMISSION_PCT
---------------------------------------- --------------
Oliver Tuvault                                      .15
Danielle Greene                                     .15
Mattea Marvins                                       .1
David Lee                                            .1
Sundar Ande                                          .1
Amit Banda                                           .1
William Smith                                       .15
Elizabeth Bates                                     .15
Sundita Kumar                                        .1
Kimberely Grant                                     .15
Charles Johnson                                      .1

11 rows selected.
```

>= (Greater Than or Equal to)

The >= operator evaluates to TRUE if the left side (expression or value) of the operator is greater than or equal to the right side of the operator.

```
SELECT first_name || ' ' || last_name "Name", commission_pct
FROM   employees
WHERE  commission_pct >= .35;
```

```
Name                                      COMMISSION_PCT
----------------------------------------- --------------
John Russell                                          .4
Janette King                                         .35
Patrick Sully                                        .35
Allan McEwen                                         .35
```

ANY or SOME

You can use the ANY or SOME operator to compare a value to each value in a list or subquery. The ANY and SOME operators always must be preceded by one of the following comparison operators: =, !=, <, >, <=, or >=.

```
SELECT first_name || ' ' || last_name "Name", department_id
FROM   employees
WHERE  department_id <= ANY (10, 15, 20, 25);
```

```
Name                                      DEPARTMENT_ID
----------------------------------------- -------------
Jennifer Whalen                                      10
Michael Hartstein                                    20
Pat Fay                                              20
```

ALL

You can use the ALL operator to compare a value to every value in a list or subquery. The ALL operator must always be preceded by one of the following comparison operators: =, !=, <, >, <=, or >=.

```
SELECT first_name || ' ' || last_name "Name", department_id
FROM   employees
WHERE  department_id >= ALL (80, 90, 100);
```

```
Name                                      DEPARTMENT_ID
----------------------------------------- -------------
Nancy Greenberg                                     100
Daniel Faviet                                       100
John Chen                                           100
Ismael Sciarra                                      100
Jose Manuel Urman                                   100
Luis Popp                                           100
Shelley Higgins                                     110
William Gietz                                       110

8 rows selected.
```

For all the comparison operators discussed, if one side of the operator is NULL, the result is NULL.

Logical Operators

Logical operators are used to combine the results of two comparison conditions (compound conditions) to produce a single result or to reverse the result of a single comparison. NOT, AND, and OR are the logical operators. When a logical operator is applied to NULL, the result is UNKNOWN. UNKNOWN acts similarly to FALSE; the only difference is that NOT FALSE is TRUE, whereas NOT UNKNOWN is also UNKNOWN.

NOT

You can use the NOT operator to reverse the result. It evaluates to TRUE if the operand is FALSE, and it evaluates to FALSE if the operand is TRUE. NOT returns NULL if the operand is NULL.

```
WHERE  !(department_id >= 30)
       *
ERROR at line 3:
SELECT first_name, department_id
FROM   employees
WHERE  not (department_id >= 30);

FIRST_NAME           DEPARTMENT_ID
-------------------- -------------
Jennifer                        10
Michael                         20
Pat                             20
```

AND

The AND operator evaluates to TRUE if both operands are TRUE. It evaluates to FALSE if either operand is FALSE. Otherwise, it returns NULL.

```
SELECT first_name, salary
FROM   employees
WHERE  last_name = 'Smith'
AND    salary    > 7500;

FIRST_NAME               SALARY
-------------------- ----------
Lindsey                    8000
```

OR

The OR operator evaluates to TRUE if either operand is TRUE. It evaluates to FALSE if both operands are FALSE. Otherwise, it returns NULL.

```
SELECT first_name, last_name
FROM   employees
WHERE  first_name = 'Kelly'
OR     last_name  = 'Smith';

FIRST_NAME           LAST_NAME
-------------------- -------------------------
Lindsey              Smith
William              Smith
Kelly                Chung
```

Logical Operator Truth Tables

The following tables are the truth tables for the three logical operators.

Table 1.7 is a truth table for the AND operator.

TABLE 1.7 AND Truth Table

AND	TRUE	FALSE	UNKNOWN
TRUE	TRUE	FALSE	UNKNOWN
FALSE	FALSE	FALSE	FALSE
UNKNOWN	UNKNOWN	FALSE	UNKNOWN

Table 1.8 is the truth table for the OR operator.

TABLE 1.8 OR Truth Table

OR	TRUE	FALSE	UNKNOWN
TRUE	TRUE	TRUE	TRUE
FALSE	TRUE	FALSE	UNKNOWN
UNKNOWN	TRUE	UNKNOWN	UNKNOWN

Table 1.9 is the truth table for the NOT operator.

TABLE 1.9 NOT Truth Table

NOT	
TRUE	FALSE
FALSE	TRUE
UNKNOWN	UNKNOWN

Other Operators

In the following sections, I will discuss all the operators that can be used in the WHERE clause of the SQL statement that were not discussed earlier.

IN and NOT IN

You can use the IN and NOT IN operators to test a membership condition. IN is equivalent to the =ANY operator, which evaluates to TRUE if the value exists in the list or the result set from a subquery. The NOT IN operator is equivalent to the !=ALL operator, which evaluates to TRUE if the value does not exist in the list or the result set from a subquery. The following examples demonstrate how to use these two operators:

```
SELECT first_name, last_name, department_id
FROM   employees
WHERE  department_id IN (10, 20, 90);

FIRST_NAME           LAST_NAME                 DEPARTMENT_ID
-------------------- ------------------------- ----------
Steven               King                              90
Neena                Kochhar                           90
Lex                  De Haan                           90
Jennifer             Whalen                            10
Michael              Hartstein                         20
Pat                  Fay                               20

6 rows selected.

SELECT first_name, last_name, department_id
FROM   employees
WHERE  department_id NOT IN
       (10, 30, 40, 50, 60, 80, 90, 110, 100);
```

```
FIRST_NAME           LAST_NAME                 DEPARTMENT_ID
-------------------- ---------------------- -------------
Michael              Hartstein                          20
Pat                  Fay                                20
Hermann              Baer                               70
SQL>
```

When using the NOT IN operator, if any value in the list or the result returned from the subquery is NULL, the NOT IN condition is evaluated to FALSE. For example, last_name not in ('Smith', 'Thomas', NULL) evaluates to last_name != 'Smith' AND last_name != 'Thomas' AND last_name != NULL. Any comparison on a NULL value results in NULL. So, the previous condition does not return any row even through there may be some rows with LAST_NAME as Smith or Thomas.

BETWEEN

You can use the BETWEEN operator to test a range. BETWEEN A AND B evaluates to TRUE if the value is greater than or equal to *A* and less than or equal to *B*. If NOT is used, the result is the reverse. The following example lists all the employees whose salary is between $5,000 and $6,000:

```
SELECT first_name, last_name, salary
FROM   employees
WHERE  salary BETWEEN 5000 AND 6000;

FIRST_NAME           LAST_NAME                     SALARY
-------------------- ------------------------- ----------
Bruce                Ernst                           6000
Kevin                Mourgos                         5800
Pat                  Fay                             6000
```

EXISTS

The EXISTS operator is always followed by a subquery in parentheses. EXISTS evaluates to TRUE if the subquery returns at least one row. The following example lists the employees who work for the administration department. Here is an example of using EXISTS. Don't worry if you do not understand the SQL for now; subqueries are discussed in detail in Chapter 4, "Using Joins and Subqueries."

```
SELECT last_name, first_name, department_id
FROM   employees e
WHERE  EXISTS (select 1 FROM departments d
```

```
WHERE  d.department_id = e.department_id
AND    d.department_name = 'Administration');

LAST_NAME                FIRST_NAME            DEPARTMENT_ID
------------------------ --------------------- -------------
Whalen                   Jennifer                         10
SQL>
```

IS NULL and IS NOT NULL

To find the NULL values or NOT NULL values, you need to use the IS NULL operator. The = or != operator will not work with NULL values. IS NULL evaluates to TRUE if the value is NULL. IS NOT NULL evaluates to TRUE if the value is not NULL. To find the employees who do not have a department assigned, use this query:

```
SELECT last_name, department_id
FROM   employees
WHERE  department_id IS NULL;

LAST_NAME                 DEPARTMENT_ID
------------------------- -------------
Grant

SQL>
SELECT last_name, department_id
FROM employees
WHERE department_id = NULL;

no rows selected
```

LIKE

Using the LIKE operator, you can perform pattern matching. The pattern-search character % is used to match any character and any number of characters. The pattern-search character _ is used to match any single character. If you are looking for the actual character % or _ in the pattern search, you can include an escape character in the search string and notify Oracle using the ESCAPE clause.

The following query searches for all employees whose first name begins with *Su* and last name does not begin with *S*:

```
SELECT first_name, last_name
FROM   employees
WHERE  first_name LIKE 'Su%'
AND    last_name NOT LIKE 'S%';
```

```
FIRST_NAME           LAST_NAME
-------------------- -------------------------
Sundar               Ande
Sundita              Kumar
Susan                Mavris
```

The following example looks for all JOB_ID values that begin with *AC_*. Since _ is a pattern-matching character, you must qualify it with an escape character. Oracle does not have a default escape character.

```
SELECT job_id, job_title
FROM   jobs
WHERE  job_id like 'AC\_%' ESCAPE '\';

JOB_ID     JOB_TITLE
---------- -----------------------------------
AC_MGR     Accounting Manager
AC_ACCOUNT Public Accountant
```

Table 1.10 shows more examples of pattern matching.

TABLE 1.10 Pattern-Matching Examples

Pattern	Matches	Does Not Match
%SONI_1	SONIC1, ULTRASONI21	SONICS1, SONI315
_IME	TIME, LIME	IME, CRIME
\%SONI_1 ESCAPE '\'	%SONIC1, %SONI91	SONIC1, ULTRASONIC1
%ME_ _ _LE ESCAPE '\'	CRIME_FILE, TIME_POLE	CRIMESPILE, CRIME_ALE

Sorting Rows

The SELECT statement may include the ORDER BY clause to sort the resulting rows in a specific order based on the data in the columns. Without the ORDER BY clause, there is no guarantee that the rows will be returned in any specific order. If an ORDER BY clause is specified, by default the rows are returned by ascending order of the columns specified. If you need to sort the rows in descending order, use the keyword DESC next to the column name. You can specify the keyword ASC to explicitly state to sort in ascending order, although it is the default. The ORDER BY clause follows the FROM clause and the WHERE clause in the SELECT statement.

To retrieve all employee names of department 90 from the EMPLOYEES table ordered by last name, use this query:

```
SELECT first_name || ' ' || last_name "Employee Name"
FROM   employees
WHERE  department_id = 90
ORDER BY last_name;

Employee Name
----------------------------------------------
Lex De Haan
Steven King
Neena Kochhar
SQL>
```

You can specify more than one column in the ORDER BY clause. In this case, the result set will be ordered by the first column in the ORDER BY clause, then the second, and so on. Columns or expressions not used in the SELECT clause can also be used in the ORDER BY clause. The following example shows how to use DESC and multiple columns in the ORDER BY clause:

```
SELECT first_name, hire_date, salary, manager_id mid
FROM   employees
WHERE  department_id IN (110,100)
ORDER BY mid ASC, salary DESC, hire_date;

FIRST_NAME           HIRE_DATE     SALARY        MID
-------------------- --------- ---------- ----------
Shelley              07-JUN-94      12000        101
Nancy                17-AUG-94      12000        101
Daniel               16-AUG-94       9000        108
John                 28-SEP-97       8200        108
Jose Manuel          07-MAR-98       7800        108
Ismael               30-SEP-97       7700        108
Luis                 07-DEC-99       6900        108
William              07-JUN-94       8300        205

8 rows selected.
SQL>
```

You can use column alias names in the ORDER BY clause.

If the DISTINCT keyword is used in the SELECT clause, you can use only those columns listed in the SELECT clause in the ORDER BY clause. If you have used any operators on columns in the SELECT clause, the ORDER BY clause also should use them. Here is an example:

```
SELECT DISTINCT 'Region ' || region_id
FROM   countries
ORDER BY region_id;

ORDER BY region_id
         *
ERROR at line 3:
ORA-01791: not a SELECTed expression

SELECT DISTINCT 'Region ' || region_id
FROM   countries
ORDER BY 'Region ' || region_id;

'REGION'||REGION_ID
----------------------------------------------
Region 1
Region 2
Region 3
Region 4
```

Not only can you use the column name or column alias to sort the result set of a query, but you can also sort the results by specifying the position of the column in the SELECT clause. This is useful if you have a lengthy expression in the SELECT clause and you need the results sorted on this value. The following example sorts the result set using positional values:

```
SELECT first_name, hire_date, salary, manager_id mid
FROM   employees
WHERE  department_id IN (110,100)
ORDER BY 4, 2, 3;

FIRST_NAME           HIRE_DATE     SALARY        MID
-------------------- --------- ---------- ----------
Shelley              07-JUN-94      12000        101
```

```
Nancy               17-AUG-94    12000       101
Daniel              16-AUG-94     9000       108
John                28-SEP-97     8200       108
Ismael              30-SEP-97     7700       108
Jose Manuel         07-MAR-98     7800       108
Luis                07-DEC-99     6900       108
William             07-JUN-94     8300       205

8 rows selected.
```

The ORDER BY clause cannot have more than 255 columns or expressions.

Sorting NULLs

By default, in an ascending-order sort, the NULL values appear at the bottom of the result set; that is, NULLs are sorted higher. For descending-order sorts, NULL values appear at the top of the result set—again, NULL values are sorted higher. You can change the default behavior by using the NULLS FIRST or NULLS LAST keyword, along with the column names (or alias names or positions). The following examples demonstrate how to use NULLS FIRST in an ascending sort:

```
SELECT last_name, commission_pct
FROM   employees
WHERE  last_name LIKE 'R%'
ORDER BY commission_pct ASC, last_name DESC;

LAST_NAME                 COMMISSION_PCT
------------------------- --------------
Russell                               .4
Rogers
Raphaely
Rajs

SELECT last_name, commission_pct
FROM   employees
WHERE  last_name LIKE 'R%'
ORDER BY commission_pct ASC NULLS FIRST, last_name DESC;
```

```
LAST_NAME                 COMMISSION_PCT
------------------------- --------------
Rogers
Raphaely
Rajs
Russell                               .4
SQL>
```

Why Do You Limit and Sort Rows?

The power of an RDBMS and SQL lies in getting exactly what you want from the database. The sample tables you considered under the HR schema are small, so even if you get all the information from the table, you can still find the specific data you're seeking. But what if you have a huge transaction table with millions of rows?

You know how easy it is to look through a catalog in the library to find a particular book or to search through an alphabetical listing to find your name. When querying a large table, make sure you know what you want.

The WHERE clause lets you query for exactly what you're looking for. The ORDER BY clause lets you sort rows. The following steps can be used as an approach to query data from single table:

1. Know the columns of the table. You can issue the DESCRIBE command to get the column names and datatype. Understand which column has what information.
2. Pick the column names you are interested in including in the query. Use these columns in the SELECT clause.
3. Identify the column or columns where you can limit the rows, or the columns that can show you only the rows of interest. Use these columns in the WHERE clause of the query, and supply the values as well as the appropriate operator.
4. If the query returns more than a few rows, you may be interested in having them sorted in a particular order. Specify the column names and the sorting order in the ORDER BY clause of the query.

Let's consider a table named PURCHASE_ORDERS. First, use the DESCRIBE command to list the columns:

```
SQL> DESCRIBE purchase_orders

Name                  Null?    Type
--------------------- -------- --------------
ORDER#                NOT NULL NUMBER (16)
ORDER_DT              NOT NULL DATE
```

```
CUSTOMER#                NOT NULL VARCHAR2 (12)
BACK_ORDER                        CHAR (1)
ORD_STATUS                        CHAR (1)
TOTAL_AMT                NOT NULL NUMBER (18,4)
SALES_TAX                         NUMBER (12,2)
```

The objective of the query is to find the completed orders that do not have any sales tax. You want to see the order number and total amount of the order. The corresponding columns that appear in the SELECT clause are ORDER# and TOTAL_AMT. Since you're interested in only the rows with no sales tax in the completed orders, the columns to appear in the WHERE clause are SALES_TAX (checking for zero sales tax) and ORD_STATUS (checking for the completeness of the order, which is status code C). Since the query returns multiple rows, you want to order them by the order number. Notice that the SALES_TAX column can be NULL, so you want to make sure you get all rows that have a sales tax amount of zero or NULL.

```
SELECT order#, total_amt
FROM   purchase_orders
WHERE  ord_status = 'C'
AND    (sales_tax IS NULL
OR      sales_tax = 0)
ORDER BY order#;
```

An alternative is to use the NVL function to deal with the NULL values. This function is discussed in Chapter 2.

Using Expressions

An *expression* is a combination of one or more values, operators, and SQL functions that result in a value. The result of an expression generally assumes the datatype of its components. The simple expression 5+6 evaluates to 11 and assumes a datatype of NUMBER. Expressions can appear in the following clauses:

- The SELECT clause of queries
- The WHERE clause, ORDER BY clause, and HAVING clause
- The VALUES clause of the INSERT statement
- The SET clause of the UPDATE statement

I will review the syntax of using these statements in later chapters.

You can include parentheses to group and evaluate expressions and then apply the result to the rest of the expression. When parentheses are used, the expression in the innermost parentheses is evaluated first. Here is an example of a compound expression: ((2*4)/(3+1))*10. The result of 2*4 is divided by the result of 3+1. Then the result from the division operation is multiplied by 10.

The CASE Expression

You can use the CASE expression to derive the IF…THEN…ELSE logic in SQL. Here is the syntax of the simple CASE expression:

```
CASE <expression>
WHEN <compare value> THEN <return value> … … …
[ELSE <return value>]
END
```

The CASE expression begins with the keyword CASE and ends with the keyword END. The ELSE clause is optional. The maximum number of arguments in a CASE expression is 255. The following query displays a description for the REGION_ID column based on the value:

```
SELECT country_name, region_id,
       CASE region_id WHEN 1 THEN 'Europe'
                      WHEN 2 THEN 'America'
                      WHEN 3 THEN 'Asia'
                      ELSE 'Other' END Continent
FROM   countries
WHERE  country_name LIKE 'I%';

COUNTRY_NAME          REGION_ID CONTINE
-------------------- ---------- -------
Israel                        4 Other
India                         3 Asia
Italy                         1 Europe
SQL>
```

The other form of the CASE expression is the searched CASE, where the values are derived based on a condition. Oracle evaluates the conditions top to bottom; when a condition evaluates to true, the rest of the WHEN clauses are not evaluated. This version has the following syntax:

```
CASE
WHEN <condition> THEN <return value> … … …
[ELSE <return value>]
END
```

The following example categorizes the salary as Low, Medium, and High using a searched CASE expression:

```
SELECT first_name, department_id, salary,
       CASE WHEN salary < 6000 THEN 'Low'
            WHEN salary < 10000 THEN 'Medium'
            WHEN salary >= 10000 THEN 'High' END Category
FROM   employees
WHERE department_id <= 30
ORDER BY first_name;

FIRST_NAME           DEPARTMENT_ID     SALARY CATEGO
-------------------- ------------- ---------- ------
Alexander                       30       3100 Low
Den                             30      11000 High
Guy                             30       2600 Low
Jennifer                        10       4400 Low
Karen                           30       2500 Low
Michael                         20      13000 High
Pat                             20       6000 Medium
Shelli                          30       2900 Low
Sigal                           30       2800 Low

9 rows selected.
```

Oracle uses the & (ampersand) character to substitute values at runtime. In the next section, I will discuss how to create SQL statements that can be used to get a different set of results based on values passed during execution time.

Finding the Current Sessions and Program Name

As a DBA you may have to query the V$SESSION dictionary view to find the current sessions in the database. This view has several columns that show various information about the session; often the DBA is interested in finding out the username and which program is connecting to the database. If the DBA wants to find out what SQL is executed in the session, the SID and SERIAL# columns can be queried to enable tracing using the DBMS_TRACE package.

I'll review in this example how to query the V$SESSION view using the simple SQL statements you learned in this chapter.

The following query may return several rows depending on the activity and number of users connected to the database:

```
SELECT username, sid, serial#, program
FROM v$session;
```

If you're using SQL*Plus, you may have to adjust the column width to fit the output in one line:

```
COLUMN program FORMAT a20
COLUMN username FORMAT a20
SELECT username, sid, serial#, program
FROM v$session;

USERNAME                    SID    SERIAL# PROGRAM
-------------------- ---------- ---------- -----------------
                            118       6246 ORACLE.EXE (W000)
BTHOMAS                     121        963 sqlplus.exe
DBSNMP                      124      23310 emagent.exe
DBSNMP                      148        608 emagent.exe
                            150          1 ORACLE.EXE (FBDA)
                            152          7 ORACLE.EXE (SMCO)
                            155          1 ORACLE.EXE (MMNL)
                            156          1 ORACLE.EXE (DIA0)
                            158          1 ORACLE.EXE (MMON)
                            159          1 ORACLE.EXE (RECO)
                            164          1 ORACLE.EXE (MMAN)
… … … (Output truncated)
```

As you can see, the background processes do not have usernames. To find out only the user sessions in the database, you can filter out the rows that do no have valid usernames:

```
SELECT username, sid, serial#, program
FROM v$session
WHERE username is NOT NULL;
```

If you're looking for specific information, you may want to add more filter conditions such as looking for a specific user or a specific program. The following SQL returns the rows in order of their session login time, with the most recent session on the top:

```
SELECT username, sid, serial#, program
FROM v$session
```

```
WHERE username is NOT NULL
ORDER BY logon_time;

USERNAME                    SID    SERIAL# PROGRAM
-------------------- ---------- ---------- ---------------
DBSNMP                      148        608 emagent.exe
DBSNMP                      124      23310 emagent.exe
BTHOMAS                     121        963 sqlplus.exe
SCOTT                       132         23 TOAD.EXE
SJACOB                      231         32 discoverer.exe
```

Accepting Values at Runtime

To create an interactive SQL statement, you can define variables in the SQL statement. This allows the user to supply values at runtime, further enhancing the ability to reuse the SQL scripts. An ampersand (&) followed by a variable name prompts for and accepts values at runtime. For example, the following SELECT statement queries the DEPARTMENTS table based on the department number supplied at runtime.

```
SELECT department_name
FROM   departments
WHERE  department_id = &dept;

Enter value for dept: 10
old   3: WHERE  DEPARTMENT_ID = &dept
new   3: WHERE  DEPARTMENT_ID = 10

DEPARTMENT_NAME
---------------
Administration

1 row selected.
```

Using Substitution Variables

Suppose that you have defined DEPT as a variable in your script, but you want to avoid the prompt for the value at runtime. SQL*Plus prompts you for a value only when the variable is undefined. You can define a *substitution variable* in SQL*Plus using the DEFINE command to provide a value. The variable will always have the CHAR datatype associated with it. Here is an example of defining a substitution variable:

```
SQL> DEFINE DEPT = 20
SQL> DEFINE DEPT
DEFINE DEPT             = "20" (CHAR)
SQL> LIST
  1  SELECT department_name
  2  FROM   departments
  3* WHERE  department_id = &DEPT
SQL> /
old   3: WHERE  DEPARTMENT_ID = &DEPT
new   3: WHERE  DEPARTMENT_ID = 20

DEPARTMENT_NAME
---------------
Marketing

1 row selected.
SQL>
```

Using the DEFINE command without any arguments shows all the defined variables.

A . (dot) is used to append characters immediately after the substitution variable. The dot separates the variable name and the literal that follows immediately. If you need a dot to be part of the literal, provide two dots continuously. For example, the following query appends _REP to the user input when seeking a value from the JOBS table:

```
SQL> SELECT job_id, job_title FROM jobs
  2* WHERE  job_id = '&JOB._REP'
SQL> /
Enter value for job: MK
old   2: WHERE  JOB_ID = '&JOB._REP'
new   2: WHERE  JOB_ID = 'MK_REP'

JOB_ID     JOB_TITLE
---------- ------------------------
MK_REP     Marketing Representative

1 row selected.
SQL>
```

The old line with the variable and the new line with the substitution are displayed. You can turn off this display by using the command SET VERIFY OFF.

Saving a Variable for a Session

Consider the following SQL, saved to a file named ex01.sql. When you execute this script file, you will be prompted for the COL1 and COL2 values multiple times:

```
SQL> SELECT &COL1, &COL2
  2  FROM   &TABLE
  3  WHERE  &COL1 = '&VAL'
  4  ORDER BY &COL2
  5
SQL> SAVE ex01
Created file ex01.sql
SQL> @ex01
Enter value for col1: FIRST_NAME
Enter value for col2: LAST_NAME
old   1: SELECT &COL1, &COL2
new   1: SELECT FIRST_NAME, LAST_NAME
Enter value for table: EMPLOYEES
old   2: FROM   &TABLE
new   2: FROM   EMPLOYEES
Enter value for col1: FIRST_NAME
Enter value for val: John
old   3: WHERE  &COL1 = '&VAL'
new   3: WHERE  FIRST_NAME = 'John'
Enter value for col2: LAST_NAME
old   4: ORDER BY &COL2
new   4: ORDER BY LAST_NAME

FIRST_NAME           LAST_NAME
-------------------- ---------
John                 Chen
John                 Russell
John                 Seo

3 rows selected.
SQL>
```

The user can enter different or wrong values for each prompt. To avoid multiple prompts, use && (double ampersand), where the variable is saved for the session.

To clear a defined variable, you can use the UNDEFINE command. Let's edit the ex01.sql file to make it look like this:

```
SELECT &&COL1, &&COL2
FROM   &TABLE
WHERE  &COL1 = '&VAL'
ORDER BY &COL2
/
Enter value for col1: first_name
Enter value for col2: last_name
old   1: SELECT &&COL1, &&COL2
new   1: SELECT first_name, last_name
Enter value for table: employees
old   2: FROM &TABLE
new   2: FROM employees
Enter value for val: John
old   3: WHERE &COL1 = '&VAL'
new   3: WHERE first_name = 'John'
old   4: ORDER BY &COL1
new   4: ORDER BY first_name

FIRST_NAME           LAST_NAME
-------------------- -------------------------
John                 Chen
John                 Russell
John                 Seo

UNDEFINE COL1 COL2
```

Using Positional Notation for Variables

Instead of variable names, you can use positional notation, where each variable is identified by &1, &2, and so on. The values are assigned to the variables by position. Do this by putting an ampersand (&), followed by a numeral, in place of a variable name. Consider the following query:

```
SQL> SELECT department_name, department_id
  2  FROM   departments
  3  WHERE  &1 = &2;
Enter value for 1: DEPARTMENT_ID
Enter value for 2: 10
old   3: WHERE  &1 = &2
new   3: WHERE  DEPARTMENT_ID = 10
```

```
DEPARTMENT_NAME                DEPARTMENT_ID
------------------------------ -------------
Administration                            10

1 row selected.
SQL>
```

If you save the SQL as a script file, you can submit the substitution-variable values while invoking the script (as command-line arguments). Each time you run this command file, `START` replaces each `&1` in the file with the first value (called an *argument*) after `START` ***`filename`***, then replaces each `&2` with the second value, and so forth. Here is an example of saving and running the previous query:

```
SQL> SAVE ex02
Created file ex02.sql
SQL> SET VERIFY OFF
SQL> @ex02 department_id 20

DEPARTMENT_NAME                DEPARTMENT_ID
------------------------------ -------------
Marketing                                 20

1 row selected.
SQL>
```

Although I did not specify two ampersands for positional substitution variables, SQL*Plus keeps the values of these variables for the session (since we passed the values as parameters to a script file). Next time you run any script with positional substitution variables, Oracle uses these values to execute the script.

Summary

This chapter started off with reviewing the fundamentals of SQL. You also saw an overview of SQL*Plus in this chapter. SQL*Plus is Oracle's native tool to interact with the database. You got a quick introduction to the Oracle datatypes, operators, and literals. You learned to write simple queries using the `SELECT` statement. You also learned to use the `WHERE` clause and the `ORDER BY` clause in this chapter.

The CHAR and VARCHAR2 datatypes are used to store alphanumeric information. The NUMBER datatype is used to store any numeric value. Date values can be stored using the DATE or TIMESTAMP datatypes. Oracle has a wide range of operators: arithmetic, concatenation, comparison, membership, logical, pattern matching, range, existence, and `NULL` checking. The `CASE` expression is used to bring conditional logic to SQL.

SQL*Plus supports all SQL statements and has its own formatting and enhancement commands. Using this tool, you can produce interactive SQL statements and formatted reports. SQL*Plus is the command-line interface to the database widely used by DBAs. SQL*Plus has its own buffer where SQL statements are buffered. You can edit the buffer using SQL*Plus editing commands. The DESCRIBE command is used to get information on a table, view, function, or procedure. Multiple SQL and SQL*Plus commands can be stored in a file and can be executed as a unit. Such files are called script files.

Data in the Oracle database is managed and accessed using SQL. A SELECT statement is the basic form of querying or reading records from the database table. You can limit or filter the rows using the WHERE clause. You can use the AND and OR logical operators to join multiple filter conditions. The ORDER BY clause is used to sort the result set in a particular order. You can use an ampersand (&) character to substitute a value at runtime.

Exam Essentials

Understand the operators. Know the various operators that can be used in queries. The parentheses around an expression change the precedence of the operators.

Understand the WHERE clause. The WHERE clause specifies a condition to limit the number or rows returned. You cannot use column alias names in this clause.

Understand the ORDER BY clause. The ORDER BY clause is used to sort the result set from a query. You can specify ascending order or descending order for the sort. Ascending order is the default. Also know that column alias names can be used in the ORDER BY clause. You can also specify columns by their position.

Know how to specify string literals using the Q/q operator. You can use the Q or q operator to specify the quote delimiters in string literals. Understand the difference between using the (, <, {, and [characters and other delimiters.

Know the order of clauses in the SELECT statement. The SELECT statement must have a FROM clause. The WHERE clause, if it exists, should follow the FROM clause and precede the ORDER BY clause.

Know the use of the DUAL table. The DUAL table is a dummy table in Oracle with one column and one row. This table is commonly used to get the values of system variables such as SYSDATE or USER.

Know the characters used for pattern matching. The % character is used to match zero or more characters. The _ character is used to match one, and only one, character. The SQL operator used with a pattern-matching character is LIKE.

Know the sort order of NULL values in queries with ORDER BY clause. By default, in an ascending-order sort, the NULL values appear at the bottom of the result set; that is, NULLs are sorted higher. For descending-order sorts, NULL values appear at the top of the result set—again, NULL values are sorted higher.

Review Questions

1. You issue the following query:

```
SELECT salary "Employee Salary"
FROM employees;
```

How will the column heading appear in the result?

A. EMPLOYEE SALARY

B. EMPLOYEE_SALARY

C. Employee Salary

D. employee_salary

2. The EMP table is defined as follows:

Column	Datatype	Length
EMPNO	NUMBER	4
ENAME	VARCHAR2	30
SALARY	NUMBER	14,2
COMM	NUMBER	10,2
DEPTNO	NUMBER	2

You perform the following two queries:

```
1. SELECT empno enumber,  ename
   FROM emp ORDER BY 1;
2. SELECT empno,  ename
   FROM emp ORDER BY  empno ASC;
```

Which of the following is true?

A. Statements 1 and 2 will produce the same result in data.

B. Statement 1 will execute; statement 2 will return an error.

C. Statement 2 will execute; statement 1 will return an error.

D. Statements 1 and 2 will execute but produce different results.

3. You issue the following SELECT statement on the EMP table shown in question 2.

```
SELECT (200+((salary*0.1)/2)) FROM emp;
```

What will happen to the result if all the parentheses are removed?

A. No difference, because the answer will always be NULL.

B. No difference, because the result will be the same.

C. The result will be higher.

D. The result will be lower.

4. In the following SELECT statement, which component is a literal? (Choose all that apply.)

```
SELECT 'Employee Name: ' || ename
FROM emp where deptno = 10;
```

A. 10

B. ename

C. Employee Name:

D. ||

5. When you try to save 34567.2255 into a column defined as NUMBER(7,2), what value is actually saved?

A. 34567.00

B. 34567.23

C. 34567.22

D. 3456.22

6. What is the default display length of the DATE datatype column?

A. 18

B. 9

C. 19

D. 6

7. What will happen if you query the EMP table shown in question 2 with the following?

```
SELECT empno, DISTINCT ename, salary FROM emp;
```

A. EMPNO, unique values of ENAME, and then SALARY are displayed.

B. EMPNO and unique values of the two columns, ENAME and SALARY, are displayed.

C. DISTINCT is not a valid keyword in SQL.

D. No values will be displayed because the statement will return an error.

8. Which clause in a query limits the rows selected?

A. ORDER BY

B. WHERE

C. SELECT

D. FROM

9. The following listing shows the records of the EMP table:

EMPNO	ENAME	SALARY	COMM	DEPTNO
7369	SMITH	800		20
7499	ALLEN	1600	300	30
7521	WARD	1250	500	30
7566	JONES	2975		20
7654	MARTIN	1250	1400	30
7698	BLAKE	2850		30
7782	CLARK	2450	24500	10
7788	SCOTT	3000		20
7839	KING	5000	50000	10
7844	TURNER	1500	0	30
7876	ADAMS	1100		20
7900	JAMES	950		30
7902	FORD	3000		20
7934	MILLER	1300	13000	10

When you issue the following query, which value will be displayed in the first row?

```
SELECT empno
FROM emp
WHERE deptno = 10
ORDER BY ename DESC;
```

A. MILLER

B. 7934

C. 7876

D. No rows will be returned because ename cannot be used in the ORDER BY clause.

10. Refer to the listing of records in the EMP table in question 9. How many rows will the following query return?

```
SELECT * FROM emp WHERE ename BETWEEN 'A' AND 'C'
```

A. 4

B. 2

C. A character column cannot be used in the BETWEEN operator.

D. 3

11. Refer to the EMP table in question 2. When you issue the following query, which line has an error?

```
1. SELECT empno "Enumber", ename "EmpName"
2. FROM emp
3. WHERE deptno = 10
4. AND  "Enumber" = 7782
5. ORDER BY "Enumber";
```

A. 1

B. 5

C. 4

D. No error; the statement will finish successfully.

12. You issue the following query:

```
SELECT empno, ename
FROM emp
WHERE empno = 7782 OR empno = 7876;
```

Which other operator can replace the OR condition in the WHERE clause?

A. IN

B. BETWEEN .. AND ..

C. LIKE

D. <=

E. >=

13. The following are clauses of the SELECT statement:

```
1. WHERE
2. FROM
3. ORDER BY
```

In which order should they appear in a query?

A. 1, 3, 2

B. 2, 1, 3

C. 2, 3, 1

D. The order of these clauses does not matter.

14. Which statement searches for PRODUCT_ID values that begin with DI_ from the ORDERS table?

A.
```
SELECT * FROM ORDERS
WHERE PRODUCT_ID = 'DI%';
```

B.
```
SELECT * FROM ORDERS
WHERE PRODUCT_ID LIKE 'DI_' ESCAPE '\';
```

C.
```
SELECT * FROM ORDERS
WHERE PRODUCT_ID LIKE 'DI\_%' ESCAPE '\';
```

D.
```
SELECT * FROM ORDERS
WHERE PRODUCT_ID LIKE 'DI\_' ESCAPE '\';
```

E.
```
SELECT * FROM ORDERS
WHERE PRODUCT_ID LIKE 'DI_%' ESCAPE '\';
```

15. COUNTRY_NAME and REGION_ID are valid column names in the COUNTRIES table. Which one of the following statements will execute without an error?

A.
```
SELECT country_name, region_id,
CASE region_id = 1 THEN 'Europe',
     region_id = 2 THEN 'America',
     region_id = 3 THEN 'Asia',
     ELSE 'Other' END Continent
FROM   countries;
```

B.
```
SELECT country_name, region_id,
CASE (region_id WHEN 1 THEN 'Europe',
                WHEN 2 THEN 'America',
                WHEN 3 THEN 'Asia',
                ELSE 'Other') Continent
FROM   countries;
```

C.
```
SELECT country_name, region_id,
CASE region_id WHEN 1 THEN 'Europe'
               WHEN 2 THEN 'America'
               WHEN 3 THEN 'Asia'
               ELSE 'Other' END Continent
FROM   countries;
```

D.
```
SELECT country_name, region_id,
CASE region_id WHEN 1 THEN 'Europe'
               WHEN 2 THEN 'America'
               WHEN 3 THEN 'Asia'
               ELSE 'Other' Continent
FROM   countries;
```

16. Which special character is used to query all the columns from the table without listing each column by name?

A. %

B. &

C. @

D. *

17. The EMPLOYEE table has the following data:

```
EMP_NAME   HIRE_DATE       SALARY
---------- --------- ----------
SMITH      17-DEC-90        800
ALLEN      20-FEB-91       1600
WARD       22-FEB-91       1250
JONES      02-APR-91       5975
WARDEN     28-SEP-91       1250
BLAKE      01-MAY-91       2850
```

What will be the value in the first row of the result set when the following query is executed?

```
SELECT hire_date FROM employee
ORDER BY salary, emp_name;
```

A. 02-APR-91

B. 17-DEC-90

C. 28-SEP-91

D. The query is invalid, because you cannot have a column in the ORDER BY clause that is not part of the SELECT clause.

18. Which SQL statement will query the EMPLOYEES table for FIRST_NAME, LAST_NAME, and SALARY of all employees in DEPARTMENT_ID 40 in the alphabetical order of last name?

A.
```
SELECT first_name last_name salary
FROM   employees
ORDER BY last_name
WHERE  department_id = 40;
```

B.
```
SELECT first_name, last_name, salary
FROM   employees
ORDER BY last_name ASC
WHERE  department_id = 40;
```

C.
```
SELECT first_name last_name salary
FROM  employees
WHERE  department_id = 40
ORDER BY last_name ASC;
```

D.
```
SELECT first_name, last_name, salary
FROM   employees
WHERE  department_id = 40
ORDER BY last_name;
```

E.
```
SELECT first_name, last_name, salary
FROM   TABLE employees
WHERE  department_id IS 40
ORDER BY last_name ASC;
```

19. When doing pattern matching using the LIKE operator, which character is used as the default escape character by Oracle?

A. |

B. /

C. \

D. There is no default escape character in Oracle.

20. Column alias names cannot be used in which clause?

A. SELECT clause

B. WHERE clause

C. ORDER BY clause

D. None of the above

21. What is wrong with the following statements submitted in SQL*Plus?

```
DEFINE V_DEPTNO = 20
SELECT LAST_NAME, SALARY
FROM    EMPLOYEES
WHERE DEPARTMENT_ID = V_DeptNo;
```

A. Nothing is wrong. The query lists the employee name and salary of the employees who belong to department 20.

B. The DEFINE statement declaration is wrong.

C. The substitution variable is not preceded with the & character.

D. The substitution variable in the WHERE clause should be V_DEPTNO instead of V_DeptNo.

22. Which two statements regarding substitution variables are true?

A. &*variable* is defined by SQL*Plus, and its value will be available for the duration of the session.

B. &&*variable* is defined by SQL*Plus, and its value will be available for the duration of the session.

C. &*n* (where *n* is a any integer) variables are defined by SQL*Plus when values are passed in as arguments to the script, and their values will be available for the duration of the session.

D. &&*variable* is defined by SQL*Plus, and its value will be available only for every reference to that variable in the current SQL.

23. Look at the data in table PRODUCTS. Which SQL will list the items on the BL shelves? (Show the result with the most available quantity at the top row.)

```
PRODUCT_ID PRODUCT_NAME         SHELF  AVAILABLE_QTY
---------- -------------------- ------ -------------
      1001 CREST                BL36             354
      1002 COLGATE              BL36              54
      1003 AQUAFRESH            BL37              43
      2002 SUNNY-D              LA21              53
      2003 CAPRISUN             LA22              45
```

A.
```
SELECT * FROM products
WHERE shelf like '%BL'
ORDER BY available_qty SORT DESC;
```

B.
```
SELECT * FROM products
WHERE shelf like 'BL%';
```

C.
```
SELECT * FROM products
WHERE shelf = 'BL%'
ORDER BY available_qty DESC;
```

D.
```
SELECT * FROM products
WHERE shelf like 'BL%'
ORDER BY available_qty DESC;
```

E.
```
SELECT * FROM products
WHERE shelf like 'BL%'
ORDER BY available_qty SORT;
```

24. The EMP table has the following data:

```
     EMPNO ENAME             SAL       COMM
---------- ---------- ---------- ----------
      7369 SMITH             800
      7499 ALLEN            1600        300
      7521 WARD             1250        500
      7566 JONES            2975
      7654 MARTIN           1250       1400
      7698 BLAKE            2850
      7782 CLARK            2450
      7788 SCOTT            3000
      7839 KING             5000
      7844 TURNER           1500          0
      7876 ADAMS            1100
      7900 JAMES             950
      7902 FORD             3000
      7934 MILLER           1300
```

Consider the following two SQL statements:

```
1. SELECT empno, ename, sal, comm
   FROM emp WHERE comm IN (0, NULL);
2. SELECT empno, ename, sal, comm
   FROM emp WHERE comm = 0 OR comm IS NULL;
```

A. 1 and 2 will produce the same result.

B. 1 will error; 2 will work fine.

C. 1 and 2 will produce different results.

D. 1 and 2 will work but will not return any rows.

Answers to Review Questions

1. C. Column alias names enclosed in quotation marks will appear as typed. Spaces and mixed case appear in the column alias name only when the alias is enclosed in double quotation marks.

2. A. Statements 1 and 2 will produce the same result. You can use the column name, column alias, or column position in the ORDER BY clause. The default sort order is ascending. For a descending sort, you must explicitly specify that order with the DESC keyword.

3. B. In the arithmetic evaluation, multiplication and division have precedence over addition and subtraction. Even if you do not include the parentheses, salary*0.1 will be evaluated first. The result is then divided by 2, and its result is added to 200.

4. A, C. Character literals in the SQL statement are enclosed in single quotation marks. Literals are concatenated using ||. Employee Name: is a character literal, and 10 is a numeric literal.

5. B. Since the numeric column is defined with precision 7 and scale 2, you can have five digits in the integer part and two digits after the decimal point. The digits after the decimal are rounded.

6. B. The default display format of DATE column is DD-MON-YY, whose length is 9.

7. D. DISTINCT is used to display a unique result row, and it should follow immediately after the keyword SELECT. Uniqueness is identified across the row, not a single column.

8. B. The WHERE clause is used to limit the rows returned from a query. The WHERE clause condition is evaluated, and rows are returned only if the result is TRUE. The ORDER BY clause is used to display the result in certain order.

9. B. There are three records belonging to DEPTNO 10: EMPNO 7934 (MILLER), 7839 (KING), and 7782 (CLARK). When you sort their names by descending order, MILLER is the first row to display. You can use alias names and columns that are not in the SELECT clause in the ORDER BY clause.

10. D. Here, a character column is compared against a string using the BETWEEN operator, which is equivalent to ename >= 'A' AND ename <= 'C'. The name CLARK will not be included in this query, because 'CLARK' is > 'C'.

11. C. Column alias names cannot be used in the WHERE clause. They can be used in the ORDER BY clause.

12. A. The IN operator can be used. You can write the WHERE clause as WHERE empno IN (7782, 7876);.

13. B. The FROM clause appears after the SELECT statement, followed by WHERE and ORDER BY clauses. The FROM clause specifies the table names, the WHERE clause limits the result set, and the ORDER BY clause sorts the result.

14. C. Since _ is a special pattern-matching character, you need to include the ESCAPE clause in LIKE. The % character matches any number of characters including 0, and _ matches a single character.

15. C. A CASE expression begins with the keyword CASE and ends with the keyword END.

16. D. An asterisk (*) is used to denote all columns in a table.

17. B. The default sorting order for a numeric column is ascending. The columns are sorted first by salary and then by name, so the row with the lowest salary is displayed first. It is perfectly valid to use a column in the ORDER BY clause that is not part of the SELECT clause.

18. D. In the SELECT clause, the column names should be separated by commas. An alias name may be provided for each column with a space or using the keyword AS. The FROM clause should appear after the SELECT clause. The WHERE clause appears after the FROM clause. The ORDER BY clause comes after the WHERE clause.

19. D. There is no default escape character in Oracle for pattern matching. If your search includes pattern-matching characters such as _ or %, define an escape character using the ESCAPE keyword in the LIKE operator.

20. B. Column alias names cannot be used in the WHERE clause of the SQL statement. In the ORDER BY clause, you can use the column name or alias name, or you can indicate the column by its position in the SELECT clause.

21. C. The query will return an error, because the substitution variable is used without an ampersand (&) character. In this query, Oracle treats V_DEPTNO as another column name from the table and returns an error. Substitution variables are not case sensitive.

22. B, C. When a variable is preceded by double ampersands, SQL*Plus defines that variable. Similarly, when you pass values to a script using START *script_name arguments*, SQL*Plus defines those variables. Once a variable is defined, its value will be available for the duration of the session or until you use UNDEFINE *variable*.

23. D. % is the wild character to pattern-match for any number of characters. Option A is almost correct, except for the SORT keyword in the ORDER BY clause, which will produce an error since it is not a valid syntax. Option B will produce results but will sort them in the order you want. Option C will not return any rows because LIKE is the operator for pattern matching, not =. Option E has an error similar to Option A.

24. C. In the first SQL, the comm IN (0, NULL) will be treated as comm = 0 OR comm = NULL. For all NULL comparisons, you should use IS NULL instead of = NULL. The first SQL will return only one row where comm = 0, whereas the second SQL will return all the rows that have comm = NULL as well as comm = 0.

Using Single-Row Functions

ORACLE DATABASE 11*g*: SQL FUNDAMENTALS I EXAM OBJECTIVES COVERED IN THIS CHAPTER:

✓ **Using Single-Row Functions to Customize Output**

- Describe various types of functions available in SQL
- Use character, number, and date functions in SELECT statements

✓ **Using Conversion Functions and Conditional Expressions**

- Describe various types of conversion functions that are available in SQL
- Use the TO_CHAR, TO_NUMBER, and TO_DATE conversion functions
- Apply conditional expressions in a SELECT statement

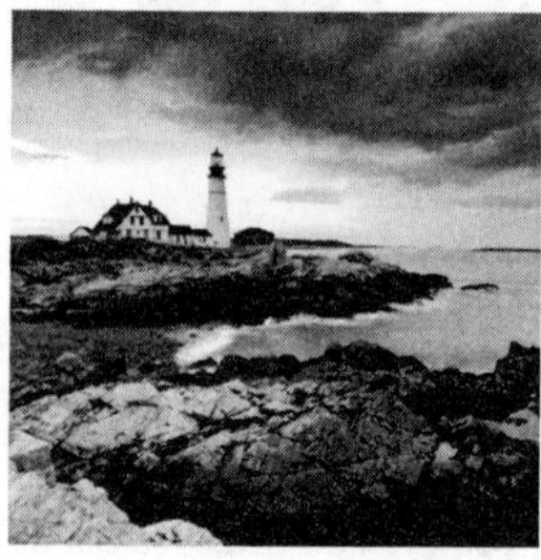

Functions are programs that take zero or more arguments and return a single value. Oracle has built a number of functions into SQL, and these functions can be called from SQL statements. The functions could be classified into many groups:

- Single-row functions
- Aggregate functions (also known as *group functions*)
- Analytical functions and regular expression functions
- National-language functions
- Object-reference functions
- Programmer-defined functions

The certification exam focuses on single-row and aggregate functions, so only those types are covered in this book. Single-row functions are covered in this chapter, and aggregate functions are covered in Chapter 3, "Using Group Functions."

Single-row functions operate on expressions derived from columns or literals, and they are executed once for each row retrieved. In this chapter, I will cover which single-row functions are available, the rules for how to use them, and what to expect on the exam regarding single-row functions.

Single-row functions also include conversion functions. Conversion functions are used to convert the datatype of the input value to a different datatype. The Oracle database has conditional expressions and functions. I discussed the conditional expression CASE in Chapter 1, "Introducing SQL." In this chapter, I will discuss the conditional function DECODE.

Single-Row Function Fundamentals

Many types of single-row functions are built into SQL. These include character, numeric, date, conversion, and miscellaneous single-row functions, as well as programmer-written stored functions.

All single-row functions can be incorporated into SQL (and PL/SQL). You can use these single-row functions in the SELECT, WHERE, and ORDER BY clauses of SELECT statements. For example, the following query includes the TO_CHAR, UPPER, and SOUNDEX single-row functions:

```
SELECT first_name, TO_CHAR(hire_date,'Day, DD-Mon-YYYY')
FROM employees
```

```
WHERE UPPER(first_name) LIKE 'AL%'
ORDER BY SOUNDEX(first_name);
```

Single-row functions also can appear in other types of statements, such as the SET clause of an UPDATE statement, the VALUES clause of an INSERT statement, and the WHERE clause of a DELETE statement. The certification exam tends to focus on using functions in SELECT statements, so I will use examples of SELECT statements in this chapter.

The built-in functions presented in this chapter are grouped by topic (character functions, date functions, and so on), and within each topic they appear in alphabetical order. Before I get into the different types of functions, I'll start with the functions that are used to handle NULL values.

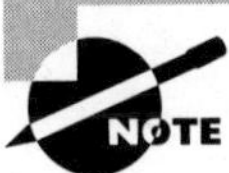

Functions can be nested so that the output from one function is used as input to another. Nested functions can include single-row functions nested within group functions or group functions nested within either single-row functions or other group functions.

Functions for NULL Handling

One area in which beginners frequently have difficulty and where even veterans sometimes stumble is the treatment of NULLs. You can expect at least one question on the exam to address the use of NULLs, but it probably won't look like a question on the use of NULLs.

NULL values represent unknown data or a lack of data. Any operation on a NULL results in a NULL. This NULL-in/NULL-out model is followed for most functions, as well. Oracle 11*g* has five NULL-handling functions; I'll give special attention to the NVL, NVL2, and COALESCE functions because these are commonly used.

NVL

The NVL function is used to replace a NULL value with a literal value. NVL takes two arguments, NVL(*x1*, *x2*), where *x1* and *x2* are expressions. The NVL function returns *x2* if *x1* is NULL. If *x1* is not NULL, then *x1* is returned. The arguments x1 and x2 can be of any datatype. If *x1* and *x2* are not of the same datatype, Oracle tries to convert them to the same datatype before performing the comparison.

For example, suppose you need to calculate the total compensation in the EMPLOYEES table, which contains SALARY and COMMISSION_PCT columns:

```
SELECT first_name, salary, commission_pct,
       salary + (salary * commission_pct) compensation
FROM employees
WHERE first_name LIKE 'T%';
```

```
FIRST_NAME               SALARY COMMISSION_PCT COMPENSATION
-------------------- ---------- -------------- ------------
TJ                         2100
Trenna                     3500
Taylor                     9600             .2        11520
Timothy                    2900
```

You see that only Taylor had the total compensation calculated in the SQL; all others have their total compensation as NULL. This is because any operation on NULL results in a NULL.

You can use the NVL function to substitute a zero in place of any NULL you encounter, like this:

```
SELECT first_name, salary, commission_pct,
       salary + (salary * NVL(commission_pct,0)) compensation
FROM employees
WHERE first_name LIKE 'T%';
```

```
FIRST_NAME               SALARY COMMISSION_PCT COMPENSATION
-------------------- ---------- -------------- ------------
TJ                         2100                        2100
Trenna                     3500                        3500
Tayler                     9600             .2        11520
Timothy                    2900                        2900
```

When you used the NVL function to substitute zero for NULL, you got the total compensation calculated correctly. For the employees who do not have a commission, the salary and compensation are the same.

NVL2

The function NVL2 is a variation of NVL. NVL2 takes three arguments, NVL2(*x1, x2, x3*), where *x1*, *x2*, and *x3* are expressions. NVL2 returns *x3* if *x1* is NULL, and *x2* if *x1* is not NULL.

For the example presented in the previous section, you could also use the NVL2 function and write the code a bit differently:

```
SELECT first_name, salary, commission_pct, NVL2(commission_pct,
       salary + salary * commission_pct, salary) compensation
FROM employees
WHERE first_name LIKE 'T%';
```

```
FIRST_NAME               SALARY COMMISSION_PCT COMPENSATION
-------------------- ---------- -------------- ------------
TJ                         2100                        2100
Trenna                     3500                        3500
Tayler                     9600             .2        11520
Timothy                    2900                        2900
```

Using the NVL2 function, if COMMISSION_PCT is not NULL, then salary + salary * commission_pct is returned. If COMMISSION_PCT is NULL, then just SALARY is returned.

The NVL function allows you to perform some value substitution for NULLs. The NVL2 function, on the other hand, allows you to implement an IF...THEN...ELSE construct based on the nullity of data. Both are useful tools to deal with NULL values.

Be prepared for a possible exam question that tests your knowledge of when to use an NVL function in a calculation. Such a question probably won't mention NVL and may not look like it is testing your knowledge of NULLs. If sample data is given as an exhibit, be sure to look for data columns with NULL values and whether they are used in the SQL presented to you.

COALESCE

COALESCE is a generalization of the NVL function. COALESCE(*exp_list*) takes more than one argument, where *exp_list* is a list of arguments separated by comma. This function returns the first non-NULL value in *exp_list*. If all expressions in *exp_list* are NULL, then NULL is returned. Each expression in *exp_list* should be the same datatype, or else Oracle tries to convert them implicitly.

For example, COALESCE(x1, x2, x3) would be evaluated as the following:

- If x1 is NULL, check x2, or else return x1. Stop.
- If x2 is NULL, check x3, or else return x2. Stop.
- If x3 is NULL, return NULL, or else return x3. Stop.

Consider the following example. The objective is to find the total salary based on COMMISSION_PCT. If COMMISSION_PCT is not NULL, calculate SALARY using COMMISSION_PCT. If COMMISSION_PCT is NULL, then give $100 as commission. If SALARY is not defined (NULL) for an employee, give the minimum salary of $900.

```
SELECT last_name, salary, commission_pct AS comm,
       COALESCE(salary+salary*commission_pct,
                salary+100, 900) compensation
FROM employees
WHERE last_name like 'T%';

LAST_NAME                     SALARY       COMM COMPENSATION
------------------------- ---------- ---------- ------------
Taylor                          8600         .2        10320
Taylor                          3200                    3300
Tobias                                                   900
Tucker                         10000         .3        13000
Tuvault                         7000        .15         8050
```

As you can see in the example, using the COALESCE function helps you avoid writing several IF…THEN conditions. You could write the same SQL using the CASE statement you learned about in Chapter 1 as follows:

```
SELECT last_name, salary, commission_pct AS comm,
       (CASE WHEN salary IS NULL THEN 900
         WHEN commission_pct IS NOT NULL
             THEN salary+salary*commission_pct
         WHEN commission_pct IS NULL THEN salary+100
         ELSE 0 END) AS compensation
 FROM employees
 WHERE last_name like 'T%';

LAST_NAME                     SALARY       COMM COMPENSATION
------------------------- ---------- ---------- ------------
Taylor                          8600         .2        10320
Taylor                          3200                    3300
Tobias                                                   900
Tucker                         10000         .3        13000
Tuvault                         7000        .15         8050
```

Try using WHEN salary IS NULL as the third condition in the CASE statement (instead of the first condition), and find out whether you see any difference in the result.

Using Single-Row Character Functions

Single-row character functions operate on character data. Most have one or more character arguments, and most return character values. Character functions take the character input value and return a character or numeric value. If the input to the function is a literal, be sure to enclose it in single quotes. The exam focuses on many commonly used character functions such as SUBSTR, INSTR, and LENGTH. When reading about these functions, pay particular attention to the commonly used functions. Even experienced programmers get confused with the REPLACE and TRANSLATE functions. In the following sections, I will review the single-row character functions in detail.

Character Function Overview

Table 2.1 summarizes the single-row character functions. I will cover each of these functions in the "Character Function Descriptions" section.

TABLE 2.1 Character Function Summary

Function	Description
ASCII	Returns the ASCII decimal equivalent of a character
CHR	Returns the character given the decimal equivalent
CONCAT	Concatenates two strings; same as the operator ||
INITCAP	Returns the string with the first letter of each word in uppercase
INSTR	Finds the numeric starting position of a string within a string
INSTRB	Same as INSTR but counts bytes instead of characters
LENGTH	Returns the length of a string in characters
LENGTHB	Returns the length of a string in bytes
LOWER	Converts a string to all lowercase
LPAD	Left-fills a string to a set length using a specified character
LTRIM	Strips leading characters from a string
REPLACE	Performs substring search and replace
RPAD	Right-fills a string to a set length using a specified character
RTRIM	Strips trailing characters from a string
SOUNDEX	Returns a phonetic representation of a string
SUBSTR	Returns a section of the specified string, specified by numeric character positions
SUBSTRB	Returns a section of the specified string, specified by numeric byte positions
TRANSLATE	Performs character search and replace
TRIM	Strips leading, trailing, or both leading and trailing characters from a string
UPPER	Converts a string to all uppercase

The functions ASCII, INSTR, LENGTH, and REGEXP_INSTR return number values, though they take character datatype as the input.

Character Function Descriptions

Over the years, Oracle has added several functions to its library to make the lives of developers easy so that they do not have to write built-in functions. Oracle has a function for most of the day-to-day programming needs. Before you write your own custom-developed piece of code, it is always a good idea to scan the Oracle documentation on built-in functions.

The character functions in the following sections are arranged in alphabetical order, with descriptions and examples of each one.

ASCII

ASCII(*c1*) takes a single argument, where *c1* is a character string. This function returns the ASCII decimal equivalent of the first character in *c1*. See also CHR() for the inverse operation.

```
SELECT ASCII('A') Big_A, ASCII('z') Little_Z, ASCII('AMER')
FROM dual;

     BIG_A   LITTLE_Z ASCII('AMER')
---------- ---------- -------------
        65        122            65
```

CHR

CHR(*i* [USING NCHAR_CS]) takes a single argument, where *i* is an integer. This function returns the character equivalent of the decimal (binary) representation of the character. If the optional USING NCHAR_CS is included, the character from the national character set is returned. The default behavior is to return the character from the database character set.

```
SELECT CHR(65), CHR(122), CHR(223)
FROM dual;

CHAR65 CHAR122 CHAR233
------ ------- -------
A      z       ß
```

CONCAT

CONCAT(*c1*, *c2*) takes two arguments, where *c1* and *c2* are both character strings. This function returns *c2* appended to *c1*. If *c1* is NULL, then *c2* is returned. If *c2* is NULL, then *c1* is returned. If both *c1* and *c2* are NULL, then NULL is returned. CONCAT returns the same results as using the concatenation operator: *c1||c2*. In the following example, notice the use of the nested function—a function inside a function—as an argument:

```
SELECT CONCAT(CONCAT(first_name, ' '), last_name) employee_name,
       first_name || ' ' || last_name AS alternate_method
FROM employees
WHERE department_id = 30;

EMPLOYEE_NAME             ALTERNATE_METHOD
------------------------- ------------------
Den Raphaely              Den Raphaely
Alexander Khoo            Alexander Khoo
Shelli Baida              Shelli Baida
Sigal Tobias              Sigal Tobias
Guy Himuro                Guy Himuro
Karen Colmenares          Karen Colmenares
```

INITCAP

INITCAP(*c1*) takes a single argument, where *c1* is a character string. This function returns *c1* with the first character of each word in uppercase and all others in lowercase. Words are delimited by white space or characters that are not alphanumeric.

```
SELECT data_value, INITCAP(data_value) initcap_example
FROM sample_data;

DATA_VALUE           INITCAP_EXAMPLE
-------------------- --------------------
THE three muskETeers The Three Musketeers
ali and*41*thieves   Ali And*41*Thieves
mississippi          Mississippi
mister INDIA         Mister India
```

INSTR

INSTR(*c1*,*c2*[,*i*[,*j*]]) takes four arguments, where *c1* and *c2* are character strings and *i* and *j* are integers. This function returns the numeric character position in *c1* where the *j* occurrence of *c2* is found. The search begins at the *i* character position in *c1*. INSTR returns a 0 when the requested string is not found. If *i* is negative, the search is performed backward, from right to left, but the position is still counted from left to right. Both *i* and *j* default to 1, and *j* cannot be negative.

The following example finds the first occurrence of i in the string starting from the fourth position of the string:

```
SELECT data_value, INSTR(data_value,'i',4,1) instr_example
FROM sample_data;

DATA_VALUE           INSTR_EXAMPLE Comment
-------------------- ------------- ------------------------------------------
THE three muskETeers             0 There is no "i" in the data value; so "0"
ali and*41*thieves              14 The first "i" is skipped, since we start
                                   at the 4th position. So the "i" in the 14th
                                   position is picked
mississippi                      5 the first i in 2nd position is skipped
mister INDIA                     0 INDIA has an "I" (upper case); so no
                                   match for "i"
```

Here is another example using a negative argument for the beginning character position. The search for the is string will start at the fourth position from the end and move to the left.

```
SELECT data_value, INSTR(data_value,'is',-4,1) instr_example
FROM sample_data;

DATA_VALUE           INSTR_EXAMPLE
-------------------- -------------
THE three muskETeers             0
ali and*41*thieves               0
mississippi                      5
mister INDIA                     2
```

INSTRB

INSTRB(*c1*,*c2*[,*i*[,*j*]]) is the same as INSTR(), except it returns bytes instead of characters. For single-byte character sets, INSTRB() is equivalent to INSTR().

LENGTH

LENGTH(*c*) takes a single argument, where *c* is a character string. This function returns the numeric length in characters of *c*. If *c* is NULL, a NULL is returned.

```
SELECT data_value, LENGTH(data_value) length_example
FROM sample_data;
```

```
DATA_VALUE           LENGTH_EXAMPLE
-------------------- --------------
THE three muskETeers             20
ali and*41*thieves               18
mississippi                      11
mister INDIA                     12
```

LENGTHB

LENGTHB(*c*) is the same as LENGTH(), except it returns bytes instead of characters. For single-byte character sets, LENGTHB() is equivalent to LENGTH().

LOWER

LOWER(*c*) takes a single argument, where *c* is a character string. This function returns the character string *c* with all characters in lowercase. See also UPPER for the inverse operation.

```
SELECT data_value, LOWER(data_value) lower_example
FROM sample_data;

DATA_VALUE           LOWER_EXAMPLE
-------------------- --------------------
THE three muskETeers the three musketeers
ali and*41*thieves   ali and*41*thieves
mississippi          mississippi
mister INDIA         mister india
```

LPAD

LPAD(*c1*, *i* [,*c2*]) takes three arguments, where *c1* and *c2* are character strings and *i* is an integer. This function returns the character string *c1* expanded in length to *i* characters, using *c2* to fill in space as needed on the left side of *c1*. If *c1* is more than *i* characters, it is truncated to *i* characters. *c2* defaults to a single space. See also RPAD.

The following example adds * to the SALARY column toward the left side. Since it does not specify a fill-in character when LPAD is applied to last_name, Oracle uses the default space as the fill-in character.

```
SELECT LPAD(last_name,10) lpad_lname,
       LPAD(salary,8,'*') lpad_salary
FROM employees
WHERE last_name like 'J%';
```

```
LPAD_LNAME LPAD_SAL
---------- --------
   Johnson ****6200
     Jones ****2800
```

LTRIM

LTRIM(*c1* [,*c2*]) takes two arguments, where *c1* and *c2* are character strings. This function returns *c1* without any leading characters that appear in *c2*. If no *c2* characters are leading characters in *c1*, then *c1* is returned unchanged. *c2* defaults to a single space. See also RTRIM and TRIM.

```
SELECT LTRIM('Mississippi','Mis') test1
      ,LTRIM('Rpadded          ') test2
      ,LTRIM('          Lpadded') test3
      ,LTRIM('     Lpadded', 'Z') test4
FROM dual;

TES TEST2             TEST3   TEST4
--- ----------------- ------- ------------
ppi Rpadded           Lpadded      Lpadded
```

In the previous example, all occurrences of the trimmed characters M, i, and s are trimmed from the input string Mississippi, beginning on the left (with M) and continuing until the first character that is not an M, i, or s is encountered. Note that the trailing i is not trimmed; only the leading characters are removed. In TEST4, there is no occurrence of Z, so the input string is returned unchanged.

REPLACE

REPLACE(*c1*, *c2* [,*c3*]) takes three arguments, where *c1*, *c2*, and *c3* are character strings. This function returns *c1* with all occurrences of *c2* replaced with *c3*. *c3* defaults to NULL. If *c3* is NULL, all occurrences of *c2* are removed. If *c2* is NULL, then *c1* is returned unchanged. If *c1* is NULL, then NULL is returned.

```
SELECT REPLACE('uptown','up','down') FROM dual;

REPLACE(
--------
downtown
```

This function can come in handy when you need to do some dynamic substitutions. For example, suppose you have a number of indexes that were created in the _DATA tablespace instead of in the _INDX tablespace:

```
SELECT index_name, tablespace_name
FROM user_indexes
WHERE tablespace_name like '%DATA%';

INDEX_NAME       TABLESPACE_NAME
---------------- ----------------
PK_DEPT          HR_DATA
PK_PO_MASTER     PO_DATA
```

You can generate the Data Definition Language (DDL) to rebuild these misplaced indexes in the correct location. In this scenario, you know your tablespace naming convention has an INDX tablespace for every DATA tablespace. You use the REPLACE function to generate the new tablespace name, replacing DATA with INDX. So, the HR index is rebuilt in the HR_INDX tablespace, and the PO index is rebuilt in the PO_INDX tablespace.

```
SELECT 'ALTER INDEX '||index_name||
                    ' rebuild tablespace '||
REPLACE(tablespace_name, 'DATA', 'INDX')|| '; ' DDL
FROM user_indexes
WHERE tablespace_name LIKE '%DATA%';

DDL
---------------------------------------------------
ALTER INDEX PK_DEPT rebuild tablespace HR_INDX;
ALTER INDEX PK_PO_MASTER rebuild tablespace PO_INDX;
```

RPAD

RPAD(*c1*, *i* [, *c2*]) takes three arguments, where *c1* and *c2* are character strings and *i* is an integer. This function returns the character string *c1* expanded in length to *i* characters, using *c2* to fill in space as needed on the right side of *c1*. If *c1* is more than *i* characters, it is truncated to *i* characters. *c2* defaults to a single space. See also LPAD.

```
SELECT RPAD(first_name,15,'.') rpad_fname, lpad(job_id,12,'.') lpad_jid
FROM employees
WHERE first_name like 'B%';

RPAD_FNAME      LPAD_JID
--------------- ------------
Bruce.......... .....IT_PROG
Britney........ ....SH_CLERK
```

RTRIM

RTRIM(*c1* [,*c2*]) takes two arguments, where *c1* and *c2* are character strings. This function returns *c1* without any trailing characters that appear in *c2*. If no *c2* characters are trailing characters in *c1*, then *c1* is returned unchanged. *c2* defaults to a single space. See also LTRIM and TRIM.

```
SELECT RTRIM('Mississippi','ip') test1
      ,RTRIM('Rpadded          ') test2
      ,RTRIM('Rpadded     ', 'Z') test3
      ,RTRIM('          Lpadded') test4
FROM dual;

TEST1   TEST2   TEST3       TEST4
------- ------- ----------- ----------------
Mississ Rpadded Rpadded              Lpadded
```

SOUNDEX

SOUNDEX(*c1*) takes a single argument, where *c1* is a character string. This function returns the Soundex phonetic representation of *c1*. The SOUNDEX function is usually used to locate names that sound alike. The example returns the records with first names that sound like "Stevan."

```
SELECT first_name, last_name
FROM employees
WHERE SOUNDEX(first_name) = SOUNDEX('Stevan');

FIRST_NAME           LAST_NAME
-------------------- -------------------------
Steven               King
Steven               Markle
Stephen              Stiles
```

SUBSTR

SUBSTR(*c1*, *x* [, *y*]) takes three arguments, where *c1* is a character string and both *x* and *y* are integers. This function returns the portion of *c1* that is *y* characters long, beginning at position *x*. If *x* is negative, the position is counted backward (that is, right to left). This function returns NULL if *y* is 0 or negative. *y* defaults to the remainder of string *c1*.

```
SELECT SUBSTR('The Three Musketeers',1,3) Part1
      ,SUBSTR('The Three Musketeers',5,5) Part2
```

```
       ,SUBSTR('The Three Musketeers',11)  Part3
       ,SUBSTR('The Three Musketeers',-5)  Part4
FROM dual;

PAR PART2 PART3      PART4
--- ----- ---------- -----
The Three Musketeers teers
```

Real World Scenario

Parsing the Filename from the Whole Path

Let's look at a real example from the life of a DBA. Suppose you want to extract only the filename from dba_data_files without the path name; you could use the following SQL. Here the INSTR function is nested inside a SUBSTR function. Single-row functions can be nested to any level. When functions are nested, the innermost function is evaluated first. The INSTR function is used to find the character position where the last \ appears in the filename string (looking for the first occurrence from the end). This position is passed into the SUBSTR function as the start position.

```
SELECT file_name,
       SUBSTR(file_name, INSTR(file_name,'\', -1,1)+1) name
FROM dba_data_files;

FILE_NAME                                NAME
---------------------------------------- -------------
C:\ORACLE\ORADATA\W11GR1\USERS01.DBF     USERS01.DBF
C:\ORACLE\ORADATA\W11GR1\UNDOTBS01.DBF   UNDOTBS01.DBF
C:\ORACLE\ORADATA\W11GR1\SYSAUX01.DBF    SYSAUX01.DBF
C:\ORACLE\ORADATA\W11GR1\SYSTEM01.DBF    SYSTEM01.DBF
C:\ORACLE\ORADATA\W11GR1\EXAMPLE01.DBF   EXAMPLE01.DBF
```

To perform the same operation on Unix or Linux databases, replace \ in the INSTR function with / because / is used on Linux/Unix to separate directories.

Let's review another example using the Linux or Unix platform. Suppose you want to find out all the file systems (mount points) used by your database; you could use the following SQL:

```
SELECT DISTINCT
       SUBSTR(file_name, 1, INSTR(file_name,'/', 1,2)-1) fs_name
FROM dba_data_files;
```

```
FS_NAME
----------------------------
/u01
/u05
/ora_temp
/ora_undo
```

In this example, you started looking for the second occurrence of / using the INSTR function and used SUBSTR to extract only the characters from 1 through the location before the second occurrence of / in the filename (hence the –1).

SUBSTRB

SUBSTRB(*c1*, *i*[, *j*]) takes three arguments, where *c1* is a character string and both *i* and *j* are integers. This function is the same as SUBSTR, except *i* and *j* are counted in bytes instead of characters. For single-byte character sets, they are equivalent.

TRANSLATE

TRANSLATE(*c1*, *c2* ,*c3*) takes three arguments, where *c1*, *c2*, and *c3* are character strings. This function returns *c1* with all occurrences of characters in *c2* replaced with the positionally corresponding characters in *c3*. A NULL is returned if any of *c1*, *c2*, or *c3* is NULL. If *c3* has fewer characters than *c2*, the unmatched characters in *c2* are removed from *c1*. If *c2* has fewer characters than *c3*, the unmatched characters in *c3* are ignored. TRANSLATE is similar to the REPLACE function. REPLACE substitutes a single string from another string, whereas TRANSLATE makes several single-character one-to-one substitutions.

The following example substitutes * for a, # for e, and $ for i, and it removes o and u from the last_name column:

```
SELECT last_name, TRANSLATE(last_name, 'aeiou', '*#$') no_vowel
FROM employees
WHERE last_name like 'S%';

LAST_NAME                 NO_VOWEL
------------------------- -------------
Sarchand                  S*rch*nd
Sciarra                   Sc$*rr*
Seo                       S#
Smith                     Sm$th
Sullivan                  Sll$v*n
Sully                     Slly
```

Here is another example, where the case is reversed; uppercase letters are converted to lowercase, and lowercase letters are converted to uppercase:

```
SELECT data_value, TRANSLATE(data_value,
'abcdefghijklmnopqrstuvwxyzABCDEFGHIJKLMNOPQRSTUVWXYZ',
'ABCDEFGHIJKLMNOPQRSTUVWXYZabcdefghijklmnopqrstuvwxyz')
FROM sample_data;

DATA_VALUE           TRANSLATE(DATA_VALUE
-------------------- --------------------
THE three muskETeers the THREE MUSKetEERS
ali and*41*thieves   ALI AND*41*THIEVES
mississippi          MISSISSIPPI
mister INDIA         MISTER india
```

TRIM

TRIM([[*c1*] *c2* FROM] *c3*) can take three arguments, where *c2* and *c3* are character strings. If present, *c1* can be one of the following literals: LEADING, TRAILING, or BOTH. This function returns *c3* with all *c1* (leading, trailing, or both) occurrences of characters in c2 removed. A NULL is returned if any of *c1*, *c2*, or *c3* is NULL. *c1* defaults to BOTH. *c2* defaults to a space character. *c3* is the only mandatory argument. If *c2*or *c3* is NULL, the function returns a NULL. It's equivalent to applying both LTRIM and RTRIM on the string *c3*.

```
SELECT TRIM('   fully padded   ') test1
      ,TRIM('   left padded') test2
      ,TRIM('right padded   ') test3
FROM dual;

TEST1        TEST2       TEST3
------------ ----------- ------------
fully padded left padded right padded
```

UPPER

UPPER(*c*) takes a single argument, where *c* is a character string. This function returns the character string *c* with all characters in uppercase. UPPER frequently appears in WHERE clauses, when you're not sure of the case of the data in the table. See also LOWER.

```
SELECT first_name, last_name
FROM employees
WHERE UPPER(first_name) = 'JOHN';
```

```
FIRST_NAME           LAST_NAME
-------------------- --------------------
John                 Chen

SELECT data_value, UPPER(data_value) upper_data
FROM sample_data;

DATA_VALUE           UPPER_DATA
-------------------- --------------------
THE three muskETeers THE THREE MUSKETEERS
ali and*41*thieves   ALI AND*41*THIEVES
mississippi          MISSISSIPPI
mister INDIA         MISTER INDIA
```

Using Single-Row Numeric Functions

When you think of numeric functions, the tasks that come to mind are finding a total, finding the average, counting the number of records, and so on. These numeric functions are group functions that operate on one or more rows. I'll discuss group functions in Chapter 3, "Using Group Functions."

In the following sections, I will review the numeric functions used on single rows. Single-row numeric functions operate on numeric data and perform some kind of mathematical or arithmetic manipulation. When using a literal in a numeric function, do not enclose it in single quotes. Literals in single quotes are treated as a character datatype.

Numeric Function Overview

Table 2.2 summarizes the single-row numeric functions in Oracle 11g. I will cover each of these functions in the "Numeric Function Descriptions" section.

TABLE 2.2 Numeric Function Summary

Function	Description
ABS	Returns the absolute value
ACOS	Returns the arc cosine
ASIN	Returns the arc sine
ATAN	Returns the arc tangent

TABLE 2.2 Numeric Function Summary *(continued)*

Function	Description
ATAN2	Returns the arc tangent; takes two inputs
BITAND	Returns the result of a bitwise AND on two inputs
CEIL	Returns the next higher integer
COS	Returns the cosine
COSH	Returns the hyperbolic cosine
EXP	Returns the base of natural logarithms raised to a power
FLOOR	Returns the next smaller integer
LN	Returns the natural logarithm
LOG	Returns the logarithm
MOD	Returns the modulo (remainder) of a division operation
NANVL	Returns an alternate number if the value is Not a Number (NaN) for BINARY_FLOAT and BINARY_DOUBLE numbers
POWER	Returns a number raised to an arbitrary power
REMAINDER	Returns the remainder in a division operation
ROUND	Rounds a number
SIGN	Returns an indicator of sign: negative, positive, or zero
SIN	Returns the sine
SINH	Returns the hyperbolic sine
SQRT	Returns the square root of a number
TAN	Returns the tangent
TANH	Returns the hyperbolic tangent
TRUNC	Truncates a number
WIDTH_BUCKET	Creates equal-width histograms

Numeric Function Descriptions

Numeric functions have numeric arguments and return numeric values. The trigonometric functions all operate on radians, not degrees.

The numeric functions are arranged in alphabetical order, with descriptions and examples of each one.

SIGN, ROUND, and TRUNC are most commonly used numeric functions—pay particular attention to them. FLOOR, CEIL, MOD, and REMAINDER are also important functions that can appear in the test. TRUNC and ROUND functions can take numeric input or a datetime input. These two functions are discussed in the "Using Single-Row Date Functions" section to illustrate their behavior with a datetime datatype input.

ABS

ABS(*n*) takes a single argument, where *n* is a numeric datatype (NUMBER, BINARY_FLOAT or BINARY_DOUBLE). This function returns the absolute value of *n*.

```
SELECT ABS(-52) negative, ABS(52)  positive
FROM dual;

  NEGATIVE   POSITIVE
---------- ----------
        52         52
```

ACOS

ACOS(*n*) takes a single argument, where *n* is a numeric datatype between –1 and 1. This function returns the arc cosine of *n* expressed in radians, accurate to 30 digits of precision.

```
SELECT ACOS(-1) PI, ACOS(0) ACOSZERO,
       ACOS(.045) ACOS045, ACOS(1) ZERO
FROM dual;

        PI   ACOSZERO    ACOS045       ZERO
---------- ---------- ---------- ----------
3.14159265 1.57079633 1.52578113          0
```

ASIN

ASIN(*n*) takes a single argument, where *n* is a numeric datatype between –1 and 1. This function returns the arc sine of *n* expressed in radians, accurate to 30 digits of precision.

```
SELECT ASIN(1) high, ASIN(0) middle, ASIN(-1) low
FROM dual;
```

```
      HIGH     MIDDLE        LOW
---------- ---------- ----------
1.57079633          0 -1.5707963
```

ATAN

`ATAN(n)` takes a single argument, where *n* is a numeric datatype. This function returns the arc tangent of *n* expressed in radians, accurate to 30 digits of precision.

```
SELECT ATAN(9E99) high, ATAN(0) middle, ATAN(-9E99) low
FROM dual;

      HIGH     MIDDLE        LOW
---------- ---------- ----------
1.57079633          0 -1.5707963
```

ATAN2

`ATAN2(n1, n2)` takes two arguments, where *n1* and *n2* are numbers. This function returns the arc tangent of *n1* and *n2* expressed in radians, accurate to 30 digits of precision. `ATAN2(n1,n2)` is equivalent to `ATAN(n1/n2)`.

```
SELECT ATAN2(9E99,1) high, ATAN2(0,3.1415) middle, ATAN2(-9E99,1) low
FROM dual;

      HIGH     MIDDLE        LOW
---------- ---------- ----------
1.57079633          0 -1.5707963
```

BITAND

`BITAND(n1, n2)` takes two arguments, where *n1* and *n2* are positive integers or zero. This function performs a bitwise `AND` operation on the two input values and returns the results, also an integer. It is used to examine bit fields.

Here are two examples of `BITAND`. The first one performs a bitwise `AND` operation on 6 (binary 0110) and 3 (binary 0011). The result is 2 (binary 0010). Similarly, the bitwise `AND` between 8 (binary 1000) and 2 (binary 0010) is 0 (0000).

```
SELECT BITAND(6,3) T1, BITAND(8,2) T2
FROM dual;

        T1         T2
---------- ----------
         2          0
```

CEIL

CEIL(*n*) takes a single argument, where *n* is a numeric datatype. This function returns the smallest integer that is greater than or equal to *n*. CEIL rounds up to a whole number. See also FLOOR.

```
SELECT CEIL(9.8), CEIL(-32.85), CEIL(0), CEIL(5)
FROM dual;

CEIL(9.8) CEIL(-32.85)    CEIL(0)    CEIL(5)
---------- ------------ ---------- ----------
        10          -32          0          5
```

COS

COS(*n*) takes a single argument, where *n* is a numeric datatype in radians. This function returns the cosine of *n*, accurate to 36 digits of precision.

```
SELECT COS(-3.14159) FROM dual;

COS(-3.14159)
-------------
           -1
```

COSH

COSH(*n*) takes a single argument, where *n* is a numeric datatype. This function returns the hyperbolic cosine of *n*, accurate to 36 digits of precision.

```
SELECT COSH(1.4) FROM dual;

 COSH(1.4)
----------
2.15089847
```

EXP

EXP(*n*) takes a single argument, where *n* is a numeric datatype. This function returns e (the base of natural logarithms) raised to the *n* power, accurate to 36 digits of precision.

```
SELECT EXP(1) "e" FROM dual;

         e
----------
2.71828183
```

FLOOR

`FLOOR(n)` takes a single argument, where *n* is a numeric datatype. This function returns the largest integer that is less than or equal to *n*. `FLOOR` rounds down to a whole number. See also `CEIL`.

```
SELECT FLOOR(9.8), FLOOR(-32.85), FLOOR(137)
FROM dual;

FLOOR(9.8) FLOOR(-32.85) FLOOR(137)
---------- ------------- ----------
         9           -33        137
```

LN

`LN(n)` takes a single argument, where *n* is a numeric datatype greater than 0. This function returns the natural logarithm of *n*, accurate to 36 digits of precision.

```
SELECT LN(2.7) FROM dual;

   LN(2.7)
----------
.993251773
```

LOG

`LOG(n1, n2)` takes two arguments, where *n1* and *n2* are numeric datatypes. This function returns the logarithm base *n1* of *n2*, accurate to 36 digits of precision.

```
SELECT LOG(8,64), LOG(3,27), LOG(2,1024), LOG(2,8)
FROM dual;

 LOG(8,64)  LOG(3,27) LOG(2,1024)   LOG(2,8)
---------- ---------- ----------- ----------
         2          3          10          3
```

MOD

`MOD(n1, n2)` takes two arguments, where *n1* and *n2* are any numeric datatype. This function returns *n1* modulo *n2*, or the remainder of *n1* divided by *n2*. If *n1* is negative, the result is negative. The sign of *n2* has no effect on the result. If n2 is zero, the result is `n1`. See also `REMAINDER`.

```
SELECT MOD(14,5), MOD(8,2.5), MOD(-64,7), MOD(12,0)
FROM dual;
```

```
 MOD(14,5) MOD(8,2.5) MOD(-64,7) MOD(12,0)
---------- ---------- ---------- ---------
         4         .5         -1        12
```

NANVL

This function is used with BINARY_FLOAT and BINARY_DOUBLE datatype numbers to return an alternate value if the input is NaN.

The following example defines the `NULL` display as ? to show `NULL` value. The `TO_BINARY_FLOAT` function (discussed later in the chapter) is used to convert input to a BINARY_FLOAT datatype number.

```
SET NULL ?
SELECT NANVL(TO_BINARY_FLOAT('NaN'), 0) T1,
       NANVL(TO_BINARY_FLOAT('NaN'), NULL) T2
FROM dual;

        T1         T2
---------- ----------
         0 ?
```

POWER

`POWER(`*n1*, *n2*) takes two arguments, where *n1* and *n2* are numeric datatypes. This function returns *n1* to the *n2* power.

```
SELECT POWER(2,10), POWER(3,3), POWER(5,3), POWER(2,-3)
FROM dual;

POWER(2,10) POWER(3,3) POWER(5,3) POWER(2,-3)
----------- ---------- ---------- -----------
       1024         27        125        .125
```

REMAINDER

`REMAINDER(`*n1*, *n2*) takes two arguments, where *n1* and *n2* are any numeric datatype. This function returns the remainder of *n1* divided by *n2*. If *n1* is negative, the result is negative. The sign of *n2* has no effect on the result. If `n2` is zero and the datatype of `n1` is NUMBER, an error is returned; if the datatype of *n1* is BINARY_FLOAT or BINARY_DOUBLE, NaNis returned. See also MOD.

```
SELECT REMAINDER(13,5), REMAINDER(12,5), REMAINDER(12.5, 5)
FROM dual;
```

```
REMAINDER(13,5) REMAINDER(12,5) REMAINDER(12.5,5)
--------------- --------------- -----------------
             -2               2               2.5
```

The difference between MOD and REMAINDER is that MOD uses the FLOOR function, whereas REMAINDER uses the ROUND function in the formula. If you apply MOD function to the previous example, the results are the same except for the first column:

```
SELECT MOD(13,5), MOD(12,5), MOD(12.5, 5)
FROM dual;

 MOD(13,5)  MOD(12,5) MOD(12.5,5)
---------- ---------- -----------
         3          2         2.5
```

Here is another example of using REMAINDER with a BINARY_FLOAT number, having *n2* as zero:

```
SELECT REMAINDER(TO_BINARY_FLOAT('13.0'), 0) RBF
from dual;

       RBF
----------
       Nan
```

ROUND

ROUND(*n1* [,*n2*]) takes two arguments, where *n1* is a numeric datatype and *n2* is an integer. This function returns *n1* rounded to *n2* digits of precision to the right of the decimal. If *n2* is negative, *n1* is rounded to the left of the decimal. If n2 is omitted, the default is zero. This function is similar to TRUNC.

```
SELECT ROUND(123.489), ROUND(123.489, 2),
       ROUND(123.489, -2), ROUND(1275, -2)
FROM dual;

ROUND(123.489) ROUND(123.489,2) ROUND(123.489,-2) ROUND(1275,-2)
-------------- ---------------- ----------------- --------------
           123           123.49               100           1300
```

SIGN

SIGN(*n*) takes a single argument, where *n* is a numeric datatype. This function returns –1 if *n* is negative, 1 if *n* is positive, and 0 if *n* is 0.

```
SELECT SIGN(-2.3), SIGN(0), SIGN(47)
FROM dual;

SIGN(-2.3)    SIGN(0)   SIGN(47)
---------- ---------- ----------
        -1          0          1
```

SIN

SIN(*n*) takes a single argument, where *n* is a number in radians. This function returns the sine of *n*, accurate to 36 digits of precision.

```
SELECT SIN(1.57079) FROM dual;

SIN(1.57079)
------------
           1
```

SINH

SINH(*n*) takes a single argument, where *n* is a number. This function returns the hyperbolic sine of *n*, accurate to 36 digits of precision.

```
SELECT SINH(1) FROM dual;

   SINH(1)
----------
1.17520119
```

SQRT

SQRT(*n*) takes a single argument, where *n* is a numeric datatype. This function returns the square root of *n*.

```
SELECT SQRT(64), SQRT(49), SQRT(5)
FROM dual;

  SQRT(64)   SQRT(49)    SQRT(5)
---------- ---------- ----------
         8          7 2.23606798
```

TAN

TAN(*n*) takes a single argument, where *n* is a numeric datatype in radians. This function returns the tangent of *n*, accurate to 36 digits of precision.

```
SELECT TAN(1.57079633/2) "45_degrees"
FROM dual;

45_Degrees
----------
         1
```

TANH

TANH(*n*) takes a single argument, where *n* is a numeric datatype. This function returns the hyperbolic tangent of *n*, accurate to 36 digits of precision.

```
SELECT TANH( ACOS(-1) ) hyp_tan_of_pi
FROM dual;

HYP_TAN_OF_PI
-------------
   .996272076
```

TRUNC

TRUNC(*n1* [,*n2*]) takes two arguments, where *n1* is a numeric datatype and *n2* is an integer. This function returns *n1* truncated to *n2* digits of precision to the right of the decimal. If *n2* is negative, *n1* is truncated to the left of the decimal. See also ROUND.

```
SELECT TRUNC(123.489), TRUNC(123.489, 2),
       TRUNC(123.489, -2), TRUNC(1275, -2)
FROM dual;

TRUNC(123.489) TRUNC(123.489,2) TRUNC(123.489,-2) TRUNC(1275,-2)
-------------- ---------------- ----------------- --------------
           123           123.48               100           1200
```

WIDTH_BUCKET

You can use WIDTH_BUCKET(*n1*, *min_val*, *max_val*, *buckets*) to build histograms of equal width. The first argument *n1* can be an expression of a numeric or datetime datatype. The second and third arguments, *min_val* and *max_val*, indicate the end points for the histogram's range. The fourth argument, *buckets*, indicates the number of buckets.

The following example divides the salary into a 10-bucket histogram within the range 2,500 to 11,000. If the salary falls below 2500, it will be in the underflow bucket (bucket 0), and if the salary exceeds 11,000, it will be in the overflow bucket (*buckets* + 1).

```
SELECT first_name, salary,
       WIDTH_BUCKET(salary, 2500, 11000, 10) hist
FROM employees
WHERE first_name like 'J%';

FIRST_NAME               SALARY       HIST
-------------------- ---------- ----------
Jennifer                   4400          3
John                       8200          7
Jose Manuel                7800          7
Julia                      3200          1
James                      2400          0
James                      2500          1
Jason                      3300          1
John                       2700          1
Joshua                     2500          1
John                      14000         11
Janette                   10000          9
Jonathon                   8600          8
Jack                       8400          7
Jean                       3100          1
Julia                      3400          2
Jennifer                   3600          2
```

Using Single-Row Date Functions

Single-row date functions operate on *datetime* datatypes. A datetime is a coined word to identify datatypes used to define dates and times. The datetime datatypes in Oracle 11*g* are DATE, TIMESTAMP, and INTERVAL. Most have one or more date arguments, and most return a datetime value. Date data is stored internally as numbers. The whole-number portion is the number of days since January 1, 4712 BC, and the decimal portion is the fraction of a day (for example, 0.5=12 hours).

Date-Format Conversion

National-language support (NLS) parameters and arguments allow you to internationalize your Oracle database system. NLS internationalizations include date representations, character sets, alphabets, and alphabetical ordering.

Oracle will implicitly or automatically convert its numeric date data to and from character data using the format model specified with NLS_DATE_FORMAT. The default format is *DD-MON-RR* (see Table 2.7). You can change this date-format model for each session with the ALTER SESSION SET NLS_DATE_FORMAT command. Here's an example:

```
SQL> SELECT SYSDATE FROM dual;

SYSDATE
---------
31-MAR-08

SQL> ALTER SESSION SET NLS_DATE_FORMAT='DD-Mon-YYYY HH24:MI:SS';

Session altered.

SQL> SELECT SYSDATE FROM dual;

SYSDATE
--------------------
31-Mar-2008 10:19:11
```

This ALTER SESSION command will set the *implicit conversion* mechanism to display date data in the format specified, such as 12-Dec-2002 15:45:32. This conversion works both ways. If the character string '30-Nov-2002 20:30:00' were inserted, updated, or assigned to a date column or variable, the correct date would be entered.

If the format model were *DD/MM/YY* or *MM/DD/YY*, there could be some ambiguity in the conversion of some dates, such as 12 April 2000 (04/12/00 or 12/04/00). To avoid problems with implicit conversions, Oracle provides explicit date/character-conversion functions: TO_DATE, TO_CHAR, TO_TIMESTAMP, TO_TIMESTAMP_TZ, TO_DSINTERVAL, and TO_YMINTERVAL. These explicit conversion functions are covered in the "Using Single-Row Conversion Functions" section later in this chapter.

Date-Function Overview

Table 2.3 summarizes the single-row date functions. I will cover each of these functions in the "Date-Function Descriptions" section.

TABLE 2.3 Date-Function Summary

Function	Description
ADD_MONTHS	Adds a number of months to a date
CURRENT_DATE	Returns the current date and time in a DATE datatype
CURRENT_TIMESTAMP	Returns the current date and time in a TIMESTAMP datatype
DBTIMEZONE	Returns the database's time zone
EXTRACT	Returns a component of a date/time expression
FROM_TZ	Returns a timestamp with time zone for a given timestamp
LAST_DAY	Returns the last day of a month
LOCALTIMESTAMP	Returns the current date and time in the session time zone
MONTHS_BETWEEN	Returns the number of months between two dates
NEW_TIME	Returns the date/time in a different time zone
NEXT_DAY	Returns the next day of a week following a given date
ROUND	Rounds a date/time
SESSIONTIMEZONE	Returns the time zone for the current session
SYS_EXTRACT_UTC	Returns the UTC (GMT) for a timestamp with a time zone
SYSDATE	Returns the current date and time in the DATE datatype
SYSTIMESTAMP	Returns the current timestamp in the TIMESTAMP datatype
TRUNC	Truncates a date to a given granularity
TZ_OFFSET	Returns the offset from UTC for a time zone name

Date-Function Descriptions

The date functions are arranged in alphabetical order except the first three, with descriptions and examples of each one. SYSDATE, SYSTIMESTAMP, and LOCALTIMESTAMP are used in many examples, and hence I'll discuss them first.

SYSDATE

SYSDATE takes no arguments and returns the current date and time to the second for the operating-system host where the database resides. The value is returned in a DATE datatype. The format that the value returned is based on NLS_DATE_FORMAT, which can be altered for the session using the ALTER SESSION SET NLS_DATE_FORMAT command. The format mask for dates and timestamps are discussed later in the chapter.

```
ALTER SESSION SET NLS_DATE_FORMAT='DD-MON-YYYY HH:MI:SS AM';
Session altered.

SELECT SYSDATE FROM dual;

SYSDATE
-----------------------
31-MAR-2008 12:00:13 PM
```

SYSDATE is one of the most commonly used Oracle functions. There's a good chance you'll see it on the exam. Since the SYSDATE value is returned based on the time of the host server where the database resides, the result will be the same for a user sitting in New York or one in Hong Kong.

SYSTIMESTAMP

SYSTIMESTAMP takes no arguments and returns a TIMESTAMP WITH TIME ZONE for the current database date and time (the time of the host server where the database resides). The fractional second is returned with six digits of precision. The format of the value returned is based on NLS_TIMESTAMP_TZ_FORMAT, which can be altered for the session using the ALTER SESSION SET NLS_TIMESTAMP_TZ_FORMAT command.

```
SQL> SELECT SYSDATE, SYSTIMESTAMP FROM dual;

SYSDATE
SYSTIMESTAMP
-------------------------------------
31-MAR-08
31-MAR-08 12.01.49.280000 PM -05:00

ALTER SESSION SET NLS_DATE_FORMAT='DD-MON-YYYY HH24:MI:SS';
Session altered.
```

```
ALTER SESSION SET
      NLS_TIMESTAMP_TZ_FORMAT='YYYY-MON-DD HH:MI:SS.FF TZR';
Session altered.

SELECT SYSDATE, SYSTIMESTAMP FROM dual;

SYSDATE
SYSTIMESTAMP
------------------------------------
31-MAR-2008 12:09:51
2008-MAR-31 12:09:51.429000 -05:00
```

LOCALTIMESTAMP

LOCALTIMESTAMP([*p*]) returns the current date and time in the session's time zone to *p* digits of precision. *p* can be 0 to 9 and defaults to 6. This function returns the value in the datatype TIMESTAMP. You can set the client time zone using the ALTER SESSION SET TIME_ZONE command.

The following example illustrates LOCALTIMESTAMP and how to change the time zone for the session. The database is in U.S./Central time zone, and the client is in U.S./Eastern time zone. See also CURRENT_TIMESTAMP.

```
SELECT SYSTIMESTAMP, LOCALTIMESTAMP FROM dual;

SYSTIMESTAMP
LOCALTIMESTAMP
----------------------------------------------------
31-MAR-08 01.02.49.272000 PM -05:00
31-MAR-08 02.02.49.272000 PM

ALTER SESSION SET TIME_ZONE = '-8:00';
```

ADD_MONTHS

ADD_MONTHS(*d*, *i*) takes two arguments, where *d* is a date and *i* is an integer. This function returns the date *d* plus *i* months. If *i* is a decimal number, the database will implicitly convert it to an integer by truncating the decimal portion (for example, 3.9 becomes 3). If *<d>* is the last day of the month or the resulting month has fewer days, then the result is the last day of the resulting month.

```
SELECT SYSDATE, ADD_MONTHS(SYSDATE, -1) PREV_MONTH,
       ADD_MONTHS(SYSDATE, 12) NEXT_YEAR
FROM dual;
```

```
SYSDATE   PREV_MONT NEXT_YEAR
--------- --------- ---------
31-MAR-08 29-FEB-08 31-MAR-09
```

CURRENT_DATE

CURRENT_DATE takes no arguments and returns the current date in the Gregorian calendar for the session's (client) time zone. This function is similar to SYSDATE, whereas SYSDATE returns the current date for the database's (host's) time zone. You can set the client time zone using the ALTER SESSION SET TIME_ZONE command.

The following example illustrates CURRENT_DATE and how to change the time zone for the session. The database is in U.S./Central time zone, and the client is in U.S./Mountain time zone.

```
ALTER SESSION SET NLS_DATE_FORMAT='DD-Mon-YYYY HH24:MI:SS';
Session altered.

SELECT SYSDATE, CURRENT_DATE FROM dual;

SYSDATE              CURRENT_DATE
-------------------- --------------------
31-Mar-2008 10:52:34 31-Mar-2008 09:52:35

ALTER SESSION SET TIME_ZONE = 'US/Eastern';
Session altered.

SELECT SYSDATE, CURRENT_DATE FROM dual;

SYSDATE              CURRENT_DATE
-------------------- --------------------
31-Mar-2008 10:53:46 31-Mar-2008 11:53:47
```

CURRENT_TIMESTAMP

CURRENT_TIMESTAMP([*p*]) returns the current date and time in the session's time zone to *p* digits of precision. *p* can be an integer 0 through 9 and defaults to 6. See also LOCALTIMESTAMP. This function is similar to CURRENT_DATE. CURRENT_DATE returns result in the DATE datatype, whereas CURRENT_TIMESTAMP returns the result in the TIMESTAMP WITH TIME ZONE datatype.

```
SQL> SELECT CURRENT_DATE, CURRENT_TIMESTAMP FROM dual;

CURRENT_DATE
CURRENT_TIMESTAMP
---------------------------------------
31-Mar-2008 12:23:43
31-MAR-08 12.23.43.305000 PM US/EASTERN
```

DBTIMEZONE

DBTIMEZONE returns the database's time zone, as set by the latest CREATE DATABASE or ALTER DATABASE SET TIME_ZONE statement. Note that after changing the database time zone with the ALTER DATABASE statement, the database must be bounced (restarted) for the change to take effect. The time zone is a character string specifying the hours and minutes offset from UTC (Coordinated Universal Time, also known as GMT, or Greenwich mean time) or a time zone region name. The valid time zone region names can be found in the TZNAME column of the view V$TIMEZONE_NAMES. The default time zone for the database is UTC (00:00) if you do not explicitly set the time zone during database creation.

```
SQL> SELECT DBTIMEZONE FROM dual;

DBTIME
------
+00:00
```

EXTRACT

EXTRACT(*c* FROM *dt*) extracts and returns the specified component *c* of date/time or interval expression *dt*. The valid components are YEAR, MONTH, DAY, HOUR, MINUTE, SECOND, TIMEZONE_HOUR, TIMEZONE_MINUTE, TIMEZONE_REGION, and TIMEZONE_ABBR. The specified component must exist in the expression. So, to extract a TIMEZONE_HOUR, the date/time expression must be a TIMESTAMP WITH TIME ZONE datatype.

Though HOUR, MINUTE, and SECOND exist in the DATE datatype, you can extract only YEAR, MONTH, and DAY from the DATE dataype expressions.

```
SELECT SYSDATE, EXTRACT(YEAR FROM SYSDATE) year_d
FROM dual;

SYSDATE                  YEAR_D
-------------------- ----------
31-MAR-2008 12:29:02       2008
```

You can extract YEAR, MONTH, DAY, HOUR, MINUTE, and SECOND from the TIMESTAMP datatype expression. You can extract all the components from the TIMESTAMP WITH TIMEZONE datatype expression.

```
SELECT LOCALTIMESTAMP,
       EXTRACT(YEAR FROM LOCALTIMESTAMP) YEAR_TS,
       EXTRACT(DAY FROM LOCALTIMESTAMP) DAY_TS,
       EXTRACT(SECOND FROM LOCALTIMESTAMP) SECOND_TS
FROM dual;

LOCALTIMESTAMP                 YEAR_TS DAY_TS  SECOND_TS
---------------------------- ------- ------- ---------
31-MAR-08 02.09.32.972000 PM    2008      31    32.972
```

FROM_TZ

FROM_TZ(*ts*, *tz*) returns a TIMESTAMP WITH TIME ZONE for the timestamp *ts* using time zone value *tz*. The character string *tz* specifies the hours and minutes offset from UTC or is a time zone region name. The valid time zone region names can be found in the TZNAME column of the view V$TIMEZONE_NAMES.

```
SELECT LOCALTIMESTAMP, FROM_TZ(LOCALTIMESTAMP, 'Japan') Japan,
FROM_TZ(LOCALTIMESTAMP, '-5:00') Central
FROM dual;

LOCALTIMESTAMP
JAPAN
CENTRAL
-------------------------------------
31-MAR-08 03.17.38.447000 PM
31-MAR-08 03.17.38.447000 PM JAPAN
31-MAR-08 03.17.38.447000 PM -05:00
```

LAST_DAY

LAST_DAY(*d*) takes a single argument, where *d* is a date. This function returns the last day of the month for the date *d*. The return datatype is DATE.

```
SELECT SYSDATE,
       LAST_DAY(SYSDATE)  END_OF_MONTH,
       LAST_DAY(SYSDATE)+1 NEXT_MONTH
FROM dual;

SYSDATE     END_OF_MONTH NEXT_MONTH
----------- ------------ -----------
09-SEP-2007 30-SEP-2007  01-OCT-2007
```

MONTHS_BETWEEN

`MONTHS_BETWEEN(d1, d2)` takes two arguments, where *d1* and *d2* are both dates. This function returns the number of months that *d2* is later than *d1*. A whole number is returned if *d1* and *d2* are the same day of the month or if both dates are the last day of a month.

```
SELECT MONTHS_BETWEEN('31-MAR-08', '30-SEP-08') E1,
       MONTHS_BETWEEN('11-MAR-08', '30-SEP-08') E2,
       MONTHS_BETWEEN('01-MAR-08', '30-SEP-08') E3,
       MONTHS_BETWEEN('31-MAR-08', '30-SEP-07') E4
FROM dual;

        E1         E2         E3         E4
---------- ---------- ---------- ----------
        -6 -6.6129032 -6.9354839          6
```

NEW_TIME

`NEW_TIME(d>, tz1, tz2)` takes three arguments, where *d* is a date and both *tz1* and *tz2* are one of the time zone constants. This function returns the date in time zone *tz2* for date *d* in time zone *tz1*.

```
SELECT SYSDATE Dallas, NEW_TIME(SYSDATE, 'CDT', 'HDT') Hawaii
FROM dual;

DALLAS               HAWAII
-------------------- --------------------
31-MAR-2008 14:34:03 31-MAR-2008 10:34:03
```

Table 2.4 lists the time zone constraints.

TABLE 2.4 Time Zone Constants

Code	Time Zone
GMT	Greenwich mean time
NST	Newfoundland standard time
AST	Atlantic standard time
ADT	Atlantic daylight time
BST	Bering standard time

TABLE 2.4 Time Zone Constants *(continued)*

Code	Time Zone
BDT	Bering daylight time
CST	Central standard time
CDT	Central daylight time
EST	Eastern standard time
EDT	Eastern daylight time
MST	Mountain standard time
MDT	Mountain daylight time
PST	Pacific standard time
PDT	Pacific daylight time
YST	Yukon standard time
YDT	Yukon daylight time
HST	Hawaii-Alaska standard time
HDT	Hawaii-Alaska daylight time

NEXT_DAY

NEXT_DAY(*d*, *dow*) takes two arguments, where *d* is a date and *dow* is a text string containing the full or abbreviated day of the week in the session's language. This function returns the next *dow* following *d*. The time portion of the return date is the same as the time portion of *d*.

```
SELECT SYSDATE, NEXT_DAY(SYSDATE,'Thu') NEXT_THU,
       NEXT_DAY('31-OCT-2008', 'Tue') Election_Day
FROM dual;

SYSDATE              NEXT_THU             ELECTION_DAY
-------------------- -------------------- --------------------
31-MAR-2008 14:53:54 03-APR-2008 14:53:54 04-NOV-2008 00:00:00
```

ROUND

ROUND(<*d*> [,*fmt*]) takes two arguments, where *d* is a date and *fmt* is a character string containing a date-format string. This function returns *d* rounded to the granularity specified in *fmt*. If fmt is omitted, d is rounded to the nearest day.

```
SELECT SYSDATE, ROUND(SYSDATE,'HH24') ROUND_HOUR,
       ROUND(SYSDATE) ROUND_DATE, ROUND(SYSDATE,'MM') NEW_MONTH,
       ROUND(SYSDATE,'YY') NEW_YEAR
FROM dual;

SYSDATE              ROUND_HOUR           ROUND_DATE
NEW_MONTH            NEW_YEAR
-------------------- -------------------- --------------------
31-MAR-2008 14:59:58 31-MAR-2008 15:00:00 01-APR-2008 00:00:00
01-APR-2008 00:00:00 01-JAN-2008 00:00:00
```

SESSIONTIMEZONE

SESSIONTIMEZONE takes no arguments and returns the database's time zone offset as per the last ALTER SESSION statement. SESSIONTIMEZONE will default to DBTIMEZONE if it is not changed with an ALTER SESSION statement.

```
SELECT DBTIMEZONE, SESSIONTIMEZONE
FROM dual;

DBTIMEZONE  SESSIONTIMEZONE
----------- ---------------
US/Central  -05:00
```

SYS_EXTRACT_UTC

SYS_EXTRACT_UTC(*ts*) takes a single argument, where *ts* is a TIMESTAMP WITH TIME ZONE. This function returns the UTC (GMT) time for the timestamp *ts*.

```
SELECT CURRENT_TIMESTAMP local,
       SYS_EXTRACT_UTC(CURRENT_TIMESTAMP) GMT
FROM dual;

LOCAL
GMT
---------------------------------------
31-MAR-08 04.06.53.731000 PM US/EASTERN
31-MAR-08 08.06.53.731000 PM
```

TRUNC

TRUNC(*d* [,*fmt*]) takes two arguments, where *d* is a date and *fmt* is a character string containing a date-format string. This function returns *d* truncated to the granularity specified in *fmt*. See also ROUND.

```
SELECT SYSDATE, TRUNC(SYSDATE,'HH24') CURR_HOUR,
       TRUNC(SYSDATE) CURR_DATE, TRUNC(SYSDATE,'MM') CURR_MONTH,
       TRUNC(SYSDATE,'YY') CURR_YEAR
FROM dual;

SYSDATE              CURR_HOUR            CURR_DATE
CURR_MONTH           CURR_YEAR
-------------------- -------------------- --------------------
31-MAR-2008 15:04:21 31-MAR-2008 15:00:00 31-MAR-2008 00:00:00
01-MAR-2008 00:00:00 01-JAN-2008 00:00:00
```

TZ_OFFSET

TZ_OFFSET(*tz*) takes a single argument, where *tz* is a time zone offset or time zone name. This function returns the numeric time zone offset for a textual time zone name. The valid time zone names can be obtained from the TZNAME column in the V$TIMEZONE_NAMES view.

```
SELECT TZ_OFFSET(SESSIONTIMEZONE) NEW_YORK,
       TZ_OFFSET('US/Pacific') LOS_ANGELES,
       TZ_OFFSET('Europe/London') LONDON,
       TZ_OFFSET('Asia/Singapore') SINGAPORE
FROM dual;

NEW_YOR LOS_ANG LONDON  SINGAPO
------- ------- ------- -------
-04:00  -07:00  +01:00  +08:00
```

Using Single-Row Conversion Functions

Single-row *conversion functions* operate on multiple datatypes. The TO_CHAR and TO_NUMBER functions have a significant number of formatting codes that can be used to display date and number data in a wide assortment of representations.

You can use the conversion functions to convert a numeric value to a character or a character value to a numeric or datetime value. Character datatypes in Oracle 11*g* are CHAR, VARCHAR2, NCHAR, NVARCHAR2, and CLOB. Numeric datatypes in Oracle

11*g* are NUMBER, BINARY_DOUBLE, and BINARY_FLOAT. Datetime datatypes in Oracle 11*g* are DATE, TIMESTAMP, and INTERVAL.

Datatype conversion are required and used extensively in day-to-day SQL use. When a user enters data, it may be in character format, which you may need to convert to a date or number. Sometimes the data is in a specific format and you have to tell Oracle how to treat the data using conversion functions and format codes. In the following sections, you will learn the various conversions and how to use them.

The exam may include a question that tests your recollection of some of the nuances of these formatting codes. General usage in a professional setting would afford you the opportunity to look them up in a reference. In the test setting, however, you must recall them on your own.

Conversion-Function Overview

Table 2.5 summarizes the single-row conversion functions. I will cover each of these functions in the "Conversion-Function Descriptions" section.

TABLE 2.5 Conversion-Function Summary

Function	Description
ASCIISTR	Converts characters to ASCII
BIN_TO_NUM	Converts a string of bits to a number
CAST	Converts datatypes
CHARTOROWID	Casts a character to the ROWID datatype
COMPOSE	Converts to Unicode
CONVERT	Converts from one character set to another
DECOMPOSE	Decomposes a Unicode string
HEXTORAW	Casts a hexadecimal to a raw
NUMTODSINTERVAL	Converts a number value to an interval day to second literal
NUMTOYMINTERVAL	Converts a number value to an interval year to month literal
RAWTOHEX	Casts a raw to a hexadecimal

TABLE 2.5 Conversion-Function Summary *(continued)*

Function	Description
ROWIDTOCHAR	Casts a ROWID to a character
SCN_TO_TIMESTAMP	Converts an SCN to corresponding timestamp of the change
TIMESTAMP_TO_SCN	Converts timestamp to an SCN
TO_BINARY_DOUBLE	Converts input into a BINARY_DOUBLE number
TO_BINARY_FLOAT	Converts input into a BINARY_FLOAT number
TO_CHAR	Converts and formats a date into a string
TO_CLOB	Converts character input or NCLOB input to CLOB
TO_DATE	Converts a string to a date, specifying the format
TO_DSINTERVAL	Converts a character string value to an interval day to second literal
TO_LOB	Converts LONG or LONG RAW values to CLOB or BLOB datatype
TO_MULTIBYTE	Converts a single-byte character to its corresponding multibyte equivalent
TO_NUMBER	Converts a string to a number, specifying the format
TO_SINGLE_BYTE	Converts a multibyte character to its corresponding single-byte equivalent
TO_TIMESTAMP	Converts character string to a TIMESTAMP value
TO_TIMESTAMP_TZ	Converts character string to a TIMESTAMP WITH TIME ZONE value
TO_YMINTERVAL	Converts a character string value to an interval year to month literal
UNISTR	Converts UCS2 Unicode

Conversion-Function Descriptions

The conversion functions are arranged in alphabetical order, with descriptions and examples of each one. Oracle 11*g* includes functions to convert from one datatype to another datatype. Most of the functions have only one argument. Many functions used to convert to/from numeric or datetime datatypes have three arguments; the second argument will tell Oracle what format the input given in the first argument should be. The third argument may be to specify an NLS string. You can use NLS parameters to tell Oracle what character set or language should be used when performing the conversion. The format mask and NLS parameters are always optional.

Pay particular attention to the TO_CHAR, TO_NUMBER, and TO_DATE functions. The format codes associated with numbers and dates are always a favorite on OCP certification exams.

ASCIISTR

ASCIISTR(*c1*) takes a single argument, where *c1* is a character string. This function returns the ASCII equivalent of all the characters in *c1*. This function leaves ASCII characters unchanged, but non-ASCII characters are returned in the format *xxxx* where *xxxx* represents a UTF-16 code unit.

```
SELECT ASCIISTR('cañon') E1, ASCIISTR('faß') E2
FROM dual;

E1        E2
--------- -------
ca\00F1on fa\00DF
```

BIN_TO_NUM

BIN_TO_NUM(*b*) takes a single argument, where *b* is a comma-delimited list of bits. This function returns the numeric representation of all the bit-field set *b*. It essentially converts a base 2 number into a base 10 number. Bit fields are the most efficient structure to store simple yes/no and true/false data. You can combine numerous bit fields into a single numeric column. Using bit fields departs from a normalized relational model, since one column represents more than one value, but this encoding can enhance performance and/or reduce disk-space usage. See also BITAND.

To understand the number returned from the BIN_TO_NUM function, recall from base 2 (binary) counting that the rightmost digit counts the 1s, the next counts the 2s, the next counts the 4s, then the 8s, and so on. Thus, 13 is represented in binary as 1101. There are one 1, zero 2s, one 4, and one 8, which add up to 13 in base 10.

```
SELECT BIN_TO_NUM(1,1,0,1) bitfield1,
       BIN_TO_NUM(0,0,0,1) bitfield2,
       BIN_TO_NUM(1,1) bitfield3
FROM dual;

BITFIELD1  BITFIELD2  BITFIELD3
---------- ---------- ----------
        13          1          3
```

CAST

`CAST(c AS t)` takes two arguments, where `c` is an expression, subquery, or `MULTISET` clause and `t` is a datatype. This function converts the expression `c` into the datatype `t`. The *CAST* function is most frequently used to convert data into programmer-defined datatypes, but it can also be used to convert data to built-in datatypes. No translation is performed; only the datatype is converted. Table 2.6 shows the datatypes that can be converted using CAST.

TABLE 2.6 CAST Datatype Conversions

Convert From/To	BINARY_ FLOAT, BINARY_ DOUBLE	CHAR, VARCHAR2	NCHAR, NVARCHAR2	DATE, TIMESTAMP, INTERVAL	NUMBER	RAW	ROWID, UROWID
BINARY_ FLOAT BINARY_ DOUBLE	Yes	Yes	Yes	No	Yes	No	No
CHAR, VARCHAR2	Yes	Yes	No	Yes	Yes	Yes	Yes
NCHAR, NVARCHAR2	Yes	No	Yes	Yes	Yes	Yes	Yes
DATE, TIMESTAMP, INTERVAL	No	Yes	No	Yes	No	No	No
NUMBER	Yes	Yes	No	No	Yes	No	No
RAW	No	Yes	No	No	No	Yes	No
ROWID, UROWID	No	Yes	No	No	No	No	Yes

The following example shows datatype conversion using the CAST function.

```
SELECT CAST(SYSDATE AS TIMESTAMP WITH LOCAL TIME ZONE) DT_2_TS
FROM dual;

DT_2_TS
----------------------------
31-MAR-08 04.43.43.000000 PM
```

CHARTOROWID

CHARTOROWID(*c*) takes a single argument, where *c* is a character string. This function returns *c* as a ROWID datatype. No translation is performed; only the datatype is converted.

```
SELECT rowid, first_name
FROM employees
WHERE first_name = 'Sarath';

ROWID              FIRST_NAME
------------------ --------------------
AAARAgAAFAAAABYAA9 Sarath

SELECT first_name, last_name
FROM employees
WHERE rowid = CHARTOROWID('AAARAgAAFAAAABYAA9');

FIRST_NAME           LAST_NAME
-------------------- -------------------------
Sarath               Sewall
```

Each row in the database is uniquely identified by a ROWID. ROWID shows the physical location of the row stored in the database. The pseudocolumn ROWID shows the address of the row.

COMPOSE

COMPOSE(*c*) takes a single argument, where *c* is a character string. This function returns *c* as a Unicode string in its fully normalized form, in the same character set as c. The COMPOSE and DECOMPOSE functions support Unicode 3.0. The Unicode 3.0 standard allows you to combine, or *compose*, a valid character from a base character and a modifier.

CONVERT

CONVERT(*c*, *dset* [,*sset*]) takes three arguments, where *c* is a character string and *dset* and *sset* are character-set names. This function returns the character string *c* converted from the source character set *sset* to the destination character set *dset*. No translation is performed. If the character does not exist in both character sets, the replacement character for the character set is used. *sset* defaults to the database character set.

```
select convert ('vis-à-vis','AL16UTF16','AL32UTF8')
from dual;
```

```
CONVERT('VIS-?-VIS','AL16UTF
----------------------------------------
 v i s -?? - v i s
```

DECOMPOSE

`DECOMPOSE(c)` takes a single argument, where *c* is a character string. This function returns *c* as a Unicode string after canonical decomposition in the same character set as *c*. The `COMPOSE` and `DECOMPOSE` functions support Unicode 3.0.

HEXTORAW

`HEXTORAW(x)` takes a single argument, where *x* is a hexadecimal string. This function returns the hexadecimal string *x* converted to a RAW datatype. No translation is performed; only the datatype is changed.

NUMTODSINTERVAL

`NUMTODSINTERVAL(x , c)` takes two arguments, where *x* is a number and *c* is a character string denoting the units for *x*. This function converts the number *x* into an INTERVAL DAY TO SECOND datatype. Valid units are `DAY`, `HOUR`, `MINUTE`, and `SECOND`. *c* can be uppercase, lowercase, or mixed case.

```
SELECT SYSDATE,
       SYSDATE+NUMTODSINTERVAL(2,'HOUR') "2 hours later",
       SYSDATE+NUMTODSINTERVAL(30,'MINUTE') "30 minutes later"
FROM dual;

SYSDATE              2 hours later        30 minutes later
-------------------- -------------------- --------------------
31-MAR-2008 23:06:23 01-APR-2008 01:06:23 31-MAR-2008 23:36:23
```

NUMTOYMINTERVAL

`NUMTOYMINTERVAL(x , c)` takes two arguments, where *x* is a number and *c* is a character string denoting the units for *x*. This function converts the number *x* into an INTERVAL YEAR TO MONTH datatype. Valid units are `YEAR` and `MONTH`. *c* can be uppercase, lowercase, or mixed case.

```
SELECT SYSDATE,
       SYSDATE+NUMTOYMINTERVAL(2,'YEAR') "2 years later",
       SYSDATE+NUMTOYMINTERVAL(5,'MONTH') "5 months later"
```

```
FROM dual;

SYSDATE              2 years later        5 months later
-------------------- -------------------- --------------------
31-MAR-2008 23:13:07 31-MAR-2010 23:13:07 31-AUG-2008 23:13:07
```

RAWTOHEX

`RAWTOHEX(x)` takes a single argument, where *x* is a raw string. This function returns the raw string *x* converted to hexadecimal. No translation is performed; only the datatype is changed.

ROWIDTOCHAR

`ROWIDTOCHAR(x)` takes a single argument, where *x* is a character string in the datatype ROWID. This function returns the ROWID string *x* converted to a VARCHAR2 datatype. No translation is performed; only the datatype is changed. The resulting string is always 18 characters long.

```
SELECT ROWIDTOCHAR(ROWID) Char_RowID, first_name
FROM employees
WHERE first_name = 'Sarath';

CHAR_ROWID         FIRST_NAME
------------------ --------------------
AAARAgAAFAAAABYAA9 Sarath
```

SCN_TO_TIMESTAMP

`SCN_TO_TIMESTAMP (n)` takes a single argument, where *n* is a numeric datatype representing a system change number (SCN) in the database. This function returns the timestamp associated with the SCN. The return datatype is TIMESTAMP.

```
SELECT SCN_TO_TIMESTAMP(8569432113130) UPD_TIME
from dual;

UPD_TIME
---------------------------------------------------
25-MAR-08 12.16.49.000000000 PM
```

An SCN is a number that gets incremented when a commit occurs in the database. The SCN identifies the state of the database uniquely, is recorded in the redo log files, and will be used in case instance recovery is needed. Please see Chapter 8, "Introducing Oracle 11*g* Components and Architecture," for more information.

Oracle provides the ORA_ROWSCN pseudocolumn to identify the SCN when the block containing the row was last modified. Using the ORA_ROWSCN pseudocolumn, you can identify the approximate time when the row was last modified. I say *approximate* because the SCN is associated with a block, and all the rows in the block will have the same SCN associated with them. This is useful in identifying the last modified time of a table, because a block can belong to only one table. Please see Chapter 10, "Allocating Database Storage and Creating Schema Objects," for more information on blocks.

```
SELECT SCN_TO_TIMESTAMP(ORA_ROWSCN) mod_time, last_name
FROM employees
WHERE first_name = 'Lex';

MOD_TIME                               LAST_NAME
-----------------------------------  -----------
27-MAR-08 10.20.56.000000000 AM       De Haan
```

TIMESTAMP_TO_SCN

TIMESTAMP_TO_SCN (<ts>) is used to identify the SCN associated with a particular timestamp. The function takes one argument, *ts*, which is of datatype TIMESTAMP. The return datatype is NUMBER.

```
SELECT TIMESTAMP_TO_SCN('25-MAR-08 09.52.20') DB_SCN
FROM dual;

         DB_SCN
---------------
  8569432102308
```

TO_BINARY_DOUBLE

TO_BINARY_DOUBLE(<*expr*> [,<*fmt*> [,<*nlsparm*>]]) takes three arguments, where *expr* is a character or numeric string, *fmt* is a format string specifying the format that *c* appears in, and *nlsparm* specifies language- or location-formatting conventions. This function returns a binary double-precision floating-point number of datatype BINARY_DOUBLE represented by *expr*. The *fmt* and *nlsparm* arguments are valid only if *expr* is a character expression. You can also use 'INF', '-INF' and 'NaN' to represent positive infinity, negative infinity, and NaN in *expr*.

The valid *fmt* numeric format conventions are listed in Table 2.9.

```
SELECT TO_BINARY_DOUBLE('1234.5678','999999.9999') CHR_FMT_DOUBLE,
       TO_BINARY_DOUBLE('1234.5678') CHR_DOUBLE,
       TO_BINARY_DOUBLE(1234.5678) NUM_DOUBLE,
       TO_BINARY_DOUBLE('INF') INF_DOUBLE
FROM dual;

 CHR_FMT_DOUBLE      CHR_DOUBLE       NUM_DOUBLE       INF_DOUBLE
--------------- --------------- --------------- ---------------
 1.2345678E+003  1.2345678E+003  1.2345678E+003             Inf
```

TO_BINARY_FLOAT

`TO_BINARY_FLOAT(<expr> [,<fmt> [,<nlsparm>] ])` takes three arguments, where *expr* is a character or numeric string, *fmt* is a format string specifying the format that *c* appears in, and *nlsparm* specifies language- or location-formatting conventions. This function returns a binary single-precision floating-point number of datatype BINARY_FLOAT represented by *expr*. The *fmt* and *nlsparm* arguments are valid only if *expr* is a character expression. You can also use 'INF', '-INF' and 'NaN' to represent positive infinity, negative infinity, and NaN in *expr*.

```
SELECT TO_BINARY_FLOAT('1234.5678','999999.9999') CHR_FMT_FLOAT,
       TO_BINARY_FLOAT('1234.5678') CHR_FLOAT,
       TO_BINARY_FLOAT(1234.5678) NUM_FLOAT,
       TO_BINARY_FLOAT('INF') INF_FLOAT
FROM dual;

  CHR_FMT_FLOAT       CHR_FLOAT       NUM_FLOAT       INF_FLOAT
--------------- --------------- --------------- ---------------
1.23456775E+003 1.23456775E+003 1.23456775E+003             Inf
```

Converting from a character or NUMBER to BINARY_FLOAT and BINARY_DOUBLE may not be exact since BINARY_FLOAT and BINARY_DOUBLE use binary precision, whereas NUMBER uses decimal precision. Converting from BINARY_FLOAT to BINARY_DOUBLE is always exact; converting BINARY_DOUBLE to BINARY_FLOAT may lose precision if BINARY_DOUBLE uses more bits of precision.

TO_CHAR

TO_CHAR(<*expr*> [,<*fmt* >[,<*nlsparm*>]]) takes three arguments, where *expr* is a date or a number or a character datatype, *fmt* is a *format model* specifying the format that expr will appear in, and *nlsparm* specifies language- or location-formatting conventions. This function returns *expr* converted into a character string (the VARCHAR2 datatype).

You can use the TO_CHAR function to convert a datetime or numeric datatype value to character. When the input is not in the default format expected by the database, you have to provide the format of the input data as the second argument. In this section I'll show how a datetime datatype value and a numeric datatype value can be converted to a character datatype.

Date Conversion

If *expr* is a date or timestamp value, *fmt* is a date-format code, and *nlsparm* is an NLS_DATE_LANGUAGE specification, if included. Note that the spelled-out numbers always appear in English, while the day or month may appear in the NLS language.

```
SELECT TO_CHAR(SYSDATE,'Day Ddspth,Month YYYY'
              ,'NLS_DATE_LANGUAGE=German') Today_Heute
FROM dual;

TODAY_HEUTE
----------------------------------------
Dienstag  First,April    2008

SELECT TO_CHAR(SYSDATE
              ,'"On the "Ddspth" day of "Month, YYYY') Today
FROM dual;

TODAY
--------------------------------------------
On the First day of April    , 2008
```

Table 2.7 lists the date-format codes.

TABLE 2.7 Date-Format Codes

Date Code	Format-Code Description
AD or BC	Epoch indicator.
A.D. or B.C.	Epoch indicator with periods.
AM or PM	Meridian indicator.
A.M. or P.M.	Meridian indicator with periods.
DY	Day of week abbreviated.
DAY	Day of week spelled out.
D	Day of week (1–7).
DD	Day of month (1–31).
DDD	Day of year (1–366).
DL	Long date format.
DS	Short date format.
TS	Time in short format.
FF	Fractional seconds.
J	Julian day (days since 4712 BC).
W	Week of the month (1–5).
WW, IW	Week of the year, ISO week of the year.
MM	Two-digit month.
MON	Month name abbreviated.
MONTH	Month name spelled out.
Q	Quarter.

TABLE 2.7 Date-Format Codes *(continued)*

Date Code	Format-Code Description
RM	Roman numeral month (I–XII).
YYYY, YYY, YY, Y	Four-digit year; last 3, 2, 1 digits in the year.
YEAR	Year spelled out.
SYYYY	If BC, year is shown as negative.
RR	Used for data input with only two digits for the year to store 20th-century dates in the 21st century.
RRRR	Used for data input. If a two-digit year is entered, this works like RR. If a four-digit year is entered, it works like YYYY.
CC, SCC	Century.
HH, HH12	Hour of the half-day (1–12).
HH24	Hour of the day (0–23).
MI	Minutes of the hour (0–59).
SS	Seconds of the minute (0–59).
SSSSS	Seconds of the day (0–86399).
TZD	Time zone daylight savings; must correspond to TZR.
TZH	Time zone hour, together with TZM is time zone offset.
TZM	Time zone minute, together with TZH is time zone offset.
TZR	Time zone region.
, . / - ; :	Punctuation.
'text'	Quoted text.
FM	Returns value with no leading or trailing blanks (fill mode).
FX	Requires exact match for the format model.

The RR code is used for data input with only two digits for the year. It is intended to deal with two-digit years before and after 2000. It rounds the century based on the current year and the two-digit year, entered as follows:

- If the current year is greater than or equal to 50 and the two-digit year is less than 50, the century is rounded up to the next century.
- If the current year is greater than or equal to 50 and the two-digit year is greater than or equal to 50, the century is unchanged.
- If the current year is less than 50 and the two-digit year is less than 50, the century is unchanged.
- If the current year is less than 50 and the two-digit year is greater than or equal to 50, the century is rounded down to the previous century.

So if the current year is 2009 (less than 50) and the two-digit year is entered as 62 (greater than or equal to 50), the year is interpreted as 1962.

For any of the numeric codes, the ordinal and/or spelled-out representation can be displayed with the modifier codes th (for ordinal) and sp (for spelled out). Here is an example:

```
SELECT SYSDATE,
       TO_CHAR(SYSDATE,'Mmspth') Month,
       TO_CHAR(SYSDATE,'DDth') Day,
       TO_CHAR(SYSDATE,'Yyyysp') Year
FROM dual;

SYSDATE   MONTH    DAY  YEAR
--------- -------- ---- -------------------
01-APR-08 Fourth   01ST Two Thousand Eight
```

For any of the spelled-out words or ordinals, case follows the pattern of the first two characters in the code. If the first two characters are uppercase, the spelled-out words are all uppercase. If the first two characters are lowercase, the spelled-out words are all lowercase. If the first two characters are uppercase and then lowercase, the spelled-out words have the first letter in uppercase and the remaining characters in lowercase.

```
SELECT TO_CHAR(SYSDATE,'MONTH') upperCase,
       TO_CHAR(SYSDATE,'Month') mixedCase,
       TO_CHAR(SYSDATE,'month') lowerCase
FROM dual;

UPPERCASE MIXEDCASE LOWERCASE
--------- --------- ---------
APRIL     April     april
```

Table 2.8 shows several examples of using the different date-format models with the TO_CHAR function. Please pay close attention to the format model and result to understand the format-model characteristics. The format model is applied to the date Tuesday 01-APR-2008.

TABLE 2.8 Date-Format Examples for Tuesday 01-APR-2008

Format Model	Result
'CCth "Century" BC'	21ST Century AD
'"On the "DDSpth" Day of "MONTH", "YYYY'	On the FIRST Day of APRIL, 2008
'"On the "DdSpth" Day of "FMMonth", "YYYY'	On the First Day of April, 2008
'DS TS'	4/1/2008 01:41:32 PM
'"Today is week" WW "and day" DDD'	Today is week 14 and day 092
'Year'	Two Thousand Eight
'W WW WW D DD DDD Y YY YYY YYYY'	1 14 14 3 01 092 8 08 008 2008

Number Conversion

If *expr* is a number, *fmt* is a numeric format code. Table 2.9 lists these codes.

TABLE 2.9 Numeric Format Codes

Numeric Code	Format-Code Description
9	Numeric digits with a leading space if positive and a leading – (minus) if negative.
0	Leading and/or trailing zeros.
,	Comma, for use as a group separator. It cannot appear after a period or decimal code.
G	Local group separator; could be comma (,) or period (.).
.	Period, for use as the decimal character. It cannot appear more than once or to the left of a group separator.
D	Local decimal character; could be comma (,) or period (.). Only one D is allowed in the format model.
$	Dollar-sign currency symbol.
C	ISO currency symbol (USD for $).
L	Local currency symbol.
FM	No leading or trailing blanks.

TABLE 2.9 Numeric Format Codes *(continued)*

Numeric Code	Format-Code Description
EEEE	Scientific notation.
MI	Negative as a trailing minus. Can appear only in the last position of the format model.
PR	Negative in angle brackets (< >). Can appear only in the last position of the format model.
S	Negative as a leading minus. Can appear only in the first or last position of the format model.
RN	Uppercase Roman numeral.
rn	Lowercase Roman numeral.
X	Hexadecimal
V	Returns value multiplied by 10^n, where n is the number of 9s after the V.
B	Returns blanks for a fixed-point number if the integer part is zero.

`nlsparm` can include `NLS_NUMERIC_CHARACTERS` for specifying decimal and grouping symbols (format symbols `D` and `G`, respectively), `NLS_CURRENCY` for specifying the currency symbol (format symbol `L`), and `NLS_ISO_CURRENCY` for specifying the ISO international currency symbol (format symbol `C`). The `NLS_CURRENCY` symbol and the `NLS_ISO_CURRENCY` mnemonic are frequently different. For example, the `NLS_CURRENCY` symbol for U.S. dollars is `$`, but this symbol is not uniquely American, so the ISO symbol for U.S. dollars is `USD`.

```
SELECT TO_CHAR(-1234.56,'L099G999D99MI',
                 'NLS_NUMERIC_CHARACTERS='',.''
                  NLS_CURRENCY=''DM''
                  NLS_ISO_CURRENCY=''GERMANY''
                 ') Balance
FROM dual;

BALANCE
------------------
    DM001.234,56-
```

Table 2.10 shows several examples of using the different numeric format models. Please pay close attention to the format model and result to understand the format-model characteristics.

TABLE 2.10 Numeric Format Examples

Numeric Format	Source Value	Result Value
'C099G999D99'	-1234.56	-USD001,234.56
'099.99'	1234.56	#######
'09G999V99'	1234.56	01,23456
'09G999D99'	1234.56	01,234.56
'09G999D99PR'	-1234.56	<01,234.56>
'999.99EEEE'	-1234.56	-1.23E+03
'$9999.999S'	-1234.56	$1234.560-
'$9999.999S'	1234.56	$1234.560+
'RN'	141	CXLI
'L99G999D99MI'	1234	$1,234.00

TO_CLOB

TO_CLOB ('<x>') converts input value to a CLOB datatype value. The argument *x* can be of type CHAR, VARCHAR2, NCLOB, NCHAR, NVARCHAR2, or CLOB. CLOB datatypes are discussed in Chapter 6, "Creating Tables and Constraints."

TO_DATE

TO_DATE(<*c*> [,<*fmt*> [,<*nlsparm*>]]) takes three arguments, where *c* is a character string, *fmt* is a format string specifying the format that *c* appears in (refer to Table 2.7, "Date-Format Codes"), and *nlsparm* specifies language- or location-formatting conventions. This function returns *c* converted into the DATE datatype.

If you omit *fmt*, *c* should be in the default date format (as defined in NLS_DATE_FORMAT or derived from NLS_TERRITORY). It is always a good practice to specify the format mask when using the TO_DATE function.

```
alter session set nls_date_format = 'DD-MON-RR HH24:MI:SS';
Session altered.

SELECT TO_DATE('30-SEP-2007', 'DD/MON/YY') DateExample
FROM dual;
```

```
DATEEXAMPLE
------------------
30-SEP-07 00:00:00

SELECT TO_DATE('SEP-2007 13', 'MON/YYYY HH24') DateExample
FROM dual;

DATEEXAMPLE
------------------
01-SEP-07 13:00:00
```

When you use the TO_DATE function and specify a format mask, Oracle will try some additional formats if the data in the input string does not match the original format. For the MM format, Oracle will try the MON and MONTH formats. The MON or MONTH formats can be used interchangeably. For the YY and RR formats, Oracle will try YYYY and RRRR.

Adding the FX format model to the TO_DATE function will require the input be given in the exact format, including spaces and punctuation characters.

Table 2.11 shows examples of the TO_DATE function and their resulting dates.

TABLE 2.11 Date-Conversion Examples

Function	Resulting Date
TO_DATE('01-01-08','DD-MM-RR')	01-JAN-2008
TO_DATE('01-01-1908','DD-MM-RR')	01-JAN-1908
TO_DATE('01-MAR-1998','DD-MONTH-YY')	01-MAR-1998
TO_DATE('01-01-98','DD-MM-YY')	01-JAN-2098
TO_DATE('01-01-98','DD-MM-YYYY')	01-JAN-0098
TO_DATE('01-01-98','DD-MM-RRRR')	01-JAN-1998
TO_DATE('01-MARCH-98','DD-MM-RRRR')	01-MAR-1998
TO_DATE('01-MAR-08','DD-MONTH-RRRR')	01-MAR-2008
TO_DATE('01-MAR-1998','fxDD/MON/YYYY')	ORA-01861 error
TO_DATE('13 MAY 2003','fxDD MON YYYY')	ORA-01841 error

Real World Scenario

Converting Numbers to Words

Once I had to debug a PL/SQL function developed by a programmer to convert numeric input to words. His program unit was very lengthy; basically, it defined the numbers from 1 through 20, tens, hundreds, thousands, and millions in words. He was using a complicated logic to split each digit from the input and was assigning a word for each digit. I told him there is a neat single-line SQL function that could replace his tens of lines of PL/SQL code. When I showed him the SQL, he was amazed with the power of simple SQL functions. I don't remember exactly where I came across this piece of magic code in my career to convert a number to words.

Using the J format along with the TO_CHAR and TO_DATE functions, you can display any number between 1 and 5,373,484 in words. The limit is because Oracle supports dates between January 1, 4712 BC, and December 31, 9999 AD.

The J format is used to display the date in Julian numbers.

```
SELECT SYSDATE, TO_CHAR(SYSDATE, 'J') Julian
FROM dual;

SYSDATE   JULIAN
--------- -------
06-APR-08 2454563
```

The SP format will spell the date. By combining the J and JSP formats, you call spell a number. Notice the use of & in the SQL. You run the SQL multiple times to input different values. Negative numbers cannot be converted to Julian dates.

```
SQL> SET VERIFY OFF
SQL> SELECT TO_CHAR(TO_DATE(&NUM, 'J'), 'jsp') num_to_spell
  2  FROM dual;
Enter value for num: 346

NUM_TO_SPELL
-----------------------
three hundred forty-six

SQL> /
Enter value for num: 5023456

NUM_TO_SPELL
-------------------------------------------------------
five million twenty-three thousand four hundred fifty-six
```

```
SQL> /
Enter value for num: -456
SELECT TO_CHAR(TO_DATE(-456, 'J'), 'jsp') num_to_spell
                        *
ERROR at line 1:
ORA-01854: julian date must be between 1 and 5373484
```

TO_DSINTERVAL

`TO_DSINTERVAL(<c> [,<nlsparm>])` takes two arguments, where *c* is a character string and *nlsparm* specifies the decimal and group separator characters. This function returns *c* converted into an INTERVAL DAY TO SECOND datatype.

```
SELECT SYSDATE,
       SYSDATE+TO_DSINTERVAL('007 12:00:00') "+7 1/2 days",
       SYSDATE+TO_DSINTERVAL('030 00:00:00') "+30 days"
FROM dual;

SYSDATE            +7 1/2 days        +30 days
------------------ ------------------ ------------------
01-APR-08 14:45:34 09-APR-08 02:45:34 01-MAY-08 14:45:34
```

TO_LOB

`TO_LOB (<long>)` converts a LONG or LONG RAW datatype to a CLOB or BLOB datatype. LONG values are converted to a CLOB datatype, and LONG RAW values are converted to a BLOB datatype. To learn more about CLOB and BLOB datatypes, see Chapter 6.

TO_MULTI_BYTE

`TO_MULTI_BYTE(<c>)` takes a single argument, where *c* is a character string. This function returns a character string containing *c* with all single-byte characters converted to their multibyte counterparts. This function is useful only in databases using character sets with both single-byte and multibyte characters. See also `TO_SINGLE_BYTE`.

TO_NUMBER

`TO_NUMBER(<expr> [,<fmt> [,<nlsparm>] ])` takes three arguments, where *expr* is a character or numeric string, *fmt* is a format string specifying the format that *expr* appears in, and *nlsparm* specifies language- or location-formatting conventions. This function returns the numeric value represented by *expr*. Table 2.9 lists all the format models that can be used with the `TO_NUMBER` function. The return datatype is NUMBER.

```
SELECT TO_NUMBER('234.89'), TO_NUMBER(1E-3) FROM dual;
```

```
TO_NUMBER('234.89') TO_NUMBER(1E-3)
------------------- ----------------
             234.89             .001
```

TO_SINGLE_BYTE

TO_SINGLE_BYTE(<*c*>) takes a single argument, where *c* is a character string. This function returns a character string containing *c* with all multibyte characters converted to their single-byte counterparts. This function is useful only in databases using character sets with both single-byte and multibyte characters. See also TO_MULTI_BYTE.

TO_TIMESTAMP

TO_TIMESTAMP(<*c*> [,<*fmt*> [,<*nlsparm*>]]) takes three arguments, where *c* is a character string, *fmt* is a format string specifying the format that *c* appears in, and *nlsparm* specifies language- or location-formatting conventions. If *c* is in default timestamp format (as defined in NLS_TIMESTAMP_FORMAT or derived from NLS_TERRITORY), then *fmt* need not be specified. The return value is of the TIMESTAMP datatype.

```
SELECT TO_TIMESTAMP('30-SEP-2007 08:51:23.456',
                    'DD-MON-YYYY HH24:MI:SS.FF')
FROM dual;

TO_TIMESTAMP('30-SEP-200708:51:23.456','DD-MON-YYYYHH24:MI:SS.FF')
---------------------------------------------------------------------------
30-SEP-07 08.51.23.456000000 AM
```

TO_TIMESTAMP_TZ

TO_TIMESTAMP(<*c*> [,<*fmt*> [,<*nlsparm*>]]) takes three arguments, where *c* is a character string, *fmt* is a format string specifying the format that *c* appears in, and *nlsparm* specifies language- or location-formatting conventions. This function has the same behavior as the TO_TIMESTAMP function, except you can specify a time zone. The return datatype is TIMESTAMP WITH TIME ZONE.

```
SELECT TO_TIMESTAMP_TZ('30-SEP-2007 08:51:23.456',
                    'DD-MON-YYYY HH24:MI:SS.FF') TS_TZ_Example
FROM dual;

TS_TZ_EXAMPLE
---------------------------------------
30-SEP-07 08.51.23.456000000 AM -05:00
```

TO_YMINTERVAL

TO_YMINTERVAL(<*c*>) takes a single argument, where *c* is a character string. This function returns *c* converted into an INTERVAL YEAR TO MONTH datatype.

```
SELECT SYSDATE,
       SYSDATE+TO_YMINTERVAL('01-03') "+15 months",
       SYSDATE-TO_YMINTERVAL('00-03') "-3 months"
FROM dual;

SYSDATE   +15 month -3 months
--------- --------- ---------
01-APR-08 01-JUL-09 01-JAN-08
```

Table 2.12 shows examples to demonstrate the difference between using the ADD_MONTHS function and the TO_YMINTERVAL function.

TABLE 2.12 Compare ADD_MONTHS and TO_YMINTERVAL

Expression	Result
TO_DATE('28-FEB-2007')+ TO_YMINTERVAL('01-00')	28-FEB-2008
ADD_MONTHS('28-FEB-2007',12)	29-FEB-2008
TO_DATE('29-FEB-2008')+ TO_YMINTERVAL('01-00')	Error: ORA-01839
ADD_MONTHS('29-FEB-2008',12)	28-FEB-2009
TO_DATE('30-APR-2008')+ TO_YMINTERVAL('00-04')	30-AUG-2008
ADD_MONTHS('30-APR-2008',04)	31-AUG-2008
TO_DATE('31-JAN-2008')+ TO_YMINTERVAL('00-03')	Error: ORA-01839

UNISTR

UNISTR(<*c*>) takes a single argument, where *c* is a character string. This function returns *c* in Unicode in the database Unicode character set. Include UCS2 characters by prepending a backslash (\) to the character's numeric code. Include the backslash character by specifying two backslashes (\\).

```
SELECT UNISTR('\00A3'), UNISTR('\00F1'), UNISTR('ca\00F1on')
FROM dual;
```

```
UN UN UNISTR('CA
-- -- ----------
 £  ñ  c a ñ o n
```

Using Other Single-Row Functions

This is the catchall category to include all the single-row functions that don't fit into the other categories. Some are incredibly useful, such as DECODE. DECODE is a very special function and the most widely used function. Most likely, you'll see a question on the certification exam about the DECODE function.

The NULLIF function is included in this category and not with other NULL-related functions. The NULLIF function returns a NULL value, whereas the NULL-related functions I discussed earlier take NULL as one of the inputs and give a value as a result.

Miscellaneous-Function Overview

Table 2.13 summarizes the single-row miscellaneous functions. I will cover each of these functions in the "Miscellaneous-Function Descriptions" section.

TABLE 2.13 Miscellaneous-Function Summary

Function	Description
BFILENAME	Returns the BFILE locator for the specified file and directory
DECODE	Acts as an inline CASE statement (emulating IF...THEN...ELSE logic)
DUMP	Returns a raw substring in the specified encoding (octal/hex/character/decimal)
EMPTY_BLOB	Returns an empty BLOB locator
EMPTY_CLOB	Returns an empty CLOB locator
GREATEST	Sorts the arguments and returns the largest
LEAST	Sorts the arguments and returns the smallest
NULLIF	Returns NULL if two expressions are equal
ORA_HASH	Returns the hash value for an expression

TABLE 2.13 Miscellaneous-Function Summary *(continued)*

Function	Description
SYS_CONTEXT	Returns various session attributes, such as IP address, terminal, and current user
SYS_GUID	Generates a globally unique identifier as a RAW value
UID	Returns the numeric user ID for the current session
USER	Returns the username for the current session
USERENV	Returns information about the current session
VSIZE	Returns the internal size in bytes for an expression

Miscellaneous-Function Descriptions

The miscellaneous functions are arranged in alphabetical order, with descriptions and examples of each one.

BFILENAME

`BFILENAME(`*`dir`*`, `*`file`*`)` takes two arguments, where *`dir`* is a directory and *`file`* is a filename. This function returns an empty BFILE locator. This function is used to initialize a BFILE variable or BFILE column in a table. When this function is used, the BFILE is instantiated. Neither *`dir`* nor *`file`* needs to exist at the time `BFILENAME` is called, but both must exist when the locator is used. I'll discuss the BFILE datatype in Chapter 6.

DECODE

`DECODE` is a conditional function. I discussed the `CASE` conditional expression in Chapter 1.

`DECODE(`*`x`*` ,`*`m1`*`, `*`r1`*` [,`*`m2`*` ,`*`r2`*`]…[,`*`d`*`])` can use multiple arguments. *`x`* is an expression. *`m1`* is a matching expression to compare with *`x`*. If *`m1`* is equivalent to *`x`*, then *`r1`* is returned; otherwise, additional matching expressions (*`m2`*, *`m3`*, *`m4`*, and so on) are compared, if they are included, and the corresponding result (*`r2`*, *`r3`*, *`r4`*, and so on) is returned. If no match is found and the default expression *`d`* is included, then *`d`* is returned. This function acts like a `case` statement in C, Pascal, or Ada. `DECODE` is a powerful tool that can make SQL very efficient—or very dense and nonintuitive. Let's look at some examples to help clarify its use.

The following example queries the `COUNTRIES` table and displays a region name based on the `region_id` column value. If the `region_id` column value does not match the values in the list, you want to display `Other`. To limit the rows in the output, you use the `SUBSTR` function to identify the country codes that begin with `I` or end with `R`.

```
SELECT country_id, country_name, region_id,
       DECODE(region_id, 1, 'Europe',
                         2, 'Americas',
                         3, 'Asia',
                            'Other') Region
FROM countries
WHERE SUBSTR(country_id,1,1) = 'I'
   OR SUBSTR(country_id,2,1) = 'R';

CO COUNTRY_NA        REGION_ID REGION
-- ---------- ---------------- --------
AR Argentina                 2 Americas
BR Brazil                    2 Americas
FR France                    1 Europe
IL Israel                    4 Other
IN India                     3 Asia
IT Italy                     1 Europe
```

DECODE does not have to return a value; it can return NULL if the optional *d* argument is not provided. In the previous example, if Other is omitted, the region name for Israel will be NULL.

```
SELECT country_id, country_name, region_id,
       DECODE(region_id, 1, 'Europe',
                         2, 'Americas',
                         3, 'Asia') Region
FROM countries
WHERE SUBSTR(country_id,1,1) = 'I'
   OR SUBSTR(country_id,2,1) = 'R';
```

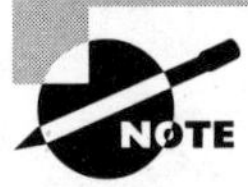

In the DECODE function, Oracle treats two NULL values as equal. Hence, you can represent the NVL function using DECODE, as in DECODE(<string>, NULL, <new_value>, <string>).

DUMP

DUMP(*x* [,*fmt* [,*n1* [,*n2*]]]) can take four arguments, where *x* is an expression. *fmt* is a format specification for octal (8), decimal (10), hexadecimal (16), or single characters (17). Decimal is the default. If you add 1000 to the format specification, the character set name is also returned (for example, 1008 for octal). *n1* is the starting byte offset within *x*, and *n2* is the length in bytes to dump. This function returns a character string containing the datatype of *x* in numeric notation (for example, 2=number, 12=date), the length in bytes of *x*, and the internal representation of x. This function is mainly used for troubleshooting data problems.

```
SELECT last_name, DUMP(last_name) DUMP_EX
FROM employees
WHERE last_name like 'J%';

LAST_NAME    DUMP_EX
------------ -----------------------------------------------
Johnson      Typ=1 Len=7: 74,111,104,110,115,111,110
Jones        Typ=1 Len=5: 74,111,110,101,115

SELECT last_name, DUMP(last_name, 1017, 3, 3) DUMP_EX
FROM employees
WHERE last_name like 'J%';

LAST_NAME    DUMP_EX
------------ -----------------------------------------------
Johnson      Typ=1 Len=7 CharacterSet=WE8MSWIN1252: h,n,s
Jones        Typ=1 Len=5 CharacterSet=WE8MSWIN1252: n,e,s
```

EMPTY_BLOB

`EMPTY_BLOB()` takes no arguments. This function returns an empty BLOB locator. This function is used to initialize a BLOB variable or BLOB column in a table. When used, the BLOB is instantiated but not populated.

EMPTY_CLOB

`EMPTY_CLOB()` takes no arguments. This function returns an empty CLOB locator. This function is used to initialize a CLOB variable or CLOB column in a table. When used, the CLOB is instantiated but not populated.

GREATEST

`GREATEST(`*`exp_list`*`)` takes one argument, where *exp_list* is a list of expressions. This function returns the expression that sorts highest in the datatype of the first expression. If the first expression is any of the character datatypes, a VARCHAR2 is returned, and the comparison rules for VARCHAR2 are used for character-literal strings. A `NULL` in the expression list results in a `NULL` being returned.

The following example shows you that the list was treated as a character list and not a date, even though you had all date values as input:

```
SELECT GREATEST('01-ARP-08','30-DEC-01','12-SEP-09')
FROM dual;

GREATEST(
---------
30-DEC-01
```

In the following example, since the first argument is numeric, Oracle tries to convert the rest of the list to numeric and encounters an error:

```
SELECT GREATEST(345, 'XYZ', 2354) FROM dual;
ERROR at line 1:
ORA-01722: invalid number
```

In the next example, I changed the order to have the character string as the first entry in the list; hence, Oracle considers the rest of the list to be characters and does not produce an error:

```
SELECT GREATEST('XYZ', 345, 2354) FROM dual;

GRE
---
XYZ
```

LEAST

LEAST(*exp_list*) takes one argument, where *exp_list* is a list of expressions. This function returns the expression that sorts lowest in the datatype of the first expression. If the first expression is any of the character datatypes, a VARCHAR2 is returned.

```
SELECT LEAST(SYSDATE,'15-MAR-2002','17-JUN-2002') oldest
FROM dual;

OLDEST
---------
15-MAR-02
```

The following SQL is used to calculate a bonus of 15 percent of salary to employees, with a maximum bonus at 500 and a minimum bonus at 400:

```
SELECT last_name, salary,
       GREATEST(LEAST(salary*0.15, 500), 400) bonus
FROM employees
WHERE department_id IN (30, 10)
ORDER BY last_name;
```

```
LAST_NAME              SALARY           BONUS
------------ ---------------- ----------------
Baida                    2900             435
Colmenares               2500             400
Himuro                   2600             400
Khoo                     3100             465
Raphaely                11000             500
Whalen                   4400             500
```

The comparison rules used by GREATEST and LEAST on character literals order trailing spaces higher than no spaces. This behavior follows the nonpadded comparison rules of the VARCHAR2 datatype. Note the ordering of the leading and trailing spaces: trailing spaces are greatest and leading spaces are least.

```
SELECT GREATEST(' Yes','Yes','Yes ')
        ,LEAST(' Yes','Yes','Yes ')
FROM dual;

GREA LEAST
---- -----
Yes   Yes
```

To remember the comparison rules for trailing and leading space in character literals, think "leading equals least."

NULLIF

NULLIF(*x1* , *x2*) takes two arguments, where *x1* and *x2* are expressions. This function returns NULL if *x1* equals *x2*; otherwise, it returns *x1*. If *x1* is NULL, NULLIF returns NULL.

To facilitate visualizing a NULL, the following example has the NULL indicator set to ?. So, a ? in the query results that follow represents a NULL:

```
SET NULL ?
SELECT ename, mgr, comm
       NULLIF(comm,0) test1,
       NULLIF(0,comm) test2,
       NULLIF(mgr,comm) test3
FROM scott.emp
WHERE empno IN (7844,7839,7654,7369);
```

```
ENAME       MGR  COMM  TEST1  TEST2  TEST3
---------- ---- ---- ----- ----- -----
SMITH       7902    ?     ?      0   7902
MARTIN      7698 1400  1400      0   7698
KING           ?    ?     ?      0      ?
TURNER      7698    0     ?      ?   7698
```

ORA_HASH

ORA_HASH (expr [,max_bucket [,seed]]) can take three arguments. The first argument, *expr*, is an expression whose hash value will be calculated and assigned to a bucket. The maximum bucket value is determined by the second argument, *max_bucket*; the default and maximum is 4,294,967,295. The *seed* argument enables Oracle to generate many different results for the same sets of data. The hash function is applied to *expr* and *seed*. The *seed* can be between 0 and 4,294,967,295.

This function is useful for getting a random sample of rows from table. In the following example, you can get few random rows from the EMPLOYEES table. Notice the difference in result for each run and with different seed values. The rows in the table are divided into 20 buckets (0 through 19) based on the hash value, and you are selecting the rows from bucket 0.

```
SELECT department_id, last_name, salary
FROM employees
WHERE ORA_HASH(last_name || first_name, 19, 2) = 0;

  DEPARTMENT_ID LAST_NAME              SALARY
--------------- ------------ ---------------
             80 Errazuriz               12000
             80 Tuvault                  7000
             50 Feeney                   3000

SELECT department_id, last_name, salary
FROM employees
WHERE ORA_HASH(last_name || first_name, 19, 5) = 0;

  DEPARTMENT_ID LAST_NAME              SALARY
--------------- ------------ ---------------
             90 Kochhar                 17000
            100 Sciarra                  7700
             80 Vishney                 10500
                Grant                    7000
             50 Chung                    3800
```

```
SELECT department_id, last_name, salary
FROM employees
WHERE ORA_HASH(last_name || first_name, 19) = 0;

   DEPARTMENT_ID LAST_NAME                  SALARY
---------------- ------------ ----------------
              70 Baer                        10000
              30 Colmenares                   2500
              50 Mallin                       3300
              50 Taylor                       3200
```

SYS_CONTEXT

SYS_CONTEXT(*n* , *p* [, *length*]) can take three arguments, where *n* is a namespace, *p* is a parameter associated with namespace *n*, and *length* is the length of the return value in bytes. *length* defaults to 256. The built-in namespace in Oracle is called USERENV, which describes the current session. The return datatype is VARCHAR2.

```
SELECT SYS_CONTEXT('USERENV','IP_ADDRESS')
FROM dual;

SYS_CONTEXT('USERENV','IP_ADDRESS')
------------------------------------
192.168.1.100
```

Table 2.14 lists the parameters available in the USERENV namespace for the SYS_CONTEXT function.

TABLE 2.14 Parameters in the USERENV Namespace

Parameter	Description
ACTION	Returns the position in the module (application).
AUDITED_CURSORID	Returns the cursor ID of the SQL that triggered the auditing.
AUTHENTICATED_IDENTITY	Returns the identity used in the authentication.
AUTHENTICATION_DATA	Returns the data used to authenticate a logged-in user.
AUTHENTICATION_METHOD	Returns the method used to authenticate a user. The return value can be DATABASE for database-authenticated accounts, OS for externally identified accounts, NETWORK for globally identified accounts, and so on.

TABLE 2.14 Parameters in the USERENV Namespace *(continued)*

Parameter	Description
BG_JOB_ID	Returns the job ID (that is, DBA_JOBS) if the session was created by a background process. Returns NULL if the session is a foreground session. See also FG_JOB_ID.
CLIENT_IDENTIFIER	Returns the client session identifier in the global context. It can be set with the DBMS_SESSION built-in package.
CLIENT_INFO	Returns the 64 bytes of user session information stored by DBMS_APPLICATION_INFO.
CURRENT_BIND	Returns bind variables for fine-grained auditing.
CURRENT_SCHEMA	Returns the current schema as set by ALTER SESSION SET CURRENT_SCHEMA or, by default, the login schema/ID.
CURRENT_SCHEMAID	Returns the numeric ID for CURRENT_SCHEMA.
CURRENT_SQL	Returns the SQL that triggered fine-grained auditing (use only within scope inside the event handler for fine-grained auditing).
CURRENT_SQL_LENGTH	Returns the length of the current SQL that triggered fine-grained auditing.
DB_DOMAIN	Returns the contents of the DB_DOMAIN init.ora parameter.
DB_NAME	Returns the contents of the DB_NAME init.ora parameter.
DB_UNIQUE_NAME	Returns the contents of the DB_UNIQUE_NAME init.ora parameter.
ENTRYID	Returns the auditing entry identifier
ENTERPRISE_IDENTITY	Returns OID DN for enterprise users, for local users NULL.
FG_JOB_ID	Returns the job ID of the current session if a foreground process created it. Returns NULL if the session is a background session. See also BG_JOB_ID.
GLOBAL_CONTEXT_MEMORY	Returns the number in the SGA by the globally accessible context.
GLOBAL_UID	Returns the global user ID from OID.
HOST	Returns the hostname of the machine from where the client connected. This is not the same terminal in V$SESSION.

TABLE 2.14 Parameters in the USERENV Namespace *(continued)*

Parameter	Description
IDENTIFICATION_TYPE	Returns how the user is set to authenticate in the database: LOCAL, EXTERNAL, or GLOBAL.
INSTANCE	Returns the instance number for the instance to which the session is connected. This is always 1 unless you are running Oracle Real Application Clusters.
INSTANCE_NAME	Returns the name of the instance.
IP_ADDRESS	Returns the IP address of the machine from where the client connected.
ISDBA	Returns TRUE if the user connected AS SYSDBA.
LANG	Returns the ISO abbreviation for the language name.
LANGUAGE	Returns a character string containing the language and territory used by the session and the database character set in the form language_territory.characterset.
MODULE	Returns the application name set through DBMS_APPLICATION_INFO.
NETWORK_PROTOCOL	Returns the network protocol being used as specified in the PROTOCOL= section of the connect string or tnsnames.ora definition.
NLS_CALENDAR	Returns the calendar for the current session.
NLS_CURRENCY	Returns the currency for the current session.
NLS_DATE_FORMAT	Returns the date format for the current session.
NLS_DATE_LANGUAGE	Returns the language used for displaying dates.
NLS_SORT	Returns the binary or linguistic sort basis.
NLS_TERRITORY	Returns the territory for the current session.
OS_USER	Returns the operating-system username for the current session.
POLICY_INVOKER	Returns the invoker of row-level security-policy functions.
PROXY_ENTERPRISE_IDENTITY	Returns OID DN when the proxy user is an enterprise user.

TABLE 2.14 Parameters in the USERENV Namespace *(continued)*

Parameter	Description
PROXY_GOLBAL_UID	Returns the global user ID from OID for Enterprise User Security proxy users.
PROXY_USER	Returns the name of the database user who opened the current session for the session user.
PROXY_USERID	Returns the numeric ID for the database user who opened the current session for the session user.
SERVER_HOST	Returns the hostname of the machine where the instance is running.
SERVICE_NAME	Returns the name of the service where the session is connected.
SESSION_USER	Returns the database username for the current session.
SESSION_USERID	Returns the numeric database user ID for the current session.
SESSIONID	Returns the auditing session identifier AUDSID. This parameter is out of scope for distributed queries.
SID	Returns the session number (same as the SID from V$SESSION).
STATEMENT_ID	Returns the auditing statement identifier.
TERMINAL	Returns the terminal identifier for the current session. This is the same as the terminal in V$SESSION.

Here are few more examples of SYS_CONTEXT in the USERENV namespace:

```
SELECT SYS_CONTEXT('USERENV', 'OS_USER'),
       SYS_CONTEXT('USERENV', 'CURRENT_SCHEMA'),
       SYS_CONTEXT('USERENV', 'HOST'),
       SYS_CONTEXT('USERENV', 'NLS_TERRITORY')
FROM dual;

SYS_CONTEXT('USERENV','OS_USER')
SYS_CONTEXT('USERENV','CURRENT_SCHEMA')
SYS_CONTEXT('USERENV','HOST')
SYS_CONTEXT('USERENV','NLS_TERRITORY')
----------------------------------------
```

```
oracle
HR
linux04.mycompany.corp
AMERICA
```

SYS_GUID

SYS_GUID() generates a globally unique identifier as a RAW value. This function is useful for creating a unique identifier to identify a row. SYS_GUID() returns a 32-bit hexadecimal representation of the 16-byte RAW value.

```
SELECT SYS_GUID() FROM DUAL;

SYS_GUID()
--------------------------------
CDA78A020D6E43A6AB743A5CE8CB8C55

SELECT SYS_GUID() FROM DUAL;

SYS_GUID()
--------------------------------
DC7C19A3AD264CE184C64194E65F83E5
```

UID

UID takes no parameters and returns the integer user ID for the current user connected to the session. The user ID uniquely identifies each user in a database and can be selected from the DBA_USERS view.

```
SQL> SHOW USER
USER is "BTHOMAS"

SELECT username, account_status
FROM dba_users
WHERE user_id = UID;

USERNAME          ACCOUNT_STATUS
---------------- ---------------
BTHOMAS          OPEN
```

USER

USER takes no parameters and returns a character string containing the username for the current user.

```
SELECT default_tablespace, temporary_tablespace
FROM dba_users
WHERE username = USER;

DEFAULT_TABLESPACE             TEMPORARY_TABLESPACE
------------------------------ ---------------------
USERS                          TEMP
```

USERENV

USERENV(*opt*) takes a single argument, where *opt* is one of the following options:

- ISDBA returns TRUE if the SYSDBA role is enabled in the current session.
- SESSIONID returns the AUDSID auditing session identifier.
- ENTRYID returns the auditing entry identifier if auditing is enabled for the instance (the init.ora parameter AUDIT_TRAIL is set to TRUE).
- INSTANCE returns the instance identifier to which the session is connected. This option is useful only if you are running the Oracle Parallel Server and have multiple instances.
- LANGUAGE returns the language, territory, and database character set. The delimiters are an underscore (_) between language and territory and a period (.) between the territory and character set.
- LANG returns the ISO abbreviation of the session's language.
- TERMINAL returns a VARCHAR2 string containing information corresponding to the operating system identifier for the current session's terminal.

The option can appear in uppercase, lowercase, or mixed case. The USERENV function has been deprecated since Oracle 9*i*. It is recommended to use the SYS_CONTEXT function with the built-in USERENV namespace instead.

VSIZE

VSIZE(*x*) takes a single argument, where *x* is an expression. This function returns the size in bytes of the internal representation of the *x*.

```
SELECT last_name, first_name,
       VSIZE(last_name) ln_size, VSIZE(first_name) fn_size
FROM employees
WHERE last_name like 'K%';
```

```
LAST_NAME    FIRST_NAME              LN_SIZE    FN_SIZE
------------ -------------------- ---------- ----------
Kaufling     Payam                         8          5
Khoo         Alexander                     4          9
King         Janette                       4          7
King         Steven                        4          6
Kochhar      Neena                         7          5
Kumar        Sundita                       5          7
```

Since the database character set is single-byte, the byte used for each character is 1; hence, the size shown here is actually the number of characters in the input. For multibyte characters, this would be different.

Summary

This chapter introduced single-row functions. It started by discussing the functions available in Oracle 11*g* to handle NULLs. Then it discussed the single-row functions available in Oracle 11*g* by grouping them into character, numeric, date, and conversion functions.

You learned that single-row functions return a value for each row as it is retrieved from the table. You can use single-row functions to interpret NULL values, format output, convert datatypes, transform data, perform date arithmetic, give environment information, and perform trigonometric calculations.

You can use single-row functions in the SELECT, WHERE, and ORDER BY clauses of SELECT statements. I covered the rich assortment of functions available in each datatype category and some functions that work on any datatype.

The NVL, NVL2, and COALESCE functions interpret NULL values.

The single-row character functions operate on character input. The INSTR function returns the position of a substring within the string. The SUBSTR function returns a portion of the string. INSTR and SUBSTR are great for extracting part of the input string. REPLACE and TRANSLATE transform the input.

Single-row numeric functions operate on numeric input. FLOOR, CEIL, ROUND, and TRUNC get the nearest number. FLOOR, CEIL, and ROUND return the nearest integer, whereas ROUND returns a value rounded to certain digits of precision. REMAINDER and MOD are similar functions.

Date functions operate on datetime values. SYSDATE and SYSTIMESTAMP values return the current date and time. MONTHS_BETWEEN finds the number of months between two date values. ADD_MONTHS is a commonly used function and can add months to or subtract months from a date. You can use ROUND and TRUNC on datetime values to find the nearest date, month, or year.

Of the conversion functions, TO_CHAR and TO_DATE are the most commonly used. I also reviewed the format codes that can be used with numeric and datetime values.

The DECODE function evaluates a condition, and you can easily build IF…THEN…ELSE logic into SQL using the DECODE function.

Exam Essentials

Understand where single-row functions can be used. Single-row functions can be used in the SELECT, WHERE, and ORDER BY clauses of SELECT statements.

Know the effects that NULL values can have on arithmetic and other functions. Any arithmetic operation on a NULL results in a NULL. This is true of most functions as well. Use the NVL, NVL2, and COALESCE functions to deal with NULLs.

Review the character-manipulation functions. Understand the arguments and the result of using character-manipulation functions such as INSTR, SUBSTR, REPLACE, and TRANSLATE.

Understand the numeric functions. Know the effects of using TRUNC and ROUND with -n as the second argument. Also practice using LENGTH and INSTR, which return a numeric result, inside SUBSTR and other character functions.

Know how date arithmetic works. When adding or subtracting numeric values from a DATE datatype, whole numbers represent days. Also, the date/time intervals INTERVAL YEAR TO MONTH and INTERVAL DAY TO SECOND can be added or subtracted from date/time datatypes. You need to know how to interpret and create expressions that add intervals to or subtract intervals from dates.

Know the datatypes for the various date/time functions. Oracle has many date/time functions to support the date/time datatypes. You need to know the return datatypes for these functions. SYSDATE and CURRENT_DATE return a DATE datatype. CURRENT_TIMESTAMP and SYSTIMESTAMP return a TIMESTAMP WITH TIME ZONE datatype. LOCALTIMESTAMP returns a TIMESTAMP datatype.

Know the format models for converting dates to/from character strings. In practice, you can simply look up format codes in a reference. For the certification exam, you must have them memorized.

Understand the use of the DECODE function. DECODE acts like a case statement in C, Pascal, or Ada. Learn how this function works and how to use it.

Review Questions

1. You want to display each project's start date as the day, week, number, and year. Which statement will give output like the following?

   `Tuesday  Week 23, 2008`

   A. `SELECT proj_id, TO_CHAR(start_date, 'DOW  Week WOY YYYY') FROM projects;`

   B. `SELECT proj_id, TO_CHAR(start_date,'Day'||' Week'||' WOY, YYYY') FROM projects;`

   C. `SELECT proj_id, TO_CHAR(start_date, 'Day" Week" WW, YYYY') FROM projects;`

   D. `SELECT proj_id, TO_CHAR(start_date, 'Day Week# , YYYY') FROM projects;`

   E. You can't calculate week numbers with Oracle.

2. What will the following statement return?

   ```
   SELECT last_name, first_name, start_date
   FROM employees
   WHERE hire_date < TRUNC(SYSDATE) - 5;
   ```

   A. Employees hired within the past five hours

   B. Employees hired within the past five days

   C. Employees hired more than five hours ago

   D. Employees hired more than five days ago

3. Which assertion about the following statements is most true?

   ```
   SELECT name, region_code||phone_number
   FROM customers;
   SELECT name, CONCAT(region_code,phone_number)
   FROM customers;
   ```

   A. If `REGION_CODE` is `NULL`, the first statement will not include that customer's `PHONE_NUMBER`.

   B. If `REGION_CODE` is `NULL`, the second statement will not include that customer's `PHONE_NUMBER`.

   C. Both statements will return the same data.

   D. The second statement will raise an error if `REGION_CODE` is `NULL` for any customer.

4. Which single-row function could you use to return a specific portion of a character string?

   A. `INSTR`

   B. `SUBSTR`

   C. `LPAD`

   D. `LEAST`

5. The data in the PRODUCT table is as described here. The bonus amount is calculated as the lesser of 5 percent of the base price or 20 percent of the surcharge.

sku	name	division	base_price	surcharge
1001	PROD-1001	A	200	50
1002	PROD-1002	C	250	
1003	PROD-1003	C	240	20
1004	PROD-1004	A	320	
1005	PROD-1005	C	225	40

Which of the following statements will achieve the desired results?

A.
```
SELECT sku, name, LEAST(base_price * 1.05, surcharge * 1.2)
FROM products;
```

B.
```
SELECT sku, name, LEAST(NVL(base_price,0) * 1.05, surcharge * 1.2)
FROM products;
```

C.
```
SELECT sku, name,  COALESCE(LEAST(base_price*1.05, surcharge * 1.2),
base_price * 1.05)
FROM products;
```

D. A, B, and C will all achieve the desired results.

E. None of these statements will achieve the desired results.

6. Which function(s) accept arguments of any datatype? (Choose all that apply.)

A. SUBSTR

B. NVL

C. ROUND

D. DECODE

E. SIGN

7. What will be returned by SIGN(ABS(NVL(-32,0)))?

A. 1

B. 32

C. -1

D. 0

E. NULL

8. The SALARY table has the following data:

```
LAST_NAME    FIRST_NAME               SALARY
------------ -------------------- ----------
Mavris       Susan                      6500
Higgins      Shelley                   12000
Tobias       Sigal
Colmenares   Karen                      2500
Weiss        Matthew                    8000
Mourgos      Kevin                      5800
Rogers       Michael                    2900
Stiles       Stephen                    3200
```

Consider the following SQL, and choose the best option:

```
SELECT last_name, NVL2(salary, salary, 0) N1,
       NVL(salary,0) N2
FROM salary;
```

A. Column N1 and N2 will have different results.

B. Column N1 will show zero for all rows, and column N2 will show the correct salary values, and zero for Tobias.

C. The SQL will error out because the number of arguments in the NVL2 function is incorrect.

D. Columns N1 and N2 will show the same result.

9. Which two functions could you use to strip leading characters from a character string? (Choose two.)

A. LTRIM

B. SUBSTR

C. RTRIM

D. INSTR

E. STRIP

10. What is the result of MOD(x1, 4), if x1 is 11?

A. -1

B. 3

C. 1

D. REMAINDER(11,4)

11. Which two SQL statements will replace the last two characters of `last_name` with 'XX' in the `employees` table when executed? (Choose two.)

    A. `SELECT RTRIM(last_name, SUBSTR(last_name, LENGTH(last_name)-1)) || 'XX' new_col FROM employees;`

    B. `SELECT REPLACE(last_name, SUBSTR(last_name, LENGTH(last_name)-1), 'XX') new_col FROM employees;`

    C. `SELECT REPLACE(SUBSTR(last_name, LENGTH(last_name)-1), 'XX') new_col FROM employees;`

    D. `SELECT CONCAT(SUBSTR(last_name, 1,LENGTH(last_name)-2), 'XX') new_col FROM employees;`

12. Which date components does the CURRENT_TIMESTAMP function display?

    A. Session date, session time, and session time zone offset

    B. Session date and session time

    C. Session date and session time zone offset

    D. Session time zone offset

13. Using the SALESPERSON_REVENUE table described here, which statements will properly display the TOTAL_REVENUE (CAR_SALES + WARRANTY_SALES) of each salesperson?

Column Name	salesperson_id	car_sales	warranty_sales
Key Type	pk		
NULLs/Unique	NN	NN	
FK Table			
Datatype	NUMBER	NUMBER	NUMBER
Length	10	11,2	11,2

A.
```
SELECT salesperson_id, car_sales, warranty_sales, car_sales + warranty_
sales total_sales
FROM salesperson_revenue;
```

B.
```
SELECT salesperson_id, car_sales, warranty_sales, car_sales +
NVL2(warranty_sales,0) total_sales
FROM salesperson_revenue;
```

C.
```
SELECT salesperson_id, car_sales, warranty_sales, NVL2(warranty_sales,
car_sales + warranty_sales, car_sales) total_sales
FROM salesperson_revenue;
```

D.
```
SELECT salesperson_id, car_sales, warranty_sales, car_sales +
COALESCE(car_sales, warranty_sales, car_sales + warranty_sales) total_
sales
FROM salesperson_revenue;
```

14. What will be the result of executing the following SQL, if today's date is February 28, 2009?

```
SELECT ADD_MONTHS('28-FEB-09', -12) from dual;
```

A. 28-FEB-10

B. 28-FEB-08

C. 29-FEB-08

D. 28-JAN-08

15. Consider the following two SQL statements, and choose the best option:

```
1. SELECT TO_DATE('30-SEP-07','DD-MM-YYYY')  from dual;
2. SELECT TO_DATE('30-SEP-07','DD-MON-RRRR') from dual;
```

A. Statement 1 will error; 2 will produce result.

B. The resulting date value from the two statements will be the same.

C. The resulting date value from the two statements will be different.

D. Both statements will generate an error.

16. What will the following SQL statement return?

```
SELECT COALESCE(NULL,'Oracle ','Certified') FROM dual;
```

A. NULL

B. Oracle

C. Certified

D. Oracle Certified

17. Which expression will always return the date one year later than the current date?

A. SYSDATE + 365

B. SYSDATE + TO_YMINTERVAL('01-00')

C. CURRENT_DATE + 1

D. NEW_TIME(CURRENT_DATE,1,'YEAR')

E. None of the above

18. Which function will return a TIMESTAMP WITH TIME ZONE datatype?

A. CURRENT_TIMESTAMP

B. LOCALTIMESTAMP

C. CURRENT_DATE

D. SYSDATE

19. Which statement would change all occurrences of the string `'IBM'` to the string `'SUN'` in the `DESCRIPTION` column of the `VENDOR` table?

A. `SELECT TRANSLATE(description, 'IBM', 'SUN') FROM vendor`

B. `SELECT CONVERT(description, 'IBM', 'SUN') FROM vendor`

C. `SELECT EXTRACT(description, 'IBM', 'SUN') FROM vendor`

D. `SELECT REPLACE(description, 'IBM', 'SUN') FROM vendor`

20. Which function implements `IF...THEN...ELSE` logic?

A. `INITCAP`

B. `REPLACE`

C. `DECODE`

D. `IFELSE`

Answers to Review Questions

1. C. Double quotation marks must surround literal strings like "Week".

2. D. The TRUNC function removes the time portion of a date by default, and whole numbers added to or subtracted from dates represent days added or subtracted from that date. TRUNC(SYSDATE) -5 means five days ago at midnight.

3. C. The two statements are equivalent.

4. B. SUBSTR returns part of the string. INSTR returns a number. LPAD adds to a character string. LEAST does not change an input string.

5. C. Options A and B do not account for NULL surcharges correctly and will set the bonus to NULL where the surcharge is NULL. In option B, the NVL function is applied to the base_price column instead of the surcharge column. In option C, the LEAST function will return a NULL if surcharge is NULL, in which case BASE_PRICE * 1.05 would be returned from the COALESCE function.

6. B, D. ROUND does not accept character arguments. SUBSTR accepts only character arguments. SIGN accepts only numeric arguments.

7. A. The functions are evaluated from the innermost to outermost, as follows:
   SIGN(ABS(NVL(-32,0))) = SIGN(ABS(-32)) = SIGN(32) = 1

8. D. The NVL function returns zero if the salary value is NULL, or else it returns the original value. The NVL2 function returns the second argument if the salary value is not NULL. If NULL, the third argument is returned.

9. A, B. RTRIM removes trailing (not leading) characters. INSTR returns a number. STRIP is not a valid Oracle function. SUBSTR with second argument greater than 1 removes leading characters from a string.

10. B. MOD returns the number remainder after division. The REMAINDER function is similar to MOD but will use the ROUND function in the algorithm; hence, the result of REMAINDER(11,4) would be -1. MOD uses FLOOR in the algorithm.

11. A, D. The SUBSTR function in option A would return the last two characters of the last name. These two characters are right-trimmed using the RTRIM function. The result would be the first portion of the last name and is concatenated to 'XX'. Option B also would do the same as A, but would replace all the occurrences of the last two characters (Paululul will be PaXXXXXX instead of PaululXX). Option C would return only the last two characters of the last name. The SUBSTR function in option D would return the first character through the last –2 characters. 'XX' is concatenated to the result.

12. A. The CURRENT_TIMESTAMP function returns the session date, session time, and session time zone offset. The return datatype is TIMESTAMP WITH TIME ZONE.

13. C. Option A will result in NULL TOTAL_SALES for rows where there are NULL WARRANTY_SALES. Option B is not the correct syntax for NVL2, because it requires three arguments. With option C, if WARRANTY_SALES is NULL, then CAR_SALES is returned; otherwise, CAR_SALES+WARRANTY_SALES is returned. The COALESCE function returns the first non-NULL argument and could be used to obtain the desired results, but the first argument here is CAR_SALES, which is not NULL, and therefore COALESCE will always return CAR_SALES.

14. C. The ADD_MONTHS function returns the date *d* plus *i* months. If <*d*> is the last day of the month or the resulting month has fewer days, then the result is the last day of the resulting month.

15. C. Statement 1 will result in 30-SEP-0007, and statement 2 will result in 30-SEP-2007. The RR and RRRR formats derive the century based on the current date if the century is not specified. The YY format will use the current century, and the YYYY format expects the century in the input.

16. B. The COALESCE function returns the first non-NULL parameter, which is the character string 'Oracle '.

17. E. Option A will not work if there is a February 29 (leap year) in the next 365 days. Option B will always add one year to the present date, except if the current date is February 29 (leap year). Option C will return the date one day later. NEW_TIME is used to return the date/time in a different time zone. ADD_MONTHS (SYSDATE,12) can be used to achieve the desired result.

18. A. LOCALTIMESTAMP does not return the time zone. CURRENT_DATE and SYSDATE return neither fractional seconds nor a time zone; they both return the DATE datatype.

19. D. CONVERT is used to change from one character set to another. EXTRACT works on date/time datatypes. TRANSLATE changes all occurrences of each character with a positionally corresponding character, so 'I like IBM' would become 'S like SUN'.

20. C. The INITCAP function capitalizes the first letter in each word. The REPLACE function performs search-and-replace string operations. There is no IFELSE function. The DECODE function is the one that implements IF...THEN...ELSE logic.

Chapter 3

Using Group Functions

ORACLE DATABASE 11*g*: SQL FUNDAMENTALS I EXAM OBJECTIVES COVERED IN THIS CHAPTER:

✓ **Reporting Aggregated Data Using the Group Functions**

- Identify the available group functions
- Describe the use of group functions
- Group data by using the GROUP BY clause
- Include or exclude the grouped rows by using the HAVING clause

As explained in the previous chapter, *functions* are programs that take zero or more arguments and return a single value. The exam focuses on two types of functions: single-row and aggregate (group) functions. Single-row functions were covered in Chapter 2, "Using Single-Row Functions." Group functions are covered in this chapter.

Group functions differ from single-row functions in how they are evaluated. Single-row functions are evaluated once for each row retrieved. Group functions are evaluated on groups of one or more rows at a time.

In this chapter, you will explore which group functions are available in SQL, the rules for how to use them, and what to expect on the exam about aggregating data and group functions. You will also explore nesting function calls together. SQL allows you to nest group functions within calls to single-row functions, as well as nest single-row functions within calls to group functions.

Group-Function Fundamentals

Group functions are sometimes called *aggregate functions* and return a value based on a number of inputs. The exact number of inputs is not determined until the query is executed and all rows are fetched. This differs from single-row functions, in which the number of inputs is known at parse time—before the query is executed. Because of this difference, group functions have slightly different requirements and behavior than single-row functions.

Group functions do not consider NULL values, except the COUNT(*) and GROUPING functions. You may apply the NVL function to the argument of the group function to substitute a value for NULL and hence be included in the processing of the group function. If the dataset contains all NULL values or there are no rows in the dataset, the group function returns NULL (the only exception to this rule is COUNT—it returns zero).

Most of the group functions can be applied either to ALL values or to only the DISTINCT values for the specified expression. When ALL is specified, all non-NULL values are applied to the group function. When DISTINCT is specified, only one of each non-NULL value is applied to the function. If you do not specify ALL or DISTINCT, the default is ALL.

To better understand the difference of ALL vs. DISTINCT, let's look at a few rows from the EMPLOYEES table:

```
SELECT first_name,  salary
FROM employees
WHERE first_name LIKE 'D%'
ORDER BY salary;
```

```
FIRST_NAME                SALARY
-------------------- ----------
Donald                      2600
Douglas                     2600
Diana                       4200
David                       4800
David                       6800
Daniel                      9000
David                       9500
Danielle                    9500
Den                        11000
```

The SALARY column contains nine values. Two employees have 2,600 and 9,500 each. When you count unique entries in the SALARY column, there are seven, since two are duplicates. The following SQL shows a few examples. The COUNT function is used to get a count, and the SUM function is used to find the total. (I'll discuss these functions later in the chapter.) When the UNIQUE keyword is used, the 2,600 and 9,500 are included in the result only once.

```
SELECT COUNT(salary) cnt_nu, COUNT(DISTINCT salary) cnt_uq,
       SUM(salary) sum_nu, SUM(DISTINCT salary) sum_uq
FROM employees
WHERE first_name LIKE 'D%';

    CNT_NU     CNT_UQ     SUM_NU     SUM_UQ
---------- ---------- ---------- ----------
         9          7      60000      47900
```

Unlike with single-row functions, you cannot use programmer-written functions on grouped data.

Utilizing Aggregate Functions

As with single-row functions, Oracle offers a rich variety of aggregate functions. These functions can appear in the SELECT, ORDER BY, or HAVING clauses of SELECT statements. When used in the SELECT clause, they usually require a GROUP BY clause as well. If no GROUP BY clause is specified, the default grouping is for the entire result set. Group functions cannot appear in the WHERE clause of a SELECT statement. The GROUP BY and HAVING clauses of SELECT statements are associated with grouping data. I'll discuss the GROUP BY clause before you learn about the various group functions.

You almost certainly will encounter a certification-exam question that tests whether you will incorrectly put a group function in the WHERE clause.

Grouping Data with GROUP BY

As the name implies, group functions work on data that is grouped. You tell the database how to group or categorize the data with a GROUP BY clause. Whenever you use a group function in the SELECT clause of a SELECT statement, you must place all nongrouping/nonconstant columns in the GROUP BY clause. If no GROUP BY clause is specified (only group functions and constants appear in the SELECT clause), the default grouping becomes the entire result set. When the query executes and the data is fetched, it is grouped based on the GROUP BY clause, and the group function is applied.

The basic syntax of using a group function in the SELECT statement is as follows:

```
SELECT [column names], group_function (column_name), … … …
FROM table
[WHERE condition]
[GROUP BY column names]
[ORDER BY column names]
```

In the following example, you find the total number of employees from the EMPLOYEES table:

```
SELECT COUNT(*) FROM employees;

  COUNT(*)
----------
       107
```

Since you did not have any other column in the SELECT clause, you didn't need to specify the GROUP BY clause. Suppose you want to find out the number of employees in each department; you can include department_id in the SELECT clause:

```
SELECT department_id, COUNT(*) "#Employees"
FROM employees;
SELECT department_id, COUNT(*) "#Employees"
       *
ERROR at line 1:
ORA-00937: not a single-group group function
```

Since you used an aggregate function and nonaggregated column, Oracle gave an error and is telling you to group the data. Here you have to use the GROUP BY clause. If you include a group function in the SELECT clause, you cannot select individual results unless you use the GROUP BY clause. Make sure all the columns in the SELECT clause that are not part of a group function are included in the GROUP BY clause. The following SQL lists the number of employees by their department:

```
SELECT department_id, COUNT(*) "#Employees"
FROM employees
GROUP BY department_id;

DEPARTMENT_ID #Employees
------------- ----------
          100          6
           30          6
                       1
           20          2
           70          1
           90          3
          110          2
           50         45
           40          1
           80         34
           10          1
           60          5
```

Notice that the rows are returned in no specific order. If you want the rows to be arranged in the order of the number of employees, you can either specify the aggregate function in the ORDER BY clause or use the position of the column, like so:

```
SELECT department_id, COUNT(*) "#Employees"
FROM employees
GROUP BY department_id
ORDER BY count(*) DESC, department_id;

SELECT department_id, COUNT(*) "#Employees"
FROM employees
GROUP BY department_id
ORDER BY 2 DESC, department_id;
```

```
DEPARTMENT_ID #Employees
------------- ----------
           50         45
           80         34
           30          6
          100          6
           60          5
           90          3
           20          2
          110          2
           10          1
           40          1
           70          1
                       1
```

You cannot use a column alias name or column position in the GROUP BY clause (as you can in the ORDER BY clause). The following SQL is using the column position in the GROUP BY clause and hence is giving an error:

```
SELECT department_id, COUNT(*) "#Employees"
FROM employees
GROUP BY 1;
SELECT department_id, COUNT(*) "#Employees"
       *
ERROR at line 1:
ORA-00979: not a GROUP BY expression
```

The following is another invalid SQL statement. In this example, the GROUP BY clause is using a column alias, which is not supported. Pay particular attention to GROUP BY questions on the certification exam, because you might see one with a column alias or column position used.

```
SELECT department_id di, COUNT(*) emp_cnt
FROM employees
GROUP BY di;
GROUP BY di
         *
ERROR at line 3:
ORA-00904: "DI": invalid identifier
```

The GROUP BY column does not have to be in the SELECT clause. In most cases, the result may not make much sense, but you might need it. In the following example, you are calculating the average salary of employees in each department; you do not want to share which department the average salary belongs to, and all you are interested in is knowing the average salaries in the company by department:

```
SELECT AVG(salary) average_salary
FROM employees
GROUP BY department_id;
```

```
AVERAGE_SALARY
--------------
          8600
          4420
          7000
          9500
         10000
    19333.3333
         10150
    3475.55556
          6500
    8955.88235
          4400
          5760
```

If you have more than one column in the GROUP BY clause, Oracle creates groups within groups. The order of columns in the GROUP BY clause determines the grouping. Multiple columns in the GROUP BY clause are required when you have more than one nonaggregate column in the SELECT clause. In the following example, the rows are grouped by the department_id, and within each department they are grouped by the job_id. The SQL shows the number of different jobs within each department:

```
SELECT department_id, job_id, COUNT(*)
FROM employees
GROUP BY department_id, job_id
ORDER BY 1, 2;

DEPARTMENT_ID JOB_ID       COUNT(*)
------------- ---------- ----------
           10 AD_ASST             1
           20 MK_MAN              1
           20 MK_REP              1
           30 PU_CLERK            5
           30 PU_MAN              1
           40 HR_REP              1
           50 SH_CLERK           20
           50 ST_CLERK           20
           50 ST_MAN              5
           60 IT_PROG             5
           70 PR_REP              1
           80 SA_MAN              5
           80 SA_REP             29
```

```
 90 AD_PRES            1
 90 AD_VP              2
100 FI_ACCOUNT         5
100 FI_MGR             1
110 AC_ACCOUNT         1
110 AC_MGR             1
    SA_REP             1
```

The GROUP BY clause groups data, but Oracle does not guarantee the order of the result set by the grouping order. To order the data in any specific order, you must use the ORDER BY clause.

Group-Function Overview

Tables 3.1 and 3.2 summarize the group functions discussed in this chapter. I will cover each of these functions in the "Group-Function Descriptions" sections. Table 3.1 summarizes the group functions that are most likely to appear on the OCP certification exam.

TABLE 3.1 Group-Function Summary: Part 1

Function	Description
AVG	Returns the statistical mean
COUNT	Returns the number of non-NULL rows
MAX	Returns the largest value
MEDIAN	Returns a middle value
MIN	Returns the smallest value
STDDEV	Returns the standard deviation
SUM	Adds all values and returns the result
VARIANCE	Returns the sample variance, or 1 for sample size 1

Table 3.2 summarizes the group functions available in Oracle Database 11*g* that are not included in Table 3.1. Although they are less likely to appear on the certification exam, they are still important to review.

TABLE 3.2 Group-Function Summary: Part 2

Function	Description
CORR	Returns the coefficient of correlation of number pairs
COVAR_POP	Returns the population covariance of number pairs
COVAR_SAMP	Returns the sample covariance of number pairs
CUME_DIST	Returns the cumulative distribution of values within groupings
DENSE_RANK	Returns the ranking of rows within an ordered group, without skipping ranks on ties
FIRST	Modifies other aggregate functions to return expressions based on the ordering of the second-column expression
GROUP_ID	Returns a group identifier used to uniquely identify duplicate groups
GROUPING	Returns 0 for nonsummary rows or 1 for summary rows
GROUPING_ID	Helps determine group by levels when CUBE or ROLLUP is used.
KEEP	Modifies other aggregate functions to return the first or last value in a grouping
LAST	Modifies other aggregate functions to return expressions based on ordering of the second-column expression
PERCENTILE_CONT	Returns the interpolated value that would fall in the specified percentile position using a continuous model
PERCENTILE_DISC	Returns the interpolated value that would fall in the specified percentile position using a discrete model
PERCENT_RANK	Returns the percentile ranking of the specified value
RANK	Returns the ranking of rows within an ordered group, skipping ranks when ties occur
STDDEV_POP	Returns the population standard deviation
STDDEV_SAMP	Returns the sample standard deviation
VAR_POP	Returns the population variance
VAR_SAMP	Returns the sample variance

Group-Function Descriptions: Part 1

I divided the group functions into two sections. The group functions included in the following sections are commonly used in everyday SQL and are most likely to appear on the OCP certification exam. I discuss each of these functions and include descriptions and examples of each.

For the certification exam, concentrate more on the group functions covered in the Part 1 discussion than those in the Part 2 discussion.

AVG

This function has the syntax `AVG([{DISTINCT | ALL}] n)`, where *n* is a numeric expression. The `AVG` function returns the average of the expression *n*.

```
SELECT job_id, AVG(salary)
FROM employees
WHERE job_id like 'AC%'
GROUP BY job_id;

JOB_ID     AVG(SALARY)
---------- -----------
AC_ACCOUNT        8300
AC_MGR           12000
```

You can use an expression or formula in the group functions. In the following example, the average compensation including commission is calculated for department 30 from the `SCOTT.EMP` table. The expression will be evaluated first, and its result will be used to calculate the mean. The data in department 30 is listed for understanding the example better.

```
SELECT deptno, sal, comm
FROM scott.emp
WHERE deptno = 30;

    DEPTNO        SAL       COMM
---------- ---------- ----------
        30       1600        300
        30       1250        500
        30       1250       1400
        30       2850
        30       1500          0
        30        950
```

```
SELECT deptno, AVG(sal + NVL(comm,0)) avg_comp
FROM scott.emp
WHERE deptno = 30
GROUP BY deptno;

    DEPTNO   AVG_COMP
---------- ----------
        30 1933.33333
```

Remember that group functions ignore NULL values. If the NVL function is not used, the employees with no commission are not included in the mean calculation. See the result difference in the following example without the NVL use:

```
SELECT deptno, AVG(sal + comm) avg_comp
FROM scott.emp
WHERE deptno = 30
GROUP BY deptno;

    DEPTNO   AVG_COMP
---------- ----------
        30       1950
```

COUNT

This function has the syntax COUNT({* | [DISTINCT | ALL] <*x*>}), where *x* is an expression. The COUNT function returns the number of rows in the query. If an expression is given and neither DISTINCT nor ALL is specified, the default is ALL. The asterisk (*) is a special quantity—it counts all rows in the result set, regardless of NULLs.

In the example that follows, you can count the number of rows in the EMPLOYEES table (the number of employees), the number of departments that have employees in them (DEPT_COUNT), and the number of employees that have a department (NON_NULL_DEPT_COUNT). You can see from the results that one employee is not assigned to a department, and the other 106 are assigned to one of 11 departments.

```
SELECT COUNT(*) emp_count,
       COUNT(DISTINCT department_id) dept_count,
       COUNT(ALL department_id) non_null_dept_count
FROM hr.employees;

EMP_COUNT  DEPT_COUNT  NON_NULL_DEPT_COUNT
---------- ----------  -------------------
       107         11                  106
```

This next example looks at the number of employees drawing a commission, as well as the distinct number of commissions drawn. You can see that 35 out of 107 employees draw a commission and that 7 different commission levels are in use.

```
SELECT COUNT(*),
       COUNT(commission_pct) comm_count,
       COUNT(DISTINCT commission_pct) distinct_comm
FROM hr.employees;

  COUNT(*) COMM_COUNT DISTINCT_COMM
---------- ---------- -------------
       107         35             7
```

MAX

This function has the syntax `MAX([{DISTINCT | ALL}] <x>)`, where *x* is an expression. This function returns the highest value in the expression *x*. *x* can be a datetime, numeric, or character value. The result of the `MAX` operation on the three groups of datatypes is as follows:

- If the expression *x* is a datetime datatype, it returns a DATE. For dates, the maximum is the latest date.
- If the expression *x* is a numeric datatype, it returns a NUMBER. For numbers, the maximum is the largest number.
- If the expression is a character datatype, it returns a VARCHAR2. For character strings, the maximum is the one that sorts highest based on the database character set.

Although the inclusion of either `DISTINCT` or `ALL` is syntactically acceptable, their use does not affect the calculation of a `MAX` function; the largest distinct value is the same as the largest of all values.

```
SELECT MAX(hire_date),
       MAX(salary),
       MAX(last_name)
FROM hr.employees;

MAX(HIRE_DA MAX(SALARY) MAX(LAST_NAME)
----------- ----------- --------------
21-APR-2000       24000 Zlotkey
```

MIN

This function has the syntax `MIN([{DISTINCT | ALL}] <x>)`, where *x* is an expression. This function returns the lowest value in the expression *x*. Similar to the `MAX` function, the *x* in `MIN` can also be a numeric, datetime, or character datatype.

- If the expression *x* is a datetime datatype, it returns a DATE. For dates, the minimum is the earliest date.

- If the expression *x* is a numeric datatype, it returns a NUMBER. For numbers, the minimum is the smallest number.
- If the expression is a character datatype, it returns a VARCHAR2. For character strings, the minimum is the one that sorts lowest based on the database character set.

Although the inclusion of either `DISTINCT` or `ALL` is syntactically acceptable, their use does not affect the calculation of a `MIN` function: the smallest distinct value is the same as the smallest value.

```
SELECT job_id, MIN(hire_date) oldest, MIN(salary) low_sal,
       MAX(salary) high_sal
FROM hr.employees
WHERE job_id like '%CLERK'
GROUP BY job_id;

JOB_ID     OLDEST      LOW_SAL   HIGH_SAL
---------- --------- ---------- ----------
PU_CLERK   18-MAY-95       2500       3100
SH_CLERK   27-JAN-96       2500       4200
ST_CLERK   14-JUL-95       2100       3600
```

SUM

This function has the syntax `SUM([{DISTINCT | ALL}] <x>)`, where *x* is a numeric expression. This function returns the sum of the expression *x*.

```
SELECT SUBSTR(phone_number, 1,3) area_code,
       SUM(salary) total_sal, ROUND(AVG(salary)) avg_sal
FROM employees
GROUP BY SUBSTR(phone_number, 1,3);

ARE  TOTAL_SAL    AVG_SAL
--- ---------- ----------
515     185900       9295
590      28800       5760
603       6000       6000
011     311500       8900
650     156400       3476
```

MEDIAN

`MEDIAN (<x>)` is an inverse distribution function that returns a middle value after the values in the expression are sorted. The argument *x* is an expression of numeric or datetime value.

```
SELECT job_id, MEDIAN(Salary) median, AVG(salary) average,
       MIN(salary) low_sal, MAX(salary) high_sal
```

```
FROM hr.employees
WHERE job_id like '%CLERK'
GROUP BY job_id;

JOB_ID         MEDIAN    AVERAGE    LOW_SAL   HIGH_SAL
---------- ---------- ---------- ---------- ----------
PU_CLERK         2750       2775       2500       3100
SH_CLERK         3100       3215       2500       4200
ST_CLERK         2700       2785       2100       3600
```

STDDEV

This function has the syntax STDDEV([{DISTINCT | ALL}] <*x*>), where *x* is a numeric expression. The STDDEV function returns the numeric standard deviation of the expression *x*.

The standard deviation is calculated as the square root of the variance:

```
SELECT department_id,
       COUNT(salary) emp_cnt,
       MIN(salary) minimum,
       MAX(salary) maximum,
       AVG(salary) mean,
       STDDEV(salary) deviation
FROM employees
GROUP BY department_id
ORDER BY department_id;

DEPARTMENT_ID    EMP_CNT    MINIMUM    MAXIMUM       MEAN  DEVIATION
------------- ---------- ---------- ---------- ---------- ----------
           10          1       4400       4400       4400          0
           20          2       6000      13000       9500 4949.74747
           30          5       2500      11000       4420  3686.0548
           40          1       6500       6500       6500          0
           50         45       2100       8200 3475.55556 1488.00592
           60          5       4200       9000       5760 1925.61678
           70          1      10000      10000      10000          0
           80         34       6100      14000 8955.88235  2033.6847
           90          3      17000      24000 19333.3333 4041.45188
          100          6       6900      12000       8600 1801.11077
          110          2       8300      12000      10150 2616.29509
                       1       7000       7000       7000          0
```

VARIANCE

This function has the syntax VARIANCE([{DISTINCT | ALL}] <*x*>), where *x* is a numeric expression. This function returns the variance of the expression *x*.

```
SELECT department_id,
       COUNT(*),
       VARIANCE(salary)
FROM hr.employees
GROUP BY department_id
ORDER BY department_id;

DEPARTMENT_ID   COUNT(*) VARIANCE(SALARY)
------------- ---------- ----------------
           10          1                0
           20          2         24500000
           30          6         13587000
           40          1                0
           50         45       2214161.62
           60          5          3708000
           70          1                0
           80         34       4135873.44
           90          3       16333333.3
          100          6          3244000
          110          2          6845000
                       1                0
```

Exploring DBA Queries Using Aggregate Functions

As a DBA, you often need to find out the space allocated for a schema and how much is free. You are not interested in seeing the space used by all the tables or indexes used in the schema, but it would be nice to have the summary broken down into tablespace-wise schema storage space. Let's write few SQL statements using the group functions that you can use to calculate space usage in a database.

The DBA_SEGMENTS dictionary view shows the segments allocated in the database—each table or index created in the database must have at least one segment created. The columns you are interested in for the query are `tablespace_name`, owner (or the schema name), and bytes (allocated space in bytes).

The first SQL just gives the total space used by all the objects in the database. This is a simple SQL statement, on all the rows in the view:

```
SELECT SUM(bytes)/1048576 size_mb
FROM dba_segments;
```

```
   SIZE_MB
----------
 1564.8125
```

Now, let's break down this space into the next level; see the space used in each tablespace. Since you are not interested in any aggregate function over the entire database but want to break it down by tablespaces, you must have the GROUP BY clause:

```
SELECT tablespace_name, SUM(bytes)/1048576 size_mb
FROM dba_segments
GROUP BY tablespace_name;

TABLESPACE_NAME                   SIZE_MB
------------------------------ ----------
SYSAUX                            716.375
UNDOTBS1                            48.25
USERS                               21.25
SYSTEM                            701.625
EXAMPLE                           77.3125
```

To find out the space allocated to each schema owner within the tablespaces, all you have to do is add the owner column to the query. Remember, since you are not performing any aggregate function on owner, that column also should be part of the GROUP BY clause. You will also include an ORDER BY clause so that the rows returned are in the order of tablespace name.

```
SELECT tablespace_name, owner, SUM(bytes)/1048576 size_mb
FROM dba_segments
GROUP BY tablespace_name, owner
ORDER BY 1, 2;

TABLESPACE_NAME                OWNER                             SIZE_MB
------------------------------ ------------------------------ ----------
EXAMPLE                        HR                                 1.5625
EXAMPLE                        IX                                  1.625
EXAMPLE                        OE                                   6.25
EXAMPLE                        PM                                 11.875
EXAMPLE                        SH                                     56
SYSAUX                         CTXSYS                             5.4375
… … …
USERS                          HR                                  .1875
USERS                          OE                                  2.625
```

```
USERS                              SCOTT                                .375
USERS                              SH                                      2
```

If you want to know the space allocated to the objects owned by each schema, you can run the following query:

```
SELECT owner, SUM(bytes)/1048576 size_mb
FROM dba_segments
GROUP BY owner
ORDER BY 1;

OWNER                             SIZE_MB
------------------------------ ----------
BTHOMAS                           16.0625
CTXSYS                             5.4375
DBSNMP                                1.5
EXFSYS                              3.875
FLOWS_030000                     100.6875
FLOWS_FILES                         .4375
HR                                   1.75
… … …
```

Group-Function Descriptions: Part 2

The group functions discussed in the following sections are included in this chapter for completeness of the group-functions discussion. The likelihood of these appearing in the OCP certification exam is minimal, but it helps to know these functions to write better SQL queries.

Many group functions discussed in this group (and AVG, COUNT, MAX, MIN, STDDEV, SUM, and VARIANCE) can be used as analytic functions. Analytic functions are commonly used in data-warehouse environments. They compute an aggregate based on a group of rows, called a *window*. Since the OCP certification exam does not include analytic functions, I won't discuss them in this chapter.

CORR

CORR(*y*, *x*) takes two arguments, where *y* and *x* are numeric expressions representing the dependent and independent variables, respectively. This function returns the coefficient of the correlation of a set of number pairs.

The coefficient of correlation is a measure of the strength of the relationship between the two numbers. CORR can return a NULL. The coefficient of the correlation is calculated from those *x*, *y* pairs that are both not NULL using the formula COVAR_POP(*y*,*x*) / (STDDEV_POP(*y*) * STDDEV_POP(*x*)).

```
SELECT CORR(list_price,min_price) correlation,
       COVAR_POP(list_price,min_price) covariance,
       STDDEV_POP(list_price) stddev_popy,
       STDDEV_POP(min_price) stddev_popx
FROM oe.product_information
WHERE list_price IS NOT NULL
AND  min_price IS NOT NULL;

CORRELATION   COVARIANCE STDDEV_POPY STDDEV_POPX
----------- ------------ ----------- -----------
  .99947495   206065.903  496.712198  415.077696
```

The previous output shows that there is a 99.947 percent change that the list price depends on the minimum price. So when the minimum price moves by *x* percent, there is a 99.947 percent chance that the list price will also move by *x* percent.

COVAR_POP

COVAR_POP(*y*, *x*) takes two arguments, where *y* and *x* are numeric expressions. This function returns the population covariance of a set of number pairs, which can be NULL.

The covariance is a measure of how two sets of data vary in the same way. The population covariance is calculated from those *y*, *x* pairs that are both not NULL using the formula (SUM(*y***x*) - SUM(*y*) * SUM(*x*) / COUNT(*x*)) / COUNT(*x*).

```
SELECT category_id,
       COVAR_POP(list_price,min_price) population,
       COVAR_SAMP(list_price,min_price) sample
FROM oe.product_information
GROUP BY category_id;

CATEGORY_ID POPULATION     SAMPLE
----------- ---------- ----------
         22         45       67.5
         25   27670.25 31623.1429
         13  25142.125 26465.3947
         11 92804.9883 98991.9875
         29    3446.75 3574.40741
         14 17982.9924 18800.4012
         21 21.5306122 25.1190476
         31 1424679.17    1709615
         24 109428.285 114639.156
         32    4575.06 4815.85263
```

```
17 5466.14286    5739.45
33        945       1134
12 26472.3333 29781.375
15 7650.84375     8160.9
16     431.38 479.311111
19 417343.887 426038.551
39 1035.14059 1086.89762
```

COVAR_SAMP

COVAR_SAMP(*y*, *x*) takes two arguments, where *y* and *x* are numeric expressions representing the dependent and independent variables, respectively. This function returns the sample covariance of a set of number pairs, which can be NULL.

The covariance is a measure of how two sets of data vary in the same way. The sample covariance is calculated from those *x*, *y* pairs that are both not NULL using the formula (SUM(*y**x*) - SUM(*y*) * SUM(*x*) / COUNT(*x*)) / (COUNT(*x*)-1).

```
SELECT SUM(list_price*min_price) sum_xy,
       SUM(list_price) sum_y,
       SUM(min_price) sum_x,
       COVAR_SAMP(list_price,min_price) COVARIANCE
FROM oe.product_information;

    SUM_XY      SUM_Y      SUM_X COVARIANCE
---------- ---------- ---------- ----------
  73803559      71407      60280 206791.488
```

CUME_DIST

This function has the syntax

CUME_DIST(<*val_list*>) WITHIN GROUP (ORDER BY *col_list*
[ASC|DESC] [NULLS {first|last}])

where *val_list* is a comma-delimited list of expressions that evaluate to numeric constant values and *col_list* is the comma-delimited list of column expressions. CUME_DIST returns the cumulative distribution of a value in *val_list* within a distribution in *col_list*.

The cumulative distribution is a measure of ranking within the ordered group and will be in the range 0 < CUME_DIST <= 1. See also PERCENT_RANK.

```
SELECT department_id,
       COUNT(*) emp_count,
       AVG(salary) mean,
       PERCENTILE_CONT(0.5) WITHIN GROUP
           (ORDER BY salary DESC) Median,
       CUME_DIST(10000) WITHIN GROUP
```

```
        (ORDER BY salary DESC) Cume_Dist_10K
FROM hr.employees
GROUP BY department_id;

DEPARTMENT_ID  EMP_COUNT       MEAN     MEDIAN CUME_DIST_10K
------------- ---------- ---------- ---------- -------------
           10          1       4400       4400            .5
           20          2       9500       9500    .666666667
           30          6       4420       2900    .428571429
           40          1       6500       6500            .5
           50         45 3475.55556       3100     .02173913
           60          5       5760       4800    .166666667
           70          1      10000      10000             1
           80         34 8955.88235       8900    .342857143
           90          3 19333.3333      17000             1
          100          6       8600       8000    .285714286
          110          2      10150      10150    .666666667
                       1       7000       7000            .5
```

DENSE_RANK

This function has the syntax

```
DENSE_RANK(val_list) WITHIN GROUP (ORDER BY col_list
[ASC|DESC] [NULLS {first|last}])
```

where *val_list* is a comma-delimited list of numeric constant expressions (expressions that evaluate to numeric constant values) and *col_list* is the comma-delimited list of column expressions. DENSE_RANK returns the row's rank within an ordered group. The ranks are consecutive integers starting with 1. The rank values are the number of unique values returned by the query. When there are ties, ranks are not skipped. For example, if there are three items tied for first, then second and third will not be skipped. See also RANK.

```
SELECT department_id,
       COUNT(*) emp_count,
       AVG(salary) mean,
       DENSE_RANK(10000) WITHIN GROUP
           (ORDER BY salary DESC) dense_rank_10K
FROM hr.employees
GROUP BY department_id;
```

```
DEPARTMENT_ID  EMP_COUNT       MEAN DENSE_RANK_10K
------------- ---------- ---------- --------------
           10          1       4400              1
           20          2       9500              2
           30          6       4420              3
           40          1       6500              1
           50         45 3475.55556              1
           60          5       5760              1
           70          1      10000              1
           80         34 8955.88235              7
           90          3 19333.3333              3
          100          6       8600              2
          110          2      10150              2
                       1       7000              1
```

To understand this ranking, let's look closer at department 80. You can see that 10,000 is the 7th-highest salary in department 80. Even though there are 11 employees that make 10,000 or more, the duplicates are not counted for ranking purposes.

```
SELECT salary, COUNT(*)
FROM hr.employees
WHERE department_id=80
GROUP BY salary
ORDER BY salary DESC;

    SALARY   COUNT(*)
---------- ----------
     14000          1
     13500          1
     12000          1
     11500          1
     11000          2
     10500          2
     10000          3
      9600          1
… … … (output truncated)
```

FIRST

See KEEP.

GROUP_ID

GROUP_ID( ) takes no arguments and requires a GROUP BY clause. GROUP_ID returns a numeric identifier that can be used to uniquely identify duplicate groups. For *i* duplicate groups, GROUP_ID will return values 0 through i-*1*.

GROUPING

GROUPING(*x*) takes a single argument, where *x* is an expression in the GROUP BY clause of the query. The GROUPING function is applicable only for queries that have a GROUP BY clause and a ROLLUP or CUBE clause. The ROLLUP and CUBE clauses create summary rows (sometimes called *superaggregates*) containing NULL in the grouped expressions. The GROUPING function returns a 1 for these summary rows and a 0 for the nonsummary rows, and it is used to distinguish the summary rows from the nonsummary rows.

GROUPING is discussed in detail in the section "Creating Superaggregates with CUBE and ROLLUP" later in this chapter.

GROUPING_ID

This function has the syntax GROUPING_ID (<col_list>) and is applicable only in SELECT statements with a GROUP BY clause with CUBE or ROLLUP. If the query contains many expressions in the GROUP BY clause, determining the GROUP BY level will require many GROUPING functions. The GROUPING_ID eliminates such a need. See the section "Creating Superaggregates with CUBE and ROLLUP" later in this chapter for a more detailed discussion on GROUPING_ID.

KEEP

The KEEP function has the syntax

agg_function KEEP(DENSE_RANK {FIRST|LAST}
ORDER BY *col_list* [ASC|DESC] [NULLS {first|last}]))

where *agg_function* is an aggregate function (COUNT, SUM, AVG, MIN, MAX, VARIANCE, or STDDEV) and *col_list* is a list of columns to be ordered for the grouping.

This function is sometimes referred to as either the FIRST or LAST function, and it is actually a modifier for one of the other group functions, such as COUNT or MIN. The KEEP function returns the first or last row of a sorted group. It is used to avoid the need for a self-join, looking for the minimum or maximum.

```
SELECT department_id,
       MIN(hire_date) earliest,
       MAX(hire_date) latest,
       COUNT(salary) KEEP
            (DENSE_RANK FIRST ORDER BY hire_date) FIRST,
       COUNT(salary) KEEP
            (DENSE_RANK LAST ORDER BY hire_date) LAST
FROM hr.employees
GROUP BY department_id;
```

```
DEPARTMENT_ID EARLIEST    LATEST        FIRST   LAST
------------- ----------- ----------- ------- ------
           10 17-Sep-1987 17-Sep-1987       1      1
           20 17-Feb-1996 17-Aug-1997       1      1
           30 07-Dec-1994 10-Aug-1999       1      1
           40 07-Jun-1994 07-Jun-1994       1      1
           50 01-May-1995 08-Mar-2000       1      1
           60 03-Jan-1990 07-Feb-1999       1      1
           70 07-Jun-1994 07-Jun-1994       1      1
           80 30-Jan-1996 21-Apr-2000       1      2
           90 17-Jun-1987 13-Jan-1993       1      1
          100 16-Aug-1994 07-Dec-1999       1      1
          110 07-Jun-1994 07-Jun-1994       2      2
              24-May-1999 24-May-1999       1      1
```

You can see from the previous query that department 80's earliest and latest anniversary dates are 30-Jan-1996 and 21-Apr-2000. The FIRST and LAST columns show us that there was one employee hired on the earliest anniversary date (30-Jun-1996) and two hired on the latest anniversary date (21-Apr-2000). Likewise, you can see that department 110 has two employees hired on the earliest anniversary date (07-Jun-1994) and two on the latest anniversary date (07-Jun-1994). If you look at the following detailed data, this becomes clearer:

```
SELECT department_id,hire_date
FROM hr.employees
WHERE department_id IN (80,110)
ORDER BY 1,2;

DEPARTMENT_ID HIRE_DATE
------------- -----------
           80 30-Jan-1996
           80 04-Mar-1996
           80 24-Jan-2000
           80 29-Jan-2000
... … … (output truncated)
           80 23-Feb-2000
           80 24-Mar-2000
           80 21-Apr-2000
           80 21-Apr-2000
          110 07-Jun-1994
          110 07-Jun-1994
```

LAST

See KEEP.

PERCENT_RANK

The PERCENT_RANK function has the syntax

```
PERCENT_RANK(<val_list>) WITHIN GROUP (ORDER BY col_list
[ASC|DESC] [NULLS {first|last}])
```

where *val_list* is a comma-delimited list of expressions that evaluate to numeric constant values and *col_list* is the comma-delimited list of column expressions. PERCENT_RANK returns the percent ranking of a value in *val_list* within a distribution in *col_list*. The percent rank *x* will be in the range 0 <= *x* <= 1.

The main difference between PERCENT_RANK and CUME_DIST is that PERCENT_RANK will always return a 0 for the first row in any set, while the CUME_DIST function cannot return a 0. You can use the PERCENT_RANK and CUME_DIST functions to examine the rankings of employees with salaries of more than 10,000 in the HR.EMPLOYEES table. Notice the different results for departments 40 and 70.

```
SELECT DEPARTMENT_ID DID,
       COUNT(*) emp_count,
       AVG(salary) mean,
       PERCENTILE_CONT(0.5) WITHIN GROUP
           (ORDER BY salary DESC) median,
       PERCENT_RANK(10000) WITHIN GROUP
           (ORDER BY salary DESC)*100 pct_rank_10K,
       CUME_DIST(10000) WITHIN GROUP
           (ORDER BY salary DESC)*100 cume_dist_10K
FROM hr.employees
GROUP BY department_id;
```

```
DID  EMP_COUNT    MEAN MEDIAN PCT_RANK_10K CUME_DIST_10K
--- ---------- ------- ------ ------------ -------------
 10          1    4400   4400            0            50
 20          2    9500   9500           50    66.6666667
 30          6    4420   2900   33.3333333    42.8571429
 40          1    6500   6500            0            50
 50         45 3475.55   3100            0    2.17391304
 60          5    5760   4800            0    16.6666667
 70          1   10000  10000            0           100
 80         34 8955.88   8900   23.5294118    34.2857143
 90          3 19333.3  17000          100           100
100          6    8600   8000   16.6666667    28.5714286
110          2   10150  10150           50    66.6666667
             1    7000   7000            0            50
```

PERCENTILE_CONT

PERCENTILE_CONT has the syntax

```
PERCENTILE_CONT(<x>) WITHIN GROUP (ORDER BY col_list
[ASC|DESC])
```

where *x* is a percentile value in the range 0 < *x* < 1 and *col_list* is the sort specification. PERCENTILE_CONT returns the interpolated value that would fall in percentile position *x* within the sorted group *col_list*.

This function assumes a continuous distribution and is most useful for obtaining the median value of an ordered group. The median value is defined to be the midpoint in a group of ordered numbers—half of the values are greater than the median, and half of the values are less than the median.

The median together with the mean or average are the two most common measures of a central tendency used to analyze data. See the AVG function for more information on calculating the mean.

For this example, you will use the SCOTT.EMP table, ordered by department number:

```
SELECT ename ,deptno ,sal
FROM scott.emp
ORDER BY deptno ,sal;

ENAME          DEPTNO        SAL
---------- ---------- ----------
MILLER             10       1300
CLARK              10       2450
KING               10       5000
SMITH              20        800
ADAMS              20       1100
JONES              20       2975
SCOTT              20       3000
FORD               20       3000
JAMES              30        950
WARD               30       1250
MARTIN             30       1250
TURNER             30       1500
ALLEN              30       1600
BLAKE              30       2850
```

You can see that for department 10, there are three SAL values: 1300, 2450, and 5000. The median would be 2450, because there is one value greater than this number and one value less than this number. The median for department 30 is not so straightforward, since there are six values and the middle value is actually between the two data points 1250 and 1500. To get the median for department 30, you need to interpolate the midpoint.

Two common techniques are used to interpolate this median value: one technique uses a continuous model, and one uses a discrete model. In the continuous model, the midpoint is assumed to be the value halfway between the 1250 and 1500, which is 1375. Using the discrete model, the median must be an actual data point, and depending on whether the data is ordered ascending or descending, the median would be 1250 or 1500.

```
SELECT deptno,
      PERCENTILE_CONT(0.5) WITHIN GROUP
            (ORDER BY sal DESC) "CONTINUOUS",
      PERCENTILE_DISC(0.5) WITHIN GROUP
            (ORDER BY sal DESC) "DISCRETE DESC",
      PERCENTILE_DISC(0.5) WITHIN GROUP
            (ORDER BY sal ASC) "DISCRETE ASC",
      AVG(sal) mean
FROM scott.emp
GROUP BY deptno;

DEPTNO CONTINUOUS DISCRETE DESC DISCRETE ASC       MEAN
------ ---------- ------------- ------------ ----------
    10       2450          2450         2450 2916.66667
    20       2975          2975         2975       2175
    30       1375          1500         1250 1566.66667
```

PERCENTILE_DISC

PERCENTILE_DISC has the syntax

PERCENTILE_DISC(<*x*>) WITHIN GROUP (ORDER BY *col_list*
[ASC|DESC])

where *x* is a percentile value in the range 0 < *x* < 1 and *col_list* is the sort specification. PERCENTILE_DISC returns the smallest cumulative distribution value from the *col_list* set that is greater than or equal to value *x*.

This function assumes a discrete distribution. Sometimes data cannot be averaged in a meaningful way. Date data, for example, cannot be averaged, but you can calculate the median date in a group of dates. For example, to calculate the median hire date for employees in each department, you could run the following query:

```
SELECT department_id did,
       COUNT(*) emp_count,
       MIN(HIRE_DATE) first,
       MAX(HIRE_DATE) last,
```

```
       PERCENTILE_DISC(0.5) WITHIN GROUP
           (ORDER BY HIRE_DATE) median
FROM hr.employees
GROUP BY department_id;

  DID  EMP_COUNT FIRST     LAST      MEDIAN
----- ---------- --------- --------- ---------
   10          1 17-SEP-87 17-SEP-87 17-SEP-87
   20          2 17-FEB-96 17-AUG-97 17-FEB-96
   30          6 07-DEC-94 10-AUG-99 24-JUL-97
   40          1 07-JUN-94 07-JUN-94 07-JUN-94
   50         45 01-MAY-95 08-MAR-00 15-MAR-98
   60          5 03-JAN-90 07-FEB-99 25-JUN-97
   70          1 07-JUN-94 07-JUN-94 07-JUN-94
   80         34 30-JAN-96 21-APR-00 23-MAR-98
   90          3 17-JUN-87 13-JAN-93 21-SEP-89
  100          6 16-AUG-94 07-DEC-99 28-SEP-97
  110          2 07-JUN-94 07-JUN-94 07-JUN-94
               1 24-MAY-99 24-MAY-99 24-MAY-99
```

RANK

RANK has the syntax

```
RANK(<val_list>) WITHIN GROUP (ORDER BY col_list
[ASC|DESC] [NULLS {first|last}])
```

where *val_list* is a comma-delimited list of numeric constant expressions (expressions that evaluate to numeric constant values) and *col_list* is the comma-delimited list of column expressions. RANK returns the row's rank within an ordered group.

When there are ties, ranks of equal value are assigned equal rank, and the number of tied rows is skipped before the next rank is assigned. For example, if there are three items tied for first, the second and third items will be skipped, and the next will be the fourth.

```
SELECT department_id DID,
       COUNT(*) emp_count,
       AVG(salary) mean,
       DENSE_RANK(10000) WITHIN GROUP
           (ORDER BY salary DESC) dense_rank_10K
FROM hr.employees
GROUP BY department_id;
```

```
       DID  EMP_COUNT       MEAN DENSE_RANK_10K
---------- ---------- ---------- --------------
        10          1       4400              1
        20          2       9500              2
        30          6       4420              3
        40          1       6500              1
        50         45 3475.55556              1
        60          5       5760              1
        70          1      10000              1
        80         34 8955.88235              7
        90          3 19333.3333              3
       100          6       8600              2
       110          2      10150              2
                    1       7000              1
```

To understand this ranking, let's look closer at department 80. You can see that 10,000 is the 7th-highest salary in department 80. But since there are 8 employees who make more than 10,000, the rank of 10,000 is 9. The duplicates are counted for ranking purposes.

```
SELECT salary, COUNT(*)
FROM hr.employees
WHERE department_id=80
 AND  salary > 9000
GROUP BY salary
ORDER BY salary DESC;

    SALARY   COUNT(*)
---------- ----------
     14000          1
     13500          1
     12000          1
     11500          1
     11000          2
     10500          2
     10000          3
      9600          1
      9500          3
```

STDDEV_POP

STDDEV_POP(<x>) takes a single argument, where *x* is a numeric expression. This function returns the numeric population standard deviation of the expression *x*. The population standard deviation is calculated as the square root of the population variance VAR_POP.

```
SELECT department_id DID,
       STDDEV(salary) STD,
       STDDEV_POP(salary) STDPOP,
       STDDEV_SAMP(salary) STDSAMP
FROM hr.employees
GROUP BY department_id;

  DID        STD     STDPOP    STDSAMP
----- ---------- ---------- ----------
  100 1801.11077 1644.18166 1801.11077
   30  3686.0548 3296.90764  3686.0548
               0          0
   20 4949.74747       3500 4949.74747
   70          0          0
   90 4041.45188 3299.83165 4041.45188
  110 2616.29509       1850 2616.29509
   50 1488.00592 1471.37963 1488.00592
   40          0          0
   80  2033.6847 2003.55437  2033.6847
   10          0          0
   60 1925.61678 1722.32401 1925.61678
```

STDDEV_SAMP

STDDEV_SAMP(<*x*>) takes a single argument, where *x* is a numeric expression. This function returns the numeric sample standard deviation of the expression *x*.

The sample standard deviation is calculated as the square root of the sample variance VAR_SAMP. *STDDEV* is similar to the STDDEV_SAMP function, except STDDEV will return 1 when there is only one row of input, while STDDEV_SAMP will return NULL.

See the description of STDDEV_POP for an example.

VAR_POP

VAR_POP(<*x*>) takes a single argument, where *x* is a numeric expression. This function returns the numeric population variance of *x*. The population variance is calculated with the formula (SUM(*x***x*) - SUM(*x*) * SUM(*x*) / COUNT(*x*)) / COUNT(*x*).

```
SELECT department_id,
       VARIANCE(salary),
       VAR_POP(salary),
       VAR_SAMP(salary)
FROM hr.employees
GROUP BY department_id;
```

```
DEPARTMENT_ID VARIANCE(SALARY) VAR_POP(SALARY) VAR_SAMP(SALARY)
------------- ---------------- --------------- ----------------
          100          3244000      2703333.33          3244000
           30         13587000        10869600         13587000
                             0               0
           20         24500000        12250000         24500000
           70                0               0
           90       16333333.3      10888888.9       16333333.3
          110          6845000         3422500          6845000
           50       2214161.62      2164958.02       2214161.62
           40                0               0
           80       4135873.44       4014230.1       4135873.44
           10                0               0
           60          3708000         2966400          3708000
```

VAR_SAMP

VAR_SAMP(<x>) takes a single argument, where *x* is a numeric expression. This function returns the numeric sample variance of *x*. The sample variance is calculated with the formula (SUM(*x***x*) – SUM(*x*) * SUM(*x*) / COUNT(*x*)) / (COUNT(*x*)-1). When the number of expressions (COUNT(*x*)) = 1, VARIANCE returns a 0, whereas VAR_SAMP returns NULL. When (COUNT(*x*)) = 0, they both return NULL. See the description of VAR_POP for an example.

Limiting Grouped Data with HAVING

A SELECT statement includes a HAVING clause to filter the grouped data. I discussed the GROUP BY clause and various group functions earlier in this chapter. The group functions cannot be used in the WHERE clause. For example, if you want to query the total salary by department excluding department 50 and return only those rows with more than 10,000 in total salary column, you would have trouble with the following query:

```
SELECT department_id, sum(salary) total_sal
FROM employees
WHERE department_id != 50
AND SUM(salary) > 10000
GROUP BY department_id;
```

The database doesn't know what the sum is when extracting the rows from the table—remember that the grouping is done after all rows have been fetched. You get an exception when you try to use SUM in the WHERE clause. The correct way to get the requested information is to instruct the database to group all the rows and then limit the output of those grouped rows. You do this by using the HAVING clause. The HAVING clause is used to restrict the groups of returned rows to those groups where the specified condition is satisfied.

```
SELECT department_id, sum(salary) total_sal
FROM employees
WHERE department_id != 50
GROUP BY department_id
HAVING SUM(salary) > 10000;

DEPARTMENT_ID  TOTAL_SAL
------------- ----------
          100      51600
           30      22100
           20      19000
           90      58000
          110      20300
           80     304500
           60      28800
```

As you can see in the previous query, a SQL statement can have both a WHERE clause and a HAVING clause. WHERE filters data before grouping; HAVING filters data after grouping.

If the SELECT statement includes a WHERE clause and a GROUP BY clause, the GROUP BY (and HAVING) clause should come after the WHERE clause. HAVING and GROUP BY clauses can appear in any order.

Creating Superaggregates with CUBE and ROLLUP

The CUBE and ROLLUP modifiers to the GROUP BY clause allow you to create aggregations of aggregates, or *superaggregates*. These superaggregates or summary rows are included with the result set in a way similar to using the COMPUTE statement on control breaks in SQL*Plus; that is, they are included in the data and contain NULL values in the aggregated columns:

- ROLLUP creates hierarchical aggregates.
- CUBE creates aggregates for all combinations of columns specified.

The key advantages of CUBE and ROLLUP are that they will allow more robust aggregations than COMPUTE and they work with any SQL-enabled tool.

These superaggregations can be visualized with a simple example using the OE.CUSTOMERS table. For this example, say you are interested in two columns —MARITAL_STATUS, which has value single or married, and GENDER, which has the value M or F. Let's write some SQL to find the total number or rows by GENDER and MARITAL_STATUS:

```
SELECT gender, marital_status, count(*) num_rec
FROM oe.customers
GROUP BY gender, marital_status;
```

```
G MARITAL_STATUS          NUM_REC
- -------------------- ----------
M married                     117
M single                       92
F single                       47
F married                      63
```

But suppose you want subtotals for each gender—a count of all female customers regardless of marital status and a count of all male customers regardless of marital status. You could remove the MARITAL_STATUS column from the previous query, which would give you the desired result, but what if you want to display the subtotals along with the original query? Oracle introduced the ROLLUP modifier to accomplish this task.

Using ROLLUP

ROLLUP is used in SELECT statements with GROUP BY clauses to calculate multiple levels of subtotals. It also provides a grand total. The ROLLUP extension adds only minimal overhead to the overall query performance. ROLLUP creates subtotals from the most detailed level to a grand total based on the grouping list provided with the ROLLUP modifier. It creates subtotals moving left to right using the columns provided in ROLLUP. The grand total is provided only if the ROLLUP modifier includes all the columns in the GROUP BY clause.

Using the previous example, you could use the ROLLUP modifier to roll up the MARITAL_STATUS column, leaving subtotals on the grouped column GENDER. Here we have not included GENDER in the ROLLUP; hence, the grand total is not provided:

```
SELECT gender, marital_status, count(*) num_rec
FROM oe.customers
GROUP BY gender, ROLLUP(marital_status);

G MARITAL_STATUS          NUM_REC
- -------------------- ----------
F single                       47
F married                      63
F                             110   <- Subtotal
M single                       92
M married                     117
M                             209   <- Subtotal
```

In the previous example, you do not have any NULL value in the MARITAL_STATUS column. If you add another record with GENDER = 'F' and a NULL value for MARITAL_STATUS, the result would be as follows:

```
SELECT gender, marital_status, count(*) num_rec
FROM oe.customers
GROUP BY gender, ROLLUP(marital_status);
```

```
G MARITAL_STATUS           NUM_REC
- -------------------- ----------
F single                       47
F married                      63
F                               1   <- Null Marital_Status
F                             111   <- Subtotal
M single                       92
M married                     117
M                             209   <- Subtotal
```

On the OCA certification exam, this can appear as a trick question to confuse you about which line is the subtotal. You may use an NVL function to display meaningful data in the result.

Now, if you want to add an aggregation for all genders as well, you put the GENDER column into the ROLLUP modifier, as follows:

```
SELECT gender, marital_status, count(*) num_rec
FROM oe.customers
GROUP BY  ROLLUP(gender, marital_status);

G MARITAL_STATUS           NUM_REC
- -------------------- ----------
F single                       47
F married                      63
F                             110   <- Subtotal
M single                       92
M married                     117
M                             209   <- Subtotal
                              319   <- Grand total
```

The order of the columns in the ROLLUP modifier is significant, because this order determines where Oracle produces subtotals. ROLLUP creates hierarchical aggregations, so the order of the expressions in the ROLLUP clause is significant. The ordering follows the same conventions used in the GROUP BY clause—most general to most specific. When you reverse the order in the example, you get different subtotals:

```
SELECT gender, marital_status, count(*) num_rec
FROM oe.customers
GROUP BY  ROLLUP(marital_status, gender);

G MARITAL_STATUS           NUM_REC
- -------------------- ----------
F single                       47
M single                       92
  single                      139   <- Subtotal
F married                      63
M married                     117
```

```
  married                        180   <- Subtotal
                                 319   <- Grand total
```

Suppose you want all these subtotals, both by GENDER and by MARITAL_STATUS. This requirement calls for the CUBE modifier, which will produce all possible aggregations, not just those in the hierarchy of columns specified.

Using CUBE

The CUBE modifier in the GROUP BY clause creates subtotals for all possible combinations of grouping columns. Let's try the previous example using the CUBE modifier:

```
SELECT gender, marital_status, count(*) num_rec
FROM oe.customers
GROUP BY  CUBE(gender, marital_status);

G MARITAL_STATUS          NUM_REC
- -------------------- ----------
                              319   <- Grand total
  single                      139   <- Subtotal Marital_Status
  married                     180   <- Subtotal Marital_Status
F                             110   <- Subtotal Gender
F single                       47
F married                      63
M                             209   <- Subtotal Gender
M single                       92
M married                     117
```

The number of aggregations created by the CUBE modifier is the number of distinct combinations of data values in all the columns that appear in the CUBE clause. CUBE creates aggregations for all combinations of columns, so unlike ROLLUP, the order of expressions in a CUBE is not significant. As you can see, the result set is the same, but the order of rows (grouping) is different:

```
SELECT gender, marital_status, count(*) num_rec
FROM oe.customers
GROUP BY  CUBE(marital_status, gender);

G MARITAL_STATUS          NUM_REC
- -------------------- ----------
                              319
F                             110
M                             209
  single                      139
```

```
F single                    47
M single                    92
  married                  180
F married                   63
M married                  117
```

More DBA Queries

In the "Exploring DBA Queries Using Aggregate Functions" sidebar, you saw some queries written to find out the space allocated by tablespace, the space allocated by schema, and the space allocated by tablespace and schema. These were written using three different SQL statements. You can see the power of CUBE in the following SQL. The results from all the three SQL statements you tried before are in this summary report, showing the different levels of aggregation.

```
SELECT tablespace_name, owner, SUM(bytes)/1048576 size_mb
FROM dba_segments
GROUP BY CUBE (tablespace_name, owner);

TABLESPACE_NAME  OWNER              SIZE_MB
---------------- --------------- ----------
                                  1564.8125  <- Grand Total
                 HR                    1.75  <- Subtotal HR schema
                 IX                   1.625  <- Subtotal IX schema
                 OE                   8.875
… … …
                 FLOWS             100.6875  <- Subtotal FLOWS schema
USERS                                 21.25  <- Subtotal USERS tablespace
USERS            HR                   .1875  <- HR schema in USERS
tablespace
USERS            OE                   2.625  <- OE schema in USERS
tablespace
USERS            SH                       2
USERS            SCOTT                 .375
USERS            BTHOMAS            16.0625
SYSAUX                              716.375  <- Subtotal SYSAUX tablespace
… … …
SYSAUX           FLOWS             100.6875
SYSTEM                              701.625  <- Subtotal SYSTEM tablespace
SYSTEM           SYS               685.1875
```

```
SYSTEM          OUTLN           .5625
SYSTEM          SYSTEM         15.875
EXAMPLE                       77.3125
EXAMPLE         HR             1.5625
... ... ...
```

As you can see in the result, the space used by each schema in each tablespace is shown as well as the total space used in each tablespace and the total space used by each schema. The total space used in the database (including all tablespaces) is also shown in the very first line.

Three functions come in handy with the ROLLUP and CUBE modifiers of the GROUP BY clause—GROUPING, GROUP_ID, and GROUPING_ID.

In the examples you have seen using the ROLLUP and CUBE modifiers, there was no way of telling which row is a subtotal and which row is a grand total. You can use the GROUPING function to overcome this problem. Review the following SQL example:

```
SELECT gender, marital_status, count(*) num_rec,
       GROUPING (gender) g_grp, GROUPING (marital_status) ms_grp
FROM oe.customers
GROUP BY  CUBE(marital_status, gender);

G MARITAL_STATUS          NUM_REC      G_GRP     MS_GRP
- -------------------- ---------- ---------- ----------
                              319          1          1
F                             110          0          1
M                             209          0          1
  single                      139          1          0
F single                       47          0          0
M single                       92          0          0
  married                     180          1          0
F married                      63          0          0
M married                     117          0          0
```

The G_GRP column has a 1 for NULL values generated by the CUBE or ROLLUP modifier for GENDER column. Similarly, the MS_GRP column has a 1 when NULL values are generated in the MARITAL_STATUS column. Using a DECODE function on the result of the GROUPING function, you can produce a more meaningful result set, as in the following example:

```
SELECT DECODE(GROUPING (gender), 1, 'Multi-Gender',
              gender) gender,
       DECODE(GROUPING (marital_status), 1,
```

```
          'Multi-MaritalStatus', marital_status) marital_status,
       count(*) num_rec
FROM oe.customers
GROUP BY  CUBE(marital_status, gender);

GENDER       MARITAL_STATUS          NUM_REC
------------ -------------------- ----------
Multi-Gender Multi-MaritalStatus         319
F            Multi-MaritalStatus         110
M            Multi-MaritalStatus         209
Multi-Gender single                      139
F            single                       47
M            single                       92
Multi-Gender married                     180
F            married                      63
M            married                     117
```

You can use the GROUPING function in the HAVING clause to filter out rows. You can display only the summary results using the GROUPING function in the HAVING clause.

The GROUPING_ID function returns the exact level of the group. It is derived from the GROUPING function by concatenating the GROUPING levels together as bits, and gives the GROUPING_ID. Review the following example closely to understand this:

```
SELECT gender, marital_status, count(*) num_rec,
       GROUPING (gender) g_grp, GROUPING (marital_status) ms_grp,
       GROUPING_ID (gender, marital_status) groupingid
FROM oe.customers
GROUP BY  CUBE(gender, marital_status);

G MARITAL_STATUS          NUM_REC      G_GRP     MS_GRP GROUPINGID
- -------------------- ---------- ---------- ---------- ----------
                              319          1          1          3
  single                      139          1          0          2
  married                     180          1          0          2
F                             110          0          1          1
F single                       47          0          0          0
F married                      63          0          0          0
M                             209          0          1          1
M single                       92          0          0          0
M married                     117          0          0          0
```

In this example, you can clearly identify the level of grouping using the GROUPING_ID function. The GROUP_ID function is used to distinguish the duplicate groups. In the following example, the GROUP_ID() value is 1 for duplicate groups. When writing complex aggregates, you can filter out the duplicate rows by using the HAVING GROUP_ID = 0 clause in the SELECT statement.

```
SELECT gender, marital_status, count(*) num_rec,
       GROUPING_ID (gender, marital_status) groupingid,
       GROUP_ID() groupid
FROM oe.customers
GROUP BY  gender, CUBE(gender, marital_status);

G MARITAL_STATUS          NUM_REC GROUPINGID    GROUPID
- -------------------- ---------- ---------- ----------
F single                       47          0          0
F married                      63          0          0
M single                       92          0          0
M married                     117          0          0
F single                       47          0          1
F married                      63          0          1
M single                       92          0          1
M married                     117          0          1
F                             110          1          0
M                             209          1          0
F                             110          1          1
M                             209          1          1
```

Nesting Functions

Functions can be *nested* so that the output from one function is used as input to another. Operators have an inherent precedence of execution such as * before +, but function precedence is based on position only. Functions are evaluated innermost to outermost and left to right. This nesting technique is common with some functions, such as DECODE (covered in Chapter 2), where it can be used to implement limited IF...THEN...ELSE logic within a SQL statement.

For example, the V$SYSSTAT view contains one row for each of three interesting sort statistics. If you want to report all three statistics on a single line, you can use DECODE combined with SUM to filter out data in the SELECT clause. This filtering operation is usually done in the WHERE or HAVING clause, but if you want all three statistics on one line, you can issue this command:

```
SELECT SUM (DECODE
        (name,'sorts (memory)',value,0)) in_memory,
```

```
       SUM (DECODE
        (name,'sorts (disk)',  value,0)) on_disk,
       SUM (DECODE
        (name,'sorts (rows)',  value,0)) rows_sorted
FROM v$sysstat;

IN_MEMORY ON_DISK ROWS_SORTED
--------- ------- -----------
      728      12      326714
```

What happens in the previous statement is a single pass through the V$SYSSTAT table. The presummary result set would have the same number of rows as V$SYSSTAT (232, for instance). Of these 232 rows, all rows and columns have zeros, except for one row in each column that has the data of interest. Table 3.3 shows the data that was used in this example. The summation operation then adds all the zeros to your interesting data and gives you the results you want.

TABLE 3.3 Presummarized Result Set

in_memory	on_disk	rows_sorted
0	0	0
0	12	0
0	0	0
0	0	326714
728	0	0
0	0	0

Nesting Single-Row Functions with Group Functions

Nested functions can include single-row functions nested within group functions, as you've just seen, or group functions nested within either single-row functions or other group functions. For example, suppose you need to report on the departments in the EMP table, showing either the number of jobs or the number of managers, whichever is greater. You would enter the following:

```
SELECT deptno, GREATEST(
       COUNT(DISTINCT job),
       COUNT(DISTINCT mgr)) cnt,
       COUNT(DISTINCT job) jobs,
```

```
       COUNT(DISTINCT mgr) mgrs
FROM scott.emp
GROUP BY deptno;

    DEPTNO        CNT       JOBS       MGRS
---------- ---------- ---------- ----------
        10          3          3          2
        20          4          3          4
        30          3          3          2
```

Nesting Group Functions

You can also nest group functions within group functions. Only one level of nesting is allowed when nesting a group function within a group function. To report the maximum number of jobs in a single department, you would query the following:

```
SELECT MAX(COUNT (DISTINCT job_id))
FROM employees
GROUP BY department_id;

MAX(COUNT(DISTINCTJOB_ID))
--------------------------
                         3
```

Group functions can be nested only one level. If you try to nest more than one level of nested group functions, you will encounter an error. Also, there is no reason to do so. Here is an example to show the error, though the SQL does not mean much:

```
SELECT MIN (MAX (COUNT (DISTINCT job_id)))
FROM employees
GROUP BY department_id;

SELECT MIN (MAX (COUNT (DISTINCT job_id)))
                 *
ERROR at line 1:
ORA-00935: group function is nested too deeply
```

Summary

Though this chapter is small in terms of OCA certification exam content, this chapter is very important for the test. It is important to understand the concept of grouping data, where GROUP BY and HAVING clauses can be used, and the rules associated with using these clauses. I started this chapter by discussing the group-function fundamentals and reviewed the group functions by concentrating on the functions that are important for the test.

I also discussed how group functions can be used in the SELECT, HAVING, and ORDER BY clauses of SELECT statements. Most group functions can be applied to all data values or only to the distinct data values. Except for COUNT(*), group functions ignore NULLs. Programmer-written functions cannot be used as group functions. COUNT, SUM, and AVG are the most commonly used group functions.

When using group functions or aggregate functions in a query, the columns that do not have any aggregate function applied to them must appear in the GROUP BY clause of the query. The HAVING clause is used to filter out data after the aggregates are calculated. Group functions cannot be used in the WHERE clause.

You can create superaggregates using the CUBE and ROLLUP modifiers in the GROUP BY clause.

Exam Essentials

Understand the usage of DISTINCT in group functions. When DISTINCT is specified, only one of each non-NULL value is applied to the function. To apply all non-NULL values, the keyword ALL should be used.

Know where group functions can be used. Group functions can be used in GROUP BY, ORDER BY, and HAVING clauses. They cannot be used in WHERE clauses.

Know how MIN and MAX sort date and character data. Older dates evaluate to lower values, while newer dates evaluate to higher values. Character data, even if it contains numbers, is sorted according to the NLS_SORT specification.

Know which expressions in a SELECT list must appear in a GROUP BY clause. If any grouping is performed, all nongroup function expressions and nonconstant expressions must appear in the GROUP BY clause.

Know the order of precedence for evaluating nested functions. You may need to evaluate an expression containing nested functions. Make sure you understand the left-to-right order of precedence used to evaluate these expressions.

Review Questions

1. How will the results of the following two statements differ?

```
Statement 1:
SELECT MAX(longitude), MAX(latitude)
FROM zip_state_city;

Statement 2:
SELECT MAX(longitude), MAX(latitude)
FROM zip_state_city
GROUP BY state;
```

   A. Statement 1 will fail because it is missing a GROUP BY clause.

   B. Statement 2 will return one row, and statement 1 may return more than one row.

   C. Statement 2 will fail because it does not have the columns used in the GROUP BY clause in the SELECT clause.

   D. Statement 1 will display two columns, and statement 2 will display two values for each state.

2. Using the SALES table described here, you need to report the following:

   - Gross, net, and earned revenue for the second and third quarters of 1999
   - Gross, net, and earned revenue for sales in the states of Illinois, California, and Texas (codes IL, CA, and TX)

Column Name	state_code	sales_date	gross	net	earned
Key Type	PK	PK			
Nulls/Unique	NN	NN	NN	NN	NN
FK Table					
Datatype	VARCHAR2	DATE	NUMBER	NUMBER	NUMBER
Length	2		11,2	11,2	11,2

   Will all the requirements be met with the following SQL statement?

```
SELECT state_code, SUM(ALL gross), SUM(net), SUM(earned)
FROM sales_detail
WHERE TRUNC(sales_date,'Q') BETWEEN
                  TO_DATE('01-Apr-1999','DD-Mon-YYYY')
              AND TO_DATE('01-Sep-1999','DD-Mon-YYYY')
 AND  state_cd IN ('IL','CA','TX')
GROUP BY state_code;
```

A. The statement meets all three requirements.

B. The statement meets two of the three requirements.

C. The statement meets one of the three requirements.

D. The statement meets none of the three requirements.

E. The statement will raise an exception.

3. Which line in the following SQL has an error?

```
1 SELECT department_id, SUM(salary)
2 FROM employees
3 WHERE department_id <> 40
4 ORDER BY department_id;
```

A. 1

B. 3

C. 4

D. No errors in SQL

4. John is trying to find out the average salary of employees in each department. He noticed that the `SALARY` column can have `NULL` values, and he does not want the `NULL`s included when calculating the average. Identify the correct SQL that will produce the desired results.

A.
```
SELECT department_id, AVG(salary)
FROM employees
GROUP BY department_id;
```

B.
```
SELECT department_id, AVG(NVL(salary,0))
FROM employees
GROUP BY department_id;
```

C.
```
SELECT department_id, NVL(AVG(salary), 0)
FROM employees
GROUP BY department_id;
```

D.
```
SELECT department_id, AVG(salary)
FROM employees
GROUP BY department_id
HAVING salary IS NOT NULL;
```

5. Review the following two SQL statements, and choose the appropriate option.

```
1.     SELECT department_id, COUNT(*)
FROM employees
HAVING COUNT(*) > 10
GROUP BY department_id;
2.     SELECT department_id, COUNT(*)
FROM employees
WHERE COUNT(*) > 10
GROUP BY department_id;
```

   A. Statement 1 and statement 2 will produce the same results.
   B. Statement 1 will succeed, and statement 2 will fail.
   C. Statement 2 will succeed, and statement 1 will fail.
   D. Both statements fail.

6. Read the following SQL carefully, and choose the appropriate option. The JOB_ID column shows the various jobs.

```
SELECT  MAX(COUNT(*))
FROM employees
GROUP BY  job_id, department_id;
```

   A. Aggregate functions cannot be nested.
   B. The columns in the GROUP BY clause must appear in the SELECT clause for the query to work.
   C. The GROUP BY clause is not required in this query.
   D. The SQL will produce the highest number of jobs within a department.

7. Identify the SQL that produces the correct result.

   A.
```
SELECT department_id, SUM(salary)
FROM employees
WHERE department_id <> 50
GROUP BY department_id
HAVING COUNT(*) > 30;
```

   B.
```
SELECT department_id, SUM(salary) sum_sal
FROM employees
WHERE department_id <> 50
GROUP BY department_id
HAVING sum_sal > 3000;
```

C.
```
SELECT department_id, SUM(salary) sum_sal
FROM employees
WHERE department_id <> 50
AND sum_sal > 3000
GROUP BY department_id;
```

D.
```
SELECT department_id, SUM(salary)
FROM employees
WHERE department_id <> 50
AND SUM(salary) > 3000
GROUP BY department_id;
```

8. Consider the following SQL, and choose the most appropriate option.

```
SELECT COUNT(DISTINCT SUBSTR(first_name, 1,1))
FROM employees;
```

A. A single-row function nested inside a group function is not allowed.

B. The GROUP BY clause is required to successfully run this query.

C. Removing the DISTINCT qualifier will fix the error in the query.

D. The query will execute successfully without any modification.

9. The sales order number (ORDER_NO) is the primary key in the table SALES_ORDERS. Which query will return the total number of orders in the SALES_ORDERS table?

A. `SELECT COUNT(ALL order_no) FROM sales_orders;`

B. `SELECT COUNT(DISTINCT order_no) FROM sales_orders;`

C. `SELECT COUNT(order_no) FROM sales_orders;`

D. `SELECT COUNT(NVL(order_no,0) FROM sales_orders;`

E. All of the above

F. A and C

10. Sheila wants to find the highest salary within each department of the EMPLOYEES table. Which query will help her get what she wants?

A. `SELECT MAX(salary) FROM employees;`

B. `SELECT MAX(salary BY department_id) FROM employees;`

C. `SELECT department_id, MAX(salary) max_sal FROM employees;`

D. `SELECT department_id, MAX(salary) FROM employees GROUP BY department_id;`

E. `SELECT department_id, MAX(salary) FROM employees USING department_id;`

11. Which assertion about the following queries is true?

```
SELECT COUNT(DISTINCT mgr), MAX(DISTINCT salary)
FROM emp;

SELECT COUNT(ALL mgr), MAX(ALL salary)
FROM emp;
```

   A. They will always return the same numbers in columns 1 and 2.

   B. They may return different numbers in column 1 but will always return the same number in column 2.

   C. They may return different numbers in both columns 1 and 2.

   D. They will always return the same number in column 1 but may return different numbers in column 2.

12. Which clauses in the SELECT statement can use single-row functions nested in aggregate functions? (Choose all that apply.)

   A. SELECT

   B. ORDER BY

   C. WHERE

   D. GROUP BY

13. Consider the following two SQL statements. Choose the most appropriate option.

   1. `select substr(first_name, 1,1) fn, SUM(salary) FROM employees GROUP BY first_name;`

   2. `select substr(first_name, 1,1) fn, SUM(salary) FROM employees GROUP BY substr(first_name, 1,1);`

   A. Statement 1 and 2 will produce the same result.

   B. Statement 1 and 2 will produce different results.

   C. Statement 1 will fail.

   D. Statement 2 will fail, but statement 1 will succeed.

14. How will the results of the following two SQL statements differ?

```
Statement 1:
SELECT COUNT(*), SUM(salary)
FROM hr.employees;

Statement 2:
SELECT COUNT(salary), SUM(salary)
FROM hr.employees;
```

A. Statement 1 will return one row, and statement 2 may return more than one row.

B. Both statements will fail because they are missing a GROUP BY clause.

C. Both statements will return the same results.

D. Statement 2 may return a smaller COUNT value than statement 1.

15. Why does the following SELECT statement fail?

```
SELECT colorname Colour, MAX(cost)
FROM itemdetail
WHERE UPPER(colorname) LIKE '%WHITE%'
GROUP BY colour
HAVING COUNT(*) > 20;
```

A. A GROUP BY clause cannot contain a column alias.

B. The condition COUNT(*) > 20 should be in the WHERE clause.

C. The GROUP BY clause must contain the group functions used in the SELECT list.

D. The HAVING clause can contain only the group functions used in the SELECT list.

16. What will the following SQL statement return?

```
select max(prod_pack_size)
from sh.products
where min(prod_weight_class) = 5;
```

A. An exception will be raised.

B. The largest PROD_PACK_SIZE for rows containing PROD_WEIGHT_CLASS of 5 or higher

C. The largest PROD_PACK_SIZE for rows containing PROD_WEIGHT_CLASS of 5

D. The largest PROD_PACK_SIZE in the SH.PRODUCTS table

17. Why will the following query raise an exception?

```
select dept_no, avg(distinct salary),
       count(job) job_count
from emp
where mgr like 'J%'
  or  abs(salary) > 10
having count(job) > 5
order by 2 desc;
```

A. The HAVING clause cannot contain a group function.

B. The GROUP BY clause is missing.

C. ABS() is not an Oracle function.

D. The query will not raise an exception.

18. Which clause will generate an error when the following query is executed?

```
SELECT department_id, AVG(salary) avg_sal
FROM employees
GROUP BY department_id
HAVING TRUNC(department_id) > 50;
```

A. The GROUP BY clause, because it is missing the group function.

B. The HAVING clause, because single-row functions cannot be used.

C. The HAVING clause, because the AVG function used in the SELECT clause is not used in the HAVING clause.

D. None of the above. The SQL statement will not return an error.

19. Which statements are true? (Choose all that apply.)

A. A group function can be used only if the GROUP BY clause is present.

B. Group functions along with nonaggregated columns can appear in the SELECT clause as long as a GROUP BY clause and a HAVING clause are present.

C. The HAVING clause is optional when the GROUP BY clause is used.

D. The HAVING clause and the GROUP BY clause are mutually exclusive; you can use only one clause in a SELECT statement.

20. Read the following two statements, and choose the best option.

1. HAVING clause should always appear after the GROUP BY clause.
2. GROUP BY clause should always appear after the WHERE clause.

A. Statement 1 and 2 are false.

B. Statement 1 is true, and statement 2 is false.

C. Statement 1 is false, and statement 2 is true.

D. Statements 1 and 2 are true.

Answers to Review Questions

1. D. Though you do not have a `state` column in the SELECT clause, having it in the GROUP BY clause will group the results by state, so you end up getting two values (two columns) for each state.

2. A. All requirements are met. The gross-, net-, and earned-revenue requirements are satisfied with the SELECT clause. The second- and third-quarter sales requirement is satisfied with the first predicate of the WHERE clause—the sales date will be truncated to the first day of a quarter; thus, 01-Apr-1999 or 01-Jul-1999 for the required quarters (which are both between 01-Apr-1999 and 01-Sep-1999). The state codes requirement is satisfied by the second predicate in the WHERE clause. This question is intentionally misleading, but so are some exam questions (and, unfortunately, some of the code in some shops).

3. C. Since the `department_id` column does not have any aggregate function applied to it, it must appear in the GROUP BY clause. The ORDER BY clause in the SQL must be replaced with a GROUP BY clause to make the query work.

4. A. Since group functions do not include NULL values in their calculation, you do not have to do anything special to exclude the NULL values. Only COUNT(*) includes NULL values.

5. B. An aggregate function is not allowed in the WHERE clause. You can have the GROUP BY and HAVING clauses in any order, but they must appear after the WHERE clause.

6. D. The SQL will work fine and produce the result. Since group functions are nested, a GROUP BY clause is required.

7. A. It is perfectly alright to have one function in the SELECT clause and another function in the HAVING clause of the query. Options B and C are trying to use the alias name, which is not allowed. Option D has a group function in the WHERE clause, which is also not allowed.

8. D. The query will return how many distinct alphabets are used to begin names in the EMPLOYEES table. You can nest a group function inside a single-row function, and vice versa.

9. E. All the queries will return the same result. Since ORDER_NO is the primary key, there cannot be NULL values in the column. Hence, ALL and DISTINCT will give the same result.

10. D. Option A will display the highest salary of all the employees. Options B and E use invalid syntax keywords. Option C does not have a GROUP BY clause.

11. B. The first column in the first query is counting the distinct MGR values in the table. The first column in the second query is counting all MGR values in the table. If a manager appears twice, the first query will count her one time, but the second will count her twice. Both the first query and the second query are selecting the maximum salary value in the table.

12. A, B. A group function is not allowed in GROUP BY or WHERE clauses, whether you use it as nested or not.

13. B. Both statements are valid. The first statement will produce the number of rows equal to the number of unique first_name values. The second statement will produce the number of rows equal to the unique number of first characters in the first_name column.

14. D. COUNT(*) will count all rows in the table. COUNT(salary) will count only the number of salary values that appear in the table. If there are any rows with a NULL salary, statement 2 will not count them.

15. A. A GROUP BY clause must contain the column or expressions on which to perform the grouping operation. It cannot use column aliasing.

16. A. You cannot place a group function in the WHERE clause. Instead, you should use a HAVING clause.

17. B. There is at least one column in the SELECT list that is not a constant or group function, so a GROUP BY clause is mandatory.

18. D. The HAVING clause filters data after the group function is applied. If an aggregate function is not used in the HAVING clause, the column used must be part of the SELECT clause.

19. C. The HAVING clause can be used in a SELECT statement only if the GROUP BY clause is present. The optional HAVING clause filters data after the rows are summarized.

20. C. The GROUP BY and HAVING clauses can appear in any order in the SELECT clause. If a WHERE clause is present, it must be before the GROUP BY clause.

Using Joins and Subqueries

ORACLE DATABASE 11*g:* SQL FUNDAMENTALS I EXAM OBJECTIVES COVERED IN THIS CHAPTER

✓ **Displaying data from multiple tables**

- Write SELECT statements to access data from more than one table using equijoins and nonequijoins
- Join a table to itself by using a self-join
- View data that generally does not meet a join condition by using outer joins
- Generate a Cartesian product of all rows from two or more tables

✓ **Using subqueries to solve queries**

- Define subqueries
- Describe the types of problems that the subqueries can solve
- List the types of subqueries
- Write single-row and multiple-row subqueries

✓ **Using the Set operators**

- Describe set operators
- Use a set operator to combine multiple queries into a single query
- Control the order of rows returned

A database has many tables that store data. In Chapter 1, "Introducing SQL," you learned how to write simple queries that select data from one table. Although this information is essential to passing the certification exam, the ability to join two or more related tables and access information is the core strength of relational databases. Using the SELECT statement, you can write advanced queries that satisfy user requirements.

This chapter focuses on querying data from more than one table using table joins and subqueries. When you use two or more tables or views in a single query, it is a join query. You'll need to understand how the various types of joins and subqueries work, as well as the proper syntax, for the certification exam.

Set operators in Oracle let you combine results from two or more SELECT statements. The results of each SELECT statement are considered a set, and Oracle provides UNION, INTERSECT, and MINUS operators to get the desired results. You will learn how these operators work in this chapter.

Writing Multiple-Table Queries

In relational database management systems (RDBMSs), related data can be stored in multiple tables. You use the power of SQL to relate the information and query data. A SELECT statement has a mandatory SELECT clause and FROM clause. The SELECT clause can have a list of columns, expressions, functions, and so on. The FROM clause tells you in which table(s) to look for the required information. In Chapter 1, you learned to query data using simple SELECT statements from a single table. In this chapter, you will learn how to retrieve data from more than one table.

To query data from more than one table, you need to identify common columns that relate the two tables. Here's how you do it:

1. In the SELECT clause, you list the columns you are interested in from all the related tables.
2. In the FROM clause, you include all the table names separated by commas.
3. In the WHERE clause, you define the relationship between the tables listed in the FROM clause using comparison operators.

You can also specify the relationship using a JOIN clause instead of the WHERE clause. The JOIN clause introduced by Oracle in Oracle *9i* was then added to conform to the ISO/ANSI

SQL1999 standard. Throughout this section, you'll see examples of queries using the Oracle native syntax as well as the ISO/ANSI SQL1999 standard. A query from multiple tables without a relationship or common column is known as a Cartesian join or cross join and is discussed later in this chapter.

A *join* is a query that combines rows from two or more tables or views. Oracle performs a join whenever multiple tables appear in the query's FROM clause. The query's SELECT clause can have the columns or expressions from any or all of these tables.

If multiple tables have the same column names, the duplicate column names should be qualified in the queries with their table name or table alias.

Inner Joins

Inner joins return only the rows that satisfy the join condition. The most common operator used to relate two tables is the equality operator (=). If you relate two tables using an equality operator, it is an *equality join*, also known as an *equijoin*. This type of join combines rows from two tables that have equivalent values for the specified columns.

Simple Inner Joins

A simple inner join has only the join condition specified, without any other filtering conditions. For example, let's consider a simple join between the DEPARTMENTS and LOCATIONS tables of the HR schema. The common column in these tables is LOCATION_ID. You will query these tables to get the location ID, city name, and department names in that city:

```
SELECT locations.location_id, city, department_name
FROM   locations, departments
WHERE  locations.location_id = departments.location_id;
```

Here, you are retrieving data from two tables—two columns from the LOCATIONS table and one column from the DEPARTMENTS table. These two tables are joined in the WHERE clause using an equality operator on the LOCATION_ID column. It is not necessary for the column names in both tables to have the same name to have a join. Notice that the LOCATION_ID column is qualified with its table name for every occurrence. This is to avoid ambiguity; it is not necessary to qualify each column, but it increases the readability of the query. If the same column name appears in more than one table used in the query, you must qualify the column name with the table name or table alias.

To execute a join of three or more tables, Oracle takes these steps:

1. Oracle joins two of the tables based on the join conditions, comparing their columns.
2. Oracle joins the result to another table, based on join conditions.
3. Oracle continues this process until all tables are joined into the result.

Complex Inner Joins

Apart from specifying the join condition in the WHERE clause, you may have another condition to limit the rows retrieved. Such joins are known as *complex joins*. For example, to continue with the example in the previous section, if you are interested only in the departments that are outside the United States, use this query:

```
SELECT locations.location_id, city, department_name
FROM   locations, departments
WHERE  locations.location_id = departments.location_id
AND    country_id != 'US';

LOCATION_ID CITY                 DEPARTMENT_NAME
----------- -------------------- -----------------
       1800 Toronto              Marketing
       2400 London               Human Resources
       2700 Munich               Public Relations
       2500 Oxford               Sales
```

Using Table Aliases

Like columns, tables can have alias names. Table aliases increase the readability of the query. You can also use them to shorten long table names with shorter alias names. Specify the *table alias name* next to the table, separated with a space. You can rewrite the query in the previous section using alias names, as follows:

```
SELECT l.location_id, city, department_name
FROM   locations l, departments d
WHERE  l.location_id = d.location_id
AND    country_id != 'US';
```

When tables (or views or materialized views) are specified in the FROM clause, Oracle looks for the object in the schema (or user) connected to the database. If the table belongs to another schema, you must qualify it with the schema name. (You may avoid this by using synonyms, which are discussed in Chapter 7, "Creating Schema Objects.") You can use the schema owner to qualify a table; you can also use the table owner and schema owner to qualify a column. Here is an example:

```
SELECT locations.location_id, hr.locations.city
      ,department_name
FROM   hr.locations, hr.departments
WHERE  locations.location_id = departments.location_id;
```

Keep in mind that you can qualify a column name with its schema and table only when the table name is qualified with the schema. In the previous SQL, you qualified the column

CITY with the schema HR. This is possible only if you qualify the LOCATIONS table with the schema. The following SQL will produce an error:

```
SELECT locations.location_id, hr.locations.city
       ,department_name
FROM  locations, hr.departments
WHERE locations.location_id = departments.location_id;

SELECT locations.location_id, hr.locations.city
                                   *
ERROR at line 1:
ORA-00904: "HR"."LOCATIONS"."CITY": invalid identifier
```

When you use table alias names, you must qualify the column names with the alias name only; qualifying the columns with the table name will produce an error, as in this example:

```
SELECT locations.location_id, city, department_name
FROM   locations l, hr.departments d
WHERE  locations.location_id = d.location_id;

WHERE  locations.location_id = d.location_id
       *
ERROR at line 3:
ORA-00904: "LOCATIONS"."LOCATION_ID": invalid identifier
```

The correct syntax is to replace `locations.location_id` with `l.location_id` in the SELECT and WHERE clauses.

If there are no common column names between the two tables used in the join (the FROM clause), you don't need to qualify the columns. However, if you qualify the columns, you are telling the Oracle database engine where exactly to find the column; hence, you are improving the performance of the query.

If there are column names common to multiple tables used in a join query, you must qualify the column name with a table name or table alias. This is true for column names appearing in SELECT, WHERE, ORDER BY, GROUP BY, and HAVING clauses. When using the ANSI syntax, the rule is different. The ANSI syntax is discussed in the next section.

When joining columns using the traditional syntax or ANSI syntax, if the column datatypes are different, Oracle tries to perform an implicit datatype conversion. This may affect your query performance. It is better if the columns used in the join condition have the same datatype or if you use the explicit conversion functions you learned in Chapter 2, "Using Single-Row Functions."

Using the ANSI Syntax

The difference between traditional Oracle join syntax and the ANSI/ISO SQL1999 syntax is that in ANSI, the join type is specified explicitly in the FROM clause. Using the ANSI syntax is clearer and is recommended over the traditional Oracle syntax. Simple joins can have the following forms:

```
<table name> NATURAL [INNER] JOIN <table name>

<table name> [INNER] JOIN <table name> USING (<columns>)

<table name> [INNER] JOIN <table name> ON <condition>
```

The following sections discuss each of the syntax forms in detail. In all three syntaxes, the keyword INNER is optional and is the default.

NATURAL JOIN

The NATURAL keyword indicates a *natural join*, where the join is based on all columns that have same name in both tables. In this type of join, you should not qualify the column names with the table name or table alias name. Let's return to the example of querying the DEPARTMENTS and LOCATIONS tables using LOCATION_ID as the join column. The new Oracle syntax is as follows:

```
SELECT location_id, city, department_name
FROM   locations NATURAL JOIN departments;
```

The common column in these two tables is LOCATION_ID, and that column is used to join the tables. When specifying NATURAL JOIN, the columns with the same name in both tables should also have same datatype. The following query will return the same results:

```
SELECT location_id, city, department_name
FROM   departments NATURAL JOIN locations;
```

Notice that even though the LOCATION_ID column is in both tables, you did not qualify this column in the SELECT clause. You cannot qualify the column names used for the join when using the NATURAL JOIN clause. The following query will result in an error:

```
SELECT l.location_id, city, department_name
FROM   departments NATURAL JOIN locations l;
SELECT l.location_id, city, department_name
       *
ERROR at line 1:
ORA-25155: column used in NATURAL join cannot have qualifier
```

The following query will not return an error because the qualifier is used on a column that's not part of the join condition:

```
SELECT location_id, city, d.department_name
FROM   departments d NATURAL JOIN locations l;
```

If you use SELECT *, common columns are listed only once in the result set. The following example demonstrates this. The common column in the COUNTRIES table and the REGIONS table is the REGION_ID.

```
SQL> DESCRIBE regions
 Name                    Null?    Type
 ----------------------- -------- ------------
 REGION_ID               NOT NULL NUMBER
 REGION_NAME                      VARCHAR2(25)

SQL> DESCRIBE countries
 Name                    Null?    Type
 ----------------------- -------- ------------
 COUNTRY_ID              NOT NULL CHAR(2)
 COUNTRY_NAME                     VARCHAR2(40)
 REGION_ID                        NUMBER

SELECT *
FROM   regions NATURAL JOIN countries;

 REGION_ID REGION_NAME      CO COUNTRY_NAME
---------- ---------------- -- ------------------
         1 Europe           UK United Kingdom
         1 Europe           NL Netherlands
         1 Europe           IT Testing Update
         1 Europe           FR France
… … …
```

Here is another example, which joins three tables:

```
SELECT region_id, region_name, country_id, country_name,
       location_id, city
FROM   regions
NATURAL JOIN countries
NATURAL JOIN locations;
```

When specifying more than two tables using NATURAL JOIN syntax, it is a good idea to use parentheses to increase readability. The previous SQL can be interpreted in two ways:

- Join the REGIONS table and the COUNTRIES table, and join the result to the LOCATIONS table.
- Join the COUNTRIES table to the LOCATIONS table, and join the result to the REGIONS table.

If you do not use parentheses, Oracle uses left associativity by pairing the tables from left to right (as in the first scenario). By using parentheses, you can make the query less ambiguous, as shown here:

```
SELECT region_id, region_name, country_id, country_name,
       location_id, city
FROM   locations
NATURAL JOIN (regions
NATURAL JOIN countries);
```

The same query written in traditional Oracle syntax is as follows:

```
SELECT regions.region_id, region_name, countries.country_id, country_name,
       location_id, city
FROM   regions, countries, locations
WHERE  regions.region_id = countries.region_id
AND    countries.country_id = locations.country_id;
```

Though NATURAL JOIN syntax is easy to read and use, its usage should be discouraged in good coding practice. Since NATURAL JOIN joins the tables by all the identical column names, you could end up having a wrong join condition if you're not careful. It is always better to explicitly specify the join condition using the syntaxes available.

JOIN...USING

If there are many columns that have the same names in the tables you are joining and they do not have the same datatype, or you want to specify the columns that should be considered for an equijoin, you can use the JOIN...USING syntax. The USING clause specifies the column names that should be used to join the tables. Here is an example:

```
SELECT location_id, city, department_name
FROM   locations JOIN departments USING (location_id);
```

The column names used in the USING clause should not be qualified with a table name or table alias. The column names not appearing in the USING clause can be qualified. If there are other common column names in the tables and if those column names are used in the query, they must be qualified.

Let's consider this syntax with joining more than two tables:

```
SELECT region_name, country_name, city
FROM   regions
JOIN   countries USING (region_id)
JOIN   locations USING (country_id);
```

Here, the REGIONS table is joined with the COUNTRIES table using the REGION_ID column, and its result is joined with the LOCATIONS table using the COUNTRY_ID column.

The following query will result in an error because there is no common column between the REGIONS and LOCATIONS tables:

```
SELECT region_name, country_name, city
FROM   regions
JOIN   locations USING (country_id)
JOIN   countries USING (region_id);

JOIN   locations USING (country_id)
                      *
ERROR at line 3:
ORA-00904: "REGIONS"."COUNTRY_ID": invalid identifier
```

You can add a WHERE clause to limit the number of rows and an ORDER BY clause to sort the rows retrieved along with any type of join operation:

```
SELECT region_name, country_name, city
FROM   regions
JOIN   countries USING (region_id)
JOIN   locations USING (country_id)
WHERE  country_id = 'US'
ORDER BY 1;
```

Remember that you cannot use alias or table names to qualify the column names on the columns used in the join operation anywhere in the query when using the NATURAL JOIN or JOIN USING syntax. You may see questions in the certification exam testing this rule.

JOIN...ON

When you do not have common column names between tables to make a join or if you want to specify arbitrary join conditions, you can use the JOIN…ON syntax. This syntax specifically defines the join condition using the column names. You can qualify column names with a table name or alias name. If the column name is common to multiple tables involved in the query, those column names must be qualified.

Using the JOIN ON syntax over the traditional join method separates the table joins from the other conditions. Since this syntax explicitly states the join condition, it is easier to read and understand. Here is the three-table example you used in the previous section, written using the JOIN…ON syntax. Notice the use of qualifier on the COUNTRY_ID column; this is required because COUNTRY_ID appears in COUNTRIES and LOCATIONS tables.

```
SELECT region_name, country_name, city
FROM   regions r
JOIN   countries c ON r.region_id = c.region_id
JOIN   locations l ON c.country_id = l.country_id
WHERE  c.country_id = 'US';
```

Multitable Joins

A *multitable join* is a join of more than two tables. In the ANSI syntax, joins are performed from left to right. The first join condition can reference columns from only the first and second tables; the second join condition can reference columns from the first, second, and third tables; and so on. Consider the following example:

```
SELECT first_name, department_name, city
FROM   employees e
JOIN   departments d
ON (e.department_id = d.department_id)
JOIN   locations l
ON (d.location_id = l.location_id);
```

The first join to be performed is EMPLOYEES and DEPARTMENTS. The first join condition can reference columns in EMPLOYEES and DEPARTMENTS but cannot reference columns in LOCATIONS. The second join condition can reference columns from all three tables.

Real World Scenario

How Do You Specify Join Conditions When You Have More Than One Column to Join?

Company XYZ was keeping detailed information about customer geography in its purchase-orders database. Consider the tables and data shown here. For simplicity, I've reduced the number of columns in the tables to the interesting ones for this example. For this demonstration, say you are interested in three tables: COUNTRY, STATE, and CITY.

```
SQL> SELECT * FROM country;

  CNT_CODE CNT_NAME               CONTINENT
---------- ---------------------- ----------
         1 UNITED STATES          N.AMERICA
        91 INDIA                  ASIA
        65 SINGAPORE              ASIA

SQL> SELECT * FROM state;

  CNT_CODE ST ST_NAME
---------- -- ---------------
         1 TX TEXAS
         1 CA CALIFORNIA
         1 TN TENNESSE
        91 TN TAMIL NADU
        91 KL KERALA
```

```
SQL> SELECT * FROM city;

  CNT_CODE ST   CTY_CODE CTY_NAME
---------- -- ---------- --------------------
         1 TX       1001 DALLAS
         1 CA       8099 LOS ANGELES
        91 TN       2243 CHENNAI

SQL>
```

The CNT_CODE column relates the COUNTRY table and the STATE table. The ST_CODE and CNT_CODE columns relate the STATE table and CITY table. The following examples show how to join the STATE and CITY tables to get information on the country code, state name, and city name.

Traditional Oracle Join

```
SQL> SELECT s.cnt_code, st_name, cty_name
  2  FROM   state s, city c
  3  WHERE  s.cnt_code  = c.cnt_code
  4  AND    s.st_code   = c.st_code
  5  AND    s.cnt_code  = 1;
  CNT_CODE ST_NAME              CTY_NAME
---------- -------------------- -------------
         1 CALIFORNIA           LOS ANGELES
         1 TEXAS                DALLAS
SQL>
```

ANSI Natural Join

```
SQL> SELECT cnt_code, st_name, cty_name
  2  FROM   state NATURAL JOIN city
  3  WHERE  cnt_code  = 1;
  CNT_CODE ST_NAME              CTY_NAME
---------- -------------------- --------------
         1 TEXAS                DALLAS
         1 CALIFORNIA           LOS ANGELES
SQL>
```

ANSI Using JOIN...USING

```
SQL> SELECT cnt_code, st_name, cty_name
  2  FROM   state JOIN city USING (cnt_code, st_code)
  3  WHERE  cnt_code  = 1;
```

```
  CNT_CODE ST_NAME              CTY_NAME
---------- -------------------- ----------------
         1 TEXAS                DALLAS
         1 CALIFORNIA           LOS ANGELES
SQL>
```

ANSI Using JOIN...ON

```
SQL> SELECT s.cnt_code, s.st_name, c.cty_name
  2  FROM   state s
  3  JOIN   city c ON s.cnt_code = c.cnt_code
  4  AND    s.st_code  = c.st_code
  5* WHERE  s.cnt_code  = 1;
  CNT_CODE ST_NAME              CTY_NAME
---------- -------------------- ----------------
         1 CALIFORNIA           LOS ANGELES
         1 TEXAS                DALLAS
SQL>
```

Cartesian Joins

A *Cartesian join* occurs when data is selected from two or more tables and there is no common relation specified in the WHERE clause. If you do not specify a join condition for the tables listed in the FROM clause, Oracle joins each row from the first table to every row in the second table. If the first table has 3 rows and the second table has 4 rows, the result will have 12 rows. If you add another table with 2 rows without specifying a join condition, the result will have 24 rows.

For the most part, Cartesian joins happen when there are many tables in the FROM clause and developers forget to include the join condition or they specify a wrong join condition. You should therefore avoid them. To avoid a Cartesian join, there should be at least n–1 join conditions when joining n tables. Sometimes you intentionally use Cartesian joins to generate large amounts of data, especially when testing applications.

Consider the following example:

```
SELECT region_name, country_name
FROM   regions, countries
WHERE  countries.country_id LIKE 'I%';

REGION_NAME               COUNTRY_NAME
------------------------- -------------
Europe                    Israel
Americas                  Israel
```

```
Asia                      Israel
Middle East and Africa    Israel
Europe                    India
Americas                  India
Asia                      India
Middle East and Africa    India
Europe                    Italy
Americas                  Italy
Asia                      Italy
Middle East and Africa    Italy
```

Although there is a WHERE clause, you did not specify a join condition between the COUNTRIES and REGIONS tables. The query returns all the matching rows from the COUNTRIES table based on the WHERE clause and retrieves one row from the REGIONS table for every row from the COUNTRIES table. There are four rows in the REGIONS table and three rows in the COUNTRIES table with a country name beginning with *I*.

If a Cartesian join is made between a table having *m* rows and another table having *n* rows, the resulting query will have $m \times n$ rows.

Using the ANSI Syntax

A Cartesian join in ANSI syntax is known as a *cross join*. A cross join is represented in ANSI/ISO SQL1999 syntax using the CROSS JOIN keywords. You can code the previous example using the ANSI syntax as follows:

```
SELECT region_name, country_name
FROM   countries
CROSS JOIN regions
WHERE  countries.country_id LIKE 'I%';

REGION_NAME               COUNTRY_NAME
------------------------- -------------
Europe                    Israel
Americas                  Israel
Asia                      Israel
Middle East and Africa    Israel
Europe                    India
Americas                  India
Asia                      India
Middle East and Africa    India
Europe                    Italy
```

```
Americas                  Italy
Asia                      Italy
Middle East and Africa    Italy
```

Outer Joins

So far, you have seen only inner joins, which return just the matched rows. Sometimes, however, you might want to see the data from one table, even if there is no corresponding row in the joining table. Oracle provides the *outer join* mechanism for this. An outer join returns results based on the inner join condition, as well as the unmatched rows from one or both of the tables.

In traditional Oracle syntax, the plus symbol surrounded by parentheses, (+), denotes an outer join in the query. Enter (+) beside the column name of the table in the WHERE clause where there may not be a corresponding row. For example, to write a query that performs an outer join of tables A and B and returns all rows from A, apply the outer join operator (+) to all columns of B in the join condition. For all rows in A that have no matching rows in B, the query returns NULL values for the columns in B.

Consider an example using the COUNTRIES and LOCATIONS tables. Say you want to list the country name and location city, and you also want to see all the countries in the COUNTRIES table. To perform this outer join, you place an outer join operator beside all columns referencing LOCATIONS in the WHERE clause:

```
SELECT c.country_name, l.city
FROM   countries c, locations l
WHERE  c.country_id = l.country_id (+);

COUNTRY_NAME                             CITY
---------------------------------------- --------------------
Australia                                Sydney
Brazil                                   Sao Paulo
Canada                                   Toronto
Canada                                   Whitehorse
Switzerland                              Geneva
Switzerland                              Bern
China                                    Beijing
Germany                                  Munich
India                                    Bombay
Italy                                    Rome
Italy                                    Venice
Japan                                    Tokyo
Japan                                    Hiroshima
Mexico                                   Mexico City
Netherlands                              Utrecht
```

```
Singapore                          Singapore
United Kingdom                     London
United Kingdom                     Oxford
United Kingdom                     Stretford
United States of America           Southlake
United States of America           South San Francisco
United States of America           South Brunswick
United States of America           Seattle
Argentina
Israel
Nigeria
Egypt
Kuwait
France
Hong Kong
Belgium
Zimbabwe
Zambia
Denmark
```

The order of tables in the query's FROM clause determines whether the join is a left outer join or a right outer join. In the previous example, you are selecting all the rows from the table appearing on the left (COUNTRIES); hence this query is using a left outer join.

If tables A and B are outer-joined (FROM A, B) and you need all rows from B, the outer join operator is placed beside all columns of A. This is a right outer join, because you are retrieving all rows from the table on the right side (table B). In outer-join syntax using the (+) operator, the placement of the outer join operator, (+), is what determines the table from where all the rows are retrieved, not the order of tables; the order of tables determines whether it is a left or right outer join. When using the ANSI syntax, the left outer join and right outer join syntaxes depend on the table order.

The outer join operator, (+), can appear only in the WHERE clause. If there are multiple join conditions between the tables, the outer join operator should be used against all the conditions. Consider the following query:

```
SELECT c.country_name, l.city
FROM   countries c, locations l
WHERE  c.country_id = l.country_id (+)
AND    l.city LIKE 'B%';

COUNTRY_NAME                         CITY
------------------------------------ --------
China                                Beijing
India                                Bombay
Switzerland                          Bern
```

Even though you included the outer join operator, Oracle just ignored it, and did not provide unmatched rows in the query result. This is because you did not place the outer join operator beside all the columns from the LOCATIONS table. The following query will return the desired result:

```
SELECT c.country_name, l.city
FROM   countries c, locations l
WHERE  c.country_id = l.country_id (+)
AND    l.city (+) LIKE 'B%';
```

An outer join (containing the (+) operator) cannot be combined with another condition using the OR or IN logical operators. For example, the following query is not valid:

```
SELECT c.country_name, l.city
FROM   countries c, locations l
WHERE  c.country_id = l.country_id (+)
OR    l.city (+) LIKE 'B%';


OR    l.city (+) LIKE 'B%'
                  *
ERROR at line 4:
ORA-01719: outer join operator (+) not allowed in operand of OR or IN
```

The following query works because the outer join operator is used on the LOCATIONS table and the IN condition is used on the column from the COUNTRIES table:

```
SELECT c.country_name, l.city
FROM   countries c, locations l
WHERE  c.country_id = l.country_id (+)
AND    c.country_name IN ('India','Israel');

COUNTRY_NAME                          CITY
----------------------------------- --------
Israel
India                                  Bombay
```

Using the ANSI Syntax

The ANSI syntax allows you to specify three types of outer joins:

- Left outer join
- Right outer join
- Full outer join

Left Outer Joins

A *left outer join* is a join between two tables that returns rows based on the matching condition, as well as unmatched rows from the table to the left of the JOIN clause. For example, the following query returns the country name and city name from the COUNTRIES and LOCATIONS tables, as well as the entire country names from the COUNTRIES table.

```
SELECT c.country_name, l.city
FROM   countries c LEFT OUTER JOIN locations l
ON  c.country_id = l.country_id;
```

The keyword OUTER between LEFT and JOIN is optional. LEFT JOIN will return the same result, as in the following example:

```
SELECT country_name, city
FROM   countries LEFT JOIN locations
USING (country_id);
```

The same query can be written using NATURAL JOIN, since COUNTRY_ID is the only column common to both tables.

```
SELECT country_name, city
FROM   countries NATURAL LEFT JOIN locations;
```

In traditional Oracle outer join syntax, the query is written as follows:

```
SELECT c.country_name, l.city
FROM   countries c, locations l
WHERE  l.country_id (+) = c.country_id;
```

Right Outer Joins

A *right outer join* is a join between two tables that returns rows based on the matching condition, as well as unmatched rows from the table to the right of the JOIN clause. Let's rewrite the previous example using RIGHT OUTER JOIN:

```
SELECT country_name, city
FROM   locations NATURAL RIGHT OUTER JOIN countries;
```

or:

```
SELECT c.country_name, l.city
FROM   locations l RIGHT JOIN countries c
ON  c.country_id = l.country_id;
```

You cannot specify the traditional outer join operator, (+), in a query when the ANSI JOIN syntax is used.

Full Outer Joins

A *full outer join* is possible when using the ANSI syntax. It is not available using the (+) operator. This is a join between two tables that returns rows based on the matching condition, as well as unmatched rows from the table on the right and left of the JOIN clause. Suppose you want to list all the employees' last names with their department names. You want to include all the employees, even if they have not been assigned a department. You also want to include all the departments, even if no employees are working for that department. Here's the query:

```
SELECT e.employee_id, e.last_name,
       d.department_id, d.department_name
FROM   employees e FULL OUTER JOIN departments d
ON     e.department_id = d.department_id;
```

Trying to perform a similar query with the outer join operator will produce an error:

```
SELECT e.employee_id, e.last_name, d.department_name
FROM   employees e, departments d
WHERE  e.department_id (+) = d.department_id (+);

WHERE  e.department_id (+) = d.department_id (+)
                           *

ERROR at line 3:
ORA-01468: a predicate may reference only one outer-joined table
```

You can achieve the full outer join using the UNION operator and the outer join operator, as in the following query:

```
SELECT e.employee_id, e.last_name, d.department_name
FROM   employees e, departments d
WHERE  e.department_id (+) = d.department_id
UNION
SELECT e.employee_id, e.last_name, d.department_name
FROM   employees e, departments d
WHERE  e.department_id = d.department_id (+);
```

If you do not specify a join type before the JOIN keyword, Oracle assumes the default value of INNER. To specify an outer join, you must use the LEFT, RIGHT, or FULL keyword.

Other Multiple-Table Queries

In this section, you will consider other methods used to retrieve data from more than one table. These methods include using self-joins and using nonequality joins. Using set operators in queries can also retrieve rows from multiple tables. Set operators are discussed in the next section.

Self-Joins

A *self-join* joins a table to itself. The table name appears in the FROM clause twice, with different alias names. The two aliases are treated as two different tables, and they are joined as you would join any other tables, using one or more related columns. The following example lists the employees' names and their manager names from the EMPLOYEES table:

```
SELECT e.last_name Employee, m.last_name Manager
FROM   employees e, employees m
WHERE  m.employee_id = e.manager_id;
```

When performing self-joins in the ANSI syntax, you must always use the JOIN…ON syntax. You cannot use NATURAL JOIN and JOIN…USING. In the following example, the keyword INNER is optional. The certification example also includes an additional WHERE clause to filter the records.

```
SELECT e.last_name Employee, m.last_name Manager
FROM   employees e INNER JOIN employees m
ON     m.employee_id = e.manager_id
WHERE  e.last_name like 'R%';

EMPLOYEE                  MANAGER
------------------------- -------------------------
Russell                   King
Raphaely                  King
Rogers                    Kaufling
Rajs                      Mourgos
```

Nonequality Joins

If the query is relating two tables using an equality operator (=), it is an equality join, also known as an *inner join* or an *equijoin*, as discussed earlier in this chapter. If any other operator is used to join the tables in the query, it is a *nonequality join*. Let's consider an example of a nonequality join. The EMPLOYEES table has a column named SALARY; the GRADES table has the range of salary values that correspond to each grade.

```
SELECT * FROM grades;

GRADE  LOW_SALARY HIGH_SALARY
------ ---------- -----------
P5              0        3000
P4           3001        5000
P3           5001        7000
P2           7001       10000
P1          10001
```

To find out which grade each employee belongs to, use the following query. You limit the rows returned by using `last_name LIKE 'R%'`.

```
SELECT last_name, salary, grade
FROM   employees, grades
WHERE  last_name LIKE 'R%'
AND    salary >= low_salary
AND    salary <= NVL(high_salary, salary);

LAST_NAME                     SALARY GRADE
------------------------- ---------- ------
Raphaely                       11000 P1
Rogers                          2900 P5
Rajs                            3500 P4
Russell                        14000 P1
```

You can write the same query using the ANSI syntax as follows:

```
SELECT last_name, salary, grade
FROM   employees JOIN grades
ON     salary >= low_salary
AND    salary <= NVL(high_salary, salary)
WHERE  last_name LIKE 'R%';
```

Using Set Operators

You can use *set operators* to select data from multiple tables. Set operators basically combine the result of two queries into one. These queries are known as *compound queries*. All set operators have equal precedence. When multiple set operators are present in the same query, they are evaluated from left to right, unless another order is specified by using parentheses. The datatypes of the resulting columns, as well as the number of columns, should match in both queries. Oracle has four set operators, which are listed in Table 4.1.

TABLE 4.1 Oracle Set Operators

Operator	Description
UNION	Returns all unique rows selected by either query
UNION ALL	Returns all rows, including duplicates selected by either query

TABLE 4.1 Oracle Set Operators *(continued)*

Operator	Description
INTERSECT	Returns rows selected from both queries
MINUS	Returns unique rows selected by the first query but not the rows selected from the second query

I'll discuss all of these in a bit, but let's first consider the EMPLOYEE table and the following two queries to illustrate the use of set operators:

```
SELECT last_name, hire_date
FROM   employees
WHERE  department_id = 90;

LAST_NAME                 HIRE_DATE
------------------------- ---------
King                      17-JUN-87
Kochhar                   21-SEP-89
De Haan                   13-JAN-93

SELECT last_name, hire_date
FROM   employees
WHERE  last_name LIKE 'K%';

LAST_NAME                 HIRE_DATE
------------------------- ---------
King                      17-JUN-87
Kochhar                   21-SEP-89
Khoo                      18-MAY-95
Kaufling                  01-MAY-95
King                      30-JAN-96
Kumar                     21-APR-00
```

The UNION Operator

The UNION operator is used to return rows from either query, without any duplicate rows.

```
SELECT last_name, hire_date
FROM   employees
WHERE  department_id = 90
```

```
UNION
SELECT last_name, hire_date
FROM   employees
WHERE  last_name LIKE 'K%';

LAST_NAME                 HIRE_DATE
------------------------- ---------
De Haan                   13-JAN-93
Kaufling                  01-MAY-95
Khoo                      18-MAY-95
King                      17-JUN-87
King                      30-JAN-96
Kochhar                   21-SEP-89
Kumar                     21-APR-00
```

Notice that even though there is a total of nine rows in both queries, the UNION query returned only unique values. The employees with the last name King appear twice, but their hire dates are different.

The UNION ALL Operator

The UNION ALL operator does not sort or filter the result set; it returns all rows from both queries. Let's consider this SQL:

```
SELECT last_name, hire_date
FROM   employees
WHERE  department_id = 90
UNION ALL
SELECT last_name, hire_date
FROM   employees
WHERE  last_name LIKE 'K%';

LAST_NAME                 HIRE_DATE
------------------------- ---------
King                      17-JUN-87
Kochhar                   21-SEP-89
De Haan                   13-JAN-93
King                      17-JUN-87
Kochhar                   21-SEP-89
Khoo                      18-MAY-95
Kaufling                  01-MAY-95
King                      30-JAN-96
Kumar                     21-APR-00
```

The INTERSECT Operator

The INTERSECT operator is used to return the rows returned by both queries. Let's find the employees common to both queries:

```
SELECT last_name, hire_date
FROM   employees
WHERE  department_id = 90
INTERSECT
SELECT last_name, hire_date
FROM   employees
WHERE  last_name LIKE 'K%';

LAST_NAME                 HIRE_DATE
------------------------- ---------
King                      17-JUN-87
Kochhar                   21-SEP-89
```

The MINUS Operator

Now, let's find the employees from the first query but not in the second query. You can use the MINUS operator here:

```
SELECT last_name, hire_date
FROM   employees
WHERE  department_id = 90
MINUS
SELECT last_name, hire_date
FROM   employees
WHERE  last_name LIKE 'K%';

LAST_NAME                 HIRE_DATE
------------------------- ---------
De Haan                   13-JAN-93
```

Putting It All Together

Each query appearing with the set operators is an independent query and will work by itself. You can have join conditions and all the SQL options and functions in these independent queries. There can be only one ORDER BY clause in the query at the very end; you cannot specify an ORDER BY clause for each query appearing with the set operators. For example, the following query will produce an error:

```
SELECT last_name, hire_date
FROM   employees
WHERE  department_id = 90
ORDER BY last_name
UNION ALL
SELECT first_name, hire_date
FROM   employees
WHERE  first_name LIKE 'K%'
ORDER BY first_name;

UNION ALL
*
ERROR at line 5:
ORA-00933: SQL command not properly ended
```

You can use the column name or alias name used in the first query or positional notation in the ORDER BY clause. Here are two examples (the result is the same for both queries):

```
SELECT last_name, hire_date "Join Date"
FROM   employees
WHERE  department_id = 90
UNION ALL
SELECT first_name, hire_date
FROM   employees
WHERE  first_name LIKE 'K%'
ORDER BY last_name, "Join Date";

SELECT last_name, hire_date "Join Date"
FROM   employees
WHERE  department_id = 90
UNION ALL
SELECT first_name, hire_date
FROM   employees
WHERE  first_name LIKE 'K%'
ORDER BY 1, 2;

LAST_NAME                 Join Date
------------------------- ---------
De Haan                   13-JAN-93
Karen                     05-JAN-97
```

```
Karen                       10-AUG-99
Kelly                       14-JUN-97
Kevin                       23-MAY-98
Kevin                       16-NOV-99
Ki                          12-DEC-99
Kimberely                   24-MAY-99
King                        17-JUN-87
Kochhar                     21-SEP-89
```

When using set operators, the number of columns in the SELECT clause of the queries appearing on either side of the set operator should be the same. The column datatypes should be compatible. If the datatypes are different, Oracle tries to do an implicit conversion of data.

Subqueries

A *subquery* is a query within a query. A subquery answers the queries that have multiple parts; the subquery answers one part of the question, and the parent query answers the other part. When you nest many subqueries, the innermost query is evaluated first. Subqueries can be used with all Data Manipulation Language (DML) statements.

Using subqueries in the `FROM` clause of a top-level query is known as an *inline view*. You can nest any number of such queries; Oracle does not have a limit. Using the inline view, you can write queries to find top-*n* values. This is possible because Oracle allows an `ORDER BY` clause in the inline view. See Chapter 7 for details.

There are three types of subqueries:

- A subquery in the `WHERE` clause of a query is called a *nested subquery*. You can have 255 levels of nested subqueries.
- When a column from the table used in the parent query is referenced in the subquery, it is known as a *correlated subquery*. For each row processed in the parent query, the correlated subquery is evaluated once.
- A *scalar subquery* returns a single row and a single column value. Scalar subqueries can be used anywhere a column name or expression can be used.

If the columns in the subquery have the same name as the columns in the containing SQL statement, it is a good idea to qualify the column names with table names or table aliases to avoid ambiguity. A subquery must be enclosed in parentheses and must be placed on the right side of the comparison operator when used in the `WHERE` clause.

Single-Row Subqueries

Single-row subqueries return only one row of result. A single-row subquery uses a single-row operator; the common operator is the equality operator (=). Consider an example using the tables from the HR schema. To find the name of the employee with the highest salary, you first need to find the highest salary using a subquery. Then you can execute the parent query with the result from the subquery.

```
SELECT last_name, first_name, salary
FROM   employees
WHERE  salary = (SELECT MAX(salary) FROM employees);

LAST_NAME                 FIRST_NAME                SALARY
------------------------- -------------------- ----------
King                      Steven                    24000
```

The parent query of a single-row subquery can return more than one row. For example, to find the names and salaries of employees who work in the accounting department, you need to find the department number for accounting in a subquery and then execute the parent query:

```
SELECT last_name, first_name, salary
FROM   employees
WHERE  department_id = (SELECT department_id
       FROM   departments
       WHERE  department_name = 'Accounting');

LAST_NAME                 FIRST_NAME                SALARY
------------------------- -------------------- ----------
Higgins                   Shelley                   12000
Gietz                     William                    8300
```

All single-row comparison operators can be used in the single-row subquery (=, >, >=, <, <=, or <>). The following example uses two subqueries. So, there are three query blocks in total. The two inner query blocks (subqueries) are executed first, and their result is passed on to the outer query (parent query) to complete its processing.

```
SELECT last_name, first_name, department_id
FROM employees
WHERE department_id < (SELECT MAX(department_id)
                       FROM departments
                       WHERE location_id = 1500)
AND hire_date >= (SELECT MIN(hire_date)
                  FROM employees
                  WHERE department_id = 30);
```

Similar to the WHERE clause, a subquery can be used in the HAVING clause. The following query lists the latest hire dates by departments that have hired an employee after the first employee was hired in department 80:

```
SELECT department_id, MAX(hire_date)
FROM employees
GROUP BY department_id
HAVING MAX(hire_date) > (SELECT MIN(hire_date)
                         FROM employees
                         WHERE department_id = 80);

DEPARTMENT_ID MAX(HIRE_
------------- ---------
          100 07-DEC-99
           30 10-AUG-99
              24-MAY-99
           20 17-AUG-97
           50 08-MAR-00
           80 21-APR-00
           60 07-FEB-99
```

Multiple-Row Subqueries

Multiple-row subqueries return more than one row of results from the subquery. It is safer to provide the multiple-row operators in the subqueries if you are not sure of the results. In the previous query, if there is more than one department ID with the name accounting, the query will fail.

The following query returns three rows from the subquery. It lists all the employees who work for the same department as John does.

```
SELECT last_name, first_name, department_id
FROM   employees
WHERE  department_id = (SELECT department_id
       FROM   employees
       WHERE  first_name = 'John');

WHERE  department_id = (SELECT department_id
                       *
ERROR at line 3:
ORA-01427: single-row subquery returns more than one row
```

The query failed because you used a single-row operator with a multiple-row subquery. Change the = to a multiple-row operator to make the query work:

```
SELECT last_name, first_name, department_id
FROM   employees
WHERE  department_id IN (SELECT department_id
       FROM    employees
       WHERE   first_name = 'John');
```

IN is the most commonly used multiple-row subquery operator. Other operators are EXISTS, ANY, SOME, and ALL. You may use NOT with the IN and EXISTS operators.

ANY and SOME are synonymous operators. ANY, SOME, and ALL operators must always be preceded by any of the single-row conditional operators (=, >, >=, <, <= or <>) and are used to compare a value to each value returned by the subquery. Table 4.2 lists the meaning of the ANY and ALL operators when used with different conditional operators.

TABLE 4.2 ANY and ALL Operator Meaning

Operation	Meaning
<ANY	Less than the maximum
<=ANY	Less than or equal to the maximum
>ANY	More than the minimum
=ANY	Equivalent to the IN operator
<ALL	Less than the minimum
>ALL	More than the maximum
<>ALL	Equivalent to the NOT IN operator

Let's review the ANY and ALL operators using examples. The following query will be used in the next subquery using the ANY operator. The subquery returns the 12000 and 8300 values. The minimum is 8,300. The second query returns salaries equal to or above 8,300 that do not belong to department 80.

```
SELECT salary FROM employees WHERE department_id = 110;
```

```
    SALARY
----------
     12000
      8300

SELECT last_name, salary, department_id
FROM employees
WHERe salary >= ANY (SELECT salary FROM employees
                     WHERE department_id = 110)
AND department_id != 80;

LAST_NAME                     SALARY DEPARTMENT_ID
------------------------- ---------- -------------
King                           24000            90
De Haan                        17000            90
Kochhar                        17000            90
Hartstein                      13000            20
Higgins                        12000           110
Greenberg                      12000           100
Raphaely                       11000            30
Baer                           10000            70
Faviet                          9000           100
Hunold                          9000            60
Gietz                           8300           110
```

The following example lists only the salaries that are more than the maximum (12,000) returned from the subquery:

```
SELECT last_name, salary, department_id
FROM employees
WHERe salary > ALL (SELECT salary FROM employees
                    WHERE department_id = 110)
AND department_id != 80;

LAST_NAME                     SALARY DEPARTMENT_ID
------------------------- ---------- -------------
Hartstein                      13000            20
De Haan                        17000            90
Kochhar                        17000            90
King                           24000            90
```

You can use the DISTINCT keyword in the subquery when using ANY or ALL operators to prevent rows from being selected multiple times.

Subquery Returns No Rows

If the subquery returns no rows, a NULL value is returned to the parent query. Since NULL is not equal to another NULL, the parent query may not return any row even if there are NULL values in the column used in the WHERE clause of the subquery.

As shown in the following SQL, there is one record in the EMPLOYEES table where you have a NULL DEPARTMENT_ID:

```
SQL> SELECT last_name, first_name, salary
  2  FROM employees
  3  WHERE department_id IS NULL;

LAST_NAME                 FIRST_NAME               SALARY
------------------------- -------------------- ----------
Grant                     Kimberely                  7000
```

Let's use this column in the subquery and see what happens:

```
SQL> SELECT last_name, first_name, salary
  2  FROM employees
  3  WHERE department_id = (SELECT department_id
  4                         FROM departments
  5                         WHERE department_name = 'JustDummy');

no rows selected

SQL>
```

In the previous example, the outer query will return a value only if the DEPARTMENT_ID column matches some value. Although the inner query returned NULL, the outer query will not match for NULL, since NULL ≠ NULL. Let's review another example. In the following query, only Tobias has a NULL salary value:

```
SQL> SELECT last_name, salary
  2  FROM employees
  3  WHERE department_id = 30;

LAST_NAME                     SALARY
------------------------- ----------
Raphaely                       11000
Khoo                            3100
Baida                           2900
Tobias
Himuro                          2600
Colmenares                      2500
```

When you use this subquery, you expect to see some results, because you know the `EMPLOYEES` table has more than the five different salary values:

```
SQL> SELECT first_name, last_name, salary
  2  FROM employees
  3  WHERE salary NOT IN (
  4        SELECT salary
  5        FROM employees
  6        WHERE department_id = 30);

no rows selected

SQL>
```

The SQL does not return any rows because one of the rows returned by the inner query is `NULL`. So, be careful when using `NOT IN` conditions with subqueries that could have a `NULL` value. This is not a problem when you use the `IN` operator. The `IN` operator is equivalent to `=ANY`, and the `NOT IN` operator is equivalent to `<> ALL`. If you include one more condition in the `WHERE` clause of the inner query, the SQL would work as expected:

```
SELECT first_name, last_name, salary
FROM employees
WHERE salary NOT IN (
      SELECT salary
      FROM employees
      WHERE department_id = 30
      AND salary is NOT NULL);
```

Correlated Subqueries

Oracle performs a *correlated subquery* when the subquery references a column from a table referred to in the parent statement. A correlated subquery is evaluated once for each row processed by the parent statement. The parent statement can be a `SELECT`, `UPDATE`, or `DELETE` statement. In the following example, the highest-paid employee of each department is selected. The subquery is executed for each row returned in the parent query. Notice that the parent table column is used inside the subquery.

```
SELECT department_id, last_name, salary
FROM   employees e1
WHERE  salary = (SELECT MAX(salary)
       FROM employees e2
       WHERE e1.department_id = e2.department_id)
ORDER BY 1, 2, 3;
```

```
DEPARTMENT_ID LAST_NAME                      SALARY
------------- ------------------------- ----------
           10 Whalen                          4400
           20 Hartstein                      13000
           30 Raphaely                       11000
           40 Mavris                          6500
           50 Fripp                           8200
           60 Hunold                          9000
           70 Baer                           10000
           80 Russell                        14000
           90 King                           24000
          100 Greenberg                      12000
          110 Higgins                        12000
```

The following example shows a correlated subquery using the EXISTS operator. The EXISTS operator checks for the existence of a row in the subquery based on the condition. The column results of the SELECT clause in the subquery are ignored when using the EXISTS operator. The query lists the names of employees who work with John (in the same department). The subquery selects a dummy value of 'x', which is ignored.

```
SELECT last_name, first_name, department_id
FROM   employees e1
WHERE  EXISTS (SELECT 'x'
       FROM   employees e2
       WHERE  first_name = 'John'
       AND    e1.department_id = e2.department_id);
```

The column names in the parent queries are available for reference in subqueries. The column names from the tables in the subquery cannot be used in the parent queries. The scope is only the current query level and its subqueries.

Scalar Subqueries

A *scalar subquery* returns exactly one column value from one row. You can use scalar subqueries in most places where you would use a column name or expression, such as in a single-row function as an argument, in the VALUES clause of an INSERT statement, in an ORDER BY clause, in a WHERE clause, and in a SELECT clause. You can also use scalar subqueries in CASE expressions. Scalar subqueries cannot be used in GROUP BY or HAVING clauses. The following sections review a few examples of using scalar subqueries.

A Scalar Subquery in a CASE Expression

To list the city name, the country code, and whether the city is in India, you use a CASE expression with a subquery to return the country code for India from the COUNTRIES table. To limit the rows, let's select only the cities that begin with *B*:

```
SELECT city, country_id, (CASE
       WHEN country_id IN (SELECT country_id
                 FROM   countries
                 WHERE  country_name = 'India')
       THEN 'Indian'
       ELSE 'Non-Indian'
       END) "INDIA?"
FROM   locations
WHERE  city LIKE 'B%';

CITY                           CO INDIA?
------------------------------ -- ----------
Beijing                        CN Non-Indian
Bombay                         IN Indian
Bern                           CH Non-Indian
```

A Scalar Subquery in a SELECT Clause

To report the employee name, the department, and the highest salary in that department, you use a subquery in the SELECT clause. This is also a correlated subquery.

```
SELECT last_name, department_id,
     (SELECT MAX(salary)
      FROM   employees sq
      WHERE  sq.department_id = e.department_id) HSAL
FROM   employees e
WHERE  last_name like 'R%';

LAST_NAME                 DEPARTMENT_ID       HSAL
------------------------- ------------- ----------
Raphaely                             30      11000
Rogers                               50       8200
Rajs                                 50       8200
Russell                              80      14000
```

A Scalar Subquery in SELECT and WHERE Clauses

The following query may be confusing, but pay close attention to the flexibility of using subqueries to solve your queries. A scalar subquery is used in the SELECT clause as well as in the WHERE clause. A multiple-row subquery is also used in the WHERE clause, after the IN operator. The purpose of the query is to find the department names and their manager names for all departments that are in the United States or Canada. Since the country information is not available in the DEPARTMENTS table, you need to get this information from the LOCATIONS table. Also, you do not know the country IDs of the United States and Canada, so you use a subquery to get them. The query also limits the number of rows retrieved by checking whether a manager is assigned to the department (d.manager_id IS NOT NULL).

```
SELECT department_name, manager_id, (SELECT last_name
    FROM employees e
    WHERE e.employee_id = d.manager_id) MGR_NAME
FROM  departments d
WHERE ((SELECT country_id FROM locations l
    WHERE  d.location_id = l.location_id)
    IN (SELECT country_id FROM countries c
    WHERE  c.country_name = 'United States of America'
    OR     c.country_name = 'Canada'))
AND   d.manager_id IS NOT NULL;

DEPARTMENT_NAME      MANAGER_ID MGR_NAME
-------------------- ---------- --------------
Administration              200 Whalen
Marketing                   201 Hartstein
Purchasing                  114 Raphaely
Shipping                    121 Fripp
IT                          103 Hunold
Executive                   100 King
Finance                     108 Greenberg
Accounting                  205 Higgins
```

A Scalar Subquery in an ORDER BY Clause

You can also use scalar subqueries in the ORDER BY clause. The following example sorts the city names by their country-name order. Notice that the country name is not included in the SELECT clause.

```
SELECT country_id, city, state_province
FROM   locations l
ORDER BY (SELECT country_name
          FROM   countries c
          WHERE  l.country_id = c.country_id);
```

If the scalar subquery returns more than one row, the query will fail. If the scalar subquery returns no rows, the value is NULL.

Finding Total Space and Free Space Using Dictionary Views

The following dictionary views are best friends of a DBA. They show the most critical aspect of the database from the user perspective—the space allocated and free. If the DBA is not monitoring the growth and free space available in the database, it is likely that they might get calls from the user community that they ran out of space in the tablespace. Let's build a query using four dictionary views (you may need the SELECT_CATALOG_ROLE privilege to query these views).

- DBA_TABLESPACES: Shows the tablespace name, type, and so on.
- DBA_DATA_FILES: Shows the data files associated with a permanent or undo tablespace and the size of the data file. The total size of all data files associated with a tablespace gives the total size of the tablespace.
- DBA_TEMP_FILES: Shows the temporary files associated with a temporary tablespace and their size.
- DBA_FREE_SPACE: Shows the unallocated space (free space) in each tablespace.

The query to get the tablespace names and type of tablespace would be as follows:

```
column tablespace_name format a18
SELECT tablespace_name, contents
FROM dba_tablespaces;

TABLESPACE_NAME    CONTENTS
------------------ ---------
SYSTEM             PERMANENT
SYSAUX             PERMANENT
UNDOTBS1           UNDO
TEMP               TEMPORARY
USERS              PERMANENT
EXAMPLE            PERMANENT
```

To find the total space allocated to each tablespace, you need to query DBA_DATA_FILES and DBA_TEMP_FILES. Since you are using a group function (SUM) along with a nonaggregated column (tablespace_name), the GROUP BY clause is a must. Notice the use of an arithmetic operation on the aggregated result to display the bytes in megabytes.

```
SELECT tablespace_name, SUM(bytes)/1048576 MBytes
FROM dba_data_files
```

```
GROUP BY tablespace_name;

TABLESPACE_NAME        MBYTES
------------------ ----------
UNDOTBS1                  730
SYSAUX               800.1875
USERS                  201.75
SYSTEM                    710
EXAMPLE                   100

SELECT tablespace_name, SUM(bytes)/1048576 MBytes
FROM dba_temp_files
GROUP BY tablespace_name;

TABLESPACE_NAME        MBYTES
------------------ ----------
TEMP                  50.0625
```

You can find the total free space in each tablespace using the DBA_FREE_SPACE view. Notice that the free space from temporary tablespace is not shown in this query.

```
SELECT tablespace_name, SUM(bytes)/1048576 MBytesFree
FROM dba_free_space
GROUP BY tablespace_name;

TABLESPACE_NAME    MBYTESFREE
------------------ ----------
SYSAUX                  85.25
UNDOTBS1             718.6875
USERS                180.4375
SYSTEM                 8.3125
EXAMPLE                22.625
```

Let's now try to display the total size of the tablespaces and their free space side-by-side using a UNION ALL query. UNION ALL is used to avoid sorting. UNION will produce the same result.

```
SELECT tablespace_name, SUM(bytes)/1048576 MBytes, 0 MBytesFree
FROM dba_data_files
GROUP BY tablespace_name
UNION ALL
SELECT tablespace_name, SUM(bytes)/1048576 MBytes, 0
FROM dba_temp_files
```

```
GROUP BY tablespace_name
UNION ALL
SELECT tablespace_name, 0, SUM(bytes)/1048576
FROM dba_free_space
GROUP BY tablespace_name;

TABLESPACE_NAME        MBYTES MBYTESFREE
------------------ ---------- ----------
UNDOTBS1                  730          0
SYSAUX               800.1875          0
USERS                  201.75          0
SYSTEM                    710          0
EXAMPLE                   100          0
TEMP                  50.0625          0
SYSAUX                      0      85.25
UNDOTBS1                    0   718.6875
USERS                       0   180.4375
SYSTEM                      0     8.3125
EXAMPLE                     0     22.625
```

You got the result, but it's not exactly as you expected. You want to see the free-space information beside each tablespace. Let's join the results of the total space with the free space and see what happens. Here you are creating two subqueries (inline views totalspace and freespace) and joining them together using the tablespace_name column.

```
SELECT tablespace_name, MBytes, MBytesFree
FROM
 (SELECT tablespace_name, SUM(bytes)/1048576 MBytes
  FROM dba_data_files
  GROUP BY tablespace_name
  UNION ALL
  SELECT tablespace_name, SUM(bytes)/1048576 MBytes
  FROM dba_temp_files
  GROUP BY tablespace_name) totalspace
JOIN
 (SELECT tablespace_name, 0, SUM(bytes)/1048576 MBytesFree
  FROM dba_free_space
  GROUP BY tablespace_name) freespace
USING (tablespace_name);
```

```
TABLESPACE_NAME         MBYTES MBYTESFREE
------------------ ---------- ----------
SYSAUX                800.1875      85.25
UNDOTBS1                   730   718.6875
USERS                   201.75   180.4375
SYSTEM                     710     8.3125
EXAMPLE                    100     22.625
```

You are almost there; the only item missing is information about the temporary tablespace. Since the temporary-tablespace free-space information is not included in the `freespace` subquery and you used an INNER join condition, the result set did not include temporary tablespaces. Now if you change the `INNER JOIN` to an `OUTER JOIN`, you get the desired result:

```
SELECT tablespace_name, MBytes, MBytesFree
FROM
 (SELECT tablespace_name, SUM(bytes)/1048576 MBytes
  FROM dba_data_files
  GROUP BY tablespace_name
  UNION ALL
  SELECT tablespace_name, SUM(bytes)/1048576 MBytes
  FROM dba_temp_files
  GROUP BY tablespace_name) totalspace
LEFT OUTER JOIN
 (SELECT tablespace_name, 0, SUM(bytes)/1048576 MBytesFree
  FROM dba_free_space
  GROUP BY tablespace_name) freespace
USING (tablespace_name)
ORDER BY 1;

TABLESPACE_NAME         MBYTES MBYTESFREE
------------------ ---------- ----------
EXAMPLE                    100     22.625
SYSAUX                800.1875    85.0625
SYSTEM                     710     8.3125
TEMP                   50.0625
UNDOTBS1                   730   718.6875
USERS                   201.75   180.4375
```

Another method to write the same query would be to use the query you built earlier and aggregate its result using an outer query, as shown here:

```
SELECT tsname, sum(MBytes) MBytes, sum(MBytesFree) MBytesFree
FROM (
  SELECT tablespace_name tsname, SUM(bytes)/1048576 MBytes, 0 MBytesFree
  FROM dba_data_files
  GROUP BY tablespace_name
  UNION ALL
  SELECT tablespace_name, SUM(bytes)/1048576 MBytes, 0
  FROM dba_temp_files
  GROUP BY tablespace_name
  UNION ALL
  SELECT tablespace_name, 0, SUM(bytes)/1048576
  FROM dba_free_space
  GROUP BY tablespace_name)
GROUP BY tsname
ORDER BY 1;

TSNAME                             MBYTES MBYTESFREE
------------------------------ ---------- ----------
EXAMPLE                               100     22.625
SYSAUX                           800.1875    85.0625
SYSTEM                                710     8.3125
TEMP                              50.0625          0
UNDOTBS1                              730   718.6875
USERS                              201.75   180.4375
```

Multiple-Column Subqueries

A subquery is multiple-column when you have more than one column in the SELECT clause of the subquery. *Multiple-column subqueries* are generally used to compare column conditions or in an UPDATE statement. Let's consider a simple example using the STATE and CITY tables shown here:

```
SQL> SELECT * FROM state;

  CNT_CODE ST_CODE    ST_NAME
---------- -------    ------------
         1 TX         TEXAS
         1 CA         CALIFORNIA
```

```
        91 TN         TAMIL NADU
         1 TN         TENNESSE
        91 KL         KERALA
SQL> SELECT * FROM city;

  CNT_CODE ST_CODE   CTY_CODE  CTY_NAME
---------- -------   --------  --------------
         1 TX            1001  DALLAS
        91 TN            2243  MADRAS
         1 CA            8099  LOS ANGELES
```

List the cities in Texas using a subquery on the STATE table:

```
SELECT cty_name
FROM   city
WHERE  (cnt_code, st_code) IN
       (SELECT cnt_code, st_code
        FROM   state
        WHERE  st_name = 'TEXAS');

CTY_NAME
----------
DALLAS
```

Subqueries in Other DML Statements

You can use subqueries in DML statements such as INSERT, UPDATE, DELETE, and MERGE. DML statements and their syntax are discussed in Chapter 5, "Manipulating Data." The following are some examples of subqueries in DML statements:

- To update the salary of all employees to the maximum salary in the corresponding department (correlated subquery), use this:

```
UPDATE employees e1
SET   salary = (SELECT MAX(salary)
      FROM   employees e2
      WHERE e1.department_id = e2.department_id);
```

- To delete the records of employees whose salary is less than the average salary in the department (using a correlated subquery), use this:

```
DELETE FROM employees e
WHERE salary < (SELECT AVG(salary) FROM employees
      WHERE  department_id = e.department_id);
```

- To insert records to a table using a subquery, use this:

  ```
  INSERT INTO employee_archive
  SELECT * FROM employees;
  ```

- To specify a subquery in the VALUES clause of the INSERT statement, use this:

  ```
  INSERT INTO departments
         (department_id, department_name)
  VALUES ((SELECT MAX(department_id)
            +10 FROM departments), 'EDP');
  ```

You can also have a subquery in the INSERT, UPDATE, and DELETE statements in place of the table name. Here is an example:

```
DELETE FROM
(SELECT * FROM departments
 WHERE department_id < 20)
WHERE department_id = 10;
```

The subquery can have an optional WITH clause. WITH READ ONLY specifies that the subquery cannot be updated. WITH CHECK OPTION specifies that if the subquery is used in place of a table in an INSERT, UPDATE, or DELETE statement, Oracle will not allow any changes to the table that would produce rows that are not included in the subquery. Let's look at an example:

```
INSERT INTO (SELECT department_id, department_name
      FROM departments
      WHERE department_id < 20)
VALUES (35, 'MARKETING');

1 row created.

INSERT INTO (SELECT department_id, department_name
      FROM departments
      WHERE department_id < 20 WITH CHECK OPTION)
VALUES (45, 'EDP')
SQL> /
      FROM departments
           *
ERROR at line 2:
ORA-01402: view WITH CHECK OPTION where-clause violation
SQL>
```

Summary

In this chapter, you learned to retrieve data from multiple tables. I started off discussing table joins. You also learned how to use subqueries and set operators.

Joins are used to relate two or more tables (or views). In a relational database, it is common to have a requirement to join data. The tables are joined by using a common column in the tables in the WHERE clause of the query. Oracle supports ISO/ANSI SQL1999 syntax for joins. Using this syntax, the tables are joined using the JOIN keyword, and a condition can be specified using the ON clause.

If the join condition uses the equality operator (= or IN), it is known as an equality join. If any other operator is used to join the tables, it is a nonequality join. If you do not specify any join condition between the tables, the result will be a Cartesian product: each row from the first table joined to every row in the second table. To avoid Cartesian joins, there should be at least *n*-1 join conditions in the WHERE clause when there are *n* tables in the FROM clause. A table can be joined to itself. If you want to select the results from a table, even if there are no corresponding rows in the joined table, you can use the outer join operator: (+). In the ANSI syntax, you can use the NATURAL JOIN, CROSS JOIN, LEFT JOIN, RIGHT JOIN, and FULL JOIN keywords to specify the type of join.

A subquery is a query within a query. Writing subqueries is a powerful way to manipulate data. You can write single-row and multiple-row subqueries. Single-row subqueries must return zero or one row; multiple-row subqueries return zero or more rows. IN and EXISTS are the most commonly used subquery operators. Subqueries can appear in the WHERE clause or in the FROM clause. They can also replace table names in SELECT, DELETE, INSERT, and UPDATE statements. Subqueries that return one row and one column result are known as scalar subqueries. Scalar subqueries can be used in most places where you would use an expression.

Set operators are used to combine the results of more than one query into one. Each query is separate and will work on its own. Four set operators are available in Oracle: UNION, UNION ALL, MINUS, and INTERSECT.

Exam Essentials

Understand joins. Make sure you know the different types of joins. Understand the difference between natural, cross, simple, complex, and outer joins.

Know the different outer join clauses. You can specify outer joins using LEFT, RIGHT, or FULL. Know the syntax of each type of join.

Be sure of the join syntax. Spend time practicing each type of join using the ANSI syntax. Understand the restrictions of using each ANSI keyword in the JOIN and their implied column-naming conventions.

Know how to write subqueries. Understand the use and flexibility of subqueries. Practice using scalar subqueries and correlated subqueries.

Understand the use of the ORDER BY clause in the subqueries. You can use the ORDER BY clause in all subqueries, except the subqueries appearing in the WHERE clause of the query. You can use the GROUP BY clause in the subqueries.

Know the set operators. Understand the set operators that can be used in compound queries. Know the difference between the UNION and UNION ALL operators.

Understand where you can specify the ORDER BY clause when using set operators. When using set operators to join two or more queries, the ORDER BY clause can appear only at the very end of the query. You can specify the column names as they appear in the top query or use positional notation.

Review Questions

1. Which line of code has an error?

   A. `SELECT dname, ename`

   B. `FROM   emp e, dept d`

   C. `WHERE  emp.deptno = dept.deptno`

   D. `ORDER BY 1, 2;`

2. What will be the result of the following query?

```
SELECT c.cust_id, c.cust_name, o.ord_date, o.prod_id
FROM   customers c, orders o
WHERE  c.cust_id = o.cust_id (+);
```

   A. List all the customer names in the CUSTOMERS table and the orders they made from the ORDERS table, even if the customer has not placed an order.

   B. List only the names of customers from the CUSTOMERS table who have placed an order in the ORDERS table.

   C. List all orders from the ORDERS table, even if there is no valid customer record in the CUSTOMERS table.

   D. For each record in the CUSTOMERS table, list the information from the ORDERS table.

3. The CUSTOMERS and ORDERS tables have the following data:

```
SQL> SELECT * FROM customers;

CUST_ CUST_NAME            PHONE           CITY
----- -------------------- --------------- -----------
A0101 Abraham Taylor Jr.                   Fort Worth
B0134 Betty Baylor         972-555-5555    Dallas
B0135 Brian King                           Chicago

SQL> SELECT * FROM orders;

ORD_DATE     PROD_ID CUST_ID   QUANTITY      PRICE
--------- ---------- ------- ---------- ----------
20-FEB-00       1741 B0134            5       65.5
02-FEB-00       1001 B0134           25    2065.85
02-FEB-00       1001 B0135            3      247.9
```

   When the following query is executed, what will be the value of PROD_ID and ORD_DATE for the customer Abraham Taylor Jr.?

```
SELECT c.cust_id, c.cust_name, o.ord_date, o.prod_id
FROM   customers c, orders o
WHERE  c.cust_id = o.cust_id (+);
```

A. NULL, 01-JAN-01

B. NULL, NULL

C. 1001, 02-FEB-00

D. The query will not return customer Abraham Taylor Jr.

4. When using ANSI join syntax, which clause is used to specify a join condition?

A. JOIN

B. USING

C. ON

D. WHERE

5. The EMPLOYEES table has EMPLOYEE_ID, DEPARTMENT_ID, and FULL_NAME columns. The DEPARTMENTS table has DEPARTMENT_ID and DEPARTMENT_NAME columns. Which two of the following queries return the department ID, name, and employee name, listing department names even if there is no employee assigned to that department? (Choose two.)

A.
```
SELECT d.department_id, d.department_name, e.full_name
FROM   departments d
NATURAL LEFT OUTER JOIN employees e;
```

B.
```
SELECT department_id, department_name, full_name
FROM   departments
NATURAL LEFT JOIN employees;
```

C.
```
SELECT d.department_id, d.department_name, e.full_name
FROM   departments d
LEFT OUTER JOIN employees e
USING (d.department_id);
```

D.
```
SELECT d.department_id, d.department_name, e.full_name
FROM   departments d
LEFT OUTER JOIN employees e
ON  (d.department_id = e.department_id);
```

6. Which two operators are not allowed when using an outer join operator in the query? (Choose two.)

A. OR

B. AND

C. IN

D. =

7. Which SQL statements do not give an error? (Choose all that apply.)

A.
```
SELECT last_name, e.hire_date, department_id
FROM employees e
JOIN (SELECT max(hire_date) max_hire_date
        FROM employees ORDER BY 1) me
ON (e.hire_date = me.max_hire_date)
```

B.
```
SELECT last_name, e.hire_date, department_id
FROM employees e
WHERE hire_date =
(SELECT max(hire_date) max_hire_date
       FROM employees ORDER BY 1)
```

C.
```
SELECT last_name, e.hire_date, department_id
FROM employees e
WHERE (department_id, hire_date) IN
(SELECT department_id, max(hire_date) hire_date
       FROM employees GROUP BY department_id)
```

D.
```
SELECT last_name, e.hire_date, department_id
FROM employees e JOIN
(SELECT department_id, max(hire_date) hire_date
FROM employees GROUP BY department_id) me
USING (hire_date)
```

8. The columns of the EMPLOYEES, DEPARTMENTS, and JOBS tables are shown here:

Table	Column Names	Datatype
EMPLOYEES	EMPLOYEE_ID	NUMBER (6)
	FIRST_NAME	VARCHAR2 (25)
	LAST_NAME	VARCHAR2 (25)
	SALARY	NUMBER (8,2)
	JOB_ID	VARCHAR2 (10)
	MANAGER_ID	NUMBER (6)
	DEPARTMENT_ID	NUMBER (2)
DEPARTMENTS	DEPARTMENT_ID	NUMBER (2)
	DEPARTMENT_NAME	VARCHAR2 (30)
	MANAGER_ID	NUMBER (6)
	LOCATION_ID	NUMBER (4)
JOBS	JOB_ID	VARCHAR2 (10)
	JOB_TITLE	VARCAHR2 (30)

Which assertion about the following query is correct?

```
1 SELECT e.last_name, d.department_name, j.job_title
2 FROM   jobs j
3 INNER JOIN employees e
4 ON (e.department_id = d.department_id)
5 JOIN departments d
6 ON (j.job_id = e.job_id);
```

A. The query returns all the rows from the EMPLOYEE table, where there is a corresponding record in the JOBS table and the DEPARTMENTS table.

B. The query fails with an invalid column name error.

C. The query fails because line 3 specifies INNER JOIN, which is not a valid syntax.

D. The query fails because line 5 does not specify the keyword INNER.

E. The query fails because the column names are qualified with the table alias.

9. The columns of the EMPLOYEES and DEPARTMENTS tables are shown in question 8. Consider the following three queries using those tables.

```
1. SELECT last_name, department_name
FROM   employees e, departments d
WHERE  e.department_id = d.department_id;
2. SELECT last_name, department_name
FROM   employees NATURAL JOIN departments;
3. SELECT last_name, department_name
FROM   employees JOIN departments
USING (department_id);
```

Which of the following assertions best describes the results?

A. Queries 1, 2, and 3 produce the same results.

B. Queries 2 and 3 produce the same result; query 1 produces a different result.

C. Queries 1, 2, and 3 produce different results.

D. Queries 1 and 3 produce the same result; query 2 produces a different result.

10. The data in the STATE table is as shown here:

```
SQL> SELECT * FROM state;

  CNT_CODE ST_CODE ST_NAME
---------- ------- ------------
         1 TX      TEXAS
         1 CA      CALIFORNIA
        91 TN      TAMIL NADU
         1 TN      TENNESSE
        91 KL      KERALA
```

Consider the following query.

```
SELECT cnt_code
FROM   state
WHERE  st_name = (SELECT st_name FROM state
                  WHERE  st_code = 'TN');
```

Which of the following assertions best describes the results?

A. The query will return the CNT_CODE for the ST_CODE value 'TN'.

B. The query will fail and will not return any rows.

C. The query will display 1 and 91 as CNT_CODE values.

D. The query will fail because an alias name is not used.

11. The data in the STATE table is shown in question 10. The data in the CITY table is as shown here:

```
SQL> SELECT * FROM city;

  CNT_CODE ST_CODE    CTY_CODE CTY_NAME
---------- ------- ---------- -------------
         1      TX       1001 DALLAS
        91      TN       2243 MADRAS
         1      CA       8099 LOS ANGELES
```

What is the result of the following query?

```
SELECT st_name "State Name"
FROM   state
WHERE  (cnt_code, st_code) =
       (SELECT cnt_code, st_code
        FROM   city
        WHERE  cty_name = 'DALLAS');
```

A. TEXAS

B. The query will fail because CNT_CODE and ST_CODE are not in the WHERE clause of the subquery.

C. The query will fail because more than one column appears in the WHERE clause.

D. TX

12. Which line of the code has an error?

```
1 SELECT department_id, count(*)
2 FROM   employees
3 GROUP BY department_id
4 HAVING COUNT(department_id) =
5 (SELECT max(count(department_id))
6  FROM employees
7  GROUP BY department_id);
```

A. Line 3

B. Line 4

C. Line 5

D. Line 7

E. No error

13. Which of the following is a correlated subquery?

A.
```
select cty_name from city
 where  st_code in (select st_code from state
 where st_name = 'TENNESSEE'
 and  city.cnt_code = state.cnt_code);
```

B.
```
select cty_name
 from   city
 where  st_code in (select st_code from state
 where st_name = 'TENNESSEE');
```

C.
```
select cty_name
 from city, state
 where  city.st_code = state.st_code
 and    city.cnt_code = state.cnt_code
 and    st_name = 'TENNESSEE';
```

D.
```
select cty_name
 from city, state
 where  city.st_code = state.st_code (+)
 and    city.cnt_code = state.cnt_code (+)
 and    st_name = 'TENNESSEE';
```

14. The COUNTRY table has the following data:

```
SQL> SELECT * FROM country;

  CNT_CODE CNT_NAME          CONTINENT
---------- ----------------- ----------
         1 UNITED STATES     N.AMERICA
        91 INDIA             ASIA
        65 SINGAPORE         ASIA
```

What value is returned from the subquery when you execute the following?

```
SELECT CNT_NAME
FROM   country
WHERE  CNT_CODE =
(SELECT MAX(cnt_code) FROM country);
```

A. INDIA

B. 65

C. 91

D. SINGAPORE

15. Which line in the following query contains an error?

```
1  SELECT deptno, ename, sal
2  FROM   emp e1
3  WHERE  sal = (SELECT MAX(sal) FROM emp
4                WHERE  deptno = e1.deptno
5                ORDER BY deptno);
```

A. Line 2

B. Line 3

C. Line 4

D. Line 5

16. Consider the following query:

```
SELECT deptno, ename, salary salary, average,
       salary-average difference
FROM   emp,
(SELECT deptno dno, AVG(salary) average FROM emp
 GROUP BY deptno)
WHERE  deptno = dno
ORDER BY 1, 2;
```

Which of the following statements is correct?

A. The query will fail because no alias name is provided for the subquery.

B. The query will fail because a column selected in the subquery is referenced outside the scope of the subquery.

C. The query will work without errors.

D. GROUP BY cannot be used inside a subquery.

17. The COUNTRY table has the following data:

```
SQL> SELECT * FROM country;

  CNT_CODE CNT_NAME             CONTINENT
---------- -------------------- ----------
         1 UNITED STATES        N.AMERICA
        91 INDIA                ASIA
        65 SINGAPORE            ASIA
```

What will be result of the following query?

```
INSERT INTO (SELECT cnt_code FROM country
             WHERE continent = 'ASIA')
VALUES (971, 'SAUDI ARABIA', 'ASIA');
```

A. One row will be inserted into the COUNTRY table.

B. WITH CHECK OPTION is missing in the subquery.

C. The query will fail because the VALUES clause is invalid.

D. The WHERE clause cannot appear in the subqueries used in INSERT statements.

18. Review the SQL code, and choose the line number that has an error.

```
1 SELECT DISTINCT department_id
2 FROM employees
3 ORDER BY department_id
4 UNION ALL
5 SELECT department_id
6 FROM departments
7 ORDER BY department_id
```

A. 1

B. 3

C. 6

D. 7

E. No error

19. Consider the following queries:

```
1. SELECT last_name, salary,
        (SELECT (MAX(sq.salary) - e.salary)
        FROM   employees sq
        WHERE  sq.department_id = e.department_id) DSAL
FROM   employees e
WHERE  department_id = 20;
2. SELECT last_name, salary, msalary - salary dsal
FROM   employees e,
       (SELECT department_id, MAX(salary) msalary
        FROM   employees
        GROUP BY department_id) sq
WHERE e.department_id = sq.department_id
AND   e.department_id = 20;
```

```
3. SELECT last_name, salary, msalary - salary dsal
FROM    employees e INNER JOIN
        (SELECT department_id, MAX(salary) msalary
         FROM   employees
         GROUP BY department_id) sq
ON       e.department_id = sq.department_id
WHERE    e.department_id = 20;
4. SELECT last_name, salary, msalary - salary dsal
FROM    employees INNER JOIN
        (SELECT department_id, MAX(salary) msalary
         FROM   employees
         GROUP BY department_id) sq
USING    (department_id)
WHERE    department_id = 20;
```

Which of the following assertions best describes the results?

A. Queries 1 and 2 produce identical results, and queries 3 and 4 produce identical results, but queries 1 and 3 produce different results.

B. Queries 1, 2, 3, and 4 produce identical results.

C. Queries 1, 2, and 3 produce identical results; query 4 will produce errors.

D. Queries 1 and 3 produce identical results; queries 2 and 4 will produce errors.

E. Queries 1, 2, 3, and 4 produce different results.

F. Queries 1 and 2 are valid SQL; queries 3 and 4 are not valid.

20. The columns of the EMPLOYEES and DEPARTMENTS tables are shown in question 8. Which query will show you the top five highest-paid employees in the company?

A.
```
SELECT last_name, salary
FROM   employees
WHERE ROWNUM <= 5
ORDER BY salary DESC;
```

B.
```
SELECT last_name, salary
FROM (SELECT *
FROM   employees
WHERE ROWNUM <= 5
ORDER BY salary DESC )
WHERE ROWNUM <= 5;
```

C.
```
SELECT * FROM
(SELECT last_name, salary
FROM   employees
ORDER BY salary)
WHERE ROWNUM <= 5;
```

D.
```
SELECT * FROM
(SELECT last_name, salary
FROM   employees
ORDER BY salary DESC)
WHERE ROWNUM <= 5;
```

Answers to Review Questions

1. C. When table aliases are defined, you should qualify the column names with the table alias only. In this case, the table name cannot be used to qualify column names. The line in option C should read WHERE e.deptno = d.deptno.

2. A. An outer join operator (+) indicates an outer join and is used to display the records, even if there are no corresponding records in the table mentioned on the other side of the operator. Here, the outer join operator is next to the ORDERS table, so even if there are no corresponding orders from a customer, the result set will have the customer ID and name.

3. B. When an outer join returns values from a table that does not have corresponding records, a NULL is returned.

4. C. The join condition is specified in the ON clause. The JOIN clause specifies the table to be joined. The USING clause specifies the column names that should be used in the join. The WHERE clause is used to specify additional search criteria to restrict the rows returned.

5. B, D. Option A does not work because you cannot qualify column names when using a natural join. Option B works because the only common column between these two tables is DEPARTMENT_ID. The keyword OUTER is optional. Option C does not work, again because you cannot qualify column names when specifying the USING clause. Option D works because it specifies the join condition explicitly in the ON clause.

6. A, C. OR and IN are not allowed in the WHERE clause on the columns where an outer join operator is specified. You can use AND and = in the outer join.

7. A, C. Options A and B have an ORDER BY clause used in the subquery. An ORDER BY clause can be used in the subquery appearing in the FROM clause, but not in the WHERE clause. Options C and D use the GROUP BY clause in the subquery, and its use is allowed in FROM as well as WHERE clauses. Option D will give an error because the DEPARTMENT_ID in the SELECT clause is ambiguous and hence doesn't need to be qualified as e.DEPARTMENT_ID. Another issue with option D is that since you used the USING clause to join, the column used in the USING clause cannot be qualified; e.hire_date in the SELECT clause should be hire_date.

8. B. The query fails because the d.DEPARTMENT_ID column is referenced before the DEPARTMENTS table is specified in the JOIN clause. A column can be referenced only after its table is specified.

9. D. Since DEPARTMENT_ID and MANAGER_ID are common columns in the EMPLOYEES and DEPARTMENTS tables, a natural join will relate these two tables using the two common columns.

10. B. There are two records in the STATE table with the ST_CODE value as 'TN'. Since you are using a single-row operator for the subquery, it will fail. Option C would be correct if it used the IN operator instead of = for the subquery.

11. A. The query will succeed, because there is only one row in the CITY table with the CTY_NAME value 'DALLAS'.

12. E. There is no error in the statement. The query will return the department number where the most employees are working and the number of employees in that department.

13. A. A subquery is correlated when a reference is made to a column from a table in the parent statement.

14. C. The subquery returns 91 to the main query.

15. D. You cannot have an ORDER BY clause in the subquery used in a WHERE clause.

16. C. The query will work fine, producing the difference between the employee's salary and average salary in the department. You do not need to use the alias names, because the column names returned from the subquery are different from the column names returned by the parent query.

17. C. Because only one column is selected in the subquery to which you are doing the insert, only one column value should be supplied in the VALUES clause. The VALUES clause can have only CNT_CODE value (971).

18. B. When using set operators, the ORDER BY clause can appear only on the SQL at the very end. You can use the column names (or aliases) appearing in the top query or use positional columns.

19. B. All four queries produce the same result. The first query uses a scalar subquery in the SELECT clause. The rest of queries use an inline view. All the queries display the last name, salary, and difference of salary from the highest salary in the department for all employees in department 20.

20. D. To find the top *n* rows, you can select the necessary columns in an inline view with an ORDER BY DESC clause. An outer query limiting the rows to *n* will give the result. ROWNUM returns the row number of the result row.

Manipulating Data

ORACLE DATABASE 11*g*: SQL FUNDAMENTALS I EXAM OBJECTIVES COVERED IN THIS CHAPTER:

✓ **Manipulating Data**

- Describe each data manipulation language (DML) statement
- Insert rows into a table
- Update rows in a table
- Delete rows from a table
- Control transactions

In this chapter, I will cover how to manipulate data. In an Oracle Database, this means using SQL data manipulation language (DML) statements. You will also learn how to coordinate multiple changes using transactions. I will discuss how to insert new data into a table, update existing data, and delete existing data from a table.

Because Oracle is a multiuser database and more than one user or session can change data at the same time, I will also need to cover locks and how they are used to control this concurrency. I will also cover another effect of a multiuser database, which is that data can change during the execution of statements. You can exercise some control over the consistency or visibility of these changes within a transaction, which is covered later in the chapter.

The certification exam will assess your knowledge of how to change data and control these changes. This chapter will solidify your understanding of these concepts in preparation for the certification exam.

Using DML Statements

DML is a subset of SQL that is employed to change data in a database table. Since SQL is English-like, meaning it's not cryptic like C or Perl, the statements used to perform data manipulation are easy to remember. The `INSERT` statement is used to add new rows to a table. The `UPDATE` statement is used modify rows in a table, and the `DELETE` statement is used to remove rows from a table.

Oracle also has the `MERGE` statement to perform an insert or update on the table from an existing source of data (table or view). `MERGE` also can include an optional clause to delete rows when certain conditions are met. At the time of publishing this book, however, `MERGE` is not part of the Oracle Database 11*g* SQL Fundamentals I test. Table 5.1 summarizes the DML statements that Oracle supports.

TABLE 5.1 DML Statements Supported by Oracle

Statement	Purpose
`INSERT`	Adds rows to a table
`UPDATE`	Changes the value stored in a table
`DELETE`	Removes rows from a table
`MERGE`	Updates or inserts rows from one table into another

Inserting Rows into a Table

The INSERT statement is used to add rows to one or more tables. The syntax for a simple INSERT statement is as follows:

```
INSERT INTO [schema.]table_name [(column_list)]
VALUES (data_values)
```

In the syntax, *table_name* is the name of the table where you want to add new rows. *table_name* may be qualified with the schema name. *column_list* is the name of the columns in the table, separated by commas, that you want to populate. *data_values* is the corresponding values separated by commas. Using this syntax, you can add only one row at a time.

column_list is optional. If *column_list* is not included, Oracle includes all columns in the order specified when creating the table. *data_values* in the VALUES clause must match the number of columns and datatype in *column_list* (or the number of columns and datatype in the table if *column_list* is omitted). For clarity, it is a good practice to include *column_list* when using the INSERT statement.

If you omit columns in *column_list*, those columns will have NULL values if no default value is defined for the column. If a default value is defined for the column, the column will get the default value. You can insert the default value using the DEFAULT keyword. The SQL statements in the following example show two methods to insert the default value into the MYACCOUNTS table if a default value of C is defined on the DR_CR column:

```
DESCRIBE MYACCOUNTS
Name          Null?    Type
------------- -------- -------------------
ACC_NO        NOT NULL NUMBER(5)
ACC_DT        NOT NULL DATE
DR_CR                  CHAR
AMOUNT                 NUMBER(15,2)

INSERT INTO myaccounts (acc_no, acc_dt, amount)
VALUES (120003, TRUNC(SYSDATE), 400);

INSERT INTO myaccounts (acc_no, acc_dt, dr_cr, amount)
VALUES (120003, TRUNC(SYSDATE), DEFAULT, 400);
```

When specifying *data_values*, enclose character and datetime values in single quotes. For date values, if the value is not in the default date format, you may have to use the TO_DATE function. When you enclose a value in single quotes, Oracle considers it character data and performs an implicit conversion if the column datatype is not a character; hence, do not enclose numeric values in single quotes.

You can find out the order of columns in a table by using the USER_TAB_COLUMNS view. The COLUMN_ID column shows the order of columns in the table. When you use the DESCRIBE command to list the table columns, the columns are listed in that order.

I'll use the ACCOUNTS table to demonstrate the INSERT statements. The column names, their order, and their datatype can be displayed using the DESCRIBE statement, as shown here:

```
SQL> DESCRIBE accounts
 Name                          Null?    Type
 ----------------------------- -------- -------------
 CUST_NAME                              VARCHAR2(20)
 ACC_OPEN_DATE                          DATE
 BALANCE                                NUMBER(15,2)
```

To insert rows into the ACCOUNTS table, you can use the INSERT statement in its simplest form, as shown here:

```
SQL> INSERT INTO accounts VALUES ('John', '13-MAY-68', 2300.45);
1 row created.
```

The following are some more examples of using INSERT statements. When you use the column list, they can appear in any order. If the DATE value is not in the default date format specified by NLS_DATE_FORMAT parameter, you should use the TO_DATE function with the format mask. The examples also include some errors generated from INSERT to help you understand the statement rules. Notice that you can explicitly insert a NULL value, or if you omit a column in the column list, a NULL value is inserted into that column, provided the column is nullable—in other words, NOT NULL constraint is not defined on the column.

```
SQL> INSERT INTO hr.accounts (cust_name, acc_open_date)
  2  VALUES (Shine, 'April-23-2001');
VALUES (Shine, 'April-23-2001')
        *
ERROR at line 2:
ORA-00984: column not allowed here


SQL> INSERT INTO hr.accounts (cust_name, acc_open_date)
  2  VALUES ('Shine', 'April-23-2001');
VALUES ('Shine', 'April-23-2001')
                 *
ERROR at line 2:
ORA-01858: a non-numeric character was found where a numeric was expected


SQL> INSERT INTO hr.accounts (cust_name, acc_open_date)
  2  VALUES ('Shine', TO_DATE('April-23-2001','Month-DD-YYYY'));
1 row created.
```

```
SQL> INSERT INTO accounts VALUES ('Jishi', '4-AUG-72');
INSERT INTO accounts VALUES ('Jishi', '4-AUG-72')
            *
ERROR at line 1:
ORA-00947: not enough values
```

You can also use functions like SYSDATE or USER in the INSERT statement. See these examples:

```
SQL> SHOW USER
USER is "HR"
SQL> INSERT INTO accounts VALUES (USER, SYSDATE, 345);
1 row created.

SQL> SELECT * FROM accounts;
CUST_NAME            ACC_OPEN_    BALANCE
-------------------- --------- ----------
John                 13-MAY-68    2300.45
Shine                23-APR-01
Jishi                12-SEP-99
HR                   23-APR-08        345
```

You can add rows with specific data values, as you have seen in the examples, or you can create rows from existing data using a subquery.

Inserting Rows from a Subquery

You can insert data into a table from an existing table or view using a subquery. To perform the subquery insert, replace the VALUES clause with the subquery. You cannot have both a VALUES clause and a subquery. The columns in the column list should match the number of columns selected in the subquery as well as their datatype. Here are a few examples:

```
SQL> INSERT INTO accounts
  2  SELECT first_name, hire_date, salary
  3  FROM hr.employees
  4  WHERE first_name like 'R%';
3 rows created.

SQL> INSERT INTO accounts (cust_name, balance)
  2  SELECT first_name, hire_date, salary
  3  FROM hr.employees
  4  WHERE first_name like 'T%';
```

```
INSERT INTO accounts (cust_name, balance)
            *
ERROR at line 1:
ORA-00913: too many values

SQL> INSERT INTO accounts (cust_name, acc_open_date)
  2  SELECT UPPER(first_name), ADD_MONTHS(hire_date,2)
  3  FROM hr.employees
  4  WHERE first_name like 'T%';
4 rows created.

SQL> SELECT * FROM accounts;
CUST_NAME            ACC_OPEN_     BALANCE
-------------------- --------- ----------
John                 13-MAY-68    2300.45
Shine                23-APR-01
Jishi                04-AUG-72
Renske               14-JUL-95       3600
Randall              15-MAR-98       2600
Randall              19-DEC-99       2500
TJ                   10-JUN-99
TRENNA               17-DEC-95
TAYLER               24-MAR-98
TIMOTHY              11-SEP-98
10 rows selected.
```

You can use `SELECT * FROM` if the source and destination table have the same structure, as shown in the following example:

```
INSERT INTO old_employees
SELECT * FROM employees;

107 rows created.
```

Inserting Rows into Multiple Tables

You can also use the `INSERT` statement to add rows to more than one table at a time. This multiple-table insert is useful for efficiently loading data, because you can add the data to multiple target tables via a single pass through the source table, with a minimum of database calls. The syntax for the multiple-table `INSERT` statement is as shown here:

```
INSERT [ALL | FIRST] {WHEN <condition> THEN INTO <insert_clause> … … …} [ELSE
<insert_clause>}
```

The keyword ALL tells Oracle to evaluate each and every WHEN clause, whether or not any evaluate to TRUE. In contrast, the FIRST keyword tells Oracle to stop evaluating WHEN clauses after encountering the first one that evaluates to TRUE. The WHEN clause and the INTO clause can be repeated.

Suppose that your company, Sales Inc., sells books, videos, and audio CDs. You have a SALES_DETAIL table that contains information about all the sales and is used by the selling system. You need to load this information into three other tables that focus specifically on the three product categories: Book, Audio, and Video. These category-specific tables are used by the analysis systems. Here are the structure and contents of the source SALES_DETAIL table:

```
Name                           Null?    Type
------------------------------ -------- ------------
TXN_ID                         NOT NULL NUMBER
PRODUCT_ID                              NUMBER
PROD_CATEGORY                           VARCHAR2(2)
CUSTOMER_ID                             VARCHAR2(10)
SALE_DATE                               DATE
SALE_QTY                                NUMBER
SALE_PRICE                              NUMBER

SELECT * FROM sales_detail;

TXN_ID PRODUCT_ID PR CUST SALE_DATE  SALE_QTY SALE_PRICE
------ ---------- -- ---- --------- -------- ----------
     1  304329743 B  43   17-JUN-02         2       19.1
     2  304943209 B  22   17-JUN-02         1       8.95
     3  211524098 A  16   17-JUN-02         1       11.4
     4  413354981 V  41   17-JUN-02         1      12.95
     5  304957315 B  48   17-JUN-02         1       38.5
     6  304183648 B  32   17-JUN-02         2       17.9
     7  211681559 A  32   18-JUN-02         1       11.4
     8  211944553 A  21   18-JUN-02         1       11.4
     9  304155687 B  26   18-JUN-02         1       8.95
    10  304776352 B  18   18-JUN-02         3      48.45
    11  413753861 V  30   18-JUN-02         1      12.95
    12  413159654 V  29   18-JUN-02         1      19.99
    13  304357689 B  11   18-JUN-02         2       72.3
    14  211153246 A  14   18-JUN-02         2       26.4
    15  304852369 B  44   18-JUN-02         1      15.95
```

The target table structures are described in the following output:

```
DESC book_sales

Name                          Null?    Type
----------------------------- -------- ------------
PROD_ID                       NOT NULL NUMBER
CUST_ID                       NOT NULL VARCHAR2(10)
QTY_SOLD                      NOT NULL NUMBER
AMT_SOLD                      NOT NULL NUMBER
ISBN                                   VARCHAR2(24)

DESC video_sales
Name                          Null?    Type
----------------------------- -------- ------------
PROD_ID                       NOT NULL NUMBER
CUST_ID                       NOT NULL VARCHAR2(10)
QTY_SOLD                      NOT NULL NUMBER
AMT_SOLD                      NOT NULL NUMBER
RATING                                 VARCHAR2(5)
YEAR_RELEASED                          NUMBER

DESC audio_sales
Name                          Null?    Type
----------------------------- -------- ------------
PROD_ID                       NOT NULL NUMBER
CUST_ID                       NOT NULL VARCHAR2(10)
QTY_SOLD                      NOT NULL NUMBER
AMT_SOLD                      NOT NULL NUMBER
ARTIST                                 VARCHAR2(64)
```

The multiple-table insert that follows selects from the SALES_DETAIL table and, based on the value of PROD_CATEGORY, inserts a row into the BOOK_SALES, VIDEO_SALES, or AUDIO_SALES table:

```
INSERT ALL
WHEN prod_category='B' THEN
  INTO book_sales(prod_id,cust_id,qty_sold,amt_sold)
      VALUES(product_id,customer_id,sale_qty,sale_price)
WHEN prod_category='V' THEN
  INTO video_sales(prod_id,cust_id,qty_sold,amt_sold)
      VALUES(product_id,customer_id,sale_qty,sale_price)
```

```
WHEN prod_category='A' THEN
  INTO audio_sales(prod_id,cust_id,qty_sold,amt_sold)
      VALUES(product_id,customer_id,sale_qty,sale_price)
SELECT prod_category ,product_id ,customer_id ,sale_qty
      ,sale_price
FROM sales_detail;
```

This multiple-table insert will create eight rows in the BOOK_SALES table, four rows in the AUDIO_SALES table, and three rows in the VIDEO_SALES table.

In most SQL statements, you can prefix column names with a table alias. In fact, this aids readability even if it's not strictly required for parsing. If you try to use an alias for the table name and then prefix the column names with either this alias or the schema-qualified table name in a multiple-table insert, you may raise an exception.

Updating Rows in a Table

The UPDATE statement is used to modify existing rows in a table. The basic syntax for the UPDATE statement is as follows:

```
UPDATE <table_name>
SET <column> = <value>
  [,<column> = <value> … … …]
[WHERE <condition>]
```

You can update more than one row at a time. If the WHERE clause is omitted, all the rows in the table are updated.

If an employee named Jennifer got transferred to another department, you can change the department_id column in the employees table for that employee. Since you know the employee ID for Jennifer, you can use the employee ID to identify Jennifer's row in the table.

```
SELECT first_name, last_name, department_id
FROM employees
WHERE employee_id = 200;

FIRST_NAME           LAST_NAME                 DEPARTMENT_ID
-------------------- ------------------------- -------------
Jennifer             Whalen                               10
```

```
UPDATE employees
SET department_id = 20
WHERE employee_id = 200;

1 row updated.

SELECT first_name, last_name, department_id
FROM employees
WHERE employee_id = 200;

FIRST_NAME           LAST_NAME                 DEPARTMENT_ID
-------------------- ------------------------- -------------
Jennifer             Whalen                               20
```

You can update more than one column in the same row by including the columns and values in the SET clause separated by commas. To remove a value from the column, you can update the column as NULL. The following example demonstrates how to update more than one column of the same row as well as update using NULL. Since no WHERE clause is included, all rows in the table are updated.

```
UPDATE old_employees
SET manager_id = NULL,
    commission_pct = 0;

107 rows updated.
```

Updating Rows Using a Subquery

When updating a column in the table, the value can be derived using a subquery. In the following example, the job_id values of all employees in department 30 are changed to match the job_id of employee 114:

```
SELECT first_name, last_name, job_id
FROM employees
WHERE department_id = 30;

FIRST_NAME           LAST_NAME                 JOB_ID
-------------------- ------------------------- ----------
Den                  Raphaely                  PU_MAN
Alexander            Khoo                      PU_CLERK
Shelli               Baida                     PU_CLERK
Sigal                Tobias                    PU_CLERK
```

```
Guy                  Himuro                    PU_CLERK
Karen                Colmenares                PU_CLERK

6 rows selected.

UPDATE employees
SET job_id = (SELECT job_id
              FROM employees
              WHERE employee_id = 114)
WHERE department_id = 30;

6 rows updated.

SELECT first_name, last_name, job_id
FROM employees
WHERE department_id = 30;

FIRST_NAME           LAST_NAME                 JOB_ID
-------------------- ------------------------- ----------
Den                  Raphaely                  PU_MAN
Alexander            Khoo                      PU_MAN
Shelli               Baida                     PU_MAN
Sigal                Tobias                    PU_MAN
Guy                  Himuro                    PU_MAN
Karen                Colmenares                PU_MAN

6 rows selected.
```

You may have more than one column in the SET clause to update more than one column of the same row using a subquery. If you specify more than one column, they must be enclosed in parentheses, and the subquery should have the same number of columns in the SELECT clause.

```
UPDATE order_rollup
SET (qty, price) = (SELECT SUM(qty), SUM(price)
                    FROM order_lines
                    WHERE customer_id = 'KOHL')
WHERE customer_id = 'KOHL'
 AND  order_period = TO_DATE('01-Oct-2001');
```

Using a Correct WHERE Clause in UPDATE

Once a developer came to me with a problem—he was trying to update one row in a table, and it was taking forever. He was sure he was using the primary key of the table in the WHERE clause and was expecting the result to come back in seconds.

The table he was updating had the following columns (some columns have been omitted):

ORDER_HEADER

```
ORDER#  VARCHAR2 (20) - Primary Key
ORDER_DT DATE
CUSTOMER# VARCHAR2 (12)
TOTAL_AMOUNT NUMBER
```

The update was performed using the value derived from another table named ORDER_TRANSACTIONS. It had the following structure:

ORDER_TRANSACTIONS

```
ORDER# VARCHAR2 (20) - Primary Key
ITEM# VARCHAR2 (20) - Primary Key
SHIP_DATE DATE
ITEM_AMOUNT NUMBER
```

The developer was trying to update the total_amount column in the ORDER_HEADER table with the sum of all the order items from the ORDER_TRANSACTIONS table using a subquery. This was the SQL he used:

```
UPDATE order_header oh
SET total_amount = (SELECT SUM(item_amount)
                    FROM order_transactions ot
                    WHERE oh.order# = ot.order#
                    AND oh.order# = 'W2H3004FU');
```

Can you see what is wrong with this statement? By the way, the table has about 2 million rows.

Though the developer thought he was updating only one row in the ORDER_HEADER table and querying only three rows from the ORDER_TRANSACTIONS table, Oracle was in fact updating all the 2 million rows in the table. Why?

Look carefully at the UPDATE statement; it is missing a WHERE clause for the UPDATE statement. The WHERE clause is present as part of the correlated subquery. So, the result of this update would have been the TOTAL_AMOUNT column updated to NULL for all rows except for order W2H3004FU. When executing the correct SQL statement, the update completed in less than one second.

```
UPDATE order_header oh
SET total_amount = (SELECT SUM(item_amount)
                    FROM order_transactions ot
                    WHERE oh.order# = ot.order#
                    AND ot.order# = 'W2H3004FU')
WHERE oh.order# = 'W2H3004FU';
```

Since we are updating a specific order# in the table and we are using the order number in the WHERE clause, it is safe to remove the join condition inside the subquery as in the following code.

```
UPDATE order_header oh
SET total_amount = (SELECT SUM(item_amount)
                    FROM order_transactions ot
                    WHERE ot.order# = 'W2H3004FU')
WHERE oh.order# = 'W2H3004FU';
```

The moral of this story is to be careful when updating tables using subqueries. Always make sure you have the correct WHERE clause for the UPDATE statement.

Deleting Rows from a Table

The DELETE statement is used to remove rows from a table. The syntax for a basic DELETE statement is as follows:

```
DELETE [FROM] <table>
[WHERE <condition>]
```

The FROM keyword is optional, included to add readability to the statement. Similar to the UPDATE statement, if the WHERE clause is omitted, all the rows in the table will be deleted.

Here are some examples of the DELETE statement. The two hyphens (--) are used as comments.

```
--Remove old orders shipped to some states
DELETE FROM po_lines
WHERE ship_to_state IN ('TX','NY','IL')
 AND  order_date < TRUNC(SYSDATE) - 90
```

```
--Remove customer Gomez
DELETE FROM customers
WHERE customer_id = 'GOMEZ';

--Remove duplicate line_detail_ids
--Note keyword FROM is not needed
DELETE line_details
WHERE rowid NOT IN (SELECT MAX(rowid)
                    FROM line_detail
                    GROUP BY line_detail_id)

--Remove all rows from the table order_staging
DELETE FROM order_staging;
```

Removing all rows from a large table can take a long time and require significant rollback segment space. If you are deleting all rows from a table, consider using the TRUNCATE statement, as described in the next section. TRUNCATE is not included in the Oracle Database 11*g* SQL Fundamentals I exam, but I've included it here for completeness.

Truncating a Table

Truncating a table can accomplish the same task as deleting if you're deleting all rows from the table, although it is sometimes a better choice. If you want to empty a table of all rows, consider using the Data Definition Language (DDL) statement TRUNCATE. Like a DELETE statement without a WHERE clause, TRUNCATE will remove all rows from a table. However, TRUNCATE is not DML—it is DDL, and therefore, it has different characteristics from the DELETE statement. DDL is the subset of SQL that is employed to define database objects. One of the key differences between DML and DDL is that DDL statements will implicitly perform a commit, not only affecting the change in object definition but also committing any pending DML. A DDL statement cannot be rolled back; only DML statements can be rolled back.

For example, to remove all rows from the ORDER_STAGING table, truncate the table as follows:

```
TRUNCATE TABLE order_staging;
```

TRUNCATE vs. DELETE

The TRUNCATE statement is similar to a DELETE statement without a WHERE clause, except for the following:

- TRUNCATE is very fast on both large and small tables. DELETE will generate undo information if a rollback is issued, but TRUNCATE will not generate undo information.
- TRUNCATE is DDL and, like all DDL, performs an implicit commit—you cannot roll back a TRUNCATE. Any uncommitted DML changes within the session will also be committed with the TRUNCATE operation.

- TRUNCATE resets the high-water mark in the table and all indexes. Since full-table scans and index fast-full scans read all data blocks up to the high-water mark, full-scan performance after a DELETE will not improve; after a TRUNCATE, it will be very fast.
- TRUNCATE does not fire any DELETE triggers.
- There is no object privilege that can be granted to allow a user to truncate another user's table. The DROP ANY TABLE system privilege is required to truncate a table in another schema. See Chapter 12, "Implementing Security and Auditing," for more information about getting around this limitation.
- When a table is truncated, the storage for the table and all indexes can be reset to the initial size. A DELETE will never shrink the size of a table or its indexes.
- You cannot truncate the parent table from an enabled referential integrity constraint. You must first disable the foreign key constraints that reference the parent table, and then you can truncate the parent table.

Merging Rows

Though the MERGE statement is not part of the test, to complete the DML discussion I will give you an introduction to the MERGE statement.

MERGE is a very powerful statement available in Oracle 11*g* (it was introduced in Oracle 9*i*) that can insert or update rows based on a condition. The statement also has an option to delete rows when certain conditions are met. The MERGE statement has a join specification that describes how to determine whether an update or insert should be executed. MERGE is a convenient way to combine multiple operations in one statement instead of writing a complex PL/SQL program.

The basic syntax of the MERGE statement is as follows:

```
MERGE INTO <table_or_view>
USING <table_or_view_or_subquery>
ON <join_condition>
WHEN MATCHED THEN UPDATE SET <update_clause> [<where clause>] [DELETE
where_clause]
WHEN NOT MATCHED THEN INSERT <insert_columns> VALUES <insert_columns>
```

The INTO clause specifies the target table where the update/insert/delete operation will be performed. The USING clause specifies the data source. The ON clause has the join condition between the source and target tables. The WHEN MATCHED THEN UPDATE clause specifies which columns to update when the ON condition is matched. You can also include an optional WHERE clause. The optional DELETE clause can delete the row if the WHERE condition specified in the DELETE clause is met. The WHEN NOT MATCHED THEN INSERT clause is used to add rows to the target table from the source table.

Let's look at a few examples. Consider two tables, ORDERS1 and ORDERS2. The rows in the tables are listed using the following SQL statements:

```
SQL> SELECT * FROM orders1;

  ORDER_ID ORDER_MO CUSTOMER_ID ORDER_TOTAL
---------- -------- ----------- -----------
      2414 channel          102     10794.6
      2397 direct           102     42283.2
      2432 channel          102       10523
      2431 direct           102      5610.6
      2454 direct           103      6653.4
      2415 direct           103         310
      2433 channel          103          78
      2437 direct           103       13550

8 rows selected.

SQL> SELECT * FROM orders2;

  ORDER_ID CUSTOMER_ID ORDER_TOTAL
---------- ----------- -----------
      2414         102       35982
      2397         102      140944
      2432         102    35076.67
      2431         102           0
      2450         147        1636
      2425         147      1500.8
      2385         147      295892
      2451         148     10474.6
      2386         148     21116.9

9 rows selected.

SQL>
```

The task before you is to merge the rows in ORDERS2 to ORDERS1. If ORDER_ID and CUSTOMER_ID match between the two tables, you need to update the ORDER_TOTAL value with the value from the ORDERS2 table and update the ORDER_MODE value to modified. For the rows in ORDERS2 where ORDER_ID and CUSTOMER_ID do not match with existing rows in ORDERS1, you need to insert the values from ORDERS2 to ORDERS1. For such rows, the ORDER_MODE value should be merged. You also want to delete the row from ORDERS1 if the new order's total value is zero. The following SQL can accomplish all these tasks using the MERGE statement:

```
MERGE INTO orders1 o1
USING orders2 o2
```

```
ON (o1.order_id = o2.order_id
    AND o1.customer_id = o2.customer_id)
WHEN MATCHED THEN UPDATE SET o1.order_total = o2.order_total,
                             o1.order_mode = 'modified'
     DELETE WHERE o2.order_total = 0
WHEN NOT MATCHED THEN INSERT
     VALUES (o2.order_id, 'merged', o2.customer_id, o2.order_total);

9 rows merged.

select * from orders1;

  ORDER_ID ORDER_MO CUSTOMER_ID ORDER_TOTAL
---------- -------- ----------- -----------
      2414 modified         102       35982
      2397 modified         102      140944
      2432 modified         102    35076.67
      2454 direct           103      6653.4
      2415 direct           103         310
      2433 channel          103          78
      2437 direct           103       13550
      2450 merged           147        1636
      2385 merged           147      295892
      2386 merged           148     21116.9
      2451 merged           148     10474.6
      2425 merged           147      1500.8

12 rows selected.
```

As you can see from the result, Oracle updated four rows that matched the `ON` condition and inserted five new rows that did not match the `ON` condition, which is why you get the "9 rows merged" feedback. Since you had the `DELETE` clause to delete any rows that had order total zero (of the four rows that matched the `ON` condition), one of them matched the `DELETE` condition and hence was removed from the table.

Understanding Transaction Control

Transaction control involves coordinating multiple concurrent accesses to the same data. When one session is changing data that another session is accessing, Oracle uses *transactions* to control which users have visibility to changing data and when they can see the changed data. Transactions represent an atomic unit of work. All changes to data in a transaction are applied together or rolled back (undone) together. Transactions provide data consistency in the event of a user-process failure or system failure.

A transaction can include one or more DML statements. A transaction ends when you save the transaction (`COMMIT`) or undo the changes (`ROLLBACK`). When DDL statements are executed, Oracle implicitly ends the previous transaction by saving the changes. It also begins a new transaction for the DDL and ends the transaction after the DDL is completed. Hence, DDL statements cannot be undone.

A number of statements in SQL let the programmer control transactions. Using transaction-control statements, the programmer can do the following:

- Explicitly begin a transaction, choosing statement-level consistency or transaction-level consistency
- Set undo savepoints and undo changes back to a savepoint
- End a transaction by making the changes permanent or undoing the changes

Table 5.2 summarizes the transaction-control statements.

TABLE 5.2 Transaction-Control Statements

Statement	Purpose
`COMMIT`	Ends the current transaction, making data changes permanent and visible to other sessions
`ROLLBACK`	Undoes all data changes in the current transaction
`ROLLBACK TO SAVEPOINT`	Undoes all data changes in the current transactions going chronologically backward to the optionally named savepoint
`SAVEPOINT`	Set an optional marker in within the transaction to be able to go back to this position if needed
`SET TRANSACTION`	Enables transaction or statement consistency

Throughout this section, I will use a banking example to clarify transactional concepts and the control statements used to ensure data is changed as designed. In this example, say you have a banking customer named Sara who has a checking account and a brokerage account with her bank.

When Sara transfers $5,000 from her checking account to her brokerage account, the balance in her checking account is reduced by $5,000, and the cash balance in her brokerage account is increased by $5,000. You cannot allow only one account to change—either both must change or neither must change.

Consider the following statements to complete the transaction. All the statements in the group must be completed, or no changes should be recorded in the database. The `INSERT` statements are used to log the transaction in the log table.

```
UPDATE checking
SET balance = balance - 5000
WHERE account = 'SARA1001';
```

```
INSERT INTO checking_log (action_date, action, amount)
VALUES (SYSDATE, 'Withdrawal', 5000);

UPDATE brokerage
SET balance = balance + 5000
WHERE account = 'SARA1001';

INSERT INTO brokerage_log (action_date, action, amount)
VALUES (SYSDATE, 'Deposit', 5000);
```

You issued the two UPDATE statements and the two INSERT statements in a single transaction. If there is any failure in one of these four statements (say, perhaps, the CHECKING_LOG table ran out of room in the tablespace), then none of the changes should go through. When all the previous statements are successful, you can issue a COMMIT statement to save the work to the database. The changes will be committed and made permanent only if all four statements succeed. If only part of the SQL statements were successful, you can issue a ROLLBACK statement to undo the changes.

A transaction will implicitly begin with a DML statement. The transaction will always end with either an implicit or explicit COMMIT or ROLLBACK statement. A ROLLBACK TO SAVEPOINT statement will not end a transaction. The following actions will end a transaction:

- A COMMIT or ROLLBACK statement is issued.
- A DDL statement, such as TRUNCATE or CREATE, is issued (an implicit COMMIT is performed).
- Exit out of a SQL*Plus (an implicit COMMIT is performed).
- Abnormal termination of a SQL*Plus session, such as closing the window (the transaction is rolled back).
- Machine failure or database crash (the transaction is rolled back).

If a DML statement fails, the transaction is not rolled back. The changes made from the successful DML statements before the failed statement are still valid. To undo those changes, you have to explicitly execute a ROLLBACK statement.

Savepoints and Partial Rollbacks

A ROLLBACK statement will undo all the changes made in the transaction. If you have to undo part of the changes in a transaction, you can set up savepoints or markers in the transaction and go back to a savepoint when needed. Savepoints are intermediate fallback positions in SQL code. The ROLLBACK TO SAVEPOINT statement is used to undo changes chronologically back to the last savepoint or to the named savepoint. Savepoints are not labels for goto statements, and ROLLBACK TO SAVEPOINT is not a goto. The code after a savepoint does not get reexecuted after a ROLLBACK TO SAVEPOINT—only the data changes made since that savepoint are undone.

Savepoints are not used extensively by programmers. However, you must understand them because there will likely be a question related to savepoints on the certification exam.

Consider a transaction with various DML statements and savepoints, as in Figure 5.1.

FIGURE 5.1 Transaction control

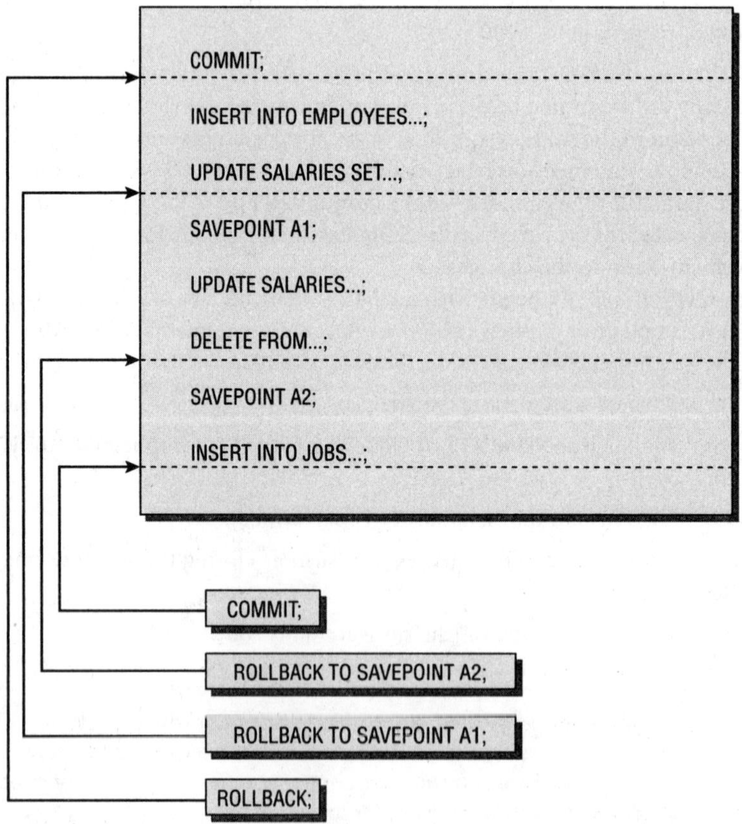

A new transaction begins after a `COMMIT` statement. Various DML statements are executed in the transaction. You have also set savepoints in between. After all the statements are successfully executed, the user has the option to issue the `ROLLBACK TO SAVEPOINT`, `ROLLBACK`, or `COMMIT` statement. The arrows in the figure show the effect of issuing the transaction-control statements.

If you create a second savepoint with the same name as an earlier savepoint, the earlier savepoint is deleted, and Oracle keeps only the later savepoint.

Again, an example will help clarify. Sara tries to withdraw $100 from her checking account. You want to log her request in the ATM activity log, but if she has insufficient funds, you don't want to change her balance and will deny her request (part of a PL/SQL block is shown here; the IF statement is PL/SQL).

```
INSERT INTO ATM_LOG(who, when, what, where)
  VALUES('Kiesha', SYSDATE, 'Withdrawal of $100','ATM54');
SAVEPOINT ATM_logged;

UPDATE checking
  SET balance = balance - 100
  WHERE account = 'SARA1001';

SELECT balance INTO new_balance
  FROM checking
  WHERE account = 'SARA1001';

IF new_balance < 0
THEN
  ROLLBACK TO ATM_logged; -- undo update
  COMMIT; -- keep changes prior to savepoint (insert)
  RAISE insufficient_funds; -- Raise error/deny request
END IF;
COMMIT; -- keep insert and update
```

The keyword SAVEPOINT is optional, so the following two statements are equivalent:

```
ROLLBACK TO ATM_logged;
ROLLBACK TO SAVEPOINT ATM_logged;
```

Because savepoints are not frequently used, always include the keyword SAVEPOINT in any ROLLBACK TO SAVEPOINT statement. That way, anyone reading the code will be reminded of the keyword SAVEPOINT, making it easier to recognize that a partial rollback has occurred.

Data Visibility

When DML operations are performed in a transaction, the changes are visible only to the session performing the DML operations. The changes are visible to other users in the database only when a COMMIT is issued (or a DDL statement causes an implicit commit).

All data changes made in a transaction are temporary until the transaction is committed. The Oracle Database has a read-consistency mechanism to ensure that each user sees the data as it existed at the last commit.

When DML operations are performed on existing rows (through UPDATE, DELETE, or MERGE operations), the affected rows are locked by Oracle, and hence no other user can perform a DML operation on those rows. The rows updated or deleted by a transaction can be queried by another session.

When changes are committed, they are made permanent to the database. All locks on the affected rows are released, and all savepoints are removed. The previous state of the data is lost (the undo segments may be overwritten). All users can view the changed data.

When changes are rolled back, data changes are undone and the previous state of data is restored. All locks on the affected rows are released.

Oracle uses read consistency to make sure you do not see the changes made to data after your query is started. Also, Oracle uses a locking mechanism to make sure that no two users are modifying data in the same row at the same time. Data consistency and the locking mechanism are discussed in the next sections.

Consistency and Transactions

Data consistency is one of the key concepts underlying the use of transaction-control statements. Understanding Oracle's consistency model will enable you to employ transaction control appropriately and answer exam questions about transaction control correctly. Oracle implements consistency to guarantee that the data seen by a statement or transaction does not change until that statement or transaction completes. This support is germane only to multiuser databases, where one database session can change (and commit) data that is being read by another session.

Oracle always uses statement-level consistency, which ensures that the data visible to a statement does not change during the life of that statement. Transactions can consist of one or more statements. When used, transaction-level consistency will ensure that the data visible to all statements in a transaction does not change for the life of the transaction. The banking example will help clarify.

Matt starts running a total-balance report against the checking account table at 10 a.m.; this report takes five minutes. During those five minutes, the data he is reporting on changes when Sara transfers $5,000 from her checking account to her brokerage account. When Matt's session gets to Sara's checking-account record, it will need to reconstruct what the record looked like at 10 a.m. Matt's session will examine the *undo segment* that Sara used during her account-transfer transaction and re-create the image of what the checking-account table looked like at 10 a.m.

Next, at 10:05 a.m., Matt runs a total balance report on the cash in the brokerage account table. If he is using transaction-level consistency, his session will re-create what the brokerage account table looked like at 10 a.m. (and exclude Sara's transfer). If Matt's session is using the default statement-level consistency, his session will report on what the brokerage account table looked like at 10:05 a.m. (and include Sara's transfer).

Oracle never uses locks for reading operations, since reading operations will never block writing operations. Instead, the undo segments (also known as *rollback segments*) are used to re-create the image needed. Undo segments are released for reuse when the transaction writing to them commits or if `undo_management` is set to `auto` and the `undo_retention` period is exceeded, so sometimes a consistent image cannot be re-created. When this happens, Oracle raises a "snapshot too old" exception. Using this example, if Matt's transaction can't locate Sara's transaction in the rollback segments because it was overwritten, Matt's transaction will not be able to re-create the 10 a.m. image of the table and will fail.

Oracle implements consistency internally through the use of system change numbers (SCNs). An SCN is a time-oriented, database-internal key. The SCN only increases, never decreases, and represents a point in time for comparison purposes. So, in the previous example, Oracle internally assigns Matt's first statement the current SCN when it starts reading the checking-account table. This starting SCN is compared to each data block's SCN. If the data-block SCN is higher (newer), then the rollback segments are examined to find the older version of the data.

Undo segments, concurrency, and SCN are discussed in detail in Chapter 13, "Managing Data and Undo."

Locking Mechanism

Locks are implemented by Oracle Database to prevent destructive interaction between concurrent transactions. Locks are acquired automatically by Oracle when a DML statement is executed; no user intervention or action is needed. Oracle uses the lowest level of restrictiveness when locking data for DML statements—only the rows affected by the DML operation are locked.

Locks are held for the duration of the transaction. A commit or rollback will release all the locks. There are two types of locks: explicit and implicit.

The locks acquired by Oracle automatically when DML operations are performed are called *implicit locks*. There is no implicit lock for `SELECT` statements.

If the user locks data manually, it is called *explicit locking*. The `LOCK TABLE` statement and `SELECT…FOR UPDATE` statements are used for explicitly locking the data.

The `SELECT…FOR UPDATE` statement is used to lock specific rows, preventing other sessions from changing or deleting those locked rows. When the rows are locked, other sessions can select these rows, but they cannot change or lock these rows. The syntax for this statement is identical to a `SELECT` statement, except you append the keywords `FOR UPDATE` to the statement. The locks acquired for a `SELECT FOR UPDATE` will not be released until the transaction ends with a `COMMIT` or `ROLLBACK`, even if no data changes.

```
SELECT product_id, warehouse_id, quantity_on_hand
FROM   oe.inventories
WHERE  quantity_on_hand < 5
FOR UPDATE;
```

The `LOCK` statement is used to lock an entire table, preventing other sessions from performing most or all DML on it. Locking can be in either shared or exclusive mode. Shared mode prevents other sessions from acquiring an exclusive lock but allows other sessions to acquire a shared lock. Exclusive mode prevents other sessions from acquiring either a shared lock or an exclusive lock. The following is an example of using the `LOCK` statement:

```
LOCK TABLE inventories IN EXCLUSIVE MODE;
```

Oracle employs both table and row locks. Table locks can be obtained in either share or exclusive mode. *Share locks* prevent other exclusive locks but allow other share locks. Exclusive locks prevent both other share locks and other exclusive locks. However, no DML locks prevent read access. To change data, Oracle must acquire an exclusive row-level lock on the rows that are changed. INSERT, UPDATE, DELETE, MERGE, and SELECT FOR UPDATE statements implicitly acquire the necessary row locks. Even if the DML operation affects all the rows in a table, Oracle Database never escalates the row-level lock to a table-level lock; and furthermore, users or developers shouldn't explicitly lock unless there is a very good reason—Oracle handles it automatically 99.9% of the time.

Summary

I started this chapter discussing DML statements in Oracle. I reviewed the INSERT, UPDATE, DELETE, and MERGE statements to add, modify, and delete data in tables. You also learned how transactions and locking work in Oracle.

The INSERT statement is used to add new rows to the table. The VALUES clause in the INSERT statement is used to add a single row at a time. Subqueries can be used to add rows to a table from an existing row source.

The UPDATE statement is used to change existing data in a table. The DELETE statement is used to remove rows from a table. Both the UPDATE and DELETE statements can have WHERE clauses to limit the data changes to specific rows. The MERGE statement allows you to insert or update rows based on a condition.

When an update or delete operation is performed on a table, the previous state of data is written to undo segments to build a read-consistent image of data. Oracle shows only committed data to users.

DML operations lock the affected rows of the table. The locks are held until the transaction is either committed or rolled back. Until the changes are committed, data changes are not visible to other users in the database.

Exam Essentials

Know the syntax for the INSERT statement. When a subquery is used to add rows to a table, the VALUES clause should not be used.

Practice UPDATE statements The UPDATE statement can update multiple columns in the same row using a subquery. Multiple subqueries can also be used to update columns in a single row.

Understand what will begin and end a transaction. A transaction will begin with an INSERT, UPDATE, DELETE, MERGE, or SELECT FOR UPDATE statement. A COMMIT or ROLLBACK will end a transaction. A DDL statement can also end a transaction.

Know how to set and roll back to savepoints. Savepoints are set with the SAVEPOINT statement. Data changes made after a savepoint are undone when a ROLLBACK TO SAVEPOINT statement is executed. ROLLBACK TO SAVEPOINT is a partial undo operation.

Understand the scope of data changes and consistency. Statement-level consistency is automatic and will ensure that each SELECT will see an image of the database consistent with the beginning of the statement's execution. Transaction-level consistency will ensure that all SELECT statements within a transaction will see an image of the database consistent with the beginning of the transaction.

Review Questions

1. Jim is trying to add records from the ORDER_DETAILS table to ORDER_DETAIL_HISTORY for orders placed before the current year. Which insert statement would accomplish his task?

   A.
   ```
   INSERT INTO ORDER_DETAIL_HISTORY
   VALUES (SELECT * FROM ORDER_DETAIL
   WHERE ORDER_DATE < TRUNC(SYSDATE,'YY'));
   ```
   B.
   ```
   INSERT FROM ORDER_DETAIL
   INTO ORDER_DETAIL_HISTORY
   WHERE ORDER_DATE < TRUNC(SYSDATE,'YY');
   ```
   C.
   ```
   INSERT INTO ORDER_DETAIL_HISTORY
   FROM ORDER_DETAIL
   WHERE ORDER_DATE < TRUNC(SYSDATE,'YY');
   ```
   D.
   ```
   INSERT INTO ORDER_DETAIL_HISTORY
   SELECT * FROM ORDER_DETAIL
   WHERE ORDER_DATE < TRUNC(SYSDATE,'YY');
   ```

2. Which of the following statements will not implicitly begin a transaction?

   A. INSERT

   B. UPDATE

   C. DELETE

   D. SELECT FOR UPDATE

   E. None of the above; they all implicitly begin a transaction, if not started already.

3. Consider the following UPDATE statement. Which UPDATE statements from the options will accomplish the same task? (Choose two.)

   ```
   UPDATE ACCOUNTS
   SET LAST_UPDATED = SYSDATE,
       UPDATE_USER = USER;
   ```

   A.
   ```
   UPDATE ACCOUNTS
   SET (LAST_UPDATED, UPDATE_USER) =
           (SYSDATE, USER);
   ```
   B.
   ```
   UPDATE ACCOUNTS
   SET LAST_UPDATED =
      (SELECT SYSDATE FROM DUAL),
   UPDATE_USER = (SELECT USER FROM DUAL);
   ```

C.
```
UPDATE ACCOUNTS
SET (LAST_UPDATED, UPDATE_USER) =
(SELECT SYSDATE, USER FROM DUAL);
```

D.
```
UPDATE ACCOUNTS
SET LAST_UPDATED = SYSDATE
AND UPDATE_USER = USER;
```

4. Which of the following statements do not end a transaction? (Choose two.)

A. SELECT

B. COMMIT

C. TRUNCATE TABLE

D. UPDATE

5. Sara wants to update the SALARY column in the OLD_EMPLOYEES table with the value from the EMPLOYEES table for employees in department 90. Which SQL will accomplish the task?

A.
```
UPDATE old_employees a
SET salary = (SELECT salary FROM employees b
              WHERE a.employee_id = b.employee_id)
WHERE department_id = 90;
```

B.
```
UPDATE old_employees
SET salary = (SELECT salary FROM employees)
WHERE department_id = 90;
```

C.
```
UPDATE old_employees a
FROM employees b
SET a.salary = b.salary
WHERE department_id = 90;
```

D.
```
UPDATE old_employees a
SET salary = (SELECT salary FROM employees b
              WHERE a.employee_id = b.employee_id
AND department_id = 90);
```

6. Review the following code snippet. Which line has an error?

```
1 UPDATE EMPLOYEES
2 WHERE EMPLOYEE_ID = 127
3 SET SALARY = SALARY * 1.25,
4 COMMISSION_PCT = 0
```

A 1

B. 2

C. 4

D. There is no error

7. Jim executes the following SQL statement. What will be the result?

```
DELETE salary, commission_pct
FROM employees
WHERE department_id = 30;
```

A. The salary and commission_pct columns for all records with department_id 30 are deleted (changed to NULL).

B. All the rows belonging to department_id 30 are deleted from the table.

C. The salary and commission_pct columns are deleted from the employees table.

D. The statement will produce an error.

8. Consider the following three SQL statements. Choose the most appropriate option.

```
1. DELETE FROM CITY WHERE CNT_CODE = 1;
2. DELETE CITY WHERE CNT_CODE = 1;
3. DELETE (SELECT * FROM CITY WHERE CNT_CODE = 1);
```

A. Statements 1 and 2 will produce the same result, statement 3 will error out.

B. Statements 1 and 2 will produce the same result; statement 3 will produce a different result.

C. Statements 1, 2, and 3 will produce the same result.

D. Statements 1, 2, and 3 will produce different results.

9. Consider the following code segment. How many rows will be in the CARS table after all these statements are executed?

```
SELECT COUNT(*) FROM CARS;
COUNT(*)
--------
      30

DELETE FROM CARS WHERE MAKE = 'TOYOTA';
2 rows deleted.
```

```
SAVEPOINT A;
Savepoint creted.

INSERT INTO CARS VALUES ('TOYOTA','CAMRY',4,220);
1 row created.

SAVEPOINT A;

INSERT INTO CARS VALUES ('TOYOTA','COROLLA',4,180);
1 row created.

ROLLBACK TO SAVEPOINT A;
Rollback complete.
```

A. 30

B. 29

C. 28

D. 32

10. Jim noticed that the HIRE_DATE and START_DATE columns in the EMPLOYEES table had date and time values, and hence when he is trying to find employees hired on a certain date, he is not getting the desired result. Which SQL statement will update all the rows in the EMPLOYEES table with no time portion in the HIRE_DATE and START_DATE columns (00:00:00).

A. UPDATE EMPLOYEES SET HIRE_DATE = TRUNC(HIRE_DATE) AND START_DATE = TRUNC(START_DATE);

B. UPDATE TABLE EMPLOYEES SET TRUNC(HIRE_DATE) AND TRUNC(START_DATE);

C. UPDATE EMPLOYEES SET HIRE_DATE = TRUNC(HIRE_DATE), START_DATE = TRUNC(START_DATE);

D. UPDATE HIRE_DATE = TRUNC(HIRE_DATE), START_DATE = TRUNC(START_DATE) IN EMPLOYEES;

11. Sara wants to update the SALARY column in the EMPLOYEE table from the SALARIES table, based on the JOB_ID value for all employees in department 22. The SALARIES table and the EMPLOYEE table have the following structure. Which is the correct UPDATE statement of the following options?

```
DESC EMPLOYEE
EMPLOYEE_ID    NUMBER (3),
EMP_NAME       VARCHAR2 (40),
JOB_ID         VARCHAR2 (4),
DEPT_ID        NUMBER
SALARY         NUMBER
```

```
DESC SALARIES
JOB_ID          VARCHAR2 (4),
SALARY          NUMBER
```

A. `UPDATE SALARIES A SET SALARY = (SELECT SALARY FROM EMPLOYEES B WHERE A.JOB_ID = B.JOB_ID WHERE DEPT_ID = 22);`

B. `UPDATE EMPLOYEE E SET SALARY = (SELECT SALARY FROM SALARIES S WHERE E.JOB_ID = S.JOB_IB AND DEPT_ID = 22);`

C. `UPDATE EMPLOYEE E SET SALARY = (SELECT SALARY FROM SALARIES S WHERE E.JOB_ID = S.JOB_IB) AND DEPT_ID = 22;`

D. `UPDATE EMPLOYEE E SET SALARY = (SELECT SALARY FROM SALARIES S WHERE E.JOB_ID = S.JOB_IB) WHERE DEPT_ID = 22);`

12. The `FIRED_EMPLOYEE` table has the following structure:

```
EMPLOYEE_ID  NUMBER (4)
FIRE_DATE DATE
```

How many rows will be counted from the last SQL statement in the code segment?

```
SELECT COUNT(*) FROM FIRED_EMPLOYEES;
COUNT(*)
--------
     105

INSERT INTO FIRED_EMPLOYEE VALUES (104, TRUNC(SYSDATE);
SAVEPOINT A;
INSERT INTO FIRED_EMPLOYEE VALUES (106, TRUNC(SYSDATE);
SAVEPOINT B;
INSERT INTO FIRED_EMPLOYEE VALUES (108, TRUNC(SYSDATE);
ROLLBACK TO A;
INSERT INTO FIRED_EMPLOYEE VALUES (104, TRUNC(SYSDATE);
COMMIT;
SELECT COUNT(*) FROM FIRED_EMPLOYEES;
```

A. 109

B. 106

C. 105

D. 107

13. The following table describes the DEPARTMENTS table:

Column Name	dept_id	dept_name	mgr_id	location_id
Key Type	pk			
Nulls/Unique	NN			
FK Table				
Datatype	NUMBER	VARCHAR2	NUMBER	NUMBER
Length	4	30	6	4
Default Value	None	None	None	99

Which of the following INSERT statements will raise an exception?

A. INSERT INTO departments (dept_id, dept_name, location_id)
VALUES(280,'Security',1700);

B. INSERT INTO departments
VALUES(280,'Security',1700);

C. INSERT INTO departments
VALUES(280,'Corporate Giving',266,1700);

D. None of these statements will raise an exception.

14. Refer to the DEPARTMENTS table structure in question 13. Two SQL statements are shown here. Choose the best option that describes the SQL statements.

```
1.INSERT INTO departments (dept_id, dept_name, mgr_id)
VALUES(280,'Security',1700);

2.INSERT INTO departments (dept_id, dept_name, mgr_id, location_id)
VALUES(280,'Security',1700, NULL);
```

A. Statements 1 and 2 insert the same values to all columns in the table.

B. Statements 1 and 2 insert different values to at least one column in the table.

C. The location_id column must be included in the column list of statement 1.

D. A NULL value cannot be inserted explicitly in statement 2.

15. The SALES table contains the following data:

```
SELECT channel_id, COUNT(*)
FROM sales
GROUP BY channel_id;

C  COUNT(*)
- ----------
T     12000
I     24000
```

How many rows will be inserted into the NEW_CHANNEL_SALES table with the following SQL statement?

```
INSERT FIRST
 WHEN channel_id ='C' THEN
   INTO catalog_sales (prod_id,time_id,promo_id
                      ,amount_sold)
       VALUES (prod_id,time_id,promo_id,amount_sold)
 WHEN channel_id ='I' THEN
   INTO internet_sales (prod_id,time_id,promo_id
                       ,amount_sold)
       VALUES (prod_id,time_id,promo_id,amount_sold)
 WHEN  channel_id IN ('I','T') THEN
   INTO new_channel_sales (prod_id,time_id,promo_id
                          ,amount_sold)
       VALUES (prod_id,time_id,promo_id,amount_sold)
SELECT channel_id,prod_id,time_id,promo_id,amount_sold
FROM sales;
```

A. 0

B. 12,000

C. 24,000

D. 36,000

16. How many rows will be counted in the last SQL statement that follows?

```
SELECT COUNT(*) FROM emp;
120 returned

INSERT INTO emp (emp_id)
   VALUES (140);
SAVEPOINT emp140;
```

```
INSERT INTO emp (emp_id)
   VALUES (141);
INSERT INTO emp (emp_id)
   VALUES (142);
INSERT INTO emp (emp_id)
   VALUES (143);
TRUNCATE TABLE employees;
INSERT INTO emp (emp_id)
   VALUES (144);

ROLLBACK;

SELECT COUNT(*) FROM emp;
```

A. 121

B. 0

C. 124

D. 143

17. Which is the best option that describes the following SQL statement?

```
1.UPDATE countries
2.CNT_NAME = UPPER(CNT_NAME)
3.WHERE country_code BETWEEN 1 and 99;
```

A. The statement is missing the keyword SET, but the statement will work just fine because SET is an optional keyword.

B. The BETWEEN operator cannot be used in the WHERE clause used in an UPDATE statement.

C. The function UPPER(CNT_NAME) should be changed to UPPER('CNT_NAME').

D. The statement is missing keyword SET; hence, the statement will fail.

18. The table ORDERS has 35 rows. The following UPDATE statement updates all 35 rows. Which is the best option?

```
UPDATE orders
SET ship_date = TRUNC(ship_date)
WHERE ship_date != TRUNC(ship_date)
```

A. When all rows in a table are updated, the LOCK TABLE orders IN EXCLUSIVE MODE statement must be executed before the UPDATE statement.

B. No other session can query from the table until the transaction ends.

C. Since all rows are updated, there is no need for any locking, and hence Oracle does not lock the records.

D. The statement locks all the rows until the transaction ends.

19. Which of the following INSERT statements will raise an exception?

A. INSERT INTO EMP SELECT * FROM NEW_EMP;

B. INSERT FIRST WHEN DEPT_NO IN (12,14) THEN INSERT INTO EMP SELECT * FROM NEW_EMP;

C. INSERT FIRST WHEN DEPT_NO IN (12,14) THEN INTO EMP SELECT * FROM NEW_EMP;

D. INSERT ALL WHEN DEPT_NO IN (12,14) THEN INTO EMP SELECT * FROM NEW_EMP;

20. What will the salary of employee Arsinoe be at the completion of the following SQL statements?

```
UPDATE emp
  SET salary = 1000
  WHERE name = 'Arsinoe';
SAVEPOINT Point_A;

UPDATE emp
  SET  salary = salary * 1.1
  WHERE name = 'Arsinoe';
SAVEPOINT Point_B;

UPDATE emp
  SET  salary = salary * 1.1
  WHERE name = 'Berenike';
SAVEPOINT point_C;

ROLLBACK TO SAVEPOINT point_b;
COMMIT;
UPDATE emp
  SET salary = 1500
  WHERE name = 'Arsinoe';
SAVEPOINT point_d;

ROLLBACK TO point_d;

COMMIT;
```

A. 1000

B. 1100

C. 1111

D. 1500

Answers to Review Questions

1. D. When inserting from another table using a subquery, the VALUES clause should not be included. Options B and C are invalid syntaxes for the INSERT statement.

2. E. If a transaction is not currently open, any INSERT, UPDATE, MERGE, DELETE, SELECT FOR UPDATE, or LOCK statement will implicitly begin a transaction.

3. B, C. Option A will error out because when using columns in set, a subquery must be used as in option C. Option D is wrong because AND is used instead of a comma to separate columns in the SET clause.

4. A, D. COMMIT, ROLLBACK, and any DDL statement end a transaction—DDL is automatically committed. INSERT, UPDATE, and DELETE statements require a commit or rollback.

5. A. Option A uses a correlated subquery to match the correct employee. Option B selects all the rows in the subquery and hence will generate an error. Option C is not valid syntax. Option D will update all the rows in the table since the UPDATE statement does not have a WHERE clause. The WHERE clause preset belongs to the subquery.

6. B. In an UPDATE statement, the WHERE clause should come after the SET clause.

7. D. When deleting a row from a table, do not use column names. To change column values to NULL, use the UPDATE statement.

8. C. The FROM keyword in the DELETE statement is optional. Statement 3 is first building a subquery with the necessary condition and deleting the rows from the subquery.

9. B. When two savepoints are created with the same name, Oracle erases the older savepoint. In the code segment, the DELETE and the first INSERT are not rolled back.

10. C. When updating more than one column in a single UPDATE statement, separate the columns by a comma; do not use the AND operator.

11. D. Option A is updating the wrong table. Option B has the right syntax but will update all the rows in the EMPLOYEE table since there is no WHERE clause for the UPDATE statement. Since the WHERE clause is in the subquery, all the rows that do not belong to department 22 will be updated with a NULL. Options C and D are similar, except for the AND keyword instead of WHERE.

12. D. The first INSERT statement and the last INSERT statement will be saved in the database. The ROLLBACK TO A statement will undo the second and third inserts.

13. B. Option B will raise an exception because there are not enough column values for the implicit column list (all columns).

14. B. Since the location_id column is defined with a default value of 99, statement 1 will insert 99 for location_id. In statement 2, a NULL is explicitly inserted into the location_id column; Oracle will not replace the NULL with the default value defined.

15. B. The FIRST clause tells Oracle to execute only the first WHEN clause that evaluates to TRUE for each row. Since no rows have a channel_id of C, no rows would be inserted into the catalog_sales table; 24,000 rows have channel_id of I, so control would pass to the second WHEN clause 24,000 times, and the internet_sales table would get 24,000 rows. Since the second WHEN clause evaluates to TRUE and the INSERT FIRST option is specified, these rows would not make it to the third WHEN clause and would not be inserted into the new_channel_sales table. Had the INSERT ALL option been used, these 24,000 rows would also get inserted into the new_channel_sales table; 12,000 rows have a channel_id of T, so control would pass all the way to the third WHEN clause for these rows, and 12,000 rows would get inserted into new_channel_sales.

16. C. The TRUNCATE statement is DDL and performs an implicit commit. After the TRUNCATE statement on the employees table, there are 124 rows in the emp table. The one row that got inserted was removed when the ROLLBACK statement was executed.

17. D. You must have the SET keyword in an UPDATE statement. The BETWEEN operator and any other valid operators are allowed in the WHERE clause.

18. D. When DML operations are performed, Oracle automatically locks the rows. You can query (read) the rows, but no other DML operation is allowed on those rows. When you read the rows, Oracle constitutes a read-consistent view using the undo segments.

19. B. The keywords INSERT INTO are required in single-table INSERT statements but are not valid in multiple-table INSERT statements.

20. D. The final rollback (to point_d) will roll the changes back to just after setting the salary to 1500.

Creating Tables and Constraints

ORACLE DATABASE 11*g*: SQL FUNDAMENTALS I EXAM OBJECTIVES COVERED IN THIS CHAPTER:

✓ **Using DDL Statements to Create and Manage Tables**

- Categorize the main database objects
- Review the table structure
- List the data types that are available for columns
- Create a simple table
- Explain how constraints are created at the time of table creation
- Describe how schema objects work

An Oracle database has many different types of objects. Related objects are logically grouped together in a schema, which consists of various types of objects. The basic types of objects in an Oracle Database are tables, indexes, constraints, sequences, and synonyms. Though this chapter discusses tables and constraints, I will start the chapter with an overview of the main database objects in Oracle.

The table is the basic structure of data storage in Oracle. A table has columns as part of the definition and stores rows of data. In a relational database, the data in various tables may be related. A constraint can be considered as a rule or policy defined in the database to enforce data integrity and business rules. In this chapter, I will discuss creating tables and using constraints. Since the table is the most important type of object in an Oracle Database, it is important to know how to create tables and constraints on tables.

Database Objects Overview

Data in the Oracle Database is stored in tables. A *table* is the main database object. Many other database objects, whether or not they store data, are generally based on the tables. Let's review the main database objects in Oracle that are relevant for this certification exam:

Table A *table* is defined with columns and stores rows of data. A table should have at least one column. In Oracle, a table normally refers to a relational table. You can also create object tables. Object tables are created with user-defined datatypes. Temporary tables (called *global temporary tables* in Oracle) are used to hold temporary data specific to a transaction or session. A table can store a wide variety of data. Apart from storing text and numeric information, you can store date, timestamp, binary, or raw data (such as images, documents, and information about external files). A table can have *virtual columns*. As the name indicates, these types of columns do not consume storage space on disk; the database derives values in virtual columns from normal columns. Tables are discussed in the next sections of this chapter.

View A *view* is a customized representation of data from one or more tables and/or views. Views are used as a window to show information from tables in a certain way or to restrict the information. Views are queries stored in the database that select data from one or more tables. They also provide a way to restrict data from certain users, thus providing an additional level of security.

Sequence A *sequence* is a way to generate continuous numbers. Sequences are useful for generating unique serial numbers or key values. The sequence definition is stored in the data dictionary. Sequence numbers are generated independently of other database objects.

Synonym A *synonym* is an alias for any table, view, sequence, or other accessible database object. Because a synonym is simply an alias, it requires no storage other than its definition in the data dictionary. Synonyms are useful because they hide the identity of the underlying object. The object can even be part of another database. A public synonym is accessible to all users of the database, and a private synonym is accessible only to its owner.

Index An *index* is a structure associated with tables used to speed up the queries. An index is an access path to reach the desired row faster. Oracle has B-tree and bitmap indexes. Creating/dropping indexes does not affect the storage of data in the underlying tables. You can create unique or nonunique indexes. Unique indexes are created automatically by Oracle when you create a primary key or a unique key constraint in a table. A composite index has more than one column in the index.

Views, sequences, synonyms, and indexes are discussed in Chapter 7, "Creating Schema Objects."

Oracle 11*g* has a wide array of database objects to suit various application requirements. These objects are not discussed in this book because they are not part of the certification exam at this time. Some of the other database objects that may be used in application development are clusters, dimensions, directories, functions, Java sources/classes, libraries, materialized views, and types. To learn more about the various Oracle 11*g* database schema objects, please refer to the Oracle documentation called "Oracle Database Administrators Guide 11g Release 1 (11.) Part Number B28310-04," which is available online at `www.oracle.com/pls/db111/db111.homepage`.

Schema Objects

A *schema* is a collection of related database objects grouped together. For example, a schema can have tables, views, triggers, synonyms, and PL/SQL programs such as procedures. A schema is owned by a database user and has the same name as the user. If the database user does not own any database objects, then no schema is associated with the user. A schema is a logical grouping of database objects.

A database user can have only one schema associated and is created when you create any database object. They may include any or all the basic database objects discussed earlier. Oracle 11*g* may also include the following types of structures in the schema. These objects are listed here only to give you an overview of schemas; creating and managing these objects are not part of the certification exam at this time. For the certification exam, prepare to know the schema objects discussed in this chapter and in Chapter 7.

Materialized view *Materialized views* are objects used to summarize and replicate data. They are similar to views but occupy storage space. Materialized views are mainly used in data-warehouse environments where data needs to be aggregated and stored so that queries and reports run faster. Materialized views can also be used to replicate data from another database.

Dimension A *dimension* is a logical structure to define the relationship between columns in a table. Dimensions are defined in the data dictionary and do not occupy any storage space. The columns in a dimension can be from a single table or from multiple tables. An example of a dimension would be the relationship between country, state, and city in a table that stores address information.

Cluster A *cluster* is a method of storing data from related tables at a common physical location. You can share the storage of rows in related tables for performance reasons if the access to the rows in the tables always involves join operations on the tables. For example, if you have an orders table and a customers table in the schema, you can query the orders table always joining the customers table, because that's where you get the customer name associated with the customer ID. A cluster may be created for the orders and customers tables so that the rows associated with the same customer are stored in the same physical storage area (block). Database storage and blocks are discussed in Chapter 8, "Introducing Oracle 11*g* Components and Architecture."

Database links A *database link* is a schema object that enables you to access an object from a different database. SQL queries can reference tables and views belonging to the remote database by appending `@db_link_name` to the table or view. For example, to access the `CUSTOMER_ORDERS` table using a database link named `LONDON_SALES`, you would use `CUSTOMER_ORDERS@LONDON_SALES`.

Triggers A *trigger* is a stored PL/SQL program that gets executed when a specified condition occurs. A trigger can be defined on a table to "fire" when an insert, update, or delete operation occurs on the table. A trigger may also be defined on the database to "fire" when certain database conditions occur, such as starting the database, or when a database error occurs.

Java objects Oracle Database 11*g* includes *Java objects* such as Java classes, Java sources, and Java resources. Java stored programs can be created using the different Java object types.

PL/SQL programs *PL/SQL stored programs* include procedures, functions, and packages. A *procedure* is a PL/SQL programmatic construct. A *function* is similar to a procedure but always returns a value. A *package* is a grouping of related PL/SQL objects.

Built-in Datatypes

When creating tables, you must specify a *datatype* for each column you define. Oracle 11*g* is rich with various datatypes to store different kinds of information. By choosing the appropriate datatype, you will be able to store and retrieve data without compromising its integrity. A datatype associates a predefined set of properties with the column.

The datatypes in Oracle 11*g* can be classified into five major categories. Figure 6.1 shows the categories and the datatype names.

FIGURE 6.1 Oracle built-in datatypes

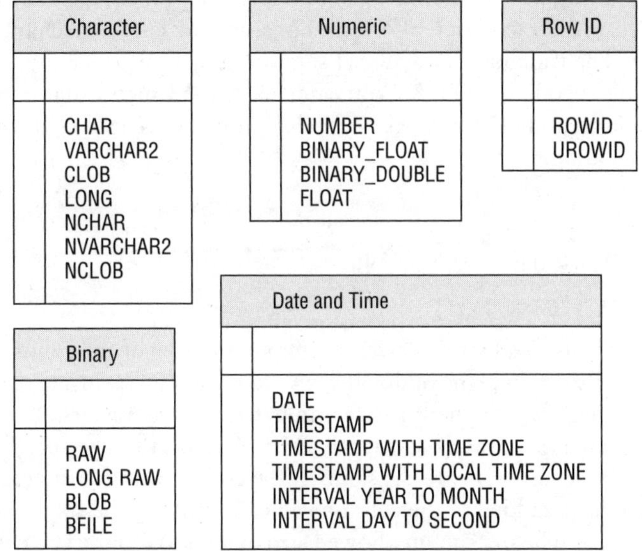

Chapter 1, "Introducing SQL," introduced four basic datatypes: CHAR, VARCHAR2, NUMBER, and DATE. Here, I will review those datatypes and describe the other datatypes that you can specify while creating a table.

Character Datatypes

Seven character datatypes can be used for defining columns in a table:

- CHAR
- NCHAR
- VARCHAR2
- NVARCHAR2
- CLOB
- NCLOB
- LONG

Character datatypes store alphanumeric data in the database character set or in the Unicode character set. You define the database character set when you create the database.

The character set determines which languages can be represented in the database. For example, US7ASCII is a 7-bit ASCII character set that can represent the English language and any other language that uses the English alphabet set. WE8ISO8859P1 is an 8-bit character set that can support multiple European languages such as English, German, French, Albanian, Spanish, Portuguese, Irish, and so on, because they all use a similar writing script. Unicode, the Universal Character Set, allows you to store any language character using a single character set. The Unicode character set supported by Oracle is either 16-bit encoding (UTF-16) or 8-bit encoding (UTF-8). You can choose the Unicode datatypes to be used in the database while creating the database. The default is the AL16UTF16 character set, which is UTF-16 encoding.

CHAR

The syntax for the CHAR datatype is as follows:

```
CHAR [(<size> [BYTE | CHAR ] ) ]
```

The CHAR datatype is fixed-length, with the maximum size of the column specified in parentheses. You can also include the optional keyword BYTE or CHAR inside the parentheses along with the size to indicate whether the size is in bytes or in characters. BYTE is the default.

For single-byte-database character sets (such as US7ASCII), the size specified in bytes and the size specified in characters are the same. If the column value is shorter than the size defined, trailing spaces are added to the column value. Specifying the size is optional, and the default size is 1 byte. The maximum allowed size in a CHAR datatype column is 2,000 bytes. Here are few examples of specifying a CHAR datatype column:

```
employee_id  CHAR (5)
employee_name CHAR (100 CHAR)
employee_sex CHAR
```

NCHAR

The syntax for the NCHAR datatype is as follows:

```
NCHAR [ ( <size> ) ]
```

The NCHAR datatype is similar to CHAR, but it is used to store Unicode character-set data. The NCHAR datatype is fixed-length, with a maximum size of 2,000 bytes and a default size of a character.

The size in the NCHAR datatype definition is always specified in characters. Trailing spaces are added if the value inserted into the column is shorter than the column's maximum length. Here is an example of specifying an NCHAR datatype column:

```
emp_name NCHAR (100)
```

Several built-in Oracle 11*g* functions have options to represent NCHAR data. An NCHAR string may be represented by prefixing the string with `N`, as in this example:

```
SELECT  emp_name FROM employee_records
WHERE emp_name = N'John Smith';
```

VARCHAR2 or VARCHAR

The syntax for the VARCHAR2 datatype is as follows:

```
VARCHAR2 (<size> [BYTE | CHAR] )
```

VARCHAR2 and VARCHAR are synonymous datatypes. VARCHAR2 specifies variable-length character data. A maximum size for the column should be defined; Oracle 11*g* will not assume any default value. Unlike CHAR columns, VARCHAR2 columns are not blank-padded with trailing spaces if the column value is shorter than its maximum specified length. You can specify the size in bytes or characters; by default, the size is in bytes. The range of values allowed for size is from 1 to 4,000 bytes. For storing variable-length data, Oracle recommends using VARCHAR2 rather than VARCHAR, because the behavior of the VARCHAR datatype may change in a future release.

NVARCHAR2

The syntax for the NVARCHAR2 datatype is as follows:

```
NVARCHAR2 (<size>)
```

The NVARCHAR2 datatype is used to store Unicode variable-length data. The size is specified in characters, and the maximum size allowed is 4,000 bytes.

If you try to insert a value into a character datatype column that is larger than its maximum specified size, Oracle will return an error. Oracle will not chop or truncate the inserted value to store it in the database column.

CLOB

The syntax for the CLOB datatype is as follows:

```
CLOB
```

CLOB is one of the Large Object datatypes provided to store variable-length character data. The maximum amount of data you can store in a CLOB column is based on the block size of the database. CLOB can store up to (4GB–1)*(database block size). You do not specify the size with this datatype definition.

NCLOB

The syntax for the NCLOB datatype is as follows:

```
NCLOB
```

NCLOB is one of the Large Object datatypes and stores variable-length Unicode character data. The maximum amount of data you can store in a NCLOB column is (4GB–1)* (database block size). You do not specify the size with this datatype definition.

LONG

The syntax for the LONG datatype is as follows:

```
LONG
```

Using the LONG datatype is discouraged in Oracle Database 11*g*. It is provided only for backward compatibility. You should use the CLOB datatype instead of LONG. LONG columns can store up to 2GB of character data. There can be only one LONG column in the table definition. A LONG datatype column can be used in the `SELECT` clause of a query, the `SET` clause of the `UPDATE` statement, and the `VALUES` clause of the `INSERT` statement. You can also create a `NOT NULL` constraint on a LONG column.

LONG datatype columns cannot appear in the following:

- The `WHERE`, `GROUP BY`, or `ORDER BY` clauses
- A `SELECT` clause if the `DISTINCT` operator is used
- A `SELECT` list of subqueries used in `INSERT` statements
- A `SELECT` list of subqueries used with the `UNION`, `INTERSECT`, or `MINUS` operator
- A `SELECT` list of queries with the `GROUP BY` clause

Numeric Datatypes

Four built-in numeric datatypes can be used for defining numeric columns in a table:

- NUMBER
- BINARY_FLOAT
- BINARY_DOUBLE
- FLOAT

Numeric datatypes are used to store integer and floating-point numbers. The NUMBER datatype can store all types of numeric data, but BINARY_FLOAT and BINARY_DOUBLE give better performance with floating-point numbers. FLOAT is a subtype of NUMBER.

NUMBER

The syntax for the NUMBER datatype is as follows:

```
NUMBER [ (<precision> [, <scale>] )]
```

You can represent all non-Oracle numeric datatypes such as float, integer, decimal, double, and so on, using the NUMBER datatype. The NUMBER datatype can store both fixed-point and floating-point numbers. Oracle 11*g* introduced two new datatypes to support floating-point numbers—specifically, BINARY_FLOAT and BINARY_DOUBLE.

BINARY_FLOAT

The syntax for the BINARY_FLOAT datatype is as follows:

```
BINARY_FLOAT
```

The BINARY_FLOAT datatype represents a 32-bit floating-point number. There is no precision defined in the definition of this datatype because it uses binary precision. BINARY_FLOAT uses 5 bytes for storage.

A floating-point number can have a decimal point anywhere or can have no decimal point. Oracle stores NUMBER datatype values using decimal precision, whereas floating-point numbers (BINARY_FLOAT and BINARY_DOUBLE) are stored using binary precision. Oracle has three special values that can be used with floating-point numbers:

`INF`: Positive infinity

`-INF`: Negative infinity

`NaN`: Not a Number (NaN is not the same as `NULL`)

BINARY_DOUBLE

The syntax for the BINARY_DOUBLE datatype is as follows:

```
BINARY_DOUBLE
```

The BINARY_DOUBLE datatype represents a 64-bit floating-point number. BINARY_DOUBLE uses 9 bytes for storage. All the characteristics of BINARY_FLOAT are applicable to BINARY_DOUBLE.

FLOAT

The syntax for the FLOAT datatype is as follows:

```
FLOAT [(precision)]
```

The FLOAT datatype is a subtype of NUMBER and is internally represented as NUMBER. There is no scale for FLOAT numbers; only precision can be optionally included. The precision can range from 1 to default binary digits. In the NUMBER datatype the precision and scale are represented in decimal digits, whereas in FLOAT the precision is represented in binary digits. In Oracle 11*g* it is recommended you use BINARY_FLOAT or BINARY_DOUBLE instead of the FLOAT datatype.

Date and Time Datatypes

In pre–Oracle9*i* databases, the only datetime datatype available was DATE, which stores the date and time. Oracle9*i* Database introduced the TIMESTAMP and INTERVAL datatypes to enhance the storage and manipulation of date and time data. Six datetime datatypes in Oracle 11*g* can be used for defining columns in a table:

- DATE
- TIMESTAMP
- TIMESTAMP WITH TIME ZONE

- TIMESTAMP WITH LOCAL TIME ZONE
- INTERVAL YEAR TO MONTH
- INTERVAL DAY TO SECOND

The interval datatypes are used to represent a measure of time. They store the number of months or number of days/hours between two time points. All interval components are integers except the seconds, which may have fractional seconds represented.

DATE

The syntax for the DATE datatype is as follows:

```
DATE
```

The DATE datatype stores date and time information. You can store the dates from January 1, 4712 BC to December 31, 9999 AD. If you specify a date value without the time component, the default time is 12 a.m. (midnight, 00:00:00 hours). If you specify a date value without the date component, the default value is the first day of the current month. The DATE datatype stores century, year, month, date, hour, minute, and seconds internally. You can display the dates in various formats using the `NLS_DATE_FORMAT` parameter or by specifying a format mask with the `TO_CHAR` function. The various date-format masks are discussed in Chapter 2, "Using Single-Row Functions."

TIMESTAMP

The syntax for `TIMESTAMP` datatype is as follows:

```
TIMESTAMP [(<precision>)]
```

The TIMESTAMP datatype stores date and time information with fractional seconds precision. The only difference between the DATE and TIMESTAMP datatypes is the ability to store fractional seconds up to a precision of nine digits. The default precision is 6 and can range from 0 to 9.

TIMESTAMP WITH TIME ZONE

The syntax for the TIMESTAMP WITH TIME ZONE datatype is as follows:

```
TIMESTAMP [(<precision>)] WITH TIME ZONE
```

The TIMESTAMP WITH TIME ZONE datatype is similar to the TIMESTAMP datatype, but it stores the *time-zone displacement*. Displacement is the difference between the local time and the Coordinated Universal Time (UTC, also known as *Greenwich mean time*). The displacement is represented in hours and minutes. Two TIMESTAMP WITH TIME ZONE values are considered identical if they represent the same time in UTC. For example, 5 p.m. CST is equal to 6 p.m. EST or 3 p.m. PST.

TIMESTAMP WITH LOCAL TIME ZONE

The syntax for the TIMESTAMP WITH LOCAL TIME ZONE datatype is as follows:

```
TIMESTAMP [(<precision>)] WITH LOCAL TIME ZONE
```

The TIMESTAMP WITH LOCAL TIME ZONE datatype is similar to the TIMESTAMP datatype, but like the TIMESTAMP WITH TIME ZONE datatype, it also includes the time-zone displacement. TIMESTAMP WITH LOCAL TIME ZONE does not store the displacement information in the database but stores the time as a normalized form of the database time zone. The data is always stored in the database time zone, but when the user retrieves data, it is shown in the user's local-session time zone.

The following example demonstrates how the DATE, TIMESTAMP, TIMESTAMP WITH TIME ZONE, and TIMESTAMP WITH LOCAL TIME ZONE datatypes store data. The `NLS_xx_FORMAT` parameter is explicitly set to display the values in the nondefault format. The data is inserted at Central Daylight Time (CDT), which is seven hours behind UTC. (The output shown in the example was reformatted for better readability.)

```
CREATE TABLE date_time_demo (
r_no         NUMBER (2),
c_date       DATE DEFAULT SYSDATE,
c_timezone   TIMESTAMP DEFAULT SYSTIMESTAMP,
c_timezone2  TIMESTAMP (2) DEFAULT SYSTIMESTAMP,
c_ts_wtz     TIMESTAMP (0) WITH TIME ZONE
                           DEFAULT SYSTIMESTAMP,
c_ts_wltz    TIMESTAMP (9) WITH LOCAL TIME ZONE
                           DEFAULT SYSTIMESTAMP);

Table created.

INSERT INTO date_time_demo (r_no) VALUES (1);
1 row created.

ALTER SESSION SET NLS_DATE_FORMAT = 'YYYY-MM-DD HH24:MI:SS';
Session altered.

ALTER SESSION SET NLS_TIMESTAMP_FORMAT  = 'YYYY-MM-DD HH24:MI:SS.FF';
Session altered.

ALTER SESSION SET NLS_TIMESTAMP_TZ_FORMAT = 'YYYY-MM-DD HH24:MI:SS.FFTZH:TZM';
Session altered.

SELECT * FROM date_time_demo;

R_NO C_DATE              C_TIMEZONE
---------------------    --------------------------
1 2008-10-24 13:09:14    2008-10-24 13:09:14. 000001
```

```
C_TIMEZONE2               C_TS_WTZ
----------------------    --------------------------
2008-10-24 13:09:14.00    2008-10-24 13:09:14.-07:00

C_TS_WLTZ
-----------------------------
2008-10-24 13:09:14.000001000
```

INTERVAL YEAR TO MONTH

The syntax for the INTERVAL YEAR TO MONTH datatype is as follows:

```
INTERVAL YEAR [(precision)] TO MONTH
```

The INTERVAL YEAR TO MONTH datatype is used to represent a period of time as years and months. *precision* specifies the precision needed for the year field, and its default is 2. Valid precision values are from 0 to 9. This datatype can be used to store the difference between two datetime values, where the only significant portions are the year and month.

INTERVAL DAY TO SECOND

The syntax for the INTERVAL DAY TO SECOND datatype is as follows:

```
INTERVAL DAY [(precision)] TO SECOND
```

The INTERVAL DAY TO SECOND datatype is used to represent a period of time as days, hours, minutes, and seconds. *precision* specifies the precision needed for the day field, and its default is 6. Valid precision values are from 0 to 9. Larger precision values allow a greater difference between the dates; for example, a precision of 2 allows values from 0 through 99, and a precision of 4 allows values from 0 through 9999. This datatype can be used to store the difference between two datetime values, including seconds.

The following example demonstrates the INTERVAL datatypes. It creates a table with the INTERVAL datatypes, inserts data to it, and selects data from the table.

```
CREATE TABLE interval_demo (
ts1    TIMESTAMP (2),
iy2m   INTERVAL YEAR (3) TO MONTH,
id2s   INTERVAL DAY (4) TO SECOND);
Table created.

INSERT INTO interval_demo VALUES (
TO_TIMESTAMP('080101-102030.45', 'YYMMDD-HH24MISS.FF'),
TO_YMINTERVAL('3-7'),
TO_DSINTERVAL('4 02:20:30.30'));
1 row created.
```

```
SELECT * FROM interval_demo;
TS1                        IY2M      ID2S
------------------------- -------- ---------------------
2008-01-01 10:20:30.45     +003-07  +0004 02:20:30.300000
```

Date Arithmetic

Datetime datatypes can be used in expressions with the + or - operator. You can use the +, -, *, and / operators with the INTERVAL datatypes. Dates are stored in the database as Julian numbers with a fraction component for the time. A *Julian date* refers to the number of days since January 1, 4712 BC. Because of the time component of the date, comparing dates can result in fractional differences, even though the date is the same. Oracle provides a number of functions, such as TRUNC, that help you remove the time component when you want to compare only the date portions.

Adding 1 to the date simply moves the date ahead one day. You can add time to the date by adding a fraction of a day. One day equals 24 hours, or 24 × 60 minutes, or 24 × 60 × 60 seconds. Table 6.1 shows the numbers used to add or subtract time for a datetime datatype.

TABLE 6.1 Date Arithmetic

Time to Add or Subtract	Fraction	Date Difference
1 day	1	1
1 hour	1/24	1/24
1 minute	1/(24×60)	1/1440
1 second	1/(24×60×60)	1/86400

Subtracting two dates gives you the difference between the dates in days. This usually results in a fractional component that represents the time difference. If the time components are the same, there will be no fractional results.

A datetime value operation using a numeric value results in a datetime value. The following example adds 2 days and 12 hours to a date value:

```
ALTER SESSION SET NLS_DATE_FORMAT = 'YYYY-MM-DD HH24:MI:SS';

SELECT TO_DATE('2008-10-24 13:09:14') + 2.5 EXAMP
FROM dual;

EXAMP
-------------------
2008-10-27 01:09:14
```

This example subtracts six hours from a timestamp value:

```
SELECT TO_TIMESTAMP('2008-10-24 13:09:14.05') - 0.25 EXAMP
FROM dual;

EXAMP
-------------------
2008-10-24 07:09:14
```

A datetime value subtracted from another datetime value results in a numeric value (the difference in days). You cannot add two datetime values. Here is an example that results in the difference between dates as a fraction of a day:

```
SELECT SYSDATE,
       SYSDATE - TO_DATE('2007-10-24 13:09:14')
FROM dual;

SYSDATE             SYSDATE-TO_DATE('2007-10-2413:09:14')
------------------- -------------------------------------
2008-05-11 23:34:06                            200.433935
```

This example converts the fraction of days to hours, minutes, and seconds using the NUMTODSINTERVAL function:

```
SELECT SYSDATE,
       NUMTODSINTERVAL(SYSDATE - TO_DATE('2008-10-24 13:09:14'), 'DAY')
FROM DUAL;

SYSDATE              NUMTODSINTERVAL(SYSDATE
-------------------  -----------------------------
2008-10-24 15:53:04  +000000000 02:43:49.999999999
```

A datetime value operation using an interval value results in a datetime value. The following example adds one year and three months to today's date:

```
SELECT TRUNC(SYSDATE),
       TRUNC(SYSDATE)+TO_YMINTERVAL('1-3')
FROM dual;
TRUNC(SYSDATE)      TRUNC(SYSDATE)+TO_Y
------------------- -------------------
2008-10-24 00:00:00 2009-01-24 00:00:00
```

An interval datatype operation on another interval or numeric value results in an interval value. You can use + and – between two interval datatypes and use * and / between interval and numeric values. The following example converts a string (which represents

1 day, 3 hours, and 30 minutes) to an INTERVAL DAY TO SECOND datatype and multiplies that value by 2, which results in 2 days and 7 hours:

```
SELECT TO_DSINTERVAL('1 03:30:00.0') * 2 FROM dual;

TO_DSINTERVAL('103:30:00.0')*2
--------------------------------
+000000002 07:00:00.000000000
```

The following example shows arithmetic between two INTERVAL DAY TO SECOND datatype values. The interval value of 3 hours and 30 minutes is subtracted from 1 day, 3 hours, and 30 minutes, resulting in 1 day.

```
SELECT TO_DSINTERVAL('1 03:30:00.0')
             - TO_DSINTERVAL('0 03:30:00.0')
FROM dual;

TO_DSINTERVAL('103:30:00.0')-TO_DSINTERVAL('003:30:00.0')
---------------------------------------------------------
+000000001 00:00:00.000000000
```

Binary Datatypes

Binary datatypes store information without converting it to the database's character set. This type of storage is required to store images, audio/video, executable files, and similar data. Four datatypes are available to store binary data:

- RAW
- LONG RAW
- BLOB
- BFILE

RAW

The syntax for the RAW datatype is as follows:

```
RAW (<size>)
```

RAW is used to store binary information up to 2,000 bytes. You must specify the maximum size of the column in bytes. RAW is a variable-length datatype.

LONG RAW

The syntax for the LONG RAW datatype is as follows:

```
LONG RAW
```

It's the same as RAW but with up to 2GB of storage and you can't specify a maximum size. LONG RAW is supported in Oracle 11*g* for backward compatibility. Use BLOB instead. You can have only one LONG RAW or LONG column in a table.

BLOB

The syntax for the BLOB datatype is as follows:

```
BLOB
```

BLOB can store binary data up to 4GB. There is no size specification for this datatype.

BFILE

The syntax for the BFILE datatype is as follows:

```
BFILE
```

BFILE is used to store information on external files. The external file size can be up to 4GB. Oracle stores only the file pointer in the database. The actual file is stored on the operating system. Of the four Large Object datatypes (CLOB, BLOB, NCLOB, and BFILE), only BFILE stores actual data outside the Oracle Database.

Row ID Datatypes

Physical storage of each row in a table can be represented using a unique value called the ROWID. Every table has a pseudocolumn called the ROWID. To store such values, Oracle provides two datatypes:

- ROWID
- UROWID

ROWID

The syntax for the ROWID datatype is as follows:

```
ROWID
```

ROWID can store the physical address of a row. Physical ROWIDs store the addresses of rows in ordinary tables (excluding index-organized tables), clustered tables, table partitions and subpartitions, indexes, and index partitions and subpartitions. Logical ROWIDs store the addresses of rows in index-organized tables. Physical ROWIDs provide the fastest possible access to a row of a given table.

UROWID

The syntax for the UROWID datatype is as follows:

```
UROWID
```

UROWID can store the logical ROWIDs of index-organized tables or non-Oracle Database tables. Oracle creates logical ROWIDs based on an index-organized table's primary key. The logical ROWIDs do not change as long as the primary key does not change.

Creating Tables

Now that you have learned about the various datatypes that you can use to store table data, you are ready to create a table. You can think of a table as a spreadsheet with columns and rows. It is a structure that holds data in a relational database. The table is created with a name to identify it and columns defined with valid column names and column attributes, such as the datatype and size. CREATE TABLE is a comprehensive statement with many options. The certification exam covers creating and managing a simple relational table only. Here is the simplest format to use to create a table:

```
CREATE TABLE products
( prod_id    NUMBER (4),
  prod_name  VARCHAR2 (20),
  stock_qty  NUMBER (15,3)
);

Table created.
```

You specify the table name following the keywords CREATE TABLE. The previous example creates a table named PRODUCTS under the user (schema) connected to the database. The table name can be qualified with the username; you must qualify the table when creating a table in another user's schema. Table and column names are discussed in more detail in the next section.

The column definitions are enclosed in parentheses. The table created by the previous code has three columns, each identified by a name and datatype. Commas separate the column definitions. This table has two columns with the NUMBER datatype and one column with the VARCHAR2 datatype. A datatype must be specified for each column.

When creating tables, you can specify the following:

- Default values for columns
- Constraints for the columns and/or table (discussed later in this chapter in the "Managing Constraints" section)
- The type of table: relational (heap), temporary, index-organized, external, or object (Index-organized and object tables are not covered on the certification exam.)
- Table storage, including any index storage and storage specification for the Large Object columns (LOBs) in the table
- The tablespace where the table/index should be stored
- Any partitioning and subpartitioning information

Naming Tables and Columns

Table names are used to identify each table. You should make table names as descriptive as possible. Table and column names are *identifiers* and can be up to 30 characters long. An identifier name should begin with a letter and can contain numeric digits. The only special characters allowed in an identifier name are the dollar sign ($), the underscore (_), and the number sign (#). The underscore can be used for meaningful separation of the words in an identifier name. These names are case insensitive. If, however, you enclose the identifier name in double quotation marks ("), it will be case sensitive in the Oracle dictionary.

Creating table names enclosed in quotation marks with mixed case can cause serious problems when you query the database if you do not know the exact case of the table name.

You can use the DESCRIBE or DESC (SQL*Plus) command to list all the columns in the table, along with their datatype, size, nullity, and order. The syntax is DESCRIBE *<table name>*. The case sensitivity of names and describing tables are illustrated in the following examples:

```
CREATE TABLE MyTable (
 Column_1  NUMBER,
 Column_2  CHAR);
Table created.

DESC mytable
 Name                  Null?    Type
 ------------------- -------- --------
 COLUMN_1                       NUMBER
 COLUMN_2                       CHAR(1)

SELECT table_name FROM user_tables
WHERE  table_name = 'MyTable';
no rows selected

CREATE TABLE "MyTable" (
 "Column1" number,
 "Column2" char);
Table created.

DESC "MyTable"
 Name                  Null?    Type
 ------------------- -------- --------
 Column1                        NUMBER
 Column2                        CHAR(1)
```

```
SELECT table_name FROM user_tables
WHERE  upper(table_name) = 'MYTABLE';

TABLE_NAME
------------------------------
MYTABLE
MyTable
```

It is a good practice to give the other objects directly related to a table a name that reflects the table name. For example, consider the EMPLOYEE table. The primary key of the table may be named PK_EMPLOYEE, indexes might be named EMPLOYEE_NDX1 and EMPLOYEE_NDX2, a check constraint could be named CK_EMPLOYEE_STATUS, a trigger could be named TRG_EMPLOYEE_HIRE, and so on.

Creating a Temporary Table

When you create a table without any specific keywords to indicate the type of the table, the table created is a relational table that is permanent. If you include the keywords GLOBAL TEMPORARY, Oracle creates a temporary relational table known as the *global temporary table* (GTT) whose definition is available to all sessions in the database, but the data is available only to the session that inserted data to it. The GTT is truly a temporary table. On other flavors of RDBMS, a permanent table created to hold temporary data is called a *temporary table*. You can do the same with Oracle, but Oracle provides true temporary tables with GTT.

The data inserted by a session is visible only to the session. Normally when you commit the data changes or new rows added to a table, the data is visible to all other sessions. When using GTTs, the data is truly temporary—it is not written permanently anywhere. The ON COMMIT clause can be included to specify whether the data in the temporary table is session-specific (ON COMMIT PRESERVE ROWS) or transaction-specific (ON COMMIT DELETE ROWS). ON COMMIT DELETE ROWS is the default. If the definition is for session-specific data, the inserted data will be available throughout the session. If the GTT is defined as transaction-specific, then when a COMMIT or ROLLBACK is performed, the data in the table is cleared. Here is an example of creating a temporary table whose inserted data will be available throughout the session:

```
CREATE GLOBAL TEMPORARY TABLE emp_bonus_temp  (
emp_id  NUMBER (10),
bonus   NUMBER (15,2))
ON COMMIT PRESERVE ROWS;
```

Specifying Default Values for Columns

When creating or altering a table, you can specify *default values* for columns. The default value specified will be used when you do not specify any value for the column while inserting data. The default value specified in the definition should satisfy the datatype and length of the column. If a default value is not explicitly set, the default for the column is implicitly set to NULL. Default values cannot refer to another column, and they cannot have the pseudocolumns LEVEL, NEXTVAL, CURRVAL, ROWNUM, or PRIOR. The default values can include SYSDATE, USER, USERENV, and UID.

In the following example, the table ORDERS is created with a column STATUS that has a default value of PENDING:

```
CREATE TABLE orders (
order_number NUMBER (8),
status       VARCHAR2 (10) DEFAULT 'PENDING');

Table created.

INSERT INTO orders (order_number) VALUES (4004);

1 row created.

SELECT * FROM orders;

ORDER_NUMBER STATUS
------------ ----------
        4004 PENDING
```

Here is an example of creating a table that includes default values for two columns:

```
CREATE TABLE emp_punch (
emp_id      NUMBER (6) NOT NULL,
time_in     DATE,
time_out    DATE,
updated_by  VARCHAR2 (30) DEFAULT USER,
update_time TIMESTAMP WITH LOCAL TIME ZONE
                                   DEFAULT SYSTIMESTAMP
);

Table created.

DESCRIBE emp_punch
```

```
 Name                          Null?    Type
 ----------------------------- -------- -------------------
 EMP_ID                        NOT NULL NUMBER(6)
 TIME_IN                                DATE
 TIME_OUT                               DATE
 UPDATED_BY                             VARCHAR2(30)
 UPDATE_TIME                            TIMESTAMP(6) WITH
                                        LOCAL TIME ZONE

INSERT INTO emp_punch (emp_id, time_in)
VALUES (1090, TO_DATE('062801-2121','MMDDYY-HH24MI'));

1 row created.

SELECT * FROM emp_punch;

EMP_ID TIME_IN   TIME_OUT  UPDATED_BY UPDATE_TIME
------ --------- --------- ---------- ------------------
1090   28-JUN-01           JOHN       02.55.58.000000 PM
```

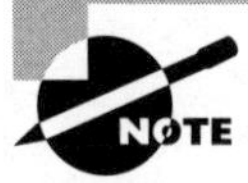

This example uses a NOT NULL constraint in the table definition. A NOT NULL constraint prevents NULL values from being entered into the column. Constraints are discussed in detail in the "Managing Constraints" section later in this chapter.

If you explicitly insert a NULL value for a column with DEFAULT defined, the value in the DEFAULT clause will not be used. You can explicitly specify DEFAULT in the INSERT statement to use the DEFAULT value, as in the following example:

```
INSERT INTO emp_punch
VALUES (104, TO_DATE('062801-2121','MMDDYY-HH24MI'),
        DEFAULT, DEFAULT, NULL);

1 row created.

SELECT * FROM emp_punch;
```

```
EMP_ID TIME_IN   TIME UPDATED UPDATE_TIME
                 _OUT  _BY
------ --------- ---- ------- ----------------------------
1090   28-JUN-01      JOHN    29-JUN-01 02.55.58.000000 PM
 104   28-JUN-01      JOHN
SQL>
```

Adding Comments

It is a good practice to document the purpose and any information on the type of data stored in the table in the database itself so that developers and administrators working on the database know the importance of the table/data. Oracle provides the COMMENT statement to add documentation to a table or a column.

Comments on tables are added using the COMMENT ON TABLE statement, and comments on table columns are added using the COMMENT ON COLUMN statement. The following example provides comments for the sample table:

```
COMMENT ON TABLE mytable IS
   'Oracle 11g Study Guide Example Table';
Comment created.

COMMENT ON COLUMN mytable.column_1 is
  'First column in MYTABLE';
Comment created.
```

You can query the table and column information from the Oracle dictionary using the following views: USER_TABLES, ALL_TABLES, USER_TAB_COLUMNS, and ALL_TAB_COLUMNS.

Creating a Table from Another Table

You can create a table using a query based on one or more existing tables or views. The column datatype and width will be determined by the query result. A table created in this fashion can select all the columns from another table (you can use *) or a subset of columns or expressions and functions applied on columns (these are called *derived columns*). The syntax for creating a table using an existing table is as follows:

```
CREATE TABLE <table characteristics> AS SELECT <query>
```

This syntax is generally known as CTAS (the abbreviated form of CREATE TABLE AS SELECT). The table characteristics include the new table name and its storage properties.

For example, suppose you need to duplicate the structure and data of the EMP table in the EMPLOYEES table. You can use CTAS, like this:

```
CREATE TABLE employees
AS SELECT * FROM emp;

Table created.
```

You can have complex query statements in the CREATE TABLE statement. The table is created with no rows if the query returned no rows. If you just want to copy the structure of the table, make sure the query returns no rows:

```
CREATE TABLE Y AS SELECT * FROM X WHERE 1 = 2;
```

You can provide column alias names to have different column names in the newly created table. The following example shows a table structure, displays the data, and then creates a new table with the data and displays it:

```
DESCRIBE city

 Name                    Null?    Type
 ------------------- -------- -------------
 CNT_CODE                NOT NULL NUMBER(4)
 ST_CODE                 NOT NULL VARCHAR2(2)
 CTY_CODE                NOT NULL NUMBER(4)
 CTY_NAME                         VARCHAR2(20)
 POPULATION                       NUMBER

SELECT COUNT(*) FROM city;

  COUNT(*)
----------
         3
CREATE TABLE new_city AS
SELECT cty_code CITY_CODE, cty_name CITY_NAME
FROM city;

Table created.

SELECT COUNT(*) FROM new_city;
```

```
  COUNT(*)
----------
         3
DESC new_city
 Name                    Null?    Type
 ------------------- -------- -------------
 CITY_CODE               NOT NULL NUMBER(4)
 CITY_NAME                        VARCHAR2(20)
```

The CREATE TABLE … AS SELECT … statement will not work if the query refers to columns of the LONG datatype.

When you create a table using the subquery, only the NOT NULL constraints associated with the columns are copied to the new table. Other constraints and column default definitions are not copied. This almost certainly will be an OCA certification exam question.

Modifying Tables

After you've created a table, you might want to modify it for several reasons. You can modify a table to change its column definition or default values, add a new column, rename a column, or drop an existing column. You can also drop and rename tables.

You might also modify a table if you need to change or add constraint definitions. You can make a table read-only so that no modifications are possible on the data in the table. The ALTER TABLE statement is used to change table definitions. Similar to the CREATE TABLE statement, the ALTER TABLE statement has several options. In the following sections, I will concentrate on the options that are pertinent to the OCA certification exam.

Adding Columns

Sometimes it is necessary to add a column to an existing table because there may be enhancements made to the application or because the developer just did not plan it completely well. To add a column to an existing table, you don't need to drop and re-create the table. Using the ALTER TABLE statement, you can easily add a column to the table. All columns added to the table using the ALTER TABLE ADD statement are added to the end of the table definition. Here is the syntax to add a new column to an existing table:

```
ALTER TABLE [<schema>.]<table_name> ADD <column_definitions>;
```

When a new column is added, it is always at the bottom of the table. For the existing rows, the new column value will be NULL.

Let's add a new column, ORDER_DATE, to the ORDERS table. Notice that the column is added to the end of the table definition. You cannot insert a new column in between other columns in a table. If you have such a requirement, the table has to be dropped and re-created.

```
DESCRIBE orders
 Name                Null?    Type
 ------------------- -------- -------------
 ORDER_NUMBER        NOT NULL NUMBER(8)
 STATUS                       VARCHAR2(10)

SELECT * FROM orders;

ORDER_NUMBER STATUS
------------ ----------
        4004 PENDING
        5005 COMPLETED

ALTER TABLE orders ADD order_date DATE;

Table altered.

DESC orders
 Name                Null?    Type
 ------------------- -------- ---------------
 ORDER_NUMBER        NOT NULL NUMBER(8)
 STATUS                       VARCHAR2(10)
 ORDER_DATE                   DATE

SELECT * FROM orders;

ORDER_NUMBER STATUS     ORDER_DAT
------------ ---------- ---------
        4004 PENDING
        5005 COMPLETED
```

If you are adding more than one column, the column definitions should be enclosed in parentheses and separated by commas. If you specify a DEFAULT value for a newly added column, all the rows in the table will have the default value automatically assigned. The following example adds two more columns to the ORDERS table:

```
ALTER TABLE orders ADD
 (quantity NUMBER (13,3),
  update_dt DATE DEFAULT SYSDATE);

Table altered.

SELECT * FROM orders;

ORDER_NUMBER STATUS     ORDER_DAT   QUANTITY UPDATE_DT
------------ ---------- --------- ---------- ---------
        4004 PENDING                         23-MAR-02
        5005 COMPLETED                       23-MAR-02
```

When adding a new column, you cannot specify the NOT NULL constraint if the table already has rows. To add a NOT NULL column, you need to follow three steps:

1. Modify the table to add the column.
2. Update the column with values for all the existing rows.
3. Add a NOT NULL constraint.

You may add a NOT NULL constraint with a DEFAULT clause, even if the table has rows. Here is an example:

```
ALTER TABLE orders
       ADD updated_by VARCHAR2 (30) NOT NULL;

ERROR at line 1:
ORA-01758: table must be empty to add mandatory
(NOT NULL) column

ALTER TABLE orders ADD updated_by VARCHAR2 (30)
  DEFAULT 'JOHN' NOT NULL;

Table altered.
```

In Oracle 11*g*, when you add a column with the NOT NULL constraint and the DEFAULT value, Oracle 11*g* does not update all the existing rows in the table with the default value. Oracle 11*g* simply updates the dictionary and gets you the value from the dictionary when you query the newly added column.

Modifying Columns

On many occasions, you may be required to change the table definition. The common definition changes are to add or remove a NOT NULL constraint to/from a column, changing the datatype of a column or changing the length of the column. The syntax to modify an existing column in a table is as follows:

```
ALTER TABLE [<schema>.]<table_name>
MODIFY <column_name> <new_attributes>;
```

If you omit any of the parts of the column definition (datatype, default value, or column constraint), the omitted parts remain unchanged. If you are modifying more than one column at a time, enclose the column definitions in parentheses. For example, to modify the ORDERS table, increasing the STATUS column to 15 and reducing the QUANTITY column to 10,3, do this:

```
ALTER TABLE orders MODIFY (quantity NUMBER (10,3),
                           status VARCHAR2 (15));
```

You can add or drop constraints in the column and modify the DEFAULT values for the column. The DEFAULT value included using the MODIFY clause affects only the new rows inserted to the table; the existing rows with NULL column values are not affected. To remove the DEFAULT value for a column, redefine the DEFAULT clause with a NULL value. For example, the following statement removes the default SYSDATE value from the UPDATE_DT column of the ORDERS table:

```
ALTER TABLE orders
MODIFY update_dt DEFAULT NULL;
```

These are the rules for modifying column definitions:

- You can increase the length of the character column and precision of the numeric column. If your table has many rows, increasing the length of a CHAR column will require a lot of resources, because the column data for all the rows needs to blank-padded with the additional length.
- You can decrease the length of a VARCHAR2 column and reduce the precision or increase the scale of a numeric column if all the data in the column fits the new length.
- You can decrease the length of a nonempty CHAR column if the parameter BLANK_TRIMMING is set to TRUE.
- The column values must be NULL to change the column's datatype. If you do not reduce the length, you can change the datatype from CHAR to VARCHAR2, or vice versa, even if the column is not empty.

Renaming Columns

Renaming column is not a common task, but sometimes you may have to change the name of a column because there was a typo in the script or the developers decided to store different data in the column. Renaming a column does not affect its data or datatype. The syntax to rename an existing column in a table is as follows:

```
ALTER TABLE [<schema>.]<table_name>
RENAME COLUMN <column_name> TO <new_name>;
```

When renaming a column, the column name must not be the same as an existing column in the table. The following example renames the DATA_VALUE column of the SAMPLE_DATA table to SAMPLE_VALUE:

```
DESCRIBE sample_data
 Name                                      Null?    Type
 ----------------------------------------- -------- ---------------
 DATA_VALUE                                         VARCHAR2(20)
 DATA_TYPE                                          VARCHAR2(10)

ALTER TABLE sample_data
RENAME COLUMN data_value to sample_value;

Table altered.

DESCRIBE sample_data
 Name                                      Null?    Type
 ----------------------------------------- -------- ---------------
 SAMPLE_VALUE                                       VARCHAR2(20)
 DATA_TYPE                                          VARCHAR2(10)
```

Dropping Columns

Similar to renaming columns, dropping columns is not a common activity for the DBA, but you should know how to drop a column in case you need to do it. You can drop a column that is not used, or you can mark the column as not used and drop it later. Here is the syntax for dropping a column:

```
ALTER TABLE [<schema>.]<table_name>
DROP {COLUMN <column_name> | (<column_names>)}
[CASCADE CONSTRAINTS]
```

DROP COLUMN drops the column name specified from the table. You can provide more than one column name separated by commas inside parentheses. The indexes and constraints on the column are also dropped. You must specify CASCADE CONSTRAINTS if the dropped column is part of a multicolumn constraint; the constraint will be dropped.

The syntax for marking a column as unused is as follows:

```
ALTER TABLE [<schema>.]<table_name>
SET UNUSED {COLUMN <column_name> | (<column_names>)}
[CASCADE CONSTRAINTS]
```

You usually mark a column as unused instead of dropping it immediately, especially at peak hours, if the table is very large, because it takes a lot of resources. In such cases, you would mark the column as unused and drop it later. Once the column is marked as unused, you will not see it as part of the table definition. Let's mark the UPDATE_DT column in the ORDERS table as unused:

```
ALTER TABLE orders SET UNUSED COLUMN update_dt;

Table altered.

DESCRIBE orders
 Name                 Null?    Type
 -------------------- -------- -------------
 ORDER_NUMBER         NOT NULL NUMBER(8)
 STATUS                        VARCHAR2(15)
 ORDER_DATE                    DATE
 QUANTITY                      NUMBER(10,3)
```

Here is the syntax for dropping a column already marked as unused:

```
ALTER TABLE [<schema>.]<table_name>
DROP {UNUSED COLUMNS | COLUMNS CONTINUE}
```

Use the COLUMNS CONTINUE clause to continue a DROP operation that was previously interrupted. The DROP UNUSED COLUMNS clause will drop all the columns that are marked as unused. You cannot selectively drop column names after marking them as unused. The following example clears data from the UPDATE_DT column in the ORDERS table:

```
ALTER TABLE orders DROP UNUSED COLUMNS;
```

The data dictionary views DBA_UNUSED_COL_TABS, ALL_UNUSED_COL_TABS, and USER_UNUSED_COL_TABS provide the names of tables in which you have columns marked as unused.

Dropping Tables

When application designs change, some tables become orphaned or unused. You can use the DROP TABLE statement to drop an existing table. The syntax of the DROP TABLE statement is as follows:

```
DROP TABLE [schema.]table_name [CASCADE CONSTRAINTS]
```

When you drop a table, you remove the data and definition of the table. The indexes, constraints, triggers, and privileges on the table are also dropped. Once you drop a table, you cannot undo the action.

Oracle does not drop the views, materialized views, or other stored programs that reference the table, but it marks them as invalid. You must specify the CASCADE CONSTRAINTS clause if there are referential integrity constraints referring to the primary key or unique key of this table. Here's how to drop the table TEST owned by the user SCOTT:

```
DROP TABLE scott.test;
```

A method for emptying a table of all rows is to use the TRUNCATE statement. This is different from dropping and re-creating a table, because TRUNCATE does not invalidate dependent objects or drop indexes, triggers, or referential integrity constraints. See Chapter 5 for more information about using TRUNCATE.

Renaming Tables

Tables and other database schema objects can be renamed in Oracle. The RENAME statement is used to rename a table and other database objects, such as views, private synonyms, or sequences. The syntax for the RENAME statement is as follows:

```
RENAME old_name TO new_name;
```

Here, *old_name* and *new_name* are the names of a table, view, private synonym, or sequence.

When you rename a table, Oracle automatically transfers integrity constraints, indexes, and grants on the old table to the new table. Oracle invalidates all objects that depend on the renamed table, such as views, synonyms, stored procedures, and functions.

The following example renames the ORDERS table to PURCHASE_ORDERS:

```
RENAME orders TO purchase_orders;

Table renamed.
```

```
DESCRIBE purchase_orders
 Name                   Null?    Type
 ------------------ -------- ---------------
 ORDER_NUMBER           NOT NULL NUMBER(8)
 STATUS                          VARCHAR2(15)
 ORDER_DATE                      DATE
 QUANTITY                        NUMBER(10,3)
```

You can use the RENAME statement to rename only the objects you own. You cannot rename an object owned by another user.

You can also use the RENAME TO clause of the ALTER TABLE statement to rename a table. Using this technique, you can qualify the table name with the schema. You must use the ALTER TABLE statement to rename a table owned by another user (and you need the ALTER privilege on the table or the ALTER ANY TABLE system privilege). Here is an example:

```
ALTER TABLE scott.purchase_orders
RENAME TO orders;

Table altered.
```

Making Tables Read-Only

Often the DBA gets requests from users to make a table read-only. Many configuration tables can be made read-only after the initial application setup is completed so that accidental changes can be avoided. To place a table in read-only mode, use the READ ONLY clause of the ALTER TABLE statement.

The following statement makes the PRODUCTS table read-only:

```
ALTER TABLE products READ ONLY;

Table altered.
```

Once the table is marked as read-only, any operation on the table that changes its data is not allowed. Many DDL operations on the table are allowed. The following operations on the read-only table are not allowed:

- INSERT, UPDATE, DELETE, or MERGE statements
- The TRUNCATE operation
- Adding, modifying, renaming, or dropping a column
- Flashing back a table
- SELECT FOR UPDATE

The following operations are allowed on the read-only table:

- SELECT
- Creating or modifying indexes
- Creating or modifying constraints
- Changing the storage characteristics of the table
- Renaming the table
- Dropping the table

The following examples demonstrate some operations that are not allowed on a read-only table:

```
TRUNCATE TABLE products;
TRUNCATE TABLE products
               *
ERROR at line 1:
ORA-12081: update operation not allowed on table "HR"."PRODUCTS"

DELETE FROM products;
DELETE FROM products
            *
ERROR at line 1:
ORA-12081: update operation not allowed on table "HR"."PRODUCTS"

INSERT INTO products VALUES (200, 'TESTING', 'X1',0);
INSERT INTO products VALUES (200, 'TESTING', 'X1',0)
            *
ERROR at line 1:
ORA-12081: update operation not allowed on table "HR"."PRODUCTS"
```

To change a read-only table to read-write, use the READ WRITE clause of the ALTER TABLE statement. The following example makes the PRODUCTS table writable:

```
ALTER TABLE products READ WRITE;

Table altered.
```

Managing Constraints

Constraints are created in the database to enforce a business rule in the database and to specify relationships between various tables. You can also enforce business rules using database triggers and application code. *Integrity constraints* prevent bad data from being entered into the database. Oracle supports five types of integrity constraints, as shown in Table 6.2.

TABLE 6.2 Integrity Constraints

Constraint	Description
NOT NULL	Prevents NULL values from being entered into the column. These types of constraints are defined on a single column. By default, Oracle allows NULL values in any column.
CHECK	Checks whether the condition specified in the constraint is satisfied.
UNIQUE	Ensures that there are no duplicate values for the column(s) specified. Every value or set of values is unique within the table.
PRIMARY KEY	Uniquely identifies each row of the table and prevents NULL values. A table can have only one primary key constraint.
FOREIGN KEY	Establishes a parent-child relationship between tables by using common columns. The foreign key defined on a table refers to the primary key or unique key of another table.

Creating Constraints

Constraints are created using the CREATE TABLE or ALTER TABLE statements. You can specify the constraint definition at the column level if the constraint is defined on a single column. Multiple-column constraints must be defined at the table level; the columns should be specified in parentheses and separated by commas.

If you do not provide a name for the constraints, Oracle assigns a system-generated unique name that begins with SYS_. A name is provided for the constraint by specifying the keyword CONSTRAINT followed by the constraint name.

You should not rely on system-generated names for constraints. If you want to compare table characteristics, such as between production and test databases, the inconsistent system-generated names will make this comparison difficult.

In the following sections, I will define the rules for each constraint type and provide examples of creating constraints.

NOT NULL Constraint

A NOT NULL constraint is defined at the column level; it cannot be defined at the table level. The syntax for a NOT NULL constraint is as follows:

```
[CONSTRAINT <constraint name>] [NOT] NULL
```

The following example creates a table with two columns that have NOT NULL constraints:

```
CREATE TABLE orders (
 order_num    NUMBER (4) CONSTRAINT nn_order_num NOT NULL,
 order_date   DATE NOT NULL,
 product_id   NUMBER (6))
```

The example provides a name for the constraint on the ORDER_NUM column. Since no name is specified for the constraint on the ORDER_DATE column, it will get a system-generated name.

Use ALTER TABLE MODIFY to add or remove a NOT NULL constraint on the columns of an existing table. The following examples remove a constraint and add a constraint to an existing table:

```
ALTER TABLE orders MODIFY order_date NULL;
ALTER TABLE orders MODIFY product_id NOT NULL;
```

Check Constraints

You can define a check constraint at the column level or table level. For both the column and table levels, the syntax is as follows:

```
[CONSTRAINT <constraint name>] CHECK ( <condition> )
```

The condition specified in the CHECK clause should evaluate to a Boolean result and can refer to values in other columns of the same row; the condition cannot use queries. Environment functions (such as SYSDATE, USER, USERENV, and UID) and pseudocolumns (such as ROWNUM, CURRVAL, NEXTVAL, and LEVEL) cannot be used to evaluate the check condition. One column can have more than one check constraint defined.

The following are examples of check constraints defined at the table level:

```
CREATE TABLE bonus (
 emp_id     VARCHAR2 (40) NOT NULL,
 salary     NUMBER (9,2),
 bonus      NUMBER (9,2),
CONSTRAINT ck_bonus check (bonus > 0));

ALTER TABLE bonus
ADD CONSTRAINT ck_bonus2 CHECK (bonus < salary);
```

The check constraint can be defined at the column level if the constraint refers to only that column.

You cannot use the ALTER TABLE MODIFY clause to add or modify check constraints (only NOT NULL constraints can be modified this way). Column-level constraints can be defined when using the CREATE TABLE statement or when using the ALTER TABLE statement with the ADD clause. Here is an example:

```
ALTER TABLE orders ADD cust_id number (5)
CONSTRAINT ck_cust_id CHECK (cust_id > 0);
```

You can use the check constraint to implement a NOT NULL constraint also. This is especially useful if you need to disallow NULL values in multiple columns together. For example, the following constraint definition for the BONUS table allows a NULL value for the BONUS and SALARY columns if both column values are NULL, or else both columns should have a valid non-NULL value.

```
ALTER TABLE bonus ADD CONSTRAINT ck_sal_bonus
CHECK ((bonus IS NULL AND salary IS NULL) OR
      (bonus IS NOT NULL AND salary IS NOT NULL));
```

Unique Constraints

A unique constraint protects one or more columns in a table, ensuring that no two rows contain duplicate data in the protected columns. Unique constraints can be defined at the column level for single-column unique keys. Here is the column-level syntax:

```
[CONSTRAINT <constraint name>] UNIQUE
```

For a multiple-column unique key (a *composite* key; the maximum number of columns specified can be 32), the constraint should be defined at the table level. Here is the table-level syntax:

```
[CONSTRAINT <constraint name>]
UNIQUE (<column>, <column>, ...)
```

Oracle creates a unique index on the unique key columns to enforce uniqueness. If a unique index or nonunique index already exists on the table with the same column-order prefix, Oracle uses the existing index. To use the existing nonunique index for enforcing uniqueness, there must not be any duplicate values in the unique key columns.

Unique constraints allow NULL values in the constraint columns. The following example defines a unique constraint with two columns:

```
ALTER TABLE employee
ADD CONSTRAINT uq_emp_id UNIQUE (dept, emp_id);
```

The next example adds a new column to the EMP table and creates a unique key at the column level:

```
ALTER TABLE employee ADD
ssn VARCHAR2 (11) CONSTRAINT uq_ssn unique;
```

Primary Key Constraints

All characteristics of the unique key are applicable to the primary key constraint, except that NULL values are not allowed in the primary key columns. A table can have only one primary key. The column-level syntax is as follows:

```
[CONSTRAINT <constraint name>] PRIMARY KEY
```

Here is the table-level syntax:

```
[CONSTRAINT <constraint name>]
PRIMARY KEY (<column>, <column>, …)
```

Oracle creates a unique index and NOT NULL constraints for each column in the key. The following example defines a primary key when creating the table:

```
CREATE TABLE employee (
 dept_no VARCHAR2 (2),
 emp_id  NUMBER (4),
 name    VARCHAR2 (20) NOT NULL,
 ssn     VARCHAR2 (11),
 salary  NUMBER (9,2) CHECK (salary > 0),
CONSTRAINT pk_employee primary key (dept_no, emp_id),
CONSTRAINT uq_ssn unique (ssn))
```

To add a primary key to an existing table, use the ALTER TABLE statement. Here is an example:

```
ALTER TABLE employee
ADD CONSTRAINT pk_employee PRIMARY KEY (dept_no, emp_id);
```

Indexes created to enforce unique keys and primary keys can be managed in the same way as any other index. However, these indexes cannot be dropped explicitly using the DROP INDEX statement.

Foreign Key Constraints

A foreign key constraint protects one or more columns in a table by ensuring that for each non-NULL value there is data available elsewhere in the database with a primary or unique key. The foreign key is the column or columns in the table (child table) where the constraint is created. The referenced key is the primary key or unique key column or columns in the table (parent table) that is referenced by the constraint. The column datatypes in the parent table and the child table should match.

You can define a foreign key constraint at the column level or table level. Here is the syntax for the column-level constraint:

```
[CONSTRAINT <constraint name>]
REFERENCES [<schema>.]<table> [(<column>, <column>, …]
[ON DELETE {CASCADE | SET NULL}]
```

Multiple-column foreign keys should be defined at the table level. Here is the table-level syntax:

```
[CONSTRAINT <constraint name>]
FOREIGN KEY (<column>, <column>, …)
REFERENCES [<schema>.]<table> [(<column>, <column>, …]
[ON DELETE {CASCADE | SET NULL}]
```

The foreign key column(s) and referenced key column(s) can be in the same table (self-referential integrity constraint). NULL values are allowed in the foreign key columns.

The following is an example of creating a foreign key constraint on the COUNTRY_CODE and STATE_CODE columns of the CITY table, which refers to the COUNTRY_CODE and STATE_CODE columns of the STATE table (the composite primary key of the STATE table).

```
ALTER TABLE city ADD CONSTRAINT fk_state
FOREIGN KEY (country_code, state_code)
REFERENCES state (country_code, state_code);
```

You can omit the column listing of the referenced table if referring to the primary key of the table. For example, if the COUNTRY_CODE and STATE_CODE columns are the primary key of the STATE table, the previous statement could be written like this:

```
ALTER TABLE city ADD CONSTRAINT fk_state
FOREIGN KEY (country_code, state_code)
REFERENCES state;
```

The ON DELETE clause specifies the action to be taken when a row in the parent table is deleted and child rows exist for the deleted parent primary key. You can delete the child rows (CASCADE) or set the foreign key column values to NULL (SET NULL). If you omit this clause, Oracle will not allow you to delete from the parent table if child records exist. You must delete the child rows first and then delete the parent row. The following are two examples of specifying the delete action in a foreign key:

```
ALTER TABLE city ADD CONSTRAINT fk_state
 FOREIGN KEY (country_code, state_code)
 REFERENCES state (country_code, state_code)
 ON DELETE CASCADE;

ALTER TABLE city ADD CONSTRAINT fk_state
 FOREIGN KEY (country_code, state_code)
 REFERENCES state (country_code, state_code)
 ON DELETE SET NULL;
```

You can query the constraint information from the Oracle dictionary using the following views: USER_CONSTRAINTS, ALL_CONSTRAINTS, USER_CONS_COLUMNS, and ALL_CONS_COLUMNS.

Disabled Constraints

When a constraint is created, it is enabled automatically. You can create a *disabled* constraint by specifying the DISABLE keyword after the constraint definition. Here is an example:

```
ALTER TABLE city ADD CONSTRAINT fk_state
 FOREIGN KEY (country_code, state_code)
 REFERENCES state (country_code, state_code) DISABLE;

ALTER TABLE bonus
ADD CONSTRAINT ck_bonus CHECK (bonus > 0) DISABLE;
```

Dropping Constraints

Dropping a constraint defined on a table may be necessary if you find out that business data does not always meet strict data validations using constraints. In such instances it may be necessary to drop a constraint. Constraints are dropped using the ALTER TABLE statement. Any constraint can be dropped by specifying the constraint name, as in this example:

```
ALTER TABLE bonus DROP CONSTRAINT ck_bonus2;
```

To drop the NOT NULL constraint, use the ALTER TABLE MODIFY statement, like this:

```
ALTER TABLE employee MODIFY employee_name NULL;
```

To drop unique key constraints with referenced foreign keys, specify the CASCADE clause to drop the foreign key constraints and the unique constraint. Specify the unique key columns(s). Here is an example:

```
ALTER TABLE employee DROP UNIQUE (emp_id) CASCADE;
```

To drop primary key constraints with referenced foreign key constraints, use the CASCADE clause to drop all foreign key constraints and then the primary key. Here is an example:

```
ALTER TABLE bonus DROP PRIMARY KEY CASCADE;
```

Enabling and Disabling Constraints

When you create a constraint, the constraint is automatically enabled (unless you specify the DISABLE clause). You can disable a constraint by using the DISABLE clause of the ALTER TABLE statement. When you disable unique or primary key constraints, Oracle drops the associated unique index. When you reenable these constraints, Oracle builds the index.

You can disable any constraint by specifying the clause DISABLE CONSTRAINT followed by the constraint name. Specifying UNIQUE and the column name(s) can disable unique keys, and specifying PRIMARY KEY can disable the table's primary key. You cannot disable a primary key or unique key if foreign keys that are enabled reference it. To disable all the referenced foreign keys and the primary or unique key, specify CASCADE. The following three examples demonstrate disabling constraints:

```
ALTER TABLE bonus DISABLE CONSTRAINT ck_bonus;

ALTER TABLE employee DISABLE CONSTRAINT uq_employee;

ALTER TABLE state DISABLE PRIMARY KEY CASCADE;
```

Using the ENABLE clause of the ALTER TABLE statement enables a constraint. When you enable a disabled unique or primary key, Oracle creates an index if an index with the unique or primary key columns does not already exist. You can specify storage for the unique or primary key while enabling these constraints, as in this example:

```
ALTER TABLE state ENABLE PRIMARY KEY USING INDEX
TABLESPACE user_INDEX STORAGE (INITIAL 2M NEXT 2M);
```

Validated Constraints

You have seen how to enable and disable a constraint. ENABLE and DISABLE affect only future data that will be added or modified in the table. In contrast, the VALIDATE and NOVALIDATE keywords in the ALTER TABLE statement act on the existing data. Therefore, a constraint can have four states, as shown in Table 6.3.

TABLE 6.3 Constraints

Constraint	Description
ENABLE VALIDATE	This is the default for the ENABLE clause. The existing data in the table is validated to verify that it conforms to the constraint.
ENABLE NOVALIDATE	This does not validate the existing data but enables the constraint for future constraint checking.
DISABLE VALIDATE	The constraint is disabled (any index used to enforce the constraint is also dropped), but the constraint is kept valid. No DML operation is allowed on the table because future changes cannot be verified.
DISABLE NOVALIDATE	This is the default for the DISABLE clause. The constraint is disabled, and no checks are done on future or existing data.

Suppose you have a large data-warehouse table, where bulk data loads are performed every night. The primary key of this table is enforced using a nonunique index because Oracle does not drop the nonunique index when disabling the constraint. When you do batch loads, you can disable the primary key constraint as follows:

```
ALTER TABLE wh01 MODIFY CONSTRAINT pk_wh01
DISABLE NOVALIDATE;
```

After the batch load completes, you can enable the primary key like this:

```
ALTER TABLE wh01 MODIFY CONSTRAINT pk_wh01
ENABLE NOVALIDATE;
```

Oracle does not allow any INSERT, UPDATE, or DELETE operations on a table with a DISABLE VALIDATE constraint. This is a quick way to make a table read-only in releases prior to Oracle 11*g*. In Oracle 11*g*, you can use the READ ONLY clause of the ALTER TABLE statement to make a table read-only.

Deferring Constraint Checks

By default, Oracle checks whether the data conforms to the constraint when the statement is executed. Oracle allows you to change this behavior if the constraint is created using the DEFERRABLE clause (NOT DEFERRABLE is the default). It specifies that the transaction can set the constraint-checking behavior.

INITIALLY IMMEDIATE specifies that the constraint should be checked for conformance at the end of each SQL statement (this is the default). INITIALLY DEFERRED specifies that the constraint should be checked for conformance at the end of the transaction.

The DEFERRABLE status of a constraint cannot be changed using ALTER TABLE MODIFY CONSTRAINT; you must drop and re-create the constraint. You can change the INITIALLY {DEFERRED|IMMEDIATE} clause using ALTER TABLE.

If the constraint is DEFERRABLE, you can set the behavior by using the SET CONSTRAINTS command or by using the ALTER SESSION SET CONSTRAINT command. You can enable or disable deferred constraint checking by listing all the constraints or by specifying the ALL keyword. The SET CONSTRAINTS command is used to set the constraint-checking behavior for the current transaction, and the ALTER SESSION command is used to set the constraint-checking behavior for the current session.

As an example, let's create a primary key constraint on the CUSTOMER table and a foreign key constraint on the ORDERS table as DEFERRABLE. Although the constraints are created as DEFERRABLE, they are not deferred because of the INITIALLY IMMEDIATE clause.

```
ALTER TABLE customer ADD CONSTRAINT pk_cust_id
PRIMARY KEY (cust_id) DEFERRABLE
INITIALLY IMMEDIATE;

ALTER TABLE orders ADD CONSTRAINT fk_cust_id
FOREIGN KEY (cust_id)
REFERENCES customer (cust_id)
ON DELETE CASCADE DEFERRABLE;
```

If you try to add a row to the ORDERS table with a CUST_ID value that is not available in the CUSTOMER table, Oracle returns an error immediately, even though you plan to add the CUSTOMER row soon. Since the constraints are verified for conformance as each SQL statement is executed, you must insert the row in the CUSTOMER table first and then add it to the

ORDERS table. Since the constraints are defined as DEFERRABLE, you can change this behavior by using this command:

```
SET CONSTRAINTS ALL DEFERRED;
```

Now you can insert rows to these tables in any order. Oracle checks the constraint conformance only at commit time.

If you want deferred constraint checking as the default, create or modify the constraint by using INITIALLY DEFERRED, as in this example:

```
ALTER TABLE customer MODIFY CONSTRAINT pk_cust_id
INITIALLY DEFERRED;
```

Real World Scenario

Creating Tables and Constraints for an Application

Here's a scenario you may find yourself in one day. You have been provided the following information to create tables and constraints for an application developed in your company to maintain geographic information:

- The COUNTRY table stores the country name and country code. The country code uniquely identifies each country. The country name must be present.
- The STATE table stores the state code, name, and its capital. The country code in this table refers to a valid entry in the COUNTRY table. The state name must be present. The state code and country code together uniquely identify each state.
- The CITY table stores the city code, name, and population. The city code uniquely identifies each city. The state and country where the city belongs are also stored in the table, which refers to the STATE table. The city name must be present.
- Each table should have a column identifying the created-on timestamp, with the system date as the default.
- The user should not be able to delete from the COUNTRY table if there are records in the STATE table for that country.
- The records in the CITY table should be automatically removed when their corresponding state is removed from the STATE table.
- All foreign and primary key constraints should be provided with meaningful names.

Let's start by creating the COUNTRY table:

```
SQL> CREATE TABLE country (
  2  code   NUMBER (4) PRIMARY KEY,
  3  name   VARCHAR2 (40));
Table created.
SQL>
```

Oops—CODE and NAME are not very descriptive column names, and you also have other columns in tables to store codes and names. Let's rename the columns to COUNTRY_CODE and COUNTRY_NAME:

```
SQL> ALTER TABLE country RENAME COLUMN
  2  code TO country_code;
Table altered.

SQL> ALTER TABLE country RENAME COLUMN
  2  name TO country_name;
Table altered.

SQL>
```

You also forgot to provide a name for the primary key constraint. Since the table was created with a system-generated name, you have to find the name first to rename the constraint:

```
SQL> SELECT constraint_name, constraint_type
  2  FROM user_constraints
  3  WHERE table_name = 'COUNTRY';

CONSTRAINT_NAME                C
------------------------------ -
SYS_C0010893                   P

SQL> ALTER TABLE country RENAME CONSTRAINT SYS_C0010893 TO pk_country;
Table altered.

SQL>
```

Oops again—the table should include a column to store the created-on date, and the country name cannot be NULL.

Before you continue, realize that if you have a good logical and physical design before you start creating tables, you will not have any of these problems. This is not the typical or recommended approach to creating tables for the application. The objective here is to demonstrate the various options available.

```
SQL> ALTER TABLE country MODIFY country_name NOT NULL
  2  ADD created  DATE DEFAULT SYSDATE;
Table altered.
SQL>
```

Review the table created:

```
SQL> DESCRIBE country
 Name                  Null?    Type
 ------------------ -------- ------------
 COUNTRY_CODE          NOT NULL NUMBER(4)
 COUNTRY_NAME          NOT NULL VARCHAR2(40)
 CREATED                        DATE
SQL>
```

Let's create the STATE table. Notice that multiple column constraints can be defined only at the table level.

```
SQL> CREATE TABLE state (
  2  state_code    VARCHAR2 (3),
  3  state_name    VARCHAR2 (40) NOT NULL,
  4  country_code  NUMBER (4) REFERENCES country,
  5  capital_city  VARCHAR2 (40),
  6  created       DATE DEFAULT SYSDATE,
  7  CONSTRAINT pk_state PRIMARY KEY
  8    (country_code, state_code));
Table created.
SQL>
```

Since you did not provide a name for the COUNTRY_CODE foreign key, Oracle assigns a name. To rename this constraint to provide a meaningful name, you can use the ALTER TABLE statement as you did before. To demonstrate dropping a constraint and re-creating it using ALTER TABLE, let's drop this constraint and then add it. So, find the constraint name from the USER_CONSTRAINTS view to drop and re-create it:

```
SQL> SELECT constraint_name, constraint_type
  2  FROM   user_constraints
  3  WHERE  table_name = 'STATE';
CONSTRAINT_NAME                C
------------------------------ -
SYS_C002811                    C
PK_STATE                       P
SYS_C002813                    R
SQL> ALTER TABLE state DROP CONSTRAINT SYS_C002813;
Table altered.
SQL> ALTER TABLE state ADD CONSTRAINT fk_state
  2  FOREIGN KEY (country_code) REFERENCES country;
Table altered.
SQL>
```

Now you'll create the CITY table. Notice the foreign key constraint is created with the ON DELETE CASCADE clause:

```
SQL> CREATE TABLE city (
     city_code    VARCHAR2 (6),
     city_name    VARCHAR2 (40) NOT NULL,
     country_code NUMBER (4) NOT NULL,
     state_code   VARCHAR2 (3) NOT NULL,
     population   NUMBER (15),
     created      DATE DEFAULT SYSDATE,
     constraint   pk_city PRIMARY KEY (city_code),
     constraint   fk_cigy FOREIGN KEY
                  (country_code, state_code)
                  REFERENCES state ON DELETE CASCADE);
Table created.
SQL>
```

Summary

Tables are the basic structure of data storage. A table comprises columns and rows, as in a spreadsheet. Each column has a characteristic that restricts and verifies the data it stores. You can use several datatypes to define columns. CHAR, NCHAR, VARCHAR2, CLOB, and NCLOB are the character datatypes. BLOB, BFILE, and RAW are the binary datatypes. DATE, TIMESTAMP, and INTERVAL are the date datatypes. TIMESTAMP datatypes can store the time-zone information also. NUMBER, BINARY_FLOAT, and BINARY_DOUBLE are the numeric datatypes.

You use the CREATE TABLE statement to create a new table. A table should have at least one column, and a datatype should be assigned to the column. The table name and column name should begin with a letter and can contain letters, numbers, or special characters. You can create a new table from an existing table using the CREATE TABLE...AS SELECT... (CTAS) statement. You can add, modify, or drop columns from an existing table using the ALTER TABLE statement.

Constraints are created in the database to enforce a business rule and to specify relationships between various tables. NOT NULL constraints can be defined only with a column definition and are used to prevent NULL values (an absence of data). Check constraints are used to verify whether the data conforms to certain conditions. Primary key constraints uniquely identify a row in the table. There can be only one primary key for a table, and the columns in the primary key cannot have NULL values. A unique key is similar to a primary key, but you can have more than one unique key in a table, as well as NULL values in the unique key columns.

You can enable and disable constraints using the ALTER TABLE statement. The constraint can be in four different states. ENABLE VALIDATE is the default state.

Exam Essentials

Understand datatypes. Know each datatype's limitations and accepted values. Concentrate on the new TIMESTAMP and INTERVAL datatypes.

Know how date arithmetic works. Know the resulting datatype of date arithmetic, especially between INTERVAL and DATE datatypes.

Know how to modify column characteristics. Understand how to change datatypes, add and modify constraints, and make other modifications.

Understand the rules associated with changing datatype definitions of columns with rows in a table. When the table is not empty, you can change a datatype only from CHAR to VARCHAR2, and vice versa. Reducing the length is allowed only if the existing data fits in the new length specified.

Understand the `DEFAULT` clause on the column definition. The `DEFAULT` clause provides a value for the column if the `INSERT` statement omits a value for the column. When modifying a column to have default values, the existing rows with `NULL` values in the table are not updated with the default value.

Know the actions permitted on read-only tables Understand the various actions that are permitted on a read-only table. Any operation that changes the data in the table is not allowed on a read-only table. Most DDL statements are allowed, including `DROP TABLE`.

Understand constraints. Know the difference between a primary key and a unique key constraint, and understand how to use a nonunique index for primary/unique keys.

Know how a constraint can be defined. You can use the `CREATE TABLE` or `ALTER TABLE` statement to define a constraint on the table.

Review Questions

1. The STATE table has the following constraints (the constraint status is shown in parentheses):

Primary key	pk_state (enabled)
Foreign key	COUNTRY table: fk_state (enabled)
Check constraint	ck_cnt_code (disabled)
Check constraint	ck_st_code (enabled)
NOT NULL constraint	nn_st_name (enabled)

   You execute the following SQL:

```
CREATE TABLE STATE_NEW AS SELECT * FROM STATE;
```

   How many constraints will there be in the new table?

   A. 0
   B. 1
   C. 3
   D. 5
   E. 2

2. Which line of code has an error?

```
1  CREATE TABLE FRUITS_VEGETABLES
2  (FRUIT_TYPE VARCHAR2,
3   FRUIT_NAME CHAR (20),
4   QUANTITY   NUMBER);
```

   A. 1
   B. 2
   C. 3
   D. 4

3. Which statement successfully adds a new column, ORDER_DATE, to the table ORDERS?

   A. `ALTER TABLE ORDERS ADD COLUMN ORDER_DATE DATE;`
   B. `ALTER TABLE ORDERS ADD ORDER_DATE (DATE);`
   C. `ALTER TABLE ORDERS ADD ORDER_DATE DATE;`
   D. `ALTER TABLE ORDERS NEW COLUMN ORDER_DATE TYPE DATE;`

4. What are the special characters allowed in a table name? (Choose all that apply.)
   - A. &
   - B. #
   - C. @
   - D. $

5. Consider the following statement:

```
CREATE TABLE MY_TABLE (
1ST_COLUMN  NUMBER,
2ND_COLUMN  VARCHAR2 (20));
```

   Which of the following best describes this statement?
   - A. Tables cannot be created without a defining a primary key. The table definition here is missing the primary key.
   - B. The reserved word COLUMN cannot be part of the column name.
   - C. The column names are invalid.
   - D. There is no maximum length specified for the first column definition. You must always specify a length for character and numeric columns.
   - E. There is no error in the statement.

6. Which dictionary view would you query to list only the tables you own?
   - A. ALL_TABLES
   - B. DBA_TABLES
   - C. USER_TABLES
   - D. USR_TABLES

7. The STATE table has six rows. You issue the following command:

```
ALTER TABLE STATE ADD UPDATE_DT DATE DEFAULT SYSDATE;
```

   Which of the following is correct?
   - A. A new column, UPDATE_DT, is added to the STATE table, and its contents for the existing rows are NULL.
   - B. Since the table is not empty, you cannot add a new column.
   - C. The DEFAULT value cannot be provided if the table has rows.
   - D. A new column, UPDATE_DT, is added to STATE and is populated with the current system date and time.

8. The `HIRING` table has the following data:

```
EMPNO       HIREDATE
---------   ----------
1021        12-DEC-00
3400        24-JAN-01
2398        30-JUN-01
```

What will be result of the following query?

`SELECT hiredate+1 FROM hiring WHERE empno = 3400;`

A. 4-FEB-01

B. 25-JAN-01

C. N-02

D. None of the above

9. What is the default length of a CHAR datatype column if no length is specified in the table definition?

A. 256

B. 1,000

C. 64

D. 1

E. You must always specify a length for CHAR columns.

10. Which statement will remove the column `UPDATE_DT` from the table `STATE`?

A. `ALTER TABLE STATE DROP COLUMN UPDATE_DT;`

B. `ALTER TABLE STATE REMOVE COLUMN UPDATE_DT;`

C. `DROP COLUMN UPDATE_DT FROM STATE;`

D. `ALTER TABLE STATE SET UNUSED COLUMN UPDATE_DT;`

E. You cannot drop a column from the table.

11. Which actions are allowed on a table that is marked as read-only? (Choose all that apply.)

A. Truncating a table

B. Inserting new data

C. Dropping a constraint

D. Dropping an index

E. Dropping a table

12. Which of the following statements will create a primary key for the CITY table with the columns STATE_CD and CITY_CD?
    - A. CREATE PRIMARY KEY ON CITY (STATE_CD, CITY_CD);
    - B. CREATE CONSTRAINT PK_CITY PRIMARY KEY ON CITY (STATE_CD, CITY_CD);
    - C. ALTER TABLE CITY ADD CONSTRAINT PK_CITY PRIMARY KEY (STATE_CD, CITY_CD);
    - D. ALTER TABLE CITY ADD PRIMARY KEY (STATE_CD, CITY_CD);
    - E. ALTER TABLE CITY ADD PRIMARY KEY CONSTRAINT PK_CITY ON (STATE_CD, CITY_CD);
13. Which of the following check constraints will raise an error? (Choose all that apply.)
    - A. CONSTRAINT ck_gender CHECK (gender IN ('M', 'F'))
    - B. CONSTRAINT ck_old_order CHECK (order_date > (SYSDATE - 30))
    - C. CONSTRAINT ck_vendor CHECK (vendor_id IN (SELECT vendor_id FROM vendors))
    - D. CONSTRAINT ck_profit CHECK (gross_amt > net_amt)
14. Consider the datatypes DATE, TIMESTAMP (TS), TIMESTAMP WITH LOCAL TIME ZONE (TSLTZ), INTERVAL YEAR TO MONTH (IY2M), and INTERVAL DAY TO SECOND (ID2S). Which operations are not allowed by Oracle Database 11g? (Choose all that apply.)
    - A. DATE+DATE
    - B. TSLTZ–DATE
    - C. TSLTZ+IY2M
    - D. TS*5
    - E. ID2S/2
    - F. IY2M+IY2M
    - G. ID2S+IY2M
    - H. DATE–IY2M
15. A constraint is created with the DEFERRABLE INITIALLY IMMEDIATE clause. What does this mean?
    - A. Constraint checking is done only at commit time.
    - B. Constraint checking is done after each SQL statement is executed, but you can change this behavior by specifying SET CONSTRAINTS ALL DEFERRED.
    - C. Existing rows in the table are immediately checked for constraint violation.
    - D. The constraint is immediately checked in a DML operation, but subsequent constraint verification is done at commit time.
16. What is the default precision for fractional seconds in a TIMESTAMP datatype column?
    - A. 0
    - B. 2
    - C. 6
    - D. 9

17. Which datatype shows the time-zone information along with the date value?

    A. TIMESTAMP

    B. TIMESTAMP WITH LOCAL TIME ZONE

    C. TIMESTAMP WITH TIME ZONE

    D. DATE

    E. Both options B and C

18. You have a large job that will load many thousands of rows into your `ORDERS` table. To speed up the loading process, you want to temporarily stop enforcing the foreign key constraint `FK_ORDERS`. Which of the following statements will satisfy your requirement?

    A. `ALTER CONSTRAINT FK_ORDERS DISABLE;`

    B. `ALTER TABLE ORDERS DISABLE FOREIGN KEY FK_ORDERS;`

    C. `ALTER TABLE ORDERS DISABLE CONSTRAINT FK_ORDERS;`

    D. `ALTER TABLE ORDERS DISABLE ALL CONSTRAINTS;`

19. You are connected to the database as user `JOHN`. You need to rename a table named `NORDERS` to `NEW_ORDERS`, owned by `SMITH`. Consider the following two statements:

    1. `RENAME SMITH.NORDERS TO NEW_ORDERS;`

    2. `ALTER TABLE SMITH.NORDERS RENAME TO NEW_ORDERS;`

    Which of the following is correct?

    A. Statement 1 will work; statement 2 will not.

    B. Statements 1 and 2 will work.

    C. Statement 1 will not work; statement 2 will work.

    D. Statements 1 and 2 will not work.

20. Tom executed the following SQL statement.

    ```
    create table xx (n number, x long, y clob);
    ```

    Choose the best option.

    A. A table named `xx` will be created.

    B. Single-character column names are not allowed in table definitions.

    C. When using the LONG datatype, other LOB datatypes cannot be used in table definitions.

    D. One of the datatypes used in the column definition needs the size specified.

Answers to Review Questions

1. B. When you create a table using CTAS (CREATE TABLE AS SELECT), only the NOT NULL constraints are copied.

2. B. A VARCHAR2 datatype should always specify the maximum length of the column.

3. C. The correct statement is C. When adding only one column, the column definition doesn't need to be enclosed in parentheses.

4. B, D. Only three special characters ($, _, and #) are allowed in table names along with letters and numbers.

5. C. All identifiers (column names, table names, and so on) must begin with an alphabetic character. An identifier can contain alphabetic characters, numbers, and the special characters $, #, and _.

6. C. The USER_TABLES view provides information on the tables owned by the user who has logged on that session. DBA_TABLES will have all the tables in the database, and ALL_TABLES will have the tables owned by you as well as the tables to which you have access. USR_TABLES is not a valid dictionary view.

7. D. When a default value is specified in the new column added, the column values for the existing rows are populated with the default value. If you include the NOT NULL constraint with the DEFAULT value, only the dictionary is updated.

8. B. In date arithmetic, adding 1 is equivalent to adding 24 hours. To add 6 hours to a date value with time, add 0.25.

9. D. If you do not specify a length for a CHAR datatype column, the default length of 1 is assumed.

10. A. You can use the DROP COLUMN clause with the ALTER TABLE statement to drop a column. There is no separate DROP COLUMN statement or a REMOVE clause in the ALTER TABLE statement. The SET UNUSED clause is used to mark the column as unused. This column can be dropped later using the DROP UNUSED COLUMNS clause.

11. C, D, E. All actions that do not modify the data in the table are permitted on a read-only table. The actions of creating/dropping a constraint, creating/dropping an index, and dropping a table are allowed. Though truncating is a DDL action, it is not permitted since the data in the table is affected.

12. C, D. The ALTER TABLE statement is used to create and remove constraints. CREATE PRIMARY KEY and CREATE CONSTRAINT are invalid statements. A constraint is always added to an existing table using the ALTER TABLE statement.

13. B, C. Check constraints cannot reference the SYSDATE function or other tables.

14. A, D, G. You cannot add two DATE datatypes, but you can subtract to find the difference in days. Multiplication and division operators are permitted only on INTERVAL datatypes. When adding or subtracting INTERVAL datatypes, both INTERVAL datatypes should be of the same category.

15. B. `DEFERRABLE` specifies that the constraint can be deferred using the `SET CONSTRAINTS` command. `INITIALLY IMMEDIATE` specifies that the constraint's default behavior is to validate the constraint for each SQL statement executed.

16. C. The default precision is 6 digits. The precision can range from 0 to 9.

17. C. Only TIMESTAMP WITH TIME ZONE stores the time-zone information as a displacement from UTC. TIMESTAMP WITH LOCAL TIME ZONE adjusts the time to the database's time zone before storing it.

18. C. You can disable a constraint by specifying its constraint name. You may enable the constraint after the load and avoid the constraint checking while enabling using the `ALTER TABLE ORDERS MODIFY CONSTRAINT FK_ORDERS ENABLE NOVALIDATE;` command.

19. C. `RENAME` can be used to rename objects owned by the user. `ALTER TABLE` should be used to rename tables owned by another user. To do so, you must have the `ALTER` privilege on the table or the `ALTER ANY TABLE` privilege.

20. A. The table will be created without error. A table cannot have more than one LONG column, but LONG and multiple LOB columns can exist together. If a LONG or LONG RAW column is defined, another LONG or LONG RAW column cannot be used.

Creating Schema Objects

ORACLE DATABASE 11*g*: SQL FUNDAMENTALS I EXAM OBJECTIVES COVERED IN THIS CHAPTER:

✓ **Creating Other Schema Objects**

- Create simple and complex views
- Retrieve data from views
- Create, maintain, and use sequences
- Create and maintain indexes
- Create private and public synonyms

An Oracle database can contain far more objects than simply tables. Chapter 6, "Creating Tables and Constraints," gave you an overview of all the major objects that can be in an Oracle schema. In this chapter, you will learn in detail some of the schema objects, concentrating of course on the OCP certification exam objectives. You will be learning about creating and managing four types of schema objects in this chapter: views, sequences, indexes, and synonyms. These four types of objects with tables are the most commonly used schema objects in an Oracle Database.

A view is a logical representation of data from one or more tables or views. You can think of a view as a query stored in the database. You can consider it a logical table, with rows and columns. Oracle 11*g* allows you to create constraints on the views and restrict the operations on views. In this chapter, I will discuss the uses of views, how they are created and managed, and how to retrieve data from views.

You can use a sequence to generate artificial keys or serial numbers. Synonyms provide aliases for objects. Indexes provide an access path to the table data. Several types of indexes can be deployed to enhance the performance of queries. Views, sequences, synonyms, and indexes are basic database objects that you'll need to understand for the certification exam, as well as for your database administration work.

Creating and Modifying Views

A *view* is a customized representation of data from one or more tables and/or views. The tables that the view is referencing are known as *base tables*. A view can be considered as a stored query or a virtual table. Only the query is stored in the Oracle data dictionary; the actual data is not copied anywhere. This means that creating views does not take any storage space other than the space in the dictionary.

Use the CREATE VIEW statement to create a view. The query that defines the view can refer to one or more tables, to materialized views, or to other views. Let's begin by creating a simple view. This example will use the EMPLOYEES table of the HR schema as the base table:

```
SQL> DESCRIBE employees
 Name                          Null?    Type
 ----------------------------- -------- -------------
 EMPLOYEE_ID                   NOT NULL NUMBER(6)
 FIRST_NAME                             VARCHAR2(20)
```

```
 LAST_NAME                  NOT NULL VARCHAR2(25)
 EMAIL                      NOT NULL VARCHAR2(25)
 PHONE_NUMBER                        VARCHAR2(20)
 HIRE_DATE                  NOT NULL DATE
 JOB_ID                     NOT NULL VARCHAR2(10)
 SALARY                              NUMBER(8,2)
 COMMISSION_PCT                      NUMBER(2,2)
 MANAGER_ID                          NUMBER(6)
 DEPARTMENT_ID                       NUMBER(4)
```

The following code creates a view named ADMIN_EMPLOYEES, with the employee information for employees who belong to the administration department (department 10). Notice that the LAST_NAME and FIRST_NAME columns are combined to display just a NAME column. You can rename columns by using alias names in the view definition. The datatype of the view's columns is derived by Oracle.

```
CREATE VIEW admin_employees AS
SELECT first_name || last_name NAME,
       email, job_id POSITION
FROM   employees
WHERE  department_id = 10;

View created.

SQL> DESCRIBE admin_employees
 Name                          Null?    Type
 ----------------------------- -------- ------------
 NAME                                    VARCHAR2(45)
 EMAIL                          NOT NULL VARCHAR2(25)
 POSITION                       NOT NULL VARCHAR2(10)
SQL>
```

If you qualify the view name with a schema name, the view will be created in that schema. You must have the CREATE ANY VIEW privilege to create a view in someone else's schema.

The views that actually copy data from base tables and take up storage are called *materialized* views. Materialized views are commonly used in data-warehouse environments. In earlier versions of Oracle, materialized views were called *snapshots*, and they are sometimes still called snapshots.

When numeric operations are performed using numeric datatypes in the view definition, the resulting column will be a floating datatype, which is NUMBER without any precision or scale. The following example uses SALARY (defined NUMBER (8,2)) and COMMISSION_PCT (defined NUMBER (2,2)) in an arithmetic operation. The resulting column value is the NUMBER datatype.

```
CREATE VIEW emp_sal_comm AS
SELECT employee_id, salary,
       salary * NVL(commission_pct,0) commission
FROM   employees;

View created.

SQL> DESCRIBE emp_sal_comm
 Name                      Null?    Type
 ------------------------- -------- ----------
 EMPLOYEE_ID               NOT NULL NUMBER(6)
 SALARY                             NUMBER(8,2)
 COMMISSION                         NUMBER
SQL>
```

The maximum number of columns that can be defined in a view is 1,000, just as for a table.

Using Defined Column Names

You can also specify the column names immediately following the view name to have different column names in the view. Let's create another view using defined column names. This view joins the DEPARTMENTS table to the EMPLOYEES table, uses a function on the HIRE_DATE column, and also derives a new column named COMMISSION_AMT. Notice the ORDER BY clause in the view definition. The derived column COMMISSION_AMT is the NUMBER datatype, so there is no maximum length.

```
CREATE VIEW emp_hire
(employee_id, employee_name, department_name,
 hire_date, commission_amt)
AS SELECT employee_id, first_name || ' ' || last_name,
    department_name, TO_CHAR(hire_date,'DD-MM-YYYY'),
    salary * NVL(commission_pct, .5)
```

```
FROM employees JOIN departments USING (department_id)
ORDER BY first_name || ' ' || last_name;

View created.

SQL> DESC emp_hire
 Name                          Null?    Type
 ----------------------------- -------- ------------
 EMPLOYEE_ID                   NOT NULL NUMBER(6)
 EMPLOYEE_NAME                          VARCHAR2(46)
 DEPARTMENT_NAME               NOT NULL VARCHAR2(30)
 HIRE_DATE                              VARCHAR2(10)
 COMMISSION_AMT                         NUMBER
SQL>
```

If you use an asterisk (*) to select all columns from a table in the query to create a view and you later modify the table to add columns, you should re-create the view to reflect the new columns. When * is used, Oracle expands it to the column list and stores the definition in the database.

Creating Views with Errors

If the CREATE VIEW statement generates an error, the view will not be created. You can create views with errors using the FORCE option (NO FORCE is the default). Normally, if the base tables do not exist, the view will not be created. If, however, you need to create the view with errors, you can do so. The view will be INVALID. Later, you can fix the error, such as creating the underlying table, and then the view can be recompiled. Oracle recompiles invalid views automatically when the view is accessed.

As an example, suppose you try to create a new view named TEST_VIEW on a nonexistent base table named TEST_TABLE:

```
CREATE VIEW test_view AS
SELECT c1, c2 FROM test_table;
SELECT c1, c2 FROM test_table
                   *
ERROR at line 2:
ORA-00942: table or view does not exist
```

Since you did not use the FORCE option, the view was not created. When you use the FORCE option, Oracle creates the view. However, trying to access the view gives an error, because the table TEST_TABLE does not exist yet:

```
CREATE FORCE VIEW test_view AS
SELECT c1, c2 FROM test_table;

Warning: View created with compilation errors.

SELECT * FROM test_view;
SELECT * FROM test_view
              *
ERROR at line 1:
ORA-04063: view "HR.TEST_VIEW" has errors
```

Now, let's create the TEST_TABLE and access the view:

```
CREATE TABLE test_table (
 c1 NUMBER (10),
 c2 VARCHAR2 (20));

Table created.

SQL> SELECT * FROM test_view;

no rows selected
SQL>
```

This time, it works!

The subquery that defines the view cannot contain the FOR UPDATE clause, and the columns should not reference the CURRVAL or NEXTVAL pseudocolumn. These pseudocolumns are discussed later in the chapter in the "Creating and Managing Sequences" section.

Creating Read-Only Views

You can create a view as read-only using the WITH READ ONLY option. Such views can be used only in queries; no DML operations can be performed on such views. Let's create a read-only view:

```
CREATE VIEW all_locations
AS SELECT country_id, country_name, location_id, city
FROM  locations NATURAL JOIN countries
WITH READ ONLY;

View created.
```

Creating Constraints on Views

Oracle 11*g* allows you to create constraints on views. Constraints on views are not enforced—they are *declarative constraints*. To enforce constraints, you must define them on the base tables. When creating constraints on views, you must always include the `DISABLE NOVALIDATE` clause. You can define primary key, unique key, and foreign key constraints on views. The syntax for creating constraints on views is the same as for creating constraints on a table (see Chapter 6).

The following example creates a view with constraints. Line 2 defines a column-level foreign key constraint, line 5 defines a column-level unique constraint, and line 7 defines a view-level foreign key constraint. The column-level constraint is called an *inline* constraint, and the view-level constraint is called an *out-of-line* constraint.

```
SQL> CREATE VIEW emp_details
  2  (employee_no CONSTRAINT fk_employee_no
  3               REFERENCES employees DISABLE NOVALIDATE,
  4   manager_no,
  5   phone_number CONSTRAINT uq_email unique
  6                DISABLE NOVALIDATE,
  7   CONSTRAINT fk_manager_no FOREIGN KEY (manager_no)
  8               REFERENCES employees DISABLE NOVALIDATE)
  9  AS SELECT employee_id, manager_id, phone_number
 10  FROM   employees
 11  WHERE  department_id = 40
SQL> /

View created.
SQL>
```

Modifying Views

To change the definition of the view, use the `CREATE VIEW` statement with the `OR REPLACE` option. The `ALTER VIEW` statement can be used to compile an invalid view or to add and drop constraints. Sometimes views become invalid when their underlying objects change.

Changing a View's Definition

When using the OR REPLACE option, if the view exists it will be replaced with the new definition; otherwise, a new view will be created. When you use the CREATE OR REPLACE option instead of dropping and re-creating the view, the privileges granted on the view are preserved. The dependent stored programs and views become invalid if the column list in the old view definition differs from the new view definition and the dependent object is using the changed/dropped column.

In the ADMIN_EMPLOYEES view defined earlier, you didn't include a space between the first name and last name of the employee. Let's fix that now using the OR REPLACE option:

```
CREATE OR REPLACE VIEW admin_employees AS
 SELECT first_name ||' '|| last_name NAME,
        email, job_id
 FROM   employees
 WHERE  department_id = 10;

View created.
```

Recompiling a View

Views become invalid when the base tables are altered. Oracle automatically recompiles the view when it is accessed, but you can explicitly recompile the view using the ALTER VIEW statement. When the view is recompiled, the objects dependent on the view become invalid.

Let's change the length of a column in the TEST_TABLE table created earlier. The TEST_VIEW view is dependent on this table. You can see the status of the database objects in the USER_OBJECTS view. The following example queries the status of the view, modifies the table, queries the status of the view, compiles the view, and again queries the status of the view:

```
SQL> SELECT last_ddl_time, status FROM user_objects
  2  WHERE  object_name = 'TEST_VIEW';

LAST_DDL_TIME           STATUS
----------------------- -------
25-OCT-2001 11:17:24 AM VALID


SQL> ALTER TABLE test_table MODIFY c2 VARCHAR2 (8);
Table altered.

SQL> SELECT last_ddl_time, status FROM user_objects
  2  WHERE  object_name = 'TEST_VIEW';
```

```
LAST_DDL_TIME           STATUS
----------------------- -------
25-OCT-2001 11:17:24 AM INVALID

SQL> ALTER VIEW test_view compile;
View altered.

SQL> SELECT last_ddl_time, status FROM user_objects
  2  WHERE  object_name = 'TEST_VIEW';

LAST_DDL_TIME           STATUS
----------------------- -------
25-OCT-2001 05:47:46 PM VALID
SQL>
```

The syntax for adding or dropping constraints on a view is similar to that for modifying the constraints on a table, but you use the ALTER VIEW statement instead of the ALTER TABLE statement. The following example adds a primary key constraint on the TEST_VIEW view:

```
ALTER VIEW hr.test_view
ADD CONSTRAINT pk_test_view
PRIMARY KEY (C1) DISABLE NOVALIDATE;

View altered.
```

The next example drops the constraint you just added:

```
ALTER VIEW test_view DROP CONSTRAINT pk_test_view;

View altered.
```

Dropping a View

To drop a view, use the DROP VIEW statement. The view definition is dropped from the dictionary, and the privileges and grants on the view are also dropped. Other views and stored programs that refer to the dropped view become invalid.

```
SQL> DROP VIEW test_view;

View dropped.
SQL>
```

Once a view is dropped, there is no rollback, and the view is not available in the Recycle Bin. So, be sure before dropping the view.

Using Views

You can use a view in most places where a table is used, such as in queries and in DML operations. If certain conditions are met, most single-table views and many join views can be used to insert, update, and delete data from the base table. All operations on views affect the data in the base tables; therefore, they should satisfy any integrity constraints defined on the base tables.

The following are some common uses of views:

To represent a subset of data For security reasons, you may not want certain users to see all the rows of your table. You may create a view on the columns that the users need to access with a WHERE clause to limit the rows and then grant privileges on the view.

To represent a superset of data You can use views to represent information from multiple normalized tables in one unnormalized view.

To hide complex joins Since views are stored queries, you can have complex queries defined as views, where the end user doesn't need to worry about the relationship between tables or know SQL.

To provide more meaningful names for columns If your tables are defined with short and cryptic column names, you may create a view and provide more meaningful column names that the users will understand better.

To minimize application and data-source changes You may develop an application referring to views, and if the data source changes or the data is derived in a different manner, only the view needs to be changed.

Using Views in Queries

You can use views in queries and subqueries. You can use all SQL functions and all the clauses of the SELECT statement when querying against a view, as you would when querying against a table.

When you issue a query against a view, most of the time Oracle merges the query with the query that defines the view and then executes the resulting query as if the query were issued directly against the base tables. This helps you use the indexes, if there are any defined on the table.

Let's query the results of the EMPLOYEE_DETAILS view created earlier:

```
SQL> SELECT * FROM emp_details;

EMPLOYEE_NO MANAGER_NO PHONE_NUMBER
----------- ---------- -------------
        203        101 515.123.7777
```

Let's consider another example using a WHERE clause and a GROUP BY clause. This example finds the total commission paid for each department from the EMP_HIRE view for all commissions greater than $100:

```
SELECT department_name, SUM(commission_amt) comm_amt
FROM   emp_hire
WHERE  commission_amt > 100
GROUP BY department_name;

DEPARTMENT_NAME                  COMM_AMT
------------------------------ ----------
Accounting                          10150
Administration                       2200
Executive                           29000
Finance                             25800
Human Resources                      3250
IT                                  14400
Marketing                            9500
Public Relations                     5000
Purchasing                          12450
Sales                               72640
Shipping                            78200
```

Inserting, Updating, and Deleting Data through Views

You can update, insert, and delete rows through a view, but with some restrictions. You can perform DML statements on a view only if the view definition does not have the following:

- A DISTINCT clause
- A GROUP BY clause
- A START WITH clause
- A CONNECT BY clause
- A ROWNUM clause
- Set operators (UNION, UNION ALL, INTERSECT, or MINUS)
- A subquery in the SELECT clause

All DML operations on the view are performed on the base tables.

Let's create a simple view based on the DEPARTMENTS table. The following view includes all the columns that are part of any constraint in the DEPARTMENTS table, so you can insert a row through the view without violating any constraints:

```
CREATE OR REPLACE VIEW dept_above_250
AS SELECT department_id DID, department_name
```

```
FROM    departments
WHERE   department_id > 250;

View created.

SELECT * FROM dept_above_250;

       DID DEPARTMENT_NAME
---------- -----------------
       260 Recruiting
       270 Payroll
```

Let's insert a new department through the view and verify that the department is added to the DEPARTMENTS table. (The SET NULL * SQL*Plus command displays an asterisk whenever the column value is NULL.)

```
SET NULL *
INSERT INTO dept_above_250
VALUES (199, 'Temporary Dept');

1 row created.

SELECT * FROM departments
WHERE  department_id = 199;

DEPARTMENT_ID DEPARTMENT_NAME      MANAGER_ID LOCATION_ID
------------- -------------------- ---------- -----------
          199 Temporary Dept       *          *
```

Although the view is defined with a WHERE clause to verify DEPARTMENT_ID is greater than 250, Oracle did not enforce this condition when you inserted a new row. If you want the DML statements through the view to conform to the view definition, use the WITH CHECK OPTION clause. The WITH CHECK OPTION clause creates a check constraint on the view to enforce the condition (such constraints will have the constraint type "V" when you query the USER_CONSTRAINTS view).

Let's re-create the DEPT_ABOVE_250 view to include the WITH CHECK OPTION clause. The CONSTRAINT keyword can be followed by a constraint name. If you do not provide a constraint name, Oracle creates a constraint whose name begins with SYS_C, followed by a unique string.

```
CREATE OR REPLACE VIEW dept_above_250
AS SELECT department_id DID, department_name
```

```
FROM   departments
WHERE  department_id > 250
WITH CHECK OPTION;

View created.

INSERT INTO dept_above_250
VALUES (199, 'Temporary Dept');
INSERT INTO dept_above_250
            *
ERROR at line 1:
ORA-01402: view WITH CHECK OPTION where-clause violation

SELECT constraint_name, table_name
FROM   user_constraints
WHERE  constraint_type = 'V';

CONSTRAINT_NAME                TABLE_NAME
------------------------------ ----------------
SYS_C002779                    DEPT_ABOVE_250
```

Let's provide a name for the constraint and query the USER_CONSTRAINTS view again:

```
CREATE OR REPLACE VIEW dept_above_250
AS SELECT department_id DID, department_name
FROM   departments
WHERE  department_id > 250
WITH CHECK OPTION CONSTRAINT check_dept_250;

View created.

SELECT constraint_name, table_name
FROM   user_constraints
WHERE  constraint_type = 'V';

CONSTRAINT_NAME                TABLE_NAME
------------------------------ ---------------
CHECK_DEPT_250                 DEPT_ABOVE_250
SQL>
```

Real World Scenario

Controlling Access Using a View

Say you have an HR application that has a requirement: an employee can see only their own record; all other records must be invisible. You can use a view to control access to personal records.

The EMPLOYEE_INFO table in the HRMS schema holds the personal information of employees. The business requirement is for the employees to be able to view or update their own address information. EMPLOYEE_ID is the primary key of this table.

The SQL variable USER gives the username used to connect to the database. Use this variable to restrict the rows available to the user. The EMPLOYEE_INFO table has a column named LOGIN_ID. The view is defined as follows:

```
CREATE OR REPLACE VIEW employee_address AS
SELECT employee_id, first_name, last_name, middle_initial,
       street, city, zip, home_phone, email
FROM   employee_info
WHERE  login_id = USER
WITH CHECK OPTION;
```

For updating the address, the user is given UPDATE privileges on the view, not on the base table. You add the WITH CHECK OPTION clause so that the user cannot add new records to the base table.

Using Join Views

A *join view* is a view with more than one base table in the top-level FROM clause. An *updatable join view* (or modifiable join view) is a view that can be used to update the base tables through the view. Any INSERT, UPDATE, or DELETE operation on the join view can modify data from only one base table in any single SQL operation.

A table in the join view is *key-preserved* if the primary and unique keys of the table are unique on the view's result set. For example, let's create a view using the base tables COUNTRIES and REGIONS:

```
CREATE OR REPLACE VIEW country_region AS
SELECT a.country_id, a.country_name, a.region_id,
       b.region_name
FROM   countries a, regions b
WHERE  a.region_id = b.region_id;
```

```
View created.

SQL> DESC country_region
 Name                                      Null?    Type
 ----------------------------------------- -------- ------------
 COUNTRY_ID                                NOT NULL CHAR(2)
 COUNTRY_NAME                                       VARCHAR2(40)
 REGION_ID                                          NUMBER
 REGION_NAME                                        VARCHAR2(25)
SQL>
```

In the COUNTRY_REGION view, the COUNTRIES table is key-preserved because it is the primary key in the COUNTRIES table and its uniqueness is kept in the view also. The REGIONS table is not key-preserved because its primary key REGION_ID is duplicated several times for each country.

You can update only a key-preserved table through a view. If the view is defined with the WITH CHECK OPTION clause, you cannot update the columns that join the base tables. For example, if you define the COUNTRY_REGION view with the WITH CHECK OPTION clause, even though the COUNTRY table is key-preserved, you will not be able to update the REGION_ID column.

INSERT statements cannot refer to any columns of the non–key-preserved table. If the view is created with the WITH CHECK OPTION clause, no INSERT operation is permitted on the view.

Let's try a few examples. Updating the REGION_NAME column in the COUNTRY_REGION view produces an error:

```
UPDATE country_region
SET    region_name = 'Testing Update'
WHERE  region_id = 1;
SET    region_name = 'Testing Update'
       *
ERROR at line 2:
ORA-01779: cannot modify a column which maps to a non key-preserved table
```

Updating the REGION_ID column does not cause an error because the column belongs to a key-preserved table:

```
UPDATE country_region
SET    region_id = 1
WHERE  country_id = 'EG';

1 row updated.
```

Let's redefine the COUNTRY_REGION view with the WITH CHECK OPTION clause and try the same UPDATE statement again:

```
CREATE OR REPLACE VIEW country_region AS
SELECT a.country_id, a.country_name, a.region_id,
       b.region_name
FROM   countries a, regions b
WHERE  a.region_id = b.region_id
WITH CHECK OPTION;

View created.

UPDATE country_region
SET    region_id = 1
WHERE  country_id = 'EG';
SET    region_id = 1
       *
ERROR at line 2:
ORA-01733: virtual column not allowed here
```

Viewing Allowable DML Operations

Oracle provides data dictionary views with information about what DML operations are allowed on each column of the view: the USER_UPDATABLE_COLUMNS view has information on columns of the views owned by the user, the ALL_UPDATABLE_COLUMNS view has information on the columns of views to which the user has access, and the DBA_UPDATABLE_COLUMNS view has information on columns of all the views in the database.

Let's query the USER_UPDATABLE_COLUMNS view to see what information is available on the COUNTRY_REGION view:

```
SELECT column_name, updatable, insertable, deletable
FROM   user_updatable_columns
WHERE  owner = 'HR'
AND    table_name = 'COUNTRY_REGION';

COLUMN_NAME                    UPD INS DEL
------------------------------ --- --- ---
COUNTRY_ID                     YES YES YES
COUNTRY_NAME                   YES YES YES
REGION_ID                      YES YES YES
REGION_NAME                    NO  NO  NO
```

You can query information on the views from the data dictionary using USER_VIEWS (or DBA_VIEWS or ALL_VIEWS). This view contains the view definition SQL. The column names of the view can be queried from USER_TAB_COLUMNS.

Using Inline Views

A subquery can appear in the FROM clause of the SELECT statement. This is similar to defining and using a view, which is why it's called an inline view. The subquery in the FROM clause is enclosed in parentheses and may be given an alias name. The columns selected in the subquery can be referenced in the parent query, just as you would select from any normal table or view.

Inline views can be considered temporary views; you don't need to create these views to use them in queries. You access the columns of the inline-view result set in the same way you access the columns of a view in DML statements.

Let's consider an example using the EMPLOYEES table of the sample HR schema. You can use the following query to report the employee names, their salaries, and the average salary in their department. I'll limit the result set to the employees whose names begin with *B*:

```
SELECT first_name, salary, avg_salary
FROM   employees, (SELECT department_id,
       AVG(salary) avg_salary FROM employees e2
       GROUP BY department_id) dept
WHERE  employees.department_id = dept.department_id
AND    first_name like 'B%';

FIRST_NAME                SALARY AVG_SALARY
-------------------- ---------- ----------
Britney                    3900 3475.55556
Bruce                      6000       5760
```

The same query written using the ANSI syntax is as follows:

```
SELECT first_name, salary, avg_salary
FROM   employees
NATURAL JOIN (SELECT department_id,
        AVG(salary) avg_salary FROM employees e2
        GROUP BY department_id) dept
WHERE  first_name like 'B%';

FIRST_NAME                SALARY AVG_SALARY
-------------------- ---------- ----------
Britney                    3900 3475.55556
Bruce                      6000       5760
```

You cannot have an ORDER BY clause in the subquery appearing in a WHERE clause. A FROM clause subquery (inline view) can have an ORDER BY clause.

As another example, suppose you want to find the newest employee in each department. You need to get the MAX(HIRE_DATE) value for all employees in each department and get the name of employee, as follows:

```
SELECT department_name, first_name, last_name,
       hire_date
FROM   employees JOIN departments
       USING (department_id)
JOIN   (SELECT department_id, max(hire_date) hire_date
        FROM   employees
        GROUP BY department_id)
USING  (department_id, hire_date);

DEPARTMENT_NAME   FIRST_NAME LAST_NAME  HIRE_DATE
----------------- ---------- ---------- ---------
Administration    Jennifer   Whalen     17-SEP-87
Marketing         Pat        Fay        17-AUG-97
Purchasing        Karen      Colmenares 10-AUG-99
Human Resources   Susan      Mavris     07-JUN-94
Shipping          Steven     Markle     08-MAR-00
IT                Diana      Lorentz    07-FEB-99
Public Relations  Hermann    Baer       07-JUN-94
Sales             Sundita    Kumar      21-APR-00
Sales             Amit       Banda      21-APR-00
Executive         Lex        De Haan    13-JAN-93
Finance           Luis       Popp       07-DEC-99
Accounting        William    Gietz      07-JUN-94
Accounting        Shelley    Higgins    07-JUN-94
```

The same query written using standard Oracle join syntax looks like this:

```
SELECT d.department_name, e.first_name, e.last_name,
       mhd.hire_date
FROM   employees e, departments d,
       (SELECT department_id, max(hire_date) hire_date
        FROM   employees
        GROUP BY department_id) mhd
WHERE e.department_id = d.department_id
AND   e.department_id = mhd.department_id
AND   e.hire_date     = mhd.hire_date;
```

```
DEPARTMENT_NAME   FIRST_NAME LAST_NAME  HIRE_DATE
----------------- ---------- ---------- ---------
Executive         Lex        De Haan    13-JAN-93
IT                Diana      Lorentz    07-FEB-99
Finance           Luis       Popp       07-DEC-99
Purchasing        Karen      Colmenares 10-AUG-99
Shipping          Steven     Markle     08-MAR-00
Sales             Amit       Banda      21-APR-00
Sales             Sundita    Kumar      21-APR-00
Administration    Jennifer   Whalen     17-SEP-87
Marketing         Pat        Fay        17-AUG-97
Human Resources   Susan      Mavris     07-JUN-94
Public Relations  Hermann    Baer       07-JUN-94
Accounting        Shelley    Higgins    07-JUN-94
Accounting        William    Gietz      07-JUN-94
```

Performing Top-*n* Analysis

Using an inline view, you can write queries to find top-*n* values. This is possible because Oracle allows an ORDER BY clause in the inline view. So, you sort the rows in the inline view and retrieve the top rows using the ROWNUM variable. The ROWNUM variable gives the row number; the row number is assigned only when the query is fetched. For example, here is a query intended to find the top five highest-paid employees:

```
SELECT last_name, salary
FROM   employees
WHERE  rownum <= 5
ORDER BY salary DESC ;

LAST_NAME                     SALARY
------------------------- ----------
King                           24000
Kochhar                        17000
De Haan                        17000
Hunold                          9000
Ernst                           6000
```

Since the ROWNUM is assigned only when each row is returned, the result set is not right. What you got is just five rows from the table sorted by salary. The following query will return the top five highest-paid employees:

```
SELECT * FROM
  (SELECT last_name, salary
   FROM   employees
   ORDER BY salary DESC)
WHERE ROWNUM <= 5;

LAST_NAME                     SALARY
------------------------- ----------
King                           24000
Kochhar                        17000
De Haan                        17000
Russell                        14000
Partners                       13500
```

The Oracle 11*g* Optimizer recognizes the top-*n* analysis queries and hence does not sort all the rows in the subquery.

Creating and Managing Sequences

An Oracle *sequence* is a named sequential-number generator. Sequence numbers are serial numbers incremented with a specific interval. Sequences are often used for artificial keys or to order rows that otherwise have no order. Like constraints (discussed in Chapter 6), sequences exist only in the data dictionary. They do not take up any storage space. Sequences can be configured to increase or decrease without bounds or to repeat (cycle) upon reaching a boundary value.

Creating and Dropping Sequences

Sequences are created with the CREATE SEQUENCE statement. The following statement creates a sequence in the HR schema:

```
CREATE SEQUENCE hr.employee_identity START WITH 2001;
```

You can use the following keywords in the CREATE SEQUENCE statement when creating a sequence:

START WITH Defines the first number that the sequence will generate. The default is MAXVALUE for descending sequences, which is –1, and MINVALUE for ascending sequences, which is 1.

INCREMENT BY Defines the increase or decrease amount for subsequently generated numbers. To specify a decreasing sequence, use a negative INCREMENT BY value. The default is 1.

MINVALUE Defines the lowest number the sequence will generate. This is the bounding value in a decreasing sequence. The default MINVALUE is NOMINVALUE, which evaluates to 1 for an increasing sequence and to -10^{26} for a decreasing sequence.

MAXVALUE Defines the largest number that the sequence will generate. This is the bounding value in the default, increasing sequence. The default MAXVALUE is the NOMAXVALUE, which evaluates to 10^{27} for an increasing sequence and to –1 for a decreasing sequence.

CYCLE Configures the sequence to repeat numbers after reaching the bounding value.

NOCYCLE Configures the sequence to not repeat numbers after reaching the bounding value. This is the default. When you try to generate MAXVALUE+1, an exception will be raised.

CACHE Defines the size of the block of sequence numbers held in memory. The default is 20.

NOCACHE Forces the data dictionary to be updated for each sequence number generated, guaranteeing no gaps in the generated numbers but decreasing the performance of the sequence.

When you create the sequence, the START WITH value must be equal to or greater than MINVALUE. Sequence numbers can be configured so that a set of numbers is fetched from the data dictionary and cached or held in memory for use. Caching the sequence improves its performance because the data dictionary table does not need to be updated for each generated number, only for each set of numbers. Sequences are removed with the DROP SEQUENCE statement:

```
DROP SEQUENCE sequence_name;
```

When the database instance terminates abnormally or the DBA performs SHUTDOWN ABORT on the database instance, the sequence numbers cached are lost. Hence, you could have gaps in the sequence.

Using Sequences

To access the next number in the sequence, you simply select from it, using the pseudocolumn NEXTVAL. To get the last sequence number your session has generated, you select from it using the pseudocolumn CURRVAL. If your session has not yet generated a new sequence number, CURRVAL will be undefined.

The syntax for accessing the next sequence number is as follows:

```
sequence_name.nextval
```

Here is the syntax for accessing the last-used sequence number:

```
sequence_name.currval
```

Sequence Initialization

The sequence is initialized in the session when you select the NEXTVAL from the sequence. One problem that you may encounter using sequences involves selecting CURRVAL from the sequence before initializing it within your session by selecting NEXTVAL from it. Here is an example:

```
CREATE SEQUENCE emp_seq NOMAXVALUE NOCYCLE;

Sequence created.

SELECT emp_seq.currval FROM dual;

ERROR at line 1:
ORA-08002: sequence POLICY_SEQ.CURRVAL is not yet defined
in this session
```

Make sure your code initializes a sequence within your session by selecting its NEXTVAL before you try to reference CURRVAL:

```
SELECT emp_seq.nextval FROM dual;

   NEXTVAL
----------
         1

SELECT emp_seq.currval FROM dual;

   CURRVAL
----------
         1
```

Sequences can be used in the SET clause of the UPDATE statement to assign a value to a column in an existing row. They can be used in the VALUES clause of the INSERT statement also. In Oracle 11g, you can also assign the value of a sequence to a variable. Here is an example using a small PL/SQL block:

```
SQL> VARIABLE v1 NUMBER
SQL> begin
  2   :v1 := emp_seq.nextval;
  3  end;
SQL> /

PL/SQL procedure successfully completed.
```

```
SQL> print v1

        V1
----------
         3

SQL>
```

Missing Sequence Values

Another potential problem in the use of sequences involves "losing" sequence values when a rollback occurs. A sequence's NEXTVAL increments outside any user transactions, so a rollback will not put the selected sequence values back into the sequence. These rolled-back values simply disappear and may create a gap in the use of the sequence numbers. This is not a bad thing—you don't want one session's use of a sequence to block others until it commits. However, you do need to understand how gaps happen. To demonstrate this, suppose you have a table with the old Acme employee identifiers and you need to assign new employee IDs to them using your new EMP_SEQ sequence:

```
SELECT * FROM old_acme_employees;

 EMP_ID ACME_ID          HOLDER_NAME
------- ---------------- -----------
        C23              Joshua
        C24              Elizabeth
        D31              David
        D34              Sara
        A872             Jamie
        A891             Jeff
        A884             Jennie

UPDATE old_acme_employees SET emp_id = emp_seq.nextval;

7 rows updated.

SELECT * FROM old_acme_employees;

    EMP_ID ACME_ID          HOLDER_NAME
---------- ---------------- -----------
         5 C23              Joshua
         6 C24              Elizabeth
```

```
         7 D31              David
         8 D34              Sara
         9 A872             Jamie
        10 A891             Jeff
        11 A884             Jennie
```

Now suppose you encounter an error, such as a rollback segment unable to extend, before you commit these changes, and this error causes the process to roll back. You can simulate the error and rollback by simply executing a rollback before the update is committed:

```
ROLLBACK;
```

After you fix the problem and run the update again, you find that there are "missing" sequence values (values 5, 6, 7, and so on):

```
UPDATE old_acme_employees SET emp_id = emp_seq.nextval;

7 rows updated.

SELECT * FROM old_acme_employees;

    EMP_ID ACME_ID          HOLDER_NAME
---------- ---------------- ------------
        12 C23              Joshua
        13 C24              Elizabeth
        14 D31              David
        15 D34              Sara
        16 A872             Jamie
        17 A891             Jeff
        18 A884             Jennie

COMMIT;
```

Maximum and Minimum Values

Another potential pitfall occurs when you reach MAXVALUE on an ascending sequence (or MINVALUE on a descending sequence). If the sequence is set to NOCYCLE, Oracle will raise an exception if you try to select NEXTVAL after the sequence reaches MAXVALUE:

```
CREATE SEQUENCE emp_seq MAXVALUE 10 NOCYCLE;

Sequence created.
```

```
SELECT  emp_seq.nextval
FROM hr.employees;

ERROR:
ORA-08004: sequence EMP_SEQ.NEXTVAL exceeds MAXVALUE
and cannot be instantiated
```

Altering Sequences

A common problem with sequences is how to go about altering them to change the NEXTVAL. You cannot simply alter the sequence and set the NEXTVAL. If you use a sequence to generate keys in your table and reload the development table from production, your sequence may be out of sync with the table. You may get primary-key violations when you run the application in development and it tries to insert key values that already exist.

You cannot directly alter the sequence and change its NEXTVAL. Instead, you can take one of the following approaches:

- Drop and re-create it (invalidating all dependent objects and losing the grants).
- Select NEXTVAL from it enough times to bring the sequence up to a desired value.
- Alter the sequence by changing the INCREMENT BY value to a large number, select NEXTVAL from the sequence to make it increment by the large number, and then alter the INCREMENT BY value back down to the original small value.

The following session log shows an example of the third technique. Start with the sequence SALE_SEQ that has a LAST_NUMBER value of 441:

```
SELECT sequence_name, cache_size, last_number
FROM user_sequences;

SEQUENCE_NAME  CACHE_SIZE LAST_NUMBER
-------------- ---------- -----------
SALE_SEQ               20         441
```

The SALES table needs this sequence to be larger than 111555888. So, you alter the sequence's INCREMENT BY value, increment it with a SELECT of its NEXTVAL, and then alter the INCREMENT BY value back to 1. Now the program won't try to generate duplicate keys and will work fine in development:

```
SELECT sequence_name, cache_size, last_number
FROM user_sequences;

SEQUENCE_NAME  CACHE_SIZE LAST_NUMBER
-------------- ---------- -----------
SALE_SEQ               20         441
```

```
ALTER SEQUENCE sale_seq INCREMENT BY 111555888;

Sequence altered.

SELECT sale_seq.nextval FROM dual;

   NEXTVAL
----------
 111556309

ALTER SEQUENCE sale_seq INCREMENT BY 1;

Sequence altered.

SELECT sequence_name, cache_size, last_number
FROM user_sequences;

SEQUENCE_NAME  CACHE_SIZE LAST_NUMBER
-------------- ---------- -----------
SALE_SEQ               20   111556310
```

The sequence can be dropped using the `DROP SEQUENCE` statement. Once dropped, the sequence definition is permanently deleted from the data dictionary. The following example shows dropping `sale_seq` from the database:

```
DROP SEQUENCE hr.sale_seq;
```

Creating and Managing Synonyms

A *synonym* is an alias for another database object. A *public synonym* is available to all users, while a *private synonym* is available only to the owner or to the accounts to whom that owner grants privileges. Both of these are discussed more fully later in this section.

A synonym can point to a table, view, sequence, procedure, function, or package in the local database or, via a database link, to an object in another database. Synonyms are frequently used to simplify SQL by giving a universal name to a local or remote object. Synonyms also can be used to give different or multiple names to individual objects. Unlike views or stored SQL, synonyms don't become invalid if the objects they point to are dropped. Likewise, you can create a synonym that points to an object that does not exist or for which the owner does not have privileges.

For example, the user `SCOTT` owns a table named `EMP`. All users log in to the database under their own username and so must reference the table with the owner as `SCOTT.EMP`.

But when you create a public synonym EMP for SCOTT.EMP, then anyone who has privileges on the table can simply reference it in their SQL (or PL/SQL) as EMP, without needing to specify the owner. When the statement is parsed, Oracle will resolve the name EMP via the synonym to SCOTT.EMP.

Creating and Dropping Synonyms

You can create private synonyms with the CREATE SYNONYM statement. Public synonyms are created using the CREATE PUBLIC SYNONYM statement. Public synonyms are owned by the PUBLIC user. PUBLIC is not a regular database user but is an internal user-like structure, similar to a group. Every user in the database is a member of PUBLIC.

The syntax for creating a private synonym is as follows:

```
CREATE SYNONYM [schema.]synonym_name
FOR [schema.]object[@db_link];
```

The syntax for creating a public synonym is as follows:

```
CREATE PUBLIC SYNONYM synonym name
FOR [schema.]object[@db_link];
```

To create a public synonym called EMPLOYEES for the table HR.EMPLOYEES, execute the following statement:

```
CREATE PUBLIC SYNONYM employees FOR hr.employees;
```

Alternatively, to create a private synonym called EMPLOYEES for the table HR.EMPLOYEES, you simply remove the keyword PUBLIC, as in the following statement. The synonym will be created in the user's schema. It is called private because the synonym is available only to that user. Let's run the following SQL as the SCOTT user:

```
CREATE SYNONYM employees FOR hr.employees;
```

To remove a synonym, use the DROP SYNONYM statement. For a public synonym, you need to make sure you include the keyword PUBLIC, as in this example:

```
DROP PUBLIC SYNONYM employees;
```

To drop a private synonym, issue the DROP SYNONYM statement without the PUBLIC keyword:

```
DROP SYNONYM employees;
DROP SYNONYM scott.employees;
```

Public Synonyms

Public synonyms are used to identify objects such as tables, views, materialized views, sequences, Java classes, procedures, functions, and packages. The data dictionary views are good examples of public synonyms. These synonyms are created when you run catalog.sql at database-creation time. When you write SQL code that references the dictionary view ALL_TABLES, you do not need to select from SYS.ALL_TABLES; you can simply select from ALL_TABLES. Your code can use the fully qualified SYS.ALL_TABLES or the unqualified ALL_TABLES and resolve to the same view, owned by user SYS. When you reference SYS.ALL_TABLES, you explicitly denote the object owned by user SYS. When you reference ALL_TABLES, you actually denote the public synonym ALL_TABLES, which then resolves to SYS.ALL_TABLES. Sound confusing? Let's look at some examples to help clarify this concept.

Suppose the DBA creates a public synonym EMPLOYEES for the HR table EMPLOYEES:

```
CREATE PUBLIC SYNONYM employees FOR hr.employees;
```

Now the user SCOTT, who does not own an EMPLOYEES table but has SELECT privileges on the HR.EMPLOYEES table, can reference that table without including the schema owner (HR):

```
SELECT COUNT(*) FROM employees;

  COUNT(*)
----------
       107
```

As another example, suppose you want to create a public synonym NJ_EMPLOYEES for the HR.EMPLOYEES table in the New_Jersey database (using the database link New_Jersey). To create this synonym, execute the following statement:

```
CREATE PUBLIC SYNONYM nj_employees for hr.employees@new_jersey;
```

When the object referenced by the synonym is dropped, the synonym will remain in the data dictionary. Its status will be changed from VALID to INVALID. When a synonym is dropped, all objects that reference the synonym will become INVALID.

Private Synonyms

Private synonyms can be created for objects that you own or objects that are owned by other users. You can even create a private synonym for an object in another database by incorporating a database link.

Private synonyms can be useful when a table is renamed and both the old and new names are needed. The synonym can be either the old or new name, with both the old and new names referencing the same object.

Private synonyms are also useful in a development environment. A developer can own a modified local copy of a table, create a private synonym that points to this local table, and test code and table changes without affecting everyone else. For example, a developer named Derek runs the following statements to set up a private version of the HR.EMPLOYEES table so he can test some new functionality without affecting anyone else using the HR.EMPLOYEES table:

```
CREATE TABLE my_employees AS SELECT * FROM hr.employees;
ALTER TABLE my_employees ADD pager_nbr VARCHAR2(10);
CREATE SYNONYM employees FOR my_employees;
```

Now Derek can test changes to his program that will use the new PAGER_NBR column. The code in the program will reference the table as EMPLOYEES, but Derek's private synonym will redirect Derek's access to the MY_EMPLOYEES table. When the code is tested and then promoted, the code won't need to change, but the reference to EMPLOYEES will resolve via the public synonym to the HR.EMPLOYEES table.

Use of a private synonym is not restricted to the owner of that synonym. If another user has privileges on the underlying object, she can reference the private synonym as if it were an object itself. For example, the user HR grants SELECT privileges on the EMPLOYEES table to both ALICE and CHACKO:

```
GRANT SELECT ON employees TO alice, chacko;
```

Then user CHACKO creates a private synonym to alias this HR-owned object:

```
CREATE SYNONYM emp_tbl FOR hr.employees;
```

User ALICE can now reference CHACKO's private synonym:

```
SELECT COUNT(*) FROM chacko.empl_tbl;

  COUNT(*)
----------
       107
```

This redirection can be a useful technique to change the objects that SQL code references, without changing the code itself. At the same time, this kind of redirection can add layers of obfuscation to code. Exercise care in the use of private synonyms.

Resolving Object References

Assume you have a table and a public synonym with the same name. When you select from this object name, is Oracle going to use the table referenced in the public synonym, or is it going to get the data from the table owned by the user? The key to avoiding confusion is to know the order that Oracle follows when trying to resolve object references. When your code references an unqualified table, view, procedure, function, or package, Oracle will look in three places for the referenced object, in this order:

1. An object owned by the current user
2. A private synonym owned by the current user
3. A public synonym

Creating Database Links

An Oracle Database link is an object that gives you visibility into another database. Unlike other objects, a database link cannot be used by itself. Instead, it acts as a modifier for a table or view reference in a remote database. The syntax for creating a database link is as follows:

```
CREATE [SHARED] [PUBLIC] DATABASE LINK link_name
[CONNECT TO username IDENTIFIED BY password] USING 'tns_name';
```

Synonyms can be used to mask the location of the table or view. The source data can reside in a totally different database. Data from another database is accessed using a database link.

Like a synonym, the keyword PUBLIC makes the database link available to all users in the database. When the CONNECT TO clause is used, it specifies the username and password that will be used to establish a session in the remote database. This password is stored in the data dictionary in an unencrypted form, which is visible only in the data dictionary view USER_DB_LINKS or directly in the SYS.LINK$ table. By default, only user SYS has SELECT privileges on SYS.LINK$. The tns_name parameter specifies the service name for the remote database. The keyword SHARED tells Oracle that all users of a public database link should share a single network connection to the remote database.

To create a public database link called NEW_JERSEY that connects as the HOME_OFFICE user with the password SECRET in the NJ database, execute the following:

```
CREATE PUBLIC DATABASE LINK new_jersey
 CONNECT TO home_office IDENTIFIED BY secret USING 'NJ';
```

If you don't want everyone to share the same username in the remote database, create the database link without the CONNECT TO clause, like this:

```
CREATE PUBLIC DATABASE LINK new_jersey USING 'NJ';
```

This will tell Oracle that each user should connect to the NJ database via their own username and password. Each user that references the database link must then have an account in both the local and remote databases.

Unlike a private synonym, a private database link really is private and is not available to other users. So if user SYSTEM created a private database link to the NJ database that specifically connected to user SYSTEM in the NJ database, the DBA would not need to worry about non-DBA user BERNICE accessing the NJ database with DBA privileges. She could not use SYSTEM's private database link.

Creating and Managing Indexes

Indexes are data structures that can offer improved performance in obtaining specific rows over the default full-table scan. Indexes do not always improve performance, however. You may create many indexes on a table, as long as the combination of columns differs. You may also use the same column in many indexes as long as the combination of columns differs. In the following sections, I will review the indexing technologies covered on the certification exam: B-tree and bitmap. I'll also cover when and how indexes can improve performance.

You can create and drop indexes without affecting the base data in the table—indexes and table data are independent. Oracle maintains the indexes automatically when new rows are added to the table or existing rows are updated or deleted.

You can create indexes using a single column from the table (simple index), or you can use multiple columns from the table to create a concatenated or *composite index*.

How Indexes Work

Indexes are used to access data more quickly than reading the whole table, and they reduce disk I/O considerably when the queries use the available indexes. Oracle retrieves rows from a table in only one of two ways:

- By ROWID
- By full-table scan

Both B-tree and bitmap indexes map column data to ROWIDs for the columns of interest, but they do so in different ways. When one or more indexes are accessed, Oracle will use the known column values to find the corresponding ROWIDs. The rows can then be retrieved by ROWID.

Indexes may improve the performance of SELECT, UPDATE, and DELETE operations. You can use an index if a subset of the indexed columns appear in the SELECT or WHERE clause. Additionally, if all the columns needed to satisfy a query appear in an index, Oracle can access only the index and not the table. As an example, consider the HR.EMPLOYEES table, which has an index on the columns (LAST_NAME and FIRST_NAME). If you run the following query to get a count of the employees named Taylor, Oracle needs to access only the index, not the table, because all the necessary columns are in the index:

```
SELECT COUNT(*)
FROM hr.employees
WHERE last_name = 'Taylor';
```

Although indexes can improve the performance of data retrieval, they degrade performance for data changes (DML). This is because the indexes must be updated in addition to the table.

Using B-Tree Indexes

B-tree indexes are the most common index type, as well as the default. The B-tree indexes include index column values and the ROWID of the row. The ROWID uniquely identifies a row in the table.

B-tree indexes provide the best performance on *high-cardinality* columns, which are columns that have many distinct values. For example, in the HR.EMPLOYEES table, the columns LAST_NAME and PHONE_NUMBER are high-cardinality columns. JOB_ID is a low-cardinality column.

B-tree indexes offer an efficient method to retrieve a small number of interesting rows. However, if more than about 10 percent of the table must be examined, a full-table scan may be the preferred method, depending on the data. You can create the following types of B-tree indexes:

Nonunique This is the default B-tree index; the column values are not unique.

Unique Create this type of B-tree index by specifying the UNIQUE keyword in the CREATE INDEX statement. In unique indexes, each column value entry is unique. Oracle guarantees that the combination of all index column values in the composite index is unique. Oracle returns an error if you try to insert two rows with the same index column values.

Oracle does not include the rows with all NULL values in the indexed columns when storing a B-tree index. Bitmap indexes store NULL values.

The CREATE INDEX statement creates a nonunique B-tree index on the columns specified. You must specify a name for the index, and the table name on which the index should be built. For example, to create an index on the ORDER_DATE column of the ORDERS table, specify the following SQL:

```
CREATE INDEX orders_ind1
ON orders (order_date);
```

To create a unique index, you must specify the keyword UNIQUE immediately after the CREATE. Here's an example:

```
CREATE UNIQUE INDEX orders_ind2
ON oe.orders (order_num);
```

You can create an index with multiple columns. Such an index is called a *composite* index. Specify the column names separated by comma. The following SQL creates a nonunique composite index on the OE.ORDERS table:

```
CREATE INDEX oe.order_ind4 ON oe.orders
  (customer_id, sales_rep_id);
```

Using Bitmap Indexes

Bitmap indexes are primarily used for decision-support systems or static data, because they do not support row-level locking. Bitmap indexes can be *simple* (one column) or *concatenated* (multiple columns), but in practice, bitmap indexes are almost always simple.

Bitmap indexes are best used for low- to medium-cardinality columns where multiple bitmap indexes can be combined with AND and OR conditions. Each key value has a bitmap, which contains a TRUE, FALSE, or NULL value for every row in the table. The bitmap index is constructed by storing the bitmaps in the leaf nodes of a B-tree structure. The B-tree structure makes it easy to find the bitmaps of interest quickly. Additionally, the bitmaps are stored in a compressed format, so they take up significantly less disk space than regular B-tree indexes.

To create a bitmap index, you must specify the keyword BITMAP immediately after CREATE. Bitmap indexes cannot be unique. The following SQL creates a bitmap index named ORDERS_IND3 on the ORDERS table using the STATUS column:

```
CREATE BITMAP INDEX orders_ind3
ON oe.orders (status);
```

Dropping Indexes

You can drop an index using the DROP INDEX statement. Use this statement to drop unique, nonunique, or bitmap indexes. Oracle frees up all the space used by the index when the index is dropped. When a table is dropped, the indexes built on the table are automatically dropped. The following SQL drops the ORDERS_IND3 index:

```
DROP INDEX oe.orders_ind3;
```

You cannot drop indexes used to enforce uniqueness or the primary key of the table. Such indexes can be dropped only after disabling the primary or unique key.

How to Find Out Whether the Index Is Being Used by the Optimizer

Oracle provides multiple ways to see how a query is being executed—the execution plan decided by the Oracle Optimizer. For this demonstration, you will use the tracing features of SQL*Plus.

The SET statement in SQL*Plus has an option to turn on tracing. The SET AUTOTRACE statement is used to turn on or off tracing. SET AUTOTRACE ON will show the query results, the execution plan, and the statistics associated with the execution. Since you are interested only in the execution plan here to verify index usage, you are interested in the result of the query. Hence, you can use SET AUTOTRACE TRACEONLY.

First, let's examine the columns and indexes on the OE.INVENTORIES table. You can query the DBA_INDEXES dictionary view to see the indexes on the table. The UNIQUENESS column tells whether the index is unique. The INDEX_TYPE column indicates the type of index—NORMAL is a B-tree index. For bitmap indexes, you will see BITMAP in this column.

```
SQL> DESCRIBE oe.inventories
 Name                                       Null?    Type
 ----------------------------------------- -------- ------------
 PRODUCT_ID                                 NOT NULL NUMBER(6)
 WAREHOUSE_ID                               NOT NULL NUMBER(3)
 QUANTITY_ON_HAND                           NOT NULL NUMBER(8)

SQL> SELECT index_name, uniqueness, index_type
  2  FROM dba_indexes
  3  WHERE table_owner = 'OE'
  4  AND table_name = 'INVENTORIES'
SQL> /

INDEX_NAME           UNIQUENES INDEX_TYPE
-------------------- --------- ------------------
INVENTORY_IX         NONUNIQUE NORMAL
INV_PRODUCT_IX       NONUNIQUE NORMAL

SQL>
```

You have two indexes on the table. You can query the DBA_IND_COLUMNS dictionary view to get the index name and index columns:

```
SQL> SELECT index_name, column_name, column_position
  2  FROM dba_ind_columns
  3  WHERE table_name = 'INVENTORIES'
  4  AND table_owner = 'OE'
  5  ORDER BY index_name, column_position
SQL> /

INDEX_NAME           COLUMN_NAME          COLUMN_POSITION
-------------------- -------------------- ---------------
INVENTORY_IX         WAREHOUSE_ID                       1
INVENTORY_IX         PRODUCT_ID                         2
INV_PRODUCT_IX       PRODUCT_ID                         1

SQL>
```

INVENTORY_IX is a composite index with two columns: WAREHOUSE_ID and PRODUCT_ID. WAREHOUSE_ID is the leading column in this index (position 1). INV_PRODUCT_IX is an index on the PRODUCT_ID column. The third column in the table, QUANTITY_ON_HAND, does not have any index.

There is one more piece of information you need to know before running the queries. Let's find out whether there is a primary key constraint defined on this table and which index is used to enforce the primary key. From the DESCRIBE you did earlier, you know that all the columns have a NOT NULL constraint defined. You can query the DBA_CONSTRAINTS dictionary view, as in the following SQL:

```
SQL> SELECT constraint_name, index_name
  2  FROM dba_constraints
  3  WHERE table_name = 'INVENTORIES'
  4  AND owner = 'OE'
  5  AND constraint_type = 'P';

CONSTRAINT_NAME        INDEX_NAME
---------------------- ----------------
INVENTORY_PK           INVENTORY_IX

SQL>
```

Let's run a few SQL statements against the OE.INVENTORIES table and learn when indexes are used:

```
SQL> SET AUTOTRACE TRACEONLY
SQL> SELECT COUNT(*) FROM oe.inventories;

Execution Plan
------------------------------------------------------
Plan hash value: 2210865566

------------------------------------------------------
| Id  | Operation             | Name          | Rows  |
------------------------------------------------------
|   0 | SELECT STATEMENT      |               |     1 |
|   1 |  SORT AGGREGATE       |               |     1 |
|   2 |   INDEX FAST FULL SCAN| INVENTORY_IX  |  1112 |
------------------------------------------------------
```

Oracle used the INVENTORY_IX index to get the result. You can see here that Oracle did not read the table to get the result; only the index is read. Let's look at another SQL statement:

```
SQL> SELECT * FROM oe.inventories
  2  WHERE product_id = 12345;
```

```
Execution Plan
----------------------------------------------------------
Plan hash value: 751505330

----------------------------------------------------------
| Id  | Operation                    | Name            |
----------------------------------------------------------
|   0 | SELECT STATEMENT             |                 |
|   1 |  TABLE ACCESS BY INDEX ROWID| INVENTORIES     |
|*  2 |   INDEX RANGE SCAN           | INV_PRODUCT_IX |
----------------------------------------------------------
```

Since PRODUCT_ID is in the WHERE clause, Oracle used the index on the PRODUCT_ID column. If you change the columns in the SELECT clause and include only the columns that are in the INVENTORY_IX index, Oracle will not read the table, as in the following example:

```
SQL> SELECT warehouse_id FROM oe.inventories
  2  WHERE product_id = 12345;

Execution Plan
--------------------------------------------------
Plan hash value: 253941387

--------------------------------------------------
| Id  | Operation             | Name          |
--------------------------------------------------
|   0 | SELECT STATEMENT      |               |
|*  1 |  INDEX FAST FULL SCAN| INVENTORY_IX |
--------------------------------------------------
```

What if you did not have the single column index on the PRODUCT_ID column? Oracle 11*g* provides option to hide the index from the Optimizer using the INVISIBLE clause of the ALTER INDEX statement (this was not discussed in the main section of the chapter because it is not one of the test objectives). Let's try the same SQL and watch how the Optimizer behaves:

```
SQL> alter index oe.inv_product_ix invisible;

Index altered.

SQL> SELECT * FROM oe.inventories
  2  WHERE product_id = 12345;
```

```
Execution Plan
----------------------------------------
Plan hash value: 3778774871

----------------------------------------
| Id  | Operation         | Name        |
----------------------------------------
|   0 | SELECT STATEMENT  |             |
|*  1 |  TABLE ACCESS FULL| INVENTORIES |
----------------------------------------

SQL> SELECT warehouse_id FROM oe.inventories
  2  WHERE product_id = 12345;

Execution Plan
--------------------------------------------
Plan hash value: 253941387

--------------------------------------------
| Id  | Operation            | Name         |
--------------------------------------------
|   0 | SELECT STATEMENT     |              |
|*  1 |  INDEX FAST FULL SCAN| INVENTORY_IX |
--------------------------------------------
```

Though PRODUCT_ID is part of the INVENTORY_IX index, Oracle did not use the index in the first SQL. It is doing a full-table scan. Optimizer compared the cost of accessing the index and table vs. accessing the table alone and decided to go with full-table scan, whereas when you included only the columns part of the index in the SELECT clause, Oracle uses the index.

This chapter completes the Oracle Database 11*g*: SQL Fundamentals I OCP certification exam materials. Chapters 8 through 17 will cover the Oracle Database 11*g*: Administration I test objectives. Good luck with your SQL certification exam. You are halfway through obtaining the prestigious Oracle 11*g* OCA certification.

Summary

In this chapter, you learned about four types of Oracle Database objects: views, sequences, synonyms, and indexes.

A view is a tailored representation of data from one or more tables or views. The view is a stored query. Views can be used to present a different perspective of data, to limit the data access, or to hide a complex query. Views can be used as you would use tables in queries. You can update, delete, and insert into the base tables through the view (with restrictions), but the operation can affect only one table at a time if there is more than one table in the view definition.

To change the definition of the view, you must re-create the view using the `CREATE OR REPLACE` statement. To recompile a view or add or drop constraints, use the `ALTER VIEW` statement. An inline view is a query that can be used instead of a table or view in the `FROM` clause of a query. By using the `ORDER BY` clause in views (and inline views), you can perform top-*n* analysis.

Sequences are number generators, and you can use them with the `NEXTVAL` and `CURRVAL` keywords. Sequences can be used in queries, or you can directly assign a sequence value to a variable. The sequence is created using a `CREATE SEQUENCE` statement. The next value of the sequence cannot be altered, but its increment value can be altered.

Oracle synonyms are a mechanism to alias other objects, either locally or in another database accessed through database links. Synonyms can be globally available (public) or restricted to limited users (private). Synonyms are widely used in Oracle Databases to ease data access so that the user does not have to know which schema or which database the data is coming from.

Indexes are used to get to the table row quickly. The two main types of Oracle indexes are B-tree and bitmap indexes. B-tree indexes are suitable for high-cardinality columns, whereas bitmap indexes are suitable for low-cardinality columns with mostly static data. B-tree indexes are the default and are widely used. Bitmap indexes are used in data warehouse environments.

This chapter completes the lessons for the OCA certification exam Oracle 11*g*: SQL Fundamentals I. I hope you have learned a lot from these chapters and have tried the review questions in each chapter. Do not forget to try the practice tests on the CD before taking the test. Good luck!

You will start learning the materials relevant to Oracle 11*g*: Administration I certification exam in the next chapter.

Exam Essentials

Understand how join views work. Know the restrictions on the columns that can be updated in a join view.

Understand how constraints are used with views. Understand the type of constraints that can be defined on a table.

Understand how inline views are used. Inline views are subqueries used in the `FROM` clause. These subqueries can have an `ORDER BY` clause.

Know how to change the definition of a view. The `CREATE OR REPLACE VIEW` statement is used to change the definition of the view. The `ALTER VIEW` statement is used to recompile a view or to manage constraints on a view.

Know the precise syntax for obtaining sequence values. You should understand how to use *sequence_name*.NEXTVAL and *sequence_name*.CURRVAL to obtain the next and most recently generated number from a sequence.

Understand when indexes degrade performance. Know that indexes degrade the performance of DML operations (`INSERT`, `UPDATE`, and `DELETE`).

Know when a bitmap index is more appropriate than a B-tree index. Bitmap indexes work best on low- to medium-cardinality columns where row-level locking is not needed. In contrast, B-tree indexes work best on high- to medium-cardinality columns and do support row-level locking.

Know how Oracle will resolve table references. Oracle will first search for a table or view that matches the referenced name. If no table or view is found, private synonyms are then examined. Finally, public synonyms are examined. If no matching name is found, Oracle will raise an exception.

Review Questions

1. How do you remove the view USA_STATES from the schema?
   - **A.** ALTER VIEW USA_STATES REMOVE;
   - **B.** DROP VIEW USA_STATES;
   - **C.** DROP VIEW USA_STATES CASCADE;
   - **D.** DROP USA_STATES;

2. In a join view, on how many base tables can you perform a DML operation (UPDATE/INSERT/DELETE) in a single step?
   - **A.** One
   - **B.** The number of base tables in the view definition
   - **C.** The number of base tables minus one
   - **D.** None

3. The following code is used to define a view. The EMP table does not have a primary key or any other constraints.

```
CREATE VIEW MYVIEW AS
SELECT DISTINCT ENAME, SALARY
FROM   EMP
WHERE  DEPT_ID = 10;
```

   Which operation is allowed on the view?
   - **A.** SELECT, INSERT, UPDATE, DELETE
   - **B.** SELECT, UPDATE
   - **C.** SELECT, INSERT, DELETE
   - **D.** SELECT
   - **E.** SELECT, UPDATE, DELETE

4. Which statements are used to modify a view definition? (Choose all that apply.)
   - **A.** ALTER VIEW
   - **B.** CREATE OR REPLACE VIEW
   - **C.** REPLACE VIEW
   - **D.** CREATE FORCE VIEW
   - **E.** CREATE OR REPLACE FORCE VIEW

5. You create a view based on the EMPLOYEES table using the following SQL.

```
CREATE VIEW MYVIEW AS SELECT * FROM EMPLOYEES;
```

You modify the table to add a column named EMP_SSN. What do you need to do to have this new column appear in the view?

A. Nothing. Since the view definition is selecting all columns, the new column will appear in the view automatically.

B. Recompile the view using ALTER VIEW MYVIEW RECOMPILE.

C. Re-create the view using CREATE OR REPLACE VIEW.

D. Add the column to the view using ALTER VIEW MYVIEW ADD EMP_SSN.

6. Which is a valid status of a constraint created on a view?

A. DISABLE VALIDATE

B. DISABLE NOVALIDATE

C. ENABLE NOVALIDATE

D. All of the above

7. The SALARY column of the EMPLOYEE table is defined as NUMBER(8,2), and the COMMISSION_PCT column is defined as NUMBER(2,2). A view is created with the following code:

```
CREATE VIEW EMP_COMM AS
SELECT LAST_NAME,
SALARY * NVL(COMMISSION_PCT,0) Commission
FROM    EMPLOYEES;
```

What is the datatype of the COMMISSION column in the view?

A. NUMBER (8,2)

B. NUMBER (10,2)

C. NUMBER

D. FLOAT

8. Which clause in the SELECT statement is not supported in a view definition subquery?

A. GROUP BY

B. HAVING

C. CUBE

D. FOR UPDATE OF

E. ORDER BY

9. The EMPLOYEE table has the following columns:

```
EMP_ID      NUMBER (4)
EMP_NAME    VARCHAR2 (30)
SALARY      NUMBER (6,2)
DEPT_ID     VARCHAR2 (2)
```

Which query will show the top five highest-paid employees?

A.
```
SELECT * FROM
(SELECT EMP_NAME, SALARY
 FROM   EMPLOYEE
 ORDER BY SALARY ASC)
WHERE ROWNUM <= 5;
```

B.
```
SELECT EMP_NAME, SALARY FROM
(SELECT *
 FROM   EMPLOYEE
 ORDER BY SALARY DESC)
WHERE ROWNUM < 5;
```

C.
```
SELECT * FROM
(SELECT EMP_NAME, SALARY
 FROM   EMPLOYEE
 ORDER BY SALARY DESC)
WHERE ROWNUM <= 5;
```

D.
```
SELECT EMP_NAME, SALARY
(SELECT *
 FROM   EMPLOYEE
 ORDER BY SALARY DESC)
WHERE ROWNUM = 5;
```

10. The EMPLOYEE table has the following columns:

```
EMP_ID      NUMBER (4) PRIMARY KEY
EMP_NAME    VARCHAR2 (30)
SALARY      NUMBER (6,2)
DEPT_ID     VARCHAR2 (2)
```

A view is defined using the following SQL:

```
CREATE VIEW EMP_IN_DEPT10 AS
SELECT * FROM EMPLOYEE
WHERE  DEPT_ID = 'HR';
```

Which INSERT statement will succeed through the view?

A. `INSERT INTO EMP_IN_DEPT10 VALUES (1000, 'JOHN',1500,'HR');`

B. `INSERT INTO EMP_IN_DEPT10 VALUES (1001, NULL,1700,'AM');`

C. `INSERT INTO EMP_IN_DEPT10 VALUES (1002, 'BILL',2500,'AC');`

D. All of the above

11. To be able to modify a join view, the view definition should not contain which of the following in the top-level query? (Choose all that apply.)

A. A DISTINCT operator

B. An ORDER BY clause

C. Aggregate functions such as SUM, AVG, and COUNT

D. A WHERE clause

E. A GROUP BY clause

F. A ROWNUM pseudocolumn

12. Which statement will create a sequence that starts with 0 and gets smaller one whole number at a time?

A. `create sequence desc_seq start with 0 increment by -1 maxvalue 1;`

B. `create sequence desc_seq increment by -1;`

C. `create sequence desc_seq start with 0 increment by -1;`

D. Sequences can only increase.

13. Which statement is most correct in describing what happens to a synonym when the underlying object is dropped?

A. The synonym's status is changed to INVALID.

B. You can't drop the underlying object if a synonym exists unless the CASCADE clause is used in the DROP statement.

C. The synonym is automatically dropped with the underlying object.

D. Nothing happens to the synonym.

14. There is a public synonym named PLAN_TABLE for SYSTEM.PLAN_TABLE. Which of the following statements will remove this public synonym from the database?

    A. `drop table system.plan_table;`

    B. `drop synonym plan_table;`

    C. `drop table system.plan_table cascade;`

    D. `drop public synonym plan_table;`

15. A developer reports that she is receiving the following error:

```
SELECT key_seq.currval FROM dual;

ERROR at line 1:
ORA-08002: sequence KEY_SEQ.CURRVAL is not yet defined
```

    Which of the following statements does the developer need to run to fix this condition?

    A. `create sequence key_seq;`

    B. `create synonym key_seq;`

    C. `select key_seq.nextval from dual;`

    D. `grant create sequence to public;`

16. Bitmapped indexes are best suited to which type of environment?

    A. High-cardinality columns

    B. Online transaction processing (OLTP) applications

    C. Full-table scan access

    D. Low- to medium-cardinality columns

17. Which clauses in a SELECT statement can an index be used for? (Choose all that apply.)

    A. SELECT

    B. FROM

    C. WHERE

    D. HAVING

18. You need to generate artificial keys for each row inserted into the PRODUCTS table. You want the first row to use a sequence value of 1000, and you want to make sure that no sequence value is skipped. Which of the following statements will meet these requirements?

    A.
    ```
    CREATE SEQUENCE product_key2
    START WITH 1000
    INCREMENT BY 1
    NOCACHE;
    ```

    B.
    ```
    CREATE SEQUENCE product_key2
    START WITH 1000
    NOCACHE;
    ```

    C.
    ```
    CREATE SEQUENCE product_key2
    START WITH 1000
    NEXTVAL 1
    NOCACHE;
    ```

    D. Options A and B meet the requirements.

    E. None of the above statements meet all the requirements.

19. Which statement will display the last number generated from the EMP_SEQ sequence?

    A. `select emp_seq.curr_val from dual;`

    B. `select emp_seq.currval from dual;`

    C. `select emp_seq.lastval from dual;`

    D. `select last_number from all_sequences where sequence_name ='EMP_SEQ';`

    E. You cannot get the last sequence number generated.

20. Which statement will create a sequence that will rotate through 100 values in a round-robin manner?

    A. `create sequence roundrobin cycle maxvalue 100;`

    B. `create sequence roundrobin cycle to 100;`

    C. `create sequence max_value 100 roundrobin cycle;`

    D. `create rotating sequence roundrobin min 1 max 100;`

Answers to Review Questions

1. B. A view is dropped using the DROP VIEW *view_name*; command.

2. A. You can perform an INSERT, UPDATE, or DELETE operation on the columns involving only one base table at a time. There are also some restrictions on the DML operations you perform on a join view.

3. D. Since the view definition includes a DISTINCT clause, only queries are allowed on the view.

4. B, E. The OR REPLACE option in the CREATE VIEW statement is used to modify the definition of the view. The FORCE option can be used to create the view with errors. The ALTER VIEW statement is used to compile a view or to add or modify constraints on the view.

5. C. When you modify the base table, the view becomes invalid. Oracle will recompile the view the first time it is accessed. Recompiling the view will make it valid, but the new column will not be available in the view. This is because when you create the view using *, Oracle expands the column names and stores the column names in the dictionary.

6. B. Since the constraints on the view are not enforced by Oracle, the only valid status of a constraint can be DISABLE NOVALIDATE. You must specify this status when creating constraints on a view.

7. C. When numeric operations are performed using numeric datatypes in the view definition, the resulting column will be a floating datatype, which is NUMBER without any precision or scale.

8. D. The FOR UPDATE OF clause is not supported in the view definition. The FOR UPDATE clause locks the rows, so it is not allowed.

9. C. You can find the top five salaries using an inline view with the ORDER BY clause. The Oracle 11*g* Optimizer understands the top-*n* rows query. Option B would have been correct if you had ROWNUM <= 5 in the WHERE clause.

10. D. The view is based on a single table, and the only constraint on the table is the primary key. Although the view is defined with a WHERE clause, you have not enforced that check while using DML statements through the WITH CHECK OPTION clause.

11. A, C, E, F. To be able to update a base table using the view, the view definition should not have a DISTINCT clause, a GROUP BY clause, a START WITH clause, a CONNECT BY clause, ROWNUM, set operators (UNION, UNION ALL, INTERSECT, or MINUS), or a subquery in the SELECT clause.

12. A. For a descending sequence, the default START WITH value is –1, and the default MAXVALUE value is –1. To start the sequence with 0, you must explicitly override both of these defaults.

13. A. When the underlying object is dropped, the synonym will become INVALID. You can see the status of the synonym by querying the USER_OBJECTS dictionary view.

14. D. To remove a public synonym, use the DROP PUBLIC SYNONYM statement. The DROP TABLE statement will remove a table from the database but will not drop any synonyms on the table. The synonym will become invalid.

15. C. A sequence is not yet initialized if NEXTVAL has not yet been selected from it within the current session. It has nothing to do with creating a sequence, creating a synonym, or granting privileges.

16. D. Bitmapped indexes are not suited for high-cardinality columns (those with highly selective data). OLTP applications tend to need row-level locking, which is not available with bitmap indexes. Full-table scans do not use indexes. Bitmap indexes are best suited to multiple combinations of low- to medium-cardinality columns.

17. A, C. The obvious answer is C, but an index also can be used for the SELECT clause. If an index contains all the columns needed to satisfy the query, the table does not need to be accessed.

18. D. Both options A and B produce identical results, because the INCREMENT BY 1 clause is the default if it is not specified. Option C is invalid because NEXTVAL is not a valid keyword within a CREATE SEQUENCE statement.

19. B. Option D is close, but it shows the greatest number in the cache, not the latest generated. The correct answer is from the sequence itself, using the pseudocolumn CURRVAL.

20. A. The keyword CYCLE will cause the sequence to wrap and reuse numbers. The keyword MAXVALUE will set the largest value the sequence will cycle to. The name roundrobin is there to confuse to you.

Oracle Database 11*g*: Administration I

Introducing Oracle Database 11*g* Components and Architecture

ORACLE DATABASE 11*g*: ADMINISTRATION I EXAM OBJECTIVES COVERED IN THIS CHAPTER:

✓ **Exploring the Oracle Database Architecture**

- Explain the Memory Structures
- Describe the Process Structures
- Overview of Storage Structures

✓ **Preparing the Database Environment**

- Identify the tools for Administering an Oracle Database
- Plan an Oracle Database installation
- Install the Oracle software by using Oracle Universal Installer (OUI)

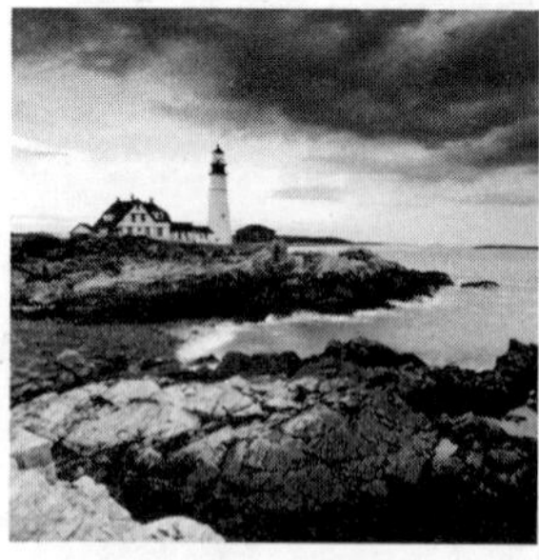

With this chapter, you'll start learning Oracle Database 11*g* (Oracle 11*g*) database administration. This chapter and the remaining chapters of the book will discuss the objectives for the Oracle 11*g* Administration I OCA certification exam.

With the release of Oracle 11*g*, Oracle Corporation has delivered a powerful and feature-rich database that can meet the performance, availability, recoverability, application-testing, and security requirements of any mission-critical application. As the Oracle DBA, you are responsible for managing and maintaining the Oracle Database 11*g* throughout its life cycle, from initial installation, creation, and configuration to final deployment. Performing these tasks requires a solid understanding of Oracle's product offerings so that you can apply the proper tools and features to the application. You must also use relational database concepts to design, implement, and maintain the tables that store the application data. At the heart of these activities is the need for a thorough understanding of the Oracle architecture and the tools and techniques used to monitor and manage the components of this architecture.

I will begin the chapter by reviewing the Oracle Database basics. You will learn what constitutes the Oracle Database 11*g*—an overview of the memory structures, the processes that manage the database, and how data is stored in the database. I will also discuss the tools used to administer the Oracle Database 11*g* and how to install the Oracle 11*g* software.

Exam objectives are subject to change at any time without prior notice and at Oracle's sole discretion. Please visit Oracle's Training and Certification website at `http://education.oracle.com/pls/web_prod-plq-dad/db_pages.getpage?page_id=41&p_exam_id=1Z0_052` for the most current exam-objectives listing.

Oracle Database Fundamentals

Databases store data. The data itself is composed of related logical units of information. The *database management system* (DBMS) facilitates the storage, modification, and retrieval of this data. Some early database technologies used flat files or hierarchical file structures to store application data. Others used networks of connections between sets of data to store and locate information. The early DBMS architecture mixed the physical manipulation of data with its logical manipulation. When the location of data changed, the application referencing the data had to be updated. Relational databases brought a revolutionary change to this architecture. Relational DBMS introduced data independence, which separated the physical model of the data from its logical model. Oracle is a relational DBMS.

All releases of Oracle's database products have used a relational DBMS model to store data in the database. This relational model is based on the groundbreaking work of Dr. Edgar Codd, which was first published in 1970 in his paper "A Relational Model of Data for Large Shared Data Banks." IBM Corporation, which was then an early adopter of Dr. Codd's model, helped develop the computer language that is used to access all relational databases today—Structured Query Language (SQL). The great thing about SQL is that you can use it to easily interact with relational databases without having to write complex computer programs and without needing to know where or how the data is physically stored on disk. You saw several SQL statements in the previous chapters.

Relational Databases

The concept of a *relational database management system* (RDBMS) is that the data consists of a set of relational objects. The basic storage of data in a database is a table. The relations are implemented in tables, where data is stored in rows and columns. Figure 8.1 shows such a relationship.

FIGURE 8.1 Relational tables

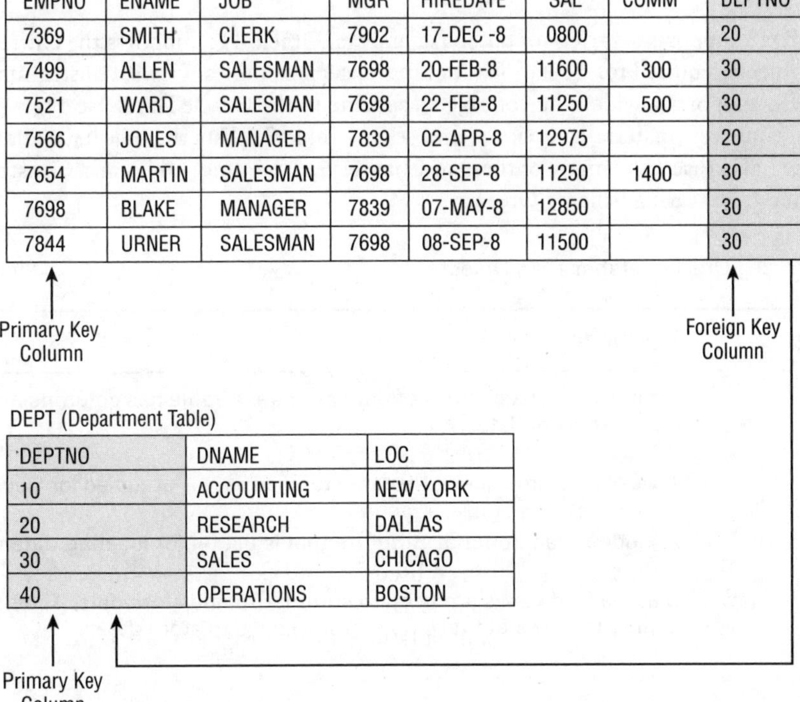
EMP (Employee Table)

EMPNO	ENAME	JOB	MGR	HIREDATE	SAL	COMM	DEPTNO
7369	SMITH	CLERK	7902	17-DEC -8	0800		20
7499	ALLEN	SALESMAN	7698	20-FEB-8	11600	300	30
7521	WARD	SALESMAN	7698	22-FEB-8	11250	500	30
7566	JONES	MANAGER	7839	02-APR-8	12975		20
7654	MARTIN	SALESMAN	7698	28-SEP-8	11250	1400	30
7698	BLAKE	MANAGER	7839	07-MAY-8	12850		30
7844	URNER	SALESMAN	7698	08-SEP-8	11500		30

DEPT (Department Table)

DEPTNO	DNAME	LOC
10	ACCOUNTING	NEW YORK
20	RESEARCH	DALLAS
30	SALES	CHICAGO
40	OPERATIONS	BOSTON

The DEPT table in the lower part of the figure stores information about departments in the company. Each department is identified by the department ID. Along with the ID, the name and location of the department are also stored in the table. The EMP table stores information about the employees in the company. Each employee is identified by a unique employee ID. This table includes employee information such as hire date, salary, manager, and so on. The DEPTNO column in both tables then provides a relationship between the tables. A department may have many employees, but an employee can work for only one department.

Since the user accessing this data doesn't need to know how or where the row is stored in the database, there must be a way to uniquely identify the rows in the tables. In our example, the department is uniquely identified by department number, and an employee is identified by an employee ID. The column (or set of columns) that uniquely identifies a row is known as the *primary key*. According to relational theory, each table in a relational database must have a primary key.

When relating tables together, the primary key of one table is placed in another table. For example, the primary key of the DEPT table is a column in the EMP table. In RDBMS terminology, this is known as a *foreign key*. A foreign key states that the data value in the column exists in another table and should continue to exist in the other table to keep the relationship between tables. The table where the column is a primary key is known as the *parent table*, and the table where the foreign key column exists is known as the *child table*. Oracle enforces the parent-child relationship between tables using *constraints*.

Oracle Database 11*g* Objects

Every RDBMS supports a variety of database objects. Oracle 11*g* supports the entire set of database objects required for a relational database, such as tables, views, constraints, and so on. It also supports a wide range of objects specific to the Oracle Database 11g, such as packages, sequences, materialized views, and so on. Table 8.1 lists the objects available in Oracle 11g. I also discussed many of these in Chapter 6, "Creating Tables and Constraints," and Chapter 7, "Creating Schema Objects."

TABLE 8.1 Oracle Database 11*g* Objects

Object Type	Description
Table	A table is the basic form of data storage. A table has columns and stores rows of data.
View	A view is a stored query. No data-storage space is occupied for view data.
Index	An index is an optional structure that is useful for locating data faster.
Materialized view	Materialized views are used to summarize and store data. They are similar to views but take up storage space to store data.

TABLE 8.1 Oracle Database 11*g* Objects *(continued)*

Object Type	Description
Index-organized table	An index-organized table use a primary key and stores the table data in the index segment.
Cluster	A cluster is a group of tables that share the same storage blocks.
Constraint	A constraint is a stored rule to enforce data integrity.
Sequence	A sequence provides a mechanism for the continuous generation of numbers.
Synonym	A synonym is an alias for a database schema object.
Triggers	A trigger is a PL/SQL program unit that gets executed when an event occurs.
Stored function	Stored functions are PL/SQL programs that can be used to create user-defined functions to return a value.
Stored procedure	Stored procedures are PL/SQL programs to define a business process.
Package	A package is a collection of procedures, functions, and other program constructs.
Java	Stored Java procedures can be created in Oracle to define business processes.
Database link	Database links are used to communicate between databases to share data.

You use SQL to create database objects and to interact with application data. In the next section, I will discuss the tools available to access and administer Oracle 11g database.

Interacting with Oracle 11*g*

SQL is the language used to interact with the Oracle 11*g* database. Many tools are available for the DBA to administer an Oracle 11*g* database. The common tools are as follows:

- SQL*Plus, which is a command-line interface utility
- SQL Developer, a GUI tool
- Oracle Enterprise Manager Database Control, a GUI tool

Using SQL*Plus and SQL Developer, you interact directly with the Oracle 11*g* database using SQL statements and a superset of commands such as `STARTUP`, `SHUTDOWN`, and so on. Using Enterprise Manager, you interact indirectly with the Oracle 11*g* database.

SQL*Plus

SQL*Plus is the primary tool for an Oracle DBA to administer the database using SQL commands. Before you can run SQL statements, you must connect to the Oracle 11*g* database. You can start SQL*Plus from a Windows command prompt using the `SQLPLUS.EXE` executable or using the `$ORACLE_HOME/bin/sqlplus` executable on the Unix/Linux platform. Figure 8.2 shows connecting to SQL*Plus from a Linux workstation.

FIGURE 8.2 SQL*Plus login in Linux

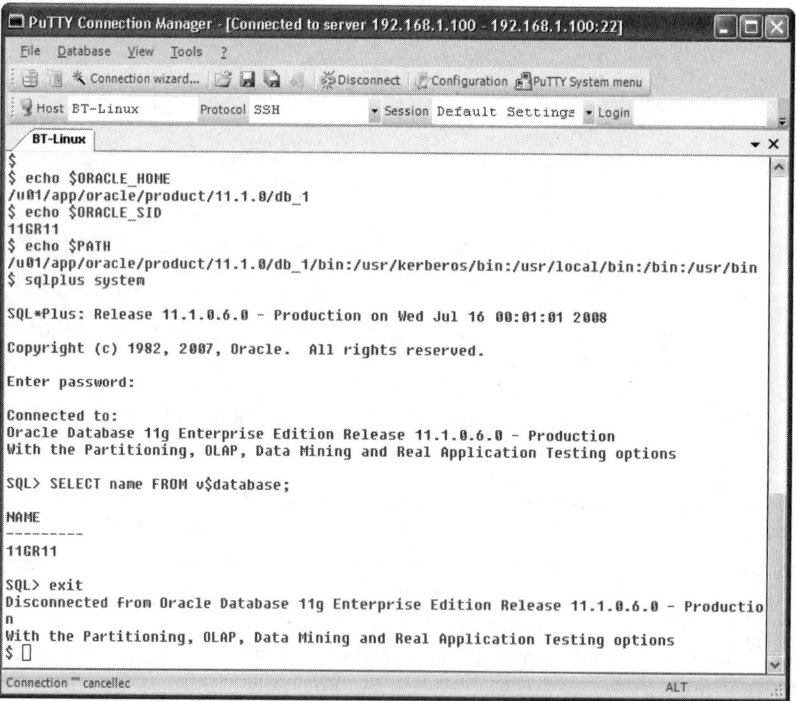

To get an overview of SQL*Plus and how to connect to the database using SQL*Plus, please refer to Chapter 1, "Introducing SQL."

SQL Developer

SQL Developer is a free GUI database-development tool. With SQL Developer, you can create and view the database objects, make changes to the objects, run SQL statements, run PL/SQL programs, create and edit PL/SQL programs, and perform PL/SQL debugging.

SQL Developer also includes a migration utility to migrate Microsoft Access and Microsoft SQL Server databases to Oracle 11*g*. Figure 8.3 shows the object browser screen of SQL Developer.

FIGURE 8.3 SQL Developer screen

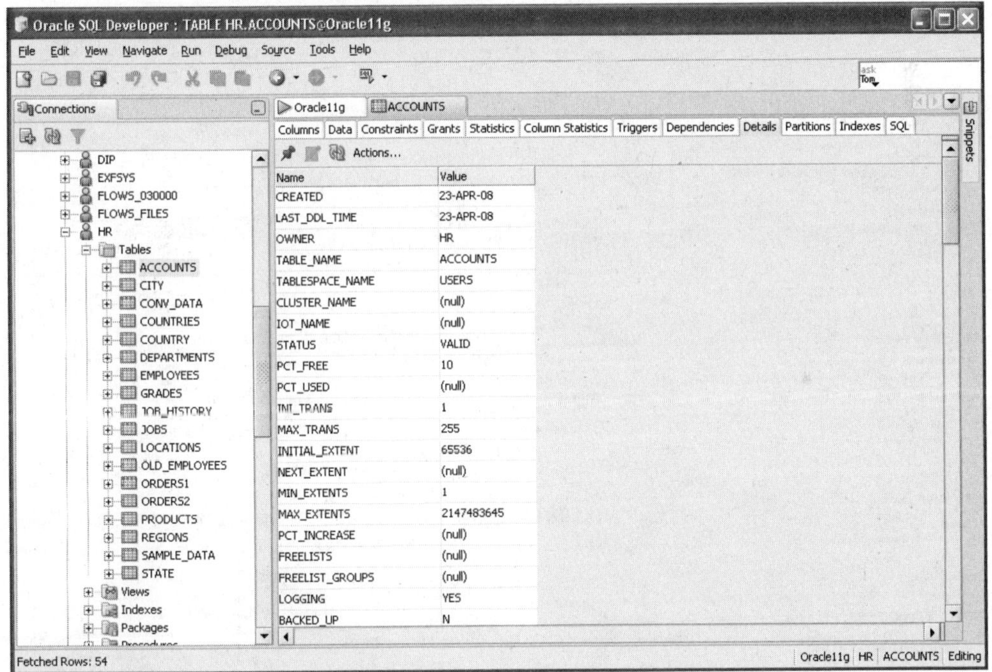

You can download and learn more about SQL Developer on the OTN website (`http://www.oracle.com/technology/products/database/sql_developer/index.html`).

Enterprise Manager Database Control

Oracle Enterprise Manager Database Control is a web-based database management tool that is bundled with the Oracle 11*g* database. This is a graphical tool specifically designed to administer the Oracle database. The Enterprise Manager Database Control is used to manage a single database, whereas the Enterprise Manager Grid Control can manage multiple databases and other services and applications, such as OAS, and even non-Oracle applications at the same time. Figure 8.4 shows the Enterprise Manager Database Control home screen, where an overview of the database is shown.

FIGURE 8.4 Enterprise Manager home screen

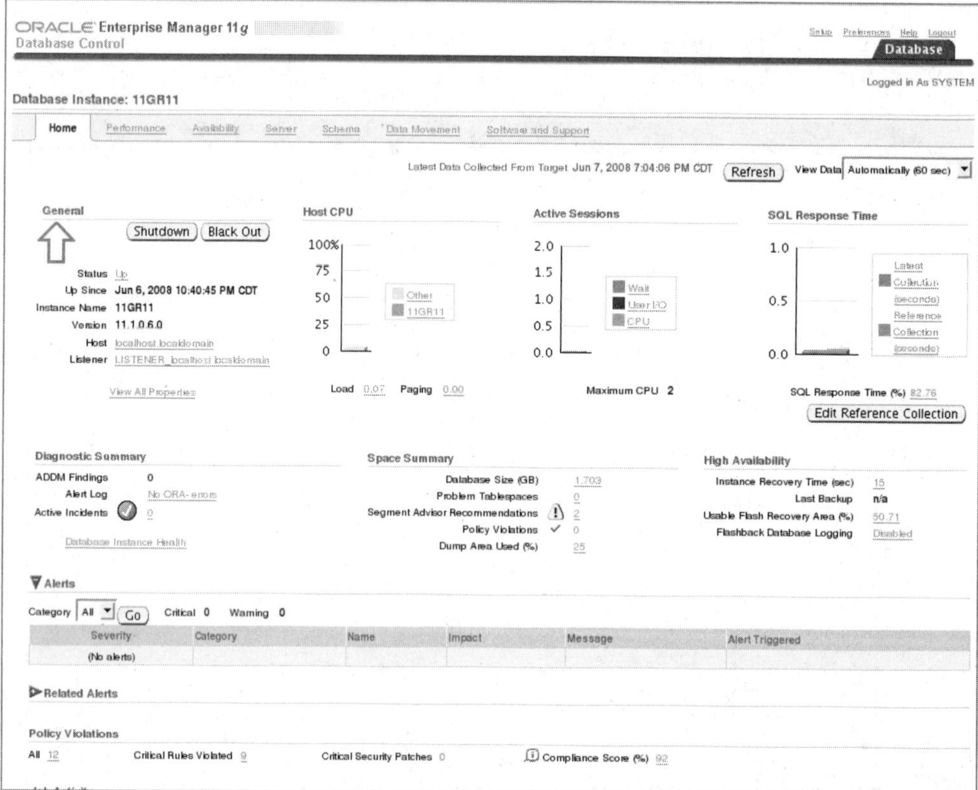

For all the database-administration examples in this chapter, you may use either SQL*Plus to perform the SQL command line or use the GUI tool Enterprise Manager (EM) Database Control. Before learning to administer the Oracle 11*g* database, let's start with the basics. In the next section, you'll learn about Oracle 11*g* architecture.

Oracle 11*g* Architecture

Each database-administration and -development tool described previously allows a user to interact with the database. Using these tools requires that user accounts be created in the database and that connectivity to the database be in place across the network. Users must also have adequate storage capacity for the data they insert, and they need recovery mechanisms for restoring the transactions they are performing in the event of a hardware failure. As the DBA, you take care of each of these tasks, as well as others, which include the following:

- Selecting the server hardware on which the database software will run
- Installing and configuring the Oracle 11*g* software on the server hardware
- Creating the Oracle 11*g* database
- Creating and managing the tables and other objects used to manage the application data
- Creating and managing database users
- Establishing reliable backup and recovery processes for the database
- Monitoring and tuning database performance

The remainder of this book is dedicated to helping you understand how to perform these and other important Oracle database-administration tasks. But first, to succeed as an Oracle DBA, you need to completely understand Oracle's underlying architecture and its mechanisms. Understanding the relationship between Oracle's memory structures, background processes, and I/O activities is critical before learning how to manage these areas.

The Oracle server architecture can be described in three categories:

- User-related processes
- Logical memory structures that are collectively called an *Oracle instance*
- Physical file structures that are collectively called a *database*

You will also see how the physical structures map to the logical structures of the database you are familiar with, such as tables and indexes.

Database is a confusing term that is often used to represent different things on different platforms; the only commonality is that it is something related to storing data. In Oracle, however, the term *database* represents the physical files that store data. An instance is composed of the memory structures and background processes. Each database should have at least one instance associated with it. It is possible for multiple instances to access a single database; such a configuration is known as Real Application Clusters (RAC). In this book, however, you'll concentrate only on single-instance databases because RAC is not part of the certification exam.

Figure 8.5 shows all the parts of an Oracle instance and database.

Although the architecture in Figure 8.5 may at first seem complex, each of these architecture components is described in more detail in the following sections, beginning with the user-related processes, and is actually fairly simple. This figure is an important piece of fundamental information when learning about the Oracle 11*g* architecture.

The key database components are memory structures, process structures, and storage structures. Process and memory structures together are called an *instance*; the storage structure is called a *database*. Taken together, the instance and the database are called an *Oracle server*.

FIGURE 8.5 The Oracle 11*g* architecture

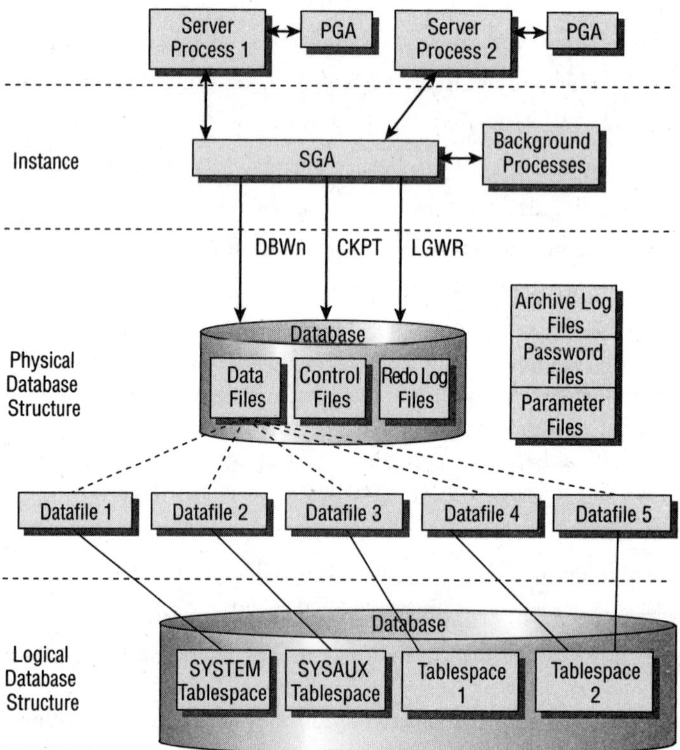

User Processes

At the user level, two types of processes allow a user to interact with the instance and, ultimately, with the database: the *user process* and the *server process*.

Whenever a user runs an application, such as a human-resources or order-taking application, Oracle starts a user process to support the user's connection to the instance. Depending on the technical architecture of the application, the user process exists either on the user's own computer or on the middle-tier application server. The user process then initiates a connection to the instance. Oracle calls the process of initiating and maintaining communication between the user process and the instance a *connection*. Once the connection is made, the user establishes a *session* in the instance.

After establishing a session, each user starts a server process on the host server itself. It is this server process that is responsible for performing the tasks that actually allow the user to interact with the database.

Examples of these interactions include sending SQL statements to the database, retrieving needed data from the database's physical files, and returning that data to the user.

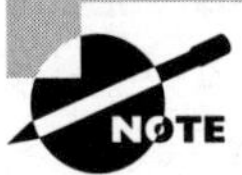

Server processes generally have a one-to-one relationship with user processes—in other words, each user process connects to one and only one server process. However, in some Oracle configurations, multiple user processes can share a single server process. We will discuss Oracle connection configurations in Chapter 11, "Understanding Network Architecture."

In addition to the user and server processes that are associated with each user connection, an additional memory structure called the *program global area* (PGA) is also created for each user. The PGA stores user-specific session information such as bind variables and session variables. Every server process on the server has a PGA memory area. Figure 8.6 shows the relationship between a user process, server processes, and the PGA.

FIGURE 8.6 The relationship between user and server processes and the PGA

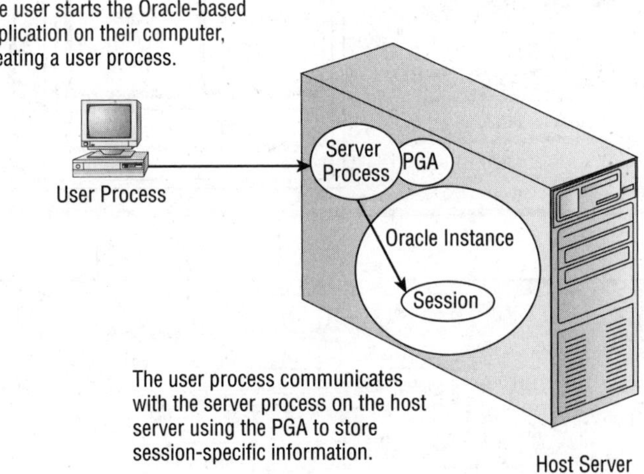

PGA memory is not shared. Each server process has a PGA associated with it and is exclusive. As a DBA, you set the total memory that can be allocated to all the PGA memory allocated to all server and background processes.

The server process communicates with the Oracle instance on behalf of the user. The Oracle instance is examined in the next section.

The Oracle Instance

An Oracle database instance consists of Oracle's main memory structure, called the *system global area* (SGA), and several Oracle background processes. It is with the SGA that the server process communicates when the user accesses the data in the database. Figure 8.7 shows the components of the SGA.

FIGURE 8.7 SGA components

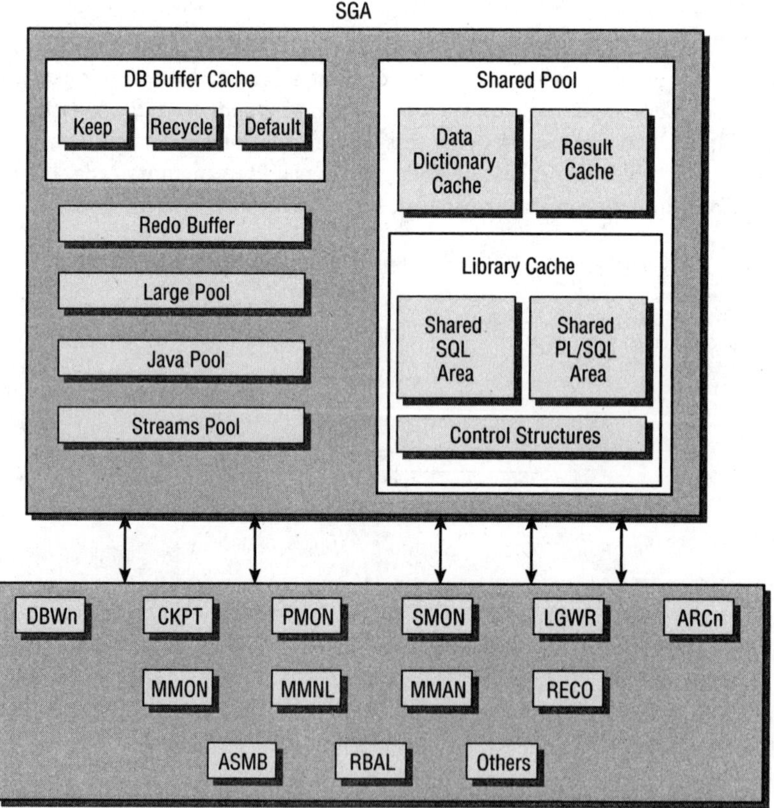

The components of the instance are described in the following sections.

Oracle Memory Structures

The SGA is a shared memory area. All the users of the database share the information maintained in this area. Oracle allocates memory for the SGA when the instance is started and deallocates it when the instance is shut down. The SGA consists of three required components and four optional components. Table 8.2 describes the required components.

TABLE 8.2 Required SGA Components

SGA Component	Description
Shared pool	Caches the most recently used SQL statements that have been issued by database users
Database buffer cache	Caches the data that has been most recently accessed by database users
Redo log buffer	Stores transaction information for recovery purposes

Table 8.3 describes the optional components.

TABLE 8.3 Optional SGA Components

SGA Component	Description
Java pool	Caches the most recently used Java objects and application code when Oracle's JVM option is used.
Large pool	Caches data for large operations such as Recovery Manager (RMAN) backup and restore activities and Shared Server components.
Streams pool	Caches the data associated with queued message requests when Oracle's Advanced Queuing option is used.
Result cache	This new area is introduced in the Oracle 11*g* database and stores results of SQL queries and PL/SQL functions for better performance.

Oracle 11*g* can manage the components of the SGA dynamically, without exceeding the value specified by the DBA for the parameter `SGA_MAX_SIZE`, but only for `ASSM`. Memory in the SGA is allocated in units of contiguous memory called *granules*. The size of a granule depends on the parameter `MEMORY_MAX_TARGET`. If `MEMORY_MAX_TARGET` is larger than 1024MB, the granule size is either 16MB or 4MB. `MEMORY_MAX_TARGET` is discussed in detail in Chapter 14, "Maintaining the Database and Managing Performance." A minimum of three granules must be allocated to SGA—one each for the required components in Table 8.2.

The sizes of these SGA components can be managed in two ways: manually or automatically. If you choose to manage these components manually, you must specify the size of each SGA component and then increase or decrease the size of each component according to the needs of the application. If these components are managed automatically, the instance itself will monitor the utilization of each SGA component and adjust their sizes accordingly, relative to a predefined maximum allowable aggregate SGA size.

Oracle 11*g* provides several dynamic performance views to see the components and sizes of SGA; you can use V$SGA and V$SGAINFO, as shown here:

```
SQL> SELECT * FROM v$sga;

NAME                      VALUE
-------------------- ----------
Fixed Size              1303916
Variable Size         570428052
Database Buffers      377487360
Redo Buffers            4935680
SQL>
```

Alternatively, you may use the SHOW SGA command from SQL*Plus, as shown here:

```
SQL> SHOW SGA

Total System Global Area  954155008 bytes
Fixed Size                  1303916 bytes
Variable Size             570428052 bytes
Database Buffers          377487360 bytes
Redo Buffers                4935680 bytes
SQL>
```

The output from this query shows that the total size of the SGA is 954,155,008 bytes. This total size is composed of the variable space that is composed of the shared pool, the large pool, the Java pool (570428052 bytes), the database buffer cache (377487360 bytes), the redo log buffer (4935680 bytes), and some additional space (1,303,916 bytes) that stores information used by the instance's background processes. The V$SGAINFO view displays additional details about the allocation of space within the SGA, as shown in the following query:

```
SQL> SELECT * FROM v$sgainfo;

NAME                                  BYTES RESIZEABLE
-------------------------------- ---------- ----------
Fixed SGA Size                      1303916 No
Redo Buffers                        4935680 No
Buffer Cache Size                 352321536 Yes
Shared Pool Size                  339738624 Yes
Large Pool Size                     4194304 Yes
Java Pool Size                     12582912 Yes
Streams Pool Size                         0 Yes
Shared IO Pool Size                       0 Yes
```

```
Granule Size                           4194304 No
Maximum SGA Size                     954155008 No
Startup overhead in Shared Pool       46137344 No
Free SGA Memory Available            239075328

12 rows selected.

SQL>
```

The results of this query show in detail how much space is occupied by each component in the shared pool. The components with the `RESIZEABLE` column with a value of `Yes` can be managed dynamically by Oracle 11g.

You can also use EM Database Control to view the sizes of each of the SGA components, as shown in Figure 8.8. From the home screen, go to the Server tab and click Memory Advisors to see this.

FIGURE 8.8 EM Database Control showing SGA components

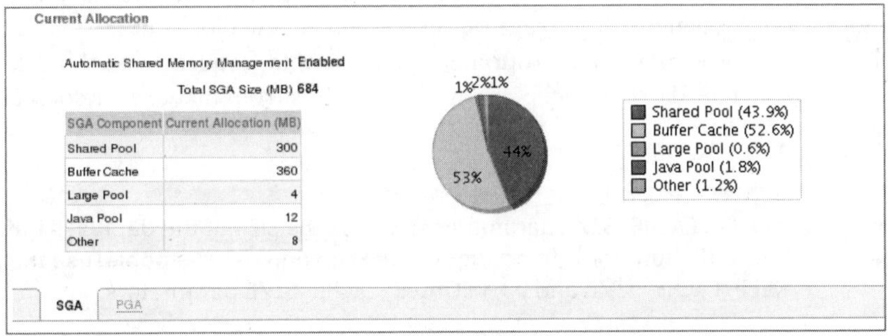

You'll learn more about the components in the SGA in the next sections.

Database Buffer Cache

The *database buffer cache* is the area in SGA that caches the database data, holding blocks from the data files that have been read recently. The database buffer cache is shared among all the users connected to the database. There are three types of buffers:

- *Dirty buffers* are the buffer blocks that need to be written to the data files. The data in these buffers has changed and has not yet been written to the disk.
- *Free buffers* do not contain any data or are free to be overwritten. When Oracle reads data from the disk, free buffers hold this data.
- *Pinned buffers* are the buffers that are currently being accessed or explicitly retained for future use.

Oracle uses a *least recently used algorithm* (LRU algorithm) to manage the contents of the shared pool and database buffer cache. When a user's server process needs to put a SQL statement into the shared pool or copy a database block into the buffer cache, Oracle uses the space in memory that is occupied by the least recently accessed SQL statement or buffer to hold the requested SQL or block copy. Using this technique, Oracle keeps frequently accessed SQL statements and database buffers in memory longer, improving the overall performance of the server by minimizing parsing and physical disk I/O.

The background process DBW*n* writes the database blocks from the database buffer cache to the data files. Dirty buffers contain data that changed and must be written to disk.

To manage the buffer cache better, Oracle 11*g* provides three buffer caches. The DEFAULT cache is the default and is required. The KEEP cache and the RECYCLE cache can be optionally configured. By default all the data read from the disk is written to the DEFAULT pool. If you want certain data not to be aged from memory, you can configure the KEEP pool and use the ALTER TABLE statement to specify which tables should use the KEEP pool. Similarly, if you do not want to age out good data from the default cache for temporary data, you may specify such tables to have the RECYCLE pool instead of the default. The blocks in the KEEP pool also follow the LRU algorithm to age out blocks when new blocks need space in the KEEP pool. By sizing the KEEP pool appropriately, you can hold frequently used blocks longer in the KEEP pool. The RECYCLE cache removes the buffers from memory as soon as they are not needed.

The DB_CACHE_SIZE parameter specifies the size of the database buffer cache default pool. To configure the keep and recycle pools, use the DB_KEEP_CACHE_SIZE and DB_RECYCLE_CACHE_SIZE parameters.

Redo Log Buffer

The *redo log buffer* is a circular buffer in the SGA that holds information about the changes made to the database data. The changes are known as *redo entries* or *change vectors* and are used to redo the changes in case of a failure. DML and DDL statements are used to make changes to the database data. The parameter LOG_BUFFER determines the size of the redo log buffer cache.

The background process LGWR writes the redo log information to the online redo log files.

Shared Pool

The *shared pool* portion of the SGA holds information such as SQL, PL/SQL procedures and packages, the data dictionary, locks, character-set information, security attributes, and so on. The shared pool consists of the library cache and the data dictionary cache.

The *library cache* contains the shared SQL areas, private SQL areas, PL/SQL programs, and control structures such as locks and library cache handles.

The *shared SQL area* is used for maintaining recently executed SQL statements and their execution plans. Oracle divides each SQL statement that it executes into a shared SQL area and a private SQL area. When two users are executing the same SQL, the information in the shared SQL area is used for both. The shared SQL area contains the parse tree and execution plan, whereas the private SQL area contains values for the bind variables (persistent area) and runtime buffers (runtime area). Oracle creates the runtime area as the first step of an execute request. For INSERT, UPDATE, and DELETE statements, Oracle frees the runtime area after the statement has been executed. For queries, Oracle frees the runtime area only after all rows have been fetched or the query has been canceled.

Oracle processes PL/SQL program units the same way it processes SQL statements. When a PL/SQL program unit is executed, the code is moved to the *shared PL/SQL area*, and the individual SQL commands within the program unit are moved to the shared SQL area. Again, the shared program units are maintained in memory with an LRU algorithm.

The third area in the library cache is used to store control information and is maintained internally by Oracle. Various locks, latches, and other control structures reside here, and any server process that requires this information can access it.

The *data dictionary cache* holds the most recently used database dictionary information. The data dictionary cache is also known as the *row cache* because it holds data as rows instead of buffers (which hold entire blocks of data).

The *result cache* is new in Oracle 11g and is used to hold the SQL and PL/SQL function results. Executions of similar SQL statements can use the cached results to answer query requests. Because retrieving results from the SQL query result cache is faster than rerunning a query, frequently run queries experience a significant performance improvement when their results are cached.

The parameter SHARED_POOL_SIZE determines the size of the shared pool.

Large Pool

The *large pool* is an optional area in the SGA that the DBA can configure to provide large memory allocations for specific database operations such as an RMAN backup or restore. The large pool allows Oracle to request large memory allocations from a separate pool to prevent contention from other applications for the same memory. The large pool does not have an LRU list. The parameter LARGE_POOL_SIZE determines the size of the large pool.

Java Pool

The *Java pool* is another optional area in the SGA that the DBA can configure to provide memory for Java operations, just as the shared pool is provided for processing SQL and PL/SQL statements. The parameter JAVA_POOL_SIZE determines the size of the Java pool.

Streams Pool

The *streams pool* is exclusively used by Oracle streams. The parameter STREAMS_POOL_SIZE determines the size of the streams pool.

If any SGA component size is set smaller than the granule size, the size of the component is rounded to the nearest granule size.

Oracle 11*g* can manage all the components of the SGA and PGA automatically; there is no need for the DBA to configure each pool individually. You will learn more about automatic memory management in Chapter 14.

Oracle Processes Structures

Many types of Oracle background processes exist. Each performs a specific job in helping to manage an instance. Five Oracle background processes are required by the Oracle instance, and several background processes are optional. The required background processes are found in all Oracle instances. Optional background processes may or may not be used, depending on the features that are being used in the database. Table 8.4 describes the required background processes.

TABLE 8.4 Required Oracle Background Processes

Process Name	OS Process	Description
Database Writer	DBW*n*	Writes modified database blocks from the SGA's database buffer cache to the data files on disk
Checkpoint	CKPT	Updates the data file headers following a checkpoint event
Log Writer	LGWR	Writes transaction recovery information from the SGA's redo log buffer to the online redo log files on disk
Process Monitor	PMON	Cleans up failed user database connections
System Monitor	SMON	Performs instance recovery following an instance crash, coalesces free space in the database, and manages space used for sorting

Table 8.5 describes some of the optional background processes.

TABLE 8.5 Optional Oracle Background Processes

Process Name	OS Process	Description
Archiver	ARC*n*	Copies the transaction recovery information from the redo log files to the archive location. Nearly all production databases use this optional process. You can have up to 30 archival processes (ARC0-ARC9, ARCa-ARCt).
Recoverer	RECO	Recovers failed transactions that are distributed across multiple databases when using Oracle's distributed database feature.
ASM Disk	ASMB	Present on databases using Automatic Storage Management disks.
ASM Balance	RBAL	Coordinates rebalance activity of disks in an ASM disk group.
Job Queue Monitor	CJQ*n*	Assigns jobs to the job queue processes when using Oracle's job scheduling feature.
Job Queue	J*nnn*	Executes database jobs that have been scheduled using Oracle's job-scheduling feature.
Queue Monitor	QMN*n*	Monitors the messages in the message queue when Oracle's Advanced Queuing feature is used.
Diagnosability	DIAG	Performs diagnostic dumps.
Diagnosablilty	DIA0	Diagnostic process responsible for hang detection and deadlock resolution.
Event Monitor	EMNC	Process responsible for event-management coordination and notification.
Flashback Data Archive	FBDA	Archives historical records from table when the flashback data archive feature is used.
Parallel Query Slave	Q*nnn*	Carries out portions of a larger overall query when Oracle's Parallel Query feature is used.
Dispatcher	D*nnn*	Assigns user's database requests to a queue where they are then serviced by shared server processes when Oracle's Shared Server feature is used. See Chapter 11 for details on using shared servers.
Shared Server	S*nnn*	Server processes that are shared among several users when Oracle's Shared Server feature is used. See Chapter 11 for details on using shared servers.

TABLE 8.5 Optional Oracle Background Processes *(continued)*

Process Name	OS Process	Description
Memory Manager	MMAN	Manages the size of each individual SGA component when Oracle's Automatic Shared Memory Management feature is used. See Chapter 14 for more information on using this feature.
Memory Monitor	MMON	Gathers and analyzes statistics used by the Automatic Workload Repository feature. See Chapter 14 for more information on using this feature.
Memory Monitor Light	MMNL	Gathers and analyzes statistics used by the Automatic Workload Repository feature. See Chapter 14 for more information on using this feature.
Recovery Writer	RVWR	Writes recovery information to disk when Oracle's Flashback Database feature is used. See Chapter 15, "Implementing Database Backups," for details on how to use the Flashback Database feature.
Change Tracking Writer	CTWR	Keeps track of which database blocks have changed when Oracle's incremental Recovery Manager feature is used. See Chapter 15 for details on using Recovery Manager to perform backups.

On Unix systems, you can view these background processes from the operating system using the ps command, as shown here:

```
$ ps -ef | grep 11GR11
oracle    2517     1  0 20:22 ?        00:00:00 ora_j000_11GR11
oracle    3436     1  0 Jun06 ?        00:00:01 ora_pmon_11GR11
oracle    3438     1  0 Jun06 ?        00:00:00 ora_vktm_11GR11
oracle    3442     1  0 Jun06 ?        00:00:00 ora_diag_11GR11
oracle    3444     1  0 Jun06 ?        00:00:00 ora_dbrm_11GR11
oracle    3446     1  0 Jun06 ?        00:00:01 ora_psp0_11GR11
oracle    3450     1  0 Jun06 ?        00:00:24 ora_dia0_11GR11
oracle    3452     1  0 Jun06 ?        00:00:00 ora_mman_11GR11
oracle    3454     1  0 Jun06 ?        00:00:03 ora_dbw0_11GR11
oracle    3456     1  0 Jun06 ?        00:00:10 ora_lgwr_11GR11
oracle    3458     1  0 Jun06 ?        00:00:02 ora_ckpt_11GR11
oracle    3460     1  0 Jun06 ?        00:00:05 ora_smon_11GR11
oracle    3462     1  0 Jun06 ?        00:00:00 ora_reco_11GR11
oracle    3464     1  0 Jun06 ?        00:00:05 ora_mmon_11GR11
oracle    3466     1  0 Jun06 ?        00:00:01 ora_mmnl_11GR11
oracle    3468     1  0 Jun06 ?        00:00:00 ora_d000_11GR11
```

```
oracle    3470    1  0 Jun06 ?          00:00:00 ora_s000_11GR11
oracle    3482    1  0 Jun06 ?          00:00:01 ora_arc0_11GR11
oracle    3484    1  0 Jun06 ?          00:00:01 ora_arc1_11GR11
oracle    3486    1  0 Jun06 ?          00:00:00 ora_arc2_11GR11
oracle    3488    1  0 Jun06 ?          00:00:00 ora_arc3_11GR11
oracle    3490    1  0 Jun06 ?          00:00:00 ora_smco_11GR11
oracle    3492    1  0 Jun06 ?          00:00:00 ora_fbda_11GR11
oracle    3494    1  0 Jun06 ?          00:00:00 ora_qmnc_11GR11
oracle    3510    1  0 Jun06 ?          00:00:00 ora_q000_11GR11
oracle    3512    1  0 Jun06 ?          00:00:00 ora_q001_11GR11
oracle    3744    1  0 Jun06 ?          00:00:02 ora_cjq0_11GR11
oracle    9616    1  0 14:01 ?          00:00:00 ora_w000_11GR11
$
```

This output shows that several background processes are running on the Linux server for the 11GR11 database.

The dynamic view `V$BGPROCESS` shows the background processes available. The following query lists multiple child processes only once to save space. To see all the processes, remove the `WHERE` clause and execute.

```
SQL> SELECT name, description
  2  FROM v$bgprocess
  3  WHERE SUBSTR(name, 4, 1) NOT BETWEEN '1' AND '9'
  4  AND SUBSTR(name, 4, 1) NOT BETWEEN 'a' AND 'z'
  5  ORDER BY name;

NAME  DESCRIPTION
----- ------------------------------------------------
ACMS  Atomic Controlfile to Memory Server
ARB0  ASM Rebalance 0
ARBA  ASM Rebalance 10
ARC0  Archival Process 0
ASMB  ASM Background
CJQ0  Job Queue Coordinator
CKPT  checkpoint
CTWR  Change Tracking Writer
DBRM  Resource Manager process
DBW0  db writer process 0
DIA0  diagnosibility process 0
DIAG  diagnosibility process
DMON  DG Broker Monitor Process
DSKM  slave DiSKMon process
EMNC  EMON Coordinator
```

```
FBDA  Flashback Data Archiver Process
FMON  File Mapping Monitor Process
FSFP  Data Guard Broker FSFO Pinger
GMON  diskgroup monitor
GTX0  Global Txn process 0
INSV  Data Guard Broker INstance SlaVe Process
KATE  Konductor of ASM Temporary Errands
LCK0  Lock Process 0
LGWR  Redo etc.
LMD0  global enqueue service daemon 0
LMON  global enqueue service monitor
LMS0  global cache service process 0
LNS0  Network Server 0
LSP0  Logical Standby
MARK  mark AU for resync koordinator
MMAN  Memory Manager
MMNL  Manageability Monitor Process 2
MMON  Manageability Monitor Process
MRP0  Managed Standby Recovery
NSV0  Data Guard Broker NetSlave Process 0
OFSC  OFS CSS
PING  interconnect latency measurement
PMON  process cleanup
PSP0  process spawner 0
QMNC  AQ Coordinator
RBAL  ASM Rebalance master
RCBG  Result Cache: Background
RECO  distributed recovery
RMS0  rac management server
RSM0  Data Guard Broker Resource Guard Process 0
RSMN  Remote Slave Monitor
RVWR  Recovery Writer
SMCO  Space Manager Process
SMON  System Monitor Process
VBG0  Volume BG 0
VDBG  Volume Driver BG
VKTM  Virtual Keeper of TiMe process

52 rows selected.
SQL>
```

Knowing the purpose of the required background processes is a must for the OCA certification exam. Let's discuss them in the next subsections.

Database Writer (DBW*n*)

The purpose of the *database writer process* (DBW*n*) is to write the contents of the dirty buffers to the data files. By default, Oracle starts one database writer process when the instance starts. For multiuser and busy systems, you can have up to 20 database writer processes (`DBW0-9`, `DBWa-j`) to improve performance. The parameter `DB_WRITER_PROCESSES` determines the additional number of database writer processes to be started. Having more DBW*n* processes than the number of CPUs is normally not beneficial.

The DBW*n* process writes the modified buffer blocks to disk, so more free buffers are available in the buffer cache. Writes are always performed in bulk to reduce disk contention; the number of blocks written in each I/O is operating system-dependent.

When Does Database Writer Write?

The DBW*n* background process writes to the data files whenever one of the following events occurs:

- A user's server process has searched too long for a free buffer when reading a buffer into the buffer cache.
- The number of modified and committed, but unwritten, buffers in the database buffer cache is too large.
- At a database checkpoint event. See Chapter 15 for information on checkpoints.
- The instance is shut down using any method other than a shutdown abort.
- A tablespace is placed into backup mode.
- A tablespace is taken offline to make it unavailable or is changed to `READ ONLY`.
- A segment is dropped.

Checkpoint (CKPT)

A *checkpoint* is when the DBW*n* process writes all the dirty buffers to the data files. When a checkpoint occurs, Oracle must update the headers of all data files as well as the control file to record the checkpoint. This update is done by the *checkpoint process* (CKPT); the DBW*n* process writes the actual data blocks to the data files.

Checkpoints help reduce the time required for instance recovery. If checkpoints occur too frequently, disk contention becomes a problem with the data file updates. If checkpoints occur too infrequently, the time required to recover a failed database instance can be significantly longer. Checkpoints occur automatically when an online redo log file is full (a log switch happens).

Log Writer (LGWR)

The *log writer process* (LGWR) writes the blocks in the redo log buffer of the SGA to the online redo log files. When the LGWR writes log buffers to disk, Oracle server processes can write new entries in the redo log buffer. LGWR writes the entries to the disk fast enough to ensure that room is available for the server process to write redo entries.

If the redo log files are multiplexed, LGWR writes simultaneously to all the members of the redo log group. Even if one of the log files in the group is damaged, LGWR writes the redo information to the available files. LGWR writes to the redo log files sequentially so that transactions can be applied in order in the event of a failure.

When Does Log Writer Write?

The LGWR background process writes to the current redo log group under any of the following conditions:

- Every three seconds
- When a user commits a transaction
- When the redo log buffer is a third full
- When the redo log buffer contains 1MB worth of redo information
- Whenever a database checkpoint occurs

As soon as a transaction commits, the information is written to redo log files. By writing the committed transaction immediately to the redo log files, the change to the database is never lost. Even if the database crashes, committed changes can be recovered from the online redo log files and applied to the data files.

Process Monitor (PMON)

The *process monitor process* (PMON) cleans up failed user processes and frees up all the resources used by the failed process. It resets the status of the active transaction table and removes the process ID from the list of active processes. It reclaims all the resources held by the user and releases all locks on tables and rows held by the user. PMON wakes up periodically to check whether it is needed. Other processes can call PMON if they detect a need for a PMON process.

PMON also checks on some optional background processes and restarts them if any have stopped.

System Monitor (SMON)

The *system monitor process* (SMON) performs instance or crash recovery at database startup by using the online redo log files. SMON is also responsible for cleaning up temporary segments in the tablespaces that are no longer used and for coalescing the contiguous free space in the dictionary-managed tablespaces. If any dead transactions were skipped during instance recovery because of file-read or offline errors, SMON recovers them when the tablespace or data file is brought back online. SMON wakes up regularly to check whether it is needed. Other processes can call SMON if they detect a need for an SMON process.

In Windows environments, a Windows service called `OracleService`*`InstanceName`* is also associated with each instance. This service must be started in order to start up the instance in Windows environments.

Oracle Storage Structures

An instance is a memory structure, but the Oracle database consists of a set of physical files that reside on the host server's disk drives. The physical storage structures include three types of files. These files are called *control files*, *data files*, and *redo log files*. The additional physical files that are associated with the Oracle Database but are not technically part of the database are as follows: the *password file*, the *parameter file*, and any *archived redo log files*. The Oracle Net configuration files are also required for connectivity to the Oracle database. Table 8.6 summarizes the role that each of these files plays in the database architecture.

TABLE 8.6 Oracle Physical Files

File Type	Information Contained in Files
Control	Locations of other physical files, database name, database block size, database character set, and recovery information. These files are required to open the database.
Data	All application data and internal metadata.
Redo log	Record of all changes made to the database; used for instance recovery.
Parameter (pfile or spfile)	Configuration parameters for the SGA, optional Oracle features, and background processes.
Archived redo log	Copy of the contents of online redo logs, used for database recovery.
Password	Optional file used to store names of users who have been granted the SYSDBA and SYSOPER privileges. See Chapter 12, "Implementing Security and Auditing," for details on SYSDBA and SYSOPER privileges.
Oracle Net	Entries that configure the database listener and client-to-database connectivity. See Chapter 11 for details.

The three files that make up a database—the control file, the data file, and the redo log file—are described in the following sections.

Control Files

Control files are critical components of the database because they store important information that is not available anywhere else. This information includes the following:

- The name of the database
- Database-creation timestamp
- The names, locations, and sizes of the data files and redo log files
- Tablespace information
- Redo log information used to recover the database in the case of a disk failure or user error
- Archived log information
- RMAN backup information
- Checkpoint information

The control files are created when the database is created in the locations specified in the `control_files` parameter in the parameter file. Because a loss of the control files negatively impacts the ability to recover the database, most production databases multiplex their control files to multiple locations. Oracle uses the CKPT background process to automatically update each of these files as needed, keeping the contents of all copies of the control synchronized. You can use the dynamic performance view `V$CONTROLFILE` to display the names and locations of all the database's control files. A sample query on `V$CONTROLFILE` is shown here:

```
SQL> SELECT name FROM v$controlfile;

NAME
--------------------------------------------
/u02/oradata/PROD/control01.ctl
/u03/oradata/PROD/control02.ctl
/u05/oradata/PROD/control03.ctl

SQL>
```

This query shows that the database has three control files, called `control01.ctl`, `control02.ctl`, and `control03.ctl`, which are stored in the directories `/u02/oradata/PROD/`, `/u03/oradata/PROD/`, and `/u05/oradata/PROD/`, respectively. The control files can be stored in any directory; `/u02`, `/u03`, and `/u05` used in the example shows that they are physically stored on different disks. You can also monitor control files using EM Database Control (on the Server tab, choose Control Files under Storage, as shown in Figure 8.9).

Control files are usually the smallest files in the database, generally between 1MB and 5MB in size. However, they can be larger depending on the PFILE/SPFILE setting for `CONTROLFILE_RECORD_KEEP_TIME` when the Recovery Manager feature is used.

FIGURE 8.9 EM Database Control showing control files

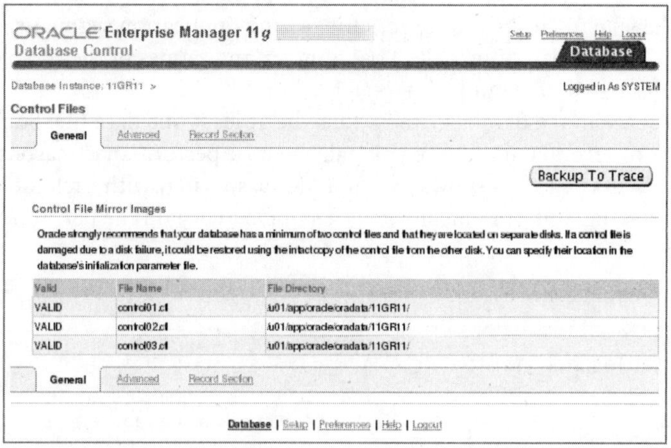

In the database, the control files keep track of the names, locations, and sizes of the database data files. Data files, and their relationship to another database structure called a *tablespace*, are examined in the next section.

Data Files

Data files are the physical files that actually store the data that has been inserted into each table in the database. The size of the data files is directly related to the amount of table data that they store. Data files are the physical structure behind another database storage area called a *tablespace*. A tablespace is a logical storage area within the database. Tablespaces group logically related segments. For example, all the tables for the Accounts Receivable application might be stored together in a tablespace called AR_TAB, and the indexes on these tables might be stored in a tablespace called AR_IDX.

By default, every Oracle 11*g* database must have at least three tablespaces. Table 8.7 describes these tablespaces.

TABLE 8.7 Required Tablespaces in Oracle 11*g*

Tablespace Name	Description
SYSTEM	Stores the data dictionary tables and PL/SQL code.
SYSAUX	Stores segments used for database options such as the Automatic Workload Repository, Online Analytical Processing (OLAP), and Spatial.
TEMP	Used for performing large sort operations. TEMP is required when the SYSTEM tablespace is created as a locally managed tablespace; otherwise, it is optional. See Chapter 10, "Allocating Database Storage and Creating Schema Objects," for details.

In addition to these three required tablespaces, most databases have tablespaces for storing other database segments such as undo and application data. Many production databases often have many more tablespaces for storing application segments. Either you or the application vendor determines the total number and names of these tablespaces. Tablespaces are discussed in detail in Chapter 10.

For each tablespace in the database, there must be at least one data file. Some tablespaces may be composed of several data files for management or performance reasons. The data dictionary view `DBA_DATA_FILES` shows the data files associated with each tablespace in the database. The following SQL statement shows a sample query on the `DBA_DATA_FILES` data dictionary view:

```
SQL> SELECT tablespace_name, file_name
  2  FROM dba_data_files
  3  ORDER BY tablespace_name;

TABLESPACE_N FILE_NAME
------------ ---------------------------------------------
APPL_DATA    /u01/app/oracle/oradata/11GR11/appl_data01.dbf
APPL_DATA    /u01/app/oracle/oradata/11GR11/appl_data02.dbf
EXAMPLE      /u01/app/oracle/oradata/11GR11/example01.dbf
SYSAUX       /u01/app/oracle/oradata/11GR11/sysaux01.dbf
SYSTEM       /u01/app/oracle/oradata/11GR11/system01.dbf
UNDOTBS1     /u01/app/oracle/oradata/11GR11/undotbs01.dbf
USERS        /u01/app/oracle/oradata/11GR11/users01.dbf

7 rows selected.
SQL>
```

The output shows that the `APPL_DATA` tablespace is comprised of two data files; all other tablespaces have one data file. You can also monitor data files using EM, as shown in Figure 8.10.

Data files are usually the largest files in the database, ranging from megabytes to gigabytes or terabytes in size.

When a user performs a SQL operation on a table, the user's server process copies the affected data from the data files into the database buffer cache in the SGA. If the user has performed a committed transaction that modifies that data, the database writer process (DBW*n*) ultimately writes the modified data back to the data files.

FIGURE 8.10 EM Database Control showing data files

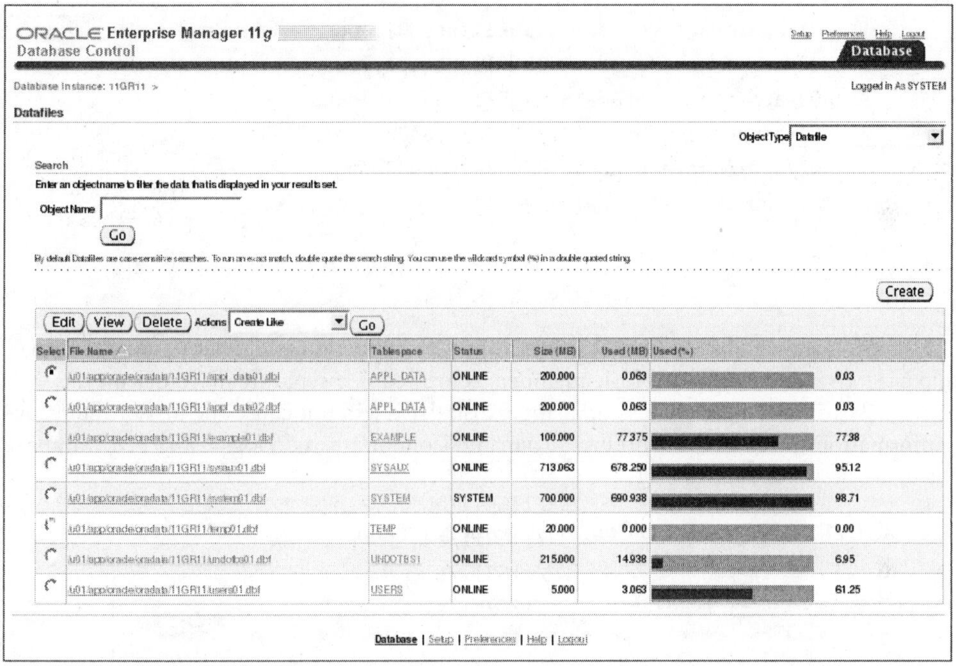

Redo Log Files

Whenever a user performs a transaction in the database, the information needed to reproduce this transaction in the event of a database failure and the user does not get a confirmation of the COMMIT until the transaction is successfully written to the redo log files.

Because of the important role that redo logs play in Oracle's recovery mechanism, they are usually multiplexed. This means that each redo log contains one or more copies of itself in case one of the copies becomes corrupt or is lost because of a hardware failure. Collectively, these sets of redo logs are referred to as *redo log groups*. Each multiplexed file within the group is called a *redo log group member*. Oracle automatically writes to all members of the redo log group to keep the files in sync. Each redo log group must be composed of one or more members. Each database must have a minimum of two redo log groups because redo logs are used in a circular fashion.

You can use the V$LOGFILE dynamic performance view to view the names of the redo log groups and the names and locations of their members, as shown here:

```
SQL> SELECT group#, member
  2  FROM v$logfile
  3  ORDER BY group#;
```

```
    GROUP# MEMBER
---------- ---------------------------------------------
         1 /u01/app/oracle/oradata/11GR11/redo01.log
         1 /u02/app/oracle/oradata/11GR11/redo01.log
         2 /u02/app/oracle/oradata/11GR11/redo02.log
         2 /u01/app/oracle/oradata/11GR11/redo02.log
         3 /u02/app/oracle/oradata/11GR11/redo03.log
         3 /u01/app/oracle/oradata/11GR11/redo03.log

6 rows selected.
SQL>
```

This output shows that the database has a total of three redo log groups and that each group has two members. Each of the members is located in a separate directory on the server's disk drives so that the loss of a single disk drive will not cause the loss of the recovery information stored in the redo logs. You can also monitor redo logs using EM Database Control, as shown in Figure 8.11.

FIGURE 8.11 EM Database Control showing redo logs

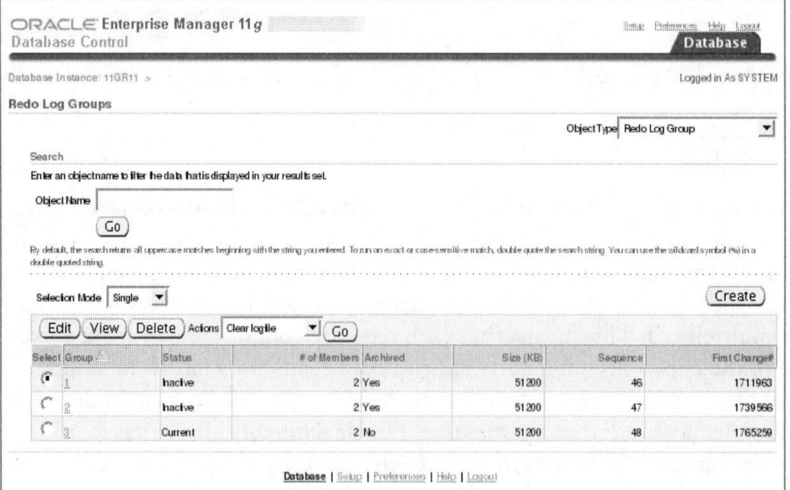

When a user performs a DML activity on the database, the recovery information for this transaction is written to the redo log buffer by the user's server process. LGWR eventually writes this recovery information to the active redo log group until that log group is filled. Once the current log fills with transaction information, LGWR switches to the next redo log until that log group fills with transaction information, and so on, until all available redo logs are used. When the last redo log is used, LGWR wraps around and starts using the first redo log again. As shown in the following query, you can use the `V$LOG` dynamic performance view to display which redo log group is currently active and being written to by LGWR:

```
SQL> SELECT group#, members, status
  2  FROM v$log
  3  ORDER BY group#;

    GROUP#    MEMBERS STATUS
---------- ---------- ----------------
         1          2 CURRENT
         2          2 INACTIVE
         3          2 INACTIVE
```

This output shows that redo log group number 1 is currently active and being written to by LGWR. Once redo log group 3 is full, LGWR switches to redo log group 4.

When LGWR wraps around from the last redo log group back to the first redo log group, any recovery information previously stored in the first redo log group is overwritten and therefore no longer available for recovery purposes. However, if the database is operating in *archive log mode*, the contents of these previously used logs are copied to a secondary location before the log is reused by LGWR. If this archiving feature is enabled, it is the job of the ARC*n* background process described in the previous section to copy the contents of the redo log to the archive location. These copies of old redo log entries are called *archive logs*. Figure 8.12 shows this process graphically.

FIGURE 8.12 How ARC*n* copies redo log entries to disk

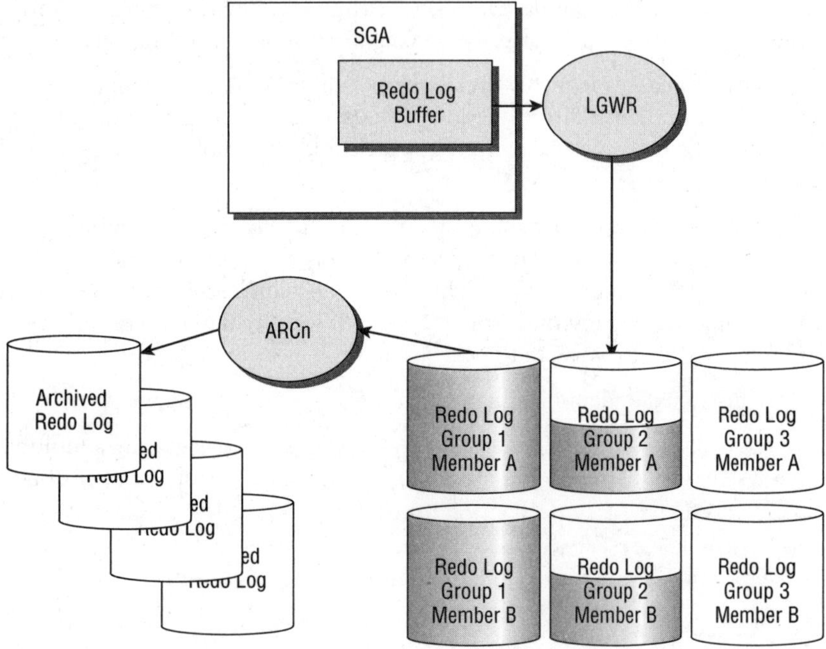

In Figure 8.12, the first redo log group has been filled, and LGWR has moved on to redo log group 2. As soon as LGWR switches from redo log group 1 to redo log group 2, the ARC*n* process starts copying the contents of redo log group 1 to the archive log file location. Once the first redo log group is safely archived, LGWR is free to wrap around and reuse the first redo log group once redo log group 3 is filled.

Nearly all production databases run in archive-log mode because they need to be able to redo all transactions since the last backup in the event of a hardware failure or user error that damages the database.

A database can have multiple archive processes and multiple archive destinations. I will discuss more about archiving and how the archived redo logs are used for database recovery in Chapter 15.

If LGWR needs to write to the redo log group that ARC*n* is trying to copy but cannot because the destination is full, the database hangs until space is cleared on the drive.

The Logical Structure

In the previous section, you saw how the Oracle database is configured physically. The obvious question is where and how your table is stored in a database. Let's now try to relate the physical storage to the logical structures you know, such as tables and indexes.

Oracle logically divides the database into smaller units to manage, store, and retrieve data efficiently. The following paragraphs give you an overview of the logical structures:

Tablespaces The database is logically divided into smaller units at the highest level, called *tablespaces*. A tablespace has a direct relation to the physical structure—a data file can belong to one and only one tablespace. A tablespace could have more than one data file associated with it.

A tablespace commonly groups related logical structures together. For example, you might group data specific to an application in a tablespace. This will ease the management of the application from the DBA's point of view. This logical division helps administer a portion of the database without affecting the rest of it. Each Oracle 11*g* database must have at least three tablespaces: `SYSTEM`, `SYSAUX`, and `TEMP`.

Tablespaces are discussed in detail in Chapter 10.

Blocks A *block* is the smallest unit of storage in Oracle. A block is usually a multiple of the operating-system block size. A data block corresponds to a specific number of bytes of storage space. The block size is based on the parameter DB_BLOCK_SIZE and determined when the database is created.

Extents An *extent* is the next level of logical grouping. It is a grouping of contiguous blocks, allocated in one chunk.

Segments A *segment* is a set of extents allocated for logical structures such as tables, indexes, clusters, table partitions, materialized views, and so on. Whenever you create a logical structure that stores data, Oracle allocates a segment, which contains at least one extent, which in turn has at least one block. A segment can be associated to only one tablespace.

Figure 8.13 shows the relationship between data files, tablespaces, segments, extents, and blocks.

FIGURE 8.13 Logical database structure

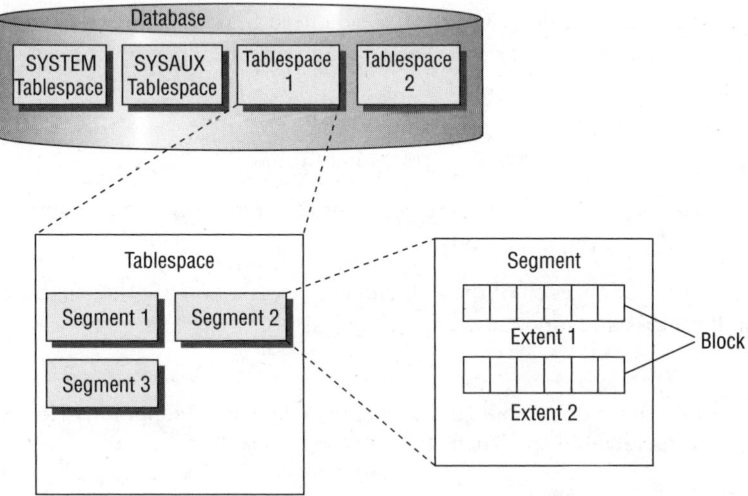

A schema is a logical structure that groups the database objects. A schema is not directly related to a tablespace or to any other logical storage structure. The objects that belong to a schema can reside in different tablespaces, and a tablespace can have objects that belong to multiple schemas. Schema objects include structures such as tables, indexes, synonyms, procedures, triggers, database links, so on.

The next section talks about how to install and configure the Oracle 11*g* software on your server so that you can then create a database. Creating a database is described in detail in Chapter 2, "Using Single-Row Functions."

Installing Oracle 11*g*

One of your duties as an Oracle DBA is to install and configure the Oracle 11*g* software on the server so that a database can be created to store application data. This section discusses each of the steps that you must perform in order to successfully install Oracle 11*g*.

The examples in this section are for a Linux server, but most of the concepts apply equally to Windows platforms. Any significant differences between Linux and Windows are noted.

Review the Documentation

Before beginning an installation of Oracle 11*g*, you need to review several documents so that you completely understand the installation requirements. These documents include the following:

- The installation guide for your operating system
- The general release notes for the version of Oracle you are installing
- The operating system–specific release notes for the version of Oracle you are installing
- Any "quick start" installation guides

Before you begin, review each of these documents so that you are thoroughly familiar with the install process and any known associated issues.

All these documents are available on Oracle's Technology Network website located at `http://otn.oracle.com/index.html`.

Review the System Requirements

The next task is to review your server-hardware specifications to see whether they meet or exceed the specifications in the install documentation. Minimally, this means you must confirm that your server meets the installation requirements in these four areas:

- The operating system is of the proper release level.
- The server has adequate memory to perform the install and run an instance.
- The server has adequate CPU resources to perform the install and run an instance.
- The server has adequate disk storage space to perform the install and run a database.

Table 8.8 shows the recommended minimum hardware requirements for an Oracle 11*g* installation.

TABLE 8.8 Recommended Minimum Hardware Requirements for Oracle 11*g*

Hardware Component	Recommended Requirement
Memory	1GB.
Swap space	1.5GB or equal to the amount of RAM.
Temp space	200MB of free space in the `/tmp` directory on Unix systems.
Free disk space	1.5GB to 3.5GB of disk space is required for the base Oracle 11*g* installation.

The Oracle Universal Installer, which is described in the subsequent section "Using the Oracle Universal Installer," will perform a quick system check prior to starting an installation to see whether your system meets the specific requirements for your operating system. If your system does not meet the minimum requirements, the installer returns an error and aborts.

On Unix systems, you must examine one critical system requirement before installation: Unix kernel parameters. Unix kernel parameters are used to configure the Unix operating-system settings for operating system–level operations that impact Oracle-related activities such as the following:

- The maximum size allowed for a sharable memory segment on the server, which can impact the SGA size
- The maximum number of files that can be open on the server at one time, which impacts the total number of users and files in the database
- The number of processes that can run concurrently on the server, which impacts the number of users and the ability to use some optional features

The systems administrator usually makes Unix kernel changes, which may require a server reboot in order to take effect. The install guide and/or release notes provide details on the appropriate kernel setting for your operating system. In addition to kernel settings, the system administrator may have to configure the server's disk storage system and backup hardware before installing the Oracle software.

Plan Your Install

Once you review the documentation and system requirements, you are ready to begin planning your installation. This is the last step before actually running the Oracle Universal Installer.

One way to simplify installation planning is to adopt the Optimal Flexible Architecture (OFA) model that Oracle recommends as a best-practice methodology for managing Oracle installations in Unix environments (and to a lesser extent, Windows environments). Cary Millsap designed the OFA model to produce database installations that are easier to manage, upgrade, and back up, while at the same time minimizing problems associated with database growth. The OFA model addresses four areas:

- Naming conventions for Unix file systems and mount points
- Naming conventions for directory paths
- Naming conventions for database files
- Standardized locations for Oracle-related files

In addition to using the OFA model, planning your install also means answering the following questions:

- Which operating-system user will own the installed Oracle software?
- On which disk drive and directory will the Oracle software be installed?
- What directory structure will be used to store the Oracle software, its related configuration files, and the database itself?
- How should the database files be laid out so that the maximum performance benefits will be realized?
- How should the database files be laid out so that the maximum recoverability benefits will be realized?

Creating the Oracle User Account

On Unix systems, every file is owned by an operating-system user account. Therefore, before you can install the Oracle software, you must create a Unix user account that will own the Oracle binaries. The username for this account can be anything, but common Oracle usernames include `oracle`, `ora11g`, and `ora111`. Each Unix user is also in one or more operating-system groups. Create a new operating-system group for the Oracle Unix user. This group is usually called `dba`, and you will be prompted for it later during the installation.

On Windows systems, you can choose an account that has administrative privileges on the server.

Naming Volumes and Mount Points

Unless Oracle's Automatic Storage Management feature or raw devices are used, almost all files on a Unix server are stored on logical storage areas called *volumes* that are attached, or *mounted*, to directories, or *mount points*, by the Unix system administrator. The OFA model suggests that these mount points be given a name that consists of a combination of a character and numeric values. Common OFA mount points for Unix systems include the following:

- /u01
- /mnt01
- /du01
- /d01

Notice that the naming convention for these mount points is generic. The mount point's name has no relationship to what type of file it will ultimately hold. The OFA model recommends this generic naming convention because it provides the greatest flexibility for future management of the server's file systems.

The concept of mount points does not apply directly to Windows environments. Windows environments assign a standard Windows drive letter (for example, C:, D:) to each volume.

Creating OFA Directory Paths

The OFA model prescribes that the directory structures under the mount points use a consistent and meaningful naming convention. In addition to this naming convention, the OFA model also assigns standard operating-system environment variable names to some of these directory paths as "nicknames" to aid in navigation and to ensure the portability of the directory structures in the event that they need to be moved to new file systems.

Table 8.9 shows the two operating-system environment variables used in the OFA model, along with the directories with which the variables are associated, for Unix systems.

TABLE 8.9 Comparison of Unix Directory Paths and Variables

Environment Variable	Directory Path	Description
$ORACLE_BASE	/u01/app/oracle	Top-level directory for Oracle software on the host server
$ORACLE_HOME	/u01/app/oracle/product/11.1.0/db_1	Directory into which the Oracle 11*g* software will be installed

Table 8.10 shows the variables and directories used in the OFA model for Windows systems.

TABLE 8.10 Comparison of Windows Directory Paths and Variables

Environment Variable	Directory Path	Description
`%ORACLE_BASE%`	`D:\ORACLE`	Top-level directory for Oracle software on the host server
`%ORACLE_HOME%`	`D:\ORACLE\ORA111\DB_1`	Directory into which the Oracle 11*g* software will be installed

These environment variables are used extensively when installing, patching, upgrading, and managing Oracle systems. Table 8.11 shows several examples of how these variables define the locations of other Oracle directories.

TABLE 8.11 Common Uses of `ORACLE_BASE` and `ORACLE_HOME`

Directory	Description
`$ORACLE_HOME/dbs`	Default location for pfiles and spfiles on Unix systems
`%ORACLE_HOME%\database`	Default location for pfiles and spfiles on Windows systems
`$ORACLE_BASE/admin/PROD/pfile`	Location of the pfile for a database called `PROD` on Unix systems
`%ORACLE_BASE%\admin\PROD\pfile`	Location of the pfile for a database called `PROD` on Windows systems
`$ORACLE_HOME/network/admin`	Default location for Oracle Net configuration files on Unix systems
`%ORACLE_HOME%\network\admin`	Default location for Oracle Net configuration files on Windows systems
`$ORACLE_HOME/rdbms/admin`	Location of many Oracle database-configuration scripts on Unix systems
`%ORACLE_HOME%\rdbms\admin`	Location of many database-configuration scripts on Windows systems

For Unix systems, Table 8.11 says `$ORACLE_HOME/dbs` is the default location for the pfile and spfile but then says that pfiles should be stored in `$ORACLE_BASE/admin/<instance>/pfile`. Windows systems are similar. This implies that the same file needs to be in two locations at the same time. You can accomplish this using two tricks. Which you use depends on your operating system.

The following examples use 11GR11 as the database (and instance) name. On Unix systems, you can create the pfile in the $ORACLE_BASE/admin/11GR11/pfile directory and then create a symbolic link in $ORACLE_HOME/dbs that points to the file in $ORACLE_BASE/admin/11GR11/pfile using this syntax:

```
ln -s $ORACLE_BASE/admin/11GR11/pfile/init11GR11.ora
   $ORACLE_HOME/dbs/initPROD.ora
```

On Windows systems, you can create the pfile in the %ORACLE_BASE%\admin\11GR11\pfile directory and then put another pfile in %ORACLE_HOME%\dbs that contains a single entry that points to the other pfile in %ORACLE_BASE%\admin\11GR11\pfile like this:

```
ifile=D:\oracle\admin\11GR11\pfile\init11GR11.ora
```

Using these techniques allows you to put the initialization parameter files in their default locations under $ORACLE_HOME but also in their desired location under $ORACLE_BASE.

Why should the "real" copy of the pfiles be stored under $ORACLE_BASE instead of $ORACLE_HOME? Well, it is a good idea to keep only version-specific files under $ORACLE_HOME. That way, when you eventually uninstall the software from an old $ORACLE_HOME, you won't lose your carefully tailored initialization files.

In addition to $ORACLE_BASE and $ORACLE_HOME, a few other non-OFA-related operating-system environment variables on Unix and Windows systems are important to be aware of. These are described in Table 8.12.

TABLE 8.12 Common Non-OFA Environment Variables

Operating-System Variable	Description
$ORACLE_SID	Defines which instance a Unix user session should be connecting to on the server.
%ORACLE_SID%	Defines which instance a Windows user session should connect to on the server.
$TNS_ADMIN	Specifies where the Oracle Net configuration files are stored on Unix systems—if they are to be stored outside their default location of $ORACLE_HOME/network/admin.
%TNS_ADMIN%	Specifies where the Oracle Net configuration files are stored on Windows systems—if they are to be stored outside their default location of %ORACLE_HOME%\network\admin.

TABLE 8.12 Common Non-OFA Environment Variables *(continued)*

Operating-System Variable	Description
$TWO_TASK	Establishes a default Oracle Net connection string that will be used if none is specified by the user.
%LOCAL%	Establishes a default Oracle Net connection string that will be used if none is specified by the user.
$LD_LIBRARY_PATH	Specifies the locations of the Oracle shared object libraries. This variable usually points to $ORACLE_HOME/lib or $ORACLE_HOME/lib32 on Unix systems.
$PATH	Tells the operating system in which directories to look for executable files on Unix systems.
%PATH%	Tells the operating system in which directories to look for executable files on Windows systems.

There is no need to set any of these variables for an Oracle 11*g* install, except for ORACLE_BASE. These variables are important when you're ready to create a database.

For complete preinstallation checks and detailed commands to create Oracle software owner and groups on the Linux platform, please read the Oracle documentation's Oracle Database Installation Guide 11*g* Release 1 for Linux, specifically, Chapter 2, "Oracle Database Pre-installation Requirements." As mentioned earlier, all Oracle documentation is available at `http://tahiti.oracle.com`.

Using the Oracle Universal Installer

You use the Oracle Universal Installer (OUI) to install and configure the Oracle 11*g* software. The OUI is a Java-based application that provides the same installation look and feel no matter which operating system the install is being run on. The OUI process consists of seven primary operations:

- Mounting the CD and starting the OUI
- Performing preinstallation checks
- Responding to server-specific prompts for file locations, names, and so on
- Selecting the products you want to install

- Copying the files from the install media to `$ORACLE_HOME`
- Compiling the Oracle binaries
- Performing post-install operations using configuration assistants

Mounting the CD and Starting the OUI

To begin the install process, insert the Oracle 11*g* CD in the server. On some Unix systems, you may have to use the appropriate operating-system command to mount the CD in your server before it is accessible.

After mounting the CD, you may want to copy its contents to a staging directory so that you can install from there instead of from the CD. If you download software from the OTN, you don't need to mount the CD. You can start the install from the disk.

OUI installations on Unix systems must also set the X Windows `DISPLAY` environment variable; otherwise, the OUI will not appear.

Performing Preinstallation Checks

Start the OUI using the `runInstaller.sh` command, as shown in Figure 8.14.

FIGURE 8.14 Invoking Oracle 11*g* install

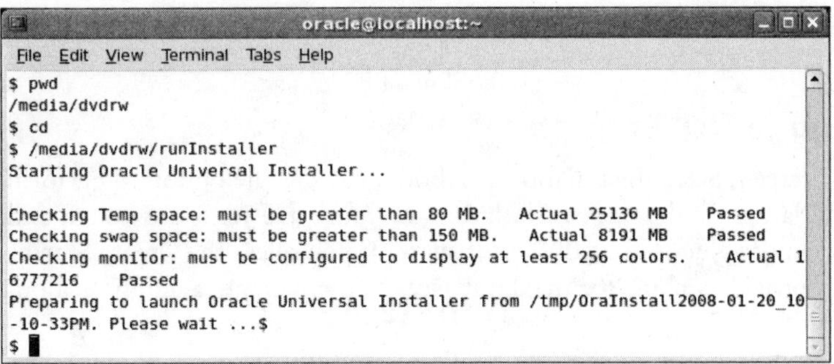

Notice that the output shows that the OUI checked the server's operating-system version, available RAM, temporary and swap space, and so on.

If needed, you can turn off the system verification that occurs prior to the installation by using the `-ignoreSysPrereqs` option of the `runInstaller` command.

Once the preinstallation tests are completed and passed, the OUI displays the initial OUI screen shown in Figure 8.15.

Choose the Oracle Database 11g option, and click the Next button on the OUI screen to proceed with the installation.

FIGURE 8.15 The initial OUI installation screen

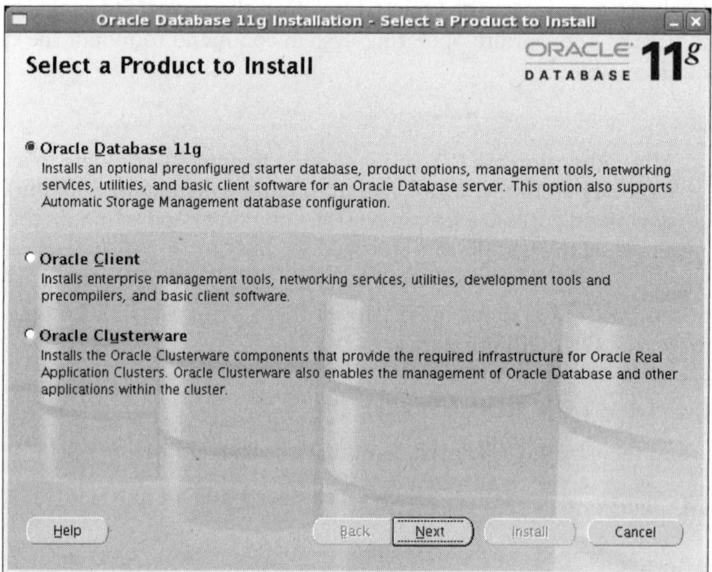

Responding to OUI Prompts

The next OUI screen, Select Installation Method, provides the option to perform a basic or advanced installation. In the basic installation, no more questions are asked, and the OUI takes all the default values to install the software. If you select the Create Starter Database check box and provide a name for the database, OUI will create a database along with the software install.

For this example, choose Advanced installation on this screen, as shown in Figure 8.16.

The next OUI screen, Specify Inventory Directory and Credentials, prompts you for two pieces of information:

- The location for the inventory files that the OUI uses to keep track of which Oracle products are installed on the server
- The name of the operating-system group of which the user doing the install is a member

You can see both items in Figure 8.17.

FIGURE 8.16 Select Installation Method screen

Oracle Database 11g Installation - Select Installation Method

ORACLE DATABASE 11g

Select Installation Method

Basic Installation

Perform full Oracle Database 11g installation with standard configuration options requiring minimal input.This option uses file system for storage, and a single password for all database accounts.

Oracle Base Location: /u01/app/oracle Browse...

Oracle Home Location: /u01/app/oracle/product/11.1.0/db_1 Browse...

Installation Type: Enterprise Edition (3.3GB)

UNIX DBA Group: dba

Create Starter Database (additional 1482MB)

Global Database Name: orcl

Database Password: Confirm Password:

This password is used for the SYS, SYSTEM, SYSMAN, and DBSNMP accounts.

Advanced Installation

Allows advanced selections such as different passwords for the SYS, SYSTEM, SYSMAN, and DBSNMP accounts, database character set, product languages, automated backups, custom installation, and alternative storage options such as Automatic Storage Management.

Help Back Next Install Cancel

FIGURE 8.17 Specify Inventory Directory and Credentials screen

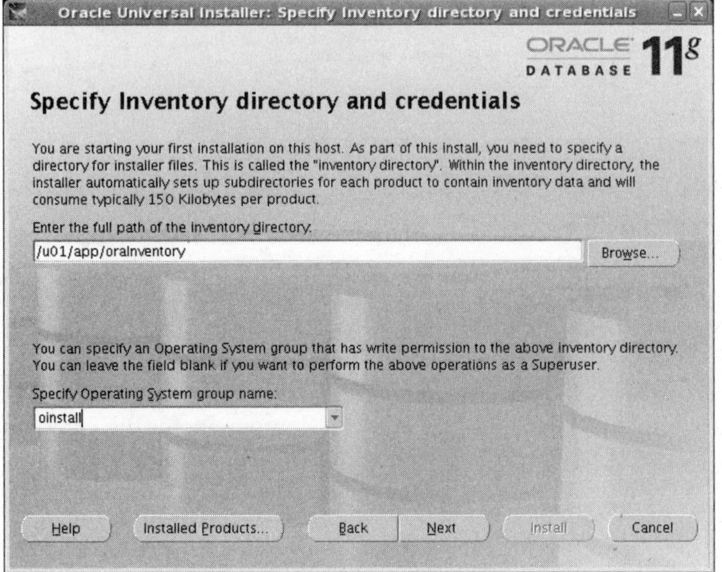

The value suggested for the `oraInventory` location, `/u01/app/oraInventory`, was selected based on the `$ORACLE_BASE` environment variable. The value suggested for the operating-system group, `oinstall`, is the Oracle default value. Because both settings are correct for our example environment, click the Next button to continue the installation.

Selecting Products to Install

The next screen, Select Installation Type, prompts you to select the type of installation to perform. In this example, I selected the Enterprise Edition option, as shown in Figure 8.18. Choose Enterprise Edition or Standard Edition based on the license you purchased. You may also choose Custom, if you want to pick and choose the products.

FIGURE 8.18 Select Installation Type screen

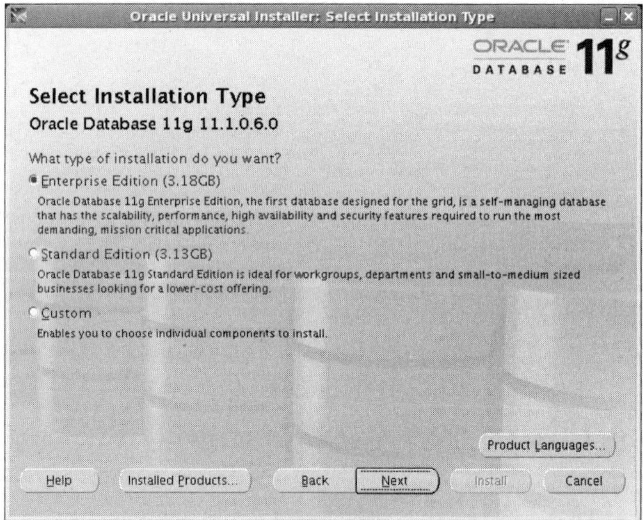

The next screen, Install Location, sets the software installation locations, as shown in Figure 8.19.

On the screen shown in Figure 8.19, the default values are populated based on the `ORACLE_BASE` variable. Click the Next button to open the next screen, which is shown in Figure 8.20.

The OUI goes through a second round of installation checks that confirm that the server's operating-system version and configuration are appropriate for the Enterprise Edition installation of Oracle 11*g*. If all the verification checks complete successfully, click the Next button to open the Select Configuration Option screen, as shown in Figure 8.21.

If these operating-system checks do not succeed, you must correct the areas that are failing the checks before continuing.

FIGURE 8.19 Install Location screen

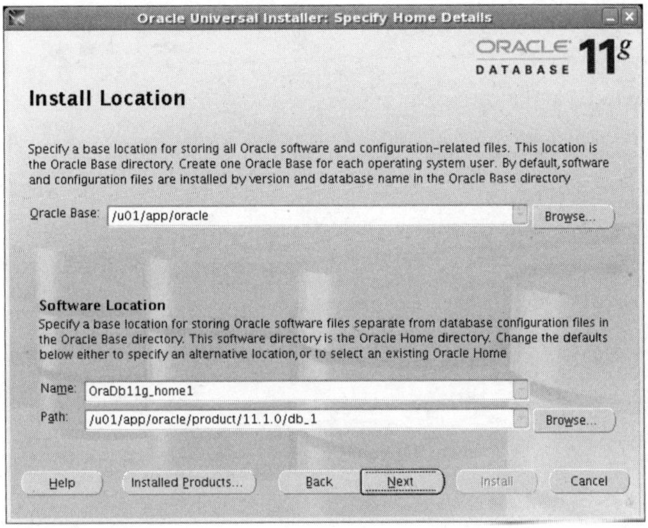

FIGURE 8.20 Prerequisite checks

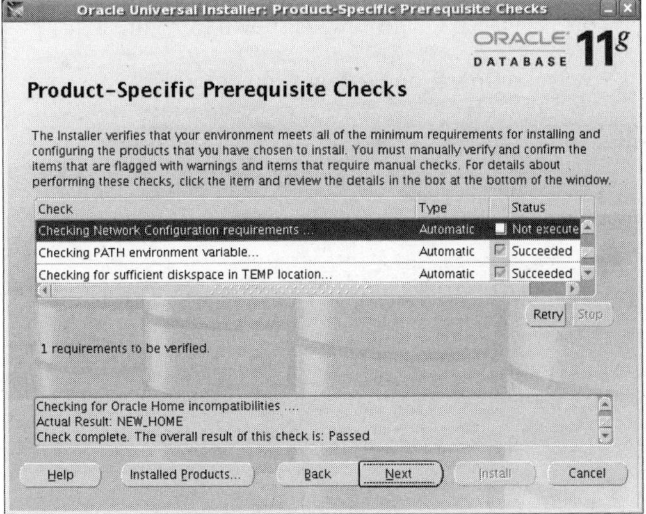

FIGURE 8.21 Select Configuration Option screen

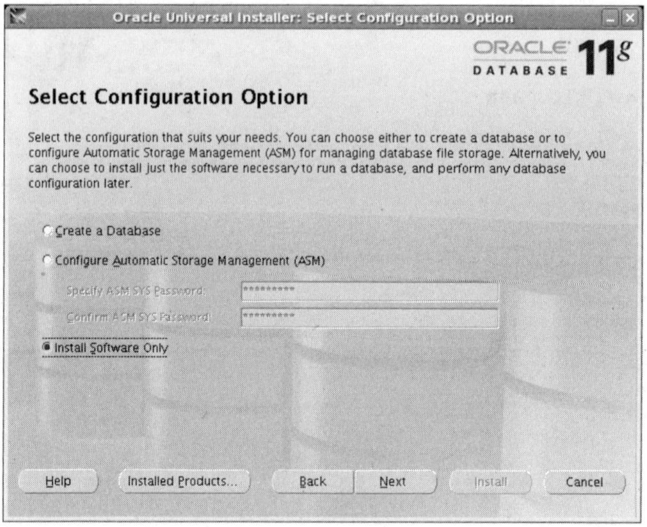

The next screen, Privileged Operating System Groups, asks whether you want to create a database following the installation process. Because creating a database is covered in Chapter 2, you'll skip this step for now. Choose the Install Software Only option, and then click Next to specify the privileged OS groups, as shown in Figure 8.22.

FIGURE 8.22 Privileged Operating System Groups screen

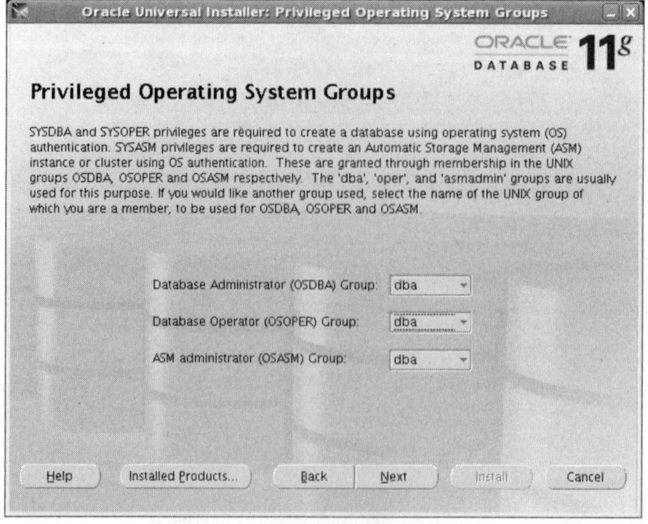

You can choose the defaults or specify specific OS groups for each function. Click Next to open the Summary screen, as shown in Figure 8.23.

FIGURE 8.23 The Summary screen

This screen summarizes all the options you selected and all the components that will be installed. If you need to make changes, click the Back button to modify your previous selections. If you are satisfied with your selections, click the Next button to start copying the Oracle binaries to the `$ORACLE_HOME` directory.

Copying and Compiling Files

The OUI displays status information while the installation and setup is in progress. Once the file-copy portion of the installation is complete, the OUI begins linking the binaries to create the executable files needed to make the Oracle 11*g* software run on the server. On Unix systems, after the linking process, you are prompted to execute configuration scripts as the superuser root from the Unix command line, as shown in Figure 8.24.

FIGURE 8.24 Running the script as root

Execute Configuration scripts

The following configuration scripts need to be executed as the "root" user.

Scripts to be executed:

Number	Script Location
1	/u01/app/oraInventory/orainstRoot.sh
2	/u01/app/oracle/product/11.1.0/db_1/root.sh

To execute the configuration scripts:
1. Open a terminal window
2. Log in as "root"
3. Run the scripts
4. Return to this window and click "OK" to continue

Help OK

The orainstRoot.sh script creates the inventory location and necessary inventory directory. The following example shows this orainstRoot.sh script being executed from another session:

```
$ su -
Password:
# cd /u01/app/oraInventory
./orainstRoot.sh
Creating the Oracle inventory pointer file (/etc/oraInst.loc)
Changing permissions of /u01/app/oraInventory to 770.
Changing groupname of /u01/app/oraInventory to oinstall.
The execution of the script is complete
$
```

Running the script creates some directory structures that are used to support the Oracle installation and sets the proper file permissions on those directories as well as other files. Once the orainstRoot.sh script executes, click the Continue button to choose the installation type.

On Unix and Linux platforms, the orainstRoot.sh script creates a file named /etc/oraInst.loc, which has information about the Oracle Inventory location and the software installation owner name. The content of the /etc/oraInst.loc is as follows:

```
$ cat /etc/oraInst.loc
inventory_loc=/u01/app/oraInventory
inst_group=oinstall
$
```

The root.sh script should be executed as root. Executing the root.sh script copies some files to a location outside $ORACLE_HOME and sets the permissions on several files inside and outside $ORACLE_HOME. Once the root.sh script executes successfully, click OK to continue the installation.

One important file created by the root.sh script is the /etc/oratab file (the /var/opt/oracle/oratab file on Solaris). When databases are created on this server, this file will have information about the database and which oracle home directory is used by the database.

If you have multiple installations to perform, you can speed up the process and minimize errors by building an OUI response file. This text file contains all the necessary responses to the OUI prompts so that an unattended, silent install is possible.

Performing Postinstall Tasks

Once the `root.sh` script has completed, the OUI will perform some brief postinstallation configuration activities before displaying the End of Installation screen, as shown in Figure 8.25.

FIGURE 8.25 End of Installation screen

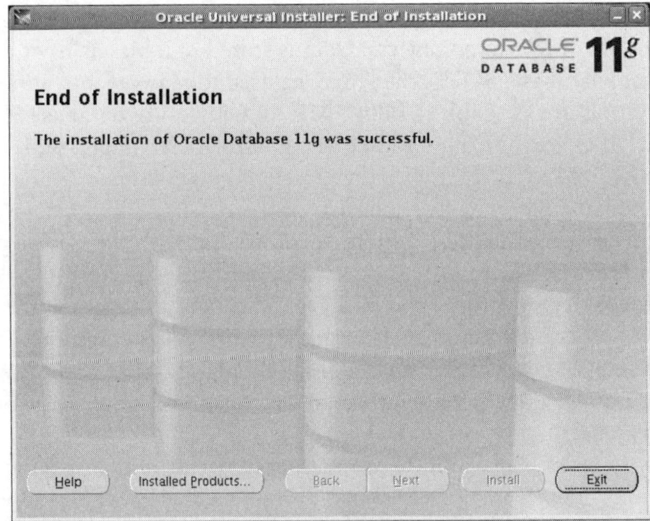

Click the Exit button and then the OK button on the pop-up screen to exit the OUI and return to the Unix prompt.

The OUI on Windows systems also offers a Basic Installation mode in which only a few installation questions are asked before the file copying begins. If you select the Advanced Installation mode, the prompts will closely follow those shown for Unix in this section.

Once the OUI is complete, you should have a completely installed and configured `$ORACLE_HOME`. You'll use this software to create your first database in Chapter 9, "Creating and Oracle 11*g* Database."

Summary

This chapter introduced you to the Oracle 11*g* database architecture and installing the Oracle 11*g* software. First I covered the Oracle database fundamentals and the Oracle database components, and then I showed how to create the database by installing the Oracle 11*g* software.

Most popular databases today are relational databases. Relational databases consist of data composed of a set of relational objects. Data is stored in tables as rows and columns. Oracle is a relational database. SQL is the language used to manage and administer Oracle databases. Several tools are available to administer an Oracle 11*g* database. The most common ones used by DBAs are SQL*Plus and Oracle Enterprise Manager. SQL Developer is a GUI tool that can be used to interact with the Oracle 11*g* database.

The Oracle 11*g* database architecture consists of three major components: memory, processes, and storage. A user process initiates a connection with the Oracle database and starts a server process. The server process is responsible for performing the tasks on the database. The memory structures and background processes together are an Oracle instance. The server process communicates with the memory structure known as the system global area. The SGA consists of a shared pool, database buffer cache, and redo log buffer. The shared pool also includes components such as a Java pool, large pool, result cache, and streams pool.

There are many types of background processes, each performing a specific job to maintain and manage the database instance. All databases have five background processes: database writer, checkpoint writer, log writer, process monitor, and system monitor. Depending on the configuration of the database, there may be other background processes such as archiver, ASM balancing, and so on.

The physical data structure consists of several files stored on disk. The most important file is the control file, which keeps track of several important pieces of information such as database name, names of data files and redo log files, backup information, so on. The CKPT process is responsible for keeping the control file updated. Redo log files contain information from the redo log buffer. The LGWR process is responsible for writing the redo log buffer contents to the redo log files. Oracle metadata and application data are stored in data files. The DBW*n* process is responsible for writing dirty blocks from the database buffer cache to the data files.

Looking at the logical structure of the database, a tablespace is the highest level of logical unit. A tablespace consists of several segments. A segment consists of one or more extents. An extent is a contiguous allocation of blocks. A block is the smallest unit of storage in an Oracle database.

Installing the Oracle 11*g* software is a relatively easy task once the preinstall checks and hardware requirements are met. Installing Oracle 11*g* is a joint task between the system administrator and DBA, because certain scripts need to be run as root on Linux/Unix platforms.

Exam Essentials

Describe the Oracle tools and what they are used for. Know which tools are available for connecting to and interacting with an Oracle database. Understand how these tools differ from one another.

Understand the Oracle architecture components. Be able to describe the logical and physical components of the Oracle architecture and the components that make up each. Know the relationship between segments, extents, database blocks, and operating-system blocks.

Know the background processes Understand the Oracle 11*g* background processes and how they are used. The important ones to know are DBWn, SMON, CKPT, PMON, LGWR, ARCn, RBAL, and ASMB.

Identify the three types of database files that constitute the database. Understand the purpose and key differences between the control files, data files, and redo log files.

Explain and categorize the SGA memory structures. Identify the SGA areas along with the subcomponents contained within each of these areas.

Explain Oracle 11*g* system requirements. Know what the requirements are for available server disk space and memory prior to performing an Oracle 11*g* installation.

Describe the Optimal Flexible Architecture. Be able to explain the concepts associated with the OFA model and how to implement an OFA-compliant installation and database directory structure.

Describe the steps for installation and configuration. Know how to set up the Oracle installation environment so that the OUI can be used to install and configure the Oracle 11*g* software.

Review Questions

1. What are the benefits of using the OFA standard for installing Oracle 11*g*? (Choose all that apply.)

   A. Helps eliminate fragmentation of free space in the SYSTEM tablespace

   B. Helps improve the database performance

   C. Facilitates routine administrative tasks such as software backups

   D. Helps avoid data-block corruption

2. You are trying to install Oracle 11*g* and the OUI prerequisite check failed. What should you do?

   A. Ignore the error, and proceed with installation.

   B. Cancel the installation, and try to install on a different server.

   C. Correct the underlying issue, and retry the installation.

   D. Cancel the installation, correct the underlying issue, and restart the installation.

3. When installing Oracle 11*g* on the Linux platform, which file is created by executing the `orainstRoot.sh` script as root?

   A. `/etc/oratab`

   B. `/etc/oraInst.loc`

   C. `$ORACLE_HOME/root.sh`

   D. None—the `orainstRoot.sh` script starts background processes required to start the OUI.

4. Which component is not part of the Oracle instance?

   A. System global area

   B. Process monitor

   C. Control file

   D. Shared pool

   E. None

5. Which background process guarantees that committed data is saved even when the changes have not been recorded in data files?

   A. DBW*n*

   B. PMON

   C. LGWR

   D. CKPT

   E. ARC*n*

6. You've just been hired as a DBA for a large company. During the interview process, you were shown the job description for the position. Which of the following tasks might have been included in this job description?

   A. Install and configure Oracle 11*g* software.

   B. Implement database installations according to OFA guidelines.

   C. Use OFA-compliant naming conventions for database files and directories.

   D. Any of the above may have been included on the DBA job description.

7. Which of the following best describes a RAC configuration?

   A. One database, multiple instances

   B. One instance, multiple databases

   C. Multiple databases on multiple servers

   D. Multiple shared server processes catering one database

8. Which component of the SGA contains the parsed SQL code?

   A. Database buffer cache

   B. Dictionary cache

   C. Library cache

   D. Parse cache

9. Which are the tasks accomplished by the SMON process? (Choose all that apply.)

   A. Performs recovery at instance startup

   B. Performs cleanup after a user session is terminated

   C. Starts any server process that stopped running

   D. Coalesces contiguous free space in dictionary-managed tablespaces

10. Choose the best statement from the options related to segments.

    A. A contiguous set of blocks constitutes a segment.

    B. A nonpartitioned table can have only one segment.

    C. A segment can belong to more than one tablespace.

    D. All of the above are true.

11. The Oracle Universal Installer prompts for which variable if not set?

    A. `ORACLE_HOME`

    B. `ORACLE_SID`

    C. `ORACLE_BASE`

    D. `ORACLE_INSTALL_BASE`

12. Which SGA component will you increase or configure so that RMAN backups are not using area from the shared pool?
    - A. Java pool
    - B. Streams pool
    - C. Recovery pool
    - D. Large pool

13. When a user session is terminated, which processes are responsible for cleaning up and releasing locks? (Choose all that apply.)
    - A. DBW*n*
    - B. LGWR
    - C. MMON
    - D. PMON
    - E. SMON

14. The LRU algorithm is used to manage what part of the Oracle architecture?
    - A. Users who log on to the database infrequently and may be candidates for being dropped
    - B. The data file that stores the least amount of information and will need the least frequent backup
    - C. The tables that users rarely access so that they can be moved to a less active tablespace
    - D. The shared pool and database buffer cache portions of the SGA

15. Two structures make up an Oracle server: an instance and a database. Which of the following best describes the difference between an Oracle instance and a database?
    - A. An instance consists of memory structures and processes, whereas a database is composed of physical files.
    - B. An instance is used only during database creation; after that, the database is all that is needed.
    - C. An instance is started whenever the demands on the database are high, but the database is used all the time.
    - D. An instance is configured using a pfile, whereas a database is configured using an spfile.

16. Which of the following is the proper order of Oracle's storage hierarchy, from smallest to largest?
    - A. Operating-system block, database block, segment, extent
    - B. Operating-system block, database block, extent, segment
    - C. Segment, extent, database block, operating-system block
    - D. Segment, database block, extent, operating-system block

17. You've been asked to install Oracle 11*g* on a new Unix server. You're likely to ask the Unix system administrator to do all but which of the following for you in order to get the new server ready for Oracle?

A. Modify the server's kernel parameters.

B. Create a new Unix user to own the Oracle software.

C. Create the mount points and directory structure using the OFA model.

D. Determine which directory will be used for `$ORACLE_HOME`.

18. Oracle's OFA model specifies a naming convention for all but which of the following?

A. Database name

B. Mount points

C. Directory paths

D. Database filenames

19. The Oracle Universal Installer is started by executing which program?

A. `emctl`

B. `runInstaller`

C. `ouistart`

D. `isqlplusctl`

20. On Unix systems, the script `root.sh` must be executed during the installation process. What is the purpose of this script?

A. It creates the root user in the database.

B. It creates the root directory for the server.

C. It grants root superuser privileges to the Oracle Unix account.

D. It copies files and sets permissions on files outside `$ORACLE_HOME`.

Answers to Review Questions

1. A, C. The OFA standard helps in administering the Oracle software installation and all related Oracle files, such as alert logs and data files. OFA recommends that separate tablespaces be created to store application data; the SYSTEM tablespace should be used only for the data dictionary. By separating the software from database files, backups are made easy.

2. C. On the prerequisite check screen, you have the option to retry a failed test. So, you can fix the underlying issue and let OUI perform the test again to continue the installation.

3. B. If an Oracle installation is performed the first time on a server, the `orainstRoot.sh` script needs to be executed to create the `/etc/oraInst.loc` file. The `oraInst.loc` file specifies the Oracle inventory location.

4. C. Control file, data file, and redo log files are part of the Oracle database. The Oracle instance constitutes the memory structures and background processes.

5. C. The log writer (LGWR) process writes the redo log buffer information to the online redo log files. A commit operation is completed only after the redo buffer is written to online redo log files.

6. D. The tasks that a DBA performs encompass all these areas plus managing database storage, security, and availability.

7. A. With Real Application Clusters, multiple instances (known as *nodes*) can mount one database. One instance can be associated with only one database.

8. C. The shared SQL area is stored in the library cache in a shared pool and is shared between users. If a query is executed again before it is aged out of the library cache, Oracle will use the parsed code and execution plan from the library cache. The database buffer cache has the data blocks cached. The dictionary cache caches data dictionary information. There is no SGA component called the parse cache.

9. A, D. SMON is responsible for performing instance recovery using the online redo log files and for coalescing contiguous free space in tablespaces. The PMON is responsible for session cleanup and for freeing up all resources after a user session is terminated.

10. B. A table or index has a segment. A segment consists of one or more extents. A segment can belong to only one tablespace, but it can span across multiple data files.

11. C. To better conform to the OFA standard, the Oracle 11*g* OUI prompts for the ORACLE_BASE value if the ORACLE_BASE environment variable is not already set. The ORACLE_HOME value is derived from ORACLE_BASE, but you have the option to change the derived value.

12. D. The large pool is configured to have RMAN not use the shared pool; hence, the shared pool is totally dedicated to application space.

13. D. PMON is responsible for cleaning up failed user processes. It reclaims all the resources held by the user and releases all locks on tables and rows held by the user. No other process is involved in the session cleanup.

14. D. The LRU mechanism ensures that each user's server process can find free space in the shared pool and database buffer cache whenever they need it, but it also keeps frequently used objects cached in those memory areas.

15. A. The instance consists of the SGA and all the Oracle background processes. The database is composed of the control files, data files, and redo logs.

16. B. Multiple operating-system blocks make up database blocks, contiguous chunks of which make up extents. A segment consists of one or more extents.

17. D. Although the Unix system administrator is responsible for creating volume groups and mount points, the DBA generally decides where the Oracle binaries will be installed—the location derived from `$ORACLE_BASE` or designated by the `$ORACLE_HOME` environment variable.

18. A. The OFA model does not include any reference to naming conventions for the database or things inside the database, such as users, tables, or tablespaces.

19. B. The `runInstaller` executable performs a preinstall check of the operating system and hardware resources before starting the OUI graphical tool.

20. D. The `root.sh` script copies configuration files to directories outside `$ORACLE_HOME` and sets the permissions on those files accordingly.

Creating an Oracle 11*g* Database

ORACLE DATABASE 11*g*: ADMINISTRATION I EXAM OBJECTIVES COVERED IN THIS CHAPTER:

✓ **Creating an Oracle Database**

- Create a database by using the Database Configuration Assistant (DBCA)

✓ **Managing the Oracle Instance**

- Setting database initialization parameters
- Describe the stages of database startup and shutdown
- Using alert log and trace files
- Using data dictionary and dynamic performance views

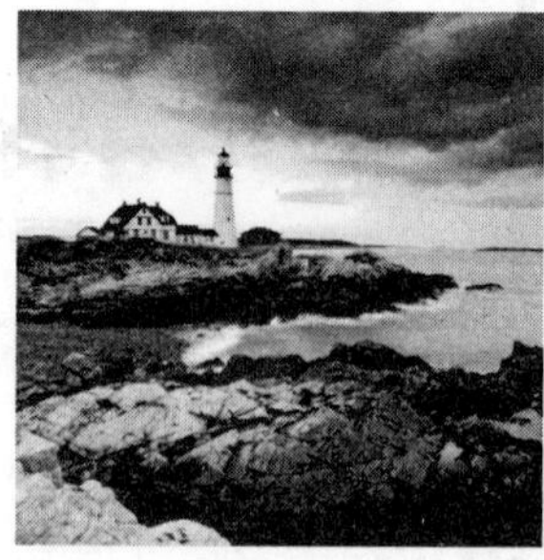

As a DBA, you are responsible for creating and managing Oracle databases and services within your organization. Oracle provides a comprehensive and cohesive set of tools to help DBAs perform these tasks. It is important for you to understand these tools and how to use them properly.

Oracle has been using Java-based tools to manage the Oracle Database because Java gives the same look and feel for the tools across all platforms. In this chapter, I will cover how to use the Oracle Database Configuration Assistant tool, which creates and removes Oracle Databases, and how you can use templates to create databases.

After creating the database using DBCA, the database will be up and running. I will then cover how to shut down and restart the database for some configuration changes, apply patches, perform server maintenance, and so on. I'll describe the various database startup and shutdown options and explain the circumstances under which you use these options.

You will also learn more about the Oracle data dictionary, including how the dictionary is created, where it is created, and so on. Finally, I will cover initialization parameter files and discuss how you can use them to manage, locate, and view the database alert log.

Using DBCA to Create Oracle 11*g* Databases

The Oracle Database Configuration Assistant (DBCA) is a Java-based tool used to create Oracle Databases. If you've been a DBA for a few years, you probably remember the days of writing and maintaining scripts to create databases. Although it is still possible to manually create a database, the DBCA provides a flexible and robust environment in which you not only can create databases but also can generate templates containing the definitions of the databases created. This provides you with the ease of using a GUI-based interface with the flexibility of Oracle-generated XML-based templates that you can use to maintain a library of database definitions.

You can also use the DBCA to add options to a running database or to remove a database. In recent years, I have seen many diehard command-line DBAs switching to the DBCA tool to create databases, mainly because of its flexibility and ease of use.

You can also use the DBCA to create a database while the Oracle software is installed, or you can invoke the DBCA later to manually create a database. In the following sections, I will show you the steps necessary to create an Oracle Database using the DBCA tool.

Invoking the Database Configuration Assistant

You can invoke the DBCA from a command line in the Unix environment or as an application in a Windows 2000 environment. If you are using the Windows XP environment, choose Start ➢ All Programs ➢ Oracle *Oracle Home* ➢ Configuration and Migration Tools ➢ Database Configuration Assistant.

If you are in a Unix environment or would prefer to work from the command line in Windows, type **dbca** from the `$ORACLE_HOME/bin` location.

After you open the DBCA, you should see the Welcome screen, as shown in Figure 9.1. The Welcome screen will be different on a node that belongs to a RAC cluster, where you will have the option to create a single-instance database or a RAC database. Since RAC is not part of the certification exam, you will be using a node that is not part of the RAC.

FIGURE 9.1 DBCA Welcome screen

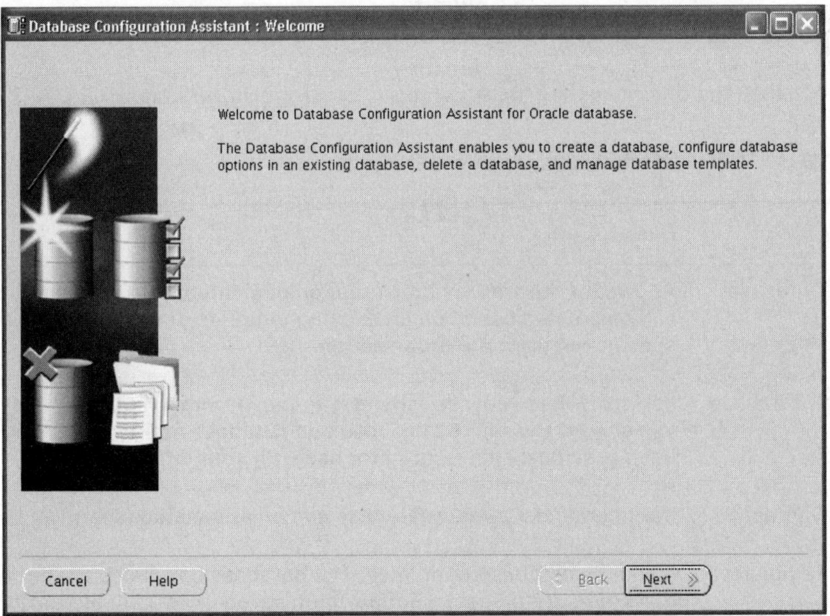

Click Next to open the Operations screen, as shown in Figure 9.2. You can create a database, configure database options, delete a database, manage templates, and configure automatic storage management.

FIGURE 9.2 DBCA Operations screen

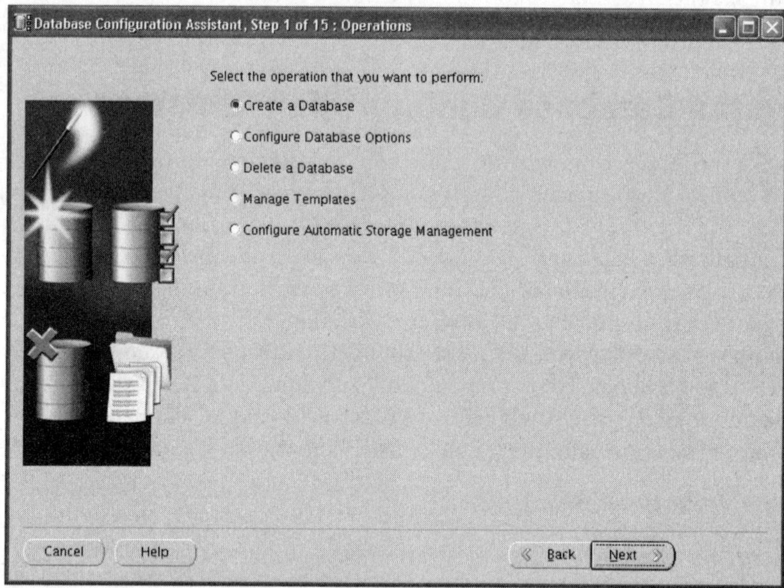

Table 9.1 lists and describes the DBCA database-management options.

TABLE 9.1 DBCA Database Management Options

Option	Description
Create a Database	Allows for the step-by-step creation of a database. The database can be created based on an existing template or customized for the specific needs of the organization.
Configure Database Options	Performs the necessary changes to move from a dedicated server to a shared server. You can also add database options that have not been previously configured for use with your database.
Delete a Database	Completely removes a database and all associated files.
Manage Templates	Manages database templates. The database templates are definitions of your database configuration saved in an XML file format on your local hard disk. You can choose from several predefined templates, or you can create customized templates.

TABLE 9.1 DBCA Database Management Options *(continued)*

Option	Description
Configure Automatic Storage Management (ASM)	Using ASM, Oracle manages the file placement and naming automatically. You provide a set of disks to the Oracle 11*g* database to use, and the provisioning and optimization are automatically handled by ASM. ASM is not covered in this book. When you're ready to take the OCP certification exam, refer to *OCP: Oracle Database 11g Administrator Certified Professional Study Guide* (Sybex, 2009).

Choose Create a Database, and click Next to open the Database Templates screen. In the coming sections, I will discuss database templates and the various screens in the DBCA to create a database.

Database Templates

The DBCA comes with two preconfigured database templates. These XML-based documents contain the information necessary to create the Oracle Database. You can choose one of these predefined templates, or you can build a custom database definition. The predefined database templates are Data Warehouse and General Purpose or Transaction Processing (see Figure 9.3). These templates were designed to create databases that are optimized for a particular type of workload. When you choose Custom Database, you will have more flexibility to create tablespaces and decide which components to install. The screens that are different when choosing the Custom Database option are identified later in the section.

FIGURE 9.3 DBCA Database Templates screen

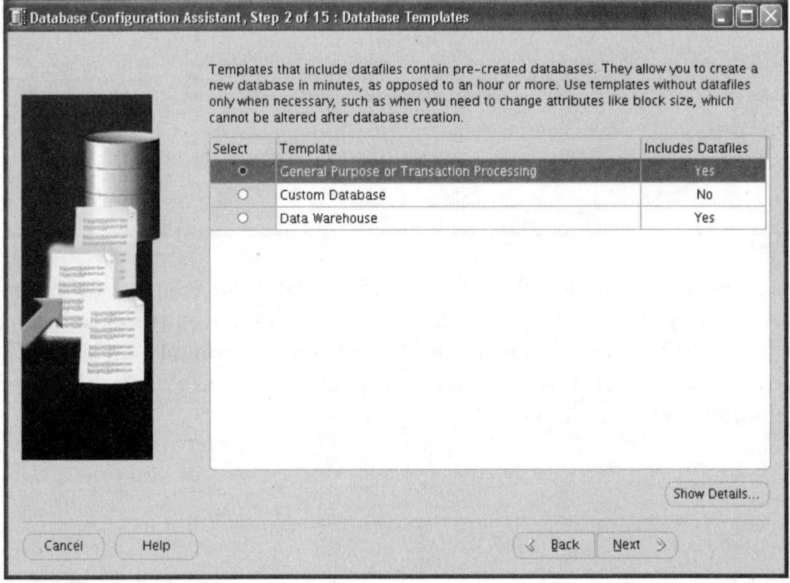

To display the configuration definitions for these preconfigured databases, click Show Details. Figure 9.4 shows the details of the General Purpose or Transaction Processing template. You have the option of saving the details as an HTML file using the button at the bottom-right corner. Before creating the database, you will get the summary information, and you will have the option to save the database create scripts as well as a similar HTML file with all the options and parameter values.

FIGURE 9.4 DBCA Templates Details screen

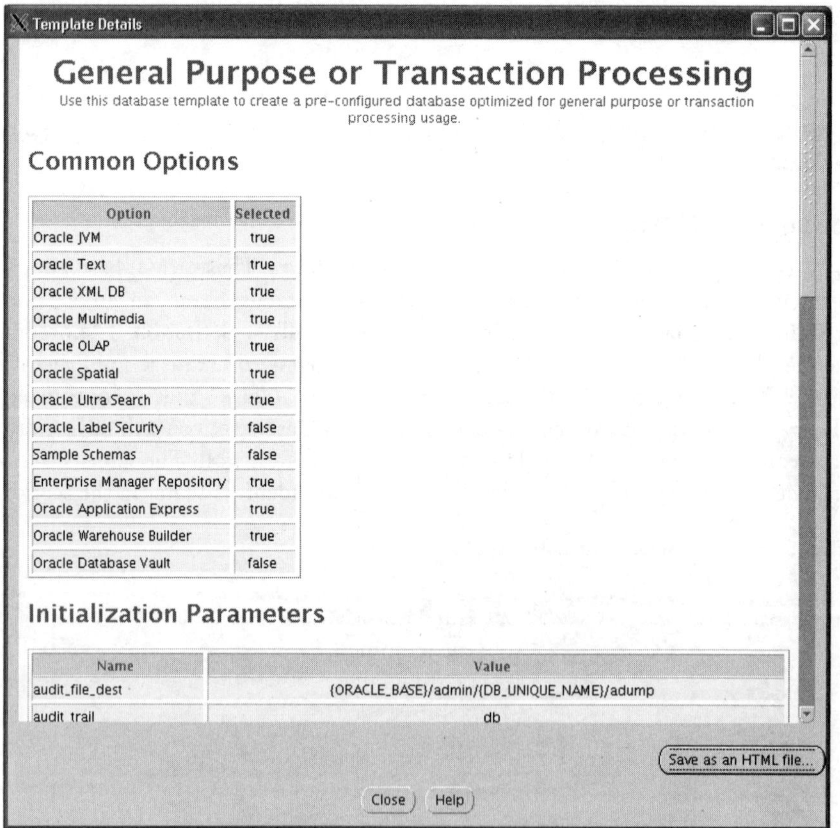

Table 9.2 displays information about what is contained in the template definition shown in Figure 9.4. When you scroll down, you'll see multiple sections on the page. Each section of the page gives further information about the template. For example, under the Common Options section, you will see a list of each of the database options that gets installed for the template definition you have chosen.

TABLE 9.2 Template Definition Details

Section	Description
Common Options	Displays which databases options will be installed
Initialization Parameters	Displays the common initialization parameters and their settings
Character Sets	Displays character sets to be used
Control Files	Displays filenames and locations for control files
Tablespaces	Displays names and types of tablespace
Datafiles	Displays filenames and size for each tablespace
Redo Log Groups	Displays group number and size

Choosing the Custom Database template option on the DBCA Database Templates screen gives you the fullest flexibility. For other templates, the database data files are prebuilt with certain Oracle options. Also, the database block size cannot be changed from 8KB. A No value in the Includes Datafiles column in the Database Templates screen shows which templates are fully customizable.

After you have chosen the appropriate template to use, click Next. You will then be presented with the Database Identification screen.

Database Identification

The Database Identification screen (see Figure 9.5) allows you to enter the global database name and Oracle system identification name (commonly referred to as the *Oracle SID*).

The global database name is the fully qualified name of the database in the enterprise. It is composed of a database name and a database domain and takes the format `database_name.database_domain`; for example, `sales.company.com`.

In this example, the first part of the global database name, `OCA11G`, is the name of your database. Since I have not specified the domain name, there is no default domain name assigned. Normally, the database domain is the same as the network domain within the enterprise. A global database name must be unique within a given network domain. The database name can be up to eight characters and can include letters, numbers, and the special characters $, _, and #.

FIGURE 9.5 DBCA Database Identification screen

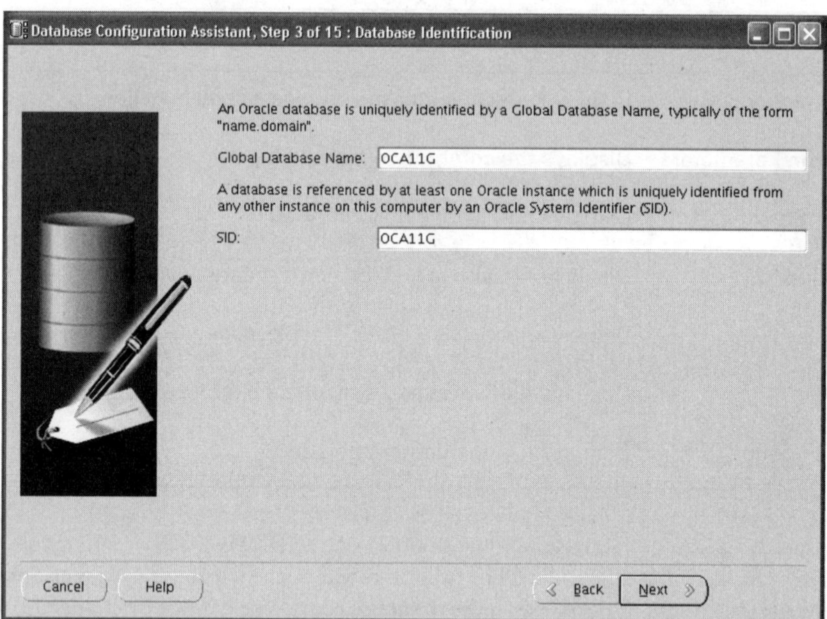

The Oracle SID is the name of the instance associated with the database. Usually this name is the same as the database name. For RAC databases where you have multiple instances associated with the database, the instance name is usually different from the database name. The Oracle SID can be a maximum of 12 characters and must be unique on the server. For example, you cannot have two Oracle SIDs called `PROD` on a single server.

Management Options

After you choose the database name, you can configure Enterprise Manager to monitor and manage your database using the DBCA Management Options screen (see Figure 9.6).

You can choose from two options: you can centrally manage all your databases from a single management console if the Management Agent is installed on the database server, or you can manage each database individually.

If the Oracle Management *Agent* is installed, the DBCA detects its presence and lists the name of the agent service. You can select this name if you want this existing agent to manage this database. Your new database then becomes one of the managed targets for the existing agent.

If you don't have an agent installed or are not doing centralized database management, you can still use Enterprise Manager to monitor and maintain the database. Choose the Use Database Control for Database Management radio button if you want to install Enterprise Manager and configure it locally.

FIGURE 9.6 DBCA Management Options screen

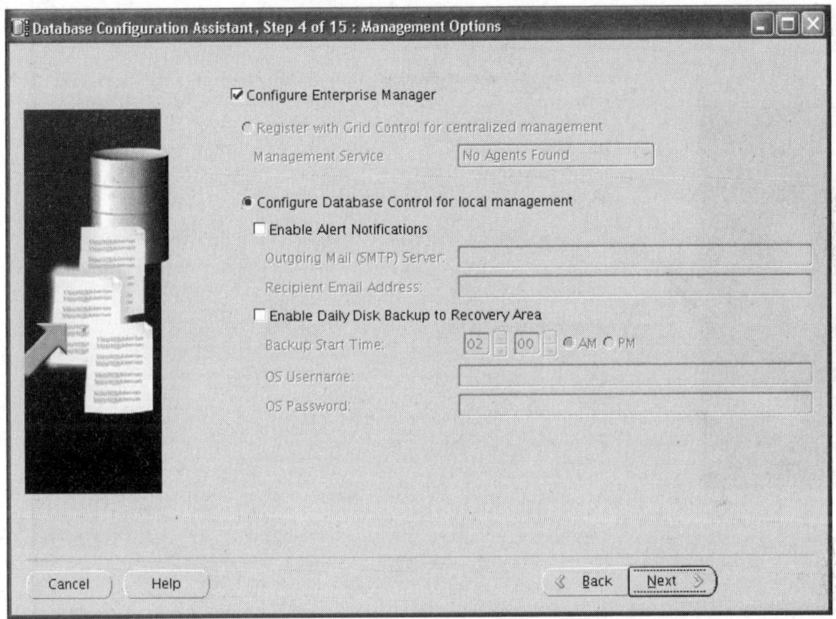

On the Management Options screen, you can also configure email notifications from Enterprise Manager. Email notifications are generated when certain database thresholds are reached, such as the maximum number of database sessions or low free space on a tablespace. After installing Enterprise Manager, you can configure notification of these database thresholds. To get these email notifications, you'll need the name of your SMTP mail server and the email address to which you want the email notifications sent.

Finally, using the Management Options screen, you can configure backups of your database. If you select Enable Daily Backup, Enterprise Manager backs up your database based on the start time you enter. The database is backed up to a designated area on your system that is specified later in the configuration process. You have to supply an operating-system username and password that Enterprise Manager will log in as to perform the backup. This user should have the proper write authorization to the area of the disk where you want the backup stored.

Database Credentials

You use the Database Credentials screen (see Figure 9.7) to configure passwords for the various administrative accounts that are set up automatically when the database is configured. You can select the same password for all the critical accounts, or you can elect to have a different password for each of the preconfigured accounts. How you elect to set your passwords may depend on the policies of your particular organization. Typically, the same critical passwords are set for these accounts, and the accounts that you won't need to access are selectively locked.

FIGURE 9.7 DBCA Database Credentials screen

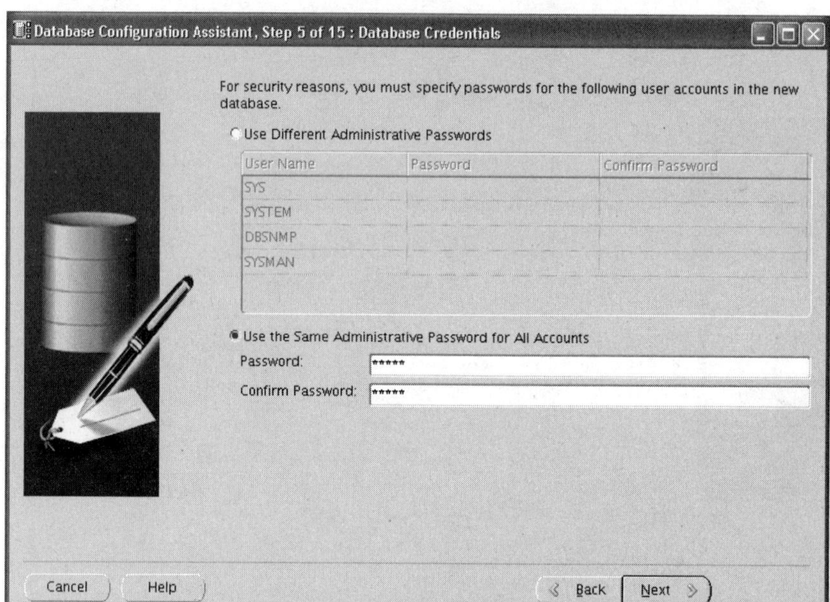

Four accounts are preconfigured when you set up your database:

SYS The SYS user owns all the internal Oracle tables that constitute the data dictionary. Normally, you should not perform any actions as the SYS user and should ensure that this account password is properly protected. Also, don't manually modify the underlying objects owned by the SYS user.

SYSTEM SYSTEM is an administrative user that contains additional administrative tables and views. Many DBAs use this account to administer the database, but ideally this account also should be locked and secured.

DBSNMP DBSNMP is a login used by the Enterprise Manager facility to monitor and gather performance statistics about the database.

SYSMAN SYSMAN is the equivalent of the SYS user for the Enterprise Manager facility. This Enterprise Manager administrator can create and modify other Enterprise Manager administrator accounts, as well as administer the database instance.

Once you have completed the Database Credentials page, click Next. You will now be presented with the Storage Options screen.

Storage Options

The Storage Options screen (see Figure 9.8) is used to define how you want to configure the disk storage areas used by the database. You have three choices:

- File System
- Automatic Storage Management (ASM)
- Raw Devices

FIGURE 9.8 DBCA Storage Options screen

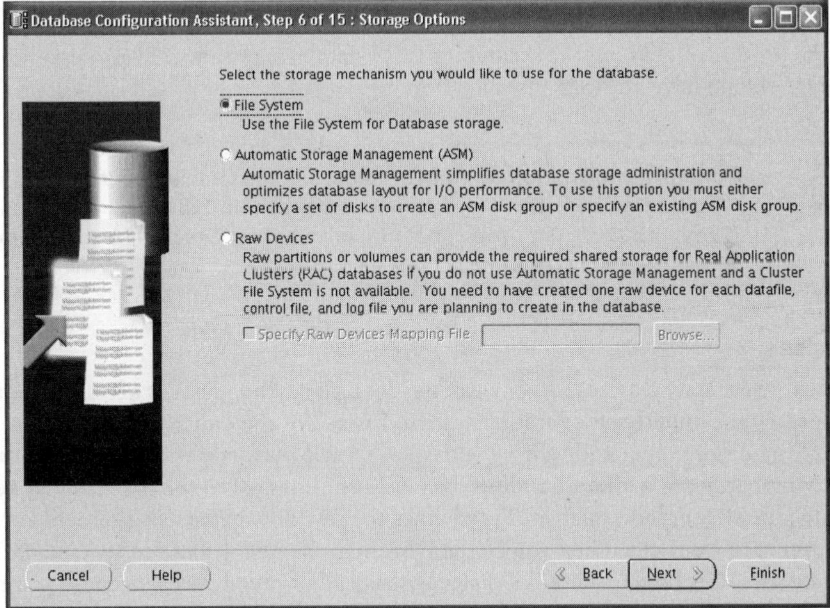

Let's take a look at these options in more detail.

File System Storage

File system storage is the most common type of storage configuration for many Oracle Databases. This type of storage definition relies on the underlying operating system to maintain and manage the actual files you as the DBA define. When you choose this option, the DBCA suggests a set of data filenames and directory locations for those files. You can modify this information at the database-storage step later in the database-creation process.

The DBCA uses the Optimal Flexible Architecture (OFA) directory design for laying out the suggested file locations. The OFA is an Oracle-recommended method for designing a flexible directory structure and naming convention for your Oracle Database files.

ASM Storage

Automatic Storage Management (ASM) is a newer type of storage mechanism available since Oracle 10*g*. ASM is designed to relieve the burden of disk and storage management and relies on Oracle to maintain your database storage. Instead of managing many individual database files, ASM allows you to define disk groups for file management.

Using disk groups, you can define one or more groups of disks as a logical unit that Oracle views as a single unit of storage. This concept is similar in nature to the way that some operating systems, including various flavors of Unix, define volume groups.

Oracle manages the storage definitions of the database within a second instance used exclusively by ASM to keep track of the diskgroup allocations. When you create a database and select the ASM option in the Storage Options screen, a series of screens guides you through the process of defining the secondary ASM database instance. Every server using ASM storage should have an ASM instance running.

For more information on ASM storage, see the Oracle documentation "Oracle Database Storage Administrator's Guide 11*g* Release 1 (11.1) Part Number B31107-04." You can find this and other Oracle 11*g* documentation at `www.oracle.com/pls/db111`.

Raw Devices

You can also select Raw Devices as your storage definition. *Raw devices* are disks that are not managed by the underlying operating system. Instead of the underlying operating system controlling disk reading and writing activities, Oracle performs the actions directly on the underlying hardware without handing the responsibilities off to the operating system.

Typically, the systems administrator predefines the raw disk partitions that will constitute the specific raw devices. Then you as the DBA map the raw devices to specific data files and redo log files. It is better to use ASM storage instead of raw devices, because you have better load-balancing options and monitoring features available with ASM.

Since the OCA certification exam is based on databases created using file-system storage, I will not be discussing ASM and raw devices in this book. Choose File System on the DBCA Storage Options screen, and click Next to specify the file locations.

Database File Locations

After you define the type of storage you want to use for your database, you need to define where you want to put the files that will constitute the database. Depending on the type of storage option you choose, you may have more or fewer location options available. Figure 9.9 shows the DBCA screen accepting the file locations.

FIGURE 9.9 DBCA Database File Locations screen

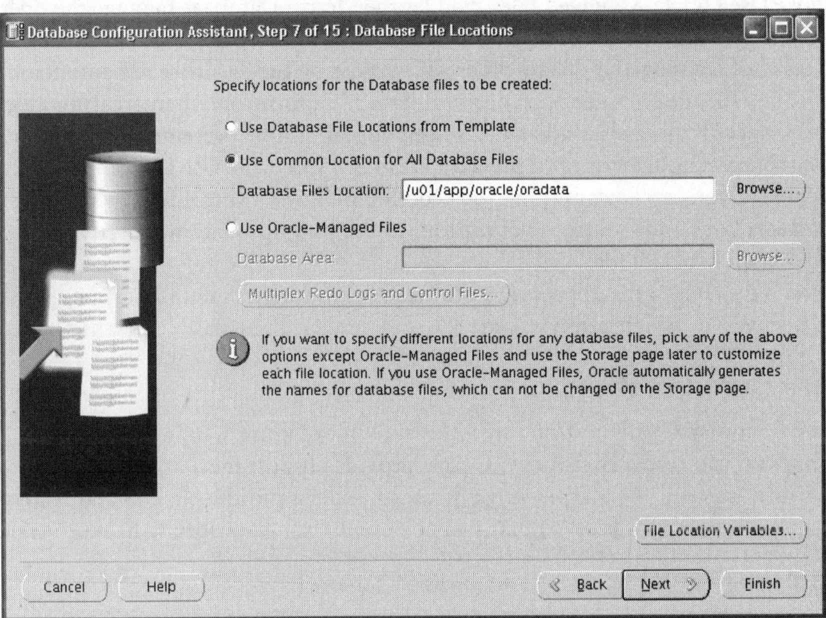

You are presented with three options on the Database File Locations screen:

- Use Database File Locations from Template
- Use Common Location for All Database Files
- Use Oracle-Managed Files

The following are descriptions of each of these options.

Use Database File Locations from Template

If you chose one of the predefined database templates to use for this database, Oracle uses the previously defined locations from the template as the basis for the database file locations. You still have the opportunity later in the database-definition process to review and modify the filenames and locations even if you choose this option.

Use Common Location for all Database Files

If you choose this option, you can specify a new directory for all your database files. Again, even if you choose this option, you can change the filenames and locations later in the database-definition process.

Use Oracle-Managed Files

If you choose Use Oracle-Managed Files, you let the Oracle Database manage the operating-system files comprising the database. As a DBA, you just specify the location of the database files. The tasks of creating and deleting files as required by the database are automatically managed—the DBA doesn't need to specify a data file's location when creating a new tablespace or specify the size or filename. Since you will not be presented with an option to change the storage characteristics of the data files later when the Use Oracle-Managed Files option is chosen, you can have multiplexed redo log files and control files by clicking the Multiplex Redo Logs and Control Files button. In the pop-up window, specify the location of the redo log and control files.

Once you have chosen the appropriate storage option for your database, click Next to get to the Recovery Configuration screen.

Recovery Configuration

You use the Recovery Configuration screen, as shown in Figure 9.10, to set up your database backup and recovery strategy. Oracle provides robust mechanisms for full point-of-failure recovery. As a DBA, it is critical to understand the backup and recovery requirements of your application so that you can choose the appropriate backup strategy.

FIGURE 9.10 DBCA Recovery Configuration screen

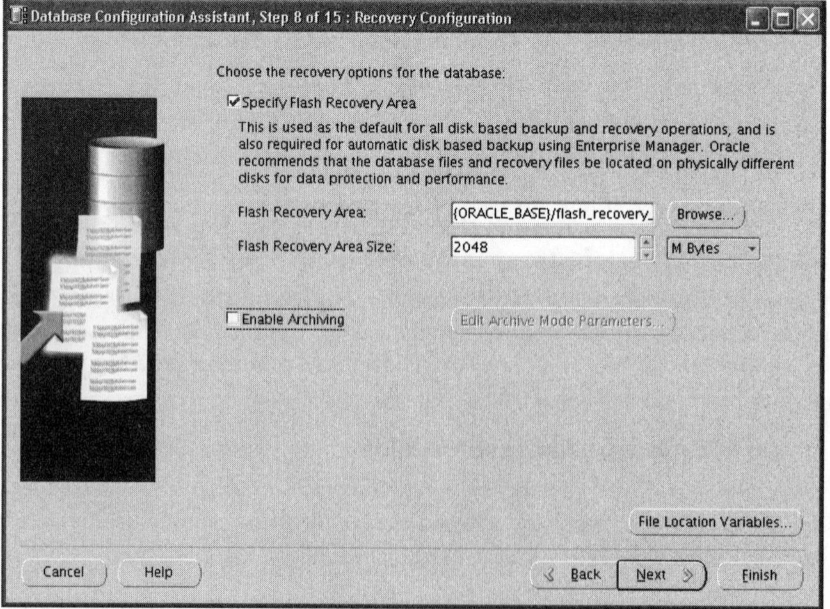

You can configure several options on this screen, including specifying the flash recovery area and size. You can also enable archive-log mode for the database and specify archive-log parameters. Let's take a look at each of these options.

Flash Recovery

Oracle flash recovery is an option available since Oracle 10*g*. It is the foundation of the new automated disk-based recovery feature. Flash recovery is designed to simplify your life in terms of Oracle backups by providing a centralized location to maintain and manage all the files related to database backups.

The flash recovery area is an area of the disk dedicated to the storage and management of files needed for recovering an Oracle Database. This area is completely separate from the other components of the Oracle Database, such as the data files, redo logs, and control files.

Oracle uses the flash recovery area to store and manage the archive logs. Enterprise Manager can store its backups in the flash recovery area and use it when restoring files during media recovery. The Oracle Recovery Manager (RMAN) uses the flash recovery area and ensures that the database is recoverable based on the files being stored in the flash recovery area. All files necessary to recover the database following a media failure are part of the flash recovery area.

You will explore the flash recovery area in more detail in Chapter 15, "Implementing Database Backups."

You can specify the directory location and the size of the disk area you want to dedicate to the flash recovery area. The default location of the directory provided by DBCA is `ORACLE_BASE\flash_recovery_area`. You can click File Location Variables on the Recovery Configuration screen to display a summary of the Oracle file location parameters, including the current setting of the `ORACLE_BASE` parameter. The size of the flash recovery area defaults to 2048MB and can be set larger or smaller by changing the Flash Recovery Size setting.

Enable Archive Logging

On the Recovery Configuration screen, you also have the ability to enable the Oracle archive-logging feature. Archive logging is the mechanism Oracle uses to enable you to perform a point-of-failure recovery of a database. To enable archive logging, select the Enable Archiving check box. Once you do so, the button Edit Archive Mode Parameters will be enabled. If you click this button, you are presented with a screen that enables you to set the various parameters that are used to configure archive logging (see Figure 9.11).

We will explore archive logging in more detail in Chapter 15.

FIGURE 9.11 DBCA Edit Archive Mode Parameters dialog box

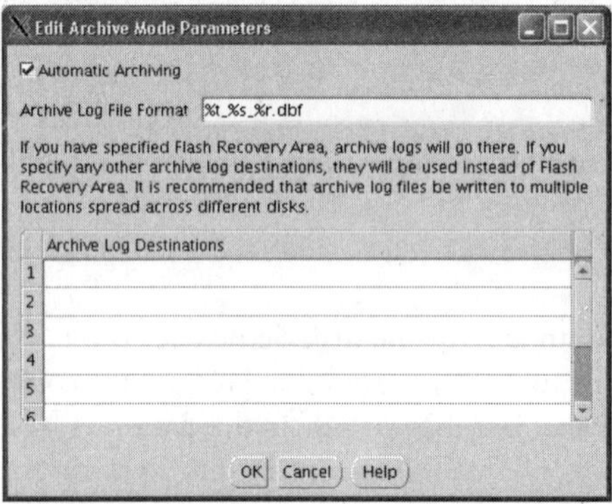

After completing the Recovery Configuration screen, click Next. You will then be presented with the Database Content screen.

Database Content

If you chose a predefined template (OLTP or Data Warehouse), you will be presented with the Database Content screen shown in Figure 9.12. You will then have the option to add sample schemas to the database, which is explored in the next section, "Sample Schemas and Custom Scripts."

FIGURE 9.12 DBCA Database Content Screen for predefined database template

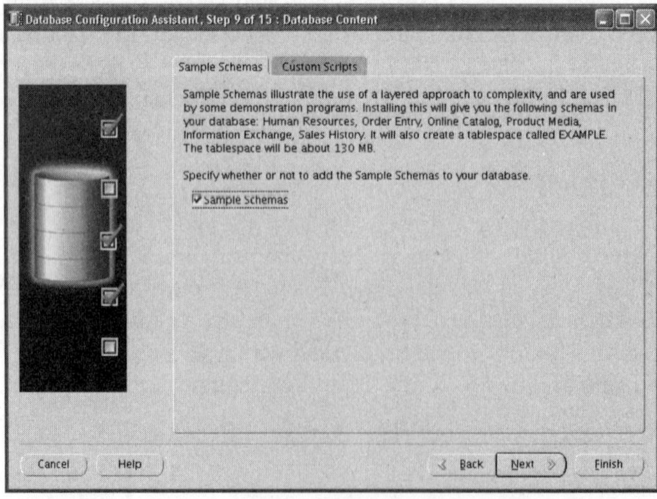

If you chose to create a custom database on the Database Templates screen, you will be presented with the Database Content screen shown in Figure 9.13.

FIGURE 9.13 The DBCA Database Content screen for custom database template

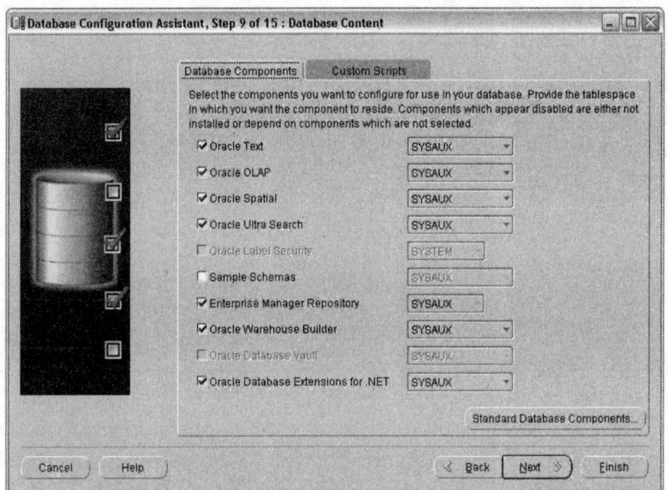

You use the options on this screen to specify which Oracle Database components you want to install. Table 9.3 describes the components that can be included and configured automatically by the DBCA.

TABLE 9.3 Oracle Optional Components

Component	Description
Oracle Text	Provides support for multimedia content such as audio and video.
Oracle OLAP	Provides facilities for creating and deploying online analytical processing applications.
Oracle Spatial	Provides the components and infrastructure for Oracle to manage and maintain geographic and spatial information such as map coordinates.
Oracle Ultra Search	Provides capabilities to perform extended text and searches within the Oracle Database.
Oracle Label Security	Manages and controls access to sensitive information within the database. This option will be enabled if the Label Security option is installed in the Oracle software home.
Sample Schemas	Installs some example data that can be used for learning purposes.

TABLE 9.3 Oracle Optional Components *(continued)*

Component	Description
Enterprise Manager Repository	Specifies the location of the schema used to manage the content of the OEM repository. If you chose to do local management of your database, this schema is required.
Oracle Warehouse Builder	Enables the ETL process and integrates various application data.
Oracle Database Vault	Addresses a security solution for regulatory compliance and security controls. This option will be enabled if the database vault option is installed in the Oracle software home.

Click the Standard Database Components button to display any additional standard features that Oracle will automatically configure for you and recommend as part of a standard database installation (see Figure 9.14). These features are the Oracle JVM, Oracle XML DB, Oracle Multimedia, and Oracle Application Express.

FIGURE 9.14 DBCA standard database components

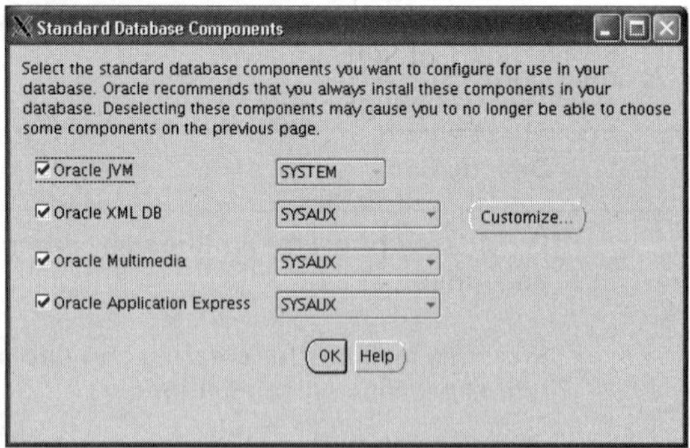

What Is a Schema?

When you are working with Oracle, you will often hear the words *schema* and *user* used interchangeably. Is there a difference between the two? Yes and no. A user is a defined database entity that has a set of abilities to perform activities based on their granted rights. A schema, which is associated with a user entity, is more appropriately defined as a collection of database objects. Some examples of database objects are tables, indexes, and views.

A schema can be related to a real person, such as a user of your Sales database who may have a user ID and password that they use to access the database. This user may or may not own any schema objects.

Because a schema is a collection of objects, DBAs often define a schema to represent a collection of objects associated with an application. For example, a DBA might create a schema called SALES and create objects owned by that schema. Then, they can grant access to other database users who need the ability to access the SALES schema.

In this way, the schema becomes a logical collection of objects associated with an application and is not tied to any specific user. This ability makes it easy to logically group common objects that are related to specific applications or tasks using a common schema name.

The main difference is that users are the entities that perform work, and schemas are the collections of objects that users perform work on.

Sample Schemas and Custom Scripts

The DBCA also lets you install examples of actual working databases. Oracle provides a set of example schemas and applications that use these schemas. You can install these sample schemas now or later by running a series of SQL scripts.

These sample schemas include the following:

- Human Resources (HR)
- Order Entry (OE)
- Product Media (PM)
- Sales History (SH)
- Queued Shipping (QS)

These schemas are designed to provide you with working examples of how to use and implement a variety of features within Oracle. For example, the Product Media schema shows how to use the Oracle Intermedia option, which is used to manage binary large objects (BLOBs) such as images and sound clips.

If you choose to create the sample schemas, Oracle creates a tablespace called EXAMPLE and stores all the necessary tables within that tablespace. Be aware that this adds about 130MB to your database definition. The examples shown in Chapters 1 through 7 mostly used the tables that belonged to the sample schema HR.

You can also run custom scripts as part of the database-creation process. Click the Custom Scripts tab on the Database Content screen to enter the names and locations of the custom scripts that you want to run at database creation (see Figure 9.15).

FIGURE 9.15 DBCA Database Content screen's Custom Scripts tab

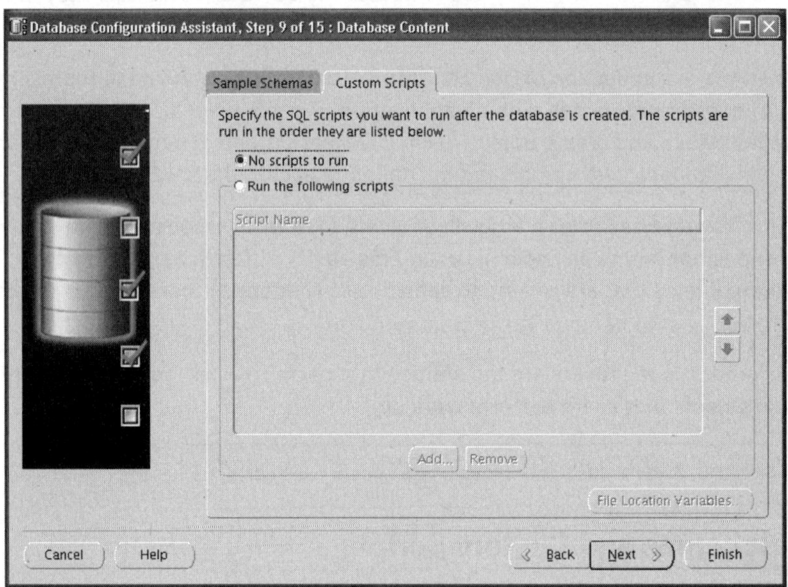

For example, you might want the DBCA to automatically create the schema and define the tables that you will use for this database. You can create a script that performs all the necessary work and have the DBCA run the script as part of the database-creation process. The custom scripts are run using the command-line utility SQL*Plus, so you will have to define a user ID and password within the body of the script. For example, your script might contain the following line:

```
connect some_userid/some_password
```

This line directs Oracle to connect to the current Oracle Database, which is determined by your `ORACLE_SID` environment variable using the supplied user ID and password.

After completing the Database Content screen, click Next. You will then be presented with the Initialization Parameters screen.

Initialization Parameters

You use the Initialization Parameters screen to define the various initialization-parameter settings used to configure size and set up the characteristics of the Oracle instance. The following four tabs are categorized according to the parameters used to manage the Oracle instance:

- Memory
- Sizing
- Character Sets
- Connection Mode

Let's take a look at each of these tabs and what settings you can manage on each one.

The Memory Tab

You use the options on the Memory tab to control the size of the database parameters that configure the overall memory footprint of the Oracle instance (see Figure 9.16). There are two general approaches to managing the memory database parameters: Oracle can set and manage most of the parameters for you, or you can customize each of the initialization parameters for your specific database.

If you choose the Typical setting, Oracle allocates memory to the various components within the Oracle system global area (SGA) and process global area (PGA). This memory allocation is automatic and is a percentage of the overall physical memory available on the server. The default is 30 percent of the total memory available, but you can change this setting by specifying the memory size or by sliding the bar to appropriate size. If you choose this setting, click the Show Memory Distribution button to see how Oracle will allocate the memory between the SGA and the PGA (see Figure 9.17).

FIGURE 9.16 Memory tab on the Initialization Parameters screen

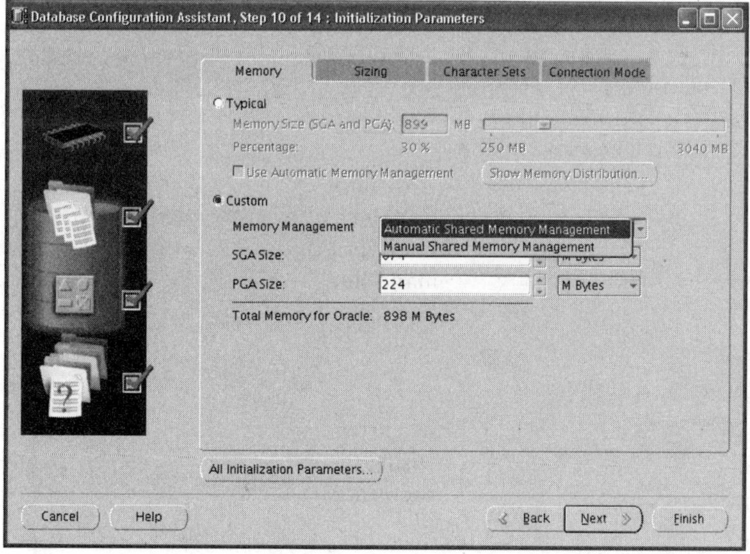

FIGURE 9.17 Memory distribution for SGA and PGA for the Typical setting

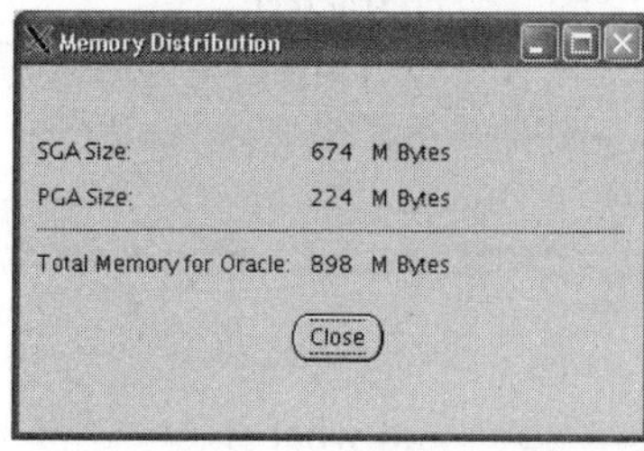

If you choose the Use Automatic Memory Management option under Typical, Oracle will manage the total memory automatically, including the SGA and PGA. The memory distribution will show differently, as in Figure 9.18, if this option is selected.

FIGURE 9.18 Memory distribution for Automatic Memory Management

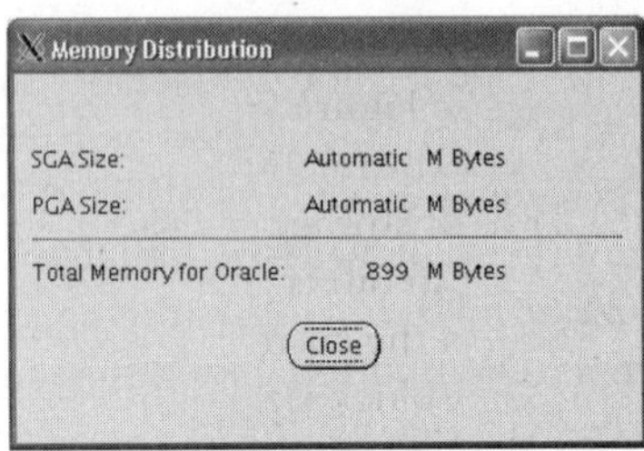

If you choose the Custom option, you will again have two options: Automatic Shared Memory Management and Manual Shared Memory Management. With automatic shared memory management, you specify only the SGA size and the PGA size. Each component inside the SGA is configured automatically by Oracle. With manual shared memory management, you have full control over how much each of the specific areas of the SGA will take. The main areas that you will configure are the shared pool, buffer cache, Java pool, large pool, and PGA size. Each of the settings maps to a specific Oracle parameter. Figure 9.19 shows the options.

FIGURE 9.19 DBCA showing manual shared memory management options

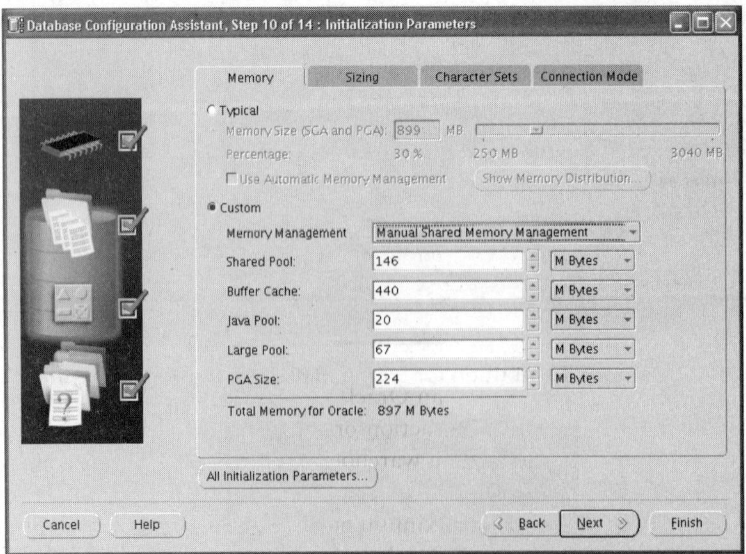

Memory management and the parameters associated with memory are discussed in detail in Chapter 14, "Maintaining the Database and Managing Performance."

The Sizing Tab

You use the options on the Sizing tab (see Figure 9.20) to configure the block size of your database and the number of processes that can connect to this database. The Block Size setting corresponds to the smallest unit of storage within the Oracle Database. All storage of database objects (tables, indexes, and so on) is governed by the block size. The block size defaults to 8KB, but you can modify it in the custom template only. Once the database is created, you cannot modify the database block size.

FIGURE 9.20 Sizing tab on the Initialization Parameters screen

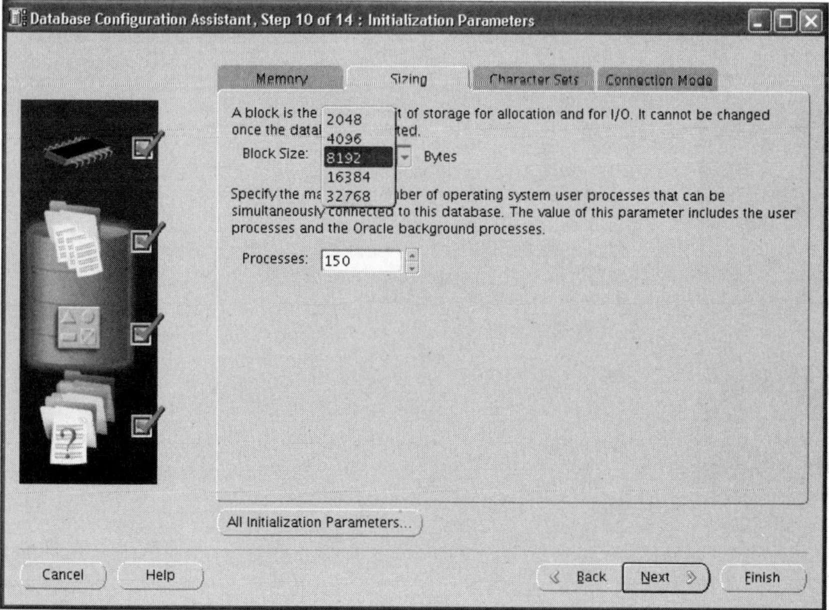

The maximum and minimum size of an Oracle block depends on the operating system. Generally, 8KB is sufficient for most transaction-oriented applications, and larger block sizes, such as 16KB and higher, are used in data warehouse–type applications. The block size can be 2KB, 4KB, 8KB, 16KB, or 32KB.

The Processes setting specifies the maximum number of simultaneous operating-system processes that can be connected to this Oracle Database. If you are not sure of the number of processes needed, you can start with the default value of 150. This parameter does have a bearing on the overall size of your Oracle instance. The larger you make this number, the more room Oracle must reserve in the SGA to track the processes.

The Character Sets Tab

You use the options on the Character Sets tab to configure the character sets you will use within your database (see Figure 9.21). You will determine the database character set, the national character set, the default language, and the default date format.

Specifying a database character set defines the type of encoding scheme that Oracle uses to determine how characters are displayed and stored within your Oracle environment. The character set you choose determines the languages that can be represented in your environment. It also controls other nuances, such as how your database interacts with your operating system and how much storage is required for your data. The default character set is based on the language setting of the operating system.

FIGURE 9.21 Character Sets tab on the Initialization Parameters screen

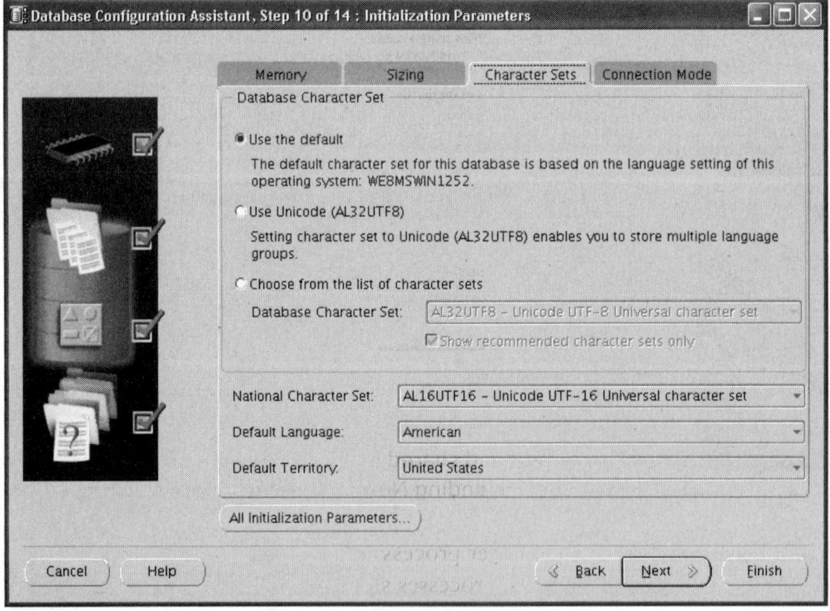

Specifying a national character set defines how your database represents Unicode characters in a database that does not use a Unicode-enabled character set.

You use the Default Language setting to manage certain aspects of how your database represents information pertaining to different locales. For example, this setting determines how your database displays time and monetary values.

You use the Default Date setting to specify how Oracle displays dates by default. For example, the AMERICA setting shows dates in the DD-MON-YYYY format by default.

The Connection Mode Tab

You use the options on the Connection Mode tab to specify the type of connections to use for this database (see Figure 9.22). You can choose Dedicated Server Mode or Shared Server Mode. The default connection mode is Dedicated Server Mode.

FIGURE 9.22 The Connection Mode tab on the Initialization Parameters screen

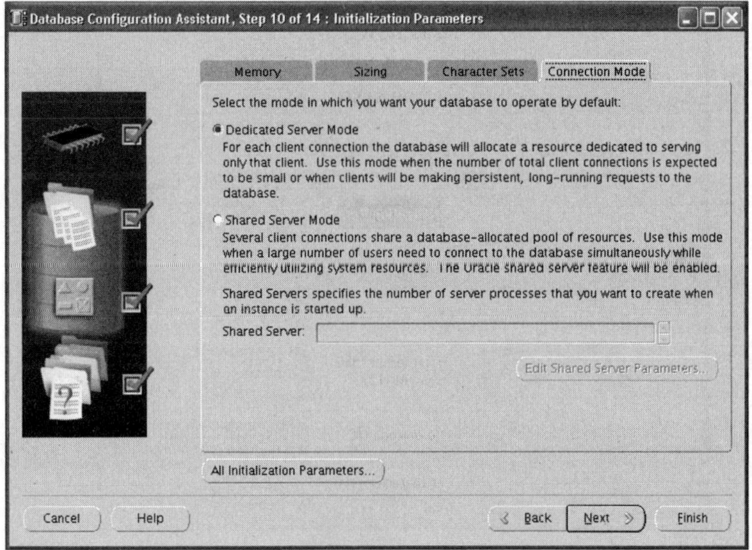

The dedicated server and shared server modes are covered in more detail in Chapter 11, "Understanding Network Architecture."

In the dedicated server mode, each user process will have a dedicated server process. In the shared process mode, many user processes share a server process.

If you want to review the initialization parameters and make any changes, click the All Initialization Parameters button. The screen shown in Figure 9.23 details the basic parameters. From this screen, you can view/edit the advanced parameters using the Show Advanced Parameters button. You have the option to edit a value on this screen.

After completing the Initialization Parameters screen, click Next. You will then be presented with the Security Settings screen.

FIGURE 9.23 DBCA Initialization Parameters screen

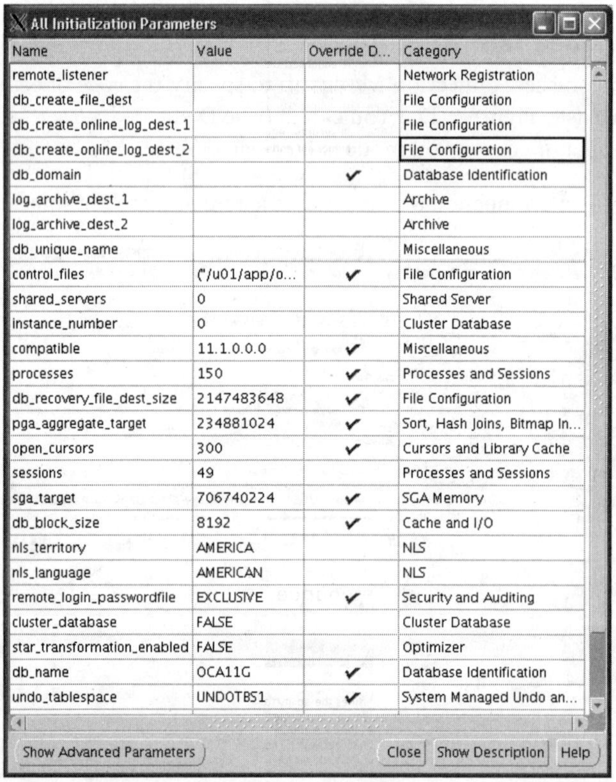

All Initialization Parameters

Name	Value	Override D...	Category
remote_listener			Network Registration
db_create_file_dest			File Configuration
db_create_online_log_dest_1			File Configuration
db_create_online_log_dest_2			File Configuration
db_domain		✔	Database Identification
log_archive_dest_1			Archive
log_archive_dest_2			Archive
db_unique_name			Miscellaneous
control_files	("/u01/app/o...	✔	File Configuration
shared_servers	0		Shared Server
instance_number	0		Cluster Database
compatible	11.1.0.0.0	✔	Miscellaneous
processes	150	✔	Processes and Sessions
db_recovery_file_dest_size	2147483648	✔	File Configuration
pga_aggregate_target	234881024	✔	Sort, Hash Joins, Bitmap In...
open_cursors	300	✔	Cursors and Library Cache
sessions	49		Processes and Sessions
sga_target	706740224	✔	SGA Memory
db_block_size	8192	✔	Cache and I/O
nls_territory	AMERICA		NLS
nls_language	AMERICAN		NLS
remote_login_passwordfile	EXCLUSIVE	✔	Security and Auditing
cluster_database	FALSE		Cluster Database
star_transformation_enabled	FALSE		Optimizer
db_name	OCA11G	✔	Database Identification
undo_tablespace	UNDOTBS1	✔	System Managed Undo an...

Show Advanced Parameters | Close | Show Description | Help

Security and Maintenance Settings

Oracle 11*g* has new and improved security settings such as case-sensitive passwords, more rigorous profile options, and so on. If you're not ready to use the Oracle 11*g* security options, choose the Revert to Pre-11g Default Security Settings option. Figure 9.24 shows the DBCA Security Settings screen.

When you click Next on the Security Settings screen, you will be presented with an option to configure automatic maintenance tasks, as shown in Figure 9.25.

On the next screen, you will be presented with options to review storage specifications for tablespaces, data files, control files, and redo log files.

FIGURE 9.24 DBCA Security Settings screen

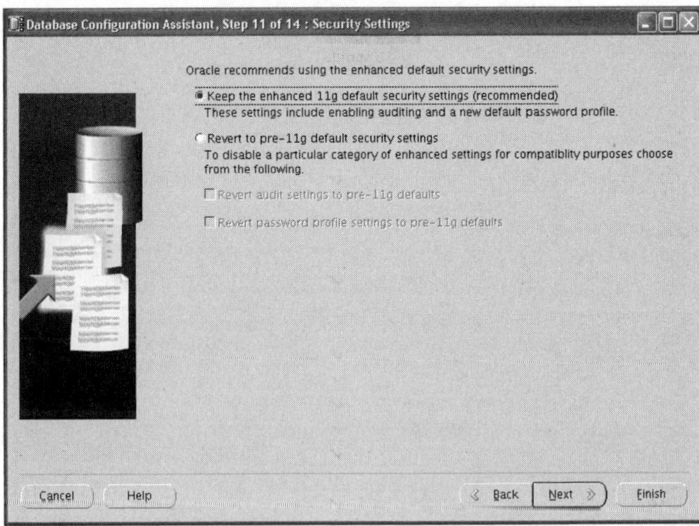

FIGURE 9.25 DBCA Automatic Maintenance Tasks screen

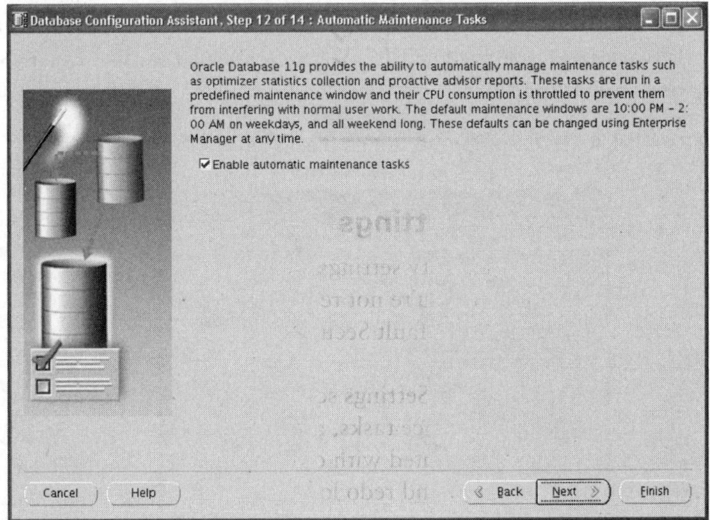

Database Storage

The Database Storage screen provides you with the opportunity to review and change the locations of the actual objects that compose the Oracle Database; namely, the data files, control files, and redo logs (see Figure 9.26).

FIGURE 9.26 The DBCA Database Storage initial screen

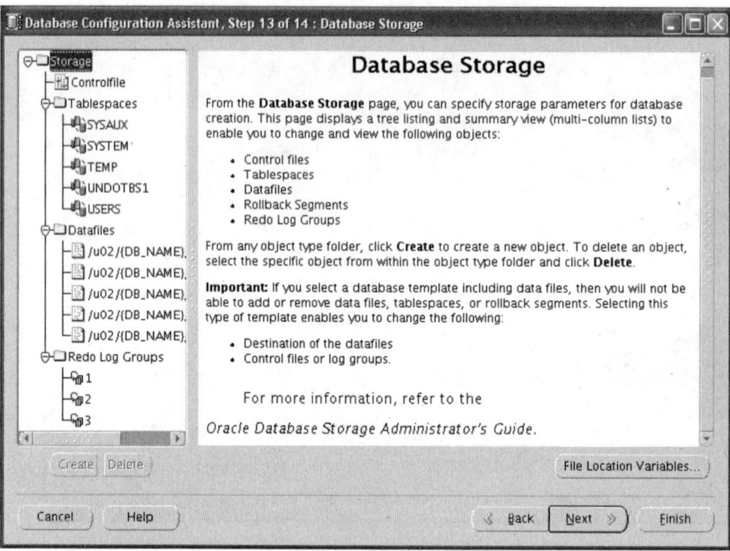

This screen displays a tree structure in the left pane. You can click the various elements within the tree to expand and display the details of each component. As with many of the other screens in the DBCA, you can click the File Location Variables button to display the settings for the various Oracle file location parameters, such as the `ORACLE_BASE` and `ORACLE_HOME` settings (see Figure 9.27).

FIGURE 9.27 DBCA File Location Variables dialog box

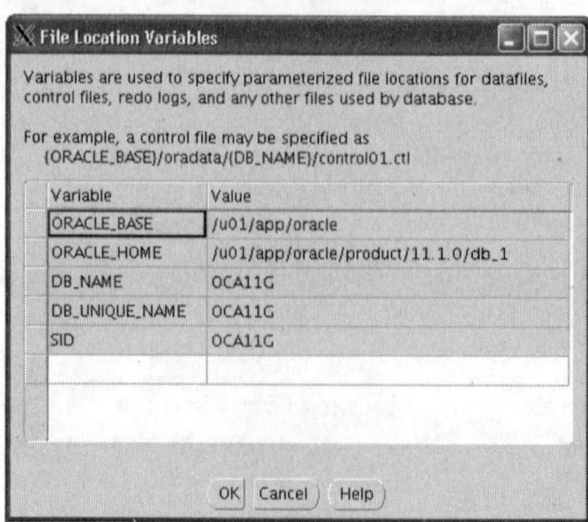

Selecting an element displays details about the element in the pane on the right. For example, clicking Controlfile displays a summary of the controlfile names and locations in the right pane. You can make manual changes to the names and locations of the control files in the right pane. Figure 9.28 shows the storage options available to configure a tablespace.

FIGURE 9.28 DBCA Database Storage tablespace storage screen

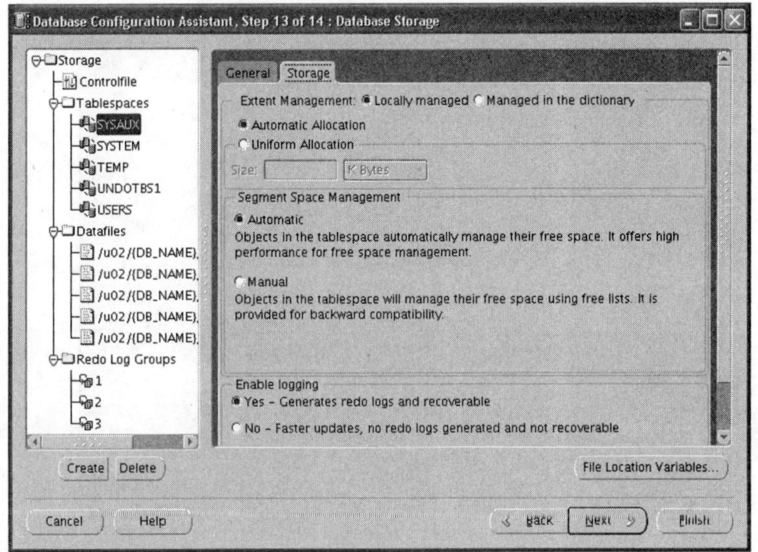

If you are creating a custom database definition that does not use a template, you can add new objects to a particular group. For example, clicking the Tablespaces folder and then clicking Create lets you add new tablespaces to your database definition. If you selected a database template that included data file definitions, you cannot add or remove data files, tablespaces, or rollback segments, but you can modify the location of the data files, control files, and redo log groups.

Chapter 10, "Allocating Database Storage and Creating Schema Objects," covers configuring and managing tablespaces and data files in detail.

After completing the Database Storage screen, click Next to create your database.

Creation Options

The Creation Options screen (see Figure 9.29) provides you with three options, and you can choose all three if needed.

Create Database Use this option to have the DBCA immediately create your database.

Save as a Database Template You actually have two choices with this option. You can elect to save your database definition to a template and create the database at a later time, or you can have the DBCA create the template and immediately create your database.

Generate Database Creation Scripts This option will generate scripts for you to create the database at a later time without using the DBCA.

FIGURE 9.29 The DBCA Creation Options screen

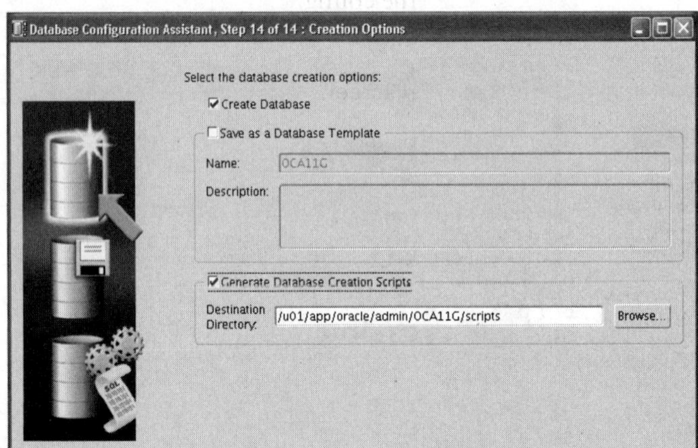

If you elect to create your database immediately, the DBCA uses the information you have provided in the previous screens to create all the necessary components of your database, populate the database with sample schemas if they were chosen, start your database, and allow you to configure the network components of your database, such as the Oracle Net listener.

I will discuss the listener component in more detail in Chapter 11.

If you elect to save your database to a template definition, this definition is added to the list of database definitions that you can select on subsequent executions of the DBCA.

You can also let the DBCA create a set of scripts that you can run manually to create the database. You can choose a location to store your scripts, and then you can run the scripts manually to generate your database. If you choose a manual creation process, you will also have to manually configure several items, including the Oracle Internet Directory Service if you elect to use centralized naming and your listener. Also, depending on your operating system, you will have to configure or modify the `oratab` file (under `/etc` or `/var/opt/oracle` depending on the platform) on Unix or create a service in the Windows environment.

When preparing for the test, create the database using a predefined template as well as a custom template. Save the database-creation scripts, and go through the scripts to understand what statements are executed behind the scenes by the DBCA to create the database. When using a custom template, a new database will be created using the CREATE DATABASE statement, whereas when using a predefined template, Oracle does not create a new database from scratch; instead, it clones an existing database from the template.

If you elect to have the DBCA create the database immediately, click Finish. You will see the Confirmation screen that summarizes the configuration options that you chose for this database (see Figure 9.30).

FIGURE 9.30 The DBCA Confirmation screen

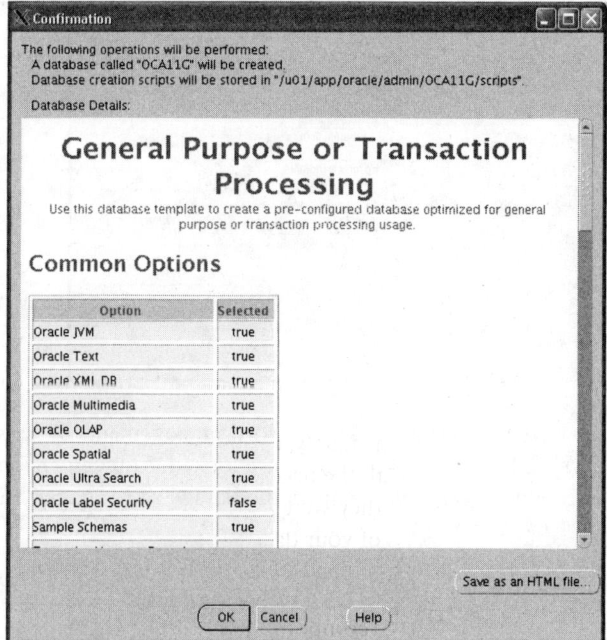

You can scroll down the window to examine the following:

- Options to install into the database
- The initialization-parameter settings
- Character-set settings
- Names and locations for data files
- Names and locations for redo logs
- Names and locations for control files

You can save this summary screen as an HTML file for later reference.

Once you start the database-creation process, Oracle creates the database as you have specified. It starts the instance, creates all the necessary database components, and configures all the database options you specified. Depending on how large a database you create and how many options you are installing, the process can take anywhere from several minutes to an hour or more.

After the database creation is complete, DBCA shows a summary screen, as shown in Figure 9.31. Note the information on this screen, especially the URL to invoke Enterprise Manager Database Control and the server parameter file location.

FIGURE 9.31 DBCA result summary screen

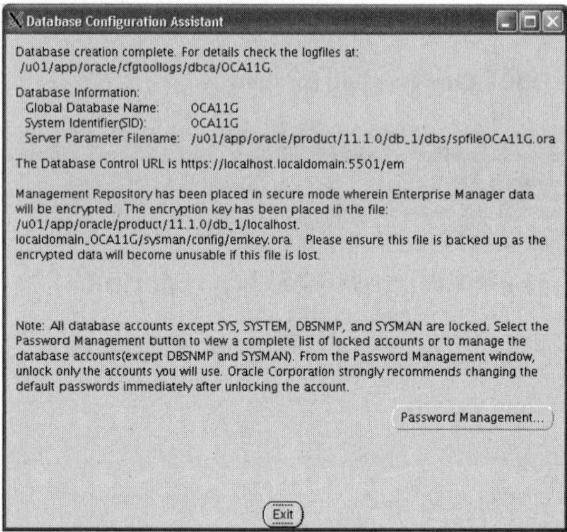

On this screen, you have the option to do password management. By default, all the accounts except SYS, SYSTEM, SYSMAN, and DBSNMP are locked. You can change the password and unlock selective accounts. Figure 9.32 shows the Password Management dialog box.

FIGURE 9.32 DBCA Password Management dialog box

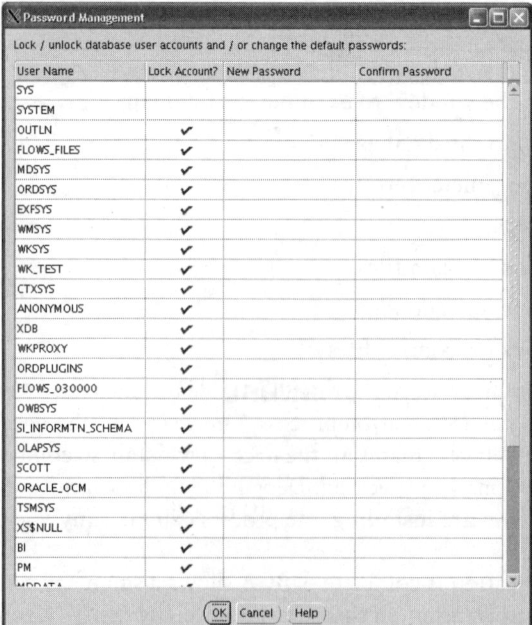

When the creation process is complete, connect to the database with one of the tools such as SQL*Plus or Enterprise Manager to ensure that all the database options and components were installed properly. Logging into Enterprise Manager will give you an overview of the new database. By using the URL specified in Figure 9.31, you can invoke the Database Control home page. Log in using the SYSMAN account with the password you supplied in Figure 9.7. Figure 9.33 shows the home screen of Enterprise Manager Database Control.

FIGURE 9.33 Enterprise Manager Database Control home page

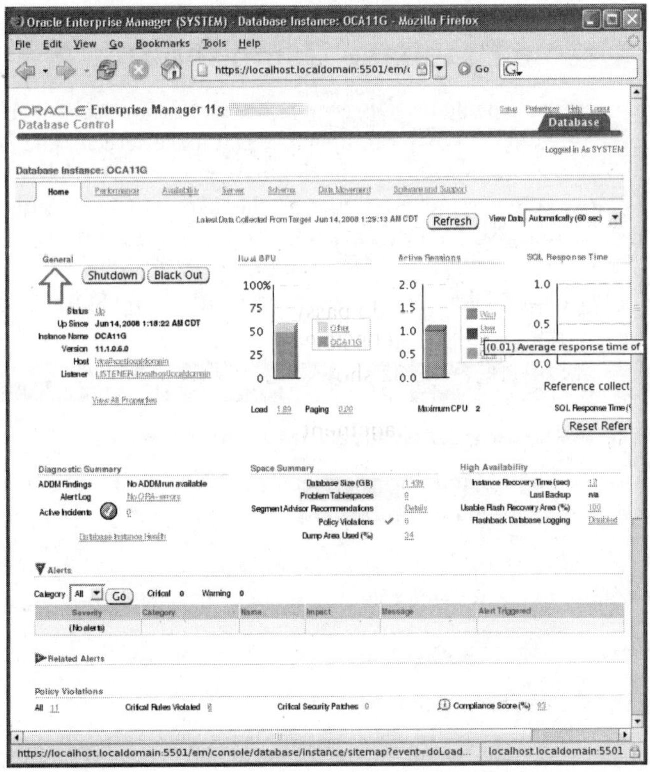

Configuring an Oracle Database Using the DBCA

The DBCA lets you change various aspects of an existing database. To change the database configuration, select Configure Database Options on the DBCA Operations screen (shown earlier in this chapter in Figure 9.2). If the database is not started, the DBCA starts it for you automatically. You must connect to the database as a user who has DBA authority.

Once you have selected and started the database, you can add options that may not have been previously included in the database. Using DBCA you can perform the following changes to database configuration:

- Add database components (refer to Figure 9.13).
- Change database security settings from pre-11*g* default security setting to 11*g* enhanced security settings, or vice versa (refer Figure 9.24).
- Change the default connection mode for the database. You can change from dedicated server mode to shared server mode, or vice versa (refer Figure 9.22).

Deleting an Oracle Database Using the DBCA

You can also delete a database using the DBCA. On the Operations screen (Figure 9.2), choose Delete a Database, and click Next to open the Database screen. The DBCA lists all the databases available for deletion. Choose the database you want to delete.

If you click Finish, the DBCA removes all files on the disk associated with the database you have chosen. If you are using Windows, the DBCA also removes the service associated with the database.

Exercise 9.1 shows you how to delete a database manually using SQL*Plus.

EXERCISE 9.1

Delete or Remove an Oracle Database Manually

Some DBAs prefer to use a command-line interface to perform their tasks. You can delete a database using the command-line tool SQL*Plus.

To do so, first connect to SQL*Plus as an administrator who has the ability to start up the database; that is, an administrator with either the SYSOPER or SYSDBA privilege.

Here's an example:

```
/u01/app/oracle>sqlplus sys/**** as sysdba
```

Once you are connected, you need to put the database in MOUNT mode. Issue the following command if the database is not running:

```
Startup mount;
```

Next, issue the following command:

```
Drop database;
```

This command deletes all the files associated with the database. If you are using raw disk devices, the special files created for these devices are not deleted. Also, you may have to remove any archived logs from the database archive area using the appropriate operating-system command.

Managing Database Templates Using the DBCA

As I explained earlier in this chapter, the DBCA can store and use XML-based templates to create your Oracle Database. As the DBA, you can manage these database-definition templates. Saving a definition of your database in a template format makes it easier to perform various tasks. For example, you can copy a preexisting template to modify new database definitions. The template definition is normally stored in the `$ORACLE_HOME/assistants/dbca/templates` directory on Unix and in the `%ORACLE_HOME%\assistants\dbca\templates` directory on Windows systems.

The DBCA can use two types of templates: seed and nonseed. *Seed* templates are template definitions that contain database-definition information and the actual data files and redo log files. The advantage of a seed template is that the DBCA makes a copy of the data files and redo logs included in the definition file. These prebuilt data files include all schema information, which makes for a faster database-creation process. The seed templates carry a `.dbc` extension. The associated predefined data files are stored as files having a `.dfb` extension. When you use a seed template, you can change the database name, the data-file locations, the number of control files and redo log groups, and the initialization parameters.

Nonseed templates contain custom-defined database definitions. Unlike seed templates, they do not come with preconfigured data files and redo logs. Nonseed templates carry a `.dbt` extension.

Now I'll cover the various options you have to manage templates.

Creating Template Definitions Using the DBCA

You can use the DBCA interface to create new database templates. When you connect to the DBCA, select Manage Templates on the Operations screen (see Figure 9.2, shown earlier in this chapter), and click Next to open the Template Management screen, as shown in Figure 9.34.

FIGURE 9.34 The DBCA Template Management screen

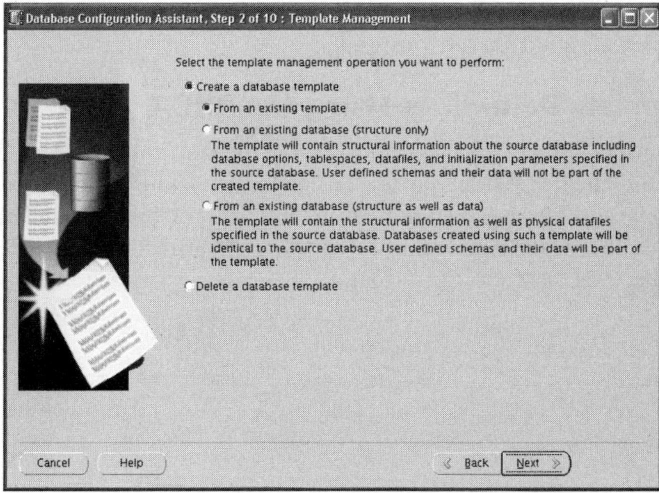

You have three choices for creating templates. Table 9.4 summarizes your options.

TABLE 9.4 Template-Creation Options

Selection	Description
From an Existing Template	Creates a new template definition from a preexisting template. This allows you to modify a variety of template settings, including parameters and data file storage characteristics.
From an Existing Database (Structure Only)	Creates a new template based on the structural characteristics of an existing database. The data files are created from scratch and will not include data from the original database. Choose this option when you want a database that is structurally like another database but does not contain any data. The database you are copying from can reside anywhere in your network.
From an Existing Database (Structure As Well As Data)	Creates a new template based on the structural characteristics of an existing database. The data files and all corresponding user data are included in the new database. Choose this option when you want an exact copy of an existing database. The database you are copying must reside on the same physical server as the new database you are creating.

Depending on the option selected, you are presented with a set of forms to save your template definition. If you elect to create a template from an existing database, you will have to connect to the database so that the DBCA can obtain information about the database. You must connect to the database as a user who has DBA credentials to perform this task.

If you are copying a definition from an existing template, you can configure the template by following a series of screens that are similar to those used to create a database. These screens allow you to configure the various aspects of the template, including initialization parameters and data file and redo log locations.

Deleting Template Definitions Using the DBCA

You can also delete an existing template definition. On the Operations screen (see Figure 9.2, shown earlier in this chapter), click Manage Templates. You will be presented with the Template Management screen (see Figure 9.34). Select the option Delete a Database Template. You can then choose the template to delete. When you remove the template, the DBCA removes the XML file from the system.

Working with Oracle 11*g* Metadata

In addition to tables such as DEPARTMENTS and EMPLOYEES that store important business data, Oracle Databases also contain system tables that store data about the database. Examples of the type of information in these system tables include the names of all the tables in the database, the column names and datatypes of those tables, the number of rows those tables contain, and security information about which users are allowed to access those tables. This "data about the database" is referred to as *metadata*. As a DBA, you will frequently use this metadata when performing your administration tasks.

An Oracle 11*g* database contains two types of metadata views:

- Data dictionary views
- Dynamic performance views

The SYS user owns the data dictionary and dynamic performance views in the Oracle 11*g* database, and they are stored in the SYSTEM tablespace. During normal database operation, Oracle uses the data dictionary frequently and updates the dictionary with the current status of the database components. The dictionary is also immediately updated when a DDL statement is executed.

Data dictionary views and dynamic performance views are described in the next section.

Data Dictionary Views

Data dictionary views provide information about the database and its objects. Depending on which features are installed and configured, an Oracle 11*g* database can contain more than 1,600 data dictionary views. Data dictionary views have names that begin with DBA_, ALL_, and USER_. Oracle creates public synonyms on many data dictionary views so users can access the views conveniently.

The difference between the DBA_, ALL_, and USER_ views can be illustrated using the DBA_TABLES data dictionary view as an example. The DBA_TABLES view shows information on all the tables in the database. The corresponding ALL_TABLES view, despite its name, shows only the tables that a particular database user owns or can access. For example, if you were logged into the database as a user named SCOTT, the ALL_TABLES view would show all the tables owned by the user SCOTT and the tables to which SCOTT has been granted access by other users. The USER_TABLES view shows only those objects owned by a user. If the user SCOTT were to examine the USER_TABLES view, only those tables he owns would be displayed. Figure 9.35 shows a graphical representation of the relationship between the DBA_, ALL_, and USER_ views.

Because the DBA_ views provide the broadest metadata information, they are generally the data dictionary views used by DBAs. Table 9.5 provides examples of DBA_ data dictionary views.

FIGURE 9.35 A comparison of data dictionary views

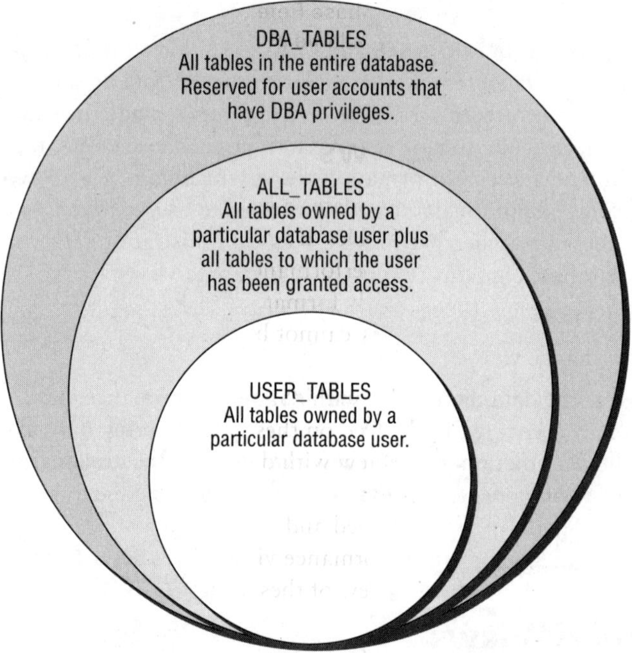

TABLE 9.5 Examples of Data Dictionary Views

Dictionary View	Description
DBA_TABLES	Shows the names and physical storage information about all the tables in the database
DBA_USERS	Shows information about all the users in the database
DBA_VIEWS	Shows information about all the views in the database
DBA_TAB_COLUMNS	Shows all the names and datatypes of the table columns in the database
DATABASE_PROPERTIES	Displays database properties such as NLS parameters, default temporary and permanent tablespace names, database time zone, so on
GLOBAL_NAME	Shows the global database name

You can find a complete list of the Oracle 11*g* data dictionary views in Part II of the "Oracle Database Reference 11*g* Release 1 (11.1) Part Number B28320-01" document available at `http://tahiti.oracle.com`.

Dynamic Performance Views

Throughout database operation, Oracle updates a set of virtual tables to record the current database activity and status. These tables are called *dynamic performance tables*. Views are created on top of the dynamic performance tables for better grouping of information and to have names in a user-friendly format. The dynamic performance views are sometimes called *fixed views*, because they cannot be altered or removed by the database administrator.

The dynamic performance tables begin with `X$`. The dynamic performance view names begin with `V_$`. Public synonyms are created on these views, and they begin with `V$`. For example, the dynamic performance view with data file information is `v_$datafile`, whereas the public synonym is `v$datafile`.

Depending on which features are installed and configured, an Oracle 11*g* database can contain approximately 480 dynamic performance views. Most of these views have names that begin with `V$`. Table 9.6 describes a few of these dynamic performance views.

TABLE 9.6 Examples of Dynamic Performance Views

Dynamic Performance View	Description
`V$DATABASE`	Contains information about the database, such as the database name and when the database was created
`V$VERSION`	Shows which software version the database is using
`V$OPTION`	Displays which optional components are installed in the database
`V$SQL`	Displays information about the SQL statements that database users have been issuing

You can find a complete list of the Oracle 11*g* data dictionary views in Part III of the "Oracle Database Reference 11*g* Release 1 (11.1) Part Number B28320-01" document available at `http://tahiti.oracle.com`.

Although the contents of the DBA_ and V$ metadata views are similar, there are some important differences between the two types. Table 9.7 compares these two types.

TABLE 9.7 Data Dictionary vs. Dynamic Performance Views

Data Dictionary Views	Dynamic Performance Views
The DBA_ views usually have plural names (for example, DBA_DATA_FILES).	The names of the V$ views are generally singular (for example, V$DATAFILE).
The DBA_ views are available only when the database is open and running.	Some V$ views are available even when the database is not fully open and running.
The data contained in the DBA_ views is static and is not cleared when the database is shut down.	The V$ views contain dynamic statistical data that is lost each time the database is shut down.

The data dictionary view DICTIONARY shows information about the data dictionary and dynamic performance views in the database. DICT is a synonym for the DICTIONARY view. The COMMENTS column shows the purpose or contents of the view. The V$FIXED_TABLE view lists the dynamic performance tables and views in the database.

The Oracle data dictionary and dynamic performance views are created while creating the database. The scripts to create the metadata are stored in the $ORACLE_HOME/rdbms/admin directory. Several scripts are in this directory, and the script that creates the base dictionary objects is called catalog.sql. The catproc.sql script creates the PL/SQL packages and functionality to support PL/SQL in the database.

You are not allowed to log in as SYS and modify the data dictionary views or update information directly using SQL. The only SYS-owned table you are allowed to delete records from is AUD$. This table is used to keep database audit information.

Managing Initialization-Parameter Files

Oracle uses initialization-parameter files to store information about initialization parameters used when an Oracle instance starts. Oracle reads the parameter file to obtain information about how the Oracle instance should be sized and configured upon startup.

The parameter file can be a plain text file, commonly referred to as a *pfile*, or it can be a binary parameter file, commonly referred to as an *spfile*. You can use either type of file to configure instance and database options; however, there are some important differences between the two types of configuration files, as shown in Table 9.8.

TABLE 9.8 Pfiles vs. Spfiles

Pfile	Spfile
Text file that can be edited using a text editor.	Binary file that cannot be edited directly.
When changes are made to the pfile, the instance must be shut down and restarted before it takes effect.	Parameter changes made to the database using `ALTER SYSTEM` are updated in the spfile.
Is called `init`*`instance_name`*`.ora`.	Is called `spfile`*`instance_name`*`.ora`.
Oracle instance reads only from pfile.	Oracle instance reads and writes to the spfile.
Can be created from an spfile using the `create pfile from spfile` command.	Can be created from a pfile using the `create spfile from pfile` command.

You can specify more than 285 documented configuration parameters in the pfile or spfile. Oracle 11*g* divides these parameters into two categories: basic and advanced. Oracle recommends you set only the basic initialization parameters manually. Oracle also recommends you do not modify the remaining parameters unless directed to do so by Oracle Support or to meet the specific needs of your application. Table 9.9 describes the basic initialization parameters . A "Yes" in the Static column indicates that the parameter is static and cannot be modified dynamically without a database restart.

TABLE 9.9 Oracle 11*g* Basic Initialization Parameters

Parameter Name	Static	Description
`CLUSTER_DATABASE`	Yes	Tells the instance whether it is part of a clustered environment.
`COMPATIBLE`	Yes	Specifies the release level and feature set you want to be active in the instance.
`CONTROL_FILES`	Yes	Designates the physical location of the database control files.
`DB_BLOCK_SIZE`	Yes	Specifies the default database block size. The database block size specified at database creation cannot be changed.

TABLE 9.9 Oracle 11*g* Basic Initialization Parameters *(continued)*

Parameter Name	Static	Description
DB_CREATE_FILE_DEST	No	Specifies the directory location where database data files will be created if the Oracle-Managed Files feature is used.
DB_CREATE_ONLINE_LOG_DEST_*n*	No	Specifies the location(s) where the database redo log files will be created if the Oracle-Managed Files feature is used.
DB_DOMAIN	Yes	Specifies the logical location of the database on the network.
DB_NAME	Yes	Specifies the name of the database that is mounted by the instance.
DB_RECOVERY_FILE_DEST	No	Specifies the location where recovery files will be written if the flash recovery feature is used.
DB_RECOVERY_FILE_DEST_SIZE	No	Specifies the amount of disk space available for storing flash recovery files.
DB_UNIQUE_NAME	Yes	Specifies a globally unique name for the database within the enterprise.
INSTANCE_NUMBER	Yes	Identifies the instance in a Real Application Clusters (RAC) environment.
LDAP_DIRECTORY_SYSAUTH	Yes	Enables or disables Oracle Internet directory–based authentication for SYSDBA and SYSOPER connections to the database.
LOG_ARCHIVE_DEST_*n*	No	Specifies as many as nine locations where archived redo log files are to be written.
LOG_ARCHIVE_DEST_STATE_*n*	No	Indicates how the specified locations should be used for log archiving.
NLS_LANGUAGE	Yes	Specifies the default language of the database.
NLS_TERRITORY	Yes	Specifies the default region or territory of the database.
OPEN_CURSORS	No	Sets the maximum number of cursors that an individual session can have open at one time.
PGA_AGGREGATE_TARGET	No	Establishes the overall amount of memory that all PGA processes are allowed to consume.
PROCESSES	Yes	Specifies the maximum number of operating-system processes that can connect to the instance.
REMOTE_LISTENER	No	Specifies a network name that points to the address or list of addresses of remote Oracle Net listeners.

TABLE 9.9 Oracle 11*g* Basic Initialization Parameters *(continued)*

Parameter Name	Static	Description
REMOTE_LOGIN_ PASSWORDFILE	Yes	Determines whether the instance uses a password file and what type.
ROLLBACK_SEGMENTS	Yes	Specifies the rollback-segment names, only if Automatic Undo Management is not being used.
SESSIONS	Yes	Determines the maximum number of sessions that can connect to the database.
SGA_TARGET	No	Establishes the maximum size of the SGA, within which space is automatically allocated to each SGA component when Automatic Memory Management is used.
SHARED_SERVERS	No	Specifies the number of shared server processes to start when the instance is started. See Chapter 11 for details.
STAR_TRANSFORMATION_ ENABLED	No	Determines whether the optimizer will consider star transformations when queries are executed. See Chapter 14 for details on the optimizer.
UNDO_MANAGEMENT	Yes	Establishes whether system undo is automatically or manually managed. See Chapter 8, "Introducing Oracle 11*g* Components and Architecture," for details on undo segments.
UNDO_TABLESPACE	No	Specifies which tablespace stores undo segments if the Automatic Undo Management option is used. See Chapter 13, "Managing Data and Undo," for details on undo management.

Any parameters not specified in the pfile or spfile take on their default values. The following is an example of the contents of a typical Oracle 11*g* pfile that contains both basic and advanced parameters:

```
audit_file_dest='/u01/app/oracle/admin/OCA11G/adump'
audit_trail='db'
compatible='11.1.0.0.0'
control_files=('/u01/app/oracle/oradata/OCA11G/control01.ctl'
,'/u01/app/oracle/oradata/OCA11G/control02.ctl'
,'/u01/app/oracle/oradata/OCA11G/control03.ctl')
db_block_size=8192
db_domain=''
db_name='OCA11G'
db_recovery_file_dest='/u01/app/oracle/flash_recovery_area'
```

```
db_recovery_file_dest_size=2147483648
diagnostic_dest='/u01/app/oracle'
dispatchers='(PROTOCOL=TCP) (SERVICE=OCA11GXDB)'
memory_target=1G
open_cursors=300
processes=150
remote_login_passwordfile='EXCLUSIVE'
undo_tablespace='UNDOTBS1'
```

In this sample pfile, the sizes of the shared pool, database buffer cache, large pool, and Java pool are not individually specified. Instead, Oracle 11*g*'s Automatic Memory Management features allow you to simply set one configuration parameter—`MEMORY_TARGET`—to establish the total amount of memory allocated to the SGA and PGA. I will discuss this parameter in Chapter 14.

On production databases, if your Oracle license is based on the number of named users, you can enforce the license compliance by setting the `LICENSE_MAX_USERS` parameter. The default for this parameter is 0, which means you can create any number of users in the database and the license compliance is not enforced.

Real World Scenario

Handle with Care: Undocumented Configuration Parameters

You've just read a performance-tuning tip posted to the Oracle newsgroup at `comp.databases.oracle.server`. The person posting the tip suggests setting the undocumented pfile parameter `_dyn_sel_est_num_blocks` to a value of 200 in order to boost your database's performance. Should you implement this suggestion?

More than 1,000 undocumented configuration parameters are available in Oracle 11*g*. Undocumented configuration parameters are distinguished from their documented counterparts by the underscore that precedes their name, as with the parameter described in the newsgroup posting.

I do not recommend utilizing undocumented pfile or spfile parameters on any of your systems because knowing the appropriate reasons to use these parameters, and the appropriate values to set these parameters to, is almost pure speculation because of their undocumented nature. Although some undocumented parameters are relatively harmless (such as `_trace_files_public`), using others incorrectly can cause unforeseen database problems. What does the `_dyn_sel_est_num_blocks` parameter do, and what value should you set it to? Only the engineers of the Oracle 11*g* kernel code know for sure.

One exception to this suggestion is when you are directed to use an undocumented configuration parameter by Oracle Support. Oracle Support occasionally uses these parameters to enhance the generation of debug information or to work around a bug in the kernel code.

Locating the Default Parameter File

The default location that Oracle searches to find the pfile and spfile parameter files is `$ORACLE_HOME/dbs` on Unix systems and `%ORACLE_HOME%\database` on Windows systems.

Oracle uses a search hierarchy when a `startup` command is issued without specifying either a pfile or an spfile. Oracle looks for files with the following names in the default directory to start the instance:

- `spfile$ORACLE_SID.ora`
- `spfile.ora`
- `init$ORACLE_SID.ora`

Oracle first looks for a parameter file called `spfile$ORACLE_SID.ora`. If it doesn't find that, it searches for `spfile.ora`. Finally, it searches for a traditional text pfile with the default name of `init$ORACLE_SID.ora`.

If the parameter files do not exist in the default location or you want to use a different parameter file to start your database, you can specify a parameter file to use when you issue a `startup` command to start the Oracle Database.

You will see examples of how database startup is performed later in this chapter in the section "Starting Up and Shutting Down an Oracle Instance."

Modifying Initialization-Parameter Values

In some instances, you may need to change the initialization parameters. For example, you might need to increase the number of sessions allowed to connect to the database because you are adding users. Whatever the case, you need to know how to make these changes. There are a few options to change the initialization-parameter value, based on the type of parameter file used. Here they are:

- If `PFILE` is used, edit the pfile using an OS editor, and make appropriate changes.
- If `SPFILE` is used, connect to the instance, and make changes using the `ALTER SYSTEM SET parameter_name = value` statement.
- Use EM Database Control to make changes.

Using EM Database Control

To use the EM Database Control tool to modify existing database parameters, navigate to the Server menu. In the Database Configuration section, you can modify your initialization parameters. The SPFile tab shows the parameters as set in the spfile. You can also use the filters to find the exact parameter that needs to be modified. The Category drop-down is a very useful feature. Figure 9.36 shows the EM screen to change initialization parameters.

The Initialization Parameters screen has two tabs:

Current tab This tab displays all the currently active settings for initialization parameters for the database instance. If a parameter is marked Dynamic, you can modify it, and this modification immediately affects the parameter that affects the currently running instance without stopping the database. The changes you make on the Current tab are not permanent, so the next time the database is stopped and restarted, the settings revert to their original values.

SPFile tab If you are using a server parameter file, you will see the SPFile tab. This tab also lets you change existing database parameters. The difference between changing parameters on this tab and changing parameters on the Current tab is that changes to the spfile are persistent across database startups and shutdowns because the changes are saved to the spfile definition. You can also apply your changes to the spfile only or to the spfile and the currently running instance.

FIGURE 9.36 The EM Database Control Initialization Parameters screen

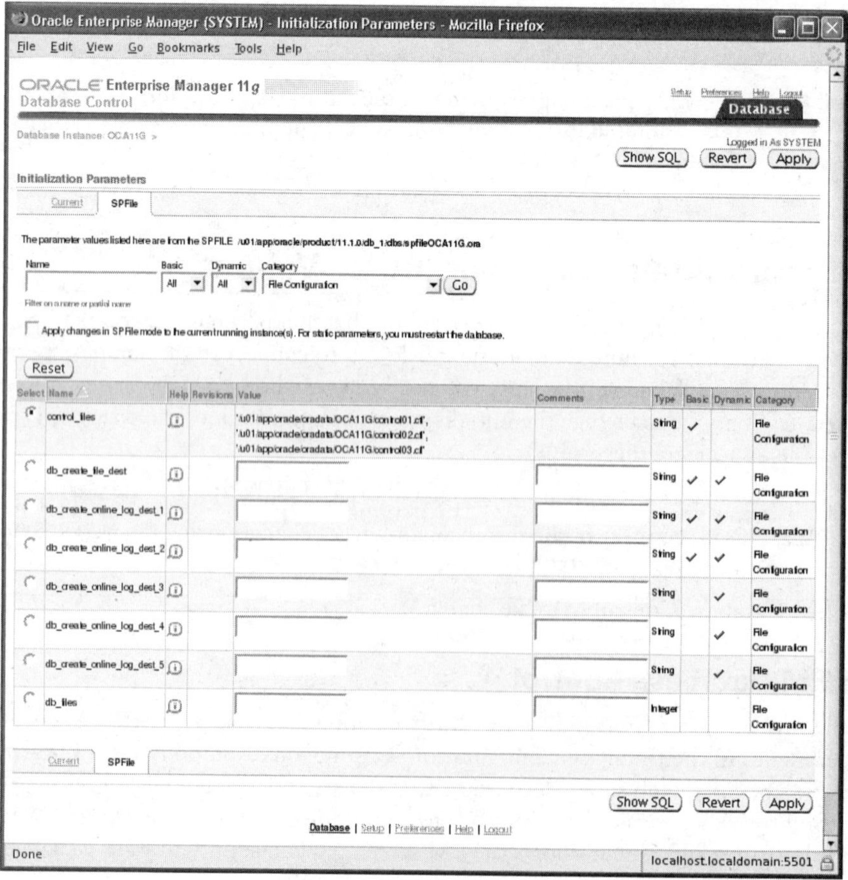

Using SQL*Plus

Though EM Database Control is a handy tool to modify the initialization parameters, sometimes it is convenient to use SQL*Plus and make changes to the parameters. You should know about two dynamic performance views: V$PARAMETER and V$SPPARAMETER.

V$PARAMETER

The V$PARAMETER view shows information about the initialization parameters that are currently in effect. This view has several useful columns. Table 9.10 lists some of the columns in V$PARAMETER and how they can be used in queries.

TABLE 9.10 V$PARAMETER Columns

Column Name	Description
NAME	This specifies the name of the initialization parameter.
VALUE	This specifies the current value of the parameter.
DISPLAY_VALUE	This specifies the current value in a more user-friendly format.
DESCRIPTION	This gives a short description about the parameter.
ISBASIC	TRUE indicates that the parameter is categorized as a basic parameter.
ISDEFAULT	FALSE indicates that the parameter was specified in the pfile or spfile during instance startup.
ISMODIFIED	FALSE indicates that the parameter has not been modified since the instance started.
ISSES_MODIFIABLE	TRUE indicates that the parameter can be modified using an ALTER SESSION statement.
ISSYS_MODIFIABLE	FALSE indicates that the parameter cannot be modified using an ALTER SYSTEM statement. Such parameters can be changed only using the SCOPE=SPFILE clause.

V$SPPARAMETER

The V$SPPARAMETER view shows the contents of the spfile used to start the instance. A TRUE value for the ISSPECIFIED column shows whether the parameter was specified in the spfile. If a pfile was used to start the instance, all the rows will have FALSE for the ISSPECIFIED column. Sometimes, querying the V$SPPARAMETER can produce readable output for parameters that take multiple values.

V$PARAMETER vs. V$SPPARAMETER

The following SQL example shows the difference in the result from the V$PARAMETER and V$SPPARAMETER views:

```
SQL> SELECT name, value
  2  FROM v$parameter
  3  WHERE name LIKE 'control%'
  4  AND isdefault = 'FALSE';

NAME                 VALUE
-------------------- ---------------------------------------------
control_files        /u01/app/oracle/oradata/OCA11G/control01.ctl, /u
                     01/app/oracle/oradata/OCA11G/control02.ctl,/u01/
                     app/oracle/oradata/OCA11G/control03.ctl


SQL> SELECT name, value
  2  FROM v$spparameter
  3  WHERE name LIKE 'control%'
  4  AND isspecified = 'TRUE';

NAME                 VALUE
-------------------- ---------------------------------------------
control_files        /u01/app/oracle/oradata/OCA11G/control01.ctl
control_files        /u01/app/oracle/oradata/OCA11G/control02.ctl
control_files        /u01/app/oracle/oradata/OCA11G/control03.ctl

SQL>
```

You can use the ALTER SESSION statement to change the value of a parameter in the current session. For example, if you want to change the default date-display format for the session only, use the following statement:

```
SQL> ALTER SESSION SET NLS_DATE_FORMAT = 'DD-MON-YYYY HH24:MI:SS';

Session altered.

SQL>
```

You can use the ALTER SYSTEM statement to change the value of a parameter system-wide or in the spfile, or both. You use the SCOPE clause to define where you want to change the parameter value: MEMORY, SPFILE, and BOTH are the valid values for the SCOPE clause.

A value of DEFERRED or IMMEDIATE in the ISSYS_MODIFIABLE column shows that the parameter can be dynamically changed using ALTER SYSTEM. The DEFERRED value indicates that the change you make does not take effect until a new session is started; the existing sessions will use the current value. IMMEDIATE indicates that as soon as you change the value of the parameter, it is available to all sessions in the instance. A *session* is a job or task that Oracle manages. When you log in to the database using SQL*Plus or any other tool, you start a session.

If you want to change a parameter value for the current instance but do not want the change to persist across database shutdowns, you can specify SCOPE=MEMORY, as in the following example:

```
SQL> ALTER SYSTEM SET UNDO_RETENTION = 3600 SCOPE=MEMORY;

System altered.
SQL>
```

Some parameters values can be set only at instance startup; they are not modifiable when the instance is running. Such parameter changes can be made with the SCOPE=SPFILE clause. Oracle will make the change only to the spfile, which takes effect after you restart the database:

```
SQL> ALTER SYSTEM SET UNDO_MANAGEMENT = MANUAL;
ALTER SYSTEM SET UNDO_MANAGEMENT = MANUAL
                 *
ERROR at line 1:
ORA-02095: specified initialization parameter cannot be modified

SQL> ALTER SYSTEM SET UNDO_MANAGEMENT = MANUAL SCOPE=SPFILE;

System altered.
SQL>
```

Most of the times when you make a parameter change, you want it to take effect immediately in memory as well as persist the change across database shutdowns. You can use the SCOPE=BOTH clause, which is the default, for this purpose. So if you omit the SCOPE clause, Oracle will make changes to the memory and to the spfile. If a pfile is used to start the instance, the change will be in memory only for the current running instance.

```
SQL> ALTER SYSTEM SET SGA_TARGET=500M SCOPE=BOTH;

System altered.
SQL>
```

You can use the SQL*Plus command SHOW PARAMETER to view the current value of an initialization parameter. You can specify the full parameter name or part of the name. For example, to view all parameters related to undo, you can do this:

```
SQL> SHOW PARAMETER undo

NAME                                 TYPE        VALUE
------------------------------------ ----------- -----------
undo_management                      string      AUTO
undo_retention                       integer     3600
undo_tablespace                      string      UNDOTBS1
SQL>
```

In the next section, I will discuss the options to start up and shut down a database.

Starting Up and Shutting Down an Oracle Instance

As a DBA, you are responsible for the startup and shutdown of the Oracle instance. Oracle gives authorized administrators the ability to perform this task using a variety of interfaces. It is important to understand the options that are available to you to start up and shut down the Oracle instance and when the various options can or should be used. The stages of instance startup and the startup options appear frequently on OCA certification exams.

To start up or shut down an Oracle instance, you need to be connected to the database with the appropriate privileges. Two special connection account authorizations are available for startup and shutdown: SYSDBA and SYSOPER. The SYSDBA authorization is an all-empowering authorization that allows you to perform any database task. The SYSOPER authorization is a less powerful authorization that allows startup and shutdown abilities but restricts other administrative tasks, such as access to nonadministrative schema objects. These authorizations are managed either through a passwords file or via operating-system control.

When a database is initially installed, only the SYS schema can connect to the database with the SYSDBA authorization. You can grant this authorization and the SYSOPER authorization to give others the ability to perform these tasks without connecting as the SYS user.

Now I will discuss how to perform a database startup.

Starting Up an Oracle 11*g* Database

As described in Chapter 8, the Oracle instance is composed of a set of logical memory structures and background processes that users interact with to communicate with the Oracle Database. When Oracle is started, these memory structures and background processes are initialized and started so that users can communicate with the Oracle Database.

Whenever an Oracle Database is started, it goes through a series of steps to ensure database consistency. When it starts up, a database passes through three modes: NOMOUNT, MOUNT, and OPEN. I will review each of these *startup* modes and other special startup options such as FORCE and RESTRICT and discuss when you need to use these options. I'll then discuss how to use the available interfaces to start up an Oracle instance.

STARTUP NOMOUNT This starts the instance without mounting the database. When a database is started in this mode, the parameter file is read, and the background processes and memory structures are initiated, but they are not attached or communicating with the disk structures of the database. When the instance is in this state, the database is not available for use.

If a database is started in NOMOUNT mode, only the background processes and instance are started. The instance is not associated with any database. This state is used to create a database or to create a database control file.

At times, a database may not be able to go to the next mode (called MOUNT mode) and remains in NOMOUNT mode. For example, this can occur if Oracle has a problem accessing the control file structures, which contain important information to continue with the startup process. If these structures are damaged or not available, the database startup process cannot continue until the problem is resolved.

If STARTUP NOMOUNT fails, the most likely cause is that the parameter file cannot be read or is not in the default location. Other causes include OS resource limits that prevent memory or process allocation.

STARTUP MOUNT This performs all the work of the STARTUP NOMOUNT option but also attaches and interacts with the database structures. At this point, Oracle obtains information from the control files that it uses to locate and attach to the main database structures. The control file contains the name of the database, all the data file names, and the redo log files associated with the database.

Certain administrative tasks can be performed while the database is in this mode, including renaming data files, enabling or disabling archive logging, renaming and adding redo log files, and recovering the database.

STARTUP OPEN This is the default startup mode if no mode is specified on the STARTUP command line. STARTUP OPEN performs all the steps of the STARTUP NOMOUNT and STARTUP MOUNT options. This option makes the database available to all users.

When opening the database, you can use a couple of options. STARTUP OPEN READ ONLY opens the database in read-only mode. STARTUP OPEN RECOVER opens the database and performs a database recovery.

Although you typically use the STARTUP NOMOUNT, STARTUP MOUNT, and STARTUP OPEN options, a few other startup options are available that you can use in certain situations: STARTUP FORCE and STARTUP RESTRICT. These are discussed next.

STARTUP FORCE You can use the STARTUP FORCE startup option if you are experiencing difficulty starting the database in a normal fashion. For example, if a database server lost power and the database stopped abruptly, it can leave the database in a state in which a STARTUP FORCE startup is necessary. This type of startup should not normally be required but can be used if a normal startup does not work. What is also different about STARTUP FORCE is that it can be issued no matter what mode the database is in. STARTUP FORCE does a shutdown abort and then restarts the database.

STARTUP RESTRICT The STARTUP RESTRICT option starts up the database and places it in OPEN mode but gives access only to users who have the RESTRICTED SESSION privilege. You might want to open a database using the RESTRICTED option when you want to perform maintenance on the database while it is open but ensure that users cannot connect and perform work on the database. You might also want to open the database using the RESTRICTED option to perform database exports or imports and guarantee that no users are accessing the system during these activities. After you are done with your work, you can disable the restricted session, ALTER SYSTEM DISABLE RESTRICTED SESSION, so everyone can connect to the database.

Starting Up Oracle Using EM Database Control

Now that you understand the various startup options, let's look at how to use the EM Database Control to start up the Oracle instance.

When you invoke the Enterprise Manager console, you are notified that the database instance is down (see Figure 9.37).

FIGURE 9.37 The EM Database Control database status screen

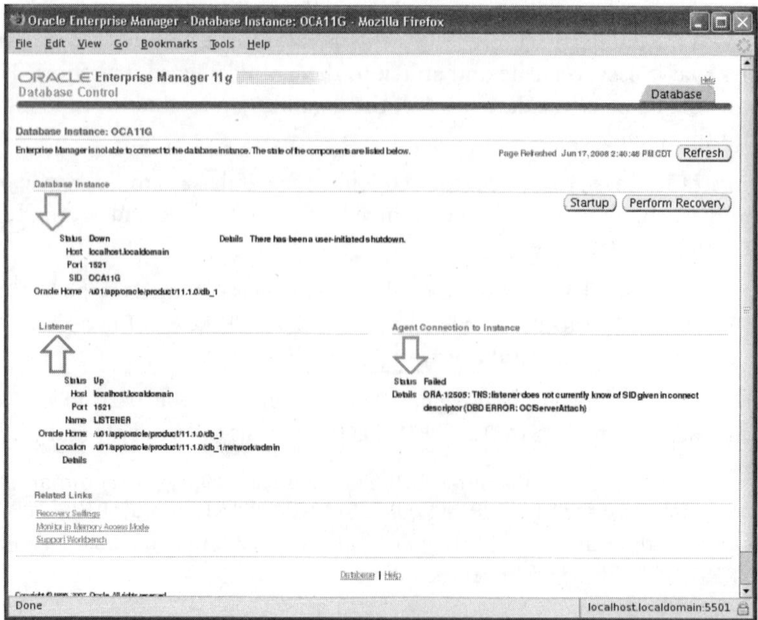

Perform the following steps to start the Oracle instance:

1. Click the Startup button located on the Database Control screen to open the Startup/Shutdown: Specify Host and Target Database Credentials screen (see Figure 9.38).
2. On the Startup/Shutdown: Specify Host and Target Database Credentials screen, you need to supply an operating-system username and password and an Oracle user ID and password that has either the SYSDBA or SYSOPER account authentication. After you enter the appropriate user ID and password information, click OK to open the Startup/Shutdown: Confirmation screen.
3. On the Startup/Shutdown: Confirmation screen, you can click Yes to continue, No to cancel, or Advanced Options to select advanced startup options.

If you click Advanced Options, you can select the type of startup you want. You can choose your startup mode (NOMOUNT, MOUNT, or OPEN), you can choose the parameter file to use, and you can choose to force database startup or to start the database in RESTRICTED mode. Click OK to return to the previous screen. By default, Oracle starts with the OPEN option and uses the default initialization file.

FIGURE 9.38 Startup/Shutdown: Specify Host and Target Database Credentials screen

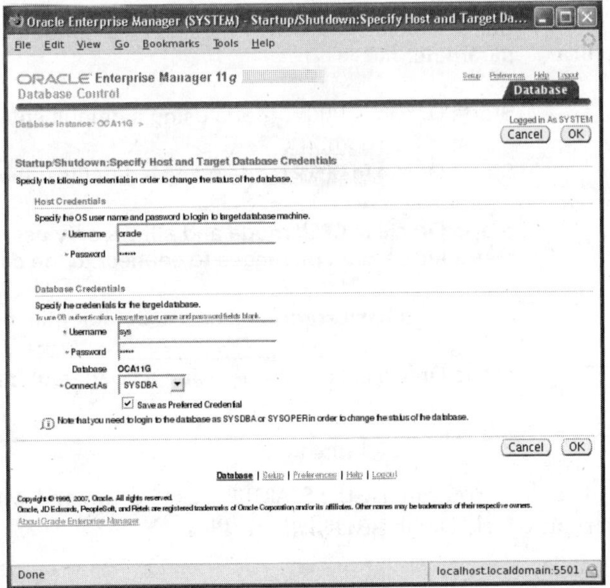

You can also click Show SQL to see the actual startup command that will be executed.

After you choose the type of startup, click Yes. The startup process may take some time to complete, depending on the system speed and whether Oracle has to perform any recovery operations during the startup process. You will be presented with a screen indicating that the database is being started. If Oracle does not encounter any problems with the startup process, you will be notified that the database is now open and available.

Starting Oracle Using SQL*Plus

You can also use the command-line facility SQL*Plus to start the Oracle Database. You will need to connect to SQL*Plus as a user with SYSOPER or SYSDBA privileges. Here is the syntax of the startup options available:

```
STARTUP [NOMOUNT|MOUNT|OPEN] [PFILE/SPFILE=] [RESTRICT]
```

Table 9.11 shows some examples of startup commands that you can use from within SQL*Plus.

TABLE 9.11 SQL*Plus DB Startup-Command Examples

Command	Description
STARTUP NOMOUNT pfile=/u01/oracle/init.ora	Starts Oracle in NOMOUNT mode using a nondefault parameter file
STARTUP MOUNT	Starts Oracle in MOUNT mode using a default spfile or pfile
STARTUP OPEN	Starts Oracle in OPEN mode using a default spfile or pfile
STARTUP RESTRICT	Starts Oracle in OPEN mode and allows only users with restricted session privileges to connect to the database
STARTUP FORCE	Forces database startup using the default pfile or spfile
STARTUP OPEN PFILE=/u01/sp01.ora	Starts Oracle in OPEN mode using a nondefault parameter file

Here is an example of how you can use the STARTUP FORCE command with a nondefault parameter file to start an Oracle Database using SQL*Plus:

```
$ sqlplus / as sysdba
SQL*Plus: Release 11.1.0.6.0 - Production on Tue Jun 17 15:00:42 2008
Copyright (c) 1982, 2007, Oracle.  All rights reserved.
Connected to an idle instance.
SQL> startup force pfile=/home/oracle/pfile1.ora
ORACLE instance started.
Total System Global Area  707244032 bytes
```

```
Fixed Size                  1302260 bytes
Variable Size             306184460 bytes
Database Buffers          394264576 bytes
Redo Buffers                5492736 bytes
Database mounted.
Database opened.
SQL>
```

If you are running Oracle on Windows, you can also start the database when you start the associated Oracle service. Starting the Oracle service automatically starts the Oracle Database.

Changing Database Startup States Using SQL

When the database is in the NOMOUNT or MOUNT state, you can go to the next state by using the ALTER DATABASE statement instead of shutting down the database and starting with the appropriate state option. The following SQL statements show how to perform database-availability state changes.

- To mount a database to an instance, use ALTER DATABASE MOUNT;.
- To open a database from nomount or mount state, use ALTER DATABSE OPEN;.
- To open a database in read-only mode, use ALTER DATABASE OPEN READ ONLY;.
- To enable restricted mode, use ALTER SYSTEM ENABLE RESTRICTED SESSION;.
- To disable restricted mode, use ALTER SYSTEM DISABLE RESTRICTED SESSION;.

If the database is already open, you cannot return to the MOUNT or NOMOUNT state. You have to shut down the database and start with the appropriate state.

Shutting Down an Oracle 11*g* Database

In some instances, you will need to shut down a database, such as to perform regularly scheduled cold backups of the database, to perform database upgrades, or to change a non-dynamic initialization parameter. Just as with starting the database, several options as well as a variety of interfaces are available for database shutdown:

SHUTDOWN NORMAL A normal shutdown is the default type of shutdown that Oracle performs if no shutdown options are provided. You need to be aware of the following when doing a normal shutdown:

- No new Oracle connections are allowed from the time the SHUTDOWN NORMAL command is issued.
- The database will wait until all users are disconnected to proceed with the shutdown process.

Because Oracle waits until all users are disconnected before shutting down, you can find yourself waiting indefinitely for a client who may be connected but is no longer doing any work or may have left for the day. This can require extra work, identifying which connections are still active and either notifying the users to disconnect or forcing the client disconnections by killing their session. This type of shutdown is also known as a *clean* shutdown because when you start Oracle again, no recovery is necessary.

SHUTDOWN TRANSACTIONAL A transactional shutdown of the database is a bit more aggressive than a normal shutdown. The characteristics of the transactional shutdown are as follows:

- No new Oracle connections are allowed from the time the `SHUTDOWN TRANSACTIONAL` command is issued.
- No new transactions are allowed to start from the time the `SHUTDOWN TRANSACTIONAL` command is issued.
- Once all active transactions on the database have completed, all client connections are disconnected.

A transactional shutdown does allow client processes to complete prior to the disconnection. This can prevent a client from losing work and can be valuable especially if the database has long-running transactions that need to be completed prior to shutdown. This type of shutdown is also a clean shutdown and does not require any recovery on a subsequent startup.

SHUTDOWN IMMEDIATE The immediate shutdown method is the next most aggressive option. An immediate shutdown is characterized as follows:

- No new Oracle connections are allowed from the time the `SHUTDOWN IMMEDIATE` command is issued.
- Any uncommitted transactions are rolled back. Thus, a user in the middle of a transaction will lose all the uncommitted work.
- Oracle does not wait for clients to disconnect. Any unfinished transactions are rolled back, and their database connections are terminated.

This type of shutdown works well if you want to perform unattended or scripted shutdowns of the database and you need to ensure that the database will shut down without getting hung up during the process by clients who are connected. Even though Oracle is forcing transactions to roll back and disconnecting users, an immediate shutdown is still a clean shutdown. No recovery activity takes place when Oracle is subsequently restarted.

SHUTDOWN ABORT A shutdown abort is the most aggressive type of shutdown and has the following characteristics:

- No new Oracle connections are allowed from the time the `SHUTDOWN ABORT` command is issued.
- Any SQL statements currently in progress are terminated, regardless of their state.
- Uncommitted work is not rolled back.
- Oracle disconnects all client connections immediately upon the issuance of the `SHUTDOWN ABORT` command.

Do not use SHUTDOWN ABORT regularly. Use it only if the other options for database shutdown fail or if you are experiencing some type of database problem that is preventing Oracle from performing a clean shutdown. This type of shutdown is not a clean shutdown and requires instance recovery when the database is subsequently started. Instance recovery is performed automatically when you do the startup—no manual intervention required. During instance recovery the uncommitted changes are rolled back from the database, and committed changes are written to the data files. Oracle uses the redo log files and undo segments to construct the instance recovery information.

Shutting Down Oracle Using EM Database Control

You can use the EM Database Control to shut down the Oracle Database. To do so, invoke the EM Database Control from your web browser:

1. Click the Shutdown button in the Database Control home screen, next to the green up arrow.
2. After you click Shutdown, you are presented with the Startup/Shutdown: Specify Host and Target Database Credentials screen (similar to the screen you had when doing startup in Figure 9.37). You must supply an OS user ID and password to log into the target database machine. If you are not using operating-system authentication, you must also enter an Oracle user ID and password that has SYSDBA authority.
3. After you authenticate, the Startup/Shutdown: Confirmation screen appears. The default shutdown selected when you are using the EM Database Control is SHUTDOWN IMMEDIATE. Oracle also displays the current status of the database on this form.

To perform a nondefault type of shutdown, click the Advanced Options button. On the Startup/Shutdown: Advanced Shutdown Options screen (see Figure 9.39), you can select the type of shutdown.

FIGURE 9.39 The Startup/Shutdown: Advanced Shutdown Options screen

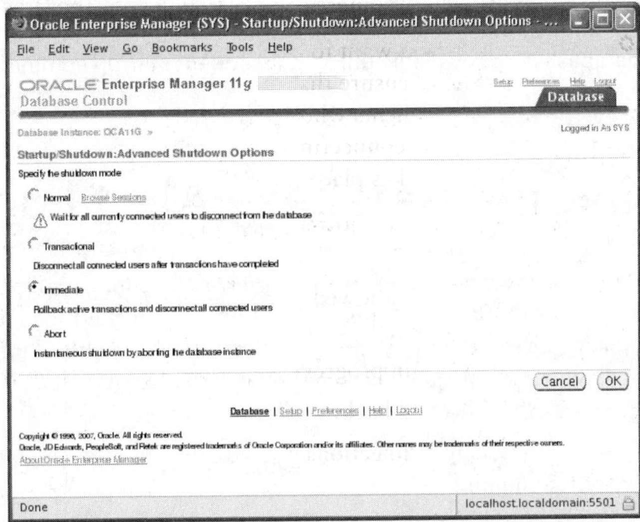

After you select the type of shutdown, click OK, and then click Yes on the Startup/Shutdown: Confirmation screen to open a screen informing you that the database shutdown is in progress. Once the process has completed, click the Refresh button, and you will see that the database is now shut down. On this EM Database Control status screen, you can start the database.

Shutting Down Oracle Using SQL*Plus

You can also use the command-line facility SQL*Plus to shut down the Oracle Database. You will need to connect to SQL*Plus as a user with the SYSOPER or SYSDBA privilege. Here is the syntax of the shutdown options available to you:

```
SHUTDOWN [NORMAL|TRANSACTIONAL|IMMEDIATE|ABORT]
```

Here is an example of how to use the SHUTDOWN IMMEDIATE command to shut down an Oracle Database using SQL*Plus:

```
$ sqlplus / as sysdba
SQL*Plus: Release 11.1.0.6.0 - Production on Tue Jun 17 15:00:04 2008
Copyright (c) 1982, 2007, Oracle.  All rights reserved.
Connected to:
Oracle Database 11g Enterprise Edition Release 11.1.0.6.0 - Production
With the Partitioning, OLAP, Data Mining and Real Application Testing options
SQL> shutdown immediate;
Database closed.
Database dismounted.
ORACLE instance shut down.
SQL>
```

If you are running in a Windows environment and shut down the database using either the Database Control or SQL*Plus tool, the Oracle service will continue to run. Even though the Oracle Windows service is running, the database is not available until a subsequent startup command is issued.

Monitoring the Database Alert Log

The database *alert log*, sometimes referred to as the *alert file*, contains information about certain activities and errors that occur within your database. The alert log contains a chronological summary of these events. The alert log contains a wealth of information that you can use to diagnose system problems and review the history of activities that have occurred on the system. Some of the events and actions recorded in the alert log include the following:

- Startup and shutdown information, including a record of every time a database is started or shut down
- Certain types of administrative actions, such as the `ALTER SYSTEM` and `ALTER DATABASE` commands
- Certain types of database errors, such as internal Oracle errors (ORA-600 errors) or space errors (ORA-1542, for example)
- Messages that are errors about shared servers and dispatchers
- Errors during materialized view refreshes
- The values of initialization parameters that have values different from their default values at instance startup

Here is an excerpt from an Oracle 11*g* alert log:

```
Tue Jun 17 11:50:48 2008
ALTER SYSTEM SET memory_target='1G' SCOPE=SPFILE;
Tue Jun 17 12:43:37 2008
ALTER SYSTEM SET undo_retention=3600 SCOPE=MEMORY;
Tue Jun 17 12:47:07 2008
ALTER SYSTEM SET sga_target='500M' SCOPE=BOTH;
Tue Jun 17 15:00:46 2008
… … …
Tue Jun 17 16:32:20 2008
Starting ORACLE instance (normal)
LICENSE_MAX_SESSION = 0
LICENSE_SESSIONS_WARNING = 0
Picked latch-free SCN scheme 2
Using LOG_ARCHIVE_DEST_1 parameter default value as
  /u01/app/oracle/product/11.1.0/db_1/dbs/arch
Using LOG_ARCHIVE_DEST_10 parameter default value as USE_DB_RECOVERY_FILE_DEST
Autotune of undo retention is turned on.
IMODE=BR
ILAT =18
LICENSE_MAX_USERS = 0
SYS auditing is disabled
Starting up ORACLE RDBMS Version: 11.1.0.6.0.
Using parameter settings in server-side spfile
  /u01/app/oracle/product/11.1.0/db_1/dbs/spfileOCA11G.ora
```

```
System parameters with non-default values:
  processes                = 150
  sga_target               = 676M
  control_files            = "/u01/app/oracle/oradata/OCA11G/control01.ctl"
  control_files            = "/u01/app/oracle/oradata/OCA11G/control02.ctl"
  control_files            = "/u01/app/oracle/oradata/OCA11G/control03.ctl"
  db_block_size            = 8192
  compatible               = "11.1.0.0.0"
  db_recovery_file_dest    = "/u01/app/oracle/flash_recovery_area"
  db_recovery_file_dest_size= 2G
  undo_tablespace          = "UNDOTBS1"
  remote_login_passwordfile= "EXCLUSIVE"
  db_domain                = ""
  dispatchers              = "(PROTOCOL=TCP) (SERVICE=OCA11GXDB)"
  audit_file_dest          = "/u01/app/oracle/admin/OCA11G/adump"
  audit_trail              = "DB"
  db_name                  = "OCA11G"
  open_cursors             = 300
  pga_aggregate_target     = 224M
  diagnostic_dest          = "/u01/app/oracle"
Tue Jun 17 16:32:20 2008
PMON started with pid=2, OS id=1353
Tue Jun 17 16:32:20 2008
VKTM started with pid=3, OS id=1355 at elevated priority
VKTM running at (20)ms precision
Tue Jun 17 16:32:20 2008
… … …
RECO started with pid=13, OS id=1379
Tue Jun 17 16:32:20 2008
MMON started with pid=14, OS id=1381
starting up 1 dispatcher(s) for network address
  '(ADDRESS=(PARTIAL=YES)(PROTOCOL=TCP))'...
Tue Jun 17 16:32:20 2008
MMNL started with pid=15, OS id=1383
starting up 1 shared server(s) ...
ORACLE_BASE from environment = /u01/app/oracle
Tue Jun 17 16:32:20 2008
ALTER DATABASE   MOUNT
Setting recovery target incarnation to 2
Successful mount of redo thread 1, with mount id 3172855255
```

```
Database mounted in Exclusive Mode
Lost write protection disabled
Completed: ALTER DATABASE   MOUNT
Tue Jun 17 16:32:27 2008
ALTER DATABASE OPEN
Beginning crash recovery of 1 threads
 parallel recovery started with 2 processes
Started redo scan
Completed redo scan
 636 redo blocks read, 107 data blocks need recovery
Started redo application at
 Thread 1: logseq 46, block 18524
Recovery of Online Redo Log: Thread 1 Group 1 Seq 46 Reading mem 0
  Mem# 0: /u01/app/oracle/oradata/OCA11G/redo01.log
Completed redo application
Completed crash recovery at
 Thread 1: logseq 46, block 19160, scn 1756449
 107 data blocks read, 107 data blocks written, 636 redo blocks read
Thread 1 advanced to log sequence 47
Thread 1 opened at log sequence 47
  Current log# 2 seq# 47 mem# 0: /u01/app/oracle/oradata/OCA11G/redo02.log
Successful open of redo thread 1
MTTR advisory is disabled because FAST_START_MTTR_TARGET is not set
SMON: enabling cache recovery
Successfully onlined Undo Tablespace 2.
Verifying file header compatibility for 11g tablespace encryption..
Verifying 11g file header compatibility for tablespace encryption completed
SMON: enabling tx recovery
Database Characterset is WE8MSWIN1252
Opening with internal Resource Manager plan
Starting background process SMCO
Tue Jun 17 16:32:28 2008
SMCO started with pid=21, OS id=1401
Starting background process FBDA
replication_dependency_tracking turned off (no async multimaster replication
found)
Tue Jun 17 16:32:29 2008
FBDA started with pid=23, OS id=1408
Starting background process QMNC
Tue Jun 17 16:32:29 2008
```

```
QMNC started with pid=22, OS id=1416
db_recovery_file_dest_size of 2048 MB is 0.00% used. This is a
user-specified limit on the amount of space that will be used by this
database for recovery-related files, and does not reflect the amount of
space available in the underlying filesystem or ASM diskgroup.
Completed: ALTER DATABASE OPEN
```

This excerpt shows a successful startup of a database. Notice the section that lists the nondefault initialization parameters. Also notice that Oracle performed an automatic recovery of the database. This indicates that the database was not shut down cleanly prior to this startup. You can also see that Oracle is starting dispatcher processes, which indicates I am running Oracle Shared Server.

The parameter that governs the location of the alert log is `DIAGNOSTIC_DEST`. This parameter is set to a path that designates where Oracle should place the log. The default value for `DIAGNOSTIC_DEST` is the `ORACLE_BASE` environment value, if set when starting the database. If `ORACLE_BASE` is not set, `DIAGNOSTIC_DEST` will default to the directory of `ORACLE_HOME/log`.

Oracle 11*g* supports two types of alert log files. The XML version of the file is located in the `DIANOSTIC_DEST/rdbms/dbname/instancename/alert` directory. The text file is in the `DIANOSTIC_DEST/rdbms/`*`dbname/instancename/`*`trace` directory. The alert log file is always named *`alert_<instancename>.log`*. For example, the alert log file name for the `OCA11G` database would be `alert_oca11g.log`.

The dictionary view `V$DIAG_INFO` shows the exact location of the alert log file for the instance. Here is an example from the `OCA11G` database running on a Linux server:

```
SQL> SELECT name, value FROM v$diag_info;

NAME                      VALUE
------------------------- ---------------------------------------------
Diag Enabled              TRUE
ADR Base                  /u01/app/oracle
ADR Home                  /u01/app/oracle/diag/rdbms/oca11g/OCA11G
Diag Trace                /u01/app/oracle/diag/rdbms/oca11g/OCA11G/trace
Diag Alert                /u01/app/oracle/diag/rdbms/oca11g/OCA11G/alert
Diag Incident             /u01/app/oracle/diag/rdbms/oca11g/OCA11G/incident
Diag Cdump                /u01/app/oracle/diag/rdbms/oca11g/OCA11G/cdump
Health Monitor            /u01/app/oracle/diag/rdbms/oca11g/OCA11G/hm
Default Trace File        /u01/app/oracle/diag/rdbms/oca11g/OCA11G/trace/OCA
                          11G_ora_9018.trc
Active Problem Count      0
Active Incident Count     0
```

The `ADR Base` value is the directory specified (or derived by the instance using `ORACLE_BASE` or `ORACLE_HOME`) for `DIGNOSTIC_DEST`. The Diag Trace location is where the text version of the alert log file located.

The alert log is continuously appended to, so it is a good idea to periodically purge it. Many DBAs do so daily or weekly, saving a copy of the current alert log to a backup and clearing the current alert log. It is a good idea to save the log contents. You can use it to review when any initialization parameters have changed and to review database errors or problems recorded in the log.

You can view the alert log content using the EM Database Control. From the Server screen, click on the alert log contents link at the bottom under Related Links. Figure 9.40 shows the contents of alert log from EM.

The alert log file of an Oracle database 11*g* is part of the advanced fault diagnosability infrastructure known as the Automatic Diagnostic Repository (ADR). To learn more about ADR, read Chapter 8 of the "Oracle Database Administrator's Guide 11*g* Release 1 (11.1) Part Number B28310-03" document. All Oracle documentation can be accessed online at `http://tahiti.oracle.com`.

FIGURE 9.40 EM View Alert Log Contents screen

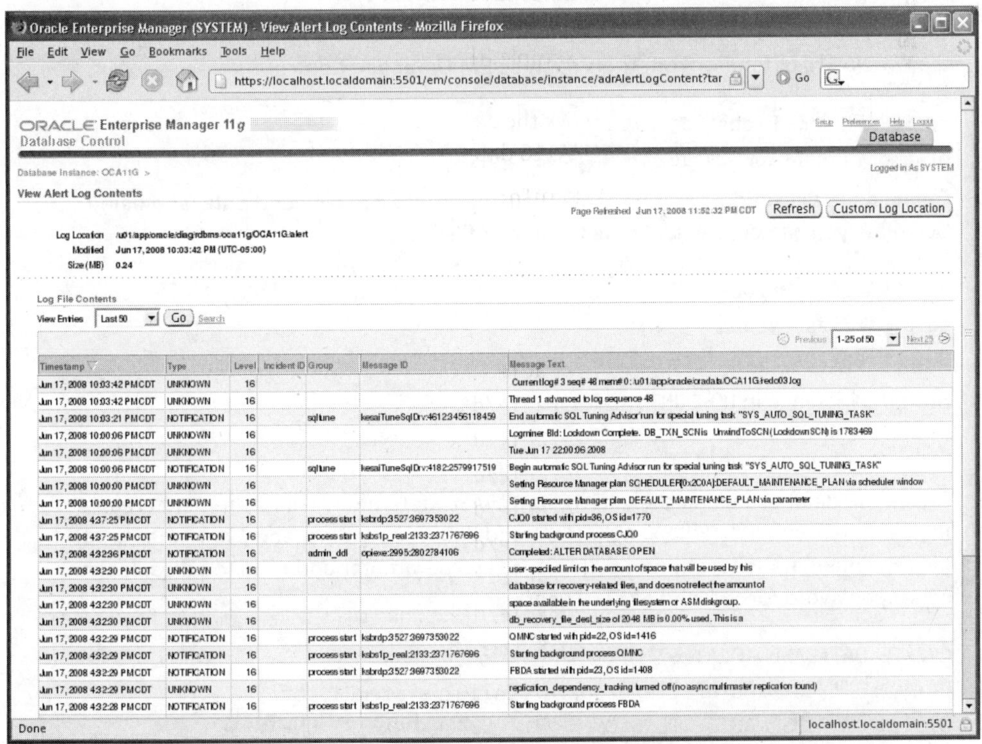

In Exercise 9.2, you'll learn to create an Oracle Database 11g without using DBCA.

EXERCISE 9.2

Creating an Oracle 11*g* database

You have learned to use the DBCA to create a database, learned to start and stop a database, and learned about alert log files and Oracle dictionary. Though the DBCA does all the background work and creates a database for you, it's good to know the stages in database creation and any relevant scripts needed if you decide to create the database manually. Here are the steps to create an Oracle 11*g* database on the Linux platform:

1. Set up the relevant environment variables before creating the database. The three important variables are ORACLE_SID, ORACLE_BASE, and ORACLE_HOME. The ORACLE_SID variable is the instance identifier, which can be up to 12 characters. On Unix platforms, the instance identifier is case sensitive. The ORACLE_BASE parameter decides where the trace file and dump file directories will be located. ORACLE_HOME is the location where the Oracle 11*g* software is installed.

```
export ORACLE_SID=OCA11G2
export ORACLE_BASE=/u01/app/oracle
export ORACLE_HOME=/u01/app/oracle/product/11.1.0
```

2. Create a password file using the ORAPWD utility. This allows administrative logins to the Oracle 11*g* database from tools such as EM Database Control.

```
cd $ORACLE_HOME/dbs
orapwd file=orapwOCA11G2
```

3. Create an initialization-parameter file. You can create a text-based pfile, and using SQL*Plus you can create the spfile from the pfile.

```
cd $ORACLE_HOME/dbs
sqlplus / as sysdba
SQL> create spfile from pfile;
```

4. Start the instance in NOMOUNT mode:

```
SQL> startup nomount;
```

5. Create the database using the CREATE DATABASE statement. This statement creates the database with SYSTEM, SYSAUX, TEMP, and UNDOTBS1 tablespaces. It creates control files specified in the location of CONTROL_FILES parameter and redo log files. It also sets a password for SYS and SYSTEM users.

```
CREATE DATABASE "OCA11G2"
DATAFILE '/u01/app/oracle/oradata/OCA11G2/system01.dbf'
SIZE 300M REUSE AUTOEXTEND ON NEXT  10240K MAXSIZE UNLIMITED
EXTENT MANAGEMENT LOCAL
```

EXERCISE 9.2 *(continued)*

```
SYSAUX DATAFILE '/u01/app/oracle/oradata/OCA11G2/sysaux01.dbf'
SIZE 120M REUSE AUTOEXTEND ON NEXT  10240K MAXSIZE UNLIMITED
SMALLFILE DEFAULT TEMPORARY TABLESPACE TEMP TEMPFILE '/u01/app/oracle/
oradata/OCA11G2/temp01.dbf'
SIZE 20M REUSE AUTOEXTEND ON NEXT  640K MAXSIZE UNLIMITED
SMALLFILE UNDO TABLESPACE "UNDOTBS1" DATAFILE '/u01/app/oracle/oradata/
OCA11G2/undotbs01.dbf'
SIZE 200M REUSE AUTOEXTEND ON NEXT  5120K MAXSIZE UNLIMITED
CHARACTER SET WE8MSWIN1252
LOGFILE GROUP 1 ('/u01/app/oracle/oradata/OCA11G2/redo01.log') SIZE
51200K,
GROUP 2 ('/u01/app/oracle/oradata/OCA11G2/redo02.log') SIZE 51200K
USER SYS IDENTIFIED BY mypwd USER SYSTEM IDENTIFIED BY mypwd;
```

6. Create additional tablespaces if any are needed:

```
CREATE TABLESPACE "USERS"
DATAFILE '/u01/app/oracle/oradata/OCA11G2/users01.dbf' SIZE 5M;
```

7. Build data dictionary views and public synonyms (? in SQL*Plus refers to the ORACLE_HOME directory):

```
SQL> @?/rdbms/admin/catalog.sql
```

8. Build the PL/SQL packages:

```
SQL> @?/rdbms/admin/catproc.sql
```

9. If you want to install additional options such as JVM or Oracle Ultra Search, run the relevant scripts:

```
SQL> @?/javavm/install/initjvm.sql;
```

10. Create an EM repository in the database:

```
SQL> @?/sysman/admin/emdrep/sql/emreposcre $ORACLE_HOME SYSMAN mypwd
TEMP ON
```

11. Configure EM Database Control:

```
$ORACLE_HOME/bin/emca -config dbcontrol db
```

Summary

In this chapter, you started off by learning how to create an Oracle 11*g* database using the Database Configuration Assistant. Then I discussed the Oracle metadata dictionary and parameter files. You also learned about database startup and shutdown as well as the alert log file.

You can use the DBCA to create databases. You can choose from preexisting database definitions stored as XML templates or create a database definition from a custom template. All aspects of the database, including database name, file location, sizing, and initialization-parameter settings, are defined within the DBCA. You can create a database after completing the database definition, or you can save the definition as a template or series of scripts to be run at a later time. You can also use the DBCA to remove databases or add options to existing databases.

You can manage and create new template definitions using the DBCA interface. This is advantageous because it serves as a way to centrally manage all your database definitions. You can also create new databases from existing databases with the DBCA by using templates.

Oracle uses initialization-parameter files to store information about initialization parameters used when an Oracle instance starts. Oracle reads the parameter file to obtain information about how the Oracle instance should be sized and configured upon startup. The parameter file can be either a plain-text file, commonly referred to as a pfile, or a binary file that is referred to as an spfile. You can use the EM Database Control facility to change existing database parameters.

The data dictionary contains information about the database and database objects. The data dictionary is created when the database is created using the script `catalog.sql`. The data dictionary views have static data, whereas the dynamic performance views have data that does not persist across database shutdowns.

The database needs to be started in order for work to be done against it. You can start up the database in one of several modes: `MOUNT`, `NOMOUNT`, and `OPEN`. You can also start up the database with the `RESTRICT` option to restrict general access to the database. You can also start up a database using the `FORCE` option if other startup methods fail.

You can shut down the database using one of several options: `NORMAL`, `TRANSACTIONAL`, `IMMEDIATE`, and `ABORT`. The `NORMAL`, `TRANSACTIONAL`, and `IMMEDIATE` options are considered clean shutdowns because no recovery is necessary upon a subsequent startup. You can start up and shut down the database using a variety of interfaces, including the EM Database Control utility and SQL*Plus.

The alert log contains information about certain activities and errors that occur within your database. The alert log contains a chronological summary of these events and a wealth of information that you can use to diagnose system problems and review histories of activities that occurred on the system. The `DIGNOSTIC_DEST` parameter determines the location of the alert log.

Exam Essentials

Be able to create a database using the DBCA. Describe the steps involved in creating a database using the Oracle Database Configuration Assistant (DBCA). Understand how the DBCA uses templates to store information about databases and how templates are used by the DBCA to create databases. Be familiar with the various options available to you when creating an Oracle Database using the DBCA.

Know how to manage DBCA templates. Understand how to use the DBCA to manage templates and the various options available when creating new database templates. Understand what each option is and when it should be used.

Describe the database startup modes. Understand the various modes of database startup. Understand what each database startup option is and when you might use the option.

Recognize how to start up an Oracle Database. Understand how to use the database tools to start up an Oracle Database.

Describe the database-shutdown modes. Understand the various modes of database shutdown. Understand what each database-shutdown option is and when you might use the option.

Be able to shut down an Oracle Database. Understand how to use the database tools to shut down an Oracle Database.

Know how to manage the Oracle parameter file. Be able to identify the Oracle parameter file and the different types of parameter files. Also understand how you can change the parameter files.

View and understand the contents of the Oracle alert log. Be able to identify the Oracle alert log and the kinds of information Oracle writes to the alert log. Be able to identify the database initialization parameter that provides the location of the alert log.

Be familiar with the metadata dictionary. Understand the difference between the static data dictionary and dynamic performance views.

Review Questions

1. You noticed that the current value of the UNDO_RETENTION parameter is 900 and is too low for some of your transactions. You issue the following statement:

   ALTER SYSTEM SET UNDO_RETENTION=4800;

   Which option is true?

   A. UNDO_RETENTION is a static parameter and hence cannot be changed using ALTER SYSTEM.

   B. The change will be available to the instance only after a database cycle.

   C. The value is changed in memory, and when the database restarts the next time, the new value will be preserved when using the spfile.

   D. The value is changed only in memory, and the server parameter file needs to be updated for the change to persist across database shutdowns.

2. You need to find the directory where the Oracle alert log is being written. Which initialization parameter contains this information?

   A. ALERT_LOG_DEST

   B. BACKGROUND_DUMP_DEST

   C. DIAGNOSTIC_DEST

   D. INIT_LOG_DUMP_DEST

3. Which data dictionary view is used to view the current values of parameters?

   A. V$DATABASE

   B. V$SPPARAMETER

   C. V$PARAMETER

   D. V$SYSPARAMETER

4. Which startup options must be used to start the instance when you're creating a new database?

   A. STARTUP FORCE

   B. STARTUP MOUNT

   C. STARTUP RESTRICT

   D. STARTUP NOMOUNT

5. The `DIAGNOSTIC_DEST` parameter is not set up in the initialization-parameter file. The value of the `ORACLE_HOME` environment variable is `/u01/app/oracle/product/11.1.0`, and the value of `ORACLE_BASE` is `/u01/app/oracle`. The database name is `xyz`, so what is the location of the text-alert log file for the `xyz` database?

   A. `/u01/app/oracle/product/11.1.0/log/rdbms/xyz/xyz/trace`

   B. `/u01/app/oracle/diag/rdbms/xyz/xyz/trace`

   C. `/u01/app/oracle/diag/rdbms/xyz/xyz/alert`

   D. `/u01/app/oracle/product/11.1.0/diag/rdbms/xyz/xyz/trace`

   E. `/u01/app/oracle/log/rdbms/xyz/xyz/trace`

6. You want to create a database using the DBCA with `DB_BLOCK_SIZE` as 32KB. Which statement is true?

   A. A block size of 32KB is not allowed in Oracle 11*g*.

   B. You must choose the Data Warehouse template in the DBCA.

   C. You must choose the Custom template in the DBCA.

   D. You must set the environment variable `DB_BLOCK_SIZE` to 32768.

7. All the following are database-management options within the Database Configuration Assistant except which one?

   A. Change Database Initialization Parameters

   B. Create a Database

   C. Manage Templates

   D. Delete a Database

8. Which of the following is another term for the fully qualified name of a database?

   A. ORACLE SID

   B. Global database name

   C. Global identifier

   D. Oracle global name

   E. ORACLE ID

9. Which of the following Oracle accounts is not automatically configured by the DBCA?

   A. `SYS`

   B. `SYSTEM`

   C. `SYSMAN`

   D. `DBSNMP`

   E. All these accounts are configured automatically by DBCA.

10. Your database name is OCA11G. The options show the files that are available in the $ORACLE_HOME/dbs directory. Which file is used to start up the database instance when you issue the STARTUP command?

    A. initOCA11G.ora
    B. OCA11Gspfile.ora
    C. spfile.ora
    D. init.ora

11. Which initialization parameter cannot be changed after creating the database?

    A. DB_BLOCK_SIZE
    B. DB_NAME
    C. CONTROL_FILES
    D. None. All parameters can be changed as and when required.

12. Which script creates the database dictionary?

    A. dictionary.sql
    B. catdict.sql
    C. catproc.sql
    D. catalog.sql

13. If your database name is PROD and your instance name is PROD1, what would be the name of the text-alert log file?

    A. alertPROD.log
    B. alert_PROD1.log
    C. PROD1alert.log
    D. PROD_alert.log

14. Your database is not responding and is in a hung state. You want to shut down and start the database to release all resources. Which statements would you use?

    A. STARTUP AFTER SHUTDOWN
    B. STARTUP FORCE
    C. SHUTDOWN FORCE
    D. SHUTDOWN ABORT and STARTUP

15. Which of the following startup options does not perform a database recovery?

    A. STARTUP
    B. STARTUP FORCE RESTRICT
    C. STARTUP NOMOUNT
    D. STARTUP OPEN
    E. STARTUP RESTRICT

16. Which of the following shutdown statements does not perform a clean shutdown?

    A. `SHUTDOWN ABORT`

    B. `SHUTDOWN TRANSACTIONAL`

    C. `SHUTDOWN`

    D. `SHUTDOWN IMMEDIATE`

    E. All of these are considered clean shutdowns.

17. You would like to export the system and limit access to only the DBA staff during the export process. Which of the following startup options should you use?

    A. `STARTUP NOMOUNT RESTRICT`

    B. `STARTUP RESTRICT`

    C. `STARTUP MOUNT RESTRICT`

    D. `STARTUP MOUNT FORCE RESTRICT`

18. You want to start up the database using a binary initialization file. What is another name for this file?

    A. Configfile

    B. Pfile

    C. Spfile

    D. `init_pfile.ora`

19. Under normal circumstances, which of the following actions or events is not found in the Oracle alert log?

    A. Database startup and shutdown information

    B. Nondefault initialization parameters

    C. ORA-00600 errors

    D. New columns added to a user table

20. Which of the following is true about EM Database Control? (Choose all that apply.)

    A. You can start up and shut down a database using Database Control.

    B. You can read the contents of the alert log file.

    C. You can modify static initialization parameters.

    D. The `CREATE DATABASE` statement creates the Database Control repository in the database.

Answers to Review Questions

1. C. When using ALTER SYSTEM to change parameter values, the change is made to the server parameter file (spfile) too, because the default for the SCOPE clause is BOTH. Option D would have been correct, if the pfile was used to start up the database.

2. C. DIAGNOSTIC_DEST is the initialization parameter that determines where the Automatic Diagnostic Repository home is. The alert log file would be in the *<diagnostic_dest>*/diag/rdbms/*<dbname>*/*<instancename>*/alert directory. A text version of the alert log is in the *<diagnostic_dest>*/diag/rdbms/*<dbname>*/*<instancename>*/trace directory.

3. C. V$PARAMETER shows information about the parameters and their current value in the database. V$SPPARAMTER shows the information as read from the spfile.

4. D. When creating a new database or creating a control file, the database should be in the NOMOUNT state.

5. B. The alert log file in Oracle 11g is saved in the $ORACLE_BASE/diag/rdbms/*<dbname>*/*<instancename>*/trace directory. The XML version of the alert-log file is in the $ORACLE_BASE/diag/rdbms/*<dbname>*/*<instancename>*/alert directory.

6. C. The Custom template lets you choose the database block size in the DBCA. If the template includes data files, the block size of the template cannot be changed. The predefined templates that come with data files have the block size at 8KB.

7. A. The Database Configuration Assistant lets you create databases, manage templates, add database options, and delete databases. Although you can change initialization parameters when you are defining a database, this is not one of the management options available.

8. B. The *global database name* is another term for the fully qualified name of a database. The global database name is composed of the database name and database domain.

9. E. The DBCA configures the SYS, SYSTEM, SYSMAN, and DBSNMP accounts by default. You can unlock the accounts and set the initial password.

10. C. When starting the instance, Oracle looks for spfileOCA11G.ora file. If it could not find that file, it looks for spfile.ora. If that file is not found, Oracle looks for the initOCA11G.ora file.

11. A. The block size of the database cannot be changed after database creation. The database name can be changed after re-creating the control file with a new name, and the CONTROL_FILES parameter can be changed after copying the control files to the new location.

12. D. The catalog.sql script creates the data dictionary views, dynamic performance views, and synonyms.

13. B. The text-alert log file has the name alert_<instancename>.log. For most non-RAC databases, the instance name and database name would be the same.

14. B, D. STARTUP FORCE will perform a SHUTDOWN ABORT and STARTUP of the database. SHUTDOWN ABORT will terminate all sessions and processes and shut down the instance.

15. C. The recovery of a database occurs when the database moves from the MOUNT mode to the OPEN mode. All these options attempt to start up and open the database except for option C, which only puts the database in NOMOUNT mode.

16. A. Any time you perform a SHUTDOWN ABORT, Oracle does not perform a clean shutdown. All other types of shutdowns are considered clean shutdowns because Oracle will not have to perform recovery on a subsequent database startup.

17. B. The STARTUP RESTRICT choice opens the database and allows only users with RESTRICTED database access to connect and use it.

18. C. A pfile is another term for a server-side binary file that Oracle reads when a database startup is performed. This binary file contains all the nondefault initialization parameters used at startup.

19. D. The Oracle alert log contains a chronological history of administrative events and actions and certain types of database errors that occur within the database. Adding a column to a user table is not an administrative action and is not recorded in the alert log.

20. A, B, C. The Database Control repository is not created when the CREATE DATABASE statement is executed. DBCA creates the Database Control repository and configures Database Control for you.

Chapter 10

Allocating Database Storage and Creating Schema Objects

ORACLE DATABASE 11*g*: ADMINISTRATION I EXAM OBJECTIVES COVERED IN THIS CHAPTER:

✓ **Managing Database Storage Structures**

- Overview of tablespace and datafiles
- Create and manage tablespaces
- Space management in tablespaces

✓ **Managing Schema Objects**

- Create and Modify tables
- Manage Constraints
- Create indexes
- Create and use temporary tables

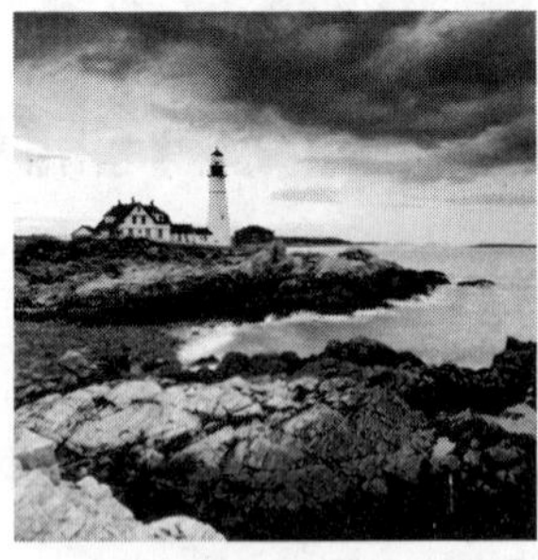

In this chapter, you will learn more about the physical and logical storage structures. To start, you'll explore how a tablespace is the highest level of logical structure in an Oracle Database 11g, whereas a data file is a physical structure that is associated with a tablespace. I will also discuss how tables and indexes are logical structures that reside in a tablespace.

Additionally, you will learn about creating and managing tablespaces and how space is allocated and managed within tablespaces. I discussed creating tables and indexes in Chapter 6, "Creating Tables and Constraints," and Chapter 7, "Creating Schema Objects." Finally, you will learn how to create these structures specifying storage attributes.

Tablespaces and Data Files Overview

The database's data is stored logically in tablespaces and physically in data files that correspond to the tablespaces. The logical storage management is independent of the physical storage of the data files. A tablespace can have more than one data file associated with it, whereas one data file belongs to only one tablespace. A database has more than one tablespace. Figure 10.1 shows the relationship between the database, tablespaces, data files, and objects within the tablespace. Any object (such as a nonpartitioned table or index) created in the database is stored on a single tablespace, but the object's physical storage can be on multiple data files belonging to that tablespace. A segment is created when a table or index is created and is stored on a single tablespace.

I discussed the logical structures block, extent, and segment in Chapter 8, "Introducing Oracle Database 11g Components and Architecture." Here is a brief refresher of what you learned in Chapter 8. Starting with the highest level of Oracle disk-space management are tablespaces. Drilling down, you find *segments* that can reside in only one tablespace. Each segment is constructed from one or more *extents*. Each of these extents can reside in only one *data file*. Thus, for a segment to straddle multiple data files, it must be constructed from multiple extents that are located in separate data files. An extent is composed of a contiguous set of *data blocks*, which is at the lowest level of space management. A data block is a fixed number of bytes of disk space.

The size of the tablespace is the total size of all the data files belonging to that tablespace. The size of the database is the total size of all tablespaces in the database, which is the total size of all data files in the database. Changing the size of the data files belonging to a tablespace can change the size of that tablespace. You can add more space to a tablespace by adding more data files to the tablespace. You can then add more space to the database either by adding more tablespaces, by adding more data files to the existing tablespaces, or by increasing the size of the existing data files.

FIGURE 10.1 Tablespaces and data files

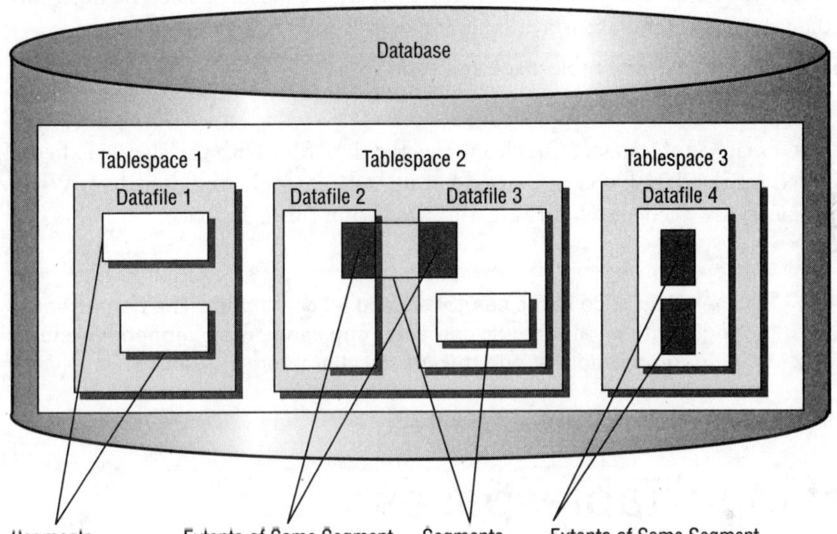

When you create a database, Oracle creates the SYSTEM tablespace. All the data dictionary objects are stored in this tablespace. You can add more space to the SYSTEM tablespace after you create the database by adding more data files or by increasing the size of the data files. The PL/SQL program units (such as procedures, functions, packages, or triggers) created in the database are also stored in the SYSTEM tablespace.

The SYSTEM tablespace is a special tablespace that is required to be online all the time for the database to function properly. SYSAUX is an auxiliary tablespace always created when an Oracle 11*g* database is created. The SYSAUX and SYSTEM tablespaces cannot be renamed or dropped.

Oracle recommends not creating any objects other than the Oracle data dictionary in the SYSTEM tablespace. By having multiple tablespaces, you can do the following:

- Separate the Oracle dictionary from other database objects. Doing so reduces contention between dictionary objects and database objects for the same data file.
- Control I/O by allocating separate physical storage disks for different tablespaces.
- Manage space quotas for users on tablespaces.
- Have separate tablespaces for temporary segments (TEMP) and undo management (rollback segments). You can also create a tablespace for a specific activity; for example, you can place high-update tables in a separate tablespace. When creating the database, you can specify tablespace names for temporary tablespaces and undo tablespaces.

- Group application-related or module-related data together so that when maintenance is required for the application's tablespace, only that tablespace need be taken offline, and the rest of the database is available for users.
- Back up the database one tablespace at a time.
- Make part of the database read-only.

When you create a tablespace, Oracle creates the data files with the size specified. The space reserved for the data file is formatted but does not contain any user data. Whenever spaces for objects are needed, extents are allocated from this free space.

The tablespace name cannot exceed 30 characters. The name should begin with an alphabetic character and can contain alphabetic characters, numeric characters, and the special characters #, _, and $.

Managing Tablespaces

Tablespaces logically group schema objects for administration convenience. Tablespaces can store zero or more segments. *Segments* are schema objects that require storage outside the data dictionary. Tables and indexes are examples of segments. *Constraints* and sequences are examples of schema objects that do not store data outside the data dictionary and are therefore not segments.

You can place the tables and indexes associated with an application into a set of tablespaces in order to manage that data more easily. You can take a tablespace offline and recover it (potentially to a different point in time), separate from the rest of the database. You can also move it to another database and configure it as read-only so that you do not have to make additional backups of static data.

In the following sections, you will learn how to create and manage tablespaces in your database.

Identifying Default Tablespaces

The SYSTEM tablespace is used for the data dictionary and should not be used to store schema objects other than those that the installation places there. The SYSAUX tablespace stores schema objects associated with Oracle-provided features, such as the spatial data option, Extended Markup Language Database (XMLDB), or Oracle Multimedia (formerly known as Intermedia).

The SYSTEM and SYSAUX tablespaces are always created when the database is created. One or more temporary tablespaces are usually created in a database as well as an undo tablespace and several application tablespaces. Because SYSTEM and SYSAUX are the only tablespaces always created with the database, SYSTEM is the default tablespace for temporary and user data if another tablespace is not defined. You should not, however, continue to use them as the default tablespace for your users or applications. In the following sections, you will learn how to create additional tablespaces and enable their use as better defaults.

Creating and Maintaining Tablespaces

You create tablespaces using either the CREATE DATABASE or CREATE TABLESPACE statement. You must make several choices when creating a tablespace:

- Whether to make the tablespace bigfile or smallfile
- Whether to manage extents locally or with the dictionary
- Whether to manage segment space automatically or manually

Additionally, there are specialized tablespaces for temporary segments and undo segments.

A tablespace is created with the CREATE TABLESPACE statement. The following statement creates a tablespace named HR_DATA. The data file associated with the tablespace is physically stored on the disk at /u02/oradata/11GR11/hr_data01.dbf and has a size of 20MB.

```
SQL> CREATE TABLESPACE HR_DATA
  2  DATAFILE '/u02/oradata/11GR11/hr_data01.dbf'
  3  SIZE 20M;

Tablespace created.
SQL>
```

In the following sections, I will discuss the various options available when creating a tablespace.

Creating Bigfile and Smallfile Tablespaces

Bigfile tablespaces are built on a single data file (or temp file), which can be as many as 2^{32} data blocks in size. So, a bigfile tablespace that uses 8KB data blocks can be as much as 32TB in size (the maximum size is 128TB for a 32KB block size).

Bigfile tablespaces are intended for very large databases. When a very large database has thousands of read-write data files, operations that must update the data file headers, such as checkpoints, can take a relatively long time. If you reduce the number of data files, these operations can complete faster.

To create a bigfile tablespace, use the keyword BIGFILE in the CREATE statement, like this:

```
CREATE BIGFILE TABLESPACE PO_ARCHIVE
DATAFILE '/u02/oradata/11GR11/po_archive.dbf' size 25G;
```

Smallfile tablespace is the new name for the old Oracle tablespace data file option. With a smallfile tablespace, you can have multiple data files for a tablespace. Each data file can be as many as 2^{22} data blocks in size. So, data files in a smallfile tablespace that uses 8KB data blocks are limited to 32GB. The smallfile tablespace can have as many as 1,022 data files, limiting the 8KB data block tablespace to slightly less than 32TB—about the same as a bigfile tablespace.

To create a smallfile tablespace, either omit the keyword BIGFILE or explicitly use the keyword SMALLFILE, like this:

```
CREATE SMALLFILE TABLESPACE PO_DETAILS
DATAFILE '/u02/oradata/11GR11/po_details.dbf' size 2G;
```

By default, Oracle Database 11*g* creates SMALLFILE tablespaces so that you do not have to specify SMALLFILE in the CREATE TABLESPACE statement. The DATABASE_PROPERTIES dictionary view shows what is the default tablespace type for your Oracle 11*g* database (look for the property name DEFAULT_TBS_TYPE). You can use the ALTER DATABASE statement to change the default behavior.

Working with Oracle Managed File Tablespaces

The Oracle Managed Files (OMF) feature can ease the administration of files used by an Oracle 11*g* database. Using the OMF feature, you specify operations in terms of tablespaces and not operating-system files. You don't explicitly name data files or temp files; the database does this for you.

To enable the OMF feature, set the initialization parameter DB_CREATE_FILE_DEST to the directory where you want the database to create and manage your data and temp files, like this:

```
ALTER SYSTEM SET
  db_create_file_dest = '/u02/oradata/'  SCOPE=BOTH;
```

When creating a tablespace using the OMF feature, you simply omit the filename:

```
CREATE TABLESPACE hr_data;
```

Oracle creates a tablespace using a unique filename, such as o1_mf_hr_data_46n3ck5t_.dbf under the /u02/oradata/11GR11/datafile directory. Notice that Oracle 11*g* adds the subdirectories DBNAME/datafile in the DB_CREATE_FILE_DEST directory. This data file will have autoextend enabled and be 100MB unless you specify a different size. By default, the tablespace is a smallfile tablespace, but you can specify a bigfile tablespace by including the keyword BIGFILE.

The OMF feature is discussed later in the chapter.

Choosing Extent Management

When Oracle allocates space to an object in a tablespace, it is allocated in chunks of contiguous database blocks known as *extents*. Each object is allocated a segment, which has one or more extents. Oracle maintains the extent information such as extents free, extent size, extents allocated, and so on, either in the data dictionary or in the tablespace itself.

If you store the *extent management* information in the dictionary for a tablespace, that tablespace is called a *dictionary-managed tablespace*. Whenever an extent is allocated or freed, the information is updated in the corresponding dictionary tables. Such updates also generate undo information.

With dictionary extent management, the database tracks free and used extents in the data dictionary, changing the FET$ and UET$ tables with recursive SQL. With local extent management, the free/used extent information is maintained in a bitmap pattern in the header of the data file. So, Oracle has to check in the local bitmap instead of making trips to the UET$ or FET$ table. Local extent management is the default if not specified and is generally the preferred technique.

A simple example of a dictionary-managed tablespace creation command is as follows:

```
CREATE TABLESPACE APPL_DATA
DATAFILE '/disk3/oradata/DB01/appl_data01.dbf' SIZE 100M
EXTENT MANAGEMENT DICTIONARY;
```

This statement creates a tablespace named APPL_DATA; the data file specified is created with a size of 100MB. You can specify more than one file under the DATAFILE clause separated by commas; you may need to create more files if there are any operating-system limits on the file size. For example, if you need to have 6GB allocated for the tablespace and the operating system allows only 2GB as the maximum file size, you need three data files for the tablespace. The statement will be as follows:

```
CREATE TABLESPACE APPL_DATA
DATAFILE '/disk3/oradata/DB01/appl_data01.dbf' SIZE 2000M,
         '/disk3/oradata/DB01/appl_data02.dbf' SIZE 2000M,
         '/disk4/oradata/DB01/appl_data03.dbf' SIZE 2000M
EXTENT MANAGEMENT DICTIONARY;
```

The options available when creating and reusing a data file are discussed in the section "Managing Data Files" later in this chapter.

If you store the management information in the tablespace by using bitmaps in each data file, such a tablespace is known as a *locally managed tablespace*. Each bit in the bitmap corresponds to a block or a group of blocks. When an extent is allocated or freed for reuse, Oracle changes the bitmap values to show the new status of the blocks. These changes do not generate rollback information because they do not update tables in the data dictionary.

With locally managed tablespaces, you have two options for how extents are allocated: UNIFORM and AUTOALLOCATE. The UNIFORM option tells the database to allocate and deallocate extents in the tablespace with the same unvarying size that you can specify or let extents default to 1MB. UNIFORM is the default for temporary tablespaces and cannot be specified for undo tablespaces. To create consistent 10MB extents, use the clause EXTENT MANAGEMENT LOCAL UNIFORM SIZE 10M in the CREATE TABLESPACE statement. Here is an example:

```
CREATE TABLESPACE hr_index
DATAFILE '/u02/oradata/11GR11/hr_index01.dbf' SIZE 2G
EXTENT MANAGEMENT LOCAL UNIFORM SIZE 10M;
```

The minimum extent size for a locally managed tablespace with AUTOALLOCATE is 64KB.

AUTOALLOCATE, on the other hand, tells the database to vary the size of extents for each segment. For example, on Windows and Linux with 8KB data blocks, each segment starts out with 64KB extents for the first 16 extents, and then the extents increase in size to 1MB for the next 63 extents. The size then increases to 8MB for the next 120 extents, then 64MB, and so on, as the segment grows. This algorithm allows small segments to remain small and large segments to grow without gaining too many extents. AUTOALLOCATE is best used for a general-purpose mixture of small and large tables. Here is an example of creating a tablespace using AUTOALLOCATE:

```
CREATE TABLESPACE hr_index
DATAFILE '/u02/oradata/11GR11/hr_index01.dbf' SIZE 2G
EXTENT MANAGEMENT LOCAL AUTOALLOCATE;
```

Bigfile tablespaces are created as locally managed; you cannot specify the EXTENT MANAGEMENT DICTIONARY clause for bigfile tablespaces. You can convert a smallfile tablespace from dictionary extent management to local extent management and back with the Oracle-supplied PL/SQL package DBMS_SPACE_ADMIN.

When the SYSTEM tablespace is created as a locally managed tablespace, you cannot create dictionary-managed tablespaces in the database. The Oracle 11*g* DBCA tool by default creates the SYSTEM tablespace as locally managed.

Choosing Segment Space Management

For tablespaces that have local extent management, you can use either manual or automatic *segment space management*. Manual segment space management exists for backward compatibility and uses free-block lists to identify the data blocks available for inserts together with the parameters PCTFREE and PCTUSED, which control when a block is made available for inserts.

After each INSERT or UPDATE, the database compares the remaining free space in that data block with the segment's PCTFREE setting. If the data block has less than PCTFREE free space (meaning it is almost full), it is taken off the free-block list and is no longer available for inserts. The remaining free space is reserved for update operations that may increase the size of rows in that data block. After each UPDATE or DELETE, the database compares the used space in that data block with that segment's PCTUSED setting. If the data block has less than PCTUSED used space, the data block is deemed empty enough for inserts and is placed on the free block list.

To specify manual segment space management, use the SEGMENT SPACE MANAGEMENT MANUAL clause of the CREATE TABLESPACE statement, or simply omit the SEGMENT SPACE

MANAGEMENT AUTO clause. Oracle strongly recommends AUTOMATIC segment space management for permanent locally managed tablespaces, and the default behavior of Oracle 11*g* is AUTO. Here is a statement that creates a tablespace with manual segment space management:

```
CREATE TABLESPACE hr_index
DATAFILE '/u02/oradata/11GR11/hr_index01.dbf'  SIZE 2G
EXTENT MANAGEMENT LOCAL AUTOALLOCATE
SEGMENT SPACE MANAGEMENT MANUAL;
```

When automatic segment space management is specified, bitmaps are used instead of free lists to identify which data blocks are available for inserts. The parameters PCTFREE and PCTUSED are ignored for segments in tablespaces with automatic segment space management. Automatic segment space management is available only on tablespaces configured for local extent management; it is not available for temporary or system tablespaces. Automatic segment space management performs better and reduces your maintenance tasks, making it the preferred technique.

To specify automatic segment space management, use the SEGMENT SPACE MANAGEMENT AUTO clause of the CREATE TABLESPACE statement like this or do not include the SEGMENT SPACE MANAGEMENT clause (it is the default):

```
CREATE TABLESPACE hr_index
DATAFILE '/u02/oradata/11GR11/hr_index01.dbf'  SIZE 2G
EXTENT MANAGEMENT LOCAL AUTOALLOCATE
SEGMENT SPACE MANAGEMENT AUTO;
```

When automatic segment space management is used, Oracle ignores the storage parameters PCTUSED, FREELISTS, and FREELIST GROUPS when creating objects.

Although the name *segment space management* sounds similar to extent management, it is quite different and can be more accurately regarded as block space management.

Choosing Other Tablespace Options

Several options are available to use when creating a tablespace. You learned to create BIGFILE or SMALLFILE tablespaces and use the EXTENT MANAGEMENT and SEGMENT SPACE MANAGEMENT options in the previous sections. In this section, you will learn the other options available while creating a tablespace:

- Specifying nondefault block size
- Specifying default storage characteristics
- Specifying logging and flashback clauses
- Creating offline tablespaces

The following example shows the optional clauses you can use while creating a dictionary-managed tablespace:

```
CREATE TABLESPACE APPL_DATA
   DATAFILE '/disk3/oradata/DB01/appl_data01.dbf'
      SIZE 100M
   DEFAULT STORAGE (
                   INITIAL 256K
                   NEXT 256K
                   MINEXTENTS 2
                   PCTINCREASE 0
                   MAXEXTENTS 4096)
   BLOCKSIZE 16K
   MINIMUM EXTENT 256K
   LOGGING
   ONLINE
   FORCE LOGGING
   FLASHBACK ON
   EXTENT MANAGEMENT DICTIONARY
   SEGMENT SPACE MANAGEMENT MANUAL;
```

The following example shows the optional clauses you can use while creating a locally managed tablespace:

```
CREATE TABLESPACE APPL_DATA
   DATAFILE '/disk3/oradata/DB01/appl_data01.dbf'
      SIZE 100M
   DEFAULT STORAGE COMPRESS
   BLOCKSIZE 16K
   LOGGING
   ONLINE
   FORCE LOGGING
   FLASHBACK ON
   EXTENT MANAGEMENT LOCAL
   SEGMENT SPACE MANAGEMENT AUTO;
```

Though Oracle manages the tablespace characteristics very efficiently with its default values, you can specify several clauses to a finer level of control. The clauses in the CREATE TABLESPACE command can specify the following:

DEFAULT STORAGE clause The DEFAULT STORAGE clause specifies the default storage parameters for new objects that are created in the tablespace. If an explicit storage clause is specified when creating an object, the tablespace defaults are not used for the specified storage parameters. The storage parameters are specified within parentheses; no parameter is mandatory, but if you specify the DEFAULT STORAGE clause, you must specify at least one parameter inside the parentheses. The storage parameters are valid only for dictionary-managed tablespaces; for locally managed tablespaces, you can specify only the COMPRESS option. I will discuss the storage parameters later in the chapter in the section "Creating a Table."

BLOCKSIZE clause Oracle allows a tablespace to have a different block size than the default standard database block size. The database block size is specified when you create the database using the initialization parameter DB_BLOCK_SIZE. This is the block size used for the SYSTEM tablespace and is known as the *standard block size*. The valid sizes of the nonstandard block size are 2KB, 4KB, 8KB, 16KB, and 32KB. If you do not specify a block size for the tablespace, the database block size is assumed. Multiple block sizes in the database are beneficial for large databases with OLTP and Decision Support System (DSS) data stored together and for storing large tables. The restrictions on specifying nonstandard block sizes along with the tablespace creation are discussed in the section "Using Nonstandard Block Sizes."

MINIMUM EXTENT clause The MINIMUM EXTENT clause specifies that the extent sizes should be a multiple of the size specified. You can use this clause to control fragmentation in the tablespace by allocating extents of at least the size specified; this clause is always a multiple of the size specified. In the CREATE TABLESPACE example, all the extents allocated in the tablespace would be a multiple of 256KB. The INITIAL and NEXT extent sizes specified should be a multiple of MINIMUM EXTENT. This clause is valid only for dictionary-managed tablespaces.

LOGGING/NOLOGGING clause The LOGGING/NOLOGGING clause specifies that the DDL operations and direct-load INSERT should be recorded in the redo log files. This is the default, and the clause can be omitted. When you specify NOLOGGING, data is modified with minimal logging, and hence the commands complete faster. Since the changes are not recorded in the redo log files, you need to apply the commands again in the case of a media recovery. You can specify LOGGING or NOLOGGING in the individual object creation statement, and it overrides the tablespace default.

FORCE LOGGING clause You must specify this clause to log all changes irrespective of the LOGGING mode for individual objects in the tablespace. You can specify the NOLOGGING clause and FORCE LOGGING clause together when creating a tablespace. If you do so, the objects will be created in NOLOGGING mode and will be overridden by the FORCE LOGGING mode. When you take the tablespace out of the FORCE LOGGING mode, the NOLOGGING attribute for objects goes into effect.

ONLINE/OFFLINE clause This clause specifies that the tablespace should be made online or available as soon as it is created. This is the default, and hence the clause can be omitted. If you do not want the tablespace to be available, you can specify OFFLINE.

FLASHBACK ON/OFF clause FLASHBACK ON puts the tablespace in the flashback mode and is the default. The OFF option turns flashback off, and hence Oracle will not save any flashback data. I will discuss flashback operations in Chapter 15, "Implementing Database Backups."

The clauses related to encrypting the tablespace are not discussed here because they are beyond the scope for this book.

Using Nonstandard Block Sizes

The block size used while creating the database is specified in the initialization parameter using the DB_BLOCK_SIZE parameter. This is known as the *standard block size* for the database. You must choose a block size that suits most of your tables as the standard block size. In most databases, this is the only block size you will ever need. Oracle gives you the option of having multiple block sizes, which is especially useful when you're transporting tablespaces from another database with a different block size.

The DB_CACHE_SIZE parameter defines the buffer cache size that is associated with the standard block size. To create tablespaces with nonstandard block size, you must set the appropriate initialization parameter to define a buffer cache size for the block size. The initialization parameter is DB_*n*K_CACHE_SIZE, where *n* is the nonstandard block size. *n* can have values 2, 4, 8, 16, or 32 but cannot have the size of the standard block size. For example, if your standard block size is 8KB, you cannot set the parameter DB_8K_CACHE_SIZE. If you need to create a tablespace that uses a different block size, say 16KB, you must set the DB_16K_CACHE_SIZE parameter. By default, the value for DB_*n*K_CACHE_SIZE parameters is 0MB.

The temporary tablespaces created should have the standard block size.

The DB_*n*K_CACHE_SIZE parameter is dynamic; you can alter its value using the ALTER SYSTEM statement.

Creating Temporary Tablespaces

Oracle can manage space for sort operations more efficiently by using *temporary tablespaces*. By exclusively designating a tablespace for temporary segments, Oracle eliminates the allocation and deallocation of temporary segments in a permanent tablespace. A temporary tablespace can be used only for sort segments. A temporary tablespace is used for temporary segments, which are created, managed, and dropped by the database as needed. These temporary segments are most commonly generated during sorting operations such as ORDER BY, GROUP BY, and CREATE INDEX. They are also generated during other operations such as hash joins or inserts into temporary tables.

You create a temporary tablespace at database creation time with the DEFAULT TEMPORARY TABLESPACE clause of the CREATE DATABASE statement or after the database is created with the CREATE TEMPORARY TABLESPACE statement, like this:

```
CREATE TEMPORARY TABLESPACE temp
TEMPFILE '/u01/oradata/11GR1/temp01.dbf' SIZE 1G;
```

Notice that the keyword TEMPFILE is used instead of DATAFILE. Temp files are available only with temporary tablespaces, they never need to be backed up, and they do not log data changes in the redo logs. The EXTENT MANAGEMENT LOCAL clause is optional and can be omitted; you can provide it to improve readability. If you do not specify the extent size by using the UNIFORM SIZE clause, the default size used will be 1MB.

Although it is always good practice to create a separate temporary tablespace, it is required when the SYSTEM tablespace is locally managed.

Temporary tablespaces are created using temp files instead of data files. Temp files are allocated slightly differently than data files. Although data files are completely allocated and initialized at creation time, temp files are not always guaranteed to allocate the disk space specified. This means that on some Unix systems a temp file will not actually allocate disk space until a sorting operation requires it. Although this delayed allocation approach allows rapid file creation, it can cause problems down the road if you have not reserved the space that may be needed at runtime.

Each user is assigned a temporary tablespace when the user is created. By default, the default tablespace (where the user creates objects) and the temporary tablespace (where the user's sort operations are performed) are both the SYSTEM tablespace. No user should have SYSTEM as their default or temporary tablespace. This will unnecessarily increase fragmentation in the SYSTEM tablespace.

When creating a database, you can also create a temporary tablespace using the DEFAULT TEMPORARY TABLESPACE clause of the CREATE DATABASE statement. If the default temporary tablespace is defined in the database, all new users will have that tablespace assigned as the temporary tablespace by default if you do not specify another tablespace for the users' temporary tablespace. You can also designate a data tablespace for application tables during database creation using the DEFAULT TABLESPACE clause.

If there are multiple temporary tablespaces in a database and if you want to utilize the space in multiple temporary tablespaces to a user's sort operation, you can use the temporary tablespace groups. When creating the temporary tablespace, use the TABLESPACE GROUP clause as in the following example:

```
CREATE TEMPORARY TABLESPACE TEMP01
TEMPFILE '/u01/oradata/11GR1/temp01a.dbf' size 200M
EXTENT MANAGEMENT LOCAL UNIFORM SIZE 5M
TABLESPACE GROUP ALL_TEMPS;
```

In this example, the tablespace is made part of the ALL_TEMPS temporary tablespace group. Tablespace groups are applicable only to temporary tablespaces. If the group does not exist, Oracle creates the group and adds the tablespace to the group.

When creating a temporary tablespace, you can use only the EXTENT MANAGEMENT and TABLESPACE GROUP clauses along with TEMPFILE clause. All other options are invalid for temporary tablespaces.

Creating Undo Tablespaces

An undo tablespace stores undo segments, which are used by the database for several purposes, including the following:

- Rolling back a transaction explicitly with a ROLLBACK statement
- Rolling back a transaction implicitly (for example, through the recovery of a failed transaction)
- Reconstructing a read-consistent image of data
- Recovering from logical corruptions

To create an undo tablespace at database creation time, set the initialization parameter UNDO_MANAGEMENT=AUTO (default), and include an UNDO TABLESPACE clause in your CREATE DATABASE statement, like this:

```
CREATE DATABASE "TEST1"
DATAFILE '/u01/app/oracle/oradata/TEST1/system01.dbf'
    SIZE 300M REUSE AUTOEXTEND ON NEXT 10240K MAXSIZE UNLIMITED
    EXTENT MANAGEMENT LOCAL
SYSAUX DATAFILE '/u01/app/oracle/oradata/TEST1/sysaux01.dbf'
    SIZE 120M REUSE AUTOEXTEND ON NEXT  10240K MAXSIZE UNLIMITED
SMALLFILE DEFAULT TEMPORARY TABLESPACE TEMP
    TEMPFILE '/u01/app/oracle/oradata/TEST1/temp01.dbf'
    SIZE 20M REUSE AUTOEXTEND ON NEXT  640K MAXSIZE UNLIMITED
SMALLFILE UNDO TABLESPACE "UNDOTBS1"
    DATAFILE '/u01/app/oracle/oradata/TEST1/undotbs01.dbf'
    SIZE 200M REUSE AUTOEXTEND ON NEXT  5120K MAXSIZE UNLIMITED
DEFAULT TABLESPACE "USERS"
    DATAFILE '/u01/app/oracle/oradata/TEST1/users01.dbf'
    SIZE 5M REUSE AUTOEXTEND ON NEXT  1280K MAXSIZE UNLIMITED
    EXTENT MANAGEMENT LOCAL SEGMENT SPACE MANAGEMENT  AUTO
CHARACTER SET WE8MSWIN1252
NATIONAL CHARACTER SET AL16UTF16
LOGFILE
   GROUP 1 ('/u01/app/oracle/oradata/TEST1/redo01.log') SIZE 51200K,
   GROUP 2 ('/u01/app/oracle/oradata/TEST1/redo02.log') SIZE 51200K,
   GROUP 3 ('/u01/app/oracle/oradata/TEST1/redo03.log') SIZE 51200K
SET DEFAULT SMALLFILE TABLESPACE
USER SYS IDENTIFIED BY mysupersekret
USER SYSTEM IDENTIFIED BY supersekret;
```

You can create an undo tablespace after database creation with the CREATE UNDO TABLESPACE statement, like this:

```
CREATE UNDO TABLESPACE undo
DATAFILE '/ORADATA/PROD/UNDO01.DBF' SIZE 2G;
```

When creating undo tablespace, you can specify the undo retention clause. The RETENTION GUARANTEE option specifies that Oracle should preserve unexpired undo data until the period of time specified by the UNDO_RETENTION initialization parameter. This setting is useful for flashback query operations. RETENTION NOGUARANTEE is the default.

The only tablespace clauses available to specify are EXTENT MANAGEMENT LOCAL and DATAFILE when creating undo tablespaces. Undo management and retention are discussed in Chapter 13, "Managing Data and Undo."

Although it is always good practice to create a separate undo tablespace, it is required when the SYSTEM tablespace is locally managed.

Removing Tablespaces

Tablespaces that are not needed in the database can be dropped. Once a tablespace is dropped, there is no rollback. Though you can drop a tablespace with objects in it, it may be safer to drop the objects first and then drop the tablespace. To remove a tablespace from the database, use the DROP TABLESPACE statement:

```
DROP TABLESPACE USER_DATA;
```

If the tablespace is not empty, you should specify the optional clause INCLUDING CONTENTS to recursively remove any segments (tables, indexes, and so on) in the tablespace, like this:

```
DROP TABLESPACE dba_sandbox INCLUDING CONTENTS;
```

If there are referential integrity constraints from the objects on other tablespaces referring to the objects in the tablespace that is being dropped, you must specify the CASCADE CONSTRAINTS clause:

```
DROP TABLESPACE USER_DATA INCLUDING CONTENTS CASCADE CONSTRAINTS;
```

When you drop a tablespace, the control file is updated with the tablespace and data file information.

Dropping a tablespace does not automatically remove the data files from the file system. Use the additional clause INCLUDING CONTENTS AND DATAFILES to remove the underlying data files as well as the stored objects, like this:

```
DROP TABLESPACE hr_data INCLUDING CONTENTS AND DATAFILES;
```

If the Oracle Managed Files feature is used for the tablespace, such files will be removed automatically when you drop the tablespace. For files that are not Oracle managed, if you need to free up the disk space, you can either use OS commands to remove the data files belonging to the dropped tablespace or use the AND DATAFILES clause.

You cannot drop the SYSTEM tablespace.

Modifying Tablespaces

Use an ALTER TABLESPACE statement to modify the attributes of a tablespace. These are some of the actions you can perform on tablespaces:

- Change the default storage clauses and the MINIMUM_EXTENT of a dictionary-managed tablespace.
- Change the extent allocation and LOGGING/NOLOGGING modes.
- Change the availability of the tablespace.
- Make the tablespace read-only or read-write.
- Coalesce the contiguous free space.
- Add more space by adding new data files or temporary files.
- Resize the data files or temporary files.
- Rename a tablespace or rename files belonging to the tablespace.
- Shrink temporary files or shrink space in the tablespace.
- Change flashback on or off and change retention guarantee.
- Begin and end a backup.

The following sections detail common modifications you can perform on the tablespaces.

Changing Storage Defaults

Changing the default storage or MINIMUM_EXTENT or LOGGING/NOLOGGING does not affect the existing objects in the tablespace. The DEFAULT STORAGE and LOGGING/NOLOGGING clauses are applied to the newly created segments if such a clause is not explicitly specified when creating new objects. For example, to change the storage parameters, use the following statement:

```
ALTER TABLESPACE APPL_DATA
DEFAULT STORAGE (INITIAL 2M NEXT 2M);
```

Only the INITIAL and NEXT values of the storage STORAGE are changed; the other storage parameters such as PCTINCREASE or MINEXTENTS remain unaltered.

Adding a Data File to a Tablespace

Smallfile tablespaces can have multiple data files and can thus be spread over multiple file systems without engaging a logical volume manager. To add a data file to a smallfile tablespace, use an ADD clause with the ALTER TABLESPACE statement. For example, the following statement adds a 2GB data file on the /u02 file system to the receivables tablespace:

```
ALTER TABLESPACE receivables ADD DATAFILE
  '/u02/oradata/ORA10/receivables01.dbf'
  SIZE 2G;
```

Taking a Tablespace Offline or Online

You can control the availability of certain tablespaces by altering the tablespace to be offline or online. When you make a tablespace offline, the segments in that tablespace are not accessible. The data stored in other tablespaces is available for use. When making a tablespace unavailable, you can use these four options:

NORMAL This is the default. Oracle writes all the dirty buffer blocks in the SGA to the data files of the tablespace and closes the data files. All data files belonging to the tablespace must be online. You need not do a media recovery when bringing the tablespace online. For example:

```
ALTER TABLESPACE USER_DATA ONLINE;
```

TEMPORARY Oracle performs a checkpoint on all online data files. It does not ensure that the data files are available. You may need to perform a media recovery on the offline data files when the tablespace is brought online. For example:

```
ALTER TABLESPACE USER_DATA OFFLINE TEMPORARY;
```

IMMEDIATE Oracle does not perform a checkpoint and does not make sure that all data files are available. You must perform a media recovery when the tablespace is brought back online. For example:

```
ALTER TABLESPACE USER_DATA OFFLINE IMMEDIATE;
```

FOR RECOVER This makes the tablespace offline for point-in-time recovery. You can copy the data files belonging to the tablespace from a backup and apply the archive log files. For example:

```
ALTER TABLESPACE USER_DATA OFFLINE FOR RECOVER;
```

You cannot make the SYSTEM tablespace offline because the data dictionary must always be available for the functioning of the database. If a tablespace is offline when you shut down the database, it remains offline when you start up the database. You can make a tablespace offline by using the following statement:

```
ALTER TABLESPACE USER_DATA OFFLINE
```

When a tablespace is taken offline, SQL statements cannot reference any objects contained in that tablespace. If there are unsaved changes when you take the tablespace offline, Oracle saves rollback data corresponding to those changes in a deferred rollback segment in the SYSTEM tablespace. When the tablespace is brought back online, Oracle applies the rollback data to the tablespace, if needed.

Making a Tablespace Read-Only

If a tablespace contains static data, it can be marked read-only. Tablespaces that contain historic or reference data are typical candidates for read-only. When a tablespace is read-only, it does not have to be backed up with the nightly or weekly database backups. One backup after being marked read-only is all that is needed for future recoveries. Tables in a read-only tablespace can only be selected from; their rows cannot be inserted, updated, or deleted.

You cannot make the SYSTEM tablespace read-only. When you make a tablespace read-only, all the data files must be online, and the tablespace can have no active transactions. You can drop objects such as tables or indexes from a read-only tablespace, but you cannot create new objects in a read-only tablespace.

Use a READ ONLY clause with an ALTER TABLESPACE statement to mark a tablespace read-only. For example, to mark the SALES2007 tablespace read-only, execute the following:

```
ALTER TABLESPACE sales2007 READ ONLY;
```

If you need to make changes to a table in a read-only tablespace, make it read writable again with the keywords READ WRITE, like this:

```
ALTER TABLESPACE sales2007 READ WRITE;
```

Oracle normally checks the availability of all data files belonging to the database when starting up the database. If you are storing your read-only tablespace on offline storage media or on a CD-ROM, you might want to skip the data file availability checking when starting up the database by setting the parameter READ_ONLY_OPEN_DELAYED to TRUE. Oracle checks the availability of data files belonging to read-only tablespaces only at the time of access to an object in the tablespace. A missing or bad read-only file will not be detected at database startup time.

Putting a Tablespace in Backup Mode

If you perform non-RMAN online backups, sometimes called *user-managed backups*, you need to put a tablespace in backup mode before you begin to copy the data files using an operating-system program. While the tablespace is in backup mode, the database continues to write data to the data files (checkpoints occur), but the occurrences of these checkpoints are not recorded in the header blocks of the data files. This omission tells the database that recovery may be needed if the database instance gets terminated abruptly.

While a tablespace is in backup mode, some additional information is written to the redo logs to assist with recovery, if needed.

See Chapter 15 for more information on backups, and see Chapter 16, "Recovering the Database," for more information about recovery.

Some companies perform backups by splitting a third mirror, mounting these mirrored file systems onto another server, and then copying them to tape. To safely split the mirror, alter all your tablespaces into backup mode, make the split, and then alter all the tablespaces out of backup mode. Put them into backup mode like this:

```
ALTER TABLESPACE system BEGIN BACKUP;
```

Use the keywords END BACKUP to take a tablespace out of backup mode, like this:

```
ALTER TABLESPACE system END BACKUP;
```

If you forget to take a tablespace out of backup mode, the next time you bounce your database, it will see that the checkpoint number in the control file is later than the one in the data file headers and report that media recovery is required.

Obtaining Tablespace Information

DBAs often need to find the space used and available in a tablespace as well as query the tablespace characteristics. The data dictionary is the place to go for obtaining tablespace information. You can use the command-line utility SQL*Plus to query the information from data dictionary tables, or you can use Enterprise Manager Grid Control. We will review both in this section.

Obtaining Tablespace Information Using SQL*Plus

Many data dictionary views can provide information about tablespaces in a database, such as the following:

- DBA_TABLESPACES
- DBA_DATA_FILES
- DBA_TEMP_FILES
- V$TABLESPACE

The DBA_TABLESPACES view has one row for each tablespace in the database and provides the following information:

- The tablespace block size
- The tablespace status: online, offline, or read-only
- The contents of the tablespace: undo, temporary, or permanent
- Whether it uses dictionary-managed or locally managed extents
- Whether the segment space management is automatic or manual
- Whether it is a bigfile or smallfile tablespace

To get a listing of all the tablespaces in the database, their status, contents, extent management policy, and segment management policy, run the following query:

```
SELECT tablespace_name, status,contents
     ,extent_management extents
     ,segment_space_management free_space
FROM dba_tablespaces

TABLESPACE_NAME    STATUS    CONTENTS  EXTENTS   FREE_SPACE
------------------ --------- --------- --------- ----------
SYSTEM             ONLINE    PERMANENT LOCAL     MANUAL
UNDOTBS1           ONLINE    UNDO      LOCAL     MANUAL
```

```
SYSAUX               ONLINE    PERMANENT LOCAL     AUTO
TEMP                 ONLINE    TEMPORARY LOCAL     MANUAL
USERS                ONLINE    PERMANENT LOCAL     AUTO
EXAMPLE              ONLINE    PERMANENT LOCAL     AUTO
DATA                 ONLINE    PERMANENT LOCAL     AUTO
INDX                 ONLINE    PERMANENT LOCAL     AUTO
```

The V$TABLESPACE view also has one row per tablespace, but it includes some information other than DBA_TABLESPACES, such as whether the tablespace participates in database flashback operations:

```
SELECT name, bigfile, flashback_on
FROM v$tablespace;

NAME       BIGFILE  FLASHBACK_ON
---------- -------- ------------
SYSTEM     NO       YES
UNDOTBS1   NO       YES
SYSAUX     NO       YES
USERS      NO       YES
TEMP       NO       YES
EXAMPLE    NO       YES
DATA       NO       YES
INDX       NO       YES
```

See Chapter 15 for more information on flashback operations.

The DBA_DATA_FILES and DBA_TEMP_FILES views contain information on data files and temp files, respectively. This information includes the tablespace name, filename, file size, and autoextend settings.

```
SELECT tablespace_name, file_name, bytes/1024 kbytes
FROM dba_data_files
UNION ALL
SELECT tablespace_name, file_name, bytes/1024 kbytes
FROM dba_temp_files;

TABLESPACE FILE_NAME                                  KBYTES
---------- ---------------------------------------- -------
USERS      C:\ORACLE\ORADATA\ORA11\USERS01.DBF       102400
SYSAUX     C:\ORACLE\ORADATA\ORA11\SYSAUX01.DBF      256000
```

```
UNDOTBS1   C:\ORACLE\ORADATA\ORA11\UNDOTBS01.DBF      51200
SYSTEM     C:\ORACLE\ORADATA\ORA11\SYSTEM01.DBF      460800
EXAMPLE    C:\ORACLE\ORADATA\ORA11\EXAMPLE01.DBF     153600
INDX       C:\ORACLE\ORADATA\ORA11\INDX01.DBF        102400
TEMP       C:\ORACLE\ORADATA\ORA11\TEMP01.DBF         51200
```

In addition to in the data dictionary, you can obtain tablespace information from several sources. Some of these sources are the DDL and the Enterprise Manager.

Generating DDL for a Tablespace

Another way to quickly identify the attributes of a tablespace is to ask the database to generate DDL to re-create the tablespace. The CREATE TABLESPACE statement that results contains the attributes for the tablespace. Use the PL/SQL package DBMS_METADATA to generate DDL for your database objects. For example, to generate the DDL for the USERS tablespace, execute this:

```
SELECT DBMS_METADATA.GET_DDL('TABLESPACE','USERS')
FROM dual;
```

The output from this statement is a CREATE TABLESPACE statement that contains all the attributes for the USERS tablespace:

```
CREATE TABLESPACE "USERS" DATAFILE
'/u01/app/oracle/oradata/11GR11/users01.dbf' SIZE 5242880
AUTOEXTEND ON NEXT 1310720 MAXSIZE 32767M
LOGGING ONLINE PERMANENT BLOCKSIZE 8192
EXTENT MANAGEMENT LOCAL AUTOALLOCATE SEGMENT SPACE MANAGEMENT AUTO;
```

Obtaining Tablespace Information Using the EM Database Control

Instead of querying the data dictionary views with a command-line tool such as SQL*Plus, you can use the interactive GUI tool EM Database Control to monitor and manage database structures, including tablespaces. The EM Database Control is an alternative to a command-line interface.

To use the Database Control, follow these steps:

1. Point your browser to the Enterprise Manager URL for your database (similar to `https://`*`hostname`*`:5500/em/console`).
2. Log in to EM, and navigate to the Server tab of the main screen, which is shown in Figure 10.2.
3. Click the Tablespaces link under the heading Storage to display a list of tablespaces like that shown in Figure 10.3.

FIGURE 10.2 The Enterprise Manager Server tab

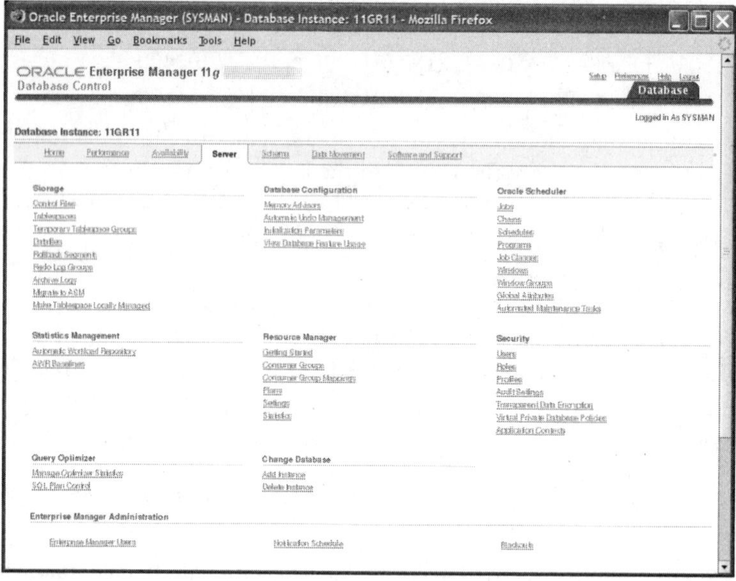

FIGURE 10.3 The Enterprise Manager Tablespaces screen

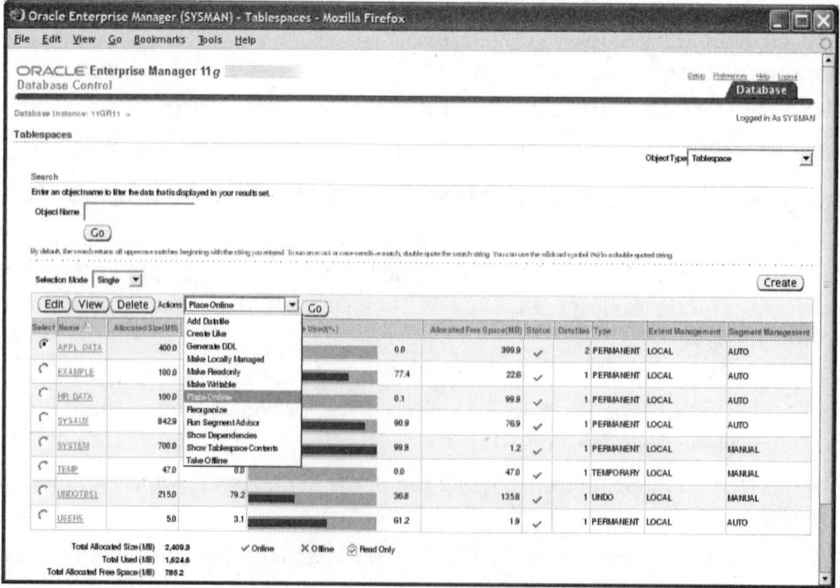

4. Click the radio button next to the tablespace you want to work with, and then click the Edit button. You can navigate to the tablespace General, Storage, and Thresholds edit screens, as shown in Figure 10.4.

FIGURE 10.4 The Enterprise Manager tablespace editor

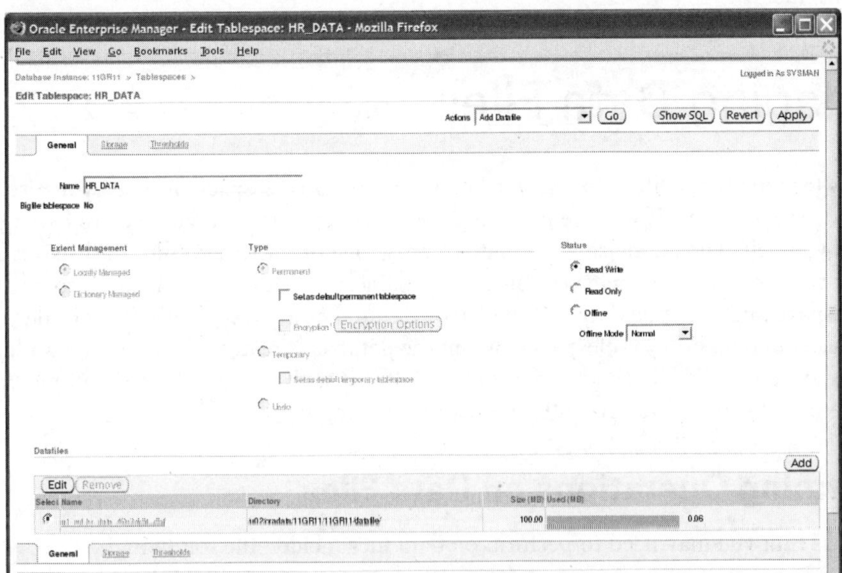

You use the screens and options in the EM Database Control to manipulate and change your tablespaces with many of the same options that the command-line interface supports. For example, to increase the size of the data file in the HR_DATA tablespace, click the Edit button next to the data file. The EM Database Control displays the tablespace edit screen, as shown in Figure 10.5.

FIGURE 10.5 Editing the data file size

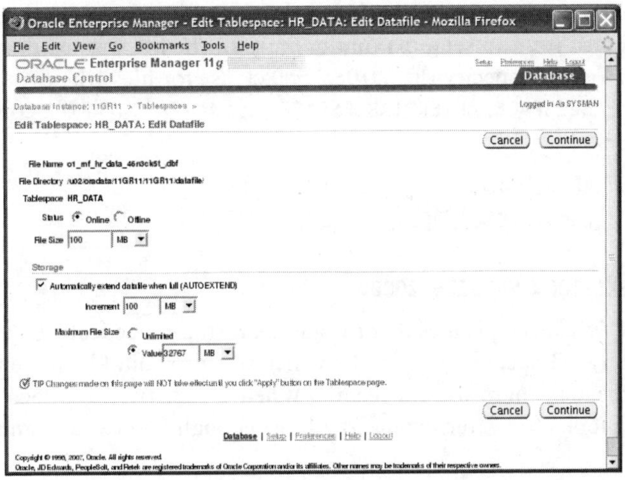

Edit the File Size field, increasing it to 100MB. The change will be applied when you click Continue.

Managing Data Files

Data files (or temporary files) are made when you create a tablespace or when you alter a tablespace to add files. If you are not using the OMF feature, you will need to manage data files yourself. The database will create or reuse one or more data files in the sizes and locations that you specify whenever you create a tablespace. A data file belongs to only one tablespace and only one database at a time. Temp files are a special variety of data file that are used in temporary tablespaces. When the database creates or reuses a data file, the operating-system file is allocated and initialized—filled with a regular pattern of mostly binary zeros. This initialization will not occur with temp files.

Performing Operations on Data Files

Operations that you may need to perform on data files include the following:

- Resizing them
- Taking them offline or online
- Moving (renaming) them

Sizing Files

You can specify that the data file (or temporary file) will grow automatically whenever space is needed in the tablespace. This is accomplished by specifying the AUTOEXTEND clause for the file. This functionality enables you to have fewer data files per tablespace and can simplify the administration of data files. The AUTOEXTEND clause can be ON or OFF; you can also specify file size increments. You can set a maximum limit for the file size; by default, the file size limit is UNLIMITED. You can specify the AUTOEXTEND clause for files when you run the CREATE DATABASE, CREATE TABLESPACE, ALTER TABLESPACE, and ALTER DATAFILE commands. For example:

```
CREATE TABLESPACE APPL_DATA
DATAFILE '/disk2/oradata/DB01/appl_data01.dbf'
SIZE 500M
AUTOEXTEND ON NEXT 100M MAXSIZE 2000M;
```

The AUTOEXTEND ON clause specifies that the automatic file-resize feature should be enabled for the specified file; NEXT specifies the size by which the file should be incremented, and MAXSIZE specifies the maximum size for the file. When Oracle tries to allocate an extent in the tablespace, it looks for a free extent. If a large enough free extent cannot be located (even after coalescing), Oracle increases the data file size by 100MB and tries to allocate the new extent.

The following statement disables the automatic file-extension feature:

```
ALTER DATABASE
DATAFILE '/disk2/oradata/DB01/appl_data01.dbf'
AUTOEXTEND OFF;
```

If the file already exists in the database, and you want to enable the autoextension feature, use the ALTER DATABASE command. For example, you can use the following statement:

```
ALTER DATABASE
DATAFILE '/disk2/oradata/DB01/appl_data01.dbf'
AUTOEXTEND ON NEXT 100M MAXSIZE 2000M;
```

You can increase or decrease the size of a data file or temporary file (thus increasing or decreasing the size of the tablespace) by using the RESIZE clause of the ALTER DATABASE DATAFILE command. For example, to redefine the size of a file, use the following statement:

```
ALTER DATABASE
DATAFILE '/disk2/oradata/DB01/appl_data01.dbf'
RESIZE 1500M;
```

When decreasing the file size, Oracle returns an error if it finds data beyond the new file size. You cannot reduce the file size below the high-water mark in the file. Reducing the file size helps reclaim unused space.

Making Files Online and Offline

Sometimes you may have to make data files unavailable to the database if there is a file corruption. You can use the ONLINE and OFFLINE clauses of the ALTER DATABASE statement to take a data file online or offline. You can specify the filename or specify the unique identifier number that represents the data file. This identifier can be found in the FILE# column of V$DATAFILE or the FILE_ID column of the DBA_DATA_FILES view.

To take a data file offline, use the OFFLINE clause. If the database is in NOARCHIVELOG mode, then you must specify the FOR DROP clause along with the OFFLINE clause. The data file will be taken offline and marked with status OFFLINE. You can remove the data file using OS commands, if you want to get rid of the data file. If the database is in ARCHIVELOG mode, you don't need to specify the FOR DROP clause when taking a data file offline. When you're ready to bring the data file online, Oracle performs media recovery on the data file to make it consistent with the database. Also, the FOR DROP clause is ignored if the database is in ARCHIVELOG mode. Here is an example of taking a data file offline:

```
ALTER DATABASE DATAFILE '/u01/oradata/11gr1/tools02.dbf' OFFLINE;
```

The following statement brings the data file online:

```
ALTER DATABASE DATAFILE '/u01/oradata/11gr1/tools02.dbf' ONLINE;
```

Renaming Files

You can rename data files using the RENAME FILE clause of the ALTER DATABASE command. You can also rename data files by using the RENAME DATAFILE clause of the ALTER TABLESPACE command. The RENAME functionality is used to logically move tablespaces from one location to another. To rename or relocate data files belonging to a non-SYSTEM tablespace, you should follow certain steps. Consider the following example.

Your tablespace USER_DATA has three data files named, such as the following:

- /disk1/oradata/DB01/user_data01.dbf
- /disk1/oradata/DB01/userdata2.dbf
- /disk1/oradata/DB01/user_data03.dbf

Renaming a Data File

If you need to rename one of these, say the second file, follow these steps:

1. Take the tablespace offline:

```
ALTER TABLESPACE USER_DATA OFFLINE;
```

2. Copy or move the file to the new location, or rename the file by using operating-system commands.
3. Rename the file in the database by using one of the following two commands:

```
ALTER DATABASE RENAME FILE
'/disk1/oradata/DB01/userdata2.dbf' TO
'/disk1/oradata/DB01/user_data02.dbf';
```

or

```
ALTER TABLESPACE USER_DATA RENAME DATAFILE
'/disk1/oradata/DB01/userdata2.dbf' TO
'/disk1/oradata/DB01/user_data02.dbf';
```

4. Bring the tablespace online:

```
ALTER TABLESPACE USER_DATA ONLINE;
```

Relocating a Tablespace

You may also determine that you need to relocate the tablespace from disk 1 to disk 2. If so, you should follow the same steps. You can also rename all the files in the tablespace by using a single command. The steps are as follows:

1. Take the tablespace offline:

```
ALTER TABLESPACE USER_DATA OFFLINE;
```

2. Copy the file to the new location by using OS commands on the disk.

3. Rename the files in the database by using one of the following two commands. The number of data files specified before the keyword TO should be equal to the number of files specified after the keyword.

```
ALTER DATABASE RENAME FILE
'/disk1/oradata/DB01/user_data01.dbf',
'/disk1/oradata/DB01/userdata2.dbf',
'/disk1/oradata/DB01/user_data03.dbf'
 TO
'/disk2/oradata/DB01/user_data01.dbf',
'/disk2/oradata/DB01/user_data02.dbf',
'/disk2/oradata/DB01/user_data03.dbf';
```

or

```
ALTER TABLESPACE USER_DATA RENAME DATAFILE
'/disk1/oradata/DB01/user_data01.dbf',
'/disk1/oradata/DB01/userdata2.dbf',
'/disk1/oradata/DB01/user_data03.dbf'
 TO
'/disk2/oradata/DB01/user_data01.dbf',
'/disk2/oradata/DB01/user_data02.dbf',
'/disk2/oradata/DB01/user_data03.dbf';
```

4. Bring the tablespace online:

```
ALTER TABLESPACE USER_DATA ONLINE;
```

Renaming or Relocating Files Belonging to Multiple Tablespaces

If you need to rename or relocate files belonging to multiple tablespaces or if the file belongs to the SYSTEM tablespace, you must follow these steps:

1. Shut down the database. A complete backup is recommended before making any structural changes.
2. Copy or rename the files on the disk by using OS commands.
3. Start up and mount the database (STARTUP MOUNT).
4. Rename the files in the database by using the ALTER DATABASE RENAME FILE command.
5. Open the database by using ALTER DATABASE OPEN.

Moving Read-Only Tablespaces

If you need to move read-only tablespaces to a CD-ROM or any write-once read-many device, follow these steps:

1. Make the tablespace read-only.
2. Copy the data files belonging to the tablespace to the read-only device.
3. Rename the files in the database by using the ALTER DATABASE RENAME FILE command.

Real World Scenario

Moving a Data File from the H Drive to the G Drive

Your operating-system administrator informed you that he is seeing lot of contention on the H drive and is seeking options to move some of the reads off the H drive and to G drive. As a DBA, you can move one of the hot files belonging to the `receivables` tablespace to the G drive.

You need to take a tablespace offline to perform some maintenance operations, such as recovering the tablespace or moving the data files to a new location. Use the `OFFLINE` clause with an `ALTER TABLESPACE` statement to take a tablespace offline. Follow these steps to rename or move a data file:

1. Take the `receivables` tablespace offline:

```
ALTER TABLESPACE receivables OFFLINE;
```

2. Use an operating-system program to physically move the file, such as Copy in Microsoft Windows or cp in Unix.
3. Tell the database about the new location:

```
ALTER TABLESPACE receivables RENAME DATAFILE
      'H:\ORACLE\ORADATA\ORA10\RECEIVABLES02.DBF'
  TO 'G:\ORACLE\ORADATA\ORA10\RECEIVABLES02.DBF' ;
```

4. Bring the tablespace back online:

```
ALTER TABLESPACE receivables ONLINE;
```

Using the Oracle Managed Files Feature

The Oracle Managed Files feature is appropriate for smaller nonproduction databases or databases on disks using Logical Volume Manager (LVM). LVM is software available with most disk systems to combine partitions of multiple physical disks to one logical volume. LVM can use mirroring, striping, RAID 5, and so on. Using the OMF feature has the following benefits:

Error prevention Since Oracle removes the files associated with the tablespace, the DBA cannot make a mistake by removing a file belonging to an active tablespace.

A standard naming convention The files created using the OMF method have unique and standard filenames.

Space retrieval When tablespaces are removed, Oracle removes the files associated with the tablespace, thus freeing up space immediately on the disk. The DBA may forget to remove the file from disk.

Easy script writing Application vendors need not worry about the syntax of specifying directory names in the scripts when porting the application to multiple platforms. The same script can be used to create tablespaces on different OS platforms.

The OMF feature can be used to create files and to remove them when the corresponding object (redo log group or tablespace) is dropped from the database. For managing OMF-created files, such as renaming or resizing, you need to use the traditional methods.

Enabling the Oracle Managed Files Feature

To enable the creation of Oracle-managed data files, you need to set the parameter DB_CREATE_FILE_DEST. You can specify this parameter in the initialization-parameter file or set/change it using the ALTER SYSTEM or ALTER SESSION statement. The DB_CREATE_FILE_DEST parameter defines the directory where Oracle can create data files. Oracle must have read-write permission on this directory. The directory must exist on the server where the database is located. Oracle will not create the directory; it will create create only the data file.

You can use the OMF feature to create data files when using the CREATE DATABASE, CREATE TABLESPACE, and ALTER TABLESPACE statements. In the CREATE DATABASE statement, you don't need to specify the filenames for the SYSTEM, UNDO, or TEMPORARY tablespaces. In the CREATE TABLESPACE statement, you can omit the DATAFILE clause. In the ALTER TABLESPACE ADD DATAFILE statement, you can omit the filename.

The data files created using the OMF feature will have a standard format. For data files, the format is ora_%t_%u.dbf, and for temp files, the format is ora_%t_%u.tmp, where %t is the tablespace name and %u is a unique eight-character string derived by Oracle. If the tablespace name is longer than eight characters, only the first eight characters are used. The filenames generated by Oracle are reported in the alert log file.

You can also use the OMF feature for the control files and redo log files of the database. Since these two types of files can be multiplexed, Oracle provides another parameter to specify the location of files, DB_CREATE_ONLINE_LOG_DEST_*n*, where *n* can be 1, 2, 3, 4, or 5. These initialization parameters also can be altered using ALTER SYSTEM or ALTER SESSION. If you set the parameters DB_CREATE_ONLINE_LOG_DEST_1 and DB_CREATE_ONLINE_LOG_DEST_2 in the parameter file when creating a database, Oracle creates two control files (one in each directory) and creates two online redo log groups with two members each (one member each in both directories).

The redo log file names created will have the format ora_%g_%u.log, where %g is the log group number and %u is an eight-character string. The control file will have a format of ora_%u.ctl, where %u is an eight-character string.

In the following sections, you will see examples of using the OMF feature while creating a database as well as creating additional tablespaces in a database.

Creating Databases Using the OMF Feature

Let's consider an example of creating a database. The following parameters are set in the initialization-parameter file:

```
UNDO_MANAGEMENT = AUTO
DB_CREATE_ONLINE_LOG_DEST_1 = '/ora1/oradata/MYDB'
```

```
DB_CREATE_ONLINE_LOG_DEST_2 = '/ora2/oradata/MYDB'
DB_CREATE_FILE_DEST = '/ora1/oradata/MYDB'
```

You do not have the CONTROL_FILES parameter set. Create the database using the following statement:

```
CREATE DATABASE MYDB
DEFAULT TEMPORARY TABLESPACE TEMP;
```

The following files will be created: the SYSTEM tablespace data file in /ora1/oradata/MYDB, the TEMP tablespace temp file in /ora1/oradata/MYDB, one control file in /ora1/oradata/MYDB and another control file in /ora2/oradata/MYDB, one member of the first redo log group in /ora1/oradata/MYDB and a second member in /ora2/oradata/MYDB, and one member of second redo log group in /ora1/oradata/MYDB and a second member in /ora2/oradata/MYDB. Since you specified the UNDO_MANAGEMENT clause and did not specify a name for the undo tablespace, Oracle creates the SYS_UNDOTBS tablespace as an undo tablespace and creates its data file in /ora1/oradata/MYDB. If you omit the DEFAULT TEMPORARY TABLESPACE clause, Oracle will not create a temporary tablespace.

When using the OMF feature to create control files, you must get the names of control files from the alert log and add them to the initialization-parameter file using the CONTROL_FILES parameter for the instance to start again.

The data files and temp files created by the OMF feature will have a default size of 100MB, be autoextensible, and have no maximum file size. Each redo log member will be 100MB in size by default.

Creating Tablespaces Using the OMF Feature

Let's consider another example that creates two tablespaces. The data file for the APP_DATA tablespace will be stored in the directory /ora5/oradata/MYDB. The data file for the APP_INDEX tablespace will be stored in the directory /ora6/oradata/MYDB.

```
ALTER SESSION SET DB_CREATE_FILE_DEST = '/ora5/oradata/MYDB';
CREATE TABLESPACE APP_DATA
EXTENT MANAGEMENT DICTIONARY;
ALTER SESSION SET DB_CREATE_FILE_DEST = '/ora6/oradata/MYDB';
CREATE TABLESPACE APP_INDEX;
```

If you do not specify the DB_CREATE_ONLINE_LOG_DEST_*n* parameter when creating a database or when adding a redo log group, the OMF feature creates one control file and two groups with one member each for redo log files in the DB_CREATE_FILE_DEST directory. If the DB_CREATE_FILE_DEST parameter is also not set and you did not provide filenames for data files and redo logs, Oracle creates the files in a default directory (mostly $ORACLE_HOME/dbs), but they will not be Oracle managed. This is the default behavior of the database.

Overriding the Default File Size

If you want to have different sizes for the files created by the OMF feature, you can do so by specifying the DATAFILE clause without a filename. You can also turn off the autoextensible feature of the data file. The following statement creates a tablespace of size 10MB and turns off the autoextensible feature:

```
CREATE TABLESPACE PAY_DATA DATAFILE SIZE 10M
AUTOEXTEND OFF;
```

Here is another example that creates multiple data files for the tablespace. The second and third data files are autoextensible.

```
CREATE TABLESPACE PAY_INDEX
DATAFILE SIZE 20M AUTOEXTEND OFF,
SIZE 30M AUTOEXTEND ON MAXSIZE 1000M,
SIZE 1M;
```

The following example adds files to an existing tablespace:

```
ALTER SYSTEM SET DB_CREATE_FILE_DEST = '/ora5/oradata/MYDB';
ALTER TABLESPACE USERS ADD DATAFILE;
ALTER SYSTEM SET DB_CREATE_FILE_DEST = '/ora8/oradata/MYDB';
ALTER TABLESPACE APP_DATA
ADD DATAFILE SIZE 200M AUTOEXTEND OFF;
```

Once created, Oracle Managed Files are treated like other database files. You can rename and resize them and must back them up. Archive log files cannot be managed by OMF.

How Do You Create a Database and its Associated Tablespaces with OMF?

You have been asked by your manager to create a test database for a new application your company just bought. The database is for testing the functionality of the application. The vendor told you it needs four tablespaces, namely, SJC_DATA, SJC_INDEX, WKW_DATA, and WKW_INDEX. The index tablespaces must be uniform extent sizes of 512KB and should have minimum sizes of 500MB. The vendor needs the SJC_DATA tablespace to be dictionary managed with the minimum and extent size multiple to be 128KB and the tablespace size to be 1GB. The SJC_DATA tablespace should be 250MB.

Since this is a test database for testing the functionality of the application, you decide to use the Oracle Managed Files feature, which makes your life easier by creating and cleaning the files belonging to the database.

Let's create the database. Your system administrator has given you four disks—namely, /ora1, /ora2, /ora3, and /ora4—each with 900MB of space.

Make sure you include the following in the parameter file:

```
UNDO_MANAGEMENT = AUTO
DB_CREATE_FILE_DEST = /ora1
```

```
DB_CREATE_ONLINE_LOG_DEST_1 = /ora1
DB_CREATE_ONLINE_LOG_DEST_2 = /ora2
```

Create the database using the following statement:

```
CREATE DATABASE SJCTEST
LOGFILE SIZE 20M
DEFAULT TEMPORARY TABLESPACE TEMP
TEMPFILE SIZE 200M
EXTENT MANAGEMENT LOCAL UNIFORM SIZE 2M
UNDO TABLESPACE UNDO_TBS SIZE 200M;
```

The previous statement creates a database named SJCTEST. The SYSTEM tablespace, undo tablespace, and temporary tablespace are created in /ora1. The SYSTEM tablespace has the default size of 100MB, and the undo tablespace and temporary tablespace will have the size of 200MB. Since you do not want each log file member to be 100MB, you specify a smaller size for online redo log members.

Two control files are created, and redo log files with two members are created. Each member is stored in /ora1 and /ora2.

After running the necessary scripts to create the catalog and packages, you create the tablespaces for the application:

```
ALTER SYSTEM SET DB_CREATE_FILE_DEST = "/ora2";
CREATE TABLESPACE SJC_DATA
EXTENT MANAGEMENT DICTIONARY
MINIMUM EXTENT 128K
DATAFILE SIZE 800M;
ALTER SYSTEM SET DB_CREATE_FILE_DEST = "/ora3";
ALTER TABLESPACE SJC_DATA ADD DATAFILE SIZE 200M;
CREATE TABLESAPCE WKW_INDEX
EXTENT MANAGEMENT LOCAL UNIFORM SIZE 512K
DATAFILE SIZE 500M;
ALTER SYSTEM SET DB_CREATE_FILE_DEST = "/ora4";
CREATE TABLESPACE WKW_DATA;
CREATE TABLESPACE SJC_INDEX
EXTENT MANAGEMENT LOCAL UNIFORM SIZE 512K
DATAFILE SIZE 500M;
```

Since you have only 900MB in each file system, to allocate 1GB to the SJC_DATA tablespace, you needed two data files. This is accomplished in two steps.

Querying Data File Information

Similar to gathering tablespace information, you can use SQL*Plus as well as the EM Grid Control to get information about data files and temporary files. In the following sections, you will query a few dictionary views that hold data file and temporary-file information. You can obtain the same information using the EM Grid Control by drilling down the tablespaces shown in Figure 10.5. You can query data file and temporary-file information by using the following views.

V$DATAFILE

This view shows data file information from the control file:

```
SELECT FILE#, RFILE#, STATUS, BYTES, BLOCK_SIZE
FROM V$DATAFILE;

     FILE#     RFILE# STATUS       BYTES BLOCK_SIZE
---------- ---------- ------- ---------- ----------
         1          1 SYSTEM   734003200       8192
         2          2 ONLINE   883818496       8192
         3          3 ONLINE   225443840       8192
         4          4 ONLINE     5242880       8192
         5          5 ONLINE   104857600       8192
         6          6 ONLINE   209715200       8192
         7          7 ONLINE   209715200       8192
         8          8 ONLINE   104857600       8192
```

V$TEMPFILE

Similar to V$DATAFILE, this view shows information about the temporary files:

```
SELECT FILE#, RFILE#, STATUS, BYTES, BLOCK_SIZE
FROM V$TEMPFILE;

     FILE#     RFILE# STATUS       BYTES BLOCK_SIZE
---------- ---------- ------- ---------- ----------
         1          1 ONLINE    49283072       8192
```

DBA_DATA_FILES

This view shows information about the filenames, associated tablespace names, size, status, and so on:

```
SELECT TABLESPACE_NAME, FILE_NAME, BYTES,
         AUTOEXTENSIBLE
FROM DBA_DATA_FILES;
```

```
TABLESPACE FILE_NAME                                     BYTES AUT
---------- ---------------------------------------- ---------- ---
USERS      /u01/app/oracle/oradata/11GR11/users01.d    5242880 YES
           bf
UNDOTBS1   /u01/app/oracle/oradata/11GR11/undotbs01  225443840 YES
           .dbf
SYSAUX     /u01/app/oracle/oradata/11GR11/sysaux01.  883818496 YES
           dbf
SYSTEM     /u01/app/oracle/oradata/11GR11/system01.  734003200 YES
           dbf
EXAMPLE    /u01/app/oracle/oradata/11GR11/example01  104857600 YES
           .dbf
APPL_DATA  /u01/app/oracle/oradata/11GR11/appl_data  209715200 NO
           01.dbf
APPL_DATA  /u01/app/oracle/oradata/11GR11/appl_data  209715200 NO
           02.dbf
HR_DATA    /u02/oradata/11GR11/11GR11/datafile/o1_m  104857600 YES
           f_hr_data_46n3ck5t_.dbf
```

DBA_TEMP_FILES

This view shows information similar to that of DBA_DATA_FILES for the temporary files in the database:

```
SELECT TABLESPACE_NAME, FILE_NAME, BYTES,
       AUTOEXTENSIBLE
FROM DBA_TEMP_FILES;

TABLESPACE FILE_NAME                                     BYTES AUT
---------- ---------------------------------------- ---------- ---
TEMP       /u01/app/oracle/oradata/11GR11/temp01.dbf   49283072 NO
```

The maximum number of data files per tablespace is OS dependent, but on most operating systems, it is 1,022. The maximum number of data files per database is 65,533. The MAXDATAFILES clause in the CREATE DATABASE and CREATE CONTROLFILE statements also limits the number of data files per database. The maximum data file size is OS dependent. There is no limit on the number of tablespaces per database. Because only 65,533 data files are allowed per database, you cannot have more than 65,533 tablespaces, because each tablespace needs at least one data file.

A useful technique for managing disk space used by data files is to enable AUTOEXTEND for application tablespaces, which tells the database to automatically enlarge a data file when the tablespace runs out of free space. The AUTOEXTEND attribute applies to individual data files and not to the tablespace.

To resize a data file manually, use the ALTER DATABASE DATAFILE statement, like this:

```
ALTER DATABASE DATAFILE
   '/u01/app/oracle/oradata/11GR11/example01.dbf' RESIZE 2000M;
```

To configure a data file to automatically enlarge as needed by adding 100MB at a time up to a maximum of 8000MB, execute the following:

```
ALTER DATABASE DATAFILE
   'C:\ORACLE\ORADATA\ORA10\DATA01.DBF'
AUTOEXTEND ON NEXT 100M MAXSIZE 8000M;
```

If you plan to use the AUTOEXTEND option for the data files, use MAXSIZE to limit the file size to the disk space available. Also, it is not advised to enable AUTOEXTEND for temporary and undo tablespaces because user error can fill up the available disk space.

Working with Schema Objects

A *schema* is collection of database objects owned by a specific database user. In an Oracle 11*g* database, the schema has the same name as the database user, so the two terms are synonymous. Schema objects include the segments (tables, indexes, and so on) you have seen in tablespaces as well as nonsegment database objects owned by a user. These nonsegment objects include constraints, views, synonyms, procedures, and packages. Database objects that are not owned by one user and thus are not schema objects include roles, tablespaces, and directories. The schema objects you need to learn for the certification exam are tables, indexes, and constraints.

In Chapter 6, you learned to create tables, what datatypes can be used, and how to modify the table structure. In the following sections, you will learn to create tables with the storage clause. You also learned in Chapter 6 the various types of constraints and how constraints are used. In Chapter 7, you learned to create indexes and learned that they are similar to tables in that you can specify storage parameters when creating them. In this chapter, you will take this a step further, creating indexes that specify storage clauses. To fully prepare for the OCA certification exam, you must understand Chapters 6 and 7 before moving on in this one.

A Little Background on Creating Tables

Tables are the primary data storage containers in an Oracle Database. You can think of a table as a spreadsheet having column headings and many rows of information. A schema or a user in the database owns the table. The table columns have a defined datatype—the data stored in the columns should satisfy the characteristics of the column. You can also define rules for storing data in the columns using integrity constraints.

Data in a table is organized into rows and columns. Each column is named and has a specific datatype and size, such as CHAR(16), VARCHAR2(50), TIMESTAMP(6), or NUMBER. A row is a single occurrence of this set of columns. You can think of columns as fields, and you can think of rows as records.

When you create a table, you must give it a name as well as specify the column names and datatypes. You can optionally specify many additional attributes, such as column default values, extent sizes, which tablespace to use, and so on. Table and column names have the following requirements:

- They must be from 1 to 30 bytes in length.
- They must begin with a letter.
- They can include letters, numbers, the underscore symbol (_), the number symbol (#), and the dollar symbol ($). (However, Oracle discourages the use of number and dollar symbols in names.)
- They cannot be a reserved word such as NUMBER or INDEX.

Table names in Oracle are not case sensitive. This is good so you do not have to keep track of case. If you enclose the table name in double quotation marks, the case of the table name is preserved. You must enclose the table name in double quotation marks if the table name contains characters that are not uppercase.

If the name is enclosed in double quotation marks (" "), the only requirement is that the name be from 1 to 30 bytes long and not contain an embedded double quotation mark. Each column name must be unique within a table. The table name must be unique within the schema; you cannot have same name for a table and a view in a schema. The following are the types of tables available in Oracle 11*g*:

Heap table Simply known as a table, this is the most common method of storing data. These tables are permanent and can be partitioned for easy storage management. Partitioning allows the table to be broken into multiple smaller pieces for easy management and better performance. The CREATE TABLE … ORGANIZATION HEAP statement is used to create a relational table. Since ORGANIZATION HEAP is the default, it can be omitted.

Temporary table Temporary tables store private data or data that is specific to a session. This data cannot be shared with other users in the database. They're used for temporary data manipulation or for storing intermediary results. The CREATE GLOBAL TEMPORARY TABLE statement is used to create a temporary table.

Index-organized table (IOT) Index-organized tables store the data in a structured primary key sorted manner. Each IOT must have a primary key defined. These tables are similar to a relational table with a primary key, but they do not use separate storage for the table and primary key like the relational tables do. The CREATE TABLE … ORGANIZATION INDEX statement is used to create an index-organized table.

External table As the name indicates, data is stored outside the Oracle Database in flat files. External tables are read-only. No indexes are allowed on external tables. Column names defined in the Oracle Database are mapped to the columns in the external file. The default driver used to read an external table is SQL*Loader. The CREATE TABLE … ORGANIZATION EXTERNAL statement is used to create an external table.

Object table Object tables are special kind of tables that support the object-oriented features of the Oracle 11*g* database. In an object table, each row represents an object.

In the following sections, you will see how to create and manage tables.

Creating a Table

To create a table, use the CREATE TABLE statement. At a minimum, you need to list the column names and datatypes for the table. You can create a table under the username used to connect to the database, or with proper privileges you can create a table under another username. A database user can be referred to as a *schema*, or as an *owner* when the user owns objects in the database. The simplest form of creating a table is as follows:

```
CREATE TABLE ORDERS (
ORDER_NUM     NUMBER,
ORDER_DATE    DATE,
PRODUCT_CD    VARCHAR2 (10),
QUANTITY      NUMBER (10,3),
STATUS        CHAR);
```

ORDERS is the table name; the columns in the table are specified in parentheses separated by commas. The table is created under the username used to connect to the database; to create the table under another schema, you need to qualify the table with the schema name. For example, if you want to create the ORDERS table as being owned by SCOTT, create the table by using CREATE TABLE SCOTT.ORDERS (   ), you must have the CREATE ANY TABLE privilege to do so.

A column name and a datatype identify each column. For certain datatypes, you can specify a maximum width. You can specify any Oracle built-in datatype or user-defined datatype for the column definition. When specifying user-defined datatypes, the user-defined type must exist before creating the table. You can add several attributes to your table definition such as the tablespace in which you want your table stored.

If you create a table without specifying the storage parameters and tablespace, the table will be created in the default tablespace of the user, and the storage parameters used will be those of the default specified for the tablespace. It is always better to estimate the size of the table and specify appropriate storage parameters when creating the table. If the table is too large, you might need to consider partitioning or creating the table in a separate tablespace. This helps you manage the table.

What Is Partitioning?

When tables are very large, you can manage them better by using partitioning. *Partitioning* is breaking a large table into manageable pieces based on the values in a column (or multiple columns) known as the *partition key*. If you have a very large table spread across many data files and one disk fails, you have to recover the entire table. However, if the table is partitioned, you need to recover only that partition. SQL statements can access the required partition(s) rather than reading the entire table. Partitioning improves performance and makes managing tables easier. Partitioning is not part of the certification exam. To learn more about partitioning, read "Oracle 11*g* Administrators Guide" in the Oracle documentation (`http://tahiti.oracle.com`).

Oracle allocates a segment to the table when the table is created. This segment will have the number of extents specified by the storage parameter `MINEXTENTS`. Oracle allocates new extents to the table as required. Though you can have an unlimited number of extents for a segment, a little planning can improve the performance of the table. Having numerous extents affects the operations on the table, such as when the table is truncated or full table scans are performed. A larger number of extents may cause additional I/Os in the data file and therefore may affect performance.

To create the `ORDERS` table using explicit storage parameters in the `USER_DATA` tablespace, use the following:

```
CREATE TABLE JAKE.ORDERS (
ORDER_NUM     NUMBER,
ORDER_DATE    DATE,
PRODUCT_CD    VARCHAR2 (10),
QUANTITY      NUMBER (10,3),
STATUS        CHAR)
TABLESPACE USER_DATA
PCTFREE    5
PCTUSED    75
INITRANS   1
STORAGE   (INITIAL 512K   NEXT 512K   PCTINCREASE 0
           MINEXTENTS 1   MAXEXTENTS 100
           FREELISTS 1    FREELIST GROUPS 1
           BUFFER_POOL KEEP);
```

The table will be owned by `JAKE` and will be created in the `USER_DATA` tablespace (`JAKE` should have appropriate space quota privileges in the tablespace). None of the storage parameters is mandatory to create a table; Oracle assigns default values if you omit them. Let's discuss the clauses used in the table creation.

TABLESPACE specifies the location where the table should be created. If you omit the STORAGE clause or any parameters in the STORAGE clause, the default will be taken from the tablespace's default storage (if applicable). If you omit the TABLESPACE clause, the table will be created in the default tablespace of the user.

PCTFREE and PCTUSED are block storage parameters. PCTFREE specifies the amount of free space that should be reserved in each block of the table for future updates. In this example, you specify a low PCTFREE for the ORDERS table, because there are not many updates to the table that increase the row length. PCTUSED specifies when the block should be considered for inserting new rows once the PCTFREE threshold is reached. Here you specified 75, so when the used space falls to less than 75 (because of updates or deletes), new rows will be added to the block.

INITRANS specifies the number of concurrent transactions that can update each block of the table. Oracle reserves space in the block header for the INITRANS number of concurrent transactions. For each additional concurrent transaction, Oracle allocates space from the free space—which has an overhead of dynamically allocating transaction entry space. If the block is full and no space is available, the transaction waits until a transaction entry space is available.

The STORAGE clause specifies the extent sizes, free lists, and buffer pool values. The INITIAL, NEXT, MINEXTENTS, MAXEXTENTS, and PCTINCREASE parameters control the size of the extents allocated to the table. If the table is created on a locally managed uniform extent tablespace, these storage parameters are ignored.

FREELIST GROUPS specifies the number of free list groups that should be created for the table. The default and minimum value is 1. Each free list group uses one data block (that's why the minimum value for INITIAL is two database blocks) known as the *segment header*, which has information about the extents, free blocks, and high-water mark of the table.

FREELISTS specifies the number of lists for each free list group. The default and minimum value is 1. The free list manages the list of blocks that are available to add new rows. A block is removed from the free list if the free space in the block is less than PCTFREE. The block remains out of the free list as long as the used space is greater than PCTUSED. Create more free lists if the volume of inserts to the table is great. An appropriate number would be the number of concurrent transactions performing inserts to the table. Oracle recommends having FREELISTS and INITRANS be the same value. The FREELIST GROUPS parameter is mostly used for RAC configuration, where you can specify a group for each instance.

The BUFFER_POOL parameter of the STORAGE clause specifies the area of the database buffer cache to keep the blocks of the table when read from the data file while querying or for update/delete. There are three buffer pools: KEEP, RECYCLE, and DEFAULT. The default value is DEFAULT. Specify KEEP if the table is small and is frequently accessed. The blocks in the KEEP pool are always available in the SGA, so I/O will be faster. The blocks assigned to the RECYCLE buffer pool are removed from memory as soon as they are not needed. Specify RECYCLE for large tables or tables that are seldom accessed. If you do not specify KEEP or RECYCLE, the blocks are assigned to the DEFAULT pool, where they will be aged out using an LRU algorithm.

If the tablespace is created with the SEGMENT SPACE MANAGEMENT AUTO clause, the parameters PCTUSED, FREELISTS, and FREELIST GROUPS are ignored.

When a table is created, you can specify several optional clauses to improve efficiency of the table based on the purpose for which the table is created. You can specify storage parameters for the table, for its indexes, and for its LOB structures. In the following sections, you will learn how to specify storage for LOB structures and the various clauses available to specify table storage.

Storing LOB Structures

A table can contain columns of type CLOB, BLOB, or NCLOB. These internal LOB columns can have different storage settings than those of the table and can be stored in a different tablespace for easy management and performance improvement. The following example specifies storage for a LOB column when creating the table:

```
CREATE TABLE LICENSE_INFO
(DRIVER_ID   VARCHAR2 (20),
 DRIVER_NAME VARCHAR2 (30),
 DOB         DATE,
 PHOTO       BLOB)
TABLESPACE APP_DATA STORAGE (INITIAL 4M NEXT 4M PCTINCREASE 0)
LOB (PHOTO) STORE AS PHOTO_LOB
    (TABLESPACE APP_LARGE_DATA
    DISABLE STORAGE IN ROW
    STORAGE (INITIAL 128M NEXT 128M PCTINCREASE 0)
    CHUNK 4000
    PCTVERSION 20
    NOCACHE LOGGING);
```

The table LICENSE_INFO is created with a BLOB datatype column. The table is stored in the APP_DATA tablespace, and the BLOB column PHOTO is stored in the APP_LARGE_DATA tablespace. I'll now discuss the various clauses specified for the LOB storage.

The LOB segment is given the name PHOTO_LOB. If a name is not given, Oracle generates a name. You can specify multiple LOB columns in parentheses following the LOB keyword, if they all have the same storage characteristics. In such cases, you cannot specify a name for the LOB segment. For example, if the table has three LOB columns and all the LOB columns have the same characteristics, you may specify the following:

```
LOB (PHOTO, VIDEO, AUDIO) STORE AS
(TABLESPACE APP_LARGE_DATA
 CACHE READS NOLOGGING);
```

`TABLESPACE` specifies the tablespace where the LOB segment(s) should be stored. The tablespace can be locally or dictionary managed. If the LOB column is larger than 4,000 bytes, data is stored in the LOB segment. Storing data in the LOB segment is known as *out-of-line* storage. If the LOB column data is less than 4,000 bytes, it is stored *inline*, along with the other column data of the table. If the `TABLESPACE` clause is omitted, the LOB segment is created in the table's tablespace.

`DISABLE/ENABLE STORAGE IN ROW` specifies whether LOB data should be stored inline or out of line. `ENABLE` is the default and stores LOB data along with the other columns if the LOB data is smaller than 4,000 bytes. `DISABLE` stores the LOB data in the LOB segment irrespective of its size. Whether the LOB data is stored inline or out of line, the LOB locator is always stored along with the row.

`STORAGE` specifies the extent sizes and growth parameters. These parameters are the same as you would use with a table.

`CHUNK` specifies the total bytes of data that will be read or written during LOB manipulation. `CHUNK` must be a multiple of the database block size. If you specify a value other than a multiple of the block size, Oracle uses the next higher value that is a multiple of the block size. For example, if you specify 4000 for `CHUNK` and the database block size is 2048, Oracle will take the value of 4096. The default value for `CHUNK` is the database block size, and the maximum value is 32KB. The `INITIAL` and `NEXT` values specified in the `STORAGE` clause must be higher than the value for `CHUNK`.

`PCTVERSION` specifies the percentage of all used LOB data space that can be occupied by old versions of LOB data pages. Since LOB data changes are not written to the rollback segments, `PCTVERSION` specifies the percentage of old information that should be kept in the LOB segment for consistent reads. The default is 10 and can range from 0 through 100.

`CACHE/NOCACHE/CACHE READS` specifies whether to cache the LOB reads. If the LOB is read and updated frequently, use the `CACHE` clause. `NOCACHE` is the default, and it is useful for a LOB that is read infrequently and never updated. `CACHE READS` caches only the read operation. This is useful for a LOB that is read frequently but never updated.

`LOGGING / NOLOGGING` specifies whether redo information should be generated for LOB data. `NOLOGGING` does not write redo and is useful for faster data loads. You cannot specify `CACHE` and `NOLOGGING` together.

Using Other Create Clauses

The other clauses you can specify while creating a table (which may appear on the certification exam) are listed here. These clauses help you manage various types of operations on the table.

`LOGGING/NOLOGGING` `LOGGING` is the default for the table and tablespace, but if the tablespace is defined as `NOLOGGING`, then the table uses `NOLOGGING`. `LOGGING` specifies that table creation and direct-load inserts should be logged to the redo log files. Creating the table by using a subquery and the `NOLOGGING` clause can improve the table creation time dramatically for large tables. If the table creation, initial data population (using a subquery), and direct-load inserts are not logged to the redo log files when using the NOLOGGING clause, you must back up the table (or better yet, the entire tablespace) after such operations are performed. Media recovery will not create or load tables created with the NOLOGGING attribute. You can also specify a separate LOGGING or NOLOGGING attribute for indexes and LOB storage of the table, independent of the table's attribute. The following example creates a table with the NOLOGGING clause:

```
CREATE TABLE MY_ORDERS (    )
TABLESPACE USER_DATA STORAGE (    )
NOLOGGING;
```

PARALLEL/NOPARALLEL NOPARALLEL is the default. PARALLEL causes the table creation (if created using a subquery) and the DML statements on the table to execute in parallel. Normally, a single-server process performs operations on tables in a transaction (serial operation). When the PARALLEL attribute is set, Oracle uses multiple processes to complete the operation for a full-table scan. You can specify a degree for the parallelism; if not specified, Oracle calculates the optimum degree of parallelism. The parameter PARALLEL_THREADS_PER_CPU determines the number for parallel degree per CPU; usually the default is 2. If you do not specify the degree, Oracle calculates the degree based on this parameter and the number of CPUs available. The following example creates a table by using a subquery. The table creation will not be logged in the redo log file, and multiple processes will query the JAKE.ORDERS table and create the MY_ORDERS table.

```
CREATE TABLE MY_ORDERS (    )
TABLESPACE USER_DATA STORAGE (    )
NOLOGGING PARALLEL
AS SELECT * FROM JAKE.ORDERS;
```

CACHE/NOCACHE NOCACHE is the default. For small lookup tables that are frequently accessed, you can specify the CACHE clause to have the blocks retrieved using a full table scan placed at the MRU end of the LRU list in the buffer cache; the blocks are not aged out of the buffer cache immediately. The default behavior (NOCACHE) is to place the blocks from a full-table scan at the tail end of the LRU list, where they are moved out of the list as soon as a different process or query needs these blocks for storing another table's blocks in the cache.

Creating a Table Using a Subquery

You can create a table using existing tables or views by specifying a subquery instead of defining the columns. The subquery can refer to more than one table or view. The table will be created with the rows returned from the subquery. You can specify new column names for the table, but Oracle derives the datatype and maximum width based on the query result—you cannot specify the datatype with this method. You can specify the storage parameters for the tables created by using the subquery.

For example, let's create a new table from the ORDERS table for the orders that are accepted. Notice that the new column names are specified.

```
CREATE TABLE ACCEPTED_ORDERS
  (ORD_NUMBER, ORD_DATE, PRODUCT_CD, QTY)
  TABLESPACE USERS
  PCTFREE 0
  STORAGE (INITIAL 128K NEXT 128K PCTINCREASE 0)
AS
  SELECT ORDER_NUM, ORDER_DATE, PRODUCT_CD, QUANTITY
  FROM   ORDERS
  WHERE  STATUS = 'A';
```

The CREATE TABLE…AS SELECT… will not work if the query refers to columns of the LONG datatype. When you create a table using the subquery, only the NOT NULL constraints associated with the columns are copied to the new table. Other constraints and column default definitions are not copied.

Creating a Temporary Table

Temporary tables hold information that is available only to the session that created the data. The definition of the temporary table is available to all sessions. A temporary table is created using the CREATE GLOBAL TEMPORARY TABLE statement. The data in the table can be session specific or transaction specific. The ON COMMIT clause specifies this. The following statement creates a temporary table that is transaction specific:

```
CREATE GLOBAL TEMPORARY TABLE INVALID_ORDERS
(ORDER#   NUMBER (8),
 ORDER_DT DATE,
 VALUE    NUMBER (12,2))
ON COMMIT DELETE ROWS
TABLESPACE TEMP_TABLES;
```

Oracle deletes rows or truncates the table after each commit. To define the table as session specific, use the ON COMMIT PRESERVE ROWS clause.

Storage for temporary tablespace is allocated in the temporary tablespace of the user if the TABLESPACE clause is omitted. Segments are created only when the first insert statement is performed on the table. The temporary segments allocated to temporary tables are deallocated at the end of the transaction for transaction-specific tables and at the end of session for session-specific tables.

You can create indexes on temporary tables. DML statements on temporary tables do not generate redo information, but undo information is generated. Programs can manipulate data in temporary tables or join them to permanent tables in the same manner as any other table.

Refer to Chapter 6 to learn about setting default values, modifying tables, renaming tables, and dropping tables.

Reorganizing Tables

You can use the MOVE clause of the ALTER TABLE command on a nonpartitioned table to reorganize or to move from one tablespace to another. The table is reorganized to reduce the number of extents by specifying larger extent sizes or to prevent row migration. When you move a table, Oracle creates a new segment for the table, copies the data, and drops the old segment. The new segment can be in the same tablespace or in a different tablespace. Since the old segment is dropped only after creating the new segment, you need to make sure you have sufficient space in the tablespace if you're not changing to a different tablespace. The MOVE clause can specify a new tablespace, new storage parameters for the table, new free-space management parameters, and new transaction-entry parameters. You can use the NOLOGGING clause to speed up the reorganization by not writing the changes to the redo log file.

The following example moves the ORDERS table to another tablespace named NEW_DATA. New storage parameters are specified, and the operation is not logged in the redo log files (NOLOGGING).

```
ALTER TABLE ORDERS MOVE
TABLESPACE NEW_DATA
STORAGE (INITIAL 50M NEXT 5M PCTINCREASE 0)
PCTFREE 0 PCTUSED 50
INITRANS 2 NOLOGGING;
```

Queries are allowed on the table while the move operation is in progress, but no insert, update, or delete operations are allowed. The granted permissions on the table are retained.

The DROP TABLE statement can include the PURGE clause, which will not place the table in the Recycle Bin.

Truncating a Table

The TRUNCATE statement is similar to the DROP statement, but it does not remove the structure of the table, so none of the indexes, constraints, triggers, and privileges on the table are dropped. By default, the space allocated to the table and indexes is freed. If you do not want to free up the space, include the REUSE STORAGE clause. You cannot roll back a truncate operation. Also, you cannot selectively delete rows using the TRUNCATE statement. The syntax of TRUNCATE statement is as follows:

```
TRUNCATE {TABLE|CLUSTER} [<schema>.]<name>
[{DROP|REUSE} STORAGE]
```

You cannot truncate the parent table of an enabled referential integrity constraint. You must first disable the constraint and then truncate the table, even if the child table has no rows. The following example demonstrates this:

```
SQL> CREATE TABLE t1 (
 2   t1f1 NUMBER CONSTRAINT pk_t1 PRIMARY KEY);
```

```
Table created.

SQL> CREATE TABLE t2 (t2f1 NUMBER CONSTRAINT fk_t2
                          REFERENCES t1 (t1f1));
Table created.

SQL> TRUNCATE TABLE t1;
truncate table t1
               *
ERROR at line 1:
ORA-02266: unique/primary keys in table referenced by enabled foreign keys

SQL> ALTER TABLE t2 DISABLE CONSTRAINT fk_t2;
Table altered.

SQL> TRUNCATE TABLE t1;
Table truncated.

SQL>
```

Use the TRUNCATE statement to delete all rows from a large table; it does not write the undo entries and is much faster than the DELETE statement when deleting large number of rows.

Using Namespaces

When you refer an object in the SQL statement, Oracle locates the object in the appropriate namespace. A table can have the same name as an index or a constraint. The namespace is simply the domain of allowable names for the set of schema objects that it serves. The following are the namespaces available in Oracle 11*g*:

- Tables, views, private synonyms
- Constraints
- Indexes
- Clusters
- Database triggers
- Private database links
- Dimensions
- Roles
- Public synonyms

- Public database links
- Tablespaces
- Profiles

For example, if you have a view named BOOKS, you cannot name a table BOOKS (tables and views share a namespace), although you can create an index named BOOKS (indexes and tables have separate namespaces) and a constraint named BOOKS (constraints and tables have separate namespaces).

Working with Constraints

Constraints enforce business rules in the database. In other words, they limit the acceptable data values for a table. Constraints are optional schema objects that depend on tables. Although you can have a table without any constraints, you cannot create a constraint without a table.

Oracle lets you create several types of constraints on your tables to enforce your business rules, including the following:

- NOT NULL
- CHECK
- UNIQUE
- PRIMARY KEY
- FOREIGN KEY

You can create constraints together with the table in the CREATE TABLE statement. After you create a table, you add or remove a constraint from a table with an ALTER TABLE statement. You specify the constraint information with either the inline syntax as a column attribute or the out-of-line syntax as part of the table definition. Constraints do not require a name; if you do not name the constraint, Oracle generates one for you. However, the generated names are simply numbers prefixed with SYS_C and may not be very meaningful.

In the following sections, I will discuss the rules for each constraint type and show examples of creating constraints.

NOT NULL

NOT NULL constraints have the following characteristics:

- The constraint is defined at the column level.
- Use CREATE TABLE to define constraints when creating the table. The following example shows a named constraint on the ORDER_NUM column; for ORDER_DATE, Oracle generates a name:

```
CREATE TABLE ORDERS (
 ORDER_NUM   NUMBER (4) CONSTRAINT NN_ORDER_NUM NOT NULL,
```

```
 ORDER_DATE  DATE NOT NULL,
 PRODUCT_ID)
```

- Use ALTER TABLE MODIFY to add or remove a NOT NULL constraint on the columns of an existing table. The following code shows examples of removing a constraint and adding a constraint:

```
ALTER TABLE ORDERS MODIFY ORDER_DATE NULL;
ALTER TABLE ORDERS MODIFY PRODUCT_ID NOT NULL;
```

CHECK

CHECK constraints have the following characteristics:

- The constraint can be defined at the column level or the table level.
- The condition specified in the CHECK clause should evaluate to a Boolean result and can refer to values in other columns of the same row; the condition cannot use queries.
- Environmental functions such as SYSDATE, USER, USERENV, UID, and pseudocolumns such as ROWNUM, CURRVAL, NEXTVAL, and LEVEL cannot be used to evaluate the check condition.
- One column can have more than one CHECK constraint defined. The column can have a NULL value.
- The constraint can be created using CREATE TABLE or ALTER TABLE:

```
CREATE TABLE BONUS (
 EMP_ID    VARCHAR2 (40) NOT NULL,
 SALARY    NUMBER (9,2),
 BONUS     NUMBER (9,2),
CONSTRAINT CK_BONUS CHECK (BONUS > 0));

ALTER TABLE BONUS
ADD CONSTRAINT CK_BONUS2 CHECK (BONUS < SALARY);
```

UNIQUE

UNIQUE constraints have the following characteristics:

- The constraint can be defined at the column level for single-column unique keys. For a multiple-column unique key (for a composite key, the maximum number of columns specified can be 32), the constraint should be defined at the table level.
- Oracle creates a unique index on the unique key columns to enforce uniqueness. If a unique index or nonunique index already exists on the table with the same columns in the index, Oracle uses the existing index. To use the existing nonunique index, there must not be any duplicate keys in the table.
- Unique constraints allow NULL values in the constraint columns.

- Storage can be specified for the implicit index created when creating the key. If no storage is specified, the index is created on the default tablespace with the default storage parameters of the tablespace. You can specify the LOGGING and NOSORT clauses, as you would when creating an index. The index created can be a local or global partitioned index. The index will have the same name as the unique constraint. The following are two examples. The first one defines a unique constraint with two columns and specifies the storage parameters for the index. The second example adds a new column to the EMP table and creates a unique key at the column level.

```
ALTER TABLE BONUS
ADD CONSTRAINT UQ_EMP_ID UNIQUE (DEPT, EMP_ID)
USING INDEX TABLESPACE INDX
STORAGE (INITIAL 32K NEXT 32K PCTINCREASE 0);

ALTER TABLE EMP ADD
SSN VARCHAR2 (11) CONSTRAINT UQ_SSN UNIQUE;
```

PRIMARY KEY

PRIMARY KEY constraints have the following characteristics:

- All characteristics of the UNIQUE key are applicable except that NULL values are not allowed in the primary key columns.
- A table can have only one primary key.
- Oracle creates a unique index and NOT NULL constraints for each column in the key. Oracle can use an existing index if all the columns of the primary key are in the index. The following example defines a primary key when creating the table. Storage parameters are specified for both the table and the primary key index.

```
CREATE TABLE EMPLOYEE (
 DEPT_NO VARCHAR2 (2),
 EMP_ID  NUMBER (4),
 NAME    VARCHAR2 (20) NOT NULL,
 SSN     VARCHAR2 (11),
 SALARY  NUMBER (9,2) CHECK (SALARY > 0),
CONSTRAINT PK_EMPLOYEE PRIMARY KEY (DEPT_NO, EMP_ID)
 USING INDEX TABLESPACE INDX
 STORAGE (INITIAL 64K NEXT 64K)
 NOLOGGING,
CONSTRAINT UQ_SSN UNIQUE (SSN)
 USING INDEX TABLESPACE INDX)
TABLESPACE USERS
STORAGE (INITIAL 128K NEXT 64K);
```

- Indexes created to enforce unique keys and primary keys can be managed as any other index. However, these indexes cannot be dropped explicitly.

FOREIGN KEY

The foreign key is the column or columns in the table (child table) where the constraint is created; the referenced key is the primary key or unique key column or columns in the table (parent table) that is referenced by the constraint. The following rules are applicable to foreign key constraints:

- A foreign key constraint can be defined at the column level or the table level. Multiple-column foreign keys should be defined at the table level.
- The foreign key column(s) and referenced key column(s) can be in the same table (self-referential integrity constraint).
- NULL values are allowed in the foreign key columns. The following is an example of creating a foreign key constraint on the COUNTRY_CODE and STATE_CODE columns of the CITY table, which refers to the COUNTRY_CODE and STATE_CODE columns of the STATE table (the composite primary key of the STATE table).

```
ALTER TABLE CITY ADD CONSTRAINT FK_STATE
 FOREIGN KEY (COUNTRY_CODE, STATE_CODE)
 REFERENCES STATE (COUNTRY_CODE, STATE_CODE);
```

- The ON DELETE clause specifies the action to be taken when a row in the parent table is deleted and child rows exist with the deleted parent primary key. You can delete the child rows (CASCADE) or set the foreign key column values to NULL (SET NULL). If you omit this clause, Oracle will not allow you to delete from the parent table if child records exist. You must delete the child rows first and then the parent row. The following are two examples of specifying the delete action in a foreign key:

```
ALTER TABLE CITY ADD CONSTRAINT FK_STATE
 FOREIGN KEY (COUNTRY_CODE, STATE_CODE)
 REFERENCES STATE (COUNTRY_CODE, STATE_CODE)
 ON DELETE CASCADE;

ALTER TABLE CITY ADD CONSTRAINT FK_STATE
 FOREIGN KEY (COUNTRY_CODE, STATE_CODE)
 REFERENCES STATE (COUNTRY_CODE, STATE_CODE)
 ON DELETE SET NULL;
```

Refer to Chapter 6 to learn more about constraints.

Deferred Constraint Checking

By default, Oracle checks whether the data conforms to the constraint when the statement is executed. Oracle allows you to change this behavior if the constraint is created using the DEFERRABLE clause (NOT DEFERRABLE is the default). It specifies that the transaction can set the constraint-checking behavior. INITIALLY IMMEDIATE specifies that the constraint should be checked for conformance at the end of each SQL statement (this is the default). INITIALLY DEFERRED specifies that the constraint should be checked for conformance at the end of the transaction. The DEFERRABLE status of a constraint cannot be changed using ALTER TABLE MODIFY CONSTRAINT; you must drop and re-create the constraint, and you can change the INITIALLY [DEFERRED/IMMEDIATE] clause using ALTER TABLE.

If the constraint is DEFERRABLE, you can set the behavior by using the SET CONSTRAINTS command or by using the ALTER SESSION SET CONSTRAINT command. You can enable or disable deferred constraint checking by listing all the constraints or by specifying the ALL keyword. The SET CONSTRAINTS command is used to set the constraint-checking behavior for the current transaction, and the ALTER SESSION command is used to set the constraint-checking behavior for the current session.

For example, if you hire a new employee and create a new department for that person to manage, you need to add a row to both the EMPLOYEES table (which references the new department) and the DEPARTMENTS table (which references the new employee). Although this temporary violation will not go against the intent of the business rule, you will need to create the constraints with some additional options, like this:

```
ALTER TABLE employees
   ADD CONSTRAINT emp_dept_fk FOREIGN KEY (dept_nbr)
     REFERENCES departments(dept_nbr) ON DELETE CASCADE
     DEFERRABLE;

ALTER TABLE departments ADD CONSTRAINT
   dept_mgr_fk FOREIGN KEY (manager_id) REFERENCES
     employees(employee_id) ON DELETE SET NULL
     DEFERRABLE INITIALLY DEFERRED;
```

By default, the database checks that a FOREIGN KEY constraint is satisfied at the end of each statement. You define this behavior with the keywords INITIALLY IMMEDIATE. Also, by default, the database will not allow programs to defer constraint checking to the end of the transaction. You define this behavior with the keywords NOT DEFERRABLE.

When you create a constraint, you can tell the database to allow either immediate or deferred constraint checking by specifying the keyword DEFERRABLE. If you normally want a DEFERRABLE constraint to be deferred, create it with the INITIALLY DEFERRED option. Only DEFERRABLE constraints can be set to INITIALLY DEFERRED. Once you create a constraint, you cannot change its deferability (for example, from NOT DEFERRABLE to DEFERABLE); instead, you must drop and re-create the constraint with the new specification.

Working with Indexes

Indexes are optional data structures built on tables. Indexes can improve data retrieval performance by providing a direct access method instead of the default full-table scan retrieval method. You can build B-tree or bitmap indexes on one or more columns in a table. An *index key* is defined as one data value stored in the index. A B-tree index sorts the keys into a binary tree and stores these keys together with the table's ROWIDs. In a bitmap index, a bitmap is created for each key. There is a bit in each bitmap for every ROWID in the table, forming the equivalent of a two-dimensional matrix. The bits are set if the corresponding row in the bitmap exists.

B-tree indexes are the default index type and are appropriate for medium- to high-cardinality columns (*high cardinality* means those having many distinct values). B-tree indexes support row-level locking and so are appropriate for multiuser, transactional applications. The indexes supporting PRIMARY KEY and UNIQUE constraints are B-tree indexes. The following are the types of B-tree indexes you can create:

Nonunique index This is the default; the index column values are not unique.

Unique index This is created by specifying the UNIQUE keyword: each column value entry of the index is unique. For composite indexes, Oracle guarantees that the combination of all index column values in the composite index is unique. Oracle returns an error if you try to insert two rows with the same index column values.

Reverse key index The reverse key index is created by specifying the REVERSE keyword. The bytes of each column indexed are reversed, while keeping the column order. For example, if column ORDER_NUM has value 54321, Oracle reverses the bytes to 12345 and then adds it to the index. This type of indexing can be used for unique indexes when inserts to the table are always in the ascending order of the indexed columns. This helps distribute the adjacent valued columns to different leaf blocks of the index and as a result improves performance by retrieving fewer index blocks. *Leaf blocks* are the blocks at the lowest level of the B-tree.

Function-based index The function-based index can be created on columns with expressions. For example, creating an index on the SUBSTR(EMPID, 1,2) can speed up the queries using SUBSTR(EMPID, 1, 2) in the WHERE clause.

Bitmap indexes, on the other hand, are best for multiple combinations of low- to medium-cardinality columns (you cannot create a unique bitmap index), and they do not support row-level locking. Bitmap indexes are best in environments in which changes to data are limited and controlled, such as many data warehousing applications. Because bitmap indexes cannot efficiently make changes to the indexed data, they are often dropped prior to data loading and then re-created after a data load.

Oracle does not include the rows with NULL values in the index columns when storing the index.

Refer to Chapter 7 to learn more about creating and modifying indexes.

Specifying Storage

If you do not specify the TABLESPACE clause in the CREATE INDEX statement, Oracle creates the index in the default tablespace of the user. If the STORAGE clause is not specified, Oracle inherits the default storage parameters defined for the tablespace. All the storage parameters discussed in the "Creating a Table" section are applicable to indexes and have the same meaning except for PCTUSED. The PCTUSED parameter cannot be specified for indexes. Keep the INITRANS parameter for the index more than the INITRANS specified for the corresponding table, because the index blocks can hold a larger number of rows than a table.

Here is an example of creating an index and specifying the storage:

```
CREATE UNIQUE INDEX IND2_ORDERS
ON ORDERS (ORDER_NUM)
TABLESPACE USER_INDEX
PCTFREE    25
INITRANS   2
MAXTRANS   255
STORAGE   (INITIAL 128K   NEXT 128K   PCTINCREASE 0
           MINEXTENTS 1   MAXEXTENTS 100
           FREELISTS 1    FREELIST GROUPS 1
           BUFFER_POOL KEEP);
```

When creating indexes for a table with rows, Oracle writes the data blocks with index values up to PCTFREE. The free space reserved by specifying PCTFREE is used when inserting into the table a new row (or updating a row that changes the corresponding index key column value) that needs to be placed between two index key values of the leaf node. If no free space is available in the block, Oracle uses a new block. If many new rows are inserted into the table, keep the PCTFREE parameter of the index high.

Using Other Create Clauses

You can specify NOLOGGING to make the index creation faster and therefore not write information to the redo log files. The default is LOGGING.

It is possible to collect statistics about the index while creating the index by specifying the COMPUTE STATISTICS clause. This avoids another ANALYZE on the index later.

The ONLINE clause specifies that the table will be available for DML operations when the index is built.

If data is loaded to the table in the order of an index, you can specify the NOSORT clause. Oracle does not sort the rows, but if the data is not sorted, Oracle returns an error. Specifying this clause saves time and temporary space.

For multicolumn indexes, eliminating the repeating key columns can save storage space. Specify the COMPRESS clause when creating the index. NOCOMPRESS is the default. This clause can be used only with nonpartitioned indexes. Index performance may be affected when using this clause.

Specify PARALLEL to create the index using multiple server processes. NOPARALLEL is the default.

The following is an example of creating an index by specifying some of the miscellaneous clauses:

```
SQL> CREATE INDEX IND5_ORDERS ON ORDERS
  2  (ORDER_NUM, ORDER_DATE)
  3  TABLESPACE INDX
```

```
NOLOGGING
NOSORT
COMPRESS
SORT
COMPUTE STATISTICS;

Index created.

SQL>
```

Reverse Key Indexes

Specifying the REVERSE keyword creates a reverse key index. Reverse key indexes improve performance of certain OLTP applications using the parallel server. The following example creates a reverse key index on the ORDER_NUM and ORDER_DATE columns of the ORDERS table:

```
CREATE UNIQUE INDEX IND2_ORDERS
ON ORDERS (ORDER_DATE, ORDER_NUM)
TABLESPACE USER_INDEX
REVERSE;
```

Function-Based Indexes

Function-based indexes are created as regular B-tree or bitmap indexes. Specify the expression or function when creating the index. Oracle precalculates the value of the expression and creates the index. For example, this creates a function based on

```
SUBSTR(PRODUCT_ID,1,2):
CREATE INDEX IND4_ORDERS
ON ORDERS (SUBSTR(PRODUCT_ID,1,2))
TABLESPACE USER_INDEX;
```

To use the function-based index, you must set the instance initialization parameter QUERY_REWRITE_ENABLED to TRUE and QUERY_REWRITE_INTEGRITY to TRUSTED. Also, the COMPATIBLE parameter should be set to 8.1.0 or higher. A query can use this index if its WHERE clause specifies a condition by using SUBSTR(PRODUCT_ID,1,2), as in the following example:

```
SELECT * FROM ORDERS
WHERE SUBSTR(PRODUCT_ID,1,2) = 'BT';
```

Index-Organized Tables

You can store index and table data together in a structure known as an *index-organized table*. IOTs are suitable for tables in which the data access is mostly through its primary key, such as lookup tables, where you have a code and a description. An IOT is a B-tree index, and instead of storing the ROWID of the table where the row belongs, the entire row is stored as part of the index. You can build additional indexes on the columns of an IOT. The data in an IOT is accessed the same way you would access the data in a table.

Since the row is stored along with the B-tree index, there is no physical `ROWID` for each row. The primary key identifies the rows in an IOT. Oracle "guesses" the location of the row and assigns a logical `ROWID` for each row, which permits the creation of secondary indexes. You can partition an IOT, but the partition columns should be a subset of the primary key columns.

To build additional indexes on the IOT, Oracle uses a logical `ROWID`, which is derived from the primary key values of the IOT. The logical `ROWID` can include a guessed physical location of the row in the data files. This guessed location is not valid when a row is moved from one block to another. If the logical `ROWID` does not include the guessed location of the `ROWID`, Oracle has to perform two index scans when using the secondary index. The logical `ROWIDs` can be stored in columns with the datatype `UROWID`.

An index-organized table is created using the `CREATE TABLE` command with the `ORGANIZATION INDEX` keyword. You must specify the primary key for the table when creating the table.

```
SQL> CREATE TABLE IOT_EXAMPLE (
     PK_COL1    NUMBER (4),
     PK_COL2    VARCHAR2 (10),
     NON_PK_COL1 VARCHAR2 (40),
     NON_PK_COL2 DATE,
     CONSTRAINT PK_IOT PRIMARY KEY
            (PK_COL1, PK_COL2))
     ORGANIZATION INDEX
     TABLESPACE INDX
     STORAGE (INITIAL 32K NEXT 32K PCTINCREASE 0);

Table created.

SQL>
```

 **Real World Scenario**

Creating Tables, Indexes, and Constraints for a Customer-Maintenance Application

Let's consider an example of creating tables that are needed to manage a customer database. The objective of this example is to give you the various options available when defining tables, indexes, and constraints. The DBA is given the physical structure of the tables and the relationship between tables by the development team:

- The DBA reviews the columns of the CUSTOMER_MASTER table and the type of data stored. CUST_ID is the unique identifier of the table, the primary key. This table contains the customer name, email address, date of birth, primary contact address type, and status flag.

- The CUSTOMER_ADDRESS table keeps the addresses of the customer. The customer can have up to four different addresses: business1, business2, home1, and home2.
- The CUSTOMER_REFERENCES table keeps information about the new customers introduced by a customer. This table simply keeps the customer ID of the referring and new customers.
- Each table has a record creation date, created username, update date, and update username.

The DBA decided to keep the tables and indexes in separate tablespaces and is using the uniform-extent feature of the tablespace. This helps manage the space on the tablespace more effectively. Data is kept in the CUST_DATA tablespace, and indexes are maintained in the CUST_INDX tablespace. Let's create the tablespaces:

```
CREATE TABLESPACE CUST_DATA DATAFILE
'C:\ORACLE\ORADATA\CUST_DATA01.DBF' SIZE 512K
AUTOEXTEND ON NEXT 128K MAXSIZE 2000K
EXTENT MANAGEMENT LOCAL UNIFORM SIZE 256K
SEGMENT SPACE MANAGEMENT AUTO;
CREATE TABLESPACE CUST_INDX DATAFILE
'C:\ORACLE\ORADATA\CUST_INDX.DBF' SIZE 256K
AUTOEXTEND ON NEXT 128K MAXSIZE 2000K
EXTENT MANAGEMENT LOCAL UNIFORM SIZE 128K
SEGMENT SPACE MANAGEMENT AUTO;
```

Now create the CUSTOMER_MASTER table. The table needs to have the primary key CUST_ID and the unique key EMAIL. A nonunique index is created on the EMAIL column and is used for the UNIQUE key enforcement. The DBA also wants to create an index on the DOB column because the firm sends out birthday greetings to all its customers every week. The check constraint on the ADD_TYPE makes sure no other values get inserted into the column.

```
CREATE TABLE CUSTOMER_MASTER (
CUST_ID       VARCHAR2 (10),
CUST_NAME     VARCHAR2 (30),
EMAIL         VARCHAR2 (30),
DOB           DATE,
ADD_TYPE      CHAR (2) CONSTRAINT CK_ADD_TYPE
              CHECK (ADD_TYPE IN ('B1','B2','H1','H2')),
CRE_USER      VARCHAR2 (5) DEFAULT USER,
CRE_TIME      TIMESTAMP (3) DEFAULT SYSTIMESTAMP,
MOD_USER      VARCHAR2 (5),
MOD_TIME      TIMESTAMP (3),
CONSTRAINT PK_CUSTOMER_MASTER PRIMARY KEY (CUST_ID)
  USING INDEX TABLESPACE CUST_INDX)
```

```
TABLESPACE CUST_DATA;
CREATE INDEX CUST_EMAIL ON CUSTOMER_MASTER (EMAIL)
TABLESPACE CUST_INDX;
ALTER TABLE CUSTOMER_MASTER ADD CONSTRAINT UQ_CUST_EMAIL
UNIQUE (EMAIL) USING INDEX CUST_EMAIL;
```

Create the CUSTOMER_ADDRESSES table. Let's create the table first and then add the primary key and foreign key. The foreign key is created with an option to defer its checking until commit time.

```
CREATE TABLE CUSTOMER_ADDRESSES (
CUST_ID     VARCHAR2 (10),
ADD_TYPE    CHAR (2),
ADD_LINE1   VARCHAR2 (40) NOT NULL,
ADD_LINE2   VARCHAR2 (40),
CITY        VARCHAR2 (40) NOT NULL,
STATE       VARCHAR2 (2) NOT NULL,
ZIP         NUMBER (5) NOT NULL)
TABLESPACE CUST_DATA;
ALTER TABLE CUSTOMER_ADDRESSES ADD CONSTRAINT
PK_CUST_ADDRESSES PRIMARY KEY (CUST_ID, ADD_TYPE)
USING INDEX TABLESPACE CUST_INDX;
ALTER TABLE CUSTOMER_ADDRESSES ADD CONSTRAINT
FK_CUST_ADDRESSES FOREIGN KEY (CUST_ID)
REFERENCES CUSTOMER_MASTER;
ALTER TABLE CUSTOMER_ADDRESSES ADD CONSTRAINT
CK_ADD_TYPE2 CHECK (ADD_TYPE IN ('B1','B2','H1','H2'));
```

The DBA forgot to enable the constraint DEFERRABLE clause and to delete records from the CUSTOMER_ADDRESSES table when the row was deleted from the CUSTOMER_MASTER table.

```
ALTER TABLE CUSTOMER_ADDRESSES
DROP CONSTRAINT FK_CUST_ADDRESSES;
ALTER TABLE CUSTOMER_ADDRESSES ADD CONSTRAINT
FK_CUST_ADDRESSES FOREIGN KEY (CUST_ID)
REFERENCES CUSTOMER_MASTER
ON DELETE CASCADE DEFERRABLE INITIALLY IMMEDIATE;
```

Create the CUSTOMER_REFERENCES table. Since this table row never grows with updates, the DBA sets the PCTFREE parameter of the table to 0.

```
CREATE TABLE CUSTOMER_REFERENCES (
CUST_ID       VARCHAR2 (10) REFERENCES CUSTOMER_MASTER,
CUST_REF_ID   VARCHAR2 (10) REFERENCES CUSTOMER_MASTER,
```

```
CRE_USER      VARCHAR2 (5),
CRE_TIME      TIMESTAMP (3) DEFAULT SYSTIMESTAMP,
MOD_USER      VARCHAR2 (5) DEFAULT USER,
MOD_TIME      TIMESTAMP (3),
CONSTRAINT PK_CUST_REFS PRIMARY KEY (CUST_ID, CUST_REF_ID))
TABLESPACE CUST_DATA
PCTFREE 0;
```

By reviewing the creating, the DBA found that the CUSTOMER_ADDRESSES table does not have the created and modified user information and the CUSTOMER_REFERENCES table has a DEFAULT value assigned to the wrong column. Let's fix these problems:

```
ALTER TABLE CUSTOMER_ADDRESSES ADD (
CRE_USER      VARCHAR2 (5) DEFAULT USER,
CRE_TIME      TIMESTAMP (3) DEFAULT SYSTIMESTAMP,
MOD_USER      VARCHAR2 (5),
MOD_TIME      TIMESTAMP (3));
ALTER TABLE CUSTOMER_REFERENCES MODIFY
MOD_USER DEFAULT NULL;
ALTER TABLE CUSTOMER_REFERENCES MODIFY
CRE_USER DEFAULT USER;
```

Also, the primary key for the CUSTOMER_REFERENCES table did not specify a tablespace for the primary key index, so it got created in the default tablespace of the table.

```
SQL> SELECT TABLESPACE_NAME FROM DBA_INDEXES WHERE
  2  INDEX_NAME = 'PK_CUST_REFS';
TABLESPACE_NAME
------------------------------
CUST_DATA
SQL> ALTER INDEX PK_CUST_REFS REBUILD TABLESPACE CUST_INDX;
Index altered.
SQL> SELECT TABLESPACE_NAME FROM DBA_INDEXES WHERE
  2  INDEX_NAME = 'PK_CUST_REFS';
TABLESPACE_NAME
------------------------------
CUST_INDX
SQL>
```

Query the dictionary views to see the table information:

```
SQL> SELECT TABLE_NAME, TABLESPACE_NAME
  2  FROM   USER_TABLES
  3  WHERE  TABLE_NAME LIKE 'CUST%';
```

```
TABLE_NAME                     TABLESPACE_NAME
------------------------------ ------------------------
CUSTOMER_ADDRESSES             CUST_DATA
CUSTOMER_MASTER                CUST_DATA
CUSTOMER_REFERENCES            CUST_DATA
SQL> SELECT SEGMENT_NAME, SEGMENT_TYPE, TABLESPACE_NAME, BYTES
  2  FROM   DBA_SEGMENTS
  3  WHERE  OWNER = 'CM'
  4  AND    SEGMENT_NAME LIKE '%CUST%';
SEGMENT_NAME         SEGMENT_TYPE       TABLESPACE      BYTES
-------------------- ------------------ ---------- ----------
CUSTOMER_MASTER      TABLE              CUST_DATA       65536
CUSTOMER_ADDRESSES   TABLE              CUST_DATA       65536
CUSTOMER_REFERENCES  TABLE              CUST_DATA       65536
PK_CUSTOMER_MASTER   INDEX              CUST_INDX       32768
CUST_EMAIL           INDEX              CUST_INDX       32768
PK_CUST_ADDRESSES    INDEX              CUST_INDX       32768
PK_CUST_REFS         INDEX              CUST_INDX       65536
7 rows selected.
SQL>
SQL> SELECT INDEX_NAME, COLUMN_NAME, COLUMN_POSITION
  2  FROM   USER_IND_COLUMNS
  3  WHERE  INDEX_NAME LIKE '%CUST%'
  4  ORDER BY 1,3;
INDEX_NAME           COLUMN_NAME          COLUMN_POSITION
-------------------- -------------------- ---------------
CUST_EMAIL           EMAIL                              1
PK_CUSTOMER_MASTER   CUST_ID                            1
PK_CUST_ADDRESSES    CUST_ID                            1
PK_CUST_ADDRESSES    ADD_TYPE                           2
PK_CUST_REFS         CUST_ID                            1
PK_CUST_REFS         CUST_REF_ID                        2
6 rows selected.
SQL>
```

Query the dictionary views to see the constraint information. Notice that the two foreign key constraints on the CUSTOMER_REFERENCES table and the NOT NULL constraints in the CUSTOMER_ADDRESSES table have system-generated names.

```
SQL> SELECT CONSTRAINT_NAME, CONSTRAINT_TYPE, TABLE_NAME,
  2         R_CONSTRAINT_NAME
```

```
  3  FROM    USER_CONSTRAINTS
  4  WHERE   TABLE_NAME LIKE 'CUST%';
CONSTRAINT_NAME      C TABLE_NAME           R_CONSTRAINT_NAME
-------------------- - -------------------- --------------------
SYS_C002792          C CUSTOMER_ADDRESSES
SYS_C002793          C CUSTOMER_ADDRESSES
SYS_C002794          C CUSTOMER_ADDRESSES
SYS_C002795          C CUSTOMER_ADDRESSES
PK_CUST_ADDRESSES    P CUSTOMER_ADDRESSES
FK_CUST_ADDRESSES    R CUSTOMER_ADDRESSES   PK_CUSTOMER_MASTER
CK_ADD_TYPE2         C CUSTOMER_ADDRESSES
CK_ADD_TYPE          C CUSTOMER_MASTER
PK_CUSTOMER_MASTER   P CUSTOMER_MASTER
UQ_CUST_EMAIL        U CUSTOMER_MASTER
PK_CUST_REFS         P CUSTOMER_REFERENCES
SYS_C002804          R CUSTOMER_REFERENCES  PK_CUSTOMER_MASTER
SYS_C002805          R CUSTOMER_REFERENCES  PK_CUSTOMER_MASTER
13 rows selected.
SQL>
SQL> SELECT CONSTRAINT_NAME, GENERATED, INDEX_NAME
  2  FROM    USER_CONSTRAINTS
  3  WHERE   TABLE_NAME LIKE 'CUST%';
CONSTRAINT_NAME      GENERATED      INDEX_NAME
-------------------- -------------- --------------------
SYS_C002792          GENERATED NAME
SYS_C002793          GENERATED NAME
SYS_C002794          GENERATED NAME
SYS_C002795          GENERATED NAME
PK_CUST_ADDRESSES    USER NAME      PK_CUST_ADDRESSES
FK_CUST_ADDRESSES    USER NAME
CK_ADD_TYPE2         USER NAME
CK_ADD_TYPE          USER NAME
PK_CUSTOMER_MASTER   USER NAME      PK_CUSTOMER_MASTER
UQ_CUST_EMAIL        USER NAME      CUST_EMAIL
PK_CUST_REFS         USER NAME      PK_CUST_REFS
SYS_C002804          GENERATED NAME
SYS_C002805          GENERATED NAME
13 rows selected.
SQL>
```

Summary

This chapter discussed the most important aspect of the Oracle Database: storing data. You learned to create both tablespaces and data files as well as to create schema objects that store the data. You found out how to create and manage tablespaces as well as how Oracle stores some schema objects as segments that are comprised of extents and data blocks. In addition, you learned how to create and modify tables, indexes, and constraints. I also covered deferred constraint checking and how to configure foreign key constraints to support either deferrable or not deferrable implementations.

A data file belongs to one tablespace, and a tablespace can have one or more data files. The size of the tablespace is the total size of all the data files belonging to that tablespace. The size of the database is the total size of all tablespaces in the database, which is the same as the total size of all data files in the database. Tablespaces are logical storage units used to group data depending on their type or category. Understand the relationship between data files and tablespaces because that is important information to know for the certification.

Tablespaces can handle the extent management through the Oracle dictionary or locally in the data files that belong to the tablespace. Locally managed tablespaces can have uniform extent sizes; this reduces fragmentation and wasted space. You can also make Oracle do the entire extent sizing for locally managed tablespaces.

A temporary tablespace is used only for sorting; no permanent objects can be created in a temporary tablespace. Only one sort segment will be created for each instance in the temporary tablespace. Multiple transactions can use the same sort segment, but one transaction can use only one extent. Although temporary files are part of the database, they do not appear in the control file, and the block changes do not generate any redo information because all the segments created on locally managed temporary tablespaces are temporary segments.

You learned about tables, indexes, and constraints in this chapter. Also study Chapters 6 and 7 before taking the certification exam. Tables are created using the `CREATE TABLE` command. By default, the table will be created in the current schema. To create the table in another schema, you should qualify the table with the schema name. Storage parameters can be specified when creating the table. Tables can be moved or reorganized using the `MOVE` clause.

Indexes can be created as B-tree or bitmap. Bitmap indexes save storage space for low-cardinality columns. You can create reverse key or function-based indexes. An index-organized table stores the index and row data in the B-tree structure. Tablespace and storage should be specified when creating indexes. Indexes can be created `ONLINE`; that is, the table will be available for insert/update/delete operations while the indexing is in progress. The `REBUILD` clause of the `ALTER INDEX` command can be used to move the index to a different tablespace or to reorganize the index.

Constraints are created on the tables to enforce business rules. There are five types of constraints: `NOT NULL`, `CHECK`, `UNIQUE`, `PRIMARY KEY`, and `FOREIGN KEY`.

The constraints can be created to check the conformance at each SQL statement or when committing the changes—checking for conformance at each statement is the default. You can enable and disable constraints. Constraints can be enabled with the `NOVALIDATE` clause to save time after large data loads.

Exam Essentials

Know the relationship of data files to tablespaces. Tablespaces are built on one or more data files—bigfile tablespaces on a single data file and smallfile tablespaces on one or more data files.

Understand the statements needed to create, modify, and drop tablespaces. Use a CREATE TABLESPACE, ALTER TABLESPACE, and DROP TABLESPACE statement to create, modify, and drop a tablespace, respectively.

Know how to take tablespaces offline and what consequences the OFFLINE IMMEDIATE option poses. Use an ALTER TABLESPACE statement to take a tablespace offline or bring it online. If you use the OFFLINE IMMEDIATE option, you must perform media recovery when you bring it back online.

Understand the default tablespaces for the database. When the database is created, if you do not specify the DEFAULT TABLESPACE and DEFAULT TEMPORARY TABLESPACE clauses, the SYSTEM tablespace will be the default for user objects and temporary segments.

Know how to use the EM Database Control to view tablespace information. The EM Database Control can be used to view tablespace information as well as perform various administrative tasks. A working knowledge of this tool is required.

Know the difference between segment space management and extent management. Extent management deals with segment-level space allocations, and segment space management deals with data block-level space allocations.

Know which initialization parameter controls OMF placement. The DB_CREATE_FILE_DEST parameter tells the database where to place Oracle Managed Files.

Know the different types of constraints and which have dependencies with others. There are the CHECK, NOT NULL, UNIQUE, PRIMARY KEY, and FOREIGN KEY constraints. A PRIMARY KEY constraint implicitly includes NOT NULL and UNIQUE constraints. A FOREIGN KEY constraint must refer to a PRIMARY KEY or UNIQUE constraint.

Know the types of indexes and when they are appropriate. B-tree indexes are medium- to high-cardinality columns in applications in which data can change frequently. Bitmap indexes are best for low- to medium-cardinality columns in applications that control data changes, usually in batches.

Review Questions

1. Which of the following statements about tablespaces is true?
   - A. A tablespace is the physical implementation of logical structure called a namespace.
   - B. A tablespace can hold the objects of only one schema.
   - C. A bigfile tablespace can have only one data file.
   - D. The SYSAUX tablespace is an optional tablespace created only if you install certain database options.

2. Automatic segment space management on the tablespace causes which of the following table attributes in that tablespace to be ignored?
   - A. The whole storage clause
   - B. NEXT and PCTINCREASE
   - C. BUFFERPOOL and FREEPOOL
   - D. PCTFREE and PCTUSED

3. Which is not a type of segment that is stored in a tablespace?
   - A. Undo
   - B. Redo
   - C. Permanent
   - D. Temporary

4. Can a table name ever include the special metacharacter dollar sign ($)?
   - A. No
   - B. Yes
   - C. Only if the table name is enclosed in double quotes
   - D. Only if the table name is enclosed in single quotes

5. Which operation can you not do to a table that is created with the following SQL statement?

```
CREATE TABLE properties
("Location"  NUMBER primary key
,value       NUMBER(15)
,lot         varchar2(12)
,constraint positive_value check
   (value > 0)
);
```

A. Rename the primary key to `properties`.

B. Insert a `null` into the `value` column.

C. Add a column named `owner`.

D. Rename the index-supporting primary key to `properties`.

E. None of the above.

6. Which constraint-checking model is the default?

A. Initially immediate and deferrable

B. Initially immediate and not deferrable

C. Initially deferred and not immediately

D. Initially deferrable and not immediate

7. Which allocation unit is the smallest?

A. Data file

B. Extent

C. Data block

D. Segment

8. Which of the following is not a valid Oracle 11*g* datatype?

A. TIMESTAMP WITH LOCAL TIMEZONE

B. BINARY

C. BLOB

D. UROWID

9. How do you specify that a temporary table will be emptied at the end of a user's session?

A. Create the temporary table with the `ON COMMIT PRESERVE ROWS` option.

B. Create the temporary table with the `ON DISCONNECT PRESERVE ROWS` option.

C. Create the temporary table with the `ON DISCONNECT PURGE ROWS` option.

D. Create the temporary table with the `ON COMMIT DELETE ROWS` option.

10. You performed the following statement in the database. What actions can you perform on the table `CUST_INFO` in the `CUST_DATA` tablespace. (Choose all that apply.)

```
ALTER TABLESPACE CUST_DATA READ ONLY;
```

A. `ALTER TABLE CUST_INFO DROP COLUMN xx;`

B. `TRUNCATE TABLE CUST_INFO;`

C. `INSERT INTO CUST_INFO VALUES (…);`

D. `DROP TABLE CUST_INFO;`

E. `RENAME CUST_INFO TO CUSTOMER_INFO;`

11. Which statements should be executed to make the USERS tablespace read-only, if the tablespace is offline? (Choose all that apply.)

- **A.** ALTER TABLESPACE USERS READ ONLY
- **B.** ALTER DATABASE MAKE TABLESPACE USERS READ ONLY
- **C.** ALTER TABLESPACE USERS ONLINE
- **D.** ALTER TABLESPACE USERS TEMPORARY

12. How would you add more space to a tablespace? (Choose all that apply.)

- **A.** ALTER TABLESPACE *<TABLESPACE NAME>* ADD DATAFILE SIZE *<N>*
- **B.** ALTER DATABASE DATAFILE *<FILENAME>* RESIZE *<N>*
- **C.** ALTER DATAFILE *<FILENAME>* RESIZE *<N>*
- **D.** ALTER TABLESPACE *<TABLESPACE NAME>* DATAFILE *<FILENAME>* RESIZE *<N>*

13. The database is using automatic memory management. The standard block size for the database is 8KB. You need to create a tablespace with a block size of 16KB. Which initialization parameter should be set?

- **A.** DB_8K_CACHE_SIZE
- **B.** DB_16K_CACHE_SIZE
- **C.** DB_CACHE_SIZE
- **D.** None of the above

14. Which data dictionary view can be queried to obtain information about the files that belong to locally managed temporary tablespaces?

- **A.** DBA_DATA_FILES
- **B.** DBA_TABLESPACES
- **C.** DBA_TEMP_FILES
- **D.** DBA_LOCAL_FILES

15. How would you drop a tablespace if the tablespace were not empty?

- **A.** Rename all the objects in the tablespace, and then drop the tablespace.
- **B.** Remove the data files belonging to the tablespace from the disk.
- **C.** Use ALTER DATABASE DROP *<TABLESPACE NAME>* CASCADE.
- **D.** Use DROP TABLESPACE *<TABLESPACE NAME>* INCLUDING CONTENTS.

16. Which command is used to enable the autoextensible feature for a file if the file is already part of a tablespace?

- **A.** ALTER DATABASE.
- **B.** ALTER TABLESPACE.
- **C.** ALTER DATA FILE.
- **D.** You cannot change the autoextensible feature once the data file created.

17. Which statement is true regarding the SYSTEM tablespace?

 A. It can be made read-only.

 B. It can be offline.

 C. Data files can be renamed.

 D. Data files cannot be resized.

18. The following statement is issued against the primary key constraint (PK_BONUS) of the BONUS table. Which statements are true? (Choose all that apply.)

```
ALTER TABLE BONUS MODIFY CONSTRAINT PK_BONUS DISABLE VALIDATE;
```

 A. No new rows can be added to the BONUS table.

 B. Existing rows of the BONUS table are validated before disabling the constraint.

 C. Rows can be modified, but the primary key columns cannot change.

 D. The unique index created when defining the constraint is dropped.

19. Which clause in the ALTER TABLE command is used to reorganize a table?

 A. REORGANIZE

 B. REBUILD

 C. RELOCATE

 D. MOVE

20. Which keyword should be used in the CREATE INDEX command to create a function-based index?

 A. CREATE FUNCTION INDEX

 B. CREATE INDEX ORGANIZATION INDEX

 C. CREATE INDEX FUNCTION BASED

 D. None of the above

Answers to Review Questions

1. C. Bigfile tablespaces can have only a single data file. The traditional or smallfile tablespace can have many data files.

2. D. Segment space management refers to free-space management, with automatic segment space management using bitmaps instead of FREELISTS, PCTFREE, and PCTUSED.

3. B. Redo information is not stored in a segment; it is stored in the redo logs. Undo segments are stored in the undo tablespace, temporary segments are in the temporary tablespace, and permanent segments go into all the other tablespaces.

4. B. Objects in an Oracle 11*g* database can always include letters, numbers, and the characters $, _, and # (dollar sign, underscore, and number sign). Names can include any other character only if they are enclosed in double quotes. The character dollar sign is not a special metacharacter in an Oracle 11*g* database.

5. E. You can rename both a constraint and an index to the same name as a table—they are in separate namespaces. Columns can be added, and `owner` is a valid column name. If the check constraint condition evaluates to `FALSE`, the data value will not be allowed; if the condition evaluates to either `TRUE` or `NULL`, the value is allowed.

6. B. Constraints can be created as deferrable and initially deferred, but deferred constraint checking is not the default.

7. C. An extent is composed of two or more data blocks; a segment is composed of one or more extents, and a data file houses all these.

8. B. Although BINARY_FLOAT and BINARY_DOUBLE are valid datatypes, BINARY is not.

9. A. The options for temporary tables are either `ON COMMIT DELETE ROWS`, which causes the table to flush at the end of each transaction, or `ON COMMIT PRESERVE ROWS`, which causes the table to flush at the end of each session.

10. B, D, E. When a tablespace is read-only, DML operations and operations that affect data in the table are not allowed. Truncate and drop operations are allowed, and you can also rename the table using the `RENAME` statement or the `ALTER TABLE` statement.

11. C, A. To make a tablespace read-only, all the data files belonging to the tablespace must be online and available. So, bring the tablespace online and then make it read-only.

12. A, B. You can add more space to a tablespace either by adding a data file or by increasing the size of an existing data file. Option A does not have a file name specified; it uses the OMF feature to generate filename.

13. B. `DB_CACHE_SIZE` doesn't need to be set for the standard block size since automatic memory management is used. If you set `DB_CACHE_SIZE`, its value will be used as the minimum. `DB_16K_CACHE_SIZE` should be set for the nonstandard block size. You must not set the `DB_8K_CACHE_SIZE` parameter because the standard block size is 8KB.

14. C. Locally managed temporary tablespaces are created using the CREATE TEMPORARY TABLESPACE command. The data files (temporary files) belonging to these tablespaces are in the DBA_TEMP_FILES view. The EXTENT_MANAGEMENT column of the DBA_TABLESPACES view shows the type of the tablespace. The data files belonging to locally managed permanent tablespaces and dictionary-managed (permanent and temporary) tablespaces can be queried from DBA_DATA_FILES. Locally managed temporary tablespaces reduce contention on the data dictionary tables.

15. D. The INCLUDING CONTENTS clause is used to drop a tablespace that is not empty. Oracle does not remove the data files that belong to the tablespace if the files are not Oracle managed; you need to do it manually using an OS command. Oracle updates only the control file. To remove the files, you can include the INCLUDING CONTENTS AND DATAFILES clause.

16. A. You can use the ALTER TABLESPACE command to rename a file that belongs to the tablespace, but all other file-management operations are done through the ALTER DATABASE command. To enable autoextension, use ALTER DATABASE DATAFILE *<FILENAME>* AUTOEXTEND ON NEXT *<INTEGER>* MAXSIZE *<INTEGER>*.

17. C. The data files belonging to the SYSTEM tablespace can be renamed when the database is in the MOUNT state by using the ALTER DATABASE RENAME FILE statement.

18. A, D. DISABLE VALIDATE disables the constraint and drops the index but keeps the constraint valid. No DML operations are allowed on the table.

19. D. The MOVE clause is used to reorganize a table. You can specify new tablespace and storage parameters. Queries are allowed on the table, but no DML operations are allowed during the move.

20. D. No keyword needs to be specified to create a function-based index other than to specify the function itself. To permit the Oracle optimizer to use a function-based index, you must set the parameter QUERY_REWRITE_ENABLED to TRUE and QUERY_REWRITE_INTEGRITY to TRUSTED.

Understanding Network Architecture

ORACLE DATABASE 11*g*: ADMINISTRATION I EXAM OBJECTIVES COVERED IN THIS CHAPTER:

✓ **Configuring the Oracle Network Environment**

- Configure and Manage the Oracle Network
- Using the Oracle Shared Server architecture

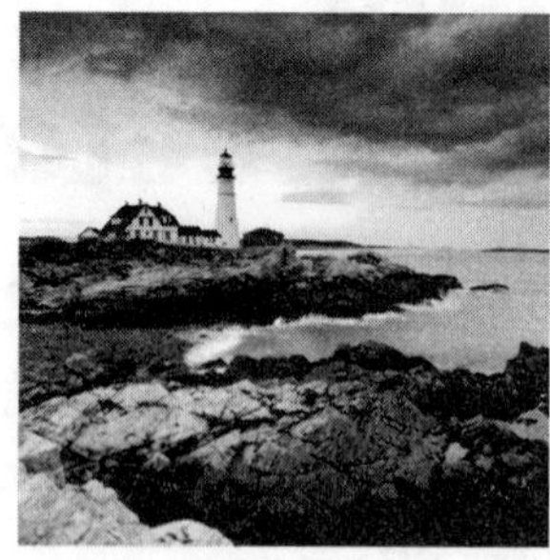

Networks have evolved from simple terminal-based systems to complex multi-tiered systems. Today's networks can comprise many computers on multiple operating systems using a wide variety of protocols and communicating across wide geographic areas. Although networks have become increasingly complex, they also have become easier to use and manage. For instance, we all take advantage of the Internet without knowing or caring about the components that make this communication possible, because the complexity of this huge network is completely hidden from us.

The experienced Oracle database administrator has seen this maturation process in the Oracle network architecture as well. From the first version of SQL*Net to the latest releases of Oracle Net, Oracle has evolved its network strategy and infrastructure to meet the demands of the rapidly changing landscape of network communications.

This chapter highlights the areas you need to consider when implementing an Oracle network strategy and when managing an Oracle 11*g* network. I'll also discuss the most common network configurations. The chapter introduces the features of Oracle Net—the connectivity-management software that is the backbone of the Oracle network architecture. I'll explain how to configure the main client- and server-side components of Oracle Net, and I'll discuss the tools you have at your disposal to perform these tasks.

As the number of users connecting to Oracle Databases in the enterprise grows, the system requirements of the servers increase—particularly the memory and process requirements. When a system starts to encounter these capacity issues, you need to know which alternatives are available within the Oracle environment that can address the problem. One configuration alternative that may help to overcome this capacity problem is Oracle Shared Server.

This chapter also discusses Oracle Shared Server and its benefits. You will learn about the client connection process and how Oracle Shared Server processes user requests. You will also learn how to configure Oracle Shared Server.

Introducing Network Configurations

You can select from three basic types of network configurations when designing an Oracle infrastructure:

- Single-tier
- Two-tier
- *n*-tier

Single-tier is the simplest type. It has been around for years and is characterized by the use of terminals for serial connections to the Oracle server. The two-tier configuration is also referred to as the *client/server* architecture, and more recently the *n*-tier architecture has been introduced. Let's take a look at each of these configuration alternatives.

Single-Tier Architecture

Single-tier architecture was the standard for many years before the birth of the personal computer. Applications using single-tier architecture are sometimes referred to as *green-screen* applications because most of the terminals that used them, such as the IBM 3270, had green screens. Single-tier architecture is commonly associated with mainframe-type applications.

This architecture is still in use today for many mission-critical applications, such as order processing and fulfillment and inventory control, because it is the simplest architecture to configure and administer. Because the terminals are directly connected to the host computer, the complexities of network protocols and multiple operating systems don't exist.

When single-tier architecture is used—for example, in mainframes—users interact with the database using terminals, which are nongraphical, character-based devices. In this type of architecture, client terminals are directly connected to larger server systems such as mainframes. All the intelligence exists on the mainframe, and all the processing takes place there. Simple serial connections also exist on the mainframe. Although no complex network architecture is necessary, a single-tier architecture is somewhat limiting in terms of scalability and flexibility (see Figure 11.1).

FIGURE 11.1 Single-tier architecture

Two-Tier Architecture

Two-tier architecture gained popularity with the introduction of the personal computer and is commonly referred to as *client/server* computing. In a two-tier environment, clients connect to servers over a network using a network protocol, which is the agreed-upon method for the client to communicate with the server. Transmission Control Protocol/Internet Protocol (TCP/IP) is a popular network protocol and has become the de facto standard of network computing. Whether you choose TCP/IP or some other network protocol, both the client and the server must be able to understand it. Figure 11.2 shows an example of two-tier architecture.

FIGURE 11.2 Two-tier architecture

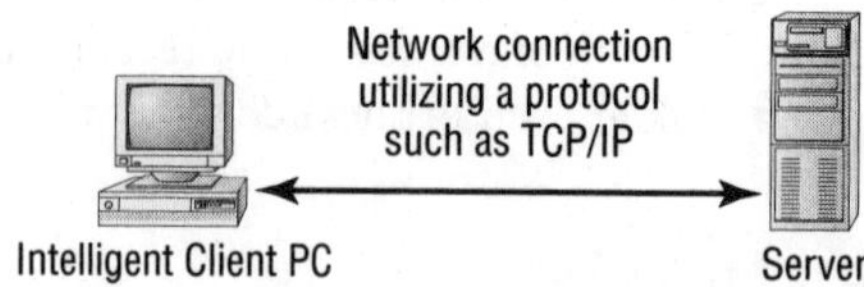

This architecture has definite benefits over single-tier architecture. First, client/server computing introduces the graphical user interface (GUI). This interface is easier to understand and learn, and it offers more flexibility than the traditional character-based interfaces of the single-tier architecture. Also, two-tier architecture allows the client computer to share the application process load. To a certain degree, this reduces the processing requirements of the server.

The two-tier architecture does have some faults, even though at one time, this configuration was thought to be the panacea of all networking architectures. Unfortunately, the main problem—that being scalability—persists. Notice that the term *client/server* contains a slash (/). The slash represents the invisible component of the two-tier architecture and the one that is often overlooked: the network! The limitation of client/server computing is one of scalability.

When prototyping projects, many developers fail to consider the network component and soon find out that what worked well in a small environment does not scale effectively to larger, more complex systems. The two-tier architecture model was subject to a great deal of redundancy because application software was required on every desktop. As a result, many companies end up with bloated computers and large servers that still do not perform adequately. What is needed is a more scalable model for network communications. That is what *n*-tier architecture provides.

n-Tier Architecture

n-*tier architecture* is the next logical step after two-tier architecture. Instead of dividing application processing work between a client and a server, you divide the work among three or more machines. The *n*-tier architecture introduces *middleware* components, such as application servers or web servers, situated between the client and the database server, which can be used for a variety of tasks, including the following:

- Moving data between machines that work with different network protocols
- Serving as firewalls that can control client access to the servers
- Offloading processing of the business logic from the clients and servers to the middle tier
- Executing transactions and monitoring activity between clients and servers to balance the load among multiple servers
- Acting as a gateway to bridge existing systems to new systems

The Internet is an example of the ultimate *n*-tier architecture, with the user's browser providing a consistent presentation interface. This common interface means less training of staff and also increases the potential reuse of client-side application components.

n-tier architecture is rapidly becoming the architecture of choice for enterprise networks. This model is scalable and divides the tasks of presentation, business logic and routing, and database processing among many machines, which means that this model accommodates large applications. Many factors are driving *n*-tier computing, such as the Internet and Oracle grid computing, which uses a large number of back-end processors to scale database services and connectivity.

By reducing the processing load on the database servers, those servers can do more work with the same number of resources. Also, the transaction servers can balance the flow of network transactions intelligently, and application servers can reduce the processing and memory requirements of the client (see Figure 11.3).

FIGURE 11.3 Connection requests in *n*-tier architecture

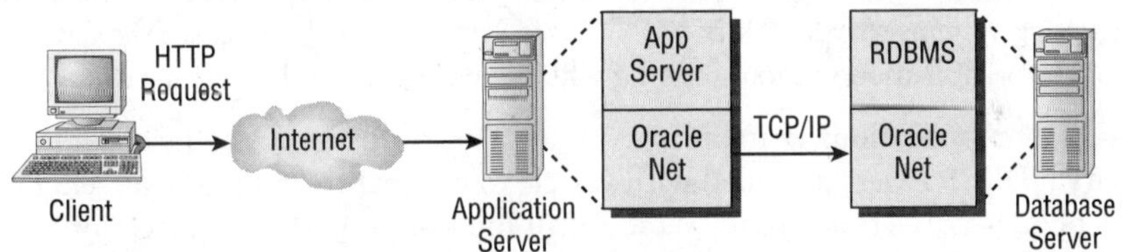

An Overview of Oracle Net Features

Oracle Net is the glue that bonds the Oracle network together. It is responsible for handling client-to-server and server-to-server communications, and it can be configured on the client, the middle-tier application, web servers, and the Oracle server.

Oracle Net manages the flow of information in the Oracle network infrastructure. First it establishes the initial connection to the Oracle server, and then it acts as the messenger, passing requests from the client back to the server or passing them between two Oracle servers. Oracle Net handles all negotiations between the client and server during the client connection.

In addition to functioning as an information manager, Oracle Net supports the use of middleware products such as Oracle Application Server and Oracle Connection Manager. These products allow *n*-tier architectures to be used in the enterprise, which increases the flexibility and performance of application designs.

To provide a further understanding of the features of Oracle Net, the following sections discuss in detail the five categories of networking solutions that Oracle Net addresses:

- Connectivity
- Manageability
- Scalability

- Security
- Accessibility

Connectivity

A client can interact with an Oracle Database in many ways. A client can be running a PC-based application or a dumb terminal application, or perhaps the client is connecting to the database via the Internet. Let's take a look at how Oracle supports connectivity to the database through these and other interfaces:

Multiprotocol support Oracle Net supports a wide range of industry-standard protocols such as TCP/IP and named pipes. This support is handled transparently and allows Oracle Net to connect to a wide range of computers and a wide range of operating environments.

Multiple operating systems Oracle Net can run on many operating systems, from Windows XP to all variants of Unix to large mainframe-based operating systems. This range allows users to bridge existing systems to other Unix or PC-based systems, which increases the data access flexibility of the organization without making wholesale changes to the existing systems.

Java and JDBC Applications written in Java can take advantage of the Java Database Connectivity (JDBC) drivers provided with Oracle to connect to an Oracle server. The two basic types of JDBC drivers are JDBC Oracle Call Interface (OCI) and JDBC thin.

The JDBC OCI driver is a client-side installed driver that is used if the Java application is resident on a client computer. This driver is also called a *type II* driver because the driver software is installed on the computer that is using the application. It uses OCI to interact with the Oracle Net infrastructure. Figure 11.4 shows how a client and server communicate when using a JDBC OCI connection.

FIGURE 11.4 Oracle JDBC OCI connection

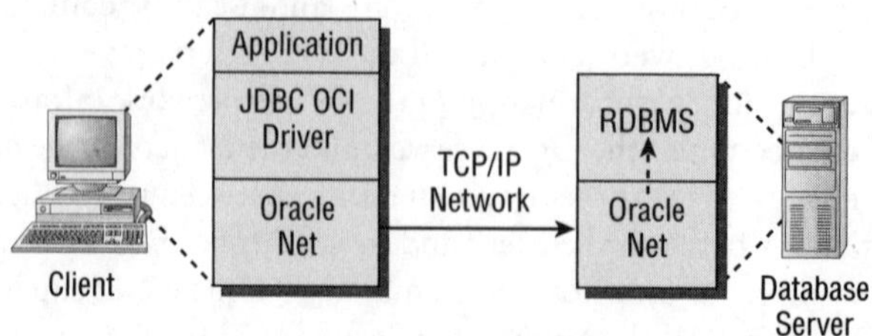

In this example, the Java application installed on the client uses the JDBC OCI driver and Oracle Database server. When an application makes a database request, it uses the JDBC OCI driver to translate the JDBC calls and send them to Oracle Net. Oracle Net is used on both the client and the server to broker all communications between the two end points.

The JDBC thin driver is written entirely in Java and, as such, is platform independent. It does not have to be installed on a client computer (which is why it's called a *thin driver*). The driver interfaces directly with a layer of the Oracle Net infrastructure called the *two-task common layer.*

Manageability

Oracle Net provides a variety of features that allow you to manage the components of an Oracle network. Let's review the key manageability features of Oracle Net.

Web Applications

Oracle Net supports a variety of connectivity solutions from a web browser interface. Connections can be made through a middle-tier web or application server or directly from a web browser to an Oracle service.

When a middle-tier solution is used, the web browser uses HTTP to contact a database service and request information. Typically, an application or web server receives this request and hands it off to Oracle Net, which manages the connection between the web server and the database server. Once the database server receives the connection request, the request is processed and passed back to the web server. The web server then sends the response to the client's web browser. This type of request fulfillment requires that the middle-tier application server be loaded with the Oracle Net software, but the client does not require any additional software.

Oracle also supports web connectivity directly from a web client. For example, a Java applet running within a web browser can use a JDBC driver to connect directly to an Oracle server without the need for an application or web server.

Location Transparency

Oracle Net provides the infrastructure to manage the database location. This is important especially in large organizations that support many databases and clients. Each database in the organization is represented as one or more services. Database services are defined by one or more service names. The actual definition of the service names is managed within Oracle Net. The definition holds information about the type and location of the service on the network. This layer of abstraction provides location transparency to the client and centralizes the management of connection information within Oracle Net, which simplifies the job of managing the network.

Directory Naming

Directory naming allows service names to be resolved through a centralized naming repository. The central repository takes the form of a Lightweight Directory Access Protocol (LDAP)–compliant server. LDAP is a protocol and language that defines a standard method for storing, identifying, and retrieving services. It provides a simplified way to manage directories of information, whether this information is about users in an organization or Oracle services connected to a network. The LDAP server allows for a standard form of managing and resolving names in an Oracle environment. The quality of these services excels because LDAP provides a single, industry-standard interface to a directory service such as Oracle Internet Directory (OID). By using OID, you ensure the security and reliability of the directory information because information is stored in the Oracle Database.

Scalability

Many enterprise systems are growing rapidly, supporting larger and larger databases and user communities. Your network capabilities need to be able to support this growth. Oracle Net provides features that allow you to expand your network reach and maximize your system resources to meet these demands.

Oracle Shared Server

Oracle Shared Server is an optional configuration of the Oracle server that allows support for a large number of concurrent connections without increasing physical resource requirements. This is accomplished by sharing resources among groups of users.

Oracle Shared Server is discussed in detail later in the chapter in the section "An Overview of Oracle Shared Server."

Connection Manager

Oracle Connection Manager is a middleware solution that provides three additional scalability features:

Multiplexing Connection Manager can group many client connections and send them as a single multiplexed network connection to the Oracle server. This reduces the total number of network connections that the server has to manage.

Network access You can configure Connection Manager with rules that restrict access by IP address. You can set up this rules-based configuration to accept or reject client connection requests. Also, connections can be restricted by point of origin, destination server, or Oracle server.

Cross-protocol connectivity This feature allows clients and servers that use different network protocols to communicate. Connection Manager acts as a translator, providing two-way protocol conversion.

Oracle Connection Manager is controlled by a set of background processes that manage the communications between clients and servers. Figure 11.5 provides an overview of the Connection Manager architecture.

Security

The threat of data tampering and database security is an issue of major concern in many organizations as network systems continue to grow in number and complexity and as users gain increasing access to systems. Sensitive business transactions are being conducted with greater frequency and, in many cases, are not protected from unauthorized tampering or message interception. Oracle Net is capable of providing organizations with a secure network environment to conduct business transactions. I'll now discuss the tools available in Oracle 11*g* to protect sensitive information.

FIGURE 11.5 Connection Manager architecture

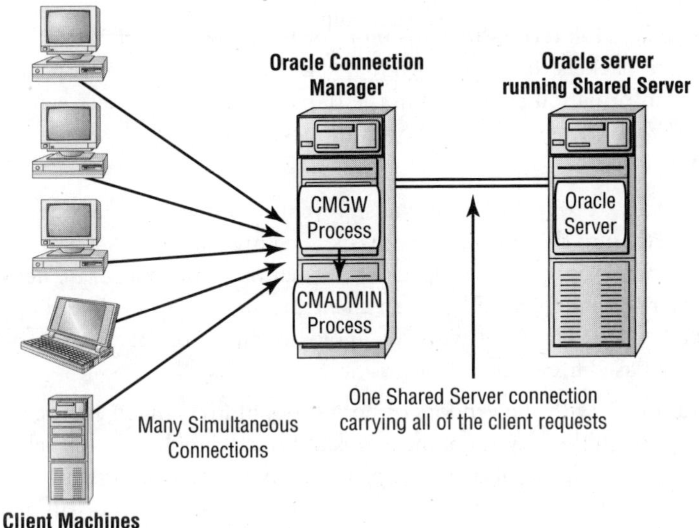

Advanced Security

Oracle Advanced Security, formerly known as the Advanced Security Option and the Advanced Networking Option, not only provides the tools necessary to ensure secure transmissions of sensitive information, but it also provides mechanisms to confidently identify and authenticate users in the Oracle enterprise.

When configured on the client and the Oracle server, Oracle Advanced Security supports secured data transmissions by encrypting and optionally checksumming the transmission of information that is sent in a transaction. Oracle supports encryption and checksumming by taking advantage of industry-standard algorithms, such as RSA RC4, Standard DES and Triple DES, and MD5 checksumming. These security features ensure that data transmitted from the client has not been altered during transmission to the Oracle server.

Oracle Advanced Security also gives you the ability to authenticate users connecting to the Oracle servers. In fact, a number of authentication features ensure that users really are who they claim to be. These are offered in the form of token cards, which use a physical card and a user-identifying PIN to gain access to the system; retina scans also supported now, which uses fingerprint technology to authenticate user connection requests; public key; and certificate-based authentication.

Firewall Support

Firewalls are an important security mechanism in corporate networks. Firewalls are generally a combination of hardware and software that is used to control network traffic and prevent intruders from compromising corporate network security. Firewalls fall into two broad categories:

IP-filtering firewalls IP-filtering firewalls monitor the network packet traffic on IP networks and filter out packets that either originated or did not originate from specific groups of machines. The information contained in the IP packet header is interrogated to obtain this information. Vendors of this type of firewall include Network Associates and Axent Communications.

Proxy-based firewalls Proxy-based firewalls prevent information from outside the firewall from flowing directly into the corporate network. The firewall acts as a gatekeeper, inspecting packets and sending only the appropriate information to the corporate network. This prevents any direct communication between clients outside the firewall and applications inside the firewall. Check Point Software Technologies and Cisco are examples of vendors that market proxy-based firewalls.

Oracle works closely with the vendors of both types of firewalls to ensure support of database traffic through these types of mechanism. Oracle supplies the Oracle Net Application Proxy Kit to the firewall vendors. This product can be incorporated into the firewall architecture to allow database packets to pass through the firewall and still maintain a high degree of security.

Real World Scenario

Know Thy Firewall

It is important to understand your network infrastructure, the network routes you are using to obtain database connections, and the type of firewall products you are using. In more than one situation, I've seen firewalls cause connectivity issues between a client and an Oracle server.

For instance, a small patch was applied to a firewall when a friend of mine was working as a DBA for one of his former employers. In this case, employees started experiencing intermittent disconnects from the Oracle Database. After many days of investigation and network tracing, the team pinned down the exact problem. The database team then contacted the firewall vendor, who sent a new patch that corrected the problem.

In another instance, the development staff started experiencing a similar connection problem. It turned out that the networking routes for the development staff had been modified to connect through a new firewall, with connections timing out after 20 minutes. This timeout was too short for this department. Increasing the timeout parameter solved the problem.

These are examples of the types of network changes you need to be aware of to avoid unnecessary downtime and to avoid wasting staff time and resources.

Accessibility

In many organizations, workers need to be able to communicate across a variety of systems and databases. They spend a lot of time bringing together data from different systems. The accessibility features of Oracle Net have capabilities that allow you to communicate with nondatabase data sources. This ability opens up new opportunities to provide customers with accurate and timely information. I'll now discuss the options available in Oracle 11*g* to access data that resides in a non-Oracle database and to execute programs that are not SQL or PL/SQL.

Heterogeneous Services

The Heterogeneous Services component provides the ability to communicate with non-Oracle databases and services. These services allow organizations to leverage and interact with their existing data stores without having to necessarily move the data to an Oracle server.

The suite of Heterogeneous Services comprises the Oracle Transparent Gateway and Generic Connectivity. These products allow Oracle to communicate with non-Oracle data sources in a seamless configuration. Heterogeneous Services also integrates existing systems with the Oracle environment, which allows you to leverage your investment in those systems. These services also allow for two-way communication and replication from Oracle data sources to non-Oracle data sources.

External Procedures

In some development efforts, interfacing with procedures that reside outside the database may be necessary. These procedures are typically written in a third-generation language, such as C. Oracle Net provides the ability to invoke such external procedures from Oracle PL/SQL callouts. When a call is made, a process is started that acts as an interface between Oracle and the external procedure. This callout process defaults to the name `extproc`. The listener is then responsible for supplying information, such as a library or procedure name and any parameters, to the called procedure. These programs are then loaded and executed under the control of the `extproc` process.

Configuring Oracle Net on the Server

Now that you understand the basic features Oracle Net provides, you need to understand how to configure the major components of Oracle Net. You must configure Oracle Net on the server in order for client connections to be established. The following sections will focus on how to configure the network elements of the Oracle server. It will also describe the types of connection methods that Oracle Net supports. We will then discuss how to manage Oracle Net on the server and troubleshoot connections from the server if clients experience connection problems.

Understanding the Oracle Listener

The Oracle *listener* is the main server-side Oracle networking component that allows connections to be established between client computers and an Oracle Database. You can think of the listener as a big ear that listens for connection requests to Oracle services.

The type of Oracle service being requested is part of the connection descriptor information supplied by the process requesting a connection, and the service name resolves to an Oracle Database. The listener can listen for any number of databases configured on the server, and it is able to listen for requests being transported on a variety of protocols. A client connection can be initiated from the same machine that the listener resides on, or it may come from some remote location.

The listener is controlled by a centralized file called `listener.ora`. Though only one `listener.ora` file is configured per machine, there may be numerous listeners on a server, and this file contains all the configuration information for every listener configured on the server. If multiple listeners are configured on a single server, they are usually set up for failover purposes or to balance connection requests and minimize the burden of connections on a single listener.

The content and structure of the `listener.ora` file is discussed later in this chapter in the section "Managing Oracle Listeners."

Every listener is a named process that runs on either a middle-tier server or the database server. The default name of the Oracle listener is `LISTENER`, and it is typically created when you install Oracle. If you configure multiple listeners, each has a unique name.

Now that you have a basic understanding of the Oracle listener, let's explore the main function of the listener, which is responding to client connection requests.

How Do Listeners Respond to Connection Requests?

A listener can respond to a client request for a connection in several ways. The response depends on several factors, such as how the server-side network components are configured and what type of connection the client is requesting. The listener then responds to the connection request in one of two ways.

The listener can spawn a new process and pass control of the client session to the process. In a *dedicated server* environment, every client connection is serviced by its own server-side process. Server-side processes are not shared among clients. Two types of dedicated connection methods are possible: direct and redirect. Each method results in a separate process that handles client processing, but the mechanics of the actual connection-initiation process are different. For remote clients to use dedicated connections, the listener process must be running on the same physical server as the database or databases for which it is listening.

The listener can also pass control of a connection request to a dispatcher. This type of connection takes place in an Oracle Shared Server environment. There are also two types of connection methods when using Oracle Shared Server: direct and redirect.

Let's take a look at each of these connection-method types.

Dedicated Connections: Direct Handoff Method

Direct handoff connections are possible when the client and database exist on the same server. For example, a direct handoff method is used when the client connection request originates from the same machine on which the listener and database are running.

Another name for direct handoff connections is *bequeath connections*.

The following steps, which show the connection process for the bequeath connections, are illustrated in Figure 11.6:

1. The client contacts the Oracle listener after resolving the service name.
2. The listener starts a dedicated process, and the client connection inherits the dedicated server process network connect end point from the listener.
3. The client now has an established connection to the dedicated server process.

FIGURE 11.6 Dedicated connections: direct handoff method

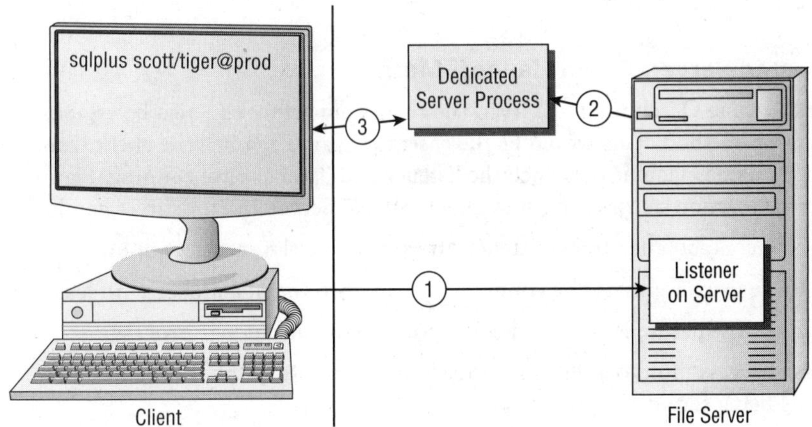

Dedicated Connections: Redirect Method

Redirect connections occur in a dedicated server environment when the client exists on a machine that is separate from the listener and database server. The listener must inform the client of the address of the spawned process in order for the process to contact the newly created dedicated server process.

The following steps, which show the connection process for redirect connections in a dedicated server environment, are illustrated in Figure 11.7:

1. The client contacts the Oracle listener after resolving the service name.
2. The listener starts a dedicated process.

3. The listener sends an acknowledgment back to the client with the address of the dedicated server connect end point on the database server to which the client will connect.
4. The client establishes a connection to the dedicated server connect end point.

FIGURE 11.7 Dedicated connections: redirect method

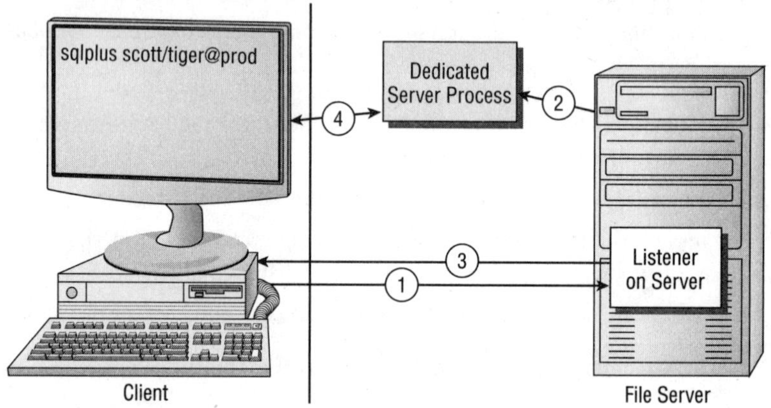

Oracle Shared Server: Direct Handoff Method

When you are using Oracle Shared Server, the client connection can also be established using a direct handoff method. This would be the case, for example, when the client request originates from the same machine on which the listener and database are running. Figure 11.8 outlines the connection steps when using Oracle Shared Server and the direct handoff method:

1. The client contacts the Oracle listener after resolving the service name.
2. The Oracle listener passes the connection request to the dispatcher with least load.
3. The client now has an established connection to the dispatcher process.
4. PMON (process monitor) sends information to the listener about the number of connections being serviced by the dispatchers.

FIGURE 11.8 Oracle Shared Server: direct handoff method

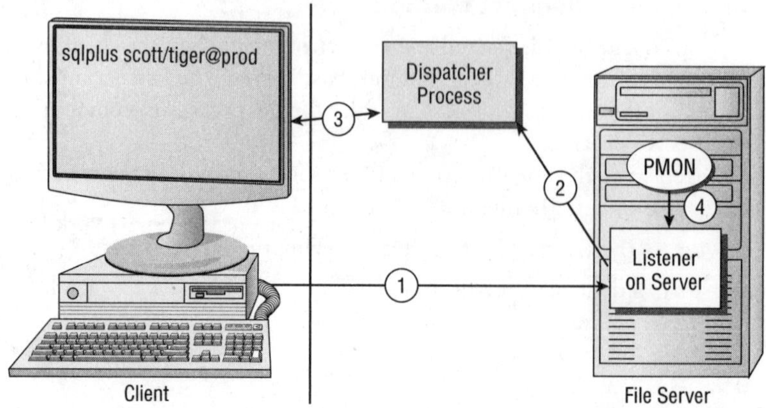

Oracle Shared Server: Redirect Method

The listener can also redirect the user to a server process or a dispatcher process when using Oracle Shared Server. This type of connection can occur when the operating system does not directly support direct handoff connections or the listener is not on the same physical machine as the Oracle server.

The following steps are illustrated in Figure 11.9:

1. The client contacts the Oracle server after resolving the service name.
2. The listener sends information to the client, redirecting the client to the dispatcher port. The original network connection between the listener and the client is disconnected.
3. The client then sends a connect signal to the server or dispatcher process to establish a network connection.
4. The dispatcher or server process sends an acknowledgment to the client.
5. PMON sends information to the listener about the number of connections being serviced by the dispatchers. The listener uses this information to maintain consistent loads between the dispatchers.

FIGURE 11.9 Oracle Shared Server: redirect connection method

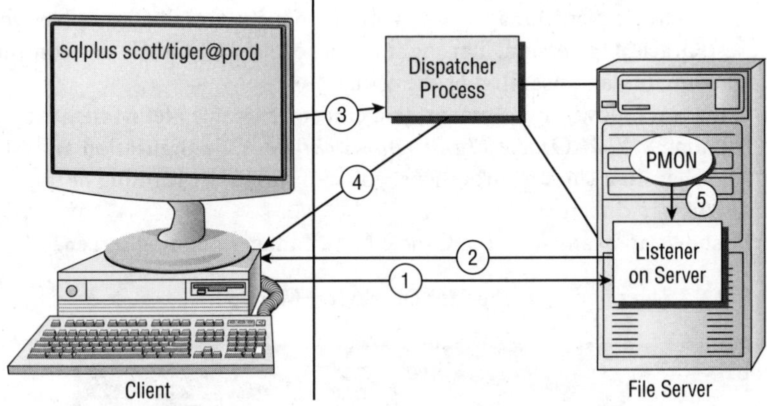

Managing Oracle Listeners

You can configure the server-side listener files in a number of ways. As part of the initial Oracle installation process, the installer prompts you to create a default listener. If you choose this method, the installer uses the set of screens that are part of the Oracle Net Configuration Assistant to do the initial listener configuration. Figure 11.10 shows an example of the opening screen for this assistant.

If you want to set up more than just basic configurations of Oracle network files, you will have to use Oracle Net Manager, the web-based tool Oracle Enterprise Manager (EM), or the command-line facility `lsnrctl`. In the next few sections, you will learn how to use these tools to configure the server-side network files.

FIGURE 11.10 Oracle Net Configuration Assistant opening screen

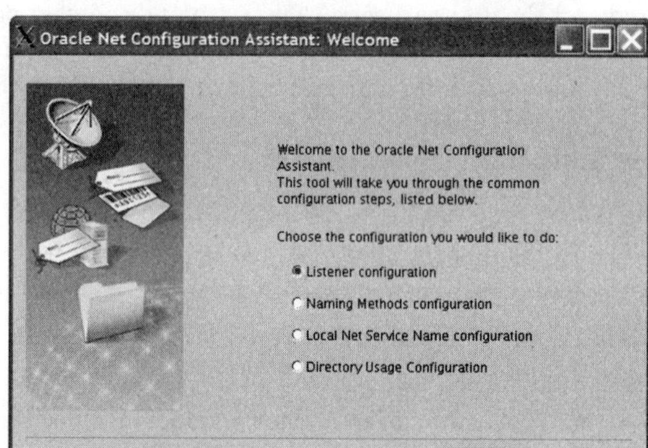

Managing Listeners with Oracle Net Manager

Oracle Net Manager is a tool you can use to create and manage most client- and server-side configuration files. Oracle Net Manager has evolved from the Oracle 7 tool, Network Manager, to the latest Oracle 11*g* version. Throughout this evolution, Oracle has continued to enhance the functionality and usability of the tool.

If you are using a Windows environment, you can start Oracle Net Manager by choosing Start ➤ Programs ➤ *Your Oracle 11g Programs choice* ➤ Configuration and Migration Tools ➤ Net Manager. In a Unix environment, you can start it by running `netmgr` from your `$ORACLE_HOME/bin` directory.

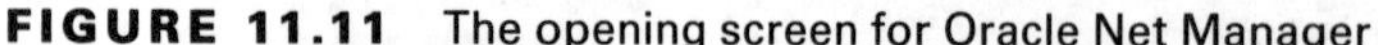

Figure 11.11 shows an example of the Oracle Net Manager opening screen.

FIGURE 11.11 The opening screen for Oracle Net Manager

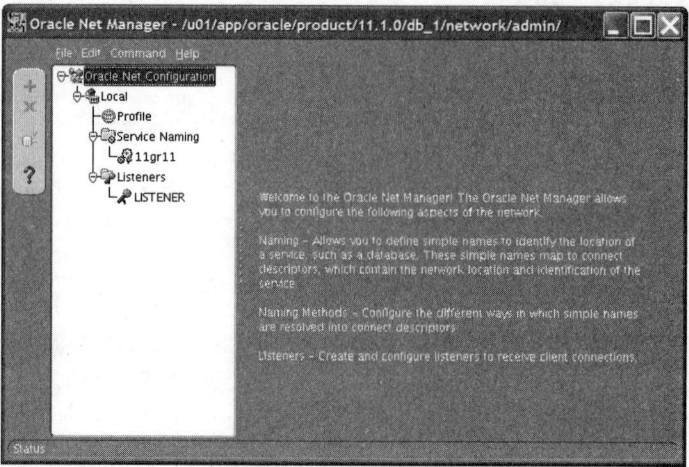

Configuring Listener Services Using Oracle Net Manager

Oracle Net Manager provides an easy-to-use graphical interface for configuring most of the network files you will be using. By using Oracle Net Manager, you can ensure that the files are created in a consistent format, which will reduce the potential for connection problems.

When you first start Oracle Net Manager, the opening screen displays a tree structure with a top level called Oracle Net Configuration. If you click the plus (+) sign next to this icon, you will see the Local folder. The choices under the Local folder relate to different network configuration files. Here are the network file choices and what each configures:

Icon	File Configured
Profile	`sqlnet.ora`
Service Naming	`tnsnames.ora`
Listeners	`listener.ora`

Creating the Listener

Earlier I said that, by default, Oracle creates a listener called `LISTENER` when it is initially installed. The default settings that Oracle uses for the `listener.ora` file are as follows:

Section of the File	Setting
Listener name	`LISTENER`
Port	`1521`
Protocols	`TCP/IP and IPC`
Hostname	`Default Host Name`
SID name	`Default Instance`

You can use Oracle Net Manager to create a nondefault listener or change the definition of existing listeners. Oracle Net Manager has a wizard interface for creating most of the basic network elements, such as the `listener.ora` and `tnsnames.ora` files.

Follow these steps to create the listener:

1. Click the plus (+) sign next to the Local icon.
2. Click the Listeners folder.
3. Click the plus sign icon, or choose Edit ➤ Create to open the Choose Listener Name dialog box.
4. Oracle Net Manager defaults to `LISTENER` or to `LISTENER1` if the default listener is already created. Click OK if this is correct, or enter a new name and then click OK to open the Listening Locations screen, as shown in Figure 11.12.

FIGURE 11.12 The Listening Locations screen

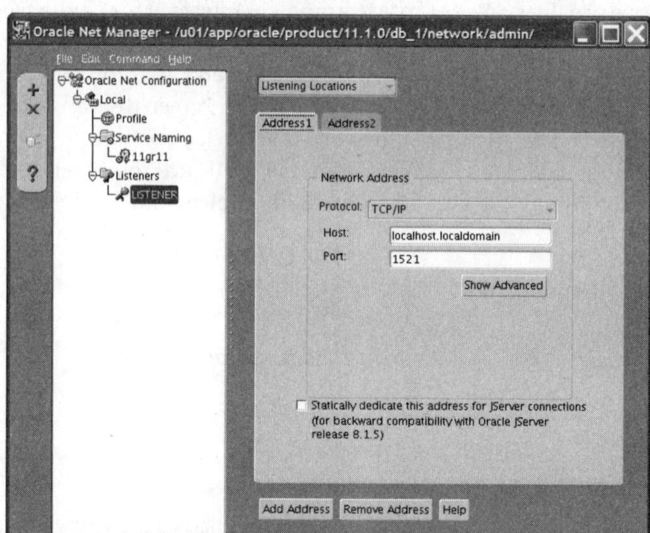

5. To configure the listening locations, click the Listening Locations drop-down list, and make your selection. Then click the Add Address button at the bottom of the screen to open a new window.

   The prompts on this screen depend on your protocol. By default, TCP/IP information is displayed. If you are using TCP/IP, the Host and Port fields are filled in for you. The *host* is the name of the machine in which the listener is running, and the *port* is the listening location for TCP/IP connections. The default value for the port is 1521.

6. To save your information, choose File ➤ Save Network Configuration, and then look in the directory where the file was saved.

You can also add listeners by following these steps. Listeners must have unique names and listen on separate ports, so assign the listener a new name and a new port (1522, for example). You also must assign service names to the listener. You'll see how to add service information in the next section.

Oracle Net Manager actually creates three files in this process: `listener.ora`, `tnsnames.ora`, and `sqlnet.ora`. The `tnsnames.ora` file does not contain any information. The `sqlnet.ora` file may contain a few entries at this point, but you can ignore them for the time being. The `listener.ora` file contains information, as shown in the following code:

```
# listener.ora Network Configuration File:
# /u01/app/oracle/product/11.1.0/db_1/network/admin/listener.ora
# Generated by Oracle configuration tools.

LISTENER =
  (DESCRIPTION_LIST =
```

```
(DESCRIPTION =
  (ADDRESS = (PROTOCOL = TCP)(HOST = localhost.localdomain)(PORT = 1521))
  (ADDRESS = (PROTOCOL = IPC)(KEY = EXTPROC1521))
 )
)
```

To figure out where the files are stored, just look at the top banner of the Oracle Net Manager screen.

Adding Service-Name Information to the Listener

After you create the listener with the name, protocol, and listening location information, you can define the network services to which the listener is responsible for connecting. This is called *static service registration*, because Oracle is not automatically registering the service with the listener. In releases of Oracle prior to Oracle8*i*, static service registration was the only method to associate services with a listener.

A listener can listen to an unlimited number of network service names. Follow these steps to add the service-name information:

1. To select the listener to configure, click the Listeners icon, and highlight the name of the listener that you want to configure.
2. From the drop-down list at the top right of the screen, select Database Services.
3. Click the Add Database button at the bottom of the screen. This opens the window that allows you to add the database (see Figure 11.13).

FIGURE 11.13 The Database Services screen

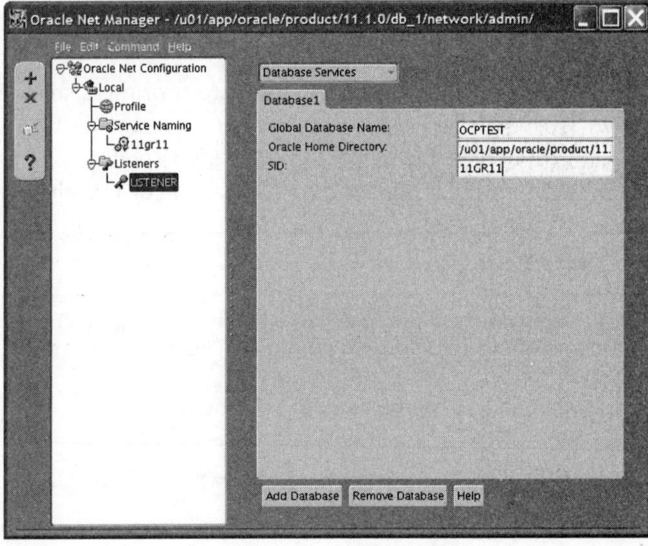

4. Enter values in the Global Database Name, Oracle Home Directory, and SID fields. The entries for SID and Global Database Name are the same if you are using a flat naming convention.
5. Choose File ➤ Save to save your configuration.

Here is an example of the completed `listener.ora` file:

```
# listener.ora Network Configuration File:
# /u01/app/oracle/product/11.1.0/db_1/network/admin/listener.ora
# Generated by Oracle configuration tools.

SID_LIST_LISTENER =
  (SID_LIST =
    (SID_DESC =
      (GLOBAL_DBNAME = OCPTEST)
      (ORACLE_HOME = /u01/app/oracle/product/11.1.0/db_1)
      (SID_NAME = 11GR11)
    )
  )

LISTENER =
  (DESCRIPTION_LIST =
    (DESCRIPTION =
      (ADDRESS = (PROTOCOL = TCP)(HOST = localhost.localdomain)(PORT = 1521))
    )
    (DESCRIPTION =
      (ADDRESS = (PROTOCOL = IPC)(KEY = EXTPROC1521))
    )
  )
```

Table 11.1 describes each of the `listener.ora` parameters for the Listening Location section of the `listener.ora` file.

TABLE 11.1 Parameters for the Listening Location Section of `listener.ora`

Parameter	Description
LISTENER	Indicates the starting point of a listener definition. This is actually the name of the listener being defined. The default name is LISTENER.
DESCRIPTION	Describes each of the listening locations.

TABLE 11.1 Parameters for the Listening Location Section of `listener.ora` *(continued)*

Parameter	Description
ADDRESS	Contains address information about the locations where the listener is listening.
PROTOCOL	Designates the protocol for this listening location.
HOST	Holds the name of the machine on which the listener resides.
PORT	Contains the address on which the listener is listening.
SID_LIST_*LISTENER*	Defines the list of Oracle services for which the listener (named LISTENER) is configured.
SID_DESC	Describes each Oracle SID.
GLOBAL_DBNAME	Identifies the global database name. This entry should match the SERVICE_NAMES entry in the `init.ora` file for the Oracle service.
ORACLE_HOME	Shows the location of the Oracle executables on the server.
SID_NAME	Contains the name of the Oracle SID for the Oracle instance.

Understanding Service Registration

Oracle 11*g* allows two types of service registration. Static service registration occurs when entries are added to the `listener.ora` file manually by using one of the Oracle tools. It is static because you are adding this information manually. Static service registration is necessary if you will be connecting to pre-Oracle8*i* instances using Oracle Enterprise Manager or if you will be connecting to external services.

Another way to manage listeners that does not require manual updating of service information in the `listener.ora` file is called *dynamic service registration*. Dynamic service registration allows an Oracle instance to automatically register itself with an Oracle listener. The benefit of this feature is that it does not require you to perform any updates of server-side network files when new Oracle instances are created. Dynamic service registration will be covered in more detail later in this chapter in the section "Dynamically Registering Services."

Optional *listener.ora* Parameters

You can set optional parameters that add functionality to the listener. To do so, select a parameter from the General Parameters drop-down list at the top right of the screen. Table 11.2 describes these parameters and where you can find them in Oracle Net Manager.

TABLE 11.2 Optional `listener.ora` Parameter Definitions

Net Manager Prompt	`listener.ora` Parameter	Description
Startup Wait Time	STARTUP_WAIT_TIME	Defines how long a listener will wait before it responds to a STATUS command in the `lsnrctl` command-line utility.
Save Configuration On Shutdown	CONNECT_TIMEOUT	Defines how long a listener will wait for a valid response from a client once a session is initiated. The default is 10 seconds.
Unavailable from Net Manager	SAVE_CONFIG_ON_STOP	Specifies whether modifications made during an `lsnrctl` session should be saved when exiting.
Log File	LOG_FILE. Will not be in the `listener.ora` file if the default setting is used. By default, listener logging is enabled with the log created in the default location	Specifies where a listener will write log information. This is ON by default and defaults to $ORACLE_HOME/network/ `log/listener.log`.
Trace Level	TRACE_LEVEL. Not present if tracing is disabled. The default is OFF	Sets the level of detail if listener connections are being traced. Valid values include `Off`, `User`, `Support`, and `Admin`.
Trace File	TRACE_FILE	Specifies the location of listener trace information. Defaults to $ORACLE_ HOME/network/trace/`listener.trc`.
Require A Password For Listener Operations	PASSWORDS	Specifies password required to perform administrative tasks in the `lsnrctl` command-line utility.

As you will see, you cannot add some parameters directly from the Oracle Net Manager and must do so manually. These optional parameters also have the listener name appended to them so that you can identify the listener definition to which they belong. For example, if the parameter `STARTUP_WAIT_TIME` is set for the default listener, the parameter created is `STARTUP_WAIT_TIME_LISTENER`.

Managing Listeners with Oracle Enterprise Manager

Oracle Enterprise Manager (EM) is a web-based tool that allows you to manage many aspects of an Oracle 11*g* server. Being able to perform administrative functions via a web interface lets you administer the database from any location where a web browser is available.

You can also manage Oracle Net using EM. On the Database Control home page, notice under the General section a list of listeners that are available to manage. Click a listener to display a screen (see Figure 11.14) that gives you details about that listener, including when the listener was started, the Oracle Net address and port information for the listener, and the listening location information.

FIGURE 11.14 The Oracle Enterprise Manager listener console

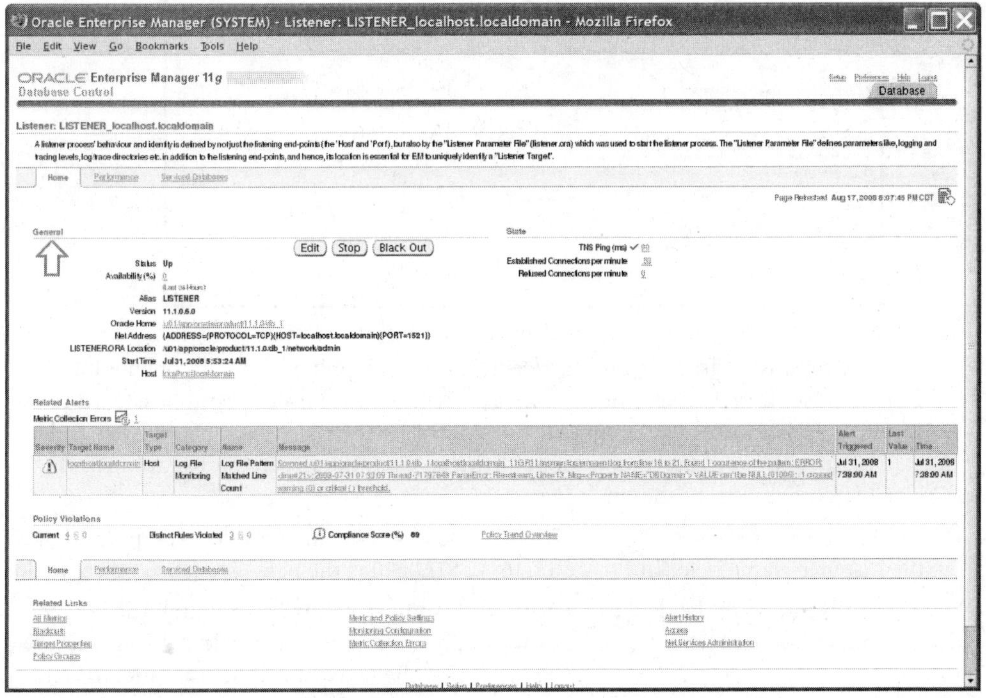

You can also add and edit listeners using the Database Control interface. Let's take a look at how to do so using the Oracle Enterprise Manager Database Control console.

Adding a Listener Using Enterprise Manager Database Control

You can use Enterprise Manager Database Control to add a listener by following these steps:

1. To add a new listener using the Database Control, select the Net Services Administration option listed under the Related Links section to open the Net Services Administration screen, as shown in Figure 11.15.

FIGURE 11.15 The Oracle Enterprise Manager Net Services Administration screen

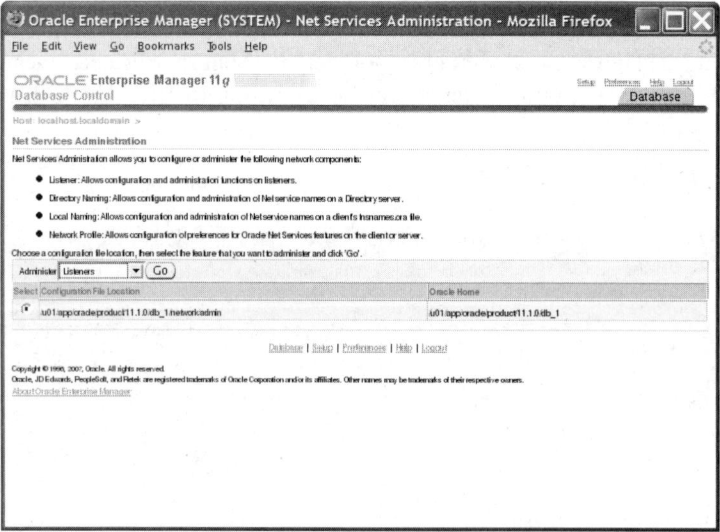

2. From the Administer drop-down list, select the listener, and click Go to open a login screen. Connect to the server with a valid operating-system user ID and password to open the listener control screen. In this example, a listener is already configured and named `LISTENER`. To create an additional listener, click the Create button to open the Create Listener screen, as shown in Figure 11.16.
3. Choose a name for the listener. Oracle will choose a new name for you and place that in the Listener Name field. In Figure 11.16, `LISTENER0` is the new listener to be created.

You can fully configure the new listener using this interface. At a minimum, the listener needs listening address information. Click the Add button to open the Add Address screen. You can choose a protocol, such as TCP/IP, for which the listener will be listening. You also need to designate a listening port and host where the listener will be listening for connections. The other parameters, the send and receive buffer size, are optional advanced parameters. Click OK to save your information.

FIGURE 11.16 The Oracle Enterprise Manager Create Listener screen

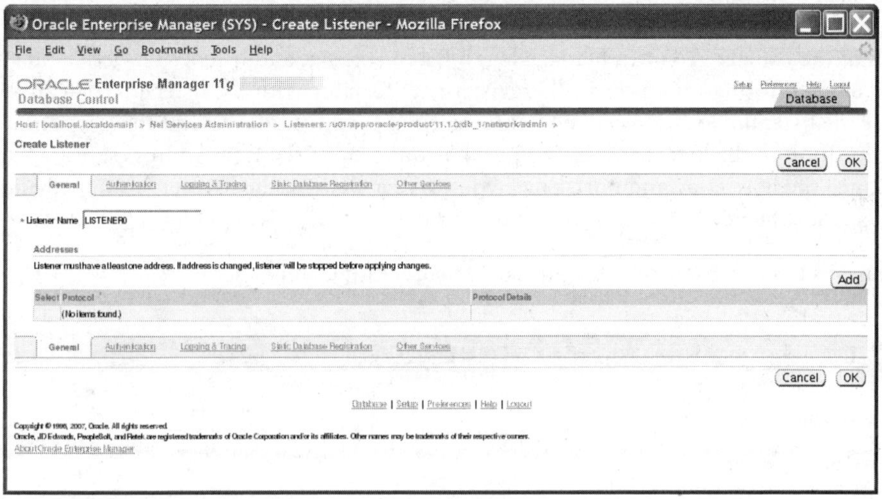

Editing Existing Listeners Using EM Database Control

From the Oracle Enterprise Manager Listener console, you can also make changes to an existing listener. Choose Edit to modify the `listener.ora` parameters, and save this information to the existing `listener.ora` file. To perform these functions, you must be logged in to the machine on which the listener file is located. From the login screen, enter the appropriate user ID and password for the machine and choose Login.

Once you are connected to the machine, you can administer all aspects of the listener. Figure 11.17 shows the main Oracle Enterprise Manager Listeners administration screen.

FIGURE 11.17 The Oracle Enterprise Manager Listeners administration screen

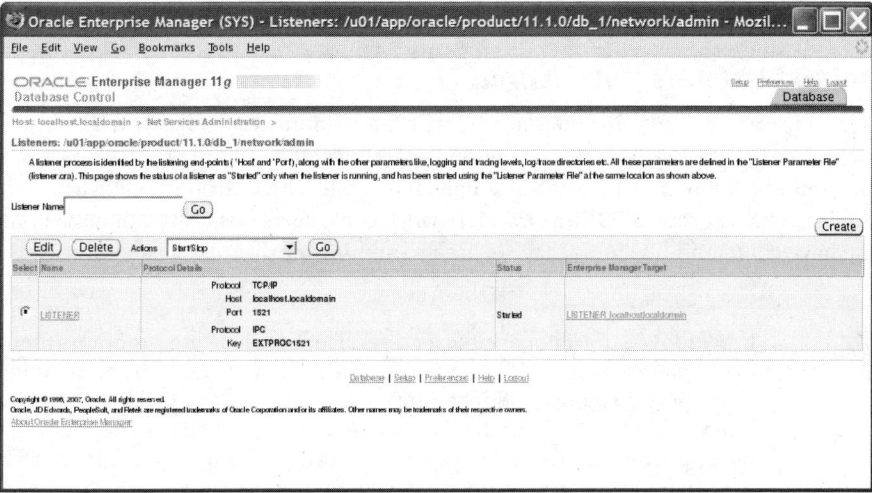

Use the Actions drop-down list to start or stop the listener as well as perform other actions such as tracing. Click the Edit button to configure the listener (see Figure 11.18). You use the tabs across the top of the listener administration screen to configure various aspects of the listener. You can manage logging and tracing, add listener services, and enter service-name information to statically register new services with the listener. You can also manage the listening location and port information. If you choose to edit the port or listening location of the listener, click the Edit button to open the Edit Address screen. You can change the hostname and port. Once you make a change, the listener is stopped and restarted with the new configuration information.

FIGURE 11.18 The Oracle Enterprise Manager Edit Listener screen

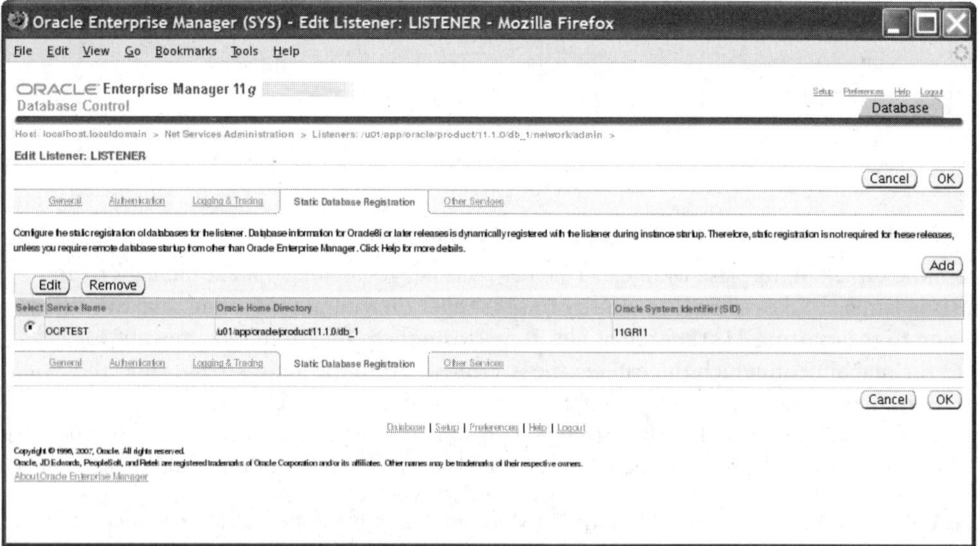

Managing Listeners with *lsnrctl*

You can also use a command-line interface, `lsnrctl`, to administer the listener. This tool gives you full configuration and administration capabilities. If you have been using Oracle, this tool should be familiar. This command-line interface has been around since the early releases of the Oracle product. Other Oracle network components, such as Connection Manager, also have command-line tools that are used to administer their associated processes.

In Windows, the listener runs as a service. Services are programs that run in the background in Windows. You can start the listener from the Windows Services panel. Choose Start ➢ Settings ➢ Control Panel ➢ Services. Then select the name of the listener service from the list of services. If the name of your listener is `Listener`, for example, look for an entry such as `OracleOra11gListener`. Select the listener name, and click Start.

To invoke the command-line utility, type **lsnrctl** at the command line. The following code shows a resulting login screen:

```
$ pwd
/u01/app/oracle/product/11.1.0/db_1/bin
$ ./lsnrctl

LSNRCTL for Linux: Version 11.1.0.6.0 - Production on 17-AUG-2008 20:50:36

Copyright (c) 1991, 2007, Oracle.  All rights reserved.

Welcome to LSNRCTL, type "help" for information.

LSNRCTL>
```

You can perform a variety of functions from within the `lsnrctl` utility. Let's take a look at the most common functions you'll perform on the listener using this utility.

Starting the Listener

The listener has commands to perform various functions. You can type **help** at the LSNRCTL> prompt to display a list of these commands. To start the default listener named LISTENER, type **start** at the prompt. To start a different listener, type **start** and then that listener name. For example, typing **start listener1** starts the LISTENER1 listener.

The following code shows the results of starting the default listener:

```
$ lsnrctl start

LSNRCTL for Linux: Version 11.1.0.6.0 - Production on 17-AUG-2008 20:51:49

Copyright (c) 1991, 2007, Oracle.  All rights reserved.

Starting /u01/app/oracle/product/11.1.0/db_1/bin/tnslsnr: please wait...

TNSLSNR for Linux: Version 11.1.0.6.0 - Production
System parameter file is /u01/app/oracle/product/11.1.0/db_1/network/admin/
listener.ora
Log messages written to /u01/app/oracle/diag/tnslsnr/localhost/listener/alert/
log.xml
Listening on: (DESCRIPTION=(ADDRESS=(PROTOCOL=tcp)(HOST=localhost.localdomain)
(PORT=1521)))
Listening on: (DESCRIPTION=(ADDRESS=(PROTOCOL=ipc)(KEY=EXTPROC1521)))

Connecting to (DESCRIPTION=(ADDRESS=(PROTOCOL=TCP)(HOST=localhost.localdomain)
(PORT=1521)))
```

```
STATUS of the LISTENER
------------------------
Alias                     LISTENER
Version                   TNSLSNR for Linux: Version 11.1.0.6.0 - Production
Start Date                17-AUG-2008 20:51:49
Uptime                    0 days 0 hr. 0 min. 0 sec
Trace Level               off
Security                  ON: Local OS Authentication
SNMP                      OFF
Listener Parameter File   /u01/app/oracle/product/11.1.0/db_1/network/admin/
listener.ora
Listener Log File         /u01/app/oracle/diag/tnslsnr/localhost/listener/
alert/log.xml
Listening Endpoints Summary...
  (DESCRIPTION=(ADDRESS=(PROTOCOL=tcp)(HOST=localhost.localdomain)(PORT=1521)))
  (DESCRIPTION=(ADDRESS=(PROTOCOL=ipc)(KEY=EXTPROC1521)))
Services Summary...
Service "OCPTEST" has 1 instance(s).
  Instance "11GR11", status UNKNOWN, has 1 handler(s) for this service...
The command completed successfully
$
```

This listing shows a summary of information, including the services that the listener is listening for, the log locations, and whether tracing is enabled for the listener.

Reloading the Listener

If the listener is running and modifications are made to the `listener.ora` file manually, with Oracle Net Manager or with Enterprise Manager, you must reload the listener to refresh the listener with the most current information. The `reload` command rereads the `listener.ora` file for the new definitions. As you can see, it is not necessary to stop and start the listener to reload it. Although stopping and restarting the listener can also accomplish a reload, using the `reload` command is better because the listener is not actually stopped, which makes this process more efficient. The following code shows an example of the `reload` command:

```
$ lsnrctl reload

LSNRCTL for Linux: Version 11.1.0.6.0 - Production on 17-AUG-2008 20:53:45

Copyright (c) 1991, 2007, Oracle.  All rights reserved.

Connecting to (DESCRIPTION=(ADDRESS=(PROTOCOL=TCP)(HOST=localhost.localdomain)
(PORT=1521)))
The command completed successfully
$
```

Reloading the listener has no effect on clients connected to the Oracle server.

In the previous code example, Oracle has reread the `listener.ora` file and applied any changes you made to the file against the currently running listener process. You can see the address, protocol, and port designation of the default listener. Notice that this listener is listening on the default port of 1521.

Showing the Status of the Listener

You can display the status of the listener by using the `status` command. The `status` command shows whether the listener is active, the locations of the logs and trace files, how long the listener has been running, and the services for the listener. This is a quick way to verify that the listener is up and running with no problems.

The following code shows the result of the `lsnrctl status` command:

```
$ lsnrctl status


LSNRCTL for Linux: Version 11.1.0.6.0 - Production on 17-AUG-2008 20:54:58


Copyright (c) 1991, 2007, Oracle.  All rights reserved.


Connecting to (DESCRIPTION=(ADDRESS=(PROTOCOL=TCP)(HOST=localhost.localdomain)
(PORT=1521)))
STATUS of the LISTENER
------------------------
Alias                     LISTENER
Version                   TNSLSNR for Linux: Version 11.1.0.6.0 - Production
Start Date                17-AUG-2008 20:51:49
Uptime                    0 days 0 hr. 3 min. 8 sec
Trace Level               off
Security                  ON: Local OS Authentication
SNMP                      OFF
Listener Parameter File   /u01/app/oracle/product/11.1.0/db_1/network/admin/
listener.ora
Listener Log File         /u01/app/oracle/diag/tnslsnr/localhost/listener/
alert/log.xml
Listening Endpoints Summary...
  (DESCRIPTION=(ADDRESS=(PROTOCOL=tcp)(HOST=localhost.localdomain)(PORT=1521)))
  (DESCRIPTION=(ADDRESS=(PROTOCOL=ipc)(KEY=EXTPROC1521)))
Services Summary...
Service "11GR11" has 1 instance(s).
  Instance "11GR11", status READY, has 1 handler(s) for this service...
Service "11GR11XDB" has 1 instance(s).
  Instance "11GR11", status READY, has 1 handler(s) for this service...
```

```
Service "11GR11_XPT" has 1 instance(s).
  Instance "11GR11", status READY, has 1 handler(s) for this service...
Service "010GR21" has 1 instance(s).
  Instance "010GR21", status READY, has 1 handler(s) for this service...
Service "010GR21XDB" has 1 instance(s).
  Instance "010GR21", status READY, has 1 handler(s) for this service...
Service "010GR21_XPT" has 1 instance(s).
  Instance "010GR21", status READY, has 1 handler(s) for this service...
Service "OCPTEST" has 1 instance(s).
  Instance "11GR11", status UNKNOWN, has 1 handler(s) for this service...
The command completed successfully
$
```

This code example depicts a listener that has recently been started. You also see what the log file and parameter file locations are for the listener. This is a good facility to use to get a quick listing of vital information for the listener.

Use `lsnrctl status` to see how long the listener was up. Look for `Uptime`.

Listing the Services for the Listener

The `lsnrctl services` command displays information about the services, such as whether the services have any dedicated, prespawned server processes or dispatched processes associated with them, and how many connections have been accepted and rejected per service. Use this method to check whether a listener is listening for a particular service.

The following code shows an example of running the `services` command:

```
$ lsnrctl services


LSNRCTL for Linux: Version 11.1.0.6.0 - Production on 17-AUG-2008 20:56:05


Copyright (c) 1991, 2007, Oracle.  All rights reserved.


Connecting to (DESCRIPTION=(ADDRESS=(PROTOCOL=TCP)(HOST=localhost.localdomain)
(PORT=1521)))
Services Summary...
Service "11GR11" has 1 instance(s).
  Instance "11GR11", status READY, has 1 handler(s) for this service...
    Handler(s):
      "DEDICATED" established:0 refused:0 state:ready
         LOCAL SERVER
Service "11GR11XDB" has 1 instance(s).
  Instance "11GR11", status READY, has 1 handler(s) for this service...
```

```
    Handler(s):
      "D000" established:0 refused:0 current:0 max:1022 state:ready
         DISPATCHER <machine: localhost.localdomain, pid: 3375>
         (ADDRESS=(PROTOCOL=tcp)(HOST=localhost.localdomain)(PORT=30767))
Service "OCPTEST" has 1 instance(s).
  Instance "11GR11", status UNKNOWN, has 1 handler(s) for this service...
    Handler(s):
      "DEDICATED" established:0 refused:0
         LOCAL SERVER
The command completed successfully
$
```

In this example, you can see that the listener is listening for connections to the service OCPTEST. The line "DEDICATED" established:0 refused:0 shows you how many connections to this service have been accepted or rejected by the listener. One reason why a listener may reject servicing a request is if the database is not available.

Other Commands in lsnrctl

You can run other commands in lsnrctl. Table 11.3 summarizes these other commands. Type the command at the LSNRCTL> prompt to execute it.

TABLE 11.3 A Summary of the lsnrctl Commands

Command	Definition
change_password	Allows a user to change the password needed to stop the listener.
Exit	Exits the lsnrctl utility.
Quit	Performs the same function as exit.
save_config	Copies the listener.ora file called listener.bak when changes are made to the listener.ora file from lsnrctl.
Services	Lists a summary of services and details information about the number of connections established and the number of connections refused for each protocol service handler.
start listener	Starts the named listener.
status listener	Shows the status of the named listener.
stop listener	Stops the named listener.
Trace	Turns on tracing for the listener.
Version	Displays the version of the Oracle Net software and protocol adapters.

Using the set Commands in lsnrctl

The lsnrctl utility also has commands called set commands. To issue these commands, type **set *commandname*** at the LSNRCTL> prompt. You use the set commands to modify the listener.ora file. For example, you can use this command to set up logging and tracing. You can set most of these parameters using the Oracle Net Manager.

To display the current setting of a parameter, use the show command, which displays the current settings of the parameters set using the set command. Table 11.4 summarizes the lsnrctl set commands. Type **set** or **show** to display a listing of all the commands.

TABLE 11.4 A Summary of the lsnrctl set Commands

Command	Description
current_listener	Sets the listener to modify or shows the name of the current listener.
displaymode	Sets display for the lsnrctl utility to RAW, COMPACT, NORMAL, or VERBOSE.
log_status	Shows whether logging is on or off for the listener.
log_file	Shows the name of listener log file.
log_directory	Shows the log directory location.
rawmode	Shows more detail on STATUS and SERVICES when set to ON. Values are ON or OFF.
startup_waittime	Sets the length of time that a listener will wait to respond to a status command in the lsnrctl command-line utility.
spawn	Starts external services that the listener is listening for and that are running on the server.
save_config_on_stop	Saves changes to the listener.ora file when exiting lsnrctl.
trc_level	Sets the trace level to OFF, USER, ADMIN, or SUPPORT.
trc_file	Sets the name of the listener trace file.
trc_directory	Sets the name of the listener trace directory.

Stopping the Listener

To stop the listener, you must issue the lsnrctl stop command. This command stops the default listener. To stop a nondefault listener, include the name of the listener. For example, to stop LISTENER1, type **lsnrctl stop listener1**. If you are in the lsnrctl> facility, you will stop the current listener defined by the current_listener setting. To see what the current listener is set to, use the show command. The default value is LISTENER.

Stopping the listener does not affect clients connected to the database. It only means that no new connections can use this listener until the listener is restarted.

The following code shows what the stop command looks like:

```
$ lsnrctl stop

LSNRCTL for Linux: Version 11.1.0.6.0 - Production on 17-AUG-2008 20:59:32

Copyright (c) 1991, 2007, Oracle.  All rights reserved.

Connecting to (DESCRIPTION=(ADDRESS=(PROTOCOL=TCP)(HOST=localhost.localdomain)
(PORT=1521)))
The command completed successfully
$
```

Dynamically Registering Services

Oracle 11*g* databases can automatically register their presence with an existing listener. The instance registers with the listener defined on the local machine. Dynamic service registration allows you to take advantage of other features, such as load balancing and automatic failover. The PMON process is responsible for registering this information with the listener.

When dynamic service registration is used, you will not see the service listed in the listener.ora file. To see the service listed, run the lsnrctl services command. Be aware that if the listener is started after the Oracle instance, there may be a time lag before the instance actually registers information with the listener.

For an instance to automatically register with a listener, the listener must be configured as a default listener, or you must specify the init.ora parameter LOCAL_LISTENER. The LOCAL_LISTENER parameter defines the location of the listener with which you want the Oracle server to register. This is a default listener definition:

```
Listener Name = LISTENER
Port = 1521
Protocol = TCP/IP
```

You must configure two other init.ora parameters to allow an instance to register information with the listener. Two parameters are used to allow automatic registration: INSTANCE_NAME and SERVICE_NAMES.

The INSTANCE_NAME parameter is set to the name of the Oracle instance you want to register with the listener. The SERVICE_NAMES parameter is a combination of the instance name and the domain name. The domain name is set to the value of the DB_DOMAIN initialization parameter. For example, if your DB_DOMAIN is set to BJS.COM and your Oracle instance is DBA, set the parameters as follows:

```
Instance_name = DBA
Service_names = DBA.BJS.COM
```

If you are not using domain names, set the INSTANCE_NAME and SERVICE_NAMES parameters to the same values.

Oracle Net Logging and Tracing on the Server

If a network problem persists, you can use *logging* and *tracing* to help resolve it. Oracle generates information into log files and trace files that can assist you in tracking down network connection problems. You can use logging to find out general information about the success or failure of certain components of the Oracle network. You can use tracing to get in-depth information about specific network connections.

By default, Oracle produces logs for clients and the Oracle listener.

- *Logging* records significant events, such as starting and stopping the listener, along with certain kinds of network errors. Errors are generated in the log in the form of an error stack. The listener log records information such as the version number, connection attempts, and the protocols for which it is listening. You can enable logging at the client, middle-tier, and server locations.
- *Tracing*, which you can also enable at the client, middle-tier, or server location, records all events that occur on a network, even when an error does not occur. The trace file provides a great deal of information that logs do not, such as the number of network round-trips made during a network connection or the number of packets sent and received during a network connection. Tracing enables you to collect a thorough listing of the actual sequence of the statements as a network connection is being processed. This gives you a much more detailed picture of what is occurring with connections that the listener is processing.

Real World Scenario

Use Tracing Sparingly

Use tracing only as a last resort if you are having connectivity problems between the client and server. Complete all the server-side checks described earlier before you resort to tracing. The tracing process generates a significant amount of overhead, and depending on the trace level set, it can create some rather large files. This activity will impede system I/O performance because of all the information that is written to the logs, and if left unchecked, it could fill your disk or file system.

> I was once involved with a large project that was using JDBC to connect to the Oracle server. We were having difficulty with connections being periodically dropped between the JDBC client and the Oracle server. We enabled tracing to try to find the problem. We did eventually correct the problem (it was with how our DNS names server was configured), but the tracing was left on inadvertently. When the system eventually went into production, the trace files grew so large that they filled the disk where tracing was being collected. To prevent this from happening, periodically ensure that the trace parameters are not turned on, and if they are, turn them off.

Use Oracle Net Manager to enable most logging and tracing parameters. Many of the logging and tracing parameters are found in the `sqlnet.ora` file. Let's take a look at how to enable logging and tracing for the various components in an Oracle network.

Server Logging

By default, the listener is configured to enable the generation of a log file. The log file records information about listener startup and shutdown, successful and unsuccessful connection attempts, and certain types of network errors. Here's what everything means by default:

- The listener log location is *<DIAGNOSTIC_DEST>*`/diag/tnslsnr/`*<hostname>*`/listener/trace` on Unix.
- The default name of the file is `listener.log`.
- The XML version of the listener log is under *<DIAGNOSTIC_DEST>*`/diag/tnslsnr/`*<hostname>*`/listener/alert`, and the filename is `log.xml`.
- If the `DIAGNOSTIC_DEST` parameter is not defined, Oracle defaults it to `$ORACLE_BASE`.

Information in the `listener.log` file contains information about connection attempts, the name of the program executing the request, and the name of the client attempting to connect. The last field contains a zero if a request was successfully completed.

Server Tracing

As mentioned earlier, tracing gathers information about the flow of traffic across a network connection. Data is transmitted back and forth in the form of packets. A packet contains sender information, receiver information, and data. Even a single network request can generate a large number of packets.

In the trace file, each line starts with the name of the procedure executed in one of the Oracle Net layers and is followed by a set of hexadecimal numbers. The hexadecimal numbers are the actual data transmitted. If you are not encrypting the data, sometimes you will see the actual data after the hexadecimal numbers.

If you are doing server-to-server communications and have a `sqlnet.ora` file on the server, you can enter information in the Server Information section located on the Tracing tab of the Profile screen in Oracle Net Manager tracing. This provides tracing information for server-to-server communications.

Enabling Server Tracing

You can enable server tracing from the same Oracle Net Manager screens shown earlier. Simply click the Tracing Enabled radio button. The default trace file location is `$DIAGNOSTIC_DEST/diag/tnslsnr/hostname/listener/trace` in Unix. You can set the trace level to `OFF`, `USER`, `ADMIN`, or `SUPPORT`. The `USER` level detects specific user errors. The `ADMIN` level contains all the user-level information along with installation-specific errors. `SUPPORT` is the highest level and can produce information that might be beneficial to Oracle Support personnel. This level also can produce large trace files.

The following example shows a section of the `listener.ora` file with the logging and tracing parameters enabled:

```
TRACE_LEVEL_LISTENER = ADMIN
TRACE_FILE_LISTENER = LISTENER.trc
LOGGING_LISTENER = ON
LOG_FILE_LISTENER = LISTENER.log
```

Configuring Oracle Net for the Client

Once the Oracle server is properly configured, you can focus on configuring the clients to allow for connectivity to the Oracle server. It is important to understand how to configure Oracle clients because without proper knowledge of how to do this, you are limited in your connection choices to the server. As a DBA, you must understand the network needs of the organization, the type of connectivity that is required, and client/server connections vs. *n*-tier connectivity, for example, in order to make the appropriate choices about client-side configuration. This section should help clarify the client-side connectivity options available to you and show you how to troubleshoot client connection problems.

Client-Side Names Resolution Options

When a client needs to connect to an Oracle server, the client must supply three pieces of information: their user ID, password, and net service name. The net service name provides the necessary information, in the form of a connect descriptor, to locate an Oracle service in a network.

This connect descriptor describes the path to the Oracle server and its service name, which is an alias for an Oracle Database. The location where this information is kept depends on the names resolution method you choose. The five methods of net service name resolution are Oracle Internet Directory, external naming, host naming, Oracle Easy Connect, and local naming. Normally, you choose just one of these methods, but you can use any combination.

Oracle Internet Directory is advantageous when you are dealing with complex networks that have many Oracle servers. When you choose this method, you can configure and manage net service names and connect descriptor information in a central location.

External naming uses a non-Oracle facility to manage and resolve Oracle service names. For example, if an organization uses an external names resolution method such as Network Information Service (NIS), the database service information could be stored in this external location and used by clients to resolve service names.

You need to be only casually familiar with the Oracle Internet Directory and the external naming resolution options. For a more detailed description of how to configure and use external naming, please consult "Oracle Database Net Services Administrator's Guide 11*g* Release 1 (11.1) Part Number B28316-04." You can find the Oracle documentation at `http://tahiti.oracle.com`.

In the following sections, we will take a closer look at the host naming, Oracle Easy Connect, and local naming methods.

The Host Naming Method

In small networks with few Oracle servers to manage, you can take advantage of the *host naming method*. Host naming is advantageous when you want to reduce the amount of configuration work necessary. Host naming saves you from configuring the clients, although it does have limitations. The following are the four prerequisites to using host naming:

- You must use TCP/IP as your network protocol.
- You must not use any advanced networking features, such as Oracle Connection Manager.
- You must have an external naming service, such as DNS, or a `HOSTS` file available to the client.
- The listener must be set up with the `GLOBAL_DBNAME` parameter equal to the name of the machine.

Now let's discuss how to configure this naming method.

Configuring the Host Naming Method

By default, Oracle attempts to use the host naming method from the client only after it attempts connections using local naming. To override this default search path for resolving names, set the `NAMES.DIRECTORY_PATH` parameter in the `sqlnet.ora` file on the client so that it searches for host naming only. The following is an example of the `sqlnet.ora` file:

```
# SQLNET.ORA Network Configuration File:
# Generated by Oracle configuration tools.

NAMES.DEFAULT_DOMAIN = bjs.com
NAMES.DIRECTORY_PATH= (HOSTNAME)
```

The host naming and the Oracle Easy Connect methods do not require any client-side configuration files. We'll discuss these connection methods later in this section.

You can check TCP/IP connectivity from the client using the TCP/IP utility `ping`. The `ping` utility attempts to contact the server by sending a small request packet. The server responds in kind with an acknowledgment.

The server must be configured with a listener running TCP/IP, and the listener must be listening on the default port of 1521. If the instance has not been dynamically registered with the listener, you must configure the listener with the `GLOBAL_DBNAME` parameter.

The Oracle Easy Connect Method

The Oracle Easy Connect method is a connection resolution technique introduced in Oracle 10*g*. This method is similar to the host naming method described in the previous section but adds parameters that allow for a port and service-name specification. By default, the Oracle Easy Connect names resolution method is configured when Oracle Net is installed.

Like the host naming method, the Oracle Easy Connect method eliminates the need for any connection information to be configured on the client. This makes for less setup and administrative work. It enhances the host naming method by allowing for a port and service specification. Remember from the previous section that the host naming method requires a listener to be listening on the default port of 1521. Allowing a port specification addresses one of the limitations of the host naming method. Using the Oracle Easy Connect method requires that certain conditions be met:

- Oracle Net Services 10*g* or 11*g* must be installed on the client.
- Oracle Net TCP/IP services must be enabled and supported on both the client and the server.
- No advanced connection descriptor features are allowed such as connection pooling or external procedure calls.

Table 11.5 describes the connect descriptor components when you are using the Oracle Easy Connect method.

TABLE 11.5 Easy Connect Components

Syntax Component	Description
//	Optional: Used when you are connecting via a URL.
Host	Required: The host or IP address to connect to.
Port	Optional: The port to connect to. The default is 1521.

TABLE 11.5 Easy Connect Components *(continued)*

Syntax Component	Description
Service name	The service name for the database. The default is the hostname of the computer on which the database resides. If the database name is different from the hostname, enter the service name.

Here is an example of how to connect to a database using the Easy Connect method:

```
CONNECT scott/tiger@myhostname:1521/11GR11
```

The example shows how a user connects to the database service 11GR11 that is running on the myhostname server and has an Oracle listener listening for TCP/IP connections on port 1521. As stated previously, this method is configured automatically when you install Oracle Net. If you want the Oracle Easy Connect method to be the first method chosen by a client when a connection request is made, you can modify the NAMES.DIRECTORY_PATH parameter in the sqlnet.ora file. The following discussion shows how to do this.

You can use the Oracle Net Manager tool to configure the Easy Connect method as the default names resolution method. Start the Oracle Net Manager tool, and then follow these steps:

1. Choose Local ➤ Profile Pane in the Navigator pane.
2. Select Naming from the panel on the right.
3. Select the Methods tab.
4. Select EZCONNECT in the Selected Methods list. You can click the promote arrows to move EZCONNECT to the top of the Selected Methods list.
5. Choose File ➤ Save Network Configuration to save your changes.

   When you check your sqlnet.ora file, you should see the following entry:

   ```
   NAMES.DIRECTORY_PATH=(EZCONNECT,TNSNAMES)
   ```

The Local Naming Method

The *local naming method* is probably the most widely used and well-known method for resolving net service names. Most users know this method as the tnsnames.ora method because it uses the tnsnames.ora file.

To use the local naming method, you must configure the tnsnames.ora file, which can be in any location, as long as the client can get to it. The default location for the tnsnames.ora file and the sqlnet.ora file is %ORACLE_HOME%\network\admin in Windows and $ORACLE_HOME/network/admin in Unix systems. If you want to change the location of this file, set the environmental variable TNS_ADMIN. In Unix-based systems, you can export TNS_ADMIN to the user's shell environment or in the user's profile. In Windows, this setting is in the registry. The Windows registry key that stores the TNS_ADMIN depends on your particular setup. Generally, it is somewhere under Hkey_local_machine/software/oracle, but it may be at a lower level depending on your configuration.

Most installations probably keep the files in these default locations on the client and server. Some users create shared disks and place the tnsnames.ora and sqlnet.ora files in this shared location to take a centralized approach to managing these files. If server-to-server communication is necessary, these files need to be on the server. The default location on the server is the same as the default location on the client.

Now that you have an understanding of the local naming method, I will discuss how to configure this method using Oracle Net Manager.

Configuring the Local Naming Method Using Oracle Net Manager

To configure the local naming method, you use Oracle Net Manager. To start this configuration, open Net Manager, and select Service Naming on the Local tab. Click the plus sign on the left side of the screen, or choose Edit ➤ Create.

The Oracle Net Manager starts the net service name wizard, which guides you through the process of creating the net service names definition. The following steps detail how to configure the local naming method:

1. When you configure a client to use the local naming method, you must first choose a *net service name*. This is the name that users enter when they are referring to the location to which they want to connect. The name you supply here should not include the domain portion if you are using the hierarchical naming mode. Figure 11.19 shows an example of choosing the net service name. Click the Next button to continue.

FIGURE 11.19 Choosing a net service name

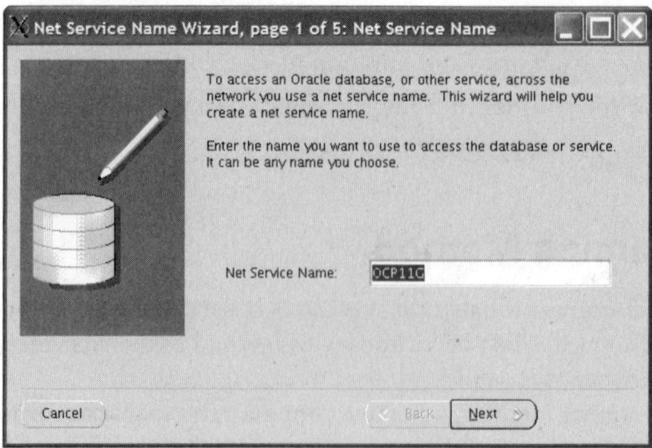

2. The next step is to enter the type of protocol that the client should use when they connect to the server for this net service name. By default, TCP/IP is chosen (see Figure 11.20). The list of protocols depends on your platform. Click the Next button to continue.

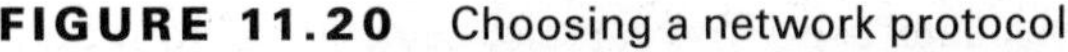

FIGURE 11.20 Choosing a network protocol

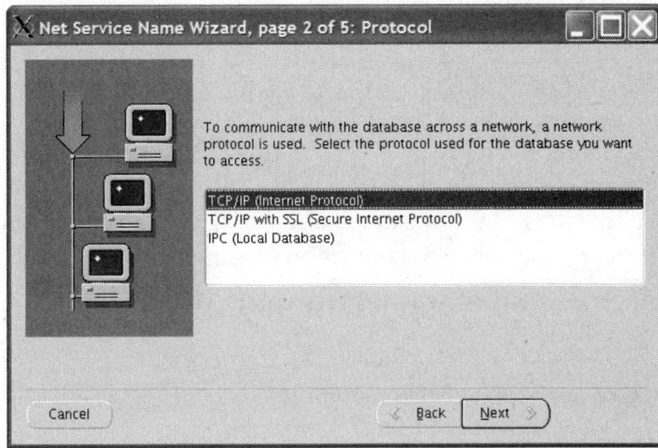

3. The next step is to choose the hostname and port. This step depends on the protocol you chose in the previous step. If you chose TCP/IP, you are prompted for the hostname and the port number. The hostname is the name of the machine on which the listener process is running. The port number is the listening location for the listener. The default port is 1521 (see Figure 11.21).

FIGURE 11.21 Choosing a hostname and a port

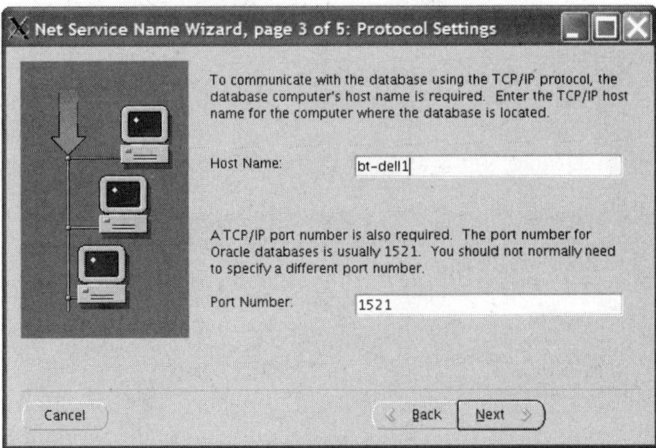

4. The next step is to define the service name. For Oracle 11g, the service name does not have to be the same as the `ORACLE_SID` because a database can have multiple service names. In Oracle 11g, the service name is normally the same as the global database name. This is the service name that is supplied to the listener, so the listener has to be listening for this service. You can also choose whether this service is for Oracle8*i* or

later databases or Oracle8*i* and previous databases. You can also select the connection type from one of these choices:

- Database Default
- Shared Server
- Dedicated Server

Figure 11.22 shows an example of the Oracle Net Manager service name screen.

5. The last step is to test the net service name and verify that all the connection information entered is correct. Click the Test button to test the network connection.

Click Finish button to create the `tnsnames.ora` entry. You can edit the entry, as shown in Figure 11.23.

FIGURE 11.22 Choosing the service name

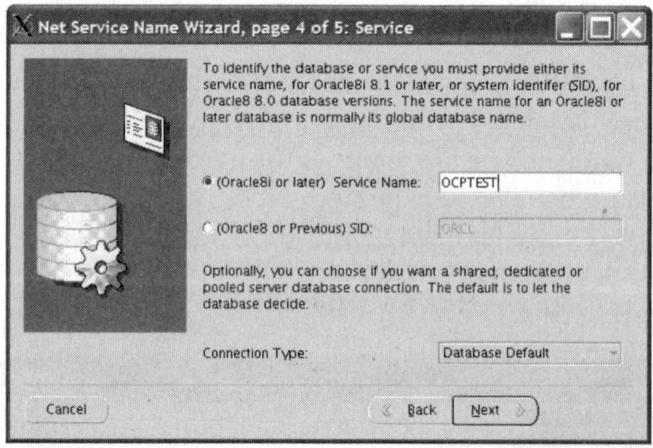

FIGURE 11.23 The Oracle Net Manager `tnsnames.ora` wizard

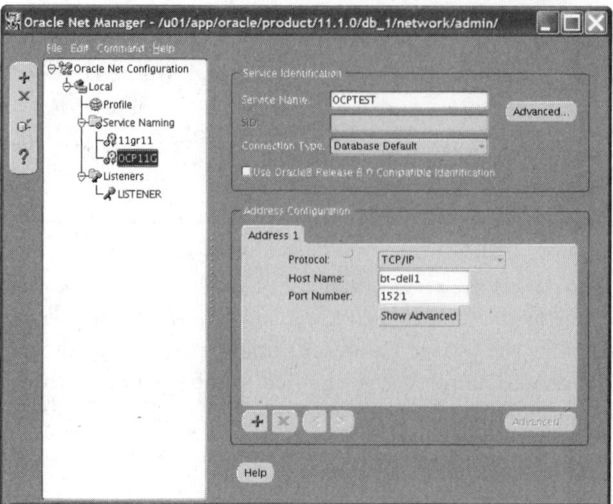

After you complete all this, save your changes by choosing File ➤ Save Network Configuration. This creates and saves the `tnsnames.ora` file.

Contents and Structure of the *tnsnames.ora* File

You created the `tnsnames.ora` file using the Oracle Net Manager, so open the `tnsnames.ora` file to view its contents. The `tnsnames.ora` file is located at the location the `TNS_ADMIN` variable is set to, which defaults to the `$ORACLE_HOME/network/admin` directory. Here is an example of the `tnsnames.ora` file:

```
OCP11G =
  (DESCRIPTION =
    (ADDRESS_LIST =
      (ADDRESS = (PROTOCOL = TCP)(HOST = bt-dell1)(PORT = 1521))
    )
    (CONNECT_DATA =
      (SERVICE_NAME = OCPTEST)
    )
  )
```

Table 11.6 summarizes the parameters in the `tnsnames.ora` file.

TABLE 11.6 The `tnsnames.ora` Parameters

Parameter	Description
DESCRIPTION	Starts the connect descriptor section of the file.
ADDRESS_LIST	Starts a list of all connect descriptor address information.
ADDRESS	Specifies the connect descriptor for the net service name.
PROTOCOL	Specifies the protocol used, such as TCP/IP.
HOST	Specifies the name of the machine on which the listener is running. An IP address can also be specified in TCP/IP.
PORT	Specifies the listening location of the listener specific to TCP/IP.
CONNECT_DATA	Starts the services section for this net service name.
SERVICE_NAME	Replaces the SID parameter from older releases of Oracle. Defines which service to connect to, which can be the same as the ORACLE_SID or the global database name. Databases can now be referred to by more than a single service name.

Configuring Local Naming Using Enterprise Manager

You can also use Oracle Enterprise Manager to configure local naming. You do so from the Net Services Administration screen as described in the "Adding a Listener Using Enterprise Manager Database Control" section earlier in this chapter. You will see the screen shown in Figure 11.15. Choose Local Naming from the Administer drop-down list, and click Go to open the Local Naming screen, as shown in Figure 11.24.

FIGURE 11.24 Using Enterprise Manager to configure local naming

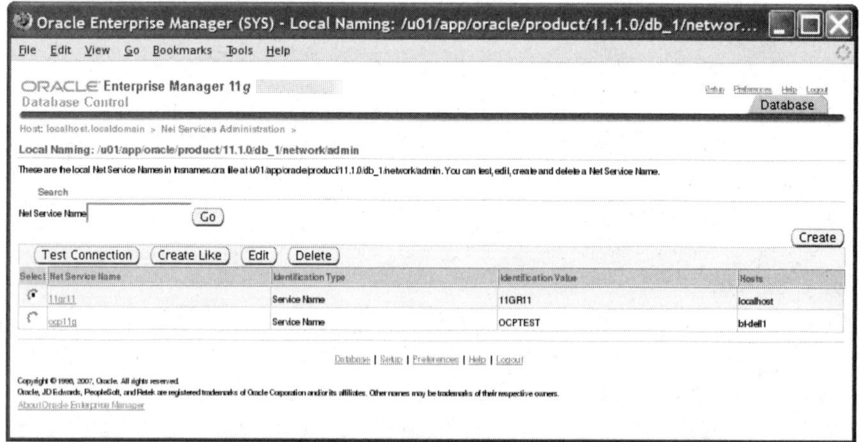

1. Click the Create button to open the Create Net Service Name page. Here you can enter the unique service name that you want users to use to connect to this Oracle service. This can also be the Oracle SID.
2. Select the type of connection to use for this service: a dedicated server, shared server, or the database default.
3. Specify the address information. This includes the protocol, port, and host used by the service being connected to.
4. Click the Add button under Addresses to open the Add Address screen to fill in the appropriate information.

On the Create New Service Name page, there is a section to configure failover and load balancing options. Five choices are listed under the Connect Time Failover and Load Balancing section. Table 11.7 summarizes these prompts. If you have multiple listeners listening for this service or are using Oracle Connection Manager, you can select from this list. The default is to use the first address only; this is the case where a single listener is being used.

Source routing is used with Oracle Connection Manager. Oracle passes control from the first address listed to the next address, and so on, until the ultimate destination is reached. Every address listed is used in the case of source routing.

TABLE 11.7 Advanced-Features Summary

Option	Advanced Feature
Try each address, in order, until one succeeds.	Failover
Try each address, randomly, until one succeeds.	Failover Load Balancing
Try one address, selected at random.	Load Balancing
Use each address in order until you reach the destination.	Source Routing
Use only the first address.	None

Troubleshooting Client-Side Connection Problems

Connection problems can also occur from the Oracle client. Several areas affect the ability of a client to connect successfully to the server. The client must be able to contact both the computer on which the Oracle server is located and the listener listening for connections to the Oracle server. The client must also be able to resolve the net service name. Let's look at the checks to perform on the client to verify connectivity to the Oracle server and to detect and troubleshoot client-side connection problems. Use the following list to help you systematically check various aspects of the client connection process:

- Verify that the client can contact the server.
- Determine the network route that the client is taking to the server.
- Verify local naming configuration files.
- Check for multiple-client network configuration files.
- Check network file locations.
- Check the `NAMES.DIRECTORY_PATH` parameter.
- Check the `NAMES.DEFAULT_DOMAIN` parameter.
- Check the client protocol adapters installed.
- Check for any common client-side error codes.

Oracle provides the `tnsping` utility to verify that the local naming entry defined in the `tnsnames.ora` file can talk to the service name defined in the `listener.ora` file. You can find `tnsping` in the `$ORACLE_HOME/bin` directory. It also provides the time it took to reach the listener in milliseconds.

Checking Network File Locations

One of the most common problems encountered is clients moving network files and not setting the TNS_ADMIN environmental variable to the new file location. Oracle expects the tnsnames.ora and sqlnet.ora files to be in the default location. If it cannot locate the files and you have not set TNS_ADMIN, you receive an ORA-12154 error message. You also receive this error if the supplied net service name is invalid or the NAMES.DEFAULT_DOMAIN value is mismatched in tnsnames.ora and sqlnet.ora files. The following code shows an example of this error message:

```
$ sqlplus system@ocp11r1

SQL*Plus: Release 11.1.0.6.0 - Production on Sun Aug 17 23:47:17 2008

Copyright (c) 1982, 2007, Oracle.  All rights reserved.

Enter password:
ERROR:
ORA-12154: TNS: could not resolve the connect identifier specified
```

If you decide to move network files, be sure to set the TNS_ADMIN environmental variable to the location of the files. Oracle first searches the default location for the files and then searches the TNS_ADMIN location for the files.

Checking NAMES.DIRECTORY_PATH

Make sure the client has the proper names resolution setting. The NAMES.DIRECTORY_PATH parameter in the sqlnet.ora file controls the order in which the client resolves net service names. If the parameter is not set, the default is local naming, OID, and then host naming.

If this parameter is set incorrectly, the client may never check the appropriate names resolution type. For example, if you are using local naming and the parameter is set to HOSTNAMES, the tnsnames.ora file will never be used to resolve the net service name. You will receive an ORA-12154 "Could Not Resolve the Connect Identifier Specified" error message.

Checking NAMES.DEFAULT_DOMAIN

NAMES.DEFAULT_DOMAIN is another common error. It was more common in older releases of Oracle because the parameter defaulted to the value WORLD. Check the client sqlnet.ora file to see whether the parameter is set. If the parameter has a value and you are using unqualified net service names, the parameter value is appended to the end of the net service name. An unqualified service name is a service name that does not contain domain information.

For example, if you entered **sqlplus matt/casey@PROD** and the NAMES.DEFAULT_DOMAIN is set to WORLD, Oracle appends .WORLD to the net service name; as a result, Oracle passes the command as `sqlplus matt/casey@PROD.WORLD`. You will receive an ORA-12154 "Could Not Resolve the Connect Identifier Specified" error message if the service name should not include the `.WORLD` domain extension. You use this parameter only if you are using a hierarchical naming convention.

Checking for Client-Side Error Codes

You should next check for client-side error codes. Here is a summary of some of the common client-side Oracle error messages you might encounter. They are discussed in detail in the following sections.

```
ORA-12154 "TNS: could not resolve connect identifier specified"
ORA-12198 "TNS: could not find path to destination"
ORA-12203 "TNS: Unable to connect to destination"
ORA-12533 "TNS: illegal address parameters"
ORA-12541 "TNS: No listener"
```

ORA-12154 This indicates that the client cannot find the service listed in the `tnsnames.ora` file. Some of the causes of this were previously described, such as the file is not in the proper directory or the `TNS_ADMIN` variable is not specified or specified incorrectly.

ORA-12198 and ORA-12203 This indicates that the client found an entry for the service in the `tnsnames.ora` file but the service specified was not found. Check to make sure the service specified in the `tnsnames.ora` file actually points to a valid database service.

ORA-12533 This indicates that you have configured the `ADDRESS` section of the `tnsnames.ora` file incorrectly. Check to make sure the syntax is correct, or re-create the definition using the Oracle Net Manager tool.

ORA-12541 This indicates that the client contacted a server that does not have a listener running on the specified port. Make sure the listener is started on the server and that the listening port specifications on the client and the server match.

An Overview of Oracle Shared Server

Oracle Shared Server is an optional configuration of Oracle Server that allows the server to support a larger number of concurrent connections without increasing physical resource requirements. It does so by sharing resources among groups of users.

Shared Server is suitable for *high-think* applications. High-think applications are composed of small transactions with natural pauses in the transaction patterns, which makes them good candidates for Oracle Shared Server connections. Many web-based applications fit this model. These types of applications are typically form-based and involve submissions of small amounts of information to the database with small result sets returned to the client.

Oracle manages dedicated server and shared server connections differently. As a DBA, you need to be able to identify these differences. This knowledge will help you better understand the advantages and disadvantages of Oracle Shared Server and when it might be advantageous to use Oracle Shared Server in your environment.

Dedicated Server vs. Shared Server

If you have ever gone to an upscale restaurant, you may have had your own personal waitperson. That waitperson is there to greet you and escort you to your seat. They take your order for food and drinks and even help prepare your order. No matter how many other patrons enter the restaurant, your waitperson is responsible for serving only your requests. Therefore, your service is consistent—if the person is a good waitperson.

A *dedicated server* environment works in much the same way. Every client connection is associated with a dedicated server process, sometimes called a *shadow process,* on the machine where the Oracle server exists. No matter how many other connections are made to the server, the same dedicated server is always responsible for processing only your requests. You use the services of that server process until you disconnect from the Oracle server.

Most restaurants operate more like shared servers. When you walk in, you are assigned a waitperson, but they may be responsible for serving many other tables. This is good for the restaurant because they can serve more customers without increasing the staff. It may be fine for you as well, if the restaurant is not too busy and the waitperson is not responsible for too many tables. Also, if most of the orders are small, the staff can keep up with the requests, and the service will be as good as if you had your own waitperson.

In a diner, things work slightly different; the waitperson takes your order and places it on a turnstile. If the diner has multiple cooks, the order is picked up from the turnstile and prepared by one of the available cooks. When the cook completes the preparation of the dinner, it is placed in a location where the waitperson can pick it up and bring it to your table.

This is how an Oracle Shared Server environment works. In an Oracle Shared Server environment, *dispatcher* processes are responsible for servicing client requests. These processes are capable of handling requests from many clients. This is different from the dedicated server environment, where a single client process is handled by a single server process. Like the waitperson in the diner, a dispatcher can be responsible for taking the orders of many clients.

When using Oracle Shared Server, idle connections can be reused and allow several users to connect to the database, thus improving scalability.

When you request something from the server, it is the dispatcher's responsibility to take your request and place it in a location called a *request queue*. The request queue functions like the turnstile in the diner analogy. All dispatcher processes place their client requests in one request queue, which is a structure contained in the system global area (SGA).

Shared Server *processes*, like cooks in a diner, are responsible for fulfilling the client requests. The Oracle Shared Server process executes the request and places the result into an area of the SGA called a *response queue*. Every dispatcher has its own response queue. The dispatcher picks up the completed request from the response queue and returns the results to the client. Figure 11.25 illustrates the following processing steps for a Shared Server request:

1. The client passes a request to the dispatcher serving it.
2. The dispatcher places the request on a request queue in the SGA.
3. One of the Shared Server processes executes the request.
4. The Shared Server places the completed request on the dispatchers' response queue of the SGA.
5. The dispatcher picks up the completed request from the response queue.
6. The completed request is passed back to the client.

FIGURE 11.25 Request processing in Shared Server

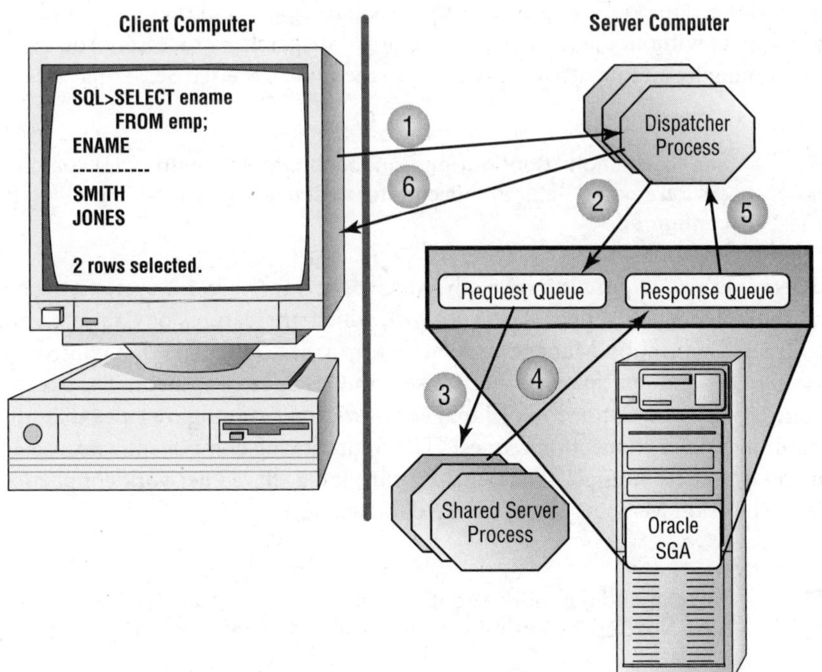

Requests placed in the request queue are processed on a first-in, first-out basis (FIFO). Currently, there is no way to prioritize requests within the queue.

Advantages and Disadvantages of Shared Server

Oracle Shared Server is used when server resources, such as memory and active processes, become constrained. People tend to throw more hardware at problems such as these; this will likely remedy the problem, but it may be an unnecessary expense.

If your system is experiencing these problems, Oracle Shared Server allows you to support the same number or a greater number of connections without requiring additional hardware. As a result, Oracle Shared Server tends to decrease the overall memory and process requirements on the server. Because clients are sharing processes, the total number of processes is reduced. This translates into resource savings on the server.

Shared Server also allows for connection pooling. Connection pooling enables the database server to disconnect an idle Oracle Shared Server connection to service an incoming request. The idle connection is still active and is reenabled once the client makes the next request. The connection pooling feature of Oracle Shared Server allows it to handle a larger number of requests without having to start additional dispatcher processes. You configure connection pooling by adding attributes to one of the Oracle Shared Server parameters.

See the section "Configuring Connection Pooling with the Dispatchers Parameter" later in this chapter to see how connection pooling is configured.

Shared Server is also required to take advantage of certain network options, such as connection multiplexing and client access control, which are features of Oracle Connection Manager. Oracle Connection Manager is a facility provided by Oracle that controls access to database services and multiplex connections in an Oracle environment. The access control component of Oracle Connection Manager allows you to configure rules that allow or disallow fulfillment of a connection request. The multiplexing component acts as a concentrator feature. It funnels multiple client sessions through a shared network connection from the Oracle Connection Manager server to the database server.

You can find out more about Oracle Connection Manager in "Oracle Database Net Services Administrators Guide 11*g* Release 1 (11.1) Part Number B28316-04."

Oracle Shared Server also has some disadvantages. Applications that generate a significant amount of network traffic or result in large result sets are not good candidates for Shared Server connections. Think of the earlier diner analogy. Your service is fine until two parties of twelve people show up. All of a sudden, the waitperson is overwhelmed with work from these two other tables, and your service begins to suffer. The same thing would happen in a Shared Server environment. If requests for large quantities of information start going to the dispatchers, the dispatchers can become overwhelmed, and you can see performance suffer for the other clients connected to the dispatcher. This, in turn, increases your response times. Dedicated processes better serve these types of applications.

Some functions are not allowed when you are using an Oracle Shared Server connection. You cannot start up, shut down, or perform certain kinds of recovery of an Oracle server when you are connected via a shared server.

Also, you should not perform certain administrative tasks using Oracle Shared Server connections, including bulk loads of data, index and table rebuilds, and table analysis. These types of tasks deal with manipulating large data sets and should use dedicated connections.

Oracle Shared Server is a scalability enhancement option, not a performance enhancement option. If you are looking for a performance increase, Shared Server is not what you should be configuring. Use Shared Server only if you are experiencing the system constraint problems discussed earlier in this chapter. You will always have equal or better performance in a dedicated server environment.

Oracle Shared Server Infrastructure

As described in the previous section, you manage client connections quite differently when using Oracle Shared Server as opposed to using a dedicated server. To accommodate the change, several modifications take place inside the internal memory structures of the Oracle server. The way in which the database and listener interact is also affected when using Oracle Shared Server. It is important to understand these changes when configuring and managing Oracle Shared Server.

Certain changes are necessary to the memory structures within Oracle to provide the Shared Server capability. Let's see what changes within the Oracle infrastructure are necessary to provide this support.

PGA and SGA Changes When Using Oracle Shared Server

When Oracle Shared Server is configured, Oracle adds two new types of structures to the SGA: request queues and response queues. These structures do not exist in a dedicated server environment. There is one request queue for all dispatchers, but each dispatcher has its own response queue. Therefore, if you have four dispatchers, you will have one request queue and four response queues. The request queue is located in the SGA where the dispatcher places client requests. A Shared Server process executes each request and places the completed request in the dispatcher's response queue.

In a dedicated server environment, each server has a memory segment called a *program global area* (PGA). The PGA is an area of memory where information about each client session is maintained. This information includes bind variables, cursor information, and the client's sort area. In an Oracle Shared Server environment, this information is moved from the PGA to an area of the SGA called the *user global area* (UGA). You can configure a special area of the SGA called the *large pool* to accommodate the bulk of the UGA.

Figure 11.26 shows how the SGA and PGA structures differ between a dedicated server and an Oracle Shared Server environment.

Each connection being serviced by a dispatcher is bound to a shared memory segment and forms a *virtual circuit*. The dispatcher uses the shared memory segment to manage communications between the client and the Oracle Database. The Oracle Shared Server processes use the virtual circuits to send and receive information to the appropriate dispatcher process.

To limit the amount of UGA memory a session can allocate, set the PRIVATE_SGA resource limit in the user's profile.

The Role of the Listener in an Oracle Shared Server Environment

The listener plays an important role in the Oracle Shared Server environment. The listener supplies the client with the address of the dispatcher to connect to when a user requests connections to an Oracle Shared Server. The listener maintains a list of dispatchers available from the Oracle Shared Server. The Oracle background process PMON notifies the listener as to which dispatcher is responsible for servicing each virtual circuit. The listener is then aware of the number of connections that the dispatcher is managing. This information allows the listener to take advantage of dispatcher load balancing.

Load balancing allows the listener to make intelligent decisions about which dispatcher to redirect client connections to so that no one dispatcher becomes overburdened. When the listener receives a connection request, it looks at the current connection load for each dispatcher and redirects the client connection request to the least-loaded dispatcher. The listener determines the least-loaded dispatcher for all nodes if Real Application Clusters (RAC) are being used, followed by the least-loaded instance for the node, and finally by the least-loaded dispatcher for the instance. By doing so, the listener ensures that connections are evenly distributed across dispatchers.

The listener can either redirect the client connection to an available dispatcher or directly hand off the request to the dispatcher. The latter is performed whenever possible and is done typically when the listener and database service exist on the same node. When the listener and database service exist on different nodes, the redirection method is used.

FIGURE 11.26 SGA/PGA comparison of dedicated server and shared server

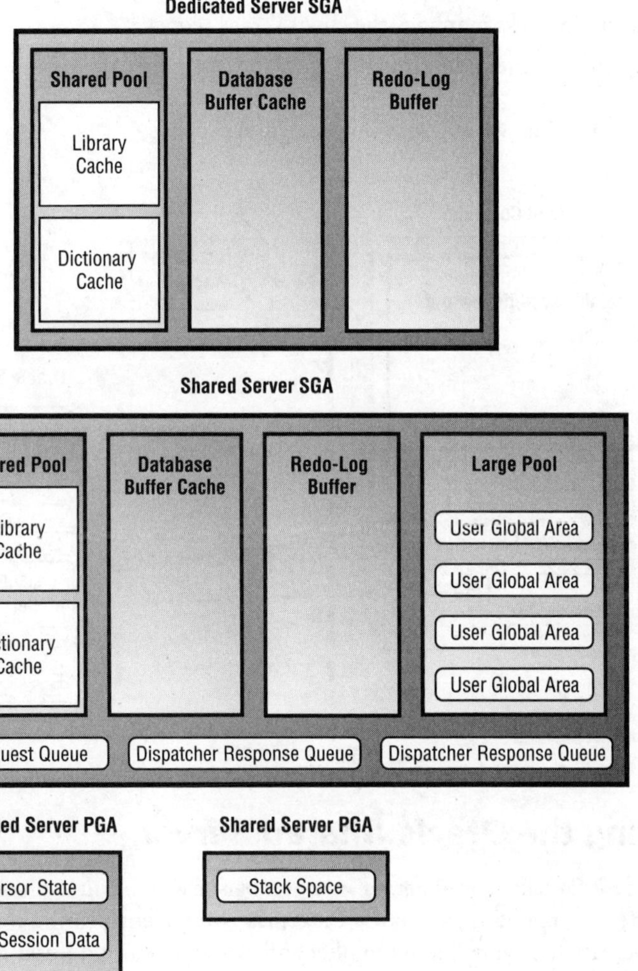

When a client connection terminates, the listener is updated to reflect the change in the number of connections that the dispatcher is handling.

Figure 11.27 illustrates the following steps in the Oracle Shared Server connection process after the database has been started and the dispatcher processes have been started:

1. The client contacts the Oracle Database server after resolving the service name.
2. The listener validates the Oracle service name supplied by the client and hands off or redirects the client connection to the least-busy dispatcher.

3. The listener sends information to the client so the client can redirect the connection to the appropriate dispatcher process.
4. The dispatcher process manages the client server request.
5. PMON registers connection information with the listener.

FIGURE 11.27 The Shared Server connection process

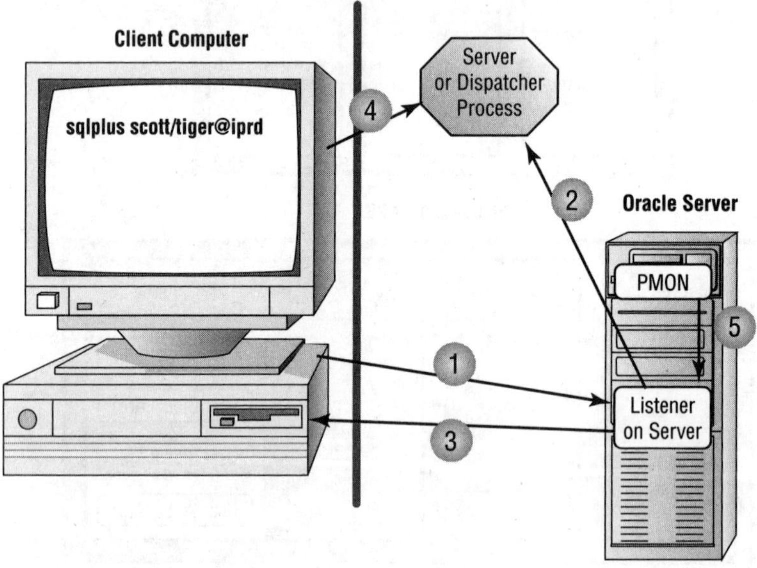

Configuring the Oracle Shared Server

You can configure Oracle Shared Server in a number of ways. You can configure it at the time the database is created, you can use Enterprise Manager to configure it after the database has been created, or you can manually configure it by editing initialization parameters. I'll discuss the parameters necessary to configure Oracle Shared Server. I'll also give examples of how to configure Shared Server at database creation or after the database is created using EM.

Defining the Shared Server Parameters

You configure Oracle Shared Server by adding parameters to the Oracle initialization file. These parameters identify the number and type of dispatchers, the number of shared servers, and the name of the database you want to associate with Shared Server.

One advantage of Oracle 11*g* is that all the parameters necessary to manage Oracle Shared Server can be changed dynamically. This fulfills one of your primary goals of ensuring the highest degree of database availability possible. Let's take a look at the parameters used to manage Oracle Shared Server.

Using the *DISPATCHERS* Parameter

The DISPATCHERS parameter defines the number of dispatchers that should start when the instance is started. This parameter specifies the number of dispatchers and the type of protocol to which the dispatchers can respond. If you configured your database using the Database Configuration Assistant, this parameter may already be configured.

You can add dispatchers dynamically using the ALTER SYSTEM command.

The DISPATCHERS parameter has a number of optional attributes. Table 11.8 describes several of them. You need to specify only ADDRESS, DESCRIPTION, or PROTOCOL for a DISPATCHERS definition. All the attributes for this parameter can be abbreviated.

TABLE 11.8 Summary of DISPATCHER Attributes

Attribute	Abbreviations	Description
ADDRESS	ADD or ADDR	Specifies the network protocol address of the end point on which the dispatchers listen.
CONNECTIONS	CON or CONN	The maximum number of network connections per dispatcher. The default value varies by operating system.
DESCRIPTION	DES or DESC	The network description of the end point where the dispatcher is listening, including the protocol being listened for.
DISPATCHERS	DIS or DISP	The number of dispatchers to start when the instance is started. The default is 1.
LISTENER	LIS or LIST	The address of the listener to which PMON sends connection information. This attribute needs to be set only when the listener is nonlocal, it uses a port other than 1521, the default port and the LOCAL_LISTENER parameter have not been specified, or the listener is resident on a different network node.
PROTOCOL	PRO or PROT	The network protocol for the dispatcher to listen for. This is the only required attribute.
SESSIONS	SES or SESS	The maximum number of network sessions allowable for this dispatcher. This will vary by operating system but predominantly defaults to 16KB.
SERVICE	SER or SERV	The Oracle net service name that the dispatcher registers with the listener. If it is not supplied, the dispatcher registers with the services listed in the SERVICE_NAMES initialization parameter.
POOL	POO	Provides connection pooling capabilities to provide the ability to handle a larger number of connections.

The two main attributes are DISPATCHERS and PROTOCOL. For example, if you want to configure three TCP/IP dispatchers and two IPC dispatchers, you set the parameter as follows:

```
DISPATCHERS = "(PRO=TCP)(DIS=3)(PRO=IPC)(DIS=2)"
```

You must consider several factors (discussed in the following section) when determining the appropriate setting for the DISPATCHERS parameter.

DETERMINING THE NUMBER OF DISPATCHERS TO START

The number of dispatchers you start depends on your particular configuration. Your operating system may place a limit on the number of connections that one dispatcher can handle. Consult your operating-system documentation to obtain this information.

When determining the number of dispatchers to start, consider the type of work that the database sessions will be performing and the number of concurrent connections that your database will be supporting. The more data-intensive the operations and the larger the number of concurrent connections, the fewer sessions each dispatcher should handle. Generally speaking, a starting point is to allow 50 concurrent sessions for each dispatcher.

You can use the following formula to determine the number of dispatchers to configure initially:

```
Number of Dispatchers = CEIL  (maximum number of concurrent sessions /
   connections per dispatcher)
```

For example, if you have 500 concurrent TCP/IP connections and you want each dispatcher to manage 50 concurrent connections, you need 10 dispatchers. You set your DISPATCHERS parameter as follows:

```
DISPATCHERS = "(PRO=TCP)(DIS=10)"
```

You can determine the number of concurrent connections by querying the V$SESSION view. This view shows you the number of clients currently connected to the Oracle server. Here is an example of the query:

```
SQL> select sid,serial#,username,server,program from v$session
  2  where username is not null;
      SID    SERIAL# USERNAME   SERVER     PROGRAM
--------- --------- ---------- --------- ---------------
        7        13      SCOTT  DEDICATED SQLPLUS.EXE
        8        12      SCOTT  DEDICATED SQLPLUS.EXE
        9         4     SYSTEM  DEDICATED SQLPLUS.EXE
```

In this example, three users are connected to the server. You can ignore any sessions that do not have a username because these would be the Oracle background processes such as PMON and SMON. If you take a sampling of this view over a typical work period, you get an idea of the average number of concurrent connections for your system. You can then use this number as a guide when you establish the starting number of dispatchers.

MANAGING THE NUMBER OF DISPATCHERS

You can start additional dispatchers or remove dispatchers dynamically using the ALTER SYSTEM command. You can start any number of dispatchers up to the MAX_DISPATCHERS setting, which is discussed next. Here is an example of adding three TCP/IP dispatchers to a system configured with two TCP/IP dispatchers:

```
ALTER SYSTEM SET DISPATCHERS="(PRO=TCP)(DIS=5)";
```

Notice that you set the number to the total number of dispatchers you want, not to the number of dispatchers you want to add.

You use additional attributes to the DISPATCHERS parameter to configure connection pooling.

CONFIGURING CONNECTION POOLING WITH THE DISPATCHERS PARAMETER

Connection pooling gives Oracle Shared Server the ability to handle a larger volume of connections by automatically disconnecting idle connections and using the idle connections to service incoming client requests. If the idle connections become active again, the connection to the dispatchers is automatically reestablished. This provides added scalability to Oracle Shared Server. If you manage applications that have a large number of possible client connections but also have a large number of idle connections, you might want to consider configuring this Oracle Shared Server option. Web applications are good candidates for connection pooling because they are typically composed of a large client base with small numbers of concurrent connections.

You enable connection pooling by adding attributes to the DISPATCHERS parameter. The POOL attribute specifies that a dispatcher is allowed to perform connection pooling. Set this attribute to the value ON to enable connection pooling for a dispatcher. You also need to specify the TICK attribute, which sets the number of 10-minute increments of inactivity for a connection to be considered idle.

Here is an example that turns on connection pooling:

```
DISPATCHERS="(PROTOCOL=tcp)(DISPATCHERS=1)(POOL=on)(TICK=1)
  (CONNECTIONS=500)(SESSIONS=1000)"
```

In this example, you want to turn on connection pooling. An idle connection is considered any connection with 10 minutes of inactivity. You want the TCP/IP dispatcher to handle a maximum of 500 concurrent connections and a maximum of 1,000 sessions per dispatcher.

Using the *MAX_DISPATCHERS* Parameter

You set the MAX_DISPATCHERS parameter to the maximum number of dispatchers you anticipate needing for Oracle Shared Server. In Oracle 11g, this parameter can be set dynamically using the ALTER SYSTEM command. The maximum number of processes that a dispatcher can run concurrently is operating system–dependent. Use the following formula to set this parameter:

```
MAX_DISPATCHERS = (maximum number of concurrent sessions/connections
     per dispatcher)
```

Here is an example of the parameter and adjusting the parameter using the ALTER SYSTEM command:

```
ALTER SYSTEM SET MAX_DISPATCHERS=10;
```

In the ALTER SYSTEM example, the MAX_DISPATCHERS parameter is being set to 10. This will be the maximum number of dispatchers that Oracle Shared Server can start simultaneously.

Using the *SHARED_SERVERS* Parameter

The SHARED_SERVERS parameter specifies the minimum number of shared servers to start and retain when the Oracle instance is started. A setting of 0 or no setting means that shared servers will not be used. If dispatchers have been configured, the default value of SHARED_SERVERS is 1. This parameter can be changed dynamically, so even if shared servers are not configured when the instance starts, they can be configured without bringing the Oracle instance down and restarting it.

The number of servers necessary depends on the type of activities your users are performing. Oracle monitors the response queue loads, starts additional shared servers as needed, and removes these shared servers when the servers are no longer needed. Generally, for the types of high-think applications that will be using shared server connections, 25 concurrent connections per shared server should be adequate. If the users are going to require larger result sets or are doing more intensive processing, you'll want to reduce this ratio.

Here is an example of setting the SHARED_SERVERS parameter:

```
SHARED_SERVERS = 3
```

You can start additional Oracle shared servers or reduce the number of Oracle shared servers dynamically using the ALTER SYSTEM command. You can start any number of Oracle shared servers up to the MAX_SERVERS setting. Here is an example of adding three additional Oracle shared servers to a system initially configured with two shared servers:

```
ALTER SYSTEM SET SHARED_SERVERS = 5;
```

Notice that you set the number to the total number of Oracle shared servers you want, not to the number of Oracle shared servers you want to add.

Using the *SHARED_SERVER_SESSIONS* Parameter

The SHARED_SERVER_SESSIONS parameter specifies the total number of Oracle Shared Server sessions that are allowed for the Oracle instance. If the number of Oracle Shared Server client connections reaches this limit, any clients that attempt to connect via an Oracle Shared Server connection will receive the following error message:

```
ERROR:
ORA-00018 maximum number of sessions exceeded
```

Once the number of Oracle Shared Server connections falls below this number, additional Shared Server connections can be established. Using this parameter limits the total number of Shared Server sessions. Dedicated server connections are still allowed if this limit is reached. This parameter can be set in the Oracle initialization file and can be modified dynamically using the ALTER SYSTEM command. Here is an example of how you specify the initialization parameter:

```
SHARED_SERVER_SESSIONS = 2
```

Here is an example of how to dynamically modify the parameter using the ALTER SYSTEM command:

```
ALTER SYSTEM SET SHARED_SERVER_SESSIONS = 5;
```

Using the *MAX_SHARED_SERVERS* Parameter

The MAX_SHARED_SERVERS parameter sets the maximum number of Oracle shared servers that can be running concurrently. This number can be modified dynamically using the ALTER SYSTEM command. Generally, you should set this parameter to accommodate your heaviest work times. If no value is specified for MAX_SHARED_SERVERS, the number of Oracle shared servers that can be started is unlimited, which is also the default setting.

The V$SHARED_SERVER_MONITOR view can assist in determining the maximum number of Oracle shared servers that have been started since the Oracle instance was started.

Here is an example of the parameter and the ALTER SYSTEM command that will change the value MAX_SHARED_SERVER to 20:

```
ALTER SYSTEM SET MAX_SHARED_SERVERS = 20;
```

Using the *CIRCUITS* Parameter

The CIRCUITS parameter manages the total number of virtual circuits allowed for all incoming and outgoing network sessions. There is no default value for this parameter, and it does influence the total size of the SGA at system startup. Generally, you do not manually configure this parameter unless there is a need to specifically limit the number of virtual circuits.

Here is an example of the parameter:

```
CIRCUITS = 200
```

You can also use the ALTER SYSTEM command to change the parameter as follows:

```
ALTER SYSTEM SET CIRCUITS = 300;
```

Now that you understand the parameters that are needed to use the Oracle Shared Server, you need to know how to configure these parameters.

Managing a Shared Server

If the Oracle Shared Server parameters were configured dynamically using the ALTER SYSTEM command or at database creation, it isn't necessary to stop and start the server. After you configure the Oracle Shared Server parameters, you need to understand how to view information about Oracle Shared Server. Oracle provides a set of dynamic performance views that you can use to gather information about the Oracle Shared Server configuration and the performance of Oracle Shared Server. You can also gather information about Oracle Shared Server connections by using the lsnrctl utility.

In the following sections, I will explain how to display information about Oracle Shared Server connections using the listener utility and discuss the various dynamic performance views used to manage Shared Server.

Displaying Information about Shared Server Connections Using the Listener Utility

You can use the `lsnrctl` command-line listener utility to display information about the dispatcher processes. Remember from the previous section that the Oracle background process PMON registers dispatcher information with the listener. The listener keeps track of the current connection load for all the dispatchers.

Use the `lsnrctl services` query to view information about dispatchers. The following example shows a listener listening for two TCP/IP dispatchers:

```
$ lsnrctl services

LSNRCTL for Linux: Version 11.1.0.6.0 - Production on 18-AUG-2008 00:01:47

Copyright (c) 1991, 2007, Oracle.  All rights reserved.

Connecting to (DESCRIPTION=(ADDRESS=(PROTOCOL=TCP)(HOST=localhost.localdomain)
(PORT=1521)))
Services Summary...
Service "11GR11" has 1 instance(s).
  Instance "11GR11", status READY, has 2 handler(s) for this service...
    Handler(s):
      "DEDICATED" established:21 refused:0 state:ready
         LOCAL SERVER
      "D000" established:0 refused:0 current:0 max:1000 state:ready
         DISPATCHER <machine: localhost.localdomain, pid: 3375>
         (ADDRESS=(PROTOCOL=tcp)(HOST=localhost.localdomain)(PORT=30767))
Service "11GR11XDB" has 1 instance(s).
  Instance "11GR11", status READY, has 0 handler(s) for this service...
```

Notice that the listing displays how many connections each dispatcher is managing, the listening location of the dispatcher, and the process ID of the dispatcher. The display also shows how many total client connections were established and how many were refused by each dispatcher since the time it was started. This summary information can be helpful when looking at how well the connections are balanced across all the dispatchers. It also can be helpful to see how many connections were refused. A connection can be refused if a user supplies an invalid user ID or password or reaches the `MAX_SHARED_SERVER` limit.

Requesting a Dedicated Connection in a Shared Server Environment

You can configure Oracle Shared Server connections and dedicated server connections to connect to a single Oracle server. This is advantageous if you have a mix of database activity. Some types of activities are well suited to Oracle Shared Server connections, and other types of activities are better suited to dedicated connections.

By default, if Oracle Shared Server is configured, a client is connected to a dispatcher unless the client explicitly requests a dedicated connection. As part of the connection descriptor, the client has to send information requesting a dedicated connection. Clients can request dedicated connections if the names resolution method is local naming. You cannot use this option with host naming. If local naming is being used, you can make the necessary changes to the `tnsnames.ora` file to allow dedicated connections. You can make these changes manually, or you can use Oracle Net Manager.

Configuring Dedicated Connections Manually

If you are using local naming, you can add a parameter to the service-name entry in the `tnsnames.ora` file. The parameter `(SERVER=DEDICATED)` is added to the DBA net service name. Here is an example of the entry in the `tnsnames.ora` file:

```
ORCL =
  (DESCRIPTION =
    (ADDRESS = (PROTOCOL = TCP)(HOST = XYZ01)(PORT = 1521))
    (CONNECT_DATA =
      (SERVICE_NAME = orcl)
      (SERVER = DEDICATED)  # Request a dedicated connection for DBA
    )
  )
```

Configuring Dedicated Connections Using Oracle Net Manager

You can use Oracle Net Manager to modify the connection type for a service. In Windows, Oracle Net Manager is a tool; in Unix, you open Oracle Net Manager by executing `netmgr`.

After you start Oracle Net Manager, follow these steps:

1. Under Service Naming in the left pane, select the service name you want to modify.
2. Click the Connection Type drop-down list in the Service Identification section, and choose Dedicated Server.

Choosing the Appropriate Connection Method Makes a Difference

As a DBA, you've configured Oracle Shared Server and are monitoring the dispatchers and shared server performance daily. The Shared Server environment has been running smoothly for months, but your monitoring starts to indicate that the wait times have increased significantly over the past week. You are also starting to receive complaints from the user community regarding system response time.

You start to investigate whether there have been any significant changes to the hardware, the network, or the database application. You confer with the systems administration and network group and find that no changes have taken place. Then your discussion with the applications group reveals that a new ad hoc reporting utility has been installed and a small number of administrators are starting to use the tool. These users are connecting via Oracle Shared Server and are requesting large data sets via the ad hoc reporting tool.

You suggest to the applications team that the administrators connect to the database using dedicated connections to alleviate the load on the shared servers. After modifying the appropriate network files, you again monitor the shared server wait times and discover that the waits have fallen back in line with what you were seeing prior to the deployment of the ad hoc reporting tool.

Summary

This chapter provided the foundation of knowledge you will need when you are designing, configuring, and managing the Oracle network infrastructure. Oracle Net manages the flow of information from client computers to Oracle servers and forms the foundation of all networked computing in the Oracle environment. Oracle Net provides services that can be divided into five main categories: connectivity, directory services, scalability, security, and accessibility.

Oracle Net provides support to *n*-tier architecture, where middleware components such as application servers are situated between the client and database server.

The listener is the main server-side component in the Oracle Net environment. Listener configuration information is stored in the `listener.ora` file, and you manage the listener using the `lsnrctl` command-line utility. You configure the listener by using the Oracle Net Manager. The Oracle Net Manager provides a graphical interface for creating most of the Oracle Net files you will use for Oracle, including the `listener.ora` file. If multiple listeners are configured, each one has a separate entry in the `listener.ora` file.

Depending on your network environment, the client configuration setups can vary from no work to configuring a number of files on the client. Local naming is the most popular of the names resolution methods, and it uses the `tnsnames.ora` file, which is typically located on each client, to resolve net service names. The client looks up the net service name in the `tnsnames.ora` file and uses the resulting connect descriptor information to connect to the Oracle server.

Shared Server is a configuration of the Oracle server that allows you to support a greater number of connections without the need for additional resources. In this configuration, user connections share processes called *dispatchers*. Dispatchers replace the dedicated server processes in a dedicated server environment. The Oracle Server is also configured with shared server processes that can process the requests of many clients. You add a number of parameters to the `init.ora` file to configure Shared Server. You can add dispatchers and shared servers dynamically after the Oracle server is started. You can add more shared servers and dispatchers up to the maximum value specified.

Exam Essentials

Understand what Oracle Net is and the functionality it provides. Be able to list the five categories of functionality that Oracle Net provides and explain the functionality that falls into each category. Also understand what functionality the Oracle Shared Server and Oracle Connection Manager options provide. In addition, be able to define Oracle Advanced Security and know when to use it.

Be able to define the main responsibilities of the Oracle listener. To fully understand the function of the Oracle listener, you should understand how the listener responds to client connection requests. In addition, know the difference between bequeath connections and redirect connections, and know under what circumstances the listener will use each. Also, be able to outline the steps involved in using each of these connection types.

Be able to define the `listener.ora` file and the ways in which the file is created. To understand the purpose of this file, know its default contents and how to change it using the various Oracle tools. In addition, be able to define the sections of the file and know the definitions of the optional parameters it contains. Also understand the structure of the `listener.ora` file when one or more listeners are configured.

Understand how to use the `lsnrctl` command-line utility. To start up and shut down the listener, know how to use the `lsnrctl` command-line utility. Be able to explain the command-line options for the `lsnrctl` utility, such as `services`, `status`, and `reload`. When using this utility, also know the options available to you, and be able to define the various `set` commands.

Understand the concepts of static and dynamic service registration. Be able to define the difference between static service registration and dynamic service registration and know the advantages of using dynamic service registration over static service registration. Also, be aware of the situations in which you have to use static service registration. Lastly, be familiar with the initialization parameters that you will need to set in order to enable dynamic service registration.

Define the Oracle client-side names resolution options. Be able to define the Oracle client-side names resolution options. Know in which situations to use local naming, Oracle Easy Connect, host naming, and OID.

Define the local naming method. In addition to knowing the meaning of the local naming method and what it does, understand how to use the Oracle Net Manager to configure this names resolution method. Understand the primary file used in the local naming method, the `tnsnames.ora` file.

Define the contents and structure of the `tnsnames.ora` file. Be able to describe the `tnsnames.ora` file and the various sections of the file and to explain how the file is used. Understand the contents of the `tnsnames.ora` file so that you can identify syntax problems with the structure of entries in the file. Be familiar with the common locations of this file and how to set the `TNS_ADMIN` parameter to override the default location of this and the other client-side network files.

Define and correct client-side errors. Understand the types of client-side connection errors that can occur. Be able to define these errors and understand the situations in which a client might encounter them.

Define Oracle Shared Server. Be able to list the advantages of Shared Server vs. a dedicated server and when it is appropriate to consider both options.

Understand the architecture of Oracle Shared Server. Be able to summarize the steps that a client takes to initiate a connection with a shared server and the processes behind those steps. Understand what happens during client request processing, and outline the steps.

Understand the changes that are made in the SGA and the PGA. Make sure you understand that in a Shared Server environment, many PGA structures are moved in the large pool inside the SGA. This means the SGA will become larger and that the large pool will need to be configured in the `init.ora` file.

Know how to configure Oracle Shared Server. Be able to define each of the parameters involved in the configuration of Oracle Shared Server. Know what parameters can be dynamically modified and what parameters require the Oracle instance to be restarted to take effect.

Know how to configure clients running in Shared Server mode. Be able to configure clients that need a dedicated connection to Oracle if it is running in Shared Server mode.

Review Questions

1. All of the following are examples of networking architectures except which one?
   A. Client/server.
   B. *n*-tier.
   C. Single-tier.
   D. Two-tier.
   E. All the above are examples of network architectures.

2. Which of the following files must be present on the Oracle server to start a nondefault Oracle listener?
   A. `listener.ora`
   B. `lsnrctl.ora`
   C. `sqlnet.ora`
   D. `tnsnames.ora`

3. Which of the following is the correct way to start a listener called `LISTENER`?
   A. `lsnrctl startup listener`
   B. `lsnrctl start`
   C. `listener start`
   D. `listener start listener`

4. When dynamic service registration is used, you will not see the service listed in which of the following files where it would normally be located?
   A. `sqlnet.ora`
   B. `tnsnames.ora`
   C. `listener.ora`
   D. None of the above

5. What are the ways in which a client can resolve a net service name? (Choose all that apply.)
   A. Local naming
   B. Host naming
   C. Easy Connect
   D. Oracle Global Naming
   E. All the above

6. Connection Manager provides which of the following?
   A. Multiplexing
   B. Cross-protocol connectivity
   C. Network access control
   D. All the above

7. Which is a requirement for using host naming?
   - A. You must use `tnsnames.ora` on the client.
   - B. You must be using TCP/IP.
   - C. You must have an OID present.
   - D. You must have a `sqlnet.ora` file present on the client.
   - E. None of the above.

8. Which of the following statements about `tnsnames.ora` is false?
   - A. It is used to resolve an Oracle service name.
   - B. It can exist on the client.
   - C. It is used for local naming.
   - D. It does not support TCP/IP.

9. A client receives the following error message:

   `"ORA-12154 TNS:could not resolve the connect identifier specified"`

   Which of the following could be possible causes of the error? (Choose all that apply.)
   - A. The listener is not running on the Oracle server.
   - B. The user entered an invalid net service name.
   - C. The user supplied the correct net service name, but the net service name is misspelled in the `tnsnames.ora` on the client file.
   - D. The listener is not configured to listen for this service.

10. What portion of the `tnsnames.ora` file specifies the name or IP address of the server where the listener process is listening?
    - A. CONNECT_DATA
    - B. PORT
    - C. SERVICE_NAME
    - D. HOST

11. A client wants to connect to the database `dbprod.com` located on the `dbprod.com` server to a nondefault port using Oracle Easy Connect. Which of the following connect strings is the best choice for the client use?
    - A. `CONNECT scott/tiger@dbprod.com:1522`
    - B. `CONNECT scott/tiger@1521:dbprod.com/dbprod.com`
    - C. `CONNECT scott/tiger@dbprod.com/1522:dbprod.com`
    - D. `CONNECT scott/tiger@dbprod.com:1521/dbprod.com`
    - E. `CONNECT scott/tiger@dbprod.com:1522/dbprod.com`

12. All the following are reasons to configure the server using Shared Server *except* which one?
    A. Overall memory utilization is reduced.
    B. The system is predominantly used for decision support with large result sets returned.
    C. The system is predominantly used for small transactions with many users.
    D. The number of idle connections on the server is reduced.

13. Which of the following is true about Shared Server?
    A. Dedicated connections cannot be made when Shared Server is configured.
    B. It is recommended that index rebuilds be performed when connected via Shared Server.
    C. The database can be started when connected via Shared Server.
    D. The database cannot be stopped when connected via Shared Server.

14. The administrator wants to allow a user to connect via a dedicated connection into a database configured in Shared Server mode. Which of the following lines accomplishes this?
    A. `(SERVER=DEDICATED)`
    B. `(CONNECT=DEDICATED)`
    C. `(INSTANCE=DEDICATED)`
    D. `(MULTITHREADED=FALSE)`
    E. None of the above

15. In which of the following files would you find the Shared Server configuration parameters?
    A. `listener.ora`
    B. `mts.ora`
    C. `init.ora`
    D. `tnsnames.ora`
    E. `sqlnet.ora`

16. What is the first step that the dispatcher performs after it receives a request from the user?
    A. Pass the request to a shared server.
    B. Place the request in a request queue in the PGA.
    C. Place the request in a request queue in the SGA.
    D. Process the request.

17. When configured in Shared Server mode, which of the following is contained in the PGA?
    A. Cursor state
    B. Sort information
    C. User session data
    D. Stack space
    E. None of the above

18. Which of the following is false about request queues?

A. They reside in the SGA.

B. They are shared by all the dispatchers.

C. Each dispatcher has its own request queue.

D. The shared server processes remove requests from the request queue.

19. What is the process that notifies the listener after a database connection is established?

A. SMON

B. DBWR

C. PMON

D. LGWR

20. Which command can you execute to get details about the number of sessions connected via Shared Server?

A. `lsnrctl sessions`

B. `lsnrctl conn`

C. `lsnrctl status`

D. `lsnrctl services`

E. None of the above

Answers to Review Questions

1. E. All these are examples of network connectivity configurations. Networking can be as simple as a dumb terminal connected directly to a server via a serial connection. It can also be as complex as an *n*-tier architecture that involves clients, middleware, the Internet, and database servers.

2. A. The listener is the process that manages incoming connection requests. The `listener.ora` file is used to configure the listener and must be configured to start a nondefault listener. The `sqlnet.ora` file is an optional client- and server-side file. The `tnsnames.ora` file is used for doing local naming resolution. There is no such file as `lsnrctl.ora`. You do not need the `listener.ora` file to start a default listener on port 1521.

3. B. Because the default listener name is LISTENER, simply enter **`lsnrctl start`**. The name LISTENER is assumed to be the listener to start in this case.

4. C. When services are dynamically registered with the listener, their information is not present in the `listener.ora` file.

5. A, B, C. Oracle uses service names in networks in much the same way it uses synonyms in the database. Service names provide location transparency and hide the complexity of connect string information. You can configure Oracle Net to connect in several ways, including host naming, local naming, OID, and Oracle Easy Connect. Oracle Global Naming is not a valid Oracle option.

6. D. Connection Manager is a middleware solution that provides for the multiplexing of connections, cross-protocol connectivity, and network access control. All the answers describe Connection Manager.

7. B. Host naming is typically used in small installations that have few Oracle Databases. This is an attractive option when you want to minimize client-side configuration. TCP/IP is a requirement when you use host naming.

8. D. A `tnsnames.ora` file is configured when you want to use local naming, and it typically exists on the client workstation. It is also used to resolve a service name. The `tnsnames.ora` file used in local naming does indeed support TCP/IP.

9. B, C. Supplying a net service name that is not contained in the `tnsnames.ora` file can cause this error. Problems with the `tnsnames.ora` file can cause this error too. Listener problems will not cause this error.

10. D. The HOST portion specifies the name of the server to contact. CONNECT_DATA specifies the database service to connect to. The PORT portion specifies the location where the listener is listening on the HOST. Option C, SERVICE_NAME, is the name of the actual database service.

11. A. The correct syntax to use with the Oracle Easy Connect method when you are connecting to a non-URL location is *`connect username/password@host:port/service_name`*. If the service name and the host are identical, you do not have to include the service name. If the port is any port other than the default port of 1521, it must be specified. Because you

want to connect to a nondefault port where the database name and the hostname are the same, the best answer is A.

12. B. Shared Server is a scalability option of Oracle. It provides a way to increase the number of supported user processes while reducing the overall memory usage. This configuration is well suited to high-volume, small-transaction–oriented systems with many users connected. Because users share processes, the number of overall idle processes is also reduced. It is not well suited for large data retrieval type applications such as decision support.

13. D. Users can still request dedicated connections in a Shared Server configuration. Bequeath and dedicated connections are one and the same. The database cannot be stopped or started by the DBA when connected over a Shared Server connection.

14. A. A user must explicitly request a dedicated connection when a server is configured in Shared Server mode. Otherwise, the user gets a Shared Server connection. The correct parameter is `(SERVER=DEDICATED)`.

15. C. The Shared Server configuration parameters exist in the `init.ora` or the `SPFILE` file on the Oracle Server machine.

16. C. Once a dispatcher receives a request from the user process, it places the request on the request queue. Remember that in a Shared Server environment, a request can be handled by a shared server process. This is made possible by placing the request and user information in the SGA.

17. D. A small PGA is maintained even though most of the user-specific information is moved to the SGA (specifically called the UGA in the shared pool or the large pool). The only information left in the reduced PGA is stack space.

18. C. Request queues reside in the SGA, and there is one request queue per instance. This is where shared server processes pick up requests that are made by users. Dispatchers have their own response queues, but they *share* a single request queue.

19. C. The PMON process notifies the listener after a client connection is established. This is so that the listener can keep track of the number of connections being serviced by each dispatcher.

20. D. Dispatchers register with listeners so that when a listener redirects a connection to a dispatcher, the listener knows how many active connections the dispatcher is serving. The `lsnrctl services` command summarizes the number of connections established, connections currently active, and other valuable information regarding Shared Server. The `lsnrctl status` command summarizes only dispatchers and does not display any details about connections.

Implementing Security and Auditing

ORACLE DATABASE 11*g*: ADMINISTRATION I EXAM OBJECTIVES COVERED IN THIS CHAPTER:

- ✓ **Administering User Security**
  - Create and manage database user accounts
  - Grant and revoke privileges
  - Create and manage roles
  - Create and manage profiles
- ✓ **Implementing Oracle Database Security**
  - Database security and principle of least privilege
  - Work with standard database auditing

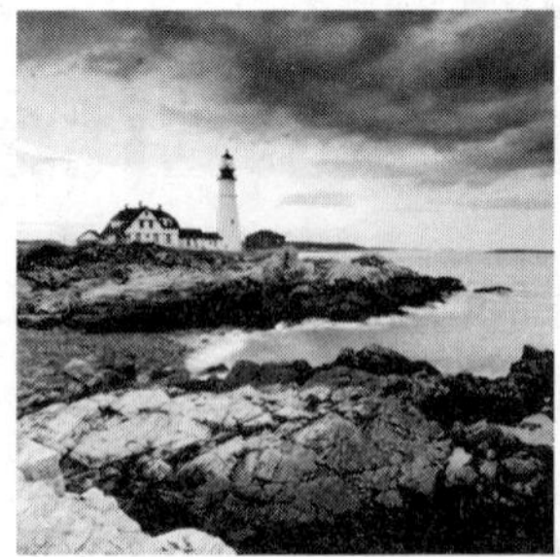

One of the key functions of a DBA is to protect your data and database by controlling database access; DBAs must also keep track of key database activities. They must maintain the security, integrity, performance, and availability of their databases. In this chapter, you will learn about managing database security, including how to manage user accounts; implement password expiration and complexity rules; and configure security policies using object, system, and role privileges. To further enhance your ability to monitor and manage database access, you will also learn how to use auditing mechanisms to fine-tune your security policy, identify attempts to access areas of your database that a user is not authorized to visit, and identify intrusion attempts.

Creating and Managing User Accounts

One of the most basic administrative requirements for a DBA is to identify and manage the users. The first step to doing this is to make sure that each user who connects to the Oracle Database 11*g* has an *account*. An account shared between many users is difficult to troubleshoot and audit and is therefore a poor security practice that should be avoided.

You create a new database account with the CREATE USER statement. When you create a new account, at a minimum the user should have a unique username and authentication method. You can optionally assign additional attributes to the user account with the CREATE USER statement. To change or assign new attributes to an existing user account, use the ALTER USER statement.

The terms *user account*, *account*, *user*, and *schema* are all interchangeable and refer to a database user account. A *schema* is a user who owns objects. All schemas are users, but not all users are schemas.

The following is an example of the CREATE USER statement with all the optional clauses available:

```
SQL> CREATE USER james
  2  IDENTIFIED BY mia0101
  3  DEFAULT TABLESPACE users
  4  TEMPORARY TABLESPACE temp
  5  QUOTA UNLIMITED ON users
  6  PROFILE default
```

```
  7  PASSWORD EXPIRE
  8  ACCOUNT UNLOCK
SQL> /

User created.

SQL>
```

In the following sections, you'll learn about the clauses presented in the CREATE USER statement.

Configuring Authentication

When a user connects to an Oracle Database instance, the user account must be authenticated. *Authentication* involves validating the identity of the user and confirming that the user has the authority to use the database. Oracle offers three authentication methods for your user accounts: password authentication (the most common), external authentication, and global authentication.

I'll cover each of these authentication methods in the following sections.

Password-Authenticated Users

When a user with password authentication attempts to connect to the database, the database verifies that the username is a valid database account and that the password supplied matches that user's password as stored in the database.

Password-authenticated user accounts are the most common and are sometimes referred to as *database-authenticated* accounts. With a password-authenticated account, the database stores the encrypted password in the data dictionary. For example, to create a password-authenticated user named rajesh with a password of welcome, you execute the following:

```
CREATE USER rajesh IDENTIFIED BY welcome;
```

The keywords IDENTIFIED BY *password* (in this case, *password* is welcome) tell the database that this user account is a password-authenticated account.

The user password in the Oracle 11*g* database is case sensitive. In earlier releases of Oracle, user passwords were case insensitive.

Externally Authenticated Users

When an externally identified user attempts to connect to the database, the database verifies that the username is a valid database account and trusts that the operating system has performed authentication.

Externally authenticated user accounts do not store or validate a password in the database. These accounts are sometimes referred to as *OPS$ accounts*, because when Oracle introduced them in Oracle 6, the account had to be prefixed with the keyword OPS$. With all releases of the database since then, including Oracle 11g, you can configure this OS_AUTHENT_PREFIX in the initialization file or spfile. For example, to create an externally authenticated user named oracle using the default OS_AUTHENT_PREFIX, you execute the following:

```
CREATE USER ops$oracle IDENTIFIED EXTERNALLY;
```

The keywords IDENTIFIED EXTERNALLY tell the database that this user account is an externally authenticated account. If you log in to the server as user **oracle**, you can log in to the database without providing a username or password, as shown here:

```
$ sqlplus /

SQL*Plus: Release 11.1.0.6.0 - Production on Mon Sep 1 17:07:46 2008
Copyright (c) 1982, 2007, Oracle.  All rights reserved.
Connected to:
Oracle Database 11g Enterprise Edition Release 11.1.0.6.0 - Production
With the Partitioning, OLAP, Data Mining and Real Application Testing options

SQL>
```

Externally authenticated accounts are frequently used for administrative scripts so that a password does not have to be embedded in a human-readable script.

Globally Authenticated Users

When a globally identified user attempts to connect to the database, the database verifies that the username is valid and passes the connection information to the advanced security option for authentication. The advanced security option supports several mechanisms for authentication, including biometrics, X.509 certificates, Kerberos, and RADIUS.

Globally authenticated user accounts do not store or validate a password in the database as a password-authenticated account does. These accounts rely on authentication provided by a service supported through the advanced security option.

The syntax for creating a globally authenticated account depends on the service called, but all use the keywords IDENTIFIED GLOBALLY, which tells the database to engage the advanced security option for authentication. Here is an example:

```
CREATE USER spy_master IDENTIFIED GLOBALLY AS 'CN=spy_master, OU=tier2,
    O=security, C=US';
```

Assigning Tablespaces and Quotas

Every user is assigned a default tablespace. When a user creates tables or indexes, they are created on the tablespace specified by the TABLESPACE clause. If the TABLESPACE clause is not provided, the segments will be created on the user's *default tablespace*. If you execute a CREATE TABLE statement and do not explicitly specify a tablespace, the database uses your default tablespace.

If you do not explicitly assign a default tablespace to a user at the time you create the user, the database assigns the database's default tablespace to the new user account. To assign a default tablespace to either a new user via a CREATE USER statement or an existing user, use the keywords DEFAULT TABLESPACE *tablespace_name*, like this:

```
CREATE USER rajesh IDENTIFIED BY welcome
DEFAULT TABLESPACE users;
```

Or use an ALTER USER statement:

```
ALTER USER rajesh
DEFAULT TABLESPACE users;
```

By default, the database default tablespace is SYSTEM. To change the database default tablespace (the value that users inherit if no default tablespace is provided), use the ALTER DATABASE statement, like this:

```
ALTER DATABASE DEFAULT TABLESPACE users;
```

Assigning a Temporary Tablespace

Every user is assigned a temporary tablespace in which the database stores temporary segments. Temporary segments are created during large sorting operations, such as ORDER BY, GROUP BY, SELECT DISTINCT, MERGE JOIN, or CREATE INDEX.

Temporary segments are also used when a temporary table is used. The database creates and drops temporary segments transparently to the user. Because of the transitory nature of temporary segments, you must use a dedicated tablespace of type TEMPORARY for your user's temporary tablespace setting.

If you do not explicitly assign a temporary tablespace at user creation time, the database assigns the database default temporary tablespace to the new user account. Use the keywords TEMPORARY TABLESPACE *tablespace_name* to assign a temporary tablespace either to a new user via the CREATE USER statement:

```
CREATE USER rajesh IDENTIFIED BY welcome
DEFAULT TABLESPACE users
TEMPORARY TABLESPACE temp;
```

or to an existing user via an ALTER USER statement:

```
ALTER USER rajesh
TEMPORARY TABLESPACE temp;
```

If the SYSTEM tablespace is locally managed at the time of database creation, you're required to provide a non-SYSTEM temporary-type tablespace as the database default temporary tablespace. To change the database default temporary tablespace, use the ALTER DATABASE statement, like this:

```
ALTER DATABASE DEFAULT TEMPORARY TABLESPACE temp;
```

You can query the data dictionary view DATABASE_PROPERTIES to view the current default tablespace and temporary tablespace assignment for the database.

Assigning Space Quotas

By default, Oracle 11*g* does not allocate any *space quota* in any tablespace when the user is created. To create segments (tables, indexes, and so on) in any tablespace, the user must have space quota granted on the tablespace. Tablespace quotas limit the amount of disk space that a user can consume. The default quota is none, which is why you need to assign a quota before you can create objects in a tablespace. You can assign a space usage quota at the same time you create a user, with the CREATE USER statement:

```
CREATE USER chip IDENTIFIED BY "Seek!r3t"
QUOTA 100M ON USERS;
```

Or you can assign it after the user has been created with the ALTER USER statement:

```
ALTER USER bart
QUOTA UNLIMTED ON USERS;
```

The special keyword UNLIMITED tells the database that the user should not have a preset limit on the amount of space that their objects can consume.

The user can create objects in any tablespace if the user has the UNLIMITED TABLESPACE system privilege. You will learn system privileges later in the chapter in the section "Granting System Privileges."

Assigning a Profile and Account Settings

In addition to default and temporary tablespaces, every user is assigned a profile. A profile serves two purposes:

- It can limit the resource usage of some resources.
- It can enforce password-management rules.

The default profile is appropriately named default. To explicitly assign a profile to a user, include the keywords PROFILE *profile_name* in the CREATE USER or ALTER USER statement. For example, to assign the profile named resource_profile to the new user jiang as well as to the existing user hamish, execute the following SQL:

```
CREATE USER jiang IDENTIFIED BY "kneehow.ma"
DEFAULT TABLESPACE users
TEMPORARY TABLESPACE temp
PROFILE resource_profile;

ALTER USER hamish
PROFILE resource_profile;
```

If you want users to change the password the first time they log in to the database, you can set the PASSWORD EXPIRE option. Each user will be forced to change the password at the first login. Here is an example of creating the user with an expired password:

```
SQL> CREATE USER shelly IDENTIFIED BY welcome
  2  PASSWORD EXPIRE;
```

```
User created.

SQL> GRANT CONNECT TO shelly;
SQL> connect shelly/welcome
ERROR:
ORA-28001: the password has expired

Changing password for shelly
New password:
Retype new password:
SQL> SHOW user
SQL> USER is "SHELLY"
```

By default, the user account is unlocked at creation. To lock the user account, use the ACCOUNT LOCK option.

To create and manage user accounts using EM Database Control, click the Server tab, and choose Users under the Security heading, as shown in Figure 12.1.

FIGURE 12.1 Database Control's server-administration screen

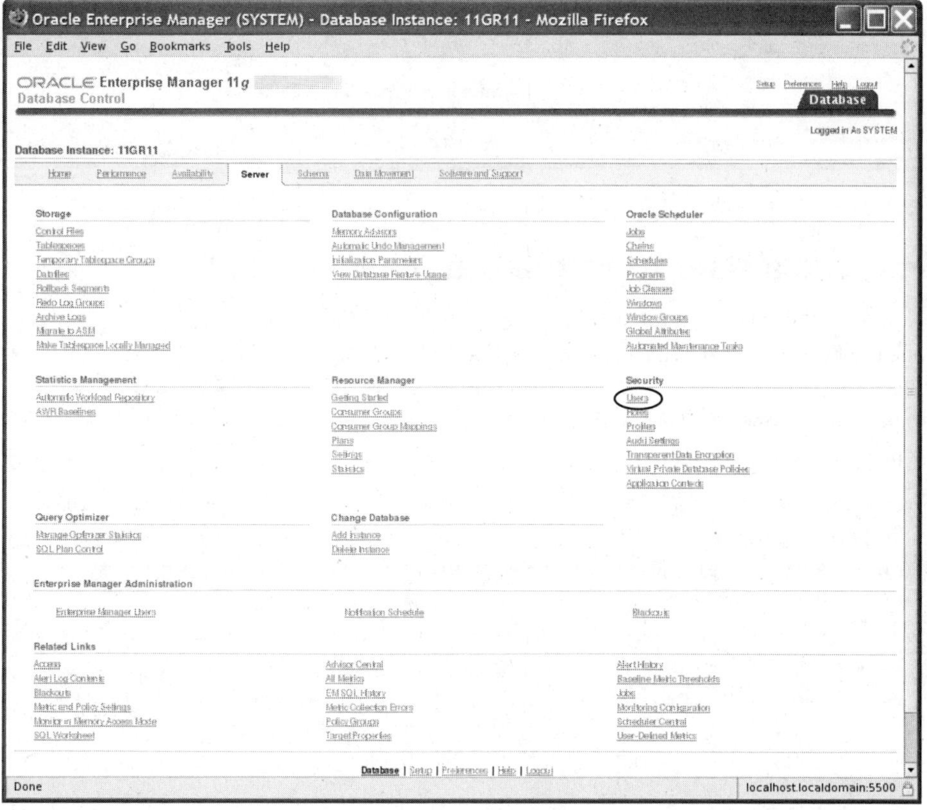

Click the Users link to get a listing of all users in the database. Clicking the Create button on this screen opens the screen to create the user, as shown in Figure 12.2.

FIGURE 12.2 Grid Control's Create User screen

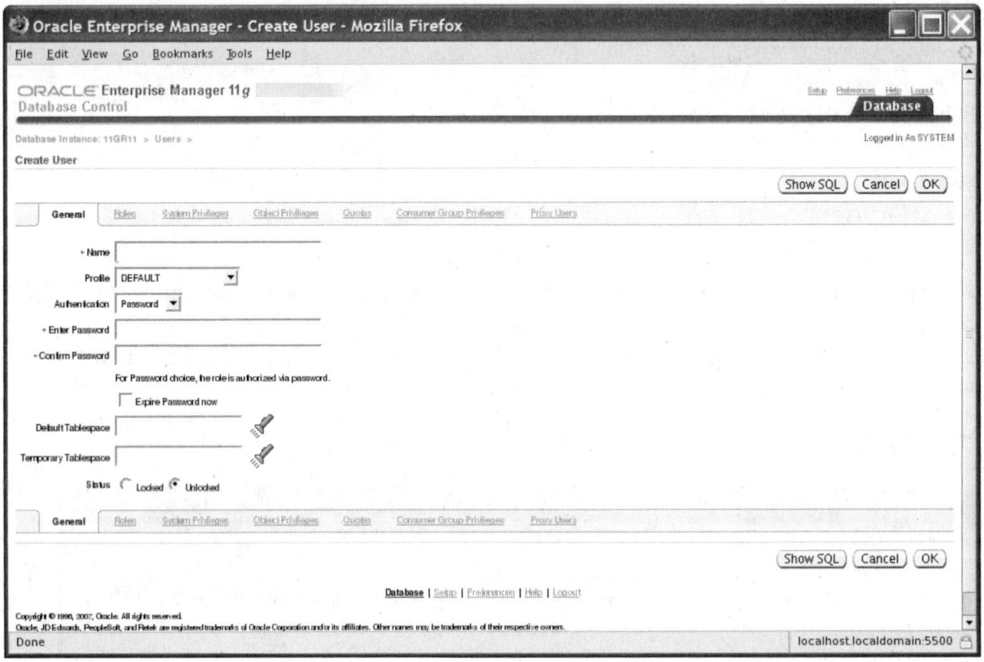

Removing a User from the Database

You use the DROP USER statement to remove a user from the database. You can optionally include the keyword CASCADE to tell the database to recursively drop all objects owned by that user.

To drop both user `rajesh` and all the objects he owns, execute the following:

```
DROP USER rajesh CASCADE;
```

Dropping a user implicitly drops any object privileges (but not role or system privileges) in which the user was the grantor. The data dictionary records both grantee and grantor for object privileges, but only the grantee is recorded for role and system privileges.

Managing Default User Accounts

The SYS and SYSTEM user accounts are always created with an Oracle 11*g* database. Additionally, the SYSMAN and DBSNMP accounts are created together with a database via the Database Configuration Assistant (DBCA).

Other special accounts can be created to support installed products, such as Recovery Manager (RMAN) or XMLDB. When created via the DBCA, these special accounts are locked and expired, leaving only SYS, SYSTEM, SYSMAN, and DBSNMP open. The SYS and SYSTEM accounts are the data dictionary owner and an administrative account, respectively. SYSMAN and DBSNMP are used by Enterprise Manager.

If your database is created via any means other than the DBCA, ensure that the accounts are locked and expired and that the default passwords are changed. You expire and lock an account using the ALTER USER statement like this:

```
ALTER USER mdsys PASSWORD EXPIRE ACCOUNT LOCK;
```

Depending on the functionality installed in your Oracle 11*g* database, you may need to lock and expire several default user accounts. Your database-created user accounts may include the following:

- ANONYMOUS
- APEX_PUBLIC_USER
- BI
- CTXSYS
- DBSNMP
- DIP
- EXFSYS
- FLOWS_030000
- FLOWS_FILES
- HR
- IX
- MDDATA
- MDSYS
- MGMT_VIEW
- OE
- OLAPSYS
- ORACLE_OCM
- ORDPLUGINS
- ORDSYS
- OUTLN
- OWBSYS
- PM
- SCOTT
- SH
- SI_INFORMTN_SCHEMA
- SPATIAL_CSW_ADMIN_USR
- SPATIAL_WFS_ADMIN_USR
- SYS
- SYSMAN
- SYSTEM
- TSMSYS
- WKPROXY
- WKSYS
- WK_TEST
- WMSYS
- XDB
- XS$NULL

Granting and Revoking Privileges

Privileges allow a user to access database objects or execute stored programs that are owned by another user. Privileges also enable a user to perform system-level operations, such as connecting to the database, creating a table, or altering the database.

Privileges are assigned to a user, to the special user PUBLIC, or to a role with the GRANT statement and can be rescinded with the REVOKE statement.

The Oracle 11*g* database has three types of privileges:

Object privileges These include permissions on schema objects such as tables, views, sequences, procedures, and packages. To use a schema object owned by another user, you need privileges on that object.

System privileges These include permissions on database-level operations, such as connecting to the database, creating users, altering the database, consuming unlimited amounts of tablespace, and querying all tables in the database.

Role privileges These include permissions granted to a user by way of a role. A *role* is a named group of privileges. Object and system privileges can be granted to a role.

I'll cover each of these privileges and how to grant them in the following sections.

Granting Object Privileges

Object privileges bestow upon the grantee the permission to use a schema object owned by another user in a particular way. As you'll see, there are several types of object privileges, some of which apply only to certain schema objects. For example, the INDEX privilege applies only to tables, and the SELECT privilege applies to tables, views, and sequences.

The following object privileges can be granted individually, can be granted grouped in a list, or can be granted with the keyword ALL to implicitly grant all available object privileges for a particular schema object.

Be careful when using ALL. It may implicitly grant powerful privileges.

Table Object Privileges

Oracle 11*g* provides several object privileges for tables. These privileges give the table owner considerable flexibility in controlling how schema objects are used and by whom.

Commonly Granted Privileges

The following privileges are commonly granted, and you should know them well:

SELECT This is the most commonly used privilege for tables. With this privilege, the table owner permits the grantee to query the specified table with a SELECT statement.

INSERT This permits the grantee to create new rows in the specified table with an INSERT statement.

UPDATE This permits the grantee to modify existing rows in the specified table with an UPDATE statement.

DELETE This permits the grantee to remove rows from the specified table with a DELETE statement.

Powerful Administrative Privileges on Tables

The following are powerful administrative privileges on tables; grant them cautiously:

ALTER This permits the grantee to execute an ALTER TABLE statement on the specified table. This privilege can be used to add, modify, or rename columns in the table, to move the table to another tablespace, or even to rename the specified table.

DEBUG This permits the grantee to access, via a debugger, the PL/SQL code in any triggers on the specified table.

INDEX This permits the grantee to create new indexes on the table. These new indexes will be owned by a different user than the table, which is an unusual practice. In most cases, the indexes on a table are owned by the same user who owns the table.

REFERENCES This permits the grantee to create foreign key constraints that reference the specified table.

View Object Privileges

Oracle 11*g* offers a smaller set of object privileges for views than it does for tables:

SELECT This is the most commonly used privilege for views. With this privilege, the view owner permits the grantee to query the view.

INSERT This permits the grantee to execute an INSERT statement on the specified view to create new rows.

UPDATE This permits the grantee to modify existing rows in the specified view with an UPDATE statement.

DELETE This permits the grantee to execute a DELETE statement on the specified view to remove rows.

DEBUG This permits the grantee to access, via a debugger, the PL/SQL code in the body of any trigger on this view.

REFERENCES This permits the grantee to create foreign key constraints on the specified view.

Sequence Object Privileges

Oracle 11*g* provides only two object privileges for sequences:

SELECT This permits the grantee to access the current and next values (CURRVAL and NEXTVAL) of the specified sequence.

ALTER This permits the grantee to change the attributes of the specified sequence with an ALTER statement.

Stored Functions, Procedures, Packages, and Java Object Privileges

Oracle 11*g* provides only two object privileges for stored PL/SQL programs:

DEBUG This permits the grantee to access, via a debugger, all the public and private variables and types declared in the specified program. If the specified object is a package, both the specification and the body are accessible to the grantee. The grantee can also use a debugger to place breakpoints in the specified program.

EXECUTE This permits the grantee to execute the specified program. If the specified object is a package, any program, variable, type, cursor, or record declared in the package specification is accessible to the grantee.

How to Grant Privileges

You use the GRANT statement to confer object privileges on either a user or a role. The optional keywords WITH GRANT OPTION additionally allow the grantee to confer these privileges on other users and roles. For example, to give SELECT, INSERT, UPDATE, and DELETE privileges on the table CUSTOMERS to the role SALES_MANAGER, execute the following statement while connected as the owner of table CUSTOMERS:

```
GRANT SELECT,INSERT,UPDATE,DELETE ON customers TO sales_manager;
```

If you grant privileges to the special user PUBLIC, you make them available to all current and future database users. For example, to give all database users the SELECT privilege on table CUSTOMERS, execute the following while connected as the owner of the table:

```
GRANT SELECT ON customers TO public;
```

When you extend a privilege to another user or role, you can also extend the ability for that grantee to turn around and grant the privilege to others. To extend this extra option, include the keywords WITH GRANT OPTION in the GRANT statement. For example, to give the SELECT privilege on table SALES.CUSTOMERS to the user SALES_ADMIN together with the permission for SALES_ADMIN to grant the SELECT privilege to others, execute the following:

```
GRANT SELECT ON sales.customers TO sales_admin WITH GRANT OPTION;
```

You can include the WITH GRANT OPTION keywords only when the grantee is a user or the special account PUBLIC. You cannot use WITH GRANT OPTION when the grantee is a role.

If you grant an object privilege using the WITH GRANT OPTION keywords and later revoke that privilege, the revoke cascades, and the privileges created by the grantee are also revoked. For example, Mary grants SELECT privileges on her table clients to Zachary with the WITH GRANT OPTION keywords. Zachary then creates a view based on the table mary.clients and grants the SELECT privilege on it to Rex. If Mary revokes the SELECT privilege from Zachary, the revoke cascades and removes the privilege from Rex. See Figure 12.3 for an illustration of this example.

FIGURE 12.3 The revoking of object privilege cascades.

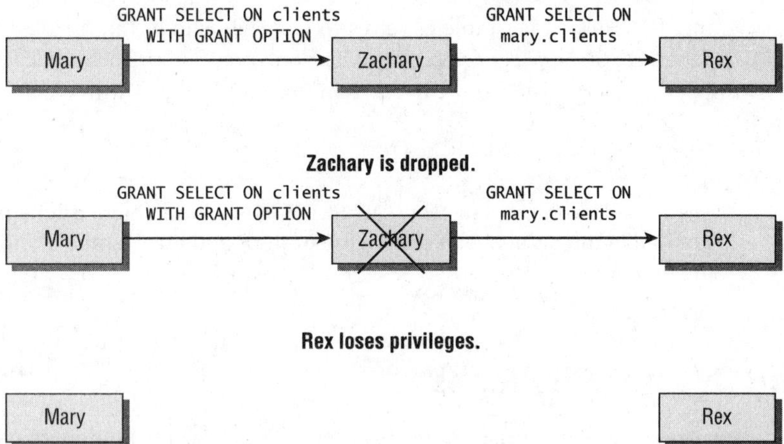

With object privileges, the database records both the grantor and the grantee. Therefore, a grantee can obtain a privilege from more than one grantor. When this multiple grant of the same privilege occurs, revoking one of these grants does not remove the privilege. To remove the privilege, all grants must be revoked, as shown in Figure 12.4.

FIGURE 12.4 The revoking of an object privilege with multiple grant paths

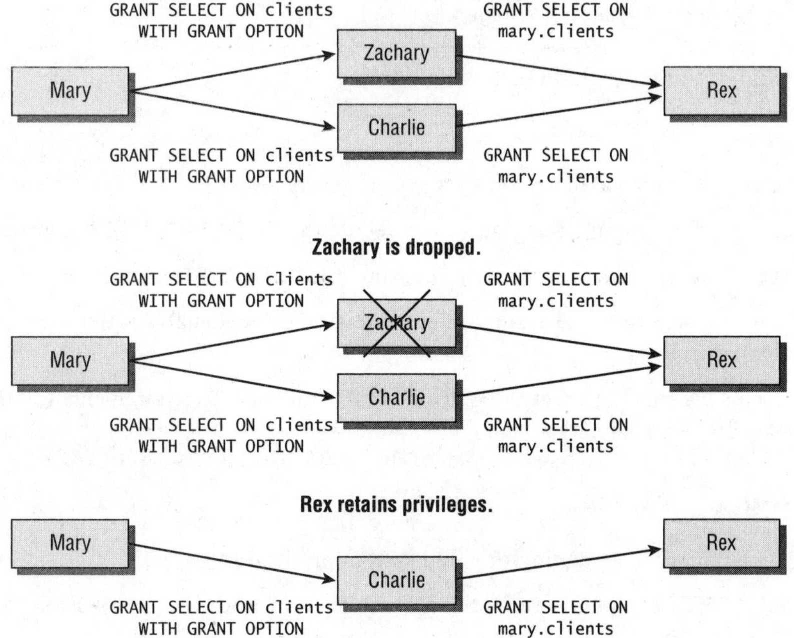

Continuing with our example, Mary has granted SELECT on her table clients to Zachary using WITH GRANT OPTION. Zachary has then granted SELECT on mary.clients to Rex. Mary has also granted SELECT on her table clients to Charlie, who has in turn granted to Rex. Rex now has the SELECT privilege from more than one grantee. If Zachary leaves and his account is dropped, the privilege from Charlie remains and Rex can still select from mary.clients.

The data dictionary view DBA_TAB_PRIVS lists all the object privileges granted in the database. It shows the grantor and the grantee along with the privilege.

Granting System Privileges

In general, *system privileges* permit the grantee to execute Data Definition Language (DDL) statements—such as CREATE, ALTER, and DROP—or Data Manipulation Language (DML) statements system-wide. Oracle 11*g* has more than 200 system privileges, all of which are listed in the data dictionary view SYSTEM_PRIVILEGE_MAP.

You will not be required to know all these privileges for the certification exam (thank goodness!), because many are for features that fall outside the scope of the exam. Pay attention to the database-related and table-related system privileges.

You should be familiar with the following groups.

Database

Oracle 11*g* gives you four database-oriented system privileges:

ALTER DATABASE This permits the grantee to execute the ALTER DATABASE statement.

ALTER SYSTEM This permits the grantee to execute the ALTER SYSTEM statement.

AUDIT SYSTEM This permits the grantee to execute AUDIT and NOAUDIT statements to perform statement auditing.

AUDIT ANY This permits the grantee to execute AUDIT and NOAUDIT statements to perform object auditing on objects in any schema.

Debugging

Oracle 11*g* gives you two debugging-oriented system privileges.

DEBUG CONNECT SESSION This permits the grantee to connect the current session to a debugger.

DEBUG ANY PROCEDURE This permits the grantee to debug all PL/SQL and Java code in the database. This system privilege is equivalent to granting the object privilege DEBUG for every applicable object in the database.

Indexes

Oracle 11*g* gives you three system privileges related to indexes:

CREATE ANY INDEX This permits the grantee to create an index in any schema.

ALTER ANY INDEX This permits the grantee to alter indexes in any schema.

DROP ANY INDEX This permits the grantee to drop indexes from any schema.

Job Scheduler

Oracle 11*g* gives you several system privileges related to the job scheduler:

CREATE JOB This permits the grantee to create jobs, programs, or schedules in their own schema.

CREATE ANY JOB This permits the grantee to create jobs, programs, or schedules in any schema.

The CREATE ANY JOB privilege gives the grantee the ability to execute programs using any other user's credentials. Grant it cautiously.

EXECUTE ANY PROGRAM This permits the grantee to use any program in a job in their own schema.

EXECUTE ANY CLASS This permits the grantee to specify any job class for jobs in their own schema.

MANAGE SCHEDULER This permits the grantee to create, alter, or delete any job class, window, or window group.

Procedures

Oracle 11*g* gives you several system privileges related to stored procedures:

CREATE PROCEDURE This permits the grantee to create procedures in their own schema.

CREATE ANY PROCEDURE This permits the grantee to create procedures in any schema.

ALTER ANY PROCEDURE This permits the grantee to recompile any procedure in the database.

DROP ANY PROCEDURE This permits the grantee to remove procedures from any schema.

EXECUTE ANY PROCEDURE This permits the grantee to run any procedure in any schema.

Profiles

Oracle 11*g* gives you three system privileges related to user profiles:

CREATE PROFILE This permits the grantee to create profiles. Causing a profile to be used requires an ALTER USER statement (which requires the ALTER USER privilege).

ALTER PROFILE This permits the grantee to modify existing profiles.

DROP PROFILE This permits the grantee to drop profiles from the database.

Roles

Oracle 11*g* gives you several system privileges related to roles. Because roles deal with security, some of these privileges are very powerful.

CREATE ROLE This permits the grantee to create new roles.

ALTER ANY ROLE This permits the grantee to change the password for any role in the database.

DROP ANY ROLE This permits the grantee to remove any role from the database.

GRANT ANY ROLE This permits the grantee to grant any role to any user or revoke any role from any user or role.

The GRANT ANY ROLE privilege permits grantees to assign or rescind powerful administrative roles, such as SCHEDULER_ADMIN and IMP_FULL_DATABASE, to or from any user, including themselves or other DBAs. Grant it cautiously.

Sequences

Oracle 11*g* gives you several system privileges to manage sequences:

CREATE SEQUENCE This permits the grantee to create new sequences in their own schema.

CREATE ANY SEQUENCE This permits the grantee to create new sequences in any schema.

ALTER ANY SEQUENCE This permits the grantee to change the characteristics of any sequence in the database.

DROP ANY SEQUENCE This permits the grantee to remove any sequence from any schema in the database.

SELECT ANY SEQUENCE This permits the grantee to select from any sequence.

Sessions

Oracle 11*g* gives you four session-oriented system privileges:

CREATE SESSION This permits the grantee to connect to the database. This privilege is required for user accounts but may be undesirable for application owner accounts.

ALTER SESSION This permits the grantee to execute ALTER SESSION statements.

ALTER RESOURCE COST This permits the grantee to change the way that Oracle calculates resource cost for resource restrictions in a profile.

For more information on managing resource consumption, see the section "Controlling Resource Usage by Users" later in this chapter.

RESTRICTED SESSION This permits the grantee to connect when the database has been opened in RESTRICTED SESSION mode, typically for administrative purposes. User accounts should not normally be granted this privilege.

Synonyms

Oracle 11*g* gives you several system privileges related to synonyms:

CREATE SYNONYM This permits the grantee to create new synonyms in their own schema.

CREATE ANY SYNONYM This permits the grantee to create new synonyms in any schema.

CREATE PUBLIC SYNONYM This permits the grantee to create new public synonyms, which are accessible to all users in the database.

DROP ANY SYNONYM This permits the grantee to remove any synonyms in any schema.

DROP PUBLIC SYNONYM This permits the grantee to remove any public synonym from the database.

Tables

Oracle 11*g* gives you several system privileges for managing tables:

CREATE TABLE This permits the grantee to create new tables in their own schema.

CREATE ANY TABLE This permits the grantee to create new tables in any schema.

ALTER ANY TABLE This permits the grantee to alter existing tables in any schema.

DROP ANY TABLE This permits the grantee to drop tables from any schema.

COMMENT ANY TABLE This permits the grantee to assign table or column comments to any table or view in any schema.

SELECT ANY TABLE This permits the grantee to query any table or view in any schema.

INSERT ANY TABLE This permits the grantee to insert new rows into any table in any schema.

UPDATE ANY TABLE This permits the grantee to modify rows in any table in any schema.

DELETE ANY TABLE This permits the grantee to delete rows from tables in any schema.

LOCK ANY TABLE This permits the grantee to execute a LOCK TABLE statement to explicitly lock a table in any schema.

FLASHBACK ANY TABLE This permits the grantee to execute a SQL flashback query, using the AS OF syntax, on any table or view in any schema.

See Chapter 15, "Implementing Database Backups," for more information on using flashback queries.

Tablespaces

Oracle 11*g* gives you four system privileges to control tablespace management:

CREATE TABLESPACE This permits the grantee to create new tablespaces.

ALTER TABLESPACE This permits the grantee to alter existing tablespaces with the ALTER TABLESPACE statement.

DROP TABLESPACE This permits the grantee to delete tablespaces from the database.

MANAGE TABLESPACE This permits the grantee to alter a tablespace ONLINE, OFFLINE, BEGIN BACKUP, or END BACKUP.

UNLIMITED TABLESPACE This permits the grantee to consume unlimited disk quota in any tablespace. This system privilege is equivalent to granting unlimited quota in each tablespace to the specified grantee.

Triggers

Oracle 11*g* gives you several system privileges to control trigger management:

CREATE TRIGGER This permits the grantee to create new triggers on tables in their own schema.

CREATE ANY TRIGGER This permits the grantee to create new triggers on tables in any schema.

ALTER ANY TRIGGER This permits the grantee to enable, disable, or compile existing triggers on tables in any schema.

DROP ANY TRIGGER This permits the grantee to remove triggers from tables in any schema.

ADMINISTER DATABASE TRIGGER This permits the grantee to create new ON DATABASE triggers. The grantee must also have the CREATE TRIGGER or CREATE ANY TRIGGER privilege before they can create an ON DATABASE trigger.

Users

Oracle 11*g* gives you several system privileges to control who can manage user accounts:

CREATE USER This permits the grantee to create new database users.

ALTER USER This permits the grantee to change the authentication method or password and assign quotas, temporary tablespaces, default tablespaces, or profiles for any user in the database. All users can change their own password without this privilege.

The ALTER USER privilege allows the grantee to change the authentication method or password for any user (and also change it back). This makes it possible for the grantee to masquerade as another user. Grant this privilege cautiously.

DROP USER This permits the grantee to remove users together with any objects they own from a database.

Views

Oracle 11*g* gives you several system privileges to manage views. Note that some of these privileges include the word TABLE and not VIEW. These privileges apply to either tables or views.

CREATE VIEW This permits the grantee to create new views in their own schema.

CREATE ANY VIEW This permits the grantee to create new views in any schema.

DROP ANY VIEW This permits the grantee to remove views from any schema.

COMMENT ANY TABLE This permits the grantee to assign table or column comments to any table or view in any schema.

FLASHBACK ANY TABLE This permits the grantee to execute a SQL flashback query, using the AS OF syntax, on any table or view in any schema.

Others

Oracle 11*g* gives you several system privileges for managing your database that don't fit into the other categories. These privileges include powerful administrative capabilities and should not be granted lightly.

ANALYZE ANY This permits the grantee to execute an ANALYZE statement on tables, indexes, or clusters in any schema.

GRANT ANY OBJECT PRIVILEGE This permits the grantee to assign object privileges on any object in any schema.

GRANT ANY PRIVILEGE This permits the grantee to assign any system privilege to other users or roles.

GRANT ANY ROLE This permits the grantee to assign any role to other users or roles. This privilege also gives the grantee permission to revoke any role.

SELECT ANY DICTIONARY This permits the grantee to select from the SYS-owned data dictionary tables, such as TAB$ or SYSAUTH$.

SYSDBA The most powerful system privilege, this permits the grantee to create, alter, start up, or shut down databases; enable ARCHIVELOG and NOARCHIVELOG mode; recover a database; and create an spfile; in addition to having all the system privileges the database has to offer, including RESTRICTED SESSION.

SYSOPER Only slightly less powerful than SYSDBA, this privilege permits the grantee to start up, shut down, alter, mount, back up, and recover a database. The grantee can create or alter an spfile and enter restricted session mode.

SYSASM Similar to the SYSDBA privilege, this gives the grantee privilege to manage an ASM instance. This privilege is new to Oracle 11*g*.

How to Grant System Privileges

As with object privileges, you use the GRANT statement to confer system privileges on either a user or a role. Unlike object privileges, the optional keywords WITH ADMIN OPTION are required to additionally allow the grantee to confer these privileges on other users and roles. For example, to give the CREATE USER, ALTER USER, and DROP USER privileges to the role APPL_DBA, you execute the following statement:

```
GRANT create user, alter user, drop user TO appl_dba;
```

System and role privileges require the wording WITH ADMIN OPTION; object privileges require the wording WITH GRANT OPTION. Because the function is so similar but the syntax is different, be sure you know when to use ADMIN and when to use GRANT—a question involving this subtle difference may appear on the exam.

As with object privileges, you can grant system privileges to the special user PUBLIC. Granting privileges to PUBLIC allows anyone with a database account and the CONNECT privilege to exercise this privilege. In general, because system privileges are more powerful than object privileges, take care when granting a system privilege to PUBLIC. For example, to give all current and future database users the FLASHBACK ANY TABLE privilege, execute the following:

```
GRANT flashback any table TO public;
```

To give the INDEX ANY TABLE privilege to the role APPL_DBA together with the permission to allow anyone with the role APPL_DBA to grant this privilege to others, execute the following:

```
GRANT index any table TO appl_dba WITH ADMIN OPTION;
```

If you grant a system privilege WITH ADMIN OPTION and later revoke that privilege, the privileges created by the grantee will not be revoked. Unlike object privileges, the revocation of system privileges does not cascade. Think of it this way: WITH GRANT OPTION includes the keyword GRANT and so implies that a revoke cascades, but WITH ADMIN OPTION does not mention GRANT, so a revoke has no effect. Here's an example. Mary grants the SELECT ANY TABLE privilege to new DBA Zachary with ADMIN OPTION. Zachary then grants this privilege to Rex. Later, Zachary gets promoted and leaves the department, so Mary revokes the SELECT ANY TABLE privilege from Zachary. Rex's privilege remains unaffected. You can see this in Figure 12.5.

FIGURE 12.5 The revoking of system privileges

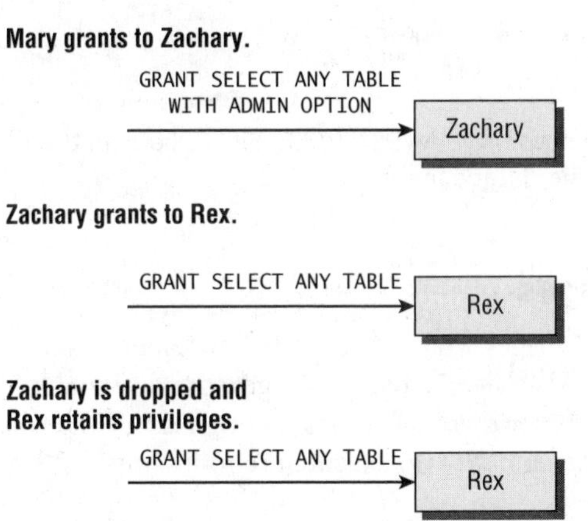

This behavior differs from object privileges, because the database does not record both grantor and grantee for system privileges—only the grantee is recorded.

The data dictionary view DBA_SYS_PRIVS lists all the system privileges granted in the database.

Role Privileges

Role privileges confer on the grantee a group of system, object, and other role privileges. Users who have been granted a role inherit the privileges that have been granted to that role. Roles can be password protected, so users may have a role granted to them yet not be able to use that role in all database sessions. I'll cover roles and role privileges—including how to grant them—in the following section, "Creating and Managing Roles."

Creating and Managing Roles

A *role* is a tool for administering privileges. Privileges can be granted to a role, and then that role can be granted to other roles and users. Users can thus inherit privileges via roles. Roles serve no other purpose than to administer privileges.

To create a role, use the CREATE ROLE statement. You can optionally include an IDENTIFIED BY clause that requires users to authenticate themselves before enabling the role. Roles requiring authentication are typically used inside an application, where a user's activities are controlled by the application. To create the role APPL_DBA, execute the following:

```
CREATE ROLE appl_dba;
```

To enable a role, execute a SET ROLE statement, like this:

```
SET ROLE appl_dba IDENTIFIED BY seekwrit;
```

The data dictionary view DBA_ROLE_PRIVS lists all the role privileges granted in the database.

Granting Role Privileges

As with object and system privileges, you use the GRANT statement to confer role privileges on either a user or another role. Also, like system privileges, the optional keywords WITH ADMIN OPTION allow the grantee to confer these privileges on other users and roles. For example, to give the OEM_MONITOR role to user charlie, execute the following:

```
GRANT oem_monitor TO charlie;
```

As with the other privileges, you can grant role privileges to the special user PUBLIC. Granting privileges to PUBLIC allows anyone with a database account to exercise this privilege. For example, to give all current and future database users use of the plustrace role, execute the following:

```
GRANT plustrace TO public;
```

To give the INDEX ANY TABLE privilege to the role APPL_DBA together with the permission to allow anyone with the role APPL_DBA to grant this privilege to others, execute the following:

```
GRANT index any table TO appl_dba WITH ADMIN OPTION;
```

When it comes to granting a role WITH ADMIN OPTION, roles behave like system privileges, and subsequent revocations do not cascade.

If the role granted to a user is not the default role, the user must enable the role in the session to be able to use the role. In the following sections, you will learn to work with roles in a session.

Enabling Roles

Roles can be enabled—or disabled, for that matter—selectively in each database session. If you have two concurrent sessions, the roles in effect for each session can be different.

Use the `SET ROLE` *role_list* statement to enable one or more roles. *role_list* is a comma-delimited list of roles to enable. This list can include the keyword `ALL`, which enables all the roles granted to the user. You can optionally append a list of roles to exclude from the `ALL` list by specifying `ALL EXCEPT` *exclusion_list*.

If a role has a password associated with it, the keywords `IDENTIFIED BY` *password* must immediately follow the role name in the *role_list*.

For example, to enable the password-protected role `HR_ADMIN`, together with the unprotected role `EMPLOYEE`, execute the following:

```
SET ROLE hr_admin IDENTIFIED BY "my!seekrit", employee;
```

To enable all roles except `HR_ADMIN`, run this:

```
SET ROLE ALL EXCEPT hr_admin;
```

You can enable as many roles as have been granted to you, up to the `MAX_ENABLED_ROLES` initialization parameter.

Identifying Enabled Roles

The roles that are enabled in your session are listed in the data dictionary view `SESSION_ROLES`. To identify these enabled roles for your session, run the following:

```
SELECT role FROM session_roles;
```

These roles include the roles that have been granted to you, the roles that have been granted to the special user `PUBLIC`, and the roles that you have inherited by way of other roles. To identify the roles granted to either user or the special user `PUBLIC`, run the following:

```
SELECT granted_role FROM user_role_privs
WHERE username IN (USER, 'PUBLIC');
```

The role `DBA` includes the role `SCHEDULER_ADMIN`, which in turn has system privileges (such as `CREATE ANY JOB`). A user who has been granted the `DBA` role inherits the `SCHEDULER_ADMIN` role indirectly. To identify the roles that are both enabled in your session and granted directly to you or `PUBLIC` but not those roles that you inherited, run this:

```
SELECT role FROM session_roles
INTERSECT
SELECT granted_role FROM user_role_privs
WHERE username IN (USER, 'PUBLIC');
```

In your sessions, you can disable only these directly granted and public roles.

Disabling Roles

Roles can be disabled in a database session either en masse or by exception. Use the `SET ROLE NONE` statement to disable all roles. Use the `SET ROLE ALL EXCEPT` *role_list* statement to enable all roles except those in the comma-delimited *role_list*.

There is no way to selectively disable a single role. Also, you cannot disable roles that you inherit by way of another role without disabling the parent role. For example, if you have been granted the `DBA`, `RESOURCE`, and `CONNECT` roles, you inherit several roles through the DBA role when it is enabled. If you want to disable the SCHEDULER_ADMIN role you inherited through the DBA role, you cannot do that. The options you have are that you can disable the DBA role or you can create a new role similar to the DBA role without the SCHEDULER_ADMIN role and use that role.

Setting Default Roles

Roles that are enabled by default when you log on are called *default roles*. You do not need to specify a password for default roles and do not have to execute a SET ROLE statement to enable a default role. Change the default roles for a user account with an ALTER USER DEFAULT ROLE *role_list* statement. The *role_list* can include the keywords ALL, NONE, and EXCEPT, in the same manner as with a SET ROLE statement.

Including a password-protected role in the *role_list* defeats the purpose of password protecting the role because it is automatically enabled without the password. When you create a role, you are implicitly granted that role with the admin option, and it is configured as a default role for your account.

For example, to create the role EMPLOYEE, grant it to user scott, and configure all of scott's roles except PLUSTRACE as default roles, run the following:

```
CREATE ROLE employee;
GRANT employee TO scott;
ALTER USER scott DEFAULT ROLE ALL EXCEPT plustrace;
```

Because the creator of a role automatically has that role assigned as a default role, administrative users (such as SYS or SYSTEM) who create many roles may need to alter their default role list. If you attempt to log on with more default roles than allowed by the MAX_ENABLED_ROLES initialization parameter, you will raise an exception, and your logon will fail.

Real World Scenario

A Password-Protected Role

Lucinda works in HR and needs to be able to modify an employee's salary after they have a review and their raise is approved. The HR application ensures that the raise is approved and falls within corporate guidelines. Although Lucinda needs to be able to change employee salaries, she should be allowed to do so only from within the HR application, because it ensures that business rules are followed.

You wisely choose to use a password-protected role to satisfy these requirements. Update privilege on the salary table is granted to the password-protected role salary_admin. Lucinda is then granted the salary_admin role, but she is not told the password for it. The HR application has the password encoded within it, so when Lucinda runs the HR application, unknown to her, a SET ROLE salary_admin IDENTIFY BY *password* statement is executed, enabling the role and allowing her to change the salary.

If Lucinda tries to execute an UPDATE statement on the salary table from SQL*Plus, she will get an insufficient privileges error.

Default Database Roles

When you create a new Oracle 11*g* database, Oracle creates several roles in the database based on the options you chose at the database creation. The following are few of the important roles that are created automatically during database creation:

CONNECT This role has only one privilege, CREATE SESSION.

RESOURCE This role has the privileges required to create common objects in the user's schema.

DBA This is the most powerful role in the database. Only database administrators should be given this role. This role has all the system privileges and several administrative privileges.

SELECT_CATALOG_ROLE This role gives the user access to query the data dictionary views.

EXECUTE_CATALOG_ROLE This role gives the user privileges to execute the packages and procedures in the data dictionary.

DELETE_CATALOG_ROLE This role gives the user the ability to delete records from the system audit table (SYS.AUD$).

To list all the roles defined in the database, query the data dictionary view DBA_ROLES. To view the system privileges granted to a role, query the DBA_SYS_PRIVS dictionary view. For example, the following query lists the system privileges granted to the RESOURCE role:

```
SQL> SELECT grantee, privilege, admin_option
  2  FROM dba_sys_privs
  3  WHERE grantee = 'RESOURCE'
SQL> /

GRANTEE              PRIVILEGE            ADM
-------------------- -------------------- ---
RESOURCE             CREATE TRIGGER       NO
RESOURCE             CREATE SEQUENCE      NO
RESOURCE             CREATE TYPE          NO
RESOURCE             CREATE PROCEDURE     NO
RESOURCE             CREATE CLUSTER       NO
RESOURCE             CREATE OPERATOR      NO
RESOURCE             CREATE INDEXTYPE     NO
RESOURCE             CREATE TABLE         NO

8 rows selected.
SQL>
```

Applying the Principle of Least Privilege

The principle of least privilege states that each user should be given only the minimal privileges needed to perform their job. This principle is a central tenet to the *initially closed philosophy* whereby all access is initially closed or unavailable and access is opened on a need-to-know basis. Highly secure environments typically operate under an initially closed philosophy. The contrasting philosophy is an initially open philosophy, whereby all access is by default open to all users and only sensitive areas are closed. Academic or learning environments typically operate under an initially open philosophy.

Many IT organizations want the most secure policies for production systems, which calls for the initially closed approach to security. To support the need for administrators and programmers to quickly learn new technology, these shops frequently create "sandbox" systems that follow the initially open philosophy. These sandbox systems afford their limited users the learning benefit of the initially open approach, while not storing or giving gateway access to any sensitive information elsewhere in the enterprise.

To implement the principle of least privilege on your production or development systems, you should take several actions, or best practices, while setting up or locking down the database. Let's take a look at these:

Protect the data dictionary Ensure that users with the SELECT ANY TABLE privilege cannot access the tables that underlie the data dictionary by setting O7_DICTIONARY_ACCESSIBILITY = FALSE. This is the default setting.

Revoke unnecessary privileges from PUBLIC By default, several packages and roles are granted to the special user PUBLIC. Review these privileges, and revoke the EXECUTE privilege from PUBLIC if these packages are not necessary. Some of these packages include the following:

UTL_TCP This permits the grantee to establish a network connection to any waiting TCP/IP network service. Once a connection is established, arbitrary information can be sent and received directly from the database to and from the other TCP services on your network. If your organization is concerned about information exchange over TCP/IP, revoke the EXECUTE privilege on this package from PUBLIC. Grant privileges on this package only to those users who need it.

UTL_SMTP This permits the grantee to send arbitrary email. If your organization is concerned about information exchange via email, revoke the EXECUTE privilege on this package from PUBLIC. Grant privileges on this package only to those users who need it.

UTL_HTTP This permits the grantee to send and receive arbitrary data via the HTTP protocol. If your organization is concerned about information exchange via HTTP, revoke the EXECUTE privilege on this package from PUBLIC. Grant privileges on this package only to those users who need it.

UTL_FILE This permits the grantee to read and write text data to and from arbitrary operating-system files that are in the designated directories. UTL_FILE does not manage concurrency, so multiple user sessions can step on each other, overwriting changes via UTL_FILE. Consider revoking the EXECUTE privilege on this package from PUBLIC.

DBMS_OBFUSCATION_TOOLKIT and DBMS_CRYPTO These permit the grantee to employ encryption technologies. In a managed environment using encryption, the keys are stored and managed. If encryption keys are lost, the encrypted data is undecipherable. Consider revoking the EXECUTE privilege on these packages from PUBLIC.

You can revoke the EXECUTE privileges like this:

```
REVOKE EXECUTE ON utl_tcp FROM PUBLIC;
REVOKE EXECUTE ON utl_smtp FROM PUBLIC;
REVOKE EXECUTE ON utl_http FROM PUBLIC;
REVOKE EXECUTE ON utl_file FROM PUBLIC;
REVOKE EXECUTE ON dbms_obfuscation_toolkit
    FROM PUBLIC;
REVOKE EXECUTE ON dbms_crypto FROM PUBLIC;
```

You can query the data dictionary to see what other packages may need to be locked down by revoking the EXECUTE privilege from PUBLIC. Here is a query to list the packages, owned by user SYS, that have the EXECUTE privilege granted to PUBLIC:

```
SELECT table_name
FROM dba_tab_privs p
    ,dba_objects   o
WHERE p.owner=o.owner
AND   p.table_name = o.object_name
AND   p.owner = 'SYS'
AND   p.privilege = 'EXECUTE'
AND   p.grantee = 'PUBLIC'
AND   o.object_type='PACKAGE';
```

Limit the users who have administrative privileges Grant administrative privileges to user accounts cautiously. Some powerful administrative privileges and roles to exercise caution with include the following:

SYSDBA This gives the grantee the highest level of privileges with the Oracle Database software. A clever user with the SYSDBA role can circumvent most database security measures. There is usually no good reason to grant this role to any account except SYS, and the SYS password should be both cautiously guarded and changed regularly. Also, guard operating-system accounts carefully. If you are logged on to the database server using a privileged operating-system account, you might be able to connect to the database with SYSDBA authority and no password by entering **connect / as sysdba** in SQL*Plus.

DBA This permits the grantee to assign privileges and manipulate data throughout the database. A clever user with the DBA role can circumvent most database security measures. Grant this role only to those users who need it.

The ANY system privileges SELECT ANY TABLE, GRANT ANY ROLE, DELETE ANY TABLE, and so on, permit the grantee to assign privileges and manipulate data throughout the database. A malicious user with the one of these roles can wreak havoc in your database. Grant these privileges only to those users who need them.

Do not enable REMOTE_OS_AUTHENT The default setting for the initialization parameter REMOTE_OS_AUTHENT is FALSE. There is rarely a reason to enable this feature. When set to TRUE, this parameter tells the database to trust any client to authenticate externally authenticated accounts. For example, if you have an externally identified account named ORACLE that has DBA privileges for use in administrative scripts running on the database server (a common practice), setting this parameter to TRUE will allow someone with a notebook or desktop PC with a locally created ORACLE account to connect to your database with DBA credentials and no password.

Controlling Resource Usage by Users

An Oracle 11*g* database lets you limit some resources that your user accounts consume. Disk-space limits are governed by tablespace quotas (discussed in "Assigning Tablespace and Quotas" earlier in the chapter); CPU and memory limits are implemented with *profiles*.

CPU and session-oriented resource limits are managed through profiles. Profiles let you set limits for several resources, including CPU time, memory, and the number of logical reads performed during a user session or database call. A database call is either a parse, an execute, or a fetch. Usually, the database implicitly performs these calls for you. You can explicitly make these database calls from Java, PL/SQL, or Oracle Call Interface (OCI) programs.

A logical read is a measure of the amount of work that the database performs while executing SQL statements. Statements that generate more logical reads require the database to perform more work than statements generating fewer logical reads. Technically, a logical read is counted for each row accessed via ROWID (index access) and for each data block accessed via a multiblock read (full-table scan or index fast full scan).

To enable resource limit restrictions with profiles, first enable them in the database by setting the initialization parameter resource_limit to TRUE, like this:

```
ALTER SYSTEM SET resource_limit = TRUE SCOPE = BOTH;
```

To assign resource limits to a profile, use the CREATE PROFILE or ALTER PROFILE statement with one or more of the kernel resource parameters. The following is an example of the CREATE PROFILE statement, with all the resources that can be controlled. A resource value of DEFAULT indicates that the value is derived from the DEFAULT profile. Initially, the DEFAULT profile has all the system resources set to UNLIMITED.

```
CREATE PROFILE "TEST1" LIMIT
CPU_PER_SESSION DEFAULT
CPU_PER_CALL DEFAULT
CONNECT_TIME DEFAULT
IDLE_TIME 10
```

```
SESSIONS_PER_USER DEFAULT
LOGICAL_READS_PER_SESSION DEFAULT
LOGICAL_READS_PER_CALL 250000
PRIVATE_SGA 25000
COMPOSITE_LIMIT DEFAULT;
```

Each resource is explained here:

CONNECT_TIME This limits any session established by a user having this profile set to the specified number of minutes. Connection time is sometimes called *wall clock time* to differentiate it from CPU time. When a session exceeds the specified number of minutes, the database rolls back any uncommitted changes and terminates the session. The next call to the database raises an exception. You can use the special value UNLIMITED to tell the database that there is no limit to a session's duration. Set this parameter in a CREATE PROFILE or ALTER PROFILE statement like this:

```
CREATE PROFILE agent LIMIT CONNECT_TIME 10;
ALTER PROFILE data_analyst LIMIT CONNECT_TIME UNLIMITED;
```

CPU_PER_CALL This limits the amount of CPU time that can be consumed by any single database call in any session established by a user with this profile. The specified value is in hundredths of a second and applies to a parse, an execute, or a fetch call. These calls are implicitly performed by the database for any SQL statement executed in SQL*Plus and can be explicitly called from OCI, Java, and PL/SQL programs. When this limit is breached, the statement fails and is automatically rolled back, and an exception is raised. The user can then commit or roll back any uncommitted changes in the transaction. Set this parameter in a CREATE PROFILE or ALTER PROFILE statement like this:

```
CREATE PROFILE agent LIMIT CPU_PER_CALL 3000;
ALTER PROFILE data_analyst LIMIT CPU_PER_CALL UNLIMITED;
```

CPU_PER_SESSION This limits the amount of CPU time that can be consumed in any session established by a user with this profile. The specified value is in hundredths of a second and applies to a parse, an execute, or a fetch. When this limit is breached, the current statement fails, the transaction is automatically rolled back, and an exception is raised. The user can then commit or roll back any uncommitted changes in the transaction before logging off. Set this parameter in a CREATE PROFILE or ALTER PROFILE statement like this:

```
CREATE PROFILE agent LIMIT CPU_PER_CALL 30000;
ALTER PROFILE data_analyst LIMIT CPU_PER_CALL UNLIMITED;
```

IDLE_TIME This limits the duration of time between database calls to the specified number of minutes. If a user having this profile exceeds this setting, the next statement fails, and the user is allowed to either commit or roll back any uncommitted changes before logging off. Long-running statements are not affected by this setting. Set IDLE_TIME in a CREATE PROFILE or ALTER PROFILE statement like this:

```
CREATE PROFILE agent LIMIT IDLE_TIME 10;
ALTER PROFILE daemon LIMIT IDLE_TIME UNLIMITED;
```

LOGICAL_READS_PER_CALL This caps the amount of work that any individual database call performs to the specified number of logical reads. The database call is either a parse, an execute, or a fetch. If the limit is exceeded, the database rolls back the statement, returns an error to the calling program, and allows the user to either commit or roll back any uncommitted changes. Logical reads are computed as the sum of consistent gets plus current mode gets. Set this parameter in a CREATE PROFILE or ALTER PROFILE statement like this:

```
CREATE PROFILE agent LIMIT LOGICAL_READS_PER_CALL 2500;
ALTER PROFILE data_analyst LIMIT LOGICAL_READS_PER_CALL 1000000;
```

LOGICAL_READS_PER_SESSION This limits the amount of database work that a user's session can consume to the specified number of logical reads. When the limit is exceeded, the current statement fails and an exception is raised, and the user must either commit or roll back the transaction and end the session. Logical reads are computed as the sum of consistent gets plus current mode gets. Set this parameter in a CREATE PROFILE or ALTER PROFILE statement like this:

```
CREATE PROFILE agent LIMIT LOGICAL_READS_PER_SESSION 250000;
ALTER PROFILE data_analyst
   LIMIT LOGICAL_READS_PER_SESSION 35000000;
```

PRIVATE_SGA This limits the amount of system global area (SGA) memory in bytes that a user connecting with shared servers (via a multithreaded server [MTS]) can allocate to the persistent area in the program global area (PGA). This area contains bind information among other items. Set this parameter in a CREATE PROFILE or ALTER PROFILE statement like this:

```
CREATE PROFILE agent LIMIT PRIVATE_SGA 2500;
ALTER PROFILE data_analyst LIMIT PRIVATE_SGA UNLIMITED;
```

SESSIONS_PER_USER This restricts a user with this profile to the specified number of database sessions. This setting can be useful to discourage DBAs from all connecting to a shared administrative account to do their work when corporate policy indicates that they should be connecting to their individual accounts. Set this parameter in a CREATE PROFILE or ALTER PROFILE statement like this:

```
CREATE PROFILE admin_profile LIMIT SESSIONS_PER_USER 2;
ALTER PROFILE data_analyst LIMIT SESSIONS_PER_USER 6;
```

COMPOSITE_LIMIT This limits the number of service units that can be consumed during a user session. Service units are calculated as the weighted sum of CPU_PER_SESSION, LOGICAL_READS_PER_SESSION, CONNECT_TIME, and PRIVATE_SGA values. The weightings are established with the ALTER RESOURCE COST statement and can be viewed from the RESOURCE_COST data dictionary view. This COMPOSITE_LIMIT allows you to cap the resource consumption of user groups in more complex ways than a single resource limit. Set this parameter in a CREATE PROFILE or ALTER PROFILE statement like this:

```
CREATE PROFILE admi_profile LIMIT COMPOSITE_LIMIT UNLIMITED;
ALTER PROFILE data_analyst LIMIT COMPOSITE_LIMIT 100000;
```

To enforce the resource limits established with profiles, you must enable them by setting the initialization parameter RESOURCE_LIMIT to TRUE. The default setting is FALSE. Set this parameter with the ALTER SYSTEM statement, like this:

```
ALTER SYSTEM SET resource_limit = TRUE SCOPE=BOTH;
```

You can also use profiles to manage passwords, which is discussed in the next section.

Implementing Password Security Features

For users who are configured for database authentication, password-security rules are enforced with profiles and password complexity rules with verification functions. Profiles have a set of standard rules that define how long a password can remain valid, the elapsed time, the number of password changes before a password can be reused, the number of failed login attempts that will lock the account, and how long the account will remain locked.

If you want a parameter to inherit the setting from the DEFAULT profile, set the parameter's value to the keyword DEFAULT. Explicitly assign password rules to a profile using the CREATE PROFILE or ALTER PROFILE statement. The following is an example of the CREATE PROFILE statement, with all the password features that can be controlled:

```
CREATE PROFILE "TEST2" LIMIT
PASSWORD_LIFE_TIME 60
PASSWORD_GRACE_TIME 7
PASSWORD_REUSE_MAX 2
PASSWORD_REUSE_TIME 4
PASSWORD_LOCK_TIME DEFAULT
FAILED_LOGIN_ATTEMPTS 5
PASSWORD_VERIFY_FUNCTION DEFAULT;
```

Each option is discussed in detail here with examples:

FAILED_LOGIN_ATTEMPTS and PASSWORD_LOCK_TIME The FAILED_LOGIN_ATTEMPTS parameter specifies how many times in a row the user can fail password authentication. If this limit is breached, the account is locked for PASSWORD_LOCK_TIME days. If the PASSWORD_LOCK_TIME parameter is set to UNLIMITED and a user exceeds FAILED_LOGIN_ATTEMPTS, the account must be manually unlocked. You can set these parameters in a CREATE PROFILE or ALTER PROFILE statement like this:

```
-- lock account for 10 minutes if 3 consecutive logins fail
CREATE PROFILE agent LIMIT
   FAILED_LOGIN_ATTEMPTS 3
   PASSWORD_LOCK_TIME 10/1440;

-- remove failed login restrictions
ALTER PROFILE student LIMIT FAILED_LOGIN_ATTEMPTS UNLIMITED;
```

```
-- manually unlock an account
ALTER USER scott ACCOUNT UNLOCK;
```

The default value for FAILED_LOGIN_ATTEMPTS in Oracle 11*g* is 10 and for PASSWORD_LOCK_TIME is 1 day.

PASSWORD_LIFE_TIME and PASSWORD_GRACE_TIME The PASSWORD_LIFE_TIME parameter specifies the maximum number of days that a password can remain in force, and PASSWORD_GRACE_TIME is the number of days after the first successful login following password expiration during which the user will be reminded to change their password but allowed to log in. After the PASSWORD_GRACE_TIME limit is reached, the user must change their password. If you set PASSWORD_LIFE_TIME to a value and set PASSWORD_GRACE_TIME to UNLIMITED, users will be reminded to change their password every time they log in but never forced to actually do so. You can set these two parameters in a CREATE PROFILE or ALTER PROFILE statement like this:

```
-- limit the password lifetime to 90 days
-- during the last 14 days the user will be reminded
-- to change the password
CREATE PROFILE agent LIMIT
   PASSWORD_LIFE_TIME 90 - 14
   PASSWORD_GRACE_TIME 14;

-- set no limit to password lifetime
ALTER PROFILE student LIMIT
   PASSWORD_LIFE_TIME UNLIMITED
   PASSWORD_GRACE_TIME DEFAULT;
```

The default value for PASSWORD_LIFE_TIME in Oracle 11*g* is 180 days and for PASSWORD_GRACE_TIME is 7 days.

PASSWORD_REUSE_TIME and PASSWORD_REUSE_MAX The PASSWORD_REUSE_TIME parameter specifies the minimum number of days that must transpire before a password can be reused. PASSWORD_REUSE_MAX specifies the minimum number of password changes that must occur before a password can be reused. If you specify a value for one of these two parameters and UNLIMITED for the other, passwords can never be reused. If you set both PASSWORD_REUSE_TIME and PASSWORD_REUSE_MAX to UNLIMITED (the default), these parameters are essentially disabled. You can set these password parameters in a CREATE PROFILE or ALTER PROFILE statement like this:

```
-- require at least 4 password changes and 1 year
-- before a password may be reused.
CREATE PROFILE agent LIMIT
   PASSWORD_REUSE_TIME 365
   PASSWORD_REUSE_MAX 4;
```

```
-- remove password reuse constraints
ALTER PROFILE student LIMIT
   PASSWORD_REUSE_TIME UNLIMITED
   PASSWORD_REUSE_MAX UNLIMITED;
```

Real World Scenario

Setting Password Lock Time to Two Hours

Several password attributes are durations expressed in days. These durations are normally set with integer values, such as 1, 15, 30, 90, or 365 days.

The default password lock time for Oracle 11*g* is 1 day, and the unit used to express the lock time is in days. A few of the clients I worked for needed the password lock to go away after two hours if the user tried to enter incorrect password too many times. How do you set the value in hours or minutes when the unit is in days?

All these password profile attributes take fractional values as well; hence, you can represent hours and minutes. Since there are 1,440 minutes in a day, you can represent 5 minutes as 5/1440 days and represent 5 seconds as 5/86400 days. The following code sets the password lock time to two hours:

```
ALTER PROFILE student LIMIT PASSWORD_LOCK_TIME 2/24;
```

You can represent the value using decimal numbers; for example, the following code sets the password lock time to six hours:

```
ALTER PROFILE student LIMIT PASSWORD_LOCK_TIME .25;
```

Using a fractional number of days is a great way to try combinations of values and observe the results of setting these password rules.

PASSWORD_VERIFY_FUNCTION The PASSWORD_VERIFY_FUNCTION parameter lets you codify additional rules that will be verified when a password is changed. These rules usually verify password complexity such as minimal password length or check that a password does not appear in a dictionary. The PL/SQL function used in the PASSWORD_VERIFY_FUNCTION parameter must be created under the user SYS and must have three parameters of type VARCHAR2. These parameters must contain the username in the first parameter, the new password in the second, and the old password in the third. You can set this parameter in a CREATE PROFILE or ALTER PROFILE statement like this:

```
-- use a custom password function
CREATE PROFILE agent LIMIT PASSWORD_VERIFY_FUNCTION my_function;
```

```
-- disable use of a custom function
ALTER PROFILE student LIMIT PASSWORD_VERIFY_FUNCTION DEFAULT;
```

Implementing a Corporate Password-Security Policy

Many companies have security policies requiring that several password complexity rules be followed. For your Oracle 11*g* database, these rules can be incorporated into a password verify function. This real-world scenario highlights an example of three password complexity requirements and how they are satisfied through a password verify function named MY_PASSWORD_VERIFY.

The first rule specifies that the password must be at least six characters in length. The second rule disallows passwords containing some form of either the username or the word *password*. The third rule requires the password to contain at least one alphabetic character, at least one digit, and at least one punctuation character. If the new password fails any of these tests, the function raises an exception, and the password change fails.

After creating this function as user SYS, assign it to a profile, like this:

```
ALTER PROFILE student LIMIT password_verify_function my_password_verify;
```

Any user having the `student` profile will need to abide by the password rules enforced by the `my_password_verify` function:

```
CREATE OR REPLACE FUNCTION my_password_verify
   (username VARCHAR2
   ,password VARCHAR2
   ,old_password VARCHAR2
   ) RETURN BOOLEAN
IS

BEGIN
   -- Check for the minimum length of the password
   IF LENGTH(password) < 6 THEN
      raise_application_error(-20001
         ,'Password must be at least 6 characters long');
   END IF;

   -- Check that the password does not contain any
   -- upper/lowercase version of either the user name
   -- or the keyword PASSWORD
```

```
   IF (    regexp_like(password,username,'i')
       OR regexp_like(password,'password','i')) THEN
      raise_application_error(-20002
         ,'Password cannot contain username or PASSWORD');
   END IF;

   -- Check that the password contains at least one letter,
   -- one digit and one punctuation character
   IF NOT(     regexp_like(password,'[[:digit:]]')
          AND regexp_like(password,'[[:alpha:]]')
          AND regexp_like(password,'[[:punct:]]')
         ) THEN
      raise_application_error(-20003
         ,'Password must contain at least one digit '||
          'and one letter and one punctuation character');
   END IF;

   -- password is okey dokey
   RETURN(TRUE);
END;
/
```

Oracle 11*g* provides the PL/SQL code to create a password complexity verify function. The script is called `utlpwdmg.sql` and is in the `$ORACLE_HOME/rdbms/admin` directory. The name of the function created using this script is called `verify_function_11g`.

Auditing Database Activity

Auditing involves monitoring and recording specific database activity. An Oracle 11*g* database supports four levels of auditing:

- Statement
- Privilege
- Object
- Fine-grained access

These afford you two locations for recording these activities. Audit records can be stored in either of these locations.

- Database
- Operating-system files

You tell the Oracle Database where to record audit trail records by setting the initialization parameter `audit_trail`. The default is `DB`, as in `AUDIT_TRAIL=DB`, which tells the database to record audit records in the database. `AUDIT_TRAIL=DB,EXTENDED` tells the database to record audit records in the database together with bind variables (`SQLBIND`) and the SQL statement triggering the audit entry (`SQLTEXT`). `AUDIT_TRAIL=OS` tells the database to record audit records in operating-system files. You cannot change this parameter in memory, only in your pfile or spfile. For example, the following statement will change the location of audit records in the spfile:

```
ALTER SYSTEM SET audit_trail=DB SCOPE=SPFILE;
```

The `audit_trail` parameter can also have values `XML` and `XML,EXTENDED`. With these two options, audit records are written to OS files in XML format. The value of `NONE` disables auditing.

After changing the `audit_trail` parameter, you will need to bounce (shut down and start up) your database instance for the change to take effect.

When recorded in the database, most audit entries are recorded in the `SYS.AUD$` table. On Unix systems, operating-system audit records are written into files in the directory specified by the initialization parameter `audit_file_dest` (which is set to `$ORACLE_BASE/admin/$ORACLE_SID/adump` if the database is created using DBCA). On Windows systems, these audit records are written to the Event Viewer log file.

The four levels of auditing are described in the following sections.

Certain database activities are always recorded in the OS audit files. Database connections using administrator privileges such as SYSDBA and SYSOPER are recorded. Database startup and shutdown are also recorded in the OS audit files.

Managing Statement Auditing

Statement auditing involves monitoring and recording the execution of specific types of SQL statements. In the following sections, you will learn how to enable and disable statement auditing as well as identify what statement auditing options are enabled.

Enabling Statement Auditing

You enable auditing of specific SQL statements with an `AUDIT` statement. For example, to audit the SQL statements `CREATE TABLE`, `DROP TABLE`, and `TRUNCATE TABLE`, use the `TABLE` audit option like this:

```
AUDIT table;
```

To record audit entries for specific users only, include a `BY USER` clause in the `AUDIT` statement. For example, to audit `CREATE`, `DROP`, and `TRUNCATE TABLE` statements for user `juanita` only, execute the following:

```
AUDIT table BY juanita;
```

Frequently, you want to record only attempts that fail—perhaps to look for users who are probing the system to see what they can get away with. To further limit auditing to only these unsuccessful executions, use a `WHENEVER` clause like this:

```
AUDIT table BY juanita WHENEVER NOT SUCCESSFUL;
```

You can alternately specify `WHENEVER SUCCESSFUL` to record only successful statements. If you do not include a `WHENEVER` clause, both successful and unsuccessful statements trigger audit records.

You can further configure non-DDL statements to record one audit entry for the triggering session or one entry for each auditable action during the session. Specify `BY ACCESS` or `BY SESSION` in the `AUDIT` statement, like this:

```
AUDIT INSERT TABLE BY juanita BY ACCESS;
```

There are many auditing options other than `TABLE` or `INSERT TABLE`. Table 12.1 shows all the statement-auditing options.

TABLE 12.1 Statement-Auditing Options

Statement-Auditing Option	Triggering SQL Statements
ALTER SEQUENCE	ALTER SEQUENCE
ALTER TABLE	ALTER TABLE
COMMENT TABLE	COMMENT ON TABLE COMMENT ON COLUMN
DATABASE LINK	CREATE DATABASE LINK DROP DATABASE LINK
DELETE TABLE	DELETE
EXECUTE PROCEDURE	Execution of any procedure or function or access to any cursor or variable in a package
GRANT PROCEDURE	GRANT on a function, package, or procedure
GRANT SEQUENCE	GRANT on a sequence
GRANT TABLE	GRANT on a table or view

TABLE 12.1 Statement Audit Options *(continued)*

Statement-Auditing Option	Triggering SQL Statements
INDEX	CREATEINDEX
INSERT TABLE	INSERT into table or view
LOCK TABLE	LOCK
NOT EXISTS	All SQL statements
PROCEDURE	CREATE FUNCTION DROP FUNCTION CREATE PACKAGE CREATE PACKAGE BODY DROP PACKAGE CREATE PROCEDURE DROP PROCEDURE
PROFILE	CREATE PROFILE ALTER PROFILE DROP PROFILE
ROLE	CREATE ROLE ALTER ROLE DROP ROLE SET ROLE
SELECT SEQUENCE	SELECT on a sequence
SELECT TABLE	SELECT from table or view
SEQUENCE	CREATE SEQUENCE DROP SEQUENCE
SESSION	LOGON
SYNONYM	CREATE SYNONYM DROP SYNONYM
SYSTEM AUDIT	AUDIT NOAUDIT
SYSTEM GRANT	GRANT REVOKE

TABLE 12.1 Statement Audit Options *(continued)*

Statement-Auditing Option	Triggering SQL Statements
TABLE	CREATE TABLE DROP TABLE TRUNCATE TABLE
TABLESPACE	CREATE TABLESPACE ALTER TABLESPACE DROP TABLESPACE
TRIGGER	CREATE TRIGGER ALTER TRIGGER (to enable or disable) ALTER TABLE (to enable all or disable all)
UPDATE TABLE	UPDATE on a table or view
USER	CREATE USER ALTER USER DROP USER
VIEW	CREATE VIEW DROP VIEW

Identifying Enabled Statement-Auditing Options

You can identify the statement-auditing options that have been enabled in your database by querying the DBA_STMT_AUDIT_OPTS data dictionary view. For example, the following example shows that SESSION auditing is enabled for all users, NOT EXISTS auditing is enabled for all users, and TABLE auditing WHENEVER NOT SUCCESSFUL is enabled for user juanita:

```
SELECT audit_option, failure, success, user_name
FROM dba_stmt_audit_opts
ORDER BY audit_option, user_name;

AUDIT_OPTION         FAILURE    SUCCESS    USER_NAME
-------------------- ---------- ---------- -------------
CREATE SESSION       BY ACCESS  BY ACCESS
NOT EXISTS           BY ACCESS  BY ACCESS
TABLE                BY ACCESS  NOT SET    JUANITA
```

Oracle Database 11*g* comes with the following auditing enabled by default:

- ALTER ANY PROCEDURE
- ALTER ANY TABLE
- ALTER DATABASE
- ALTER PROFILE
- ALTER SYSTEM
- ALTER USER
- CREATE ANY JOB
- CREATE ANY LIBRARY
- CREATE ANY PROCEDURE
- CREATE ANY TABLE
- CREATE EXTERNAL JOB
- CREATE PUBLIC DATABASE LINK
- CREATE SESSION
- CREATE USER
- DROP ANY PROCEDURE
- DROP ANY TABLE
- DROP PROFILE
- DROP USER
- EXEMPT ACCESS POLICY
- GRANT ANY OBJECT PRIVILEGE
- GRANT ANY PRIVILEGE
- GRANT ANY ROLE
- ROLE
- SYSTEM AUDIT

You can enable administrator auditing by setting the initialization parameter AUDIT_SYS_OPERATIONS=TRUE. All the activities performed connected as SYS or SYSDBA/SYSOPER privileges are recorded in the OS audit trail.

Disabling Statement Auditing

To disable auditing of a specific SQL statement, use a NOAUDIT statement, which allows the same BY and WHENEVER options as the AUDIT statement. If you enable auditing for a specific user, specify that user in the NOAUDIT statement as well. However, it is not necessary to include the WHENEVER NOT SUCCESSFUL clause in the NOAUDIT statement.

For example, to disable the three audit options in the previous section, execute the following three statements:

```
NOAUDIT session;
NOAUDIT not exists;
NOAUDIT table BY juanita;
```

Examining the Audit Trail

Statement, privilege, and object audit records are written to the SYS.AUD$ table and made available via the data dictionary views DBA_AUDIT_TRAIL and USER_AUDIT_TRAIL. These data dictionary views cannot contain values for every record because this view is used for three different types of audit records. For example, you can view the user, time, and type of statement audited for user juanita by executing the following:

```
SELECT username, timestamp, action_name
FROM dba_audit_trail
WHERE username = 'JUANITA';

ORA USER         TIMESTAMP             ACTION_NAME
---------------- --------------------- -------------
JUANITA          15-Jun-2004 18:43:52  LOGON
JUANITA          15-Jun-2004 18:44:19  LOGOFF
JUANITA          15-Jun-2004 18:46:01  LOGON
JUANITA          15-Jun-2004 18:46:40  CREATE TABLE
```

If you enable AUDIT SESSION, the database creates one audit record when a user logs on and updates that record when the user logs off successfully. These session audit records contain some valuable information that can help you narrow the focus of your tuning efforts. Among the information recorded in the audit records are the username, logon time, logoff time, and the number of physical reads and logical reads performed during the session. By looking for sessions with high counts of logical or physical reads, you can identify high-resource-consuming jobs and narrow the focus of your tuning efforts.

Managing Privilege Auditing

Privilege auditing involves monitoring and recording the execution of SQL statements that require a specific system privilege, such as SELECT ANY TABLE or GRANT ANY PRIVILEGE. You can audit any system privilege. In the following sections, you will learn how to enable and disable privilege auditing as well as identify which privilege-auditing options are enabled in your database.

Enabling Privilege Auditing

You enable privilege auditing with an AUDIT statement, specifying the system privilege that you want to monitor. For example, to audit statements that require the system privilege CREATE ANY TABLE, execute the following:

```
AUDIT create any table;
```

To record audit entries for specific users only, include a BY *USER clause* in the AUDIT statement. For example, to audit SQL statements made by user juanita that require the CREATE ANY TABLE privilege, execute the following:

```
AUDIT create any table BY juanita;
```

Just as you do with statement auditing, you can further configure non-DDL privileges to record one audit entry for the triggering session or one for each auditable action during the session by specifying BY ACCESS or BY SESSION in the AUDIT statement, like this:

```
AUDIT DELETE ANY TABLE BY juanita BY ACCESS;
```

Identifying Enabled Privilege-Auditing Options

You can report on the privilege auditing that has been enabled in your database by querying the DBA_PRIV_AUDIT_OPTS data dictionary view. For example, the following report shows that ALTER PROFILE auditing is enabled for all users and that ALTER USER and DELETE ANY TABLE auditing is enabled for user juanita:

```
SELECT privilege, user_name
FROM dba_priv_audit_opts
ORDER BY privilege, user_name;

PRIVILEGE            USER_NAME
-------------------- ----------------
ALTER PROFILE
DELETE ANY TABLE     JUANITA
ALTER USER           JUANITA
```

Disabling Privilege Auditing

To disable auditing of a system privilege, use a NOAUDIT statement. The NOAUDIT statement allows the same BY options as the AUDIT statement. If you enable auditing for a specific user, you need to specify that user in the NOAUDIT statement. For example, to disable the three audit options in the previous section, execute the following three statements:

```
NOAUDIT alter profile;
NOAUDIT delete any table BY juanita;
NOAUDIT alter user BY juanita;
```

Managing Object Auditing

Object auditing involves monitoring and recording the execution of SQL statements that require a specific object privilege, such as SELECT, INSERT, UPDATE, DELETE, or EXECUTE.

Unlike either statement or system privilege auditing, schema object auditing cannot be restricted to specific users—it is enabled for all users or no users. In the following sections, you will learn how to enable and disable object-auditing options as well as identify which object-auditing options are enabled.

Enabling Object Auditing

You enable object auditing with an AUDIT statement, specifying both the object and object privilege that you want to monitor. For example, to audit SELECT statements on the HR.EMPLOYEE_SALARY table, execute the following:

```
AUDIT select ON hr.employee_salary;
```

You can further configure these audit records to record one audit entry for the triggering session or one for each auditable action during the session by specifying BY ACCESS or BY SESSION in the AUDIT statement. This access/session configuration can be defined differently for successful or unsuccessful executions. For example, to make one audit entry per auditable action for successful SELECT statements on the HR.EMPLOYEE_SALARY table, execute the following:

```
-- one audit entry for each trigging statement
AUDIT select ON hr.employee_salary
   BY ACCESS WHENEVER SUCCESSFUL;

-- one audit entry for the session experiencing one or more
-- triggering statements
AUDIT select ON hr.employee_salary
   BY SESSION WHENEVER NOT SUCCESSFUL;
```

Identifying Enabled Object-Auditing Options

The object-auditing options that are enabled in the database are recorded in the DBA_OBJ_AUDIT_OPTS data dictionary view. Unlike the statement and privilege _AUDIT_OPTS views, the DBA_OBJ_AUDIT_OPTS data dictionary view always has one row for each auditable object in the database. There are columns for each object privilege that auditing can be enabled on, and in each of these columns, a code is reported that shows the auditing options. For example, the following report on the HR.EMPLOYEES table shows that no auditing is enabled for the INSERT object privilege and that the SELECT object privilege has auditing enabled with one audit entry for each access when the access is successful and one audit entry for each session when the access is not successful:

```
SELECT owner, object_name, object_type, ins, sel
FROM dba_obj_audit_opts
WHERE owner='HR'
AND   object_name='EMPLOYEE_SALARY';
```

```
OWNER        OBJECT_NAME              OBJECT_TY INS SEL
------------ ------------------------ --------- --- ---
HR           EMPLOYEE_SALARY          TABLE     -/- A/S
```

The coding for the object privilege columns contains one of three possible values: a hyphen (-) to indicate no auditing is enabled, an A to indicate BY ACCESS, or an S to indicate BY SESSION. The first code (preceding the slash) denotes the action for successful statements, and the second code (after the slash) denotes the action for unsuccessful statements.

Disabling Object Auditing

To disable object auditing, use a NOAUDIT statement, which allows the same WHENEVER options as the AUDIT statement. For example, to disable the auditing of unsuccessful SELECT statements against the HR.EMPLOYEES table, execute the following:

```
NOAUDIT select ON hr.employee_salary  WHENEVER NOT SUCCESSFUL;
```

Purging the Audit Trail

Database audit records for statement, privilege, and object auditing are stored in the table SYS.AUD$. Depending on how extensive your auditing and retention policies are, you will need to periodically delete old audit records from this table. The database does not provide an interface to assist in deleting rows from the audit table, so you will need to do so yourself. To purge audit records older than 90 days, execute the following as user SYS:

```
DELETE FROM sys.aud$ WHERE timestamp# < SYSDATE -90;
```

You might want to copy the audit records into a different table for historical retention or export them to an operating-system file before removing them. It is a good practice to audit changes to the AUD$ table so that you can identify when changes were made.

Only the user SYS, a user with the DELETE ANY TABLE privilege, or a user to whom SYS granted the DELETE privilege on SYS.AUD$ can delete the audit trail records from the SYS.AUD$ table.

Oracle 11*g* audits all DML statements against the SYS.AUD$ table. The INSERT, UPDATE, MERGE, and DELETE statements against the SYS.AUD$ table are not deleted from the SYS.AUD$ table. You have to truncate the SYS.AUD$ table to remove such records.

You can also use EM Grid Control to enable and disable auditing. On the Server tab (as shown earlier in Figure 12.1), click the Audit Settings link under Security. As shown in Figure 12.6, the Audit Settings screen shows the audit location, enabled audits, and audit trail information.

FIGURE 12.6 EM Grid Control Audit Settings screen

Managing Fine-Grained Auditing

Fine-grained auditing (FGA) lets you monitor and record data access based on the content of the data. With FGA, you define an audit policy on a table and optionally a column. When the specified condition evaluates to TRUE, an audit record is created, and an optional event-handler program is called. You use the PL/SQL package DBMS_FGA to configure and manage FGA.

In the following sections, you will learn how to create, drop, enable, and disable fine-grained auditing policies.

Creating an FGA Policy

To create a new FGA policy, use the packaged procedure DBMS_FGA.ADD_POLICY. This procedure has the following parameters:

object_schema This is the owner of the object to be audited. The default is NULL, which tells the database to use the current user.

object_name This is the name of the object to be monitored.

policy_name This is a unique name for the new policy

audit_condition This is a SQL expression that evaluates to a Boolean. When this condition evaluates to either TRUE or NULL (the default), an audit record can be created. This condition cannot directly use the SYSDATE, UID, USER, or USERENV functions, it cannot use subqueries or sequences, and it cannot reference the pseudocolumns LEVEL, PRIOR, and ROWNUM.

audit_column This is a comma-delimited list of columns that the database will look to access. If a column in audit_column is referenced in the SQL statement and the audit_condition is not FALSE, an audit record is created. Columns appearing in audit_column do not have to also appear in the audit_condition expression. The default value is NULL, which tells the database that any column being referenced should trigger the audit record.

handler_schema This is the owner of the event handler procedure. The default is NULL, which tells the database to use the current schema.

handler_module This is the name of the event handler procedure. The default NULL tells the database to not use an event handler. If the event handler is a packaged procedure, the handler_module must reference both the package name and the program, using dot notation, like this:

```
UTL_MAIL.SEND_ATTACH_RAW
```

enable This is a Boolean that tells the database whether this policy should be in effect. The default is TRUE.

statement_types This tells the database which types of statements to monitor. Valid values are a comma-delimited list of SELECT, INSERT, UPDATE, and DELETE. The default is SELECT.

audit_trail This parameter tells the database whether to record the SQL statement and bind variables for the triggering SQL in the audit trail. The default value DBMS_FGA.DB_EXTENDED indicates that the SQL statement and bind variables should be recorded in the audit trail. Set this parameter to DBMS_FGA.DB to save space by not recording the SQL statement or bind variables in the audit trail.

audit_column_ops This parameter has only two valid values: DBMS_FGA.ALL_COLUMNS and DBMS_FGA.ANY_COLUMNS. When set to DBMS_FGA.ALL_COLUMNS, this parameter tells the database that all columns appearing in the audit_column parameter must be referenced in order to trigger an audit record. The default is DBMS_FGA.ANY_COLUMNS, which tells the database that if any column appearing in the audit_column also appears in the SQL statement, an audit record should be created.

To create a new disabled audit policy named COMPENSATION_AUD that looks for SELECT statements that access the HR.EMPLOYEES table and references either SALARY or COMMISSION_PCT, execute the following:

```
DBMS_FGA.ADD_POLICY(object_schema=>'HR'
   ,object_name=>'EMPLOYEES'
   ,policy_name=>'COMPENSATION_AUD'
   ,audit_column=>'SALARY, COMMISSION_PCT'
   ,enable=>FALSE
   ,statement_types=>'SELECT');
```

Enabling an FGA Policy

Use the procedure DBMS_FGA.ENABLE_POLICY to enable an FGA policy. This procedure will not raise an exception if the policy is already enabled. For example, you can enable the COMPENSATION_AUD policy added in the previous section like this:

```
DBMS_FGA.ENABLE_POLICY(object_schema=>'HR'
   ,object_name=>'EMPLOYEES'
   ,policy_name=>'COMPENSATION_AUD');
```

If you use direct path inserts, be careful with FGA. If an FGA policy is enabled on a table participating in a direct path insert, the auditing overrides the hint, disabling the direct path access and causing conventional inserts. As with all hints, the database does not directly tell you that your hint is being ignored.

Disabling an FGA Policy

To turn off an FGA, use the DBMS_FGA.DISABLE_POLICY procedure. Here is an example:

```
DBMS_FGA.DISABLE_POLICY(object_schema=>'HR'
   ,object_name=>'EMPLOYEES'
   ,policy_name=>'COMPENSATION_AUD');
```

Dropping an FGA Policy

To remove an FGA policy, use the DBMS_FGA.DROP_POLICY procedure. For example, to drop the COMPENSATION_AUD policy used in this section, run this:

```
DBMS_FGA.DROP_POLICY(object_schema=>'HR'
   ,object_name=>'EMPLOYEES'
   ,policy_name=>'COMPENSATION_AUD');
```

Identifying FGA Policies in the Database

Query the DBA_AUDIT_POLICIES data dictionary view to report on the FGA policies defined in your database. For example, the following report shows that the policy named COMPENSATION_AUD on the column SALARY in the table HR.EMPLOYEES is defined but not enabled:

```
SELECT policy_name ,object_schema||'.'||
      object_name object_name
      ,policy_column
      ,enabled ,audit_trail
FROM dba_audit_policies;
```

```
POLICY_NAME      OBJECT_NAME  POLICY ENABLED AUDIT_TRAIL
---------------- ------------ ------ ------- -----------
COMPENSATION_AUD HR.EMPLOYEES SALARY NO      DB_EXTENDED
```

Audit records from this policy, when enabled, capture the standard auditing information as well as the text of the SQL statement that triggered the auditing (DB_EXTENDED).

Reporting on the FGA Audit Trail Entries

The DBA_FGA_AUDIT_TRAIL data dictionary view is used in reporting on the FGA audit entries that have been recorded in the database. The following example shows audit trail entries for the COMPENSATION_AUD policy, listing the database username and the timestamp of the audit record and computer from which the database connection was made:

```
SELECT db_user, timestamp, userhost
FROM dba_fga_audit_traiL
WHERE policy_name='COMPENSATION_AUD'

DB_USER      TIMESTAMP            USERHOST
------------ -------------------- --------------------
CHIPD        10-Jun-2004 09:48:14 XYZcorp\CHIPNOTEBOOK
JUANITA      19-Jun-2004 14:50:47 XYZcorp\HR_PC2
```

Summary

Oracle 11*g* gives you a well-stocked toolkit for managing users and securing the database. You create and manage user accounts with the CREATE, ALTER, and DROP USER statements. User passwords in Oracle 11*g* are case sensitive. You can assign tablespace resources to be used for sorting that are different than those for tables or indexes. You can limit the disk, CPU, and memory resources that your users consume by employing tablespace quotas and kernel resource limits in user profiles.

To protect data from unwanted access or manipulation, you can employ object and system privileges. You can create and use roles to make managing these database privileges easier. You can enable object, statement, privilege, and fine-grained auditing to help you monitor and record sensitive database activity. By default, DBCA enables several key auditing features when you create an Oracle 11*g* database.

The Oracle 11*g* database has several powerful features (user accounts and packages) that will need to be locked down in your production systems, and in this chapter you learned which user accounts need to be locked, as well as which standard packages should be locked down to better protect your company's data.

Exam Essentials

Be familiar with the authentication methods. Database accounts can be authenticated by the database (identified by password), by the operating system (identified externally), or by an enterprise security service (identified globally).

Know how to assign default and temporary tablespace to users. Assign default and temporary tablespaces with either a CREATE USER statement or an ALTER USER statement. Understand which tablespace would be assigned if you omitted the DEFAULT TABLESPACE clause when creating a user.

Be able to identify and grant object, system, and role privileges. Know the difference between these types of privileges and when to use each type.

Know the differences between the WITH ADMIN OPTION and WITH GRANT OPTION keywords. The ADMIN option applies to role or system privileges, but the GRANT option applies to object privileges.

Know how to enable roles. Know when a role needs to be enabled and how to enable it.

Be able to secure your database. Make sure you know how to lock down your database. Know which packages should be secured and how to secure them.

Know how to implement password security. An Oracle 11*g* database gives you several standard password-security settings. Know what is available in a profile and what needs to be implemented in a password-verifying function.

Know how to enable, disable, and identify enabled auditing options. Be able to describe the types of auditing, how to enable them, and how to report on the audit trail.

Review Questions

1. Which of the following statements creates an Oracle account but lets the operating system authenticate logons?

   A. `create user ops$admin identified by os;`

   B. `create user ops$admin identified externally;`

   C. `create user ops$admin nopassword;`

   D. `create user ops$admin authenticated by os;`

2. If you want to capture the SQL statement and bind variables when performing statement auditing, which value should the `AUDIT_TRAIL` parameter have?

   A. `NONE`

   B. `DB`

   C. `DB,EXTENDED`

   D. `OS`

   E. `OS,EXTENDED`

3. Which of the following statements gives user `desmond` the ability to alter table `gl.accounts`?

   A. `grant alter on gl.accounts to desmond;`

   B. `grant alter to desmond on gl.accounts;`

   C. `grant alter table to desmond;`

   D. `allow desmond to alter table gl.accounts;`

4. Which of the following statements gives user `desmond` the ability to alter table `gl.accounts` as well as give this ability to other accounts?

   A. `grant alter any table with grant option to desmond;`

   B. `grant alter on gl.accounts to desmond with admin option;`

   C. `grant alter any table to desmond with grant option;`

   D. `grant alter any table to desmond with admin option;`

5. Examine the `CREATE USER` statement, and choose which of the following options best applies.

```
CREATE USER JOHN IDENTIFIED BY JOHNNY
DEFAULT TABLESPACE INDEX01
PASSWORD EXPIRE
QUOTA UNLIMITED ON DATA01
QUOTA UNLIMITED ON INDEX01;
GRANT CONNECT TO JOHN;
```

A. JOHN will not be able to log in to the database using SQL*Plus until the DBA changes his password.

B. JOHN is authenticated by the database.

C. When creating tables, if JOHN did not specify the TABLESPACE clause, the table will be created on the DATA01 tablespace.

D. Specifying unlimited space quota on INDEX01 is a redundant step since INDEX01 is JOHN's default tablespace.

6. User system granted SELECT on sh.products to user ian using WITH GRANT OPTION. Ian then granted SELECT on sh.products to user stuart. Ian has left the company, and his account has been dropped. What happens to Stuart's privileges on sh.products?

A. Stuart loses his SELECT privilege on sh.products.

B. Stuart retains his SELECT privilege on sh.products.

C. Stuart loses his SELECT privilege if Ian was dropped with the CASCADE REVOKE option.

D. Stuart retains his SELECT privilege if Ian was dropped with the NOCASCADE REVOKE option.

7. User system granted SELECT ANY TABLE to user ian using WITH ADMIN OPTION. Ian then granted SELECT ANY TABLE to user stuart. Ian has left the company, and his account has been dropped. What happens to Stuart's privileges?

A. Stuart loses his privileges.

B. Stuart retains his privileges.

C. Stuart loses his privileges if Ian was dropped with the CASCADE REVOKE option.

D. Stuart retains his privileges if Ian was dropped with the NOCASCADE REVOKE option.

8. Which of the following system privileges can allow the grantee to masquerade as another user and therefore should be granted judiciously?

A. CREATE ANY JOB

B. ALTER USER

C. CREATE ANY PROCEDURE

D. All of the above

9. Which of the following statements enables the role user_admin in the current session?

A. `alter session enable role user_admin;`

B. `alter session set role user_admin;`

C. `alter role user_admin enable;`

D. `set role user_admin;`

10. Which of the following SQL statements allows user `augustin` to use the privileges associated with the password-protected role `info_czar` that has been granted to him?

    A. `set role all;`

    B. `alter user augustin default role all;`

    C. `alter session enable role info_czar;`

    D. `alter session enable info_czar identified by brozo`

11. By default, how much space can any account use for a new table?

    A. None

    B. Up to the current free space in the tablespace

    C. Unlimited space, including autoextends

    D. Up to the default quota established at tablespace creation time

12. Which of the following SQL statements results in a disconnection after a session is idle for 30 minutes?

    A. `alter session set idle_timeout=30;`

    B. `alter session set idle_timeout=1800;`

    C. `alter profile default limit idle_time 30;`

    D. `alter profile default set idle_timeout 30;`

13. Which of the following prevents a user from reusing a password when they change their password?

    A. Setting the initialization parameter `NO_PASSWORD_REUSE` to `TRUE`

    B. Altering that user's profile to `UNLIMITED` for `PASSWORD_REUSE_TIME` and 1 for `PASSWORD_REUSE_MAX`

    C. Altering that user's profile to `UNLIMITED` for both `PASSWORD_REUSE_TIME` and `PASSWORD_REUSE_MAX`

    D. Using a password verify function to record the new password and comparing the new passwords to those recorded previously

14. Examine the code, and choose the best option that describes the reason for error.

```
CREATE USER JOHN IDENTIFIED BY JOHN1;
CREATE ROLE HR_QUERY;
GRANT CONNECT, OEQUERY, SELECT ANY TABLE TO HR_QUERY;
ALTER USER JOHN DEFAULT ROLE ALL EXCEPT HR_QUERY;
GRANT HR_QUERY TO JOHN;
CONNECT JOHN/JOHN1
SELECT COUNT(*) FROM HR.EMPLOYEES;
Error: ORA-01031: insufficient privileges
```

A. John needs the SELECT_CATALOG_ROLE privilege.

B. HR_QUERY is not a default role for John.

C. The SELECT privilege on the HR.EMPLOYEES table is not granted to JOHN or HR_QUERY.

D. John should enable the role using the SET ROLE statement and a password.

15. You created a database user using the following statement. Which option will connect the user successfully to the database?

```
CREATE USER JOHN IDENTIFIED BY John1;
GRANT CONNECT TO JOHN;
```

A. CONNECT JOHN/JOHN1

B. CONNECT JOHN/john1

C. CONNECT john/John1

D. All of the above

16. What is the default value for the AUDIT_TRAIL parameter?

A. NONE

B. DB

C. DB,EXTENDED

D. XML

17. Which of the following SQL statements limits attempts to guess passwords by locking an account after three failed logon attempts?

A. `alter profile default limit failed_login_attempts 3;`

B. `alter system set max_logon_failures = 3 scope=both;`

C. `alter user set failed_login_attempts = 3;`

D. `alter system set failed_login_attempts = 3 scope=both;`

18. Where can the database write audit_trail records?

A. In a database table

B. In a file outside the database

C. Both in the database and in an operating-system file

D. Either in the database or in an operating-system file

19. User JAMES has a table named JOBS created on the tablespace USERS. When you issue the following statement, what effect will it have on the JOBS table?

    ALTER USER JAMES QUOTA 0 ON USERS;

    A. No more rows can be added to the JOBS table.
    B. No new blocks can be allocated to the JOBS table.
    C. No new extents can be allocated to the JOBS table.
    D. The table JOBS cannot be accessed.
    E. The table is truncated.

20. How do you manage fine-grained auditing?
    A. With the AUDIT and NOAUDIT statements
    B. With the DBMS_FGA package
    C. With the GRANT and REVOKE statements
    D. With the CREATE, ALTER, and DROP statements

Answers to Review Questions

1. B. Authentication by the operating system is called external authentication, and the Oracle account name must match the operating-system account name prefixed with the OS_AUTHENT_PREFIX string.

2. C. The AUDIT_TRAIL parameter with the value DB,EXTENDED enables capturing SQL statements and bind variables in auditing. OS,EXTENDED is not a valid value for AUDIT_TRAIL.

3. A. Altering a table in another user's schema requires either the object privilege ALTER on that object or the system privilege ALTER ANY TABLE. Option A has the correct syntax for granting the object privilege on ALTER gl.accounts to user desmond. Although option C would allow user desmond to alter his own tables, he would need the ALTER ANY TABLE privilege to alter another user's table.

4. D. Either the ALTER ANY TABLE system privilege or the ALTER object privilege is required. Conferring the ability to further grant the privilege requires the keywords WITH ADMIN OPTION for system or role privileges or the keywords WITH GRANT OPTION for object privileges. Only option D has both the correct syntax and the correct keywords.

5. B. JOHN will be able to log in to the database using SQL*Plus, and Oracle will prompt for new password when John logs in the first time. Since John's default tablespace is INDEX01, the tables and indexes created will be on the INDEX01 tablespace if the TABLESPACE clause is omitted. Though INDEX01 is the default tablespace, to create objects on INDEX01 or any other tablespace, a specific space quota needs to be defined, or the user should have the UNLIMITED TABLESPACE system privilege.

6. A. When object privileges are granted through an intermediary, they are implicitly dropped when the intermediary is dropped. CASCADE REVOKE and NOCASCADE REVOKE are not part of the GRANT statement syntax.

7. B. When system privileges are granted through an intermediary, they are not affected when the intermediary is dropped. CASCADE REVOKE and NOCASCADE REVOKE are not part of the GRANT statement syntax.

8. D. The CREATE ANY JOB and CREATE ANY PROCEDURE system privileges allow the grantee to create and run programs with the privileges of another user. The ALTER USER privilege allows the grantee to change a user's password, connect as that user, and then change the password back. These are all powerful system privileges and should be restricted to as few administrative users as practical.

9. D. The SET ROLE statement enables or disables roles in the current session.

10. B. To enable a password-protected role, you need to either execute a SET ROLE statement specifying the password or alter the user to make the role a default role. Default roles do not require a set role statement or a password to become enabled.

11. A. By default, user accounts have no quota in any tablespace. Before a user can create a table or an index, you need to either give the user a quota in one or more specific

tablespaces or grant the UNLIMITED TABLESPACE system privilege to give an unlimited quota (including autoextends) in all tablespaces.

12. C. Profiles limit the amount of idle time, CPU time, logical reads, or other resource-oriented session limits. Option C uses the correct syntax to limit idle time for a session to 30 minutes.

13. B. Although option D could also work, it involves storing the passwords in a table in the database, which could be a security concern. It also takes a lot more effort to configure and maintain. The better technique is to use the standard database profile features PASSWORD_REUSE_TIME and PASSWORD_REUSE_MAX. Setting one of these profile parameters to UNLIMITED and the other to a specific value prevents passwords from being reused. If both of these profile parameters are set to UNLIMITED, these parameters are essentially disabled. There is no initialization parameter called NO_PASSWORD_REUSE.

14. B. Since HR_QUERY has the SELECT ANY TABLE privilege, no other privilege is required to query user tables in the database. To avoid the error, HR_QUERY must be defined as a default role for John, or John should use the SET ROLE statement. A password is not needed for SET ROLE because the role is not password protected.

15. C. In Oracle 11*g* user passwords are case sensitive. The username is not case sensitive if you did not enclose it in double quotes.

16. B. In Oracle 11*g*, the default value for AUDIT_TRAIL parameter is DB. By default, Oracle 11*g* enables several key database-auditing features.

17. A. You limit the number of failed logon attempts with a profile.

18. D. The destination of audit_trail records is controlled by the initialization parameter audit_trail. Setting this parameter to DB or DB,EXTENDED causes the audit trail to be written to a database table. Setting the parameter to OS or XML causes the audit trail to be written to an operating-system file.

19. C. When a space quota is exceeded or quota is removed from a user on a tablespace, the tables remain in the tablespace, but no new extents can be allocated. New rows can be inserted into the table as long as the table does not require Oracle to allocate a new extent in the table.

20. B. Fine-grained auditing is managed using the DBMS_FGA package. The AUDIT and NOAUDIT statements are used to manage statement, privilege, and object auditing. The GRANT and REVOKE statements are used to manage system, object, and role privileges. The CREATE, ALTER, and DROP statements are used to manage several types of database objects and settings.

Managing Data and Undo

ORACLE DATABASE 11*g*: ADMINISTRATION I EXAM OBJECTIVES COVERED IN THIS CHAPTER:

✓ **Managing Data and Concurrency**

- Manage data using DML
- Identify and administer PL/SQL objects
- Monitor and resolve locking conflicts

✓ **Managing Undo Data**

- Overview of Undo
- Transactions and undo data
- Managing undo

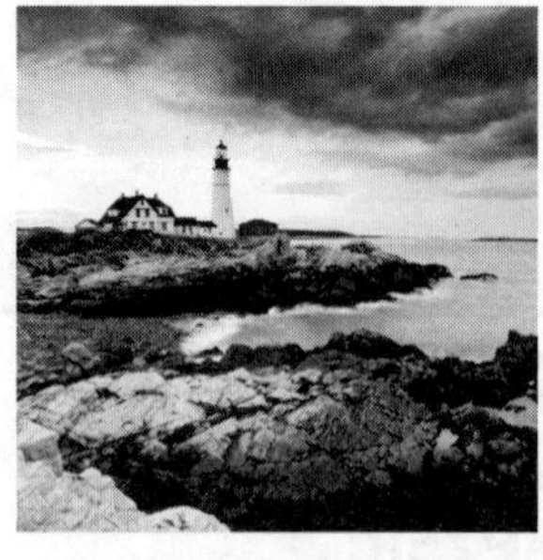

Oracle supports manipulating data via several interfaces, but the most common are SQL and PL/SQL. Understanding how to use and manage PL/SQL programs is an important skill for any DBA. Some database functionality is delivered only as PL/SQL programs, such as fine-grained auditing, and other functionality is available in both a command-line version and as a PL/SQL program, such as Data Pump export and Data Pump import. As you gain experience, you will increasingly rely on using PL/SQL to manage your databases. So, you need to have a solid grasp of SQL and PL/SQL fundamentals to be a successful Oracle DBA.

In Chapter 5, "Manipulating Data," you learned to add, change, and remove information from an Oracle Database using SQL DML statements. In this chapter, you will review DML statements and learn how to administer PL/SQL stored objects. You will also understand what "undo" is in Oracle and how Oracle uses undo information to build consistent results.

Manipulating Data through SQL

The Structured Query Language (SQL) includes Data Definition Language (DDL) statements, Data Control Language (DCL) statements, and Data Manipulation Language (DML) statements. You learned to add, modify, and delete information from the Oracle Database using DML statements in Chapter 5. You also learned how to create, alter, and delete objects using DDL statements in Chapters 6, 7, and 10. In Chapter 12, "Implementing Security and Auditing," you learned how to use the DCL statements `GRANT` and `REVOKE` to give and take privileges on database objects. To provide complete coverage of the main OCP objective "Managing Data and Concurrency," in this chapter I will explain the DML statements `INSERT`, `UPDATE`, and `DELETE` for adding, modifying, and removing data from your tables.

After using DML statements to add rows to a table, update rows in a table, or delete rows from a table, you must make these changes permanent by executing a `COMMIT` command. Alternatively, you can undo the DML changes with a `ROLLBACK` command. Until you commit the changes, other database sessions will not be able to see your changes.

Read Chapter 5 to understand DML statements completely. This chapter reviews only the `INSERT`, `UPDATE`, and `DELETE` statements.

Using the INSERT Statement

You use the INSERT statement to add rows in one or more tables. You can create these rows with specific data values or copy them from existing tables using a subquery.

Inserting into a Single Table

When using SQL, the only way to add rows in an Oracle 11*g* table is with an INSERT statement, and the most common variety of INSERT statement is the single table insert. The syntax for a simple INSERT statement is as follows:

```
INSERT INTO [schema.]table_name [(column_list)]
VALUES (data_values)
```

In the syntax, *table_name* is the name of the table where you want to add new rows, and it can be qualified with the schema name. *column_list* is the name of columns in the table, each separated by a comma, that you want to populate. The *data_values* are the corresponding values for each column in the *column_list*, each separated by a comma. Using this syntax you add one row at a time to the table.

column_list is optional, with the default being a list of all columns in the table in COLUMN_ID order. See the data dictionary views USER_TAB_COLUMNS, ALL_TAB_COLUMNS, or DBA_TAB_COLUMNS for the COLUMN_ID. Although inserting into a table is more common, you can also insert into a view, as long as the view does not contain one of the following:

- A DISTINCT operator
- A set operator (UNION, MINUS, and so on)
- An aggregate function (SUM, COUNT, AVG, and so on)
- A GROUP BY, ORDER BY, or CONNECT BY clause
- A subquery in the SELECT list

Here are some examples of using the INSERT statement to insert rows into a single table. The following inserts one row, channel 3, in the channels table:

```
INSERT INTO channels (channel_id ,channel_desc
   ,channel_class ,channel_class_id
   ,channel_total ,channel_total_id)
VALUES (3 ,'Direct Sales' ,'Direct'
   ,12 ,'Channel total' ,1);
```

The following inserts one row, channel 5, in the channels table:

```
INSERT INTO channels VALUES
  (5 ,'Catalog' ,'Indirect' ,13 ,'Channel total' ,1);
```

You can also add rows to a table based on the result from a subquery. The following example copies zero or more rows from the `territories` table in the `home_office` database to the `regions` table. `home_office` is the name of the database link.

```
INSERT INTO regions (region_id ,region_name)
  SELECT region_seq.NEXTVAL , terr_name
  FROM territories@home_office
WHERE class = 'R';
```

The number and datatypes of values in the `VALUES` list must match the number and datatypes in the column list. The database will perform implicit datatype conversion if necessary to convert the values into the datatype of the target.

To understand database links, read the sidebar "Creating Database Links" in Chapter 7, "Creating Schema Objects."

Inserting into Multiple Tables

Most `INSERT` statements are the single-table variety, but Oracle also supports a multiple-table `INSERT` statement. You'll most frequently use multitable inserts in data warehouse Extract, Transform, and Load (ETL) routines.

With a multitable insert, you can make a single pass through the source data and load the data into more than one table. By reducing the number of passes through the source data, you can reduce the overall work and thus achieve faster throughput.

The syntax for the multiple-table `INSERT` statement is as follows:

```
INSERT [ALL | FIRST] {WHEN <condition>
THEN INTO <insert_clause> … … …}
[ELSE <insert_clause>]
```

If a `WHEN` condition evaluates to `TRUE`, the corresponding `INTO` clause is executed. If no `WHEN` condition evaluates to `TRUE`, the `ELSE` clause is executed. The keyword `ALL` tells the database to check each `WHEN` condition. On the other hand, the keyword `FIRST` tells the database to stop checking `WHEN` conditions after finding the first `TRUE` condition.

In the following example, an insurance company has policies for both property and casualty in the `policy` table, but in its data mart, the company might break out these policy types into separate fact tables. During the monthly load, new policies are added to both the `property_premium_fact` and `casualty_premium_fact` tables. You can use a multitable `INSERT` to add these rows more efficiently than two separate `INSERT` statements. A multitable `INSERT` looks like this:

```
INSERT FIRST
WHEN policy_type = 'P' THEN
  INTO property_premium_fact(policy_id ,
      policy_nbr ,premium_amt)
```

```
  VALUES (property_premium_seq.nextval ,
         policy_number ,gross_premium)
WHEN p.policy_type = 'C' THEN
  INTO property_premium_fact(policy_id ,
      policy_nbr ,premium_amt)
  VALUES (property_premium_seq.nextval ,
         policy_number ,gross_premium)
SELECT policy_nbr ,gross_premium ,policy_type
FROM policies
WHERE policy_date >=
      TRUNC(SYSDATE,'MM') - TO_YMINTERVAL('00-01');
```

By using this multitable INSERT statement instead of two separate statements, the code makes a single pass through the policy table instead of two and thus saves a significant amount of I/O and processing time.

Using the UPDATE Statement

You use an UPDATE statement to change existing rows in a table. The basic syntax for the UPDATE statement is as follows:

```
UPDATE <table_name>
SET <column_list> = <values>
  [,<column_list> = <values> … … …]
[WHERE <condition>]
```

The column list can be either a single column or a comma-delimited list of columns. A single list of columns lets you assign single values—either literals or from a subquery. The following updates customer XYZ's phone and fax numbers and sets their quantity based on their orders:

```
UPDATE order_rollup r
SET phone = '3125551212'
   ,fax   = '7735551212'
   ,qty   = (SELECT SUM(d.qty)
             FROM order_details d
             WHERE d.customer_id = r.customer_id)
WHERE r.customer_id = 'XYZ';
```

When you use a comma-delimited list of columns, you must enclose them in parentheses. The comma-delimited list lets you assign multiple values from a subquery. The following updates both the quantity and the price for customer XYZ for the order they placed on October 1, 2008:

```
UPDATE order_rollup
SET (qty, price) = (SELECT SUM(qty), SUM(price)
```

```
                    FROM order_details
                    WHERE customer_id = 'XYZ')
WHERE customer_id = 'XYZ'
 AND  order_period = TO_DATE('01-Oct-2008');
```

Assigning multiple values from a single subquery can save you from having to perform multiple subqueries, thus improving the efficiency of your SQL.

Using the MERGE Statement

The MERGE statement is used to both update and insert rows in a table. The MERGE statement has a join specification that describes how to determine whether an update or insert should be executed. The syntax of a simple MERGE statement is as follows:

```
MERGE INTO <table>
USING <subquery or table>
ON <condition>
[WHEN MATCHED THEN UPDATE SET <column> = <expression> [WHERE <condition>]]
[WHEN NOT MATCHED THEN INSERT <column_list> VALUES <values_list> [WHERE
<condition>]]
[WHERE <condition>]
```

The WHEN MATCHED predicate specifies how to update the existing rows. The WHEN NOT MATCHED predicate specifies how to create rows that do not exist.

The following example has a new pricing sheet for products in category 33. This new pricing data has been loaded into the NEW_PRICES table. You need to update the PRODUCT_INFORMATION table with these new prices. The NEW_PRICES table contains updates to existing rows in the PRODUCT_INFORMATION table as well as new products. The new products need to be inserted, and the existing products need to be updated.

```
SELECT product_id,category_id,list_price,min_price
FROM oe.product_information
WHERE category_id=33;

PRODUCT_ID CATEGORY_ID LIST_PRICE  MIN_PRICE
---------- ----------- ---------- ----------
      2986          33        125        111
      3163          33         35         29
      3165          33         40         34
      3167          33         55         47
      3216          33         30         26
      3220          33         45         36

SELECT *
FROM new_prices;
```

```
PRODUCT_ID LIST_PRICE  MIN_PRICE
---------- ---------- ----------
      2986        135        121
      3163         40         32
      3164         40         35
      3165         40         37
      3166         50         45
      3167         55         50
      3216         30         26
      3220         45         36
```

You can use the MERGE statement to perform an update/insert of the new pricing data into the PRODUCT_INFORMATION table, as follows:

```
MERGE INTO oe.product_information pi
USING (SELECT product_id, list_price, min_price
    FROM new_prices) NP
ON (pi.product_id = np.product_id)
WHEN MATCHED THEN UPDATE SET pi.list_price =np.list_price
                            ,pi.min_price = np.min_price
WHEN NOT MATCHED THEN INSERT (pi.product_id,pi.category_id
                            ,pi.list_price,pi.min_price)
  VALUES (np.product_id, 33,np.list_price, np.min_price);
```

```
PRODUCT_ID CATEGORY_ID LIST_PRICE  MIN_PRICE
---------- ----------- ---------- ----------
      2986          33        135        121 (updated)
      3163          33         40         32 (updated)
      3164          33         40         35 (inserted)
      3165          33         40         37 (updated)
      3166          33         50         45 (inserted)
      3167          33         55         50 (updated)
      3216          33         30         26 (updated)
      3220          33         45         36 (updated)
```

Using the DELETE Statement

You use the DELETE statement to remove rows from a table. The syntax for a basic DELETE statement is as follows:

```
DELETE [FROM] <table>
[WHERE <condition>]
```

Here are some examples of a DELETE statement. The following removes orders from certain states:

```
DELETE FROM orders
WHERE state IN ('TX','NY','IL')
 AND  order_date < TRUNC(SYSDATE) - 90
```

The following removes customer GOMEZ:

```
DELETE FROM customers
WHERE customer_name = 'GOMEZ';
```

The following removes duplicate line_detail_id values. Note that the keyword FROM is not needed.

```
DELETE line_details
WHERE rowid NOT IN (SELECT MAX(rowid)
                    FROM line_detail
                    GROUP BY line_detail_id)
```

The following example removes all rows from table order_staging:

```
DELETE FROM order_staging;
```

The WHERE clause is optional, and when it is not present, all rows from the table are removed. If you need to remove all rows from a table, consider using the TRUNCATE statement. TRUNCATE is a DDL statement and, unlike the DELETE statement, does not support a ROLLBACK. Using TRUNCATE, unlike using DELETE, does not generate undo and executes much faster for a large table.

When you perform the TRUNCATE operation, Oracle performs an implicit commit since it is a DDL and also requires an exclusive lock on the table. To read more about the difference between DELETE and TRUNCATE, see the section "Truncating a Table" in Chapter 5.

Identifying PL/SQL Objects

PL/SQL is Oracle's procedural language extension to SQL. This Oracle proprietary language was derived from Ada and has evolved to include a robust feature set, including sequential and conditional controls, looping constructs, exception handling, records, and collections, as well as object-oriented features such as methods, overloading, upcasting, and type inheritance.

Full knowledge of the PL/SQL language is well beyond the scope of the OCA/OCP exams, and more developers than DBAs create PL/SQL programs. But a significant number of database features are delivered as PL/SQL programs, and knowing how to identify and work with these programs is crucial to your effectiveness. In this section, you will learn what kinds of PL/SQL programs are available, when each is appropriate, and what configuration options are applicable to working with PL/SQL programs.

The exam covers five types of named PL/SQL programs, which are usually stored in the database: functions, procedures, packages, package bodies, and triggers. Each of these program types is covered in the following sections. The name and source code for each stored PL/SQL program is available from the data dictionary views DBA_SOURCE and DBA_TRIGGERS, although some packages are supplied *wrapped*, which means that the source code is a binary form. You can wrap your programs as well with the wrap utility.

Wrap is an Oracle-provided utility used to hide the PL/SQL source code, which helps protect your intellectual property. See Appendix A in the Oracle documentation "Oracle Database PL/SQL Language Reference 11*g* Release 1 (11.1) Part Number B28370-02" for details on using Wrap. You can access the Oracle documentation at http://tahiti.oracle.com. You can also use the subprograms available in the DBMS_DDL package to wrap code.

Working with Functions

Functions are PL/SQL programs that execute zero or more statements and return a value through a RETURN statement. Functions can also receive or return zero or more values through their parameters. Oracle provides several built-in functions such as the commonly used SYSDATE, COUNT, and SUBSTR functions. Several SQL functions and hundreds of PL/SQL functions come with Oracle Database 11*g*. We discussed several of the SQL functions in Chapter 2, "Using Single-Row Functions," and Chapter 3, "Using Group Functions." Because functions have a return value, a datatype is associated with them. Functions can be invoked anywhere an expression of the same datatype is allowed. Here are some examples:

- As a default value:
  ```
  DECLARE
    today  DATE DEFAULT SYSDATE;
  ```
- In an assignment:
  ```
  today := SYSDATE;
  ```
- In a Boolean expression:
  ```
  IF TO_CHAR(SYSDATE,'Day') = 'Monday'
  ```
- In a SQL expression:
  ```
  SELECT COUNT(*)
  FROM employees
  WHERE hire_date > SYSDATE-30;
  ```
- In the parameter list of another procedure or function:
  ```
  SELECT TRUNC(SYSDATE)
  ```

Create a function with the CREATE FUNCTION statement, like this:

```
CREATE OR REPLACE FUNCTION is_weekend(
  check_date IN DATE DEFAULT SYSDATE)
  RETURN VARCHAR2 AS
BEGIN
   CASE TO_CHAR(check_date,'DY')
   WHEN 'SAT' THEN
      RETURN 'YES';
   WHEN 'SUN' THEN
      RETURN 'YES';
   ELSE
      RETURN 'NO';
   END CASE;
END;
```

Functions, like all named PL/SQL, have the `OR REPLACE` keywords available in the `CREATE` statement. When present, `OR REPLACE` tells the database to not raise an exception if the object already exists. This behavior differs from a `DROP` and `CREATE`, in that privileges are not lost during a `REPLACE` operation and any objects that reference this object will not become invalid.

Working with Procedures

Procedures are PL/SQL programs that execute one or more statements. Procedures can receive and return values only through their parameter lists. You create a procedure with the `CREATE PROCEDURE` statement, like this:

```
CREATE OR REPLACE PROCEDURE archive_orders
   (cust_id   IN NUMBER
   ,retention IN NUMBER) IS
BEGIN

   INSERT INTO orders_archive
   SELECT * FROM orders
   WHERE customer = cust_id
   AND   order_date < SYSDATE - retention;

   DELETE orders
   WHERE customer = cust_id
   AND   order_date < SYSDATE - retention;

   INSERT INTO maint_log
```

```
    (action, action_date, who) VALUES
    ('archive orders '||retention||' for '||cust_id
    ,SYSDATE ,USER);
END;
```

The keyword IS, in the third line, is synonymous with the keyword AS, shown in the third line of the last example function in the previous section. Both are syntactically valid for all named SQL.

You invoke a procedure as a stand-alone statement within a PL/SQL program or by using the CALL or EXEC command. Here is an example:

```
EXEC DBMS_OUTPUT.PUT_LINE('Hello world!');
Hello world!

PL/SQL procedure successfully completed.

CALL  DBMS_OUTPUT.PUT_LINE('Hello world!');
Hello world!

Call completed.
```

A function or procedure by default is executed with the privileges of its owner, not of its invoker. If you create the procedure or function with a clause AUTHID CURRENT_USER, then the procedure or function will be executed with the privileges of the invoker. To be able to execute a procedure or function owned by another user, you must have been given the EXECUTE privilege or should have the EXECUTE ANY system privilege.

Working with Packages

A *package* is a container for functions, procedures, and data structures such as records, cursors, variables, and constants. A package has a publicly visible portion, called the *specification* (or *spec* for short) and a private portion called the *package body*. The package spec describes the programs and data structures that can be accessed from other programs. The package body contains the implementation of the procedures and functions. The package spec is identified in the data dictionary as the type PACKAGE, and the package body is identified as the type PACKAGE BODY.

To create a package spec, use the CREATE PACKAGE statement. In the following example, the package spec table_util contains one function and one procedure:

```
CREATE OR REPLACE PACKAGE table_util IS
  FUNCTION version RETURN VARCHAR2;
  PROCEDURE truncate (table_name IN VARCHAR2);
```

```
END table_util;
```

Privileges on a package are granted at the package-spec level. The EXECUTE privilege on a package allows the grantee to execute any program or use any data structure declared in the package specification. You cannot grant the EXECUTE privilege on only some of the programs declared in the spec.

Creating a Package Body

A package body depends on a package spec having the same name. The package body can be created only after the spec. The package body implements the programs that were declared in the package spec and can optionally contain private programs and data accessible only from within the package body.

To create a package body, use the CREATE PACKAGE BODY statement:

```
CREATE OR REPLACE PACKAGE BODY table_util IS
```

Here is an example of a private variable that can be referenced only in the package body:

```
version_string VARCHAR2(8) := '1.0.0';
```

Here is the code for the version function:

```
FUNCTION version RETURN VARCHAR2 IS
  BEGIN
     RETURN version_string;
  END;
```

Here is the code for the truncate procedure:

```
PROCEDURE truncate (table_name IN VARCHAR2) IS
  BEGIN
     IF  UPPER(table_name) = 'ORDER_STAGE'
      OR UPPER(table_name) = 'SALES_ROLLUP'
     THEN
        EXECUTE IMMEDIATE 'truncate table ' ||
           UPPER(table_name);
     ELSE
        RAISE_APPLICATION_ERROR(-20010
           ,'Invalid table for truncate: '|| table_name);
     END IF;
  END;
END table_util;
```

The package name following the END statement is optional but encouraged because it improves readability.

Working with Triggering Events and Managing Triggers

Triggers are PL/SQL programs that are invoked in response to an event in the database. Three sets of events can be hooked, allowing you to integrate your business logic with the database in an event-driven manner. Triggers can be created on DML events, DDL events, and database events. These three trigger event classes provide developers and you, the DBA, with a robust toolkit with which to design, build, and troubleshoot systems.

I will cover each of these events in more detail in the following sections. I will also discuss how to enable and disable triggers.

DML Trigger Events

DML triggers are invoked, or *fired*, when the specified DML events occur. If the keywords FOR EACH ROW are included in the trigger definition, the trigger fires once for each row that is changed. If these keywords are missing, the trigger fires once for each statement that causes the specified change. If the DML event list includes the UPDATE event, the trigger can be further restricted to fire only when updates of specific columns occur.

The following example creates a trigger that fires before any insert and before an update to the HIRE_DATE column of the EMPLOYEE table:

```
CREATE OR REPLACE TRIGGER employee_trg
 BEFORE INSERT OR UPDATE OF hire_date
 ON employees FOR EACH ROW
BEGIN
   log_update(USER,SYSTIMESTAMP);
   IF INSERTING THEN -- if fired due to insert
     :NEW.create_user :=  USER;
     :NEW.create_ts   :=  SYSTIMESTAMP;
   ELSIF UPDATING THEN -- if fired due to update
     IF :OLD.hire_date <> :NEW.hire_date THEN
        RAISE_APPLICATION_ERROR(-20013,
          'update of hire_date not allowed');
     END IF;
   END IF;
END;
```

This trigger will fire once for each row affected, because the keywords FOR EACH ROW are included. When the triggering event is an INSERT, two columns are forced to the specific values returned by USER and SYSTIMESTAMP. DML triggers cannot be created on SYS-owned objects. Table 13.1 shows the DML trigger events.

TABLE 13.1 DML Trigger Events

Event	When It Fires
INSERT	When a row is added to a table or a view.
UPDATE	When an UPDATE statement changes a row in a table or view. Update triggers can also specify an OF clause to limit the scope of changes that fire this type of trigger.
DELETE	When a row is removed from a table or a view.

Multiple triggers on a table fire in the following order:

1. Before statement triggers
2. Before row triggers
3. After row triggers
4. After statement triggers

Until Oracle 11*g*, if you had two or more triggers defined for the same statement for the same timing point, the order of trigger execution was unpredictable. In Oracle 11*g*, the FOLLOWS clause removes that restriction.

DDL Trigger Events

DDL triggers fire either for DDL changes to a specific schema or to all schemas in the database. The keywords ON DATABASE specify that the trigger will fire for the specified event on any schema in the database.

The following is an example of a trigger that fires for a DDL event in only one schema:

```
CREATE OR REPLACE TRIGGER NoGrantToPublic
BEFORE GRANT ON engineering.SCHEMA
DECLARE
   grantee_list    dbms_standard.ora_name_list_t;
   counter         BINARY_INTEGER;
BEGIN
   -- get the list of grantees
   counter := GRANTEE(grantee_list);
   FOR loop_counter IN
     grantee_list.FIRST..grantee_list.LAST
   LOOP
      -- if PUBLIC is on the grantee list, stop the action
      IF REGEXP_LIKE(grantee_list(loop_counter)
            ,'public','i') THEN
         RAISE_APPLICATION_ERROR(-20113
```

```
            ,'No grant to PUBLIC allowed for '
             ||DICTIONARY_OBJ_OWNER||'.'
             ||DICTIONARY_OBJ_NAME);
      END IF;
   END LOOP;
END;
```

In the preceding example, the DDL event is a GRANT statement issued by user engineering. The code examines the grantee list, and if it finds the special user/role PUBLIC, an exception is raised, causing the grant to fail. Table 13.2 shows the DDL trigger events.

TABLE 13.2 DDL Trigger Events

Event	When It Fires
[BEFORE/AFTER] ALTER	When an ALTER statement changes a database object
[BEFORE/AFTER] ANALYZE	When the database gathers or deletes statistics or validates the structure of an object
[BEFORE/AFTER] ASSOCIATE STATISTICS	When the database associates a statistic with a database object with an ASSOCIATE STATISTICS statement
[BEFORE/AFTER] AUDIT	When the database records an audit action (except FGA)
[BEFORE/AFTER] COMMENT	When a comment on a table or column is modified
[BEFORE/AFTER] CREATE	When the database object is created
[BEFORE/AFTER] DDL	In conjunction with any of the following: ALTER, ANALYZE, ASSOCIATE STATISTICS, AUDIT, COMMENT, CREATE, DISASSOCIATE STATISTICS, DROP GRANT, NOAUDIT, RENAME, REVOKE, or TRUNCATE
[BEFORE/AFTER] DISASSOCIATE STATISTICS	When a database disassociates a statistic type from a database object with a DISASSOCIATE STATISTICS statement
[BEFORE/AFTER] DROP	When a DROP statement removes an object from the database
[BEFORE/AFTER] GRANT	When a GRANT statement assigns a privilege
[BEFORE/AFTER] NOAUDIT	When a NOAUDIT statement changes database auditing
[BEFORE/AFTER] RENAME	When a RENAME statement changes an object name
[BEFORE/AFTER] REVOKE	When a REVOKE statement rescinds a privilege
[BEFORE/AFTER] TRUNCATE	When a TRUNCATE statement purges a table

Database Trigger Events

Database event triggers fire when the specified database-level event occurs. Most of these triggers are available only before or after the database event, but not both.

The following example creates an after-server error trigger that sends an email notification when an ORA-01555 error occurs:

```
CREATE OR REPLACE TRIGGER Email_on_1555_Err
AFTER SERVERERROR ON DATABASE
DECLARE
   mail_conn         UTL_SMTP.connection;
   smtp_relay        VARCHAR2(32) := 'mailserver';
   recipient_address VARCHAR2(64) := 'DBA@hotmail.com';
   sender_address    VARCHAR2(64) := 'oracle@sybex.com';
   mail_port         NUMBER := 25;
   msg               VARCHAR2(200);
BEGIN
   IF USER = 'SYSTEM' THEN
      -- Ignore this error
      NULL;
   ELSIF IS_SERVERERROR (1555) THEN
     -- compose the message
     msg := 'Subject: ORA-1555 error';
     msg := msg||'Snapshot too old err at '||systimestamp;
     -- send email notice
     mail_conn := UTL_SMTP.open_connection(smtp_relay
           ,mail_port);
     UTL_SMTP.HELO(mail_conn, smtp_relay);
     UTL_SMTP.MAIL(mail_conn, sender_address);
     UTL_SMTP.RCPT(mail_conn, recipient_address);
     UTL_SMTP.DATA(mail_conn, msg);
     UTL_SMTP.QUIT(mail_conn);
   END IF;
END;
```

Be careful when using database triggers. Fully test them in development before deploying them to production. Table 13.3 shows the database trigger events.

TABLE 13.3 Database Trigger Events

Event	When It Fires
AFTER LOGON	When a database session is established—only the AFTER trigger is allowed
BEFORE LOGOFF	When a database session ends normally—only the BEFORE trigger is allowed

TABLE 13.3 Database Trigger Events *(continued)*

Event	When It Fires
AFTER STARTUP	When the database is opened—only the AFTER trigger is allowed
BEFORE SHUTDOWN	When the database is closed—only the BEFORE trigger is allowed
AFTER SERVERERROR	When a database exception is raised—only the AFTER trigger is allowed
AFTER SUSPEND	When a server error causes a transaction to be suspended—only the AFTER trigger is allowed

Enabling and Disabling Triggers

The database automatically enables a trigger when you create it. After creating a trigger, you can disable (temporarily prevent it from firing) or reenable it. You can disable and enable triggers by name with an ALTER TRIGGER statement. Here are two examples:

```
ALTER TRIGGER after_ora60 DISABLE;

ALTER TRIGGER load_packages ENABLE;
```

Alternatively, you can enable and disable multiple DML triggers with an ALTER TABLE statement, like this:

```
ALTER TABLE employees DISABLE ALL TRIGGERS;
ALTER TABLE employees ENABLE ALL TRIGGERS;
```

You can also create a trigger with the ENABLE or DISABLE clause. ENABLE is the default.

You can query the STATUS column of the DBA_TRIGGERS view to find out whether a trigger is enabled or disabled.

Using and Administering PL/SQL Programs

Oracle 11*g* comes bundled with hundreds of built-in packages that give you significant capabilities for administering your database. Many features in the database are implemented through one or more of these built-in packages. To use the job scheduler, collect and manage optimizer statistics, implement fine-grained auditing, send email from the database, and use Data Pump or Log Miner, you must engage built-in packages. As you gain experience, you will use these built-in packages more extensively.

These are some of the commonly used built-in catalog packages:

- DBMS_STATS
- DBMS_METADATA
- DBMS_MONITOR

- UTL_FILE
- UTL_MAIL

To view the names and parameter lists for stored programs (except triggers), use the SQL*Plus DESCRIBE command like this:

```
describe dbms_monitor
-- some output is deleted for brevity

PROCEDURE SESSION_TRACE_DISABLE
 Argument Name   Type                In/Out Default?
 --------------- ------------------- ------ --------
 SESSION_ID      BINARY_INTEGER      IN     DEFAULT
 SERIAL_NUM      BINARY_INTEGER      IN     DEFAULT

PROCEDURE SESSION_TRACE_ENABLE
 Argument Name   Type                In/Out Default?
 --------------- ------------------- ------ --------
 SESSION_ID      BINARY_INTEGER      IN     DEFAULT
 SERIAL_NUM      BINARY_INTEGER      IN     DEFAULT
 WAITS           BOOLEAN             IN     DEFAULT
 BINDS           BOOLEAN             IN     DEFAULT
 PLAN_STAT       VARCHAR2            IN     DEFAULT
```

You can see in this output from DESCRIBE that the packaged procedure DBMS_MONITOR contains several procedures, including SESSION_TRACE_DISABLE and SESSION_TRACE_ENABLE. Furthermore, you can see the names, datatypes, and in/out mode for each parameter (SESSION_ID, SERIAL_NUM, and so on).

An extensive list of Oracle built-in PL/SQL packages is available in the manual "Oracle Database PL/SQL Packages and Types Reference 11*g* Release 1 (11.1) Part Number B28419-03." Fortunately, you don't have to know all these programs for the certification exam!

A PL/SQL program may be invalidated when a dependent object is changed through the ALTER command. The database automatically recompiles the package body the next time it is called, but you can choose to compile invalid PL/SQL programs yourself and thus eliminate the costly recompile during regular system processing. To explicitly compile a named SQL program, use the ALTER...COMPILE statement, like this:

```
ALTER PROCEDURE archive_orders COMPILE;
ALTER FUNCTION is_weekend COMPILE;
ALTER PACKAGE table_util COMPILE;
```

```
ALTER PACKAGE table_util COMPILE BODY;
ALTER TRIGGER fire_me COMPILE;
```

Other objects, such as views or types, are similarly compiled.

Oracle 11*g* implements a finer-grained dependency control; hence, if the package specification is not changed, the PL/SQL objects that reference the functions and procedures of the package are not invalidated when only the package body is changed.

Monitoring Locks and Resolving Lock Conflicts

In any database with many users, you will eventually have to deal with locking conflicts when two or more users try to change the same row in the database. In the following sections, I'll present an overview of how locking works in the Oracle Database, how users are queued for a particular resource once it is locked, and how Oracle classifies lock types in the database. Then, I'll show you a number of ways to detect and resolve locking issues; I'll also cover a special type of lock situation: the deadlock.

Understanding Locks and Transactions

Locks prevent multiple users from changing the same data at the same time. Before one or more rows in a table can be changed, the user executing the DML statement must obtain a lock on the row or rows; a *lock* gives the user exclusive control over the data until the user has committed or rolled back the transaction that is changing the data.

In Oracle 11g, a transaction can lock one row, multiple rows, or an entire table. Although you can manually lock rows, Oracle can automatically lock the rows needed at the lowest possible level to ensure data integrity and minimize conflicts with other transactions that may need to access other rows in the table.

In Table 13.4, both updates to the EMPLOYEES table return to the command prompt immediately after the UPDATE because the locks are on different rows in the EMPLOYEES table and neither session is waiting for the other lock to be released.

TABLE 13.4 Concurrent Transactions on Different Rows of the Same Table

Session 1	Time	Session 2
update employees set salary = salary * 1.2 where employee_id = 102;	11:29	update employees set manager = 100 where employee_id = 109;
commit;	11:30	commit;

Real World Scenario

Packaged Applications and Locking

The HR department recently purchased a benefits-management package that interfaced well with our existing employee-management tables; however, once HR started using the application, other users who accessed the employee tables started complaining of severe slowdowns in updates to the employee information.

Reviewing the CPU and I/O usage of the instance did not reveal any problems, and it wasn't until we looked at the locking information that we noticed a table lock on the employees table whenever the benefits-management features were being used! The benefits-management application was written to work on a number of database platforms, and the least capable of those platforms did not support row locking. As a result, no one could make changes to the employees table whenever an employee's benefits were being changed, and everyone had to wait for the benefits changes to complete. Fortunately, the parameter file for the benefits-management package had an option to specify Oracle as the target platform; after setting the specific database version in the package's parameter file, the package was smart enough to use row locking instead of table locking whenever the employee table needed to be updated.

Queries never require a lock. Even if another transaction has locked several rows or an entire table, a query always succeeds, using the prelock image of the data stored in the undo tablespace.

If multiple users require a lock on a row or rows in a table, the first user to request the lock obtains it, and the remaining users are enqueued using a first-in, first-out (FIFO) method. At a `SQL>` command prompt, a DML statement (`INSERT`, `UPDATE`, `DELETE`, or `MERGE`) that is waiting for a lock on a resource appears to hang, unless the `NOWAIT` keyword is used in a `LOCK` statement.

The `WAIT` and `NOWAIT` keywords are explained in the next section, "Maximizing Data Concurrency."

At the end of a transaction, when either a `COMMIT` or a `ROLLBACK` is issued (either explicitly by the user or implicitly when the session terminates normally or abnormally), all locks are released.

Maximizing Data Concurrency

Rows of a table are locked either explicitly by the user at the beginning of a transaction or implicitly by Oracle, usually at the row level, depending on the operation. If a table must be locked for performance reasons (which is rare), you can use the LOCK TABLE command, specifying the level at which the table should be locked.

In the following example, you lock the EMPLOYEES and DEPARTMENTS tables at the highest possible level, EXCLUSIVE:

```
SQL> lock table hr.employees, hr.departments
     in exclusive mode;
Table(s) Locked.
```

Until the transaction with the LOCK statement either commits or rolls back, only queries are allowed on the EMPLOYEES or DEPARTMENTS table.

In the sections that follow, I will review the lock modes, as well as show you how to avoid the lock enqueue process and terminate the command if the requested resource is already locked.

Lock Modes

Lock modes provide a way for you to specify how much and what kinds of access other users have on tables that you are using in DML commands. In Table 13.5, you can see the types of locks that can be obtained at the table level.

TABLE 13.5 Table Lock Modes

Table Lock Mode	Description
ROW SHARE	Permits concurrent access to the locked table but prohibits other users from locking the entire table for exclusive access.
ROW EXCLUSIVE	Same as ROW SHARE but also prohibits locking in SHARE mode. This type of lock is obtained automatically with standard DML commands such as UPDATE, INSERT, or DELETE.
SHARE	Permits concurrent queries but prohibits updates to the table; this mode is required to create an index on a table and is automatically obtained when using the CREATE INDEX statement.
SHARE ROW EXCLUSIVE	Used to query a whole table and to allow other users to query the table but to prevent other users from locking the table in SHARE mode or updating rows.
EXCLUSIVE	The most restrictive locking mode; permits queries on the locked table but prohibits DML by any other users. This mode is required to drop the table and is automatically obtained when using the DROP TABLE statement.

Manual lock requests wait in the same queue as implicit locks and are satisfied in a FIFO manner as each request releases the lock with an implicit or explicit COMMIT or ROLLBACK.

You can explicitly obtain locks on individual rows by using the SELECT ... FOR UPDATE statement, as you can see in the following example:

```
SQL> select * from hr.employees
     where manager_id = 100
     for update;
```

Not only does this query show the rows that satisfy the query conditions, but it also locks the selected rows and prevents other transactions from locking or updating these rows until a COMMIT or ROLLBACK occurs.

NOWAIT Mode

Using NOWAIT in a LOCK TABLE statement returns control to the user immediately if any locks already exist on the requested resource, as you can see in the following example:

```
SQL> lock table hr.employees
     in share row exclusive mode
     nowait;
lock table hr.employees
           *
ERROR at line 1:
ORA-00054: resource busy and acquire with NOWAIT specified or timeout expired


SQL>
```

This is especially useful in a PL/SQL application if an alternate execution path can be followed if the requested resource is not yet available. NOWAIT can also be used in the SELECT ... FOR UPDATE statement.

WAIT Mode

You can tell Oracle 11*g* to wait a specified number of seconds to acquire a DML lock. If you do not specify a NOWAIT or WAIT clause, then the database waits indefinitely if the table is locked by another user. In the following example, Oracle will wait for 60 seconds to acquire the lock. If the lock is not acquired within 60 seconds, an error is returned.

```
SQL> lock table hr.employees
     in share row exclusive mode
     wait 60;
```

DDL Lock Waits

When DML statements have rows locked in a table or if the table is manually locked by a user, DDL statements on the table fail with the ORA-00054 error. To have the DDL statements wait for a specified number of seconds before throwing the ORA-00054 error, you can set the initialization parameter DDL_LOCK_TIMEOUT. The default value is 0, which means the error is issued immediately. You can specify a value up to 1,000,000 seconds.

```
SQL> alter table hr.employees modify salary number (15,2);
alter table hr.employees modify salary number (15,2)
            *
ERROR at line 1:
ORA-00054: resource busy and acquire with NOWAIT specified or timeout expired

SQL> show parameter ddl_lock
NAME                                 TYPE        VALUE
------------------------------------ ----------- ------------------------------
ddl_lock_timeout                     integer     0
SQL>
```

Detecting and Resolving Lock Conflicts

Although locks are a common and sometimes unavoidable occurrence in many databases, they are usually resolved by waiting in the queue. In some cases, you may need to resolve the lock problem manually (such as if a user makes an update at 4:59 p.m. and does not perform a COMMIT before leaving for the day).

In the next few sections, I will describe in more detail some of the reasons that lock conflicts occur and how to detect lock conflicts, and I'll discuss a more specific and serious type of lock conflict: a deadlock.

Understanding Lock Conflicts

In addition to the proverbial user who makes a change at 4:59 p.m. and forgets to perform a COMMIT before leaving for the day, other more typical lock conflicts are caused by long-running transactions that perform hundreds, thousands, or even hundreds of thousands of DML commands in the overnight batch run but are not finished updating the tables when the normal business day starts. The uncommitted transactions from the overnight batch jobs may lock tables that need to be updated by clerical staff during the business day, causing a lock conflict.

Another typical cause of lock conflicts is using unnecessarily high locking levels. In the "Packaged Applications and Locking" sidebar earlier in this chapter, we described a third-party application that routinely locked resources at the table level instead of at the row level to be compatible with every SQL-based database on the market. Developers may unnecessarily code updates to tables with higher locking levels than required by Oracle 11*g*.

Detecting Lock Conflicts

Detecting locks in Oracle 11*g* using EM Database Control makes your job easy; you don't need to query against V$SESSION, V$TRANSACTION, V$LOCK, and V$LOCKED_OBJECT to see who is locking what resource. You can click the Instance Locks link on the Performance tab of EM Grid Control. In Figure 13.1, you can see the tables locked by the user SCOTT after executing the following statement:

```
SQL> lock table hr.employees, hr.departments
     in exclusive mode;
Table(s) Locked.
```

FIGURE 13.1 The Instance Locks screen in EM Database Control

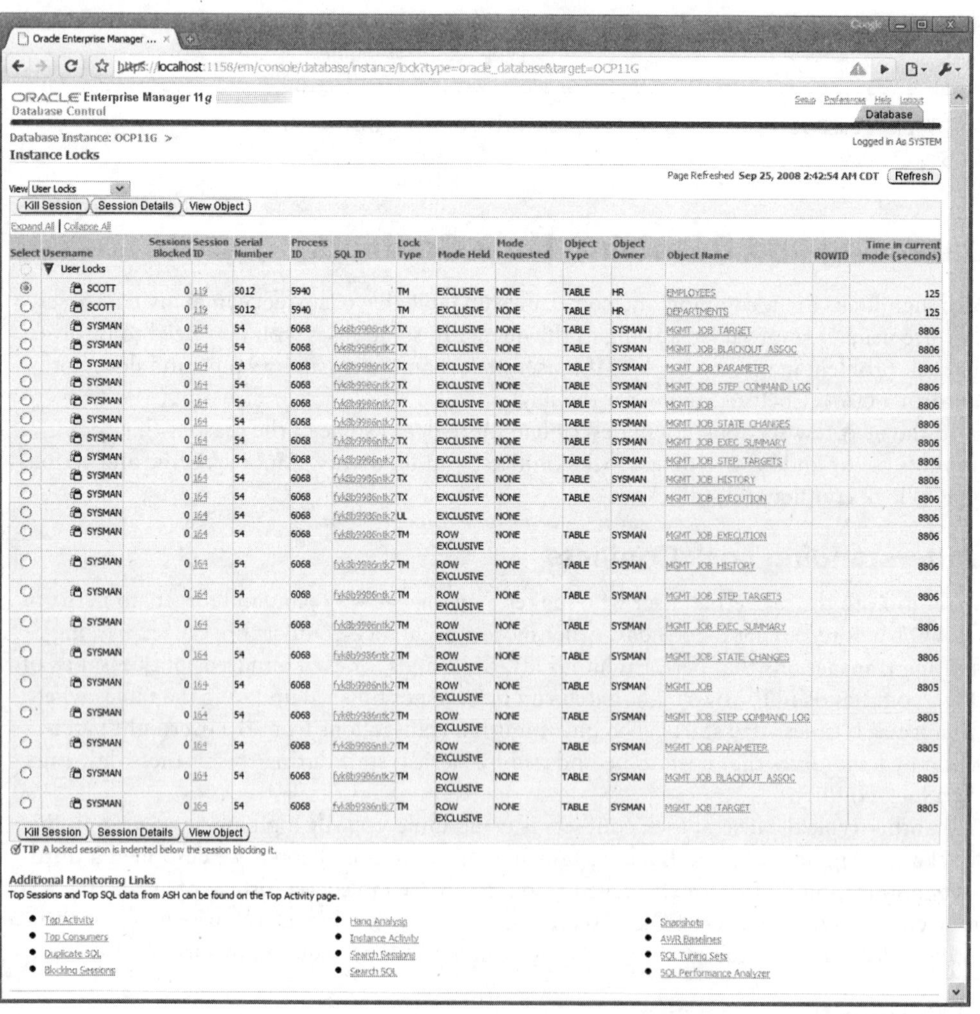

SCOTT has an EXCLUSIVE lock on both the EMPLOYEES and DEPARTMENTS tables. You can drill down on the locked object by clicking one of the links in the Object Name column; similarly, you can review other information about SCOTT's session by clicking one of the links in the Session ID column.

If the HR user performs the following SQL, HR's session will wait until the SCOTT user releases the locks:

```
SQL> UPDATE employees SET salary = 0 WHERE salary IS NULL;
```

On the EM Grid Control screen, choose Blocking Locks from the drop-down view, and you can see that user SCOTT is blocking the HR user, as shown in Figure 13.2.

FIGURE 13.2 The blocking locks shown in EM Database Control

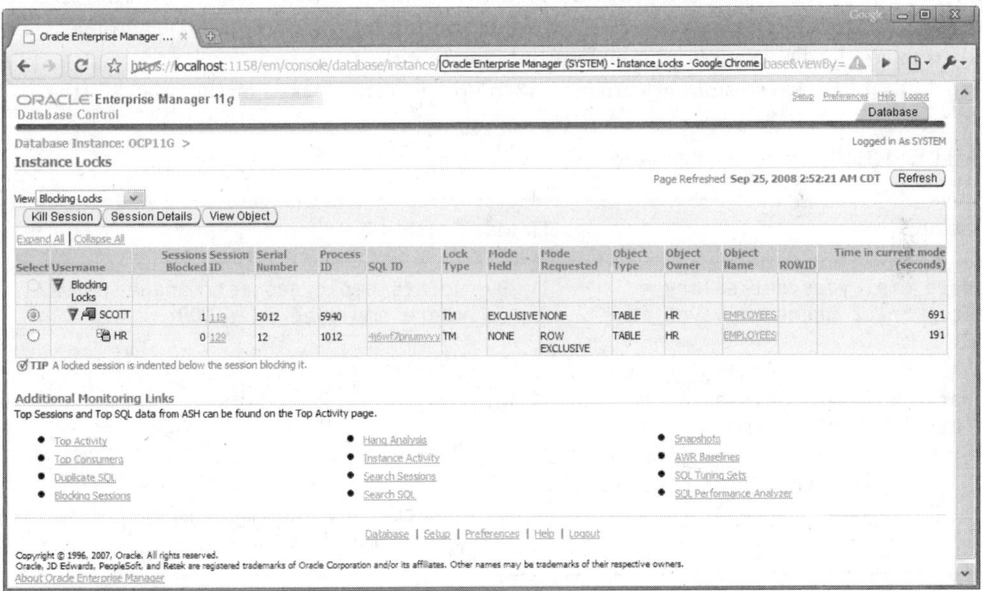

The data dictionary view DBA_LOCK is very handy for the DBA to look for locks and whether any session is blocking other users. A session with value of `Blocking` in the BLOCKING_OTHERS column may have to be manually terminated using the `ALTER SYSTEM KILL SESSION` statement. DBA_WAITERS is another view that shows only the sessions that are waiting on a lock. This view shows the holding session and the waiting session.

Understanding and Resolving Deadlocks

Resolving a lock conflict, the user can either COMMIT or ROLLBACK the current transaction. If you cannot contact the user and it is an emergency, you can select the session holding the lock and click the Kill Session button on the Instance Locks screen of the EM Database Control (refer to Figure 13.1, earlier in this chapter). The next time the user whose session has been killed tries to execute a command, the error message "ORA-00028: Your session has been killed" is returned. Again, this is an option of last resort: you'll lose all the statements executed in the session since the last COMMIT.

A more serious type of lock conflict is a deadlock. A *deadlock* is a special type of lock conflict in which two or more users are waiting for a resource locked by the other users. As a result, neither transaction can complete without some kind of intervention: the session that first detects a deadlock rolls back the statement waiting on the resource with the error message "ORA-00060: Deadlock detected while waiting for resource." Oracle automatically resolves deadlocks without user/DBA intervention.

In Table 13.6, two sessions are attempting to update a row locked by the other session.

TABLE 13.6 Deadlock Scenario

Session 1	Time	Session 2
`update employees set salary = salary * 1.2 where employee_id = 102;`	11:29	`update employees set manager = 100 where employee_id = 109;`
`update employees set salary = salary * 1.2 where employee_id = 109;`	11:44	
	11:50	`update employees set manager = 100 where employee_id = 102;`

Prior to 11:44, session 1 and session 2 updated two different rows in the database and did not commit the transaction. At 11:44, session 1 issued an UPDATE statement against the same row locked by session 2. This causes session 1 to hang, waiting for the lock to be released by session 2. The lock held by session 2 will be released only when session 2 performs a commit or rollback. At 11:50, when session 2 is trying to update a row already locked by session 1, you have a deadlock situation: session 1 waiting on session 2 and session 2 waiting on session 1. When this situation forms, Oracle throws out the ORA-00060 error and fails the statement. Remember, the transaction is not rolled back, because only the statement is in error. In our example, session 2 will get the ORA-00060 error when the update at 11:50 is issued, but session 1 will wait until session 2 commits or rolls back.

Leveraging Undo Management

Whenever a process or a user session changes data in the database, Oracle saves the old value as it existed before it was modified as undo data. This provides a number of benefits to the database user:

- It lets the user change their minds and roll back, or undo, the change to the database.
- It supports read-consistent queries. Once a query starts, any changes to the query's underlying tables are not reflected in the query's results.
- It supports flashback query, an Oracle feature introduced in Oracle9*i*. Flashback query allows a user to see how a table looked at some point in the past. As long as the undo data still exists for the requested point of time, flashback queries are possible.

In the following sections, I present all aspects of undo management. First, I will show how transactions are related to undo management and how undo records are stored in an undo tablespace along with some of the features supported by undo records. Next, I will show you how to set up the initialization parameters to specify a target for how much undo is retained in the undo tablespace; in addition, I will show you the commands needed to guarantee that undo space is available for SELECT statements at the expense of DML commands.

Monitoring an undo tablespace is not unlike monitoring any other tablespace: you want to make sure you have enough undo space in the tablespace to satisfy all types of user transactions but not so much that you're wasting space that can be used for objects in other tablespaces. Therefore, I will present some methods to accurately calculate the optimal amount of undo space you will need. Finally, I will review the notification methods you can use to proactively alert you to problems with the undo tablespace.

Understanding Undo Segments

Undo segments, also known as *rollback segments*, are similar to other segments in the database, such as table or index segments, in that an undo segment consists of extents, which in turn consist of data blocks. Also, an undo segment contains data similar to that stored in a table. However, that is where the similarity ends. Undo segments must be stored in a special type of tablespace called an *undo tablespace*. Although a database can have more than one undo tablespace, only one undo tablespace can be active at any one time. Undo segments contain undo information about one or many tables involved in a transaction. Also, undo segments automatically grow and shrink as needed, acting as a circular buffer—transactions that fill up the extents in an undo segment can wrap around to the beginning of the segment if the first extent is not being used by an active transaction.

At the beginning of a transaction—in other words, when the first DML command is issued after a previous COMMIT or a user first connects to the database—the transaction is assigned to an undo segment in the undo tablespace. Any changes to any table in the transaction are recorded in the assigned undo segment. The names of the current active undo segments can be retrieved from the dynamic performance view V$ROLLNAME, as you can see in the following query:

```
SQL> select * from v$rollname;

       USN NAME
---------- ----------------------
         0 SYSTEM
         1 _SYSSMU1_1192467665$
         2 _SYSSMU2_1192467665$
         3 _SYSSMU3_1192467665$
         4 _SYSSMU4_1192467665$
         5 _SYSSMU5_1192467665$
         6 _SYSSMU6_1192467665$
         7 _SYSSMU7_1192467665$
         8 _SYSSMU8_1192467665$
         9 _SYSSMU9_1192467665$
        10 _SYSSMU10_1192467665$

11 rows selected.
```

The data dictionary view DBA_ROLLBACK_SEGS shows both active (online) and inactive (offline) undo segments in both the SYSTEM and undo tablespaces.

The undo segment with an undo segment number (USN) of 0 is an undo segment reserved for exclusive use by system users such as SYS or SYSTEM or if no other undo segments are online and the data being changed resides in the SYSTEM tablespace. In this example, nine other undo segments are available in the undo tablespace for user transactions.

The dynamic performance view V$TRANSACTION shows the relationship between a transaction and the undo segments. In the following query, you begin a transaction and then join V$TRANSACTION to V$ROLLNAME to find out the name of the undo segment assigned to the transaction:

```
SQL> set transaction name 'Update clerk salaries';
Transaction set.

SQL> update hr.employees set salary = salary * 1.25
     where job_id like '%CLERK';
44 rows updated.
```

```
SQL> select xid, status, start_time, xidusn seg_num,
            r.name seg_name
     from v$transaction t join v$rollname r
            on t.xidusn = r.usn
     where t.name = 'Update clerk salaries';

XID              STATUS  START_TIME        SEG_NUM SEG_NAME
---------------- ------- ----------------- ------- --------------------
05001100DD020000 ACTIVE  09/25/08 03:03:34       5 _SYSSMU5_1192467665$

1 row selected.
```

The column XID is the internally assigned, unique transaction number assigned to this transaction, and it is assigned the undo segment _SYSSMU5_1192467665$. The column XIDUSN (aliased as SEG_NUM in the query) is the undo segment number for _SYSSMU5_1192467665$. A transaction can reside in only one undo segment; it cannot be moved to another undo segment. However, many different transactions can use the same undo segment.

If an extent in the assigned undo segment fills up and more space is required, the next available extent is used; if all extents in the segment are needed for current transactions, a new extent is allocated for the undo segment.

All undo segments are owned by SYS, regardless of who is making changes in a transaction. Each segment must have a minimum of two extents; the maximum number of extents in an undo segment is high: for an undo tablespace with a block size of 8KB, the default maximum number of extents per undo segment is 32,765.

During a media failure with an undo tablespace, the tablespace can be recovered using archived and online redo log files just as with any other tablespace; however, the instance must be in a MOUNT state to recover an undo tablespace.

Tablespace recovery is discussed in Chapter 16, "Recovering the Database."

Using Undo Data

Undo data is the old value of data when a process or user changes data in a table or an index. Undo data serves four purposes in an Oracle Database:

- User rollback of a transaction
- Read consistency of DML operations and queries
- Database recovery operations
- Flashback functionality

User Transaction Rollback

In Chapter 8, "Introducing Oracle Database 11*g* Components and Architecture," you learned about transactions and how they are managed within the database architecture. At the user level, you might have one or hundreds of DML commands (such as DELETE, INSERT, UPDATE, or MERGE) within a particular transaction that need to be undone by a user or a process that is making changes to one or more tables. Undoing the changes within a transaction is called *rolling back* part or all of the transaction. The undo information needed to roll back the changes is called, appropriately, the *rollback information* and is stored in a special type of tablespace called an *undo tablespace*.

When an entire transaction is rolled back, Oracle undoes all the changes since the beginning of the transactions, using the saved undo information in the undo tablespace, releases any locks on rows involved in the transaction, and ends the transaction.

If a failure occurs on the client or a network, abnormally terminating the user's connection to the database, undo information is used in much the same way as if the user explicitly rolled back the transaction, and Oracle undoes all the changes since the beginning of the transaction, using information saved in the undo tablespace.

Read Consistency

Undo also provides read consistency for users who are querying rows involved in a DML transaction by another user or session. When one user starts to make changes to a table after another user has already begun a query against the table, the user issuing the query will not see the changes to the table until after the query has completed and the user issues a new query against the table. Undo segments in an undo tablespace are used to reconstruct the data blocks belonging to the table to provide the previous values of the rows for any user issuing SELECT statements against the table before the DML statements' transaction commits.

For example, the user KELSIEJ begins a transaction at 3 p.m. that contains several long-running DML statements against the EMPLOYEES table; the statements aren't expected to finish until 3:15 p.m. As each DML command is issued, the previous values of each row are saved in the transaction's undo segment. At 3:05 p.m., the user SARAHCR issues a SELECT against the EMPLOYEES table; none of the changes made so far by KELSIEJ are visible to SARAHCR. The undo tablespace provides the previous values of the EMPLOYEES table to SARAHCR and any other users querying the EMPLOYEES table between 3 p.m. and 3:15 p.m. Even if SARAHCR's query is still running at 3:20 p.m., the query still appears as it did at 3 p.m. before KELSIEJ started making changes.

INSERT statements use little space in an undo segment; only the pointer to the new row is stored in the undo tablespace. To undo an INSERT statement, the pointer locates the new row and deletes it from the table if the transaction is rolled back.

In a few situations, either SARAHCR's query or KELSIEJ's DML statements might fail, because the undo tablespace is not sized correctly or because the undo retention period is too short.

You can also apply read consistency to an entire transaction instead of just a single SELECT statement by using the SET TRANSACTION statement as follows:

```
SQL> set transaction read only;
Transaction set.
```

Until the transaction is either rolled back or committed, all queries in the transaction see only those changes to other tables that were committed before the transaction began. Only the following statements are permitted in a read-only transaction:

- SELECT statements without the FOR UPDATE clause
- LOCK TABLE
- SET ROLE
- ALTER SESSION
- ALTER SYSTEM

In other words, a read-only transaction cannot contain any statement that changes data in a table, regardless of where the table resides. For example, although an ALTER USER command does not change data in the USERS or any other non-SYSTEM tablespace, it does change the data dictionary tables and therefore cannot be used in a read-only transaction.

Monitoring, Configuring, and Administering Undo

Compared with configuring rollback operations in releases previous to Oracle9*i*, managing undo in later versions of Oracle requires little intervention. However, two particular situations will trigger intervention: either not enough undo space to handle all active transactions or not enough undo space to satisfy long-running queries that need undo information for read consistency. Running out of undo space for transactions generates messages such as "ORA-01650: Unable to extend rollback segment"; long-running queries whose undo entries have been reused by current transactions typically receive the "ORA-01555: Snapshot too old" message.

In the following sections, I will show you how to configure the undo tablespace using two initialization parameters: UNDO_MANAGEMENT and UNDO_TABLESPACE. I will also present the methods available for monitoring the health of the undo tablespace, as well as using EM Database Control's Undo Advisor to size or resize the undo tablespace. Using the dynamic performance view V$UNDOSTAT, you can calculate an optimal size for the undo tablespace if the Undo Advisor is not available. Finally, I will show you how to guarantee that long-running queries will have undo entries available, even if it means that a DML transaction fails, by using the RETENTION GUARANTEE option.

Configuring the Undo Tablespace

Manual undo management is not recommended, although it is still available in Oracle 11*g*. Instead, use manual undo management only for compatibility with Oracle8*i* or earlier. Automatic undo management is the default for the Oracle 11*g* database. To configure automatic undo management, use the initialization parameters UNDO_MANAGEMENT, UNDO_TABLESPACE, and UNDO_RETENTION.

UNDO_MANAGEMENT

The parameter UNDO_MANAGEMENT specifies the way in which undo data is managed in the database: either manually using rollback segments or automatically using a single tablespace to hold undo information.

The allowed values for UNDO_MANAGEMENT are MANUAL and AUTO. To change the undo-management mode, you must restart the instance. This parameter is not dynamic, as you can see in the following example:

```
SQL> alter system
     set undo_management = manual;

set undo_management = manual
    *
ERROR at line 2:
ORA-02095: specified initialization parameter cannot be modified
```

If you are using an spfile, you can change the value of this parameter in the spfile only and then restart the instance for the parameter to take effect, as follows:

```
SQL> alter system
     set undo_management = manual scope=spfile;
System altered.
```

UNDO_TABLESPACE

The parameter UNDO_TABLESPACE specifies the name of the undo tablespace to use for read consistency and transaction rollback.

You can create an undo tablespace when the database is created; you can resize it later or create a new one later. In any case, only one undo tablespace can be active at any given time, unless the value of UNDO_TABLESPACE is changed while the old undo tablespace still contains active transactions. In this case, the old undo tablespace remains active until the last transaction using the old undo tablespace either commits or rolls back; all new transactions use the new undo tablespace.

If UNDO_TABLESPACE is not defined but at least one undo tablespace exists in the database, the first undo tablespace discovered by the Oracle instance at startup is assigned to

UNDO_TABLESPACE. You can find out the name of the current undo tablespace with the SHOW PARAMETER command, as in the following example:

```
SQL> show parameter undo_tablespace

NAME                     TYPE        VALUE
------------------------ ----------- --------------------
undo_tablespace          string      UNDOTBS1
```

For most platforms, if an undo tablespace is not explicitly created in the CREATE DATABASE command, Oracle automatically creates one with the name SYS_UNDOTBS.

Here is an example of how you can switch the undo tablespace from UNDOTBS1 to UNDO_BATCH:

```
SQL> show parameter undo_tablespace

NAME                         TYPE        VALUE
---------------------------- ----------- --------------------
undo_tablespace              string      UNDOTBS1

SQL> alter system set undo_tablespace=undo_batch;
System altered.

SQL> show parameter undo_tablespace

NAME                         TYPE        VALUE
---------------------------- ----------- --------------------
undo_tablespace              string      UNDO_BATCH
```

UNDO_RETENTION

The parameter UNDO_RETENTION specifies, in seconds, how long undo information that has already been committed should be retained until it can be overwritten. This is not a guaranteed limit: if the number of seconds specified by UNDO_RETENTION has not been reached and if a transaction needs undo space, already committed undo information can be overwritten.

```
SQL> show parameter undo

NAME                                 TYPE        VALUE
------------------------------------ ----------- ----------
undo_management                      string      AUTO
undo_retention                       integer     900
undo_tablespace                      string      UNDOTBS1
```

To guarantee undo retention, you can use the RETENTION GUARANTEE keywords for the undo tablespace, as you will see later in this chapter in the section "Guaranteeing Undo Retention."

Setting UNDO_RETENTION to zero turns on automatic undo retention tuning. Oracle continually adjusts this parameter to retain just enough undo information to satisfy the longest-running query to date. If the undo tablespace is not big enough for the longest-running query, automatic undo retention retains as much as possible without extending the undo tablespace. In any case, automatic undo retention attempts to maintain at least 900 seconds, or 15 minutes, of undo information.

Regardless of how long undo information is retained, it falls into one of three categories:

Uncommitted undo information This is undo information that is still supporting an active transaction and is required in the event of a ROLLBACK or a transaction failure. This undo information is never overwritten.

Committed undo information Also known as *unexpired undo*, this is undo information that is no longer needed to support an active transaction but is still needed to satisfy the undo retention interval, as defined by UNDO_RETENTION. This undo can be overwritten, however, if an active transaction needs undo space.

Expired undo information This is undo information that is no longer needed to support an active transaction and is overwritten when space is required by an active transaction.

Here is an example of how you can change undo retention from its current value to 12 hours:

```
SQL> show parameter undo_retention

NAME                TYPE        VALUE
------------------ ----------- -----------------------
undo_retention      integer     600

SQL> alter system set undo_retention = 43200;
System altered.

SQL> show parameter undo_retention

NAME                TYPE        VALUE
------------------ ----------- -----------------------
undo_retention      integer     43200
```

Unless you use the SCOPE parameter in the ALTER SYSTEM command, the change to UNDO_RETENTION takes effect immediately and stays in effect the next time the instance is restarted.

Monitoring the Undo Tablespace

Undo tablespaces are monitored just like any other tablespace: if a specific set of space thresholds is not defined, the database default values are used; otherwise, a specific set of thresholds can be assigned. When an undo tablespace's data files do not have the AUTOEXTEND attribute set, transactions can fail because too many transactions are vying for too little undo space.

Although you can allow the data files in your undo tablespace to autoextend initially, turn off autoextend on its data files once you believe that the undo tablespace has been sized correctly. This prevents a single user from accidentally using up large amounts of disk space in the undo tablespace by neglecting to commit transactions as frequently as possible.

Figure 13.3 shows the Automatic Undo Management screen in EM Database Control (click the Server tab and choose Automatic Undo Management under Database Configuration). The current size of the undo tablespace is 270MB, and during the last seven days, the size of this undo tablespace has been sufficient to support the maximum undo generation.

FIGURE 13.3 The Automatic Undo Management screen in EM Database Control

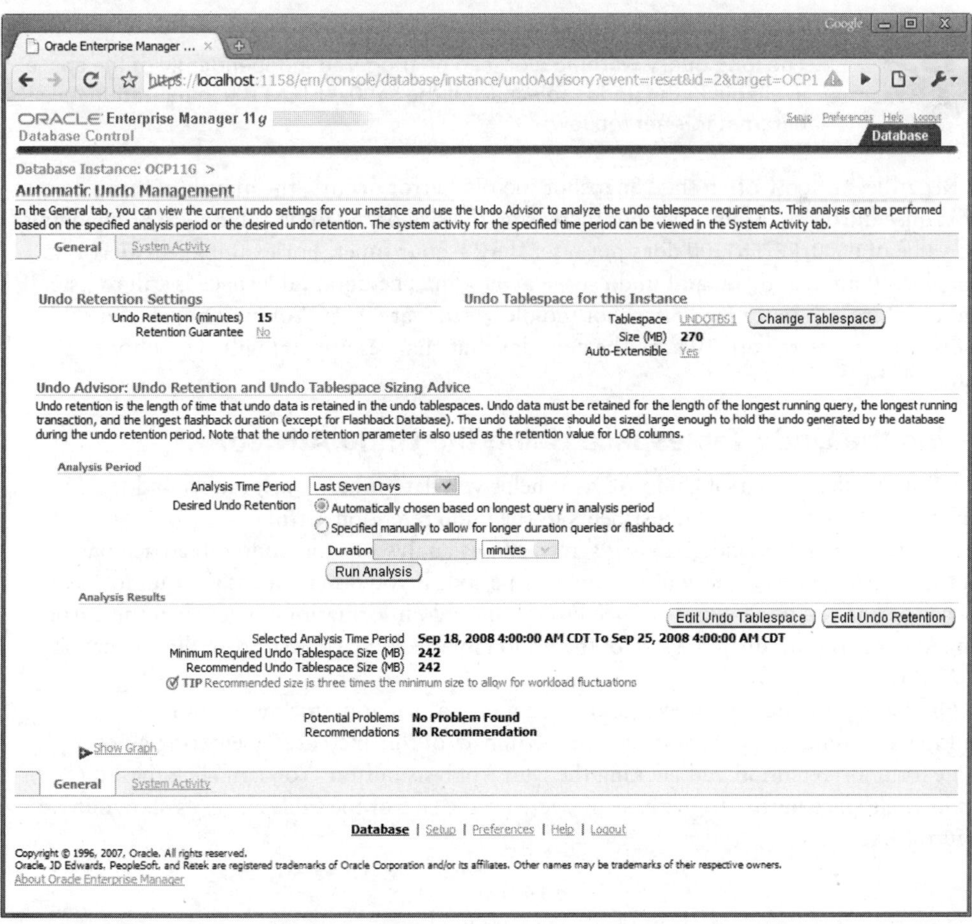

EM Database Control uses the data dictionary view V$UNDOSTAT to calculate the undo usage rate and provide recommendations. V$UNDOSTAT collects 10-minute snapshots of the undo space consumption and, in conjunction with UNDO_RETENTION and the database block size, can provide an optimal undo tablespace size.

Running out of space in an undo tablespace can also trigger an "ORA-01555: Snapshot too old" error. Long-running queries that need a read-consistent view of one or more tables can be at odds with ongoing transactions that need undo space. Unless the undo tablespace is defined with the RETENTION GUARANTEE parameter (described later in this chapter in the section "Guaranteeing Undo Retention"), ongoing DML can use undo space that is needed for long-running queries. As a result, a "Snapshot too old" error is returned to the user executing the query, and an alert is generated. This alert is also known as a *long query warning alert*.

The long query warning alert can be triggered independently of the space available in the undo tablespace if the UNDO_RETENTION initialization parameter is set too low.

Regardless of how often the "Snapshot too old" error occurs, the alert is generated at most once during a 24-hour period. Increasing the size of the undo tablespace or changing the value of UNDO_RETENTION does not reset the 24-hour timer. For example, an alert is generated at 10 a.m., and you add undo space at 11 a.m. The undo tablespace is still too small, and users are still receiving "Snapshot too old" errors at 2 p.m. You will not receive a long query warning alert until 10 a.m. the next day, but chances are you will get a phone call before then!

Sizing the Undo Tablespace Using the Undo Advisor

The EM Database Control Undo Advisor helps you determine how large an undo tablespace should be, given adjustments to the undo retention setting.

In Figure 13.3, the Undo Advisor screen shows analysis of the undo tablespace based on the longest-running query in the analysis period. If you don't expect your undo usage to increase or you don't expect to need to retain undo information longer than the current longest one, you can drop the size of the undo tablespace to 242MB from the current size of 270MB.

On the other hand, if you expect to need undo information for more than the current longest-running query, you can see the impact of this increase by entering a new value for undo retention and clicking the Run Analysis button. You can click the Edit Undo Tablespace button to increase or decrease the size of the tablespace, as shown in Figure 13.4.

FIGURE 13.4 Edit Tablespace screen in EM Database Control

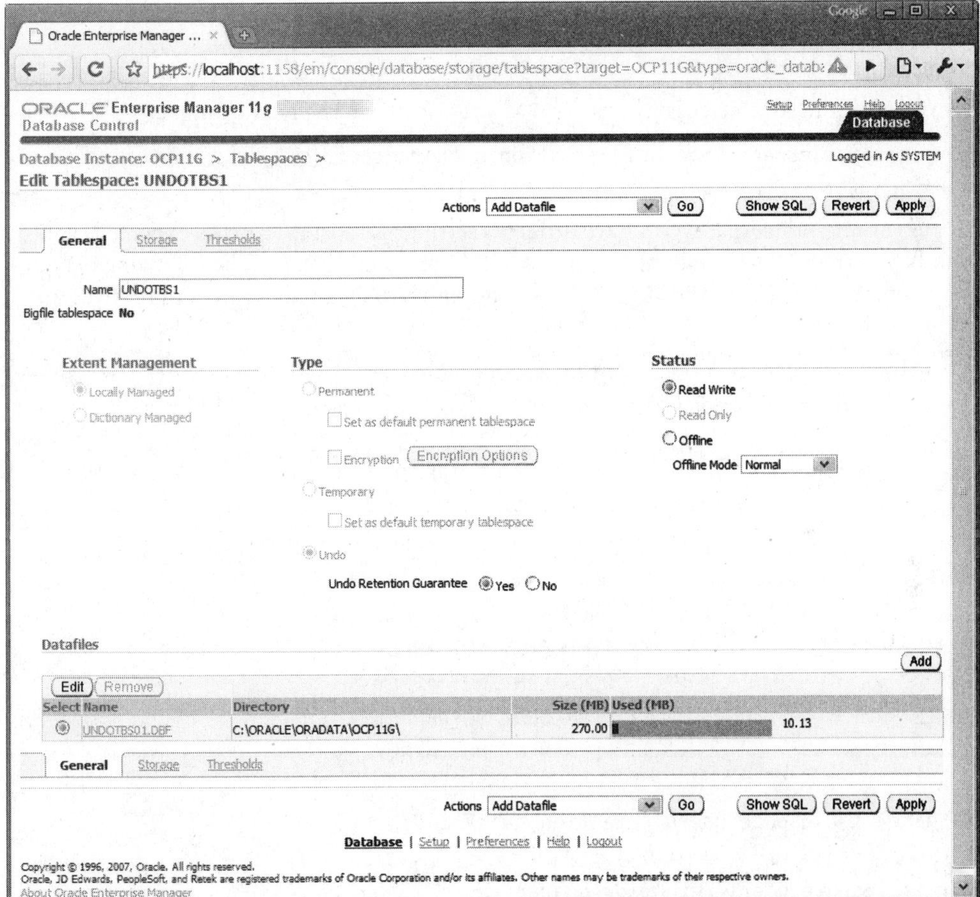

Guaranteeing Undo Retention

By default, undo information from committed transactions (unexpired undo) is overwritten before a transaction fails because of a lack of expired undo. If your database requirements are such that you want long-running queries to succeed at the expense of DML in a transaction, such as in a data warehouse environment where a query can run for hours or even days, you can set the `RETENTION GUARANTEE` parameter for the undo tablespace.

This parameter is not available as an initialization parameter. You can set retention guarantee using the Edit Tablespace EM Database Control screen shown in Figure 13.4

by choosing Yes for Undo Retention Guarantee. You can also use ALTER TABLESPACE at the command line to set it, as in the following example:

```
SQL> alter tablespace undotbs1 retention guarantee;
Tablespace altered.
```

Turning off the parameter is just as easy, as you can see in the next example:

```
SQL> alter tablespace undotbs1 retention noguarantee;
Tablespace altered.
```

Different undo tablespaces can have different settings for RETENTION. As expected, you cannot set RETENTION for a tablespace that is not an undo tablespace. The following example is attempting to change the RETENTION setting for the USERS tablespace and receives an error message:

```
SQL> select tablespace_name, contents,
  2     retention from dba_tablespaces;

TABLESPACE_NAME                CONTENTS  RETENTION
------------------------------ --------- -----------
SYSTEM                         PERMANENT NOT APPLY
UNDOTBS1                       UNDO      NOGUARANTEE
SYSAUX                         PERMANENT NOT APPLY
TEMP                           TEMPORARY NOT APPLY
USERS                          PERMANENT NOT APPLY
EXAMPLE                        PERMANENT NOT APPLY
OE_TRANS                       PERMANENT NOT APPLY

SQL> alter tablespace users retention guarantee;

alter tablespace users retention guarantee
*
ERROR at line 1:
ORA-30044: 'Retention' can only be specified for undo tablespace
```

Summary

In this chapter, you learned how to use the SQL DML statements to manipulate data as well as how to identify, execute, and compile PL/SQL programs, including triggers. You also learned how locks work in Oracle 11*g* database and how undo is managed.

To create, change, and remove data from an Oracle Database, use the `INSERT`, `UPDATE`, `MERGE`, and `DELETE` statements.

Although Oracle usually manages locks at the minimum level to ensure that two sessions do not try to simultaneously update the same row in a table, you can explicitly lock a table at a number of levels. In addition, you can lock a subset of rows in a table to prevent updates or locks from other transactions with the `FOR UPDATE` clause in the `SELECT` statement.

You learned some reasons that lock conflicts occur and how to resolve them; a special kind of lock conflict, a deadlock, occurs when two users are waiting on a resource locked by the other user. Deadlocks, unlike other types of lock conflicts, are resolved quickly and automatically by Oracle long before any manual lock resolution is attempted.

I presented the undo tablespace and its importance for the two types of database users: those who want to query a table and receive consistent results and those who want to make changes to a table and have the option to roll back the data to its state when the transaction started.

You can configure an undo tablespace with a handful of initialization parameters. `UNDO_MANAGEMENT` defines the mode in which undo is managed and can be either `MANUAL` or `AUTO`. `UNDO_TABLESPACE` identifies the current undo tablespace, which can be switched while the database is open to users; however, only one undo tablespace can be active at a time.

You can use EM Database Control to both proactively monitor and resize the undo tablespace. For databases whose long-running queries have priority over successful DML transactions, you can specify that an undo tablespace retain expired undo information at the expense of failed transactions.

Exam Essentials

Know the syntax for how to insert data with either a list of values or a subquery. A list of values requires the keyword VALUES, while a subquery does not.

Know that PL/SQL functions have a RETURN clause. Functions have a datatype and a RETURN clause. The other PL/SQL programs do not.

Know how to enable and disable triggers. Use the ALTER TRIGGER statement to enable or disable any individual trigger and the ALTER TABLE ENABLE ALL TRIGGERS or ALTER TABLE DISABLE ALL TRIGGERS statement to enable or disable triggers en masse. You can also specify the ENABLE or DISABLE clause at the time of trigger creation.

Know the purpose of the Undo Advisor. Optimize the UNDO_RETENTION parameter as well as the size of the undo tablespace by using Undo Advisor. Use the graph on the Undo Advisor screen to perform what-if analyses given the undo retention requirements.

Be able to monitor locking and resolve lock conflicts. Identify the reasons for database lock conflicts, and explain how to resolve them. Show an example of a more serious type of lock conflict, a deadlock.

Understand the options to wait for acquiring a lock. The LOCK TABLE statement includes the WAIT clause to specify how long to wait to acquire a lock. You can set the initialization parameter DDL_LOCK_TIMEOUT to specify the number of seconds to wait when trying to acquire a DDL lock.

List the features supported by undo data in an undo tablespace. Enumerate the four primary uses for undo data: rollback, read consistency, database recovery, and flashback operations. Show how the rollback requirements for users who perform long transactions can interfere with read consistency required for query users. Be able to identify and use the method to preserve expired undo at the expense of transactions.

Summarize the steps for monitoring, configuring, and administering the undo tablespace. Set the initialization parameters required to use an undo tablespace. Be able to review the status of the undo tablespace using EM Database Control, and use the Undo Advisor to resize the undo tablespace when conditions warrant it. Alter the initialization parameter UNDO_RETENTION to configure how long undo information needs to be retained for long-running queries.

List the types of lock modes available when locking a table. Identify the locks available, from least restrictive to most restrictive. Be able to request a lock with either a LOCK or SELECT statement and return immediately if the lock is not available.

Review Questions

1. Changes made with an UPDATE statement are permanent in the database after what occurs?
   - A. DBWR flushes the changes to disk.
   - B. You issue a SAVEPOINT statement.
   - C. You issue a COMMIT statement.
   - D. A checkpoint occurs.

2. Why would you execute a CREATE OR REPLACE PROCEDURE statement instead of a DROP PROCEDURE statement and a CREATE PROCEDURE statement?
   - A. It is less typing.
   - B. There is no difference between the two.
   - C. CREATE OR REPLACE PROCEDURE does not invalidate dependent objects.
   - D. DROP PROCEDURE and CREATE PROCEDURE require regranting of privileges.

3. Which of the following is not a trigger event?
   - A. UPDATE
   - B. SELECT
   - C. NOAUDIT
   - D. SERVERERROR

4. You need to let an application role execute the SLEEP procedure in the DBMS_LOCK package but do not want to let an application role have access to the other more powerful capabilities of the DBMS_LOCK package. How can you satisfy these requirements best?
   - A. Grant EXECUTE on dbms_lock to the user system. Then create a procedure in the system schema that calls DBMS_LOCK.SLEEP. Finally, grant EXECUTE on this procedure to the application role.
   - B. Grant EXECUTE on DBMS_LOCK to the application role.
   - C. Grant EXECUTE on DMBS_LOCK.SLEEP to the application role.
   - D. Write your own procedure to mimic the functionality of the DBMS_LOCK.SLEEP procedure.

5. Which of the following INSERT statements raises an exception?
   - A. INSERT INTO ORDERS SELECT * FROM STANDING_ORDERS
   - B. INSERT FIRST WHEN ORDER_TYPE IN (2,5,12) THEN INSERT INTO ORDERS SELECT * FROM STANDING_ORDERS
   - C. INSERT FIRST WHEN ORDER_TYPE IN (2,5,12) THEN INTO ORDERS SELECT * FROM STANDING_ORDERS
   - D. INSERT INTO ALL WHEN ORDER_TYPE IN (2,5,12) THEN INTO ORDERS SELECT * FROM STANDING_ORDERS

6. What will be the salary of employee number 189 at the completion of the following SQL statements?

```
update emp set salary = 1000 where employee_num = 189;
savepoint save_1;
update emp set salary = salary * 1.1 where employee_num = 189;
savepoint save_2;
update emp set salary = salary * 1.1 where employee_num = 189;
savepoint save_3;
rollback to savepoint save_2;
commit;
update emp set salary = 1500 where employee_num = 189;
savepoint save_4;
rollback to save_4;
commit;
```

   A. 1,000
   B. 1,100
   C. 1,111
   D. 1,500

7. Which of the following commands returns an error if the transaction starts with SET TRANSACTION READ ONLY?
   A. ALTER SYSTEM
   B. SET ROLE
   C. ALTER USER
   D. None of the above

8. Guaranteed undo retention can be specified for which of the following objects?
   A. A tablespace
   B. A table
   C. The database
   D. A transaction
   E. The instance

9. Which of the following lock modes permits concurrent queries on a table but prohibits updates to the locked table?
   A. ROW SHARE
   B. ROW EXCLUSIVE
   C. EXCLUSIVE
   D. SHARE ROW EXCLUSIVE
   E. SHARE

10. Select the statement that is *not* true regarding undo tablespaces.

    A. Undo tablespaces will not be created if they are not specified in the CREATE DATABASE command.

    B. Two undo tablespaces can be active if a new undo tablespace was specified and the old one contains pending transactions.

    C. You can switch from one undo tablespace to another while the database is online.

    D. UNDO_MANAGEMENT cannot be changed dynamically while the instance is running.

11. To resolve a lock conflict, which of the following methods can you use? (Choose all that apply.)

    A. Oracle automatically resolves the lock after a short but predefined time period by killing the session that is holding the lock.

    B. The DBA can kill the session holding the lock.

    C. The user can either roll back or commit the transaction that is holding the lock.

    D. Oracle automatically resolves the lock after a short but predefined period by killing the session that is requesting the lock.

12. If all extents in an undo segment fill up, which of the following occurs next? (Choose all that apply.)

    A. A new extent is allocated in the undo segment if all existing extents still contain active transaction data.

    B. Other transactions using the segment are moved to another existing segment with enough free space.

    C. A new undo segment is created, and the transaction that filled up the undo segment is moved in its entirety to another undo segment.

    D. The first extent in the segment is reused if the undo data in the first extent is not needed.

    E. The transaction that filled up the undo segment spills over to another undo segment.

13. Which of the following commands returns control to the user immediately if a table is already locked by another user?

    A. `LOCK TABLE HR.EMPLOYEES IN EXCLUSIVE MODE WAIT DEFERRED;`

    B. `LOCK TABLE HR.EMPLOYEES IN SHARE MODE NOWAIT;`

    C. `LOCK TABLE HR.EMPLOYEES IN SHARE MODE WAIT DISABLED;`

    D. `LOCK TABLE HR.EMPLOYEES IN EXCLUSIVE MODE NOWAIT DEFERRED;`

14. Two transactions occur at the wall clock times in the following table. What happens at 10:05?

Session 1	Time	Session 2
`update customer set region = 'H' where state='WI' and county='GRANT';`	9:51	
	9:59	`update customer set mgr=201 where state='IA' and county='JOHNSON';`
`update customer set region='H' where state='IA' and county='JOHNSON';`	10:01	
	10:05	`update customer set mgr=201 where state='WI' and county='GRANT';`

   A. Session 2 will wait for session 1 to commit or roll back.
   B. Session 1 will wait for session 2 to commit or roll back.
   C. A deadlock will occur, and both sessions will hang unless one of the users cancels their statement or the DBA kills one of the sessions.
   D. A deadlock will occur, and Oracle will cancel one of the statements.
   E. Neither session is updating the same column, so no waiting or deadlock will occur.

15. Undo information falls into all the following categories except for which one?
   A. Uncommitted undo information
   B. Undo information required in case an instance crash requires a rollforward operation when the instance is restarted
   C. Committed undo information required to satisfy the undo retention interval
   D. Expired undo information that is no longer needed to support a running transaction

16. Undo segments are owned by which user?
   A. SYSTEM
   B. The user who initiated the transaction
   C. SYS
   D. The user who owns the object changed by the transaction

17. The EM Database Control Undo Advisor uses ____________ to recommend the new size of the undo tablespace.

A. the value of the parameter `UNDO_RETENTION`

B. the number of "Snapshot too old" errors

C. the current size of the undo tablespace

D. the desired amount of time to retain undo data

E. the most recent undo generation rate

18. A developer wants to write a PL/SQL program that inserts new data into the `cust_trans` table, for which `cust_id` is the primary key. The data is to read from the `new_cust_info` table, which is populated daily. If `cust_id` already exists in the `cust_trans` table, he wants to update the row with new information. Which option would you recommend?

A. Include the `EXCEPTION` clause in the PL/SQL program.

B. Use the `UPSERT` SQL statement instead of PL/SQL.

C. Use the `MERGE` SQL statement instead of PL/SQL.

D. Delete the rows from the `cust_trans` table that exist in the `new_cust_info` table, and then perform an insert from the `new_cust_info` table.

19. Choose the option that is true regarding locks in the Oracle 11*g* database.

A. When session 1 has a table locked using the `LOCK TABLE...EXCLUSIVE MODE` statement, all DML statements and queries wait until session1 does a `COMMIT` or `ROLLBACK`.

B. When `SELECT...FOR UPDATE` is performed, the table is locked.

C. The `DDL_LOCK_TIMEOUT` parameter can be set to `TRUE` to not return the ORA-00054 error.

D. The `LOCK TABLE` statement can include the `WAIT` clause to specify the number of seconds to wait for acquiring the lock.

20. Which can be used to execute a user-defined PL/SQL function named `IS_CREDIT_OK`? (Choose all that apply.)

A. `X := IS_CREDIT_OK`

B. `SELECT IS_CREDIT_OK INTO X FROM DUAL`

C. `EXECUTE IS_CREDIT_OK`

D. `RUN IS_CREDIT_OK`

Answers to Review Questions

1. C. A commit makes pending DML changes permanent. When a checkpoint occurs, DBWR flushes dirty buffers to disk, which is independent of transaction boundaries.

2. D. Using CREATE OR REPLACE PROCEDURE is less typing, but, more important, when you drop an object, all privileges granted on that object are dropped as well. When you perform a CREATE OR REPLACE PROCEDURE, you do not lose privileges granted on that object. When you drop and create a procedure, it invalidates all dependent objects, whereas if you re-create, the dependent objects are invalidated only if the procedure specification is changed.

3. B. You can create a trigger for just about any database event that involves a change to data, but you cannot create a SELECT trigger in Oracle 11g.

4. A. You cannot grant privileges on only one packaged procedure. You can grant EXECUTE only on the whole package. To be more restrictive in granting privileges, you need to create an intermediate procedure that calls the single procedure you want and grant EXECUTE on that intermediate procedure to the grantee. Granting a privilege to a role does not allow the role grantee to use that privilege in a PL/SQL program.

5. D. Single-table inserts must begin with the keywords INSERT INTO and cannot contain the keywords THEN INTO. Multitable INSERT statements cannot begin with the keywords INSERT INTO and may contain the keywords THEN INTO. Option D contains an invalid combination of keywords and will thus raise an exception.

6. D. The last ROLLBACK statement rolls back all DML statements since SAVEPOINT SAVE_4. The last UPDATE was executed before the SAVEPOINT to SAVE_4; therefore, the change made by the last UPDATE is unchanged, and the salary remains 1,500.

7. D. When you use SET TRANSACTION READ ONLY, no data changes can be made in the transaction. You can do DDL changes though. DDL statements does an implicit COMMIT and ends the transaction. ALTER USER is a DDL statement.

8. A. Guaranteed undo retention can be set at the tablespace level by using the RETENTION GUARANTEE clause with either the CREATE TABLESPACE or ALTER TABLESPACE command. Only undo tablespaces can have this attribute.

9. E. SHARE mode permits concurrent queries but prohibits updates to the locked table. SHARE mode is required to create an index on the table.

10. A. If an undo tablespace is not explicitly created in the CREATE DATABASE command, Oracle automatically creates one with the name SYS_UNDOTBS.

11. B, C. Locks are resolved at the user level by either committing or rolling back the transaction holding the lock. Also, the DBA can kill the session holding the lock as a last resort.

12. A, D. If a transaction fills up an undo segment, either a new extent is allocated for the undo segment or other extents in the segment are reused if the undo data in those extents is no longer needed by other transactions using the same undo segment. Transactions cannot cross segment boundaries in an undo tablespace, and they cannot move to another segment.

13. B. Regardless of the type of lock requested, NOWAIT is required if you want the command with the lock request to terminate immediately if a lock is already held on the table.

14. D. At 10:01, session 1 waits for session 2. At 10:05, a deadlock will occur; Oracle detects the deadlock and cancels one of the statements.

15. B. Undo information is required for instance recovery but only to roll back uncommitted transactions after the online redo logs roll forward.

16. C. Undo segments are always owned by SYS.

17. D. The Undo Advisor uses the desired time period for undo data retention and analyzes the impact of the desired undo retention setting.

18. C. Though options A and D can be used to achieve the same result, they are not the most efficient. There is no UPSERT statement in Oracle 11*g*. The MERGE statement is used to conditionally update or insert rows into a table.

19. D. In Oracle, locks never block readers. Option A is true, if it did not include the word *queries* in it. Only DML statements wait when the table is locked in exclusive mode. SELECT...FOR UPDATE locks only the rows returned by the SELECT clause; it does not lock the table. The DDL_LOCK_TIMEOUT parameter is used to specify the number of seconds to wait when DDL statements on locked objects are executed. The LOCK TABLE statement can include the WAIT clause to specify the number of seconds to wait to acquire the lock.

20. A, B. A function always returns a value; hence, the function can be used in the SELECT statements and assignments. Functions can also be used in PL/SQL constructs such as IF statements. EXECUTE is used to run a procedure. RUN is used to execute a SQL or PL/SQL script file.

Maintaining the Database and Managing Performance

ORACLE DATABASE 11*g*: ADMINISTRATION I EXAM OBJECTIVES COVERED IN THIS CHAPTER:

✓ **Database Maintenance**

- Use and manage Optimizer Statistics
- Use and manage Automatic Workload Repository (AWR)
- Use Advisory Framework
- Manage Alerts and Thresholds

✓ **Performance Management**

- Use Automatic Memory Management
- Use Memory Advisors
- Troubleshoot invalid and unusable objects

Successful database administrators are always on the lookout for potential database problems that could adversely impact the availability or performance of the systems they manage. Fortunately, Oracle 11*g* comes with an array for proactive performance monitoring and an alert mechanism to help you do this.

The Oracle Database 11*g* periodically collects statistics on the database objects and uses the statistics to find the best execution plan for a SQL statement. The Automatic Workload Repository collects, analyzes, and maintains the performance statistics of the database. Oracle 11*g* also offers several advisors that help DBAs fine-tune the database components. One new tool is Automatic Memory Management, which greatly simplifies memory management. In this chapter, you will learn about all the database-management and performance-management tools available to DBAs for better database administration.

Proactive Database Maintenance

You can monitor your systems for management and performance problems in essentially two ways:

- *Reactive monitoring* involves monitoring a database environment after a performance or management issue has arisen. For example, you start gathering performance statistics using third-party tools, EM, or homegrown scripts after users call to tell you that the system is slow. Obviously, this type of monitoring leaves a lot to be desired because a problem has already arisen and the users of the system are already impacted. You can use the techniques discussed in this chapter for reactive monitoring, but they are most effective when used to perform proactive monitoring.
- *Proactive monitoring* allows you to identify and respond to common database-performance and -management issues before they occur. Most of the features in Enterprise Manager Database Control are geared toward proactive monitoring.

The database-maintenance framework in Oracle 11*g* consists of these proactive tool sets:

- Automated tasks, such as collecting optimizer statistics
- Automatic Workload Repository
- Advisory Framework
- Server alerts and thresholds

Automatic Diagnostic Repository, where the alert log and trace information are kept, is used for reactive database maintenance.

The monitoring tools available in EM Database Control collect their information from a variety of sources including data dictionary views, dynamic performance views, and the operating system. Oracle 11*g* also makes extensive use of the cost-based optimizer statistics for its proactive monitoring. But discussing all the database-maintenance options available in Oracle 11*g* is not in the scope of this book; it is a large topic that warrants its own book. In the following section, you will instead learn the database-maintenance options available in Oracle 11*g* that are relevant to the OCP certification exam.

Managing Optimizer Statistics

Optimizer statistics are a collection of important statistical data that describe the contents of the database. The query optimizer uses the optimizer statistics to find the best way to get to the row of data the query wants to find. The database collects statistics on objects that have segments allocated as well as overall system statistics. The optimizer uses the statistics to decide how to do the following:

- Access data and determine which indexes to use
- Join tables
- Evaluate expressions and conditions

The *cost-based optimizer* (CBO) uses these statistics to formulate efficient execution plans for each SQL statement that is issued by application users. For example, the CBO may have to decide whether to use an available index when processing a query. The CBO can only make an effective guess at the proper execution plan when it knows the number of rows in the table, the size and type of indexes on that table, and how many rows the CBO expects to be returned by a query. Because of this, the statistics gathered and stored in the data dictionary views are sometimes called optimizer statistics.

The following are some of the statistics collected:

- Table and index statistics
  - Total number of rows in table and average row length
  - Total number of blocks used
  - Levels and number of leaf blocks for indexes
- Column statistics
  - Number of distinct values in a column
  - Number of `NULL` values
  - Low value and high value for a column
  - Data distribution and data skew
- System statistics
  - Disk I/O performance
  - CPU performance

You can use the `DBMS_STATS` package to collect optimizer statistics in the database. `DBMS_STATS` has several subprograms (procedures and functions) to collect and manage statistics. In the following sections, you will learn how to collect optimizer statistics and what management options are available to maintain the statistics.

Optimizer statistics are a snapshot of statistical information at a specific point in time. They are persistent across instance restarts because they are stored in the data dictionary tables.

Collecting Statistics

In an Oracle 11*g* database, you'll rarely need to manually collect statistics. The default collection frequency and options are good for most of the database environments. You may have to collect statistics manually when you bulk load data into a table or when you delete several rows from the table. Sometimes you may have to create histograms for the optimizer to be able to make better execution plans based on the query.

When you create the Oracle 11*g* database using DBCA, gathering optimizer statistics is automatically set up and enabled using the Automated Maintenance Tasks (AutoTask) infrastructure. AutoTask schedules maintenance tasks to run automatically, using the Oracle Scheduler, during maintenance windows. Automatic optimizer statistics are collected using the procedure `DBMS_STATS.GATHER_DATABASE_STATS_JOB_PROC`. This procedure collects statistics on objects that have no statistics collected or have stale statistics. Oracle Database considers statistics stale when more than 10 percent of data in the table has changed since statistics were gathered on the table. This procedure also prioritizes the objects that need the statistics collected and processes them first.

You can enable and disable the automatic optimizer statistics gathering by using the `DBMS_AUTO_TASK` package. To disable the automatic statistics gathering, use the `DISABLE` subprogram as shown here:

```
BEGIN
  DBMS_AUTO_TASK_ADMIN.DISABLE (
       client_name=>'auto optimizer stats collection',
       operation=>NULL, window_name=>NULL);
END;
```

If you disable the automatic statistics gathering, make sure you collect statistics manually so that the optimizer produces intelligent execution plans. To enable automatic statistics gathering, use the `ENABLE` subprogram as follows:

```
BEGIN
  DBMS_AUTO_TASK_ADMIN.ENABLE (
       client_name=>'auto optimizer stats collection',
       operation=>NULL, window_name=>NULL);
END;
```

To view the status of AutoTask jobs, you can run the following query:

```
SQL> SELECT client_name, status FROM dba_autotask_client;
```

```
CLIENT_NAME                              STATUS
---------------------------------------- --------
auto optimizer stats collection          ENABLED
auto space advisor                       ENABLED
sql tuning advisor                       ENABLED
```

You can collect the statistics manually using the DBMS_STATS procedure from SQL*Plus or using EM Database Control.

Manually Collecting Stats Using SQL*Plus

Collecting manual statistics is useful for tables and indexes whose storage characteristics change frequently or that need to be analyzed outside the normal analysis window. Manual statistics may also need to be collected if the data in the table is highly volatile, such as when you truncate and load the table often. For such tables, you can collect the statistics when the table is fully loaded and lock the statistics so that subsequent statistics-gathering jobs do not override the statistics. The following example shows collecting statistics on a table and locking the statistics:

```
BEGIN
  DBMS_STATS.GATHER_TABLE_STATS('HR','EMPLOYEES', cascade=>TRUE);
  DBMS_STATS.LOCK_TABLE_STATS('HR','EMPLOYEES');
END;
```

Procedures are available to collect optimizer statistics at the database, schema, table, or index level. Table 14.1 shows the optimizer's statistics-gathering procedures.

TABLE 14.1 DBMS_STATS Statistics-Gathering Procedures

Procedure Name	Purpose
GATHER_TABLE_STATS	Collects table, column, and index stats
GATHER_INDEX_STATS	Collects index stats
GATHER_SCHEMA_STATS	Collects stats on all objects in the schema
GATHER_DATABASE_STATS	Collects stats on all objects in all schemas of the database
GATHER_DICTIONARY_STATS	Collects statistics on SYS-owned dictionary objects

The following example collects statistics on all objects owned by the HR schema, sampling 10 percent of rows for the statistics gathering:

```
SQL> EXEC DBMS_STATS.GATHER_SCHEMA_STATS('HR',estimate_percent=>10);
PL/SQL procedure successfully completed.
SQL>
```

For complete details of the many options available in the DBMS_STATS package, see Chapter 127 of the "Oracle Database PL/SQL Packages and Types Reference 11*g* Release 1 (11.1) Part Number B28419-03" documentation, available at `http://tahiti.oracle.com`.

Manually Collecting Stats Using EM Grid Control

You can use the EM Gather Statistics Wizard to manually collect statistics for individual segments, schemas, or the database as a whole. To start the wizard, click the Server tab on the EM Database Control screen, and click the Manage Optimizer Statistics link under Query Optimizer (Figure 14.1).

FIGURE 14.1 Server tab in EM Grid Control

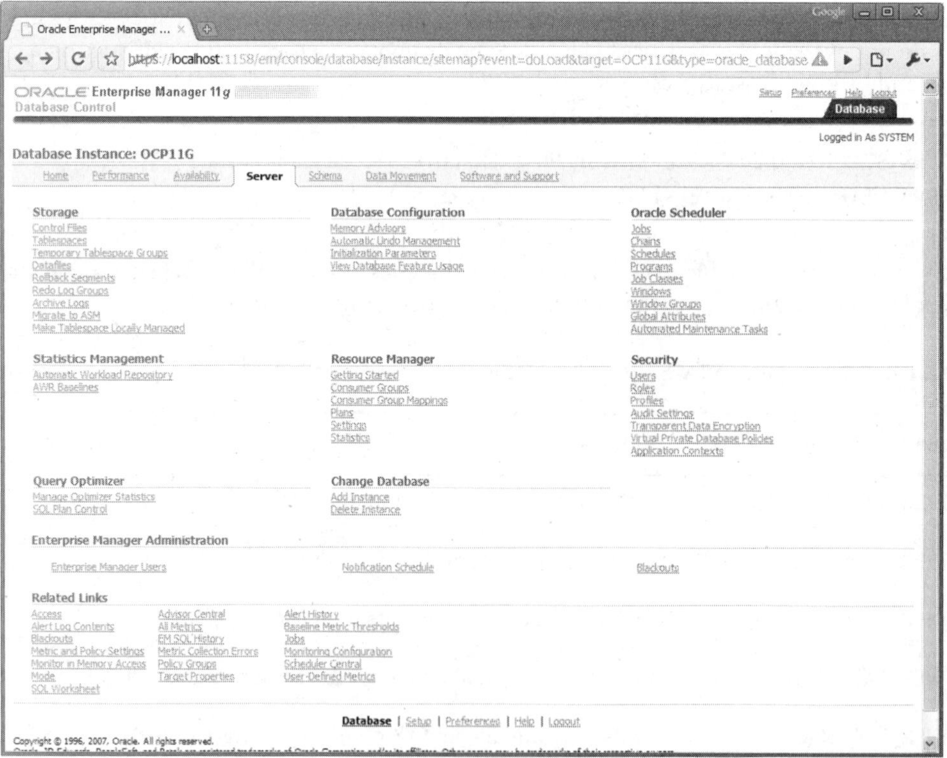

You can choose from several options in addition to gathering optimizer statistics, as shown on the Manage Optimizer Statistics screen (Figure 14.2). Whenever you collect statistics, existing statistics are saved to history tables and preserved for 31 days. You can click the Restore Optimizer Statistics link to restore old statistics. You can also lock, unlock, and delete statistics.

FIGURE 14.2 Manage Optimizer Statistics screen in EM Grid Control

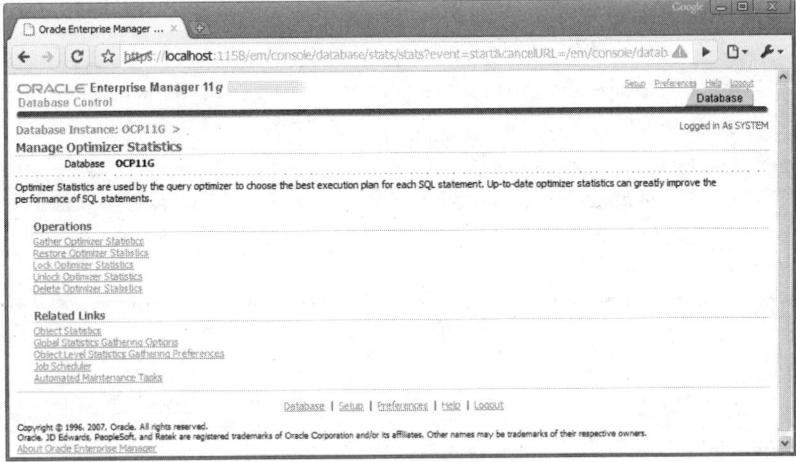

Click the Gather Optimizer Statistics link on the Manage Optimizer Statistics screen. You can collect statistics at the database, schema, object, or system level. Choose the options needed to collect statistics, as shown in Figure 14.3.

FIGURE 14.3 Gather Optimizer Statistics screen in EM Database Control

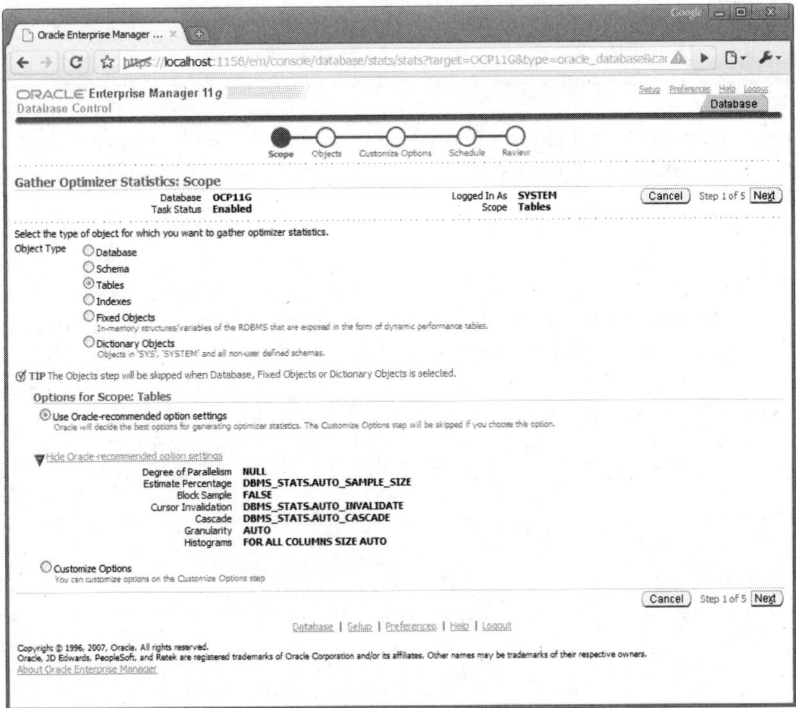

You will be taken through scope, objects, options, schedule, and review screens. Provide the options needed for the statistics collection. If you have chosen to customize the options shown in Figure 14.3, you will get a screen similar to Figure 14.4 for choosing options.

FIGURE 14.4 Customize Options for the Gather Optimizer Statistics screen in EM Database Control

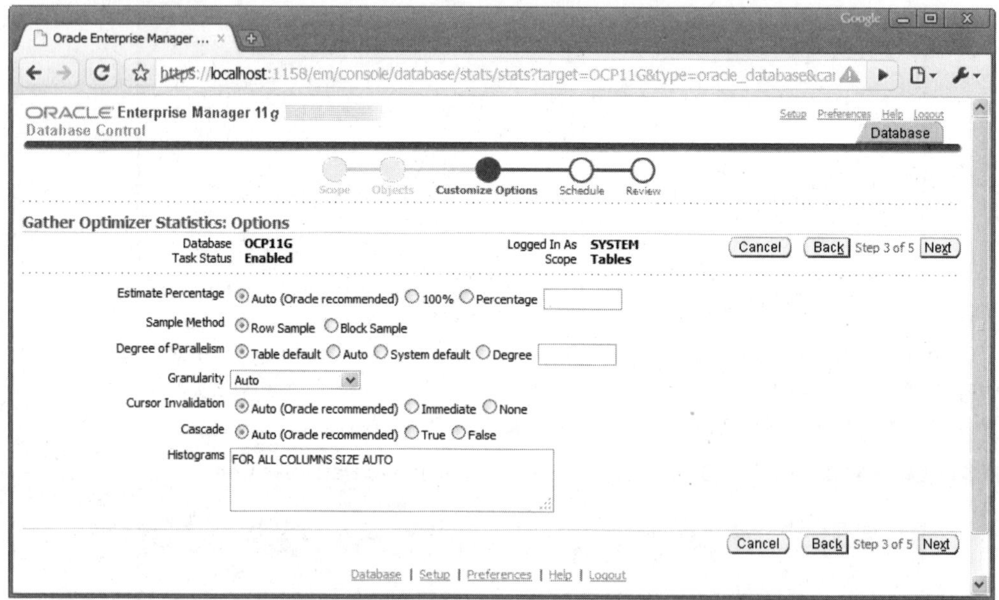

You can also view the SQL behind the options you have chosen by clicking the Show SQL button. Figure 14.5 shows the code behind a statistics-gathering job for two HR-owned tables.

To read more about collecting and managing optimizer statistics, read Chapter 13 from the "Oracle Database Performance Tuning Guide 11*g* Release 1 (11.1) Part Number B28274-01" Oracle documentation.

In the next section, you will learn how to set preferences for statistics gathering.

FIGURE 14.5 Show SQL for the Gather Optimizer Statistics screen in EM Grid Control

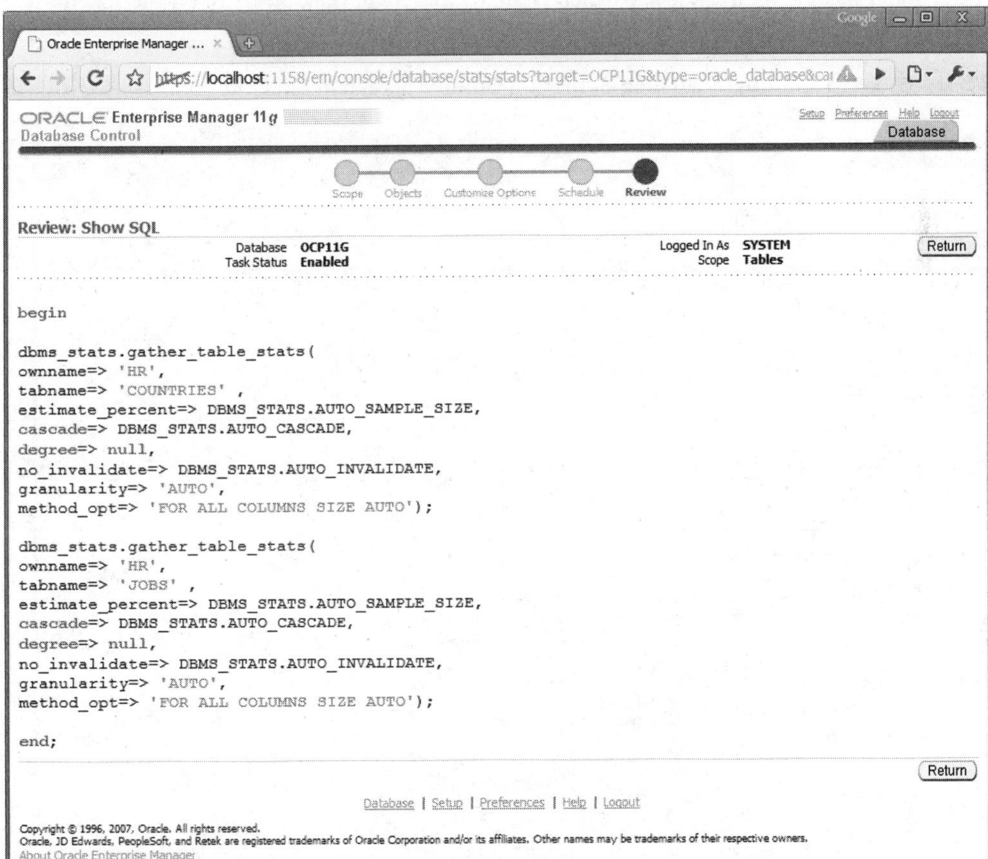

Defining Statistics Preferences

The default staleness percentage for statistics gathering is 10; if you want to change this and other default options, you can set the preferences for statistics gathering using EM Grid Control or using DBMS_STATS directly. In this section, you will learn how to set preferences using EM Database Control, and using the Show SQL option, you can see the DBMS_STATS code behind it.

On the EM Database Control Manage Optimizer statistics screen (shown earlier in Figure 14.2), you can click the Global Statistics Gathering and Object Level Statistics Gathering Preferences links.

Figure 14.6 shows the Global Statistics Gathering Options screen. Using this screen, you set the preferences at a global level, which is applicable to all the objects in all the schemas, unless specific schema or object level preferences are set.

FIGURE 14.6 Global Statistics Gathering Options screen in EM Grid Control

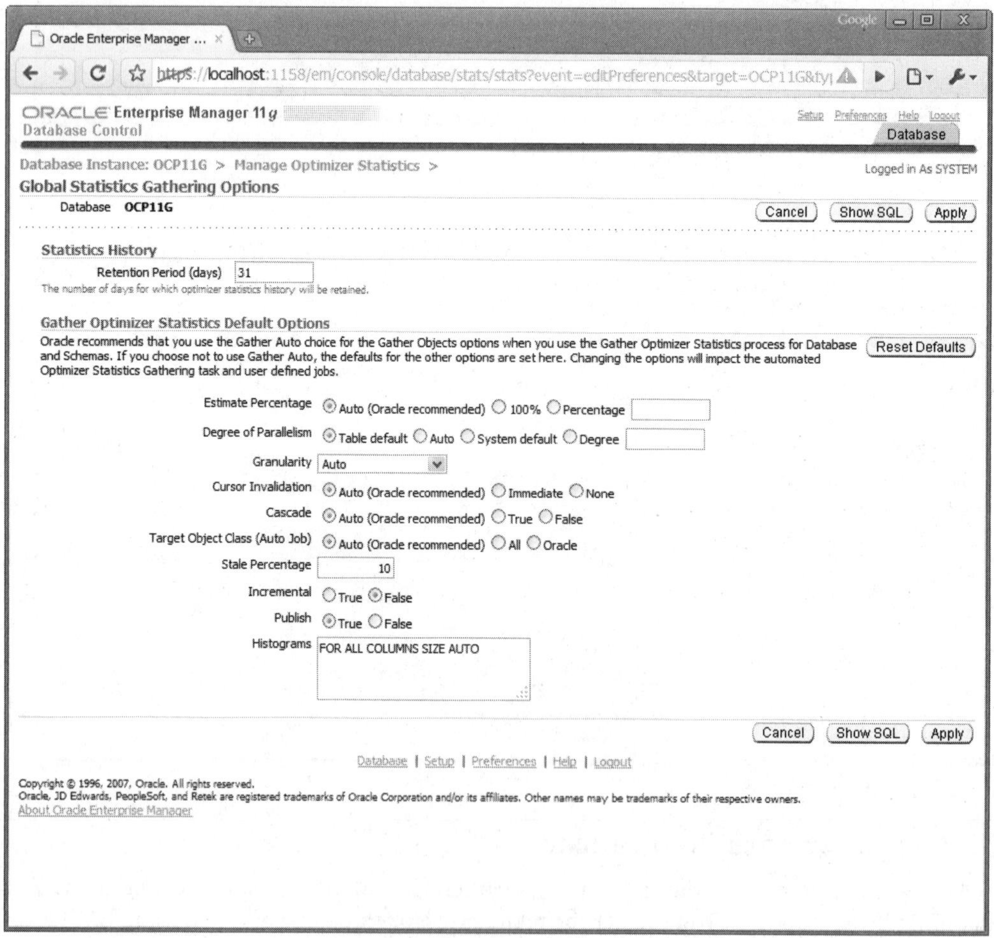

Here you can change the retention period for how long optimizer statistics history is kept in the database (DBMS_STATS.ALTER_STATS_HISTORY_RETENTION), as well as other default options (DBMS_STATS.SET_GLOBAL_PREFS). Table 14.2 shows the EM Grid Control option and its corresponding preference name when using DBMS_SQL.

If you want to minimize the time required to collect table statistics for partitioned tables, you can set the global preference INCREMENTAL to TRUE, where only statistics on a (new) partition are gathered and the table statistics are adjusted accordingly:

```
EXEC DBMS_STATS.SET_GLOBAL_PREFS ('INCREMENTAL', 'TRUE');
```

TABLE 14.2 DBMS_STATS.SET_GLOBAL_PREFS Preferences

Preference Parameter	EM Database Control Option	Purpose
ESTIMATE_PERCENT	Estimate Percent	Sets the percentage of rows in the table to consider when estimating statistics
DEGREE	Degree of Parallelism	Specifies how many parallel processes are used to gather stats
GRANULARITY	Granularity	Determines granularity of statistics to collect for partitioned tables
NO_INVALIDATE	Cursor Invalidation	Determines whether dependent cursors should be made invalid
CASCADE	Cascade	Determines whether index statistics should be gathered when table statistics are gathered
AUTOSTATS_TARGET	Target Object Class	Determines which objects are considered for automatic statistics collection
STALE_PERCENT	Stale Percent	Sets the percentage of rows that need to change before statistics are gathered again
INCREMENTAL	Incremental	Gives global stats on the partitioned table maintained without doing a full scan
PUBLISH	Publish	Determines whether newly gathered stats are published immediately
METHOD_OPT	Histograms	Sets options for collecting histograms

Similar to global stats preferences, you can also set preferences on a table or schema. Click the Object Level Statistics Gathering Preferences link on the Manage Optimizer Statistics screen (Figure 14.2). Figure 14.7 shows the Object Level Statistics Gathering Preferences screen.

FIGURE 14.7 Object Level Statistics Gathering Preferences screen in EM Grid Control

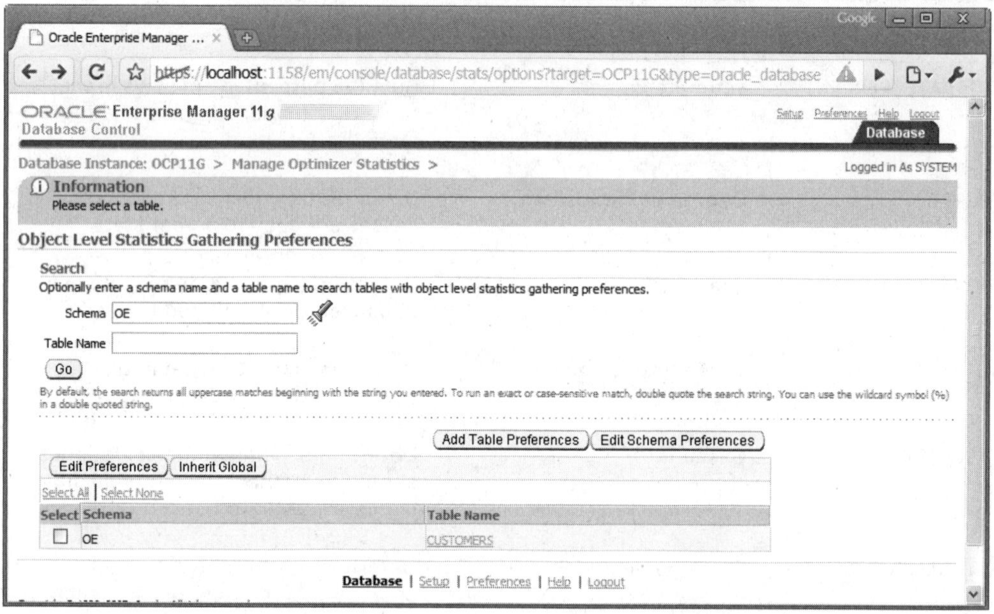

To view the tables where preferences are set, enter the filters, if any (schema and/or table name), and click Go. You have the following options on this screen:

- Select existing tables, and click Edit Preferences to edit (this runs DBMS_STATS.SET_TABLE_PREFS).
- Select existing tables, and click Inherit Global to remove preferences (this runs DBMS_STATS.DELETE_TABLE_PREFS).
- Click Add Table Preferences to set table preferences on a new table (this runs DBMS_STATS.SET_TABLE_PREFS).
- Click Edit Schema Preferences to add/edit schema preferences (this runs DBMS_STATS.SET_SCHEMA_PREFS).

The data dictionary view DBA_TAB_STAT_PREFS (or ALL_ or USER_) gives the tables with a preference set. Remember, when you use the SET_SCHEMA_PREFS procedure, DBMS_STATS adds an entry to this view for each table under the schema. When you use the SET_DATABASE_PREFS procedure, DBMS_STATS adds an entry to this view for each table in the database except system tables. To include system tables, set the third parameter to TRUE.

Let's explore two important features of Oracle 11*g* statistics gathering using the table preferences.

Changing the Default Staleness Threshold

Since Oracle10*g*, tables have had the default MONITORING enabled. The statistics-collection job looks for staleness of 10 percent or more for it to reanalyze the table. In Oracle 11*g*, you can specify the threshold value for each table if you want to override the 10 percent default using SET_TABLE_PREFS. Here's an example:

```
SQL> exec dbms_stats.set_table_prefs('SH','CUSTOMERS','STALE_PERCENT','20');
PL/SQL procedure successfully completed.

SQL> DESCRIBE dba_tab_stat_prefs
 Name                          Null?    Type
 ----------------------------- -------- ----------------------------
 OWNER                         NOT NULL VARCHAR2(30)
 TABLE_NAME                    NOT NULL VARCHAR2(30)
 PREFERENCE_NAME                        VARCHAR2(30)
 PREFERENCE_VALUE                       VARCHAR2(1000)

SQL> SELECT table_name, preference_name, preference_value
     FROM dba_tab_stat_prefs;

TABLE_NAME     PREFERENCE_NAME        PREFERENCE_VALUE
-------------- ---------------------- -------------------
CUSTOMERS      STALE_PERCENT          20
```

You can also use the function GET_PREFS to verify the preference value. The function returns the custom defined preference value. And if no such value is defined, it returns the default.

```
SQL> SELECT dbms_stats.get_prefs('STALE_PERCENT','SH','CUSTOMERS')
     FROM dual;

DBMS_STATS.GET_PREFS('STALE_PERCENT','SH','CUSTOMERS')
---------------------------------------------------------------
20

SQL> SELECT dbms_stats.get_prefs('STALE_PERCENT','HR','EMPLOYEES')
     FROM dual;

DBMS_STATS.GET_PREFS('STALE_PERCENT','HR','EMPLOYEES')
----------------------------------------------------------------
10
```

Pending Statistics

In Oracle 11*g*, the statistics gathering is divided into two steps—collect statistics and publish. By default, the behavior is like pre–Oracle 11*g* databases; the statistics will be available (published) to all users as soon as the stats are gathered. If you want to test the implications of the new statistics before making it available to all users in the database, you can do so. This is helpful to test the new statistics to make sure they do not affect the database negatively.

To test with the new statistics before making them available to all users, perform these steps:

1. Set the table preference parameter PUBLISH to FALSE. If you're messing with many tables, you can use the SET_SCHEMA_PREFS, SET_DATABASE_PREFS, or SET_GLOBAL_PREFS procedure. For demonstrating the example, the statistics on table HR.EMPLOYEES are deleted:

```
SQL> select table_name, num_rows, last_analyzed from dba_tables
  2  where owner = 'HR' and table_name = 'EMPLOYEES';
TABLE_NAME NUM_ROWS   LAST_ANAL
---------- ---------- ---------
EMPLOYEES

SQL> select dbms_stats.get_prefs('PUBLISH','HR','EMPLOYEES')
     from dual;
DBMS_STATS.GET_PREFS('PUBLISH','HR','EMPLOYEES')
-----------------------------------------------------------
TRUE

SQL> exec dbms_stats.set_table_prefs('HR','EMPLOYEES','PUBLISH','FALSE');
PL/SQL procedure successfully completed.
```

2. Gather table statistics as you normally would using the DBMS_STATS package. Since the PUBLISH preference is set to FALSE, you do not see the statistics:

```
SQL> exec dbms_stats.gather_table_stats('HR','EMPLOYEES');
PL/SQL procedure successfully completed.

SQL> select num_rows, last_analyzed from dba_tables
  2  where owner = 'HR' and table_name = 'EMPLOYEES';
  NUM_ROWS LAST_ANAL
---------- ---------
```

3. You can verify the pending statistics by querying DBA_TAB_PENDING_STATS:

```
SQL> select table_name, num_rows, blocks, sample_size
  2  from dba_tab_pending_stats;
```

```
TABLE_NAME          NUM_ROWS     BLOCKS SAMPLE_SIZE
---------------- ---------- ---------- -----------
EMPLOYEES                107          5         107
```

4. Test your SQL by making the pending statistics visible:

```
SQL> alter session set optimizer_use_pending_statistics = true;
```

5. When you're ready to publish the statistics, perform the following:

```
SQL> exec dbms_stats.publish_pending_stats('HR','EMPLOYEES');
PL/SQL procedure successfully completed.

SQL> select num_rows, last_analyzed from dba_tables
  2  where owner = 'HR' and table_name = 'EMPLOYEES';
  NUM_ROWS LAST_ANAL
---------- ---------
       107 15-FEB-08

SQL> select table_name, num_rows, blocks, sample_size
  2  from dba_tab_pending_stats;
no rows selected
```

The PUBLISH_PENDING_STATS procedure accepts the schema name and table name as the first two parameters. If you specify NULL for the schema name, the default user's schema will be used. If you specify NULL for the table name, all pending stats on all tables in the schema are published.

Extended Statistics

In Oracle 11*g*, you can tell the optimizer the relationship between columns by using the *extended statistics* feature (multicolumn statistics). The extended statistics feature also includes statistics on columns where a function is applied (function-based statistics). By collecting extended statistics on columns, the optimizer will be able to estimate the selectivity better.

To collect multicolumn statistics (extended histograms), use the GATHER_TABLE_STATS procedure with the METHOD_OPT option like you would collect normal histogram statistics.

To create multicolumn statistics and function-based statistics, follow these two steps:

1. Create an extended statistics group using the DBMS_STATS.CREATE_EXTENDED_STATS function. The function returns the name of the extended stat group created. This function has three arguments: the owner, the table name, and the extension. The "extension" could be a combination of columns, up to 32 or expression on column (for function-based statistics, discussed later).
2. Collect histogram statistics on the table using the GATHER_TABLE_STATS procedure. FOR ALL COLUMNS SIZE SKEWONLY is a good option because Oracle collects histograms only on columns with large data distribution.

Collecting Extended Table Statistics: An Example

I'll now demonstrate the extended statistics feature of Oracle 11*g* with an example. The CUSTOMERS table is populated and has about 91,000 rows. Statistics are collected on the table with the FOR ALL ROWS SIZE AUTO option:

```
SQL> select column_name, num_distinct, histogram
  2  from dba_tab_col_statistics
  3  where owner = 'BTHOMAS' and table_name = 'CUSTOMERS';

COLUMN_NAME                    NUM_DISTINCT HISTOGRAM
------------------------------ ------------ ---------------
CUST_COUNTRY                              3 FREQUENCY
CUST_STATE                                6 FREQUENCY
CUST_NAME                             47692 NONE

SQL>
SQL> select * from customers where cust_country = 'India' and cust_state =
'TN';

-------------------------------------------------------------------------------
| Id  | Operation          | Name      | Rows  | Bytes | Cost (%CPU)| Time     |
-------------------------------------------------------------------------------
|   0 | SELECT STATEMENT   |           |  1447 | 41963 |   137   (1)| 00:00:02 |
|*  1 |  TABLE ACCESS FULL| CUSTOMERS |  1447 | 41963 |   137   (1)| 00:00:02 |
-------------------------------------------------------------------------------

Predicate Information (identified by operation id):
---------------------------------------------------

   1 - filter("CUST_STATE"='TN' AND "CUST_COUNTRY"='India')


SQL> SELECT dbms_stats.create_extended_stats('BTHOMAS','CUSTOMERS',
              '(CUST_COUNTRY, CUST_STATE)') EXTSTAT
     FROM dual;
```

```
EXTSTAT
--------------------------------
SYS_STUZVS6GX30A0GN_5YRYSD2LPM


SQL>
SQL> exec dbms_stats.gather_table_stats(null, 'customers',
         method_opt=>'for all columns size skewonly');

PL/SQL procedure successfully completed.

SQL> select column_name, num_distinct, histogram
  2  from user_tab_col_statistics
  3* where table_name = 'CUSTOMERS'
SQL> /

COLUMN_NAME                    NUM_DISTINCT HISTOGRAM
------------------------------ ------------ ---------------
CUST_NAME                             47692 HEIGHT BALANCED
CUST_STATE                                6 FREQUENCY
CUST_COUNTRY                              3 FREQUENCY
SYS_STUZVS6GX30A0GN_5YRYSD2LPM            8 FREQUENCY

SQL> select * from customers where cust_country = 'India' and cust_state =
'TN';

----------------------------------------------------------------------------
| Id  | Operation         | Name      | Rows  | Bytes | Cost (%CPU)| Time     |
----------------------------------------------------------------------------
|   0 | SELECT STATEMENT  |           |    86 |  2580 |   137   (1)| 00:00:02 |
|*  1 |  TABLE ACCESS FULL| CUSTOMERS |    86 |  2580 |   137   (1)| 00:00:02 |
----------------------------------------------------------------------------

Predicate Information (identified by operation id):
---------------------------------------------------
   1 - filter("CUST_STATE"='TN' AND "CUST_COUNTRY"='India')
```

As you can see in the example, before extended statistics were collected, the estimated number of rows was 1447, whereas after the extended statistics collection, the number of rows optimizer estimated to return is 86.

To drop the extend statistics, use the DROP_EXTENDED_STATISTICS procedure:

```
SQL> exec dbms_stats.drop_extended_stats(null,'CUSTOMERS',
        '(CUST_COUNTRY, CUST_STATE)');
PL/SQL procedure successfully completed.
SQL>
```

To define the extension and collect statistics in one step, you can do the following:

```
SQL> exec dbms_stats.gather_table_stats(null, 'customers',
          method_opt=>'for all columns size skewonly
          for columns (cust_country, cust_state)');
PL/SQL procedure successfully completed.

SQL> select extension_name, extension from user_stat_extensions
  2  where table_name = 'CUSTOMERS';

EXTENSION_NAME                       EXTENSION
------------------------------------ -----------------------------
SYS_STUZVS6GX30A0GN_5YRYSD2LPM       ("CUST_COUNTRY","CUST_STATE")
```

In the next section, you'll learn to enable and disable the automatic statistics collection as well as perform other AutoTask jobs.

Configuring Automated Maintenance Tasks Using EM

The following are three default automated maintenance tasks:

- Gathering optimizer statistics
- Running the Segment Advisor
- Running the SQL Tuning Advisor

You can also enable and disable the AutoTask jobs using EM Grid Control. On the Server tab, choose Automated Maintenance Tasks under Oracle Scheduler. Figure 14.8 shows the Automated Maintenance Tasks screen.

By clicking the Configure button, you can enable or disable the default AutoTask jobs, as well as adjust the days on which these tasks are run, as shown in Figure 14.9.

To learn more about Automated Maintenance Tasks and Oracle Scheduler, read the "Oracle Database Administrator's Guide 11*g* Release 1 (11.1) Part Number B28310-04" Oracle documentation.

FIGURE 14.8 Automated Maintenance Tasks screen

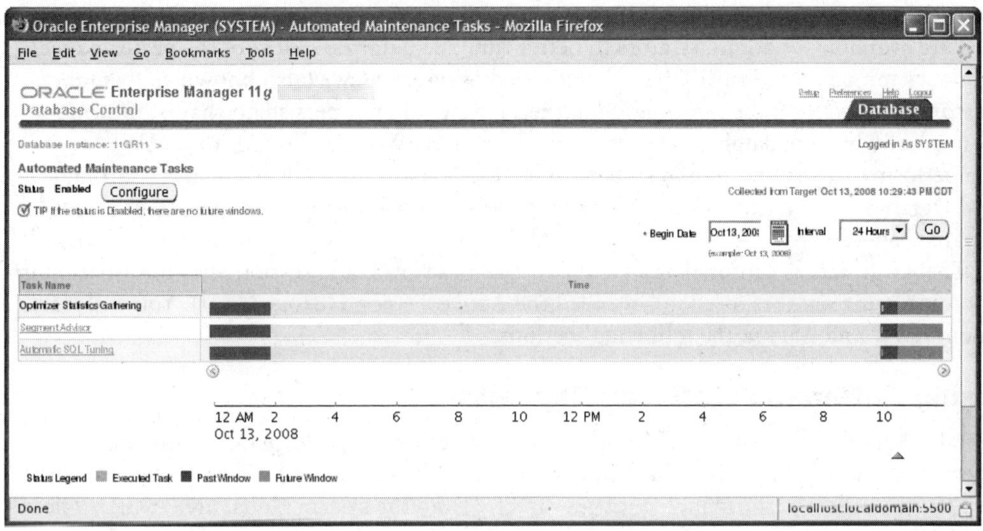

FIGURE 14.9 Configure Automated Maintenance Tasks screen

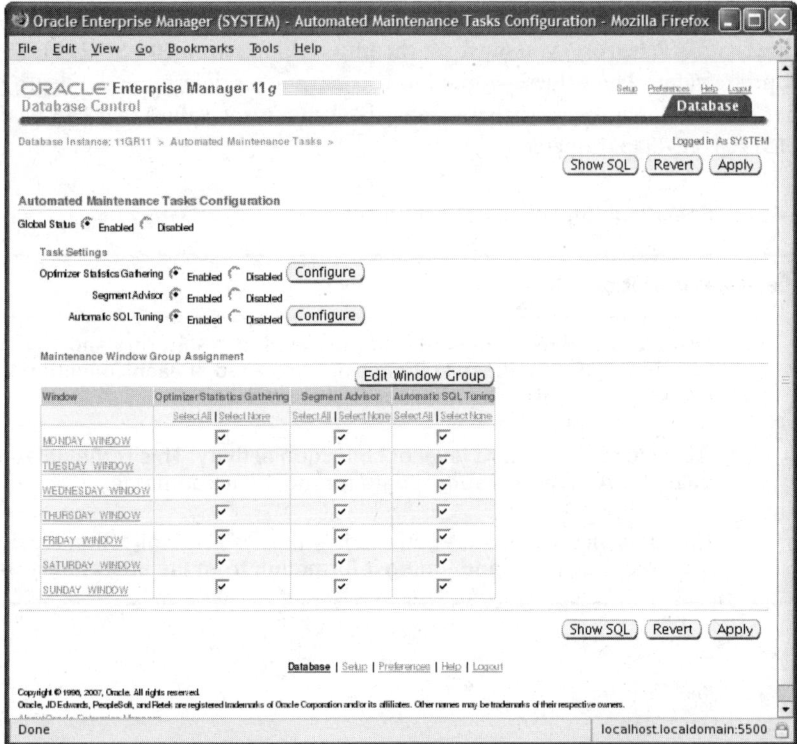

Gathering Performance Statistics

Oracle Database generates several performance statistics that are used for self-tuning purposes and are available for administrators to better tune the database. Most of the performance statistics information is available through V$ dictionary views (also known as *dynamic performance views*). The information in the V$ views are not persistent; that is, information is lost when the database is shut down. Automatic Workload Repository (AWR) saves the performance information in system tables and is made available for analysis through EM Database Control and other third-party tools. AWR information is persistent across database shutdowns.

The AWR data is captured at a system or database level, and session-level information is captured using another mechanism called the Active Session History (ASH). You will learn about AWR and ASH in the following sections.

Using Automatic Workload Repository

Two background processes are responsible for collecting the performance statistics: Memory Monitor (MMON) and Memory Monitor Light (MMNL). These processes work together to collect performance statistics directly from the system global area (SGA). The MMON process does most of the work by waking up every 60 minutes and gathering statistical information from the data dictionary views, dynamic performance views, and optimizer and then storing this information in the database. The tables that store these statistics are the Automatic Workload Repository. These tables are owned by the user SYSMAN and are stored in the SYSAUX tablespace.

To activate the AWR feature, you must set the pfile/spfile's parameter STATISTICS_LEVEL to the appropriate value. The values assigned to this parameter determine the depth of the statistics that the MMON process gathers. Table 14.3 shows the values that can be assigned to the STATISTICS_LEVEL parameter.

TABLE 14.3 Specifying Statistics Collection Levels

Collection Level	Description
BASIC	Disables the AWR and most other diagnostic monitoring and advisory activities. Few database statistics are gathered at each collection interval when operating the instance in this mode.
TYPICAL	Activates the standard level of collection activity. This is the default value for AWR and is appropriate for most environments.
ALL	Captures all the statistics gathered by the TYPICAL collection level, plus the execution plans and timing information from the operating system.

Once gathered, the statistics are stored in the AWR for a default duration of eight days. However, you can modify both the frequency of the snapshots and the duration for which they are saved in the AWR. One way to modify these intervals is by using the Oracle-supplied package DBMS_WORKLOAD_REPOSITORY. The following SQL command shows the DBMS_WORKLOAD_REPOSITORY package being used to change the AWR collection interval to 1 hour and the retention period to 30 days:

```
SQL> execute dbms_workload_repository.modify_snapshot_settings
            (interval=>60,retention=>43200);
PL/SQL procedure successfully completed.
```

The 30-day retention value shown here is expressed in minutes: 60 minutes per hour × 24 hours per day × 30 days = 43,200 minutes.

You can also change the AWR collection interval, retention period, and collection depth using EM Database Control. Choose the Server tab, and click Automatic Workload Repository under Statistics Management (see Figure 14.10).

FIGURE 14.10 AWR statistics collection and retention using EM

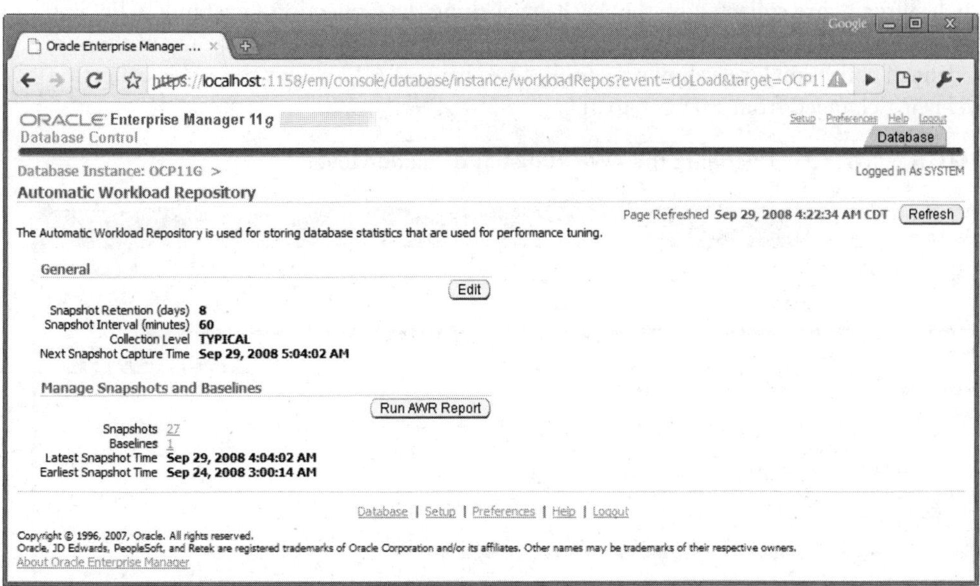

Click the Edit button to change the settings, as shown in Figure 14.11.

FIGURE 14.11 Changing AWR statistics collection and retention using EM

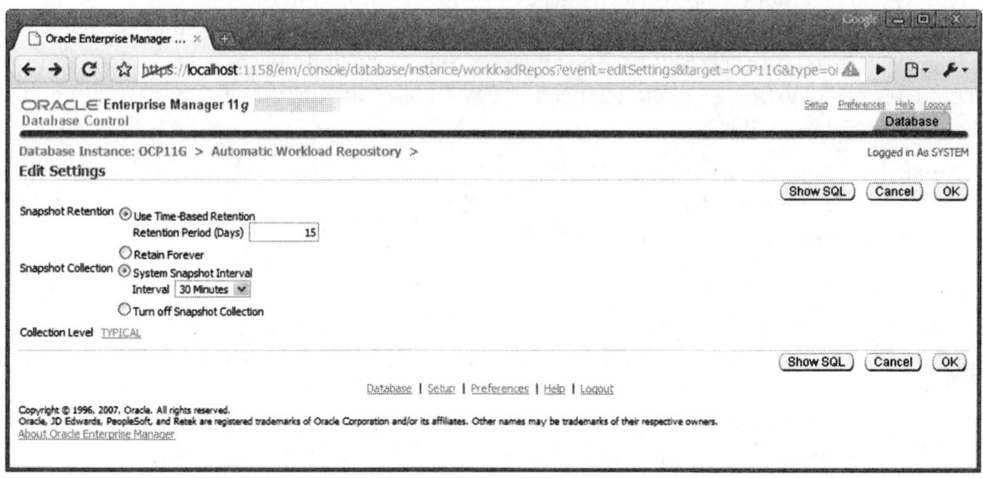

In Figure 14.11, the retention period for statistics gathered by the MMON process is set to 15 days, and statistics are collected every 30 minutes. You can also modify the depth at which statistics are collected by the AWR by clicking the Collection Level link. Clicking this link opens the Initialization Parameters screen where you can specify any of the three predefined collection levels shown in Table 14.3. Figure 14.12 shows the AWR collection level being changed from TYPICAL to ALL.

FIGURE 14.12 Changing the AWR statistics collection level

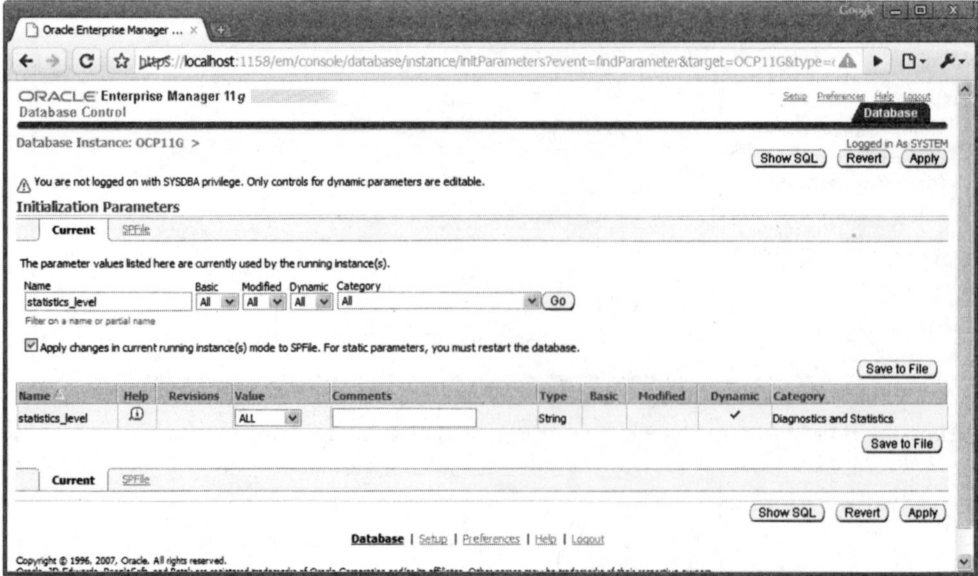

Take care when specifying the AWR statistics collection interval. Gathering snapshots too frequently requires additional space in the SYSAUX tablespace and adds database overhead each time the statistics are collected. AWR does not use any space in the SGA.

Using EM Database Control, you can view the AWR report. Click the Run AWR Report button on the Automatic Workload Repository screen shown earlier in Figure 14.10. You can get the same report using SQL*Plus by running the script `$ORACLE_HOME/rdbms/admin/awrrpt.sql`.

You can manage the AWR snapshots with SQL*Plus by utilizing the `DBMS_WORKLOAD_REPOSITORY` package, as described in the next section.

Managing AWR Snapshots Manually

You can create AWR snapshots by using the `CREATE_SNAPSHOT` procedure, as shown here:

```
SQL> EXECUTE DBMS_WORKLOAD_REPOSITORY.CREATE_SNAPSHOT ();
PL/SQL procedure successfully completed.
SQL>
```

You can use the `DROP_SNAPSHOT_RANGE` procedure to delete a range of snapshots, and you can query valid snapshot IDs from the `DBA_HIST_SNAPSHOT` view. The following example shows how to query the `DBA_HIST_SNAPSHOT` view:

```
SQL> SELECT snap_id, begin_interval_time, end_interval_time
  2  FROM dba_hist_snapshot
  3  ORDER BY snap_id;

   SNAP_ID BEGIN_INTERVAL_TIME            END_INTERVAL_TIME
---------- ------------------------------ ------------------------------
         1 24-SEP-08 02.06.11.000 AM      24-SEP-08 03.00.14.156 AM
         2 25-SEP-08 12.06.26.000 AM      25-SEP-08 12.17.55.437 AM
         3 25-SEP-08 12.17.55.437 AM      25-SEP-08 01.00.51.296 AM
         4 25-SEP-08 01.00.51.296 AM      25-SEP-08 02.00.22.109 AM
… … …
        27 27-SEP-08 07.03.17.375 PM      29-SEP-08 04.03.47.687 AM
        28 29-SEP-08 04.03.47.687 AM      29-SEP-08 05.00.39.437 AM
        29 29-SEP-08 05.00.39.437 AM      29-SEP-08 05.42.13.718 AM
```

To delete snapshots in the range 5–15, you can execute the following code. Note that the ASH (discussed in the next section) data is also purged between the time periods specified by the snapshot range.

```
SQL> BEGIN
  2   DBMS_WORKLOAD_REPOSITORY.DROP_SNAPSHOT_RANGE (5, 15);
  3  END;
  4  /
PL/SQL procedure successfully completed.
SQL>
```

Once AWR snapshots are taken and stored in the database, the Automatic Database Diagnostic feature uses the AWR data, as described in the "Automatic Database Diagnostic Monitoring" section.

Active Session History

ASH is sampled data at specified intervals from the current state of all active sessions. The data is collected in memory and can be accessed by V$ views. The ASH information is also written to a persistent store by the AWR snapshots.

The V$ACTIVE_SESSION_HISTORY provides the information collected by the ASH sampler. The sessions are sampled every second and are stored in a circular buffer in SGA. Each session is stored as a row. The current and historical information is available in the data dictionary view DBA_HIST_ACTIVE_SESS_HISTORY. ASH information also includes the execution plan for each SQL captured.

Oracle provides a script to generate an ASH report, $ORACLE_HOME/rdbms/admin/ashrpt.sql. You will be prompted for the report type (HTML or text), the begin time in minutes prior to SYSDATE, the duration in minutes for the report, and a name for the report. You can also use EM Database Control to generate the ASH report.

On the EM Database Control home screen, click the Performance tab, and click the Run ASH Report button, as shown in Figure 14.13.

FIGURE 14.13 Performance screen in EM Database Control

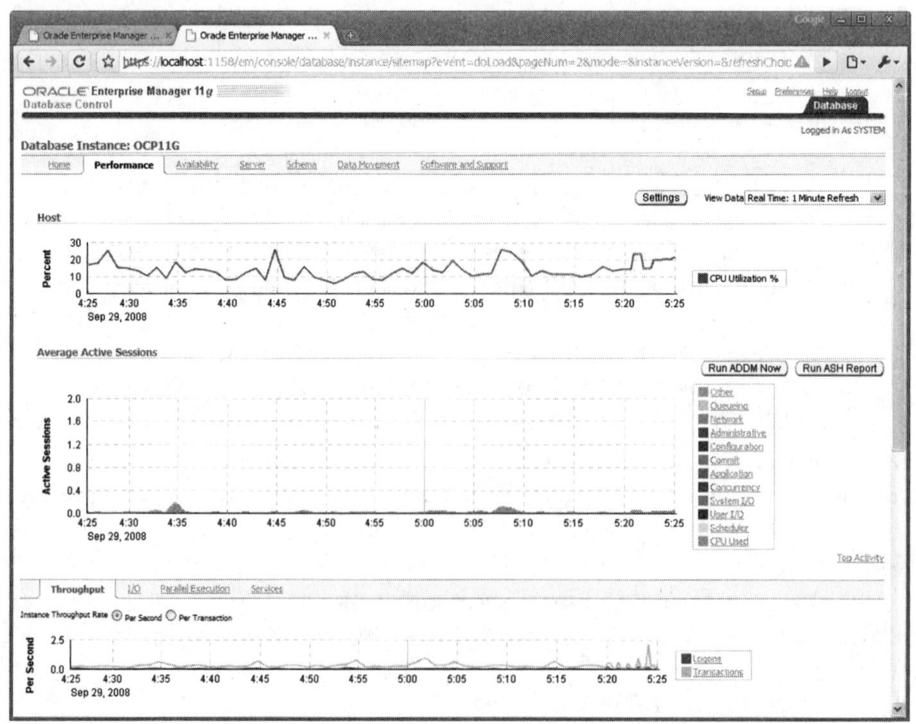

The screen shown in Figure 14.14 captures parameters for the ASH report. Specify the start time and end time for the report, and click the Generate Report button.

FIGURE 14.14 ASH report parameters

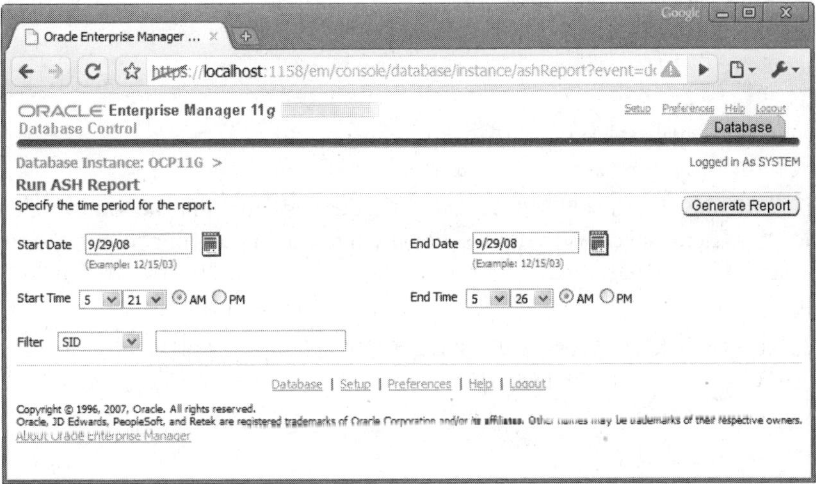

Any session that is connected to the database and does not wait for a wait event that belongs to the idle wait class is considered as an active session.

AWR Baselines

It is a good practice to baseline your database when everything is working as expected. When things go south, you can use this baseline to compare system statistics and performance metrics. *AWR baselines* contain performance data from a specific time period that is preserved for comparison when problems occur. This baseline data is excluded from the AWR purging process.

You can create two types of baselines: a *single* baseline and a *repeating* baseline. A single baseline is captured at a single fixed-time interval, such as October 5 between 10 a.m. and 1 p.m. A repeating baseline repeats during a time interval for a specific period, such as every Friday between 10 a.m. and 1 p.m. You can create and delete AWR baselines using EM Database Control or SQL*Plus.

Managing AWR Baselines Using SQL*Plus

To create a single baseline, use the `CREATE_BASELINE` procedure as shown in the following code. You can include the optional `expiration` parameter to automatically delete the snapshot after the specified number of days.

```
SQL> BEGIN
   DBMS_WORKLOAD_REPOSITORY.CREATE_BASELINE(
    start_snap_id => 27,
    end_snap_id => 29,
    baseline_name => 'OCP Example',
    expiration => 21);
 END;
SQL> /
PL/SQL procedure successfully completed.
SQL>
```

To drop a baseline, use the DROP_BASELINE procedure as shown in the following code. The cascade parameter specifies that only the baseline should be dropped, not the snapshots associated with the baseline.

```
SQL> BEGIN
   DBMS_WORKLOAD_REPOSITORY.DROP_BASELINE(
    baseline_name => 'OCP Example',
    cascade => FALSE);
 END;
SQL> /
PL/SQL procedure successfully completed.
SQL>
```

You can create a baseline for the future date and time. These are called *baseline templates*. The following code creates a baseline template:

```
SQL> BEGIN
   DBMS_WORKLOAD_REPOSITORY.CREATE_BASELINE_TEMPLATE(
      start_time => TO_DATE('01-JAN-09 05.00.00','DD-MON-YY HH.MI.SS'),
      end_time => TO_DATE('01-JAN-09 08.00.00','DD-MON-YY HH.MI.SS'),
      baseline_name => 'baseline_090101',
      template_name => 'template_090101',
      expiration => 21);
 END;
SQL> /
PL/SQL procedure successfully completed.
SQL>
```

AWR baselines and baseline templates are never dropped automatically (or purged) from the database unless explicitly dropped by the DBA or the expiration period ends.

Managing AWR Baselines Using EM Database Control

Using EM Database Control to create, rename, and drop AWR baselines is easier than using SQL*Plus and error-free. From the database home page, click the Server tab (shown earlier in Figure 14.1). Click the AWR Baselines link under Statistics Management. The current baselines are displayed, as shown in Figure 14.15.

FIGURE 14.15 AWR Baselines screen

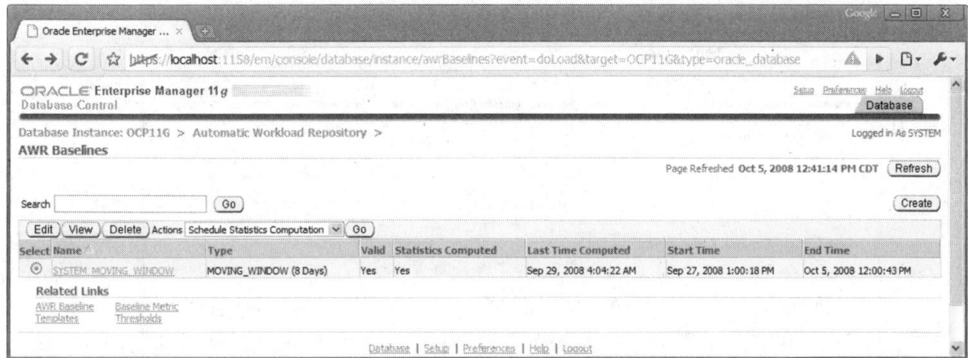

Click the Create button to create a new baseline. You will be presented with the option to create a single baseline or a repeating baseline. If you choose a single baseline, you will be presented with the screen shown in Figure 14.16. Enter the name of the baseline. You can specify the snapshots to include in the baseline by using the snapshot IDs or using a time range.

FIGURE 14.16 AWR Create Single Baseline screen

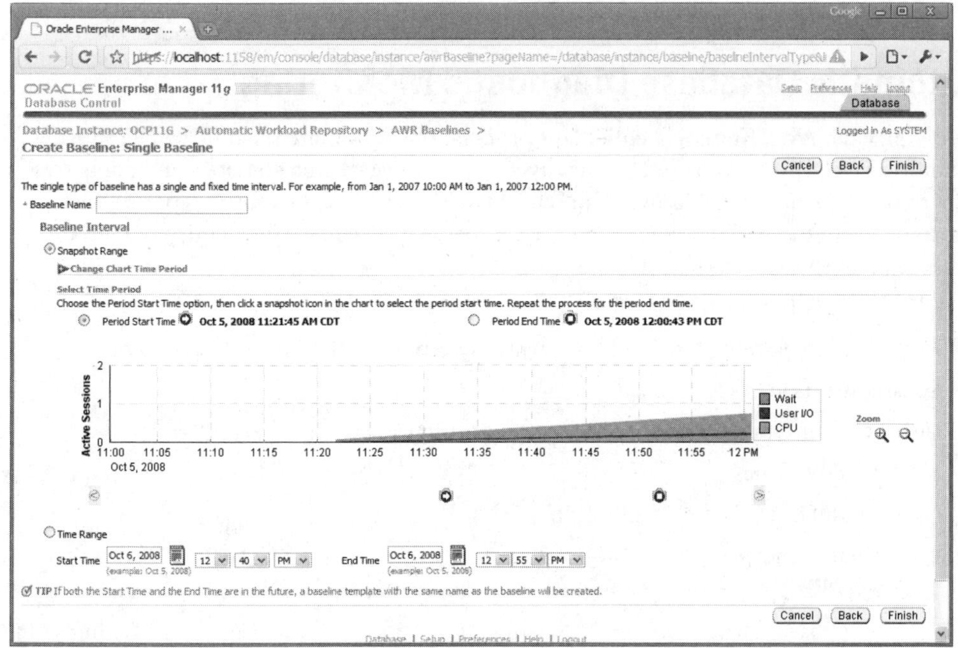

If you choose to create a repeating baseline, you'll see the screen shown in Figure 14.17. Enter a baseline name, and specify the frequency.

FIGURE 14.17 AWR Create Repeating Baseline screen

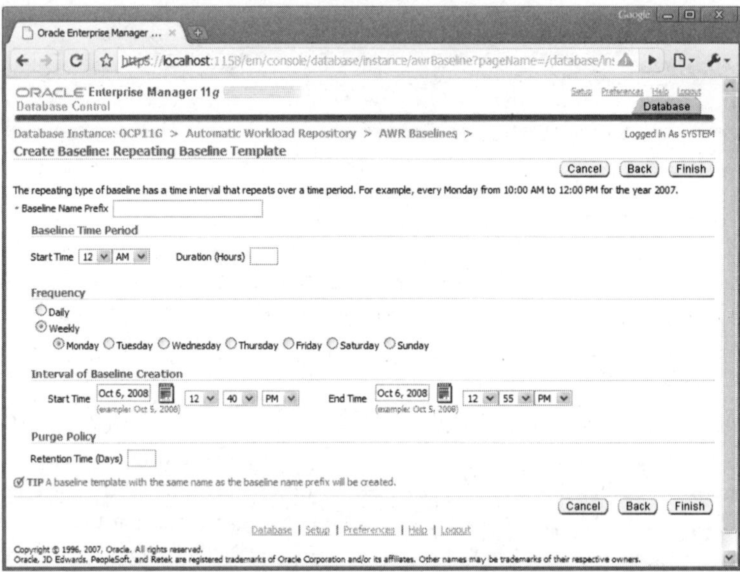

You can drop a baseline by choosing the baseline and clicking the Delete button on the AWR Baselines screen (Figure 14.15).

Automatic Database Diagnostic Monitoring

Following each AWR statistics-collection process, the Automated Database Diagnostic Monitoring (ADDM) feature automatically analyzes the gathered statistics and compares them to the statistics gathered by the previous two AWR snapshots. By comparing the current statistics to these two previous snapshots, the ADDM can easily identify potential database problems such as these:

- CPU and I/O bottlenecks
- Resource-intensive SQL or PL/SQL or Java execution
- Lock contention
- Utilization of Oracle's memory structures within the SGA
- RAC-specific issues
- Issues with Oracle Net configuration
- Data-concurrency issues

Based on these findings, the ADDM may recommend possible remedies. The goal of these recommendations is to minimize DB Time. DB Time is composed of two types of time measures for nonidle database users: CPU time and wait time. This information is stored as the cumulative time that all database users have spent either using CPU resources or waiting for access to resources such as CPU, I/O, or Oracle's memory structures. High or increasing values for DB Time indicate that users are requesting increasingly more server resources and may also be experiencing waits for those resources, which can lead to less than optimal performance. In this way, minimizing DB Time is a much better way to measure overall database performance than Oracle's old ratio-based tuning methodologies.

DB Time is calculated by combining all the times from all nonidle user sessions into one number. Therefore, it is possible for the DB Time value to be larger than the total time that the instance has been running.

Once ADDM completes its comparison of the newly collected statistics to the previously collected statistics, the results are stored in the AWR. You can use these statistics to establish baselines against which future performance will be compared, and you can use deviations from these baseline measures to identify areas that need attention. In this manner, ADDM allows you to not only better detect and alert yourself to potential management and performance problems in the database but also allows you to automatically take corrective actions to rectify those problems quickly and with little or no manual intervention.

The following sections introduce the interfaces, features, and functionality of ADDM and explain how you can use this utility to monitor and manage database storage, security, and performance. We'll begin by examining the EM Database Control tools you can use to view the results of ADDM analysis.

Using EM Database Control to View ADDM Analysis

EM Database Control graphically displays the results of the ADDM analysis on several screens, including the following:

- The Performance Findings link under the Diagnostic Summary section of the EM Database Control main screen
- The Performance tab of the EM Database Control main screen
- The ADDM screen located by clicking the Advisor Central link at the bottom of the EM Database Control main screen

You'll see sample output from each of the EM Database Control screens in the following sections.

The EM Database Control Performance Findings Link

The EM Database Control home screen contains a section called Diagnostic Summary. One of the links under this section is ADDM Findings. Figure 14.18 shows this section.

FIGURE 14.18 The Diagnostic Summary section of the EM Database Control home screen

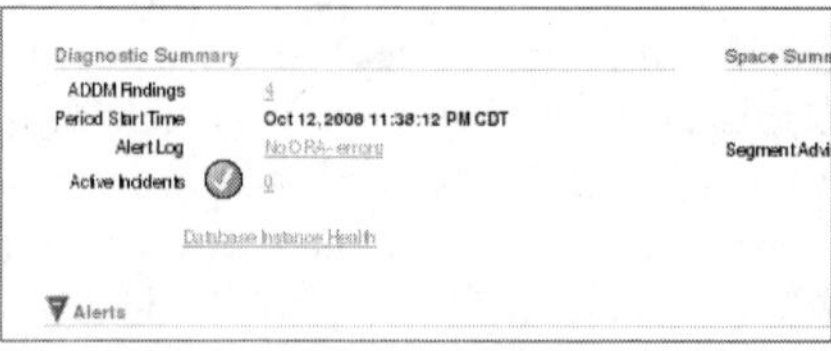

The output in Figure 14.18 shows that ADDM discovered four performance-related findings. Clicking the link for these four performance findings displays the ADDM summary screen, at the bottom of which is the Performance Analysis section, as shown in Figure 14.19.

The Findings section on this screen shows the ADDM analysis and the recommendation to resolve the issue.

FIGURE 14.19 ADDM summary screen

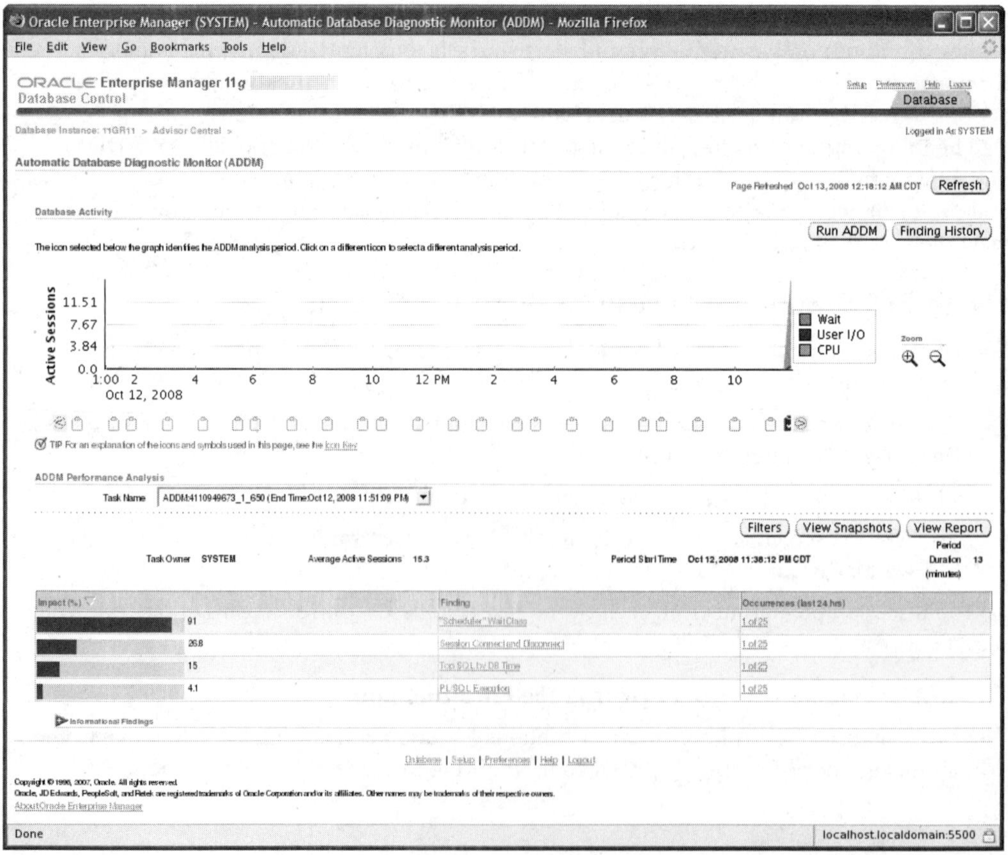

The EM Database Control Performance Tab

You can also click the Performance tab on the EM Database Control main screen to view performance data collected by AWR and analyzed by ADDM. You can click the Run ADDM Now button to take an AWR snapshot and perform ADDM analysis. Figure 14.20 shows the Performance tab of EM Database Control.

FIGURE 14.20 EM Database Control Performance tab

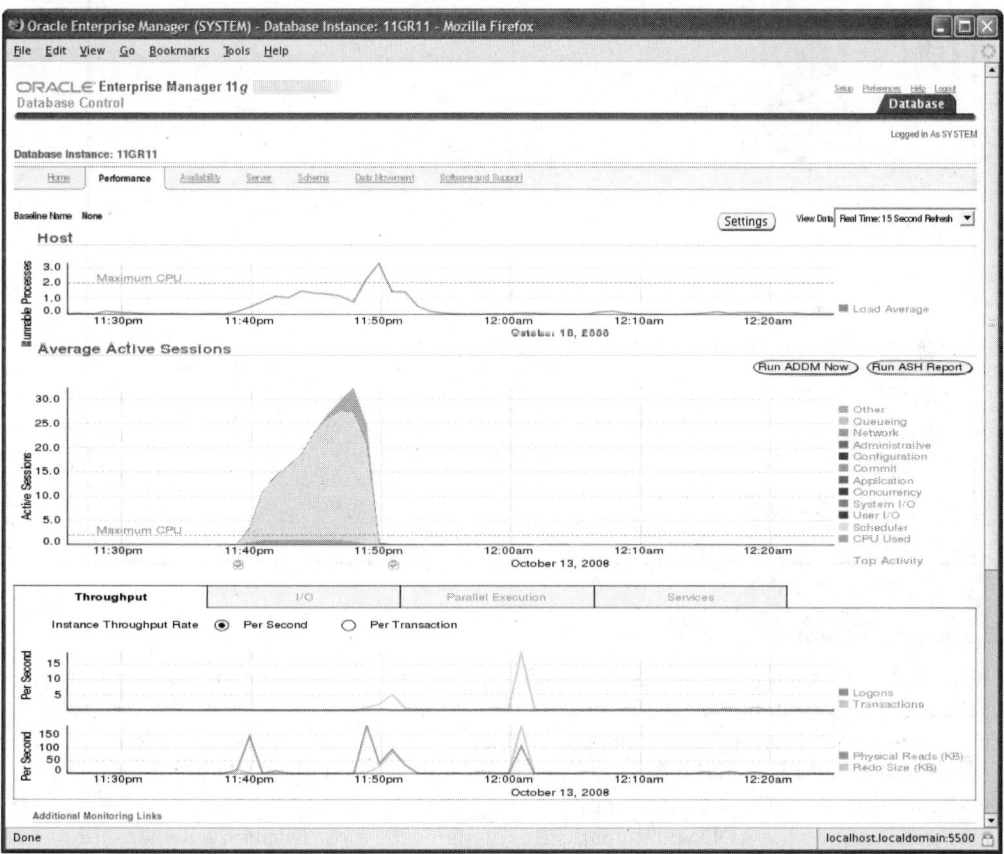

Using Active Sessions of the Performance tab, you can drill down into detailed information that has been identified as having an impact on performance. Click the Scheduler link, which will take you to the screen shown in Figure 14.21.

FIGURE 14.21 Detailed performance information

The Advisor Central Screen

The Advisor Central screen also contains ADDM findings. The link for the Advisor Central screen is at the bottom of the EM Database Control home screen. Click this link to display the Advisor Central screen, shown in Figure 14.22.

Click the ADDM link in the Advisors section of this screen to display a graph that shows all the recent AWR snapshots taken by the MMON process.

As stated earlier, the ADDM automatically compares the most recent AWR snapshot with the last two AWR snapshots when formulating its recommendations. However, you can use this Create ADDM Task screen to manually select any two AWR snapshot times and formulate ADDM recommendations for activity that occurred between those two points in time. To start this process, click the Period Start Time radio button, and then select a start date and time by clicking the point in the graph's timeline that corresponds to the beginning period that you want to use. Repeat this process to specify the end-process timestamp.

You can also manually perform an ADDM analysis without EM Database Control by using the `addmrpt.sql` script located in the `$ORACLE_HOME/rdbms/admin` directory.

FIGURE 14.22 The Advisor Central screen

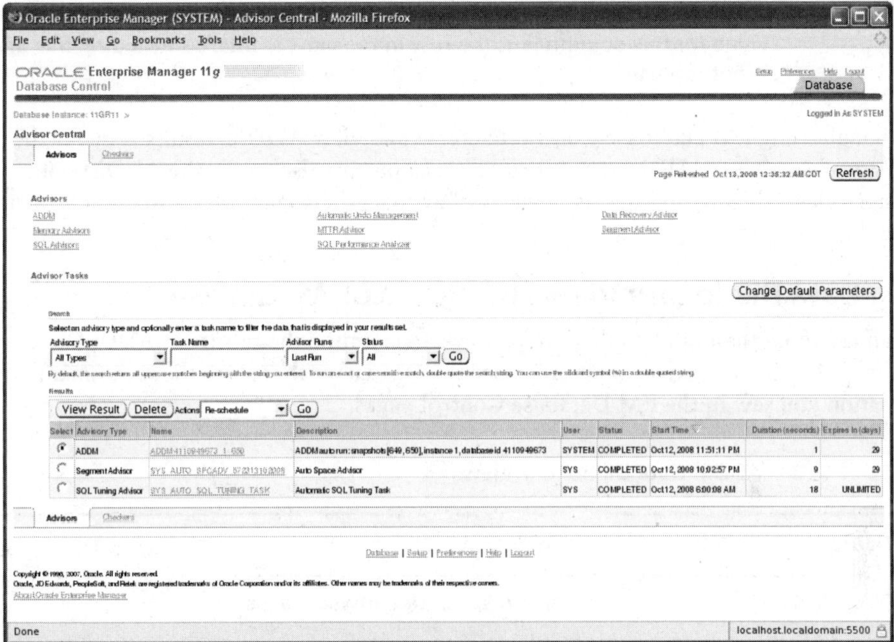

You can use the DBMS_ADDM package to manually analyze AWR snapshots. Table 14.4 shows some of the subprograms in DBMS_ADDM that can be used to manually manage ADDM analysis.

TABLE 14.4 Partial List of DBMS_ADDM Subprograms

Procedure Name	Description
ANALYZE_DB	Creates an ADDM analysis by specifying the begin and end AWR snapshot IDs
DELETE	Deletes an ADDM task
INSERT_FINDING_DIRECTIVE	Excludes certain findings from ADDM reporting
INSERT_SEGMENT_DIRECTIVE	Excludes a certain schema, object, or segment from ADDM reporting (do not run Segment Advisor on these segments)
INSERT_SQL_DIRECTIVE	Excludes certain SQL from ADDM reporting

The DBA_ADVISOR_FINDINGS, DBA_ADVISOR_RECOMMENDATIONS, and DBA_ADVISOR_ACTIONS dictionary views have a column named FILTERED. If the value for this column is Y, the row in the view is filtered by a directive and is not reported.

Although using EM Database Control to create and view ADDM results is by far the simplest way to review ADDM recommendations, you can also query the ADDM data dictionary views directly. I'll discuss some of these data dictionary views in the following section.

Using Data Dictionary Views to View ADDM Analysis

You can use more than 20 data dictionary views to examine the results of ADDM's activities. Table 14.5 describes five commonly used ADDM views that store the recommendation information you saw in the EM Database Control pages.

TABLE 14.5 ADDM Data Dictionary Views

View Name	Description
DBA_ADDM_TASKS	Displays executed advisor tasks
DBA_ADDM_FINDINGS	Describes the findings identified by the ADDM analysis
DBA_ADVISOR_OBJECTS	Describes the objects that are referenced in the ADDM findings and recommendations
DBA_ADVISOR_RECOMMENDATIONS	Describes the recommendations made based on ADDM findings
DBA_ADVISOR_RATIONALE	Describes the rationale behind each ADDM finding

DBA_ADDM_TASKS, DBA_ADDM_INSTANCES, and DBA_ADDM_FINDINGS are extensions of the corresponding DBA_ADVISOR_ views but are specific for ADDM tasks and findings.

The following SQL statement shows a sample query on the DBA_ADVISOR_FINDINGS data dictionary view that identifies the type of performance problem that is causing the most impact on the database:

```
SQL> SELECT task_id, type, message
  2  FROm dba_advisor_findings
  3  WHERE impact= (select MAX(impcat) FROM dba_advisor_findings);
```

```
TASK_ID TYPE       MESSAGE
------- ---------  ----------------------------------------------------
    164 PROBLEM    SQL statements consuming significant database time
                   were found.
```

The output from this query shows that SQL statements being executed in the database are contributing to the poor database performance. By itself, the DBA_ADVISOR_FINDINGS table does not identify which SQL statements are consuming the database time. Instead, these are shown in the DBA_ADVISOR_OBJECTS data dictionary view and are identified by the TASK_ID value shown in the query on DBA_ADVISOR_FINDINGS. A query on that view, using the TASK_ID of 164 returned by the ADDM session that had the potential for the greatest database impact, returns the SQL statements shown here:

```
SQL> SELECT attr4
  2  FROM dba_advisor_objects
  3  WHERE task_id = 164;

ATTR4
-------------------------------------------------------------------
UPDATE customers SET credit_limit=credit_limit*1.15 WHERE cust_id = :B1

DELETE FROM sales WHERE time_id BETWEEN '01-JAN-00' and '01-JAN-01';

UPDATE sales_history SET quantity_sold = quantity_sold+10 WHERE
   CHANNEL_ID := B1

SELECT COUNT(*) FROM Sales_history;

SELECT DISTINCT channel_id FROM sales_history;
```

This query shows all the SQL statements that were captured by the AWR during the snapshot period and that were used in the ADDM analysis for that same period.

The DBA_ADVISOR_ACTIONS data dictionary view shows the ADDM recommendations for each finding. The following query shows the recommendations for correcting the performance issues associated with TASK_ID 164, which was identified earlier as being the costliest database activity:

```
SQL> SELECT TRIM(attr1) ATTR1, TRIM(attr2) ATTR2, TRIM(attr3) ATTR3
  2  FROM dba_advisor_actions
  3  WHERE task_id = 164;

ATTR1          ATTR2    ATTR3
----------     ------   ----------
log_buffer     262144   15728640
db_cache_size  25165824 50331648
undo_retention 900      363
```

This output indicates that ADDM recommends that the values for LOG_BUFFER, DB_CACHE_SIZE, and UNDO_RETENTION all be changed from their current values to 15,728,640 bytes; 50,331,648 bytes; and 363 seconds, respectively.

If you want to see the rationale behind each of the actions shown in DBA_ADVISOR_ACTIONS, query the DBA_ADVISOR_RATIONALE data dictionary view. The DBA_ADVISOR_RATIONALE view stores the ADDM recommendations that ADDM has formulated based on the AWR data like those stored in DBA_ADVISOR_FINDINGS and DBA_ADVISOR_OBJECTS. The following example shows a sample query on the DBA_ADVISOR_RATIONALE view using the TASK_ID of 164 identified earlier:

```
SQL> SELECT message
  2  FROM dba_advisor_rationale
  3  WHERE task_id = 164;

MESSAGE
----------------------------------------------------------------------
Buffer cache writes due to small log files were consuming significant
   database time.

The buffer cache was undersized causing significant read I/O.

The value of "undo retention" was 900 seconds and the longest running
  query lasted only 330 seconds. This extra retention caused
  unnecessary I/O.
```

As you can see from the complexity of these examples, examining the ADDM results via EM Database Control is much easier than accessing the data dictionary views via SQL. From a practical standpoint, you would run SQL queries against these ADDM views only if EM Database Control were unavailable.

To gain further insight into the recommendations and information gathered by the ADDM, Oracle 11*g* also provides several advisor utilities in EM Database Control. I will discuss these advisors in the next section.

The Advisory Framework

Oracle 11*g* comes with several advisors to help proactively manage the database. The top portion of Figure 14.22 shows the advisors available in Oracle 11*g* and how to invoke them.

Advisors provide recommendations that are key for a DBA to manage the database effectively. The advisors can be classified into various categories. The following are the advisors:

- Memory
  - SGA Advisor
  - PGA Advisor
  - Shared Pool Advisor
  - Buffer Cache Advisor
- SQL
  - SQL Tuning Advisor
  - SQL Access Advisor
- Automatic Undo Management
  - Undo Advisor
- Recovery
  - MTTR Advisor
  - Data Recovery Advisor
- Space
  - Segment Advisor

The purpose of each advisor is explained next. Since the OCA certification exam expects you to only be familiar with the general purpose of the advisors, I won't go into detail of each advisor in this book. You can click each advisor's link on the Advisor Central screen and familiarize yourself with the contents.

Memory advisors Memory advisors provide the optimal size for various memory parameters. If AMM is enabled, the advisor provides the target amount of memory to allocate to the instance. If AMM is disabled but ASMM is enabled, the advisor provides recommendations on the optimal sizes for SGA and PGA. If no automatic memory features are enabled, you can get the sizes for individual SGA components such as shared pool and buffer cache. AMM and ASMM are discussed later in the chapter.

SQL Tuning Advisor This provides SQL tuning advice. You may use the top activity or current session's graphs to drill down to the SQL statement to tune. You can tune one statement or multiple statements. The advice includes restructuring SQL statements, creating additional indexes, using materialized views, partitioning tables, refreshing the optimizer statistics, and so on.

SQL Access Advisor The SQL Access Advisor provides recommendations on schema modifications. It recommends indexes and materialized views to optimize SQL queries.

Undo Advisor The Undo Advisor recommends the optimal size for the undo tablespace based on the undo retention and flashback requirements.

MTTR Advisor The MTTR Advisor provides the optimal value for the FAST_START_MTTR_TARGET initialization parameter. This parameter determines the amount of time required by the instance to start in the event of an instance crash. Instance failure can occur when the host server crashes, when any critical SGA background process fails, or if the instance is shut down using the ABORT option. Instance recovery occurs automatically on the first startup following the instance failure. During instance recovery, Oracle uses the online redo logs to roll back any uncommitted transactions that were "in flight" when the instance crashed to ensure that all committed transactions are written to disk. As a DBA, you often try to minimize the time it takes to perform this instance recovery so that you can bring up the database quickly.

Data Recovery Advisor The Data Recovery Advisor helps diagnose and repair data failures and corruptions. It analyzes the failure based on the symptoms and determines the repair strategies.

Segment Advisor The Segment Advisor identifies whether a segment is a good candidate for a shrink operation based on the level of fragmentation within the segment. The advisor also keeps historical growth of the segment, which can be used for capacity planning. Segments that can be shrunk are those that the Segment Advisor has found to need less space than they are currently allocated. By shrinking or compressing these segments, space is returned to the database for use by other objects, and the total number of I/Os needed to access these objects is reduced, potentially improving the performance of SQL statements that access these objects.

In the next section, you'll learn about another tool in the Oracle 11*g* database that helps you proactively monitor the database with timely alerts.

Monitoring Server-Generated Alerts

In addition to monitoring and making recommendations on SQL, memory, mean time to recover, segments, and undo activity, an Oracle 11*g* database can also proactively monitor itself for other types of problems related to configuration, security, and space management. To do so, you use the server-generated alerts feature.

A *server-generated alert* is an alert from the Oracle 11*g* database that says it suspects a problem with the database. These alerts are also an integral part of the ADDM architecture. They notify you when a management or performance issue occurs and begin taking corrective actions—if you configured such actions. By default, the alert notifications are sent to a predefined persistent queue named ALERT_QUE owned by SYS. EM Grid Control reads this queue.

There are two types of server-generated alerts: threshold based and event based. *Threshold* alerts are triggered when a specified threshold is met, such as when a tablespace has reached certain capacity. Threshold alerts can be fired at a warning level (for example, 85 percent tablespace capacity) or at a critical level (for example, 97 percent tablespace capacity). *Event* alerts are triggered when a specified event occurs, such as a database error.

Viewing and Configuring Alerts Using EM Database Control

The EM Database Control home page displays the alerts when they are triggered. Figure 14.23 shows the Alerts section of the Database Control home page.

FIGURE 14.23 Alerts section of the Database Control home page

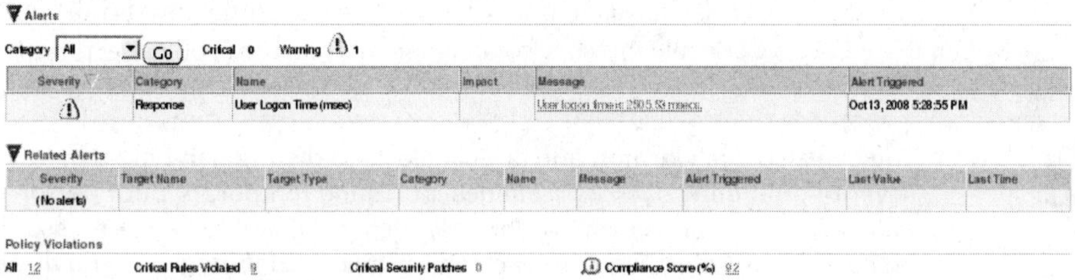

You can see the alert history by clicking the Alert link. You can configure the alerts by clicking the Metric and Policy Settings link under Related Links. Figure 14.24 shows the top portion of the Metric and Policy Settings screen.

FIGURE 14.24 Metric and Policy Settings screen

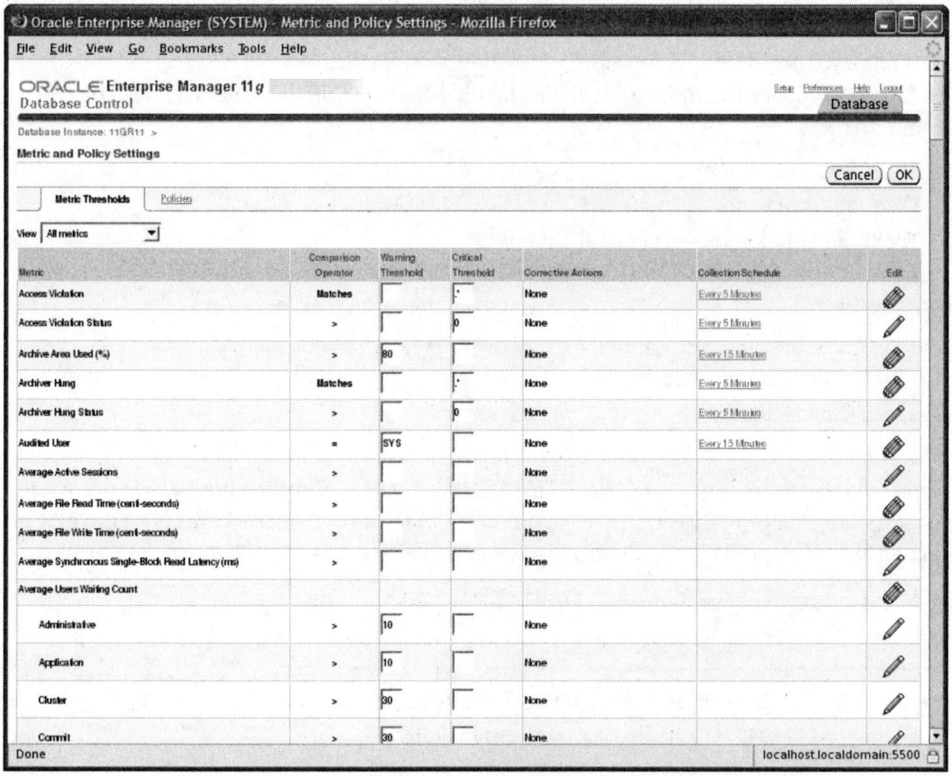

As you can see in Figure 14.24, each alert can have two levels of severity: Warning and Critical. These two alert levels allow you to achieve greater granularity. For example, you might want two thresholds set up with regard to the archive destination. One might be a warning threshold that triggers an alert when the archive destination is 80 percent full—causing a message to be displayed on the EM Database Control main screen. In addition, you might want to set up a critical threshold so that you receive an email whenever the archive destination device is 90 percent full. In this manner, you can escalate a potential problem from an EM Database Control console message to an email alert as the problem gets worse.

You can also use warning and critical alerts to distinguish between lower-severity problems, such as statistics indicating temporary poor performance, and higher-severity problems, such as ORA-0600 error messages in the database alert log. You can achieve this by defining warning thresholds only for lower-severity alerts and defining warning and critical alerts for higher-severity problems.

Viewing and Configuring Alerts Using SQL

You can use SQL*Plus to configure the alert thresholds and to view the alerts. The DBMS_SERVER_ALERT package has the subprograms to define and query the thresholds. The SET_THRESHOLD procedure is used to define the threshold, and the GET_THRESHOLD procedure is used to retrieve threshold information.

You can also query the thresholds from the DBA_THRESHOLDS dictionary view. The following is an example:

```
SQL> SELECT metrics_name, warning_value, critical_value
  2  FROM dba_thresholds
  3  WHERE metrics_name like 'Tablespace%'
SQL> /
METRICS_NAME                        WARNING_VA CRITICAL_V
----------------------------------- ---------- ----------
Tablespace Bytes Space Usage        0          0
Tablespace Space Usage              85         97
SQL>
```

Threshold alerts are written to DBA_OUTSTANDING_ALERTS. Nonthreshold alerts are written only to DBA_ALERT_HISTORY. Entries from DBA_OUTSTANDING_ALERTS are cleared when the alert condition is cleared. The following is a query from the DBA_OUTSTANDING_ALERTS view:

```
SQL> SELECT reason FROM dba_outstanding_alerts;
REASON
-------------------------------------------------------
db_recovery_file_dest_size of 4395630592 bytes is 97.27%
used and has 119794176 remaining bytes available.
```

```
Metrics "Database Time Spent Waiting (%)" is at 36.84571
for event class "Concurrency"
```

The V$METRIC view shows system-level metric values. Metric history is saved in the V$METRIC_HISTORY view.

So far, you have seen several tools that help DBAs proactively monitor the database. I cannot possible identify all the potential issues and how to proactively avoid them. Errors and database corruptions do happen. The Oracle 11*g* database has a reporting mechanism to analyze the problem reactively and take measures to avoid it in the future. You'll learn about the Automatic Diagnostic Repository in the next section.

Understanding Automatic Diagnostic Repository

The Automatic Diagnostic Repository (ADR) is a file-based repository for database diagnostic data such as alert log files, trace files, core dump files, health monitor reports, and so on. In prior releases of Oracle, the trace and dump files were traditionally saved in directories specified by the _DUMP_DIRECTORY parameters. Starting with Oracle 11*g*, these files and much more are saved under the ADR framework.

ADR replaces the BACKGROUND_DUMP_DEST, CORE_DUMP_DEST, and USER_DUMP_DEST locations. A new parameter, DIAGNOSTIC_DEST, specifies the base directory for the ADR. The default for DIAGNOSTIC_DEST is $ORACLE_BASE if available; otherwise, it's $ORACLE_HOME/log. ADR is a vast topic and is not covered here in its entirety.

Within ADR base, there can be multiple ADR homes. Each ADR home is the base directory for all the files belonging to an instance. The ADR home directory for an instance is $DIAGNOSTIC_DEST/diag/rdbms/<dbname>/<instance name>.

The subdirectories under the DIAGNOSTIC_DEST are as follows:

```
DIAGNOSTIC_DEST/diag
    rdbms
        <db_name>
            <instance_name>
                alert
                cdump
                hm
                incident
                incpkg
                ir
                lck
                metadata
                stage
                sweep
                trace
```

```
DIAGNOSTIC_DEST/diag
    tnslsnr
        <machine_name>
            <listener_name>
                alert
                cdump
                incident
                incpkg
                lck
                metadata
                stage
                sweep
                trace
```

In Oracle 11g, an alert log file is written in XML format as well as in text format. The XML-format file is under the `alert` directory, whereas the text-format file is under the `trace` directory. Table 14.6 shows where to look for log and trace files in Oracle 11g.

TABLE 14.6 Alert File and Trace File Locations

Type of File	Pre–Oracle 11*g* Location	Oracle 11*g* Location
Alert log (text)	BACKGROUND_DUMP_DEST	<ADR_HOME>/trace
Alert log (XML)	None	<ADR_HOME>/alert
Server trace files	BACKGROUND_DUMP_DEST	<ADR_HOME>/trace
User trace files	USER_DUMP_DEST	<ADR_HOME>/trace
Core dump files	CORE_DUMP_DEST	<ADR_HOME>/cdump
Incident dumps	USER_DUMP_DEST, BACKGROUND_DUMP_DEST	<ADR_HOME>/incident/incdir_n

The values for _DUMP_DEST parameters are ignored by Oracle 11g. The new view V$DIAG_INFO gives file locations:

```
SQL> SELECT name, value FROM v$diag_info;

NAME                      VALUE
------------------------- ---------------------------------------------
Diag Enabled              TRUE
ADR Base                  c:\oracle
ADR Home                  c:\oracle\diag\rdbms\w11gr1\w11gr1
Diag Trace                c:\oracle\diag\rdbms\w11gr1\w11gr1\trace
Diag Alert                c:\oracle\diag\rdbms\w11gr1\w11gr1\alert
Diag Incident             c:\oracle\diag\rdbms\w11gr1\w11gr1\incident
Diag Cdump                c:\oracle\diag\rdbms\w11gr1\w11gr1\cdump
Health Monitor            c:\oracle\diag\rdbms\w11gr1\w11gr1\hm
Default Trace File        c:\...\w11gr1\trace\w11gr1_ora_6036.trc
Active Problem Count      0
Active Incident Count     0
```

The standard directory structure and diagnostic framework enables DBAs to package and send trace-file and log information to Oracle Support for timely resolution to issues. The ADR command interface (ADRCI) is a command-line tool available to view the ADR information and to package incident and problem information into a zip file.

Using ADRCI to View the Alert Log File

You invoke the ADRCI command-line tool with the executable `adrci`, and you use the `show alert` command to view the alert log file. You can use options such as `-tail` to view the end of the file or `-P` to filter the output. You can also use the `SPOOL` command similar to SQL*Plus to write the output to a file.

The `help` command in `adrci` displays all the available commands in ADRCI. Invoke ADRCI using the `adrci.exe` executable on Windows or using the `adrci` executable on Unix/Linux platforms.

```
$ adrci

ADRCI: Release 11.1.0.6.0 - Beta on Wed Oct 15 06:53:26 2008
Copyright (c) 1982, 2007, Oracle.  All rights reserved.
ADR base = "/u01/app/oracle"

adrci> help
 HELP [topic]
   Available Topics:
        CREATE REPORT
        ECHO
        EXIT
        HELP
        HOST
        IPS
        PURGE
        RUN
        SET BASE
        SET BROWSER
        SET CONTROL
        SET ECHO
        SET EDITOR
        SET HOMES | HOME | HOMEPATH
        SET TERMOUT
        SHOW ALERT
        SHOW BASE
        SHOW CONTROL
        SHOW HM_RUN
        SHOW HOMES | HOME | HOMEPATH
        SHOW INCDIR
```

```
        SHOW INCIDENT
        SHOW PROBLEM
        SHOW REPORT
        SHOW TRACEFILE
        SPOOL
 There are other commands intended to be used directly by Oracle, type
 "HELP EXTENDED" to see the list
adrci>
```

To find out the purpose and get detailed syntax information on a specific command, do `help <command>`:

```
adrci> help show alert


  Usage: SHOW ALERT [-p <predicate_string>]  [-term]
                    [ [-tail [num] [-f]] | [-file <alert_file_name>] ]
  Purpose: Show alert messages.
  Options:
    [-p <predicate_string>]: The predicate string must be double quoted.
    The fields in the predicate are the fields:
        ORIGINATING_TIMESTAMP         timestamp
        NORMALIZED_TIMESTAMP          timestamp
        ORGANIZATION_ID               text(65)
        COMPONENT_ID                  text(65)
        HOST_ID                       text(65)
        HOST_ADDRESS                  text(17)
        MESSAGE_TYPE                  number
        MESSAGE_LEVEL                 number
        MESSAGE_ID                    text(65)
        MESSAGE_GROUP                 text(65)
        CLIENT_ID                     text(65)
        MODULE_ID                     text(65)
        PROCESS_ID                    text(33)
        THREAD_ID                     text(65)
        USER_ID                       text(65)
        INSTANCE_ID                   text(65)
        DETAILED_LOCATION             text(161)
        UPSTREAM_COMP_ID              text(101)
        DOWNSTREAM_COMP_ID            text(101)
```

```
    EXECUTION_CONTEXT_ID              text(101)
    EXECUTION_CONTEXT_SEQUENCE        number
    ERROR_INSTANCE_ID                 number
    ERROR_INSTANCE_SEQUENCE           number
    MESSAGE_TEXT                      text(2049)
    MESSAGE_ARGUMENTS                 text(129)
    SUPPLEMENTAL_ATTRIBUTES           text(129)
    SUPPLEMENTAL_DETAILS              text(129)
    PROBLEM_KEY                       text(65)

  [-tail [num] [-f]]: Output last part of the alert messages and
  output latest messages as the alert log grows. If num is not specified,
  the last 10 messages are displayed. If "-f" is specified, new data
  will append at the end as new alert messages are generated.

  [-term]: Direct results to terminal. If this option is not specified,
  the results will be open in an editor.
  By default, it will open in emacs, but "set editor" can be used
  to set other editors.

  [-file <alert_file_name>]: Allow users to specify an alert file which
  may not be in ADR. <alert_file_name> must be specified with full path.
  Note that this option cannot be used with the -tail option

 Examples:
  show alert
  show alert -p "message_text like '%incident%'"
  show alert -tail 20

adrci>
```

Using EM to View the Alert Log File

You can also use EM Database Control to view the alert log contents. On the Database Control home page, click the Alert Log Contents link under Related Links. You can view the last 50, 100, or up to 2,000 lines of the alert log. See Figure 14.25.

FIGURE 14.25 View Alert Log Contents screen in Database Control

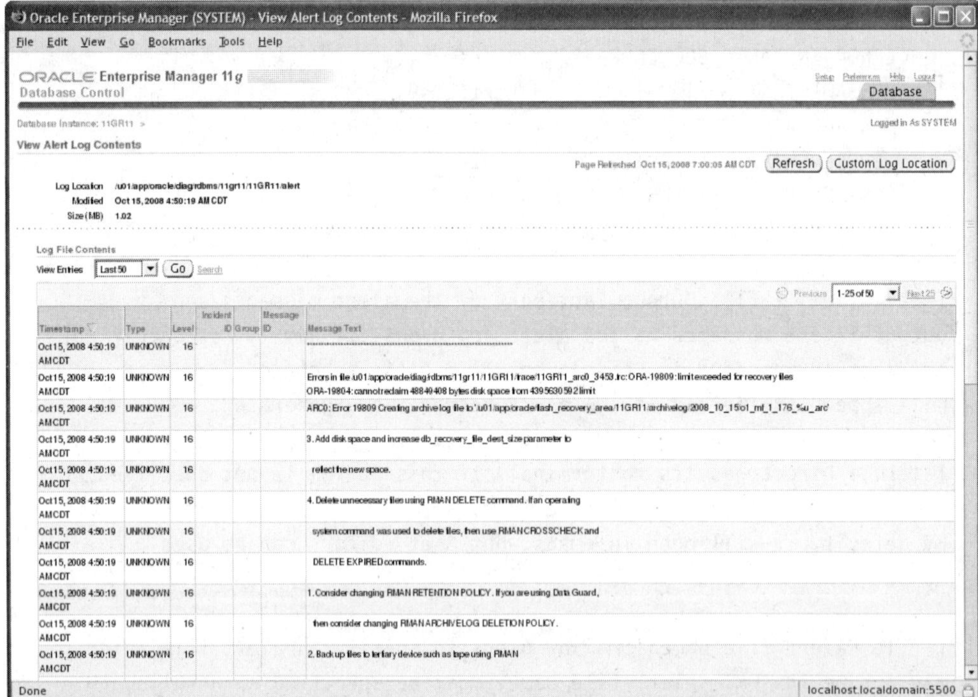

In the next section, you will learn the tools available to monitor the performance of the database.

Managing Performance

Although AWR, ADDM, advisors, and ADR all help you proactively monitor and manage your databases, you can use additional performance-specific features of EM Database Control to further enhance the performance of your database. When thinking about tuning, you should consider the following areas:

- Memory-allocation issues
- I/O contention (disk/SAN configuration)
- CPU contention
- Network issues
- SQL problems (bad SQL, optimizer plans)

Several dictionary and dynamic performance views are available in Oracle 11*g* that help you tune and gather system information. When it comes to tuning, managing the instance memory is very important. How much memory should you allocate for all the various SGA components? In the following sections, you will learn how Oracle 11*g* can help you take the guesswork out of database administration and tune the database.

Sources of Tuning Information

EM Database Control provides a wealth of information for improving database monitoring and management, but you also need to be aware of several other sources of information about database performance, including the following:

- The alert log
- Background and user trace files
- Dynamic performance views
- Data dictionary views

The Alert Log

The Oracle alert log records informational and error messages for a variety of activities that have occurred against the database during its operation. These activities are recorded in chronological order from the oldest to most recent. You can find the alert log in the ADR directory that you learned about earlier.

The alert log frequently indicates whether gross tuning problems exist in the database. Tables that are unable to acquire additional storage, sorts that are failing, and problems with rollback segments are all examples of tuning problems that can show up as messages in the alert log. Most of these messages are accompanied by an Oracle error message.

Background and User Trace Files

Oracle trace files are text files that contain session information for the process that created them. Trace files can be generated by the Oracle background processes, through the use of trace events, or by user server processes. These trace files can contain useful information for performance tuning and system troubleshooting. Trace files are also located in the ADR directories.

You can generate user trace files for a particular session by using the `DBMS_MONITOR` package. Many subprograms are available in this package to enable and disable trace; the most common ones are `SESSION_TRACE_ENABLE` to start the tracing and `SESSION_TRACE_DISABLE` to stop the tracing.

To use the `SESSION_TRACE_ENABLE` procedure, you must know the `SID` and `SERIAL#` on the session, which you can get by querying the `V$SESSION` view. The third argument to the procedure is `waits`, which is `TRUE` by default. The fourth argument is `binds`, which is `FALSE` by default. By enabling the waits, the wait information is written to the trace file. By enabling the binds, the bind variable values are also written to the trace file. Once you have the SID and SERIAL#, you can enable trace for the session by doing the following:

```
SQL> BEGIN
       DBMS_MONITOR.SESSION_TRACE_ENABLE(session_id=>324,
                                         serial_num=>54385,
                                         waits=>TRUE,
                                         binds=>TRUE);
     END;
```

To stop tracing, you have to pass in the SID and SERIAL# as parameters:

```
SQL> BEGIN
       DBMS_MONITOR.SESSION_TRACE_DISABLE(session_id=>324,
                                          serial_num=>54385);
     END;
```

You can also use EM Database Control to enable and disable trace. To see the sessions in the instance, you can choose any of the following links under the Additional Monitoring Links on the Performance tab in Database Control (see Figure 14.26):

- Top Consumers
- Blocking Sessions
- Instance Locks
- Search Sessions

FIGURE 14.26 Additional Monitoring Links section on the Performance tab

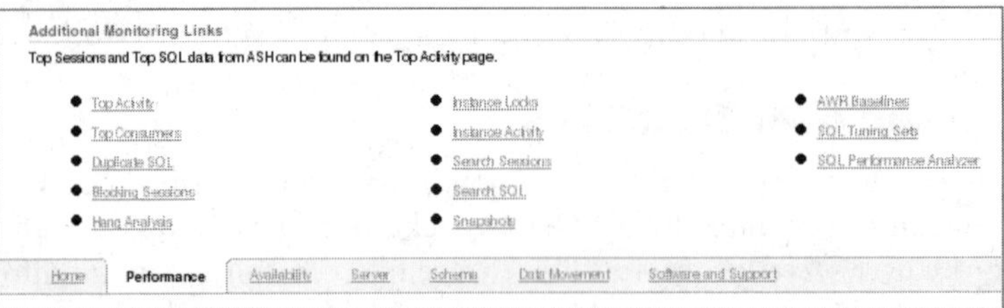

When you click Top Consumers, you will get an overview of the consumers. Click Top Sessions to view the sessions in the instance, as shown in Figure 14.27.

You can use the Enable SQL Trace and Disable SQL Trace buttons on this screen to enable and disable tracing.

The 10046 trace event, which can be activated at the instance or session level, is particularly useful for finding performance bottlenecks. See Note 171647.1 at `http://metalink.oracle.com` for a discussion of using the 10046 trace event as a tuning technique.

FIGURE 14.27 Top Sessions screen on EM

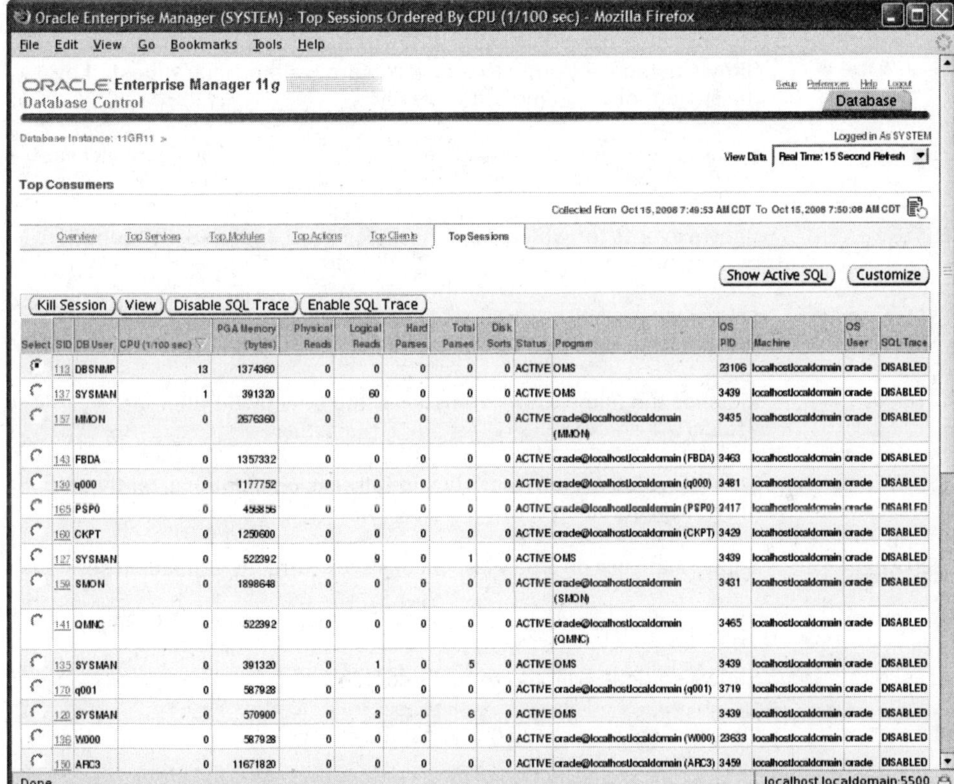

Dynamic Performance Views

As described in Chapter 8, "Introducing Oracle Database 11*g* Components and Architecture," Oracle Database 11*g* contains several dynamic performance views. Table 14.7 contains a partial listing of some of the V$ views that are frequently used in performance tuning and troubleshooting.

TABLE 14.7 A Partial Listing of Dynamic Performance Views

Name	Description
V$SGAINFO	Shows information about the size of the SGA's components
V$PGASTAT	Shows information about PGA memory usage

TABLE 14.7 A Partial Listing of Dynamic Performance Views *(continued)*

Name	Description
V$EVENT_NAME	Shows database events that may require waits when requested by the system or by an individual session
V$SYSTEM_EVENT	Shows events for which waits have occurred for all sessions accessing the system
V$SESSION_EVENT	Shows events for which waits have occurred, individually identified by session
V$SESSION_WAIT	Shows events for which waits are currently occurring, individually identified by session
V$STATNAME	Matches the name to the statistics listed only by number in V$SESSTAT and V$SYSSAT
V$SYSSTAT	Shows overall system statistics for all sessions, both currently and previously connected
V$SESSTAT	Shows statistics on a per-session basis for currently connected sessions
V$SESSION	Shows current connection information on a per-session basis
V$WAITSTAT	Shows statistics related to block contention
V$LOCK	Lists the locks currently in the database
V$PARAMETER	Shows the initialization-parameter values that are currently in effect
V$SPPARAMETER	Shows the contents of the server parameter file (spfile); look for value TRUE in column ISSPECIFIED to see if the parameter was explicitly specified in the spfile, as opposed to default values.
V$FILESTAT	Shows number of reads/writes and timing statistics for data files
V$DATAFILE	Shows data file properties
V$TEMPFILE	Shows temporary file properties
V$TEMPSEG_USAGE	Displays temporary segment usage by session

In general, queries that incorporate V$SYSSTAT show statistics for the entire instance since the time it was started. By joining this view to the other relevant views, you get the overall picture of performance in the database. Alternatively, queries that incorporate V$SESSTAT show statistics for a particular session. These queries are better suited for examining the performance of an individual operation or process. EM Database Control makes extensive use of these views when creating performance-related graphs.

Data Dictionary Views

Depending on the features and options installed, an Oracle 11*g* database has hundreds of data dictionary views. Table 14.8 contains a partial listing of some of the DBA views that are used when you tune performance on a database.

TABLE 14.8 A Partial Listing of Data Dictionary Views for Tuning and Troubleshooting

Name	Description
DBA_TABLES	Table storage, row, and block information
DBA_INDEXES	Index storage, row, and block information
INDEX_STATS	Index depth and dispersion information
DBA_DATA_FILES	Data file location, naming, and size information
DBA_SEGMENTS	General information about any space-consuming segment in the database
DBA_HISTOGRAMS	Table and index histogram definition information
DBA_OBJECTS	General information about all objects in the database, including tables, indexes, triggers, sequences, and partitions
DBA_WAITERS	Shows sessions that are waiting for another session to release a lock
DBA_TABLESPACES	Shows tablespaces in the database and their properties
DBA_FREE_SPACE	Shows the free space available in all tablespaces in the database

The DBA_OBJECTS data dictionary view contains a STATUS column that indicates, through the use of a VALID or INVALID value, whether a database object is valid and ready to be used or is invalid and in need of some attention before it can be used. Invalid and unusable objects are discussed in the next section.

Compiling Invalid and Unusable Objects

Invalid PL/SQL objects and unusable indexes have an impact on database performance. Common examples of invalid objects are PL/SQL code that contains errors or references to other invalid objects and indexes that are unusable because of maintenance operations or failed direct-path load processes. Some invalid objects, such as PL/SQL stored procedures and functions, dynamically recompile the next time they are accessed, and they then take on a status of VALID again. This approach has a cost associated, because users experience a slight delay while the object is being recompiled. But you must manually correct other invalid objects, such as unusable indexes. Therefore, proactive database-management techniques dictate that you identify and remedy invalid objects before they cause problems for database users.

Identifying Unusable Objects Using the Data Dictionary

One way to identify invalid PL/SQL objects is to query the DBA_OBJECTS data dictionary view and then correct them using the commands shown here. The following query identifies the invalid objects in the database:

```
SQL> SELECT owner, object_name, object_type
  2  FROM dba_objects
  3  WHERE status = 'INVALID';

OWNER           OBJECT_NAME                    OBJECT_TYPE
--------------- ------------------------------ ------------
SH              P_UPDATE_SALES_HISTORY         PROCEDURE
WHSE            LOAD_DATASTAGE                 PACKAGE BODY
OE              SAMPLE_VIEW                    VIEW
```

As you can see in the query, few objects are invalid in the database. To compile these invalid objects, you can use the ALTER *object_name* command. For example, to compile the view and procedure, do the following:

```
SQL> ALTER VIEW oe.sample_view COMPILE;

View altered.

SQL> ALTER PROCEDURE sh.p_update_sales_history COMPILE;

Procedure altered.
```

You can use the same syntax to compile a view, procedure, function, package specification, or trigger. To compile a package body, the syntax is slightly different:

```
SQL> ALTER PACKAGE whse.load_datastage COMPILE BODY;

Package body altered.
```

Indexes may be left in the unusable state, where direct-load operations on the table fail for some reason. Unusable indexes are ignored by the optimizer. You can identify such indexes by querying the DBA_INDEXES view. If the index is partitioned, you must query DBA_INDEX_PARTITIONS:

```
SQL> SELECT owner, index_name, index_type
  2  FROM dba_indexes
  3  WHERE status = 'UNUSABLE';
OWNER           INDEX_NAME                     INDEX_TYPE
--------------- ------------------------------ ----------
HR              JOB_ID_PK                      NORMAL
```

To fix the issue, you can rebuild the index:

```
SQL> ALTER INDEX hr.job_id_pk REBUILD;
```

When rebuilding an index using the REBUILD command, the amount of space used by the index is temporarily larger than the actual space needed to store the index. Make sure that adequate space exists in the tablespace before starting the rebuild process. This is because when you rebuild the index, Oracle builds a new index at a new location and drops the unusable index after the new index is built. You may specify the TABLESPACE clause and ONLINE clause for the index rebuild. By specifying the TABLESPACE clause, you can rebuild the index to a new tablespace. The ONLINE clause makes sure that users can perform DML operations on the table while the index is rebuilt. If ONLINE is not specified, users wait for the index rebuild to complete.

By default, Oracle 11*g* checks for invalid object metrics every 24 hours.

Identifying Unusable Objects Using EM

EM Database Control also offers a mechanism for fixing invalid database objects. Figure 14.28 shows the Schema tab in EM Database Control. You can see various types of objects under the Database Objects group and the Programs group.

FIGURE 14.28 Schema tab in EM Database Control

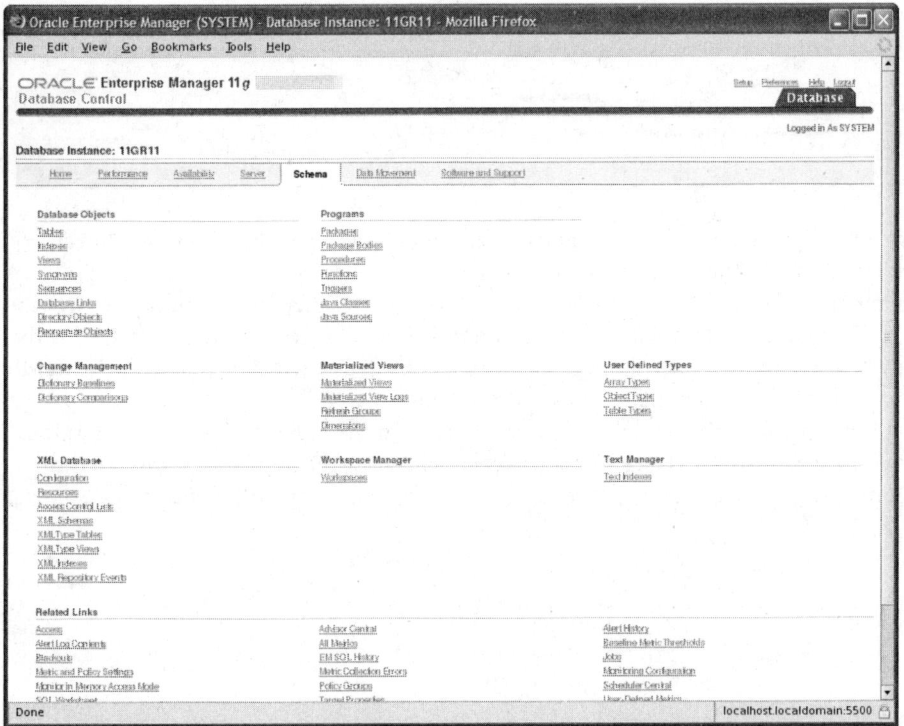

You can get a list of PL/SQL objects and their status by clicking any of the PL/SQL object types under Programs. To list the views and their status, click the Views link under Database Objects. Figure 14.29 shows that the object list is filtered by the HR schema, and you can see that the view is invalid. To compile the view, choose Compile in the Actions drop-down, and click Go.

FIGURE 14.29 Compile Invalid View using EM Database Control

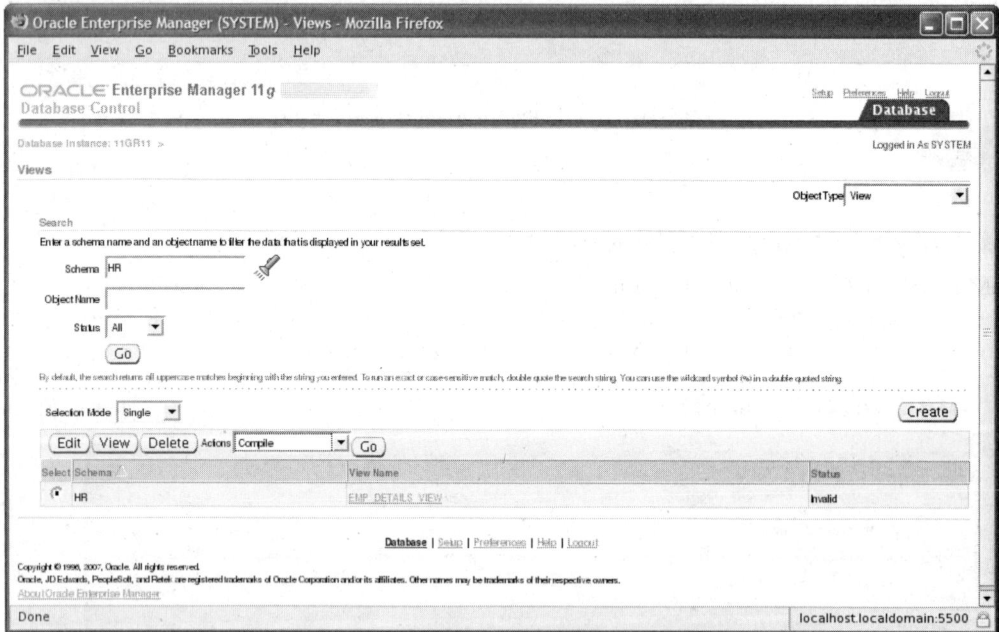

Using the same screen, you can choose a different object type by using the Object Type drop-down, rather than going back and forth on the EM screen.

To rebuild an index, choose the Reorganize action after picking the index you want to rebuild. EM guides you through a six-step interview process to set new attributes for the index when rebuilt. EM provides an impact report in step 4, which is particularly useful in analyzing the space requirements, as shown in Figure 14.30.

EM Database Control will generate a job to rebuild the index and submit it at a time specified by you in step 5. The summary screen will show the SQL statements used to rebuild the index as well as the procedures submitted to schedule the rebuild task.

FIGURE 14.30 Impact Report for rebuilding the index

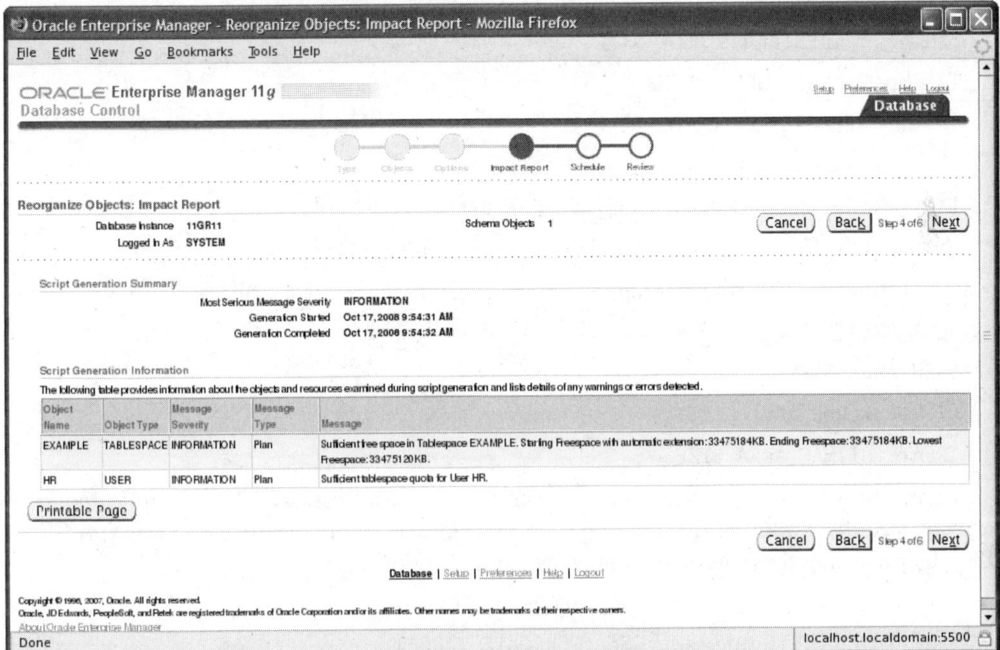

Tuning Memory

In Chapter 8 you learned about the architecture of Oracle 11*g*. An Oracle instance consists of memory structures and background processes. The memory structure comprises SGA and PGA, and it is important to size the SGA and PGA appropriately for better database performance.

Fortunately, Oracle 11*g* provides a variety of automatic options to tune memory so that DBAs don't need to worry about tuning the individual memory components such as the Java pool and the shared pool. In the following sections, you will revisit the memory components and learn the options available to tune and manage.

Memory Components

The two primary memory components are SGA and PGA. SGA consists of the following components. The parameters that control these pools are also provided for your reference.

- Shared pool: `SHARED_POOL_SIZE`
- Database buffer cache: `DB_CACHE_SIZE`

- Large pool: LARGE_POOL_SIZE
- Java pool: JAVA_POOL_SIZE
- Streams pool: STREAMS_POOL_SIZE
- Log buffer: LOG_BUFFER_SIZE
- Result Cache: RESULT_CACHE_SIZE
- Database keep buffer cache: DB_KEEP_CACHE_SIZE
- Database recycle buffer cache: DB_RECYCLE_CACHE_SIZE
- Buffer cache for nonstandard block size: DB_nK_CACHE_SIZE

The parameters that can be configured to manage the PGA are as follows:

- SORT_AREA_SIZE
- HASH_AREA_SIZE
- BITMAP_MERGE_AREA_SIZE
- CREATE_BITMAP_AREA_SIZE

As you can see from the previous components and parameters, it can get complicated to correctly size these pools and memory parameters. Oracle 11*g* takes the pain away from DBAs by providing these automatic memory-tuning options:

- Automatic SGA tuning using SGA_TARGET
- Automatic PGA tuning using PGA_AGGREGATE_TARGET
- Automatic Memory tuning (PGA and SGA) using MEMORY_TARGET

The following advisors views are available in Oracle 11*g* to tune the individual components of memory:

- V$DB_CACHE_ADVICE to size the database buffer cache
- V$SHARED_POOL_ADVICE to size the shared pool
- V$JAVA_POOL_ADVICE to size the Java pool
- V$STREAMS_POOL_ADVICE to size the streams pool

Automatic Shared Memory Management

Automatic Shared Memory Management (ASMM) was introduced in Oracle 10*g* and can automatically tune five important SGA components as well as the area required (fixed size) for internal allocations:

- SHARED_POOL_SIZE
- DB_CACHE_SIZE
- LARGE_POOL_SIZE
- JAVA_POOL_SIZE
- STREAMS_POOL_SIZE

To enable ASMM, you set the SGA_TARGET parameter, where you specify the total size for the SGA. You still have to manually size the other SGA components, which in most cases do not need much tuning. These components are as follows:

- LOG_BUFFER
- DB_KEEP_CACHE_SIZE
- DB_RECYCLE_CACHE_SIZE
- DB_nK_CACHE_SIZE

SGA_TARGET is a dynamic parameter; you can increase it to the maximum size specified by the static parameter SGA_MAX_SIZE.

You can change a dynamic initialization parameter by using the ALTER SYSTEM statement, whereas you should change static parameters in the spfile or init.ora first. The instance needs to be restarted for the new value to take effect.

You can still specify sizes for the five pools when using ASMM. Oracle will use the values specified as the minimum size for the components. To get full automatic tuning, the five SGA components must be set to zero or not specified in the initialization file.

The parameter STATISTICS_LEVEL must be set to TYPICAL or ALL for the Automatic Shared Memory Management feature to function.

You can tune the appropriate size of SGA_TARGET using the advisor view V$SGA_TARGET_ADVICE. The V$SGAINFO view shows the sizes of various SGA components.

```
SQL> SELECT * FROM v$sgainfo;

NAME                                  BYTES RES
-------------------------------- ---------- ---
Fixed SGA Size                      1303916 No
Redo Buffers                        4935680 No
Buffer Cache Size                 318767104 Yes
Shared Pool Size                  352321536 Yes
Large Pool Size                    25165824 Yes
Java Pool Size                     12582912 Yes
Streams Pool Size                         0 Yes
Shared IO Pool Size                       0 Yes
Granule Size                        4194304 No
Maximum SGA Size                  954155008 No
Startup overhead in Shared Pool    46137344 No
Free SGA Memory Available         239075328
```

```
SQL> SELECT * FROM v$sga_target_advice;

  SGA_SIZE SGA_SIZE_FACTOR ESTD_DB_TIME ESTD_DB_TIME_FACTOR ESTD_PHYSICAL_READS
---------- --------------- ------------ ------------------- -------------------
       684               1          301                   1               27924
       342              .5          323              1.0731               31035
       513             .75          301                   1               27924
       855            1.25          278               .9236               24657
      1026             1.5          278               .9236               24657
      1197            1.75          278               .9236               24657
      1368               2          278               .9236               24657
```

Automatic SQL Execution Memory Management

You can use Automatic SQL Execution Memory Management to tune the PGA using the PGA_AGGREGATE_TARGET and WORKAREA_SIZE_POLICY parameters. Both parameters can be dynamically modified.

PGA_AGGREGATE_TARGET specifies the target amount of memory available to the instance (PGA memory) for all server processes. Setting a nonzero value for PGA_AGGREGATE_TARGET automatically sets the WORKAREA_SIZE_POLICY parameter to AUTO, which means the _AREA_SIZE parameters are automatically sized.

If you set PGA_AGGREGATE_TARGET=0 and set WORKAREA_SIZE_POLICY to AUTO, Oracle 11*g* will throw an ORA-04032 error at startup.

You can tune PGA performance by using the advisor view V$PGA_TARGET_ADVICE. The advice is generated by simulating past workload.

Automatic Memory Management

Automatic Memory Management (AMM) is new to Oracle 11*g* and further eases the memory management. AMM automatically tunes the SGA and PGA components. All you have to do is to specify the total memory available to the instance by using the MEMORY_TARGET parameter.

When AMM is used, Oracle automates the sizing of SGA and PGA, and it causes the indirect transfer of memory from SGA to PGA, and vice versa, as required by the workload. The default for SGA is 60 percent and the default for PGA is 40 percent allocation when the instance is started.

MEMORY_TARGET is a dynamic parameter; you can increase it up to the maximum specified by the static parameter MEMORY_MAX_TARGET. By default, AMM is not enabled in Oracle 11*g*—the default value for MEMORY_TARGET is zero.

You still can set SGA_TARGET, PGA_AGGREGATE_TARGET, and the various SGA pool parameters in the initialization file. Oracle 11*g* will use these values as the minimum when configuring the various pools. Table 14.9 shows some rules when you have configured the AMM and ASMM memory parameters.

TABLE 14.9 Memory-Tuning Parameters Dependency

MEMORY_TARGET (**MT**)	SGA_TARGET (**ST**)	**Result**
MT=0 AMM is disabled	AMM is disabled ASMM is disabled	ST=0 Must specify values for individual pools.
MT=0	AMM is disabled ASMM is enabled	ST>0 Individual pools will be automatically tuned. SGA and PGA memory will be treated separately.
MT>0	AMM is enabled ASMM is disabled	ST=0 Full automatic tuning of SGA and PGA.
MT>0	AMM is enabled ASMM is enabled	ST>0 Automatic tuning of SGA and PGA, but SGA will keep the minimum value specified by ST.

You can adjust the MEMORY_TARGET parameter size after reviewing the advisor view V$MEMORY_TARGET_ADVICE:

```
SQL> SELECT * FROM v$memory_target_advice;

MEMORY_SIZE MEMORY_SIZE_FACTOR ESTD_DB_TIME ESTD_DB_TIME_FACTOR    VERSION
----------- ------------------ ------------ ------------------- ----------
        912                  1          303                   1          0
        456                 .5          304                   1          0
        684                .75          304                   1          0
       1140               1.25          304                   1          0
       1368                1.5          304                   1          0
       1596               1.75          304                   1          0
       1824                  2          304                   1          0
```

If you want to know the size of all the AMM memory components, you can query the V$MEMORY_DYNAMIC_COMPONENTS view:

```
SQL> SELECT component, current_size, min_size, max_size
  2  FROM v$memory_dynamic_components;

COMPONENT                      CURRENT_SIZE   MIN_SIZE   MAX_SIZE
------------------------------ ------------ ---------- ----------
shared pool                       352321536  352321536  352321536
large pool                         25165824    8388608   25165824
java pool                          12582912   12582912   12582912
streams pool                              0          0          0
SGA Target                        717225984  717225984  717225984
DEFAULT buffer cache              318767104  318767104  335544320
KEEP buffer cache                         0          0          0
RECYCLE buffer cache                      0          0          0
DEFAULT 2K buffer cache                   0          0          0
DEFAULT 4K buffer cache                   0          0          0
DEFAULT 8K buffer cache                   0          0          0
DEFAULT 16K buffer cache                  0          0          0
DEFAULT 32K buffer cache                  0          0          0
Shared IO Pool                            0          0          0
PGA Target                        239075328  239075328  239075328
ASM Buffer Cache                          0          0          0
```

The V$MEMORY_RESIZE_OPS view has a circular history of the last 800 SGA resize requests, both manual and automatic.

Managing Memory Using EM Database Control

You can use EM Database Control to enable and disable various memory-tuning options as well as monitor the memory components and their performance. You can use the information on this screen to decide whether your Oracle 11*g* database needs more memory allocated for better performance. On the Server tab, click the Memory Advisors link on the Database Configuration section. This takes you to the Memory Advisors screen, as shown in Figure 14.31.

This screen shows the current status of memory usage as well as gives you the option to enable or disable Automatic Memory Management. Click the Advice button, and you can view the memory size advice.

FIGURE 14.31 Memory Advisors screen in EM

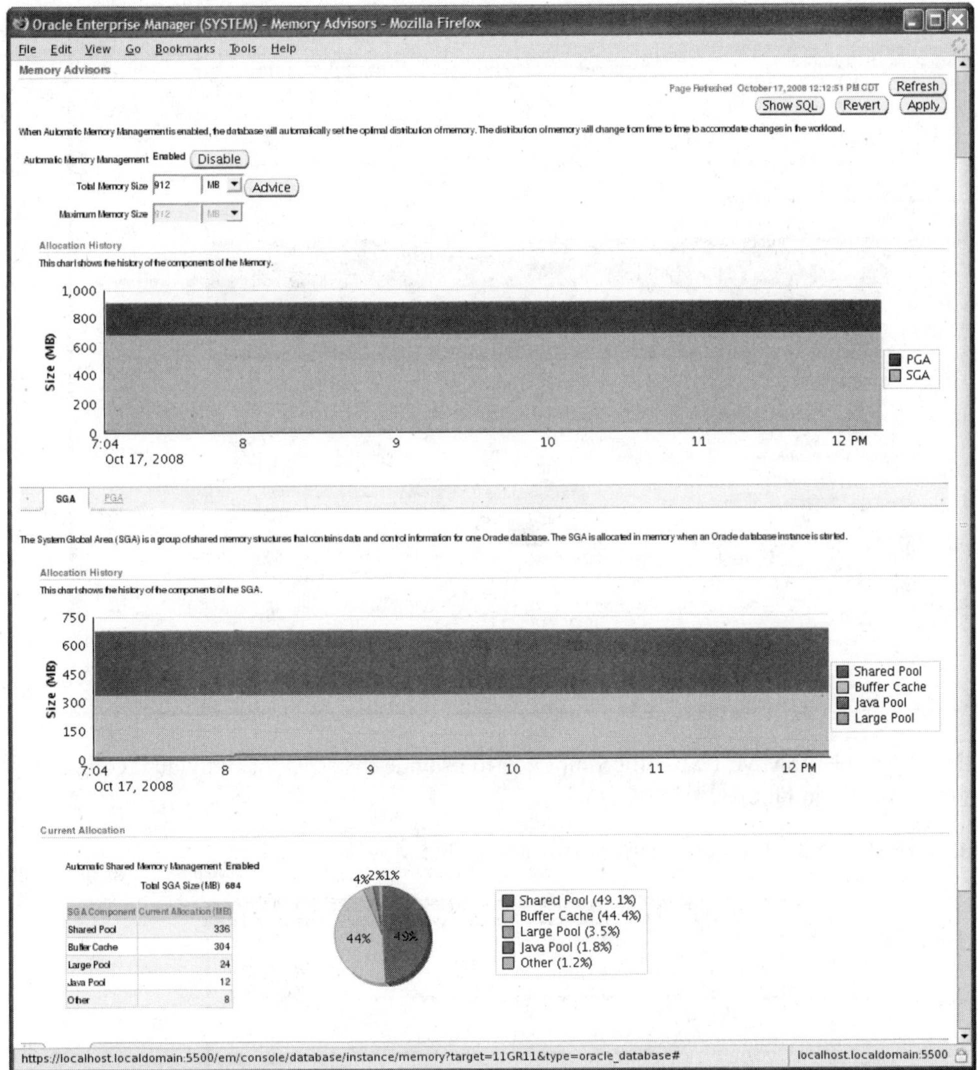

If you disable AMM using the Disable button, EM automatically enables ASMM, as shown in Figure 14.32.

FIGURE 14.32 ASMM screen in EM

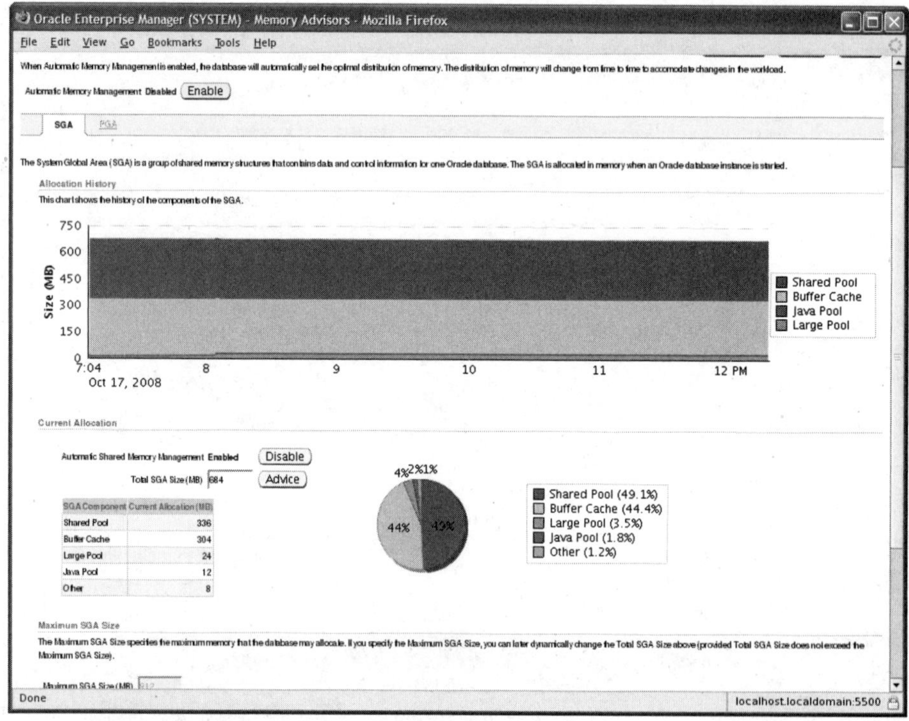

If you disable ASMM, EM will prompt you to provide the sizes for individual components, as shown in Figure 14.33.

FIGURE 14.33 Memory Components screen in EM

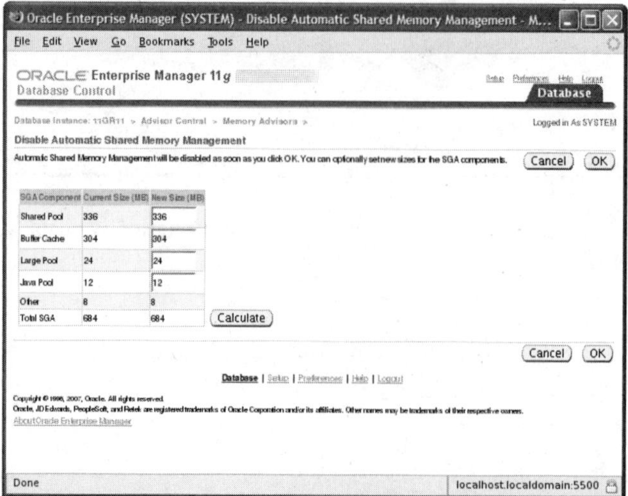

You can also get to the Memory Advisor screen from Advisor Central. EM also shows several important performance metrics, discussed in the next section.

Important Performance Metrics

Throughput is another example of a statistical performance metric. *Throughput* is the amount of processing that a computer or system can perform in a given amount of time, for example, the number of customer deposits that can be posted to the appropriate accounts in four hours under regular workloads. Throughput is an important measure when considering the scalability of the system. *Scalability* refers to the degree to which additional users can be added to the system without system performance declining significantly. New features such as Oracle Database 10g's Grid Computing capabilities make Oracle one of the most scalable database platforms on the market.

Performance considerations for transactional systems usually revolve around throughput maximization.

Another important metric related to performance is response time. *Response time* is the amount of time it takes for a single user's request to return the desired result when using an application, for example, the time it takes for the system to return a listing of all the customers who purchased products that require service contracts.

Performance-tuning considerations for decision-support systems usually revolve around response time minimization.

You can use EM Database Control to both monitor and react to sudden changes in performance metrics such as throughput and response time.

Using EM Database Control to View Performance Metrics

EM Database Control provides a graphical view of throughput, response time, I/O, and other important performance metrics. The Performance tab in EM Database Control gives a good overview of database performance, as shown earlier in this chapter in Figure 14.13. On this screen you can see session performance and host performance, as well as throughput, I/O, and concurrency. The Additional Monitoring Links section on this screen takes you to various performance-tuning screens, shown earlier in Figure 14.26.

Click Top Activity to view the top sessions in the instance. You can drill down to a particular wait category. This screen is useful to figure out whether there was a performance problem and if you want to know what happened in the last few minutes, as shown in Figure 14.34.

FIGURE 14.34 Top Activity screen on EM

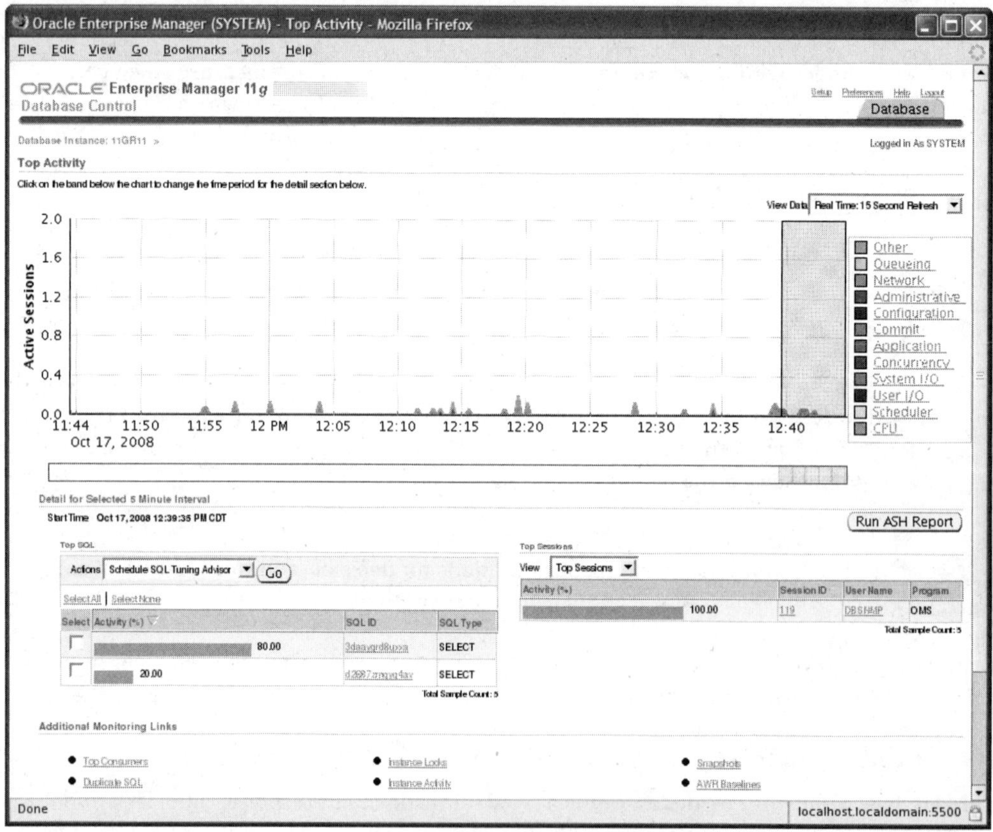

The Top Consumers link is another very useful tool. When you click this link, an Overview tab is displayed, as shown in Figure 14.35.

FIGURE 14.35 Top Consumers overview on EM

This tab shows the following sections:

- Top Services
- Top Modules
- Top Actions
- Top Clients
- Top Sessions

The Top Sessions area shows the CPU usage and I/O operations for each session, as shown previously in Figure 14.27.

Summary

Oracle 11*g* provides many tools for proactively identifying and fixing potential performance and management problems in the database. In this chapter, you learned about tools such as AWR, ADDR, ADR, AMM, and ASMM.

At the core of the monitoring system is the Automatic Workload Repository, which uses the MMON background process to gather statistics from the SGA and store them in a collection of tables owned by the user `SYSMAN`.

Following each AWR statistics collection interval, the Automatic Database Diagnostic Monitoring feature examines the newly gathered statistics and compares them with the two previous AWR statistics to establish baselines in an attempt to identify poorly performing components of the database. The ADDM then summarizes these findings on the EM Database Control main screen and Performance tab. Using these screens, you can identify and examine the SQL statements that are contributing the most to DB Time. You can further explore the opportunities for improving the performance or manageability of your database using the EM Database Control advisors, which include the SQL Tuning Advisor, SQL Access Advisor, Memory Advisor, Mean Time To Recover Advisor, Segment Advisor, and Undo Management Advisor.

In addition to alerts, you can find indicators of database performance in the database alert log, user and background trace files, data dictionary views, and dynamic performance views. Some data dictionary views do not contain accurate information about the segments in the database until after statistics are collected on those objects. Therefore, you can automatically collect segment statistics through the use of EM Database Control jobs.

Invalid and unusable database objects also have a negative impact on performance and manageability. You can monitor and repair invalid and unusable objects using the data dictionary and the EM Database Control Administration screen.

Memory tuning is simplified in Oracle 11*g* using Automatic Memory Management. AMM is configured using the `MEMORY_TARGET` parameter. If other memory parameters are specified, they will be considered as the minimum for those components.

EM Database Control summarizes several important performance metrics on the EM Database Control main screen. These metrics include performance statistics for the host server, user sessions, and instance throughput.

Exam Essentials

Understand the Automatic Workload Repository. Describe the components of the AWR and how they are used to collect and store database performance statistics.

Describe the role of Automatic Database Diagnostic Monitor. Know how ADDM uses the AWR statistics to formulate tuning recommendations using historical and baseline metrics.

Explain how each advisor is used to improve performance. Describe how you can use each of the EM Database Control advisors shown on the Advisor Central screen to improve database performance and manageability.

Describe how alerts are used to monitor performance. Show how you can configure the EM Database Control alert system to alert you via the console or via email whenever a monitored event occurs in the database.

Remember the location of alert log file. Starting in Oracle 11g, the alert log file location is determined by the `DIAGNOSTIC_DEST` parameter. Learn the location of the text alert log file and XML alert log file.

Identify and fix invalid or unusable objects. Understand the techniques you can use to identify invalid procedures, functions, triggers, and views and how to validate them. Know how to find unusable indexes and how to fix them.

Understand Automatic Memory Management. Know the parameters that control the memory management and how the pools are allocated.

Understand sources of tuning information. Know in which dynamic performance views, data dictionary views, and log files tuning information can be found outside the EM Database Control monitoring system.

Review Questions

1. Which of the following components of the Oracle architecture stores the statistics gathered by the MMON process?

   A. ADDM

   B. AWR

   C. ASMM

   D. ADR

2. Which of the following options for the pfile/spfile's STATISTICS_LEVEL parameter turns off AWR statistics gathering and ADDM advisory services?

   A. OFF

   B. TYPICAL

   C. ALL

   D. BASIC

3. Which parameter is used to enable Automatic Memory Management?

   A. AMM_TARGET

   B. MEMORY_TARGET

   C. SGA_TARGET

   D. All of the above

4. Which statement about an index with the status UNUSABLE in DBA_INDEXES is true?

   A. The index will be automatically fixed the next time it is used.

   B. The Oracle optimizer throws an error when it tries to use the index.

   C. The index must be recompiled using the ALTER INDEX...RECOMPILE statement.

   D. The index must be reorganized using the ALTER INDEX...REBUILD statement before it can be used again.

5. Suppose you have used EM Database Control to drill down into ADDM findings and have found that a single SQL statement is causing the majority of I/O on your system. Which of the following advisors is best suited to troubleshoot this SQL statement?

   A. SQL Tuning Advisor

   B. SQL Access Advisor

   C. Both A and B

   D. Neither A nor B

6. You found out that few procedures in the APPS schema have an INVALID status in the DBA_OBJECTS view. What are your options to fix the issue? (Choose the best two answers.)

   A. Do nothing. When the procedure is accessed the next time, Oracle will try to recompile.

   B. Drop the procedure so that users get a valid error.

   C. Recompile the procedure using ALTER PROCEDURE…COMPILE.

   D. Contact the developer or vendor to get the source code and re-create the procedure.

7. Which procedure is used to tell Oracle that the statistics gathered should not be published?

   A. DBMS_STATS.PUBLISH_STATS

   B. DBMS_STATS.SET_TABLE_PREFS

   C. DBMS_STATS.PENDING_STATS

   D. DBMS_STATS.GATHER_TABLE_STATS

8. Which data dictionary view contains information explaining why ADDM made its recommendations?

   A. DBA_ADVISOR_FINDINGS

   B. DBA_ADVISOR_OBJECTS

   C. DBA_ADVISOR_RECOMMENDATIONS

   D. DBA_ADVISOR_RATIONALE

9. Which of the following advisors determines whether the space allocated to the shared pool, large pool, or buffer cache is adequate?

   A. SQL Tuning Advisor

   B. SGA Tuning Advisor

   C. Memory Advisor

   D. Pool Advisor

10. Which of the following advisors determines whether the estimated instance-recovery duration is within the expected service-level agreements?

    A. Undo Management Advisor

    B. SQL Access Advisor

    C. SQL Tuning Advisor

    D. MTTR Advisor

11. If no email address is specified, where will alert information be displayed?

    A. In the DBA_ALERTS data dictionary view.

    B. In the V$ALERTS dynamic performance view.

    C. In the EM Database Control main screen.

    D. No alert information is sent or displayed.

12. When you configure an alert, which of the following types of alert thresholds can you use to monitor a tablespace for diminishing free space?

A. Warning threshold

B. Critical threshold

C. Both A and B

D. Neither A nor B

13. Multiple baseline metrics can be gathered and stored in the AWR. Why might you want more than one metrics baseline?

A. You might want a separate baseline metric for each user.

B. You might want a separate baseline metric for daytime usage vs. off-hours usage.

C. You might want a separate baseline metric for each schema.

D. You would never want more than one baseline metric, even though it is possible to gather and store them.

14. Using EM Database Control, you discover that two application PL/SQL functions and a view are currently invalid. Which of the following might you use to fix these objects? (Choose two.)

A. Shut down and restart the database.

B. Use EM Database Control to recompile the object.

C. Export the invalid objects, drop them, and then import them.

D. Use the `ALTER FUNCTION...COMPILE` and `ALTER VIEW...COMPILE` commands.

15. Which statement about `MEMORY_TARGET` parameter is not true?

A. It is a dynamic initialization parameter.

B. It represents the total maximum memory that can be allocated to the instance memory (PGA and SGA combined).

C. Its default value is zero.

D. You will not get an error when `SGA_TARGET` and `PGA_AGGREGATE_TARGET` parameters are set to nonzero values.

16. Which of the following is a performance metric that could be defined as "the amount of work that a system can perform in a given amount of time"?

A. Response time

B. Uptime

C. Throughput

D. Runtime

17. Which of the following is typically not one of the three primary sources of performance metric information on the EM Database Control Performance tab?

    A. Host

    B. Session

    C. Instance

    D. Network

18. By default, how long will database statistics be retained in the AWR?

    A. 7 days

    B. 30 days

    C. 7 hours

    D. Indefinitely

19. Your users have called to complain that system performance has suddenly decreased markedly. Where would be the most likely place to look for the cause of the problem in EM Database Control?

    A. Main screen

    B. Performance tab

    C. Administration tab

    D. Maintenance tab

20. Using EM Database Control, you've identified that the following SQL statement is the source of a high amount of disk I/O:

    ```
    SELECT NAME, LOCATION, CREDIT_LIMIT FROM CUSTOMERS
    ```

    What might you do first to try to improve performance?

    A. Run the SQL Tuning Advisor.

    B. Run the SQL Access Advisor.

    C. Check the EM Database Control main screen for alerts.

    D. Click the Alert Log Content link in the EM Database Control main screen.

Answers to Review Questions

1. B. The MMON process gathers statistics from the SGA and stores them in the AWR. The ADDM process then uses these statistics to compare the current state of the database with baseline and historical performance metrics before summarizing the results on the EM Database Control screens.

2. D. Setting STATISTICS_LEVEL = BASIC disables the collection and analysis of AWR statistics. TYPICAL is the default setting, and ALL gathers information for the execution plan and operating-system timing. OFF is not a valid value for this parameter.

3. B. Automatic Memory Management is enabled by setting a nonzero value for the MEMORY_TARGET parameter. The default value for this parameter is zero. SGA_TARGET enables the ASSM (Automatic Shared Memory Management) feature.

4. D. Unusable indexes must be manually rebuilt by the DBA, or the user owning the index can rebuild or drop/recreate as well, before the index can be used. The Oracle optimizer ignores the unusable index.

5. C. You can use the SQL Tuning Advisor and SQL Access Advisor together to determine whether I/O can be minimized and overall DB Time reduced to the targeted SQL statement.

6. A, C. Invalid PL/SQL objects will be automatically recompiled the next time they are accessed. The DBA can manually recompile the procedure. Manual recompilation is the recommended approach.

7. B. The DBMS_STATS.SET_TABLE_PREFS procedure is used to set the PUBLISH preference to FALSE. To be able to use the pending statistics, the OPTIMIZER_USE_PENDING_STATISTICS parameter must be set to TRUE in the session.

8. D. DBA_ADVISOR_RATIONALE provides the rationale for each ADDM recommendation. The ADDM findings are stored in DBA_ADVISOR_FINDINGS. The objects related to the findings are shown in DBA_ADVISOR_OBJECTS. The actual ADDM recommendations are found in DBA_ADVISOR_RECOMMENDATIONS.

9. C. The Memory Advisor can help determine whether the overall size of the SGA is appropriate and whether memory is properly allocated to the SGA components.

10. D. The Mean Time To Recover (MTTR) Advisor provides recommendations that you can use to configure the database so that the instance-recovery time fits within the service levels that you specified.

11. C. By default, alerts are displayed in the Alerts section of the EM Database Control main screen, even when email notifications are not configured.

12. C. You can specify both warning and critical thresholds for monitoring the available free space in a tablespace. In this situation, the warning threshold is generally a lower number than the critical threshold.

13. B. Because many transactional systems run batch processing during off-hours, having a relevant baseline for each type of usage pattern yields better results in terms of alerts and ADDM recommendations.

14. B, D. After fixing the issue that originally caused the invalid status, you can use both EM Database Control and SQL to compile an invalid object. Starting and stopping the database will not fix invalid objects. Export/import is also not an appropriate technique for recompiling invalid objects.

15. B. MEMORY_TARGET represents the total size allocated for SGA and PGA components. The maximum that can be allocated for these structures is determined by the MEMORY_MAX_TARGET parameter. You still can set the SGA_TARGET and PGA_AGGREGATE_TARGET parameters; Oracle will use these as the minimums.

16. C. Throughput is an important performance metric because it is an overall measure of performance that can be compared against similar measures taken before and after tuning changes are implemented.

17. D. Network information may be contained in the Session Information section of the EM Database Control Performance screen, but only if network issues contributed to session wait times.

18. A. By default, database statistics are retained in the AWR for seven days. You can change the default duration using the EM Database Control Automatic Workload Repository link on the Performance tab or using the DBMS_WORKLOAD_REPOSITORY PL/SQL package.

19. B. The Performance tab of EM Database Control provides a quick overview of how the host system, user sessions, and throughput are impacted by the system slowdown. You can also drill down into any of these three areas to take a look at details about this slowdown.

20. A. Running the SQL Tuning Advisor provides the most information about how the performance of this SQL statement might be improved. The SQL Access Advisor is run only after the output from the SQL Tuning Advisor indicates that it will be useful. EM Database Control does not store detailed information about I/O activity in either its alerts or the alert log.

Implementing Database Backups

ORACLE DATABASE 11*g*: ADMINISTRATION I EXAM OBJECTIVES COVERED IN THIS CHAPTER:

✓ **Backup and Recovery Concepts**

- Identify the importance of checkpoints, redo log files, and archived log files
- Overview of flash recovery area
- Configure ARCHIVELOG mode

✓ **Performing Database Backups**

- Create consistent database backups
- Back up your database without shutting it down
- Create incremental backups
- Automate database backups
- Manage backups, view backup reports and monitor the flash recovery area

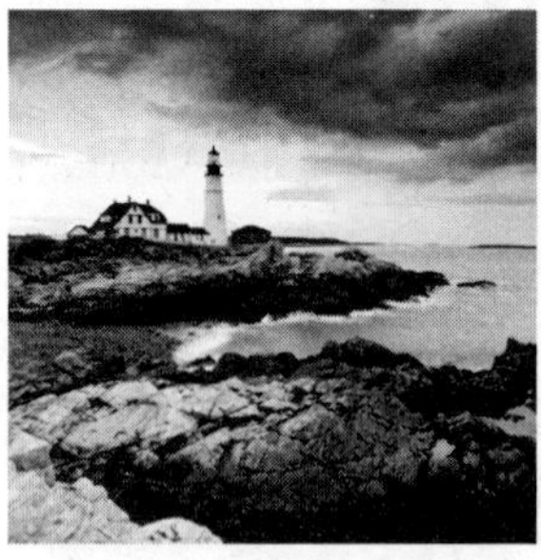

Oracle's administration tool, Enterprise Manager Database Control, makes configuring and performing backups easier. Most, if not all, of the functionality available with the command-line interface is available in a graphical user interface to save time and make backup operations less error-prone.

Oracle Database 11*g* makes it easy for you to configure your database to be highly available and reliable. In other words, you want to configure your database to minimize the amount of downtime while at the same time being able to recover quickly and without losing any committed transactions when the database becomes unavailable for reasons that may be beyond your control.

In this chapter, I will first describe the components you will use to minimize or eliminate data loss in your database while at the same time keeping availability high. Specifically, I will cover the following:

- Checkpoints
- Redo log files
- Archived redo log files
- The flash recovery area

Next, you will learn how to configure your database for recovery. This will include a discussion of `ARCHIVELOG` mode and other required initialization parameters. Once your environment is configured, you will need to know how to actually back it up, using both operating-system commands and the RMAN utility. You will also learn how to automate and manage your backups as well as how to monitor one of the key components in your backup strategy: the flash recovery area. In Chapter 16, "Recovering the Database," you will then learn how to use the files created and maintained during your backups to quickly recover the database in the event of a database failure.

Understanding and Configuring Recovery Components

As a database administrator, your primary goal is to keep the database open and available for users, usually 24 hours a day, 7 days a week. Your partnership with the server's system administrator includes the following tasks:

- Proactively solving common causes of failures
- Increasing the mean time between failure (MTBF)

- Ensuring a high level of hardware redundancy
- Increasing availability by using Oracle options such as Real Application Clusters (RAC) and Oracle Streams (an advanced replication technology)
- Decreasing the mean time to recover (MTTR) by setting the appropriate Oracle initialization parameters and ensuring that backups are readily available in a recovery scenario
- Minimizing or eliminating loss of committed transactions by using archived redo logs, standby databases, and Oracle Data Guard

A number of structures and events in the database directly support backup and recovery operations. The control files maintain the list of database files in the database, along with a record of the most recent database backups (if you are using RMAN for your backups). The checkpoint (CKPT) background process works in concert with the database writer (DBW*n*) process to manage the amount of time required for instance recovery; during instance recovery, the redo log files are used to synchronize the data files. For more serious types of failures, such as media failures, archived redo log files are applied to a restored backup copy of a data file to synchronize the data files and ensure that no committed transactions are lost. Finally, the flash recovery area, introduced in Oracle 10*g*, is a common area for all recovery-related files that makes your job much easier when backing up or recovering your database.

To maximize your database's availability, it almost goes without saying that you want to perform regularly scheduled backups. Most media failures require some kind of restoration of a data file from a disk or tape backup before you can initiate media recovery.

In addition to regularly scheduled backups (see the section "Performing Backups" later in this chapter), you can configure a number of other features to maximize your database's availability and minimize recovery time, such as multiplexing control files, multiplexing redo log files, configuring the database in `ARCHIVELOG` mode, and using a flash recovery area.

Understanding Control Files

The control file is one of the smallest, yet also one of the most critical, files in the database. Recovering from the loss of one copy of a control file is relatively straightforward; recovering from the loss of your only control file or all control files is more of a challenge and requires more-advanced recovery techniques.

In the following section, you will get an overview of the control file architecture. You will then learn how maximize the recoverability of the control file in the section "Multiplexing Control Files."

Control File Architecture

The control file is a relatively small (in the megabyte range) binary file that contains information about the structure of the database. You can think of the control file as a metadata repository for the physical database. It has the structure of the database, meaning the data files and redo log files constitute a database. The control file is created when the database is created and is updated with the physical changes, for example, whenever you add or rename a file.

The control file is updated continuously and should be available at all times. Don't edit the contents of the control file; only Oracle processes should update its contents. When you start up the database, Oracle uses the control file to identify and to open the data files and redo log files. Control files play a major role when recovering a database.

The contents of the control file include the following:

- The database name to which the control file belongs. A control file can belong to only one database.
- The database-creation timestamp.
- The name, location, and online/offline status information of the data files.
- The name and location of the redo log files.
- Redo log archive information.
- Tablespace names.
- The current log sequence number, which is a unique identifier that is incremented and recorded when an online redo log file is switched.
- The most recent checkpoint information.
- The beginning and ending of undo segments.
- Recovery Manager's backup information. Recovery Manager (RMAN) is the Oracle utility you use to back up and recover databases.

The control file size is determined by the `MAX` clauses you provide when you create the database:

- `MAXLOGFILES`
- `MAXLOGMEMBERS`
- `MAXLOGHISTORY`
- `MAXDATAFILES`
- `MAXINSTANCES`

Oracle preallocates space for these maximums in the control file. Therefore, when you add or rename a file in the database, the control file size does not change.

When you add a new file to the database or relocate a file, an Oracle server process immediately updates the information in the control file. Back up the control file after any structural changes. The log writer (LGWR) process updates the control file with the current log sequence number. The CKPT process updates the control file with the recent checkpoint information. When the database is in `ARCHIVELOG` mode, the archiver (ARC*n*) process updates the control file with information such as the archive log filename and log sequence number.

The control file contains two types of record sections: reusable and not reusable. RMAN information is kept in the reusable section. Items such as the names of the backup data files are kept in this section, and once this section fills up, the entries are reused in a circular fashion after the number of days specified by the initialization parameter `CONTROL_FILE_RECORD_KEEP_TIME` is reached. Therefore, the control file can continue to grow because of new RMAN backup information recorded in the control file before `CONTROL_FILE_RECORD_KEEP_TIME`.

You can query the control file names and their status by using EM Database Control. On the Server tab, click the Control Files link under Storage. You will see the Control Files screen, as shown in Figure 15.1.

FIGURE 15.1 Control Files screen of EM

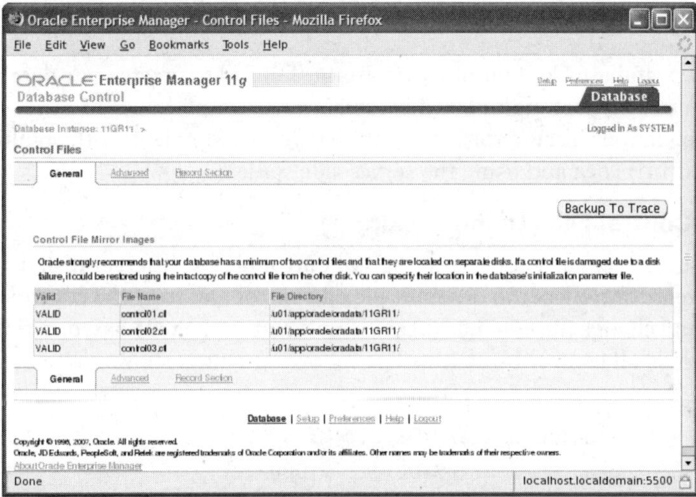

The Record Section tab on this screen shows the record information from the control file, as shown in Figure 15.2. It shows the size used in the control file for each section, the total number of records that can be saved with the current size of the control file, and the number or records used.

FIGURE 15.2 Control Files screen's Record Section tab

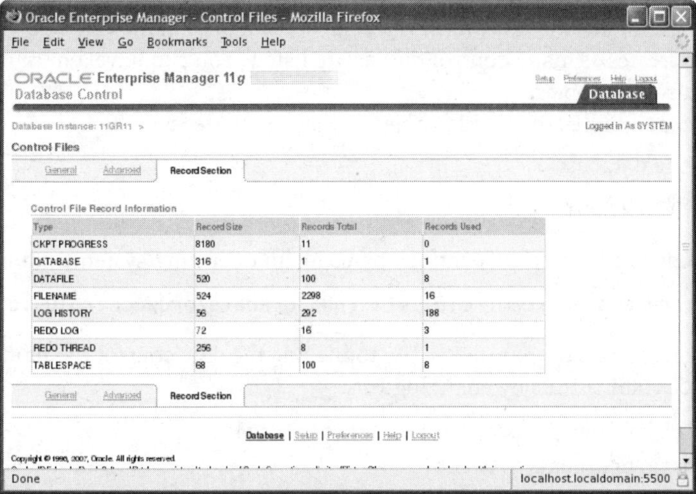

Multiplexing Control Files

Because the control file is critical for database operation, at a minimum you must have two copies of the control file; Oracle recommends a minimum of three copies. You duplicate the control file on different disks either by using the multiplexing feature of Oracle or by using the mirroring feature of your operating system. If you have multiple disk controllers on your server, at least one copy of the control file should reside on a disk managed by a different disk controller.

If you use the Database Configuration Assistant (DBCA) to create your database, three copies of the control files are multiplexed by default.

The next two sections discuss the two ways that you can implement the multiplexing feature: using an `init.ora` and using the server-side spfile.

Multiplexing Control Files Using init.ora

Multiplexing means keeping a copy of the same control file on different disk drives and ideally on different controllers too. To multiplex a control file, copy the control file to multiple locations and change the `CONTROL_FILES` parameter in the text-based initialization file `init.ora` to include all control filenames. The following syntax shows three multiplexed control files:

```
CONTROL_FILES = ('/ora01/oradata/MYDB/ctrlMYDB01.ctl',
                 '/ora02/oradata/MYDB/ctrlMYDB02.ctl',
                 '/ora03/oradata/MYDB/ctrlMYDB03.ctl')
```

By storing the control file on multiple disks, you avoid the risk of a single point of failure. When multiplexing control files, updates to the control file can take a little longer, but that is insignificant when compared with the benefits. If you lose one control file, you can restart the database after copying one of the other control files or after changing the `CONTROL_FILES` parameter in the initialization file.

When multiplexing control files, Oracle updates all the control files at the same time but uses only the first control file listed in the `CONTROL_FILES` parameter for reading.

When creating a database, you can list the control file names in the `CONTROL_FILES` parameter, and Oracle creates as many control files as are listed. You can have a maximum of eight multiplexed control file copies.

If you need to add more control file copies, follow these steps:

1. Shut down the database.

   ```
   SQL> SHUTDOWN NORMAL
   ```

2. Copy the control file to more locations by using an operating-system command:

   ```
   $ cp /u02/oradata/ord/control01.ctl /u05/oradata/ord/control04.ctl
   ```

3. Change the initialization-parameter file to include the new control file name(s) in the parameter `CONTROL_FILES` by changing this:

   ```
   CONTROL_FILES=('/u02/oradata/ord/control01.ctl',
   '/u03/oradata/ord/control02.ctl',
   '/u04/oradata/ord/control03.ctl')
   ```

to this:

```
CONTROL_FILES=('/u02/oradata/ord/control01.ctl',
'/u03/oradata/ord/control02.ctl',
'/u04/oradata/ord/control03.ctl',
'/u05/oradata/ord/control04.ctl')
```

4. Start the instance:

```
SQL> STARTUP
```

This procedure is somewhat similar to the procedure for recovering from the loss of a control file.

You can find examples of control file recovery in Chapter 16.

After creating the database, you can change the location of the control files, rename the control files, or drop certain control files. You must have at least one control file for each database. To add, rename, or delete control files, you need to follow the preceding steps. Basically, you shut down the database, use the operating-system copy command (copying, renaming, or deleting the control files accordingly), modify the `init.ora` parameter file, and start up the database.

Multiplexing Control Files Using an Spfile

Multiplexing using a binary spfile is similar to multiplexing using `init.ora`. The major difference is in how the `CONTROL_FILES` parameter is changed. Follow these steps:

1. Alter the spfile while the database is still open:

```
SQL> ALTER SYSTEM SET CONTROL_FILES =
        '/ora01/oradata/MYDB/ctrlMYDB01.ctl',
        '/ora02/oradata/MYDB/ctrlMYDB02.ctl',
        '/ora03/oradata/MYDB/ctrlMYDB03.ctl',
        '/ora04/oradata/MYDB/ctrlMYDB04.ctl' SCOPE=SPFILE;
```

   This parameter change takes effect only after the next instance restart by using the `SCOPE=SPFILE` qualifier. The contents of the binary spfile are changed immediately, but the old specification of `CONTROL_FILES` is used until the instance is restarted.

2. Shut down the database:

```
SQL> SHUTDOWN NORMAL
```

3. Copy an existing control file to the new location:

```
$ cp /ora01/oradata/MYDB/ctrlMYDB01.ctl /ora04/oradata/MYDB/ctrlMYDB04.ctl
```

4. Start the instance:

```
SQL> STARTUP
```

Understanding Checkpoints

The CKPT process controls the amount of time required for instance recovery. During a checkpoint, CKPT updates the control file and the header of the data files to reflect the last successful transaction by recording the last system change number (SCN). The SCN, which is a number sequentially assigned to each transaction in the database, is also recorded in the control file against the data file name that is taken offline or made read-only.

A checkpoint occurs automatically every time a redo log file switch occurs, either when the current redo log file fills up or when you manually switch redo log files. The DBW*n* processes in conjunction with CKPT routinely write new and changed buffers to advance the checkpoint from where instance recovery can begin, thus reducing the MTTR.

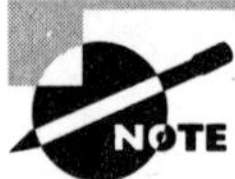

You can find more information on tuning the MTTR and how often checkpointing occurs in Chapter 16.

Understanding Redo Log Files

A redo log file records all changes to the database, in most cases before the changes are written to the data files.

To recover from an instance or a media failure, redo log information is required to roll data files forward to the last committed transaction. Ensuring that you have at least two members for each redo log file group dramatically reduces the likelihood of data loss because the database continues to operate if one member of a redo log file is lost.

In the following sections, I will give you an architectural overview of redo log files, as well as show you how to add redo log groups, add or remove redo log group members, and clear a redo log group in case one of the redo log group's members becomes corrupted.

Redo Log File Architecture

Online redo log files are filled with redo records. A redo record, also called a *redo entry*, consists of a group of change vectors, each of which describes a change made to a single block in the database. Redo entries record data that you can use to reconstruct all changes made to the database, including the undo segments. When you recover the database by using redo log files, Oracle reads the change vectors in the redo records and applies the changes to the relevant blocks.

The LGWR process writes redo information from the redo log buffer to the online redo log files under a variety of circumstances:

- When a user commits a transaction, even if this is the only transaction in the log buffer
- When the redo log buffer becomes one-third full
- When the buffer contains approximately 1MB of *changed* records; this total does not include deleted or inserted records
- When a database checkpoint is performed

LGWR always writes its records to the online redo log file *before* DBW*n* writes new or modified database buffer cache records to the data files.

Each database has its own set of online redo log groups. A redo log group can have one or more redo log members (each member is a single operating-system file). If you have a RAC configuration, in which multiple instances are mounted to one database, each instance has one online redo thread. That is, the LGWR process of each instance writes to the same online redo log files, and hence Oracle has to keep track of the instance from where the database changes are coming. Single-instance configurations will have only one thread, and that thread number is 1. The redo log file contains both committed and uncommitted transactions. Whenever a transaction is committed, a system change number is assigned to the redo records to identify the committed transaction.

The redo log group is referenced by an integer; you can specify the group number when you create the redo log files—either when you create the database or when you create a redo log group after you create the database. You can also change the redo log configuration (adding, dropping, or renaming files) by using database commands. The following example shows a CREATE DATABASE command:

```
CREATE DATABASE "MYDB01"
… … …
LOGFILE '/ora02/oradata/MYDB01/redo01.log' SIZE 10M,
        '/ora03/oradata/MYDB01/redo02.log' SIZE 10M;
```

This example creates two log-file groups; the first file is assigned to group 1, and the second file is assigned to group 2. You can have more files in each group; this practice is known as the *multiplexing* of redo log files, which I'll discuss later in this chapter in the section "Multiplexing Redo Log Files." You can specify any group number—the range will be between 1 and the initialization parameter MAXLOGFILES. Oracle recommends that all redo log groups be the same size. The following is an example of creating the log files by specifying the group number:

```
CREATE DATABASE "MYDB01"
… … …
LOGFILE GROUP 1 '/ora02/oradata/MYDB01/redo01.log' SIZE 10M,
        GROUP 2 '/ora03/oradata/MYDB01/redo02.log' SIZE 10M;
```

Log Switch Operations

The LGWR process writes to only one redo log file group at any time. The file that is actively being written to is known as the *current* log file. The log files that are required for instance recovery are known as the *active* log files. The other log files are known as *inactive*. Oracle automatically recovers an instance when starting up the instance by using the online redo log files. Instance recovery can be needed if you do not shut down the database cleanly or if your database server crashes.

The log files are written in a circular fashion. A log switch occurs when Oracle finishes writing to one log group and starts writing to the next log group. A log switch always occurs when the current redo log group is completely full and log writing must continue. You can force a log switch by using the ALTER SYSTEM command. A manual log switch can be necessary when performing maintenance on the redo log files by using the ALTER SYSTEM SWITCH LOGFILE command.

Whenever a log switch occurs, Oracle allocates a sequence number to the new redo log group before writing to it. As stated earlier, this number is known as the *log sequence number*. If there are lots of transactions or changes to the database, the log switches can occur too frequently. Size the redo log files appropriately to avoid frequent log switches. Oracle writes to the alert log file whenever a log switch occurs.

Redo log files are written sequentially on the disk, so the I/O will be fast if there is no other activity on the disk. (The disk head is always properly positioned.) Keep the redo log files on a separate disk for better performance. If you have to store a data file on the same disk as the redo log file, do not put the SYSTEM, UNDOTBS, SYSAUX, or any very active data or index tablespace file on this disk. A commit cannot complete until a transaction's information has been written to the redo logs, so maximizing the throughput of the redo log files is a top priority.

Database checkpoints are closely tied to redo log file switches. You learned about checkpoints earlier in the chapter in the section "Understanding Checkpoints." A checkpoint is an event that flushes the modified data from the buffer cache to the disk and updates the control file and data files. The CKPT process updates the headers of data files and control files; the actual blocks are written to the file by the DBW*n* process. A checkpoint is initiated when the redo log file is filled and a log switch occurs; when the instance is shut down with NORMAL, TRANSACTIONAL, or IMMEDIATE; when a tablespace status is changed to read-only or put into BACKUP mode; or when other values specified by certain parameters (discussed later in this section) are reached.

You can force a checkpoint if needed, as shown here:

```
ALTER SYSTEM CHECKPOINT;
```

Forcing a checkpoint ensures that all changes to the database buffers are written to the data files on disk.

Another way to force a checkpoint is by forcing a log-file switch:

```
ALTER SYSTEM SWITCH LOGFILE;
```

The size of the redo log affects the checkpoint performance. If the size of the redo log is smaller and the transaction volume is high, a log switch occurs often, and so does the checkpoint. The DBW*n* process writes the dirty buffer blocks whenever a checkpoint occurs. This situation might reduce the time required for instance recovery, but it might also affect the runtime performance. You can adjust checkpoints primarily by using the initialization parameter FAST_START_MTTR_TARGET. It is used to ensure that recovery time at instance startup (if required) will not exceed a certain number of seconds.

You can use the FAST_START_MTTR_TARGET parameter to tune checkpoint frequency; its value determines how long an instance can take to start after an instance crash.

Multiplexing Redo Log Files

You can keep multiple copies of the online redo log file to safeguard against damage to these files. When multiplexing online redo log files, LGWR concurrently writes the same redo log information to multiple identical online redo log files, thereby eliminating a single point of redo log failure. All copies of the redo file are the same size and are known as a *redo group*, which is identified by an integer. Each redo log file in the group is known as a *redo member*. You must have at least two redo log groups for normal database operation.

When multiplexing redo log files, keeping the members of a group on different disks is preferable so that one disk failure will not affect the continuing operation of the database. If LGWR can write to at least one member of the group, database operation proceeds as normal; an entry is written to the alert log file. If all members of the redo log file group are not available for writing, Oracle hangs, crashes, or shuts down. An instance recovery or media recovery can be needed to bring up the database, and you can lose committed transactions.

You can create multiple copies of the online redo log files when you create the database. For example, the following statement creates two redo log file groups with two members in each:

```
CREATE DATABASE "MYDB01"
... ... ...
LOGFILE
  GROUP 1 ('/ora02/oradata/MYDB01/redo0101.log',
           '/ora03/oradata/MYDB01/redo0102.log') SIZE 50M,
  GROUP 2 ('/ora02/oradata/MYDB01/redo0201.log',
           '/ora03/oradata/MYDB01/redo0202.log') SIZE 50M;
```

The maximum number of log file groups is specified in the clause MAXLOGFILES, and the maximum number of members is specified in the clause MAXLOGMEMBERS. You can separate the filenames (members) by using a space or a comma.

In the following sections, you will learn how to create a new redo log group, add a new member to an existing group, rename a member, and drop a member from an existing group. In addition, I'll show you how to drop a group and clear all members of a group in certain circumstances.

Redo Log Troubleshooting

In the case of redo log groups, it's best to be generous with the number of groups and the number of members for each group. After estimating the number of groups that would be appropriate for your installation, add one more. The slight additional work involved in maintaining either additional or larger redo logs is small in relation to the time needed to fix a problem when the number of users and concurrent active transactions increase.

The space needed for additional log file groups is minimal and is well worth the effort up front to avoid the undesirable situation in which writes to the redo log file are waiting on the completion of writes to the database files or the archived log file destination.

Creating New Groups

You can create and add more redo log groups to the database by using the `ALTER DATABASE` command. The following statement creates a new log file group with two members:

```
ALTER DATABASE ADD LOGFILE
  GROUP 3 ('/ora02/oradata/MYDB01/redo0301.log',
           '/ora03/oradata/MYDB01/redo0302.log') SIZE 10M;
```

If you omit the `GROUP` clause, Oracle assigns the next available number. For example, the following statement also creates a multiplexed group:

```
ALTER DATABASE ADD LOGFILE
    ('/ora02/oradata/MYDB01/redo0301.log',
     '/ora03/oradata/MYDB01/redo0302.log') SIZE 10M;
```

To create a new group without multiplexing, use the following statement:

```
ALTER DATABASE ADD LOGFILE
    '/ora02/oradata/MYDB01/redo0301.log' REUSE;
```

You can add more than one redo log group by using the `ALTER DATABASE` command—just use a comma to separate the groups.

If the redo log files you create already exist, use the REUSE option, and don't specify the size. The new redo log size will be the same as that of the existing file.

Adding a new redo log group is straightforward using EM Database Control. To do so, click the Server tab, and then click the Redo Log Groups link under Storage. You can view the current redo log groups and add another redo log group using the Create button, as you can see in Figure 15.3 on the Redo Log Groups screen.

FIGURE 15.3 The Redo Log Groups maintenance screen

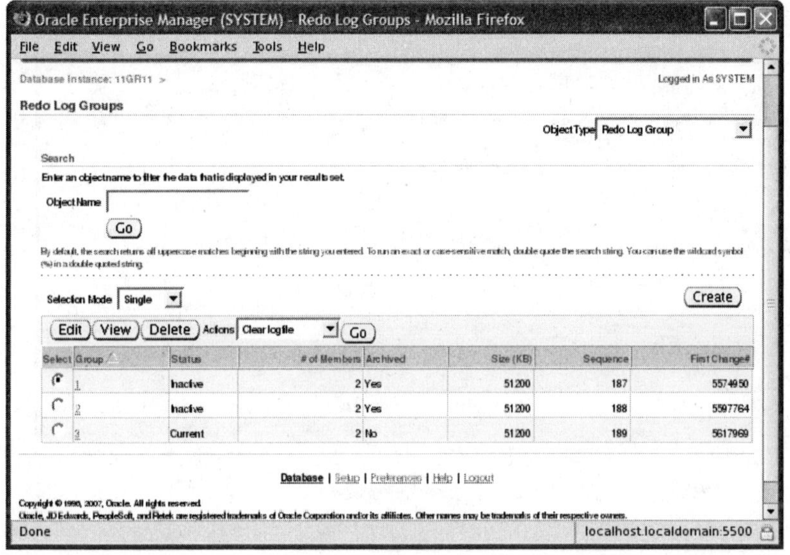

Adding New Members

If you forgot to multiplex the redo log files when creating the database (multiplexing redo log files is the default when you use DBCA) or if you need to add more redo log members, you can do so by using the ALTER DATABASE command. When adding new members, you do not specify the file size, because all group members will have the same size.

If you know the group number, use the following statement to add a member to group 2:

```
ALTER DATABASE ADD LOGFILE MEMBER
'/ora04/oradata/MYDB01/redo0203.log' TO GROUP 2;
```

You can also add group members by specifying the names of other members in the group, instead of specifying the group number. Specify all the existing group members with this syntax:

```
ALTER DATABASE ADD LOGFILE MEMBER
 '/ora04/oradata/MYDB01/redo0203.log' TO
('/ora02/oradata/MYDB01/redo0201.log',
 '/ora03/oradata/MYDB01/redo0202.log');
```

You can add a new member to a group in EM Database Control by clicking the Edit button shown in Figure 15.3 and then clicking Add. Figure 15.4 shows the Edit Redo Log Group screen, where you can add or remove redo log group members.

FIGURE 15.4 The Edit Redo Log Group screen

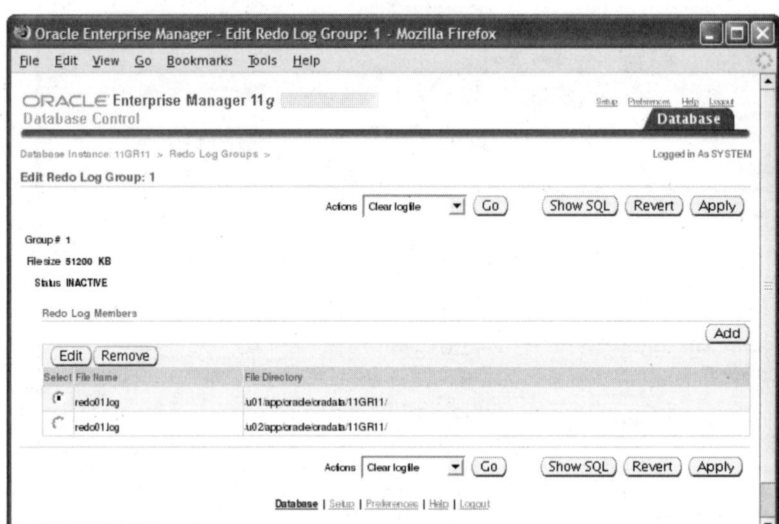

Renaming Log Members

If you want to move the log file member from one disk to another or just want a more meaningful name, you can rename a redo log member. Before renaming the online redo log members, the new (target) online redo files should exist. The SQL commands in Oracle change only the internal pointer in the control file to a new log file; they do not change or rename the operating-system file. You must use an operating-system command to rename or move the file. Follow these steps to rename a log member:

1. Shut down the database.
2. Copy/rename the redo log file member to the new location by using an operating-system command.
3. Start up the instance, and mount the database (`STARTUP MOUNT`).
4. Rename the log file member in the control file. Use `ALTER DATABASE RENAME FILE 'old_redo_file_name' TO 'new_redo_file_name';`.
5. Open the database (`ALTER DATABASE OPEN`).
6. Back up the control file.

Another way to achieve the same result is to add a new member to the group and then drop the old member from the group, as discussed in the "Adding New Members" section earlier in this chapter and the "Dropping Redo Log Groups" section, which is next.

You can rename a log-group member in EM Database Control by clicking the Edit button shown in Figure 15.4 and then changing the filename in the File Name box.

Dropping Redo Log Groups

You can drop a redo log group and its members by using the ALTER DATABASE command. Remember that you should have at least two redo log groups for the database to function normally. The group that is to be dropped should not be the active group or the current group—that is, you can drop only an inactive log-file group. If the log file to be dropped is not inactive, use the ALTER SYSTEM SWITCH LOGFILE command.

To drop the log-file group 3, use the following SQL statement:

```
ALTER DATABASE DROP LOGFILE GROUP 3;
```

When an online redo log group is dropped from the database, the operating-system files are not deleted from disk. The control files of the associated database are updated to drop the members of the group from the database structure. After dropping an online redo log group, make sure the drop is completed successfully, and then use the appropriate operating-system command to delete the dropped online redo log files.

You can delete an entire redo log group in EM Database Control by clicking the Delete button (see Figure 15.3, shown earlier) and then confirming the delete by clicking the Yes button.

Dropping Redo Log Members

In much the same way that you drop a redo log group, you can drop only the members of an inactive redo log group. Also, if there are only two groups, the log member to be dropped should not be the last member of a group. Each redo log group can have a different number of members, though this is not advised. For example, say you have three log groups, each with two members. If you drop a log member from group 2 and a failure occurs to the sole member of group 2, the instance will hang, crash, and potentially cause the loss of committed transactions when attempts are made to write to the missing redo log group, as I discussed earlier in this chapter. Even if you drop a member for maintenance reasons, ensure that all redo log groups have the same number of members.

To drop a redo log member, use the DROP LOGFILE MEMBER clause of the ALTER DATABASE command:

```
ALTER DATABASE DROP LOGFILE MEMBER

'/ora04/oradata/MYDB01/redo0203.log';
```

The operating-system file is not removed from the disk; only the control file is updated. Use an operating-system command to delete the redo log file member from disk.

If a database is running in ARCHIVELOG mode, redo log members cannot be deleted unless the redo log group has been archived.

You can drop a member of a redo log group in EM Database Control by clicking the Edit button (see Figure 15.4, shown earlier), selecting the member to be dropped, and then clicking the Remove button.

Clearing Online Redo Log Files

Under certain circumstances, a redo log group member (or all members of a log group) can become corrupted. To solve this problem, you can drop and add the log-file group or group member again. It is much easier, however, to use the ALTER DATABASE CLEAR LOGFILE command. The following example clears the contents of redo log group 3 in the database:

```
ALTER DATABASE CLEAR LOGFILE GROUP 3;
```

Another distinct advantage of this command is that you can clear a log group even if the database has only two log groups and only one member in each group. Additionally, by using the UNARCHIVED keyword, you can clear a log-group member even if it has not been archived. In this case, it is advisable to do a full database backup at the earliest convenience, because the unarchived redo log file is no longer usable for database recovery.

You can clear the redo logs by choosing Clear Logfile from the Actions drop-down box and clicking Go (as shown earlier in Figure 15.3). The other options available in the drop-down box are as follows:

- Create Like
- Force Checkpoint
- Generate DDL
- Sizing Advice
- Switch Logfile

Understanding Archived Redo Log (ARCHIVELOG) Files

If you use only online redo log files, your database is protected against instance failure but not media failure. Although saving the redo log files before they are overwritten takes additional disk space and management, the increased recoverability of the database outweighs the slight additional overhead and maintenance costs.

In the following sections, I will present an overview of how archived redo log files work, how to set the location for saving the archived redo log files, and how to enable archiving in the database.

Archived Redo Log File Architecture

An archived redo log file is a copy of a redo log file before it is overwritten by new redo information. Because the online redo log files are reused in a circular fashion, you have no way of bringing a backup of a data file up to the latest committed transaction unless you configure the database in ARCHIVELOG mode.

The process of copying is called *archiving*. The ARC*n* background processes do this archiving. By archiving the redo log files, you can use them later to recover a database, update a standby database, or use the LogMiner utility to audit the database activities.

When an online redo log file is full and LGWR starts writing to the next redo log file, ARC*n* copies the completed redo log file to the archive destination. It is possible to specify more than one archive destination. The LGWR process waits for the ARC*n* process to complete the copy operation before overwriting any online redo log file. As with LGWR, the failure of one of the ARC*n* backup processes will cause instance failure, but no committed transactions will be lost because the "Commit Complete" message is not returned to the user or calling program until LGWR successfully records the transaction in the online redo log file group.

When the archiver process is copying the redo log files to another destination, the database is said to be in `ARCHIVELOG` mode. If archiving is not enabled, the database is said to be in `NOARCHIVELOG` mode. In production systems, you cannot afford to lose data and should therefore run the database in `ARCHIVELOG` mode so that in the event of a failure, you can recover the database to the time of failure or to a point in time. You can achieve this ability to recover by restoring the database backup and applying the database changes by using the archived log files.

Real World Scenario

Archive-Logging Space Issues

After you configure the database for `ARCHIVELOG` mode, your job is only half complete. You need to continually make sure there is enough room for the archived log files. Otherwise, the database will hang. At least once in your DBA career, you will get a phone call from some users saying that the database is "hung." It's not until you check the alert log that you discover the archiving process cannot find disk space for a newly filled log file in the archiving destinations.

There should be enough space available for online archived redo log files to recover and roll forward from the last full backup of each data file that is also online; the remaining archived logs and any previous data file backups can be moved to another disk or to tape.

Remembering your zero-transaction-loss strategy (which should be every DBA's strategy), make sure you do not misplace or delete an archived log file before it is backed up to tape; otherwise, you will not be able to perform a complete recovery because of a media failure.

If you use RMAN and the flash recovery area for all your backup files, then you can further automate this process by directing RMAN to maintain enough backups to satisfy a recovery-window policy (number of days) or a redundancy policy (multiple copies of each backup). Once an archived log or other backup file is no longer needed for the policy, the files are automatically deleted from the flash recovery area.

Setting the Archive Destination

You specify the archive destination in the initialization-parameter file. To change the archive destination parameters during normal database operation, you use the ALTER SYSTEM command. The following sections cover some of the parameters associated with archive-log destinations and the archiver process. You can find a complete list of initialization parameters in the Oracle documentation "Oracle 11*g* Reference" at http://tahiti.oracle.com.

LOG_ARCHIVE_DEST_n

Using this parameter, you can specify at most 10 archiving destinations. These locations can be on the local machine or on a remote machine where the standby database is located. The syntax for specifying this parameter in the initialization file is as follows:

```
LOG_ARCHIVE_DEST_n =  "null_string" |
((SERVICE = tnsnames_name |
  LOCATION = 'directory_name')
 [MANDATORY | OPTIONAL]
 [REOPEN [= integer]])
```

For example, the following specifies a location for the archive-log files on the local machine at /archive/MYDB01. The MANDATORY clause specifies that writing to this location must succeed.

```
LOG_ARCHIVE_DEST_1 = ((LOCATION='/archive/MYDB01') MANDATORY)
```

Here is another example, which applies the archive logs to a standby database on a remote computer:

```
LOG_ARCHIVE_DEST_2 = (SERVICE=STDBY01) OPTIONAL REOPEN 60;
```

In this example, STDBY01 is the Oracle Net connect string used to connect to the remote database. Because writing is optional, the database activity continues even if ARC*n* could not write the archive-log file. It tries the writing operation again because the REOPEN clause is specified. The REOPEN clause specifies when the next attempt to write to this location should be made if the first attempt does not succeed. The default value is 300 seconds.

You can also use the EM Database Control web pages to configure the backup and recovery settings by choosing the Availability tab of EM Database Control. Figure 15.5 shows the Backup/Recovery section on the Availability tab.

FIGURE 15.5 Backup/Recovery section options in EM

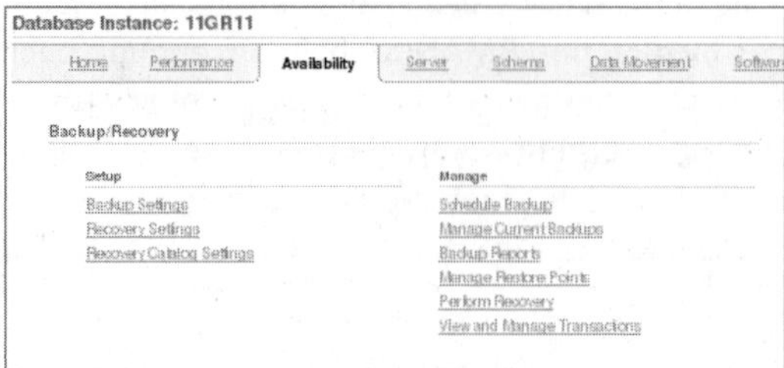

By clicking the Recovery Settings link, you can configure the archive-log destinations using the Media Recovery section. For the database shown in the example, only one archive location is set up, as shown in Figure 15.6.

FIGURE 15.6 The log-archive destinations

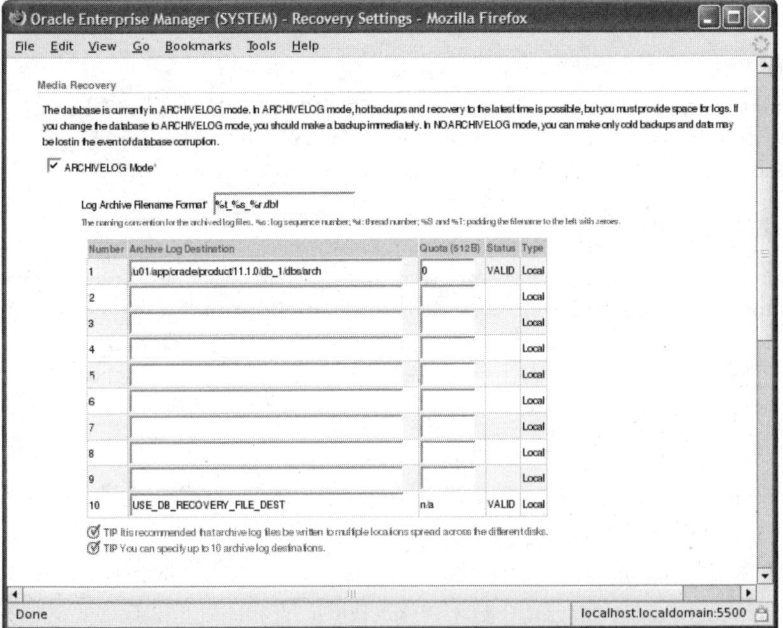

Destination 10 is the flash recovery area using the string `USE_DB_RECOVERY_FILE_DEST`.

The flash recovery area is discussed in the section "Understanding the Flash Recovery Area," later in this chapter.

LOG_ARCHIVE_MIN_SUCCEED_DEST

This parameter specifies the number of destinations that the ARC*n* process should successfully write at a minimum to proceed with overwriting the online redo log files. The default value of this parameter is 1. This parameter cannot exceed the total number of enabled destinations. If this parameter value is less than the number of `MANDATORY` destinations, the parameter is ignored.

LOG_ARCHIVE_FORMAT

This parameter specifies the format in which to write the filename of the archived redo log files. To ensure that the log files are not overwritten, you use predefined substitution variables to construct the name of each archived redo log file. You can provide a text string and any of the predefined substitution variables. The variables are as follows:

- %s: This is the log sequence number.
- %t: This is the thread number.
- %r: This is the reset log's ID, which ensures uniqueness even after using advanced recovery techniques that reset the log sequence numbers.
- %d: This is the database ID.

The format you provide must include at least %s, %t, and %r. If you use the same archived redo log location for multiple databases, you must also use %d. In Figure 15.6, shown previously, the log-archive filename format is defined as %t_%s_%r.dbf.

Setting ARCHIVELOG

Specifying these parameters does not start writing the archive-log files. To enable archiving of the redo log files, place the database in ARCHIVELOG mode. You can specify the ARCHIVELOG clause while creating the database. However, you might prefer to create the database first and then enable ARCHIVELOG mode. To enable ARCHIVELOG mode, follow these steps:

1. Shut down the database.
2. Set up the appropriate initialization parameters.
3. Start up and mount the database; you can change ARCHIVELOG mode only when the database is in the MOUNT state.
4. Enable ARCHIVELOG mode by using the command ALTER DATABASE ARCHIVELOG.
5. Open the database by using ALTER DATABASE OPEN.
6. Back up the database.

To disable ARCHIVELOG mode, follow these steps:

1. Shut down the database.
2. Start up and mount the database.
3. Disable ARCHIVELOG mode by using the command ALTER DATABASE NOARCHIVELOG.
4. Open the database by using ALTER DATABASE OPEN.

The dynamic performance view V$DATABASE tells you whether you are in ARCHIVELOG mode, as you can see in this query:

```
SQL> SELECT dbid, name, created, log_mode
     FROM v$database;

      DBID NAME      CREATED   LOG_MODE
---------- --------- --------- ------------
1387044942 ORD       03-MAR-04 ARCHIVELOG
```

Understanding the Flash Recovery Area

As the price of disk space drops, the difference in its price compared with tape is offset by the advantages of using a disk as the primary backup medium. Even a slow disk can be accessed randomly faster than a tape drive. This rapid access means that any database-recovery operation takes only minutes instead of hours.

Using disk space as the primary medium for all database-recovery operations is the key component of the Oracle 11*g* database's flash recovery area. The flash recovery area is a single, unified storage area for all recovery-related files and recovery activities in an Oracle database.

The flash recovery area can be a single directory, an entire file system, or an Automatic Storage Management (ASM) disk group. To further optimize the use of disk space for recovery operations, a flash recovery area can be shared by more than one database.

In the following sections, I will cover all the major aspects of a flash recovery area: what can and should be kept in the flash recovery area and how to set up a flash recovery using initialization parameters and SQL commands. Also, as with other aspects of Oracle 11*g*, I will show how you can manage most parts of the flash recovery area using EM Database Control, and I'll introduce some of the more advanced management techniques.

Flash Recovery Area Occupants

All the files needed to recover a database from a media failure or a logical error are contained in the flash recovery area. The flash recovery area can contain the following:

Control files A copy of the control file is created in the flash recovery area when the database is created. This copy of the control file can be used as one of the mirrored copies of the control file to ensure that at least one copy of the control file is available after a media failure.

Archived log files When the flash recovery area is configured, the initialization parameter `LOG_ARCHIVE_DEST_10` is automatically set to the flash recovery area location. The corresponding ARC*n* processes create archived log files in the flash recovery area and any other defined `LOG_ARCHIVE_DEST_`*n* locations.

Flashback logs If the flashback database is enabled, its flashback logs are stored in the flash recovery area.

Control file and spfile autobackups The flash recovery area holds control file and spfile autobackups generated by RMAN if RMAN is configured for control file autobackup. When RMAN backs up data file 1, which is part of the `SYSTEM` tablespace, the control file is automatically included in the RMAN backup.

Data file copies For RMAN `BACKUP AS COPY` image files, the default destination for the data file copies is the flash recovery area.

RMAN backup sets By default, RMAN uses the flash recovery area for both backup sets and image copies. In addition, RMAN puts restored archived log files from tape into the flash recovery area in preparation for a recovery operation.

The Flash Recovery Area and SQL Commands

You must define two initialization parameters to set up the flash recovery area: DB_RECOVERY_FILE_DEST_SIZE and DB_RECOVERY_FILE_DEST. Because both of these are dynamic parameters, the instance doesn't need to be shut down and restarted for the flash recovery area to be usable.

DB_RECOVERY_FILE_DEST_SIZE, which must be defined before DB_RECOVERY_FILE_DEST, defines the size of the flash recovery area. To maximize the benefits of the flash recovery area, it should be large enough to hold a copy of all data files, incremental backups, online redo logs, archived redo logs not yet backed up to tape, control files, and control file autobackups. At a bare minimum, you need enough space to hold the archived log files not yet copied to tape.

Here is an example of configuring DB_RECOVERY_FILE_DEST_SIZE:

```
SQL> ALTER SYSTEM SET
     db_recovery_file_dest_size = 8g SCOPE=both;
```

The size of the flash recovery area will be 8GB, and because this example uses the SCOPE=BOTH parameter in the ALTER SYSTEM command, the initialization parameter takes effect immediately and stays in effect even after a database restart.

The parameter DB_RECOVERY_FILE_DEST specifies the physical location where all flash recovery files are stored. The ASM disk group or file system must have at least as much space as the amount specified with DB_RECOVERY_FILE_DEST_SIZE, and it can have significantly more. DB_RECOVERY_FILE_DEST_SIZE, however, can be increased on the fly if more space is needed and the file system where the flash recovery area resides has the space available.

The following example uses the directory /OraFlash for the flash recovery area, like so:

```
SQL> ALTER SYSTEM SET
     db_recovery_file_dest = '/OraFlash' SCOPE=both;
```

Clearing the value of DB_RECOVERY_FILE_DEST disables the flash recovery area; the parameter DB_RECOVERY_FILE_DEST_SIZE cannot be cleared until the DB_RECOVERY_FILE_DEST parameter has been cleared.

The Flash Recovery Area and EM Database Control

You can create and maintain the flash recovery area using EM Database Control. Click the Availability tab, and then click the Recovery Settings link to display the Configure Recovery Settings screen. Figure 15.7 shows the Flash Recovery section.

In the Flash Recovery section, the flash recovery area has been configured for a database in the file system /u01/app/oracle/flash_recovery_area, with a maximum size of 15,000MB (15GB). Just more than 4GB of space is currently used in the flash recovery area. Flashback logging has not yet been enabled for this database.

FIGURE 15.7 Flash Recovery section of the Recovery Settings screen

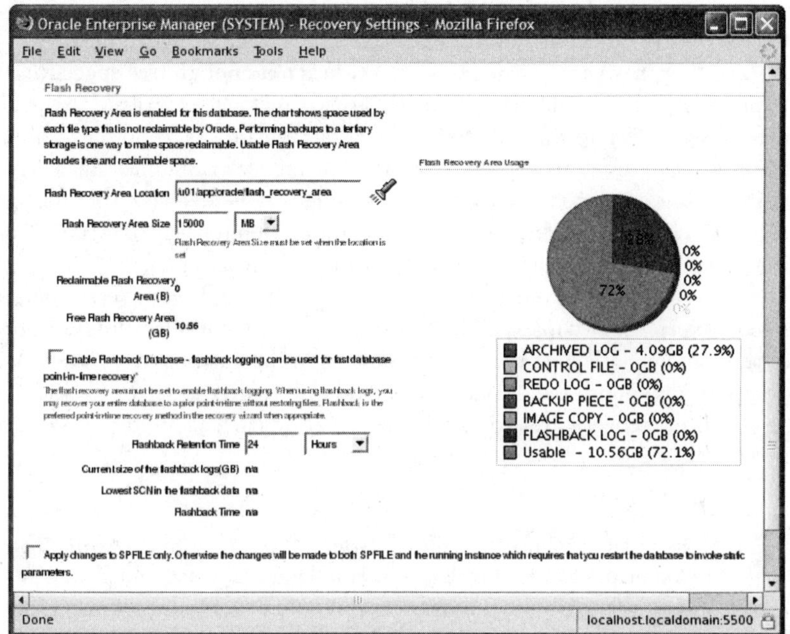

You can enable flashback logging by selecting the Enable Flashback Database box. Oracle's flashback features complement the media-recovery options in the database. Using the `FLASHBACK DATABASE` command in RMAN, you can revert the data file contents to a state at a prior time. This operation is much faster than recovering from a full database backup and applying the archive logs to recover the database to a point in time. The flashback logs contain the past versions of the data blocks.

You can enable flashback database using SQL*Plus. The steps needed are as follows:

1. Make sure the database is in `ARCHIVELOG` mode and the flash recovery area is configured using the `DB_RECOVERY_FILE_DEST` and `DB_RECOVERY_FILE_DEST_SIZE` parameters.
2. Specify the length of desired flashback window using the `DB_FLASHBACK_RETENTION_TARGET` parameter.
3. Shut down the database, and start in `MOUNT` state.
4. Enable the flashback database feature using the `ALTER DATABASE FLASHBACK ON` statement.
5. Open the database.

You can find more information about configuring and using flashback logs with flashback database in *OCP: Oracle Database 11*g *Administrator Certified Professional Study Guide* (Sybex, 2009).

Flash Recovery Area Management

Because the space in the flash recovery area is limited by the initialization parameter DB_RECOVERY_FILE_DEST_SIZE, the Oracle database keeps track of which files are no longer needed on disk so that they can be deleted when there is not enough free space for new files. Each time a file is deleted from the flash recovery area, a message is written to the alert log.

A message is also written to the alert log in other circumstances. If no files can be deleted and the recovery area's used space is at 85 percent, a warning message is issued. When the space used is at 97 percent, a critical warning is issued. These warnings are recorded in the alert log file, can be viewed in the data dictionary view DBA_OUTSTANDING_ALERTS, and are available on the main screen of EM Database Control.

When you receive these alerts, you have a number of options. If your retention policy can be adjusted to keep fewer copies of data files or reduce the number of days in the recovery window, this can help alleviate the space problems in the flash recovery area. Assuming your retention policy is sound, you should instead add more disk space or back up some of the files in the flash recovery area to another destination such as another disk or a tape device.

If the flash recovery area is full, Oracle 11*g* will write ORA-19809 and ORA-19804 errors to the alert log file. The flash recovery area is automatically cleared based on the retention specified. To manually clear the flash recovery area, you must perform BACKUP RECOVERY AREA to back up the flash recovery area files and to delete the files.

Performing Backups

Your backup strategy depends on the activity of your database, the level of availability required by your service-level agreements (SLAs), and how much downtime you can tolerate during a recovery effort.

In this section, I'll first review some terminology, and then I will show you a way to back up the control file to a text file that you can edit and use in case of the loss of all control files. I will then discuss how to back up the database using OS utilities. Finally, I will introduce Recovery Manager and show you how to make some of the backups described in the terminology review.

Understanding Backup Terminology

You can make a *whole* backup, which backs up the entire database, or you can back up only part of the database, which is called a *partial* backup. Whole backups and partial backups are known as Oracle *backup strategies*. The backup type can be divided into two general categories: *full* backups and *incremental* backups. Depending on whether you make your database backups when the database is open or closed, backups can be further categorized into the backup modes known as *consistent* backup and *inconsistent* backup.

Your backups can be managed using operating-system and SQL commands or entirely by RMAN. Many backup types are available using RMAN only, such as incremental backups; unless you have some specific requirements, it is highly recommended that you use RMAN to implement your backup strategy.

The following are definitions for whole database backups, partial database backups, full backups, incremental backups, consistent backups, and inconsistent backups:

Whole database A whole database backup includes all data files and at least one control file. Online redo log files are never backed up; restoring backed-up redo log files and replacing the current redo log files will result in loss of data during media recovery. Only one of the control files needs to be backed up; all copies of the control file are identical.

Partial database A partial database backup includes zero or more tablespaces, which in turn includes zero or more data files; a control file is optional in a partial database backup. As you may infer, a partial database backup that includes no tablespaces and does not include the control file backs up 0 bytes of data to the backup destination.

Full A full backup includes all blocks of every data file backed up in a whole or partial database backup.

Incremental An incremental backup makes a copy of all data blocks that have changed since a previous backup. Though Oracle11*g* supports five levels of incremental backups from 0 to 4, 0 and 1 are most commonly used. An incremental backup at level 0 is considered a baseline backup; it is the equivalent of a full backup and contains all data blocks in the data file(s) that are backed up. Although incremental backups can take less time, the potential downside is that you must first restore the baseline backup and then apply all incremental backups performed since the baseline backup.

Consistent A consistent backup, also known as an *offline backup*, is performed while the database is not open. These backups are consistent because the SCN in the control file matches the SCN in every data file's header. Although recovering using a consistent backup requires no additional recovery operation after a failure, you reduce your database's availability during a consistent backup as well as risk the loss of committed transactions performed since the consistent backup.

Inconsistent Although the term *inconsistent backup* may sound like something you might avoid in a database, it is a way to maintain the availability of the database while performing backups. An inconsistent backup, also known as an *online backup*, is performed while the database is open and available to users. The backup is inconsistent because the SCN in the control file is most likely out of sync with the SCN in the header of the data files. Inconsistent backups require recovery when they are used for recovering from a media failure, but they keep availability high because the database is open while the backup is performed.

Backups can be performed using two methods: using user-managed backup or using Oracle's backup and recovery tool called Recovery Manager. RMAN backups are easier to create, and the recovery operations are pretty much automated. I discuss RMAN backups in the section "Using RMAN to Create Backups."

In the next sections, you will learn to back up the control file, back up the database, and use Recovery Manager.

Backing Up the Control File

In addition to multiplexing the control file, you can guard against the loss of all control files by backing up the control file. You can back up the control using three methods:

- An editable text file; this backup is called a *backup to trace.*
- A binary backup of the control file.
- RMAN backup of the control file.

Text Backup of Control File

The text backup is created using the `ALTER DATABASE BACKUP CONTROLFILE TO TRACE` statement, and the file is created in the trace directory under `<ADR_HOME>/trace`. The trace file format is *`sid`*`_ora_`*`pid`*`.trc`, where *`sid`* is the session database ID and *`pid`* is the process ID of the user creating the trace backup. This special backup of the control file is not a trace file per se; in other words, it is not a dump file or an error report for a failed user or system process. It is a proactive rather than reactive report of the contents of the control file, and the report happens to end up in a directory with other trace files.

Back up the control file to trace after any change to the structure of the database, such as adding or dropping a tablespace or creating a new redo log file group. Using the command line to create a backup of the control file is almost as easy as clicking the Backup to Trace button within EM Database Control (see Figure 15.1 earlier in the chapter):

```
SQL> alter database backup controlfile to trace;
Database altered.
```

If you want to create the control file create statement in a named file, rather than an Oracle-generated trace file name, you can do this:

```
SQL> alter database backup controlfile to trace as '/tmp/mydbcontrol.txt';
Database altered.
```

The control file create statements are created in the file */tmp/mydbcontrol.txt*.

Here is an excerpt from the output of the command; note that a lot of editing might be required before using this file to re-create the control file:

```
--
-- The following are current System-scope REDO Log Archival related
-- parameters and can be included in the database initialization file.
--
-- LOG_ARCHIVE_DEST=''
```

```
-- LOG_ARCHIVE_DUPLEX_DEST=''
--
-- LOG_ARCHIVE_FORMAT=%t_%s_%r.dbf
--
-- DB_UNIQUE_NAME="11GR11"
--
-- LOG_ARCHIVE_CONFIG='SEND, RECEIVE, NODG_CONFIG'
-- LOG_ARCHIVE_MAX_PROCESSES=4
-- STANDBY_FILE_MANAGEMENT=MANUAL
-- STANDBY_ARCHIVE_DEST=?/dbs/arch
-- FAL_CLIENT=''
-- FAL_SERVER=''
--
-- LOG_ARCHIVE_DEST_10='LOCATION=USE_DB_RECOVERY_FILE_DEST'
-- LOG_ARCHIVE_DEST_10='OPTIONAL REOPEN=300 NODELAY'
-- LOG_ARCHIVE_DEST_10='ARCH NOAFFIRM NOEXPEDITE NOVERIFY SYNC'
-- LOG_ARCHIVE_DEST_10='REGISTER NOALTERNATE NODEPENDENCY'
-- LOG_ARCHIVE_DEST_10='NOMAX_FAILURE NOQUOTA_SIZE NOQUOTA_USED NODB_UNIQUE_
NAME'
-- LOG_ARCHIVE_DEST_10='VALID_FOR=(PRIMARY_ROLE,ONLINE_LOGFILES)'
-- LOG_ARCHIVE_DEST_STATE_10=ENABLE
--
-- LOG_ARCHIVE_DEST_1='LOCATION=/u01/app/oracle/product/11.1.0/db_1/dbs/arch'
-- LOG_ARCHIVE_DEST_1='MANDATORY NOREOPEN NODELAY'
-- LOG_ARCHIVE_DEST_1='ARCH NOAFFIRM EXPEDITE NOVERIFY SYNC'
-- LOG_ARCHIVE_DEST_1='NOREGISTER NOALTERNATE NODEPENDENCY'
-- LOG_ARCHIVE_DEST_1='NOMAX_FAILURE NOQUOTA_SIZE NOQUOTA_USED NODB_UNIQUE_
NAME'
-- LOG_ARCHIVE_DEST_1='VALID_FOR=(PRIMARY_ROLE,ONLINE_LOGFILES)'
-- LOG_ARCHIVE_DEST_STATE_1=ENABLE
--
-- The following commands will create a new control file and use it
-- to open the database.
-- Data used by Recovery Manager will be lost.
-- The contents of online logs will be lost and all backups will
-- be invalidated. Use this only if online logs are damaged.
-- After mounting the created controlfile, the following SQL
-- statement will place the database in the appropriate
-- protection mode:
--  ALTER DATABASE SET STANDBY DATABASE TO MAXIMIZE PERFORMANCE
```

```
STARTUP NOMOUNT
CREATE CONTROLFILE REUSE DATABASE "11GR11" RESETLOGS  ARCHIVELOG
    MAXLOGFILES 16
    MAXLOGMEMBERS 3
    MAXDATAFILES 100
    MAXINSTANCES 8
    MAXLOGHISTORY 292
LOGFILE
  GROUP 1 (
    '/u01/app/oracle/oradata/11GR11/redo01.log',
    '/u02/app/oracle/oradata/11GR11/redo01.log'
  ) SIZE 50M,
  GROUP 2 (
    '/u01/app/oracle/oradata/11GR11/redo02.log',
    '/u02/app/oracle/oradata/11GR11/redo02.log'
  ) SIZE 50M,
  GROUP 3 (
    '/u01/app/oracle/oradata/11GR11/redo03.log',
    '/u02/app/oracle/oradata/11GR11/redo03.log'
  ) SIZE 50M
-- STANDBY LOGFILE
DATAFILE
  '/u01/app/oracle/oradata/11GR11/system01.dbf',
  '/u01/app/oracle/oradata/11GR11/sysaux01.dbf',
  '/u01/app/oracle/oradata/11GR11/undotbs01.dbf',
  '/u01/app/oracle/oradata/11GR11/users01.dbf',
  '/u01/app/oracle/oradata/11GR11/example01.dbf',
  '/u01/app/oracle/oradata/11GR11/appl_data01.dbf',
  '/u01/app/oracle/oradata/11GR11/appl_data02.dbf'
CHARACTER SET WE8MSWIN1252
;
-- Commands to re-create incarnation table
-- Below log names MUST be changed to existing filenames on
-- disk. Any one log file from each branch can be used to
-- re-create incarnation records.
-- ALTER DATABASE REGISTER LOGFILE '/u01/app/oracle/ ↵
flash_recovery_area/11GR11/archivelog/2008_10_26/o1_mf_1_1_%u_.arc';
-- ALTER DATABASE REGISTER LOGFILE '/u01/app/oracle/ ↵
flash_recovery_area/11GR11/archivelog/2008_10_26/o1_mf_1_1_%u_.arc';
-- Recovery is required if any of the datafiles are restored backups,
```

```
-- or if the last shutdown was not normal or immediate.
RECOVER DATABASE USING BACKUP CONTROLFILE
-- Database can now be opened zeroing the online logs.
ALTER DATABASE OPEN RESETLOGS;
-- Files in read-only tablespaces are now named.
ALTER DATABASE RENAME FILE 'MISSING00008'
  TO '/u02/oradata/11GR11/11GR11/datafile/o1_mf_hr_data_46n3ck5t_.dbf';
-- Online the files in read-only tablespaces.
ALTER TABLESPACE "HR_DATA" ONLINE;
-- Commands to add tempfiles to temporary tablespaces.
-- Online tempfiles have complete space information.
-- Other tempfiles may require adjustment.
ALTER TABLESPACE TEMP ADD TEMPFILE '/u01/app/oracle/oradata/11GR11/temp01.dbf'
     SIZE 400M  REUSE AUTOEXTEND ON NEXT 100M  MAXSIZE 4000M;
-- End of tempfile additions.
--
```

Binary Backup of Control File

Another way to back up your control file is to make a binary copy of it using the similar ALTER DATABASE command, as in the following example:

```
SQL> alter database backup controlfile to
                '/ora_backup/11GR11/ctlfile20040911.bkp';
Database altered.
```

You can then copy the binary backup of the control file to a backup device.

RMAN Backup of Control File

Using RMAN, you can back up the control file using the BACKUP CURRENT CONTROLFILE statement, as shown here. This backup is also a binary backup.

```
RMAN> BACKUP CURRENT CONTROLFILE;

Starting backup at 26-OCT-08
using target database control file instead of recovery catalog
allocated channel: ORA_DISK_1
channel ORA_DISK_1: SID=123 device type=DISK
channel ORA_DISK_1: starting full datafile backup set
channel ORA_DISK_1: specifying datafile(s) in backup set
including current control file in backup set
channel ORA_DISK_1: starting piece 1 at 26-OCT-08
channel ORA_DISK_1: finished piece 1 at 26-OCT-08
```

```
piece handle=/u01/app/oracle/flash_recovery_area/ ↵
11GR11/backupset/2008_10_26/o1_mf_ncnnf_TAG20081026T225337_4jbgtcgs_.bkp ↵
tag=TAG20081026T225337 comment=NONE
channel ORA_DISK_1: backup set complete, elapsed time: 00:00:02
Finished backup at 26-OCT-08

RMAN>
```

Backing Up the Database

An Oracle 11*g* database can be backed using different modes, depending on the ARCHIVELOG setting of the database. If the database is in ARCHIVELOG mode, you can perform an online database backup (also known as an *inconsistent* or *hot* backup) or offline database backup (also known as a *consistent* or *cold* backup). If the database is in NOARCHIVELOG mode, you can perform an offline backup only.

You can use OS utilities to perform the database backup or use the RMAN. Using RMAN is the preferred and easier method of backup. In the following sections, you will learn how to back up the database using OS utilities (user-managed backups). RMAN backups are discussed in the next section.

User-Managed Cold Backups

Cold backups are performed after shutting down the database. Shut down the database cleanly using the SHUTDOWN IMMEDIATE or SHUTDOWN TRANSACTIONAL statement, and copy all control files and data files to another location or to your tape management system using OS commands. You can also copy the redo logs, but this is not needed if the database shutdown is clean. You also need to back up the parameter file (init file or spfile) and password file.

You can identify the control files in the database using the dynamic performance view V$CONTROLFILE. The data files that need to be backed up can be identified by using the view V$DATAFILE.

User-Managed Hot Backups

To perform a hot backup, the database must be in ARCHIVELOG mode. Before starting to copy the data files belonging to a tablespace, you must place the tablespace in backup mode using the BEGIN BACKUP clause. For example, if you want to back up the USERS tablespace, perform the following:

```
SQL> ALTER TABLESPACE user BEGIN BACKUP;
```

When a tablespace is placed in the backup mode, data-block changes are written to the redo log files. After you take the tablespace out of the backup mode, the database advances the data file checkpoint SCN to the current database-checkpoint SCN.

When a tablespace is in backup mode, use OS utilities to copy the data files belonging to the tablespace to another location or to the tape management system. To take the tablespace out of the backup mode, use the END BACKUP clause as in the following example:

```
SQL> ALTER TABLESPACE user END BACKUP;
```

If your database is small or if you plan to place all the tablespaces in backup mode for the hot backup, instead of placing each tablespace in backup mode, you can use the ALTER DATABASE statement to make the whole database in backup mode, as in the following example:

```
SQL> ALTER DATABASE BEGIN BACKUP;
```

You cannot perform incremental backups using user-managed backups. You must use RMAN for incremental backups.

Using RMAN to Create Backups

RMAN is the primary component of the Oracle database used to perform backup and recovery operations. You can use RMAN to back up all types: whole or partial databases, full or incremental, and consistent or inconsistent. RMAN is closely integrated with EM Database Control.

RMAN has a command-line interface for advanced configuration and backup operations; the most common backup functions are available via a GUI within EM Database Control. It includes a scripting language to make it easy to automate backups, and it can back up the most critical types of files in your database except for online redo log files (which you should not back up anyway), password files, and text-based init.ora files. Data files, control files, archived log files, and spfiles can be backed up using RMAN. In other words, RMAN is a "one-stop shopping" solution for all your backup and recovery needs. In the rare circumstance that you have to back up outside RMAN, you can register the file created during this backup with RMAN for future use in an RMAN recovery scenario.

Because of the relatively static nature of password files and text-based init.ora files, these can be included in the regular operating-system backups, or you can back them up manually whenever they are changed.

In the following sections, I will explain the difference between image copies and backup sets and how RMAN handles each of these backup types. After learning some of the RMAN configuration settings, I will show you some examples of how RMAN performs full and incremental backups, using both the command line and the graphical user interface.

Configuring RMAN Backup Settings

Configuring RMAN backup settings is straightforward using EM Database Control. On the Availability tab, click Backup Settings to open the Device tab screen, as shown in Figure 15.8.

FIGURE 15.8 The Backup Settings: Device screen

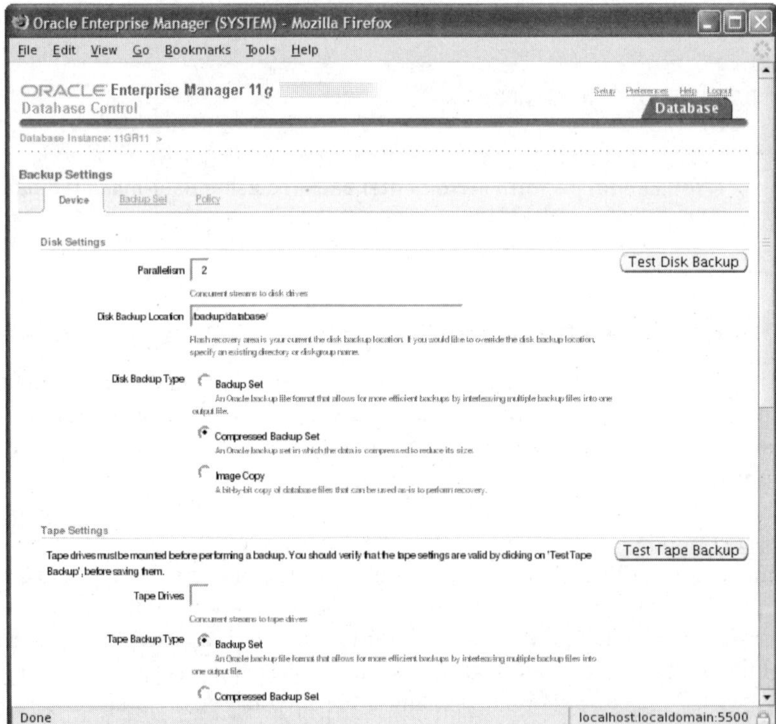

There is a separate section in this screen for your disk device and any tape devices. Under the Disk Settings section, you can control the following parameters:

Parallelism To take advantage of multiple CPUs or disk controllers, increase the value of this parameter to reduce the overall backup time by performing different portions of the backup in parallel.

Disk Backup Location If you are not backing up to the flash recovery area, change this value to the location where you want the backups stored.

Disk Backup Type You can choose image copy, backup set, or compressed backup set.

Under the Tape settings, you can specify whether you want the backups to be written directly to the tape or media management tool. You also have the option to configure the Oracle Secure Backup (OSB) tool on this screen. OSB is a separately licensed product from Oracle to manage the backups and tape libraries. Using OSB, you can back up any type of OS files anywhere on the network.

Click the Backup Set tab, and specify the maximum size for a backup-set piece (a single file), as shown in Figure 15.9. In this case, set the maximum backup-set piece size to 2GB to make it easier to move files around on file systems whose file-size limit is 2GB.

FIGURE 15.9 The Backup Settings: Backup Set screen

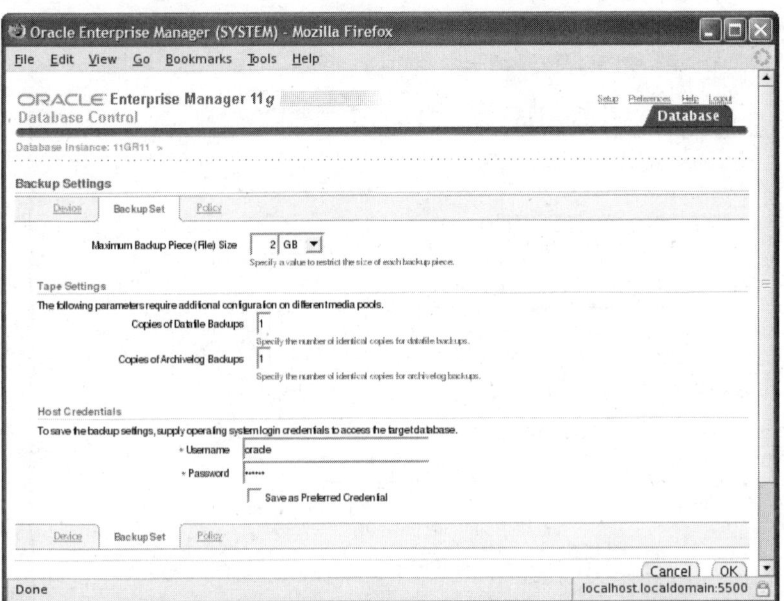

You use the last tab on the Backup Settings screen, the Policy tab, to set a number of other default backup settings, such as automatically backing up the control file with each backup, skipping read-only and offline data files, and using a block-change tracking file. A block-change tracking file keeps track of changed blocks in each tablespace so that incremental backups need not read every block in every data file to determine which blocks need to be backed up during an incremental backup. Figure 15.10 shows an example of the Policy tab with a block-change tracking file specified.

Always enable the automatic backup of control files and spfiles. This is an Oracle-recommended best practice.

Infrequently used parameters, such as the control file autobackup filename format and the snapshot control file destination filename, are not available from the graphical user interface; you must use the RMAN command-line interface to change these values.

You can invoke the RMAN command line by using the executable `rman`. RMAN can optionally use a catalog database where the backup information is kept. If a catalog database is not used, RMAN uses the database control file to perform the backup and recovery operations.

FIGURE 15.10 The Backup Settings: Policy screen

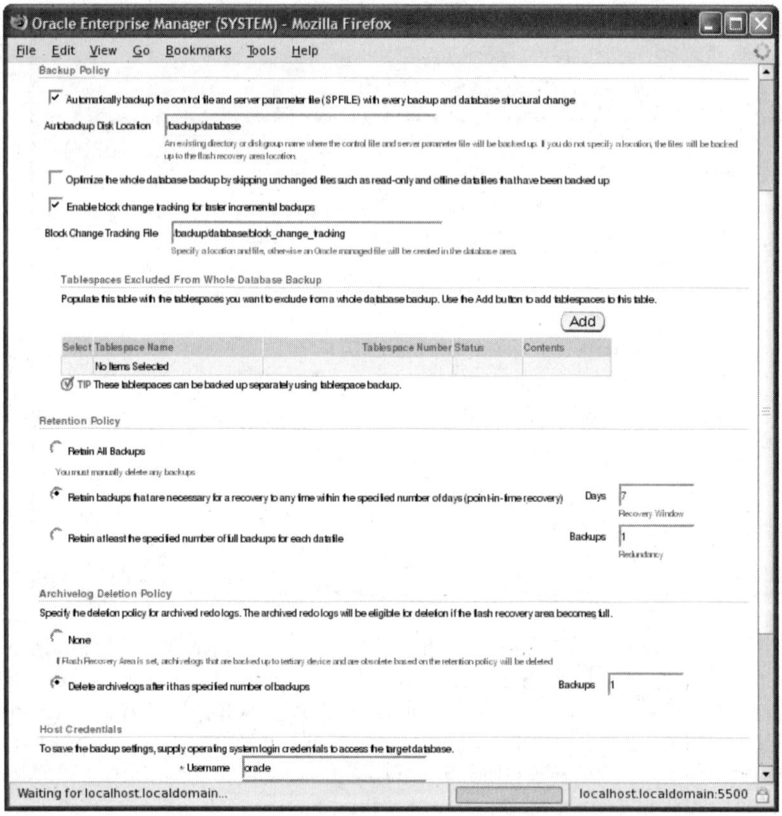

The following RMAN command-line session uses the RMAN `SHOW ALL` command to display all default RMAN backup settings:

```
$ rman target / nocatalog
Recovery Manager: Release 11.1.0.6.0 - Production on Sun Oct 26 23:51:53 2008
Copyright (c) 1982, 2007, Oracle.  All rights reserved.
connected to target database: 11GR11 (DBID=4110949673)
using target database control file instead of recovery catalog

RMAN> SHOW ALL;

RMAN configuration parameters for database with db_unique_name 11GR11 are:
CONFIGURE RETENTION POLICY TO RECOVERY WINDOW OF 7 DAYS;
CONFIGURE BACKUP OPTIMIZATION OFF; # default
CONFIGURE DEFAULT DEVICE TYPE TO DISK; # default
```

```
CONFIGURE CONTROLFILE AUTOBACKUP ON;
CONFIGURE CONTROLFILE AUTOBACKUP FORMAT
FOR DEVICE TYPE DISK TO '/backup/database/%F';
CONFIGURE DEVICE TYPE DISK BACKUP TYPE TO COMPRESSED BACKUPSET PARALLELISM 2;
CONFIGURE DATAFILE BACKUP COPIES FOR DEVICE TYPE DISK TO 1; # default
CONFIGURE ARCHIVELOG BACKUP COPIES FOR DEVICE TYPE DISK TO 1; # default
CONFIGURE CHANNEL DEVICE TYPE DISK FORMAT
   '/backup/database/%U' MAXPIECESIZE 2 G;
CONFIGURE MAXSETSIZE TO UNLIMITED; # default
CONFIGURE ENCRYPTION FOR DATABASE OFF; # default
CONFIGURE ENCRYPTION ALGORITHM 'AES128'; # default
CONFIGURE COMPRESSION ALGORITHM 'BZIP2'; # default
CONFIGURE ARCHIVELOG DELETION POLICY TO BACKED UP 1 TIMES TO 'SBT_TAPE';
CONFIGURE SNAPSHOT CONTROLFILE NAME TO
'/u01/app/oracle/product/11.1.0/db_1/dbs/snapcf_11GR11.f'; # default

RMAN>
```

You can enable block-change tracking in the database by using the SQL statement ALTER DATABASE ENABLE BLOCK CHANGE TRACKING.

Understanding Image Copies and Backup Sets

Image copies are duplicates of data files or archived redo log files, which means that every block of every file is backed up; you can use RMAN or operating-system commands to make image copies. In contrast, backup sets are copies of one or more data files or archived redo log files that are stored in a proprietary format readable only by RMAN; backup sets consist of one or more physical files and do not include never-used blocks in the data files being backed up. Backup sets can save even more space by using a compression algorithm designed specifically for the type of data found in an Oracle data file.

Another difference between image copies and backup sets is that image copies can be copied only to a disk location; backup sets can be written to disk or directly to a tape or other secondary storage device.

Creating Full and Incremental Backups

The Oracle-recommended backup strategy uses RMAN to make a one-time, whole-database, baseline incremental level-zero online backup weekly and then a level-one incremental backup for the other days of the week. You can easily fine-tune this strategy for your own needs by making, for example, a level-two incremental backup at noon during the weekdays if heavy Data Manipulation Language (DML) is occurring in the database.

Using RMAN, you can accomplish this backup strategy with just a couple of the RMAN commands that follow. First, here is the baseline level-one backup at the RMAN command prompt:

```
RMAN> backup incremental level 0
      as compressed backupset database;
```

This backs up the entire database using compression to save disk space in addition to the space savings already gained by using backup sets instead of image copies.

Starting with a baseline level-zero incremental backup, you can make level-one incremental backups during the rest of the week, as in the following example:

```
RMAN> backup incremental level 1

      as compressed backupset database;
```

The options are the same as in the previous example, except that only the blocks that have changed since the last backup are copied to the backup set.

Another variation is to make an incrementally updated backup. An incrementally updated backup uses an incremental backup and updates the changed blocks in an existing image copy as if the entire image copy were backed up. In a recovery scenario, you can restore the image copy of the data file(s) without using an incremental backup; the incremental backup is already applied, saving a significant amount of time during a recovery operation. The following RMAN script shows how an incrementally updated backup works at the command line:

```
run
{
   recover copy of database with tag 'inc_upd_img';
   backup incremental level 1 for
      recover of copy with tag 'inc_upd_img' database;
}
```

This short and cryptic script demonstrates the advantages of using a graphical user interface to perform incrementally updated backups. As you can see in Figure 15.11, on the Schedule Backup: Options screen, you can click a check box to perform an incrementally updated backup in addition to the full backup or incremental backup discussed previously in this section. The Schedule backup link is under the Manage section on the Availability screen (see Figure 15.5 earlier in the chapter).

The Oracle-suggested backup is provided on the right side of the screen. If you want to enable this policy for backups, click the Schedule Oracle-Suggested Backup button. To customize the backups according to your company policy, click the Schedule Customized Backup button. You will be provided with four screens to schedule the backup. The first screen is to specify the backup options, as shown in Figure 15.12.

FIGURE 15.11 Scheduling the backup and specifying the backup type

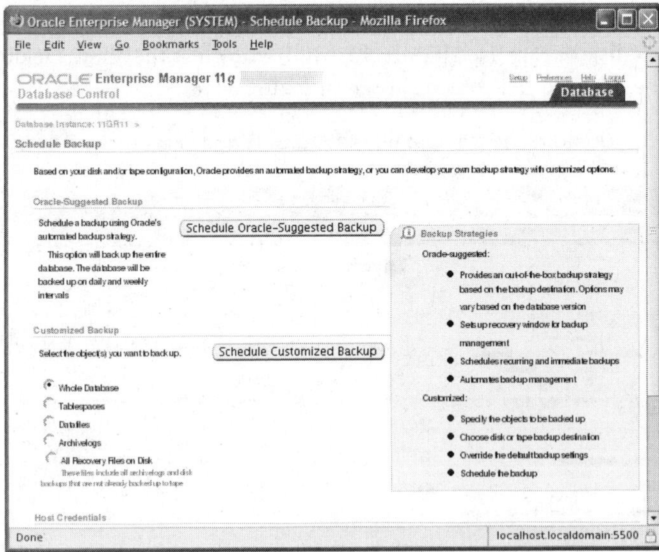

FIGURE 15.12 Customized backup schedule: Options screen

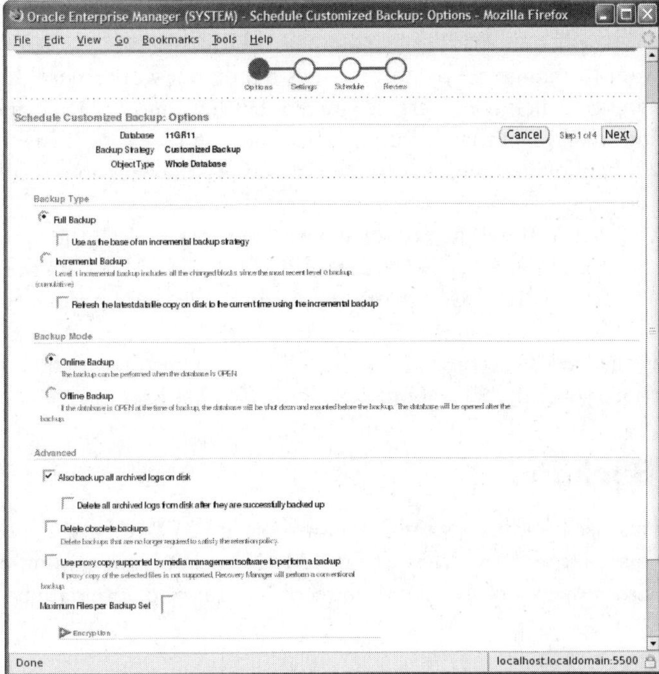

On this screen, you can specify the backup type (full backup or incremental), backup mode (online or offline), and whether to back up archive logs. Click the Next button to advance to the next screen, where you specify the backup settings. Specify whether you want to back up to disk or tape (see Figure 15.13). If you click the View Default Settings button, you will be taken to the screen shown in Figure 15.8.

FIGURE 15.13 Customized backup schedule: Settings screen

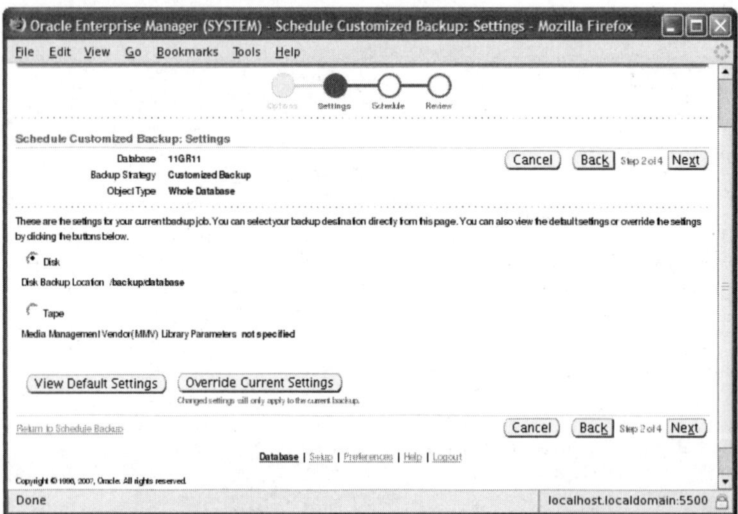

If you do not want to change the default settings but do not want to use the default location for backups, you can click the Override Current Settings button. The Schedule screen gives you the option to perform the backup one time or on a repeating basis. If you choose Repeating, you will be provided with the options to specify the backup repeating schedules, as shown in Figure 15.14.

On the Review screen, you will be provided with a summary of all the options you chose in the previous screens and the RMAN script that will be used to back up the database, as shown in Figure 15.15. You also have the option to edit the RMAN script before scheduling the job.

After reviewing the backup settings, click the Submit Job button to schedule the backup. In the next section, you will learn about managing RMAN backups.

Managing Backups

Managing your database backups is straightforward using EM Database Control. In the following sections, you will get an overview of the RMAN backup- and catalog-maintenance commands and learn how to monitor the flash recovery area and automate backups using the Scheduler.

FIGURE 15.14 Customized backup schedule: Schedule screen

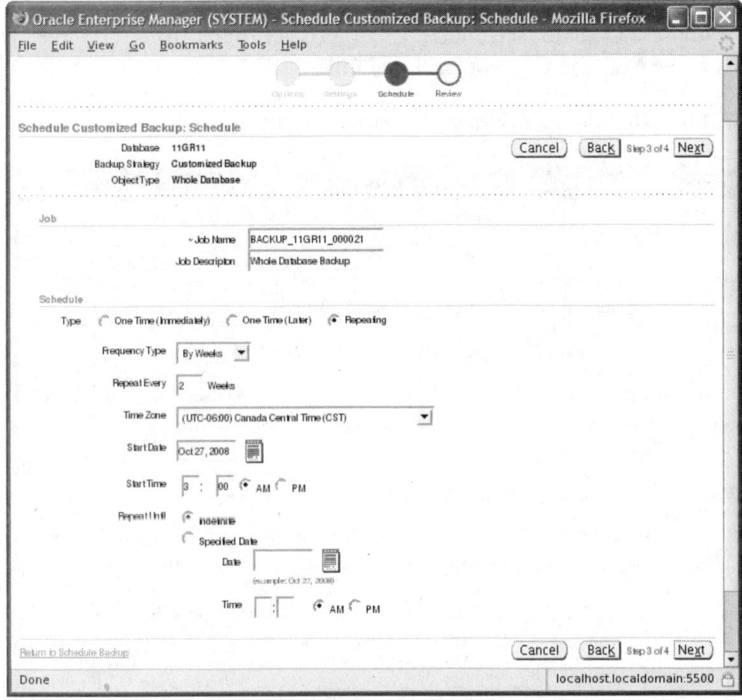

FIGURE 15.15 Customized backup schedule: Review screen

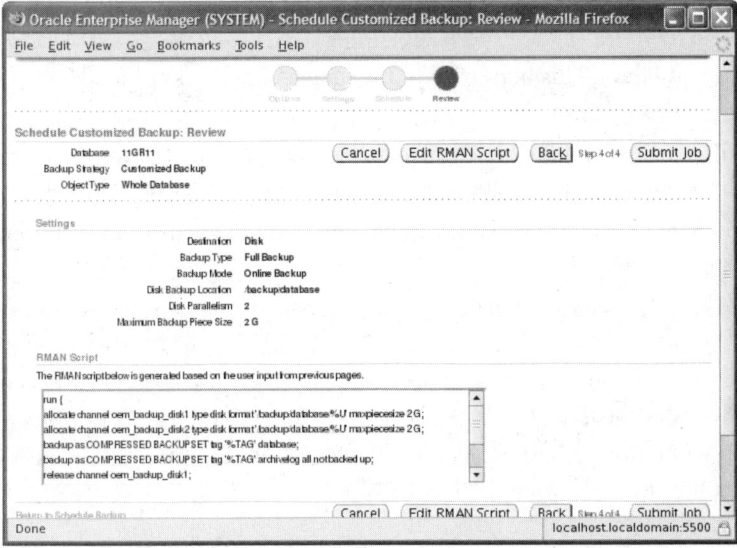

Catalog Maintenance

A number of backup-management functions are available on the Manage Current Backups screen in EM Database Control (see Figure 15.16). To get there, from the screen shown in Figure 15.5, click the Manage Current Backups link.

FIGURE 15.16 The Manage Current Backups screen

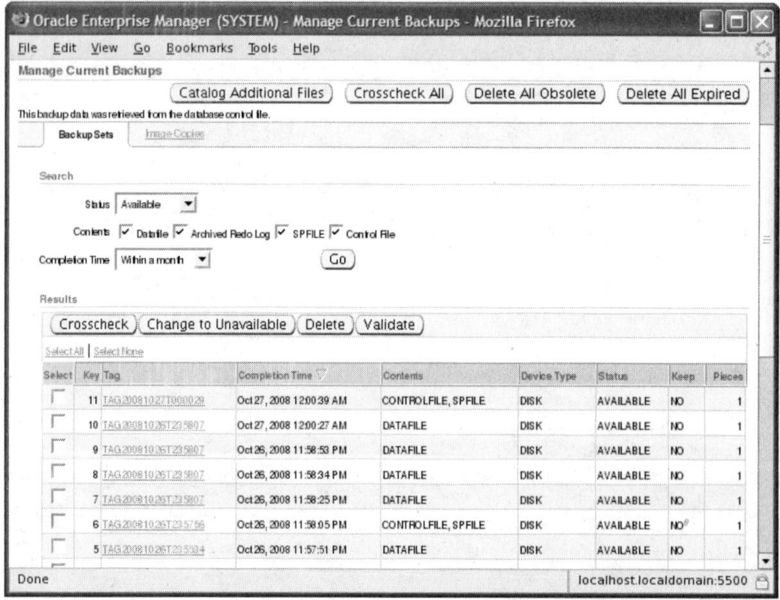

This screen shows you the current backups based on the search criteria entered. The four buttons at the top perform the following functions:

Catalog Additional Files This button adds any image-copy backups made outside RMAN to the RMAN catalog.

Crosscheck All This button double-checks the backup files listed in the catalog (or control file) against the actual files on disk (or tape) to make sure they are all available.

Delete All Obsolete This button deletes all backup files not needed to satisfy the existing retention policy.

Delete All Expired This button deletes the catalog entry for any backups not found when a crosscheck was performed.

Viewing Backup Reports

On the screen shown in Figure 15.5, click the Backup Reports link to show the View Backup Report screen, as shown in Figure 15.17.

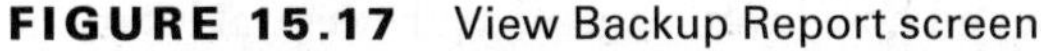

FIGURE 15.17 View Backup Report screen

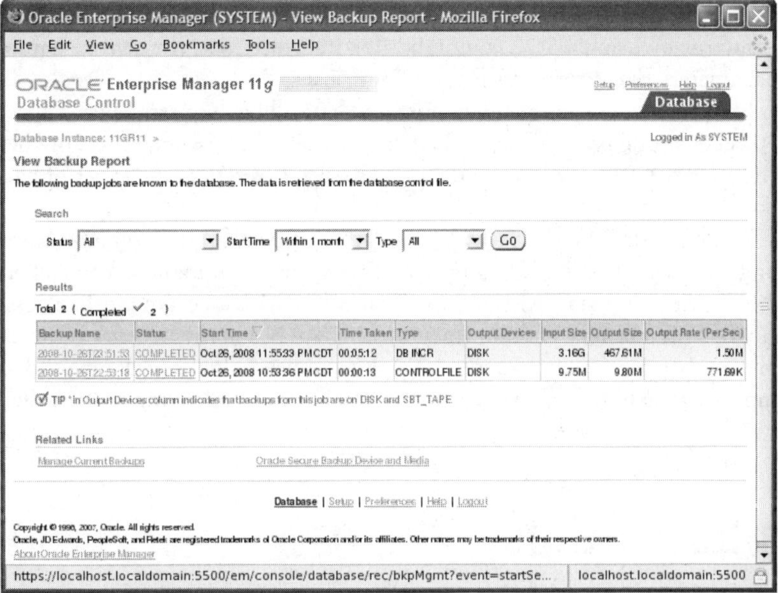

Click the name of the backup in the Backup Name column to display a detailed status report of the backup, including what is being backed up (data files, control files, spfiles), the size of the backup, the backup start and end times, and the backup pieces.

Summary

In this chapter, you learned the database structures that are key elements to ensure a smooth recovery in the event of a database failure: control files, online redo log files, and archived redo log files. You learned to back up the various pieces of the database and learned how to schedule and manage backups using EM Database Control.

The control files contain the metadata about every other structure in the database. The online redo log files provide performance benefits to ongoing transactions and ensure that no committed transactions are lost after an instance failure; being able to change the number of redo log groups and the number of members in each group enhances both the availability and performance of the database. Archived redo log files make copies of online redo log files to one or more destinations before they are overwritten by new transactions. The common thread through all three of these structures is multiplexing: creating redundant copies of database components or redundant archival locations to minimize the impact of a media failure.

You learned about the flash recovery area and how it can be used as the central location for backups of all database files, control files, initialization-parameter files, and archived redo log files in the database. You can manage the flash recovery area via the EM Database Control interface or by using a SQL command-line interface to set or change database initialization parameters that control its location and size.

Before making database backups, you must understand backup strategies, types, and modes. ARCHIVELOG mode provides many benefits and few downsides, especially in a production environment; NOARCHIVELOG mode, in many ways, restricts the types of backups you can make.

Recovery Manager, or RMAN, provides a number of benefits over manual backup methods using a combination of SQL and operating-system commands. You can access most RMAN functionality via EM Database Control or with a command-line version for advanced backup and recovery techniques. One of RMAN's many benefits is the ability to create compressed backup sets, which not only skips unused blocks in database data files but also compresses the blocks before writing to the backup set, saving I/O bandwidth and disk space.

Exam Essentials

Identify the purpose of the redo log files. Describe the redo log file architecture. Provide details about how to create new redo log file groups and add new members to redo log file groups. Be able to drop redo log group members. Know how to clear online redo log file groups when a log file member becomes corrupted.

Be able to multiplex a control file. List the steps required to create additional copies of the control file, for both an `init.ora` file and an spfile.

Describe the basic differences between operating a database in ARCHIVELOG mode and in NOARCHIVELOG mode. Identify the initialization parameters and commands that control the archive process. Briefly describe how archive-log information is recorded in the control file.

Identify and discuss backup terminology. Enumerate the backup strategies, the backup types, and the backup modes. Give examples of how you can combine the strategies, types, and modes in different scenarios.

List the benefits of using RMAN to create backups. Show how to configure RMAN backup settings via the EM Database Control interface. Differentiate image copies from backup sets. Provide examples of an incremental backup strategy.

Explain the benefits of the flash recovery area. Show how you can access the characteristics and status of the flash recovery area using EM Database Control as well as via dynamic performance views. Describe the database components that can be stored in the flash recovery area. Enumerate the initialization parameters that control the location and size of the flash recovery area.

Know how flashback database option works. The flashback database option can greatly reduce the time required to rewind the database to a prior point in time. Understand the parameters associated with flashback database.

Understand backup catalog maintenance. Show how the EM Database Control interface simplifies cataloging, crosschecking, and cleaning up.

Review Questions

1. Among the failure events, which is the most serious?
   - **A.** The loss of an entire redo log file group but no loss in any other group
   - **B.** The loss of one member of each redo log file group
   - **C.** The failure of the ARC0 background process
   - **D.** The failure of the LGWR background process

2. To enable the flashback database option, the database must be in which of the following modes?
   - **A.** `NOARCHIVELOG` mode
   - **B.** `ARCHIVELOG` mode
   - **C.** `FLASHBACK LOG` mode
   - **D.** `BEGIN BACKUP` mode

3. When the database is in `ARCHIVELOG` mode, database recovery is possible up to which event or time?
   - **A.** The last redo log file switch
   - **B.** The last checkpoint position
   - **C.** The last commit
   - **D.** The last incremental backup using RMAN

4. From the following, choose the true statement regarding image copies and backup sets.
   - **A.** An image copy stores one data file per image copy, and a backup set can store all data files in a single file.
   - **B.** An image copy stores one data file per image copy, and a backup set consists of one file per data file backed up.
   - **C.** Both image copies and backup sets use a single file to store all objects to be backed up.
   - **D.** A backup set stores each data file in its own backup file, but an image copy places all data files into a single output file.

5. The option on the EM Database Control backup-scheduling options screen that allows you to refresh an image copy on disk with an incremental backup is known as which RMAN feature?
   - **A.** Incrementally updated backups
   - **B.** Incremental level-zero backups
   - **C.** Compressed image-copy refresh
   - **D.** Compressed incremental backups

6. When should the DBA make a trace copy of the control file using `ALTER DATABASE BACKUP CONTROLFILE TO TRACE`?

   A. After every backup

   B. After multiplexing the control files

   C. Whenever restarting the instance

   D. Whenever the physical structure of the database changes

7. Which of the following is not a step in configuring your database to archive redo log files?

   A. Place the database in `ARCHIVELOG` mode.

   B. Multiplex the online redo log files.

   C. Specify a destination for archived redo log files.

   D. Specify a naming convention for your archived redo log files.

8. Why are online backups known as inconsistent backups?

   A. Because not all control files are synchronized to the same SCN until the database is shut down

   B. Because both committed and uncommitted transactions are included in a backup when the database is online

   C. Because a database failure while an online backup is in progress can leave the database in an inconsistent state

   D. Because online backups make copies of data files while they are not consistent with the control files

9. Which parameter is used to specify the archive-log destination?

   A. `ARCHIVE_LOG_DEST_`*n*

   B. `LOG_ARCHIVE_DEST_`*n*

   C. `DB_CREATE_FILE_DEST`

   D. `DB_RECOVERY_FILE_DEST_`*n*

10. Which of the following initialization parameters specifies the location where the control file trace backup is sent?

    A. `DIAGNOSTIC_DEST`

    B. `BACKGROUND_DUMP_DEST`

    C. `LOG_ARCHIVE_DEST`

    D. `CORE_DUMP_DEST`

11. Which of the following pieces of information is not available in the control file?

    A. Instance name

    B. Database name

    C. Tablespace names

    D. Log sequence number

12. Which data dictionary view shows that the database is in ARCHIVELOG mode?
    - A. V$INSTANCE
    - B. V$LOG
    - C. V$DATABASE
    - D. V$THREAD

13. Which file records all changes made to the database and is used only when recovering an instance?
    - A. Archive-log file
    - B. Redo log file
    - C. Control file
    - D. Alert log file

14. Which initialization parameter contains the value used as the default for archived log file destination 10?
    - A. LOG_ARCHIVE_DEST
    - B. STANDBY_ARCHIVE_DEST
    - C. LOG_ARCHIVE_DUPLEX_DEST
    - D. DB_RECOVERY_FILE_DEST
    - E. USE_DB_RECOVERY_FILE_DEST

15. Which of the following commands is a key step in multiplexing control files using an spfile?
    - A. ALTER SYSTEM SET CONTROL_FILES= '/u01/oradata/PRD/cntrl01.ctl', '/u01/oradata/PRD/cntrl02.ctl' SCOPE=SPFILE;
    - B. ALTER SYSTEM SET CONTROL_FILES= '/u01/oradata/PRD/cntrl01.ctl', '/u01/oradata/PRD/cntrl02.ctl' SCOPE=MEMORY;
    - C. ALTER SYSTEM SET CONTROL_FILES= '/u01/oradata/PRD/cntrl01.ctl', '/u01/oradata/PRD/cntrl02.ctl' SCOPE=BOTH;
    - D. The number of control files is fixed when the database is created.

16. Which statement adds a member /logs/redo22.log to redo log file group 2?
    - A. ALTER DATABASE ADD LOGFILE '/logs/redo22.log' TO GROUP 2;
    - B. ALTER DATABASE ADD LOGFILE MEMBER '/logs/redo22.log' TO GROUP 2;
    - C. ALTER DATABASE ADD MEMBER '/logs/redo22.log' TO GROUP 2;
    - D. ALTER DATABASE ADD LOGFILE '/logs/redo22.log';

17. What is the biggest advantage of having the control files on different disks?
    - A. Database performance.
    - B. Guards against failure.
    - C. Faster archiving.
    - D. Writes are concurrent, so having control files on different disks speeds up control file writes.

18. To place the database into ARCHIVELOG mode, in which state must you start the database?

A. MOUNT

B. NOMOUNT

C. OPEN

D. SHUTDOWN

E. Any of the above

19. Which of the following commands places the database in ARCHIVELOG mode?

A. ALTER SYSTEM ARCHIVELOG;

B. ALTER DATABASE ARCHIVELOG;

C. ALTER SYSTEM SET ARCHIVELOG=TRUE;

D. ALTER DATABASE ENABLE ARCHIVELOG MODE;

E. ALTER DATABASE ARCHIVELOG MODE;

20. Which of the following substitution-variable formats are always required for specifying the names of the archived redo log files? (Choose all that apply.)

A. %d

B. %s

C. %r

D. %t

Answers to Review Questions

1. A. Losing an entire redo log file group can result in losing committed transactions that may not yet have been written to the database files. Losing all members of a redo log file group except for one does not affect database operation and does not result in lost data. A message is placed in the alert log file. The failure of LGWR or ARC0 causes an instance failure, but you do not lose any committed transaction data.

2. B. To enable the flashback database option, the database must be in `ARCHIVELOG` mode. `FLASHBACK LOG` mode is not a valid mode of database operation. `BEGIN BACKUP` mode is used to perform hot backups without using RMAN.

3. C. In `ARCHIVELOG` mode, recovering the database is possible up to the last `COMMIT` statement; in other words, no committed transactions are lost in `ARCHIVELOG` mode.

4. A. Image copies are duplicate data and log files in OS format. Backup sets are binary compressed files in Oracle proprietary format. In addition to storing multiple data files in a single output file, backup sets do not contain unused blocks.

5. A. Incrementally updated backups save time during a recovery operation because fewer incremental backups need to be applied to the restored image copy.

6. D. In the rare event that all multiplexed copies of the control file are lost, having a trace copy of the control file reduces the possibility of data loss and reduces downtime during a recovery operation. The preferred and recommended way to back up a control file is to enable control file autobackup using RMAN.

7. B. Although it is recommended that you multiplex your online redo log files, it is not required to enable `ARCHIVELOG` mode of the database.

8. D. During an online backup, even if all data files are backed up at the same time, they are rarely, if ever, in sync with the control file.

9. B. `LOG_ARCHIVE_DEST_n` specifies the archive-log location. You can configure up to 10 archive-log destinations. `LOG_ARCHIVE_DEST_10` is reserved for the flash recovery area, which is specified by the parameter `DB_RECOVERY_FILE_DEST`.

10. A. The trace backup is created in a subdirectory under the location specified by the `DIAGNOSTIC_DEST` parameter—`$DIAGNOSTIC_DEST/diag/<dbname>/<instancename>/trace directory`.

11. A. The instance name is not in the control file. The control file has information about the physical database structure.

12. C. The `V$DATABASE` view in the column `LOG_MODE` shows whether the database is in `ARCHIVELOG` mode or in `NOARCHIVELOG` mode.

13. B. The redo log file records all changes made to the database. The LGWR process writes the redo log buffer entries to the redo log files. These entries are used to roll forward, or to update, the data files during an instance recovery. Archive log files are used for media recovery.

14. D. DB_RECOVERY_FILE_DEST points to the flash recovery area, and this is the default for archived log-file destination number 10.

15. A. The location of the new control files is not valid until an operating-system copy is made of the current control file to the new location(s) and the instance is restarted. The SCOPE=SPFILE option specifies that the parameter change will not take place until a restart. Specifying either MEMORY or BOTH causes an error, because CONTROL_FILES is not a dynamic parameter.

16. B. When adding log-file members, specify the group number, or specify all the existing group members.

17. B. Having the control files on different disks ensures that even if you lose one disk, you lose only one control file. If you lose one of the control files, you can shut down the database and copy a control file, or you can change the CONTROL_FILES parameter and restart the database.

18. A. To put the database into ARCHIVELOG mode, the database must be in the MOUNT state; the control files and all data files that are not offline must be available to change the database to ARCHIVELOG mode.

19. B. You use the ALTER DATABASE ARCHIVELOG command while the database is in the MOUNT state to enable archiving of online redo log files.

20. B, C, D. The substitution variable %d, which represents the database ID, is required only if multiple databases share the same archive-log destination.

Recovering the Database

ORACLE DATABASE 11*g*: ADMINISTRATION I EXAM OBJECTIVES COVERED IN THIS CHAPTER:

✓ **Backup and Recovery Concepts**

- Identify the types of failure that can occur in an Oracle database
- Describe ways to tune instance recovery

✓ **Performing Database Recovery**

- Overview of Data Recovery Advisor
- Use Data Recovery Advisor to Perform recovery (Control file, Redo log file, and Data file)

Oracle Database 11*g* makes it easy for you to recover from a number of database failures. In Chapter 15, "Implementing Database Backups," I emphasized the importance of checkpoints, redo log files, and archived log files to maintain a high level of availability and recoverability. I also showed you how to use the flash recovery area and several ways to back up your database. In this chapter, I'll show you how to use those backups effectively when some kind of failure inevitably occurs.

First, you'll understand the kinds of failures that can occur in an Oracle database and explore how they can occur because of mistakes by users or DBAs or because of hardware or software failures that are out of your direct control. Each of these failures can require little or no action whatsoever, as in the case of an instance failure, but at the other end of the spectrum, a crash of the disk containing the `SYSTEM` tablespace requires a recovery effort.

To balance performance with recoverability, you will learn how to tune instance recovery to minimize the amount of time Oracle will require to recover from an instance failure while still providing a reasonable response time for ongoing transactions. In a nutshell, your job is to increase the mean time between failures (MTBF) by providing redundant components where possible and leveraging other Oracle high-availability features such as Real Application Clusters (RAC) and Streams (an advanced replication technology). Hand in hand with increasing MTBF is decreasing the mean time to recovery (MTTR) to ensure compliance with any service-level agreements you have in place. Last, but certainly not least, these efforts should help you minimize data loss in such a way that committed transactions are never lost.

In this chapter, you will also learn the steps required to recover from the loss of both system-critical and non-system-critical data files for databases that are operating in both `ARCHIVELOG` and `NOARCHIVELOG` modes. I'll also show you how to recover from the loss of a control file or a redo log file.

The Data Recovery Advisor was introduced in Oracle 11g, which automates most of the recovery tasks and is integrated with Enterprise Manager (EM) Database Control. As with most DBA operations in the database, EM Database Control makes many of these administration tasks easier and less error-prone.

Understanding Types of Database Failure

Database-related failures fall into six general categories. Understanding which category a failure belongs in will help you more quickly understand the nature of the recovery effort you need to use to reverse the effects of the failure and maintain a high level of availability and performance in your database. The six general categories of failures are as follows:

Statement A single database operation fails, such as a Data Manipulation Language (DML) statement—INSERT, UPDATE, and so on.

User process A single database connection fails.

Network A network component between the client and the database server fails, and the session is disconnected from the database.

User error An error message is not generated, but the operation's result, such as dropping a table, is not what the user intended.

Instance The database instance crashes unexpectedly.

Media One or more of the database files is lost, deleted, or corrupted.

In the next six sections, I'll provide details on these failure types and suggest some possible solutions for each one. For one particular type of failure, media failure, I'll provide more detailed solutions for recovery later in this chapter.

Statement Failures

Statement failures occur when a single database operation fails, such as a single INSERT statement or the creation of a table. Table 16.1 shows the most common problems that occur when a statement fails, along with their solutions.

TABLE 16.1 Common Problems and Solutions for When a Statement Fails

Problem	Solution
Attempts to access tables without the appropriate privileges	Provide the appropriate privileges, or create views on the tables and grant privileges on the view.
Running out of space	Add space to the tablespace, increase the user's quota on the tablespace, or enable resumable-space allocation.
Entering invalid data	If constraints and triggers are not in place to enforce data integrity, entering bad data may succeed and cause application issues. DBAs need to work with users to validate and correct data.
Logic errors in applications	Work with developers to correct program errors or provide additional logic in the application to recover gracefully from unavoidable errors.

Although granting user privileges or additional quotas within a tablespace solves many of these problems, also consider whether there are any gaps in the user education process that might lead to some of these problems in the first place.

User-Process Failures

The abnormal termination of a user session is categorized as a *user-process failure*. After a user-process failure, any uncommitted transaction must be cleaned up. The PMON (process monitor) background process periodically checks all user processes to ensure that the session is still connected. If the `PMON` finds a disconnected session, it rolls back the uncommitted transaction and releases all locks held by the disconnected process. Causes for user-process failures typically fall into one of these categories:

- A user closes their SQL*Plus window without logging out.
- The workstation reboots suddenly before the application can be closed.
- The application program causes an exception and closes before the application can be terminated normally.

A small percentage of user-process failures is generally no cause for concern unless it becomes chronic. A failure may be a sign that user education is lacking—for example, training users to terminate the application gracefully before shutting down their workstation. A DBA intervention is not needed for user-process failures, but administrators must watch for trends, and if happens too often, they need to investigate because there may be application problems or network issues that cause an excessive number of user-process failures. More information may be available in the alert log file showing whether the user process is hitting a bug and whether there are any trace files written.

Network Failures

Depending on the locations of your workstation and your server, getting from your workstation to the server over the network might involve a number of hops; for example, you might traverse several local switches and WAN routers to get to the database. From a network perspective, this configuration provides a number of points where failure can occur. These types of failures are called *network failures*.

In addition to hardware failures between the server and client, a listener process on the Oracle server can fail, or the network card on the server itself can fail. To guard against these kinds of failures, you can provide redundant network paths from your clients to the server, as well as additional listener connections on the Oracle server and redundant network cards on the server.

User-Error Failures

Even if all your redundant hardware is at peak performance and your users have been trained to disconnect from their Oracle sessions properly, users can still inadvertently delete or modify data in tables or drop an index. This is known as a *user-error failure*. Although these operations succeed from a statement point of view, they might not be logically correct: the DROP TABLE command worked fine, but you really didn't want to drop that table!

If data was inadvertently deleted from a table and not yet committed, a ROLLBACK statement will undo the damage. If a COMMIT has already been performed, you have a number of options at your disposal, such as using data in the undo tablespace for a flashback query or using data in the archived and online redo logs with the LogMiner utility, available as a command-line interface or a graphical user interface.

You can recover a dropped table using Oracle's recycle-bin functionality. A dropped table is stored in a special structure in the tablespace and is available for retrieval as long as the space occupied by the table in the tablespace is not needed for new objects. Even if the table is no longer in the tablespace's recycle bin, depending on the criticality of the dropped table, you can use either tablespace point-in-time recovery (TSPITR) or flashback database recovery to recover the table, taking into consideration the potential data loss for other objects stored in the same tablespace for TSPITR or in the database if you use flashback database recovery.

TSPITR and flashback database recovery are beyond the scope of this book but are covered in more detail in *OCP: Oracle Database 11*g *Administrator Certified Professional Study Guide* (Sybex, 2009).

If the inadvertent changes are limited to a small number of tables that have few or no interdependencies with other database objects, flashback-table functionality is most likely the right tool to bring back the table to a certain point in time.

Later in this chapter, in the section "Performing Recovery Operations," I'll show you how to recover dropped tables from the recycle bin using the flashback drop functionality, retrieve deleted rows from a table using the flashback query functionality, use the flashback table functionality to bring a table back to a specific point in time along with its dependent objects, and use LogMiner to query online and archived redo logs for the previous state of modified rows.

The Oracle 11*g* database provides flashback technology, which is aimed to recover from user errors.

Instance Failures

An *instance failure* occurs when the instance shuts down without synchronizing all the database files to the same system change number (SCN), requiring a recovery operation the next time the instance is started. Many of the reasons for an instance failure are out of your direct control; in these situations, you can minimize the impact of these failures by tuning instance recovery. You will learn how to tune instance recovery later in this chapter, in the section "Tuning Instance Recovery."

Here are a few causes for instance failure:

- A power outage
- A server-hardware failure
- Failure of an Oracle background process
- Emergency shutdown procedures (intentional power outage or SHUTDOWN ABORT)

In all these scenarios, the solution is easy: run the STARTUP command, and let Oracle automatically perform instance recovery using the online redo logs and undo data in the undo tablespace. If the cause of the instance failure is related to an Oracle background-process failure, you can use the alert log and process-specific trace files to debug the problem. EM Database Control makes it easy to review the contents of the alert log and any other alerts generated right before the point of failure.

Media Failures

Another type of failure that is somewhat out of your control is media failure. A *media failure* is any type of failure that results in the loss of one or more database files: data files, control files, or redo log files. Although the loss of other database-related files such as an `init.ora` file or a server-parameter file (spfile) is of great concern, Oracle Corporation does not consider it a media failure. The database file can be lost or corrupted for a number of reasons:

- Failure of a disk drive
- Failure of a disk controller
- Inadvertent deletion or corruption of a database file

Following the best practices defined in Chapter 15—in other words, adequately mirroring control files and redo log files and ensuring that full backups and their subsequent archived redo log files are available—will keep you prepared for any type of media failure.

In the next section, I will show you how to recover from the loss of control files, data files, and redo log files.

Performing Recovery Operations

Once the inevitable database failure occurs, you can perform a relatively quick and painless recovery operation if you have followed the backup guidelines presented in Chapter 15 and clearly understand the types of failures presented earlier in this chapter.

Before I show you how to perform recovery, however, it is important for you to understand how an Oracle instance starts up and what kinds of failures can occur at each startup phase. Understanding the startup phases is important, because some types of recovery operations must occur in a particular phase. Once a database is started, the instance will fail under a number of conditions that I will describe in detail.

Next, I will describe how instance recovery works and how to tune instance recovery, and then show you ways to easily recover from several types of user errors. Finally, I will show you how to recover from media failures due to the loss of both critical and non–system-critical data files.

Understanding Instance Startup

Starting up a database involves several phases, from being shut down to being open and available to users. If certain prerequisites are not present, the database startup halts, and you must take some kind of remedial action to permit the startup to proceed. In the following list are the four basic database states along with their prerequisites after you type the STARTUP command at the SQL*Plus prompt:

SHUTDOWN No background processes are active. A STARTUP command is used when the database is in this state; the STARTUP command fails if you are in any other state unless you are using STARTUP FORCE to restart an instance.

NOMOUNT Also known as the STARTED state, the instance must be able to access the initialization-parameter file, either as a text-based `init.ora` file or as an spfile.

MOUNT In this state, the instance checks that all control files listed in the initialization-parameter file are present and identical. Even if one of the multiplexed control files is unavailable or corrupted, the instance does not enter the MOUNT state and stays in the NOMOUNT state.

OPEN Most of the time spent in the instance startup occurs during this phase. All redo log groups must have at least one member available, and all data files that are marked as online must be available.

You are notified in a number of ways that a redo log group member is missing or a data file is missing. If a data file is missing or corrupted, you will get a message while you are running the STARTUP command, as in this example:

```
SQL> startup

ORACLE instance started.

Total System Global Area  197132288 bytes
Fixed Size                   778076 bytes
Variable Size             162537636 bytes
Database Buffers           33554432 bytes
Redo Buffers                 262144 bytes
Database mounted.
```

```
ORA-01157: cannot identify/lock data file 4 - see DBWR trace file
ORA-01110: data file 4: '/u05/oradata/ord/users01.dbf'

SQL>
```

The message in SQL*Plus shows only the first data file that needs attention. You will have to use the dynamic performance view `V$RECOVER_FILE` to list all the files that need attention. Here is a query against the view `V$RECOVER_FILE` and a second query joining `V$RECOVER_FILE` and `V$DATAFILE` given the previous `STARTUP` command:

```
SQL> select file#, error from v$recover_file;

     FILE# ERROR
---------- -----------------------------------------------------------
         4 FILE NOT FOUND
        11 FILE NOT FOUND

SQL> select file#, name from
  2       v$datafile join v$recover_file using (file#);

     FILE# NAME
---------- -------------------------------------------------------
         4 /u05/oradata/ord/users01.dbf
        11 /u08/oradata/ord/idx02.dbf

SQL>
```

If a data file is offline or taken offline, the instance can still start as long as the data file does not belong to the `SYSTEM` or `UNDO` tablespace. Once the instance is started, you can proceed to recover the missing or corrupted data file and subsequently bring it online. If all files are available but out of sync, automatic instance recovery is performed as long as the online redo log files can bring all data files to the same SCN. Otherwise, media recovery is required using archived redo log files.

If a redo log group member is missing, a message is generated in the alert log, but the database will still open.

Keeping an Instance from Failing

Media failures are not always critical, depending on which type of data file is lost. If any of the multiplexed copies of the control file are lost, an entire redo log group is lost, or any data file from the `SYSTEM` or `UNDO` tablespace is lost, the instance will fail.

In some cases, the instance becomes unavailable to users but will not shut down; in this case, you can use `SHUTDOWN ABORT` to force the instance to shut down without resynchronizing the data files with the control file. The next time the instance is started, instance recovery will be performed. If you plan on starting up the instance right after using SHUTDOWN ABORT, you can instead use STARTUP FORCE as shorthand for a SHUTDOWN ABORT and a STARTUP.

Later in this chapter, I will show you how to recover from the loss of a control file, a redo log file member, or one or more data files.

Recovering from Instance Failure

As I discussed earlier, in the section "Instance Failures," an instance failure is any kind of failure that prevents the synchronization of the database's data files and control files before the instance is shut down.

Oracle automatically recovers from instance failure during *instance recovery*. Instance recovery is initiated by simply starting up the database with the STARTUP command.

Instance recovery is also known as *crash recovery*.

During a STARTUP operation, Oracle first attempts to read the initialization file, and then it mounts the control file and attempts to open the data files referenced in the control files. If the data files are not synchronized, instance recovery is initiated.

Instance recovery occurs in phases:

Phase 1 Find data files that are out of sync with the control file.

Phase 2 Use the online redo log files to restore the data files to the state before instance failure in a rollforward operation. After the rollforward, data files have committed and uncommitted data.

Phase 3 Open the database. Once the rollforward operation completes, the database is open to users.

Phase 4 Oracle then uses the undo segments to roll back any uncommitted transactions. The rollback operation uses data in the undo tablespace; without a consistent undo tablespace, the rollback operation cannot succeed. After the rollback phase, the data files contain only committed data.

Tuning Instance Recovery

Before a user receives a "Commit complete" message, the new or changed data must be successfully written to a redo log file. At some point in the future, the same information must be used to update the data files; this operation usually lags behind the redo log file write because sequential writes to the redo log file are by nature faster than random writes to one or more data files on disk.

As I discussed in Chapter 15, checkpoints keep track of what still needs to be written from the redo log files to the data files. Any transactions not yet written to the data files are at an SCN after the last checkpoint.

The amount of time required for instance recovery depends on how long it takes to bring the data files up-to-date from the last checkpoint position to the latest SCN in the control file. To prevent performance problems, the distance between the checkpoint position and the end of the redo log group cannot be more than 90 percent of the size of the redo log group.

You can tune instance recovery by setting an MTTR target, in seconds, using the initialization parameter FAST_START_MTTR_TARGET. The default value for this parameter is zero; the maximum is 3,600 seconds (1 hour).

A setting of zero disables the target, which reduces the likelihood of redo logs waiting for writes to the data files. However, if FAST_START_MTTR_TARGET is set to a low nonzero value, writes to the redo logs most likely have to wait for writes to the data files. Although this reduces the amount of time it takes to recover the instance in the case of an instance failure, it affects performance and response time. Setting this value too high can result in an unacceptable amount of time needed to recover the instance after an instance failure.

Two other parameters control instance recovery time:

LOG_CHECKPOINT_TIMEOUT This is the maximum number of seconds that any new or modified block in the buffer cache waits until it is written to disk.

FAST_START_IO_TARGET This is similar to FAST_START_MTTR_TARGET, except that the recovery operation is specified as the number of I/Os instead of the number of seconds to finish instance recovery.

Setting either of these parameters overrides FAST_START_MTTR_TARGET. As part of the enhanced manageability features introduced with Oracle9*i*, setting FAST_START_MTTR_TARGET is the easiest and most straightforward way to define your database's recovery time given the time-based constraints included in most typical SLAs.

The EM Database Control interface makes it easy to adjust FAST_START_MTTR_TARGET. On the Availability screen of Database Control, choose Recovery Settings. Figure 16.1 shows the Instance Recovery setting, which you can find in the top section of the Recovery Settings screen.

FIGURE 16.1 Adjusting MTTR for instance recovery

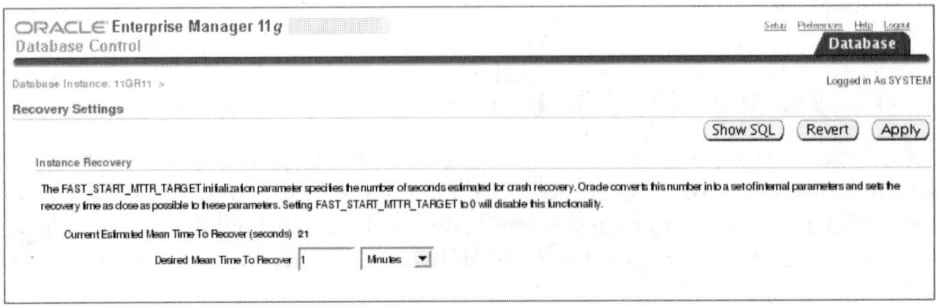

Enter the desired value using seconds or minutes. When you click the Apply button, the new value for FAST_START_MTTR_TARGET goes into effect immediately and stays in effect when the instance is restarted.

Using the SQL*Plus command line, you can accomplish this task by using the ALTER SYSTEM command, as in this example:

```
SQL> alter system set fast_start_mttr_target=60 scope=both;
System altered.
```

Using SCOPE=BOTH, the new value of the parameter takes effect immediately and stays in effect the next time the instance is restarted.

Recovering from User Errors

Earlier in this chapter, in the section "User-Error Failures," you learned a number of scenarios in which a user's data was inadvertently changed or deleted or a table was dropped. In the following sections, you'll learn quite a few helpful tasks, such as how to do the following:

- Use flashback query to retrieve selected rows from a previous state of a table
- Recover a table using flashback drop and a tablespace's recycle bin
- Bring an entire table and its dependent objects (such as indexes) back to a specific point in time using flashback table
- Roll back a specific transaction and its dependent transactions using flashback transaction
- Query previous transactions in the online and archived redo logs using the LogMiner utility

Using Flashback Query

One of the features introduced in Oracle9*i* was called *flashback query*. It allows a user to "go back in time" and view the contents of a table as it existed at some point in the recent past. A flashback query looks a lot like a standard SQL SELECT statement, with the addition of the AS OF TIMESTAMP clause.

Before users can take advantage of the flashback query feature, you, the DBA, must perform two tasks:

- Make sure there is an undo tablespace in the database that is large enough to retain changes made by all users for a specified period of time. This is the same tablespace that is used to support COMMIT and ROLLBACK functionality (discussed in Chapter 13, "Managing Data and Undo").
- Specify how long the undo information will be retained for use by flashback queries by using the initialization parameter UNDO_RETENTION. This parameter is specified in seconds; therefore, if you specify UNDO_RETENTION=172800 (default is 900), the undo information for flashback queries can be available for up to two days.

The key to the flashback query functionality is using the AS OF TIMESTAMP clause in the SELECT statement; you can specify the timestamp as any valid expression that evaluates to a date or timestamp value. In the following example, you want to query the EMPLOYEES table as it existed 15 minutes ago:

```
SQL> SELECT employee_id, last_name, email
     FROM hr.employees
     AS OF TIMESTAMP (systimestamp - interval '15' minute)
     WHERE employee_id = 101;

EMPLOYEE_ID LAST_NAME                 EMAIL
----------- --------------------- -------------------
        101 Kochhar                   NKOCHHAR
```

You can just as easily specify an absolute time of day to retrieve the contents of the row at that time, as in this example:

```
SQL> SELECT employee_id, last_name, email
     FROM hr.employees
     AS OF TIMESTAMP
        (to_timestamp ('01-Sep-04 16:18:57.845993',
                       'DD-Mon-RR HH24:MI:SS.FF'))
     WHERE employee_id = 101;

EMPLOYEE_ID LAST_NAME                 EMAIL
----------- --------------------- -------------------
        101 Kochhar                   NTKOCHHAR
```

If your flashback query requires undo data that is no longer available in the undo tablespace, you will receive an error message:

```
SQL> SELECT employee_id, last_name, email
     FROM hr.employees
     AS OF TIMESTAMP (systimestamp - interval '10' month)
     WHERE employee_id = 101;

select employee_id, last_name, email
       *
ERROR at line 1:
ORA-08180: no snapshot found based on specified time
```

Real World Scenario

Using Flashback Query to Retrieve Missing Rows

Recently an application administrator in my company inadvertently deleted a bunch of rows from a database table and committed the transaction. He learned about the deletion with the wrong WHERE clause only when users started calling him about the missing data on their screens and the various errors they were getting.

Panicked, the application administrator called his manager and told her about what happened, and they planned an outage for the affected application and a couple of other applications hosted in the same database.

In our company, the DBA is the last person to know about issues, but by the time a problem comes to the DBA, it is a crisis.

The application administrator told the DBA team that there was a recovery situation and that he had arranged for all the outages and notifications. One of our DBAs asked the application administrator the time of the data deletion and the table name. The DBA did a query similar to the following to show the records the administrator deleted. Luckily, there were not many transactions going on in the database, because users were getting errors and the changed rows were still available in the undo. If there were many transactions, Oracle could have overwritten the committed transaction's rollback space (depending on the UNDO_RENTENTION setting):

```
SELECT * FROM vms.dvbt606a
AS OF TIMESTAMP to_timestamp ('12-Sep-08 12:20', 'DD-Mon-RR HH24:MI');
```

Then the DBA got the WHERE clause from the administrator to filter out the rows that the administrator deleted and inserted those rows into the original table using the following SQL statement:

```
INSERT INTO vms.dvbt606a
SELECT * FROM vms.dvbt606a
AS OF TIMESTAMP to_timestamp ('12-Sep-08 12:20', 'DD-Mon-RR HH24:MI')
WHERE TRANS_DATE BETWEEN TO_DATE('01-MAY-08','DD-MON-YY')
      AND TO_DATE('31-MAY-08','DD-MON-YY');
```

We did not have to take any applications offline, and the whole recovery operation took less than 15 minutes after coming to the DBA. We could have also used the FLASHBACK TABLE feature, which would have made the recovery sooner (and there would be no need to know the WHERE clause used for deletion), but nobody thought of it.

Using Flashback Drop and the Recycle Bin

Another user-recovery flashback feature, *flashback drop*, lets you restore a dropped table without using tablespace point-in-time recovery. Although tablespace point-in-time recovery could effectively restore a table and its contents to a point in time before it was dropped, it is potentially time-consuming and has the side effect of losing work from other transactions that occurred within the same tablespace after the table was dropped.

In the following sections, I will talk about the new logical structure available in each tablespace—the recycle bin—and how you can query the recycle bin and retrieve dropped objects from it. I will also describe some minor limitations involved in using the recycle bin.

Recycle-Bin Concepts

The *recycle bin* is a logical structure within each tablespace that holds dropped tables and objects related to the tables, such as indexes. The space associated with the dropped table is not immediately available but shows up in the data dictionary view DBA_FREE_SPACE. When space pressure occurs in the tablespace, objects in the recycle bin are deleted in a first-in, first-out (FIFO) fashion, maximizing the amount of time that the most recently dropped object remains in the recycle bin.

The dropped object still belongs to the owner and still counts against the quota for the owner in the tablespace; in fact, the table itself is still directly accessible from the recycle bin, as you will see in subsequent examples.

Retrieving Dropped Tables from the Recycle Bin

You retrieve a dropped table from the recycle bin at the SQL command line by using the FLASHBACK TABLE...TO BEFORE DROP command. In the following example, the user retrieves the table ORDER_ITEMS from the recycle bin after discovering that the table was inadvertently dropped:

```
SQL> select order_id, line_item_id, product_id
  2  from order_items
  3  where rownum < 5;
from order_items
     *
ERROR at line 2:
ORA-00942: table or view does not exist


SQL> flashback table order_items to before drop;

Flashback complete.

SQL> select order_id, line_item_id, product_id
  2  from order_items
  3  where rownum < 5;
```

```
  ORDER_ID LINE_ITEM_ID PRODUCT_ID
---------- ------------ ----------
      2355            1       2289
      2356            1       2264
      2357            1       2211
      2358            1       1781

SQL>
```

If the table ORDER_ITEMS was re-created after it was dropped, Gary would add the RENAME TO clause in the FLASHBACK TABLE command to give the restored table a new name, as in the following example:

```
SQL> drop table order_items;

Table dropped.

SQL> flashback table order_items to before drop
  2      rename to order_items_old_version;

Flashback complete.

SQL> select order_id, line_item_id, product_id
  2  from order_items_old_version
  3  where rownum < 5;

  ORDER_ID LINE_ITEM_ID PRODUCT_ID
---------- ------------ ----------
      2355            1       2289
      2356            1       2264
      2357            1       2211
      2358            1       1781

SQL>
```

If the table to be retrieved from the recycle bin was dropped more than once and you want to retrieve an incarnation of the table before the most recent one, you can use the name of the table in the recycle bin; you can query the view RECYCLEBIN or use the SHOW RECYCLEBIN command.

Recycle-Bin Considerations and Limitations

A few limitations are associated with the recycle bin:

- Only non-SYSTEM locally managed tablespaces can have a recycle bin. However, dependent objects in a dictionary-managed tablespace are protected if the dropped object is in a locally managed tablespace.

- A table's dependent objects are saved in the recycle bin when the table is dropped, except for bitmap join indexes, referential integrity constraints (foreign key constraints), and materialized view logs.
- Indexes are protected only if the table is dropped first; explicitly dropping an index does not place the index into the recycle bin.

Using Flashback Table

Flashback table allows you to recover one or more tables to a specific point in time without having to use more time-consuming recovery operations such as tablespace point-in-time recovery or flashback database that can also affect the availability of the rest of the database. Flashback table works in place by rolling back only the changes made to the table or tables and their dependent objects, such as indexes. Flashback table is different from flashback drop; flashback table undoes recent transactions to an existing table, whereas flashback drop recovers a dropped table. Flashback table uses data in the undo tablespace, whereas flashback drop uses the recycle bin.

The FLASHBACK TABLE command brings one or more tables back to a point in time before any number of logical corruptions have occurred on the tables. To be able to flash back a table, you must enable row movement for the table. Because DML operations are used to bring the table back to its former state, the row IDs in the table change. As a result, flashback table is not a viable option for applications that depend on the table's row IDs to remain constant.

In the following example, you find out that someone in the HR department has accidentally deleted all the employees in department 60, the IT department, along with the row for IT in the DEPARTMENTS table. Because this happened less than 15 minutes ago, you are sure that there is enough undo information to support a flashback table operation.

Before running the FLASHBACK TABLE command, you confirm that the row in DEPARTMENTS for the IT department is still missing using this query:

```
SQL> SELECT * FROM hr.departments
     WHERE department_name = 'IT';


no rows selected
```

Next, you flash back the table to 15 minutes ago, specifying both tables in the same command, as follows:

```
SQL> FLASHBACK TABLE hr.employees, hr.departments
     TO TIMESTAMP systimestamp - interval '15' minute;


Flashback complete.
```

Finally, you check to see whether the IT department is truly back in the table:

```
SQL> SELECT * FROM hr.departments
     WHERE department_name = 'IT';

DEPARTMENT_ID DEPARTMENT_NAME     MANAGER_ID LOCATION_ID
------------- ------------------ ---------- -----------
           60 IT                        103        1400
```

If you flash back either too far or not far enough, you can simply rerun the FLASHBACK TABLE command with a different timestamp or SCN, as long as the undo data is still available.

Although the rest of the database is unaffected by a flashback table operation, the FLASHBACK TABLE command acquires exclusive DML locks on the tables involved in the flashback. This is usually not an availability issue, because the users who would normally use the table are waiting for the flashback operation to complete anyway!

Integrity constraints are not violated when one or more tables are flashed back; this is why you typically group tables related by integrity constraints or parent-child relationships in the FLASHBACK TABLE command. When a flashback operation is in progress, the triggers on the table are disabled. If you want the triggers to fire during the flashback operation, add the ENABLE TRIGGERS clause to the FLASHBACK TABLE statement, as in the following example.

```
SQL> FLASHBACK TABLE hr.employees
     TO TIMESTAMP TO_TIMESTAMP('02NOV08 22:00'. 'DDMONYY HH24:MI')
     ENABLE TRIGGERS;
```

To be able to perform a flashback table operation, the table must have ROW MOVEMENT enabled. Enable row movement using ALTER TABLE <name> ENABLE ROW MOVEMENT.

Using EM Database Control to Perform Table Recovery

You can perform recovery operations using EM Database Control. On the Availability screen, choose Perform Recovery under the Manage section of Backup/Recovery. On the Perform Recovery screen, choose Tables as the recovery scope. As you can see in Figure 16.2, choosing Tables as the recovery scope gives you two options:

- Flashback Existing Tables
- Flashback Dropped Tables

FIGURE 16.2 Table recovery screen

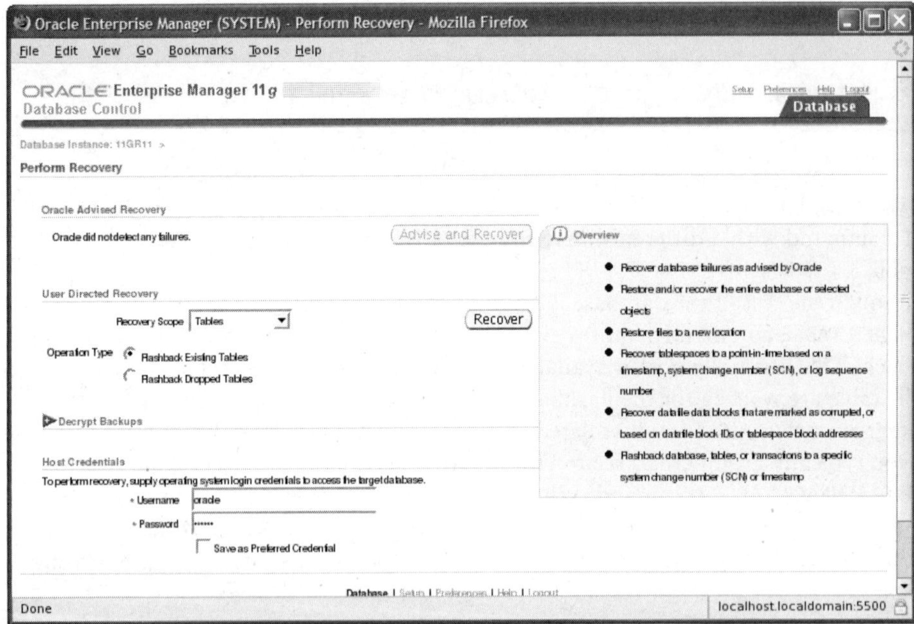

Choose Flashback Existing Tables to roll back the table to a previous state. Click Recover to get to the Perform Object Level Recovery screen, as shown in Figure 16.3. Here you have four options to choose from:

- Evaluate Row Changes and Transactions to Decide on a Point in Time
- Flashback to a Timestamp
- Flashback to a Restore Point
- Flashback to a Known SCN

Based on the option you choose, you will be presented with one of three screens. Choose Flashback to a Timestamp for this example. You will be presented with a screen to choose the tables that you want to flash back, as shown in Figure 16.4.

Choose the tables you want to perform flashback on, and click Next. A summary screen will be shown for you to review the specifications such as timestamp, corresponding SCNs, and table names. Click Submit to perform the flashback operation.

To retrieve a dropped table, choose Flashback Dropped Tables from the screen shown earlier, in Figure 16.2. You will be presented with all the tables that are in the recycle bin, as shown in Figure 16.5. Choose the table(s) you want to restore, and click Next.

FIGURE 16.3 Perform Object Level Recovery screen

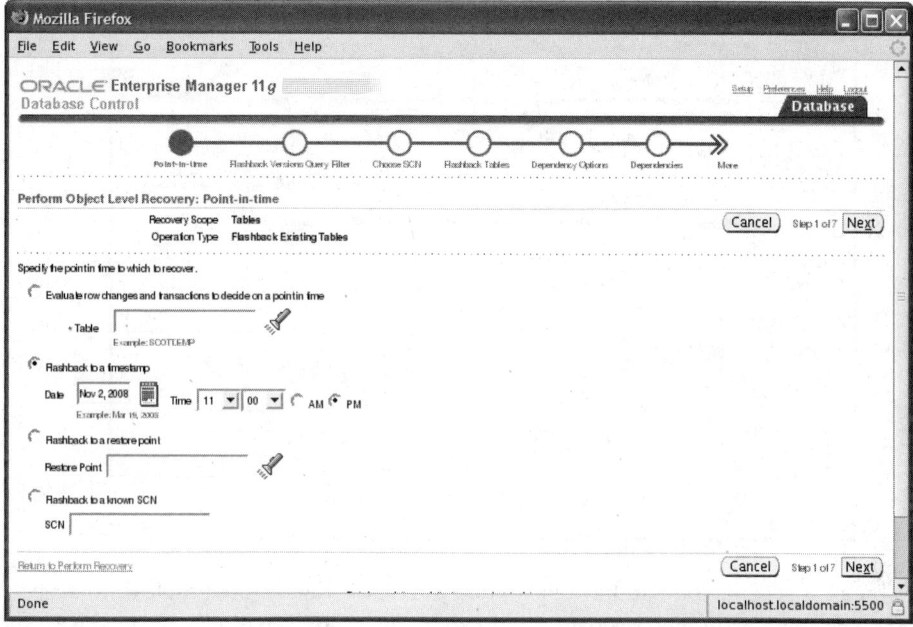

FIGURE 16.4 Perform Object Level Recovery: Flashback Tables screen

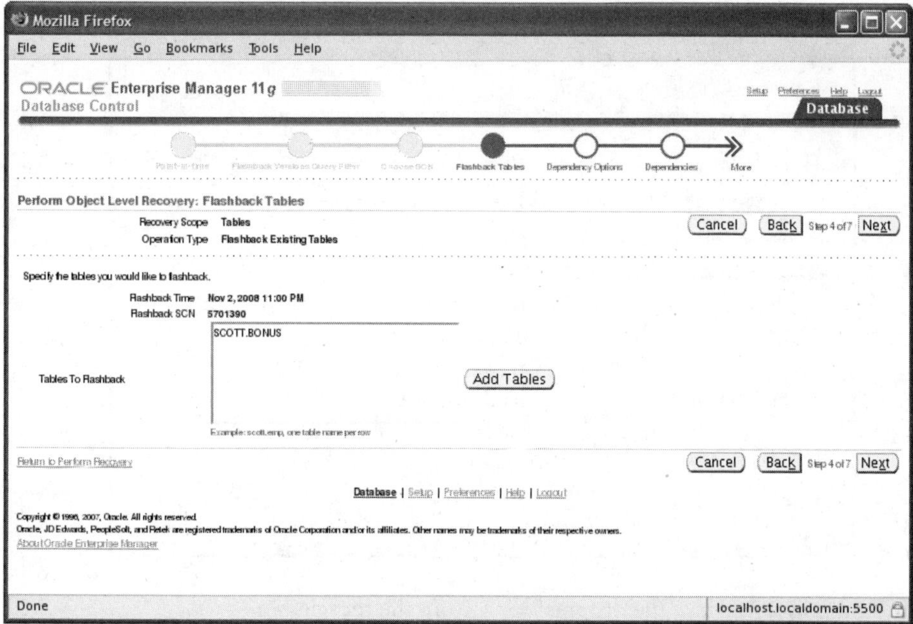

FIGURE 16.5 Perform Object Level Recovery: Dropped Objects Selection screen

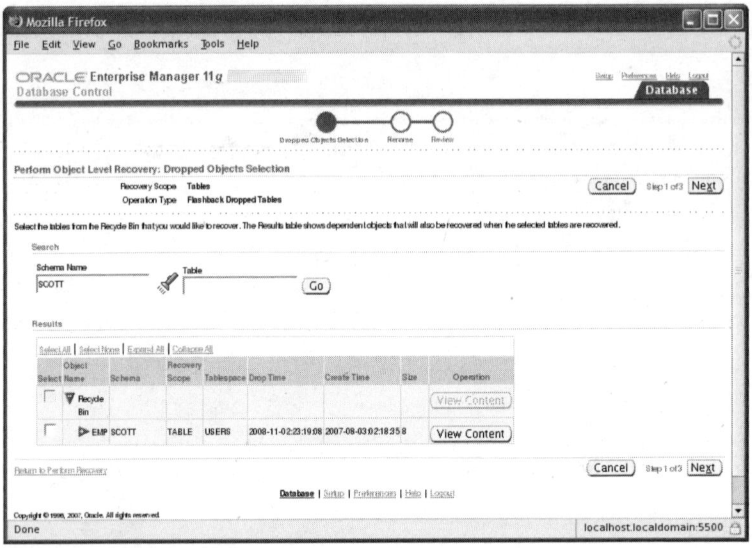

On the next screen, you will have the option to rename the restored table or to keep the original name. A summary screen, as shown in Figure 16.6, will be displayed with the impact analysis.

FIGURE 16.6 Perform Object Level Recovery: Review screen

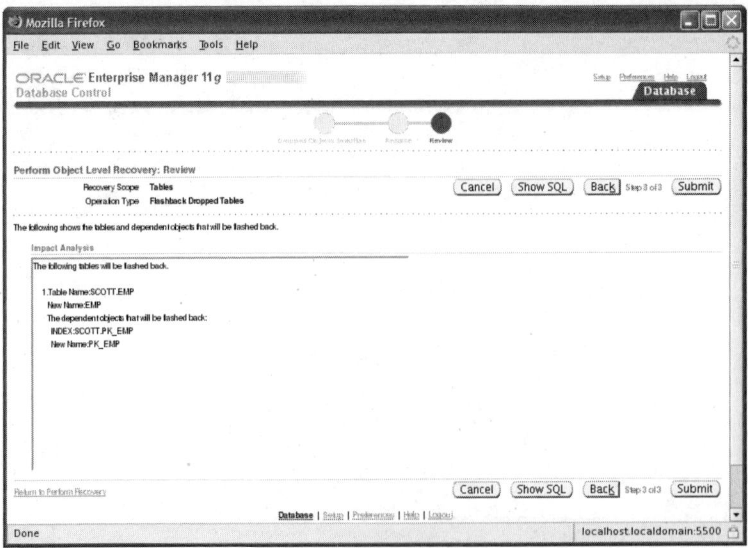

Click Submit to retrieve the dropped table from the recycle bin.

Using Flashback Transaction

You can use the flashback transaction technology to undo a transaction and its dependent transactions. The DBMS_FLASHBACK.TRANSACTION_BACKOUT procedure is used to accomplish this task.

You must meet the following prerequisites to perform a flashback transaction on an Oracle 11*g* database:

- The database must be in ARCHIVELOG mode.
- Supplemental logging must be enabled in the database using ALTER DATABASE ADD SUPPLEMENTAL LOG DATA.
- A supplemental log data primary key should be created using the statement ALTER DATABASE ADD SUPPLEMENTAL LOG DATA (PRIMARY KEY) COLUMNS.
- The user performing the flashback transaction must have the SELECT ANY TRANSACTION privilege.
- The user should have the EXECUTE privilege on DBMS_FLASHBACK.
- The user also should have appropriate DML privileges on the tables (such as INSERT/UPDATE/DELETE).

Using EM Database Control, you can perform the flashback transaction. In the Perform Recovery screen (shown earlier, in Figure 16.2), choose Transactions as the recovery scope. You will be presented with the screen shown in Figure 16.7.

FIGURE 16.7 Flashback Transaction: Perform Query screen

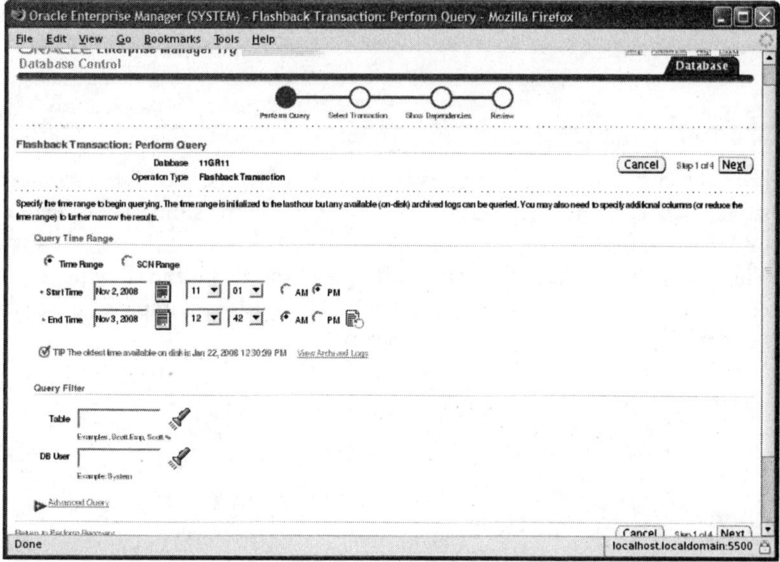

Specify the time range of transactions you want to recover. If your database is very active, you will be able to restrict the number of transactions retrieved for the time range by specifying a query filter using the table name or username. When you click Next, Oracle will mine the transactions that happened between the time range and give you the screen shown in Figure 16.8.

FIGURE 16.8 Flashback Transaction: Select Transaction screen

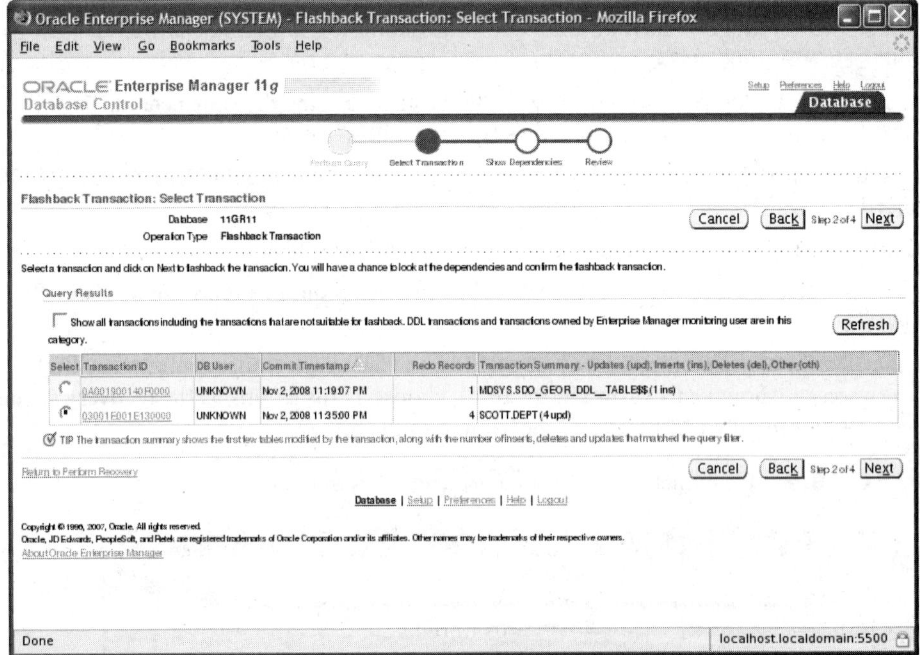

Here you can select the transaction you want to revert. To see the SQL statements that made the change, click the transaction ID. Click Next to see the summary screen, as shown in Figure 16.9.

Here clicking the Show Undo SQL Script button will show you the statements that are run to undo the changes made in the transaction. Click Finish to complete the flashback-transaction operation.

FIGURE 16.9 Flashback Transaction: Review screen

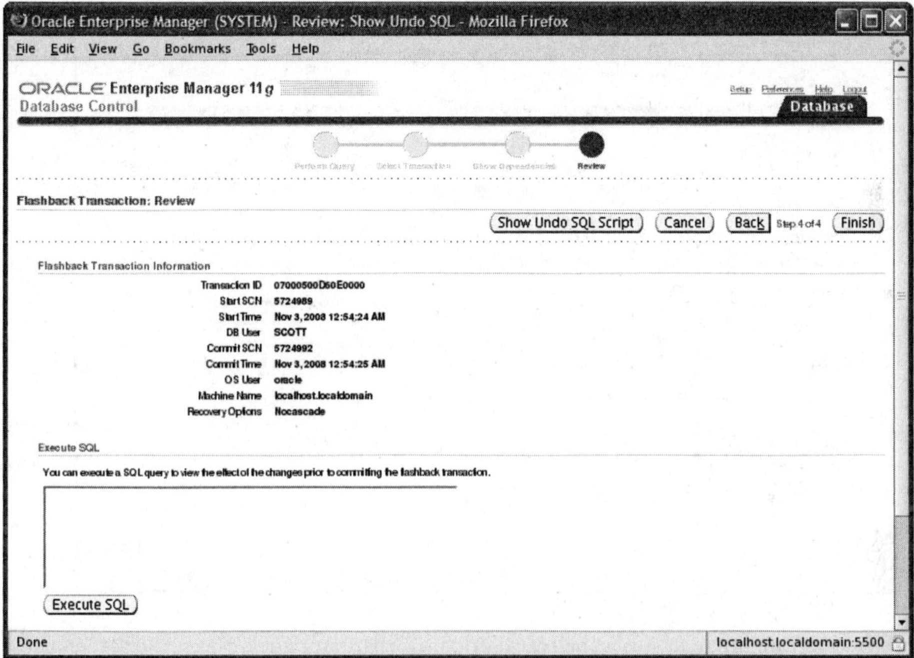

Using LogMiner

Oracle LogMiner is another tool you can use to view past activity in the database. The LogMiner tool can help find changed records in redo log files by using a set of PL/SQL procedures and functions. LogMiner extracts all DDL and DML activity from the redo log files for viewing via the dynamic performance view `V$LOGMNR_CONTENTS`. In addition to extracting the DDL and DML statements used to change the database, the `V$LOGMNR_CONTENTS` view also contains the DML statements needed to reverse the change made to the database. This is a good tool for not only pinpointing when changes were made to a table but also for automatically generating the SQL statements needed to reverse those changes.

LogMiner works differently from Oracle's flashback query feature. The flashback query feature allows a user to see the contents of a table at a specified time in the past, while LogMiner can search a time period for all changes against the table. A flashback query uses the undo information stored in the undo tablespace; LogMiner uses redo logs, both online and archived. Both tools can be useful for tracking down how and when changes to database objects took place.

You can configure and use LogMiner either by using a SQL command line or by using EM Database Control (choose View and Manage Transactions from the Availability screen). Figure 16.10 shows the Log Miner screen.

FIGURE 16.10 LogMiner screen

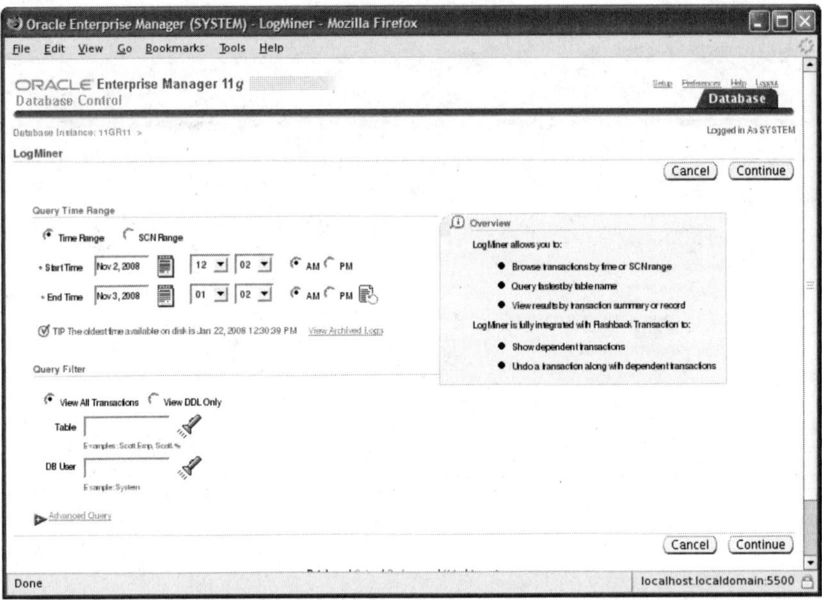

Specify the time range to mine the transactions. When you click Next, the screen shown in Figure 16.11 will be displayed with all the SQL statements that went into the database during the time range. Click the transaction ID to see all the related SQL statements in the transaction.

FIGURE 16.11 LogMiner Results screen

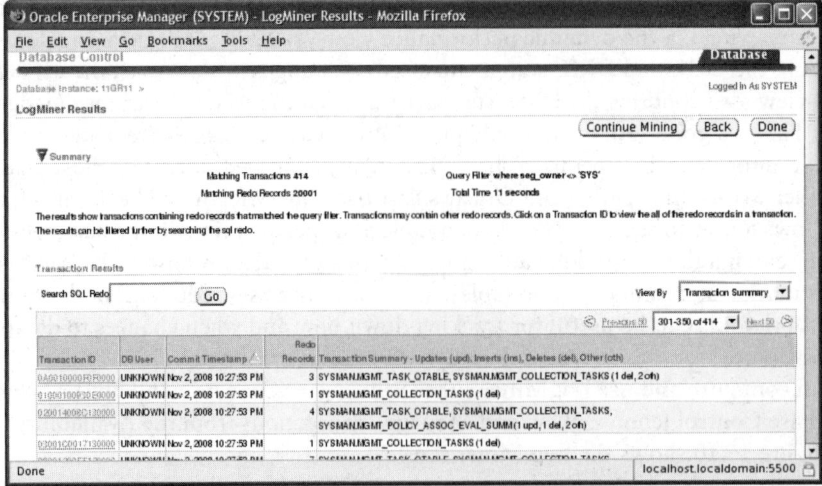

When you click a transaction, you can see all the related transactions and have the option to flash back the transaction. Click the Flashback Transaction button to undo the changes made in that transaction. You can view the SQL statements that are executed in that transaction using the SQL Redo column, as shown in Figure 16.12.

FIGURE 16.12 LogMiner's Transaction Details screen

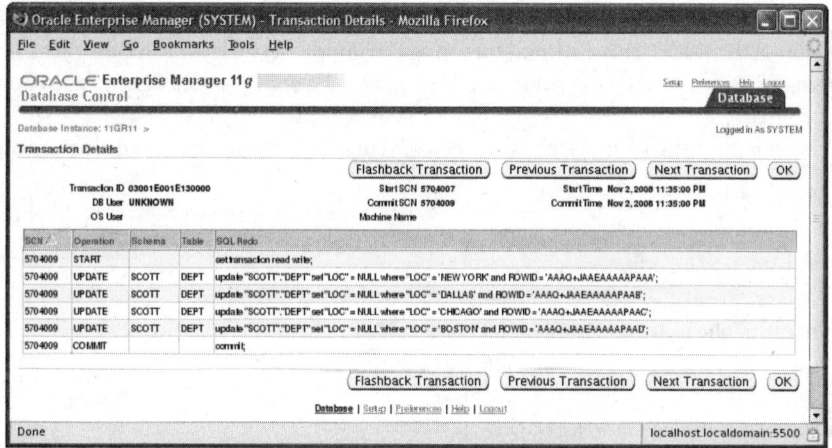

LogMiner does not actually undo the change; it only provides the statements that you can use to undo the change. You can extract and run any or all DML commands you find in the redo logs, keeping in mind any integrity constraints in place for the tables you are modifying. The Flashback Transaction button on the LogMiner screen invokes the flashback transaction feature of the database discussed earlier in the chapter.

Recovering from Loss of a Control File

Losing one of the multiplexed control files immediately aborts the instance. Assuming you have not lost every control file, recovering from this failure is fairly straightforward.

Here are the steps to recover from the loss of a control file:

1. If the instance is not shut down, use `SHUTDOWN ABORT` to force a complete shutdown.
2. Copy one of the good copies of the control file to the location of the corrupted or missing control file. If the corrupted or missing control file resided on a failed disk, copy it to another suitable location instead, and update the initialization-parameter file to update the control-file reference. Alternatively, you can temporarily remove the reference from the initialization-parameter file until you find a suitable location. However, it is

highly desirable to maintain at least two, if not more, copies of the control file available in the case of another media failure.

3. Start the instance with STARTUP.

In the following example, you use a server-parameter file (spfile) for initialization parameters, and you decide to temporarily do without a third multiplexed control file until the disk containing the lost control file is repaired. You'll change the initialization-parameter CONTROL_FILES using the ALTER SYSTEM … SCOPE=SPFILE command when the instance is started in NOMOUNT mode. You cannot start in MOUNT mode because that mode checks for the existence of all copies of the control file, and as far as the spfile is concerned, you are still missing a control file.

The first step is to start the database in NOMOUNT mode, as you can see in this example:

```
SQL> startup nomount

ORACLE instance started.

Total System Global Area  188743680 bytes
Fixed Size                   778036 bytes
Variable Size             162537676 bytes
Database Buffers           25165824 bytes
Redo Buffers                 262144 bytes
SQL>
```

Looking at the dynamic performance view V$SPPARAMETER, you can see that you still have three copies of the control file referenced, but the disk containing the third copy has failed:

```
SQL> select name, value from v$spparameter
     where name = 'control_files';

NAME            VALUE
--------------- -------------------------------------------------
control_files   /u02/oradata/ord/control01.ctl
control_files   /u06/oradata/ord/control02.ctl
control_files   /u07/oradata/ord/control03.ctl
```

In the next step, you change the value of CONTROL_FILES in the spfile and restart the instance, as you can see here:

```
SQL> alter system set control_files =
     '/u02/oradata/ord/control01.ctl',
     '/u06/oradata/ord/control02.ctl'
     scope = spfile;

System altered.
```

```
SQL> shutdown immediate
ORA-01507: database not mounted
ORACLE instance shut down.

SQL> startup
ORACLE instance started.

Total System Global Area  188743680 bytes
Fixed Size                   778036 bytes
Variable Size             162537676 bytes
Database Buffers           25165824 bytes
Redo Buffers                 262144 bytes
Database mounted.
Database opened.
SQL>
```

Once the instance is restarted successfully, you confirm that the control file is no longer being referenced, as you can see in this query:

```
SQL> select name, value from v$spparameter
     where name = 'control_files';

NAME            VALUE
--------------- ---------------------------------------
control_files   /u02/oradata/ord/control01.ctl
control_files   /u06/oradata/ord/control02.ctl
```

You still have two multiplexed copies of the control file; therefore, you are covered in case of a media failure of the disk containing one of the remaining control files.

Using the Data Recovery Advisor

The Data Recovery Advisor (DRA) is a new tool introduced in the Oracle 11*g* database that automatically diagnoses database failures and determines the appropriate recovery options. In addition to recommending the recovery options available, it can perform the recovery after the DBA confirms the operation. DRA can proactively check for failures, before the database process detects corruption and signals an error.

DRA has user interfaces through the GUI of EM Database Control and through the command-line utility RMAN. DRA in Oracle 11*g* Release 1 supports only single-instance databases; it does not support RAC databases.

You can invoke the Data Recovery Advisor from EM Database Control using any of the following methods:

- Using the Perform Recovery screen shown earlier in Figure 16.2. If there are any failures detected, the Advise and Recover button will be enabled, as shown in Figure 16.13. It will also display a summary of failures with the failure description.

FIGURE 16.13 Invoking DRA from Perform Recovery screen

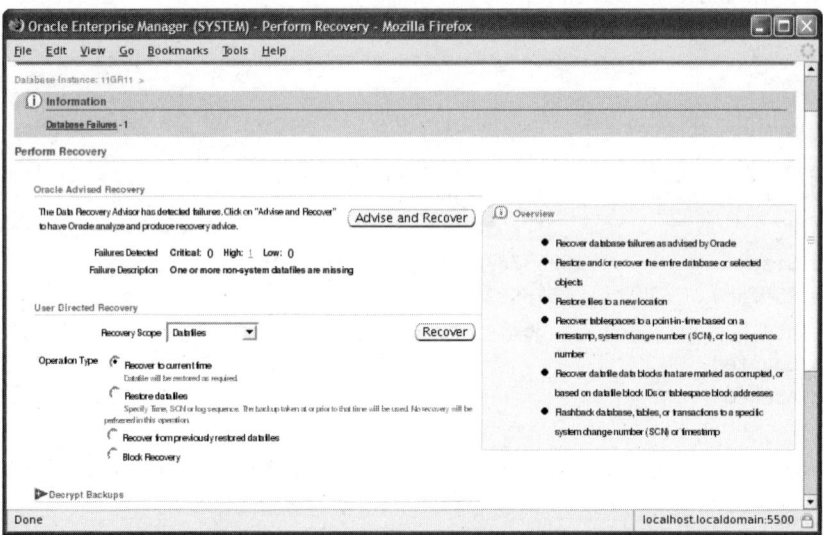

- Using the Support Workbench. Support Workbench is invoked from the Software and Support tab of EM Database Control. The Checker Findings tab in Support Workbench shows the failures in the database, as shown in Figure 16.14. By clicking the Launch Recovery Advisor button, you can invoke DRA.
- Using the Advisor Central page by clicking the Data Recovery Advisor link under Advisors.

FIGURE 16.14 Invoking DRA from the Support Workbench screen

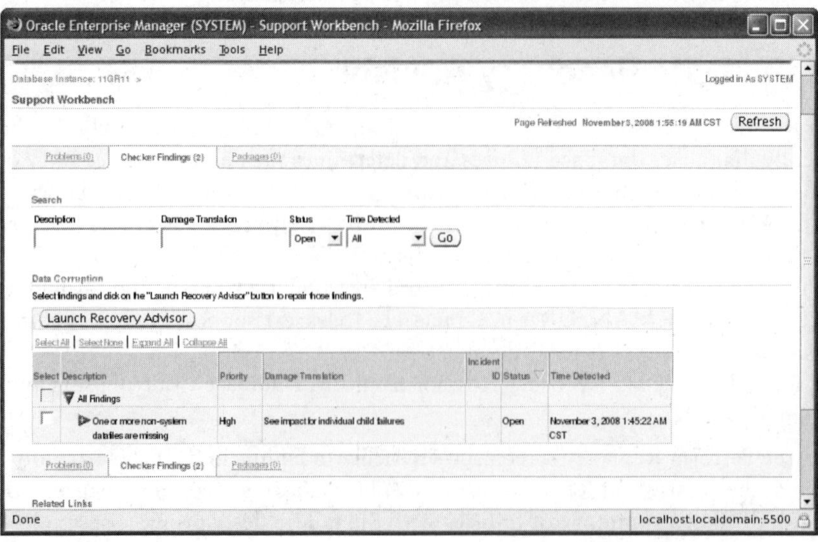

The Health Monitor (HM) tool in the Oracle 11*g* database proactively monitors the health of the database. It assesses data failures and reports to the Data Recovery Advisor. DRA consolidates the findings of HM into failures and assigns a priority based on the failure.

Failure checks in the database can be reactive or proactive. When an error occurs in the database, reactive checks are automatically executed. The following are examples of data failures where the DRA can analyze and suggest repair options:

- Missing data files
- Data files with incorrect OS permissions
- Offline tablespaces
- Corrupted data files (physical corruption)
- Corrupt index entry or dictionary entry (logical corruption)
- I/O failures
- Number of open files exceeded

In the following sections, you will look at the various scenarios of media-failure errors and see how DRA can help analyze and fix errors.

Recovering from the Loss of a Redo Log File

A database instance stays up as long as at least one member of a redo log group is available. The alert log records the loss of a redo log group member; as with most database status information, EM Database Control allows you to easily review the contents of the alert log.

The dynamic performance view `V$LOGFILE` provides the status of each member of each redo log file member of each redo log group; the `STATUS` column is defined as follows:

`INVALID` The file is corrupted or missing.

`STALE` This redo log file member is new and has never been used.

`DELETED` The file is no longer being used.

<blank> The redo log file is in use and is not corrupted.

When you are aware of a missing or deleted redo log group member, follow these three steps to ensure that you maintain a maximum level of redundancy. Losing the remaining member(s) of the redo log group will cause the instance to fail.

1. Verify which redo log group member is missing.
2. Archive the redo log group's contents; if you clear this redo log group before archiving it, you must back up the full database to ensure maximum recoverability of the database in case of the loss of a data file. Use the command `ALTER SYSTEM ARCHIVE LOG GROUP` *`groupnum`*`;` to force the archive operation. (*`groupnum`* refers to the redo log group that you want to archive.)
3. Clear the log group to re-create the missing redo log file members using the command `ALTER DATABASE CLEAR LOGFILE GROUP` *`groupnum`*`;`. Alternatively, you can replace the missing member by copying one of the good group members to the location of the

missing member; using ALTER DATABASE CLEAR LOGFILE GROUP has the advantage of being platform-independent.

In this example, you lose a redo log file group member and check the status of the redo log file groups using V$LOGFILE:

```
SQL> select * from v$logfile
     order by group#;

    GROUP# STATUS  TYPE   MEMBER                          IS_
---------- ------- ------ ---------------------------- ---
         1         ONLINE /u07/oradata/ord/redo01.log  NO
         1         ONLINE /u08/oradata/ord/redo01.log  NO
         2         ONLINE /u07/oradata/ord/redo02.log  NO
         2         ONLINE /u08/oradata/ord/redo02.log  NO
         3         ONLINE /u07/oradata/ord/redo03.log  NO
         3         ONLINE /u08/oradata/ord/redo03.log  NO


SQL> ! rm /u08/oradata/ord/redo01.log

SQL> select * from v$logfile order by group#;

    GROUP# STATUS  TYPE   MEMBER                          IS_
---------- ------- ------ ---------------------------- ---
         1         ONLINE /u07/oradata/ord/redo01.log  NO
         1 INVALID ONLINE /u08/oradata/ord/redo01.log  NO
         2         ONLINE /u07/oradata/ord/redo02.log  NO
         2         ONLINE /u08/oradata/ord/redo02.log  NO
         3         ONLINE /u07/oradata/ord/redo03.log  NO
         3         ONLINE /u08/oradata/ord/redo03.log  NO
```

It appears that group number 1 has a missing member, so you want to archive group number 1 using the ALTER SYSTEM ARCHIVE command:

```
SQL> alter system archive log group 1;
```

Finally, you can re-create the missing redo log file group member using the ALTER DATABASE command mentioned in step 3:

```
SQL> alter database clear logfile group 1;

Database altered.
```

Checking the view V$LOGFILE again, you can see that the redo log group member is no longer invalid:

```
SQL> select * from v$logfile order by group#;

    GROUP# STATUS  TYPE   MEMBER                          IS_
---------- ------- ------ ------------------------------ ---
         1         ONLINE /u07/oradata/ord/redo01.log    NO
         1         ONLINE /u08/oradata/ord/redo01.log    NO
         2         ONLINE /u07/oradata/ord/redo02.log    NO
         2         ONLINE /u08/oradata/ord/redo02.log    NO
         3         ONLINE /u07/oradata/ord/redo03.log    NO
         3         ONLINE /u08/oradata/ord/redo03.log    NO

6 rows selected.
```

By reviewing the contents of the alert log using either the EM Database Control interface by clicking the Alert Log Content link at the bottom of the Database Control home page or by reviewing the file $ORACLE_BASE/admin/ord/bdump/alert_ord.log, you can see the failures associated with the missing redo log group member:

```
Sun Sep 12 17:31:43 2008
ARC1: Evaluating archive   log 1 thread 1 sequence 2500
Sun Sep 12 17:31:43 2008
Errors in file
/u01/app/oracle/diag/rdbms/11gr11/11GR11/trace/11GR11_ora_3506.trc:
ORA-00313: open failed for members of log group 1 of thread 1
ORA-00312: online log 1 thread 1: '/u02/app/oracle/oradata/11GR11/redo01.log'
ORA-27037: unable to obtain file status
Linux Error: 2: No such file or directory
Additional information: 3
```

The Database Recovery Advisor knows about the failure. You can see the error reported on the EM Database Control home page, as shown in Figure 16.15.

FIGURE 16.15 Critical errors in the Alerts section of home page

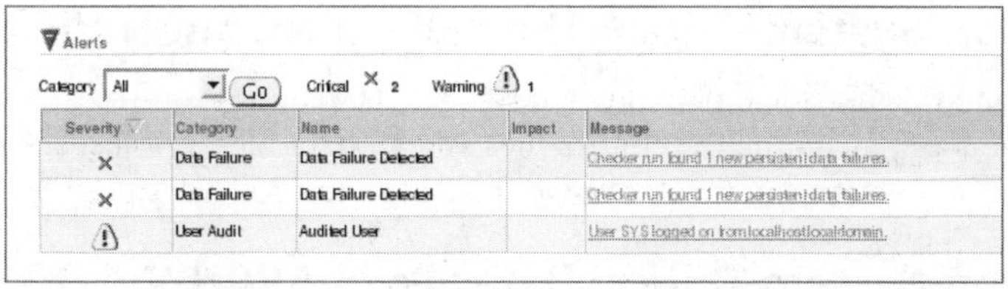

When you invoke DRA, you can see more details about these failures. As shown in Figure 16.16, you can click the Advise button to see more information about how this failure could have happened and how to remediate the failure.

FIGURE 16.16 View and Manage Failures screen

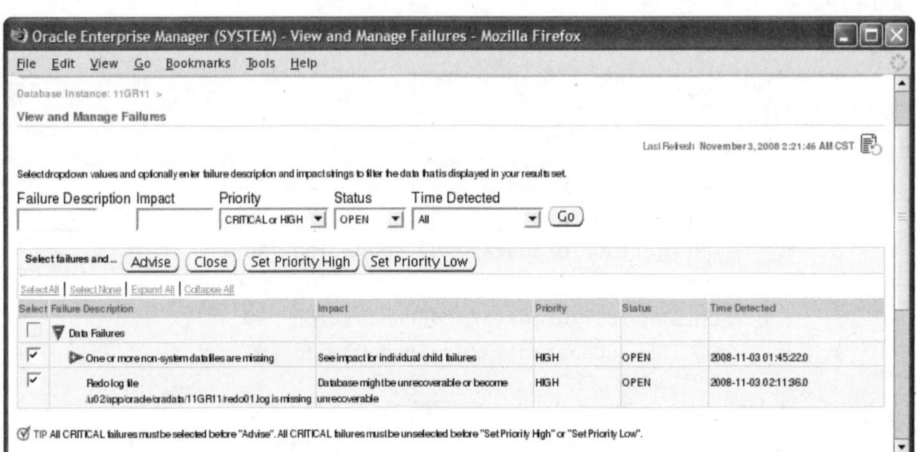

You can increase or decrease the priority of a failure by using the Set Priority High and Set Priority Low buttons. If you have taken care of the issue or if you do not want to resolve a noncritical failure, you can use the Close button to close the failure incident.

To fix a missing redo log group member, you can use the actions such as Switch Log File and Clear Log File on the Redo Log Groups screen.

Recovering from the Loss of a Non–System-Critical Data File

If you lose a non-system-critical data file (in other words, not the SYSTEM or UNDO tablespace), your options are similar to those when you lose a system-critical data file, except that most of your recovery effort in ARCHIVELOG mode can occur while the database is open to users, who can use tablespaces other than the one being recovered.

Loss of a Non-System-Critical Data File in NOARCHIVELOG Mode

The loss of a non-system-critical data file in NOARCHIVELOG mode requires the complete restoration of the database, including the control files and all data files, not just the missing data files. As a result, you must reenter any changes made to the database since the last backup.

Loss of a Non-System-Critical Data File in ARCHIVELOG Mode

The loss of a non-system-critical data file in ARCHIVELOG mode affects only objects that are in the missing file, and recovery can proceed while the rest of the database is online.

Because you are in ARCHIVELOG mode, no committed transactions in the lost data file will have to be reentered.

Recovering from the loss of a non–system-critical data file is not quite as complicated as the recovery from a system-critical data file, which I will cover in the next section; the database is continuously available to all users, except for the data files being recovered.

In the EM Database Control interface, invoke the Data Recovery Advisor. Choose the failure you want to fix, and click the Advice button. Figure 16.17 shows the Manual Actions screen.

FIGURE 16.17 Manual Actions screen of DRA

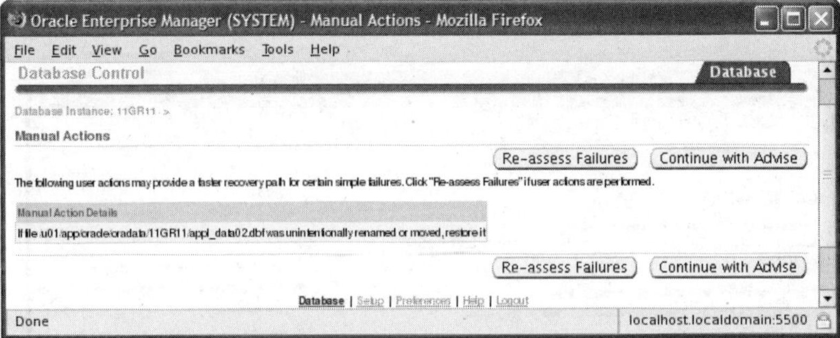

Click the Continue with Advise button to see the recovery advice. DRA generates a RMAN script to execute, as shown in Figure 16.18. You can run this script manually using the RMAN command line with no modification.

FIGURE 16.18 Recovery Advice screen of DRA

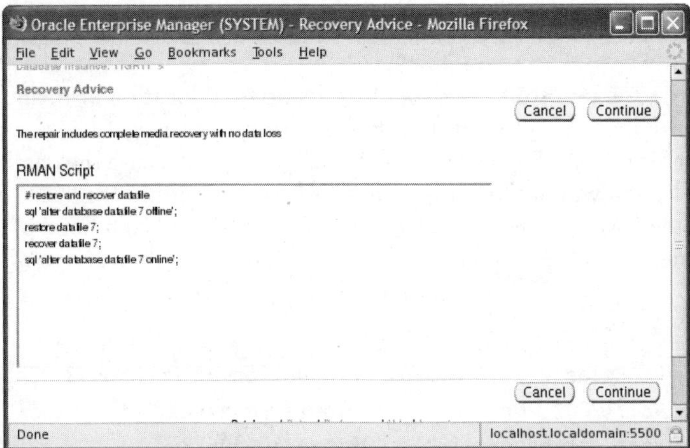

Click Continue to review and submit a job to start the restore and recovery.

You can also recover from the failure without using DRA. On the Perform Recovery screen, choose Datafiles as the recovery scope. You will be presented with four options to recover, as shown in Figure 16.19:

- Recover to Current Time: Restore the data file from backup, and recover the data file using archive log and redo log files.
- Restore Datafiles: No recovery is performed.
- Recover from Previously Restored Datafile: Continue recovery after the data file restore.
- Block Recovery: Recover the corrupted blocks in a data file.

FIGURE 16.19 User-directed recovery of a data file

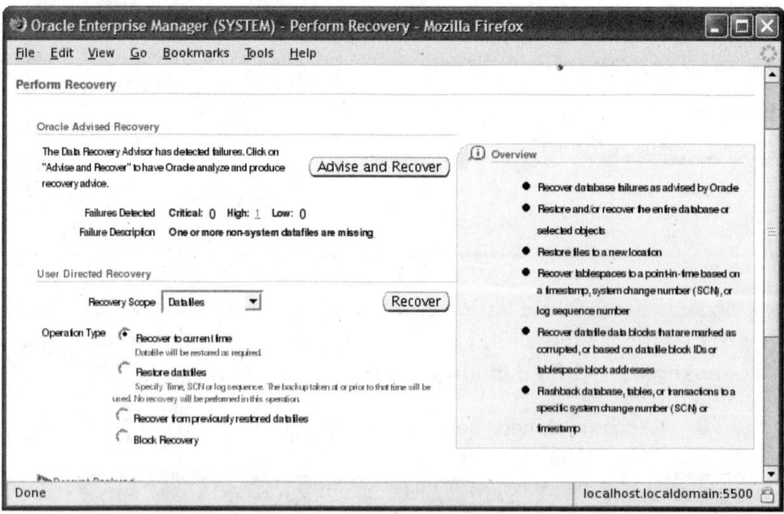

You have the option to restore the data file to its original location or to another location. You also have the option to edit the RMAN script generated. When you click Submit, the RMAN script is executed, and the data file is recovered. Because the database is in `ARCHIVELOG` mode, you will not lose any committed transactions in the `USERS` tablespace.

You can run the RMAN statement `LIST FAILURE` at the `RMAN` command prompt, and you will see output similar to the following:

```
$ rman target /

Recovery Manager: Release 11.1.0.6.0 - Production on Mon Nov 3 02:57:39 2008
Copyright (c) 1982, 2007, Oracle.  All rights reserved.
connected to target database: 11GR11 (DBID=4110949673)
```

```
RMAN> list failure;

using target database control file instead of recovery catalog
List of Database Failures
=========================

Failure ID Priority Status    Time Detected Summary
---------- -------- --------- ------------- -------
482        HIGH     OPEN      03-NOV-08
        One or more non-system datafiles are missing

RMAN>
```

The ADVISE FAILURE commands lists the failures. You can list all failures, or you can specify options such as CRITICAL, HIGH, so on. Here is some output from the ADVISE FAILURE statement:

```
RMAN> advise failure all;

List of Database Failures
=========================

Failure ID Priority Status    Time Detected Summary
---------- -------- --------- ------------- -------
482        HIGH     OPEN      03-NOV-08
        One or more non-system datafiles are missing

analyzing automatic repair options; this may take some time
using channel ORA_DISK_1
using channel ORA_DISK_2
analyzing automatic repair options complete

Mandatory Manual Actions
========================
no manual actions available

Optional Manual Actions
=======================
1. If file /u01/app/oracle/oradata/11GR11/appl_data02.dbf
was unintentionally renamed or moved, restore it
```

```
Automated Repair Options
========================
Option Repair Description
------ ------------------
1      Restore and recover datafile 7
  Strategy: The repair includes complete media recovery with no data loss
  Repair script: /u01/app/oracle/diag/rdbms/11gr11/11GR11/hm/reco_2087308400.hm

RMAN>
```

To fix the failures using DRA, you can use the command `REPAIR FAILURE`, as shown next. It asks for your confirmation before performing the restore and recovery. If you do not want the confirmation, include the `NOPROMPT` clause, which will automatically repair all `HIGH` and `CRITICAL` priority failures. The `REPAIR FAILURE` command can be executed only after performing the `ADVISE FAILURE`.

```
RMAN> repair failure;

Strategy: The repair includes complete media recovery with no data loss
Repair script: /u01/app/oracle/diag/rdbms/11gr11/11GR11/hm/reco_2087308400.hm

contents of repair script:
   # restore and recover datafile
   sql 'alter database datafile 7 offline';
   restore datafile 7;
   recover datafile 7;
   sql 'alter database datafile 7 online';

Do you really want to execute the above repair (enter YES or NO)? YES
executing repair script

sql statement: alter database datafile 7 offline

Starting restore at 03-NOV-08
using channel ORA_DISK_1
using channel ORA_DISK_2

channel ORA_DISK_1: starting datafile backup set restore
channel ORA_DISK_1: specifying datafile(s) to restore from backup set
channel ORA_DISK_1: restoring datafile 00007 to
/u01/app/oracle/oradata/11GR11/appl_data02.dbf
channel ORA_DISK_1: reading from backup piece /backup/database/0ejunlkq_1_1
```

```
channel ORA_DISK_1: piece handle=/backup/database/0ejunlkq_1_1
 tag=BACKUP_11GR11_0000_110208102644
channel ORA_DISK_1: restored backup piece 1
channel ORA_DISK_1: restore complete, elapsed time: 00:00:07
Finished restore at 03-NOV-08

Starting recover at 03-NOV-08
using channel ORA_DISK_1
using channel ORA_DISK_2

starting media recovery

archived log for thread 1 with sequence 193 is already on disk as file
 /flash_recovery_area/11GR11/archivelog/2008_11_02/o1_mf_1_193_4jwzm1yv_.arc
… … …
media recovery complete, elapsed time: 00:00:01
Finished recover at 03-NOV-08

sql statement: alter database datafile 7 online
repair failure complete

RMAN>
```

When you run REPAIR FAILURE, the Data Recovery Advisor closes the failure after successfully repairing the failure. As you saw in the Figure 16.16, you can increase or decrease the priority of a failure by using the CHANGE FAILURE command in RMAN. You can also close a failure using this command.

```
RMAN> CHANGE FAILURE 2 PRIORITY LOW;
RMAN> CHANGE FAILURE 5 CLOSE;
```

Data Recovery Advisor Views

The Data Recovery Advisor added four new views to the Oracle 11*g* data dictionary. These views start with V$IR_.

- V$IR_FAILURE: List of all the failures in the database (the same result you see with the LIST FAILURE command)
- V$IR_MANUAL_CHECKLIST: List of the manual-actions section of ADVISE FAILURE
- V$IR_REPAIR: Repair recommendations as provided by the ADVISE FAILURE command
- V$IR_FAILURE_SET: Link between V$IR_REPAIR and V$IR_FAILURE

Recovering from the Loss of a System-Critical Data File

When you lose a system-critical data file (in other words, a file from the SYSTEM or UNDO tablespace), the kinds of recovery available depend on whether you are operating in ARCHIVELOG mode or NOARCHIVELOG mode. Oracle strongly recommends operating in ARCHIVELOG mode for any production database that is not read-only.

Loss of a System-Critical Data File in NOARCHIVELOG Mode

The loss of a system-critical data file in NOARCHIVELOG mode requires a complete restoration of the database, including the control files and all data files, not just the missing data files. As a result, you must reenter any changes made to the database since the last backup, which must have been a cold backup.

Loss of a System-Critical Data File in ARCHIVELOG Mode

The loss of a system-critical data file in ARCHIVELOG mode cannot proceed while the database is open; recovery must be performed while the database is in the MOUNT state. Because the database is operating in ARCHIVELOG mode, you will not have to reenter any committed transactions in the database.

When a system-critical data file is lost, such as the data file for the SYSTEM tablespace, the instance will abort; in the rare circumstance that this does not happen, shut down the database, and start it in MOUNT mode, as in this example:

```
SQL> shutdown abort
ORACLE instance shut down.
SQL> startup mount
ORACLE instance started.

Total System Global Area  197132288 bytes
Fixed Size                   778076 bytes
Variable Size             162537636 bytes
Database Buffers           33554432 bytes
Redo Buffers                 262144 bytes
Database mounted.
SQL>
```

Once the database is mounted, you can restore and recover the missing data file. After the recovery is completed, open the database.

To use the Data Recovery Advisor for the recovery, invoke Perform Recovery from the Availability screen of EM Database Control. Select Datafiles as the recovery scope, choose Restore to Current Time, and add the files that need recovery. Submit the job to complete the recovery operation. After the recovery operation is completed, open the database using ALTER DATABASE OPEN.

Users are not required to reenter any data because the recovery is up to the time of the last commit in the database.

The difference between recovering from the loss of a system-critical data file and non–system-critical data file is the state of the database. To recover a system-critical data file, the database must be in MOUNT state, not OPEN.

Summary

In this chapter, you learned about the types of failures that can occur in the database. You learned the stages in instance startup and how to improve the instance recovery time. You also learned to recover from failures using the Data Recovery Advisor framework.

Understanding failure is critical to deciding the type of action required to recover from the failure. This chapter reviewed the six types of failures in a database: statement, user process, network, user error, instance, and media.

In addition to knowing how an instance fails, you need to know what is required to keep a database up and running: all control files, at least one member of each redo log group, and all data files for the SYSTEM and UNDO tablespaces. For instance failures, you want to know how long the database will take to recover. You can use the initialization parameter FAST_START_MTTR_TARGET to specify the target recovery time, making it easier to meet service-level agreements.

You learned ways to recover from three of the failure types: instance, user errors, and media. In the discussion on instance failures, you learned the steps required to successfully start up the database, identifying the prerequisites that must be in place for the startup phase to complete.

In many cases, users themselves can solve their errors; flashback query can retrieve rows that have been deleted from a table in the past, even after a COMMIT has been performed. Dropped tables are kept in the recycle bin, which lets a user bring back the entire table as long as the space occupied by the table in the tablespace was not overwritten by new objects. Flashback table brings a table back to a given point in time without affecting other objects or users in the database; flashback query and flashback table are often used as complementary tools when many rows or even a few rows in a table have been lost or inadvertently deleted. Flashback transaction is used to flash back an entire transaction and its dependent transactions. Finally, you can access previous transactions against a table from the online and archived redo logs when the self-service recovery tools are not successful in recovering user data.

Also in this chapter, I presented scenarios of media failures and how to recover from such failures using the Data Recovery Advisor. If the database is in ARCHIVELOG mode, you can recover the database from these failures without losing any committed transactions. If the database is in NOARCHIVELOG mode, you can recover only to the last good cold backup. RMAN includes several commands to support the Data Recovery Advisor.

Exam Essentials

Identify the initialization parameters used to tune instance recovery. Be able to define the possible values for FAST_START_MTTR_TARGET, FAST_START_IO_TARGET, and LOG_CHECKPOINT_TIMEOUT. Show the relationship between these parameters and in which situations each is most appropriately used.

List the phases of instance startup. Show how the database instance moves from SHUTDOWN to NOMOUNT to MOUNT to OPEN, and describe the conditions required in each step before the instance can proceed to the next phase.

Be able to list the types of failures that can occur in a database. Identify the six types of failures: statement, user process, network, user error, instance, and media.

List the features supported by Oracle to help users fix their own errors. Describe each type of user-error recovery solution: flashback query, flashback table, flashback transaction, and flashback drop.

Be able to use flashback query to retrieve previous table data. Show how flashback query can help a user look at the contents of a table at some point in time in the past. Demonstrate the flexibility in specifying the date at which the flashback query is executed.

Describe how flashback drop is used. Describe the components of flashback drop, such as the recycle bin, and show how it can store a deleted table unless space pressure occurs in the tablespace. Be able to identify the restrictions on the types of objects that can be saved in the recycle bin.

Understand how many control files and redo log members are required for the database to function. When you use multiplexed control files and redo log files, Oracle Database 11*g* requires all control files to be available and at least one member of the redo log group to be available for the database to function.

Understand the failures that can be identified and repaired by the Data Recovery Advisor. The Data Recovery Advisor can detect and repair all types of media failures and logical corruption. It cannot detect user errors or network issues.

Identify the three types of database files affected by media failures. Compare and contrast the loss of control files, redo log file group members, and data files, and describe how to recover from the loss of each of these files. Understand how the loss of certain types of data files may have a larger impact on availability and recoverability than others.

Familiarize yourself with the commands you can use to identify and perform recovery using RMAN. RMAN commands such as LIST FAILURE, ADVISE FAILURE, REPAIR FAILURE, and CHANGE FAILURE are used to support the Data Recovery Advisor actions.

Review Questions

1. The distance between the checkpoint position in a redo log group and the end of the redo log group can never be what percentage of the smallest redo log group?

   A. 15

   B. 100

   C. 50

   D. 90

   E. None of the above; the distance is relative to the size of the largest redo log group.

2. A database user tries to add a new row to a table, but the tablespace where the table resides is out of space. This type of failure is considered a ___________ failure, and the DBA can solve this problem by _________________.

   A. user error; providing additional user privileges

   B. user error; increasing the user's quota

   C. statement failure; enabling resumable-space allocation

   D. statement failure; changing the application logic

3. Which of the following initialization parameters controls the mean time to recover the database, in seconds, after an instance failure?

   A. FAST_START_IO_TARGET

   B. LOG_CHECKPOINT_TIMEOUT

   C. FAST_START_MTTR_TARGET

   D. MTTR_TARGET_ADVICE

   E. FAST_START_TARGET_MTTR

4. What background process frees up locks and rolls back uncommitted changes for an abnormally disconnected session?

   A. ORB0

   B. RBAL

   C. SMON

   D. PMON

5. Which of the following is not an example of a user-process failure?

   A. A user's PC suddenly reboots.

   B. The network or an application develops problems.

   C. The DBA kills the user session.

   D. Users terminate SQL*Plus without logging out.

6. Which of the following can help prevent database network failures? (Choose all that apply.)
   - **A.** Configure a backup listener process on the server.
   - **B.** Open more than one session when updating the database.
   - **C.** Configure multiple network cards on the server.
   - **D.** Create a standby database.

7. Identify the statement that is not true regarding the loss of a control file.
   - **A.** A damaged control file can be repaired by using one of the remaining undamaged control files, assuming there are at least two copies of the control file.
   - **B.** The missing or damaged control file can be replaced while the instance is still active.
   - **C.** You can temporarily run the instance with one fewer control file, as long as you remove one of the references to the missing control file in the spfile or `init.ora` file.
   - **D.** An instance typically fails when one of the multiplexed control files is lost or damaged.

8. Which failures can be detected by the Data Recovery Advisor, which then provides repair recommendations? (Choose all that apply.)
   - **A.** Instance failure
   - **B.** Accidental deletion of a data file
   - **C.** Disk containing one redo log member is offline
   - **D.** User accidentally dropped a table

9. The instance can still be started even if some data files are missing; this rule does not apply to which tablespaces? (Choose all that apply.)
   - **A.** USERS
   - **B.** SYSTEM
   - **C.** TEMP
   - **D.** SYSAUX
   - **E.** UNDO

10. Select the statement that is *not* true regarding media failure. A media failure occurs when
    - **A.** the network card on the server fails.
    - **B.** the DBA accidentally deletes one of the data files for the SYSTEM tablespace.
    - **C.** there is a head crash on all physical drives in the RAID controller box.
    - **D.** a corrupted track on a CD containing a read-only tablespace causes a query to fail.

11. Choose the correct statement about the Data Recovery Advisor.
    - **A.** The Data Recovery Advisor is a stand-alone tool.
    - **B.** The Data Recovery Advisor does not support RAC databases.
    - **C.** The `CHANGE FAILURE` command can be used in SQL*Plus session.
    - **D.** The `REPAIR FAILURE` command works only after `LIST FAILURE`.

12. To recover a data file from the SYSTEM or UNDO tablespace, the instance must be in which database state?
    - A. NOMOUNT
    - B. OPEN
    - C. ABORT
    - D. MOUNT
13. The STATUS column of the dynamic performance view V$LOGFILE contains what value if one of the redo log file group members has been lost because of a media failure?
    - A. INVALID
    - B. STALE
    - C. DELETED
    - D. The column contains a NULL value.
14. Place the following events or actions leading up to and during instance recovery in the correct order.
    1. The database is opened and available.
    2. Oracle uses undo segments in the undo tablespace to roll back uncommitted transactions.
    3. The DBA issues the STARTUP command at the SQL*Plus prompt.
    4. Oracle applies the information in the online redo log files to the data files.
    - A. 4, 3, 2, 1
    - B. 3, 4, 1, 2
    - C. 2, 1, 3, 4
    - D. 2, 1, 4, 3
    - E. 3, 2, 4, 1
    - F. 3, 4, 2, 1
15. You noticed that when your instance crashes, it takes a long time to start up the database. Which advisor can be used to tune this situation?
    - A. The Undo Advisor
    - B. The SQL Tuning Advisor
    - C. The Database Tuning Advisor
    - D. The MTTR Advisor
    - E. The Instance Tuning Advisor
16. If a data file is missing when the instance is started, where is the error message recorded?
    - A. Only in the alert log.
    - B. All missing files are returned directly to the administrator in the SQL*Plus session.
    - C. The first missing file is returned directly to the administrator in the SQL*Plus session, and the rest of the missing files are identified in V$RECOVER_FILE.
    - D. Only in the alert log and in the DBWR background-process trace files.

17. In ARCHIVELOG mode, the loss of a data file for any tablespace other than the SYSTEM or UNDO tablespace affects which objects in the database?
    - A. The loss affects only objects whose extents reside in the lost data file.
    - B. The loss affects only the objects in the affected tablespace, and work can continue in other tablespaces.
    - C. The loss will not abort the instance but will prevent other transactions in any tablespace other than SYSTEM or UNDO until the affected tablespace is recovered.
    - D. The loss affects only those users whose default tablespace contains the lost or damaged data file.
18. Which dynamic performance view shows the data files either needing media recovery or missing at instance startup?
    - A. V$RECOVER_FILE
    - B. V$DATAFILE
    - C. V$TABLESPACE
    - D. V$RECOVERY_FILE_DEST
    - E. V$RECOVERY_FILE_STATUS
19. A fire breaks out in the server room near the routers, and the operations manager cuts off power to all servers, including the database servers. Before the fire is put out, the disk drive containing the SYSTEM tablespace and both network cards on the Oracle Database 11*g* server are destroyed. The user SCOTT was about to create a new table, but the connection was dropped after the power was disconnected from the server. This scenario is primarily an example of what kind of failure?
    - A. Network
    - B. Instance
    - C. Statement
    - D. Media
    - E. User error
    - F. User process
20. Which of the following conditions prevents the instance from progressing through the NOMOUNT, MOUNT, and OPEN states?
    - A. One of the redo log file groups is missing a member.
    - B. The instance was previously shut down uncleanly with SHUTDOWN ABORT.
    - C. Either the spfile or `init.ora` file is missing.
    - D. One of the five multiplexed control files is damaged.
    - E. The USERS tablespace is offline, with one of its data files deleted.

Answers to Review Questions

1. D. The distance (in bytes) between the checkpoint position in a redo log group and the end of the current redo log group can never be more than 90 percent of the size of the smallest redo log group.

2. C. The failure of one statement is considered a statement failure, and one way to solve the problem is to enable resumable-space allocation. When resumable space is enabled, Oracle generates an alert and places the session in a suspended state.

3. C. The parameter FAST_START_MTTR_TARGET specifies the desired time, in seconds, to recover a single instance from a crash or instance failure. The parameters LOG_CHECKPOINT_TIMEOUT and FAST_START_IO_TARGET can still be used in Oracle 11*g* but should be used only together with an advanced-tuning scenario or for compatibility with older versions of Oracle. MTTR_TARGET_ADVICE and FAST_START_TARGET_MTTR are not valid initialization parameters.

4. D. The PMON process periodically polls server processes to make sure their sessions are still connected.

5. C. A DBA's disconnection of a session is an intentional process termination, not a failure. If a user's PC reboots, the user does not get a chance to log off, and the session is cleaned up by PMON; similarly, disconnecting from the application or SQL*Plus before logging out is considered a user-process failure. A network problem can prematurely disconnect a user session, causing a user-process failure. In all cases, PMON performs the session cleanup, whether the disconnection was intentional or not.

6. A, C. In addition to configuring a backup listener process and installing multiple network cards, you can implement connect-time failover and a backup network connection to reduce the possibility of network failures.

7. B. The instance must be shut down, if it is not already down, to repair or replace the missing or damaged control file.

8. B, C. Media failure, physical corruption, logical corruption, and missing data files all can be identified by the Data Recovery Advisor, which also provides recommendations for repair.

9. B, E. If a tablespace is taken offline because a data file is missing, the instance can still be started as long as the missing data file does not belong to the SYSTEM or UNDO tablespace.

10. A. If a network card fails, the failure type is network; the actual media containing the database files are not affected.

11. B. The Data Recovery Advisor in Oracle 11*g* Release 1 does not support RAC databases. It is integrated with EM Database Control and with RMAN. CHANGE FAILURE and other commands can be executed using RMAN. The ADVISE FAILURE command must be run before you can perform REPAIR FAILURE.

12. D. Unlike recovery of non–system-critical tablespaces other than SYSTEM or UNDO that can be recovered with the database in OPEN state, the database must be in MOUNT state to recover either the SYSTEM or UNDO tablespace.

13. A. If the redo log file group member has been lost because of a media failure or inadvertent deletion, the STATUS column is set to INVALID when an attempt is made to write redo information to that member.

14. B. Instance recovery, also known as crash recovery, occurs when the DBA attempts to open the database but the files were not synchronized to the same SCN when the database was shut down. Once the DBA issues the STARTUP command, Oracle uses information in the redo log files to restore the data files (including the undo tablespace's data files) to the state before the instance failure. Oracle then uses undo data in the undo tablespace after the database has been opened and made available to users to roll back uncommitted transactions.

15. D. The MTTR Advisor can tell the DBA the most effective value for the FAST_START_MTTR_TARGET parameter. This parameter specifies the maximum time required in seconds to perform instance recovery.

16. C. In addition to reporting the first missing file to the administrator and listing all the missing files in the dynamic performance view V$RECOVER_FILE, the missing data file(s) are noted in the DBWR background-process trace files.

17. B. The loss of one or more of a tablespace's data files does not prevent other users from doing their work in other tablespaces. Recovering the affected data files can continue while the database is still online and available.

18. A. The dynamic performance view V$RECOVER_FILE contains a list of the data files that either need media recovery or are missing when the instance is started.

19. B. The primary failure in this scenario is instance. Subsequently, a network failure will occur when connections are attempted through the burned-out router. However, no connections are possible until the network card in the server is replaced; the instance cannot start because of a media failure on the disk containing the SYSTEM tablespace.

20. D. All copies of the control files as defined in the spfile or the `init.ora` file must be identical and available. If one of the redo log file groups is missing a member, a warning is recorded in the alert log, but instance startup still proceeds. If the instance was previously shut down with SHUTDOWN ABORT, instance recovery automatically occurs during startup. Only an spfile or an `init.ora` file is needed to enter the NOMOUNT state, not both. If a tablespace is offline, the status of its data files is not checked until an attempt is made to bring it online; therefore, it will not prevent instance startup.

Moving Data and Using EM Tools

ORACLE DATABASE 11*g*: ADMINISTRATION I EXAM OBJECTIVES COVERED IN THIS CHAPTER:

✓ **Moving Data**

- Describe and use methods to move data (Directory objects, SQL*Loader, External Tables)
- Explain the general architecture of Oracle Data Pump
- Use Data Pump Export and Import to move data between Oracle databases

✓ **Intelligent Infrastructure Enhancements**

- Use the Enterprise Manager Support Workbench
- Managing Patches

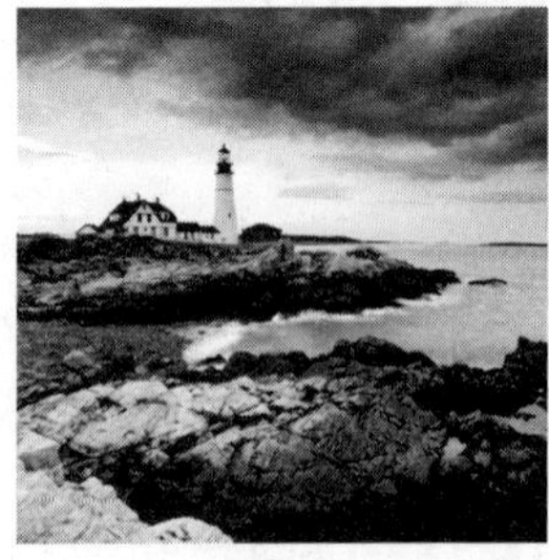

As a DBA, you are often required to move data between databases, extract data, or load data received from external sources. Oracle 11*g* provides tools to move data. You can use these tools to back up data from a table or a schema before making changes for quick recovery. Oracle Data Pump is a high-performance data-movement tool that you can use to unload and load data between Oracle databases, and you can use the SQL*Loader tool to load data received from external sources such as flat files.

In this chapter you will also learn about contacting Oracle Support through Enterprise Manager Support Workbench. EM Support Workbench is new in Oracle 11*g* and can be used to examine a database problem and contact Oracle Support for a resolution. EM can also alert you when database patches are ready. You will learn to use EM to stage and apply a patch.

Understanding Data Pump

The Data Pump facility is a high-speed mechanism for transferring data or metadata from one database to another or from operating-system files. Data Pump employs direct path unloading and direct path loading technologies. Unlike the older export and import programs (`exp` and `imp`), which operated on the client side of a database session, the Data Pump facility runs on the server. Thus, you must use a database directory to specify dump-file and log-file locations.

You can use Data Pump to copy data from one schema to another between two databases or within a single database. You can also use it to extract a logical copy of the entire database, a list of schemas, a list of tables, or a list of tablespaces to portable operating-system files. Data Pump can also transfer or extract the metadata (DDL statements) for a database, schema, or table.

You can call Data Pump from the command-line programs `expdp` and `impdp` or through the `DBMS_DATAPUMP PL/SQL` package, or you can invoke it from EM.

Data Pump export extracts data and metadata from your database, and Data Pump import loads this extracted data into the same database or into a different database, optionally transforming metadata along the way. These transformations let you, for example, copy tables from one schema to another or remap a tablespace from one database to another.

These are some of the key features of Data Pump:

- A fine-grained object selection using `INCLUDE` and `EXCLUDE` options
- An option to specify a lower-compatibility version so only supported object types are exported

- The ability to perform export and import in using parallel processes
- The ability to detach and attach to a job from the client session, allowing the DBA to close the export/import session and yet have the ability to administer the jobs
- An option to change target table names, tablespace names, and schema names
- Another option to compress metadata or data or both during export
- A tablespace metadata export to support the transportable tablespace feature of the database
- An option to append data to an existing table or to truncate and load data to an existing table
- The automatic use of direct path export whenever possible
- The ability to copy data from one database to another using a network
- The ability to specify a sample percentage to unload only a subset of data
- The ability to monitor job progress; job status can be queried from the database or using EM
- An option to restart or terminate failed export and import jobs

Architecture of Data Pump

In Oracle 11*g* Data Pump, the database does all the work. This is a major deviation from the architecture of export/import utilities, which previously ran as clients and did the major part of the work. The dump files for export/import were stored at the client, whereas the Data Pump files are stored at the server. Figure 17.1 shows the Data Pump architecture.

Data Pump Components

Data Pump consists of the following components:

Data Pump API `DBMS_DATAPUMP` is the PL/SQL API for Data Pump, which is the engine. Data Pump jobs are created and monitored using this API.

Metadata API The `DBMS_METADATA` API provides the database object definition to the Data Pump processes.

Client Tools Data Pump client tools `expdp` and `impdp` use the procedures provided by the `DBMS_DATAPUMP` package. These tools make calls to the Data Pump API to initiate and monitor Data Pump operations.

Data-movement APIs Data Pump uses the Direct Path API (DPAPI) to move data. Certain circumstances do not allow the use of DPAPI; in those cases, the Oracle external table with the `ORACLE_DATADUMP` access driver API is used.

FIGURE 17.1 Data Pump architecture

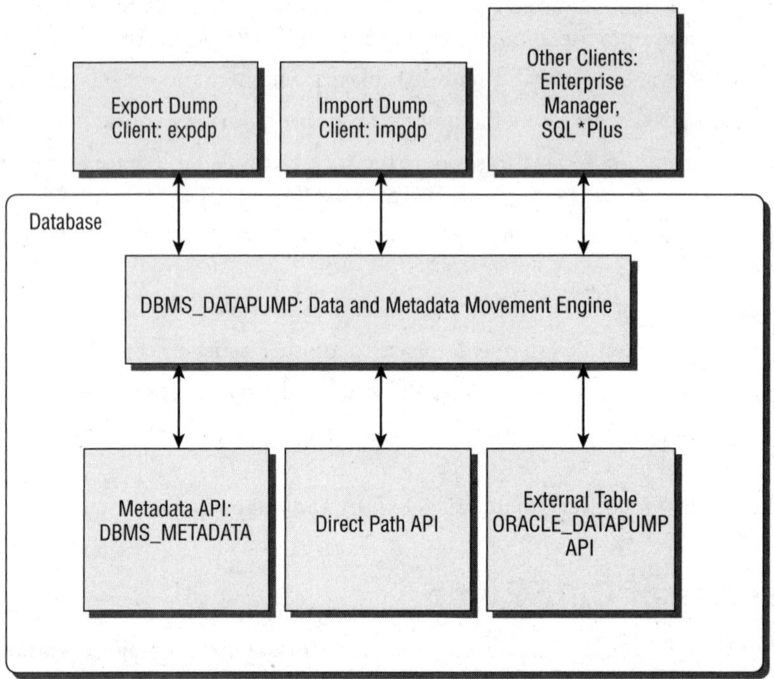

Data Pump Processes

Oracle Data Pump jobs, once started, are performed by various processes on the database server. The following are the processes involved in the Data Pump operation:

Client process This process is initiated by the client utility—`expdp`, `impdp`, or other clients—to make calls to the Data Pump API. Since Data Pump is completely integrated into the database, once the Data Pump job is initiated, this process is not necessary for the progress of the job.

Shadow process When a client logs into the Oracle Database, a foreground process is created (a standard feature of Oracle). This shadow process services the client data dump API requests. This process creates the master table and creates Advanced Queries (AQ) queues used for communication. Once the client process ends, the shadow process goes away too.

Master control process (MCP) The *master control process* controls the execution of the Data Pump job; there is one MCP per job. MCP divides the Data Pump job into various metadata and data-load or -unload jobs and hands them over to the worker processes. The MCP has a process name of the format `<ORACLE_SID>_DMnn_<PROCESS_ID>`. It maintains the job state, job description, restart information, and file information in the master table.

Worker process The MCP creates the worker processes based on the value of the PARALLEL parameter. The workers perform the tasks requested by the MCP, mainly loading or unloading data and metadata. The worker processes have the format <ORACLE_SID>_DWnn_<PROCESS_ID>. The worker processes maintain the current status in the master table that can be used to restart a failed job.

Parallel query (PQ) processes The worker processes can initiate parallel-query processes if an external table is used as the data-access method for loading or unloading. These are standard parallel-query slaves of the parallel-execution architecture.

Oracle Data Pump cannot be used to load data into a database from data exported using the exp utility.

Let's consider the example of an export Data Pump operation and see all the activities and processes involved. Say user A invokes the expdp client, which initiates the shadow process. The client calls the DBMS_DATAPUMP.OPEN procedure to establish the kind of export to be performed. The OPEN call starts the MCP process and creates two AQ queues.

The first queue is the status queue, used to send the status of the job, which includes logging information and errors. Clients interested in the status of the job can query this queue. This is strictly a unidirectional queue—the MCP posts the information to the queue, and the clients consume the information. The second queue is the command-and-control queue, which is used to control the worker processes established by the MCP and to perform API commands and file requests. This is a bidirectional queue where the MCP listens and writes. The commands are sent to this queue by the DBMS_DATAPUMP methods or by using the parameters of the expdp client.

Once all the components (parameters and filters) of the job are defined, the client (expdp) invokes DBMS_DATAPUMP.START_JOB. Based on the number of parallel processes requested, the MCP starts the worker processes. The MCP directs one of the worker processes to do the metadata extraction using the DBMS_METADATA API.

During the operation, a master table is maintained in the schema of the user who initiated the Data Pump export. The master table has the same name as the name of the Data Pump job. This table maintains one row per object with status information. In the event of a failure, Data Pump uses the information in this table to restart the job. The master table is the heart of every Data Pump operation; it maintains all the information about the job. Data Pump uses the master table to restart a failed or suspended job. The master table is dropped (by default) when the Data Pump job finishes successfully.

The master table is written to the dump file set as the last step of the export dump operation and is removed from the user's schema. For an import dump operation, the master table is loaded from the dump file set to the user's schema as the first step and is used to sequence the objects being imported.

While the export job is underway, the original client who invoked the export job can detach from the job without aborting the job. This is especially useful when performing long-running data export jobs. Users can attach the job at any time using the DBMS_DATAPUMP methods and query the status or change the parallelism of the job.

Since the master table is created in the Data Pump user's schema as a table, if there is an existing table in the schema with the Data Pump job name, the job fails. The user must have appropriate privileges to create the table and have appropriate tablespace quotas.

Data Access Methods

Data Pump chooses the most appropriate data-access method. Two methods are supported: direct path access and external table access. Direct path export has been supported since Oracle 7.3. External tables were introduced in Oracle9*i*, and support for writing to external tables has been available since Oracle 10*g*. Data Pump provides an external-tables access driver (ORACLE_DATAPUMP) that can be used to read and write files. The format of the file is the same as the direct path methods; hence, it's possible to load data that is unloaded in another method. Data Pump uses the Direct Load API whenever possible. The following are the exceptions when an external tables method will be used:

- Tables with fine-grained access control are enabled in insert and select operations.
- A domain index exists for a LOB column.
- A global index on multipartition table exists during a single-partition load.
- Clustered table or table has an active trigger during import.
- A table contains BFILE columns.
- A referential integrity constraint is present during import.
- A table contains a VARRAY column with an embedded opaque type.
- Loading and unloading very large tables and partitions, where the PARALLEL SQL clause can be used to an advantage.
- Loading tables that are partitioned differently at load time and unload time.

Using Data Pump Clients

Oracle 11*g* comes with the expdp utility to invoke Data Pump for export and comes with impdp for import. The Data Pump export utility (expdp) unloads data and metadata to a set of OS files called *dump files*. The Data Pump import utility (impdp) loads data and metadata stored in an export dump file to a target database. expdp and impdp accept parameters that are then passed to the DBMS_DATAPUMP program. The command-line executable name for Data Pump export is expdp and for Data Pump import is impdp on Windows as well as Unix platforms. For a user to invoke expdp/impdp, they need to set up a directory where the dump files will be stored and they must have appropriate privileges to perform Data Pump export/import. In the next section, I will discuss how to set up the export dump location.

Setting Up the Dump Location

Since Data Pump is server-based, directory objects must be created in the database where the Data Pump files will be stored. Directory objects are named directory locations on the database server representing the physical location on the server's file system. Directories are used with several database features, including BFILEs, external tables, utl_file, SQL*Loader, and Data Pump.

The directory object contains the location of a specific operating-system directory. By using a named directory object, you do not have to hard-code the directory path in programs, and you get file-management flexibility.

Under Unix, you create directories with the CREATE DIRECTORY statement, like this:

```
CREATE DIRECTORY dump_dir AS '/oracle/data_pump/dumps';
CREATE DIRECTORY log_dir  AS '/oracle/data_pump/logs';
```

Under Windows, you create directories like this:

```
CREATE DIRECTORY dpump_dir  AS 'G:\datadumps';
```

Directories are not schema objects, like tables or synonyms, because they are not owned by a schema. Instead, directories are like profiles or roles in that they are owned by the database. To control access to a directory, you need to grant the READ or WRITE object privilege on that directory, like this:

```
GRANT read,write ON DIRECTORY dump_dir TO PUBLIC;
```

To create directories, you must have the CREATE ANY DIRECTORY system privilege. By default, only the users SYSTEM and SYS have this privilege. Be careful in granting this system privilege to users, because the database employs the operating-system credentials of the database-instance owner.

Directory objects are owned by the SYS user; thus, the directory names must be unique across the database.

The user executing Data Pump must have been granted permissions on the directory. READ permission is required to import, and WRITE permission is required to export and to create log files or SQL files.

Note that the oracle user (who owns the software installation and database files) must have read and write OS privileges on the directory. The user SCOTT, for example, need not have any OS privileges on the directory for Data Pump to succeed.

A default directory can be created for Data Pump operations in the database. Privileged users (with the EXP_FULL_DATABASE or IMP_FULL_DATABASE privilege) need not specify a directory object name when performing the Data Pump operation. The name of the default directory must be DATA_PUMP_DIR. Also, the privileged users need not have explicit READ or WRITE permission on DATA_PUMP_DIR.

Using EM Database Control, you can create and edit directory objects. On the Database Control Schema page, click Directory Objects under Database Objects. Figure 17.2 shows the Directory Objects screen that appears.

FIGURE 17.2 Directory Objects screen of EM

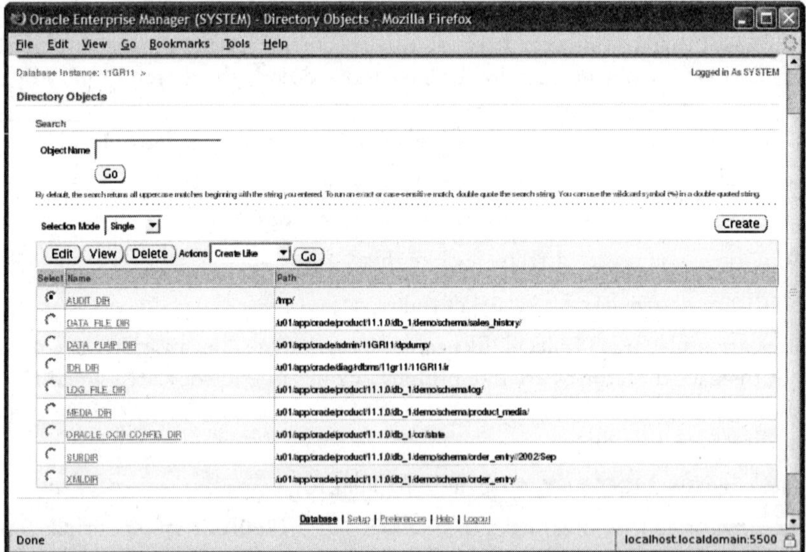

Click the Edit button to change the physical directory. You can also use the Delete button to delete an existing directory and the Create button to create a new directory.

Data Pump can write three types of files to the OS directory defined in the database. Remember that absolute paths are not supported; Data Pump can write only to a directory defined by a directory database object. The file types are as follows:

Dump files These contain data and metadata information.

Log files These record the standard output to a file and contain job progress and status information.

SQL files Data-dump import can extract the metadata information from a dump file, which can be used to create database objects without using the Data Pump import utility.

You can specify the location of the files to the Data Pump clients using three methods (given in the order of precedence):

- Prefix the filename with the directory name separated by a colon; for example, `DUMPFILE=dumplocation:myfile.dmp`.
- Use the `DIRECTORY` parameter on the OS environment.
- Define the `DATA_DUMP_DIR` directory in the database for privileged users.

The export and import done using the `expdp` and `impdp` tools can have different modes based on the requirement. The next section discusses this.

Specifying Export and Import Modes

Export and import using the Data Pump clients can be performed in five different modes to unload or load different portions of the database. When performing the dump-file import, specifying the mode is optional; when no mode is specified, the entire dump file is loaded with the mode automatically set to the one used for export.

Table 17.1 describes the export and import modes.

TABLE 17.1 Export and Import Modes in Data Pump

Mode	Description	Export	Import
Database	Performed by specifying the FULL=Y parameter	The export user requires the EXP_FULL_DATABASE role.	The import user requires the IMP_FULL_DATABASE role.
Tablespace	Performed by specifying the TABLESPACES parameter	Data and metadata for only those objects contained in the specified tablespaces are unloaded. The export user requires the EXP_FULL_DATABASE role.	All objects contained in the specified tablespaces are loaded. The import user requires the IMP_FULL_DATABASE privilege. The source dump file can be exported in database, tablespace, schema, or table mode.
Schema	Performed by specifying the SCHEMAS parameter. This is the default mode	Only objects belonging to the specified schema are unloaded. The EXP_FULL_DATABASE role is required to specify a list of schemas.	All objects belonging to the specified schema are loaded. The source can be a database or schema-mode export. The IMP_FULL_DATABASE role is required to specify a list of schema.
Table	Performed by specifying the TABLES parameter	Only the specified table, its partitions, and its dependent objects are unloaded. The export user must have the SELECT privilege on the tables.	Only the specified table, its partitions, and its dependent objects are loaded. This requires the IMP_FULL_DATABASE role to specify tables belonging to a different user.
Transport tablespace	Performed by specifying the TRANSPORT_TABLESPACES parameter	Only metadata for tables and their dependent objects within the specified set of tablespaces are unloaded. Use this mode to transport tablespaces from one database to another.	Metadata from a transport tablespace export is loaded.

In a database-mode export, the entire database is exported to operating-system files, including user accounts, public synonyms, roles, and profiles. In a schema-mode export, all data and metadata for a list of schemas is exported. At the most granular level is the table-mode export, which includes the data and metadata for a list of tables. A tablespace-mode export extracts both data and metadata for all objects in a tablespace list as well as any object dependent on those in the specified tablespace list. Therefore, if a table resides in your specified tablespace list, all its indexes are included whether or not they also reside in the specified tablespace list. In each of these modes, you can further specify that only data or only metadata be exported. The default is to export both data and metadata.

With some objects, such as indexes, only the metadata is exported; the actual internal structures contain physical addresses and are always rebuilt on import.

The files created by a Data Pump export are called *dump files*, and one or more of these files can be created during a single Data Pump export job. Multiple files are created if your Data Pump job has a parallel degree greater than 1 or if a single dump file exceeds the `filesize` parameter. All the export dump files from a single Data Pump export job are called a *dump-file set*.

Using expdp

You use the `expdp` utility to perform Data Pump exports. Any user can export objects or a complete schema owned by the user without any additional privileges. Nonprivileged users must have `WRITE` permission on the directory object and must specify the `DIRECTORY` parameter or specify the directory object name along with the dump filename.

Here is an example to perform an export by user `SCOTT`. Since Scott is not a privileged user, he must specify the `DIRECTORY` object name.

```
$ expdp scott/tiger


Export: Release 11.1.0.6.0 - Production on Saturday, 15 November, 2008
13:50:05
Copyright (c) 2003, 2007, Oracle.  All rights reserved.
Connected to: Oracle Database 11g Enterprise Edition Release 11.1.0.6.0 -
Production
With the Partitioning, OLAP, Data Mining and Real Application Testing options
ORA-39002: invalid operation
ORA-39070: Unable to open the log file.
ORA-39145: directory object parameter must be specified and non-null
```

Let's create a directory for user `SCOTT` and grant read and write privileges on this directory:

```
SQL> CREATE DIRECTORY dumplocation AS '/u02/dpump';
Directory created.
```

```
SQL> GRANT READ, WRITE on DIRECTORY dumplocation TO scott;
Grant succeeded.
```

Now, let's try the export specifying the directory:

```
$ expdp scott/tiger directory=dumplocation
Export: Release 11.1.0.6.0 - Production on Saturday, 15 November, 2008
16:04:22
Copyright (c) 2003, 2007, Oracle.  All rights reserved.
Connected to: Oracle Database 11g Enterprise Edition Release 11.1.0.6.0 -
Production
With the Partitioning, OLAP, Data Mining and Real Application Testing options
FLASHBACK automatically enabled to preserve database integrity.
Starting "SCOTT"."SYS_EXPORT_SCHEMA_01":  scott/********
directory=dumplocation
Estimate in progress using BLOCKS method...
Processing object type SCHEMA_EXPORT/TABLE/TABLE_DATA
Total estimation using BLOCKS method: 192 KB
Processing object type SCHEMA_EXPORT/PRE_SCHEMA/PROCACT_SCHEMA
Processing object type SCHEMA_EXPORT/TABLE/TABLE
Processing object type SCHEMA_EXPORT/TABLE/INDEX/INDEX
Processing object type SCHEMA_EXPORT/TABLE/CONSTRAINT/CONSTRAINT
Processing object type SCHEMA_EXPORT/TABLE/INDEX/STATISTICS/INDEX_STATISTICS
Processing object type SCHEMA_EXPORT/TABLE/COMMENT
Processing object type SCHEMA_EXPORT/TABLE/STATISTICS/TABLE_STATISTICS
Processing object type SCHEMA_EXPORT/POST_SCHEMA/PROCACT_SCHEMA
. . exported "SCOTT"."DEPT"                              5.914 KB       4 rows
. . exported "SCOTT"."EMP"                               8.570 KB      14 rows
. . exported "SCOTT"."SALGRADE"                          5.867 KB       5 rows
. . exported "SCOTT"."BONUS"                                 0 KB       0 rows
Master table "SCOTT"."SYS_EXPORT_SCHEMA_01" successfully loaded/unloaded
******************************************************************************
Dump file set for SCOTT.SYS_EXPORT_SCHEMA_01 is:
  /u02/dpump/expdat.dmp
Job "SCOTT"."SYS_EXPORT_SCHEMA_01" successfully completed at 16:04:55
$
```

Since you did not specify any other parameters, expdp used default values for the filenames (expdat.dmp and export.log), did schema-level export (login schema), calculated job estimation using the blocks method, used a default job name (SYS_EXPORT_SCHEMA_01), and exported both data and metadata.

Data Pump Export Parameters

You can use various parameters while invoking expdp. You can obtain a list of parameters by specifying expdp help=y:

```
$ expdp help=y
Export: Release 11.1.0.6.0 - Production on Saturday, 15 November, 2008
16:54:49
Copyright (c) 2003, 2007, Oracle.  All rights reserved.

The Data Pump export utility provides a mechanism for transferring data
objects
between Oracle databases. The utility is invoked with the following command:

   Example: expdp scott/tiger DIRECTORY=dmpdir DUMPFILE=scott.dmp

You can control how Export runs by entering the 'expdp' command followed
by various parameters. To specify parameters, you use keywords:

   Format:  expdp KEYWORD=value or KEYWORD=(value1,value2,...,valueN)
   Example: expdp scott/tiger DUMPFILE=scott.dmp DIRECTORY=dmpdir
SCHEMAS=scott
              or TABLES=(T1:P1,T1:P2), if T1 is partitioned table

USERID must be the first parameter on the command line.

Keyword               Description (Default)
------------------------------------------------------------------------------
ATTACH                Attach to existing job, e.g. ATTACH [=job name].
COMPRESSION           Reduce size of dumpfile contents where valid keyword.
                      values are: ALL, (METADATA_ONLY), DATA_ONLY and NONE.
CONTENT               Specifies data to unload where the valid keyword
                      values are: (ALL), DATA_ONLY, and METADATA_ONLY.
DATA_OPTIONS          Data layer flags where the only valid value is:
                      XML_CLOBS-write XML datatype in CLOB format
DIRECTORY             Directory object to be used for dumpfiles and logfiles.
DUMPFILE              List of destination dump files (expdat.dmp),
                      e.g. DUMPFILE=scott1.dmp, scott2.dmp, dmpdir:scott3.dmp.
ENCRYPTION            Encrypt part or all of the dump file where valid keyword
                      values are: ALL, DATA_ONLY, METADATA_ONLY,
                      ENCRYPTED_COLUMNS_ONLY, or NONE.
ENCRYPTION_ALGORITHM  Specify how encryption should be done where valid
                      keyword values are: (AES128), AES192, and AES256.
ENCRYPTION_MODE       Method of generating encryption key where valid keyword
                      values are: DUAL, PASSWORD, and (TRANSPARENT).
```

```
ENCRYPTION_PASSWORD   Password key for creating encrypted column data.
ESTIMATE              Calculate job estimates where the valid keyword
                      values are: (BLOCKS) and STATISTICS.
ESTIMATE_ONLY         Calculate job estimates without performing the export.
EXCLUDE               Exclude specific object types, e.g. EXCLUDE=TABLE:EMP.
FILESIZE              Specify the size of each dumpfile in units of bytes.
FLASHBACK_SCN         SCN used to set session snapshot back to.
FLASHBACK_TIME        Time used to get the SCN closest to the specified time.
FULL                  Export entire database (N).
HELP                  Display Help messages (N).
INCLUDE               Include specific object types, e.g. INCLUDE=TABLE_DATA.
JOB_NAME              Name of export job to create.
LOGFILE               Log file name (export.log).
NETWORK_LINK          Name of remote database link to the source system.
NOLOGFILE             Do not write logfile (N).
PARALLEL              Change the number of active workers for current job.
PARFILE               Specify parameter file.
QUERY                 Predicate clause used to export a subset of a table.
REMAP_DATA            Specify a data conversion function,
                      e.g. REMAP_DATA=EMP.EMPNO:REMAPPKG.EMPNO.
REUSE_DUMPFILES       Overwrite destination dump file if it exists (N).
SAMPLE                Percentage of data to be exported;
SCHEMAS               List of schemas to export (login schema).
STATUS                Frequency (secs) job status is to be monitored where
                      the default (0) will show new status when available.
TABLES                Identifies a list of tables to export - one schema only.
TABLESPACES           Identifies a list of tablespaces to export.
TRANSPORTABLE         Specify whether transportable method can be used where
                      valid keyword values are: ALWAYS, (NEVER).
TRANSPORT_FULL_CHECK  Verify storage segments of all tables (N).
TRANSPORT_TABLESPACES List of tablespaces from which metadata will be
                      unloaded.
VERSION               Version of objects to export where valid keywords are:
                      (COMPATIBLE), LATEST, or any valid database version.

The following commands are valid while in interactive mode.
Note: abbreviations are allowed

Command               Description
------------------------------------------------------------------------------
ADD_FILE              Add dumpfile to dumpfile set.
CONTINUE_CLIENT       Return to logging mode. Job will be re-started if idle.
```

```
EXIT_CLIENT          Quit client session and leave job running.
FILESIZE             Default filesize (bytes) for subsequent ADD_FILE commands.
HELP                 Summarize interactive commands.
KILL_JOB             Detach and delete job.
PARALLEL             Change the number of active workers for current job.
                     PARALLEL=<number of workers>.
REUSE_DUMPFILES      Overwrite destination dump file if it exists (N).
START_JOB            Start/resume current job.
STATUS               Frequency (secs) job status is to be monitored where
                     the default (0) will show new status when available.
                     STATUS[=interval]
STOP_JOB             Orderly shutdown of job execution and exits the client.
                     STOP_JOB=IMMEDIATE performs an immediate shutdown of the
                     Data Pump job.

$
```

FLASHBACK_SCN and FLASHBACK_TIME are mutually exclusive parameters.

The DUMPFILE parameter can specify more than one file. The filenames can be comma-separated, or you can use the %U substitution variable. If you specify %U in the DUMPFILE filename, the number of files initially created is based on the value of the PARALLEL parameter. Preexisting files that match the name of the files generated are not overwritten; an error is flagged. To forcefully overwrite the files, use the REUSE_DUMPFILES=Y parameter. The FILESIZE parameter determines the size of each file. Table 17.2 shows some examples.

You can specify all the parameters in a file and specify the filename with the PARFILE parameter. The only exception is the PARFILE parameter inside the parameter file. Recursive PARFILE is not supported.

The SAMPLE parameter is useful to get a subset of data unloaded from the source table. Specify the percentage of rows that need to be unloaded using this parameter. The SAMPLE parameter is not valid for network exports.

In the next section, I will discuss the impdp utility, which does the import from a dump file created using expdp.

TABLE 17.2 Data Pump DUMPFILE Examples

Parameter Examples	File Characteristics
DUMPFILE=exp%U.dmp FILESIZE=200M	Initially the exp01.dmp file will be created; once the file is 200MB, the next file will be created.
DUMPFILE=exp%U_%U.dmp PARALLEL=3	Initially three files will be created: exp01_01.dmp, exp02_02.dmp, and exp03_03.dmp. Notice that every occurrence of the substitution variable is incremented each time. Since there is no FILESIZE, no more files will be created.
DUMPFILE=DMPDIR1:exp%U.dmp, DMPDIR2:exp%U.dmp FILESIZE=100M	This method is especially useful if you do not have enough space in one directory to perform the complete export job. The dump files are stored in directories defined by DMPDIR1 and DMPDIR2.

Using Impdp

The Data Pump import program impdp is the utility that can read and apply the dump file created by the expdp utility. The directory permission and privileges for using impdp are similar to those for expdp.

impdp has several modes of operation, including full, schema, table, and tablespace. In the full mode, the entire content of an export file set is loaded. In a schema-mode import, all content for a list of schemas in the specified file set is loaded. The specified file set for a schema-mode import can be from either a database or a schema-mode export. With a table-mode import, only the specified table and dependent objects are loaded from the export file set. With a tablespace-mode import, all objects in the export file set that were in the specified tablespace list are loaded.

With all these modes, the source can be a live database instead of a set of export files. Table 17.3 shows the supported mapping of export mode to import mode.

TABLE 17.3 Export to Import Modes

Source Export Mode	Import Mode
Database Schema Table Tablespace Live database	Full

TABLE 17.3 Export to Import Modes *(continued)*

Source Export Mode	Import Mode
Database Schema Live database	Schema
Database Schema Table Tablespace Live database	Table
Database Schema Table Tablespace Live database	Tablespace

The IMP_FULL_DATABASE role is required if the source is a live database or the export session required the EXP_FULL_DATABASE role.

Data Pump Import Parameters

You can use various parameters while invoking impdp. You can obtain a list of parameters by specifying impdp help=y:

```
$ impdp help=y

Import: Release 11.1.0.6.0 - Production on Saturday, 15 November, 2008
21:13:53

Copyright (c) 2003, 2007, Oracle.  All rights reserved.


The Data Pump Import utility provides a mechanism for transferring data
objects
between Oracle databases. The utility is invoked with the following command:

     Example: impdp scott/tiger DIRECTORY=dmpdir DUMPFILE=scott.dmp

You can control how Import runs by entering the 'impdp' command followed
by various parameters. To specify parameters, you use keywords:

     Format:  impdp KEYWORD=value or KEYWORD=(value1,value2,...,valueN)
     Example: impdp scott/tiger DIRECTORY=dmpdir DUMPFILE=scott.dmp

USERID must be the first parameter on the command line.
```

```
Keyword               Description (Default)
------------------------------------------------------------------------------
ATTACH                Attach to existing job, e.g. ATTACH [=job name].
CONTENT               Specifies data to load where the valid keywords are:
                      (ALL), DATA_ONLY, and METADATA_ONLY.
DATA_OPTIONS          Data layer flags where the only valid value is:
                      SKIP_CONSTRAINT_ERRORS-constraint errors are not fatal.
DIRECTORY             Directory object to be used for dump, log, and sql
                      files.
DUMPFILE              List of dumpfiles to import from (expdat.dmp),
                      e.g. DUMPFILE=scott1.dmp, scott2.dmp, dmpdir:scott3.dmp.
ENCRYPTION_PASSWORD   Password key for accessing encryptß  ed column data.
                      This parameter is not valid for network import jobs.
ESTIMATE              Calculate job estimates where the valid keywords are:
                      (BLOCKS) and STATISTICS.
EXCLUDE               Exclude specific object types, e.g. EXCLUDE=TABLE:EMP.
FLASHBACK_SCN         SCN used to set session snapshot back to.
FLASHBACK_TIME        Time used to get the SCN closest to the specified time.
FULL                  Import everything from source (Y).
HELP                  Display help messages (N).
INCLUDE               Include specific object types, e.g. INCLUDE=TABLE_DATA.
JOB_NAME              Name of import job to create.
LOGFILE               Log file name (import.log).
NETWORK_LINK          Name of remote database link to the source system.
NOLOGFILE             Do not write logfile.
PARALLEL              Change the number of active workers for current job.
PARFILE               Specify parameter file.
PARTITION_OPTIONS     Specify how partitions should be transformed where the
                      valid keywords are: DEPARTITION, MERGE and (NONE)
QUERY                 Predicate clause used to import a subset of a table.
REMAP_DATA            Specify a data conversion function,
                      e.g. REMAP_DATA=EMP.EMPNO:REMAPPKG.EMPNO
REMAP_DATAFILE        Redefine datafile references in all DDL statements.
REMAP_SCHEMA          Objects from one schema are loaded into another schema.
REMAP_TABLE           Table names are remapped to another table,
                      e.g. REMAP_TABLE=EMP.EMPNO:REMAPPKG.EMPNO.
REMAP_TABLESPACE      Tablespace object are remapped to another tablespace.
REUSE_DATAFILES       Tablespace will be initialized if it already exists (N).
SCHEMAS               List of schemas to import.
SKIP_UNUSABLE_INDEXES Skip indexes that were set to the Index Unusable state.
SQLFILE               Write all the SQL DDL to a specified file.
STATUS                Frequency (secs) job status is to be monitored where
                      the default (0) will show new status when available.
```

```
STREAMS_CONFIGURATION Enable the loading of Streams metadata
TABLE_EXISTS_ACTION   Action to take if imported object already exists.
                      Valid keywords: (SKIP), APPEND, REPLACE and TRUNCATE.
TABLES                Identifies a list of tables to import.
TABLESPACES           Identifies a list of tablespaces to import.
TRANSFORM             Metadata transform to apply to applicable objects.
                      Valid transform keywords: SEGMENT_ATTRIBUTES, STORAGE,
                      OID, and PCTSPACE.
TRANSPORTABLE         Options for choosing  transportable data movement.
                      Valid keywords: ALWAYS and (NEVER).
                      Only valid in NETWORK_LINK mode import operations.
TRANSPORT_DATAFILES   List of datafiles to be imported by transportable mode.
TRANSPORT_FULL_CHECK  Verify storage segments of all tables (N).
TRANSPORT_TABLESPACES List of tablespaces from which metadata will be loaded.
                      Only valid in NETWORK_LINK mode import operations.
VERSION               Version of objects to export where valid keywords are:
                      (COMPATIBLE), LATEST, or any valid database version.
                      Only valid for NETWORK_LINK and SQLFILE.

The following commands are valid while in interactive mode.
Note: abbreviations are allowed

Command               Description (Default)
------------------------------------------------------------------------------

CONTINUE_CLIENT       Return to logging mode. Job will be re-started if idle.
EXIT_CLIENT           Quit client session and leave job running.
HELP                  Summarize interactive commands.
KILL_JOB              Detach and delete job.
PARALLEL              Change the number of active workers for current job.
                      PARALLEL=<number of workers>.
START_JOB             Start/resume current job.
                      START_JOB=SKIP_CURRENT will start the job after skipping
                      any action which was in progress when job was stopped.
STATUS                Frequency (secs) job status is to be monitored where
                      the default (0) will show new status when available.
                      STATUS[=interval]
STOP_JOB              Orderly shutdown of job execution and exits the client.
                      STOP_JOB=IMMEDIATE performs an immediate shutdown of the
                      Data Pump job.

$
```

You must include one parameter to specify the mode, either full, schemas, tables, or tablespaces. You can include several other parameters on the command line or place them in a file and use the parfile= parameter to instruct impdp where to find them. Here are some examples of imports:

- Read the dump file FULL.DMP and extract all DDL, placing it in the file FULL.SQL. Do not write a log file.

```
impdp system/password full=y dumpfile=dumplocation:FULL.DMP
   nologfile=y sqlfile= dumplocation:FULL.SQL
```

- Read the data accessed via the database link PROD, and import schema HR into schema HR_TEST, importing only metadata, writing the log file to the database directory chap7, and naming this log file HR_TEST.imp.

```
impdp system/password network_link=prod schemas="HR"
   remap_schema="HR:HR_TEST" content=metadata_only
   logfile= dumplocation:HR_TEST.imp
```

- Read the dump file HR.DMP, and write to the SQL file HR_proc_give.sql all the DDL to create any procedures with the name LIKE 'GIVE%'. Do not write a log file.

```
impdp system/password full=y dumpfile= dumplocation:HR.DMP
   nologfile=y sqlfile= dumplocation:HR_proc_give.SQL
   include=PROCEDURE:"LIKE 'GIVE%'"
```

The combinations of parameters you can use in copying data and metadata give you, the DBA, flexibility in administering your databases.

When using the schema-level import with the SCHEMAS parameter, if the schema does not exist in the target database, the import operation creates it with the same attributes from the source. The schema created by the import operation will need to have the password reset.

You can use the CONTENT, INCLUDE, and EXCLUDE parameters in the impdp utility to filter the metadata objects. Their behavior is the same as in the expdp utility. I'll discuss them in detail in the "Data and Metadata Filters" section. In the next section, I will discuss methods to use a different target for tablespaces, schemas, and data files.

Import Transformations

While performing the import, you can specify a different target name for data files, tablespaces, or schemas. These transformations are possible because the object metadata is stored in the dump file as XML. The REMAP_ parameters are used to specify this. When any one of the three REMAP_ parameters is used, Data Pump makes transformations to the metadata DDL during import. The IMP_FULL_DATABASE role is required to use these parameters. You can use these parameters multiple times if there is more than one transformation to be made, but the same source cannot be repeated more than once. The following are the parameters you can use to specify a different target name for each type of object:

REMAP_DATAFILES Using this parameter, you can specify a different name for the data file. The filename referenced could be in a CREATE TABLESPACE, CREATE LIBRARY, or CREATE DIRECTORY statement. REMAP_DATAFILES is especially useful when performing a full database import, when the tablespaces are being created by impdp and the source directories do not exist in the target database server, or when the source and target platforms are different (VMS, Windows, Unix). The syntax is as follows:

```
REMAP_DATAFILE=source_datafile:target_datafile
```

REMAP_SCHEMA Using this parameter, you can load all the objects belonging to the source schema to a target schema. Multiple source schemas can map to the same target schema. If the target schema specified does not exist, the import operation creates the schema and performs the load. The syntax is as follows:

```
REMAP_SCHEMA=source_schema:target_schema
```

REMAP_TABLE Using this parameter, you can rename a table while performing the import. Only the table is renamed; its dependent indexes, triggers, constraints, and columns are not renamed. The syntax is as follows:

```
REMAP_TABLE=source_table:target_table
```

REMAP_TABLESPACE Using this parameter, you can create the objects that belong to a tablespace in the source to another in the target. The syntax is as follows:

```
REMAP_TABLESPACE=source_tablespace:target_tablespace
```

TRANSFORM Using the TRANSFORM parameter, you can specify that the storage clause should not be generated in the DDL for import. This is useful if the storage characteristics of the source and target databases are different. TRANSFORM has the following syntax:

```
TRANSFORM=name:boolean_value[:object_type]
```

The name of the transform can be either SEGMENT_ATTRIBUTES or STORAGE. STORAGE removes the STORAGE clause from the CREATE statement DDL, whereas SEGMENT_ATTRIBUTES removes physical attributes, tablespaces, logging, and storage attributes. boolean_value can be Y or N; the default is Y. The type of object is optional; the valid values are TABLE and INDEX.

For example, if you want to ignore the storage characteristics during the import and use the defaults for the tablespace, you can do the following:

```
impdp dumpfile=scott.dmp  transform=storage:N:table exclude=indexes
```

The next example will remove all the segment attributes; the import will use the user's default tablespace and its default storage characteristics:

```
impdp dumpfile=scott.dmp  transform=segment_attributes:N
```

In the next section, I will discuss how data can be copied from one database to another without using a dump file.

Network-Mode Import

NETWORK_LINK enables the network-mode import using a database link. The database link must be created before performing the import. Export is performed on the source database based on the various parameters; the data and metadata are passed to the source database using the database link and loaded. To get a consistent export from the source database, you can use the FLASHBACK_SCN or FLASHBACK_TIME parameter.

Using FLASHBACK_SCN, FLASHBACK_TIME, ESTIMATE, or TRANSPORT_TABLESPACES requires the NETWORK_LINK parameter to also be specified. Here is an example of how to copy the SCOTT schema in the source (remote) database to LARRY in the target (local) database. Scott's objects are stored in the USERS tablespace; in the target, you will create Larry's objects in the EXAMPLE tablespace. The database link name is NEW_DB.

```
$ impdp schemas=scott network_link=new_db remap_schema=scott:larry ↵
  remap_tablespace=users:example
```

The network mode import is different from using SQL*Net to perform the import: impdp username/password@database.

In the next example, data is read via the database link PROD, and it imports only the data from HR.DEPARTMENTS into schema HR_TEST.DEPARTMENTS. Write a log file to file DEPT_DATA.log.

```
impdp system/password network_link=prod schemas="HR"
    remap_schema="HR:HR_TEST" content=data_only
    include=TABLE:"= 'DEPARTMENTS'"
    logfile= dumplocation:HR_TEST.imp
```

Using Network Mode to Refresh Test Data from Production

Consider that you periodically refresh the Oracle10*g* test database with production data. Since you have to preserve all the grants on the test schema, you can perform the following steps using SQL*Plus and exp/imp tools to perform the data refresh:

1. Disable all the foreign keys.
2. Disable all the primary keys.
3. Drop the indexes so that the import goes faster.
4. Truncate the tables.
5. Export the data from the production database.

6. Import the data to the test database using parameters:

```
COMMIT=Y
BUFFERS=10485760
FROMUSER=SCHEMAPROD
TOUSER=SCHEMATEST
IGNORE=Y
GRANTS=N
```

You can achieve the same results in a single step using impdp with the following parameters (TEST_SCHEMA is the name of database link and must exist):

```
SCHEMAS=SCHEMAPROD
NETWORK_LINK=TEST_SCHEMA
REMAP_SCHEMA=SCHEMAPROD:SCHEMATEST
TABLE_EXISTS_ACTION=REPLACE
EXCLUDE=OBJECT_GRANT
```

Data and Metadata Filters

The Data Pump provides fine-grained object selection to filter the metadata objects during export and import. You can specify the EXCLUDE and INCLUDE parameters with expdp and impdp clients to filter metadata objects. You can use the CONTENT parameter to specify whether you need to export/import just data, just metadata, or both. You can use the QUERY parameter to filter data rows.

The EXCLUDE and INCLUDE parameters are mutually exclusive. Also, when you specify either parameter, you cannot specify CONTENT=DATA_ONLY. The QUERY, EXCLUDE, and INCLUDE parameters have the following syntax:

```
QUERY=[schema.][table_name:]"query clause"
EXCLUDE=object_type[:"object names"]
INCLUDE=object_type[:"object names"]
```

Table 17.4 shows examples of data and metadata filter usage. Though the explanations in the Accomplishes column refer to unloading, it is applicable to loading also.

TABLE 17.4 Data Pump Metadata Filter Examples

Parameter Examples	Accomplishes
schemas=traing content=metadata_only	Unloads the metadata information for all objects owned by the TRAING schema. No data row will be unloaded.

TABLE 17.4 Data Pump Metadata Filter Examples *(continued)*

Parameter Examples	Accomplishes

`content=data_only`
`schemas=traing`
`query=traing.student:"where ee_dept = 'IST'"`
	No metadata will be unloaded; only data rows will be unloaded. All data rows will be unloaded for all tables owned by TRAING, except the STUDENT table, where only the rows that belong to the IST dept is unloaded.

`content=data_only`
`tables=traing.student`
`query="where ee_dept = 'IST'"`
	Only rows in the STUDENT table that belong to the IST department are unloaded.

`schemas=traing`
`exclude=view,package,procedure,function,grant,trigger`
`exclude=index:"like 'S%'"`
	Table rows will be unloaded. Metadata definitions for view, trigger, procedure, function, grants, packages, and indexes that begin with *S* are not unloaded.

`Content=data_only`
`schemas=hr`
`include=table:"in ('EMPLOYEES','DEPARTMENTS')"`
`query="where DEPARTMENT_ID = 10"`
	Only rows belonging to the department 10 are unloaded from the EMPLOYEES and DEPARTMENTS tables.

You can obtain the parameter values for INCLUDE and EXCLUDE by querying the OBJECT_PATH column from the following data dictionary views:

- DATABASE_EXPORT_OBJECTS for full-database export parameters
- SCHEMA_EXPORT_OBJECTS for schema-level export parameters
- TABLE_EXPORT_OBJECTS for table-level export parameters

The following query shows the values that can be used with the INCLUDE/EXCLUDE parameters when performing a schema-level export that is related to packages:

```
SQL> select object_path, comments
     from schema_export_objects
     where object_path like '%PACKAGE%';

OBJECT_PATH        COMMENTS
------------------ ----------------------------------------------
ALTER_PACKAGE_SPEC Recompile package specifications in the selected
                   schemas
PACKAGE            Packages (both specification and body) in sele-
                   cted schemas and their dependent grants and audits
```

```
PACKAGE_BODY        Package bodies in the selected schemas
PACKAGE_SPEC        Package specifications in the selected schemas
… … …
SQL>
```

Data Pump has the ability to monitor the jobs and make adjustments to the jobs. The jobs initiated by impdp and expdp can be monitored and modified by using the same clients. In the next section, I will discuss managing the jobs using expdp and impdp.

Managing Data Pump Jobs

Data Pump clients expdp and impdp provide an interactive command interface. Since each export and import operation has a job name, you can attach to that job from any computer and monitor the job or make adjustments to the job. Table 17.5 lists the parameters that can be used interactively.

TABLE 17.5 Data Pump Interactive Parameters

Parameter	Purpose
ADD_FILE	Adds another file or a file set to the DUMPFILE set.
CONTINUE_CLIENT	Changes mode from interactive client to logging mode.
EXIT_CLIENT	Leaves the client session and discontinues logging but leaves the current job running.
KILL_JOB	Detaches all currently attached client sessions and terminates the job.
PARALLEL	Increases or decreases the number of threads.
START_JOB	Starts (restarts) a job that is not currently running. The SKIP_CURRENT option can be used to skip the recent failed DDL statement that caused the job to stop.
STOP_JOB	Stops the current job; the job can be restarted later.
STATUS	Displays detailed status of the job; the refresh interval can be specified in seconds. The detailed status is displayed to the output screen but not written to the log file.

The data dictionary view DBA_DATAPUMP_JOBS shows the active job information along with its current state, the number of threads, and the number of client sessions attached. You can join this view with DBA_DATAPUMP_SESSIONS to get the SADDR column of the sessions attached and can join the SADDR column with V$SESSION to get more information. The

V$SESSION_LONGOPS view also has an entry showing the progress of the job. Use the SID and SERIAL# columns from V$SESSOIN to query V$SESSION_LONGOPS.

The following example should help you understand the parameters more clearly. Say you have an export dump job to be performed. You start the job with the following parameters in a parameter file:

```
DIRECTORY=DUMPLOCATION
DUMPFILE=volest.dmp
LOGFILE=volest.exp.log
SCHEMAS=volest
JOB_NAME=VOLEST_EXP_TEST
```

A table with name VOLEST_EXP_TEST is created in your schema. This is the master control table. Querying the DBA_DATAPUMP_JOBS view will show the status of the jobs running:

```
SQL> SELECT job_name, state
  2  FROM dba_datapump_jobs;

JOB_NAME                       STATE
------------------------------ ----------------
VOLEST_EXP_TEST                EXECUTING

SQL>
```

By pressing Ctrl+C, you can stop the logging screen, and you can enter interactive mode. If you find that the job is halfway through and is consuming resources on the server, you can suspend the job and restart it later when the server is less busy:

```
Export> stop_job
Are you sure you wish to stop this job ([y]/n): y
oracle@linux>
```

Let's say you went home and logged back in to your company network. From home, you see the status of the job; the job is in suspended mode. Now, you may use more processing power available in the server to resume the job, so the first step is to attach to the job:

```
oracle@linux:> expdp bill/billthedba attach=VOLEST_EXP_TEST

Export: Release 11.1.0.6.0 - Production on Saturday, 15 November, 2008
23:33:18
Copyright (c) 2003, 2007, Oracle.  All rights reserved.
Connected to: Oracle Database 11g Enterprise Edition Release 11.1.0.6.0 -
Production
With the Partitioning, OLAP, Data Mining and Real Application Testing options
```

```
Job: VOLEST_EXP_TEST
  Owner: BILL
  Operation: EXPORT
  Creator Privs: FALSE
  GUID: D8C25554B641EF14E030007F0200562C
  Start Time: Friday, 23 April, 2004 15:16
  Mode: SCHEMA
  Instance: BT10GNF1
  Max Parallelism: 1
  EXPORT Job Parameters:
  Parameter Name      Parameter Value:
     CLIENT_COMMAND        bill/******** parfile=volest.par
     DATA_ACCESS_METHOD    AUTOMATIC
     ESTIMATE              BLOCKS
     INCLUDE_METADATA      1
     LOG_FILE_DIRECTORY    DUMPLOCATION
     LOG_FILE_NAME         volest.exp.log
     TABLE_CONSISTENCY     0
     USER_METADATA         1
  State: IDLING
  Bytes Processed: 730,622,512
  Percent Done: 69
  Current Parallelism: 1
  Job Error Count: 0
  Dump File: /oradata/dumpfiles/volest.dmp
    bytes written: 733,958,144

Worker 1 Status:
  State: UNDEFINED

Export> parallel=4

Export> status=60

Job: VOLEST_EXP_TEST
  Operation: EXPORT
  Mode: SCHEMA
  State: IDLING
  Bytes Processed: 730,622,512
```

```
  Percent Done: 69
  Current Parallelism: 4
  Job Error Count: 0
  Dump File: /oradata/dumpfiles/volest.dmp
    bytes written: 733,958,144

Worker 1 Status:
  State: UNDEFINED

Export> start_job

Export> continue_client
```

After attaching to the job, you increased the threads to 4 from 1 (`parallel=4`), set up to display detailed status to the screen every minute (`status=60`), restarted the job (`start_job`), and let the output display on the screen (`continue_client`).

Multiple clients (sessions) can attach to a job.

You can use Enterprise Manager Grid Control or Database Control to perform the Data Pump export and import. You can also do the job monitoring using OEM. The next section discusses using the Data Pump Wizard in EM.

Real World Scenario

Using Fine-Grained Object Selection

The fine-grained object selection in Data Pump export came as a real boon for DBAs. As DBAs, we perform daily exports on the OLTP database excluding certain large (maybe I should say "huge") tables. This particular database includes tables that are DSS in nature in addition to the OLTP tables. In Oracle8*i* and Oracle9*i*, I had to re-create one of the dictionary views to exclude certain multimillion-row transaction tables. I'm not listing the view name here because changing SYS-owned data dictionary views isn't supported.

In Oracle 10*g* and Oracle 11*g*, you do not have to mess with the dictionary views anymore to perform a selective export excluding certain objects. After upgrading the database, I did a tablespace reorganization to better group the tables. I organized the tables into multiple tablespaces based on the expected size of the tables. The tablespaces have a naming convention of %LARGE, %MED, and %SMALL.

While performing the daily export dump using expdp, you simply use `EXCLUDE=TABLESPACE:"like '%LARGE'"`, which excludes all the objects created in the %LARGE tablespaces.

Using the Data Pump Wizard

You can use EM Database Control as a menu-driven interface to Data Pump export jobs. This program steps you through several options and then shows you the PL/SQL code that it will execute. Therefore, you can also use EM Database Control to learn more about using the PL/SQL interface. From the Database Control home page, click the Data Movement tab. Under Move Row Data, you will see links related to Data Pump operations:

- Export to Export Files
- Import from Export Files
- Import from Database
- Monitor Export and Import Jobs

Figure 17.3 shows the Data Movement tab in EM Database Control.

FIGURE 17.3 Data Movement tab in EM

Click the Export to Export Files link to start a Data Pump export job. The export and import both support database, schema, table, and tablespace modes. On the first screen, you choose the mode of export. The screen shown on Figure 17.4 appears when you choose the Database export mode. Here you have the option to estimate the disk space required for the dump file as well as the number of threads (PARALLEL) required.

You can expand the Show Advanced Options link to specify whether you want data-only export or metadata-only export, to include or exclude objects, to export a consistent view of data as of a timestamp or SCN, and to filter rows using a query. On the next two screens, you can specify the location of the dump file and job schedule. You have the option to run the job immediately, to run the job at a later time, or to repeatedly run the job. The final screen shows a review of the Data Pump export, as shown in Figure 17.5. Click Submit Job to start the Data Pump export.

FIGURE 17.4 Data Pump Export: Options screen in EM

Oracle Enterprise Manager (SYSTEM) - Export: Options - Mozilla Firefox
File Edit View Go Bookmarks Tools Help
Database Control
Database
Options Files Schedule Review
Export: Options
Database 11GR11
Cancel Finish Step 1 of 4 Next
Maximum Number of Threads in Export Job 1
This option allows you to make tradeoffs between resource consumption and elapsed time. Parallelism is only available in Enterprise Edition.
Estimate Disk Space
Calculates an estimate of how much disk space the export job will consume (in bytes). The estimate is for table row data only and does not include metadata.
Blocks
Estimate will be calculated by multiplying the number of database blocks used by the target objects times the appropriate block sizes. This method will provide the quickest rough estimate.
Statistics
Estimate will be calculated using per-table statistics. This method will provide the most accuracy if all target tables have been recently analyzed.
Estimate Disk Space Now
Calculate the estimate of space that will be consumed without actually performing the export operation. This may take a few minutes.
Optional File
Generate Log File
Directory Object AUDIT_DIR Create Directory Object
Log File EXPDAT.LOG
Show Advanced Options
Cancel Finish Step 1 of 4 Next
https://localhost.localdomain:5500/em/console/database/home
localhost.localdomain:5500

FIGURE 17.5 Data Pump Export: Review screen in EM

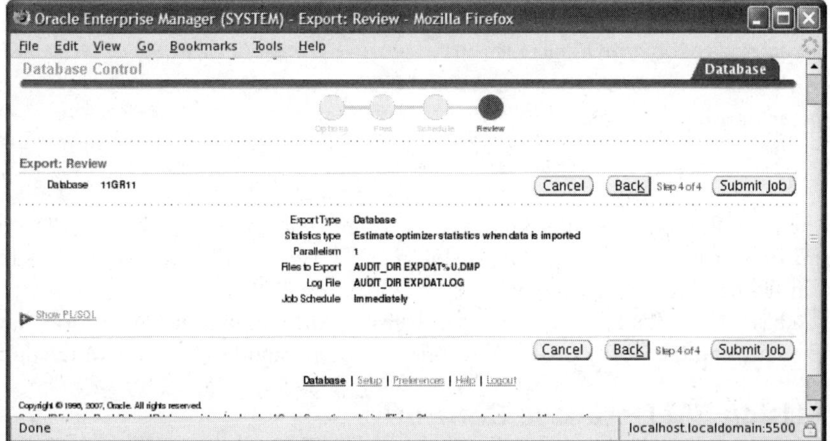

Click the Show PL/SQL link to see the PL/SQL code behind the export job. You can run this code using SQL*Plus to perform the export job. Here is an example:

```
declare
  h1   NUMBER;
begin
  h1 := dbms_datapump.open (
        operation => 'EXPORT',
        job_mode => 'FULL',
        job_name => 'EXPORT000041',
        version => 'COMPATIBLE');
  dbms_datapump.set_parallel(handle => h1, degree => 1);
  dbms_datapump.add_file(handle => h1,
        filename => 'EXPDAT.LOG',
        directory => 'AUDIT_DIR', filetype => 3);
  dbms_datapump.set_parameter(handle => h1,
        name => 'KEEP_MASTER', value => 0);
  dbms_datapump.add_file(handle => h1,
        filename => 'EXPDAT%U.DMP',
        directory => 'AUDIT_DIR', filetype => 1);
  dbms_datapump.set_parameter(handle => h1,
        name => 'INCLUDE_METADATA', value => 1);
  dbms_datapump.set_parameter(handle => h1,
        name => 'DATA_ACCESS_METHOD', value => 'AUTOMATIC');
  dbms_datapump.set_parameter(handle => h1,
        name => 'ESTIMATE', value => 'BLOCKS');
  dbms_datapump.start_job(handle => h1,
        skip_current => 0, abort_step => 0);
  dbms_datapump.detach(handle => h1);
end;
/
```

Once the Data Pump job is submitted, you can view its progress by clicking the Monitor Export and Import Jobs link on the Data Movement screen. A summary of the job appears, as shown in Figure 17.6.

Here you have the option to increase the parallelism of the job; use the Change Job State button to stop or suspend the job. You also have option to specify another location for the dump file.

Import Using EM Database Control

Click the Import from Export Files link on the Data Movement screen to invoke the Data Pump Import Wizard. Similar to export, import also has four modes: database, schema, table, and tablespace. After you choose the type of import, the next screen lets you choose the dump file to import from. On the next screen, you have the option to remap the schema and tablespace. On the import schema screen shown in Figure 17.7, HR schema objects are imported to the JAMES schema, and the objects in the EXAMPLE tablespace are moved to the USERS tablespace.

FIGURE 17.6 Data Pump export job run status

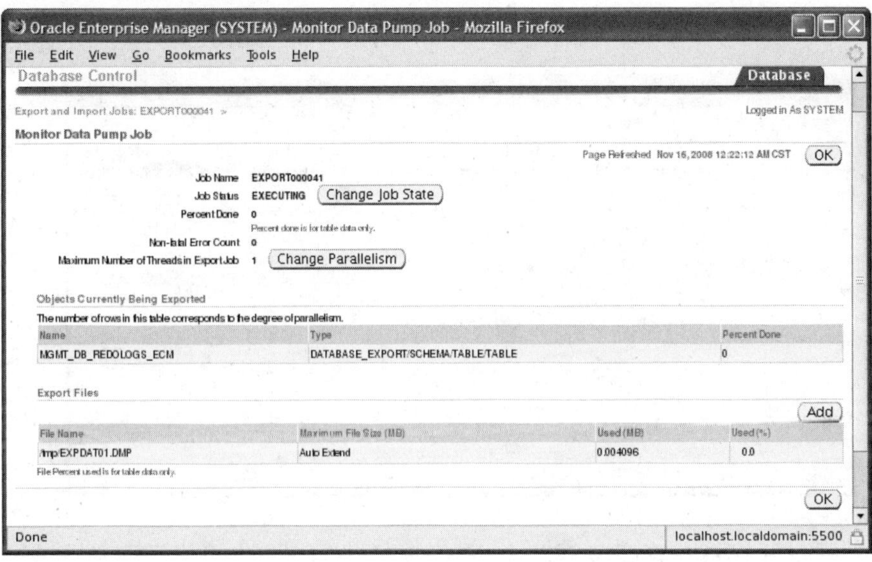

FIGURE 17.7 Data Pump Import: Re-mapping screen

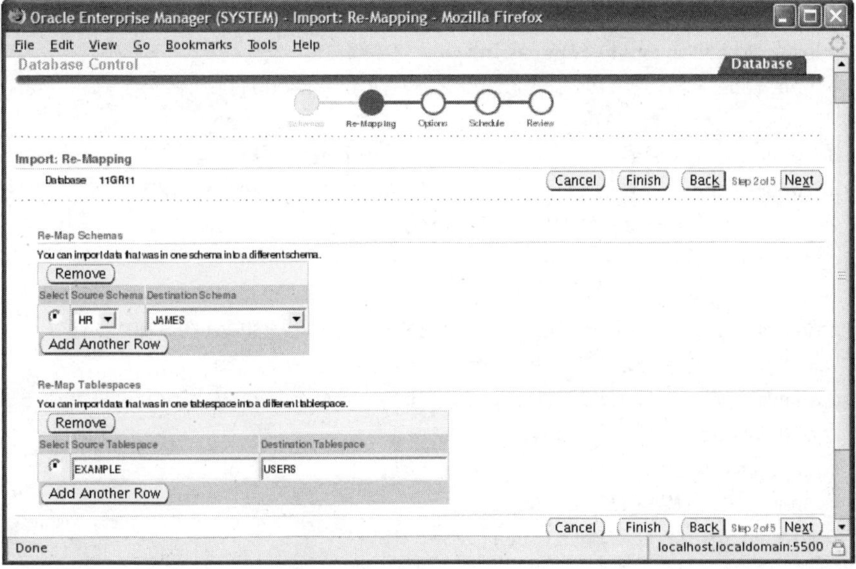

On the next screen, you can specify the number of parallel processes and the log-file destination directory. Similar to export, you can specify to run the job immediately or at a later time. By clicking the Submit Job button on the Review screen, as shown in Figure 17.8, you submit the import job.

FIGURE 17.8 Data Pump Import: Review screen

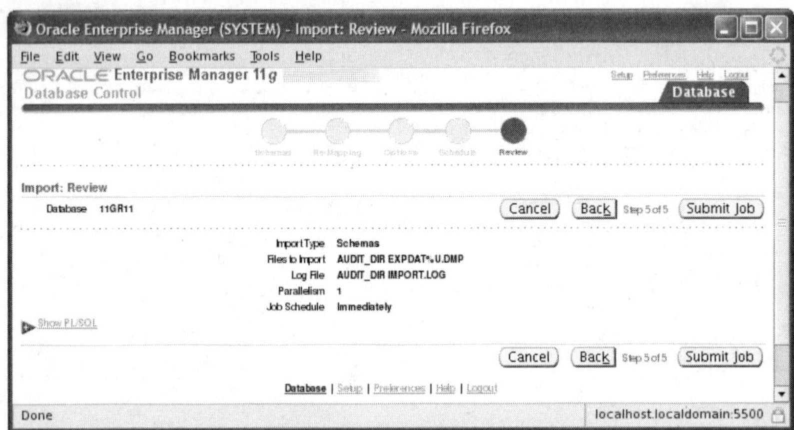

Similar to export, clicking the Show PL/SQL link shows the PL/SQL code behind the import:

```
declare
  h1   NUMBER;
begin
  h1 := dbms_datapump.open (operation => 'IMPORT',
         job_mode => 'SCHEMA', job_name => 'IMPORT000043',
         version => 'COMPATIBLE');
  dbms_datapump.set_parallel(handle => h1, degree => 1);
  dbms_datapump.add_file(handle => h1, filename => 'IMPORT.LOG',
         directory => 'AUDIT_DIR', filetype => 3);
  dbms_datapump.set_parameter(handle => h1,
         name => 'KEEP_MASTER', value => 0);
  dbms_datapump.add_file(handle => h1, filename => 'EXPDAT%U.DMP',
         directory => 'AUDIT_DIR', filetype => 1);
  dbms_datapump.metadata_remap(handle => h1, name => 'REMAP_SCHEMA',
         old_value => 'HR', value => 'JAMES');
  dbms_datapump.metadata_remap(handle => h1,
         name => 'REMAP_TABLESPACE',
         old_value => 'EXAMPLE', value => 'USERS');
```

```
  dbms_datapump.metadata_filter(handle => h1,
        name => 'SCHEMA_EXPR', value => 'IN(''HR'')');
  dbms_datapump.set_parameter(handle => h1,
       name => 'INCLUDE_METADATA', value => 1);
  dbms_datapump.set_parameter(handle => h1,
       name => 'DATA_ACCESS_METHOD', value => 'AUTOMATIC');
  dbms_datapump.set_parameter(handle => h1,
       name => 'SKIP_UNUSABLE_INDEXES', value => 0);
  dbms_datapump.start_job(handle => h1, skip_current => 0,
       abort_step => 0);
  dbms_datapump.detach(handle => h1);
end;
/
```

Loading Data with SQL*Loader

SQL*Loader is a program that reads data files in many possible formats, parses the data (breaks it into meaningful pieces), and loads the data into database tables. Like Data Pump, myriad options are available and a hefty book could be devoted to its use. The Oracle Database Utilities manual devotes several hundred pages of reference material to SQL*Loader alone. This section will not be so comprehensive or attempt to cram all possible uses of SQL*Loader into a few short pages. Instead, I will cover the basics and teach you what is necessary for the exam.

SQL*Loader uses the following file types:

Log This is a mandatory file. If you do not specify a log file, SQL*Loader will try to create one in the current directory with the name of your control file and a `.log` filename extension. If SQL*Loader cannot create the log file, execution is aborted. The log file contains a summary of the SQL*Loader session, including any errors that were generated.

Control This is a mandatory file. This file tells SQL*Loader where the other files are, how to parse and load the data, and which tables to load the data into, and this file can contain the data as well.

Data Data files are optional and, if included, hold the data that SQL*Loader reads and loads into the database. The data can be located in the control file, so these files are optional.

Bad This holds the "bad" data records—those that did not pass validation by either SQL*Loader or the database. Bad files are created only if one or more records fail validation. Just as with the log file, if you do not specify a bad file, the database will create one, with the name of your control file and a `.bad` filename extension.

Discard This holds data records that did not get loaded because they did not satisfy the record-selection criteria in the control file. Discard files are created only if data records were discarded because they did not satisfy the selection criteria.

SQL*Loader provides a robust toolkit to build data-loading programs for your Oracle 11*g* database. It can operate either on the database server or on a client machine.

The following section will show you how to employ SQL*Loader to load data into your database tables.

Specifying SQL*Loader Command-Line Parameters

To invoke the SQL*Loader program, use the command `sqlldr` followed by one or more command-line parameters. These parameters can be identified positionally on the command line or with a *keyword=value* pair. You can mix positional and keyword notation provided that all the keyword-notation parameters appear after all the positional parameters.

For example, to invoke SQL*Loader, telling it to use the connect string `system/password` and use the control file `regions.ctl`, you can execute any of the following command lines:

```
sqlldr system/password regions.ctl
sqlldr control=regions.ctl userid=system/password
sqlldr system/password control=regions.ctl
```

The command-line parameters include those shown here, by executing the `sqlldr` command with no parameters:

```
$ sqlldr


SQL*Loader: Release 11.1.0.6.0 - Production on Sun Nov 16 00:46:00 2008
Copyright (c) 1982, 2007, Oracle.  All rights reserved.
Usage: SQLLDR keyword=value [,keyword=value,...]

Valid Keywords:
    userid -- ORACLE username/password
   control -- control file name
       log -- log file name
       bad -- bad file name
      data -- data file name
   discard -- discard file name
discardmax -- number of discards to allow          (Default all)
      skip -- number of logical records to skip    (Default 0)
      load -- number of logical records to load    (Default all)
    errors -- number of errors to allow            (Default 50)
```

```
      rows -- number of rows in conventional path bind array
              or between direct path data saves
               (Default: Conventional path 64, Direct path all)
  bindsize -- size of conventional path bind array in bytes  (Default 256000)
    silent -- suppress messages during run
              (header,feedback,errors,discards,partitions)
    direct -- use direct path                      (Default FALSE)
   parfile -- parameter file: name of file that contains
              parameter specifications
  parallel -- do parallel load                     (Default FALSE)
      file -- file to allocate extents from
skip_unusable_indexes -- disallow/allow unusable indexes or
                         index partitions  (Default FALSE)
skip_index_maintenance -- do not maintain indexes, mark affected
                          indexes as unusable  (Default FALSE)
commit_discontinued -- commit loaded rows when load
                       is discontinued  (Default FALSE)
readsize -- size of read buffer                  (Default 1048576)
external_table -- use external table for load;
                  NOT_USED, GENERATE_ONLY, EXECUTE  (Default NOT_USED)
columnarrayrows -- number of rows for direct path column array  (Default 5000)
streamsize -- size of direct path stream buffer in bytes  (Default 256000)
multithreading -- use multithreading in direct path
resumable -- enable or disable resumable for current session  (Default FALSE)
resumable_name -- text string to help identify resumable statement
resumable_timeout -- wait time (in seconds) for RESUMABLE  (Default 7200)
date_cache -- size (in entries) of date conversion cache  (Default 1000)

PLEASE NOTE: Command-line parameters may be specified either by
position or by keywords.  An example of the former case is 'sqlldr
scott/tiger foo'; an example of the latter is 'sqlldr control=foo
userid=scott/tiger'.  One may specify parameters by position before
but not after parameters specified by keywords.  For example,
'sqlldr scott/tiger control=foo logfile=log' is allowed, but
'sqlldr scott/tiger control=foo log' is not, even though the
position of the parameter 'log' is correct.
$
```

Many of the command-line parameters can also appear in the control file. When they appear as both command-line parameters and in the control file, the command-line options take precedence.

Specifying Control File Options

The control file contains commands to tell SQL*Loader where to find the data, how to parse it, how to load it, what to do when errors occur, and what to do with records that fail validation. A control file has two or three main sections. The first contains session-wide information, such as log filename, bind size, and whether direct or conventional path loading will be used. The second section contains one or more `INTO TABLE` blocks. These blocks specify the target tables and columns. The third section, if present, is the actual data. Comments can appear anywhere in the control files (except in the data lines) and should be used liberally. The control file language can be somewhat cryptic, so generous use of comments is encouraged. Comments in a control file start with a double dash and end with a new line. The control file must begin with the line `LOAD DATA` or `CONTINUE LOAD DATA` and also have an `INTO TABLE` clause, together with directions on how to parse the data and load it into which columns.

The best way to learn how to construct a control file is to look at examples and then use variations of them to build your control file. This section gives you several examples but is certainly not a comprehensive sampling. Again, the intent is to present you with enough information to get you going.

For a comprehensive reference, see the Oracle manual "Oracle Database Utilities 11*g* Release 1."

The first example is rather simple and straightforward. The control file contains both control file commands and the data. The command line is as follows:

```
sqlldr hr/hr control=regions.ctl
```

The control file `regions.ctl` contains the following:

```
LOAD DATA
-- Control file begins with LOAD DATA
INFILE *
-- The * tells SQL*Loader the data is inline
INTO TABLE regions TRUNCATE
-- truncate the target table before loading
FIELDS TERMINATED BY ',' OPTIONALLY ENCLOSED BY '"'
-- how to parse the data
 (region_id, region_name)
-- positional mapping of data file fields to table columns
-- lines following BEGINDATA are loaded
-- no comments are allowed after BEGINDATA
BEGINDATA
1,"Europe"
2,"Americas"
3,"Asia"
4,"Middle East and Africa"
```

The LOAD DATA command tells SQL*Loader that you are beginning a new data load. If you are continuing a data load that was interrupted, specify CONTINUE LOAD DATA. The command INFILE * tells SQL*Loader that the data will appear in the control file. The table REGIONS is loaded. The keyword TRUNCATE tells SQL*Loader to truncate the table before loading it. Instead of TRUNCATE, you can specify INSERT (the default), which requires the table to be empty at the start of the load. APPEND tells SQL*Loader to add the data to any existing data in the table. REPLACE tells SQL*Loader to issue a DELETE to empty out the table before loading. DELETE differs from a TRUNCATE; for DELETE the DML triggers fire and DELETE can be rolled back.

The lines in the control file that follow the BEGINDATA contain the data to parse and load. The parsing specification tells SQL*Loader that the data fields are comma-delimited and that text data can be enclosed by double quotation marks. These double quotation marks should not be loaded as part of the data. The list of columns enclosed in parentheses are the table columns that will be loaded with the data fields.

In the second example, the same data is loaded into the same table, but it is located in a stand-alone file called regions.dat and is in the following pipe-delimited, fixed format:

```
1|Europe                |
2|Americas              |
3|Asia                  |
4|Middle East and Africa |
```

The command line is as follows:

```
sqlldr hr/hr control=regions.ctl
```

The content of the control file is as follows:

```
LOAD DATA
INFILE  '/apps/seed_data/regions.dat'
BADFILE '/apps/seed_data/regions.bad'
DISCARDFILE '/apps/seed_data/regions.dsc'
OPTIONS (DIRECT=TRUE)
-- data file spec
INTO TABLE regions APPEND
-- add this data to the existing target table
(region_id   POSITION(1)    INTEGER EXTERNAL
,region_name POSITION(3:25) NULLIF region_name = BLANKS
) -- how to parse the data
```

The control file tells SQL*Loader where to find the data file (INFILE) as well as the bad and discard files (BADFILE and DISCARDFILE). The OPTIONS line specifies direct path loading. With fixed-format data, the column specification identifies the starting and ending positions. A numeric datatype can be identified as INTEGER EXTERNAL. The directive

`NULLIF region_name = BLANKS` tells SQL*Loader to set the `region_name` column to `NULL` if the data field contains only white space.

You shouldn't have to know the minutiae of how to tell SQL*Loader precisely how to parse data—the options are far too arcane to expect you to recite them off the top of your head for an exam—but knowing the SQL*Loader capabilities of reading fixed-format and variable-format data is essential. More important to your job is knowing about direct path loads and unusable indexes, which are discussed in the next section.

Using Direct Path Loading

Direct path loading is a SQL*Loader option that allows you, under certain conditions, to use the direct path interface to load data into a table. The direct path interface can be significantly faster than conventional path loading. With conventional loading, SQL*Loader loads data into a bind array and passes it to the database engine to process with an `INSERT` statement. Full undo and redo mechanisms operate on conventional path loads. Direct path loading is enabled by specifying the `DIRECT=Y` parameter.

With direct path loading, SQL*Loader reads data, passing it to the database via the direct path API. The API formats it directly into Oracle data blocks in memory and then flushes these blocks, en masse, directly to the data files using multiblock I/O, bypassing the buffer cache, as well as redo and undo mechanisms. Direct path loads always write to a table above the high-water mark; thus, always increase the number of data blocks that a table is actually using.

The important thing to remember about direct path load is that it is fast but has restrictions, including the following:

- Indexes are rebuilt at the end of a direct path load. If unique constraint violations are found, the unique index is left in an unusable state. To correct the index, you must find and remove the constraint violations and then rebuild the index.

Unusable indexes are a possible result of direct path loading. Make sure you know what causes an unusable index and how to fix it.

- Direct path load cannot occur if there are active transactions against the table being loaded.
- Triggers do not fire during direct path loads.
- Direct path loading into clustered tables is not supported.
- During direct path loads, foreign key constraints are disabled at the beginning of the load and then reenabled after the load.

- Only primary key, unique, and `NOT NULL` constraints are enforced.
- Direct path load prevents other users from making changes to the table while the direct load operation is in progress.

Using EM to Load Data

You can invoke the SQL*Loader API from EM Database Control using the Load Data from User Files link on the Data Movement screen (shown earlier in Figure 17.3). You have the option to generate a control file using the wizard or to use an existing control file. The EM Wizard uses seven screens to collect information to build a control file.

Figure 17.9 shows the first screen, where you specify the file locations. You can specify the location on the database server (using directory objects) or on the local machine.

FIGURE 17.9 SQL*Loader data file location

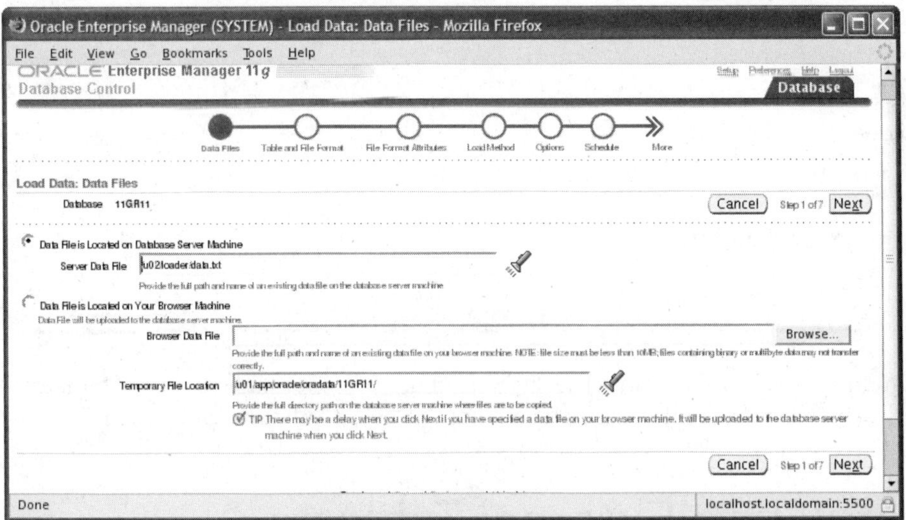

On the next screen, you specify the table to load data into as well as the file format. A sample of the data file appears for you to preview. On the File Format Attributes screen, you can specify the delimiter used to separate columns and have the option to verify the column mappings. On the next screen (Load Method), you specify whether you want to use conventional load or direct load. You can also choose Parallel Direct Load, which is the fastest of all loading options.

Figure 17.10 shows the loading options. Here you can specify the discard file, bad file, and log file. You can also specify a variety of other options.

FIGURE 17.10 SQL*Loader options

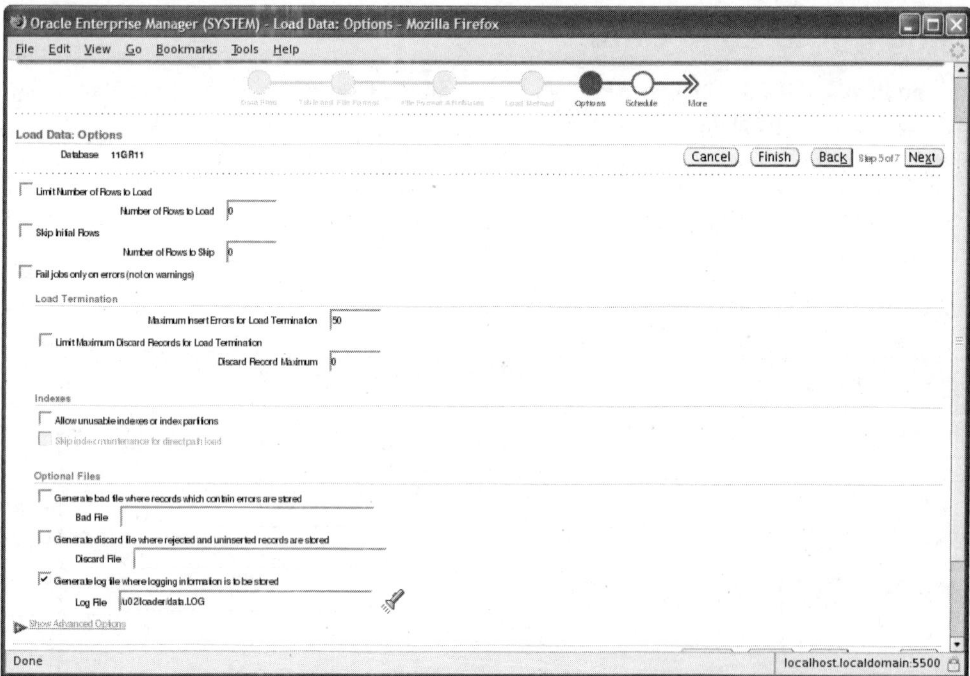

On the next screen, you can schedule the load operation for immediately or for later. Finally, you'll have a chance to review your options before submitting the load job.

Populating External Tables

External tables were introduced in Oracle9*i* and were read-only from the Oracle Database. In Oracle 10*g*, external tables were made writable. In Oracle9*i*, ORACLE_LOADER was the only access driver available for external tables; Oracle 10*g* introduced the ORACLE_DATAPUMP access driver. The external tables that use the ORACLE_LOADER access driver are read-only—they read ASCII flat files from the OS. Only the external tables created with the ORACLE_DATAPUMP access driver can be written to. The resulting file is in proprietary format (Oracle native external representation, DPAPI), which only Data Pump can read. You can use this file to load to another Oracle Database.

You may ask how is this beneficial—why don't you use the Oracle Data Pump clients to generate the file? Well, though Oracle Data Pump can handle a certain level of filtering, join operations with another table are not possible. Using the external table ORACLE_DATAPUMP access driver, you can unload data that is derived from complex queries. This is useful in loading data marts from data warehouse or similar applications. Data from external tables can be used in SQL queries.

In the following sections, you will learn how to populate an external table using the ORACLE_DATAPUMP and ORACLE_LOADER DPAPI.

Loading External Tables Using Data Pump

You use the ORACLE_DATAPUMP access driver to unload data from an Oracle Database to a flat file (DPAPI format) using the external table method. The external table must be created using the CREATE TABLE...AS SELECT... (CTAS) method. You can specify the PARALLEL clause when creating the table; the ORACLE_DATAPUMP access driver unloads data into multiple flat files at the same time. One parallel execution server will write to only one file at a time. Unloading data in the context of an external table means creating an external table using the CTAS method.

During the unload (or populate) operation, the data goes from the subquery to the SQL engine for the data to be processed and is extracted in the DPAPI format to write to the flat file. The external table to unload data can be created only using the CTAS method with the ORACLE_DATAPUMP access driver. The unload operation does not include the metadata for the tables. You can use the VERSION clause when unloading the data to make sure it loads correctly on the target database.

I'll now demonstrate how to unload data using the ORACLE_DATAPUMP access driver. You will join the EMPLOYEES and DEPARTMENTS tables of the HR schema to unload data. The following statement creates the table in the database as well as creates two files, empl_comm1.dmp and empl_comm2.dmp, in the OS:

```
SQL> CREATE TABLE empl_commission
     ORGANIZATION EXTERNAL (TYPE ORACLE_DATAPUMP
     DEFAULT DIRECTORY work_dir
     LOCATION ('empl_comm1.dmp','empl_comm2.dmp'))
     PARALLEL 2
     AS
     SELECT employee_id,
            first_name || ' ' || last_name employee_name,
            department_name,
            TO_CHAR(hire_date,'DD-MM-YYYY') hire_date,
            salary * NVL(commission_pct, 0.5) commission
     FROM hr.employees JOIN hr.departments USING (department_id)
     ORDER BY first_name || ' ' || last_name
SQL> /

Table created.
```

```
SQL> SELECT department_name, sum(commission) total_comm
  2  FROM   empl_commission
  3  GROUP BY department_name;

DEPARTMENT_NAME                TOTAL_COMM
------------------------------ ----------
Accounting                          10150
Finance                             25800
Human Resources                      3250
Marketing                            9500
Purchasing                          12450
Sales                               72640
Shipping                            78200
Administration                       2200
Executive                           29000
IT                                  14400
Public Relations                     5000

11 rows selected.

SQL>
```

ORGANIZATION EXTERNAL specifies that the resulting table is an external table. TYPE ORACLE_DATAPUMP specifies that the Data Pump access driver should be used. DEFAULT DIRECTORY specifies the location of the dump files. The LOCATION parameter specifies the filenames. Most often when external tables are used, a very large amount of data is unloaded; hence, using the PARALLEL clause will speed up the operation. If the parallel clause is used, the number of files specified in the LOCATION clause must match the PARALLEL degree. If you did not specify enough files to match the degree of parallelism, Oracle decreases the parallelism to match the number of files provided.

The files created using the ORACLE_DATAPUMP access driver can be read-only by Oracle 11*g* because the data is unloaded in a proprietary format. You can use this method to move data from one database to another.

You can copy the dump files to another Oracle 10*g* or 11*g* database and load it using the Data Pump utility, or you can create an external table on these dump files and load from it. Let's create an external table using these dump files and query it:

```
SQL> CREATE TABLE new_empl_commission (
  2  employee_id  NUMBER (6),
  3  employee_name VARCHAR2 (40),
  4  department_name VARCHAR2 (30),
  5  hire_date VARCHAR2 (10),
```

```
  6  commission NUMBER)
  7  ORGANIZATION EXTERNAL (TYPE ORACLE_DATAPUMP
  8  DEFAULT DIRECTORY work_dir
  9  ACCESS PARAMETERS (
 10  LOGFILE 'new_empl_commission.log')
 11  LOCATION ('empl_comm1.dmp', 'expl_comm2.dmp'));

Table created.
```

The data dictionary views DBA_EXTERNAL_TABLES and DBA_EXTERNAL_LOCATIONS can be queried to view the characteristics, location, and filenames of external tables.

Loading External Tables Using Loader

You use the ORACLE_LOADER access driver to load data to an Oracle database from a flat file using the external table method. You can specify the PARALLEL clause when creating the table; the ORACLE_LOADER access driver divides the large flat file into chunks that can be processed separately. Loading data in the context of external table means reading data from the external table (flat file) and loading to a table in the database using the INSERT statement.

Let's create an external table using the ORACLE_LOADER access driver; say the user already has privilege to read from and write to the directory WORK_DIR. The source data file is employee.dat, which has fixed column data (name, title, and salary). The following code shows the contents of the employee.dat file, creates the external table using the ORACLE_LOADER driver, and queries the external table. You can use the data from this external table to load other tables using INSERT statements.

```
linux:oracle>cat employee.dat
SMITH   CLERK    800
SCOTT   ANALYST  3000
ADAMS   CLERK    1100
MILLER  CLERK    1300
linux:oracle>
SQL> CREATE TABLE employees (
  2  ename  VARCHAR2 (10),
  3  title  VARCHAR2 (10),
  4  salary NUMBER (8))
  5  ORGANIZATION EXTERNAL (
  6  TYPE ORACLE_LOADER
```

```
DEFAULT DIRECTORY WORK_DIR
ACCESS PARAMETERS (RECORDS DELIMITED BY NEWLINE FIELDS (
ename CHAR(10),
title CHAR(10),
salary CHAR(8)))
LOCATION ('employee.dat'))
PARALLEL
SQL> /

Table created.

SQL> SELECT * FROM employees;

ENAME      TITLE          SALARY
---------- ---------- ----------
SMITH      CLERK             800
SCOTT      ANALYST          3000
ADAMS      CLERK            1100
MILLER     CLERK            1300

SQL>
```

Only SELECT statements are allowed on external tables; no INSERT, UPDATE, or DELETE operation is permitted on external tables.

You have learned to move data to and from a database using various tools. Next, you will learn the infrastructure enhancements available in Enterprise Manager to contact Oracle Support and to manage patches.

Using EM Support Workbench

Oracle 11*g* comes with an advanced fault diagnostic infrastructure framework for detecting, diagnosing and resolving database problems. The problems that are targeted are critical errors that affect the health of the database (such as ORA-600, ORA-7445, and so on).

When a critical error occurs in the database, Oracle flags them as incidents and assigns an incident number. All the diagnostic data such as trace files, alert log information, and dumps related to the error are captured and tagged with the incident number. This data is then stored in the Automatic Diagnostic Repository, where it can be retrieved using the ADRCI utility or using EM Database Control.

The EM Database Control feature that enables you to interact with the fault diagnostic infrastructure of the database is called EM Support Workbench. With Support Workbench, you can investigate, report, diagnose, and repair the problem. In the following sections, you will learn how the Support Workbench works by going through the phases of a problem.

Identifying a Problem

The Health Check framework of Oracle 11*g* performs proactive checks on the database periodically. Upon detecting a critical error, the fault diagnostic infrastructure runs a few more checks to analyze the critical error. These errors are then tagged as incidents and reported. You can view active incident counts on the Database Control home page, as shown in Figure 17.11.

FIGURE 17.11 Database Control home page showing active incidents and alerts

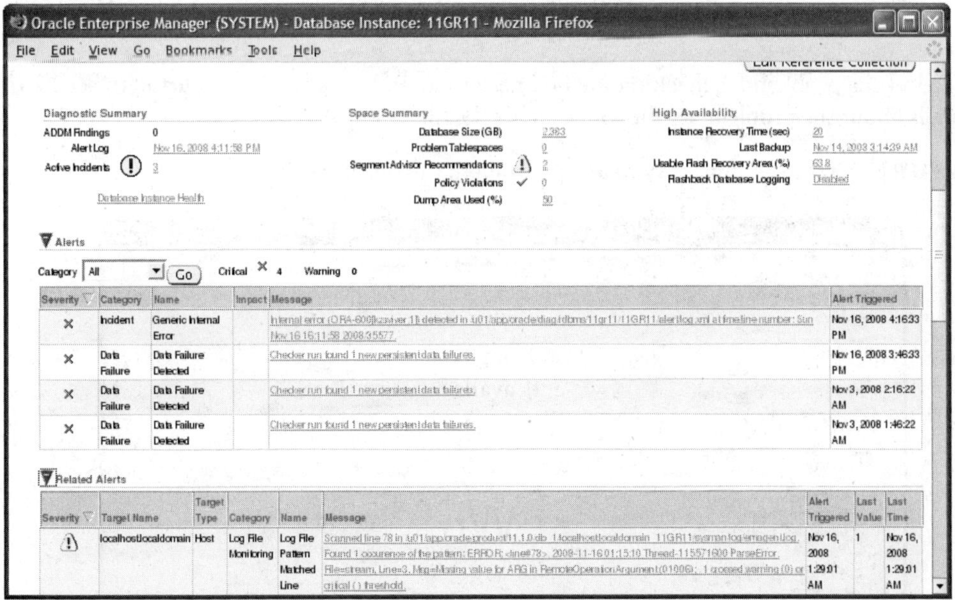

By clicking the Active Incidents count, you will be taken to the Support Workbench home page. You can also invoke the Support Workbench using the Software and Support page in Database Control. The Support Workbench groups similar incidents together and calls it a *problem*. As you can see in Figure 17.12, there are three incidents of the ORA-600 error, and they are grouped together as one problem.

FIGURE 17.12 Support Workbench Problems screen

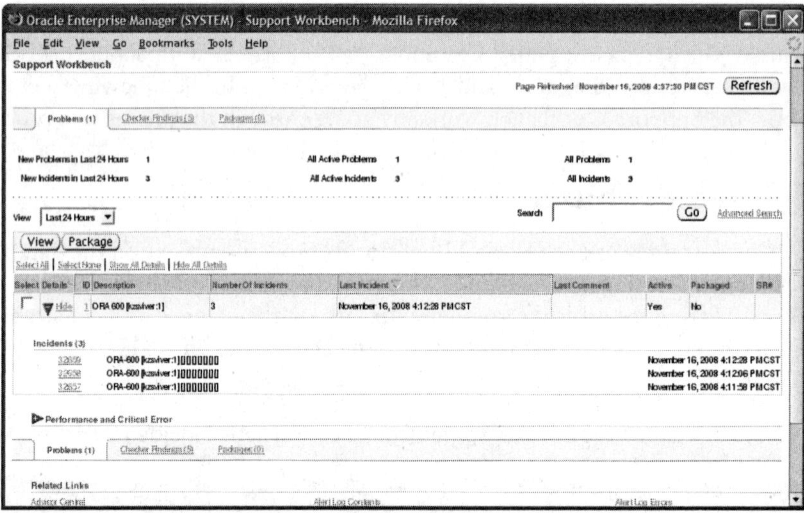

Select the problem by checking the box next to it, and click the View button to see more details about the problem, as shown in Figure 17.13.

FIGURE 17.13 Support Workbench Problem Details screen

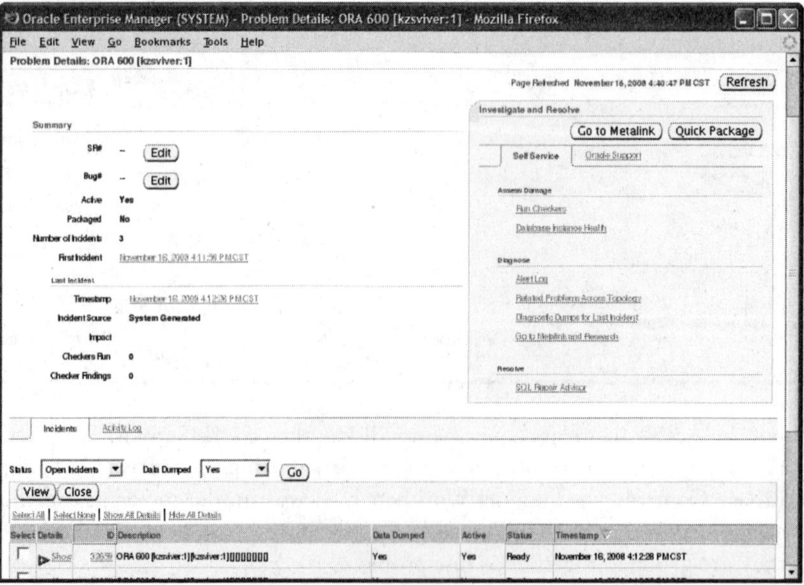

In the next section, you will learn how to gather more information about the problem.

Gathering Additional Diagnostic Information

On the Problem Details screen, under the Investigate and Resolve section, you have various options. On the Self Service tab, you have links available to gather more information about the problem. If you prefer self-service, you can run more checks on the database, diagnose the current problem, or resolve the issue by running the SQL Repair Advisor (if the error is caused by a SQL Statement). The following are your options on the Self Service tab:

- Assess Damage
  - Run Checkers: Run the database health check again to find more issues.
  - Database Instance Health: Show the database health screen, which shows the number of incidents and problems by hour for the last 24 hours.
- Diagnose
  - Alert Log: Shows the alert log entries related to the incident.
  - Related Problems Across Topology: Shows any other incidents that may be related to the current problem.
  - Diagnostic Dumps for Last Incident: Shows the dump and trace files associated with the incident.
  - Go to Metalink and Research: Metalink is Oracle's support site, where you can search and find solutions to the issue.
- Resolve:
  - SQL Repair Advisor: Since the problem is caused by a SQL statement, you can run the SQL Repair Advisor to fix the SQL issue.

You can use the tools under Diagnose to gather more information about the incident and problem. If you have identified the SQL causing the problem and you find an issue with the SQL, you can resolve the problem by yourself. You may also get an answer by searching Oracle's support website, Metalink. Contacting Metalink is discussed later in the chapter.

After self-service, if you could not resolve the problem or could not find more information about the problem of symptoms, you can contact Oracle Support. EM Support Workbench makes contacting Oracle Support easy without having to remember the URL or phone number and gathers all the information that would be of help to the support analyst. Let's go through the next steps of Support Workbench to contact Oracle Support for a resolution to the example problem.

Creating a Service Request

If you cannot identify or resolve the issue yourself, the next logical step is to contact Oracle Support for help. On the Problem Details page shown in Figure 17.13, click the Oracle Support tab under the Investigate and Resolve section. Figure 17.14 shows the Oracle Support tab.

FIGURE 17.14 Contacting the Oracle Support section of Support Workbench

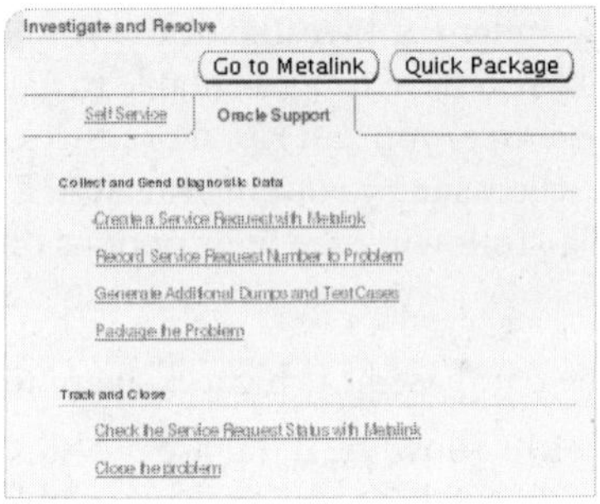

The Create a Service Request with Metalink link takes you to the Metalink login page, where you can log in and enter a service request. The URL for Metalink is `https://metalink.oracle.com`. Once the service request (SR) is created, you can use the Edit button on the Problem Details screen to update the SR number.

After you create the SR, the next step is to send relevant trace and dump files to Oracle for analysis. Support Workbench provides a packaging service to make this task easier for the DBA.

Oracle Support Services (OSS) is a 24/7 operation providing support to all Oracle customers throughout the world. The primary method of contacting OSS is using the web page at `https://metalink.oracle.com`. You have to register for an account first and provide information such as the customer service identifier (CSI) number, your contact information, so on.

Once you log in to Metalink, you can find a wealth of information, including the following:

- Searches for known issues
- Forum to discuss various issues
- Opening an SR
- Patches and updates
- Product certification
- Bug information
- Knowledge Base articles
- User documentation
- Electronic technical reference documents

The Metalink forums enable you to interact with other customers to share ideas and provide solutions. You can download patches and patch documentation.

See Metalink note 166650.1, "Global Customer Support Working Effectively with Support," for more information on using the Oracle Support Services.

Packaging Diagnostic Data

You can invoke packaging in two ways. On the Support Workbench page, you can select the problem and click the Package button. This gives you the option to create a quick package or a custom package. A *quick package* gathers information for a single problem with all the default options. With a *custom package*, you have the option to edit the package contents, remove any sensitive data, and add more traces and test cases. Another option to invoke packages is from the Problem Details screen, where you can invoke quick packaging for the problem. You can also optionally upload the packaged information to Oracle under the service request number. Figure 17.15 shows the Quick Packaging screen.

FIGURE 17.15 Quick Packaging screen

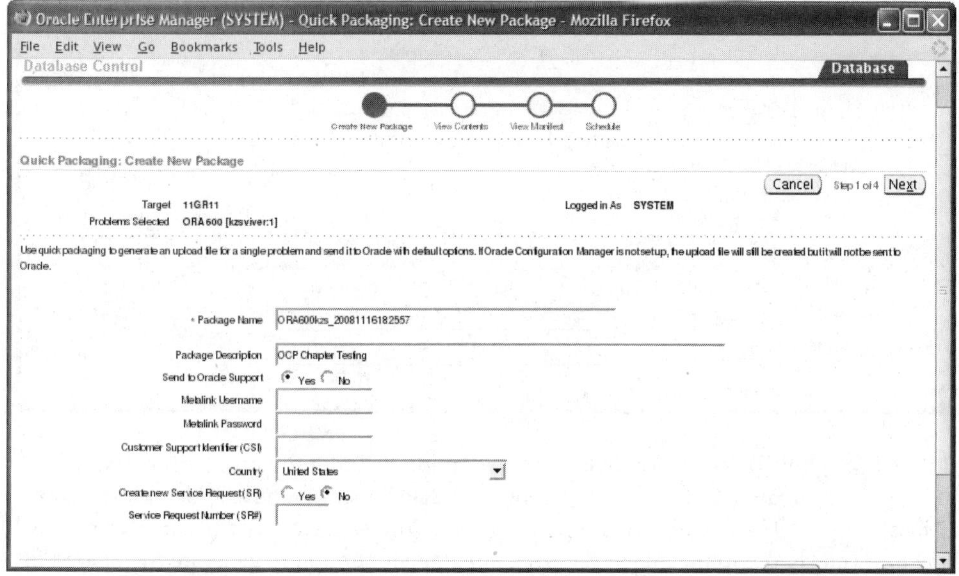

On this screen, you have the option to upload the created package to Oracle Support. If you want Support Workbench to upload the information, provide your Metalink username and password along with the CSI number. If you have not created an SR yet, you have the option to create a new SR from this screen. Enter the SR number for uploading diagnostic information for an existing SR.

If you choose custom packaging, the screen will look like Figure 17.16. Here Oracle will show you all the incidents to report and the files that are being packaged. You can exclude the files you do not want to send. Also, you have the option to add more incidents to the same package.

FIGURE 17.16 Customize Package screen

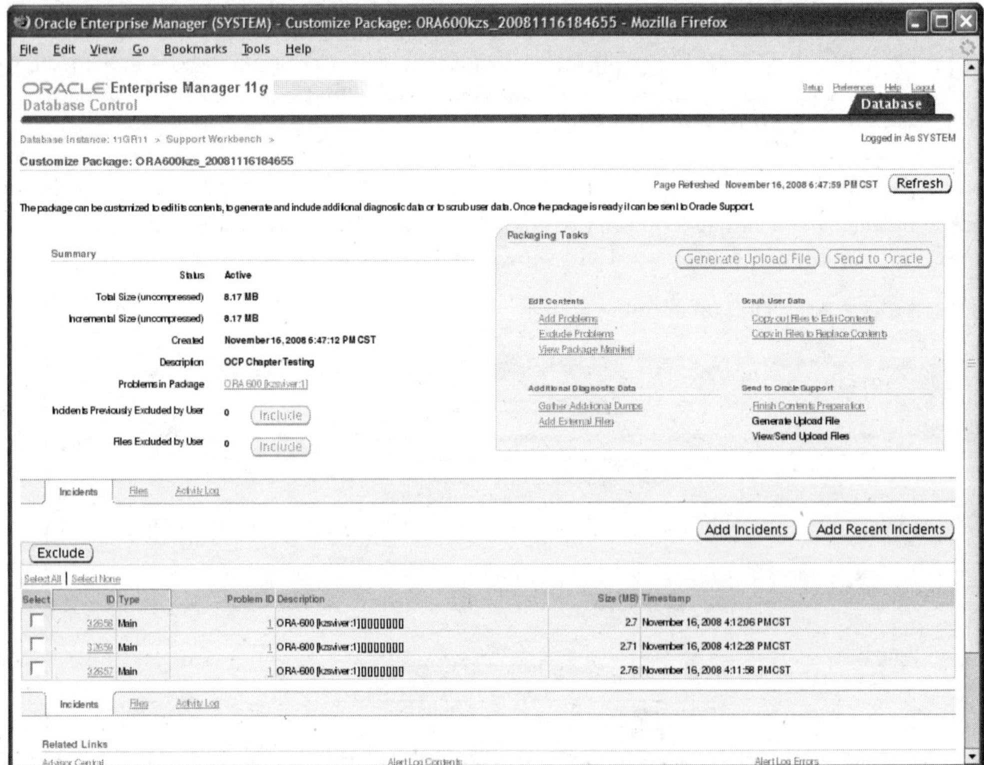

In the Packaging Tasks section, you have the option to add more problems or exclude problems. You can also edit the files you sent to Oracle. Once you have added all the necessary files, click the Finish Contents Preparation link. You will see a confirmation screen with all the files you choose to include in the packaging and an option to generate the upload file. After the file is generated, the Send to Oracle button will be enabled, and you can use it to send the information to Oracle.

Configuring Incident Packaging

You can customize the package-retention and -configuration rules by using the Incident Packaging Configuration link in the Related Links section of the Support Workbench screen. Figure 17.17 shows the default retention and packaging settings.

FIGURE 17.17 Incident packaging configuration

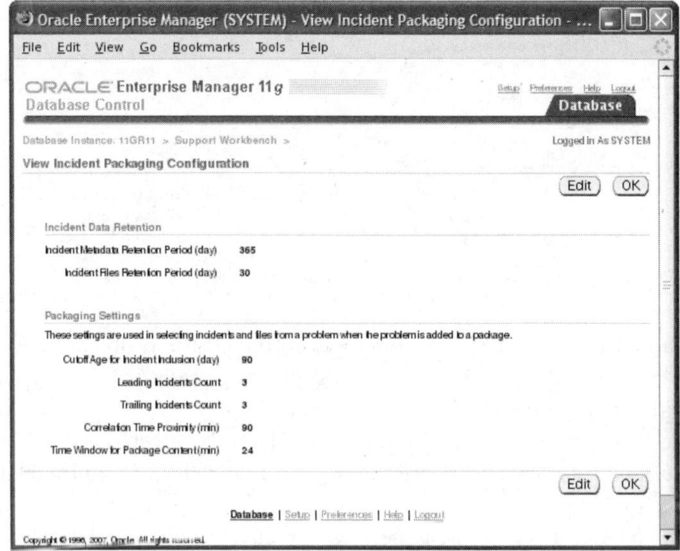

Click the Edit button to change the defaults. You can change the following values:

Incident Metadata Retention Period Information such as the incident ID, time, and problem are known as the *metadata*. The default is to keep this information for 365 days.

Incident Files Retention Period Specify how long you want to keep the files (data) related to an incident; the default is 30 days.

Cutoff Age for Incident Inclusion Include the incidents that are not older than the value specified here in days.

Leading Incidents Count and Trailing Incidents Count If a problem has several incidents, the packaging by default includes only three incidents from the time it started occurring and three incidents from the latest occurrence.

Correlation Time Proximity Specify the interval in minutes that should be treated as "happened at the same time" for related incidents. The default is 90 minutes.

Time Window for Package Content This is the time in minutes to include incidents in the package; the default is 24 minutes.

Tracking and Closing the Incident

You can track the progress of the incident by adding comments to the activity log. The activity log is available on the Problem Details screen as well as on the packaging screens. The Activity Log tab shows the system-generated operations that have occurred on the problem so far. This tab enables you to add your own comments while investigating the problem. Figure 17.18 shows the Activity Log tab.

FIGURE 17.18 Problem activity log

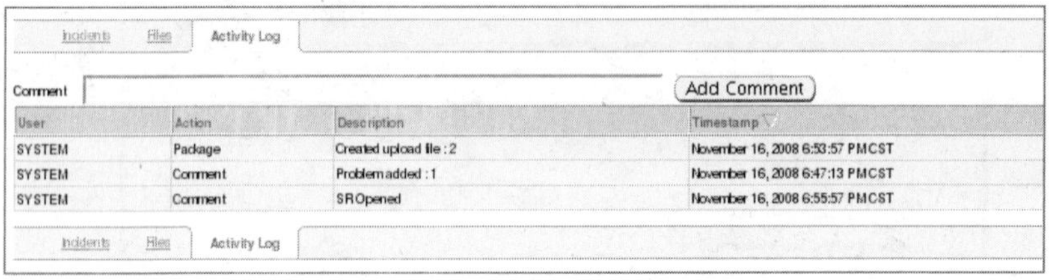

Incidents | Files | Activity Log

Comment [ ] (Add Comment)

User	Action	Description	Timestamp
SYSTEM	Package	Created upload file : 2	November 16, 2008 6:53:57 PMCST
SYSTEM	Comment	Problem added : 1	November 16, 2008 6:47:13 PMCST
SYSTEM	Comment	SR Opened	November 16, 2008 6:55:57 PMCST

Incidents | Files | Activity Log

You can add an entry using the Add Comment button. If the problem is related to an Oracle bug, you can add the bug number on the Problem Details screen by clicking the Edit button (shown earlier in Figure 17.13).

As you saw on the Self Service tab of the Problem Details screen, the Oracle advisors that can help you repair critical errors are the SQL Repair Advisor and the Data Recovery Advisor.

When you have a resolution for the issue, you can close the incident by clicking the Close button on the Support Workbench screen or by clicking the Close the Problem link on the Problem Details screen.

By default closed incidents are not shown on the Problem Details screen. All incidents (open and closed) are purged after 30 days. You can disable the incident purging on the Incident Details page. You can get to the Incident Details page by clicking the incident ID on the Problem Details screen (shown earlier in Figure 17.13). Click the Disable Purging button to disable the purging of the incident.

In the next section, you will learn how Enterprise Manager can help DBAs manage patches.

Using EM to Manage Patches

As a DBA, you have several reasons to download and apply patches. In Oracle 11g, Oracle has made the patch research and application easier by integrating OSS with Enterprise Manager. Oracle Corporation releases the following types of patches for its database product:

Patch release A patch release is a major patch that changes the version number of the database. Oracle release numbers have the format 11.1.0.6.0, where 11 is the major release number, 1 is the maintenance release number, 0 is the application-server release number, 6 is the component-specific release number, and 0 is the platform-specific release number. When a patch release is applied, the component-specific release number will change. Patch releases go through rigorous regression testing. Patch releases are cumulative, which means the latest patch release will include most interim patches and critical patch updates, as well as lower patch releases.

Interim patches Interim patches are one-off patches to fix a specific issue on a platform. The Oracle release numbers do not change when applying interim patches. Interim patches do not go through regression testing.

Critical patch updates Critical patch updates (CPUs) include security patches and other patches that depend on the security patches. CPUs are cumulative, which means previous CPUs are included. CPUs go through regression testing, and they do not advance the release numbers.

Patch releases are installed using the Oracle Universal Installer (OUI). You can install interim patches and CPUs using the OPatch utility. You can use `opatch lsinventory` to review all the patches applied to an Oracle Home installation:

```
$ $ORACLE_HOME/OPatch/opatch lsinventory
Invoking OPatch 11.1.0.6.0

Oracle Interim Patch Installer version 11.1.0.6.0
Copyright (c) 2007, Oracle Corporation.  All rights reserved.

Oracle Home       : /u01/app/oracle/product/11.1.0/db_1
Central Inventory : /u01/app/oraInventory
   from           : /etc/oraInst.loc
OPatch version    : 11.1.0.6.0
OUI version       : 11.1.0.6.0
OUI location      : /u01/app/oracle/product/11.1.0/db_1/oui
Log file location : /u01/app/oracle/product/11.1.0/db_1/ ↵
 cfgtoollogs/opatch/opatch2008-11-16_23-08-22PM.log
Lsinventory Output file location :
/u01/app/oracle/product/11.1.0/db_1/cfgtoollogs/opatch/ ↵
 lsinv/lsinventory2008-11-16_23-08-22PM.txt

------------------------------------------------------------------------------
Installed Top-level Products (1):
Oracle Database 11g                                                 11.1.0.6.0
There are 1 products installed in this Oracle Home.
```

```
Interim patches (1) :

Patch  6529615      : applied on Sun Nov 16 23:08:05 CST 2008
   Created on 7 Nov 2008, 04:01:26 hrs US/Pacific
   Bugs fixed:
     6529615
--------------------------------------------------------------------------------
OPatch succeeded.
$
```

To apply a patch using OPatch, first read the README.txt file accompanying each patch for instructions. Most of the patches are installed by using the opatch apply statement, from the patch staging directory. Enterprise Manager can be used to review, download, and apply patches. The patch-management links are in the Database Software Patching section on the Software and Support tab of Database Control, as shown in Figure 17.19.

FIGURE 17.19 Database Software Patching links on EM

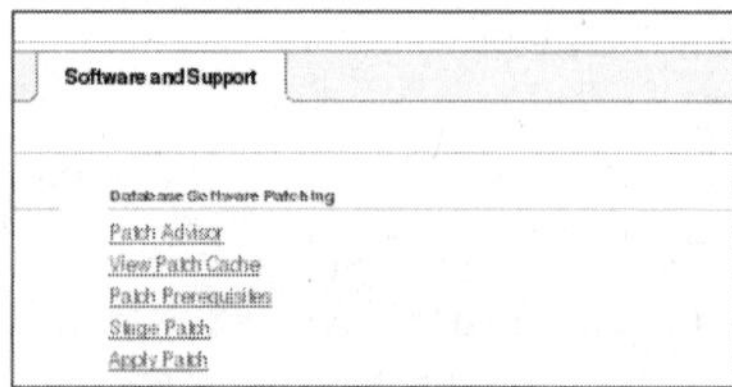

I will discuss each link in the following sections.

Using the Patch Advisor

The Patch Advisor shows the critical patch updates and the recommended patches for the release of the database on your server. Before you can use the Patch Advisor, you must set up Metalink login credentials and perform Metalink integration with EM. You can do this in two steps:

1. Enter the Metalink username and password. Click the Setup link on the top-right corner of EM Database Control. Click Patching Setup on the left menu, as shown in Figure 17.20.
2. Run the Refresh from Metalink job. Under the Related Links section on the Database Control home page, click the Jobs link to invoke the Job Activity screen. Under the Create drop-down list, choose Refresh from Metalink, and click Go, as shown in Figure 17.21.

Click the Patch Advisor link on the screen shown in Figure 17.19. The Patch Advisor screen shows critical security patches that need to be applied to ORACLE_HOME and recommended patches, as shown in Figure 17.22. Oracle can show the recommended patches based on the features used in the database. Select All from the drop-down box to show all the recommended patches.

FIGURE 17.20 Software patching setup in EM

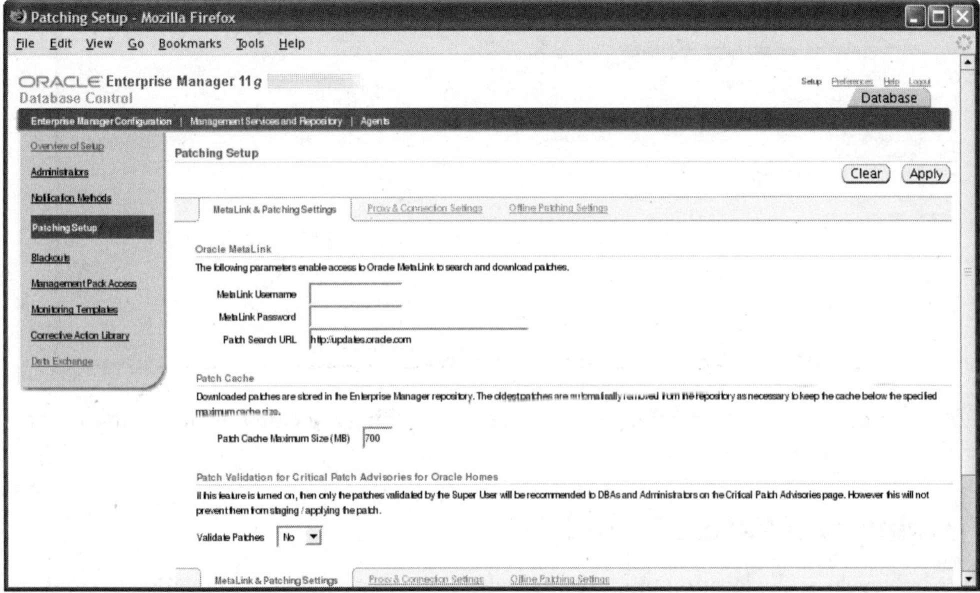

FIGURE 17.21 Refresh from Metalink job setup in EM

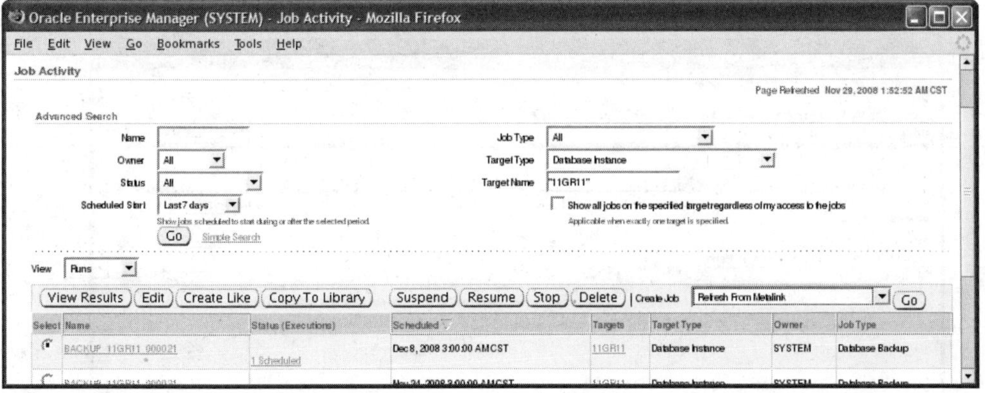

FIGURE 17.22 Patch Advisor screen on EM

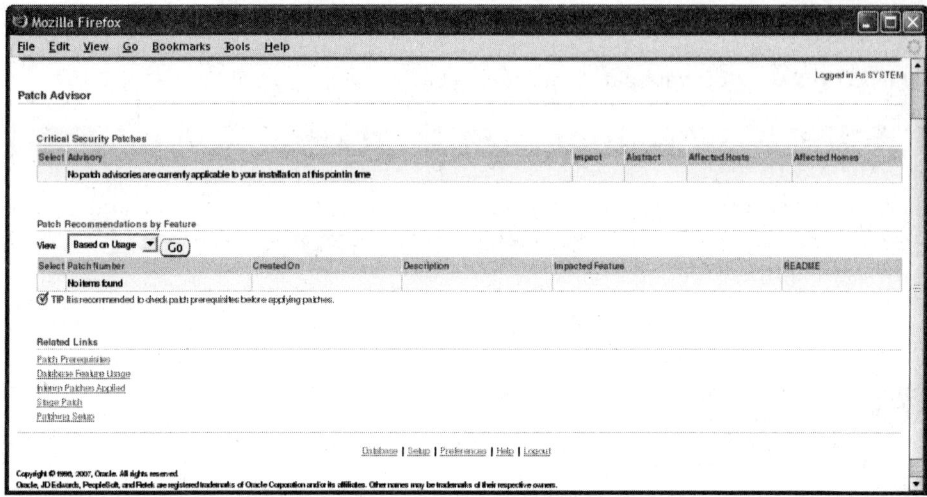

You can also invoke the patching setup screen by clicking the Patching Setup link in the Related Links section.

Viewing the Patch Cache

The patch cache is the location on the server where all your patches are downloaded and kept. One advantage of having the patch cache is that you can apply the patch to multiple Oracle Homes from one download. Figure 17.23 shows the Patch Cache screen.

FIGURE 17.23 Patch Cache screen in EM

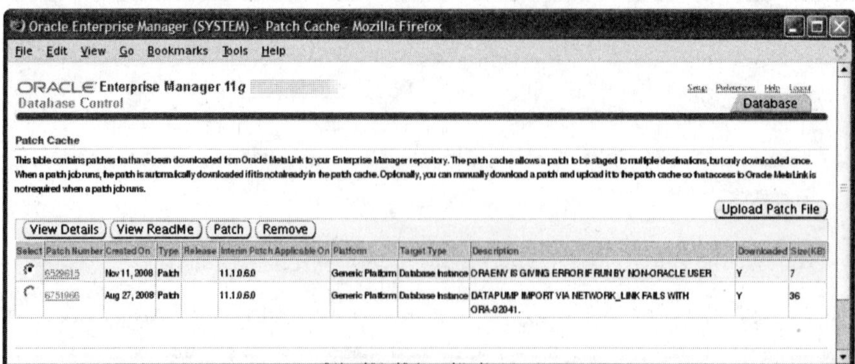

You can click the View ReadMe button to read the patch application details, and you can click the Patch button to apply the patch.

Finding the Patch Prerequisites

Click the Patch Prerequisite Check link to get the screen to evaluate the standard prerequisite checks on Oracle Home and Server with deployment-specific checks. Figure 17.24 shows the Patch prerequisite checker screen.

FIGURE 17.24 Patch Prerequisite Checker screen in EM

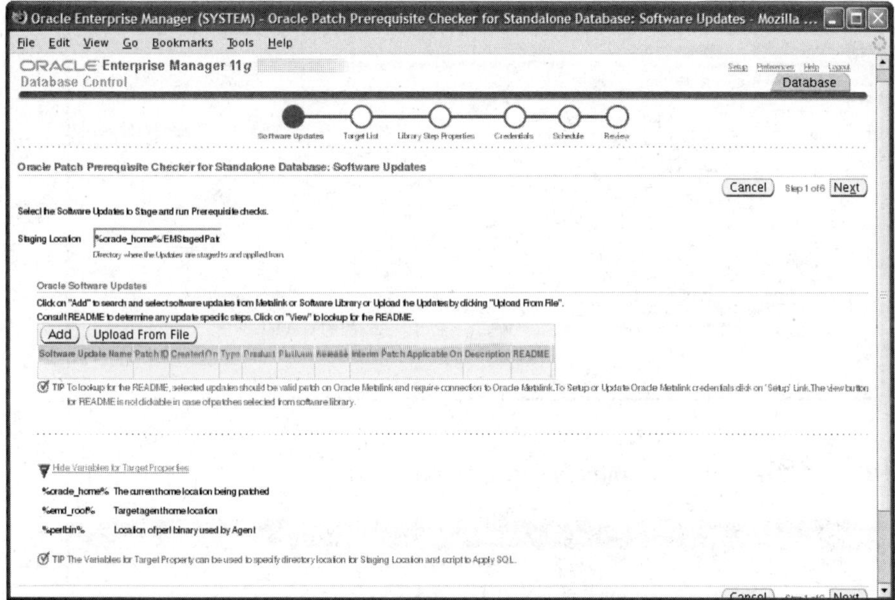

Staging a Patch

You can download patches from Metalink and stage them for later application. Figure 17.25 shows the staging patch screen.

You can select the patch to download by specifying the patch number or by specifying the product and release-number criteria. When the patches are displayed, choose the patch you want to stage. Click Next to prepare for staging or applying the patch.

On the next screen, specify the targets or destination of the patch. You can choose the Oracle Instance name or the Oracle home location. On the Set Credentials screen, specify the host operating-system username and password. On the Stage or Apply screen, you can choose to download the patch or to apply the patch after downloading. On the Schedule screen, specify whether you want the patch to be downloaded immediately or at a later time. Figure 17.26 shows the Summary screen. Review the patch sizes, where the patches will be applied, and so on, and click the Finish button to download the patch.

FIGURE 17.25 Staging patch screen in EM

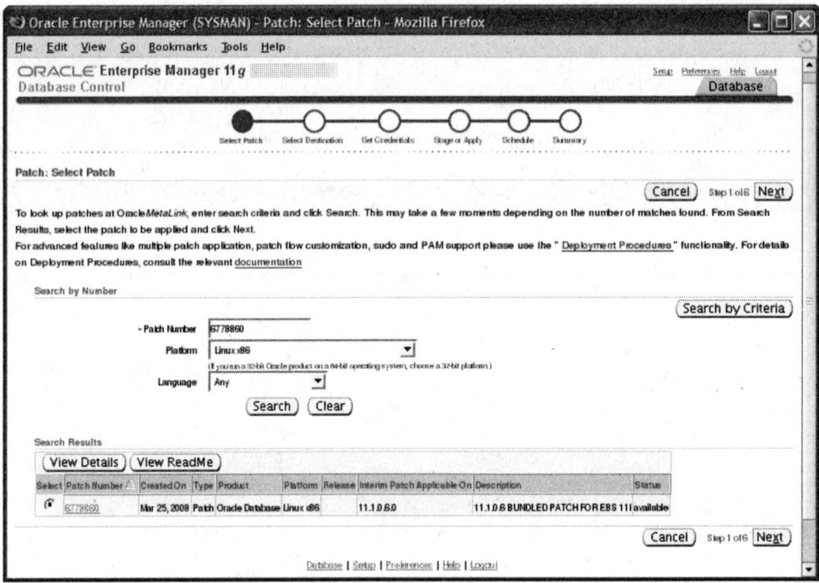

FIGURE 17.26 Patch: Summary screen in EM

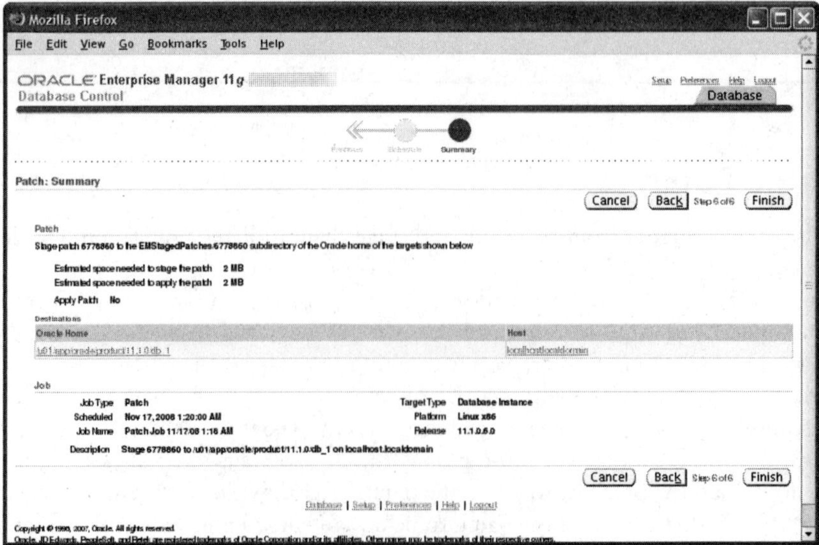

Staged patches are stored under the `$ORACLE_HOME/EMStagedPatches` directory in this example.

Applying a Patch

When you click the Apply Patch link on the Software and Support page, you invoke the Patch Wizard. Figure 17.27 shows the first screen, where the wizard prompts you to select the patches.

FIGURE 17.27 Apply Patch Wizard in EM

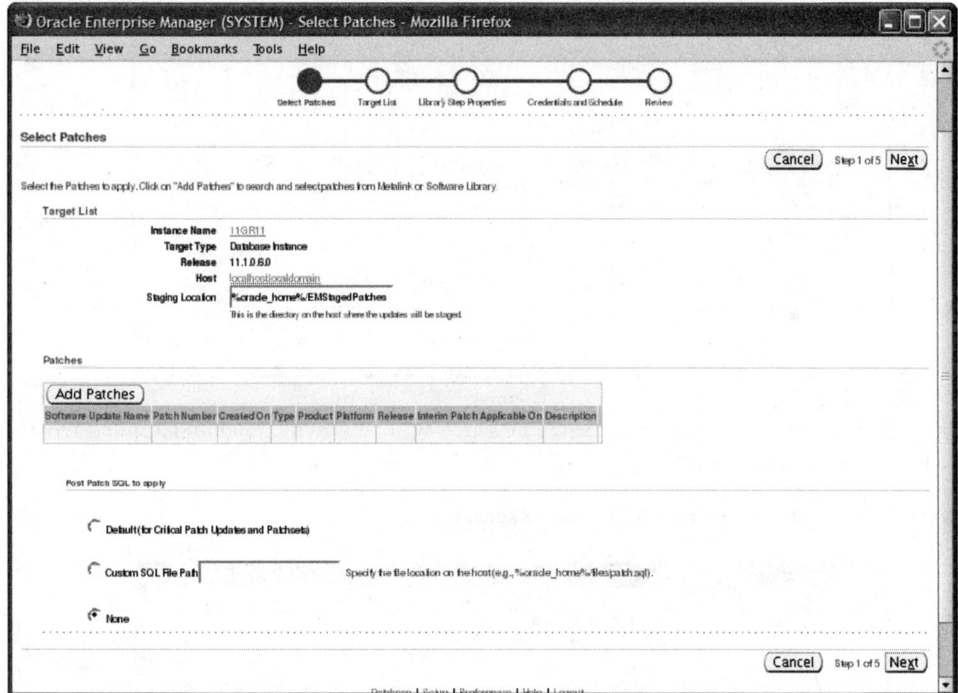

Click the Add Patches button to select the patches to apply. The Add Patches button brings you to the page shown in Figure 17.28, where you can search for patches and select the patch.

The Target List step is skipped for non-RAC instances; the Library Step Properties step is also skipped most of the time, unless you have customized the deployment procedures. The Credentials and Schedule screen prompts you to enter the Oracle software-owner username and password. For the schedule, you can specify one time (immediately), one time (later), or repeating.

FIGURE 17.28 Searching for and selecting patches in EM

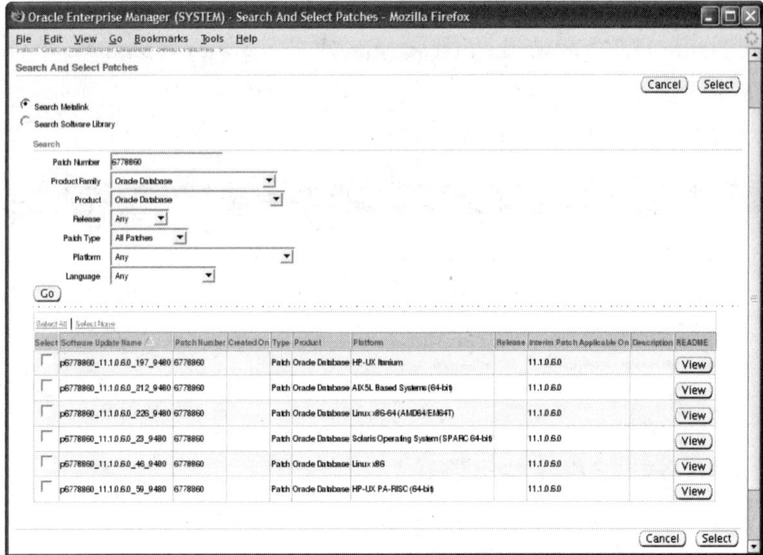

Figure 17.29 shows the review screen. The patch will be downloaded and applied when you click the Finish button.

FIGURE 17.29 Apply patch Summary screen in EM

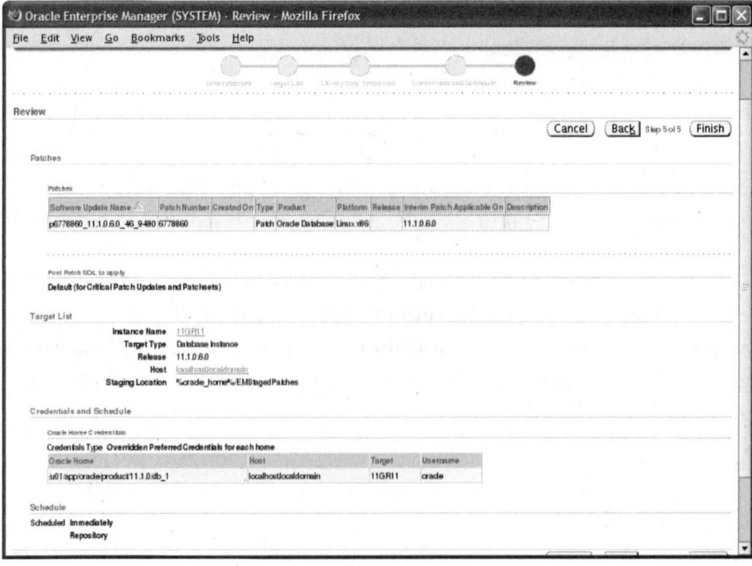

As you can see from the previous screens and options, EM Database Control helps DBAs be proactive about the critical and recommended patches they need.

Summary

In this chapter, I discussed how to move data using Oracle Data Pump, using SQL*Loader, and using external tables. You also learned how to use Enterprise Manger to diagnose and contact Oracle Support as well as manage patches.

Data Pump is a very high-speed infrastructure for data and metadata movement. The client utilities `expdp` and `impdp` are used to unload and load data and metadata. The Data Pump architecture includes the data and metadata movement engine `DBMS_DATAPUMP`, the Direct Path API that supports a stream interface, the metadata API `DBMS_METADATA`, the external tables API, and the client utilities.

Data Pump export and import are performed on the server. You can attach to a job from any computer and monitor its progress or make resource adjustments. In the interactive mode, you can add a file to export a dump-file set, kill a job, stop a job, change the parallelism, and enable detailed status logging.

SQL*Loader is used to load ASCII files to the Oracle database. You can invoke Data Pump and SQL*Loader using EM Database Control.

You can also use external tables to move data. You can use the `ORACLE_DATAPUMP` access driver to write data into an external table, and you can use the `ORACLE_LOADER` access driver to read flat files into Oracle Database.

EM Database Control infrastructure enhancements include Support Workbench and patch management. Using Support Workbench, you can identify, investigate, diagnose, and resolve incidents. The Patch Advisor provides the patches that are needed on the database and can be used to stage and apply patches.

Exam Essentials

Know how to create database directory objects. Directory objects are required for use in the Data Pump export and Data Pump import programs.

Know that directory objects are not owned by individual schema. Directory objects are not schema objects. Instead, they are owned by the database like roles or profiles.

Be aware of the Data Pump export and import modes. Data Pump export has database, schema, table, and tablespace modes, and Data Pump import has full, schema, table, and tablespace modes. Although these modes sound similar, they differ between the two tools.

Be familiar with the Data Pump options that let you transfer both data and metadata from one schema to another. The `content=` parameter controls whether data, metadata, or both are copied. The `remap_schema` parameter allows you to transfer data from one schema to another.

Be aware of the limitations of SQL*Loader direct-path mode, including unusable indexes. SQL*Loader direct-path mode has several limitations, the most prominent being that it locks the table in exclusive mode for the duration of the load. Unique indexes are marked unusable if unique violations are found after a direct path load. These unique violations must be resolved before the index can be rebuilt.

Know the external table access drivers. ORACLE_DATAPUMP and ORACLE_LOADER are the access drivers used with external tables. The ORACLE_DATAPUMP access driver can be used to read and write to an external table. The ORACLE_LOADER access driver is read-only.

Understand Support Workbench's capabilities. Support Workbench can identify, diagnose, and package an incident to contact Oracle Support Services for help.

Be familiar with the Patch Advisor and patch staging screens. EM Database Control makes patch management easy. You can get information about the patches relevant to the database, you can stage patches, and you can apply patches.

Review Questions

1. Which two PL/SQL packages are used by Oracle Data Pump?

   A. `UTL_DATAPUMP`

   B. `DBMS_METADATA`

   C. `DBMS_DATAPUMP`

   D. `UTL_FILE`

   E. `DBMS_SQL`

2. These options list the benefits of Oracle Data Pump; pick two that are not true.

   A. Data Pump supports fine-grained object selection using the `EXCLUDE`, `INCLUDE`, and `CONTENT` options.

   B. Data Pump has the ability to specify the target version of the database so that the objects exported are compatible. This is useful in moving data from Oracle 10*g* to Oracle9*i*.

   C. Data Pump has the ability to specify the maximum number of threads to unload data.

   D. The DBA can choose to perform the export using direct path or external tables.

   E. The Data Pump job can be monitored from another computer on the network.

3. The Data Pump job maintains a master control table with information about Data Pump. Choose the right statement.

   A. The master table is the heart of Data Pump operation and is maintained in the `SYS` schema.

   B. The master table contains one row for the operation that keeps track of the object being worked so that the job can be restarted in the event of failure.

   C. During the export, the master table is written to the dump file set at the beginning of export operation.

   D. The Data Pump job runs in the schema of the job creator with that user's rights and privileges.

   E. All of the above.

4. When using the `expdp` and `impdp` clients, the parameters `LOGFILE`, `DUMPFILE`, and `SQLFILE` need a directory object where the files will be written to or read from. Choose the non-supported method for non-privileged users.

   A. Specify the `DIRECTORY` parameter.

   B. Specify the filename parameters with `directory:file_name`.

   C. Use the initialization parameter `DATA_PUMP_DIR`.

   D. None of the above (all are supported).

5. Which command-line parameter of expdp and impdp clients connects you to an existing job?
   A. CONNECT_CLIENT
   B. CONTINUE_CLIENT
   C. APPEND
   D. ATTACH
6. Which option unloads the data and metadata of the SCOTT user, except the tables that begin with TEMP? The dump file also should have the DDL to create the user.
   A. CONTENT=BOTH TABLES=(not like 'TEMP%') SCHEMAS=SCOTT
   B. SCHEMAS=SCOTT EXCLUDE=TABLE:"LIKE 'TEMP%'"
   C. INCLUDE=METADATA EXCLUDE=TABLES:"NOT LIKE 'TEMP%'" SCHEMAS=SCOTT
   D. TABLES="NOT LIKE 'TEMP%'" SCHEMAS=SCOTT
7. Which parameter is not a valid one for using the impdp client?
   A. REMAP_INDEX
   B. REMAP_TABLE
   C. REMAP_SCHEMA
   D. REMAP_TABLESPACE
   E. REMAP_DATAFILE
8. When do you use the FLASHBACK_TIME parameter in the impdp utility?
   A. To load data from the dump file that was modified after a certain time.
   B. To discard data from the dump file that was modified after a certain time.
   C. When the NETWORK_LINK parameter is used.
   D. FLASHBACK_TIME is valid only with expdp, not with impdp.
9. To perform a Data Pump import from a live database, which parameter needs to be set?
   A. db_link
   B. network_link
   C. dumpfile
   D. directory
10. Choose two statements about EM Support Workbench that are true.
   A. It can identify problems, contact Oracle Support, and resolve problems automatically.
   B. It helps collect diagnostic data and package it to send to Oracle Support.
   C. Multiple incidents of similar nature are combined as a problem.
   D. It is primarily used to track service requests created with Oracle Support.

11. Which types of patches do not undergo rigorous testing?
    - A. Interim patches
    - B. Critical patch updates
    - C. Patch releases
    - D. None of the above
12. When is it most appropriate to use external table?
    - A. When you need to read binary files (PDF and photos) into Oracle Database
    - B. To query a large file without loading the data into the database
    - C. When the `expdp` and `impdp` utilities are not licensed for use
    - D. To load a large file into the database quickly
13. Which constraint is not enforced during the direct path load using SQL*Loader?
    - A. Primary key.
    - B. Unique key.
    - C. Not null.
    - D. Check.
    - E. All the constraints are enforced.
    - F. No constraints are enforced.
14. Which utility can be used to identify the patches applied to your Oracle Database home location?
    - A. ADRCI
    - B. OPatch
    - C. Oracle Universal Installer (OUI)
    - D. All of the above
15. Choose the correct statement about Oracle Support Services.
    - A. Support can be contacted using the `metalink.oracle.com` web page.
    - B. Anyone can register and search Oracle Support's Knowledge Base.
    - C. There is no published phone number to contact OSS.
    - D. Support analysts are available only during U.S. Pacific time zone work hours.
16. When using EM Database Control to load data into Oracle Database from a flat file, you should do which of the following?
    - A. Cut and paste the file content into the data text box.
    - B. Always build your own control file and specify it for the data load.
    - C. Keep the log file, bad file, and data file in the same directory.
    - D. Load the data file from the server or on your client machine.
    - E. Load the data from the client machine.

17. Choose the statement that is *not* true from the following about direct path load.
    - A. Direct path load cannot occur if active transactions against the table are being loaded.
    - B. Triggers do not fire during direct path loads.
    - C. During direct path loads, foreign key constraints are disabled at the beginning of the load and then reenabled after the load.
    - D. Only primary key, unique, and `NOT NULL` constraints are enforced.
    - E. Direct path load allows other users to perform DML operations on the table while the direct load operation is in progress.
18. Which two advisors can help you repair critical errors?
    - A. SQL Tuning Advisor
    - B. SQL Repair Advisor
    - C. SQL Syntax Advisor
    - D. Data Recovery Advisor
19. When using EM Support Workbench, how is a problem closed?
    - A. When the error is no longer appearing
    - B. When Oracle Support Services closes the SR in Metalink
    - C. When the DBA manually closes the incident
    - D. All of the above
20. To register for Oracle Support Services Metalink access, you must do which of the following? (Choose all that apply.)
    - A. Have a valid driver's license
    - B. Be an Oracle customer with a valid CSI number
    - C. Get approval from the CSI administrator
    - D. Be a member of the IOUG or OAUG user group

Answers to Review Questions

1. B, C. The DBMS_METADATA package provides the database object definitions to the export worker process in the proper order of their creation. The DBMS_DATAPUMP package has the API for high-speed export and import for bulk data and metadata loading and unloading.

2. B, D. Oracle Data Pump is known to versions 10*g* and newer; Oracle9*i* does not support Data Pump. Though Data Pump can perform data access using the direct-path or external-table method, Data Pump makes the decision automatically; the DBA cannot specify the data-access method. Data Pump also supports network mode to import directly from the source database and can estimate the space requirements for the dump file.

3. D. The master table is the heart of the Data Pump operation and is maintained in the schema of the job creator. It bears the name of the job, contains one row for each object and each operation, and keeps status. Using this information helps restart a failed job or suspend and resume a job. The master table is written to the dump file as the last step of the export and is loaded to the schema of the user as the first step of the import.

4. C. If a directory object is created with name DATA_PUMP_DIR, the privileged users can use this location as the default location for Data Pump files. Privileged users are users with EXP_FULL_DATABASE or IMP_FULL_DATABASE roles. Using %U in the filename generates multiple files for parallel unloads with each parallel process writing to one file.

5. D. The ATTACH parameter lets you attach or connect to an existing Data Pump job and places you in interactive mode. ATTACH without any parameters attaches to the currently running job, if there is only one job from the user. Otherwise, you must specify the job name when using the ATTACH parameter.

6. B. If the CONTENT parameter is not specified, both data and metadata will be unloaded. The valid values for CONTENT are METADATA_ONLY, DATA_ONLY, and ALL. If Scott is performing the export, SCHEMAS=SCOTT is optional.

7. A. REMAP_DATAFILE changes the name of the source data file to the target data filename in all DDL statements where the source data file is referenced. REMAP_SCHEMA loads all objects from the source schema into the destination schema. When using REMAP_TABLESPACE, all objects selected for import with persistent data in the source tablespace are remapped to be created in the destination tablespace. REMAP_TABLE changes the name of the table. Since the dump file is in XML format, Data Pump can make these transformations easily. REMAP_INDEX is an invalid parameter.

8. C. You can specify the FLASHBACK_TIME or FLASHBACK_SCN parameter only when performing a network import where the source is a database.

9. B. The network_link parameter specifies a database link to the source database.

10. B, C. Oracle Support Workbench can help DBAs diagnose the problem, collect more information and related traces, and dump files into a package to send to Oracle Support for analysis.

11. A. Interim patches are also known as one-off patches, created for a specific problem. CPU and patch releases undergo rigorous testing.

12. B. External tables can be used to read ASCII flat files without loading into the database. The external table must be created with the `ORACLE_LOADER` access driver.

13. D. Primary key, unique key, and not null constraints are enforced during direct path load. Check and foreign key constraints are not enforced.

14. B. OPatch is used to apply the CPU and interim patches. The `lsinventory` option of the `$ORACLE_HOME/OPatch/opatch` command is used to query patches.

15. A. OSS can be contacted via phone or the Web. The Web is the preferred method of contact.

16. D. The data file, log file, and bad file can be on the database server or on the client machine. When using a database server, you must specify the file location using directory objects.

17. E. While the direct path load is in progress, users cannot run any DML statements against the table. Only queries are allowed.

18. B, D. The SQL Repair Advisor can be invoked to diagnose issues arising out of SQL statements. The Data Recovery Advisor can be used to recover from block corruptions and missing data files.

19. C. Problems are closed manually by the DBA. If the retention periods are not changed, incident data will be purged from the Automatic Diagnostic Repository after 30 days, and Metadata will be kept for 1 year.

20. B, C. You must have a valid customer support identifier to register and use the OSS web page.

About the Companion CD

IN THIS APPENDIX:

- What you'll find on the CD
- System requirements
- Using the CD
- Troubleshooting

What You'll Find on the CD

The following sections are arranged by category and summarize the software and other goodies you'll find on the CD. If you need help with installing the items provided on the CD, refer to the installation instructions in the "Using the CD" section of this appendix.

Some programs on the CD might fall into one of these categories:

Shareware programs are fully functional, free, trial versions of copyrighted programs. If you like particular programs, register with their authors for a nominal fee and receive licenses, enhanced versions, and technical support.

Freeware programs are free, copyrighted games, applications, and utilities. You can copy them to as many computers as you like—for free—but they offer no technical support.

GNU software is governed by its own license, which is included inside the folder of the GNU software. There are no restrictions on distribution of GNU software. See the GNU license at the root of the CD for more details.

Trial, *demo*, or *evaluation* versions of software are usually limited either by time or by functionality (such as not letting you save a project after you create it).

Sybex Test Engine

For Windows

The CD contains the Sybex test engine, which includes all the assessment test and chapter review questions in electronic format, as well as two bonus exams located only on the CD.

PDF of the Book

For Windows

We have included an electronic version of the text in `.pdf` format. You can view the electronic version of the book with Adobe Reader.

Adobe Reader

For Windows

We've also included a copy of Adobe Reader so you can view PDF files that accompany the book's content. For more information on Adobe Reader or to check for a newer version, visit Adobe's website at `www.adobe.com/products/reader/`.

Electronic Flashcards

For PC, Pocket PC, and Palm

These handy electronic flashcards are just what they sound like. One side contains a question or fill-in-the-blank question, and the other side shows the answer.

System Requirements

Make sure your computer meets the minimum system requirements shown in the following list. If your computer doesn't match up to most of these requirements, you may have problems using the software and files on the companion CD. For the latest and greatest information, please refer to the ReadMe file located at the root of the CD-ROM.

- A PC running Microsoft Windows 98, Windows 2000, Windows NT4 (with SP4 or later), Windows Me, Windows XP, or Windows Vista
- An Internet connection
- A CD-ROM drive

Using the CD

To install the items from the CD to your hard drive, follow these steps:

1. Insert the CD into your computer's CD-ROM drive. The license agreement appears.
2. Read the license agreement, and then click the Accept button if you want to use the CD.

The CD interface appears. The interface allows you to access the content with just one or two clicks.

Windows users: The interface won't launch if you have autorun disabled. In that case, click Start ➤ Run (for Windows Vista, Start ➤ All Programs ➤ Accessories ➤ Run). In the dialog box that appears, type **`D:\Start.exe`**. (Replace *D* with the proper letter if your CD drive uses a different letter. If you don't know the letter, see how your CD drive is listed under My Computer.) Click OK.

Troubleshooting

Wiley has attempted to provide programs that work on most computers with the minimum system requirements. Alas, your computer may differ, and some programs may not work properly for some reason.

The two likeliest problems are that you don't have enough memory (RAM) for the programs you want to use or you have other programs running that are affecting installation or running of a program. If you get an error message such as "Not enough memory" or "Setup cannot continue," try one or more of the following suggestions and then try using the software again:

Turn off any antivirus software running on your computer. Installation programs sometimes mimic virus activity and may make your computer incorrectly believe that it's being infected by a virus.

Close all running programs. The more programs you have running, the less memory is available to other programs. Installation programs typically update files and programs; so if you keep other programs running, installation may not work properly.

Have your local computer store add more RAM to your computer. This is, admittedly, a drastic and somewhat expensive step. However, adding more memory can really help the speed of your computer and allow more programs to run at the same time.

Customer Care

If you have trouble with the book's companion CD-ROM, please call the Wiley Product Technical Support phone number at (800) 762-2974. Outside the United States, call +1 (317) 572-3994. You can also contact Wiley Product Technical Support at `http://sybex.custhelp.com`. John Wiley & Sons will provide technical support only for installation and other general quality-control items. For technical support on the applications themselves, consult the program's vendor or author.

To place additional orders or to request information about other Wiley products, please call (877) 762-2974.

Glossary

A

Active Session History (ASH) Sampled data at specified intervals from the current state of all active sessions. The data is collected in memory and can be accessed by V$ views.

ADDM *See* Automated Database Diagnostic Monitoring (ADDM).

aggregate functions Functions that operate on groups of rows, also known as group functions. The exact number of inputs for aggregate functions is not determined until the query is executed and all rows are fetched. This differs from *single-row functions*, in which the number of inputs is known at parse time, before the query is executed.

alert log file A file where Oracle Database writes information about the database start-ups, shutdown, check points, redo log switches, errors, and warning information.

anonymous block An unnamed PL/SQL program.

archived redo log file A file that contains the contents of a previously used redo log file. It's created only when the database is operating in ARCHIVELOG mode.

ARCHIVELOG **mode** A database configuration in which redo log files are copied to the archive log destination, which ensures that they won't be overwritten and lost. These archived logs are used primarily for media recovery.

ARC*n* An Oracle background process that copies the online redo log files to an archived log destination.

arithmetic operators Operators used to manipulate information in the arithmetic expressions. Addition (+), subtraction (–), multiplication (*), and division (/) are the arithmetic operators.

ASM *See* Automated Storage Management (ASM).

auditing The monitoring and recording of specific database activities.

Automated Database Diagnostic Monitoring (ADDM)
The process that analyzes the data in the Automatic Workload Repository (AWR) to identify sources of potential performance bottlenecks and that recommends solutions for correcting the problem. *See also* Automatic Workload Repository (AWR).

automated maintenance tasks Tasks performed by Oracle Database to gather database statistics, run the segment-space advisor periodically, and so on.

Automated Storage Management (ASM) A type of storage mechanism that is new in Oracle 10*g*. Oracle manages the storage definitions of the database within a second database used exclusively by ASM to keep track of the disk allocations for your databases.

Automatic Memory Management (AMM) A mechanism to manage the memory requirement automatically by allocating the total memory to Oracle. Oracle will manage the SGA and PGA based on demand.

Automatic Shared Memory Management (ASMM) A mechanism to manage the shared memory requirement automatically by allocating the memory to Oracle. Oracle will manage the individual pools in SGA based on demand.

Automatic Workload Repository (AWR) The collection of tables, owned by the SYSMAN schema, that stores the performance statistics gathered from the system global area (SGA) by the Memory Monitor (MMON) background process.

AWR *See* Automatic Workload Repository (AWR).

B

B-tree index An index database object that organizes table data in a binary tree format.

back up to trace A method of backing up the control file contents to a text file in the location specified.

backup sets A set of Recovery Manager (RMAN) files that contains the saved data from a backup.

base tables The tables used to define a view.

baseline metrics A collection of performance statistics against which current or future database performance is measured to determine whether a significant performance deviation has occurred.

bigfile tablespace A tablespace built on a single data file that can be up to 2^{32} data blocks in size.

binary operators Operators that take two operands. All operators are binary, except the + or – used to represent the sign of a numeric value.

bitmap index An index database object that organizes table data in a series of bitmaps. A bitmap index is analogous to a two-dimensional matrix, where index keys and table rows are the axes.

block The smallest unit of data storage in the database.

block change tracking file A file that tracks the blocks changed since the last incremental backup, saving time during an incremental backup because not all blocks in every data file need to be checked for changes.

C

cardinality The number of distinct values. If a table has a cardinality of 1,000, it has 1,000 rows. If a column has a cardinality of 30, it has 30 distinct values (there may be 1,000 rows but only 30 distinct values).

Cartesian join A join that joins two tables with no common condition, also known as a cross join. Each row from the first table is joined against every row in the second table.

CASE An expression that can be used to derive IF...THEN...ELSE logic in SQL.

change vectors A description of a change made to a single block in the database.

CHAR Datatype used to store fixed-length character data.

checkpoint An event during which the dirty data-block buffers are flushed to disk and database files are updated to reflect this action. The database is put into a consistent state.

checkpoint (CKPT) process The Oracle background process that updates the control file and the data file headers to reflect the last successful transaction by recording the last system change number (SCN).

CKPT *See* checkpoint (CKPT) process.

column The vertical space in a table or a view that holds a specific domain of data. In the relational model, an entity has attributes. When this model is implemented in an Oracle Database, an entity becomes a table, and an attribute becomes a column.

column alias Another name for the column to display with the query results. Alias names can provide meaningful names for the result set.

COMMIT The SQL command for making permanent the changes made during a transaction.

comparison operators Operators that compare two values or expressions and give a Boolean result of TRUE, FALSE, or NULL.

complex join A join that includes additional filter criteria along with the join conditions in the WHERE clause.

compound query A query that includes a set operator to join two or more queries.

concatenation operator Operator used to join two text strings. The operator is ||.

concurrency The condition where many users/sessions can access and modify data at the same time.

connection The communication channel between the user process and the server process. *See also* server process; user process.

Connection Manager *See* Oracle Connection Manager.

consistency A state maintained by the database. A statement/transaction sees a time-consistent image of the data plus any uncommitted data from the statement/transaction.

consistent backup A backup performed while the database is shut down and unavailable. This is also referred to as offline backup.

constraint An optional schema object that restricts values in the dependent table to a specified condition. Constraints enforce business rules about data.

control file A small binary file that contains metadata about the physical structure of the database, such as the database name, locations of the data files and redo logs, and recovery information.

conversion functions Single-row functions used to convert the datatype of input between numeric, character, and datetime values.

correlated subquery A subquery that references the column names of the parent query.

cost-based optimizer The Oracle optimizer mode that uses statistics about the size, selectivity, and dispersion of the tables and indexes in the database to formulate the most efficient execution plan.

cross join A join that joins two tables with no common condition, also known as a Cartesian join. Each row from the first table is joined against every row in the second table.

`CURRVAL` The sequence pseudocolumn that will return the last number generated from the sequence-number generator.

D

data block The smallest unit of disk allocation in data or temp files, composed of one or more file-system blocks.

Data Control Language (DCL) The category of SQL commands that control access to database objects, including the `GRANT` and `REVOKE` commands.

Data Definition Language (DDL) The category of SQL commands used to create objects in the database, including `CREATE`, `ALTER`, and `DROP`.

Data Manipulation Language (DML) The category of SQL commands used to create, modify, or remove data from a table, including `INSERT`, `UPDATE`, and `DELETE`.

Data Recovery Advisor A tool to identify failures, recommend resolution, and perform recovery action.

database A collection of control files, data files, and redo logs.

database buffer cache The portion of the system global area (SGA) where copies of the data blocks are cached in memory. *See also* system global area (SGA).

Database Configuration Assistant (DBCA)
A Java-based tool you can use to create Oracle databases. The DBCA can store and manage definitions of your databases in the form of templates that can be used to make copies of a database.

Database Control A web-based component of the Enterprise Management Framework for managing Oracle Database 10*g*. Database Control allows you to monitor and administer a single Oracle Database instance or a single Real Application Clusters (RAC) environment.

database templates XML-based documents that the DBCA creates to store information about database definitions. The documents contain everything the DBCA needs to create a database. *See also* Database Configuration Assistant (DBCA).

Database Writer (DBW*n*) The Oracle background process that is responsible for writing changed data-block buffers from the database buffer cache back to the data files on disk.

data files The physical database files that store the database's segments, such as tables, indexes, rollback, and partition.

datatype A characteristic assigned to each column in a table that defines what type of data can be stored in the column and its valid values.

DATE Datatype used to store date and time information.

DB Time A cumulative measure of time spent by the database responding to user requests, including wait times for access to resources such as memory, disk, and CPU for all nonidle user sessions.

DBCA *See* Database Configuration Assistant (DBCA).

DBMS_DATAPUMP The Procedural Language SQL (PL/SQL) package that is an API to Data Pump.

DBW*n* *See* Database Writer (DBW*n*).

DCL *See* Data Control Language (DCL).

DDL *See* Data Definition Language (DDL).

deadlock A special kind of lock conflict that prevents two or more transactions from completing because each transaction has a lock on a resource needed by the other transaction.

declarative constraints Constraints that are not enforced. These constraints will have a state of `DISABLE NOVALIDATE`.

dedicated server A type of connection in which every client connection has an associated dedicated server process on the machine where the Oracle server exists. *See also* shared server process.

default role A role initially enabled for every user session.

default tablespace The tablespace where a user's tables and indexes are stored if not declared explicitly.

deferred constraint checking Constraint checking that is deferred to a transaction level. By default, constraints are checked at the statement level.

DELETE SQL statement used to remove rows from a table.

DIAGNOSTIC_DEST Parameter specifying the location of the parent directory where all trace, log, and dump files will be written on the server.

directory object A database object that identifies a file-system location. Directory objects are used by Data Pump jobs.

dispatcher A process in an Oracle Shared Server environment that manages requests from one or more client connections.

DML *See* Data Manipulation Language (DML).

DUAL A dummy table in the Oracle Database. DUAL has one column and one row. It is mainly used to query the system variables such as SYSDATE and USER.

dynamic service registration The ability of an Oracle instance to automatically register its existence with a listener.

E

Emctl The command-line utility used to stop and start the Oracle Management agent.

Enterprise Manager (EM) Database Control The web-based GUI tool for managing Oracle environments.

environment variables Variables that define the SQL*Plus environment. These variables are set using the SET command. The SHOW command is used to display the value of the variables.

equality join (equijoin) A join in which two tables are joined with an equality operator or an IN operator. Natural joins and JOIN...USING are examples of equality joins.

escape character A character used to prefix a pattern-matching character, such as % or _, to allow the inclusion of the pattern-matching character in the string.

exclusive lock A table lock that will block all changes to data and all other table locks.

expression A combination of one or more values, operators, and SQL functions that result in a value.

extent management Defines how free and used extents are managed in a tablespace.

extents A group of contiguous data blocks allocated to a segment.

Extproc The default name of the callout process that is used when executing external procedures from Oracle.

F

FAST_START_MTTR_TARGET An initialization parameter that specifies the desired amount of time, in seconds, to perform instance recovery after an instance failure.

FGA *See* fine-grained auditing (FGA).

fine-grained auditing (FGA) Special auditing that allows custom rules to be used in monitoring and capturing audit records.

firewall Generally, a combination of hardware and software that controls network traffic and prevents intruders from compromising corporate network security.

flash recovery area A single, unified storage area for all recovery-related files and recovery activities in an Oracle database.

flashback database A flashback feature that lets you recover the entire database to a specific point in time in the past.

flashback drop A flashback feature that retrieves a table after it has been dropped without using other more complicated and disruptive recovery techniques such as point-in-time recovery or flashback database.

flashback query A feature of the Oracle database that allows a user to view the contents of a table as of a user-specified point in time in the past. How far in the past a flashback query can retrieve rows depends on the size of the undo tablespace and on the setting of the `UNDO_RETENTION` system parameter.

flashback table A flashback feature that allows you to recover one or more existing tables to a specific point in time. Flashback table is done in place by rolling back only the changes made to the table or tables and their dependent objects, such as indexes.

foreign key A relationship between two tables. The foreign key defined on a table refers to the primary key or unique key of another table.

full backup A backup that includes all blocks of every data file backed up in a whole or partial database backup.

full outer join A join between two tables that returns rows based on the matching condition, as well as unmatched rows from the table on the right and left of the `JOIN` clause.

function A PL/SQL program that returns a value and is called in an expression.

G

Generic Connectivity One of the Heterogeneous Services offered by Oracle that allows for connectivity solutions based on third-party connection options such as OLEDB (a Microsoft standard) and Open Database Connectivity (ODBC). *See also* Heterogeneous Services.

granule The unit of contiguous memory used within the system global area (SGA) for allocating space to the shared pool, database buffer cache, Java pool, and large pool.

grid computing The concept of spreading Oracle's memory structures across two or more computers on an as-needed basis in order to maximize the performance of the application during peak usage and minimize the use of resources during low usage.

Grid Control
A web-based user interface that communicates with and centrally manages all the components within the Oracle enterprise. From a centralized location, Grid Control lets you monitor and administer the entire computing environment, including hosts, databases, listeners, application servers, HTTP servers, and web applications.

`GROUP BY` Clause used in queries to group aggregate data.

H

`HAVING` Clause used in queries to filter out aggregated results.

Health Monitor Component of Oracle Database to proactively monitor the health of database.

Heterogeneous Services The facility that lets you communicate with non-Oracle databases and services.

host The physical machine on which the Oracle server is located. This can be an IP address or a real name that is resolved via some external naming solution, such as DNS.

host string The database alias name used to connect to the Oracle database. You connect to the database by supplying a username, a password, and a host string. The host string can be omitted if the database is local.

hostnaming method A name-resolution method for small networks that minimizes the amount of configuration work you must perform.

I

identifiers Names used in the database, such as table names, column names, and so on. An identifier must begin with an alphabetic character and can contain alphabetic characters, digits, and three special characters: #, $, and _.

image copies A bit-for-bit duplicate of data files or archived redo log files in a database. You can create image copies using operating-system commands or Recovery Manager (RMAN).

inconsistent backup A backup performed when the database is open and the system change number (SCN) in the data files and the control file do not necessarily match. This is also referred to as an online backup.

incremental backup A backup that makes a copy of all data blocks that have changed since a previous baseline backup.

incrementally updated backup A backup that applies an incremental backup to an image copy, reducing the amount of time required in the event of media recovery.

index A data structure that physically organizes data from a table in order to improve table access speed.

index key A single occurrence of an index value.

inline view A subquery that appears in the `FROM` clause. This type of subquery is similar to selecting from a view.

inner join A join that selects only matching rows of both tables. This is the default type of join.

`INSERT` SQL statement used to add rows to a table.

instance The Oracle system global area (SGA) and all the Oracle background processes. *See also* system global area (SGA).

instance failure A circumstance in which the database instance fails unexpectedly because of a power outage or the failure of an Oracle background process.

instance recovery The process of synchronizing the contents of each data file with the control file during instance startup using the online redo log files and data in the undo tablespace.

integrity constraints Constraints that protect the data integrity. They are business rules defined in the database.

IP-filtering firewalls A type of firewall that monitors the network packet traffic on IP networks and filters out packets that either originated or did not originate from specific groups of machines.

J

Java pool The system global area (SGA) memory structure where Java code is cached. *See also* system global area (SGA).

Java Virtual Machine (JVM) The software that interprets and executes Java code inside the database.

join A relationship between two tables specified by using common columns or a condition to join two tables together.

Julian date A date that refers to the number of days since January 1, 4712 BC.

JVM *See* Java Virtual Machine (JVM).

K

key A distinct value in an index or a unique combination of columns in a table to identify the primary key.

key-preserved A state of a table in a join view. A table in the join view is key-preserved if the primary and unique keys of the table are unique to the view's result set.

L

large pool An optional area in the system global area (SGA) used for specific database operations such as backup or recovery. *See also* system global area (SGA); user global area (UGA).

least recently used (LRU) algorithm The mechanism that the Oracle kernel uses to manage the shared pool and database buffer caches, whereby the SQL or buffers that have been least recently accessed are those that are overwritten to make room for new SQL or buffers when these requests are made by user server processes.

left outer join A join between two tables that returns rows based on the matching condition, as well as unmatched rows from the table to the left of the `JOIN` clause.

LGWR *See* log writer (LGWR).

listener A server-side process that is responsible for listening and establishing connections to an Oracle server in response to a client connection request.

`listener.ora` The configuration file for the Oracle listener located on the Oracle server.

literals Values that represent a fixed value (constant). There are four types of literals: integer, character, number, and interval.

load balancing The ability of the Oracle listener to balance the number of connections between a group of dispatcher processes in an Oracle Shared Server environment.

local naming method A name-resolution method that relies on resolving an Oracle Net service name via the `tnsnames.ora` file.

log sequence number An identifier unique to the database that is incremented and recorded when an online redo log file is switched.

log writer (LGWR) The background process that writes redo log entries from the redo log buffer to the online redo logs. *See also* redo log buffer.

logging The recording of the Data Manipulation Language (DML) statements, creation of new objects, and other changes in the redo logs. The process also records significant events, such as starting and stopping the listener, along with certain kinds of network errors. *See also* Data Manipulation Language (DML).

logical operators Operators that are used to combine the results of two comparison conditions to produce a single result or to reverse the result of a single comparison. `NOT`, `AND`, and `OR` are the logical operators.

long query warning alert An alert generated when a query issues an "ORA-01555: snapshot too old error" message. This error usually occurs either when there is not enough space in the undo tablespace to hold the previous values of changed data or when the undo retention period for the database is set too low.

`lsnrctl` The command-line utility to manage the Oracle listener.

M

managed targets Entities that can be monitored and managed within the Oracle Management Framework. These entities include databases, application servers, web servers, applications, and Oracle agents such as the Oracle Net listener and Connection Manager. *See also* Oracle Connection Manager.

mean time to recovery (MTTR) The average amount of time it takes to recover the database and make it available after an instance failure occurs.

media failure A failure in which one or more database files is damaged. Media failure applies to control files, redo log files, temp files, and data files.

metadata Data that describes data. Metadata includes table definitions, stored PL/SQL program code, and privileges but not the information found in tables.

metric A measurement that is collected and stored in the Automatic Workload Recovery (AWR) repository. *See also* Automatic Workload Recovery (AWR).

middleware Software and hardware that sits between a client and the Oracle server. Middleware can provide a variety of functions, such as load balancing, security, and application-specific business-logic processing.

MTTR *See* mean time to recovery (MTTR).

multiple-column subquery A subquery that selects multiple columns in the subquery. Such subqueries are generally used in `UPDATE` statements or in the `WHERE` clause.

multiple-row subquery A subquery that returns no rows or more than one row.

multiplexing Creating multiple copies of a redo log file or control file in different locations so that the loss of one copy does not significantly affect your ability to recover a database.

multitable join A join that joins more than two tables in a query.

N

NAMES.DIRECTORY_PATH An entry found in the sqlnet.ora file that defines the net service name search method hierarchy for a client.

natural join A join that joins two tables using the columns with the same name and datatype in both tables.

nested subquery A subquery within another subquery.

Net Service Names The name of an Oracle service on the network. This is the name the user enters when referring to an Oracle service.

network failure A failure in the network connection between the client and the database; for example, a router reboot or a failure of a network card in the server.

NEXTVAL The sequence pseudocolumn that will cause the generation of the next number from the sequence-number generator.

NOARCHIVELOG mode A database mode in which redo log files are not written to an archive destination before they are overwritten. A database in NOARCHIVELOG mode can recover only from an instance failure.

nonequality join A join that joins two tables with a nonequality operator.

***n*-tier architecture** A network architecture involving at least three computers, typically a client computer, a middle-tier computer, and a database server.

NULL A value that represents unknown or missing data. Most functions return NULL when called with a NULL argument.

NUMBER Datatype used to store numeric values in table.

O

object privilege A database privilege that allows the grantee to perform a specific operation on a database object, such as a SELECT, an UPDATE, or a DELETE operation on a table.

OFA *See* Optimal Flexible Architecture (OFA).

Optimal Flexible Architecture (OFA) A model for organizing mount points, directory structures, and files so that they will be easier to manage, maintain, and back up.

optimizer statistics Measures such as number of rows, average row length, number of leaf blocks, and degree of selectivity that are stored as metadata whenever statistics are automatically or manually collected for database tables and indexes.

Oracle Connection Manager A networking solution from Oracle with connection multiplexing, access control and multiprotocol support. It enables a large number of users to connect to a database with a minimal number of network connections.

Oracle flash recovery area A component of the new automated disk-based recovery mechanisms in Oracle 10*g*. Flash recovery is designed to simplify your life in terms of Oracle backups by providing a centralized location to maintain and manage all the files related to database backups.

Oracle Management Agent A process that identifies and collects data about entities of interest within the Oracle Management Framework.

Oracle Management Framework An integrated set of tools that lets you perform traditional tasks more easily and efficiently as well as provides an effective mechanism for monitoring components within the enterprise.

Oracle Net Networking software that establishes a connection between Oracle Database and a client session.

Oracle server The combination of an Oracle instance and database.

Oracle Services Oracle Corporation's nonsoftware offerings, such as education and consulting services.

Oracle Shared Server A connection configuration that enhances the scalability of the Oracle Server through the use of dispatcher processes and Shared Server resources. Shared Server allows the server to support a larger number of lightweight concurrent connections by allowing them to share resources.

Oracle Transparent Gateway A connectivity product that seamlessly extends the reach of Oracle to non-Oracle data stores and allows you to treat non-Oracle data sources as if they were part of the Oracle environment.

Oracle Universal Installer (OUI) The Java-based installation tool for installing Oracle software.

OUI *See* Oracle Universal Installer (OUI).

outer join A join used to select data from a table even if there is no matching row in the joined table. These are the rows that are not returned by using a simple join. An outer join is specified by the outer-join operator (+) or the `FULL OUTER JOIN` keywords.

P

package A container for bundling procedures, functions, and data structures.

package body The part of a package that contains the program implementation.

package specification The part of a package that declares its external interface.

partial database backup A backup that includes zero or more tablespaces, which in turn include zero or more data files; a control file is optional in a partial database backup.

password A secret word associated with each user ID to authenticate a database connection.

password file The encrypted file that contains the usernames and passwords of users who have been granted SYSDBA and SYSOPER privileges.

pfile A plain-text file that contains database-initialization parameters. Oracle reads this file at startup and uses the information to configure various aspects of the Oracle instance and database.

PGA *See* program global area (PGA).

ping A TCP/IP utility that checks basic network connectivity between two computers.

PMON *See* Process Monitor (PMON).

port Used with TCP/IP to name the ends of logical connections, which carry conversations between two computers.

primary key A column or combination of column values that can identify a row uniquely. Primary key columns cannot have NULL values.

principle of least privilege Permits only the minimal set of privileges that are required for the situation.

private synonym A restricted alias to another object.

privileges The assigned permissions to create, modify, remove, or use a database object or a feature.

proactive monitoring Monitoring the Oracle server for potential issues before they occur, thus avoiding the impact on the database's performance, availability, or manageability.

procedure A PL/SQL program that is invoked as a stand-alone statement.

Process Monitor (PMON) The background process that cleans up failed user connections.

profile A set of limits on database resources or password characteristics.

program global area (PGA) An area of memory in which information for each client session is maintained. PGA includes bind variable, cursor information, and the client's sort area.

proxy-based firewall A firewall that prevents information from outside the firewall from flowing directly into the corporate network. The firewall acts as a gatekeeper, inspecting packets and sending only the appropriate information to the corporate network.

public synonym A global alias to another object.

Q

query A category of SQL statement that retrieves rows from database tables.

R

raw device A disk that does not contain an operating system–managed file system. Instead of a file system managing the reading and writing activities, Oracle does so.

reactive monitoring Monitoring the Oracle server for issues after they have occurred, too late to avoid impacting the database's performance, availability, or manageability.

read consistency Oracle's read consistency uses undo data to ensure that a statement (or a transaction) sees a set of data that does not change during its execution.

recycle bin A logical container in each tablespace holding dropped tables that can be retrieved by a database user as long as the space occupied by the deleted object is not required for new objects in the tablespace.

redo entry A group of *change vectors*. Redo entries record data that you can use to reconstruct all changes made to the database, including the undo segments. This is also referred to as a redo record.

redo log The physical files on disk that store the transaction recovery information written from the redo log buffer by the LGWR (log writer) process. *See also* log writer (LGWR).

redo log buffer The portion of the system global area (SGA) where transaction recovery information is stored until it can be written to the redo log files. *See also* system global area (SGA).

redo log file One of the files that constitutes a redo log group. This is also referred to as a redo log member.

redo log group A collection of multiplexed (mirrored) redo log files that contain information about changes in the database.

redo log group member One of the redo logs within a redo log group.

referential integrity Enforcing business rules within or between tables using primary key constraints and foreign key constraints.

refuse packet A packet sent via TCP/IP that acknowledges the refusal of some network request.

request queue A location in the system global area (SGA) in an Oracle Shared Server environment in which the dispatcher process places client requests. The shared server process then processes these requests. See also system global area (SGA).

response queue The location in the system global area (SGA) in an Oracle Shared Server environment where a shared server process places a completed client request. The dispatcher process then picks up the completed request and sends it back to the client.

response time The time it takes for a single user's request to return the desired result while using an application. Frequently used as a performance measure in data warehouse systems.

right outer join A join between two tables that returns rows based on the matching condition, as well as unmatched rows from the table to the right of the `JOIN` clause.

role A mechanism for grouping privileges for ease in administering them.

role privilege A database privilege that, by proxy, gives the grantee any combination of object, system, or other role privileges. Some role privileges that are included with all Oracle databases are DBA, resource, and java_admin.

rollforward The first phase of instance recovery, during which information in the online redo log files is applied to the data files (including the undo tablespace) to bring the data files up to their state before the instance failed.

ROLLBACK The SQL statement to undo a transaction.

rollback The second phase of instance recovery, during which uncommitted transactions are backed out from the data files.

rollback segments Manually managed segments for storing undo information. This information is used for read consistency and recovery purposes. Rollback segments were replaced by system-managed undo segments when automatic undo management was used.

rolling back The process of undoing one or more changes to data within a transaction.

row A single instance of data in a table. In the relational model, a row is analogous to a tuple.

row exclusive lock A table lock that is implicitly acquired with an `INSERT`, an `UPDATE`, a `MERGE`, or a `DELETE` statement.

row share lock A table lock that is implicitly acquired with a `SELECT FOR UPDATE` statement.

ROWID A pseudocolumn in every table that is the physical address of a row in the database.

S

savepoint An intermediate point within a transaction to which changes can be rolled back, without rolling back the entire transaction.

scalability The ability of a system to continue to provide adequate performance as the amount of data, the number of users, or both increases.

scalar subquery A subquery that returns one row and one column value. If the scalar subquery returns no rows, the resulting value is NULL.

SCN *See* system change number (SCN).

script file One or more SQL and/or SQL*Plus commands saved in a file for reuse.

segment A schema object that stores data outside the data dictionary. Tables and indexes are segments, while constraints and sequences are not.

segment space management Defines how free space within a segment is managed.

SELECT The SQL statement used to query data. This is the most commonly used statement in Oracle.

self join A join in which a table is joined to itself in a query.

self-referencing foreign key A foreign key constraint that refers to the primary key column of the same table.

sequence A named sequential-number generator.

server parameter file (spfile) A binary, dynamically modifiable file that stores a list of instance configuration parameters.

server process The operating-system process that executes on the host server on behalf of the user. The server process is responsible for parsing and placing SQL statements into the shared pool, copying database blocks into the database buffer cache, and placing transaction-recovery information into the redo log buffer.

session The term used to describe a user's connection to an instance.

set operators Operators used to write compound queries. UNION, UNION ALL, MINUS, and INTERSECT are the set operators.

SGA *See* system global area (SGA).

shadow process Another name for a dedicated server process. *See also* shared server process.

share lock A table lock that will block all changes to data and exclusive locks but will allow other share locks.

share row exclusive lock A table lock that will block all changes to data and other locks, except other row share locks.

shared server process Processes in an Oracle Shared Server configuration that executes the client requests.

shared pool The portion of the system global area (SGA) where cached SQL statements and supported metadata are stored.

single-row functions Functions that operate on a single row at a time. These functions know how many arguments they will operate on at compile time, before any data is fetched.

single-row subquery A subquery that returns only one row.

single-tier architecture A network architecture in which the client and server processes all run on the same computer.

smallfile tablespace A traditional tablespace that can have multiple data files, each limited to 2^{22} data blocks in size.

spfile *See* server parameter file (spfile).

SQL *See* Structured Query Language (SQL).

SQL buffer A buffer where the previously executed SQL statement is stored. SQL in the buffer can be edited, or it can be run using the / command.

SQL*Loader The Oracle bulk load program to load data from a flat file.

statement A single SQL command that can include subqueries.

statement failure The failure of a single database operation such as a Data Manipulation Language (DML) statement; for example, `INSERT`, `UPDATE`, and so on. *See also* Data Manipulation Language (DML).

static service registration The inputting of service-name information directly into the `listener.ora` file.

Streams pool The portion of the system global area (SGA) that is used to cache Oracle queuing information when the Oracle Streams feature is used. *See also* system global area (SGA).

Structured Query Language (SQL) The English-like language developed to allow users to easily query and manipulate the data stored in relational databases.

subquery A query within another query. A subquery answers queries that have multiple parts. The subquery answers one part of the question, and the parent query answers the other part.

substitution variable A variable that will accept values from the user during execution of the SQL.

superaggregates Summary rows (created by the `ROLLUP` and `CUBE` clauses) containing `NULL` in the grouped expressions. The `GROUPING` function returns a 1 for these summary rows and a 0 for the nonsummary rows, and it is used to distinguish the summary rows from the nonsummary rows.

Support Workbench Support Workbench can be used to examine a database problem and contact Oracle Support for a resolution.

synonym An alias to another object.

SYSASM A special database authorization given to users to manage ASM instances.

SYSDATE A built-in function to get the current system date and time.

SYSDBA A special all-empowering database authorization assigned to users that allows them to perform any database task.

SYSOPER A special database authorization assigned to users that allows them to perform a variety of database tasks, such as startup and shutdown. Its capabilities are not as encompassing as SYSDBA.

system change number (SCN) A unique number sequentially assigned to each transaction in the database.

system global area (SGA) The shared memory structure that Oracle uses to cache application users' SQL statements, data, index, and rollback buffers, Java, and redo information.

system monitor (SMON) The background process that is responsible for instance recovery, temporary tablespace management, and space management.

system privilege A database privilege that allows the grantee to perform a specific system operation, such as creating a session or altering any table.

T

table The basic structure in the database to store data. Tables are defined with columns and contain rows of data.

table alias name An alias name for a table in queries generally used to qualify ambiguous columns to tell Oracle specifically to which table the column belongs.

tablespace A logical storage area for database segments.

temporary tablespace The tablespace in which a user's temporary segments are stored.

throughput The amount of work that an application or the database can perform in a specified amount of time. This is frequently used as a performance measure in systems.

time-zone displacement The difference between the time zone and UTC (Coordinated Universal Time zone).

TIMESTAMP Datatype used to storage datetime data with a fraction of seconds, and optional time-zone information.

tnsnames.ora The name of the physical file that is used to resolve an Oracle Net service name when you are using the local naming resolution method.

tnsping An Oracle-supplied utility used to test basic connectivity from an Oracle client to an Oracle listener.

tracing A configuration that records all events that occur on a network, even when an error does not occur. This facility can be established at the client, the middle tier, or the server location.

transaction A unit of work within a series of SQL statements. A statement begins with the user's first Data Manipulation Language (DML) statement and ends with a COMMIT or ROLLBACK command. *See also* Data Manipulation Language (DML).

trigger A Procedural Language/SQL (PL/SQL) program that is invoked in response to a database event.

two-tier architecture A network architecture that is characterized by a client computer and a back-end server that communicate using some type of network protocol, such as TCP/IP.

U

UGA *See* user global area (UGA).

Undo Advisor A tool within the Oracle advisory framework that uses past undo usage to recommend settings for the UNDO_RETENTION parameter as well as an optimal size for the undo tablespace.

undo data The data blocks changed or updated, along with pointers to rows inserted that are stored in an undo tablespace to support read consistency, rolling back, and recovery from failed transactions or an instance crash. This is also referred to as rollback information.

undo segment The segment that stores the before image of modified data. This is used for rollback or transaction-recovery purposes.

undo tablespace A special type of tablespace that holds undo data. Only one undo tablespace can be active in the database at any given time.

Unicode A multibyte character set that can represent characters from any language. Unicode can, for example, represent characters from English, Greek, Urdu, and Japanese within a single character set.

updatable join view A view that queries from more than one table and can be used to update the base tables through the view.

UPDATE SQL statement used to modify existing rows in a table.

user error A user operation that does not generate an error message, but whose result was unintended, such as accidentally dropping a table.

user global area (UGA) An area in either the system global area (SGA) or program global area (PGA) used to keep track of session-specific information. *See also* program global area (PGA); system global area (SGA).

user process The process that runs on the client computer or application server and connects to the instance using a server process.

user-process failure The failure of a single connection to the database.

username A unique identification to connect to Oracle Database.

V

VARCHAR2 Datatype used to store variable-length character data.

view A customized representation of data from one or more tables. Views can be used to present a different perspective of data, to limit the data access, or to hide a complex query.

W

WHERE A clause used with SQL statements to limit the number of rows retrieved.

whole-database backup A database backup that includes all data files and at least one control file.

Index

Note to the Reader: Throughout this index **boldfaced** page numbers indicate primary discussions of a topic. *Italicized* page numbers indicate illustrations.

A

B

C

D

E

F

H

I

J

M

N

O

P

Q

R

S

V

W

Wiley Publishing, Inc.
End-User License Agreement

READ THIS. You should carefully read these terms and conditions before opening the software packet(s) included with this book "Book". This is a license agreement "Agreement" between you and Wiley Publishing, Inc. "WPI". By opening the accompanying software packet(s), you acknowledge that you have read and accept the following terms and conditions. If you do not agree and do not want to be bound by such terms and conditions, promptly return the Book and the unopened software packet(s) to the place you obtained them for a full refund.

1. License Grant. WPI grants to you (either an individual or entity) a nonexclusive license to use one copy of the enclosed software program(s) (collectively, the "Software," solely for your own personal or business purposes on a single computer (whether a standard computer or a workstation component of a multi-user network). The Software is in use on a computer when it is loaded into temporary memory (RAM) or installed into permanent memory (hard disk, CD-ROM, or other storage device). WPI reserves all rights not expressly granted herein.

2. Ownership. WPI is the owner of all right, title, and interest, including copyright, in and to the compilation of the Software recorded on the physical packet included with this Book "Software Media". Copyright to the individual programs recorded on the Software Media is owned by the author or other authorized copyright owner of each program. Ownership of the Software and all proprietary rights relating thereto remain with WPI and its licensers.

3. Restrictions On Use and Transfer.

(a) You may only (i) make one copy of the Software for backup or archival purposes, or (ii) transfer the Software to a single hard disk, provided that you keep the original for backup or archival purposes. You may not (i) rent or lease the Software, (ii) copy or reproduce the Software through a LAN or other network system or through any computer subscriber system or bulletin-board system, or (iii) modify, adapt, or create derivative works based on the Software.

(b) You may not reverse engineer, decompile, or disassemble the Software. You may transfer the Software and user documentation on a permanent basis, provided that the transferee agrees to accept the terms and conditions of this Agreement and you retain no copies. If the Software is an update or has been updated, any transfer must include the most recent update and all prior versions.

4. Restrictions on Use of Individual Programs. You must follow the individual requirements and restrictions detailed for each individual program in the About the CD-ROM appendix of this Book or on the Software Media. These limitations are also contained in the individual license agreements recorded on the Software Media. These limitations may include a requirement that after using the program for a specified period of time, the user must pay a registration fee or discontinue use. By opening the Software packet(s), you will be agreeing to abide by the licenses and restrictions for these individual programs that are detailed in the About the CD-ROM appendix and/or on the Software Media. None of the material on this Software Media or listed in this Book may ever be redistributed, in original or modified form, for commercial purposes.

5. Limited Warranty.

(a) WPI warrants that the Software and Software Media are free from defects in materials and workmanship under normal use for a period of sixty (60) days from the date of purchase of this Book. If WPI receives notification within the warranty period of defects in materials or workmanship, WPI will replace the defective Software Media.

(b) WPI AND THE AUTHOR(S) OF THE BOOK DISCLAIM ALL OTHER WARRANTIES, EXPRESS OR IMPLIED, INCLUDING WITHOUT LIMITATION IMPLIED WARRANTIES OF MERCHANTABILITY AND FITNESS FOR A PARTICULAR PURPOSE, WITH RESPECT TO THE SOFTWARE, THE PROGRAMS, THE SOURCE CODE CONTAINED THEREIN, AND/OR THE TECHNIQUES DESCRIBED IN THIS BOOK. WPI DOES NOT WARRANT THAT THE FUNCTIONS CONTAINED IN THE SOFTWARE WILL MEET YOUR REQUIREMENTS OR THAT THE OPERATION OF THE SOFTWARE WILL BE ERROR FREE.

(c) This limited warranty gives you specific legal rights, and you may have other rights that vary from jurisdiction to jurisdiction.

6. Remedies.

(a) WPI's entire liability and your exclusive remedy for defects in materials and workmanship shall be limited to replacement of the Software Media, which may be returned to WPI with a copy of your receipt at the following address: Software Media Fulfillment Department, Attn.: OCA Oracle Database 11g Administrator Certified Associate Study Guide, Wiley Publishing, Inc., 10475 Crosspoint Blvd., Indianapolis, IN 46256, or call 1-800-762-2974. Please allow four to six weeks for delivery. This Limited Warranty is void if failure of the Software Media has resulted from accident, abuse, or misapplication. Any replacement Software Media will be warranted for the remainder of the original warranty period or thirty (30) days, whichever is longer.

(b) In no event shall WPI or the author be liable for any damages whatsoever (including without limitation damages for loss of business profits, business interruption, loss of business information, or any other pecuniary loss) arising from the use of or inability to use the Book or the Software, even if WPI has been advised of the possibility of such damages.

(c) Because some jurisdictions do not allow the exclusion or limitation of liability for consequential or incidental damages, the above limitation or exclusion may not apply to you.

7. U.S. Government Restricted Rights. Use, duplication, or disclosure of the Software for or on behalf of the United States of America, its agencies and/or instrumentalities "U.S. Government" is subject to restrictions as stated in paragraph (c)(1)(ii) of the Rights in Technical Data and Computer Software clause of DFARS 252.227-7013, or subparagraphs (c) (1) and (2) of the Commercial Computer Software - Restricted Rights clause at FAR 52.227-19, and in similar clauses in the NASA FAR supplement, as applicable.

8. General. This Agreement constitutes the entire understanding of the parties and revokes and supersedes all prior agreements, oral or written, between them and may not be modified or amended except in a writing signed by both parties hereto that specifically refers to this Agreement. This Agreement shall take precedence over any other documents that may be in conflict herewith. If any one or more provisions contained in this Agreement are held by any court or tribunal to be invalid, illegal, or otherwise unenforceable, each and every other provision shall remain in full force and effect.

The Best OCA: Oracle Database 11*g* Book/CD Package on the Market!

Get ready for your Oracle Certified Administrator for Oracle Database 11g certification with the most comprehensive and challenging sample tests anywhere!

The Sybex Test Engine features:

- All the review questions, as covered in each chapter of the book.
- Challenging questions representative of those you'll find on the real exam.
- Four full-length bonus exams—two each for exams 1Z0-501 and 1Z0-502—available only on the CD.
- An Assessment Test to narrow your focus to certain objective groups.

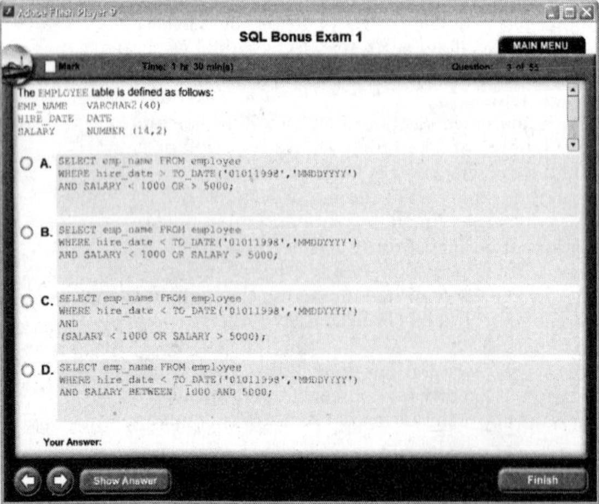

Search through the complete book in PDF!

- Access the entire *OCA: Oracle Database 11*g *Administrator Certified Associate Study Guide* complete with figures and tables, in electronic format.
- Search the *OCA: Oracle Database 11*g *Administrator Certified Associate Study Guide* chapters to find information on any topic in seconds.

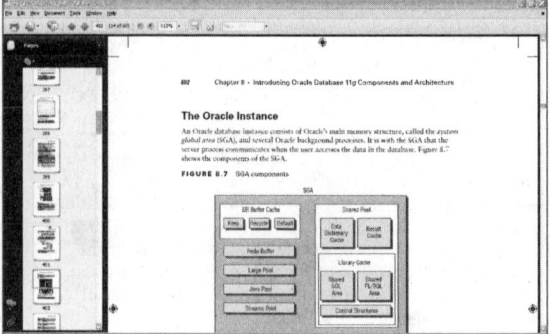

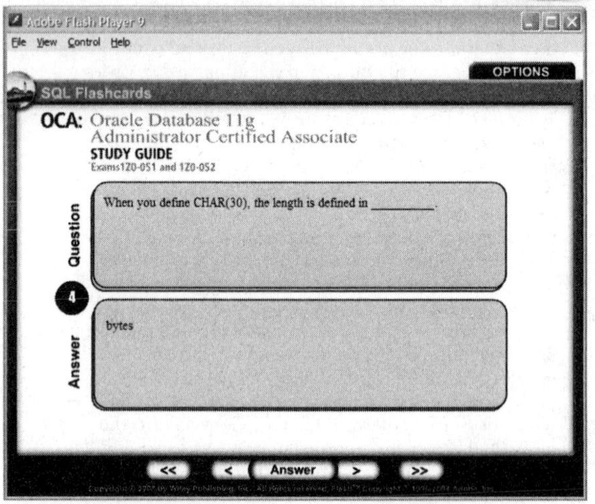

Use the Electronic Flashcards for PCs or Palm devices to jog your memory and prep last-minute for the exam!

- Reinforce your understanding of key concepts with these hardcore flashcard-style questions.
- Download the Flashcards to your Palm device and go on the road. Now you can study for the Oracle Database 11*g*: SQL Fundamentals I (1Z0-051) and Oracle Database 11*g*: Administration I (1Z0-052) exams anytime, anywhere.

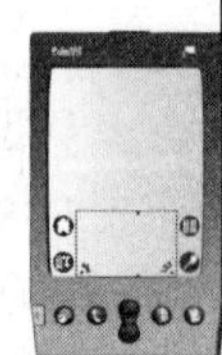